W·H·O·L·E·S·A·L·E AND RETAIL TRADE USA

Industry Analyses, Statistics, and Leading Companies

ISSN 1084-8622

W·H·O·L·E·S·A·L·E AND RETAIL TRADE USA

Second Edition

Industry Analyses, Statistics, and Leading Companies

- A comprehensive guide to economic activity in 133 distribution industries
- Provides unique analysis and synthesis of federal statistics
- Includes more than 4,300 leading companies
- Offers details on local distribution industries activity in 370 major metropolitan areas

Arsen J. Darnay,
Joyce Piwowarski, Editors

DETROIT • LONDON

Arsen J. Darnay and Joyce Piwowarski, *Editors*

Editorial Code and Data, Inc. Staff

Sherae R. Carroll, *Data Entry Associate*

Gale Research Inc. Staff

Amanda Quick, *Editorial Coordinator*

Mary Beth Trimper, *Production Manager*
Cindy Range, *Production Assistant*

Cynthia Baldwin, *Product Design Manager*
Kathleen A. Hourdakis, *Cover Designer*
C. J. Jonik, *Keyliner*
Todd Nessel, *Macintosh Artists*

This book is printed on acid-free paper that meets the minimum requirements of American National Standard for Information Sciences—Permanence Paper for Printed Library Materials, ANSI Z39.48-1984.

This book is printed on recycled paper that meets Environmental Protection Agency standards.

British Library Cataloguing in Publication Data
Wholesale and retail trade USA: industry analyses, statistics, and leading companies.
I. Darnay, Arsen J and Piwowarski, Joyce
338.40973

ISBN 0-7876-1664-8
ISSN 1084-8622

Printed in the United States of America
Published in the United States by The Gale Group

Contents

Introduction

Wholesale and Retail Trade USA: Industry Analyses, Statistics, and Leading Companies (*WRTUSA*), now in its 2nd edition, presents statistics on 69 wholesale and 64 retail industries drawn from a variety of federal sources and combined with information on leading public and private corporations. National, state, and metro level data are presented in a comprehensive, pre-analyzed format. Specific features include—

- 133 distribution industries at the 4-digit standard industrial classification (SIC) level, showing statistics and participants.
- The most currently available national statistical data for 1982, 1987, 1992, and beyond, with data extrapolated or projected for years with no federal reporting.
- Detailed state-level statistics for each industry for 1995 and 1992, with ratios.
- Coverage of 370 metropolitan statistical areas, including ratios.
- More than 4,300 public and private companies that participate in the wholesale and retail industries.
- More than 160 occupational groups employed by the services sector in 1996 with projections to the year 2006.
- State and regional maps.
- Preanalyzed format, including tables for indices of change and six industry ratios.
- Indexes for SICs, Subjects, Companies, Metropolitan Areas, and Occupations.
- Textual description of each industry in the appendix.

'The Most Current Data Available'

WRTUSA reports the most current data available at the time of the book's preparation. The objective is to present the best available information—data based on surveys by authoritative bodies—for all wholesale and retail industries on a comparable basis. Some industry associations collect more recent data. Analysts also publish estimates on one or another of these industries based on investigation and educated guessing. These data are rarely in the same format as the federal data and are not available for a large cross section of industry. Therefore, the data in *WRTUSA* are, indeed, the most current at this level of detail and spanning the entirety of wholesale and retail activity (see next section).

Scope and Coverage

WRTUSA covers all wholesale and retail distribution, the range of industries included in SICs 5012-5199 (wholesale) and 5200-5999 (retail). The industries covered include a part of business activity least visible to the public—wholesale trade—as well as that portion which is the most visible of all—retail trade, including stores, catalog companies, and restaurants and bars.

The last category, especially fast food restaurants, is popularly treated as part of the "services" sector. It could be argued—since food is "produced" on site—that this component should be in manufacturing. Officially, restaurants and bars are part of retail trade.

The sequence of presentation is wholesale followed by retail—following the logic of distribution itself. Products move from a producer to a wholesaler, from the wholesaler to the retailer, and from retailer to consumer. This, of course, is a gross generalization. Many products bypass the wholesale level altogether (e.g., pleasure boats). Others may bypass both the wholesale and retail level, being sold directly by one company to the other (e.g., industrial components) or by a producer to the customer (e.g., farmer selling pumpkins at a roadside stand).

The Appendix, SIC Descriptions, provides definitions for the economic activity included under each SIC.

SIC Coverage

The definition of the wholesale and the retail trade sectors, as used in *WRTUSA*, is that provided by the Standard Industrial Classification Manual, 1987, Executive Office of the President, Office of Management and Budget[1]. The sectors are defined as ranging from *SIC 5012 - Automobiles and other motor vehicles* to *SIC 5199 - Nondurable goods, nec* (not elsewhere classified) and *SIC 5211 - Lumber and other building materials* to *SIC 5999 - Miscellaneous retail stores, nec.*

Years Covered

WRTUSA includes data for 1982, 1987, and 1992 from Economic Census, Department of Commerce. Data on establishments, employment, and payroll for 1983-86, 1988-91, and 1993-95 are

[1] The North American Industry Classification System (NAICS) will be the coding system of the future. This book will begin to reflect NAICS coding as soon as data in NAICS format become available.

included from the *County Business Patterns* for those years; 1992 is the most recently available year for revenue information, 1995 for other data elements.

Geographical Coverage

WRTUSA shows statistical data nationally for the 1982-1995 period for all industries by state (Part I). Part II reports statistics on Metropolitan Statistical Areas (MSAs) and Primary Metropolitan Statistical Areas (PMSAs). MSAs are large population nuclei that, with adjacent communities, have a high degree of socioeconomic integration; PMSAs are coherent urban areas *within* a major urban region. Data are for 1994 and 1995.

Organization and Content

WRTUSA is divided into two parts as follows; five indexes provide access to the contents.

Part I - National and State Data

The first half of the book is organized by 4-digit wholesale and retail trade category. For each industry, data are presented in the following sequence:

General Statistics	Table of national statistics.
Indices of Change	Table of national data in index format.
Selected Ratios	Table of 6 industry ratios.
Leading Companies	Table of up to 50 companies in the industry.
Occupations	Table of occupations employed by the industry group.
Maps	Graphics showing states where the industry is disproportionately large and regions where the industry predominates.
State-level Statistics	Table showing statistics by state.

Each industry begins on a new page. The order of graphics and tables is invariable.

Part II - Metropolitan Area Data

The second half of the book presents tables for 370 metro areas. Organization is alphabetical by metro area. Within each table, data are placed in SIC order. Only industries for which employment, establishment, and payroll data were reported are included. Data are drawn from the *County Business Patterns* for 1994 and 1995.

Indexes

WRTUSA features five indexes as follows:

- **SIC Index**. Shows SICs in numerical and in alphabetical order with page references.
- **Subject Index**. Shows more than 2,400 products or types of organizations by page and SIC reference in alphabetical order.
- **Company Index**. Shows more than 4,300 companies in alphabetical order with page and SIC references.
- **Metropolitan Area Index**. The index shows 370 metro areas in two arrangements: alphabetically and alphabetically by state. Page references are provided.
- **Occupational Index**. Shows, in alphabetical order, the more than 160 occupations included in *WRTUSA*. Page and SIC references are given.

For detailed information on *WRTUSA*'s industry profiles, city and metro area tables, and indexes, please consult "Overview of Content and Sources."

Appendix

The Appendix, SIC Descriptions, provides a brief description of each of the 4-digit SICs included in *WRTUSA*.

Comments and Suggestions Are Welcome

Comments on *WRTUSA* and suggestions for its improvement are always welcome. Although every effort is made to maintain accuracy, errors may occasionally occur; the editors will be grateful if these are called to their attention. Please contact:

Editors
Wholesale and Retail Trade USA
Gale Research
27500 Drake Rd.
Farmington Hills, MI 48331-3535
Phone: (248) 699-GALE
(800) 347-GALE
Fax: (248) 699-8069

Overview of Content and Sources

Part I - National and State Data

The first part of *Wholesale and Retail Trade USA* is organized by industry; the profile of each industry is presented in eight parts, as follows:

General Statistics

This table shows national statistics for the industry for the years 1982-1995 under seven categories. For the Wholesale Sector, these categories are: Establishments, Employment, Payroll, Sales, Expenses, Beginning Inventory, and Ending Inventory. For the Retail Sector, the last three categories are not available; in their place, three ratios are reported: Employees per Establishment, Sales per Establishment, and Payroll per Employee. Values are in actual counts or in dollars, as shown above each column. For columns expressing values in millions of dollars, a figure like 9,538.7 stands for 9,538,700,000. Payroll per Employee figures are in dollars and reflect annual pay per person.

Values shown may be followed by an italicized lower case *e* or *p*. These markers indicate that a value is either ***e***xtrapolated or ***p***rojected. Extrapolations are used to fill in series where values between two Economic Census years are unavailable. Projections are used to extend a series of actual or extrapolated values to the year 1998. A more complete discussion of this subject is provided below.

Data in the General Statistics tables combine census data (Economic Census) and data from the *County Business Patterns* (CBP). Methods of collecting these data are very different. Data for 1982, 1987, and 1992, derived from the Economic Census, are the most complete and reliable. They are based on a 100 percent national sample. CBP data are partial surveys.

Indices of Change

The data presented in the General Statistics table are restated as indices in the Indices of Change table. The purpose of the table is to show the user rapidly how different categories have changed since 1992. The year 1992 is used as the base and is therefore shown as 100 in every category. The values for other years are expressed in relation to the 1992 value. For example, total establishments in *SIC 5012 - Automobiles and Other Motor Vehicles* was 7,899. This value is taken as the base for the total establishments column of the Indices of Change table. In 1988, the industry had 6,750 establishments. That value, divided by 7,899 and multiplied by 100, is 85.5—the index for total establishments for 1988. In years other than 1992, a value of 100 means same as 1992, higher or lower values mean better or worse performance than 1992.

Selected Ratios

To aid the user in understanding the industries, 6 ratios are presented in the Selected Ratios table for each industry and for the average of all industries in the sector under consideration; an index, comparing the two categories, is provided as well. All ratios are for 1992.

The categories— "Employees per Establishment," "Payroll per Establishment," etc.—represent a division between the first and the second element (Employees divided by Establishments).

The first column of values represents the **Average of all Wholesale** or **Retail**. These ratios are calculated by (1) adding all categories for Wholesale or Retail and (2) following the method for ratio or percentage calculation described above.

The second column of values shows the ratios for the **Analyzed Industry**, i.e., the industry currently under consideration.

The third column is an **Index** comparing the Analyzed Industry to the Average of All Wholesale or Retail Industries. The index is useful for determining quickly and consistently how the Analyzed Industry stands in relation to all services. Index values of 100 mean that the Analyzed Industry, within a given ratio, is identical to the average of all industries reported. An index value of 500 means that the Analyzed Industry is five times the average—for instance, it has five times as many employees per establishment. An index value of 50 would indicate half the average of all industries (50%).

Leading Companies

The table of *Leading Companies* shows up to 50 companies that participate in the industry. The listings are sorted in descending order of sales and show the company name, address, name of the chief executive officer, telephone, company type, sales (in millions of dollars) and employment (in thousands of employees). The number of companies shown, their total sales, and total employment are summed at the top of the table for the user's convenience.

The data are from the *Ward's Business Directory of U.S. Private and Public Companies* for 1998. Public and private corporations, divisions, subsidiaries, joint ventures, and corporate groups are shown. Thus a listing for an industry may show the parent company as well as important divisions and subsidiaries of the same company (usually in a different location).

While this method of presentation has the disadvantage of duplication (the sales of a parent corporation include the sales of any divisions listed separately), it has the advantage of providing the user with information on major components of an enterprise at different locations. In any event, the user should not assume that the sum of the sales (or employment) shown in the Leading Companies table represents the total sales (or employment) of an industry. The Sales column of the General Statistics table is a better guide to industry sales/income.

The company's type (private, public, division, etc.) is shown on the table under the column headed "Co Type," thus providing the user with a means of roughly determining the total "net" sales (or employment) represented in the table; this can be accomplished by adding the values and then deducting values corresponding to divisions and subsidiaries of parent organizations also shown in the table. The code used is as follows:

P	Public Corporation
R	Private Corporation
S	Subsidiary
D	Division
J	Joint Venture
G	Corporate Group

An asterisk (*) placed behind the sales volume indicates an estimate; the absence of an asterisk indicates that the sales value has been obtained from annual reports, other formal submissions to regulatory bodies, or from the corporation. The symbol "<" appears in front of some employment values to indicate that the actual value is "less than" the value shown. Thus the value of "<0.1" means that the company employs fewer than 100 people.

Occupations Employed by Industry Group

Wholesale and Retail Trade USA presents data on nearly 100 occupational categories employed by the two sectors. The information presented is an extract from the *Industry-Occupation Matrix* produced by the Bureau of Labor Statistics (BLS), Department of Labor, in 1998.

The table on Occupations Employed presents an extract; showing the entire matrix would have required too much space. Thus only those occupations are included that represent 1% or more of total employment in an industry. The advantage of this method is that the data are kept manageable while most of an industry's employment is defined by occupation. The disadvantage is that certain occupations, although employed by an industry, do not make the "cutoff" of 1% of total employment.

The data are shown for 1996 in percent of Total Employment for an industry group (3-digit industry level or groupings of 3-digit industries). Also shown is the Bureau of Labor Statistics' projection of the anticipated growth or decline of the occupation to the year 2006. This value is reported as a Percent Change to 2006; a value of 5.5, for instance, means that overall employment, in the industry group, will increase 5.5% between 1996 and 2006; a negative value indicates a corresponding decline. Note that these are not rates of annual change.

BLS does not provide occupational data at the 4-digit SIC level. Consequently, the same table of Occupations Employed is reproduced for each industry which is in the same 3-digit grouping. This approach has been adopted so that the user will find the occupations associated with a 4-digit industry with other data on that industry.

The user should note the following:

- As already stated, the occupations shown are a subset of total occupations employed: those that account for 1% or more of employment in the industry group.
- Since the data are for groups, some occupations listed will appear out of place in a particular 4-digit industry; that is because those occupations are employed by a related 4-digit industry in the same group.
- Growth or decline indicated for an occupation within an industry group does not mean that the occupation is growing or declining overall. The overall pattern is that service occupations, especially those associated with medicine and health, are growing. Manufacturing occupations, especially those associated with old industries or those threatened by the overseas migration of their jobs, are declining.

Maps

The geographical presentation of data begins with two maps titled **State and Regional Concentration**. The first map shows states which have proportionately greater representation in the industry than would be indicated by the state's population. The ratio is based on total revenues or number of establishments; number of establishments is used when revenue data are suppressed. A state's total revenues are divided by total revenues in 1992 for the industry to get the first ratio. Then the state's population (for 1992) is divided by total U.S. population to get the second ratio. If the first ratio is greater than the second, the state map is shaded.

In the second map, the industry's concentration is shown by Census Region. The two maps, together, tell the user at a glance where the industry is especially active and which regions rank first, second, and third in revenues or in number of establishments. Establishment counts are used for ranking in those industries where revenue data are withheld (the (D) symbol) for the majority of states. The data for ranking are taken from the Industry Data by State table.

The regional boundaries are those of the Census Regions and are named as follows:

1 - Pacific (includes Alaska and Hawaii)
2 - Mountain
3 - West North Central
4 - West South Central
5 - East North Central
6 - East South Central
7 - New England
8 - Middle Atlantic
9 - South Atlantic

In the case of the Pacific region, all parts of the region are shaded (including Alaska and Hawaii), even if the basis for the ranking is the industry's predominance in California (the usual case).

Although regional data are only graphed and not reported in a separate table, the table of Industry Data by State provides all the necessary information for constructing a regional table.

Industry Data by State

The table on Industry Data by State provides 14 data elements for each state in which the industry is active. The data are drawn from the *County Business Patterns*, 1995, and the Economic Census, 1992. Even in this series, certain data elements are suppressed by the Bureau of the Census to prevent disclosure of competitive information. This may come about in instances where only a few operations are present in the state or they are operated by a small number of companies. The states are shown in descending order of total revenues. The categories of Establishments, Employment, Payroll, and Sales are the same as those used in the General Statistics table. Their subdivisions are as follows:

- Establishment and Employment data are shown as totals; each state is then shown as percent of U.S. establishments or employment in the industry for 1995 (if available). Employment per Establishment is shown as well. Employment data are sometimes available only as a range of numbers, e.g., 100-249.

- Payroll is shown in millions of dollars and per employee in dollars for 1995.

- Total sales are shown for 1992 in millions of dollars, as percent of U.S. total revenues, and in dollars per establishment.

The symbol (D) is used when data are withheld to prevent disclosure. Dashes are used to indicate that the corresponding data element cannot be calculated because some portion of the ratio is missing or withheld.

Projected Data Series

The General Statistics table for most industries holds trend projections of data series from 1996 to 1998, with the base year of the projections being 1982 or 1987.

How Projections Were Made

Projections are based on a curve-fitting algorithm using the least-squares method. In essence, the algorithm calculates a trend line for the data using existing data points. Extensions of the trend line are used to predict future years of data. The method is illustrated in the chart on the next page. It shows actual data values plotted for 1982 through 1992 and the least-squares trend line drawn to overlay the points. The trend line is extended through 1996. The values for 1993 through 1996 represent the "trend" of the earlier years.

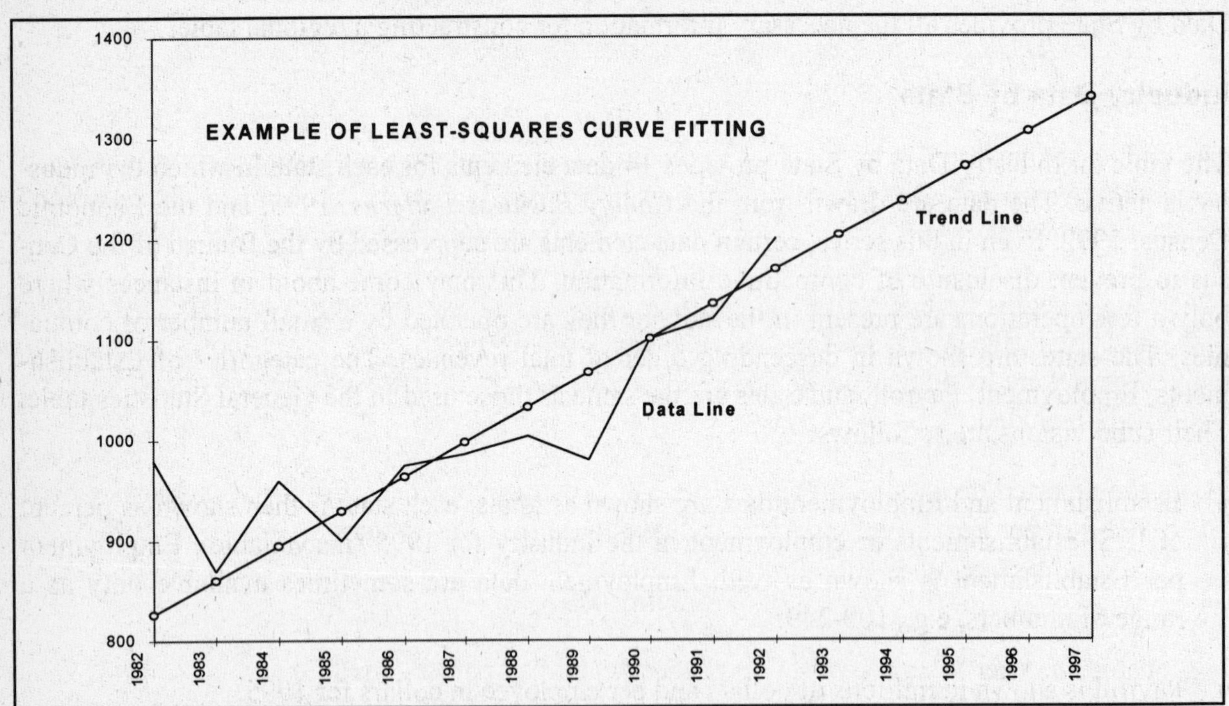

What Values Were Projected

For the wholesale sector, all values in the table were subject to projection, including establishments, employment, payroll, sales, expenses, beginning inventory, and ending inventory. In the retail sector tables, only the first four columns were subject to projections. The other columns represent ratios calculated from government data.

In many cases, values extrapolated from base years (for the years 1983-1986 and 1988-1991) are incorporated into the trend calculations.

Limitations of Projections

Projections are simply means of detecting trends—that may or may not hold in the future. The projections in *WRTUSA*, therefore, are not as reliable as actual survey data. Most analysts trying to project the future routinely turn to trend projection. In *WRTUSA*, the work of doing the projections has been done for the user in advance.

Part II - Metropolitan Area Data

Part II of *WRTUSA* is a presentation of statistics for metropolitan statistical areas drawn from *County Business Patterns* (CBP) for 1994 and 1995.

All told, statistics for 370 metro areas are shown. The information is organized alphabetically by name of the metro area. The state or states where the entity is located are shown. The Metropolitan Area Index may be used to identify all metro areas that are located in one state.

Each table begins by showing summary data for the Wholesale categories followed by 4-digit SIC data; next, the Retail total is presented, followed by retail SICs. Only those industries for which data were available for all three CBP categories (establishments, employment, and payroll) were included.

Data are reported on Number of Establishments, Total Employment, Employment per Establishment, Payroll per Employee, and total Annual Payroll (in 1,000 dollars).

Indexes

To enable the user to find industries, products, and companies rapidly and easily, *WRTUSA* is thoroughly indexed. Page and SIC references are provided in all five *WRTUSA* indexes.

SIC Index

Part One of the index is ordered numerically using the 1987 SIC sequence beginning with the first wholesale industry. This part is followed immediately by an alphabetical listing by industry name. Each industry name is followed by its SIC and then the page number on which it begins.

Subject Index

The index holds the names of more than 2,400 products sold by the wholesale and retail sectors as well as names of types of stores. Each term is followed by a page number and SIC code.

Company Index

This index shows more than 4,300 company names arranged in alphabetical order. Company names are followed by page references and a listing of SICs (within brackets).

Metropolitan Area Index

This index shows every metropolitan area that appears in *WRTUSA*. The first part of the index is arranged alphabetically by metro area; the second part is alphabetically by state and, within states, alphabetically by metro area. A metro area that includes more than one state will appear under each state in which a part of it is located. Page references are provided.

Occupation Index

The Occupation Index shows the occupations listed in *WRTUSA*. The occupational groups included as entries in the industry tables are here separated into individual occupations so that they are easier to locate alphabetically. This index does not attempt to refer the user to every industry in which an occupation occurs; that approach would render the index unwieldy; rather, the total number of 3-digit industries employing the occupation is shown, in parentheses, following the name of the occupation; thereafter, the top ten (or fewer) industry groups are shown in their order of importance; the most important group (that which employs the largest number) is shown first.

User's Guide

Wholesale and Retail Trade USA (*WRTUSA*) profiles the distribution sectors of the U.S. economy in a manner designed to help the user in relatively straight-forward reference work as well as in complex tasks of planning and analysis.

The user may be interested in the distribution sector alone. In that case, most of the necessary information is provided in this volume. He or she may also be engaged in a more complex investigation. In that case, it is recommended that the other volumes in Gale's "USA" series be consulted as well.

No attempt is made to give an exhaustive catalog of *WRTUSA*'s uses. To a large extent, the user's own unique context and situation will dictate the best use of the book. In what follows, a brief summary of the sectors is presented. Next come some examples of possible uses of the book as a reference tool and as an analytical tool.

Summary of the Sectors

Wholesale trade is a major industrial sector, with sales of $3.25 trillion in 1992, an increase of nearly 29 percent over 1987. Nearly 500,000 establishments employ 5.8 million people, just shy of 12 people per establishment; employment per establishment has undergone virtually no change since 1987. Sales are $6.6 million per establishment and $561,000 per employee. Income per employee was $29,746 in 1992, up 28% since 1987—a growth that parallels sales. The first table on the next page profiles the wholesale sector[1].

The Retail Trade sector is smaller—$1.895 trillion in 1992. It has grown at a slightly slower rate than the wholesale sector, 27 percent since 1987. With more than three times as many establishments (1.5 million) as wholesale, retail employs 18.4 million people, slightly more than

---

[1] Census data charting revenues for wholesale and retail become available every five years. The 1997 results were not yet available as of publication time. Data in this volume update many series to 1995 and provide projections to 1998. However, these comparisons are updated only when new census data are published.

12 people per establishment. Earnings in the industry are less than half that of earnings in the wholesale sector—$12,107 per employee per year; earnings also have grown at a slower rate. Sales are $1,241,555 per establishment and $102,941 per employee. The second table on the next page profiles the sector.

WHOLESALE TRADE	1987	1992	% Change
Establishments	469,539	495,457	5.52
Employment	5,609,024	5,791,401	3.25
Payroll ($ million)	130,000	172,272	32.52
Sales ($ million)	2,524,727	3,249,874	28.72
Payroll per Employee ($)	23,177	29,746	28.34
RETAIL TRADE	**1987**	**1992**	**% Change**
Establishments	1,503,593	1,526,215	15.05
Employment	17,779,942	18,407,453	3.5
Payroll ($ million)	177,547	222,868	25.53
Sales ($ million)	1,493,309	1,894,880	26.89
Payroll per Employee ($)	9,986	12,107	21.24

Using *WRTUSA* as a Reference Tool

WRTUSA is a convenient "look-up" tool for the reference librarian, information specialist, provider of technical information, or consultant who needs to respond rapidly to a telephone query from a client or constituent—someone who needs a quick answer and few details. Some examples follow.

Finding an SIC

The simplest use of *WRTUSA* is to define the SIC for a wholesale or retail category. The caller may be an accountant, calling on behalf of a client, who is "in the tobacco business." He wants to know his client's SIC. The Subject Index provides references to SICs 5194, 5912, and 5993 when consulted on "tobacco." The caller, when questioned, reveals that the client is an exporter of expensive tobacco leaves but also runs three tobacco shops. The answer is SIC 5159 for the export business and SIC 5993 for the tobacco shops.

Providing Magnitude Information

How big is a particular industry? How big is it in a particular geography? Staying with tobacco as an industry, *WRTUSA* can be used to answer a journalistic question, say, on the size of the tobacco industry. Magnitude of the tobacco production industry can be obtained from Gale's *Manufacturing USA* ($31.9 billion). The wholesale distribution of this industry was $39.239 billion in 1992 and projected to be $52.536 billion in 1998. Retail sales through tobacco stores and stands were $781.8 million in 1992, suggesting that the vast majority of tobacco products pass through wholesale distribution and are then sold through grocery and drug stores.

A look at Industry Data by State indicates that the largest wholesale activity in tobacco is concentrated in Kentucky, New York, and California, in that order.

New York, California, and Illinois have both the largest cities in the United States and (not surprisingly) the largest number of tobacco stands.

Comparing Industries

Another caller is a student writing a paper. Its theme is a perceived demise of books in favor of computers. She wants to see how computer stores and book stores are doing—to get a feel for trends.

WRTUSA provides data to help in this analysis. *SIC 5734 - Computer and Software Stores* shows that sales of this industry's products were $6.550 billion in 1992. By contrast, book store sales (SIC 5942) were $8.015 billion, indicating that books are not dead yet. But what about rates of growth? *WRTUSA* shows that, since 1987, computer and software sales have increased 59.5 percent and book store sales by 36.2 percent. Computers are growing faster than books, but the growth rate of books is impressive—especially for such an ancient technology. It appears that the gloomy theme of that paper will be difficult to support with these figures.

Answering Locational Questions

An entrepreneur, thinking of expanding a chain of Minnesota-based computer stores to nearby states, is hesitating over priorities. Should he target Wisconsin, Iowa, or Illinois? The State and Regional Concentration map shows that the penetration of computer stores is higher in Illinois than in the other two states. At first glance, Wisconsin may have a favorable profile: labor costs appear to be lower; Wisconsin also has larger sales volumes, per store, than Iowa.

The planner of a new mall in Cleveland wants to contact local book sellers to take space in his mall. *WRTUSA*'s Leading Companies table for *SIC 5942 - Books Stores* provides three companies in Ohio, two of which are near (Wit and Wisdom in Beachwood and J.R. Holcomb and Co. in Cleveland).

Helping Buyers, Sellers, and Job Seekers

Using a combination of the Subject Index and the Leading Companies table, the user can rapidly help a caller identify companies—whatever the context: finding a vendor, finding a customer, or finding a job. Corporate sales and employment data help, additionally, to narrow the field of search. And in either case, addresses and telephone numbers are usually available.

Using the Occupation Index, the user can identify industries that employ a caller's skills and, once the industries are located, the company tables can identify potential employers by city and state.

Using *WRTUSA* as a Research Tool

Scope and Limitations

WRTUSA represents the distribution sectors of the U.S. economy and, consequently, shows but a piece of the "economic puzzle." A few components of this industry (*SIC 5812 - Eating Places*) are relatively autonomous. The vast majority of the rest depend on the activities of the manufacturing, mining, and/or of the agricultural sectors for their stock in trade. Using *WRTUSA* alone, therefore, restricts the user to investigations that relate strictly to distribution. Those with broader scope, of course, can easily use other Gale titles in the "USA" series to trace economic activity beyond the wholesale and retail sectors.

Market Analysis, Strategy, and Planning

Multi-year trend data are generally available for every industry, permitting the user to track trends uniformly, at least in the 1987-1995 period. In most instances, *WRTUSA* provides three benchmark years, 1982, 1987, and 1992. Statistics from 1987 forward are available in those cases where industry definitions changed radically in the 1987 SIC revisions. Also useful for marketing planning and the evolution of strategy are the essentially complete data sets for state activity (Industry Data by State) and the Metro Area tables in Part II of *WRTUSA*. Market penetration is well marked in the state maps, identifying (depending on the point of view) states where a service activity may have saturated the market or where that particular service can anticipate a favorable environment and resources. Although not provided in *WRTUSA*, market penetration data can be derived easily from the Metro Area tables as well. Since nearly 400 city tables are availabie, listing all major wholesale and retail industries, valuable work with a local focus is possible.

Locational Analysis

The key resources provided for locational analysis are the Industry Data by State tables and, within these, data on employment, payroll, and revenues. Employment per establishment is provided in precalculated form; this datum, combined with payroll per employee (usually the key cost element in the wholseale and retail trades) and sales per establishment are helpful in identifying the strengths and weaknesses of different states as an element in locational planning. The state map, as discussed above, provides an at-a-glance view of market penetration, which can be augmented by an examination of key cities/metro areas (easily located in the second part of the Metropolitan Area Index).

Diversification, Mergers, and Acquisitions

Especially when working with *WRTUSA*'s companion book, *Manufacturing USA*, which has a nearly identical organization, the user can identify distribution and manufacturing categories that, together, can create desired synergies. The Leading Companies tables from each book provide lists of candidates or first contacts in desired locations.

Employment Analysis

The occupational data in *WRTUSA* are shown by 3-digit industry group—somewhat of a limitation; at the same time, they show projections of growth or decline to the year 2006, which is useful in planning corporate, governmental, and educational activities.

Conclusions

The discussion, above, was presented to illustrate some uses *of Wholesale and Retail Trade USA: Industry Analyses, Statistics, and Leading Companies*. Many other analyses and evaluations are possible using the data in *WRTUSA*. Comments on this User's Guide, including suggestions on other cases that should be illustrated in future editions, are welcome.

Abbreviations, Codes, and Symbols

U.S. State Postal Codes

AK	Alaska
AL	Alabama
AR	Arkansas
AZ	Arizona
CA	California
CO	Colorado
CT	Connecticut
CZ	Canal Zone
DC	District of Columbia
DE	Delaware
FL	Florida
GA	Georgia
GU	Guam
HI	Hawaii
IA	Iowa
ID	Idaho
IL	Illinois
IN	Indiana
KS	Kansas
KY	Kentucky
LA	Louisiana
MA	Massachusetts
MD	Maryland
ME	Maine
MI	Michigan
MN	Minnesota
MO	Missouri
MS	Mississippi
MT	Montana
NC	North Carolina
ND	North Dakota
NE	Nebraska
NH	New Hampshire
NJ	New Jersey
NM	New Mexico
NV	Nevada
NY	New York
OH	Ohio
OK	Oklahoma
OR	Oregon
PA	Pennsylvania
PR	Puerto Rico
RI	Rhode Island
SC	South Carolina
SD	South Dakota
TN	Tennessee
TX	Texas
UT	Utah
VA	Virginia
VI	Virgin Islands
VT	Vermont
WA	Washington
WI	Wisconsin
WV	West Virginia
WY	Wyoming

Miscellaneous Abbreviations

APt	Airport
Assn	Association
Assoc	Association
CH	Court House
Cmte	Committee
Co	Company
Com	Community
Cons	Consumer
Coop	Cooperative
Corp	Corporation
Devel	Development
E	East
Fdn	Foundation
Ft	Fort
Inc	Incorporated
Ind	Industries
Intl	International
Inst	Institute
Ltd	Limited
Mfg	Manufacturing
Mont	Montana
Mt	Mount
N	North
Nec	Not elsewhere classified
Pub	Publishing
S	South
SE	South East
Svc	Service
Svcs	Services
Univ	University
Vil	Village
W	West

Codes and Symbols

P	Publicly Held
R	Privately Held
D	Division
S	Subsidiary
J	Joint Venture
A	Affiliate
G	Group
T	Subject to Federal Income Tax
X	Exempt from Federal Income Tax
(D)	Data withheld to prevent disclosure of competitive information
<	Less Than
*	Sales estimated by Ward's

Part I

NATIONAL AND STATE DATA

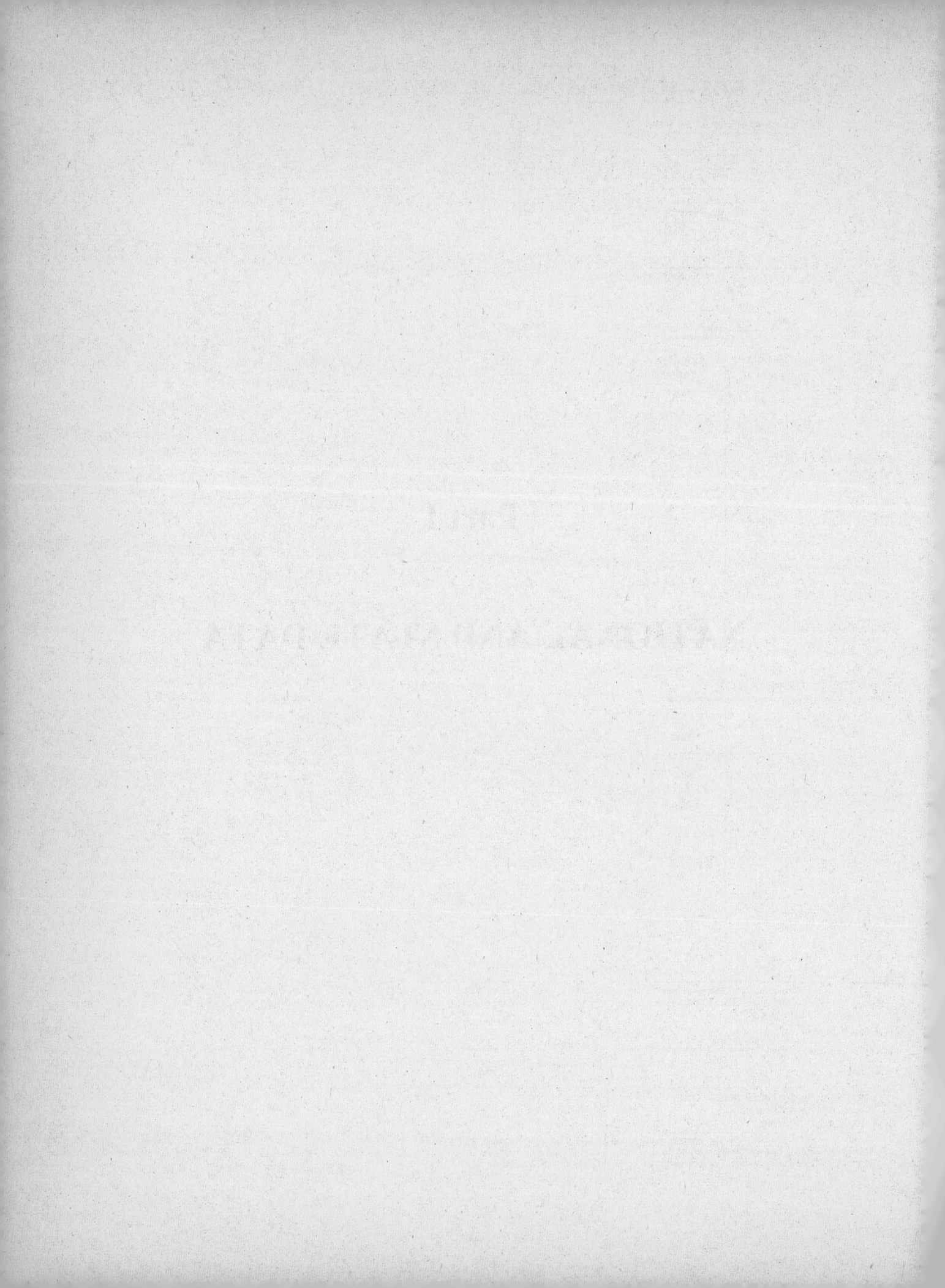

5012 - AUTOMOBILES AND OTHER MOTOR VEHICLES

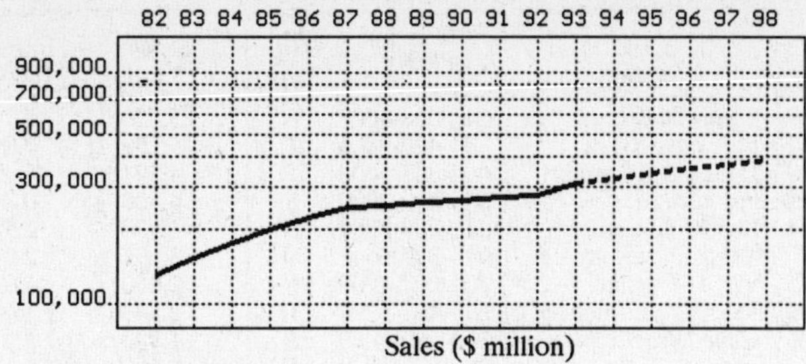

Sales ($ million)

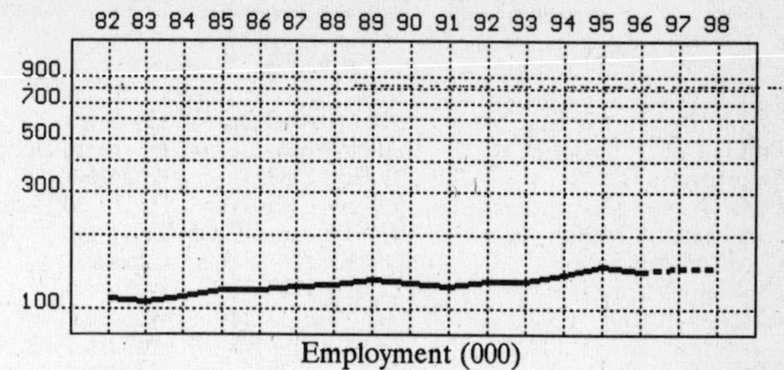

Employment (000)

GENERAL STATISTICS

Year	Establishments (number)	Employment (number)	Payroll ($ million)	Sales ($ million)	Expenses ($ million)	Beginning Inventory ($ million)	Ending Inventory ($ million)
1982	6,685	111,198	2,170.2	130,132.9	-	-	-
1983	6,504	106,459	2,239.0	153,493.0e	-	-	-
1984	6,381	112,495	2,524.2	176,853.0e	-	-	-
1985	6,296	118,530	2,754.9	200,213.1e	-	-	-
1986	6,211	119,636	2,841.0	223,573.1e	-	-	-
1987	7,125	124,448	2,910.5	246,933.2	7,657.2	8,313.6	9,882.9
1988	6,750	126,535	3,174.5	253,329.1e	7,680.6e	8,447.8e	9,725.0e
1989	6,549	131,501	3,250.7	259,725.0e	7,704.1e	8,582.0e	9,567.0e
1990	6,433	127,118	3,175.7	266,121.0e	7,727.5e	8,716.2e	9,409.1e
1991	6,427	123,654	3,140.7	272,516.9e	7,750.9e	8,850.4e	9,251.2e
1992	7,899	130,098	3,519.9	278,912.9	7,774.4	8,984.6	9,093.3
1993	7,771	129,436	3,657.9	313,068.3p	7,797.8p	9,118.8p	8,935.4p
1994	7,956	138,918	4,185.4	327,946.2p	7,821.2p	9,253.0p	8,777.4p
1995	8,123	150,554	4,605.5	342,824.2p	7,844.7p	9,387.2p	8,619.5p
1996	7,879p	143,753p	4,323.9p	357,702.2p	7,868.1p	9,521.4p	8,461.6p
1997	8,005p	146,248p	4,479.9p	372,580.2p	7,891.5p	9,655.6p	8,303.7p
1998	8,131p	148,743p	4,636.0p	387,458.2p	7,915.0p	9,789.8p	8,145.7p

Sources: Economic Census of the United States, 1982, 1987, and 1992. Establishment counts, employment, and payroll are from *County Business Patterns* for non-Census years. Values followed by a 'p' are projections by the editors. Sales and expense data for non-Census years are extrapolations, marked by 'e'. Industries reclassified in 1987 will not have data for prior years. Data are the most recent available at this level of detail.

INDICES OF CHANGE

Year	Establishments (number)	Employment (number)	Payroll ($ million)	Sales ($ million)	Expenses ($ million)	Beginning Inventory ($ million)	Ending Inventory ($ million)
1982	84.6	85.5	61.7	46.7	-	-	-
1983	82.3	81.8	63.6	55.0e	-	-	-
1984	80.8	86.5	71.7	63.4e	-	-	-
1985	79.7	91.1	78.3	71.8e	-	-	-
1986	78.6	92.0	80.7	80.2e	-	-	-
1987	90.2	95.7	82.7	88.5	98.5	92.5	108.7
1988	85.5	97.3	90.2	90.8e	98.8e	94.0e	106.9e
1989	82.9	101.1	92.4	93.1e	99.1e	95.5e	105.2e
1990	81.4	97.7	90.2	95.4e	99.4e	97.0e	103.5e
1991	81.4	95.0	89.2	97.7e	99.7e	98.5e	101.7e
1992	100.0	100.0	100.0	100.0	100.0	100.0	100.0
1993	98.4	99.5	103.9	112.2p	100.3p	101.5p	98.3p
1994	100.7	106.8	118.9	117.6p	100.6p	103.0p	96.5p
1995	102.8	115.7	130.8	122.9p	100.9p	104.5p	94.8p
1996	99.8p	110.5p	122.8p	128.2p	101.2p	106.0p	93.1p
1997	101.3p	112.4p	127.3p	133.6p	101.5p	107.5p	91.3p
1998	102.9p	114.3p	131.7p	138.9p	101.8p	109.0p	89.6p

Sources: Same as General Statistics. The values shown reflect change from the base year, 1992. Values above 100 mean greater than 1992, values below 100 mean less than 1992, and a value of 100 in the 1982-91 or 1993-98 period means same as 1992. Values followed by a 'p' are projections by the editors; 'e' stands for extrapolation. Data are the most recent available at this level of detail.

SELECTED RATIOS

For 1992	Avg. of All Wholesale	Analyzed Industry	Index	For 1992	Avg. of All Wholesale	Analyzed Industry	Index
Employees per Establishment	12	16	141	Sales per Employee	561,172	2,143,868	382
Payroll per Establishment	349,729	445,613	127	Sales per Establishment	6,559,346	35,309,900	538
Payroll per Employee	29,919	27,056	90	Expenses per Establishment	723,071	984,226	136

Sources: Same as General Statistics. The 'Average of All Manufacturing' column represents the average of all manufacturing industries reported for the most recent complete year available. The Index shows the relationship between the Average and the Analyzed Industry. For example, 100 means that they are equal; 500 that the Analyzed Industry is five times the average; 50 means that the Analyzed Industry is half the national average. The abbreviation 'na' is used to show that data are 'not available'.

LEADING COMPANIES

Number shown: **50** Total sales ($ mil): **69,577** Total employment (000): **107.6**

Company Name	Address				CEO Name	Phone	Co. Type	Sales ($ mil)	Empl. (000)
Toyota Motor Sales U.S.A. Inc.	19001 S Western	Torrance	CA	90509	Shinji Sakai	310-618-4000	S	25,030 •	15.7
JM Family Enterprises Inc.	100 Northwest 12th	Deerfield Beach	FL	33442	Patricia Moran	954-429-2000	R	5,200	2.8
Cox Enterprises Inc.	PO Box 105357	Atlanta	GA	30348	James C Kennedy	404-843-5000	R	4,591 •	44.0
Southeast Toyota Distributors	100 NW 12th Ave	Deerfield Beach	FL	33442	Pat Moran	305-429-2000	S	4,500	0.8
American Honda Motor	1919 Torrance Blvd	Torrance	CA	90504	Koichi Amemiya	310-783-2000	S	3,970	2.5
Mitsubishi Motor Sales	6400 Katella Ave	Cypress	CA	90630	Takashi Sonobe	714-372-6000	S	3,691	2.0
BMW of North America Inc.	PO Box 1227	Westwood	NJ	07675	Victor Doolen	201-307-4000	S	2,690 •	1.0
Chevrolet Motor Div.	30007 Van Dyke	Warren	MI	48090	John G Middlebrook	810-492-5290	D	2,540	1.6
Volkswagen of America Inc.	3800 Hamlin Rd	Auburn Hills	MI	48326	Clive Warrillow	313-340-5000	S	1,930 •	1.2
Gulf States Toyota Inc.	PO Box 40306	Houston	TX	77040	Jerry Pyle	713-744-3300	R	1,740 •	1.1
Volvo Cars of North America	PO Box 913	Rockleigh	NJ	07647	Helge Alten	201-768-7300	S	1,740 •	0.6
ADT Ltd.	PO Box 5035	Boca Raton	FL	33431	Michael A Ashcroft	561-988-3600	P	1,704	16.0
Subaru of America Inc.	PO Box 6000	Cherry Hill	NJ	08034	George Muller	609-488-8500	S	1,500 •	0.7
Mazda Motor of America Inc.	PO Box 19734	Irvine	CA	92623	George Toyama	714-727-1990	S	1,230 •	0.8
Kawasaki Motors Corp USA	PO Box 25252	Santa Ana	CA	92799	M. Tsurutami	714-770-0400	S	830 •	0.4
Saab Cars USA Inc.	4405-A Int'l Blvd	Norcross	GA	30093	Joel Manby	770-279-0100	S	600	0.2
Mel Farr Automotive Group	24750 Greenfield	Oak Park	MI	48237	Mel Farr Sr	248-967-3700	R	535 •	0.9
Transnational Motors Inc.	PO Box 2008	Grand Rapids	MI	49501	Robert L Hooker	616-949-7570	R	500	0.1
ADT Automotive Inc.	435 Metroplex Dr	Nashville	TN	37211	M J Richardson	615-333-1400	S	433	6.0
Central Atlantic Toyota	6710 Baymeadow	Glen Burnie	MD	21060	Dennis Clemens	410-760-1500	D	410 •	0.3
Porsche Cars North America	PO Box 30911	Reno	NV	89520	Frederick J Schwab	702-348-3000	S	381 •	0.2
Subaru	PO Box 11293	Portland	OR	97211	Tim Parzybok	503-287-4171	D	280	<0.1
Minneapolis Northstar Auto	4908 Val Industl Bl	Shakopee	MN	55379	Kelly Conger	612-445-5544	S	270	0.2
Kia Motors America Inc.	PO Box 52410	Irvine	CA	92619	W K Kim	714-470-7000	S	240 •	0.2
Geo. Byers Sons Inc.	PO Box 16513	Columbus	OH	43216	George W Byers III	614-228-5111	R	237	0.5
Kansas City Auto Auction Inc.	3901 N Skiles	Kansas City	MO	64161	Jamie Porter	816-452-4084	R	230 •	0.2
Land Rover North America Inc.	PO Box 1503	L Seabrook	MD	20706	Charles R Hughes	301-731-6523	S	230 •	0.2
Arrow Truck Sales Inc.	3200 Manchester	Kansas City	MO	64129	Jerome Nerman	816-923-5000	R	200 •	0.2
W.D. Larson Companies Limited	8050 Hwy 101	Shakopee	MN	55379	William D Larson	612-445-1312	R	175	0.5
Dallas Auto Auction Inc.	5333 W Keist Blvd	Dallas	TX	75236	Barry Roop	214-330-1800	R	170 •	0.3
Houston Peterbilt Inc.	5219 I-45 N	Houston	TX	77022	Walter C Golden	713-691-4511	S	160	0.3
Dothan Auto Auction Inc.	3664 S Oates St	Dothan	AL	36301	M J Richardson	334-792-1115	S	150 •	0.1
Manning Equipment Inc.	PO Box 23229	Louisville	KY	40223	Michael Stich	502-426-5210	R	130 •	<0.1
Consumers Financial Corp.	PO Box 26	Camp Hill	PA	17001	James C Robertson	717-761-4230	P	115	<0.1
Oldsmobile Div.	920 Townsend St	Lansing	MI	48921	Darwin E Clark	517-377-5000	D	110 •	0.6
B/T Western Corp.	4 Upper Newportz	Newport Beach	CA	92660	Ronald W Barley	714-476-8424	R	100	<0.1
ADESA Corp.	1919 S Post Rd	Indianapolis	IN	46239	Michael Hockett	317-862-7220	S	94	3.0
Berge Ford Inc.	PO Box 4008	Mesa	AZ	85211	Craig Berge	602-497-1111	R	91 •	0.3
Peugeot Motors of America	1 Peugeot Plz	Lyndhurst	NJ	07071	Pascal Henault	201-935-8400	S	87	0.2
Engs Motor Truck Co.	1550 S McCarran	Sparks	NV	89431	Edward W Engs III	702-359-8840	R	85	0.3
Big Sky Auto Auction Inc.	1236 Cordova St	Billings	MT	59101	Howard H Bohl	406-259-5999	R	80	0.1
W.W. Wallwork Inc.	PO Box 1819	Fargo	ND	58107	W W Wallwork III	701-282-2350	R	80 •	0.2
ADESA Auctions	PO Box 130	Moody	AL	35004	Billy Noles	205-640-1010	S	73 •	0.2
Truck Equipment Inc.	680 Potts Ave	Green Bay	WI	54304	Isadore L Kwaterski	414-494-7451	R	71 •	<0.1
Texas Kenworth Co.	PO Box 560049	Dallas	TX	75356	VE Salvino	214-920-7300	R	70 •	0.3
Kenworth of Tennessee Inc.	Spence Ln & I-40 E	Nashville	TN	37210	Lester Turner Jr	615-366-5454	R	68	0.2
Joyserv Company Ltd.	1751 Talleyrand	Jacksonville	FL	32206	Gary Hall	904-354-5000	S	63 •	0.3
Darlings	153 Perry Rd	Bangor	ME	04401	JB Darling	207-941-1240	R	60	0.2
O'Connor Truck Sales Inc.	H & Hunting Pk Av	Philadelphia	PA	19124	Perry Mangioni	215-744-8500	R	60	<0.1
Sadisco of Florence	PO Box 6525	Florence	SC	29502	Charles H Powers	803-669-1941	R	54 •	0.1

Source: Ward's Business Directory of U.S. Private and Public Companies, 1998. The company type code used is as follows: P - Public, R - Private, S - Subsidiary, D - Division, J - Joint Venture, A - Affiliate, G - Group. Sales are in millions of dollars, employees are in thousands. An asterisk (*) indicates an estimated sales volume. The symbol < stands for 'less than'.

OCCUPATIONS EMPLOYED BY SIC 501 - MOTOR VEHICLES, PARTS, AND SUPPLIES

Occupation	% of Total 1996	Change to 2006	Occupation	% of Total 1996	Change to 2006
Sales & related workers nec	19.1	12.5	Salespersons, retail	2.2	2.3
Truck drivers light & heavy	9.3	53.4	Helpers, laborers nec	2.2	2.3
General managers & top executives	5.5	-0.9	Driver/sales workers	2.1	2.3
Stock clerks	4.7	2.3	Assemblers, fabricators, hand workers nec	2.0	2.3
General office clerks	4.0	-12.0	Blue collar worker supervisors	1.7	-1.3
Bus & truck mechanics	3.8	-8.0	Secretaries, except legal & medical	1.6	-18.9
Marketing & sales worker supervisors	3.4	2.3	Transportation equipment operators nec	1.4	2.3
Automotive mechanics	3.0	-8.0	Clerical supervisors & managers	1.4	2.3
Traffic, shipping, receiving clerks	3.0	2.3	Industrial truck & tractor operators	1.4	2.3
Order fillers, wholesale & retail sales	2.9	2.3	Order clerks	1.0	-7.9
Bookkeeping, accounting, & auditing clerks	2.7	-18.2	Purchasing managers	1.0	2.3
Freight, stock, & material movers, hand	2.3	-7.9			

Source: Industry-Occupation Matrix, Bureau of Labor Statistics. These data relate to one or more 3-digit SIC industry groups rather than to a single 4-digit SIC. The change reported for each occupation to the year 2006 is a percent of growth or decline as estimated by the Bureau of Labor Statistics. The abbreviation nec stands for 'not elsewhere classified'.

STATE AND REGIONAL CONCENTRATION

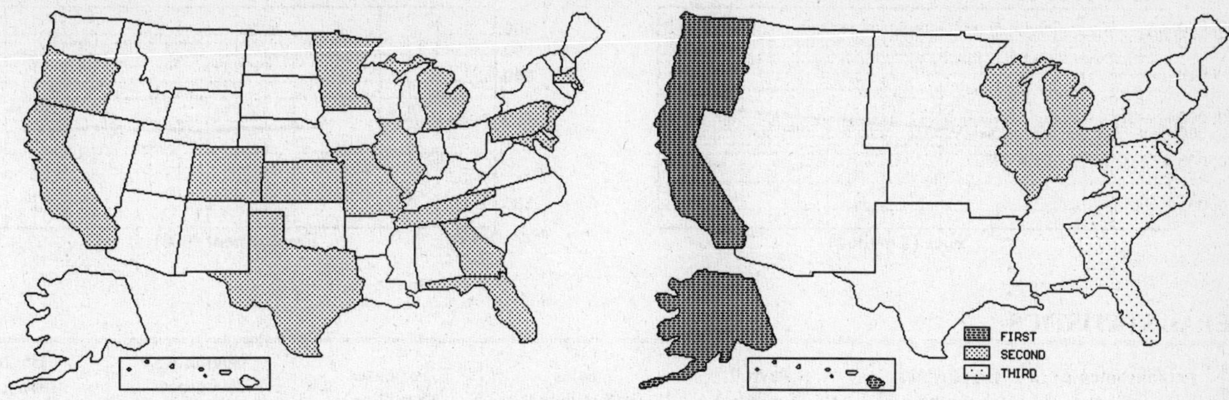

INDUSTRY DATA BY STATE

State	Establishments - 1995 Total (number)	Establishments - 1995 % of U.S.	Employment - 1995 Total (number)	Employment - 1995 % of U.S.	Employment - 1995 Per Estab.	Payroll - 1995 Total ($ mil.)	Payroll - 1995 Per Empl. ($)	Sales - 1992 Total ($ mil.)	Sales - 1992 % of U.S.	Sales - 1992 Per Estab ($)
California	719	8.9	17,109	11.4	24	719.7	42,065	56,786.4	20.4	3,487,465
Michigan	281	3.5	5,573	3.7	20	218.3	39,168	20,282.8	7.3	4,993,292
New Jersey	292	3.6	5,652	3.8	19	213.6	37,795	19,695.6	7.1	3,858,849
Texas	541	6.7	9,782	6.5	18	271.1	27,713	19,528.4	7.0	2,298,544
Illinois	269	3.3	6,729	4.5	25	240.9	35,798	18,423.2	6.6	3,146,038
Florida	635	7.8	9,139	6.1	14	230.4	25,207	16,856.8	6.0	2,166,124
Georgia	258	3.2	4,708	3.1	18	156.9	33,328	15,298.7	5.5	3,584,516
Pennsylvania	387	4.8	7,784	5.2	20	196.0	25,174	14,418.6	5.2	2,133,871
New York	412	5.1	5,577	3.7	14	147.3	26,410	10,832.0	3.9	2,087,886
Ohio	323	4.0	7,022	4.7	22	189.2	26,944	10,545.6	3.8	2,014,060
Maryland	121	1.5	2,410	1.6	20	89.5	37,126	8,415.3	3.0	3,182,810
Massachusetts	115	1.4	1,980	1.3	17	70.8	35,782	7,818.1	2.8	4,281,542
Missouri	231	2.8	5,093	3.4	22	148.0	29,064	7,070.0	2.5	1,458,028
Tennessee	200	2.5	3,963	2.6	20	124.5	31,406	6,433.0	2.3	2,016,611
Minnesota	156	1.9	3,296	2.2	21	105.6	32,041	5,474.6	2.0	2,175,919
Colorado	140	1.7	2,555	1.7	18	80.3	31,442	5,160.6	1.9	2,521,041
North Carolina	277	3.4	4,571	3.0	17	119.0	26,033	4,811.9	1.7	1,317,599
Virginia	190	2.3	3,214	2.1	17	86.7	26,972	4,151.2	1.5	1,495,398
Oregon	113	1.4	1,905	1.3	17	65.6	34,414	3,314.7	1.2	1,821,284
Kansas	101	1.2	1,622	1.1	16	48.7	30,017	3,211.4	1.2	2,320,384
Washington	166	2.0	2,407	1.6	15	72.0	29,901	3,002.9	1.1	1,389,584
Wisconsin	173	2.1	4,499	3.0	26	123.0	27,331	2,509.3	0.9	674,714
Indiana	238	2.9	5,440	3.6	23	138.3	25,425	2,237.6	0.8	471,674
Alabama	194	2.4	2,677	1.8	14	72.4	27,033	1,286.8	0.5	604,706
Connecticut	84	1.0	1,109	0.7	13	42.7	38,523	1,054.7	0.4	1,162,850
Louisiana	96	1.2	1,284	0.9	13	30.1	23,426	999.1	0.4	1,084,780
South Carolina	155	1.9	1,780	1.2	11	40.2	22,610	957.4	0.3	660,749
Oklahoma	108	1.3	2,106	1.4	20	47.7	22,633	927.5	0.3	627,536
Iowa	111	1.4	2,329	1.5	21	69.9	30,031	835.4	0.3	448,642
Kentucky	127	1.6	2,098	1.4	17	50.9	24,252	822.2	0.3	450,769
Nebraska	73	0.9	1,606	1.1	22	44.6	27,740	818.1	0.3	558,397
Arizona	116	1.4	2,114	1.4	18	48.5	22,954	770.6	0.3	503,021
Mississippi	94	1.2	1,419	0.9	15	36.9	25,985	682.6	0.2	587,460
Arkansas	111	1.4	1,497	1.0	13	40.0	26,699	636.6	0.2	485,954
Utah	48	0.6	1,508	1.0	31	44.2	29,330	561.4	0.2	452,369
New Mexico	39	0.5	524	0.3	13	14.0	26,655	333.2	0.1	697,006
Montana	40	0.5	716	0.5	18	15.9	22,261	281.7	0.1	336,591
West Virginia	41	0.5	837	0.6	20	18.8	22,405	221.2	0.1	304,279
Idaho	43	0.5	666	0.4	15	15.9	23,892	200.8	0.1	263,488
Nevada	34	0.4	573	0.4	17	20.3	35,356	182.2	0.1	442,318
North Dakota	38	0.5	709	0.5	19	16.3	22,962	165.1	0.1	277,548
New Hampshire	39	0.5	531	0.4	14	17.2	32,478	160.9	0.1	327,792
Hawaii	16	0.2	115	0.1	7	4.3	37,652	155.3	0.1	947,146
Maine	52	0.6	672	0.4	13	16.1	23,946	139.4	0.1	275,484
Delaware	21	0.3	298	0.2	14	8.2	27,594	99.8	0.0	316,756
South Dakota	28	0.3	537	0.4	19	12.6	23,371	90.3	0.0	222,426
Vermont	24	0.3	301	0.2	13	8.1	26,824	66.8	0.0	285,517
Wyoming	12	0.1	167	0.1	14	3.5	21,228	31.6	0.0	229,123
Alaska	6	0.1	82	0.1	14	2.8	34,537	29.4	0.0	279,771
Rhode Island	30	0.4	229	0.2	8	6.5	28,406	(D)	-	-
D.C.	5	0.1	40	0.0	8	1.8	44,525	(D)	-	-

Source: *County Business Patterns, 1995* and *Economic Census of the U.S., 1992*. Data are sorted by 1992 revenues and, if revenues are unavailable, by establishments in 1995. The symbol (D) indicates that data are withheld by the source to avoid disclosure of competitive information. A dash (-) indicates that data are not available or undisclosed because they do not meet statistical validity standards. Shaded *states* on the state map indicate those states which have proportionately greater representation in the industry than would be indicated by the state's population; the ratio is based on total revenues or number of establishments. Shaded *regions* indicate where the industry is regionally most concentrated.

5013 - MOTOR VEHICLE SUPPLIES AND NEW PARTS

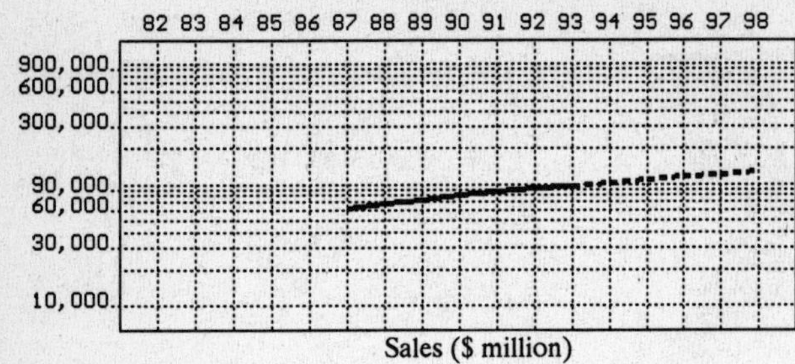

Sales ($ million)

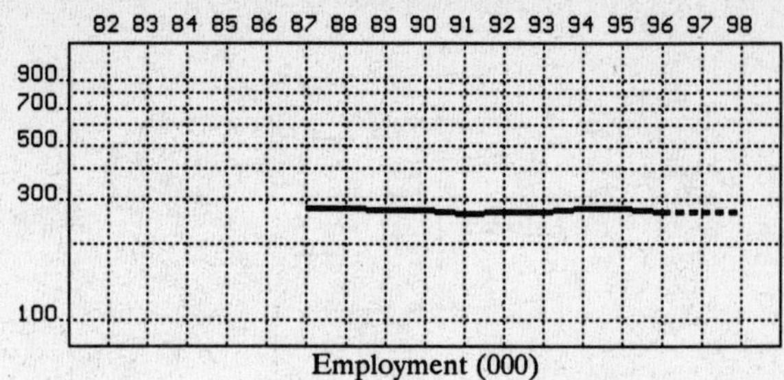

Employment (000)

GENERAL STATISTICS

Year	Establishments (number)	Employment (number)	Payroll ($ million)	Sales ($ million)	Expenses ($ million)	Beginning Inventory ($ million)	Ending Inventory ($ million)
1982	-	-	-	-	-	-	-
1983	-	-	-	-	-	-	-
1984	-	-	-	-	-	-	-
1985	-	-	-	-	-	-	-
1986	-	-	-	-	-	-	-
1987	28,902	279,562	5,478.0	62,455.8	10,628.7	8,547.1	8,970.6
1988	27,206	274,840	5,900.8	68,240.3e	11,107.0e	9,012.6e	9,355.8e
1989	26,345	274,041	6,113.8	74,024.9e	11,585.4e	9,478.2e	9,741.0e
1990	25,674	272,029	6,343.8	79,809.4e	12,063.8e	9,943.7e	10,126.2e
1991	25,158	262,213	6,259.8	85,594.0e	12,542.1e	10,409.2e	10,511.4e
1992	28,002	271,270	6,545.5	91,378.5	13,020.5	10,874.7	10,896.6
1993	27,123	268,217	6,845.5	97,163.1p	13,498.9p	11,340.3p	11,281.8p
1994	27,140	274,902	7,126.8	102,947.6p	13,977.3p	11,805.8p	11,667.0p
1995	24,649	274,818	7,437.9	108,732.2p	14,455.6p	12,271.3p	12,052.2p
1996	25,578p	269,833p	7,548.8p	114,516.7p	14,934.0p	12,736.9p	12,437.4p
1997	25,356p	269,313p	7,768.5p	120,301.3p	15,412.4p	13,202.4p	12,822.6p
1998	25,134p	268,793p	7,988.2p	126,085.8p	15,890.7p	13,667.9p	13,207.8p

Sources: *Economic Census of the United States*, 1982, 1987, and 1992. Establishment counts, employment, and payroll are from *County Business Patterns* for non-Census years. Values followed by a 'p' are projections by the editors. Sales and expense data for non-Census years are extrapolations, marked by 'e'. Industries reclassified in 1987 will not have data for prior years. Data are the most recent available at this level of detail.

INDICES OF CHANGE

Year	Establishments (number)	Employment (number)	Payroll ($ million)	Sales ($ million)	Expenses ($ million)	Beginning Inventory ($ million)	Ending Inventory ($ million)
1982	-	-	-	-	-	-	-
1983	-	-	-	-	-	-	-
1984	-	-	-	-	-	-	-
1985	-	-	-	-	-	-	-
1986	-	-	-	-	-	-	-
1987	103.2	103.1	83.7	68.3	81.6	78.6	82.3
1988	97.2	101.3	90.2	74.7e	85.3e	82.9e	85.9e
1989	94.1	101.0	93.4	81.0e	89.0e	87.2e	89.4e
1990	91.7	100.3	96.9	87.3e	92.7e	91.4e	92.9e
1991	89.8	96.7	95.6	93.7e	96.3e	95.7e	96.5e
1992	100.0	100.0	100.0	100.0	100.0	100.0	100.0
1993	96.9	98.9	104.6	106.3p	103.7p	104.3p	103.5p
1994	96.9	101.3	108.9	112.7p	107.3p	108.6p	107.1p
1995	88.0	101.3	113.6	119.0p	111.0p	112.8p	110.6p
1996	91.3p	99.5p	115.3p	125.3p	114.7p	117.1p	114.1p
1997	90.6p	99.3p	118.7p	131.7p	118.4p	121.4p	117.7p
1998	89.8p	99.1p	122.0p	138.0p	122.0p	125.7p	121.2p

Sources: Same as General Statistics. The values shown reflect change from the base year, 1992. Values above 100 mean greater than 1992, values below 100 mean less than 1992, and a value of 100 in the 1982-91 or 1993-98 period means same as 1992. Values followed by a 'p' are projections by the editors; 'e' stands for extrapolation. Data are the most recent available at this level of detail.

SELECTED RATIOS

For 1992	Avg. of All Wholesale	Analyzed Industry	Index	For 1992	Avg. of All Wholesale	Analyzed Industry	Index
Employees per Establishment	12	10	83	Sales per Employee	561,172	336,854	60
Payroll per Establishment	349,729	233,751	67	Sales per Establishment	6,559,346	3,263,285	50
Payroll per Employee	29,919	24,129	81	Expenses per Establishment	723,071	464,985	64

Sources: Same as General Statistics. The 'Average of All Manufacturing' column represents the average of all manufacturing industries reported for the most recent complete year available. The Index shows the relationship between the Average and the Analyzed Industry. For example, 100 means that they are equal; 500 that the Analyzed Industry is five times the average; 50 means that the Analyzed Industry is half the national average. The abbreviation 'na' is used to show that data are 'not available'.

LEADING COMPANIES

Number shown: **50** Total sales ($ mil): **74,007** Total employment (000): **377.7**

Company Name	Address				CEO Name	Phone	Co. Type	Sales ($ mil)	Empl. (000)
Delphi Automotive Systems	5725 Delphi Dr	Troy	MI	48098	JT Battenberg	248-813-2500	D	28,400	216.0
Genuine Parts Co.	2999 Circle 75 Pkwy	Atlanta	GA	30339	Larry L Prince	770-953-1700	P	6,005	24.5
GM Service Parts Operations	6060 W Bristol Rd	Flint	MI	48554	WJ Lovejoy	313-635-5412	D	5,000	15.0
Southeast Toyota Distributors	100 NW 12th Ave	Deerfield Bch	FL	33442	Pat Moran	305-429-2000	S	4,500	0.8
Johnson Controls	PO Box 8010	Plymouth	MI	48170	John Barth	313-454-5000	D	3,800	23.0
Hitachi America Ltd.	50 Prospect Ave	Tarrytown	NY	10591	T Shimayama	914-332-5800	S	3,500	6.0
AC-Delco/GM Service Parts	PO Box 6020	Grand Blanc	MI	48439	WJ Lovejoy	810-606-2000	D	3,160	13.0
Mannesmann Capital Corp.	450 Park Ave	New York	NY	10022	Peter P Wittgenstein	212-826-0040	S	3,000	9.0
Siemens Automotive Corp.	2400 Exec Hills	Auburn Hills	MI	48326	George R Perry	248-253-1000	S	2,700	15.6
Gulf States Toyota Inc.	PO Box 40306	Houston	TX	77040	Jerry Pyle	713-744-3300	R	1,740 *	1.1
CARQUEST Corp.	12596 W Bayaud	Lakewood	CO	80228	Peter Kornafel	303-984-2000	R	1,614 *	14.0
Lacy Diversified Industries	54 Monument Cir	Indianapolis	IN	46204	Andre Lacy	317-237-2251	R	866 *	3.0
General Parts Inc.	PO Box 26006	Raleigh	NC	27611	N Joe Owen	919-573-3000	R	850 *	3.5
TBC Corp.	PO Box 18342	Memphis	TN	38181	Louis S DiPasqua	901-363-8030	P	643	0.6
A.P.S. Inc.	15710 J F Kennedy	Houston	TX	77032	Mark S Hoffman	713-507-1100	S	604	6.8
Aisin World Corporation	24330 Garnier St	Torrance	CA	90505	Tetsuro Senga	310-326-8681	S	590	1.1
Fisher Auto Parts Inc.	512 Greenville Ave	Staunton	VA	24401	Art Fisher	703-885-8905	R	550 *	1.1
Transnational Motors Inc.	PO Box 2008	Grand Rapids	MI	49501	Robert L Hooker	616-949-7570	R	500	0.1
PACCAR Inc. Parts Div.	750 Houser Way N	Renton	WA	98055	Bob Christensen	425-251-7400	D	420 *	0.7
ZF Industries Inc.	7310 Turfway Rd	Florence	KY	41042	Jim Orchard	606-282-4300	S	420	1.5
U.S. Oil Company Inc.	425 S Washington	Comb. Locks	WI	54113	Tom Schmidt	414-739-6101	R	400	1.0
Myers Industries Inc.	1293 S Main St	Akron	OH	44301	Stephen E Myers	330-253-5592	P	340	1.9
ASEC Manufacturing	PO Box 580970	Tulsa	OK	74158	Edwin L Yoder	918-266-1400	J	250	0.5
Dana World Trade Div.	PO Box 405	Toledo	OH	43697	Karl Nitsch	419-867-2105	D	250	0.1
Ezon Inc.	1900 Exeter Rd	Germantown	TN	38138	Barry Gomez	901-755-5555	R	250	0.5
ZEXEL USA Corp.	625 Southside Dr	Decatur	IL	62521	A Tanaka	217-362-2300	S	235	1.1
Bowman Distribution	PO Box 6908	Cleveland	OH	44101	Leonard M Carlucci	216-416-7200	D	213	1.2
Banks Lumber Company Inc.	PO Box 2299	Elkhart	IN	46515	William Banks	219-294-5671	R	200	1.0
Itco Tire Co.	PO Box 641	Wilson	NC	27893	A Burwell Jr	919-291-8900	R	200 *	0.5
Keystone Automotive Industries	700 E Bonita Ave	Pomona	CA	91767	Charles Hogarty	909-624-8041	P	194	1.5
Ed Tucker Distributor Inc.	1775 Hurd Dr	Irving	TX	75038	Robert Gregg	214-580-0555	S	190	0.4
Piasa Motor Fuels Inc.	PO Box 484	Alton	IL	62002	R William Schrimpf	618-254-7341	R	165	0.1
Automotive Diagnostics	8001 Angling Rd	Kalamazoo	MI	49002	Ron Ortiz	616-329-7600	S	160	1.6
Republic Automotive Parts Inc.	PO Box 2088	Brentwood	TN	37024	Keith M Thompson	615-373-2050	P	155	1.3
Beck-Arnley Worldparts Corp.	PO Box 110910	Nashville	TN	37222	Ira Davis	615-834-8080	S	150	0.6
Pam Oil Inc.	PO Box 5200	Sioux Falls	SD	57117	William G Pederson	605-336-1788	R	150	0.4
Hahn Automotive Warehouse	415 W Main St	Rochester	NY	14608	Michael Futerman	716-235-1595	P	142	1.1
Big O Tires Inc.	11755 E Peakview	Englewood	CO	80111	Steven P Cloward	303-790-2800	P	142	0.2
Coast Distribution System	1982 Zanker Rd	San Jose	CA	95112	Thomas R McGuire	408-436-8611	P	139	0.4
CCI Corp.	PO Box 582800	Tulsa	OK	74158	JM Klein	918-836-0151	R	130 *	0.6
Manning Equipment Inc.	PO Box 23229	Louisville	KY	40223	Michael Stich	502-426-5210	R	130 *	<0.1
Kraco Enterprises Inc.	505 E Euclid Ave	Compton	CA	90224	Lawrence M Kraines	213-774-2550	R	120 *	0.5
Universal Coach Parts Inc.	105 E Oakton St	Des Plaines	IL	60018	John Brignon	847-803-8900	S	120 *	0.3
Strafco Inc.	PO Box 600	San Antonio	TX	78292	Jack D Trawick	210-226-0101	R	113	1.1
Fiat Auto U.S.A. Inc.	250 Sylvan Ave	Englewood Clfs	NJ	07632	Gian L Buitoni	201-816-2600	S	110 *	<0.1
Auto Parts Club Inc.	5825 Oberlin Dr	San Diego	CA	92121	Steve Kirby	619-622-5050	R	100	0.7
Champion Auto Stores Inc.	9353 Jefferson Hwy	Maple Grove	MN	55369	Gary D Bebeau	612-391-6655	R	100	0.9
Cummins Southern Plains Inc.	600 Watson Dr	Arlington	TX	76004	RD Gillikin	817-640-6801	R	100	0.5
Stant Manufacturing Inc.	1620 Columbia Ave	Connersville	IN	47331	Lou Braga	765-825-3121	S	100 *	0.8
Automotive Supply Associates	129 Manchester	Concord	NH	03301	George Segal	603-225-4000	R	97 *	0.4

Source: Ward's Business Directory of U.S. Private and Public Companies, 1998. The company type code used is as follows: P - Public, R - Private, S - Subsidiary, D - Division, J - Joint Venture, A - Affiliate, G - Group. Sales are in millions of dollars, employees are in thousands. An asterisk (*) indicates an estimated sales volume. The symbol < stands for 'less than'.

OCCUPATIONS EMPLOYED BY SIC 501 - MOTOR VEHICLES, PARTS, AND SUPPLIES

Occupation	% of Total 1996	Change to 2006	Occupation	% of Total 1996	Change to 2006
Sales & related workers nec	19.1	12.5	Salespersons, retail	2.2	2.3
Truck drivers light & heavy	9.3	53.4	Helpers, laborers nec	2.2	2.3
General managers & top executives	5.5	-0.9	Driver/sales workers	2.1	2.3
Stock clerks	4.7	2.3	Assemblers, fabricators, hand workers nec	2.0	2.3
General office clerks	4.0	-12.0	Blue collar worker supervisors	1.7	-1.3
Bus & truck mechanics	3.8	-8.0	Secretaries, except legal & medical	1.6	-18.9
Marketing & sales worker supervisors	3.4	2.3	Transportation equipment operators nec	1.4	2.3
Automotive mechanics	3.0	-8.0	Clerical supervisors & managers	1.4	2.3
Traffic, shipping, receiving clerks	3.0	2.3	Industrial truck & tractor operators	1.4	2.3
Order fillers, wholesale & retail sales	2.9	2.3	Order clerks	1.0	-7.9
Bookkeeping, accounting, & auditing clerks	2.7	-18.2	Purchasing managers	1.0	2.3
Freight, stock, & material movers, hand	2.3	-7.9			

Source: Industry-Occupation Matrix, Bureau of Labor Statistics. These data relate to one or more 3-digit SIC industry groups rather than to a single 4-digit SIC. The change reported for each occupation to the year 2006 is a percent of growth or decline as estimated by the Bureau of Labor Statistics. The abbreviation nec stands for 'not elsewhere classified'.

STATE AND REGIONAL CONCENTRATION

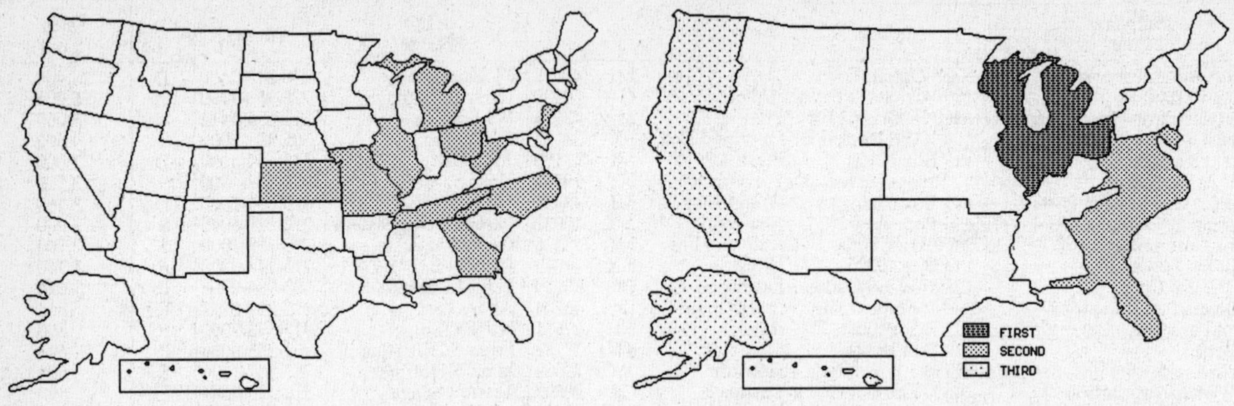

INDUSTRY DATA BY STATE

State	Establishments - 1995 Total (number)	Establishments - 1995 % of U.S.	Employment - 1995 Total (number)	Employment - 1995 % of U.S.	Employment - 1995 Per Estab.	Payroll - 1995 Total ($ mil.)	Payroll - 1995 Per Empl. ($)	Sales - 1992 Total ($ mil.)	Sales - 1992 % of U.S.	Sales - 1992 Per Estab ($)
Michigan	1,188	4.8	21,160	7.7	18	889.8	42,050	23,274.9	25.5	1,216,416
California	2,446	9.9	29,595	10.8	12	815.3	27,547	9,514.5	10.4	323,634
Texas	1,480	6.0	18,147	6.6	12	523.2	28,830	5,374.7	5.9	319,848
Ohio	1,073	4.4	13,539	4.9	13	375.4	27,726	4,644.7	5.1	314,168
Illinois	1,022	4.1	13,281	4.8	13	416.4	31,350	4,619.2	5.1	348,648
Georgia	770	3.1	8,235	3.0	11	246.4	29,919	3,885.8	4.3	465,867
New York	1,474	6.0	13,604	5.0	9	340.0	24,994	3,518.5	3.9	243,410
Florida	1,438	5.8	14,033	5.1	10	340.0	24,227	3,299.9	3.6	242,962
New Jersey	748	3.0	9,512	3.5	13	283.5	29,807	2,879.1	3.2	332,765
North Carolina	689	2.8	6,158	2.2	9	149.7	24,302	2,568.5	2.8	407,827
Tennessee	553	2.2	7,608	2.8	14	199.4	26,209	2,566.9	2.8	335,854
Pennsylvania	1,152	4.7	12,485	4.5	11	286.8	22,970	2,452.9	2.7	210,691
Missouri	692	2.8	7,911	2.9	11	206.9	26,148	2,134.7	2.3	323,684
Massachusetts	598	2.4	6,718	2.4	11	172.2	25,637	1,582.5	1.7	253,120
Minnesota	514	2.1	5,231	1.9	10	138.7	26,519	1,384.4	1.5	265,507
Indiana	627	2.5	6,638	2.4	11	156.2	23,532	1,360.7	1.5	191,323
Wisconsin	523	2.1	5,609	2.0	11	132.9	23,698	1,326.9	1.5	252,793
Washington	423	1.7	4,641	1.7	11	131.4	28,303	1,123.8	1.2	229,482
Virginia	652	2.6	5,725	2.1	9	125.4	21,906	1,103.9	1.2	189,805
Kansas	305	1.2	3,158	1.1	10	82.3	26,072	935.6	1.0	331,776
Colorado	328	1.3	3,518	1.3	11	86.7	24,646	919.8	1.0	240,901
Oregon	316	1.3	3,974	1.4	13	104.4	26,264	869.5	1.0	213,795
Maryland	417	1.7	4,360	1.6	10	106.6	24,450	827.5	0.9	190,545
Kentucky	356	1.4	4,182	1.5	12	91.6	21,914	789.3	0.9	202,595
West Virginia	192	0.8	1,472	0.5	8	34.7	23,552	694.7	0.8	390,949
Alabama	363	1.5	3,754	1.4	10	85.7	22,816	677.0	0.7	192,449
South Carolina	293	1.2	2,449	0.9	8	51.1	20,870	664.3	0.7	245,580
Connecticut	303	1.2	3,184	1.2	11	79.3	24,901	563.1	0.6	169,550
Louisiana	368	1.5	3,339	1.2	9	78.4	23,488	555.9	0.6	156,318
Arizona	341	1.4	3,622	1.3	11	78.4	21,638	499.9	0.5	153,329
Iowa	371	1.5	3,017	1.1	8	62.3	20,658	470.5	0.5	148,293
Oklahoma	323	1.3	2,917	1.1	9	60.8	20,827	438.5	0.5	166,811
Mississippi	229	0.9	2,043	0.7	9	43.3	21,196	385.3	0.4	175,681
Nevada	113	0.5	1,239	0.5	11	32.8	26,454	371.5	0.4	262,013
Nebraska	225	0.9	2,073	0.8	9	45.6	21,994	355.9	0.4	151,241
Utah	170	0.7	2,159	0.8	13	52.1	24,120	351.9	0.4	165,933
Arkansas	283	1.1	2,256	0.8	8	46.0	20,386	345.8	0.4	144,375
New Hampshire	159	0.6	1,590	0.6	10	37.0	23,242	248.8	0.3	177,473
Delaware	71	0.3	694	0.3	10	19.4	27,971	246.3	0.3	366,012
Maine	138	0.6	1,284	0.5	9	29.6	23,051	184.1	0.2	151,870
Montana	88	0.4	825	0.3	9	17.5	21,185	179.7	0.2	149,263
New Mexico	109	0.4	1,089	0.4	10	23.1	21,186	164.0	0.2	141,282
Hawaii	73	0.3	1,065	0.4	15	25.2	23,700	162.8	0.2	150,719
Idaho	146	0.6	1,183	0.4	8	23.3	19,697	150.1	0.2	120,965
Alaska	51	0.2	564	0.2	11	18.9	33,427	134.6	0.1	203,634
South Dakota	85	0.3	893	0.3	11	20.1	22,512	128.0	0.1	139,274
Rhode Island	86	0.3	824	0.3	10	20.7	25,163	127.9	0.1	144,540
North Dakota	114	0.5	1,009	0.4	9	23.1	22,936	126.7	0.1	119,170
Vermont	111	0.5	781	0.3	7	16.8	21,549	99.7	0.1	149,099
Wyoming	46	0.2	352	0.1	8	8.6	24,574	70.8	0.1	144,506
D.C.	14	0.1	119	0.0	9	3.1	26,210	22.4	0.0	174,015

Source: County Business Patterns, 1995 and *Economic Census of the U.S., 1992.* Data are sorted by 1992 revenues and, if revenues are unavailable, by establishments in 1995. The symbol (D) indicates that data are withheld by the source to avoid disclosure of competitive information. A dash (-) indicates that data are not available or undisclosed because they do not meet statistical validity standards. Shaded *states* on the state map indicate those states which have proportionately greater representation in the industry than would be indicated by the state's population; the ratio is based on total revenues or number of establishments. Shaded *regions* indicate where the industry is regionally most concentrated.

5014 - TIRES AND TUBES

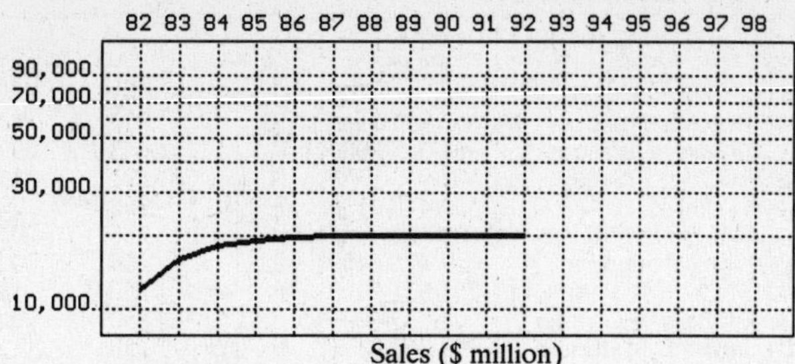

Sales ($ million)

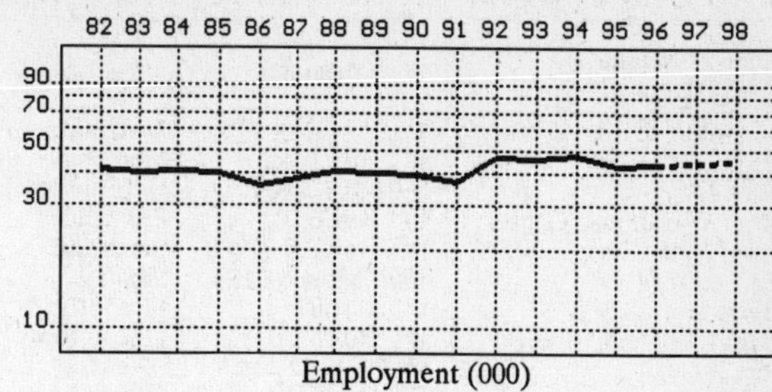

Employment (000)

GENERAL STATISTICS

Year	Establishments (number)	Employment (number)	Payroll ($ million)	Sales ($ million)	Expenses ($ million)	Beginning Inventory ($ million)	Ending Inventory ($ million)
1982	3,695	41,200	780.6	11,964.2	-	-	-
1983	3,655	40,436	817.7	-	-	-	-
1984	3,525	40,745	842.7	-	-	-	-
1985	3,434	39,938	854.0	-	-	-	-
1986	3,307	36,352	795.3	-	-	-	-
1987	3,746	(D)	(D)	(D)	(D)	(D)	-
1988	3,532	40,732	1,001.0	-	-	-	-
1989	3,417	40,504	1,012.2	-	-	-	-
1990	3,365	39,815	1,044.3	-	-	-	-
1991	3,297	37,339	966.3	-	-	-	-
1992	4,146	46,341	1,260.2	20,093.6	2,509.9	2,015.7	2,076.2
1993	3,943	45,539	1,267.7	-	-	-	-
1994	3,930	47,053	1,373.5	-	-	-	-
1995	3,434	42,743	1,267.0	-	-	-	-
1996	3,718*p*	43,506*p*	1,327.4*p*	-	-	-	-
1997	3,734*p*	44,177*p*	1,378.9*p*	-	-	-	-
1998	3,749*p*	44,848*p*	1,430.3*p*	-	-	-	-

Sources: *Economic Census of the United States*, 1982, 1987, and 1992. Establishment counts, employment, and payroll are from *County Business Patterns* for non-Census years. Values followed by a 'p' are projections by the editors. Sales and expense data for non-Census years are extrapolations, marked by 'e'. Industries reclassified in 1987 will not have data for prior years. Data are the most recent available at this level of detail.

INDICES OF CHANGE

Year	Establishments (number)	Employment (number)	Payroll ($ million)	Sales ($ million)	Expenses ($ million)	Beginning Inventory ($ million)	Ending Inventory ($ million)
1982	89.1	88.9	61.9	59.5	-	-	-
1983	88.2	87.3	64.9	-	-	-	-
1984	85.0	87.9	66.9	-	-	-	-
1985	82.8	86.2	67.8	-	-	-	-
1986	79.8	78.4	63.1	-	-	-	-
1987	90.4	(D)	(D)	(D)	(D)	(D)	-
1988	85.2	87.9	79.4	-	-	-	-
1989	82.4	87.4	80.3	-	-	-	-
1990	81.2	85.9	82.9	-	-	-	-
1991	79.5	80.6	76.7	-	-	-	-
1992	100.0	100.0	100.0	100.0	100.0	100.0	100.0
1993	95.1	98.3	100.6	-	-	-	-
1994	94.8	101.5	109.0	-	-	-	-
1995	82.8	92.2	100.5	-	-	-	-
1996	89.7*p*	93.9*p*	105.3*p*	-	-	-	-
1997	90.1*p*	95.3*p*	109.4*p*	-	-	-	-
1998	90.4*p*	96.8*p*	113.5*p*	-	-	-	-

Sources: Same as General Statistics. The values shown reflect change from the base year, 1992. Values above 100 mean greater than 1992, values below 100 mean less than 1992, and a value of 100 in the 1982-91 or 1993-98 period means same as 1992. Values followed by a 'p' are projections by the editors; 'e' stands for extrapolation. Data are the most recent available at this level of detail.

SELECTED RATIOS

For 1992	Avg. of All Wholesale	Analyzed Industry	Index	For 1992	Avg. of All Wholesale	Analyzed Industry	Index
Employees per Establishment	12	11	96	Sales per Employee	561,172	433,603	77
Payroll per Establishment	349,729	303,956	87	Sales per Establishment	6,559,346	4,846,503	74
Payroll per Employee	29,919	27,194	91	Expenses per Establishment	723,071	605,379	84

Sources: Same as General Statistics. The 'Average of All Manufacturing' column represents the average of all manufacturing industries reported for the most recent complete year available. The Index shows the relationship between the Average and the Analyzed Industry. For example, 100 means that they are equal; 500 that the Analyzed Industry is five times the average; 50 means that the Analyzed Industry is half the national average. The abbreviation 'na' is used to show that data are 'not available'.

LEADING COMPANIES

Number shown: **50** Total sales ($ mil): **5,653** Total employment (000): **21.2**

Company Name	Address				CEO Name	Phone	Co. Type	Sales ($ mil)	Empl. (000)
Reinalt-Thomas Corp.	14631 N Scottsdale	Scottsdale	AZ	85254	Bruce T Halle	602-951-1938	R	810 *	5.0
TBC Corp.	PO Box 18342	Memphis	TN	38181	Louis S DiPasqua	901-363-8030	P	643	0.6
SF Services Inc.	3001 JFK Blvd	N. Little Rock	AR	72116	Michael P Sadler	501-945-2371	R	591	1.3
Les Schwab Warehouse Center	PO Box 667	Prineville	OR	97754	G Phil Wick	503-447-4136	R	352	2.2
Dunlap and Kyle Company Inc.	PO Box 720	Batesville	MS	38606	Robert H Dunlap	601-563-7601	R	280	0.7
Hercules/CEDCO	1300 Morrical Blvd	Findlay	OH	45840	Craig Anderson	419-425-6400	S	265	0.3
Brad Ragan Inc.	PO 240587	Charlotte	NC	28224	Michael R Thomann	704-521-2100	P	252	1.8
J.H. Heafner Company Inc.	PO Box 837	Lincolnton	NC	28092	William H Gaither	704-735-3003	R	250 *	0.5
Merchants Inc.	9073 Euclid Ave	Manassas	VA	20110	James L Matthews	703-368-3171	R	250	1.8
Itco Tire Co.	PO Box 641	Wilson	NC	27893	A Burwell Jr	919-291-8900	R	200 *	0.5
Ganin Tire Company Inc.	1421 38th St	Brooklyn	NY	11218	Saul Ganin	718-633-0600	R	150	0.2
Big O Tires Inc.	11755 E Peakview	Englewood	CO	80111	Steven P Cloward	303-790-2800	P	142	0.2
Reliable Tire Distributors Inc.	PO Box 560	Camden	NJ	08101	Richard Betz	609-365-6500	R	93	0.1
Friend Tire Co.	11 Industrial Dr	Monett	MO	65708	Donald L Isbell	417-235-7836	S	89	0.2
Kumho U.S.A. Inc.	14605 Miller Ave	Fontana	CA	92336	Jong G Kahng	909-428-3999	R	83	<0.1
T.O. Haas Tire Company Inc.	PO Box 81067	Lincoln	NE	68501	Randall Haas	402-473-1415	S	80	0.3
Bauer Built Inc.	Hwy 25 S, Box 248	Durand	WI	54736	Jerry M Bauer	715-672-4295	R	79	0.4
LeMans Corp.	PO Box 5222	Janesville	WI	53547	Fred Fox	608-758-1111	R	79 *	0.3
Dean Tire and Rubber Co.	2103 Production Dr	Louisville	KY	40299	RJ Burns Sr	502-491-1450	R	70	<0.1
Allied Oil and Supply Inc.	PO Box 3687	Omaha	NE	68103	RC Heinson	402-344-4343	R	60	0.2
Target Tire and Automotive	2221 Lejeune Blvd	Jacksonville	NC	28540	LB Stein	919-353-4300	R	60	0.2
Bridgestone/Firestone Tire	1 Bridgestone Park	Nashville	TN	37214	John Lampe	615-391-0088	D	58	0.6
El Dorado Tire Co.	1120 E Long Lake	Troy	MI	48098	HR Calamari	313-528-3020	R	49	<0.1
Jetzon Tire and Rubber	1050 Bethelem Pike	Montgomeryv	PA	18936	Marc Hoffman	215-643-2300	R	42	<0.1
Johnson Cooperative Grain Co.	PO Box 280	Johnson	KS	67855	Thomas P Ryan	316-492-6210	R	36 *	<0.1
Capital Tire Inc.	1001 Cherry St	Toledo	OH	43608	Thomas B Geiger Sr	419-241-5111	R	35 *	0.1
Don Olson Tire and Auto	2021 Sunnydale	Clearwater	FL	34625	Larry Morgan	813-441-3727	R	35	0.9
Howard Tire Service Inc.	120 El Camino Real	Belmont	CA	94002	Alfred Howard	415-592-3200	R	34 *	<0.1
Tires, Wheels, Etc. Wholesale	3910 Cherry Ave	Long Beach	CA	90807	Hank Feldman	310-981-2686	R	32	<0.1
California Tire Co.	38503 Cherry St	Newark	CA	94560	Michael C Largent	510-487-5777	S	30	<0.1
Donald B. Rice Tire Co.	909 East St	Frederick	MD	21701	K Rice	301-662-0166	R	30 *	0.1
Jack Williams Tire Co.	PO Box 3655	Scranton	PA	18505	William C Williams	717-457-5000	R	29	0.2
H.C. Lewis Oil Co.	PO Box 649	Welch	WV	24801	HC Lewis Jr	304-436-2148	R	28	<0.1
Tire Service Company Inc.	500 S Gravers Rd	Plym. Meeting	PA	19462	RD Avellino	215-825-0404	R	26	0.3
Redburn Tire	3801 W Clarendon	Phoenix	AZ	85019	A Wigg	602-272-7601	R	25	0.1
Jim Paris Tire City of Montbello	1800 Bassett St	Denver	CO	80202	James T Paris	303-297-3600	R	23	0.1
H.C. Gabler Inc.	PO Box 220	Chambersburg	PA	17201	Harold C Gabler Jr	717-264-4184	R	22 *	0.3
Deas Tire Co.	2314 25th Ave	Gulfport	MS	39501	Louise Deas	601-863-5072	R	21 *	<0.1
Southern Nevada T.B.A. Supply	1701 Las Vegas S	Las Vegas	NV	89104	Ted Wiens Jr	702-732-2382	R	20	0.2
Berry Tire Company Inc.	9229 W Grand	Franklin Park	IL	60131	RL Berry	708-451-2200	R	20	0.1
Johnny Antonelli Tire Company	156 Ames St	Rochester	NY	14611	Joseph A DePaolis	716-235-8600	R	20	0.2
S and M Co.	2101 Kennedy NE	Minneapolis	MN	55413	John P Sieff	612-331-6680	S	19	0.1
Superior Tire Inc.	2320 Western Ave	Las Vegas	NV	89102	Marlo D Reimer	702-384-2937	R	19 *	0.1
Prior Tire Enterprises Inc.	PO Box 54264	Atlanta	GA	30379	Robert H Goldstein	404-522-8866	R	19	0.1
Farmers Cooperative Co.	PO Box 505	Glidden	IA	51443	Joe Daniels	712-659-2227	R	19	<0.1
Apollo Tire Company Inc.	21339 Saticoy	Canoga Park	CA	91304	S Bostanian	818-348-6142	R	18 *	0.1
Gay Johnson's Inc.	PO Box 1829	Grand Junction	CO	81502	Bert Johnson	970-245-7992	R	18	<0.1
Magnum Tire Corp.	724 N 1st St	Minneapolis	MN	55401	Steven Wallack	612-338-8861	R	18	<0.1
United Distributing Co.	101 N Kings Hwy	Cape Girardeau	MO	63701	Fred R Wilferth	314-335-3341	R	16 *	<0.1
Ball Tire and Gas Inc.	620 Ripley Blvd	Alpena	MI	49707	James Ball	517-354-4186	R	15	0.1

Source: *Ward's Business Directory of U.S. Private and Public Companies*, 1998. The company type code used is as follows: P - Public, R - Private, S - Subsidiary, D - Division, J - Joint Venture, A - Affiliate, G - Group. Sales are in millions of dollars, employees are in thousands. An asterisk (*) indicates an estimated sales volume. The symbol < stands for 'less than'.

OCCUPATIONS EMPLOYED BY SIC 501 - MOTOR VEHICLES, PARTS, AND SUPPLIES

Occupation	% of Total 1996	Change to 2006	Occupation	% of Total 1996	Change to 2006
Sales & related workers nec	19.1	12.5	Salespersons, retail	2.2	2.3
Truck drivers light & heavy	9.3	53.4	Helpers, laborers nec	2.2	2.3
General managers & top executives	5.5	-0.9	Driver/sales workers	2.1	2.3
Stock clerks	4.7	2.3	Assemblers, fabricators, hand workers nec	2.0	2.3
General office clerks	4.0	-12.0	Blue collar worker supervisors	1.7	-1.3
Bus & truck mechanics	3.8	-8.0	Secretaries, except legal & medical	1.6	-18.9
Marketing & sales worker supervisors	3.4	2.3	Transportation equipment operators nec	1.4	2.3
Automotive mechanics	3.0	-8.0	Clerical supervisors & managers	1.4	2.3
Traffic, shipping, receiving clerks	3.0	2.3	Industrial truck & tractor operators	1.4	2.3
Order fillers, wholesale & retail sales	2.9	2.3	Order clerks	1.0	-7.9
Bookkeeping, accounting, & auditing clerks	2.7	-18.2	Purchasing managers	1.0	2.3
Freight, stock, & material movers, hand	2.3	-7.9			

Source: *Industry-Occupation Matrix*, Bureau of Labor Statistics. These data relate to one or more 3-digit SIC industry groups rather than to a single 4-digit SIC. The change reported for each occupation to the year 2006 is a percent of growth or decline as estimated by the Bureau of Labor Statistics. The abbreviation nec stands for 'not elsewhere classified'.

STATE AND REGIONAL CONCENTRATION

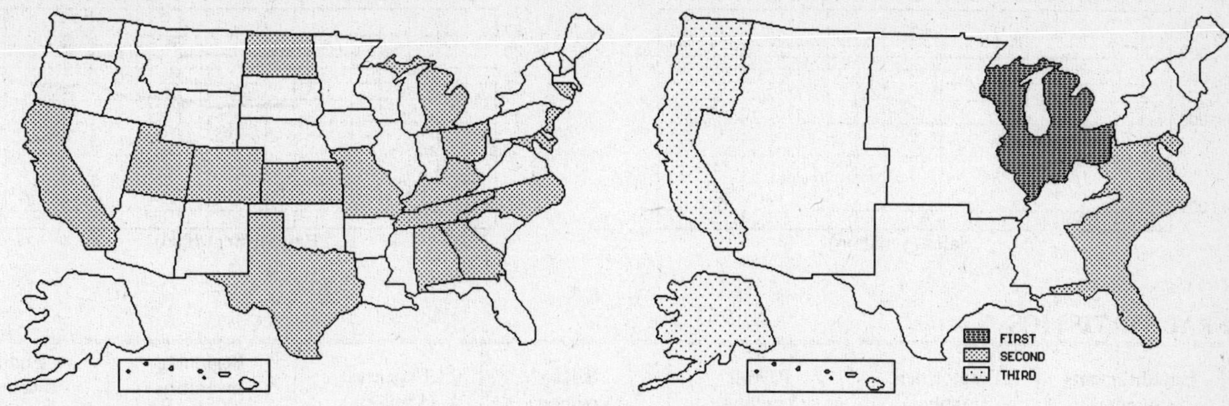

INDUSTRY DATA BY STATE

State	Establishments - 1995 Total (number)	Establishments - 1995 % of U.S.	Employment - 1995 Total (number)	Employment - 1995 % of U.S.	Employment - 1995 Per Estab.	Payroll - 1995 Total ($ mil.)	Payroll - 1995 Per Empl. ($)	Sales - 1992 Total ($ mil.)	Sales - 1992 % of U.S.	Sales - 1992 Per Estab ($)
California	338	9.8	3,805	8.9	11	125.5	32,981	2,380.9	12.4	502,407
Ohio	149	4.3	2,193	5.1	15	71.8	32,726	2,029.6	10.6	679,465
Texas	228	6.6	2,446	5.7	11	67.8	27,713	1,484.6	7.7	499,695
Maryland	50	1.5	810	1.9	16	22.6	27,894	1,057.8	5.5	1,035,006
Michigan	103	3.0	1,107	2.6	11	31.6	28,580	1,003.3	5.2	885,485
Tennessee	92	2.7	1,282	3.0	14	37.7	29,425	918.2	4.8	657,287
New Jersey	102	3.0	1,212	2.8	12	43.1	35,572	907.5	4.7	746,936
Illinois	135	3.9	1,844	4.3	14	57.3	31,086	833.3	4.3	457,872
Georgia	110	3.2	1,629	3.8	15	54.0	33,135	814.1	4.2	503,778
Connecticut	29	0.8	466	1.1	16	17.2	36,931	778.9	4.1	1,497,883
New York	147	4.3	1,645	3.8	11	44.9	27,274	653.7	3.4	392,854
Florida	200	5.8	1,839	4.3	9	56.4	30,644	647.1	3.4	328,994
Pennsylvania	164	4.8	2,141	5.0	13	54.7	25,561	627.3	3.3	276,240
North Carolina	116	3.4	1,765	4.1	15	53.4	30,245	530.8	2.8	297,555
Alabama	70	2.0	871	2.0	12	22.3	25,659	495.1	2.6	524,487
Missouri	100	2.9	1,167	2.7	12	29.7	25,472	400.3	2.1	300,294
Kentucky	55	1.6	740	1.7	13	20.7	27,915	333.8	1.7	393,205
Kansas	38	1.1	498	1.2	13	14.3	28,627	324.7	1.7	504,259
Colorado	58	1.7	650	1.5	11	19.8	30,468	308.6	1.6	445,299
Indiana	74	2.2	1,053	2.5	14	31.1	29,493	283.2	1.5	258,669
Virginia	79	2.3	1,306	3.1	17	33.5	25,629	220.0	1.1	188,500
Arizona	57	1.7	685	1.6	12	19.5	28,466	202.6	1.1	296,706
Washington	61	1.8	540	1.3	9	16.2	30,013	195.8	1.0	314,260
Utah	28	0.8	411	1.0	15	12.6	30,696	180.9	0.9	398,348
Mississippi	37	1.1	666	1.6	18	17.5	26,225	178.1	0.9	289,060
Oregon	59	1.7	599	1.4	10	15.7	26,250	174.8	0.9	256,695
Iowa	63	1.8	668	1.6	11	17.8	26,573	171.6	0.9	215,011
Wisconsin	60	1.7	785	1.8	13	20.9	26,623	165.7	0.9	168,061
Massachusetts	46	1.3	558	1.3	12	16.8	30,048	162.6	0.8	290,860
South Carolina	45	1.3	1,233	2.9	27	53.7	43,569	136.5	0.7	242,510
Oklahoma	40	1.2	527	1.2	13	14.1	26,820	131.4	0.7	204,673
Arkansas	37	1.1	373	0.9	10	10.4	27,954	95.5	0.5	201,392
Nevada	23	0.7	279	0.7	12	9.9	35,541	80.8	0.4	323,092
New Hampshire	31	0.9	239	0.6	8	5.9	24,874	62.2	0.3	215,381
North Dakota	21	0.6	276	0.6	13	6.8	24,529	55.4	0.3	178,193
New Mexico	18	0.5	176	0.4	10	4.9	27,676	44.6	0.2	236,989
South Dakota	16	0.5	201	0.5	13	5.7	28,597	40.1	0.2	213,106
Maine	23	0.7	247	0.6	11	5.8	23,510	39.5	0.2	166,532
Hawaii	15	0.4	134	0.3	9	3.9	28,754	34.0	0.2	183,000
Alaska	7	0.2	50	0.1	7	2.3	45,920	20.5	0.1	269,868
Minnesota	67	2.0	871	2.0	13	26.7	30,670	(D)	-	-
Louisiana	60	1.7	664	1.6	11	17.3	26,114	(D)	-	-
Montana	41	1.2	351	0.8	9	8.8	25,177	(D)	-	-
West Virginia	40	1.2	573	1.3	14	12.8	22,267	(D)	-	-
Nebraska	38	1.1	507	1.2	13	14.1	27,901	(D)	-	-
Idaho	28	0.8	283	0.7	10	6.5	22,848	(D)	-	-
Vermont	12	0.3	93	0.2	8	2.6	28,387	(D)	-	-
Delaware	9	0.3	106	0.2	12	2.8	26,670	(D)	-	-
Wyoming	9	0.3	119	0.3	13	3.7	31,160	(D)	-	-
Rhode Island	6	0.2	60	0.1	10	1.8	30,600	(D)	-	-

Source: County Business Patterns, 1995 and *Economic Census of the U.S., 1992*. Data are sorted by 1992 revenues and, if revenues are unavailable, by establishments in 1995. The symbol (D) indicates that data are withheld by the source to avoid disclosure of competitive information. A dash (-) indicates that data are not available or undisclosed because they do not meet statistical validity standards. Shaded *states* on the state map indicate those states which have proportionately greater representation in the industry than would be indicated by the state's population; the ratio is based on total revenues or number of establishments. Shaded *regions* indicate where the industry is regionally most concentrated.

5015 - MOTOR VEHICLE PARTS, USED

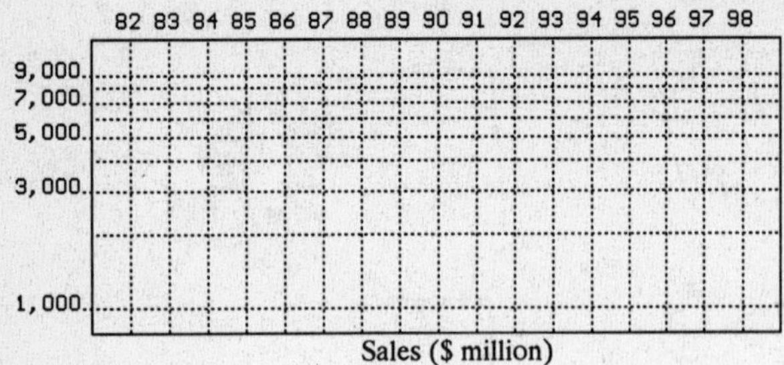

Sales ($ million)

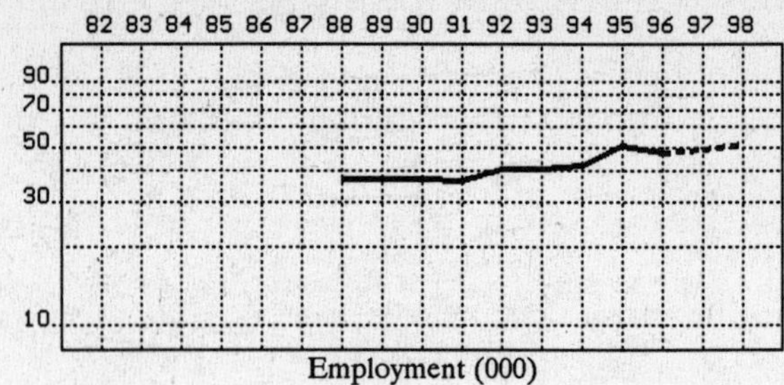

Employment (000)

GENERAL STATISTICS

Year	Establishments (number)	Employment (number)	Payroll ($ million)	Sales ($ million)	Expenses ($ million)	Beginning Inventory ($ million)	Ending Inventory ($ million)
1982	-	-	-	-	-	-	-
1983	-	-	-	-	-	-	-
1984	-	-	-	-	-	-	-
1985	-	-	-	-	-	-	-
1986	-	-	-	-	-	-	-
1987	6,075	(D)	(D)	(D)	(D)	(D)	-
1988	5,852	37,219	603.8	-	-	-	-
1989	5,546	37,519	622.4	-	-	-	-
1990	5,727	37,453	647.2	-	-	-	-
1991	5,837	36,491	656.1	-	-	-	-
1992	7,227	40,893	739.2	3,719.3	1,457.9	435.5	456.8
1993	7,098	41,024	773.2	-	-	-	-
1994	6,976	42,485	828.6	-	-	-	-
1995	7,795	50,419	1,029.4	-	-	-	-
1996	7,697p	47,528p	977.0p	-	-	-	-
1997	7,945p	49,103p	1,030.2p	-	-	-	-
1998	8,192p	50,679p	1,083.4p	-	-	-	-

Sources: Economic Census of the United States, 1982, 1987, and 1992. Establishment counts, employment, and payroll are from *County Business Patterns* for non-Census years. Values followed by a 'p' are projections by the editors. Sales and expense data for non-Census years are extrapolations, marked by 'e'. Industries reclassified in 1987 will not have data for prior years. Data are the most recent available at this level of detail.

INDICES OF CHANGE

Year	Establishments (number)	Employment (number)	Payroll ($ million)	Sales ($ million)	Expenses ($ million)	Beginning Inventory ($ million)	Ending Inventory ($ million)
1982	-	-	-	-	-	-	-
1983	-	-	-	-	-	-	-
1984	-	-	-	-	-	-	-
1985	-	-	-	-	-	-	-
1986	-	-	-	-	-	-	-
1987	84.1	(D)	(D)	(D)	(D)	(D)	-
1988	81.0	91.0	81.7	-	-	-	-
1989	76.7	91.7	84.2	-	-	-	-
1990	79.2	91.6	87.6	-	-	-	-
1991	80.8	89.2	88.8	-	-	-	-
1992	100.0	100.0	100.0	100.0	100.0	100.0	100.0
1993	98.2	100.3	104.6	-	-	-	-
1994	96.5	103.9	112.1	-	-	-	-
1995	107.9	123.3	139.3	-	-	-	-
1996	106.5p	116.2p	132.2p	-	-	-	-
1997	109.9p	120.1p	139.4p	-	-	-	-
1998	113.4p	123.9p	146.6p	-	-	-	-

Sources: Same as General Statistics. The values shown reflect change from the base year, 1992. Values above 100 mean greater than 1992, values below 100 mean less than 1992, and a value of 100 in the 1982-91 or 1993-98 period means same as 1992. Values followed by a 'p' are projections by the editors; 'e' stands for extrapolation. Data are the most recent available at this level of detail.

SELECTED RATIOS

For 1992	Avg. of All Wholesale	Analyzed Industry	Index	For 1992	Avg. of All Wholesale	Analyzed Industry	Index
Employees per Establishment	12	6	48	Sales per Employee	561,172	90,952	16
Payroll per Establishment	349,729	102,283	29	Sales per Establishment	6,559,346	514,640	8
Payroll per Employee	29,919	18,076	60	Expenses per Establishment	723,071	201,730	28

Sources: Same as General Statistics. The 'Average of All Manufacturing' column represents the average of all manufacturing industries reported for the most recent complete year available. The Index shows the relationship between the Average and the Analyzed Industry. For example, 100 means that they are equal; 500 that the Analyzed Industry is five times the average; 50 means that the Analyzed Industry is half the national average. The abbreviation 'na' is used to show that data are 'not available'.

LEADING COMPANIES

Number shown: **13** Total sales ($ mil): **3,561** Total employment (000): **16.3**

Company Name	Address				CEO Name	Phone	Co. Type	Sales ($ mil)	Empl. (000)
CARQUEST Corp.	12596 W Bayaud	Lakewood	CO	80228	Peter Kornafel	303-984-2000	R	1,614 *	14.0
Mazda Motor of America Inc.	PO Box 19734	Irvine	CA	92623	George Toyama	714-727-1990	S	1,230 *	0.8
Tube City Inc.	PO Box 2000	Glassport	PA	15045	Michael Coslov	412-678-6141	R	320	0.3
Auto Parts Club Inc.	5825 Oberlin Dr	San Diego	CA	92121	Steve Kirby	619-622-5050	R	100	0.7
Atlas Supply Co.	2625 Cumberland	Atlanta	GA	30339	Hugh D Hanna	404-431-3880	R	75	<0.1
O'Connor Truck Sales Inc.	H & Hunting Pk Av	Philadelphia	PA	19124	Perry Mangioni	215-744-8500	R	60	<0.1
Neil Parts Distribution Corp.	PO Box 787	Medford	NY	11763	Neil Feldstein	516-758-1144	R	52 *	0.1
Blonders of Hartford	741 Windsor St	Hartford	CT	06120	Gary Blonder	203-522-1104	R	31 *	<0.1
Autoline Industries Inc.	625 Enterprise Dr	Oak Brook	IL	60523	Michael Winter	630-990-3200	R	30	<0.1
H.C. Lewis Oil Co.	PO Box 649	Welch	WV	24801	HC Lewis Jr	304-436-2148	R	28	<0.1
Barker-Jennings Corp.	PO Box 11289	Lynchburg	VA	24506	Fred C Thomas	804-846-8471	R	13	<0.1
Pik-A-Nut Div.	PO Box 587	Huntington	IN	46750	Joe Hohe	219-356-0100	D	5	<0.1
Danville Gasoline and Oil	201 W Main St	Danville	IL	61832	WT Leverenz IV	217-446-8500	R	3	<0.1

Source: *Ward's Business Directory of U.S. Private and Public Companies*, 1998. The company type code used is as follows: P - Public, R - Private, S - Subsidiary, D - Division, J - Joint Venture, A - Affiliate, G - Group. Sales are in millions of dollars, employees are in thousands. An asterisk (*) indicates an estimated sales volume. The symbol < stands for 'less than'.

OCCUPATIONS EMPLOYED BY SIC 501 - MOTOR VEHICLES, PARTS, AND SUPPLIES

Occupation	% of Total 1996	Change to 2006	Occupation	% of Total 1996	Change to 2006
Sales & related workers nec	19.1	12.5	Salespersons, retail	2.2	2.3
Truck drivers light & heavy	9.3	53.4	Helpers, laborers nec	2.2	2.3
General managers & top executives	5.5	-0.9	Driver/sales workers	2.1	2.3
Stock clerks	4.7	2.3	Assemblers, fabricators, hand workers nec	2.0	2.3
General office clerks	4.0	-12.0	Blue collar worker supervisors	1.7	-1.3
Bus & truck mechanics	3.8	-8.0	Secretaries, except legal & medical	1.6	-18.9
Marketing & sales worker supervisors	3.4	2.3	Transportation equipment operators nec	1.4	2.3
Automotive mechanics	3.0	-8.0	Clerical supervisors & managers	1.4	2.3
Traffic, shipping, receiving clerks	3.0	2.3	Industrial truck & tractor operators	1.4	2.3
Order fillers, wholesale & retail sales	2.9	2.3	Order clerks	1.0	-7.9
Bookkeeping, accounting, & auditing clerks	2.7	-18.2	Purchasing managers	1.0	2.3
Freight, stock, & material movers, hand	2.3	-7.9			

Source: *Industry-Occupation Matrix*, Bureau of Labor Statistics. These data relate to one or more 3-digit SIC industry groups rather than to a single 4-digit SIC. The change reported for each occupation to the year 2006 is a percent of growth or decline as estimated by the Bureau of Labor Statistics. The abbreviation nec stands for 'not elsewhere classified'.

STATE AND REGIONAL CONCENTRATION

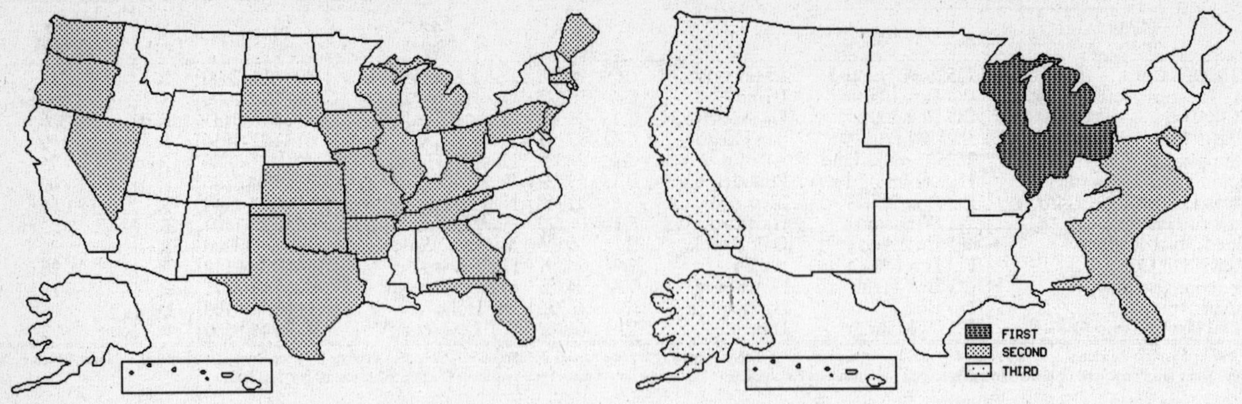

INDUSTRY DATA BY STATE

State	Establishments - 1995 Total (number)	Establishments - 1995 % of U.S.	Employment - 1995 Total (number)	Employment - 1995 % of U.S.	Employment - 1995 Per Estab.	Payroll - 1995 Total ($ mil.)	Payroll - 1995 Per Empl. ($)	Sales - 1992 Total ($ mil.)	Sales - 1992 % of U.S.	Sales - 1992 Per Estab ($)
California	797	10.2	5,673	11.3	7	116.3	20,501	427.7	12.1	94,948
Texas	626	8.0	4,004	7.9	6	82.5	20,611	296.1	8.4	94,789
New York	416	5.3	3,266	6.5	8	72.4	22,156	228.5	6.5	96,470
Florida	471	6.0	2,818	5.6	6	55.7	19,777	207.6	5.9	98,287
Illinois	251	3.2	2,294	4.5	9	52.1	22,705	176.8	5.0	92,484
Pennsylvania	373	4.8	2,022	4.0	5	40.1	19,827	173.0	4.9	102,991
Ohio	350	4.5	2,280	4.5	7	47.6	20,862	164.8	4.7	91,474
Michigan	270	3.5	1,983	3.9	7	40.0	20,152	141.7	4.0	96,464
New Jersey	199	2.6	1,338	2.7	7	33.0	24,697	135.9	3.8	136,421
Massachusetts	176	2.3	1,172	2.3	7	28.5	24,299	105.5	3.0	110,971
Georgia	235	3.0	1,452	2.9	6	28.9	19,921	101.4	2.9	95,805
North Carolina	218	2.8	1,275	2.5	6	24.1	18,925	94.9	2.7	83,857
Missouri	209	2.7	1,032	2.0	5	20.9	20,265	87.7	2.5	87,273
Washington	155	2.0	1,153	2.3	7	23.8	20,628	82.4	2.3	74,540
Wisconsin	180	2.3	1,295	2.6	7	24.8	19,122	76.2	2.2	72,130
Virginia	194	2.5	1,503	3.0	8	32.7	21,786	75.5	2.1	76,042
Tennessee	196	2.5	819	1.6	4	14.8	18,115	75.5	2.1	92,484
Indiana	171	2.2	1,263	2.5	7	23.8	18,851	74.5	2.1	68,203
Kentucky	131	1.7	784	1.6	6	14.1	17,972	70.5	2.0	103,757
Maryland	91	1.2	977	1.9	11	22.9	23,472	63.4	1.8	74,292
Oklahoma	149	1.9	889	1.8	6	16.0	17,978	63.4	1.8	88,145
Oregon	111	1.4	711	1.4	6	15.1	21,277	61.9	1.7	93,149
Alabama	152	1.9	670	1.3	4	12.6	18,770	56.5	1.6	91,354
Arizona	130	1.7	645	1.3	5	13.4	20,705	50.5	1.4	81,047
Kansas	114	1.5	604	1.2	5	11.6	19,129	49.0	1.4	87,605
Colorado	151	1.9	758	1.5	5	14.4	18,960	48.4	1.4	80,818
Iowa	103	1.3	677	1.3	7	12.7	18,696	46.6	1.3	85,374
South Carolina	113	1.4	612	1.2	5	11.4	18,706	44.3	1.3	75,776
Arkansas	105	1.3	533	1.1	5	9.2	17,340	42.0	1.2	95,820
Connecticut	71	0.9	482	1.0	7	10.5	21,822	35.8	1.0	81,781
Louisiana	102	1.3	515	1.0	5	9.5	18,538	34.8	1.0	75,665
Mississippi	96	1.2	529	1.0	6	8.0	15,170	31.3	0.9	73,479
Maine	32	0.4	193	0.4	6	3.5	18,269	19.5	0.6	111,469
Nevada	36	0.5	288	0.6	8	5.8	20,014	19.3	0.5	74,949
South Dakota	36	0.5	247	0.5	7	4.9	19,895	17.3	0.5	94,830
Utah	47	0.6	320	0.6	7	5.0	15,634	15.3	0.4	57,250
New Mexico	58	0.7	325	0.6	6	5.0	15,265	13.6	0.4	66,107
New Hampshire	31	0.4	269	0.5	9	6.2	22,963	11.1	0.3	90,967
Alaska	8	0.1	74	0.1	9	2.3	30,919	6.5	0.2	101,937
North Dakota	28	0.4	112	0.2	4	1.8	15,830	6.5	0.2	68,421
D.C.	5	0.1	36	0.1	7	0.7	18,306	2.5	0.1	66,342
Hawaii	9	0.1	17	0.0	2	0.5	30,353	2.1	0.1	71,138
Minnesota	127	1.6	798	1.6	6	15.8	19,823	(D)	-	-
Nebraska	57	0.7	424	0.8	7	9.3	21,960	(D)	-	-
West Virginia	49	0.6	271	0.5	6	4.0	14,624	(D)	-	-
Idaho	37	0.5	240	0.5	6	4.3	18,042	(D)	-	-
Rhode Island	34	0.4	283	0.6	8	8.0	28,110	(D)	-	-
Montana	32	0.4	139	0.3	4	2.3	16,187	(D)	-	-
Delaware	31	0.4	196	0.4	6	3.8	19,378	(D)	-	-
Vermont	17	0.2	81	0.2	5	1.5	19,086	(D)	-	-
Wyoming	15	0.2	78	0.2	5	1.3	16,910	(D)	-	-

Source: County Business Patterns, 1995 and *Economic Census of the U.S., 1992*. Data are sorted by 1992 revenues and, if revenues are unavailable, by establishments in 1995. The symbol (D) indicates that data are withheld by the source to avoid disclosure of competitive information. A dash (-) indicates that data are not available or undisclosed because they do not meet statistical validity standards. Shaded *states* on the state map indicate those states which have proportionately greater representation in the industry than would be indicated by the state's population; the ratio is based on total revenues or number of establishments. Shaded *regions* indicate where the industry is regionally most concentrated.

5021 - FURNITURE

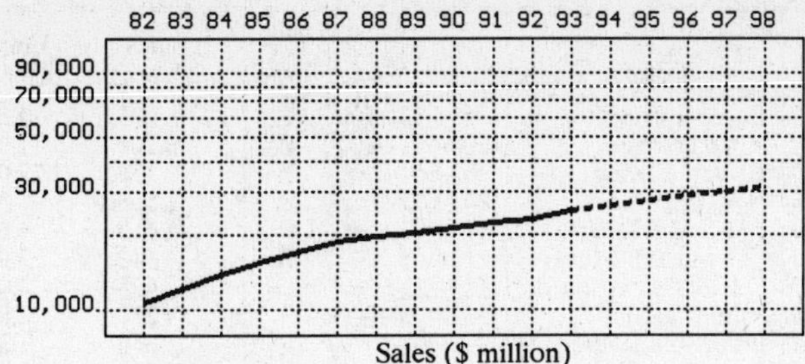

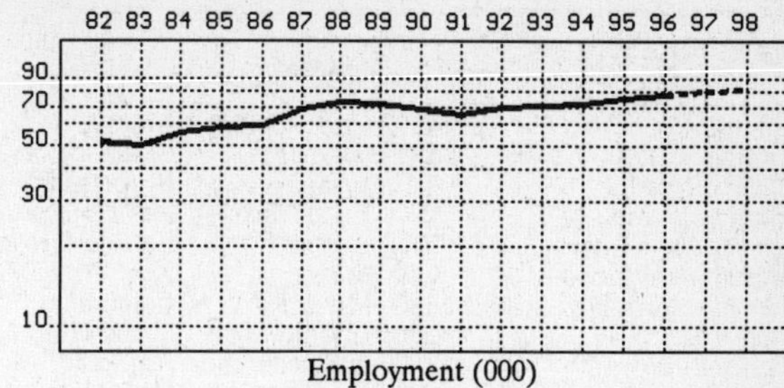

GENERAL STATISTICS

Year	Establishments (number)	Employment (number)	Payroll ($ million)	Sales ($ million)	Expenses ($ million)	Beginning Inventory ($ million)	Ending Inventory ($ million)
1982	5,763	51,287	970.3	10,672.6	-	-	-
1983	5,612	49,708	1,019.7	12,264.1e	-	-	-
1984	5,541	55,404	1,195.5	13,855.5e	-	-	-
1985	5,536	58,430	1,311.7	15,447.0e	-	-	-
1986	5,491	59,102	1,389.1	17,038.4e	-	-	-
1987	6,819	68,995	1,704.3	18,629.9	3,402.2	1,095.6	1,219.7
1988	6,470	72,848	1,922.5	19,508.9e	3,508.0e	1,140.6e	1,238.0e
1989	6,170	71,462	1,912.6	20,387.9e	3,613.9e	1,185.6e	1,256.2e
1990	6,125	68,882	1,910.7	21,266.9e	3,719.7e	1,230.6e	1,274.4e
1991	6,035	64,972	1,803.9	22,146.0e	3,825.5e	1,275.6e	1,292.7e
1992	7,342	69,186	1,985.6	23,025.0	3,931.3	1,320.6	1,310.9
1993	7,179	71,075	2,090.7	25,069.8p	4,037.1p	1,365.6p	1,329.1p
1994	7,197	72,037	2,231.3	26,305.1p	4,142.9p	1,410.6p	1,347.3p
1995	7,230	74,898	2,417.3	27,540.3p	4,248.8p	1,455.6p	1,365.6p
1996	7,381p	78,007p	2,489.2p	28,775.5p	4,354.6p	1,500.5p	1,383.8p
1997	7,522p	79,758p	2,593.8p	30,010.8p	4,460.4p	1,545.6p	1,402.0p
1998	7,663p	81,508p	2,698.4p	31,246.0p	4,566.2p	1,590.6p	1,420.3p

Sources: *Economic Census of the United States*, 1982, 1987, and 1992. Establishment counts, employment, and payroll are from *County Business Patterns* for non-Census years. Values followed by a 'p' are projections by the editors. Sales and expense data for non-Census years are extrapolations, marked by 'e'. Industries reclassified in 1987 will not have data for prior years. Data are the most recent available at this level of detail.

INDICES OF CHANGE

Year	Establishments (number)	Employment (number)	Payroll ($ million)	Sales ($ million)	Expenses ($ million)	Beginning Inventory ($ million)	Ending Inventory ($ million)
1982	78.5	74.1	48.9	46.4	-	-	-
1983	76.4	71.8	51.4	53.3e	-	-	-
1984	75.5	80.1	60.2	60.2e	-	-	-
1985	75.4	84.5	66.1	67.1e	-	-	-
1986	74.8	85.4	70.0	74.0e	-	-	-
1987	92.9	99.7	85.8	80.9	86.5	83.0	93.0
1988	88.1	105.3	96.8	84.7e	89.2e	86.4e	94.4e
1989	84.0	103.3	96.3	88.5e	91.9e	89.8e	95.8e
1990	83.4	99.6	96.2	92.4e	94.6e	93.2e	97.2e
1991	82.2	93.9	90.8	96.2e	97.3e	96.6e	98.6e
1992	100.0	100.0	100.0	100.0	100.0	100.0	100.0
1993	97.8	102.7	105.3	108.9p	102.7p	103.4p	101.4p
1994	98.0	104.1	112.4	114.2p	105.4p	106.8p	102.8p
1995	98.5	108.3	121.7	119.6p	108.1p	110.2p	104.2p
1996	100.5p	112.7p	125.4p	125.0p	110.8p	113.6p	105.6p
1997	102.5p	115.3p	130.6p	130.3p	113.5p	117.0p	107.0p
1998	104.4p	117.8p	135.9p	135.7p	116.2p	120.4p	108.3p

Sources: Same as General Statistics. The values shown reflect change from the base year, 1992. Values above 100 mean greater than 1992, values below 100 mean less than 1992, and a value of 100 in the 1982-91 or 1993-98 period means same as 1992. Values followed by a 'p' are projections by the editors; 'e' stands for extrapolation. Data are the most recent available at this level of detail.

SELECTED RATIOS

For 1992	Avg. of All Wholesale	Analyzed Industry	Index	For 1992	Avg. of All Wholesale	Analyzed Industry	Index
Employees per Establishment	12	9	81	Sales per Employee	561,172	332,799	59
Payroll per Establishment	349,729	270,444	77	Sales per Establishment	6,559,346	3,136,066	48
Payroll per Employee	29,919	28,699	96	Expenses per Establishment	723,071	535,454	74

Sources: Same as General Statistics. The 'Average of All Manufacturing' column represents the average of all manufacturing industries reported for the most recent complete year available. The Index shows the relationship between the Average and the Analyzed Industry. For example, 100 means that they are equal; 500 that the Analyzed Industry is five times the average; 50 means that the Analyzed Industry is half the national average. The abbreviation 'na' is used to show that data are 'not available'.

LEADING COMPANIES
Number shown: **50** Total sales ($ mil): **21,147** Total employment (000): **95.4**

Company Name	Address				CEO Name	Phone	Co. Type	Sales ($ mil)	Empl. (000)
Genuine Parts Co.	2999 Circle 75 Pkwy	Atlanta	GA	30339	Larry L Prince	770-953-1700	P	6,005	24.5
B J's Wholesale Club Inc.	PO Box 9601	Natick	MA	01760	John J Nugent	508-651-7400	P	3,200	11.0
Corporate Express Inc.	1 Env Way	Broomfield	CO	80021	Robert L King	303-664-2000	P	3,196	27.0
United Stationers Inc.	2200 E Golf Rd	Des Plaines	IL	60016	R W Larrimore	847-699-5000	P	2,558	5.5
BT Office Products Intern.	2150 E Lake Cook	Buffalo Grove	IL	60089	Frans H J Koffrie	847-793-7500	P	1,619	6.6
Joyce International Inc.	114 5th Ave	New York	NY	10019	G Lynn Schostack	212-463-9044	R	540 *	3.0
Value City Furniture Div.	1800 Moler Rd	Columbus	OH	43207	David Thompson	614-221-9200	D	425	4.0
Office Depot Inc.	3366 E Willow St	Signal Hill	CA	90806	John Maloney	562-490-1000	S	350 *	2.0
School Specialties Inc.	1000 N Bluemound	Appleton	WI	54914	Dave VandeZden	920-734-5712	P	350	1.3
Warehouse Club Inc.	7235 N Linder Ave	Skokie	IL	60077	Everett L Buckardt	708-679-6800	P	215	0.9
La Salle-Deitch Company Inc.	PO Box 2347	Elkhart	IN	46515	A Clark Peters	219-294-2661	S	200	0.5
ATD-American Co.	135 Greenwood	Wyncote	PA	19095	Jerome Zaslow	215-576-1000	R	190	0.1
TAB Products Co.	1400 Page Mill Rd	Palo Alto	CA	94304	Philip C Kantz	650-852-2400	P	155	1.1
Farmers Furniture Company	1851 Telefair	Dublin	GA	31021	Sherwin Glass	912-275-3150	S	120 *	0.2
National Business Furniture	PO Box 92952	Milwaukee	WI	53202	George Mosher	414-276-8511	R	115	0.1
Champion Industries Inc.	PO Box 2968	Huntington	WV	25728	Marshall T Reynolds	304-528-2791	P	108	0.9
Coaster Company of America	12928 Sandoval St	Santa Fe Sprgs	CA	90670	Norman Dinner	562-944-7899	R	100	0.2
International Business Interiors	800 South St	Waltham	MA	02154	Steven Karol	617-891-6660	S	87	0.6
Wasserstrom Co.	477 S Front St	Columbus	OH	43215	R Wasserstrom	614-228-6525	R	81 *	0.3
AIG Designs Inc.	11415 Old Roswell	Alpharetta	GA	30201	Billy R Pate	404-664-3585	S	75	<0.1
Business Resource Group	2150 N 1st St, #101	San Jose	CA	95131	John W Peth	408-325-3200	P	73	0.2
Rucker Fuller Co.	731 Sansome St	San Francisco	CA	94111	Lee Pierce	415-627-4600	R	66	0.2
Furniture Consultants Inc.	11 W 19th St	New York	NY	10011	John Varacchi	212-229-4500	R	65	0.2
Thomas W. Ruff and Co.	1114 Dublin Rd	Columbus	OH	43215	Michael Gorman	614-487-4000	R	65	0.2
Contract Interiors Carson	10 Oak Hollow St	Southfield	MI	48034	Robert Spradlin	313-356-6550	R	61	0.2
Corporate Express	7700 Port Capital	Baltimore	MD	21227	Rick Nelson	410-799-7700	S	60	0.4
Modern Business Machines Inc.	505 N 22nd St	Milwaukee	WI	53233	Marvin Cooper	414-344-1000	S	58	0.3
Dancker, Sellew and Douglas	53 Park Pl	New York	NY	10007	J Scott Douglas	212-619-7171	R	55	0.2
Walker and Zanger Inc.	31 Warren Pl	Mount Vernon	NY	10550	Leon Zanger	914-667-1600	R	55	<0.1
Silvers Inc.	151 W Fort St	Detroit	MI	48232	Ira Silver	313-963-0000	R	52	0.3
Globe Business Resources Inc.	1925 Greenwood	Cincinnati	OH	45246	David D Hoguet	513-771-8221	P	50	0.4
Desks Inc. (Chicago, Illinois)	2323 W Pershing	Chicago	IL	60609	Robert A Stacey	312-664-8500	R	50	<0.1
General Office Products Co.	2050 Old Hwy 8	New Brighton	MN	55112	Thomas J Reaser	612-639-4700	S	50	0.3
J.A. Kindel Co.	605 N Wayne Ave	Cincinnati	OH	45215	John Berning	513-733-9600	S	50	0.1
Philadelphia Stationers Inc.	10551 Decatur Rd	Philadelphia	PA	19154	Herman Marx	215-632-5200	R	50 *	0.3
Continental Office Furniture	2061 Silver Dr	Columbus	OH	43211	John Lucks	614-262-8088	R	45 *	0.3
Office Environments Inc.	3925 Rose Lake Dr	Charlotte	NC	28217	Thomas McAnallen	704-357-3800	R	45 *	0.2
Andrews Office Supply	8400 A Ardmore	Landover	MD	20785	Jay Mutschler	301-322-5300	S	42	0.2
Corporate Environments	PO Box 29725	Atlanta	GA	30359	John R Harris	404-679-8999	R	41	<0.1
Facility Systems Inc.	6423 City West	Eden Prairie	MN	55344	Duane Frederiksen	612-829-4300	R	40	0.1
Lincoln Office Supply Company	7707 N Knoxville	Peoria	IL	61614	Thomas E Spuegeon	309-693-2444	R	40	0.2
Office Resources Inc.	PO Box 1689	Louisville	KY	40201	Stephen Zink	502-589-5900	R	40	0.2
United Restaurant Equ Co.	PO Box 1460	Woonsocket	RI	02895	Robert Halpern	401-769-1000	R	40	0.1
Carithers-Wallace-Courtenay	4343 Northeast	Atlanta	GA	30301	GM Brandon	770-493-8200	S	40	0.1
Fashion Bed Group	5950 W 51st St	Chicago	IL	60638	Joe Geiger	708-458-1800	S	39 *	0.1
Fraenkel Wholesale Furniture	PO Box 15385	Baton Rouge	LA	70895	Harvey Hoffman	504-275-8111	R	39 *	0.2
Hilton Equipment Corp.	9336 Civic Ctr Dr	Beverly Hills	CA	90210	Donald Royal	310-278-4321	S	39 *	<0.1
A.Y. McDonald Supply	PO Box 1390	Dubuque	IA	52004	John McDonald III	319-583-2558	S	38	0.2
Amarillo Hardware Co.	PO Box 1891	Amarillo	TX	79172	Joe Wildman	806-376-4722	R	35	0.2
Space Designs Inc.	2490 Charleston Rd	Mountain View	CA	94043	Boyd Baugh	415-960-0915	R	35	<0.1

Source: *Ward's Business Directory of U.S. Private and Public Companies*, 1998. The company type code used is as follows: P - Public, R - Private, S - Subsidiary, D - Division, J - Joint Venture, A - Affiliate, G - Group. Sales are in millions of dollars, employees are in thousands. An asterisk (*) indicates an estimated sales volume. The symbol < stands for 'less than'.

OCCUPATIONS EMPLOYED BY SIC 502 - WHOLESALE TRADE, OTHER

Occupation	% of Total 1996	Change to 2006	Occupation	% of Total 1996	Change to 2006
Sales & related workers nec	19.5	20.2	Clerical supervisors & managers	1.9	20.2
General managers & top executives	5.9	16.4	Order clerks	1.9	8.2
Truck drivers light & heavy	5.4	20.2	Helpers, laborers nec	1.7	20.2
General office clerks	3.6	3.4	Electrical & electronic technicians	1.4	18.8
Traffic, shipping, receiving clerks	3.6	16.7	Blue collar worker supervisors	1.4	16.0
Stock clerks	3.5	-3.9	Wholesale & retail buyers, except farm products	1.3	17.0
Freight, stock, & material movers, hand	3.3	8.2	Office machine & cash register servicers	1.3	20.2
Marketing & sales worker supervisors	3.1	20.2	Hand packers & packagers	1.2	-3.9
Order fillers, wholesale & retail sales	3.0	16.7	Maintenance repairers, general utility	1.1	12.0
Bookkeeping, accounting, & auditing clerks	2.9	-3.9	Industrial truck & tractor operators	1.1	20.2
Salespersons, retail	2.5	20.2	Purchasing managers	1.1	20.2
Secretaries, except legal & medical	2.5	-4.7	Receptionists & information clerks	1.0	20.2
Assemblers, fabricators, hand workers nec	2.0	-3.9			

Source: *Industry-Occupation Matrix*, Bureau of Labor Statistics. These data relate to one or more 3-digit SIC industry groups rather than to a single 4-digit SIC. The change reported for each occupation to the year 2006 is a percent of growth or decline as estimated by the Bureau of Labor Statistics. The abbreviation nec stands for 'not elsewhere classified'.

STATE AND REGIONAL CONCENTRATION

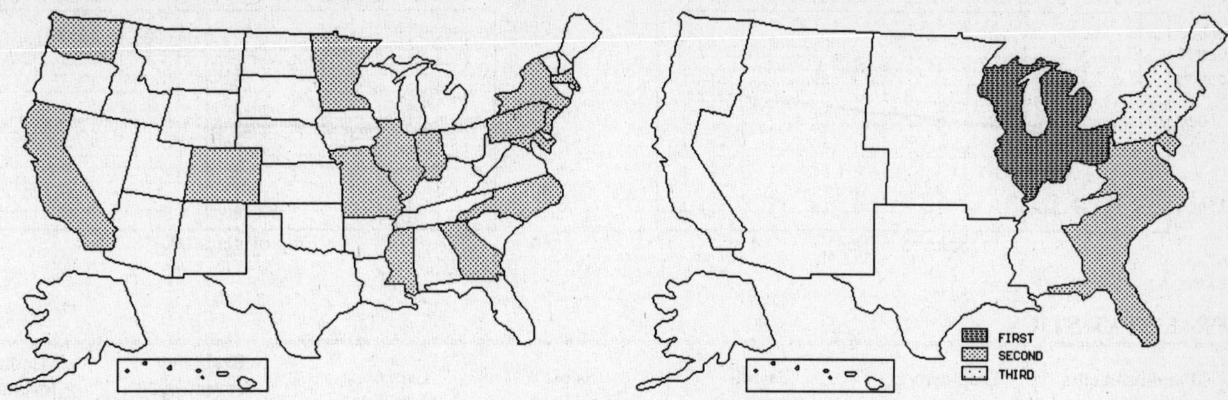

INDUSTRY DATA BY STATE

State	Establishments - 1995 Total (number)	Establishments - 1995 % of U.S.	Employment - 1995 Total (number)	Employment - 1995 % of U.S.	Employment - 1995 Per Estab.	Payroll - 1995 Total ($ mil.)	Payroll - 1995 Per Empl. ($)	Sales - 1992 Total ($ mil.)	Sales - 1992 % of U.S.	Sales - 1992 Per Estab ($)
California	1,017	14.1	10,645	14.2	10	328.8	30,886	2,982.1	13.2	300,042
Illinois	406	5.6	3,604	4.8	9	147.2	40,836	2,103.5	9.3	567,129
New York	580	8.0	5,519	7.4	10	203.2	36,825	1,795.8	7.9	326,037
Texas	529	7.3	5,881	7.9	11	181.7	30,893	1,455.7	6.4	283,990
Pennsylvania	270	3.7	3,657	4.9	14	108.5	29,669	1,371.6	6.1	396,315
Florida	543	7.5	4,285	5.7	8	122.7	28,642	1,042.3	4.6	277,785
New Jersey	273	3.8	2,757	3.7	10	107.7	39,051	1,039.8	4.6	344,064
North Carolina	305	4.2	2,849	3.8	9	87.1	30,571	990.2	4.4	429,570
Georgia	288	4.0	2,576	3.4	9	81.9	31,778	980.8	4.3	422,925
Ohio	233	3.2	2,611	3.5	11	81.1	31,056	771.8	3.4	301,592
Massachusetts	151	2.1	1,379	1.8	9	56.6	41,027	708.4	3.1	496,087
Michigan	187	2.6	2,508	3.4	13	98.3	39,207	678.8	3.0	314,114
Minnesota	156	2.2	1,671	2.2	11	66.6	39,877	668.8	3.0	498,022
Indiana	109	1.5	1,728	2.3	16	63.0	36,437	636.3	2.8	431,989
Washington	173	2.4	1,807	2.4	10	52.8	29,200	562.1	2.5	335,984
Missouri	130	1.8	1,636	2.2	13	54.0	33,027	519.6	2.3	362,114
Maryland	147	2.0	1,855	2.5	13	58.5	31,542	468.6	2.1	228,135
Virginia	167	2.3	1,570	2.1	9	46.2	29,405	413.9	1.8	257,700
Colorado	158	2.2	1,412	1.9	9	44.7	31,691	413.0	1.8	356,621
Tennessee	120	1.7	1,265	1.7	11	39.8	31,430	399.8	1.8	297,270
Mississippi	72	1.0	971	1.3	13	24.5	25,228	318.1	1.4	350,746
Wisconsin	95	1.3	1,196	1.6	13	39.7	33,201	306.2	1.4	286,659
D.C.	30	0.4	212	0.3	7	9.9	46,637	222.3	1.0	685,963
Arizona	121	1.7	1,341	1.8	11	35.0	26,115	211.9	0.9	271,951
Oregon	64	0.9	457	0.6	7	14.4	31,400	185.3	0.8	271,231
Alabama	106	1.5	1,357	1.8	13	31.8	23,416	177.8	0.8	172,154
Kentucky	66	0.9	923	1.2	14	24.5	26,549	147.9	0.7	214,378
South Carolina	74	1.0	724	1.0	10	18.9	26,166	134.1	0.6	218,682
Louisiana	66	0.9	511	0.7	8	13.1	25,734	133.3	0.6	244,092
Iowa	46	0.6	666	0.9	14	20.4	30,673	126.4	0.6	217,167
Utah	46	0.6	343	0.5	7	10.2	29,633	96.6	0.4	266,033
Nebraska	22	0.3	455	0.6	21	12.5	27,413	75.8	0.3	200,005
Hawaii	32	0.4	265	0.4	8	7.4	27,774	71.9	0.3	244,684
Oklahoma	44	0.6	544	0.7	12	15.0	27,621	69.7	0.3	222,534
New Hampshire	27	0.4	286	0.4	11	8.3	28,864	55.6	0.2	212,981
Arkansas	44	0.6	372	0.5	8	9.4	25,390	51.6	0.2	180,252
New Mexico	28	0.4	357	0.5	13	10.0	28,003	39.6	0.2	178,194
Delaware	14	0.2	57	0.1	4	2.1	36,439	27.0	0.1	228,653
Idaho	18	0.2	163	0.2	9	4.2	25,951	25.2	0.1	221,175
Rhode Island	11	0.2	132	0.2	12	3.6	26,992	23.7	0.1	257,870
Nevada	20	0.3	158	0.2	8	5.1	32,108	20.5	0.1	176,784
Vermont	10	0.1	61	0.1	6	1.4	23,311	18.6	0.1	197,947
Maine	15	0.2	90	0.1	6	3.1	34,900	18.0	0.1	216,795
South Dakota	10	0.1	124	0.2	12	3.0	24,460	16.9	0.1	222,500
Alaska	5	0.1	20-99	-	-	(D)	-	10.1	0.0	177,421
Montana	13	0.2	89	0.1	7	2.0	22,337	9.0	0.0	112,325
Wyoming	7	0.1	20-99	-	-	(D)	-	2.3	0.0	120,789
Connecticut	89	1.2	952	1.3	11	33.2	34,881	(D)	-	-
Kansas	56	0.8	388	0.5	7	12.7	32,791	(D)	-	-
West Virginia	27	0.4	293	0.4	11	6.8	23,184	(D)	-	-
North Dakota	10	0.1	126	0.2	13	3.2	25,452	(D)	-	-

Source: County Business Patterns, 1995 and *Economic Census of the U.S., 1992*. Data are sorted by 1992 revenues and, if revenues are unavailable, by establishments in 1995. The symbol (D) indicates that data are withheld by the source to avoid disclosure of competitive information. A dash (-) indicates that data are not available or undisclosed because they do not meet statistical validity standards. Shaded *states* on the state map indicate those states which have proportionately greater representation in the industry than would be indicated by the state's population; the ratio is based on total revenues or number of establishments. Shaded *regions* indicate where the industry is regionally most concentrated.

5023 - HOMEFURNISHINGS

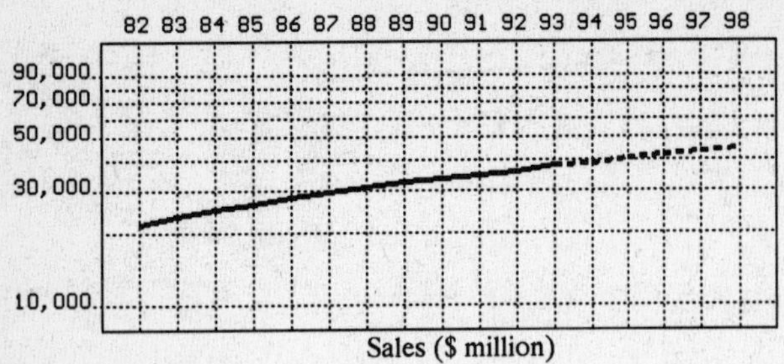

Sales ($ million)

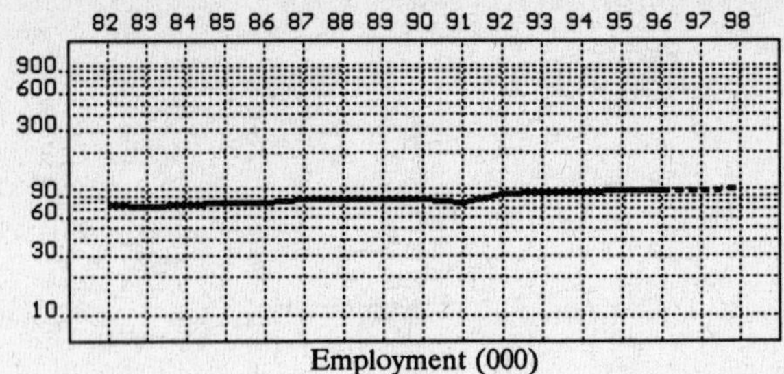

Employment (000)

GENERAL STATISTICS

Year	Establishments (number)	Employment (number)	Payroll ($ million)	Sales ($ million)	Expenses ($ million)	Beginning Inventory ($ million)	Ending Inventory ($ million)
1982	7,361	74,817	1,396.2	21,778.9	-	-	-
1983	6,835	73,145	1,493.9	23,321.6*e*	-	-	-
1984	6,878	76,961	1,610.8	24,864.4*e*	-	-	-
1985	6,754	78,266	1,756.7	26,407.1*e*	-	-	-
1986	6,511	77,912	1,751.8	27,949.9*e*	-	-	-
1987	7,702	84,050	1,948.1	29,492.6	4,481.1	2,343.7	2,492.1
1988	7,200	82,925	2,073.7	30,774.4*e*	4,765.8*e*	2,540.4*e*	2,699.1*e*
1989	6,852	83,971	2,159.4	32,056.2*e*	5,050.6*e*	2,737.0*e*	2,906.2*e*
1990	6,867	83,042	2,217.8	33,338.0*e*	5,335.4*e*	2,933.7*e*	3,113.2*e*
1991	6,771	79,248	2,150.1	34,619.8*e*	5,620.2*e*	3,130.3*e*	3,320.3*e*
1992	9,115	92,274	2,626.7	35,901.6	5,905.0	3,326.9	3,527.3
1993	8,890	93,981	2,754.2	37,610.4*p*	6,189.8*p*	3,523.6*p*	3,734.4*p*
1994	8,824	97,024	2,942.8	39,022.6*p*	6,474.5*p*	3,720.2*p*	3,941.4*p*
1995	8,442	98,253	2,995.0	40,434.9*p*	6,759.3*p*	3,916.9*p*	4,148.5*p*
1996	8,638*p*	97,561*p*	3,057.0*p*	41,847.2*p*	7,044.1*p*	4,113.5*p*	4,355.5*p*
1997	8,789*p*	99,371*p*	3,180.1*p*	43,259.5*p*	7,328.9*p*	4,310.2*p*	4,562.6*p*
1998	8,941*p*	101,180*p*	3,303.1*p*	44,671.7*p*	7,613.7*p*	4,506.8*p*	4,769.6*p*

Sources: *Economic Census of the United States*, 1982, 1987, and 1992. Establishment counts, employment, and payroll are from *County Business Patterns* for non-Census years. Values followed by a 'p' are projections by the editors. Sales and expense data for non-Census years are extrapolations, marked by 'e'. Industries reclassified in 1987 will not have data for prior years. Data are the most recent available at this level of detail.

INDICES OF CHANGE

Year	Establishments (number)	Employment (number)	Payroll ($ million)	Sales ($ million)	Expenses ($ million)	Beginning Inventory ($ million)	Ending Inventory ($ million)
1982	80.8	81.1	53.2	60.7	-	-	-
1983	75.0	79.3	56.9	65.0*e*	-	-	-
1984	75.5	83.4	61.3	69.3*e*	-	-	-
1985	74.1	84.8	66.9	73.6*e*	-	-	-
1986	71.4	84.4	66.7	77.9*e*	-	-	-
1987	84.5	91.1	74.2	82.1	75.9	70.4	70.7
1988	79.0	89.9	78.9	85.7*e*	80.7*e*	76.4*e*	76.5*e*
1989	75.2	91.0	82.2	89.3*e*	85.5*e*	82.3*e*	82.4*e*
1990	75.3	90.0	84.4	92.9*e*	90.4*e*	88.2*e*	88.3*e*
1991	74.3	85.9	81.9	96.4*e*	95.2*e*	94.1*e*	94.1*e*
1992	100.0	100.0	100.0	100.0	100.0	100.0	100.0
1993	97.5	101.8	104.9	104.8*p*	104.8*p*	105.9*p*	105.9*p*
1994	96.8	105.1	112.0	108.7*p*	109.6*p*	111.8*p*	111.7*p*
1995	92.6	106.5	114.0	112.6*p*	114.5*p*	117.7*p*	117.6*p*
1996	94.8*p*	105.7*p*	116.4*p*	116.6*p*	119.3*p*	123.6*p*	123.5*p*
1997	96.4*p*	107.7*p*	121.1*p*	120.5*p*	124.1*p*	129.6*p*	129.4*p*
1998	98.1*p*	109.7*p*	125.8*p*	124.4*p*	128.9*p*	135.5*p*	135.2*p*

Sources: Same as General Statistics. The values shown reflect change from the base year, 1992. Values above 100 mean greater than 1992, values below 100 mean less than 1992, and a value of 100 in the 1982-91 or 1993-98 period means same as 1992. Values followed by a 'p' are projections by the editors; 'e' stands for extrapolation. Data are the most recent available at this level of detail.

SELECTED RATIOS

For 1992	Avg. of All Wholesale	Analyzed Industry	Index	For 1992	Avg. of All Wholesale	Analyzed Industry	Index
Employees per Establishment	12	10	87	Sales per Employee	561,172	389,076	69
Payroll per Establishment	349,729	288,173	82	Sales per Establishment	6,559,346	3,938,738	60
Payroll per Employee	29,919	28,466	95	Expenses per Establishment	723,071	647,833	90

Sources: Same as General Statistics. The 'Average of All Manufacturing' column represents the average of all manufacturing industries reported for the most recent complete year available. The Index shows the relationship between the Average and the Analyzed Industry. For example, 100 means that they are equal; 500 that the Analyzed Industry is five times the average; 50 means that the Analyzed Industry is half the national average. The abbreviation 'na' is used to show that data are 'not available'.

LEADING COMPANIES Number shown: 50 Total sales ($ mil): 8,428 Total employment (000): 25.8

Company Name	Address				CEO Name	Phone	Co. Type	Sales ($ mil)	Empl. (000)
Truserv Corp.	8600 W Bryn Mawr	Chicago	IL	60631	Dan A Cotter	773-695-5000	R	3,846 *	6.0
GE Supply	2 Corporate Dr	Shelton	CT	06484	WL Meddaugh	203-944-3000	D	1,100 *	2.2
LD Brinkman and Co.	1655 Waters Ridge	Lewisville	TX	75057	Levon Ezell	972-353-3500	S	270 *	1.0
La Salle-Deitch Company Inc.	PO Box 2347	Elkhart	IN	46515	A Clark Peters	219-294-2661	S	200	0.5
Decorative Home Accents Inc.	PO Box 11877	Abbeville	SC	29620	Murphy L Fontenot	864-446-2123	R	177	2.0
Home Innovations Inc.	295 Fifth Ave	New York	NY	10016	Chip Fontenot	212-686-2080	S	170 *	2.0
Independent Distribution	3000 Waterview	Baltimore	MD	21230	James L Zamoiski	410-539-3000	R	160	0.5
Kerr Group Inc.	500 New Holland	Lancaster	PA	17602	D. Gordon Strickland	717-299-6511	P	107	0.9
Wilton Industries Inc.	2240 W 75th St	Woodridge	IL	60517	VA Naccarato	630-963-7100	R	104 *	0.5
Koval Marketing Inc.	11208 47th Ave W	Mukilteo	WA	98275	Roy Koval	425-347-4249	R	100	<0.1
L. Powell Co.	PO Box 1408	Culver City	CA	90232	Richard Powell	310-204-2224	R	100 *	<0.1
Lifetime Hoan Corp.	1 Merrick Ave	Westbury	NY	11590	Milton L Cohen	516-683-6000	P	100	0.5
Crystal Clear Industries Inc.	2 Bergen Tpk	Ridgefield Park	NJ	07660	Abraham Lefkowitz	201-440-4200	R	97	0.3
Universal International Inc.	5000 Winnetka N	New Hope	MN	55428	Mark H Ravich	612-533-1169	P	88	1.2
Bradshaw International Inc.	9303 Greenleaf Ave	Santa Fe Sprgs	CA	91730	Mike Rodrigue	310-946-7466	S	84 *	<0.1
Hoboken Wood Flooring Corp.	70 Demarest Dr	Wayne	NJ	07470	John Sakosits	201-694-2888	R	77	0.2
Lowy Group Inc.	4001 N Khiway	St. Louis	MO	63115	M James Cerruti	314-383-2055	R	75	0.5
Conso Products Co.	PO Box 326	Union	SC	29379	SD Southerland	864-427-9004	P	73	1.5
Fitz and Floyd Silvestri	501 Corporateive	Lewisville	TX	75057	Arthur Bylin	972-918-0098	R	63 *	0.3
Bomaine Corp.	2716 Ocean Pk Blvd	Santa Monica	CA	90405	GM Bronstein	310-450-2303	R	61 *	0.7
Building Plastics Inc.	3263 Sharpe Ave	Memphis	TN	38111	Alexander R Hill	901-744-6414	R	61	0.2
Dansk Intern. Designs Ltd.	Radio Circle Rd	Mount Kisco	NY	10549	James Soloman	914-666-2121	S	60	<0.1
Jaydon Inc.	PO Box 4990	Rock Island	IL	61201	Jay M Gellerman	309-787-4492	R	60	0.4
Phoenix Textile Corp.	13652 Lakefront Dr	St. Louis	MO	63045	Pam Reynolds	314-291-2151	R	60 *	0.1
Stark Carpet Corp.	979 3rd Ave	New York	NY	10022	John S Stark	212-752-9000	R	60	0.3
Wedgwood U.S.A. Inc.	PO Box 1454	Wall	NJ	07719	Chris McGillary	908-938-5800	S	60	0.1
Cain and Bultman Inc.	PO Box 2815	Jacksonville	FL	32203	MA Sandifer	904-356-4812	R	52	0.1
H.W. Baker Linen Co.	PO Box 544	Mahwah	NJ	07430	DE Hymans	201-825-2000	R	51 *	0.2
Noritake Company Inc.	75 Seaview Dr	Secaucus	NJ	07094	K Tomita	201-319-0600	S	51 *	0.2
Otagiri Mercantile Company	475 Ecceles Ave	S. San Francisco	CA	94080	T Hirokawa	415-871-4080	R	51	0.2
Bennett Brothers Inc.	30 E Adams St	Chicago	IL	60603	GK Bennett	312-263-4800	R	50	0.1
Tash Inc.	11190 White Birch	R. Cucamonga	CA	91730	Ron Jones	909-945-9566	R	50 *	0.3
Ostrow Textile L.L.C.	PO Box 10550	Rock Hill	SC	29731	Joel J Ostrow	803-324-4284	R	46 *	0.5
Noury and Sons Ltd.	5 Sampson St	Saddle Brook	NJ	07663	Paul Peykar	201-867-6900	R	45	0.1
M. Block and Sons Inc.	2355 S Blue Island	Chicago	IL	60608	Bennet S Levy	312-247-8400	R	42	0.1
Adleta Corp.	1645 Diplomat Dr	Carrollton	TX	75006	Jack Adleta	214-620-5600	R	41	<0.1
Allison-Erwin Co.	2920 N Tryon St	Charlotte	NC	28232	PD McMillan	704-334-8621	R	40	0.1
Cooper Distributors Inc.	7122 NW 74th Ave	Miami	FL	33166	J Cooper	305-888-3910	S	40	0.2
George H. Lehleitner and Co.	PO Box 23707	Harahan	LA	70183	Tom P Hoy Jr	504-734-0530	R	40	0.2
Misco Shawnee Inc.	2200 Forte Ct	Maryland H.	MO	63043	Courtney A Gould	314-739-3337	R	40	0.1
USCP-Wesco Inc.	4444 Ayers Ave	Los Angeles	CA	90023	Lou Bernardi	213-269-0292	S	40	0.2
Villeroy&Boch Tableware Ltd.	5 Fawn DR, #303	Princeton	NJ	08540	Safford Sweatt	609-734-7800	R	40 *	<0.1
Craftmade International Inc.	PO Box 1037	Coppell	TX	75019	James R Ridings	972-393-3800	P	40	<0.1
Fashion Bed Group	5950 W 51st St	Chicago	IL	60638	Joe Geiger	708-458-1800	S	39 *	0.1
B.R. Funsten and Co.	2045 Evans Ave	San Francisco	CA	94124	Jim Funsten	415-641-1200	R	38 *	<0.1
First National Trading Company	295 5th Ave	New York	NY	10001	Paul Shen	212-725-7265	S	38	0.2
Wanke Cascade	6330 N Cutter Cir	Portland	OR	97217	Brian Radditz	503-289-8609	R	37 *	0.1
Fetco International Corp.	PO Box 165	Randolph	MA	02368	Kenneth McCord	617-871-2000	R	35	<0.1
William M. Bird and Company	PO Box 20040	Charleston	SC	29413	D Maybank Hagood	803-722-5930	R	35	<0.1
Orders Distributing Company	PO Box 17189	Greenville	SC	29606	C Micheal Smith	803-288-4220	R	34 *	0.2

Source: *Ward's Business Directory of U.S. Private and Public Companies*, 1998. The company type code used is as follows: P - Public, R - Private, S - Subsidiary, D - Division, J - Joint Venture, A - Affiliate, G - Group. Sales are in millions of dollars, employees are in thousands. An asterisk (*) indicates an estimated sales volume. The symbol < stands for 'less than'.

OCCUPATIONS EMPLOYED BY SIC 502 - WHOLESALE TRADE, OTHER

Occupation	% of Total 1996	Change to 2006	Occupation	% of Total 1996	Change to 2006
Sales & related workers nec	19.5	20.2	Clerical supervisors & managers	1.9	20.2
General managers & top executives	5.9	16.4	Order clerks	1.9	8.2
Truck drivers light & heavy	5.4	20.2	Helpers, laborers nec	1.7	20.2
General office clerks	3.6	3.4	Electrical & electronic technicians	1.4	18.8
Traffic, shipping, receiving clerks	3.6	16.7	Blue collar worker supervisors	1.4	16.0
Stock clerks	3.5	-3.9	Wholesale & retail buyers, except farm products	1.3	17.0
Freight, stock, & material movers, hand	3.3	8.2	Office machine & cash register servicers	1.3	20.2
Marketing & sales worker supervisors	3.1	20.2	Hand packers & packagers	1.2	-3.9
Order fillers, wholesale & retail sales	3.0	16.7	Maintenance repairers, general utility	1.1	12.0
Bookkeeping, accounting, & auditing clerks	2.9	-3.9	Industrial truck & tractor operators	1.1	20.2
Salespersons, retail	2.5	20.2	Purchasing managers	1.1	20.2
Secretaries, except legal & medical	2.5	-4.7	Receptionists & information clerks	1.0	20.2
Assemblers, fabricators, hand workers nec	2.0	-3.9			

Source: *Industry-Occupation Matrix*, Bureau of Labor Statistics. These data relate to one or more 3-digit SIC industry groups rather than to a single 4-digit SIC. The change reported for each occupation to the year 2006 is a percent of growth or decline as estimated by the Bureau of Labor Statistics. The abbreviation nec stands for 'not elsewhere classified'.

STATE AND REGIONAL CONCENTRATION

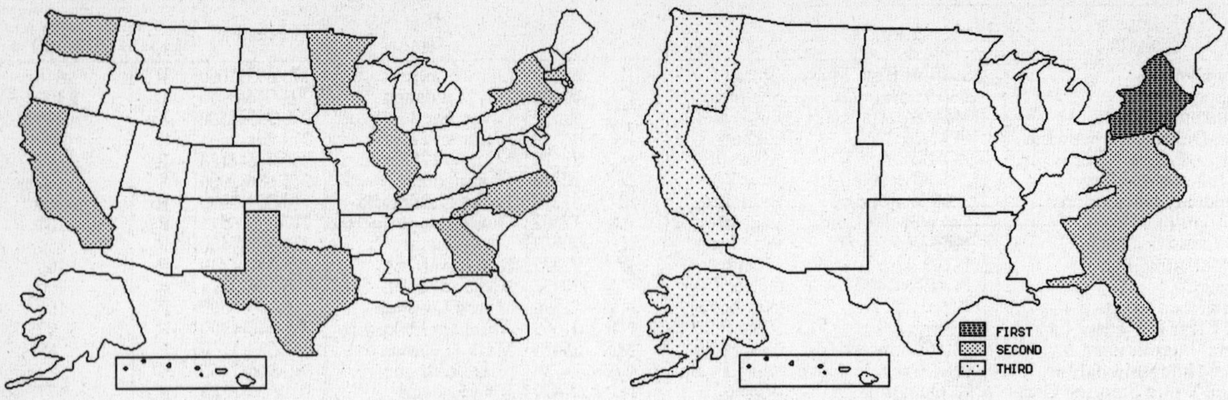

INDUSTRY DATA BY STATE

State	Establishments - 1995 Total (number)	% of U.S.	Employment - 1995 Total (number)	% of U.S.	Per Estab.	Payroll - 1995 Total ($ mil.)	Per Empl. ($)	Sales - 1992 Total ($ mil.)	% of U.S.	Per Estab ($)
New York	1,053	12.5	9,943	10.1	9	394.8	39,708	5,328.5	14.9	514,131
California	1,147	13.6	13,151	13.4	11	375.1	28,523	4,896.6	13.7	340,351
Georgia	467	5.5	7,048	7.2	15	200.0	28,379	3,731.8	10.4	621,140
New Jersey	400	4.7	8,486	8.6	21	298.7	35,202	3,064.3	8.6	441,798
Texas	592	7.0	6,891	7.0	12	198.3	28,779	2,906.6	8.1	484,520
Illinois	388	4.6	5,491	5.6	14	201.1	36,623	2,472.8	6.9	476,359
Pennsylvania	250	3.0	3,485	3.5	14	101.8	29,210	1,306.0	3.7	310,370
Ohio	235	2.8	3,288	3.3	14	100.8	30,653	1,281.9	3.6	424,762
Florida	663	7.9	4,627	4.7	7	119.2	25,768	1,221.6	3.4	295,206
North Carolina	230	2.7	2,146	2.2	9	67.8	31,612	1,077.9	3.0	561,408
Massachusetts	217	2.6	1,880	1.9	9	63.8	33,913	905.9	2.5	458,697
Washington	235	2.8	2,387	2.4	10	72.6	30,401	768.2	2.1	323,979
Michigan	170	2.0	2,147	2.2	13	61.7	28,719	720.0	2.0	415,460
Minnesota	172	2.0	1,510	1.5	9	49.4	32,715	660.1	1.8	454,608
Missouri	148	1.8	2,157	2.2	15	64.6	29,938	647.2	1.8	291,814
Maryland	158	1.9	1,838	1.9	12	57.4	31,220	626.8	1.8	324,109
Colorado	133	1.6	1,324	1.3	10	36.5	27,575	374.4	1.0	313,816
Tennessee	138	1.6	1,993	2.0	14	55.1	27,634	336.7	0.9	268,481
Virginia	143	1.7	1,460	1.5	10	41.9	28,705	285.5	0.8	231,526
Arizona	134	1.6	1,748	1.8	13	44.4	25,427	259.2	0.7	216,750
Connecticut	94	1.1	812	0.8	9	25.3	31,187	253.0	0.7	304,141
South Carolina	83	1.0	1,799	1.8	22	47.9	26,641	252.5	0.7	201,966
Alabama	81	1.0	1,248	1.3	15	29.4	23,559	249.3	0.7	196,928
Oregon	110	1.3	1,082	1.1	10	29.9	27,672	237.3	0.7	292,970
Indiana	126	1.5	1,119	1.1	9	26.5	23,659	227.9	0.6	230,680
Wisconsin	106	1.3	967	1.0	9	26.7	27,638	220.7	0.6	226,177
Louisiana	58	0.7	698	0.7	12	17.2	24,711	169.7	0.5	212,683
Rhode Island	23	0.3	410	0.4	18	13.5	32,941	116.4	0.3	330,662
Utah	58	0.7	813	0.8	14	17.5	21,565	111.8	0.3	170,434
Oklahoma	65	0.8	604	0.6	9	14.4	23,810	110.7	0.3	176,287
Kentucky	57	0.7	582	0.6	10	14.3	24,552	104.2	0.3	186,797
Arkansas	45	0.5	481	0.5	11	12.2	25,464	97.6	0.3	305,853
Hawaii	42	0.5	497	0.5	12	13.3	26,781	94.3	0.3	257,727
Iowa	37	0.4	572	0.6	15	12.5	21,911	92.4	0.3	214,422
Nevada	28	0.3	260	0.3	9	7.0	26,823	83.2	0.2	239,876
New Hampshire	31	0.4	190	0.2	6	5.0	26,232	60.1	0.2	488,935
Maine	26	0.3	362	0.4	14	8.9	24,622	59.4	0.2	206,829
Mississippi	31	0.4	445	0.5	14	10.1	22,685	57.8	0.2	176,274
Nebraska	24	0.3	264	0.3	11	6.6	25,087	48.4	0.1	162,889
West Virginia	19	0.2	228	0.2	12	5.3	23,434	37.8	0.1	148,996
New Mexico	32	0.4	327	0.3	10	6.9	21,006	36.9	0.1	165,552
Delaware	23	0.3	173	0.2	8	6.0	34,792	35.2	0.1	247,951
South Dakota	9	0.1	86	0.1	10	1.9	22,384	30.6	0.1	205,074
D.C.	17	0.2	82	0.1	5	3.8	46,146	29.4	0.1	288,471
Idaho	21	0.2	160	0.2	8	4.0	25,069	23.4	0.1	156,120
Montana	11	0.1	73	0.1	7	1.3	17,575	13.4	0.0	196,368
Alaska	8	0.1	20-99	-	-	(D)	-	11.0	0.0	182,817
Vermont	13	0.2	97	0.1	7	2.1	21,845	7.9	0.0	108,438
Wyoming	3	0.0	20-99	-	-	(D)	-	1.6	0.0	53,533
Kansas	82	1.0	668	0.7	8	17.4	26,046	(D)	-	-
North Dakota	6	0.1	73	0.1	12	1.6	21,411	(D)	-	-

Source: County Business Patterns, 1995 and *Economic Census of the U.S., 1992*. Data are sorted by 1992 revenues and, if revenues are unavailable, by establishments in 1995. The symbol (D) indicates that data are withheld by the source to avoid disclosure of competitive information. A dash (-) indicates that data are not available or undisclosed because they do not meet statistical validity standards. Shaded *states* on the state map indicate those states which have proportionately greater representation in the industry than would be indicated by the state's population; the ratio is based on total revenues or number of establishments. Shaded *regions* indicate where the industry is regionally most concentrated.

5031 - LUMBER, PLYWOOD, AND MILLWORK

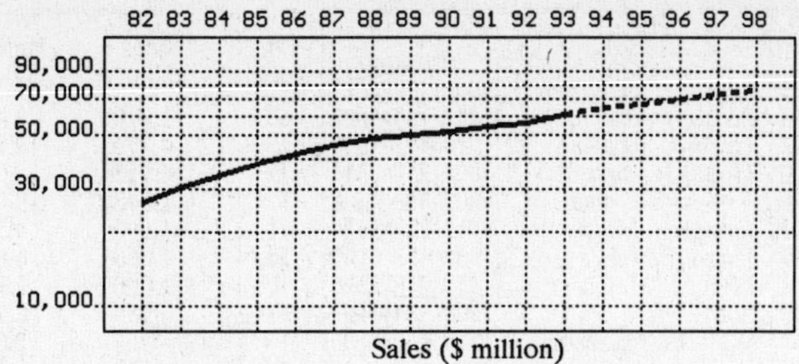

Sales ($ million)

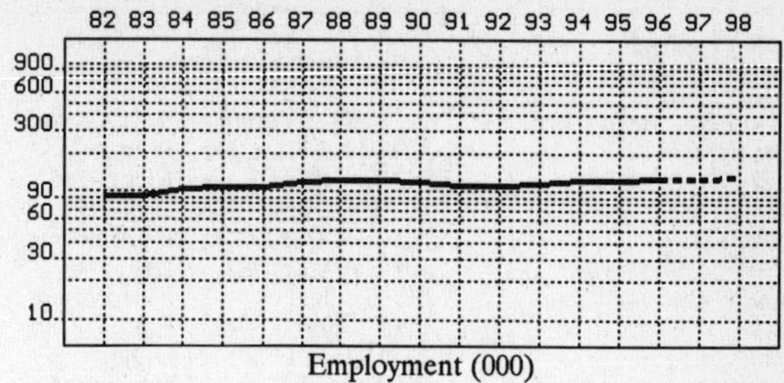

Employment (000)

GENERAL STATISTICS

Year	Establishments (number)	Employment (number)	Payroll ($ million)	Sales ($ million)	Expenses ($ million)	Beginning Inventory ($ million)	Ending Inventory ($ million)
1982	7,245	91,656	1,674.4	26,465.1	-	-	-
1983	7,259	92,272	1,919.8	30,347.5e	-	-	-
1984	6,882	104,188	2,198.4	34,230.0e	-	-	-
1985	6,853	106,462	2,358.2	38,112.5e	-	-	-
1986	6,800	108,358	2,529.5	41,995.0e	-	-	-
1987	8,098	119,796	2,812.4	45,877.5	5,554.5	2,990.2	3,352.0
1988	7,808	123,333	3,091.0	47,902.8e	5,713.0e	3,144.1e	3,515.1e
1989	7,633	122,607	3,159.2	49,928.2e	5,871.5e	3,298.0e	3,678.2e
1990	7,677	118,902	3,134.7	51,953.6e	6,030.0e	3,451.9e	3,841.3e
1991	7,594	109,438	2,982.5	53,979.0e	6,188.6e	3,605.8e	4,004.5e
1992	8,364	111,626	3,242.3	56,004.4	6,347.1	3,759.7	4,167.6
1993	8,377	115,391	3,591.8	61,068.6p	6,505.6p	3,913.6p	4,330.7p
1994	8,604	122,835	3,876.1	64,022.6p	6,664.2p	4,067.4p	4,493.9p
1995	8,584	122,769	3,794.6	66,976.5p	6,822.7p	4,221.3p	4,657.0p
1996	8,667p	126,616p	4,055.4p	69,930.4p	6,981.2p	4,375.2p	4,820.1p
1997	8,796p	128,549p	4,211.7p	72,884.4p	7,139.7p	4,529.1p	4,983.2p
1998	8,925p	130,483p	4,368.0p	75,838.3p	7,298.3p	4,683.0p	5,146.4p

Sources: Economic Census of the United States, 1982, 1987, and 1992. Establishment counts, employment, and payroll are from *County Business Patterns* for non-Census years. Values followed by a 'p' are projections by the editors. Sales and expense data for non-Census years are extrapolations, marked by 'e'. Industries reclassified in 1987 will not have data for prior years. Data are the most recent available at this level of detail.

INDICES OF CHANGE

Year	Establishments (number)	Employment (number)	Payroll ($ million)	Sales ($ million)	Expenses ($ million)	Beginning Inventory ($ million)	Ending Inventory ($ million)
1982	86.6	82.1	51.6	47.3	-	-	-
1983	86.8	82.7	59.2	54.2e	-	-	-
1984	82.3	93.3	67.8	61.1e	-	-	-
1985	81.9	95.4	72.7	68.1e	-	-	-
1986	81.3	97.1	78.0	75.0e	-	-	-
1987	96.8	107.3	86.7	81.9	87.5	79.5	80.4
1988	93.4	110.5	95.3	85.5e	90.0e	83.6e	84.3e
1989	91.3	109.8	97.4	89.2e	92.5e	87.7e	88.3e
1990	91.8	106.5	96.7	92.8e	95.0e	91.8e	92.2e
1991	90.8	98.0	92.0	96.4e	97.5e	95.9e	96.1e
1992	100.0	100.0	100.0	100.0	100.0	100.0	100.0
1993	100.2	103.4	110.8	109.0p	102.5p	104.1p	103.9p
1994	102.9	110.0	119.5	114.3p	105.0p	108.2p	107.8p
1995	102.6	110.0	117.0	119.6p	107.5p	112.3p	111.7p
1996	103.6p	113.4p	125.1p	124.9p	110.0p	116.4p	115.7p
1997	105.2p	115.2p	129.9p	130.1p	112.5p	120.5p	119.6p
1998	106.7p	116.9p	134.7p	135.4p	115.0p	124.6p	123.5p

Sources: Same as General Statistics. The values shown reflect change from the base year, 1992. Values above 100 mean greater than 1992, values below 100 mean less than 1992, and a value of 100 in the 1982-91 or 1993-98 period means same as 1992. Values followed by a 'p' are projections by the editors; 'e' stands for extrapolation. Data are the most recent available at this level of detail.

SELECTED RATIOS

For 1992	Avg. of All Wholesale	Analyzed Industry	Index	For 1992	Avg. of All Wholesale	Analyzed Industry	Index
Employees per Establishment	12	13	114	Sales per Employee	561,172	501,715	89
Payroll per Establishment	349,729	387,649	111	Sales per Establishment	6,559,346	6,695,887	102
Payroll per Employee	29,919	29,046	97	Expenses per Establishment	723,071	758,859	105

Sources: Same as General Statistics. The 'Average of All Manufacturing' column represents the average of all manufacturing industries reported for the most recent complete year available. The Index shows the relationship between the Average and the Analyzed Industry. For example, 100 means that they are equal; 500 that the Analyzed Industry is five times the average; 50 means that the Analyzed Industry is half the national average. The abbreviation 'na' is used to show that data are 'not available'.

LEADING COMPANIES Number shown: 50 Total sales ($ mil): 35,358 Total employment (000): 93.8

Company Name	Address				CEO Name	Phone	Co. Type	Sales ($ mil)	Empl. (000)
Nissho Iwai American Corp.	1211 of the Amer	New York	NY	10036	Akira Yokouchi	212-704-6500	S	11,910	0.4
HomeBase Inc.	3345 Michelson Dr	Irvine	CA	92612	Herbert J Zarkin	714-442-5000	P	4,376	19.5
Universal Corp.	PO Box 25099	Richmond	VA	23260	Henry H Harrell	804-359-9311	P	4,113	25.0
Crane Co.	100 1st Stamford Pl	Stamford	CT	06902	Robert S Evans	203-363-7300	P	1,848	10.0
84 Lumber Co.	Rte 519, Box 8484	Eighty Four	PA	15384	Joseph A Hardy	412-228-8820	R	1,600	4.5
Carter Lumber Co.	601 Talmadge Rd	Kent	OH	44240	Brian Carter	330-673-6100	R	1,060 *	4.0
Hardware Wholesalers Inc.	PO Box 868	Fort Wayne	IN	46801	Michael McClelland	219-748-5300	R	1,000	1.1
Boise Cascade Corp.	1111 Jefferson Sq	Boise	ID	83702	Stan Bell	208-384-6161	D	956 *	5.2
Cameron Ashley	11651 Plano Rd	Dallas	TX	75243	Walter J Muratori	214-860-5100	P	762	2.0
Builder Marts of America Inc.	PO Box 47	Greenville	SC	29602	Brian S MacKenzie	864-297-6101	R	547	0.1
Rugby USA Inc.	570 Lake Cook Rd	Deerfield	IL	60015	Dave Stry	847-405-0850	R	500	1.3
Furman Lumber Inc.	PO Box 130	Nutting Lake	MA	01865	Barry L Kronick	508-670-3800	R	455	0.3
Wolohan Lumber Co.	PO Box 3235	Saginaw	MI	48605	James L Wolohan	517-793-4532	P	425	1.5
Patrick Industries Inc.	PO Box 638	Elkhart	IN	46515	Mervin D Lung	219-294-7511	P	404	1.5
Timber Products Co.	PO Box 269	Springfield	OR	97477	Joseph H Gonyea	541-747-4577	R	360 *	1.0
Tumac Lumber Company Inc.	529 SW 3rd Ave	Portland	OR	97204	Michael Blanchat	503-226-6661	R	318	0.2
Anderson Lumber Co.	PO Box 9459	Ogden	UT	84409	James C Beardall	801-479-3400	R	285	1.6
AMRE Inc.	8585 Nemmons Fwy	Dallas	TX	75219	Robert M Swartz	214-929-4088	P	271	3.1
Morgan Distribution Inc.	PO Box 2003	Mechanicsburg	PA	17055	Joseph LaCroix	717-697-1151	S	250	0.8
Roberts and Dybdahl Inc.	Box 1908	Des Moines	IA	50306	Howard L Roberts	515-283-7100	R	230	0.3
Allied Building Stores Inc.	PO Box 8030	Monroe	LA	71211	Laddie Woods	318-343-7200	R	226	<0.1
Banks Lumber Company Inc.	PO Box 2299	Elkhart	IN	46515	William Banks	219-294-5671	R	200	1.0
Hampton Lumber Sales Co.	9400 SW Barnes Rd	Portland	OR	97225	Michael Phillips	503-297-7691	S	200 *	0.5
Canal Industries Inc.	PO Box 260001	Conway	SC	29526		803-347-4251	R	190 *	0.4
Forest City Trading Group Inc.	PO Box 4209	Portland	OR	97208	Milan Stoyanov	503-246-8500	S	180 *	0.6
American Intern. Forest Products	5560 SW 107th St	Beaverton	OR	97005	John W Judy	503-641-1611	S	150	0.1
Dixieline Lumber Co.	3250 Sports Arena	San Diego	CA	92110	William S Cowling II	619-224-4120	R	150	0.7
Diamond Hill Plywood Co.	600 E Broad St	Darlington	SC	29532	John Ramsey	803-393-2803	S	130	0.4
Miller and Company Inc.	500 Hooper Dr	Selma	AL	36701	Bill Deramus	205-874-8271	R	130 *	0.4
Millman Lumber Co.	9264 Manchester	St. Louis	MO	63144	Richard G Millman	314-968-1700	R	130 *	0.4
Redwood Empire Inc.	PO Box 1300	Morgan Hill	CA	95038	Rodger A Burch	408-779-7354	R	130 *	0.4
Geneva Corp.	PO Box 21962	Greensboro	NC	27420	F James Becher	910-275-9936	R	125	0.6
OREPAC Building Products	30170 OREPAC	Wilsonville	OR	97070	Glen Hart	503-682-5050	R	120	0.5
Futter Lumber Corp.	PO Box 347	Rockville Centre	NY	11571	Bernard Futter	516-764-4445	R	116	<0.1
Frank Paxton Co.	6311 St John Ave	Kansas City	MO	64114	Roger Davis	816-483-3007	S	110	0.7
Stringfellow Lumber Co.	PO Box 1117	Birmingham	AL	35201	Donald R Fisher	205-731-9400	S	110	<0.1
Allied Plywood Corp.	200 Baker Ave	Concord	MA	01742	Robert H Nassau	508-371-3399	S	100	0.2
Brockway-Smith Co.	146 Dascomb Rd	Andover	MA	01810	Rodolph P Gagnon	508-475-7100	R	100	0.5
Crestland Cooperative	PO Box 329	Creston	IA	50801	Larry E Crosser	515-782-6411	R	100	0.2
Builderway Inc.	PO Drawer 27107	Greenville	SC	29616	Newell LaVoy	803-297-6266	R	98 *	0.4
Pan American Trade Dev Corp.	310 Madison Ave	New York	NY	10017	Peter Slotta	212-599-3500	R	98 *	0.4
Brookharts Inc.	704 S Sierra Madre	Co Springs	CO	80907	TW Watt	719-471-4500	R	96 *	0.4
J.E. Higgins Lumber Co.	PO Box 4124	Concord	CA	94524	Jonathan R Long	510-674-9300	R	95	0.4
Thomas R. Hopson Broker Inc.	PO Box 7295	Marietta	GA	30065	Steve Hopson	404-578-2400	R	94	0.5
Lumberman's Inc.	4433 Stafford St	Grand Rapids	MI	49548	Henry Bouma	616-538-5180	R	90	0.2
Patrick Lumber Company Inc.	828 SW 1st St	Portland	OR	97204	R D McCracken	503-222-9671	R	85	<0.1
Philadelphia Reserve Supply Co.	400 Mack Dr	Croydon	PA	19021	Frank J Dalinsky	215-785-3141	R	85	<0.1
Snavely Forest Products Inc.	PO Box 9808	Pittsburgh	PA	15227	SV Snavely	412-885-4000	R	85	0.1
International Industries Inc.	PO Drawer D	Gilbert	WV	25621	James Harless	304-664-3227	R	84 *	0.3
Kogel-Giant Builders	390 Rte 25	Middle Island	NY	11953	Larry Kogel	516-924-0500	R	83 *	0.3

Source: Ward's Business Directory of U.S. Private and Public Companies, 1998. The company type code used is as follows: P - Public, R - Private, S - Subsidiary, D - Division, J - Joint Venture, A - Affiliate, G - Group. Sales are in millions of dollars, employees are in thousands. An asterisk (*) indicates an estimated sales volume. The symbol < stands for 'less than'.

OCCUPATIONS EMPLOYED BY SIC 503 - WHOLESALE TRADE, OTHER

Occupation	% of Total 1996	Change to 2006	Occupation	% of Total 1996	Change to 2006
Sales & related workers nec	19.5	20.2	Clerical supervisors & managers	1.9	20.2
General managers & top executives	5.9	16.4	Order clerks	1.9	8.2
Truck drivers light & heavy	5.4	20.2	Helpers, laborers nec	1.7	20.2
General office clerks	3.6	3.4	Electrical & electronic technicians	1.4	18.8
Traffic, shipping, receiving clerks	3.6	16.7	Blue collar worker supervisors	1.4	16.0
Stock clerks	3.5	-3.9	Wholesale & retail buyers, except farm products	1.3	17.0
Freight, stock, & material movers, hand	3.3	8.2	Office machine & cash register servicers	1.3	20.2
Marketing & sales worker supervisors	3.1	20.2	Hand packers & packagers	1.2	-3.9
Order fillers, wholesale & retail sales	3.0	16.7	Maintenance repairers, general utility	1.1	12.0
Bookkeeping, accounting, & auditing clerks	2.9	-3.9	Industrial truck & tractor operators	1.1	20.2
Salespersons, retail	2.5	20.2	Purchasing managers	1.1	20.2
Secretaries, except legal & medical	2.5	-4.7	Receptionists & information clerks	1.0	20.2
Assemblers, fabricators, hand workers nec	2.0	-3.9			

Source: Industry-Occupation Matrix, Bureau of Labor Statistics. These data relate to one or more 3-digit SIC industry groups rather than to a single 4-digit SIC. The change reported for each occupation to the year 2006 is a percent of growth or decline as estimated by the Bureau of Labor Statistics. The abbreviation nec stands for 'not elsewhere classified'.

STATE AND REGIONAL CONCENTRATION

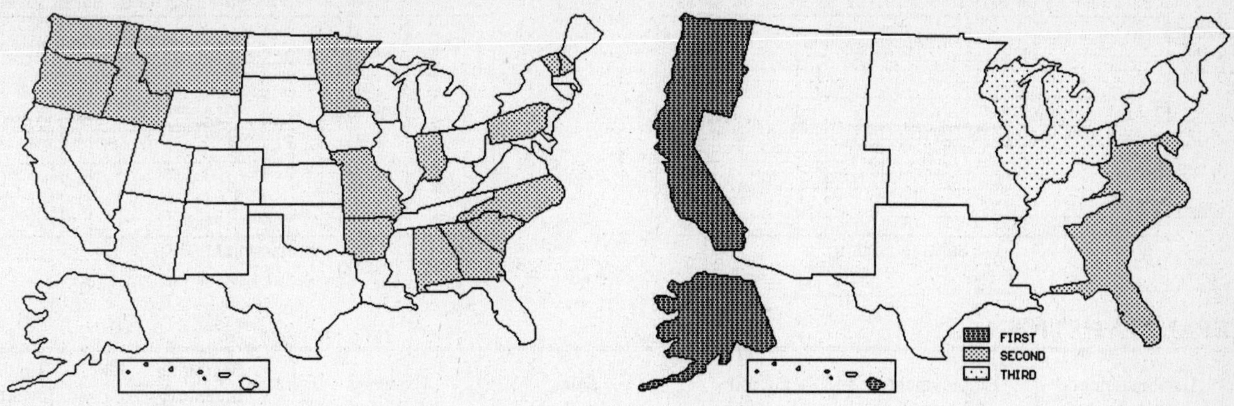

INDUSTRY DATA BY STATE

	Establishments - 1995		Employment - 1995			Payroll - 1995		Sales - 1992		
State	Total (number)	% of U.S.	Total (number)	% of U.S.	Per Estab.	Total ($ mil.)	Per Empl. ($)	Total ($ mil.)	% of U.S.	Per Estab ($)
California	742	8.6	9,939	8.1	13	331.5	33,352	5,016.3	9.1	453,065
Oregon	388	4.5	4,865	4.0	13	196.8	40,445	4,794.0	8.7	1,219,860
Washington	361	4.2	3,934	3.2	11	134.2	34,108	3,553.4	6.4	889,007
Texas	453	5.3	7,599	6.2	17	224.4	29,524	3,205.8	5.8	541,429
Pennsylvania	340	4.0	5,670	4.6	17	170.1	29,993	3,080.0	5.6	446,379
New York	457	5.3	5,792	4.7	13	186.9	32,266	2,400.6	4.3	397,976
Florida	493	5.7	6,077	5.0	12	166.0	27,310	2,378.9	4.3	437,146
Minnesota	189	2.2	2,899	2.4	15	109.5	37,772	2,144.7	3.9	941,492
North Carolina	406	4.7	6,457	5.3	16	173.0	26,799	2,006.9	3.6	413,202
Indiana	219	2.6	3,659	3.0	17	104.3	28,503	1,922.7	3.5	647,145
Illinois	335	3.9	4,320	3.5	13	148.3	34,340	1,655.0	3.0	454,550
Michigan	268	3.1	3,510	2.9	13	121.3	34,549	1,653.2	3.0	462,174
Georgia	292	3.4	4,720	3.8	16	145.1	30,749	1,518.4	2.7	396,555
Ohio	318	3.7	4,293	3.5	14	122.5	28,546	1,506.7	2.7	425,872
Idaho	65	0.8	775	0.6	12	23.0	29,693	1,384.1	2.5	1,453,885
Virginia	210	2.4	3,912	3.2	19	107.7	27,519	1,382.9	2.5	396,925
Massachusetts	176	2.1	2,622	2.1	15	96.0	36,606	1,236.5	2.2	474,287
Missouri	179	2.1	2,721	2.2	15	76.6	28,143	1,167.7	2.1	452,429
Alabama	216	2.5	3,092	2.5	14	80.0	25,878	1,144.1	2.1	456,548
New Jersey	196	2.3	2,847	2.3	15	101.5	35,637	1,098.4	2.0	381,652
Tennessee	226	2.6	3,268	2.7	14	87.0	26,611	1,038.1	1.9	333,142
South Carolina	105	1.2	1,842	1.5	18	52.4	28,421	898.0	1.6	596,699
Wisconsin	183	2.1	2,649	2.2	14	80.2	30,263	826.8	1.5	374,110
Maryland	152	1.8	2,588	2.1	17	75.2	29,051	778.0	1.4	318,332
Louisiana	104	1.2	1,625	1.3	16	41.2	25,361	716.8	1.3	564,448
Arkansas	75	0.9	700	0.6	9	21.1	30,184	694.4	1.3	1,039,572
Colorado	146	1.7	2,298	1.9	16	72.4	31,515	633.2	1.1	361,431
Kentucky	137	1.6	1,949	1.6	14	50.8	26,073	553.3	1.0	319,290
Arizona	130	1.5	2,187	1.8	17	64.8	29,631	526.7	1.0	378,893
Connecticut	97	1.1	1,379	1.1	14	46.1	33,426	518.1	0.9	445,843
Mississippi	87	1.0	1,198	1.0	14	33.1	27,645	502.5	0.9	436,203
New Hampshire	52	0.6	775	0.6	15	26.7	34,427	473.0	0.9	802,971
Iowa	90	1.0	1,355	1.1	15	35.9	26,528	434.0	0.8	358,693
Utah	61	0.7	944	0.8	15	29.7	31,421	323.4	0.6	460,670
Montana	62	0.7	597	0.5	10	19.9	33,362	289.4	0.5	534,980
Hawaii	46	0.5	569	0.5	12	21.1	37,128	256.6	0.5	301,167
Oklahoma	67	0.8	913	0.7	14	21.5	23,604	235.3	0.4	333,803
New Mexico	50	0.6	818	0.7	16	23.6	28,883	230.0	0.4	366,759
Maine	46	0.5	584	0.5	13	15.0	25,639	214.3	0.4	368,290
Nebraska	42	0.5	497	0.4	12	33.0	66,447	212.0	0.4	304,191
Vermont	35	0.4	346	0.3	10	9.8	28,376	172.4	0.3	504,231
North Dakota	20	0.2	386	0.3	19	10.7	27,723	129.0	0.2	367,578
Nevada	54	0.6	641	0.5	12	20.1	31,303	122.1	0.2	278,141
South Dakota	20	0.2	387	0.3	19	10.0	25,721	107.0	0.2	307,526
West Virginia	50	0.6	666	0.5	13	12.4	18,574	105.0	0.2	256,724
Rhode Island	20	0.2	150	0.1	8	5.3	35,393	76.4	0.1	279,766
Wyoming	15	0.2	100-249	-	-	(D)	-	61.0	0.1	500,115
Alaska	12	0.1	81	0.1	7	2.2	27,506	24.6	0.0	379,154
D.C.	2	0.0	20-99	-	-	(D)	-	11.6	0.0	242,146
Kansas	69	0.8	1,104	0.9	16	36.9	33,455	(D)	-	-
Delaware	26	0.3	439	0.4	17	12.6	28,795	(D)	-	-

Source: *County Business Patterns, 1995* and *Economic Census of the U.S., 1992*. Data are sorted by 1992 revenues and, if revenues are unavailable, by establishments in 1995. The symbol (D) indicates that data are withheld by the source to avoid disclosure of competitive information. A dash (-) indicates that data are not available or undisclosed because they do not meet statistical validity standards. Shaded *states* on the state map indicate those states which have proportionately greater representation in the industry than would be indicated by the state's population; the ratio is based on total revenues or number of establishments. Shaded *regions* indicate where the industry is regionally most concentrated.

5032 - BRICK, STONE, & RELATED MATERIALS

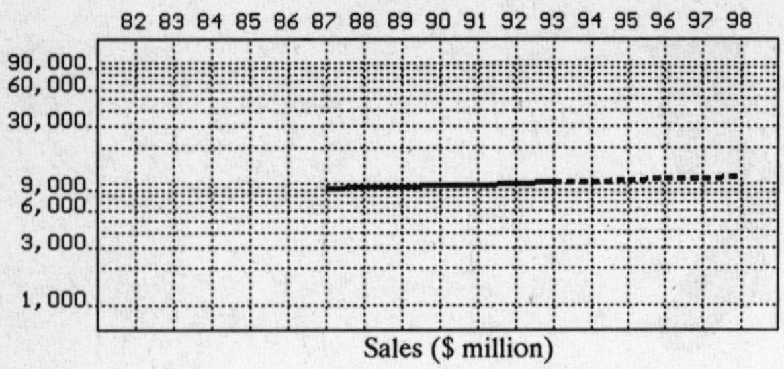

Sales ($ million)

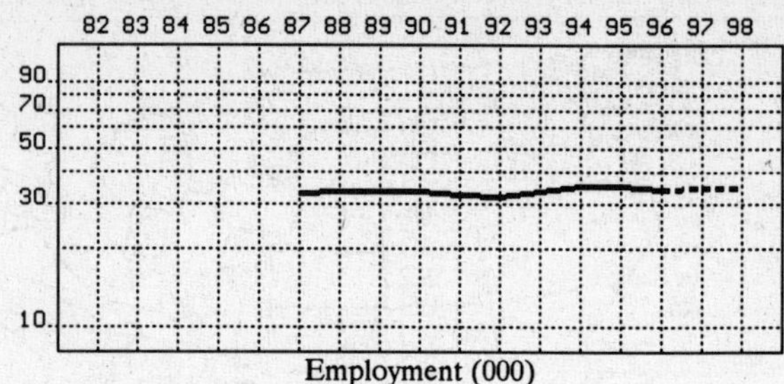

Employment (000)

GENERAL STATISTICS

Year	Establishments (number)	Employment (number)	Payroll ($ million)	Sales ($ million)	Expenses ($ million)	Beginning Inventory ($ million)	Ending Inventory ($ million)
1982	-	-	-	-	-	-	-
1983	-	-	-	-	-	-	-
1984	-	-	-	-	-	-	-
1985	-	-	-	-	-	-	-
1986	-	-	-	-	-	-	-
1987	3,880	33,252	800.2	9,094.1	1,838.2	630.3	686.1
1988	3,754	33,941	878.7	9,298.8e	1,874.6e	677.9e	721.1e
1989	3,622	33,352	969.8	9,503.5e	1,911.0e	725.6e	756.2e
1990	3,746	33,415	929.4	9,708.2e	1,947.4e	773.3e	791.2e
1991	3,892	32,419	889.8	9,912.9e	1,983.7e	820.9e	826.2e
1992	4,285	32,062	924.8	10,117.7	2,020.1	868.6	861.2
1993	4,434	33,468	981.5	10,322.4p	2,056.5p	916.3p	896.2p
1994	4,618	35,532	1,116.7	10,527.1p	2,092.9p	963.9p	931.2p
1995	4,375	35,141	1,103.8	10,731.8p	2,129.3p	1,011.6p	966.2p
1996	4,629p	34,554p	1,117.2p	10,936.5p	2,165.7p	1,059.3p	1,001.3p
1997	4,741p	34,741p	1,149.7p	11,141.2p	2,202.1p	1,106.9p	1,036.3p
1998	4,853p	34,928p	1,182.2p	11,345.9p	2,238.4p	1,154.6p	1,071.3p

Sources: *Economic Census of the United States*, 1982, 1987, and 1992. Establishment counts, employment, and payroll are from *County Business Patterns* for non-Census years. Values followed by a 'p' are projections by the editors. Sales and expense data for non-Census years are extrapolations, marked by 'e'. Industries reclassified in 1987 will not have data for prior years. Data are the most recent available at this level of detail.

INDICES OF CHANGE

Year	Establishments (number)	Employment (number)	Payroll ($ million)	Sales ($ million)	Expenses ($ million)	Beginning Inventory ($ million)	Ending Inventory ($ million)
1982	-	-	-	-	-	-	-
1983	-	-	-	-	-	-	-
1984	-	-	-	-	-	-	-
1985	-	-	-	-	-	-	-
1986	-	-	-	-	-	-	-
1987	90.5	103.7	86.5	89.9	91.0	72.6	79.7
1988	87.6	105.9	95.0	91.9e	92.8e	78.0e	83.7e
1989	84.5	104.0	104.9	93.9e	94.6e	83.5e	87.8e
1990	87.4	104.2	100.5	96.0e	96.4e	89.0e	91.9e
1991	90.8	101.1	96.2	98.0e	98.2e	94.5e	95.9e
1992	100.0	100.0	100.0	100.0	100.0	100.0	100.0
1993	103.5	104.4	106.1	102.0p	101.8p	105.5p	104.1p
1994	107.8	110.8	120.8	104.0p	103.6p	111.0p	108.1p
1995	102.1	109.6	119.4	106.1p	105.4p	116.5p	112.2p
1996	108.0p	107.8p	120.8p	108.1p	107.2p	122.0p	116.3p
1997	110.6p	108.4p	124.3p	110.1p	109.0p	127.4p	120.3p
1998	113.3p	108.9p	127.8p	112.1p	110.8p	132.9p	124.4p

Sources: Same as General Statistics. The values shown reflect change from the base year, 1992. Values above 100 mean greater than 1992, values below 100 mean less than 1992, and a value of 100 in the 1982-91 or 1993-98 period means same as 1992. Values followed by a 'p' are projections by the editors; 'e' stands for extrapolation. Data are the most recent available at this level of detail.

SELECTED RATIOS

For 1992	Avg. of All Wholesale	Analyzed Industry	Index	For 1992	Avg. of All Wholesale	Analyzed Industry	Index
Employees per Establishment	12	7	64	Sales per Employee	561,172	315,567	56
Payroll per Establishment	349,729	215,823	62	Sales per Establishment	6,559,346	2,361,190	36
Payroll per Employee	29,919	28,844	96	Expenses per Establishment	723,071	471,435	65

Sources: Same as General Statistics. The 'Average of All Manufacturing' column represents the average of all manufacturing industries reported for the most recent complete year available. The Index shows the relationship between the Average and the Analyzed Industry. For example, 100 means that they are equal; 500 that the Analyzed Industry is five times the average; 50 means that the Analyzed Industry is half the national average. The abbreviation 'na' is used to show that data are 'not available'.

LEADING COMPANIES

Number shown: **50** Total sales ($ mil): **9,718** Total employment (000): **28.1**

Company Name	Address				CEO Name	Phone	Co. Type	Sales ($ mil)	Empl. (000)
Petrofina Delaware Inc.	PO Box 2159	Dallas	TX	75221	Ron W Haddock	214-750-2400	S	4,081	2.7
Lafarge Corp.	PO Box 4600	Reston	VA	22090	John M Piecuch	703-264-3600	P	1,806	7.3
Boise Cascade Corp.	1111 Jefferson Sq	Boise	ID	83702	Stan Bell	208-384-6161	D	956*	5.2
Rugby USA Inc.	570 Lake Cook Rd	Deerfield	IL	60015	Dave Stry	847-405-0850	R	500	1.3
Wolohan Lumber Co.	PO Box 3235	Saginaw	MI	48605	James L Wolohan	517-793-4532	P	425	1.5
Material Service Corp.	222 N La Salle St	Chicago	IL	60601	Walter Serwa	312-372-3600	S	130*	1.2
Granite Rock Co.	PO Box 50001	Watsonville	CA	95077	Bruce W Woolpert	408-768-2000	R	110*	0.4
Arundel Corp.	PO Box 5000	Sparks	MD	21152	Scott McCaleb	410-329-5000	S	100	0.6
Jack B. Parson Cos.	PO Box 3429	Ogden	UT	84409	John W Parson	801-731-1111	S	100	0.9
Head & Engguist Equipment L.L	PO Box 52945	Baton Rouge	LA	70892	John Engquist	504-356-6113	R	82	0.2
Holmes Limestone Co.	PO Box 295	Berlin	OH	44610	Merle Mulet	216-893-2721	R	80*	0.1
Vaughan and Sons Inc.	PO Box 17258	San Antonio	TX	78217	Curtis Vaughan III	210-352-1300	R	78*	0.3
Maxco Inc.	PO Box 80737	Lansing	MI	48908	Max A Coon	517-321-3130	P	74	0.6
Hudson Cos.	1 Service Rd	Providence	RI	02905	Thomas F Hudson	401-781-5200	R	70*	0.2
Livingston-Graham Inc.	16080 Arrow Hwy	Irwindale	CA	91706	David Hummel	818-856-6700	S	70	0.3
Builders General Supply Co.	PO Box 95	Little Silver	NJ	07739	Timothy J Shaheen	908-747-0808	R	60	0.2
Pacific Coast Cement Corp.	PO Box 4120	Ontario	CA	91761	Jon T Pawley	909-390-7600	S	60	<0.1
J.H. Shears Sons Inc.	819 W 1st St	Hutchinson	KS	67501	Charles L Jarvis	316-662-3307	R	55*	0.5
Walker and Zanger Inc.	31 Warren Pl	Mount Vernon	NY	10550	Leon Zanger	914-667-1600	R	55	<0.1
Acme Materials	PO Box 2503	Spokane	WA	99220	Steve Robinson	509-535-3081	S	50	0.5
Keystone Cement Co.	PO Box A	Bath	PA	18014	Gary L Pechota	610-837-1881	S	50*	0.2
Stancorp Inc.	PO Box 500	Youngstown	OH	44501	RT Beeghly	216-747-5444	R	50	0.9
Cooper Distributors Inc.	7122 NW 74th Ave	Miami	FL	33166	J Cooper	305-888-3910	S	40	0.2
Unimast Inc.	9595 Grand Ave	Franklin Park	IL	60131	Garen W Smith	708-451-1410	S	40	0.4
Rio Grande Co.	PO Box 17227	Denver	CO	80217	Bruce Peterson	303-825-2211	R	39*	0.1
Thorpe Corp.	PO Box 330403	Houston	TX	77233	Gerald Scott	713-644-1247	R	39*	0.1
Wildish Land Co.	PO Box 7428	Eugene	OR	97401	James A Wildish	503-485-1700	R	37*	0.1
Empire Sand and Gravel	PO Box 1215	Billings	MT	59103	Meredith Reiter	406-252-8465	R	30*	0.2
Revere Products	4529 Indrial Pkwy	Cleveland	OH	44135	Jack Nesser	216-671-5500	D	26*	0.1
Big River Industries Inc.	375 Northridge Rd	Atlanta	GA	30350	BJ Burks	404-804-8070	R	25	0.2
Clay Ingels Company Inc.	PO Box 2120	Lexington	KY	40594	WS Chapman Jr	606-252-0836	R	25*	<0.1
Cooperative Reserve Supply	PO Box 39	Belmont	MA	02178	Richard Hosterman	617-864-1444	R	25	<0.1
Transit Mix Concrete Co.	PO Box 1030	Co Springs	CO	80901	Bud Herskind	719-475-0700	S	25*	0.2
Carter-Waters Corp.	PO Box 412676	Kansas City	MO	64141	Jeff Hanes	816-471-2570	R	24	0.1
E.L. Gardner Inc.	1914 Forest Dr	Annapolis	MD	21401	EL Gardner Jr	410-721-2550	R	23*	0.2
Kuhlman Corp. (Toledo, Ohio)	PO Box 714	Toledo	OH	43697	TL Goligoski	419-243-2121	R	22	0.1
Corriveau-Routhier Inc.	266 Clay St	Manchester	NH	03103	David J Corriveau	603-627-3805	R	21	<0.1
Allen Company Inc.	PO Box 537	Winchester	KY	40392	JB Allen	606-744-3361	R	20	0.2
Breckenridge Material	2833 Breckenridge	St. Louis	MO	63144	GR McKean	314-962-1234	R	20	0.1
Riverton Coal Co.	US 23 S Box 17840	Catlettsburg	KY	41129	Steve Issacs	606-739-4136	R	20	<0.1
Capeletti Brothers Inc.	PO Box 4944	Miami Lakes	FL	33014	Joe Capeletti	305-823-9500	R	20*	<0.1
R.C.P. Block and Brick Inc.	PO Box 579	Lemon Grove	CA	91946	Marvin H Finch	619-460-7250	R	19	0.2
Badger Corrugating Co.	PO Box 1837	La Crosse	WI	54601	Michael J Sexauer	608-788-0100	R	18	<0.1
Cen-Cal Wallboard Supply Co.	880 S River Rd	W. Sacramento	CA	95691	Dave Schlachton	916-372-2320	S	18	<0.1
Intile Designs Inc.	PO Box 55645	Houston	TX	77255	CW Cox	713-468-8400	R	18	<0.1
Ontario Stone Corp.	34301 Chardon Rd	Willoughby Hls	OH	44094	Carl Barricelli	216-631-3645	R	18	<0.1
Roofers Supplies Inc.	PO Box 126	Bergenfield	NJ	07621	Robert G Austin	201-384-4224	R	18	<0.1
Pozzolanic Northwest Inc.	7525 SE 24th St	Mercer Island	WA	98040	G. A Peabody Jr	206-232-9320	R	16	<0.1
George F. Pettinos Inc.	123 Coulter Ave	Ardmore	PA	19003	Lewis Pettinos	610-649-6210	R	15	<0.1
Yahara Materials Inc.	PO Box 277	Waunakee	WI	53597	Larry Burcalow	608-849-4162	R	15	<0.1

Source: *Ward's Business Directory of U.S. Private and Public Companies*, 1998. The company type code used is as follows: P - Public, R - Private, S - Subsidiary, D - Division, J - Joint Venture, A - Affiliate, G - Group. Sales are in millions of dollars, employees are in thousands. An asterisk (*) indicates an estimated sales volume. The symbol < stands for 'less than'.

OCCUPATIONS EMPLOYED BY SIC 503 - WHOLESALE TRADE, OTHER

Occupation	% of Total 1996	Change to 2006	Occupation	% of Total 1996	Change to 2006
Sales & related workers nec	19.5	20.2	Clerical supervisors & managers	1.9	20.2
General managers & top executives	5.9	16.4	Order clerks	1.9	8.2
Truck drivers light & heavy	5.4	20.2	Helpers, laborers nec	1.7	20.2
General office clerks	3.6	3.4	Electrical & electronic technicians	1.4	18.8
Traffic, shipping, receiving clerks	3.6	16.7	Blue collar worker supervisors	1.4	16.0
Stock clerks	3.5	-3.9	Wholesale & retail buyers, except farm products	1.3	17.0
Freight, stock, & material movers, hand	3.3	8.2	Office machine & cash register servicers	1.3	20.2
Marketing & sales worker supervisors	3.1	20.2	Hand packers & packagers	1.2	-3.9
Order fillers, wholesale & retail sales	3.0	16.7	Maintenance repairers, general utility	1.1	12.0
Bookkeeping, accounting, & auditing clerks	2.9	-3.9	Industrial truck & tractor operators	1.1	20.2
Salespersons, retail	2.5	20.2	Purchasing managers	1.1	20.2
Secretaries, except legal & medical	2.5	-4.7	Receptionists & information clerks	1.0	20.2
Assemblers, fabricators, hand workers nec	2.0	-3.9			

Source: *Industry-Occupation Matrix*, Bureau of Labor Statistics. These data relate to one or more 3-digit SIC industry groups rather than to a single 4-digit SIC. The change reported for each occupation to the year 2006 is a percent of growth or decline as estimated by the Bureau of Labor Statistics. The abbreviation nec stands for 'not elsewhere classified'.

STATE AND REGIONAL CONCENTRATION

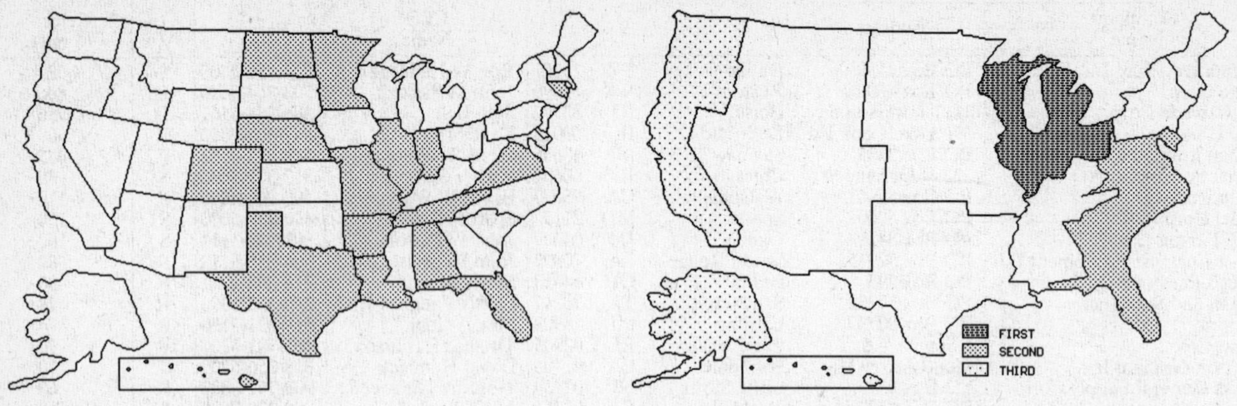

INDUSTRY DATA BY STATE

State	Establishments - 1995 Total (number)	% of U.S.	Employment - 1995 Total (number)	% of U.S.	Per Estab.	Payroll - 1995 Total ($ mil.)	Per Empl. ($)	Sales - 1992 Total ($ mil.)	% of U.S.	Per Estab ($)
California	467	10.7	4,006	11.4	9	112.3	28,037	1,151.6	11.5	272,433
Texas	400	9.1	3,632	10.3	9	102.5	28,230	799.9	8.0	292,795
Florida	379	8.7	3,069	8.7	8	86.5	28,173	719.5	7.2	277,370
New York	274	6.3	1,808	5.2	7	67.7	37,442	621.2	6.2	291,634
Illinois	157	3.6	1,305	3.7	8	44.9	34,434	619.8	6.2	429,510
Ohio	167	3.8	1,797	5.1	11	60.7	33,783	416.5	4.1	308,749
Minnesota	79	1.8	734	2.1	9	30.9	42,128	389.6	3.9	488,880
Pennsylvania	139	3.2	936	2.7	7	28.7	30,632	353.6	3.5	320,915
Tennessee	75	1.7	635	1.8	8	19.1	30,083	337.2	3.4	458,837
Michigan	144	3.3	1,182	3.4	8	43.5	36,766	318.7	3.2	340,896
Alabama	71	1.6	586	1.7	8	17.3	29,601	306.7	3.1	557,691
New Jersey	135	3.1	905	2.6	7	35.4	39,066	268.2	2.7	273,413
Georgia	146	3.3	1,002	2.9	7	29.9	29,845	260.8	2.6	276,030
Virginia	81	1.9	658	1.9	8	20.8	31,669	259.6	2.6	384,665
Indiana	84	1.9	676	1.9	8	21.3	31,521	246.1	2.5	385,197
Missouri	73	1.7	618	1.8	8	21.4	34,600	240.0	2.4	365,280
Massachusetts	89	2.0	773	2.2	9	28.1	36,344	194.1	1.9	286,336
Washington	107	2.4	902	2.6	8	29.8	33,084	190.3	1.9	210,723
Louisiana	82	1.9	766	2.2	9	21.2	27,730	184.8	1.8	285,110
Wisconsin	77	1.8	510	1.5	7	18.7	36,584	181.0	1.8	352,920
Colorado	77	1.8	750	2.1	10	25.9	34,552	164.4	1.6	358,115
North Carolina	117	2.7	796	2.3	7	22.9	28,729	145.6	1.5	260,458
Maryland	66	1.5	594	1.7	9	20.0	33,697	138.0	1.4	288,724
Connecticut	57	1.3	457	1.3	8	16.4	35,796	135.1	1.3	258,745
Arizona	107	2.4	745	2.1	7	22.1	29,662	132.0	1.3	208,880
Hawaii	23	0.5	108	0.3	5	3.5	32,407	117.2	1.2	1,065,064
Kentucky	51	1.2	432	1.2	8	12.8	29,572	114.2	1.1	334,827
South Carolina	52	1.2	400	1.1	8	11.4	28,603	113.6	1.1	371,193
Arkansas	45	1.0	233	0.7	5	6.1	26,146	106.5	1.1	686,974
Nebraska	33	0.8	223	0.6	7	5.9	26,668	95.3	0.9	517,870
Kansas	38	0.9	272	0.8	7	7.5	27,397	83.7	0.8	367,281
Iowa	38	0.9	355	1.0	9	11.7	32,986	78.7	0.8	254,728
Oregon	45	1.0	371	1.1	8	12.6	33,976	76.1	0.8	235,529
Utah	43	1.0	280	0.8	7	8.3	29,482	69.0	0.7	363,384
Mississippi	39	0.9	366	1.0	9	11.6	31,590	66.2	0.7	248,951
Oklahoma	53	1.2	375	1.1	7	9.5	25,376	54.9	0.5	203,270
Nevada	35	0.8	287	0.8	8	7.8	27,345	52.6	0.5	275,178
New Mexico	41	0.9	566	1.6	14	14.4	25,463	44.3	0.4	230,719
North Dakota	15	0.3	64	0.2	4	3.1	48,375	38.2	0.4	636,350
West Virginia	14	0.3	146	0.4	10	4.0	27,164	34.8	0.3	145,548
New Hampshire	30	0.7	159	0.5	5	5.0	31,415	24.0	0.2	173,833
Montana	16	0.4	44	0.1	3	1.4	32,159	18.8	0.2	587,625
Idaho	28	0.6	161	0.5	6	3.9	24,099	18.6	0.2	202,087
Alaska	10	0.2	25	0.1	3	2.0	80,200	18.3	0.2	388,489
Vermont	25	0.6	109	0.3	4	3.1	28,835	17.6	0.2	199,818
South Dakota	7	0.2	20-99	-	-	(D)	-	10.1	0.1	265,816
Maine	9	0.2	27	0.1	3	1.1	40,185	10.1	0.1	139,833
Rhode Island	17	0.4	136	0.4	8	4.2	30,559	(D)	-	-
Delaware	13	0.3	108	0.3	8	3.4	31,269	(D)	-	-
Wyoming	3	0.1	3	0.0	1	0.1	47,667	(D)	-	-
D.C.	2	0.0	0-19	-	-	(D)	-	(D)	-	-

Source: County Business Patterns, 1995 and *Economic Census of the U.S., 1992*. Data are sorted by 1992 revenues and, if revenues are unavailable, by establishments in 1995. The symbol (D) indicates that data are withheld by the source to avoid disclosure of competitive information. A dash (-) indicates that data are not available or undisclosed because they do not meet statistical validity standards. Shaded *states* on the state map indicate those states which have proportionately greater representation in the industry than would be indicated by the state's population; the ratio is based on total revenues or number of establishments. Shaded *regions* indicate where the industry is regionally most concentrated.

5033 - ROOFING, SIDING, & INSULATION

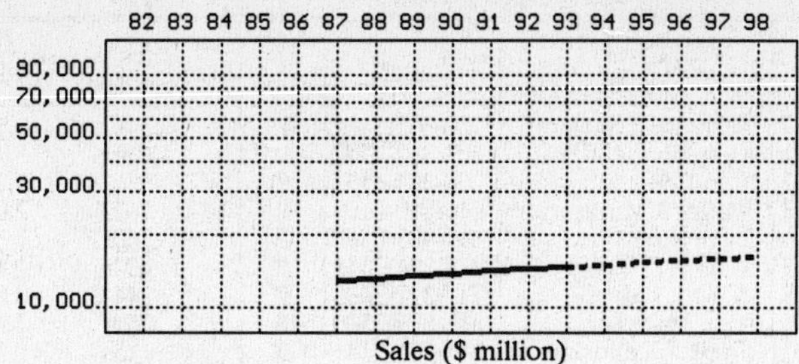

Sales ($ million)

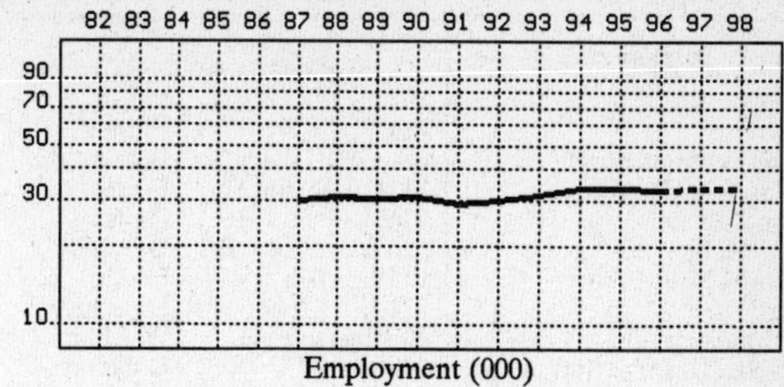

Employment (000)

GENERAL STATISTICS

Year	Establishments (number)	Employment (number)	Payroll ($ million)	Sales ($ million)	Expenses ($ million)	Beginning Inventory ($ million)	Ending Inventory ($ million)
1982	-	-	-	-	-	-	-
1983	-	-	-	-	-	-	-
1984	-	-	-	-	-	-	-
1985	-	-	-	-	-	-	-
1986	-	-	-	-	-	-	-
1987	2,684	30,208	767.5	12,901.2	1,640.7	761.2	841.1
1988	2,631	30,743	845.8	13,206.1e	1,704.0e	791.3e	868.5e
1989	2,491	30,715	865.5	13,511.1e	1,767.3e	821.5e	895.8e
1990	2,442	30,878	895.3	13,816.1e	1,830.5e	851.6e	923.2e
1991	2,486	29,462	865.1	14,121.1e	1,893.8e	881.7e	950.6e
1992	2,848	30,060	921.9	14,426.1	1,957.0	911.9	978.0
1993	2,835	31,689	1,041.5	14,731.1p	2,020.3p	942.0p	1,005.4p
1994	2,902	33,514	1,135.2	15,036.0p	2,083.5p	972.1p	1,032.8p
1995	2,854	33,652	1,164.3	15,341.0p	2,146.8p	1,002.3p	1,060.2p
1996	2,901p	33,148p	1,180.8p	15,646.0p	2,210.1p	1,032.4p	1,087.6p
1997	2,945p	33,535p	1,228.1p	15,951.0p	2,273.3p	1,062.5p	1,115.0p
1998	2,988p	33,922p	1,275.3p	16,256.0p	2,336.6p	1,092.7p	1,142.4p

Sources: Economic Census of the United States, 1982, 1987, and 1992. Establishment counts, employment, and payroll are from *County Business Patterns* for non-Census years. Values followed by a 'p' are projections by the editors. Sales and expense data for non-Census years are extrapolations, marked by 'e'. Industries reclassified in 1987 will not have data for prior years. Data are the most recent available at this level of detail.

INDICES OF CHANGE

Year	Establishments (number)	Employment (number)	Payroll ($ million)	Sales ($ million)	Expenses ($ million)	Beginning Inventory ($ million)	Ending Inventory ($ million)
1982	-	-	-	-	-	-	-
1983	-	-	-	-	-	-	-
1984	-	-	-	-	-	-	-
1985	-	-	-	-	-	-	-
1986	-	-	-	-	-	-	-
1987	94.2	100.5	83.3	89.4	83.8	83.5	86.0
1988	92.4	102.3	91.7	91.5e	87.1e	86.8e	88.8e
1989	87.5	102.2	93.9	93.7e	90.3e	90.1e	91.6e
1990	85.7	102.7	97.1	95.8e	93.5e	93.4e	94.4e
1991	87.3	98.0	93.8	97.9e	96.8e	96.7e	97.2e
1992	100.0	100.0	100.0	100.0	100.0	100.0	100.0
1993	99.5	105.4	113.0	102.1p	103.2p	103.3p	102.8p
1994	101.9	111.5	123.1	104.2p	106.5p	106.6p	105.6p
1995	100.2	111.9	126.3	106.3p	109.7p	109.9p	108.4p
1996	101.9p	110.3p	128.1p	108.5p	112.9p	113.2p	111.2p
1997	103.4p	111.6p	133.2p	110.6p	116.2p	116.5p	114.0p
1998	104.9p	112.8p	138.3p	112.7p	119.4p	119.8p	116.8p

Sources: Same as General Statistics. The values shown reflect change from the base year, 1992. Values above 100 mean greater than 1992, values below 100 mean less than 1992, and a value of 100 in the 1982-91 or 1993-98 period means same as 1992. Values followed by a 'p' are projections by the editors; 'e' stands for extrapolation. Data are the most recent available at this level of detail.

SELECTED RATIOS

For 1992	Avg. of All Wholesale	Analyzed Industry	Index	For 1992	Avg. of All Wholesale	Analyzed Industry	Index
Employees per Establishment	12	11	90	Sales per Employee	561,172	479,910	86
Payroll per Establishment	349,729	323,701	93	Sales per Establishment	6,559,346	5,065,344	77
Payroll per Employee	29,919	30,669	103	Expenses per Establishment	723,071	687,149	95

Sources: Same as General Statistics. The 'Average of All Manufacturing' column represents the average of all manufacturing industries reported for the most recent complete year available. The Index shows the relationship between the Average and the Analyzed Industry. For example, 100 means that they are equal; 500 that the Analyzed Industry is five times the average; 50 means that the Analyzed Industry is half the national average. The abbreviation 'na' is used to show that data are 'not available'.

LEADING COMPANIES

Number shown: **50** Total sales ($ mil): **8,332** Total employment (000): **20.5**

Company Name	Address				CEO Name	Phone	Co. Type	Sales ($ mil)	Empl. (000)
T.J.T. Inc.	PO Box 278	Emmett	ID	83617	Terrence J Sheldon	208-365-5321	P	2,544	<0.1
American Builders Supply	One ABC Pkwy	Beloit	WI	53511	Kenneth Hendricks	608-362-7777	R	1,416*	3.4
Boise Cascade Corp.	1111 Jefferson Sq	Boise	ID	83702	Stan Bell	208-384-6161	D	956*	5.2
Cameron Ashley	11651 Plano Rd	Dallas	TX	75243	Walter J Muratori	214-860-5100	P	762	2.0
Rugby USA Inc.	570 Lake Cook Rd	Deerfield	IL	60015	Dave Stry	847-405-0850	R	500	1.3
Patrick Industries Inc.	PO Box 638	Elkhart	IN	46515	Mervin D Lung	219-294-7511	P	404	1.5
Irex Corp.	PO Box 1268	Lancaster	PA	17608	W Kirk Liddell	717-397-3633	P	244	0.5
Harvey Industries Inc.	43 Emerson Rd	Waltham	MA	02154	Alan Marlow	617-899-3500	R	160*	1.1
Philadelphia Reserve Supply Co.	400 Mack Dr	Croydon	PA	19021	Frank J Dalinsky	215-785-3141	R	85	<0.1
GLS Corp.	723 W Algonquin	Arlington H.	IL	60006	Steven L Dehmlow	847-437-0200	R	73*	0.2
Roofing Wholesale Company	1918 W Grant St	Phoenix	AZ	85009	Harley Lisherness	602-258-3794	R	70	0.2
Seven D Wholesale	PO Box 67	Gallitzin	PA	16641	Donald A DeGol Sr	814-886-8151	R	67*	0.2
Builders General Supply Co.	PO Box 95	Little Silver	NJ	07739	Timothy J Shaheen	908-747-0808	R	60	0.2
Gulfside Supply Inc.	PO Box 11475	Tampa	FL	33609	James Resch	813-247-4560	R	60	0.2
Young Sales Corp.	1054 Central Indrial	St. Louis	MO	63110	W Todd McCane	314-771-3080	R	60	0.7
Building Products Inc.	PO Box 1390	Watertown	SD	57201	Lee Schull	605-886-3495	R	53	0.1
MacArthur Co.	2400 Wycliff St	St. Paul	MN	55114	R. C Lockwood	612-646-2773	R	50	0.3
Sunniland Corp.	PO Box 8001	Sanford	FL	32772	Tomas W Moore	407-322-2424	R	50*	0.2
Shook & Fletcher Insulation Co.	PO Box 380501	Birmingham	AL	35238	Wayne W Killion	205-991-7606	R	45	0.3
Dallas Wholesale Builders	PO Box 271023	Dallas	TX	75227	Byron Potter	214-381-2200	R	43*	0.1
Standard Roofings Inc.	PO Box 1410	Tinton Falls	NJ	07724	William B Higginson	908-542-3300	R	40*	0.2
Midwest Sales Company of Iowa	1700 W 29th St	Kansas City	MO	64108	Barry Shepherd	816-753-0586	R	35	0.1
Rhodes Supply Company Inc.	Hwy 303 S, Rte 3	Mayfield	KY	42066	Gene Rhodes	502-382-2185	R	34	<0.1
E.J. Bartells Co.	PO Box 997	Renton	WA	98057	EA Jensen	206-228-4111	R	30	0.4
Wesco Cedar Inc.	PO Box 2566	Eugene	OR	97404	LF Plummer	503-688-5020	R	30	<0.1
Brock White Co.	2575 Kasota Ave	St. Paul	MN	55108	Richard Garland	612-647-0950	R	28*	<0.1
SG Wholesale Roofing Supply	PO Box 1464	Santa Ana	CA	92702	Roger Glazer	714-953-7376	R	28	<0.1
Revere Products	4529 Indrial Pkwy	Cleveland	OH	44135	Jack Nesser	216-671-5500	D	26*	0.1
Cooperative Reserve Supply	PO Box 39	Belmont	MA	02178	Richard Hosterman	617-864-1444	R	25	<0.1
H. Verby Company Inc.	186-14 Jamaica Ave	Jamaica	NY	11423	Stanley M Verby	718-454-5522	R	25	<0.1
Carter-Waters Corp.	PO Box 412676	Kansas City	MO	64141	Jeff Hanes	816-471-2570	R	24	0.1
Southern Sash Sales	PO Box 471	Sheffield	AL	35660	EH Darby	205-383-3261	R	24*	0.4
Pan Am Distributing Inc.	1833 Hormel St	San Antonio	TX	78219	Ken Hamill	210-225-3892	R	20*	<0.1
Badger Corrugating Co.	PO Box 1837	La Crosse	WI	54601	Michael J Sexauer	608-788-0100	R	18	<0.1
Nailite International Inc.	1251 NW 165th St	Miami	FL	33169	Ken Ude	305-620-6200	R	18	<0.1
Roofers Supplies Inc.	PO Box 126	Bergenfield	NJ	07621	Robert G Austin	201-384-4224	R	18	<0.1
Eikenhout and Sons Inc.	346 Wealthy St SW	Grand Rapids	MI	49501	Henry Schierbeek	616-459-4523	R	16	<0.1
Wimsatt Brothers Inc.	PO Box 32488	Louisville	KY	40232	Raymond J Paulin Jr	502-458-3221	R	16*	<0.1
Bennett Supply Co.	19th & Main St	Pittsburgh	PA	15215	David Bennett III	412-782-4500	R	15*	<0.1
Branton Industries Inc.	PO Box 10536	Jefferson	LA	70181	Harold T Branton	504-733-7770	R	15*	0.2
Dealers Supply Co.	110 SE Washington	Portland	OR	97214	P Francis	503-236-1195	R	15*	<0.1
Industrial Roofing Co.	35 N John St	Haledon	NJ	07508	S Komito	201-791-7300	R	15	0.1
Jett Supply Company Inc.	PO Box 2400	Pueblo	CO	81004	Daniel Perko	719-561-2713	S	15*	<0.1
Mid-South Building Supply	5640 P Sunnyside	Beltsville	MD	20705	J Briggs	301-937-5200	R	15	<0.1
Polycoat Systems Inc.	5 Depot St	Hudson Falls	NY	12839	George Carruthers	518-747-0654	R	15	<0.1
Western Products Inc.	2001 1st Ave N	Fargo	ND	58102	M Bullinger	701-293-5310	R	15	0.1
Brauer Supply Co.	4260 Forest Park	St. Louis	MO	63108	Jim Truesdell	314-534-7150	R	14	<0.1
Burton Building Products Inc.	PO Box 4159	Little Rock	AR	72204	Steven Burton	501-663-7700	R	14	<0.1
Corken Steel Products Co.	PO Box 2650	Covington	KY	41012	DI Corken	606-291-4664	R	14*	<0.1
Western Materials Inc.	PO Box 430	Yakima	WA	98907	Stan Martinkus	509-575-3000	R	14	<0.1

Source: *Ward's Business Directory of U.S. Private and Public Companies*, 1998. The company type code used is as follows: P - Public, R - Private, S - Subsidiary, D - Division, J - Joint Venture, A - Affiliate, G - Group. Sales are in millions of dollars, employees are in thousands. An asterisk (*) indicates an estimated sales volume. The symbol < stands for 'less than'.

OCCUPATIONS EMPLOYED BY SIC 503 - WHOLESALE TRADE, OTHER

Occupation	% of Total 1996	Change to 2006	Occupation	% of Total 1996	Change to 2006
Sales & related workers nec	19.5	20.2	Clerical supervisors & managers	1.9	20.2
General managers & top executives	5.9	16.4	Order clerks	1.9	8.2
Truck drivers light & heavy	5.4	20.2	Helpers, laborers nec	1.7	20.2
General office clerks	3.6	3.4	Electrical & electronic technicians	1.4	18.8
Traffic, shipping, receiving clerks	3.6	16.7	Blue collar worker supervisors	1.4	16.0
Stock clerks	3.5	-3.9	Wholesale & retail buyers, except farm products	1.3	17.0
Freight, stock, & material movers, hand	3.3	8.2	Office machine & cash register servicers	1.3	20.2
Marketing & sales worker supervisors	3.1	20.2	Hand packers & packagers	1.2	-3.9
Order fillers, wholesale & retail sales	3.0	16.7	Maintenance repairers, general utility	1.1	12.0
Bookkeeping, accounting, & auditing clerks	2.9	-3.9	Industrial truck & tractor operators	1.1	20.2
Salespersons, retail	2.5	20.2	Purchasing managers	1.1	20.2
Secretaries, except legal & medical	2.5	-4.7	Receptionists & information clerks	1.0	20.2
Assemblers, fabricators, hand workers nec	2.0	-3.9			

Source: *Industry-Occupation Matrix*, Bureau of Labor Statistics. These data relate to one or more 3-digit SIC industry groups rather than to a single 4-digit SIC. The change reported for each occupation to the year 2006 is a percent of growth or decline as estimated by the Bureau of Labor Statistics. The abbreviation nec stands for 'not elsewhere classified'.

STATE AND REGIONAL CONCENTRATION

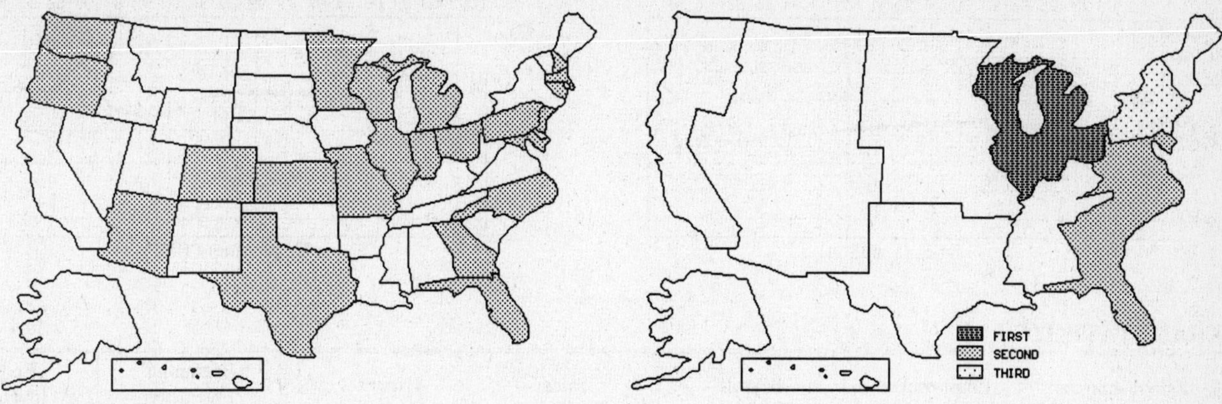

INDUSTRY DATA BY STATE

State	Establishments - 1995 Total (number)	Establishments - 1995 % of U.S.	Employment - 1995 Total (number)	Employment - 1995 % of U.S.	Employment - 1995 Per Estab.	Payroll - 1995 Total ($ mil.)	Payroll - 1995 Per Empl. ($)	Sales - 1992 Total ($ mil.)	Sales - 1992 % of U.S.	Sales - 1992 Per Estab ($)
California	175	6.1	2,404	7.2	14	83.9	34,891	1,403.4	9.9	499,616
Texas	169	5.9	2,137	6.4	13	84.5	39,527	1,159.9	8.2	578,504
Pennsylvania	154	5.4	2,311	6.9	15	85.0	36,773	964.2	6.8	460,215
Florida	190	6.7	1,897	5.7	10	53.6	28,274	844.2	6.0	502,515
Ohio	161	5.6	2,170	6.5	13	86.9	40,041	790.5	5.6	476,798
Michigan	113	4.0	1,284	3.8	11	47.4	36,892	741.1	5.3	669,436
New Jersey	101	3.5	1,541	4.6	15	58.6	38,029	717.3	5.1	473,139
Illinois	136	4.8	1,432	4.3	11	54.7	38,205	677.2	4.8	538,707
Georgia	90	3.2	945	2.8	10	33.3	35,270	567.4	4.0	713,675
New York	129	4.5	1,432	4.3	11	51.1	35,681	545.4	3.9	338,146
North Carolina	97	3.4	892	2.7	9	29.7	33,275	504.9	3.6	677,740
Minnesota	56	2.0	846	2.5	15	31.2	36,902	450.8	3.2	614,229
Massachusetts	48	1.7	498	1.5	10	24.1	48,363	373.0	2.6	680,600
Missouri	77	2.7	955	2.9	12	29.9	31,275	359.7	2.5	338,089
Indiana	90	3.2	1,011	3.0	11	30.5	30,120	328.2	2.3	419,105
Wisconsin	70	2.5	1,039	3.1	15	39.1	37,635	308.7	2.2	310,265
Washington	86	3.0	890	2.7	10	32.7	36,756	306.5	2.2	432,880
Maryland	63	2.2	969	2.9	15	33.0	34,094	293.9	2.1	413,948
Virginia	80	2.8	1,007	3.0	13	32.2	32,012	282.8	2.0	405,709
Tennessee	76	2.7	520	1.6	7	15.9	30,533	253.9	1.8	511,976
Colorado	48	1.7	582	1.7	12	19.9	34,179	230.7	1.6	578,271
Connecticut	38	1.3	693	2.1	18	23.4	33,714	224.5	1.6	532,000
Arizona	38	1.3	539	1.6	14	13.7	25,436	217.6	1.5	437,781
Oregon	46	1.6	561	1.7	12	18.7	33,278	180.0	1.3	362,821
Kansas	34	1.2	369	1.1	11	12.8	34,575	179.0	1.3	795,609
Iowa	44	1.5	438	1.3	10	11.4	25,961	143.8	1.0	379,377
Alabama	41	1.4	360	1.1	9	11.2	31,222	133.8	0.9	493,701
South Carolina	53	1.9	392	1.2	7	10.9	27,929	126.1	0.9	408,052
Oklahoma	28	1.0	299	0.9	11	9.6	32,247	114.8	0.8	352,104
Louisiana	41	1.4	349	1.0	9	11.3	32,358	102.7	0.7	355,343
Utah	33	1.2	311	0.9	9	8.3	26,640	97.7	0.7	374,425
Kentucky	24	0.8	389	1.2	16	10.5	27,018	95.1	0.7	336,141
New Hampshire	17	0.6	161	0.5	9	6.1	38,106	65.4	0.5	359,593
Maine	16	0.6	216	0.6	14	6.6	30,444	46.4	0.3	324,741
Nebraska	22	0.8	122	0.4	6	3.1	25,230	45.8	0.3	428,000
Idaho	12	0.4	95	0.3	8	2.8	29,726	45.5	0.3	275,958
New Mexico	15	0.5	150	0.4	10	3.9	25,953	39.2	0.3	326,650
Hawaii	12	0.4	121	0.4	10	3.8	31,587	35.2	0.2	314,571
Mississippi	16	0.6	94	0.3	6	3.4	36,043	33.7	0.2	340,192
South Dakota	6	0.2	250-499	-	-	(D)	-	27.6	0.2	412,687
West Virginia	16	0.6	94	0.3	6	3.0	31,957	19.8	0.1	336,000
Montana	7	0.2	37	0.1	5	1.1	30,541	11.4	0.1	207,855
Vermont	5	0.2	47	0.1	9	1.3	28,383	9.5	0.1	256,270
D.C.	3	0.1	0-19	-	-	(D)	-	7.7	0.1	589,308
Wyoming	3	0.1	6	0.0	2	0.1	22,667	2.4	0.0	484,800
Arkansas	24	0.8	298	0.9	12	8.4	28,034	(D)	-	-
Delaware	16	0.6	212	0.6	13	6.9	32,401	(D)	-	-
Nevada	11	0.4	121	0.4	11	3.0	24,736	(D)	-	-
Rhode Island	9	0.3	57	0.2	6	2.5	43,088	(D)	-	-
Alaska	8	0.3	38	0.1	5	1.5	40,526	(D)	-	-
North Dakota	7	0.2	40	0.1	6	1.1	26,725	(D)	-	-

Source: *County Business Patterns, 1995* and *Economic Census of the U.S., 1992*. Data are sorted by 1992 revenues and, if revenues are unavailable, by establishments in 1995. The symbol (D) indicates that data are withheld by the source to avoid disclosure of competitive information. A dash (-) indicates that data are not available or undisclosed because they do not meet statistical validity standards. Shaded *states* on the state map indicate those states which have proportionately greater representation in the industry than would be indicated by the state's population; the ratio is based on total revenues or number of establishments. Shaded *regions* indicate where the industry is regionally most concentrated.

5039 - CONSTRUCTION MATERIALS, NEC

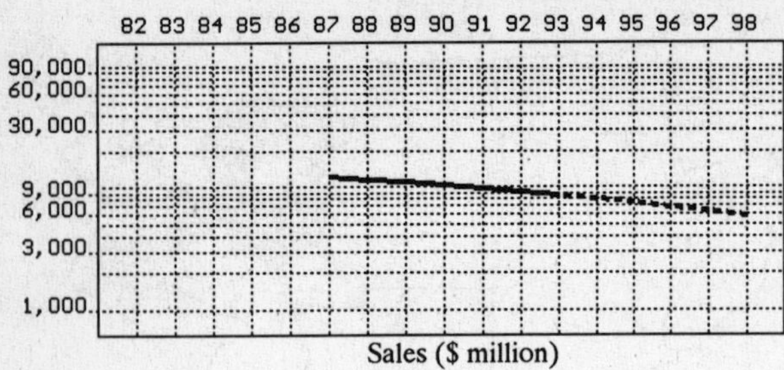

Sales ($ million)

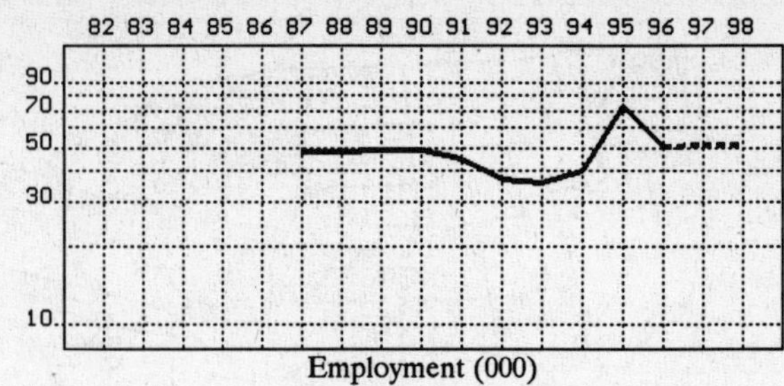

Employment (000)

GENERAL STATISTICS

Year	Establishments (number)	Employment (number)	Payroll ($ million)	Sales ($ million)	Expenses ($ million)	Beginning Inventory ($ million)	Ending Inventory ($ million)
1982	-	-	-	-	-	-	-
1983	-	-	-	-	-	-	-
1984	-	-	-	-	-	-	-
1985	-	-	-	-	-	-	-
1986	-	-	-	-	-	-	-
1987	4,413	47,892	1,096.1	12,073.3	2,190.5	709.7	760.1
1988	4,134	47,887	1,175.5	11,501.8e	2,138.3e	707.0e	742.5e
1989	4,194	48,350	1,192.3	10,930.4e	2,086.2e	704.3e	724.9e
1990	4,170	48,675	1,231.9	10,358.9e	2,034.0e	701.6e	707.4e
1991	4,175	44,999	1,164.1	9,787.5e	1,981.9e	698.9e	689.8e
1992	4,049	36,978	970.9	9,216.0	1,929.7	696.2	672.3
1993	4,008	35,761	1,013.1	8,644.5p	1,877.6p	693.5p	654.7p
1994	3,982	39,930	1,192.5	8,073.1p	1,825.4p	690.9p	637.2p
1995	6,871	72,757	2,178.6	7,501.6p	1,773.2p	688.2p	619.6p
1996	5,184p	50,252p	1,559.6p	6,930.2p	1,721.1p	685.5p	602.1p
1997	5,332p	50,897p	1,622.3p	6,358.7p	1,668.9p	682.8p	584.5p
1998	5,480p	51,542p	1,684.9p	5,787.3p	1,616.8p	680.1p	567.0p

Sources: Economic Census of the United States, 1982, 1987, and 1992. Establishment counts, employment, and payroll are from *County Business Patterns* for non-Census years. Values followed by a 'p' are projections by the editors. Sales and expense data for non-Census years are extrapolations, marked by 'e'. Industries reclassified in 1987 will not have data for prior years. Data are the most recent available at this level of detail.

INDICES OF CHANGE

Year	Establishments (number)	Employment (number)	Payroll ($ million)	Sales ($ million)	Expenses ($ million)	Beginning Inventory ($ million)	Ending Inventory ($ million)
1982	-	-	-	-	-	-	-
1983	-	-	-	-	-	-	-
1984	-	-	-	-	-	-	-
1985	-	-	-	-	-	-	-
1986	-	-	-	-	-	-	-
1987	109.0	129.5	112.9	131.0	113.5	101.9	113.1
1988	102.1	129.5	121.1	124.8e	110.8e	101.6e	110.4e
1989	103.6	130.8	122.8	118.6e	108.1e	101.2e	107.8e
1990	103.0	131.6	126.9	112.4e	105.4e	100.8e	105.2e
1991	103.1	121.7	119.9	106.2e	102.7e	100.4e	102.6e
1992	100.0	100.0	100.0	100.0	100.0	100.0	100.0
1993	99.0	96.7	104.3	93.8p	97.3p	99.6p	97.4p
1994	98.3	108.0	122.8	87.6p	94.6p	99.2p	94.8p
1995	169.7	196.8	224.4	81.4p	91.9p	98.9p	92.2p
1996	128.0p	135.9p	160.6p	75.2p	89.2p	98.5p	89.6p
1997	131.7p	137.6p	167.1p	69.0p	86.5p	98.1p	86.9p
1998	135.4p	139.4p	173.5p	62.8p	83.8p	97.7p	84.3p

Sources: Same as General Statistics. The values shown reflect change from the base year, 1992. Values above 100 mean greater than 1992, values below 100 mean less than 1992, and a value of 100 in the 1982-91 or 1993-98 period means same as 1992. Values followed by a 'p' are projections by the editors; 'e' stands for extrapolation. Data are the most recent available at this level of detail.

SELECTED RATIOS

For 1992	Avg. of All Wholesale	Analyzed Industry	Index	For 1992	Avg. of All Wholesale	Analyzed Industry	Index
Employees per Establishment	12	9	78	Sales per Employee	561,172	249,229	44
Payroll per Establishment	349,729	239,788	69	Sales per Establishment	6,559,346	2,276,118	35
Payroll per Employee	29,919	26,256	88	Expenses per Establishment	723,071	476,587	66

Sources: Same as General Statistics. The 'Average of All Manufacturing' column represents the average of all manufacturing industries reported for the most recent complete year available. The Index shows the relationship between the Average and the Analyzed Industry. For example, 100 means that they are equal; 500 that the Analyzed Industry is five times the average; 50 means that the Analyzed Industry is half the national average. The abbreviation 'na' is used to show that data are 'not available'.

LEADING COMPANIES

Number shown: **50** Total sales ($ mil): **14,617** Total employment (000): **61.3**

Company Name	Address				CEO Name	Phone	Co. Type	Sales ($ mil)	Empl. (000)
HomeBase Inc.	3345 Michelson Dr	Irvine	CA	92612	Herbert J Zarkin	714-442-5000	P	4,376	19.5
84 Lumber Co.	Rte 519, Box 8484	Eighty Four	PA	15384	Joseph A Hardy	412-228-8820	R	1,600	4.5
Boise Cascade Corp.	1111 Jefferson Sq	Boise	ID	83702	Stan Bell	208-384-6161	D	956 •	5.2
Cameron Ashley	11651 Plano Rd	Dallas	TX	75243	Walter J Muratori	214-860-5100	P	762	2.0
Sun Distributors L.P.	1 Logan Sq	Philadelphia	PA	19103	Donald T Marshall	215-665-3650	P	656	4.3
Norandex Inc.	8450 S Bedford Rd	Macedonia	OH	44056	Daniel Dietzel	330-468-2200	S	650	3.2
VVP America Inc.	965 Ridgelake Blvd	Memphis	TN	38120	Mark Burke	901-767-7111	S	650	2.5
L and W Supply Corp.	125 S Franklin St	Chicago	IL	60606	Frank R Wall	312-606-5400	S	500	1.7
Wolohan Lumber Co.	PO Box 3235	Saginaw	MI	48605	James L Wolohan	517-793-4532	P	425	1.5
Patrick Industries Inc.	PO Box 638	Elkhart	IN	46515	Mervin D Lung	219-294-7511	P	404	1.5
Anderson Lumber Co.	PO Box 9459	Ogden	UT	84409	James C Beardall	801-479-3400	R	285	1.6
Fontaine Industries Inc.	1950 Stonegate Dr	Birmingham	AL	35242	Kelly Dier	205-969-1119	S	255 •	1.0
Binswanger Glass Co.	PO Box 171173	Memphis	TN	38187	Mark Burke	901-767-7111	S	222	2.1
Mendez and Company Inc.	PO Box 363348	San Juan	PR	00936	S Alvarez-Mendez	809-793-8888	R	200	0.3
A.P.I. Inc.	2366 Rose Pl	St. Paul	MN	55113	Lee R Anderson	612-636-4320	R	190 •	0.5
Apex Supply Company Inc.	2500 B Gwinnett	Atlanta	GA	30340	Clyde Rodbell	404-449-7000	R	140 •	0.4
United Hardware	5005 Nathan Ln	Plymouth	MN	55442	David A Heider	612-559-1800	R	136	0.4
Redwood Empire Inc.	PO Box 1300	Morgan Hill	CA	95038	Rodger A Burch	408-779-7354	R	130 •	0.4
Rugby Building Products	53 Perimeter Ctr E	Atlanta	GA	30346	Sherman L Griffith	404-551-8900	S	130	0.5
Irving Materials Inc.	8032 N State Rd 9	Greenfield	IN	46140	Fred R Irving	317-326-3101	R	120	0.6
Acoustical Material Services	1620 S Maple Ave	Montebello	CA	90640	Max Gondon	213-721-9011	R	100	0.4
Lyman-Richey Corp.	4315 Cuming St	Omaha	NE	68131	Tom Baughman	402-558-2727	R	100	0.4
Pan American Trade Dev Corp.	310 Madison Ave	New York	NY	10017	Peter Slotta	212-599-3500	R	98 •	0.4
Georgia Marble Co.	1201 Roberts BlvdB	Kennesaw	GA	30144	AL Gay Jr	404-421-6500	R	97	0.8
Dairyman's Supply Co.	PO Box 528	Mayfield	KY	42066	John E Cook	502-247-5642	R	94	<0.1
Standard Supply and Hardware	PO Box 60620	New Orleans	LA	70160	Evans Hadden	504-586-8400	R	75	0.3
Maxco Inc.	PO Box 80737	Lansing	MI	48908	Max A Coon	517-321-3130	P	74	0.6
E.C. Barton and Co.	PO Box 4040	Jonesboro	AR	72403	Niel Crowson	501-932-6673	R	71	0.4
Prudential Metal Supply Corp.	171 Milton St	Dedham	MA	02026	Robert Kolikof	617-329-3232	R	65 •	0.3
Eagle Supply Inc.	PO Box 75305	Tampa	FL	33675	Thomas Havnes	813-248-4918	S	65	0.2
TDA Industries Inc.	122 E 42nd St	New York	NY	10168	Douglas P Fields	212-972-1510	R	65	0.4
Canfor U.S.A. Corp.	PO Box 674	Meridian	ID	83642	Harold E Unruh	208-888-2456	S	61	0.2
Builders General Supply Co.	PO Box 95	Little Silver	NJ	07739	Timothy J Shaheen	908-747-0808	R	60	0.2
Lofland Co.	PO Box 35446	Dallas	TX	75235	Blake Irwin	214-631-5250	R	60	0.3
Lumbermen's Merchandising	137 W Wayne Ave	Wayne	PA	19087	Anthony J DeCarlo	215-293-7000	R	60 •	0.2
Mervis Industries Inc.	PO Box 827	Danville	IL	61834	Louis L Mervis	217-442-5300	R	60	0.3
Spahn and Rose Lumber Co.	PO Box 149	Dubuque	IA	52004	CD Spahn	319-582-3606	R	56	0.2
Carry Safe Ltd.	920 Davis Rd, #101	Elgin	IL	60123	Guy David	708-931-4771	R	52 •	0.2
H.W. Jenkins Co.	PO Box 18347	Memphis	TN	38181	HW Jenkins Jr	901-363-7641	R	50	0.1
Ted Lansing Corp.	8501 Sanford Dr	Richmond	VA	23228	JC Lansing	804-266-8893	R	50	0.3
Mid-AM Building Supply Inc.	100 W Sparks	Moberly	MO	65270	JI Knaebel	816-263-2140	R	47	0.1
Fischer Lime and Cement Co.	PO Box 18383	Memphis	TN	38181	Thomas J Sheppard	901-363-4986	R	45	0.4
Henry Bacon Building Materials	PO Box 7012	Issaquah	WA	98027	Richard Carroll	206-391-8000	R	44	0.4
Dallas Wholesale Builders	PO Box 271023	Dallas	TX	75227	Byron Potter	214-381-2200	R	43 •	0.1
Midpac Lumber Company Ltd.	1001 Ahua St	Honolulu	HI	96819	Michael K Yoshida	808-836-8111	R	41	0.2
Rogers Group Inc. Louisville	600 N Englishation	Louisville	KY	42203	Frank Warren	502-456-6930	D	41 •	0.2
Dana Kepner Co.	700 Alcott	Denver	CO	80204	Wayne E Johnson	303-623-6161	R	40	<0.1
Tews Co.	6200 W Center St	Milwaukee	WI	53210	William Tews	414-442-8000	R	40	<0.1
Pritchard Paint and Glass Co.	PO Box 30547	Charlotte	NC	28230	Donald R Beard	704-376-8561	R	39 •	0.2
Riggs Supply Co.	320 Cedar St	Kennett	MO	63857	Aldolfis Riggs III	314-888-4639	R	39 •	0.2

Source: *Ward's Business Directory of U.S. Private and Public Companies*, 1998. The company type code used is as follows: P - Public, R - Private, S - Subsidiary, D - Division, J - Joint Venture, A - Affiliate, G - Group. Sales are in millions of dollars, employees are in thousands. An asterisk (•) indicates an estimated sales volume. The symbol < stands for 'less than'.

OCCUPATIONS EMPLOYED BY SIC 503 - WHOLESALE TRADE, OTHER

Occupation	% of Total 1996	Change to 2006	Occupation	% of Total 1996	Change to 2006
Sales & related workers nec	19.5	20.2	Clerical supervisors & managers	1.9	20.2
General managers & top executives	5.9	16.4	Order clerks	1.9	8.2
Truck drivers light & heavy	5.4	20.2	Helpers, laborers nec	1.7	20.2
General office clerks	3.6	3.4	Electrical & electronic technicians	1.4	18.8
Traffic, shipping, receiving clerks	3.6	16.7	Blue collar worker supervisors	1.4	16.0
Stock clerks	3.5	-3.9	Wholesale & retail buyers, except farm products	1.3	17.0
Freight, stock, & material movers, hand	3.3	8.2	Office machine & cash register servicers	1.3	20.2
Marketing & sales worker supervisors	3.1	20.2	Hand packers & packagers	1.2	-3.9
Order fillers, wholesale & retail sales	3.0	16.7	Maintenance repairers, general utility	1.1	12.0
Bookkeeping, accounting, & auditing clerks	2.9	-3.9	Industrial truck & tractor operators	1.1	20.2
Salespersons, retail	2.5	20.2	Purchasing managers	1.1	20.2
Secretaries, except legal & medical	2.5	-4.7	Receptionists & information clerks	1.0	20.2
Assemblers, fabricators, hand workers nec	2.0	-3.9			

Source: *Industry-Occupation Matrix*, Bureau of Labor Statistics. These data relate to one or more 3-digit SIC industry groups rather than to a single 4-digit SIC. The change reported for each occupation to the year 2006 is a percent of growth or decline as estimated by the Bureau of Labor Statistics. The abbreviation nec stands for 'not elsewhere classified'.

STATE AND REGIONAL CONCENTRATION

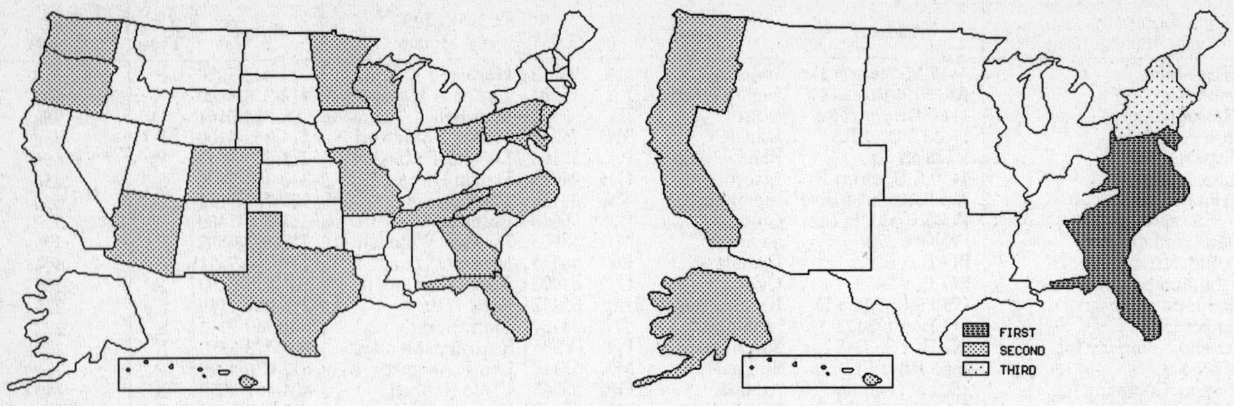

INDUSTRY DATA BY STATE

State	Establishments - 1995 Total (number)	% of U.S.	Employment - 1995 Total (number)	% of U.S.	Per Estab.	Payroll - 1995 Total ($ mil.)	Per Empl. ($)	Sales - 1992 Total ($ mil.)	% of U.S.	Per Estab ($)
California	612	8.9	6,102	8.4	10	192.3	31,507	971.7	10.9	253,517
Georgia	240	3.5	2,989	4.1	12	98.2	32,837	785.0	8.8	345,068
Texas	498	7.2	6,383	8.8	13	171.8	26,918	694.7	7.8	260,680
Florida	496	7.2	4,398	6.1	9	122.6	27,877	561.7	6.3	243,881
New Jersey	218	3.2	2,745	3.8	13	97.9	35,665	486.9	5.5	322,908
Pennsylvania	300	4.4	3,747	5.2	12	113.4	30,272	455.1	5.1	230,551
New York	393	5.7	3,406	4.7	9	104.8	30,775	428.0	4.8	245,684
Ohio	275	4.0	3,463	4.8	13	98.0	28,303	400.3	4.5	324,908
Illinois	270	3.9	3,005	4.1	11	102.1	33,993	378.9	4.2	228,529
North Carolina	189	2.8	2,070	2.8	11	60.3	29,131	323.2	3.6	317,223
Washington	243	3.5	2,250	3.1	9	70.5	31,322	241.9	2.7	240,501
Maryland	138	2.0	1,918	2.6	14	59.5	31,025	226.8	2.5	213,174
Michigan	207	3.0	2,100	2.9	10	70.3	33,496	210.7	2.4	300,970
Missouri	155	2.3	1,715	2.4	11	54.4	31,716	207.2	2.3	286,516
Tennessee	151	2.2	1,694	2.3	11	52.7	31,081	203.0	2.3	308,967
Wisconsin	145	2.1	1,583	2.2	11	49.5	31,288	189.0	2.1	202,749
Colorado	142	2.1	1,482	2.0	10	44.8	30,246	185.9	2.1	219,164
Massachusetts	143	2.1	1,340	1.8	9	47.3	35,318	176.0	2.0	261,504
Minnesota	132	1.9	1,132	1.6	9	37.1	32,795	168.3	1.9	264,972
Indiana	154	2.2	1,415	1.9	9	43.2	30,553	151.1	1.7	263,775
Arizona	150	2.2	1,600	2.2	11	46.3	28,961	148.0	1.7	196,251
Virginia	146	2.1	1,435	2.0	10	44.7	31,176	145.4	1.6	225,493
Alabama	99	1.4	1,005	1.4	10	25.5	25,378	141.8	1.6	297,813
Oregon	103	1.5	1,355	1.9	13	41.2	30,410	136.9	1.5	219,418
Louisiana	98	1.4	1,237	1.7	13	28.8	23,308	119.6	1.3	150,685
Connecticut	74	1.1	604	0.8	8	22.2	36,705	114.8	1.3	303,743
South Carolina	87	1.3	1,053	1.4	12	27.7	26,285	93.5	1.0	200,991
Kentucky	107	1.6	1,122	1.5	10	27.4	24,381	89.5	1.0	172,703
Oklahoma	84	1.2	711	1.0	8	16.3	22,975	69.7	0.8	168,755
Iowa	91	1.3	806	1.1	9	21.1	26,201	61.0	0.7	153,329
Utah	62	0.9	1,157	1.6	19	28.5	24,646	50.7	0.6	149,593
Hawaii	43	0.6	231	0.3	5	8.5	36,887	48.9	0.5	208,902
New Mexico	61	0.9	520	0.7	9	14.8	28,454	41.2	0.5	157,240
West Virginia	35	0.5	256	0.4	7	6.0	23,449	39.4	0.4	192,371
Nebraska	53	0.8	565	0.8	11	14.7	26,103	34.2	0.4	144,114
Idaho	32	0.5	293	0.4	9	7.0	24,003	33.7	0.4	285,958
New Hampshire	40	0.6	233	0.3	6	7.6	32,721	24.6	0.3	236,385
South Dakota	26	0.4	226	0.3	9	5.5	24,257	21.8	0.2	495,477
Montana	29	0.4	207	0.3	7	5.2	25,164	19.7	0.2	161,525
Mississippi	44	0.6	445	0.6	10	12.0	27,004	19.6	0.2	124,682
Vermont	18	0.3	126	0.2	7	3.9	30,833	14.0	0.2	280,540
Maine	24	0.3	163	0.2	7	4.9	29,988	7.7	0.1	150,745
Kansas	80	1.2	652	0.9	8	18.0	27,580	(D)	-	-
Arkansas	57	0.8	710	1.0	12	15.0	21,070	(D)	-	-
Nevada	43	0.6	407	0.6	9	13.1	32,123	(D)	-	-
North Dakota	21	0.3	199	0.3	9	5.9	29,422	(D)	-	-
Rhode Island	20	0.3	79	0.1	4	2.4	30,165	(D)	-	-
Delaware	17	0.2	219	0.3	13	6.4	29,333	(D)	-	-
Wyoming	13	0.2	20-99	-	-	(D)	-	(D)	-	-
Alaska	10	0.1	82	0.1	8	3.1	37,890	(D)	-	-
D.C.	3	0.0	20-99	-	-	(D)	-	(D)	-	-

Source: County Business Patterns, 1995 and *Economic Census of the U.S., 1992*. Data are sorted by 1992 revenues and, if revenues are unavailable, by establishments in 1995. The symbol (D) indicates that data are withheld by the source to avoid disclosure of competitive information. A dash (-) indicates that data are not available or undisclosed because they do not meet statistical validity standards. Shaded *states* on the state map indicate those states which have proportionately greater representation in the industry than would be indicated by the state's population; the ratio is based on total revenues or number of establishments. Shaded *regions* indicate where the industry is regionally most concentrated.

5043 - PHOTOGRAPHIC EQUIPMENT AND SUPPLIES

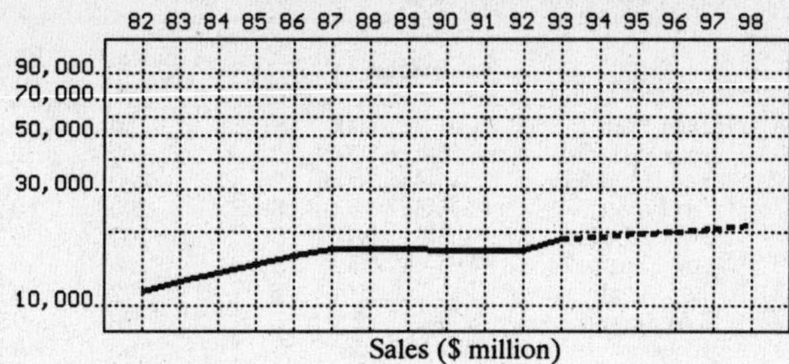

Sales ($ million)

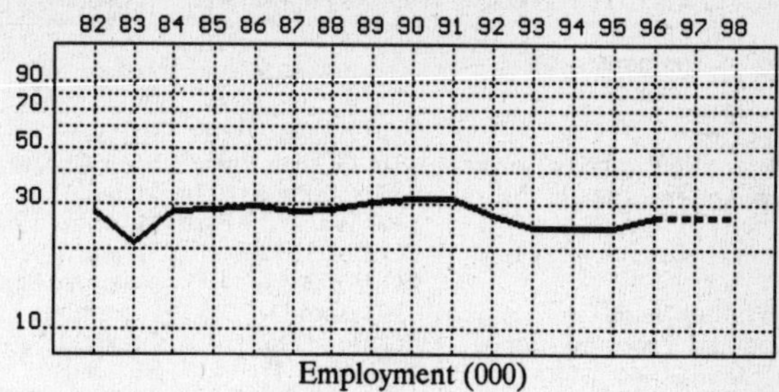

Employment (000)

GENERAL STATISTICS

Year	Establishments (number)	Employment (number)	Payroll ($ million)	Sales ($ million)	Expenses ($ million)	Beginning Inventory ($ million)	Ending Inventory ($ million)
1982	1,480	28,157	671.9	11,366.5	-	-	-
1983	1,425	21,188	473.4	12,506.3e	-	-	-
1984	1,367	28,126	743.5	13,646.2e	-	-	-
1985	1,319	28,607	793.4	14,786.0e	-	-	-
1986	1,263	29,745	838.9	15,925.9e	-	-	-
1987	1,556	28,123	846.3	17,065.7	1,893.3	1,094.4	1,048.8
1988	1,483	28,840	967.0	16,986.9e	1,963.0e	1,099.8e	1,065.3e
1989	1,427	30,599	963.2	16,908.2e	2,032.6e	1,105.3e	1,081.8e
1990	1,372	31,529	1,069.8	16,829.4e	2,102.3e	1,110.7e	1,098.3e
1991	1,374	31,375	1,119.0	16,750.7e	2,171.9e	1,116.1e	1,114.8e
1992	1,461	27,372	999.6	16,671.9	2,241.6	1,121.5	1,131.3
1993	1,402	24,645	953.6	18,587.2p	2,311.3p	1,127.0p	1,147.9p
1994	1,387	24,494	959.9	19,117.8p	2,380.9p	1,132.4p	1,164.4p
1995	1,386	24,541	1,032.4	19,648.3p	2,450.6p	1,137.8p	1,180.9p
1996	1,401p	27,165p	1,142.5p	20,178.9p	2,520.3p	1,143.2p	1,197.4p
1997	1,400p	27,098p	1,176.4p	20,709.4p	2,589.9p	1,148.7p	1,213.9p
1998	1,399p	27,031p	1,210.3p	21,239.9p	2,659.6p	1,154.1p	1,230.4p

Sources: *Economic Census of the United States*, 1982, 1987, and 1992. Establishment counts, employment, and payroll are from *County Business Patterns* for non-Census years. Values followed by a 'p' are projections by the editors. Sales and expense data for non-Census years are extrapolations, marked by 'e'. Industries reclassified in 1987 will not have data for prior years. Data are the most recent available at this level of detail.

INDICES OF CHANGE

Year	Establishments (number)	Employment (number)	Payroll ($ million)	Sales ($ million)	Expenses ($ million)	Beginning Inventory ($ million)	Ending Inventory ($ million)
1982	101.3	102.9	67.2	68.2	-	-	-
1983	97.5	77.4	47.4	75.0e	-	-	-
1984	93.6	102.8	74.4	81.9e	-	-	-
1985	90.3	104.5	79.4	88.7e	-	-	-
1986	86.4	108.7	83.9	95.5e	-	-	-
1987	106.5	102.7	84.7	102.4	84.5	97.6	92.7
1988	101.5	105.4	96.7	101.9e	87.6e	98.1e	94.2e
1989	97.7	111.8	96.4	101.4e	90.7e	98.6e	95.6e
1990	93.9	115.2	107.0	100.9e	93.8e	99.0e	97.1e
1991	94.0	114.6	111.9	100.5e	96.9e	99.5e	98.5e
1992	100.0	100.0	100.0	100.0	100.0	100.0	100.0
1993	96.0	90.0	95.4	111.5p	103.1p	100.5p	101.5p
1994	94.9	89.5	96.0	114.7p	106.2p	101.0p	102.9p
1995	94.9	89.7	103.3	117.9p	109.3p	101.5p	104.4p
1996	95.9p	99.2p	114.3p	121.0p	112.4p	101.9p	105.8p
1997	95.8p	99.0p	117.7p	124.2p	115.5p	102.4p	107.3p
1998	95.8p	98.8p	121.1p	127.4p	118.6p	102.9p	108.8p

Sources: Same as General Statistics. The values shown reflect change from the base year, 1992. Values above 100 mean greater than 1992, values below 100 mean less than 1992, and a value of 100 in the 1982-91 or 1993-98 period means same as 1992. Values followed by a 'p' are projections by the editors; 'e' stands for extrapolation. Data are the most recent available at this level of detail.

SELECTED RATIOS

For 1992	Avg. of All Wholesale	Analyzed Industry	Index	For 1992	Avg. of All Wholesale	Analyzed Industry	Index
Employees per Establishment	12	19	160	Sales per Employee	561,172	609,086	109
Payroll per Establishment	349,729	684,189	196	Sales per Establishment	6,559,346	11,411,294	174
Payroll per Employee	29,919	36,519	122	Expenses per Establishment	723,071	1,534,292	212

Sources: Same as General Statistics. The 'Average of All Manufacturing' column represents the average of all manufacturing industries reported for the most recent complete year available. The Index shows the relationship between the Average and the Analyzed Industry. For example, 100 means that they are equal; 500 that the Analyzed Industry is five times the average; 50 means that the Analyzed Industry is half the national average. The abbreviation 'na' is used to show that data are 'not available'.

LEADING COMPANIES

Number shown: **47** Total sales ($ mil): **4,439** Total employment (000): **10.0**

Company Name	Address				CEO Name	Phone	Co. Type	Sales ($ mil)	Empl. (000)
Minolta Corp.	101 Williams Dr	Ramsey	NJ	07446	Hiroshi Fujii	201-825-4000	S	1,150	3.0
VWR Scientific Products Corp.	1310 Goshen Pkwy	West Chester	PA	19380	Jerrold B Harris	215-431-1700	P	1,117	2.1
Olympus America Inc.	2 Corporate Ctr Dr	Melville	NY	11747	Sidney Braginsky	516-844-5000	S	800	1.5
Nikon Inc.	1300 Walt Whitman	Melville	NY	11747	Hideo Fukushi	516-547-4200	S	290 •	0.5
Fuji Medical Systems USA Inc.	PO Box 120035	Stamford	CT	06907	Charles J Leslie	203-353-0300	S	200	0.3
Vivitar Corp.	PO Box 2559	Newbury Park	CA	91319	Victor Chernick	805-498-7008	S	110 •	0.1
Young-Phillips Sales Co.	6399 Amp Dr	Clemmons	NC	27012	Richard Blair	910-766-7070	R	72	0.2
Anderson and Vreeland Inc.	PO Box 1246	Fairfield	NJ	07007	WK Anderson	973-227-2270	R	70	0.2
Samsung Opto-Electronics	40 Seaview Dr	Secaucus	NJ	07094	Steve Lee	201-902-0347	S	60	<0.1
Konica U.S.A. Inc.	440 Silvan Ave	Englewood Clfs	NJ	07632	Richard Carter	201-568-3100	S	58	0.2
Jungkind Photo-Graphic Inc.	PO Box 1509	Little Rock	AR	72203	R L Bumgardner	501-376-3481	R	45	0.2
Ricom Electronics Ltd.	PO Box 17882	Milwaukee	WI	53217	Marcia Rose	414-357-8181	R	45 •	<0.1
Arriflex Corp.	617 Rte 303	Blauvelt	NY	10913	Volker Bahnemann	914-353-1400	S	43	0.1
Cantel Industries Inc.	1135 Broad St	Clifton	NJ	07013	James P Reilly	973-470-8700	P	35	0.2
Fred P. Gattas Company Inc.	5000 Summer Ave	Memphis	TN	38122	Fred Gattas Jr	901-767-2930	R	28	0.1
Omega Acquisition Corp.	191 Shaeffer Ave	Westminster	MD	21158	Charles Ezrine	410-857-6353	R	25	0.1
Sinar-Bron Inc.	17 Progress St	Edison	NJ	08820	Jim Bellina	908-754-5800	R	24 •	<0.1
Recognition Systems Inc..	30 Harbor Park Dr	P. Washington	NY	11050	John E McCusker	516-625-5000	R	23 •	<0.1
Comprehensive Video Group	55 Ruta Ct	S. Hackensack	NJ	07606	Shelly Goldstein	201-229-0025	R	20 •	<0.1
Mamiya America Corp.	8 Westchester Plaza	Elmsford	NY	10523	Henry Froehlich	914-347-3300	R	19	<0.1
Koyo Internationalorporated	315 Allen St	Cumming	GA	30130	Kim Mizuno	404-889-2858	S	18 •	<0.1
Showscan Entertainment Inc.	3939 Landmark St	Culver City	CA	90232	Dennis Pope	310-558-0150	P	18	<0.1
Chilcote Co.	2140 Superior Ave	Cleveland	OH	44114	D Hein	216-781-6000	R	15	0.1
GMI Photographic Inc.	125 Schmitt Blvd	Farmingdale	NY	11735	Joseph Gallen	516-752-0066	R	13 •	<0.1
Mahalick Corp.	PO Box 40	Yonkers	NY	10703	Brian Roberts	914-963-1100	R	13	<0.1
Murphy Co. (Columbus, Ohio)	455 W Broad St	Columbus	OH	43215	John L Murphy	614-221-7731	R	13	<0.1
USI Inc.	98 Fort Path Rd	Madison	CT	06443	David R Polastri	203-245-8586	R	13 •	<0.1
Eye Communication Systems	455 E Industrial Dr	Hartland	WI	53029	John Bessent	414-367-1360	R	13	0.1
Don McAlister Camera Co.	1454 W Lane Ave	Columbus	OH	43221	RE Longenbaker	614-488-1865	R	10 •	0.1
Savage Universal Corp.	550 W Elliot Rd	Chandler	AZ	85225	Richard Pressman	602-632-1320	R	10	<0.1
Great Lakes Technologies Corp.	PO Box 4005	Kalamazoo	MI	49003	Robin L Marshall	616-385-2200	S	9	<0.1
Wittco Systems Inc.	PO Box 230306	Portland	OR	97223	Bill Witt	503-620-9887	R	9	<0.1
Cushing and Company Inc.	325 W Huron St	Chicago	IL	60610	Cathleen Duff	312-266-8228	R	9	<0.1
Pako Corp.	2440 Fernbrook	Minneapolis	MN	55447	Richard Reedy	612-559-7600	R	7	0.1
JOS Projection Systems Inc.	17512 Von Karman	Irvine	CA	92614	Alice Schellin	714-476-2222	R	6	<0.1
Supercircuits Inc.	1 Supercircuitsaza	Leander	TX	78645	Steve Klindworth	512-260-0333	R	6	<0.1
Beta Screen Corp.	707 Commercial	Carlstadt	NJ	07072	A Serchuk	201-939-2400	R	4	<0.1
Dot Line	9420 Eton Ave	Chatsworth	CA	91311	Walter A Reeves Jr	214-631-9730	R	3 •	<0.1
Santa Barbara Instrument Group	PO Box 50437	Santa Barbara	CA	93150	Richard Schwartz	805-969-1851	R	3	<0.1
UV Process Supply Inc.	1229 W Cortland St	Chicago	IL	60614	Stephen B Siggel	312-248-0099	R	3 •	<0.1
Vanguard Imaging Corp.	55 Cabot Ct	Hauppauge	NY	11788	Harry Warring	516-435-2100	S	3 •	<0.1
Hoag Enterprises Inc.	PO Box 4406	Springfield	MO	65808	Charles Hoag	417-883-8300	R	3	<0.1
Options International Inc.	913 18th Ave S	Nashville	TN	37212	Donna Reid	615-327-8090	R	2	<0.1
Central Audio Visual Equipment	271 E Helen Rd	Palatine	IL	60067	Michael Bashir	708-776-9200	R	1	<0.1
D/A Mid South Inc.	9000 Jameel, #100	Houston	TX	77040	Richard J Gunn	713-895-0090	R	1	<0.1
Kinetronics Corp.	PO Box 6178	Sarasota	FL	34278	Bill Stelcher	813-388-2432	R	1	<0.1
Distributing Inc.	7046 W Greenfield	West Allis	WI	53214	David Gray	414-774-4949	R	1	<0.1

Source: *Ward's Business Directory of U.S. Private and Public Companies*, 1998. The company type code used is as follows: P - Public, R - Private, S - Subsidiary, D - Division, J - Joint Venture, A - Affiliate, G - Group. Sales are in millions of dollars, employees are in thousands. An asterisk (*) indicates an estimated sales volume. The symbol < stands for 'less than'.

OCCUPATIONS EMPLOYED BY SIC 504 - WHOLESALE TRADE, OTHER

Occupation	% of Total 1996	Change to 2006	Occupation	% of Total 1996	Change to 2006
Sales & related workers nec	19.5	20.2	Clerical supervisors & managers	1.9	20.2
General managers & top executives	5.9	16.4	Order clerks	1.9	8.2
Truck drivers light & heavy	5.4	20.2	Helpers, laborers nec	1.7	20.2
General office clerks	3.6	3.4	Electrical & electronic technicians	1.4	18.8
Traffic, shipping, receiving clerks	3.6	16.7	Blue collar worker supervisors	1.4	16.0
Stock clerks	3.5	-3.9	Wholesale & retail buyers, except farm products	1.3	17.0
Freight, stock, & material movers, hand	3.3	8.2	Office machine & cash register servicers	1.3	20.2
Marketing & sales worker supervisors	3.1	20.2	Hand packers & packagers	1.2	-3.9
Order fillers, wholesale & retail sales	3.0	16.7	Maintenance repairers, general utility	1.1	12.0
Bookkeeping, accounting, & auditing clerks	2.9	-3.9	Industrial truck & tractor operators	1.1	20.2
Salespersons, retail	2.5	20.2	Purchasing managers	1.1	20.2
Secretaries, except legal & medical	2.5	-4.7	Receptionists & information clerks	1.0	20.2
Assemblers, fabricators, hand workers nec	2.0	-3.9			

Source: *Industry-Occupation Matrix*, Bureau of Labor Statistics. These data relate to one or more 3-digit SIC industry groups rather than to a single 4-digit SIC. The change reported for each occupation to the year 2006 is a percent of growth or decline as estimated by the Bureau of Labor Statistics. The abbreviation nec stands for 'not elsewhere classified'.

STATE AND REGIONAL CONCENTRATION

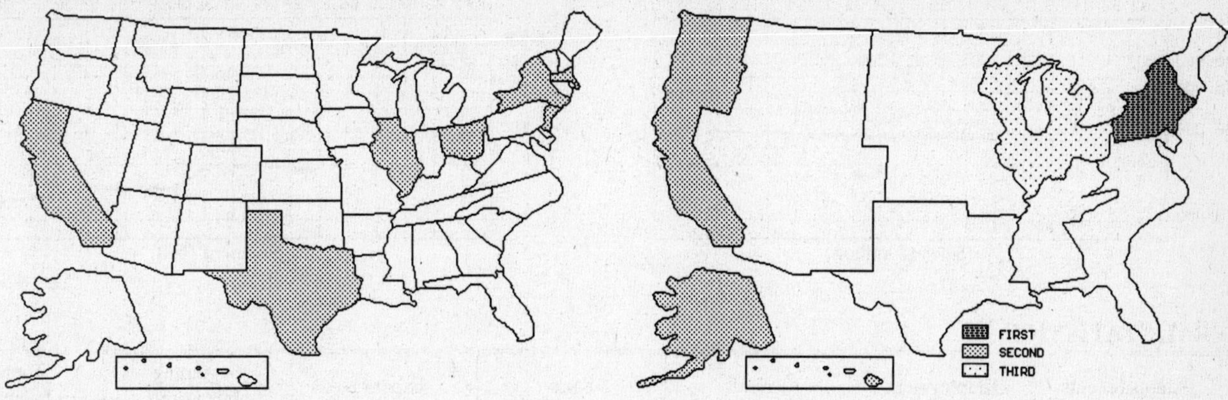

INDUSTRY DATA BY STATE

	Establishments - 1995		Employment - 1995			Payroll - 1995		Sales - 1992		
State	Total (number)	% of U.S.	Total (number)	% of U.S.	Per Estab.	Total ($ mil.)	Per Empl. ($)	Total ($ mil.)	% of U.S.	Per Estab ($)
California	219	15.8	4,731	19.4	22	214.3	45,302	2,972.6	19.5	611,270
New York	193	13.9	4,188	17.2	22	197.8	47,221	2,499.2	16.4	572,808
New Jersey	85	6.1	2,058	8.4	24	98.5	47,877	2,044.1	13.4	882,616
Illinois	98	7.1	2,429	10.0	25	106.3	43,769	1,564.2	10.3	581,072
Massachusetts	44	3.2	784	3.2	18	29.6	37,699	1,168.9	7.7	1,106,869
Texas	75	5.4	1,224	5.0	16	50.8	41,524	1,058.4	7.0	595,928
Ohio	50	3.6	786	3.2	16	28.8	36,701	791.5	5.2	842,018
Florida	90	6.5	1,019	4.2	11	35.9	35,190	413.6	2.7	510,035
Virginia	28	2.0	373	1.5	13	12.9	34,456	337.6	2.2	452,534
Pennsylvania	37	2.7	436	1.8	12	13.0	29,844	263.4	1.7	412,274
Minnesota	22	1.6	548	2.2	25	21.7	39,608	254.5	1.7	444,143
North Carolina	22	1.6	453	1.9	21	19.0	41,949	253.4	1.7	610,590
Michigan	34	2.5	297	1.2	9	8.5	28,768	197.7	1.3	428,000
Colorado	28	2.0	327	1.3	12	13.9	42,560	183.7	1.2	507,348
Indiana	23	1.7	324	1.3	14	13.1	40,537	159.5	1.0	390,922
Maryland	28	2.0	252	1.0	9	8.7	34,671	157.2	1.0	430,800
Washington	19	1.4	144	0.6	8	4.2	29,229	156.9	1.0	454,710
Tennessee	24	1.7	294	1.2	12	9.9	33,714	129.9	0.9	320,812
Kansas	15	1.1	488	2.0	33	23.0	47,074	128.9	0.8	484,519
Connecticut	24	1.7	314	1.3	13	12.0	38,061	128.3	0.8	427,700
Arizona	13	0.9	134	0.5	10	3.5	26,060	114.9	0.8	520,086
Louisiana	9	0.6	88	0.4	10	1.9	21,886	94.1	0.6	435,486
Oklahoma	8	0.6	91	0.4	11	3.0	32,901	41.3	0.3	389,472
Wisconsin	14	1.0	133	0.5	10	4.0	29,827	36.8	0.2	237,484
Utah	10	0.7	98	0.4	10	3.3	33,939	19.1	0.1	302,413
Iowa	11	0.8	97	0.4	9	1.7	17,825	13.3	0.1	148,078
Alabama	12	0.9	128	0.5	11	2.8	22,070	11.7	0.1	143,000
Nebraska	4	0.3	44	0.2	11	0.9	20,886	5.1	0.0	223,870
Delaware	4	0.3	20-99	-	-	(D)	-	4.5	0.0	151,133
South Carolina	6	0.4	54	0.2	9	1.0	18,907	3.5	0.0	80,465
Vermont	2	0.1	0-19	-	-	(D)	-	3.2	0.0	264,333
Rhode Island	4	0.3	0-19	-	-	(D)	-	1.6	0.0	319,800
New Mexico	2	0.1	0-19	-	-	(D)	-	0.6	0.0	93,667
Georgia	43	3.1	1,010	4.1	23	51.3	50,814	(D)	-	-
Missouri	29	2.1	537	2.2	19	18.1	33,669	(D)	-	-
Oregon	14	1.0	141	0.6	10	4.2	29,574	(D)	-	-
Hawaii	11	0.8	171	0.7	16	5.9	34,538	(D)	-	-
Kentucky	7	0.5	130	0.5	19	3.0	23,438	(D)	-	-
Nevada	6	0.4	20-99	-	-	(D)	-	(D)	-	-
Arkansas	4	0.3	26	0.1	7	0.5	20,154	(D)	-	-
D.C.	4	0.3	0-19	-	-	(D)	-	(D)	-	-
New Hampshire	4	0.3	19	0.1	5	1.1	55,368	(D)	-	-
Maine	3	0.2	10	0.0	3	0.1	13,200	(D)	-	-
Idaho	1	0.1	0-19	-	-	(D)	-	(D)	-	-
North Dakota	1	0.1	20-99	-	-	(D)	-	(D)	-	-
West Virginia	1	0.1	0-19	-	-	(D)	-	(D)	-	-
Wyoming	1	0.1	0-19	-	-	(D)	-	(D)	-	-

Source: County Business Patterns, 1995 and *Economic Census of the U.S., 1992*. Data are sorted by 1992 revenues and, if revenues are unavailable, by establishments in 1995. The symbol (D) indicates that data are withheld by the source to avoid disclosure of competitive information. A dash (-) indicates that data are not available or undisclosed because they do not meet statistical validity standards. Shaded *states* on the state map indicate those states which have proportionately greater representation in the industry than would be indicated by the state's population; the ratio is based on total revenues or number of establishments. Shaded *regions* indicate where the industry is regionally most concentrated.

5044 - OFFICE EQUIPMENT

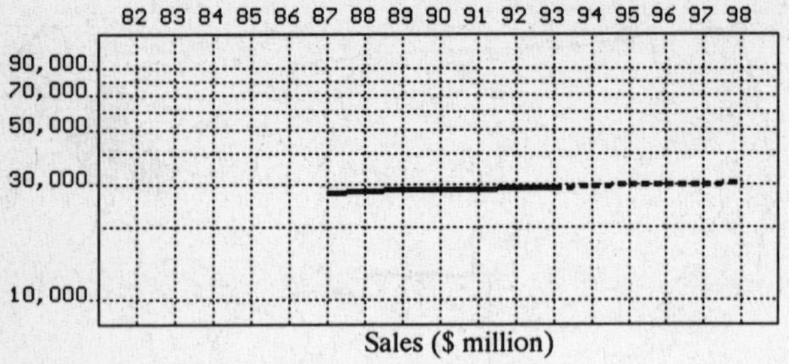

Sales ($ million)

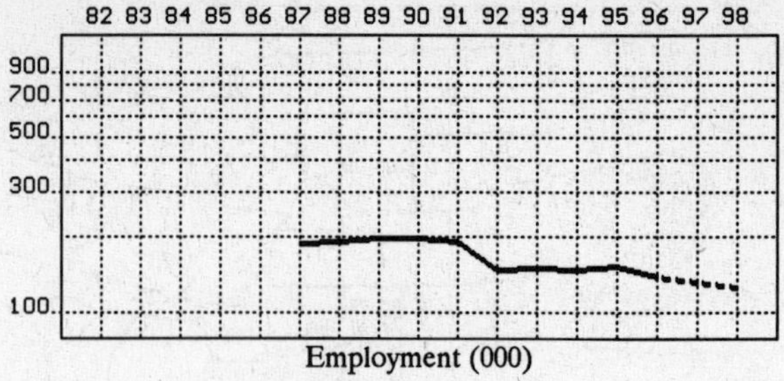

Employment (000)

GENERAL STATISTICS

Year	Establishments (number)	Employment (number)	Payroll ($ million)	Sales ($ million)	Expenses ($ million)	Beginning Inventory ($ million)	Ending Inventory ($ million)
1982	-	-	-	-	-	-	-
1983	-	-	-	-	-	-	-
1984	-	-	-	-	-	-	-
1985	-	-	-	-	-	-	-
1986	-	-	-	-	-	-	-
1987	11,524	188,982	4,766.2	27,762.5	8,336.0	2,385.6	2,458.6
1988	11,040	191,610	5,184.3	27,990.8*e*	8,405.9*e*	2,427.8*e*	2,503.1*e*
1989	10,192	196,289	5,449.4	28,219.0*e*	8,475.8*e*	2,470.0*e*	2,547.6*e*
1990	10,103	196,197	5,582.2	28,447.3*e*	8,545.8*e*	2,512.2*e*	2,592.1*e*
1991	10,051	192,070	5,699.6	28,675.6*e*	8,615.7*e*	2,554.4*e*	2,636.6*e*
1992	8,631	148,991	4,721.4	28,903.8	8,685.7	2,596.6	2,681.1
1993	8,703	152,097	5,008.1	29,132.1*p*	8,755.6*p*	2,638.8*p*	2,725.6*p*
1994	8,734	149,132	5,068.4	29,360.4*p*	8,825.5*p*	2,681.0*p*	2,770.1*p*
1995	8,996	152,963	5,444.7	29,588.7*p*	8,895.5*p*	2,723.2*p*	2,814.6*p*
1996	7,985*p*	140,334*p*	5,265.7*p*	29,816.9*p*	8,965.4*p*	2,765.4*p*	2,859.1*p*
1997	7,627*p*	133,549*p*	5,276.1*p*	30,045.2*p*	9,035.3*p*	2,807.6*p*	2,903.6*p*
1998	7,269*p*	126,764*p*	5,286.5*p*	30,273.5*p*	9,105.3*p*	2,849.8*p*	2,948.1*p*

Sources: *Economic Census of the United States*, 1982, 1987, and 1992. Establishment counts, employment, and payroll are from *County Business Patterns* for non-Census years. Values followed by a 'p' are projections by the editors. Sales and expense data for non-Census years are extrapolations, marked by 'e'. Industries reclassified in 1987 will not have data for prior years. Data are the most recent available at this level of detail.

INDICES OF CHANGE

Year	Establishments (number)	Employment (number)	Payroll ($ million)	Sales ($ million)	Expenses ($ million)	Beginning Inventory ($ million)	Ending Inventory ($ million)
1982	-	-	-	-	-	-	-
1983	-	-	-	-	-	-	-
1984	-	-	-	-	-	-	-
1985	-	-	-	-	-	-	-
1986	-	-	-	-	-	-	-
1987	133.5	126.8	100.9	96.1	96.0	91.9	91.7
1988	127.9	128.6	109.8	96.8*e*	96.8*e*	93.5*e*	93.4*e*
1989	118.1	131.7	115.4	97.6*e*	97.6*e*	95.1*e*	95.0*e*
1990	117.1	131.7	118.2	98.4*e*	98.4*e*	96.7*e*	96.7*e*
1991	116.5	128.9	120.7	99.2*e*	99.2*e*	98.4*e*	98.3*e*
1992	100.0	100.0	100.0	100.0	100.0	100.0	100.0
1993	100.8	102.1	106.1	100.8*p*	100.8*p*	101.6*p*	101.7*p*
1994	101.2	100.1	107.3	101.6*p*	101.6*p*	103.3*p*	103.3*p*
1995	104.2	102.7	115.3	102.4*p*	102.4*p*	104.9*p*	105.0*p*
1996	92.5*p*	94.2*p*	111.5*p*	103.2*p*	103.2*p*	106.5*p*	106.6*p*
1997	88.4*p*	89.6*p*	111.7*p*	103.9*p*	104.0*p*	108.1*p*	108.3*p*
1998	84.2*p*	85.1*p*	112.0*p*	104.7*p*	104.8*p*	109.8*p*	110.0*p*

Sources: Same as General Statistics. The values shown reflect change from the base year, 1992. Values above 100 mean greater than 1992, values below 100 mean less than 1992, and a value of 100 in the 1982-91 or 1993-98 period means same as 1992. Values followed by a 'p' are projections by the editors; 'e' stands for extrapolation. Data are the most recent available at this level of detail.

SELECTED RATIOS

For 1992	Avg. of All Wholesale	Analyzed Industry	Index	For 1992	Avg. of All Wholesale	Analyzed Industry	Index
Employees per Establishment	12	17	148	Sales per Employee	561,172	193,997	35
Payroll per Establishment	349,729	547,028	156	Sales per Establishment	6,559,346	3,348,836	51
Payroll per Employee	29,919	31,689	106	Expenses per Establishment	723,071	1,006,338	139

Sources: Same as General Statistics. The 'Average of All Manufacturing' column represents the average of all manufacturing industries reported for the most recent complete year available. The Index shows the relationship between the Average and the Analyzed Industry. For example, 100 means that they are equal; 500 that the Analyzed Industry is five times the average; 50 means that the Analyzed Industry is half the national average. The abbreviation 'na' is used to show that data are 'not available'.

LEADING COMPANIES

Number shown: **50** Total sales ($ mil): **17,727** Total employment (000): **62.0**

Company Name	Address				CEO Name	Phone	Co. Type	Sales ($ mil)	Empl. (000)
Sharp Electronics Corp.	PO Box 650	Mahwah	NJ	07430	Sueyuki Hirooka	201-529-8200	S	3,500 *	2.3
United Stationers Inc.	2200 E Golf Rd	Des Plaines	IL	60016	R W Larrimore	847-699-5000	P	2,558	5.5
Danka Business Systems PLC	11201 Danka Cir N	St. Petersburg	FL	33716	Daniel Doyle	813-576-6003	P	2,101	21.8
BT Office Products Intern.	2150 E Lake Cook	Buffalo Grove	IL	60089	Frans H J Koffrie	847-793-7500	P	1,619	6.6
Lanier Worldwide Inc.	2300 Pklake Dr NE	Atlanta	GA	30345	Wesley E Cantrell	404-496-9500	S	1,270 *	7.0
Minolta Corp.	101 Williams Dr	Ramsey	NJ	07446	Hiroshi Fujii	201-825-4000	S	1,150	3.0
Konica Business Machines	500 Day Hill Rd	Windsor	CT	06095	Teruo Nakazawa	860-683-2222	S	640	2.4
Casio Inc.	570 Mt Pleasant	Dover	NJ	07801	John J McDonald	973-361-5400	D	630	0.3
Astro Business Solutions Inc.	110 W Walnut St	Gardena	CA	90248	Ollie Hatch Jr	310-217-3000	S	523 *	0.7
A.B. Dick Co.	5700 W Touhy Ave	Niles	IL	60714	Ron Peterson	708-763-1900	S	400	0.2
CHS Promark (Miami, Florida)	2153 NW 86th Ave	Miami	FL	33126	Alvin Perlman	305-594-4990	R	400	0.3
Oce-USA Inc.	5450 N Cumberland	Chicago	IL	60656	Giovanni Pelizzari	773-714-8500	S	400 *	2.5
Servco Pacific Inc.	PO Box 2788	Honolulu	HI	96803	Mark H Fukunaga	808-521-6511	R	361	0.9
Funai Corp.	100 North St	Teterboro	NJ	07608	Masawo Suwa	201-288-2063	S	360	<0.1
Quill Corp.	100 Shelter Rd	Lincolnshire	IL	60069	Jack Miller	708-634-4850	R	270 *	1.0
Brother International Corp.	200 Cottontail Lane	Somerset	NJ	08875	Hiromi Gunji	908-704-1700	S	160	0.5
Gestetner Corp.	599 W Putnam Ave	Greenwich	CT	06836	C Rajaratnarm	203-625-7600	S	130 *	0.6
AM Multigraphics Div.	431 Lakeview Ct	Mount Prospect	IL	60056	Thomas D Rooney	847-375-1700	R	123 *	0.7
Lewan and Associates Inc.	PO Box 22855	Denver	CO	80222	Paul R Lewan	303-759-5440	R	100	0.5
T. Talbott Bond Co.	7138 Windsor Blvd	Baltimore	MD	21244	Henry Bond	410-265-8600	R	86 *	0.5
Western ResourceNet Intern	6000 N Cutter Cir	Portland	OR	97217	Jerry Lindsey	503-289-2800	S	75	0.1
Young-Phillips Sales Co.	6399 Amp Dr	Clemmons	NC	27012	Richard Blair	910-766-7070	R	72	0.2
American Loose Leaf	4015 Papin St	St. Louis	MO	63110	Gerald Holschen	314-535-1414	D	70	0.4
Louisiana Graphic Supplier Inc.	2323 Edenborn Ave	Metairie	LA	70001	Thomas Waldrup	504-837-4993	D	66 *	<0.1
Harper Brothers	PO Box 2108	Greenville	SC	29606	Glenda W Morgan	803-242-3600	D	51	0.2
CERBCO Inc.	3421 Pennsy Dr	Landover	MD	20785	Robert W Erickson	301-773-1784	P	51	0.3
McRae Industries Inc.	402 N Main St	Mount Gilead	NC	27306	Branson J McRae	910-439-6147	P	49	0.9
Lincoln Office Supply Company	7707 N Knoxville	Peoria	IL	61614	Thomas E Spuegeon	309-693-2444	R	40	0.2
Ohio Business Machines Inc.	1728 Saint Claire	Cleveland	OH	44114	Sal Spagnola	216-579-1300	R	40	0.3
Select Copy Systems	6229 Santos Diaz St	Irwindale	CA	91706	Frank Mendicina	818-334-0383	R	32	0.2
Imagetech RICOH Corp.	192 Nickerson St	Seattle	WA	98109	Warren White	206-298-1600	S	30 *	0.2
Shredex Inc.	49 Natcon Dr	Shirley	NY	11967	Michael J Falco Jr	516-345-0300	R	27	<0.1
Standard Duplicating Machine	10 Connector Rd	Andover	MA	01810	L Guy Reny	508-470-1920	R	27 *	<0.1
Milner Document Products Inc.	2845 Amwiler Rd	Atlanta	GA	30360	Gene Milner	770-263-5300	R	24 *	0.2
Pacific Stationery & Printing Co.	8303 Killingsworth	Portland	OR	97220	John A Stirek	503-255-8900	R	24	0.1
Open Plan Systems Inc.	4299 Carolina Ave	Richmond	VA	23222	Stan A Fischer	804-228-5600	P	22	0.3
Advance Business Systems	PO Box 627	Cockeysville	MD	21030	Alan I Elkin	410-252-4800	R	22 *	0.1
Forms and Supplies Inc.	PO Box 18694	Memphis	TN	38181	Richard Mason	901-365-1249	R	22	0.1
Capitol Copy Products Inc.	12000 Baltimore	Beltsville	MD	20705	A. A Manoogian	301-937-5030	S	20	<0.1
Ames Supply Co.	2537 Curtiss St	Downers Grove	IL	60515	R C Hildebrandt	630-964-2440	R	20 *	0.1
Cash Register Sales Inc.	2909 Anthony	Minneapolis	MN	55418	David Sanders	612-781-3474	R	20 *	<0.1
Everything for the Office Inc.	8201 54th Ave N	New Hope	MN	55428	Edward Lloyd	612-533-0100	R	20	0.1
Personal Financial Assistant	5130 Pkwayaza Blvd	Charlotte	NC	28217	John DiNiro	704-357-8004	S	19 *	0.1
Cotey Workplace Environments	PO Box 1206	Northbrook	IL	60062	William Cotey	847-564-4606	R	18	<0.1
Office Equipment and Supply	495 New Rochelle	Bronxville	NY	10708	Michael Maglio	718-823-4254	R	16 *	0.1
BT Office Products Intern.	28241 Mound Rd	Warren	MI	48092	Richard M Beaudin	810-573-8877	D	15 *	<0.1
HPS Office Systems	8020 Zionsville Rd	Indianapolis	IN	46268	William A Boncosky	317-875-9000	D	15	<0.1
Eltrex Industries Inc.	65 Sullivan St	Rochester	NY	14605	Matthew Augustine	716-454-6100	R	14 *	0.1
USI Inc.	98 Fort Path Rd	Madison	CT	06443	David R Polastri	203-245-8586	R	13 *	<0.1
Eye Communication Systems	455 E Industrial Dr	Hartland	WI	53029	John Bessent	414-367-1360	R	13	0.1

Source: *Ward's Business Directory of U.S. Private and Public Companies*, 1998. The company type code used is as follows: P - Public, R - Private, S - Subsidiary, D - Division, J - Joint Venture, A - Affiliate, G - Group. Sales are in millions of dollars, employees are in thousands. An asterisk (*) indicates an estimated sales volume. The symbol < stands for 'less than'.

OCCUPATIONS EMPLOYED BY SIC 504 - WHOLESALE TRADE, OTHER

Occupation	% of Total 1996	Change to 2006	Occupation	% of Total 1996	Change to 2006
Sales & related workers nec	19.5	20.2	Clerical supervisors & managers	1.9	20.2
General managers & top executives	5.9	16.4	Order clerks	1.9	8.2
Truck drivers light & heavy	5.4	20.2	Helpers, laborers nec	1.7	20.2
General office clerks	3.6	3.4	Electrical & electronic technicians	1.4	18.8
Traffic, shipping, receiving clerks	3.6	16.7	Blue collar worker supervisors	1.4	16.0
Stock clerks	3.5	-3.9	Wholesale & retail buyers, except farm products	1.3	17.0
Freight, stock, & material movers, hand	3.3	8.2	Office machine & cash register servicers	1.3	20.2
Marketing & sales worker supervisors	3.1	20.2	Hand packers & packagers	1.2	-3.9
Order fillers, wholesale & retail sales	3.0	16.7	Maintenance repairers, general utility	1.1	12.0
Bookkeeping, accounting, & auditing clerks	2.9	-3.9	Industrial truck & tractor operators	1.1	20.2
Salespersons, retail	2.5	20.2	Purchasing managers	1.1	20.2
Secretaries, except legal & medical	2.5	-4.7	Receptionists & information clerks	1.0	20.2
Assemblers, fabricators, hand workers nec	2.0	-3.9			

Source: *Industry-Occupation Matrix*, Bureau of Labor Statistics. These data relate to one or more 3-digit SIC industry groups rather than to a single 4-digit SIC. The change reported for each occupation to the year 2006 is a percent of growth or decline as estimated by the Bureau of Labor Statistics. The abbreviation nec stands for 'not elsewhere classified'.

STATE AND REGIONAL CONCENTRATION

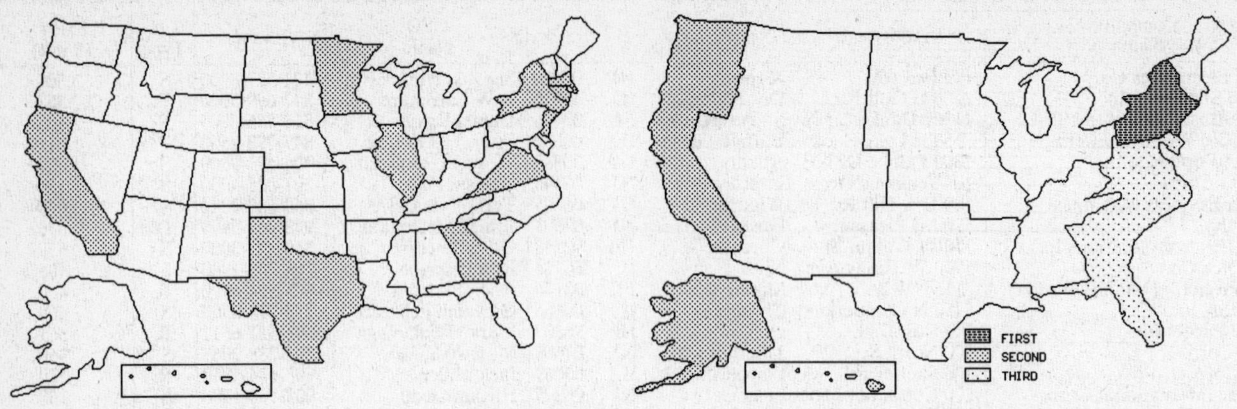

INDUSTRY DATA BY STATE

State	Establishments - 1995 Total (number)	Establishments - 1995 % of U.S.	Employment - 1995 Total (number)	Employment - 1995 % of U.S.	Employment - 1995 Per Estab.	Payroll - 1995 Total ($ mil.)	Payroll - 1995 Per Empl. ($)	Sales - 1992 Total ($ mil.)	Sales - 1992 % of U.S.	Sales - 1992 Per Estab ($)
California	920	10.2	18,082	11.9	20	667.7	36,924	4,653.0	16.3	259,540
New Jersey	302	3.4	7,550	5.0	25	322.9	42,766	2,718.9	9.5	352,237
New York	520	5.8	11,014	7.2	21	438.8	39,842	2,303.9	8.1	218,382
Texas	698	7.8	11,482	7.5	16	401.2	34,938	2,110.6	7.4	182,360
Illinois	397	4.4	7,210	4.7	18	271.5	37,663	1,585.4	5.6	208,857
Florida	568	6.3	8,383	5.5	15	259.6	30,972	1,459.9	5.1	175,403
Massachusetts	189	2.1	4,570	3.0	24	217.1	47,497	1,279.3	4.5	249,862
Georgia	257	2.9	5,227	3.4	20	197.6	37,800	1,177.8	4.1	247,014
Ohio	345	3.8	6,714	4.4	19	231.8	34,522	1,121.9	3.9	168,852
Pennsylvania	401	4.5	7,024	4.6	18	228.7	32,556	1,033.0	3.6	157,013
Virginia	220	2.4	4,352	2.9	20	171.0	39,301	852.3	3.0	197,804
Connecticut	152	1.7	2,634	1.7	17	106.9	40,567	663.1	2.3	271,440
Michigan	227	2.5	4,091	2.7	18	143.9	35,176	627.3	2.2	153,826
Minnesota	162	1.8	3,725	2.4	23	138.4	37,141	546.3	1.9	171,853
North Carolina	260	2.9	3,477	2.3	13	120.8	34,744	494.5	1.7	144,252
Missouri	216	2.4	3,356	2.2	16	103.3	30,790	462.7	1.6	143,796
Washington	208	2.3	2,686	1.8	13	102.7	38,218	431.5	1.5	164,400
Maryland	172	1.9	2,840	1.9	17	91.2	32,096	393.6	1.4	152,485
Tennessee	204	2.3	2,903	1.9	14	93.9	32,329	378.9	1.3	143,895
Colorado	159	1.8	2,620	1.7	16	90.9	34,710	371.3	1.3	161,854
Indiana	201	2.2	3,099	2.0	15	98.2	31,677	349.5	1.2	124,638
Wisconsin	172	1.9	2,571	1.7	15	86.4	33,624	343.6	1.2	142,736
Arizona	152	1.7	2,320	1.5	15	77.5	33,403	304.6	1.1	125,385
Alabama	153	1.7	1,953	1.3	13	60.7	31,087	239.7	0.8	129,335
Louisiana	150	1.7	1,968	1.3	13	64.3	32,679	235.5	0.8	111,500
Kansas	98	1.1	1,635	1.1	17	54.3	33,191	233.9	0.8	152,960
Oklahoma	134	1.5	1,700	1.1	13	48.3	28,388	214.4	0.8	134,682
Oregon	134	1.5	1,971	1.3	15	63.0	31,965	209.8	0.7	134,219
South Carolina	126	1.4	1,746	1.1	14	47.1	26,963	208.2	0.7	145,693
Iowa	117	1.3	1,472	1.0	13	46.6	31,651	181.5	0.6	130,667
Kentucky	106	1.2	1,397	0.9	13	42.0	30,065	166.9	0.6	125,700
Utah	63	0.7	1,131	0.7	18	37.4	33,039	128.7	0.5	118,594
New Hampshire	49	0.5	620	0.4	13	20.5	33,129	121.3	0.4	196,903
New Mexico	70	0.8	881	0.6	13	26.1	29,614	112.1	0.4	131,896
Hawaii	38	0.4	748	0.5	20	26.4	35,356	98.3	0.3	135,038
Nebraska	59	0.7	772	0.5	13	22.7	29,358	93.5	0.3	124,355
West Virginia	60	0.7	757	0.5	13	20.9	27,653	91.1	0.3	133,187
Mississippi	71	0.8	587	0.4	8	16.8	28,612	90.5	0.3	115,775
Arkansas	98	1.1	979	0.6	10	25.5	26,033	89.7	0.3	105,327
Nevada	53	0.6	695	0.5	13	19.1	27,462	79.8	0.3	111,113
Alaska	24	0.3	347	0.2	14	15.1	43,556	64.1	0.2	212,245
Maine	39	0.4	455	0.3	12	12.9	28,420	41.5	0.1	94,699
Idaho	40	0.4	338	0.2	8	9.3	27,482	41.4	0.1	94,390
Montana	39	0.4	356	0.2	9	7.6	21,298	28.8	0.1	103,341
North Dakota	30	0.3	306	0.2	10	8.3	26,984	26.3	0.1	93,390
South Dakota	31	0.3	291	0.2	9	7.2	24,756	22.5	0.1	91,251
Wyoming	27	0.3	100-249	-	-	(D)	-	21.5	0.1	85,804
Vermont	15	0.2	100-249	-	-	(D)	-	7.7	0.0	104,568
Rhode Island	37	0.4	640	0.4	17	23.3	36,448	(D)	-	-
Delaware	27	0.3	446	0.3	17	21.3	47,661	(D)	-	-
D.C.	6	0.1	500-999	-	-	(D)	-	(D)	-	-

Source: *County Business Patterns, 1995* and *Economic Census of the U.S., 1992*. Data are sorted by 1992 revenues and, if revenues are unavailable, by establishments in 1995. The symbol (D) indicates that data are withheld by the source to avoid disclosure of competitive information. A dash (-) indicates that data are not available or undisclosed because they do not meet statistical validity standards. Shaded *states* on the state map indicate those states which have proportionately greater representation in the industry than would be indicated by the state's population; the ratio is based on total revenues or number of establishments. Shaded *regions* indicate where the industry is regionally most concentrated.

5045 - COMPUTERS, PERIPHERALS & SOFTWARE

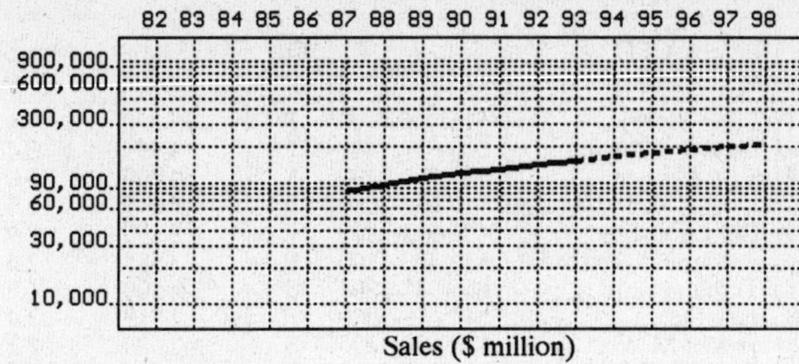

Sales ($ million)

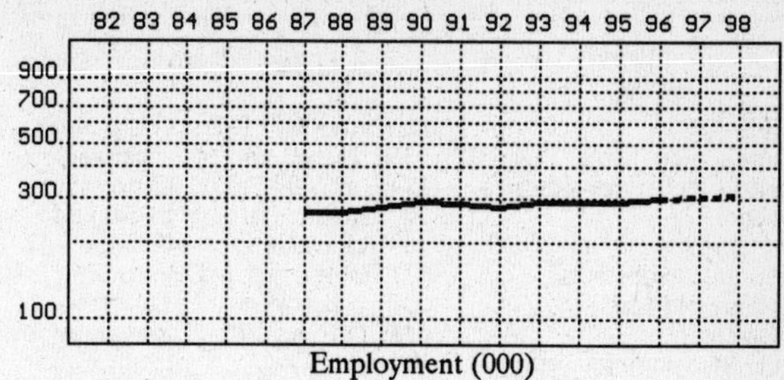

Employment (000)

GENERAL STATISTICS

Year	Establishments (number)	Employment (number)	Payroll ($ million)	Sales ($ million)	Expenses ($ million)	Beginning Inventory ($ million)	Ending Inventory ($ million)
1982	-	-	-	-	-	-	-
1983	-	-	-	-	-	-	-
1984	-	-	-	-	-	-	-
1985	-	-	-	-	-	-	-
1986	-	-	-	-	-	-	-
1987	12,821	266,018	8,889.6	84,515.4	17,199.3	3,773.5	4,399.1
1988	12,405	264,192	10,378.4	95,756.6e	18,566.8e	4,454.5e	5,029.1e
1989	11,754	277,242	11,702.8	106,997.8e	19,934.2e	5,135.5e	5,659.0e
1990	12,514	288,723	12,080.4	118,239.0e	21,301.6e	5,816.5e	6,288.9e
1991	13,436	285,473	12,283.3	129,480.2e	22,669.1e	6,497.5e	6,918.8e
1992	17,578	279,686	12,597.3	140,721.4	24,036.5	7,178.5	7,548.8
1993	18,598	293,970	13,929.1	151,962.7p	25,403.9p	7,859.5p	8,178.7p
1994	19,559	292,339	13,870.2	163,203.9p	26,771.3p	8,540.5p	8,808.6p
1995	19,332	292,072	14,546.7	174,445.1p	28,138.8p	9,221.5p	9,438.5p
1996	20,854p	299,947p	15,425.9p	185,686.3p	29,506.2p	9,902.5p	10,068.5p
1997	21,959p	303,498p	16,060.4p	196,927.5p	30,873.6p	10,583.5p	10,698.4p
1998	23,063p	307,049p	16,695.0p	208,168.7p	32,241.1p	11,264.5p	11,328.3p

Sources: Economic Census of the United States, 1982, 1987, and 1992. Establishment counts, employment, and payroll are from *County Business Patterns* for non-Census years. Values followed by a 'p' are projections by the editors. Sales and expense data for non-Census years are extrapolations, marked by 'e'. Industries reclassified in 1987 will not have data for prior years. Data are the most recent available at this level of detail.

INDICES OF CHANGE

Year	Establishments (number)	Employment (number)	Payroll ($ million)	Sales ($ million)	Expenses ($ million)	Beginning Inventory ($ million)	Ending Inventory ($ million)
1982	-	-	-	-	-	-	-
1983	-	-	-	-	-	-	-
1984	-	-	-	-	-	-	-
1985	-	-	-	-	-	-	-
1986	-	-	-	-	-	-	-
1987	72.9	95.1	70.6	60.1	71.6	52.6	58.3
1988	70.6	94.5	82.4	68.0e	77.2e	62.1e	66.6e
1989	66.9	99.1	92.9	76.0e	82.9e	71.5e	75.0e
1990	71.2	103.2	95.9	84.0e	88.6e	81.0e	83.3e
1991	76.4	102.1	97.5	92.0e	94.3e	90.5e	91.7e
1992	100.0	100.0	100.0	100.0	100.0	100.0	100.0
1993	105.8	105.1	110.6	108.0p	105.7p	109.5p	108.3p
1994	111.3	104.5	110.1	116.0p	111.4p	119.0p	116.7p
1995	110.0	104.4	115.5	124.0p	117.1p	128.5p	125.0p
1996	118.6p	107.2p	122.5p	132.0p	122.8p	137.9p	133.4p
1997	124.9p	108.5p	127.5p	139.9p	128.4p	147.4p	141.7p
1998	131.2p	109.8p	132.5p	147.9p	134.1p	156.9p	150.1p

Sources: Same as General Statistics. The values shown reflect change from the base year, 1992. Values above 100 mean greater than 1992, values below 100 mean less than 1992, and a value of 100 in the 1982-91 or 1993-98 period means same as 1992. Values followed by a 'p' are projections by the editors; 'e' stands for extrapolation. Data are the most recent available at this level of detail.

SELECTED RATIOS

For 1992	Avg. of All Wholesale	Analyzed Industry	Index	For 1992	Avg. of All Wholesale	Analyzed Industry	Index
Employees per Establishment	12	16	136	Sales per Employee	561,172	503,141	90
Payroll per Establishment	349,729	716,651	205	Sales per Establishment	6,559,346	8,005,541	122
Payroll per Employee	29,919	45,041	151	Expenses per Establishment	723,071	1,367,420	189

Sources: Same as General Statistics. The 'Average of All Manufacturing' column represents the average of all manufacturing industries reported for the most recent complete year available. The Index shows the relationship between the Average and the Analyzed Industry. For example, 100 means that they are equal; 500 that the Analyzed Industry is five times the average; 50 means that the Analyzed Industry is half the national average. The abbreviation 'na' is used to show that data are 'not available'.

LEADING COMPANIES

Number shown: **50** Total sales ($ mil): **65,904** Total employment (000): **86.6**

Company Name	Address				CEO Name	Phone	Co. Type	Sales ($ mil)	Empl. (000)
Avent Inc.	80 Cutter Mill Rd	Great Neck	NY	11021	Leon Machiz	516-466-7000	P	5,390	9.4
Tech Data Corp.	5350 Tech Data Dr	Clearwater	FL	34620	Steven A Raymund	813-539-7429	P	4,599	3.4
Mitsubishi Electronics America	PO Box 6007	Cypress	CA	90630	Aira Katayama	714-220-2500	S	4,400	3.0
Merisel Inc.	200 Continental	El Segundo	CA	90245	Dwight A Steffensen	310-615-3080	P	4,049	2.3
InaCom Corp.	10810 Farnam Dr	Omaha	NE	68154	Bill L Fairfield	402-392-3900	P	3,900	2.9
Intelligent Electronics Inc.	411 Eagleview Blvd	Exton	PA	19341	Richard D Sanford	610-458-5500	P	3,588	2.6
Hitachi America Ltd.	50 Prospect Ave	Tarrytown	NY	10591	T Shimayama	914-332-5800	S	3,500	6.0
Comdisco Inc.	6111 N River Rd	Rosemont	IL	60018	Jack Slevin	847-698-3000	P	2,819	2.4
Hitachi Data Systems Corp.	PO Box 54996	Santa Clara	CA	95056	Steven M West	408-970-1000	S	2,000	2.3
CompuCom Systems Inc.	10100 N Central	Dallas	TX	75230	Edward R Anderson	214-265-3600	P	1,995	3.7
CHS Electronics Inc.	2153 NW 86th Ave	Miami	FL	33122	Claudio Osorio	305-716-8273	P	1,855	2.3
Ingram Book Group Inc.	1 Ingram Blvd	La Vergne	TN	37086	Lee Synnott	615-793-5000	S	1,820 *	2.5
Pioneer-Standard Electronics	4800 E 131st St	Cleveland	OH	44105	James L Bayman	216-587-3600	P	1,509	2.1
AmeriData Technologies Inc.	700 Canal St	Stamford	CT	06902	Gerald A Poch	203-357-1464	S	1,500	3.5
Lanier Worldwide Inc.	2300 Pklake Dr NE	Atlanta	GA	30345	Wesley E Cantrell	404-496-9500	S	1,270 *	7.0
Wyle Electronics	15370 Barranca	Irvine	CA	92718	Ralph L Ozorkiewicz	714-753-9953	P	1,245	1.5
Decision Data Inc.	400 Horsham Rd	Horsham	PA	19044	Anthony Bamber	215-956-6700	R	1,240 *	2.5
Marshall Industries	9320 Telstar Ave	El Monte	CA	91731	Robert Rodin	818-307-6000	P	1,185	1.4
Handleman Co.	500 Kirts Blvd	Troy	MI	48084	Stephen Strome	248-362-4400	P	1,181	3.5
Access Graphics Inc.	1426 Pearl St	Boulder	CO	80302	Perry Monych	303-938-9333	S	1,032 *	0.6
Ingram Micro Inc.	1600 E Andrew Pl	Santa Ana	CA	92705	John L Stead	714-566-1000	P	990 *	2.0
Satellite Information Systems	7464 Arapahoe Rd	Boulder	CO	80303	Michael J Ellis	303-449-0442	P	838	<0.1
Avnet Computer Inc.	3011 S 52nd St	Tempe	AZ	85282	Rich Ward	602-414-6700	S	800	0.6
Software Spectrum Inc.	PO Box 479501	Garland	TX	75047	Judy O Sims	214-840-6600	P	796	1.6
Hamilton Hallmark Div.	10950 W Wash	Culver City	CA	90232	Leon Machiz	310-665-2600	D	744	0.6
Comark Inc.	444 Scott Dr	Bloomingdale	IL	60108	Charles S Wolande	600-351-9700	R	700 *	0.6
SED International Inc.	4916 Roy Atlanta	Atlanta	GA	30085	Gerald Diamond	770-491-8962	S	646	0.4
Casio Inc.	570 Mt Pleasant	Dover	NJ	07801	John J McDonald	973-361-5400	D	630	0.3
Electronic Arts Inc.	1450 Fashion Island	San Mateo	CA	94404	L F Probst III	650-571-7171	P	625	1.7
Daisytek International Corp.	500 N Central	Plano	TX	75074	Mark C Layton	214-881-4700	P	604	0.7
MAG Innovision Inc.	2801 S Yale St	Santa Ana	CA	92704	William Wang	714-751-2008	R	600	0.3
Government Technology Services	4100 Lafayette Ctr	Chantilly	VA	22021	Dendy Young	703-502-2000	P	527	0.4
Astro Business Solutions Inc.	110 W Walnut St	Gardena	CA	90248	Ollie Hatch Jr	310-217-3000	S	523 *	0.7
El Camino Resources Intern.	21051 Warner Ctr	Woodland Hills	CA	91367	David Harmon	818-226-6600	R	515 *	0.5
NECX Inc.	4 Technology Dr	Peabody	MA	01960	Henry Bertolon	978-538-8000	R	501	0.3
En Pointe Technologies Inc.	100 N Sepulveda	El Segundo	CA	90245	Attiazaz Din	310-725-5200	P	491	0.4
SAP America, Inc.	701 Lee Rd, Ste 200	Wayne	PA	19087	Paul Wahl	610-725-4500	S	479 *	1.8
Dataflex Corp.	3920 Park Ave	Edison	NJ	08820	Richard C Rose	908-791-2200	S	472	0.8
Liuski International Inc.	6585 Crescent Dr	Norcross	GA	30071	Morries Liu	770-447-9454	P	422	0.5
Computer Integration Corp.	15720 J J Delaney	Charlotte	NC	28277	John E Paget	704-714-4000	P	418	0.4
CHS Promark (Miami, Florida)	2153 NW 86th Ave	Miami	FL	33126	Alvin Perlman	305-594-4990	R	400	0.3
TEAC America Inc.	7733 Telegraph Rd	Montebello	CA	90640	Hajime Yamaguchi	213-726-0303	S	380	0.2
D and H Distributing Co.	2525 N 7th St	Harrisburg	PA	17110	Izzy Schwab	717-236-8001	R	375	0.4
Motor Sound Corp.	541 Division St	Campbell	CA	95008	William W Topper	408-374-7900	R	375	0.3
GT Interactive Software Corp.	16 East 40th St	New York	NY	10016	R W Chaimowitz	212-726-6500	P	365	1.0
Funai Corp.	100 North St	Teterboro	NJ	07608	Masawo Suwa	201-288-2063	S	360	<0.1
Cummins Electronics Company	2851 State St	Columbus	IN	47201	EW Booth	812-377-8601	S	320	0.7
GBC Technologies Inc.	6110 110th St W	Bloomington	MN	55438	Robert Zakheim	612-947-1000	S	319	0.4
Gates/FA Distributing Inc.	39 Pelham Ridge	Greenville	SC	29615	Philip D Ellett	803-234-0736	S	307	0.4
Computer Data Systems Inc.	1 Curie Court	Rockville	MD	20850	Peter A Bracken	301-921-7000	P	304	3.9

Source: *Ward's Business Directory of U.S. Private and Public Companies*, 1998. The company type code used is as follows: P - Public, R - Private, S - Subsidiary, D - Division, J - Joint Venture, A - Affiliate, G - Group. Sales are in millions of dollars, employees are in thousands. An asterisk (*) indicates an estimated sales volume. The symbol < stands for 'less than'.

OCCUPATIONS EMPLOYED BY SIC 504 - WHOLESALE TRADE, OTHER

Occupation	% of Total 1996	Change to 2006	Occupation	% of Total 1996	Change to 2006
Sales & related workers nec	19.5	20.2	Clerical supervisors & managers	1.9	20.2
General managers & top executives	5.9	16.4	Order clerks	1.9	8.2
Truck drivers light & heavy	5.4	20.2	Helpers, laborers nec	1.7	20.2
General office clerks	3.6	3.4	Electrical & electronic technicians	1.4	18.8
Traffic, shipping, receiving clerks	3.6	16.7	Blue collar worker supervisors	1.4	16.0
Stock clerks	3.5	-3.9	Wholesale & retail buyers, except farm products	1.3	17.0
Freight, stock, & material movers, hand	3.3	8.2	Office machine & cash register servicers	1.3	20.2
Marketing & sales worker supervisors	3.1	20.2	Hand packers & packagers	1.2	-3.9
Order fillers, wholesale & retail sales	3.0	16.7	Maintenance repairers, general utility	1.1	12.0
Bookkeeping, accounting, & auditing clerks	2.9	-3.9	Industrial truck & tractor operators	1.1	20.2
Salespersons, retail	2.5	20.2	Purchasing managers	1.1	20.2
Secretaries, except legal & medical	2.5	-4.7	Receptionists & information clerks	1.0	20.2
Assemblers, fabricators, hand workers nec	2.0	-3.9			

Source: *Industry-Occupation Matrix*, Bureau of Labor Statistics. These data relate to one or more 3-digit SIC industry groups rather than to a single 4-digit SIC. The change reported for each occupation to the year 2006 is a percent of growth or decline as estimated by the Bureau of Labor Statistics. The abbreviation nec stands for 'not elsewhere classified'.

STATE AND REGIONAL CONCENTRATION

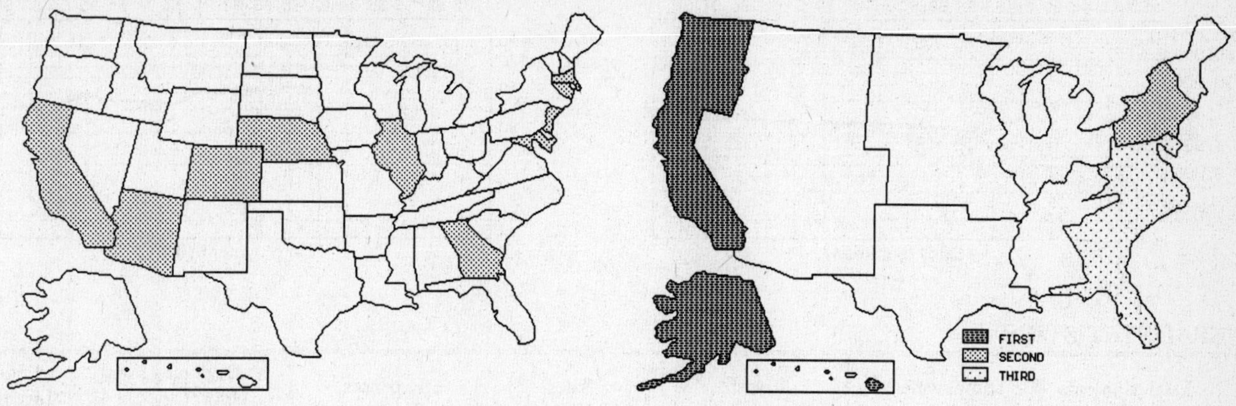

INDUSTRY DATA BY STATE

State	Establishments - 1995 Total (number)	Establishments - 1995 % of U.S.	Employment - 1995 Total (number)	Employment - 1995 % of U.S.	Employment - 1995 Per Estab.	Payroll - 1995 Total ($ mil.)	Payroll - 1995 Per Empl. ($)	Sales - 1992 Total ($ mil.)	Sales - 1992 % of U.S.	Sales - 1992 Per Estab ($)
California	3,536	18.3	60,386	20.7	17	3,019.7	50,006	43,746.1	31.5	697,271
New York	1,089	5.6	16,405	5.6	15	907.0	55,288	9,101.0	6.5	558,415
Illinois	776	4.0	16,760	5.7	22	981.4	58,554	9,095.7	6.5	518,185
Texas	1,518	7.9	22,306	7.6	15	1,136.2	50,936	9,025.6	6.5	452,706
Massachusetts	704	3.6	13,243	4.5	19	713.4	53,873	6,587.7	4.7	554,332
New Jersey	858	4.4	12,537	4.3	15	638.3	50,916	5,701.8	4.1	508,587
Colorado	420	2.2	8,232	2.8	20	391.6	47,574	5,229.2	3.8	756,535
Florida	1,234	6.4	15,629	5.4	13	713.1	45,629	4,375.3	3.1	407,723
Georgia	697	3.6	11,825	4.0	17	631.8	53,431	4,115.8	3.0	444,188
Maryland	403	2.1	9,579	3.3	24	555.8	58,019	4,002.2	2.9	439,126
Pennsylvania	671	3.5	9,076	3.1	14	433.5	47,763	3,802.7	2.7	387,364
Ohio	644	3.3	9,754	3.3	15	461.2	47,282	3,491.4	2.5	364,141
Virginia	506	2.6	8,314	2.8	16	418.2	50,300	3,456.6	2.5	401,188
Michigan	484	2.5	7,009	2.4	14	367.3	52,407	2,939.6	2.1	377,207
Arizona	332	1.7	5,511	1.9	17	237.7	43,135	2,767.3	2.0	709,387
Minnesota	508	2.6	8,399	2.9	17	412.0	49,054	2,355.6	1.7	377,799
Washington	463	2.4	5,003	1.7	11	246.0	49,176	2,017.2	1.5	388,902
Connecticut	277	1.4	3,703	1.3	13	200.3	54,096	1,950.6	1.4	512,103
North Carolina	375	1.9	4,987	1.7	13	232.1	46,534	1,730.8	1.2	352,225
Nebraska	95	0.5	1,386	0.5	15	56.1	40,499	1,555.5	1.1	1,107,102
Indiana	277	1.4	2,876	1.0	10	127.3	44,263	1,513.1	1.1	464,432
Wisconsin	304	1.6	4,023	1.4	13	173.4	43,111	1,225.9	0.9	312,015
Oregon	255	1.3	2,570	0.9	10	116.9	45,497	997.2	0.7	377,710
Tennessee	264	1.4	3,283	1.1	12	136.5	41,580	930.3	0.7	266,091
Alabama	206	1.1	2,146	0.7	10	88.3	41,149	894.8	0.6	323,152
Oklahoma	163	0.8	1,961	0.7	12	69.0	35,170	661.4	0.5	315,118
Louisiana	149	0.8	1,563	0.5	10	55.6	35,573	611.8	0.4	370,764
Kansas	196	1.0	2,450	0.8	13	108.4	44,232	525.4	0.4	312,943
Utah	170	0.9	1,898	0.6	11	78.7	41,450	485.3	0.3	287,816
Arkansas	91	0.5	968	0.3	11	42.4	43,833	467.1	0.3	394,874
New Hampshire	169	0.9	2,053	0.7	12	95.7	46,616	441.1	0.3	341,909
Iowa	136	0.7	1,479	0.5	11	48.6	32,829	413.5	0.3	336,751
D.C.	20	0.1	291	0.1	15	23.1	79,323	390.5	0.3	2,324,232
Kentucky	144	0.7	1,722	0.6	12	67.9	39,419	342.4	0.2	203,305
South Carolina	121	0.6	1,161	0.4	10	48.9	42,105	335.2	0.2	256,844
New Mexico	89	0.5	927	0.3	10	39.1	42,211	316.8	0.2	280,813
Rhode Island	49	0.3	703	0.2	14	34.4	48,967	211.5	0.2	287,020
Hawaii	42	0.2	481	0.2	11	27.1	56,437	177.1	0.1	224,206
Mississippi	73	0.4	760	0.3	10	25.4	33,445	162.2	0.1	250,258
Nevada	100	0.5	847	0.3	8	32.3	38,119	160.4	0.1	223,780
Maine	59	0.3	483	0.2	8	17.9	37,060	123.0	0.1	193,406
West Virginia	55	0.3	348	0.1	6	14.1	40,569	105.6	0.1	224,206
Montana	42	0.2	353	0.1	8	10.5	29,802	105.4	0.1	266,159
Vermont	32	0.2	258	0.1	8	8.6	33,213	90.6	0.1	177,931
North Dakota	38	0.2	427	0.1	11	14.7	34,407	87.8	0.1	199,936
Idaho	51	0.3	547	0.2	11	21.4	39,086	86.1	0.1	210,555
Alaska	38	0.2	292	0.1	8	12.7	43,592	83.3	0.1	256,418
South Dakota	42	0.2	367	0.1	9	13.3	36,161	66.6	0.0	178,102
Wyoming	14	0.1	93	0.0	7	1.6	17,108	12.6	0.0	113,315
Missouri	307	1.6	4,049	1.4	13	209.0	51,615	(D)	-	-
Delaware	46	0.2	649	0.2	14	31.2	48,012	(D)	-	-

Source: County Business Patterns, 1995 and *Economic Census of the U.S., 1992*. Data are sorted by 1992 revenues and, if revenues are unavailable, by establishments in 1995. The symbol (D) indicates that data are withheld by the source to avoid disclosure of competitive information. A dash (-) indicates that data are not available or undisclosed because they do not meet statistical validity standards. Shaded *states* on the state map indicate those states which have proportionately greater representation in the industry than would be indicated by the state's population; the ratio is based on total revenues or number of establishments. Shaded *regions* indicate where the industry is regionally most concentrated.

5046 - COMMERCIAL EQUIPMENT, NEC

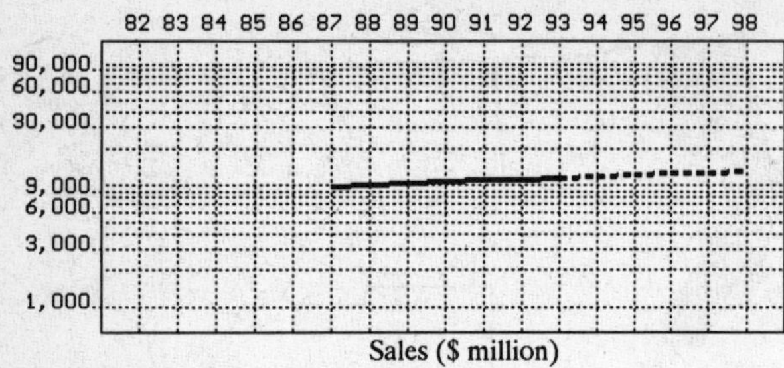

Sales ($ million)

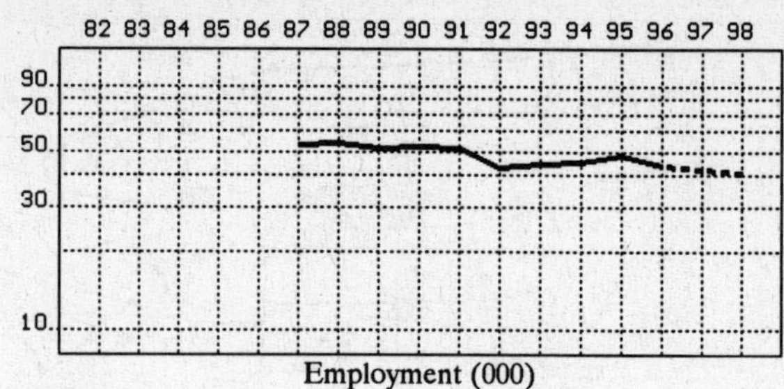

Employment (000)

GENERAL STATISTICS

Year	Establishments (number)	Employment (number)	Payroll ($ million)	Sales ($ million)	Expenses ($ million)	Beginning Inventory ($ million)	Ending Inventory ($ million)
1982	-	-	-	-	-	-	-
1983	-	-	-	-	-	-	-
1984	-	-	-	-	-	-	-
1985	-	-	-	-	-	-	-
1986	-	-	-	-	-	-	-
1987	5,587	53,157	1,214.5	9,654.8	2,323.3	810.6	848.1
1988	5,331	53,412	1,337.4	9,964.4e	2,345.2e	840.4e	880.4e
1989	4,813	51,486	1,338.2	10,274.1e	2,367.1e	870.2e	912.6e
1990	4,801	52,073	1,388.7	10,583.8e	2,389.0e	900.0e	944.9e
1991	4,880	51,581	1,418.1	10,893.4e	2,410.9e	929.8e	977.1e
1992	4,998	42,924	1,207.9	11,203.1	2,432.8	959.6	1,009.4
1993	5,011	44,271	1,274.5	11,512.8p	2,454.7p	989.4p	1,041.6p
1994	5,039	45,117	1,353.7	11,822.5p	2,476.6p	1,019.2p	1,073.9p
1995	5,141	47,772	1,491.0	12,132.1p	2,498.5p	1,049.0p	1,106.1p
1996	4,895p	43,254p	1,406.6p	12,441.8p	2,520.4p	1,078.8p	1,138.4p
1997	4,860p	42,088p	1,420.7p	12,751.5p	2,542.3p	1,108.6p	1,170.6p
1998	4,826p	40,921p	1,434.8p	13,061.1p	2,564.2p	1,138.4p	1,202.9p

Sources: *Economic Census of the United States*, 1982, 1987, and 1992. Establishment counts, employment, and payroll are from *County Business Patterns* for non-Census years. Values followed by a 'p' are projections by the editors. Sales and expense data for non-Census years are extrapolations, marked by 'e'. Industries reclassified in 1987 will not have data for prior years. Data are the most recent available at this level of detail.

INDICES OF CHANGE

Year	Establishments (number)	Employment (number)	Payroll ($ million)	Sales ($ million)	Expenses ($ million)	Beginning Inventory ($ million)	Ending Inventory ($ million)
1982	-	-	-	-	-	-	-
1983	-	-	-	-	-	-	-
1984	-	-	-	-	-	-	-
1985	-	-	-	-	-	-	-
1986	-	-	-	-	-	-	-
1987	111.8	123.8	100.5	86.2	95.5	84.5	84.0
1988	106.7	124.4	110.7	88.9e	96.4e	87.6e	87.2e
1989	96.3	119.9	110.8	91.7e	97.3e	90.7e	90.4e
1990	96.1	121.3	115.0	94.5e	98.2e	93.8e	93.6e
1991	97.6	120.2	117.4	97.2e	99.1e	96.9e	96.8e
1992	100.0	100.0	100.0	100.0	100.0	100.0	100.0
1993	100.3	103.1	105.5	102.8p	100.9p	103.1p	103.2p
1994	100.8	105.1	112.1	105.5p	101.8p	106.2p	106.4p
1995	102.9	111.3	123.4	108.3p	102.7p	109.3p	109.6p
1996	97.9p	100.8p	116.4p	111.1p	103.6p	112.4p	112.8p
1997	97.2p	98.1p	117.6p	113.8p	104.5p	115.5p	116.0p
1998	96.6p	95.3p	118.8p	116.6p	105.4p	118.6p	119.2p

Sources: Same as General Statistics. The values shown reflect change from the base year, 1992. Values above 100 mean greater than 1992, values below 100 mean less than 1992, and a value of 100 in the 1982-91 or 1993-98 period means same as 1992. Values followed by a 'p' are projections by the editors; 'e' stands for extrapolation. Data are the most recent available at this level of detail.

SELECTED RATIOS

For 1992	Avg. of All Wholesale	Analyzed Industry	Index	For 1992	Avg. of All Wholesale	Analyzed Industry	Index
Employees per Establishment	12	9	73	Sales per Employee	561,172	260,999	47
Payroll per Establishment	349,729	241,677	69	Sales per Establishment	6,559,346	2,241,517	34
Payroll per Employee	29,919	28,140	94	Expenses per Establishment	723,071	486,755	67

Sources: Same as General Statistics. The 'Average of All Manufacturing' column represents the average of all manufacturing industries reported for the most recent complete year available. The Index shows the relationship between the Average and the Analyzed Industry. For example, 100 means that they are equal; 500 that the Analyzed Industry is five times the average; 50 means that the Analyzed Industry is half the national average. The abbreviation 'na' is used to show that data are 'not available'.

LEADING COMPANIES

Number shown: **50** Total sales ($ mil): **7,056** Total employment (000): **18.0**

Company Name	Address				CEO Name	Phone	Co. Type	Sales ($ mil)	Empl. (000)
Gordon Food Service Inc.	PO Box 1787	Grand Rapids	MI	49501	Daniel Gordon	616-530-7000	R	1,970 •	3.8
Performance Food Group Co.	6800 Paragon Place	Richmond	VA	23230	Robert C Sledd	804-285-7340	P	1,230	2.0
SYSCO Food Services	20701 E Currier Rd	Walnut	CA	91789	Bruce J Schwartz	909-595-9595	S	500 •	1.0
International Dairy Queen Inc.	7505 Metro Blvd	Minneapolis	MN	55439	Michael P Sullivan	612-830-0200	P	411	0.6
Nobel/Sysco Food Services Co.	PO Box 5566	Denver	CO	80217	Michael L Kauffman	303-458-4000	S	400	0.9
Norstan Inc.	605 N Hwy 169	Plymouth	MN	55441	Paul Baszucki	612-513-4500	P	321	1.8
Quality Foods Inc.	PO Box 4908	Little Rock	AR	72214	Don Kirkpatrick	501-568-3141	R	280	0.8
Sysco Food Service of Seattle	PO Box 97054	Kent	WA	98064	Robert M Jenson	206-622-2261	S	280 •	0.7
Pegler-Sysco Food Services Co.	1700 Ctr Park Rd	Lincoln	NE	68512	Donald H Pegler III	402-423-1031	S	150	0.4
Lady Baltimore Foods Inc.	1601 Fairfax	Kansas City	KS	66117	Melvin Cosner	913-371-8300	P	121	0.5
Allen Foods Inc.	8543 Page Ave	St. Louis	MO	63114	Stanley Allen	314-426-4100	R	120	0.5
Kenneth O. Lester Company	PO Box 340	Lebanon	TN	37087	Thomas Hoffman	615-444-2963	S	98	0.2
Syndicate Systems Inc.	PO Box 70	Middlebury	IN	46540	JL Burris	219-825-9561	R	84	0.9
Wasserstrom Co.	477 S Front St	Columbus	OH	43215	R Wasserstrom	614-228-6525	R	81 •	0.3
Burrows Co.	230 West Palatine	Wheeling	IL	60090	George J Burrows	847-537-7300	R	80	0.3
Superior Products Mfg Co.	500 W County D	St. Paul	MN	55112	Robert M Kurek	612-636-1110	R	80	0.2
H. Betti Industries Inc.	303 Paterson Plank	Carlstadt	NJ	07072	Joe Cirillo	201-438-1300	R	68 •	0.2
IJ Co. Tri-Cities Div.	PO Box 8099	Gray	TN	37615	Tim Keller	423-239-9441	D	52 •	0.1
Brady Distributing Co.	PO Box 19269	Charlotte	NC	28219	Jon P Brady	704-357-6284	R	50 •	0.1
Hubert Co.	9555 Dry Fork Rd	Harrison	OH	45030	HG Thomas	513-367-8600	R	48 •	0.3
FWB Inc.	1555 Adams Dr	Menlo Park	CA	94025	Norman Fong	415-325-4392	R	40	<0.1
United Restaurant Equ Co.	PO Box 1460	Woonsocket	RI	02895	Robert Halpern	401-769-1000	R	40	0.1
Hilton Equipment Corp.	9336 Civic Ctr Dr	Beverly Hills	CA	90210	Donald Royal	310-278-4321	S	39 •	<0.1
M. Tucker Company Inc.	900 S 2nd St	Harrison	NJ	07029	Stephen Tucker	201-484-1200	R	35	<0.1
Singer Equipment Company	PO Box 13668	Reading	PA	19612	HD Singer	610-929-8000	R	35	0.1
Electronic Label Technology	708 W Kenosha	Broken Arrow	OK	74012	Tim Wright	918-258-2121	R	30	0.1
Palm Brothers Inc.	2727 Nicollet Ave	Minneapolis	MN	55408	Reuben Palm	612-871-2727	R	29 •	0.2
APW/Wyott Food Service	729 3rd Ave	Dallas	TX	75226	Hylton Jonas	214-421-7366	R	28	0.3
Rave Computer Association	36960 Metro Ct	Sterling H.	MI	48312	F Darter	810-939-8230	R	26	<0.1
Boelter Companies Inc.	11100 W Silver Spr	Milwaukee	WI	53225	FW Boelter	414-461-3400	R	25	0.2
Douron Inc.	30 New Plant Ct	Owings Mills	MD	21117	Ronald W Hux	410-363-2600	R	25	<0.1
American Locker Security	608 Allen St	Jamestown	NY	14701	Harold J Ruttenberg	716-664-9600	S	23	<0.1
Houston's Inc.	3939 SE 26th St	Portland	OR	97202	John Houston	503-230-1985	R	21	<0.1
H.D. Sheldon and Company	19 Union Sq W	New York	NY	10003	Robert Metros	212-924-6920	R	20	<0.1
PBI Market Equipment Inc.	2667 Gundry Ave	Signal Hill	CA	90806	TL Everson	310-595-4785	R	20	<0.1
Atlanta Fixture and Sails Co.	3185 NE Exp	Atlanta	GA	30341	Paul Klein	404-455-8844	R	19 •	0.1
Battery Shop Inc.	PO Box 51647	New Berlin	WI	53151	Robert Levy	414-789-5100	R	18	<0.1
National Products Co.	113-131 N 2nd St	Philadelphia	PA	19106	Stanley B Caplen	215-627-5000	R	18	0.1
Haldeman-Homme Inc.	430 Industrial Blvd	Minneapolis	MN	55413	Ernie Stalock	612-331-4880	R	17	<0.1
Maines Paper and Food Service	PO Box 438	Conklin	NY	13748	David Maines	607-772-0055	D	17	<0.1
Frank P. Corso Inc.	PO Box 488	Biloxi	MS	39533	Elizabeth Joachim	601-436-4697	R	15	<0.1
Buffalo Hotel Supply Company	PO Box 646	Amherst	NY	14226	James M Bedard	716-691-8080	R	15	<0.1
Le Creuset of America Inc.	PO Box 575	Yemassee	SC	29945	Finn Schjorring	803-943-4308	S	12	<0.1
Regional Supply Inc.	3571 S 300 W	Salt Lake City	UT	84115	DC Mendenhall	801-262-6451	R	12	0.1
Bintz Distributing Co.	PO Box 1350	Salt Lake City	UT	84115	B Williams	801-363-5821	R	10	<0.1
George R. Ruhl and Son Inc.	7451 Race Rd	Hanover	MD	21076	George R Ruhl	410-796-0203	R	9 •	<0.1
National Equipment	7220 W Frontage	Shawnee Msn	KS	66203	Norma Smith	913-262-8200	R	9	<0.1
Yamato Corp.	PO Box 60159	Co Springs	CO	80960	Shozo Kawanishi	719-527-1500	S	9	<0.1
Dixie Store Fixtures and Sales	2425 1st Ave N	Birmingham	AL	35203	Francis G Cypress	205-322-2442	R	8 •	<0.1
J.A.H. Enterprises Inc.	PO Box 336	Livingston	LA	70754	Jeffrey Henderson	504-686-2252	R	8	<0.1

Source: *Ward's Business Directory of U.S. Private and Public Companies*, 1998. The company type code used is as follows: P - Public, R - Private, S - Subsidiary, D - Division, J - Joint Venture, A - Affiliate, G - Group. Sales are in millions of dollars, employees are in thousands. An asterisk (*) indicates an estimated sales volume. The symbol < stands for 'less than'.

OCCUPATIONS EMPLOYED BY SIC 504 - WHOLESALE TRADE, OTHER

Occupation	% of Total 1996	Change to 2006	Occupation	% of Total 1996	Change to 2006
Sales & related workers nec	19.5	20.2	Clerical supervisors & managers	1.9	20.2
General managers & top executives	5.9	16.4	Order clerks	1.9	8.2
Truck drivers light & heavy	5.4	20.2	Helpers, laborers nec	1.7	20.2
General office clerks	3.6	3.4	Electrical & electronic technicians	1.4	18.8
Traffic, shipping, receiving clerks	3.6	16.7	Blue collar worker supervisors	1.4	16.0
Stock clerks	3.5	-3.9	Wholesale & retail buyers, except farm products	1.3	17.0
Freight, stock, & material movers, hand	3.3	8.2	Office machine & cash register servicers	1.3	20.2
Marketing & sales worker supervisors	3.1	20.2	Hand packers & packagers	1.2	-3.9
Order fillers, wholesale & retail sales	3.0	16.7	Maintenance repairers, general utility	1.1	12.0
Bookkeeping, accounting, & auditing clerks	2.9	-3.9	Industrial truck & tractor operators	1.1	20.2
Salespersons, retail	2.5	20.2	Purchasing managers	1.1	20.2
Secretaries, except legal & medical	2.5	-4.7	Receptionists & information clerks	1.0	20.2
Assemblers, fabricators, hand workers nec	2.0	-3.9			

Source: *Industry-Occupation Matrix*, Bureau of Labor Statistics. These data relate to one or more 3-digit SIC industry groups rather than to a single 4-digit SIC. The change reported for each occupation to the year 2006 is a percent of growth or decline as estimated by the Bureau of Labor Statistics. The abbreviation nec stands for 'not elsewhere classified'.

STATE AND REGIONAL CONCENTRATION

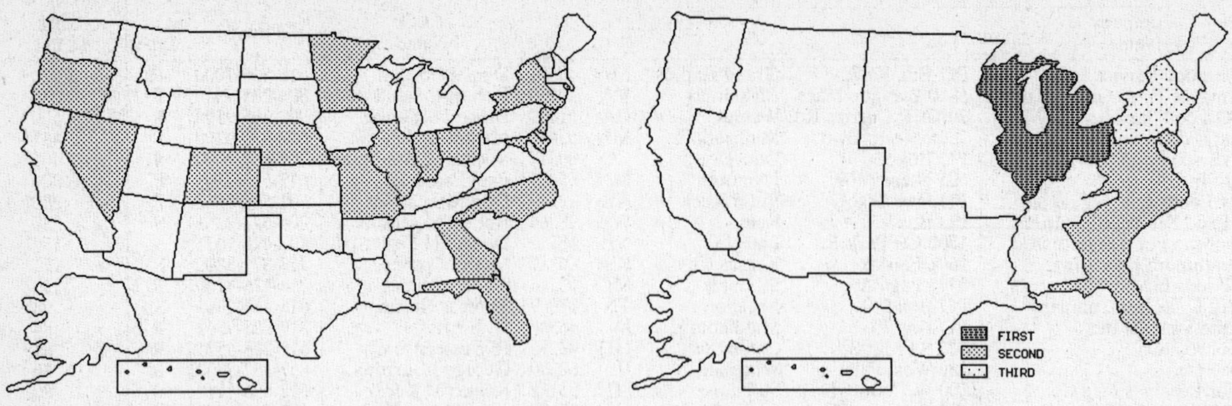

INDUSTRY DATA BY STATE

State	Establishments - 1995 Total (number)	Establishments - 1995 % of U.S.	Employment - 1995 Total (number)	Employment - 1995 % of U.S.	Employment - 1995 Per Estab.	Payroll - 1995 Total ($ mil.)	Payroll - 1995 Per Empl. ($)	Sales - 1992 Total ($ mil.)	Sales - 1992 % of U.S.	Sales - 1992 Per Estab ($)
California	546	10.6	4,868	10.2	9	158.3	32,517	1,245.5	12.1	277,636
Illinois	273	5.3	3,654	7.7	13	131.0	35,857	979.2	9.5	319,362
New York	405	7.9	3,072	6.4	8	100.1	32,601	810.1	7.9	281,295
Florida	372	7.2	2,790	5.8	8	80.2	28,742	678.6	6.6	232,148
Texas	352	6.8	3,041	6.4	9	92.8	30,522	669.5	6.5	261,636
New Jersey	216	4.2	2,085	4.4	10	74.6	35,798	577.9	5.6	267,445
Ohio	204	4.0	2,892	6.1	14	90.2	31,197	566.2	5.5	214,799
Georgia	175	3.4	1,814	3.8	10	59.2	32,626	390.6	3.8	247,668
Minnesota	107	2.1	1,247	2.6	12	43.8	35,157	377.2	3.7	324,348
Pennsylvania	212	4.1	1,823	3.8	9	50.8	27,872	373.0	3.6	208,754
Michigan	167	3.2	1,369	2.9	8	44.2	32,278	314.8	3.1	217,860
Nebraska	21	0.4	234	0.5	11	5.6	24,068	291.6	2.8	721,886
North Carolina	126	2.5	1,153	2.4	9	36.5	31,651	285.5	2.8	248,439
Maryland	100	1.9	1,170	2.5	12	40.7	34,806	270.7	2.6	262,265
Indiana	99	1.9	1,153	2.4	12	38.2	33,091	268.4	2.6	315,788
Missouri	127	2.5	1,204	2.5	9	32.9	27,346	243.5	2.4	275,154
Washington	135	2.6	1,148	2.4	9	35.0	30,527	198.4	1.9	229,944
Colorado	103	2.0	838	1.8	8	24.3	29,055	181.8	1.8	243,023
Tennessee	106	2.1	971	2.0	9	31.4	32,363	168.5	1.6	193,286
Oregon	77	1.5	790	1.7	10	25.3	31,976	139.1	1.3	215,345
Wisconsin	87	1.7	658	1.4	8	19.5	29,641	129.6	1.3	185,464
South Carolina	59	1.1	550	1.2	9	16.5	30,080	109.9	1.1	270,800
Connecticut	70	1.4	538	1.1	8	17.8	33,091	105.7	1.0	226,779
Virginia	92	1.8	689	1.4	7	18.8	27,280	100.2	1.0	173,341
Kansas	59	1.1	610	1.3	10	18.4	30,120	98.4	1.0	305,724
Arizona	81	1.6	598	1.3	7	14.8	24,744	95.7	0.9	209,495
Alabama	56	1.1	545	1.1	10	15.3	27,996	80.5	0.8	166,623
Nevada	48	0.9	431	0.9	9	13.1	30,371	78.7	0.8	180,915
Utah	32	0.6	379	0.8	12	9.5	25,150	69.2	0.7	166,841
Iowa	41	0.8	317	0.7	8	9.0	28,356	68.3	0.7	231,488
Oklahoma	54	1.1	646	1.4	12	17.2	26,667	66.5	0.6	148,098
Rhode Island	26	0.5	329	0.7	13	11.3	34,441	63.9	0.6	228,164
Louisiana	63	1.2	570	1.2	9	12.0	21,000	57.7	0.6	121,476
Arkansas	40	0.8	262	0.5	7	5.6	21,485	34.5	0.3	100,516
Hawaii	28	0.5	219	0.5	8	5.4	24,808	34.5	0.3	187,359
New Mexico	25	0.5	285	0.6	11	7.0	24,611	25.5	0.2	140,994
Idaho	18	0.4	143	0.3	8	3.0	21,028	15.8	0.2	141,964
West Virginia	19	0.4	127	0.3	7	2.7	21,291	12.2	0.1	109,757
Maine	17	0.3	91	0.2	5	1.9	20,835	10.4	0.1	147,000
North Dakota	11	0.2	80	0.2	7	2.2	27,000	10.3	0.1	155,970
Alaska	6	0.1	39	0.1	7	1.1	28,205	10.1	0.1	253,225
Massachusetts	130	2.5	1,146	2.4	9	40.3	35,169	(D)	-	-
Kentucky	46	0.9	476	1.0	10	14.8	31,151	(D)	-	-
Mississippi	34	0.7	283	0.6	8	7.0	24,572	(D)	-	-
New Hampshire	24	0.5	125	0.3	5	4.1	32,544	(D)	-	-
Montana	19	0.4	125	0.3	7	2.6	20,592	(D)	-	-
Delaware	11	0.2	69	0.1	6	2.0	29,203	(D)	-	-
South Dakota	11	0.2	64	0.1	6	1.6	25,719	(D)	-	-
Vermont	5	0.1	6	0.0	1	0.2	33,667	(D)	-	-
Wyoming	4	0.1	20-99	-	-	(D)	-	(D)	-	-
D.C.	2	0.0	20-99	-	-	(D)	-	(D)	-	-

Source: County Business Patterns, 1995 and *Economic Census of the U.S., 1992*. Data are sorted by 1992 revenues and, if revenues are unavailable, by establishments in 1995. The symbol (D) indicates that data are withheld by the source to avoid disclosure of competitive information. A dash (-) indicates that data are not available or undisclosed because they do not meet statistical validity standards. Shaded *states* on the state map indicate those states which have proportionately greater representation in the industry than would be indicated by the state's population; the ratio is based on total revenues or number of establishments. Shaded *regions* indicate where the industry is regionally most concentrated.

5047 - MEDICAL AND HOSPITAL EQUIPMENT

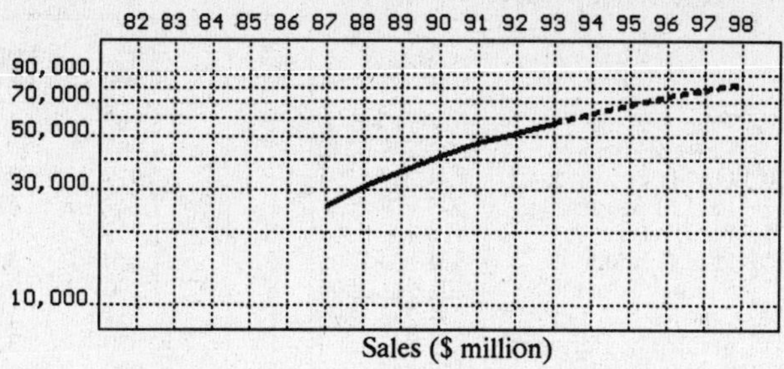

Sales ($ million)

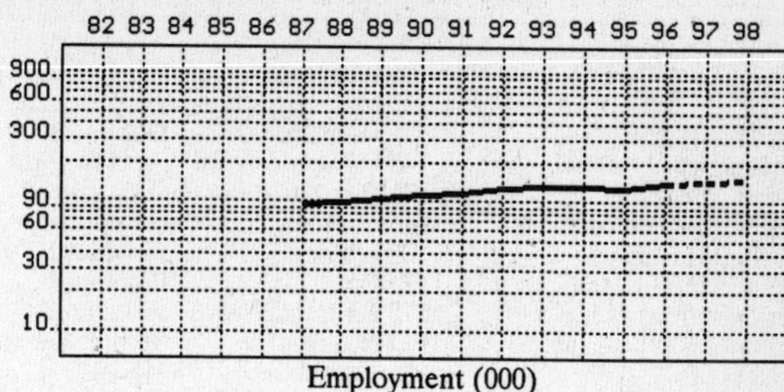

Employment (000)

GENERAL STATISTICS

Year	Establishments (number)	Employment (number)	Payroll ($ million)	Sales ($ million)	Expenses ($ million)	Beginning Inventory ($ million)	Ending Inventory ($ million)
1982	-	-	-	-	-	-	-
1983	-	-	-	-	-	-	-
1984	-	-	-	-	-	-	-
1985	-	-	-	-	-	-	-
1986	-	-	-	-	-	-	-
1987	7,747	96,848	2,598.6	25,243.3	5,111.4	2,236.0	2,364.0
1988	7,330	99,822	3,065.2	30,537.6e	6,035.3e	2,594.1e	2,765.8e
1989	7,024	104,575	3,385.5	35,832.0e	6,959.1e	2,952.1e	3,167.6e
1990	7,528	109,464	3,713.0	41,126.4e	7,883.0e	3,310.1e	3,569.3e
1991	8,112	115,407	4,082.1	46,420.8e	8,806.9e	3,668.1e	3,971.1e
1992	9,521	125,470	5,083.3	51,715.2	9,730.7	4,026.2	4,372.9
1993	10,323	130,905	5,151.7	57,009.6p	10,654.6p	4,384.2p	4,774.7p
1994	10,593	132,032	5,289.3	62,304.0p	11,578.5p	4,742.2p	5,176.4p
1995	9,989	127,780	5,522.8	67,598.4p	12,502.3p	5,100.2p	5,578.2p
1996	10,964p	139,897p	6,149.5p	72,892.8p	13,426.2p	5,458.3p	5,980.0p
1997	11,420p	144,714p	6,537.3p	78,187.2p	14,350.1p	5,816.3p	6,381.8p
1998	11,876p	149,531p	6,925.2p	83,481.6p	15,273.9p	6,174.3p	6,783.5p

Sources: *Economic Census of the United States*, 1982, 1987, and 1992. Establishment counts, employment, and payroll are from *County Business Patterns* for non-Census years. Values followed by a 'p' are projections by the editors. Sales and expense data for non-Census years are extrapolations, marked by 'e'. Industries reclassified in 1987 will not have data for prior years. Data are the most recent available at this level of detail.

INDICES OF CHANGE

Year	Establishments (number)	Employment (number)	Payroll ($ million)	Sales ($ million)	Expenses ($ million)	Beginning Inventory ($ million)	Ending Inventory ($ million)
1982	-	-	-	-	-	-	-
1983	-	-	-	-	-	-	-
1984	-	-	-	-	-	-	-
1985	-	-	-	-	-	-	-
1986	-	-	-	-	-	-	-
1987	81.4	77.2	51.1	48.8	52.5	55.5	54.1
1988	77.0	79.6	60.3	59.0e	62.0e	64.4e	63.2e
1989	73.8	83.3	66.6	69.3e	71.5e	73.3e	72.4e
1990	79.1	87.2	73.0	79.5e	81.0e	82.2e	81.6e
1991	85.2	92.0	80.3	89.8e	90.5e	91.1e	90.8e
1992	100.0	100.0	100.0	100.0	100.0	100.0	100.0
1993	108.4	104.3	101.3	110.2p	109.5p	108.9p	109.2p
1994	111.3	105.2	104.1	120.5p	119.0p	117.8p	118.4p
1995	104.9	101.8	108.6	130.7p	128.5p	126.7p	127.6p
1996	115.2p	111.5p	121.0p	141.0p	138.0p	135.6p	136.8p
1997	119.9p	115.3p	128.6p	151.2p	147.5p	144.5p	145.9p
1998	124.7p	119.2p	136.2p	161.4p	157.0p	153.4p	155.1p

Sources: Same as General Statistics. The values shown reflect change from the base year, 1992. Values above 100 mean greater than 1992, values below 100 mean less than 1992, and a value of 100 in the 1982-91 or 1993-98 period means same as 1992. Values followed by a 'p' are projections by the editors; 'e' stands for extrapolation. Data are the most recent available at this level of detail.

SELECTED RATIOS

For 1992	Avg. of All Wholesale	Analyzed Industry	Index	For 1992	Avg. of All Wholesale	Analyzed Industry	Index
Employees per Establishment	12	13	113	Sales per Employee	561,172	412,172	73
Payroll per Establishment	349,729	533,904	153	Sales per Establishment	6,559,346	5,431,698	83
Payroll per Employee	29,919	40,514	135	Expenses per Establishment	723,071	1,022,025	141

Sources: Same as General Statistics. The 'Average of All Manufacturing' column represents the average of all manufacturing industries reported for the most recent complete year available. The Index shows the relationship between the Average and the Analyzed Industry. For example, 100 means that they are equal; 500 that the Analyzed Industry is five times the average; 50 means that the Analyzed Industry is half the national average. The abbreviation 'na' is used to show that data are 'not available'.

LEADING COMPANIES

Number shown: **50** Total sales ($ mil): **32,902** Total employment (000): **82.5**

Company Name	Address				CEO Name	Phone	Co. Type	Sales ($ mil)	Empl. (000)
Cardinal Health Inc.	5555 Glendon	Dublin	OH	43016	John C Kane	614-717-5000	P	8,862	4.8
Allegiance Corp.	1430 Waukegan Rd	McGaw Park	IL	60085	Lester B Knight	847-578-4240	P	4,387	20.7
Owens and Minor Inc.	PO Box 27626	Glen Allen	VA	23060	G Gilmer Minor III	804-747-9794	P	3,019	3.0
Fisher Scientific International	Liberty Ln	Hampton	NH	03842	Paul M Montrone	603-929-2650	P	2,144	6.6
Fisher Scientific Co.	2000 Park Ln	Pittsburgh	PA	15275	Paul Patek	412-490-8300	S	1,299 *	4.0
McKesson General Medical	PO Box 27452	Richmond	VA	23261	Paul C Julian	804-264-7500	S	1,200 *	3.0
Neuman Distributors Inc.	175 Railroad Ave	Ridgefield	NJ	07657	Samuel Toscano Jr	201-941-2000	S	1,200	0.8
Durr-Fillauer Medical Inc.	PO Box 244009	Montgomery	AL	36124	Charles E Adair	334-213-8800	P	951	1.4
Henry Schein Inc.	135 Duryea Rd	Melville	NY	11747	Stanley M Bergman	516-843-5500	P	830	3.2
Olympus America Inc.	2 Corporate Ctr Dr	Melville	NY	11747	Sidney Braginsky	516-844-5000	S	800	1.5
Patterson Dental Co.	1031 Mendota Hght	St. Paul	MN	55120	Peter L Frechette	612-686-1600	P	662	2.9
Hill's Pet Nutrition Inc.	PO Box 148	Topeka	KS	66601	Robert C Wheeler	913-354-8523	S	600 *	2.5
W.A. Butler Co.	5000 Bradenton	Dublin	OH	43017	Steven A Ritt Jr	614-761-9095	R	500 *	0.7
Physician Sales and Service Inc.	7800 Belford Pkwy	Jacksonville	FL	32256	Patrick C Kelly	904-281-0011	P	483	2.1
Auto Suture Company U.S.A.	150 Glover Ave	Norwalk	CT	06856	Turi Josefen	203-845-1000	S	410 *	1.4
Le Bonheur Health Systems	50 N Dunlap St	Memphis	TN	38103	Eugene Cashman	901-572-3000	R	400	1.4
Philips Medical Systems	PO Box 860	Shelton	CT	06484	Jack E Price	203-926-7674	S	373 *	1.6
Stuart Medical Inc.	Donohue & Luxor	Greensburg	PA	15601	Richard P Byington	412-837-5700	R	350 *	1.2
Carl Zeiss Inc.	1 Zeiss Dr	Thornwood	NY	10594	Thomas J Miller	914-747-1800	S	300 *	0.4
Moore Medical Corp.	PO Box 1500	New Britain	CT	06050	Mark E Karp	860-826-3600	P	286	0.5
RDIS Corp.	55 E Monroe St	Chicago	IL	60603	CW Engle	312-849-2990	R	280 *	1.6
Consolidated Companies Inc.	PO Box 6096	Metairie	LA	70009	Victor J Kurzweg	504-834-4082	R	260 *	0.5
Vallen Corp.	PO Box 3587	Houston	TX	77253	James W Thompson	713-462-8700	P	258	1.0
Sullivan Dental Products Inc.	10920 W Lincoln	West Allis	WI	53227	Robert E Doering	414-321-8881	P	242	1.0
Nova Technologies Inc.	89 Cabot Ct, Unit L	Hauppauge	NY	11788	Stephen Fisher	516-434-8811	P	220	<0.1
Redline Healthcare Corp.	8121 10th Ave N	Golden Valley	MN	55427	Rob Carr	612-545-5757	R	220 *	0.8
Geriatric&Medical Companies	5601 Chestnut St	Philadelphia	PA	19139	Daniel Veloric	215-476-2250	P	192	5.3
ATD-American Co.	135 Greenwood	Wyncote	PA	19095	Jerome Zaslow	215-576-1000	R	190	0.1
Symphony Pharmacy Services	5350 Alla Rd	Los Angeles	CA	90066	Eileen Goodis	310-823-1616	S	160 *	0.2
Pegler-Sysco Food Services Co.	1700 Ctr Park Rd	Lincoln	NE	68512	Donald H Pegler III	402-423-1031	S	150	0.4
ALARIS Medical Systems Inc.	10221 Wateridge	San Diego	CA	92121	William J Mercer	619-458-7000	S	141 *	1.4
Perfusion Services	16818 Campo Ct	San Diego	CA	92127	King Nelson	619-485-5599	S	140 *	1.0
Micro Bio-Medics Inc.	846 Pelham Pkwy	Pelham Manor	NY	10803	Bruce J Haber	914-738-8400	P	122	0.3
Gulf South Medical Supply Inc.	426 Christine Dr	Ridgeland	MS	39157	Thomas G Hixon	601-856-5900	P	120	0.3
Veratex Group	PO Box 4031	Troy	MI	48007	James H Devlin	313-588-2970	S	97 *	0.5
Suburban Ostomy Supply	75 October Hill Rd	Holliston	MA	01746	Donald H Benovitz	508-429-1000	P	94	0.3
Midmark Corp.	60 Vista Dr	Versailles	OH	45380	Louis Fischer	937-526-3662	R	91	0.7
Gainor Medical U.S.A. Inc.	PO Box 353	McDonough	GA	30253	Mark Gainor	404-474-0474	R	90 *	<0.1
L.D. Caulk Co.	PO Box 359	Milford	DE	19963	TL Whiting	302-422-4511	D	90	0.5
Hitachi Medical Systems America	1963 Case Pkwy	Twinsburg	OH	44087	Richard Ernst	216-425-1313	S	85	0.1
Burrows Co.	230 West Palatine	Wheeling	IL	60090	George J Burrows	847-537-7300	R	80	0.3
Leica Inc.	111 Deer Lake Rd	Deerfield	IL	60015	Henry B Smith III	847-405-0123	S	76 *	0.3
Midwest Veterinary Supply Inc.	11965 Larc Indrial	Burnsville	MN	55337	Russell R Wiley	612-894-4350	R	70	0.2
Gensia Sicor Inc.	9360 Towne Centre	San Diego	CA	92121	David F Hale	619-546-8300	P	60	1.0
Smith and Davis Mfg Co.	4203 Earth City	Earth City	MO	63045	Bevil Hogg	314-512-7000	S	60	0.3
Zee Service Inc.	22 Corporate Park	Irvine	CA	92714	D Taylor	714-252-9500	S	60	0.3
Midwest Medical Supply	160 Corp Woods Ct	Bridgeton	MO	63044	Merrill Klearman	314-291-2900	R	55	0.2
Charles Leich Div.	PO Box 869	Evansville	IN	47708	RM Leich Jr	812-428-6700	D	50	<0.1
Binson's Hospital Supplies Inc.	26834 Lawrence	Center Line	MI	48015	Jim Binson	810-755-2300	R	48 *	0.2
Anabolic Laboratories Inc.	17802 Gillette Ave	Irvine	CA	92614	Steven Brown	714-863-0340	R	44 *	0.3

Source: *Ward's Business Directory of U.S. Private and Public Companies*, 1998. The company type code used is as follows: P - Public, R - Private, S - Subsidiary, D - Division, J - Joint Venture, A - Affiliate, G - Group. Sales are in millions of dollars, employees are in thousands. An asterisk (*) indicates an estimated sales volume. The symbol < stands for 'less than'.

OCCUPATIONS EMPLOYED BY SIC 504 - WHOLESALE TRADE, OTHER

Occupation	% of Total 1996	Change to 2006	Occupation	% of Total 1996	Change to 2006
Sales & related workers nec	19.5	20.2	Clerical supervisors & managers	1.9	20.2
General managers & top executives	5.9	16.4	Order clerks	1.9	8.2
Truck drivers light & heavy	5.4	20.2	Helpers, laborers nec	1.7	20.2
General office clerks	3.6	3.4	Electrical & electronic technicians	1.4	18.8
Traffic, shipping, receiving clerks	3.6	16.7	Blue collar worker supervisors	1.4	16.0
Stock clerks	3.5	-3.9	Wholesale & retail buyers, except farm products	1.3	17.0
Freight, stock, & material movers, hand	3.3	8.2	Office machine & cash register servicers	1.3	20.2
Marketing & sales worker supervisors	3.1	20.2	Hand packers & packagers	1.2	-3.9
Order fillers, wholesale & retail sales	3.0	16.7	Maintenance repairers, general utility	1.1	12.0
Bookkeeping, accounting, & auditing clerks	2.9	-3.9	Industrial truck & tractor operators	1.1	20.2
Salespersons, retail	2.5	20.2	Purchasing managers	1.1	20.2
Secretaries, except legal & medical	2.5	-4.7	Receptionists & information clerks	1.0	20.2
Assemblers, fabricators, hand workers nec	2.0	-3.9			

Source: *Industry-Occupation Matrix*, Bureau of Labor Statistics. These data relate to one or more 3-digit SIC industry groups rather than to a single 4-digit SIC. The change reported for each occupation to the year 2006 is a percent of growth or decline as estimated by the Bureau of Labor Statistics. The abbreviation nec stands for 'not elsewhere classified'.

STATE AND REGIONAL CONCENTRATION

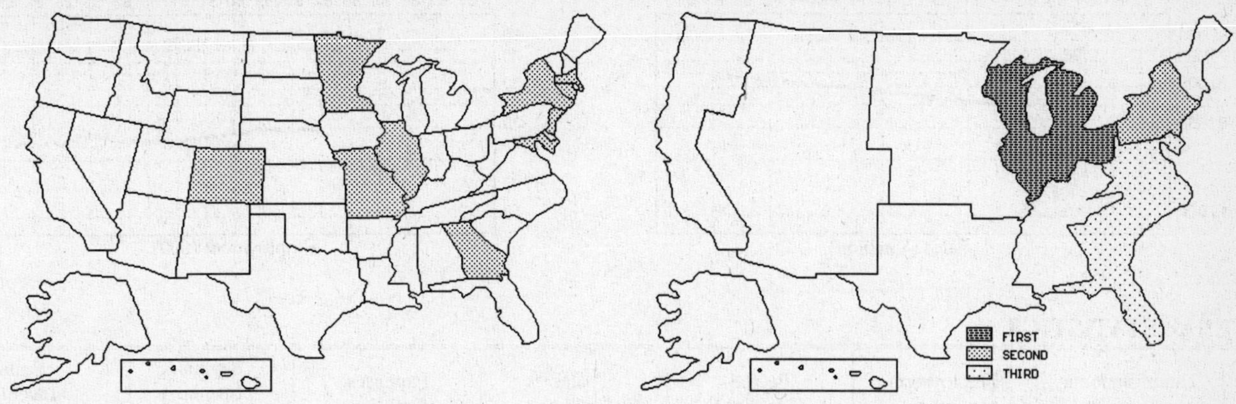

INDUSTRY DATA BY STATE

State	Establishments - 1995 Total (number)	Establishments - 1995 % of U.S.	Employment - 1995 Total (number)	Employment - 1995 % of U.S.	Employment - 1995 Per Estab.	Payroll - 1995 Total ($ mil.)	Payroll - 1995 Per Empl. ($)	Sales - 1992 Total ($ mil.)	Sales - 1992 % of U.S.	Sales - 1992 Per Estab ($)
Illinois	494	4.9	9,937	7.8	20	462.3	46,523	6,108.2	11.9	686,541
California	1,114	11.2	14,767	11.6	13	632.4	42,826	5,224.7	10.2	348,968
New Jersey	414	4.1	8,213	6.4	20	409.5	49,859	4,390.1	8.5	497,805
New York	670	6.7	10,109	7.9	15	459.4	45,448	3,726.6	7.2	392,769
Texas	727	7.3	7,360	5.8	10	293.0	39,813	2,791.6	5.4	369,067
Georgia	328	3.3	4,846	3.8	15	222.3	45,882	2,650.3	5.2	527,636
Florida	903	9.0	8,176	6.4	9	313.6	38,354	2,490.8	4.8	318,885
Pennsylvania	416	4.2	5,720	4.5	14	256.6	44,853	2,398.8	4.7	376,691
Massachusetts	251	2.5	4,047	3.2	16	218.9	54,095	2,168.7	4.2	541,104
Ohio	408	4.1	4,838	3.8	12	188.2	38,890	1,961.5	3.8	370,444
Connecticut	131	1.3	2,509	2.0	19	172.6	68,789	1,699.7	3.3	567,522
Maryland	179	1.8	3,127	2.4	17	130.3	41,656	1,485.4	2.9	459,729
Michigan	278	2.8	4,533	3.5	16	185.4	40,907	1,435.2	2.8	369,523
Missouri	258	2.6	3,176	2.5	12	130.8	41,189	1,383.6	2.7	410,552
Minnesota	225	2.3	4,361	3.4	19	218.1	50,015	1,099.2	2.1	376,580
North Carolina	228	2.3	2,683	2.1	12	107.7	40,139	1,022.2	2.0	416,725
Indiana	157	1.6	2,771	2.2	18	142.4	51,392	902.7	1.8	406,091
Tennessee	228	2.3	2,563	2.0	11	101.1	39,438	774.2	1.5	325,701
Washington	202	2.0	2,240	1.8	11	94.1	42,000	772.8	1.5	361,304
Wisconsin	155	1.6	1,573	1.2	10	65.0	41,304	755.2	1.5	407,566
Colorado	205	2.1	1,862	1.5	9	77.6	41,701	738.0	1.4	369,192
Virginia	181	1.8	1,667	1.3	9	67.5	40,521	631.5	1.2	392,489
Louisiana	154	1.5	1,364	1.1	9	50.3	36,856	600.5	1.2	403,594
Arizona	174	1.7	1,474	1.2	8	54.4	36,890	549.5	1.1	353,392
Alabama	158	1.6	1,614	1.3	10	55.4	34,300	407.0	0.8	267,052
Kentucky	127	1.3	1,310	1.0	10	39.9	30,431	345.9	0.7	291,396
Oregon	118	1.2	1,057	0.8	9	38.4	36,303	326.6	0.6	341,677
South Carolina	104	1.0	905	0.7	9	34.7	38,301	318.9	0.6	359,171
Kansas	111	1.1	948	0.7	9	37.9	39,931	306.8	0.6	315,619
Oklahoma	124	1.2	912	0.7	7	27.9	30,605	260.3	0.5	257,479
Nebraska	70	0.7	860	0.7	12	29.0	33,771	227.1	0.4	281,768
Utah	96	1.0	694	0.5	7	24.1	34,742	206.3	0.4	361,250
Mississippi	59	0.6	651	0.5	11	19.6	30,072	198.7	0.4	287,142
Arkansas	77	0.8	839	0.7	11	23.5	27,977	190.8	0.4	256,847
Rhode Island	36	0.4	398	0.3	11	17.3	43,560	176.6	0.3	456,320
Iowa	66	0.7	760	0.6	12	25.8	33,970	169.0	0.3	248,219
New Hampshire	42	0.4	294	0.2	7	9.3	31,687	97.3	0.2	352,475
West Virginia	42	0.4	357	0.3	9	9.6	27,006	95.1	0.2	254,214
Maine	27	0.3	358	0.3	13	10.6	29,715	69.8	0.1	204,088
Hawaii	36	0.4	235	0.2	7	8.6	36,396	67.8	0.1	277,852
New Mexico	41	0.4	251	0.2	6	9.7	38,542	65.9	0.1	218,159
South Dakota	20	0.2	161	0.1	8	5.2	32,391	36.0	0.1	207,075
Idaho	27	0.3	173	0.1	6	6.1	35,133	33.8	0.1	268,405
Montana	20	0.2	189	0.1	9	4.8	25,217	26.4	0.1	201,588
Vermont	15	0.2	118	0.1	8	4.0	34,186	21.1	0.0	271,051
Alaska	5	0.1	46	0.0	9	1.4	29,652	14.9	0.0	303,408
D.C.	7	0.1	20-99	-	-	(D)	-	12.1	0.0	327,351
Nevada	44	0.4	322	0.3	7	12.7	39,382	(D)	-	-
Delaware	17	0.2	161	0.1	9	3.9	24,043	(D)	-	-
North Dakota	14	0.1	208	0.2	15	7.9	37,899	(D)	-	-
Wyoming	6	0.1	0-19	-	-	(D)	-	(D)	-	-

Source: County Business Patterns, 1995 and *Economic Census of the U.S., 1992.* Data are sorted by 1992 revenues and, if revenues are unavailable, by establishments in 1995. The symbol (D) indicates that data are withheld by the source to avoid disclosure of competitive information. A dash (-) indicates that data are not available or undisclosed because they do not meet statistical validity standards. Shaded *states* on the state map indicate those states which have proportionately greater representation in the industry than would be indicated by the state's population; the ratio is based on total revenues or number of establishments. Shaded *regions* indicate where the industry is regionally most concentrated.

5048 - OPHTHALMIC GOODS

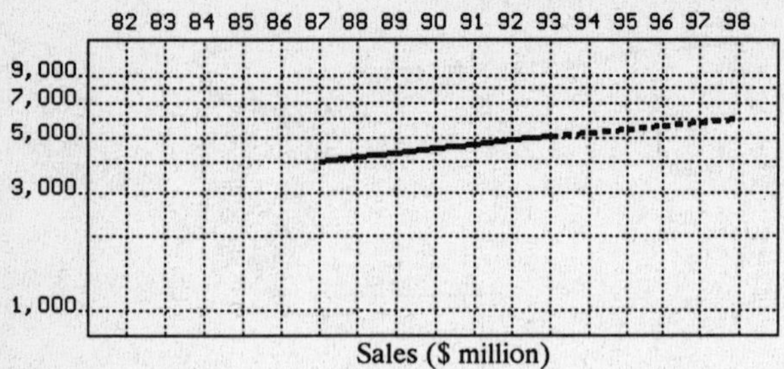

Sales ($ million)

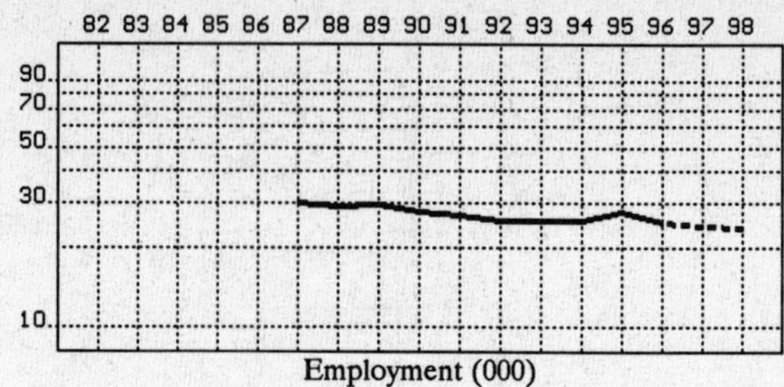

Employment (000)

GENERAL STATISTICS

Year	Establishments (number)	Employment (number)	Payroll ($ million)	Sales ($ million)	Expenses ($ million)	Beginning Inventory ($ million)	Ending Inventory ($ million)
1982	-	-	-	-	-	-	-
1983	-	-	-	-	-	-	-
1984	-	-	-	-	-	-	-
1985	-	-	-	-	-	-	-
1986	-	-	-	-	-	-	-
1987	1,899	30,134	591.9	4,026.3	1,290.2	520.6	538.9
1988	1,782	29,289	613.7	4,203.0e	1,317.8e	553.6e	575.3e
1989	1,613	29,573	654.9	4,379.6e	1,345.4e	586.6e	611.6e
1990	1,603	27,998	652.2	4,556.3e	1,373.0e	619.7e	648.0e
1991	1,568	27,149	675.5	4,732.9e	1,400.6e	652.7e	684.3e
1992	1,783	25,561	654.4	4,909.6	1,428.2	685.7	720.7
1993	1,752	25,552	678.9	5,086.2p	1,455.9p	718.8p	757.0p
1994	1,740	25,571	716.6	5,262.9p	1,483.5p	751.8p	793.4p
1995	1,739	27,880	828.9	5,439.5p	1,511.1p	784.8p	829.7p
1996	1,694p	25,080p	783.0p	5,616.2p	1,538.7p	817.9p	866.1p
1997	1,689p	24,569p	804.8p	5,792.8p	1,566.3p	850.9p	902.4p
1998	1,684p	24,058p	826.6p	5,969.5p	1,593.9p	883.9p	938.8p

Sources: *Economic Census of the United States*, 1982, 1987, and 1992. Establishment counts, employment, and payroll are from *County Business Patterns* for non-Census years. Values followed by a 'p' are projections by the editors. Sales and expense data for non-Census years are extrapolations, marked by 'e'. Industries reclassified in 1987 will not have data for prior years. Data are the most recent available at this level of detail.

INDICES OF CHANGE

Year	Establishments (number)	Employment (number)	Payroll ($ million)	Sales ($ million)	Expenses ($ million)	Beginning Inventory ($ million)	Ending Inventory ($ million)
1982	-	-	-	-	-	-	-
1983	-	-	-	-	-	-	-
1984	-	-	-	-	-	-	-
1985	-	-	-	-	-	-	-
1986	-	-	-	-	-	-	-
1987	106.5	117.9	90.4	82.0	90.3	75.9	74.8
1988	99.9	114.6	93.8	85.6e	92.3e	80.7e	79.8e
1989	90.5	115.7	100.1	89.2e	94.2e	85.5e	84.9e
1990	89.9	109.5	99.7	92.8e	96.1e	90.4e	89.9e
1991	87.9	106.2	103.2	96.4e	98.1e	95.2e	94.9e
1992	100.0	100.0	100.0	100.0	100.0	100.0	100.0
1993	98.3	100.0	103.8	103.6p	101.9p	104.8p	105.0p
1994	97.6	100.0	109.5	107.2p	103.9p	109.6p	110.1p
1995	97.5	109.1	126.7	110.8p	105.8p	114.5p	115.1p
1996	95.0p	98.1p	119.7p	114.4p	107.7p	119.3p	120.2p
1997	94.7p	96.1p	123.0p	118.0p	109.7p	124.1p	125.2p
1998	94.4p	94.1p	126.3p	121.6p	111.6p	128.9p	130.3p

Sources: Same as General Statistics. The values shown reflect change from the base year, 1992. Values above 100 mean greater than 1992, values below 100 mean less than 1992, and a value of 100 in the 1982-91 or 1993-98 period means same as 1992. Values followed by a 'p' are projections by the editors; 'e' stands for extrapolation. Data are the most recent available at this level of detail.

SELECTED RATIOS

For 1992	Avg. of All Wholesale	Analyzed Industry	Index	For 1992	Avg. of All Wholesale	Analyzed Industry	Index
Employees per Establishment	12	14	123	Sales per Employee	561,172	192,074	34
Payroll per Establishment	349,729	367,022	105	Sales per Establishment	6,559,346	2,753,561	42
Payroll per Employee	29,919	25,602	86	Expenses per Establishment	723,071	801,010	111

Sources: Same as General Statistics. The 'Average of All Manufacturing' column represents the average of all manufacturing industries reported for the most recent complete year available. The Index shows the relationship between the Average and the Analyzed Industry. For example, 100 means that they are equal; 500 that the Analyzed Industry is five times the average; 50 means that the Analyzed Industry is half the national average. The abbreviation 'na' is used to show that data are 'not available'.

LEADING COMPANIES

Number shown: **25** Total sales ($ mil): **624** Total employment (000): **2.4**

Company Name	Address				CEO Name	Phone	Co. Type	Sales ($ mil)	Empl. (000)
Carl Zeiss Inc.	1 Zeiss Dr	Thornwood	NY	10594	Thomas J Miller	914-747-1800	S	300 *	0.4
BEC Group Inc.	555 T Fremd	Rye	NY	10580	William T Sullivan	914-967-9400	P	67	0.4
Bonneau Co.	1601 Val View Ln	Dallas	TX	75234	John H Flynn Jr	972-241-3484	S	60	0.1
Charmant Incorporated USA	400 American Rd	Morris Plains	NJ	07950	Masao Otani	201-538-1511	S	40	0.2
Bolle America Inc.	3890 Elm St	Denver	CO	80207	Bill Humes	303-321-4300	S	20 *	<0.1
Moonlight Products Inc.	10401 Roselle St	San Diego	CA	92121	David W Knight	619-625-0300	R	20	<0.1
Irwin International Inc.	PO Box 4000	Corona	CA	91720	James Irwin	909-372-9555	R	15 *	<0.1
Neostyle Eyewear Corp.	2605 State St	San Diego	CA	92103	Helmut Igel	619-299-0755	R	14	<0.1
Midwest Vision Distributors	Hwy 23 E, Box 1167	St. Cloud	MN	56301	Myrel A Neumann	612-252-6006	R	11	0.2
Newton Professional Purchasing	PO Box 900	Newton	IA	50208	James Bond	515-792-9962	R	10 *	<0.1
Ocean Optique Distributors	14250 SW 122nd	Miami	FL	33186	Ray Hyman Sr	305-255-3272	P	10	<0.1
Con-Cise Lens Co.	PO Box 2198	San Leandro	CA	94577	CF Moore	510-483-9400	R	8	<0.1
Oliver Peoples Inc.	8600 Sunset Blvd	Los Angeles	CA	90069	Thomas M Werner	310-657-5475	R	8 *	<0.1
Al Nyman and Son	1500 SW 66th Ave	Hollywood	FL	33023	Al Nyman	305-592-2900	R	7	0.2
Cumberland Optical Company	806 Olympic St	Nashville	TN	37203	Kenneth W Wyatt	615-254-5868	R	7	<0.1
Schneider Corp.	400 Crossways Pk	Woodbury	NY	11797	Ron Leven	516-496-8500	S	6	<0.1
Global Optics Inc.	PO Box 8008	Green Bay	WI	54308	Amos Williams	414-432-1502	R	4	<0.1
Joy Optical Co.	1104 53rd Court S	Mangonia Park	FL	33407	Alexandra Shelton	561-863-3205	R	4	<0.1
Optical Advantage	8009 34th Ave S	Minneapolis	MN	55425	Jim Leto	612-854-6109	D	4	0.3
Universal/Univis Inc.	110 Frank Mossveig	Attleboro	MA	02703	J Charles Hoff	508-226-9630	R	3	<0.1
Marine Optical Inc.	5 Hampden Dr	South Easton	MA	02375	Michael Ferrara	508-238-8700	R	2	0.1
Combine Optical Associates	36 Main St	P. Washington	NY	11050	Neil Glachman	516-883-2528	R	1 *	<0.1
Coyote Vision USA	PO Box 277	Pittsford	NY	14534	Steven Carhart	716-385-7580	R	1 *	<0.1
Europa Time Inc.	3030 Hampton Pl	Boca Raton	FL	33434	Ralph Jacobson	407-241-8097	R	1	<0.1
Distributing Inc.	7046 W Greenfield	West Allis	WI	53214	David Gray	414-774-4949	R	1	<0.1

Source: *Ward's Business Directory of U.S. Private and Public Companies*, 1998. The company type code used is as follows: P - Public, R - Private, S - Subsidiary, D - Division, J - Joint Venture, A - Affiliate, G - Group. Sales are in millions of dollars, employees are in thousands. An asterisk (*) indicates an estimated sales volume. The symbol < stands for 'less than'.

OCCUPATIONS EMPLOYED BY SIC 504 - WHOLESALE TRADE, OTHER

Occupation	% of Total 1996	Change to 2006	Occupation	% of Total 1996	Change to 2006
Sales & related workers nec	19.5	20.2	Clerical supervisors & managers	1.9	20.2
General managers & top executives	5.9	16.4	Order clerks	1.9	8.2
Truck drivers light & heavy	5.4	20.2	Helpers, laborers nec	1.7	20.2
General office clerks	3.6	3.4	Electrical & electronic technicians	1.4	18.8
Traffic, shipping, receiving clerks	3.6	16.7	Blue collar worker supervisors	1.4	16.0
Stock clerks	3.5	-3.9	Wholesale & retail buyers, except farm products	1.3	17.0
Freight, stock, & material movers, hand	3.3	8.2	Office machine & cash register servicers	1.3	20.2
Marketing & sales worker supervisors	3.1	20.2	Hand packers & packagers	1.2	-3.9
Order fillers, wholesale & retail sales	3.0	16.7	Maintenance repairers, general utility	1.1	12.0
Bookkeeping, accounting, & auditing clerks	2.9	-3.9	Industrial truck & tractor operators	1.1	20.2
Salespersons, retail	2.5	20.2	Purchasing managers	1.1	20.2
Secretaries, except legal & medical	2.5	-4.7	Receptionists & information clerks	1.0	20.2
Assemblers, fabricators, hand workers nec	2.0	-3.9			

Source: *Industry-Occupation Matrix*, Bureau of Labor Statistics. These data relate to one or more 3-digit SIC industry groups rather than to a single 4-digit SIC. The change reported for each occupation to the year 2006 is a percent of growth or decline as estimated by the Bureau of Labor Statistics. The abbreviation nec stands for 'not elsewhere classified'.

STATE AND REGIONAL CONCENTRATION

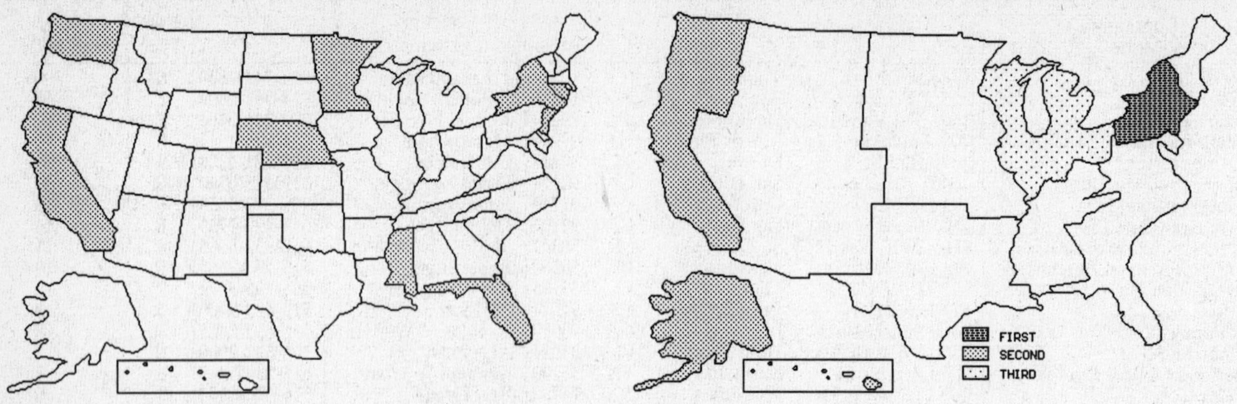

INDUSTRY DATA BY STATE

State	Establishments - 1995		Employment - 1995			Payroll - 1995		Sales - 1992		
	Total (number)	% of U.S.	Total (number)	% of U.S.	Per Estab.	Total ($ mil.)	Per Empl. ($)	Total ($ mil.)	% of U.S.	Per Estab ($)
New York	193	11.1	3,269	12.0	17	138.1	42,239	1,044.7	22.3	348,476
New Jersey	77	4.4	3,525	12.9	46	109.2	30,984	686.4	14.7	250,405
California	241	13.9	3,685	13.5	15	122.3	33,185	670.3	14.3	173,926
Florida	163	9.4	1,930	7.1	12	63.1	32,703	338.3	7.2	207,821
Texas	92	5.3	2,413	8.9	26	62.0	25,678	195.8	4.2	138,283
Illinois	70	4.0	939	3.4	13	22.4	23,834	179.5	3.8	246,254
Ohio	46	2.6	967	3.5	21	23.7	24,497	137.3	2.9	121,060
Pennsylvania	60	3.5	812	3.0	14	21.8	26,865	128.4	2.7	130,589
Washington	33	1.9	365	1.3	11	9.0	24,540	117.6	2.5	274,133
Connecticut	29	1.7	615	2.3	21	19.5	31,748	108.7	2.3	184,813
Minnesota	40	2.3	639	2.3	16	16.5	25,776	103.6	2.2	147,779
Michigan	52	3.0	763	2.8	15	18.5	24,210	89.5	1.9	122,574
Tennessee	31	1.8	534	2.0	17	13.3	24,824	78.2	1.7	119,555
Wisconsin	24	1.4	577	2.1	24	13.1	22,674	76.1	1.6	155,071
Indiana	42	2.4	417	1.5	10	10.3	24,588	67.0	1.4	144,420
Georgia	43	2.5	401	1.5	9	11.5	28,661	63.6	1.4	204,527
North Carolina	37	2.1	489	1.8	13	12.4	25,337	53.3	1.1	107,328
Virginia	18	1.0	316	1.2	18	11.6	36,630	51.8	1.1	207,276
Mississippi	12	0.7	173	0.6	14	4.0	23,254	51.3	1.1	356,438
Iowa	24	1.4	306	1.1	13	6.5	21,082	50.8	1.1	210,888
Oregon	18	1.0	217	0.8	12	5.6	25,631	49.0	1.0	206,088
Kentucky	16	0.9	276	1.0	17	7.3	26,504	45.7	1.0	155,442
Kansas	10	0.6	310	1.1	31	8.0	25,719	43.4	0.9	106,188
Nebraska	18	1.0	337	1.2	19	7.3	21,638	35.8	0.8	124,564
Arizona	26	1.5	282	1.0	11	7.8	27,816	33.6	0.7	108,487
Missouri	31	1.8	318	1.2	10	6.6	20,692	31.8	0.7	105,295
Colorado	28	1.6	170	0.6	6	5.9	34,624	31.5	0.7	165,094
Oklahoma	22	1.3	310	1.1	14	6.9	22,190	29.8	0.6	110,814
Rhode Island	5	0.3	104	0.4	21	2.3	22,490	14.9	0.3	148,660
South Carolina	18	1.0	150	0.6	8	3.5	23,367	14.8	0.3	116,520
Louisiana	17	1.0	148	0.5	9	2.6	17,885	12.6	0.3	71,181
Alabama	16	0.9	113	0.4	7	2.4	20,920	9.9	0.2	90,227
Hawaii	10	0.6	127	0.5	13	2.6	20,189	8.4	0.2	78,103
Arkansas	15	0.9	130	0.5	9	2.2	17,146	7.8	0.2	63,504
New Hampshire	3	0.2	64	0.2	21	1.4	22,203	6.3	0.1	105,367
North Dakota	7	0.4	20-99	-	-	(D)	-	4.9	0.1	76,641
Maine	10	0.6	83	0.3	8	1.4	16,325	4.4	0.1	58,960
New Mexico	4	0.2	20-99	-	-	(D)	-	3.1	0.1	54,982
Vermont	5	0.3	20-99	-	-	(D)	-	3.0	0.1	72,167
Massachusetts	52	3.0	496	1.8	10	16.9	34,155	(D)	-	-
Maryland	26	1.5	346	1.3	13	9.6	27,725	(D)	-	-
Utah	12	0.7	92	0.3	8	1.8	19,043	(D)	-	-
Nevada	10	0.6	100-249	-	-	(D)	-	(D)	-	-
Idaho	7	0.4	20-99	-	-	(D)	-	(D)	-	-
Montana	7	0.4	20-99	-	-	(D)	-	(D)	-	-
South Dakota	7	0.4	43	0.2	6	0.9	22,023	(D)	-	-
West Virginia	5	0.3	20-99	-	-	(D)	-	(D)	-	-
Wyoming	4	0.2	20-99	-	-	(D)	-	(D)	-	-
Delaware	3	0.2	100-249	-	-	(D)	-	(D)	-	-

Source: *County Business Patterns, 1995* and *Economic Census of the U.S., 1992*. Data are sorted by 1992 revenues and, if revenues are unavailable, by establishments in 1995. The symbol (D) indicates that data are withheld by the source to avoid disclosure of competitive information. A dash (-) indicates that data are not available or undisclosed because they do not meet statistical validity standards. Shaded *states* on the state map indicate those states which have proportionately greater representation in the industry than would be indicated by the state's population; the ratio is based on total revenues or number of establishments. Shaded *regions* indicate where the industry is regionally most concentrated.

5049 - PROFESSIONAL EQUIPMENT, NEC

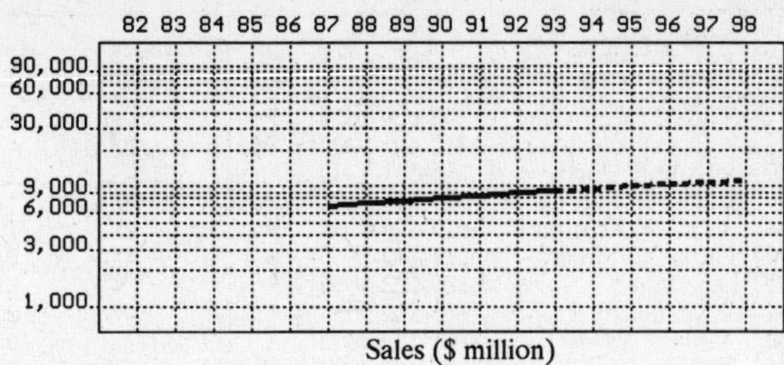

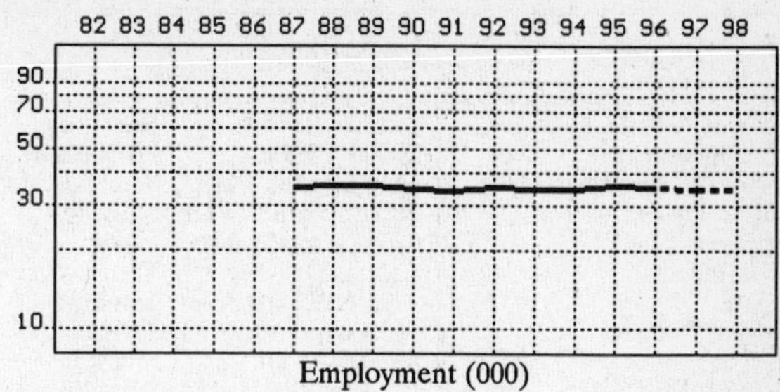

GENERAL STATISTICS

Year	Establishments (number)	Employment (number)	Payroll ($ million)	Sales ($ million)	Expenses ($ million)	Beginning Inventory ($ million)	Ending Inventory ($ million)
1982	-	-	-	-	-	-	-
1983	-	-	-	-	-	-	-
1984	-	-	-	-	-	-	-
1985	-	-	-	-	-	-	-
1986	-	-	-	-	-	-	-
1987	3,114	35,054	820.8	6,881.3	1,675.6	681.9	707.4
1988	3,031	36,038	1,014.5	7,274.9e	1,778.3e	723.9e	749.5e
1989	2,733	35,994	978.2	7,668.5e	1,880.9e	765.8e	791.6e
1990	2,629	34,698	988.4	8,062.1e	1,983.6e	807.8e	833.7e
1991	2,633	33,965	1,017.6	8,455.7e	2,086.2e	849.8e	875.8e
1992	2,820	35,088	1,116.2	8,849.4	2,188.9	891.7	917.9
1993	2,778	34,721	1,107.8	9,243.0p	2,291.5p	933.7p	960.0p
1994	2,730	34,656	1,127.9	9,636.6p	2,394.2p	975.6p	1,002.2p
1995	2,779	36,170	1,229.4	10,030.2p	2,496.8p	1,017.6p	1,044.3p
1996	2,642p	35,001p	1,241.4p	10,423.8p	2,599.5p	1,059.6p	1,086.4p
1997	2,609p	34,970p	1,280.7p	10,817.4p	2,702.1p	1,101.5p	1,128.5p
1998	2,576p	34,939p	1,320.1p	11,211.0p	2,804.8p	1,143.5p	1,170.6p

Sources: *Economic Census of the United States*, 1982, 1987, and 1992. Establishment counts, employment, and payroll are from *County Business Patterns* for non-Census years. Values followed by a 'p' are projections by the editors. Sales and expense data for non-Census years are extrapolations, marked by 'e'. Industries reclassified in 1987 will not have data for prior years. Data are the most recent available at this level of detail.

INDICES OF CHANGE

Year	Establishments (number)	Employment (number)	Payroll ($ million)	Sales ($ million)	Expenses ($ million)	Beginning Inventory ($ million)	Ending Inventory ($ million)
1982	-	-	-	-	-	-	-
1983	-	-	-	-	-	-	-
1984	-	-	-	-	-	-	-
1985	-	-	-	-	-	-	-
1986	-	-	-	-	-	-	-
1987	110.4	99.9	73.5	77.8	76.5	76.5	77.1
1988	107.5	102.7	90.9	82.2e	81.2e	81.2e	81.7e
1989	96.9	102.6	87.6	86.7e	85.9e	85.9e	86.2e
1990	93.2	98.9	88.6	91.1e	90.6e	90.6e	90.8e
1991	93.4	96.8	91.2	95.6e	95.3e	95.3e	95.4e
1992	100.0	100.0	100.0	100.0	100.0	100.0	100.0
1993	98.5	99.0	99.2	104.4p	104.7p	104.7p	104.6p
1994	96.8	98.8	101.0	108.9p	109.4p	109.4p	109.2p
1995	98.5	103.1	110.1	113.3p	114.1p	114.1p	113.8p
1996	93.7p	99.8p	111.2p	117.8p	118.8p	118.8p	118.4p
1997	92.5p	99.7p	114.7p	122.2p	123.4p	123.5p	122.9p
1998	91.4p	99.6p	118.3p	126.7p	128.1p	128.2p	127.5p

Sources: Same as General Statistics. The values shown reflect change from the base year, 1992. Values above 100 mean greater than 1992, values below 100 mean less than 1992, and a value of 100 in the 1982-91 or 1993-98 period means same as 1992. Values followed by a 'p' are projections by the editors; 'e' stands for extrapolation. Data are the most recent available at this level of detail.

SELECTED RATIOS

For 1992	Avg. of All Wholesale	Analyzed Industry	Index	For 1992	Avg. of All Wholesale	Analyzed Industry	Index
Employees per Establishment	12	12	106	Sales per Employee	561,172	252,206	45
Payroll per Establishment	349,729	395,816	113	Sales per Establishment	6,559,346	3,138,085	48
Payroll per Employee	29,919	31,811	106	Expenses per Establishment	723,071	776,206	107

Sources: Same as General Statistics. The 'Average of All Manufacturing' column represents the average of all manufacturing industries reported for the most recent complete year available. The Index shows the relationship between the Average and the Analyzed Industry. For example, 100 means that they are equal; 500 that the Analyzed Industry is five times the average; 50 means that the Analyzed Industry is half the national average. The abbreviation 'na' is used to show that data are 'not available'.

LEADING COMPANIES

Number shown: **50** Total sales ($ mil): **7,058** Total employment (000): **21.0**

Company Name	Address				CEO Name	Phone	Co. Type	Sales ($ mil)	Empl. (000)
Fisher Scientific International	Liberty Ln	Hampton	NH	03842	Paul M Montrone	603-929-2650	P	2,144	6.6
Fisher Scientific Co.	2000 Park Ln	Pittsburgh	PA	15275	Paul Patek	412-490-8300	S	1,299 *	4.0
VWR Scientific Products Corp.	1310 Goshen Pkwy	West Chester	PA	19380	Jerrold B Harris	215-431-1700	P	1,117	2.1
Olympus America Inc.	2 Corporate Ctr Dr	Melville	NY	11747	Sidney Braginsky	516-844-5000	S	800	1.5
Anacomp Inc.	12365 Crosthwaite	Poway	CA	92064	Ralph W Koehrer	619-679-9736	P	463	2.7
Carl Zeiss Inc.	1 Zeiss Dr	Thornwood	NY	10594	Thomas J Miller	914-747-1800	S	300 *	0.4
VGC Corp.	5701 NW 94th Ave	Tamarac	FL	33321	Leo Bohan	305-722-3000	S	130 *	0.5
Mitutoyo/MTI Corp.	965 Corporate Blvd	Aurora	IL	60504	K Nakanishi	708-820-9666	S	89 *	0.3
Philips Electronic	85 McKee Dr	Mahwah	NJ	07430	William A Enser	201-529-3800	S	80	0.4
Thomas Scientific	PO Box 99	Swedesboro	NJ	08085	EB Patterson Jr	609-467-2000	R	76 *	0.3
Crocker Fels Co.	1900 Section Rd	Cincinnati	OH	45242	John B Armstrong	513-458-2300	R	38	0.1
Cantel Industries Inc.	1135 Broad St	Clifton	NJ	07013	James P Reilly	973-470-8700	P	35	0.2
North Coast Medical Inc.	187 Stauffer Blvd	San Jose	CA	95125	Mark Biehl	408-283-1900	R	35 *	0.1
Briggs-Weaver Inc.	306 Airline Dr	Coppell	TX	75019	A Lee Mulkey	972-304-7200	S	30 *	0.1
Ben Meadows Company Inc.	3589 Broad St	Atlanta	GA	30341	F Karl Hube	404-455-0907	R	28	<0.1
Alvin and Company Inc.	PO Box 188	Windsor	CT	06095	Joe Miller	203-243-8991	R	25	0.2
Daigger and Company Inc.	675 Heathrow Dr	Lincolnshire	IL	60069	Jane Woldenberg	847-520-7000	R	25	<0.1
Perstorp Analytical Inc.	12101 Tech Rd	Silver Spring	MD	20904	Donald Webster	301-680-0001	S	25	0.1
ReCellular Inc.	PO Box 391	Dexter	MI	48130	Charles Newman	313-426-0800	R	25 *	0.2
Sargent-Welch Scientific Co.	911 Commerce Ct	Buffalo Grove	IL	60089	Jerrold Harrold	708-459-6625	S	23 *	<0.1
U.S.-China Industrial Exchange	7201 Wisconsin Ave	Bethesda	MD	20814	Roberta Lipson	301-215-7777	P	23	0.1
Central Scientific Co.	3300 Cenco Pkwy	Franklin Park	IL	60131	John Currey	708-451-0150	R	21	<0.1
Missco Corporation of Jackson	2510 Lakeland Ter	Jackson	MS	39216	Victor L Smith	601-948-8600	R	21	0.1
Paul H. Gesswein and Co.	255 Hancock Ave	Bridgeport	CT	06605	Dwight Gesswein	203-366-5400	R	20 *	<0.1
Duo-Fast Corp.	20 Corporate Dr	Orangeburg	NY	10962	Stephen Leber	914-365-2400	D	19	<0.1
Western Graphtec Inc.	11 Vanderbilt	Irvine	CA	92618	Kunio Minejima	714-454-2800	S	15	<0.1
Videomedia Inc.	175 Lewis Rd, #23	San Jose	CA	95111	Donald Bennett	408-227-9977	R	14	<0.1
Caxton Printers Ltd.	312 Main St	Caldwell	ID	83605	Gordon Gipson	208-459-7421	R	13	<0.1
HB Instruments Inc.	53 W Century Rd	Paramus	NJ	07652	Chip Ganz	201-265-7865	S	12 *	<0.1
Intermountain Scientific Corp.	PO Box 380	Kaysville	UT	84037	Cynthia A Lindberg	801-547-5047	R	10	<0.1
Broadcasters General Store	2480 SE 52nd St	Ocala	FL	34480	David Kerstin	352-622-7700	R	9	<0.1
Cushing and Company Inc.	325 W Huron St	Chicago	IL	60610	Cathleen Duff	312-266-8228	R	9	<0.1
Cameca Instruments Inc.	204 Spring Hill Rd	Trumbull	CT	06611	Claude Conty	203-459-0623	S	8	<0.1
Geotronics of North America	911 Hawthorn Dr	Itasca	IL	60143	Frank Larsson	708-285-1400	S	7	<0.1
Graphic Resources Corp.	12311 Industry St	Garden Grove	CA	92641	Stephen Beko	714-891-1003	R	7 *	<0.1
School Specialty Inc.	5800 NE Hassalo St	Portland	OR	97213	Dan Spalding	503-281-1193	S	7	<0.1
F-D-C Corp.	PO Box 1047	Elk Grove Vill.	IL	60009	RI Hawley	708-437-3990	R	6	<0.1
MacAlaster Bicknell Company	181 Henry St	New Haven	CT	06510	John M Bee Jr	203-624-4191	R	6	<0.1
Sony Magnescale America Inc.	137 Bristol Ln	Orange	CA	92665	Thomas J Moran	714-921-0630	S	6	<0.1
Worldwide Environmental	430 S Cataract Ave	San Dimas	CA	91773	William Delaney	909-599-6431	R	6 *	<0.1
Chiral Technologies Inc.	PO Box 564	Exton	PA	19341	Thomas B Lewis	215-594-2100	R	4 *	<0.1
Pagel Safety Inc.	1687 Westwood	Waukesha	WI	53186	Bruce S Pagel	414-544-8060	R	4	<0.1
Selsi Company Inc.	PO Box 10	Midland Park	NJ	07432	W Silbernagel Sr	201-612-9200	R	4	<0.1
Vector Engineering Inc.	12438 Loma Rica	Grass Valley	CA	95945	Mark E Smith	916-272-2448	R	4	<0.1
A and B Smith Co.	PO Box 1776	Pittsburgh	PA	15230	Stuart Smith	412-858-5400	R	3	<0.1
California Surveying	4733 Auburn Blvd	Sacramento	CA	95841	Tom Kubo	916-344-0232	R	3	<0.1
Santa Barbara Instrument Group	PO Box 50437	Santa Barbara	CA	93150	Richard Schwartz	805-969-1851	R	3	<0.1
Trend Scientific Inc.	PO Box 120266	St. Paul	MN	55112	David Taus	612-633-0925	R	3	<0.1
Protein Databases Inc.	405 Oakwood Rd	Huntington St	NY	11746	Stephen H Blose	516-673-3939	P	3	<0.1
Arun Technology Inc.	PO Box 2947	Dearborn	MI	48123	Paul K Penney	313-277-8186	S	2	<0.1

Source: *Ward's Business Directory of U.S. Private and Public Companies*, 1998. The company type code used is as follows: P - Public, R - Private, S - Subsidiary, D - Division, J - Joint Venture, A - Affiliate, G - Group. Sales are in millions of dollars, employees are in thousands. An asterisk (*) indicates an estimated sales volume. The symbol < stands for 'less than'.

OCCUPATIONS EMPLOYED BY SIC 504 - WHOLESALE TRADE, OTHER

Occupation	% of Total 1996	Change to 2006	Occupation	% of Total 1996	Change to 2006
Sales & related workers nec	19.5	20.2	Clerical supervisors & managers	1.9	20.2
General managers & top executives	5.9	16.4	Order clerks	1.9	8.2
Truck drivers light & heavy	5.4	20.2	Helpers, laborers nec	1.7	20.2
General office clerks	3.6	3.4	Electrical & electronic technicians	1.4	18.8
Traffic, shipping, receiving clerks	3.6	16.7	Blue collar worker supervisors	1.4	16.0
Stock clerks	3.5	-3.9	Wholesale & retail buyers, except farm products	1.3	17.0
Freight, stock, & material movers, hand	3.3	8.2	Office machine & cash register servicers	1.3	20.2
Marketing & sales worker supervisors	3.1	20.2	Hand packers & packagers	1.2	-3.9
Order fillers, wholesale & retail sales	3.0	16.7	Maintenance repairers, general utility	1.1	12.0
Bookkeeping, accounting, & auditing clerks	2.9	-3.9	Industrial truck & tractor operators	1.1	20.2
Salespersons, retail	2.5	20.2	Purchasing managers	1.1	20.2
Secretaries, except legal & medical	2.5	-4.7	Receptionists & information clerks	1.0	20.2
Assemblers, fabricators, hand workers nec	2.0	-3.9			

Source: *Industry-Occupation Matrix*, Bureau of Labor Statistics. These data relate to one or more 3-digit SIC industry groups rather than to a single 4-digit SIC. The change reported for each occupation to the year 2006 is a percent of growth or decline as estimated by the Bureau of Labor Statistics. The abbreviation nec stands for 'not elsewhere classified'.

STATE AND REGIONAL CONCENTRATION

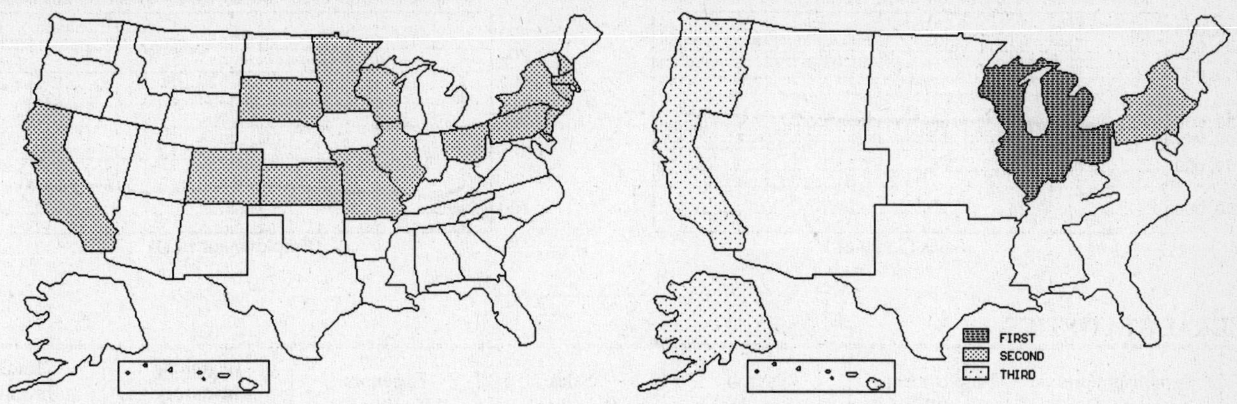

INDUSTRY DATA BY STATE

State	Establishments - 1995 Total (number)	Establishments - 1995 % of U.S.	Employment - 1995 Total (number)	Employment - 1995 % of U.S.	Employment - 1995 Per Estab.	Payroll - 1995 Total ($ mil.)	Payroll - 1995 Per Empl. ($)	Sales - 1992 Total ($ mil.)	Sales - 1992 % of U.S.	Sales - 1992 Per Estab ($)
California	319	11.5	4,966	13.8	16	183.8	37,002	1,459.9	17.9	312,806
Illinois	152	5.5	2,987	8.3	20	104.5	34,988	847.0	10.4	282,817
New York	177	6.4	2,624	7.3	15	102.7	39,141	694.6	8.5	256,678
Ohio	100	3.6	1,505	4.2	15	44.3	29,409	641.8	7.9	386,890
New Jersey	141	5.1	2,345	6.5	17	91.7	39,093	591.6	7.3	275,928
Massachusetts	99	3.6	1,626	4.5	16	71.4	43,929	493.3	6.1	293,454
Pennsylvania	121	4.4	1,314	3.7	11	47.4	36,080	426.9	5.2	320,260
Texas	182	6.5	1,854	5.2	10	54.3	29,304	379.7	4.7	250,653
Florida	160	5.8	1,311	3.6	8	42.2	32,169	236.9	2.9	201,309
Minnesota	60	2.2	813	2.3	14	24.5	30,177	230.5	2.8	235,939
Missouri	56	2.0	937	2.6	17	25.7	27,424	219.7	2.7	221,678
North Carolina	69	2.5	1,206	3.4	17	36.4	30,210	215.1	2.6	162,740
Colorado	63	2.3	663	1.8	11	27.8	41,917	178.8	2.2	214,131
Wisconsin	43	1.5	824	2.3	19	25.4	30,778	171.6	2.1	167,407
Connecticut	59	2.1	846	2.4	14	34.1	40,270	155.3	1.9	214,536
Michigan	65	2.3	832	2.3	13	23.5	28,230	151.9	1.9	171,829
Washington	59	2.1	568	1.6	10	18.0	31,690	145.6	1.8	191,634
Delaware	18	0.6	307	0.9	17	11.6	37,847	113.2	1.4	639,734
Kansas	38	1.4	650	1.8	17	17.8	27,395	97.0	1.2	162,832
Virginia	66	2.4	420	1.2	6	12.3	29,355	79.4	1.0	212,775
Indiana	57	2.1	572	1.6	10	14.0	24,509	74.2	0.9	198,906
Arizona	50	1.8	381	1.1	8	13.1	34,446	54.8	0.7	219,884
Louisiana	44	1.6	297	0.8	7	7.8	26,175	54.4	0.7	189,554
Tennessee	41	1.5	467	1.3	11	12.7	27,244	53.2	0.7	153,245
Mississippi	15	0.5	191	0.5	13	7.4	38,712	52.6	0.6	225,747
Alabama	36	1.3	576	1.6	16	15.1	26,255	45.8	0.6	152,219
South Carolina	26	0.9	325	0.9	13	10.0	30,658	43.4	0.5	171,585
New Hampshire	11	0.4	125	0.3	11	3.4	27,408	38.4	0.5	181,052
South Dakota	11	0.4	89	0.2	8	3.9	43,764	36.6	0.4	410,854
Iowa	18	0.6	186	0.5	10	7.4	40,043	36.4	0.4	176,039
Nebraska	22	0.8	184	0.5	8	3.9	21,370	31.7	0.4	153,927
New Mexico	19	0.7	105	0.3	6	3.0	28,200	29.8	0.4	301,263
Oklahoma	24	0.9	213	0.6	9	7.8	36,676	26.6	0.3	192,638
West Virginia	13	0.5	91	0.3	7	2.0	22,484	21.0	0.3	179,538
Montana	14	0.5	100-249	-	-	(D)	-	12.8	0.2	118,963
Georgia	83	3.0	1,194	3.3	14	42.0	35,198	(D)	-	-
Maryland	68	2.4	679	1.9	10	30.1	44,364	(D)	-	-
Kentucky	36	1.3	476	1.3	13	9.0	18,983	(D)	-	-
Oregon	34	1.2	275	0.8	8	8.6	31,091	(D)	-	-
Arkansas	15	0.5	59	0.2	4	2.1	36,102	(D)	-	-
Nevada	14	0.5	164	0.5	12	3.8	23,317	(D)	-	-
Utah	14	0.5	142	0.4	10	3.7	26,366	(D)	-	-
Rhode Island	13	0.5	234	0.7	18	6.0	25,577	(D)	-	-
Idaho	11	0.4	20-99	-	-	(D)	-	(D)	-	-
Hawaii	10	0.4	93	0.3	9	2.6	28,140	(D)	-	-
North Dakota	10	0.4	146	0.4	15	3.3	22,445	(D)	-	-
Vermont	8	0.3	20-99	-	-	(D)	-	(D)	-	-
Alaska	6	0.2	34	0.1	6	0.8	24,706	(D)	-	-
Maine	4	0.1	30	0.1	8	1.0	32,733	(D)	-	-
Wyoming	4	0.1	9	0.0	2	0.1	13,444	(D)	-	-
D.C.	1	0.0	0-19	-	-	(D)	-	-	-	-

Source: *County Business Patterns, 1995* and *Economic Census of the U.S., 1992*. Data are sorted by 1992 revenues and, if revenues are unavailable, by establishments in 1995. The symbol (D) indicates that data are withheld by the source to avoid disclosure of competitive information. A dash (-) indicates that data are not available or undisclosed because they do not meet statistical validity standards. Shaded *states* on the state map indicate those states which have proportionately greater representation in the industry than would be indicated by the state's population; the ratio is based on total revenues or number of establishments. Shaded *regions* indicate where the industry is regionally most concentrated.

5051 - METALS SERVICE CENTERS AND OFFICES

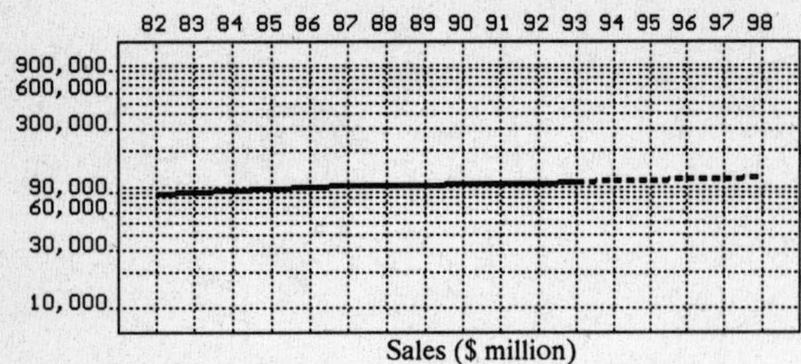

Sales ($ million)

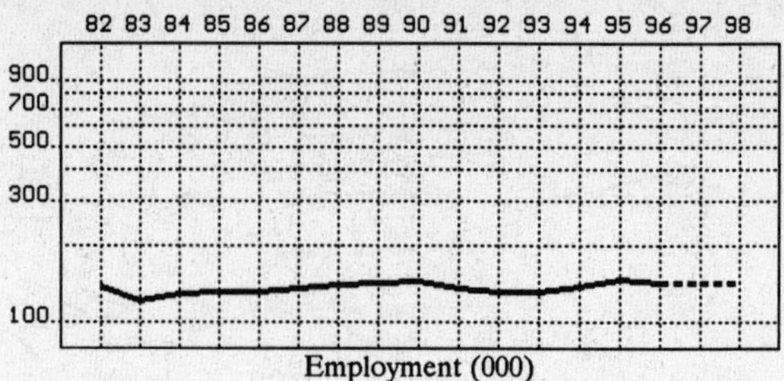

Employment (000)

GENERAL STATISTICS

Year	Establishments (number)	Employment (number)	Payroll ($ million)	Sales ($ million)	Expenses ($ million)	Beginning Inventory ($ million)	Ending Inventory ($ million)
1982	9,676	139,796	3,155.9	87,764.0	-	-	-
1983	9,354	123,091	3,042.6	90,439.9e	-	-	-
1984	9,155	130,125	3,388.8	93,115.7e	-	-	-
1985	8,939	132,894	3,482.2	95,791.6e	-	-	-
1986	8,843	131,512	3,509.5	98,467.5e	-	-	-
1987	10,281	137,009	3,854.4	101,143.3	8,028.9	7,795.4	8,020.0
1988	9,814	141,598	4,354.9	102,081.5e	8,270.2e	8,050.4e	8,245.6e
1989	9,629	143,818	4,555.4	103,019.6e	8,511.4e	8,305.5e	8,471.3e
1990	9,673	144,931	4,646.5	103,957.7e	8,752.7e	8,560.5e	8,697.0e
1991	9,537	137,645	4,431.9	104,895.9e	8,994.0e	8,815.6e	8,922.6e
1992	10,426	132,741	4,458.1	105,834.0	9,235.2	9,070.6	9,148.3
1993	10,250	132,320	4,667.7	109,615.7p	9,476.5p	9,325.7p	9,374.0p
1994	10,246	138,724	5,104.7	111,422.7p	9,717.8p	9,580.7p	9,599.6p
1995	10,331	146,921	5,623.2	113,229.7p	9,959.1p	9,835.8p	9,825.3p
1996	10,385p	142,255p	5,486.0p	115,036.7p	10,200.3p	10,090.8p	10,051.0p
1997	10,474p	143,002p	5,662.4p	116,843.7p	10,441.6p	10,345.9p	10,276.6p
1998	10,562p	143,749p	5,838.9p	118,650.7p	10,682.9p	10,600.9p	10,502.3p

Sources: Economic Census of the United States, 1982, 1987, and 1992. Establishment counts, employment, and payroll are from *County Business Patterns* for non-Census years. Values followed by a 'p' are projections by the editors. Sales and expense data for non-Census years are extrapolations, marked by 'e'. Industries reclassified in 1987 will not have data for prior years. Data are the most recent available at this level of detail.

INDICES OF CHANGE

Year	Establishments (number)	Employment (number)	Payroll ($ million)	Sales ($ million)	Expenses ($ million)	Beginning Inventory ($ million)	Ending Inventory ($ million)
1982	92.8	105.3	70.8	82.9	-	-	-
1983	89.7	92.7	68.2	85.5e	-	-	-
1984	87.8	98.0	76.0	88.0e	-	-	-
1985	85.7	100.1	78.1	90.5e	-	-	-
1986	84.8	99.1	78.7	93.0e	-	-	-
1987	98.6	103.2	86.5	95.6	86.9	85.9	87.7
1988	94.1	106.7	97.7	96.5e	89.6e	88.8e	90.1e
1989	92.4	108.3	102.2	97.3e	92.2e	91.6e	92.6e
1990	92.8	109.2	104.2	98.2e	94.8e	94.4e	95.1e
1991	91.5	103.7	99.4	99.1e	97.4e	97.2e	97.5e
1992	100.0	100.0	100.0	100.0	100.0	100.0	100.0
1993	98.3	99.7	104.7	103.6p	102.6p	102.8p	102.5p
1994	98.3	104.5	114.5	105.3p	105.2p	105.6p	104.9p
1995	99.1	110.7	126.1	107.0p	107.8p	108.4p	107.4p
1996	99.6p	107.2p	123.1p	108.7p	110.5p	111.2p	109.9p
1997	100.5p	107.7p	127.0p	110.4p	113.1p	114.1p	112.3p
1998	101.3p	108.3p	131.0p	112.1p	115.7p	116.9p	114.8p

Sources: Same as General Statistics. The values shown reflect change from the base year, 1992. Values above 100 mean greater than 1992, values below 100 mean less than 1992, and a value of 100 in the 1982-91 or 1993-98 period means same as 1992. Values followed by a 'p' are projections by the editors; 'e' stands for extrapolation. Data are the most recent available at this level of detail.

SELECTED RATIOS

For 1992	Avg. of All Wholesale	Analyzed Industry	Index	For 1992	Avg. of All Wholesale	Analyzed Industry	Index
Employees per Establishment	12	13	109	Sales per Employee	561,172	797,297	142
Payroll per Establishment	349,729	427,594	122	Sales per Establishment	6,559,346	10,150,969	155
Payroll per Employee	29,919	33,585	112	Expenses per Establishment	723,071	885,786	123

Sources: Same as General Statistics. The 'Average of All Manufacturing' column represents the average of all manufacturing industries reported for the most recent complete year available. The Index shows the relationship between the Average and the Analyzed Industry. For example, 100 means that they are equal; 500 that the Analyzed Industry is five times the average; 50 means that the Analyzed Industry is half the national average. The abbreviation 'na' is used to show that data are 'not available'.

LEADING COMPANIES

Number shown: **50** Total sales ($ mil): **83,168** Total employment (000): **99.3**

Company Name	Address				CEO Name	Phone	Co. Type	Sales ($ mil)	Empl. (000)
Marubeni America Corp.	450 Lexington Ave	New York	NY	10017	Katsuo Koh	212-450-0100	S	29,000 *	2.2
Nissho Iwai American Corp.	1211 of the Amer	New York	NY	10036	Akira Yokouchi	212-704-6500	S	11,910	0.4
Inland Steel Industries Inc.	30 W Monroe St	Chicago	IL	60603	Robert J Darnall	312-346-0300	P	4,584	14.7
Ryerson Tull Inc.	2621 West 15thace	Chicago	IL	60608	Neil S Novich	773-762-2121	P	2,789	5.4
Pechiney Corp.	475 Steamboat Rd	Greenwich	CT	06830	Michel Simonnard	203-661-4600	S	2,780 *	28.0
Tomen America Inc.	1285 of the Amer	New York	NY	10019	Hajime Kawamura	212-397-4600	S	2,645	0.9
Kanematsu U.S.A. Inc.	114 W 47th St	New York	NY	10036	Minoru Inoue	212-704-9400	S	2,250	1.0
Thyssen Inc.	400 Renaissance	Detroit	MI	48243	Kenneth Graham	313-567-5600	S	1,950	3.0
Wesco Financial Corp.	301 E Colorado	Pasadena	CA	91101	Charles T Munger	818-585-6700	P	1,818	0.3
O'Neal Steel Inc.	PO Box 2623	Birmingham	AL	35202	Max DeJonge	205-599-8000	R	1,773 *	2.4
Joseph T. Ryerson and Son Inc.	PO Box 8000	Chicago	IL	60680	Carl G Lusted	773-762-2121	S	1,666 *	5.0
Tang Industries Inc.	1965 Pratt Blvd	Elk Grove Vill.	IL	60007	Cyrus Tang	708-806-7200	R	1,560 *	2.1
Renco Corp.	30 Rockefeller Plz	New York	NY	10112	Ira Rennert	212-541-6000	R	1,170 *	7.0
Earle M. Jorgensen Co.	3050 E Birch St	Brea	CA	92821	Maurice S Nelson Jr	714-579-8823	S	1,000	2.2
National Material L.P.	1965 Pratt Blvd	Elk Grove Vill.	IL	60007	Michael Tang	847-806-7200	S	891 *	1.2
Edgcomb Metals Co.	555 State Rd	Bensalem	PA	19020	Francois Faijean	215-245-3300	S	800	1.3
Alro Steel Corp.	PO Box 927	Jackson	MI	49204	Mark Alyea	517-787-5500	R	780 *	1.0
Reynolds Aluminum Supply Co.	6603 W Broad St	Richmond	VA	23230	Donald T Cowles	804-281-2000	D	750 *	0.9
Tradearbed Inc.	825 3rd Ave	New York	NY	10022	F Lamesch	212-486-9890	S	750	0.3
A.M. Castle and Co.	3400 N Wolf Rd	Franklin Park	IL	60131	Richard G Mork	708-455-7111	P	673	1.5
Reliance Steel&Aluminum Co.	PO Box 60482	Los Angeles	CA	90060	Joe D Crider	213-582-2272	P	654	1.4
Cambridge-Lee Industries Inc.	500 Lincoln St	Allston	MA	02134	Gunther Bouer	617-783-3100	R	570 *	0.8
Olympic Steel Inc.	5080 Richmond Rd	Bedford H.	OH	44146	Michael D Siegal	216-292-3800	P	560	1.0
Vincent Metal Goods	455 85th Ave NW	Minneapolis	MN	55433	Harrison P Jones	612-717-9000	D	560 *	0.9
J.M. Tull Metals Company Inc.	PO Box 4725	Norcross	GA	30091	S E Makarewicz	404-368-4311	S	540 *	0.7
Copper and Brass Sales Inc.	17401 10 Mile Rd	Eastpointe	MI	48021	William Howenstein	810-775-7710	R	500	1.0
Francosteel Corp.	345 Hudson St	New York	NY	10014	M. Longchampt	212-633-1010	S	500	0.2
Mannesmann Pipe and Steel	1990 Post Oak Blvd	Houston	TX	77056	Rudolf Georg	713-960-1900	S	500	<0.1
Klockner Namasco Corp.	666 Old Country	Garden City	NY	11530	FW Mueller	516-237-6900	S	480 *	0.7
Pitt-Des Moines Inc.	3400 Grand Ave	Pittsburgh	PA	15225	William W, McKee	412-331-3000	P	475	2.0
Guy F. Atkinson Co.	1001 Bayhill Dr	San Bruno	CA	94066	Jack J Agresti	415-876-1000	P	468	1.1
Titan Industrial Corp.	555 Madison Ave	New York	NY	10022	Michael S Levin	212-421-6700	R	450	0.2
Hanwa American Corp.	750 3rd Ave	New York	NY	10017	T Kamoto	212-867-3160	S	441	0.1
Nomura America Corp.	60 E 42nd St	New York	NY	10165	Masami Ikeuchi	212-867-6684	S	422 *	<0.1
Familian Northwest Inc.	PO Box 17098	Portland	OR	97217	Tom Stern	503-283-3333	S	420 *	1.2
Feralloy Corp.	8755 W Higgins Rd	Chicago	IL	60631	Frank M Walker	312-380-1500	S	390	0.5
Gibraltar Steel Corp.	PO Box 2028	Buffalo	NY	14219	Brian J Lipke	716-826-6500	P	343	0.9
Ziegler Steel Service Corp.	7000 Van Dini Blvd	Los Angeles	CA	90040	GH Ziegler	213-726-7000	R	330 *	0.5
Ferro Union Inc.	1000 W Francisco	Torrance	CA	90502	S W Scheinkman	310-538-9900	S	300	0.4
Vinson Supply Co.	PO Box 702440	Tulsa	OK	74170	Robert C Mellor	918-481-8770	S	300	0.5
New Process Steel Corp.	5800 Westview Dr	Houston	TX	77055	Eugene R Fant	713-686-9631	R	290 *	0.4
Crucible Service Centers	5639 W Genesee St	Camillus	NY	13031	Harry O'Brien	315-487-0800	D	282 *	0.4
Blue Tee Corp.	250 Park Ave S	New York	NY	10003	Richard Secrist	212-598-0880	R	250 *	0.9
Southwestern Ohio Steel Inc.	PO Box 148	Hamilton	OH	45012	Jacque R Huber	513-896-2700	S	250	0.5
Marmon/Keystone Corp.	PO Box 992	Butler	PA	16001	N E Gottschalk Jr	412-283-3000	S	235	1.1
Nippon Steel U.S.A. Inc.	10 E 50th St	New York	NY	10022	Hiroshi Suetsugu	212-486-7150	S	230 *	<0.1
Kataman Metals Inc.	770 Bonhomme St	St. Louis	MO	63105	Warren J Gelman	314-863-6699	R	228 *	<0.1
L.B. Foster Co.	415 Holiday Dr	Pittsburgh	PA	15220	Lee B Foster II	412-928-3417	P	220	0.5
AFCO Metals Inc.	PO Box 95010	Little Rock	AR	72295	Steve Makarewicz	501-490-2255	S	220	0.3
Naporano Iron and Metal Co.	PO Box 5158	Newark	NJ	07105	Joseph Naporano	201-344-4570	R	220	0.3

Source: *Ward's Business Directory of U.S. Private and Public Companies*, 1998. The company type code used is as follows: P - Public, R - Private, S - Subsidiary, D - Division, J - Joint Venture, A - Affiliate, G - Group. Sales are in millions of dollars, employees are in thousands. An asterisk (*) indicates an estimated sales volume. The symbol < stands for 'less than'.

OCCUPATIONS EMPLOYED BY SIC 505 - WHOLESALE TRADE, OTHER

Occupation	% of Total 1996	Change to 2006	Occupation	% of Total 1996	Change to 2006
Sales & related workers nec	19.5	20.2	Clerical supervisors & managers	1.9	20.2
General managers & top executives	5.9	16.4	Order clerks	1.9	8.2
Truck drivers light & heavy	5.4	20.2	Helpers, laborers nec	1.7	20.2
General office clerks	3.6	3.4	Electrical & electronic technicians	1.4	18.8
Traffic, shipping, receiving clerks	3.6	16.7	Blue collar worker supervisors	1.4	16.0
Stock clerks	3.5	-3.9	Wholesale & retail buyers, except farm products	1.3	17.0
Freight, stock, & material movers, hand	3.3	8.2	Office machine & cash register servicers	1.3	20.2
Marketing & sales worker supervisors	3.1	20.2	Hand packers & packagers	1.2	-3.9
Order fillers, wholesale & retail sales	3.0	16.7	Maintenance repairers, general utility	1.1	12.0
Bookkeeping, accounting, & auditing clerks	2.9	-3.9	Industrial truck & tractor operators	1.1	20.2
Salespersons, retail	2.5	20.2	Purchasing managers	1.1	20.2
Secretaries, except legal & medical	2.5	-4.7	Receptionists & information clerks	1.0	20.2
Assemblers, fabricators, hand workers nec	2.0	-3.9			

Source: *Industry-Occupation Matrix*, Bureau of Labor Statistics. These data relate to one or more 3-digit SIC industry groups rather than to a single 4-digit SIC. The change reported for each occupation to the year 2006 is a percent of growth or decline as estimated by the Bureau of Labor Statistics. The abbreviation nec stands for 'not elsewhere classified'.

STATE AND REGIONAL CONCENTRATION

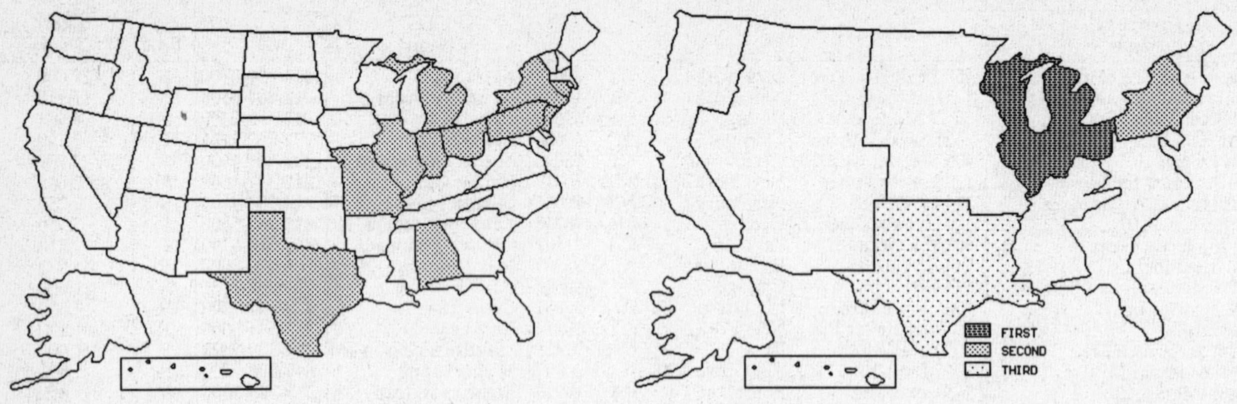

INDUSTRY DATA BY STATE

State	Establishments - 1995 Total (number)	Establishments - 1995 % of U.S.	Employment - 1995 Total (number)	Employment - 1995 % of U.S.	Employment - 1995 Per Estab.	Payroll - 1995 Total ($ mil.)	Payroll - 1995 Per Empl. ($)	Sales - 1992 Total ($ mil.)	Sales - 1992 % of U.S.	Sales - 1992 Per Estab ($)
Illinois	808	7.8	16,592	11.4	21	658.5	39,686	13,444.4	14.1	905,833
New York	636	6.2	7,378	5.1	12	382.0	51,772	11,623.1	12.2	1,765,088
Michigan	562	5.4	9,371	6.4	17	405.4	43,264	10,180.4	10.7	1,303,842
Texas	1,001	9.7	12,211	8.4	12	470.2	38,504	8,504.2	8.9	747,360
California	1,006	9.7	14,127	9.7	14	550.3	38,955	8,153.8	8.5	596,172
Pennsylvania	589	5.7	8,065	5.5	14	336.3	41,695	7,513.5	7.9	963,640
Ohio	716	6.9	11,773	8.1	16	446.5	37,923	7,440.1	7.8	727,278
New Jersey	446	4.3	4,971	3.4	11	225.3	45,318	5,345.5	5.6	1,072,095
Missouri	289	2.8	3,771	2.6	13	138.8	36,812	3,272.1	3.4	949,541
Connecticut	178	1.7	2,141	1.5	12	109.0	50,909	2,807.2	2.9	1,420,649
Indiana	261	2.5	5,064	3.5	19	165.6	32,700	2,389.7	2.5	649,207
Alabama	185	1.8	3,634	2.5	20	121.3	33,369	1,929.2	2.0	558,688
Tennessee	193	1.9	3,246	2.2	17	109.3	33,668	1,816.0	1.9	666,183
Maryland	110	1.1	1,594	1.1	14	55.6	34,875	1,493.7	1.6	844,878
Kentucky	113	1.1	1,330	0.9	12	42.4	31,883	1,305.0	1.4	976,810
Wisconsin	181	1.8	2,135	1.5	12	77.9	36,467	1,110.0	1.2	587,621
North Carolina	205	2.0	2,906	2.0	14	103.8	35,731	1,082.4	1.1	413,133
Oklahoma	153	1.5	1,986	1.4	13	61.0	30,708	906.2	0.9	539,088
Colorado	131	1.3	1,871	1.3	14	59.8	31,956	884.3	0.9	591,873
Louisiana	162	1.6	2,028	1.4	13	63.2	31,184	749.0	0.8	386,456
Virginia	101	1.0	1,475	1.0	15	61.0	41,371	716.5	0.8	491,066
Kansas	80	0.8	1,022	0.7	13	30.4	29,720	695.3	0.7	832,638
Oregon	98	0.9	1,764	1.2	18	60.7	34,430	626.6	0.7	363,007
Iowa	75	0.7	1,115	0.8	15	36.6	32,850	367.2	0.4	411,253
South Carolina	88	0.9	1,033	0.7	12	32.9	31,817	341.6	0.4	365,309
Utah	63	0.6	893	0.6	14	25.0	27,992	254.8	0.3	378,096
Nebraska	36	0.3	480	0.3	13	13.1	27,358	171.8	0.2	445,197
Delaware	17	0.2	299	0.2	18	9.5	31,692	141.1	0.1	626,973
West Virginia	30	0.3	339	0.2	11	9.0	26,640	120.3	0.1	315,753
Hawaii	22	0.2	215	0.1	10	7.6	35,265	82.0	0.1	347,407
Maine	14	0.1	100-249	-	-	(D)	-	46.7	0.0	240,495
South Dakota	6	0.1	20-99	-	-	(D)	-	8.9	0.0	444,850
Florida	469	4.5	4,329	3.0	9	143.3	33,109	(D)	-	-
Georgia	282	2.7	4,002	2.7	14	144.5	36,110	(D)	-	-
Massachusetts	206	2.0	2,643	1.8	13	102.0	38,599	(D)	-	-
Washington	192	1.9	2,556	1.8	13	87.8	34,343	(D)	-	-
Minnesota	160	1.5	2,961	2.0	19	113.7	38,415	(D)	-	-
Arizona	115	1.1	1,096	0.8	10	32.3	29,431	(D)	-	-
Arkansas	61	0.6	915	0.6	15	26.4	28,901	(D)	-	-
Mississippi	53	0.5	790	0.5	15	22.5	28,447	(D)	-	-
Rhode Island	37	0.4	567	0.4	15	17.0	30,046	(D)	-	-
New Mexico	35	0.3	250-499	-	-	(D)	-	(D)	-	-
New Hampshire	33	0.3	310	0.2	9	13.1	42,403	(D)	-	-
Idaho	31	0.3	284	0.2	9	6.8	24,077	(D)	-	-
Montana	26	0.3	339	0.2	13	7.0	20,617	(D)	-	-
Nevada	23	0.2	242	0.2	11	10.0	41,145	(D)	-	-
Wyoming	20	0.2	161	0.1	8	4.1	25,596	(D)	-	-
Alaska	14	0.1	20-99	-	-	(D)	-	(D)	-	-
Vermont	14	0.1	100-249	-	-	(D)	-	(D)	-	-
North Dakota	5	0.0	20-99	-	-	(D)	-	(D)	-	-

Source: County Business Patterns, 1995 and *Economic Census of the U.S., 1992*. Data are sorted by 1992 revenues and, if revenues are unavailable, by establishments in 1995. The symbol (D) indicates that data are withheld by the source to avoid disclosure of competitive information. A dash (-) indicates that data are not available or undisclosed because they do not meet statistical validity standards. Shaded *states* on the state map indicate those states which have proportionately greater representation in the industry than would be indicated by the state's population; the ratio is based on total revenues or number of establishments. Shaded *regions* indicate where the industry is regionally most concentrated.

5052 - COAL AND OTHER MINERALS AND ORES

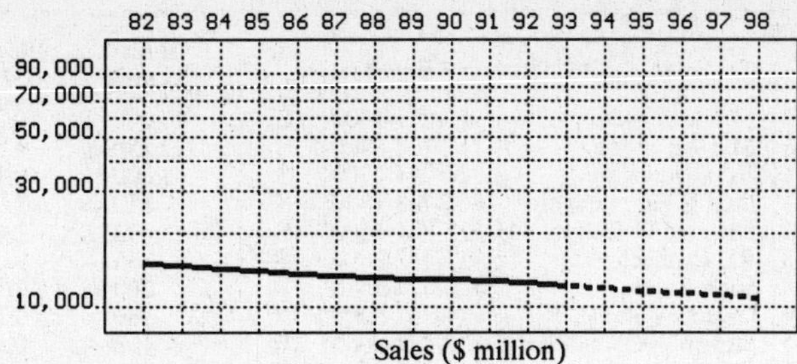

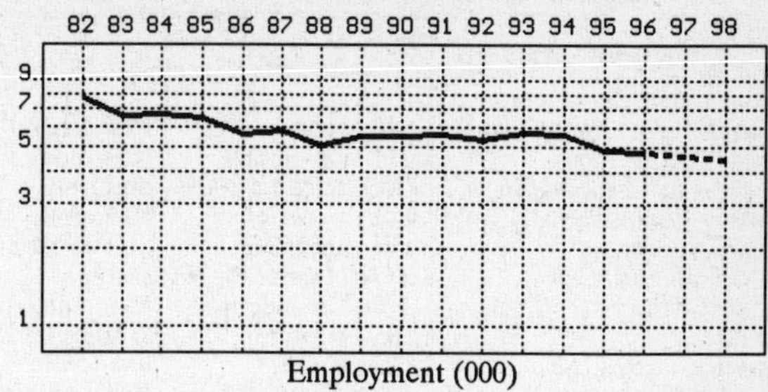

GENERAL STATISTICS

Year	Establishments (number)	Employment (number)	Payroll ($ million)	Sales ($ million)	Expenses ($ million)	Beginning Inventory ($ million)	Ending Inventory ($ million)
1982	942	7,674	203.2	14,925.7	-	-	-
1983	824	6,569	193.6	14,617.5e	-	-	-
1984	805	6,706	199.4	14,309.2e	-	-	-
1985	740	6,421	204.8	14,001.0e	-	-	-
1986	681	5,629	179.8	13,692.7e	-	-	-
1987	812	5,766	184.1	13,384.4	424.9	210.7	209.9
1988	722	5,051	187.2	13,205.1e	449.0e	273.7e	268.4e
1989	703	5,470	209.1	13,025.8e	473.1e	336.8e	326.9e
1990	679	5,487	217.3	12,846.5e	497.2e	399.8e	385.4e
1991	667	5,565	225.6	12,667.2e	521.4e	462.8e	443.9e
1992	822	5,301	225.6	12,487.9	545.5	525.8	502.5
1993	802	5,723	248.4	12,097.6p	569.6p	588.8p	561.0p
1994	766	5,557	239.3	11,853.8p	593.8p	651.9p	619.5p
1995	720	4,817	227.9	11,610.0p	617.9p	714.9p	678.0p
1996	706p	4,755p	239.4p	11,366.2p	642.0p	777.9p	736.5p
1997	698p	4,611p	243.3p	11,122.4p	666.1p	840.9p	795.0p
1998	691p	4,467p	247.1p	10,878.7p	690.3p	904.0p	853.5p

Sources: Economic Census of the United States, 1982, 1987, and 1992. Establishment counts, employment, and payroll are from *County Business Patterns* for non-Census years. Values followed by a 'p' are projections by the editors. Sales and expense data for non-Census years are extrapolations, marked by 'e'. Industries reclassified in 1987 will not have data for prior years. Data are the most recent available at this level of detail.

INDICES OF CHANGE

Year	Establishments (number)	Employment (number)	Payroll ($ million)	Sales ($ million)	Expenses ($ million)	Beginning Inventory ($ million)	Ending Inventory ($ million)
1982	114.6	144.8	90.1	119.5	-	-	-
1983	100.2	123.9	85.8	117.1e	-	-	-
1984	97.9	126.5	88.4	114.6e	-	-	-
1985	90.0	121.1	90.8	112.1e	-	-	-
1986	82.8	106.2	79.7	109.6e	-	-	-
1987	98.8	108.8	81.6	107.2	77.9	40.1	41.8
1988	87.8	95.3	83.0	105.7e	82.3e	52.1e	53.4e
1989	85.5	103.2	92.7	104.3e	86.7e	64.1e	65.1e
1990	82.6	103.5	96.3	102.9e	91.1e	76.0e	76.7e
1991	81.1	105.0	100.0	101.4e	95.6e	88.0e	88.3e
1992	100.0	100.0	100.0	100.0	100.0	100.0	100.0
1993	97.6	108.0	110.1	96.9p	104.4p	112.0p	111.6p
1994	93.2	104.8	106.1	94.9p	108.9p	124.0p	123.3p
1995	87.6	90.9	101.0	93.0p	113.3p	136.0p	134.9p
1996	85.9p	89.7p	106.1p	91.0p	117.7p	147.9p	146.6p
1997	85.0p	87.0p	107.8p	89.1p	122.1p	159.9p	158.2p
1998	84.0p	84.3p	109.5p	87.1p	126.5p	171.9p	169.9p

Sources: Same as General Statistics. The values shown reflect change from the base year, 1992. Values above 100 mean greater than 1992, values below 100 mean less than 1992, and a value of 100 in the 1982-91 or 1993-98 period means same as 1992. Values followed by a 'p' are projections by the editors; 'e' stands for extrapolation. Data are the most recent available at this level of detail.

SELECTED RATIOS

For 1992	Avg. of All Wholesale	Analyzed Industry	Index	For 1992	Avg. of All Wholesale	Analyzed Industry	Index
Employees per Establishment	12	6	55	Sales per Employee	561,172	2,355,763	420
Payroll per Establishment	349,729	274,453	78	Sales per Establishment	6,559,346	15,192,092	232
Payroll per Employee	29,919	42,558	142	Expenses per Establishment	723,071	663,625	92

Sources: Same as General Statistics. The 'Average of All Manufacturing' column represents the average of all manufacturing industries reported for the most recent complete year available. The Index shows the relationship between the Average and the Analyzed Industry. For example, 100 means that they are equal; 500 that the Analyzed Industry is five times the average; 50 means that the Analyzed Industry is half the national average. The abbreviation 'na' is used to show that data are 'not available'.

LEADING COMPANIES

Number shown: **38** Total sales ($ mil): **16,607** Total employment (000): **8.0**

Company Name	Address				CEO Name	Phone	Co. Type	Sales ($ mil)	Empl. (000)
Mitsubishi International Corp.	520 Madison Ave	New York	NY	10022	M Numaguchi	212-605-2000	S	10,000	0.7
Kanematsu U.S.A. Inc.	114 W 47th St	New York	NY	10036	Minoru Inoue	212-704-9400	S	2,250	1.0
Arch Coal Sales Company Inc.	City Place 1,e 300	St. Louis	MO	63141	John Eaves	314-994-2700	S	1,000	<0.1
A.T. Massey Coal Company	PO Box 26765	Richmond	VA	23261	Don L Blankenship	804-788-1800	S	850	2.0
Electric Fuels Corp.	PO Box 15208	St. Petersburg	FL	33733	Richard D Keller	813-824-6600	S	643*	1.4
Hickman, Williams and Co.	17370 Laurel Pk N	Livonia	MI	48152	RL Damschroder	313-462-1890	R	286	0.2
Anker Energy Corp.	2708 Cranberry Sq	Morgantown	WV	26505	John Faltis	304-594-1616	R	200	<0.1
Asoma Corp.	105 Corporate Pk	White Plains	NY	10604	Glenn W Peel	914-251-5400	R	180	<0.1
American Resources Inc.	PO Box 592	Evansville	IN	47704	Steven E Chancellor	812-424-9000	R	153	0.5
Westmoreland Coal Sales Co.	200 S Broad St	Philadelphia	PA	19102	R Page Henley Jr	215-545-2500	S	111	<0.1
ANR Coal Company L.L.C.	PO Box 1871	Roanoke	VA	24008	James Van Lanen	540-983-0222	S	100*	0.4
Connell Brothers Company Ltd.	320 California St	San Francisco	CA	94104	Frank M Brown	415-772-4000	S	90	0.2
Holmes Limestone Co.	PO Box 295	Berlin	OH	44610	Merle Mulet	216-893-2721	R	80*	0.1
Rosebud Coal Sales Co.	1000 Kiewit Plz	Omaha	NE	68131	Bruce Grewcock	402-342-2052	D	80	0.1
Alley-Cassetty Coal Co.	PO Box 23305	Nashville	TN	37202	Fred Cassetty	615-244-7077	R	53	0.2
Transocean Coal Company L.P.	599 Lexington Ave	New York	NY	10022	Lawrence Perlstein	212-370-3600	R	50	<0.1
United Eastern Coal Sales Corp.	PO Box 729	Indiana	PA	15701	Mark A Stefanov	412-349-6254	S	50	<0.1
Alabama Coal Cooperative	2870 Rocky Ridge	Birmingham	AL	35243	Randy C Johnson	205-979-5963	R	45	0.5
Peabody COALSALES Co.	701 Market St	St. Louis	MO	63101	Richard A Navarre	314-342-7600	S	43*	<0.1
ITC Inc.	PO Box 20191	Baltimore	MD	21284	Harold T Rubin	410-825-2920	R	37	<0.1
Ambrose Branch Coal Company	PO Box 806	Pound	VA	24279	Paul R Ison	703-796-4941	R	32*	<0.1
F and S Alloys and Minerals	605 3rd Ave	New York	NY	10158	Roger Engel	212-490-1356	S	31	<0.1
H.M. Royal Inc.	PO Box 28	Trenton	NJ	08601	HL Boyer Royal	609-396-9176	R	31*	<0.1
G and B Oil Company Inc.	PO Box 811	Elkin	NC	28621	Jeffery C Eidson	910-835-3607	R	30	0.1
Emerald International Corp.	7310 Turfway Rd	Florence	KY	41042	Jack J Wells Jr	606-525-2522	R	26	<0.1
Summers Fuel Inc.	28 Allegheny Ave	Baltimore	MD	21204	W N Clements II	410-825-8555	R	25	<0.1
Hawley Fuel Coal Inc.	Empireate 8004	New York	NY	10118	Jean P Ruff	212-279-1212	R	24*	<0.1
Whittaker, Clark and Daniels	1000 Coolidge St	S. Plainfield	NJ	07080	George Dippold	908-561-6100	R	23	0.1
Lambert Coal Company Inc.	PO Box 394	Nora	VA	24272	AJ Lambert	703-835-8666	R	21*	<0.1
Manhattan Brass and Copper	PO Box 780145	Maspeth	NY	11378	Mark Bernstein	718-381-5300	R	20	<0.1
River Trading Co.	3300 Bass Lake Rd	Brooklyn Ctr	MN	55429	Tom Conlan	612-561-9206	R	11*	<0.1
Transco Resources Inc.	1458 Miamisburg	Dayton	OH	45458	William J Little	513-436-0082	R	11	<0.1
James River Coal Sales Inc.	701 E Byrd St	Richmond	VA	23219	James B Crawford	804-780-3003	S	6	<0.1
Amvest Coal Sales Inc.	PO Box 5347	Charlottesville	VA	22905	William H Dickey Jr	804-977-3350	S	5	<0.1
Hydro Magnesium	21644 Melrose Ave	Southfield	MI	48075	Darryl L Albright	810-353-2629	S	4*	<0.1
Stinnes Intercoal Inc.	605 3rd Ave	New York	NY	10158	Jurgen Lorenz	212-986-1515	S	4*	<0.1
Coors Energy Co.	PO Box 467	Golden	CO	80402	D W MacDonald	303-277-6042	S	1	<0.1
General Oil Corp.	6850 Heckinger Dr	Springfield	VA	22151	George H Starke Jr	703-642-6769	R	1	<0.1

Source: *Ward's Business Directory of U.S. Private and Public Companies*, 1998. The company type code used is as follows: P - Public, R - Private, S - Subsidiary, D - Division, J - Joint Venture, A - Affiliate, G - Group. Sales are in millions of dollars, employees are in thousands. An asterisk (*) indicates an estimated sales volume. The symbol < stands for 'less than'.

OCCUPATIONS EMPLOYED BY SIC 505 - WHOLESALE TRADE, OTHER

Occupation	% of Total 1996	Change to 2006	Occupation	% of Total 1996	Change to 2006
Sales & related workers nec	19.5	20.2	Clerical supervisors & managers	1.9	20.2
General managers & top executives	5.9	16.4	Order clerks	1.9	8.2
Truck drivers light & heavy	5.4	20.2	Helpers, laborers nec	1.7	20.2
General office clerks	3.6	3.4	Electrical & electronic technicians	1.4	18.8
Traffic, shipping, receiving clerks	3.6	16.7	Blue collar worker supervisors	1.4	16.0
Stock clerks	3.5	-3.9	Wholesale & retail buyers, except farm products	1.3	17.0
Freight, stock, & material movers, hand	3.3	8.2	Office machine & cash register servicers	1.3	20.2
Marketing & sales worker supervisors	3.1	20.2	Hand packers & packagers	1.2	-3.9
Order fillers, wholesale & retail sales	3.0	16.7	Maintenance repairers, general utility	1.1	12.0
Bookkeeping, accounting, & auditing clerks	2.9	-3.9	Industrial truck & tractor operators	1.1	20.2
Salespersons, retail	2.5	20.2	Purchasing managers	1.1	20.2
Secretaries, except legal & medical	2.5	-4.7	Receptionists & information clerks	1.0	20.2
Assemblers, fabricators, hand workers nec	2.0	-3.9			

Source: *Industry-Occupation Matrix*, Bureau of Labor Statistics. These data relate to one or more 3-digit SIC industry groups rather than to a single 4-digit SIC. The change reported for each occupation to the year 2006 is a percent of growth or decline as estimated by the Bureau of Labor Statistics. The abbreviation nec stands for 'not elsewhere classified'.

STATE AND REGIONAL CONCENTRATION

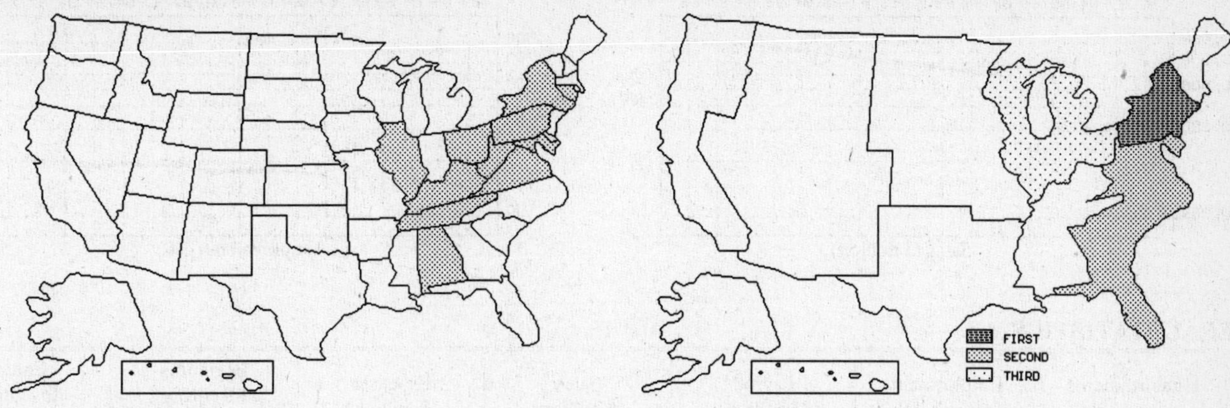

INDUSTRY DATA BY STATE

State	Establishments - 1995 Total (number)	Establishments - 1995 % of U.S.	Employment - 1995 Total (number)	Employment - 1995 % of U.S.	Employment - 1995 Per Estab.	Payroll - 1995 Total ($ mil.)	Payroll - 1995 Per Empl. ($)	Sales - 1992 Total ($ mil.)	Sales - 1992 % of U.S.	Sales - 1992 Per Estab ($)
Pennsylvania	100	13.9	660	14.2	7	23.0	34,917	1,695.5	15.0	2,140,837
New York	61	8.5	461	9.9	8	29.4	63,870	1,465.4	12.9	3,072,140
Virginia	44	6.1	212	4.6	5	12.7	60,009	1,368.8	12.1	4,318,060
Ohio	47	6.5	334	7.2	7	16.8	50,422	971.4	8.6	3,184,866
California	24	3.3	138	3.0	6	9.0	65,304	897.7	7.9	5,541,198
West Virginia	36	5.0	356	7.6	10	13.6	38,154	689.9	6.1	2,218,293
Tennessee	38	5.3	226	4.9	6	12.5	55,372	642.1	5.7	2,334,985
Illinois	23	3.2	206	4.4	9	12.4	60,277	599.2	5.3	2,261,309
Connecticut	13	1.8	85	1.8	7	7.9	92,671	509.2	4.5	6,134,639
Kentucky	75	10.4	352	7.6	5	12.1	34,494	503.8	4.5	1,339,763
Texas	21	2.9	128	2.7	6	5.4	42,281	336.8	3.0	1,216,000
Michigan	8	1.1	72	1.5	9	3.4	47,028	280.8	2.5	2,576,183
New Jersey	19	2.6	130	2.8	7	8.4	64,346	248.4	2.2	2,299,667
Alabama	24	3.3	130	2.8	5	4.8	36,554	233.7	2.1	2,225,867
Maryland	15	2.1	216	4.6	14	13.9	64,361	229.7	2.0	1,184,021
Missouri	9	1.3	35	0.8	4	3.2	91,429	114.3	1.0	1,242,446
North Carolina	8	1.1	23	0.5	3	1.2	50,478	108.1	1.0	2,921,189
Indiana	17	2.4	62	1.3	4	2.4	39,452	107.6	1.0	1,415,171
Utah	7	1.0	90	1.9	13	4.1	45,456	80.4	0.7	692,672
Colorado	11	1.5	52	1.1	5	2.1	41,308	66.1	0.6	1,468,911
Wisconsin	11	1.5	66	1.4	6	2.4	36,000	61.5	0.5	1,098,964
Louisiana	12	1.7	100-249	-	-	(D)	-	37.8	0.3	275,591
Oregon	4	0.6	14	0.3	4	0.7	46,571	24.5	0.2	3,497,714
South Carolina	7	1.0	20	0.4	3	0.7	37,000	23.8	0.2	1,254,737
Oklahoma	2	0.3	0-19	-	-	(D)	-	11.3	0.1	663,882
Kansas	2	0.3	0-19	-	-	(D)	-	9.7	0.1	1,082,000
Florida	16	2.2	77	1.7	5	3.3	43,169	(D)	-	-
Georgia	12	1.7	137	2.9	11	4.7	34,131	(D)	-	-
Arizona	10	1.4	117	2.5	12	3.7	31,726	(D)	-	-
Minnesota	6	0.8	29	0.6	5	1.0	36,138	(D)	-	-
Massachusetts	5	0.7	23	0.5	5	1.5	63,870	(D)	-	-
Washington	5	0.7	22	0.5	4	1.1	48,227	(D)	-	-
Wyoming	5	0.7	30	0.6	6	0.6	21,100	(D)	-	-
Arkansas	4	0.6	18	0.4	5	0.5	29,111	(D)	-	-
Alaska	3	0.4	0-19	-	-	(D)	-	(D)	-	-
Montana	3	0.4	5	0.1	2	0.1	16,600	(D)	-	-
Rhode Island	3	0.4	132	2.8	44	2.6	19,780	(D)	-	-
Nevada	2	0.3	0-19	-	-	(D)	-	(D)	-	-
New Mexico	2	0.3	0-19	-	-	(D)	-	(D)	-	-
D.C.	1	0.1	0-19	-	-	(D)	-	(D)	-	-
Maine	1	0.1	0-19	-	-	(D)	-	-	-	-
Nebraska	1	0.1	0-19	-	-	(D)	-	-	-	-
New Hampshire	1	0.1	0-19	-	-	(D)	-	(D)	-	-
North Dakota	1	0.1	0-19	-	-	(D)	-	(D)	-	-
Vermont	1	0.1	0-19	-	-	(D)	-	(D)	-	-

Source: County Business Patterns, 1995 and *Economic Census of the U.S., 1992*. Data are sorted by 1992 revenues and, if revenues are unavailable, by establishments in 1995. The symbol (D) indicates that data are withheld by the source to avoid disclosure of competitive information. A dash (-) indicates that data are not available or undisclosed because they do not meet statistical validity standards. Shaded *states* on the state map indicate those states which have proportionately greater representation in the industry than would be indicated by the state's population; the ratio is based on total revenues or number of establishments. Shaded *regions* indicate where the industry is regionally most concentrated.

5063 - ELECTRICAL APPARATUS AND EQUIPMENT

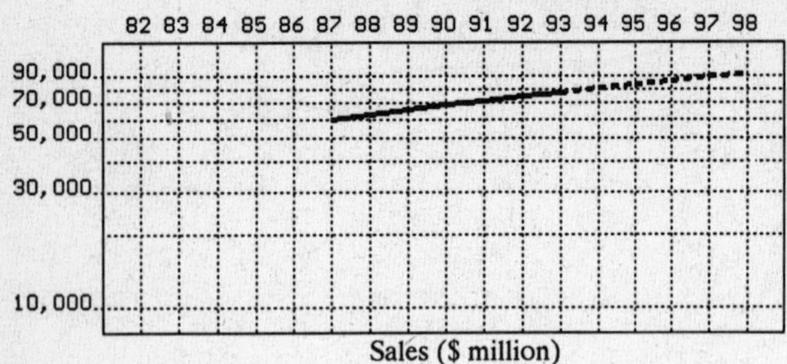

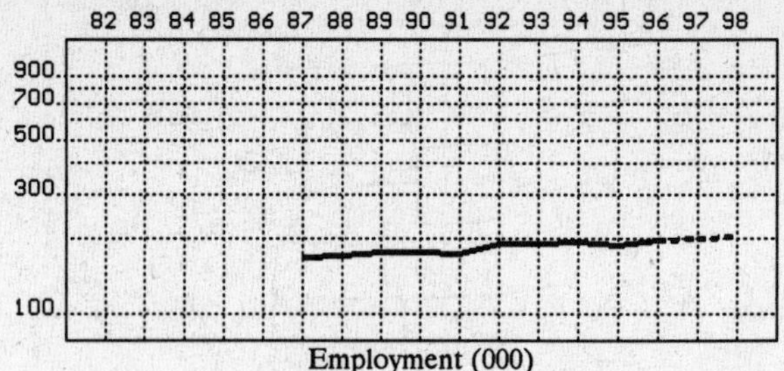

GENERAL STATISTICS

Year	Establishments (number)	Employment (number)	Payroll ($ million)	Sales ($ million)	Expenses ($ million)	Beginning Inventory ($ million)	Ending Inventory ($ million)
1982	-	-	-	-	-	-	-
1983	-	-	-	-	-	-	-
1984	-	-	-	-	-	-	-
1985	-	-	-	-	-	-	-
1986	-	-	-	-	-	-	-
1987	15,045	167,809	4,299.1	59,389.0	8,179.6	4,285.8	4,675.8
1988	14,632	169,959	4,704.4	62,459.2e	8,784.1e	4,633.6e	4,968.4e
1989	14,511	176,561	5,117.2	65,529.5e	9,388.7e	4,981.5e	5,261.0e
1990	14,824	175,660	5,243.8	68,599.7e	9,993.2e	5,329.4e	5,553.6e
1991	14,895	171,817	5,109.0	71,669.9e	10,597.7e	5,677.3e	5,846.2e
1992	18,511	190,238	6,094.1	74,740.1	11,202.3	6,025.2	6,138.8
1993	18,350	191,633	6,496.9	77,810.4p	11,806.8p	6,373.0p	6,431.4p
1994	18,264	195,300	6,918.1	80,880.6p	12,411.4p	6,720.9p	6,724.0p
1995	16,576	189,019	7,077.9	83,950.8p	13,015.9p	7,068.8p	7,016.6p
1996	18,544p	198,021p	7,453.9p	87,021.1p	13,620.5p	7,416.7p	7,309.2p
1997	19,017p	201,447p	7,810.0p	90,091.3p	14,225.0p	7,764.6p	7,601.8p
1998	19,490p	204,873p	8,166.1p	93,161.5p	14,829.5p	8,112.4p	7,894.4p

Sources: Economic Census of the United States, 1982, 1987, and 1992. Establishment counts, employment, and payroll are from *County Business Patterns* for non-Census years. Values followed by a 'p' are projections by the editors. Sales and expense data for non-Census years are extrapolations, marked by 'e'. Industries reclassified in 1987 will not have data for prior years. Data are the most recent available at this level of detail.

INDICES OF CHANGE

Year	Establishments (number)	Employment (number)	Payroll ($ million)	Sales ($ million)	Expenses ($ million)	Beginning Inventory ($ million)	Ending Inventory ($ million)
1982	-	-	-	-	-	-	-
1983	-	-	-	-	-	-	-
1984	-	-	-	-	-	-	-
1985	-	-	-	-	-	-	-
1986	-	-	-	-	-	-	-
1987	81.3	88.2	70.5	79.5	73.0	71.1	76.2
1988	79.0	89.3	77.2	83.6e	78.4e	76.9e	80.9e
1989	78.4	92.8	84.0	87.7e	83.8e	82.7e	85.7e
1990	80.1	92.3	86.0	91.8e	89.2e	88.5e	90.5e
1991	80.5	90.3	83.8	95.9e	94.6e	94.2e	95.2e
1992	100.0	100.0	100.0	100.0	100.0	100.0	100.0
1993	99.1	100.7	106.6	104.1p	105.4p	105.8p	104.8p
1994	98.7	102.7	113.5	108.2p	110.8p	111.5p	109.5p
1995	89.5	99.4	116.1	112.3p	116.2p	117.3p	114.3p
1996	100.2p	104.1p	122.3p	116.4p	121.6p	123.1p	119.1p
1997	102.7p	105.9p	128.2p	120.5p	127.0p	128.9p	123.8p
1998	105.3p	107.7p	134.0p	124.6p	132.4p	134.6p	128.6p

Sources: Same as General Statistics. The values shown reflect change from the base year, 1992. Values above 100 mean greater than 1992, values below 100 mean less than 1992, and a value of 100 in the 1982-91 or 1993-98 period means same as 1992. Values followed by a 'p' are projections by the editors; 'e' stands for extrapolation. Data are the most recent available at this level of detail.

SELECTED RATIOS

For 1992	Avg. of All Wholesale	Analyzed Industry	Index	For 1992	Avg. of All Wholesale	Analyzed Industry	Index
Employees per Establishment	12	10	88	Sales per Employee	561,172	392,877	70
Payroll per Establishment	349,729	329,215	94	Sales per Establishment	6,559,346	4,037,605	62
Payroll per Employee	29,919	32,034	107	Expenses per Establishment	723,071	605,170	84

Sources: Same as General Statistics. The 'Average of All Manufacturing' column represents the average of all manufacturing industries reported for the most recent complete year available. The Index shows the relationship between the Average and the Analyzed Industry. For example, 100 means that they are equal; 500 that the Analyzed Industry is five times the average; 50 means that the Analyzed Industry is half the national average. The abbreviation 'na' is used to show that data are 'not available'.

LEADING COMPANIES Number shown: 50 Total sales ($ mil): 32,957 Total employment (000): 82.5

Company Name	Address				CEO Name	Phone	Co. Type	Sales ($ mil)	Empl. (000)
Arrow Electronics Inc.	25 Hub Dr	Melville	NY	11747	Stephen P Kaufman	516-391-1300	P	7,001	9.0
W.W. Grainger Inc.	455 Knightsbridge	Lincolnshire	IL	60069	Richard L Keyser	847-793-9030	P	4,137	14.6
Anixter International Inc.	4711 Golf Rd	Skokie	IL	60076	Robert W Grubbs	847-677-2600	P	2,805	6.3
WESCO Distribution Inc.	4 Station Sq	Pittsburgh	PA	15219	Roy W Haley	412-454-2000	R	2,500 *	4.5
ESSROC Corp.	3251 Bath Pike Rd	Nazareth	PA	18064	Robert Rayner	610-837-6725	R	1,880 *	10.0
Marshall Industries	9320 Telstar Ave	El Monte	CA	91731	Robert Rodin	818-307-6000	P	1,185	1.4
GE Supply	2 Corporate Dr	Shelton	CT	06484	WL Meddaugh	203-944-3000	D	1,100 *	2.2
Hughes Supply Inc.	PO Box 2273	Orlando	FL	32802	David H Hughes	407-841-4755	P	1,082	3.3
Hardware Wholesalers Inc.	PO Box 868	Fort Wayne	IN	46801	Michael McClelland	219-748-5300	R	1,000	1.1
Summers Group Inc.	PO Box 1085	Addison	TX	75001	Joe Hassell	972-387-3600	S	650	1.5
Consolidated Electrical	31356 Via Colinas	Westlake Vill.	CA	91362	Keith W Colburn	818-991-9000	R	640 *	2.5
Audiovox Corp.	150 Marcus Blvd	Hauppauge	NY	11788	John J Shalam	516-231-7750	P	603	1.0
All-Phase Electric Supply Co.	875 Riverview Dr	Benton Harbor	MI	49022	Ken Renwick	616-926-0504	R	550 *	1.8
Builder Marts of America Inc.	PO Box 47	Greenville	SC	29602	Brian S MacKenzie	864-297-6101	R	547	0.1
Primus Inc.	3110 Kettering Blvd	Dayton	OH	45439	Richard F Schiewetz	513-294-6878	R	530	2.0
Cresent Electric Supply Co.	PO Box 500	East Dubuque	IL	61025		815-747-3145	R	450	1.5
Electrical Insulation Suppliers	1255 Collier NW	Atlanta	GA	30318	Steve Kendall	404-355-1651	R	440	1.0
Fastenal Co.	2001 Theurer Blvd	Winona	MN	55987	Robert A Kierlin	507-454-5374	P	398	3.1
Willcox & Gibbs	7000 NW 52nd St	Miami	FL	33166	Pete Schiller	407-841-4860	D	360	1.1
Mayer Electrical Supply Co.	PO Box 1328	Birmingham	AL	35201	Charles A Collat Sr	205-583-3500	R	300	0.7
TDK Corporation of America	1600 Feehanville Dr	Mount Prospect	IL	60056	Mitsikuni Baba	847-803-6100	S	271 *	0.2
Kirby Risk Electrical Supply	PO Box 5089	Lafayette	IN	47903	JK Risk III	317-448-4567	R	270 *	0.9
Waxman Industries Inc.	24460 Aurora Rd	Bedford H.	OH	44146	Armond Waxman	216-439-1830	P	266	0.8
Border States Electric Supply	105 25th St, N	Fargo	ND	58102	Paul Madson	701-293-5834	D	260	0.6
Stuart C. Irby Co.	PO Box 1819	Jackson	MS	39215	Stuart M Irby	601-969-1811	R	237	0.6
Essex Brownell Div.	250 N Rte 303	Congers	NY	10920	Christopher Mapes	914-267-2700	D	230	0.5
Group One Capital Inc.	1611 Des Peres Rd	St. Louis	MO	63131	Bruce A Olson	314-821-5100	R	230 *	2.0
Platt Electric Supply Inc.	10605 SW Allen	Beaverton	OR	97005	Harvey J Platt	503-641-6121	R	210 *	0.8
McNaughton-McKay Electric	1357 E Lincoln Ave	Madison H.	MI	48071	William H Bull	810-399-7500	R	190	0.3
Cetron Communications Div.	40W267 Keslinger	Lafox	IL	60147	E J Richardson	630-208-3700	D	189 *	0.5
Branch Electric Supply Co.	1049 Pr Georges	Up Marlboro	MD	20772	John Richardson	301-249-5005	R	180 *	0.6
HWC Distribution Corp.	10201 N Loop E	Houston	TX	77028	Edward W Holland	713-609-2100	S	180	0.3
NRG Generating (U.S.) Inc.	1221 Nicollet Mall	Minneapolis	MN	55403	Leonard A Bluhm	612-373-5300	P	178	0.2
Houston Wire and Cable Co.	10201 N Loop E	Houston	TX	77028	E W Holland III	281-609-2200	S	160	0.3
Kendall Electric Inc.	131 Grand Trunk	Battle Creek	MI	49015	Axel Johnson	616-963-5585	R	150 *	0.5
Sager Electronics Inc.	60 Research Rd	Hingham	MA	02043	R P Norton III	617-749-6700	R	150	0.4
Silliter/Klebes Indust Supplies	13 Hamden Pk Dr	Hamden	CT	06517	Jay Drummond	203-497-1500	D	140 *	<0.1
Turtle and Hughes Inc.	1900 Lower Rd	Linden	NJ	07036	Susan T Millard	908-574-3600	R	140	0.2
Steiner Electric Co.	1250 Touhy Rd	Elk Grove Vill.	IL	60007	Harold M Kerman	708-228-0400	R	130 *	0.5
Anicom Inc.	6133 N River Rd	Rosemont	IL	60018	Scott C Anixter	847-518-8700	P	116	0.5
Southern Electric Supply	301 46th Ct	Meridian	MS	39301	Timothy Hogan	601-693-4141	S	110	0.3
Wholesale Electric Supply	PO Box 230197	Houston	TX	77223	Clyde G Rutland	713-748-6100	R	110 *	0.3
Cummins Southern Plains Inc.	600 Watson Dr	Arlington	TX	76004	RD Gillikin	817-640-6801	R	100	0.5
Hawthorne Machinery Inc.	PO Box 708	San Diego	CA	92112	Tom J Hawthorne	619-674-7000	R	100	0.3
Crystal Clear Industries Inc.	2 Bergen Tpk	Ridgefield Park	NJ	07660	Abraham Lefkowitz	201-440-4200	R	97	0.3
Summit Electric Supply Inc.	PO Box 6409	Albuquerque	NM	87197	Victor Jury Jr	505-884-4400	R	91 *	0.3
ESD Co.	7380 Convoy Court	San Diego	CA	92111	Alan Rosenfeld	619-636-4400	D	81	0.2
Resource Electronics Inc.	PO Box 408	Columbia	SC	29202	Roy B Reynolds	803-779-5332	S	80	0.2
State Electric Supply Co.	PO Box 5397	Huntington	WV	25703	John T Spoor	304-523-7491	S	77	0.3
Raub Supply Co.	301 W James St	Lancaster	PA	17604	Joseph C Schick	717-397-6221	R	75	0.3

Source: *Ward's Business Directory of U.S. Private and Public Companies*, 1998. The company type code used is as follows: P - Public, R - Private, S - Subsidiary, D - Division, J - Joint Venture, A - Affiliate, G - Group. Sales are in millions of dollars, employees are in thousands. An asterisk (*) indicates an estimated sales volume. The symbol < stands for 'less than'.

OCCUPATIONS EMPLOYED BY SIC 506 - WHOLESALE TRADE, OTHER

Occupation	% of Total 1996	Change to 2006	Occupation	% of Total 1996	Change to 2006
Sales & related workers nec	19.5	20.2	Clerical supervisors & managers	1.9	20.2
General managers & top executives	5.9	16.4	Order clerks	1.9	8.2
Truck drivers light & heavy	5.4	20.2	Helpers, laborers nec	1.7	20.2
General office clerks	3.6	3.4	Electrical & electronic technicians	1.4	18.8
Traffic, shipping, receiving clerks	3.6	16.7	Blue collar worker supervisors	1.4	16.0
Stock clerks	3.5	-3.9	Wholesale & retail buyers, except farm products	1.3	17.0
Freight, stock, & material movers, hand	3.3	8.2	Office machine & cash register servicers	1.3	20.2
Marketing & sales worker supervisors	3.1	20.2	Hand packers & packagers	1.2	-3.9
Order fillers, wholesale & retail sales	3.0	16.7	Maintenance repairers, general utility	1.1	12.0
Bookkeeping, accounting, & auditing clerks	2.9	-3.9	Industrial truck & tractor operators	1.1	20.2
Salespersons, retail	2.5	20.2	Purchasing managers	1.1	20.2
Secretaries, except legal & medical	2.5	-4.7	Receptionists & information clerks	1.0	20.2
Assemblers, fabricators, hand workers nec	2.0	-3.9			

Source: *Industry-Occupation Matrix*, Bureau of Labor Statistics. These data relate to one or more 3-digit SIC industry groups rather than to a single 4-digit SIC. The change reported for each occupation to the year 2006 is a percent of growth or decline as estimated by the Bureau of Labor Statistics. The abbreviation nec stands for 'not elsewhere classified'.

STATE AND REGIONAL CONCENTRATION

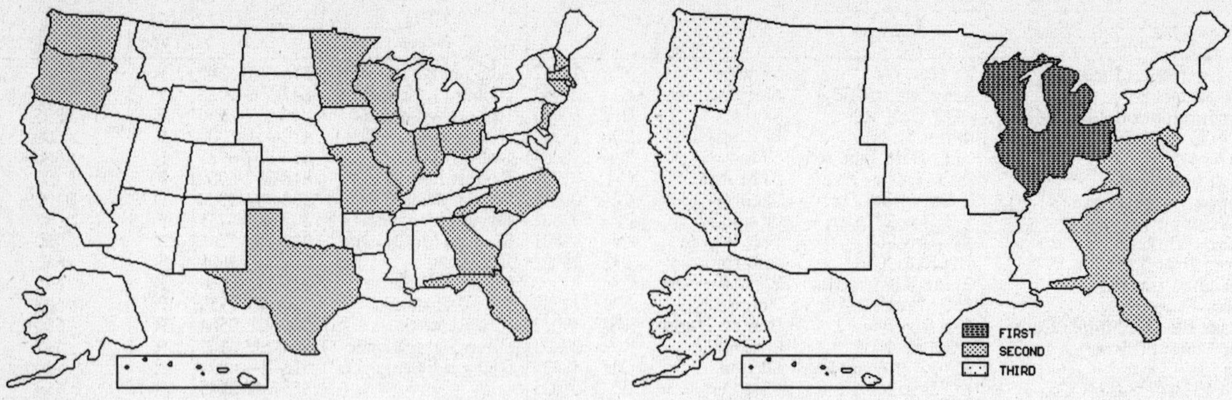

INDUSTRY DATA BY STATE

State	Establishments - 1995 Total (number)	Establishments - 1995 % of U.S.	Employment - 1995 Total (number)	Employment - 1995 % of U.S.	Employment - 1995 Per Estab.	Payroll - 1995 Total ($ mil.)	Payroll - 1995 Per Empl. ($)	Sales - 1992 Total ($ mil.)	Sales - 1992 % of U.S.	Sales - 1992 Per Estab ($)
California	1,777	10.7	22,049	11.7	12	918.5	41,657	8,648.9	11.6	376,532
Texas	1,208	7.3	13,496	7.2	11	509.0	37,714	5,596.7	7.5	424,057
New York	1,048	6.3	10,705	5.7	10	398.0	37,182	4,755.6	6.4	358,671
Illinois	838	5.1	10,317	5.5	12	409.3	39,670	4,633.6	6.2	414,228
Florida	1,020	6.2	10,090	5.4	10	351.1	34,793	4,109.7	5.5	438,368
Ohio	759	4.6	8,590	4.6	11	315.5	36,723	3,985.8	5.3	439,013
Pennsylvania	728	4.4	10,023	5.3	14	372.9	37,208	3,433.1	4.6	372,843
New Jersey	577	3.5	6,688	3.6	12	269.3	40,263	3,287.4	4.4	373,699
Georgia	516	3.1	6,313	3.4	12	239.0	37,856	2,988.1	4.0	427,117
Michigan	521	3.1	7,205	3.8	14	299.6	41,576	2,574.5	3.4	403,400
North Carolina	506	3.1	5,847	3.1	12	208.4	35,643	2,221.6	3.0	360,066
Wisconsin	332	2.0	4,101	2.2	12	147.7	36,017	2,219.9	3.0	527,049
Indiana	344	2.1	4,047	2.2	12	135.4	33,467	1,978.3	2.6	415,008
Massachusetts	394	2.4	4,647	2.5	12	173.7	37,382	1,962.2	2.6	389,944
Missouri	365	2.2	4,130	2.2	11	149.4	36,173	1,709.6	2.3	411,072
Minnesota	322	1.9	3,654	1.9	11	144.5	39,539	1,704.9	2.3	479,162
Washington	364	2.2	3,748	2.0	10	132.6	35,374	1,590.8	2.1	450,781
Tennessee	397	2.4	3,950	2.1	10	138.1	34,949	1,356.2	1.8	355,481
Maryland	265	1.6	2,865	1.5	11	112.6	39,315	1,275.4	1.7	427,997
Virginia	359	2.2	4,787	2.5	13	201.4	42,071	1,240.4	1.7	342,273
Connecticut	261	1.6	4,274	2.3	16	192.7	45,093	1,103.7	1.5	361,156
Alabama	274	1.7	3,149	1.7	11	104.5	33,193	1,019.2	1.4	341,767
Louisiana	288	1.7	2,919	1.6	10	94.3	32,309	1,007.2	1.3	345,746
Colorado	270	1.6	2,962	1.6	11	113.8	38,431	982.3	1.3	413,432
Oregon	210	1.3	2,240	1.2	11	78.9	35,204	884.8	1.2	391,699
Arizona	272	1.6	2,709	1.4	10	102.6	37,876	852.3	1.1	342,856
South Carolina	195	1.2	1,858	1.0	10	59.8	32,161	763.9	1.0	387,976
Kentucky	212	1.3	2,293	1.2	11	71.9	31,357	762.3	1.0	364,402
Iowa	164	1.0	1,681	0.9	10	59.4	35,358	588.6	0.8	395,017
Kansas	193	1.2	1,661	0.9	9	54.5	32,839	548.5	0.7	366,428
Oklahoma	209	1.3	1,573	0.8	8	48.2	30,661	500.8	0.7	338,622
Utah	138	0.8	1,487	0.8	11	48.0	32,306	462.5	0.6	349,571
Arkansas	144	0.9	1,549	0.8	11	50.0	32,283	420.9	0.6	318,128
New Hampshire	90	0.5	803	0.4	9	29.8	37,110	381.1	0.5	453,650
Nebraska	107	0.6	1,019	0.5	10	29.3	28,795	359.8	0.5	365,677
Mississippi	117	0.7	1,491	0.8	13	39.6	26,563	298.1	0.4	298,688
Maine	59	0.4	884	0.5	15	28.7	32,503	271.5	0.4	365,447
West Virginia	90	0.5	850	0.5	9	23.8	27,964	269.6	0.4	293,680
New Mexico	101	0.6	1,047	0.6	10	36.1	34,508	269.4	0.4	321,521
Nevada	94	0.6	1,084	0.6	12	40.6	37,448	260.4	0.3	249,858
Hawaii	63	0.4	608	0.3	10	21.7	35,709	254.1	0.3	426,408
Delaware	34	0.2	460	0.2	14	16.1	34,967	205.9	0.3	367,052
Idaho	66	0.4	477	0.3	7	16.5	34,583	146.9	0.2	306,664
North Dakota	34	0.2	352	0.2	10	12.5	35,582	142.1	0.2	357,121
Rhode Island	44	0.3	491	0.3	11	16.9	34,499	131.8	0.2	254,444
Alaska	42	0.3	347	0.2	8	12.2	35,170	120.7	0.2	340,893
D.C.	10	0.1	100-249	-	-	(D)	-	104.4	0.1	368,855
Montana	52	0.3	250-499	-	-	(D)	-	103.0	0.1	341,089
Vermont	44	0.3	370	0.2	8	11.7	31,622	102.9	0.1	308,060
South Dakota	31	0.2	250-499	-	-	(D)	-	99.0	0.1	291,920
Wyoming	28	0.2	191	0.1	7	5.2	27,476	49.5	0.1	291,300

Source: County Business Patterns, 1995 and *Economic Census of the U.S., 1992*. Data are sorted by 1992 revenues and, if revenues are unavailable, by establishments in 1995. The symbol (D) indicates that data are withheld by the source to avoid disclosure of competitive information. A dash (-) indicates that data are not available or undisclosed because they do not meet statistical validity standards. Shaded *states* on the state map indicate those states which have proportionately greater representation in the industry than would be indicated by the state's population; the ratio is based on total revenues or number of establishments. Shaded *regions* indicate where the industry is regionally most concentrated.

5064 - ELECTRICAL APPLIANCES, TV & RADIOS

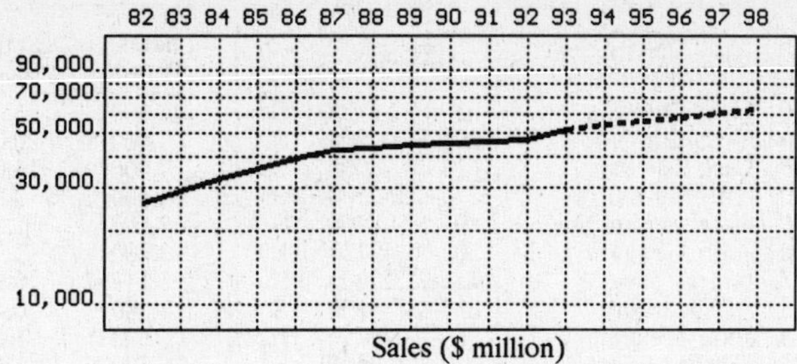

Sales ($ million)

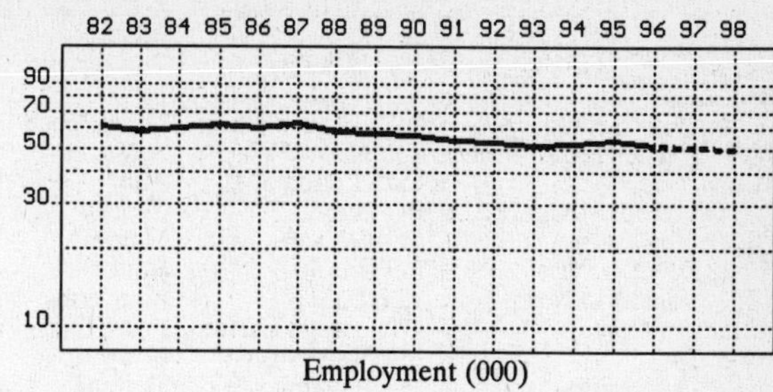

Employment (000)

GENERAL STATISTICS

Year	Establishments (number)	Employment (number)	Payroll ($ million)	Sales ($ million)	Expenses ($ million)	Beginning Inventory ($ million)	Ending Inventory ($ million)
1982	3,779	60,882	1,183.2	25,741.4	-	-	-
1983	3,695	58,562	1,285.8	29,134.5*e*	-	-	-
1984	3,472	59,788	1,387.7	32,527.5*e*	-	-	-
1985	3,372	62,344	1,487.4	35,920.6*e*	-	-	-
1986	3,234	60,181	1,484.2	39,313.7*e*	-	-	-
1987	3,740	62,722	1,663.1	42,706.7	4,920.9	4,063.1	3,933.8
1988	3,515	58,362	1,702.3	43,541.5*e*	4,905.5*e*	4,001.1*e*	3,914.5*e*
1989	3,389	57,280	1,731.4	44,376.2*e*	4,890.0*e*	3,939.1*e*	3,895.2*e*
1990	3,385	56,325	1,744.8	45,210.9*e*	4,874.6*e*	3,877.1*e*	3,876.0*e*
1991	3,354	54,018	1,731.4	46,045.6*e*	4,859.2*e*	3,815.2*e*	3,856.7*e*
1992	3,785	52,910	1,849.4	46,880.3	4,843.8	3,753.2	3,837.4
1993	3,701	51,160	1,837.4	51,901.4*p*	4,828.4*p*	3,691.2*p*	3,818.2*p*
1994	3,666	51,754	1,954.9	54,015.3*p*	4,813.0*p*	3,629.2*p*	3,798.9*p*
1995	3,674	54,080	2,090.9	56,129.2*p*	4,797.5*p*	3,567.3*p*	3,779.6*p*
1996	3,598*p*	51,267*p*	2,101.6*p*	58,243.1*p*	4,782.1*p*	3,505.3*p*	3,760.4*p*
1997	3,604*p*	50,480*p*	2,161.5*p*	60,357.0*p*	4,766.7*p*	3,443.3*p*	3,741.1*p*
1998	3,610*p*	49,692*p*	2,221.4*p*	62,470.9*p*	4,751.3*p*	3,381.3*p*	3,721.8*p*

Sources: Economic Census of the United States, 1982, 1987, and 1992. Establishment counts, employment, and payroll are from *County Business Patterns* for non-Census years. Values followed by a 'p' are projections by the editors. Sales and expense data for non-Census years are extrapolations, marked by 'e'. Industries reclassified in 1987 will not have data for prior years. Data are the most recent available at this level of detail.

INDICES OF CHANGE

Year	Establishments (number)	Employment (number)	Payroll ($ million)	Sales ($ million)	Expenses ($ million)	Beginning Inventory ($ million)	Ending Inventory ($ million)
1982	99.8	115.1	64.0	54.9	-	-	-
1983	97.6	110.7	69.5	62.1*e*	-	-	-
1984	91.7	113.0	75.0	69.4*e*	-	-	-
1985	89.1	117.8	80.4	76.6*e*	-	-	-
1986	85.4	113.7	80.3	83.9*e*	-	-	-
1987	98.8	118.5	89.9	91.1	101.6	108.3	102.5
1988	92.9	110.3	92.0	92.9*e*	101.3*e*	106.6*e*	102.0*e*
1989	89.5	108.3	93.6	94.7*e*	101.0*e*	105.0*e*	101.5*e*
1990	89.4	106.5	94.3	96.4*e*	100.6*e*	103.3*e*	101.0*e*
1991	88.6	102.1	93.6	98.2*e*	100.3*e*	101.7*e*	100.5*e*
1992	100.0	100.0	100.0	100.0	100.0	100.0	100.0
1993	97.8	96.7	99.4	110.7*p*	99.7*p*	98.3*p*	99.5*p*
1994	96.9	97.8	105.7	115.2*p*	99.4*p*	96.7*p*	99.0*p*
1995	97.1	102.2	113.1	119.7*p*	99.0*p*	95.0*p*	98.5*p*
1996	95.1*p*	96.9*p*	113.6*p*	124.2*p*	98.7*p*	93.4*p*	98.0*p*
1997	95.2*p*	95.4*p*	116.9*p*	128.7*p*	98.4*p*	91.7*p*	97.5*p*
1998	95.4*p*	93.9*p*	120.1*p*	133.3*p*	98.1*p*	90.1*p*	97.0*p*

Sources: Same as General Statistics. The values shown reflect change from the base year, 1992. Values above 100 mean greater than 1992, values below 100 mean less than 1992, and a value of 100 in the 1982-91 or 1993-98 period means same as 1992. Values followed by a 'p' are projections by the editors; 'e' stands for extrapolation. Data are the most recent available at this level of detail.

SELECTED RATIOS

For 1992	Avg. of All Wholesale	Analyzed Industry	Index	For 1992	Avg. of All Wholesale	Analyzed Industry	Index
Employees per Establishment	12	14	120	Sales per Employee	561,172	886,039	158
Payroll per Establishment	349,729	488,613	140	Sales per Establishment	6,559,346	12,385,812	189
Payroll per Employee	29,919	34,954	117	Expenses per Establishment	723,071	1,279,736	177

Sources: Same as General Statistics. The 'Average of All Manufacturing' column represents the average of all manufacturing industries reported for the most recent complete year available. The Index shows the relationship between the Average and the Analyzed Industry. For example, 100 means that they are equal; 500 that the Analyzed Industry is five times the average; 50 means that the Analyzed Industry is half the national average. The abbreviation 'na' is used to show that data are 'not available'.

LEADING COMPANIES

Number shown: **50** Total sales ($ mil): **78,846** Total employment (000): **97.2**

Company Name	Address				CEO Name	Phone	Co. Type	Sales ($ mil)	Empl. (000)
Tatung Company of America	2850 El Presidio St	Long Beach	CA	90810	Hsin-Chin Liu	310-637-2105	S	45,000	25.0
Matsushita Electric Corporation	1 Panasonic Way	Secaucus	NJ	07094	Yoshinori Kobe	201-348-7000	S	7,400	20.0
Amway Corp.	7575 Fulton St E	Ada	MI	49355	Dick DeVos	616-787-6000	R	7,000	14.0
Mitsubishi Electronics America	PO Box 6007	Cypress	CA	90630	Aira Katayama	714-220-2500	S	4,400	3.0
Sharp Electronics Corp.	PO Box 650	Mahwah	NJ	07430	Sueyuki Hirooka	201-529-8200	S	3,500 *	2.3
B J's Wholesale Club Inc.	PO Box 9601	Natick	MA	01760	John J Nugent	508-651-7400	P	3,200	11.0
Tadiran Electronic Industries	10 E 53rd St	New York	NY	10022	Israel Zamir	212-751-3600	S	1,117 *	8.3
Uniden America Corp.	4700 Amon Carter	Fort Worth	TX	76155	Al Silverberg	817-858-3300	S	760 *	0.4
Audiovox Corp.	150 Marcus Blvd	Hauppauge	NY	11788	John J Shalam	516-231-7750	P	603	1.0
Aisin World Corporation	24330 Garnier St	Torrance	CA	90505	Tetsuro Senga	310-326-8681	S	590	1.1
Pioneer Electronics (USA) Inc.	2265 E 220th St	Long Beach	CA	90810	Takofumi Sano	310-835-6177	S	432 *	0.9
TEAC America Inc.	7733 Telegraph Rd	Montebello	CA	90640	Hajime Yamaguchi	213-726-0303	S	380	0.2
D and H Distributing Co.	2525 N 7th St	Harrisburg	PA	17110	Izzy Schwab	717-236-8001	R	375	0.4
Servco Pacific Inc.	PO Box 2788	Honolulu	HI	96803	Mark H Fukunaga	808-521-6511	R	361	0.9
Funai Corp.	100 North St	Teterboro	NJ	07608	Masawo Suwa	201-288-2063	S	360	<0.1
Colorado Prime Foods	1 Michael Ave	Farmingdale	NY	11735	Bill Dordelman	516-694-1111	R	350	2.0
Distribution Holdings Inc.	4 Triad Ctr, #800	Salt Lake City	UT	84180	S Whitfield Lee	801-575-6500	R	240 *	0.5
GPX Inc. (St. Louis, Missouri)	108 Madison St	St. Louis	MO	63102	K J Berresheim	314-621-3314	S	200	0.5
Emerson Radio Corp.	PO Box 430	Parsippany	NJ	07054	Geoffrey P Jurick	973-884-5800	P	179	0.1
Helen of Troy Texas Corp.	6827 Market Ave	El Paso	TX	79915	Gerald J Rubin	915-779-6363	S	167 *	0.3
Brother International Corp.	200 Cottontail Lane	Somerset	NJ	08875	Hiromi Gunji	908-704-1700	S	160	0.5
Independent Distribution	3000 Waterview	Baltimore	MD	21230	James L Zamoiski	410-539-3000	R	160	0.5
Clarion Corporation of America	661 W Red Beach	Gardena	CA	90247	I Ishitsubo	310-327-9100	S	140 *	0.3
ABC International Traders Inc.	16730 Schoenborn	North Hills	CA	91343	Isaac Larian	818-894-2525	R	105 *	<0.1
A and A International Corp.	1200 1 Tandy Ctr	Fort Worth	TX	76102	Mark Yamatat	817-390-3011	S	100 *	0.4
Kenwood USA Corp.	PO Box 22745	Long Beach	CA	90801	Joe Richter	310-639-9000	S	98	0.2
Climatic Corp.	PO Box 25189	Columbia	SC	29224	John H Bailey	803-736-7770	R	95	0.1
Madison Electric Co.	31855 Van Dykc	Warren	MI	48093	Joseph Schneider	810-825-0200	R	90	0.2
Craig Consumer Electronics	13845 Artesia Blvd	Cerritos	CA	90703	Richard I Berger	310-926-9944	P	89	<0.1
Washington Electric	PO Box 598	Sandersville	GA	31082	TL Bray	912-552-2577	R	86 *	0.1
Toshiba America Consumer	82 Totowa Rd	Wayne	NJ	07470	Toshihide Yasui	973-628-8000	S	80 *	0.2
Arizona Wholesale Supply Co.	PO Box 2979	Phoenix	AZ	85062	TW Thomas	602-258-7901	R	73 *	0.2
AB Wholesale Co.	710 S College Ave	Bluefield	VA	24605	Kaleel A Ammar Jr	703-322-4686	S	70	0.1
Professional Housewares	29309 Clayton Ave	Wickliffe	OH	44092	Mark Fallenberg	216-944-3500	R	70	0.1
H. Betti Industries Inc.	303 Paterson Plank	Carlstadt	NJ	07072	Joe Cirillo	201-438-1300	R	68 *	0.2
Nunn Electric Supply Corp.	105-19 Polk St	Amarillo	TX	79189	Carl D Hare	806-376-4581	R	62	0.3
National Cellular Inc.	2400 E Randol Mill	Arlington	TX	76011	Ron Koonsman	817-640-4600	R	60	0.2
Sherwood Corp.	PO Box 428	La Mirada	CA	90637	Juck Hur	714-521-6100	S	60	<0.1
Tacony Corp.	1760 Gilsinn Ln	Fenton	MO	63026	Kenneth J Tacony	314-349-3000	R	60	0.2
Goldberg Company Inc.	PO Box 6126	Richmond	VA	23222	Leroy B Goldberg	804-228-5700	R	53 *	<0.1
Cain and Bultman Inc.	PO Box 2815	Jacksonville	FL	32203	MA Sandifer	904-356-4812	R	52	0.1
Blodgett Supply Company Inc.	PO Box 759	Williston	VT	05495	Sam Levin	802-864-9831	R	49 *	0.1
Masek Distributing Inc.	PO Box 130	Gering	NE	69341	Joe Masek	308-436-2100	R	47	<0.1
Durkopp Adler America Inc.	3025 Northwoods	Norcross	GA	30071	Ben Burks	404-446-8162	S	46	<0.1
Carbone of America	400 Myrtle Ave	Boonton	NJ	07005	Emilio DeBarnardo	201-334-0700	S	45	0.4
Noma International Inc.	7400 W Indrial Dr	Forest Park	IL	60130	Richard Knelstein	708-771-9400	S	45	0.1
Ricom Electronics Ltd.	PO Box 17882	Milwaukee	WI	53217	Marcia Rose	414-357-8181	R	45 *	<0.1
Hite Co.	PO Box 1754	Altoona	PA	16603	R Lee Hite	814-944-6121	R	44	0.2
Allison-Erwin Co.	2920 N Tryon St	Charlotte	NC	28232	PD McMillan	704-334-8621	R	40	0.1
Rowenta Inc.	196 Boston Ave	Medford	MA	02155	Paul Pofcher	781-396-0600	S	40 *	<0.1

Source: *Ward's Business Directory of U.S. Private and Public Companies*, 1998. The company type code used is as follows: P - Public, R - Private, S - Subsidiary, D - Division, J - Joint Venture, A - Affiliate, G - Group. Sales are in millions of dollars, employees are in thousands. An asterisk (*) indicates an estimated sales volume. The symbol < stands for 'less than'.

OCCUPATIONS EMPLOYED BY SIC 506 - WHOLESALE TRADE, OTHER

Occupation	% of Total 1996	Change to 2006	Occupation	% of Total 1996	Change to 2006
Sales & related workers nec	19.5	20.2	Clerical supervisors & managers	1.9	20.2
General managers & top executives	5.9	16.4	Order clerks	1.9	8.2
Truck drivers light & heavy	5.4	20.2	Helpers, laborers nec	1.7	20.2
General office clerks	3.6	3.4	Electrical & electronic technicians	1.4	18.8
Traffic, shipping, receiving clerks	3.6	16.7	Blue collar worker supervisors	1.4	16.0
Stock clerks	3.5	-3.9	Wholesale & retail buyers, except farm products	1.3	17.0
Freight, stock, & material movers, hand	3.3	8.2	Office machine & cash register servicers	1.3	20.2
Marketing & sales worker supervisors	3.1	20.2	Hand packers & packagers	1.2	-3.9
Order fillers, wholesale & retail sales	3.0	16.7	Maintenance repairers, general utility	1.1	12.0
Bookkeeping, accounting, & auditing clerks	2.9	-3.9	Industrial truck & tractor operators	1.1	20.2
Salespersons, retail	2.5	20.2	Purchasing managers	1.1	20.2
Secretaries, except legal & medical	2.5	-4.7	Receptionists & information clerks	1.0	20.2
Assemblers, fabricators, hand workers nec	2.0	-3.9			

Source: *Industry-Occupation Matrix*, Bureau of Labor Statistics. These data relate to one or more 3-digit SIC industry groups rather than to a single 4-digit SIC. The change reported for each occupation to the year 2006 is a percent of growth or decline as estimated by the Bureau of Labor Statistics. The abbreviation nec stands for 'not elsewhere classified'.

STATE AND REGIONAL CONCENTRATION

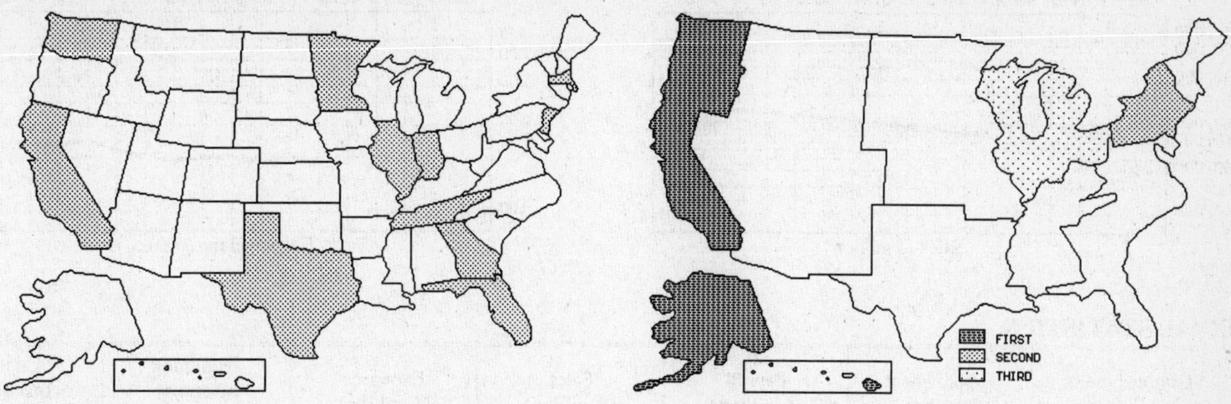

INDUSTRY DATA BY STATE

State	Establishments - 1995 Total (number)	Establishments - 1995 % of U.S.	Employment - 1995 Total (number)	Employment - 1995 % of U.S.	Employment - 1995 Per Estab.	Payroll - 1995 Total ($ mil.)	Payroll - 1995 Per Empl. ($)	Sales - 1992 Total ($ mil.)	Sales - 1992 % of U.S.	Sales - 1992 Per Estab ($)
California	574	15.6	9,242	17.1	16	384.0	41,544	8,797.1	19.1	1,006,644
New Jersey	186	5.1	7,176	13.3	39	374.3	52,161	6,841.4	14.9	969,583
Illinois	175	4.8	3,977	7.4	23	170.5	42,860	3,982.8	8.7	712,100
Texas	273	7.4	3,814	7.1	14	126.2	33,095	3,547.0	7.7	944,598
Florida	368	10.0	4,279	7.9	12	136.5	31,897	2,866.3	6.2	791,138
New York	342	9.3	2,991	5.5	9	101.5	33,939	2,375.7	5.2	741,937
Georgia	108	2.9	1,807	3.4	17	78.7	43,535	2,055.6	4.5	1,264,184
Indiana	57	1.6	956	1.8	17	46.8	48,993	1,833.6	4.0	3,097,260
Ohio	116	3.2	2,155	4.0	19	71.4	33,112	1,459.9	3.2	837,115
Massachusetts	103	2.8	1,516	2.8	15	62.7	41,375	1,380.6	3.0	1,147,627
Tennessee	67	1.8	1,139	2.1	17	35.3	30,986	1,305.2	2.8	916,605
Washington	68	1.9	976	1.8	14	40.6	41,631	1,266.2	2.8	1,166,989
Minnesota	75	2.0	920	1.7	12	42.0	45,615	1,021.1	2.2	1,074,845
Michigan	90	2.4	971	1.8	11	42.4	43,674	941.9	2.0	876,169
Pennsylvania	116	3.2	1,010	1.9	9	32.8	32,477	937.6	2.0	868,106
Missouri	74	2.0	846	1.6	11	26.8	31,691	649.9	1.4	772,754
Arizona	60	1.6	739	1.4	12	25.4	34,360	604.5	1.3	1,151,341
Virginia	60	1.6	774	1.4	13	22.8	29,422	437.6	1.0	550,472
Wisconsin	39	1.1	741	1.4	19	23.0	31,077	427.5	0.9	662,817
Colorado	65	1.8	501	0.9	8	18.0	35,830	420.6	0.9	891,081
North Carolina	56	1.5	532	1.0	10	19.5	36,669	390.7	0.8	628,114
Connecticut	41	1.1	467	0.9	11	21.7	46,535	384.1	0.8	932,216
Kansas	42	1.1	398	0.7	9	14.0	35,058	381.8	0.8	871,781
Oregon	36	1.0	532	1.0	15	14.8	27,902	261.7	0.6	521,386
Louisiana	34	0.9	635	1.2	19	15.5	24,339	251.6	0.5	585,105
Hawaii	29	0.8	348	0.6	12	10.3	29,641	159.6	0.3	396,915
Kentucky	32	0.9	336	0.6	10	7.8	23,262	152.3	0.3	581,435
Utah	33	0.9	270	0.5	8	8.1	30,022	129.9	0.3	343,579
Oklahoma	29	0.8	399	0.7	14	9.8	24,449	106.7	0.2	346,571
Arkansas	17	0.5	195	0.4	11	6.5	33,462	103.2	0.2	1,001,864
Alabama	43	1.2	543	1.0	13	13.8	25,436	96.9	0.2	389,277
Nebraska	17	0.5	258	0.5	15	5.8	22,562	76.1	0.2	349,280
South Carolina	32	0.9	270	0.5	8	5.9	21,963	75.2	0.2	240,252
Iowa	29	0.8	300	0.6	10	7.6	25,227	71.2	0.2	253,253
West Virginia	14	0.4	219	0.4	16	5.0	22,612	45.3	0.1	209,884
Mississippi	15	0.4	168	0.3	11	5.0	29,649	34.2	0.1	257,361
Alaska	6	0.2	78	0.1	13	1.9	24,513	27.3	0.1	303,689
Maine	8	0.2	106	0.2	13	4.2	39,349	27.0	0.1	191,149
New Mexico	14	0.4	76	0.1	5	2.0	26,882	16.8	0.0	300,125
South Dakota	4	0.1	0-19	-	-	(D)	-	9.1	0.0	275,091
Delaware	7	0.2	19	0.0	3	0.5	27,316	9.0	0.0	502,278
North Dakota	5	0.1	20-99	-	-	(D)	-	7.9	0.0	253,871
Idaho	12	0.3	26	0.0	2	0.8	29,885	3.2	0.0	131,833
Maryland	61	1.7	963	1.8	16	37.8	39,285	(D)	-	-
Nevada	12	0.3	171	0.3	14	4.3	24,936	(D)	-	-
Rhode Island	10	0.3	51	0.1	5	1.3	26,157	(D)	-	-
New Hampshire	9	0.2	34	0.1	4	1.4	40,029	(D)	-	-
Montana	5	0.1	20-99	-	-	(D)	-	(D)	-	-
Vermont	3	0.1	0-19	-	-	(D)	-	(D)	-	-
D.C.	2	0.1	20-99	-	-	(D)	-	(D)	-	-
Wyoming	1	0.0	0-19	-	-	(D)	-	(D)	-	-

Source: County Business Patterns, 1995 and *Economic Census of the U.S., 1992*. Data are sorted by 1992 revenues and, if revenues are unavailable, by establishments in 1995. The symbol (D) indicates that data are withheld by the source to avoid disclosure of competitive information. A dash (-) indicates that data are not available or undisclosed because they do not meet statistical validity standards. Shaded *states* on the state map indicate those states which have proportionately greater representation in the industry than would be indicated by the state's population; the ratio is based on total revenues or number of establishments. Shaded *regions* indicate where the industry is regionally most concentrated.

5065 - ELECTRONIC PARTS AND EQUIPMENT

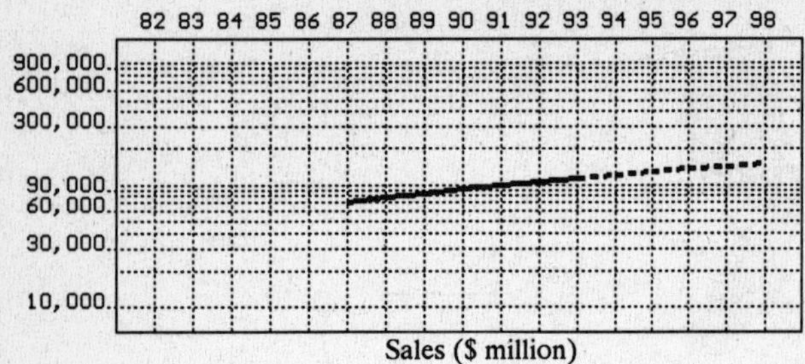

Sales ($ million)

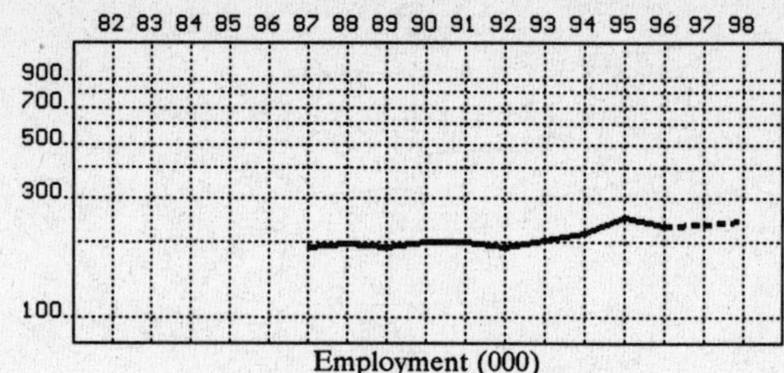

Employment (000)

GENERAL STATISTICS

Year	Establishments (number)	Employment (number)	Payroll ($ million)	Sales ($ million)	Expenses ($ million)	Beginning Inventory ($ million)	Ending Inventory ($ million)
1982	-	-	-	-	-	-	-
1983	-	-	-	-	-	-	-
1984	-	-	-	-	-	-	-
1985	-	-	-	-	-	-	-
1986	-	-	-	-	-	-	-
1987	14,724	190,845	5,563.9	71,078.1	10,914.2	4,793.8	5,292.2
1988	13,995	199,167	6,494.1	78,095.3e	11,405.4e	4,922.4e	5,402.8e
1989	13,448	192,042	6,193.1	85,112.5e	11,896.7e	5,050.9e	5,513.5e
1990	14,320	200,580	6,808.7	92,129.7e	12,387.9e	5,179.5e	5,624.1e
1991	15,072	202,642	7,260.0	99,146.9e	12,879.1e	5,308.0e	5,734.7e
1992	17,007	192,552	7,126.5	106,164.0	13,370.4	5,436.6	5,845.3
1993	17,720	204,502	8,216.8	113,181.2p	13,861.6p	5,565.1p	5,955.9p
1994	18,453	219,455	9,292.9	120,198.4p	14,352.8p	5,693.7p	6,066.6p
1995	19,488	249,965	11,481.7	127,215.6p	14,844.1p	5,822.2p	6,177.2p
1996	19,664p	231,936p	10,640.3p	134,232.8p	15,335.3p	5,950.7p	6,287.8p
1997	20,391p	237,174p	11,247.5p	141,250.0p	15,826.5p	6,079.3p	6,398.4p
1998	21,119p	242,411p	11,854.7p	148,267.2p	16,317.8p	6,207.8p	6,509.1p

Sources: *Economic Census of the United States*, 1982, 1987, and 1992. Establishment counts, employment, and payroll are from *County Business Patterns* for non-Census years. Values followed by a 'p' are projections by the editors. Sales and expense data for non-Census years are extrapolations, marked by 'e'. Industries reclassified in 1987 will not have data for prior years. Data are the most recent available at this level of detail.

INDICES OF CHANGE

Year	Establishments (number)	Employment (number)	Payroll ($ million)	Sales ($ million)	Expenses ($ million)	Beginning Inventory ($ million)	Ending Inventory ($ million)
1982	-	-	-	-	-	-	-
1983	-	-	-	-	-	-	-
1984	-	-	-	-	-	-	-
1985	-	-	-	-	-	-	-
1986	-	-	-	-	-	-	-
1987	86.6	99.1	78.1	67.0	81.6	88.2	90.5
1988	82.3	103.4	91.1	73.6e	85.3e	90.5e	92.4e
1989	79.1	99.7	86.9	80.2e	89.0e	92.9e	94.3e
1990	84.2	104.2	95.5	86.8e	92.7e	95.3e	96.2e
1991	88.6	105.2	101.9	93.4e	96.3e	97.6e	98.1e
1992	100.0	100.0	100.0	100.0	100.0	100.0	100.0
1993	104.2	106.2	115.3	106.6p	103.7p	102.4p	101.9p
1994	108.5	114.0	130.4	113.2p	107.3p	104.7p	103.8p
1995	114.6	129.8	161.1	119.8p	111.0p	107.1p	105.7p
1996	115.6p	120.5p	149.3p	126.4p	114.7p	109.5p	107.6p
1997	119.9p	123.2p	157.8p	133.0p	118.4p	111.8p	109.5p
1998	124.2p	125.9p	166.3p	139.7p	122.0p	114.2p	111.4p

Sources: Same as General Statistics. The values shown reflect change from the base year, 1992. Values above 100 mean greater than 1992, values below 100 mean less than 1992, and a value of 100 in the 1982-91 or 1993-98 period means same as 1992. Values followed by a 'p' are projections by the editors; 'e' stands for extrapolation. Data are the most recent available at this level of detail.

SELECTED RATIOS

For 1992	Avg. of All Wholesale	Analyzed Industry	Index	For 1992	Avg. of All Wholesale	Analyzed Industry	Index
Employees per Establishment	12	11	97	Sales per Employee	561,172	551,352	98
Payroll per Establishment	349,729	419,033	120	Sales per Establishment	6,559,346	6,242,371	95
Payroll per Employee	29,919	37,011	124	Expenses per Establishment	723,071	786,170	109

Sources: Same as General Statistics. The 'Average of All Manufacturing' column represents the average of all manufacturing industries reported for the most recent complete year available. The Index shows the relationship between the Average and the Analyzed Industry. For example, 100 means that they are equal; 500 that the Analyzed Industry is five times the average; 50 means that the Analyzed Industry is half the national average. The abbreviation 'na' is used to show that data are 'not available'.

LEADING COMPANIES

Number shown: 50 Total sales ($ mil): 144,596 Total employment (000): 135.7

Company Name	Address				CEO Name	Phone	Co. Type	Sales ($ mil)	Empl. (000)
Tatung Company of America	2850 El Presidio St	Long Beach	CA	90810	Hsin-Chin Liu	310-637-2105	S	45,000	25.0
View Tech Inc.	950 Flynn Rd, #F	Camarillo	CA	93012	Robert G Hatfield	805-482-8277	P	25,812	0.3
Williams Companies Inc.	1 Williams Center	Tulsa	OK	74172	Keith E Bailey	918-588-2000	P	13,879	15.0
Bergen Brunswig Corp.	4000 Metropolitan	Orange	CA	92668	Donald R Roden	714-385-4000	P	11,660	5.1
Arrow Electronics Inc.	25 Hub Dr	Melville	NY	11747	Stephen P Kaufman	516-391-1300	P	7,001	9.0
Avent Inc.	80 Cutter Mill Rd	Great Neck	NY	11021	Leon Machiz	516-466-7000	P	5,390	9.4
Intelligent Electronics Inc.	411 Eagleview Blvd	Exton	PA	19341	Richard D Sanford	610-458-5500	P	3,588	2.6
Hitachi America Ltd.	50 Prospect Ave	Tarrytown	NY	10591	T Shimayama	914-332-5800	S	3,500	6.0
Graybar Electric Company Inc.	PO Box 7231	St. Louis	MO	63177	Carl Hall	314-727-3900	R	3,300	7.0
Kanematsu U.S.A. Inc.	114 W 47th St	New York	NY	10036	Minoru Inoue	212-704-9400	S	2,250	1.0
Pioneer-Standard Electronics	4800 E 131st St	Cleveland	OH	44105	James L Bayman	216-587-3600	P	1,509	2.1
CellStar Corp.	1730 Briercroft Ct	Carrollton	TX	75006	Alan H Goldfield	214-323-0600	P	1,483	1.0
Rexel Inc.	150 Alhambra Cir	Coral Gables	FL	33134	Gilles Guinchard	305-446-8000	S	1,302 *	3.2
TDK U.S.A. Corp.	12 Harbor Park Dr	P. Washington	NY	11050	Kenjiro Kihira	516-625-0100	S	1,260 *	4.5
Wyle Electronics	15370 Barranca	Irvine	CA	92718	Ralph L Ozorkiewicz	714-753-9953	P	1,245	1.5
Marshall Industries	9320 Telstar Ave	El Monte	CA	91731	Robert Rodin	818-307-6000	P	1,185	1.4
Tadiran Electronic Industries	10 E 53rd St	New York	NY	10022	Israel Zamir	212-751-3600	S	1,117 *	8.3
Brightpoint Inc.	6402 Corporate Dr	Indianapolis	IN	46278	Robert J Laikin	317-297-6100	P	1,040	0.4
Bell Industries Inc.	11812 San Vicente	Los Angeles	CA	90049	Gordon Graham	310-826-2355	P	891	1.9
GTE Supply	5615 Highpoint Dr	Irving	TX	75038	Larry Henry	214-751-4100	D	840 *	3.0
Premier Industrial Corp.	PO Box 94884	Cleveland	OH	44101	Bruce W Johnson	216-391-8300	P	818	4.5
Hamilton Hallmark Div.	10950 W Washington	Culver City	CA	90232	Leon Machiz	310-665-2600	D	744	0.6
Sprint/North Supply	600 Industrial Pkwy	Indust Apt	KS	66031	William Obermayer	913-791-7000	S	677	1.0
Southern Electronics Corp.	4916 Roy Atlanta	Tucker	GA	30085	Gerald Diamond	770-491-8962	P	646	0.4
Audiovox Corp.	150 Marcus Blvd	Hauppauge	NY	11788	John J Shalam	516-231-7750	P	603	1.0
Xilinx Inc.	2100 Logic Dr	San Jose	CA	95124	Willem P Roelandts	408-559-7778	P	568	1.2
Bell Microproducts Inc.	1941 Ringwood Ave	San Jose	CA	95131	W Donald Bell	408-451-9400	P	534	0.7
Panasonic Industrial Co.	2 Panasonic Way	Secaucus	NJ	07094	Yoshinori Kobe	201-348-7000	S	450	1.0
Pioneer Electronics (USA) Inc.	2265 E 220th St	Long Beach	CA	90810	Takofumi Sano	310-835-6177	S	432 *	0.9
D and H Distributing Co.	2525 N 7th St	Harrisburg	PA	17110	Izzy Schwab	717-236-8001	R	375	0.4
Motor Sound Corp.	541 Division St	Campbell	CA	95008	William W Topper	408-374-7900	R	375	0.3
Pioneer-Standard Electronics	9100 Gaither Rd	Gaithersburg	MD	20877	Bruce S Tucker	301-921-3800	S	365	0.5
Funai Corp.	100 North St	Teterboro	NJ	07608	Masawo Suwa	201-288-2063	S	360	<0.1
WorldCom Network Services	PO Box 21348	Tulsa	OK	74121	Roy A Wilkins	918-588-3210	S	340 *	2.1
Thomas Nelson Inc.	501 Nelson Place	Nashville	TN	37214	Sam Moore	615-889-9000	P	332	1.3
Sterling Electronics Corp.	PO Box 1229	Houston	TX	77251	Ronald S Spolane	713-627-9800	P	322	0.7
Norstan Inc.	605 N Hwy 169	Plymouth	MN	55441	Paul Baszucki	612-513-4500	P	321	1.8
BellSouth Communication	1936 Blue Hills NE	Roanoke	VA	24012	Fredrick K Shaftman	540-983-6000	P	300	1.3
Power and Telephone Supply	2673 Yale Ave	Memphis	TN	38112	Jim Pentecost	810-238-7514	R	280	0.4
Milgray Electronics Inc.	77 Schmitt Blvd	Farmingdale	NY	11735	Herbert S Davidson	516-420-9800	S	275	0.5
TDK Corporation of America	1600 Feehanville Dr	Mount Prospect	IL	60056	Mitsikuni Baba	847-803-6100	S	271 *	0.2
Richardson Electronics, Ltd.	40W267 Keslinger	Lafox	IL	60147	E J Richardson	630-208-2200	P	255	0.7
Passive Electrical Mechanical	3254 Fraser St	Aurora	CO	80011	Cathy Morris	303-375-1300	D	243 *	0.6
Southwestern Bell Telecom	1000 Des Peres Rd	St. Louis	MO	63131	Dick Moore	314-822-6900	S	240 *	0.9
Richey Electronics Inc.	7441 Lincoln Way	Garden Grove	CA	92841	W. C Cacciatore	714-898-8288	P	226	1.1
Reptron Electronics Inc.	14401 McCormick	Tampa	FL	33626	Michael L Musto	813-854-2351	P	223	1.0
TIE Systems Inc.	8500 W 110th St	Overland Park	KS	66210	Charlie McNane	913-344-0400	S	210 *	0.8
Nu Horizons Electronics Corp.	6000 New Horizons	Amityville	NY	11701	Irving Lubman	516-226-6000	P	203	0.4
Peak Technologies Group Inc.	600 Madison Ave	New York	NY	10022	Nicholas R Toms	212-832-2833	P	185	0.8
Katy Industries Inc.	6300 S Syracuse	Englewood	CO	80111	John R Prann Jr	303-290-9300	P	171	1.1

Source: *Ward's Business Directory of U.S. Private and Public Companies*, 1998. The company type code used is as follows: P - Public, R - Private, S - Subsidiary, D - Division, J - Joint Venture, A - Affiliate, G - Group. Sales are in millions of dollars, employees are in thousands. An asterisk (*) indicates an estimated sales volume. The symbol < stands for 'less than'.

OCCUPATIONS EMPLOYED BY SIC 506 - WHOLESALE TRADE, OTHER

Occupation	% of Total 1996	Change to 2006	Occupation	% of Total 1996	Change to 2006
Sales & related workers nec	19.5	20.2	Clerical supervisors & managers	1.9	20.2
General managers & top executives	5.9	16.4	Order clerks	1.9	8.2
Truck drivers light & heavy	5.4	20.2	Helpers, laborers nec	1.7	20.2
General office clerks	3.6	3.4	Electrical & electronic technicians	1.4	18.8
Traffic, shipping, receiving clerks	3.6	16.7	Blue collar worker supervisors	1.4	16.0
Stock clerks	3.5	-3.9	Wholesale & retail buyers, except farm products	1.3	17.0
Freight, stock, & material movers, hand	3.3	8.2	Office machine & cash register servicers	1.3	20.2
Marketing & sales worker supervisors	3.1	20.2	Hand packers & packagers	1.2	-3.9
Order fillers, wholesale & retail sales	3.0	16.7	Maintenance repairers, general utility	1.1	12.0
Bookkeeping, accounting, & auditing clerks	2.9	-3.9	Industrial truck & tractor operators	1.1	20.2
Salespersons, retail	2.5	20.2	Purchasing managers	1.1	20.2
Secretaries, except legal & medical	2.5	-4.7	Receptionists & information clerks	1.0	20.2
Assemblers, fabricators, hand workers nec	2.0	-3.9			

Source: *Industry-Occupation Matrix*, Bureau of Labor Statistics. These data relate to one or more 3-digit SIC industry groups rather than to a single 4-digit SIC. The change reported for each occupation to the year 2006 is a percent of growth or decline as estimated by the Bureau of Labor Statistics. The abbreviation nec stands for 'not elsewhere classified'.

STATE AND REGIONAL CONCENTRATION

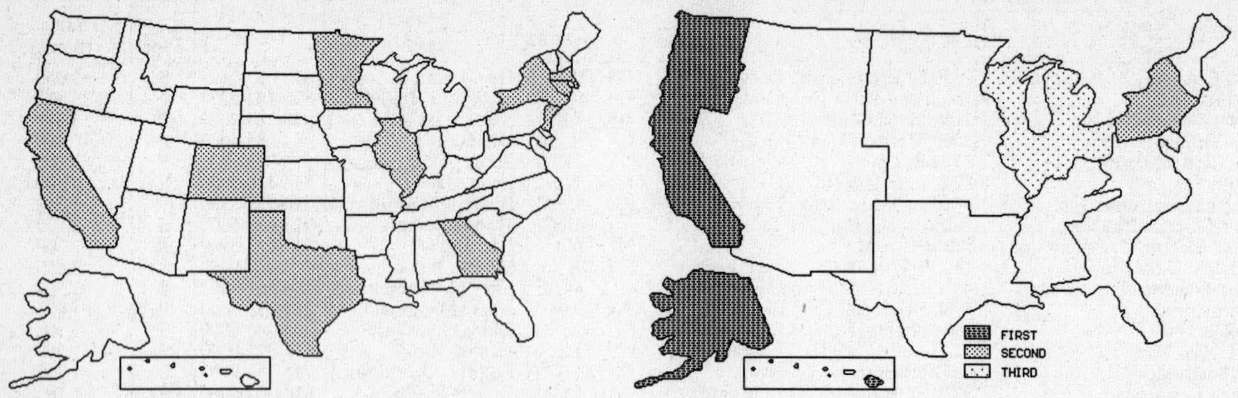

INDUSTRY DATA BY STATE

State	Establishments - 1995 Total (number)	Establishments - 1995 % of U.S.	Employment - 1995 Total (number)	Employment - 1995 % of U.S.	Employment - 1995 Per Estab.	Payroll - 1995 Total ($ mil.)	Payroll - 1995 Per Empl. ($)	Sales - 1992 Total ($ mil.)	Sales - 1992 % of U.S.	Sales - 1992 Per Estab ($)
California	3,278	16.8	54,062	21.6	16	2,834.4	52,429	27,097.3	26.4	668,655
Texas	1,506	7.7	21,282	8.5	14	1,030.3	48,412	9,091.5	8.9	621,983
New York	1,592	8.2	19,409	7.8	12	868.4	44,741	8,002.0	7.8	494,044
Illinois	990	5.1	16,830	6.7	17	845.2	50,218	7,452.1	7.3	582,829
New Jersey	875	4.5	10,989	4.4	13	553.5	50,371	6,477.0	6.3	637,186
Georgia	543	2.8	7,923	3.2	15	377.8	47,680	4,904.2	4.8	872,327
Massachusetts	690	3.5	10,415	4.2	15	522.3	50,147	4,744.6	4.6	599,515
Florida	1,373	7.0	12,526	5.0	9	462.4	36,913	4,333.4	4.2	454,715
Colorado	442	2.3	5,801	2.3	13	270.1	46,556	3,204.2	3.1	666,574
Pennsylvania	602	3.1	7,472	3.0	12	313.6	41,975	3,159.1	3.1	521,640
Ohio	691	3.5	8,057	3.2	12	323.6	40,164	2,317.0	2.3	362,543
Minnesota	452	2.3	5,414	2.2	12	239.8	44,289	2,244.3	2.2	546,846
North Carolina	419	2.2	5,483	2.2	13	238.5	43,493	2,156.1	2.1	521,669
Michigan	465	2.4	4,869	1.9	10	204.7	42,034	1,939.5	1.9	486,828
Indiana	422	2.2	4,117	1.6	10	158.6	38,516	1,881.1	1.8	588,037
Connecticut	261	1.3	3,356	1.3	13	167.4	49,867	1,787.1	1.7	580,611
Arizona	435	2.2	4,479	1.8	10	172.0	38,400	1,530.4	1.5	539,442
Washington	396	2.0	3,939	1.6	10	157.7	40,037	1,427.7	1.4	415,026
Virginia	341	1.7	4,263	1.7	13	219.0	51,379	1,323.4	1.3	354,992
Alabama	248	1.3	2,009	0.8	8	79.9	39,793	1,276.0	1.2	923,969
Missouri	321	1.6	4,049	1.6	13	153.8	37,973	1,261.8	1.2	410,487
Oregon	245	1.3	2,422	1.0	10	104.1	42,981	801.6	0.8	446,325
Kansas	179	0.9	2,107	0.8	12	91.6	43,486	653.3	0.6	326,480
Tennessee	257	1.3	2,807	1.1	11	104.2	37,118	650.4	0.6	266,660
Wisconsin	254	1.3	2,689	1.1	11	96.0	35,706	561.9	0.5	268,186
Utah	128	0.7	1,924	0.8	15	83.9	43,616	309.2	0.3	290,101
Iowa	125	0.6	1,299	0.5	10	45.2	34,761	285.3	0.3	278,603
Louisiana	165	0.8	1,438	0.6	9	49.9	34,727	259.2	0.3	182,288
Oklahoma	131	0.7	1,288	0.5	10	46.2	35,882	252.4	0.2	291,076
New Mexico	97	0.5	583	0.2	6	18.7	32,098	212.8	0.2	443,408
Nebraska	71	0.4	654	0.3	9	21.5	32,813	169.2	0.2	302,741
South Carolina	124	0.6	1,134	0.5	9	41.6	36,674	156.6	0.2	212,419
Hawaii	43	0.2	485	0.2	11	22.2	45,751	140.0	0.1	293,589
Kentucky	134	0.7	1,065	0.4	8	32.7	30,731	134.2	0.1	192,537
Arkansas	94	0.5	1,125	0.5	12	33.7	29,912	106.8	0.1	189,647
South Dakota	30	0.2	428	0.2	14	13.3	31,164	92.1	0.1	246,971
Idaho	76	0.4	616	0.2	8	20.3	32,938	65.0	0.1	183,653
Maine	39	0.2	253	0.1	6	9.2	36,225	64.8	0.1	289,094
Mississippi	87	0.4	594	0.2	7	16.0	26,995	57.5	0.1	129,763
West Virginia	64	0.3	410	0.2	6	10.9	26,546	53.0	0.1	159,611
Alaska	21	0.1	195	0.1	9	6.7	34,297	39.0	0.0	168,797
North Dakota	33	0.2	182	0.1	6	5.2	28,753	25.9	0.0	193,037
Delaware	35	0.2	225	0.1	6	8.8	38,987	23.5	0.0	147,679
Maryland	332	1.7	4,762	1.9	14	212.6	44,635	(D)	-	-
New Hampshire	135	0.7	2,116	0.8	16	95.0	44,895	(D)	-	-
Nevada	88	0.5	868	0.3	10	30.7	35,361	(D)	-	-
Rhode Island	63	0.3	662	0.3	11	27.7	41,894	(D)	-	-
Montana	33	0.2	100-249	-	-	(D)	-	(D)	-	-
Vermont	28	0.1	273	0.1	10	12.4	45,308	(D)	-	-
Wyoming	19	0.1	20-99	-	-	(D)	-	(D)	-	-
D.C.	16	0.1	418	0.2	26	23.6	56,531	(D)	-	-

Source: County Business Patterns, 1995 and *Economic Census of the U.S., 1992*. Data are sorted by 1992 revenues and, if revenues are unavailable, by establishments in 1995. The symbol (D) indicates that data are withheld by the source to avoid disclosure of competitive information. A dash (-) indicates that data are not available or undisclosed because they do not meet statistical validity standards. Shaded *states* on the state map indicate those states which have proportionately greater representation in the industry than would be indicated by the state's population; the ratio is based on total revenues or number of establishments. Shaded *regions* indicate where the industry is regionally most concentrated.

5072 - HARDWARE

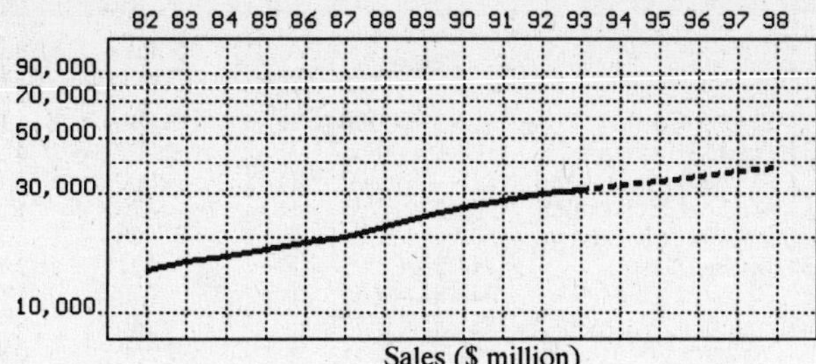

Sales ($ million)

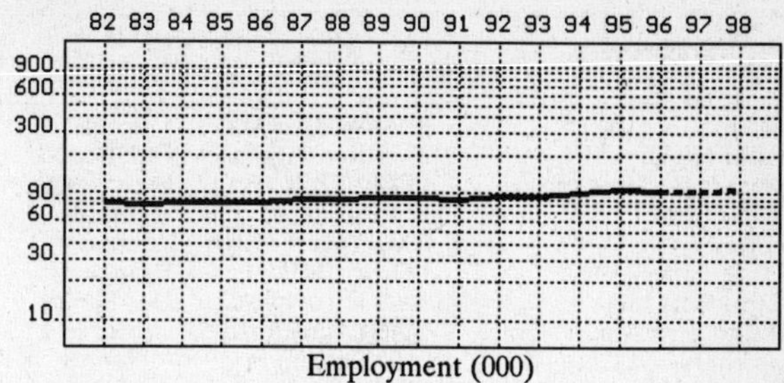

Employment (000)

GENERAL STATISTICS

Year	Establishments (number)	Employment (number)	Payroll ($ million)	Sales ($ million)	Expenses ($ million)	Beginning Inventory ($ million)	Ending Inventory ($ million)
1982	6,788	83,478	1,516.0	14,693.2	-	-	-
1983	6,725	80,419	1,590.1	15,765.4e	-	-	-
1984	6,471	82,166	1,751.4	16,837.7e	-	-	-
1985	6,837	84,314	1,875.8	17,909.9e	-	-	-
1986	6,329	84,899	1,938.4	18,982.2e	-	-	-
1987	7,552	90,160	2,110.9	20,054.4	4,157.1	2,583.3	2,777.6
1988	7,256	89,652	2,283.2	22,064.4e	4,404.8e	2,830.2e	3,010.1e
1989	7,033	91,256	2,362.4	24,074.3e	4,652.4e	3,077.1e	3,242.7e
1990	7,061	92,669	2,462.1	26,084.3e	4,900.0e	3,324.1e	3,475.2e
1991	7,083	89,680	2,419.9	28,094.3e	5,147.7e	3,571.0e	3,707.8e
1992	8,407	96,938	2,788.8	30,104.2	5,395.3	3,817.9	3,940.3
1993	8,233	96,383	2,890.5	30,579.7p	5,642.9p	4,064.9p	4,172.8p
1994	8,309	100,417	3,023.7	32,120.8p	5,890.6p	4,311.8p	4,405.4p
1995	8,723	106,360	3,326.7	33,661.9p	6,138.2p	4,558.7p	4,637.9p
1996	8,522p	103,268p	3,290.6p	35,203.0p	6,385.8p	4,805.7p	4,870.5p
1997	8,679p	104,953p	3,421.4p	36,744.1p	6,633.5p	5,052.6p	5,103.0p
1998	8,836p	106,638p	3,552.1p	38,285.2p	6,881.1p	5,299.5p	5,335.6p

Sources: Economic Census of the United States, 1982, 1987, and 1992. Establishment counts, employment, and payroll are from *County Business Patterns* for non-Census years. Values followed by a 'p' are projections by the editors. Sales and expense data for non-Census years are extrapolations, marked by 'e'. Industries reclassified in 1987 will not have data for prior years. Data are the most recent available at this level of detail.

INDICES OF CHANGE

Year	Establishments (number)	Employment (number)	Payroll ($ million)	Sales ($ million)	Expenses ($ million)	Beginning Inventory ($ million)	Ending Inventory ($ million)
1982	80.7	86.1	54.4	48.8	-	-	-
1983	80.0	83.0	57.0	52.4e	-	-	-
1984	77.0	84.8	62.8	55.9e	-	-	-
1985	81.3	87.0	67.3	59.5e	-	-	-
1986	75.3	87.6	69.5	63.1e	-	-	-
1987	89.8	93.0	75.7	66.6	77.1	67.7	70.5
1988	86.3	92.5	81.9	73.3e	81.6e	74.1e	76.4e
1989	83.7	94.1	84.7	80.0e	86.2e	80.6e	82.3e
1990	84.0	95.6	88.3	86.6e	90.8e	87.1e	88.2e
1991	84.3	92.5	86.8	93.3e	95.4e	93.5e	94.1e
1992	100.0	100.0	100.0	100.0	100.0	100.0	100.0
1993	97.9	99.4	103.6	101.6p	104.6p	106.5p	105.9p
1994	98.8	103.6	108.4	106.7p	109.2p	112.9p	111.8p
1995	103.8	109.7	119.3	111.8p	113.8p	119.4p	117.7p
1996	101.4p	106.5p	118.0p	116.9p	118.4p	125.9p	123.6p
1997	103.2p	108.3p	122.7p	122.1p	122.9p	132.3p	129.5p
1998	105.1p	110.0p	127.4p	127.2p	127.5p	138.8p	135.4p

Sources: Same as General Statistics. The values shown reflect change from the base year, 1992. Values above 100 mean greater than 1992, values below 100 mean less than 1992, and a value of 100 in the 1982-91 or 1993-98 period means same as 1992. Values followed by a 'p' are projections by the editors; 'e' stands for extrapolation. Data are the most recent available at this level of detail.

SELECTED RATIOS

For 1992	Avg. of All Wholesale	Analyzed Industry	Index	For 1992	Avg. of All Wholesale	Analyzed Industry	Index
Employees per Establishment	12	12	99	Sales per Employee	561,172	310,551	55
Payroll per Establishment	349,729	331,724	95	Sales per Establishment	6,559,346	3,580,849	55
Payroll per Employee	29,919	28,769	96	Expenses per Establishment	723,071	641,763	89

Sources: Same as General Statistics. The 'Average of All Manufacturing' column represents the average of all manufacturing industries reported for the most recent complete year available. The Index shows the relationship between the Average and the Analyzed Industry. For example, 100 means that they are equal; 500 that the Analyzed Industry is five times the average; 50 means that the Analyzed Industry is half the national average. The abbreviation 'na' is used to show that data are 'not available'.

LEADING COMPANIES

Number shown: **50** Total sales ($ mil): **14,080** Total employment (000): **40.8**

Company Name	Address				CEO Name	Phone	Co. Type	Sales ($ mil)	Empl. (000)
Truserv Corp.	8600 W Bryn Mawr	Chicago	IL	60631	Dan A Cotter	773-695-5000	R	3,846 *	6.0
Ace Hardware Corp.	2200 Kensington	Oak Brook	IL	60523	David F Wodnik	708-990-6600	R	2,907	4.5
Hardware Wholesalers Inc.	PO Box 868	Fort Wayne	IN	46801	Michael McClelland	219-748-5300	R	1,000	1.1
West Union Corp.	PO Box 3177	Memphis	TN	38173	Micheal McDonnell	901-529-5700	R	420 *	1.9
Fastenal Co.	2001 Theurer Blvd	Winona	MN	55987	Robert A Kierlin	507-454-5374	P	398	3.1
Wynn's International Inc.	PO Box 14143	Orange	CA	92613	James Carroll	714-938-3700	P	321	2.1
Lawson Products Inc.	1666 E Touhy Ave	Des Plaines	IL	60018	Bernard Kalish	847-827-9666	P	278	1.9
Waxman Industries Inc.	24460 Aurora Rd	Bedford H.	OH	44146	Armond Waxman	216-439-1830	P	266	0.8
Orgill Brothers and Co.	2100 Latham St	Memphis	TN	38109	William Fondren Jr	901-948-3381	S	260 *	0.8
Pennington Seed Inc.	PO Box 290	Madison	GA	30650	B Pennington III	706-342-1234	R	250	0.7
Bowman Distribution	PO Box 6908	Cleveland	OH	44101	Leonard M Carlucci	216-416-7200	D	213	1.2
Makita U.S.A. Inc.	14930 Northam St	La Mirada	CA	90638	Paul Fukatsu	714-522-8088	S	210 *	0.7
Copeland Lumber Yard Inc.	901 NE Glisan St	Portland	OR	97232	Helen J Whitsell	503-232-7181	R	175	1.0
Black and Decker Corp.	626 Hanover Pike	Hampstead	MD	21074	Bud Schreiber	410-239-5000	D	173 *	1.0
Katy Industries Inc.	6300 S Syracuse	Englewood	CO	80111	John R Prann Jr	303-290-9300	P	171	1.1
Barnett Inc.	PO Box 2317	Jacksonville	FL	32203	William R Pray	904-384-6530	P	160	0.6
Moore-Handley Inc.	3140 Pelham Pkwy	Pelham	AL	35124	William Riley	205-663-8011	P	146	0.4
United Hardware	5005 Nathan Ln	Plymouth	MN	55442	David A Heider	612-559-1800	R	136	0.4
Kar Products	461 N 3rd Ave	Des Plaines	IL	60016	Max Beshears	847-296-6111	S	130	1.0
Swiss Army Brands Inc.	1 Research Dr	Shelton	CT	06484	J Merrick Taggert	203-929-6391	P	130	0.2
Firmont Tamper	PO Box 415	Fairmont	MN	56031	G Robert Newman	507-235-3361	D	110 *	0.9
Pendleton Grain Growers Inc.	1000 Dorion SW	Pendleton	OR	97801	Ed Balsiger	503-276-7611	R	105	0.3
Wilmar Industries Inc.	303 Harper Dr	Moorestown	NJ	08057	William S Green	609-439-1222	P	101	0.6
Lifetime Hoan Corp.	1 Merrick Ave	Westbury	NY	11590	Milton L Cohen	516-683-6000	P	100	0.5
Louis Berkman Co.	PO Box 820	Steubenville	OH	43952	Louis Berkman	614-283-3722	R	100	0.8
Burbank Aircraft Supply Inc.	10671 Lanark St	Sun Valley	CA	91352	Terry Brenner	818-767-8560	S	98 *	0.3
Maintenance Warehouse	PO Box 85838	San Diego	CA	92186	Lucille Neeley	619-452-5555	R	98 *	0.3
VSI Fasteners Inc.	PO Box 2007	Stanton	CA	90681	Clark Higgins	714-891-8400	R	98 *	0.3
Universal Cooperative Inc.	7801 Metro Pkwy	Minneapolis	MN	55440	Patrick Finley	612-854-0800	R	94 *	0.2
Caldwell Supply Company Inc.	PO Box T	Hazleton	PA	18201	Ralph Caldwell III	717-455-7511	R	92 *	0.2
Star Stainless Screw Co.	PO Box 288	Totowa	NJ	07511	Wayne Golden	201-256-2300	R	92 *	0.3
Emery Waterhouse Co.	PO Box 659	Portland	ME	04104	Charles Hildrein Jr	207-775-2371	R	90	0.3
Monroe Hardware Co.	101 Sutherland Ave	Monroe	NC	28110	William Prince Jr	704-289-3121	R	90	0.4
Arden Industrial Products Inc.	560 Oak Grove	Vadnais H.	MN	55127	Larry A Carlson	612-490-6800	P	88	0.4
American Lock and Supply	4411 E La Palma	Anaheim	CA	92807	Sean DeForrest	714-996-8882	R	85 *	0.3
Long Lewis Inc.	430 N 9th St	Birmingham	AL	35203	Vaughan Burrell	205-322-2561	R	85	0.2
W.E. Aubuchon Company Inc.	95 Aubuchon Dr	Westminster	MA	01473	W E Aubuchon Jr	508-874-0521	R	80	0.8
California Hardware Co.	PO Box 3640	Ontario	CA	91764	Hardy Soberholm	909-390-6100	R	79	0.2
Ammar's Inc.	S College Ave	Bluefield	VA	24605	Keleel A Ammar Jr	540-322-4686	R	75	0.8
Baer Supply Co.	909 Forest Edge Dr	Vernon Hills	IL	60061		847-913-2237	S	75 *	0.3
Jensen Distribution Services	PO Box 3708	Spokane	WA	99220	Mike Jensen	509-624-1321	R	74 *	0.2
Service Supply Company Inc.	PO Box 732	Indianapolis	IN	46206	Frank N Owings Jr	317-638-2424	R	72	0.5
Allied Wholesale Inc.	13207 Bradley Ave	Sylmar	CA	91342	Timothy Florian	818-364-2333	R	70	<0.1
AB Wholesale Co.	710 S College Ave	Bluefield	VA	24605	Kaleel A Ammar Jr	703-322-4686	S	70	0.1
Dougherty Hanna Resources	6000 Harvard Ave	Cleveland	OH	44105	Marcus Hanna	216-271-1200	R	68	0.1
Frederick Trading Co.	7901 Trading Ln	Frederick	MD	21705	Nicholas M Felsh	301-662-2161	R	66	0.4
Odell Hardware Company Inc.	PO Box 20688	Greensboro	NC	27420	Tom McGoldrick	910-299-9121	S	65 *	0.2
Kruse Co.	4275 Thunderbird	Fairfield	OH	45014	G Hovekamp Jr	513-860-3600	R	59	0.2
General Fasteners Company	11820 Globe St	Livonia	MI	48150	David H Grossman	313-591-9500	R	56 *	0.2
Bostwick-Braun Co.	PO Box 912	Toledo	OH	43697	Richard E Smith	419-259-3600	R	55	0.2

Source: *Ward's Business Directory of U.S. Private and Public Companies*, 1998. The company type code used is as follows: P - Public, R - Private, S - Subsidiary, D - Division, J - Joint Venture, A - Affiliate, G - Group. Sales are in millions of dollars, employees are in thousands. An asterisk (*) indicates an estimated sales volume. The symbol < stands for 'less than'.

OCCUPATIONS EMPLOYED BY SIC 507 - WHOLESALE TRADE, OTHER

Occupation	% of Total 1996	Change to 2006	Occupation	% of Total 1996	Change to 2006
Sales & related workers nec	19.5	20.2	Clerical supervisors & managers	1.9	20.2
General managers & top executives	5.9	16.4	Order clerks	1.9	8.2
Truck drivers light & heavy	5.4	20.2	Helpers, laborers nec	1.7	20.2
General office clerks	3.6	3.4	Electrical & electronic technicians	1.4	18.8
Traffic, shipping, receiving clerks	3.6	16.7	Blue collar worker supervisors	1.4	16.0
Stock clerks	3.5	-3.9	Wholesale & retail buyers, except farm products	1.3	17.0
Freight, stock, & material movers, hand	3.3	8.2	Office machine & cash register servicers	1.3	20.2
Marketing & sales worker supervisors	3.1	20.2	Hand packers & packagers	1.2	-3.9
Order fillers, wholesale & retail sales	3.0	16.7	Maintenance repairers, general utility	1.1	12.0
Bookkeeping, accounting, & auditing clerks	2.9	-3.9	Industrial truck & tractor operators	1.1	20.2
Salespersons, retail	2.5	20.2	Purchasing managers	1.1	20.2
Secretaries, except legal & medical	2.5	-4.7	Receptionists & information clerks	1.0	20.2
Assemblers, fabricators, hand workers nec	2.0	-3.9			

Source: *Industry-Occupation Matrix*, Bureau of Labor Statistics. These data relate to one or more 3-digit SIC industry groups rather than to a single 4-digit SIC. The change reported for each occupation to the year 2006 is a percent of growth or decline as estimated by the Bureau of Labor Statistics. The abbreviation nec stands for 'not elsewhere classified'.

STATE AND REGIONAL CONCENTRATION

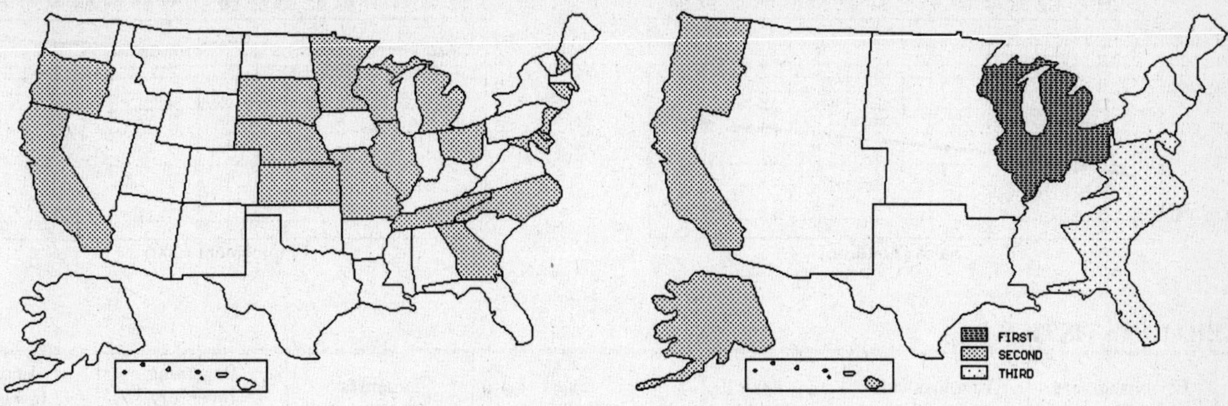

INDUSTRY DATA BY STATE

State	Establishments - 1995 Total (number)	Establishments - 1995 % of U.S.	Employment - 1995 Total (number)	Employment - 1995 % of U.S.	Employment - 1995 Per Estab.	Payroll - 1995 Total ($ mil.)	Payroll - 1995 Per Empl. ($)	Sales - 1992 Total ($ mil.)	Sales - 1992 % of U.S.	Sales - 1992 Per Estab ($)
California	1,034	11.9	14,326	13.5	14	468.7	32,717	4,103.1	13.9	303,643
Illinois	588	6.7	7,306	6.9	12	250.6	34,303	2,646.0	9.0	400,721
Texas	656	7.5	7,455	7.0	11	213.9	28,698	1,834.3	6.2	290,838
New York	587	6.7	5,838	5.5	10	204.9	35,096	1,415.0	4.8	246,216
Ohio	397	4.6	6,315	5.9	16	184.2	29,174	1,363.9	4.6	229,969
Maryland	121	1.4	1,543	1.5	13	45.0	29,152	1,312.7	4.5	722,864
Michigan	321	3.7	4,027	3.8	13	145.6	36,160	1,260.6	4.3	363,803
Georgia	263	3.0	2,714	2.6	10	77.4	28,509	1,203.6	4.1	474,417
New Jersey	351	4.0	3,879	3.6	11	165.4	42,650	1,200.9	4.1	305,035
Missouri	173	2.0	2,081	2.0	12	65.0	31,246	1,167.0	4.0	549,705
Pennsylvania	348	4.0	4,511	4.2	13	144.6	32,053	1,157.4	3.9	293,595
Florida	500	5.7	4,565	4.3	9	128.7	28,191	957.5	3.2	238,355
North Carolina	247	2.8	4,192	3.9	17	121.3	28,934	940.5	3.2	288,940
Minnesota	190	2.2	2,456	2.3	13	78.7	32,033	820.6	2.8	362,287
Tennessee	172	2.0	2,491	2.3	14	74.8	30,010	719.1	2.4	307,815
Wisconsin	177	2.0	2,718	2.6	15	79.9	29,402	679.3	2.3	297,680
Massachusetts	213	2.4	2,266	2.1	11	89.5	39,512	635.7	2.2	311,925
Indiana	204	2.3	2,469	2.3	12	74.3	30,093	612.0	2.1	268,070
Washington	202	2.3	2,188	2.1	11	67.8	31,008	527.6	1.8	234,290
Oregon	135	1.5	1,520	1.4	11	43.0	28,302	509.9	1.7	376,830
Arizona	139	1.6	1,800	1.7	13	47.8	26,534	432.2	1.5	281,728
Connecticut	115	1.3	1,301	1.2	11	42.4	32,592	413.1	1.4	351,017
Kansas	74	0.8	1,183	1.1	16	33.9	28,627	351.5	1.2	331,330
Virginia	155	1.8	1,685	1.6	11	43.3	25,725	347.5	1.2	200,182
Oklahoma	86	1.0	1,492	1.4	17	51.0	34,212	335.4	1.1	243,566
Colorado	144	1.7	1,400	1.3	10	41.0	29,283	300.9	1.0	298,773
Louisiana	107	1.2	1,123	1.1	10	28.9	25,729	271.4	0.9	249,693
South Carolina	68	0.8	976	0.9	14	28.4	29,072	262.8	0.9	329,262
Nebraska	50	0.6	994	0.9	20	20.5	20,631	232.2	0.8	270,577
Alabama	147	1.7	1,456	1.4	10	40.1	27,568	220.9	0.7	181,848
South Dakota	21	0.2	465	0.4	22	9.9	21,366	207.3	0.7	492,411
New Hampshire	38	0.4	573	0.5	15	17.3	30,145	204.6	0.7	376,882
Utah	64	0.7	845	0.8	13	21.4	25,309	144.4	0.5	256,982
Iowa	84	1.0	766	0.7	9	20.5	26,811	120.0	0.4	190,808
Maine	20	0.2	344	0.3	17	9.1	26,436	106.3	0.4	217,344
Hawaii	50	0.6	335	0.3	7	9.9	29,630	97.3	0.3	218,099
Arkansas	70	0.8	609	0.6	9	14.9	24,396	94.8	0.3	179,487
Delaware	21	0.2	196	0.2	9	7.7	39,097	87.4	0.3	475,196
Mississippi	58	0.7	404	0.4	7	10.6	26,220	62.1	0.2	178,922
Idaho	44	0.5	282	0.3	6	6.5	23,057	32.4	0.1	128,762
West Virginia	28	0.3	188	0.2	7	3.8	20,330	31.6	0.1	122,066
New Mexico	27	0.3	228	0.2	8	6.8	29,776	25.8	0.1	150,971
Montana	18	0.2	206	0.2	11	3.8	18,340	23.5	0.1	131,826
North Dakota	16	0.2	126	0.1	8	2.5	19,635	16.4	0.1	158,154
Wyoming	11	0.1	55	0.1	5	1.1	20,582	5.7	0.0	191,200
Kentucky	72	0.8	691	0.6	10	18.5	26,745	(D)	-	-
Nevada	48	0.6	606	0.6	13	18.8	30,998	(D)	-	-
Rhode Island	33	0.4	804	0.8	24	31.7	39,488	(D)	-	-
Vermont	17	0.2	99	0.1	6	2.2	21,848	(D)	-	-
D.C.	12	0.1	118	0.1	10	4.9	41,119	(D)	-	-
Alaska	7	0.1	150	0.1	21	4.2	27,813	(D)	-	-

Source: County Business Patterns, 1995 and *Economic Census of the U.S., 1992*. Data are sorted by 1992 revenues and, if revenues are unavailable, by establishments in 1995. The symbol (D) indicates that data are withheld by the source to avoid disclosure of competitive information. A dash (-) indicates that data are not available or undisclosed because they do not meet statistical validity standards. Shaded *states* on the state map indicate those states which have proportionately greater representation in the industry than would be indicated by the state's population; the ratio is based on total revenues or number of establishments. Shaded *regions* indicate where the industry is regionally most concentrated.

5074 - PLUMBING & HYDRONIC HEATING SUPPLIES

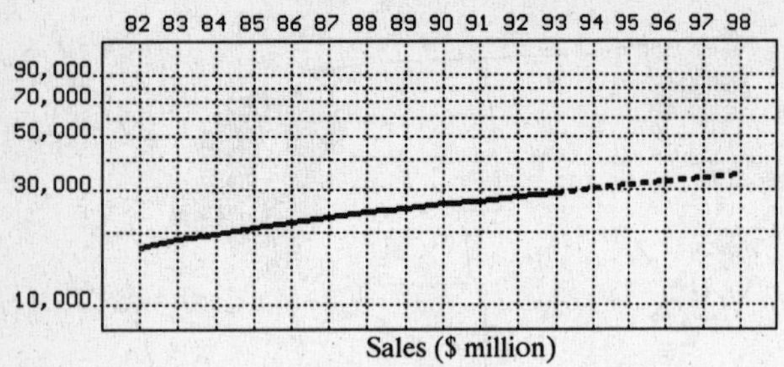

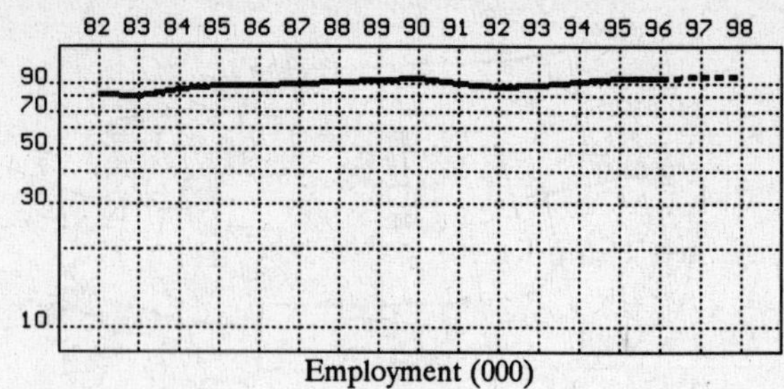

GENERAL STATISTICS

Year	Establishments (number)	Employment (number)	Payroll ($ million)	Sales ($ million)	Expenses ($ million)	Beginning Inventory ($ million)	Ending Inventory ($ million)
1982	8,820	82,459	1,501.3	17,364.1	-	-	-
1983	8,592	80,530	1,575.6	18,540.4e	-	-	-
1984	8,578	85,856	1,765.6	19,716.7e	-	-	-
1985	8,522	88,526	1,935.6	20,893.1e	-	-	-
1986	8,442	88,421	1,979.8	22,069.4e	-	-	-
1987	8,931	89,872	2,086.0	23,245.7	3,991.7	2,575.6	2,800.4
1988	8,677	90,817	2,343.7	24,175.2e	4,151.4e	2,684.0e	2,871.5e
1989	8,558	93,194	2,472.7	25,104.7e	4,311.2e	2,792.4e	2,942.7e
1990	8,659	94,194	2,541.7	26,034.3e	4,471.0e	2,900.8e	3,013.8e
1991	8,712	89,719	2,461.4	26,963.8e	4,630.7e	3,009.1e	3,085.0e
1992	9,326	87,048	2,488.7	27,893.3	4,790.5	3,117.5	3,156.1
1993	9,213	88,760	2,620.5	29,226.7p	4,950.3p	3,225.9p	3,227.3p
1994	9,341	92,224	2,845.7	30,279.6p	5,110.0p	3,334.3p	3,298.4p
1995	9,400	95,002	2,976.1	31,332.5p	5,269.8p	3,442.6p	3,369.6p
1996	9,295p	94,473p	3,058.1p	32,385.5p	5,429.6p	3,551.0p	3,440.7p
1997	9,355p	95,196p	3,164.9p	33,438.4p	5,589.3p	3,659.4p	3,511.9p
1998	9,416p	95,920p	3,271.8p	34,491.3p	5,749.1p	3,767.8p	3,583.0p

Sources: *Economic Census of the United States*, 1982, 1987, and 1992. Establishment counts, employment, and payroll are from *County Business Patterns* for non-Census years. Values followed by a 'p' are projections by the editors. Sales and expense data for non-Census years are extrapolations, marked by 'e'. Industries reclassified in 1987 will not have data for prior years. Data are the most recent available at this level of detail.

INDICES OF CHANGE

Year	Establishments (number)	Employment (number)	Payroll ($ million)	Sales ($ million)	Expenses ($ million)	Beginning Inventory ($ million)	Ending Inventory ($ million)
1982	94.6	94.7	60.3	62.3	-	-	-
1983	92.1	92.5	63.3	66.5e	-	-	-
1984	92.0	98.6	70.9	70.7e	-	-	-
1985	91.4	101.7	77.8	74.9e	-	-	-
1986	90.5	101.6	79.6	79.1e	-	-	-
1987	95.8	103.2	83.8	83.3	83.3	82.6	88.7
1988	93.0	104.3	94.2	86.7e	86.7e	86.1e	91.0e
1989	91.8	107.1	99.4	90.0e	90.0e	89.6e	93.2e
1990	92.8	108.2	102.1	93.3e	93.3e	93.0e	95.5e
1991	93.4	103.1	98.9	96.7e	96.7e	96.5e	97.7e
1992	100.0	100.0	100.0	100.0	100.0	100.0	100.0
1993	98.8	102.0	105.3	104.8p	103.3p	103.5p	102.3p
1994	100.2	105.9	114.3	108.6p	106.7p	107.0p	104.5p
1995	100.8	109.1	119.6	112.3p	110.0p	110.4p	106.8p
1996	99.7p	108.5p	122.9p	116.1p	113.3p	113.9p	109.0p
1997	100.3p	109.4p	127.2p	119.9p	116.7p	117.4p	111.3p
1998	101.0p	110.2p	131.5p	123.7p	120.0p	120.9p	113.5p

Sources: Same as General Statistics. The values shown reflect change from the base year, 1992. Values above 100 mean greater than 1992, values below 100 mean less than 1992, and a value of 100 in the 1982-91 or 1993-98 period means same as 1992. Values followed by a 'p' are projections by the editors; 'e' stands for extrapolation. Data are the most recent available at this level of detail.

SELECTED RATIOS

For 1992	Avg. of All Wholesale	Analyzed Industry	Index	For 1992	Avg. of All Wholesale	Analyzed Industry	Index
Employees per Establishment	12	9	80	Sales per Employee	561,172	320,436	57
Payroll per Establishment	349,729	266,856	76	Sales per Establishment	6,559,346	2,990,918	46
Payroll per Employee	29,919	28,590	96	Expenses per Establishment	723,071	513,671	71

Sources: Same as General Statistics. The 'Average of All Manufacturing' column represents the average of all manufacturing industries reported for the most recent complete year available. The Index shows the relationship between the Average and the Analyzed Industry. For example, 100 means that they are equal; 500 that the Analyzed Industry is five times the average; 50 means that the Analyzed Industry is half the national average. The abbreviation 'na' is used to show that data are 'not available'.

LEADING COMPANIES

Number shown: **50** Total sales ($ mil): **11,313** Total employment (000): **33.4**

Company Name	Address				CEO Name	Phone	Co. Type	Sales ($ mil)	Empl. (000)
Shaklee Corp.	444 Market St	San Francisco	CA	94111	Charles L Orr	415-954-3000	S	1,690 *	2.2
Hughes Supply Inc.	PO Box 2273	Orlando	FL	32802	David H Hughes	407-841-4755	P	1,082	3.3
Ferguson Enterprises Inc.	PO Box 2778	Newport News	VA	23609	Charles A Banks	804-874-7795	S	1,000	3.0
Bell Industries Inc.	11812 San Vicente	Los Angeles	CA	90049	Gordon Graham	310-826-2355	P	891	1.9
Cambridge-Lee Industries Inc.	500 Lincoln St	Allston	MA	02134	Gunther Bouer	617-783-3100	R	570 *	0.8
Primus Inc.	3110 Kettering Blvd	Dayton	OH	45439	Richard F Schiewetz	513-294-6878	R	530	2.0
Noland Co.	80 29th St	Newport News	VA	23607	Lloyd U Noland III	757-928-9000	P	465	1.6
Familian Northwest Inc.	PO Box 17098	Portland	OR	97217	Tom Stern	503-283-3333	S	420 *	1.2
Automatic Equipment Sales	PO Box 27305	Richmond	VA	23261	Ralph K Taylor	804-355-0651	R	325	0.6
Familian Pipe and Supply	7651 Woodman	Van Nuys	CA	91402	David Shapiro	818-786-9720	D	300 *	1.3
Hajoca Corp.	127 Coulter Ave	Ardmore	PA	19003	RF Parsons	215-649-1430	R	300 *	1.3
Waxman Industries Inc.	24460 Aurora Rd	Bedford H.	OH	44146	Armond Waxman	216-439-1830	P	266	0.8
Westburne Supply Inc.	PO Box 65013	Anaheim	CA	92815		714-491-0992	S	193 *	0.5
F.W. Webb Co.	200 Middlesex Tpk	Burlington	MA	01803	John Pope	617-272-6600	R	180	0.6
Gage Co.	PO Box 1168	Pittsburgh	PA	15230	Robert A Chute	412-255-6904	R	176	0.6
Barnett Inc.	PO Box 2317	Jacksonville	FL	32203	William R Pray	904-384-6530	P	160	0.6
Moore-Handley Inc.	3140 Pelham Pkwy	Pelham	AL	35124	William Riley	205-663-8011	P	146	0.4
Apex Supply Company Inc.	2500 Gwinnett	Atlanta	GA	30340	Clyde Rodbell	404-449-7000	R	140 *	0.4
Chicago Tube and Iron Co.	2531 W 48th St	Chicago	IL	60632	Robert B Haigh	312-523-1441	R	140	0.4
R.E. Michel Company Inc.	1 RE Michel Dr	Glen Burnie	MD	21060	JWH Michel	410-760-4000	R	130	0.7
Thos. Somerville Co.	4900 6th St NE	Washington	DC	20017	Michael McInerney	202-635-4321	R	125	0.4
Famous Enterprises Inc.	PO Box 1889	Akron	OH	44309	Jay Blaushild	216-762-9621	R	120	0.7
National Safety Associates Inc.	PO Box 18603	Memphis	TN	38181	Jay Martin	901-366-9288	R	110	0.1
Wilmar Industries Inc.	303 Harper Dr	Moorestown	NJ	08057	William S Green	609-439-1222	P	101	0.6
SPS Company Inc.	6363 Hwy 7	Minneapolis	MN	55416	Ralph Gross	612-929-1377	R	100	0.3
Chicago Furnace Supply Inc.	4929 S Lincoln	Lisle	IL	60532	Robert A Lorenz	708-971-0400	R	99	<0.1
Keenan Supply	PO Box 759	La Puente	CA	91747	Eric Augustin	818-330-1225	D	94	0.4
Gerber Plumbing Fixtures Corp.	4656 W Touhy Ave	Chicago	IL	60646	Harriet G Lewis	312-675-6570	R	90	0.9
Lyon Conklin and Company	2101 Race St	Baltimore	MD	21230	Jenny Allen	410-752-6800	R	90	0.2
Consolidated Pipe and Supply	PO Box 2472	Birmingham	AL	35201	Howard Kerr	205-323-7261	R	82 *	0.4
Raub Supply Co.	301 W James St	Lancaster	PA	17604	Joseph C Schick	717-397-6221	R	75	0.3
Keller Supply Co.	3209 17th Ave W	Seattle	WA	98119	Nick Keller	206-285-3300	R	71 *	0.3
Slakey Brothers Inc.	PO Box 15647	Sacramento	CA	95852	Frank Nisonger	916-329-3750	R	71 *	0.3
Service Supply Systems Inc.	PO Box 749	Cordele	GA	31015	CM Hunt	912-273-1112	R	70	0.2
Trumbull Industries Inc.	PO Box 30	Warren	OH	44482	Richard C Mueller	216-393-6624	R	70	0.3
Frederick Trading Co.	7901 Trading Ln	Frederick	MD	21705	Nicholas M Felsh	301-662-2161	R	66	0.4
Temperature Equipment Corp.	17725 Volbrecht Rd	Lansing	IL	60438	FA Mungo	708-418-0900	R	65	0.1
Robertson Heating Supply Co.	500 W Main St	Alliance	OH	44601	Scott Robertson	216-821-9180	R	62	0.2
Sidener Supply Co.	PO Box 28446	St. Louis	MO	63146	Lawrence E Sidener	314-432-4700	R	62 *	0.2
La Crosse Plumbing Supply Co.	106 Cameron Ave	La Crosse	WI	54601	Jerry Stahl	608-784-3839	R	60 *	0.3
Fields and Company of Lubbock	1610 5th St	Lubbock	TX	79408	Dan Law	806-762-0241	R	59 *	0.3
Ace Electric Supply Co.	5911 Phillips Hwy	Jacksonville	FL	32216	Barry Covington	904-731-5900	R	58 *	0.2
Connor Co.	2800 NE Adams St	Peoria	IL	61601	WP Collins	309-688-4406	R	55	0.2
J.H. Larson Electrical Co.	700 Colorado Ave S	Minneapolis	MN	55416	CE Pahl	612-545-1717	R	55	0.2
Columbia Pipe and Supply	1120 W Pershing	Chicago	IL	60609	WD Arenberg	312-927-6600	R	50	0.2
Heatilator Inc.	1915 W Saunders St	Mount Pleasant	IA	52641	Stan Askren	319-385-9211	S	50 *	0.4
Moore Supply Co.	PO Box 448	Conroe	TX	77305	Mark Hanley	409-756-4445	R	50	0.2
Treaty Co.	PO Box 40	Greenville	OH	45331	MM Montgomery	513-548-2181	R	50	0.8
United Pipe and Supply	PO Box 2220	Eugene	OR	97402	Taylor Ramsey	503-688-6511	R	50 *	0.2
Blodgett Supply Company Inc.	PO Box 759	Williston	VT	05495	Sam Levin	802-864-9831	R	49 *	0.1

Source: *Ward's Business Directory of U.S. Private and Public Companies*, 1998. The company type code used is as follows: P - Public, R - Private, S - Subsidiary, D - Division, J - Joint Venture, A - Affiliate, G - Group. Sales are in millions of dollars, employees are in thousands. An asterisk (*) indicates an estimated sales volume. The symbol < stands for 'less than'.

OCCUPATIONS EMPLOYED BY SIC 507 - WHOLESALE TRADE, OTHER

Occupation	% of Total 1996	Change to 2006	Occupation	% of Total 1996	Change to 2006
Sales & related workers nec	19.5	20.2	Clerical supervisors & managers	1.9	20.2
General managers & top executives	5.9	16.4	Order clerks	1.9	8.2
Truck drivers light & heavy	5.4	20.2	Helpers, laborers nec	1.7	20.2
General office clerks	3.6	3.4	Electrical & electronic technicians	1.4	18.8
Traffic, shipping, receiving clerks	3.6	16.7	Blue collar worker supervisors	1.4	16.0
Stock clerks	3.5	-3.9	Wholesale & retail buyers, except farm products	1.3	17.0
Freight, stock, & material movers, hand	3.3	8.2	Office machine & cash register servicers	1.3	20.2
Marketing & sales worker supervisors	3.1	20.2	Hand packers & packagers	1.2	-3.9
Order fillers, wholesale & retail sales	3.0	16.7	Maintenance repairers, general utility	1.1	12.0
Bookkeeping, accounting, & auditing clerks	2.9	-3.9	Industrial truck & tractor operators	1.1	20.2
Salespersons, retail	2.5	20.2	Purchasing managers	1.1	20.2
Secretaries, except legal & medical	2.5	-4.7	Receptionists & information clerks	1.0	20.2
Assemblers, fabricators, hand workers nec	2.0	-3.9			

Source: *Industry-Occupation Matrix*, Bureau of Labor Statistics. These data relate to one or more 3-digit SIC industry groups rather than to a single 4-digit SIC. The change reported for each occupation to the year 2006 is a percent of growth or decline as estimated by the Bureau of Labor Statistics. The abbreviation nec stands for 'not elsewhere classified'.

STATE AND REGIONAL CONCENTRATION

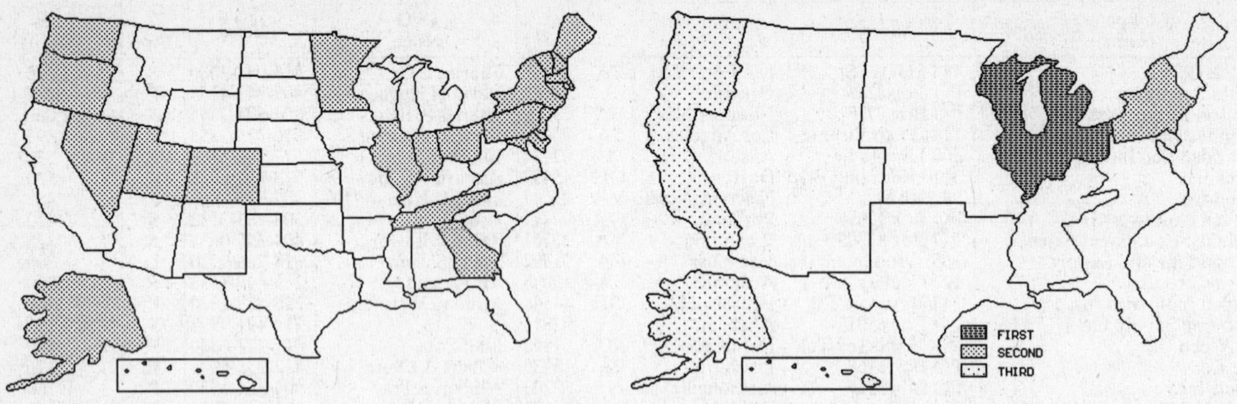

INDUSTRY DATA BY STATE

	Establishments - 1995		Employment - 1995			Payroll - 1995		Sales - 1992		
State	Total (number)	% of U.S.	Total (number)	% of U.S.	Per Estab.	Total ($ mil.)	Per Empl. ($)	Total ($ mil.)	% of U.S.	Per Estab ($)
California	829	8.8	9,058	9.6	11	291.1	32,139	3,211.8	11.6	355,756
New York	713	7.6	6,576	6.9	9	222.0	33,765	2,185.3	7.9	305,716
Illinois	380	4.0	4,546	4.8	12	169.0	37,181	1,893.3	6.8	470,504
Pennsylvania	534	5.7	6,086	6.4	11	188.1	30,911	1,702.9	6.1	284,239
Texas	608	6.5	5,447	5.7	9	161.4	29,628	1,556.5	5.6	304,481
Ohio	423	4.5	4,833	5.1	11	142.5	29,480	1,310.7	4.7	330,742
Florida	548	5.8	4,287	4.5	8	128.2	29,914	1,245.4	4.5	298,584
Massachusetts	253	2.7	3,094	3.3	12	115.1	37,199	1,037.9	3.7	357,660
New Jersey	340	3.6	3,545	3.7	10	126.4	35,669	1,013.9	3.6	291,767
Georgia	255	2.7	2,612	2.8	10	85.5	32,717	904.8	3.3	421,828
Michigan	296	3.1	3,185	3.4	11	98.7	30,986	884.3	3.2	317,538
North Carolina	278	3.0	2,473	2.6	9	76.8	31,051	726.6	2.6	346,309
Indiana	218	2.3	2,556	2.7	12	79.3	31,016	718.6	2.6	308,421
Washington	178	1.9	2,039	2.2	11	60.5	29,653	675.4	2.4	365,091
Minnesota	184	2.0	1,892	2.0	10	68.3	36,088	665.3	2.4	392,021
Maryland	174	1.9	1,858	2.0	11	58.3	31,399	632.8	2.3	374,190
Virginia	204	2.2	1,821	1.9	9	55.8	30,633	598.3	2.2	327,102
Tennessee	170	1.8	1,907	2.0	11	59.0	30,956	552.3	2.0	332,103
Wisconsin	191	2.0	2,398	2.5	13	73.7	30,716	516.2	1.9	260,328
Colorado	179	1.9	1,891	2.0	11	63.7	33,697	509.3	1.8	360,179
Missouri	242	2.6	2,156	2.3	9	64.6	29,953	457.5	1.6	265,511
Connecticut	146	1.6	1,442	1.5	10	50.7	35,131	404.5	1.5	275,351
Oregon	108	1.1	1,455	1.5	13	49.3	33,880	382.1	1.4	275,865
Arizona	141	1.5	1,323	1.4	9	37.8	28,599	353.4	1.3	305,413
Louisiana	134	1.4	1,167	1.2	9	30.1	25,802	294.9	1.1	302,809
Alabama	132	1.4	1,199	1.3	9	32.8	27,348	283.9	1.0	287,324
Kansas	123	1.3	1,118	1.2	9	29.5	26,395	271.6	1.0	423,738
Iowa	128	1.4	1,181	1.2	9	34.1	28,886	253.8	0.9	270,252
Utah	80	0.9	1,105	1.2	14	32.1	29,042	239.6	0.9	217,191
Oklahoma	118	1.3	842	0.9	7	21.3	25,274	225.5	0.8	332,056
Kentucky	123	1.3	1,155	1.2	9	28.8	24,941	224.8	0.8	235,876
South Carolina	99	1.1	925	1.0	9	26.3	28,404	192.0	0.7	211,881
New Hampshire	71	0.8	724	0.8	10	19.5	26,981	163.1	0.6	303,765
Nevada	53	0.6	771	0.8	15	24.4	31,712	159.4	0.6	286,644
Maine	64	0.7	680	0.7	11	18.3	26,874	149.9	0.5	248,552
Mississippi	68	0.7	543	0.6	8	13.8	25,422	141.6	0.5	264,667
Arkansas	97	1.0	686	0.7	7	16.3	23,730	137.4	0.5	257,732
New Mexico	67	0.7	543	0.6	8	14.9	27,409	110.7	0.4	245,933
Hawaii	43	0.5	276	0.3	6	8.4	30,362	107.8	0.4	296,978
Idaho	34	0.4	377	0.4	11	9.9	26,337	106.3	0.4	278,277
Nebraska	63	0.7	451	0.5	7	11.9	26,295	100.2	0.4	243,903
West Virginia	55	0.6	500	0.5	9	11.3	22,516	80.5	0.3	193,957
Montana	34	0.4	362	0.4	11	8.8	24,390	73.6	0.3	256,296
Alaska	37	0.4	339	0.4	9	11.7	34,590	72.9	0.3	285,980
Vermont	32	0.3	293	0.3	9	7.9	27,102	68.4	0.2	212,994
South Dakota	40	0.4	292	0.3	7	8.2	27,938	59.8	0.2	225,747
North Dakota	24	0.3	215	0.2	9	6.3	29,260	53.9	0.2	272,384
Delaware	36	0.4	280	0.3	8	8.4	29,971	51.6	0.2	234,373
Wyoming	14	0.1	20-99	-	-	(D)	-	21.3	0.1	242,205
Rhode Island	33	0.4	289	0.3	9	9.9	34,107	(D)	-	-
D.C.	6	0.1	100-249	-	-	(D)	-	(D)	-	-

Source: County Business Patterns, 1995 and *Economic Census of the U.S., 1992*. Data are sorted by 1992 revenues and, if revenues are unavailable, by establishments in 1995. The symbol (D) indicates that data are withheld by the source to avoid disclosure of competitive information. A dash (-) indicates that data are not available or undisclosed because they do not meet statistical validity standards. Shaded *states* on the state map indicate those states which have proportionately greater representation in the industry than would be indicated by the state's population; the ratio is based on total revenues or number of establishments. Shaded *regions* indicate where the industry is regionally most concentrated.

5075 - WARM AIR HEATING & AIR-CONDITIONING

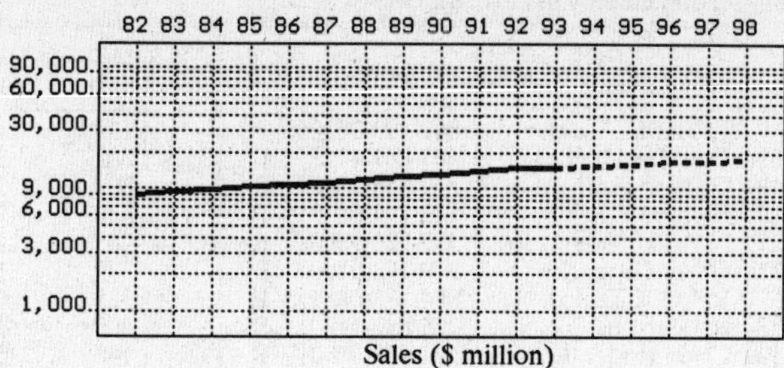

Sales ($ million)

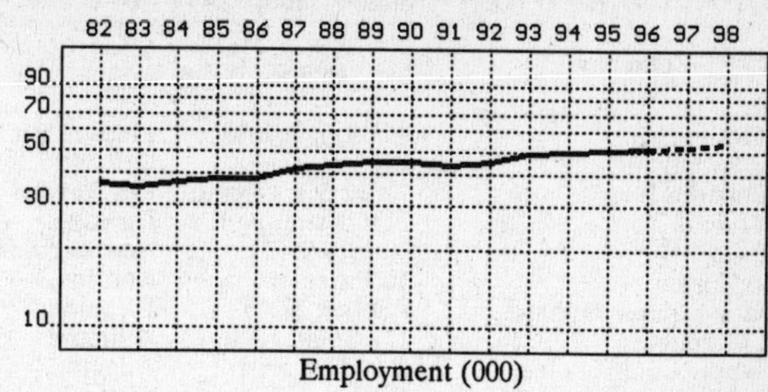

Employment (000)

GENERAL STATISTICS

Year	Establishments (number)	Employment (number)	Payroll ($ million)	Sales ($ million)	Expenses ($ million)	Beginning Inventory ($ million)	Ending Inventory ($ million)
1982	4,398	36,732	752.4	8,966.2	-	-	-
1983	4,242	35,352	800.7	9,401.4e	-	-	-
1984	4,244	37,125	912.6	9,836.7e	-	-	-
1985	4,116	38,009	977.9	10,272.0e	-	-	-
1986	4,064	38,424	1,012.3	10,707.3e	-	-	-
1987	5,101	42,414	1,109.8	11,142.6	2,167.2	1,328.6	1,429.2
1988	4,931	43,164	1,217.8	11,838.2e	2,285.0e	1,427.3e	1,537.3e
1989	4,822	44,753	1,345.0	12,533.8e	2,402.9e	1,526.0e	1,645.4e
1990	4,837	44,832	1,380.6	13,229.5e	2,520.8e	1,624.7e	1,753.5e
1991	4,868	43,900	1,377.2	13,925.1e	2,638.6e	1,723.4e	1,861.6e
1992	5,486	45,129	1,461.4	14,620.8	2,756.5	1,822.1	1,969.7
1993	5,470	48,196	1,623.1	14,890.4p	2,874.3p	1,920.8p	2,077.8p
1994	5,506	49,661	1,772.0	15,455.8p	2,992.2p	2,019.5p	2,185.9p
1995	5,571	50,314	1,852.7	16,021.3p	3,110.1p	2,118.2p	2,294.0p
1996	5,704p	51,281p	1,875.5p	16,586.8p	3,227.9p	2,216.9p	2,402.1p
1997	5,821p	52,423p	1,958.0p	17,152.2p	3,345.8p	2,315.6p	2,510.2p
1998	5,937p	53,565p	2,040.4p	17,717.7p	3,463.6p	2,414.3p	2,618.3p

Sources: *Economic Census of the United States*, 1982, 1987, and 1992. Establishment counts, employment, and payroll are from *County Business Patterns* for non-Census years. Values followed by a 'p' are projections by the editors. Sales and expense data for non-Census years are extrapolations, marked by 'e'. Industries reclassified in 1987 will not have data for prior years. Data are the most recent available at this level of detail.

INDICES OF CHANGE

Year	Establishments (number)	Employment (number)	Payroll ($ million)	Sales ($ million)	Expenses ($ million)	Beginning Inventory ($ million)	Ending Inventory ($ million)
1982	80.2	81.4	51.5	61.3	-	-	-
1983	77.3	78.3	54.8	64.3e	-	-	-
1984	77.4	82.3	62.4	67.3e	-	-	-
1985	75.0	84.2	66.9	70.3e	-	-	-
1986	74.1	85.1	69.3	73.2e	-	-	-
1987	93.0	94.0	75.9	76.2	78.6	72.9	72.6
1988	89.9	95.6	83.3	81.0e	82.9e	78.3e	78.0e
1989	87.9	99.2	92.0	85.7e	87.2e	83.7e	83.5e
1990	88.2	99.3	94.5	90.5e	91.4e	89.2e	89.0e
1991	88.7	97.3	94.2	95.2e	95.7e	94.6e	94.5e
1992	100.0	100.0	100.0	100.0	100.0	100.0	100.0
1993	99.7	106.8	111.1	101.8p	104.3p	105.4p	105.5p
1994	100.4	110.0	121.3	105.7p	108.6p	110.8p	111.0p
1995	101.5	111.5	126.8	109.6p	112.8p	116.3p	116.5p
1996	104.0p	113.6p	128.3p	113.4p	117.1p	121.7p	122.0p
1997	106.1p	116.2p	134.0p	117.3p	121.4p	127.1p	127.4p
1998	108.2p	118.7p	139.6p	121.2p	125.7p	132.5p	132.9p

Sources: Same as General Statistics. The values shown reflect change from the base year, 1992. Values above 100 mean greater than 1992, values below 100 mean less than 1992, and a value of 100 in the 1982-91 or 1993-98 period means same as 1992. Values followed by a 'p' are projections by the editors; 'e' stands for extrapolation. Data are the most recent available at this level of detail.

SELECTED RATIOS

For 1992	Avg. of All Wholesale	Analyzed Industry	Index	For 1992	Avg. of All Wholesale	Analyzed Industry	Index
Employees per Establishment	12	8	70	Sales per Employee	561,172	323,978	58
Payroll per Establishment	349,729	266,387	76	Sales per Establishment	6,559,346	2,665,111	41
Payroll per Employee	29,919	32,383	108	Expenses per Establishment	723,071	502,461	69

Sources: Same as General Statistics. The 'Average of All Manufacturing' column represents the average of all manufacturing industries reported for the most recent complete year available. The Index shows the relationship between the Average and the Analyzed Industry. For example, 100 means that they are equal; 500 that the Analyzed Industry is five times the average; 50 means that the Analyzed Industry is half the national average. The abbreviation 'na' is used to show that data are 'not available'.

LEADING COMPANIES

Number shown: **50** Total sales ($ mil): **10,818** Total employment (000): **35.9**

Company Name	Address				CEO Name	Phone	Co. Type	Sales ($ mil)	Empl. (000)
W.W. Grainger Inc.	455 Knightsbridge	Lincolnshire	IL	60069	Richard L Keyser	847-793-9030	P	4,137	14.6
Hughes Supply Inc.	PO Box 2273	Orlando	FL	32802	David H Hughes	407-841-4755	P	1,082	3.3
Bell Industries Inc.	11812 San Vicente	Los Angeles	CA	90049	Gordon Graham	310-826-2355	P	891	1.9
Primus Inc.	3110 Kettering Blvd	Dayton	OH	45439	Richard F Schiewetz	513-294-6878	R	530	2.0
Noland Co.	80 29th St	Newport News	VA	23607	Lloyd U Noland III	757-928-9000	P	465	1.6
Pameco Corp.	1000 Center Place	Norcross	GA	30093	Gerry Gurbacki	770-798-0700	P	379	1.3
Automatic Equipment Sales	PO Box 27305	Richmond	VA	23261	Ralph K Taylor	804-355-0651	R	325	0.6
Hajoca Corp.	127 Coulter Ave	Ardmore	PA	19003	RF Parsons	215-649-1430	R	300 *	1.3
Apex Supply Company Inc.	2500 Gwinnett	Atlanta	GA	30340	Clyde Rodbell	404-449-7000	R	140 *	0.4
Famous Manufacturing Co.	PO Box 1889	Akron	OH	44309	Dave Ross	216-762-9621	R	140 *	0.6
R.E. Michel Company Inc.	1 RE Michel Dr	Glen Burnie	MD	21060	JWH Michel	410-760-4000	R	130	0.7
Thos. Somerville Co.	4900 6th St NE	Washington	DC	20017	Michael McInerney	202-635-4321	R	125	0.4
Gensco Inc.	4402 20th St E	Tacoma	WA	98424	Charles E Walters	253-922-3003	R	117 *	0.5
Baker Distributing Co.	PO Box 2954	Jacksonville	FL	32203	Terry Kelly	904-733-9633	S	107	0.5
Chicago Furnace Supply Inc.	4929 S Lincoln	Lisle	IL	60532	Robert A Lorenz	708-971-0400	R	99	<0.1
Climatic Corp.	PO Box 25189	Columbia	SC	29224	John H Bailey	803-736-7770	R	95	0.1
Thermo Industries Inc.	4300 Golf Acres Dr	Charlotte	NC	28208	Robert M Teague	704-394-7311	S	92	0.2
Lyon Conklin and Company	2101 Race St	Baltimore	MD	21230	Jenny Allen	410-752-6800	R	90	0.2
Refron Inc.	38 33rd St, #18	Long Island C.	NY	11101	Jay Kestenbaum	718-392-8002	R	85	<0.1
ACR Group Inc.	3200 Wilcrest Dr	Houston	TX	77042	Alex Trevino Jr	713-780-8532	P	78	0.2
ABCO Refrigeration Supply	49-70 31st St	Long Island C.	NY	11101	JA Gottlieb	718-937-9000	R	75	0.2
Slakey Brothers Inc.	PO Box 15647	Sacramento	CA	95852	Frank Nisonger	916-329-3750	R	71 *	0.3
Coastline Distribution Inc.	601 Codisco Way	Sanford	FL	32771	Mark Nelles	407-323-8500	S	68	0.2
United Refrigeration Inc.	11401 Roosevelt	Philadelphia	PA	19154	John H Reilly	215-698-9100	R	66 *	0.3
Temperature Equipment Corp.	17725 Volbrecht Rd	Lansing	IL	60438	FA Mungo	708-418-0900	R	65	0.1
Robertson Heating Supply Co.	500 W Main St	Alliance	OH	44601	Scott Robertson	216-821-9180	R	62	0.2
J.H. Larson Electrical Co.	700 Colorado Ave S	Minneapolis	MN	55416	CE Pahl	612-545-1717	R	55	0.2
Johnson Supply and Equipment	10151 Stella Link	Houston	TX	77025	Robert E Uehlinger	713-661-6666	R	54	0.2
Columbia Pipe and Supply	1120 W Pershing	Chicago	IL	60609	WD Arenberg	312-927-6600	R	50	0.2
Mutual Mfg and Supply Co.	3300 Spring Grove	Cincinnati	OH	45225	Andrew P Barton Jr	513-541-2330	R	50	0.3
Treaty Co.	PO Box 40	Greenville	OH	45331	MM Montgomery	513-548-2181	R	50	0.8
Goodin Co.	2700 N 2nd St	Minneapolis	MN	55411	BD Reisberg	612-588-7811	R	47 *	0.2
Armstrong International Inc.	816 Maple St	Three Rivers	MI	49093	Gus Armstrong	616-273-1415	S	45 *	0.3
Hammond Sheet Metal	119 Cass Ave	St. Louis	MO	63102	GK Moser	314-241-5922	R	45	0.1
Gustave A. Larson Co.	2425 S 162nd St	New Berlin	WI	53151	J Michael McBride	414-782-2300	R	44	0.1
Actrade International Ltd.	7 Penn Plaza	New York	NY	10001	Henry N Seror	212-563-1036	P	43	<0.1
Mingledorffs Inc.	6675 Jones Mill Ct	Norcross	GA	30092	Robert M Kesterton	404-446-6311	R	43 *	0.2
Robertshaw Uni-Line	PO Box 2000	Corona	CA	91718	Gerry Wiley	909-734-2600	D	41 *	0.2
Control Resource Industries	670 Mariner Dr	Michigan City	IN	46360	John M Wojcik	219-872-5591	P	41	0.1
Habegger Corp.	4995 Winton Rd	Cincinnati	OH	45232	F Habegger	513-681-6313	R	40	0.1
Marco Sales Inc.	1100 Macklind Ave	St. Louis	MO	63110	AB Jokerst Jr	314-768-4200	R	40	<0.1
Wittichen Supply Company Inc.	1600 3rd Ave S	Birmingham	AL	35233	David P Henderson	205-251-8500	R	40	0.1
Refrigeration Sales Corp.	3405 Perkins Ave	Cleveland	OH	44114	W Farr Jr	216-881-7800	R	39	0.1
Andrews Distributing Company	PO Box 17557	Nashville	TN	37217	Peggy Andrews	615-399-1776	R	38	<0.1
Cain and Bultman Co.	4825 Fulton Indrial	Atlanta	GA	30336	V Bauer	404-691-0730	D	35 *	<0.1
Burke Engineering Company	PO Box 3427	El Monte	CA	91733	Gary W Burke	626-579-6763	R	34 *	0.1
Waltron Inc.	3989 Central NE	Minneapolis	MN	55421	Ronald Lewis	612-781-6601	R	34 *	0.1
Excelsior Mfg and Supply	1465 E Indrial Dr	Itasca	IL	60143	John Brady	708-773-5500	R	33	0.2
Weathertrol Supply Company	2600 University	Denton	TX	76201	Rick Salazar	940-387-1778	S	32	0.1
Thermal Supply Inc.	717 S Lander St	Seattle	WA	98134	Bob Monroe	206-624-4590	R	31 *	0.1

Source: *Ward's Business Directory of U.S. Private and Public Companies*, 1998. The company type code used is as follows: P - Public, R - Private, S - Subsidiary, D - Division, J - Joint Venture, A - Affiliate, G - Group. Sales are in millions of dollars, employees are in thousands. An asterisk (*) indicates an estimated sales volume. The symbol < stands for 'less than'.

OCCUPATIONS EMPLOYED BY SIC 507 - WHOLESALE TRADE, OTHER

Occupation	% of Total 1996	Change to 2006	Occupation	% of Total 1996	Change to 2006
Sales & related workers nec	19.5	20.2	Clerical supervisors & managers	1.9	20.2
General managers & top executives	5.9	16.4	Order clerks	1.9	8.2
Truck drivers light & heavy	5.4	20.2	Helpers, laborers nec	1.7	20.2
General office clerks	3.6	3.4	Electrical & electronic technicians	1.4	18.8
Traffic, shipping, receiving clerks	3.6	16.7	Blue collar worker supervisors	1.4	16.0
Stock clerks	3.5	-3.9	Wholesale & retail buyers, except farm products	1.3	17.0
Freight, stock, & material movers, hand	3.3	8.2	Office machine & cash register servicers	1.3	20.2
Marketing & sales worker supervisors	3.1	20.2	Hand packers & packagers	1.2	-3.9
Order fillers, wholesale & retail sales	3.0	16.7	Maintenance repairers, general utility	1.1	12.0
Bookkeeping, accounting, & auditing clerks	2.9	-3.9	Industrial truck & tractor operators	1.1	20.2
Salespersons, retail	2.5	20.2	Purchasing managers	1.1	20.2
Secretaries, except legal & medical	2.5	-4.7	Receptionists & information clerks	1.0	20.2
Assemblers, fabricators, hand workers nec	2.0	-3.9			

Source: *Industry-Occupation Matrix*, Bureau of Labor Statistics. These data relate to one or more 3-digit SIC industry groups rather than to a single 4-digit SIC. The change reported for each occupation to the year 2006 is a percent of growth or decline as estimated by the Bureau of Labor Statistics. The abbreviation nec stands for 'not elsewhere classified'.

STATE AND REGIONAL CONCENTRATION

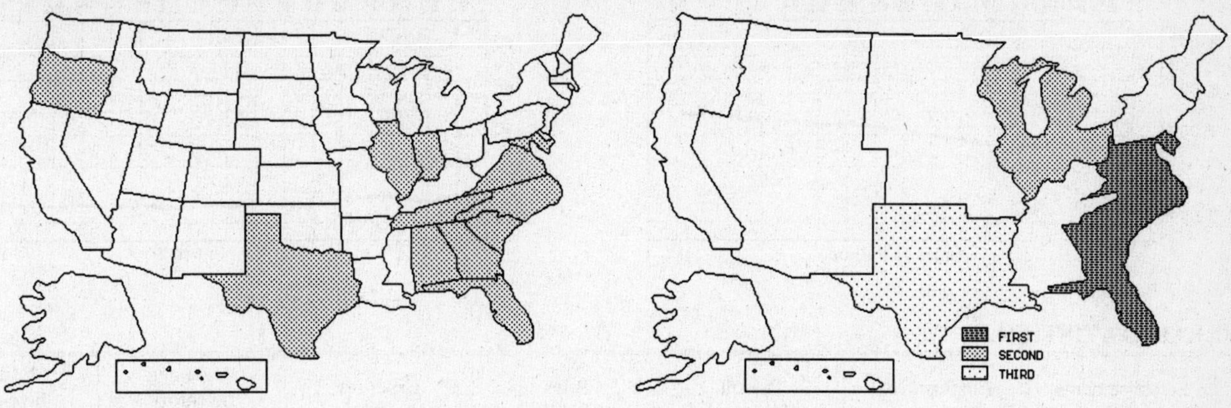

INDUSTRY DATA BY STATE

	Establishments - 1995		Employment - 1995			Payroll - 1995		Sales - 1992		
State	Total (number)	% of U.S.	Total (number)	% of U.S.	Per Estab.	Total ($ mil.)	Per Empl. ($)	Total ($ mil.)	% of U.S.	Per Estab ($)
Texas	510	9.2	5,127	10.2	10	182.5	35,591	2,014.2	14.0	431,404
California	358	6.4	3,223	6.4	9	130.7	40,555	1,160.7	8.0	344,827
New York	295	5.3	2,277	4.5	8	102.2	44,896	913.8	6.3	367,575
Florida	445	8.0	3,621	7.2	8	117.3	32,406	837.6	5.8	279,960
Illinois	248	4.5	2,450	4.9	10	98.1	40,033	771.6	5.3	352,662
Pennsylvania	234	4.2	2,466	4.9	11	92.0	37,299	636.6	4.4	262,613
North Carolina	241	4.3	1,838	3.7	8	68.0	36,972	577.0	4.0	357,039
Ohio	231	4.1	2,594	5.2	11	91.4	35,254	576.9	4.0	303,618
Georgia	220	3.9	1,968	3.9	9	71.2	36,199	516.0	3.6	317,527
Michigan	193	3.5	1,971	3.9	10	77.0	39,057	502.7	3.5	254,785
Tennessee	165	3.0	1,689	3.4	10	61.9	36,660	482.5	3.3	311,064
Maryland	131	2.4	1,166	2.3	9	42.8	36,721	433.4	3.0	363,854
New Jersey	163	2.9	1,401	2.8	9	59.6	42,521	428.0	3.0	368,287
Virginia	170	3.1	1,541	3.1	9	51.7	33,567	423.8	2.9	295,157
Indiana	126	2.3	1,219	2.4	10	46.6	38,247	354.9	2.5	293,083
South Carolina	124	2.2	986	2.0	8	34.2	34,653	287.9	2.0	330,569
Missouri	118	2.1	1,115	2.2	9	43.1	38,656	286.6	2.0	284,303
Alabama	110	2.0	929	1.8	8	27.7	29,868	283.6	2.0	324,806
Wisconsin	93	1.7	939	1.9	10	38.5	40,991	270.9	1.9	306,082
Washington	99	1.8	1,068	2.1	11	40.1	37,588	260.5	1.8	315,360
Massachusetts	90	1.6	965	1.9	11	40.6	42,050	227.7	1.6	289,718
Oregon	49	0.9	643	1.3	13	21.7	33,719	225.4	1.6	483,790
Minnesota	87	1.6	743	1.5	9	27.4	36,880	205.7	1.4	366,608
Louisiana	126	2.3	798	1.6	6	27.3	34,204	192.5	1.3	265,928
Colorado	76	1.4	836	1.7	11	30.3	36,300	189.2	1.3	328,979
Kentucky	84	1.5	946	1.9	11	28.4	30,063	181.7	1.3	234,731
Arizona	88	1.6	809	1.6	9	30.8	38,115	177.3	1.2	296,458
Oklahoma	82	1.5	592	1.2	7	18.8	31,672	120.0	0.8	229,446
Connecticut	66	1.2	385	0.8	6	17.2	44,595	117.5	0.8	344,572
Utah	43	0.8	439	0.9	10	15.0	34,223	93.3	0.6	292,580
Arkansas	47	0.8	411	0.8	9	11.1	26,934	92.5	0.6	247,890
Kansas	51	0.9	426	0.8	8	19.4	45,631	89.7	0.6	271,694
Mississippi	60	1.1	432	0.9	7	11.6	26,947	88.8	0.6	255,971
Nevada	29	0.5	240	0.5	8	8.0	33,171	75.4	0.5	237,063
Iowa	53	1.0	394	0.8	7	12.3	31,211	68.6	0.5	221,345
West Virginia	32	0.6	238	0.5	7	6.3	26,668	59.9	0.4	286,751
New Mexico	24	0.4	145	0.3	6	4.9	33,545	57.3	0.4	448,016
Idaho	27	0.5	150	0.3	6	4.8	31,687	35.6	0.2	289,187
Hawaii	12	0.2	97	0.2	8	4.0	41,247	27.2	0.2	394,754
Alaska	5	0.1	20-99	-	-	(D)	-	18.5	0.1	319,672
Maine	15	0.3	59	0.1	4	2.0	33,661	16.9	0.1	244,652
Montana	15	0.3	67	0.1	4	2.6	39,075	16.6	0.1	306,759
South Dakota	14	0.3	84	0.2	6	2.8	33,345	15.4	0.1	247,806
Vermont	6	0.1	20-99	-	-	(D)	-	7.7	0.1	263,828
North Dakota	8	0.1	34	0.1	4	0.9	27,382	6.7	0.0	185,333
Wyoming	6	0.1	20-99	-	-	(D)	-	3.5	0.0	182,053
D.C.	2	0.0	0-19	-	-	(D)	-	1.4	0.0	117,750
Nebraska	47	0.8	379	0.8	8	12.7	33,443	(D)	-	-
Delaware	22	0.4	140	0.3	6	5.0	36,064	(D)	-	-
New Hampshire	17	0.3	123	0.2	7	5.1	41,472	(D)	-	-
Rhode Island	14	0.3	61	0.1	4	2.2	35,951	(D)	-	-

Source: *County Business Patterns, 1995* and *Economic Census of the U.S., 1992*. Data are sorted by 1992 revenues and, if revenues are unavailable, by establishments in 1995. The symbol (D) indicates that data are withheld by the source to avoid disclosure of competitive information. A dash (-) indicates that data are not available or undisclosed because they do not meet statistical validity standards. Shaded *states* on the state map indicate those states which have proportionately greater representation in the industry than would be indicated by the state's population; the ratio is based on total revenues or number of establishments. Shaded *regions* indicate where the industry is regionally most concentrated.

5078 - REFRIGERATION EQUIPMENT AND SUPPLIES

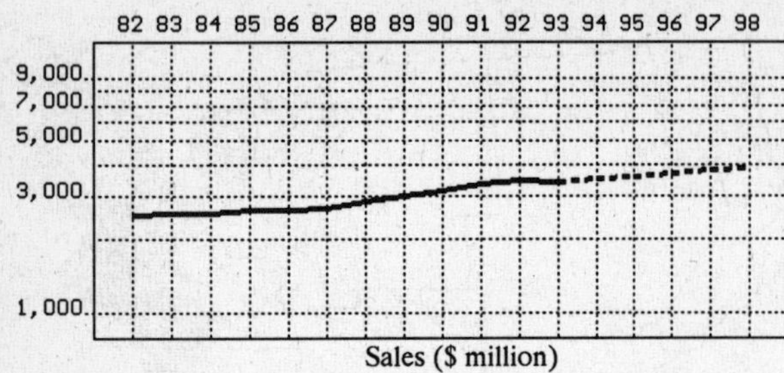

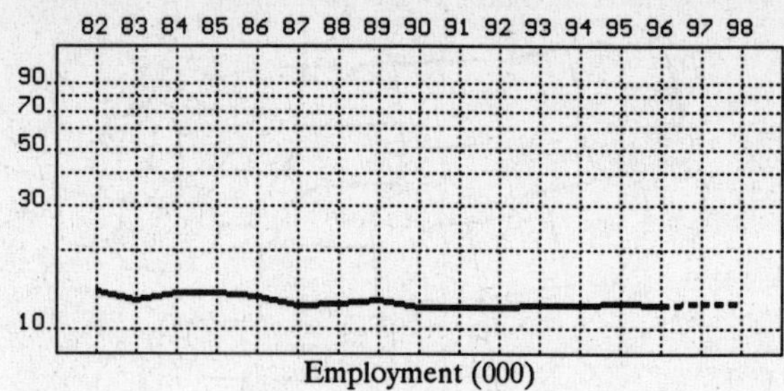

GENERAL STATISTICS

Year	Establishments (number)	Employment (number)	Payroll ($ million)	Sales ($ million)	Expenses ($ million)	Beginning Inventory ($ million)	Ending Inventory ($ million)
1982	1,599	13,927	281.2	2,505.6	-	-	-
1983	1,524	12,828	282.1	2,541.2e	-	-	-
1984	1,545	13,765	311.8	2,576.8e	-	-	-
1985	-	-	-	2,612.4e	-	-	-
1986	1,487	13,351	326.8	2,648.0e	-	-	-
1987	1,513	12,218	303.3	2,683.6	567.4	288.5	295.9
1988	1,444	12,446	340.9	2,840.8e	588.1e	299.8e	311.9e
1989	1,365	12,852	348.3	2,998.0e	608.8e	311.2e	327.8e
1990	1,340	12,097	353.2	3,155.3e	629.6e	322.6e	343.7e
1991	1,372	11,948	355.0	3,312.5e	650.3e	334.0e	359.6e
1992	1,455	11,928	366.9	3,469.7	671.1	345.4	375.5
1993	1,430	12,273	385.2	3,427.9p	691.8p	356.8p	391.4p
1994	1,421	12,152	417.7	3,524.3p	712.5p	368.1p	407.4p
1995	1,404	12,407	439.4	3,620.7p	733.3p	379.5p	423.3p
1996	1,421p	12,320p	438.9p	3,717.2p	754.0p	390.9p	439.2p
1997	1,430p	12,399p	454.5p	3,813.6p	774.7p	402.3p	455.1p
1998	1,440p	12,478p	470.0p	3,910.0p	795.5p	413.7p	471.0p

Sources: *Economic Census of the United States*, 1982, 1987, and 1992. Establishment counts, employment, and payroll are from *County Business Patterns* for non-Census years. Values followed by a 'p' are projections by the editors. Sales and expense data for non-Census years are extrapolations, marked by 'e'. Industries reclassified in 1987 will not have data for prior years. Data are the most recent available at this level of detail.

INDICES OF CHANGE

Year	Establishments (number)	Employment (number)	Payroll ($ million)	Sales ($ million)	Expenses ($ million)	Beginning Inventory ($ million)	Ending Inventory ($ million)
1982	109.9	116.8	76.6	72.2	-	-	-
1983	104.7	107.5	76.9	73.2e	-	-	-
1984	106.2	115.4	85.0	74.3e	-	-	-
1985	-	-	-	75.3e	-	-	-
1986	102.2	111.9	89.1	76.3e	-	-	-
1987	104.0	102.4	82.7	77.3	84.5	83.5	78.8
1988	99.2	104.3	92.9	81.9e	87.6e	86.8e	83.1e
1989	93.8	107.7	94.9	86.4e	90.7e	90.1e	87.3e
1990	92.1	101.4	96.3	90.9e	93.8e	93.4e	91.5e
1991	94.3	100.2	96.8	95.5e	96.9e	96.7e	95.8e
1992	100.0	100.0	100.0	100.0	100.0	100.0	100.0
1993	98.3	102.9	105.0	98.8p	103.1p	103.3p	104.2p
1994	97.7	101.9	113.9	101.6p	106.2p	106.6p	108.5p
1995	96.5	104.0	119.8	104.4p	109.3p	109.9p	112.7p
1996	97.7p	103.3p	119.6p	107.1p	112.4p	113.2p	117.0p
1997	98.3p	103.9p	123.9p	109.9p	115.4p	116.5p	121.2p
1998	99.0p	104.6p	128.1p	112.7p	118.5p	119.8p	125.4p

Sources: Same as General Statistics. The values shown reflect change from the base year, 1992. Values above 100 mean greater than 1992, values below 100 mean less than 1992, and a value of 100 in the 1982-91 or 1993-98 period means same as 1992. Values followed by a 'p' are projections by the editors; 'e' stands for extrapolation. Data are the most recent available at this level of detail.

SELECTED RATIOS

For 1992	Avg. of All Wholesale	Analyzed Industry	Index	For 1992	Avg. of All Wholesale	Analyzed Industry	Index
Employees per Establishment	12	8	70	Sales per Employee	561,172	290,887	52
Payroll per Establishment	349,729	252,165	72	Sales per Establishment	6,559,346	2,384,674	36
Payroll per Employee	29,919	30,760	103	Expenses per Establishment	723,071	461,237	64

Sources: Same as General Statistics. The 'Average of All Manufacturing' column represents the average of all manufacturing industries reported for the most recent complete year available. The Index shows the relationship between the Average and the Analyzed Industry. For example, 100 means that they are equal; 500 that the Analyzed Industry is five times the average; 50 means that the Analyzed Industry is half the national average. The abbreviation 'na' is used to show that data are 'not available'.

LEADING COMPANIES

Number shown: **45** Total sales ($ mil): **2,167** Total employment (000): **7.1**

Company Name	Address				CEO Name	Phone	Co. Type	Sales ($ mil)	Empl. (000)
Noland Co.	80 29th St	Newport News	VA	23607	Lloyd U Noland III	757-928-9000	P	465	1.6
Associated Grocers of Florida	7000 NW 32nd Ave	Miami	FL	33147	Calvin J Miller	305-696-0080	R	210 *	0.4
R.E. Michel Company Inc.	1 RE Michel Dr	Glen Burnie	MD	21060	JWH Michel	410-760-4000	R	130	0.7
Baker Distributing Co.	PO Box 2954	Jacksonville	FL	32203	Terry Kelly	904-733-9633	S	107	0.5
Refron Inc.	38 33rd St, #18	Long Island C.	NY	11101	Jay Kestenbaum	718-392-8002	R	85	<0.1
Superior Products Mfg Co.	500 W County D	St. Paul	MN	55112	Robert M Kurek	612-636-1110	R	80	0.2
ACR Group Inc.	3200 Wilcrest Dr	Houston	TX	77042	Alex Trevino Jr	713-780-8532	P	78	0.2
ABCO Refrigeration Supply	49-70 31st St	Long Island C.	NY	11101	JA Gottlieb	718-937-9000	R	75	0.2
Refrigeration Supplies	1201 Monterey Pass	Monterey Park	CA	91754	HG Martin	213-264-2800	R	68 *	0.3
United Refrigeration Inc.	11401 Roosevelt	Philadelphia	PA	19154	John H Reilly	215-698-9100	R	66 *	0.3
Temperature Equipment Corp.	17725 Volbrecht Rd	Lansing	IL	60438	FA Mungo	708-418-0900	R	65	0.1
Johnson Supply and Equipment	10151 Stella Link	Houston	TX	77025	Robert E Uehlinger	713-661-6666	R	54	0.2
Cummins Southwest Inc.	PO Box 6688	Phoenix	AZ	85009	Frank Thomas	602-252-8021	R	50	0.3
Blodgett Supply Company Inc.	PO Box 759	Williston	VT	05495	Sam Levin	802-864-9831	R	49 *	0.1
Gustave A. Larson Co.	2425 S 162nd St	New Berlin	WI	53151	J Michael McBride	414-782-2300	R	44	0.1
Actrade International Ltd.	7 Penn Plaza	New York	NY	10001	Henry N Seror	212-563-1036	P	43	<0.1
Wittichen Supply Company Inc.	1600 3rd Ave S	Birmingham	AL	35233	David P Henderson	205-251-8500	R	40	0.1
Refrigeration Sales Corp.	3405 Perkins Ave	Cleveland	OH	44114	W Farr Jr	216-881-7800	R	39	0.1
Burke Engineering Company	PO Box 3427	El Monte	CA	91733	Gary W Burke	626-579-6763	R	34 *	0.1
Weathertrol Supply Company	2600 University	Denton	TX	76201	Rick Salazar	940-387-1778	S	32	0.1
Thermal Supply Inc.	717 S Lander St	Seattle	WA	98134	Bob Monroe	206-624-4590	R	31 *	0.1
Young Supply Co.	888 W Baltimore	Detroit	MI	48202	Ronald Vallan	313-875-3280	R	30	0.1
George L. Johnston Company	1200 Holden Ave	Detroit	MI	48202	G Lenard Johnston	313-871-7000	R	25	<0.1
W.A. Roosevelt Co.	PO Box 1208	La Crosse	WI	54602	Steve W Reiman	608-781-2000	R	23	<0.1
Refrigeration Equipment Co.	820 Atlantic Ave	N. Kansas City	MO	64116	Bob Heinzinger	816-471-1466	S	20 *	0.1
Acme Refrigeration	11844 S Choctaw	Baton Rouge	LA	70815	AE Kaiser Jr	504-273-1740	R	19 *	<0.1
Convoy Servicing Company Inc.	3323 Jane Ln	Dallas	TX	75247	William Niseman	214-638-3053	R	19 *	<0.1
Southern Refrigeration Corp.	2026 Salem Ave	Roanoke	VA	24027	John S Lang Jr	703-342-3493	R	18	<0.1
William Wurzbach Company	1939 East 14th St	Oakland	CA	94606		510-261-0217	S	18	<0.1
Maines Paper and Food Service	PO Box 438	Conklin	NY	13748	David Maines	607-772-0055	D	17	<0.1
Shelby-Skipwith Inc.	PO Box 777	Memphis	TN	38101	Jon Wallace	901-948-4481	R	16	<0.1
Heating & Cooling Wholesalers	1576 S Division Ave	Grand Rapids	MI	49507	R A Hungerford	616-241-2426	R	15	<0.1
Refrigeration and Electric	1222 Spring St	Little Rock	AR	72202	Carl H Miller Jr	501-374-6373	R	15 *	<0.1
Tesco Distributors Inc.	300 Nye Ave	Irvington	NJ	07111	Arnold Blun	201-399-0333	R	15 *	<0.1
Brock-McVey Co.	PO Box 55487	Lexington	KY	40555	J M McDonald III	606-255-1412	S	14 *	0.1
Illco Inc.	PO Box 1330	Aurora	IL	60507	John P Glass III	708-892-7904	R	14	<0.1
Totaline of Florida Inc.	401 College St	Jacksonville	FL	32204	John Donahue	904-356-4975	D	11	<0.1
Hattenbach Co.	1929 E 61st St	Cleveland	OH	44103	HA Hattenbach	216-881-5200	R	10	<0.1
United States Electric Co.	301 N 1st St	Springfield	IL	62702	Paul Branham	217-522-3347	R	8	<0.1
Gardner and Benoit Inc.	PO Box 30005	Charlotte	NC	28230	HB Benoit Jr	704-332-5086	R	6	<0.1
Water Warehouse, Etc.	PO Box 123	Matawan	NJ	07747	Kenneth Siebenberg	908-739-4848	R	3	<0.1
Fetzer Company-Restaurateurs	209 E Main St	Louisville	KY	40202	Keith Fetzer	502-583-2744	R	2	<0.1
F.B. Inc.	3950 Michigan Ave	Detroit	MI	48216	Mark Fontana	313-897-4000	R	1	<0.1
Warren Equipment Co.	PO Box 2872	Beaumont	TX	77704	Marvin W Hall	409-838-3791	R	1	<0.1
Hockenberg Equipment Co.	528 36th St, #B	Des Moines	IA	50312	Betty Sue Halferty	515-255-5774	R	1 *	<0.1

Source: *Ward's Business Directory of U.S. Private and Public Companies*, 1998. The company type code used is as follows: P - Public, R - Private, S - Subsidiary, D - Division, J - Joint Venture, A - Affiliate, G - Group. Sales are in millions of dollars, employees are in thousands. An asterisk (*) indicates an estimated sales volume. The symbol < stands for 'less than'.

OCCUPATIONS EMPLOYED BY SIC 507 - WHOLESALE TRADE, OTHER

Occupation	% of Total 1996	Change to 2006	Occupation	% of Total 1996	Change to 2006
Sales & related workers nec	19.5	20.2	Clerical supervisors & managers	1.9	20.2
General managers & top executives	5.9	16.4	Order clerks	1.9	8.2
Truck drivers light & heavy	5.4	20.2	Helpers, laborers nec	1.7	20.2
General office clerks	3.6	3.4	Electrical & electronic technicians	1.4	18.8
Traffic, shipping, receiving clerks	3.6	16.7	Blue collar worker supervisors	1.4	16.0
Stock clerks	3.5	-3.9	Wholesale & retail buyers, except farm products	1.3	17.0
Freight, stock, & material movers, hand	3.3	8.2	Office machine & cash register servicers	1.3	20.2
Marketing & sales worker supervisors	3.1	20.2	Hand packers & packagers	1.2	-3.9
Order fillers, wholesale & retail sales	3.0	16.7	Maintenance repairers, general utility	1.1	12.0
Bookkeeping, accounting, & auditing clerks	2.9	-3.9	Industrial truck & tractor operators	1.1	20.2
Salespersons, retail	2.5	20.2	Purchasing managers	1.1	20.2
Secretaries, except legal & medical	2.5	-4.7	Receptionists & information clerks	1.0	20.2
Assemblers, fabricators, hand workers nec	2.0	-3.9			

Source: *Industry-Occupation Matrix*, Bureau of Labor Statistics. These data relate to one or more 3-digit SIC industry groups rather than to a single 4-digit SIC. The change reported for each occupation to the year 2006 is a percent of growth or decline as estimated by the Bureau of Labor Statistics. The abbreviation nec stands for 'not elsewhere classified'.

STATE AND REGIONAL CONCENTRATION

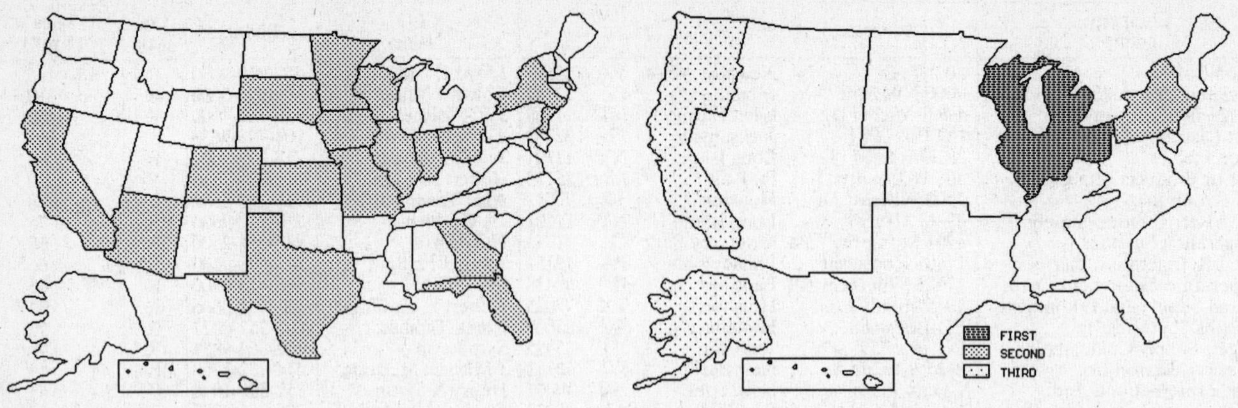

INDUSTRY DATA BY STATE

State	Establishments - 1995 Total (number)	Establishments - 1995 % of U.S.	Employment - 1995 Total (number)	Employment - 1995 % of U.S.	Employment - 1995 Per Estab.	Payroll - 1995 Total ($ mil.)	Payroll - 1995 Per Empl. ($)	Sales - 1992 Total ($ mil.)	Sales - 1992 % of U.S.	Sales - 1992 Per Estab ($)
California	181	12.9	1,820	14.7	10	68.6	37,701	416.2	12.4	239,068
Texas	112	8.0	1,114	9.0	10	36.9	33,169	266.5	7.9	242,528
New York	79	5.6	936	7.6	12	33.2	35,469	243.8	7.3	276,703
Illinois	75	5.3	640	5.2	9	25.2	39,395	239.9	7.1	403,202
Florida	84	6.0	540	4.4	6	16.0	29,691	186.1	5.5	364,174
Ohio	52	3.7	661	5.3	13	23.4	35,395	174.3	5.2	284,264
Missouri	45	3.2	385	3.1	9	14.5	37,769	171.1	5.1	529,848
Pennsylvania	62	4.4	505	4.1	8	18.2	36,137	141.2	4.2	324,566
Indiana	30	2.1	310	2.5	10	10.4	33,652	140.5	4.2	260,243
Georgia	48	3.4	307	2.5	6	11.6	37,655	137.3	4.1	411,186
New Jersey	32	2.3	264	2.1	8	8.9	33,610	126.6	3.8	439,510
Minnesota	28	2.0	234	1.9	8	10.4	44,487	104.6	3.1	471,108
Wisconsin	27	1.9	277	2.2	10	9.7	35,134	90.9	2.7	339,231
Colorado	18	1.3	173	1.4	10	6.9	40,133	76.1	2.3	380,595
Massachusetts	36	2.6	209	1.7	6	7.0	33,727	65.5	1.9	350,032
Iowa	14	1.0	297	2.4	21	12.2	41,020	63.6	1.9	184,997
Michigan	28	2.0	187	1.5	7	8.5	45,604	63.3	1.9	355,871
Arizona	31	2.2	272	2.2	9	7.2	26,386	57.3	1.7	299,990
Washington	32	2.3	247	2.0	8	9.9	40,069	57.2	1.7	306,027
Maryland	20	1.4	171	1.4	9	8.7	50,947	53.4	1.6	301,588
North Carolina	33	2.4	200	1.6	6	6.5	32,700	53.0	1.6	267,803
Virginia	27	1.9	272	2.2	10	9.3	34,265	47.4	1.4	176,160
Kansas	15	1.1	159	1.3	11	5.3	33,239	43.4	1.3	314,601
Tennessee	31	2.2	211	1.7	7	6.9	32,825	39.6	1.2	192,316
Alabama	19	1.4	219	1.8	12	8.2	37,612	36.7	1.1	169,046
Oklahoma	19	1.4	159	1.3	8	4.1	25,855	29.6	0.9	159,392
Connecticut	8	0.6	73	0.6	9	2.4	32,219	29.5	0.9	316,882
Louisiana	18	1.3	202	1.6	11	5.4	26,683	29.2	0.9	207,043
Oregon	17	1.2	99	0.8	6	3.2	31,939	28.1	0.8	295,453
Utah	12	0.9	78	0.6	7	2.9	37,397	24.0	0.7	368,800
Arkansas	19	1.4	135	1.1	7	4.0	29,585	23.3	0.7	179,154
South Dakota	5	0.4	44	0.4	9	1.9	43,864	16.0	0.5	517,484
South Carolina	13	0.9	75	0.6	6	2.5	32,680	14.9	0.4	196,461
West Virginia	13	0.9	74	0.6	6	1.5	19,824	12.6	0.4	241,365
Mississippi	9	0.6	39	0.3	4	1.1	27,923	10.7	0.3	249,000
Maine	6	0.4	26	0.2	4	0.7	27,231	9.4	0.3	363,038
Hawaii	7	0.5	35	0.3	5	1.4	39,200	9.2	0.3	241,237
Montana	9	0.6	60	0.5	7	1.5	25,250	7.9	0.2	212,811
Idaho	8	0.6	40	0.3	5	1.1	27,800	7.8	0.2	216,306
North Dakota	6	0.4	50	0.4	8	1.8	36,060	6.1	0.2	198,323
New Mexico	8	0.6	32	0.3	4	0.6	18,500	4.5	0.1	251,333
Kentucky	22	1.6	226	1.8	10	8.1	35,819	(D)	-	-
Nebraska	13	0.9	136	1.1	10	4.7	34,243	(D)	-	-
Nevada	13	0.9	51	0.4	4	1.4	26,745	(D)	-	-
Rhode Island	7	0.5	29	0.2	4	0.5	17,655	(D)	-	-
New Hampshire	5	0.4	87	0.7	17	3.4	38,851	(D)	-	-
Delaware	3	0.2	20	0.2	7	0.6	31,550	(D)	-	-
Alaska	2	0.1	0-19	-	-	(D)	-	(D)	-	-
Vermont	2	0.1	0-19	-	-	(D)	-	(D)	-	-
Wyoming	1	0.1	0-19	-	-	(D)	-	-	-	-

Source: County Business Patterns, 1995 and *Economic Census of the U.S., 1992*. Data are sorted by 1992 revenues and, if revenues are unavailable, by establishments in 1995. The symbol (D) indicates that data are withheld by the source to avoid disclosure of competitive information. A dash (-) indicates that data are not available or undisclosed because they do not meet statistical validity standards. Shaded *states* on the state map indicate those states which have proportionately greater representation in the industry than would be indicated by the state's population; the ratio is based on total revenues or number of establishments. Shaded *regions* indicate where the industry is regionally most concentrated.

5082 - CONSTRUCTION AND MINING MACHINERY

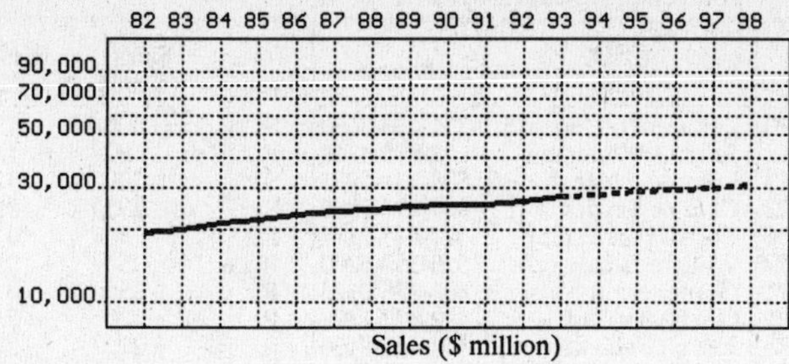

Sales ($ million)

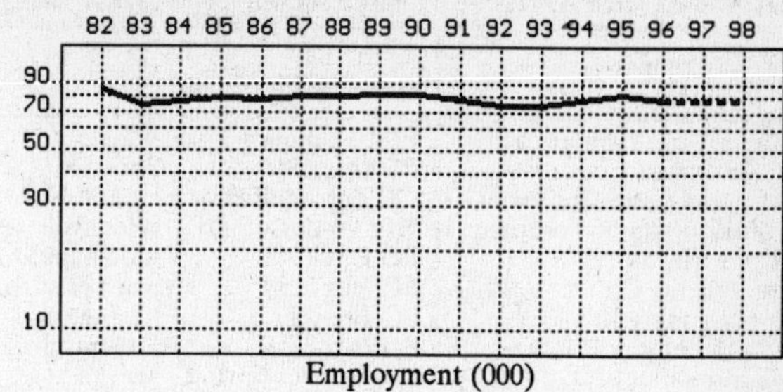

Employment (000)

GENERAL STATISTICS

Year	Establishments (number)	Employment (number)	Payroll ($ million)	Sales ($ million)	Expenses ($ million)	Beginning Inventory ($ million)	Ending Inventory ($ million)
1982	5,000	85,293	1,813.2	19,278.4	-	-	-
1983	4,907	74,005	1,729.2	20,216.9e	-	-	-
1984	4,530	76,714	1,942.3	21,155.4e	-	-	-
1985	4,388	79,028	2,092.3	22,094.0e	-	-	-
1986	4,287	77,454	2,107.2	23,032.5e	-	-	-
1987	4,983	79,720	2,208.6	23,971.0	4,198.9	6,035.5	6,426.0
1988	4,763	80,095	2,391.8	24,400.9e	4,236.1e	6,326.6e	6,610.1e
1989	4,589	82,280	2,524.7	24,830.7e	4,273.3e	6,617.7e	6,794.2e
1990	4,644	81,947	2,584.9	25,260.5e	4,310.5e	6,908.7e	6,978.3e
1991	4,624	77,663	2,431.8	25,690.3e	4,347.6e	7,199.8e	7,162.3e
1992	5,157	73,518	2,388.7	26,120.2	4,384.8	7,490.9	7,346.4
1993	5,021	73,578	2,548.7	27,382.4p	4,422.0p	7,781.9p	7,530.5p
1994	4,970	77,135	2,844.2	28,066.6p	4,459.2p	8,073.0p	7,714.6p
1995	4,987	81,881	3,162.9	28,750.8p	4,496.3p	8,364.1p	7,898.7p
1996	4,953p	77,492p	3,003.9p	29,434.9p	4,533.5p	8,655.1p	8,082.7p
1997	4,977p	77,346p	3,092.3p	30,119.1p	4,570.7p	8,946.2p	8,266.8p
1998	5,001p	77,199p	3,180.7p	30,803.3p	4,607.9p	9,237.3p	8,450.9p

Sources: Economic Census of the United States, 1982, 1987, and 1992. Establishment counts, employment, and payroll are from *County Business Patterns* for non-Census years. Values followed by a 'p' are projections by the editors. Sales and expense data for non-Census years are extrapolations, marked by 'e'. Industries reclassified in 1987 will not have data for prior years. Data are the most recent available at this level of detail.

INDICES OF CHANGE

Year	Establishments (number)	Employment (number)	Payroll ($ million)	Sales ($ million)	Expenses ($ million)	Beginning Inventory ($ million)	Ending Inventory ($ million)
1982	97.0	116.0	75.9	73.8	-	-	-
1983	95.2	100.7	72.4	77.4e	-	-	-
1984	87.8	104.3	81.3	81.0e	-	-	-
1985	85.1	107.5	87.6	84.6e	-	-	-
1986	83.1	105.4	88.2	88.2e	-	-	-
1987	96.6	108.4	92.5	91.8	95.8	80.6	87.5
1988	92.4	108.9	100.1	93.4e	96.6e	84.5e	90.0e
1989	89.0	111.9	105.7	95.1e	97.5e	88.3e	92.5e
1990	90.1	111.5	108.2	96.7e	98.3e	92.2e	95.0e
1991	89.7	105.6	101.8	98.4e	99.2e	96.1e	97.5e
1992	100.0	100.0	100.0	100.0	100.0	100.0	100.0
1993	97.4	100.1	106.7	104.8p	100.8p	103.9p	102.5p
1994	96.4	104.9	119.1	107.5p	101.7p	107.8p	105.0p
1995	96.7	111.4	132.4	110.1p	102.5p	111.7p	107.5p
1996	96.1p	105.4p	125.8p	112.7p	103.4p	115.5p	110.0p
1997	96.5p	105.2p	129.5p	115.3p	104.2p	119.4p	112.5p
1998	97.0p	105.0p	133.2p	117.9p	105.1p	123.3p	115.0p

Sources: Same as General Statistics. The values shown reflect change from the base year, 1992. Values above 100 mean greater than 1992, values below 100 mean less than 1992, and a value of 100 in the 1982-91 or 1993-98 period means same as 1992. Values followed by a 'p' are projections by the editors; 'e' stands for extrapolation. Data are the most recent available at this level of detail.

SELECTED RATIOS

For 1992	Avg. of All Wholesale	Analyzed Industry	Index	For 1992	Avg. of All Wholesale	Analyzed Industry	Index
Employees per Establishment	12	14	122	Sales per Employee	561,172	355,290	63
Payroll per Establishment	349,729	463,196	132	Sales per Establishment	6,559,346	5,064,999	77
Payroll per Employee	29,919	32,491	109	Expenses per Establishment	723,071	850,262	118

Sources: Same as General Statistics. The 'Average of All Manufacturing' column represents the average of all manufacturing industries reported for the most recent complete year available. The Index shows the relationship between the Average and the Analyzed Industry. For example, 100 means that they are equal; 500 that the Analyzed Industry is five times the average; 50 means that the Analyzed Industry is half the national average. The abbreviation 'na' is used to show that data are 'not available'.

LEADING COMPANIES

Number shown: **50** Total sales ($ mil): **7,404** Total employment (000): **24.2**

Company Name	Address				CEO Name	Phone	Co. Type	Sales ($ mil)	Empl. (000)
Atlas Copco North America	1211 Hamburg Tpk	Wayne	NJ	07470	Lennart Jo Hansson	201-633-8600	S	600	1.9
Empire Southwest Co.	PO Box 2985	Phoenix	AZ	85062	John O Whiteman	602-898-4300	R	600	1.1
Theo. H. Davies and Company	810 Kapiolani Blvd	Honolulu	HI	96813	David A Heenan	808-531-5971	S	300	3.0
American Equipment Company	2106 Anderson Dr	Greenville	SC	29602	Charles Snyder	864-295-7800	S	293	2.5
MacAllister Machinery	PO Box 1941	Indianapolis	IN	46206	Chris Macallister	317-545-2151	R	250	0.4
Peterson Tractor Co.	PO Box 5258	San Leandro	CA	94577	William E Doyle Jr	510-357-6200	R	250 *	0.4
Pioneer Machinery Inc.	PO Box 250	Lexington	SC	29071	Garner Scott	803-356-0123	R	250	0.4
Beckwith Machinery Co.	PO Box 8718	Pittsburgh	PA	15221	GN Beckwith III	412-327-1300	R	220	0.7
FABCO Equipment Inc.	11200 Silver Spring	Milwaukee	WI	53225	Joseph Fabick	414-461-9100	R	210 *	0.3
Mustang Tractor	PO Box 1373	Houston	TX	77251	F Louis Tucker Jr	713-460-2000	R	200 *	0.8
H.O. Penn Machinery Company	54 Noxon Rd	Poughkeepsie	NY	12603	C Thomas Cleveland	914-452-1200	R	180	0.3
Holt Cos.	PO Box 207916	San Antonio	TX	78220	Peter Holt	210-648-1111	R	180 *	0.5
Pearce Industries Inc.	PO Box 35068	Houston	TX	77235	Louis M Pearce III	713-723-1050	R	180 *	0.7
Southeastern Equipment	PO Box 536	Cambridge	OH	43725	W Baker	614-432-6131	R	170 *	0.3
American United Global Inc.	11634 Patton Rd	Downey	CA	90241	Robert M Rubin	310-862-8163	P	155	0.4
Polyphase Corp.	16885 Dallas Pkwy	Dallas	TX	75248	Paul A Tanner	214-732-0010	P	152	0.9
Patten Industries Inc.	635 W Lake St	Elmhurst	IL	60126	Byron C Patten Jr	708-279-4400	R	150	0.4
Bramco Inc.	PO Box 32230	Louisville	KY	40232	Charles Leis	502-493-4300	R	148 *	0.2
Western Power and Equipment	4601 NE 7th Ave	Vancouver	WA	98662	C Dean McLain	360-253-2346	P	148	0.4
RDO Equipment Co.	PO Box 7160	Fargo	ND	58109	Ronald D Offutt	701-237-6062	D	140	0.8
Road Machinery Co.	PO Box 4425	Phoenix	AZ	85030	AD Frederickson	602-252-7121	R	140 *	0.2
SMA Equipment Inc.	5230 Wilson St	Riverside	CA	92509	Vigo Carlund	909-784-1444	S	140 *	0.2
Modern Group Ltd.	PO Box 710	Bristol	PA	19007	David E Griffith	215-943-9100	R	130	0.5
Rudd Equipment Co.	PO Box 32427	Louisville	KY	40232	K Harshberger	502-456-4050	R	120	0.3
Arnold Machinery Co.	PO Box 30020	Salt Lake City	UT	84130	Alvin Richer	801-972-4000	R	110	0.3
Puckett Machinery Co.	PO Box 3170	Jackson	MS	39207	Richard Puckett	601-969-6000	R	110	0.2
M.D. Moody and Sons Inc.	4652 Phillips Hwy	Jacksonville	FL	32207	Max D Moody III	904-737-4401	R	107	0.2
Liebherr-America Inc.	PO Drawer O	Newport News	VA	23605	Ron Jacobson	804-245-5251	S	100	0.2
Carolina Tractor/CAT	PO Box 1095	Charlotte	NC	28201	E. I Weisiger Jr	704-596-6700	R	97	0.5
Wyoming Machinery Co.	PO Box 2335	Casper	WY	82602	Richard Wheeler	307-472-1000	R	93 *	0.3
Double T Holding Co.	4421 NE Columbia	Portland	OR	97218	EH Halton Jr	503-288-6411	R	90	0.4
Kubota Tractor Corp.	PO Box 2992	Torrance	CA	90509	S Majima	310-370-3370	S	88 *	0.4
North Carolina Equipment	PO Box 431	Raleigh	NC	27602	RJ Calton	919-833-4811	R	88	0.3
Scott Truck and Tractor	PO Box 4948	Monroe	LA	71211	TH Scott	318-387-4160	R	85 *	0.5
Gregory Poole Equipment Co.	4807 Beryl Rd	Raleigh	NC	27606	James G Poole Jr	919-828-0641	R	84	0.4
Head & Engguist Equipment L.L	PO Box 52945	Baton Rouge	LA	70892	John Engquist	504-356-6113	R	82	0.2
Roland Machinery Co.	PO Box 2879	Springfield	IL	62708	W. E McGreevy	217-789-7711	R	82	0.2
Cleveland Brothers Equipment	PO Box 2535	Harrisburg	PA	17105	Jay W Cleveland	717-564-2121	R	80	0.3
Dean Machinery Co.	1201 W 31st St	Kansas City	MO	64108	Curt Stokes	816-753-5300	R	80	0.2
McDonald Industries Inc.	PO Box 88000	Seattle	WA	98138	Michael O'Byrne	206-872-3500	R	72	0.2
Trax Inc.	1340 Perimeter S	Atlanta	GA	30349	Herb Humphrey	404-996-6800	R	72	0.2
Anderson Equipment Co.	PO Box 339	Bridgeville	PA	15017	RL Anderson	412-343-2300	R	70	0.2
Berry Companies Inc.	PO Box 829	Wichita	KS	67201	Walter Berry	316-832-0171	R	70	0.2
West Texas Equipment Co.	PO Box 61247	Midland	TX	79711	Scot McKinney	915-563-1863	R	70	0.3
National Mine Service Inc.	PO Box 310	Indiana	PA	15701	William S Tate	724-349-7100	R	65	0.2
E.A. Martin Machinery Co.	PO Box 988	Springfield	MO	65801	Donald G Martin Jr	417-866-6651	R	63	0.2
Chadwick-BaRoss Inc.	160 Warren Ave	Westbrook	ME	04092	R Bartlett	207-854-8411	R	60	0.2
Furnival/State Machinery Co.	PO Box 12399	Lancaster	PA	17605	Robert Thomson	717-397-7551	R	60	0.2
Nebraska Machinery Co.	401 N 12th St	Omaha	NE	68102	Jerry L Swanson	402-346-6500	R	60 *	0.3
Smith Tractor & Equipment	PO Box 2990	Tacoma	WA	98401	Scott Highland	206-922-8718	S	60	0.2

Source: *Ward's Business Directory of U.S. Private and Public Companies*, 1998. The company type code used is as follows: P - Public, R - Private, S - Subsidiary, D - Division, J - Joint Venture, A - Affiliate, G - Group. Sales are in millions of dollars, employees are in thousands. An asterisk (*) indicates an estimated sales volume. The symbol < stands for 'less than'.

OCCUPATIONS EMPLOYED BY SIC 508 - MACHINERY, EQUIPMENT, AND SUPPLIES

Occupation	% of Total 1996	Change to 2006	Occupation	% of Total 1996	Change to 2006
Sales & related workers nec	21.7	4.5	Salespersons, retail	2.2	4.5
General managers & top executives	7.4	1.3	Clerical supervisors & managers	2.0	4.5
General office clerks	3.9	-10.1	Bus & truck mechanics	1.9	4.5
Mobile heavy equipment mechanics	3.8	4.5	Order clerks	1.8	-6.0
Farm equipment mechanics	3.7	-26.9	Freight, stock, & material movers, hand	1.7	-6.0
Traffic, shipping, receiving clerks	3.3	4.5	Order fillers, wholesale & retail sales	1.6	14.9
Truck drivers light & heavy	3.3	4.5	Machinists	1.5	-20.9
Marketing & sales worker supervisors	3.2	4.5	Electrical & electronic technicians	1.2	3.3
Bookkeeping, accounting, & auditing clerks	3.2	-16.4	Wholesale & retail buyers, except farm products	1.2	1.7
Secretaries, except legal & medical	2.9	-17.1	Purchasing managers	1.1	4.5
Stock clerks	2.6	4.5	Welders & cutters	1.1	4.5
Maintenance repairers, general utility	2.5	-2.6	Helpers, laborers nec	1.0	4.5
Assemblers, fabricators, hand workers nec	2.5	4.5	Receptionists & information clerks	1.0	4.5
Blue collar worker supervisors	2.2	0.9			

Source: *Industry-Occupation Matrix*, Bureau of Labor Statistics. These data relate to one or more 3-digit SIC industry groups rather than to a single 4-digit SIC. The change reported for each occupation to the year 2006 is a percent of growth or decline as estimated by the Bureau of Labor Statistics. The abbreviation nec stands for 'not elsewhere classified'.

STATE AND REGIONAL CONCENTRATION

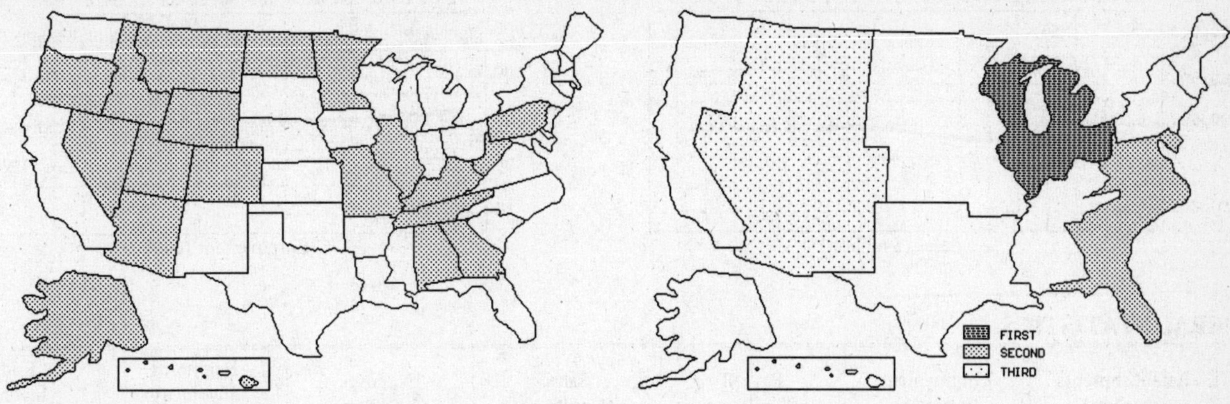

INDUSTRY DATA BY STATE

State	Establishments - 1995 Total (number)	Establishments - 1995 % of U.S.	Employment - 1995 Total (number)	Employment - 1995 % of U.S.	Employment - 1995 Per Estab.	Payroll - 1995 Total ($ mil.)	Payroll - 1995 Per Empl. ($)	Sales - 1992 Total ($ mil.)	Sales - 1992 % of U.S.	Sales - 1992 Per Estab ($)
Illinois	199	4.0	4,668	5.7	23	256.6	54,968	4,143.7	16.0	1,012,136
Pennsylvania	253	5.1	4,603	5.6	18	157.5	34,209	1,685.0	6.5	391,593
Texas	344	6.9	5,679	6.9	17	219.7	38,687	1,551.4	6.0	305,268
California	348	7.0	4,252	5.2	12	173.2	40,729	1,352.2	5.2	280,664
Colorado	111	2.2	1,737	2.1	16	63.2	36,378	1,256.3	4.9	766,058
Florida	265	5.3	4,261	5.2	16	150.9	35,416	1,224.1	4.7	339,450
Georgia	163	3.3	2,577	3.1	16	105.0	40,753	936.3	3.6	458,500
Ohio	188	3.8	3,162	3.9	17	120.9	38,241	785.7	3.0	276,834
New York	181	3.6	2,393	2.9	13	82.9	34,636	694.8	2.7	285,117
Kentucky	160	3.2	2,951	3.6	18	96.5	32,701	691.5	2.7	279,182
West Virginia	128	2.6	2,200	2.7	17	74.8	34,008	649.1	2.5	319,262
Tennessee	104	2.1	2,082	2.5	20	79.5	38,169	645.7	2.5	370,862
Virginia	172	3.4	2,312	2.8	13	82.3	35,597	598.6	2.3	267,465
Missouri	120	2.4	2,368	2.9	20	83.2	35,151	579.7	2.2	276,025
Alabama	112	2.2	2,395	2.9	21	88.0	36,742	572.3	2.2	262,906
North Carolina	146	2.9	2,500	3.1	17	93.8	37,502	532.2	2.1	225,220
Minnesota	116	2.3	1,874	2.3	16	74.7	39,878	519.7	2.0	313,256
Maryland	82	1.6	1,210	1.5	15	49.7	41,106	495.6	1.9	474,304
Michigan	121	2.4	1,797	2.2	15	80.8	44,943	474.8	1.8	299,380
Indiana	96	1.9	1,562	1.9	16	60.1	38,490	466.7	1.8	357,903
Washington	129	2.6	1,667	2.0	13	67.5	40,504	454.4	1.8	299,537
Arizona	115	2.3	1,734	2.1	15	69.2	39,926	443.6	1.7	315,484
Wisconsin	100	2.0	1,731	2.1	17	70.8	40,924	441.7	1.7	308,467
Oregon	101	2.0	1,769	2.2	18	71.0	40,141	419.7	1.6	280,721
New Jersey	100	2.0	1,430	1.7	14	60.9	42,571	380.0	1.5	315,084
Utah	58	1.2	1,317	1.6	23	51.8	39,320	349.9	1.4	316,392
Nevada	62	1.2	1,240	1.5	20	49.3	39,781	319.1	1.2	343,102
Louisiana	71	1.4	1,215	1.5	17	42.3	34,845	298.3	1.2	256,016
Iowa	64	1.3	1,030	1.3	16	37.3	36,242	257.9	1.0	288,530
South Carolina	70	1.4	1,191	1.5	17	40.7	34,166	232.7	0.9	233,828
Massachusetts	66	1.3	942	1.2	14	39.6	42,070	230.8	0.9	278,423
Arkansas	66	1.3	947	1.2	14	31.4	33,131	199.3	0.8	241,000
Oklahoma	55	1.1	859	1.0	16	26.4	30,751	196.6	0.8	249,224
Mississippi	55	1.1	761	0.9	14	28.8	37,896	176.2	0.7	267,347
New Mexico	32	0.6	558	0.7	17	23.7	42,557	160.0	0.6	270,670
Montana	39	0.8	651	0.8	17	22.0	33,796	153.0	0.6	263,404
Wyoming	29	0.6	488	0.6	17	19.8	40,600	141.0	0.5	317,644
Nebraska	33	0.7	711	0.9	22	24.5	34,437	139.9	0.5	224,256
Hawaii	17	0.3	373	0.5	22	14.5	38,925	134.5	0.5	332,109
Idaho	32	0.6	568	0.7	18	21.8	38,294	127.9	0.5	256,337
North Dakota	24	0.5	512	0.6	21	17.8	34,732	112.4	0.4	295,805
Connecticut	52	1.0	457	0.6	9	21.1	46,201	112.3	0.4	243,531
Alaska	26	0.5	425	0.5	16	21.9	51,466	109.6	0.4	315,842
Maine	29	0.6	506	0.6	17	19.0	37,626	109.1	0.4	290,909
New Hampshire	32	0.6	487	0.6	15	15.5	31,906	90.5	0.4	235,047
South Dakota	21	0.4	361	0.4	17	11.9	32,848	73.5	0.3	244,850
Vermont	13	0.3	150	0.2	12	4.1	27,393	43.5	0.2	291,685
Delaware	19	0.4	134	0.2	7	5.6	42,097	42.7	0.2	333,797
Rhode Island	9	0.2	20-99	-	-	(D)	-	23.8	0.1	226,257
Kansas	58	1.2	1,013	1.2	17	35.8	35,299	(D)	-	-
D.C.	1	0.0	0-19	-	-	(D)	-	(D)	-	-

Source: County Business Patterns, 1995 and *Economic Census of the U.S., 1992*. Data are sorted by 1992 revenues and, if revenues are unavailable, by establishments in 1995. The symbol (D) indicates that data are withheld by the source to avoid disclosure of competitive information. A dash (-) indicates that data are not available or undisclosed because they do not meet statistical validity standards. Shaded *states* on the state map indicate those states which have proportionately greater representation in the industry than would be indicated by the state's population; the ratio is based on total revenues or number of establishments. Shaded *regions* indicate where the industry is regionally most concentrated.

5083 - FARM AND GARDEN MACHINERY

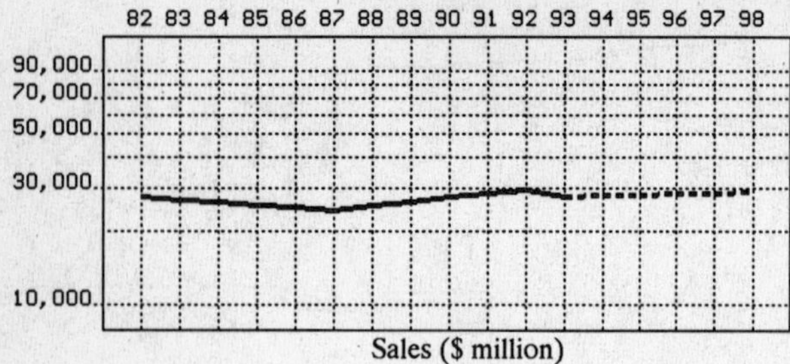

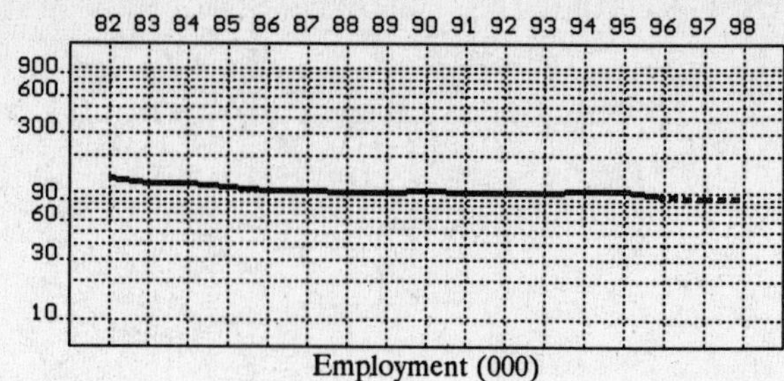

GENERAL STATISTICS

Year	Establishments (number)	Employment (number)	Payroll ($ million)	Sales ($ million)	Expenses ($ million)	Beginning Inventory ($ million)	Ending Inventory ($ million)
1982	14,425	133,148	2,116.2	27,514.6	-	-	-
1983	13,912	120,687	2,024.8	26,846.1e	-	-	-
1984	13,193	117,651	2,061.6	26,177.7e	-	-	-
1985	12,503	112,982	2,003.4	25,509.2e	-	-	-
1986	11,643	105,031	1,942.7	24,840.8e	-	-	-
1987	11,782	103,468	1,958.8	24,172.3	3,927.6	6,070.7	5,825.2
1988	11,032	102,292	2,080.7	25,237.6e	4,070.9e	6,402.6e	6,138.4e
1989	10,397	100,107	2,141.8	26,302.9e	4,214.1e	6,734.5e	6,451.6e
1990	10,314	103,114	2,294.1	27,368.2e	4,357.4e	7,066.3e	6,764.8e
1991	10,132	102,158	2,288.1	28,433.5e	4,500.6e	7,398.2e	7,078.0e
1992	10,742	102,068	2,363.3	29,498.8	4,643.9	7,730.1	7,391.2
1993	10,435	100,816	2,492.6	27,727.0p	4,787.2p	8,061.9p	7,704.4p
1994	10,280	103,375	2,684.3	27,925.4p	4,930.4p	8,393.8p	8,017.6p
1995	10,034	105,432	2,761.2	28,123.9p	5,073.7p	8,725.7p	8,330.8p
1996	9,068p	94,898p	2,638.8p	28,322.3p	5,216.9p	9,057.5p	8,644.0p
1997	8,745p	93,148p	2,693.4p	28,520.7p	5,360.2p	9,389.4p	8,957.2p
1998	8,423p	91,398p	2,748.0p	28,719.1p	5,503.4p	9,721.3p	9,270.4p

Sources: Economic Census of the United States, 1982, 1987, and 1992. Establishment counts, employment, and payroll are from *County Business Patterns* for non-Census years. Values followed by a 'p' are projections by the editors. Sales and expense data for non-Census years are extrapolations, marked by 'e'. Industries reclassified in 1987 will not have data for prior years. Data are the most recent available at this level of detail.

INDICES OF CHANGE

Year	Establishments (number)	Employment (number)	Payroll ($ million)	Sales ($ million)	Expenses ($ million)	Beginning Inventory ($ million)	Ending Inventory ($ million)
1982	134.3	130.5	89.5	93.3	-	-	-
1983	129.5	118.2	85.7	91.0e	-	-	-
1984	122.8	115.3	87.2	88.7e	-	-	-
1985	116.4	110.7	84.8	86.5e	-	-	-
1986	108.4	102.9	82.2	84.2e	-	-	-
1987	109.7	101.4	82.9	81.9	84.6	78.5	78.8
1988	102.7	100.2	88.0	85.6e	87.7e	82.8e	83.1e
1989	96.8	98.1	90.6	89.2e	90.7e	87.1e	87.3e
1990	96.0	101.0	97.1	92.8e	93.8e	91.4e	91.5e
1991	94.3	100.1	96.8	96.4e	96.9e	95.7e	95.8e
1992	100.0	100.0	100.0	100.0	100.0	100.0	100.0
1993	97.1	98.8	105.5	94.0p	103.1p	104.3p	104.2p
1994	95.7	101.3	113.6	94.7p	106.2p	108.6p	108.5p
1995	93.4	103.3	116.8	95.3p	109.3p	112.9p	112.7p
1996	84.4p	93.0p	111.7p	96.0p	112.3p	117.2p	116.9p
1997	81.4p	91.3p	114.0p	96.7p	115.4p	121.5p	121.2p
1998	78.4p	89.5p	116.3p	97.4p	118.5p	125.8p	125.4p

Sources: Same as General Statistics. The values shown reflect change from the base year, 1992. Values above 100 mean greater than 1992, values below 100 mean less than 1992, and a value of 100 in the 1982-91 or 1993-98 period means same as 1992. Values followed by a 'p' are projections by the editors; 'e' stands for extrapolation. Data are the most recent available at this level of detail.

SELECTED RATIOS

For 1992	Avg. of All Wholesale	Analyzed Industry	Index	For 1992	Avg. of All Wholesale	Analyzed Industry	Index
Employees per Establishment	12	10	81	Sales per Employee	561,172	289,011	52
Payroll per Establishment	349,729	220,006	63	Sales per Establishment	6,559,346	2,746,118	42
Payroll per Employee	29,919	23,154	77	Expenses per Establishment	723,071	432,312	60

Sources: Same as General Statistics. The 'Average of All Manufacturing' column represents the average of all manufacturing industries reported for the most recent complete year available. The Index shows the relationship between the Average and the Analyzed Industry. For example, 100 means that they are equal; 500 that the Analyzed Industry is five times the average; 50 means that the Analyzed Industry is half the national average. The abbreviation 'na' is used to show that data are 'not available'.

LEADING COMPANIES

Number shown: **50** Total sales ($ mil): **10,636** Total employment (000): **25.6**

Company Name	Address				CEO Name	Phone	Co. Type	Sales ($ mil)	Empl. (000)
Truserv Corp.	8600 W Bryn Mawr	Chicago	IL	60631	Dan A Cotter	773-695-5000	R	3,846•	6.0
Cenex/Land O'Lakes Ag Services	PO Box 64089	St. Paul	MN	55164	Noel Estenson	612-451-5151	J	2,900	3.0
Empire Southwest Co.	PO Box 2985	Phoenix	AZ	85062	John O Whiteman	602-898-4300	R	600	1.1
Tennessee Farmers Cooperative	PO Box 3003	La Vergne	TN	37086	Vernon Glover	615-793-8011	R	428•	0.7
Parts Industries Corp.	PO Box 429	Memphis	TN	38101	Kenneth Walker	901-523-7711	S	300	1.9
IIC Industries Inc.	420 Lexington Ave	New York	NY	10170	Bernard Schreier	212-297-6132	P	204	4.5
Moore-Handley Inc.	3140 Pelham Pkwy	Pelham	AL	35124	William Riley	205-663-8011	P	146	0.4
RDO Equipment Co.	PO Box 7160	Fargo	ND	58109	Ronald D Offutt	701-237-6062	D	140	0.8
United Hardware	5005 Nathan Ln	Plymouth	MN	55442	David A Heider	612-559-1800	R	136	0.4
United Dairymen of Arizona	PO Box 26877	Tempe	AZ	85285	Jim Boyle	602-966-7211	R	112•	0.2
Iowa Veterinary Supply Co.	124 Country Club	Iowa Falls	IA	50126	Thomas Kruse Sr	515-648-2529	R	104	0.2
Caldwell Supply Company Inc.	PO Box T	Hazleton	PA	18201	Ralph Caldwell III	717-455-7511	R	92•	0.2
Kubota Tractor Corp.	PO Box 2992	Torrance	CA	90509	S Majima	310-370-3370	S	88•	0.4
Scott Truck and Tractor	PO Box 4948	Monroe	LA	71211	TH Scott	318-387-4160	R	85•	0.5
Richton International Corp.	340 Main St	Madison	NJ	07940	Fred R Sullivan	201-966-0104	P	67	0.3
Tru-Part Manufacturing Corp.	232 Lothenbach	St. Paul	MN	55118	BB Calmenson	612-455-6681	R	65	0.3
Century Supply Corp.	747 E Roosevelt Rd	Lombard	IL	60148	Joe Mallahan	708-889-0800	S	59	0.3
John Fabick Tractor Co.	1 Fabick Dr	Fenton	MO	63026	HP Fabick	314-343-5900	R	58•	0.5
Sand Livestock Systems Inc.	PO Box 948	Columbus	NE	68601	Charles Sand	402-564-1211	R	57	0.3
Neowa F.S. Inc.	PO Box 127	Maynard	IA	50655	John P Flynn	319-637-2281	R	56	<0.1
Tidewater Companies Inc.	PO Box 1116	Brunswick	GA	31521	Ken S Trowbridge Jr	912-638-7726	R	55•	0.3
Pantropic Power Products Inc.	8205 NW 58th St	Miami	FL	33166	Luis Botas	305-592-4944	R	51	0.2
Maine Potato Growers Inc.	PO Box 271	Presque Isle	ME	04769	Joe Lallande	207-764-3131	R	51	0.1
Belarus Machinery Inc.	7075 W Parkland Ct	Milwaukee	WI	53223	Edward Ossinski	414-355-2000	S	50	0.1
Century Rain Aid	31691 Dequindre	Madison H.	MI	48071	Wayne R Miller	313-588-2990	R	50	0.2
Martin Tractor Company Inc.	PO Box 1698	Topeka	KS	66601	J Martin-McKinney	913-266-5770	R	50	0.2
Latshaw Enterprises Inc.	PO Box 7710	Wichita	KS	67277	John Latshaw	316-942-7266	P	48	0.5
Masek Distributing Inc.	PO Box 130	Gering	NE	69341	Joe Masek	308-436-2100	R	47	<0.1
Agri-Sales Associates Inc.	209Louise Ave	Nashville	TN	37203	Jerry R Bellar	615-329-1141	R	46	<0.1
Baker Implement Co.	RR 3	Kennett	MO	63587	Jerry Kombs	314-888-4646	R	45	0.1
Foley Tractor Company Inc.	1550 S West St	Wichita	KS	67213	PJ Foley Jr	316-943-4211	R	45	0.2
Rotary Corp.	PO Box 947	Glennville	GA	30427	Ed Nelson	912-654-3433	R	44	0.4
United Farmers Cooperative	PO Box 4	Lafayette	MN	56054	Robert Webster	507-228-8224	R	44	<0.1
Northwestern Supply Co.	PO Box 426	St. Cloud	MN	56302	Herbert Jameson Jr	320-251-0812	R	36	<0.1
Monroe Tractor and Implement	PO Box 370	Henrietta	NY	14467	Janet E Felosky	716-334-3867	R	35•	0.1
Turf Products Corp.	PO Box 1200	Enfield	CT	06083	F N Zeytoonjian	203-763-3581	R	33•	0.2
Sloan Implement Company Inc.	PO Box 80	Assumption	IL	62510	Tom Sloan	217-226-4411	R	32	<0.1
White's Herring Tractor & Truck	PO Box 3817	Wilson	NC	27893	D Steve White	919-291-0131	S	31•	0.1
Doonan Truck and Equipment	PO Box 1286	Great Bend	KS	67530	W Doonan	316-792-2491	R	30	<0.1
Morrow County Grain Growers	Hwy 207	Lexington	OR	97839	Tom Curran	503-989-8221	R	29•	<0.1
Mountainland Supply Co.	1505 W 130 S	Orem	UT	84058	RJ Rasmussen	801-224-6050	R	28	<0.1
Drake America Div.	2 Gannett Dr	White Plains	NY	10604	Edward S Dorian Jr	914-697-9800	D	26•	<0.1
Stull Enterprises Inc.	PO Box 887	Concordville	PA	19331	Rodman W Smith	610-459-8406	R	25•	<0.1
Hector Turf	1301 NW 3rd St	Deerfield Beach	FL	33442	JR Mantey	305-429-3200	R	25	<0.1
West Implement Company Inc.	PO Box 1389	Cleveland	MS	38732	Rex Morgan	601-843-5321	R	25	<0.1
Modern Distributing Co.	1610 N Topping	Kansas City	MO	64120	Joe Frazier	816-231-8500	R	23•	<0.1
Barbee-Neuhaus Implement Co.	2000 W Expwy 83	Weslaco	TX	78596	Joe D Barbee	210-968-7502	R	23	<0.1
Bucklin Tractor and Implement	Hwy 54	Bucklin	KS	67834	Kelly J Estes	316-826-3271	R	23	<0.1
Riverview FS Inc.	PO Box 5127	Rockford	IL	61125	Ron R Karlson	815-332-4956	R	22•	<0.1
Ruth Farmers Elevator Inc.	4600 Ruth Rd	Ruth	MI	48470	Paul Holdwick	517-864-3391	R	21	<0.1

Source: *Ward's Business Directory of U.S. Private and Public Companies*, 1998. The company type code used is as follows: P - Public, R - Private, S - Subsidiary, D - Division, J - Joint Venture, A - Affiliate, G - Group. Sales are in millions of dollars, employees are in thousands. An asterisk (*) indicates an estimated sales volume. The symbol < stands for 'less than'.

OCCUPATIONS EMPLOYED BY SIC 508 - MACHINERY, EQUIPMENT, AND SUPPLIES

Occupation	% of Total 1996	Change to 2006	Occupation	% of Total 1996	Change to 2006
Sales & related workers nec	21.7	4.5	Salespersons, retail	2.2	4.5
General managers & top executives	7.4	1.3	Clerical supervisors & managers	2.0	4.5
General office clerks	3.9	-10.1	Bus & truck mechanics	1.9	4.5
Mobile heavy equipment mechanics	3.8	4.5	Order clerks	1.8	-6.0
Farm equipment mechanics	3.7	-26.9	Freight, stock, & material movers, hand	1.7	-6.0
Traffic, shipping, receiving clerks	3.3	4.5	Order fillers, wholesale & retail sales	1.6	14.9
Truck drivers light & heavy	3.3	4.5	Machinists	1.5	-20.9
Marketing & sales worker supervisors	3.2	4.5	Electrical & electronic technicians	1.2	3.3
Bookkeeping, accounting, & auditing clerks	3.2	-16.4	Wholesale & retail buyers, except farm products	1.2	1.7
Secretaries, except legal & medical	2.9	-17.1	Purchasing managers	1.1	4.5
Stock clerks	2.6	4.5	Welders & cutters	1.1	4.5
Maintenance repairers, general utility	2.5	-2.6	Helpers, laborers nec	1.0	4.5
Assemblers, fabricators, hand workers nec	2.5	4.5	Receptionists & information clerks	1.0	4.5
Blue collar worker supervisors	2.2	0.9			

Source: *Industry-Occupation Matrix*, Bureau of Labor Statistics. These data relate to one or more 3-digit SIC industry groups rather than to a single 4-digit SIC. The change reported for each occupation to the year 2006 is a percent of growth or decline as estimated by the Bureau of Labor Statistics. The abbreviation nec stands for 'not elsewhere classified'.

STATE AND REGIONAL CONCENTRATION

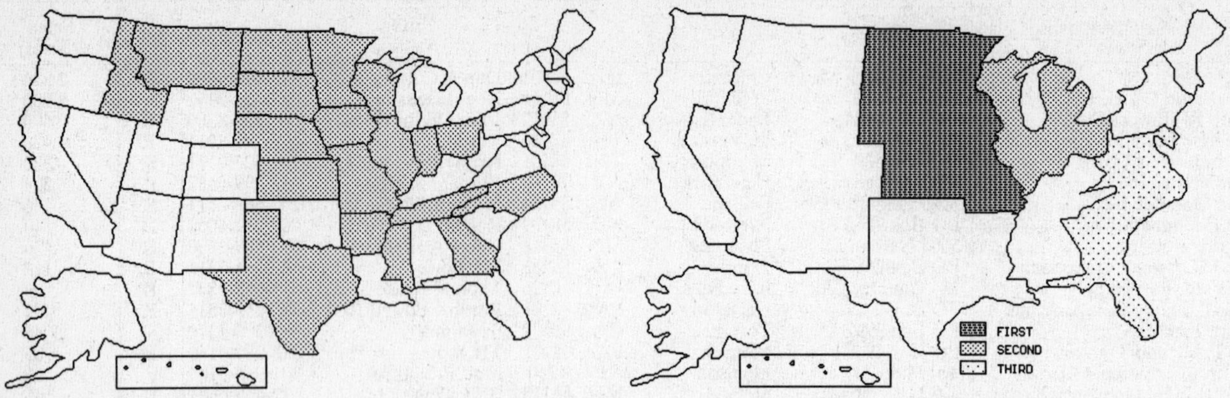

INDUSTRY DATA BY STATE

	Establishments - 1995		Employment - 1995			Payroll - 1995		Sales - 1992		
State	Total (number)	% of U.S.	Total (number)	% of U.S.	Per Estab.	Total ($ mil.)	Per Empl. ($)	Total ($ mil.)	% of U.S.	Per Estab ($)
Minnesota	462	4.6	5,174	4.9	11	153.0	29,580	2,931.4	10.0	607,422
Texas	702	7.0	7,139	6.8	10	185.8	26,020	2,380.6	8.1	349,677
California	624	6.2	6,830	6.5	11	219.7	32,161	1,814.7	6.2	256,056
Missouri	359	3.6	3,868	3.7	11	95.4	24,661	1,621.9	5.5	432,156
Illinois	473	4.7	5,742	5.5	12	156.7	27,286	1,601.2	5.4	282,401
Georgia	286	2.9	3,040	2.9	11	86.9	28,599	1,496.5	5.1	486,193
Ohio	357	3.6	4,271	4.1	12	114.5	26,816	1,440.6	4.9	362,494
Iowa	540	5.4	5,247	5.0	10	125.5	23,911	1,212.4	4.1	229,407
Wisconsin	454	4.5	4,418	4.2	10	116.6	26,392	1,199.3	4.1	265,158
North Carolina	250	2.5	3,170	3.0	13	99.5	31,394	1,046.6	3.6	342,820
Florida	351	3.5	3,057	2.9	9	79.8	26,118	905.4	3.1	273,198
Kansas	290	2.9	3,627	3.4	13	89.3	24,613	851.2	2.9	255,229
Tennessee	209	2.1	1,937	1.8	9	49.5	25,563	809.6	2.7	402,582
Pennsylvania	321	3.2	3,500	3.3	11	86.6	24,753	776.2	2.6	213,598
Nebraska	338	3.4	3,968	3.8	12	91.7	23,100	768.8	2.6	215,603
Indiana	300	3.0	3,096	2.9	10	73.3	23,682	683.5	2.3	219,633
Michigan	246	2.5	2,458	2.3	10	71.4	29,066	677.1	2.3	270,612
New York	308	3.1	2,723	2.6	9	65.4	24,030	578.6	2.0	203,959
North Dakota	219	2.2	2,408	2.3	11	58.5	24,308	544.1	1.8	269,646
Arkansas	218	2.2	2,310	2.2	11	58.6	25,379	533.2	1.8	254,157
Washington	171	1.7	2,006	1.9	12	54.1	26,956	439.4	1.5	208,037
Mississippi	165	1.6	1,622	1.5	10	40.3	24,863	405.7	1.4	258,391
South Dakota	163	1.6	1,615	1.5	10	38.8	24,028	395.2	1.3	256,969
Oregon	138	1.4	1,506	1.4	11	38.8	25,774	337.2	1.1	244,513
Alabama	180	1.8	1,620	1.5	9	35.4	21,838	320.2	1.1	233,586
Idaho	141	1.4	1,562	1.5	11	39.2	25,088	319.7	1.1	217,338
Oklahoma	185	1.8	1,552	1.5	8	33.3	21,454	316.4	1.1	208,857
Virginia	188	1.9	1,836	1.7	10	41.9	22,825	316.3	1.1	183,061
Louisiana	148	1.5	1,704	1.6	12	39.3	23,072	315.8	1.1	208,153
Kentucky	184	1.8	1,469	1.4	8	28.7	19,529	315.0	1.1	206,976
Colorado	164	1.6	1,607	1.5	10	41.8	26,032	294.4	1.0	218,741
Maryland	87	0.9	1,409	1.3	16	37.5	26,604	268.3	0.9	237,877
New Jersey	85	0.8	860	0.8	10	32.0	37,257	259.0	0.9	294,602
Montana	91	0.9	997	0.9	11	23.7	23,732	188.6	0.6	218,995
Arizona	95	0.9	1,043	1.0	11	33.5	32,104	179.1	0.6	237,562
South Carolina	103	1.0	945	0.9	9	21.2	22,397	173.6	0.6	174,447
Utah	59	0.6	762	0.7	13	18.0	23,597	149.5	0.5	224,124
Massachusetts	62	0.6	554	0.5	9	19.6	35,296	102.8	0.3	199,320
Connecticut	36	0.4	513	0.5	14	16.5	32,127	94.7	0.3	206,749
Maine	44	0.4	290	0.3	7	6.2	21,224	70.8	0.2	197,131
New Mexico	36	0.4	399	0.4	11	7.6	19,163	63.6	0.2	208,492
Wyoming	26	0.3	256	0.2	10	5.3	20,789	51.5	0.2	206,104
Delaware	23	0.2	257	0.2	11	6.0	23,198	45.8	0.2	181,623
Hawaii	15	0.1	131	0.1	9	4.6	34,962	40.9	0.1	237,826
West Virginia	42	0.4	245	0.2	6	4.1	16,624	35.8	0.1	159,107
Nevada	22	0.2	202	0.2	9	5.2	25,629	32.6	0.1	203,919
New Hampshire	20	0.2	183	0.2	9	4.4	23,891	32.4	0.1	184,318
Rhode Island	11	0.1	20-99	-	-	(D)	-	11.6	0.0	136,212
Alaska	2	0.0	0-19	-	-	(D)	-	1.2	0.0	112,909
Vermont	41	0.4	224	0.2	5	4.9	21,821	(D)	-	-

Source: County Business Patterns, 1995 and *Economic Census of the U.S., 1992.* Data are sorted by 1992 revenues and, if revenues are unavailable, by establishments in 1995. The symbol (D) indicates that data are withheld by the source to avoid disclosure of competitive information. A dash (-) indicates that data are not available or undisclosed because they do not meet statistical validity standards. Shaded *states* on the state map indicate those states which have proportionately greater representation in the industry than would be indicated by the state's population; the ratio is based on total revenues or number of establishments. Shaded *regions* indicate where the industry is regionally most concentrated.

5084 - INDUSTRIAL MACHINERY AND EQUIPMENT

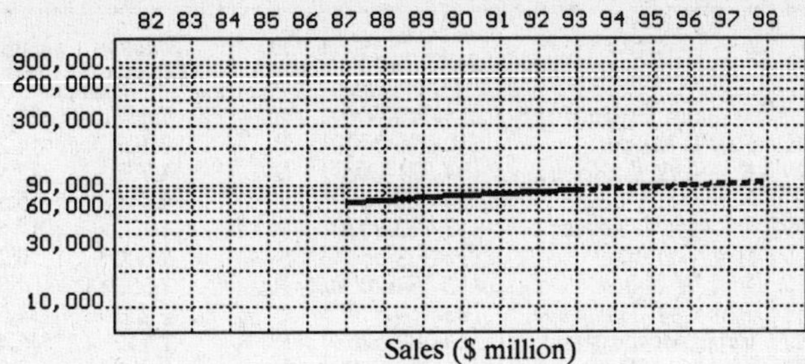

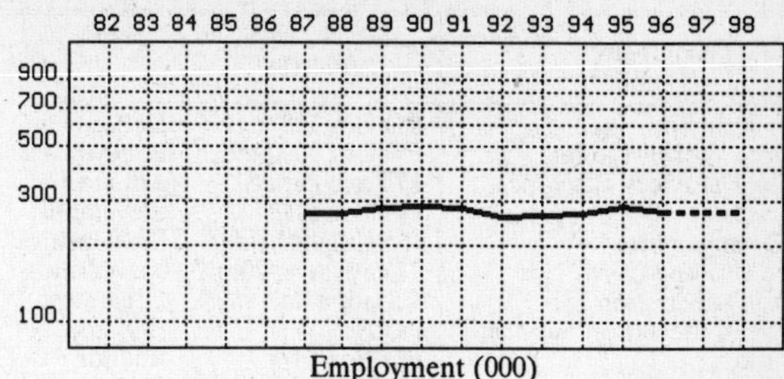

GENERAL STATISTICS

Year	Establishments (number)	Employment (number)	Payroll ($ million)	Sales ($ million)	Expenses ($ million)	Beginning Inventory ($ million)	Ending Inventory ($ million)
1982	-	-	-	-	-	-	-
1983	-	-	-	-	-	-	-
1984	-	-	-	-	-	-	-
1985	-	-	-	-	-	-	-
1986	-	-	-	-	-	-	-
1987	30,304	268,361	7,255.5	71,446.3	13,974.2	7,228.8	7,572.7
1988	28,573	270,294	8,123.1	74,486.9e	14,496.7e	7,622.8e	7,870.8e
1989	27,600	280,145	8,671.3	77,527.5e	15,019.2e	8,016.7e	8,168.9e
1990	27,809	287,075	9,169.4	80,568.1e	15,541.6e	8,410.7e	8,467.0e
1991	27,934	281,383	9,115.9	83,608.6e	16,064.1e	8,804.6e	8,765.1e
1992	30,322	259,024	8,772.6	86,649.2	16,586.6	9,198.6	9,063.2
1993	29,774	261,147	9,246.0	89,689.8p	17,109.1p	9,592.5p	9,361.3p
1994	29,854	268,073	10,062.3	92,730.4p	17,631.6p	9,986.5p	9,659.5p
1995	30,363	287,967	11,282.7	95,771.0p	18,154.0p	10,380.4p	9,957.6p
1996	30,082p	274,195p	10,967.5p	98,811.6p	18,676.5p	10,774.4p	10,255.7p
1997	30,264p	274,290p	11,345.5p	101,852.2p	19,199.0p	11,168.3p	10,553.8p
1998	30,447p	274,385p	11,723.5p	104,892.7p	19,721.5p	11,562.3p	10,851.9p

Sources: Economic Census of the United States, 1982, 1987, and 1992. Establishment counts, employment, and payroll are from *County Business Patterns* for non-Census years. Values followed by a 'p' are projections by the editors. Sales and expense data for non-Census years are extrapolations, marked by 'e'. Industries reclassified in 1987 will not have data for prior years. Data are the most recent available at this level of detail.

INDICES OF CHANGE

Year	Establishments (number)	Employment (number)	Payroll ($ million)	Sales ($ million)	Expenses ($ million)	Beginning Inventory ($ million)	Ending Inventory ($ million)
1982	-	-	-	-	-	-	-
1983	-	-	-	-	-	-	-
1984	-	-	-	-	-	-	-
1985	-	-	-	-	-	-	-
1986	-	-	-	-	-	-	-
1987	99.9	103.6	82.7	82.5	84.2	78.6	83.6
1988	94.2	104.4	92.6	86.0e	87.4e	82.9e	86.8e
1989	91.0	108.2	98.8	89.5e	90.6e	87.2e	90.1e
1990	91.7	110.8	104.5	93.0e	93.7e	91.4e	93.4e
1991	92.1	108.6	103.9	96.5e	96.8e	95.7e	96.7e
1992	100.0	100.0	100.0	100.0	100.0	100.0	100.0
1993	98.2	100.8	105.4	103.5p	103.2p	104.3p	103.3p
1994	98.5	103.5	114.7	107.0p	106.3p	108.6p	106.6p
1995	100.1	111.2	128.6	110.5p	109.4p	112.8p	109.9p
1996	99.2p	105.9p	125.0p	114.0p	112.6p	117.1p	113.2p
1997	99.8p	105.9p	129.3p	117.5p	115.7p	121.4p	116.4p
1998	100.4p	105.9p	133.6p	121.1p	118.9p	125.7p	119.7p

Sources: Same as General Statistics. The values shown reflect change from the base year, 1992. Values above 100 mean greater than 1992, values below 100 mean less than 1992, and a value of 100 in the 1982-91 or 1993-98 period means same as 1992. Values followed by a 'p' are projections by the editors; 'e' stands for extrapolation. Data are the most recent available at this level of detail.

SELECTED RATIOS

For 1992	Avg. of All Wholesale	Analyzed Industry	Index	For 1992	Avg. of All Wholesale	Analyzed Industry	Index
Employees per Establishment	12	9	73	Sales per Employee	561,172	334,522	60
Payroll per Establishment	349,729	289,315	83	Sales per Establishment	6,559,346	2,857,635	44
Payroll per Employee	29,919	33,868	113	Expenses per Establishment	723,071	547,015	76

Sources: Same as General Statistics. The 'Average of All Manufacturing' column represents the average of all manufacturing industries reported for the most recent complete year available. The Index shows the relationship between the Average and the Analyzed Industry. For example, 100 means that they are equal; 500 that the Analyzed Industry is five times the average; 50 means that the Analyzed Industry is half the national average. The abbreviation 'na' is used to show that data are 'not available'.

LEADING COMPANIES

Number shown: **50** Total sales ($ mil): **50,012** Total employment (000): **143.1**

Company Name	Address				CEO Name	Phone	Co. Type	Sales ($ mil)	Empl. (000)
Dresser Industries Inc.	PO Box 718	Dallas	TX	75221	William E Bradford	214-740-6000	P	7,458	31.3
Unisource Worldwide Inc.	PO Box 3000-0935	Berwyn	PA	19312	Ray B Mundt	610-296-4470	P	7,108	14.2
BET Plant Services USA Inc.	17 Exec Park S	Atlanta	GA	30329	Ralph A Trallo	404-321-6067	S	4,750	12.5
LTV Corp.	PO Box 6778	Cleveland	OH	44101	David H Hoag	216-622-5000	P	4,446	15.5
W.W. Grainger Inc.	455 Knightsbridge	Lincolnshire	IL	60069	Richard L Keyser	847-793-9030	P	4,137	14.6
Duferco Trading Corp.	712 5th Ave, 20th Fl	New York	NY	10019	Bruno Balfo	212-308-5544	S	3,000 *	0.2
WESCO Distribution Inc.	4 Station Sq	Pittsburgh	PA	15219	Roy W Haley	412-454-2000	R	2,500 *	4.5
Stewart and Stevenson Services	PO Box 1637	Houston	TX	77251	Robert L Hargrave	713-868-7700	P	1,234	4.5
Airgas Inc.	PO Box 6675	Radnor	PA	19087	Peter McCausland	610-687-5253	P	1,159	6.4
National-Oilwell Inc.	5555 San Felipe	Houston	TX	77056	Joel V Staff	713-960-5100	P	1,006	3.1
Olympus America Inc.	2 Corporate Ctr Dr	Melville	NY	11747	Sidney Braginsky	516-844-5000	S	800	1.5
Duferco Energy Group Inc.	8550 Katy Fwy	Houston	TX	77024	John Rupuano	713-932-9786	S	730 *	<0.1
Sun Distributors L.P.	1 Logan Sq	Philadelphia	PA	19103	Donald T Marshall	215-665-3650	P	656	4.3
General Electric Co.	1 Neumann Way	Cincinnati	OH	45215	Richard R Ruegg	513-552-5370	D	650	0.1
Atlas Copco North America	1211 Hamburg Tpk	Wayne	NJ	07470	Lennart Jo Hansson	201-633-8600	S	600	1.9
Aisin World Corporation	24330 Garnier St	Torrance	CA	90505	Tetsuro Senga	310-326-8681	S	590	1.1
Rank America Inc.	5 Concourse Pkwy	Atlanta	GA	30328	John Watson	404-392-9029	S	500	6.0
Noland Co.	80 29th St	Newport News	VA	23607	Lloyd U Noland III	757-928-9000	P	465	1.6
Kennametal Inc.	PO Box 231	Latrobe	PA	15650	Philip Weihl	724-539-5000	S	450	0.3
Wilson Industries Inc.	PO Box 1492	Houston	TX	77251	WS Wilson	713-237-3700	R	450	1.1
MSC Industrial Direct Company	151 Sunnyside Blvd	Plainview	NY	11803	Mitchell Jacobson	516-349-7100	P	438	2.0
Nomura America Corp.	60 E 42nd St	New York	NY	10165	Masami Ikeuchi	212-867-6684	S	422 *	<0.1
A.B. Dick Co.	5700 W Touhy Ave	Niles	IL	60714	Ron Peterson	708-763-1900	S	400	0.2
Fastenal Co.	2001 Theurer Blvd	Winona	MN	55987	Robert A Kierlin	507-454-5374	P	398	3.1
TEAC America Inc.	7733 Telegraph Rd	Montebello	CA	90640	Hajime Yamaguchi	213-726-0303	S	380	0.2
ResourceNet International	50 E River Ctr Blvd	Covington	KY	41011	Thomas E Costello	606-655-2000	D	320	1.0
JLK Direct Distribution Inc.	PO Box 231	Latrobe	PA	15650	Michael W Ruprich	412-539-5000	P	316	0.8
Darr Equipment Company Inc.	PO Box 540788	Dallas	TX	75354	Randall R Engstrom	214-721-2000	R	310 *	1.0
Carl Zeiss Inc.	1 Zeiss Dr	Thornwood	NY	10594	Thomas J Miller	914-747-1800	S	300 *	0.4
Star Cutter Co.	PO Box 376	Farmington Hls	MI	48332	Brad Lawton	248-474-8200	R	300 *	0.8
Vinson Supply Co.	PO Box 702440	Tulsa	OK	74170	Robert C Mellor	918-481-8770	S	300	0.5
NC Machinery Co.	PO Box 3562	Seattle	WA	98124	John Harnish	206-251-9800	R	270 *	0.9
Pioneer Machinery Inc.	PO Box 250	Lexington	SC	29071	Garner Scott	803-356-0123	R	250	0.4
Ringhaver Equipment Co.	PO Box 30169	Tampa	FL	33630	Lance Ringhaver	813-671-3700	R	250 *	0.7
Essex Brownell Div.	250 N Rte 303	Congers	NY	10920	Christopher Mapes	914-267-2700	D	230	0.5
Wrenn Brungart	PO Box 410050	Charlotte	NC	28241	Ken Brown	704-587-1003	S	230	1.0
DoAll Co.	254 N Laurel Ave	Des Plaines	IL	60016	ML Wilkie	847-824-1122	R	218 *	0.1
Tetra Laval Convenience Food	PO Box 358	Avon	MA	02322	Paul Lyqum	508-588-2600	S	200 *	0.2
H.O. Penn Machinery Company	54 Noxon Rd	Poughkeepsie	NY	12603	C Thomas Cleveland	914-452-1200	R	180	0.3
Pearce Industries Inc.	PO Box 35068	Houston	TX	77235	Louis M Pearce III	713-723-1050	R	180 *	0.7
Hope Group	PO Box 840	Northborough	MA	01532	Carey Rhoten	508-393-7660	R	160	<0.1
Toyota Tsusho America Inc.	437 Madison Ave	New York	NY	10022	Senji Fujita	212-418-0100	S	160 *	<0.1
Omega Environmental Inc.	PO Box 3005	Bothell	WA	98041	Louise J Tedesco	206-486-4800	P	152	1.0
Kelly Tractor Co.	8255 NW 58th St	Miami	FL	33166	L Patrick Kelly	305-592-5360	R	150 *	0.5
Leslie Paper Co.	2500 N Mayfair Rd	Milwaukee	WI	53226	Barry Hentz	414-771-0200	S	150 *	0.4
Production Tool Supply	PO Box 987	Warren	MI	48089	Mark Kahn	810-755-7770	R	150	0.4
Linox Gas Tech Inc.	12000 Roosevelt Rd	Hillside	IL	60162	Carl Kock	708-449-9300	R	130	0.1
Modern Group Ltd.	PO Box 710	Bristol	PA	19007	David E Griffith	215-943-9100	R	130	0.5
Alban Tractor Company Inc.	PO Box 9595	Baltimore	MD	21237	James C Alban III	410-686-7777	R	125	0.4
C and H Distributors Inc.	PO Box 04499	Milwaukee	WI	53204	David K Stark	414-271-2250	S	125	0.2

Source: *Ward's Business Directory of U.S. Private and Public Companies*, 1998. The company type code used is as follows: P - Public, R - Private, S - Subsidiary, D - Division, J - Joint Venture, A - Affiliate, G - Group. Sales are in millions of dollars, employees are in thousands. An asterisk (*) indicates an estimated sales volume. The symbol < stands for 'less than'.

OCCUPATIONS EMPLOYED BY SIC 508 - MACHINERY, EQUIPMENT, AND SUPPLIES

Occupation	% of Total 1996	Change to 2006	Occupation	% of Total 1996	Change to 2006
Sales & related workers nec	21.7	4.5	Salespersons, retail	2.2	4.5
General managers & top executives	7.4	1.3	Clerical supervisors & managers	2.0	4.5
General office clerks	3.9	-10.1	Bus & truck mechanics	1.9	4.5
Mobile heavy equipment mechanics	3.8	4.5	Order clerks	1.8	-6.0
Farm equipment mechanics	3.7	-26.9	Freight, stock, & material movers, hand	1.7	-6.0
Traffic, shipping, receiving clerks	3.3	4.5	Order fillers, wholesale & retail sales	1.6	14.9
Truck drivers light & heavy	3.3	4.5	Machinists	1.5	-20.9
Marketing & sales worker supervisors	3.2	4.5	Electrical & electronic technicians	1.2	3.3
Bookkeeping, accounting, & auditing clerks	3.2	-16.4	Wholesale & retail buyers, except farm products	1.2	1.7
Secretaries, except legal & medical	2.9	-17.1	Purchasing managers	1.1	4.5
Stock clerks	2.6	4.5	Welders & cutters	1.1	4.5
Maintenance repairers, general utility	2.5	-2.6	Helpers, laborers nec	1.0	4.5
Assemblers, fabricators, hand workers nec	2.5	4.5	Receptionists & information clerks	1.0	4.5
Blue collar worker supervisors	2.2	0.9			

Source: *Industry-Occupation Matrix*, Bureau of Labor Statistics. These data relate to one or more 3-digit SIC industry groups rather than to a single 4-digit SIC. The change reported for each occupation to the year 2006 is a percent of growth or decline as estimated by the Bureau of Labor Statistics. The abbreviation nec stands for 'not elsewhere classified'.

STATE AND REGIONAL CONCENTRATION

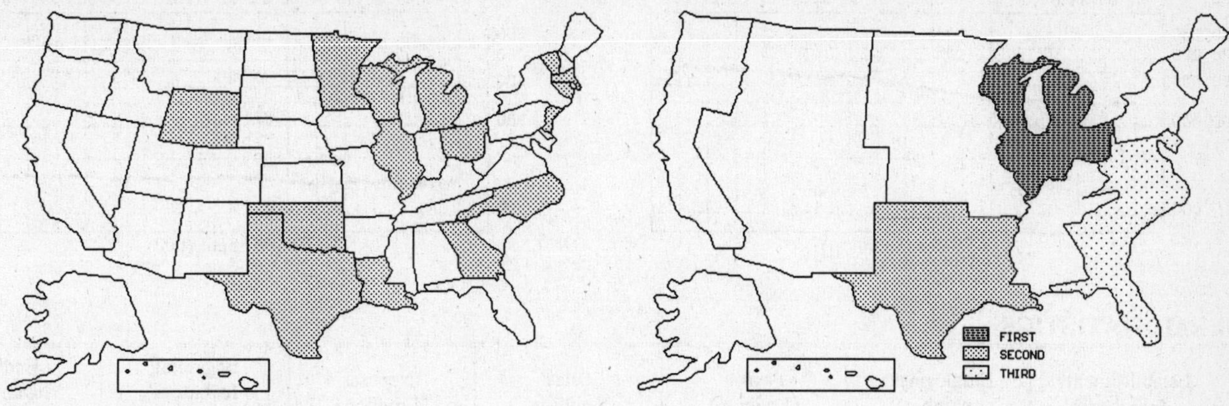

INDUSTRY DATA BY STATE

State	Establishments - 1995 Total (number)	Establishments - 1995 % of U.S.	Employment - 1995 Total (number)	Employment - 1995 % of U.S.	Employment - 1995 Per Estab.	Payroll - 1995 Total ($ mil.)	Payroll - 1995 Per Empl. ($)	Sales - 1992 Total ($ mil.)	Sales - 1992 % of U.S.	Sales - 1992 Per Estab ($)
Texas	3,464	11.4	28,977	10.1	8	1,082.1	37,344	10,074.8	11.7	370,969
California	2,772	9.1	27,567	9.6	10	1,121.1	40,668	8,525.6	9.9	323,663
Illinois	1,864	6.1	21,250	7.4	11	970.8	45,683	7,864.5	9.1	397,640
New York	1,404	4.6	11,885	4.1	8	488.5	41,106	5,041.2	5.9	413,890
Ohio	1,689	5.6	16,184	5.6	10	629.7	38,908	4,445.4	5.2	313,627
New Jersey	1,116	3.7	11,640	4.0	10	511.3	43,929	4,090.5	4.8	389,424
North Carolina	1,006	3.3	11,698	4.1	12	469.2	40,111	4,051.0	4.7	417,758
Michigan	1,261	4.2	13,416	4.7	11	590.1	43,987	3,993.1	4.6	342,429
Pennsylvania	1,318	4.3	13,345	4.6	10	508.6	38,112	3,728.2	4.3	308,016
Georgia	951	3.1	9,117	3.2	10	383.7	42,091	3,251.1	3.8	391,327
Minnesota	584	1.9	7,604	2.6	13	339.7	44,668	2,999.5	3.5	479,688
Florida	1,441	4.7	10,445	3.6	7	361.4	34,604	2,603.3	3.0	295,253
Massachusetts	689	2.3	6,524	2.3	9	302.1	46,301	2,113.7	2.5	367,786
Wisconsin	675	2.2	6,843	2.4	10	272.3	39,787	1,827.8	2.1	301,810
Louisiana	776	2.6	7,602	2.6	10	256.9	33,791	1,761.0	2.0	265,774
Missouri	596	2.0	5,861	2.0	10	236.6	40,371	1,656.1	1.9	318,913
Connecticut	505	1.7	4,437	1.5	9	203.3	45,823	1,553.2	1.8	358,962
Tennessee	561	1.8	5,628	2.0	10	195.1	34,672	1,528.2	1.8	285,747
Indiana	668	2.2	6,296	2.2	9	224.2	35,605	1,395.2	1.6	263,386
Washington	549	1.8	4,776	1.7	9	176.4	36,934	1,265.9	1.5	295,429
Oklahoma	655	2.2	5,595	1.9	9	188.2	33,645	1,231.2	1.4	259,536
South Carolina	446	1.5	4,169	1.4	9	160.0	38,368	1,164.8	1.4	330,439
Virginia	429	1.4	3,862	1.3	9	137.9	35,711	1,028.8	1.2	277,897
Colorado	477	1.6	3,706	1.3	8	140.9	38,020	955.1	1.1	315,307
Alabama	438	1.4	4,078	1.4	9	143.2	35,108	895.3	1.0	270,722
Kentucky	326	1.1	3,700	1.3	11	123.0	33,232	885.3	1.0	257,578
Maryland	319	1.1	3,360	1.2	11	129.3	38,483	804.3	0.9	269,704
Oregon	363	1.2	3,420	1.2	9	128.1	37,463	745.6	0.9	247,532
Arizona	345	1.1	3,096	1.1	9	100.9	32,606	588.8	0.7	222,032
Utah	224	0.7	2,106	0.7	9	67.3	31,976	463.8	0.5	237,485
Iowa	212	0.7	2,241	0.8	11	68.9	30,751	393.7	0.5	208,986
Arkansas	228	0.8	1,988	0.7	9	53.9	27,091	306.0	0.4	188,762
Rhode Island	106	0.3	899	0.3	8	30.8	34,217	266.0	0.3	330,797
Mississippi	178	0.6	1,440	0.5	8	40.9	28,408	257.1	0.3	222,597
New Mexico	197	0.6	1,263	0.4	6	40.3	31,888	250.2	0.3	227,836
West Virginia	137	0.5	1,640	0.6	12	50.5	30,808	240.6	0.3	186,683
Wyoming	132	0.4	744	0.3	6	27.6	37,156	205.1	0.2	270,289
Vermont	45	0.1	298	0.1	7	14.0	46,916	203.2	0.2	601,142
New Hampshire	168	0.6	1,028	0.4	6	36.0	34,993	201.2	0.2	276,718
Alaska	65	0.2	427	0.1	7	17.1	39,941	181.3	0.2	373,078
Nebraska	124	0.4	928	0.3	7	31.8	34,294	170.1	0.2	196,440
Maine	88	0.3	1,131	0.4	13	43.8	38,771	159.5	0.2	218,764
Delaware	55	0.2	473	0.2	9	17.2	36,381	121.3	0.1	230,102
Idaho	74	0.2	558	0.2	8	17.1	30,677	110.1	0.1	220,238
North Dakota	82	0.3	585	0.2	7	17.5	29,986	106.5	0.1	207,237
Hawaii	38	0.1	260	0.1	7	8.1	31,300	68.6	0.1	209,143
Nevada	72	0.2	380	0.1	5	15.2	39,892	67.1	0.1	256,095
Montana	67	0.2	295	0.1	4	7.7	26,037	62.7	0.1	217,542
South Dakota	38	0.1	434	0.2	11	11.4	26,341	56.3	0.1	209,242
Kansas	341	1.1	2,752	1.0	8	90.2	32,768	(D)	-	-
D.C.	5	0.0	16	0.0	3	0.6	36,063	(D)	-	-

Source: County Business Patterns, 1995 and *Economic Census of the U.S., 1992*. Data are sorted by 1992 revenues and, if revenues are unavailable, by establishments in 1995. The symbol (D) indicates that data are withheld by the source to avoid disclosure of competitive information. A dash (-) indicates that data are not available or undisclosed because they do not meet statistical validity standards. Shaded *states* on the state map indicate those states which have proportionately greater representation in the industry than would be indicated by the state's population; the ratio is based on total revenues or number of establishments. Shaded *regions* indicate where the industry is regionally most concentrated.

5085 - INDUSTRIAL SUPPLIES

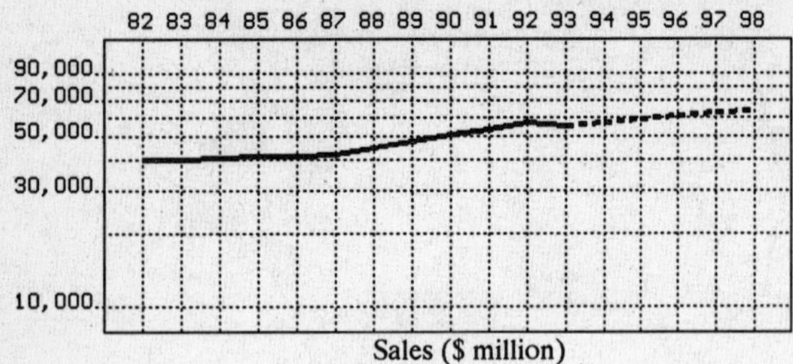

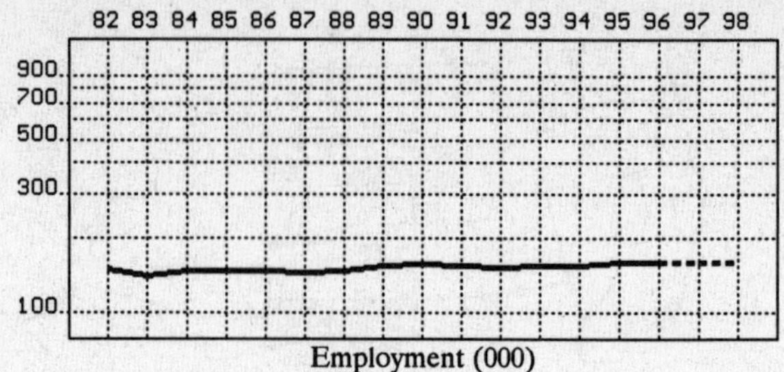

GENERAL STATISTICS

Year	Establishments (number)	Employment (number)	Payroll ($ million)	Sales ($ million)	Expenses ($ million)	Beginning Inventory ($ million)	Ending Inventory ($ million)
1982	14,825	151,067	3,036.8	39,799.9	-	-	-
1983	13,834	141,799	3,051.8	40,190.8e	-	-	-
1984	14,037	148,295	3,361.5	40,581.7e	-	-	-
1985	13,841	148,258	3,500.9	40,972.6e	-	-	-
1986	13,505	146,341	3,547.4	41,363.4e	-	-	-
1987	14,780	144,872	3,562.0	41,754.3	6,801.6	3,566.5	3,667.6
1988	14,206	148,938	4,086.9	44,740.3e	7,254.0e	3,774.2e	3,862.2e
1989	13,990	154,759	4,395.6	47,726.3e	7,706.4e	3,982.0e	4,056.9e
1990	14,070	157,159	4,693.6	50,712.3e	8,158.9e	4,189.8e	4,251.5e
1991	14,068	155,271	4,674.6	53,698.3e	8,611.3e	4,397.6e	4,446.1e
1992	16,199	152,661	4,814.2	56,684.3	9,063.7	4,605.4	4,640.8
1993	15,765	153,961	5,016.8	55,423.8p	9,516.2p	4,813.2p	4,835.4p
1994	15,678	153,968	5,267.9	57,112.2p	9,968.6p	5,021.0p	5,030.0p
1995	15,874	161,267	5,824.6	58,800.7p	10,421.0p	5,228.8p	5,224.7p
1996	15,715p	158,510p	5,752.7p	60,489.1p	10,873.4p	5,436.5p	5,419.3p
1997	15,861p	159,467p	5,959.4p	62,177.5p	11,325.9p	5,644.3p	5,613.9p
1998	16,007p	160,425p	6,166.1p	63,866.0p	11,778.3p	5,852.1p	5,808.6p

Sources: Economic Census of the United States, 1982, 1987, and 1992. Establishment counts, employment, and payroll are from *County Business Patterns* for non-Census years. Values followed by a 'p' are projections by the editors. Sales and expense data for non-Census years are extrapolations, marked by 'e'. Industries reclassified in 1987 will not have data for prior years. Data are the most recent available at this level of detail.

INDICES OF CHANGE

Year	Establishments (number)	Employment (number)	Payroll ($ million)	Sales ($ million)	Expenses ($ million)	Beginning Inventory ($ million)	Ending Inventory ($ million)
1982	91.5	99.0	63.1	70.2	-	-	-
1983	85.4	92.9	63.4	70.9e	-	-	-
1984	86.7	97.1	69.8	71.6e	-	-	-
1985	85.4	97.1	72.7	72.3e	-	-	-
1986	83.4	95.9	73.7	73.0e	-	-	-
1987	91.2	94.9	74.0	73.7	75.0	77.4	79.0
1988	87.7	97.6	84.9	78.9e	80.0e	82.0e	83.2e
1989	86.4	101.4	91.3	84.2e	85.0e	86.5e	87.4e
1990	86.9	102.9	97.5	89.5e	90.0e	91.0e	91.6e
1991	86.8	101.7	97.1	94.7e	95.0e	95.5e	95.8e
1992	100.0	100.0	100.0	100.0	100.0	100.0	100.0
1993	97.3	100.9	104.2	97.8p	105.0p	104.5p	104.2p
1994	96.8	100.9	109.4	100.8p	110.0p	109.0p	108.4p
1995	98.0	105.6	121.0	103.7p	115.0p	113.5p	112.6p
1996	97.0p	103.8p	119.5p	106.7p	120.0p	118.0p	116.8p
1997	97.9p	104.5p	123.8p	109.7p	125.0p	122.6p	121.0p
1998	98.8p	105.1p	128.1p	112.7p	130.0p	127.1p	125.2p

Sources: Same as General Statistics. The values shown reflect change from the base year, 1992. Values above 100 mean greater than 1992, values below 100 mean less than 1992, and a value of 100 in the 1982-91 or 1993-98 period means same as 1992. Values followed by a 'p' are projections by the editors; 'e' stands for extrapolation. Data are the most recent available at this level of detail.

SELECTED RATIOS

For 1992	Avg. of All Wholesale	Analyzed Industry	Index	For 1992	Avg. of All Wholesale	Analyzed Industry	Index
Employees per Establishment	12	9	81	Sales per Employee	561,172	371,308	66
Payroll per Establishment	349,729	297,191	85	Sales per Establishment	6,559,346	3,499,247	53
Payroll per Employee	29,919	31,535	105	Expenses per Establishment	723,071	559,522	77

Sources: Same as General Statistics. The 'Average of All Manufacturing' column represents the average of all manufacturing industries reported for the most recent complete year available. The Index shows the relationship between the Average and the Analyzed Industry. For example, 100 means that they are equal; 500 that the Analyzed Industry is five times the average; 50 means that the Analyzed Industry is half the national average. The abbreviation 'na' is used to show that data are 'not available'.

LEADING COMPANIES

Number shown: **50** Total sales ($ mil): **28,396** Total employment (000): **86.6**

Company Name	Address				CEO Name	Phone	Co. Type	Sales ($ mil)	Empl. (000)
Sammons Enterprises Inc.	300 Crescent Ct	Dallas	TX	75201	Robert Korba	214-210-5999	R	6,400	2.1
Genuine Parts Co.	2999 Circle 75 Pkwy	Atlanta	GA	30339	Larry L Prince	770-953-1700	P	6,005	24.5
WESCO Distribution Inc.	4 Station Sq	Pittsburgh	PA	15219	Roy W Haley	412-454-2000	R	2,500 *	4.5
Arvin Industries Inc.	PO Box 3000	Columbus	IN	47202	Byron O Pond	812-379-3000	P	2,349	14.3
Applied Industrial Technologies	PO Box 6925	Cleveland	OH	44101	John C Dannemiller	216-881-8900	P	1,160	4.1
Motion Industries Inc.	PO Box 1477	Birmingham	AL	35210	Willam Stevens	205-956-1122	S	1,021	5.0
Reynolds International Inc.	PO Box 27002	Richmond	VA	23261	R N Reynolds	804-281-2000	S	900	6.1
H. Muehlstein and Company	PO Box 5445	Norwalk	CT	06856	J Kevin Donohue	203-855-6000	R	700	0.3
All-Phase Electric Supply Co.	875 Riverview Dr	Benton Harbor	MI	49022	Ken Renwick	616-926-0504	R	550 *	1.8
Berry Bearing Co.	4242 S 1st Ave	Lyons	IL	60534	Gardner E Larned	708-442-1200	S	440 *	1.5
PrimeSource Corp.	4350 Haddonfield	Pennsauken	NJ	08109	James F Mullan	609-488-4888	P	357	0.7
Kaman Industrial Technologies	1332 Blue Hills Ave	Bloomfield	CT	06002	Richard E Moynihan	203-243-8311	S	320	1.4
JLK Direct Distribution Inc.	PO Box 231	Latrobe	PA	15650	Michael W Ruprich	412-539-5000	P	316	0.8
Fairmont Supply Co.	PO Box 501	Washington	PA	15301	Charles Whirlow	412-223-2200	S	291	0.6
Lawson Products Inc.	1666 E Touhy Ave	Des Plaines	IL	60018	Bernard Kalish	847-827-9666	P	278	1.9
Kirby Risk Electrical Supply	PO Box 5089	Lafayette	IN	47903	JK Risk III	317-448-4567	R	270 *	0.9
McJunkin Corp.	PO Box 513	Charleston	WV	25322	HB Wehrle III	304-348-5211	R	270 *	1.3
Industrial Distributors Group	2500 Royal Place	Tucker	GA	30084	Martin S Pinson	770-243-4044	P	251	0.9
Dixie Bearings Inc.	PO Box 93803	Cleveland	OH	44101	John C Dannemiller	216-881-2828	S	250 *	1.0
DoAll Co.	254 N Laurel Ave	Des Plaines	IL	60016	ML Wilkie	847-824-1122	R	218 *	0.1
Bowman Distribution	PO Box 6908	Cleveland	OH	44101	Leonard M Carlucci	216-416-7200	D	213	1.2
King Bearing Inc.	PO Box 550	Corona	CA	91720	Don Shargin	909-279-1171	S	200	0.9
Van Leeuwen Pipe and Tube	PO Box 40904	Houston	TX	77240	Roland Balkenende	713-466-9966	S	200	0.4
Gage Co.	PO Box 1168	Pittsburgh	PA	15230	Robert A Chute	412-255-6904	R	176	0.6
Norwood Promotional Products	9311 San Pedro	San Antonio	TX	78216	Frank P Krasovec	210-341-9440	P	176	1.9
Hope Group	PO Box 840	Northborough	MA	01532	Carey Rhoten	508-393-7660	R	160	<0.1
Ingram Paper Co.	PO Box 60003	City of Industry	CA	91716	Larry Stillman	818-854-5400	R	150 *	0.3
Pickands Mather Sales Inc.	1422 Euclid Ave	Cleveland	OH	44115	Sam R Zickel	216-694-5300	R	150 *	<0.1
Production Tool Supply	PO Box 987	Warren	MI	48089	Mark Kahn	810-755-7770	R	150	0.4
Silliter/Klebes Indust Supplies	13 Hamden Pk Dr	Hamden	CT	06517	Jay Drummond	203-497-1500	D	140 *	<0.1
C.R. Laurence Company Inc.	2503 E Vernon Ave	Los Angeles	CA	90058	D Friese	213-588-1281	R	130 *	0.5
C and H Distributors Inc.	PO Box 04499	Milwaukee	WI	53204	David K Stark	414-271-2250	S	125	0.2
Dillon Supply Co.	PO Box 1111	Raleigh	NC	27602	Robert L McCann	919-832-7771	R	120 *	0.4
Famous Enterprises Inc.	PO Box 1889	Akron	OH	44309	Jay Blaushild	216-762-9621	R	120	0.7
Interstate Co.	2601 E 80th St	Minneapolis	MN	55425	Jeff Caswell	612-854-2044	R	120	0.6
IBT Inc.	PO Box 2982	Shawnee Msn	KS	66201	Stephen R Cloud	913-677-3151	R	115	0.4
BMI-France Inc.	27 Noblestown Rd	Carnegie	PA	15106	Willard Bellows	412-923-2525	D	114	<0.1
Precision Industries Inc.	4611 S 96th St	Omaha	NE	68127	Dennis Circo	402-593-7000	R	100	0.5
Snyder Paper Corp.	PO Box 758	Hickory	NC	28603	Roger McGuire	704-328-2501	R	100 *	0.3
Hub Inc.	PO Box 125	Tucker	GA	30085	Ben H Camp	404-934-3101	R	80	0.3
Wilton Corp.	300 S Hicks Rd	Palatine	IL	60067	Charles Vogl	847-934-6000	R	80	0.5
Standard Supply and Hardware	PO Box 60620	New Orleans	LA	70160	Evans Hadden	504-586-8400	R	75	0.3
Water Products Co.	7887 Fuller Rd	Eden Prairie	MN	55344	Rick Klau	612-937-2907	S	72	0.3
Bertsch Co.	1655 Steele Ave SW	Grand Rapids	MI	49507	John R Bertsch	616-452-3251	R	72	0.2
Service Supply Company Inc.	PO Box 732	Indianapolis	IN	46206	Frank N Owings Jr	317-638-2424	R	72	0.5
Alamo Iron Works	PO Box 231	San Antonio	TX	78291	Tony Koch	210-223-6161	R	71	0.5
Trumbull Industries Inc.	PO Box 30	Warren	OH	44482	Richard C Mueller	216-393-6624	R	70	0.3
Goodall Rubber Co.	Quakerbridge Ctr	Lawrenceville	NJ	08648	Torgny Astrom	609-799-2000	S	68	0.3
Continental Glass and Plastic	841 W Cermak Rd	Chicago	IL	60608	Richard A Giesen	312-666-2050	R	65	0.1
OKI Systems Inc.	4665 Interstate Dr	Cincinnati	OH	45246	Gary Thompson	513-874-2600	R	65	0.3

Source: *Ward's Business Directory of U.S. Private and Public Companies*, 1998. The company type code used is as follows: P - Public, R - Private, S - Subsidiary, D - Division, J - Joint Venture, A - Affiliate, G - Group. Sales are in millions of dollars, employees are in thousands. An asterisk (*) indicates an estimated sales volume. The symbol < stands for 'less than'.

OCCUPATIONS EMPLOYED BY SIC 508 - MACHINERY, EQUIPMENT, AND SUPPLIES

Occupation	% of Total 1996	Change to 2006	Occupation	% of Total 1996	Change to 2006
Sales & related workers nec	21.7	4.5	Salespersons, retail	2.2	4.5
General managers & top executives	7.4	1.3	Clerical supervisors & managers	2.0	4.5
General office clerks	3.9	-10.1	Bus & truck mechanics	1.9	4.5
Mobile heavy equipment mechanics	3.8	4.5	Order clerks	1.8	-6.0
Farm equipment mechanics	3.7	-26.9	Freight, stock, & material movers, hand	1.7	-6.0
Traffic, shipping, receiving clerks	3.3	4.5	Order fillers, wholesale & retail sales	1.6	14.9
Truck drivers light & heavy	3.3	4.5	Machinists	1.5	-20.9
Marketing & sales worker supervisors	3.2	4.5	Electrical & electronic technicians	1.2	3.3
Bookkeeping, accounting, & auditing clerks	3.2	-16.4	Wholesale & retail buyers, except farm products	1.2	1.7
Secretaries, except legal & medical	2.9	-17.1	Purchasing managers	1.1	4.5
Stock clerks	2.6	4.5	Welders & cutters	1.1	4.5
Maintenance repairers, general utility	2.5	-2.6	Helpers, laborers nec	1.0	4.5
Assemblers, fabricators, hand workers nec	2.5	4.5	Receptionists & information clerks	1.0	4.5
Blue collar worker supervisors	2.2	0.9			

Source: *Industry-Occupation Matrix*, Bureau of Labor Statistics. These data relate to one or more 3-digit SIC industry groups rather than to a single 4-digit SIC. The change reported for each occupation to the year 2006 is a percent of growth or decline as estimated by the Bureau of Labor Statistics. The abbreviation nec stands for 'not elsewhere classified'.

STATE AND REGIONAL CONCENTRATION

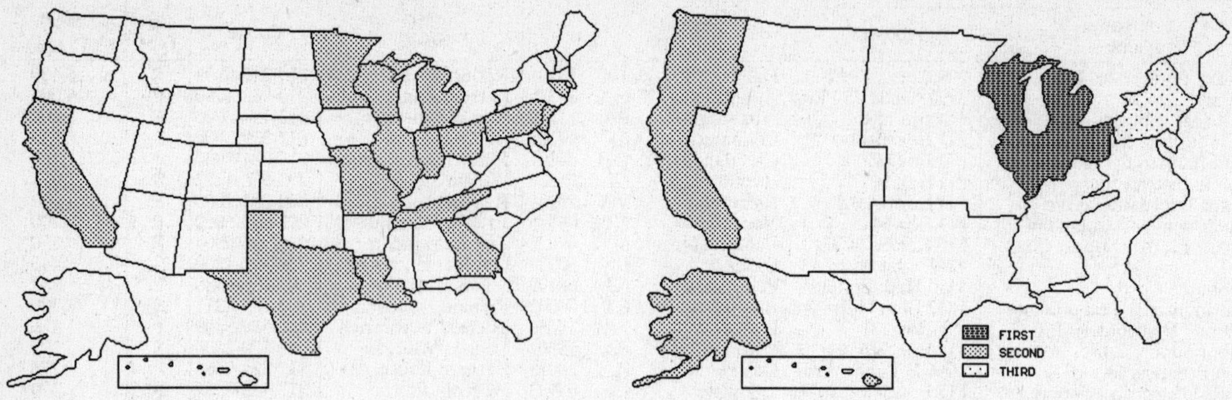

INDUSTRY DATA BY STATE

State	Establishments - 1995		Employment - 1995			Payroll - 1995		Sales - 1992		
	Total (number)	% of U.S.	Total (number)	% of U.S.	Per Estab.	Total ($ mil.)	Per Empl. ($)	Total ($ mil.)	% of U.S.	Per Estab ($)
California	1,431	9.0	14,924	9.3	10	553.6	37,096	8,002.3	14.2	520,272
Texas	1,437	9.1	15,002	9.3	10	537.0	35,795	4,737.7	8.4	316,694
Ohio	923	5.8	11,409	7.1	12	413.9	36,278	4,253.4	7.6	424,577
Illinois	839	5.3	10,065	6.3	12	398.9	39,636	3,954.1	7.0	456,487
Pennsylvania	816	5.1	8,613	5.3	11	318.1	36,938	3,847.9	6.8	425,322
Michigan	644	4.1	7,286	4.5	11	303.2	41,613	3,047.5	5.4	484,568
New Jersey	574	3.6	5,227	3.2	9	205.3	39,277	2,159.7	3.8	410,209
New York	698	4.4	6,592	4.1	9	262.6	39,831	2,154.3	3.8	319,871
Georgia	534	3.4	4,916	3.1	9	175.9	35,774	1,851.8	3.3	377,225
Wisconsin	321	2.0	4,531	2.8	14	155.6	34,336	1,549.8	2.8	379,115
Florida	669	4.2	5,183	3.2	8	165.0	31,830	1,478.6	2.6	292,151
Missouri	343	2.2	3,886	2.4	11	142.5	36,662	1,470.6	2.6	411,365
North Carolina	519	3.3	5,051	3.1	10	165.8	32,818	1,344.1	2.4	275,378
Indiana	425	2.7	4,031	2.5	9	135.0	33,484	1,280.0	2.3	349,255
Tennessee	399	2.5	3,858	2.4	10	135.2	35,036	1,272.6	2.3	367,585
Louisiana	403	2.5	3,970	2.5	10	142.2	35,807	1,270.0	2.3	295,135
Massachusetts	315	2.0	3,654	2.3	12	153.6	42,028	1,189.9	2.1	409,472
Minnesota	280	1.8	3,921	2.4	14	150.6	38,411	1,127.4	2.0	302,001
Washington	327	2.1	3,144	2.0	10	113.3	36,034	1,075.9	1.9	353,565
Connecticut	222	1.4	1,944	1.2	9	87.0	44,744	1,040.5	1.9	587,850
Alabama	327	2.1	2,891	1.8	9	99.1	34,292	809.5	1.4	278,180
Virginia	302	1.9	2,483	1.5	8	84.7	34,103	740.2	1.3	289,354
Colorado	220	1.4	2,048	1.3	9	71.7	35,019	611.6	1.1	321,564
Oregon	263	1.7	2,761	1.7	10	95.1	34,443	583.1	1.0	246,247
Kentucky	217	1.4	2,528	1.6	12	78.5	31,066	524.6	0.9	274,066
Kansas	205	1.3	1,806	1.1	9	61.8	34,232	521.8	0.9	319,149
South Carolina	238	1.5	2,174	1.4	9	69.2	31,829	511.7	0.9	227,607
Oklahoma	227	1.4	1,904	1.2	8	58.6	30,792	498.4	0.9	263,305
Iowa	168	1.1	1,715	1.1	10	54.0	31,497	442.2	0.8	319,485
Maryland	171	1.1	1,416	0.9	8	49.3	34,851	413.7	0.7	291,731
Arizona	161	1.0	1,324	0.8	8	46.1	34,832	268.9	0.5	244,015
Arkansas	169	1.1	1,308	0.8	8	35.7	27,256	256.8	0.5	236,482
Utah	98	0.6	974	0.6	10	31.1	31,965	254.8	0.5	323,717
West Virginia	120	0.8	1,183	0.7	10	35.4	29,936	239.7	0.4	226,106
Mississippi	123	0.8	1,104	0.7	9	31.6	28,662	224.5	0.4	226,092
Nebraska	88	0.6	1,052	0.7	12	33.2	31,588	202.4	0.4	218,572
Maine	75	0.5	801	0.5	11	27.0	33,683	160.1	0.3	213,697
New Hampshire	63	0.4	395	0.2	6	14.9	37,815	137.7	0.2	368,096
Nevada	68	0.4	478	0.3	7	15.0	31,389	134.7	0.2	342,690
Rhode Island	62	0.4	507	0.3	8	18.2	35,822	95.9	0.2	217,519
Idaho	69	0.4	547	0.3	8	17.3	31,669	88.6	0.2	204,711
New Mexico	70	0.4	494	0.3	7	12.8	25,919	87.3	0.2	201,972
Hawaii	44	0.3	362	0.2	8	11.8	32,657	67.5	0.1	190,686
Delaware	36	0.2	364	0.2	10	11.3	31,047	64.5	0.1	194,970
Montana	37	0.2	339	0.2	9	9.7	28,667	55.5	0.1	201,000
Alaska	29	0.2	175	0.1	6	6.7	38,406	52.4	0.1	292,844
North Dakota	23	0.1	156	0.1	7	5.5	35,346	40.0	0.1	277,562
Vermont	21	0.1	100-249	-	-	(D)	-	31.9	0.1	196,772
Wyoming	34	0.2	379	0.2	11	9.8	25,947	(D)	-	-
South Dakota	23	0.1	160	0.1	7	5.3	33,244	(D)	-	-
D.C.	4	0.0	20-99	-	-	(D)	-	(D)	-	-

Source: County Business Patterns, 1995 and *Economic Census of the U.S., 1992*. Data are sorted by 1992 revenues and, if revenues are unavailable, by establishments in 1995. The symbol (D) indicates that data are withheld by the source to avoid disclosure of competitive information. A dash (-) indicates that data are not available or undisclosed because they do not meet statistical validity standards. Shaded *states* on the state map indicate those states which have proportionately greater representation in the industry than would be indicated by the state's population; the ratio is based on total revenues or number of establishments. Shaded *regions* indicate where the industry is regionally most concentrated.

5087 - SERVICE ESTABLISHMENT EQUIPMENT

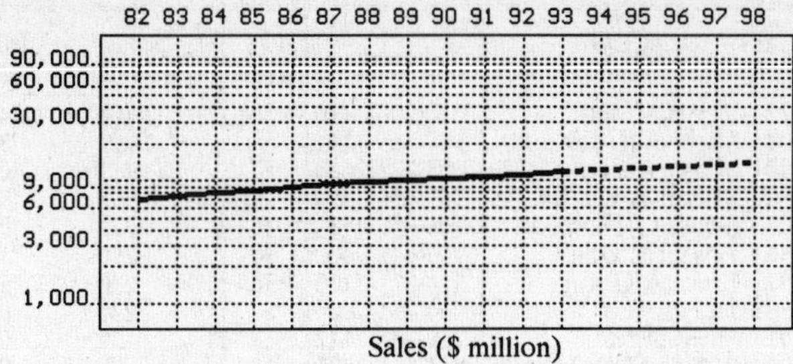

Sales ($ million)

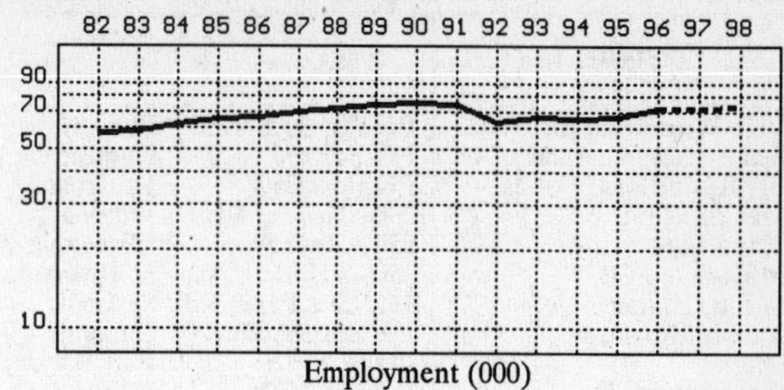

Employment (000)

GENERAL STATISTICS

Year	Establishments (number)	Employment (number)	Payroll ($ million)	Sales ($ million)	Expenses ($ million)	Beginning Inventory ($ million)	Ending Inventory ($ million)
1982	7,426	57,441	915.9	6,950.8	-	-	-
1983	7,118	57,861	979.2	7,449.1e	-	-	-
1984	7,111	62,022	1,105.4	7,947.3e	-	-	-
1985	6,907	64,580	1,175.7	8,445.6e	-	-	-
1986	7,080	66,280	1,259.6	8,943.8e	-	-	-
1987	8,467	69,217	1,330.1	9,442.1	2,529.5	920.3	980.3
1988	8,291	71,671	1,497.8	9,789.2e	2,607.8e	953.6e	1,004.0e
1989	7,992	74,320	1,594.6	10,136.4e	2,686.2e	987.0e	1,027.6e
1990	8,072	75,232	1,662.7	10,483.5e	2,764.5e	1,020.3e	1,051.3e
1991	8,125	74,563	1,682.3	10,830.7e	2,842.9e	1,053.6e	1,074.9e
1992	7,579	62,965	1,552.2	11,177.8	2,921.2	1,087.0	1,098.6
1993	7,452	66,461	1,647.5	11,772.2p	2,999.5p	1,120.3p	1,122.2p
1994	7,392	65,316	1,739.8	12,195.0p	3,077.9p	1,153.7p	1,145.9p
1995	7,279	66,730	1,818.1	12,617.7p	3,156.2p	1,187.0p	1,169.6p
1996	7,800p	71,600p	1,933.8p	13,040.4p	3,234.6p	1,220.3p	1,193.2p
1997	7,828p	72,245p	2,001.5p	13,463.1p	3,312.9p	1,253.7p	1,216.9p
1998	7,856p	72,890p	2,069.2p	13,885.8p	3,391.3p	1,287.0p	1,240.5p

Sources: *Economic Census of the United States*, 1982, 1987, and 1992. Establishment counts, employment, and payroll are from *County Business Patterns* for non-Census years. Values followed by a 'p' are projections by the editors. Sales and expense data for non-Census years are extrapolations, marked by 'e'. Industries reclassified in 1987 will not have data for prior years. Data are the most recent available at this level of detail.

INDICES OF CHANGE

Year	Establishments (number)	Employment (number)	Payroll ($ million)	Sales ($ million)	Expenses ($ million)	Beginning Inventory ($ million)	Ending Inventory ($ million)
1982	98.0	91.2	59.0	62.2	-	-	-
1983	93.9	91.9	63.1	66.6e	-	-	-
1984	93.8	98.5	71.2	71.1e	-	-	-
1985	91.1	102.6	75.7	75.6e	-	-	-
1986	93.4	105.3	81.1	80.0e	-	-	-
1987	111.7	109.9	85.7	84.5	86.6	84.7	89.2
1988	109.4	113.8	96.5	87.6e	89.3e	87.7e	91.4e
1989	105.4	118.0	102.7	90.7e	92.0e	90.8e	93.5e
1990	106.5	119.5	107.1	93.8e	94.6e	93.9e	95.7e
1991	107.2	118.4	108.4	96.9e	97.3e	96.9e	97.8e
1992	100.0	100.0	100.0	100.0	100.0	100.0	100.0
1993	98.3	105.6	106.1	105.3p	102.7p	103.1p	102.1p
1994	97.5	103.7	112.1	109.1p	105.4p	106.1p	104.3p
1995	96.0	106.0	117.1	112.9p	108.0p	109.2p	106.5p
1996	102.9p	113.7p	124.6p	116.7p	110.7p	112.3p	108.6p
1997	103.3p	114.7p	128.9p	120.4p	113.4p	115.3p	110.8p
1998	103.7p	115.8p	133.3p	124.2p	116.1p	118.4p	112.9p

Sources: Same as General Statistics. The values shown reflect change from the base year, 1992. Values above 100 mean greater than 1992, values below 100 mean less than 1992, and a value of 100 in the 1982-91 or 1993-98 period means same as 1992. Values followed by a 'p' are projections by the editors; 'e' stands for extrapolation. Data are the most recent available at this level of detail.

SELECTED RATIOS

For 1992	Avg. of All Wholesale	Analyzed Industry	Index	For 1992	Avg. of All Wholesale	Analyzed Industry	Index
Employees per Establishment	12	8	71	Sales per Employee	561,172	177,524	32
Payroll per Establishment	349,729	204,803	59	Sales per Establishment	6,559,346	1,474,838	22
Payroll per Employee	29,919	24,652	82	Expenses per Establishment	723,071	385,433	53

Sources: Same as General Statistics. The 'Average of All Manufacturing' column represents the average of all manufacturing industries reported for the most recent complete year available. The Index shows the relationship between the Average and the Analyzed Industry. For example, 100 means that they are equal; 500 that the Analyzed Industry is five times the average; 50 means that the Analyzed Industry is half the national average. The abbreviation 'na' is used to show that data are 'not available'.

LEADING COMPANIES

Number shown: **50** Total sales ($ mil): **11,677** Total employment (000): **36.0**

Company Name	Address				CEO Name	Phone	Co. Type	Sales ($ mil)	Empl. (000)
Unisource Worldwide Inc.	PO Box 3000-0935	Berwyn	PA	19312	Ray B Mundt	610-296-4470	P	7,108	14.2
Sally Beauty Company Inc.	PO Box 490	Denton	TX	76202	Michael H Renzulli	940-565-1111	S	1,291 *	8.0
Reinhart Institutional Foods	PO Box 2859	La Crosse	WI	54602	Mark Drazkowski	608-782-2660	R	415 *	0.8
Fastenal Co.	2001 Theurer Blvd	Winona	MN	55987	Robert A Kierlin	507-454-5374	P	398	3.1
Clark Food Service Inc.	950 Arthur Ave	Elk Grove Vill.	IL	60007	Donald J Hindman	708-956-1730	R	325	0.8
Edward Don and Co.	2500 S Harlem Ave	N. Riverside	IL	60546	Robert E Don	708-442-9400	R	250	1.1
Group One Capital Inc.	1611 Des Peres Rd	St. Louis	MO	63131	Bruce A Olson	314-821-5100	R	230 *	2.0
Unisource Midwest Inc.	PO Box 308001	Gahanna	OH	43230	Jack Bryant	614-251-7000	S	230 *	0.5
Fisher Paper	PO Box 1720	Fort Wayne	IN	46801	Floyd Sims	219-747-7442	D	87 *	0.2
W.S. Lee and Sons Inc.	PO Box 1631	Altoona	PA	16603	Walter J Lee Jr	814-696-3535	R	79 *	0.2
Marstan Industries Inc.	10814 Northeast	Philadelphia	PA	19116	Mark Levin	215-969-0600	R	75 *	0.5
Illinois Range Co.	708 W Central Rd	Mount Prospect	IL	60056	ET Krakowiak	708-253-4950	R	69	0.4
State Service Systems Inc.	10405-B E 55th Pl	Tulsa	OK	74146	Jamie Cheek	918-627-8000	S	60	<0.1
HP Products	4220 Saquaro Trail	Indianapolis	IN	46268	Donald Ames Shuel	317-298-9950	R	55	0.3
Wink Davis Equipment	800 Miami Cir NE	Atlanta	GA	30324	Alex Davis	404-266-2290	S	52 *	<0.1
Canover Industries Inc.	48th & Maspeth	Maspeth	NY	11378	Alfred Eisenberg	718-456-8900	R	50	0.2
Twyman Templeton Company	PO Box 4490	Columbus	OH	43204	Donald Lewis	614-272-5623	R	45	<0.1
Actrade International Ltd.	7 Penn Plaza	New York	NY	10001	Henry N Seror	212-563-1036	P	43	<0.1
Paper Mart	5631 Alexander	City of Com	CA	90040	Mary M Bush	213-726-8200	R	40 *	<0.1
Ledyard Company Inc.	1005 17th Ave	Santa Cruz	CA	95062	Richard Fontana	408-462-4400	R	38	0.1
Institutional Wholesale Co.	25 S Whitney Ave	Cookeville	TN	38501	Jimmy W Mackie	615-526-9588	R	37	0.1
Sierra Craft Inc.	18825 E San Jose	City of Industry	CA	91748	JA Unickel	818-964-2395	S	37 *	0.2
Singer Equipment Company	PO Box 13668	Reading	PA	19612	HD Singer	610-929-8000	R	35	0.1
Waltron Inc.	3989 Central NE	Minneapolis	MN	55421	Ronald Lewis	612-781-6601	R	34 *	0.1
Aerial Company Inc.	PO Box 197	Marinette	WI	54143	Ryan Hmielewski	715-735-9323	R	32 *	0.2
M. Conley Company Inc.	1312 4th St SE	Canton	OH	44701	Richard D Conley	216-456-8243	R	32	0.1
Paramount Restaurant Co.	333 Harborside	Providence	RI	02905	David Friedman	401-461-3000	R	30 *	0.1
Bark River Culvert	PO Box 10947	Green Bay	WI	54307	Fred H Lindner Jr	414-435-6676	R	29 *	0.1
R.W. Smith and Co.	PO Box 26160	San Diego	CA	92196	Ronald Woodhill	619-530-1800	R	28	<0.1
Peerless Paper Mills Inc.	1122 Longford Rd	Oaks	PA	19456	W Sheppard	215-933-9015	R	28	<0.1
Anderson Winn Paper Co.	PO Box 7609	Mission Hills	CA	91346	Sean Kim	818-898-1941	D	26	<0.1
G.A. Kayser and Sons Inc.	327 Elm St	Buffalo	NY	14203	Gerald A Kayser	716-854-8443	R	26 *	0.2
Glover Wholesale Inc.	PO Box 484	Columbus	GA	31902	Wally S Summers	706-324-3647	R	25	<0.1
Flo-Pac Corp.	700 N Washington	Minneapolis	MN	55401	JA Bowen	612-332-6240	R	23	0.2
Adams-Burch Inc.	5556 Tuxedo Rd	Hyattsville	MD	20781	Dan W Blaylock	301-341-1600	R	23	0.1
McShane Enterprises Inc.	5963 Mine Brook	Bernardsville	NJ	07924	David R McShane	908-953-0200	R	22	<0.1
Total Safety Inc.	11111 Wilcrest	Houston	TX	77017	George Fortenberry	713-941-0306	R	22	0.2
Easterday Janitorial Supply Co.	355 7th St	San Francisco	CA	94103	Paul Ridgeway	415-861-8310	D	21	0.2
Keyston Brothers	1601 N California	Walnut Creek	CA	94596	Jim Mitchell	510-945-4949	R	21	0.2
American Industrial Supply	519 Potrero Ave	San Francisco	CA	94110	George Herbst	415-826-1144	R	20 *	<0.1
Automatic Rain Co.	4060 Campbell Ave	Menlo Park	CA	94025	Willard Hayes	415-323-5161	R	20	<0.1
Kellermeyer Co.	PO Box 3357	Toledo	OH	43607	Don V Kellermeyer	419-255-3022	R	20 *	0.2
Ecolab Inc. Textile Care Div.	Ecolab Center	St. Paul	MN	55102		612-293-2233	D	20 *	0.1
Angus Fire Armour Corp.	PO Box 879	Angier	NC	27501	Robert Harcourt	919-639-6151	S	19	0.2
Columbus Paper Company Inc.	PO Box 6369	Columbus	GA	31995	Michael Greenblatt	706-689-1361	R	19	<0.1
Golden Triangle Import/Export	2807 Hoover Ave	National City	CA	91950	V de Murguia	619-551-0080	R	19 *	<0.1
Ro-Vic Inc.	PO Box 1140	Manchester	CT	06045	R Parrott Sr	203-646-3322	R	18	<0.1
Mikara Corp.	3109 Louisiana Ave	Minneapolis	MN	55427	Michael P Hicks	612-546-9500	R	17	0.2
Kranz Inc.	1717 Taylor Ave	Racine	WI	53403	Jeff Neubauer	414-637-9391	R	17	<0.1
Sanderson Safety Supply Co.	1101 SE 3rd St	Portland	OR	97214	Steven Spahr	503-238-5700	R	17	0.1

Source: *Ward's Business Directory of U.S. Private and Public Companies*, 1998. The company type code used is as follows: P - Public, R - Private, S - Subsidiary, D - Division, J - Joint Venture, A - Affiliate, G - Group. Sales are in millions of dollars, employees are in thousands. An asterisk (*) indicates an estimated sales volume. The symbol < stands for 'less than'.

OCCUPATIONS EMPLOYED BY SIC 508 - MACHINERY, EQUIPMENT, AND SUPPLIES

Occupation	% of Total 1996	Change to 2006	Occupation	% of Total 1996	Change to 2006
Sales & related workers nec	21.7	4.5	Salespersons, retail	2.2	4.5
General managers & top executives	7.4	1.3	Clerical supervisors & managers	2.0	4.5
General office clerks	3.9	-10.1	Bus & truck mechanics	1.9	4.5
Mobile heavy equipment mechanics	3.8	4.5	Order clerks	1.8	-6.0
Farm equipment mechanics	3.7	-26.9	Freight, stock, & material movers, hand	1.7	-6.0
Traffic, shipping, receiving clerks	3.3	4.5	Order fillers, wholesale & retail sales	1.6	14.9
Truck drivers light & heavy	3.3	4.5	Machinists	1.5	-20.9
Marketing & sales worker supervisors	3.2	4.5	Electrical & electronic technicians	1.2	3.3
Bookkeeping, accounting, & auditing clerks	3.2	-16.4	Wholesale & retail buyers, except farm products	1.2	1.7
Secretaries, except legal & medical	2.9	-17.1	Purchasing managers	1.1	4.5
Stock clerks	2.6	4.5	Welders & cutters	1.1	4.5
Maintenance repairers, general utility	2.5	-2.6	Helpers, laborers nec	1.0	4.5
Assemblers, fabricators, hand workers nec	2.5	4.5	Receptionists & information clerks	1.0	4.5
Blue collar worker supervisors	2.2	0.9			

Source: *Industry-Occupation Matrix*, Bureau of Labor Statistics. These data relate to one or more 3-digit SIC industry groups rather than to a single 4-digit SIC. The change reported for each occupation to the year 2006 is a percent of growth or decline as estimated by the Bureau of Labor Statistics. The abbreviation nec stands for 'not elsewhere classified'.

STATE AND REGIONAL CONCENTRATION

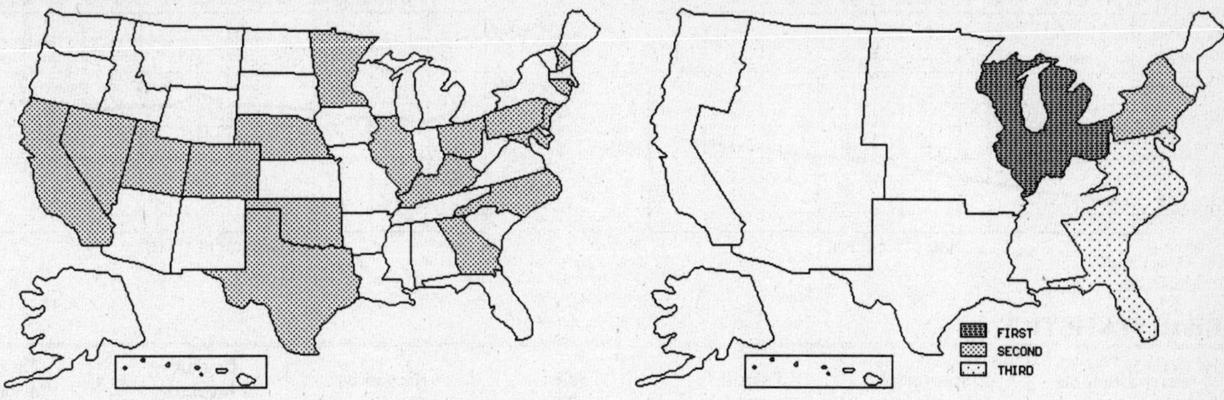

INDUSTRY DATA BY STATE

State	Establishments - 1995 Total (number)	Establishments - 1995 % of U.S.	Employment - 1995 Total (number)	Employment - 1995 % of U.S.	Employment - 1995 Per Estab.	Payroll - 1995 Total ($ mil.)	Payroll - 1995 Per Empl. ($)	Sales - 1992 Total ($ mil.)	Sales - 1992 % of U.S.	Sales - 1992 Per Estab ($)
California	691	9.5	6,664	10.0	10	197.8	29,679	1,361.1	12.3	191,703
Texas	576	7.9	4,400	6.6	8	112.8	25,632	779.7	7.0	194,052
Illinois	364	5.0	3,493	5.2	10	102.1	29,220	752.2	6.8	220,468
New York	427	5.9	3,465	5.2	8	99.3	28,655	733.9	6.6	219,589
Pennsylvania	367	5.0	3,547	5.3	10	94.1	26,543	641.2	5.8	170,527
Ohio	294	4.0	3,303	4.9	11	94.8	28,694	546.7	4.9	170,302
New Jersey	275	3.8	2,349	3.5	9	74.5	31,734	496.5	4.5	214,484
Georgia	237	3.3	2,055	3.1	9	61.5	29,912	439.1	4.0	224,735
Florida	391	5.4	2,827	4.2	7	71.5	25,293	436.3	3.9	158,370
Michigan	233	3.2	2,441	3.7	10	75.0	30,729	360.7	3.3	165,469
North Carolina	239	3.3	2,164	3.2	9	58.9	27,195	310.2	2.8	153,860
Connecticut	75	1.0	976	1.5	13	35.5	36,365	269.1	2.4	323,883
Maryland	131	1.8	1,446	2.2	11	45.7	31,633	237.0	2.1	172,595
Minnesota	112	1.5	1,526	2.3	14	51.8	33,959	229.1	2.1	191,709
Kentucky	95	1.3	1,262	1.9	13	24.1	19,100	224.6	2.0	220,214
Massachusetts	151	2.1	1,246	1.9	8	34.8	27,949	220.9	2.0	166,459
Indiana	174	2.4	1,476	2.2	8	35.3	23,899	219.0	2.0	187,460
Tennessee	152	2.1	1,246	1.9	8	35.9	28,801	201.0	1.8	158,801
Missouri	195	2.7	1,646	2.5	8	39.7	24,117	199.3	1.8	142,062
Wisconsin	129	1.8	1,662	2.5	13	34.4	20,715	186.2	1.7	160,124
Louisiana	138	1.9	1,656	2.5	12	38.6	23,283	184.0	1.7	136,005
Virginia	128	1.8	1,106	1.7	9	26.7	24,102	182.5	1.6	131,104
Washington	159	2.2	1,307	2.0	8	36.1	27,592	175.8	1.6	151,166
Colorado	147	2.0	1,222	1.8	8	33.5	27,426	172.2	1.6	169,315
Arizona	137	1.9	1,549	2.3	11	36.8	23,737	153.0	1.4	115,195
Oklahoma	99	1.4	692	1.0	7	14.9	21,578	143.3	1.3	190,007
Alabama	106	1.5	987	1.5	9	25.3	25,624	120.2	1.1	156,487
Oregon	108	1.5	918	1.4	9	25.9	28,247	118.4	1.1	137,003
South Carolina	108	1.5	836	1.3	8	21.7	25,999	110.3	1.0	134,384
Kansas	75	1.0	847	1.3	11	20.9	24,651	108.8	1.0	138,419
Utah	81	1.1	769	1.2	9	19.5	25,390	107.2	1.0	167,178
Iowa	78	1.1	791	1.2	10	17.2	21,690	82.1	0.7	136,389
Nebraska	40	0.5	714	1.1	18	18.2	25,440	81.5	0.7	125,652
Nevada	57	0.8	486	0.7	9	15.9	32,749	67.5	0.6	161,119
Mississippi	51	0.7	446	0.7	9	9.1	20,480	57.9	0.5	137,171
Arkansas	65	0.9	375	0.6	6	9.0	23,869	57.0	0.5	137,127
New Hampshire	26	0.4	395	0.6	15	11.3	28,648	55.7	0.5	159,074
Rhode Island	39	0.5	288	0.4	7	8.1	28,194	46.9	0.4	249,441
New Mexico	50	0.7	361	0.5	7	8.6	23,812	39.4	0.4	144,260
West Virginia	48	0.7	253	0.4	5	4.7	18,684	35.3	0.3	125,277
Maine	24	0.3	151	0.2	6	3.3	21,662	28.3	0.3	196,236
Idaho	29	0.4	283	0.4	10	7.5	26,647	26.2	0.2	113,303
Hawaii	26	0.4	134	0.2	5	3.0	22,388	25.7	0.2	125,385
North Dakota	26	0.4	166	0.2	6	3.5	21,313	25.4	0.2	178,761
Alaska	22	0.3	128	0.2	6	3.8	29,719	21.9	0.2	144,735
South Dakota	13	0.2	122	0.2	9	3.0	24,213	18.2	0.2	103,726
Montana	32	0.4	223	0.3	7	4.8	21,740	(D)	-	-
Delaware	21	0.3	94	0.1	4	2.2	23,500	(D)	-	-
Wyoming	15	0.2	84	0.1	6	1.7	19,869	(D)	-	-
Vermont	12	0.2	87	0.1	7	1.8	20,494	(D)	-	-
D.C.	11	0.2	66	0.1	6	2.1	31,606	(D)	-	-

Source: *County Business Patterns, 1995* and *Economic Census of the U.S., 1992*. Data are sorted by 1992 revenues and, if revenues are unavailable, by establishments in 1995. The symbol (D) indicates that data are withheld by the source to avoid disclosure of competitive information. A dash (-) indicates that data are not available or undisclosed because they do not meet statistical validity standards. Shaded *states* on the state map indicate those states which have proportionately greater representation in the industry than would be indicated by the state's population; the ratio is based on total revenues or number of establishments. Shaded *regions* indicate where the industry is regionally most concentrated.

5088 - TRANSPORTATION EQUIPMENT & SUPPLIES

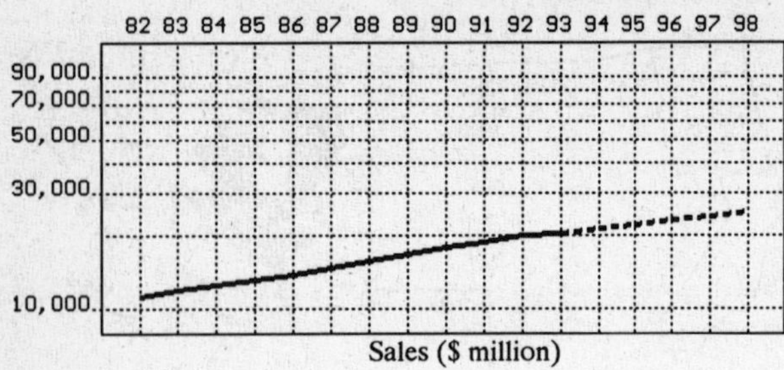

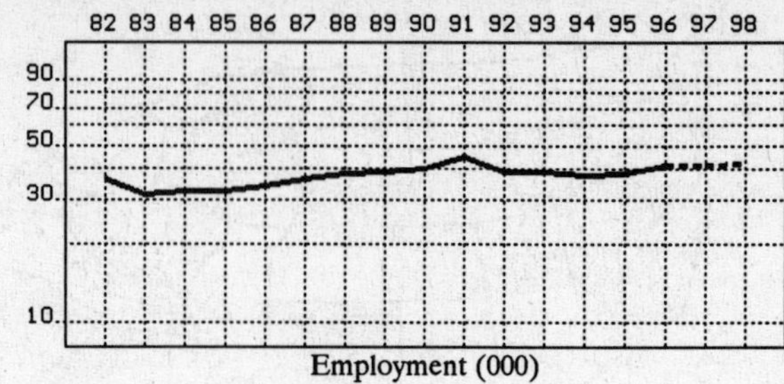

GENERAL STATISTICS

Year	Establishments (number)	Employment (number)	Payroll ($ million)	Sales ($ million)	Expenses ($ million)	Beginning Inventory ($ million)	Ending Inventory ($ million)
1982	3,131	36,645	764.3	11,103.7	-	-	-
1983	3,031	31,694	709.3	11,814.9e	-	-	-
1984	2,918	32,356	760.7	12,526.1e	-	-	-
1985	2,821	32,508	815.1	13,237.3e	-	-	-
1986	2,794	34,307	883.1	13,948.6e	-	-	-
1987	3,248	36,441	993.3	14,659.8	2,016.0	1,502.6	1,668.7
1988	3,063	38,210	1,178.8	15,702.6e	2,162.0e	1,728.1e	1,899.7e
1989	3,067	38,879	1,250.6	16,745.3e	2,308.1e	1,953.6e	2,130.7e
1990	3,148	39,940	1,326.4	17,788.1e	2,454.1e	2,179.1e	2,361.7e
1991	3,210	44,554	1,473.6	18,830.9e	2,600.1e	2,404.6e	2,592.7e
1992	3,866	39,444	1,375.9	19,873.7	2,746.2	2,630.1	2,823.7
1993	3,862	38,696	1,343.9	20,373.9p	2,892.2p	2,855.6p	3,054.6p
1994	3,820	37,569	1,374.6	21,250.9p	3,038.2p	3,081.1p	3,285.6p
1995	3,785	38,100	1,441.5	22,127.9p	3,184.2p	3,306.6p	3,516.6p
1996	3,842p	41,242p	1,604.1p	23,004.9p	3,330.3p	3,532.1p	3,747.6p
1997	3,919p	41,795p	1,668.5p	23,881.9p	3,476.3p	3,757.6p	3,978.6p
1998	3,995p	42,348p	1,732.9p	24,758.9p	3,622.3p	3,983.1p	4,209.6p

Sources: *Economic Census of the United States*, 1982, 1987, and 1992. Establishment counts, employment, and payroll are from *County Business Patterns* for non-Census years. Values followed by a 'p' are projections by the editors. Sales and expense data for non-Census years are extrapolations, marked by 'e'. Industries reclassified in 1987 will not have data for prior years. Data are the most recent available at this level of detail.

INDICES OF CHANGE

Year	Establishments (number)	Employment (number)	Payroll ($ million)	Sales ($ million)	Expenses ($ million)	Beginning Inventory ($ million)	Ending Inventory ($ million)
1982	81.0	92.9	55.5	55.9	-	-	-
1983	78.4	80.4	51.6	59.4e	-	-	-
1984	75.5	82.0	55.3	63.0e	-	-	-
1985	73.0	82.4	59.2	66.6e	-	-	-
1986	72.3	87.0	64.2	70.2e	-	-	-
1987	84.0	92.4	72.2	73.8	73.4	57.1	59.1
1988	79.2	96.9	85.7	79.0e	78.7e	65.7e	67.3e
1989	79.3	98.6	90.9	84.3e	84.0e	74.3e	75.5e
1990	81.4	101.3	96.4	89.5e	89.4e	82.9e	83.6e
1991	83.0	113.0	107.1	94.8e	94.7e	91.4e	91.8e
1992	100.0	100.0	100.0	100.0	100.0	100.0	100.0
1993	99.9	98.1	97.7	102.5p	105.3p	108.6p	108.2p
1994	98.8	95.2	99.9	106.9p	110.6p	117.1p	116.4p
1995	97.9	96.6	104.8	111.3p	115.9p	125.7p	124.5p
1996	99.4p	104.6p	116.6p	115.8p	121.3p	134.3p	132.7p
1997	101.4p	106.0p	121.3p	120.2p	126.6p	142.9p	140.9p
1998	103.3p	107.4p	125.9p	124.6p	131.9p	151.4p	149.1p

Sources: Same as General Statistics. The values shown reflect change from the base year, 1992. Values above 100 mean greater than 1992, values below 100 mean less than 1992, and a value of 100 in the 1982-91 or 1993-98 period means same as 1992. Values followed by a 'p' are projections by the editors; 'e' stands for extrapolation. Data are the most recent available at this level of detail.

SELECTED RATIOS

For 1992	Avg. of All Wholesale	Analyzed Industry	Index	For 1992	Avg. of All Wholesale	Analyzed Industry	Index
Employees per Establishment	12	10	87	Sales per Employee	561,172	503,846	90
Payroll per Establishment	349,729	355,898	102	Sales per Establishment	6,559,346	5,140,636	78
Payroll per Employee	29,919	34,882	117	Expenses per Establishment	723,071	710,347	98

Sources: Same as General Statistics. The 'Average of All Manufacturing' column represents the average of all manufacturing industries reported for the most recent complete year available. The Index shows the relationship between the Average and the Analyzed Industry. For example, 100 means that they are equal; 500 that the Analyzed Industry is five times the average; 50 means that the Analyzed Industry is half the national average. The abbreviation 'na' is used to show that data are 'not available'.

LEADING COMPANIES Number shown: **50** Total sales ($ mil): **23,051** Total employment (000): **58.2**

Company Name	Address				CEO Name	Phone	Co. Type	Sales ($ mil)	Empl. (000)
Mitsubishi International Corp.	520 Madison Ave	New York	NY	10022	M Numaguchi	212-605-2000	S	10,000	0.7
US Airways Group Inc.	2345 Crystal Dr	Arlington	VA	22227	Stephen M Wolf	703-872-7000	P	7,474	43.1
Stewart and Stevenson Services	PO Box 1637	Houston	TX	77251	Robert L Hargrave	713-868-7700	P	1,234	4.5
General Electric Co.	1 Neumann Way	Cincinnati	OH	45215	Richard R Ruegg	513-552-5370	D	650	0.1
International Lease Finance	1999nue of thears	Los Angeles	CA	90067	Steven Udvar-Hazy	310-788-1999	S	386 *	<0.1
International Air Leases Inc.	PO Box 522230	Miami	FL	33152	George Batchelor	305-889-6000	R	300	0.4
Banner Aerospace Inc.	PO Box 20260	Washington	DC	20041	Jeffrey J Steiner	202-478-5790	P	288	0.6
Labinal Inc.	881 Parkview Blvd	Lombard	IL	60148	Amaury du Fretay	630-705-5700	S	200 *	2.5
Willis Lease Finance Corp.	180 Harbor Dr	Sausalito	CA	94965	Charles F Willis IV	415-331-5281	P	198	<0.1
H.O. Penn Machinery Company	54 Noxon Rd	Poughkeepsie	NY	12603	C Thomas Cleveland	914-452-1200	R	180	0.3
Aviation Sales Co.	6905 NW 25th	Miami	FL	33122	Dale S Baker	305-592-4055	P	162	0.3
Agusta Aerospace Corp.	PO Box 16002	Philadelphia	PA	19114	Robert J Budica	215-281-1400	S	150	<0.1
Federal Express Aviation Svcs	2005 Corporate Ave	Memphis	TN	38132	James R Parker	901-395-3830	S	150 *	0.1
Azcon Corp.	224 S Michigan Ave	Chicago	IL	60604	Bert Pollan	312-362-0066	D	140	0.2
British Aerospace Holdings Inc.	15000 Conf Ctr	Chantilly	VA	20151	Paul Harris	703-227-1500	S	130	0.2
Astra Jet Corp.	4 Independence	Princeton	NJ	08540	Roy E Bergstrom	609-987-1125	S	100 *	<0.1
Argo International Corp.	140 Franklin St	New York	NY	10013	John Calicchio	212-431-1700	R	90	0.3
Gregory Poole Equipment Co.	4807 Beryl Rd	Raleigh	NC	27606	James G Poole Jr	919-828-0641	R	84	0.4
Halton Co.	4421 NE Columbia	Portland	OR	97218	Edward H Halton Jr	503-288-6411	S	80	0.4
Nelson A. Taylor Company Inc.	10 W 9th Ave	Gloversville	NY	12078	James W Taylor	518-725-0681	R	80	0.7
Aviation Service Corp.	PO Box 20735	Atlanta	GA	30349	Tom O'Neal	404-765-1850	R	64 *	0.2
Elliott Aviation Inc.	PO Box 100	Moline	IL	61266	Wynn Elliott	309-799-3183	R	60	0.3
Devtec Corp.	812 Bloomfield Ave	Windsor	CT	06095	Robert Barrack	203-688-9520	S	52	0.2
Derco Industries Inc.	PO Box 25549	Milwaukee	WI	53225	Eric Dermond	414-355-3066	R	50	0.1
Western Branch Diesel Inc.	PO Box 7788	Portsmouth	VA	23707	H A Haneman Jr	804-484-6230	R	44	0.2
Orion Aircraft Sales Inc.	9465 Wilshire Blvd	Beverly Hills	CA	90212	Leonard A Meldeau	310-000-0000	R	40	<0.1
DIFCO Inc.	PO Box 238	Findlay	OH	45839	Wayne Westlake	419-422-0525	R	38 *	0.1
Barfield Inc.	PO Box 025367	Miami	FL	33102	Marc Paganini	305-871-3900	R	35	0.3
Power Parts Co.	1860 N Wilmot Ave	Chicago	IL	60647	William Agey	312-772-4600	S	34	0.2
AMR Combs/API	3778 Distirplex Dr	Memphis	TN	38118	Peter Lasalle	901-365-3470	D	33 *	<0.1
Hawker Pacific Inc.	11310 Sherman	Sun Valley	CA	91352	David Lokken	818-765-6201	S	33 *	0.2
Medart Inc. (Fenton, Missouri)	100 L Williams	Fenton	MO	63026	J Michael Medart	314-343-0505	R	32	0.1
Continental Information Systems	PO Box 4785	Syracuse	NY	13221	Michael L Rosen	315-455-1900	P	31	<0.1
Azimuth Corp.	4209 Vineland Rd	Orlando	FL	32811	Alexander Milley	407-849-0480	R	31	0.1
Venturian Corp.	1600 2nd St S	Hopkins	MN	55343	Gary B Rappaport	612-931-2500	P	28	0.1
Airmotive Inc.	3400 Winona Ave	Burbank	CA	91504		818-845-7423	R	28	<0.1
Spencer Industries Inc.	8410 Dallas Ave	Seattle	WA	98108	Charles Harris	206-763-0210	R	28	0.1
Alco Equipment Inc.	PO Box 386	Agawam	MA	01001	David Townsend	413-789-0330	R	27	0.2
Lynton Group Inc.	9 Airport Rd	Morristown	NJ	07960	Christopher Tennant	973-292-9000	P	26	0.1
Williams and Wells Corp.	100 State St	Moonachie	NJ	07074	Stuart Margolins	201-440-1800	R	26	<0.1
Stull Enterprises Inc.	PO Box 887	Concordville	PA	19331	Rodman W Smith	610-459-8406	R	25 *	<0.1
Birmingham Rail Locomotive	PO Box 530157	Birmingham	AL	35253	Carlisle Jones Sr	205-424-7245	R	25	<0.1
Meridian Aerospace Group Ltd.	3796 Vest Mill Rd	Winston-Salem	NC	27103	William D Gardner	919-765-5454	R	25	<0.1
Saab Aircraft of America Inc.	21300 Ridgetop Cir	Sterling	VA	22170	Jack Faherty	703-406-7200	S	25	<0.1
W.S. Wilson Corp.	24 Harbor Park Dr	P. Washington	NY	11050	Harry L Baugher	516-621-8800	R	25	<0.1
Aviation Distributors Inc.	1 Wrigley Dr	Irvine	CA	92618	Osamah S Bakhit	714-586-7558	P	25	<0.1
Summit Aviation Inc.	Summit Airport	Middletown	DE	19709	Patrick J Foley	302-834-5400	R	23 *	<0.1
Intern. Airline Support Group	8095 NW 64th	Miami	FL	33166	Alexius A Dyer III	305-593-2658	P	20	<0.1
AAA Interair Inc.	PO Box 522230	Miami	FL	33152	Douglas A Potter	305-889-6111	S	20	<0.1
Gulf Marine Supplies	401 St Joseph St	New Orleans	LA	70130	Clyde Merritt	504-525-6252	R	20 *	<0.1

Source: Ward's Business Directory of U.S. Private and Public Companies, 1998. The company type code used is as follows: P - Public, R - Private, S - Subsidiary, D - Division, J - Joint Venture, A - Affiliate, G - Group. Sales are in millions of dollars, employees are in thousands. An asterisk (*) indicates an estimated sales volume. The symbol < stands for 'less than'.

OCCUPATIONS EMPLOYED BY SIC 508 - MACHINERY, EQUIPMENT, AND SUPPLIES

Occupation	% of Total 1996	Change to 2006	Occupation	% of Total 1996	Change to 2006
Sales & related workers nec	21.7	4.5	Salespersons, retail	2.2	4.5
General managers & top executives	7.4	1.3	Clerical supervisors & managers	2.0	4.5
General office clerks	3.9	-10.1	Bus & truck mechanics	1.9	4.5
Mobile heavy equipment mechanics	3.8	4.5	Order clerks	1.8	-6.0
Farm equipment mechanics	3.7	-26.9	Freight, stock, & material movers, hand	1.7	-6.0
Traffic, shipping, receiving clerks	3.3	4.5	Order fillers, wholesale & retail sales	1.6	14.9
Truck drivers light & heavy	3.3	4.5	Machinists	1.5	-20.9
Marketing & sales worker supervisors	3.2	4.5	Electrical & electronic technicians	1.2	3.3
Bookkeeping, accounting, & auditing clerks	3.2	-16.4	Wholesale & retail buyers, except farm products	1.2	1.7
Secretaries, except legal & medical	2.9	-17.1	Purchasing managers	1.1	4.5
Stock clerks	2.6	4.5	Welders & cutters	1.1	4.5
Maintenance repairers, general utility	2.5	-2.6	Helpers, laborers nec	1.0	4.5
Assemblers, fabricators, hand workers nec	2.5	4.5	Receptionists & information clerks	1.0	4.5
Blue collar worker supervisors	2.2	0.9			

Source: Industry-Occupation Matrix, Bureau of Labor Statistics. These data relate to one or more 3-digit SIC industry groups rather than to a single 4-digit SIC. The change reported for each occupation to the year 2006 is a percent of growth or decline as estimated by the Bureau of Labor Statistics. The abbreviation nec stands for 'not elsewhere classified'.

STATE AND REGIONAL CONCENTRATION

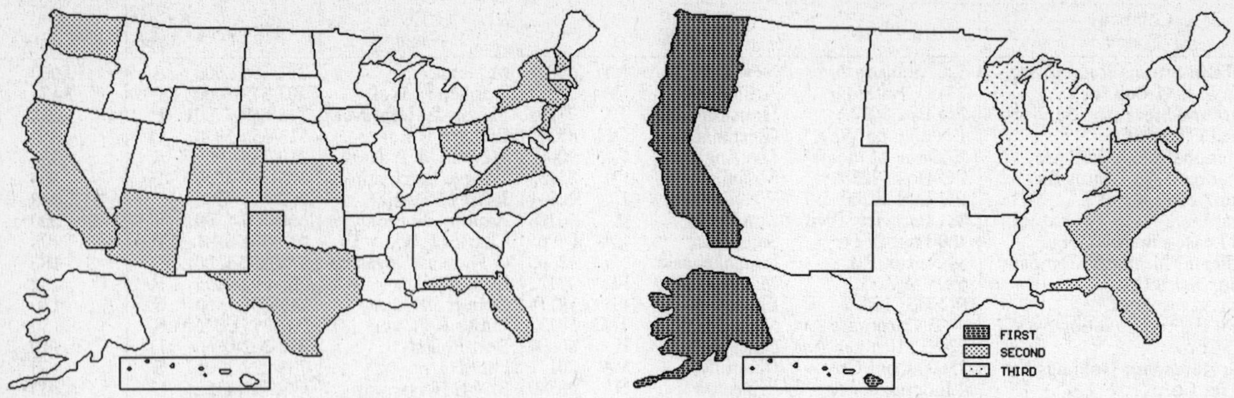

INDUSTRY DATA BY STATE

State	Establishments - 1995 Total (number)	Establishments - 1995 % of U.S.	Employment - 1995 Total (number)	Employment - 1995 % of U.S.	Employment - 1995 Per Estab.	Payroll - 1995 Total ($ mil.)	Payroll - 1995 Per Empl. ($)	Sales - 1992 Total ($ mil.)	Sales - 1992 % of U.S.	Sales - 1992 Per Estab ($)
California	582	15.4	5,380	14.2	9	218.4	40,596	2,935.6	14.8	456,978
Florida	650	17.2	5,522	14.5	8	199.1	36,055	1,926.2	9.7	358,356
New York	196	5.2	2,043	5.4	10	95.0	46,489	1,631.5	8.2	560,640
Texas	380	10.0	3,528	9.3	9	128.9	36,544	1,535.0	7.7	385,496
Virginia	88	2.3	992	2.6	11	43.6	43,917	1,527.2	7.7	1,083,913
Ohio	91	2.4	943	2.5	10	31.6	33,520	1,398.2	7.1	1,372,108
Washington	207	5.5	2,002	5.3	10	78.1	38,997	1,366.0	6.9	681,627
Illinois	122	3.2	1,854	4.9	15	74.6	40,257	890.3	4.5	740,086
New Jersey	132	3.5	1,768	4.7	13	74.7	42,241	815.0	4.1	644,758
Kansas	66	1.7	1,566	4.1	24	59.0	37,677	785.8	4.0	480,295
Arizona	57	1.5	496	1.3	9	17.9	35,998	769.1	3.9	547,821
Connecticut	72	1.9	669	1.8	9	37.0	55,280	543.6	2.7	563,303
Colorado	36	1.0	362	1.0	10	10.2	28,144	402.8	2.0	1,051,621
Missouri	83	2.2	582	1.5	7	20.8	35,667	337.4	1.7	484,784
Pennsylvania	68	1.8	693	1.8	10	25.3	36,457	307.5	1.6	356,739
Indiana	37	1.0	387	1.0	10	10.5	27,251	296.9	1.5	829,411
Georgia	83	2.2	717	1.9	9	26.5	36,925	291.4	1.5	426,690
Tennessee	58	1.5	629	1.7	11	20.8	33,051	264.1	1.3	470,822
Louisiana	85	2.2	835	2.2	10	27.3	32,679	222.5	1.1	250,869
Massachusetts	46	1.2	282	0.7	6	9.8	34,734	143.4	0.7	464,146
Michigan	64	1.7	552	1.5	9	18.3	33,107	143.3	0.7	268,333
Maryland	52	1.4	622	1.6	12	31.9	51,214	137.8	0.7	529,842
Alabama	26	0.7	284	0.7	11	9.6	33,729	133.8	0.7	224,909
Minnesota	45	1.2	566	1.5	13	16.6	29,387	133.4	0.7	290,608
Oregon	58	1.5	627	1.7	11	19.6	31,330	125.0	0.6	267,752
Oklahoma	54	1.4	918	2.4	17	33.1	36,086	116.2	0.6	332,808
Wisconsin	31	0.8	330	0.9	11	11.9	36,088	108.7	0.5	453,038
New Hampshire	15	0.4	356	0.9	24	14.0	39,424	91.4	0.5	335,853
North Carolina	51	1.3	284	0.7	6	9.6	33,947	85.7	0.4	280,173
Nebraska	19	0.5	92	0.2	5	3.1	33,185	75.2	0.4	565,098
Kentucky	23	0.6	189	0.5	8	5.7	30,365	45.1	0.2	338,887
Utah	18	0.5	275	0.7	15	6.7	24,349	35.3	0.2	156,853
South Carolina	25	0.7	166	0.4	7	3.7	22,343	28.6	0.1	181,051
Arkansas	20	0.5	461	1.2	23	9.9	21,499	28.4	0.1	189,187
Iowa	21	0.6	107	0.3	5	4.2	39,262	26.3	0.1	289,242
Alaska	16	0.4	81	0.2	5	2.7	32,815	20.9	0.1	282,676
Mississippi	19	0.5	88	0.2	5	2.0	23,182	20.0	0.1	149,231
Maine	11	0.3	114	0.3	10	2.7	23,447	18.3	0.1	175,644
West Virginia	7	0.2	378	1.0	54	15.8	41,796	14.9	0.1	204,096
Nevada	10	0.3	36	0.1	4	1.7	47,917	12.2	0.1	328,649
Rhode Island	10	0.3	28	0.1	3	0.9	33,429	10.9	0.1	494,045
New Mexico	9	0.2	33	0.1	4	0.7	21,242	9.9	0.0	309,156
Hawaii	7	0.2	35	0.1	5	0.6	18,286	6.0	0.0	181,061
Idaho	6	0.2	25	0.1	4	0.5	19,400	2.5	0.0	122,500
North Dakota	3	0.1	0-19	-	-	(D)	-	1.7	0.0	127,615
Vermont	10	0.3	20-99	-	-	(D)	-	(D)	-	-
Delaware	6	0.2	67	0.2	11	2.8	41,836	(D)	-	-
D.C.	4	0.1	0-19	-	-	(D)	-	(D)	-	-
Montana	3	0.1	20-99	-	-	(D)	-	(D)	-	-
South Dakota	2	0.1	0-19	-	-	(D)	-	(D)	-	-
Wyoming	1	0.0	20-99	-	-	(D)	-	(D)	-	-

Source: County Business Patterns, 1995 and *Economic Census of the U.S., 1992*. Data are sorted by 1992 revenues and, if revenues are unavailable, by establishments in 1995. The symbol (D) indicates that data are withheld by the source to avoid disclosure of competitive information. A dash (-) indicates that data are not available or undisclosed because they do not meet statistical validity standards. Shaded *states* on the state map indicate those states which have proportionately greater representation in the industry than would be indicated by the state's population; the ratio is based on total revenues or number of establishments. Shaded *regions* indicate where the industry is regionally most concentrated.

5091 - SPORTING & RECREATIONAL GOODS

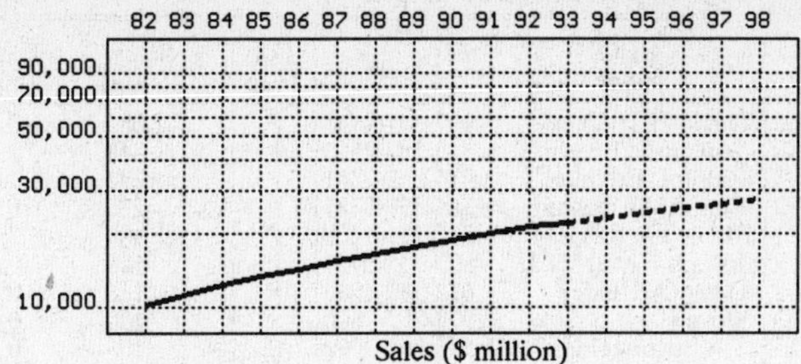

Sales ($ million)

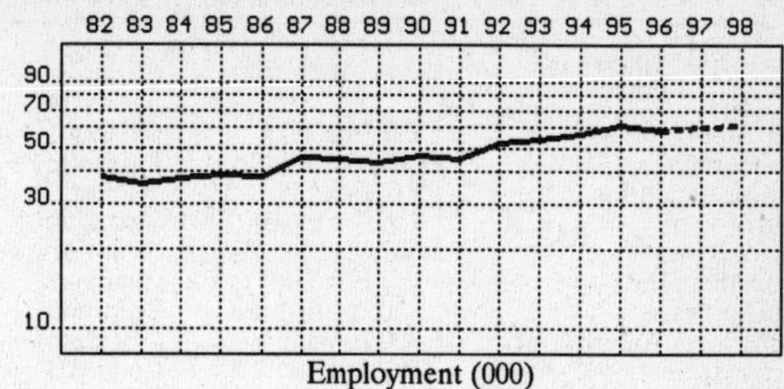

Employment (000)

GENERAL STATISTICS

Year	Establishments (number)	Employment (number)	Payroll ($ million)	Sales ($ million)	Expenses ($ million)	Beginning Inventory ($ million)	Ending Inventory ($ million)
1982	4,050	38,159	654.3	10,242.4	-	-	-
1983	3,790	35,972	645.7	11,265.8e	-	-	-
1984	3,799	37,895	697.8	12,289.2e	-	-	-
1985	3,725	39,438	761.2	13,312.6e	-	-	-
1986	3,668	38,535	779.2	14,336.0e	-	-	-
1987	4,922	45,625	957.2	15,359.4	2,289.9	1,641.0	1,874.0
1988	4,575	45,352	1,058.3	16,504.5e	2,496.6e	1,792.3e	2,021.2e
1989	4,195	43,610	1,106.6	17,649.6e	2,703.2e	1,943.7e	2,168.5e
1990	4,242	46,518	1,165.3	18,794.6e	2,909.9e	2,095.0e	2,315.8e
1991	4,290	44,480	1,198.9	19,939.7e	3,116.6e	2,246.3e	2,463.0e
1992	5,530	52,269	1,405.1	21,084.8	3,323.2	2,397.7	2,610.3
1993	5,702	53,646	1,489.1	22,030.8p	3,529.9p	2,549.0p	2,757.5p
1994	5,730	56,056	1,623.8	23,115.0p	3,736.5p	2,700.4p	2,904.8p
1995	5,745	60,790	1,748.6	24,199.3p	3,943.2p	2,851.7p	3,052.1p
1996	5,786p	58,410p	1,741.4p	25,283.5p	4,149.8p	3,003.1p	3,199.3p
1997	5,948p	60,118p	1,828.0p	26,367.7p	4,356.5p	3,154.4p	3,346.6p
1998	6,110p	61,827p	1,914.5p	27,452.0p	4,563.2p	3,305.7p	3,493.8p

Sources: *Economic Census of the United States*, 1982, 1987, and 1992. Establishment counts, employment, and payroll are from *County Business Patterns* for non-Census years. Values followed by a 'p' are projections by the editors. Sales and expense data for non-Census years are extrapolations, marked by 'e'. Industries reclassified in 1987 will not have data for prior years. Data are the most recent available at this level of detail.

INDICES OF CHANGE

Year	Establishments (number)	Employment (number)	Payroll ($ million)	Sales ($ million)	Expenses ($ million)	Beginning Inventory ($ million)	Ending Inventory ($ million)
1982	73.2	73.0	46.6	48.6	-	-	-
1983	68.5	68.8	46.0	53.4e	-	-	-
1984	68.7	72.5	49.7	58.3e	-	-	-
1985	67.4	75.5	54.2	63.1e	-	-	-
1986	66.3	73.7	55.5	68.0e	-	-	-
1987	89.0	87.3	68.1	72.8	68.9	68.4	71.8
1988	82.7	86.8	75.3	78.3e	75.1e	74.8e	77.4e
1989	75.9	83.4	78.8	83.7e	81.3e	81.1e	83.1e
1990	76.7	89.0	82.9	89.1e	87.6e	87.4e	88.7e
1991	77.6	85.1	85.3	94.6e	93.8e	93.7e	94.4e
1992	100.0	100.0	100.0	100.0	100.0	100.0	100.0
1993	103.1	102.6	106.0	104.5p	106.2p	106.3p	105.6p
1994	103.6	107.2	115.6	109.6p	112.4p	112.6p	111.3p
1995	103.9	116.3	124.4	114.8p	118.7p	118.9p	116.9p
1996	104.6p	111.7p	123.9p	119.9p	124.9p	125.2p	122.6p
1997	107.6p	115.0p	130.1p	125.1p	131.1p	131.6p	128.2p
1998	110.5p	118.3p	136.3p	130.2p	137.3p	137.9p	133.8p

Sources: Same as General Statistics. The values shown reflect change from the base year, 1992. Values above 100 mean greater than 1992, values below 100 mean less than 1992, and a value of 100 in the 1982-91 or 1993-98 period means same as 1992. Values followed by a 'p' are projections by the editors; 'e' stands for extrapolation. Data are the most recent available at this level of detail.

SELECTED RATIOS

For 1992	Avg. of All Wholesale	Analyzed Industry	Index	For 1992	Avg. of All Wholesale	Analyzed Industry	Index
Employees per Establishment	12	9	81	Sales per Employee	561,172	403,390	72
Payroll per Establishment	349,729	254,087	73	Sales per Establishment	6,559,346	3,812,803	58
Payroll per Employee	29,919	26,882	90	Expenses per Establishment	723,071	600,940	83

Sources: Same as General Statistics. The 'Average of All Manufacturing' column represents the average of all manufacturing industries reported for the most recent complete year available. The Index shows the relationship between the Average and the Analyzed Industry. For example, 100 means that they are equal; 500 that the Analyzed Industry is five times the average; 50 means that the Analyzed Industry is half the national average. The abbreviation 'na' is used to show that data are 'not available'.

LEADING COMPANIES

Number shown: **50** Total sales ($ mil): **5,061** Total employment (000): **18.6**

Company Name	Address				CEO Name	Phone	Co. Type	Sales ($ mil)	Empl. (000)
Hughes Supply Inc.	PO Box 2273	Orlando	FL	32802	David H Hughes	407-841-4755	P	1,082	3.3
Central Garden and Pet Co.	3697 Mt Diablo	Lafayette	CA	94549	William E Brown	510-283-4573	P	841	2.7
Gander Mountain Inc.	PO Box 128	Wilmot	WI	53192	Ralph L Freitag	414-862-2331	P	292	1.3
SCP Pool Corp.	128 Northpark Blvd	Covington	LA	70433	Frank J St Romain	504-892-5521	P	236	0.8
Noel Group Inc.	667 Madison Ave	New York	NY	10021	Stanley R Rawn	212-371-1400	P	189	3.4
Ellett Brothers Inc.	PO Box 128	Chapin	SC	29036	Joseph F Murray Jr	803-345-3751	P	148	0.4
United Hardware	5005 Nathan Ln	Plymouth	MN	55442	David A Heider	612-559-1800	R	136	0.4
Salomon North America Inc.	400 E Main St	Georgetown	MA	01833	Steve Bagby	978-352-7600	S	130	0.1
American Recreation Company	48 Mall Ave	Commack	NY	11725	S A Silverstein	516-864-2000	S	105	0.6
Maurice Pincoffs Company Inc.	PO Box 920919	Houston	TX	77292	John I Griffin	713-681-5461	R	100	0.1
Outdoor Sports Headquarters	967 Watertower Ln	Dayton	OH	45449	Martin S Altman	513-865-5855	S	90	0.2
AcuSport Corporation	1 Hunter Pl	Bellefontaine	OH	43311	William L Fraim	513-593-7010	S	85	0.2
Henry's Tackle L.L.C.	PO Drawer 1107	Morehead City	NC	28557	Mark Suber	919-726-6186	S	80	0.3
Nationwide Sports Distributing	70 James Way	Southampton	PA	18966	Leslie Edelman	215-322-2050	R	75	0.2
Pool Water Products	17872 Mitchell Ave	Irvine	CA	92614	Dean C Allred	714-756-1666	R	73 •	0.3
American Recreation Products	1224 Fern Ridge	St. Louis	MO	63141	George J Grabner Jr	314-576-8000	S	70	0.6
Rand Intern. Leisure Products	51 Executive Blvd	Farmingdale	NY	11735	Larry Goldmeier	516-249-6000	R	65	<0.1
Bicknell Distributors Inc.	12 Parkwood Dr	Hopkinton	MA	01748	Jon Hulme	508-435-2321	S	60	0.2
Nelson/Weather-Rite Inc.	125 Enterprise Ave	Secaucus	NJ	07096	Melvin Marx	201-348-0400	S	60	0.1
Jerry's Sport Center Inc.	PO Box 121	Forest City	PA	18421	Bernard Ziomek	717-785-9400	R	59 •	0.1
Dakco Distributors Inc.	PO Box 5009	Minot	ND	58702	RF Saunders	701-857-1140	R	58 •	<0.1
Browning	1 Browning Pl	Morgan	UT	84050	Don W Gobel	801-876-2711	S	55	0.3
Simmons Outdoor Corp.	2120 Killearney	Tallahassee	FL	32308	Larry W Bridgeman	904-878-5100	P	52	<0.1
Abu Garcia Inc.	21 Law Dr	Fairfield	NJ	07006	N Stenhoj	201-227-7666	R	50	0.1
Faber Brothers Inc.	4141 S Pulaski	Chicago	IL	60632	Wayne J Koslowski	773-376-9300	R	50	0.2
RSR Wholesale Guns Inc.	4405 Metric Dr	Winter Park	FL	32792	Bob Steger	407-677-4342	R	49 •	0.2
General Sportcraft Ltd.	140 Woodbine St	Bergenfield	NJ	07621	KJ Edelson	201-384-4242	R	47	0.1
Nordica USA Inc.	139 Harvest Ln	Williston	VT	05495	Timothy Jamieson	802-879-4644	S	44 •	<0.1
Canstar Sports USA	PO Box 716	Swanton	VT	05488	D Terreri	802-868-2711	D	40	<0.1
Folsom Corp.	43 McKee Dr	Mahwah	NJ	07430	L Feldsott	201-529-3550	R	40	0.2
Regent Sports Corp.	45 Ranick Rd	Hauppauge	NY	11788	Irving Lawner	516-234-2800	R	40	0.1
Orcal Inc.	701 N Hariton Ave	Orange	CA	92667	Ron Heffner	714-997-4780	R	39 •	0.2
Superior Pool Products Inc.	4900 E Landon Dr	Anaheim	CA	92807	Dave Chess	714-693-8035	S	36 •	0.2
Precise International	15 Corporate Dr	Orangeburg	NY	10962	Tom Higgins	914-365-3500	R	35	<0.1
V.F. Grace Inc.	605 E 13th Ave	Anchorage	AK	99501	Charles R Rush	907-272-6431	R	35	<0.1
Franklin Sports Industries Inc.	PO Box 508	Stoughton	MA	02072	Larry Franklin	781-344-1111	R	32 •	0.2
Morrow Snowboards Inc.	PO Box 12606	Salem	OR	97302	David Calapp	503-375-9300	P	32	0.3
Lew Horton Distributing Co.	PO Box 5023	Westborough	MA	01581	Lew Horton	508-366-7400	R	30	<0.1
Normark Corp.	10395 Yellow Cir	Minnetonka	MN	55343	Ronald W Weber	612-933-7060	S	30	<0.1
Roller Derby Skate Corp.	311 W Edwards St	Litchfield	IL	62056	Edwin Seltzer	217-324-3961	R	30 •	<0.1
Dynamic Classics Ltd.	230 5th Ave	New York	NY	10001	Marvin Cooper	212-571-0267	P	30	<0.1
Point Sporting Goods Inc.	2925 Welsby Ave	Stevens Point	WI	54481	William Debot	715-344-4620	R	29	0.1
Leslie Edelman of New York	75 Sherwood Ave	Farmingdale	NY	11735	Robert Ishkanian	516-249-8080	S	28 •	0.1
Morris Rothenberg and Son	25 Ranick Rd	Smithtown	NY	11788	Milton Somberg	516-234-8000	R	28	<0.1
Camfour Inc.	65 Ind Park	Westfield	MA	01085	AF Ferst	413-568-3371	R	25 •	<0.1
Go/Sportsmen's Supply Inc.	1535 Industrial Ave	Billings	MT	59104	Duane Grasulak	406-252-2109	R	25	<0.1
Lifestyle International Inc.	110 S Enterprise	Secaucus	NJ	07094	DH Palk	201-863-2426	S	25 •	<0.1
CGS Distributing Inc.	A300 E 51st Ave	Denver	CO	80216	Michael B Burgamy	303-331-0114	S	24	<0.1
G. Joannou Cycle Company	151 Ludlow Ave	Northvale	NJ	07647	Madeline Joannou	201-768-9050	R	24 •	0.1
International Armament Corp.	PO Box 208	Alexandria	VA	22313	Samuel Cummings	703-548-1400	R	24	<0.1

Source: *Ward's Business Directory of U.S. Private and Public Companies*, 1998. The company type code used is as follows: P - Public, R - Private, S - Subsidiary, D - Division, J - Joint Venture, A - Affiliate, G - Group. Sales are in millions of dollars, employees are in thousands. An asterisk (•) indicates an estimated sales volume. The symbol < stands for 'less than'.

OCCUPATIONS EMPLOYED BY SIC 509 - WHOLESALE TRADE, OTHER

Occupation	% of Total 1996	Change to 2006	Occupation	% of Total 1996	Change to 2006
Sales & related workers nec	19.5	20.2	Clerical supervisors & managers	1.9	20.2
General managers & top executives	5.9	16.4	Order clerks	1.9	8.2
Truck drivers light & heavy	5.4	20.2	Helpers, laborers nec	1.7	20.2
General office clerks	3.6	3.4	Electrical & electronic technicians	1.4	18.8
Traffic, shipping, receiving clerks	3.6	16.7	Blue collar worker supervisors	1.4	16.0
Stock clerks	3.5	-3.9	Wholesale & retail buyers, except farm products	1.3	17.0
Freight, stock, & material movers, hand	3.3	8.2	Office machine & cash register servicers	1.3	20.2
Marketing & sales worker supervisors	3.1	20.2	Hand packers & packagers	1.2	-3.9
Order fillers, wholesale & retail sales	3.0	16.7	Maintenance repairers, general utility	1.1	12.0
Bookkeeping, accounting, & auditing clerks	2.9	-3.9	Industrial truck & tractor operators	1.1	20.2
Salespersons, retail	2.5	20.2	Purchasing managers	1.1	20.2
Secretaries, except legal & medical	2.5	-4.7	Receptionists & information clerks	1.0	20.2
Assemblers, fabricators, hand workers nec	2.0	-3.9			

Source: *Industry-Occupation Matrix*, Bureau of Labor Statistics. These data relate to one or more 3-digit SIC industry groups rather than to a single 4-digit SIC. The change reported for each occupation to the year 2006 is a percent of growth or decline as estimated by the Bureau of Labor Statistics. The abbreviation nec stands for 'not elsewhere classified'.

STATE AND REGIONAL CONCENTRATION

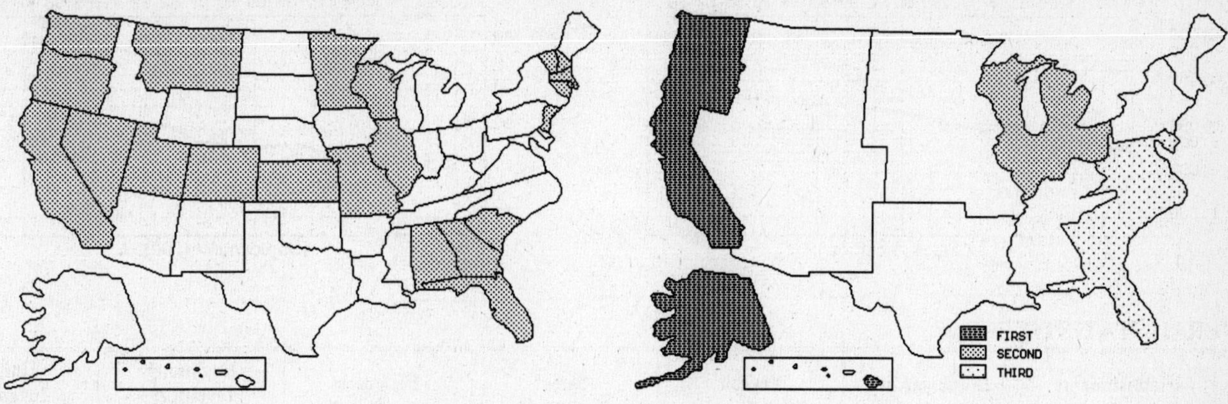

INDUSTRY DATA BY STATE

State	Establishments - 1995 Total (number)	Establishments - 1995 % of U.S.	Employment - 1995 Total (number)	Employment - 1995 % of U.S.	Employment - 1995 Per Estab.	Payroll - 1995 Total ($ mil.)	Payroll - 1995 Per Empl. ($)	Sales - 1992 Total ($ mil.)	Sales - 1992 % of U.S.	Sales - 1992 Per Estab ($)
California	850	14.8	8,824	14.5	10	285.4	32,341	3,297.2	15.6	425,887
Illinois	255	4.4	2,946	4.8	12	103.9	35,277	1,513.4	7.2	565,559
New York	298	5.2	3,316	5.5	11	103.4	31,172	1,360.3	6.5	519,215
Florida	439	7.6	3,275	5.4	7	97.4	29,736	1,180.8	5.6	392,817
Massachusetts	139	2.4	1,865	3.1	13	83.3	44,646	1,001.1	4.7	450,144
Texas	357	6.2	3,546	5.8	10	92.7	26,140	883.3	4.2	347,883
New Jersey	182	3.2	1,978	3.3	11	75.7	38,260	880.4	4.2	466,047
Pennsylvania	187	3.3	2,318	3.8	12	66.7	28,769	852.8	4.0	417,411
Wisconsin	138	2.4	1,307	2.2	9	39.8	30,438	807.7	3.8	473,142
Minnesota	172	3.0	2,583	4.3	15	58.2	22,542	717.9	3.4	504,476
Ohio	193	3.4	2,159	3.6	11	55.9	25,892	683.2	3.2	357,491
Georgia	159	2.8	1,696	2.8	11	50.1	29,548	675.9	3.2	440,343
Washington	190	3.3	1,956	3.2	10	59.4	30,344	599.9	2.8	384,772
South Carolina	76	1.3	2,144	3.5	28	53.2	24,824	587.2	2.8	409,181
Missouri	133	2.3	1,316	2.2	10	34.1	25,888	483.5	2.3	457,851
Michigan	174	3.0	1,401	2.3	8	38.7	27,643	451.5	2.1	317,275
Alabama	82	1.4	694	1.1	8	17.6	25,393	447.8	2.1	960,936
North Carolina	129	2.2	1,105	1.8	9	26.8	24,282	402.4	1.9	341,624
Utah	63	1.1	700	1.2	11	18.7	26,721	393.0	1.9	658,281
Colorado	171	3.0	1,523	2.5	9	41.7	27,370	374.5	1.8	277,201
Connecticut	67	1.2	716	1.2	11	23.4	32,627	309.8	1.5	497,207
Oregon	108	1.9	843	1.4	8	22.9	27,196	285.6	1.4	339,986
Kansas	56	1.0	1,156	1.9	21	31.6	27,341	280.3	1.3	261,755
Indiana	95	1.7	1,223	2.0	13	32.5	26,572	277.2	1.3	265,998
Vermont	26	0.5	642	1.1	25	23.1	35,910	262.1	1.2	663,476
Tennessee	107	1.9	929	1.5	9	22.2	23,899	232.0	1.1	288,601
Maryland	69	1.2	552	0.9	8	15.7	28,413	207.9	1.0	362,254
Virginia	90	1.6	682	1.1	8	20.8	30,457	166.4	0.8	252,813
Louisiana	70	1.2	1,036	1.7	15	17.3	16,681	161.1	0.8	192,956
Rhode Island	18	0.3	713	1.2	40	8.4	11,844	129.9	0.6	314,433
New Hampshire	47	0.8	402	0.7	9	13.4	33,284	126.3	0.6	410,101
Nevada	43	0.7	542	0.9	13	14.4	26,585	116.6	0.6	413,486
Kentucky	52	0.9	496	0.8	10	12.4	24,996	116.4	0.6	213,115
Iowa	50	0.9	497	0.8	10	11.4	22,845	107.3	0.5	229,261
Montana	24	0.4	223	0.4	9	4.7	21,045	104.4	0.5	476,890
Arizona	99	1.7	602	1.0	6	12.5	20,749	102.5	0.5	204,571
Arkansas	36	0.6	316	0.5	9	7.3	23,218	84.3	0.4	417,436
Oklahoma	47	0.8	462	0.8	10	9.4	20,294	79.7	0.4	216,579
Hawaii	42	0.7	219	0.4	5	6.1	28,059	63.3	0.3	299,777
Idaho	29	0.5	415	0.7	14	7.1	17,048	55.5	0.3	189,570
Mississippi	35	0.6	241	0.4	7	4.5	18,830	43.4	0.2	235,712
Maine	29	0.5	153	0.3	5	3.8	24,680	40.4	0.2	399,644
Nebraska	31	0.5	293	0.5	9	6.0	20,614	34.2	0.2	150,110
West Virginia	25	0.4	174	0.3	7	2.5	14,494	21.8	0.1	120,713
Alaska	15	0.3	97	0.2	6	2.4	25,000	20.9	0.1	326,531
South Dakota	10	0.2	100	0.2	10	2.2	22,000	16.6	0.1	213,282
North Dakota	11	0.2	92	0.2	8	2.1	23,293	16.0	0.1	246,400
New Mexico	14	0.2	120	0.2	9	2.2	18,733	11.2	0.1	124,800
Wyoming	7	0.1	179	0.3	26	3.0	16,989	10.2	0.0	59,655
Delaware	3	0.1	0-19	-	-	(D)	-	(D)	-	-
D.C.	3	0.1	0-19	-	-	(D)	-	(D)	-	-

Source: County Business Patterns, 1995 and *Economic Census of the U.S., 1992*. Data are sorted by 1992 revenues and, if revenues are unavailable, by establishments in 1995. The symbol (D) indicates that data are withheld by the source to avoid disclosure of competitive information. A dash (-) indicates that data are not available or undisclosed because they do not meet statistical validity standards. Shaded *states* on the state map indicate those states which have proportionately greater representation in the industry than would be indicated by the state's population; the ratio is based on total revenues or number of establishments. Shaded *regions* indicate where the industry is regionally most concentrated.

5092 - TOYS AND HOBBY GOODS AND SUPPLIES

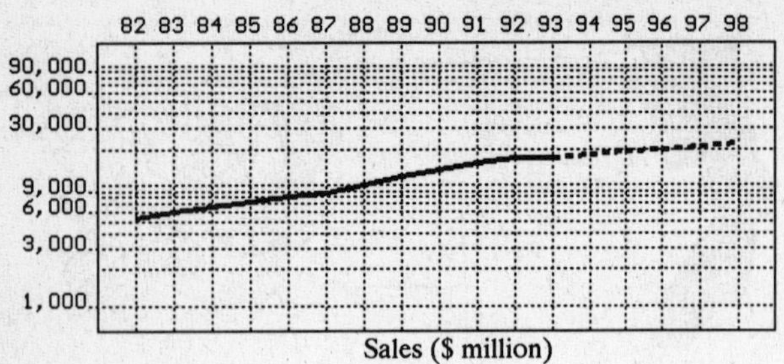

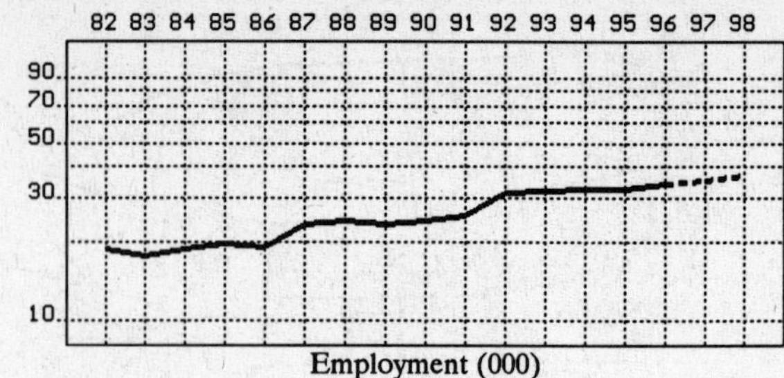

GENERAL STATISTICS

Year	Establishments (number)	Employment (number)	Payroll ($ million)	Sales ($ million)	Expenses ($ million)	Beginning Inventory ($ million)	Ending Inventory ($ million)
1982	2,054	18,847	319.4	5,371.3	-	-	-
1983	1,874	17,593	332.7	6,005.0e	-	-	-
1984	1,831	18,944	379.7	6,638.7e	-	-	-
1985	1,770	19,698	422.2	7,272.4e	-	-	-
1986	1,748	19,357	435.9	7,906.1e	-	-	-
1987	2,424	23,455	508.2	8,539.8	1,393.6	726.7	882.9
1988	2,221	24,226	557.8	10,190.3e	1,661.1e	904.8e	1,062.3e
1989	2,049	23,779	590.5	11,840.7e	1,928.6e	1,083.0e	1,241.8e
1990	2,123	24,291	637.7	13,491.2e	2,196.0e	1,261.1e	1,421.3e
1991	2,136	25,664	660.2	15,141.7e	2,463.5e	1,439.3e	1,600.8e
1992	2,738	31,685	941.9	16,792.2	2,731.0	1,617.4	1,780.2
1993	2,770	32,141	948.2	16,778.8p	2,998.5p	1,795.5p	1,959.7p
1994	2,751	32,646	970.0	17,920.9p	3,266.0p	1,973.7p	2,139.2p
1995	2,767	32,715	1,010.7	19,063.0p	3,533.4p	2,151.8p	2,318.7p
1996	2,810p	34,242p	1,055.9p	20,205.1p	3,800.9p	2,329.9p	2,498.1p
1997	2,887p	35,521p	1,113.7p	21,347.2p	4,068.4p	2,508.1p	2,677.6p
1998	2,964p	36,800p	1,171.5p	22,489.3p	4,335.9p	2,686.2p	2,857.1p

Sources: Economic Census of the United States, 1982, 1987, and 1992. Establishment counts, employment, and payroll are from *County Business Patterns* for non-Census years. Values followed by a 'p' are projections by the editors. Sales and expense data for non-Census years are extrapolations, marked by 'e'. Industries reclassified in 1987 will not have data for prior years. Data are the most recent available at this level of detail.

INDICES OF CHANGE

Year	Establishments (number)	Employment (number)	Payroll ($ million)	Sales ($ million)	Expenses ($ million)	Beginning Inventory ($ million)	Ending Inventory ($ million)
1982	75.0	59.5	33.9	32.0	-	-	-
1983	68.4	55.5	35.3	35.8e	-	-	-
1984	66.9	59.8	40.3	39.5e	-	-	-
1985	64.6	62.2	44.8	43.3e	-	-	-
1986	63.8	61.1	46.3	47.1e	-	-	-
1987	88.5	74.0	54.0	50.9	51.0	44.9	49.6
1988	81.1	76.5	59.2	60.7e	60.8e	55.9e	59.7e
1989	74.8	75.0	62.7	70.5e	70.6e	67.0e	69.8e
1990	77.5	76.7	67.7	80.3e	80.4e	78.0e	79.8e
1991	78.0	81.0	70.1	90.2e	90.2e	89.0e	89.9e
1992	100.0	100.0	100.0	100.0	100.0	100.0	100.0
1993	101.2	101.4	100.7	99.9p	109.8p	111.0p	110.1p
1994	100.5	103.0	103.0	106.7p	119.6p	122.0p	120.2p
1995	101.1	103.3	107.3	113.5p	129.4p	133.0p	130.2p
1996	102.6p	108.1p	112.1p	120.3p	139.2p	144.1p	140.3p
1997	105.4p	112.1p	118.2p	127.1p	149.0p	155.1p	150.4p
1998	108.2p	116.1p	124.4p	133.9p	158.8p	166.1p	160.5p

Sources: Same as General Statistics. The values shown reflect change from the base year, 1992. Values above 100 mean greater than 1992, values below 100 mean less than 1992, and a value of 100 in the 1982-91 or 1993-98 period means same as 1992. Values followed by a 'p' are projections by the editors; 'e' stands for extrapolation. Data are the most recent available at this level of detail.

SELECTED RATIOS

For 1992	Avg. of All Wholesale	Analyzed Industry	Index	For 1992	Avg. of All Wholesale	Analyzed Industry	Index
Employees per Establishment	12	12	99	Sales per Employee	561,172	529,973	94
Payroll per Establishment	349,729	344,010	98	Sales per Establishment	6,559,346	6,133,017	94
Payroll per Employee	29,919	29,727	99	Expenses per Establishment	723,071	997,443	138

Sources: Same as General Statistics. The 'Average of All Manufacturing' column represents the average of all manufacturing industries reported for the most recent complete year available. The Index shows the relationship between the Average and the Analyzed Industry. For example, 100 means that they are equal; 500 that the Analyzed Industry is five times the average; 50 means that the Analyzed Industry is half the national average. The abbreviation 'na' is used to show that data are 'not available'.

LEADING COMPANIES Number shown: 44 Total sales ($ mil): 9,379 Total employment (000): 51.2

Company Name	Address				CEO Name	Phone	Co. Type	Sales ($ mil)	Empl. (000)
Avon Products Inc.	1345 of the Amer	New York	NY	10105	James E Preston	212-282-5000	P	5,079	35.0
Anco Management Services Inc.	202 N Court St	Florence	AL	35630	Joel Anderson	205-766-3824	R	740•	3.0
Wang's International Inc.	4250 E Shelby Dr	Memphis	TN	38118	Robert Wang	901-362-2111	R	470•	1.0
Value Merchants Inc.	710 N Plankinton	Milwaukee	WI	53203		414-274-2575	P	363	4.8
Ben Franklin Crafts Inc.	500 E North Ave	Carol Stream	IL	60188	Bob Kendig	708-462-6100	S	350	0.2
Great Planes Model	1608 Interstate Dr	Champaign	IL	61821	Wayne Hemming	217-398-6300	R	350•	0.8
Applause Enterprises Inc.	PO Box 4183	Woodland Hills	CA	91365	Steven L Muellner	818-992-6000	R	280•	0.6
Ben Franklin Stores Inc.	PO Box 5938	Chicago	IL	60188	Robert A Kendig	630-462-6100	S	250	0.6
Diamond Comic Distributors	1966 Greenspring	Timonium	MD	21093	Stephen Geppi	410-560-7100	R	220	0.5
Sanrio Inc.	570 Eccles Ave	S San Francisco	CA	94080	K Tsuji	650-952-2880	S	150	0.5
B.J. Alan Co.	555 King Blvd	Youngstown	OH	44502	Bruce Zoldan	216-746-1064	R	110	0.3
ABC International Traders Inc.	16730 Schoenborn	North Hills	CA	91343	Isaac Larian	818-894-2525	R	105•	<0.1
Discovery Toys Inc.	6400 Brisa St	Livermore	CA	94550	Lane Nemeth	925-606-2600	S	93	0.2
Ammar's Inc.	S College Ave	Bluefield	VA	24605	Keleel A Ammar Jr	540-322-4686	R	75	0.8
Tash Inc. Western Div.	11190 White Birch	R. Cucamonga	CA	91730	Ronald Jones	909-945-9566	D	70•	0.2
M.W. Kasch Co.	5401 W Donges Bay	Mequon	WI	53092	Jeff C Kasch	414-242-5000	R	70•	0.2
Imperial Toy Corp.	2060 E 7th St	Los Angeles	CA	90021	Fred Kort	213-489-2100	R	47•	0.1
South Carolina Distributors		Cherokee Falls	SC	29702	Herbert Livingston	803-839-2766	R	47•	0.1
Strombecker Corp.	600 N Pulaski Rd	Chicago	IL	60624	Daniel B Shure	773-638-1000	R	45	0.4
Unique Industries Inc.	2400 S Weccacoe	Philadelphia	PA	19148	Everett Novak	215-336-4300	R	45	0.2
Testor Corp.	620 Buckbee St	Rockford	IL	61104	David Miller	815-962-6654	S	43	0.3
Price Stern Sloan Inc.	11150 Olympic 650	Los Angeles	CA	90064	Morton Mint	310-477-6100	P	37	0.2
Acme Premium Supply Corp.	4100 Forest Pk Blvd	St. Louis	MO	63108	Robert V Dawson	314-531-8880	R	35	0.2
United Model Distributors Inc.	301 Holbrook Dr	Wheeling	IL	60090	Richard Rovnick	708-459-6700	R	35•	0.2
S and S Worldwide Inc.	PO Box 513	Colchester	CT	06415	Stephen Schwartz	203-537-3451	R	33•	0.3
Shepher Distributors and Sales	2300 Linden Blvd	Brooklyn	NY	11208	Sid Monchik	718-649-2525	R	32	<0.1
Wm. K. Walthers Inc.	PO Box 3039	Milwaukee	WI	53201	Philip Walthers	414-527-0770	R	25	0.2
American West Marketing Inc.	2002 E McFadden	Santa Ana	CA	92705	Terry Anderson	714-550-6003	S	23•	<0.1
International Playthings Inc.	120 Riverdale Rd	Riverdale	NJ	07457	Ted Kiesewetter	201-831-1400	R	23	<0.1
Kidsview Inc.	266 Harristown Rd	Glen Rock	NJ	07452	Michael Nafash	201-493-9595	S	22	<0.1
Variety Distributors Inc.	702 Spring St	Harlan	IA	51537	Gary Simecka	712-755-2184	R	17	<0.1
Model Rectifier Corp.	200 Carter Dr	Edison	NJ	08817	Roy Gielber	908-248-0400	R	14•	<0.1
Herr's and Bernat Inc.	70 Eastgate Dr	Danville	IL	61832	Ken Cutler	217-442-4121	R	14	<0.1
R.B. Howell Co.	630 NW 10th Ave	Portland	OR	97209	Robert Howell	503-227-3125	R	14•	<0.1
Cardinal Inc.	400 Markley St	Port Reading	NJ	07064	S Darwin	908-636-6160	R	13	<0.1
Kipp Brothers Inc.	PO Box 157	Indianapolis	IN	46206	Sam Chernin	317-634-5507	R	12	<0.1
E.Z. Gregory Inc.	PO Box 44268	Madison	WI	53744	Gary Hermanson	608-271-2324	R	9	<0.1
Action Products International	344 Cypress Rd	Ocala	FL	34472	Ronald Kaplan	352-680-3516	P	6	<0.1
Action Industries Inc.	460 Nixon Rd	Cheswick	PA	15024	T Ronald Casper	412-782-4800	P	5	<0.1
Cromers Inc.	PO Box 163	Columbia	SC	29202	James Cromer	803-779-2290	R	4	<0.1
Ishi Press International	1702-H Meridian	San Jose	CA	95125	Hartland Snyder	408-271-0415	R	2•	<0.1
Dentt Inc.	4171 Marquis Way	Salt Lake City	UT	84124	Gale Hammond	801-277-7056	R	1	<0.1
Direct Connect International	266 Harristown Rd	Glen Rock	NJ	07452	Peter L Schneider	201-445-2101	P	1	<0.1
Pyrotex Inc.	3216 Belt Line Rd	Dallas	TX	75234	Randy Beckham	214-488-3011	R	0•	<0.1

Source: *Ward's Business Directory of U.S. Private and Public Companies*, 1998. The company type code used is as follows: P - Public, R - Private, S - Subsidiary, D - Division, J - Joint Venture, A - Affiliate, G - Group. Sales are in millions of dollars, employees are in thousands. An asterisk (•) indicates an estimated sales volume. The symbol < stands for 'less than'.

OCCUPATIONS EMPLOYED BY SIC 509 - WHOLESALE TRADE, OTHER

Occupation	% of Total 1996	Change to 2006	Occupation	% of Total 1996	Change to 2006
Sales & related workers nec	19.5	20.2	Clerical supervisors & managers	1.9	20.2
General managers & top executives	5.9	16.4	Order clerks	1.9	8.2
Truck drivers light & heavy	5.4	20.2	Helpers, laborers nec	1.7	20.2
General office clerks	3.6	3.4	Electrical & electronic technicians	1.4	18.8
Traffic, shipping, receiving clerks	3.6	16.7	Blue collar worker supervisors	1.4	16.0
Stock clerks	3.5	-3.9	Wholesale & retail buyers, except farm products	1.3	17.0
Freight, stock, & material movers, hand	3.3	8.2	Office machine & cash register servicers	1.3	20.2
Marketing & sales worker supervisors	3.1	20.2	Hand packers & packagers	1.2	-3.9
Order fillers, wholesale & retail sales	3.0	16.7	Maintenance repairers, general utility	1.1	12.0
Bookkeeping, accounting, & auditing clerks	2.9	-3.9	Industrial truck & tractor operators	1.1	20.2
Salespersons, retail	2.5	20.2	Purchasing managers	1.1	20.2
Secretaries, except legal & medical	2.5	-4.7	Receptionists & information clerks	1.0	20.2
Assemblers, fabricators, hand workers nec	2.0	-3.9			

Source: *Industry-Occupation Matrix*, Bureau of Labor Statistics. These data relate to one or more 3-digit SIC industry groups rather than to a single 4-digit SIC. The change reported for each occupation to the year 2006 is a percent of growth or decline as estimated by the Bureau of Labor Statistics. The abbreviation nec stands for 'not elsewhere classified'.

STATE AND REGIONAL CONCENTRATION

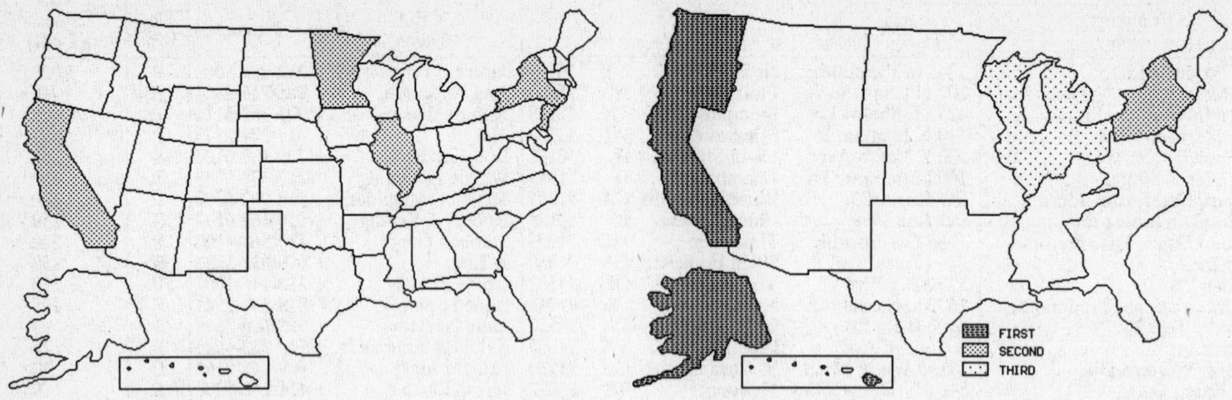

INDUSTRY DATA BY STATE

State	Establishments - 1995 Total (number)	% of U.S.	Employment - 1995 Total (number)	% of U.S.	Per Estab.	Payroll - 1995 Total ($ mil.)	Per Empl. ($)	Sales - 1992 Total ($ mil.)	% of U.S.	Per Estab ($)
California	560	20.2	7,140	22.0	13	249.7	34,969	4,493.4	30.0	622,873
New York	331	12.0	3,044	9.4	9	111.1	36,498	2,063.3	13.8	756,882
New Jersey	145	5.2	3,185	9.8	22	109.1	34,260	1,565.6	10.5	520,825
Illinois	134	4.8	2,196	6.8	16	74.8	34,071	1,553.9	10.4	793,612
Texas	148	5.3	1,534	4.7	10	43.8	28,585	866.2	5.8	517,437
Minnesota	60	2.2	521	1.6	9	18.0	34,516	623.2	4.2	1,187,070
Ohio	92	3.3	1,716	5.3	19	60.4	35,183	583.4	3.9	344,781
Pennsylvania	108	3.9	1,245	3.8	12	28.1	22,559	396.0	2.6	327,264
Florida	174	6.3	1,304	4.0	7	30.5	23,425	347.0	2.3	323,714
Georgia	42	1.5	495	1.5	12	14.8	29,802	287.2	1.9	409,669
Massachusetts	56	2.0	649	2.0	12	19.4	29,897	250.6	1.7	671,895
Indiana	43	1.6	703	2.2	16	12.1	17,245	206.8	1.4	317,611
Connecticut	30	1.1	256	0.8	9	8.9	34,918	194.0	1.3	573,976
Wisconsin	46	1.7	774	2.4	17	17.4	22,459	173.0	1.2	211,433
North Carolina	40	1.4	722	2.2	18	24.2	33,583	163.9	1.1	394,014
Missouri	61	2.2	404	1.2	7	12.0	29,735	160.4	1.1	280,926
Michigan	51	1.8	391	1.2	8	8.7	22,312	129.2	0.9	150,709
Tennessee	50	1.8	429	1.3	9	11.1	25,834	119.4	0.8	313,472
Alabama	22	0.8	771	2.4	35	16.7	21,663	84.1	0.6	256,436
Oregon	33	1.2	431	1.3	13	7.4	17,204	78.8	0.5	250,952
Colorado	48	1.7	400	1.2	8	7.7	19,290	74.4	0.5	222,149
Maryland	34	1.2	342	1.1	10	7.3	21,231	64.7	0.4	179,255
Arizona	37	1.3	191	0.6	5	3.0	15,838	56.5	0.4	211,607
Kansas	32	1.2	234	0.7	7	4.3	18,577	56.2	0.4	398,688
Virginia	30	1.1	229	0.7	8	6.9	30,066	54.1	0.4	287,872
Nevada	14	0.5	198	0.6	14	6.2	31,242	49.2	0.3	218,471
Nebraska	13	0.5	153	0.5	12	3.1	20,059	39.5	0.3	292,370
Oklahoma	14	0.5	192	0.6	14	4.0	20,755	35.2	0.2	247,908
South Carolina	19	0.7	138	0.4	7	4.8	34,812	32.4	0.2	279,121
Utah	22	0.8	146	0.4	7	2.4	16,425	30.7	0.2	207,108
Hawaii	21	0.8	85	0.3	4	1.8	21,706	25.5	0.2	194,618
Louisiana	16	0.6	127	0.4	8	2.2	17,291	17.6	0.1	147,714
South Dakota	5	0.2	100-249	-	-	(D)	-	16.4	0.1	182,344
Arkansas	12	0.4	53	0.2	4	0.7	12,906	13.4	0.1	231,655
Maine	12	0.4	128	0.4	11	2.7	20,703	11.5	0.1	189,279
New Hampshire	12	0.4	51	0.2	4	1.6	32,118	10.2	0.1	243,786
Iowa	28	1.0	125	0.4	4	3.5	27,664	9.2	0.1	70,731
Montana	10	0.4	61	0.2	6	1.2	20,426	7.0	0.0	130,167
New Mexico	9	0.3	56	0.2	6	1.0	18,554	5.5	0.0	108,314
Kentucky	16	0.6	50	0.2	3	0.9	18,540	5.3	0.0	97,815
Alaska	6	0.2	18	0.1	3	0.8	44,444	4.9	0.0	407,083
North Dakota	8	0.3	60	0.2	8	0.8	12,550	4.5	0.0	144,935
West Virginia	9	0.3	34	0.1	4	0.3	9,706	4.0	0.0	90,023
D.C.	2	0.1	0-19	-	-	(D)	-	3.0	0.0	338,333
Wyoming	4	0.1	20-99	-	-	(D)	-	2.4	0.0	62,816
Idaho	6	0.2	29	0.1	5	0.4	12,724	2.0	0.0	72,556
Mississippi	8	0.3	32	0.1	4	0.4	11,094	1.9	0.0	90,762
Vermont	5	0.2	42	0.1	8	0.6	14,357	1.6	0.0	143,000
Washington	75	2.7	1,373	4.2	18	51.8	37,698	(D)	-	-
Rhode Island	13	0.5	62	0.2	5	4.4	70,274	(D)	-	-
Delaware	1	0.0	0-19	-	-	(D)	-	-	-	-

Source: County Business Patterns, 1995 and *Economic Census of the U.S., 1992*. Data are sorted by 1992 revenues and, if revenues are unavailable, by establishments in 1995. The symbol (D) indicates that data are withheld by the source to avoid disclosure of competitive information. A dash (-) indicates that data are not available or undisclosed because they do not meet statistical validity standards. Shaded *states* on the state map indicate those states which have proportionately greater representation in the industry than would be indicated by the state's population; the ratio is based on total revenues or number of establishments. Shaded *regions* indicate where the industry is regionally most concentrated.

5093 - SCRAP AND WASTE MATERIALS

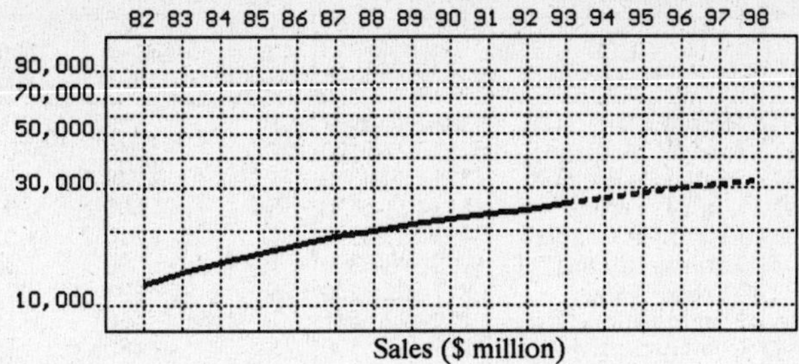

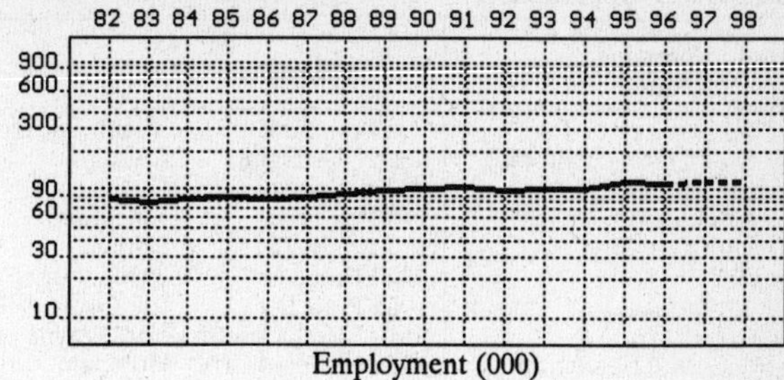

GENERAL STATISTICS

Year	Establishments (number)	Employment (number)	Payroll ($ million)	Sales ($ million)	Expenses ($ million)	Beginning Inventory ($ million)	Ending Inventory ($ million)
1982	8,403	83,708	1,212.1	12,260.3	-	-	-
1983	8,795	77,462	1,289.4	13,589.1e	-	-	-
1984	7,671	85,018	1,450.0	14,917.9e	-	-	-
1985	7,353	85,307	1,463.4	16,246.7e	-	-	-
1986	7,137	83,279	1,494.8	17,575.5e	-	-	-
1987	8,716	85,762	1,624.1	18,904.3	3,807.6	1,089.2	1,116.8
1988	8,248	93,158	2,153.3	20,015.8e	4,065.7e	1,162.8e	1,185.7e
1989	8,139	99,304	2,328.5	21,127.4e	4,323.8e	1,236.4e	1,254.6e
1990	8,628	102,179	2,389.8	22,238.9e	4,581.8e	1,310.0e	1,323.5e
1991	9,058	105,709	2,401.7	23,350.5e	4,839.9e	1,383.6e	1,392.4e
1992	8,928	98,005	2,269.1	24,462.0	5,098.0	1,457.2	1,461.3
1993	9,073	100,172	2,414.7	25,929.1p	5,356.0p	1,530.8p	1,530.2p
1994	9,079	102,395	2,668.8	27,149.2p	5,614.1p	1,604.4p	1,599.1p
1995	9,541	115,866	3,218.0	28,369.4p	5,872.2p	1,678.0p	1,668.0p
1996	9,321p	111,981p	3,058.5p	29,589.6p	6,130.2p	1,751.6p	1,736.9p
1997	9,432p	114,366p	3,196.0p	30,809.8p	6,388.3p	1,825.2p	1,805.8p
1998	9,544p	116,751p	3,333.6p	32,029.9p	6,646.4p	1,898.8p	1,874.7p

Sources: *Economic Census of the United States*, 1982, 1987, and 1992. Establishment counts, employment, and payroll are from *County Business Patterns* for non-Census years. Values followed by a 'p' are projections by the editors. Sales and expense data for non-Census years are extrapolations, marked by 'e'. Industries reclassified in 1987 will not have data for prior years. Data are the most recent available at this level of detail.

INDICES OF CHANGE

Year	Establishments (number)	Employment (number)	Payroll ($ million)	Sales ($ million)	Expenses ($ million)	Beginning Inventory ($ million)	Ending Inventory ($ million)
1982	94.1	85.4	53.4	50.1	-	-	-
1983	98.5	79.0	56.8	55.6e	-	-	-
1984	85.9	86.7	63.9	61.0e	-	-	-
1985	82.4	87.0	64.5	66.4e	-	-	-
1986	79.9	85.0	65.9	71.8e	-	-	-
1987	97.6	87.5	71.6	77.3	74.7	74.7	76.4
1988	92.4	95.1	94.9	81.8e	79.8e	79.8e	81.1e
1989	91.2	101.3	102.6	86.4e	84.8e	84.8e	85.9e
1990	96.6	104.3	105.3	90.9e	89.9e	89.9e	90.6e
1991	101.5	107.9	105.8	95.5e	94.9e	94.9e	95.3e
1992	100.0	100.0	100.0	100.0	100.0	100.0	100.0
1993	101.6	102.2	106.4	106.0p	105.1p	105.1p	104.7p
1994	101.7	104.5	117.6	111.0p	110.1p	110.1p	109.4p
1995	106.9	118.2	141.8	116.0p	115.2p	115.2p	114.1p
1996	104.4p	114.3p	134.8p	121.0p	120.2p	120.2p	118.9p
1997	105.6p	116.7p	140.9p	125.9p	125.3p	125.3p	123.6p
1998	106.9p	119.1p	146.9p	130.9p	130.4p	130.3p	128.3p

Sources: Same as General Statistics. The values shown reflect change from the base year, 1992. Values above 100 mean greater than 1992, values below 100 mean less than 1992, and a value of 100 in the 1982-91 or 1993-98 period means same as 1992. Values followed by a 'p' are projections by the editors; 'e' stands for extrapolation. Data are the most recent available at this level of detail.

SELECTED RATIOS

For 1992	Avg. of All Wholesale	Analyzed Industry	Index	For 1992	Avg. of All Wholesale	Analyzed Industry	Index
Employees per Establishment	12	11	94	Sales per Employee	561,172	249,600	44
Payroll per Establishment	349,729	254,155	73	Sales per Establishment	6,559,346	2,739,919	42
Payroll per Employee	29,919	23,153	77	Expenses per Establishment	723,071	571,013	79

Sources: Same as General Statistics. The 'Average of All Manufacturing' column represents the average of all manufacturing industries reported for the most recent complete year available. The Index shows the relationship between the Average and the Analyzed Industry. For example, 100 means that they are equal; 500 that the Analyzed Industry is five times the average; 50 means that the Analyzed Industry is half the national average. The abbreviation 'na' is used to show that data are 'not available'.

LEADING COMPANIES

Number shown: **50** Total sales ($ mil): **23,102** Total employment (000): **45.1**

Company Name	Address				CEO Name	Phone	Co. Type	Sales ($ mil)	Empl. (000)
World Fuel Services Corp.	700 Poinciana	Miami Springs	FL	33166	Jerrold Blair	305-884-2001	P	7,726	0.2
Tribune Co. (Chicago, Illinois)	435 N Michigan	Chicago	IL	60611	John W Madigan	312-222-9100	P	2,720	10.7
Commercial Metals Co.	7800emmons Frwy	Dallas	TX	75247	Stanley A Rabin	214-689-4300	P	2,248	7.2
David J. Joseph Co.	PO Box 1078	Cincinnati	OH	45201	Louis F Terhar	513-621-8770	S	1,500	0.7
Heckett Multiserv Div.	PO Box 1071	Butler	PA	16003	Richard E Chapla	412-283-5741	D	1,310	3.5
Wellman Inc.	1040 Broad St	Shrewsbury	NJ	07702	Thomas M Duff	908-542-7300	P	1,099	3.2
National Material L.P.	1965 Pratt Blvd	Elk Grove Vill.	IL	60007	Michael Tang	847-806-7200	S	891 *	1.2
OmniSource Corp.	1610 N Calhoun St	Fort Wayne	IN	46808	Daniel Rifkin	219-422-5541	R	550	1.1
International Mill Service Inc.	1155 Business Ctr	Horsham	PA	19044	Lou Guzzetti	215-956-5500	S	480 *	1.3
IMCO Recycling Inc.	5215 N O'Connor	Irving	TX	75039	Donald V Ingram	972-869-6575	P	339	1.5
Allwaste Inc.	5151 San Felipe	Houston	TX	77056	Robert M Chiste	713-623-8777	P	337	3.8
Tube City Inc.	PO Box 2000	Glassport	PA	15045	Michael Coslov	412-678-6141	R	320	0.3
Blue Diamond Materials Co.	1245 Arrow Hwy	Irwindale	CA	91706	Dave Hummel	626-303-2623	S	190	0.5
Columbia National Group Inc.	6600 Grant Ave	Cleveland	OH	44105	David Miller	216-883-4972	R	180 *	0.5
Mindis Consolidated Industries	3715 Northside	Atlanta	GA	30327	Byron Kopman	404-262-0400	S	160 *	0.5
Azcon Corp.	224 S Michigan Ave	Chicago	IL	60604	Bert Pollan	312-362-0066	D	140	0.2
Southern Scrap Material	PO Box 26087	New Orleans	LA	70186	E. L Diefenthal	504-942-0340	S	140	0.3
Image Industries Inc.	PO Box 5555	Armuchee	GA	30105	H Stanley Padgett	706-235-8444	S	135	1.4
Simsmetal USA Corp.	600 S 4th St	Richmond	CA	94804	John J Mike	510-412-5300	S	130 *	0.4
Addington Resources Inc.	771 Corporate Dr	Lexington	KY	40503	Jack T Baker	606-223-3824	P	128	0.4
D. Benedetto Inc.	420 Lexington Ave	New York	NY	10017	Peter Benedetto Sr	212-867-8484	R	110	0.2
Pacific Hide and Fur Depot Inc.	PO Box 1549	Great Falls	MT	59403	Noble E Vosburg	303-761-8801	R	110	0.5
Metalsco Inc.	2388 Schuetz Rd	St. Louis	MO	63146	Sheldon Tauben	314-997-5200	R	100	<0.1
Peltz Group Inc.	PO Box 1799	Milwaukee	WI	53217	H Peltz	414-449-3900	R	100	0.3
Sadoff and Rudoy Industries	PO Box 1138	Fond du Lac	WI	54936	Sheldon J Lasky	414-921-2070	R	100	0.3
Energy Answers Corp.	79 N Pearl St	Albany	NY	12207	Patrick F Mahoney	518-434-1227	R	98 *	0.2
Huron Valley Steel Corp.	41000 Huron River	Belleville	MI	48111	Leynold Fritz	313-697-3400	R	97 *	0.3
Atlas Inc. (Cleveland, Ohio)	8550 Aetna Rd	Cleveland	OH	44105	A J Giordano Jr	216-441-3800	R	95	0.2
Alter Trading Corp.	2117 State St	Bettendorf	IA	52722	Rob Goldstein	319-344-5200	S	94	0.3
Paper Recycling Intern. L.P.	3850 Holcomb	Norcross	GA	30092	Howard Ingram	404-449-8688	R	92	<0.1
Luntz Corp.	237 E Tuscarawas	Canton	OH	44702	Andrew Luntz	216-455-0211	R	90	0.3
Louis Padnos Iron and Metal	PO Box 1979	Holland	MI	49422	Seymour K Padnos	616-396-6521	R	76	0.3
Aerospace Metals Inc.	500 Flatbush Ave	Hartford	CT	06106	Ray Noeker	203-522-3123	R	75 *	0.2
Fairway Salvage Inc.	12428 Center St	South Gate	CA	90280	Ed Kushins	310-630-8766	R	75	<0.1
Federal International Inc.	5595 Pershing Ave	St. Louis	MO	63112	Melvin L Lefkowitz	314-367-5595	R	75	0.4
Harmon Associates Corp.	86 Garden St	Westbury	NY	11590	Norman H Harvey	516-997-3400	R	75	<0.1
Weiner Steel Corp.	8200 E Slauson Ave	Pico Rivera	CA	90660	Herman L Weiner	213-723-8327	R	75 *	0.2
Reserve Iron and Metal L.P.	4431 W 130th St	Cleveland	OH	44135	Paul D Joseph	216-671-3000	S	74	0.1
Texpack USA Inc.	1001 S Bayshore Dr	Miami	FL	33131	Joseph Artiga	305-358-9696	R	74 *	0.2
SerVaas Inc.	1000 Waterway	Indianapolis	IN	46202	Beurt Servaas	317-636-1000	R	71 *	0.6
Addlestone International Corp.	PO Drawer 979	Charleston	SC	29402	Nathan Addlestone	803-577-9300	R	69	<0.1
Metal Management Inc.	500 N Dearborn St	Chicago	IL	60610	Gerald M Jacobs	312-645-0700	P	65	0.4
Markovits and Fox	PO Box 611420	San Jose	CA	95161	Marvin B Fox	408-453-7888	R	65	0.1
Southern Foundry and Supply	PO Box 6216	Chattanooga	TN	37401	Julius Chazen	615-756-6070	R	65 *	0.2
Schiavone-Bonomo Corp.	1 Jersey Ave	Jersey City	NJ	07302	Joseph Laraja	201-333-4300	R	63	0.2
Recycling Industries Inc.	9780 S Meridian	Englewood	CO	80112	Thomas J Wiens	303-790-7372	P	62	0.3
Steelmet Inc.	PO Box 369	McKeesport	PA	15134	Juergen Mross	412-672-9200	S	61 *	0.1
Mervis Industries Inc.	PO Box 827	Danville	IL	61834	Louis L Mervis	217-442-5300	R	60	0.3
Boliden Metech Inc.	120 Main	Mapleville	RI	02839	John Cesar	401-568-0711	S	56	0.2
Empire Recycling Inc.	15729 Crabbs	Rockville	MD	20855	Barclay E Booth	301-921-9202	R	56 *	0.2

Source: Ward's Business Directory of U.S. Private and Public Companies, 1998. The company type code used is as follows: P - Public, R - Private, S - Subsidiary, D - Division, J - Joint Venture, A - Affiliate, G - Group. Sales are in millions of dollars, employees are in thousands. An asterisk (*) indicates an estimated sales volume. The symbol < stands for 'less than'.

OCCUPATIONS EMPLOYED BY SIC 509 - WHOLESALE TRADE, OTHER

Occupation	% of Total 1996	Change to 2006	Occupation	% of Total 1996	Change to 2006
Sales & related workers nec	19.5	20.2	Clerical supervisors & managers	1.9	20.2
General managers & top executives	5.9	16.4	Order clerks	1.9	8.2
Truck drivers light & heavy	5.4	20.2	Helpers, laborers nec	1.7	20.2
General office clerks	3.6	3.4	Electrical & electronic technicians	1.4	18.8
Traffic, shipping, receiving clerks	3.6	16.7	Blue collar worker supervisors	1.4	16.0
Stock clerks	3.5	-3.9	Wholesale & retail buyers, except farm products	1.3	17.0
Freight, stock, & material movers, hand	3.3	8.2	Office machine & cash register servicers	1.3	20.2
Marketing & sales worker supervisors	3.1	20.2	Hand packers & packagers	1.2	-3.9
Order fillers, wholesale & retail sales	3.0	16.7	Maintenance repairers, general utility	1.1	12.0
Bookkeeping, accounting, & auditing clerks	2.9	-3.9	Industrial truck & tractor operators	1.1	20.2
Salespersons, retail	2.5	20.2	Purchasing managers	1.1	20.2
Secretaries, except legal & medical	2.5	-4.7	Receptionists & information clerks	1.0	20.2
Assemblers, fabricators, hand workers nec	2.0	-3.9			

Source: Industry-Occupation Matrix, Bureau of Labor Statistics. These data relate to one or more 3-digit SIC industry groups rather than to a single 4-digit SIC. The change reported for each occupation to the year 2006 is a percent of growth or decline as estimated by the Bureau of Labor Statistics. The abbreviation nec stands for 'not elsewhere classified'.

STATE AND REGIONAL CONCENTRATION

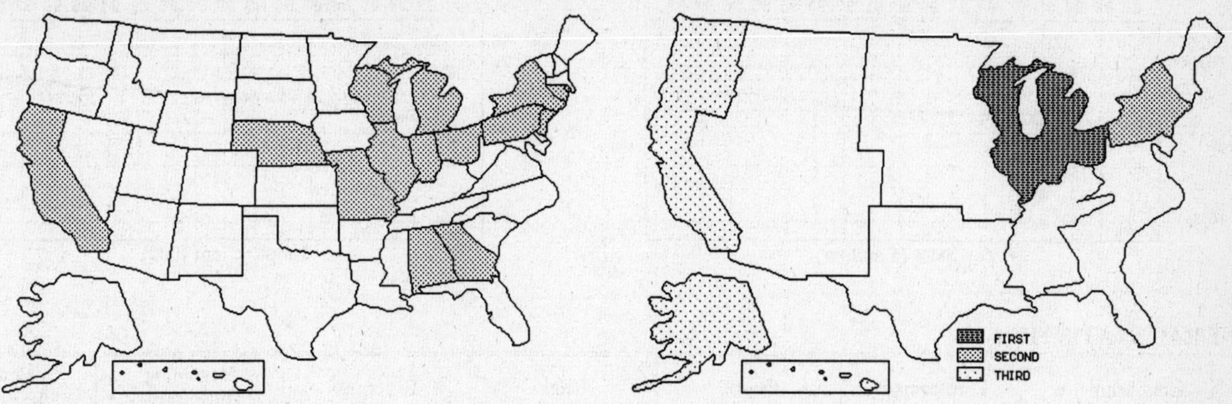

INDUSTRY DATA BY STATE

State	Establishments - 1995 Total (number)	Establishments - 1995 % of U.S.	Employment - 1995 Total (number)	Employment - 1995 % of U.S.	Employment - 1995 Per Estab.	Payroll - 1995 Total ($ mil.)	Payroll - 1995 Per Empl. ($)	Sales - 1992 Total ($ mil.)	Sales - 1992 % of U.S.	Sales - 1992 Per Estab ($)
California	1,023	10.7	13,351	11.5	13	343.8	25,748	3,269.6	13.4	264,039
Illinois	524	5.5	6,404	5.5	12	215.0	33,575	2,172.7	8.9	387,352
Pennsylvania	524	5.5	6,283	5.4	12	191.0	30,394	1,910.5	7.8	316,511
New York	679	7.1	7,860	6.8	12	214.2	27,254	1,792.6	7.3	268,192
Ohio	494	5.2	6,995	6.0	14	217.8	31,139	1,682.8	6.9	288,887
Texas	626	6.6	8,075	7.0	13	197.5	24,454	1,438.0	5.9	226,565
New Jersey	394	4.1	5,208	4.5	13	170.3	32,696	1,151.4	4.7	266,832
Michigan	329	3.4	4,001	3.5	12	146.9	36,724	915.5	3.7	241,118
Florida	390	4.1	3,757	3.2	10	93.5	24,882	849.0	3.5	273,958
Georgia	285	3.0	3,052	2.6	11	84.0	27,515	678.2	2.8	242,459
Indiana	246	2.6	3,881	3.3	16	126.2	32,518	656.9	2.7	205,409
Missouri	225	2.4	2,774	2.4	12	71.9	25,933	570.6	2.3	267,626
Alabama	190	2.0	2,798	2.4	15	74.1	26,493	553.3	2.3	261,491
Massachusetts	234	2.5	2,661	2.3	11	82.5	31,022	539.1	2.2	241,301
North Carolina	267	2.8	3,762	3.2	14	98.5	26,194	509.1	2.1	187,443
Wisconsin	230	2.4	2,950	2.5	13	87.5	29,671	495.4	2.0	193,067
Maryland	133	1.4	1,775	1.5	13	51.7	29,134	439.9	1.8	300,059
Connecticut	120	1.3	1,725	1.5	14	64.1	37,157	433.8	1.8	295,097
Tennessee	167	1.8	2,230	1.9	13	64.9	29,110	396.8	1.6	218,487
Washington	201	2.1	2,169	1.9	11	53.7	24,781	333.2	1.4	191,182
Minnesota	192	2.0	1,969	1.7	10	51.6	26,189	287.1	1.2	186,431
Virginia	155	1.6	1,921	1.7	12	49.0	25,513	280.6	1.1	161,986
South Carolina	140	1.5	1,773	1.5	13	44.3	24,997	267.4	1.1	171,627
Iowa	161	1.7	1,425	1.2	9	33.8	23,725	265.3	1.1	236,913
Oregon	130	1.4	1,738	1.5	13	42.8	24,621	254.0	1.0	208,848
Colorado	109	1.1	1,061	0.9	10	24.4	22,972	212.9	0.9	208,725
Kentucky	138	1.4	1,521	1.3	11	37.2	24,434	202.1	0.8	176,240
Louisiana	101	1.1	1,047	0.9	10	22.4	21,404	172.9	0.7	194,508
Nebraska	63	0.7	696	0.6	11	13.5	19,466	172.7	0.7	346,791
Arkansas	86	0.9	664	0.6	8	17.1	25,708	162.7	0.7	249,173
Arizona	122	1.3	1,594	1.4	13	31.6	19,816	158.8	0.6	129,190
West Virginia	87	0.9	1,101	1.0	13	23.2	21,032	157.8	0.6	216,101
Utah	59	0.6	659	0.6	11	16.5	25,009	146.4	0.6	250,603
Oklahoma	93	1.0	1,300	1.1	14	28.9	22,240	145.8	0.6	141,004
Rhode Island	45	0.5	535	0.5	12	14.0	26,249	131.0	0.5	348,279
Kansas	99	1.0	850	0.7	9	18.8	22,158	117.6	0.5	168,676
Mississippi	86	0.9	773	0.7	9	16.9	21,875	116.7	0.5	156,264
Maine	60	0.6	712	0.6	12	16.1	22,650	104.8	0.4	190,980
New Hampshire	37	0.4	283	0.2	8	8.0	28,141	45.1	0.2	167,185
Idaho	41	0.4	374	0.3	9	8.6	22,872	40.2	0.2	133,615
New Mexico	40	0.4	279	0.2	7	6.3	22,448	33.9	0.1	156,092
Montana	35	0.4	287	0.2	8	7.7	26,763	31.5	0.1	121,494
Hawaii	26	0.3	169	0.1	7	5.3	31,373	30.3	0.1	189,306
Delaware	32	0.3	276	0.2	9	5.6	20,188	27.4	0.1	102,872
South Dakota	35	0.4	269	0.2	8	5.3	19,755	24.7	0.1	121,093
North Dakota	26	0.3	244	0.2	9	4.7	19,389	23.3	0.1	112,236
Nevada	23	0.2	331	0.3	14	8.3	25,193	19.3	0.1	92,335
Vermont	16	0.2	105	0.1	7	2.1	20,095	18.7	0.1	186,860
D.C.	4	0.0	96	0.1	24	1.8	19,052	13.4	0.1	223,167
Alaska	4	0.0	60	0.1	15	2.2	36,317	4.8	0.0	91,000
Wyoming	15	0.2	43	0.0	3	0.8	18,000	4.7	0.0	156,800

Source: *County Business Patterns, 1995* and *Economic Census of the U.S., 1992*. Data are sorted by 1992 revenues and, if revenues are unavailable, by establishments in 1995. The symbol (D) indicates that data are withheld by the source to avoid disclosure of competitive information. A dash (-) indicates that data are not available or undisclosed because they do not meet statistical validity standards. Shaded *states* on the state map indicate those states which have proportionately greater representation in the industry than would be indicated by the state's population; the ratio is based on total revenues or number of establishments. Shaded *regions* indicate where the industry is regionally most concentrated.

5094 - JEWELRY & PRECIOUS STONES

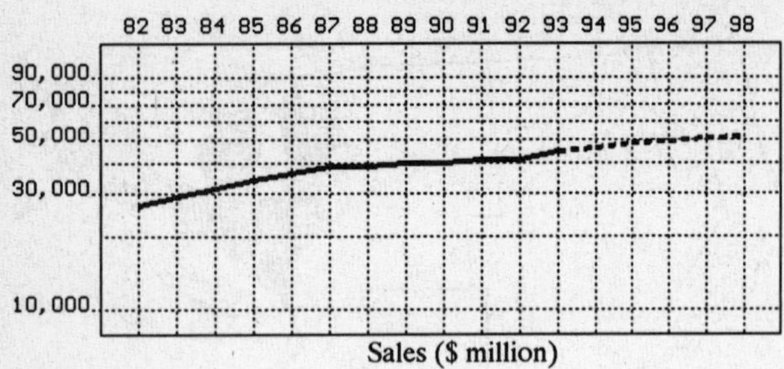

Sales ($ million)

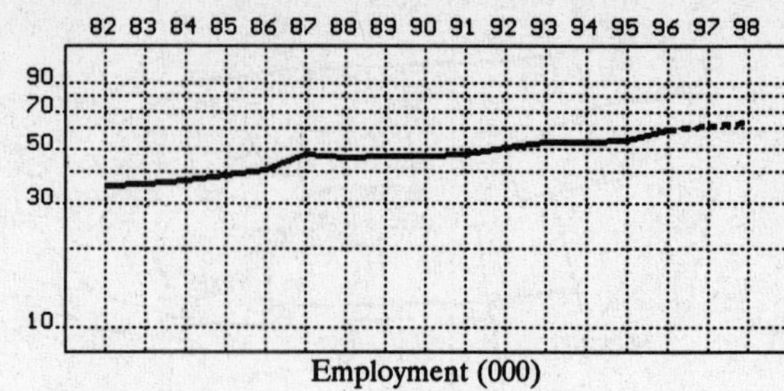

Employment (000)

GENERAL STATISTICS

Year	Establishments (number)	Employment (number)	Payroll ($ million)	Sales ($ million)	Expenses ($ million)	Beginning Inventory ($ million)	Ending Inventory ($ million)
1982	5,466	35,137	678.7	26,568.5	-	-	-
1983	5,696	36,213	718.2	28,971.1*e*	-	-	-
1984	-	-	-	31,373.8*e*	-	-	-
1985	5,243	38,804	858.0	33,776.4*e*	-	-	-
1986	5,259	40,735	930.8	36,179.0*e*	-	-	-
1987	6,927	47,062	1,093.0	38,581.6	2,615.1	2,899.0	3,087.6
1988	6,430	45,546	1,196.2	39,126.5*e*	2,778.7*e*	3,021.0*e*	3,170.4*e*
1989	6,187	46,734	1,240.2	39,671.4*e*	2,942.2*e*	3,143.1*e*	3,253.2*e*
1990	6,347	46,605	1,281.6	40,216.2*e*	3,105.7*e*	3,265.1*e*	3,336.0*e*
1991	6,292	46,764	1,299.7	40,761.1*e*	3,269.3*e*	3,387.2*e*	3,418.8*e*
1992	7,421	50,452	1,467.7	41,306.0	3,432.8	3,509.2	3,501.6
1993	7,567	52,904	1,495.0	44,890.8*p*	3,596.4*p*	3,631.3*p*	3,584.4*p*
1994	7,645	52,850	1,532.6	46,364.5*p*	3,759.9*p*	3,753.3*p*	3,667.2*p*
1995	7,670	53,330	1,584.5	47,838.3*p*	3,923.4*p*	3,875.4*p*	3,750.0*p*
1996	8,263*p*	58,968*p*	1,772.6*p*	49,312.0*p*	4,087.0*p*	3,997.4*p*	3,832.8*p*
1997	8,563*p*	61,182*p*	1,862.6*p*	50,785.8*p*	4,250.5*p*	4,119.5*p*	3,915.6*p*
1998	8,863*p*	63,395*p*	1,952.5*p*	52,259.5*p*	4,414.1*p*	4,241.5*p*	3,998.4*p*

Sources: Economic Census of the United States, 1982, 1987, and 1992. Establishment counts, employment, and payroll are from *County Business Patterns* for non-Census years. Values followed by a 'p' are projections by the editors. Sales and expense data for non-Census years are extrapolations, marked by 'e'. Industries reclassified in 1987 will not have data for prior years. Data are the most recent available at this level of detail.

INDICES OF CHANGE

Year	Establishments (number)	Employment (number)	Payroll ($ million)	Sales ($ million)	Expenses ($ million)	Beginning Inventory ($ million)	Ending Inventory ($ million)
1982	73.7	69.6	46.2	64.3	-	-	-
1983	76.8	71.8	48.9	70.1*e*	-	-	-
1984	-	-	-	76.0*e*	-	-	-
1985	70.7	76.9	58.5	81.8*e*	-	-	-
1986	70.9	80.7	63.4	87.6*e*	-	-	-
1987	93.3	93.3	74.5	93.4	76.2	82.6	88.2
1988	86.6	90.3	81.5	94.7*e*	80.9*e*	86.1*e*	90.5*e*
1989	83.4	92.6	84.5	96.0*e*	85.7*e*	89.6*e*	92.9*e*
1990	85.5	92.4	87.3	97.4*e*	90.5*e*	93.0*e*	95.3*e*
1991	84.8	92.7	88.6	98.7*e*	95.2*e*	96.5*e*	97.6*e*
1992	100.0	100.0	100.0	100.0	100.0	100.0	100.0
1993	102.0	104.9	101.9	108.7*p*	104.8*p*	103.5*p*	102.4*p*
1994	103.0	104.8	104.4	112.2*p*	109.5*p*	107.0*p*	104.7*p*
1995	103.4	105.7	108.0	115.8*p*	114.3*p*	110.4*p*	107.1*p*
1996	111.3*p*	116.9*p*	120.8*p*	119.4*p*	119.1*p*	113.9*p*	109.5*p*
1997	115.4*p*	121.3*p*	126.9*p*	123.0*p*	123.8*p*	117.4*p*	111.8*p*
1998	119.4*p*	125.7*p*	133.0*p*	126.5*p*	128.6*p*	120.9*p*	114.2*p*

Sources: Same as General Statistics. The values shown reflect change from the base year, 1992. Values above 100 mean greater than 1992, values below 100 mean less than 1992, and a value of 100 in the 1982-91 or 1993-98 period means same as 1992. Values followed by a 'p' are projections by the editors; 'e' stands for extrapolation. Data are the most recent available at this level of detail.

SELECTED RATIOS

For 1992	Avg. of All Wholesale	Analyzed Industry	Index	For 1992	Avg. of All Wholesale	Analyzed Industry	Index
Employees per Establishment	12	7	58	Sales per Employee	561,172	818,719	146
Payroll per Establishment	349,729	197,777	57	Sales per Establishment	6,559,346	5,566,096	85
Payroll per Employee	29,919	29,091	97	Expenses per Establishment	723,071	462,579	64

Sources: Same as General Statistics. The 'Average of All Manufacturing' column represents the average of all manufacturing industries reported for the most recent complete year available. The Index shows the relationship between the Average and the Analyzed Industry. For example, 100 means that they are equal; 500 that the Analyzed Industry is five times the average; 50 means that the Analyzed Industry is half the national average. The abbreviation 'na' is used to show that data are 'not available'.

LEADING COMPANIES

Number shown: **46** Total sales ($ mil): **70,457** Total employment (000): **43.0**

Company Name	Address				CEO Name	Phone	Co. Type	Sales ($ mil)	Empl. (000)
Loews Corp.	667 Madison Ave	New York	NY	10021	Laurence A Tisch	212-545-2000	P	67,683	35.3
Casio Inc.	570 Mt Pleasant	Dover	NJ	07801	John J McDonald	973-361-5400	D	630	0.3
MTB Bank	90 Broad St	New York	NY	10004	Fred Tordella	212-858-3300	R	314	0.2
K's Merchandise Mart Inc.	3103 N Charles St	Decatur	IL	62526	David K Eldridge	217-875-1440	R	288*	1.8
SMH (US) Inc.	35 E 21st St	New York	NY	10010	Roland Streule	212-505-6150	S	200	0.4
Swiss Army Brands Inc.	1 Research Dr	Shelton	CT	06484	J Merrick Taggert	203-929-6391	P	130	0.2
Bulova Corp.	1 Bulova Ave	Woodside	NY	11377	Herbert C Hofmann	718-204-3300	P	109	0.4
Citizen Watch of America	1200 Wall St W	Lyndhurst	NJ	07071	Laurence Grunstein	201-438-8150	S	100*	0.3
Bijoux Terner L.P.	7200 NW 7th St	Miami	FL	33126	Salomon Terner	305-266-9000	R	88	0.4
Gerson Company Inc.	6100 Broadmoor St	Shawnee Msn	KS	66202	Peter Gerson	913-262-7400	R	76*	0.3
Samsung Opto-Electronics	40 Seaview Dr	Secaucus	NJ	07094	Steve Lee	201-902-0347	S	60	<0.1
Towle Manufacturing Co.	144 Addison St	East Boston	MA	02128	Leonard Florence	617-568-1300	S	56*	0.2
Donald Bruce and Co.	3600 N Talman Ave	Chicago	IL	60618	Lewis Solomon	312-477-8100	R	51*	0.2
Bennett Brothers Inc.	30 E Adams St	Chicago	IL	60603	GK Bennett	312-263-4800	R	50	0.1
Simon Golub and Sons Inc.	PO Box 80866	Seattle	WA	98108	AT Harris	206-762-4800	R	50	0.2
Citra Trading Corp.	590 5th Ave	New York	NY	10036	H Chitrik	212-354-1000	R	44	<0.1
Wedlo Inc.	3200 2nd Ave N	Birmingham	AL	35203	Robert A Keller	205-322-4444	R	40	0.4
Gordon Brothers Corp.	40 Broad St, #11	Boston	MA	02100	Michael Frieze	617-426-3233	R	38*	0.2
Harry Winston Inc.	718 5th Ave	New York	NY	10019	Ronald Winston	212-245-2000	R	38	0.2
Precise International	15 Corporate Dr	Orangeburg	NY	10962	Tom Higgins	914-365-3500	R	35	<0.1
Zak Designs Inc.	S 1604 Garfield Rd	Spokane	WA	99204	Irving L Zakheim	509-244-0555	R	26*	0.1
Baume and Mercier	663 5th Ave	New York	NY	10022	Steven P Kaiser	212-593-0444	S	25*	0.1
Frank Mastoloni and Sons Inc.	608 5th Ave	New York	NY	10020	F J Mastoloni Sr	212-757-7278	R	25	<0.1
Stanley Roberts Inc.	65 Industrial Rd	Lodi	NJ	07644	Edward Pomeranz	201-778-5900	R	25*	0.1
William J. Kappel Wholesale Co.	535 Liberty Ave	Pittsburgh	PA	15222	William D Kappel	412-471-6400	R	25*	0.1
Texas Sales Co.	PO Box 1826	El Paso	TX	79949	Jack Schlusselburg	915-772-1177	R	24*	0.1
Marketing Group Inc.	294 E 155th St	Harvey	IL	60426	Michael D Gurley	708-331-0200	R	22	<0.1
Denver Merchandise Mart	451 E 58th Ave	Denver	CO	80216	Darrell Hare	303-292-6278	R	19*	<0.1
Genal Strap Inc.	31-00 47th Ave	Long Island C.	NY	11101	Aaron Greenwald	718-706-8700	R	18	<0.1
Rothenberg and Schloss Inc.	930 Broadway	Kansas City	MO	64105	Louis H Ehrlich	816-842-1100	R	18	<0.1
Time Service Inc.	245 23rd St	Toledo	OH	43624	L S Goldberg	419-241-4181	S	18	0.6
Tacoa Inc.	1337-EE 100 Oak	Charlotte	NC	28211	John F McClure	704-525-4448	S	16	0.2
Dallas Gold and Silver Exchange	2817 Forest Ln	Dallas	TX	75234	LS Smith	214-484-3662	P	14	<0.1
Cliff Weil Inc.	PO Box 427	Mechanicsville	VA	23116	AB Hutzler II	804-746-1321	R	14*	<0.1
Chatham Created Gems Inc.	111 Maiden Ln	San Francisco	CA	94108	Thomas Chatham	415-397-8450	R	13	0.1
Lory's West Inc.	314 S Beverly Dr	Beverly Hills	CA	90212	Bruce Faber	310-551-1212	R	13	<0.1
Fantasy Diamond Corp.	1550 W Carroll Ave	Chicago	IL	60607	Louis Price	312-243-3300	R	11	<0.1
Foreign Exchange Ltd.	415 Stockton St	San Francisco	CA	94108	Randy Roberts	415-677-5107	S	11	<0.1
Tobe Turpen's	1710 S 2nd St	Gallup	NM	87301	Tobe Turpen Jr	505-722-3806	R	11*	<0.1
Airmo Corp.	950 Mason St	San Francisco	CA	94106	Robert Small	415-772-5336	S	9	<0.1
A-Mark Precious Metals Inc.	100 Wilshire Blvd	Santa Monica	CA	90401	Mark Albarin	310-319-0200	S	7*	<0.1
IOA Data Corp.	383 Lafayette St	New York	NY	10003	S J Rubenstein	212-673-9300	R	4	<0.1
Roen Phillips Corp.	500 S Clinton St	Chicago	IL	60607	Sid M Phillips	312-939-3090	R	4	<0.1
J.P. Morton Company Inc.	PO Box 741188	Los Angeles	CA	90004	JP Morton	213-487-1440	R	3*	<0.1
Connor and Associates Inc.	3595 Almaden Rd	San Jose	CA	95118	Connie Connor	408-445-0911	R	1	<0.1
Europa Time Inc.	3030 Hampton Pl	Boca Raton	FL	33434	Ralph Jacobson	407-241-8097	R	1	<0.1

Source: *Ward's Business Directory of U.S. Private and Public Companies*, 1998. The company type code used is as follows: P - Public, R - Private, S - Subsidiary, D - Division, J - Joint Venture, A - Affiliate, G - Group. Sales are in millions of dollars, employees are in thousands. An asterisk (*) indicates an estimated sales volume. The symbol < stands for 'less than'.

OCCUPATIONS EMPLOYED BY SIC 509 - WHOLESALE TRADE, OTHER

Occupation	% of Total 1996	Change to 2006	Occupation	% of Total 1996	Change to 2006
Sales & related workers nec	19.5	20.2	Clerical supervisors & managers	1.9	20.2
General managers & top executives	5.9	16.4	Order clerks	1.9	8.2
Truck drivers light & heavy	5.4	20.2	Helpers, laborers nec	1.7	20.2
General office clerks	3.6	3.4	Electrical & electronic technicians	1.4	18.8
Traffic, shipping, receiving clerks	3.6	16.7	Blue collar worker supervisors	1.4	16.0
Stock clerks	3.5	-3.9	Wholesale & retail buyers, except farm products	1.3	17.0
Freight, stock, & material movers, hand	3.3	8.2	Office machine & cash register servicers	1.3	20.2
Marketing & sales worker supervisors	3.1	20.2	Hand packers & packagers	1.2	-3.9
Order fillers, wholesale & retail sales	3.0	16.7	Maintenance repairers, general utility	1.1	12.0
Bookkeeping, accounting, & auditing clerks	2.9	-3.9	Industrial truck & tractor operators	1.1	20.2
Salespersons, retail	2.5	20.2	Purchasing managers	1.1	20.2
Secretaries, except legal & medical	2.5	-4.7	Receptionists & information clerks	1.0	20.2
Assemblers, fabricators, hand workers nec	2.0	-3.9			

Source: *Industry-Occupation Matrix*, Bureau of Labor Statistics. These data relate to one or more 3-digit SIC industry groups rather than to a single 4-digit SIC. The change reported for each occupation to the year 2006 is a percent of growth or decline as estimated by the Bureau of Labor Statistics. The abbreviation nec stands for 'not elsewhere classified'.

STATE AND REGIONAL CONCENTRATION

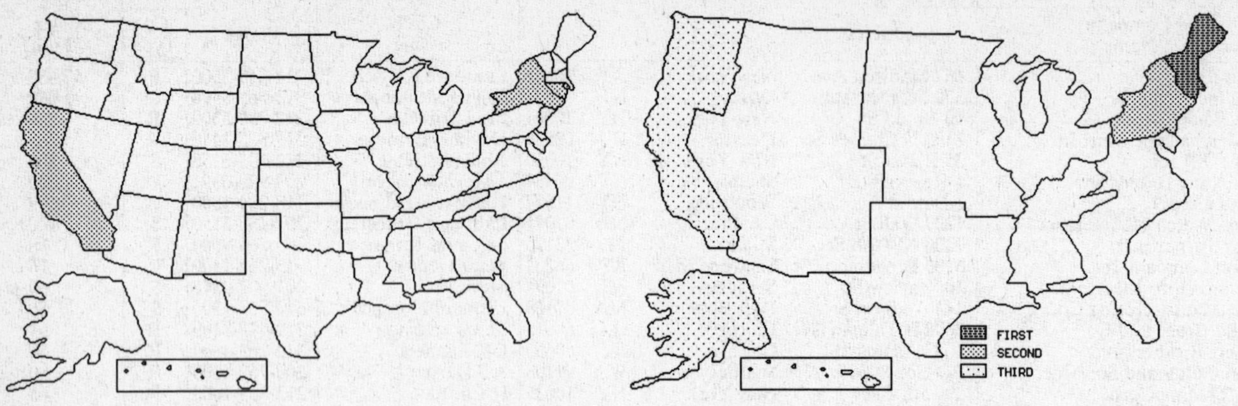

INDUSTRY DATA BY STATE

State	Establishments - 1995 Total (number)	Establishments - 1995 % of U.S.	Employment - 1995 Total (number)	Employment - 1995 % of U.S.	Employment - 1995 Per Estab.	Payroll - 1995 Total ($ mil.)	Payroll - 1995 Per Empl. ($)	Sales - 1992 Total ($ mil.)	Sales - 1992 % of U.S.	Sales - 1992 Per Estab ($)
Connecticut	60	0.8	1,163	2.2	19	70.8	60,871	18,359.2	44.7	20,674,730
New York	2,438	31.8	15,269	28.6	6	536.9	35,161	9,098.6	22.2	661,715
California	1,218	15.9	7,367	13.8	6	218.8	29,704	5,077.0	12.4	627,638
Florida	590	7.7	3,085	5.8	5	88.7	28,756	1,235.2	3.0	418,140
Illinois	296	3.9	2,465	4.6	8	74.3	30,146	1,037.4	2.5	359,211
Texas	461	6.0	2,884	5.4	6	73.1	25,348	1,034.8	2.5	382,110
New Jersey	210	2.7	1,506	2.8	7	56.4	37,429	949.9	2.3	665,680
Rhode Island	173	2.3	2,379	4.5	14	48.2	20,248	501.7	1.2	171,042
Pennsylvania	157	2.0	1,361	2.6	9	36.6	26,863	484.9	1.2	356,514
Georgia	184	2.4	985	1.8	5	24.5	24,879	370.7	0.9	489,012
Massachusetts	139	1.8	895	1.7	6	31.9	35,687	359.7	0.9	356,865
Michigan	104	1.4	774	1.5	7	24.7	31,966	252.7	0.6	366,697
Ohio	131	1.7	1,054	2.0	8	23.1	21,901	234.3	0.6	247,699
Utah	27	0.4	424	0.8	16	26.8	63,092	225.2	0.5	546,612
New Mexico	102	1.3	1,086	2.0	11	17.9	16,524	187.1	0.5	158,826
Missouri	91	1.2	764	1.4	8	17.2	22,546	141.1	0.3	187,901
Minnesota	88	1.1	1,402	2.6	16	17.9	12,799	140.2	0.3	216,055
Washington	101	1.3	633	1.2	6	16.5	26,082	129.0	0.3	220,154
Indiana	46	0.6	471	0.9	10	11.0	23,425	108.0	0.3	372,279
Arizona	116	1.5	774	1.5	7	25.7	33,214	106.6	0.3	234,874
Tennessee	82	1.1	542	1.0	7	11.9	21,959	95.5	0.2	160,289
Hawaii	82	1.1	338	0.6	4	7.6	22,538	94.8	0.2	198,379
Kansas	27	0.4	620	1.2	23	10.1	16,211	78.4	0.2	225,239
Oregon	41	0.5	288	0.5	7	6.4	22,181	77.6	0.2	338,734
Virginia	65	0.8	265	0.5	4	6.9	26,083	72.4	0.2	264,201
Wisconsin	49	0.6	445	0.8	9	10.3	23,252	70.4	0.2	191,356
South Carolina	27	0.4	118	0.2	4	3.0	25,398	69.2	0.2	641,194
Alabama	41	0.5	244	0.5	6	6.4	26,172	62.8	0.2	271,675
Colorado	87	1.1	356	0.7	4	6.9	19,295	61.1	0.1	167,816
North Carolina	68	0.9	418	0.8	6	10.6	25,256	57.9	0.1	147,617
Kentucky	30	0.4	254	0.5	8	4.5	17,634	44.2	0.1	279,494
Iowa	24	0.3	89	0.2	4	2.4	27,202	41.3	0.1	439,298
Oklahoma	33	0.4	198	0.4	6	4.5	22,955	38.7	0.1	206,064
Nevada	25	0.3	112	0.2	4	3.4	30,491	32.3	0.1	271,050
Alaska	8	0.1	28	0.1	4	1.0	36,214	29.0	0.1	764,421
Arkansas	20	0.3	126	0.2	6	2.9	22,873	27.9	0.1	296,691
South Dakota	18	0.2	224	0.4	12	6.3	28,348	23.9	0.1	126,646
Maine	18	0.2	59	0.1	3	1.2	19,983	8.3	0.0	130,047
Mississippi	13	0.2	182	0.3	14	4.4	24,242	7.5	0.0	88,341
Vermont	10	0.1	33	0.1	3	1.0	31,061	7.3	0.0	178,415
New Hampshire	11	0.1	26	0.0	2	0.6	24,038	6.9	0.0	229,400
Idaho	7	0.1	21	0.0	3	0.3	12,095	2.6	0.0	120,273
North Dakota	8	0.1	54	0.1	7	1.4	25,074	2.4	0.0	120,950
Delaware	2	0.0	0-19	-	-	(D)	-	2.3	0.0	461,200
D.C.	3	0.0	0-19	-	-	(D)	-	2.2	0.0	432,200
West Virginia	6	0.1	11	0.0	2	0.2	13,636	1.0	0.0	90,818
Wyoming	1	0.0	0-19	-	-	(D)	-	1.0	0.0	483,500
Maryland	69	0.9	226	0.4	3	5.1	22,770	(D)	-	-
Louisiana	51	0.7	1,213	2.3	24	22.8	18,818	(D)	-	-
Nebraska	9	0.1	83	0.2	9	1.1	12,675	(D)	-	-
Montana	3	0.0	7	0.0	2	0.1	11,571	(D)	-	-

Source: County Business Patterns, 1995 and *Economic Census of the U.S., 1992*. Data are sorted by 1992 revenues and, if revenues are unavailable, by establishments in 1995. The symbol (D) indicates that data are withheld by the source to avoid disclosure of competitive information. A dash (-) indicates that data are not available or undisclosed because they do not meet statistical validity standards. Shaded *states* on the state map indicate those states which have proportionately greater representation in the industry than would be indicated by the state's population; the ratio is based on total revenues or number of establishments. Shaded *regions* indicate where the industry is regionally most concentrated.

5099 - DURABLE GOODS, NEC

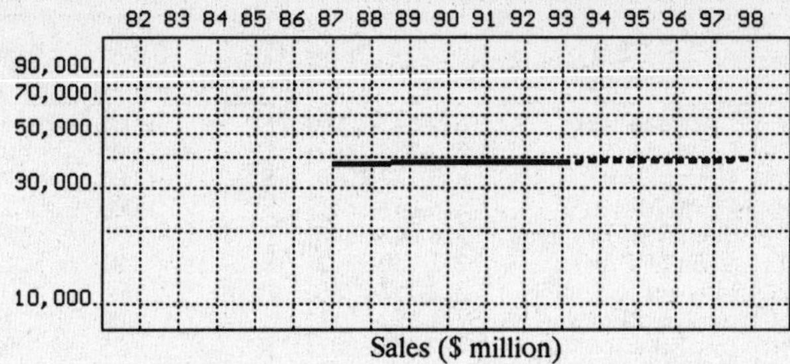

Sales ($ million)

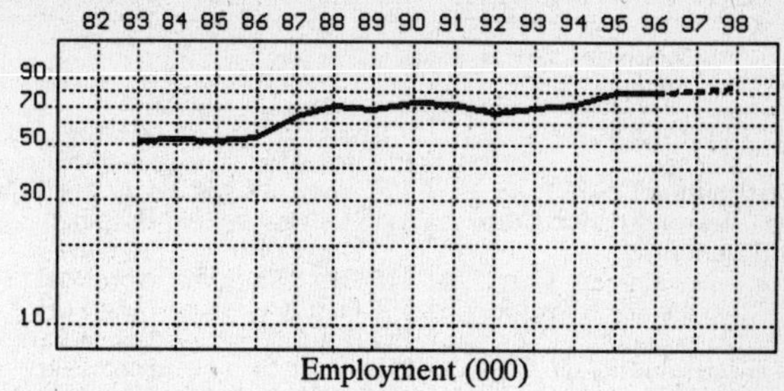

Employment (000)

GENERAL STATISTICS

Year	Establishments (number)	Employment (number)	Payroll ($ million)	Sales ($ million)	Expenses ($ million)	Beginning Inventory ($ million)	Ending Inventory ($ million)
1982	-	-	-	-	-	-	-
1983	7,415	51,245	905.8	-	-	-	-
1984	6,575	51,698	963.7	-	-	-	-
1985	6,149	51,606	1,016.4	-	-	-	-
1986	5,850	53,131	1,092.9	-	-	-	-
1987	9,348	63,972	1,375.8	37,269.1	3,230.4	1,664.5	1,899.3
1988	8,872	70,614	1,637.5	37,447.4e	3,394.8e	1,766.8e	2,014.0e
1989	8,351	68,433	1,708.3	37,625.8e	3,559.3e	1,869.1e	2,128.6e
1990	8,727	72,742	1,915.4	37,804.2e	3,723.8e	1,971.4e	2,243.3e
1991	8,529	71,422	1,914.4	37,982.6e	3,888.2e	2,073.7e	2,358.0e
1992	9,688	66,308	1,827.9	38,161.0	4,052.7	2,175.9	2,472.6
1993	10,246	69,702	1,985.8	38,339.4p	4,217.2p	2,278.2p	2,587.3p
1994	10,223	72,183	2,170.9	38,517.8p	4,381.6p	2,380.5p	2,702.0p
1995	10,820	79,701	2,456.6	38,696.1p	4,546.1p	2,482.8p	2,816.7p
1996	11,014p	80,293p	2,489.3p	38,874.5p	4,710.6p	2,585.1p	2,931.3p
1997	11,370p	82,502p	2,614.4p	39,052.9p	4,875.0p	2,687.4p	3,046.0p
1998	11,726p	84,712p	2,739.6p	39,231.3p	5,039.5p	2,789.7p	3,160.7p

Sources: Economic Census of the United States, 1982, 1987, and 1992. Establishment counts, employment, and payroll are from *County Business Patterns* for non-Census years. Values followed by a 'p' are projections by the editors. Sales and expense data for non-Census years are extrapolations, marked by 'e'. Industries reclassified in 1987 will not have data for prior years. Data are the most recent available at this level of detail.

INDICES OF CHANGE

Year	Establishments (number)	Employment (number)	Payroll ($ million)	Sales ($ million)	Expenses ($ million)	Beginning Inventory ($ million)	Ending Inventory ($ million)
1982	-	-	-	-	-	-	-
1983	76.5	77.3	49.6	-	-	-	-
1984	67.9	78.0	52.7	-	-	-	-
1985	63.5	77.8	55.6	-	-	-	-
1986	60.4	80.1	59.8	-	-	-	-
1987	96.5	96.5	75.3	97.7	79.7	76.5	76.8
1988	91.6	106.5	89.6	98.1e	83.8e	81.2e	81.5e
1989	86.2	103.2	93.5	98.6e	87.8e	85.9e	86.1e
1990	90.1	109.7	104.8	99.1e	91.9e	90.6e	90.7e
1991	88.0	107.7	104.7	99.5e	95.9e	95.3e	95.4e
1992	100.0	100.0	100.0	100.0	100.0	100.0	100.0
1993	105.8	105.1	108.6	100.5p	104.1p	104.7p	104.6p
1994	105.5	108.9	118.8	100.9p	108.1p	109.4p	109.3p
1995	111.7	120.2	134.4	101.4p	112.2p	114.1p	113.9p
1996	113.7p	121.1p	136.2p	101.9p	116.2p	118.8p	118.6p
1997	117.4p	124.4p	143.0p	102.3p	120.3p	123.5p	123.2p
1998	121.0p	127.8p	149.9p	102.8p	124.3p	128.2p	127.8p

Sources: Same as General Statistics. The values shown reflect change from the base year, 1992. Values above 100 mean greater than 1992, values below 100 mean less than 1992, and a value of 100 in the 1982-91 or 1993-98 period means same as 1992. Values followed by a 'p' are projections by the editors; 'e' stands for extrapolation. Data are the most recent available at this level of detail.

SELECTED RATIOS

For 1992	Avg. of All Wholesale	Analyzed Industry	Index	For 1992	Avg. of All Wholesale	Analyzed Industry	Index
Employees per Establishment	12	7	59	Sales per Employee	561,172	575,511	103
Payroll per Establishment	349,729	188,677	54	Sales per Establishment	6,559,346	3,938,997	60
Payroll per Employee	29,919	27,567	92	Expenses per Establishment	723,071	418,322	58

Sources: Same as General Statistics. The 'Average of All Manufacturing' column represents the average of all manufacturing industries reported for the most recent complete year available. The Index shows the relationship between the Average and the Analyzed Industry. For example, 100 means that they are equal; 500 that the Analyzed Industry is five times the average; 50 means that the Analyzed Industry is half the national average. The abbreviation 'na' is used to show that data are 'not available'.

LEADING COMPANIES

Number shown: **50** Total sales ($ mil): **10,403** Total employment (000): **19.1**

Company Name	Address				CEO Name	Phone	Co. Type	Sales ($ mil)	Empl. (000)
Eastern Enterprises	9 Riverside Rd	Weston	MA	02193	J Atwood Ives	617-647-2300	P	1,007	1.4
J.M.	PO Box 9008	Champaign	IL	61826		217-384-2800	D	1,000 *	0.9
Uni Distribution Co.	10 Universal Cityz	Universal City	CA	91608	Henry Droz	818-777-1000	S	1,000 *	1.1
Warner-Elektra-Atlantic Corp.	111 Hollywood	Burbank	CA	91505	David Mount	818-843-6311	S	1,000	1.2
Henry Schein Inc.	135 Duryea Rd	Melville	NY	11747	Stanley M Bergman	516-843-5500	P	830	3.2
Alliance Entertainment Corp.	115 East 57th St	New York	NY	10022	Alvin N Teller	212-750-2303	P	691	1.9
Perry H. Koplik and Sons Inc.	505 Park Ave	New York	NY	10022	Michael R Koplik	212-752-2288	R	500	0.2
Yamaha Corporation	PO Box 6600	Buena Park	CA	90620	Noriyuki Egawa	714-522-9011	S	500	1.0
D and H Distributing Co.	2525 N 7th St	Harrisburg	PA	17110	Izzy Schwab	717-236-8001	R	375	0.4
Jerry Bassin Inc.	15959 NW 15th Ave	Miami	FL	33169	Jerry Bassin	305-621-0070	S	320 *	0.4
Price and Pierce International	PO Box 971	Stamford	CT	06904	C E Allanson	203-328-2000	R	200	<0.1
Mazel Stores Inc.	31000 Aurora Rd	Solon	OH	44139	Reuven Dessler	216-248-5200	P	180	0.9
CD One Stop	13 Clarke Cir	Bethel	CT	06801	Allen Tuchman	203-798-6590	S	150 *	0.4
General Merchandise Services	PO Box 700	Bellefontaine	OH	43311	James W Donnelly	513-592-7025	D	150 *	0.3
Roland Corporation U.S.	7200 Dominion Cir	Los Angeles	CA	90040	Dennis Houlihan	213-685-5141	R	150	0.2
Sodak Gaming Inc.	5301 S Hwy 16	Rapid City	SD	57701	M G Wordeman	605-341-5400	P	138	<0.1
WaxWorks/VideoWorks Inc.	325 E 3rd St	Owensboro	KY	42301	Terry Woodward	502-926-0008	R	120	0.3
RED Distribution	79 5th Ave, 15th Fl	New York	NY	10003	Sal Licata	718-740-5700	S	110	0.1
Koval Marketing Inc.	11208 47th Ave W	Mukilteo	WA	98275	Roy Koval	425-347-4249	R	100	<0.1
R.S. Hughes Company Inc.	PO Box 25061	Glendale	CA	91221	Robert McCollum	818-563-1122	R	100	0.4
Airway Industries Inc.	Airway Park	Ellwood City	PA	16117	Thomas Falloon	412-752-0012	R	91 *	0.2
McGrath RentCorp	2500 Grant Ave	San Lorenzo	CA	94580	Robert P McGrath	510-276-2626	P	89	0.3
Lib-Com Ltd.	1150 Motor Pkwy	Central Islip	NY	11722	Joel Margolin	516-582-8800	R	80	<0.1
Strategic Distribution Inc.	165 Mason St	Greenwich	CT	06830	Andrew M Bursky	203-629-8750	R	80	0.4
Big State Record Distribution	4830 Lakawana	Dallas	TX	75247	Billy Emerson	214-631-1100	S	76 *	0.2
K-Tel International Inc.	2605 Fernbrook	Minneapolis	MN	55447	Philip Kives	612-559-6888	P	76	0.2
International Music Corp.	PO Box 2344	Fort Worth	TX	76113	Tommy Moore	817-336-5114	R	74	0.2
AB Wholesale Co.	710 S College Ave	Bluefield	VA	24605	Kaleel A Ammar Jr	703-322-4686	S	70	0.1
Service Supply Systems Inc.	PO Box 749	Cordele	GA	31015	CM Hunt	912-273-1112	R	70	0.2
Racing Champions Corp.	800 Rooisevelt Rd	Glen Ellyn	IL	60137	Robert E Dods	630-790-3507	P	66	<0.1
Orr Safety Corp.	PO Box 16326	Louisville	KY	40256	Clark Orr	502-774-5791	R	65	0.2
Blevins Inc.	421 Hart Ln	Nashville	TN	37216	James W Blevins	615-227-7772	R	65	0.2
Korg U.S.A. Inc.	89 Frost St	Westbury	NY	11590	Michael I Kovins	516-333-9100	S	60	<0.1
Samsung Opto-Electronics	40 Seaview Dr	Secaucus	NJ	07094	Steve Lee	201-902-0347	S	60	<0.1
Squires Timber Co.	PO Box 548	Elizabethtown	NC	28337	Nelson Squires	919-862-3533	R	60	<0.1
Brentwood Music Inc.	1 Maryland Farms	Brentwood	TN	37027	James Van Hook	615-373-3950	S	58	0.3
HP Products	4220 Saquaro Trail	Indianapolis	IN	46268	Donald Ames Shuel	317-298-9950	R	55	0.3
Central South Music Inc.	3730 Vulcan Dr	Nashville	TN	37211	Randy Davidson	615-833-5960	R	52	0.5
Reis Environmental Inc.	11022 Linpage Pl	St. Louis	MO	63132	Rudolph L Wise	314-426-5603	S	52	0.1
Bennett Brothers Inc.	30 E Adams St	Chicago	IL	60603	GK Bennett	312-263-4800	R	50	0.1
Brady Distributing Co.	PO Box 19269	Charlotte	NC	28219	Jon P Brady	704-357-6284	R	50 *	0.1
Highsmith Inc.	W5527 Hwy 106	Fort Atkinson	WI	53538	Duncan Highsmith	920-563-9571	R	50	0.2
Lathrop's Shooters Supply Inc.	5146 E Pima St	Tucson	AZ	85712	Robert Jensen	602-881-0266	R	45	0.1
Noma International Inc.	7400 W Indrial Dr	Forest Park	IL	60130	Richard Knelstein	708-771-9400	S	45	0.1
MBT International Inc.	PO Box 30819	Charleston	SC	29417	Eddie Toporek	803-763-9083	R	43	0.1
Platinum Entertainment Inc.	2001 Butterfield Rd	Downers Grove	IL	60515	Steven Devick	630-769-0033	P	43	0.1
Essex Entertainment Inc.	560 Sylvan Ave	Englewood Clfs	NJ	07632	Richard Greener	201-894-8700	R	40	<0.1
Gotham Distributing Corp.	2324 Haverford Rd	Ardmore	PA	19003	Nina Greene	215-649-7565	R	40 *	<0.1
Thomas Monahan Co.	202 N Oak St	Arcola	IL	61910	T F Monahan Jr	217-268-4955	R	40	0.2
Pacific Coast One-Stop	45 W Easy St	Simi Valley	CA	93065	Steven Kall	818-709-3640	R	38 *	<0.1

Source: *Ward's Business Directory of U.S. Private and Public Companies*, 1998. The company type code used is as follows: P - Public, R - Private, S - Subsidiary, D - Division, J - Joint Venture, A - Affiliate, G - Group. Sales are in millions of dollars, employees are in thousands. An asterisk (*) indicates an estimated sales volume. The symbol < stands for 'less than'.

OCCUPATIONS EMPLOYED BY SIC 509 - WHOLESALE TRADE, OTHER

Occupation	% of Total 1996	Change to 2006	Occupation	% of Total 1996	Change to 2006
Sales & related workers nec	19.5	20.2	Clerical supervisors & managers	1.9	20.2
General managers & top executives	5.9	16.4	Order clerks	1.9	8.2
Truck drivers light & heavy	5.4	20.2	Helpers, laborers nec	1.7	20.2
General office clerks	3.6	3.4	Electrical & electronic technicians	1.4	18.8
Traffic, shipping, receiving clerks	3.6	16.7	Blue collar worker supervisors	1.4	16.0
Stock clerks	3.5	-3.9	Wholesale & retail buyers, except farm products	1.3	17.0
Freight, stock, & material movers, hand	3.3	8.2	Office machine & cash register servicers	1.3	20.2
Marketing & sales worker supervisors	3.1	20.2	Hand packers & packagers	1.2	-3.9
Order fillers, wholesale & retail sales	3.0	16.7	Maintenance repairers, general utility	1.1	12.0
Bookkeeping, accounting, & auditing clerks	2.9	-3.9	Industrial truck & tractor operators	1.1	20.2
Salespersons, retail	2.5	20.2	Purchasing managers	1.1	20.2
Secretaries, except legal & medical	2.5	-4.7	Receptionists & information clerks	1.0	20.2
Assemblers, fabricators, hand workers nec	2.0	-3.9			

Source: *Industry-Occupation Matrix*, Bureau of Labor Statistics. These data relate to one or more 3-digit SIC industry groups rather than to a single 4-digit SIC. The change reported for each occupation to the year 2006 is a percent of growth or decline as estimated by the Bureau of Labor Statistics. The abbreviation nec stands for 'not elsewhere classified'.

STATE AND REGIONAL CONCENTRATION

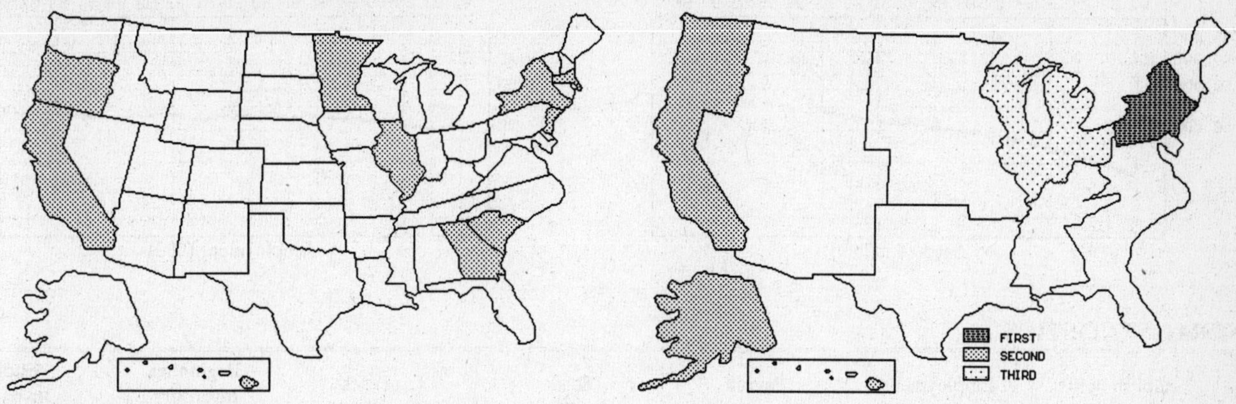

INDUSTRY DATA BY STATE

State	Establishments - 1995 Total (number)	Establishments - 1995 % of U.S.	Employment - 1995 Total (number)	Employment - 1995 % of U.S.	Employment - 1995 Per Estab.	Payroll - 1995 Total ($ mil.)	Payroll - 1995 Per Empl. ($)	Sales - 1992 Total ($ mil.)	Sales - 1992 % of U.S.	Sales - 1992 Per Estab ($)
New York	827	7.6	5,440	6.8	7	212.4	39,051	8,113.0	24.0	1,269,440
California	1,450	13.4	11,139	14.0	8	423.4	38,006	6,396.5	18.9	611,407
Illinois	507	4.7	4,248	5.3	8	130.1	30,632	1,774.0	5.2	577,294
Texas	692	6.4	5,420	6.8	8	138.0	25,461	1,628.5	4.8	397,386
Florida	1,029	9.5	5,147	6.5	5	139.0	27,013	1,396.4	4.1	352,542
Ohio	450	4.2	3,504	4.4	8	92.9	26,520	1,385.1	4.1	586,178
Massachusetts	220	2.0	1,660	2.1	8	61.0	36,758	1,315.1	3.9	1,118,320
New Jersey	352	3.3	2,781	3.5	8	103.6	37,243	1,301.0	3.8	535,189
Pennsylvania	354	3.3	3,421	4.3	10	101.8	29,766	1,234.7	3.7	448,153
Georgia	338	3.1	2,757	3.5	8	78.6	28,523	1,141.3	3.4	516,433
Oregon	167	1.5	1,000	1.3	6	30.0	29,983	1,071.4	3.2	924,431
Minnesota	217	2.0	2,904	3.6	13	107.2	36,908	821.5	2.4	473,749
Michigan	341	3.2	2,180	2.7	6	70.0	32,089	759.9	2.2	380,530
Wisconsin	162	1.5	1,261	1.6	8	35.7	28,293	504.7	1.5	504,707
North Carolina	288	2.7	2,340	2.9	8	58.5	25,010	501.2	1.5	364,481
Alabama	260	2.4	2,049	2.6	8	57.3	27,981	496.7	1.5	287,123
South Carolina	171	1.6	1,158	1.5	7	33.5	28,916	484.1	1.4	542,149
Tennessee	199	1.8	1,494	1.9	8	43.1	28,878	451.9	1.3	313,198
Arkansas	118	1.1	1,157	1.5	10	24.4	21,111	316.1	0.9	327,199
Virginia	169	1.6	1,205	1.5	7	29.5	24,452	297.2	0.9	300,818
Missouri	191	1.8	1,106	1.4	6	32.4	29,253	293.4	0.9	284,545
Colorado	168	1.6	1,208	1.5	7	30.0	24,814	290.5	0.9	316,053
Louisiana	159	1.5	1,387	1.7	9	30.0	21,613	290.1	0.9	267,390
Indiana	230	2.1	1,125	1.4	5	33.4	29,724	261.2	0.8	302,325
Mississippi	204	1.9	1,120	1.4	5	24.8	22,148	248.8	0.7	306,774
Hawaii	47	0.4	289	0.4	6	7.4	25,540	182.8	0.5	679,662
Kentucky	80	0.7	677	0.9	8	13.2	19,501	167.4	0.5	307,213
Nevada	47	0.4	587	0.7	12	18.5	31,436	120.1	0.4	251,299
Utah	65	0.6	417	0.5	6	10.6	25,374	102.2	0.3	238,308
Maine	54	0.5	221	0.3	4	5.2	23,611	79.4	0.2	372,545
Arizona	122	1.1	1,115	1.4	9	42.0	37,672	70.1	0.2	148,907
Kansas	68	0.6	296	0.4	4	9.2	31,044	65.1	0.2	222,068
Oklahoma	67	0.6	337	0.4	5	6.3	18,694	56.7	0.2	221,648
New Hampshire	46	0.4	221	0.3	5	6.1	27,443	51.7	0.2	302,187
Iowa	67	0.6	322	0.4	5	6.3	19,484	48.1	0.1	153,805
Idaho	37	0.3	265	0.3	7	5.2	19,792	30.0	0.1	137,794
Vermont	32	0.3	222	0.3	7	5.3	24,018	24.3	0.1	130,102
Alaska	16	0.1	94	0.1	6	2.8	29,319	12.0	0.0	231,096
D.C.	6	0.1	13	0.0	2	0.5	39,769	9.8	0.0	349,571
South Dakota	23	0.2	20-99	-	-	(D)	-	8.4	0.0	113,500
Wyoming	9	0.1	20-99	-	-	(D)	-	3.0	0.0	108,286
Washington	293	2.7	2,129	2.7	7	77.5	36,393	(D)	-	-
Connecticut	127	1.2	1,376	1.7	11	41.3	30,025	(D)	-	-
Maryland	125	1.2	1,412	1.8	11	41.3	29,242	(D)	-	-
West Virginia	49	0.5	145	0.2	3	3.2	22,283	(D)	-	-
Nebraska	42	0.4	296	0.4	7	8.0	27,105	(D)	-	-
Rhode Island	38	0.4	345	0.4	9	8.2	23,699	(D)	-	-
Montana	34	0.3	229	0.3	7	7.3	32,083	(D)	-	-
New Mexico	30	0.3	193	0.2	6	4.1	21,181	(D)	-	-
Delaware	21	0.2	105	0.1	5	2.3	21,876	(D)	-	-
North Dakota	12	0.1	53	0.1	4	1.0	19,811	(D)	-	-

Source: County Business Patterns, 1995 and *Economic Census of the U.S., 1992*. Data are sorted by 1992 revenues and, if revenues are unavailable, by establishments in 1995. The symbol (D) indicates that data are withheld by the source to avoid disclosure of competitive information. A dash (-) indicates that data are not available or undisclosed because they do not meet statistical validity standards. Shaded *states* on the state map indicate those states which have proportionately greater representation in the industry than would be indicated by the state's population; the ratio is based on total revenues or number of establishments. Shaded *regions* indicate where the industry is regionally most concentrated.

5111 - PRINTING AND WRITING PAPER

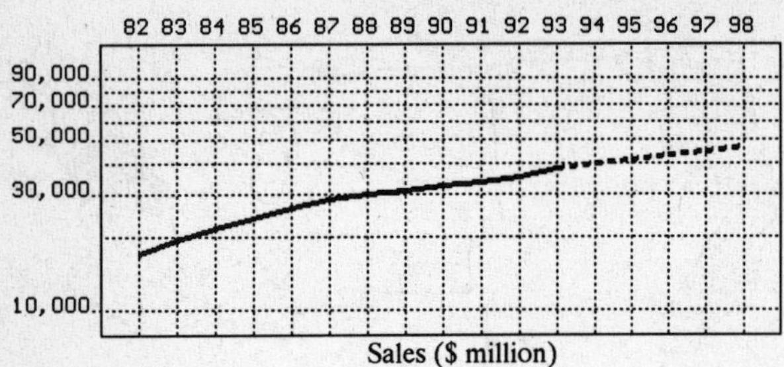

Sales ($ million)

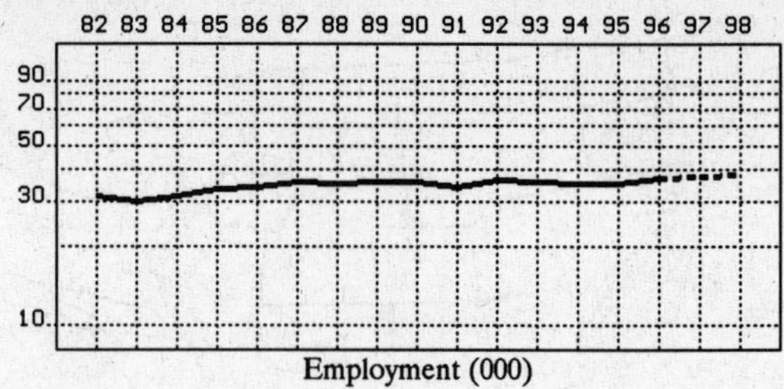

Employment (000)

GENERAL STATISTICS

Year	Establishments (number)	Employment (number)	Payroll ($ million)	Sales ($ million)	Expenses ($ million)	Beginning Inventory ($ million)	Ending Inventory ($ million)
1982	2,009	31,514	756.0	16,983.4	-	-	-
1983	1,535	30,365	787.3	19,292.9e	-	-	-
1984	1,861	31,903	899.3	21,602.3e	-	-	-
1985	1,867	33,943	981.7	23,911.8e	-	-	-
1986	1,809	34,368	1,040.6	26,221.2e	-	-	-
1987	2,074	35,900	1,100.1	28,530.6	2,104.2	1,055.2	1,078.3
1988	2,005	35,461	1,193.4	29,802.1e	2,211.6e	1,143.9e	1,156.9e
1989	1,969	35,999	1,301.7	31,073.5e	2,319.0e	1,232.6e	1,235.5e
1990	1,924	35,922	1,337.0	32,344.9e	2,426.5e	1,321.3e	1,314.1e
1991	1,851	34,460	1,274.3	33,616.3e	2,533.9e	1,409.9e	1,392.7e
1992	2,561	36,646	1,387.3	34,887.8	2,641.3	1,498.6	1,471.3
1993	2,472	36,010	1,388.9	37,857.7p	2,748.7p	1,587.3p	1,549.8p
1994	2,379	35,479	1,396.8	39,648.2p	2,856.1p	1,676.0p	1,628.4p
1995	2,335	35,447	1,622.9	41,438.6p	2,963.5p	1,764.7p	1,707.0p
1996	2,436p	37,239p	1,624.7p	43,229.0p	3,070.9p	1,853.4p	1,785.6p
1997	2,487p	37,600p	1,684.5p	45,019.5p	3,178.3p	1,942.1p	1,864.2p
1998	2,539p	37,961p	1,744.3p	46,809.9p	3,285.8p	2,030.7p	1,942.8p

Sources: Economic Census of the United States, 1982, 1987, and 1992. Establishment counts, employment, and payroll are from *County Business Patterns* for non-Census years. Values followed by a 'p' are projections by the editors. Sales and expense data for non-Census years are extrapolations, marked by 'e'. Industries reclassified in 1987 will not have data for prior years. Data are the most recent available at this level of detail.

INDICES OF CHANGE

Year	Establishments (number)	Employment (number)	Payroll ($ million)	Sales ($ million)	Expenses ($ million)	Beginning Inventory ($ million)	Ending Inventory ($ million)
1982	78.4	86.0	54.5	48.7	-	-	-
1983	59.9	82.9	56.8	55.3e	-	-	-
1984	72.7	87.1	64.8	61.9e	-	-	-
1985	72.9	92.6	70.8	68.5e	-	-	-
1986	70.6	93.8	75.0	75.2e	-	-	-
1987	81.0	98.0	79.3	81.8	79.7	70.4	73.3
1988	78.3	96.8	86.0	85.4e	83.7e	76.3e	78.6e
1989	76.9	98.2	93.8	89.1e	87.8e	82.3e	84.0e
1990	75.1	98.0	96.4	92.7e	91.9e	88.2e	89.3e
1991	72.3	94.0	91.9	96.4e	95.9e	94.1e	94.7e
1992	100.0	100.0	100.0	100.0	100.0	100.0	100.0
1993	96.5	98.3	100.1	108.5p	104.1p	105.9p	105.3p
1994	92.9	96.8	100.7	113.6p	108.1p	111.8p	110.7p
1995	91.2	96.7	117.0	118.8p	112.2p	117.8p	116.0p
1996	95.1p	101.6p	117.1p	123.9p	116.3p	123.7p	121.4p
1997	97.1p	102.6p	121.4p	129.0p	120.3p	129.6p	126.7p
1998	99.2p	103.6p	125.7p	134.2p	124.4p	135.5p	132.0p

Sources: Same as General Statistics. The values shown reflect change from the base year, 1992. Values above 100 mean greater than 1992, values below 100 mean less than 1992, and a value of 100 in the 1982-91 or 1993-98 period means same as 1992. Values followed by a 'p' are projections by the editors; 'e' stands for extrapolation. Data are the most recent available at this level of detail.

SELECTED RATIOS

For 1992	Avg. of All Wholesale	Analyzed Industry	Index	For 1992	Avg. of All Wholesale	Analyzed Industry	Index
Employees per Establishment	12	14	122	Sales per Employee	561,172	952,022	170
Payroll per Establishment	349,729	541,702	155	Sales per Establishment	6,559,346	13,622,725	208
Payroll per Employee	29,919	37,857	127	Expenses per Establishment	723,071	1,031,355	143

Sources: Same as General Statistics. The 'Average of All Manufacturing' column represents the average of all manufacturing industries reported for the most recent complete year available. The Index shows the relationship between the Average and the Analyzed Industry. For example, 100 means that they are equal; 500 that the Analyzed Industry is five times the average; 50 means that the Analyzed Industry is half the national average. The abbreviation 'na' is used to show that data are 'not available'.

LEADING COMPANIES

Number shown: **50** Total sales ($ mil): **15,525** Total employment (000): **28.6**

Company Name	Address				CEO Name	Phone	Co. Type	Sales ($ mil)	Empl. (000)
Unisource Worldwide Inc.	PO Box 3000-0935	Berwyn	PA	19312	Ray B Mundt	610-296-4470	P	7,108	14.2
WWF Paper Corp.	2 Bala Plz, #200	Bala Cynwyd	PA	19004	E. V Furlong Jr	610-667-9210	R	800	0.4
Alling and Cory Co.	PO Box 20403	Rochester	NY	14602	S T Hubbard Jr	716-581-4100	S	750	1.2
Dillard	PO Box 21767	Greensboro	NC	27420	Newell E Holt	910-299-1211	D	560 *	1.8
Ris Paper Company Inc.	7300 Turfway Rd	Florence	KY	41042	Mark Griffin	606-746-8700	R	500 *	0.6
Bradner Central Co.	333 S Des Plaines	Chicago	IL	60661	Terence J Shea	312-454-1852	R	400	0.2
Gould Paper Corp.	315 Park Ave S	New York	NY	10010	Harry E Gould Jr	212-505-1000	R	350 *	0.5
ResourceNet International	50 E River Ctr Blvd	Covington	KY	41011	Thomas E Costello	606-655-2000	D	320	1.0
Mac Papers Inc.	PO Box 5369	Jacksonville	FL	32247	FS McGehee	904-348-3300	R	310	0.8
A.T. Clayton and Company Inc.	2 Pickwick Plz	Greenwich	CT	06830	Mark Vallely Jr	203-861-1190	R	300	<0.1
Perkins-Goodwin Company Inc.	300 Atlantic St	Stamford	CT	06901	Robert T O'Hara	203-363-7800	R	300	<0.1
Unisource-Central Region Div.	1015 Corp Square	St. Louis	MO	63132	Steve Olroyd	314-919-1800	S	265	0.4
Maines Paper and Food Service	12 Terrace Dr	Conklin	NY	13748	Floyd Maines	607-772-1936	R	260 *	0.5
Unisource Midwest Inc.	PO Box 308001	Gahanna	OH	43230	Jack Bryant	614-251-7000	S	230 *	0.5
Dillard Paper Birmingham	PO Box 11367	Birmingham	AL	35202	Joe Strong	205-798-8380	D	220 *	1.0
Millcraft Paper Co.	6800 Grant Ave	Cleveland	OH	44105	Charles L Mlakar Jr	216-441-5505	R	200	0.3
Price and Pierce International	PO Box 971	Stamford	CT	06904	C E Allanson	203-328-2000	R	200	<0.1
Cincinnati Cordage & Paper Co.	PO Box 17125	Cincinnati	OH	45217	John F Church Jr	513-242-3600	R	190 *	0.2
Roosevelt Paper Co.	7601 State Rd	Philadelphia	PA	19136	Ted Kosloff	215-331-5000	R	190	0.5
Ingram Paper Co.	PO Box 60003	City of Industry	CA	91716	Larry Stillman	818-854-5400	R	150 *	0.3
Leslie Paper Co.	2500 N Mayfair Rd	Milwaukee	WI	53226	Barry Hentz	414-771-0200	S	150 *	0.4
Paper Corporation	161 of the Amer	New York	NY	10013	Daniel D Romanaux	212-645-5900	S	150	<0.1
Perez Trading Company Inc.	3490 NW 125th St	Miami	FL	33167	J Perez	305-769-0761	R	139	0.2
Spicers Paper Inc.	12310 E Slauson	Santa Fe Sprgs	CA	90670	Chris Creighton	562-698-1199	S	126 *	0.3
Marquardt and Company Inc.	161 6th Ave	New York	NY	10013	John Cooper	212-645-7200	R	100	<0.1
Seaman-Patrick Paper Co.	2000 Howard St	Detroit	MI	48216	Michael Starling	313-496-3131	S	100 *	0.1
Snyder Paper Corp.	PO Box 758	Hickory	NC	28603	Roger McGuire	704-328-2501	R	100 *	0.3
Frank Parsons Paper Co.	2270 Beaver Rd	Landover	MD	20785	Douglas T Parsons	301-386-4700	R	80	0.2
Henley Paper Co.	PO Box 20408	Greensboro	NC	27420	Nixon C Henley	919-668-0081	R	80	0.3
Kelly Paper Company	1441 E 16th St	Los Angeles	CA	90021	Ed Pearson	213-749-1311	S	80	0.2
West Coast Paper Co.	23200 64th Ave S	Kent	WA	98032	Frederick J Stabbert	206-623-1850	R	76 *	0.2
Western ResourceNet Intern	6000 N Cutter Cir	Portland	OR	97217	Jerry Lindsey	503-289-2800	S	75	0.1
Sabin Robbins Paper Co.	106 Cir Freeway Dr	Cincinnati	OH	45246	Thomas P Price Jr	513-874-5270	R	75 *	0.2
Beacon Paper Co.	8537 Chapin Indrial	St. Louis	MO	63114	Kent M Reynolds	314-423-4100	D	50	<0.1
Carpenter Paper Co.	PO Box 2709	Grand Rapids	MI	49501	James Holtsclaw	616-452-9741	S	50	0.1
Central Paper Co. Trenton	1004 Whitehead Ext	Trenton	NJ	08638	David Relles	609-883-7500	D	47	<0.1
Triangle Marketing Corp.	32 Bleecker St	New York	NY	10012	L Diamond	212-966-0100	R	45	0.1
Websource	161 of the Amer	New York	NY	10013	Donald J Heller	212-255-1600	D	44 *	<0.1
Anchor Paper Co.	480 Broadway St	St. Paul	MN	55101	Hamel Hartinger	612-298-1311	R	38	0.1
Bulkley Denton JB Papers Div.	PO Box 560	Union	NJ	07083	Jonathan Bloom	908-964-4500	D	37 *	0.1
Cole Papers Inc.	1300 38th St	Fargo	ND	58108	R Charles Perkins	701-282-5311	R	34	0.2
Jackson Paper Company Inc.	197 N Gallatin St	Jackson	MS	39207	Jim P Archer	601-352-0837	R	34	0.1
Unisource Worldwide Inc.	12601 E 38th Ave	Denver	CO	80239	Robert Keating	303-371-4260	D	33 *	<0.1
Chris Cam Corp.	808 W Cherokee St	Sioux Falls	SD	57104	D Christenson	605-336-1190	R	32	0.1
Hudson Valley Paper Co.	PO Box 1988	Albany	NY	12201	ST Jones III	518-471-5111	R	30	<0.1
Select Robinson Paper Co.	160 Fox St	Portland	ME	04101	David H Drake	207-773-2973	S	26 *	<0.1
LaSalle Paper and Packaging	2429 S 51st Ave	Phoenix	AZ	85009	Thomas P Hayes III	602-484-7337	S	25	<0.1
Tayloe Paper Co.	PO Box 580880	Tulsa	OK	74158	David L Bayles	918-835-6911	R	24	<0.1
White Rose Paper Co.	4665 Hollins Ferry	Baltimore	MD	21227	Theodore A Imbach	410-247-1900	R	22	<0.1
Executive Converting Corp.	4750 Simonton Rd	Dallas	TX	75244	Greg Wilemon	972-387-0500	S	20	<0.1

Source: *Ward's Business Directory of U.S. Private and Public Companies*, 1998. The company type code used is as follows: P - Public, R - Private, S - Subsidiary, D - Division, J - Joint Venture, A - Affiliate, G - Group. Sales are in millions of dollars, employees are in thousands. An asterisk (*) indicates an estimated sales volume. The symbol < stands for 'less than'.

OCCUPATIONS EMPLOYED BY SIC 511 - WHOLESALE TRADE, OTHER

Occupation	% of Total 1996	Change to 2006	Occupation	% of Total 1996	Change to 2006
Sales & related workers nec	19.5	20.2	Clerical supervisors & managers	1.9	20.2
General managers & top executives	5.9	16.4	Order clerks	1.9	8.2
Truck drivers light & heavy	5.4	20.2	Helpers, laborers nec	1.7	20.2
General office clerks	3.6	3.4	Electrical & electronic technicians	1.4	18.8
Traffic, shipping, receiving clerks	3.6	16.7	Blue collar worker supervisors	1.4	16.0
Stock clerks	3.5	-3.9	Wholesale & retail buyers, except farm products	1.3	17.0
Freight, stock, & material movers, hand	3.3	8.2	Office machine & cash register servicers	1.3	20.2
Marketing & sales worker supervisors	3.1	20.2	Hand packers & packagers	1.2	-3.9
Order fillers, wholesale & retail sales	3.0	16.7	Maintenance repairers, general utility	1.1	12.0
Bookkeeping, accounting, & auditing clerks	2.9	-3.9	Industrial truck & tractor operators	1.1	20.2
Salespersons, retail	2.5	20.2	Purchasing managers	1.1	20.2
Secretaries, except legal & medical	2.5	-4.7	Receptionists & information clerks	1.0	20.2
Assemblers, fabricators, hand workers nec	2.0	-3.9			

Source: *Industry-Occupation Matrix*, Bureau of Labor Statistics. These data relate to one or more 3-digit SIC industry groups rather than to a single 4-digit SIC. The change reported for each occupation to the year 2006 is a percent of growth or decline as estimated by the Bureau of Labor Statistics. The abbreviation nec stands for 'not elsewhere classified'.

STATE AND REGIONAL CONCENTRATION

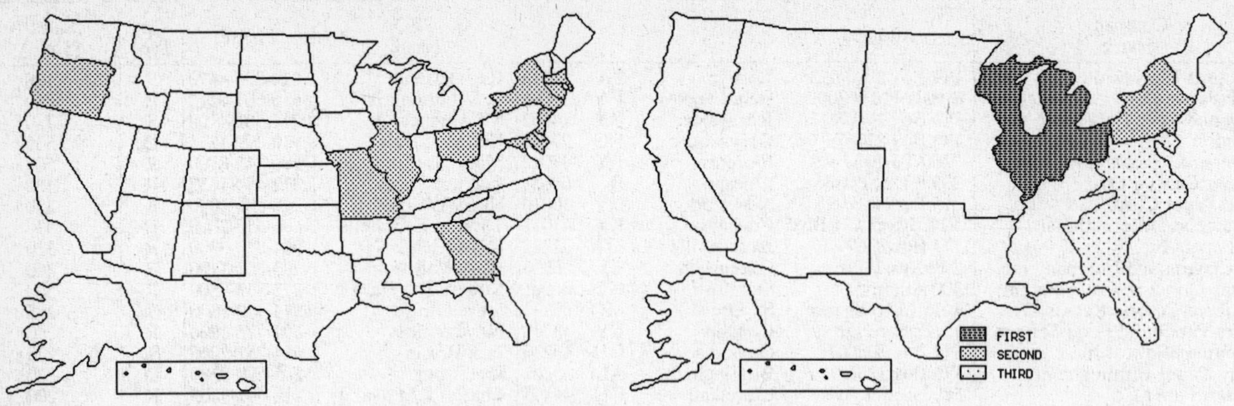

INDUSTRY DATA BY STATE

State	Establishments - 1995 Total (number)	Establishments - 1995 % of U.S.	Employment - 1995 Total (number)	Employment - 1995 % of U.S.	Employment - 1995 Per Estab.	Payroll - 1995 Total ($ mil.)	Payroll - 1995 Per Empl. ($)	Sales - 1992 Total ($ mil.)	Sales - 1992 % of U.S.	Sales - 1992 Per Estab ($)
Illinois	163	7.0	2,282	6.5	14	120.4	52,751	5,688.0	17.1	2,281,599
New York	197	8.4	2,708	7.7	14	159.4	58,866	4,727.1	14.2	1,486,027
California	290	12.4	4,155	11.7	14	189.7	45,652	3,429.6	10.3	780,514
Connecticut	54	2.3	765	2.2	14	58.9	77,039	2,303.7	6.9	3,329,107
Texas	176	7.5	2,023	5.7	11	66.3	32,791	1,767.5	5.3	751,816
Georgia	82	3.5	1,640	4.6	20	77.4	47,188	1,604.2	4.8	1,097,280
Pennsylvania	96	4.1	1,531	4.3	16	77.9	50,863	1,551.1	4.7	781,417
Ohio	116	5.0	1,708	4.8	15	67.7	39,633	1,461.0	4.4	877,984
New Jersey	117	5.0	1,780	5.0	15	86.7	48,698	1,147.8	3.5	740,516
Massachusetts	73	3.1	1,059	3.0	15	58.9	55,621	1,084.8	3.3	1,210,708
Michigan	82	3.5	1,054	3.0	13	49.5	46,923	834.9	2.5	768,105
Florida	121	5.2	1,467	4.1	12	59.9	40,802	804.7	2.4	480,729
Maryland	39	1.7	1,121	3.2	29	47.8	42,665	783.8	2.4	686,348
Virginia	32	1.4	412	1.2	13	15.3	37,228	703.2	2.1	1,238,055
Missouri	59	2.5	960	2.7	16	49.2	51,257	697.6	2.1	760,688
Wisconsin	41	1.8	744	2.1	18	33.5	45,051	608.2	1.8	689,579
Washington	38	1.6	521	1.5	14	20.5	39,397	492.9	1.5	734,528
North Carolina	45	1.9	911	2.6	20	34.9	38,290	461.9	1.4	638,887
Oregon	29	1.2	555	1.6	19	23.1	41,712	398.3	1.2	704,989
Colorado	30	1.3	653	1.8	22	27.7	42,481	374.3	1.1	548,881
Tennessee	48	2.1	583	1.6	12	25.6	43,954	310.4	0.9	502,249
South Carolina	10	0.4	161	0.5	16	6.0	37,404	280.7	0.8	1,356,188
Indiana	43	1.8	763	2.2	18	29.6	38,826	231.2	0.7	339,551
Kansas	26	1.1	462	1.3	18	17.6	38,052	213.9	0.6	578,214
Arizona	27	1.2	407	1.2	15	15.8	38,791	200.1	0.6	468,504
Kentucky	22	0.9	557	1.6	25	19.8	35,517	173.5	0.5	465,263
Oklahoma	19	0.8	321	0.9	17	12.1	37,819	151.5	0.5	425,469
Iowa	22	0.9	365	1.0	17	14.3	39,156	140.1	0.4	431,225
Alabama	27	1.2	390	1.1	14	13.2	33,821	124.9	0.4	326,217
New Hampshire	12	0.5	115	0.3	10	5.9	51,713	110.5	0.3	913,091
Maine	7	0.3	110	0.3	16	4.6	41,855	88.6	0.3	952,957
Mississippi	6	0.3	144	0.4	24	4.8	33,063	61.1	0.2	260,906
Arkansas	13	0.6	162	0.5	12	5.6	34,519	55.9	0.2	301,935
New Mexico	13	0.6	130	0.4	10	3.4	26,031	29.8	0.1	273,101
Hawaii	6	0.3	51	0.1	9	1.8	35,569	25.1	0.1	448,071
Montana	6	0.3	55	0.2	9	3.8	69,400	18.5	0.1	307,983
North Dakota	5	0.2	44	0.1	9	1.7	39,591	14.7	0.0	272,407
West Virginia	5	0.2	46	0.1	9	1.1	24,174	12.9	0.0	286,111
Vermont	3	0.1	18	0.1	6	0.6	33,778	11.1	0.0	503,773
Minnesota	54	2.3	1,168	3.3	22	54.2	46,398	(D)	-	-
Louisiana	27	1.2	397	1.1	15	12.7	31,990	(D)	-	-
Nevada	9	0.4	48	0.1	5	1.9	39,500	(D)	-	-
Rhode Island	9	0.4	102	0.3	11	4.4	42,657	(D)	-	-
Nebraska	8	0.3	279	0.8	35	9.6	34,505	(D)	-	-
Utah	8	0.3	349	1.0	44	22.3	64,017	(D)	-	-
Idaho	7	0.3	62	0.2	9	2.3	37,613	(D)	-	-
Delaware	4	0.2	35	0.1	9	0.5	15,571	(D)	-	-
D.C.	3	0.1	20-99	-	-	(D)	-	(D)	-	-
South Dakota	3	0.1	20-99	-	-	(D)	-	(D)	-	-
Alaska	2	0.1	20-99	-	-	(D)	-	(D)	-	-
Wyoming	1	0.0	0-19	-	-	(D)	-	(D)	-	-

Source: County Business Patterns, 1995 and *Economic Census of the U.S., 1992*. Data are sorted by 1992 revenues and, if revenues are unavailable, by establishments in 1995. The symbol (D) indicates that data are withheld by the source to avoid disclosure of competitive information. A dash (-) indicates that data are not available or undisclosed because they do not meet statistical validity standards. Shaded *states* on the state map indicate those states which have proportionately greater representation in the industry than would be indicated by the state's population; the ratio is based on total revenues or number of establishments. Shaded *regions* indicate where the industry is regionally most concentrated.

5112 - STATIONERY AND OFFICE SUPPLIES

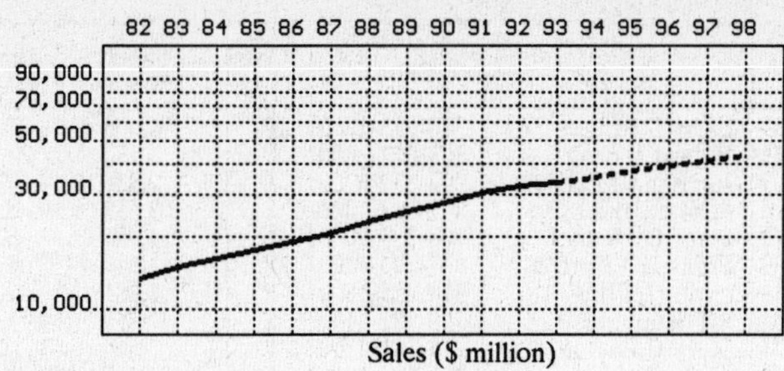

Sales ($ million)

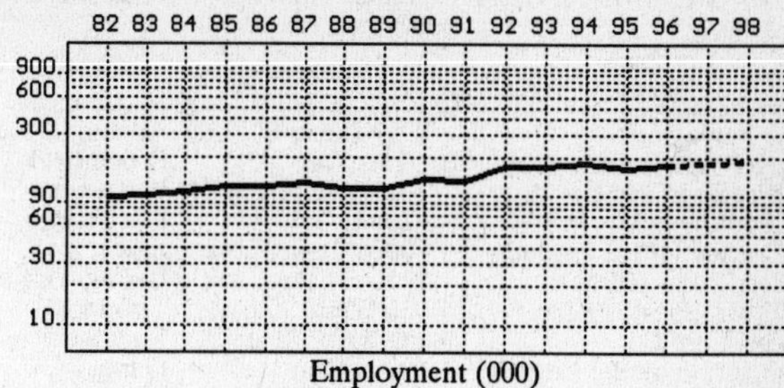

Employment (000)

GENERAL STATISTICS

Year	Establishments (number)	Employment (number)	Payroll ($ million)	Sales ($ million)	Expenses ($ million)	Beginning Inventory ($ million)	Ending Inventory ($ million)
1982	8,036	97,684	1,598.5	13,412.2	-	-	-
1983	8,336	100,504	1,754.3	14,852.6e	-	-	-
1984	7,970	106,997	1,912.4	16,293.0e	-	-	-
1985	7,847	120,138	2,194.1	17,733.4e	-	-	-
1986	7,733	118,450	2,286.4	19,173.8e	-	-	-
1987	9,778	124,634	2,303.6	20,614.2	4,364.0	1,301.6	1,374.2
1988	9,464	116,717	2,504.5	23,023.7e	4,788.0e	1,458.0e	1,528.5e
1989	9,188	116,848	2,601.8	25,433.1e	5,212.0e	1,614.4e	1,682.9e
1990	9,326	136,384	2,881.5	27,842.5e	5,636.0e	1,770.8e	1,837.3e
1991	9,113	129,912	2,687.7	30,252.0e	6,060.0e	1,927.2e	1,991.6e
1992	11,807	168,825	3,435.8	32,661.4	6,484.0	2,083.6	2,146.0
1993	11,392	168,706	3,555.3	33,485.2p	6,908.0p	2,240.1p	2,300.3p
1994	11,430	178,929	3,753.1	35,410.1p	7,332.0p	2,396.5p	2,454.7p
1995	9,967	165,437	3,768.3	37,335.0p	7,756.0p	2,552.9p	2,609.1p
1996	11,411p	177,193p	3,937.4p	39,259.9p	8,180.0p	2,709.3p	2,763.4p
1997	11,681p	183,198p	4,107.8p	41,184.9p	8,604.0p	2,865.7p	2,917.8p
1998	11,951p	189,204p	4,278.2p	43,109.8p	9,028.0p	3,022.1p	3,072.1p

Sources: Economic Census of the United States, 1982, 1987, and 1992. Establishment counts, employment, and payroll are from *County Business Patterns* for non-Census years. Values followed by a 'p' are projections by the editors. Sales and expense data for non-Census years are extrapolations, marked by 'e'. Industries reclassified in 1987 will not have data for prior years. Data are the most recent available at this level of detail.

INDICES OF CHANGE

Year	Establishments (number)	Employment (number)	Payroll ($ million)	Sales ($ million)	Expenses ($ million)	Beginning Inventory ($ million)	Ending Inventory ($ million)
1982	68.1	57.9	46.5	41.1	-	-	-
1983	70.6	59.5	51.1	45.5e	-	-	-
1984	67.5	63.4	55.7	49.9e	-	-	-
1985	66.5	71.2	63.9	54.3e	-	-	-
1986	65.5	70.2	66.5	58.7e	-	-	-
1987	82.8	73.8	67.0	63.1	67.3	62.5	64.0
1988	80.2	69.1	72.9	70.5e	73.8e	70.0e	71.2e
1989	77.8	69.2	75.7	77.9e	80.4e	77.5e	78.4e
1990	79.0	80.8	83.9	85.2e	86.9e	85.0e	85.6e
1991	77.2	77.0	78.2	92.6e	93.5e	92.5e	92.8e
1992	100.0	100.0	100.0	100.0	100.0	100.0	100.0
1993	96.5	99.9	103.5	102.5p	106.5p	107.5p	107.2p
1994	96.8	106.0	109.2	108.4p	113.1p	115.0p	114.4p
1995	84.4	98.0	109.7	114.3p	119.6p	122.5p	121.6p
1996	96.6p	105.0p	114.6p	120.2p	126.2p	130.0p	128.8p
1997	98.9p	108.5p	119.6p	126.1p	132.7p	137.5p	136.0p
1998	101.2p	112.1p	124.5p	132.0p	139.2p	145.0p	143.2p

Sources: Same as General Statistics. The values shown reflect change from the base year, 1992. Values above 100 mean greater than 1992, values below 100 mean less than 1992, and a value of 100 in the 1982-91 or 1993-98 period means same as 1992. Values followed by a 'p' are projections by the editors; 'e' stands for extrapolation. Data are the most recent available at this level of detail.

SELECTED RATIOS

For 1992	Avg. of All Wholesale	Analyzed Industry	Index	For 1992	Avg. of All Wholesale	Analyzed Industry	Index
Employees per Establishment	12	14	122	Sales per Employee	561,172	193,463	34
Payroll per Establishment	349,729	290,997	83	Sales per Establishment	6,559,346	2,766,274	42
Payroll per Employee	29,919	20,351	68	Expenses per Establishment	723,071	549,166	76

Sources: Same as General Statistics. The 'Average of All Manufacturing' column represents the average of all manufacturing industries reported for the most recent complete year available. The Index shows the relationship between the Average and the Analyzed Industry. For example, 100 means that they are equal; 500 that the Analyzed Industry is five times the average; 50 means that the Analyzed Industry is half the national average. The abbreviation 'na' is used to show that data are 'not available'.

LEADING COMPANIES

Number shown: **50** Total sales ($ mil): **26,052** Total employment (000): **116.3**

Company Name	Address				CEO Name	Phone	Co. Type	Sales ($ mil)	Empl. (000)
Genuine Parts Co.	2999 Circle 75 Pkwy	Atlanta	GA	30339	Larry L Prince	770-953-1700	P	6,005	24.5
Corporate Express Inc.	1 Env Way	Broomfield	CO	80021	Robert L King	303-664-2000	P	3,196	27.0
U.S. Office Products Co.	1025 T Jefferson St	Washington	DC	20007	Jonathan J Ledecky	202-339-6700	P	2,836	17.0
United Stationers Inc.	2200 E Golf Rd	Des Plaines	IL	60016	R W Larrimore	847-699-5000	P	2,558	5.5
Boise Cascade Office Products	800 W Bryn Mawr	Itasca	IL	60143	Peter G Danis Jr	708-773-5000	P	1,986	8.5
BT Office Products Intern.	2150 E Lake Cook	Buffalo Grove	IL	60089	Frans H J Koffrie	847-793-7500	P	1,619	6.6
Viking Office Products Inc.	950 West 190th St	Torrance	CA	90248	Irwin Helford	310-225-4500	P	1,286	2.8
Alling and Cory Co.	PO Box 20403	Rochester	NY	14602	S T Hubbard Jr	716-581-4100	S	750	1.2
Daisytek International Corp.	500 N Central	Plano	TX	75074	Mark C Layton	214-881-4700	P	604	0.7
CHS Promark (Miami, Florida)	2153 NW 86th Ave	Miami	FL	33126	Alvin Perlman	305-594-4990	R	400	0.3
Nashua Corp.	PO Box 2002	Nashua	NH	03061	Gerald G Garbacz	603-880-2323	P	390	2.4
Servco Pacific Inc.	PO Box 2788	Honolulu	HI	96803	Mark H Fukunaga	808-521-6511	R	361	0.9
Office Depot Inc.	3366 E Willow St	Signal Hill	CA	90806	John Maloney	562-490-1000	S	350*	2.0
School Specialties Inc.	1000 N Bluemound	Appleton	WI	54914	Dave VandeZden	920-734-5712	P	350	1.3
Thomas Nelson Inc.	501 Nelson Place	Nashville	TN	37214	Sam Moore	615-889-9000	P	332	1.3
Burt, Knust, McCabe Enterprises	222 Pitkin St	East Hartford	CT	06108	Don Griesdorn	203-528-9981	R	300	2.0
Staples National Advantage Div.	45 E Wesley St	S. Hackensack	NJ	07606	Evan Stern	201-488-2900	D	200	0.5
Nebraska Book Company Inc.	PO Box 80529	Lincoln	NE	68501	Mark Oppegard	402-421-7300	R	160	0.6
A.T. Cross Co.	One Albion Rd	Lincoln	RI	02865	Russell A Boss	401-333-1200	P	155	1.1
TAB Products Co.	1400 Page Mill Rd	Palo Alto	CA	94304	Philip C Kantz	650-852-2400	P	155	1.1
Lindenmeyr Munroe	PO Box 6033	Farmingdale	NY	11735	Kenneth Obletz	718-520-1586	S	150*	<0.1
Sanrio Inc.	570 Eccles Ave	S. San Francisco	CA	94080	K Tsuji	650-952-2880	S	150	0.5
Richard Young Journal Inc.	508 S Military Tr	Deerfield Beach	FL	33442	Richard Young	954-426-8100	D	140*	0.3
James Crean (USA) Inc.	12 E 41st St, #1501	New York	NY	10017	Philip Soden	212-725-5944	S	130*	0.8
Champion Industries Inc.	PO Box 2968	Huntington	WV	25728	Marshall T Reynolds	304-528-2791	P	108	0.9
Koval Marketing Inc.	11208 47th Ave W	Mukilteo	WA	98275	Roy Koval	425-347-4249	R	100	<0.1
Fisher Paper	PO Box 1720	Fort Wayne	IN	46801	Floyd Sims	219-747-7442	D	87*	0.2
Frank Parsons Paper Co.	2270 Beaver Rd	Landover	MD	20785	Douglas T Parsons	301-386-4700	R	80	0.2
Henley Paper Co.	PO Box 20408	Greensboro	NC	27420	Nixon C Henley	919-668-0081	R	80	0.3
American Loose Leaf	4015 Papin St	St. Louis	MO	63110	Gerald Holschen	314-535-1414	D	70	0.4
Tash Inc.	11190 White Birch	R. Cucamonga	CA	91730	Ronald Jones	909-945-9566	D	70*	0.2
Business Express of Boulder	1904 Pearl St	Boulder	CO	80302	Pavel Bouska	303-443-9300	R	65	0.2
Spectrum Office Products Inc.	14623 Mushroom	Rochester	NY	14692	Henry Epstein	716-424-3600	R	63*	0.3
Modern Business Machines Inc.	505 N 22nd St	Milwaukee	WI	53233	Marvin Cooper	414-344-1000	S	58	0.3
Office America Inc.	PO Box 2430	Glen Allen	VA	23058	Allan Werner	804-747-9964	R	53	0.7
Silvers Inc.	151 W Fort St	Detroit	MI	48232	Ira Silver	313-963-0000	R	52	0.3
Pantropic Power Products Inc.	8205 NW 58th St	Miami	FL	33166	Luis Botas	305-592-4944	R	51	0.2
Carpenter Paper Co.	PO Box 2709	Grand Rapids	MI	49501	James Holtsclaw	616-452-9741	S	50	0.1
General Office Products Co.	2050 Old Hwy 8	New Brighton	MN	55112	Thomas J Reaser	612-639-4700	S	50	0.3
Philadelphia Stationers Inc.	10551 Decatur Rd	Philadelphia	PA	19154	Herman Marx	215-632-5200	R	50*	0.3
Continental Office Furniture	2061 Silver Dr	Columbus	OH	43211	John Lucks	614-262-8088	R	45*	0.3
Cuna Service Group Inc.	PO Box 431	Madison	WI	53701	Brad Murphy	608-231-4000	S	45	0.5
Andrews Office Supply	8400 Ardmore	Landover	MD	20785	Jay Mutschler	301-322-5300	S	42	0.2
Business Office Supply Co.	816 E Broadway St	Louisville	KY	40204	Stephen Zink	502-589-8400	R	40*	0.2
GBS Corp.	PO Box 2340	North Canton	OH	44720	Skip Dragoiu	216-494-5330	R	40	0.1
Paper Mart	5631 Alexander	City of Com	CA	90040	Mary M Bush	213-726-8200	R	40*	<0.1
Carithers-Wallace-Courtenay	4343 Northeast	Atlanta	GA	30301	GM Brandon	770-493-8200	S	40	0.1
Disc Distributing Corp.	19430 S Van Ness	Torrance	CA	90501	Dan Hoffman	310-787-6800	R	39*	<0.1
U.S. Ring Binder Corp.	429 Church St	New Bedford	MA	02745	Eugene J Angel	508-998-1181	S	38	1.0
Fetco International Corp.	PO Box 165	Randolph	MA	02368	Kenneth McCord	617-871-2000	R	35	<0.1

Source: *Ward's Business Directory of U.S. Private and Public Companies*, 1998. The company type code used is as follows: P - Public, R - Private, S - Subsidiary, D - Division, J - Joint Venture, A - Affiliate, G - Group. Sales are in millions of dollars, employees are in thousands. An asterisk (*) indicates an estimated sales volume. The symbol < stands for 'less than'.

OCCUPATIONS EMPLOYED BY SIC 511 - WHOLESALE TRADE, OTHER

Occupation	% of Total 1996	Change to 2006	Occupation	% of Total 1996	Change to 2006
Sales & related workers nec	19.5	20.2	Clerical supervisors & managers	1.9	20.2
General managers & top executives	5.9	16.4	Order clerks	1.9	8.2
Truck drivers light & heavy	5.4	20.2	Helpers, laborers nec	1.7	20.2
General office clerks	3.6	3.4	Electrical & electronic technicians	1.4	18.8
Traffic, shipping, receiving clerks	3.6	16.7	Blue collar worker supervisors	1.4	16.0
Stock clerks	3.5	-3.9	Wholesale & retail buyers, except farm products	1.3	17.0
Freight, stock, & material movers, hand	3.3	8.2	Office machine & cash register servicers	1.3	20.2
Marketing & sales worker supervisors	3.1	20.2	Hand packers & packagers	1.2	-3.9
Order fillers, wholesale & retail sales	3.0	16.7	Maintenance repairers, general utility	1.1	12.0
Bookkeeping, accounting, & auditing clerks	2.9	-3.9	Industrial truck & tractor operators	1.1	20.2
Salespersons, retail	2.5	20.2	Purchasing managers	1.1	20.2
Secretaries, except legal & medical	2.5	-4.7	Receptionists & information clerks	1.0	20.2
Assemblers, fabricators, hand workers nec	2.0	-3.9			

Source: *Industry-Occupation Matrix*, Bureau of Labor Statistics. These data relate to one or more 3-digit SIC industry groups rather than to a single 4-digit SIC. The change reported for each occupation to the year 2006 is a percent of growth or decline as estimated by the Bureau of Labor Statistics. The abbreviation nec stands for 'not elsewhere classified'.

STATE AND REGIONAL CONCENTRATION

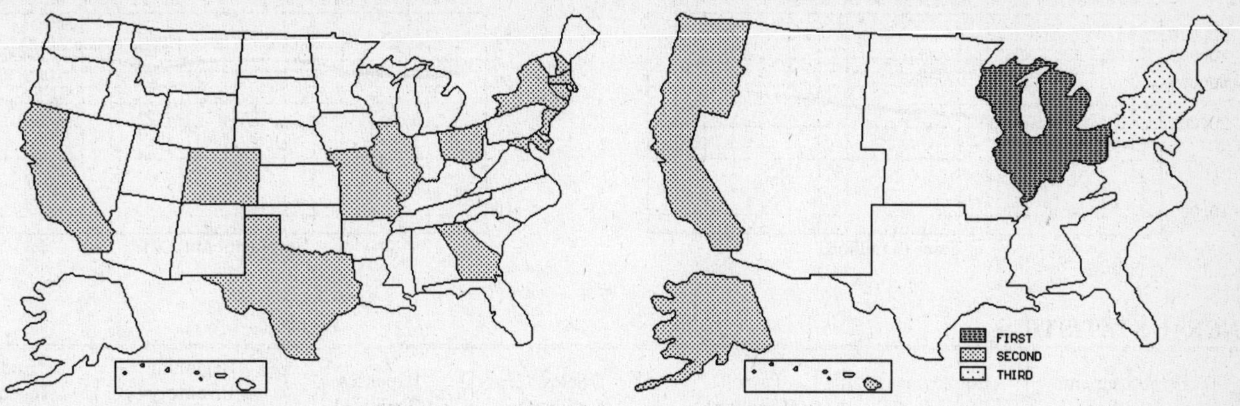

INDUSTRY DATA BY STATE

State	Establishments - 1995 Total (number)	Establishments - 1995 % of U.S.	Employment - 1995 Total (number)	Employment - 1995 % of U.S.	Employment - 1995 Per Estab.	Payroll - 1995 Total ($ mil.)	Payroll - 1995 Per Empl. ($)	Sales - 1992 Total ($ mil.)	Sales - 1992 % of U.S.	Sales - 1992 Per Estab ($)
California	1,103	11.1	23,688	14.3	21	511.3	21,586	4,867.9	15.3	198,862
Illinois	569	5.7	11,920	7.2	21	287.3	24,103	2,760.3	8.7	237,366
New York	688	6.9	10,377	6.3	15	235.9	22,732	2,602.9	8.2	230,122
Texas	755	7.6	13,483	8.1	18	284.3	21,086	2,226.8	7.0	190,279
New Jersey	414	4.2	8,879	5.4	21	199.7	22,486	2,002.4	6.3	189,156
Ohio	431	4.3	12,893	7.8	30	215.2	16,695	1,780.5	5.6	119,113
Georgia	346	3.5	10,856	6.6	31	151.2	13,929	1,776.7	5.6	186,862
Florida	561	5.6	7,879	4.8	14	162.3	20,598	1,287.6	4.1	199,759
Connecticut	152	1.5	1,992	1.2	13	63.4	31,843	1,239.8	3.9	401,995
Pennsylvania	377	3.8	4,278	2.6	11	115.9	27,095	1,022.4	3.2	192,614
Massachusetts	224	2.2	2,851	1.7	13	92.3	32,381	995.7	3.1	245,493
Missouri	251	2.5	4,544	2.7	18	130.8	28,775	882.4	2.8	217,444
Michigan	331	3.3	4,585	2.8	14	116.7	25,455	820.0	2.6	171,080
Maryland	183	1.8	2,601	1.6	14	75.3	28,951	673.5	2.1	216,287
Virginia	222	2.2	2,746	1.7	12	73.2	26,655	582.7	1.8	160,798
New Hampshire	60	0.6	573	0.3	10	15.3	26,775	560.4	1.8	929,373
North Carolina	282	2.8	3,569	2.2	13	90.4	25,338	539.7	1.7	182,098
Washington	203	2.0	2,661	1.6	13	64.3	24,159	466.3	1.5	182,788
Indiana	180	1.8	2,653	1.6	15	59.7	22,512	454.5	1.4	178,533
Colorado	202	2.0	2,464	1.5	12	51.9	21,069	443.0	1.4	199,260
Tennessee	197	2.0	2,696	1.6	14	70.2	26,049	407.6	1.3	163,552
Wisconsin	194	1.9	2,573	1.6	13	58.1	22,566	347.5	1.1	149,546
Arizona	142	1.4	2,242	1.4	16	46.9	20,935	323.0	1.0	218,836
Oregon	142	1.4	1,984	1.2	14	50.8	25,610	301.2	0.9	179,190
Alabama	130	1.3	1,479	0.9	11	30.6	20,698	296.1	0.9	175,327
Louisiana	141	1.4	1,772	1.1	13	37.8	21,335	240.0	0.8	142,836
Oklahoma	112	1.1	1,239	0.7	11	26.7	21,570	221.7	0.7	185,846
Kansas	97	1.0	1,113	0.7	11	23.6	21,187	192.5	0.6	172,301
Iowa	108	1.1	1,236	0.7	11	26.1	21,147	187.1	0.6	125,987
Kentucky	108	1.1	1,100	0.7	10	22.3	20,310	173.5	0.5	146,174
South Carolina	96	1.0	1,112	0.7	12	26.7	23,993	167.8	0.5	129,600
Hawaii	53	0.5	626	0.4	12	15.9	25,454	121.4	0.4	177,934
Nebraska	57	0.6	848	0.5	15	19.2	22,593	119.0	0.4	135,233
Arkansas	65	0.7	603	0.4	9	15.3	25,430	106.0	0.3	166,187
Nevada	60	0.6	735	0.4	12	15.8	21,529	91.8	0.3	168,165
Mississippi	68	0.7	687	0.4	10	14.4	21,022	87.5	0.3	124,407
New Mexico	52	0.5	684	0.4	13	14.0	20,485	76.8	0.2	133,812
Maine	53	0.5	565	0.3	11	14.8	26,165	72.8	0.2	113,357
West Virginia	46	0.5	430	0.3	9	9.6	22,365	53.3	0.2	127,277
Idaho	42	0.4	482	0.3	11	94.6	196,218	46.0	0.1	89,762
Vermont	30	0.3	360	0.2	12	10.5	29,247	42.7	0.1	144,858
South Dakota	30	0.3	236	0.1	8	4.7	19,847	33.8	0.1	112,916
North Dakota	20	0.2	224	0.1	11	4.5	19,987	24.7	0.1	94,210
Montana	32	0.3	199	0.1	6	4.5	22,824	24.2	0.1	95,248
D.C.	9	0.1	90	0.1	10	2.3	25,856	21.5	0.1	143,313
Wyoming	17	0.2	143	0.1	8	2.5	17,455	18.6	0.1	93,377
Minnesota	192	1.9	2,802	1.7	15	72.6	25,914	(D)	-	-
Utah	70	0.7	974	0.6	14	16.7	17,181	(D)	-	-
Rhode Island	32	0.3	260	0.2	8	6.5	25,031	(D)	-	-
Alaska	19	0.2	261	0.2	14	7.0	26,820	(D)	-	-
Delaware	19	0.2	190	0.1	10	6.2	32,879	(D)	-	-

Source: *County Business Patterns, 1995* and *Economic Census of the U.S., 1992*. Data are sorted by 1992 revenues and, if revenues are unavailable, by establishments in 1995. The symbol (D) indicates that data are withheld by the source to avoid disclosure of competitive information. A dash (-) indicates that data are not available or undisclosed because they do not meet statistical validity standards. Shaded *states* on the state map indicate those states which have proportionately greater representation in the industry than would be indicated by the state's population; the ratio is based on total revenues or number of establishments. Shaded *regions* indicate where the industry is regionally most concentrated.

5113 - INDUSTRIAL & PERSONAL SERVICE PAPER

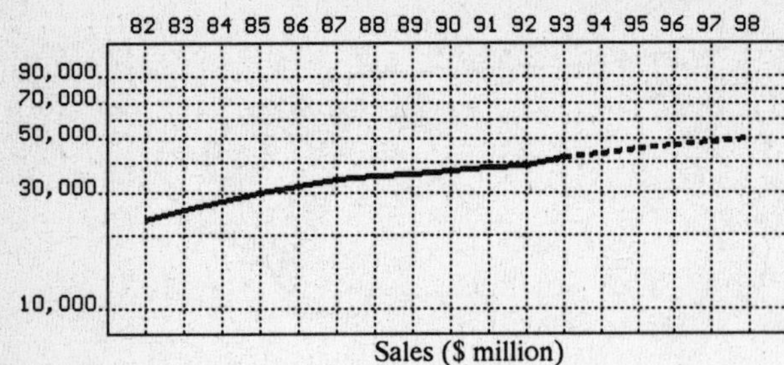

Sales ($ million)

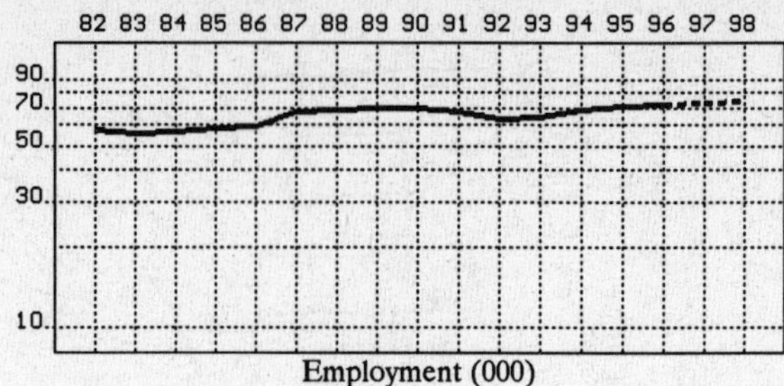

Employment (000)

GENERAL STATISTICS

Year	Establishments (number)	Employment (number)	Payroll ($ million)	Sales ($ million)	Expenses ($ million)	Beginning Inventory ($ million)	Ending Inventory ($ million)
1982	4,473	57,369	1,231.9	23,097.5	-	-	-
1983	4,168	55,152	1,248.5	25,283.6*e*	-	-	-
1984	4,160	56,236	1,367.1	27,469.6*e*	-	-	-
1985	4,105	57,895	1,453.2	29,655.6*e*	-	-	-
1986	3,999	59,329	1,509.0	31,841.7*e*	-	-	-
1987	4,956	67,142	1,798.5	34,027.7	3,351.7	1,092.1	1,188.8
1988	4,728	68,543	2,021.3	35,028.4*e*	3,491.5*e*	1,145.8*e*	1,233.0*e*
1989	4,583	69,539	2,121.2	36,029.1*e*	3,631.3*e*	1,199.5*e*	1,277.2*e*
1990	4,667	69,718	2,227.5	37,029.8*e*	3,771.1*e*	1,253.2*e*	1,321.3*e*
1991	4,619	67,215	2,176.5	38,030.6*e*	3,910.9*e*	1,306.9*e*	1,365.5*e*
1992	5,293	63,567	2,115.5	39,031.3	4,050.7	1,360.6	1,409.7
1993	5,242	64,092	2,126.4	41,971.6*p*	4,190.6*p*	1,414.3*p*	1,453.9*p*
1994	5,388	67,972	2,368.0	43,565.0*p*	4,330.4*p*	1,468.0*p*	1,498.0*p*
1995	5,466	70,805	2,675.1	45,158.4*p*	4,470.2*p*	1,521.7*p*	1,542.2*p*
1996	5,469*p*	71,715*p*	2,667.7*p*	46,751.7*p*	4,610.0*p*	1,575.4*p*	1,586.4*p*
1997	5,571*p*	72,758*p*	2,771.6*p*	48,345.1*p*	4,749.8*p*	1,629.1*p*	1,630.6*p*
1998	5,674*p*	73,800*p*	2,875.5*p*	49,938.5*p*	4,889.6*p*	1,682.8*p*	1,674.7*p*

Sources: Economic Census of the United States, 1982, 1987, and 1992. Establishment counts, employment, and payroll are from *County Business Patterns* for non-Census years. Values followed by a 'p' are projections by the editors. Sales and expense data for non-Census years are extrapolations, marked by 'e'. Industries reclassified in 1987 will not have data for prior years. Data are the most recent available at this level of detail.

INDICES OF CHANGE

Year	Establishments (number)	Employment (number)	Payroll ($ million)	Sales ($ million)	Expenses ($ million)	Beginning Inventory ($ million)	Ending Inventory ($ million)
1982	84.5	90.2	58.2	59.2	-	-	-
1983	78.7	86.8	59.0	64.8*e*	-	-	-
1984	78.6	88.5	64.6	70.4*e*	-	-	-
1985	77.6	91.1	68.7	76.0*e*	-	-	-
1986	75.6	93.3	71.3	81.6*e*	-	-	-
1987	93.6	105.6	85.0	87.2	82.7	80.3	84.3
1988	89.3	107.8	95.5	89.7*e*	86.2*e*	84.2*e*	87.5*e*
1989	86.6	109.4	100.3	92.3*e*	89.6*e*	88.2*e*	90.6*e*
1990	88.2	109.7	105.3	94.9*e*	93.1*e*	92.1*e*	93.7*e*
1991	87.3	105.7	102.9	97.4*e*	96.5*e*	96.1*e*	96.9*e*
1992	100.0	100.0	100.0	100.0	100.0	100.0	100.0
1993	99.0	100.8	100.5	107.5*p*	103.5*p*	103.9*p*	103.1*p*
1994	101.8	106.9	111.9	111.6*p*	106.9*p*	107.9*p*	106.3*p*
1995	103.3	111.4	126.5	115.7*p*	110.4*p*	111.8*p*	109.4*p*
1996	103.3*p*	112.8*p*	126.1*p*	119.8*p*	113.8*p*	115.8*p*	112.5*p*
1997	105.3*p*	114.5*p*	131.0*p*	123.9*p*	117.3*p*	119.7*p*	115.7*p*
1998	107.2*p*	116.1*p*	135.9*p*	127.9*p*	120.7*p*	123.7*p*	118.8*p*

Sources: Same as General Statistics. The values shown reflect change from the base year, 1992. Values above 100 mean greater than 1992, values below 100 mean less than 1992, and a value of 100 in the 1982-91 or 1993-98 period means same as 1992. Values followed by a 'p' are projections by the editors; 'e' stands for extrapolation. Data are the most recent available at this level of detail.

SELECTED RATIOS

For 1992	Avg. of All Wholesale	Analyzed Industry	Index	For 1992	Avg. of All Wholesale	Analyzed Industry	Index
Employees per Establishment	12	12	103	Sales per Employee	561,172	614,018	109
Payroll per Establishment	349,729	399,679	114	Sales per Establishment	6,559,346	7,374,136	112
Payroll per Employee	29,919	33,280	111	Expenses per Establishment	723,071	765,294	106

Sources: Same as General Statistics. The 'Average of All Manufacturing' column represents the average of all manufacturing industries reported for the most recent complete year available. The Index shows the relationship between the Average and the Analyzed Industry. For example, 100 means that they are equal; 500 that the Analyzed Industry is five times the average; 50 means that the Analyzed Industry is half the national average. The abbreviation 'na' is used to show that data are 'not available'.

LEADING COMPANIES

Number shown: **50** Total sales ($ mil): **53,224** Total employment (000): **60.0**

Company Name	Address				CEO Name	Phone	Co. Type	Sales ($ mil)	Empl. (000)
Marubeni America Corp.	450 Lexington Ave	New York	NY	10017	Katsuo Koh	212-450-0100	S	29,000 *	2.2
Unisource Worldwide Inc.	PO Box 3000-0935	Berwyn	PA	19312	Ray B Mundt	610-296-4470	P	7,108	14.2
Martin-Brower Co.	1020 31st St	Downers Grove	IL	60515	Herbert Heller	708-563-0141	S	1,570 *	3.0
Central National-Gottesman	3 Manhattanville	Purchase	NY	10577	James G Wallach	914-696-9000	R	1,500	0.8
Nationwide Papers Div.	1 Champion Plz	Stamford	CT	06921	Thomas V Zeuthen	203-358-7000	D	1,340	0.2
Bunzl Distribution USA	701 Emerson Rd	St. Louis	MO	63141	Rick Snellings	314-997-5959	S	1,250 *	2.5
Abitibi-Price Sales Corp.	45 Rockefeller Plz	New York	NY	10111	RY Oberlander	212-603-1400	S	1,210	1.5
McCarty-Holman Company	PO Box 3409	Jackson	MS	39207	W H Holman Jr	601-948-0361	S	1,040	10.0
Alling and Cory Co.	PO Box 20403	Rochester	NY	14602	S T Hubbard Jr	716-581-4100	S	750	1.2
Zellerbach Co.	3131 New Mark Dr	Miamisburg	OH	45342	Peter H Vogel	937-495-6000	S	685 *	2.2
Chemed Corp.	255 E 5th St	Cincinnati	OH	45202	Edward L Hutton	513-762-6900	P	684	7.9
Unijax Div.	7785 Baymeadows	Jacksonville	FL	32256	Charles F White	904-783-0550	D	600 *	1.7
Perry H. Koplik and Sons Inc.	505 Park Ave	New York	NY	10022	Michael R Koplik	212-752-2288	R	500	0.2
Conestoga Holdings Inc.	72 Cummings Pt Rd	Stamford	CT	06902	J Herbert Ogden Jr	203-977-1139	R	465	0.2
Sofco Mead Inc.	PO Box 2023	Scotia	NY	12302	Jim Gargiulo	518-374-7810	R	380	0.7
Clark Food Service Inc.	950 Arthur Ave	Elk Grove Vill.	IL	60007	Donald J Hindman	708-956-1730	R	325	0.8
ResourceNet International	50 E River Ctr Blvd	Covington	KY	41011	Thomas E Costello	606-655-2000	D	320	1.0
National Sanitary Supply Co.	255 E 5th St	Cincinnati	OH	45202	Charles White	513-762-6500	S	310	1.7
Perkins-Goodwin Company Inc.	300 Atlantic St	Stamford	CT	06901	Robert T O'Hara	203-363-7800	R	300	<0.1
Century Papers Inc.	PO Box 1908	Houston	TX	77251	W Dwight Jackson	713-921-7800	D	266 *	0.5
Unisource-Central Region Div.	1015 Corp Square	St. Louis	MO	63132	Steve Olroyd	314-919-1800	S	265	0.4
Maines Paper and Food Service	12 Terrace Dr	Conklin	NY	13748	Floyd Maines	607-772-1936	R	260 *	0.5
Unisource International	International Plz	Philadelphia	PA	19113	John R Buchanan III	610-521-3300	D	230 *	<0.1
Dillard Paper Co.	PO Box 11367	Birmingham	AL	35202	Joe Strong	205-798-8380	D	220 *	1.0
Cincinnati Cordage & Paper Co.	PO Box 17125	Cincinnati	OH	45217	John F Church Jr	513-242-3600	R	190 *	0.2
Golden State Containers Inc.	6817 E Acco St	City of Com	CA	90040	Dave Oliver	213-887-4266	R	190 *	0.4
Friedman Bag Company Inc.	PO Box 866004	Los Angeles	CA	90086	Alvin Lanfeld	213-628-2341	R	160 *	0.3
SYGMA Network	4000 Industrial Rd	Harrisburg	PA	17110	Gregory K Marshall	717-232-3111	S	160 *	0.2
Ingram Paper Co.	PO Box 60003	City of Industry	CA	91716	Larry Stillman	818-854-5400	R	150 *	0.3
Lindenmeyr Munroe	PO Box 6033	Farmingdale	NY	11735	Kenneth Obletz	718-520-1586	S	150 *	<0.1
Berlin Packaging Inc.	111 N Canal St	Chicago	IL	60606	Andrew T Berlin	847-640-4790	R	140	0.2
Perez Trading Company Inc.	3490 NW 125th St	Miami	FL	33167	J Perez	305-769-0761	R	139	0.2
Albert H. Notini and Sons Inc.	PO Box 299	Lowell	MA	01853	Alex Turshette	508-459-7151	R	130 *	0.2
Prairie Farms Dairy Supply Inc.	1800 Adams St	Granite City	IL	62040	Jim McCulloch	618-451-5600	S	130 *	0.3
Mutual Distributors Inc.	PO Box 330	Lakeland	FL	33802	William D Mills	941-688-0042	R	110 *	0.4
Fisher Paper	PO Box 1720	Fort Wayne	IN	46801	Floyd Sims	219-747-7442	D	87 *	0.2
Bunzl New Jersey Inc.	PO Box 668	Dayton	NJ	08810	Mark Brasher	908-821-7000	D	80	0.3
Henley Paper Co.	PO Box 20408	Greensboro	NC	27420	Nixon C Henley	919-668-0081	R	80	0.3
West Coast Paper Co.	23200 64th Ave S	Kent	WA	98032	Frederick J Stabbert	206-623-1850	R	76 *	0.2
Western ResourceNet Intern	6000 N Cutter Cir	Portland	OR	97217	Jerry Lindsey	503-289-2800	S	75	0.1
Acme Paper and Supply	PO Box 422	Savage	MD	20763	Edward Attman	410-792-2333	R	67 *	0.1
Continental Glass and Plastic	841 W Cermak Rd	Chicago	IL	60608	Richard A Giesen	312-666-2050	R	65	0.1
Kent H. Landsberg Co.	1640 S Greenwood	Montebello	CA	90640	Gene Shelton	213-726-7776	D	65	0.5
Ziff Co.	180 Shrewsbury St	West Boylston	MA	01583		508-835-6021	S	65	0.2
Calpine Containers Inc.	PO Box 5050	Walnut Creek	CA	94596	Ted Rathbun	510-798-3010	R	63 *	0.2
RMA/KOLKO Corp.	20 Jetview Dr	Rochester	NY	14624	Michael I Zimet	716-328-9500	R	62	0.2
K. Yamada Distributors Ltd.	2949 Koapaka St	Honolulu	HI	96819	Gil Yamada	808-836-3221	R	54 *	0.1
United Packaging Corp.	1136 Samuelson St	City of Industry	CA	91748	Gene Raper	818-968-0791	R	54	0.1
Pollock Paper Distributors	PO Box 660005	Dallas	TX	75266	L Pollock III	214-263-2126	R	52 *	0.3
Maine Potato Growers Inc.	PO Box 271	Presque Isle	ME	04769	Joe Lallande	207-764-3131	R	51	0.1

Source: Ward's Business Directory of U.S. Private and Public Companies, 1998. The company type code used is as follows: P - Public, R - Private, S - Subsidiary, D - Division, J - Joint Venture, A - Affiliate, G - Group. Sales are in millions of dollars, employees are in thousands. An asterisk (*) indicates an estimated sales volume. The symbol < stands for 'less than'.

OCCUPATIONS EMPLOYED BY SIC 511 - WHOLESALE TRADE, OTHER

Occupation	% of Total 1996	Change to 2006	Occupation	% of Total 1996	Change to 2006
Sales & related workers nec	19.5	20.2	Clerical supervisors & managers	1.9	20.2
General managers & top executives	5.9	16.4	Order clerks	1.9	8.2
Truck drivers light & heavy	5.4	20.2	Helpers, laborers nec	1.7	20.2
General office clerks	3.6	3.4	Electrical & electronic technicians	1.4	18.8
Traffic, shipping, receiving clerks	3.6	16.7	Blue collar worker supervisors	1.4	16.0
Stock clerks	3.5	-3.9	Wholesale & retail buyers, except farm products	1.3	17.0
Freight, stock, & material movers, hand	3.3	8.2	Office machine & cash register servicers	1.3	20.2
Marketing & sales worker supervisors	3.1	20.2	Hand packers & packagers	1.2	-3.9
Order fillers, wholesale & retail sales	3.0	16.7	Maintenance repairers, general utility	1.1	12.0
Bookkeeping, accounting, & auditing clerks	2.9	-3.9	Industrial truck & tractor operators	1.1	20.2
Salespersons, retail	2.5	20.2	Purchasing managers	1.1	20.2
Secretaries, except legal & medical	2.5	-4.7	Receptionists & information clerks	1.0	20.2
Assemblers, fabricators, hand workers nec	2.0	-3.9			

Source: Industry-Occupation Matrix, Bureau of Labor Statistics. These data relate to one or more 3-digit SIC industry groups rather than to a single 4-digit SIC. The change reported for each occupation to the year 2006 is a percent of growth or decline as estimated by the Bureau of Labor Statistics. The abbreviation nec stands for 'not elsewhere classified'.

STATE AND REGIONAL CONCENTRATION

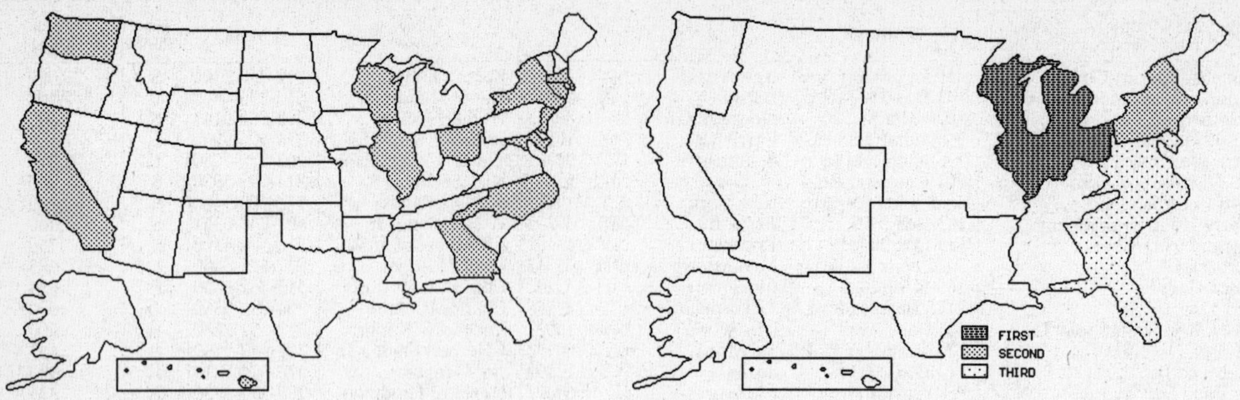

INDUSTRY DATA BY STATE

State	Establishments - 1995 Total (number)	Establishments - 1995 % of U.S.	Employment - 1995 Total (number)	Employment - 1995 % of U.S.	Employment - 1995 Per Estab.	Payroll - 1995 Total ($ mil.)	Payroll - 1995 Per Empl. ($)	Sales - 1992 Total ($ mil.)	Sales - 1992 % of U.S.	Sales - 1992 Per Estab ($)
Illinois	396	7.2	4,605	6.5	12	219.7	47,720	5,180.3	13.7	1,160,450
California	667	12.2	8,714	12.3	13	339.1	38,914	4,747.7	12.5	605,420
New Jersey	365	6.7	3,650	5.2	10	180.5	49,457	3,572.3	9.4	1,002,893
New York	577	10.6	6,880	9.7	12	271.4	39,452	3,369.3	8.9	547,585
Massachusetts	167	3.1	2,483	3.5	15	100.7	40,571	2,022.6	5.3	758,079
Georgia	180	3.3	2,644	3.7	15	119.1	45,043	1,919.0	5.1	789,389
Florida	314	5.7	3,327	4.7	11	112.0	33,662	1,795.6	4.7	549,944
Ohio	233	4.3	4,016	5.7	17	132.3	32,946	1,723.2	4.5	494,452
Pennsylvania	223	4.1	3,469	4.9	16	136.2	39,272	1,693.9	4.5	497,629
Texas	303	5.5	3,569	5.0	12	119.0	33,345	1,598.4	4.2	478,272
North Carolina	155	2.8	1,948	2.8	13	71.4	36,665	1,209.7	3.2	723,081
Washington	121	2.2	1,359	1.9	11	55.5	40,823	888.0	2.3	754,427
Wisconsin	118	2.2	2,725	3.9	23	95.0	34,845	848.6	2.2	745,687
Maryland	91	1.7	1,611	2.3	18	58.9	36,584	743.9	2.0	497,565
Missouri	129	2.4	1,716	2.4	13	61.1	35,603	658.4	1.7	422,562
Indiana	109	2.0	1,528	2.2	14	51.8	33,899	634.8	1.7	504,214
Michigan	143	2.6	1,799	2.5	13	74.8	41,575	634.5	1.7	420,744
Tennessee	95	1.7	1,194	1.7	13	40.6	34,027	615.4	1.6	640,323
Connecticut	102	1.9	1,117	1.6	11	48.3	43,198	522.4	1.4	524,517
Colorado	75	1.4	536	0.8	7	18.1	33,787	464.8	1.2	980,496
South Carolina	49	0.9	732	1.0	15	26.1	35,608	428.2	1.1	564,195
Virginia	63	1.2	694	1.0	11	24.2	34,831	283.2	0.7	344,140
Arizona	62	1.1	609	0.9	10	18.1	29,770	253.0	0.7	471,169
Oregon	52	1.0	562	0.8	11	21.8	38,849	223.6	0.6	512,851
Hawaii	28	0.5	629	0.9	22	18.8	29,944	204.3	0.5	312,356
Alabama	52	1.0	982	1.4	19	28.1	28,571	191.0	0.5	226,577
Kansas	34	0.6	437	0.6	13	14.4	33,043	179.0	0.5	498,604
Louisiana	49	0.9	480	0.7	10	14.0	29,104	165.1	0.4	257,192
Iowa	45	0.8	437	0.6	10	15.2	34,696	149.4	0.4	358,269
Utah	26	0.5	524	0.7	20	14.9	28,433	138.1	0.4	392,429
Kentucky	43	0.8	477	0.7	11	16.1	33,736	131.0	0.3	311,195
Arkansas	37	0.7	475	0.7	13	12.6	26,585	118.9	0.3	243,067
Mississippi	38	0.7	436	0.6	11	11.7	26,924	109.1	0.3	273,454
Oklahoma	33	0.6	490	0.7	15	15.4	31,359	94.5	0.2	261,837
Rhode Island	20	0.4	196	0.3	10	6.9	35,276	71.7	0.2	356,527
North Dakota	10	0.2	172	0.2	17	7.4	43,017	61.1	0.2	315,088
New Hampshire	22	0.4	231	0.3	10	9.0	38,952	52.7	0.1	273,088
Maine	23	0.4	271	0.4	12	6.8	25,129	52.4	0.1	203,093
New Mexico	20	0.4	218	0.3	11	6.3	28,894	49.4	0.1	277,562
West Virginia	15	0.3	259	0.4	17	6.5	25,127	41.8	0.1	209,095
Montana	9	0.2	122	0.2	14	2.9	23,648	16.7	0.0	166,570
Vermont	9	0.2	110	0.2	12	2.1	19,018	15.6	0.0	193,123
Minnesota	95	1.7	1,503	2.1	16	46.6	30,982	(D)	-	-
Nevada	18	0.3	105	0.1	6	3.8	35,990	(D)	-	-
Nebraska	14	0.3	181	0.3	13	3.6	20,105	(D)	-	-
Delaware	13	0.2	181	0.3	14	4.1	22,525	(D)	-	-
Idaho	13	0.2	145	0.2	11	3.9	26,876	(D)	-	-
South Dakota	4	0.1	167	0.2	42	4.1	24,599	(D)	-	-
Alaska	3	0.1	20-99	-	-	(D)	-	(D)	-	-
D.C.	3	0.1	20-99	-	-	(D)	-	(D)	-	-
Wyoming	1	0.0	0-19	-	-	(D)	-	(D)	-	-

Source: County Business Patterns, 1995 and *Economic Census of the U.S., 1992*. Data are sorted by 1992 revenues and, if revenues are unavailable, by establishments in 1995. The symbol (D) indicates that data are withheld by the source to avoid disclosure of competitive information. A dash (-) indicates that data are not available or undisclosed because they do not meet statistical validity standards. Shaded *states* on the state map indicate those states which have proportionately greater representation in the industry than would be indicated by the state's population; the ratio is based on total revenues or number of establishments. Shaded *regions* indicate where the industry is regionally most concentrated.

5122 - DRUGS, PROPRIETARIES, AND SUNDRIES

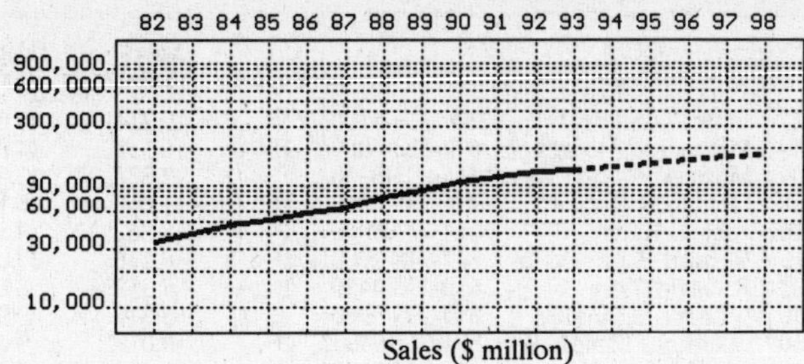

Sales ($ million)

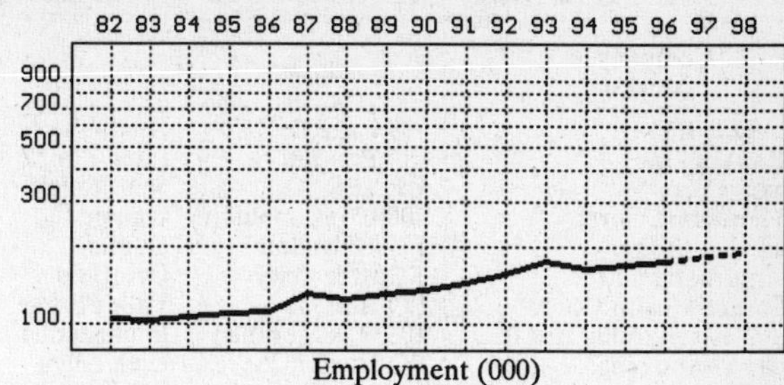

Employment (000)

GENERAL STATISTICS

Year	Establishments (number)	Employment (number)	Payroll ($ million)	Sales ($ million)	Expenses ($ million)	Beginning Inventory ($ million)	Ending Inventory ($ million)
1982	4,005	105,689	1,975.1	33,986.8	-	-	-
1983	3,953	104,832	2,101.4	40,045.5e	-	-	-
1984	3,873	107,850	2,302.2	46,104.1e	-	-	-
1985	4,031	109,647	2,485.0	52,162.8e	-	-	-
1986	4,086	113,161	2,673.1	58,221.4e	-	-	-
1987	4,912	133,102	2,967.8	64,280.1	7,122.0	4,804.5	5,492.5
1988	4,737	126,350	3,395.0	77,337.1e	8,103.9e	5,657.0e	6,350.0e
1989	4,730	133,325	3,674.0	90,394.2e	9,085.9e	6,509.4e	7,207.5e
1990	5,185	136,291	4,179.5	103,451.2e	10,067.8e	7,361.8e	8,065.0e
1991	5,247	145,964	4,775.7	116,508.3e	11,049.8e	8,214.2e	8,922.5e
1992	6,070	158,167	5,380.0	129,565.3	12,031.7	9,066.7	9,779.9
1993	6,362	175,433	6,466.0	131,170.5p	13,013.7p	9,919.1p	10,637.4p
1994	6,587	166,130	6,438.2	140,728.3p	13,995.6p	10,771.5p	11,494.9p
1995	6,891	170,587	7,160.0	150,286.2p	14,977.5p	11,623.9p	12,352.4p
1996	6,857p	178,374p	7,085.0p	159,844.0p	15,959.5p	12,476.4p	13,209.9p
1997	7,099p	184,190p	7,496.6p	169,401.9p	16,941.4p	13,328.8p	14,067.4p
1998	7,340p	190,006p	7,908.2p	178,959.7p	17,923.4p	14,181.2p	14,924.9p

Sources: Economic Census of the United States, 1982, 1987, and 1992. Establishment counts, employment, and payroll are from *County Business Patterns* for non-Census years. Values followed by a 'p' are projections by the editors. Sales and expense data for non-Census years are extrapolations, marked by 'e'. Industries reclassified in 1987 will not have data for prior years. Data are the most recent available at this level of detail.

INDICES OF CHANGE

Year	Establishments (number)	Employment (number)	Payroll ($ million)	Sales ($ million)	Expenses ($ million)	Beginning Inventory ($ million)	Ending Inventory ($ million)
1982	66.0	66.8	36.7	26.2	-	-	-
1983	65.1	66.3	39.1	30.9e	-	-	-
1984	63.8	68.2	42.8	35.6e	-	-	-
1985	66.4	69.3	46.2	40.3e	-	-	-
1986	67.3	71.5	49.7	44.9e	-	-	-
1987	80.9	84.2	55.2	49.6	59.2	53.0	56.2
1988	78.0	79.9	63.1	59.7e	67.4e	62.4e	64.9e
1989	77.9	84.3	68.3	69.8e	75.5e	71.8e	73.7e
1990	85.4	86.2	77.7	79.8e	83.7e	81.2e	82.5e
1991	86.4	92.3	88.8	89.9e	91.8e	90.6e	91.2e
1992	100.0	100.0	100.0	100.0	100.0	100.0	100.0
1993	104.8	110.9	120.2	101.2p	108.2p	109.4p	108.8p
1994	108.5	105.0	119.7	108.6p	116.3p	118.8p	117.5p
1995	113.5	107.9	133.1	116.0p	124.5p	128.2p	126.3p
1996	113.0p	112.8p	131.7p	123.4p	132.6p	137.6p	135.1p
1997	116.9p	116.5p	139.3p	130.7p	140.8p	147.0p	143.8p
1998	120.9p	120.1p	147.0p	138.1p	149.0p	156.4p	152.6p

Sources: Same as General Statistics. The values shown reflect change from the base year, 1992. Values above 100 mean greater than 1992, values below 100 mean less than 1992, and a value of 100 in the 1982-91 or 1993-98 period means same as 1992. Values followed by a 'p' are projections by the editors; 'e' stands for extrapolation. Data are the most recent available at this level of detail.

SELECTED RATIOS

For 1992	Avg. of All Wholesale	Analyzed Industry	Index	For 1992	Avg. of All Wholesale	Analyzed Industry	Index
Employees per Establishment	12	26	223	Sales per Employee	561,172	819,168	146
Payroll per Establishment	349,729	886,326	253	Sales per Establishment	6,559,346	21,345,189	325
Payroll per Employee	29,919	34,015	114	Expenses per Establishment	723,071	1,982,158	274

Sources: Same as General Statistics. The 'Average of All Manufacturing' column represents the average of all manufacturing industries reported for the most recent complete year available. The Index shows the relationship between the Average and the Analyzed Industry. For example, 100 means that they are equal; 500 that the Analyzed Industry is five times the average; 50 means that the Analyzed Industry is half the national average. The abbreviation 'na' is used to show that data are 'not available'.

LEADING COMPANIES Number shown: **50** Total sales ($ mil): **108,322** Total employment (000): **196.4**

Company Name	Address				CEO Name	Phone	Co. Type	Sales ($ mil)	Empl. (000)
Price/Costco Inc.	999 Lake Dr	Issaquah	WA	98027	James D Sinegal	206-313-8100	P	19,214	40.0
SUPERVALU Inc.	PO Box 990	Eden Prairie	MN	55440	Michael W Wright	612-828-4000	P	16,552	44.8
McKesson Corp.	1 Post St	San Francisco	CA	94104	Mark A Pulido	415-983-8300	P	12,887	13.3
Bergen Brunswig Corp.	4000 Metropolitan	Orange	CA	92668	Donald R Roden	714-385-4000	P	11,660	5.1
Cardinal Health Inc.	5555 Glendon	Dublin	OH	43016	John C Kane	614-717-5000	P	8,862	4.8
Baxter International Inc.	1 Baxter Pkwy	Deerfield	IL	60015	Vernon R Loucks Jr	847-948-2000	P	6,138	37.0
AmeriSource Health Corp.	PO Box 959	Valley Forge	PA	19482	R David Yost	610-296-4480	P	5,552	3.0
Bindley Western Industries Inc.	10333 N Meridian	Indianapolis	IN	46290	William E Bindley	317-298-9900	P	5,317	0.9
Owens and Minor Inc.	PO Box 27626	Glen Allen	VA	23060	G Gilmer Minor III	804-747-9794	P	3,019	3.0
Shaklee Corp.	444 Market St	San Francisco	CA	94111	Charles L Orr	415-954-3000	S	1,690 •	2.2
Eby-Brown Company L.P.	280 Shuman Blvd	Naperville	IL	60566	William S Wake Jr	708-778-2800	R	1,450	1.2
Grocers Supply Company Inc.	PO Box 14200	Houston	TX	77221	Milton Levit	713-747-5000	R	1,300	2.0
Nu Skin International Inc.	75 W Center St	Provo	UT	84601	Blake Roney	801-345-1000	R	1,230 •	1.6
Neuman Distributors Inc.	175 Railroad Ave	Ridgefield	NJ	07657	Samuel Toscano Jr	201-941-2000	S	1,200	0.8
Durr-Fillauer Medical Inc.	PO Box 244009	Montgomery	AL	36124	Charles E Adair	334-213-8800	P	951	1.4
Omnicare Inc.	255 East 5th St	Cincinnati	OH	45202	Joel F Gemunder	513-762-6666	P	896	5.0
Nu Skin Asia Pacific Inc.	75 W Center St	Provo	UT	84601	Steven J Lund	801-345-6100	P	679	0.9
Quality King Distributors Inc.	2060 9th Ave	Ronkonkoma	NY	11779	Bernard Nussdorf	516-737-5555	R	610 •	0.8
Affiliated Foods Inc.	PO Box 30300	Amarillo	TX	79120	Benny Cooper	806-372-3851	R	600	0.9
Drug Guild Distributors Inc.	350 Meadowland	Secaucus	NJ	07094	Roman Englander	201-348-3700	R	522 •	0.3
W.A. Butler Co.	5000 Bradenton	Dublin	OH	43017	Steven A Ritt Jr	614-761-9095	R	500 •	0.7
D and K Wholesale Drug Inc.	8000 Maryland Ave	St. Louis	MO	63105	JH Armstrong	314-727-3485	P	479	0.2
AmeriSource Corp. Paducah	PO Box 330	Paducah	KY	42001	Terry Haas	502-444-7300	D	453 •	0.3
Walco International Inc.	1701 W Northwest	Grapevine	TX	93257	Jim Robinson	209-781-3510	R	450	0.8
Clintec Nutrition Co.	3 Pkwy N, #500	Deerfield	IL	60015	Phillip Laughlin	847-317-2800	J	400 •	2.0
Kay Wholesale Drug Co.	1 Alta Rd	Wilkes-Barre	PA	18702	Howard Greenberg	717-823-5177	R	380	0.2
F. Dohmen Co.	PO Box 9	Germantown	WI	53022	John Dohmen	414-255-0022	R	340	0.3
Syncor International Corp.	20001 Prairie St	Chatsworth	CA	91311	Gene R McGrevin	818-886-7400	P	333	2.2
Moore Medical Corp.	PO Box 1500	New Britain	CT	06050	Mark E Karp	860-826-3600	P	286	0.5
Allou Health and Beauty Care	50 Emjay Blvd	Brentwood	NY	11717	Victor Jacobs	516-273-4000	P	285	0.3
Rexall Sundown Inc.	4031 NE 12th Terr	Ft. Lauderdale	FL	33334	Christian Nast	561-241-9400	P	263	0.8
Marmac Distributors Inc.	4 Craftsman Rd	East Windsor	CT	06088	John G Dewees	203-623-9926	S	240	0.1
North Carolina Mutual	PO Box 411	Durham	NC	27702	Donald Peterson	919-596-2151	R	240 •	0.2
Imperial Distributors Inc.	33 Sword St	Auburn	MA	01501	Michael Sleeper	508-756-5156	R	230 •	0.3
C.D. Smith Drug Co.	PO Box 789	St. Joseph	MO	64502	Robert Farley	816-232-5471	R	220 •	0.1
Core-Mark International Inc.	395 Oyster Pt Blvd	S. San Francisco	CA	94080	Gary L Walsh	650-589-9445	R	220	2.2
Warehouse Club Inc.	7235 N Linder Ave	Skokie	IL	60077	Everett L Buckardt	708-679-6800	P	215	0.9
Tamco Distributors Company	365 Victoria Rd	Youngstown	OH	44501	David Schwartz	216-792-2311	S	210 •	0.3
Weider Health and Fitness Inc.	21100 Erwin St	Woodland Hills	CA	91367	Eric Weider	818-884-6800	R	210 •	0.5
Cardinal Health Inc.	42 Ross Rd	Savannah	GA	31405	Larry A Shaffer Jr	912-234-7204	D	200	<0.1
Yves Saint Laurent Parfums	40 W 57th St	New York	NY	10019	Donald J Loftus	212-621-7300	D	200	0.2
Houston Foods Co.	3501 Mt Prospect	Franklin Park	IL	60131	Robert P Pesch	847-957-9191	R	196 •	0.2
Geriatric&Medical Companies	5601 Chestnut St	Philadelphia	PA	19139	Daniel Veloric	215-476-2250	P	192	5.3
Care Enterprises Inc.	2742 Dow Ave	Tustin	CA	92680	John W Adams	949-830-9322	D	192	5.7
Medi-Save Pharmacies Inc.	PO Box 1631	Baton Rouge	LA	70821	Carl J Napoli	504-293-4300	S	180	1.7
Tsumura International Inc.	300 Lighting Way	Secaucus	NJ	07096	Howard Hirsch	201-223-9000	S	180 •	0.6
Walsh Distribution Inc.	5005 State Line Ave	Texarkana	TX	75503	Ron Nelson	903-794-5141	R	180 •	0.2
AMCON Distributing Co.	PO Box 241230	Omaha	NE	68124	Kathleen Evans	402-331-3727	R	179	0.4
Albers Inc.	PO Box 51030	Knoxville	TN	37950	John M Walz	423-524-5492	R	170	0.2
Meyers and Company Inc.	PO Box 787	Tiffin	OH	44883	Robert W Meyer	419-447-7252	S	170 •	0.1

Source: *Ward's Business Directory of U.S. Private and Public Companies*, 1998. The company type code used is as follows: P - Public, R - Private, S - Subsidiary, D - Division, J - Joint Venture, A - Affiliate, G - Group. Sales are in millions of dollars, employees are in thousands. An asterisk (*) indicates an estimated sales volume. The symbol < stands for 'less than'.

OCCUPATIONS EMPLOYED BY SIC 512 - WHOLESALE TRADE, OTHER

Occupation	% of Total 1996	Change to 2006	Occupation	% of Total 1996	Change to 2006
Sales & related workers nec	19.5	20.2	Clerical supervisors & managers	1.9	20.2
General managers & top executives	5.9	16.4	Order clerks	1.9	8.2
Truck drivers light & heavy	5.4	20.2	Helpers, laborers nec	1.7	20.2
General office clerks	3.6	3.4	Electrical & electronic technicians	1.4	18.8
Traffic, shipping, receiving clerks	3.6	16.7	Blue collar worker supervisors	1.4	16.0
Stock clerks	3.5	-3.9	Wholesale & retail buyers, except farm products	1.3	17.0
Freight, stock, & material movers, hand	3.3	8.2	Office machine & cash register servicers	1.3	20.2
Marketing & sales worker supervisors	3.1	20.2	Hand packers & packagers	1.2	-3.9
Order fillers, wholesale & retail sales	3.0	16.7	Maintenance repairers, general utility	1.1	12.0
Bookkeeping, accounting, & auditing clerks	2.9	-3.9	Industrial truck & tractor operators	1.1	20.2
Salespersons, retail	2.5	20.2	Purchasing managers	1.1	20.2
Secretaries, except legal & medical	2.5	-4.7	Receptionists & information clerks	1.0	20.2
Assemblers, fabricators, hand workers nec	2.0	-3.9			

Source: *Industry-Occupation Matrix*, Bureau of Labor Statistics. These data relate to one or more 3-digit SIC industry groups rather than to a single 4-digit SIC. The change reported for each occupation to the year 2006 is a percent of growth or decline as estimated by the Bureau of Labor Statistics. The abbreviation nec stands for 'not elsewhere classified'.

STATE AND REGIONAL CONCENTRATION

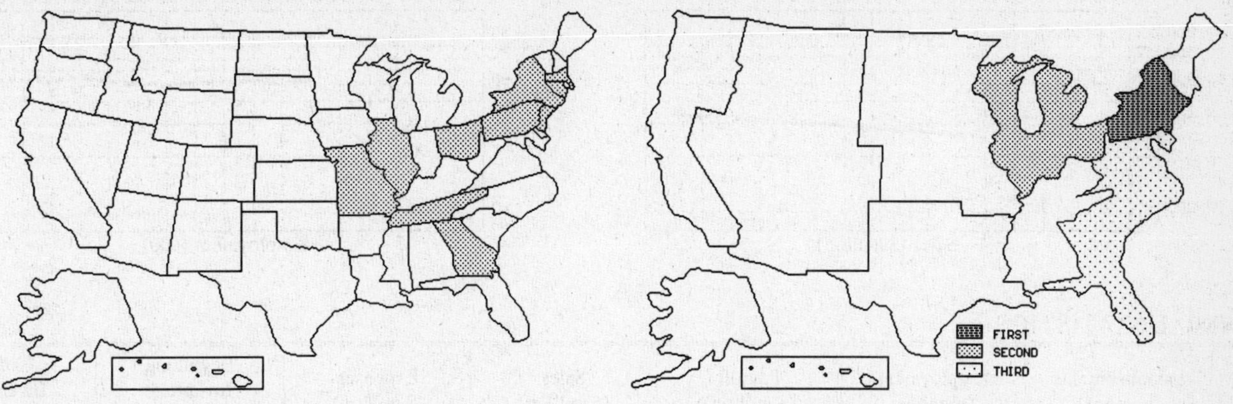

INDUSTRY DATA BY STATE

State	Establishments - 1995 Total (number)	Establishments - 1995 % of U.S.	Employment - 1995 Total (number)	Employment - 1995 % of U.S.	Employment - 1995 Per Estab.	Payroll - 1995 Total ($ mil.)	Payroll - 1995 Per Empl. ($)	Sales - 1992 Total ($ mil.)	Sales - 1992 % of U.S.	Sales - 1992 Per Estab ($)
New Jersey	478	6.9	26,609	15.6	56	1,403.6	52,749	16,375.7	12.9	999,371
California	967	14.0	18,302	10.8	19	748.0	40,869	13,567.1	10.7	758,192
Illinois	285	4.1	10,802	6.3	38	471.4	43,641	13,303.4	10.5	1,195,164
New York	719	10.4	21,516	12.6	30	920.2	42,768	12,744.2	10.0	660,219
Pennsylvania	218	3.2	7,685	4.5	35	484.4	63,034	7,441.3	5.8	928,425
Texas	491	7.1	7,197	4.2	15	306.4	42,572	7,372.3	5.8	916,612
Ohio	203	2.9	6,703	3.9	33	212.0	31,631	6,213.0	4.9	625,242
Florida	641	9.3	7,480	4.4	12	246.8	33,000	5,531.4	4.3	700,883
Georgia	181	2.6	5,841	3.4	32	287.0	49,129	5,214.3	4.1	1,217,449
Tennessee	123	1.8	3,786	2.2	31	114.9	30,362	3,604.6	2.8	801,380
Missouri	145	2.1	3,444	2.0	24	136.2	39,534	3,333.3	2.6	1,215,208
Massachusetts	122	1.8	3,274	1.9	27	116.8	35,677	3,053.7	2.4	778,025
Michigan	126	1.8	2,401	1.4	19	86.1	35,857	2,615.2	2.1	1,137,546
Indiana	106	1.5	2,432	1.4	23	77.8	31,977	2,285.2	1.8	1,171,275
North Carolina	118	1.7	2,584	1.5	22	128.4	49,673	2,199.2	1.7	740,488
Maryland	98	1.4	2,539	1.5	26	104.4	41,104	1,934.7	1.5	906,181
Alabama	88	1.3	1,924	1.1	22	66.6	34,633	1,779.5	1.4	1,153,271
Connecticut	103	1.5	3,530	2.1	34	150.4	42,596	1,731.1	1.4	543,336
Washington	117	1.7	2,472	1.5	21	98.2	39,744	1,708.1	1.3	835,271
Virginia	93	1.3	2,058	1.2	22	66.8	32,472	1,593.8	1.3	846,417
Colorado	114	1.7	1,436	0.8	13	44.2	30,784	1,371.4	1.1	619,426
Louisiana	115	1.7	1,946	1.1	17	54.8	28,174	1,274.2	1.0	761,600
Arizona	132	1.9	1,958	1.2	15	129.5	66,122	1,261.1	1.0	997,670
Minnesota	113	1.6	2,753	1.6	24	95.0	34,519	1,218.8	1.0	540,962
Oklahoma	64	0.9	1,240	0.7	19	30.5	24,565	1,070.2	0.8	927,415
Oregon	84	1.2	1,096	0.6	13	32.6	29,764	997.8	0.8	1,272,751
Utah	81	1.2	2,342	1.4	29	69.4	29,628	905.8	0.7	465,015
Wisconsin	81	1.2	1,893	1.1	23	57.7	30,498	860.0	0.7	616,460
Kansas	59	0.9	1,116	0.7	19	49.0	43,938	760.9	0.6	1,039,471
Arkansas	43	0.6	2,705	1.6	63	70.3	25,999	669.0	0.5	217,714
Iowa	43	0.6	582	0.3	14	21.8	37,405	565.2	0.4	1,066,477
South Carolina	53	0.8	731	0.4	14	19.6	26,756	401.9	0.3	546,091
Hawaii	49	0.7	620	0.4	13	22.4	36,134	349.7	0.3	518,866
Idaho	26	0.4	342	0.2	13	8.5	24,956	302.6	0.2	397,133
Mississippi	37	0.5	531	0.3	14	13.6	25,571	302.6	0.2	516,357
Nebraska	36	0.5	626	0.4	17	13.2	21,149	300.0	0.2	584,862
West Virginia	29	0.4	352	0.2	12	10.9	31,105	279.8	0.2	818,155
Nevada	69	1.0	545	0.3	8	18.9	34,639	184.7	0.1	365,073
South Dakota	10	0.1	89	0.1	9	2.5	27,539	157.9	0.1	770,317
New Mexico	28	0.4	321	0.2	11	12.0	37,352	107.3	0.1	701,216
Wyoming	14	0.2	129	0.1	9	4.5	34,574	104.0	0.1	1,351,078
Vermont	13	0.2	174	0.1	13	5.8	33,138	73.4	0.1	524,150
Montana	15	0.2	20-99	-	-	(D)	-	58.1	0.0	638,835
New Hampshire	18	0.3	100-249	-	-	(D)	-	38.5	0.0	217,763
Kentucky	57	0.8	1,905	1.1	33	53.4	28,038	(D)	-	-
Rhode Island	24	0.3	250	0.1	10	8.6	34,316	(D)	-	-
Maine	18	0.3	234	0.1	13	8.1	34,487	(D)	-	-
Delaware	16	0.2	1,585	0.9	99	55.0	34,717	(D)	-	-
North Dakota	14	0.2	99	0.1	7	2.6	26,242	(D)	-	-
Alaska	8	0.1	100-249	-	-	(D)	-	(D)	-	-
D.C.	6	0.1	100-249	-	-	(D)	-	(D)	-	-

Source: County Business Patterns, 1995 and *Economic Census of the U.S., 1992*. Data are sorted by 1992 revenues and, if revenues are unavailable, by establishments in 1995. The symbol (D) indicates that data are withheld by the source to avoid disclosure of competitive information. A dash (-) indicates that data are not available or undisclosed because they do not meet statistical validity standards. Shaded *states* on the state map indicate those states which have proportionately greater representation in the industry than would be indicated by the state's population; the ratio is based on total revenues or number of establishments. Shaded *regions* indicate where the industry is regionally most concentrated.

5131 - PIECE GOODS & NOTIONS

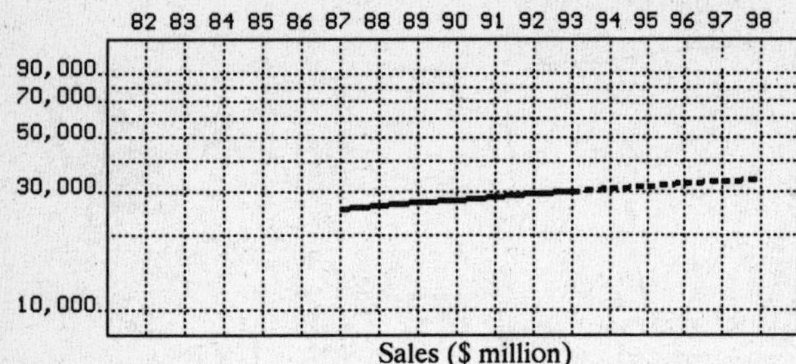

Sales ($ million)

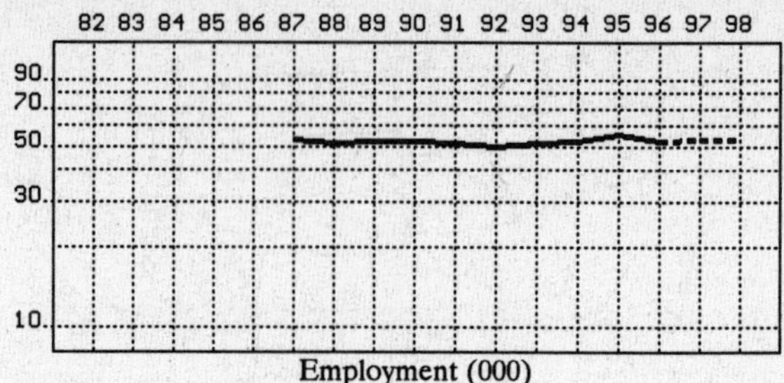

Employment (000)

GENERAL STATISTICS

Year	Establishments (number)	Employment (number)	Payroll ($ million)	Sales ($ million)	Expenses ($ million)	Beginning Inventory ($ million)	Ending Inventory ($ million)
1982	-	-	-	-	-	-	-
1983	-	-	-	-	-	-	-
1984	-	-	-	-	-	-	-
1985	-	-	-	-	-	-	-
1986	-	-	-	-	-	-	-
1987	5,696	52,780	1,424.9	25,667.8	3,058.4	1,723.3	1,908.7
1988	5,189	50,900	1,469.3	26,392.7e	3,195.5e	1,829.1e	2,026.9e
1989	4,802	52,128	1,569.3	27,117.5e	3,332.5e	1,935.0e	2,145.0e
1990	4,738	52,016	1,683.3	27,842.3e	3,469.6e	2,040.8e	2,263.2e
1991	4,755	51,343	1,714.6	28,567.1e	3,606.7e	2,146.6e	2,381.4e
1992	5,640	49,930	1,729.8	29,291.9	3,743.8	2,252.5	2,499.5
1993	5,713	51,215	1,786.8	30,016.7p	3,880.9p	2,358.3p	2,617.7p
1994	5,827	52,100	1,866.3	30,741.6p	4,018.0p	2,464.1p	2,735.9p
1995	5,967	54,971	1,949.1	31,466.4p	4,155.1p	2,570.0p	2,854.0p
1996	5,847p	52,636p	2,002.3p	32,191.2p	4,292.2p	2,675.8p	2,972.2p
1997	5,942p	52,777p	2,065.1p	32,916.0p	4,429.3p	2,781.6p	3,090.4p
1998	6,037p	52,918p	2,127.9p	33,640.8p	4,566.4p	2,887.5p	3,208.5p

Sources: Economic Census of the United States, 1982, 1987, and 1992. Establishment counts, employment, and payroll are from *County Business Patterns* for non-Census years. Values followed by a 'p' are projections by the editors. Sales and expense data for non-Census years are extrapolations, marked by 'e'. Industries reclassified in 1987 will not have data for prior years. Data are the most recent available at this level of detail.

INDICES OF CHANGE

Year	Establishments (number)	Employment (number)	Payroll ($ million)	Sales ($ million)	Expenses ($ million)	Beginning Inventory ($ million)	Ending Inventory ($ million)
1982	-	-	-	-	-	-	-
1983	-	-	-	-	-	-	-
1984	-	-	-	-	-	-	-
1985	-	-	-	-	-	-	-
1986	-	-	-	-	-	-	-
1987	101.0	105.7	82.4	87.6	81.7	76.5	76.4
1988	92.0	101.9	84.9	90.1e	85.4e	81.2e	81.1e
1989	85.1	104.4	90.7	92.6e	89.0e	85.9e	85.8e
1990	84.0	104.2	97.3	95.1e	92.7e	90.6e	90.5e
1991	84.3	102.8	99.1	97.5e	96.3e	95.3e	95.3e
1992	100.0	100.0	100.0	100.0	100.0	100.0	100.0
1993	101.3	102.6	103.3	102.5p	103.7p	104.7p	104.7p
1994	103.3	104.3	107.9	104.9p	107.3p	109.4p	109.5p
1995	105.8	110.1	112.7	107.4p	111.0p	114.1p	114.2p
1996	103.7p	105.4p	115.8p	109.9p	114.6p	118.8p	118.9p
1997	105.4p	105.7p	119.4p	112.4p	118.3p	123.5p	123.6p
1998	107.0p	106.0p	123.0p	114.8p	122.0p	128.2p	128.4p

Sources: Same as General Statistics. The values shown reflect change from the base year, 1992. Values above 100 mean greater than 1992, values below 100 mean less than 1992, and a value of 100 in the 1982-91 or 1993-98 period means same as 1992. Values followed by a 'p' are projections by the editors; 'e' stands for extrapolation. Data are the most recent available at this level of detail.

SELECTED RATIOS

For 1992	Avg. of All Wholesale	Analyzed Industry	Index	For 1992	Avg. of All Wholesale	Analyzed Industry	Index
Employees per Establishment	12	9	76	Sales per Employee	561,172	586,659	105
Payroll per Establishment	349,729	306,702	88	Sales per Establishment	6,559,346	5,193,599	79
Payroll per Employee	29,919	34,645	116	Expenses per Establishment	723,071	663,794	92

Sources: Same as General Statistics. The 'Average of All Manufacturing' column represents the average of all manufacturing industries reported for the most recent complete year available. The Index shows the relationship between the Average and the Analyzed Industry. For example, 100 means that they are equal; 500 that the Analyzed Industry is five times the average; 50 means that the Analyzed Industry is half the national average. The abbreviation 'na' is used to show that data are 'not available'.

LEADING COMPANIES

Number shown: **50** Total sales ($ mil): **47,826** Total employment (000): **19.1**

Company Name	Address				CEO Name	Phone	Co. Type	Sales ($ mil)	Empl. (000)
Marubeni America Corp.	450 Lexington Ave	New York	NY	10017	Katsuo Koh	212-450-0100	S	29,000 •	2.2
Mitsubishi International Corp.	520 Madison Ave	New York	NY	10022	M Numaguchi	212-605-2000	S	10,000	0.7
Robert Allen Fabrics Inc.	55 Cabot Blvd	Mansfield	MA	02048	Ronald Kass	508-339-9151	S	1,260	0.9
Springs Industries Inc.	PO Box 111	Lancaster	SC	29721	Jonathan Murphy	803-286-2491	D	970 •	0.5
Hanes Converting Co.	500 N McLin Creek	Conover	NC	28613	Mike Walters	704-464-4673	S	677 •	0.4
Barrow Industries	5 Dan Rd	Canton	MA	02021	Stephen Y Barrow	617-828-6750	R	670	0.4
Tingue Brown and Company	535 N Midland Ave	Saddle Brook	NJ	07663	William J Tingue	201-796-4490	R	580 •	0.3
Nomura America Corp.	60 E 42nd St	New York	NY	10165	Masami Ikeuchi	212-867-6684	S	422 •	<0.1
Hancock Fabrics Inc.	PO Box 2400	Tupelo	MS	38803	Larry G Kirk	601-842-2834	P	378	6.5
Peachtree Fabrics Inc.	1400 English St	Atlanta	GA	30318	DL Dutson Jr	404-351-5400	R	330 •	0.2
Hallwood Group Inc.	3710 Rawlans St	Dallas	TX	75219	A. J Gumbiner	214-528-5588	P	210	1.0
Arthur Sanderson and Sons	285 Grand Ave	Englewood	NJ	07631	Bill Wagner	201-894-8400	S	190 •	0.1
ATD-American Co.	135 Greenwood	Wyncote	PA	19095	Jerome Zaslow	215-576-1000	R	190	0.1
Majilite Corp.	1530 Broadway Rd	Dracut	MA	01826	Norm Lowe	508-441-6800	R	190 •	0.1
West Coast Liquidators Inc.	2430 E Del Amo	Dominguez	CA	90220	Philip L Carter	310-537-9220	S	180 •	0.5
Helen of Troy Texas Corp.	6827 Market Ave	El Paso	TX	79915	Gerald J Rubin	915-779-6363	S	167 •	0.3
Marcus Brothers Textile Inc.	1460 Broadway	New York	NY	10036	Martin Marcus	212-354-8700	R	160 •	<0.1
L.P. Muller and Company Inc.	1 S Executive Park	Charlotte	NC	28287	RW Hallman	704-552-5204	R	125	<0.1
R.S. Hughes Company Inc.	PO Box 25061	Glendale	CA	91221	Robert McCollum	818-563-1122	R	100	0.4
Symphony Fabrics Corp.	229 W 36th St	New York	NY	10018	S D Schneiderman	212-244-6700	R	100	<0.1
Greenwood Mills Marketing Co.	111 W 40th St	New York	NY	10018	Robert E Kaplan	212-398-9200	D	97 •	<0.1
Carlyle Industries	1 Palmer Terr	Carlstadt	NJ	07072	Gregory H Cheskin	20193565220	P	89	1.2
Joshua L. Baily and Company	PO Box 9501	Hoboken	NJ	07030	RI Bonsal	201-656-7777	R	87 •	<0.1
Burrows Co.	230 West Palatine	Wheeling	IL	60090	George J Burrows	847-537-7300	R	80	0.3
Mainzer Minton Company Inc.	48 W 38th St	New York	NY	10018	Arthur Fried	212-944-3630	R	80	<0.1
Fabricut Inc.	PO Box 470490	Tulsa	OK	74147	Harvey Nudelman	918-622-7700	R	75	0.5
Lucerne Textiles Inc.	519 8th Ave	New York	NY	10018	Douglas Rimsky	212-563-7800	R	75	<0.1
I. Wolfmark Inc.	221 N Washtenaw	Chicago	IL	60612	Stan Leedy	312-826-0600	R	73 •	<0.1
Chori America Inc.	1 Penn Plz, 54th Fl	New York	NY	10119	T Nakamoura	212-563-3264	R	72 •	<0.1
Brookwood Companies Inc.	10 E 39th St	New York	NY	10016	Amber Brookman	212-725-7311	S	70	0.4
ARC Mills Corp.	221 W 37th St	New York	NY	10018	Robert Bender	212-221-8400	R	70	<0.1
Maharam Fabric Corp.	PO Box 6900	Hauppauge	NY	11788	Donald H Maharam	516-582-3434	R	70	0.3
P. Kaufman Inc.	153 East 53rd St	New York	NY	10022	Ronald Kaufman	212-292-2200	R	70 •	0.1
Blumenthal-Lansing Co.	1 Palmer Ter	Carlstadt	NJ	07072	Ralph Langer	201-935-6220	S	68	0.1
Glick Textiles Inc.	PO Box 52220	Houston	TX	77052	Lanny G Glick	713-227-3956	R	67 •	<0.1
John Kaldor Fabricmaker USA	500 7th Ave	New York	NY	10018	Rick Wolf	212-221-8270	S	67 •	<0.1
Plezall Wipers Inc.	9869 NW 79th	Hialeah Grdns	FL	33016	Brian Markowitz	305-556-3744	S	67	<0.1
Atlas Textile Company Inc.	PO Box 911008	Commerce	CA	90091	Benjamin Kaye	213-888-8700	R	60	0.1
Raytex Fabrics Inc.	469 7th Ave	New York	NY	10018	Dan Reich	212-268-6001	R	60 •	<0.1
Edgars Fabrics Inc.	261 5th Ave	New York	NY	10016	Albert Rubin	212-686-2952	R	58 •	<0.1
Warren of Stafford Corp.	46 E 61st St	New York	NY	10021	Pier Guerci	212-980-7960	D	58 •	<0.1
Phillips Industries Inc.	PO Box 1350	High Point	NC	27261	S Dave Phillips	910-882-3301	R	52 •	0.5
Level Export Corp.	1460 Broadway	New York	NY	10036	Nessim Levy	212-354-2600	R	50	<0.1
Charter Fabrics Inc.	1430 Broadway	New York	NY	10018	Joseph B Sacks	212-391-8110	R	49	0.1
Prince Group Inc.	1040 of the Amer	New York	NY	10018	Irving B Prince	212-354-9393	R	48 •	<0.1
Tapetex Inc.	240 Commerce Dr	Rochester	NY	14623	J Goodman	716-334-0480	R	45	<0.1
TETKO Inc.	333 S Highland Ave	Briarcliff Manor	NY	10510	Peter Lohaus	914-941-7767	S	45	0.2
Rube P. Hoffman Company	25792 Obero Dr	Mission Viejo	CA	92691	Philip Hoffman	714-770-2922	R	43	<0.1
Loomcraft Textiles Inc.	645 N Lakeview	Vernon Hills	IL	60061	Ron Frankel	847-680-0000	R	41	<0.1
Allen Brown Industries Inc.	1720 Watterson Tr	Louisville	KY	40299	Reynold Engdahl	502-499-0628	R	40	<0.1

Source: Ward's Business Directory of U.S. Private and Public Companies, 1998. The company type code used is as follows: P - Public, R - Private, S - Subsidiary, D - Division, J - Joint Venture, A - Affiliate, G - Group. Sales are in millions of dollars, employees are in thousands. An asterisk (*) indicates an estimated sales volume. The symbol < stands for 'less than'.

OCCUPATIONS EMPLOYED BY SIC 513 - WHOLESALE TRADE, OTHER

Occupation	% of Total 1996	Change to 2006	Occupation	% of Total 1996	Change to 2006
Sales & related workers nec	19.5	20.2	Clerical supervisors & managers	1.9	20.2
General managers & top executives	5.9	16.4	Order clerks	1.9	8.2
Truck drivers light & heavy	5.4	20.2	Helpers, laborers nec	1.7	20.2
General office clerks	3.6	3.4	Electrical & electronic technicians	1.4	18.8
Traffic, shipping, receiving clerks	3.6	16.7	Blue collar worker supervisors	1.4	16.0
Stock clerks	3.5	-3.9	Wholesale & retail buyers, except farm products	1.3	17.0
Freight, stock, & material movers, hand	3.3	8.2	Office machine & cash register servicers	1.3	20.2
Marketing & sales worker supervisors	3.1	20.2	Hand packers & packagers	1.2	-3.9
Order fillers, wholesale & retail sales	3.0	16.7	Maintenance repairers, general utility	1.1	12.0
Bookkeeping, accounting, & auditing clerks	2.9	-3.9	Industrial truck & tractor operators	1.1	20.2
Salespersons, retail	2.5	20.2	Purchasing managers	1.1	20.2
Secretaries, except legal & medical	2.5	-4.7	Receptionists & information clerks	1.0	20.2
Assemblers, fabricators, hand workers nec	2.0	-3.9			

Source: Industry-Occupation Matrix, Bureau of Labor Statistics. These data relate to one or more 3-digit SIC industry groups rather than to a single 4-digit SIC. The change reported for each occupation to the year 2006 is a percent of growth or decline as estimated by the Bureau of Labor Statistics. The abbreviation nec stands for 'not elsewhere classified'.

STATE AND REGIONAL CONCENTRATION

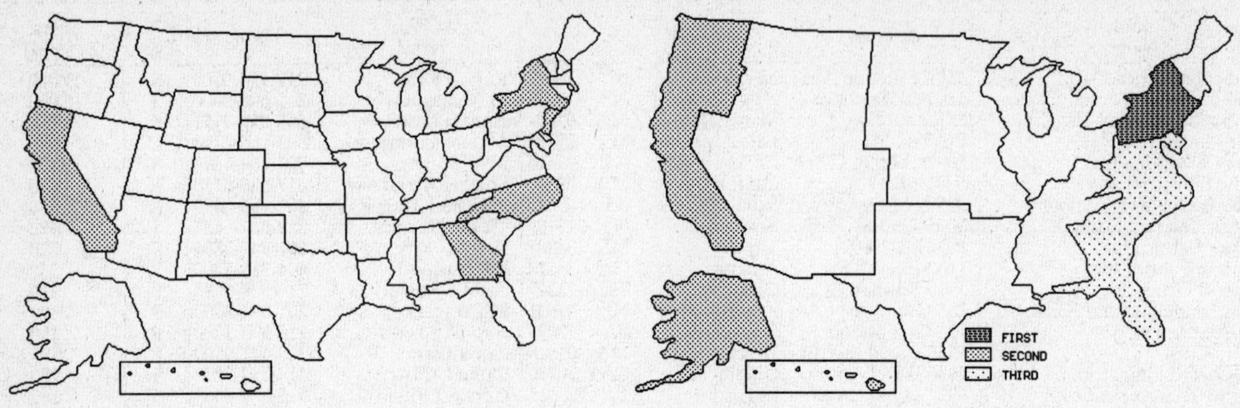

INDUSTRY DATA BY STATE

State	Establishments - 1995		Employment - 1995			Payroll - 1995		Sales - 1992		
	Total (number)	% of U.S.	Total (number)	% of U.S.	Per Estab.	Total ($ mil.)	Per Empl. ($)	Total ($ mil.)	% of U.S.	Per Estab ($)
New York	1,901	31.9	17,490	32.0	9	850.1	48,607	14,651.4	50.8	854,910
California	1,052	17.6	9,335	17.1	9	268.0	28,707	4,533.3	15.7	592,433
North Carolina	315	5.3	2,826	5.2	9	96.6	34,167	1,602.3	5.6	671,839
New Jersey	371	6.2	2,862	5.2	8	107.3	37,501	1,377.2	4.8	377,219
Illinois	183	3.1	1,724	3.2	9	61.2	35,486	937.6	3.3	577,666
Georgia	185	3.1	1,652	3.0	9	54.1	32,770	871.6	3.0	593,298
Texas	224	3.8	1,944	3.6	9	47.5	24,457	841.3	2.9	428,136
Pennsylvania	151	2.5	2,099	3.8	14	59.7	28,464	579.9	2.0	383,271
Massachusetts	105	1.8	1,461	2.7	14	49.4	33,821	572.5	2.0	434,343
Florida	297	5.0	1,862	3.4	6	45.7	24,534	501.1	1.7	278,391
Michigan	74	1.2	776	1.4	10	26.8	34,537	349.5	1.2	440,768
South Carolina	100	1.7	1,740	3.2	17	44.0	25,310	298.4	1.0	364,813
Tennessee	68	1.1	832	1.5	12	23.6	28,422	296.8	1.0	392,046
Ohio	77	1.3	584	1.1	8	18.1	30,971	215.9	0.7	430,930
Missouri	63	1.1	732	1.3	12	24.2	33,008	202.8	0.7	353,951
Mississippi	35	0.6	341	0.6	10	7.9	23,194	142.8	0.5	526,952
Maryland	37	0.6	196	0.4	5	6.2	31,714	112.7	0.4	435,297
Washington	74	1.2	356	0.7	5	14.6	40,899	109.6	0.4	237,640
Indiana	46	0.8	344	0.6	7	9.6	27,802	100.9	0.3	456,679
Connecticut	44	0.7	249	0.5	6	8.7	34,859	93.4	0.3	407,978
Rhode Island	27	0.5	526	1.0	19	14.9	28,335	67.3	0.2	273,585
Colorado	59	1.0	506	0.9	9	11.0	21,779	64.9	0.2	165,671
Oklahoma	20	0.3	441	0.8	22	10.7	24,252	61.5	0.2	121,462
New Hampshire	16	0.3	111	0.2	7	5.7	51,090	58.7	0.2	666,761
Alabama	36	0.6	266	0.5	7	6.5	24,331	54.4	0.2	230,373
Hawaii	26	0.4	185	0.3	7	5.4	29,173	49.4	0.2	211,312
Arizona	35	0.6	196	0.4	6	4.3	21,903	27.3	0.1	160,624
Wisconsin	30	0.5	202	0.4	7	5.1	25,223	27.1	0.1	237,561
D.C.	9	0.2	63	0.1	7	1.8	28,016	16.3	0.1	301,574
Iowa	10	0.2	275	0.5	28	4.3	15,458	14.0	0.0	87,450
Arkansas	12	0.2	48	0.1	4	1.0	21,479	7.7	0.0	113,735
New Mexico	12	0.2	63	0.1	5	1.0	16,159	5.3	0.0	99,057
Idaho	6	0.1	18	0.0	3	0.3	14,500	1.5	0.0	109,357
Minnesota	65	1.1	484	0.9	7	11.3	23,295	(D)	-	-
Oregon	42	0.7	512	0.9	12	10.5	20,486	(D)	-	-
Louisiana	26	0.4	202	0.4	8	4.2	21,025	(D)	-	-
Virginia	25	0.4	516	0.9	21	8.5	16,438	(D)	-	-
Kansas	23	0.4	131	0.2	6	2.9	21,931	(D)	-	-
Utah	21	0.4	212	0.4	10	4.0	19,075	(D)	-	-
Kentucky	17	0.3	129	0.2	8	2.7	21,147	(D)	-	-
Nevada	9	0.2	33	0.1	4	0.7	22,394	(D)	-	-
Vermont	9	0.2	122	0.2	14	3.0	24,623	(D)	-	-
Nebraska	7	0.1	20-99	-	-	(D)	-	(D)	-	-
Delaware	6	0.1	20-99	-	-	(D)	-	(D)	-	-
Maine	4	0.1	0-19	-	-	(D)	-	(D)	-	-
West Virginia	4	0.1	22	0.0	6	0.4	19,364	(D)	-	-
Montana	3	0.1	100-249	-	-	(D)	-	(D)	-	-
South Dakota	3	0.1	0-19	-	-	(D)	-	(D)	-	-
North Dakota	2	0.0	0-19	-	-	(D)	-	-	-	-
Alaska	1	0.0	20-99	-	-	(D)	-	(D)	-	-

Source: County Business Patterns, 1995 and *Economic Census of the U.S., 1992*. Data are sorted by 1992 revenues and, if revenues are unavailable, by establishments in 1995. The symbol (D) indicates that data are withheld by the source to avoid disclosure of competitive information. A dash (-) indicates that data are not available or undisclosed because they do not meet statistical validity standards. Shaded *states* on the state map indicate those states which have proportionately greater representation in the industry than would be indicated by the state's population; the ratio is based on total revenues or number of establishments. Shaded *regions* indicate where the industry is regionally most concentrated.

5136 - MEN'S AND BOYS' CLOTHING

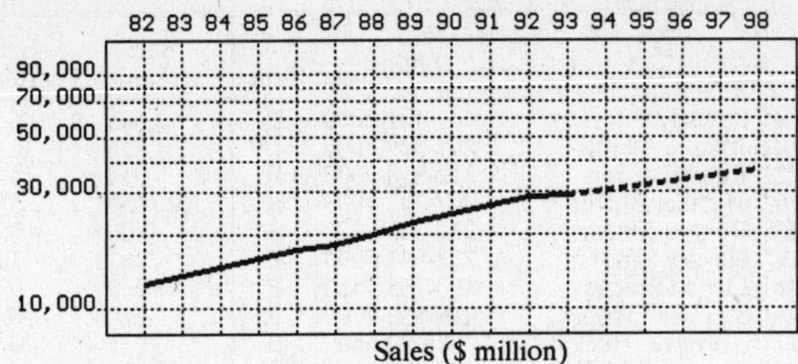

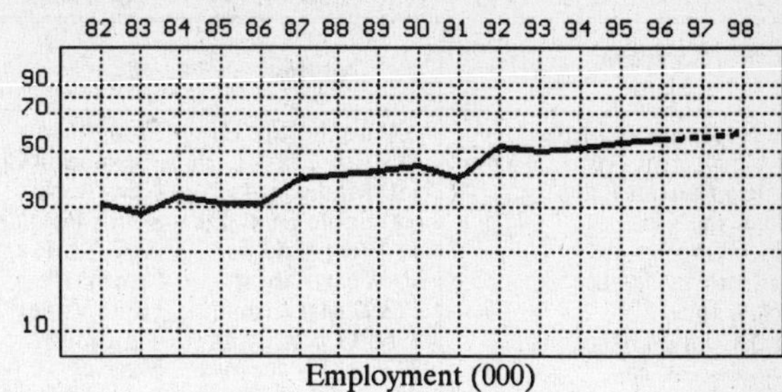

GENERAL STATISTICS

Year	Establishments (number)	Employment (number)	Payroll ($ million)	Sales ($ million)	Expenses ($ million)	Beginning Inventory ($ million)	Ending Inventory ($ million)
1982	2,977	31,074	607.9	12,424.9	-	-	-
1983	2,555	28,309	572.4	13,587.0*e*	-	-	-
1984	2,546	33,197	684.7	14,749.0*e*	-	-	-
1985	2,381	30,728	686.2	15,911.0*e*	-	-	-
1986	2,195	31,058	728.7	17,073.0*e*	-	-	-
1987	3,311	38,773	939.4	18,235.0	2,435.0	1,463.5	1,655.9
1988	2,954	39,894	1,047.5	20,220.5*e*	2,701.1*e*	1,659.5*e*	1,884.7*e*
1989	2,760	41,393	1,169.4	22,206.1*e*	2,967.3*e*	1,855.4*e*	2,113.4*e*
1990	2,765	43,271	1,194.9	24,191.6*e*	3,233.4*e*	2,051.4*e*	2,342.2*e*
1991	2,658	39,150	1,172.8	26,177.2*e*	3,499.6*e*	2,247.4*e*	2,570.9*e*
1992	4,620	51,908	1,527.2	28,162.7	3,765.7	2,443.3	2,799.7
1993	4,368	50,000	1,530.2	28,800.7*p*	4,031.8*p*	2,639.3*p*	3,028.5*p*
1994	4,312	50,764	1,607.9	30,374.4*p*	4,298.0*p*	2,835.2*p*	3,257.2*p*
1995	4,136	53,310	1,675.9	31,948.2*p*	4,564.1*p*	3,031.2*p*	3,486.0*p*
1996	4,285*p*	54,889*p*	1,772.1*p*	33,522.0*p*	4,830.3*p*	3,227.2*p*	3,714.7*p*
1997	4,432*p*	56,847*p*	1,864.2*p*	35,095.8*p*	5,096.4*p*	3,423.1*p*	3,943.5*p*
1998	4,579*p*	58,806*p*	1,956.2*p*	36,669.5*p*	5,362.6*p*	3,619.1*p*	4,172.2*p*

Sources: Economic Census of the United States, 1982, 1987, and 1992. Establishment counts, employment, and payroll are from *County Business Patterns* for non-Census years. Values followed by a 'p' are projections by the editors. Sales and expense data for non-Census years are extrapolations, marked by 'e'. Industries reclassified in 1987 will not have data for prior years. Data are the most recent available at this level of detail.

INDICES OF CHANGE

Year	Establishments (number)	Employment (number)	Payroll ($ million)	Sales ($ million)	Expenses ($ million)	Beginning Inventory ($ million)	Ending Inventory ($ million)
1982	64.4	59.9	39.8	44.1	-	-	-
1983	55.3	54.5	37.5	48.2*e*	-	-	-
1984	55.1	64.0	44.8	52.4*e*	-	-	-
1985	51.5	59.2	44.9	56.5*e*	-	-	-
1986	47.5	59.8	47.7	60.6*e*	-	-	-
1987	71.7	74.7	61.5	64.7	64.7	59.9	59.1
1988	63.9	76.9	68.6	71.8*e*	71.7*e*	67.9*e*	67.3*e*
1989	59.7	79.7	76.6	78.8*e*	78.8*e*	75.9*e*	75.5*e*
1990	59.8	83.4	78.2	85.9*e*	85.9*e*	84.0*e*	83.7*e*
1991	57.5	75.4	76.8	92.9*e*	92.9*e*	92.0*e*	91.8*e*
1992	100.0	100.0	100.0	100.0	100.0	100.0	100.0
1993	94.5	96.3	100.2	102.3*p*	107.1*p*	108.0*p*	108.2*p*
1994	93.3	97.8	105.3	107.9*p*	114.1*p*	116.0*p*	116.3*p*
1995	89.5	102.7	109.7	113.4*p*	121.2*p*	124.1*p*	124.5*p*
1996	92.7*p*	105.7*p*	116.0*p*	119.0*p*	128.3*p*	132.1*p*	132.7*p*
1997	95.9*p*	109.5*p*	122.1*p*	124.6*p*	135.3*p*	140.1*p*	140.9*p*
1998	99.1*p*	113.3*p*	128.1*p*	130.2*p*	142.4*p*	148.1*p*	149.0*p*

Sources: Same as General Statistics. The values shown reflect change from the base year, 1992. Values above 100 mean greater than 1992, values below 100 mean less than 1992, and a value of 100 in the 1982-91 or 1993-98 period means same as 1992. Values followed by a 'p' are projections by the editors; 'e' stands for extrapolation. Data are the most recent available at this level of detail.

SELECTED RATIOS

For 1992	Avg. of All Wholesale	Analyzed Industry	Index	For 1992	Avg. of All Wholesale	Analyzed Industry	Index
Employees per Establishment	12	11	96	Sales per Employee	561,172	542,550	97
Payroll per Establishment	349,729	330,563	95	Sales per Establishment	6,559,346	6,095,823	93
Payroll per Employee	29,919	29,421	98	Expenses per Establishment	723,071	815,087	113

Sources: Same as General Statistics. The 'Average of All Manufacturing' column represents the average of all manufacturing industries reported for the most recent complete year available. The Index shows the relationship between the Average and the Analyzed Industry. For example, 100 means that they are equal; 500 that the Analyzed Industry is five times the average; 50 means that the Analyzed Industry is half the national average. The abbreviation 'na' is used to show that data are 'not available'.

LEADING COMPANIES

Number shown: **50** Total sales ($ mil): **10,456** Total employment (000): **47.7**

Company Name	Address				CEO Name	Phone	Co. Type	Sales ($ mil)	Empl. (000)
Reebok International Ltd.	100 Techn Ctr Dr	Stoughton	MA	02072	Paul B Fireman	781-401-5000	P	3,643	6.9
Russell Corp. Knit Apparel Div.	PO Box 272	Alexander City	AL	35010	John C Adams	205-329-4000	D	1,228	18.0
Polo Ralph Lauren Corp.	650 Madison Ave	New York	NY	10022	Ralph Lauren	212-318-7000	R	910 *	4.0
G.H. Bass and Co.	600 Sable Oaks Dr	South Portland	ME	04116	Michael Blitzer	207-791-4000	S	450	5.0
GFT USA Corp.	11 West 42nd St	New York	NY	10036	Ronald Frafch	212-302-8871	S	400 *	0.6
Nautica Enterprises Inc.	40 West 57th St	New York	NY	10019	Harvey Sanders	212-541-5990	P	387	1.3
Fila U.S.A. Inc.	11350 McCormick	Hunt Valley	MD	21031	Enrico Frachey	410-785-7530	P	295	0.1
Diamond Comic Distributors	1966 Greenspring	Timonium	MD	21093	Stephen Geppi	410-560-7100	R	220	0.5
Warehouse Club Inc.	7235 N Linder Ave	Skokie	IL	60077	Everett L Buckardt	708-679-6800	P	215	0.9
Gulf Coast Sportswear Inc.	PO Box 1498	Lake Jackson	TX	77566	Samuel T McKnight	409-297-7552	R	180 *	0.5
West Coast Liquidators Inc.	2430 E Del Amo	Dominguez	CA	90220	Philip L Carter	310-537-9220	S	180 *	0.5
Izod Lacoste	404 5th Ave, 6th Fl	New York	NY	10018	Bob Cosky	212-502-0349	S	140 *	0.2
G-III Apparel Group Ltd.	345 W 37th St	New York	NY	10018	Morris Goldfarb	212-629-8830	P	131	0.2
Broder Brothers Co.	45555 Port St	Plymouth	MI	48170	Harold Brode	313-454-4800	R	130	0.2
Salomon North America Inc.	400 E Main St	Georgetown	MA	01833	Steve Bagby	978-352-7600	S	130	0.1
South Carolina Tees Inc.	PO Box 66	Columbia	SC	29202	William Gregg	803-256-1393	R	124 *	0.2
L and L Concession Co.	1307 Maple Rd	Troy	MI	48084	Jerome B Levy	810-689-3850	R	122 *	0.5
Amerex (USA) Inc.	350 5th Ave, #7418	New York	NY	10118	Frederick R Shretz	212-967-3330	R	110	0.2
Robert Stock Ltd.	350 5th Ave, #1111	New York	NY	10118	Steven Arnold	212-947-2895	R	100	<0.1
Perfect Industrial Uniforms Inc.	2585 Interplex Dr	Trevose	PA	19053	Steve Zalman	215-638-1330	R	97 *	0.3
Universal International Inc.	5000 Winnetka N	New Hope	MN	55428	Mark H Ravich	612-533-1169	P	88	1.2
Full Line Distributors	PO Box 105432	Atlanta	GA	30348	Isador Mitzner	770-416-4229	D	78	0.2
Ruff Hewn L.P.	827 Herman Ct	High Point	NC	27261	Gary Finkel	910-861-7000	R	75 *	0.2
L.A. T Sportswear Inc.	PO Box 926	Canton	GA	30114	Isador E Mitzner	770-479-1877	P	73	0.4
Alba-Waldensian Inc.	PO Box 100	Valdese	NC	28690	Lee N Mortenson	704-874-2191	P	60	0.9
Scope Imports Inc.	8020 Blankenship	Houston	TX	77055	Allan Finkelman	713-688-0077	R	56	<0.1
T-Shirt City Inc.	4501 W Mitchell	Cincinnati	OH	45232	Mitch Shapiro	513-542-3500	R	55 *	<0.1
Wise El Santo Company Inc.	PO Box 8360	St. Louis	MO	63132	Rudolph L Wise	314-428-3100	R	51 *	0.1
Authentic Imports Inc.	350 5th Ave, #4920	New York	NY	10118	Frank Reilly	212-736-2121	R	50	<0.1
Level Export Corp.	1460 Broadway	New York	NY	10036	Nessim Levy	212-354-2600	R	50	<0.1
Nice Man Merchandising Inc.	8752 Monticello	Osseo	MN	55369	Gary Clark	612-533-5305	D	50	0.1
Grandoe Corp.	PO Box 713	Gloversville	NY	12078	Richard J Zuckerwar	518-725-8641	R	45	0.3
Sports Specialties Corp.	20001 Ellipse	Foothill Ranch	CA	92610	Mark A, Hampton	949-768-4000	S	44 *	<0.1
B.U.M. International Inc.	20101 S Santa Fe	R. Dominguez	CA	90221	Morton Forshpan	310-537-6000	P	38	0.7
Jewel and Co.	9601 Apollo Dr	Landover	MD	20785	William P Jewel	301-925-6200	R	37	0.1
Charles Navasky & Company	PO Box 728	Philipsburg	PA	16866	Edward Navasky	814-342-1160	R	35	0.7
Pine State Knitwear Co.	PO Box 631	Mount Airy	NC	27030	Lindsay Holcomb Jr	919-789-9121	S	35	0.5
Frank L. Robinson Co.	1150 S Flower St	Los Angeles	CA	90015	Harold Robinson	213-748-8211	R	32	<0.1
Morrow Snowboards Inc.	PO Box 12606	Salem	OR	97302	David Calapp	503-375-9300	P	32	0.3
Cooper Sportswear Mfg	720 Frelinghuysen	Newark	NJ	07114	Morton Cooper	201-824-3400	R	30	0.2
Levi Strauss and Co. Henderson	501 Conestoga Way	Henderson	NV	89015	Tim McCubbin	702-564-5555	D	30 *	0.3
Sport Obermeyer Ltd.	115 AABC	Aspen	CO	81611	Klaus Obermeyer	970-925-5060	R	30	<0.1
Famous Mart Inc.	PO Box 220268	Charlotte	NC	28222	GP Sinkoe	704-333-5157	R	27	<0.1
Fairfield Line Inc.	PO Box 500	Fairfield	IA	52556	F Hunt	515-472-3191	R	25	0.2
Foremost Athletic Apparel	1307 E Maple Rd	Troy	MI	48083	John G Levy	810-689-3850	S	25	0.5
Zeiger International Inc.	625 Prospect St	Trenton	NJ	08618	Shelly Zeiger	609-394-1000	R	25 *	<0.1
C.E. Smith and Associates Inc.	PO Box 433	Carthage	MO	64836	Clayton E Smith	417-358-7985	R	24 *	<0.1
Herbert Abrams Co. Inc.	1655 Imperial Way	Thorofare	NJ	08086	Herbert Abrams	609-848-5330	R	23 *	<0.1
Joseph Abboud Co.	650 5th Ave, 27th Fl	New York	NY	10019	Joseph Abboud	212-859-9140	R	22 *	<0.1
Kolon America Inc.	350 5th Ave, #5211	New York	NY	10118	IY Ro	212-736-0120	R	22	<0.1

Source: *Ward's Business Directory of U.S. Private and Public Companies*, 1998. The company type code used is as follows: P - Public, R - Private, S - Subsidiary, D - Division, J - Joint Venture, A - Affiliate, G - Group. Sales are in millions of dollars, employees are in thousands. An asterisk (*) indicates an estimated sales volume. The symbol < stands for 'less than'.

OCCUPATIONS EMPLOYED BY SIC 513 - WHOLESALE TRADE, OTHER

Occupation	% of Total 1996	Change to 2006	Occupation	% of Total 1996	Change to 2006
Sales & related workers nec	19.5	20.2	Clerical supervisors & managers	1.9	20.2
General managers & top executives	5.9	16.4	Order clerks	1.9	8.2
Truck drivers light & heavy	5.4	20.2	Helpers, laborers nec	1.7	20.2
General office clerks	3.6	3.4	Electrical & electronic technicians	1.4	18.8
Traffic, shipping, receiving clerks	3.6	16.7	Blue collar worker supervisors	1.4	16.0
Stock clerks	3.5	-3.9	Wholesale & retail buyers, except farm products	1.3	17.0
Freight, stock, & material movers, hand	3.3	8.2	Office machine & cash register servicers	1.3	20.2
Marketing & sales worker supervisors	3.1	20.2	Hand packers & packagers	1.2	-3.9
Order fillers, wholesale & retail sales	3.0	16.7	Maintenance repairers, general utility	1.1	12.0
Bookkeeping, accounting, & auditing clerks	2.9	-3.9	Industrial truck & tractor operators	1.1	20.2
Salespersons, retail	2.5	20.2	Purchasing managers	1.1	20.2
Secretaries, except legal & medical	2.5	-4.7	Receptionists & information clerks	1.0	20.2
Assemblers, fabricators, hand workers nec	2.0	-3.9			

Source: *Industry-Occupation Matrix*, Bureau of Labor Statistics. These data relate to one or more 3-digit SIC industry groups rather than to a single 4-digit SIC. The change reported for each occupation to the year 2006 is a percent of growth or decline as estimated by the Bureau of Labor Statistics. The abbreviation nec stands for 'not elsewhere classified'.

STATE AND REGIONAL CONCENTRATION

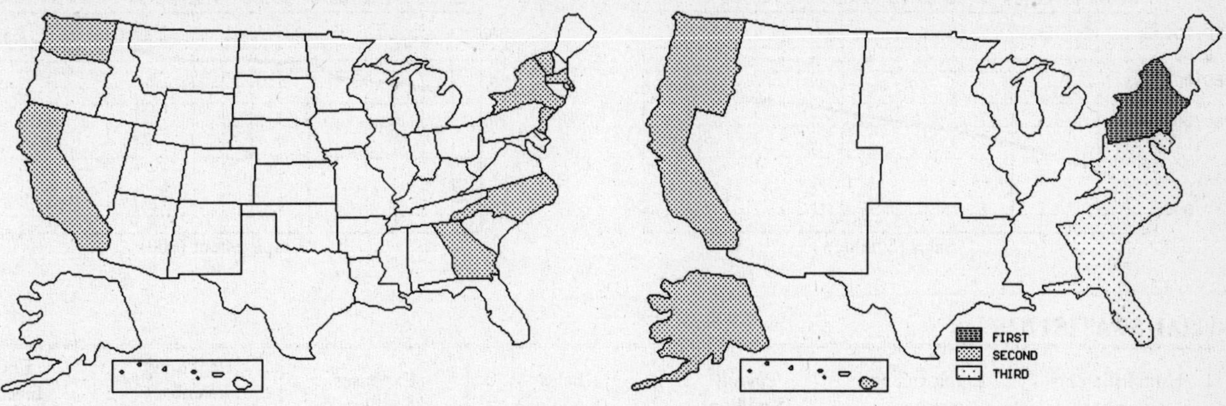

INDUSTRY DATA BY STATE

State	Establishments - 1995 Total (number)	Establishments - 1995 % of U.S.	Employment - 1995 Total (number)	Employment - 1995 % of U.S.	Employment - 1995 Per Estab.	Payroll - 1995 Total ($ mil.)	Payroll - 1995 Per Empl. ($)	Sales - 1992 Total ($ mil.)	Sales - 1992 % of U.S.	Sales - 1992 Per Estab ($)
New York	837	20.2	8,928	16.8	11	382.9	42,889	7,852.8	32.1	778,428
California	678	16.4	9,192	17.3	14	269.0	29,270	4,541.5	18.6	525,885
North Carolina	101	2.4	1,759	3.3	17	40.6	23,109	1,934.1	7.9	1,133,702
New Jersey	247	6.0	4,229	7.9	17	204.0	48,243	1,787.0	7.3	462,006
Texas	239	5.8	2,365	4.4	10	61.3	25,929	1,459.9	6.0	546,147
Georgia	130	3.1	1,831	3.4	14	53.9	29,444	977.3	4.0	563,934
Florida	246	5.9	2,167	4.1	9	54.1	24,987	691.0	2.8	329,070
Ohio	107	2.6	1,949	3.7	18	50.3	25,795	626.1	2.6	340,816
Washington	110	2.7	1,589	3.0	14	51.5	32,431	610.4	2.5	510,349
Massachusetts	91	2.2	1,068	2.0	12	35.8	33,522	605.7	2.5	321,490
Pennsylvania	123	3.0	2,199	4.1	18	61.6	28,033	578.8	2.4	244,030
Missouri	69	1.7	1,182	2.2	17	31.6	26,753	330.3	1.4	348,820
Michigan	56	1.4	1,184	2.2	21	32.7	27,628	295.9	1.2	449,664
Colorado	65	1.6	464	0.9	7	12.6	27,142	245.0	1.0	609,460
Virginia	68	1.6	1,178	2.2	17	26.8	22,784	243.1	1.0	270,087
South Carolina	31	0.7	405	0.8	13	10.9	26,815	241.0	1.0	569,688
Minnesota	71	1.7	624	1.2	9	21.7	34,846	193.5	0.8	330,841
Tennessee	58	1.4	667	1.3	11	17.0	25,426	184.8	0.8	260,230
Connecticut	41	1.0	402	0.8	10	13.1	32,652	135.1	0.6	443,066
Wisconsin	42	1.0	545	1.0	13	11.1	20,435	130.7	0.5	327,474
Arizona	37	0.9	563	1.1	15	13.5	23,972	97.3	0.4	157,689
Vermont	16	0.4	217	0.4	14	6.0	27,553	96.3	0.4	867,910
Kansas	22	0.5	161	0.3	7	6.5	40,540	83.4	0.3	261,313
Alabama	36	0.9	535	1.0	15	8.6	16,088	77.0	0.3	199,381
Hawaii	36	0.9	357	0.7	10	8.2	23,050	73.2	0.3	194,149
Louisiana	22	0.5	568	1.1	26	9.9	17,403	69.9	0.3	110,279
Indiana	44	1.1	380	0.7	9	6.6	17,295	65.0	0.3	170,236
Oklahoma	25	0.6	452	0.8	18	7.9	17,573	52.0	0.2	149,893
Utah	28	0.7	198	0.4	7	3.9	19,929	36.8	0.2	144,455
Iowa	17	0.4	259	0.5	15	4.0	15,544	23.8	0.1	106,393
D.C.	10	0.2	69	0.1	7	1.8	25,928	23.6	0.1	444,792
New Mexico	11	0.3	162	0.3	15	3.7	22,667	20.6	0.1	153,470
Arkansas	20	0.5	338	0.6	17	5.6	16,707	19.5	0.1	244,062
New Hampshire	17	0.4	126	0.2	7	2.8	22,389	18.8	0.1	189,455
Montana	10	0.2	150	0.3	15	3.5	23,347	17.9	0.1	102,684
Nebraska	13	0.3	110	0.2	8	2.2	20,273	17.1	0.1	179,547
West Virginia	5	0.1	65	0.1	13	0.8	12,015	6.5	0.0	80,185
Alaska	3	0.1	20-99	-	-	(D)	-	3.2	0.0	143,636
South Dakota	4	0.1	17	0.0	4	0.3	20,412	1.3	0.0	83,125
Illinois	161	3.9	2,364	4.4	15	73.1	30,943	(D)	-	-
Maryland	49	1.2	769	1.4	16	20.8	27,091	(D)	-	-
Oregon	35	0.8	296	0.6	8	7.0	23,672	(D)	-	-
Kentucky	32	0.8	313	0.6	10	14.2	45,243	(D)	-	-
Mississippi	22	0.5	308	0.6	14	6.8	21,984	(D)	-	-
Nevada	19	0.5	331	0.6	17	9.9	29,958	(D)	-	-
Maine	11	0.3	150	0.3	14	2.9	19,120	(D)	-	-
Rhode Island	8	0.2	22	0.0	3	0.5	20,682	(D)	-	-
North Dakota	6	0.1	47	0.1	8	0.5	11,298	(D)	-	-
Idaho	5	0.1	20	0.0	4	0.3	13,250	(D)	-	-
Delaware	2	0.0	0-19	-	-	(D)	-	(D)	-	-

Source: County Business Patterns, 1995 and *Economic Census of the U.S., 1992*. Data are sorted by 1992 revenues and, if revenues are unavailable, by establishments in 1995. The symbol (D) indicates that data are withheld by the source to avoid disclosure of competitive information. A dash (-) indicates that data are not available or undisclosed because they do not meet statistical validity standards. Shaded *states* on the state map indicate those states which have proportionately greater representation in the industry than would be indicated by the state's population; the ratio is based on total revenues or number of establishments. Shaded *regions* indicate where the industry is regionally most concentrated.

5137 - WOMEN'S AND CHILDREN'S CLOTHING

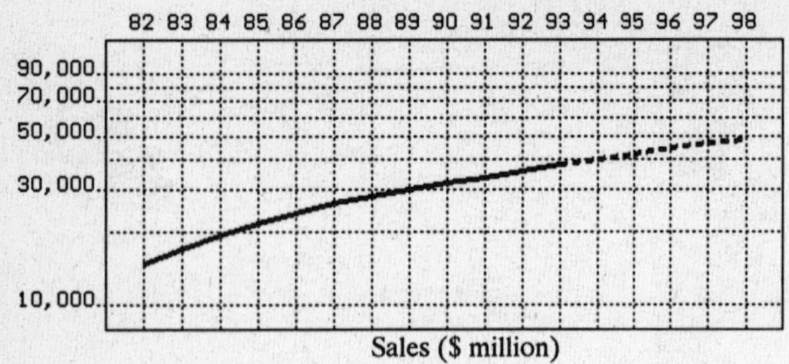

Sales ($ million)

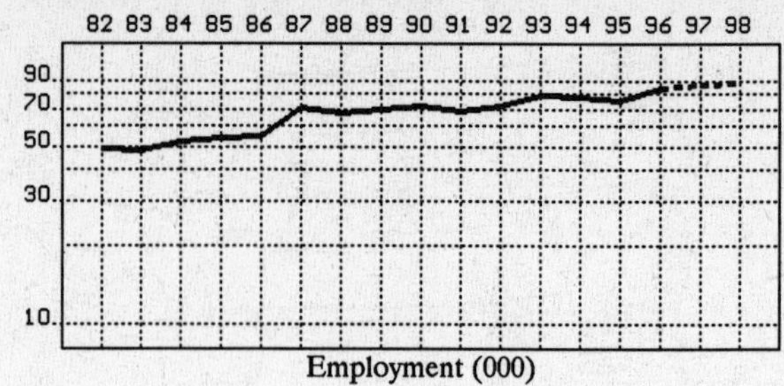

Employment (000)

GENERAL STATISTICS

Year	Establishments (number)	Employment (number)	Payroll ($ million)	Sales ($ million)	Expenses ($ million)	Beginning Inventory ($ million)	Ending Inventory ($ million)
1982	4,942	48,402	891.3	14,582.5	-	-	-
1983	4,520	47,838	947.7	16,922.0*e*	-	-	-
1984	4,405	51,699	1,075.2	19,261.6*e*	-	-	-
1985	4,156	54,257	1,181.0	21,601.1*e*	-	-	-
1986	3,933	54,862	1,292.9	23,940.6*e*	-	-	-
1987	6,234	71,059	1,708.6	26,280.2	4,394.8	2,009.3	2,302.8
1988	5,538	67,385	1,799.4	28,123.3*e*	4,653.2*e*	2,173.4*e*	2,453.9*e*
1989	5,146	69,935	1,932.9	29,966.5*e*	4,911.7*e*	2,337.5*e*	2,605.1*e*
1990	5,194	71,639	2,070.7	31,809.6*e*	5,170.2*e*	2,501.6*e*	2,756.3*e*
1991	5,088	68,742	2,097.6	33,652.8*e*	5,428.6*e*	2,665.7*e*	2,907.4*e*
1992	7,581	72,485	2,384.5	35,495.9	5,687.1	2,829.8	3,058.6
1993	7,449	79,200	2,480.1	38,151.3*p*	5,945.5*p*	2,993.9*p*	3,209.8*p*
1994	7,446	77,736	2,548.0	40,242.7*p*	6,204.0*p*	3,158.0*p*	3,360.9*p*
1995	7,082	75,634	2,534.5	42,334.0*p*	6,462.4*p*	3,322.0*p*	3,512.1*p*
1996	7,496*p*	83,717*p*	2,857.7*p*	44,425.3*p*	6,720.9*p*	3,486.1*p*	3,663.3*p*
1997	7,745*p*	86,204*p*	3,001.2*p*	46,516.7*p*	6,979.3*p*	3,650.2*p*	3,814.4*p*
1998	7,995*p*	88,691*p*	3,144.7*p*	48,608.0*p*	7,237.8*p*	3,814.3*p*	3,965.6*p*

Sources: *Economic Census of the United States*, 1982, 1987, and 1992. Establishment counts, employment, and payroll are from *County Business Patterns* for non-Census years. Values followed by a 'p' are projections by the editors. Sales and expense data for non-Census years are extrapolations, marked by 'e'. Industries reclassified in 1987 will not have data for prior years. Data are the most recent available at this level of detail.

INDICES OF CHANGE

Year	Establishments (number)	Employment (number)	Payroll ($ million)	Sales ($ million)	Expenses ($ million)	Beginning Inventory ($ million)	Ending Inventory ($ million)
1982	65.2	66.8	37.4	41.1	-	-	-
1983	59.6	66.0	39.7	47.7*e*	-	-	-
1984	58.1	71.3	45.1	54.3*e*	-	-	-
1985	54.8	74.9	49.5	60.9*e*	-	-	-
1986	51.9	75.7	54.2	67.4*e*	-	-	-
1987	82.2	98.0	71.7	74.0	77.3	71.0	75.3
1988	73.1	93.0	75.5	79.2*e*	81.8*e*	76.8*e*	80.2*e*
1989	67.9	96.5	81.1	84.4*e*	86.4*e*	82.6*e*	85.2*e*
1990	68.5	98.8	86.8	89.6*e*	90.9*e*	88.4*e*	90.1*e*
1991	67.1	94.8	88.0	94.8*e*	95.5*e*	94.2*e*	95.1*e*
1992	100.0	100.0	100.0	100.0	100.0	100.0	100.0
1993	98.3	109.3	104.0	107.5*p*	104.5*p*	105.8*p*	104.9*p*
1994	98.2	107.2	106.9	113.4*p*	109.1*p*	111.6*p*	109.9*p*
1995	93.4	104.3	106.3	119.3*p*	113.6*p*	117.4*p*	114.8*p*
1996	98.9*p*	115.5*p*	119.8*p*	125.2*p*	118.2*p*	123.2*p*	119.8*p*
1997	102.2*p*	118.9*p*	125.9*p*	131.0*p*	122.7*p*	129.0*p*	124.7*p*
1998	105.5*p*	122.4*p*	131.9*p*	136.9*p*	127.3*p*	134.8*p*	129.7*p*

Sources: Same as General Statistics. The values shown reflect change from the base year, 1992. Values above 100 mean greater than 1992, values below 100 mean less than 1992, and a value of 100 in the 1982-91 or 1993-98 period means same as 1992. Values followed by a 'p' are projections by the editors; 'e' stands for extrapolation. Data are the most recent available at this level of detail.

SELECTED RATIOS

For 1992	Avg. of All Wholesale	Analyzed Industry	Index	For 1992	Avg. of All Wholesale	Analyzed Industry	Index
Employees per Establishment	12	10	82	Sales per Employee	561,172	489,700	87
Payroll per Establishment	349,729	314,536	90	Sales per Establishment	6,559,346	4,682,219	71
Payroll per Employee	29,919	32,896	110	Expenses per Establishment	723,071	750,178	104

Sources: Same as General Statistics. The 'Average of All Manufacturing' column represents the average of all manufacturing industries reported for the most recent complete year available. The Index shows the relationship between the Average and the Analyzed Industry. For example, 100 means that they are equal; 500 that the Analyzed Industry is five times the average; 50 means that the Analyzed Industry is half the national average. The abbreviation 'na' is used to show that data are 'not available'.

LEADING COMPANIES

Number shown: **50** Total sales ($ mil): **12,945** Total employment (000): **51.5**

Company Name	Address				CEO Name	Phone	Co. Type	Sales ($ mil)	Empl. (000)
Reebok International Ltd.	100 Techn Ctr Dr	Stoughton	MA	02072	Paul B Fireman	781-401-5000	P	3,643	6.9
B J's Wholesale Club Inc.	PO Box 9601	Natick	MA	01760	John J Nugent	508-651-7400	P	3,200	11.0
Russell Corp. Knit Apparel Div.	PO Box 272	Alexander City	AL	35010	John C Adams	205-329-4000	D	1,228	18.0
Polo Ralph Lauren Corp.	650 Madison Ave	New York	NY	10022	Ralph Lauren	212-318-7000	R	910*	4.0
GFT USA Corp.	11 West 42nd St	New York	NY	10036	Ronald Frafch	212-302-8871	S	400*	0.6
Fila U.S.A. Inc.	11350 McCormick	Hunt Valley	MD	21031	Enrico Frachey	410-785-7530	P	295	0.1
Diamond Comic Distributors	1966 Greenspring	Timonium	MD	21093	Stephen Geppi	410-560-7100	R	220	0.5
Gulf Coast Sportswear Inc.	PO Box 1498	Lake Jackson	TX	77566	Samuel T McKnight	409-297-7552	R	180*	0.5
West Coast Liquidators Inc.	2430 E Del Amo	Dominguez	CA	90220	Philip L Carter	310-537-9220	S	180*	0.5
Kenneth Cole Productions Inc.	152 West 57th St	New York	NY	10019	Kenneth D Cole	212-265-1500	P	152	0.6
Izod Lacoste	404 5th Ave, 6th Fl	New York	NY	10018	Bob Cosky	212-502-0349	S	140*	0.2
G-III Apparel Group Ltd.	345 W 37th St	New York	NY	10018	Morris Goldfarb	212-629-8830	P	131	0.2
Broder Brothers Co.	45555 Port St	Plymouth	MI	48170	Harold Brode	313-454-4800	R	130	0.2
South Carolina Tees Inc.	PO Box 66	Columbia	SC	29202	William Gregg	803-256-1393	R	124*	0.2
L and L Concession Co.	1307 Maple Rd	Troy	MI	48084	Jerome B Levy	810-689-3850	R	122*	0.5
Amerex (USA) Inc.	350 5th Ave, #7418	New York	NY	10118	Frederick R Shretz	212-967-3330	R	110	0.2
Francine Browner Inc.	5500 E Olympic	Los Angeles	CA	90022	Francine Browner	213-888-6400	R	100	0.3
Robert Stock Ltd.	350 5th Ave, #1111	New York	NY	10118	Steven Arnold	212-947-2895	R	100	<0.1
Universal International Inc.	5000 Winnetka N	New Hope	MN	55428	Mark H Ravich	612-533-1169	P	88	1.2
Andrew Sports Club Inc.	1407 Broadway	New York	NY	10018	Andrew Kirpalani	212-764-6225	R	85	<0.1
Liz and Co.	1441 Broadway	New York	NY	10018	Kathryn L White	212-354-4900	D	84	<0.1
Full Line Distributors	PO Box 105432	Atlanta	GA	30348	Isador Mitzner	770-416-4229	D	78	0.2
Ruff Hewn L.P.	827 Herman Ct	High Point	NC	27261	Gary Finkel	910-861-7000	R	75*	0.2
I. Wolfmark Inc.	221 N Washtenaw	Chicago	IL	60612	Stan Leedy	312-826-0600	R	73*	<0.1
L.A. T Sportswear Inc.	PO Box 926	Canton	GA	30114	Isador E Mitzner	770-479-1877	P	73	0.4
Movie Star Inc.	136 Madison Ave	New York	NY	10016	Mark M David	212-679-7260	P	61	0.7
Tahari Ltd.	525 7th Ave, 21st Fl	New York	NY	10128	Elie Tahari	212-921-3600	R	60	0.1
T-Shirt City Inc.	4501 W Mitchell	Cincinnati	OH	45232	Mitch Shapiro	513-542-3500	R	55*	<0.1
Authentic Imports Inc.	350 5th Ave, #4920	New York	NY	10118	Frank Reilly	212-736-2121	R	50	<0.1
Bag Bazaar Ltd.	1 E 33rd St	New York	NY	10016	David Sutton	212-689-3508	R	50*	<0.1
Level Export Corp.	1460 Broadway	New York	NY	10036	Nessim Levy	212-354-2600	R	50	<0.1
Nice Man Merchandising Inc.	8752 Monticello	Osseo	MN	55369	Gary Clark	612-533-5305	D	50	0.1
North American Fur Producers	1275 Val Brook	Lyndhurst	NJ	07071	Michael Mengar	201-933-3366	R	49	0.2
Nitches Inc.	10280 Sante Fe	San Diego	CA	92121	Steven P Wyandt	619-625-2633	P	48	<0.1
Grandoe Corp.	PO Box 713	Gloversville	NY	12078	Richard J Zuckerwar	518-725-8641	R	45	0.3
Sports Specialties Corp.	20001 Ellipse	Foothill Ranch	CA	92610	Mark A, Hampton	949-768-4000	S	44*	<0.1
Ronlee Apparel Co.	165 Chubb Ave	Lyndhurst	NJ	07071	YW Lee	201-507-5300	R	43*	0.1
B.U.M. International Inc.	20101 S Santa Fe	R. Dominguez	CA	90221	Morton Forshpan	310-537-6000	P	38	0.7
Jewel and Co.	9601 Apollo Dr	Landover	MD	20785	William P Jewel	301-925-6200	R	37	0.1
Pine State Knitwear Co.	PO Box 631	Mount Airy	NC	27030	Lindsay Holcomb Jr	919-789-9121	S	35	0.5
Harry J. Rashti and Company	112 W 34th St	New York	NY	10120	Michael Rashti	212-594-2939	R	34*	0.2
French Toast	100 W 33rd St	New York	NY	10001	Samuel Gindi	212-594-4740	R	33	0.1
Honey Fashions Ltd.	417 5th Ave	New York	NY	10016	Norman Elowitz	212-686-4424	R	33*	0.1
Frank L. Robinson Co.	1150 S Flower St	Los Angeles	CA	90015	Harold Robinson	213-748-8211	R	32	<0.1
Morrow Snowboards Inc.	PO Box 12606	Salem	OR	97302	David Calapp	503-375-9300	P	32	0.3
Cooper Sportswear Mfg	720 Frelinghuysen	Newark	NJ	07114	Morton Cooper	201-824-3400	R	30	0.2
Lanz Inc.	8680 Hayden Pl	Culver City	CA	90232	Alexis Scharff	310-558-0200	R	30	0.2
Sport Obermeyer Ltd.	115 AABC	Aspen	CO	81611	Klaus Obermeyer	970-925-5060	R	30	<0.1
Terry Products Inc.	Drawer 108	Kannapolis	NC	28082	MA Kraft	704-938-3191	R	30	0.5
Famous Mart Inc.	PO Box 220268	Charlotte	NC	28222	GP Sinkoe	704-333-5157	R	27	<0.1

Source: *Ward's Business Directory of U.S. Private and Public Companies*, 1998. The company type code used is as follows: P - Public, R - Private, S - Subsidiary, D - Division, J - Joint Venture, A - Affiliate, G - Group. Sales are in millions of dollars, employees are in thousands. An asterisk (*) indicates an estimated sales volume. The symbol < stands for 'less than'.

OCCUPATIONS EMPLOYED BY SIC 513 - WHOLESALE TRADE, OTHER

Occupation	% of Total 1996	Change to 2006	Occupation	% of Total 1996	Change to 2006
Sales & related workers nec	19.5	20.2	Clerical supervisors & managers	1.9	20.2
General managers & top executives	5.9	16.4	Order clerks	1.9	8.2
Truck drivers light & heavy	5.4	20.2	Helpers, laborers nec	1.7	20.2
General office clerks	3.6	3.4	Electrical & electronic technicians	1.4	18.8
Traffic, shipping, receiving clerks	3.6	16.7	Blue collar worker supervisors	1.4	16.0
Stock clerks	3.5	-3.9	Wholesale & retail buyers, except farm products	1.3	17.0
Freight, stock, & material movers, hand	3.3	8.2	Office machine & cash register servicers	1.3	20.2
Marketing & sales worker supervisors	3.1	20.2	Hand packers & packagers	1.2	-3.9
Order fillers, wholesale & retail sales	3.0	16.7	Maintenance repairers, general utility	1.1	12.0
Bookkeeping, accounting, & auditing clerks	2.9	-3.9	Industrial truck & tractor operators	1.1	20.2
Salespersons, retail	2.5	20.2	Purchasing managers	1.1	20.2
Secretaries, except legal & medical	2.5	-4.7	Receptionists & information clerks	1.0	20.2
Assemblers, fabricators, hand workers nec	2.0	-3.9			

Source: *Industry-Occupation Matrix*, Bureau of Labor Statistics. These data relate to one or more 3-digit SIC industry groups rather than to a single 4-digit SIC. The change reported for each occupation to the year 2006 is a percent of growth or decline as estimated by the Bureau of Labor Statistics. The abbreviation nec stands for 'not elsewhere classified'.

STATE AND REGIONAL CONCENTRATION

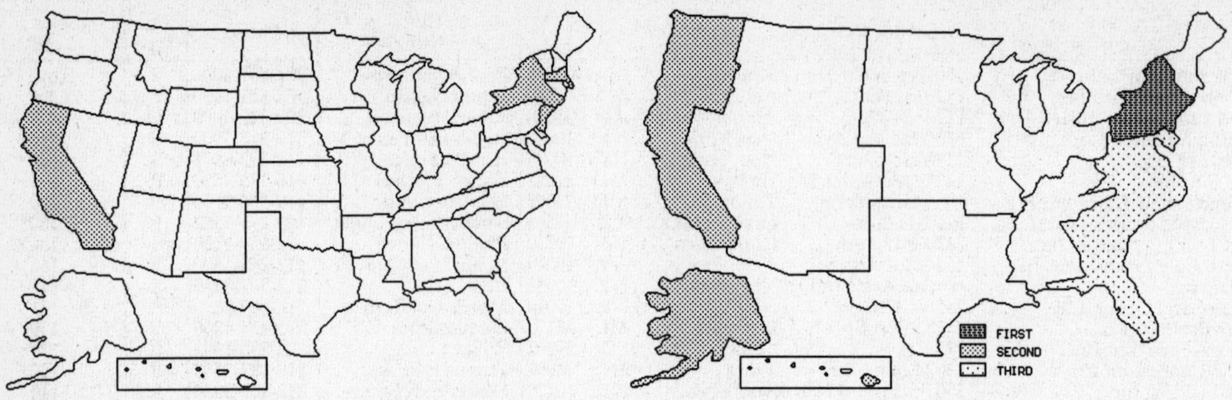

INDUSTRY DATA BY STATE

State	Establishments - 1995 Total (number)	Establishments - 1995 % of U.S.	Employment - 1995 Total (number)	Employment - 1995 % of U.S.	Employment - 1995 Per Estab.	Payroll - 1995 Total ($ mil.)	Payroll - 1995 Per Empl. ($)	Sales - 1992 Total ($ mil.)	Sales - 1992 % of U.S.	Sales - 1992 Per Estab ($)
New York	2,534	35.8	27,335	36.4	11	1,156.7	42,315	16,212.7	46.7	591,099
California	1,372	19.4	13,776	18.3	10	367.7	26,690	4,967.4	14.3	389,935
New Jersey	403	5.7	9,866	13.1	24	354.9	35,971	4,646.1	13.4	454,649
Massachusetts	127	1.8	1,614	2.1	13	76.2	47,186	1,339.4	3.9	1,045,577
Texas	403	5.7	3,141	4.2	8	68.8	21,897	1,257.7	3.6	450,479
Illinois	232	3.3	1,488	2.0	6	44.5	29,937	1,035.6	3.0	589,772
Florida	436	6.2	2,872	3.8	7	61.4	21,372	738.0	2.1	274,130
Georgia	169	2.4	1,008	1.3	6	29.1	28,847	634.5	1.8	737,760
Pennsylvania	141	2.0	1,686	2.2	12	48.1	28,509	555.5	1.6	305,399
North Carolina	132	1.9	1,602	2.1	12	32.3	20,157	500.1	1.4	406,249
Connecticut	38	0.5	558	0.7	15	43.8	78,536	360.2	1.0	957,883
Minnesota	97	1.4	695	0.9	7	18.8	27,049	340.1	1.0	429,982
Oregon	25	0.4	552	0.7	22	20.1	36,406	309.1	0.9	548,108
Virginia	39	0.6	272	0.4	7	7.8	28,651	236.3	0.7	956,603
Washington	70	1.0	818	1.1	12	18.7	22,847	225.4	0.6	210,060
Ohio	71	1.0	598	0.8	8	12.3	20,635	200.2	0.6	674,091
Tennessee	59	0.8	491	0.7	8	8.7	17,725	192.3	0.6	503,437
Colorado	78	1.1	936	1.2	12	23.7	25,353	157.1	0.5	279,482
Missouri	57	0.8	844	1.1	15	22.7	26,923	135.4	0.4	423,100
Alabama	33	0.5	402	0.5	12	8.4	20,823	134.3	0.4	467,798
Michigan	49	0.7	402	0.5	8	8.8	21,806	82.5	0.2	218,323
Kansas	21	0.3	69	0.1	3	1.8	25,435	73.5	0.2	979,360
Hawaii	39	0.6	354	0.5	9	8.6	24,226	62.7	0.2	263,613
Rhode Island	13	0.2	207	0.3	16	4.2	20,155	47.0	0.1	439,000
Arizona	42	0.6	296	0.4	7	5.5	18,449	46.9	0.1	165,774
Utah	18	0.3	290	0.4	16	5.1	17,572	38.4	0.1	297,473
Louisiana	25	0.4	160	0.2	6	2.8	17,425	30.8	0.1	221,424
Wisconsin	26	0.4	400	0.5	15	6.0	15,083	30.6	0.1	84,668
Oklahoma	19	0.3	100-249	-	-	(D)	-	30.0	0.1	138,870
Vermont	13	0.2	168	0.2	13	4.3	25,601	26.1	0.1	205,850
Indiana	41	0.6	205	0.3	5	3.5	17,312	19.8	0.1	131,026
Maine	14	0.2	100-249	-	-	(D)	-	18.0	0.1	154,128
New Hampshire	14	0.2	104	0.1	7	3.9	37,462	17.5	0.1	190,087
Arkansas	15	0.2	104	0.1	7	1.3	12,212	6.9	0.0	74,591
Iowa	18	0.3	140	0.2	8	1.5	10,914	5.3	0.0	125,357
New Mexico	12	0.2	35	0.0	3	0.6	18,000	5.0	0.0	59,107
South Dakota	6	0.1	24	0.0	4	0.2	7,167	1.9	0.0	110,353
Montana	5	0.1	18	0.0	4	0.2	10,000	0.8	0.0	67,500
South Carolina	47	0.7	579	0.8	12	18.7	32,358	(D)	-	-
Maryland	41	0.6	395	0.5	10	7.9	20,033	(D)	-	-
Mississippi	20	0.3	180	0.2	9	2.2	12,239	(D)	-	-
Nevada	18	0.3	156	0.2	9	4.9	31,340	(D)	-	-
Kentucky	16	0.2	285	0.4	18	8.0	28,098	(D)	-	-
Nebraska	8	0.1	20-99	-	-	(D)	-	(D)	-	-
Delaware	7	0.1	37	0.0	5	0.8	22,811	(D)	-	-
West Virginia	5	0.1	18	0.0	4	0.2	12,889	(D)	-	-
Idaho	4	0.1	9	0.0	2	0.1	10,444	(D)	-	-
Alaska	3	0.0	0-19	-	-	(D)	-	(D)	-	-
D.C.	3	0.0	10	0.0	3	0.1	9,600	(D)	-	-
North Dakota	3	0.0	20-99	-	-	(D)	-	(D)	-	-
Wyoming	1	0.0	0-19	-	-	(D)	-	-	-	-

Source: County Business Patterns, 1995 and *Economic Census of the U.S., 1992.* Data are sorted by 1992 revenues and, if revenues are unavailable, by establishments in 1995. The symbol (D) indicates that data are withheld by the source to avoid disclosure of competitive information. A dash (-) indicates that data are not available or undisclosed because they do not meet statistical validity standards. Shaded *states* on the state map indicate those states which have proportionately greater representation in the industry than would be indicated by the state's population; the ratio is based on total revenues or number of establishments. Shaded *regions* indicate where the industry is regionally most concentrated.

5139 - FOOTWEAR

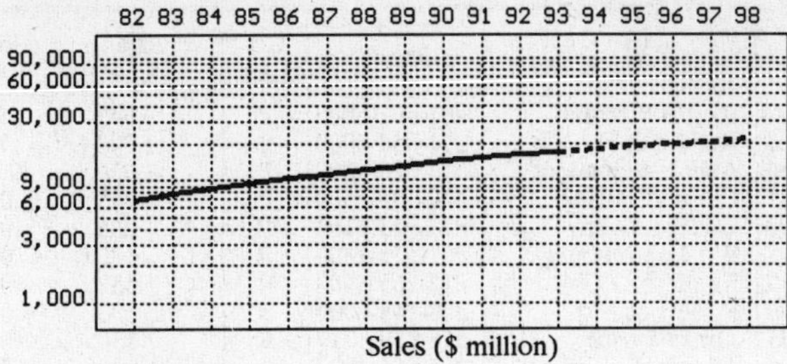

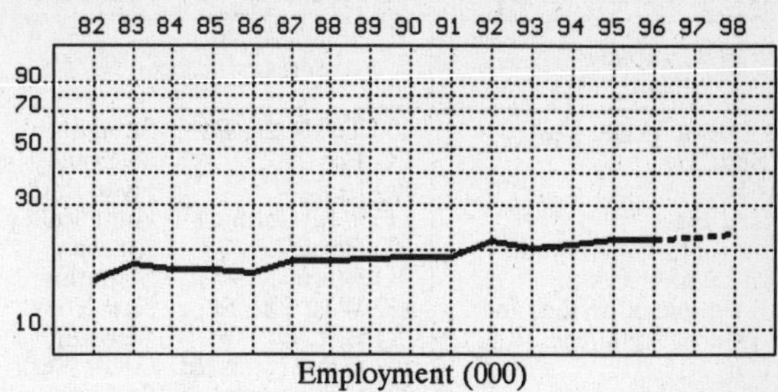

GENERAL STATISTICS

Year	Establishments (number)	Employment (number)	Payroll ($ million)	Sales ($ million)	Expenses ($ million)	Beginning Inventory ($ million)	Ending Inventory ($ million)
1982	1,503	15,395	357.4	6,881.6	-	-	-
1983	1,457	17,742	399.5	7,763.9e	-	-	-
1984	1,384	16,831	432.8	8,646.2e	-	-	-
1985	1,337	16,903	455.8	9,528.5e	-	-	-
1986	1,260	16,219	457.8	10,410.8e	-	-	-
1987	1,694	18,179	588.3	11,293.1	1,662.2	1,146.7	1,308.5
1988	1,535	18,103	610.3	12,284.9e	1,865.7e	1,309.0e	1,436.0e
1989	1,415	18,554	629.5	13,276.8e	2,069.2e	1,471.3e	1,563.5e
1990	1,386	18,775	702.6	14,268.7e	2,272.6e	1,633.6e	1,691.0e
1991	1,327	18,934	738.6	15,260.5e	2,476.1e	1,795.9e	1,818.5e
1992	1,712	21,826	880.2	16,252.4	2,679.6	1,958.3	1,946.1
1993	1,659	20,516	853.7	17,065.0p	2,883.0p	2,120.6p	2,073.6p
1994	1,665	21,191	947.1	18,002.0p	3,086.5p	2,282.9p	2,201.1p
1995	1,609	22,105	1,009.6	18,939.1p	3,290.0p	2,445.2p	2,328.6p
1996	1,629p	22,101p	1,027.0p	19,876.2p	3,493.5p	2,607.5p	2,456.2p
1997	1,646p	22,559p	1,077.6p	20,813.3p	3,696.9p	2,769.8p	2,583.7p
1998	1,664p	23,018p	1,128.2p	21,750.3p	3,900.4p	2,932.1p	2,711.2p

Sources: Economic Census of the United States, 1982, 1987, and 1992. Establishment counts, employment, and payroll are from *County Business Patterns* for non-Census years. Values followed by a 'p' are projections by the editors. Sales and expense data for non-Census years are extrapolations, marked by 'e'. Industries reclassified in 1987 will not have data for prior years. Data are the most recent available at this level of detail.

INDICES OF CHANGE

Year	Establishments (number)	Employment (number)	Payroll ($ million)	Sales ($ million)	Expenses ($ million)	Beginning Inventory ($ million)	Ending Inventory ($ million)
1982	87.8	70.5	40.6	42.3	-	-	-
1983	85.1	81.3	45.4	47.8e	-	-	-
1984	80.8	77.1	49.2	53.2e	-	-	-
1985	78.1	77.4	51.8	58.6e	-	-	-
1986	73.6	74.3	52.0	64.1e	-	-	-
1987	98.9	83.3	66.8	69.5	62.0	58.6	67.2
1988	89.7	82.9	69.3	75.6e	69.6e	66.8e	73.8e
1989	82.7	85.0	71.5	81.7e	77.2e	75.1e	80.3e
1990	81.0	86.0	79.8	87.8e	84.8e	83.4e	86.9e
1991	77.5	86.7	83.9	93.9e	92.4e	91.7e	93.4e
1992	100.0	100.0	100.0	100.0	100.0	100.0	100.0
1993	96.9	94.0	97.0	105.0p	107.6p	108.3p	106.6p
1994	97.3	97.1	107.6	110.8p	115.2p	116.6p	113.1p
1995	94.0	101.3	114.7	116.5p	122.8p	124.9p	119.7p
1996	95.1p	101.3p	116.7p	122.3p	130.4p	133.2p	126.2p
1997	96.2p	103.4p	122.4p	128.1p	138.0p	141.4p	132.8p
1998	97.2p	105.5p	128.2p	133.8p	145.6p	149.7p	139.3p

Sources: Same as General Statistics. The values shown reflect change from the base year, 1992. Values above 100 mean greater than 1992, values below 100 mean less than 1992, and a value of 100 in the 1982-91 or 1993-98 period means same as 1992. Values followed by a 'p' are projections by the editors; 'e' stands for extrapolation. Data are the most recent available at this level of detail.

SELECTED RATIOS

For 1992	Avg. of All Wholesale	Analyzed Industry	Index	For 1992	Avg. of All Wholesale	Analyzed Industry	Index
Employees per Establishment	12	13	109	Sales per Employee	561,172	744,635	133
Payroll per Establishment	349,729	514,136	147	Sales per Establishment	6,559,346	9,493,224	145
Payroll per Employee	29,919	40,328	135	Expenses per Establishment	723,071	1,565,187	216

Sources: Same as General Statistics. The 'Average of All Manufacturing' column represents the average of all manufacturing industries reported for the most recent complete year available. The Index shows the relationship between the Average and the Analyzed Industry. For example, 100 means that they are equal; 500 that the Analyzed Industry is five times the average; 50 means that the Analyzed Industry is half the national average. The abbreviation 'na' is used to show that data are 'not available'.

LEADING COMPANIES

Number shown: **48** Total sales ($ mil): **9,058** Total employment (000): **28.0**

Company Name	Address				CEO Name	Phone	Co. Type	Sales ($ mil)	Empl. (000)
Reebok International Ltd.	100 Techn Ctr Dr	Stoughton	MA	02072	Paul B Fireman	781-401-5000	P	3,643	6.9
Brown Shoe Co.	PO Box 29	St. Louis	MO	63166	Ronald A Fromm	314-854-4000	S	1,808*	3.0
J. Baker Inc.	PO Box 231	Hyde Park	MA	02136	Alan I Weinstein	617-828-9300	P	1,020	11.6
Fila U.S.A. Inc.	11350 McCormick	Hunt Valley	MD	21031	Enrico Frachey	410-785-7530	P	295	0.1
Items International Airwalk	PO Box 951	Altoona	PA	16603	George Yohn	814-943-6164	R	236*	0.1
Southern Leather Co.	PO Box 6	Memphis	TN	38101	W I Loewenberg	901-525-1200	R	180*	0.3
Kenneth Cole Productions Inc.	152 West 57th St	New York	NY	10019	Kenneth D Cole	212-265-1500	P	152	0.6
B-W-A International Inc.	PO Box 70	Webster	MA	01570	Robert M Siff	508-943-6000	R	130	<0.1
Jimlar Corp.	160 Great Neck Rd	Great Neck	NY	11021	James Tarica	516-829-1717	R	130	0.1
Pagoda Trading Co.	8300 Maryland Ave	St. Louis	MO	63105	Thomas A William	314-854-4000	S	120*	0.2
AmAsia International Ltd.	34 3rd Ave	Burlington	MA	01803	Norman Finn	781-229-6611	R	100*	0.2
Elan-Polo Inc.	1699 S Hanley Rd	St. Louis	MO	63144	Joe Russell	314-645-3018	R	100*	0.3
Chernin Shoe Inc.	1001 S Clinton St	Chicago	IL	60607	Steve Larrick	312-922-5900	R	90*	0.9
Birkenstock Footprint Sandals	PO Box 6140	Novato	CA	94948	Margot Fraser	415-892-4200	R	81*	0.1
Bostonian Shoe Co.	520 S Broad St	Kennett Square	PA	19348	Robert Landerman	215-444-6550	S	70	<0.1
Aerogroup International Inc.	201 Meadow Rd	Edison	NJ	08817	Jules Schneider	732-985-6900	R	61*	0.1
SBC/Sporto Corp.	2 Midway St	Boston	MA	02210	James Brilliant	617-426-2121	R	60*	0.1
Impo International Inc.	PO Drawer 639	Santa Maria	CA	93456	Eric Keeler	805-922-7753	R	58*	<0.1
Bally Retail Inc.	1 Bally Pl	New Rochelle	NY	10801	Merle Sloss	914-632-4444	R	54*	0.6
Iron Age Corp.	Robinsonaza Three	Pittsburgh	PA	15205	William J Mills	412-787-4100	R	50	0.4
Candie's Inc.	2975 Westchester	Purchase	NY	10577	Neil Cole	914-694-8600	P	45	<0.1
Hush Puppies Co.	9341 Courtland Dr	Rockford	MI	49351	Louis A Dubrow	616-866-5500	D	45*	<0.1
Twyman Templeton Company	PO Box 4490	Columbus	OH	43204	Donald Lewis	614-272-5623	R	45	<0.1
Lehigh Safety Shoe Co.	1100 E Main St	Endicott	NY	13760	Alan R Hutson	607-754-7980	S	40	0.2
Street Cars Inc.	35 Eastman St	South Easton	MA	02375	Charles Wang	508-230-7256	R	40*	<0.1
Jasmine Ltd.	130 Twinbridge Dr	Pennsauken	NJ	08109	Irving M Mangel	609-665-7117	P	31	<0.1
Hi-Tec Sports USA Inc.	4801 Stoddard Rd	Modesto	CA	95356	Terry MacKness	209-545-1111	R	30	<0.1
Wolff Shoe Co.	1705 L Williams	Fenton	MO	63026	Gary Wolff	314-343-7770	R	30*	<0.1
Foremost Athletic Apparel	1307 E Maple Rd	Troy	MI	48083	John G Levy	810-689-3850	S	25	0.5
Zeiger International Inc.	625 Prospect St	Trenton	NJ	08618	Shelly Zeiger	609-394-1000	R	25*	<0.1
Angel-Etts Inc.	5900 Rodeo Rd	Los Angeles	CA	90016	Louis Jackson	213-870-4637	R	24*	<0.1
Shtofman Company Inc.	PO Box 4758	Tyler	TX	75712	Norman Shtofman	903-592-0861	R	22	0.3
LJO Inc.	401 Hamburg Tpk	Wayne	NJ	07470	Leif J Ostberg	201-956-6990	R	21*	<0.1
Schwartz and Benjamin Inc.	100 Marine Blvd	Lynn	MA	01901	Arthur R Schwartz	617-595-5600	R	20	<0.1
Tober Industries Inc.	1520 Washington	St. Louis	MO	63103	Lester Tober	314-421-2030	R	20	<0.1
Baris Shoe Company Inc.	47 W 34th St	New York	NY	10001	Seth Gaffin	212-594-9750	R	17*	<0.1
B. Klitzner and Son Inc.	PO Box 1357	Rocky Mount	NC	27802	David Jay	919-442-5740	R	16*	<0.1
D. Myers and Sons Inc.	4311 Erdman Ave	Baltimore	MD	21213	E Carey Ries	410-522-7500	R	16	<0.1
Inter-Pacific Corp.	2257 Colby Ave	Los Angeles	CA	90064	Frank Arnsteine	310-473-7591	R	15*	<0.1
Kaepa Inc.	5410 Kaepa Ct	San Antonio	TX	78218	Frank Legacki	210-661-7463	R	15	<0.1
Super Shoe Stores Inc.	PO Box 239	Cumberland	MD	21502	Rick Alteer	301-759-4300	R	14*	0.2
Bob Levine Shoes Inc.	20 Aquarium Dr	Secaucus	NJ	07094	Robert Levine	201-864-2057	R	12	<0.1
Pro-Trak Corp.	PO Box 79	Prentice	WI	54556	Faye Enders	715-428-2886	R	12*	<0.1
Trans-World Shoe Import Corp.	1809 Clarkson Rd	Chesterfield	MO	63017	James Richter	314-532-3361	R	12*	<0.1
Cable and Company Worldwide	724 5th Ave	New York	NY	10019	David Albahari	212-489-9686	P	10	<0.1
Garpac Corp.	462 Seventh Ave	New York	NY	10018	David Roth	212-760-0070	R	10	<0.1
E.T. Wright and Co.	141 Longwater Dr	Norwell	MA	02061	G MacNaughton	617-878-0420	D	8	<0.1
L.B. Evans Son Co.	1 Oak Hill Rd	Fitchburg	MA	01420	Kenneth Ansin	508-342-6092	R	1*	<0.1

Source: *Ward's Business Directory of U.S. Private and Public Companies*, 1998. The company type code used is as follows: P - Public, R - Private, S - Subsidiary, D - Division, J - Joint Venture, A - Affiliate, G - Group. Sales are in millions of dollars, employees are in thousands. An asterisk (*) indicates an estimated sales volume. The symbol < stands for 'less than'.

OCCUPATIONS EMPLOYED BY SIC 513 - WHOLESALE TRADE, OTHER

Occupation	% of Total 1996	Change to 2006	Occupation	% of Total 1996	Change to 2006
Sales & related workers nec	19.5	20.2	Clerical supervisors & managers	1.9	20.2
General managers & top executives	5.9	16.4	Order clerks	1.9	8.2
Truck drivers light & heavy	5.4	20.2	Helpers, laborers nec	1.7	20.2
General office clerks	3.6	3.4	Electrical & electronic technicians	1.4	18.8
Traffic, shipping, receiving clerks	3.6	16.7	Blue collar worker supervisors	1.4	16.0
Stock clerks	3.5	-3.9	Wholesale & retail buyers, except farm products	1.3	17.0
Freight, stock, & material movers, hand	3.3	8.2	Office machine & cash register servicers	1.3	20.2
Marketing & sales worker supervisors	3.1	20.2	Hand packers & packagers	1.2	-3.9
Order fillers, wholesale & retail sales	3.0	16.7	Maintenance repairers, general utility	1.1	12.0
Bookkeeping, accounting, & auditing clerks	2.9	-3.9	Industrial truck & tractor operators	1.1	20.2
Salespersons, retail	2.5	20.2	Purchasing managers	1.1	20.2
Secretaries, except legal & medical	2.5	-4.7	Receptionists & information clerks	1.0	20.2
Assemblers, fabricators, hand workers nec	2.0	-3.9			

Source: *Industry-Occupation Matrix*, Bureau of Labor Statistics. These data relate to one or more 3-digit SIC industry groups rather than to a single 4-digit SIC. The change reported for each occupation to the year 2006 is a percent of growth or decline as estimated by the Bureau of Labor Statistics. The abbreviation nec stands for 'not elsewhere classified'.

STATE AND REGIONAL CONCENTRATION

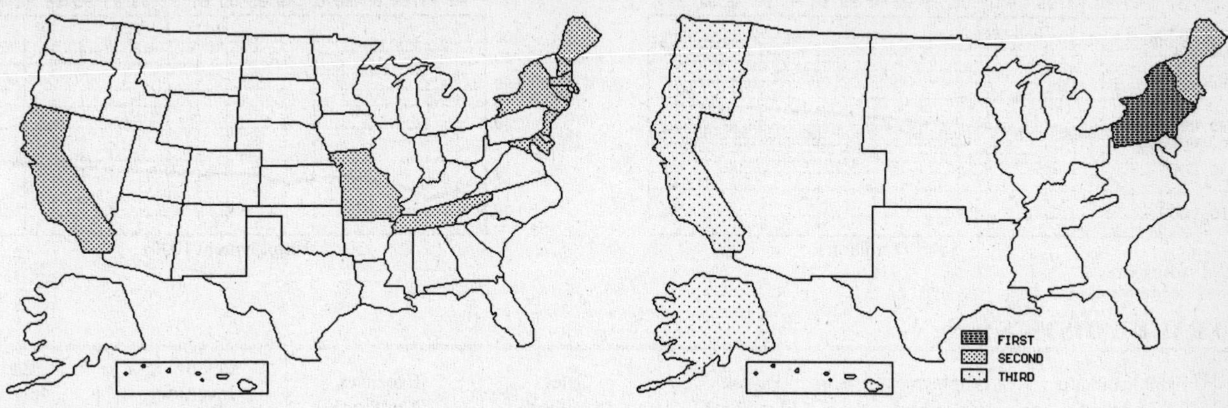

INDUSTRY DATA BY STATE

State	Establishments - 1995 Total (number)	Establishments - 1995 % of U.S.	Employment - 1995 Total (number)	Employment - 1995 % of U.S.	Employment - 1995 Per Estab.	Payroll - 1995 Total ($ mil.)	Payroll - 1995 Per Empl. ($)	Sales - 1992 Total ($ mil.)	Sales - 1992 % of U.S.	Sales - 1992 Per Estab ($)
Massachusetts	81	5.0	3,411	15.7	42	204.3	59,882	3,045.9	21.6	1,092,486
New York	343	21.3	3,359	15.5	10	179.2	53,352	2,856.0	20.2	864,409
California	283	17.6	2,957	13.6	10	101.7	34,390	2,247.5	15.9	685,433
New Jersey	109	6.8	2,170	10.0	20	72.9	33,613	1,120.2	7.9	593,933
Tennessee	33	2.1	1,465	6.8	44	43.2	29,468	724.6	5.1	573,720
Missouri	59	3.7	705	3.3	12	38.4	54,410	647.9	4.6	955,674
Texas	81	5.0	728	3.4	9	23.9	32,817	474.6	3.4	623,604
Florida	135	8.4	690	3.2	5	21.7	31,486	459.6	3.3	536,313
Connecticut	26	1.6	271	1.3	10	43.2	159,288	437.1	3.1	693,784
Michigan	18	1.1	304	1.4	17	12.7	41,931	334.1	2.4	1,246,504
Maine	4	0.2	250-499	-	-	(D)	-	307.1	2.2	348,598
Maryland	18	1.1	283	1.3	16	12.6	44,572	276.0	2.0	1,232,286
New Hampshire	17	1.1	635	2.9	37	21.4	33,672	238.6	1.7	482,093
Pennsylvania	43	2.7	509	2.3	12	27.7	54,336	221.1	1.6	295,948
North Carolina	35	2.2	454	2.1	13	15.4	33,866	142.4	1.0	228,963
Washington	30	1.9	292	1.3	10	10.8	36,908	140.5	1.0	798,347
Wisconsin	23	1.4	178	0.8	8	8.6	48,163	94.6	0.7	781,413
Minnesota	19	1.2	68	0.3	4	2.6	37,735	81.3	0.6	535,178
Georgia	30	1.9	141	0.7	5	3.9	27,730	73.8	0.5	580,827
Ohio	25	1.6	124	0.6	5	11.3	90,960	65.5	0.5	500,153
Alabama	10	0.6	55	0.3	6	1.0	18,436	47.1	0.3	760,129
Indiana	10	0.6	41	0.2	4	1.0	24,415	27.1	0.2	242,241
Colorado	11	0.7	42	0.2	4	1.7	39,524	18.7	0.1	549,206
Hawaii	15	0.9	56	0.3	4	1.2	21,196	11.6	0.1	214,185
Arkansas	5	0.3	80	0.4	16	2.8	34,775	10.0	0.1	242,854
Arizona	10	0.6	25	0.1	3	0.8	30,440	9.2	0.1	187,571
Oklahoma	3	0.2	20-99	-	-	(D)	-	2.9	0.0	205,071
Iowa	2	0.1	0-19	-	-	(D)	-	2.3	0.0	283,875
Illinois	44	2.7	277	1.3	6	12.1	43,617	(D)	-	-
Oregon	17	1.1	1,696	7.8	100	91.1	53,726	(D)	-	-
Virginia	13	0.8	211	1.0	16	10.1	47,934	(D)	-	-
South Carolina	11	0.7	251	1.2	23	7.0	27,829	(D)	-	-
Kentucky	7	0.4	71	0.3	10	1.3	18,944	(D)	-	-
Utah	6	0.4	15	0.1	3	0.3	22,267	(D)	-	-
Kansas	5	0.3	23	0.1	5	0.4	18,348	(D)	-	-
Rhode Island	5	0.3	41	0.2	8	1.1	27,000	(D)	-	-
Alaska	3	0.2	12	0.1	4	0.3	26,250	(D)	-	-
Montana	3	0.2	31	0.1	10	1.0	32,548	(D)	-	-
Nevada	3	0.2	0-19	-	-	(D)	-	(D)	-	-
Vermont	3	0.2	9	0.0	3	0.4	49,111	(D)	-	-
Delaware	2	0.1	20-99	-	-	(D)	-	(D)	-	-
Louisiana	2	0.1	0-19	-	-	(D)	-	(D)	-	-
Mississippi	2	0.1	0-19	-	-	(D)	-	(D)	-	-
Nebraska	2	0.1	0-19	-	-	(D)	-	(D)	-	-
D.C.	1	0.1	0-19	-	-	(D)	-	(D)	-	-
Idaho	1	0.1	0-19	-	-	(D)	-	(D)	-	-
North Dakota	1	0.1	20-99	-	-	(D)	-	(D)	-	-

Source: County Business Patterns, 1995 and *Economic Census of the U.S., 1992*. Data are sorted by 1992 revenues and, if revenues are unavailable, by establishments in 1995. The symbol (D) indicates that data are withheld by the source to avoid disclosure of competitive information. A dash (-) indicates that data are not available or undisclosed because they do not meet statistical validity standards. Shaded *states* on the state map indicate those states which have proportionately greater representation in the industry than would be indicated by the state's population; the ratio is based on total revenues or number of establishments. Shaded *regions* indicate where the industry is regionally most concentrated.

5141 - GROCERIES, GENERAL LINE

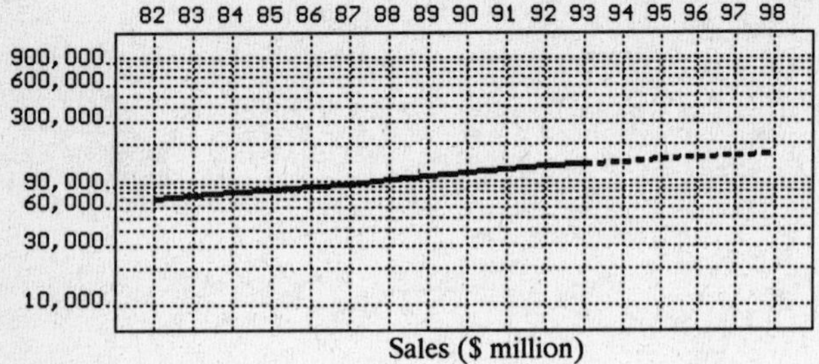

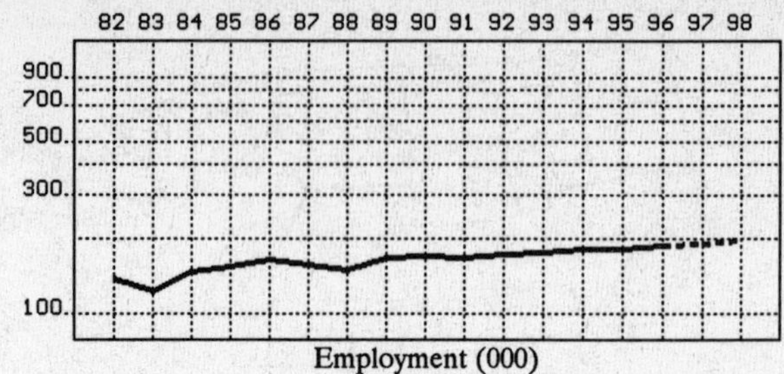

GENERAL STATISTICS

Year	Establishments (number)	Employment (number)	Payroll ($ million)	Sales ($ million)	Expenses ($ million)	Beginning Inventory ($ million)	Ending Inventory ($ million)
1982	4,267	137,695	2,774.7	70,573.7	-	-	-
1983	3,488	124,125	2,621.8	75,102.0e	-	-	-
1984	3,859	146,917	3,188.9	79,630.3e	-	-	-
1985	3,641	156,483	3,561.6	84,158.6e	-	-	-
1986	3,407	165,021	3,696.5	88,686.9e	-	-	-
1987	4,368	157,191	3,702.5	93,215.2	7,028.2	4,348.3	4,698.5
1988	3,998	151,514	3,920.1	101,092.7e	7,481.7e	4,706.8e	5,009.5e
1989	3,738	167,220	4,358.7	108,970.2e	7,935.1e	5,065.3e	5,320.4e
1990	3,751	171,302	4,574.1	116,847.6e	8,388.5e	5,423.9e	5,631.4e
1991	3,653	166,525	4,663.1	124,725.1e	8,842.0e	5,782.4e	5,942.4e
1992	4,528	172,827	5,025.8	132,602.6	9,295.4	6,140.9	6,253.3
1993	4,412	175,974	5,216.3	134,999.6p	9,748.8p	6,499.4p	6,564.3p
1994	4,653	181,304	5,572.0	141,202.5p	10,202.3p	6,858.0p	6,875.3p
1995	4,545	182,444	5,645.9	147,405.4p	10,655.7p	7,216.5p	7,186.2p
1996	4,463p	188,415p	5,930.0p	153,608.3p	11,109.1p	7,575.0p	7,497.2p
1997	4,521p	192,047p	6,163.4p	159,811.2p	11,562.6p	7,933.5p	7,808.2p
1998	4,580p	195,678p	6,396.7p	166,014.1p	12,016.0p	8,292.1p	8,119.1p

Sources: Economic Census of the United States, 1982, 1987, and 1992. Establishment counts, employment, and payroll are from *County Business Patterns* for non-Census years. Values followed by a 'p' are projections by the editors. Sales and expense data for non-Census years are extrapolations, marked by 'e'. Industries reclassified in 1987 will not have data for prior years. Data are the most recent available at this level of detail.

INDICES OF CHANGE

Year	Establishments (number)	Employment (number)	Payroll ($ million)	Sales ($ million)	Expenses ($ million)	Beginning Inventory ($ million)	Ending Inventory ($ million)
1982	94.2	79.7	55.2	53.2	-	-	-
1983	77.0	71.8	52.2	56.6e	-	-	-
1984	85.2	85.0	63.5	60.1e	-	-	-
1985	80.4	90.5	70.9	63.5e	-	-	-
1986	75.2	95.5	73.6	66.9e	-	-	-
1987	96.5	91.0	73.7	70.3	75.6	70.8	75.1
1988	88.3	87.7	78.0	76.2e	80.5e	76.6e	80.1e
1989	82.6	96.8	86.7	82.2e	85.4e	82.5e	85.1e
1990	82.8	99.1	91.0	88.1e	90.2e	88.3e	90.1e
1991	80.7	96.4	92.8	94.1e	95.1e	94.2e	95.0e
1992	100.0	100.0	100.0	100.0	100.0	100.0	100.0
1993	97.4	101.8	103.8	101.8p	104.9p	105.8p	105.0p
1994	102.8	104.9	110.9	106.5p	109.8p	111.7p	109.9p
1995	100.4	105.6	112.3	111.2p	114.6p	117.5p	114.9p
1996	98.6p	109.0p	118.0p	115.8p	119.5p	123.4p	119.9p
1997	99.9p	111.1p	122.6p	120.5p	124.4p	129.2p	124.9p
1998	101.2p	113.2p	127.3p	125.2p	129.3p	135.0p	129.8p

Sources: Same as General Statistics. The values shown reflect change from the base year, 1992. Values above 100 mean greater than 1992, values below 100 mean less than 1992, and a value of 100 in the 1982-91 or 1993-98 period means same as 1992. Values followed by a 'p' are projections by the editors; 'e' stands for extrapolation. Data are the most recent available at this level of detail.

SELECTED RATIOS

For 1992	Avg. of All Wholesale	Analyzed Industry	Index	For 1992	Avg. of All Wholesale	Analyzed Industry	Index
Employees per Establishment	12	38	327	Sales per Employee	561,172	767,256	137
Payroll per Establishment	349,729	1,109,938	317	Sales per Establishment	6,559,346	29,285,027	446
Payroll per Employee	29,919	29,080	97	Expenses per Establishment	723,071	2,052,871	284

Sources: Same as General Statistics. The 'Average of All Manufacturing' column represents the average of all manufacturing industries reported for the most recent complete year available. The Index shows the relationship between the Average and the Analyzed Industry. For example, 100 means that they are equal; 500 that the Analyzed Industry is five times the average; 50 means that the Analyzed Industry is half the national average. The abbreviation 'na' is used to show that data are 'not available'.

LEADING COMPANIES

Number shown: **50** Total sales ($ mil): **189,406** Total employment (000): **353.4**

Company Name	Address				CEO Name	Phone	Co. Type	Sales ($ mil)	Empl. (000)
Price/Costco Inc.	999 Lake Dr	Issaquah	WA	98027	James D Sinegal	206-313-8100	P	19,214	40.0
Advantage Sales and Marketing	18851 Bardeen Ave	Irvine	CA	92612	Sonny King	714-833-1200	R	18,000 •	12.0
SUPERVALU Inc.	PO Box 990	Eden Prairie	MN	55440	Michael W Wright	612-828-4000	P	16,552	44.8
Fleming Companies Inc.	PO Box 26647	Oklahoma City	OK	73126	Robert E Stauth	405-840-7200	P	16,487	41.2
SYSCO Corp.	1390 Enclave Pkwy	Houston	TX	77077	Bill M Lindig	713-584-1390	P	14,455	32.0
Nissho Iwai American Corp.	1211 of the Amer	New York	NY	10036	Akira Yokouchi	212-704-6500	S	11,910	0.4
Mitsubishi International Corp.	520 Madison Ave	New York	NY	10022	M Numaguchi	212-605-2000	S	10,000	0.7
McLane Company Inc.	PO Box 6115	Temple	TX	76503	Grady Rosier	254-771-7500	S	5,252 •	10.0
Wakefern Food Corp.	600 York St	Elizabeth	NJ	07207	Thomas Infusino	908-527-3300	R	4,600	3.2
Nash Finch Co.	PO Box 355	Minneapolis	MN	55440	Alfred N Flaten	612-832-0534	P	4,392	12.2
HomeBase Inc.	3345 Michelson Dr	Irvine	CA	92612	Herbert J Zarkin	714-442-5000	P	4,376	19.5
Richfood Holdings Inc.	PO Box 26967	Richmond	VA	23261	John E Stokely	804-746-6000	P	3,412	5.2
Penn Traffic Co.	PO Box 4737	Syracuse	NY	13221	Gary D Hirsch	315-453-7284	P	3,297	27.3
B J's Wholesale Club Inc.	PO Box 9601	Natick	MA	01760	John J Nugent	508-651-7400	P	3,200	11.0
Malone and Hyde Inc.	1991 Corporate Ave	Memphis	TN	38132	Bob Harris	901-367-8200	S	3,119	4.0
Spartan Stores Inc.	PO Box 8700	Grand Rapids	MI	49518	James D 'Meyer	616-878-2000	R	2,840 •	3.0
Tomen America Inc.	1285 of the Amer	New York	NY	10019	Hajime Kawamura	212-397-4600	S	2,645	0.9
International MultiFoods Corp.	PO Box 2942	Minneapolis	MN	55402	Gary E Costley	612-340-3300	P	2,596	7.2
Bunge Corp.	11720 Borman Dr	St. Louis	MO	63146	John E Klein	314-872-3030	R	2,570 •	3.0
Roundy's Inc.	23000 Roundy Dr	Pewaukee	WI	53072	Jerry Lestina	414-547-7999	R	2,500	5.0
Gordon Food Service Inc.	PO Box 1787	Grand Rapids	MI	49501	Daniel Gordon	616-530-7000	R	1,970 •	3.8
Rykoff-Sexton Mfg Div.	761 Terminal St	Los Angeles	CA	90021	William J Caskey	213-622-4131	S	1,700	2.8
US Foodservice Inc.	1065 Hwy 315	Wilkes-Barre	PA	18702	Frank H Bevevino	717-831-7500	S	1,700	3.9
JP Foodservice Inc.	9830 Patuxent	Columbia	MD	21046	James L Miller	410-312-7100	P	1,692	3.7
M.B.M. Corp.	PO Box 800	Rocky Mount	NC	27802	Jerry Wordsworth	919-985-7200	R	1,575	1.6
Martin-Brower Co.	1020 31st St	Downers Grove	IL	60515	Herbert Heller	708-563-0141	S	1,570 •	3.0
AmeriServe Food Distribution	17975 Sarah	Brookfield	WI	53045	Raymond Marshall	414-792-9300	R	1,519	1.7
Connell Co.	45 Cardinal Dr	Westfield	NJ	07090	Grover Connell	908-233-0700	R	1,500 •	0.1
Eby-Brown Company L.P.	280 Shuman Blvd	Naperville	IL	60566	William S Wake Jr	708-778-2800	R	1,450	1.2
PYA/Monarch Inc.	PO Box 1328	Greenville	SC	29602	James Carlson	803-676-8600	S	1,400	2.5
Super Rite Foods Inc.	PO Box 2261	Harrisburg	PA	17110	Peter Vanderveen	717-232-6821	S	1,360 •	2.6
Balfour Maclaine Corp.	61 Broadway	New York	NY	10006	A C Van Ekris	212-269-0800	P	1,312	0.8
Grocers Supply Company Inc.	PO Box 14200	Houston	TX	77221	Milton Levit	713-747-5000	R	1,300	2.0
United Grocers Inc.	PO Box 22187	Milwaukie	OR	97269	Charles E Carlbon	503-833-1000	R	1,300	1.8
Riser Foods Inc.	5300 Richmond Rd	Bedford H.	OH	44146	Anthony C Rego	216-292-7000	P	1,285	5.5
Performance Food Group Co.	6800 Paragon Place	Richmond	VA	23230	Robert C Sledd	804-285-7340	P	1,230	2.0
Super Food Services Inc.	Kettering Box 2323	Dayton	OH	45429	Jack Twyman	513-439-7500	P	1,155	1.7
C and S Wholesale Grocers Inc.	PO Box 821	Brattleboro	VT	05302	Richard Cohen	802-257-4371	R	1,150 •	2.2
Shamrock Foods Co.	2228 Black Canyon	Phoenix	AZ	85009	Kent McClelland	602-272-6721	R	1,052 •	2.0
Associated Grocers Inc.	PO Box 3763	Seattle	WA	98124	Donald Benson	206-762-2100	R	1,050	1.6
McCarty-Holman Company	PO Box 3409	Jackson	MS	39207	W H Holman Jr	601-948-0361	S	1,040	10.0
GSC Enterprises Inc.	PO Box 638	Sulphur Sprgs	TX	75483	Michael K McKenzie	903-885-7621	R	1,000	2.0
Holiday Cos.	PO Box 1224	Minneapolis	MN	55440	Ron Erickson	612-830-8700	R	1,000	5.1
J.M.	PO Box 9008	Champaign	IL	61826		217-384-2800	D	1,000 •	0.9
Shurfine International Inc.	2100 N Mannheim	Northlake	IL	60164	James R Barth	708-681-2000	R	1,000 •	0.2
SUPERVALU Inc.	PO Box 1198	Fort Wayne	IN	46801	John Gerber	219-483-2146	D	1,000	0.9
Smart and Final Stores Corp.	4700 S Boyle Ave	Vernon	CA	90058	Roger M Laverty III	213-589-1054	S	970 •	3.5
Foodland Distributors	PO Box 2886	Livonia	MI	48151	Greg Gallis	313-523-2100	S	910 •	1.0
Fleming/Gateway	3501 Marshall NE	Minneapolis	MN	55418	Dale Conklin	612-781-8051	D	900	0.6
Paul Inman Associates Inc.	PO Box 1600	Farmington Hls	MI	48333	Jerry Inman	248-626-8300	R	900	0.4

Source: *Ward's Business Directory of U.S. Private and Public Companies*, 1998. The company type code used is as follows: P - Public, R - Private, S - Subsidiary, D - Division, J - Joint Venture, A - Affiliate, G - Group. Sales are in millions of dollars, employees are in thousands. An asterisk (*) indicates an estimated sales volume. The symbol < stands for 'less than'.

OCCUPATIONS EMPLOYED BY SIC 514 - GROCERIES AND RELATED PRODUCTS

Occupation	% of Total 1996	Change to 2006	Occupation	% of Total 1996	Change to 2006
Sales & related workers nec	14.5	21.9	Industrial truck & tractor operators	2.4	21.9
Truck drivers light & heavy	12.6	10.8	Bookkeeping, accounting, & auditing clerks	2.4	-11.3
Driver/sales workers	6.1	33.0	Helpers, laborers nec	2.1	10.8
Freight, stock, & material movers, hand	4.9	-0.2	Salespersons, retail	1.7	10.8
General managers & top executives	3.7	7.4	Secretaries, except legal & medical	1.6	-12.1
Order fillers, wholesale & retail sales	3.7	10.8	Butchers & meatcutters	1.5	-11.3
Stock clerks	3.6	10.8	Blue collar worker supervisors	1.5	7.0
Hand packers & packagers	3.3	10.8	Packaging & filling machine operators	1.4	10.8
Traffic, shipping, receiving clerks	3.0	10.8	Wholesale & retail buyers, except farm products	1.4	7.9
Marketing & sales worker supervisors	2.9	10.8	Order clerks	1.2	-0.2
Agricultural, forestry, fishing workers nec	2.8	21.9	Clerical supervisors & managers	1.2	10.9
General office clerks	2.5	-4.6			

Source: *Industry-Occupation Matrix*, Bureau of Labor Statistics. These data relate to one or more 3-digit SIC industry groups rather than to a single 4-digit SIC. The change reported for each occupation to the year 2006 is a percent of growth or decline as estimated by the Bureau of Labor Statistics. The abbreviation nec stands for 'not elsewhere classified'.

STATE AND REGIONAL CONCENTRATION

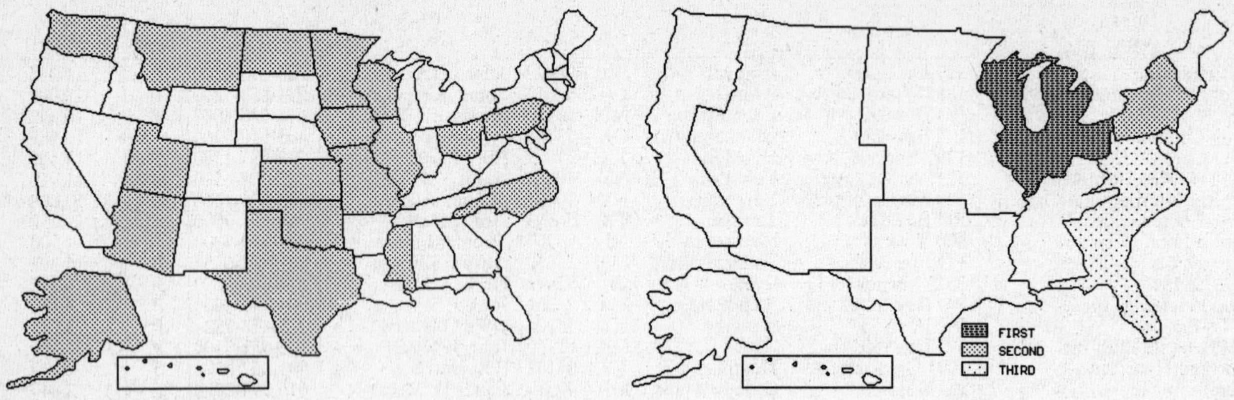

INDUSTRY DATA BY STATE

State	Establishments - 1995		Employment - 1995			Payroll - 1995		Sales - 1992		
	Total (number)	% of U.S.	Total (number)	% of U.S.	Per Estab.	Total ($ mil.)	Per Empl. ($)	Total ($ mil.)	% of U.S.	Per Estab ($)
California	693	15.2	18,065	9.9	26	580.3	32,125	12,523.9	9.8	770,462
Texas	203	4.5	12,716	7.0	63	366.0	28,786	10,829.7	8.5	853,741
Illinois	224	4.9	7,830	4.3	35	281.9	35,996	9,093.0	7.1	1,333,868
Pennsylvania	174	3.8	10,286	5.6	59	317.1	30,825	7,775.4	6.1	826,292
New York	442	9.7	8,717	4.8	20	301.1	34,547	7,184.0	5.6	865,855
Florida	276	6.1	7,018	3.8	25	228.1	32,507	5,794.8	4.6	727,899
Ohio	158	3.5	8,322	4.6	53	247.9	29,790	5,531.8	4.3	771,410
New Jersey	175	3.9	6,311	3.5	36	239.2	37,899	5,081.2	4.0	971,182
North Carolina	102	2.2	7,544	4.1	74	207.2	27,471	4,547.3	3.6	733,200
Michigan	133	2.9	7,646	4.2	57	217.6	28,458	4,216.1	3.3	673,826
Wisconsin	61	1.3	5,868	3.2	96	174.1	29,672	4,100.8	3.2	709,964
Washington	121	2.7	4,852	2.7	40	177.9	36,670	3,776.3	3.0	768,315
Missouri	78	1.7	3,523	1.9	45	116.6	33,085	3,478.0	2.7	852,664
Minnesota	50	1.1	4,130	2.3	83	143.0	34,616	3,240.1	2.5	816,363
Massachusetts	171	3.8	5,938	3.3	35	187.9	31,641	2,821.4	2.2	700,271
Indiana	66	1.5	3,463	1.9	52	99.4	28,715	2,664.3	2.1	737,000
Maryland	64	1.4	3,654	2.0	57	117.7	32,211	2,331.3	1.8	648,655
Arizona	71	1.6	3,228	1.8	45	97.8	30,288	2,246.9	1.8	805,926
Tennessee	71	1.6	3,349	1.8	47	100.5	30,002	2,237.9	1.8	669,236
Virginia	88	1.9	4,248	2.3	48	124.6	29,342	2,138.9	1.7	608,507
Kansas	38	0.8	2,506	1.4	66	82.5	32,927	2,108.4	1.7	764,461
Iowa	32	0.7	2,584	1.4	81	76.9	29,744	1,946.7	1.5	656,131
Oklahoma	50	1.1	2,471	1.4	49	74.4	30,106	1,934.4	1.5	762,767
Mississippi	31	0.7	2,644	1.4	85	68.9	26,049	1,902.0	1.5	645,626
Colorado	63	1.4	2,482	1.4	39	81.8	32,949	1,706.1	1.3	627,244
Alabama	60	1.3	2,439	1.3	41	61.4	25,173	1,694.1	1.3	687,523
Connecticut	55	1.2	1,699	0.9	31	56.3	33,118	1,630.7	1.3	616,527
Georgia	98	2.2	3,234	1.8	33	95.0	29,387	1,629.8	1.3	494,328
Louisiana	80	1.8	2,640	1.4	33	65.1	24,652	1,589.1	1.2	662,658
Kentucky	56	1.2	2,507	1.4	45	68.3	27,245	1,413.6	1.1	536,692
Utah	43	0.9	2,292	1.3	53	68.2	29,754	1,339.5	1.1	696,557
South Carolina	50	1.1	1,323	0.7	26	32.4	24,501	1,041.2	0.8	772,380
North Dakota	15	0.3	1,058	0.6	71	32.9	31,104	925.5	0.7	864,957
Arkansas	36	0.8	1,528	0.8	42	41.0	26,842	770.9	0.6	478,245
Montana	22	0.5	1,063	0.6	48	29.3	27,582	631.5	0.5	591,810
Maine	25	0.6	1,181	0.6	47	34.1	28,909	584.0	0.5	467,223
Alaska	24	0.5	697	0.4	29	26.3	37,684	580.7	0.5	861,645
Hawaii	51	1.1	786	0.4	15	19.9	25,310	376.6	0.3	468,980
New Hampshire	23	0.5	711	0.4	31	26.9	37,904	369.9	0.3	678,794
West Virginia	22	0.5	640	0.4	29	15.1	23,573	366.7	0.3	577,557
New Mexico	34	0.7	1,124	0.6	33	28.3	25,187	315.5	0.2	394,364
Nevada	41	0.9	845	0.5	21	23.3	27,588	310.3	0.2	453,029
Idaho	21	0.5	569	0.3	27	15.8	27,682	294.6	0.2	505,273
D.C.	10	0.2	142	0.1	14	3.5	24,768	80.1	0.1	468,199
Rhode Island	19	0.4	115	0.1	6	3.0	25,713	33.9	0.0	329,000
Oregon	69	1.5	2,140	1.2	31	67.3	31,440	(D)	-	-
Nebraska	29	0.6	2,113	1.2	73	57.9	27,424	(D)	-	-
Vermont	13	0.3	1,724	0.9	133	54.0	31,321	(D)	-	-
South Dakota	8	0.2	372	0.2	47	8.2	22,051	(D)	-	-
Delaware	3	0.1	52	0.0	17	1.1	20,365	(D)	-	-
Wyoming	3	0.1	55	0.0	18	0.9	15,745	(D)	-	-

Source: County Business Patterns, 1995 and *Economic Census of the U.S., 1992.* Data are sorted by 1992 revenues and, if revenues are unavailable, by establishments in 1995. The symbol (D) indicates that data are withheld by the source to avoid disclosure of competitive information. A dash (-) indicates that data are not available or undisclosed because they do not meet statistical validity standards. Shaded *states* on the state map indicate those states which have proportionately greater representation in the industry than would be indicated by the state's population; the ratio is based on total revenues or number of establishments. Shaded *regions* indicate where the industry is regionally most concentrated.

5142 - PACKAGED FROZEN FOODS

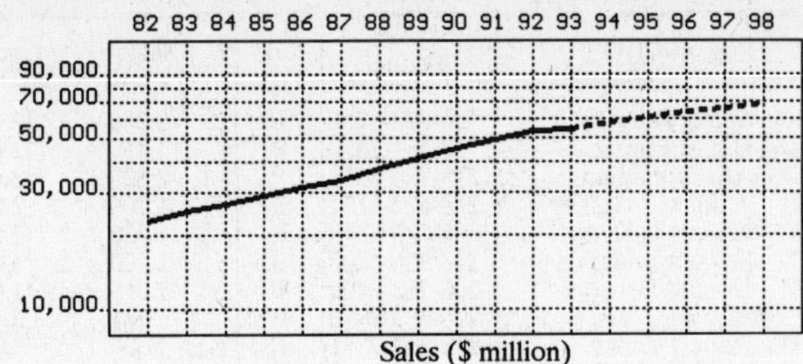

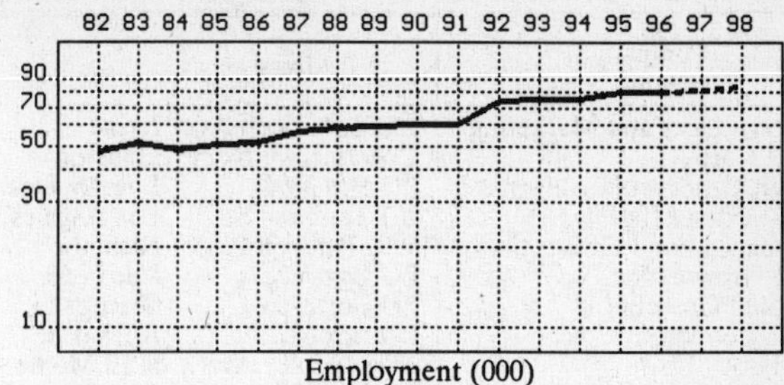

GENERAL STATISTICS

Year	Establishments (number)	Employment (number)	Payroll ($ million)	Sales ($ million)	Expenses ($ million)	Beginning Inventory ($ million)	Ending Inventory ($ million)
1982	2,676	46,997	872.3	22,628.8	-	-	-
1983	2,580	50,794	995.8	24,755.7e	-	-	-
1984	2,367	47,932	1,004.1	26,882.7e	-	-	-
1985	2,277	50,363	1,088.1	29,009.7e	-	-	-
1986	2,174	50,939	1,125.9	31,136.6e	-	-	-
1987	2,835	56,199	1,281.1	33,263.6	2,784.3	1,224.3	1,305.8
1988	2,671	58,028	1,413.7	37,262.1e	3,136.8e	1,392.2e	1,476.6e
1989	2,538	59,007	1,492.8	41,260.6e	3,489.2e	1,560.1e	1,647.5e
1990	2,438	59,865	1,588.7	45,259.0e	3,841.7e	1,728.0e	1,818.3e
1991	2,358	60,351	1,653.6	49,257.5e	4,194.1e	1,895.9e	1,989.1e
1992	3,468	73,755	2,113.9	53,256.0	4,546.6	2,063.8	2,159.9
1993	3,247	75,075	2,184.6	54,192.0p	4,899.0p	2,231.7p	2,330.8p
1994	3,054	75,345	2,304.1	57,254.7p	5,251.5p	2,399.6p	2,501.6p
1995	2,911	79,675	2,422.1	60,317.5p	5,603.9p	2,567.5p	2,672.4p
1996	3,083p	79,462p	2,461.4p	63,380.2p	5,956.4p	2,735.4p	2,843.2p
1997	3,136p	82,016p	2,584.5p	66,442.9p	6,308.8p	2,903.3p	3,014.1p
1998	3,189p	84,569p	2,707.5p	69,505.6p	6,661.3p	3,071.2p	3,184.9p

Sources: *Economic Census of the United States*, 1982, 1987, and 1992. Establishment counts, employment, and payroll are from *County Business Patterns* for non-Census years. Values followed by a 'p' are projections by the editors. Sales and expense data for non-Census years are extrapolations, marked by 'e'. Industries reclassified in 1987 will not have data for prior years. Data are the most recent available at this level of detail.

INDICES OF CHANGE

Year	Establishments (number)	Employment (number)	Payroll ($ million)	Sales ($ million)	Expenses ($ million)	Beginning Inventory ($ million)	Ending Inventory ($ million)
1982	77.2	63.7	41.3	42.5	-	-	-
1983	74.4	68.9	47.1	46.5e	-	-	-
1984	68.3	65.0	47.5	50.5e	-	-	-
1985	65.7	68.3	51.5	54.5e	-	-	-
1986	62.7	69.1	53.3	58.5e	-	-	-
1987	81.7	76.2	60.6	62.5	61.2	59.3	60.5
1988	77.0	78.7	66.9	70.0e	69.0e	67.5e	68.4e
1989	73.2	80.0	70.6	77.5e	76.7e	75.6e	76.3e
1990	70.3	81.2	75.2	85.0e	84.5e	83.7e	84.2e
1991	68.0	81.8	78.2	92.5e	92.2e	91.9e	92.1e
1992	100.0	100.0	100.0	100.0	100.0	100.0	100.0
1993	93.6	101.8	103.3	101.8p	107.8p	108.1p	107.9p
1994	88.1	102.2	109.0	107.5p	115.5p	116.3p	115.8p
1995	83.9	108.0	114.6	113.3p	123.3p	124.4p	123.7p
1996	88.9p	107.7p	116.4p	119.0p	131.0p	132.5p	131.6p
1997	90.4p	111.2p	122.3p	124.8p	138.8p	140.7p	139.5p
1998	92.0p	114.7p	128.1p	130.5p	146.5p	148.8p	147.5p

Sources: Same as General Statistics. The values shown reflect change from the base year, 1992. Values above 100 mean greater than 1992, values below 100 mean less than 1992, and a value of 100 in the 1982-91 or 1993-98 period means same as 1992. Values followed by a 'p' are projections by the editors; 'e' stands for extrapolation. Data are the most recent available at this level of detail.

SELECTED RATIOS

For 1992	Avg. of All Wholesale	Analyzed Industry	Index	For 1992	Avg. of All Wholesale	Analyzed Industry	Index
Employees per Establishment	12	21	182	Sales per Employee	561,172	722,066	129
Payroll per Establishment	349,729	609,544	174	Sales per Establishment	6,559,346	15,356,401	234
Payroll per Employee	29,919	28,661	96	Expenses per Establishment	723,071	1,311,015	181

Sources: Same as General Statistics. The 'Average of All Manufacturing' column represents the average of all manufacturing industries reported for the most recent complete year available. The Index shows the relationship between the Average and the Analyzed Industry. For example, 100 means that they are equal; 500 that the Analyzed Industry is five times the average; 50 means that the Analyzed Industry is half the national average. The abbreviation 'na' is used to show that data are 'not available'.

LEADING COMPANIES

Number shown: **50** Total sales ($ mil): **48,754** Total employment (000): **76.3**

Company Name	Address				CEO Name	Phone	Co. Type	Sales ($ mil)	Empl. (000)
Advantage Sales and Marketing	18851 Bardeen Ave	Irvine	CA	92612	Sonny King	714-833-1200	R	18,000 •	12.0
SYSCO Corp.	1390 Enclave Pkwy	Houston	TX	77077	Bill M Lindig	713-584-1390	P	14,455	32.0
Certified Grocers of California	PO Box 3396	Los Angeles	CA	90051	Alfred Plamann	213-726-2601	P	2,307	2.4
Rykoff-Sexton Mfg Div.	761 Terminal St	Los Angeles	CA	90021	William J Caskey	213-622-4131	S	1,700	2.8
Performance Food Group Co.	6800 Paragon Place	Richmond	VA	23230	Robert C Sledd	804-285-7340	P	1,230	2.0
Sunkist Growers Inc.	PO Box 7888	Van Nuys	CA	91409	Russell L Hanlin	818-986-4800	R	1,100	1.0
Associated Grocers Inc.	PO Box 3763	Seattle	WA	98124	Donald Benson	206-762-2100	R	1,050	1.6
Pro-Fac Cooperative Inc.	PO Box 682	Rochester	NY	14603	Roy A Myers	716-383-1850	P	731	3.4
Zacky Foods Co.	2000 N Tyler Ave	S. El Monte	CA	91733	Robert Zacky	818-443-9351	R	600	3.0
Fleming Foods of Ohio Inc.	PO Box 207	Massillon	OH	44648	Basil Violand	216-879-5681	S	519	0.5
Proficient Food Co.	9408 Richmond Pl	R. Cucamonga	CA	91730	Brock Partin	909-484-6100	S	485	0.5
Bozzuto's Inc.	275 Schoolhouse	Cheshire	CT	06410	Michael A Bozzuto	203-272-3511	P	378	1.0
Scot Lad-Lima Inc.	1100 Prosperity Rd	Lima	OH	45801	Stan Alexander	419-228-3141	S	350	0.5
Norpac Food Sales Inc.	4350 SW Galewood	Lake Oswego	OR	97035	Roger D Baker	503-635-9311	R	330	<0.1
Clark Food Service Inc.	950 Arthur Ave	Elk Grove Vill.	IL	60007	Donald J Hindman	708-956-1730	R	325	0.8
Southeast Frozen Food Co.	18770 NE 6th Ave	Miami	FL	33179	John Robinson	305-652-4622	R	320	0.5
Gateway Foods Inc.	PO Box 1957	La Crosse	WI	54602	Michael Karey	608-785-1330	D	300	1.0
Jordan's Meats Inc.	PO Box 588	Portland	ME	04112	James Vanan Stone	207-772-5411	R	271 •	0.8
Consolidated Companies Inc.	PO Box 6096	Metairie	LA	70009	Victor J Kurzweg	504-834-4082	R	260 •	0.5
New England Frozen Foods	1 Harvest Ln	Southborough	MA	01772	Bruce C Ginsberg	508-481-0300	R	200	0.4
Burris Foods Inc.	PO Box 219	Milford	DE	19963	Robert D Burris	302-422-4531	R	190 •	0.5
Dulin Inc.	207-K Kelsey Ln	Tampa	FL	33619	Ray E Wood	813-628-4747	R	180 •	0.4
Murry's Inc.	8300 Pennsylvania	Up Marlboro	MD	20772	I Mendelson	301-420-6400	R	180 •	1.5
Sky Brothers Inc.	PO Box 632	Altoona	PA	16603	Rocco Alianiello	814-946-1201	S	180	0.4
Ritter Sysco Food Services Inc.	640 Dowd Ave	Elizabeth	NJ	07207	Martin Ritter	908-558-2700	S	170	0.4
Troyer Foods Inc.	PO Box 608	Goshen	IN	46526	Paris Ball-Miller	219-533-0302	R	170	0.2
Grocers Specialty Co.	2601 S Eastern Ave	Los Angeles	CA	90040	Alfred Plamann	213-726-2601	S	160 •	0.2
Harker's Distribution Inc.	801 6th St SW	Le Mars	IA	51031	Ron Geiger	712-546-8171	R	160	0.5
Sherwood Food Distributors	18615 Sherwood	Detroit	MI	48234	J. Lawrence Tushman	313-366-3100	R	160 •	0.5
Ajinomoto U.S.A. Inc.	500 Frank W Burr	Teaneck	NJ	07666	Hiroshi Kurihara	201-488-1212	S	150	0.2
Tamarkin Company Inc.	375 Victoria Rd	Youngstown	OH	44515	Ray Burgo	330-792-3811	S	150	0.3
Sysco Food Service	PO Box 160	Jamestown	NY	14702	V E Wetmore Jr	716-665-5620	D	140 •	0.3
Abbott Foods Inc.	2400 Harrison Rd	Columbus	OH	43204	Lawrence C Abbott	614-272-0658	R	135	0.3
Brenham Wholesale Grocery	PO Box 584	Brenham	TX	77834	Luther Utesch	409-836-7925	R	130	0.2
California Shellfish Company	505 Beach Court	San Francisco	CA	94133	Eugene Bugatto	415-923-7400	R	130 •	0.5
Royal Cup Inc.	PO Box 170971	Birmingham	AL	35217	Hatton Smith	205-849-5836	R	130	0.5
King Provision Corp.	9009 Regency Sq	Jacksonville	FL	32211	Edward F Hicks	904-725-4122	S	120 •	0.4
Jordan's Foods	PO Box 4657	Portland	ME	04112	Richard Giles	207-871-0700	D	111	0.2
Allegiance Brokerage Co.	PO Drawer 410529	Charlotte	NC	28241	Terry Pietsch	704-529-1176	S	110	0.2
Associated Brokers Inc.	PO Box 26328	Raleigh	NC	27611	Pete Troutman	919-833-2651	R	110 •	0.2
Brown Moore and Flint Inc.	1920 Westridge	Irving	TX	75038	Tom Garrison	214-518-1442	R	110	0.2
Glazier Foods Co.	1520 Oliver St	Houston	TX	77007	Thomas A Glazier	713-869-6411	R	100 •	0.2
Barnett Brothers Brokerage	2509 74th St	Lubbock	TX	79423	Tom Barnett	806-745-7575	R	95	<0.1
Merchants Co.	PO Box 1351	Hattiesburg	MS	39403	Donald B Suber	601-583-4351	S	93	0.3
Squeri FoodService	PO Box 14180	Cincinnati	OH	45250	John Squeri	513-381-1106	R	86	0.2
G and G Produce Company	5949 S Eastern Ave	City of Com	CA	90040	Dave Kuntz	213-727-1212	S	80	0.3
Martin Brothers Distributing	PO Box 69	Cedar Falls	IA	50613	John Martin	319-266-1775	R	80	0.3
W.S. Lee and Sons Inc.	PO Box 1631	Altoona	PA	16603	Walter J Lee Jr	814-696-3535	R	79 •	0.2
Ancona Brothers Co.	PO Box 27787	Omaha	NE	68127	Mike Ancona	402-331-4900	R	78	0.2
Keeners Inc.	2900 4th Ave S	Seattle	WA	98134	Wayne V Keener	206-628-4811	R	75	0.2

Source: *Ward's Business Directory of U.S. Private and Public Companies*, 1998. The company type code used is as follows: P - Public, R - Private, S - Subsidiary, D - Division, J - Joint Venture, A - Affiliate, G - Group. Sales are in millions of dollars, employees are in thousands. An asterisk (•) indicates an estimated sales volume. The symbol < stands for 'less than'.

OCCUPATIONS EMPLOYED BY SIC 514 - GROCERIES AND RELATED PRODUCTS

Occupation	% of Total 1996	Change to 2006	Occupation	% of Total 1996	Change to 2006
Sales & related workers nec	14.5	21.9	Industrial truck & tractor operators	2.4	21.9
Truck drivers light & heavy	12.6	10.8	Bookkeeping, accounting, & auditing clerks	2.4	-11.3
Driver/sales workers	6.1	33.0	Helpers, laborers nec	2.1	10.8
Freight, stock, & material movers, hand	4.9	-0.2	Salespersons, retail	1.7	10.8
General managers & top executives	3.7	7.4	Secretaries, except legal & medical	1.6	-12.1
Order fillers, wholesale & retail sales	3.7	10.8	Butchers & meatcutters	1.5	-11.3
Stock clerks	3.6	10.8	Blue collar worker supervisors	1.5	7.0
Hand packers & packagers	3.3	10.8	Packaging & filling machine operators	1.4	10.8
Traffic, shipping, receiving clerks	3.0	10.8	Wholesale & retail buyers, except farm products	1.4	7.9
Marketing & sales worker supervisors	2.9	10.8	Order clerks	1.2	-0.2
Agricultural, forestry, fishing workers nec	2.8	21.9	Clerical supervisors & managers	1.2	10.9
General office clerks	2.5	-4.6			

Source: *Industry-Occupation Matrix*, Bureau of Labor Statistics. These data relate to one or more 3-digit SIC industry groups rather than to a single 4-digit SIC. The change reported for each occupation to the year 2006 is a percent of growth or decline as estimated by the Bureau of Labor Statistics. The abbreviation nec stands for 'not elsewhere classified'.

STATE AND REGIONAL CONCENTRATION

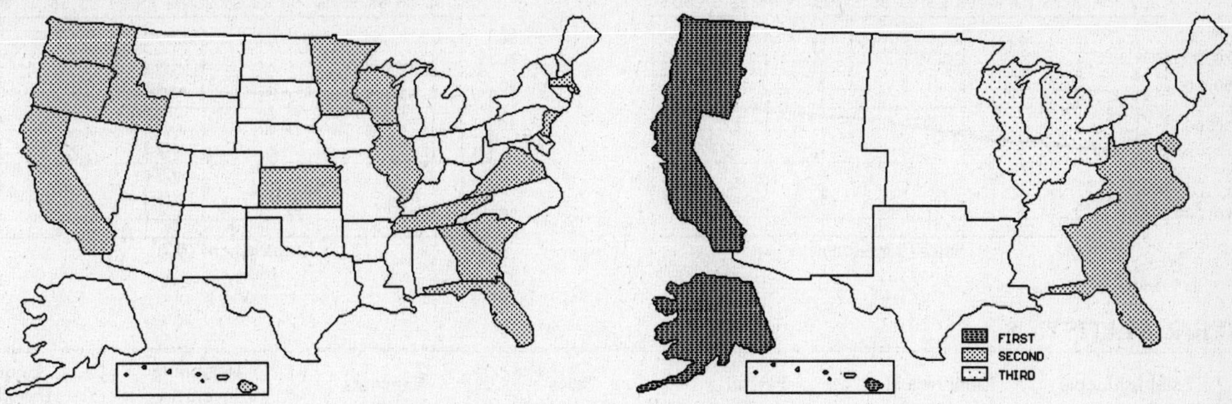

INDUSTRY DATA BY STATE

State	Establishments - 1995 Total (number)	Establishments - 1995 % of U.S.	Employment - 1995 Total (number)	Employment - 1995 % of U.S.	Employment - 1995 Per Estab.	Payroll - 1995 Total ($ mil.)	Payroll - 1995 Per Empl. ($)	Sales - 1992 Total ($ mil.)	Sales - 1992 % of U.S.	Sales - 1992 Per Estab ($)
California	370	12.7	10,884	13.8	29	327.1	30,058	8,137.0	15.6	894,176
Florida	226	7.8	4,233	5.4	19	127.3	30,083	3,268.1	6.3	745,460
New York	225	7.7	4,432	5.6	20	131.8	29,740	3,059.0	5.9	731,128
Texas	156	5.4	5,534	7.0	35	152.4	27,545	3,006.5	5.8	576,071
Illinois	152	5.2	3,997	5.1	26	133.4	33,386	2,800.1	5.4	679,310
Pennsylvania	131	4.5	3,742	4.7	29	109.9	29,375	2,356.3	4.5	692,431
Washington	93	3.2	1,137	1.4	12	47.4	41,705	2,172.5	4.2	1,417,145
Ohio	84	2.9	2,671	3.4	32	82.2	30,784	2,115.4	4.1	757,381
Georgia	85	2.9	2,688	3.4	32	88.7	33,013	2,043.7	3.9	756,348
Massachusetts	104	3.6	2,585	3.3	25	95.0	36,753	2,030.3	3.9	1,039,032
New Jersey	135	4.6	2,255	2.9	17	83.2	36,905	1,785.6	3.4	774,984
Virginia	61	2.1	2,514	3.2	41	75.7	30,101	1,626.9	3.1	829,226
Michigan	94	3.2	2,225	2.8	24	71.7	32,224	1,514.0	2.9	785,262
Wisconsin	66	2.3	3,384	4.3	51	93.2	27,538	1,349.1	2.6	561,176
Tennessee	55	1.9	2,375	3.0	43	69.1	29,079	1,339.1	2.6	594,869
Idaho	15	0.5	429	0.5	29	8.5	19,790	1,229.1	2.4	2,400,551
Minnesota	57	2.0	1,884	2.4	33	59.5	31,598	1,118.9	2.1	516,593
North Carolina	57	2.0	1,879	2.4	33	61.7	32,821	1,021.9	2.0	709,632
Maryland	49	1.7	1,039	1.3	21	29.7	28,628	889.8	1.7	846,648
South Carolina	23	0.8	1,112	1.4	48	41.8	37,591	869.3	1.7	646,351
Missouri	64	2.2	2,052	2.6	32	60.9	29,680	833.6	1.6	532,332
Oregon	45	1.5	867	1.1	19	25.6	29,584	798.2	1.5	1,184,200
Kansas	29	1.0	1,057	1.3	36	34.9	32,976	710.8	1.4	683,415
Indiana	41	1.4	1,234	1.6	30	34.2	27,723	654.4	1.3	514,458
Colorado	27	0.9	1,233	1.6	46	40.6	32,934	554.7	1.1	635,348
Connecticut	26	0.9	363	0.5	14	12.3	33,923	548.2	1.0	996,785
Louisiana	48	1.6	1,308	1.7	27	28.1	21,460	530.7	1.0	365,214
Oklahoma	30	1.0	1,815	2.3	61	45.5	25,091	527.3	1.0	412,636
Alabama	31	1.1	912	1.2	29	29.0	31,836	485.6	0.9	468,320
Kentucky	41	1.4	907	1.1	22	25.0	27,576	473.7	0.9	484,345
Arizona	36	1.2	671	0.8	19	23.6	35,116	461.0	0.9	576,305
Iowa	31	1.1	993	1.3	32	28.5	28,726	441.1	0.8	451,522
Mississippi	21	0.7	786	1.0	37	19.8	25,214	385.8	0.7	531,441
Arkansas	18	0.6	598	0.8	33	18.6	31,157	324.3	0.6	738,788
Hawaii	46	1.6	458	0.6	10	14.6	31,793	320.8	0.6	421,570
Rhode Island	14	0.5	224	0.3	16	7.9	35,183	107.2	0.2	956,893
Maine	17	0.6	432	0.5	25	11.0	25,493	105.8	0.2	273,258
Montana	5	0.2	100-249	-	-	(D)	-	72.5	0.1	480,457
Alaska	10	0.3	138	0.2	14	3.0	21,420	62.4	0.1	262,118
New Mexico	12	0.4	187	0.2	16	3.2	17,139	45.6	0.1	373,852
New Hampshire	4	0.1	80	0.1	20	2.2	27,525	25.2	0.0	382,409
South Dakota	10	0.3	570	0.7	57	14.7	25,747	13.3	0.0	182,370
D.C.	1	0.0	0-19	-	-	(D)	-	6.8	0.0	853,250
Utah	20	0.7	603	0.8	30	15.9	26,327	(D)	-	-
Nebraska	19	0.7	364	0.5	19	10.8	29,563	(D)	-	-
Nevada	13	0.4	99	0.1	8	3.8	38,556	(D)	-	-
Delaware	4	0.1	100-249	-	-	(D)	-	(D)	-	-
North Dakota	4	0.1	98	0.1	25	2.2	22,633	(D)	-	-
West Virginia	3	0.1	250-499	-	-	(D)	-	(D)	-	-
Wyoming	2	0.1	0-19	-	-	(D)	-	(D)	-	-
Vermont	1	0.0	0-19	-	-	(D)	-	(D)	-	-

Source: County Business Patterns, 1995 and *Economic Census of the U.S., 1992*. Data are sorted by 1992 revenues and, if revenues are unavailable, by establishments in 1995. The symbol (D) indicates that data are withheld by the source to avoid disclosure of competitive information. A dash (-) indicates that data are not available or undisclosed because they do not meet statistical validity standards. Shaded *states* on the state map indicate those states which have proportionately greater representation in the industry than would be indicated by the state's population; the ratio is based on total revenues or number of establishments. Shaded *regions* indicate where the industry is regionally most concentrated.

5143 - DAIRY PRODUCTS, EXC. DRIED OR CANNED

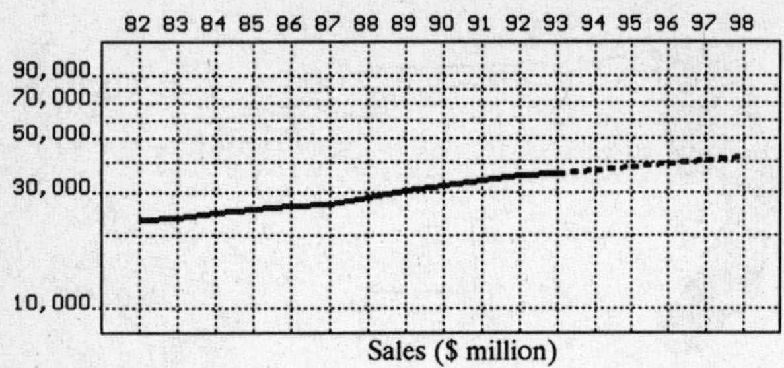

Sales ($ million)

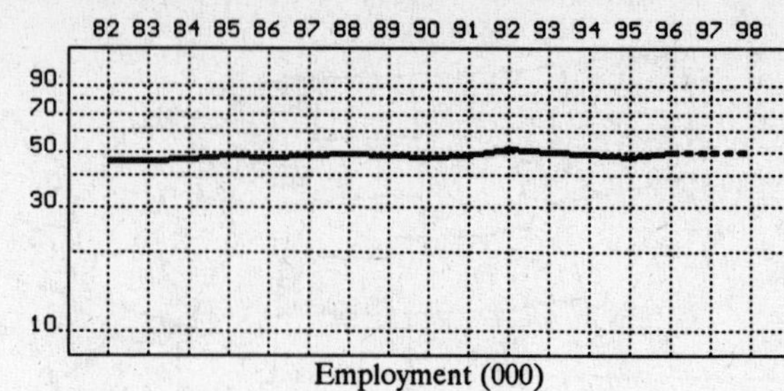

Employment (000)

GENERAL STATISTICS

Year	Establishments (number)	Employment (number)	Payroll ($ million)	Sales ($ million)	Expenses ($ million)	Beginning Inventory ($ million)	Ending Inventory ($ million)
1982	3,912	45,701	850.7	22,939.3	-	-	-
1983	3,824	45,965	885.8	23,736.7e	-	-	-
1984	3,618	46,602	965.6	24,534.2e	-	-	-
1985	3,429	48,148	1,013.0	25,331.6e	-	-	-
1986	3,272	47,387	1,040.2	26,129.1e	-	-	-
1987	3,743	48,038	1,097.1	26,926.6	2,590.8	515.3	541.3
1988	3,455	48,488	1,191.8	28,606.1e	2,750.1e	546.9e	586.8e
1989	3,245	47,830	1,190.9	30,285.6e	2,909.4e	578.5e	632.3e
1990	3,192	47,432	1,240.8	31,965.1e	3,068.7e	610.1e	677.8e
1991	3,132	48,016	1,330.8	33,644.6e	3,228.0e	641.7e	723.3e
1992	3,378	50,975	1,469.9	35,324.1	3,387.3	673.3	768.8
1993	3,191	49,924	1,531.9	35,560.2p	3,546.6p	704.9p	814.3p
1994	3,024	48,542	1,576.9	36,798.7p	3,705.9p	736.5p	859.8p
1995	2,873	46,817	1,523.3	38,037.2p	3,865.2p	768.1p	905.3p
1996	2,899p	49,384p	1,645.0p	39,275.7p	4,024.5p	799.7p	950.8p
1997	2,835p	49,589p	1,703.3p	40,514.2p	4,183.8p	831.3p	996.3p
1998	2,771p	49,794p	1,761.6p	41,752.6p	4,343.1p	862.9p	1,041.8p

Sources: Economic Census of the United States, 1982, 1987, and 1992. Establishment counts, employment, and payroll are from *County Business Patterns* for non-Census years. Values followed by a 'p' are projections by the editors. Sales and expense data for non-Census years are extrapolations, marked by 'e'. Industries reclassified in 1987 will not have data for prior years. Data are the most recent available at this level of detail.

INDICES OF CHANGE

Year	Establishments (number)	Employment (number)	Payroll ($ million)	Sales ($ million)	Expenses ($ million)	Beginning Inventory ($ million)	Ending Inventory ($ million)
1982	115.8	89.7	57.9	64.9	-	-	-
1983	113.2	90.2	60.3	67.2e	-	-	-
1984	107.1	91.4	65.7	69.5e	-	-	-
1985	101.5	94.5	68.9	71.7e	-	-	-
1986	96.9	93.0	70.8	74.0e	-	-	-
1987	110.8	94.2	74.6	76.2	76.5	76.5	70.4
1988	102.3	95.1	81.1	81.0e	81.2e	81.2e	76.3e
1989	96.1	93.8	81.0	85.7e	85.9e	85.9e	82.2e
1990	94.5	93.0	84.4	90.5e	90.6e	90.6e	88.2e
1991	92.7	94.2	90.5	95.2e	95.3e	95.3e	94.1e
1992	100.0	100.0	100.0	100.0	100.0	100.0	100.0
1993	94.5	97.9	104.2	100.7p	104.7p	104.7p	105.9p
1994	89.5	95.2	107.3	104.2p	109.4p	109.4p	111.8p
1995	85.1	91.8	103.6	107.7p	114.1p	114.1p	117.8p
1996	85.8p	96.9p	111.9p	111.2p	118.8p	118.8p	123.7p
1997	83.9p	97.3p	115.9p	114.7p	123.5p	123.5p	129.6p
1998	82.0p	97.7p	119.8p	118.2p	128.2p	128.2p	135.5p

Sources: Same as General Statistics. The values shown reflect change from the base year, 1992. Values above 100 mean greater than 1992, values below 100 mean less than 1992, and a value of 100 in the 1982-91 or 1993-98 period means same as 1992. Values followed by a 'p' are projections by the editors; 'e' stands for extrapolation. Data are the most recent available at this level of detail.

SELECTED RATIOS

For 1992	Avg. of All Wholesale	Analyzed Industry	Index	For 1992	Avg. of All Wholesale	Analyzed Industry	Index
Employees per Establishment	12	15	129	Sales per Employee	561,172	692,969	123
Payroll per Establishment	349,729	435,139	124	Sales per Establishment	6,559,346	10,457,105	159
Payroll per Employee	29,919	28,836	96	Expenses per Establishment	723,071	1,002,753	139

Sources: Same as General Statistics. The 'Average of All Manufacturing' column represents the average of all manufacturing industries reported for the most recent complete year available. The Index shows the relationship between the Average and the Analyzed Industry. For example, 100 means that they are equal; 500 that the Analyzed Industry is five times the average; 50 means that the Analyzed Industry is half the national average. The abbreviation 'na' is used to show that data are 'not available'.

LEADING COMPANIES

Number shown: **50** Total sales ($ mil): **10,357** Total employment (000): **24.8**

Company Name	Address				CEO Name	Phone	Co. Type	Sales ($ mil)	Empl. (000)
Associated Milk Producers	PO Box 455	New Ulm	MN	56073	Mark Furth	507-354-8295	R	928	1.8
Associated Milk Producers	PO Box 5040	Arlington	TX	76005	Nobel Anderson	817-461-2674	D	920 *	1.6
Tuscan Dairy Farms Inc.	750 Union Ave	Union	NJ	07083	Robert W Allen	908-686-1500	S	770	1.4
Milk Marketing Inc.	8257 Dow Cir	Strongsville	OH	44136	Donald H Schriver	216-826-4730	R	650	0.7
Michael Foods Inc.	5353 Wayzata Blvd	Minneapolis	MN	55416	Gregg A Ostrander	612-546-1500	P	616	2.7
Sargento Inc.	1 Persnickety Pl	Plymouth	WI	53073	Louis P Gentine	920-893-8484	R	580 *	1.0
Dairylea Cooperative Inc.	PO Box 4844	Syracuse	NY	13221	Richard Smith	315-433-0100	R	550	<0.1
Flav-O-Rich Inc.	316 North 4th St	Campbell	KY	42718	Steve G Conerly	502-465-8119	S	530 *	2.5
Fleming Foods of Ohio Inc.	PO Box 207	Massillon	OH	44648	Basil Violand	216-879-5681	S	519	0.5
Finevest Foods Inc.	191 Mason St	Greenwich	CT	06830	Philip J Ablove	203-629-8014	P	302	1.7
Consolidated Companies Inc.	PO Box 6096	Metairie	LA	70009	Victor J Kurzweg	504-834-4082	R	260 *	0.5
Dairy Fresh Products Co.	601 Rockefeller	Ontario	CA	91761	Jim DeKeyser	909-975-1019	S	250	0.5
New England Frozen Foods	1 Harvest Ln	Southborough	MA	01772	Bruce C Ginsberg	508-481-0300	R	200	0.4
Burris Foods Inc.	PO Box 219	Milford	DE	19963	Robert D Burris	302-422-4531	R	190 *	0.5
Dulin Inc.	207-K Kelsey Ln	Tampa	FL	33619	Ray E Wood	813-628-4747	R	180 *	0.4
Farmland Dairies Inc.	520 Main Ave	Wallington	NJ	07057	Marc Goldman	973-777-2500	R	160	0.3
Hickory Farms Inc.	PO Box 219	Maumee	OH	43537	Ike Herb	419-893-7611	R	160	2.3
M.E. Franks Inc.	150 Radnor	St. Davids	PA	19087	Donald W Street	610-902-4020	R	160 *	<0.1
Crystal Farms	6465 Wayzata Blvd	Minneapolis	MN	55426	N A Rodriquez	612-544-8101	S	156 *	0.4
Multifoods Specialty Distribution	PO Box 173773	Denver	CO	80217	Bruce Kean	303-338-6100	D	150 *	0.4
Tamarkin Company Inc.	375 Victoria Rd	Youngstown	OH	44515	Ray Burgo	330-792-3811	S	150	0.3
Maryland and Virginia Milk	1985 Newton Sq S	Reston	VA	22090	Russell Wachter	703-742-6800	R	140 *	0.3
United Dairymen of Arizona	PO Box 26877	Tempe	AZ	85285	Jim Boyle	602-966-7211	R	112 *	0.2
Melody Farms Inc.	31111 Industrial Rd	Livonia	MI	48150	MJ George	313-525-4000	R	100 *	0.5
Rockview Farms Inc.	PO Box 668	Downey	CA	90241	EJ Degroot	310-927-5511	R	100 *	0.2
Dairy Fresh Corp.	PO Box 159	Greensboro	AL	36744	Betty Gist	334-624-3041	R	95	0.5
Western Dairy Products Inc.	3625 Westwind	Santa Rosa	CA	95403	Graeme Honeyfield	707-524-6770	S	90	<0.1
Squeri FoodService	PO Box 14180	Cincinnati	OH	45250	John Squeri	513-381-1106	R	86	0.2
Crestar Food Products Inc.	750 Old Hickory	Brentwood	TN	37027	Donald J Kerr	615-377-4400	S	85	0.2
Tony's Fine Foods	PO Box 1501	W. Sacramento	CA	95605	Anthony Ingoglia Jr	916-374-4000	R	85 *	0.3
Detroit City Dairy Inc.	15004 3rd Ave	Highland Park	MI	48203	M Must	313-868-5511	R	80 *	0.2
W.S. Lee and Sons Inc.	PO Box 1631	Altoona	PA	16603	Walter J Lee Jr	814-696-3535	R	79 *	0.2
Remarks Inc.	6728 Hyland Croy	Dublin	OH	43017	Malcolm J Graves	614-889-2561	R	75	0.3
Hawaiian Grocery Stores Ltd.	2915 Kaihikapu St	Honolulu	HI	96819	Richard H Loeffler	808-839-5121	R	70	0.1
Priscilla Gold Seal Corp.	25 Charlotte Ave	Hicksville	NY	11801	Allen Newman	718-852-2500	R	69 *	0.1
Sun City Industries Inc.	5545 NW 35th Ave	Fort Lauderdale	FL	33309	Malvin Avchen	305-730-3333	P	68	0.2
Mulligan Sales Inc.	PO Box 90008	City of Industry	CA	91715	James Mulligan	818-968-9621	R	60	<0.1
Smith Brothers Farms Inc.	27441 68th Ave S	Kent	WA	98032	Alexis Koester	206-852-1000	R	60 *	0.3
Maryland Hotel Supply Co.	701 W Hamburg St	Baltimore	MD	21230	RD Niller III	410-539-7055	R	53 *	0.2
Marquez Bros.	1670 Las Plumas	San Jose	CA	95133	Gustavo Marquez	408-272-2700	R	52 *	<0.1
J. Kings Food Service	700 Furrows Rd	Holtsville	NY	11742	John King	516-289-8401	R	50	0.1
Sunbelt Distributors Inc.	4494 Campbell Rd	Houston	TX	77041	Mike Stamper	713-329-9988	R	50	0.2
Lincoln Poultry and Egg Co.	2005 M St	Lincoln	NE	68510	Richard Evnen	402-477-3757	R	47 *	0.1
Old Home Foods Inc.	370 University Ave	St. Paul	MN	55103	Richard Hanson	612-228-9035	R	45 *	0.1
Sure Winner Foods Inc.	PO Box 317	Brewer	ME	04412	Mark Irving	207-989-6447	R	40 *	<0.1
Cole Brothers and Fox Co.	252 Yandell Ave	Canton	MS	39046	William E Fox	601-859-1414	R	39 *	<0.1
Texas Health Distributors	840 Interchange	Austin	TX	78721	Craig Weller	512-385-3853	D	39 *	0.1
Kraft Food Ingredients Corp.	PO Box 398	Memphis	TN	38133	Mike Taylor	901-381-6500	D	37 *	<0.1
Prairie Farms Dairy Inc.	PO Box 10419	Fort Wayne	IN	46852	Charles Allen	219-483-6436	D	35	0.1
Zanios Foods Inc.	PO Box 27730	Albuquerque	NM	87125	Jim Zanios	505-831-1411	R	34 *	<0.1

Source: *Ward's Business Directory of U.S. Private and Public Companies*, 1998. The company type code used is as follows: P - Public, R - Private, S - Subsidiary, D - Division, J - Joint Venture, A - Affiliate, G - Group. Sales are in millions of dollars, employees are in thousands. An asterisk (*) indicates an estimated sales volume. The symbol < stands for 'less than'.

OCCUPATIONS EMPLOYED BY SIC 514 - GROCERIES AND RELATED PRODUCTS

Occupation	% of Total 1996	Change to 2006	Occupation	% of Total 1996	Change to 2006
Sales & related workers nec	14.5	21.9	Industrial truck & tractor operators	2.4	21.9
Truck drivers light & heavy	12.6	10.8	Bookkeeping, accounting, & auditing clerks	2.4	-11.3
Driver/sales workers	6.1	33.0	Helpers, laborers nec	2.1	10.8
Freight, stock, & material movers, hand	4.9	-0.2	Salespersons, retail	1.7	10.8
General managers & top executives	3.7	7.4	Secretaries, except legal & medical	1.6	-12.1
Order fillers, wholesale & retail sales	3.7	10.8	Butchers & meatcutters	1.5	-11.3
Stock clerks	3.6	10.8	Blue collar worker supervisors	1.5	7.0
Hand packers & packagers	3.3	10.8	Packaging & filling machine operators	1.4	10.8
Traffic, shipping, receiving clerks	3.0	10.8	Wholesale & retail buyers, except farm products	1.4	7.9
Marketing & sales worker supervisors	2.9	10.8	Order clerks	1.2	-0.2
Agricultural, forestry, fishing workers nec	2.8	21.9	Clerical supervisors & managers	1.2	10.9
General office clerks	2.5	-4.6			

Source: *Industry-Occupation Matrix*, Bureau of Labor Statistics. These data relate to one or more 3-digit SIC industry groups rather than to a single 4-digit SIC. The change reported for each occupation to the year 2006 is a percent of growth or decline as estimated by the Bureau of Labor Statistics. The abbreviation nec stands for 'not elsewhere classified'.

STATE AND REGIONAL CONCENTRATION

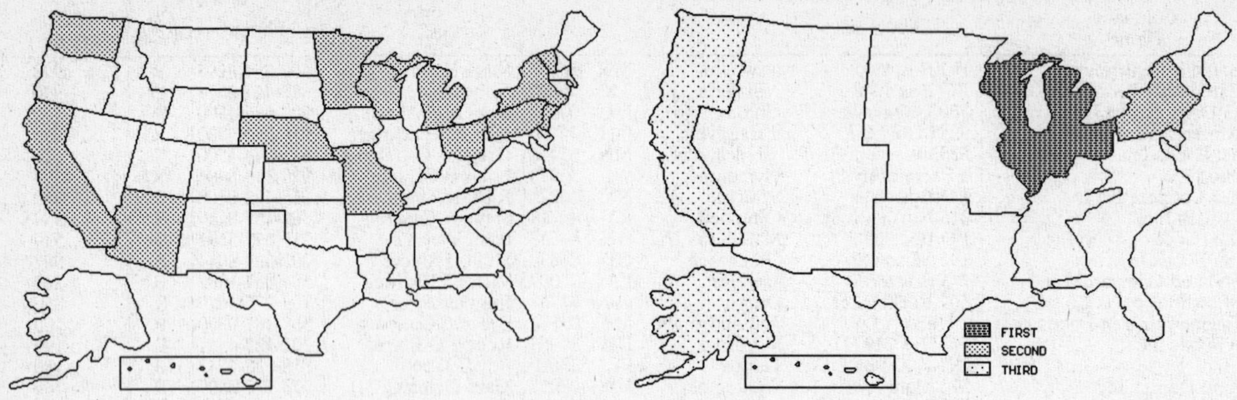

INDUSTRY DATA BY STATE

	Establishments - 1995		Employment - 1995			Payroll - 1995		Sales - 1992		
State	Total (number)	% of U.S.	Total (number)	% of U.S.	Per Estab.	Total ($ mil.)	Per Empl. ($)	Total ($ mil.)	% of U.S.	Per Estab ($)
California	324	11.3	5,742	12.3	18	211.2	36,779	4,905.9	14.0	743,878
New York	354	12.3	4,597	9.8	13	138.0	30,028	3,418.2	9.8	741,626
Wisconsin	139	4.8	2,943	6.3	21	69.5	23,600	3,396.2	9.7	1,074,736
New Jersey	143	5.0	2,271	4.9	16	92.6	40,785	2,289.9	6.5	820,179
Pennsylvania	118	4.1	2,137	4.6	18	61.8	28,898	2,013.8	5.7	961,259
Ohio	82	2.9	4,067	8.7	50	207.7	51,066	1,909.3	5.4	453,508
Florida	152	5.3	2,293	4.9	15	70.5	30,744	1,855.8	5.3	725,789
Illinois	160	5.6	2,135	4.6	13	71.8	33,611	1,512.1	4.3	730,477
Texas	120	4.2	2,240	4.8	19	64.4	28,753	1,357.7	3.9	460,704
Michigan	91	3.2	2,130	4.6	23	65.5	30,773	1,347.3	3.8	624,597
Missouri	61	2.1	1,192	2.5	20	38.1	31,966	890.2	2.5	722,584
Minnesota	84	2.9	1,001	2.1	12	34.2	34,202	870.9	2.5	692,861
Washington	76	2.6	1,008	2.2	13	32.1	31,866	837.7	2.4	706,905
North Carolina	83	2.9	1,116	2.4	13	30.6	27,387	813.3	2.3	568,325
Arizona	45	1.6	783	1.7	17	22.5	28,736	655.3	1.9	914,015
Tennessee	36	1.3	691	1.5	19	18.1	26,255	650.0	1.9	758,447
Maryland	34	1.2	808	1.7	24	23.5	29,078	635.2	1.8	702,636
Indiana	53	1.8	985	2.1	19	30.6	31,095	566.3	1.6	628,552
Massachusetts	43	1.5	753	1.6	18	30.1	39,967	535.7	1.5	711,449
Georgia	62	2.2	681	1.5	11	20.9	30,727	424.2	1.2	482,095
Connecticut	36	1.3	765	1.6	21	23.1	30,182	414.8	1.2	697,079
Virginia	33	1.1	592	1.3	18	15.5	26,135	407.2	1.2	816,044
Colorado	28	1.0	563	1.2	20	15.6	27,623	366.5	1.0	603,807
Alabama	31	1.1	339	0.7	11	8.7	25,631	325.4	0.9	1,056,344
Kansas	23	0.8	376	0.8	16	9.8	26,045	292.5	0.8	878,237
Iowa	21	0.7	129	0.3	6	4.0	30,969	289.9	0.8	1,031,651
Oregon	37	1.3	418	0.9	11	12.7	30,471	286.7	0.8	731,403
Kentucky	50	1.7	553	1.2	11	14.4	25,984	278.7	0.8	500,422
Nebraska	20	0.7	304	0.6	15	7.6	25,076	258.2	0.7	819,676
Vermont	8	0.3	173	0.4	22	5.0	29,092	200.7	0.6	809,387
Utah	18	0.6	288	0.6	16	6.0	20,951	188.5	0.5	700,807
South Carolina	37	1.3	555	1.2	15	13.5	24,277	126.4	0.4	273,688
Idaho	18	0.6	145	0.3	8	4.1	28,090	122.3	0.3	879,986
West Virginia	15	0.5	127	0.3	8	3.2	25,173	79.7	0.2	306,662
Oklahoma	22	0.8	201	0.4	9	4.7	23,284	68.8	0.2	303,251
New Hampshire	10	0.3	130	0.3	13	4.1	31,308	50.1	0.1	266,521
Mississippi	24	0.8	237	0.5	10	4.4	18,755	45.6	0.1	211,930
Hawaii	8	0.3	76	0.2	10	2.0	26,776	43.4	0.1	377,652
Delaware	1	0.0	0-19	-	-	(D)	-	42.5	0.1	363,427
Nevada	17	0.6	147	0.3	9	4.7	32,279	40.9	0.1	314,615
Maine	11	0.4	120	0.3	11	2.3	18,858	38.2	0.1	350,615
Arkansas	14	0.5	136	0.3	10	3.3	24,471	36.7	0.1	269,676
Rhode Island	10	0.3	165	0.4	16	4.1	25,073	31.2	0.1	181,349
North Dakota	24	0.8	76	0.2	3	1.1	15,118	29.3	0.1	400,959
South Dakota	12	0.4	20	0.0	2	0.6	27,750	28.7	0.1	1,104,846
New Mexico	17	0.6	90	0.2	5	2.3	26,089	25.0	0.1	231,213
Wyoming	10	0.3	39	0.1	4	0.8	20,872	18.4	0.1	485,395
Alaska	4	0.1	40	0.1	10	1.0	25,900	17.1	0.0	271,429
Montana	17	0.6	55	0.1	3	0.8	15,127	16.7	0.0	235,127
Louisiana	35	1.2	374	0.8	11	9.7	25,837	(D)	-	-
D.C.	2	0.1	0-19	-	-	(D)	-	(D)	-	-

Source: County Business Patterns, 1995 and *Economic Census of the U.S., 1992.* Data are sorted by 1992 revenues and, if revenues are unavailable, by establishments in 1995. The symbol (D) indicates that data are withheld by the source to avoid disclosure of competitive information. A dash (-) indicates that data are not available or undisclosed because they do not meet statistical validity standards. Shaded *states* on the state map indicate those states which have proportionately greater representation in the industry than would be indicated by the state's population; the ratio is based on total revenues or number of establishments. Shaded *regions* indicate where the industry is regionally most concentrated.

5144 - POULTRY AND POULTRY PRODUCTS

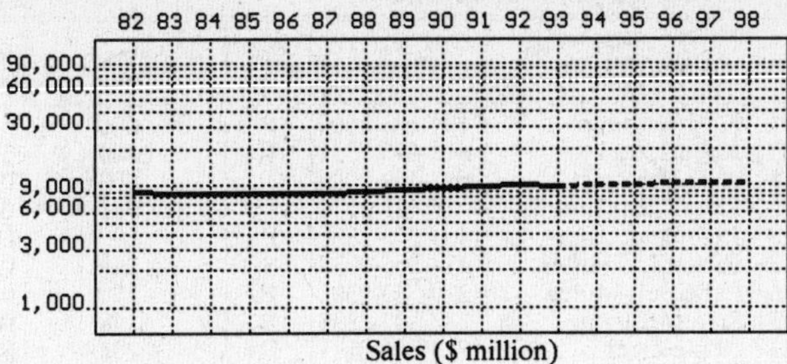

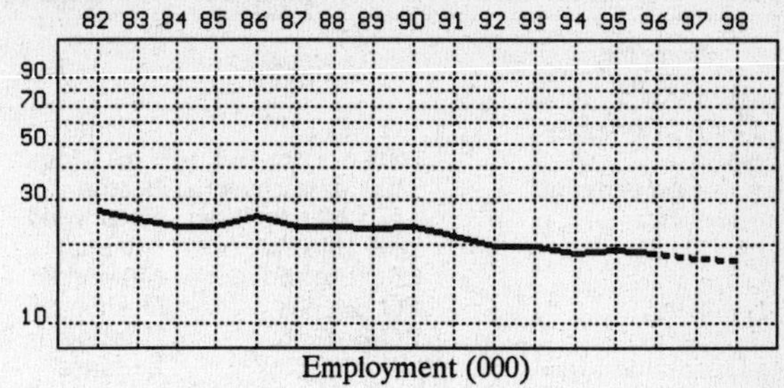

GENERAL STATISTICS

Year	Establishments (number)	Employment (number)	Payroll ($ million)	Sales ($ million)	Expenses ($ million)	Beginning Inventory ($ million)	Ending Inventory ($ million)
1982	1,630	27,280	374.3	8,752.5	-	-	-
1983	1,598	25,227	360.3	8,712.7e	-	-	-
1984	1,425	23,628	353.1	8,673.0e	-	-	-
1985	1,354	23,794	375.4	8,633.2e	-	-	-
1986	1,267	26,033	408.7	8,593.5e	-	-	-
1987	1,372	23,850	405.5	8,553.7	888.9	149.4	153.1
1988	1,298	23,720	438.3	8,866.6e	908.4e	153.6e	157.3e
1989	1,207	23,169	445.3	9,179.5e	927.9e	157.9e	161.4e
1990	1,152	23,765	477.9	9,492.4e	947.4e	162.1e	165.6e
1991	1,118	21,903	476.4	9,805.3e	966.9e	166.3e	169.8e
1992	1,224	19,916	444.3	10,118.2	986.4	170.5	174.0
1993	1,141	19,672	448.9	9,854.0p	1,005.9p	174.7p	178.2p
1994	1,069	18,488	433.3	9,990.6p	1,025.3p	179.0p	182.4p
1995	1,019	19,091	448.8	10,127.2p	1,044.8p	183.2p	186.6p
1996	968p	18,459p	481.4p	10,263.7p	1,064.3p	187.4p	190.8p
1997	927p	17,877p	489.5p	10,400.3p	1,083.8p	191.6p	195.0p
1998	886p	17,295p	497.5p	10,536.9p	1,103.3p	195.9p	199.2p

Sources: *Economic Census of the United States*, 1982, 1987, and 1992. Establishment counts, employment, and payroll are from *County Business Patterns* for non-Census years. Values followed by a 'p' are projections by the editors. Sales and expense data for non-Census years are extrapolations, marked by 'e'. Industries reclassified in 1987 will not have data for prior years. Data are the most recent available at this level of detail.

INDICES OF CHANGE

Year	Establishments (number)	Employment (number)	Payroll ($ million)	Sales ($ million)	Expenses ($ million)	Beginning Inventory ($ million)	Ending Inventory ($ million)
1982	133.2	137.0	84.2	86.5	-	-	-
1983	130.6	126.7	81.1	86.1e	-	-	-
1984	116.4	118.6	79.5	85.7e	-	-	-
1985	110.6	119.5	84.5	85.3e	-	-	-
1986	103.5	130.7	92.0	84.9e	-	-	-
1987	112.1	119.8	91.3	84.5	90.1	87.6	88.0
1988	106.0	119.1	98.6	87.6e	92.1e	90.1e	90.4e
1989	98.6	116.3	100.2	90.7e	94.1e	92.6e	92.8e
1990	94.1	119.3	107.6	93.8e	96.0e	95.1e	95.2e
1991	91.3	110.0	107.2	96.9e	98.0e	97.5e	97.6e
1992	100.0	100.0	100.0	100.0	100.0	100.0	100.0
1993	93.2	98.8	101.0	97.4p	102.0p	102.5p	102.4p
1994	87.3	92.8	97.5	98.7p	103.9p	105.0p	104.8p
1995	83.3	95.9	101.0	100.1p	105.9p	107.4p	107.2p
1996	79.1p	92.7p	108.3p	101.4p	107.9p	109.9p	109.7p
1997	75.7p	89.8p	110.2p	102.8p	109.9p	112.4p	112.0p
1998	72.4p	86.8p	112.0p	104.1p	111.8p	114.9p	114.5p

Sources: Same as General Statistics. The values shown reflect change from the base year, 1992. Values above 100 mean greater than 1992, values below 100 mean less than 1992, and a value of 100 in the 1982-91 or 1993-98 period means same as 1992. Values followed by a 'p' are projections by the editors; 'e' stands for extrapolation. Data are the most recent available at this level of detail.

SELECTED RATIOS

For 1992	Avg. of All Wholesale	Analyzed Industry	Index	For 1992	Avg. of All Wholesale	Analyzed Industry	Index
Employees per Establishment	12	16	139	Sales per Employee	561,172	508,044	91
Payroll per Establishment	349,729	362,990	104	Sales per Establishment	6,559,346	8,266,503	126
Payroll per Employee	29,919	22,309	75	Expenses per Establishment	723,071	805,882	111

Sources: Same as General Statistics. The 'Average of All Manufacturing' column represents the average of all manufacturing industries reported for the most recent complete year available. The Index shows the relationship between the Average and the Analyzed Industry. For example, 100 means that they are equal; 500 that the Analyzed Industry is five times the average; 50 means that the Analyzed Industry is half the national average. The abbreviation 'na' is used to show that data are 'not available'.

LEADING COMPANIES

Number shown: **50** Total sales ($ mil): **4,634** Total employment (000): **21.5**

Company Name	Address				CEO Name	Phone	Co. Type	Sales ($ mil)	Empl. (000)
Golden Poultry Company Inc.	PO Box 2210	Atlanta	GA	30301	K. N Whitmire	404-393-5000	P	600	5.7
Zacky Foods Co.	2000 N Tyler Ave	S. El Monte	CA	91733	Robert Zacky	818-443-9351	R	600	3.0
Agar Supply Company Inc.	1100 Massachusetts	Boston	MA	02125	Alan Bressler	617-442-8989	R	400*	0.4
Western Beef Inc.	47-05 Metropolitan	Ridgewood	NY	11385	Peter Castellana Jr	718-417-3770	P	341	2.0
Cagle's Inc.	2000 Hills Ave NW	Atlanta	GA	30318	J Douglas Cagle	404-355-2820	P	309	3.1
Entree Corp.	8200 Brown Deer	Milwaukee	WI	53223	Richard Y Fisher	414-355-0037	S	219	0.3
Troyer Foods Inc.	PO Box 608	Goshen	IN	46526	Paris Ball-Miller	219-533-0302	R	170	0.2
Randall Foods Inc.	PO Box 2669	Huntington P.	CA	90255	Stan M Bloom	213-587-2383	R	168	0.5
Harker's Distribution Inc.	801 6th St SW	Le Mars	IA	51031	Ron Geiger	712-546-8171	R	160	0.5
Crystal Farms	6465 Wayzata Blvd	Minneapolis	MN	55426	N A Rodriquez	612-544-8101	S	156*	0.4
Norbest Inc.	PO Box 1000	Midvale	UT	84047	Steven Jensen	801-566-5656	R	140	1.2
Case Farms of North Carolina	PO Box 308	Morganton	NC	28655	Thomas Shelton	704-438-6900	R	130*	0.7
Mott's of Mississippi	PO Box 708	Water Valley	MS	38965	Tom Mallalie	601-473-1771	D	90*	0.3
Petaluma Poultry Processors	PO Box 7368	Petaluma	CA	94955	Allen Shainsky	707-763-1907	R	76*	0.2
Sun City Industries Inc.	5545 NW 35th Ave	Ft Lauderdale	FL	33309	Malvin Avchen	305-730-3333	P	68	0.2
Robert Wholey and Company	1501 Penn Ave	Pittsburgh	PA	15222	Robert L Wholey	412-261-3693	R	65	0.2
Sutherland Foodservice Inc.	PO Box 786	Forest Park	GA	30051	JE Sutherland	404-366-8550	R	63*	0.2
Central Connecticut Cooperative	PO Box 8500	Manchester	CT	06040	Bob Jacquire	203-649-4523	R	55*	<0.1
J. Kings Food Service	700 Furrows Rd	Holtsville	NY	11742	John King	516-289-8401	R	50	0.1
McFarling Foods Inc.	333 W 14th St	Indianapolis	IN	46202	Don McFarling	317-635-2633	R	50	0.1
L. Craelius and Company Inc.	1100 W Fulton St	Chicago	IL	60607	Larry A Craelius	312-666-7100	R	47*	<0.1
Lincoln Poultry and Egg Co.	2005 M St	Lincoln	NE	68510	Richard Evnen	402-477-3757	R	47*	0.1
McInerney-Miller Brothers Inc.	2001 Brewster St	Detroit	MI	48207	DI Miller	313-833-4800	R	47*	0.1
Will Poultry Co.	1075 William St	Buffalo	NY	14206	Donald E Will	716-853-2000	R	47*	0.1
ConAgra Poultry Co.	2475 Meadow Brk	Duluth	GA	30096	Russ Bragg	770-232-4200	S	45	0.1
Hillandale Farms of Florida	PO Box 1703	Lake City	FL	32056	Jack E Hazen	904-755-1870	R	45	0.2
Metropolitan Poultry	1920 Stanford Ct	Landover	MD	20785	Brian C Willard	301-772-0060	R	38	0.1
Dutt and Wagner of Virginia	Hwy 11 W	Abingdon	VA	24210	Peggy Wagner	703-628-2116	R	35*	0.1
Zanios Foods Inc.	PO Box 27730	Albuquerque	NM	87125	Jim Zanios	505-831-1411	R	34*	<0.1
Hemmelgran and Sons Inc.	PO Box 169	Coldwater	OH	45828	Ronald Gross	419-678-2351	R	30	<0.1
Poultry Specialties Inc.	PO Box 2061	Russellville	AR	72811	Phil Carruth	501-968-1777	R	30	<0.1
Zephyr Egg Co.	PO Box 9005	Zephyrhills	FL	33539	Lois Linville	813-782-1521	R	30	0.2
Roberts Foods Inc.	1615 W Jefferson St	Springfield	IL	62702	Dean Robert Jr	217-793-2633	R	25	<0.1
Lambright's Inc.	PO Box 71	Lagrange	IN	46761	R D Lambright	219-463-2178	R	24	0.1
Smith Packing Company Inc.	PO Box 446	Utica	NY	13503	Wesley Smith	315-732-5125	R	17	<0.1
Jawd Associates Inc.	47-49 Little W 12th	New York	NY	10014	Robert Dee	212-989-2000	R	15*	<0.1
Jordan Meat and Livestock	1225 W 3300 S	Salt Lake City	UT	84119	Irvin Guss	801-972-8770	R	15	<0.1
Loda Poultry Company Inc.	PO Box 246	Loda	IL	60948	Beth Bauman	217-386-2381	R	15*	<0.1
Feather Crest Farms Inc.	14374 E SH 21	Bryan	TX	77808	DR Barrett	409-589-2576	R	14	<0.1
Forrest Foods Inc.	1050 Thorndale	Bensenville	IL	60106	Terry Levy	708-766-0400	R	14*	<0.1
Thayer Food Products Inc.	962 87th Ave	Oakland	CA	94621	RW Thayer Sr	510-569-7943	R	14*	<0.1
Thomas Brothers Ham Co.	1852 Gold Hill Rd	Asheboro	NC	27203	Howard M Thomas	910-672-0337	R	13	<0.1
United Meat Company Inc.	1040 Bryant St	San Francisco	CA	94103	Douglas Gee	415-864-2118	R	13	<0.1
Race Street Foods Inc.	PO Box 28385	San Jose	CA	95159	G Barsanti	408-294-6161	R	13*	0.1
Comer Packing Company Inc.	PO Box 33	Aberdeen	MS	39730	Jimmie Comer	601-369-9325	R	12	<0.1
Egg Products Inc.	PO Box 517	Muskego	WI	53150	Wayne Boldt	414-422-9700	R	10	<0.1
Gant Food Distributors Inc.	1200 Carter Rd	Owensboro	KY	42301	James Gant	502-684-2382	R	10*	<0.1
Rose Hill Distribution Inc.	81 Rose Hill Rd	Branford	CT	06405	Rae Shebell	203-488-7231	R	9*	<0.1
Vallet Food Service Inc.	1230 E 12th St	Dubuque	IA	52001	Edward G White	319-588-2347	R	9*	<0.1
Consolidated Poultry&Egg Co.	426 St Paul Ave	Memphis	TN	38126	James J Skefos	901-523-1366	R	8	<0.1

Source: *Ward's Business Directory of U.S. Private and Public Companies*, 1998. The company type code used is as follows: P - Public, R - Private, S - Subsidiary, D - Division, J - Joint Venture, A - Affiliate, G - Group. Sales are in millions of dollars, employees are in thousands. An asterisk (*) indicates an estimated sales volume. The symbol < stands for 'less than'.

OCCUPATIONS EMPLOYED BY SIC 514 - GROCERIES AND RELATED PRODUCTS

Occupation	% of Total 1996	Change to 2006	Occupation	% of Total 1996	Change to 2006
Sales & related workers nec	14.5	21.9	Industrial truck & tractor operators	2.4	21.9
Truck drivers light & heavy	12.6	10.8	Bookkeeping, accounting, & auditing clerks	2.4	-11.3
Driver/sales workers	6.1	33.0	Helpers, laborers nec	2.1	10.8
Freight, stock, & material movers, hand	4.9	-0.2	Salespersons, retail	1.7	10.8
General managers & top executives	3.7	7.4	Secretaries, except legal & medical	1.6	-12.1
Order fillers, wholesale & retail sales	3.7	10.8	Butchers & meatcutters	1.5	-11.3
Stock clerks	3.6	10.8	Blue collar worker supervisors	1.5	7.0
Hand packers & packagers	3.3	10.8	Packaging & filling machine operators	1.4	10.8
Traffic, shipping, receiving clerks	3.0	10.8	Wholesale & retail buyers, except farm products	1.4	7.9
Marketing & sales worker supervisors	2.9	10.8	Order clerks	1.2	-0.2
Agricultural, forestry, fishing workers nec	2.8	21.9	Clerical supervisors & managers	1.2	10.9
General office clerks	2.5	-4.6			

Source: *Industry-Occupation Matrix*, Bureau of Labor Statistics. These data relate to one or more 3-digit SIC industry groups rather than to a single 4-digit SIC. The change reported for each occupation to the year 2006 is a percent of growth or decline as estimated by the Bureau of Labor Statistics. The abbreviation nec stands for 'not elsewhere classified'.

STATE AND REGIONAL CONCENTRATION

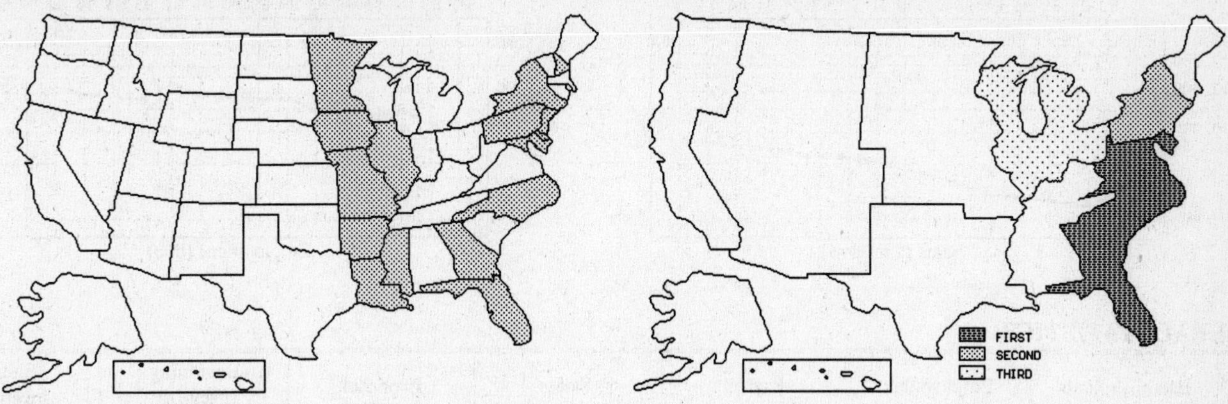

INDUSTRY DATA BY STATE

	Establishments - 1995		Employment - 1995			Payroll - 1995		Sales - 1992		
State	Total (number)	% of U.S.	Total (number)	% of U.S.	Per Estab.	Total ($ mil.)	Per Empl. ($)	Total ($ mil.)	% of U.S.	Per Estab ($)
California	102	10.0	1,916	10.2	19	52.4	27,336	1,062.4	11.0	511,257
New York	85	8.3	996	5.3	12	27.5	27,596	726.7	7.5	678,500
Texas	74	7.3	1,067	5.7	14	25.9	24,239	604.2	6.3	506,448
Pennsylvania	63	6.2	1,070	5.7	17	26.7	24,955	583.0	6.0	382,785
Illinois	49	4.8	1,048	5.6	21	27.1	25,884	568.9	5.9	510,214
North Carolina	47	4.6	832	4.4	18	23.5	28,195	568.4	5.9	532,191
Missouri	35	3.4	757	4.0	22	15.5	20,461	554.1	5.7	828,239
Florida	53	5.2	1,235	6.6	23	24.1	19,495	547.2	5.7	600,037
Georgia	52	5.1	1,251	6.6	24	26.1	20,886	377.1	3.9	293,459
Arkansas	25	2.5	730	3.9	29	17.4	23,895	374.6	3.9	415,797
New Jersey	34	3.3	452	2.4	13	14.0	30,909	305.5	3.2	763,638
Minnesota	21	2.1	406	2.2	19	9.4	23,054	305.1	3.2	938,677
Mississippi	21	2.1	103	0.5	5	4.1	39,680	292.3	3.0	2,016,000
Ohio	38	3.7	1,337	7.1	35	22.2	16,599	282.2	2.9	221,696
Maryland	15	1.5	328	1.7	22	10.1	30,848	257.6	2.7	451,086
Louisiana	7	0.7	60	0.3	9	0.7	12,367	232.3	2.4	1,191,138
Indiana	17	1.7	499	2.6	29	9.7	19,491	189.9	2.0	518,981
Washington	20	2.0	476	2.5	24	10.9	22,868	184.5	1.9	545,757
Wisconsin	13	1.3	288	1.5	22	7.0	24,420	168.8	1.8	506,829
New Hampshire	9	0.9	234	1.2	26	6.3	27,051	139.7	1.4	802,661
Michigan	15	1.5	166	0.9	11	4.7	28,440	137.4	1.4	651,237
Virginia	16	1.6	571	3.0	36	10.2	17,848	137.2	1.4	329,786
Iowa	17	1.7	400	2.1	24	6.3	15,770	131.4	1.4	453,017
Tennessee	22	2.2	251	1.3	11	6.1	24,124	116.4	1.2	444,114
Alabama	23	2.3	365	1.9	16	5.4	14,847	113.7	1.2	554,517
Connecticut	10	1.0	234	1.2	23	6.1	26,209	103.5	1.1	415,651
South Carolina	14	1.4	310	1.6	22	6.5	20,971	88.9	0.9	282,270
Arizona	11	1.1	93	0.5	8	2.2	23,839	75.3	0.8	566,481
Kentucky	11	1.1	171	0.9	16	2.9	17,000	62.8	0.7	234,187
Delaware	4	0.4	40	0.2	10	1.5	37,150	56.7	0.6	1,318,349
Kansas	9	0.9	196	1.0	22	3.8	19,633	53.8	0.6	413,477
Utah	9	0.9	67	0.4	7	1.5	23,000	53.2	0.6	542,439
Oklahoma	10	1.0	259	1.4	26	4.9	18,834	45.0	0.5	225,935
Colorado	3	0.3	23	0.1	8	0.7	31,609	42.5	0.4	989,070
D.C.	2	0.2	0-19	-	-	(D)	-	31.5	0.3	1,970,250
New Mexico	2	0.2	20-99	-	-	(D)	-	22.2	0.2	238,366
Montana	1	0.1	0-19	-	-	(D)	-	19.7	0.2	532,649
Rhode Island	2	0.2	0-19	-	-	(D)	-	16.1	0.2	460,314
South Dakota	1	0.1	0-19	-	-	(D)	-	11.7	0.1	585,250
Massachusetts	24	2.4	327	1.7	14	10.9	33,245	(D)	-	-
Hawaii	9	0.9	125	0.7	14	2.6	20,512	(D)	-	-
Oregon	5	0.5	62	0.3	12	2.2	35,161	(D)	-	-
Nebraska	4	0.4	100-249	-	-	(D)	-	(D)	-	-
Nevada	4	0.4	57	0.3	14	1.8	31,298	(D)	-	-
Idaho	3	0.3	23	0.1	8	0.3	14,565	(D)	-	-
Vermont	3	0.3	15	0.1	5	0.6	40,267	(D)	-	-
Maine	2	0.2	20-99	-	-	(D)	-	(D)	-	-
North Dakota	1	0.1	0-19	-	-	(D)	-	(D)	-	-
West Virginia	1	0.1	0-19	-	-	(D)	-	(D)	-	-
Wyoming	1	0.1	0-19	-	-	(D)	-	(D)	-	-

Source: *County Business Patterns, 1995* and *Economic Census of the U.S., 1992*. Data are sorted by 1992 revenues and, if revenues are unavailable, by establishments in 1995. The symbol (D) indicates that data are withheld by the source to avoid disclosure of competitive information. A dash (-) indicates that data are not available or undisclosed because they do not meet statistical validity standards. Shaded *states* on the state map indicate those states which have proportionately greater representation in the industry than would be indicated by the state's population; the ratio is based on total revenues or number of establishments. Shaded *regions* indicate where the industry is regionally most concentrated.

5145 - CONFECTIONERY

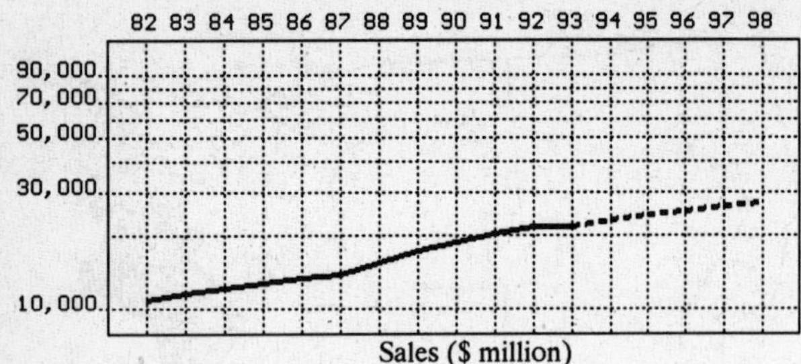

Sales ($ million)

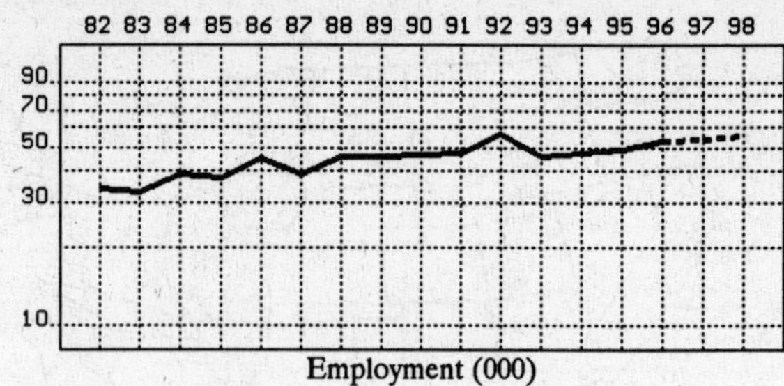

Employment (000)

GENERAL STATISTICS

Year	Establishments (number)	Employment (number)	Payroll ($ million)	Sales ($ million)	Expenses ($ million)	Beginning Inventory ($ million)	Ending Inventory ($ million)
1982	2,595	34,448	648.7	10,876.8	-	-	-
1983	2,595	33,206	616.1	11,491.8e	-	-	-
1984	2,452	39,394	786.6	12,106.9e	-	-	-
1985	2,394	37,783	749.5	12,721.9e	-	-	-
1986	2,332	45,202	832.3	13,337.0e	-	-	-
1987	2,818	39,271	828.6	13,952.0	1,581.9	558.0	576.5
1988	2,620	45,978	1,071.9	15,522.7e	1,739.6e	600.9e	616.2e
1989	2,514	45,696	1,115.2	17,093.4e	1,897.3e	643.9e	655.9e
1990	2,505	46,704	1,218.9	18,664.0e	2,055.0e	686.9e	695.7e
1991	2,454	46,899	1,263.3	20,234.7e	2,212.7e	729.9e	735.4e
1992	2,693	56,322	1,203.5	21,805.4	2,370.4	772.8	775.1
1993	2,548	45,891	1,182.4	21,812.3p	2,528.1p	815.8p	814.9p
1994	2,541	46,847	1,256.3	22,905.2p	2,685.7p	858.8p	854.6p
1995	2,464	49,075	1,330.9	23,998.0p	2,843.4p	901.7p	894.3p
1996	2,541p	52,979p	1,436.3p	25,090.9p	3,001.1p	944.7p	934.1p
1997	2,542p	54,207p	1,493.5p	26,183.7p	3,158.8p	987.7p	973.8p
1998	2,542p	55,436p	1,550.7p	27,276.6p	3,316.5p	1,030.6p	1,013.5p

Sources: Economic Census of the United States, 1982, 1987, and 1992. Establishment counts, employment, and payroll are from *County Business Patterns* for non-Census years. Values followed by a 'p' are projections by the editors. Sales and expense data for non-Census years are extrapolations, marked by 'e'. Industries reclassified in 1987 will not have data for prior years. Data are the most recent available at this level of detail.

INDICES OF CHANGE

Year	Establishments (number)	Employment (number)	Payroll ($ million)	Sales ($ million)	Expenses ($ million)	Beginning Inventory ($ million)	Ending Inventory ($ million)
1982	96.4	61.2	53.9	49.9	-	-	-
1983	96.4	59.0	51.2	52.7e	-	-	-
1984	91.1	69.9	65.4	55.5e	-	-	-
1985	88.9	67.1	62.3	58.3e	-	-	-
1986	86.6	80.3	69.2	61.2e	-	-	-
1987	104.6	69.7	68.8	64.0	66.7	72.2	74.4
1988	97.3	81.6	89.1	71.2e	73.4e	77.8e	79.5e
1989	93.4	81.1	92.7	78.4e	80.0e	83.3e	84.6e
1990	93.0	82.9	101.3	85.6e	86.7e	88.9e	89.8e
1991	91.1	83.3	105.0	92.8e	93.3e	94.4e	94.9e
1992	100.0	100.0	100.0	100.0	100.0	100.0	100.0
1993	94.6	81.5	98.2	100.0p	106.7p	105.6p	105.1p
1994	94.4	83.2	104.4	105.0p	113.3p	111.1p	110.3p
1995	91.5	87.1	110.6	110.1p	120.0p	116.7p	115.4p
1996	94.4p	94.1p	119.3p	115.1p	126.6p	122.2p	120.5p
1997	94.4p	96.2p	124.1p	120.1p	133.3p	127.8p	125.6p
1998	94.4p	98.4p	128.8p	125.1p	139.9p	133.4p	130.8p

Sources: Same as General Statistics. The values shown reflect change from the base year, 1992. Values above 100 mean greater than 1992, values below 100 mean less than 1992, and a value of 100 in the 1982-91 or 1993-98 period means same as 1992. Values followed by a 'p' are projections by the editors; 'e' stands for extrapolation. Data are the most recent available at this level of detail.

SELECTED RATIOS

For 1992	Avg. of All Wholesale	Analyzed Industry	Index	For 1992	Avg. of All Wholesale	Analyzed Industry	Index
Employees per Establishment	12	21	179	Sales per Employee	561,172	387,156	69
Payroll per Establishment	349,729	446,899	128	Sales per Establishment	6,559,346	8,097,066	123
Payroll per Employee	29,919	21,368	71	Expenses per Establishment	723,071	880,208	122

Sources: Same as General Statistics. The 'Average of All Manufacturing' column represents the average of all manufacturing industries reported for the most recent complete year available. The Index shows the relationship between the Average and the Analyzed Industry. For example, 100 means that they are equal; 500 that the Analyzed Industry is five times the average; 50 means that the Analyzed Industry is half the national average. The abbreviation 'na' is used to show that data are 'not available'.

LEADING COMPANIES

Number shown: **50** Total sales ($ mil): **7,643** Total employment (000): **18.3**

Company Name	Address				CEO Name	Phone	Co. Type	Sales ($ mil)	Empl. (000)
Eby-Brown Company L.P.	280 Shuman Blvd	Naperville	IL	60566	William S Wake Jr	708-778-2800	R	1,450	1.2
Grocers Supply Company Inc.	PO Box 14200	Houston	TX	77221	Milton Levit	713-747-5000	R	1,300	2.0
Sathers Inc.	PO Box 28	Round Lake	MN	56167	Bill Bradfield	507-945-8181	S	360 *	1.5
Vendor Supply of America Inc.	PO Box 17387	Denver	CO	80217	Devendra Mishra	303-634-1400	S	360 *	1.5
Grocery Supply Co.	PO Box 638	Sulphur Sprgs	TX	75483	Jerry Gillem	903-885-7621	S	333 *	0.8
L and L Jiroch Distributing Co.	1180 58th St	Wyoming	MI	49509	Michael Alexander	616-530-6600	S	330 *	0.4
Farner-Bocken Co.	Hwy 30 E	Carroll	IA	51401	John Norgaard	712-792-3503	R	310 *	0.6
J.T. Davenport and Sons Inc.	PO Box 1105	Sanford	NC	27330	John T Davenport Jr	919-774-9444	R	235	0.3
Core-Mark International Inc.	395 Oyster Pt Blvd	S. San Francisco	CA	94080	Gary L Walsh	650-589-9445	R	220	2.2
Warehouse Club Inc.	7235 N Linder Ave	Skokie	IL	60077	Everett L Buckardt	708-679-6800	P	215	0.9
Associated Grocers	PO Box 5200	Manchester	NH	03108	Norman J Turcotte	603-669-3250	R	200	0.3
Houston Foods Co.	3501 Mt Prospect	Franklin Park	IL	60131	Robert P Pesch	847-957-9191	R	196 *	0.2
Grocers Specialty Co.	2601 S Eastern Ave	Los Angeles	CA	90040	Alfred Plamann	213-726-2601	S	160 *	0.2
Albert H. Notini and Sons Inc.	PO Box 299	Lowell	MA	01853	Alex Turshette	508-459-7151	R	130 *	0.2
Miller and Hartman South Inc.	PO Box 218	Leitchfield	KY	42755	Wayne Jones	502-444-7246	S	130 *	0.3
L and L Concession Co.	1307 Maple Rd	Troy	MI	48084	Jerome B Levy	810-689-3850	R	122 *	0.5
Mutual Distributors Inc.	PO Box 330	Lakeland	FL	33802	William D Mills	941-688-0042	R	110 *	0.4
Burklund Distributors Inc.	2500 N Main St	East Peoria	IL	61611	Dale E Burklund	309-694-1900	R	90 *	0.1
George Melhado Co.	10 Merchant St	Sharon	MA	02067	Warren J Alberts	617-784-5550	R	88 *	0.1
James Brudnick Company Inc.	219 Medford St	Malden	MA	02148	Richard Brudnick	617-321-6800	R	77 *	0.1
Remarks Inc.	6728 Hyland Croy	Dublin	OH	43017	Malcolm J Graves	614-889-2561	R	75	0.3
Los Angeles Nut House	1601 E Olympic	Los Angeles	CA	90021	Michael Booker	213-623-2541	S	67 *	<0.1
R.H. Barringer Distributing	1620 Fairfax Rd	Greensboro	NC	27407	Mark Craig	910-854-0555	R	66 *	0.2
Old Dutch Foods Inc.	2375 Terminal Rd	Roseville	MN	55113	Vernon O Aanenson	612-633-8810	R	63	0.4
Mike-Sell's Potato Chip Co.	333 Leo St	Dayton	OH	45404	Leslie C Mapp	513-228-9400	S	60 *	0.3
Mound City Industries Inc.	1315 Cherokee St	St. Louis	MO	63118	Robert L Krekeler	314-773-5200	R	60 *	<0.1
Sunshine Nut Co.	16435 I-35	Selma	TX	78154	Chuck Taylor	210-651-5300	S	57	0.2
Tzetzo Brothers Inc.	1100 Military Rd	Buffalo	NY	14217	Perry Tzetzo	716-877-0800	R	54	0.1
Bunn Capitol Co.	PO Box 4227	Springfield	IL	62708	B Bunn	217-529-5401	R	50	0.2
Perugina Brands of America	299 Market St	Saddle Brook	NJ	07663	J Dattoli	201-587-8080	D	50	<0.1
C.J. Vitner Company Inc.	4202 W 45th St	Chicago	IL	60632	William A Vitner	312-523-7900	R	48	0.4
Consolidated Wholesale Co.	PO Box 26903	Oklahoma City	OK	73126	JJ Lehman	405-232-5593	D	46	<0.1
Safier's Inc.	8700 Harvard Ave	Cleveland	OH	44105	SJ Safier	216-341-8700	R	45 *	<0.1
Specialty Sales and Marketing	PO Box 23778	Harahan	LA	70183	Newton Harris	504-734-1001	D	42 *	<0.1
Preferred Products Inc.	11095 Viking Dr	Eden Prairie	MN	55344	Glenn Fischer	612-996-7400	S	36 *	0.2
SWD Corp.	PO Box 340	Lima	OH	45802	Carl Berger	419-227-2436	R	35	<0.1
United Candy and Tobacco Co.	7408 Tonnelle Ave	North Bergen	NJ	07047	J Choy	201-943-8675	R	35 *	<0.1
Silverado Foods Inc.	6846 S Canton	Tulsa	OK	74136	Lawrence D Field	918-496-2400	P	34	0.6
Pine Lesser and Sons Inc.	PO Box 1807	Clifton	NJ	07015	Allan G Lesser	973-478-3310	R	32 *	<0.1
Foreign Candy Company Inc.	451 Black Forest	Hull	IA	51239	Peter W De Yager	712-439-1496	R	32 *	0.1
Torn and Glasser Inc.	PO Box 21823	Los Angeles	CA	90021	Robert Glasser	213-627-6496	R	30 *	<0.1
Homa Co.	PO Box 5425	Parsippany	NJ	07054	Ali Amin	201-887-6500	R	26 *	0.1
Albert's Organics Inc.	1330 E 6th St	Los Angeles	CA	90021	Albert Lusk	213-891-1310	R	25	<0.1
Blevins Concession Supply	5000 E Acline Dr	Tampa	FL	33619	Randy Green	813-247-7116	R	25	0.1
J. Sosnick and Son	258 Littlefield Ave	S. San Francisco	CA	94080	Myron J Sosnick	415-952-2226	R	25	0.1
Fritz Company Inc.	1912 Hastings Ave	Newport	MN	55055	James Fritz	612-459-9751	R	24 *	0.1
Peter P. Dennis Inc.	1224 S Main St	Phillipsburg	NJ	08865	John Zarbatany	908-454-2141	R	24	<0.1
Shari Candies Inc.	1804 N 2nd St	Mankato	MN	56001	Arlen T Kitsis	507-387-1181	R	22 *	0.2
Benham and Company Inc.	PO Box 29	Mineola	TX	75773	Raymond Curbow	903-569-2636	S	20	<0.1
F.A. Davis and Sons Inc.	6610 Cabot Dr	Baltimore	MD	21226	Louis V Manzo	410-360-6000	R	20 *	0.2

Source: *Ward's Business Directory of U.S. Private and Public Companies*, 1998. The company type code used is as follows: P - Public, R - Private, S - Subsidiary, D - Division, J - Joint Venture, A - Affiliate, G - Group. Sales are in millions of dollars, employees are in thousands. An asterisk (*) indicates an estimated sales volume. The symbol < stands for 'less than'.

OCCUPATIONS EMPLOYED BY SIC 514 - GROCERIES AND RELATED PRODUCTS

Occupation	% of Total 1996	Change to 2006	Occupation	% of Total 1996	Change to 2006
Sales & related workers nec	14.5	21.9	Industrial truck & tractor operators	2.4	21.9
Truck drivers light & heavy	12.6	10.8	Bookkeeping, accounting, & auditing clerks	2.4	-11.3
Driver/sales workers	6.1	33.0	Helpers, laborers nec	2.1	10.8
Freight, stock, & material movers, hand	4.9	-0.2	Salespersons, retail	1.7	10.8
General managers & top executives	3.7	7.4	Secretaries, except legal & medical	1.6	-12.1
Order fillers, wholesale & retail sales	3.7	10.8	Butchers & meatcutters	1.5	-11.3
Stock clerks	3.6	10.8	Blue collar worker supervisors	1.5	7.0
Hand packers & packagers	3.3	10.8	Packaging & filling machine operators	1.4	10.8
Traffic, shipping, receiving clerks	3.0	10.8	Wholesale & retail buyers, except farm products	1.4	7.9
Marketing & sales worker supervisors	2.9	10.8	Order clerks	1.2	-0.2
Agricultural, forestry, fishing workers nec	2.8	21.9	Clerical supervisors & managers	1.2	10.9
General office clerks	2.5	-4.6			

Source: *Industry-Occupation Matrix*, Bureau of Labor Statistics. These data relate to one or more 3-digit SIC industry groups rather than to a single 4-digit SIC. The change reported for each occupation to the year 2006 is a percent of growth or decline as estimated by the Bureau of Labor Statistics. The abbreviation nec stands for 'not elsewhere classified'.

STATE AND REGIONAL CONCENTRATION

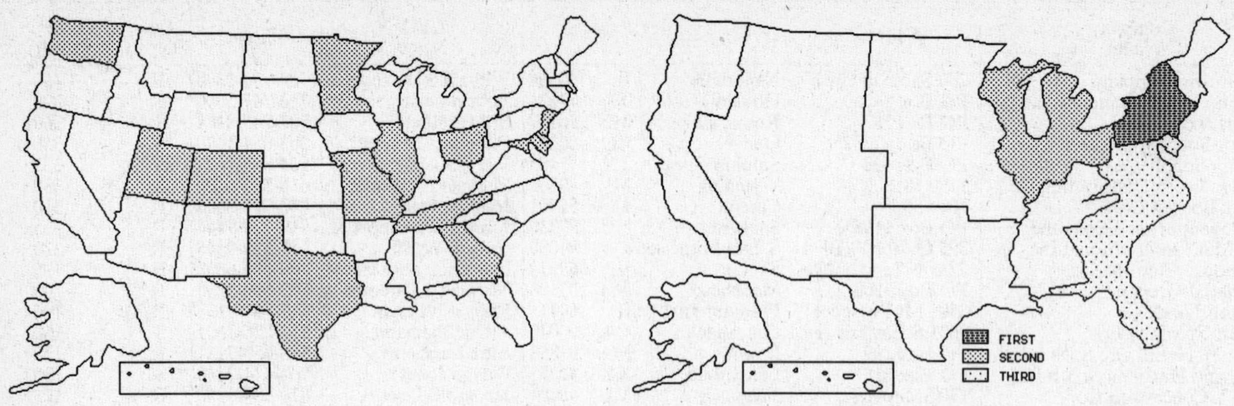

INDUSTRY DATA BY STATE

	Establishments - 1995		Employment - 1995			Payroll - 1995		Sales - 1992		
State	Total (number)	% of U.S.	Total (number)	% of U.S.	Per Estab.	Total ($ mil.)	Per Empl. ($)	Total ($ mil.)	% of U.S.	Per Estab ($)
New Jersey	103	4.2	3,124	6.4	30	122.5	39,221	3,458.3	16.0	1,117,394
California	241	9.8	5,454	11.1	23	143.2	26,264	2,314.7	10.7	363,941
Illinois	119	4.8	3,336	6.8	28	97.4	29,199	1,768.0	8.2	376,737
Texas	156	6.3	5,127	10.5	33	130.3	25,411	1,576.2	7.3	271,948
New York	212	8.6	2,197	4.5	10	63.4	28,848	1,094.1	5.1	389,367
Ohio	116	4.7	2,731	5.6	24	68.1	24,942	979.4	4.5	358,610
Pennsylvania	143	5.8	1,872	3.8	13	48.9	26,116	897.8	4.2	411,264
Georgia	79	3.2	1,731	3.5	22	48.4	27,953	873.0	4.0	416,328
Maryland	39	1.6	966	2.0	25	29.8	30,832	834.8	3.9	729,680
Florida	120	4.9	2,093	4.3	17	56.9	27,184	659.5	3.1	279,821
Missouri	56	2.3	1,228	2.5	22	29.9	24,324	612.9	2.8	419,539
Michigan	88	3.6	1,552	3.2	18	45.5	29,320	597.2	2.8	255,885
Tennessee	54	2.2	1,374	2.8	25	30.7	22,368	578.9	2.7	370,382
Minnesota	51	2.1	1,471	3.0	29	35.1	23,844	511.9	2.4	416,843
North Carolina	66	2.7	1,487	3.0	23	36.4	24,463	494.4	2.3	350,387
Massachusetts	55	2.2	965	2.0	18	25.4	26,331	481.6	2.2	490,391
Washington	56	2.3	868	1.8	15	23.9	27,528	456.1	2.1	413,924
Colorado	44	1.8	879	1.8	20	26.9	30,576	413.7	1.9	407,619
Wisconsin	52	2.1	816	1.7	16	20.0	24,471	343.3	1.6	375,154
Virginia	49	2.0	840	1.7	17	21.8	25,943	302.3	1.4	244,359
Alabama	43	1.7	817	1.7	19	21.3	26,097	244.6	1.1	274,238
Connecticut	30	1.2	358	0.7	12	11.1	31,087	213.2	1.0	411,651
Louisiana	35	1.4	719	1.5	21	19.5	27,089	202.6	0.9	252,250
Kentucky	32	1.3	413	0.8	13	10.0	24,136	178.5	0.8	381,410
Utah	23	0.9	475	1.0	21	12.6	26,596	171.0	0.8	350,447
Arizona	28	1.1	614	1.3	22	15.5	25,205	153.2	0.7	225,293
Kansas	24	1.0	370	0.8	15	9.5	25,597	149.8	0.7	350,895
Indiana	52	2.1	592	1.2	11	12.3	20,836	120.6	0.6	202,711
South Carolina	21	0.9	480	1.0	23	10.6	22,123	107.5	0.5	175,055
Oregon	35	1.4	494	1.0	14	13.2	26,684	102.6	0.5	318,696
Oklahoma	18	0.7	421	0.9	23	9.9	23,492	95.8	0.4	174,466
Hawaii	26	1.1	278	0.6	11	7.4	26,712	93.6	0.4	284,617
Arkansas	19	0.8	308	0.6	16	8.1	26,224	92.5	0.4	229,561
Iowa	14	0.6	395	0.8	28	9.0	22,841	76.2	0.4	256,468
Mississippi	29	1.2	420	0.9	14	9.8	23,255	67.3	0.3	148,282
New Hampshire	9	0.4	199	0.4	22	5.8	29,281	58.8	0.3	209,089
New Mexico	17	0.7	234	0.5	14	5.4	22,970	47.1	0.2	186,103
West Virginia	15	0.6	269	0.5	18	7.1	26,431	43.3	0.2	139,806
Vermont	5	0.2	50	0.1	10	2.0	40,820	25.4	0.1	650,333
Alaska	7	0.3	87	0.2	12	2.8	32,011	21.6	0.1	244,909
South Dakota	4	0.2	20-99	-	-	(D)	-	17.5	0.1	295,831
Maine	12	0.5	47	0.1	4	1.0	21,660	11.1	0.1	184,917
D.C.	2	0.1	20-99	-	-	(D)	-	8.4	0.0	349,500
Montana	7	0.3	25	0.1	4	0.3	10,040	6.8	0.0	322,619
Wyoming	4	0.2	20-99	-	-	(D)	-	0.8	0.0	277,667
Nebraska	16	0.6	237	0.5	15	6.5	27,506	(D)	-	-
Rhode Island	10	0.4	90	0.2	9	2.0	22,144	(D)	-	-
Nevada	9	0.4	48	0.1	5	0.5	10,208	(D)	-	-
Idaho	8	0.3	87	0.2	11	1.9	21,494	(D)	-	-
North Dakota	8	0.3	301	0.6	38	8.2	27,179	(D)	-	-
Delaware	3	0.1	20-99	-	-	(D)	-	(D)	-	-

Source: County Business Patterns, 1995 and *Economic Census of the U.S., 1992*. Data are sorted by 1992 revenues and, if revenues are unavailable, by establishments in 1995. The symbol (D) indicates that data are withheld by the source to avoid disclosure of competitive information. A dash (-) indicates that data are not available or undisclosed because they do not meet statistical validity standards. Shaded *states* on the state map indicate those states which have proportionately greater representation in the industry than would be indicated by the state's population; the ratio is based on total revenues or number of establishments. Shaded *regions* indicate where the industry is regionally most concentrated.

5146 - FISH AND SEAFOODS

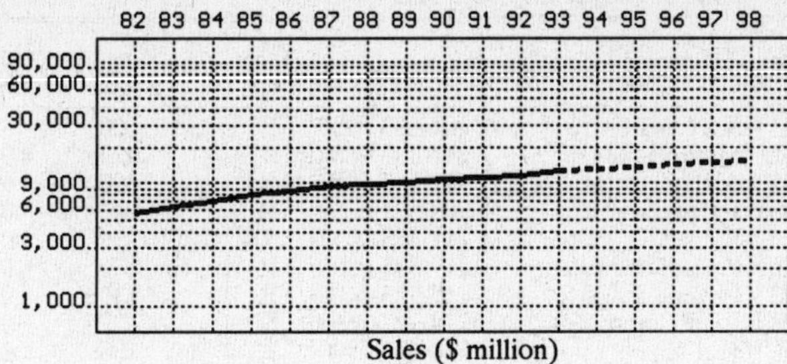

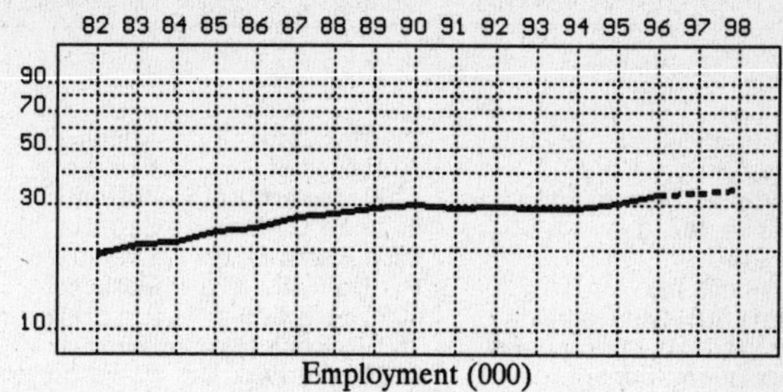

GENERAL STATISTICS

Year	Establishments (number)	Employment (number)	Payroll ($ million)	Sales ($ million)	Expenses ($ million)	Beginning Inventory ($ million)	Ending Inventory ($ million)
1982	2,174	19,096	276.1	5,706.1	-	-	-
1983	2,202	21,047	306.1	6,442.2e	-	-	-
1984	2,257	21,607	334.5	7,178.2e	-	-	-
1985	2,290	23,651	371.1	7,914.3e	-	-	-
1986	2,342	24,524	422.0	8,650.4e	-	-	-
1987	2,745	27,233	473.4	9,386.5	1,045.0	345.1	407.6
1988	2,618	28,058	536.7	9,805.5e	1,102.7e	371.6e	423.8e
1989	2,587	29,333	571.3	10,224.4e	1,160.4e	398.0e	440.1e
1990	2,606	30,028	603.4	10,643.3e	1,218.1e	424.5e	456.4e
1991	2,584	29,280	611.3	11,062.2e	1,275.8e	451.0e	472.7e
1992	3,100	29,651	591.3	11,481.2	1,333.5	477.4	489.0
1993	3,168	29,094	613.2	12,419.1p	1,391.2p	503.9p	505.3p
1994	3,223	29,511	648.7	12,996.6p	1,449.0p	530.4p	521.6p
1995	3,168	30,545	702.0	13,574.1p	1,506.7p	556.8p	537.9p
1996	3,287p	32,961p	747.1p	14,151.6p	1,564.4p	583.3p	554.2p
1997	3,372p	33,806p	779.5p	14,729.1p	1,622.1p	609.8p	570.5p
1998	3,457p	34,652p	811.8p	15,306.6p	1,679.8p	636.2p	586.8p

Sources: *Economic Census of the United States*, 1982, 1987, and 1992. Establishment counts, employment, and payroll are from *County Business Patterns* for non-Census years. Values followed by a 'p' are projections by the editors. Sales and expense data for non-Census years are extrapolations, marked by 'e'. Industries reclassified in 1987 will not have data for prior years. Data are the most recent available at this level of detail.

INDICES OF CHANGE

Year	Establishments (number)	Employment (number)	Payroll ($ million)	Sales ($ million)	Expenses ($ million)	Beginning Inventory ($ million)	Ending Inventory ($ million)
1982	70.1	64.4	46.7	49.7	-	-	-
1983	71.0	71.0	51.8	56.1e	-	-	-
1984	72.8	72.9	56.6	62.5e	-	-	-
1985	73.9	79.8	62.8	68.9e	-	-	-
1986	75.5	82.7	71.4	75.3e	-	-	-
1987	88.5	91.8	80.1	81.8	78.4	72.3	83.4
1988	84.5	94.6	90.8	85.4e	82.7e	77.8e	86.7e
1989	83.5	98.9	96.6	89.1e	87.0e	83.4e	90.0e
1990	84.1	101.3	102.0	92.7e	91.3e	88.9e	93.3e
1991	83.4	98.7	103.4	96.4e	95.7e	94.5e	96.7e
1992	100.0	100.0	100.0	100.0	100.0	100.0	100.0
1993	102.2	98.1	103.7	108.2p	104.3p	105.6p	103.3p
1994	104.0	99.5	109.7	113.2p	108.7p	111.1p	106.7p
1995	102.2	103.0	118.7	118.2p	113.0p	116.6p	110.0p
1996	106.0p	111.2p	126.4p	123.3p	117.3p	122.2p	113.3p
1997	108.8p	114.0p	131.8p	128.3p	121.6p	127.7p	116.7p
1998	111.5p	116.9p	137.3p	133.3p	126.0p	133.3p	120.0p

Sources: Same as General Statistics. The values shown reflect change from the base year, 1992. Values above 100 mean greater than 1992, values below 100 mean less than 1992, and a value of 100 in the 1982-91 or 1993-98 period means same as 1992. Values followed by a 'p' are projections by the editors; 'e' stands for extrapolation. Data are the most recent available at this level of detail.

SELECTED RATIOS

For 1992	Avg. of All Wholesale	Analyzed Industry	Index	For 1992	Avg. of All Wholesale	Analyzed Industry	Index
Employees per Establishment	12	10	82	Sales per Employee	561,172	387,211	69
Payroll per Establishment	349,729	190,742	55	Sales per Establishment	6,559,346	3,703,613	56
Payroll per Employee	29,919	19,942	67	Expenses per Establishment	723,071	430,161	59

Sources: Same as General Statistics. The 'Average of All Manufacturing' column represents the average of all manufacturing industries reported for the most recent complete year available. The Index shows the relationship between the Average and the Analyzed Industry. For example, 100 means that they are equal; 500 that the Analyzed Industry is five times the average; 50 means that the Analyzed Industry is half the national average. The abbreviation 'na' is used to show that data are 'not available'.

LEADING COMPANIES

Number shown: **50** Total sales ($ mil): **3,858** Total employment (000): **12.5**

Company Name	Address				CEO Name	Phone	Co. Type	Sales ($ mil)	Empl. (000)
Golden Poultry Company Inc.	PO Box 2210	Atlanta	GA	30301	K. N Whitmire	404-393-5000	P	600	5.7
Nomura America Corp.	60 E 42nd St	New York	NY	10165	Masami Ikeuchi	212-867-6684	S	422 *	<0.1
Agar Supply Company Inc.	1100 Massachusetts	Boston	MA	02125	Alan Bressler	617-442-8989	R	400 *	0.4
D.B. Brown Inc.	400 Port Carteret	Carteret	NJ	07008	Jeffrey Stavitsky	908-541-0200	R	340 *	0.2
Entree Corp.	8200 Brown Deer	Milwaukee	WI	53223	Richard Y Fisher	414-355-0037	S	219	0.3
Troyer Foods Inc.	PO Box 608	Goshen	IN	46526	Paris Ball-Miller	219-533-0302	R	170	0.2
California Shellfish Company	505 Beach Court	San Francisco	CA	94133	Eugene Bugatto	415-923-7400	R	130 *	0.5
Fishery Products International	18 Electronics Ave	Danvers	MA	01923	John Cummings	978-777-2660	S	127 *	0.5
Empress International Ltd.	10 Harbor Park Dr	P. Washington	NY	11050	Joel Kolen	516-621-5900	R	108	<0.1
Stavis Seafoods Inc.	7 Channel St	Boston	MA	02210	Ed Stavis	617-482-6349	R	95	<0.1
Performance Northwest Inc.	PO Box 23139	Portland	OR	97224	Jack Wynne	503-624-0624	R	78 *	0.2
Inland Seafood Corp.	1222 Menlo Dr	Atlanta	GA	30318	Joel Knox	404-350-5850	R	66 *	0.3
Robert Wholey and Company	1501 Penn Ave	Pittsburgh	PA	15222	Robert L Wholey	412-261-3693	R	65	0.2
Salasnek Fisheries Inc.	12301 Conant St	Detroit	MI	48212	Jordan Salasnek	313-368-2500	R	55	0.1
John T. Handy Company Inc.	PO Box 309	Crisfield	MD	21817	Carol Haltaman	410-968-1772	S	54 *	0.2
Chicago Fish House Inc.	1250 W Division St	Chicago	IL	60661	Jack Mitsakopoulos	312-227-7000	R	50	0.1
McFarling Foods Inc.	333 W 14th St	Indianapolis	IN	46202	Don McFarling	317-635-2633	R	50	0.1
Steuart Investment Co.	4646 40th NW	Washington	DC	20016	Guy Steuart	202-537-8940	R	50 *	0.4
McInerney-Miller Brothers Inc.	2001 Brewster St	Detroit	MI	48207	DI Miller	313-833-4800	R	47 *	0.1
Will Poultry Co.	1075 William St	Buffalo	NY	14206	Donald E Will	716-853-2000	R	47 *	0.1
Caleb Haley and Company Inc.	14 Fulton Fish Mkt	New York	NY	10038	William Smith	212-732-7474	R	45	<0.1
Becker Food Company Inc.	4160 Prt Wash Rd	Milwaukee	WI	53212	Stephen S Becker	414-964-5353	R	39 *	<0.1
Metropolitan Poultry	1920 Stanford Ct	Landover	MD	20785	Brian C Willard	301-772-0060	R	38	0.1
Dole and Bailey Inc.	PO Box 2405	Woburn	MA	01888	DM Matheson	617-935-1234	R	35	0.2
Slade Gorton and Company	225 Southampton	Boston	MA	02118	Michael C Gorton	617-442-5800	R	35 *	0.2
Seattle Fish Co.	6211 E 42nd Ave	Denver	CO	80216	Ed Iacino	303-329-9595	R	34	0.1
Zanios Foods Inc.	PO Box 27730	Albuquerque	NM	87125	Jim Zanios	505-831-1411	R	34 *	<0.1
Rymer Foods Inc.	4600 S Packers Ave	Chicago	IL	60609	P Edward Schenk	773-927-7777	P	34	0.2
Clear Springs Foods Inc.	PO Box 712	Buhl	ID	83316	L Cope	208-543-4316	R	32	0.4
Gilbert Foods Inc.	7251 Standard Dr	Hanover	MD	21076	Peter Gilbert	410-712-6000	R	30	0.2
International Oceanic	PO Box 767	Bayou La Batre	AL	36509	David A Kirpich	334-824-4193	R	27 *	0.1
Quality Meats and Seafood Inc.	PO Box 337	West Fargo	ND	58078	R Rieth	701-282-0202	R	25	0.1
Dory Seafood Inc.	2300 130th Ave	Bellevue	WA	98005	Arne Einmo	425-869-3679	R	20	<0.1
Morley Sales Company Inc.	809 W Madison St	Chicago	IL	60607	Robert G Slavik	312-829-1125	R	20	<0.1
Plus Marketing Corp.	21740 Trolley	Taylor	MI	48180	John G Schirle Jr	313-292-6666	R	20 *	<0.1
Borstein Seafood Inc.	PO Box 188	Bellingham	WA	98227	Jay Bornstein	360-734-7990	R	19	0.3
Lone Star Food Service Co.	PO Box 2005	Austin	TX	78768	Franklin Hall	512-478-3161	R	19 *	<0.1
Smith Packing Company Inc.	PO Box 446	Utica	NY	13503	Wesley Smith	315-732-5125	R	17	<0.1
Nordic Delights Foods Inc.	72 Water St	Lubec	ME	04652	Robert J Peacock	207-733-5556	R	16 *	<0.1
Bay State Lobster Company	379 Commercial St	Boston	MA	02109	Richard Faro	617-523-4588	R	15 *	<0.1
Blount Seafood Corp.	PO Box 327	Warren	RI	02885	Frederick N Blount	401-245-8800	R	15	<0.1
D.B. Berelson Co.	100 Pine St, #225	San Francisco	CA	94111	Herb Wiltsek	415-956-6600	R	15 *	<0.1
L.N. White and Company Inc.	225 W 34th St	New York	NY	10122	David White	212-239-7474	R	15 *	<0.1
Lawson Seafood Company Inc.	15 Rudds Ln	Hampton	VA	23669	Jerry L Olson	804-722-6211	R	15 *	0.1
Fresh Fish Company Inc.	8501 Page Blvd	St. Louis	MO	63114	Thomas J Hillman	314-428-7777	R	13	<0.1
Tennessee Shell Co.	PO Box 647	Camden	TN	38320	Peggy M Baker	901-584-7747	R	13 *	<0.1
Race Street Foods Inc.	PO Box 28385	San Jose	CA	95159	G Barsanti	408-294-6161	R	13 *	0.1
Sea K. Fish Company Inc.	PO Box 2040	Blaine	WA	98230	Martin Kuljis	206-332-5121	R	12	0.1
Olson-Kessler Meat Company	PO Box 9175	Corpus Christi	TX	78469	Donald P Olson	512-853-6291	R	11	<0.1
M.F. Foley Company Inc.	PO Box 3093	New Bedford	MA	02740	MF Foley	508-997-0773	R	10 *	<0.1

Source: *Ward's Business Directory of U.S. Private and Public Companies*, 1998. The company type code used is as follows: P - Public, R - Private, S - Subsidiary, D - Division, J - Joint Venture, A - Affiliate, G - Group. Sales are in millions of dollars, employees are in thousands. An asterisk (*) indicates an estimated sales volume. The symbol < stands for 'less than'.

OCCUPATIONS EMPLOYED BY SIC 514 - GROCERIES AND RELATED PRODUCTS

Occupation	% of Total 1996	Change to 2006	Occupation	% of Total 1996	Change to 2006
Sales & related workers nec	14.5	21.9	Industrial truck & tractor operators	2.4	21.9
Truck drivers light & heavy	12.6	10.8	Bookkeeping, accounting, & auditing clerks	2.4	-11.3
Driver/sales workers	6.1	33.0	Helpers, laborers nec	2.1	10.8
Freight, stock, & material movers, hand	4.9	-0.2	Salespersons, retail	1.7	10.8
General managers & top executives	3.7	7.4	Secretaries, except legal & medical	1.6	-12.1
Order fillers, wholesale & retail sales	3.7	10.8	Butchers & meatcutters	1.5	-11.3
Stock clerks	3.6	10.8	Blue collar worker supervisors	1.5	7.0
Hand packers & packagers	3.3	10.8	Packaging & filling machine operators	1.4	10.8
Traffic, shipping, receiving clerks	3.0	10.8	Wholesale & retail buyers, except farm products	1.4	7.9
Marketing & sales worker supervisors	2.9	10.8	Order clerks	1.2	-0.2
Agricultural, forestry, fishing workers nec	2.8	21.9	Clerical supervisors & managers	1.2	10.9
General office clerks	2.5	-4.6			

Source: *Industry-Occupation Matrix*, Bureau of Labor Statistics. These data relate to one or more 3-digit SIC industry groups rather than to a single 4-digit SIC. The change reported for each occupation to the year 2006 is a percent of growth or decline as estimated by the Bureau of Labor Statistics. The abbreviation nec stands for 'not elsewhere classified'.

STATE AND REGIONAL CONCENTRATION

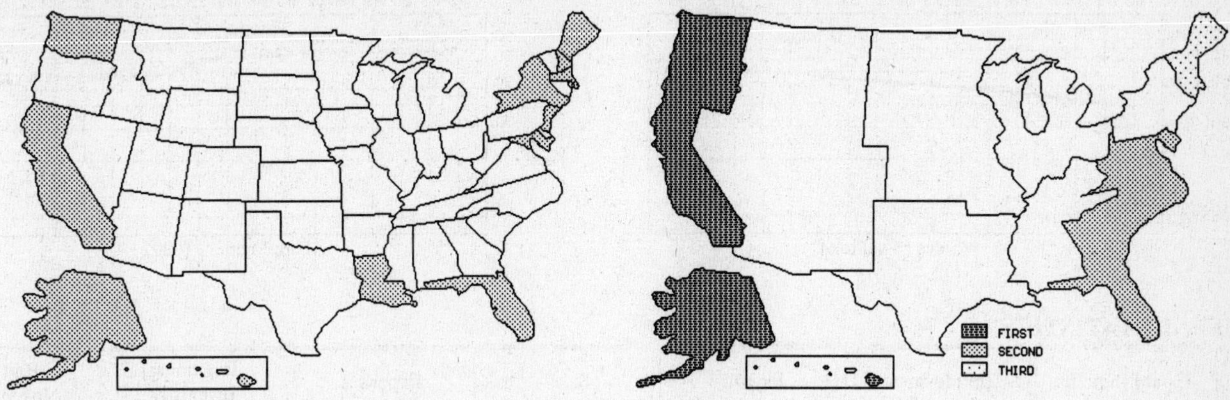

INDUSTRY DATA BY STATE

State	Establishments - 1995 Total (number)	Establishments - 1995 % of U.S.	Employment - 1995 Total (number)	Employment - 1995 % of U.S.	Employment - 1995 Per Estab.	Payroll - 1995 Total ($ mil.)	Payroll - 1995 Per Empl. ($)	Sales - 1992 Total ($ mil.)	Sales - 1992 % of U.S.	Sales - 1992 Per Estab ($)
Washington	178	5.6	2,432	8.0	14	80.1	32,955	2,121.9	18.6	884,145
California	312	9.8	3,546	11.7	11	90.8	25,605	1,547.3	13.6	427,304
Massachusetts	245	7.7	2,257	7.4	9	74.1	32,845	1,254.9	11.0	586,963
Florida	372	11.7	2,981	9.8	8	64.4	21,620	1,203.2	10.5	411,502
New York	313	9.9	2,570	8.5	8	68.7	26,739	907.7	8.0	425,134
New Jersey	101	3.2	1,262	4.2	12	25.5	20,200	435.0	3.8	445,676
Texas	119	3.8	1,288	4.2	11	26.1	20,283	409.2	3.6	336,548
Illinois	64	2.0	649	2.1	10	18.4	28,351	371.1	3.3	557,261
Maine	174	5.5	1,521	5.0	9	24.9	16,402	351.8	3.1	268,781
Louisiana	197	6.2	1,876	6.2	10	20.8	11,088	301.9	2.6	144,036
Pennsylvania	63	2.0	556	1.8	9	13.8	24,847	274.2	2.4	278,395
Maryland	100	3.2	922	3.0	9	19.6	21,248	236.5	2.1	264,558
Rhode Island	62	2.0	484	1.6	8	12.7	26,326	232.1	2.0	424,298
Virginia	105	3.3	1,329	4.4	13	16.5	12,440	197.6	1.7	136,255
North Carolina	85	2.7	957	3.2	11	15.8	16,559	195.1	1.7	157,700
Hawaii	52	1.6	457	1.5	9	11.7	25,523	161.5	1.4	335,859
Oregon	38	1.2	538	1.8	14	13.5	25,180	129.9	1.1	270,004
Georgia	53	1.7	476	1.6	9	10.6	22,309	124.6	1.1	411,353
Connecticut	29	0.9	184	0.6	6	10.7	58,005	113.0	1.0	576,684
Michigan	32	1.0	333	1.1	10	8.5	25,577	82.7	0.7	299,634
Mississippi	40	1.3	320	1.1	8	4.4	13,809	81.6	0.7	239,258
Ohio	22	0.7	280	0.9	13	7.0	24,911	74.5	0.7	222,922
Minnesota	17	0.5	116	0.4	7	2.0	17,483	70.1	0.6	604,466
Alabama	59	1.9	814	2.7	14	6.6	8,098	67.9	0.6	108,646
South Carolina	39	1.2	313	1.0	8	6.1	19,374	64.1	0.6	205,494
New Hampshire	22	0.7	92	0.3	4	2.9	31,011	61.1	0.5	522,504
Arizona	8	0.3	161	0.5	20	4.2	26,329	59.0	0.5	344,959
Colorado	12	0.4	231	0.8	19	5.5	23,961	45.6	0.4	200,903
Oklahoma	6	0.2	131	0.4	22	1.5	11,817	35.9	0.3	718,840
Indiana	11	0.3	54	0.2	5	1.3	23,481	33.3	0.3	584,860
Wisconsin	26	0.8	173	0.6	7	3.4	19,734	29.9	0.3	186,894
Alaska	107	3.4	306	1.0	3	7.7	25,065	29.9	0.3	563,736
Missouri	10	0.3	20-99	-	-	(D)	-	26.7	0.2	182,993
New Mexico	5	0.2	49	0.2	10	1.4	29,102	15.8	0.1	232,118
D.C.	6	0.2	69	0.2	11	1.6	23,696	12.9	0.1	229,750
Nebraska	3	0.1	35	0.1	12	0.8	22,400	11.2	0.1	399,250
Delaware	10	0.3	84	0.3	8	2.0	23,238	7.4	0.1	160,674
Tennessee	13	0.4	75	0.2	6	1.2	16,013	7.3	0.1	134,630
Vermont	4	0.1	38	0.1	10	1.0	25,053	7.2	0.1	134,981
Iowa	2	0.1	0-19	-	-	(D)	-	7.1	0.1	273,346
Kansas	8	0.3	31	0.1	4	0.5	17,516	4.0	0.0	198,000
West Virginia	1	0.0	20-99	-	-	(D)	-	2.6	0.0	125,476
Nevada	12	0.4	151	0.5	13	4.4	29,430	(D)	-	-
Arkansas	10	0.3	45	0.1	5	1.0	23,178	(D)	-	-
Utah	7	0.2	77	0.3	11	1.9	25,286	(D)	-	-
Kentucky	5	0.2	51	0.2	10	2.4	46,824	(D)	-	-
Montana	5	0.2	14	0.0	3	0.3	19,500	(D)	-	-
Idaho	2	0.1	20-99	-	-	(D)	-	(D)	-	-
South Dakota	1	0.0	20-99	-	-	(D)	-	(D)	-	-
Wyoming	1	0.0	0-19	-	-	(D)	-	(D)	-	-

Source: County Business Patterns, 1995 and *Economic Census of the U.S., 1992*. Data are sorted by 1992 revenues and, if revenues are unavailable, by establishments in 1995. The symbol (D) indicates that data are withheld by the source to avoid disclosure of competitive information. A dash (-) indicates that data are not available or undisclosed because they do not meet statistical validity standards. Shaded *states* on the state map indicate those states which have proportionately greater representation in the industry than would be indicated by the state's population; the ratio is based on total revenues or number of establishments. Shaded *regions* indicate where the industry is regionally most concentrated.

5147 - MEATS AND MEAT PRODUCTS

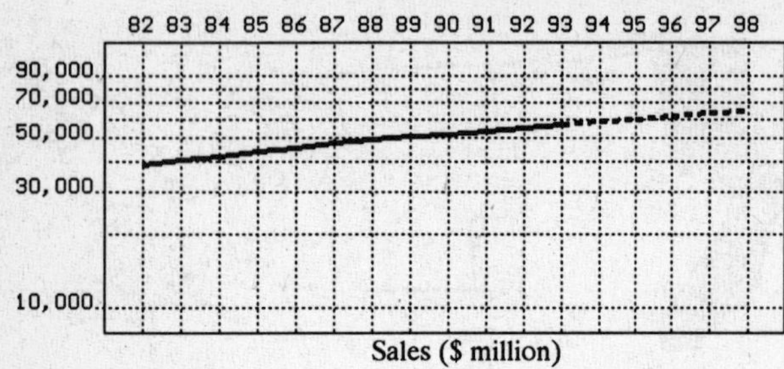

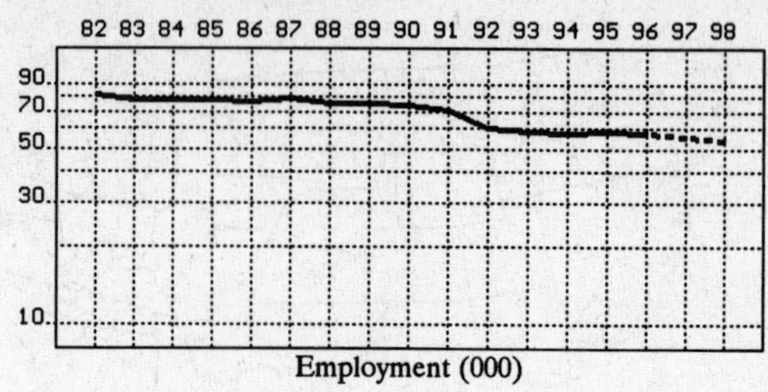

GENERAL STATISTICS

Year	Establishments (number)	Employment (number)	Payroll ($ million)	Sales ($ million)	Expenses ($ million)	Beginning Inventory ($ million)	Ending Inventory ($ million)
1982	5,088	82,181	1,492.8	38,585.1	-	-	-
1983	5,042	77,801	1,465.0	40,345.4e	-	-	-
1984	4,710	78,313	1,501.9	42,105.8e	-	-	-
1985	4,480	78,557	1,547.3	43,866.1e	-	-	-
1986	4,303	76,613	1,599.4	45,626.5e	-	-	-
1987	4,779	78,973	1,642.0	47,386.8	3,462.2	923.5	1,012.5
1988	4,439	76,216	1,686.7	48,883.7e	3,408.5e	938.5e	1,003.1e
1989	4,168	75,264	1,691.1	50,380.5e	3,354.7e	953.4e	993.7e
1990	4,045	74,230	1,728.7	51,877.4e	3,301.0e	968.3e	984.2e
1991	3,966	71,023	1,726.4	53,374.2e	3,247.3e	983.2e	974.8e
1992	4,123	60,537	1,516.5	54,871.1	3,193.6	998.1	965.4
1993	3,912	58,791	1,500.2	56,799.1p	3,139.9p	1,013.1p	956.0p
1994	3,799	57,450	1,539.4	58,427.7p	3,086.2p	1,028.0p	946.6p
1995	3,730	58,100	1,599.9	60,056.3p	3,032.4p	1,042.9p	937.2p
1996	3,583p	57,181p	1,635.9p	61,684.9p	2,978.7p	1,057.8p	927.7p
1997	3,484p	55,243p	1,642.2p	63,313.5p	2,925.0p	1,072.7p	918.3p
1998	3,384p	53,305p	1,648.5p	64,942.1p	2,871.3p	1,087.7p	908.9p

Sources: Economic Census of the United States, 1982, 1987, and 1992. Establishment counts, employment, and payroll are from *County Business Patterns* for non-Census years. Values followed by a 'p' are projections by the editors. Sales and expense data for non-Census years are extrapolations, marked by 'e'. Industries reclassified in 1987 will not have data for prior years. Data are the most recent available at this level of detail.

INDICES OF CHANGE

Year	Establishments (number)	Employment (number)	Payroll ($ million)	Sales ($ million)	Expenses ($ million)	Beginning Inventory ($ million)	Ending Inventory ($ million)
1982	123.4	135.8	98.4	70.3	-	-	-
1983	122.3	128.5	96.6	73.5e	-	-	-
1984	114.2	129.4	99.0	76.7e	-	-	-
1985	108.7	129.8	102.0	79.9e	-	-	-
1986	104.4	126.6	105.5	83.2e	-	-	-
1987	115.9	130.5	108.3	86.4	108.4	92.5	104.9
1988	107.7	125.9	111.2	89.1e	106.7e	94.0e	103.9e
1989	101.1	124.3	111.5	91.8e	105.0e	95.5e	102.9e
1990	98.1	122.6	114.0	94.5e	103.4e	97.0e	101.9e
1991	96.2	117.3	113.8	97.3e	101.7e	98.5e	101.0e
1992	100.0	100.0	100.0	100.0	100.0	100.0	100.0
1993	94.9	97.1	98.9	103.5p	98.3p	101.5p	99.0p
1994	92.1	94.9	101.5	106.5p	96.6p	103.0p	98.1p
1995	90.5	96.0	105.5	109.4p	95.0p	104.5p	97.1p
1996	86.9p	94.5p	107.9p	112.4p	93.3p	106.0p	96.1p
1997	84.5p	91.3p	108.3p	115.4p	91.6p	107.5p	95.1p
1998	82.1p	88.1p	108.7p	118.4p	89.9p	109.0p	94.1p

Sources: Same as General Statistics. The values shown reflect change from the base year, 1992. Values above 100 mean greater than 1992, values below 100 mean less than 1992, and a value of 100 in the 1982-91 or 1993-98 period means same as 1992. Values followed by a 'p' are projections by the editors; 'e' stands for extrapolation. Data are the most recent available at this level of detail.

SELECTED RATIOS

For 1992	Avg. of All Wholesale	Analyzed Industry	Index	For 1992	Avg. of All Wholesale	Analyzed Industry	Index
Employees per Establishment	12	15	126	Sales per Employee	561,172	906,406	162
Payroll per Establishment	349,729	367,815	105	Sales per Establishment	6,559,346	13,308,537	203
Payroll per Employee	29,919	25,051	84	Expenses per Establishment	723,071	774,582	107

Sources: Same as General Statistics. The 'Average of All Manufacturing' column represents the average of all manufacturing industries reported for the most recent complete year available. The Index shows the relationship between the Average and the Analyzed Industry. For example, 100 means that they are equal; 500 that the Analyzed Industry is five times the average; 50 means that the Analyzed Industry is half the national average. The abbreviation 'na' is used to show that data are 'not available'.

LEADING COMPANIES

Number shown: **50** Total sales ($ mil): **10,833** Total employment (000): **27.2**

Company Name	Address				CEO Name	Phone	Co. Type	Sales ($ mil)	Empl. (000)
Monfort International Sales	PO Box G	Greeley	CO	80632	Charles Monfort	303-353-2311	D	2,473 *	0.1
Associated Grocers Inc.	PO Box 3763	Seattle	WA	98124	Donald Benson	206-762-2100	R	1,050	1.6
SUPERVALU Inc.	PO Box 1198	Fort Wayne	IN	46801	John Gerber	219-483-2146	D	1,000	0.9
Golden Poultry Company Inc.	PO Box 2210	Atlanta	GA	30301	K. N Whitmire	404-393-5000	P	600	5.7
Affiliated Foods Cooperative	PO Box 1067	Norfolk	NE	68702	Vergil Froehlich	402-371-0555	R	560	0.5
City Market Inc.	PO Box 729	Grand Junction	CO	81502	Anthony Prinster	970-241-0750	S	460	3.7
Agar Supply Company Inc.	1100 Massachusetts	Boston	MA	02125	Alan Bressler	617-442-8989	R	400 *	0.4
Western Beef Inc.	47-05 Metropolitan	Ridgewood	NY	11385	Peter Castellana Jr	718-417-3770	P	341	2.0
D.B. Brown Inc.	400 Port Carteret	Carteret	NJ	07008	Jeffrey Stavitsky	908-541-0200	R	340 *	0.2
Cagle's Inc.	2000 Hills Ave NW	Atlanta	GA	30318	J Douglas Cagle	404-355-2820	P	309	3.1
J. Gerber and Company Inc.	11 Penn Plz	New York	NY	10001	Geoffrey Clain	212-631-1200	R	250	<0.1
Entree Corp.	8200 Brown Deer	Milwaukee	WI	53223	Richard Y Fisher	414-355-0037	S	219	0.3
Omaha Steaks International	PO Box 3300	Omaha	NE	68103	Alan Simon	402-331-1010	R	170	0.7
Troyer Foods Inc.	PO Box 608	Goshen	IN	46526	Paris Ball-Miller	219-533-0302	R	170	0.2
Randall Foods Inc.	PO Box 2669	Huntington P.	CA	90255	Stan M Bloom	213-587-2383	R	168	0.5
Earp Meat Company Inc.	6550 Kansas Ave	Kansas City	KS	66111	Donald C Earp	913-287-3311	R	160 *	0.2
Hickory Farms Inc.	PO Box 219	Maumee	OH	43537	Ike Herb	419-893-7611	R	160	2.3
Abbott Foods Inc.	2400 Harrison Rd	Columbus	OH	43204	Lawrence C Abbott	614-272-0658	R	135	0.3
Brenham Wholesale Grocery	PO Box 584	Brenham	TX	77834	Luther Utesch	409-836-7925	R	130	0.2
Cattleman's Meat Co.	1825 Scott St	Detroit	MI	48207	David S Rohtbart	313-833-2700	S	125	0.3
Midamar Corp.	PO Box 218	Cedar Rapids	IA	52406	Bill Aossey	319-362-3711	R	114 *	<0.1
J and B Wholesale Distribution	PO Box 212	St. Michael	MN	55376	Bob Hegman	612-497-3913	R	100 *	0.3
Tony's Fine Foods	PO Box 1501	W. Sacramento	CA	95605	Anthony Ingoglia Jr	916-374-4000	R	85 *	0.3
Keeners Inc.	2900 4th Ave S	Seattle	WA	98134	Wayne V Keener	206-628-4811	R	75	0.2
Remarks Inc.	6728 Hyland Croy	Dublin	OH	43017	Malcolm J Graves	614-889-2561	R	75	0.3
Doughtie's Foods Inc.	2410 Wesley St	Portsmouth	VA	23707	Vernon W Mules	804-393-6007	P	73	0.3
Dixie Saving Stores Inc.	PO Box 1637	Chattanooga	TN	37401	Herbert St Goar	423-266-5151	R	70 *	0.1
Kunzler and Company Inc.	PO Box 4747	Lancaster	PA	17604	C C Kunzler Jr	717-299-6301	R	70 *	0.4
Aurora Packing Company Inc.	PO Box 209	North Aurora	IL	60542	Marvin Fagel	630-897-0551	R	68	0.2
Robert Wholey and Company	1501 Penn Ave	Pittsburgh	PA	15222	Robert L Wholey	412-261-3693	R	65	0.2
Tennessee Dressed Beef	PO Box 23031	Nashville	TN	37202	RN Hall	615-742-5800	R	64	<0.1
Alpine Packing Co.	9900 Lower Sacr	Stockton	CA	95210	Jerry Singer	209-477-2691	R	56 *	0.1
Stone Commodities Corp.	30 S Wacker Dr	Chicago	IL	60606	William C Bachman	312-454-3000	R	54	0.1
Maryland Hotel Supply Co.	701 W Hamburg St	Baltimore	MD	21230	RD Niller III	410-539-7055	R	53 *	0.2
Mosey's Inc.	4 Mosey Dr	Bloomfield	CT	06002	Russel Pouliot	203-243-1725	S	51 *	0.2
J. Kings Food Service	700 Furrows Rd	Holtsville	NY	11742	John King	516-289-8401	R	50	0.1
McFarling Foods Inc.	333 W 14th St	Indianapolis	IN	46202	Don McFarling	317-635-2633	R	50	0.1
Fairbank Reconstruction Corp.	PO Box 170	Ashville	NY	14710	Joseph Fairbank	716-782-2000	R	45	<0.1
Vowles Farm Fresh Foods	PO Box 2868	El Cajon	CA	92021	Bill Vowles	619-448-2101	R	42	0.1
King Cotton Foods	1837 Harbor Ave	Memphis	TN	38113	Rick Lowry	901-942-3221	D	39 *	<0.1
Pioneer Snacks Inc.	30777 Northwestern	Farmington Hls	MI	48334	Robert George	810-932-9200	R	37 *	0.1
Dole and Bailey Inc.	PO Box 2405	Woburn	MA	01888	DM Matheson	617-935-1234	R	35	0.2
Great Western Meats Inc.	PO Box 568366	Orlando	FL	32856	Greg Voorhees	407-841-4270	R	34 *	<0.1
Zanios Foods Inc.	PO Box 27730	Albuquerque	NM	87125	Jim Zanios	505-831-1411	R	34 *	<0.1
Choe Meat Co.	2637 E Vernon Ave	Los Angeles	CA	90058	Harold Choe	213-589-5271	R	32	<0.1
Tusco Grocers Inc.	PO Box 240	Dennison	OH	44621	Hudson Hillyer	740-922-2223	R	30	<0.1
Glen Rose Meat Services Inc.	PO Box 58146	Vernon	CA	90058	Glen Rose	213-589-3393	R	30	<0.1
Hearn Kirkwood	7251 Standard Dr	Hanover	MD	21076	Peter D Gilbert	410-712-6000	S	30	0.1
First Choice Food Distributors	6800 Snowden Rd	Fort Worth	TX	76140	William Burgess	817-551-5704	S	26	<0.1
Maverick Ranch Lite Beef Inc.	5360 N Franklin St	Denver	CO	80216	Roy Moore	303-294-0146	R	25	0.1

Source: *Ward's Business Directory of U.S. Private and Public Companies*, 1998. The company type code used is as follows: P - Public, R - Private, S - Subsidiary, D - Division, J - Joint Venture, A - Affiliate, G - Group. Sales are in millions of dollars, employees are in thousands. An asterisk (*) indicates an estimated sales volume. The symbol < stands for 'less than'.

OCCUPATIONS EMPLOYED BY SIC 514 - GROCERIES AND RELATED PRODUCTS

Occupation	% of Total 1996	Change to 2006	Occupation	% of Total 1996	Change to 2006
Sales & related workers nec	14.5	21.9	Industrial truck & tractor operators	2.4	21.9
Truck drivers light & heavy	12.6	10.8	Bookkeeping, accounting, & auditing clerks	2.4	-11.3
Driver/sales workers	6.1	33.0	Helpers, laborers nec	2.1	10.8
Freight, stock, & material movers, hand	4.9	-0.2	Salespersons, retail	1.7	10.8
General managers & top executives	3.7	7.4	Secretaries, except legal & medical	1.6	-12.1
Order fillers, wholesale & retail sales	3.7	10.8	Butchers & meatcutters	1.5	-11.3
Stock clerks	3.6	10.8	Blue collar worker supervisors	1.5	7.0
Hand packers & packagers	3.3	10.8	Packaging & filling machine operators	1.4	10.8
Traffic, shipping, receiving clerks	3.0	10.8	Wholesale & retail buyers, except farm products	1.4	7.9
Marketing & sales worker supervisors	2.9	10.8	Order clerks	1.2	-0.2
Agricultural, forestry, fishing workers nec	2.8	21.9	Clerical supervisors & managers	1.2	10.9
General office clerks	2.5	-4.6			

Source: *Industry-Occupation Matrix*, Bureau of Labor Statistics. These data relate to one or more 3-digit SIC industry groups rather than to a single 4-digit SIC. The change reported for each occupation to the year 2006 is a percent of growth or decline as estimated by the Bureau of Labor Statistics. The abbreviation nec stands for 'not elsewhere classified'.

STATE AND REGIONAL CONCENTRATION

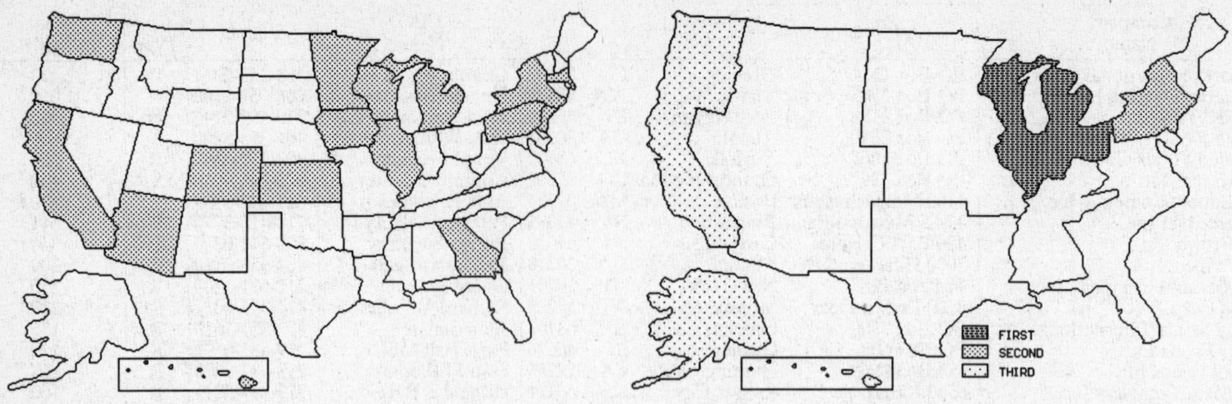

INDUSTRY DATA BY STATE

State	Establishments - 1995 Total (number)	Establishments - 1995 % of U.S.	Employment - 1995 Total (number)	Employment - 1995 % of U.S.	Employment - 1995 Per Estab.	Payroll - 1995 Total ($ mil.)	Payroll - 1995 Per Empl. ($)	Sales - 1992 Total ($ mil.)	Sales - 1992 % of U.S.	Sales - 1992 Per Estab ($)
California	461	12.4	7,752	13.4	17	223.6	28,839	5,743.9	13.8	693,704
Illinois	266	7.1	4,982	8.6	19	141.1	28,317	3,844.7	9.2	822,923
New York	553	14.8	5,152	8.9	9	155.8	30,236	3,717.5	8.9	592,996
Texas	235	6.3	3,809	6.6	16	94.4	24,791	2,659.8	6.4	708,147
Pennsylvania	161	4.3	2,781	4.8	17	82.7	29,735	2,539.8	6.1	989,405
New Jersey	223	6.0	2,113	3.6	9	82.6	39,076	2,126.3	5.1	883,734
Florida	203	5.4	2,558	4.4	13	69.5	27,177	1,927.7	4.6	662,663
Michigan	115	3.1	2,043	3.5	18	54.0	26,454	1,705.4	4.1	820,690
Ohio	92	2.5	1,946	3.4	21	49.9	25,628	1,640.9	3.9	731,244
Georgia	75	2.0	1,709	2.9	23	48.6	28,451	1,471.5	3.5	872,786
Massachusetts	91	2.4	1,561	2.7	17	53.4	34,218	1,395.4	3.3	883,169
Minnesota	64	1.7	1,359	2.3	21	41.1	30,251	1,190.5	2.9	1,010,651
Washington	87	2.3	1,166	2.0	13	33.9	29,069	1,045.7	2.5	611,515
Colorado	59	1.6	795	1.4	13	21.8	27,375	956.3	2.3	1,348,739
Wisconsin	73	2.0	1,158	2.0	16	28.1	24,266	856.4	2.1	527,998
Kansas	34	0.9	534	0.9	16	16.0	30,030	792.7	1.9	1,398,111
Maryland	32	0.9	608	1.0	19	20.7	34,054	743.5	1.8	1,017,077
Arizona	40	1.1	648	1.1	16	18.2	28,116	656.3	1.6	959,440
Iowa	55	1.5	1,104	1.9	20	25.5	23,076	650.2	1.6	724,892
Tennessee	52	1.4	1,175	2.0	23	29.5	25,125	637.8	1.5	597,727
Virginia	36	1.0	459	0.8	13	11.0	24,037	587.5	1.4	1,140,720
Missouri	77	2.1	909	1.6	12	22.4	24,655	537.0	1.3	588,777
North Carolina	73	2.0	1,244	2.1	17	28.2	22,682	510.4	1.2	406,023
Kentucky	34	0.9	695	1.2	20	15.2	21,915	500.5	1.2	670,845
Oregon	55	1.5	1,138	2.0	21	22.4	19,676	460.8	1.1	673,646
Indiana	56	1.5	910	1.6	16	21.4	23,527	455.6	1.1	571,615
Alabama	27	0.7	516	0.9	19	11.6	22,424	269.9	0.6	517,088
Louisiana	42	1.1	864	1.5	21	17.7	20,468	238.3	0.6	298,561
Oklahoma	31	0.8	435	0.7	14	10.2	23,476	236.7	0.6	429,597
Utah	22	0.6	350	0.6	16	8.0	22,900	233.5	0.6	799,620
Hawaii	23	0.6	456	0.8	20	11.7	25,757	202.9	0.5	416,612
Nevada	18	0.5	260	0.4	14	10.5	40,415	162.8	0.4	628,645
Connecticut	34	0.9	332	0.6	10	10.0	30,090	137.9	0.3	344,757
Mississippi	24	0.6	344	0.6	14	7.1	20,503	123.0	0.3	256,260
D.C.	10	0.3	266	0.5	27	8.7	32,624	99.2	0.2	364,526
Maine	7	0.2	188	0.3	27	5.8	31,090	95.1	0.2	426,578
South Carolina	30	0.8	218	0.4	7	4.5	20,564	94.1	0.2	416,376
Vermont	12	0.3	296	0.5	25	4.9	16,530	89.0	0.2	263,178
Idaho	14	0.4	178	0.3	13	3.7	20,921	74.0	0.2	281,426
Arkansas	17	0.5	153	0.3	9	2.8	18,288	67.2	0.2	369,484
West Virginia	10	0.3	250	0.4	25	4.4	17,712	62.3	0.1	253,358
New Mexico	13	0.3	88	0.2	7	2.5	28,318	48.0	0.1	495,165
Montana	15	0.4	58	0.1	4	0.9	16,241	36.1	0.1	475,197
Delaware	5	0.1	61	0.1	12	1.7	27,934	30.0	0.1	461,908
New Hampshire	8	0.2	67	0.1	8	1.3	19,985	29.4	0.1	432,441
Alaska	8	0.2	52	0.1	7	1.6	30,923	17.7	0.0	654,556
South Dakota	5	0.1	20-99	-	-	(D)	-	5.7	0.0	248,957
Wyoming	8	0.2	45	0.1	6	0.7	15,133	4.5	0.0	137,212
Nebraska	27	0.7	1,650	2.8	61	41.6	25,201	(D)	-	-
Rhode Island	17	0.5	576	1.0	34	14.5	25,215	(D)	-	-
North Dakota	1	0.0	0-19	-	-	(D)	-	(D)	-	-

Source: *County Business Patterns, 1995* and *Economic Census of the U.S., 1992*. Data are sorted by 1992 revenues and, if revenues are unavailable, by establishments in 1995. The symbol (D) indicates that data are withheld by the source to avoid disclosure of competitive information. A dash (-) indicates that data are not available or undisclosed because they do not meet statistical validity standards. Shaded *states* on the state map indicate those states which have proportionately greater representation in the industry than would be indicated by the state's population; the ratio is based on total revenues or number of establishments. Shaded *regions* indicate where the industry is regionally most concentrated.

5148 - FRESH FRUITS AND VEGETABLES

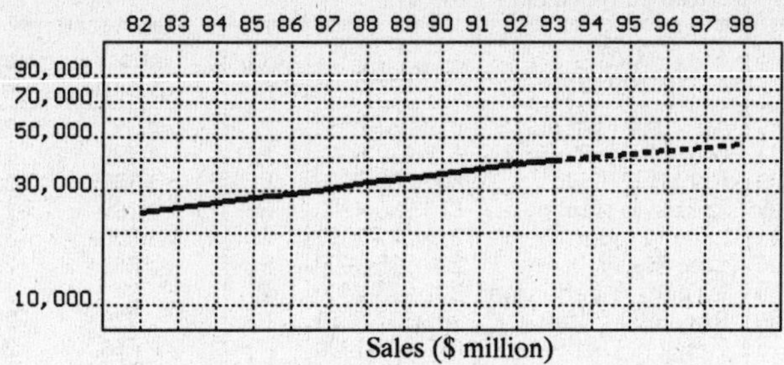

Sales ($ million)

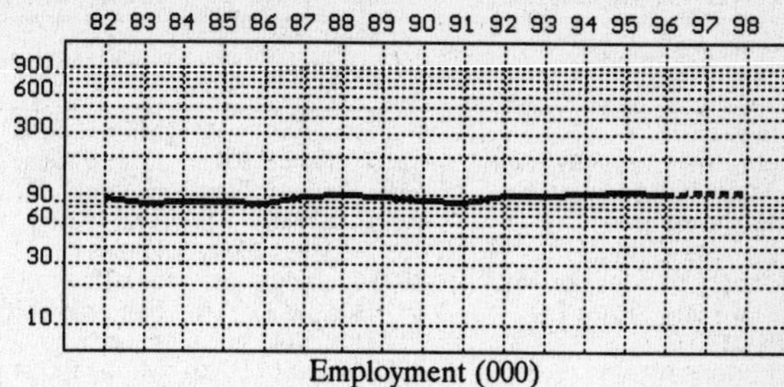

Employment (000)

GENERAL STATISTICS

Year	Establishments (number)	Employment (number)	Payroll ($ million)	Sales ($ million)	Expenses ($ million)	Beginning Inventory ($ million)	Ending Inventory ($ million)
1982	5,929	94,270	1,355.2	24,153.7	-	-	-
1983	5,516	86,918	1,402.0	25,412.9*e*	-	-	-
1984	5,278	89,022	1,503.8	26,672.1*e*	-	-	-
1985	4,967	87,932	1,537.4	27,931.3*e*	-	-	-
1986	4,678	86,365	1,566.1	29,190.5*e*	-	-	-
1987	5,838	98,870	1,810.6	30,449.7	3,922.1	309.2	325.1
1988	5,411	100,388	1,971.3	32,062.3*e*	4,133.1*e*	331.7*e*	350.6*e*
1989	5,075	98,514	2,037.2	33,674.8*e*	4,344.2*e*	354.3*e*	376.1*e*
1990	4,980	92,682	2,099.5	35,287.3*e*	4,555.2*e*	376.9*e*	401.6*e*
1991	4,848	89,811	2,098.6	36,899.8*e*	4,766.3*e*	399.4*e*	427.2*e*
1992	6,003	101,372	2,372.1	38,512.3	4,977.4	422.0	452.7
1993	5,770	101,764	2,488.7	39,546.7*p*	5,188.4*p*	444.5*p*	478.2*p*
1994	5,662	105,908	2,629.0	40,982.5*p*	5,399.5*p*	467.1*p*	503.7*p*
1995	5,422	107,572	2,713.5	42,418.4*p*	5,610.5*p*	489.7*p*	529.2*p*
1996	5,460*p*	105,495*p*	2,785.6*p*	43,854.2*p*	5,821.6*p*	512.2*p*	554.7*p*
1997	5,471*p*	106,786*p*	2,894.3*p*	45,290.1*p*	6,032.6*p*	534.8*p*	580.2*p*
1998	5,481*p*	108,077*p*	3,003.0*p*	46,726.0*p*	6,243.7*p*	557.3*p*	605.8*p*

Sources: *Economic Census of the United States*, 1982, 1987, and 1992. Establishment counts, employment, and payroll are from *County Business Patterns* for non-Census years. Values followed by a 'p' are projections by the editors. Sales and expense data for non-Census years are extrapolations, marked by 'e'. Industries reclassified in 1987 will not have data for prior years. Data are the most recent available at this level of detail.

INDICES OF CHANGE

Year	Establishments (number)	Employment (number)	Payroll ($ million)	Sales ($ million)	Expenses ($ million)	Beginning Inventory ($ million)	Ending Inventory ($ million)
1982	98.8	93.0	57.1	62.7	-	-	-
1983	91.9	85.7	59.1	66.0*e*	-	-	-
1984	87.9	87.8	63.4	69.3*e*	-	-	-
1985	82.7	86.7	64.8	72.5*e*	-	-	-
1986	77.9	85.2	66.0	75.8*e*	-	-	-
1987	97.3	97.5	76.3	79.1	78.8	73.3	71.8
1988	90.1	99.0	83.1	83.3*e*	83.0*e*	78.6*e*	77.4*e*
1989	84.5	97.2	85.9	87.4*e*	87.3*e*	84.0*e*	83.1*e*
1990	83.0	91.4	88.5	91.6*e*	91.5*e*	89.3*e*	88.7*e*
1991	80.8	88.6	88.5	95.8*e*	95.8*e*	94.6*e*	94.4*e*
1992	100.0	100.0	100.0	100.0	100.0	100.0	100.0
1993	96.1	100.4	104.9	102.7*p*	104.2*p*	105.3*p*	105.6*p*
1994	94.3	104.5	110.8	106.4*p*	108.5*p*	110.7*p*	111.3*p*
1995	90.3	106.1	114.4	110.1*p*	112.7*p*	116.0*p*	116.9*p*
1996	91.0*p*	104.1*p*	117.4*p*	113.9*p*	117.0*p*	121.4*p*	122.5*p*
1997	91.1*p*	105.3*p*	122.0*p*	117.6*p*	121.2*p*	126.7*p*	128.2*p*
1998	91.3*p*	106.6*p*	126.6*p*	121.3*p*	125.4*p*	132.1*p*	133.8*p*

Sources: Same as General Statistics. The values shown reflect change from the base year, 1992. Values above 100 mean greater than 1992, values below 100 mean less than 1992, and a value of 100 in the 1982-91 or 1993-98 period means same as 1992. Values followed by a 'p' are projections by the editors; 'e' stands for extrapolation. Data are the most recent available at this level of detail.

SELECTED RATIOS

For 1992	Avg. of All Wholesale	Analyzed Industry	Index	For 1992	Avg. of All Wholesale	Analyzed Industry	Index
Employees per Establishment	12	17	144	Sales per Employee	561,172	379,911	68
Payroll per Establishment	349,729	395,152	113	Sales per Establishment	6,559,346	6,415,509	98
Payroll per Employee	29,919	23,400	78	Expenses per Establishment	723,071	829,152	115

Sources: Same as General Statistics. The 'Average of All Manufacturing' column represents the average of all manufacturing industries reported for the most recent complete year available. The Index shows the relationship between the Average and the Analyzed Industry. For example, 100 means that they are equal; 500 that the Analyzed Industry is five times the average; 50 means that the Analyzed Industry is half the national average. The abbreviation 'na' is used to show that data are 'not available'.

LEADING COMPANIES

Number shown: **50** Total sales ($ mil): **17,473** Total employment (000): **47.5**

Company Name	Address				CEO Name	Phone	Co. Type	Sales ($ mil)	Empl. (000)
Nash Finch Co.	PO Box 355	Minneapolis	MN	55440	Alfred N Flaten	612-832-0534	P	4,392	12.2
C.H. Robinson Company Inc.	8100 Mitchell Rd	Eden Prairie	MN	55344	Daryl R Verdoorn	612-937-8500	P	1,790	1.8
Performance Food Group Co.	6800 Paragon Place	Richmond	VA	23230	Robert C Sledd	804-285-7340	P	1,230	2.0
Sunkist Growers Inc.	PO Box 7888	Van Nuys	CA	91409	Russell L Hanlin	818-986-4800	R	1,100	1.0
Albert Fisher Holdings Inc.	15303 Dallas Pkwy	Dallas	TX	75248	Lenny Pippin	214-387-2394	S	1,090 *	3.5
Food Services of America Inc.	4025 Delridge	Seattle	WA	98106	Tom Staley	206-933-5000	S	863 *	2.3
Associated Food Stores Inc.	PO Box 30430	Salt Lake City	UT	84130	Richard A Parkinson	801-973-4400	R	842	1.3
R.D. Offutt Co.	PO Box 7160	Fargo	ND	58106	Ronald D Offutt	701-237-6062	R	720 *	2.0
Michael Foods Inc.	5353 Wayzata Blvd	Minneapolis	MN	55416	Gregg A Ostrander	612-546-1500	P	616	2.7
Affiliated Foods Cooperative	PO Box 1067	Norfolk	NE	68702	Vergil Froehlich	402-371-0555	R	560	0.5
Riviana Foods Inc.	PO Box 2636	Houston	TX	77252	Joseph A Hafner Jr	713-529-3251	P	460	2.8
Fleming Companies Inc.	624 S 25th Ave	Phoenix	AZ	85009	Ray Gunther	602-269-5200	D	310 *	0.9
Fresh America Corp.	5400 LBJ Frwy	Dallas	TX	75240	David I Sheinfeld	972-774-0575	P	239	1.0
Tripifoods Inc.	PO Box 1107	Buffalo	NY	14240	CJ Tripi	716-853-7400	R	200	0.3
United Foods Inc.	10 Pictsweet Dr	Bells	TN	38006	James I Tankersley	901-422-7600	P	196	2.3
Beckman Produce Inc.	415 Grove St	St. Paul	MN	55101	Kathy Lalibete	612-222-1212	R	180	0.7
Standard Fruit and Vegetable	PO Box 225027	Dallas	TX	75222	Martin H Rutchik	214-428-3600	R	150	0.4
Tamarkin Company Inc.	375 Victoria Rd	Youngstown	OH	44515	Ray Burgo	330-792-3811	S	150	0.3
Seald-Sweet Growers Inc.	PO Box 6152	Vero Beach	FL	32961	Kenneth A Bear	561-569-2244	R	145 *	<0.1
Brenham Wholesale Grocery	PO Box 584	Brenham	TX	77834	Luther Utesch	409-836-7925	R	130	0.2
Fishery Products International	18 Electronics Ave	Danvers	MA	01923	John Cummings	978-777-2660	S	127 *	0.5
Bell-Carter Foods Inc.	3742 Mt Diablo	Lafayette	CA	94549	Tim Carter	510-284-5933	R	100	0.5
Giumarra Brothers Fruit Co.	PO Box 21218	Los Angeles	CA	90021	Donald J Corsaro	213-627-2900	R	100	0.1
Paramount Export Co.	280 17th St	Oakland	CA	94612	Nick Kukulan	510-839-0150	R	100 *	<0.1
Snokist Growers	PO Box 1587	Yakima	WA	98907	JF Grandy	509-453-5631	R	90 *	0.8
A. Levy and J. Zentner Co.	PO Box 292307	Sacramento	CA	95829	GN Thomas	916-381-7100	R	80 *	0.8
G and G Produce Company	5949 S Eastern Ave	City of Com	CA	90040	Dave Kuntz	213-727-1212	S	80	0.3
Lindemann Produce Inc.	300 E 2nd St	Reno	NV	89501	George Lindemann	702-323-2442	R	80	0.2
Park Orchards Inc.	4428 Broadview Rd	Richfield	OH	44286	David A Vaughn	216-659-6134	R	80	0.6
Castellini Co.	6000 Creek Rd	Cincinnati	OH	45242	Bill Shuller	513-936-4650	R	75 *	0.6
Club Chef	800 Bank St	Cincinnati	OH	45214	John O'Brian	513-562-4200	D	75	0.6
Naturipe Berry Growers	PO Box 1630	Watsonville	CA	95077	Larry Shikuma	408-722-2430	R	75	0.3
Nick Penachio Company Inc.	240 Food Ctr Dr	Bronx	NY	10474	Nick A Penachio	718-842-0630	R	75 *	0.2
Caro Produce	2324 Bayou Blue	Houma	LA	70364	Ricky Thibodaux	504-872-1483	S	71 *	0.4
JC Produce Inc.	PO Box 1027	W. Sacramento	CA	95691	Jim Catchot	916-372-4050	R	70	0.3
Red's Market Inc.	8801 Exchange Dr	Orlando	FL	32809	Kent Shoemaker	407-857-3930	R	70	0.4
Blue Anchor Inc.	730 Howe Ave	Sacramento	CA	95825	Pat Sanguinetti	916-929-3050	R	68	0.1
Syndex Corp.	3173 Produce Row	Houston	TX	77023	Carey Hoffman	713-923-5807	R	65	0.2
S.K.H. Management Co.	PO Box 1500	Lititz	PA	17543	Paul W Stauffer	717-626-4771	R	59	0.9
Jac Vandenberg Inc.	100 Corporate Blvd	Yonkers	NY	10701	David Schiro	914-964-5900	R	56	<0.1
Lee Ray-Tarantino Company	PO Box 2408	S. San Francisco	CA	94083	Joe Tarantino	415-871-4323	S	55	0.1
Waverly Growers Cooperative	PO Box 287	Waverly	FL	33877	NP Hansen	813-439-3602	R	55 *	0.5
West Coast Fruit & Produce Co.	PO Box 1377	Tacoma	WA	98401	Don Goodwin	206-272-1181	S	54	0.1
Maine Potato Growers Inc.	PO Box 271	Presque Isle	ME	04769	Joe Lallande	207-764-3131	R	51	0.1
Community Suffolk Inc.	304 2nd St	Everett	MA	02149	Joe Piazza	617-389-5200	R	50	<0.1
Costa Fruit and Produce Co.	414 Rutherford Ave	Charlestown	MA	02129	Manuel R Costa	617-241-8007	R	50	0.2
De Bruyn Produce Company	PO Box 76	Zeeland	MI	49464	Robert D De Bruyn	616-772-2102	R	50	0.3
Dixie Produce and Packaging	PO Box 23647	Harahan	LA	70183	Sal J Peraino	504-733-7500	R	50	0.3
Progressive Produce Co.	PO Box 911231	Los Angeles	CA	90091	James K Leimkuhler	213-890-8100	S	50	0.1
Banana Supply Company Inc.	3030 NE 2nd Ave	Miami	FL	33137	Thomas R Nest	305-573-7610	S	49 *	0.2

Source: *Ward's Business Directory of U.S. Private and Public Companies*, 1998. The company type code used is as follows: P - Public, R - Private, S - Subsidiary, D - Division, J - Joint Venture, A - Affiliate, G - Group. Sales are in millions of dollars, employees are in thousands. An asterisk (*) indicates an estimated sales volume. The symbol < stands for 'less than'.

OCCUPATIONS EMPLOYED BY SIC 514 - GROCERIES AND RELATED PRODUCTS

Occupation	% of Total 1996	Change to 2006	Occupation	% of Total 1996	Change to 2006
Sales & related workers nec	14.5	21.9	Industrial truck & tractor operators	2.4	21.9
Truck drivers light & heavy	12.6	10.8	Bookkeeping, accounting, & auditing clerks	2.4	-11.3
Driver/sales workers	6.1	33.0	Helpers, laborers nec	2.1	10.8
Freight, stock, & material movers, hand	4.9	-0.2	Salespersons, retail	1.7	10.8
General managers & top executives	3.7	7.4	Secretaries, except legal & medical	1.6	-12.1
Order fillers, wholesale & retail sales	3.7	10.8	Butchers & meatcutters	1.5	-11.3
Stock clerks	3.6	10.8	Blue collar worker supervisors	1.5	7.0
Hand packers & packagers	3.3	10.8	Packaging & filling machine operators	1.4	10.8
Traffic, shipping, receiving clerks	3.0	10.8	Wholesale & retail buyers, except farm products	1.4	7.9
Marketing & sales worker supervisors	2.9	10.8	Order clerks	1.2	-0.2
Agricultural, forestry, fishing workers nec	2.8	21.9	Clerical supervisors & managers	1.2	10.9
General office clerks	2.5	-4.6			

Source: *Industry-Occupation Matrix*, Bureau of Labor Statistics. These data relate to one or more 3-digit SIC industry groups rather than to a single 4-digit SIC. The change reported for each occupation to the year 2006 is a percent of growth or decline as estimated by the Bureau of Labor Statistics. The abbreviation nec stands for 'not elsewhere classified'.

STATE AND REGIONAL CONCENTRATION

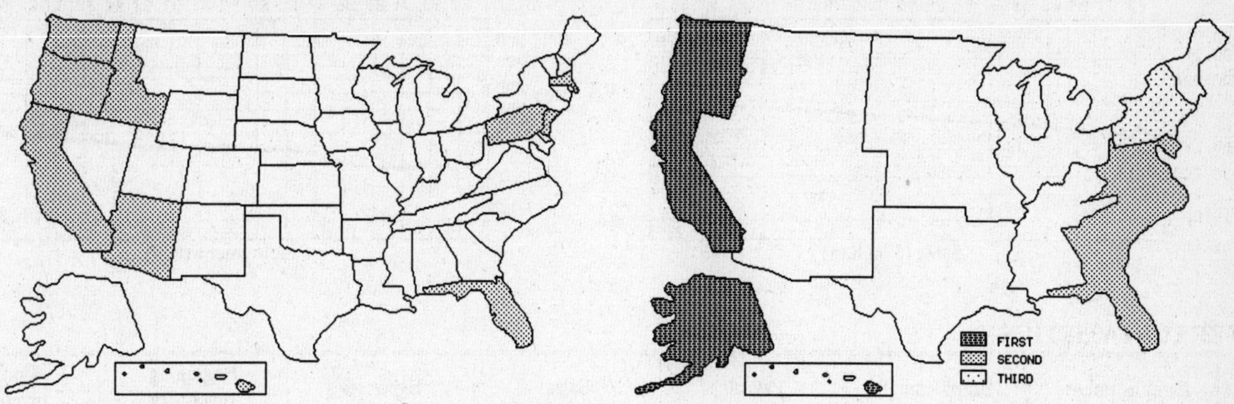

INDUSTRY DATA BY STATE

State	Establishments - 1995 Total (number)	Establishments - 1995 % of U.S.	Employment - 1995 Total (number)	Employment - 1995 % of U.S.	Employment - 1995 Per Estab.	Payroll - 1995 Total ($ mil.)	Payroll - 1995 Per Empl. ($)	Sales - 1992 Total ($ mil.)	Sales - 1992 % of U.S.	Sales - 1992 Per Estab ($)
California	1,075	19.8	23,922	22.2	22	702.9	29,381	10,674.4	27.8	493,957
Florida	583	10.8	12,418	11.5	21	250.9	20,208	3,941.9	10.3	303,619
New York	467	8.6	5,562	5.2	12	179.1	32,207	2,692.8	7.0	490,054
Texas	339	6.3	8,297	7.7	24	153.9	18,549	2,500.6	6.5	307,083
Washington	179	3.3	6,607	6.1	37	148.1	22,417	1,948.2	5.1	331,269
Pennsylvania	228	4.2	5,022	4.7	22	132.3	26,353	1,824.9	4.8	436,173
New Jersey	199	3.7	1,984	1.8	10	71.2	35,887	1,325.7	3.5	659,239
Illinois	178	3.3	2,018	1.9	11	76.0	37,650	1,174.3	3.1	588,016
Ohio	140	2.6	3,156	2.9	23	84.0	26,617	1,170.0	3.1	452,083
Arizona	157	2.9	3,684	3.4	23	65.1	17,683	1,017.6	2.7	390,929
Massachusetts	152	2.8	1,896	1.8	12	76.1	40,153	1,015.2	2.6	583,105
Michigan	152	2.8	2,224	2.1	15	65.6	29,518	1,009.4	2.6	503,460
Georgia	126	2.3	2,700	2.5	21	54.8	20,312	592.9	1.5	297,203
Minnesota	72	1.3	1,366	1.3	19	44.8	32,783	568.7	1.5	429,227
Missouri	75	1.4	1,109	1.0	15	35.7	32,177	501.8	1.3	372,500
Oregon	82	1.5	2,013	1.9	25	47.6	23,662	468.5	1.2	208,969
Maryland	61	1.1	1,075	1.0	18	34.6	32,193	460.4	1.2	402,484
Tennessee	87	1.6	1,691	1.6	19	43.9	25,955	451.0	1.2	299,285
North Carolina	88	1.6	1,440	1.3	16	32.4	22,481	437.4	1.1	328,097
Indiana	52	1.0	1,558	1.4	30	39.3	25,208	437.1	1.1	312,690
Idaho	71	1.3	3,005	2.8	42	40.7	13,552	350.9	0.9	108,543
Colorado	78	1.4	1,894	1.8	24	39.7	20,938	350.2	0.9	206,745
Wisconsin	65	1.2	1,253	1.2	19	29.8	23,791	312.9	0.8	246,764
Louisiana	49	0.9	937	0.9	19	20.9	22,254	260.7	0.7	306,742
Connecticut	46	0.8	529	0.5	11	15.9	30,057	244.2	0.6	494,273
Hawaii	50	0.9	741	0.7	15	19.7	26,619	233.5	0.6	300,150
Virginia	59	1.1	937	0.9	16	22.5	24,061	209.7	0.5	225,928
Kentucky	47	0.9	879	0.8	19	15.6	17,792	208.2	0.5	232,337
Utah	31	0.6	614	0.6	20	14.8	24,129	193.4	0.5	210,881
Alabama	44	0.8	1,252	1.2	28	22.6	18,020	191.7	0.5	212,739
Kansas	19	0.4	509	0.5	27	10.8	21,187	171.5	0.4	362,535
South Carolina	50	0.9	444	0.4	9	10.9	24,601	169.7	0.4	425,288
Iowa	21	0.4	300	0.3	14	9.3	30,923	146.0	0.4	550,947
Rhode Island	20	0.4	276	0.3	14	6.2	22,322	135.9	0.4	367,189
Maine	40	0.7	306	0.3	8	6.5	21,363	134.3	0.4	359,126
Oklahoma	39	0.7	603	0.6	15	11.6	19,158	120.3	0.3	214,369
D.C.	12	0.2	620	0.6	52	16.0	25,865	118.8	0.3	231,053
West Virginia	26	0.5	609	0.6	23	10.9	17,898	117.6	0.3	173,962
Arkansas	21	0.4	234	0.2	11	6.5	27,748	107.7	0.3	601,587
North Dakota	23	0.4	222	0.2	10	3.1	14,158	88.7	0.2	229,720
New Mexico	22	0.4	247	0.2	11	7.0	28,352	69.4	0.2	284,266
Delaware	10	0.2	47	0.0	5	1.9	40,957	65.2	0.2	1,481,136
Mississippi	28	0.5	272	0.3	10	5.3	19,625	58.0	0.2	194,527
New Hampshire	9	0.2	129	0.1	14	3.1	24,155	23.3	0.1	209,874
Alaska	5	0.1	63	0.1	13	1.8	27,984	15.3	0.0	318,896
South Dakota	3	0.1	19	0.0	6	0.7	34,789	14.8	0.0	380,462
Vermont	6	0.1	98	0.1	16	2.3	23,071	14.1	0.0	210,806
Montana	6	0.1	54	0.1	9	1.2	21,685	10.4	0.0	155,731
Nevada	15	0.3	470	0.4	31	11.1	23,679	(D)	-	-
Nebraska	11	0.2	222	0.2	20	6.1	27,293	(D)	-	-
Wyoming	4	0.1	45	0.0	11	0.6	12,600	(D)	-	-

Source: County Business Patterns, 1995 and *Economic Census of the U.S., 1992*. Data are sorted by 1992 revenues and, if revenues are unavailable, by establishments in 1995. The symbol (D) indicates that data are withheld by the source to avoid disclosure of competitive information. A dash (-) indicates that data are not available or undisclosed because they do not meet statistical validity standards. Shaded *states* on the state map indicate those states which have proportionately greater representation in the industry than would be indicated by the state's population; the ratio is based on total revenues or number of establishments. Shaded *regions* indicate where the industry is regionally most concentrated.

5149 - GROCERIES AND RELATED PRODUCTS, NEC

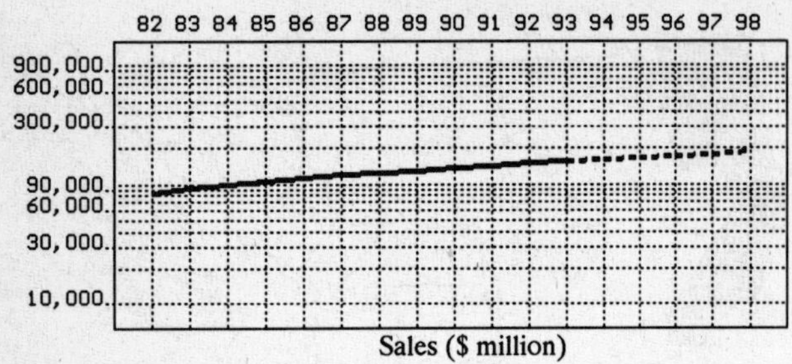

Sales ($ million)

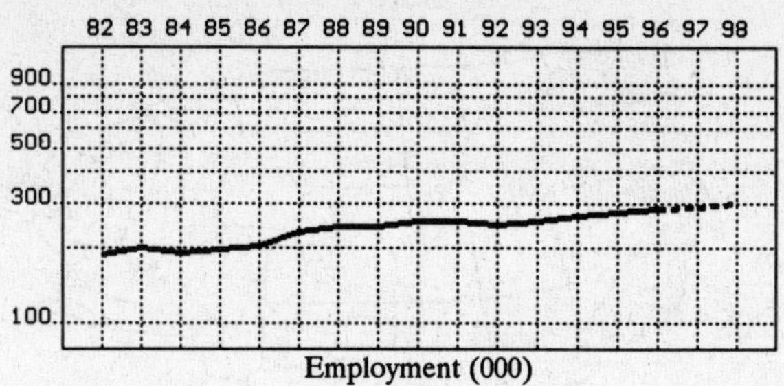

Employment (000)

GENERAL STATISTICS

Year	Establishments (number)	Employment (number)	Payroll ($ million)	Sales ($ million)	Expenses ($ million)	Beginning Inventory ($ million)	Ending Inventory ($ million)
1982	12,120	186,097	3,624.1	84,442.8	-	-	-
1983	11,818	199,851	4,117.0	91,116.3e	-	-	-
1984	11,515	192,743	4,109.9	97,789.9e	-	-	-
1985	11,307	195,625	4,408.7	104,463.5e	-	-	-
1986	11,219	203,958	4,783.6	111,137.0e	-	-	-
1987	13,577	232,888	5,488.3	117,810.6	11,452.2	3,564.0	3,709.6
1988	12,751	241,418	6,072.3	123,567.7e	12,171.2e	3,921.1e	4,087.7e
1989	12,238	241,951	6,290.3	129,324.7e	12,890.1e	4,278.2e	4,465.9e
1990	12,224	255,577	6,929.3	135,081.8e	13,609.0e	4,635.3e	4,844.0e
1991	12,088	254,111	7,117.1	140,838.9e	14,327.9e	4,992.4e	5,222.1e
1992	14,357	246,547	6,985.5	146,595.9	15,046.9	5,349.5	5,600.3
1993	14,005	254,093	7,419.0	153,852.7p	15,765.8p	5,706.6p	5,978.4p
1994	14,242	269,960	8,097.8	160,068.1p	16,484.7p	6,063.8p	6,356.5p
1995	14,099	278,012	8,474.5	166,283.4p	17,203.7p	6,420.9p	6,734.7p
1996	14,264p	284,994p	8,810.7p	172,498.7p	17,922.6p	6,778.0p	7,112.8p
1997	14,475p	292,014p	9,186.2p	178,714.0p	18,641.5p	7,135.1p	7,490.9p
1998	14,686p	299,034p	9,561.7p	184,929.3p	19,360.5p	7,492.2p	7,869.1p

Sources: *Economic Census of the United States*, 1982, 1987, and 1992. Establishment counts, employment, and payroll are from *County Business Patterns* for non-Census years. Values followed by a 'p' are projections by the editors. Sales and expense data for non-Census years are extrapolations, marked by 'e'. Industries reclassified in 1987 will not have data for prior years. Data are the most recent available at this level of detail.

INDICES OF CHANGE

Year	Establishments (number)	Employment (number)	Payroll ($ million)	Sales ($ million)	Expenses ($ million)	Beginning Inventory ($ million)	Ending Inventory ($ million)
1982	84.4	75.5	51.9	57.6	-	-	-
1983	82.3	81.1	58.9	62.2e	-	-	-
1984	80.2	78.2	58.8	66.7e	-	-	-
1985	78.8	79.3	63.1	71.3e	-	-	-
1986	78.1	82.7	68.5	75.8e	-	-	-
1987	94.6	94.5	78.6	80.4	76.1	66.6	66.2
1988	88.8	97.9	86.9	84.3e	80.9e	73.3e	73.0e
1989	85.2	98.1	90.0	88.2e	85.7e	80.0e	79.7e
1990	85.1	103.7	99.2	92.1e	90.4e	86.6e	86.5e
1991	84.2	103.1	101.9	96.1e	95.2e	93.3e	93.2e
1992	100.0	100.0	100.0	100.0	100.0	100.0	100.0
1993	97.5	103.1	106.2	105.0p	104.8p	106.7p	106.8p
1994	99.2	109.5	115.9	109.2p	109.6p	113.4p	113.5p
1995	98.2	112.8	121.3	113.4p	114.3p	120.0p	120.3p
1996	99.4p	115.6p	126.1p	117.7p	119.1p	126.7p	127.0p
1997	100.8p	118.4p	131.5p	121.9p	123.9p	133.4p	133.8p
1998	102.3p	121.3p	136.9p	126.1p	128.7p	140.1p	140.5p

Sources: Same as General Statistics. The values shown reflect change from the base year, 1992. Values above 100 mean greater than 1992, values below 100 mean less than 1992, and a value of 100 in the 1982-91 or 1993-98 period means same as 1992. Values followed by a 'p' are projections by the editors; 'e' stands for extrapolation. Data are the most recent available at this level of detail.

SELECTED RATIOS

For 1992	Avg. of All Wholesale	Analyzed Industry	Index	For 1992	Avg. of All Wholesale	Analyzed Industry	Index
Employees per Establishment	12	17	147	Sales per Employee	561,172	594,596	106
Payroll per Establishment	349,729	486,557	139	Sales per Establishment	6,559,346	10,210,761	156
Payroll per Employee	29,919	28,333	95	Expenses per Establishment	723,071	1,048,053	145

Sources: Same as General Statistics. The 'Average of All Manufacturing' column represents the average of all manufacturing industries reported for the most recent complete year available. The Index shows the relationship between the Average and the Analyzed Industry. For example, 100 means that they are equal; 500 that the Analyzed Industry is five times the average; 50 means that the Analyzed Industry is half the national average. The abbreviation 'na' is used to show that data are 'not available'.

LEADING COMPANIES Number shown: 50 Total sales ($ mil): 65,060 Total employment (000): 197.0

Company Name	Address				CEO Name	Phone	Co. Type	Sales ($ mil)	Empl. (000)
SYSCO Corp.	1390 Enclave Pkwy	Houston	TX	77077	Bill M Lindig	713-584-1390	P	14,455	32.0
Amway Corp.	7575 Fulton St E	Ada	MI	49355	Dick DeVos	616-787-6000	R	7,000	14.0
Alliant FoodService Inc.	One Parkway	Deerfield	IL	60015	James A Miller	847-405-8500	S	5,200	12.0
HomeBase Inc.	3345 Michelson Dr	Irvine	CA	92612	Herbert J Zarkin	714-442-5000	P	4,376	19.5
ProSource Services Corp.	550 Biltmore Way	Coral Gables	FL	33134	Thomas C Highland	305-740-1000	S	4,360 •	3.8
Universal Corp.	PO Box 25099	Richmond	VA	23260	Henry H Harrell	804-359-9311	P	4,113	25.0
Certified Grocers of California	PO Box 3396	Los Angeles	CA	90051	Alfred Plamann	213-726-2601	P	2,307	2.4
Perrier Group of America Inc.	777 W Putnam Ave	Greenwich	CT	06830	Kim Jeffery	203-531-4100	S	2,000	4.5
Quaker Oats Co.	PO Box 049001	Chicago	IL	60604	Barbara Allen	312-222-7111	D	1,741	9.0
Rykoff-Sexton Mfg Div.	761 Terminal St	Los Angeles	CA	90021	William J Caskey	213-622-4131	S	1,700	2.8
Shaklee Corp.	444 Market St	San Francisco	CA	94111	Charles L Orr	415-954-3000	S	1,690 •	2.2
Dial Corp.	15501 N Dial Blvd	Scottsdale	AZ	85260	Malcolm Jozoff	602-754-3425	P	1,428	2.5
Sunkist Growers Inc.	PO Box 7888	Van Nuys	CA	91409	Russell L Hanlin	818-986-4800	R	1,100	1.0
Starbucks Corp.	PO Box 34067	Seattle	WA	98124	Howard Schultz	206-447-1575	P	967	16.6
Marriot Distribution Services	10400 Fernwood Rd	Bethesda	MD	20817	Robert T Pras	301-380-3000	D	872	13.0
Pepsi Franchise Services Inc.	14841 Dallas Pkwy	Dallas	TX	75240	Bob Hunter	214-338-7000	S	850	0.7
Pro-Fac Cooperative Inc.	PO Box 682	Rochester	NY	14603	Roy A Myers	716-383-1850	P	731	3.4
Deli Universal Inc.	PO Box 25099	Richmond	VA	23261	Jaap Godthelp	804-359-9311	S	710 •	6.0
Perfection Bakeries Inc.	350 Pearl St	Fort Wayne	IN	46802	John F Popp	219-424-8245	R	696 •	1.5
Michael Foods Inc.	5353 Wayzata Blvd	Minneapolis	MN	55416	Gregg A Ostrander	612-546-1500	P	616	2.7
Schultz Sav-O Stores Inc.	PO Box 419	Sheboygan	WI	53082	James H Dickelman	920-457-4433	P	473	1.7
Riviana Foods Inc.	PO Box 2636	Houston	TX	77252	Joseph A Hafner Jr	713-529-3251	P	460	2.8
National Beverage Corp.	1 N University Dr	Plantation	FL	33324	Nick A Caporella	954-581-0922	P	385	1.2
Bozzuto's Inc.	275 Schoolhouse	Cheshire	CT	06410	Michael A Bozzuto	203-272-3511	P	378	1.0
Waldensian Bakeries Inc.	320 E Main St	Valdese	NC	28690	Richard Crow	704-874-2136	R	370 •	0.8
Sathers Inc.	PO Box 28	Round Lake	MN	56167	Bill Bradfield	507-945-8181	S	360 •	1.5
Distribution Plus Inc.	825 Green Bay Rd	Wilmette	IL	60091	Dan O'Connell	847-256-8289	R	350 •	1.0
Select Beverages Inc.	7955 S Cass Ave	Darien	IL	60561	Timothy Healy	630-241-3555	R	350 •	1.5
Atalanta Corp.	1 Atalanta Plz	Elizabeth	NJ	07206	George Gellert	908-351-8000	R	340	0.2
L and L Jiroch Distributing Co.	1180 58th St	Wyoming	MI	49509	Michael Alexander	616-530-6600	S	330 •	0.4
Norpac Food Sales Inc.	4350 SW Galewood	Lake Oswego	OR	97035	Roger D Baker	503-635-9311	R	330	<0.1
National Distributing Company	PO Box 44127	Atlanta	GA	30336	Michael C Carlos	404-696-9440	R	310 •	1.0
Allou Health and Beauty Care	50 Emjay Blvd	Brentwood	NY	11717	Victor Jacobs	516-273-4000	P	285	0.3
Quality Foods Inc.	PO Box 4908	Little Rock	AR	72214	Don Kirkpatrick	501-568-3141	R	280	0.8
Dairy Fresh Products Co.	601 Rockefeller	Ontario	CA	91761	Jim DeKeyser	909-975-1019	S	250	0.5
Millbrook Distribution Services	PO Box 790	Harrison	AR	72601	Bob Sigel	870-741-3425	S	250 •	2.0
Miesel/SYSCO Food Service	PO Box 33579	Detroit	MI	48232	Michael W Green	313-397-7990	S	239 •	0.7
Great Brands of Europe Inc.	208 Harbor Dr	Stamford	CT	06902	Mark Rodriguez	203-425-1700	S	225 •	0.2
Roma Food Enterprises Inc.	45 Stanford Rd	Piscataway	NJ	08854	Louis Piancone	908-463-7662	R	210 •	0.5
Georgia Crown Distributing Co.	PO Box 7908	Columbus	GA	31908	Don Leebern III	706-568-4580	R	200 •	0.7
Houston Foods Co.	3501 Mt Prospect	Franklin Park	IL	60131	Robert P Pesch	847-957-9191	R	196 •	0.2
JFC International Inc.	540 Forbes Blvd	S. San Francisco	CA	94080	N Enokido	415-873-8400	S	193	0.4
Topco Associates Inc.	7711 Gross Pt Rd	Skokie	IL	60077	W Steven Rubow	847-676-3030	R	189 •	0.4
High Grade Beverage	PO Box 7092	N. Brunswick	NJ	08902	Joe De Marco	908-821-7600	R	180 •	0.4
Kehe Food Distributors Inc.	900 Schmidt Rd	Romeoville	IL	60446	Jerry Kehe	815-886-0700	R	180 •	0.4
Sky Brothers Inc.	PO Box 632	Altoona	PA	16603	Rocco Alianiello	814-946-1201	S	180	0.4
Ritter Sysco Food Services Inc.	640 Dowd Ave	Elizabeth	NJ	07207	Martin Ritter	908-558-2700	S	170	0.4
National Wine and Spirits Corp.	PO Box 1602	Indianapolis	IN	46206	James Beck	317-636-6092	R	168	0.5
Indianapolis Coca-Cola Bottling	5000 W 25th St	Speedway	IN	46224	Anthony Stroinsky	317-243-3771	R	160 •	0.4
Crystal Farms	6465 Wayzata Blvd	Minneapolis	MN	55426	N A Rodriquez	612-544-8101	S	156 •	0.4

Source: *Ward's Business Directory of U.S. Private and Public Companies*, 1998. The company type code used is as follows: P - Public, R - Private, S - Subsidiary, D - Division, J - Joint Venture, A - Affiliate, G - Group. Sales are in millions of dollars, employees are in thousands. An asterisk (*) indicates an estimated sales volume. The symbol < stands for 'less than'.

OCCUPATIONS EMPLOYED BY SIC 514 - GROCERIES AND RELATED PRODUCTS

Occupation	% of Total 1996	Change to 2006	Occupation	% of Total 1996	Change to 2006
Sales & related workers nec	14.5	21.9	Industrial truck & tractor operators	2.4	21.9
Truck drivers light & heavy	12.6	10.8	Bookkeeping, accounting, & auditing clerks	2.4	-11.3
Driver/sales workers	6.1	33.0	Helpers, laborers nec	2.1	10.8
Freight, stock, & material movers, hand	4.9	-0.2	Salespersons, retail	1.7	10.8
General managers & top executives	3.7	7.4	Secretaries, except legal & medical	1.6	-12.1
Order fillers, wholesale & retail sales	3.7	10.8	Butchers & meatcutters	1.5	-11.3
Stock clerks	3.6	10.8	Blue collar worker supervisors	1.5	7.0
Hand packers & packagers	3.3	10.8	Packaging & filling machine operators	1.4	10.8
Traffic, shipping, receiving clerks	3.0	10.8	Wholesale & retail buyers, except farm products	1.4	7.9
Marketing & sales worker supervisors	2.9	10.8	Order clerks	1.2	-0.2
Agricultural, forestry, fishing workers nec	2.8	21.9	Clerical supervisors & managers	1.2	10.9
General office clerks	2.5	-4.6			

Source: *Industry-Occupation Matrix*, Bureau of Labor Statistics. These data relate to one or more 3-digit SIC industry groups rather than to a single 4-digit SIC. The change reported for each occupation to the year 2006 is a percent of growth or decline as estimated by the Bureau of Labor Statistics. The abbreviation nec stands for 'not elsewhere classified'.

STATE AND REGIONAL CONCENTRATION

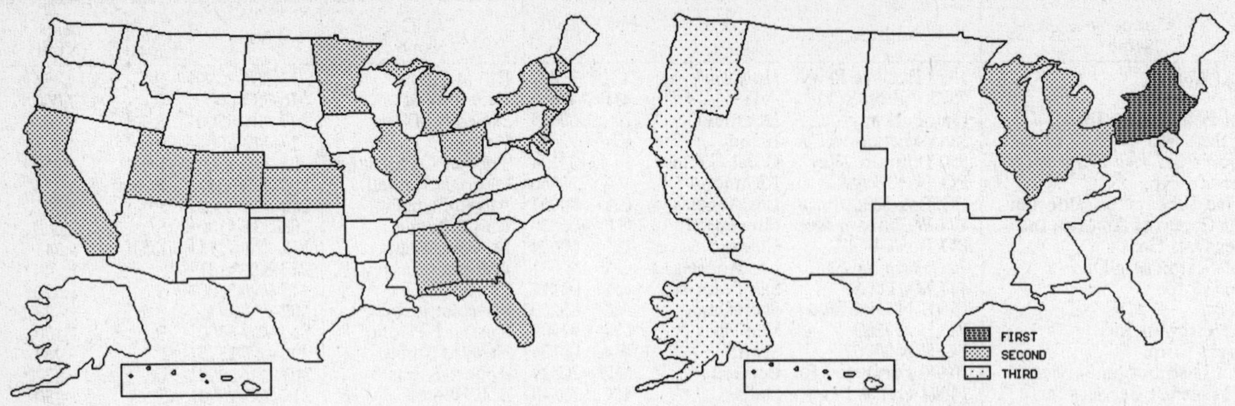

INDUSTRY DATA BY STATE

State	Establishments - 1995 Total (number)	Establishments - 1995 % of U.S.	Employment - 1995 Total (number)	Employment - 1995 % of U.S.	Employment - 1995 Per Estab.	Payroll - 1995 Total ($ mil.)	Payroll - 1995 Per Empl. ($)	Sales - 1992 Total ($ mil.)	Sales - 1992 % of U.S.	Sales - 1992 Per Estab ($)
California	1,924	13.6	36,371	13.1	19	1,202.1	33,052	19,094.1	14.4	567,383
New York	1,926	13.7	21,232	7.6	11	706.8	33,291	18,964.8	14.3	977,869
New Jersey	744	5.3	12,966	4.7	17	439.5	33,897	9,532.0	7.2	873,053
Texas	734	5.2	15,053	5.4	21	476.8	31,676	8,038.3	6.0	549,630
Florida	764	5.4	14,201	5.1	19	411.1	28,948	7,515.5	5.7	557,408
Illinois	609	4.3	14,032	5.0	23	440.3	31,376	7,119.1	5.4	696,181
Michigan	418	3.0	12,822	4.6	31	418.3	32,620	6,402.4	4.8	518,835
Ohio	427	3.0	11,093	4.0	26	323.8	29,185	6,191.1	4.7	609,784
Pennsylvania	519	3.7	12,667	4.6	24	401.5	31,694	6,094.1	4.6	492,970
Georgia	282	2.0	6,168	2.2	22	208.9	33,869	3,861.7	2.9	678,558
North Carolina	267	1.9	5,799	2.1	22	178.1	30,720	3,447.6	2.6	614,106
Maryland	246	1.7	7,644	2.7	31	213.4	27,920	3,108.0	2.3	640,690
Virginia	221	1.6	8,362	3.0	38	175.2	20,949	2,955.3	2.2	489,284
Minnesota	201	1.4	3,955	1.4	20	125.3	31,692	2,794.5	2.1	716,527
Washington	359	2.5	5,997	2.2	17	177.2	29,547	2,676.5	2.0	469,074
Tennessee	201	1.4	4,856	1.7	24	151.4	31,185	2,449.4	1.8	603,297
Missouri	283	2.0	4,510	1.6	16	132.5	29,380	2,404.3	1.8	563,600
Kansas	120	0.9	3,444	1.2	29	108.2	31,418	2,273.1	1.7	771,316
Alabama	149	1.1	4,524	1.6	30	127.0	28,078	2,264.0	1.7	561,095
Wisconsin	221	1.6	5,928	2.1	27	181.7	30,650	2,159.7	1.6	384,968
Colorado	233	1.7	3,292	1.2	14	93.1	28,272	2,101.9	1.6	813,435
Indiana	259	1.8	5,449	2.0	21	154.4	28,339	2,098.5	1.6	430,292
Connecticut	206	1.5	4,394	1.6	21	165.9	37,765	1,880.8	1.4	577,634
Utah	141	1.0	2,934	1.1	21	78.1	26,625	1,371.9	1.0	548,979
Arizona	260	1.8	4,576	1.6	18	116.1	25,375	1,217.8	0.9	330,207
Oklahoma	133	0.9	2,233	0.8	17	55.3	24,758	853.3	0.6	408,462
South Carolina	108	0.8	3,207	1.2	30	91.1	28,419	826.9	0.6	399,075
Iowa	105	0.7	2,144	0.8	20	57.3	26,745	752.5	0.6	353,959
New Hampshire	78	0.6	1,616	0.6	21	51.9	32,113	660.1	0.5	536,245
Mississippi	87	0.6	1,859	0.7	21	45.1	24,256	395.1	0.3	316,816
Alaska	30	0.2	563	0.2	19	18.7	33,160	303.3	0.2	524,785
Idaho	75	0.5	1,056	0.4	14	28.7	27,145	282.5	0.2	298,964
New Mexico	90	0.6	1,545	0.6	17	32.7	21,152	279.5	0.2	198,521
West Virginia	62	0.4	1,136	0.4	18	26.7	23,516	255.0	0.2	280,814
North Dakota	44	0.3	994	0.4	23	22.5	22,657	213.9	0.2	310,493
Wyoming	39	0.3	346	0.1	9	8.6	24,942	78.8	0.1	259,257
Massachusetts	322	2.3	7,551	2.7	23	246.7	32,676	(D)	-	-
Oregon	216	1.5	3,467	1.2	16	91.6	26,412	(D)	-	-
Louisiana	190	1.3	3,096	1.1	16	82.4	26,607	(D)	-	-
Kentucky	125	0.9	2,463	0.9	20	74.5	30,268	(D)	-	-
Arkansas	113	0.8	2,317	0.8	21	57.0	24,618	(D)	-	-
Hawaii	99	0.7	1,376	0.5	14	34.7	25,238	(D)	-	-
Maine	83	0.6	1,327	0.5	16	34.1	25,675	(D)	-	-
Nevada	82	0.6	2,025	0.7	25	56.0	27,652	(D)	-	-
Nebraska	64	0.5	1,523	0.5	24	45.8	30,066	(D)	-	-
Vermont	61	0.4	755	0.3	12	20.3	26,872	(D)	-	-
Montana	52	0.4	734	0.3	14	17.4	23,657	(D)	-	-
Rhode Island	47	0.3	924	0.3	20	30.4	32,886	(D)	-	-
Delaware	37	0.3	644	0.2	17	19.7	30,666	(D)	-	-
South Dakota	22	0.2	497	0.2	23	11.4	23,028	(D)	-	-
D.C.	21	0.1	345	0.1	16	6.9	19,997	(D)	-	-

Source: County Business Patterns, 1995 and *Economic Census of the U.S., 1992*. Data are sorted by 1992 revenues and, if revenues are unavailable, by establishments in 1995. The symbol (D) indicates that data are withheld by the source to avoid disclosure of competitive information. A dash (-) indicates that data are not available or undisclosed because they do not meet statistical validity standards. Shaded *states* on the state map indicate those states which have proportionately greater representation in the industry than would be indicated by the state's population; the ratio is based on total revenues or number of establishments. Shaded *regions* indicate where the industry is regionally most concentrated.

5153 - GRAIN AND FIELD BEANS

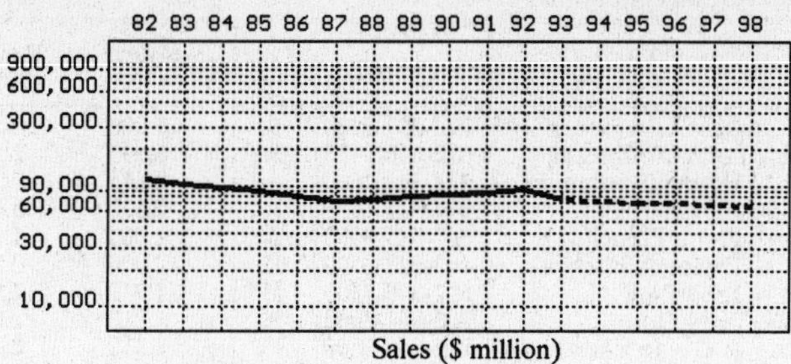

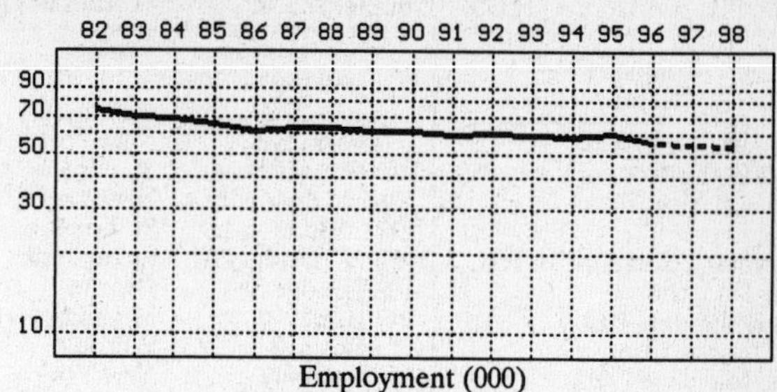

GENERAL STATISTICS

Year	Establishments (number)	Employment (number)	Payroll ($ million)	Sales ($ million)	Expenses ($ million)	Beginning Inventory ($ million)	Ending Inventory ($ million)
1982	9,118	74,189	1,280.9	110,525.7	-	-	-
1983	8,611	70,260	1,265.1	103,122.8e	-	-	-
1984	8,490	68,525	1,271.7	95,720.0e	-	-	-
1985	8,069	64,664	1,235.5	88,317.2e	-	-	-
1986	7,704	61,205	1,228.9	80,914.3e	-	-	-
1987	8,155	63,272	1,273.0	73,511.5	3,607.7	3,268.2	3,932.3
1988	7,871	63,283	1,345.7	76,989.9e	3,671.1e	3,746.8e	4,288.5e
1989	7,660	61,644	1,351.1	80,468.3e	3,734.5e	4,225.4e	4,644.7e
1990	7,426	61,082	1,375.5	83,946.8e	3,797.8e	4,704.0e	5,000.9e
1991	7,180	59,011	1,365.9	87,425.2e	3,861.2e	5,182.6e	5,357.0e
1992	7,444	60,243	1,446.2	90,903.6	3,924.6	5,661.2	5,713.2
1993	7,185	59,195	1,436.1	76,576.3p	3,988.0p	6,139.7p	6,069.4p
1994	6,960	58,117	1,478.7	74,614.1p	4,051.4p	6,618.3p	6,425.6p
1995	6,815	59,692	1,587.0	72,651.9p	4,114.7p	7,096.9p	6,781.8p
1996	6,622p	55,652p	1,522.4p	70,689.7p	4,178.1p	7,575.5p	7,138.0p
1997	6,470p	54,649p	1,545.0p	68,727.5p	4,241.5p	8,054.1p	7,494.2p
1998	6,318p	53,647p	1,567.6p	66,765.3p	4,304.9p	8,532.7p	7,850.3p

Sources: Economic Census of the United States, 1982, 1987, and 1992. Establishment counts, employment, and payroll are from *County Business Patterns* for non-Census years. Values followed by a 'p' are projections by the editors. Sales and expense data for non-Census years are extrapolations, marked by 'e'. Industries reclassified in 1987 will not have data for prior years. Data are the most recent available at this level of detail.

INDICES OF CHANGE

Year	Establishments (number)	Employment (number)	Payroll ($ million)	Sales ($ million)	Expenses ($ million)	Beginning Inventory ($ million)	Ending Inventory ($ million)
1982	122.5	123.1	88.6	121.6	-	-	-
1983	115.7	116.6	87.5	113.4e	-	-	-
1984	114.1	113.7	87.9	105.3e	-	-	-
1985	108.4	107.3	85.4	97.2e	-	-	-
1986	103.5	101.6	85.0	89.0e	-	-	-
1987	109.6	105.0	88.0	80.9	91.9	57.7	68.8
1988	105.7	105.0	93.1	84.7e	93.5e	66.2e	75.1e
1989	102.9	102.3	93.4	88.5e	95.2e	74.6e	81.3e
1990	99.8	101.4	95.1	92.3e	96.8e	83.1e	87.5e
1991	96.5	98.0	94.4	96.2e	98.4e	91.5e	93.8e
1992	100.0	100.0	100.0	100.0	100.0	100.0	100.0
1993	96.5	98.3	99.3	84.2p	101.6p	108.5p	106.2p
1994	93.5	96.5	102.2	82.1p	103.2p	116.9p	112.5p
1995	91.6	99.1	109.7	79.9p	104.8p	125.4p	118.7p
1996	89.0p	92.4p	105.3p	77.8p	106.5p	133.8p	124.9p
1997	86.9p	90.7p	106.8p	75.6p	108.1p	142.3p	131.2p
1998	84.9p	89.1p	108.4p	73.4p	109.7p	150.7p	137.4p

Sources: Same as General Statistics. The values shown reflect change from the base year, 1992. Values above 100 mean greater than 1992, values below 100 mean less than 1992, and a value of 100 in the 1982-91 or 1993-98 period means same as 1992. Values followed by a 'p' are projections by the editors; 'e' stands for extrapolation. Data are the most recent available at this level of detail.

SELECTED RATIOS

For 1992	Avg. of All Wholesale	Analyzed Industry	Index	For 1992	Avg. of All Wholesale	Analyzed Industry	Index
Employees per Establishment	12	8	69	Sales per Employee	561,172	1,508,949	269
Payroll per Establishment	349,729	194,277	56	Sales per Establishment	6,559,346	12,211,660	186
Payroll per Employee	29,919	24,006	80	Expenses per Establishment	723,071	527,217	73

Sources: Same as General Statistics. The 'Average of All Manufacturing' column represents the average of all manufacturing industries reported for the most recent complete year available. The Index shows the relationship between the Average and the Analyzed Industry. For example, 100 means that they are equal; 500 that the Analyzed Industry is five times the average; 50 means that the Analyzed Industry is half the national average. The abbreviation 'na' is used to show that data are 'not available'.

LEADING COMPANIES

Number shown: **50** Total sales ($ mil): **46,771** Total employment (000): **58.3**

Company Name	Address				CEO Name	Phone	Co. Type	Sales ($ mil)	Empl. (000)
Continental Grain Co.	277 Park Ave	New York	NY	10172	Paul J Freibourg	212-207-5100	R	15,000	14.5
Harvest States Cooperatives	PO Box 64594	St. Paul	MN	55164	John D Johnson	612-646-9433	R	6,036	2.5
Tomen America Inc.	1285 of the Amer	New York	NY	10019	Hajime Kawamura	212-397-4600	S	2,645	0.9
Bunge Corp.	11720 Borman Dr	St. Louis	MO	63146	John E Klein	314-872-3030	R	2,570 *	3.0
Countrymark Cooperative Inc.	950 N Meridian St	Indianapolis	IN	46204	Philip French	317-685-3000	R	2,000	1.6
Scoular Co., The	1027 Dodge St	Omaha	NE	68102	Duane A Fischer	402-342-3500	R	2,000	0.2
ConAgra Trading Cos.	PO Box 2910	Minneapolis	MN	55402	Fred Page	612-370-7500	D	1,710	2.0
Louis Dreyfus Corp.	PO Box 810	Wilton	CT	06897	John Goss	203-761-2000	R	1,710 *	2.0
Balfour Maclaine Corp.	61 Broadway	New York	NY	10006	A C Van Ekris	212-269-0800	P	1,312	0.8
Southern States Cooperative	PO Box 26234	Richmond	VA	23260	Wayne A Boutwell	804-281-1000	R	1,216	3.5
Andersons Inc.	480 W Dussel Dr	Maumee	OH	43537	Richard P Anderson	419-893-5050	P	1,155	3.0
Farmland Grain Div.	10100 Exec Hills	Kansas City	MO	64153	John Bernardi	816-459-3300	D	1,060 *	0.4
Seaboard Corp.	200 Boylston St	Chestnut Hill	MA	02167	HH Bresky	617-332-8492	P	1,054	12.9
Agri Grain Marketing	PO Box 8129	Des Moines	IA	50301	Peter Reed	515-224-2600	J	1,000	0.1
Tabor Grain Co.	4666 Faries Pkwy	Decatur	IL	62525	Burnell D Kraft	217-424-5200	S	878 *	1.2
ADM-Growmark Inc.	PO Box 1470	Decatur	IL	62525	Burnell Kraft	217-424-5900	S	584 *	0.7
Collingwood Grain Inc.	PO Box 2150	Hutchinson	KS	67504	Lowell Downey	316-663-7121	S	580 *	0.7
GROWMARK Inc.	1701 Towanda Ave	Bloomington	IL	61701	Norm Jones	309-557-6000	R	330	0.8
Bartlett and Co.	4800 Main St	Kansas City	MO	64112	Paul D Bartlett	816-753-6300	R	260	0.6
South Dakota Wheat Growers	PO Box 1460	Aberdeen	SD	57401	Verland Losinger	605-225-5500	R	254	0.3
Alabama Farmers Cooperative	PO Box 2227	Decatur	AL	35609	Thomas Paulk	205-353-6843	R	250	0.6
Koch Agriculture Company Inc.	PO Box 2256	Wichita	KS	67220	Larry Angel	316-828-5500	S	250 *	0.7
Farmers Cooperative Co.	PO Box 35	Farnhamville	IA	50538	Roger Koppen	515-544-3213	R	240	0.2
Demeter Inc.	PO Box 465	Fowler	IN	47944	Donald Brouillette	317-884-0600	R	200	0.2
Watonwan Farm Services Co.	PO Box 26	St. James	MN	56081	Don Gales	507-375-3355	R	170	0.2
Perdue Farms Grain Div.	PO Box 1537	Salisbury	MD	21802	Richard Willey	410-543-3650	D	163 *	0.8
Trinidad-Benham Corp.	PO Box 22139	Denver	CO	80222	Carl C Hartman	303-220-1400	R	150 *	0.5
CGB Enterprises Inc.	PO Box 249	Mandeville	LA	70470	Richard Wilcox	504-867-3500	R	140	0.8
Heartland Co-op	2829 Westown	W. Des Moines	IA	50266	Larry Petersen	515-225-1334	R	140	0.2
Pendleton Grain Growers Inc.	1000 Dorion SW	Pendleton	OR	97801	Ed Balsiger	503-276-7611	R	105	0.3
Crestland Cooperative	PO Box 329	Creston	IA	50801	Larry E Crosser	515-782-6411	R	100	0.2
Anderson Grain Corp.	PO Box 1117	Levelland	TX	79336	Buck Anderson	806-894-4982	R	96 *	0.2
JaGee Corp.	PO Box 9600	Fort Worth	TX	76147	Richard F Garvey	817-335-5881	R	95	0.3
Universal Cooperative Inc.	7801 Metro Pkwy	Minneapolis	MN	55440	Patrick Finley	612-854-0800	R	94 *	0.2
Cooperative Elevator Co.	7211 E Michigan	Pigeon	MI	48755	John P Kohr	517-453-4500	R	92	0.2
Auglaize Farmers Cooperative	PO Box 360	Wapakoneta	OH	45895	Larry Hammond	419-738-2137	R	90	0.2
Aurora Cooperative Elevator	PO Box 209	Aurora	NE	68818	Rodney Schroeder	402-694-2106	R	90 *	0.1
Farmers Cooperative Dayton	PO Box 47	Dayton	IA	50530	Roger Coppen	515-547-2813	R	85 *	0.1
Ursa Farmers Cooperative	202 W Maple St	Ursa	IL	62376	Gerald Jenkins	217-964-2111	R	82	<0.1
Wright Lorenz Grain Company	PO Box 2420	Salina	KS	67402	Don R Timmel	913-827-3687	R	80	<0.1
United Co-op Inc.	PO Box 127	Hampton	NE	68843	Jay Larson	402-725-3131	R	78 *	0.1
Albert City Elevator Inc.	PO Box 38	Albert City	IA	50510	Bruce G Anderson	712-843-2291	R	75	<0.1
Frick's Services Inc.	PO Box 40	Wawaka	IN	46794	DR Frick	219-761-3311	R	75 *	0.1
La Porte County Cooperative	PO Box 160	La Porte	IN	46350	Dean Kaesebier	219-362-2156	R	75	0.1
St. Hilaire Cooperative Elevators	PO Box 128	St. Hilaire	MN	56754	Robert E Miller	218-964-5252	R	73	<0.1
Mondovi Cooperative	735 E Main St	Mondovi	WI	54755	Paul Adams	715-926-4212	R	72 *	<0.1
AG ONE CO-OP Inc.	PO Box 2009	Anderson	IN	46018	Doug Brount	317-643-6639	R	68 *	<0.1
Farmers Coop Assoc.	PO Box 228	Jackson	MN	56143	Wayne Gordon	507-847-4160	R	63 *	<0.1
Growers Cooperative Inc.	PO Box 2196	Terre Haute	IN	47802	Keith C Bowers	812-235-8123	R	63 *	<0.1
Metamora Elevator Co.	State Rte 120	Metamora	OH	43540	Fred R Duncan	419-644-4711	R	63	<0.1

Source: *Ward's Business Directory of U.S. Private and Public Companies*, 1998. The company type code used is as follows: P - Public, R - Private, S - Subsidiary, D - Division, J - Joint Venture, A - Affiliate, G - Group. Sales are in millions of dollars, employees are in thousands. An asterisk (*) indicates an estimated sales volume. The symbol < stands for 'less than'.

OCCUPATIONS EMPLOYED BY SIC 515 - WHOLESALE TRADE, OTHER

Occupation	% of Total 1996	Change to 2006	Occupation	% of Total 1996	Change to 2006
Sales & related workers nec	19.5	20.2	Clerical supervisors & managers	1.9	20.2
General managers & top executives	5.9	16.4	Order clerks	1.9	8.2
Truck drivers light & heavy	5.4	20.2	Helpers, laborers nec	1.7	20.2
General office clerks	3.6	3.4	Electrical & electronic technicians	1.4	18.8
Traffic, shipping, receiving clerks	3.6	16.7	Blue collar worker supervisors	1.4	16.0
Stock clerks	3.5	-3.9	Wholesale & retail buyers, except farm products	1.3	17.0
Freight, stock, & material movers, hand	3.3	8.2	Office machine & cash register servicers	1.3	20.2
Marketing & sales worker supervisors	3.1	20.2	Hand packers & packagers	1.2	-3.9
Order fillers, wholesale & retail sales	3.0	16.7	Maintenance repairers, general utility	1.1	12.0
Bookkeeping, accounting, & auditing clerks	2.9	-3.9	Industrial truck & tractor operators	1.1	20.2
Salespersons, retail	2.5	20.2	Purchasing managers	1.1	20.2
Secretaries, except legal & medical	2.5	-4.7	Receptionists & information clerks	1.0	20.2
Assemblers, fabricators, hand workers nec	2.0	-3.9			

Source: *Industry-Occupation Matrix*, Bureau of Labor Statistics. These data relate to one or more 3-digit SIC industry groups rather than to a single 4-digit SIC. The change reported for each occupation to the year 2006 is a percent of growth or decline as estimated by the Bureau of Labor Statistics. The abbreviation nec stands for 'not elsewhere classified'.

STATE AND REGIONAL CONCENTRATION

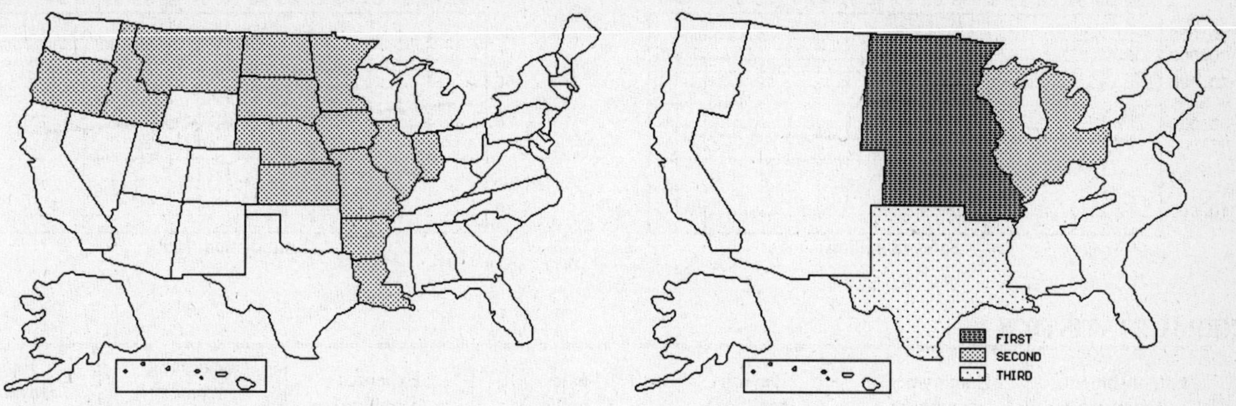

INDUSTRY DATA BY STATE

State	Establishments - 1995 Total (number)	Establishments - 1995 % of U.S.	Employment - 1995 Total (number)	Employment - 1995 % of U.S.	Employment - 1995 Per Estab.	Payroll - 1995 Total ($ mil.)	Payroll - 1995 Per Empl. ($)	Sales - 1992 Total ($ mil.)	Sales - 1992 % of U.S.	Sales - 1992 Per Estab ($)
Illinois	763	11.2	5,846	9.8	8	165.9	28,370	10,367.4	12.0	1,842,759
Minnesota	439	6.4	4,475	7.5	10	128.0	28,611	9,113.7	10.6	2,068,007
Iowa	735	10.8	8,006	13.5	11	211.2	26,384	7,146.3	8.3	921,865
Louisiana	69	1.0	1,435	2.4	21	45.5	31,721	6,243.2	7.2	5,466,914
Oregon	56	0.8	416	0.7	7	15.8	37,935	5,999.3	6.9	13,098,895
Kansas	619	9.1	4,875	8.2	8	123.8	25,401	5,985.0	6.9	1,152,079
Missouri	281	4.1	2,578	4.3	9	57.7	22,400	5,264.5	6.1	1,979,149
New York	65	1.0	498	0.8	8	20.0	40,257	5,041.2	5.8	9,405,246
Nebraska	421	6.2	4,043	6.8	10	100.6	24,872	4,197.7	4.9	807,242
Texas	384	5.6	3,236	5.4	8	82.4	25,467	3,845.7	4.5	1,123,156
Ohio	289	4.2	2,677	4.5	9	67.9	25,382	2,559.9	3.0	987,988
Indiana	331	4.9	3,056	5.1	9	86.7	28,358	2,549.1	3.0	903,287
North Dakota	346	5.1	2,273	3.8	7	55.5	24,416	2,098.6	2.4	1,076,771
Arkansas	73	1.1	771	1.3	11	18.2	23,606	1,683.1	1.9	2,334,348
Washington	172	2.5	983	1.7	6	33.3	33,860	1,666.3	1.9	1,717,826
California	126	1.8	1,284	2.2	10	40.6	31,654	1,427.5	1.7	857,356
South Dakota	230	3.4	1,762	3.0	8	40.2	22,821	1,288.3	1.5	824,280
Montana	111	1.6	630	1.1	6	13.3	21,048	983.6	1.1	1,828,340
Tennessee	59	0.9	450	0.8	8	17.8	39,527	971.3	1.1	2,471,573
Oklahoma	174	2.6	1,286	2.2	7	29.3	22,750	943.6	1.1	582,821
Michigan	150	2.2	1,577	2.7	11	43.8	27,772	931.6	1.1	678,000
Colorado	138	2.0	1,208	2.0	9	27.6	22,810	842.9	1.0	707,154
Florida	40	0.6	265	0.4	7	6.8	25,623	769.3	0.9	2,652,600
Wisconsin	76	1.1	832	1.4	11	22.0	26,492	635.0	0.7	800,763
Idaho	127	1.9	1,265	2.1	10	29.3	23,138	586.9	0.7	485,404
Kentucky	57	0.8	538	0.9	9	12.1	22,472	550.8	0.6	1,059,254
North Carolina	87	1.3	632	1.1	7	14.1	22,244	515.0	0.6	808,526
Georgia	55	0.8	381	0.6	7	8.1	21,349	502.6	0.6	1,051,483
Virginia	32	0.5	236	0.4	7	6.4	27,161	431.6	0.5	1,547,025
Pennsylvania	49	0.7	448	0.8	9	13.7	30,478	331.4	0.4	938,864
Maryland	24	0.4	214	0.4	9	4.5	21,234	262.9	0.3	1,776,473
New Jersey	18	0.3	159	0.3	9	11.9	75,006	172.8	0.2	1,199,694
Alabama	27	0.4	212	0.4	8	6.3	29,486	153.1	0.2	705,442
South Carolina	33	0.5	176	0.3	5	3.2	18,011	125.5	0.1	575,505
Utah	18	0.3	123	0.2	7	2.2	17,854	65.5	0.1	703,849
Arizona	14	0.2	137	0.2	10	2.5	17,971	55.5	0.1	702,532
New Mexico	11	0.2	70	0.1	6	1.2	17,043	21.7	0.0	395,036
Massachusetts	7	0.1	47	0.1	7	1.2	25,872	9.2	0.0	235,462
Hawaii	3	0.0	0-19	-	-	(D)	-	8.4	0.0	263,281
Maine	11	0.2	20	0.0	2	0.7	33,950	6.4	0.0	292,409
Mississippi	53	0.8	330	0.6	6	7.4	22,345	(D)	-	-
Delaware	13	0.2	20-99	-	-	(D)	-	(D)	-	-
Wyoming	11	0.2	20-99	-	-	(D)	-	(D)	-	-
Connecticut	7	0.1	20-99	-	-	(D)	-	(D)	-	-
Rhode Island	4	0.1	0-19	-	-	(D)	-	(D)	-	-
New Hampshire	2	0.0	0-19	-	-	(D)	-	(D)	-	-
Vermont	2	0.0	20-99	-	-	(D)	-	(D)	-	-
Alaska	1	0.0	0-19	-	-	(D)	-	-	-	-
D.C.	1	0.0	0-19	-	-	(D)	-	-	-	-
West Virginia	1	0.0	0-19	-	-	(D)	-	(D)	-	-

Source: County Business Patterns, 1995 and *Economic Census of the U.S., 1992*. Data are sorted by 1992 revenues and, if revenues are unavailable, by establishments in 1995. The symbol (D) indicates that data are withheld by the source to avoid disclosure of competitive information. A dash (-) indicates that data are not available or undisclosed because they do not meet statistical validity standards. Shaded *states* on the state map indicate those states which have proportionately greater representation in the industry than would be indicated by the state's population; the ratio is based on total revenues or number of establishments. Shaded *regions* indicate where the industry is regionally most concentrated.

5154 - LIVESTOCK

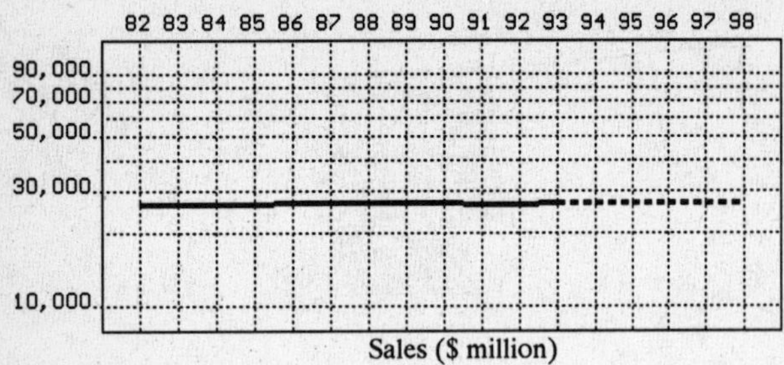

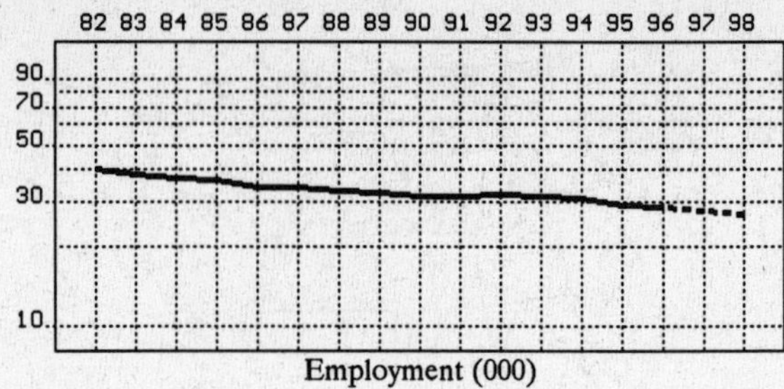

GENERAL STATISTICS

Year	Establishments (number)	Employment (number)	Payroll ($ million)	Sales ($ million)	Expenses ($ million)	Beginning Inventory ($ million)	Ending Inventory ($ million)
1982	3,157	39,954	239.9	26,089.2	-	-	-
1983	3,005	38,347	244.9	26,216.6e	-	-	-
1984	2,899	36,939	242.4	26,343.9e	-	-	-
1985	2,770	36,693	235.6	26,471.2e	-	-	-
1986	2,544	34,090	228.3	26,598.5e	-	-	-
1987	2,592	34,510	237.6	26,725.8	607.2	74.5	92.0
1988	2,433	33,147	252.0	26,665.7e	616.1e	83.4e	101.3e
1989	2,332	32,530	252.5	26,605.6e	625.0e	92.4e	110.6e
1990	2,301	31,578	258.9	26,545.5e	633.9e	101.3e	119.9e
1991	2,255	31,567	260.0	26,485.4e	642.9e	110.2e	129.1e
1992	2,316	32,034	254.8	26,425.3	651.8	119.1	138.4
1993	2,368	31,852	265.7	26,671.9p	660.7p	128.1p	147.7p
1994	2,372	31,127	270.2	26,705.5p	669.6p	137.0p	157.0p
1995	2,239	29,176	262.2	26,739.1p	678.5p	145.9p	166.2p
1996	2,059p	28,551p	269.1p	26,772.7p	687.4p	154.8p	175.5p
1997	1,995p	27,847p	271.6p	26,806.3p	696.3p	163.8p	184.8p
1998	1,930p	27,144p	274.0p	26,839.9p	705.3p	172.7p	194.1p

Sources: Economic Census of the United States, 1982, 1987, and 1992. Establishment counts, employment, and payroll are from *County Business Patterns* for non-Census years. Values followed by a 'p' are projections by the editors. Sales and expense data for non-Census years are extrapolations, marked by 'e'. Industries reclassified in 1987 will not have data for prior years. Data are the most recent available at this level of detail.

INDICES OF CHANGE

Year	Establishments (number)	Employment (number)	Payroll ($ million)	Sales ($ million)	Expenses ($ million)	Beginning Inventory ($ million)	Ending Inventory ($ million)
1982	136.3	124.7	94.2	98.7	-	-	-
1983	129.7	119.7	96.1	99.2e	-	-	-
1984	125.2	115.3	95.1	99.7e	-	-	-
1985	119.6	114.5	92.5	100.2e	-	-	-
1986	109.8	106.4	89.6	100.7e	-	-	-
1987	111.9	107.7	93.2	101.1	93.2	62.6	66.5
1988	105.1	103.5	98.9	100.9e	94.5e	70.0e	73.2e
1989	100.7	101.5	99.1	100.7e	95.9e	77.6e	79.9e
1990	99.4	98.6	101.6	100.5e	97.3e	85.1e	86.6e
1991	97.4	98.5	102.0	100.2e	98.6e	92.5e	93.3e
1992	100.0	100.0	100.0	100.0	100.0	100.0	100.0
1993	102.2	99.4	104.3	100.9p	101.4p	107.6p	106.7p
1994	102.4	97.2	106.0	101.1p	102.7p	115.0p	113.4p
1995	96.7	91.1	102.9	101.2p	104.1p	122.5p	120.1p
1996	88.9p	89.1p	105.6p	101.3p	105.5p	130.0p	126.8p
1997	86.1p	86.9p	106.6p	101.4p	106.8p	137.5p	133.5p
1998	83.4p	84.7p	107.6p	101.6p	108.2p	145.0p	140.2p

Sources: Same as General Statistics. The values shown reflect change from the base year, 1992. Values above 100 mean greater than 1992, values below 100 mean less than 1992, and a value of 100 in the 1982-91 or 1993-98 period means same as 1992. Values followed by a 'p' are projections by the editors; 'e' stands for extrapolation. Data are the most recent available at this level of detail.

SELECTED RATIOS

For 1992	Avg. of All Wholesale	Analyzed Industry	Index	For 1992	Avg. of All Wholesale	Analyzed Industry	Index
Employees per Establishment	12	14	118	Sales per Employee	561,172	824,914	147
Payroll per Establishment	349,729	110,017	31	Sales per Establishment	6,559,346	11,409,888	174
Payroll per Employee	29,919	7,954	27	Expenses per Establishment	723,071	281,434	39

Sources: Same as General Statistics. The 'Average of All Manufacturing' column represents the average of all manufacturing industries reported for the most recent complete year available. The Index shows the relationship between the Average and the Analyzed Industry. For example, 100 means that they are equal; 500 that the Analyzed Industry is five times the average; 50 means that the Analyzed Industry is half the national average. The abbreviation 'na' is used to show that data are 'not available'.

LEADING COMPANIES Number shown: 15 Total sales ($ mil): 2,419 Total employment (000): 1.7

Company Name	Address				CEO Name	Phone	Co. Type	Sales ($ mil)	Empl. (000)
Golodetz Trading Corp.	666 5th Ave	New York	NY	10103	I Suder	212-581-2400	R	1,300	0.5
Michigan Livestock Exchange	2651 Coolidge Rd	East Lansing	MI	48823	Thomas H Reed	517-337-2856	R	500 *	0.2
Producers Livestock Marketing	PO Box 540477	N. Salt Lake	UT	84054	Mike Urrutia	801-292-2424	R	140 *	0.2
Producers Livestock Association	PO Box 29800	Columbus	OH	43229	W Dennis Bolling	614-890-6666	R	76	0.1
Agri-Empire	PO Box 490	San Jacinto	CA	92581	Larry Minor	909-654-7311	R	75	0.2
Farmers Livestock Marketing	PO Box 5	Nl Stck Yrds	IL	62071	Dorris Penrod	618-875-1110	R	75	<0.1
Bales Continental	PO Box 1337	Huron	SD	57350	Jerry Bales	605-352-8682	R	61	<0.1
Stone Commodities Corp.	30 S Wacker Dr	Chicago	IL	60606	William C Bachman	312-454-3000	R	54	0.1
Central Livestock Association	PO Box 419	South St. Paul	MN	55075	DG Kampmier	612-451-1844	R	40	0.1
Garrard County Stockyard	PO Box 654	Lancaster	KY	40444	E Freeman	606-792-2118	R	30	<0.1
Vintage Sales Stables Inc.	3451 Lincoln E	Paradise	PA	17562	Robert Frame	717-442-4181	R	26 *	<0.1
Maynard Cooperative Co.	PO Box 215	Maynard	IA	50655	Lee Probert	319-637-2285	R	15	<0.1
Finger Lakes Livestock Exchange	Rte 5 & 20 E	Canandaigua	NY	14424	Ronald Parker	716-394-1515	R	14	<0.1
El Toro Land and Cattle Co.	PO Box G	Heber	CA	92249	Robert Odell	619-352-6312	R	12	<0.1
PrimeAg Inc.	1600 Genessee St	Kansas City	MO	64102	Jack Runyan	816-471-4360	R	1	<0.1

Source: *Ward's Business Directory of U.S. Private and Public Companies*, 1998. The company type code used is as follows: P - Public, R - Private, S - Subsidiary, D - Division, J - Joint Venture, A - Affiliate, G - Group. Sales are in millions of dollars, employees are in thousands. An asterisk (*) indicates an estimated sales volume. The symbol < stands for 'less than'.

OCCUPATIONS EMPLOYED BY SIC 515 - WHOLESALE TRADE, OTHER

Occupation	% of Total 1996	Change to 2006	Occupation	% of Total 1996	Change to 2006
Sales & related workers nec	19.5	20.2	Clerical supervisors & managers	1.9	20.2
General managers & top executives	5.9	16.4	Order clerks	1.9	8.2
Truck drivers light & heavy	5.4	20.2	Helpers, laborers nec	1.7	20.2
General office clerks	3.6	3.4	Electrical & electronic technicians	1.4	18.8
Traffic, shipping, receiving clerks	3.6	16.7	Blue collar worker supervisors	1.4	16.0
Stock clerks	3.5	-3.9	Wholesale & retail buyers, except farm products	1.3	17.0
Freight, stock, & material movers, hand	3.3	8.2	Office machine & cash register servicers	1.3	20.2
Marketing & sales worker supervisors	3.1	20.2	Hand packers & packagers	1.2	-3.9
Order fillers, wholesale & retail sales	3.0	16.7	Maintenance repairers, general utility	1.1	12.0
Bookkeeping, accounting, & auditing clerks	2.9	-3.9	Industrial truck & tractor operators	1.1	20.2
Salespersons, retail	2.5	20.2	Purchasing managers	1.1	20.2
Secretaries, except legal & medical	2.5	-4.7	Receptionists & information clerks	1.0	20.2
Assemblers, fabricators, hand workers nec	2.0	-3.9			

Source: *Industry-Occupation Matrix*, Bureau of Labor Statistics. These data relate to one or more 3-digit SIC industry groups rather than to a single 4-digit SIC. The change reported for each occupation to the year 2006 is a percent of growth or decline as estimated by the Bureau of Labor Statistics. The abbreviation nec stands for 'not elsewhere classified'.

STATE AND REGIONAL CONCENTRATION

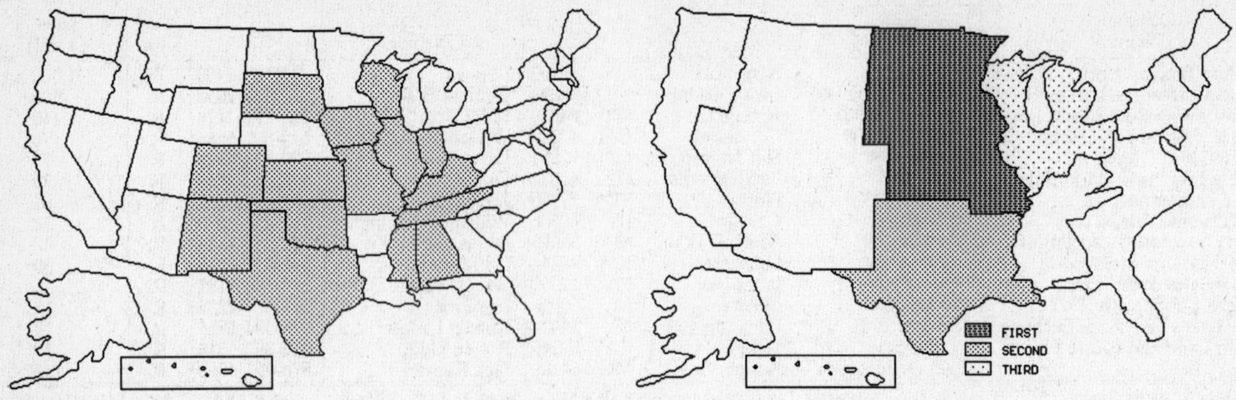

INDUSTRY DATA BY STATE

State	Establishments - 1995 Total (number)	Establishments - 1995 % of U.S.	Employment - 1995 Total (number)	Employment - 1995 % of U.S.	Employment - 1995 Per Estab.	Payroll - 1995 Total ($ mil.)	Payroll - 1995 Per Empl. ($)	Sales - 1992 Total ($ mil.)	Sales - 1992 % of U.S.	Sales - 1992 Per Estab ($)
Texas	233	10.4	4,121	14.4	18	35.3	8,565	3,081.4	14.2	745,919
Iowa	187	8.4	1,629	5.7	9	16.9	10,361	1,694.8	7.8	934,778
South Dakota	64	2.9	1,303	4.5	20	8.8	6,760	1,503.7	6.9	1,063,438
Missouri	135	6.0	1,369	4.8	10	11.8	8,639	1,417.6	6.5	883,813
Kentucky	64	2.9	965	3.4	15	10.0	10,347	1,403.3	6.5	1,548,900
Kansas	71	3.2	1,345	4.7	19	10.1	7,492	1,287.9	5.9	803,919
Oklahoma	73	3.3	1,375	4.8	19	8.0	5,854	1,195.4	5.5	732,914
Illinois	125	5.6	719	2.5	6	10.8	15,024	1,078.2	5.0	1,115,041
Colorado	29	1.3	692	2.4	24	6.8	9,892	934.8	4.3	1,337,411
Ohio	73	3.3	698	2.4	10	9.3	13,328	913.5	4.2	966,618
Wisconsin	81	3.6	681	2.4	8	7.5	11,018	767.5	3.5	1,017,954
Indiana	95	4.2	632	2.2	7	6.6	10,481	699.4	3.2	983,754
Michigan	35	1.6	394	1.4	11	4.5	11,396	669.4	3.1	1,521,389
California	70	3.1	767	2.7	11	8.3	10,808	647.9	3.0	748,984
Tennessee	66	2.9	748	2.6	11	6.2	8,295	627.4	2.9	746,898
Mississippi	39	1.7	459	1.6	12	5.2	11,270	524.4	2.4	797,014
Pennsylvania	51	2.3	732	2.6	14	6.1	8,380	505.2	2.3	672,740
Alabama	34	1.5	675	2.4	20	5.0	7,468	388.1	1.8	475,593
Virginia	45	2.0	493	1.7	11	4.6	9,363	319.3	1.5	628,563
North Carolina	41	1.8	587	2.0	14	7.2	12,206	294.5	1.4	480,484
Georgia	53	2.4	620	2.2	12	4.4	7,058	283.4	1.3	425,592
Florida	29	1.3	435	1.5	15	4.5	10,253	241.0	1.1	479,119
New Mexico	17	0.8	336	1.2	20	2.5	7,313	191.4	0.9	623,472
New York	43	1.9	366	1.3	9	4.0	10,801	186.8	0.9	476,589
Oregon	18	0.8	274	1.0	15	1.3	4,770	185.0	0.9	722,629
Washington	18	0.8	318	1.1	18	2.1	6,720	166.8	0.8	446,045
South Carolina	23	1.0	242	0.8	11	2.1	8,628	133.7	0.6	559,552
Louisiana	22	1.0	397	1.4	18	2.6	6,496	112.5	0.5	265,884
Arizona	19	0.8	65	0.2	3	1.2	17,831	83.1	0.4	1,013,402
Maryland	15	0.7	109	0.4	7	1.4	12,615	61.3	0.3	312,872
West Virginia	16	0.7	152	0.5	10	0.8	5,125	54.7	0.3	475,930
New Jersey	16	0.7	108	0.4	7	2.1	19,352	38.9	0.2	547,451
Nevada	6	0.3	55	0.2	9	0.8	14,927	26.3	0.1	797,485
Massachusetts	9	0.4	20-99	-	-	(D)	-	21.9	0.1	509,279
Minnesota	89	4.0	884	3.1	10	11.3	12,809	(D)	-	-
Nebraska	86	3.8	1,563	5.4	18	12.1	7,740	(D)	-	-
Arkansas	35	1.6	705	2.5	20	3.5	4,932	(D)	-	-
Montana	27	1.2	250-499	-	-	(D)	-	(D)	-	-
North Dakota	25	1.1	521	1.8	21	4.0	7,582	(D)	-	-
Idaho	24	1.1	701	2.4	29	3.3	4,678	(D)	-	-
Utah	11	0.5	175	0.6	16	1.0	5,709	(D)	-	-
Vermont	10	0.4	57	0.2	6	1.0	18,368	(D)	-	-
Wyoming	9	0.4	225	0.8	25	2.6	11,520	(D)	-	-
Connecticut	3	0.1	0-19	-	-	(D)	-	(D)	-	-
Maine	2	0.1	0-19	-	-	(D)	-	(D)	-	-
Alaska	1	0.0	20-99	-	-	(D)	-	(D)	-	-
Hawaii	1	0.0	0-19	-	-	(D)	-	(D)	-	-
New Hampshire	1	0.0	0-19	-	-	(D)	-	(D)	-	-

Source: *County Business Patterns, 1995* and *Economic Census of the U.S., 1992*. Data are sorted by 1992 revenues and, if revenues are unavailable, by establishments in 1995. The symbol (D) indicates that data are withheld by the source to avoid disclosure of competitive information. A dash (-) indicates that data are not available or undisclosed because they do not meet statistical validity standards. Shaded *states* on the state map indicate those states which have proportionately greater representation in the industry than would be indicated by the state's population; the ratio is based on total revenues or number of establishments. Shaded *regions* indicate where the industry is regionally most concentrated.

5159 - FARM-PRODUCT RAW MATERIALS, NEC

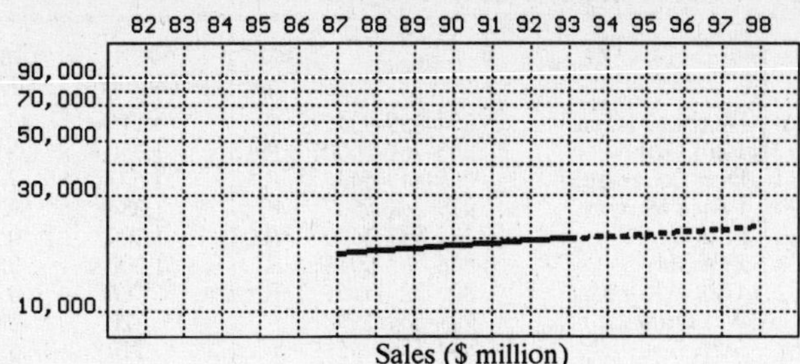

Sales ($ million)

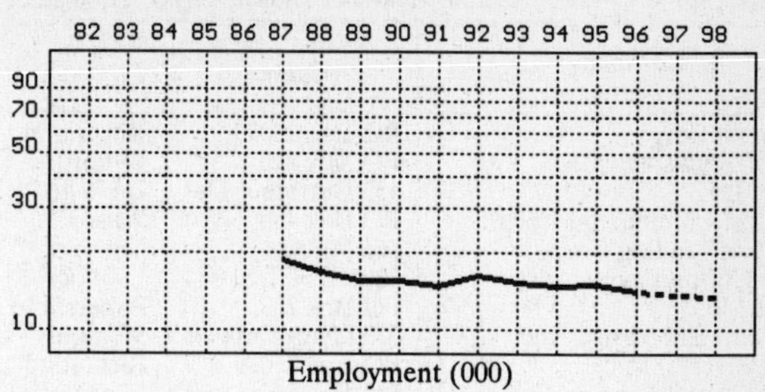

Employment (000)

GENERAL STATISTICS

Year	Establishments (number)	Employment (number)	Payroll ($ million)	Sales ($ million)	Expenses ($ million)	Beginning Inventory ($ million)	Ending Inventory ($ million)
1982	-	-	-	-	-	-	-
1983	-	-	-	-	-	-	-
1984	-	-	-	-	-	-	-
1985	-	-	-	-	-	-	-
1986	-	-	-	-	-	-	-
1987	1,830	18,944	336.4	17,368.9	866.1	1,608.0	1,986.0
1988	1,698	16,759	334.7	17,803.2e	901.6e	1,724.2e	2,000.8e
1989	1,611	15,455	338.0	18,237.5e	937.1e	1,840.4e	2,015.7e
1990	1,573	15,582	359.7	18,671.8e	972.6e	1,956.6e	2,030.5e
1991	1,558	14,896	364.2	19,106.2e	1,008.1e	2,072.8e	2,045.3e
1992	1,791	16,433	399.4	19,540.5	1,043.6	2,189.1	2,060.1
1993	1,828	15,371	408.4	19,974.8p	1,079.1p	2,305.3p	2,074.9p
1994	1,717	14,688	394.2	20,409.2p	1,114.6p	2,421.5p	2,089.7p
1995	1,699	14,971	400.0	20,843.5p	1,150.1p	2,537.7p	2,104.6p
1996	1,716p	14,115p	421.7p	21,277.8p	1,185.6p	2,653.9p	2,119.4p
1997	1,719p	13,758p	431.9p	21,712.1p	1,221.1p	2,770.1p	2,134.2p
1998	1,722p	13,401p	442.1p	22,146.5p	1,256.6p	2,886.3p	2,149.0p

Sources: Economic Census of the United States, 1982, 1987, and 1992. Establishment counts, employment, and payroll are from *County Business Patterns* for non-Census years. Values followed by a 'p' are projections by the editors. Sales and expense data for non-Census years are extrapolations, marked by 'e'. Industries reclassified in 1987 will not have data for prior years. Data are the most recent available at this level of detail.

INDICES OF CHANGE

Year	Establishments (number)	Employment (number)	Payroll ($ million)	Sales ($ million)	Expenses ($ million)	Beginning Inventory ($ million)	Ending Inventory ($ million)
1982	-	-	-	-	-	-	-
1983	-	-	-	-	-	-	-
1984	-	-	-	-	-	-	-
1985	-	-	-	-	-	-	-
1986	-	-	-	-	-	-	-
1987	102.2	115.3	84.2	88.9	83.0	73.5	96.4
1988	94.8	102.0	83.8	91.1e	86.4e	78.8e	97.1e
1989	89.9	94.0	84.6	93.3e	89.8e	84.1e	97.8e
1990	87.8	94.8	90.1	95.6e	93.2e	89.4e	98.6e
1991	87.0	90.6	91.2	97.8e	96.6e	94.7e	99.3e
1992	100.0	100.0	100.0	100.0	100.0	100.0	100.0
1993	102.1	93.5	102.2	102.2p	103.4p	105.3p	100.7p
1994	95.9	89.4	98.7	104.4p	106.8p	110.6p	101.4p
1995	94.9	91.1	100.2	106.7p	110.2p	115.9p	102.2p
1996	95.8p	85.9p	105.6p	108.9p	113.6p	121.2p	102.9p
1997	96.0p	83.7p	108.1p	111.1p	117.0p	126.5p	103.6p
1998	96.2p	81.5p	110.7p	113.3p	120.4p	131.9p	104.3p

Sources: Same as General Statistics. The values shown reflect change from the base year, 1992. Values above 100 mean greater than 1992, values below 100 mean less than 1992, and a value of 100 in the 1982-91 or 1993-98 period means same as 1992. Values followed by a 'p' are projections by the editors; 'e' stands for extrapolation. Data are the most recent available at this level of detail.

SELECTED RATIOS

For 1992	Avg. of All Wholesale	Analyzed Industry	Index	For 1992	Avg. of All Wholesale	Analyzed Industry	Index
Employees per Establishment	12	9	78	Sales per Employee	561,172	1,189,101	212
Payroll per Establishment	349,729	223,004	64	Sales per Establishment	6,559,346	10,910,385	166
Payroll per Employee	29,919	24,305	81	Expenses per Establishment	723,071	582,691	81

Sources: Same as General Statistics. The 'Average of All Manufacturing' column represents the average of all manufacturing industries reported for the most recent complete year available. The Index shows the relationship between the Average and the Analyzed Industry. For example, 100 means that they are equal; 500 that the Analyzed Industry is five times the average; 50 means that the Analyzed Industry is half the national average. The abbreviation 'na' is used to show that data are 'not available'.

LEADING COMPANIES

Number shown: **50** Total sales ($ mil): **16,392** Total employment (000): **56.3**

Company Name	Address				CEO Name	Phone	Co. Type	Sales ($ mil)	Empl. (000)
Universal Corp.	PO Box 25099	Richmond	VA	23260	Henry H Harrell	804-359-9311	P	4,113	25.0
Louis Dreyfus Corp.	PO Box 810	Wilton	CT	06897	John Goss	203-761-2000	R	1,710 *	2.0
Agway Inc.	333 Butternut Dr	De Witt	NY	13214	Don C Cararelli	315-449-6436	R	1,671	7.1
Standard Commercial Corp.	PO Box 450	Wilson	NC	27894	J Alec Murray	919-291-5507	P	1,354	2.2
Golodetz Trading Corp.	666 5th Ave	New York	NY	10103	I Suder	212-581-2400	R	1,300	0.5
Plains Cotton Cooperative	3301 E 50th St	Lubbock	TX	79408	Van May	806-763-8011	R	1,000 *	0.8
Calcot Ltd.	PO Box 259	Bakersfield	CA	93302	Tom W Smith	805-327-5961	R	786	0.2
Dunavant Enterprises Inc.	3797 New Getwell	Memphis	TN	38118	WB Dunavant	901-369-1500	R	720	2.0
Deli Universal Inc.	PO Box 25099	Richmond	VA	23261	Jaap Godthelp	804-359-9311	S	710 *	6.0
Staple Cotton Cooperative	PO Box 547	Greenwood	MS	38935	Woods E Eastland	601-453-6231	R	705	0.2
Golden Peanut Co.	1100 Johnson Ferry	Atlanta	GA	30342	James C Ielase	404-843-7850	J	310 *	0.9
Okleelanta Corp.	PO Box 86	South Bay	FL	33493	Alfonso Fanjul Jr	407-996-9072	R	200 *	5.0
Jimbo's Jumbos Inc.	PO Box 465	Edenton	NC	27932	J Tilmon Keel Jr	919-482-2193	R	190 *	0.7
Birdsong Corp.	612 Madison Ave	Suffolk	VA	23434	William J Spain Jr	804-539-3456	R	180 *	0.5
Cargill Peanut Products	PO Box 272	Dawson	GA	31742	Simon Oosterman	912-995-2111	D	140	0.3
Hohenberg Brothers Co.	PO Box 193	Memphis	TN	38101	James E Echols	901-529-4200	S	110 *	0.3
S. Shamash and Sons	42 W 39th St	New York	NY	10018	Jeff White	212-840-3111	R	100	<0.1
Weil Brothers Cotton Inc.	4444 Park Blvd	Montgomery	AL	36116	Robert S Weil Sr	205-244-1800	R	100	0.1
Young Pecan Shelling Company	PO Box 6709	Florence	SC	29502	James W Swink	803-662-2452	R	80	0.2
Casa Export Ltd.	PO Box 1337	Smithfield	NC	27577	Paolo Cavazzuti	919-934-7101	S	72 *	0.2
Chilewich Corp.	148 Madison Ave	New York	NY	10016	Simon Chilewich	212-686-1818	R	72 *	0.2
Commodity Specialists Co.	301 4th Ave	Minneapolis	MN	55415	Philip J Lindau	612-330-9889	R	65	0.1
Southwestern Irrigated Cotton	PO Box 1709	El Paso	TX	79949	David L Hand	915-581-5441	R	60	<0.1
Stone Commodities Corp.	30 S Wacker Dr	Chicago	IL	60606	William C Bachman	312-454-3000	R	54	0.1
Ohsman and Sons Co.	PO Box 1196	Cedar Rapids	IA	52406	Michael Ohsman	319-365-7546	R	50	<0.1
Thomas Monahan Co.	202 N Oak St	Arcola	IL	61910	T F Monahan Jr	217-268-4955	R	40	0.2
ABJ Enterprises Inc.	PO Box 428	Dunn	NC	28335	Alsey B Johnson	910-892-1357	R	37	<0.1
McClesky Mills Inc.	Rhodes St	Smithville	GA	31787	Jerry M Chandler	912-846-2003	R	36 *	0.1
A.J. Hollander and Company	545 Madison Ave	New York	NY	10022	Per M Hollander	212-644-0400	R	32 *	<0.1
Forte Dupee Sawyer Co.	311 Summer St	Boston	MA	02210	Donald Forte Jr	617-482-8434	R	30 *	<0.1
Sessions Company Inc.	PO Box 1095	Enterprise	AL	36331	HM Sessions Sr	334-393-0200	R	30	0.1
Pioneer Growers Co-Op	PO Box 490	Belle Glade	FL	33430	Gene Duff	407-996-5561	R	29	0.2
Montgomery Company Inc.	713 1st Ave	Opelika	AL	36801	T P Montgomery	205-749-3438	R	26	<0.1
Brown County Cooperative	Rte 5	Hiawatha	KS	66434	Harold Neher	913-742-2196	R	25	<0.1
Severn Peanut Company Inc.	PO Box 710	Severn	NC	27877	Dallas Barnes	919-585-0838	S	25 *	0.1
Campbell Tobacco Rehandling	PO Box 678	Mayfield	KY	42066	Robert J Baker	502-247-0991	R	24	<0.1
Vanguard Trading Services Inc.	320 3rd Ave NE	Issaquah	WA	98027	Craig W Stauffer	425-557-8250	R	24 *	<0.1
Jesse R. Taylor Co.	405 S 10th St	Opelika	AL	36801	Jesse R Taylor	334-745-5774	R	21	<0.1
Hog Inc.	PO Box 643	Carlinville	IL	62626	Kirby D Bates	217-854-4719	R	20	<0.1
Farmers Cooperative Compress	PO Box 2877	Lubbock	TX	79408	Rex McKinney	806-763-9431	R	19	0.2
Damascus Peanut Co.	State Hwy 200 W	Damascus	GA	31741	Joe Bryan	912-725-3353	R	17 *	0.1
Wonalancet Co.	1711 Tulle Cir NE	Atlanta	GA	30329	James J Dunn	404-633-4551	R	14	<0.1
A.M. Bickley Inc.	PO Box 91	Marshallville	GA	31057	AM Bickley Jr	912-967-2291	R	13 *	<0.1
George F. Brocke and Sons Inc.	PO Box 159	Kendrick	ID	83537	George F Brocke Jr	208-289-4231	R	13	<0.1
Juergens Produce and Feed Co.	PO Box 1027	Carroll	IA	51401	Vernis Juergens	712-792-3506	R	13	<0.1
Tobacco Supply Company Inc.	PO Box 726	Springfield	TN	37172	ML Smith Jr	615-384-2421	R	13	<0.1
W.H. Nored Cotton Co.	PO Box 1009	Greenwood	MS	38935	Bobby Nored	601-453-3772	R	13	<0.1
Jirdon Agri Chemicals Inc.	PO Box 516	Morrill	NE	69358	William L Siegel	308-247-2126	R	11	<0.1
Lexington Trotters and Breeders	PO Box 420	Lexington	KY	40585	John A Cashman Jr	606-255-0752	R	10	<0.1
American Legend Cooperative	PO Box 58308	Seattle	WA	98188	Claudia Campbell	206-251-3100	R	4	<0.1

Source: *Ward's Business Directory of U.S. Private and Public Companies*, 1998. The company type code used is as follows: P - Public, R - Private, S - Subsidiary, D - Division, J - Joint Venture, A - Affiliate, G - Group. Sales are in millions of dollars, employees are in thousands. An asterisk (*) indicates an estimated sales volume. The symbol < stands for 'less than'.

OCCUPATIONS EMPLOYED BY SIC 515 - WHOLESALE TRADE, OTHER

Occupation	% of Total 1996	Change to 2006	Occupation	% of Total 1996	Change to 2006
Sales & related workers nec	19.5	20.2	Clerical supervisors & managers	1.9	20.2
General managers & top executives	5.9	16.4	Order clerks	1.9	8.2
Truck drivers light & heavy	5.4	20.2	Helpers, laborers nec	1.7	20.2
General office clerks	3.6	3.4	Electrical & electronic technicians	1.4	18.8
Traffic, shipping, receiving clerks	3.6	16.7	Blue collar worker supervisors	1.4	16.0
Stock clerks	3.5	-3.9	Wholesale & retail buyers, except farm products	1.3	17.0
Freight, stock, & material movers, hand	3.3	8.2	Office machine & cash register servicers	1.3	20.2
Marketing & sales worker supervisors	3.1	20.2	Hand packers & packagers	1.2	-3.9
Order fillers, wholesale & retail sales	3.0	16.7	Maintenance repairers, general utility	1.1	12.0
Bookkeeping, accounting, & auditing clerks	2.9	-3.9	Industrial truck & tractor operators	1.1	20.2
Salespersons, retail	2.5	20.2	Purchasing managers	1.1	20.2
Secretaries, except legal & medical	2.5	-4.7	Receptionists & information clerks	1.0	20.2
Assemblers, fabricators, hand workers nec	2.0	-3.9			

Source: Industry-Occupation Matrix, Bureau of Labor Statistics. These data relate to one or more 3-digit SIC industry groups rather than to a single 4-digit SIC. The change reported for each occupation to the year 2006 is a percent of growth or decline as estimated by the Bureau of Labor Statistics. The abbreviation nec stands for 'not elsewhere classified'.

STATE AND REGIONAL CONCENTRATION

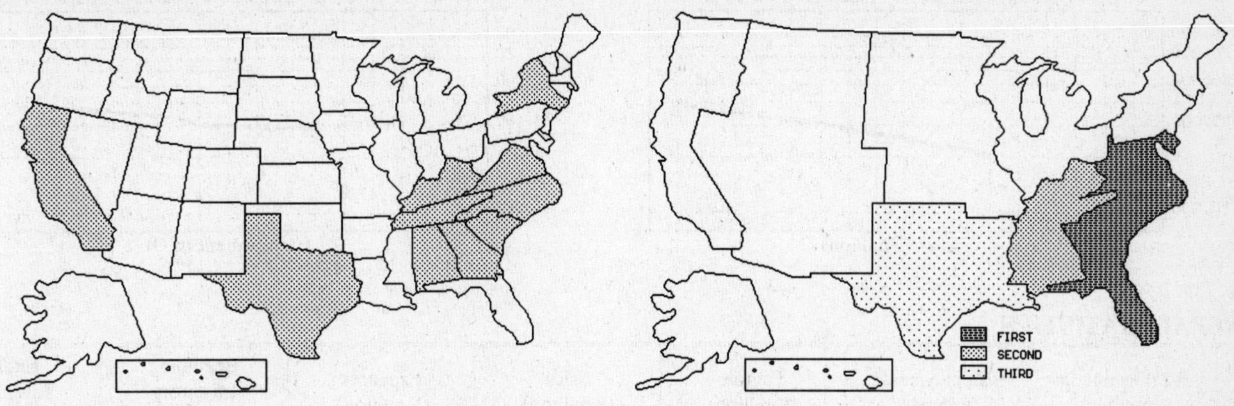

INDUSTRY DATA BY STATE

State	Establishments - 1995		Employment - 1995			Payroll - 1995		Sales - 1992		
	Total (number)	% of U.S.	Total (number)	% of U.S.	Per Estab.	Total ($ mil.)	Per Empl. ($)	Total ($ mil.)	% of U.S.	Per Estab ($)
Tennessee	82	4.8	1,090	7.3	13	44.4	40,749	2,601.5	14.5	2,399,886
California	123	7.2	1,473	9.9	12	41.6	28,219	2,569.9	14.3	1,469,358
Texas	206	12.1	1,892	12.7	9	45.2	23,914	2,449.0	13.7	1,408,265
North Carolina	148	8.7	936	6.3	6	37.5	40,116	1,568.4	8.8	1,192,719
New York	121	7.1	521	3.5	4	20.2	38,768	1,426.5	8.0	1,537,131
Virginia	63	3.7	819	5.5	13	29.6	36,094	1,229.3	6.9	1,079,261
Georgia	124	7.3	1,069	7.2	9	24.2	22,609	1,040.4	5.8	1,054,110
Kentucky	107	6.3	1,356	9.1	13	14.7	10,864	896.3	5.0	488,720
Florida	54	3.2	393	2.6	7	10.9	27,733	721.4	4.0	1,666,018
Alabama	48	2.8	439	2.9	9	11.2	25,519	658.4	3.7	1,486,126
South Carolina	40	2.4	148	1.0	4	5.2	35,311	314.2	1.8	1,331,475
Pennsylvania	29	1.7	188	1.3	6	6.6	34,989	301.7	1.7	1,621,957
Louisiana	24	1.4	137	0.9	6	2.5	18,095	261.9	1.5	1,577,717
Massachusetts	43	2.5	254	1.7	6	8.9	34,949	222.7	1.2	1,272,811
New Jersey	25	1.5	427	2.9	17	9.8	23,030	220.9	1.2	677,534
Washington	22	1.3	277	1.9	13	5.5	20,007	217.6	1.2	693,083
Illinois	28	1.6	256	1.7	9	7.4	28,734	215.6	1.2	975,606
Ohio	32	1.9	277	1.9	9	5.2	18,614	127.7	0.7	321,597
Oklahoma	20	1.2	197	1.3	10	4.0	20,137	112.7	0.6	589,953
Kansas	16	0.9	102	0.7	6	2.4	23,843	110.7	0.6	1,118,273
Iowa	29	1.7	231	1.5	8	5.0	21,723	109.1	0.6	627,167
Wisconsin	19	1.1	170	1.1	9	2.9	17,259	107.0	0.6	581,484
Missouri	29	1.7	313	2.1	11	5.2	16,661	88.5	0.5	318,360
Arizona	15	0.9	65	0.4	4	3.3	50,985	75.3	0.4	1,123,746
Michigan	20	1.2	112	0.8	6	2.1	18,911	55.1	0.3	510,509
Colorado	17	1.0	110	0.7	6	2.7	24,145	45.6	0.3	288,310
Indiana	19	1.1	124	0.8	7	1.8	14,435	42.0	0.2	341,447
New Mexico	13	0.8	113	0.8	9	2.0	17,973	40.2	0.2	744,926
Oregon	12	0.7	83	0.6	7	2.8	33,410	34.4	0.2	296,560
Maryland	11	0.6	108	0.7	10	1.3	11,750	34.0	0.2	435,487
South Dakota	13	0.8	56	0.4	4	1.0	18,732	22.0	0.1	338,369
Mississippi	28	1.6	437	2.9	16	12.4	28,355	(D)	-	-
Arkansas	24	1.4	126	0.8	5	3.0	23,802	(D)	-	-
Minnesota	18	1.1	139	0.9	8	3.0	21,482	(D)	-	-
Nebraska	15	0.9	138	0.9	9	3.1	22,167	(D)	-	-
Idaho	11	0.6	57	0.4	5	2.1	36,035	(D)	-	-
Connecticut	10	0.6	77	0.5	8	4.4	57,519	(D)	-	-
Hawaii	7	0.4	45	0.3	6	0.8	18,644	(D)	-	-
North Dakota	7	0.4	76	0.5	11	1.9	25,632	(D)	-	-
Utah	5	0.3	49	0.3	10	0.6	13,102	(D)	-	-
Maine	4	0.2	0-19	-	-	(D)	-	(D)	-	-
West Virginia	4	0.2	20-99	-	-	(D)	-	(D)	-	-
Nevada	3	0.2	39	0.3	13	0.9	23,538	(D)	-	-
Rhode Island	3	0.2	7	0.0	2	0.1	16,286	(D)	-	-
Montana	2	0.1	0-19	-	-	(D)	-	(D)	-	-
Vermont	2	0.1	0-19	-	-	(D)	-	(D)	-	-
Wyoming	2	0.1	0-19	-	-	(D)	-	(D)	-	-
Delaware	1	0.1	0-19	-	-	(D)	-	(D)	-	-
New Hampshire	1	0.1	0-19	-	-	(D)	-	(D)	-	-

Source: County Business Patterns, 1995 and *Economic Census of the U.S., 1992*. Data are sorted by 1992 revenues and, if revenues are unavailable, by establishments in 1995. The symbol (D) indicates that data are withheld by the source to avoid disclosure of competitive information. A dash (-) indicates that data are not available or undisclosed because they do not meet statistical validity standards. Shaded *states* on the state map indicate those states which have proportionately greater representation in the industry than would be indicated by the state's population; the ratio is based on total revenues or number of establishments. Shaded *regions* indicate where the industry is regionally most concentrated.

5162 - PLASTICS MATERIALS & BASIC SHAPES

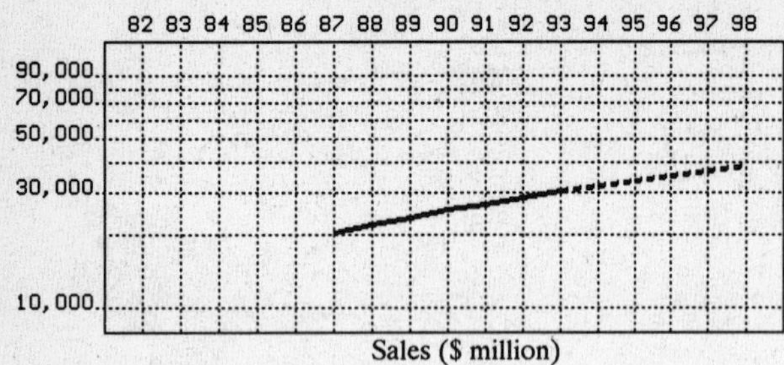

Sales ($ million)

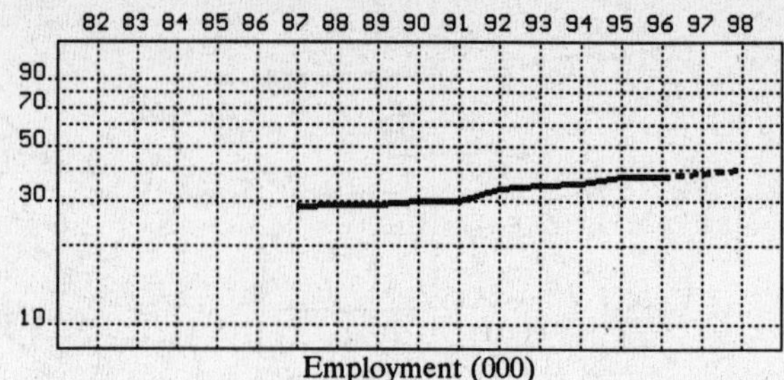

Employment (000)

GENERAL STATISTICS

Year	Establishments (number)	Employment (number)	Payroll ($ million)	Sales ($ million)	Expenses ($ million)	Beginning Inventory ($ million)	Ending Inventory ($ million)
1982	-	-	-	-	-	-	-
1983	-	-	-	-	-	-	-
1984	-	-	-	-	-	-	-
1985	-	-	-	-	-	-	-
1986	-	-	-	-	-	-	-
1987	2,744	28,453	788.4	20,307.5	1,693.3	623.7	692.8
1988	2,660	29,227	863.4	21,960.8e	1,851.0e	726.1e	791.3e
1989	2,511	29,227	926.8	23,614.0e	2,008.7e	828.5e	889.8e
1990	2,522	30,153	973.4	25,267.3e	2,166.3e	930.9e	988.3e
1991	2,581	29,898	999.1	26,920.5e	2,324.0e	1,033.3e	1,086.9e
1992	3,490	33,459	1,160.9	28,573.8	2,481.6	1,135.7	1,185.4
1993	3,509	34,936	1,225.4	30,227.1p	2,639.3p	1,238.1p	1,283.9p
1994	3,524	35,112	1,293.7	31,880.3p	2,796.9p	1,340.4p	1,382.4p
1995	3,603	37,855	1,431.4	33,533.6p	2,954.6p	1,442.8p	1,480.9p
1996	3,765p	37,868p	1,460.9p	35,186.9p	3,112.3p	1,545.2p	1,579.5p
1997	3,915p	39,034p	1,538.4p	36,840.1p	3,269.9p	1,647.6p	1,678.0p
1998	4,065p	40,201p	1,615.8p	38,493.4p	3,427.6p	1,750.0p	1,776.5p

Sources: Economic Census of the United States, 1982, 1987, and 1992. Establishment counts, employment, and payroll are from *County Business Patterns* for non-Census years. Values followed by a 'p' are projections by the editors. Sales and expense data for non-Census years are extrapolations, marked by 'e'. Industries reclassified in 1987 will not have data for prior years. Data are the most recent available at this level of detail.

INDICES OF CHANGE

Year	Establishments (number)	Employment (number)	Payroll ($ million)	Sales ($ million)	Expenses ($ million)	Beginning Inventory ($ million)	Ending Inventory ($ million)
1982	-	-	-	-	-	-	-
1983	-	-	-	-	-	-	-
1984	-	-	-	-	-	-	-
1985	-	-	-	-	-	-	-
1986	-	-	-	-	-	-	-
1987	78.6	85.0	67.9	71.1	68.2	54.9	58.4
1988	76.2	87.4	74.4	76.9e	74.6e	63.9e	66.8e
1989	71.9	87.4	79.8	82.6e	80.9e	73.0e	75.1e
1990	72.3	90.1	83.8	88.4e	87.3e	82.0e	83.4e
1991	74.0	89.4	86.1	94.2e	93.6e	91.0e	91.7e
1992	100.0	100.0	100.0	100.0	100.0	100.0	100.0
1993	100.5	104.4	105.6	105.8p	106.4p	109.0p	108.3p
1994	101.0	104.9	111.4	111.6p	112.7p	118.0p	116.6p
1995	103.2	113.1	123.3	117.4p	119.1p	127.0p	124.9p
1996	107.9p	113.2p	125.8p	123.1p	125.4p	136.1p	133.2p
1997	112.2p	116.7p	132.5p	128.9p	131.8p	145.1p	141.6p
1998	116.5p	120.1p	139.2p	134.7p	138.1p	154.1p	149.9p

Sources: Same as General Statistics. The values shown reflect change from the base year, 1992. Values above 100 mean greater than 1992, values below 100 mean less than 1992, and a value of 100 in the 1982-91 or 1993-98 period means same as 1992. Values followed by a 'p' are projections by the editors; 'e' stands for extrapolation. Data are the most recent available at this level of detail.

SELECTED RATIOS

For 1992	Avg. of All Wholesale	Analyzed Industry	Index	For 1992	Avg. of All Wholesale	Analyzed Industry	Index
Employees per Establishment	12	10	82	Sales per Employee	561,172	853,994	152
Payroll per Establishment	349,729	332,636	95	Sales per Establishment	6,559,346	8,187,335	125
Payroll per Employee	29,919	34,696	116	Expenses per Establishment	723,071	711,060	98

Sources: Same as General Statistics. The 'Average of All Manufacturing' column represents the average of all manufacturing industries reported for the most recent complete year available. The Index shows the relationship between the Average and the Analyzed Industry. For example, 100 means that they are equal; 500 that the Analyzed Industry is five times the average; 50 means that the Analyzed Industry is half the national average. The abbreviation 'na' is used to show that data are 'not available'.

LEADING COMPANIES

Number shown: **50** Total sales ($ mil): **5,308** Total employment (000): **10.6**

Company Name	Address				CEO Name	Phone	Co. Type	Sales ($ mil)	Empl. (000)
Thyssen Inc.	400 Renaissance	Detroit	MI	48243	Kenneth Graham	313-567-5600	S	1,950	3.0
H. Muehlstein and Company	PO Box 5445	Norwalk	CT	06856	J Kevin Donohue	203-855-6000	R	700	0.3
General Polymers Div.	12001 Toepfer Rd	Warren	MI	48089	Daniel W McGuire	810-755-1100	D	650	0.3
Cadillac Plastic Group Inc.	2855 Coolidge Hwy	Troy	MI	48084	Kent Darragh	248-205-3100	S	270 •	1.5
Cook Composites	820 E 14th Ave	N. Kansas City	MO	64116	Werner Bruck	816-391-6000	R	260	1.1
M.A. Hanna Resin Distribution	PO Box 428	Lemont	IL	60439	Richard Anderson	708-972-0505	S	200	<0.1
Kranson Industries	460 N Lindbergh	St. Louis	MO	63141	Kenneth Kranzberg	314-569-3633	R	110	0.2
Rapid Industrial Plastics Co.	13 Linden Ave E	Jersey City	NJ	07305	Martin Sirotkin	201-433-5500	R	100	0.2
Harrington Industrial Plastics	14480 Yorba Ave	Chino	CA	91710	William McCollum	909-597-8641	S	81	0.3
Abell Corp.	PO Box 8056	Monroe	LA	71211	G Hughes Abell	318-345-2600	R	80 •	0.2
Western ResourceNet Intern	6000 N Cutter Cir	Portland	OR	97217	Jerry Lindsey	503-289-2800	S	75	0.1
GLS Corp.	723 W Algonquin	Arlington H.	IL	60006	Steven L Dehmlow	847-437-0200	R	73 •	0.2
Plastic Distributing Corp.	Molumco Indrial	Ayer	MA	01432	Regis Magnus	508-772-0764	S	65	0.2
Ryan Herco Products Corp.	PO Box 588	Burbank	CA	91503	Frank Gibbs	818-841-1141	R	60	0.2
Lusk Metals and Plastics	PO Box 24013	Oakland	CA	94623	Jim Taylor	510-785-6400	R	40 •	<0.1
Sumitomo Plastics America Inc.	900 Lafayette St	Santa Clara	CA	95050	Yoshiaki Suzuki	408-243-8402	S	35	<0.1
Kerr Group Inc.	500 New Holland	Lancaster	PA	17602	Gordon Strickland	717-299-6511	D	32	0.2
Curbell Inc.	7 Cobham Dr	Orchard Park	NY	14127	Tom Leone	716-667-3377	R	32	0.1
AIN Plastics Inc.	PO Box 151	Mount Vernon	NY	10551	N Drucker	914-668-6800	R	30	0.2
Corr Tech Inc.	4545 Homestead	Houston	TX	77028	James Gottesman	713-674-7887	R	30 •	<0.1
FFR Inc.	261 Alpha Park	Cleveland	OH	44143	Gerald A Conway	216-473-6919	R	25	<0.1
Regal Plastic Supply Co.	111 E 10th Ave	N. Kansas City	MO	64116	R Cull	816-421-6290	R	25	0.2
Paper Products Company Inc.	36 Terminal Way	Pittsburgh	PA	15219	DR Lackner	412-481-6200	R	24	<0.1
LaVanture Products Co.	PO Box 2088	Elkhart	IN	46515	R. A Lavanture	219-264-0658	R	23	0.2
Plastic Piping Systems Inc.	3601 Tryclan Dr	Charlotte	NC	28217	LG Arnold	704-527-6494	S	23	<0.1
Port Plastics Inc.	16750 Chestnut St	City of Industry	CA	91747	Keith Piggot	818-333-7678	S	22 •	<0.1
Akrochem Corp.	255 Fountain St	Akron	OH	44304	Walton A Silver	216-535-2108	R	19	<0.1
Prime Alliance Inc.	1803 Hull Ave	Des Moines	IA	50309	Tom Irvine	515-244-4844	R	17 •	<0.1
Clark-Schwebel Distribution	PO Box 3448	Santa Fe Sprgs	CA	90760	Marvin B Fuller	310-921-9926	S	16	<0.1
Advanced Plastics Inc.	7360 Cockrill Bend	Nashville	TN	37209	Roy Abner	615-350-6500	R	15 •	<0.1
Intersystems of Delaware	93 Mason St	Greenwich	CT	06830	Herbert M Pearlman	203-629-1400	P	15	0.3
Regal Plastic Supply Inc.	PO Box 59977	Dallas	TX	75229	Don Walker	972-484-0741	R	15	<0.1
Mooney General Paper Co.	1451 Chestnut Ave	Hillside	NJ	07205	Gary Riemer	201-926-3800	R	14	<0.1
Trade Supplies	3188 E Slauson Ave	Vernon	CA	90058	Martin Sanders	213-581-3250	R	13 •	<0.1
Dielectric Corp.	N 83 W 13330 Leon	Menomonee Fls	WI	53051	Raymond Esser	414-255-2600	R	13	0.1
Texberry Container Corp.	1701 Crosspoint	Houston	TX	77233	Michael Vaughn	713-796-8800	S	13	<0.1
Ohio Valley Supply Co.	3512 Spring Grove	Cincinnati	OH	45223	Thomas E Butler	513-681-8300	R	12 •	<0.1
Regional Supply Inc.	3571 S 300 W	Salt Lake City	UT	84115	DC Mendenhall	801-262-6451	R	12	0.1
Targun Plastics Co.	899 Skokie Blvd	Northbrook	IL	60062	Jerome Targun	708-272-0869	R	12	<0.1
Greenstreak Plastic Products	PO Box 7139	St. Louis	MO	63177	Charlie Van Dyke	314-225-9400	D	11 •	<0.1
Meyer Plastics Inc.	PO Box 20902	Indianapolis	IN	46220	John R Meyer	317-259-4131	R	11	0.1
American Renolit Corp.	135 Algonquin	Whippany	NJ	07981	Peter Lowenstein	201-386-9200	R	10 •	<0.1
Beck Packaging Corp.	PO Box 20250	Lehigh Valley	PA	18002	Irwin Beck	610-264-0551	R	10	<0.1
Coral Sales Co.	PO Box 577	Clackamas	OR	97015	Douglas P Daniels	503-655-6351	R	10	<0.1
Federal Plastics Corp.	715 South Ave	Cranford	NJ	07016	Peter T Triano	908-272-5800	R	10 •	<0.1
MRC Polymers Inc.	1716 W Webster	Chicago	IL	60614	Dan Eberhardt	312-276-6345	R	10	<0.1
C. Bamberger Molding	PO Box 67	Carlstadt	NJ	07072	Claude P Bamberger	201-933-6262	R	9	<0.1
Freund Can Co.	155 W 84th St	Chicago	IL	60620	Kenneth G Freund	312-224-4230	R	9	<0.1
Oliner Fibre Company Inc.	2391 Vauxhall Rd	Union	NJ	07083	AW Oliner	908-688-5800	R	9	<0.1
Great Southern Industries Inc.	PO Box 5325	Jackson	MS	39216	WF Barnett	601-948-5700	R	9	0.1

Source: *Ward's Business Directory of U.S. Private and Public Companies*, 1998. The company type code used is as follows: P - Public, R - Private, S - Subsidiary, D - Division, J - Joint Venture, A - Affiliate, G - Group. Sales are in millions of dollars, employees are in thousands. An asterisk (*) indicates an estimated sales volume. The symbol < stands for 'less than'.

OCCUPATIONS EMPLOYED BY SIC 516 - WHOLESALE TRADE, OTHER

Occupation	% of Total 1996	Change to 2006	Occupation	% of Total 1996	Change to 2006
Sales & related workers nec	19.5	20.2	Clerical supervisors & managers	1.9	20.2
General managers & top executives	5.9	16.4	Order clerks	1.9	8.2
Truck drivers light & heavy	5.4	20.2	Helpers, laborers nec	1.7	20.2
General office clerks	3.6	3.4	Electrical & electronic technicians	1.4	18.8
Traffic, shipping, receiving clerks	3.6	16.7	Blue collar worker supervisors	1.4	16.0
Stock clerks	3.5	-3.9	Wholesale & retail buyers, except farm products	1.3	17.0
Freight, stock, & material movers, hand	3.3	8.2	Office machine & cash register servicers	1.3	20.2
Marketing & sales worker supervisors	3.1	20.2	Hand packers & packagers	1.2	-3.9
Order fillers, wholesale & retail sales	3.0	16.7	Maintenance repairers, general utility	1.1	12.0
Bookkeeping, accounting, & auditing clerks	2.9	-3.9	Industrial truck & tractor operators	1.1	20.2
Salespersons, retail	2.5	20.2	Purchasing managers	1.1	20.2
Secretaries, except legal & medical	2.5	-4.7	Receptionists & information clerks	1.0	20.2
Assemblers, fabricators, hand workers nec	2.0	-3.9			

Source: *Industry-Occupation Matrix*, Bureau of Labor Statistics. These data relate to one or more 3-digit SIC industry groups rather than to a single 4-digit SIC. The change reported for each occupation to the year 2006 is a percent of growth or decline as estimated by the Bureau of Labor Statistics. The abbreviation nec stands for 'not elsewhere classified'.

STATE AND REGIONAL CONCENTRATION

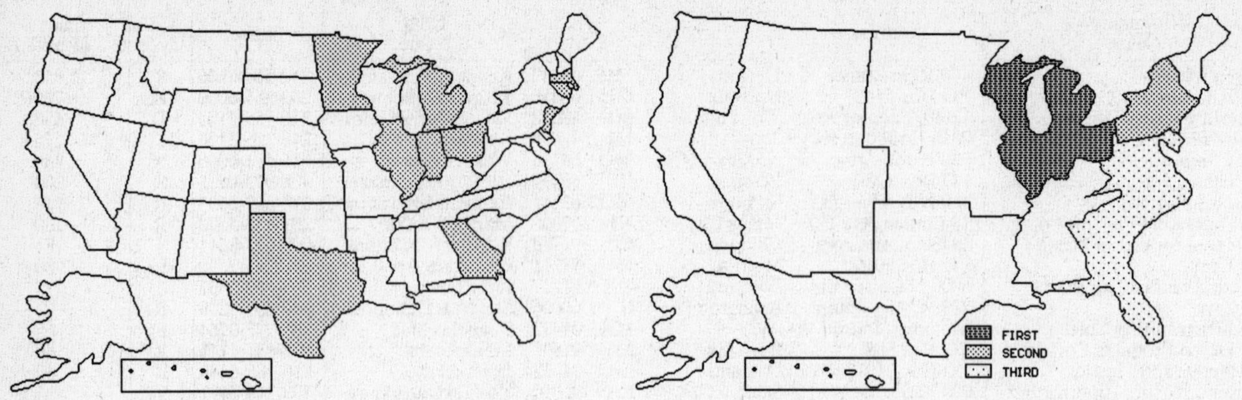

INDUSTRY DATA BY STATE

State	Establishments - 1995 Total (number)	Establishments - 1995 % of U.S.	Employment - 1995 Total (number)	Employment - 1995 % of U.S.	Employment - 1995 Per Estab.	Payroll - 1995 Total ($ mil.)	Payroll - 1995 Per Empl. ($)	Sales - 1992 Total ($ mil.)	Sales - 1992 % of U.S.	Sales - 1992 Per Estab ($)
Illinois	244	6.8	3,007	8.0	12	128.8	42,828	3,278.9	12.2	1,308,952
California	452	12.5	4,975	13.3	11	183.3	36,841	2,610.6	9.7	573,623
New Jersey	238	6.6	2,448	6.5	10	108.5	44,315	2,512.1	9.3	998,448
Texas	278	7.7	3,104	8.3	11	112.8	36,326	2,451.9	9.1	958,882
Georgia	133	3.7	1,119	3.0	8	46.3	41,362	2,397.4	8.9	2,761,992
Michigan	182	5.1	1,866	5.0	10	89.8	48,144	2,356.8	8.7	1,536,353
New York	256	7.1	1,960	5.2	8	79.3	40,473	1,530.5	5.7	702,723
Ohio	192	5.3	2,175	5.8	11	81.0	37,263	1,514.3	5.6	834,310
Indiana	79	2.2	978	2.6	12	32.4	33,145	1,256.4	4.7	1,260,208
Massachusetts	104	2.9	1,253	3.4	12	45.5	36,318	1,108.7	4.1	1,066,025
Pennsylvania	152	4.2	1,804	4.8	12	69.3	38,409	822.3	3.0	475,021
Florida	174	4.8	1,434	3.8	8	46.9	32,674	764.0	2.8	550,419
North Carolina	86	2.4	907	2.4	11	35.4	39,076	685.4	2.5	867,547
Minnesota	84	2.3	901	2.4	11	35.7	39,659	561.5	2.1	817,351
Missouri	79	2.2	808	2.2	10	26.8	33,119	452.6	1.7	683,718
Connecticut	61	1.7	640	1.7	10	35.2	55,020	402.6	1.5	808,378
Wisconsin	70	1.9	1,313	3.5	19	46.7	35,560	321.7	1.2	319,148
Kentucky	27	0.7	280	0.7	10	10.4	37,089	206.8	0.8	780,211
Washington	56	1.6	462	1.2	8	16.7	36,210	184.4	0.7	448,693
Tennessee	61	1.7	546	1.5	9	17.3	31,652	168.9	0.6	435,356
Colorado	48	1.3	442	1.2	9	14.9	33,769	164.9	0.6	486,440
Virginia	39	1.1	293	0.8	8	9.5	32,430	151.3	0.6	573,220
South Carolina	51	1.4	651	1.7	13	19.1	29,347	144.6	0.5	266,764
Arizona	49	1.4	492	1.3	10	14.6	29,612	134.0	0.5	352,568
Utah	29	0.8	352	0.9	12	10.8	30,707	109.0	0.4	437,594
Oregon	36	1.0	274	0.7	8	8.5	30,956	96.8	0.4	512,122
Louisiana	32	0.9	282	0.8	9	9.4	33,167	94.2	0.3	362,227
Kansas	25	0.7	223	0.6	9	6.4	28,664	87.3	0.3	417,689
Alabama	33	0.9	416	1.1	13	8.6	20,786	77.6	0.3	275,355
Rhode Island	16	0.4	158	0.4	10	5.9	37,335	68.8	0.3	474,690
Iowa	20	0.6	205	0.5	10	6.0	29,322	59.6	0.2	488,910
Nevada	17	0.5	118	0.3	7	3.4	29,136	39.5	0.1	419,926
Oklahoma	37	1.0	295	0.8	8	8.2	27,769	39.4	0.1	160,085
New Hampshire	19	0.5	111	0.3	6	6.6	59,189	38.2	0.1	522,712
Arkansas	18	0.5	163	0.4	9	3.5	21,331	35.8	0.1	313,632
Mississippi	15	0.4	100-249	-	-	(D)	-	31.3	0.1	230,243
New Mexico	11	0.3	71	0.2	6	1.3	18,915	16.4	0.1	282,086
Maine	7	0.2	17	0.0	2	0.4	22,882	4.3	0.0	212,700
North Dakota	4	0.1	31	0.1	8	0.8	26,645	3.3	0.0	118,214
Maryland	30	0.8	414	1.1	14	13.6	32,928	(D)	-	-
Delaware	18	0.5	100-249	-	-	(D)	-	(D)	-	-
Hawaii	9	0.2	118	0.3	13	3.6	30,797	(D)	-	-
Nebraska	8	0.2	107	0.3	13	1.9	17,514	(D)	-	-
West Virginia	8	0.2	189	0.5	24	10.1	53,175	(D)	-	-
Idaho	4	0.1	20-99	-	-	(D)	-	(D)	-	-
South Dakota	4	0.1	0-19	-	-	(D)	-	(D)	-	-
Wyoming	3	0.1	0-19	-	-	(D)	-	(D)	-	-
Alaska	2	0.1	0-19	-	-	(D)	-	(D)	-	-
Vermont	2	0.1	20-99	-	-	(D)	-	(D)	-	-
Montana	1	0.0	0-19	-	-	(D)	-	-	-	-

Source: *County Business Patterns, 1995* and *Economic Census of the U.S., 1992*. Data are sorted by 1992 revenues and, if revenues are unavailable, by establishments in 1995. The symbol (D) indicates that data are withheld by the source to avoid disclosure of competitive information. A dash (-) indicates that data are not available or undisclosed because they do not meet statistical validity standards. Shaded *states* on the state map indicate those states which have proportionately greater representation in the industry than would be indicated by the state's population; the ratio is based on total revenues or number of establishments. Shaded *regions* indicate where the industry is regionally most concentrated.

5169 - CHEMICALS & ALLIED PRODUCTS, NEC

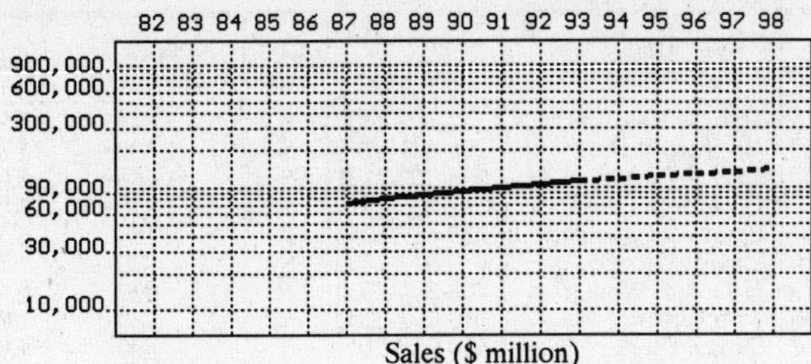

Sales ($ million)

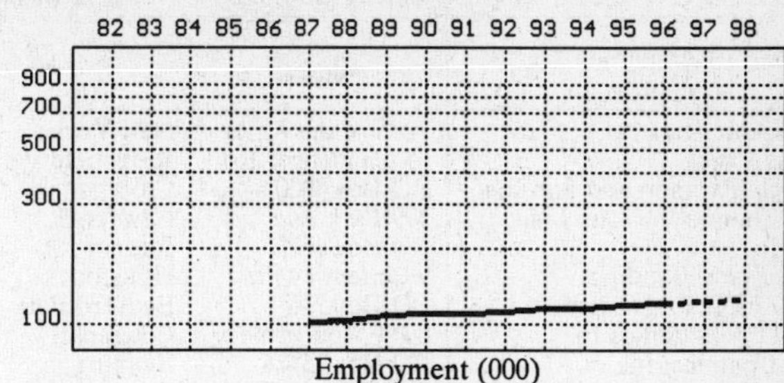

Employment (000)

GENERAL STATISTICS

Year	Establishments (number)	Employment (number)	Payroll ($ million)	Sales ($ million)	Expenses ($ million)	Beginning Inventory ($ million)	Ending Inventory ($ million)
1982	-	-	-	-	-	-	-
1983	-	-	-	-	-	-	-
1984	-	-	-	-	-	-	-
1985	-	-	-	-	-	-	-
1986	-	-	-	-	-	-	-
1987	9,961	102,989	3,058.4	74,312.2	6,840.6	2,373.6	2,525.2
1988	9,389	104,206	3,444.1	80,229.2e	7,369.6e	2,601.4e	2,732.9e
1989	9,045	109,177	3,758.1	86,146.2e	7,898.6e	2,829.2e	2,940.6e
1990	9,014	111,448	4,028.7	92,063.3e	8,427.6e	3,057.1e	3,148.3e
1991	9,230	109,727	3,997.5	97,980.3e	8,956.6e	3,284.9e	3,355.9e
1992	10,703	113,551	4,434.7	103,897.4	9,485.6	3,512.7	3,563.6
1993	10,653	116,544	4,712.6	109,814.4p	10,014.6p	3,740.5p	3,771.3p
1994	10,695	115,680	4,729.6	115,731.5p	10,543.6p	3,968.3p	3,979.0p
1995	10,733	120,698	5,197.3	121,648.5p	11,072.6p	4,196.1p	4,186.7p
1996	10,928p	121,732p	5,378.5p	127,565.5p	11,601.6p	4,423.9p	4,394.4p
1997	11,127p	123,767p	5,623.9p	133,482.6p	12,130.6p	4,651.7p	4,602.1p
1998	11,326p	125,802p	5,869.4p	139,399.6p	12,659.6p	4,879.6p	4,809.7p

Sources: Economic Census of the United States, 1982, 1987, and 1992. Establishment counts, employment, and payroll are from *County Business Patterns* for non-Census years. Values followed by a 'p' are projections by the editors. Sales and expense data for non-Census years are extrapolations, marked by 'e'. Industries reclassified in 1987 will not have data for prior years. Data are the most recent available at this level of detail.

INDICES OF CHANGE

Year	Establishments (number)	Employment (number)	Payroll ($ million)	Sales ($ million)	Expenses ($ million)	Beginning Inventory ($ million)	Ending Inventory ($ million)
1982	-	-	-	-	-	-	-
1983	-	-	-	-	-	-	-
1984	-	-	-	-	-	-	-
1985	-	-	-	-	-	-	-
1986	-	-	-	-	-	-	-
1987	93.1	90.7	69.0	71.5	72.1	67.6	70.9
1988	87.7	91.8	77.7	77.2e	77.7e	74.1e	76.7e
1989	84.5	96.1	84.7	82.9e	83.3e	80.5e	82.5e
1990	84.2	98.1	90.8	88.6e	88.8e	87.0e	88.3e
1991	86.2	96.6	90.1	94.3e	94.4e	93.5e	94.2e
1992	100.0	100.0	100.0	100.0	100.0	100.0	100.0
1993	99.5	102.6	106.3	105.7p	105.6p	106.5p	105.8p
1994	99.9	101.9	106.7	111.4p	111.2p	113.0p	111.7p
1995	100.3	106.3	117.2	117.1p	116.7p	119.5p	117.5p
1996	102.1p	107.2p	121.3p	122.8p	122.3p	125.9p	123.3p
1997	104.0p	109.0p	126.8p	128.5p	127.9p	132.4p	129.1p
1998	105.8p	110.8p	132.4p	134.2p	133.5p	138.9p	135.0p

Sources: Same as General Statistics. The values shown reflect change from the base year, 1992. Values above 100 mean greater than 1992, values below 100 mean less than 1992, and a value of 100 in the 1982-91 or 1993-98 period means same as 1992. Values followed by a 'p' are projections by the editors; 'e' stands for extrapolation. Data are the most recent available at this level of detail.

SELECTED RATIOS

For 1992	Avg. of All Wholesale	Analyzed Industry	Index	For 1992	Avg. of All Wholesale	Analyzed Industry	Index
Employees per Establishment	12	11	91	Sales per Employee	561,172	914,984	163
Payroll per Establishment	349,729	414,342	118	Sales per Establishment	6,559,346	9,707,316	148
Payroll per Employee	29,919	39,055	131	Expenses per Establishment	723,071	886,256	123

Sources: Same as General Statistics. The 'Average of All Manufacturing' column represents the average of all manufacturing industries reported for the most recent complete year available. The Index shows the relationship between the Average and the Analyzed Industry. For example, 100 means that they are equal; 500 that the Analyzed Industry is five times the average; 50 means that the Analyzed Industry is half the national average. The abbreviation 'na' is used to show that data are 'not available'.

LEADING COMPANIES

Number shown: **50** Total sales ($ mil): **18,222** Total employment (000): **42.3**

Company Name	Address				CEO Name	Phone	Co. Type	Sales ($ mil)	Empl. (000)
Tomen America Inc.	1285 of the Amer	New York	NY	10019	Hajime Kawamura	212-397-4600	S	2,645	0.9
Degussa Corp.	65 Challenger Rd	Ridgefield Park	NJ	07660	Andrew Burke	201-641-6100	S	2,300 *	1.8
Joseph T. Ryerson and Son Inc.	PO Box 8000	Chicago	IL	60680	Carl G Lusted	773-762-2121	S	1,666 *	5.0
Harris Chemical Group Inc.	399 Park Ave	New York	NY	10022	D George Harris	212-750-3510	R	1,270 *	3.0
Airgas Inc.	PO Box 6675	Radnor	PA	19087	Peter McCausland	610-687-5253	P	1,159	6.4
Coastal States Trading	9 Greenway Plz	Houston	TX	77046	David Arledge	713-877-1400	S	970	1.5
CHEMCENTRAL Corp.	PO Box 730	Bedford Park	IL	60499	H Daniel Wenstrup	708-594-7000	R	827	0.9
Simon U.S. Holdings Inc.	8044 Montgomery	Cincinnati	OH	45236	Rob Wilson	513-792-2300	S	780 *	1.8
SOCO Chemical Inc.	PO Box 13786	Reading	PA	19612	Steven Clark	610-926-6100	S	600	1.0
Sherwin-Williams Diversified	31500 Solon Rd	Solon	OH	44139	Richard Wilson	440-498-2300	D	489 *	2.5
Ellis and Everard	700 Galleria Pkwy	Atlanta	GA	30339	W J Gissendanner	404-956-5360	S	430	1.0
Stinnes Corp.	120 White Plains	Tarrytown	NY	10591	Henning Maier	914-366-7200	S	430	1.2
GATX Terminals Corp.	500 W Monroe	Chicago	IL	60661	A J Anprukaitis	312-621-6200	S	293	1.1
Lawson Products Inc.	1666 E Touhy Ave	Des Plaines	IL	60018	Bernard Kalish	847-827-9666	P	278	1.9
Cook Composites	820 E 14th Ave	N. Kansas City	MO	64116	Werner Bruck	816-391-6000	R	260	1.1
Crompton and Knowles Colors	PO Box 33188	Charlotte	NC	28233	Ed Fording	704-372-5890	S	200	0.6
Tetra Technologies Inc.	25025 I-45 N	The Woodlands	TX	77380	Allen T McInnes	713-367-1983	P	178	1.0
OSCA Inc.	PO Box 80627	Lafayette	LA	70598	Richard J Alario	318-837-6047	S	175 *	0.6
Aceto Corp.	1 Hollow Lane	Lake Success	NY	11042	Leonard S Schwartz	516-627-6000	P	169	<0.1
Kay Chemical Co.	8300 Capital Dr	Greensboro	NC	27409	Randall Kaplan	910-668-7290	D	164 *	0.4
SYGMA Network	4000 Industrial Rd	Harrisburg	PA	17110	Gregory K Marshall	717-232-3111	S	160 *	0.2
Ajinomoto U.S.A. Inc.	500 Frank W Burr	Teaneck	NJ	07666	Hiroshi Kurihara	201-488-1212	S	150	0.2
Linox Gas Tech Inc.	12000 Roosevelt Rd	Hillside	IL	60162	Carl Kock	708-449-9300	R	130	0.1
Mays Chemical Co.	5611 E 71st St	Indianapolis	IN	46220	William G Mays	317-842-8722	R	123	0.1
Lady Baltimore Foods Inc.	1601 Fairfax	Kansas City	KS	66117	Melvin Cosner	913-371-8300	P	121	0.5
Neville Chemical Co.	2800 Neville Rd	Pittsburgh	PA	15225	L Van V Dauler Jr	412-331-4200	R	120 *	0.5
Olin Hunt Specialty Products	5 Garrett Mt	West Paterson	NJ	07424	Edward B Pollak	201-977-6000	S	120	0.4
Sunox Inc.	PO Box 33871	Charlotte	NC	28233	James King	704-596-6262	R	120 *	0.5
Old World Trading Co.	4065 Commercial	Northbrook	IL	60062	Tom Hurvis	847-559-2000	R	101 *	0.1
Wilmar Industries Inc.	303 Harper Dr	Moorestown	NJ	08057	William S Green	609-439-1222	P	101	0.6
Brewer Environmental Industries	311 Pacific St	Honolulu	HI	96817	Stephen W Knoy	808-532-7400	S	100	0.2
R.S. Hughes Company Inc.	PO Box 25061	Glendale	CA	91221	Robert McCollum	818-563-1122	R	100	0.4
Textile Chemical Company Inc.	PO Box 13788	Reading	PA	19612	William E Huttner	610-926-4151	S	100	0.2
Kenneth O. Lester Company	PO Box 340	Lebanon	TN	37087	Thomas Hoffman	615-444-2963	S	98	0.2
Delta Distributors Inc.	610 Fisher Rd	Longview	TX	75604	Kevin W Kessing	903-759-7151	S	95	0.2
Universal Cooperative Inc.	7801 Metro Pkwy	Minneapolis	MN	55440	Patrick Finley	612-854-0800	R	94 *	0.2
THP United Enterprises Inc.	PO Box 1991	Milwaukee	WI	53201	Mark Wilson	414-523-6500	R	94	1.5
Golden Neo-Life Diamite Intern.	3500 Gateway Blvd	Fremont	CA	94538	James Arnott	510-651-0405	R	92 *	0.1
Connell Brothers Company Ltd.	320 California St	San Francisco	CA	94104	Frank M Brown	415-772-4000	S	90	0.2
Ecolab Inc.	Ecolab Center	St. Paul	MN	55102	Dean deBuhr	612-293-2233	D	90 *	0.7
Burris Chemical Inc.	PO Box 70788	Charleston	SC	29415	AA Burris III	803-554-7511	R	85 *	0.3
Mozel Inc.	4003 Park Ave	St. Louis	MO	63110	Peter E Macy	314-865-3115	R	81	<0.1
Transcontinental Fertilizer Co.	44 E Lancaster Ave	Ardmore	PA	19003	Alfred W Aspen	610-642-5001	R	80	<0.1
Thomas Scientific	PO Box 99	Swedesboro	NJ	08085	EB Patterson Jr	609-467-2000	R	76 *	0.3
Valley National Gases Inc.	PO Box 6628	Wheeling	WV	26003	Lawrence E Bandi	304-232-1541	P	74	0.5
Chori America Inc.	1 Penn Plz, 54th Fl	New York	NY	10119	T Nakamoura	212-563-3264	R	72 *	<0.1
Ulrich Chemical Inc.	3111 N Post Rd	Indianapolis	IN	46226	Ed M Pitkin	317-898-8632	R	70	0.2
GNI Group Inc.	PO Box 220	Deer Park	TX	77536	Carl V Rush Jr	281-930-0350	P	69	0.2
Lotepro Corp.	115 Stevens Ave	Valhalla	NY	10595	DH Kistenmacher	914-747-3500	S	67	0.1
West Agro Inc.	11100 N Congress	Kansas City	MO	64153	WM Papineau	816-891-1600	S	67	0.1

Source: *Ward's Business Directory of U.S. Private and Public Companies*, 1998. The company type code used is as follows: P - Public, R - Private, S - Subsidiary, D - Division, J - Joint Venture, A - Affiliate, G - Group. Sales are in millions of dollars, employees are in thousands. An asterisk (*) indicates an estimated sales volume. The symbol < stands for 'less than'.

OCCUPATIONS EMPLOYED BY SIC 516 - WHOLESALE TRADE, OTHER

Occupation	% of Total 1996	Change to 2006	Occupation	% of Total 1996	Change to 2006
Sales & related workers nec	19.5	20.2	Clerical supervisors & managers	1.9	20.2
General managers & top executives	5.9	16.4	Order clerks	1.9	8.2
Truck drivers light & heavy	5.4	20.2	Helpers, laborers nec	1.7	20.2
General office clerks	3.6	3.4	Electrical & electronic technicians	1.4	18.8
Traffic, shipping, receiving clerks	3.6	16.7	Blue collar worker supervisors	1.4	16.0
Stock clerks	3.5	-3.9	Wholesale & retail buyers, except farm products	1.3	17.0
Freight, stock, & material movers, hand	3.3	8.2	Office machine & cash register servicers	1.3	20.2
Marketing & sales worker supervisors	3.1	20.2	Hand packers & packagers	1.2	-3.9
Order fillers, wholesale & retail sales	3.0	16.7	Maintenance repairers, general utility	1.1	12.0
Bookkeeping, accounting, & auditing clerks	2.9	-3.9	Industrial truck & tractor operators	1.1	20.2
Salespersons, retail	2.5	20.2	Purchasing managers	1.1	20.2
Secretaries, except legal & medical	2.5	-4.7	Receptionists & information clerks	1.0	20.2
Assemblers, fabricators, hand workers nec	2.0	-3.9			

Source: *Industry-Occupation Matrix*, Bureau of Labor Statistics. These data relate to one or more 3-digit SIC industry groups rather than to a single 4-digit SIC. The change reported for each occupation to the year 2006 is a percent of growth or decline as estimated by the Bureau of Labor Statistics. The abbreviation nec stands for 'not elsewhere classified'.

STATE AND REGIONAL CONCENTRATION

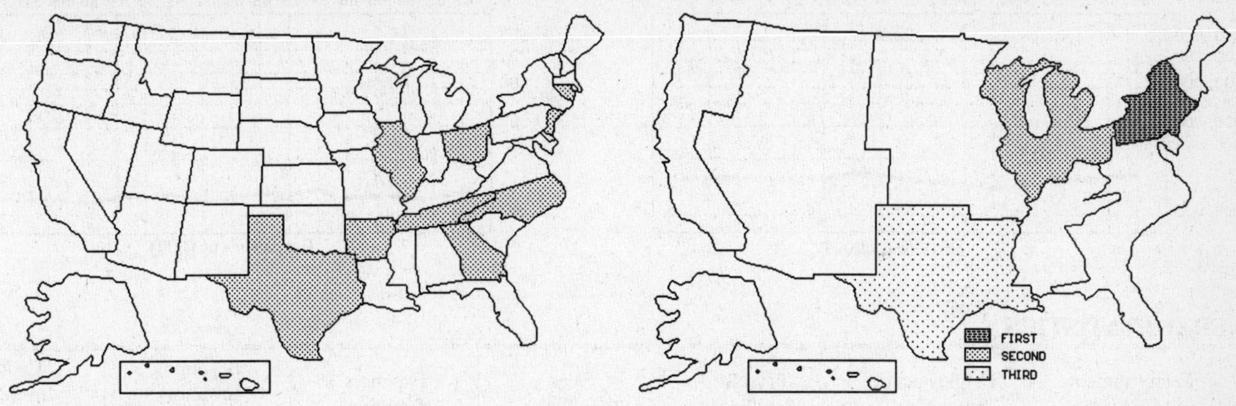

INDUSTRY DATA BY STATE

	Establishments - 1995		Employment - 1995			Payroll - 1995		Sales - 1992		
State	Total (number)	% of U.S.	Total (number)	% of U.S.	Per Estab.	Total ($ mil.)	Per Empl. ($)	Total ($ mil.)	% of U.S.	Per Estab ($)
Texas	1,071	10.0	11,693	10.0	11	532.7	45,557	13,494.9	14.1	1,189,500
California	915	8.5	10,518	9.0	11	455.7	43,323	9,088.7	9.5	907,870
New Jersey	629	5.9	6,866	5.8	11	341.5	49,743	9,030.4	9.4	1,335,075
Ohio	514	4.8	7,658	6.5	15	342.4	44,711	7,282.1	7.6	966,818
North Carolina	340	3.2	4,546	3.9	13	179.9	39,581	7,009.0	7.3	1,649,175
Illinois	554	5.2	6,646	5.7	12	290.0	43,640	6,871.5	7.2	1,054,229
New York	659	6.1	6,150	5.2	9	302.7	49,213	6,149.2	6.4	967,467
Georgia	440	4.1	5,537	4.7	13	230.3	41,587	5,800.1	6.1	1,183,456
Tennessee	213	2.0	2,414	2.1	11	96.3	39,906	3,627.1	3.8	1,583,203
Pennsylvania	428	4.0	6,711	5.7	16	318.6	47,472	3,558.1	3.7	648,697
Michigan	305	2.8	3,795	3.2	12	182.9	48,200	2,382.7	2.5	710,194
Florida	615	5.7	5,639	4.8	9	216.1	38,316	1,805.8	1.9	377,701
Arkansas	88	0.8	893	0.8	10	27.4	30,653	1,730.9	1.8	2,791,776
Massachusetts	206	1.9	2,343	2.0	11	105.0	44,832	1,723.1	1.8	591,714
Louisiana	259	2.4	2,441	2.1	9	86.0	35,224	1,583.1	1.7	704,521
Missouri	247	2.3	2,279	1.9	9	90.8	39,839	1,478.8	1.5	684,308
Connecticut	161	1.5	2,258	1.9	14	113.9	50,461	1,471.0	1.5	1,029,405
Indiana	233	2.2	2,954	2.5	13	121.4	41,097	1,438.0	1.5	571,781
Minnesota	172	1.6	2,048	1.7	12	86.4	42,164	1,287.6	1.3	754,323
Virginia	184	1.7	2,483	2.1	13	105.9	42,645	1,042.5	1.1	460,079
Oklahoma	174	1.6	1,311	1.1	8	43.9	33,465	961.0	1.0	722,010
Colorado	152	1.4	1,507	1.3	10	56.5	37,480	794.3	0.8	580,656
Alabama	137	1.3	1,341	1.1	10	53.1	39,575	743.8	0.8	611,674
Wisconsin	188	1.8	1,955	1.7	10	70.5	36,081	707.9	0.7	363,757
Washington	139	1.3	1,246	1.1	9	47.7	38,307	659.7	0.7	477,689
Iowa	113	1.1	1,172	1.0	10	41.7	35,542	618.3	0.6	631,613
Kentucky	132	1.2	1,707	1.5	13	56.8	33,269	553.0	0.6	338,039
South Carolina	183	1.7	1,730	1.5	9	60.9	35,188	518.6	0.5	438,414
Kansas	115	1.1	1,082	0.9	9	37.6	34,750	487.1	0.5	455,271
Oregon	106	1.0	958	0.8	9	32.8	34,271	469.8	0.5	561,233
Arizona	134	1.2	1,401	1.2	10	49.0	35,004	325.7	0.3	409,195
Rhode Island	57	0.5	522	0.4	9	21.1	40,395	246.2	0.3	423,043
Utah	98	0.9	1,030	0.9	11	29.8	28,956	232.5	0.2	309,589
New Hampshire	53	0.5	383	0.3	7	17.2	44,935	191.9	0.2	540,555
Nevada	48	0.4	377	0.3	8	12.3	32,698	114.9	0.1	365,841
New Mexico	68	0.6	540	0.5	8	15.1	28,048	94.1	0.1	225,695
Mississippi	68	0.6	250-499	-	-	(D)	-	90.6	0.1	215,157
Maine	30	0.3	215	0.2	7	7.5	34,944	63.3	0.1	276,493
North Dakota	37	0.3	231	0.2	6	7.5	32,446	55.5	0.1	231,200
Montana	32	0.3	100-249	-	-	(D)	-	41.4	0.0	191,009
Maryland	131	1.2	1,531	1.3	12	56.5	36,884	(D)	-	-
Nebraska	56	0.5	396	0.3	7	11.8	29,831	(D)	-	-
West Virginia	51	0.5	447	0.4	9	14.7	32,982	(D)	-	-
Wyoming	39	0.4	250-499	-	-	(D)	-	(D)	-	-
Alaska	31	0.3	230	0.2	7	9.6	41,909	(D)	-	-
Delaware	31	0.3	1000-2499	-	-	(D)	-	(D)	-	-
Hawaii	31	0.3	296	0.3	10	10.2	34,399	(D)	-	-
Idaho	27	0.3	100-249	-	-	(D)	-	(D)	-	-
South Dakota	19	0.2	100-249	-	-	(D)	-	(D)	-	-
Vermont	17	0.2	20-99	-	-	(D)	-	(D)	-	-
D.C.	3	0.0	11	0.0	4	0.8	76,727	(D)	-	-

Source: County Business Patterns, 1995 and *Economic Census of the U.S., 1992.* Data are sorted by 1992 revenues and, if revenues are unavailable, by establishments in 1995. The symbol (D) indicates that data are withheld by the source to avoid disclosure of competitive information. A dash (-) indicates that data are not available or undisclosed because they do not meet statistical validity standards. Shaded *states* on the state map indicate those states which have proportionately greater representation in the industry than would be indicated by the state's population; the ratio is based on total revenues or number of establishments. Shaded *regions* indicate where the industry is regionally most concentrated.

5171 - PETROLEUM BULK STATIONS & TERMINALS

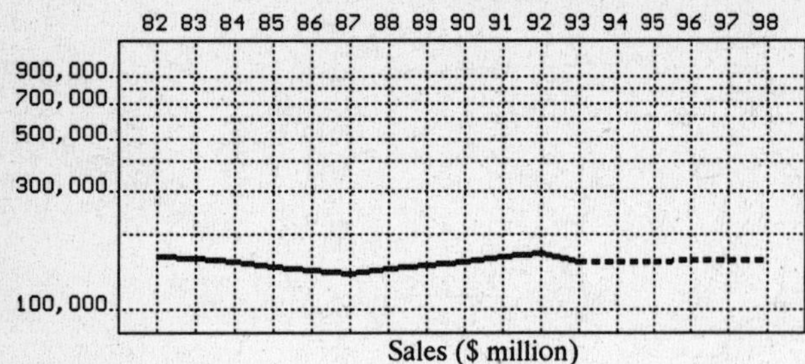

Sales ($ million)

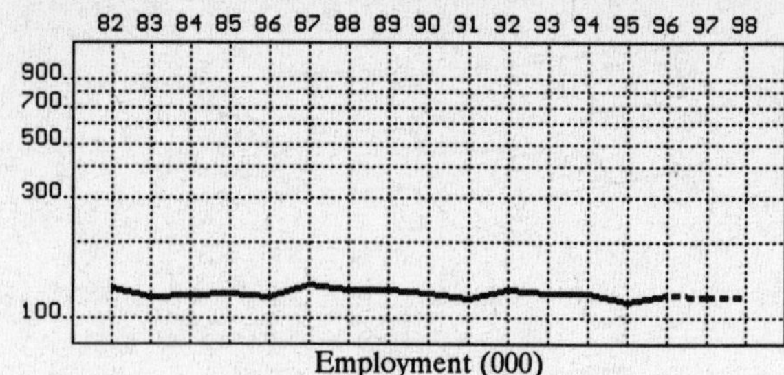

Employment (000)

GENERAL STATISTICS

Year	Establishments (number)	Employment (number)	Payroll ($ million)	Sales ($ million)	Expenses ($ million)	Beginning Inventory ($ million)	Ending Inventory ($ million)
1982	14,015	131,057	2,233.0	163,769.2	-	-	-
1983	12,457	121,489	2,129.9	158,946.4e	-	-	-
1984	11,880	124,336	2,290.6	154,123.6e	-	-	-
1985	11,232	125,536	2,365.0	149,300.8e	-	-	-
1986	10,610	122,770	2,428.4	144,478.0e	-	-	-
1987	12,353	135,923	2,689.3	139,655.2	7,222.7	5,438.4	5,878.9
1988	11,458	129,892	2,801.7	145,263.4e	7,468.6e	5,601.6e	5,998.8e
1989	10,927	128,657	2,839.5	150,871.6e	7,714.4e	5,764.8e	6,118.8e
1990	10,292	127,030	2,907.3	156,479.7e	7,960.2e	5,928.0e	6,238.7e
1991	9,784	120,425	2,875.5	162,087.9e	8,206.0e	6,091.2e	6,358.7e
1992	12,098	130,047	3,215.1	167,696.1	8,451.9	6,254.4	6,478.6
1993	11,200	126,436	3,291.8	156,235.4p	8,697.7p	6,417.7p	6,598.6p
1994	10,562	124,661	3,409.1	156,628.1p	8,943.5p	6,580.9p	6,718.5p
1995	9,241	116,150	3,363.1	157,020.7p	9,189.3p	6,744.1p	6,838.5p
1996	9,747p	123,589p	3,543.2p	157,413.4p	9,435.1p	6,907.3p	6,958.4p
1997	9,541p	123,263p	3,645.7p	157,806.1p	9,681.0p	7,070.5p	7,078.4p
1998	9,335p	122,938p	3,748.3p	158,198.8p	9,926.8p	7,233.7p	7,198.3p

Sources: Economic Census of the United States, 1982, 1987, and 1992. Establishment counts, employment, and payroll are from *County Business Patterns* for non-Census years. Values followed by a 'p' are projections by the editors. Sales and expense data for non-Census years are extrapolations, marked by 'e'. Industries reclassified in 1987 will not have data for prior years. Data are the most recent available at this level of detail.

INDICES OF CHANGE

Year	Establishments (number)	Employment (number)	Payroll ($ million)	Sales ($ million)	Expenses ($ million)	Beginning Inventory ($ million)	Ending Inventory ($ million)
1982	115.8	100.8	69.5	97.7	-	-	-
1983	103.0	93.4	66.2	94.8e	-	-	-
1984	98.2	95.6	71.2	91.9e	-	-	-
1985	92.8	96.5	73.6	89.0e	-	-	-
1986	87.7	94.4	75.5	86.2e	-	-	-
1987	102.1	104.5	83.6	83.3	85.5	87.0	90.7
1988	94.7	99.9	87.1	86.6e	88.4e	89.6e	92.6e
1989	90.3	98.9	88.3	90.0e	91.3e	92.2e	94.4e
1990	85.1	97.7	90.4	93.3e	94.2e	94.8e	96.3e
1991	80.9	92.6	89.4	96.7e	97.1e	97.4e	98.1e
1992	100.0	100.0	100.0	100.0	100.0	100.0	100.0
1993	92.6	97.2	102.4	93.2p	102.9p	102.6p	101.9p
1994	87.3	95.9	106.0	93.4p	105.8p	105.2p	103.7p
1995	76.4	89.3	104.6	93.6p	108.7p	107.8p	105.6p
1996	80.6p	95.0p	110.2p	93.9p	111.6p	110.4p	107.4p
1997	78.9p	94.8p	113.4p	94.1p	114.5p	113.0p	109.3p
1998	77.2p	94.5p	116.6p	94.3p	117.5p	115.7p	111.1p

Sources: Same as General Statistics. The values shown reflect change from the base year, 1992. Values above 100 mean greater than 1992, values below 100 mean less than 1992, and a value of 100 in the 1982-91 or 1993-98 period means same as 1992. Values followed by a 'p' are projections by the editors; 'e' stands for extrapolation. Data are the most recent available at this level of detail.

SELECTED RATIOS

For 1992	Avg. of All Wholesale	Analyzed Industry	Index	For 1992	Avg. of All Wholesale	Analyzed Industry	Index
Employees per Establishment	12	11	92	Sales per Employee	561,172	1,289,504	230
Payroll per Establishment	349,729	265,755	76	Sales per Establishment	6,559,346	13,861,473	211
Payroll per Employee	29,919	24,723	83	Expenses per Establishment	723,071	698,620	97

Sources: Same as General Statistics. The 'Average of All Manufacturing' column represents the average of all manufacturing industries reported for the most recent complete year available. The Index shows the relationship between the Average and the Analyzed Industry. For example, 100 means that they are equal; 500 that the Analyzed Industry is five times the average; 50 means that the Analyzed Industry is half the national average. The abbreviation 'na' is used to show that data are 'not available'.

LEADING COMPANIES

Number shown: **50** Total sales ($ mil): **27,568** Total employment (000): **34.7**

Company Name	Address				CEO Name	Phone	Co. Type	Sales ($ mil)	Empl. (000)
Amerada Hess Corp.	1185 of the Amer	New York	NY	10036	John B Hess	212-997-8500	P	8,930	9.1
EOTT Energy Partners L.P.	1330 Post Oak Blvd	Houston	TX	77056	Phil Hawk	713-993-5200	P	6,359	0.9
Enron Liquid Fuels Co.	1400 Smith St	Houston	TX	77002	John M Muckleroy	713-654-6161	S	2,200	1.4
Racetrac Petroleum Inc.	300 Technology Ct	Smyrna	GA	30082	Carl E Bolch Jr	770-431-7600	R	1,600	3.0
Coastal Oil New England Inc.	222 Lee Burbank	Revere	MA	02151	Sam Farooki	617-284-4490	S	745	0.1
Howell Corp.	1500 Howell Bdg	Houston	TX	77002	Donald W Clayton	713-658-4000	P	685	0.1
AmeriGas Propane Inc.	PO Box 965	Valley Forge	PA	19482	Robert Mauch	610-337-1000	S	512	5.0
Truman Arnold Co.	PO Box 1481	Texarkana	TX	75504	Truman Arnold	903-794-3835	R	500	0.3
Carlos R. Leffler Inc.	PO Box 278	Richland	PA	17087	Patrick Castagna	717-866-2105	R	450*	1.0
Colonial Oil Industries Inc.	PO Box 576	Savannah	GA	31402	Robert Demere Jr	912-236-1331	S	450*	0.4
U.S. Oil Company Inc.	425 S Washington	Comb. Locks	WI	54113	Tom Schmidt	414-739-6101	R	400	1.0
GROWMARK Inc.	1701 Towanda Ave	Bloomington	IL	61701	Norm Jones	309-557-6000	R	330	0.8
A.T. Williams Oil Co.	PO Box 7287	Winston-Salem	NC	27109	Arthur T Williams Jr	910-767-6280	R	320*	1.5
Apex Oil Co.	8182 Maryland Ave	St. Louis	MO	63105	PA Novelly	314-889-9600	R	310*	0.4
GATX Terminals Corp.	500 W Monroe	Chicago	IL	60661	A J Anprukaitis	312-621-6200	S	293	1.1
South Dakota Wheat Growers	PO Box 1460	Aberdeen	SD	57401	Verland Losinger	605-225-5500	R	254	0.3
Englefield Oil Co.	447 James Pkwy	Newark	OH	43055	F W Englefield III	614-522-1310	R	210	1.2
Lakeside Oil Company Inc.	PO Box 23440	Milwaukee	WI	53223	Herbert H Elliott	414-445-6464	R	210	<0.1
L and L Oil Company Inc.	PO Box 6984	Metairie	LA	70009	FL Levy	504-832-8600	R	200	0.2
Petroleum World Inc.	PO Box 307	Cliffside	NC	28024	Michael J Frost	704-482-0438	R	200	0.4
Meenan Oil Company L.P.	6900 Jericho Tpk	Syosset	NY	11791	Paul A Vermylen Jr	516-364-9030	R	180	0.8
Piasa Motor Fuels Inc.	PO Box 484	Alton	IL	62002	R William Schrimpf	618-254-7341	R	165	0.1
Petroleum Marketers Inc.	PO Box 12203	Roanoke	VA	24023	Terry M Phelps	703-362-4900	R	151	0.7
District Petroleum Products	1832 Milan Ave	Sandusky	OH	44870	Scott Stipp	419-625-8373	R	120*	0.3
Ayers Oil Company Inc.	PO Box 229	Canton	MO	63435	Steve Ayers	314-288-4466	R	110*	0.2
Rad Oil Company Inc.	287 Bowman Ave	Purchase	NY	10577	Donald Draizin	914-253-8945	R	100*	0.2
Toms Sierra Company Inc.	PO Box 759	Colfax	CA	95713	Nick Toms	916-346-2264	R	95	0.3
J.H. Williams Oil Company Inc.	PO Box 439	Tampa	FL	33601	J Hulon Williams III	813-228-7776	R	92*	0.3
Phoenix Fuel Company Inc.	2343 N 27th Ave	Phoenix	AZ	85009	Joseph W Wilhoit	602-278-6271	R	91	0.1
RKA Petroleum Companies	PO Box 23340	Detroit	MI	48223	Roger L Alberti	313-272-6700	R	90	0.1
Yoder Oil Company Inc.	PO Box 10	Elkhart	IN	46515	Kent J Yoder	219-264-2107	R	85	0.2
Jacobus Co.	2323 N Mayfair Rd	Milwaukee	WI	53226	CD Jacobus	414-476-0701	R	80*	0.2
Shipley Oil Co.	550 E King St	York	PA	17405	WS Shipley III	717-848-4100	R	80	0.4
Bauer Built Inc.	Hwy 25 S, Box 248	Durand	WI	54736	Jerry M Bauer	715-672-4295	R	79	0.4
Crystal Flash Petroleum Corp.	PO Box 684	Indianapolis	IN	46206	Mac Fehsenfeld	317-879-2849	R	75	0.3
Fleischli Oil Company Inc.	PO Box 487	Cheyenne	WY	82003	G Loghry	307-634-4466	R	75	<0.1
Erie Petroleum Inc.	1502 Greengarden	Erie	PA	16502	Patrick F Callahan	814-456-7516	R	72*	0.2
Hicks Oil and Hicks Gas Inc.	PO Box 98	Roberts	IL	60962	Todd M Coady	217-395-2281	R	70*	0.5
Agri Cooperative Inc.	310 Logan Rd	Holdrege	NE	68949	Ron Jurgens	308-995-8626	R	60*	0.1
Wooten Oil Co.	PO Box 1277	Goldsboro	NC	27533	SD Wooten Jr	919-734-1357	R	60	0.2
Boncosky Oil Co.	739 N State St	Elgin	IL	60123	Kevin McCarter	847-741-2577	R	52*	0.1
Olympian Oil Co.	260 Michele Ct	S San Francisco	CA	94080	Fred Bertetta	415-873-8200	R	52*	0.3
Bell Gas Inc.	PO Box 490	Roswell	NM	88202	Eugene Bell	505-622-4800	R	50	0.5
Jefferson City Oil Company	PO Box 576	Jefferson City	MO	65102	Cletus A Kolb	573-634-2025	R	50	<0.1
M.M. Fowler Inc.	PO Box 1090	Durham	NC	27705	ML Barnes	919-596-8246	R	50	<0.1
Illini F.S. Inc.	1509 E University	Urbana	IL	61801	Steve Wattnem	217-384-8300	R	47*	0.1
Phibro Inc.	500 Nyala Farms	Westport	CT	06880	Andrew J Hall	203-221-5800	S	46	0.2
Ampride	2075 Dakota S	Huron	SD	57350	Lori Ogden	605-352-6493	R	45	<0.1
Superior Cooperative	603 Railroad St	Superior	IA	51363	Garry Strube	712-858-4491	R	45	<0.1
Johnson Oil of Gaylord	507 Otesgo Rd	Gaylord	MI	49735	Dale E Johnson	517-732-2451	R	44*	<0.1

Source: *Ward's Business Directory of U.S. Private and Public Companies*, 1998. The company type code used is as follows: P - Public, R - Private, S - Subsidiary, D - Division, J - Joint Venture, A - Affiliate, G - Group. Sales are in millions of dollars, employees are in thousands. An asterisk (*) indicates an estimated sales volume. The symbol < stands for 'less than'.

OCCUPATIONS EMPLOYED BY SIC 517 - PETROLEUM AND PETROLEUM PRODUCTS

Occupation	% of Total 1996	Change to 2006	Occupation	% of Total 1996	Change to 2006
Truck drivers light & heavy	22.3	-7.3	Secretaries, except legal & medical	2.4	-26.5
Cashiers	11.5	-1.0	Clerical supervisors & managers	1.8	-7.3
General managers & top executives	7.8	-10.1	Blue collar worker supervisors	1.6	-10.5
Sales & related workers nec	6.8	2.0	Accountants & auditors	1.6	-14.1
Bookkeeping, accounting, & auditing clerks	4.6	-25.8	Salespersons, retail	1.6	-7.3
General office clerks	4.5	-20.2	Freight, stock, & material movers, hand	1.3	-16.6
Service station attendants	3.5	-76.8	Stock clerks	1.2	-7.3
Marketing & sales worker supervisors	3.4	-7.3	Driver/sales workers	1.1	-7.3
Maintenance repairers, general utility	2.8	-13.6	Management support workers nec	1.0	-7.2

Source: *Industry-Occupation Matrix*, Bureau of Labor Statistics. These data relate to one or more 3-digit SIC industry groups rather than to a single 4-digit SIC. The change reported for each occupation to the year 2006 is a percent of growth or decline as estimated by the Bureau of Labor Statistics. The abbreviation nec stands for 'not elsewhere classified'.

STATE AND REGIONAL CONCENTRATION

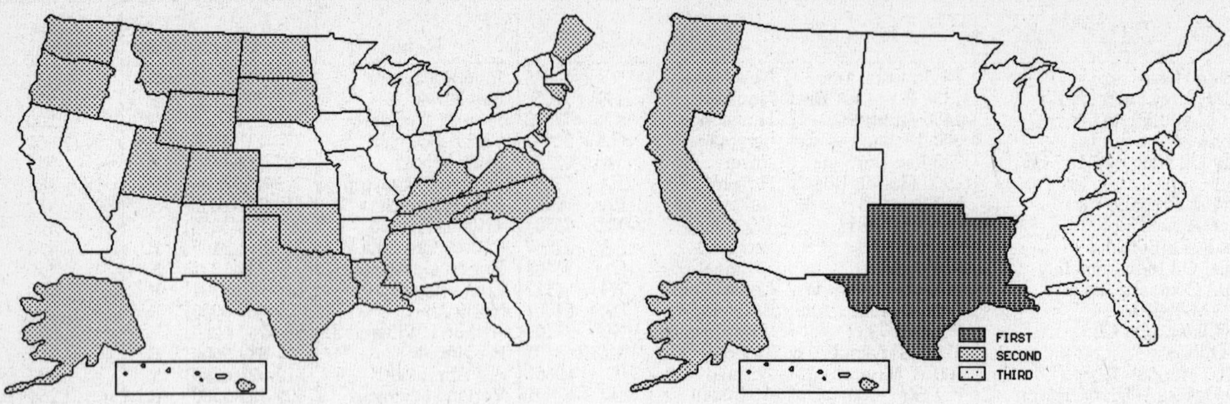

INDUSTRY DATA BY STATE

	Establishments - 1995		Employment - 1995			Payroll - 1995		Sales - 1992		
State	Total (number)	% of U.S.	Total (number)	% of U.S.	Per Estab.	Total ($ mil.)	Per Empl. ($)	Total ($ mil.)	% of U.S.	Per Estab ($)
Texas	835	9.0	9,583	8.3	11	322.5	33,654	29,828.2	18.5	2,761,101
California	499	5.4	7,398	6.4	15	280.2	37,878	17,767.3	11.0	2,199,192
Florida	327	3.5	4,162	3.6	13	121.8	29,271	6,664.4	4.1	1,280,879
New York	231	2.5	4,135	3.6	18	140.8	34,055	6,108.3	3.8	1,189,768
New Jersey	113	1.2	2,227	1.9	20	92.8	41,655	5,776.7	3.6	2,307,914
Pennsylvania	306	3.3	7,894	6.8	26	244.7	31,000	5,219.2	3.2	905,479
Oklahoma	200	2.2	1,609	1.4	8	39.2	24,366	5,031.5	3.1	2,998,509
Ohio	267	2.9	3,416	2.9	13	104.1	30,465	4,854.6	3.0	1,289,066
Louisiana	295	3.2	3,498	3.0	12	93.0	26,585	4,746.2	3.0	1,282,746
Illinois	351	3.8	4,167	3.6	12	129.4	31,065	4,711.1	2.9	1,050,879
Michigan	228	2.5	3,270	2.8	14	105.6	32,308	4,616.4	2.9	1,234,331
Virginia	220	2.4	3,949	3.4	18	105.2	26,650	4,487.6	2.8	948,947
North Carolina	343	3.7	4,183	3.6	12	106.3	25,421	4,379.7	2.7	813,761
Georgia	284	3.1	2,963	2.6	10	85.7	28,929	4,023.5	2.5	1,133,381
Tennessee	218	2.4	2,803	2.4	13	81.1	28,950	3,408.1	2.1	1,105,801
Washington	183	2.0	2,288	2.0	13	74.0	32,326	3,390.7	2.1	1,135,904
Colorado	140	1.5	1,863	1.6	13	58.0	31,133	3,362.3	2.1	1,713,700
Indiana	265	2.9	2,942	2.5	11	78.7	26,756	3,139.1	2.0	928,999
Missouri	323	3.5	2,680	2.3	8	66.5	24,795	3,055.9	1.9	893,544
Connecticut	61	0.7	991	0.9	16	43.3	43,742	2,865.1	1.8	2,160,747
Kentucky	197	2.1	2,597	2.2	13	59.2	22,804	2,644.7	1.6	1,030,656
Oregon	162	1.8	2,255	1.9	14	55.9	24,810	2,616.0	1.6	1,110,349
Alabama	226	2.4	3,094	2.7	14	65.3	21,120	2,507.5	1.6	756,400
Minnesota	305	3.3	3,087	2.7	10	64.5	20,908	2,354.1	1.5	703,359
Wisconsin	246	2.7	2,247	1.9	9	57.3	25,497	2,297.1	1.4	747,269
Utah	59	0.6	1,118	1.0	19	36.7	32,818	1,976.8	1.2	2,100,760
Mississippi	171	1.9	2,305	2.0	13	63.6	27,572	1,902.5	1.2	751,379
South Carolina	169	1.8	1,700	1.5	10	42.1	24,740	1,852.8	1.2	983,439
Kansas	188	2.0	1,364	1.2	7	28.1	20,614	1,519.5	0.9	904,460
Arizona	89	1.0	1,180	1.0	13	34.7	29,372	1,494.4	0.9	1,129,580
Iowa	247	2.7	1,806	1.6	7	38.7	21,404	1,442.2	0.9	615,781
Arkansas	199	2.2	1,814	1.6	9	36.3	20,036	1,166.1	0.7	552,153
Maine	49	0.5	793	0.7	16	22.5	28,348	920.0	0.6	806,999
Wyoming	74	0.8	478	0.4	6	12.6	26,287	874.6	0.5	1,349,738
Hawaii	26	0.3	300	0.3	12	13.0	43,453	870.7	0.5	2,568,336
Alaska	46	0.5	542	0.5	12	25.4	46,792	847.8	0.5	1,226,851
New Mexico	107	1.2	1,201	1.0	11	23.8	19,825	813.3	0.5	528,458
Nevada	33	0.4	338	0.3	10	11.8	34,970	795.5	0.5	1,850,095
Rhode Island	18	0.2	434	0.4	24	17.7	40,700	786.4	0.5	2,480,631
Nebraska	175	1.9	1,446	1.2	8	29.5	20,424	682.5	0.4	405,274
Montana	94	1.0	997	0.9	11	19.0	19,094	665.0	0.4	590,033
West Virginia	83	0.9	1,000	0.9	12	22.6	22,567	624.3	0.4	626,766
North Dakota	157	1.7	1,511	1.3	10	27.0	17,883	587.2	0.4	351,428
South Dakota	128	1.4	1,039	0.9	8	21.5	20,648	564.7	0.4	467,501
New Hampshire	23	0.2	398	0.3	17	12.6	31,716	396.0	0.2	835,418
Vermont	12	0.1	362	0.3	30	7.9	21,796	217.1	0.1	537,391
Idaho	94	1.0	1,150	1.0	12	22.2	19,331	(D)	-	-
Maryland	82	0.9	1,862	1.6	23	51.2	27,504	(D)	-	-
Massachusetts	75	0.8	1,442	1.2	19	59.9	41,542	(D)	-	-
Delaware	14	0.2	100-249	-	-	(D)	-	(D)	-	-
D.C.	4	0.0	20-99	-	-	(D)	-	(D)	-	-

Source: County Business Patterns, 1995 and *Economic Census of the U.S., 1992*. Data are sorted by 1992 revenues and, if revenues are unavailable, by establishments in 1995. The symbol (D) indicates that data are withheld by the source to avoid disclosure of competitive information. A dash (-) indicates that data are not available or undisclosed because they do not meet statistical validity standards. Shaded *states* on the state map indicate those states which have proportionately greater representation in the industry than would be indicated by the state's population; the ratio is based on total revenues or number of establishments. Shaded *regions* indicate where the industry is regionally most concentrated.

5172 - PETROLEUM PRODUCTS, NEC

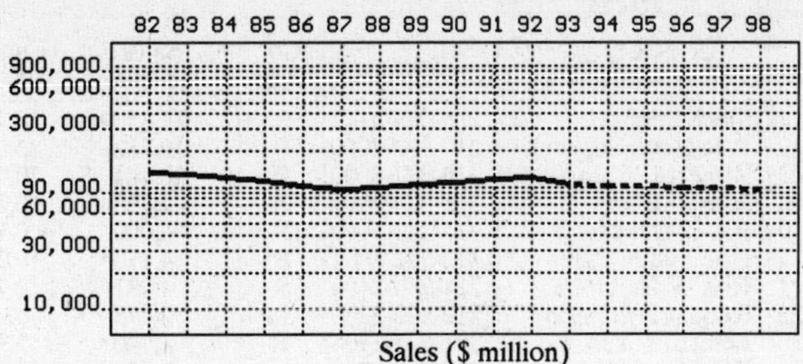

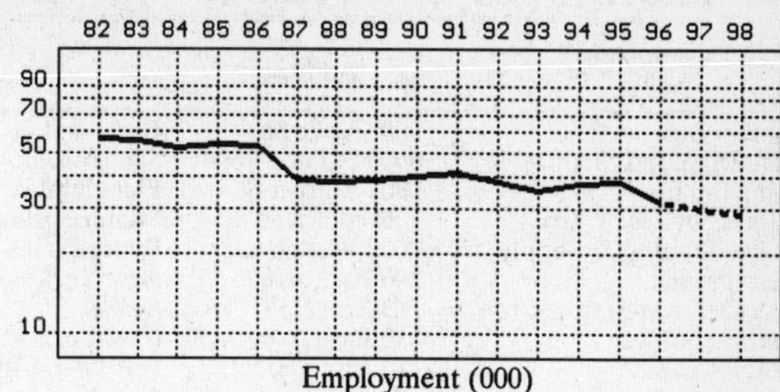

GENERAL STATISTICS

Year	Establishments (number)	Employment (number)	Payroll ($ million)	Sales ($ million)	Expenses ($ million)	Beginning Inventory ($ million)	Ending Inventory ($ million)
1982	6,287	56,680	1,199.8	133,226.0	-	-	-
1983	5,790	55,540	1,192.1	125,624.5*e*	-	-	-
1984	5,420	52,542	1,211.5	118,023.0*e*	-	-	-
1985	5,120	53,325	1,225.9	110,421.5*e*	-	-	-
1986	4,884	53,104	1,233.4	102,820.0*e*	-	-	-
1987	4,373	39,265	968.4	95,218.5	2,579.2	1,160.3	933.7
1988	3,976	38,525	1,036.0	99,991.5*e*	2,764.4*e*	1,346.7*e*	1,220.7*e*
1989	3,826	39,040	1,071.4	104,764.5*e*	2,949.7*e*	1,533.1*e*	1,507.7*e*
1990	3,835	40,257	1,155.2	109,537.5*e*	3,134.9*e*	1,719.5*e*	1,794.7*e*
1991	3,895	41,705	1,237.9	114,310.5*e*	3,320.1*e*	1,905.9*e*	2,081.7*e*
1992	3,962	38,297	1,219.9	119,083.5	3,505.3	2,092.2	2,368.7
1993	3,879	35,459	1,203.5	103,607.4*p*	3,690.5*p*	2,278.6*p*	2,655.7*p*
1994	3,864	37,663	1,344.1	102,193.1*p*	3,875.7*p*	2,465.0*p*	2,942.7*p*
1995	3,824	38,608	1,410.7	100,778.9*p*	4,060.9*p*	2,651.4*p*	3,229.7*p*
1996	3,146*p*	32,022*p*	1,274.6*p*	99,364.6*p*	4,246.2*p*	2,837.7*p*	3,516.7*p*
1997	2,966*p*	30,387*p*	1,285.4*p*	97,950.4*p*	4,431.4*p*	3,024.1*p*	3,803.7*p*
1998	2,786*p*	28,752*p*	1,296.2*p*	96,536.1*p*	4,616.6*p*	3,210.5*p*	4,090.7*p*

Sources: Economic Census of the United States, 1982, 1987, and 1992. Establishment counts, employment, and payroll are from *County Business Patterns* for non-Census years. Values followed by a 'p' are projections by the editors. Sales and expense data for non-Census years are extrapolations, marked by 'e'. Industries reclassified in 1987 will not have data for prior years. Data are the most recent available at this level of detail.

INDICES OF CHANGE

Year	Establishments (number)	Employment (number)	Payroll ($ million)	Sales ($ million)	Expenses ($ million)	Beginning Inventory ($ million)	Ending Inventory ($ million)
1982	158.7	148.0	98.4	111.9	-	-	-
1983	146.1	145.0	97.7	105.5*e*	-	-	-
1984	136.8	137.2	99.3	99.1*e*	-	-	-
1985	129.2	139.2	100.5	92.7*e*	-	-	-
1986	123.3	138.7	101.1	86.3*e*	-	-	-
1987	110.4	102.5	79.4	80.0	73.6	55.5	39.4
1988	100.4	100.6	84.9	84.0*e*	78.9*e*	64.4*e*	51.5*e*
1989	96.6	101.9	87.8	88.0*e*	84.1*e*	73.3*e*	63.7*e*
1990	96.8	105.1	94.7	92.0*e*	89.4*e*	82.2*e*	75.8*e*
1991	98.3	108.9	101.5	96.0*e*	94.7*e*	91.1*e*	87.9*e*
1992	100.0	100.0	100.0	100.0	100.0	100.0	100.0
1993	97.9	92.6	98.7	87.0*p*	105.3*p*	108.9*p*	112.1*p*
1994	97.5	98.3	110.2	85.8*p*	110.6*p*	117.8*p*	124.2*p*
1995	96.5	100.8	115.6	84.6*p*	115.9*p*	126.7*p*	136.3*p*
1996	79.4*p*	83.6*p*	104.5*p*	83.4*p*	121.1*p*	135.6*p*	148.5*p*
1997	74.9*p*	79.3*p*	105.4*p*	82.3*p*	126.4*p*	144.5*p*	160.6*p*
1998	70.3*p*	75.1*p*	106.3*p*	81.1*p*	131.7*p*	153.5*p*	172.7*p*

Sources: Same as General Statistics. The values shown reflect change from the base year, 1992. Values above 100 mean greater than 1992, values below 100 mean less than 1992, and a value of 100 in the 1982-91 or 1993-98 period means same as 1992. Values followed by a 'p' are projections by the editors; 'e' stands for extrapolation. Data are the most recent available at this level of detail.

SELECTED RATIOS

For 1992	Avg. of All Wholesale	Analyzed Industry	Index	For 1992	Avg. of All Wholesale	Analyzed Industry	Index
Employees per Establishment	12	10	83	Sales per Employee	561,172	3,109,473	554
Payroll per Establishment	349,729	307,900	88	Sales per Establishment	6,559,346	30,056,411	458
Payroll per Employee	29,919	31,854	106	Expenses per Establishment	723,071	884,730	122

Sources: Same as General Statistics. The 'Average of All Manufacturing' column represents the average of all manufacturing industries reported for the most recent complete year available. The Index shows the relationship between the Average and the Analyzed Industry. For example, 100 means that they are equal; 500 that the Analyzed Industry is five times the average; 50 means that the Analyzed Industry is half the national average. The abbreviation 'na' is used to show that data are 'not available'.

LEADING COMPANIES

Number shown: **50** Total sales ($ mil): **84,970** Total employment (000): **150.9**

Company Name	Address				CEO Name	Phone	Co. Type	Sales ($ mil)	Empl. (000)
BP America Inc.	200 Public Sq	Cleveland	OH	44114	Steve Percy	216-586-4141	S	11,550 *	12.7
Ultramar Diamond Shamrock	6000 N Loop 1604	San Antonio	TX	78249	R R Hemminghaus	210-592-2000	P	10,882	23.0
Sun Company Inc.	1801 Market St	Philadelphia	PA	19103	Robert H Campbell	215-977-3000	P	10,464	10.9
World Fuel Services Corp.	700 Poinciana	Miami Springs	FL	33166	Jerrold Blair	305-884-2001	P	7,726	0.2
Texaco Oil Trading & Supply	2000 Westchester	White Plains	NY	10650	RA O'Doherty	914-253-4000	S	6,000	<0.1
Elf Aquitaine Inc.	280 Park Ave	New York	NY	10017	Dominique Paret	212-922-3000	S	4,170 *	10.0
Petrofina Delaware Inc.	PO Box 2159	Dallas	TX	75221	Ron W Haddock	214-750-2400	S	4,081	2.7
Transammonia Inc.	350 Park Ave	New York	NY	10022	Ronald P Stanton	212-223-3200	R	2,478	0.2
Sinclair Oil Corp.	PO Box 30825	Salt Lake City	UT	84130	Peter Johnson	801-524-2700	R	1,930 *	3.9
Ogden Services Corp.	2 Penn Plz	New York	NY	10121	R Richard Ablon	212-868-6000	S	1,750	39.0
Agway Inc.	333 Butternut Dr	De Witt	NY	13214	Don C Cararelli	315-449-6436	R	1,671	7.1
Racetrac Petroleum Inc.	300 Technology Ct	Smyrna	GA	30082	Carl E Bolch Jr	770-431-7600	R	1,600	3.0
Balfour Maclaine Corp.	61 Broadway	New York	NY	10006	A C Van Ekris	212-269-0800	P	1,312	0.8
Northeast Petroleum Div.	PO Box 1090	Beverly	MA	01915	Aaron Markley	508-524-1500	D	1,250	0.2
Ferrellgas Partners L.P.	1 Liberty Plaza	Liberty	MO	64068	James E Ferrell	816-792-1600	P	1,200	3.4
Castrol North America Holdings	1500 Valley Rd	Wayne	NJ	07470	Thomas R Crane Jr	201-633-2200	S	1,160	2.0
Tauber Oil Co.	PO Box 4645	Houston	TX	77210	Jerry Tauber Jr	713-869-8700	R	1,127	<0.1
Flying J Inc.	PO Box 678	Brigham City	UT	84302	J Phillip Adams	801-734-6400	R	1,030 *	7.0
Enron Oil Trading	PO Box 4666	Houston	TX	77210	Gary W Luce	713-993-5200	S	1,000 *	0.7
Coastal States Trading	9 Greenway Plz	Houston	TX	77046	David Arledge	713-877-1400	S	970	1.5
Tesoro Petroleum Corp.	PO Box 17536	San Antonio	TX	78217	Bruce A Smith	210-828-8484	P	943	1.0
Triarc Companies Inc.	280 Park Ave	New York	NY	10017	Nelson Peltz	212-451-3000	P	861	2.0
Coastal Oil New England Inc.	222 Lee Burbank	Revere	MA	02151	Sam Farooki	617-284-4490	S	745	0.1
Agway Energy Products	PO Box 4852	Syracuse	NY	13221	Stephen B Burnett	315-449-7380	S	720 *	1.5
Kiel Brothers Oil Company Inc.	PO Box 344	Columbus	IN	47202	T Kiel	812-372-3751	R	640 *	1.3
Coastal Fuels Marketing Inc.	PO Box 025500	Miami	FL	33102	Dan Hill	305-551-5200	S	600	<0.1
Cornerstone Propane G.P. Inc.	432 Westridge Dr	Watsonville	CA	95076	Keith G Baxter	408-724-1921	S	596	1.7
SF Services Inc.	3001 JFK Blvd	N. Little Rock	AR	72116	Michael P Sadler	501-945-2371	R	591	1.3
Texaco Trading & Trans	PO Box 5568	Denver	CO	80217	JE Shamas	303-861-4475	S	470 *	0.5
Dead River Co.	PO Box 1427	Bangor	ME	04401	P Andrews Nixon	207-947-8641	R	450	0.9
Webber Oil Co.	PO Box 929	Bangor	ME	04402	Larry Mahaney	207-942-5501	R	390 *	0.8
Wainoco Oil Corp.	10000 Memorial Dr	Houston	TX	77024	James R Gibbs	713-688-9600	P	374	0.3
FFP Operating Partners L.P.	2801 Glenda Ave	Fort Worth	TX	76117	John H Harvison	817-838-4700	S	371 *	1.3
Uni-Marts Inc.	477 E Beaver Ave	State College	PA	16801	Henry D Sahakian	814-234-6000	P	352	2.8
Western Petroleum Co.	9531 W 78th St	Eden Prairie	MN	55344	James W Emison	612-941-9090	R	328	<0.1
Trans-Tec Services Inc.	500 Frank W Burr	Teaneck	NJ	07666	Michael Kasbar	201-692-9292	S	321	<0.1
A.T. Williams Oil Co.	PO Box 7287	Winston-Salem	NC	27109	Arthur T Williams Jr	910-767-6280	R	320 *	1.5
Vanguard Petroleum Corp.	1111 N Loop W	Houston	TX	77008	Tom Garner	713-802-4242	R	300	<0.1
Advance Petroleum Inc.	700 Poinciana	Miami Springs	FL	33166	Ralph R Weiser	305-883-8554	S	241	0.1
DynAir Fueling Inc.	2000 Halley	Reston	VA	22090	Hal Watson	703-264-9500	S	240 *	0.5
Gate Petroleum Co.	PO Box 23627	Jacksonville	FL	32241	Herbert Peyton	904-737-7220	R	220 *	2.0
Keystops Inc.	PO Box 2809	Franklin	KY	42135	Lester Key	502-586-8283	R	218	0.2
Lakeside Oil Company Inc.	PO Box 23440	Milwaukee	WI	53223	Herbert H Elliott	414-445-6464	R	210	<0.1
NOCO Energy Corp.	2440 Sheridan Dr	Tonawanda	NY	14150	Donald F Newman	716-874-6200	R	200	0.6
Sico Co.	15 Mount Joy St	Mount Joy	PA	17552	Franklin R Eichler	717-653-1411	R	190 *	0.4
River City Petroleum Inc.	840 Delta Ln	W. Sacramento	CA	95691	L. D Robinson	916-371-4960	R	180 *	0.2
Evans Systems Inc.	PO Box 2480	Bay City	TX	77404	Jerriel L Evans Sr	409-245-2424	P	160	0.5
Chesapeake Utilities Corp.	909 Silver Lake	Dover	DE	19904	Ralph J Adkins	302-734-6713	P	137	0.4
Castle Oil Corp.	500 Mamaroneck	Harrison	NY	10528	Mauro C Romita	914-381-6500	R	130 *	0.3
Brewer Oil Co.	PO Box 1347	Artesia	NM	88210	Don Brewer	505-748-1248	R	120 *	0.3

Source: *Ward's Business Directory of U.S. Private and Public Companies*, 1998. The company type code used is as follows: P - Public, R - Private, S - Subsidiary, D - Division, J - Joint Venture, A - Affiliate, G - Group. Sales are in millions of dollars, employees are in thousands. An asterisk (*) indicates an estimated sales volume. The symbol < stands for 'less than'.

OCCUPATIONS EMPLOYED BY SIC 517 - PETROLEUM AND PETROLEUM PRODUCTS

Occupation	% of Total 1996	Change to 2006	Occupation	% of Total 1996	Change to 2006
Truck drivers light & heavy	22.3	-7.3	Secretaries, except legal & medical	2.4	-26.5
Cashiers	11.5	-1.0	Clerical supervisors & managers	1.8	-7.3
General managers & top executives	7.8	-10.1	Blue collar worker supervisors	1.6	-10.5
Sales & related workers nec	6.8	2.0	Accountants & auditors	1.6	-14.1
Bookkeeping, accounting, & auditing clerks	4.6	-25.8	Salespersons, retail	1.6	-7.3
General office clerks	4.5	-20.2	Freight, stock, & material movers, hand	1.3	-16.6
Service station attendants	3.5	-76.8	Stock clerks	1.2	-7.3
Marketing & sales worker supervisors	3.4	-7.3	Driver/sales workers	1.1	-7.3
Maintenance repairers, general utility	2.8	-13.6	Management support workers nec	1.0	-7.2

Source: *Industry-Occupation Matrix*, Bureau of Labor Statistics. These data relate to one or more 3-digit SIC industry groups rather than to a single 4-digit SIC. The change reported for each occupation to the year 2006 is a percent of growth or decline as estimated by the Bureau of Labor Statistics. The abbreviation nec stands for 'not elsewhere classified'.

STATE AND REGIONAL CONCENTRATION

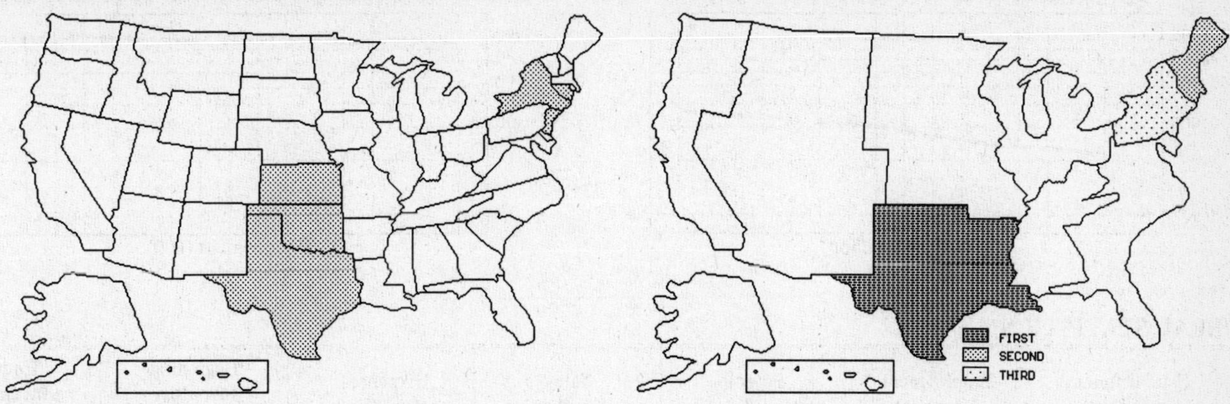

INDUSTRY DATA BY STATE

State	Establishments - 1995 Total (number)	Establishments - 1995 % of U.S.	Employment - 1995 Total (number)	Employment - 1995 % of U.S.	Employment - 1995 Per Estab.	Payroll - 1995 Total ($ mil.)	Payroll - 1995 Per Empl. ($)	Sales - 1992 Total ($ mil.)	Sales - 1992 % of U.S.	Sales - 1992 Per Estab ($)
Texas	512	13.4	6,028	15.7	12	291.0	48,272	51,365.5	43.5	9,931,452
Connecticut	50	1.3	718	1.9	14	93.0	129,581	12,949.3	11.0	11,134,376
California	267	7.0	2,733	7.1	10	111.0	40,598	10,046.1	8.5	3,234,426
New York	212	5.5	3,529	9.2	17	143.1	40,560	9,221.2	7.8	2,991,944
New Jersey	110	2.9	977	2.5	9	45.3	46,349	3,955.3	3.4	3,252,676
Georgia	130	3.4	1,166	3.0	9	36.5	31,326	2,733.6	2.3	3,152,939
Illinois	177	4.6	1,510	3.9	9	43.8	28,992	2,508.4	2.1	1,332,111
Florida	146	3.8	1,133	3.0	8	33.1	29,194	2,276.5	1.9	2,269,668
Massachusetts	65	1.7	929	2.4	14	41.7	44,847	2,212.5	1.9	3,511,875
Oklahoma	118	3.1	816	2.1	7	26.9	32,967	1,889.4	1.6	2,164,310
Missouri	92	2.4	1,029	2.7	11	34.7	33,755	1,868.7	1.6	1,043,949
Ohio	145	3.8	1,012	2.6	7	32.9	32,484	1,821.7	1.5	1,675,916
Colorado	69	1.8	963	2.5	14	30.3	31,441	1,590.7	1.3	1,811,714
Kansas	68	1.8	378	1.0	6	8.9	23,648	1,470.2	1.2	2,143,198
Michigan	86	2.2	786	2.0	9	23.4	29,831	1,204.7	1.0	1,308,045
Louisiana	88	2.3	1,048	2.7	12	33.5	31,987	1,115.6	0.9	1,173,108
Arkansas	56	1.5	415	1.1	7	11.8	28,516	1,010.1	0.9	2,775,077
Pennsylvania	108	2.8	1,042	2.7	10	33.2	31,895	834.9	0.7	843,333
Indiana	90	2.4	839	2.2	9	28.4	33,901	815.4	0.7	1,463,878
North Carolina	108	2.8	871	2.3	8	23.9	27,489	740.1	0.6	803,571
Washington	42	1.1	380	1.0	9	11.3	29,768	635.2	0.5	2,175,401
Virginia	70	1.8	979	2.6	14	35.6	36,362	628.5	0.5	731,632
Tennessee	75	2.0	596	1.6	8	17.8	29,866	606.6	0.5	1,064,207
Minnesota	75	2.0	582	1.5	8	16.1	27,735	536.6	0.5	1,064,645
Alabama	61	1.6	713	1.9	12	14.8	20,739	463.6	0.4	544,170
Oregon	34	0.9	370	1.0	11	9.8	26,384	326.4	0.3	1,121,790
Iowa	85	2.2	627	1.6	7	15.4	24,525	319.8	0.3	543,939
Kentucky	74	1.9	663	1.7	9	15.5	23,425	315.8	0.3	436,812
New Hampshire	14	0.4	148	0.4	11	7.1	48,122	302.5	0.3	2,459,073
Wisconsin	64	1.7	332	0.9	5	8.0	24,160	295.0	0.2	810,538
Mississippi	43	1.1	453	1.2	11	9.9	21,927	242.7	0.2	687,496
South Carolina	48	1.3	334	0.9	7	10.4	31,102	193.1	0.2	479,181
Maine	19	0.5	531	1.4	28	10.8	20,373	188.1	0.2	353,524
Arizona	40	1.0	650	1.7	16	11.9	18,252	181.9	0.2	436,259
Nebraska	56	1.5	318	0.8	6	7.0	21,893	179.6	0.2	471,499
Hawaii	21	0.5	323	0.8	15	12.7	39,303	153.0	0.1	784,559
Montana	23	0.6	213	0.6	9	4.2	19,737	149.2	0.1	626,740
Utah	26	0.7	429	1.1	16	6.5	15,040	128.9	0.1	372,595
New Mexico	36	0.9	263	0.7	7	6.7	25,456	126.9	0.1	293,859
North Dakota	27	0.7	148	0.4	5	2.8	18,919	104.9	0.1	754,453
West Virginia	33	0.9	245	0.6	7	5.1	21,012	75.6	0.1	402,346
Nevada	19	0.5	82	0.2	4	2.2	26,378	75.5	0.1	634,538
Vermont	8	0.2	92	0.2	11	3.0	33,065	59.5	0.1	826,181
Wyoming	24	0.6	149	0.4	6	4.4	29,765	46.5	0.0	286,895
Rhode Island	12	0.3	110	0.3	9	3.2	29,118	46.3	0.0	449,252
South Dakota	30	0.8	110	0.3	4	1.8	16,664	35.2	0.0	386,516
Alaska	12	0.3	68	0.2	6	1.6	23,632	11.4	0.0	247,913
Maryland	26	0.7	313	0.8	12	12.1	38,661	(D)	-	-
Idaho	21	0.5	246	0.6	12	8.8	35,878	(D)	-	-
Delaware	6	0.2	20-99	-	-	(D)	-	(D)	-	-
D.C.	3	0.1	100-249	-	-	(D)	-	(D)	-	-

Source: County Business Patterns, 1995 and *Economic Census of the U.S., 1992*. Data are sorted by 1992 revenues and, if revenues are unavailable, by establishments in 1995. The symbol (D) indicates that data are withheld by the source to avoid disclosure of competitive information. A dash (-) indicates that data are not available or undisclosed because they do not meet statistical validity standards. Shaded *states* on the state map indicate those states which have proportionately greater representation in the industry than would be indicated by the state's population; the ratio is based on total revenues or number of establishments. Shaded *regions* indicate where the industry is regionally most concentrated.

5181 - BEER AND ALE

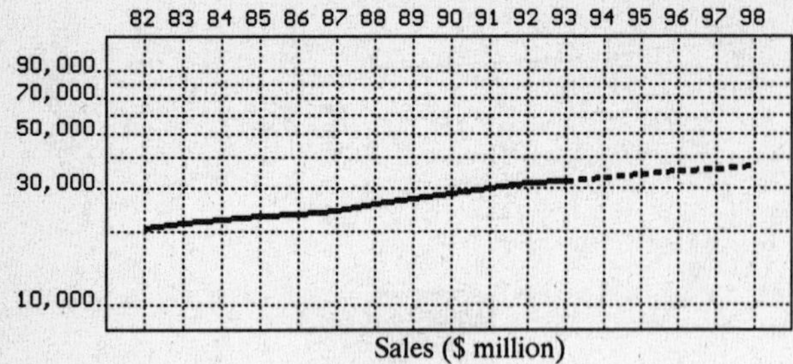

Sales ($ million)

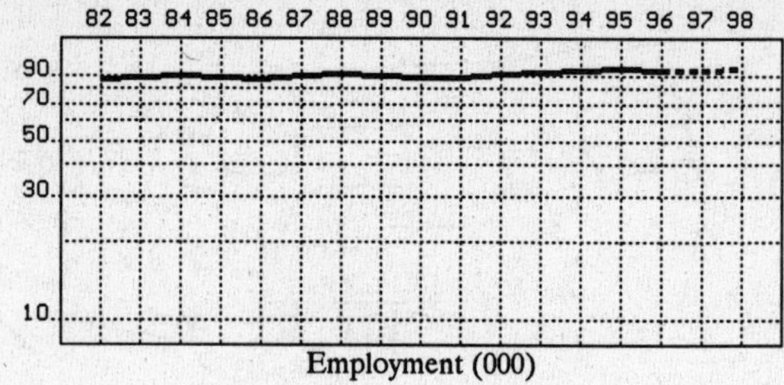

Employment (000)

GENERAL STATISTICS

Year	Establishments (number)	Employment (number)	Payroll ($ million)	Sales ($ million)	Expenses ($ million)	Beginning Inventory ($ million)	Ending Inventory ($ million)
1982	4,708	87,548	1,857.8	20,821.6	-	-	-
1983	4,522	88,057	1,967.8	21,514.9e	-	-	-
1984	4,310	90,454	2,106.0	22,208.2e	-	-	-
1985	4,078	89,386	2,188.4	22,901.4e	-	-	-
1986	3,887	87,482	2,250.8	23,594.7e	-	-	-
1987	3,934	90,091	2,314.7	24,288.0	4,791.7	1,154.0	1,171.0
1988	3,775	90,852	2,496.3	25,751.0e	5,020.7e	1,248.8e	1,257.1e
1989	3,545	89,762	2,480.7	27,214.1e	5,249.7e	1,343.6e	1,343.1e
1990	3,406	89,177	2,595.5	28,677.1e	5,478.8e	1,438.4e	1,429.1e
1991	3,284	88,880	2,680.0	30,140.2e	5,707.8e	1,533.3e	1,515.1e
1992	3,403	91,086	2,851.8	31,603.2	5,936.8	1,628.1	1,601.2
1993	3,298	94,076	2,960.6	31,806.6p	6,165.8p	1,722.9p	1,687.2p
1994	3,211	94,902	3,055.6	32,884.8p	6,394.9p	1,817.7p	1,773.2p
1995	3,123	95,892	3,130.3	33,963.0p	6,623.9p	1,912.5p	1,859.2p
1996	2,864p	94,361p	3,217.7p	35,041.1p	6,852.9p	2,007.4p	1,945.3p
1997	2,746p	94,869p	3,314.0p	36,119.3p	7,081.9p	2,102.2p	2,031.3p
1998	2,628p	95,378p	3,410.3p	37,197.4p	7,311.0p	2,197.0p	2,117.3p

Sources: *Economic Census of the United States*, 1982, 1987, and 1992. Establishment counts, employment, and payroll are from *County Business Patterns* for non-Census years. Values followed by a 'p' are projections by the editors. Sales and expense data for non-Census years are extrapolations, marked by 'e'. Industries reclassified in 1987 will not have data for prior years. Data are the most recent available at this level of detail.

INDICES OF CHANGE

Year	Establishments (number)	Employment (number)	Payroll ($ million)	Sales ($ million)	Expenses ($ million)	Beginning Inventory ($ million)	Ending Inventory ($ million)
1982	138.3	96.1	65.1	65.9	-	-	-
1983	132.9	96.7	69.0	68.1e	-	-	-
1984	126.7	99.3	73.8	70.3e	-	-	-
1985	119.8	98.1	76.7	72.5e	-	-	-
1986	114.2	96.0	78.9	74.7e	-	-	-
1987	115.6	98.9	81.2	76.9	80.7	70.9	73.1
1988	110.9	99.7	87.5	81.5e	84.6e	76.7e	78.5e
1989	104.2	98.5	87.0	86.1e	88.4e	82.5e	83.9e
1990	100.1	97.9	91.0	90.7e	92.3e	88.3e	89.3e
1991	96.5	97.6	94.0	95.4e	96.1e	94.2e	94.6e
1992	100.0	100.0	100.0	100.0	100.0	100.0	100.0
1993	96.9	103.3	103.8	100.6p	103.9p	105.8p	105.4p
1994	94.4	104.2	107.1	104.1p	107.7p	111.6p	110.7p
1995	91.8	105.3	109.8	107.5p	111.6p	117.5p	116.1p
1996	84.2p	103.6p	112.8p	110.9p	115.4p	123.3p	121.5p
1997	80.7p	104.2p	116.2p	114.3p	119.3p	129.1p	126.9p
1998	77.2p	104.7p	119.6p	117.7p	123.1p	134.9p	132.2p

Sources: Same as General Statistics. The values shown reflect change from the base year, 1992. Values above 100 mean greater than 1992, values below 100 mean less than 1992, and a value of 100 in the 1982-91 or 1993-98 period means same as 1992. Values followed by a 'p' are projections by the editors; 'e' stands for extrapolation. Data are the most recent available at this level of detail.

SELECTED RATIOS

For 1992	Avg. of All Wholesale	Analyzed Industry	Index	For 1992	Avg. of All Wholesale	Analyzed Industry	Index
Employees per Establishment	12	27	229	Sales per Employee	561,172	346,960	62
Payroll per Establishment	349,729	838,025	240	Sales per Establishment	6,559,346	9,286,865	142
Payroll per Employee	29,919	31,309	105	Expenses per Establishment	723,071	1,744,578	241

Sources: Same as General Statistics. The 'Average of All Manufacturing' column represents the average of all manufacturing industries reported for the most recent complete year available. The Index shows the relationship between the Average and the Analyzed Industry. For example, 100 means that they are equal; 500 that the Analyzed Industry is five times the average; 50 means that the Analyzed Industry is half the national average. The abbreviation 'na' is used to show that data are 'not available'.

LEADING COMPANIES

Number shown: **50** Total sales ($ mil): **7,106** Total employment (000): **19.6**

Company Name	Address				CEO Name	Phone	Co. Type	Sales ($ mil)	Empl. (000)
Ben E. Keith Co.	PO Box 2628	Fort Worth	TX	76113	Howard P Hallam	817-877-5700	R	726 *	1.4
Glazer's Wholesale Drug	14860 Landmark	Dallas	TX	75240	Bennett J Glazer	972-702-0900	R	686 *	2.2
Van Munching and Company	1270 of the Amer	New York	NY	10020	L Van Munching Jr	212-332-8500	S	500	0.2
National Distributing Company	PO Box 44127	Atlanta	GA	30336	Michael C Carlos	404-696-9440	R	310 *	1.0
Labatt USA Inc.	23 Old King's S	Darien	CT	06820	Thaine Preston	203-656-1876	R	300	0.5
Magnolia Marketing Co.	PO Box 53333	New Orleans	LA	70153	Tom Cole	504-837-1500	R	290	1.0
Vierk Distributing Co.	16745 Lathrop Ave	Harvey	IL	60426	Richard A Vierk	708-333-0084	R	273	<0.1
Georgia Crown Distributing Co.	PO Box 7908	Columbus	GA	31908	Don Leebern III	706-568-4580	R	200 *	0.7
Mendez and Company Inc.	PO Box 363348	San Juan	PR	00936	S Alvarez-Mendez	809-793-8888	R	200	0.3
High Grade Beverage	PO Box 7092	N. Brunswick	NJ	08902	Joe De Marco	908-821-7600	R	180 *	0.4
Sapporo U.S.A. Inc.	666 3rd Ave	New York	NY	10017	Mike Yazawa	212-922-9165	S	180 *	<0.1
United Liquors Ltd.	1 United Dr	W. Bridgewater	MA	02379	A Raymond Tye	508-588-2300	R	180 *	0.6
Western Distributing Co.	PO Box 5542	Denver	CO	80217	Vieri Gaines	303-292-1711	R	160 *	0.7
Ben Arnold-Heritage Beverage	PO Box 487	Columbia	SC	29202	Harvey Belson	803-251-3456	R	150	0.3
Universal Brands Inc.	3325 NW 70th Ave	Miami	FL	33122	Douglas Hrdlicka	305-591-9800	R	150	0.5
Barton Inc.	55 E Monroe St	Chicago	IL	60603	Ellis M Goodman	312-346-9200	S	140 *	0.5
Gambrinus Co.	14800 San Pedro	San Antonio	TX	78232	Carlos Alvarez	210-490-9128	R	125	<0.1
Atlanta Beverage Co.	PO Box 44008	Atlanta	GA	30336	C Mark Pirrung	404-699-6700	R	120 *	0.4
Columbia Distributing Co.	PO Box 17195	Portland	OR	97217	Edward L Maletis	503-289-9600	R	110 *	0.4
Wayne Densch Inc.	75 W Holden Ave	Orlando	FL	32839	Leonard Williams	407-851-7100	R	100 *	0.3
Zeb Pearce Cos.	PO Box 1239	Mesa	AZ	85211	Art Pearce	602-834-5527	R	98 *	0.3
Odom Corp.	PO Box 24627	Seattle	WA	98124	John P Odom	206-623-3256	R	93 *	0.3
United Distillers North America	6 Landmark Sq	Stamford	CT	06901	Walter Caldwell	203-359-7100	S	93	1.3
Whitehall Company Ltd.	750 Everett St	Norwood	MA	02062	Marvin A Gordon	617-769-6500	R	93	0.3
Mounthood Beverage Co.	3601 NW Yeon Ave	Portland	OR	97210	Richard Lytle	503-274-9990	R	90	0.4
Wirtz Corp.	680 N Lkshore Dr	Chicago	IL	60611	William Wirtz	312-943-7000	R	90 *	0.3
Hensley and Co.	4201 N 45th Ave	Phoenix	AZ	85031	Robert Delgado	602-264-1635	R	81	0.4
A. Levy and J. Zentner Co.	PO Box 292307	Sacramento	CA	95829	GN Thomas	916-381-7100	R	80 *	0.8
Halo Distributing Co.	PO Box 7370	San Antonio	TX	78207	Dennis O'Malley	210-735-1111	R	76 *	0.2
East Side Beverage Co.	1260 Grey Fox Rd	Arden Hills	MN	55112	Todd Knipping	612-482-1133	R	75	0.1
General Wholesale Co.	1271-A Tacoma Dr	Atlanta	GA	30318	William D Young Sr	404-351-3626	R	70	0.3
Coast Distributing Co.	PO Box 80758	San Diego	CA	92138	Roy D Clark	619-275-4600	R	66 *	0.2
D. Canale Beverages Inc.	45 Eh Crump W	Memphis	TN	38106	Chris W Canale	901-948-4543	R	66 *	0.2
Powers Distributing Company	2000 Pontiac Dr	Sylvan Lake	MI	48320	Jerry Powers	810-682-2010	R	66 *	0.2
R.H. Barringer Distributing	1620 Fairfax Rd	Greensboro	NC	27407	Mark Craig	910-854-0555	R	66 *	0.2
Clare Rose Inc.	72 West Ave	Patchogue	NY	11772	F Rose	516-475-1840	R	63	<0.1
B. Olinde and Sons Company	9536 Airline Hwy	Baton Rouge	LA	70815	JB Olinde	504-926-3380	R	60 *	0.2
Heineken USA Inc.	50 Main St	White Plains	NY	10606	Michael Foley	914-681-4100	S	60	0.2
Pacific Beverage Company Inc.	5305 Ekwill St	Santa Barbara	CA	93111	PC Jordano	805-964-0611	S	60	0.2
Willow Distributors Inc.	PO Box 153169	Dallas	TX	75315	Dennis Nausler	214-426-5636	R	60 *	0.2
Better Brands of Atlanta Inc.	755 NW Jefferson	Atlanta	GA	30377	Bob Bailey	404-872-4731	R	55 *	0.3
Budco of San Antonio Inc.	PO Box 937	San Antonio	TX	78294	Berkley V Dawson	210-225-3044	R	55 *	0.2
Grey Eagle Distributors Inc.	2340 Millpark Dr	Maryland H.	MO	63043	Jerry Clinton	314-429-9100	R	55 *	0.2
Miller of Dallas Inc.	2730 Irving Blvd	Dallas	TX	75207	Barry Andrews	214-630-0777	R	55 *	0.2
Grantham Distributing	2685 Hansrob Rd	Orlando	FL	32804	Varley Grantham	407-299-6446	R	54 *	0.1
Molson Breweries U.S.A. Inc.	11911 Freedom Dr	Reston	VA	20190	J J Carefoote	703-709-6600	S	54 *	0.2
General Distributing Co.	PO Box 16070	Salt Lake City	UT	84116	RE Avery	801-531-7895	R	51 *	<0.1
Star Distributors Inc.	PO Box 1200	New Haven	CT	06505	Anthony J Gallo	203-932-3636	R	50	0.2
Clement and Muller Inc.	2800 Grand Ave	Philadelphia	PA	19114	C John Muller	215-676-7575	R	46 *	0.2
Anthony Distributors Inc.	2900 E 7th Ave	Tampa	FL	33605	Sal Italiano	813-247-4000	R	45 *	0.2

Source: *Ward's Business Directory of U.S. Private and Public Companies*, 1998. The company type code used is as follows: P - Public, R - Private, S - Subsidiary, D - Division, J - Joint Venture, A - Affiliate, G - Group. Sales are in millions of dollars, employees are in thousands. An asterisk (*) indicates an estimated sales volume. The symbol < stands for 'less than'.

OCCUPATIONS EMPLOYED BY SIC 518 - WHOLESALE TRADE, OTHER

Occupation	% of Total 1996	Change to 2006	Occupation	% of Total 1996	Change to 2006
Sales & related workers nec	19.5	20.2	Clerical supervisors & managers	1.9	20.2
General managers & top executives	5.9	16.4	Order clerks	1.9	8.2
Truck drivers light & heavy	5.4	20.2	Helpers, laborers nec	1.7	20.2
General office clerks	3.6	3.4	Electrical & electronic technicians	1.4	18.8
Traffic, shipping, receiving clerks	3.6	16.7	Blue collar worker supervisors	1.4	16.0
Stock clerks	3.5	-3.9	Wholesale & retail buyers, except farm products	1.3	17.0
Freight, stock, & material movers, hand	3.3	8.2	Office machine & cash register servicers	1.3	20.2
Marketing & sales worker supervisors	3.1	20.2	Hand packers & packagers	1.2	-3.9
Order fillers, wholesale & retail sales	3.0	16.7	Maintenance repairers, general utility	1.1	12.0
Bookkeeping, accounting, & auditing clerks	2.9	-3.9	Industrial truck & tractor operators	1.1	20.2
Salespersons, retail	2.5	20.2	Purchasing managers	1.1	20.2
Secretaries, except legal & medical	2.5	-4.7	Receptionists & information clerks	1.0	20.2
Assemblers, fabricators, hand workers nec	2.0	-3.9			

Source: *Industry-Occupation Matrix*, Bureau of Labor Statistics. These data relate to one or more 3-digit SIC industry groups rather than to a single 4-digit SIC. The change reported for each occupation to the year 2006 is a percent of growth or decline as estimated by the Bureau of Labor Statistics. The abbreviation nec stands for 'not elsewhere classified'.

STATE AND REGIONAL CONCENTRATION

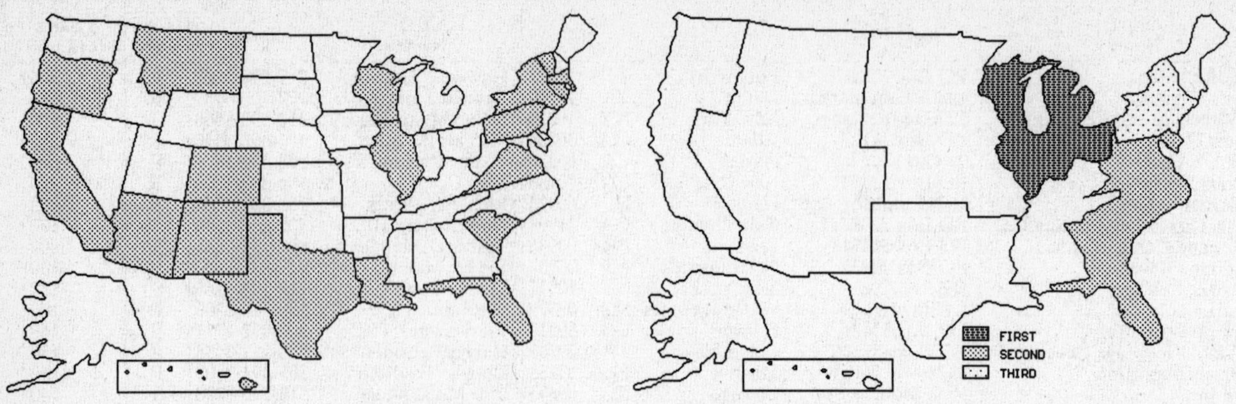

INDUSTRY DATA BY STATE

State	Establishments - 1995 Total (number)	Establishments - 1995 % of U.S.	Employment - 1995 Total (number)	Employment - 1995 % of U.S.	Employment - 1995 Per Estab.	Payroll - 1995 Total ($ mil.)	Payroll - 1995 Per Empl. ($)	Sales - 1992 Total ($ mil.)	Sales - 1992 % of U.S.	Sales - 1992 Per Estab ($)
California	183	5.9	9,697	10.4	53	319.1	32,903	3,692.9	12.5	386,932
New York	264	8.5	5,958	6.4	23	194.5	32,644	2,732.4	9.3	465,884
Texas	215	6.9	8,156	8.7	38	266.4	32,657	2,423.1	8.2	312,582
Florida	84	2.7	5,376	5.8	64	174.7	32,495	1,750.3	5.9	351,684
Pennsylvania	355	11.4	4,157	4.5	12	125.9	30,281	1,476.4	5.0	369,480
Illinois	147	4.7	3,900	4.2	27	137.6	35,283	1,389.3	4.7	362,747
Wisconsin	114	3.7	2,516	2.7	22	82.3	32,703	1,295.7	4.4	541,435
Ohio	97	3.1	3,991	4.3	41	132.3	33,139	1,201.1	4.1	319,097
Michigan	104	3.3	3,910	4.2	38	140.2	35,848	1,023.0	3.5	276,867
Virginia	71	2.3	2,827	3.0	40	88.9	31,454	911.7	3.1	346,904
New Jersey	34	1.1	2,226	2.4	65	96.2	43,227	759.8	2.6	398,647
Massachusetts	33	1.1	2,330	2.5	71	92.9	39,870	757.8	2.6	405,245
North Carolina	68	2.2	2,728	2.9	40	75.9	27,837	757.1	2.6	309,887
Georgia	54	1.7	2,544	2.7	47	82.0	32,247	727.8	2.5	299,643
Connecticut	25	0.8	1,308	1.4	52	64.3	49,196	639.9	2.2	557,922
Washington	75	2.4	2,404	2.6	32	73.5	30,562	594.6	2.0	261,367
Missouri	76	2.4	1,821	2.0	24	65.1	35,752	569.4	1.9	297,646
Louisiana	51	1.6	2,052	2.2	40	48.5	23,639	544.5	1.8	274,722
Indiana	64	2.0	1,637	1.8	26	43.3	26,478	529.8	1.8	356,313
Tennessee	35	1.1	1,837	2.0	52	64.3	35,022	513.7	1.7	296,259
Maryland	44	1.4	1,360	1.5	31	47.6	35,023	500.1	1.7	332,983
Arizona	29	0.9	1,552	1.7	54	54.1	34,868	493.1	1.7	368,780
Alabama	45	1.4	1,837	2.0	41	47.5	25,842	476.5	1.6	267,843
South Carolina	42	1.3	1,389	1.5	33	45.4	32,716	469.1	1.6	350,594
Colorado	47	1.5	1,327	1.4	28	43.6	32,864	415.0	1.4	317,740
Oregon	65	2.1	1,530	1.6	24	44.6	29,150	375.3	1.3	264,076
Oklahoma	53	1.7	1,011	1.1	19	28.2	27,849	298.9	1.0	301,305
Iowa	64	2.0	1,239	1.3	19	34.7	28,037	297.6	1.0	239,196
Kentucky	41	1.3	876	0.9	21	30.1	34,416	271.4	0.9	354,296
Kansas	41	1.3	901	1.0	22	27.9	30,952	253.4	0.9	298,138
Hawaii	12	0.4	500-999	-	-	(D)	-	253.2	0.9	457,857
Arkansas	37	1.2	714	0.8	19	22.8	31,912	221.6	0.8	305,271
New Mexico	25	0.8	607	0.7	24	18.1	29,783	216.0	0.7	399,224
West Virginia	41	1.3	716	0.8	17	23.7	33,084	189.1	0.6	271,248
Montana	34	1.1	600	0.6	18	15.2	25,307	124.5	0.4	211,078
Idaho	33	1.1	542	0.6	16	14.5	26,806	116.4	0.4	226,377
Vermont	9	0.3	250-499	-	-	(D)	-	101.0	0.3	215,258
D.C.	6	0.2	221	0.2	37	7.7	34,769	80.3	0.3	305,437
South Dakota	19	0.6	268	0.3	14	8.2	30,750	73.3	0.2	306,778
Minnesota	81	2.6	1,283	1.4	16	43.7	34,072	(D)	-	-
Mississippi	52	1.7	1,377	1.5	26	34.4	25,001	(D)	-	-
Nebraska	36	1.2	561	0.6	16	18.6	33,178	(D)	-	-
Wyoming	26	0.8	100-249	-	-	(D)	-	(D)	-	-
North Dakota	24	0.8	250-499	-	-	(D)	-	(D)	-	-
Utah	17	0.5	549	0.6	32	14.6	26,672	(D)	-	-
Nevada	13	0.4	569	0.6	44	21.2	37,223	(D)	-	-
New Hampshire	12	0.4	593	0.6	49	22.4	37,845	(D)	-	-
Maine	11	0.4	500-999	-	-	(D)	-	(D)	-	-
Alaska	7	0.2	100-249	-	-	(D)	-	(D)	-	-
Rhode Island	5	0.2	237	0.3	47	10.4	44,038	(D)	-	-
Delaware	3	0.1	250-499	-	-	(D)	-	(D)	-	-

Source: *County Business Patterns, 1995* and *Economic Census of the U.S., 1992.* Data are sorted by 1992 revenues and, if revenues are unavailable, by establishments in 1995. The symbol (D) indicates that data are withheld by the source to avoid disclosure of competitive information. A dash (-) indicates that data are not available or undisclosed because they do not meet statistical validity standards. Shaded *states* on the state map indicate those states which have proportionately greater representation in the industry than would be indicated by the state's population; the ratio is based on total revenues or number of establishments. Shaded *regions* indicate where the industry is regionally most concentrated.

5182 - WINE AND DISTILLED BEVERAGES

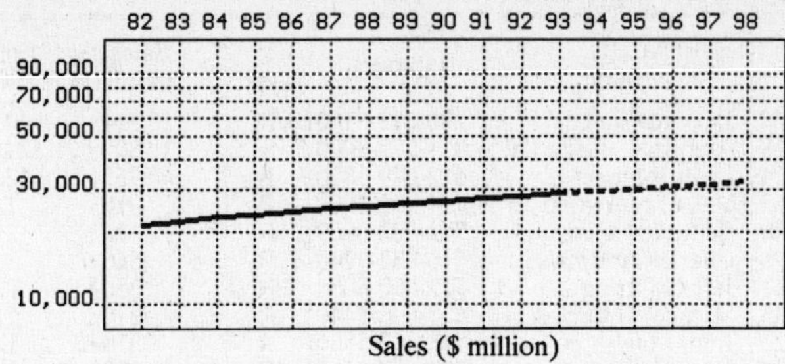

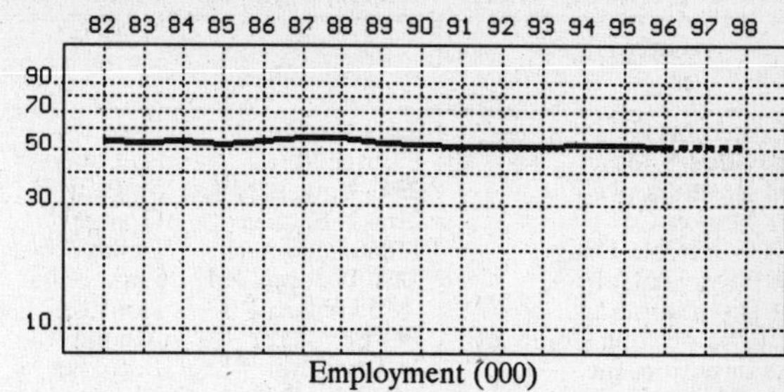

GENERAL STATISTICS

Year	Establishments (number)	Employment (number)	Payroll ($ million)	Sales ($ million)	Expenses ($ million)	Beginning Inventory ($ million)	Ending Inventory ($ million)
1982	1,958	53,738	1,233.0	21,300.5	-	-	-
1983	1,806	53,194	1,295.7	22,069.3e	-	-	-
1984	1,721	53,637	1,359.6	22,838.2e	-	-	-
1985	1,797	52,618	1,362.7	23,607.0e	-	-	-
1986	1,744	53,913	1,418.6	24,375.8e	-	-	-
1987	1,901	55,719	1,534.7	25,144.6	3,602.9	2,302.4	2,419.5
1988	1,801	55,706	1,630.3	25,692.5e	3,631.3e	2,381.8e	2,494.2e
1989	1,697	52,946	1,618.6	26,240.4e	3,659.7e	2,461.3e	2,568.9e
1990	1,653	51,782	1,692.8	26,788.3e	3,688.0e	2,540.7e	2,643.6e
1991	1,596	51,182	1,739.9	27,336.2e	3,716.4e	2,620.2e	2,718.3e
1992	1,856	50,735	1,817.8	27,884.1	3,744.8	2,699.6	2,792.9
1993	1,757	51,027	1,904.2	28,793.5p	3,773.2p	2,779.1p	2,867.6p
1994	1,779	51,684	1,947.3	29,451.9p	3,801.5p	2,858.5p	2,942.3p
1995	1,783	52,481	2,043.9	30,110.2p	3,829.9p	2,937.9p	3,017.0p
1996	1,719p	51,270p	2,073.5p	30,768.6p	3,858.3p	3,017.4p	3,091.7p
1997	1,711p	51,055p	2,134.8p	31,426.9p	3,886.7p	3,096.8p	3,166.4p
1998	1,703p	50,840p	2,196.0p	32,085.3p	3,915.0p	3,176.3p	3,241.1p

Sources: *Economic Census of the United States*, 1982, 1987, and 1992. Establishment counts, employment, and payroll are from *County Business Patterns* for non-Census years. Values followed by a 'p' are projections by the editors. Sales and expense data for non-Census years are extrapolations, marked by 'e'. Industries reclassified in 1987 will not have data for prior years. Data are the most recent available at this level of detail.

INDICES OF CHANGE

Year	Establishments (number)	Employment (number)	Payroll ($ million)	Sales ($ million)	Expenses ($ million)	Beginning Inventory ($ million)	Ending Inventory ($ million)
1982	105.5	105.9	67.8	76.4	-	-	-
1983	97.3	104.8	71.3	79.1e	-	-	-
1984	92.7	105.7	74.8	81.9e	-	-	-
1985	96.8	103.7	75.0	84.7e	-	-	-
1986	94.0	106.3	78.0	87.4e	-	-	-
1987	102.4	109.8	84.4	90.2	96.2	85.3	86.6
1988	97.0	109.8	89.7	92.1e	97.0e	88.2e	89.3e
1989	91.4	104.4	89.0	94.1e	97.7e	91.2e	92.0e
1990	89.1	102.1	93.1	96.1e	98.5e	94.1e	94.7e
1991	86.0	100.9	95.7	98.0e	99.2e	97.1e	97.3e
1992	100.0	100.0	100.0	100.0	100.0	100.0	100.0
1993	94.7	100.6	104.8	103.3p	100.8p	102.9p	102.7p
1994	95.9	101.9	107.1	105.6p	101.5p	105.9p	105.3p
1995	96.1	103.4	112.4	108.0p	102.3p	108.8p	108.0p
1996	92.6p	101.1p	114.1p	110.3p	103.0p	111.8p	110.7p
1997	92.2p	100.6p	117.4p	112.7p	103.8p	114.7p	113.4p
1998	91.8p	100.2p	120.8p	115.1p	104.5p	117.7p	116.0p

Sources: Same as General Statistics. The values shown reflect change from the base year, 1992. Values above 100 mean greater than 1992, values below 100 mean less than 1992, and a value of 100 in the 1982-91 or 1993-98 period means same as 1992. Values followed by a 'p' are projections by the editors; 'e' stands for extrapolation. Data are the most recent available at this level of detail.

SELECTED RATIOS

For 1992	Avg. of All Wholesale	Analyzed Industry	Index	For 1992	Avg. of All Wholesale	Analyzed Industry	Index
Employees per Establishment	12	27	234	Sales per Employee	561,172	549,603	98
Payroll per Establishment	349,729	979,418	280	Sales per Establishment	6,559,346	15,023,761	229
Payroll per Employee	29,919	35,829	120	Expenses per Establishment	723,071	2,017,672	279

Sources: Same as General Statistics. The 'Average of All Manufacturing' column represents the average of all manufacturing industries reported for the most recent complete year available. The Index shows the relationship between the Average and the Analyzed Industry. For example, 100 means that they are equal; 500 that the Analyzed Industry is five times the average; 50 means that the Analyzed Industry is half the national average. The abbreviation 'na' is used to show that data are 'not available'.

LEADING COMPANIES

Number shown: **50** Total sales ($ mil): **42,902** Total employment (000): **98.7**

Company Name	Address				CEO Name	Phone	Co. Type	Sales ($ mil)	Empl. (000)
Price/Costco Inc.	999 Lake Dr	Issaquah	WA	98027	James D Sinegal	206-313-8100	P	19,214	40.0
Anheuser-Busch Inc.	1 Busch Pl	St. Louis	MO	63118	August A Busch III	314-577-2000	S	12,800	24.3
Johnson Brothers	2341 University Ave	St. Paul	MN	55114	Lynn Johnson	612-649-5800	R	3,750 *	12.0
Young's Market Co.	2164 N Batavia	Orange	CA	92865	V O Underwood Jr	714-283-4933	R	910	1.5
Glazer's Wholesale Drug	14860 Landmark	Dallas	TX	75240	Bennett J Glazer	972-702-0900	R	686 *	2.2
Sunbelt Beverage Corp.	2330 W Joppa Rd	Lutherville	MD	21093	Charles Andrews	410-832-7740	R	560 *	1.8
Tarrant Distributors Inc.	9835 Genard Rd	Houston	TX	77041	Jeff Goldring	713-690-8888	R	356 *	0.8
National Distributing Company	PO Box 44127	Atlanta	GA	30336	Michael C Carlos	404-696-9440	R	310 *	1.0
Peerless Importers Inc.	16 Bridgewater St	Brooklyn	NY	11222	John Magliocco	718-383-5500	R	310 *	1.0
Magnolia Marketing Co.	PO Box 53333	New Orleans	LA	70153	Tom Cole	504-837-1500	R	290	1.0
Georgia Crown Distributing Co.	PO Box 7908	Columbus	GA	31908	Don Leebern III	706-568-4580	R	200 *	0.7
Mendez and Company Inc.	PO Box 363348	San Juan	PR	00936	S Alvarez-Mendez	809-793-8888	R	200	0.3
United Liquors Ltd.	1 United Dr	W. Bridgewater	MA	02379	A Raymond Tye	508-588-2300	R	180 *	0.6
National Wine and Spirits Corp.	PO Box 1602	Indianapolis	IN	46206	James Beck	317-636-6092	R	168	0.5
Reitman Industries	10 Patton Dr	West Caldwell	NJ	07006	Howard Jacobs	201-228-5100	R	164	0.3
Continental Distributing	9800 W Balmoral	Rosemont	IL	60018	Fred Cooper	847-671-7700	R	160	0.4
Western Distributing Co.	PO Box 5542	Denver	CO	80217	Vieri Gaines	303-292-1711	R	160 *	0.7
Ben Arnold-Heritage Beverage	PO Box 487	Columbia	SC	29202	Harvey Belson	803-251-3456	R	150	0.3
Block Distributing Company	PO Box 8157	San Antonio	TX	78208	Eddie Block	210-224-7531	R	150 *	0.3
Fedway Associates Inc.	PO Box 519	Kearny	NJ	07032	Richard Leventhal	973-624-6444	R	150	0.5
Jaydor Corp.	16 Bleeker St	Millburn	NJ	07041	M. D Silverman	201-379-1234	R	140	0.4
Columbia Distributing Co.	PO Box 17195	Portland	OR	97217	Edward L Maletis	503-289-9600	R	110 *	0.4
Olinger Distributing Co.	5337 W 78th St	Indianapolis	IN	46268	Ray Dorulla	317-876-1188	R	100 *	0.4
Odom Corp.	PO Box 24627	Seattle	WA	98124	John P Odom	206-623-3256	R	93 *	0.3
United Distillers North America	6 Landmark Sq	Stamford	CT	06901	Walter Caldwell	203-359-7100	S	93	1.3
Whitehall Company Ltd.	750 Everett St	Norwood	MA	02062	Marvin A Gordon	617-769-6500	R	93	0.3
Mounthood Beverage Co.	3601 NW Yeon Ave	Portland	OR	97210	Richard Lytle	503-274-9990	R	90	0.4
Wirtz Corp.	680 N Lkshore Dr	Chicago	IL	60611	William Wirtz	312-943-7000	R	90 *	0.3
A. Levy and J. Zentner Co.	PO Box 292307	Sacramento	CA	95829	GN Thomas	916-381-7100	R	80 *	0.8
F. Korbel and Bros. Inc.	13250 River Rd	Guerneville	CA	95446	Gary B Heck	707-887-2294	R	80	0.3
G. Raden and Sons Inc.	18289 Olympic S	Seattle	WA	98188	Gary Raden	206-251-9300	R	78 *	0.3
General Wholesale Co.	1271-A Tacoma Dr	Atlanta	GA	30318	William D Young Sr	404-351-3626	R	70	0.3
Castleton Beverage Corp.	PO Box 26368	Jacksonville	FL	32226	Felipe T Lopez	904-757-1290	S	69 *	0.2
D. Canale Beverages Inc.	45 Eh Crump W	Memphis	TN	38106	Chris W Canale	901-948-4543	R	66 *	0.2
Eber Brothers Wine and Liquor	3200 Monroe Ave	Rochester	NY	14618	Lester Eber	716-586-7700	R	62 *	0.6
Quality Brands Inc.	226 Dover Rd	Glen Burnie	MD	21060	Herbert S Kasoff	410-787-5656	R	60	0.2
Better Brands of Atlanta Inc.	755 NW Jefferson	Atlanta	GA	30377	Bob Bailey	404-872-4731	R	55 *	0.3
Grantham Distributing	2685 Hansrob Rd	Orlando	FL	32804	Varley Grantham	407-299-6446	R	54 *	0.1
Badger Liquor Company Inc.	850 S Morris St	Fond du Lac	WI	54936	Gary Sadoff	920-922-0550	R	54	0.2
Austin Nichols and Company	156 East 46th St	New York	NY	10017	M Bord	212-455-9400	S	50 *	0.2
Edison Liquor Corp.	PO Box 609	Brookfield	WI	53008	Richard Deutsch	414-821-0600	S	50 *	0.1
Phillips Products Co.	PO Box 1185	Minneapolis	MN	55440	Steve Gill	612-623-1688	S	50	<0.1
J.W. Costello Beverage Co.	PO Box 95007	Las Vegas	NV	89193	JW Costello	702-876-4000	R	46 *	0.2
Remy Amerique Inc.	1350 of the Amer	New York	NY	10019	Herve Zeller	212-399-0200	R	46 *	0.2
Merrimack Valley Distributing	PO Box 417	Danvers	MA	01923	Richard Tatelman	508-777-2213	R	45	0.1
N.K.S. Distributors Inc.	PO Box 758	New Castle	DE	19720	James V Tigani Jr	302-322-1811	R	45 *	0.2
Standard Beverage Corp.	PO Box 968	Wichita	KS	67201	L Rudd	316-838-7707	R	45	0.1
Manhattan Distributing Co.	11675 Fairgrove	Maryland H.	MO	63043	Nolan Crane	314-567-1400	R	42 *	0.1
De Luca Liquor and Wine Ltd.	2548 W Desert Inn	Las Vegas	NV	89109	Ray Norvell	702-735-9144	S	41 *	0.2
Milton S. Kronheim and Co.	2900 V St NE	Washington	DC	20018	M E Margolies	202-526-8000	R	38	<0.1

Source: *Ward's Business Directory of U.S. Private and Public Companies*, 1998. The company type code used is as follows: P - Public, R - Private, S - Subsidiary, D - Division, J - Joint Venture, A - Affiliate, G - Group. Sales are in millions of dollars, employees are in thousands. An asterisk (*) indicates an estimated sales volume. The symbol < stands for 'less than'.

OCCUPATIONS EMPLOYED BY SIC 518 - WHOLESALE TRADE, OTHER

Occupation	% of Total 1996	Change to 2006	Occupation	% of Total 1996	Change to 2006
Sales & related workers nec	19.5	20.2	Clerical supervisors & managers	1.9	20.2
General managers & top executives	5.9	16.4	Order clerks	1.9	8.2
Truck drivers light & heavy	5.4	20.2	Helpers, laborers nec	1.7	20.2
General office clerks	3.6	3.4	Electrical & electronic technicians	1.4	18.8
Traffic, shipping, receiving clerks	3.6	16.7	Blue collar worker supervisors	1.4	16.0
Stock clerks	3.5	-3.9	Wholesale & retail buyers, except farm products	1.3	17.0
Freight, stock, & material movers, hand	3.3	8.2	Office machine & cash register servicers	1.3	20.2
Marketing & sales worker supervisors	3.1	20.2	Hand packers & packagers	1.2	-3.9
Order fillers, wholesale & retail sales	3.0	16.7	Maintenance repairers, general utility	1.1	12.0
Bookkeeping, accounting, & auditing clerks	2.9	-3.9	Industrial truck & tractor operators	1.1	20.2
Salespersons, retail	2.5	20.2	Purchasing managers	1.1	20.2
Secretaries, except legal & medical	2.5	-4.7	Receptionists & information clerks	1.0	20.2
Assemblers, fabricators, hand workers nec	2.0	-3.9			

Source: *Industry-Occupation Matrix*, Bureau of Labor Statistics. These data relate to one or more 3-digit SIC industry groups rather than to a single 4-digit SIC. The change reported for each occupation to the year 2006 is a percent of growth or decline as estimated by the Bureau of Labor Statistics. The abbreviation nec stands for 'not elsewhere classified'.

STATE AND REGIONAL CONCENTRATION

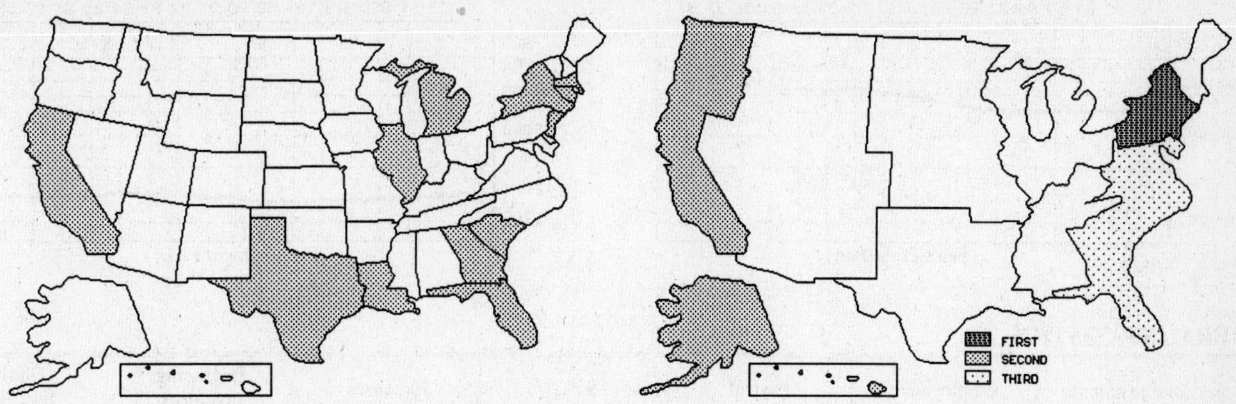

INDUSTRY DATA BY STATE

State	Establishments - 1995 Total (number)	Establishments - 1995 % of U.S.	Employment - 1995 Total (number)	Employment - 1995 % of U.S.	Employment - 1995 Per Estab.	Payroll - 1995 Total ($ mil.)	Payroll - 1995 Per Empl. ($)	Sales - 1992 Total ($ mil.)	Sales - 1992 % of U.S.	Sales - 1992 Per Estab ($)
California	262	14.7	7,187	13.9	27	317.4	44,157	4,684.9	17.6	618,547
New York	132	7.4	5,373	10.4	41	266.6	49,610	3,200.2	12.1	610,373
Florida	91	5.1	3,921	7.6	43	162.8	41,511	2,234.1	8.4	635,766
Texas	88	4.9	3,210	6.2	36	120.3	37,484	2,215.1	8.3	610,726
New Jersey	77	4.3	2,435	4.7	32	107.5	44,154	1,860.3	7.0	828,648
Illinois	84	4.7	3,180	6.1	38	124.5	39,164	1,660.2	6.3	568,564
Georgia	55	3.1	1,864	3.6	34	69.7	37,384	1,090.8	4.1	719,980
Michigan	110	6.2	1,752	3.4	16	68.2	38,917	998.9	3.8	620,071
Connecticut	32	1.8	1,369	2.6	43	70.0	51,146	880.3	3.3	565,393
Massachusetts	49	2.7	1,566	3.0	32	61.7	39,397	713.5	2.7	508,163
Ohio	56	3.1	1,168	2.3	21	33.5	28,716	591.2	2.2	447,846
Louisiana	32	1.8	1,390	2.7	43	38.6	27,794	489.2	1.8	396,455
Maryland	28	1.6	1,210	2.3	43	48.1	39,723	485.3	1.8	410,589
Indiana	19	1.1	919	1.8	48	31.0	33,751	431.7	1.6	377,696
Wisconsin	35	2.0	1,236	2.4	35	41.1	33,234	402.9	1.5	347,287
South Carolina	26	1.5	862	1.7	33	23.6	27,326	391.1	1.5	411,282
Pennsylvania	62	3.5	540	1.0	9	17.5	32,424	374.9	1.4	762,014
Colorado	30	1.7	940	1.8	31	36.2	38,459	358.8	1.4	433,364
Arizona	21	1.2	920	1.8	44	31.6	34,371	345.5	1.3	458,862
Missouri	27	1.5	923	1.8	34	35.4	38,309	344.1	1.3	372,028
Tennessee	23	1.3	741	1.4	32	28.5	38,402	340.8	1.3	458,678
Washington	51	2.9	1,034	2.0	20	37.1	35,900	318.6	1.2	372,171
North Carolina	53	3.0	1,085	2.1	20	29.3	26,962	316.8	1.2	353,125
Kentucky	31	1.7	597	1.2	19	18.8	31,506	247.9	0.9	437,995
Virginia	38	2.1	980	1.9	26	30.5	31,171	230.3	0.9	279,522
Oklahoma	15	0.8	266	0.5	18	6.5	24,609	224.4	0.8	782,049
Alabama	25	1.4	399	0.8	16	9.9	24,885	181.4	0.7	450,186
D.C.	8	0.4	366	0.7	46	14.1	38,495	151.1	0.6	452,338
Iowa	22	1.2	225	0.4	10	4.8	21,511	139.1	0.5	562,988
New Mexico	14	0.8	411	0.8	29	11.8	28,779	118.1	0.4	288,105
Arkansas	9	0.5	272	0.5	30	8.7	32,158	117.0	0.4	412,056
Kansas	15	0.8	386	0.7	26	10.3	26,591	108.9	0.4	268,342
Hawaii	18	1.0	250-499	-	-	(D)	-	95.4	0.4	387,890
Oregon	32	1.8	490	0.9	15	13.5	27,549	90.4	0.3	262,898
South Dakota	6	0.3	132	0.3	22	4.0	30,462	41.4	0.2	328,595
Idaho	14	0.8	170	0.3	12	4.4	25,947	30.0	0.1	285,419
Vermont	5	0.3	20-99	-	-	(D)	-	28.2	0.1	564,440
West Virginia	7	0.4	46	0.1	7	0.7	14,435	7.2	0.0	131,382
Montana	4	0.2	38	0.1	10	0.6	14,842	4.2	0.0	156,407
Minnesota	22	1.2	853	1.6	39	29.0	33,992	(D)	-	-
New Hampshire	9	0.5	78	0.2	9	2.7	34,821	(D)	-	-
Nevada	7	0.4	666	1.3	95	31.7	47,554	(D)	-	-
Rhode Island	7	0.4	180	0.3	26	6.9	38,467	(D)	-	-
Delaware	6	0.3	100-249	-	-	(D)	-	(D)	-	-
Nebraska	6	0.3	260	0.5	43	7.9	30,554	(D)	-	-
North Dakota	5	0.3	100-249	-	-	(D)	-	(D)	-	-
Mississippi	4	0.2	139	0.3	35	3.0	21,496	(D)	-	-
Utah	4	0.2	14	0.0	4	0.3	19,857	(D)	-	-
Alaska	3	0.2	20-99	-	-	(D)	-	(D)	-	-
Maine	2	0.1	0-19	-	-	(D)	-	(D)	-	-
Wyoming	2	0.1	0-19	-	-	(D)	-	(D)	-	-

Source: *County Business Patterns, 1995* and *Economic Census of the U.S., 1992*. Data are sorted by 1992 revenues and, if revenues are unavailable, by establishments in 1995. The symbol (D) indicates that data are withheld by the source to avoid disclosure of competitive information. A dash (-) indicates that data are not available or undisclosed because they do not meet statistical validity standards. Shaded *states* on the state map indicate those states which have proportionately greater representation in the industry than would be indicated by the state's population; the ratio is based on total revenues or number of establishments. Shaded *regions* indicate where the industry is regionally most concentrated.

5191 - FARM SUPPLIES

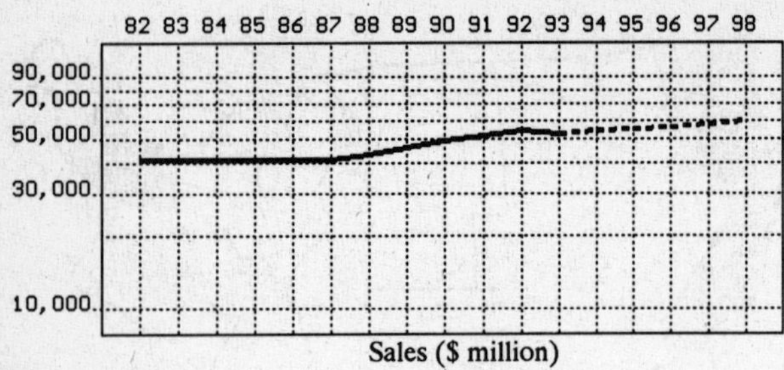

Sales ($ million)

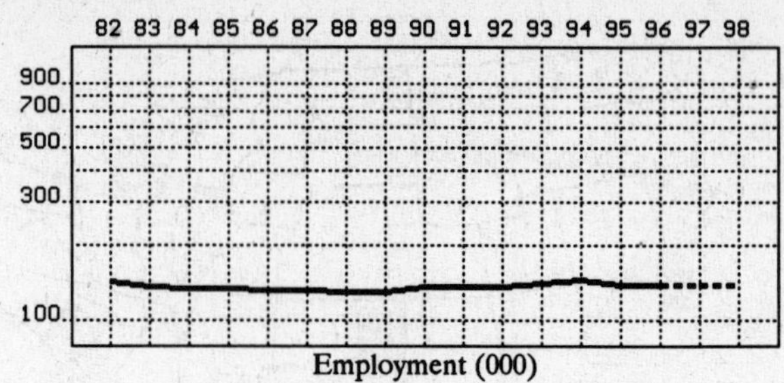

Employment (000)

GENERAL STATISTICS

Year	Establishments (number)	Employment (number)	Payroll ($ million)	Sales ($ million)	Expenses ($ million)	Beginning Inventory ($ million)	Ending Inventory ($ million)
1982	18,927	142,975	2,165.1	40,896.3	-	-	-
1983	18,886	137,457	2,149.8	40,871.9*e*	-	-	-
1984	17,759	134,669	2,239.3	40,847.5*e*	-	-	-
1985	17,114	134,304	2,296.2	40,823.2*e*	-	-	-
1986	16,635	131,025	2,311.4	40,798.8*e*	-	-	-
1987	18,321	131,146	2,371.1	40,774.4	5,533.3	3,445.5	3,592.4
1988	17,081	130,484	2,509.3	43,489.8*e*	5,875.7*e*	3,753.8*e*	3,892.0*e*
1989	16,501	130,181	2,594.5	46,205.1*e*	6,218.1*e*	4,062.1*e*	4,191.7*e*
1990	16,391	136,212	2,814.0	48,920.5*e*	6,560.5*e*	4,370.3*e*	4,491.3*e*
1991	16,268	136,182	2,888.0	51,635.8*e*	6,902.9*e*	4,678.6*e*	4,790.9*e*
1992	17,469	137,387	3,102.0	54,351.1	7,245.3	4,986.8	5,090.5
1993	17,078	140,936	3,232.7	52,583.3*p*	7,587.7*p*	5,295.1*p*	5,390.2*p*
1994	16,835	145,383	3,498.2	53,928.8*p*	7,930.1*p*	5,603.3*p*	5,689.8*p*
1995	15,792	139,460	3,473.7	55,274.3*p*	8,272.5*p*	5,911.6*p*	5,989.4*p*
1996	15,979*p*	138,911*p*	3,525.0*p*	56,619.8*p*	8,614.9*p*	6,219.9*p*	6,289.0*p*
1997	15,814*p*	139,263*p*	3,636.5*p*	57,965.3*p*	8,957.3*p*	6,528.1*p*	6,588.7*p*
1998	15,649*p*	139,615*p*	3,748.0*p*	59,310.8*p*	9,299.7*p*	6,836.4*p*	6,888.3*p*

Sources: *Economic Census of the United States*, 1982, 1987, and 1992. Establishment counts, employment, and payroll are from *County Business Patterns* for non-Census years. Values followed by a 'p' are projections by the editors. Sales and expense data for non-Census years are extrapolations, marked by 'e'. Industries reclassified in 1987 will not have data for prior years. Data are the most recent available at this level of detail.

INDICES OF CHANGE

Year	Establishments (number)	Employment (number)	Payroll ($ million)	Sales ($ million)	Expenses ($ million)	Beginning Inventory ($ million)	Ending Inventory ($ million)
1982	108.3	104.1	69.8	75.2	-	-	-
1983	108.1	100.1	69.3	75.2*e*	-	-	-
1984	101.7	98.0	72.2	75.2*e*	-	-	-
1985	98.0	97.8	74.0	75.1*e*	-	-	-
1986	95.2	95.4	74.5	75.1*e*	-	-	-
1987	104.9	95.5	76.4	75.0	76.4	69.1	70.6
1988	97.8	95.0	80.9	80.0*e*	81.1*e*	75.3*e*	76.5*e*
1989	94.5	94.8	83.6	85.0*e*	85.8*e*	81.5*e*	82.3*e*
1990	93.8	99.1	90.7	90.0*e*	90.5*e*	87.6*e*	88.2*e*
1991	93.1	99.1	93.1	95.0*e*	95.3*e*	93.8*e*	94.1*e*
1992	100.0	100.0	100.0	100.0	100.0	100.0	100.0
1993	97.8	102.6	104.2	96.7*p*	104.7*p*	106.2*p*	105.9*p*
1994	96.4	105.8	112.8	99.2*p*	109.5*p*	112.4*p*	111.8*p*
1995	90.4	101.5	112.0	101.7*p*	114.2*p*	118.5*p*	117.7*p*
1996	91.5*p*	101.1*p*	113.6*p*	104.2*p*	118.9*p*	124.7*p*	123.5*p*
1997	90.5*p*	101.4*p*	117.2*p*	106.6*p*	123.6*p*	130.9*p*	129.4*p*
1998	89.6*p*	101.6*p*	120.8*p*	109.1*p*	128.4*p*	137.1*p*	135.3*p*

Sources: Same as General Statistics. The values shown reflect change from the base year, 1992. Values above 100 mean greater than 1992, values below 100 mean less than 1992, and a value of 100 in the 1982-91 or 1993-98 period means same as 1992. Values followed by a 'p' are projections by the editors; 'e' stands for extrapolation. Data are the most recent available at this level of detail.

SELECTED RATIOS

For 1992	Avg. of All Wholesale	Analyzed Industry	Index	For 1992	Avg. of All Wholesale	Analyzed Industry	Index
Employees per Establishment	12	8	67	Sales per Employee	561,172	395,606	70
Payroll per Establishment	349,729	177,572	51	Sales per Establishment	6,559,346	3,111,289	47
Payroll per Employee	29,919	22,579	75	Expenses per Establishment	723,071	414,752	57

Sources: Same as General Statistics. The 'Average of All Manufacturing' column represents the average of all manufacturing industries reported for the most recent complete year available. The Index shows the relationship between the Average and the Analyzed Industry. For example, 100 means that they are equal; 500 that the Analyzed Industry is five times the average; 50 means that the Analyzed Industry is half the national average. The abbreviation 'na' is used to show that data are 'not available'.

LEADING COMPANIES

Number shown: **50** Total sales ($ mil): **51,591** Total employment (000): **36.6**

Company Name	Address				CEO Name	Phone	Co. Type	Sales ($ mil)	Empl. (000)
Terra International Inc.	PO Box 6000	Sioux City	IA	51102	Burton M Joyce	712-277-1340	S	29,000	4.0
Cenex/Land O'Lakes Ag Services	PO Box 64089	St. Paul	MN	55164	Noel Estenson	612-451-5151	J	2,900	3.0
Transammonia Inc.	350 Park Ave	New York	NY	10022	Ronald P Stanton	212-223-3200	R	2,478	0.2
Countrymark Cooperative Inc.	950 N Meridian St	Indianapolis	IN	46204	Philip French	317-685-3000	R	2,000	1.6
Scoular Co., The	2027 Dodge St	Omaha	NE	68102	Duane A Fischer	402-342-3500	R	2,000	0.2
Southern States Cooperative	PO Box 26234	Richmond	VA	23260	Wayne A Boutwell	804-281-1000	R	1,216	3.5
Wilbur-Ellis Co.	345 California St	San Francisco	CA	94104	Brayton Wilbur Jr	415-772-4000	R	1,200 *	2.0
Andersons Inc.	480 W Dussel Dr	Maumee	OH	43537	Richard P Anderson	419-893-5050	P	1,155	3.0
Tabor Grain Co.	4666 Faries Pkwy	Decatur	IL	62525	Burnell D Kraft	217-424-5200	S	878 *	1.2
Central Garden and Pet Co.	3697 Mt Diablo	Lafayette	CA	94549	William E Brown	510-283-4573	P	841	2.7
MFA Inc.	201 Ray Young Dr	Columbia	MO	65201	Don Copenharer	573-874-5111	R	720	1.6
SF Services Inc.	3001 JFK Blvd	N. Little Rock	AR	72116	Michael P Sadler	501-945-2371	R	591	1.3
Collingwood Grain Inc.	PO Box 2150	Hutchinson	KS	67504	Lowell Downey	316-663-7121	S	580 *	0.7
Hydro Agri North America Inc.	100 N Tampa St	Tampa	FL	33602	Bjorn Bach	813-222-5700	S	500	0.1
PM AG Products Inc.	17475 Jovanna	Homewood	IL	60430	Michael A Reed	708-206-2030	S	450	1.1
Walco International Inc.	1701 W Northwest	Grapevine	TX	93257	Jim Robinson	209-781-3510	R	450	0.8
Western Farm Service Inc.	3705 W Beechwood	Fresno	CA	93711	Herman T Wilson Jr	209-436-0450	D	400	1.0
GROWMARK Inc.	1701 Towanda Ave	Bloomington	IL	61701	Norm Jones	309-557-6000	R	330	0.8
Swiss Valley Farms Co.	PO Box 4493	Davenport	IA	52808	Eugene Quast	319-391-3341	R	300	0.7
South Dakota Wheat Growers	PO Box 1460	Aberdeen	SD	57401	Verland Losinger	605-225-5500	R	254	0.3
Pennington Seed Inc.	PO Box 290	Madison	GA	30650	B Pennington III	706-342-1234	R	250	0.7
Novartis Seeds Inc.	7500 Olson Mem	Golden Valley	MN	55427	Ed Shonsey	612-593-7333	S	207 *	0.8
Lextron Inc.	PO Box BB	Greeley	CO	80632	RC Hummel	970-353-2600	R	188 *	0.5
Watonwan Farm Services Co.	PO Box 26	St. James	MN	56081	Don Gales	507-375-3355	R	170	0.2
Ag Services of America Inc.	PO Box 668	Cedar Falls	IA	50613	Gaylen D Miller	319-277-0261	P	148	0.1
Heartland Co-op	2829 Westown	W. Des Moines	IA	50266	Larry Petersen	515-225-1334	R	140	0.2
United Suppliers Inc.	PO Box 538	Eldora	IA	50627	Maurice Hyde	515-858-2341	R	130 *	0.3
Huntting Elevator Co.	PO Box 99	Austin	MN	55912	J Huntting	507-433-3476	R	120 *	0.2
Illinois Agricultural Association	1701 Towanda Ave	Bloomington	IL	61701	Ronald Warfield	309-557-2111	S	120 *	0.3
Miles Farm Supply Inc.	2760 Keller Rd	Owensboro	KY	42301	Billy J Miles	502-926-2420	R	109	0.5
Pendleton Grain Growers Inc.	1000 Dorion SW	Pendleton	OR	97801	Ed Balsiger	503-276-7611	R	105	0.3
Iowa Veterinary Supply Co.	124 Country Club	Iowa Falls	IA	50126	Thomas Kruse Sr	515-648-2529	R	104	0.2
A.L. Gilbert Co.	PO Box 38	Oakdale	CA	95361	Robert T Gilbert	209-847-1721	R	100	0.3
Brewer Environmental Industries	311 Pacific St	Honolulu	HI	96817	Stephen W Knoy	808-532-7400	S	100	0.2
Crestland Cooperative	PO Box 329	Creston	IA	50801	Larry E Crosser	515-782-6411	R	100	0.2
Maurice Pincoffs Company Inc.	PO Box 920919	Houston	TX	77292	John I Griffin	713-681-5461	R	100	0.1
Anderson Grain Corp.	PO Box 1117	Levelland	TX	79336	Buck Anderson	806-894-4982	R	96 *	0.2
Caldwell Supply Company Inc.	PO Box T	Hazleton	PA	18201	Ralph Caldwell III	717-455-7511	R	92 *	0.2
Auglaize Farmers Cooperative	PO Box 360	Wapakoneta	OH	45895	Larry Hammond	419-738-2137	R	90	0.2
Aurora Cooperative Elevator	PO Box 209	Aurora	NE	68818	Rodney Schroeder	402-694-2106	R	90 *	0.1
Farmers Cooperative	PO Box 47	Dayton	IA	50530	Roger Coppen	515-547-2813	R	85 *	0.1
Ursa Farmers Cooperative	202 W Maple St	Ursa	IL	62376	Gerald Jenkins	217-964-2111	R	82	<0.1
Abell Corp.	PO Box 8056	Monroe	LA	71211	G Hughes Abell	318-345-2600	R	80 *	0.2
Fruit Growers Supply Co.	14130 Riverside Dr	Sherman Oaks	CA	91423	Timothy J Lindgren	818-986-6480	R	80 *	0.2
Transcontinental Fertilizer Co.	44 E Lancaster Ave	Ardmore	PA	19003	Alfred W Aspen	610-642-5001	R	80	<0.1
Wright Lorenz Grain Company	PO Box 2420	Salina	KS	67402	Don R Timmel	913-827-3687	R	80	<0.1
United Co-op Inc.	PO Box 127	Hampton	NE	68843	Jay Larson	402-725-3131	R	78 *	0.1
Albert City Elevator Inc.	PO Box 38	Albert City	IA	50510	Bruce G Anderson	712-843-2291	R	75	<0.1
Frick's Services Inc.	PO Box 40	Wawaka	IN	46794	DR Frick	219-761-3311	R	75 *	0.1
La Porte County Cooperative	PO Box 160	La Porte	IN	46350	Dean Kaesebier	219-362-2156	R	75	0.1

Source: *Ward's Business Directory of U.S. Private and Public Companies*, 1998. The company type code used is as follows: P - Public, R - Private, S - Subsidiary, D - Division, J - Joint Venture, A - Affiliate, G - Group. Sales are in millions of dollars, employees are in thousands. An asterisk (*) indicates an estimated sales volume. The symbol < stands for 'less than'.

OCCUPATIONS EMPLOYED BY SIC 519 - WHOLESALE TRADE, OTHER

Occupation	% of Total 1996	Change to 2006	Occupation	% of Total 1996	Change to 2006
Sales & related workers nec	19.5	20.2	Clerical supervisors & managers	1.9	20.2
General managers & top executives	5.9	16.4	Order clerks	1.9	8.2
Truck drivers light & heavy	5.4	20.2	Helpers, laborers nec	1.7	20.2
General office clerks	3.6	3.4	Electrical & electronic technicians	1.4	18.8
Traffic, shipping, receiving clerks	3.6	16.7	Blue collar worker supervisors	1.4	16.0
Stock clerks	3.5	-3.9	Wholesale & retail buyers, except farm products	1.3	17.0
Freight, stock, & material movers, hand	3.3	8.2	Office machine & cash register servicers	1.3	20.2
Marketing & sales worker supervisors	3.1	20.2	Hand packers & packagers	1.2	-3.9
Order fillers, wholesale & retail sales	3.0	16.7	Maintenance repairers, general utility	1.1	12.0
Bookkeeping, accounting, & auditing clerks	2.9	-3.9	Industrial truck & tractor operators	1.1	20.2
Salespersons, retail	2.5	20.2	Purchasing managers	1.1	20.2
Secretaries, except legal & medical	2.5	-4.7	Receptionists & information clerks	1.0	20.2
Assemblers, fabricators, hand workers nec	2.0	-3.9			

Source: *Industry-Occupation Matrix*, Bureau of Labor Statistics. These data relate to one or more 3-digit SIC industry groups rather than to a single 4-digit SIC. The change reported for each occupation to the year 2006 is a percent of growth or decline as estimated by the Bureau of Labor Statistics. The abbreviation nec stands for 'not elsewhere classified'.

STATE AND REGIONAL CONCENTRATION

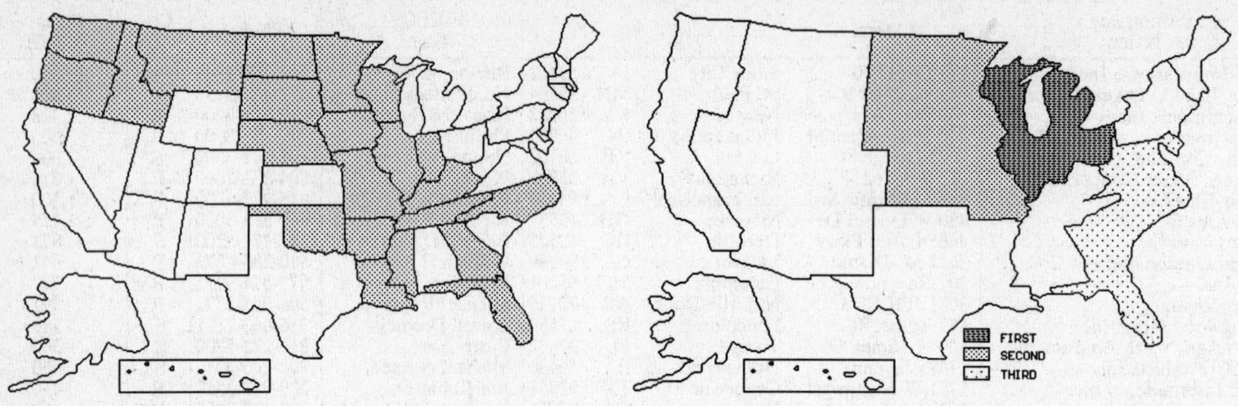

INDUSTRY DATA BY STATE

State	Establishments - 1995 Total (number)	Establishments - 1995 % of U.S.	Employment - 1995 Total (number)	Employment - 1995 % of U.S.	Employment - 1995 Per Estab.	Payroll - 1995 Total ($ mil.)	Payroll - 1995 Per Empl. ($)	Sales - 1992 Total ($ mil.)	Sales - 1992 % of U.S.	Sales - 1992 Per Estab ($)
Illinois	962	6.1	9,347	6.7	10	265.2	28,376	5,790.4	10.9	531,429
California	986	6.2	10,685	7.7	11	379.9	35,553	4,445.3	8.3	428,008
Minnesota	632	4.0	5,906	4.2	9	142.1	24,066	3,305.7	6.2	617,895
Iowa	907	5.7	8,013	5.7	9	196.2	24,479	3,271.3	6.1	440,940
Florida	530	3.4	4,073	2.9	8	113.3	27,819	2,904.2	5.4	679,975
Texas	1,280	8.1	9,657	6.9	8	208.0	21,539	2,587.7	4.9	290,848
New York	437	2.8	3,081	2.2	7	92.5	30,033	2,095.1	3.9	426,446
Indiana	554	3.5	4,587	3.3	8	118.4	25,807	1,953.3	3.7	425,268
North Carolina	481	3.0	3,479	2.5	7	84.3	24,238	1,928.3	3.6	515,165
Nebraska	488	3.1	4,417	3.2	9	108.0	24,449	1,903.2	3.6	418,462
Georgia	477	3.0	4,006	2.9	8	93.2	23,261	1,582.1	3.0	423,487
Wisconsin	635	4.0	6,294	4.5	10	145.6	23,139	1,567.9	2.9	253,206
Missouri	658	4.2	5,396	3.9	8	108.6	20,135	1,560.8	2.9	303,176
Louisiana	268	1.7	2,357	1.7	9	49.0	20,804	1,457.2	2.7	638,565
Ohio	473	3.0	4,204	3.0	9	99.3	23,625	1,411.8	2.6	370,752
Pennsylvania	384	2.4	3,844	2.8	10	98.8	25,700	1,283.8	2.4	281,836
Washington	397	2.5	4,083	2.9	10	111.4	27,279	1,261.0	2.4	320,045
Tennessee	330	2.1	3,944	2.8	12	83.3	21,124	1,143.9	2.1	305,199
Arkansas	339	2.1	3,512	2.5	10	78.4	22,331	1,088.2	2.0	358,309
Kentucky	389	2.5	3,375	2.4	9	67.5	19,994	977.0	1.8	304,822
Oregon	254	1.6	3,011	2.2	12	75.0	24,914	921.7	1.7	373,906
Mississippi	251	1.6	2,677	1.9	11	57.4	21,434	882.2	1.7	411,863
Michigan	282	1.8	2,130	1.5	8	58.3	27,352	806.7	1.5	350,913
Virginia	292	1.8	2,834	2.0	10	55.3	19,528	714.0	1.3	251,145
New Jersey	148	0.9	1,558	1.1	11	51.4	33,015	688.2	1.3	391,495
Oklahoma	285	1.8	1,980	1.4	7	38.7	19,562	684.9	1.3	380,933
Alabama	301	1.9	2,203	1.6	7	45.5	20,642	646.2	1.2	285,051
Idaho	211	1.3	2,280	1.6	11	54.3	23,807	553.9	1.0	291,510
North Dakota	147	0.9	1,183	0.8	8	33.5	28,349	543.2	1.0	528,430
Colorado	187	1.2	1,696	1.2	9	40.7	24,008	479.1	0.9	336,433
South Carolina	189	1.2	1,312	0.9	7	24.8	18,912	406.0	0.8	329,812
South Dakota	217	1.4	1,359	1.0	6	29.1	21,416	397.9	0.7	307,529
Arizona	166	1.1	1,307	0.9	8	40.4	30,913	365.2	0.7	335,385
Maryland	118	0.7	1,153	0.8	10	28.3	24,585	354.7	0.7	257,056
Montana	142	0.9	1,065	0.8	8	23.0	21,583	228.1	0.4	272,526
Massachusetts	87	0.6	674	0.5	8	18.9	28,107	168.8	0.3	234,425
New Mexico	87	0.6	598	0.4	7	10.2	17,030	141.5	0.3	262,508
Connecticut	50	0.3	385	0.3	8	16.8	43,595	132.1	0.2	282,353
Utah	82	0.5	648	0.5	8	12.9	19,931	115.5	0.2	227,309
Vermont	46	0.3	392	0.3	9	10.3	26,395	108.5	0.2	255,407
Hawaii	34	0.2	246	0.2	7	6.0	24,374	99.7	0.2	305,880
West Virginia	80	0.5	449	0.3	6	6.8	15,118	79.1	0.1	165,853
Nevada	51	0.3	321	0.2	6	7.6	23,692	72.7	0.1	278,720
Delaware	36	0.2	348	0.2	10	5.6	16,060	71.4	0.1	291,371
Wyoming	52	0.3	389	0.3	7	7.8	19,956	64.3	0.1	187,061
Maine	39	0.2	152	0.1	4	3.2	21,184	50.1	0.1	220,885
New Hampshire	23	0.1	112	0.1	5	2.7	24,437	25.4	0.0	171,784
Rhode Island	17	0.1	114	0.1	7	2.3	20,044	16.8	0.0	137,902
Alaska	5	0.0	24	0.0	5	0.3	13,292	5.8	0.0	232,840
Kansas	306	1.9	2,600	1.9	8	63.2	24,320	(D)	-	-

Source: County Business Patterns, 1995 and *Economic Census of the U.S., 1992*. Data are sorted by 1992 revenues and, if revenues are unavailable, by establishments in 1995. The symbol (D) indicates that data are withheld by the source to avoid disclosure of competitive information. A dash (-) indicates that data are not available or undisclosed because they do not meet statistical validity standards. Shaded *states* on the state map indicate those states which have proportionately greater representation in the industry than would be indicated by the state's population; the ratio is based on total revenues or number of establishments. Shaded *regions* indicate where the industry is regionally most concentrated.

5192 - BOOKS, PERIODICALS, & NEWSPAPERS

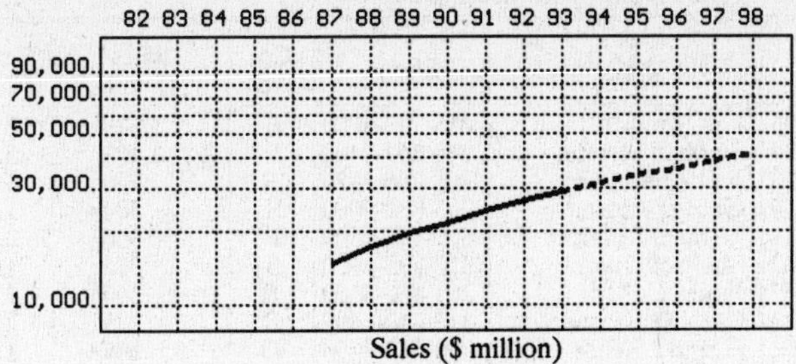

Sales ($ million)

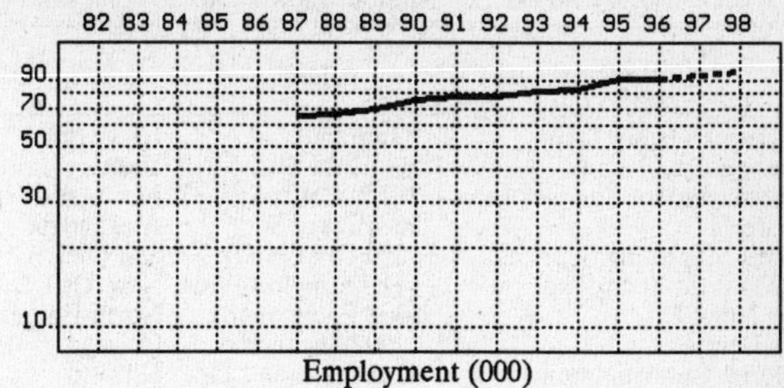

Employment (000)

GENERAL STATISTICS

Year	Establishments (number)	Employment (number)	Payroll ($ million)	Sales ($ million)	Expenses ($ million)	Beginning Inventory ($ million)	Ending Inventory ($ million)
1982	-	-	-	-	-	-	-
1983	-	-	-	-	-	-	-
1984	-	-	-	-	-	-	-
1985	-	-	-	-	-	-	-
1986	-	-	-	-	-	-	-
1987	3,935	64,837	1,367.9	14,695.6	2,794.3	830.5	896.2
1988	3,822	66,446	1,448.5	17,070.2e	3,067.6e	967.4e	1,036.8e
1989	3,621	70,297	1,654.0	19,444.9e	3,340.9e	1,104.3e	1,177.5e
1990	3,699	75,355	1,909.8	21,819.5e	3,614.3e	1,241.2e	1,318.1e
1991	3,827	77,392	1,955.5	24,194.2e	3,887.6e	1,378.1e	1,458.7e
1992	4,205	77,392	2,044.2	26,568.8	4,160.9	1,515.0	1,599.3
1993	4,220	81,794	2,293.8	28,943.5p	4,434.3p	1,651.9p	1,740.0p
1994	4,233	82,834	2,324.2	31,318.1p	4,707.6p	1,788.8p	1,880.6p
1995	4,351	91,746	2,643.1	33,692.8p	4,980.9p	1,925.7p	2,021.2p
1996	4,374p	91,607p	2,722.0p	36,067.5p	5,254.3p	2,062.6p	2,161.8p
1997	4,450p	94,638p	2,874.3p	38,442.1p	5,527.6p	2,199.5p	2,302.5p
1998	4,527p	97,668p	3,026.7p	40,816.8p	5,800.9p	2,336.4p	2,443.1p

Sources: Economic Census of the United States, 1982, 1987, and 1992. Establishment counts, employment, and payroll are from *County Business Patterns* for non-Census years. Values followed by a 'p' are projections by the editors. Sales and expense data for non-Census years are extrapolations, marked by 'e'. Industries reclassified in 1987 will not have data for prior years. Data are the most recent available at this level of detail.

INDICES OF CHANGE

Year	Establishments (number)	Employment (number)	Payroll ($ million)	Sales ($ million)	Expenses ($ million)	Beginning Inventory ($ million)	Ending Inventory ($ million)
1982	-	-	-	-	-	-	-
1983	-	-	-	-	-	-	-
1984	-	-	-	-	-	-	-
1985	-	-	-	-	-	-	-
1986	-	-	-	-	-	-	-
1987	93.6	83.8	66.9	55.3	67.2	54.8	56.0
1988	90.9	85.9	70.9	64.2e	73.7e	63.9e	64.8e
1989	86.1	90.8	80.9	73.2e	80.3e	72.9e	73.6e
1990	88.0	97.4	93.4	82.1e	86.9e	81.9e	82.4e
1991	91.0	100.0	95.7	91.1e	93.4e	91.0e	91.2e
1992	100.0	100.0	100.0	100.0	100.0	100.0	100.0
1993	100.4	105.7	112.2	108.9p	106.6p	109.0p	108.8p
1994	100.7	107.0	113.7	117.9p	113.1p	118.1p	117.6p
1995	103.5	118.5	129.3	126.8p	119.7p	127.1p	126.4p
1996	104.0p	118.4p	133.2p	135.8p	126.3p	136.1p	135.2p
1997	105.8p	122.3p	140.6p	144.7p	132.8p	145.2p	144.0p
1998	107.7p	126.2p	148.1p	153.6p	139.4p	154.2p	152.8p

Sources: Same as General Statistics. The values shown reflect change from the base year, 1992. Values above 100 mean greater than 1992, values below 100 mean less than 1992, and a value of 100 in the 1982-91 or 1993-98 period means same as 1992. Values followed by a 'p' are projections by the editors; 'e' stands for extrapolation. Data are the most recent available at this level of detail.

SELECTED RATIOS

For 1992	Avg. of All Wholesale	Analyzed Industry	Index	For 1992	Avg. of All Wholesale	Analyzed Industry	Index
Employees per Establishment	12	18	157	Sales per Employee	561,172	343,302	61
Payroll per Establishment	349,729	486,136	139	Sales per Establishment	6,559,346	6,318,383	96
Payroll per Employee	29,919	26,414	88	Expenses per Establishment	723,071	989,512	137

Sources: Same as General Statistics. The 'Average of All Manufacturing' column represents the average of all manufacturing industries reported for the most recent complete year available. The Index shows the relationship between the Average and the Analyzed Industry. For example, 100 means that they are equal; 500 that the Analyzed Industry is five times the average; 50 means that the Analyzed Industry is half the national average. The abbreviation 'na' is used to show that data are 'not available'.

LEADING COMPANIES

Number shown: **50** Total sales ($ mil): **8,006** Total employment (000): **28.7**

Company Name	Address				CEO Name	Phone	Co. Type	Sales ($ mil)	Empl. (000)
Ingram Book Group Inc.	1 Ingram Blvd	La Vergne	TN	37086	Lee Synnott	615-793-5000	S	1,820 •	2.5
Handleman Co.	500 Kirts Blvd	Troy	MI	48084	Stephen Strome	248-362-4400	P	1,181	3.5
Anco Management Services Inc.	202 N Court St	Florence	AL	35630	Joel Anderson	205-766-3824	R	740 •	3.0
Time Life Inc.	2000 Duke St	Alexandria	VA	22314	George Artandi	703-838-7000	S	500 •	1.5
Advanced Marketing Services	5880 Oberlin Dr	San Diego	CA	92121	Michael M Nicita	619-457-2500	P	386	0.4
Kable News Company Inc.	641 Lexington Ave	New York	NY	10022	Michael Duloc	212-705-4600	S	370 •	1.5
Hudson News Co.	1305 Patersonank	North Bergen	NJ	07047	James Cohen	201-867-3600	R	340 •	1.4
Charles Levy Co.	1200 N Branch	Chicago	IL	60622	Carol G Kloster	312-440-4400	R	285	2.1
Levy Home Entertainment	4201 Raymond Dr	Hillside	IL	60162	Howard Reese	708-547-4400	D	285 •	1.7
Diamond Comic Distributors	1966 Greenspring	Timonium	MD	21093	Stephen Geppi	410-560-7100	R	220	0.5
Nebraska Book Company Inc.	PO Box 80529	Lincoln	NE	68501	Mark Oppegard	402-421-7300	R	160	0.6
PennWell Publishing Co.	PO Box 1260	Tulsa	OK	74101	Joseph Wolking	918-835-3161	R	160 •	1.0
Spring Arbor Distribution	10885 Textile Rd	Belleville	MI	48111	Rick Pigott	313-481-0900	R	157	0.7
AMREP Corp.	641 Lexington Ave	New York	NY	10022	A B Gliedman	212-541-7300	P	152	1.7
Time Distribution Services Inc.	1271 of the Amer	New York	NY	10020	Larry Gunn	212-522-8437	S	140 •	0.6
MBS Textbook Exchange Inc.	2711 W Ash St	Columbia	MO	65203	RK Pugh	314-445-2243	R	120 •	0.5
Blackwell North America Inc.	6024 SW Jean Rd	Lake Oswego	OR	97035	Fred A Philipp	503-684-1140	S	110	0.4
Publishers Group West Inc.	4065 Hollis St	Emeryville	CA	94608	Randall Fleming	510-658-3453	R	100	0.2
National Association	528 E Lorain St	Oberlin	OH	44074	Garis F Distelhorst	216-775-7777	R	85 •	0.2
United Methodist Publishing	201 8th Ave S	Nashville	TN	37203	Robert K Feaster	615-749-6000	R	82	1.1
Flynt Distribution Company	9171 Wilshire Blvd	Beverly Hills	CA	90210	James Kohls	310-858-7100	S	74	0.3
PMG International Inc.	1011 N Frio St	San Antonio	TX	78207	Jack Cavaleri	210-226-6820	R	61 •	0.3
Haddon Craftsmen Inc.	1001 Wyoming Ave	Scranton	PA	18509	TF Sack	717-348-9211	S	58	0.9
Distribution Systems of America	31 Grand Blvd N	Brentwood	NY	11717	Lewis Sito	516-952-1041	S	55 •	0.2
Martin News Agency Inc.	11325 Gemini Ln	Dallas	TX	75229	Bennett T Martin	214-241-8531	R	37 •	0.2
Al-WaLi Inc.	401 Thornton Rd	Lichia Springs	GA	30057	Rich Bellezza	770-948-7845	R	31	<0.1
Follett Campus Resources	2211 N West St	River Grove	IL	60171	George Carr	708-583-2000	D	28 •	0.4
P.B.D. Inc.	1650 Bluegrass Lks	Alpharetta	GA	30201	James E Dockter	404-442-8633	R	25	0.1
George R. Klein News Co.	1771 E 30th St	Cleveland	OH	44172	Ronald Clark	216-623-0370	R	24 •	0.1
Bookpeople	7900 Edgewater Dr	Oakland	CA	94621	Gene Taback	510-632-4700	R	22	<0.1
Ballen Booksellers International	125 Ricefield Ln	Hauppauge	NY	11788	Leonard Schrift	516-952-1673	R	21 •	0.1
Ward's Natural Science	PO Box 92912	Rochester	NY	14692	Peter O'Brien	716-359-2502	R	20	0.2
Kansas City Periodical	PO Box 14948	Lenexa	KS	66285	James Brunkhardt	913-541-8600	R	17 •	<0.1
Stoeger Inc.	55 Ruta Ct	S. Hackensack	NJ	07606	Brian T Herrick	201-440-2700	R	15	<0.1
NEWSouth Distributors	PO Box 61297	Jacksonville	FL	32236	Gil Brechtel	904-783-2350	R	14	<0.1
Caxton Printers Ltd.	312 Main St	Caldwell	ID	83605	Gordon Gipson	208-459-7421	R	13	<0.1
Lectorum Publications Inc.	111 8th Ave	New York	NY	10011	Lawrence Jackel	212-929-2833	R	12	<0.1
Scherer Companies Inc.	5131 Post Rd	Dublin	OH	43017	Ronald Scherer	614-792-0777	R	12 •	<0.1
Bonneville News Company Inc.	965 Beardsley Pl	Salt Lake City	UT	84119	EL Madsen Sr	801-972-5454	R	10 •	<0.1
Quality Books Inc.	1003 W Pines Rd	Oregon	IL	61061	Harold Sterling	815-732-4450	S	10	<0.1
MILTCO Corp.	PO Box 1321	Harrisburg	PA	17105	Ken Quigley	717-541-8130	R	8	0.1
Consortium Book Sales	1045 Westgate Dr	St. Paul	MN	55114	Randall Beek	612-221-9035	R	7	<0.1
BSC Litho Inc.	3000 Canby St	Harrisburg	PA	17103	Edwin T Cosgrove	717-238-8378	S	6	<0.1
Charles E. Tuttle Company Inc.	PO Box 410	Rutland	VT	05702	Peter W Ackroyd	802-773-8930	R	6	<0.1
Action Products International	344 Cypress Rd	Ocala	FL	34472	Ronald Kaplan	352-680-3516	P	6	<0.1
Daret Inc.	33 Daret Dr	Ringwood	NJ	07456	David Muth	201-962-6001	R	5 •	<0.1
Hacker Art Books Inc.	45 W 57th St	New York	NY	10019	Seymour Hacker	212-688-7600	R	5 •	<0.1
United Learning Inc.	6633 W Howard St	Niles	IL	60714	Ronald E Reed	847-647-0600	R	5	<0.1
Moondog's Inc.	1201 Oakton St, #1	Elk Grove Vill.	IL	60007	Gary L Colabuono	708-806-6060	R	4	<0.1
D and K Enterprises Inc.	3216 Commander	Carrollton	TX	75006	Mark Rudiger	214-248-9100	R	3 •	<0.1

Source: *Ward's Business Directory of U.S. Private and Public Companies*, 1998. The company type code used is as follows: P - Public, R - Private, S - Subsidiary, D - Division, J - Joint Venture, A - Affiliate, G - Group. Sales are in millions of dollars, employees are in thousands. An asterisk (•) indicates an estimated sales volume. The symbol < stands for 'less than'.

OCCUPATIONS EMPLOYED BY SIC 519 - WHOLESALE TRADE, OTHER

Occupation	% of Total 1996	Change to 2006	Occupation	% of Total 1996	Change to 2006
Sales & related workers nec	19.5	20.2	Clerical supervisors & managers	1.9	20.2
General managers & top executives	5.9	16.4	Order clerks	1.9	8.2
Truck drivers light & heavy	5.4	20.2	Helpers, laborers nec	1.7	20.2
General office clerks	3.6	3.4	Electrical & electronic technicians	1.4	18.8
Traffic, shipping, receiving clerks	3.6	16.7	Blue collar worker supervisors	1.4	16.0
Stock clerks	3.5	-3.9	Wholesale & retail buyers, except farm products	1.3	17.0
Freight, stock, & material movers, hand	3.3	8.2	Office machine & cash register servicers	1.3	20.2
Marketing & sales worker supervisors	3.1	20.2	Hand packers & packagers	1.2	-3.9
Order fillers, wholesale & retail sales	3.0	16.7	Maintenance repairers, general utility	1.1	12.0
Bookkeeping, accounting, & auditing clerks	2.9	-3.9	Industrial truck & tractor operators	1.1	20.2
Salespersons, retail	2.5	20.2	Purchasing managers	1.1	20.2
Secretaries, except legal & medical	2.5	-4.7	Receptionists & information clerks	1.0	20.2
Assemblers, fabricators, hand workers nec	2.0	-3.9			

Source: *Industry-Occupation Matrix*, Bureau of Labor Statistics. These data relate to one or more 3-digit SIC industry groups rather than to a single 4-digit SIC. The change reported for each occupation to the year 2006 is a percent of growth or decline as estimated by the Bureau of Labor Statistics. The abbreviation nec stands for 'not elsewhere classified'.

STATE AND REGIONAL CONCENTRATION

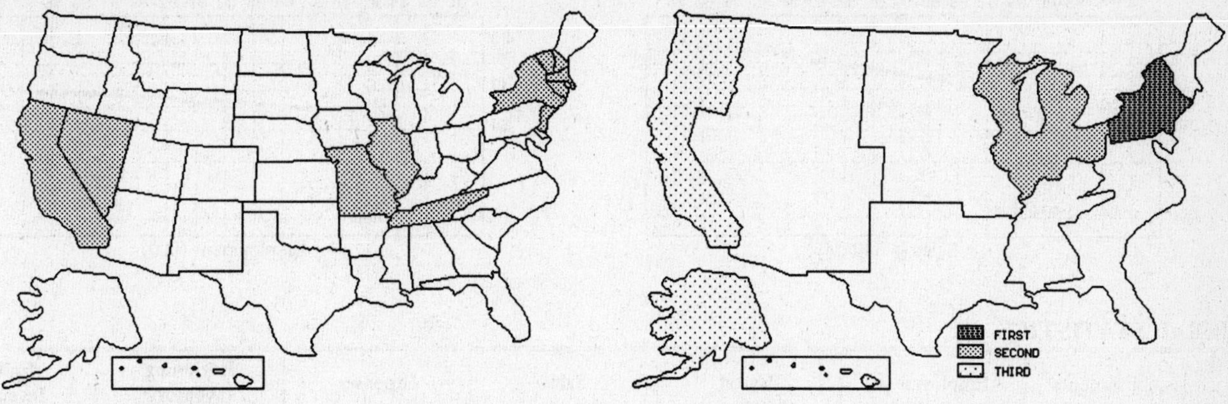

INDUSTRY DATA BY STATE

State	Establishments - 1995 Total (number)	Establishments - 1995 % of U.S.	Employment - 1995 Total (number)	Employment - 1995 % of U.S.	Employment - 1995 Per Estab.	Payroll - 1995 Total ($ mil.)	Payroll - 1995 Per Empl. ($)	Sales - 1992 Total ($ mil.)	Sales - 1992 % of U.S.	Sales - 1992 Per Estab ($)
New York	531	12.2	9,952	10.8	19	340.7	34,238	4,237.2	16.0	463,536
California	555	12.8	10,459	11.4	19	379.5	36,286	3,537.8	13.4	465,504
Illinois	241	5.5	8,963	9.8	37	248.1	27,680	2,460.9	9.3	366,803
New Jersey	173	4.0	6,077	6.6	35	218.7	35,987	1,863.3	7.1	324,788
Texas	253	5.8	3,804	4.1	15	117.1	30,790	1,807.5	6.8	460,616
Massachusetts	148	3.4	3,615	3.9	24	116.6	32,260	1,305.8	4.9	413,089
Florida	227	5.2	3,110	3.4	14	85.0	27,344	1,012.6	3.8	393,087
Connecticut	80	1.8	2,165	2.4	27	64.3	29,687	987.9	3.7	445,418
Tennessee	71	1.6	3,626	4.0	51	80.5	22,207	692.8	2.6	269,256
Missouri	87	2.0	3,197	3.5	37	63.3	19,804	687.4	2.6	267,266
Pennsylvania	177	4.1	3,356	3.7	19	89.3	26,594	678.5	2.6	223,550
Ohio	149	3.4	3,363	3.7	23	72.9	21,665	672.6	2.5	283,565
Michigan	128	2.9	2,567	2.8	20	77.4	30,155	659.5	2.5	247,856
Georgia	104	2.4	1,993	2.2	19	55.9	28,038	623.1	2.4	398,128
Virginia	95	2.2	1,512	1.6	16	32.6	21,577	571.9	2.2	460,060
Maryland	111	2.6	1,814	2.0	16	44.3	24,435	468.4	1.8	200,260
Minnesota	94	2.2	2,953	3.2	31	92.0	31,158	437.3	1.7	213,531
Washington	102	2.3	1,546	1.7	15	44.6	28,831	369.9	1.4	326,802
Colorado	74	1.7	1,576	1.7	21	35.1	22,295	298.6	1.1	294,792
Indiana	67	1.5	1,313	1.4	20	22.3	16,980	270.1	1.0	303,141
D.C.	15	0.3	457	0.5	30	23.4	51,263	252.2	1.0	609,128
Oregon	69	1.6	1,209	1.3	18	33.2	27,438	241.9	0.9	237,857
North Carolina	76	1.7	1,131	1.2	15	30.4	26,889	232.7	0.9	231,308
Wisconsin	72	1.7	1,374	1.5	19	37.6	27,334	203.9	0.8	181,537
Arizona	60	1.4	912	1.0	15	22.8	24,964	192.9	0.7	257,849
New Hampshire	30	0.7	960	1.0	32	25.4	26,422	158.9	0.6	255,878
Nevada	23	0.5	547	0.6	24	10.0	18,210	149.6	0.6	243,674
Iowa	44	1.0	914	1.0	21	17.8	19,441	139.9	0.5	151,919
Kansas	32	0.7	417	0.5	13	8.9	21,305	137.7	0.5	348,544
Alabama	45	1.0	901	1.0	20	24.6	27,312	135.7	0.5	197,177
Utah	43	1.0	675	0.7	16	16.8	24,855	104.3	0.4	215,589
Oklahoma	33	0.8	469	0.5	14	10.6	22,597	103.3	0.4	268,434
Arkansas	23	0.5	389	0.4	17	8.9	22,871	101.2	0.4	283,487
Louisiana	42	1.0	469	0.5	11	8.7	18,567	93.8	0.4	194,992
Nebraska	19	0.4	547	0.6	29	11.6	21,282	79.5	0.3	128,830
Hawaii	23	0.5	427	0.5	19	11.1	25,970	74.0	0.3	229,683
South Carolina	34	0.8	290	0.3	9	6.4	22,069	65.2	0.2	220,159
Vermont	19	0.4	414	0.5	22	7.8	18,775	63.1	0.2	198,902
Maine	17	0.4	223	0.2	13	5.0	22,623	46.4	0.2	176,517
New Mexico	20	0.5	174	0.2	9	3.2	18,345	38.4	0.1	322,765
Rhode Island	13	0.3	114	0.1	9	3.5	30,675	26.5	0.1	249,547
West Virginia	17	0.4	189	0.2	11	3.2	16,778	25.3	0.1	168,960
Alaska	9	0.2	104	0.1	12	1.9	18,519	24.1	0.1	371,323
Montana	15	0.3	246	0.3	16	4.1	16,728	23.3	0.1	113,444
Idaho	7	0.2	64	0.1	9	1.3	20,359	19.8	0.1	341,207
South Dakota	11	0.3	89	0.1	8	2.1	24,045	17.5	0.1	135,752
Mississippi	12	0.3	40	0.0	3	1.1	28,325	17.4	0.1	144,174
North Dakota	11	0.3	101	0.1	9	1.8	18,267	15.8	0.1	167,713
Wyoming	5	0.1	26	0.0	5	0.4	13,692	2.4	0.0	107,636
Kentucky	40	0.9	760	0.8	19	16.7	21,929	(D)	-	-
Delaware	5	0.1	153	0.2	31	2.6	17,203	(D)	-	-

Source: County Business Patterns, 1995 and *Economic Census of the U.S., 1992*. Data are sorted by 1992 revenues and, if revenues are unavailable, by establishments in 1995. The symbol (D) indicates that data are withheld by the source to avoid disclosure of competitive information. A dash (-) indicates that data are not available or undisclosed because they do not meet statistical validity standards. Shaded *states* on the state map indicate those states which have proportionately greater representation in the industry than would be indicated by the state's population; the ratio is based on total revenues or number of establishments. Shaded *regions* indicate where the industry is regionally most concentrated.

5193 - FLOWERS & FLORISTS' SUPPLIES

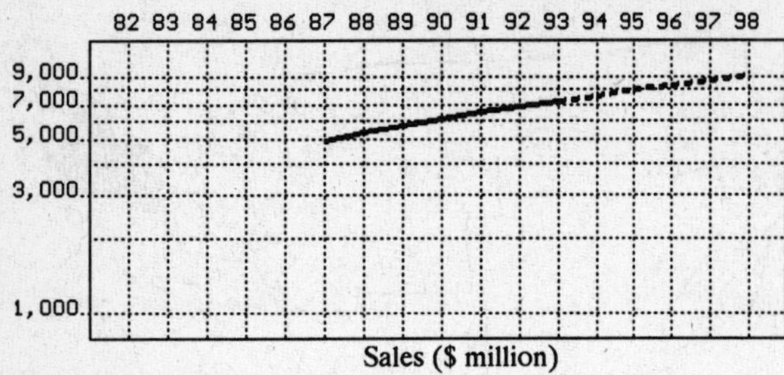

Sales ($ million)

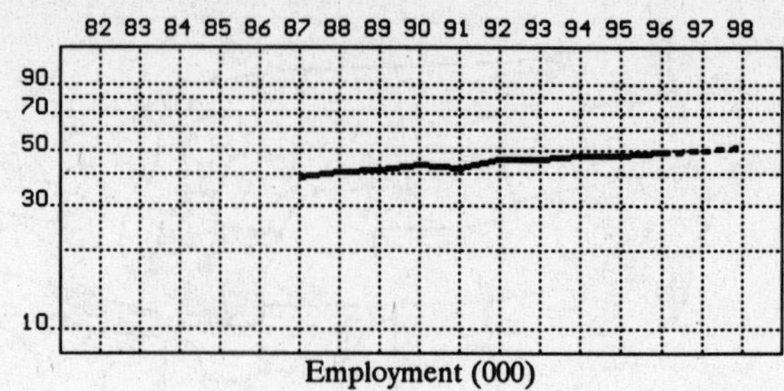

Employment (000)

GENERAL STATISTICS

Year	Establishments (number)	Employment (number)	Payroll ($ million)	Sales ($ million)	Expenses ($ million)	Beginning Inventory ($ million)	Ending Inventory ($ million)
1982	-	-	-	-	-	-	-
1983	-	-	-	-	-	-	-
1984	-	-	-	-	-	-	-
1985	-	-	-	-	-	-	-
1986	-	-	-	-	-	-	-
1987	3,573	39,042	660.5	4,985.5	1,385.6	403.8	445.5
1988	3,397	40,694	733.4	5,353.8e	1,489.0e	434.0e	476.2e
1989	3,165	41,374	770.9	5,722.1e	1,592.3e	464.2e	506.8e
1990	3,327	43,304	830.0	6,090.5e	1,695.6e	494.4e	537.5e
1991	3,341	42,234	829.3	6,458.8e	1,798.9e	524.7e	568.2e
1992	4,322	46,096	908.3	6,827.1	1,902.2	554.9	598.8
1993	4,269	45,466	910.5	7,195.4p	2,005.5p	585.1p	629.5p
1994	4,277	47,618	967.1	7,563.7p	2,108.9p	615.3p	660.1p
1995	3,887	46,946	976.2	7,932.0p	2,212.2p	645.6p	690.8p
1996	4,320p	48,922p	1,036.3p	8,300.3p	2,315.5p	675.8p	721.4p
1997	4,439p	49,978p	1,075.0p	8,668.6p	2,418.8p	706.0p	752.1p
1998	4,557p	51,034p	1,113.7p	9,037.0p	2,522.1p	736.2p	782.8p

Sources: *Economic Census of the United States*, 1982, 1987, and 1992. Establishment counts, employment, and payroll are from *County Business Patterns* for non-Census years. Values followed by a 'p' are projections by the editors. Sales and expense data for non-Census years are extrapolations, marked by 'e'. Industries reclassified in 1987 will not have data for prior years. Data are the most recent available at this level of detail.

INDICES OF CHANGE

Year	Establishments (number)	Employment (number)	Payroll ($ million)	Sales ($ million)	Expenses ($ million)	Beginning Inventory ($ million)	Ending Inventory ($ million)
1982	-	-	-	-	-	-	-
1983	-	-	-	-	-	-	-
1984	-	-	-	-	-	-	-
1985	-	-	-	-	-	-	-
1986	-	-	-	-	-	-	-
1987	82.7	84.7	72.7	73.0	72.8	72.8	74.4
1988	78.6	88.3	80.7	78.4e	78.3e	78.2e	79.5e
1989	73.2	89.8	84.9	83.8e	83.7e	83.7e	84.6e
1990	77.0	93.9	91.4	89.2e	89.1e	89.1e	89.8e
1991	77.3	91.6	91.3	94.6e	94.6e	94.6e	94.9e
1992	100.0	100.0	100.0	100.0	100.0	100.0	100.0
1993	98.8	98.6	100.2	105.4p	105.4p	105.4p	105.1p
1994	99.0	103.3	106.5	110.8p	110.9p	110.9p	110.2p
1995	89.9	101.8	107.5	116.2p	116.3p	116.3p	115.4p
1996	100.0p	106.1p	114.1p	121.6p	121.7p	121.8p	120.5p
1997	102.7p	108.4p	118.4p	127.0p	127.2p	127.2p	125.6p
1998	105.4p	110.7p	122.6p	132.4p	132.6p	132.7p	130.7p

Sources: Same as General Statistics. The values shown reflect change from the base year, 1992. Values above 100 mean greater than 1992, values below 100 mean less than 1992, and a value of 100 in the 1982-91 or 1993-98 period means same as 1992. Values followed by a 'p' are projections by the editors; 'e' stands for extrapolation. Data are the most recent available at this level of detail.

SELECTED RATIOS

For 1992	Avg. of All Wholesale	Analyzed Industry	Index	For 1992	Avg. of All Wholesale	Analyzed Industry	Index
Employees per Establishment	12	11	91	Sales per Employee	561,172	148,106	26
Payroll per Establishment	349,729	210,157	60	Sales per Establishment	6,559,346	1,579,616	24
Payroll per Employee	29,919	19,705	66	Expenses per Establishment	723,071	440,120	61

Sources: Same as General Statistics. The 'Average of All Manufacturing' column represents the average of all manufacturing industries reported for the most recent complete year available. The Index shows the relationship between the Average and the Analyzed Industry. For example, 100 means that they are equal; 500 that the Analyzed Industry is five times the average; 50 means that the Analyzed Industry is half the national average. The abbreviation 'na' is used to show that data are 'not available'.

LEADING COMPANIES

Number shown: **35** Total sales ($ mil): **4,084** Total employment (000): **17.0**

Company Name	Address				CEO Name	Phone	Co. Type	Sales ($ mil)	Empl. (000)
DIMON Inc.	PO Box 681	Danville	VA	24543	Claude B Owen Jr	804-792-7511	P	2,513	6.7
Florimex Worldwide Inc.	512 Bridge St	Danville	VA	24541	Dwight L Ferguson	804-792-7511	S	397	1.3
Celebrity Inc. (Tyler, Texas)	PO Box 6666	Tyler	TX	75707	J Patterson	903-561-3981	P	125	0.7
Ball Horticultural Co.	622 Town Rd	West Chicago	IL	60185	Anna Caroline Ball	630-231-3600	R	100*	0.5
Shemin Nurseries Inc.	641 Danbury Rd	Ridgefield	CT	06877	Robert Rankl	203-531-0540	S	86	0.3
Manatee Fruit Co.	PO Box 128	Palmetto	FL	34221	WL Preston	813-722-3279	R	79	0.3
Gerson Company Inc.	6100 Broadmoor St	Shawnee Msn	KS	66202	Peter Gerson	913-262-7400	R	76*	0.3
Pennock Co.	3027 Stokley St	Philadelphia	PA	19129	Wayne Collins	215-844-6600	R	76*	0.4
L and L Nursery Supply Inc.	PO Box 249	Chino	CA	91710	D Valois	909-591-0461	R	52	0.3
Nordlie Inc.	262 E Montcalm St	Detroit	MI	48201	Kevin Smith	313-963-2400	R	52*	0.1
Wetsel Inc.	PO Box 791	Harrisonburg	VA	22801	Floyd Grigsby	540-434-6753	S	48	0.2
Stein Garden and Gifts	5400 S 27th St	Milwaukee	WI	53221	Jack Stein	414-281-8400	R	40	0.8
Roy Houff Co.	6200 S Oak Pk Ave	Chicago	IL	60638	Roy Houff	312-586-8118	R	38	0.2
Greenleaf Wholesale Florists	PO Box 537	Brighton	CO	80601	Dwight Matsuno	303-659-8000	R	37	0.3
Reliance Trading Corporation	4949 W 65th St	Chicago	IL	60638	Ira Kleinberg	708-563-2515	R	35	0.5
Bailey Nurseries Inc.	1325 Bailey Rd	St. Paul	MN	55119	Gordon J Bailey	612-459-9744	R	28	0.4
New England Pottery Co.	1000 Washington St	Foxboro	MA	02035	Lawrence D Gititz	508-543-7700	R	23	0.1
Gardener's Supply Co.	128 Intervale Rd	Burlington	VT	05401	William Raap	802-660-3500	R	22	0.1
Valley Crest Tree Co.	24121 Ventura Blvd	Calabasas	CA	91302	Stuart J Sperber	818-223-8500	S	22	0.4
Geo. W. Hill and Company Inc.	PO Box 787	Florence	KY	41022	Dave Hill	606-371-8423	R	20	<0.1
LBK Marketing Corp.	7800 Bayberry Rd	Jacksonville	FL	32256	David M Bailys	904-737-8500	R	20	<0.1
Oregon Garden Products	3150 Minter Bridge	Hillsboro	OR	97123	Robert Terry	503-640-4633	R	20	0.6
Van Wingerden International	556 Jeffress Rd	Fletcher	NC	28732	Bert Lemkes	704-891-4116	R	20	0.3
Wight Nurseries Inc.	PO Box 390	Cairo	GA	31728	R VanLandingham	912-377-3033	R	19	0.5
Pursley Turf & Garden Centers	9049 59th Cir E	Bradenton	FL	34202	Walter L Pursley	813-756-8441	R	16	0.2
Metrolina Greenhouses Inc.	16400 Concord	Huntersville	NC	28078	T. Van Wingerden	704-875-1371	R	15	0.2
Zieger and Sons Inc.	6215 Ardleigh St	Philadelphia	PA	19138	PC Zieger	215-438-7060	R	15	0.2
Conard-Pyle Co.	372 Rose Hill Rd	West Grove	PA	19390	Steven B Hutton	215-869-2426	R	14	0.2
Rott-Keller Supply Co.	PO Box 390	Fargo	ND	58107	Herb F Rott Jr	701-235-0563	R	13*	<0.1
U.A.F. L.P.	6610 Anderson Rd	Tampa	FL	33634	Bill McClure	813-885-6936	R	13*	0.1
Hanford's Inc.	PO Box 32666	Charlotte	NC	28232	Paul Norman	704-375-2528	R	13	0.1
Rowland Nursery Inc.	7402 Menaul NE	Albuquerque	NM	87110	Reba K Rowland	505-883-5727	R	12	0.3
McGinnis Farms Inc.	5610 Ferry	Alpharetta	GA	30202	Stan Walker	404-740-1874	R	11*	0.1
Mid American Growers	Rte 89	Granville	IL	61326	N Vanwingerden	815-339-6831	R	11	0.2
International Decoratives	PO Box 777	Valley Center	CA	92082	RE Russell	619-749-2682	R	1	<0.1

Source: *Ward's Business Directory of U.S. Private and Public Companies*, 1998. The company type code used is as follows: P - Public, R - Private, S - Subsidiary, D - Division, J - Joint Venture, A - Affiliate, G - Group. Sales are in millions of dollars, employees are in thousands. An asterisk (*) indicates an estimated sales volume. The symbol < stands for 'less than'.

OCCUPATIONS EMPLOYED BY SIC 519 - WHOLESALE TRADE, OTHER

Occupation	% of Total 1996	Change to 2006	Occupation	% of Total 1996	Change to 2006
Sales & related workers nec	19.5	20.2	Clerical supervisors & managers	1.9	20.2
General managers & top executives	5.9	16.4	Order clerks	1.9	8.2
Truck drivers light & heavy	5.4	20.2	Helpers, laborers nec	1.7	20.2
General office clerks	3.6	3.4	Electrical & electronic technicians	1.4	18.8
Traffic, shipping, receiving clerks	3.6	16.7	Blue collar worker supervisors	1.4	16.0
Stock clerks	3.5	-3.9	Wholesale & retail buyers, except farm products	1.3	17.0
Freight, stock, & material movers, hand	3.3	8.2	Office machine & cash register servicers	1.3	20.2
Marketing & sales worker supervisors	3.1	20.2	Hand packers & packagers	1.2	-3.9
Order fillers, wholesale & retail sales	3.0	16.7	Maintenance repairers, general utility	1.1	12.0
Bookkeeping, accounting, & auditing clerks	2.9	-3.9	Industrial truck & tractor operators	1.1	20.2
Salespersons, retail	2.5	20.2	Purchasing managers	1.1	20.2
Secretaries, except legal & medical	2.5	-4.7	Receptionists & information clerks	1.0	20.2
Assemblers, fabricators, hand workers nec	2.0	-3.9			

Source: *Industry-Occupation Matrix*, Bureau of Labor Statistics. These data relate to one or more 3-digit SIC industry groups rather than to a single 4-digit SIC. The change reported for each occupation to the year 2006 is a percent of growth or decline as estimated by the Bureau of Labor Statistics. The abbreviation nec stands for 'not elsewhere classified'.

STATE AND REGIONAL CONCENTRATION

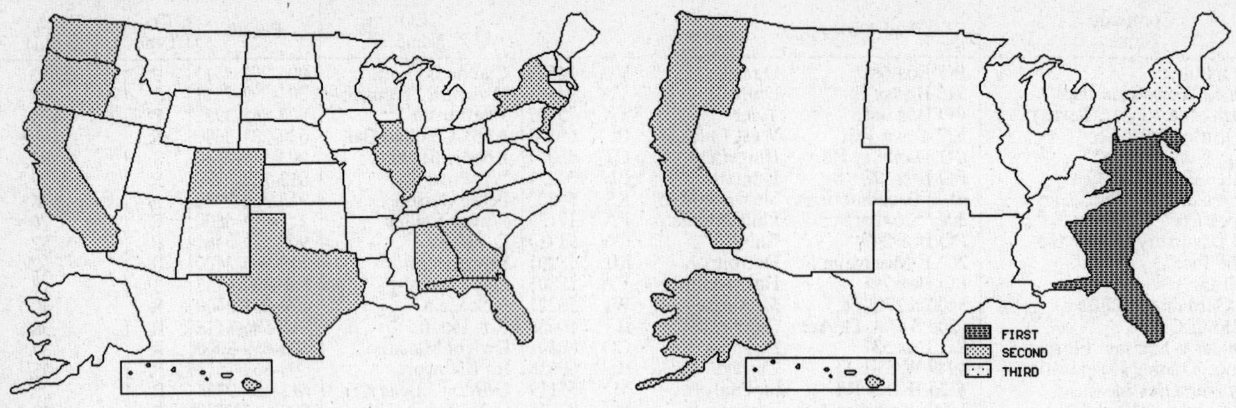

INDUSTRY DATA BY STATE

State	Establishments - 1995 Total (number)	Establishments - 1995 % of U.S.	Employment - 1995 Total (number)	Employment - 1995 % of U.S.	Employment - 1995 Per Estab.	Payroll - 1995 Total ($ mil.)	Payroll - 1995 Per Empl. ($)	Sales - 1992 Total ($ mil.)	Sales - 1992 % of U.S.	Sales - 1992 Per Estab ($)
Florida	488	12.6	5,542	11.8	11	124.7	22,493	1,058.6	15.9	210,339
California	614	15.8	7,434	15.9	12	138.1	18,578	983.4	14.8	148,408
Illinois	147	3.8	2,624	5.6	18	70.9	27,028	503.2	7.6	199,069
New York	255	6.6	2,499	5.3	10	64.2	25,686	497.7	7.5	185,934
Texas	274	7.0	3,354	7.2	12	59.9	17,848	474.5	7.1	129,722
New Jersey	129	3.3	2,368	5.1	18	67.1	28,347	403.3	6.1	146,925
Pennsylvania	145	3.7	1,770	3.8	12	38.7	21,876	281.9	4.2	134,242
Ohio	139	3.6	1,876	4.0	13	36.9	19,658	237.6	3.6	139,025
Georgia	129	3.3	1,509	3.2	12	29.9	19,820	234.8	3.5	163,252
Washington	110	2.8	1,324	2.8	12	32.5	24,517	205.1	3.1	168,551
Massachusetts	73	1.9	854	1.8	12	22.9	26,837	152.8	2.3	152,654
Michigan	88	2.3	1,092	2.3	12	22.4	20,535	150.7	2.3	150,598
Alabama	68	1.7	1,024	2.2	15	16.4	15,990	147.6	2.2	117,412
Oregon	76	2.0	685	1.5	9	16.3	23,765	110.9	1.7	160,456
Missouri	69	1.8	1,250	2.7	18	17.8	14,261	101.2	1.5	122,192
Colorado	65	1.7	801	1.7	12	16.4	20,509	95.5	1.4	123,760
North Carolina	115	3.0	974	2.1	8	17.0	17,471	93.7	1.4	114,128
Tennessee	80	2.1	632	1.3	8	12.5	19,752	90.3	1.4	116,940
Minnesota	48	1.2	735	1.6	15	14.4	19,604	79.4	1.2	119,466
Connecticut	35	0.9	451	1.0	13	10.8	23,927	79.4	1.2	165,764
Wisconsin	50	1.3	754	1.6	15	15.6	20,647	76.7	1.2	111,936
Indiana	63	1.6	684	1.5	11	14.5	21,270	73.3	1.1	93,281
Virginia	51	1.3	590	1.3	12	10.4	17,710	69.3	1.0	104,393
Arizona	66	1.7	654	1.4	10	9.9	15,203	59.5	0.9	100,636
Louisiana	39	1.0	415	0.9	11	6.4	15,352	40.3	0.6	92,733
Hawaii	32	0.8	345	0.7	11	5.4	15,559	35.9	0.5	80,392
South Carolina	40	1.0	361	0.8	9	6.3	17,432	31.4	0.5	125,568
Oklahoma	28	0.7	294	0.6	10	5.2	17,687	31.3	0.5	92,141
Utah	34	0.9	555	1.2	16	7.7	13,888	29.8	0.4	83,114
Iowa	26	0.7	442	0.9	17	6.2	14,007	29.5	0.4	96,163
Arkansas	32	0.8	295	0.6	9	3.7	12,644	29.2	0.4	90,888
Mississippi	30	0.8	283	0.6	9	5.0	17,700	26.8	0.4	106,598
Kansas	21	0.5	189	0.4	9	3.4	17,783	21.3	0.3	112,163
South Dakota	6	0.2	176	0.4	29	3.5	20,017	18.6	0.3	107,092
Nevada	21	0.5	113	0.2	5	2.4	20,938	18.4	0.3	128,462
New Hampshire	8	0.2	93	0.2	12	2.1	22,086	15.5	0.2	136,246
D.C.	7	0.2	83	0.2	12	3.5	42,723	13.7	0.2	142,208
Idaho	11	0.3	70	0.1	6	1.1	15,114	13.4	0.2	137,680
Delaware	10	0.3	93	0.2	9	1.7	18,677	13.0	0.2	140,902
West Virginia	15	0.4	84	0.2	6	1.0	11,786	6.5	0.1	57,283
Maine	10	0.3	47	0.1	5	1.3	28,489	6.2	0.1	123,860
New Mexico	15	0.4	164	0.4	11	2.1	12,872	6.0	0.1	86,329
Montana	5	0.1	40	0.1	8	0.6	14,400	5.6	0.1	185,100
Alaska	3	0.1	20-99	-	-	(D)	-	3.7	0.1	71,627
Maryland	52	1.3	645	1.4	12	14.2	21,943	(D)	-	-
Kentucky	34	0.9	316	0.7	9	6.3	19,902	(D)	-	-
Nebraska	13	0.3	116	0.2	9	2.0	16,931	(D)	-	-
Rhode Island	7	0.2	122	0.3	17	3.0	24,533	(D)	-	-
Vermont	6	0.2	36	0.1	6	0.7	20,333	(D)	-	-
North Dakota	5	0.1	20-99	-	-	(D)	-	(D)	-	-

Source: County Business Patterns, 1995 and *Economic Census of the U.S., 1992*. Data are sorted by 1992 revenues and, if revenues are unavailable, by establishments in 1995. The symbol (D) indicates that data are withheld by the source to avoid disclosure of competitive information. A dash (-) indicates that data are not available or undisclosed because they do not meet statistical validity standards. Shaded *states* on the state map indicate those states which have proportionately greater representation in the industry than would be indicated by the state's population; the ratio is based on total revenues or number of establishments. Shaded *regions* indicate where the industry is regionally most concentrated.

5194 - TOBACCO AND TOBACCO PRODUCTS

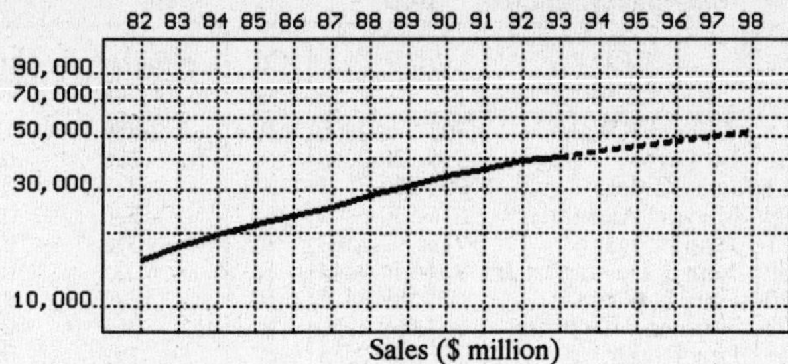

Sales ($ million)

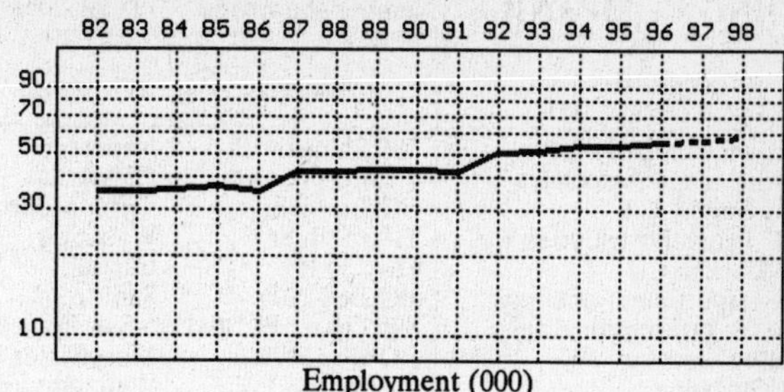

Employment (000)

GENERAL STATISTICS

Year	Establishments (number)	Employment (number)	Payroll ($ million)	Sales ($ million)	Expenses ($ million)	Beginning Inventory ($ million)	Ending Inventory ($ million)
1982	1,940	35,281	546.4	15,598.1	-	-	-
1983	1,937	35,462	596.5	17,571.5e	-	-	-
1984	1,759	35,907	621.5	19,544.8e	-	-	-
1985	1,652	36,919	649.1	21,518.2e	-	-	-
1986	1,543	35,062	638.8	23,491.6e	-	-	-
1987	1,813	42,672	784.9	25,465.0	1,739.5	1,206.4	1,394.8
1988	1,702	42,092	858.3	28,219.9e	1,902.3e	1,394.6e	1,619.1e
1989	1,577	42,975	919.2	30,974.8e	2,065.1e	1,582.8e	1,843.3e
1990	1,522	43,073	986.5	33,729.6e	2,227.9e	1,771.0e	2,067.6e
1991	1,421	42,522	1,030.1	36,484.5e	2,390.7e	1,959.2e	2,291.8e
1992	1,702	50,345	1,272.2	39,239.4	2,553.5	2,147.4	2,516.1
1993	1,620	51,459	1,347.1	40,715.5p	2,716.3p	2,335.6p	2,740.3p
1994	1,564	53,802	1,425.4	43,079.6p	2,879.1p	2,523.8p	2,964.6p
1995	1,496	54,226	1,424.4	45,443.7p	3,041.9p	2,712.0p	3,188.9p
1996	1,456p	54,876p	1,496.9p	47,807.8p	3,204.7p	2,900.2p	3,413.1p
1997	1,429p	56,461p	1,571.8p	50,172.0p	3,367.5p	3,088.4p	3,637.4p
1998	1,402p	58,047p	1,646.6p	52,536.1p	3,530.3p	3,276.6p	3,861.6p

Sources: Economic Census of the United States, 1982, 1987, and 1992. Establishment counts, employment, and payroll are from *County Business Patterns* for non-Census years. Values followed by a 'p' are projections by the editors. Sales and expense data for non-Census years are extrapolations, marked by 'e'. Industries reclassified in 1987 will not have data for prior years. Data are the most recent available at this level of detail.

INDICES OF CHANGE

Year	Establishments (number)	Employment (number)	Payroll ($ million)	Sales ($ million)	Expenses ($ million)	Beginning Inventory ($ million)	Ending Inventory ($ million)
1982	114.0	70.1	42.9	39.8	-	-	-
1983	113.8	70.4	46.9	44.8e	-	-	-
1984	103.3	71.3	48.9	49.8e	-	-	-
1985	97.1	73.3	51.0	54.8e	-	-	-
1986	90.7	69.6	50.2	59.9e	-	-	-
1987	106.5	84.8	61.7	64.9	68.1	56.2	55.4
1988	100.0	83.6	67.5	71.9e	74.5e	64.9e	64.3e
1989	92.7	85.4	72.3	78.9e	80.9e	73.7e	73.3e
1990	89.4	85.6	77.5	86.0e	87.2e	82.5e	82.2e
1991	83.5	84.5	81.0	93.0e	93.6e	91.2e	91.1e
1992	100.0	100.0	100.0	100.0	100.0	100.0	100.0
1993	95.2	102.2	105.9	103.8p	106.4p	108.8p	108.9p
1994	91.9	106.9	112.0	109.8p	112.8p	117.5p	117.8p
1995	87.9	107.7	112.0	115.8p	119.1p	126.3p	126.7p
1996	85.6p	109.0p	117.7p	121.8p	125.5p	135.1p	135.7p
1997	84.0p	112.1p	123.5p	127.9p	131.9p	143.8p	144.6p
1998	82.4p	115.3p	129.4p	133.9p	138.3p	152.6p	153.5p

Sources: Same as General Statistics. The values shown reflect change from the base year, 1992. Values above 100 mean greater than 1992, values below 100 mean less than 1992, and a value of 100 in the 1982-91 or 1993-98 period means same as 1992. Values followed by a 'p' are projections by the editors; 'e' stands for extrapolation. Data are the most recent available at this level of detail.

SELECTED RATIOS

For 1992	Avg. of All Wholesale	Analyzed Industry	Index	For 1992	Avg. of All Wholesale	Analyzed Industry	Index
Employees per Establishment	12	30	253	Sales per Employee	561,172	779,410	139
Payroll per Establishment	349,729	747,474	214	Sales per Establishment	6,559,346	23,054,877	351
Payroll per Employee	29,919	25,270	84	Expenses per Establishment	723,071	1,500,294	207

Sources: Same as General Statistics. The 'Average of All Manufacturing' column represents the average of all manufacturing industries reported for the most recent complete year available. The Index shows the relationship between the Average and the Analyzed Industry. For example, 100 means that they are equal; 500 that the Analyzed Industry is five times the average; 50 means that the Analyzed Industry is half the national average. The abbreviation 'na' is used to show that data are 'not available'.

LEADING COMPANIES

Number shown: **50** Total sales ($ mil): **5,521** Total employment (000): **10.1**

Company Name	Address				CEO Name	Phone	Co. Type	Sales ($ mil)	Empl. (000)
Eby-Brown Company L.P.	280 Shuman Blvd	Naperville	IL	60566	William S Wake Jr	708-778-2800	R	1,450	1.2
Harold Levinson Associates	1 Enterprise Pl	Hicksville	NY	11801	Ed Berro	516-822-0068	R	390	0.2
Grocery Supply Co.	PO Box 638	Sulphur Sprgs	TX	75483	Jerry Gillem	903-885-7621	S	333 *	0.8
L and L Jiroch Distributing Co.	1180 58th St	Wyoming	MI	49509	Michael Alexander	616-530-6600	S	330 *	0.4
Farner-Bocken Co.	Hwy 30 E	Carroll	IA	51401	John Norgaard	712-792-3503	R	310 *	0.6
J.T. Davenport and Sons Inc.	PO Box 1105	Sanford	NC	27330	John T Davenport Jr	919-774-9444	R	235	0.3
Core-Mark International Inc.	395 Oyster Pt Blvd	S San Francisco	CA	94080	Gary L Walsh	650-589-9445	R	220	2.2
Associated Grocers	PO Box 5200	Manchester	NH	03108	Norman J Turcotte	603-669-3250	R	200	0.3
800 JR Cigar Inc.	301 Rt 10, E	Whippany	NJ	07981	Lew Rothman	201-884-9555	P	192	0.6
AMCON Distributing Co.	PO Box 241230	Omaha	NE	68124	Kathleen Evans	402-331-3727	R	179	0.4
Grocers Specialty Co.	2601 S Eastern Ave	Los Angeles	CA	90040	Alfred Plamann	213-726-2601	S	160 *	0.2
Imperial Trading Co.	PO Box 23508	Harahan	LA	70183	R L Pierpoint Jr	504-733-1400	R	158 *	0.2
Albert H. Notini and Sons Inc.	PO Box 299	Lowell	MA	01853	Alex Turshette	508-459-7151	R	130 *	0.2
Miller and Hartman South Inc.	PO Box 218	Leitchfield	KY	42755	Wayne Jones	502-444-7246	S	130 *	0.3
Burklund Distributors Inc.	2500 N Main St	East Peoria	IL	61611	Dale E Burklund	309-694-1900	R	90 *	0.1
George Melhado Co.	10 Merchant St	Sharon	MA	02067	Warren J Alberts	617-784-5550	R	88 *	0.1
James Brudnick Company Inc.	219 Medford St	Malden	MA	02148	Richard Brudnick	617-321-6800	R	77 *	0.1
Mound City Industries Inc.	1315 Cherokee St	St. Louis	MO	63118	Robert L Krekeler	314-773-5200	R	60 *	<0.1
Birmingham Tobacco Co.	PO Box 11021	Birmingham	AL	35202	Frank P Damico Jr	205-324-2581	R	57 *	<0.1
Tzetzo Brothers Inc.	1100 Military Rd	Buffalo	NY	14217	Perry Tzetzo	716-877-0800	R	54	0.1
Republic Tobacco L.P.	5100 Ravenswd	Chicago	IL	60640	Donald Levin	312-728-1500	R	50	0.3
Consolidated Wholesale Co.	PO Box 26903	Oklahoma City	OK	73126	JJ Lehman	405-232-5593	D	46	<0.1
Safier's Inc.	8700 Harvard Ave	Cleveland	OH	44105	SJ Safier	216-341-8700	R	45 *	<0.1
Lane Ltd.	2280 Mt Ind Blvd	Tucker	GA	30084	David H Michod	404-934-8540	S	44	0.2
Cole Brothers and Fox Co.	252 Yandell Ave	Canton	MS	39046	William E Fox	601-859-1414	R	39 *	<0.1
SWD Corp.	PO Box 340	Lima	OH	45802	Carl Berger	419-227-2436	R	35	<0.1
United Candy and Tobacco Co.	7408 Tonnelle Ave	North Bergen	NJ	07047	J Choy	201-943-8675	R	35 *	<0.1
Pine Lesser and Sons Inc.	PO Box 1807	Clifton	NJ	07015	Allan G Lesser	973-478-3310	R	32 *	<0.1
Fritz Company Inc.	1912 Hastings Ave	Newport	MN	55055	James Fritz	612-459-9751	R	24 *	0.1
Peter P. Dennis Inc.	1224 S Main St	Phillipsburg	NJ	08865	John Zarbatany	908-454-2141	R	24	<0.1
Bensen Intern. Tobacco U.S.A.	26250 Corporate	Hayward	CA	94545	Thomas Bensen	510-264-4360	R	20	<0.1
Clifford D. Fite Co.	PO Box 616	Cedartown	GA	30125	Tom Steel	770-748-5315	R	20 *	<0.1
F.A. Davis and Sons Inc.	6610 Cabot Dr	Baltimore	MD	21226	Louis V Manzo	410-360-6000	R	20 *	0.2
Kaiser Wholesale Inc.	PO Box 1115	New Albany	IN	47150	JR Kaiser	812-945-2651	R	20	<0.1
Weeke Wholesale Company	1600 N 89th St	Fairview H.	IL	62208	Wayne W Week	618-397-1900	R	20	<0.1
A.W Marshall Co.	PO Box 16127	Salt Lake City	UT	84116	AW Marshall	801-328-4713	R	17	<0.1
Cullen Distributors Inc.	125 S Park St	Streator	IL	61364	John Cullen	815-672-2975	R	17 *	<0.1
New Hampshire Tobacco Corp.	130 Northeastern	Nashua	NH	03060	RA Bertland	603-882-1131	R	17 *	<0.1
Corr-Williams Co.	PO Box 2570	Jackson	MS	39207	Hal Nievanck	601-353-5871	R	16 *	<0.1
Blackburn-Russell Company	PO Box 157	Bedford	PA	15522	Robert B Blackburn	814-623-5181	R	16	<0.1
Albert Guarnieri Co.	1133-71 E Mkt St	Warren	OH	44483	A Guarnieri III	216-394-5636	R	15	<0.1
Frank P. Corso Inc.	PO Box 488	Biloxi	MS	39533	Elizabeth Joachim	601-436-4697	R	15	<0.1
Atlas Merchandising Co.	138-142 McKean	Charleroi	PA	15022	Rose Kiski	412-489-9561	R	13	<0.1
Franklin Cigar and Tobacco	PO Box 1151	Franklin	LA	70538	Keith A Landen	318-828-3208	R	13	<0.1
Lavin Candy Company Inc.	74 S Catherine St	Plattsburgh	NY	12901	Irvin C Reid	518-563-4630	R	12	<0.1
Boyd-Bluford Company Inc.	3750 Progress Rd	Norfolk	VA	23541	Bruce Melchor	804-855-6036	R	11 *	<0.1
John C. Klosterman Company	901 Portage St	Kalamazoo	MI	49001	John H Bartels	616-381-0870	R	11	<0.1
John F. Trompeter Co.	637 E Main St	Louisville	KY	40202	BA Trompeter	502-585-5852	R	11 *	<0.1
Cash and Carry Stores Inc.	PO Box 308	Elkin	NC	28621	DW Myers	910-835-4405	R	10 *	<0.1
Hattiesburg Grocery Co.	PO Box 350	Hattiesburg	MS	39403	William T Russell Jr	601-584-7544	R	10	<0.1

Source: *Ward's Business Directory of U.S. Private and Public Companies*, 1998. The company type code used is as follows: P - Public, R - Private, S - Subsidiary, D - Division, J - Joint Venture, A - Affiliate, G - Group. Sales are in millions of dollars, employees are in thousands. An asterisk (*) indicates an estimated sales volume. The symbol < stands for 'less than'.

OCCUPATIONS EMPLOYED BY SIC 519 - WHOLESALE TRADE, OTHER

Occupation	% of Total 1996	Change to 2006	Occupation	% of Total 1996	Change to 2006
Sales & related workers nec	19.5	20.2	Clerical supervisors & managers	1.9	20.2
General managers & top executives	5.9	16.4	Order clerks	1.9	8.2
Truck drivers light & heavy	5.4	20.2	Helpers, laborers nec	1.7	20.2
General office clerks	3.6	3.4	Electrical & electronic technicians	1.4	18.8
Traffic, shipping, receiving clerks	3.6	16.7	Blue collar worker supervisors	1.4	16.0
Stock clerks	3.5	-3.9	Wholesale & retail buyers, except farm products	1.3	17.0
Freight, stock, & material movers, hand	3.3	8.2	Office machine & cash register servicers	1.3	20.2
Marketing & sales worker supervisors	3.1	20.2	Hand packers & packagers	1.2	-3.9
Order fillers, wholesale & retail sales	3.0	16.7	Maintenance repairers, general utility	1.1	12.0
Bookkeeping, accounting, & auditing clerks	2.9	-3.9	Industrial truck & tractor operators	1.1	20.2
Salespersons, retail	2.5	20.2	Purchasing managers	1.1	20.2
Secretaries, except legal & medical	2.5	-4.7	Receptionists & information clerks	1.0	20.2
Assemblers, fabricators, hand workers nec	2.0	-3.9			

Source: *Industry-Occupation Matrix*, Bureau of Labor Statistics. These data relate to one or more 3-digit SIC industry groups rather than to a single 4-digit SIC. The change reported for each occupation to the year 2006 is a percent of growth or decline as estimated by the Bureau of Labor Statistics. The abbreviation nec stands for 'not elsewhere classified'.

STATE AND REGIONAL CONCENTRATION

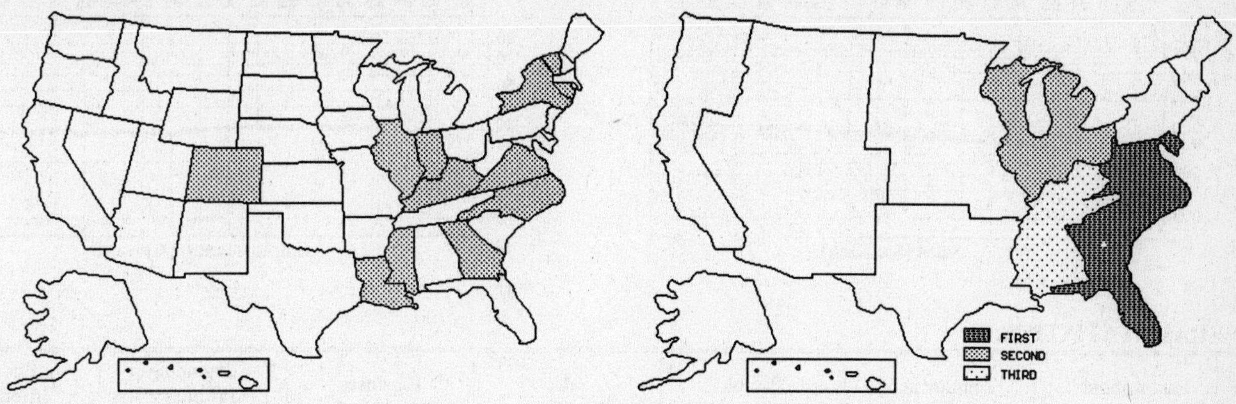

INDUSTRY DATA BY STATE

State	Establishments - 1995 Total (number)	Establishments - 1995 % of U.S.	Employment - 1995 Total (number)	Employment - 1995 % of U.S.	Employment - 1995 Per Estab.	Payroll - 1995 Total ($ mil.)	Payroll - 1995 Per Empl. ($)	Sales - 1992 Total ($ mil.)	Sales - 1992 % of U.S.	Sales - 1992 Per Estab ($)
Kentucky	54	3.6	5,675	10.5	105	159.7	28,147	3,835.8	9.8	916,550
New York	173	11.6	3,862	7.2	22	156.6	40,547	3,047.1	7.8	960,028
California	75	5.0	2,659	4.9	35	78.8	29,630	2,596.5	6.6	873,070
Texas	55	3.7	2,942	5.5	53	72.4	24,619	2,425.9	6.2	919,583
Illinois	56	3.7	2,951	5.5	53	81.9	27,770	2,195.3	5.6	919,307
Virginia	33	2.2	846	1.6	26	17.4	20,604	2,073.6	5.3	1,001,236
Florida	66	4.4	2,648	4.9	40	75.0	28,326	1,953.9	5.0	760,585
Ohio	64	4.3	1,635	3.0	26	41.8	25,578	1,541.0	3.9	752,831
North Carolina	64	4.3	2,304	4.3	36	52.6	22,838	1,473.5	3.8	690,829
Pennsylvania	75	5.0	1,871	3.5	25	45.1	24,109	1,384.5	3.5	659,301
Georgia	35	2.3	1,533	2.8	44	40.9	26,680	1,355.6	3.5	883,694
Michigan	36	2.4	2,081	3.9	58	45.1	21,686	1,282.4	3.3	821,548
Connecticut	40	2.7	1,826	3.4	46	53.2	29,151	1,244.1	3.2	1,169,296
New Jersey	77	5.1	1,303	2.4	17	34.5	26,505	1,026.6	2.6	784,885
Indiana	36	2.4	1,073	2.0	30	27.2	25,355	954.5	2.4	815,155
Massachusetts	28	1.9	1,268	2.4	45	32.7	25,791	815.7	2.1	771,020
Colorado	21	1.4	995	1.8	47	28.0	28,175	805.2	2.1	915,042
Tennessee	39	2.6	1,521	2.8	39	35.2	23,160	764.0	2.0	630,889
Louisiana	32	2.1	1,176	2.2	37	24.2	20,588	694.3	1.8	593,932
Mississippi	31	2.1	1,111	2.1	36	22.6	20,341	662.7	1.7	663,330
Wisconsin	29	1.9	1,065	2.0	37	26.7	25,024	656.5	1.7	619,948
Minnesota	28	1.9	1,114	2.1	40	30.4	27,330	644.1	1.6	588,238
Alabama	18	1.2	1,085	2.0	60	20.2	18,625	603.7	1.5	613,508
Missouri	23	1.5	700	1.3	30	15.5	22,081	546.5	1.4	855,269
Washington	21	1.4	832	1.5	40	21.9	26,323	542.9	1.4	725,783
Maryland	19	1.3	646	1.2	34	17.0	26,365	470.6	1.2	701,268
Arizona	9	0.6	408	0.8	45	12.1	29,642	373.0	1.0	1,000,056
Oregon	12	0.8	399	0.7	33	10.2	25,441	344.7	0.9	879,398
South Carolina	28	1.9	677	1.3	24	13.8	20,362	307.3	0.8	466,974
Iowa	18	1.2	513	1.0	28	15.2	29,538	300.9	0.8	544,083
West Virginia	20	1.3	425	0.8	21	9.6	22,645	245.2	0.6	553,440
Arkansas	22	1.5	537	1.0	24	10.2	18,942	220.0	0.6	409,728
Oklahoma	24	1.6	541	1.0	23	11.3	20,828	216.2	0.6	454,145
Maine	5	0.3	407	0.8	81	9.7	23,774	187.5	0.5	522,164
Kansas	20	1.3	319	0.6	16	6.1	19,254	183.0	0.5	575,522
D.C.	4	0.3	256	0.5	64	5.9	22,879	162.7	0.4	638,027
Nevada	8	0.5	198	0.4	25	5.3	26,611	147.6	0.4	696,236
Hawaii	7	0.5	100-249	-	-	(D)	-	123.6	0.3	407,789
Vermont	5	0.3	248	0.5	50	4.7	18,952	93.2	0.2	441,559
New Hampshire	4	0.3	181	0.3	45	4.2	23,193	85.8	0.2	510,756
Utah	4	0.3	505	0.9	126	9.1	17,966	84.1	0.2	384,146
Idaho	11	0.7	214	0.4	19	4.3	20,164	72.9	0.2	461,633
North Dakota	10	0.7	302	0.6	30	5.1	16,964	69.1	0.2	324,329
Delaware	7	0.5	88	0.2	13	2.6	29,511	61.2	0.2	702,920
Montana	9	0.6	237	0.4	26	5.6	23,620	53.2	0.1	350,013
New Mexico	5	0.3	143	0.3	29	3.0	20,748	45.5	0.1	459,202
South Dakota	6	0.4	146	0.3	24	2.7	18,411	45.0	0.1	365,512
Rhode Island	7	0.5	20-99	-	-	(D)	-	36.5	0.1	468,244
Wyoming	5	0.3	67	0.1	13	1.1	16,358	23.4	0.1	324,569
Nebraska	14	0.9	321	0.6	23	7.2	22,430	(D)	-	-
Alaska	4	0.3	20-99	-	-	(D)	-	(D)	-	-

Source: County Business Patterns, 1995 and *Economic Census of the U.S., 1992*. Data are sorted by 1992 revenues and, if revenues are unavailable, by establishments in 1995. The symbol (D) indicates that data are withheld by the source to avoid disclosure of competitive information. A dash (-) indicates that data are not available or undisclosed because they do not meet statistical validity standards. Shaded *states* on the state map indicate those states which have proportionately greater representation in the industry than would be indicated by the state's population; the ratio is based on total revenues or number of establishments. Shaded *regions* indicate where the industry is regionally most concentrated.

5198 - PAINTS, VARNISHES, AND SUPPLIES

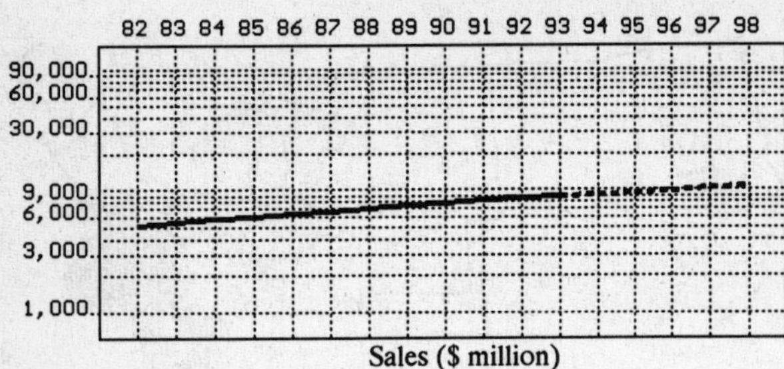

Sales ($ million)

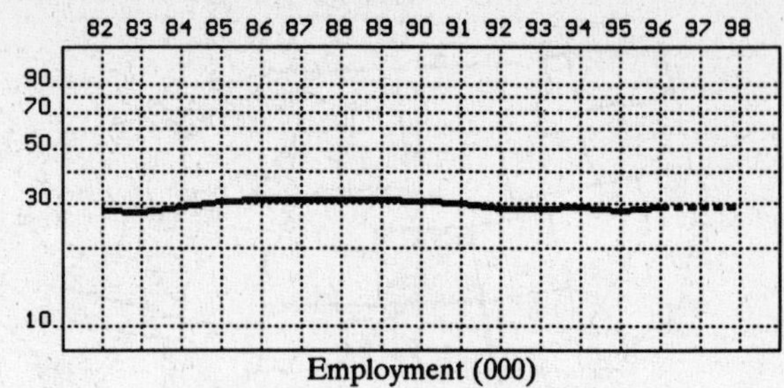

Employment (000)

GENERAL STATISTICS

Year	Establishments (number)	Employment (number)	Payroll ($ million)	Sales ($ million)	Expenses ($ million)	Beginning Inventory ($ million)	Ending Inventory ($ million)
1982	3,604	28,276	491.2	5,157.0	-	-	-
1983	3,631	27,552	524.9	5,466.0*e*	-	-	-
1984	3,455	29,318	586.6	5,774.9*e*	-	-	-
1985	3,443	30,449	630.6	6,083.9*e*	-	-	-
1986	3,468	31,280	682.5	6,392.9*e*	-	-	-
1987	3,657	30,780	660.3	6,701.8	1,502.5	607.1	647.6
1988	3,468	31,085	706.6	7,085.7*e*	1,564.5*e*	619.1*e*	656.4*e*
1989	3,460	30,917	720.6	7,469.5*e*	1,626.5*e*	631.2*e*	665.2*e*
1990	3,438	30,472	742.6	7,853.3*e*	1,688.5*e*	643.2*e*	674.0*e*
1991	3,415	29,948	759.0	8,237.2*e*	1,750.5*e*	655.2*e*	682.8*e*
1992	3,539	28,862	781.6	8,621.0	1,812.4	667.3	691.6
1993	3,465	28,493	799.5	8,882.3*p*	1,874.4*p*	679.3*p*	700.3*p*
1994	3,544	29,051	858.3	9,228.8*p*	1,936.4*p*	691.3*p*	709.1*p*
1995	3,348	28,198	855.2	9,575.2*p*	1,998.4*p*	703.4*p*	717.9*p*
1996	3,422*p*	29,442*p*	898.0*p*	9,921.6*p*	2,060.4*p*	715.4*p*	726.7*p*
1997	3,412*p*	29,418*p*	924.4*p*	10,268.0*p*	2,122.4*p*	727.4*p*	735.5*p*
1998	3,402*p*	29,394*p*	950.8*p*	10,614.4*p*	2,184.4*p*	739.5*p*	744.3*p*

Sources: Economic Census of the United States, 1982, 1987, and 1992. Establishment counts, employment, and payroll are from *County Business Patterns* for non-Census years. Values followed by a 'p' are projections by the editors. Sales and expense data for non-Census years are extrapolations, marked by 'e'. Industries reclassified in 1987 will not have data for prior years. Data are the most recent available at this level of detail.

INDICES OF CHANGE

Year	Establishments (number)	Employment (number)	Payroll ($ million)	Sales ($ million)	Expenses ($ million)	Beginning Inventory ($ million)	Ending Inventory ($ million)
1982	101.8	98.0	62.8	59.8	-	-	-
1983	102.6	95.5	67.2	63.4*e*	-	-	-
1984	97.6	101.6	75.1	67.0*e*	-	-	-
1985	97.3	105.5	80.7	70.6*e*	-	-	-
1986	98.0	108.4	87.3	74.2*e*	-	-	-
1987	103.3	106.6	84.5	77.7	82.9	91.0	93.6
1988	98.0	107.7	90.4	82.2*e*	86.3*e*	92.8*e*	94.9*e*
1989	97.8	107.1	92.2	86.6*e*	89.7*e*	94.6*e*	96.2*e*
1990	97.1	105.6	95.0	91.1*e*	93.2*e*	96.4*e*	97.5*e*
1991	96.5	103.8	97.1	95.5*e*	96.6*e*	98.2*e*	98.7*e*
1992	100.0	100.0	100.0	100.0	100.0	100.0	100.0
1993	97.9	98.7	102.3	103.0*p*	103.4*p*	101.8*p*	101.3*p*
1994	100.1	100.7	109.8	107.1*p*	106.8*p*	103.6*p*	102.5*p*
1995	94.6	97.7	109.4	111.1*p*	110.3*p*	105.4*p*	103.8*p*
1996	96.7*p*	102.0*p*	114.9*p*	115.1*p*	113.7*p*	107.2*p*	105.1*p*
1997	96.4*p*	101.9*p*	118.3*p*	119.1*p*	117.1*p*	109.0*p*	106.3*p*
1998	96.1*p*	101.8*p*	121.7*p*	123.1*p*	120.5*p*	110.8*p*	107.6*p*

Sources: Same as General Statistics. The values shown reflect change from the base year, 1992. Values above 100 mean greater than 1992, values below 100 mean less than 1992, and a value of 100 in the 1982-91 or 1993-98 period means same as 1992. Values followed by a 'p' are projections by the editors; 'e' stands for extrapolation. Data are the most recent available at this level of detail.

SELECTED RATIOS

For 1992	Avg. of All Wholesale	Analyzed Industry	Index	For 1992	Avg. of All Wholesale	Analyzed Industry	Index
Employees per Establishment	12	8	70	Sales per Employee	561,172	298,697	53
Payroll per Establishment	349,729	220,853	63	Sales per Establishment	6,559,346	2,435,999	37
Payroll per Employee	29,919	27,081	91	Expenses per Establishment	723,071	512,122	71

Sources: Same as General Statistics. The 'Average of All Manufacturing' column represents the average of all manufacturing industries reported for the most recent complete year available. The Index shows the relationship between the Average and the Analyzed Industry. For example, 100 means that they are equal; 500 that the Analyzed Industry is five times the average; 50 means that the Analyzed Industry is half the national average. The abbreviation 'na' is used to show that data are 'not available'.

LEADING COMPANIES

Number shown: **43** Total sales ($ mil): **1,826** Total employment (000): **10.0**

Company Name	Address				CEO Name	Phone	Co. Type	Sales ($ mil)	Empl. (000)
National Patent Development	9 West 57th St	New York	NY	10019	Jerome I Feldman	212-826-8500	P	235	2.0
Strafco Inc.	PO Box 600	San Antonio	TX	78292	Jack D Trawick	210-226-0101	R	113	1.1
FinishMaster Inc.	4259 40th St SE	Kentwood	MI	49512	Andre B Lacy	616-949-7604	P	108	0.7
Wilmar Industries Inc.	303 Harper Dr	Moorestown	NJ	08057	William S Green	609-439-1222	P	101	0.6
Penn Color Inc.	400 Old Dublin Pk	Doylestown	PA	18901	K Putman	215-345-6550	R	100	0.5
Seabrook Wallcoverings Inc.	1325 Farmville Rd	Memphis	TN	38122	James Seabrook Jr	901-320-3500	R	100 *	0.5
Emery Waterhouse Co.	PO Box 659	Portland	ME	04104	Charles Hildrein Jr	207-775-2371	R	90	0.3
Brewster Wallcovering Co.	67 Pacella Park Dr	Randolph	MA	02368	Kenneth Grandberg	617-963-4800	R	77	0.3
Maharam Fabric Corp.	PO Box 6900	Hauppauge	NY	11788	Donald H Maharam	516-582-3434	R	70	0.3
Mobile Paint Manufacturing Co.	4775 Hamilton Blvd	Theodore	AL	36582	Robert A Williams	334-443-6110	R	55	0.4
Masterchem Industries Inc.	PO Box 368	Barnhart	MO	63012	Robert Caldwell	314-942-2510	S	50 *	<0.1
Apollo Colors Inc.	3000 Dundee Rd	Northbrook	IL	60062	Thomas W Rogers	847-564-9190	R	50 *	0.2
Thompson PBE Florida Div.	PO Box 7470	Clearwater	FL	34618	William B Turner	813-535-6474	D	50	0.3
HPM Building Supply	380 Kanoelehua	Hilo	HI	96720	Michael K Fujimoto	808-935-0875	R	46	0.2
Soco-Lynch Corp.	3270 E Washington	Los Angeles	CA	90023	Jimmie Dunn	213-269-0191	S	42	<0.1
Clarence House Imports Ltd.	211 E 58th St	New York	NY	10021	Robin Roberts	212-752-2890	R	40	<0.1
Fred G. Anderson Inc.	5825 Excelsior Blvd	Minneapolis	MN	55416	Paul Norby	612-927-1800	R	38 *	0.2
H. Lynn White Inc.	8208 Nieman Rd	Lenexa	KS	66214	William H Hare Jr	913-492-4100	R	32 *	<0.1
Felmor Corp.	2020 Hollins Ferry	Baltimore	MD	21230	Robert Slatkin	410-669-6000	R	30 *	0.1
Cron Chemical Corp.	PO Box 14042	Houston	TX	77221	JJ Sette	713-644-7561	S	28	<0.1
Hardlines Marketing Inc.	PO Box 23080	Milwaukee	WI	53223	Tom Semrau	414-351-4700	R	27	<0.1
Forbo America Inc.	1105 N Market St	Wilmington	DE	19801	Doug Grimes	302-427-2139	R	27	<0.1
J.C. Licht Company Inc.	45 N Brandon Dr	Glendale H.	IL	60139	Gregory Licht	708-351-0400	R	25	0.3
Thompson Lacquer Company	2324 S Grand Ave	Los Angeles	CA	90007	Mort Kline	213-746-2290	R	24 *	0.3
Whittaker, Clark and Daniels	1000 Coolidge St	S. Plainfield	NJ	07080	George Dippold	908-561-6100	R	23	0.1
Ag-Land FS Inc.	1505 Valle Vista	Pekin	IL	61554	Kendall Miller	309-346-4145	R	22	<0.1
Management Supply Co.	2395 Research Dr	Farmington Hls	MI	48335	Fred Blechman	810-471-5500	S	21 *	<0.1
J.M. Lynne Company Inc.	PO Box 1010	Smithtown	NY	11787	Jonathan Landsberg	516-582-4300	R	21	0.1
Fargo Glass and Paint Co.	1801 7th Ave N	Fargo	ND	58102	Gerald Lovell	701-235-4441	R	20	0.1
Mattos Inc.	4501 Beech Rd	Camp Springs	MD	20748	Joseph G Mattos	301-423-1142	R	20	0.1
Westgate Fabrics Inc.	1000 Fountain Pkwy	Grand Prairie	TX	75050	J Jay Cassen	972-647-2323	R	20	0.1
Courtaulds Coatings Inc.	3658 Lawrenceville	Tucker	GA	30084	Tom Grant	404-938-4600	D	15 *	<0.1
Hamilton Equipment Inc.	567 S Reading Rd	Ephrata	PA	17522	R J Hamilton Jr	717-733-7951	R	15	<0.1
W.A. Wilson and Sons Inc.	6 Industrial Park	Wheeling	WV	26003	Robert H Hartong	304-232-2200	R	13	<0.1
Davis Paint Co.	PO Box 7589	Kansas City	MO	64116	Kevin C Ostby	816-471-4447	R	13	<0.1
John Seven Paint	3070 29th St SE	Grand Rapids	MI	49512	Charles K Seven	616-942-2020	R	13	<0.1
SmithChem Div.	84 Dayton Ave	Passaic	NJ	07055	Warren Klugman	201-779-5001	D	13 *	<0.1
Consolidated Coatings Corp.	PO Box 10	Brunswick	OH	44212	FP Malloy	216-220-6754	S	10	0.1
Ribelin Sales Inc.	PO Box 461673	Garland	TX	75046	Michael Ribelin	214-272-1594	R	8	<0.1
Lejere Sales Company Inc.	5 Lawrence St	Bloomfield	NJ	07003	Jeremy Blank	201-748-6502	R	7	<0.1
Columbus Wallcovering Co.	2301 Shermer Rd	Northbrook	IL	60062	Tim Schorn	708-882-7474	D	6	<0.1
RAE Products and Chemical	11630 S Cicero Ave	Alsip	IL	60658	Donna Gurenberg	708-396-1984	R	5 *	<0.1
CADCO Div.	2776 County Rd 69	Gibsonburg	OH	43431	James Herl	419-665-2367	D	4	<0.1

Source: *Ward's Business Directory of U.S. Private and Public Companies*, 1998. The company type code used is as follows: P - Public, R - Private, S - Subsidiary, D - Division, J - Joint Venture, A - Affiliate, G - Group. Sales are in millions of dollars, employees are in thousands. An asterisk (*) indicates an estimated sales volume. The symbol < stands for 'less than'.

OCCUPATIONS EMPLOYED BY SIC 519 - WHOLESALE TRADE, OTHER

Occupation	% of Total 1996	Change to 2006	Occupation	% of Total 1996	Change to 2006
Sales & related workers nec	19.5	20.2	Clerical supervisors & managers	1.9	20.2
General managers & top executives	5.9	16.4	Order clerks	1.9	8.2
Truck drivers light & heavy	5.4	20.2	Helpers, laborers nec	1.7	20.2
General office clerks	3.6	3.4	Electrical & electronic technicians	1.4	18.8
Traffic, shipping, receiving clerks	3.6	16.7	Blue collar worker supervisors	1.4	16.0
Stock clerks	3.5	-3.9	Wholesale & retail buyers, except farm products	1.3	17.0
Freight, stock, & material movers, hand	3.3	8.2	Office machine & cash register servicers	1.3	20.2
Marketing & sales worker supervisors	3.1	20.2	Hand packers & packagers	1.2	-3.9
Order fillers, wholesale & retail sales	3.0	16.7	Maintenance repairers, general utility	1.1	12.0
Bookkeeping, accounting, & auditing clerks	2.9	-3.9	Industrial truck & tractor operators	1.1	20.2
Salespersons, retail	2.5	20.2	Purchasing managers	1.1	20.2
Secretaries, except legal & medical	2.5	-4.7	Receptionists & information clerks	1.0	20.2
Assemblers, fabricators, hand workers nec	2.0	-3.9			

Source: *Industry-Occupation Matrix*, Bureau of Labor Statistics. These data relate to one or more 3-digit SIC industry groups rather than to a single 4-digit SIC. The change reported for each occupation to the year 2006 is a percent of growth or decline as estimated by the Bureau of Labor Statistics. The abbreviation nec stands for 'not elsewhere classified'.

STATE AND REGIONAL CONCENTRATION

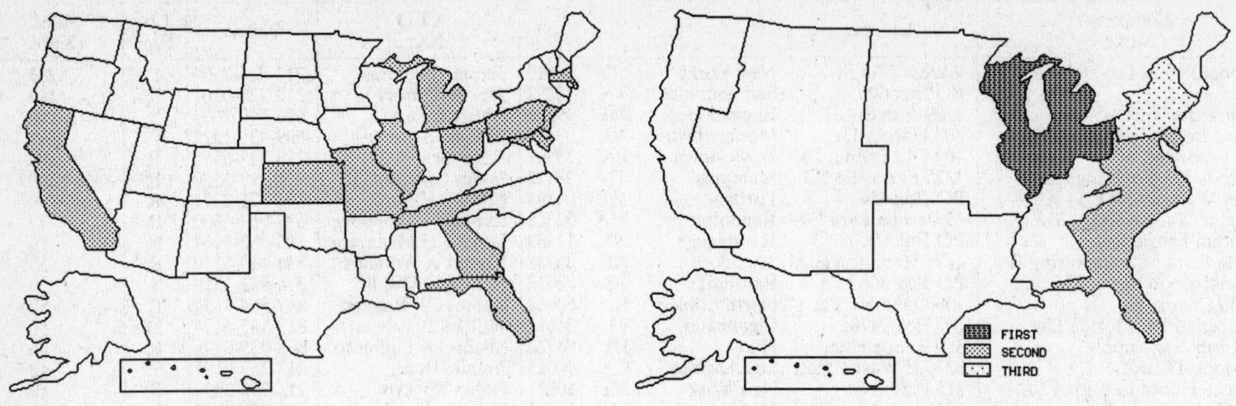

INDUSTRY DATA BY STATE

State	Establishments - 1995		Employment - 1995			Payroll - 1995		Sales - 1992		
	Total (number)	% of U.S.	Total (number)	% of U.S.	Per Estab.	Total ($ mil.)	Per Empl. ($)	Total ($ mil.)	% of U.S.	Per Estab ($)
California	352	10.5	3,266	11.6	9	108.7	33,269	1,114.9	13.0	309,444
Ohio	140	4.2	2,947	10.5	21	97.1	32,959	989.2	11.6	399,346
Pennsylvania	155	4.6	1,286	4.6	8	44.9	34,907	557.7	6.5	390,573
Texas	287	8.6	2,077	7.4	7	67.5	32,517	557.4	6.5	266,555
New York	186	5.6	1,746	6.2	9	56.4	32,285	555.4	6.5	257,845
Illinois	152	4.5	1,128	4.0	7	39.5	35,007	548.4	6.4	394,782
Florida	268	8.0	1,683	6.0	6	41.0	24,344	468.2	5.5	277,203
Georgia	156	4.7	1,185	4.2	8	33.7	28,474	378.8	4.4	325,699
New Jersey	101	3.0	1,173	4.2	12	45.6	38,841	366.4	4.3	294,994
Maryland	99	3.0	750	2.7	8	22.4	29,875	338.1	4.0	386,868
Michigan	111	3.3	1,157	4.1	10	37.5	32,375	322.2	3.8	291,074
Tennessee	64	1.9	683	2.4	11	17.4	25,488	255.6	3.0	690,708
Missouri	87	2.6	613	2.2	7	15.8	25,845	222.5	2.6	360,661
Massachusetts	49	1.5	650	2.3	13	21.8	33,506	215.6	2.5	289,364
Washington	109	3.3	661	2.4	6	19.3	29,245	158.0	1.8	226,981
North Carolina	97	2.9	592	2.1	6	16.0	27,074	129.7	1.5	252,840
Minnesota	40	1.2	340	1.2	9	8.2	23,982	118.0	1.4	227,888
Virginia	92	2.7	479	1.7	5	11.4	23,777	110.8	1.3	163,623
Colorado	55	1.6	379	1.3	7	10.8	28,443	106.2	1.2	196,619
Kansas	29	0.9	206	0.7	7	5.0	24,257	102.0	1.2	490,298
Connecticut	46	1.4	469	1.7	10	14.4	30,723	97.0	1.1	329,837
Indiana	81	2.4	554	2.0	7	15.1	27,186	97.0	1.1	180,216
Oregon	36	1.1	229	0.8	6	6.7	29,214	96.0	1.1	327,761
Kentucky	37	1.1	313	1.1	8	8.8	28,083	93.4	1.1	343,504
Wisconsin	66	2.0	562	2.0	9	12.2	21,683	91.5	1.1	157,558
Louisiana	49	1.5	335	1.2	7	9.3	27,782	66.8	0.8	210,830
South Carolina	53	1.6	358	1.3	7	9.7	27,148	66.2	0.8	163,365
Alabama	44	1.3	304	1.1	7	8.0	26,431	62.7	0.7	225,597
Arizona	59	1.8	404	1.4	7	9.5	23,525	50.7	0.6	165,166
Oklahoma	28	0.8	229	0.8	8	5.8	25,210	40.4	0.5	166,074
Utah	26	0.8	160	0.6	6	3.6	22,612	33.4	0.4	261,242
Arkansas	23	0.7	131	0.5	6	3.4	25,947	28.0	0.3	198,652
Delaware	10	0.3	49	0.2	5	1.7	34,673	22.3	0.3	297,533
Nevada	20	0.6	178	0.6	9	4.6	25,966	22.0	0.3	373,000
Iowa	17	0.5	174	0.6	10	3.4	19,713	19.5	0.2	153,283
Hawaii	18	0.5	103	0.4	6	2.6	25,670	13.8	0.2	149,739
New Mexico	12	0.4	69	0.2	6	1.8	25,768	13.2	0.2	137,427
West Virginia	8	0.2	45	0.2	6	1.3	28,844	10.2	0.1	217,085
Maine	6	0.2	0-19	-	-	(D)	-	7.1	0.1	153,913
Idaho	7	0.2	35	0.1	5	0.7	19,371	4.9	0.1	122,950
Vermont	5	0.1	0-19	-	-	(D)	-	2.6	0.0	287,333
Montana	5	0.1	20	0.1	4	0.4	18,700	2.1	0.0	192,000
Mississippi	13	0.4	110	0.4	8	3.1	27,936	(D)	-	-
Nebraska	13	0.4	80	0.3	6	2.2	27,562	(D)	-	-
D.C.	10	0.3	43	0.2	4	1.0	22,256	(D)	-	-
North Dakota	7	0.2	54	0.2	8	1.2	22,074	(D)	-	-
Rhode Island	7	0.2	57	0.2	8	1.5	26,474	(D)	-	-
Alaska	5	0.1	45	0.2	9	1.1	25,333	(D)	-	-
New Hampshire	4	0.1	20-99	-	-	(D)	-	(D)	-	-
South Dakota	4	0.1	13	0.0	3	0.3	21,538	(D)	-	-

Source: County Business Patterns, 1995 and *Economic Census of the U.S., 1992*. Data are sorted by 1992 revenues and, if revenues are unavailable, by establishments in 1995. The symbol (D) indicates that data are withheld by the source to avoid disclosure of competitive information. A dash (-) indicates that data are not available or undisclosed because they do not meet statistical validity standards. Shaded *states* on the state map indicate those states which have proportionately greater representation in the industry than would be indicated by the state's population; the ratio is based on total revenues or number of establishments. Shaded *regions* indicate where the industry is regionally most concentrated.

5199 - NONDURABLE GOODS, NEC

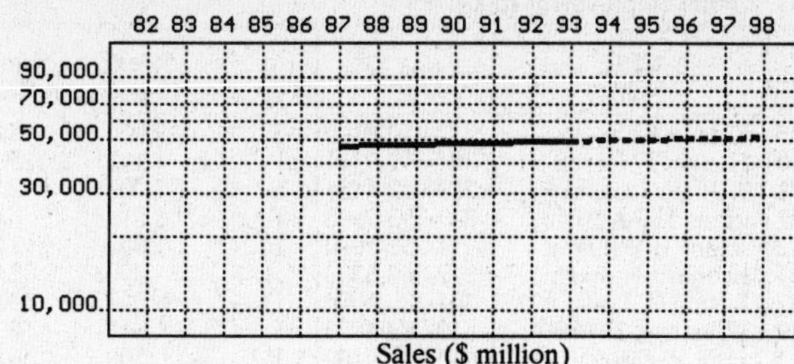

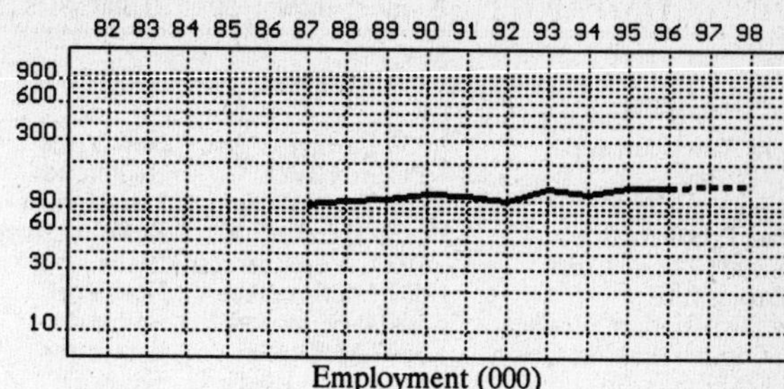

GENERAL STATISTICS

Year	Establishments (number)	Employment (number)	Payroll ($ million)	Sales ($ million)	Expenses ($ million)	Beginning Inventory ($ million)	Ending Inventory ($ million)
1982	-	-	-	-	-	-	-
1983	-	-	-	-	-	-	-
1984	-	-	-	-	-	-	-
1985	-	-	-	-	-	-	-
1986	-	-	-	-	-	-	-
1987	12,375	95,519	1,983.3	46,927.9	4,452.0	2,318.7	2,621.8
1988	11,514	101,081	2,322.5	47,336.2e	4,709.0e	2,348.3e	2,651.1e
1989	11,438	105,441	2,511.6	47,744.6e	4,965.9e	2,377.8e	2,680.5e
1990	12,796	115,968	2,795.8	48,152.9e	5,222.9e	2,407.4e	2,709.8e
1991	13,131	111,459	2,792.8	48,561.2e	5,479.8e	2,436.9e	2,739.1e
1992	15,535	101,114	2,645.4	48,969.6	5,736.8	2,466.5	2,768.5
1993	18,293	129,068	3,414.4	49,377.9p	5,993.7p	2,496.0p	2,797.8p
1994	17,778	117,097	3,176.8	49,786.2p	6,250.7p	2,525.6p	2,827.2p
1995	18,822	130,395	3,551.2	50,194.6p	6,507.6p	2,555.1p	2,856.5p
1996	19,717p	130,234p	3,673.4p	50,602.9p	6,764.6p	2,584.7p	2,885.8p
1997	20,734p	133,900p	3,848.3p	51,011.2p	7,021.5p	2,614.2p	2,915.2p
1998	21,751p	137,566p	4,023.1p	51,419.6p	7,278.5p	2,643.8p	2,944.5p

Sources: *Economic Census of the United States*, 1982, 1987, and 1992. Establishment counts, employment, and payroll are from *County Business Patterns* for non-Census years. Values followed by a 'p' are projections by the editors. Sales and expense data for non-Census years are extrapolations, marked by 'e'. Industries reclassified in 1987 will not have data for prior years. Data are the most recent available at this level of detail.

INDICES OF CHANGE

Year	Establishments (number)	Employment (number)	Payroll ($ million)	Sales ($ million)	Expenses ($ million)	Beginning Inventory ($ million)	Ending Inventory ($ million)
1982	-	-	-	-	-	-	-
1983	-	-	-	-	-	-	-
1984	-	-	-	-	-	-	-
1985	-	-	-	-	-	-	-
1986	-	-	-	-	-	-	-
1987	79.7	94.5	75.0	95.8	77.6	94.0	94.7
1988	74.1	100.0	87.8	96.7e	82.1e	95.2e	95.8e
1989	73.6	104.3	94.9	97.5e	86.6e	96.4e	96.8e
1990	82.4	114.7	105.7	98.3e	91.0e	97.6e	97.9e
1991	84.5	110.2	105.6	99.2e	95.5e	98.8e	98.9e
1992	100.0	100.0	100.0	100.0	100.0	100.0	100.0
1993	117.8	127.6	129.1	100.8p	104.5p	101.2p	101.1p
1994	114.4	115.8	120.1	101.7p	109.0p	102.4p	102.1p
1995	121.2	129.0	134.2	102.5p	113.4p	103.6p	103.2p
1996	126.9p	128.8p	138.9p	103.3p	117.9p	104.8p	104.2p
1997	133.5p	132.4p	145.5p	104.2p	122.4p	106.0p	105.3p
1998	140.0p	136.1p	152.1p	105.0p	126.9p	107.2p	106.4p

Sources: Same as General Statistics. The values shown reflect change from the base year, 1992. Values above 100 mean greater than 1992, values below 100 mean less than 1992, and a value of 100 in the 1982-91 or 1993-98 period means same as 1992. Values followed by a 'p' are projections by the editors; 'e' stands for extrapolation. Data are the most recent available at this level of detail.

SELECTED RATIOS

For 1992	Avg. of All Wholesale	Analyzed Industry	Index	For 1992	Avg. of All Wholesale	Analyzed Industry	Index
Employees per Establishment	12	7	56	Sales per Employee	561,172	484,301	86
Payroll per Establishment	349,729	170,286	49	Sales per Establishment	6,559,346	3,152,211	48
Payroll per Employee	29,919	26,163	87	Expenses per Establishment	723,071	369,282	51

Sources: Same as General Statistics. The 'Average of All Manufacturing' column represents the average of all manufacturing industries reported for the most recent complete year available. The Index shows the relationship between the Average and the Analyzed Industry. For example, 100 means that they are equal; 500 that the Analyzed Industry is five times the average; 50 means that the Analyzed Industry is half the national average. The abbreviation 'na' is used to show that data are 'not available'.

LEADING COMPANIES

Number shown: **50** Total sales ($ mil): **44,386** Total employment (000): **69.1**

Company Name	Address				CEO Name	Phone	Co. Type	Sales ($ mil)	Empl. (000)
Marubeni America Corp.	450 Lexington Ave	New York	NY	10017	Katsuo Koh	212-450-0100	S	29,000 •	2.2
Universal Corp.	PO Box 25099	Richmond	VA	23260	Henry H Harrell	804-359-9311	P	4,113	25.0
Rykoff-Sexton Mfg Div.	761 Terminal St	Los Angeles	CA	90021	William J Caskey	213-622-4131	S	1,700	2.8
BT Office Products Intern.	2150 E Lake Cook	Buffalo Grove	IL	60089	Frans H J Koffrie	847-793-7500	P	1,619	6.6
Golden State Foods Corp.	18301 Von Karman	Irvine	CA	92612	James E Williams	714-252-2000	R	1,000	1.8
Hartz Group Inc.	667 Madison Ave	New York	NY	10021	Leonard N Stern	212-308-3336	R	890 •	2.0
Marriot Distribution Services	10400 Fernwood Rd	Bethesda	MD	20817	Robert T Pras	301-380-3000	D	872	13.0
Central Garden and Pet Co.	3697 Mt Diablo	Lafayette	CA	94549	William E Brown	510-283-4573	P	841	2.7
Harold M. Pitman Co.	721 Union Blvd	Totowa	NJ	07512	John W Dreyer	973-812-0400	R	500	0.6
Wang's International Inc.	4250 E Shelby Dr	Memphis	TN	38118	Robert Wang	901-362-2111	R	470 •	1.0
Frederick Atkins Inc.	1515 Broadway	New York	NY	10036	Nancy Marino	212-840-7000	R	450	0.2
Blyth Industries Inc.	100 Field Point Rd	Greenwich	CT	06830	Robert B Goergen	203-661-1926	P	331	2.1
Houston Foods Co.	3501 Mt Prospect	Franklin Park	IL	60131	Robert P Pesch	847-957-9191	R	196 •	0.2
Friedman Bag Company Inc.	PO Box 866004	Los Angeles	CA	90086	Alvin Lanfeld	213-628-2341	R	160 •	0.3
Spring Arbor Distribution	10885 Textile Rd	Belleville	MI	48111	Rick Pigott	313-481-0900	R	157	0.7
A.T. Cross Co.	One Albion Rd	Lincoln	RI	02865	Russell A Boss	401-333-1200	P	155	1.1
General Merchandise Services	PO Box 700	Bellefontaine	OH	43311	James W Donnelly	513-592-7025	D	150 •	0.3
Imperial Commodities Corp.	17 Battery Pl	New York	NY	10004	Lee J Muenzen	212-837-9400	S	140 •	<0.1
Golden Cat	300 Airport Rd	Cape Girardeau	MO	63702	Bob Watt	573-334-6618	D	135	0.7
Kenlin Pet Supply Inc.	301 Island Rd	Mahwah	NJ	07430	Neill Hines	201-529-5050	P	100	0.4
Koval Marketing Inc.	11208 47th Ave W	Mukilteo	WA	98275	Roy Koval	425-347-4249	R	100	<0.1
Loui Michel Cie	2311 Boswell Rd	Chula Vista	CA	91914	Michael Block	619-482-2922	R	89 •	0.2
Dupey Management Corp.	9015 Sterling St	Irving	TX	75063	Michael Dupey	214-929-8595	R	85	1.7
Food Ingredients and Additives	620 Progress Ave	Waukesha	WI	53186	David Carpenter	414-547-5531	D	70	0.2
Blumenthal-Lansing Co.	1 Palmer Ter	Carlstadt	NJ	07072	Ralph Langer	201-935-6220	S	68	0.1
Consumer Products Co.	345 S High St	Muncie	IN	47305	Jack Metz	765-281-5019	S	65 •	0.1
Fitz and Floyd Silvestri	501 Corporateive	Lewisville	TX	75057	Arthur Bylin	972-918-0098	R	63 •	0.3
FSC Educational Inc.	223 S Illinois Ave	Mansfield	OH	44905	James D Miller	419-589-8222	R	54 •	0.3
Great Lakes Pet Supply Inc.	7774-A S 10th St	Oak Creek	WI	53154	James Merkel	414-570-1000	R	53 •	0.1
Wise El Santo Company Inc.	PO Box 8360	St. Louis	MO	63132	Rudolph L Wise	314-428-3100	R	51 •	0.1
Kurt S. Adler Inc.	1107 Broadway	New York	NY	10010	Kurt S Adler	212-924-0900	R	50	0.2
Texas Art Supply Co.	PO Box 66328	Houston	TX	77006	Louis K Adler	713-526-5221	R	47	0.2
Roman Inc.	555 Lawrence Ave	Roselle	IL	60172	Ronald Jedlinski	708-529-3000	R	45	0.2
Newton Manufacturing Co.	1123 1st Ave E	Newton	IA	50208	Mancil R Laidig	515-792-4121	R	41	0.2
Clarence House Imports Ltd.	211 E 58th St	New York	NY	10021	Robin Roberts	212-752-2890	R	40	<0.1
ConAgra Pet Products Co.	1 Central Park Plz	Omaha	NE	68102	Robert Scharf	402-595-7000	S	40 •	<0.1
Thomas Monahan Co.	202 N Oak St	Arcola	IL	61910	T F Monahan Jr	217-268-4955	R	40	0.2
Hahn and Phillips Grease	PO Box 130	Marshall	MO	65340	Larry R Phillips	660-886-9688	R	35	<0.1
Helveston Associates Inc.	2165 EW Park Ct	Stone Mountain	GA	30087	Steve Helveston	404-879-8334	R	35	<0.1
Sullivan's	PO Box 5361	Sioux Falls	SD	57117	Marian Sullivan	605-339-4274	R	35	<0.1
Humboldt Industries Inc.	1 Maplewood Dr	Hazleton	PA	18201	Jack Rosenzweig	717-384-5555	R	33	<0.1
Fabri Quilt Inc.	901 E 14th Ave	N. Kansas City	MO	64116	Lionel J Kunst	816-421-2000	R	32	0.2
M. Conley Company Inc.	1312 4th St SE	Canton	OH	44701	Richard D Conley	216-456-8243	R	32	0.1
Rust Wholesale Company Inc.	PO Box 230	Greensburg	IN	47240	Joseph F Rust	812-663-7394	R	32	<0.1
United Cooperative Farmers	22 Kimball Pl	Fitchburg	MA	01420	Donald Upton	508-345-4103	R	31 •	<0.1
Specialty Merchandise Corp.	9401 De Soto Ave	Chatsworth	CA	91311	Mark Schwartz	818-998-3300	R	30	0.2
W.P. Ballard and Co.	PO Box 12246	Birmingham	AL	35202	John Beeler Jr	205-251-7272	R	30	<0.1
Leather Factory Inc.	PO Box 50429	Fort Worth	TX	76105	Wray Thompson	817-496-4414	P	28	0.2
Morris Rothenberg and Son	25 Ranick Rd	Smithtown	NY	11788	Milton Somberg	516-234-8000	R	28	<0.1
George Zolton Lefton Co.	3622 S Morgan St	Chicago	IL	60609	George Z Lefton	312-254-4344	R	26 •	<0.1

Source: *Ward's Business Directory of U.S. Private and Public Companies*, 1998. The company type code used is as follows: P - Public, R - Private, S - Subsidiary, D - Division, J - Joint Venture, A - Affiliate, G - Group. Sales are in millions of dollars, employees are in thousands. An asterisk (*) indicates an estimated sales volume. The symbol < stands for 'less than'.

OCCUPATIONS EMPLOYED BY SIC 519 - WHOLESALE TRADE, OTHER

Occupation	% of Total 1996	Change to 2006	Occupation	% of Total 1996	Change to 2006
Sales & related workers nec	19.5	20.2	Clerical supervisors & managers	1.9	20.2
General managers & top executives	5.9	16.4	Order clerks	1.9	8.2
Truck drivers light & heavy	5.4	20.2	Helpers, laborers nec	1.7	20.2
General office clerks	3.6	3.4	Electrical & electronic technicians	1.4	18.8
Traffic, shipping, receiving clerks	3.6	16.7	Blue collar worker supervisors	1.4	16.0
Stock clerks	3.5	-3.9	Wholesale & retail buyers, except farm products	1.3	17.0
Freight, stock, & material movers, hand	3.3	8.2	Office machine & cash register servicers	1.3	20.2
Marketing & sales worker supervisors	3.1	20.2	Hand packers & packagers	1.2	-3.9
Order fillers, wholesale & retail sales	3.0	16.7	Maintenance repairers, general utility	1.1	12.0
Bookkeeping, accounting, & auditing clerks	2.9	-3.9	Industrial truck & tractor operators	1.1	20.2
Salespersons, retail	2.5	20.2	Purchasing managers	1.1	20.2
Secretaries, except legal & medical	2.5	-4.7	Receptionists & information clerks	1.0	20.2
Assemblers, fabricators, hand workers nec	2.0	-3.9			

Source: *Industry-Occupation Matrix*, Bureau of Labor Statistics. These data relate to one or more 3-digit SIC industry groups rather than to a single 4-digit SIC. The change reported for each occupation to the year 2006 is a percent of growth or decline as estimated by the Bureau of Labor Statistics. The abbreviation nec stands for 'not elsewhere classified'.

STATE AND REGIONAL CONCENTRATION

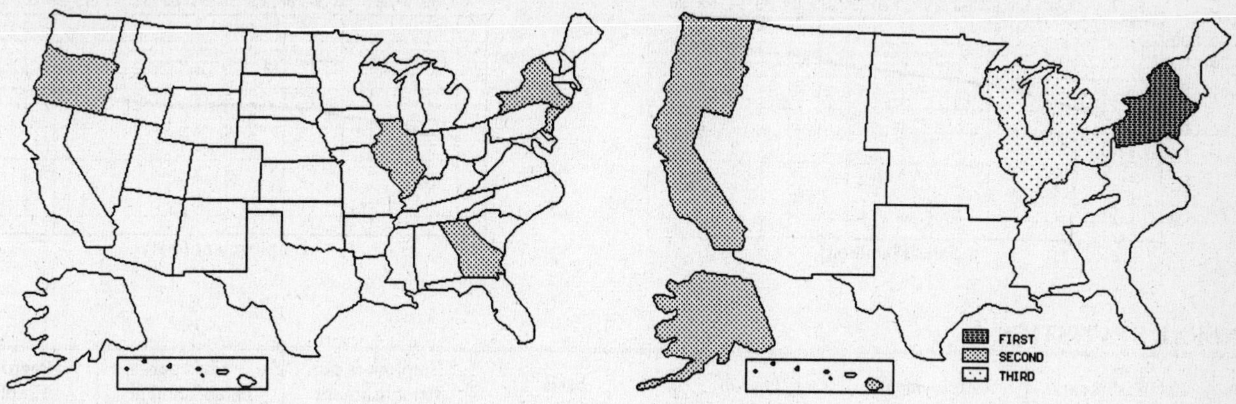

INDUSTRY DATA BY STATE

State	Establishments - 1995 Total (number)	% of U.S.	Employment - 1995 Total (number)	% of U.S.	Per Estab.	Payroll - 1995 Total ($ mil.)	Per Empl. ($)	Sales - 1992 Total ($ mil.)	% of U.S.	Per Estab ($)
New York	1,979	10.5	12,634	9.7	6	504.3	39,919	22,154.5	47.9	2,059,927
California	3,860	20.5	24,264	18.6	6	635.5	26,192	4,311.5	9.3	248,444
New Jersey	693	3.7	6,118	4.7	9	212.3	34,708	2,956.6	6.4	493,750
Illinois	872	4.6	7,626	5.8	9	250.5	32,854	2,373.1	5.1	352,508
Texas	1,143	6.1	7,939	6.1	7	193.0	24,305	1,489.4	3.2	248,818
Georgia	589	3.1	4,915	3.8	8	133.6	27,188	1,371.8	3.0	379,908
Florida	1,382	7.3	6,886	5.3	5	146.5	21,278	1,279.3	2.8	221,940
North Carolina	621	3.3	3,821	2.9	6	108.9	28,495	1,246.2	2.7	443,656
Ohio	635	3.4	5,090	3.9	8	128.5	25,251	1,143.3	2.5	286,676
Washington	324	1.7	2,107	1.6	7	50.5	23,990	924.2	2.0	575,087
Pennsylvania	772	4.1	4,016	3.1	5	97.5	24,287	885.6	1.9	282,587
Oregon	163	0.9	1,371	1.1	8	30.4	22,177	843.1	1.8	801,438
Michigan	388	2.1	2,567	2.0	7	75.9	29,559	617.7	1.3	330,843
Massachusetts	339	1.8	2,363	1.8	7	75.3	31,885	604.5	1.3	301,332
Missouri	328	1.7	2,975	2.3	9	72.3	24,298	517.2	1.1	282,327
South Carolina	177	0.9	1,284	1.0	7	32.0	24,926	508.6	1.1	417,587
Virginia	301	1.6	2,173	1.7	7	53.8	24,779	438.1	0.9	192,157
Indiana	294	1.6	1,725	1.3	6	41.2	23,901	436.2	0.9	321,239
Tennessee	273	1.5	2,129	1.6	8	46.3	21,745	410.2	0.9	245,030
Wisconsin	316	1.7	2,120	1.6	7	52.0	24,540	355.4	0.8	198,997
Colorado	281	1.5	1,478	1.1	5	32.8	22,222	209.0	0.5	175,807
Iowa	135	0.7	1,343	1.0	10	27.7	20,655	206.2	0.4	140,446
Oklahoma	124	0.7	945	0.7	8	19.0	20,142	144.5	0.3	209,787
Alabama	159	0.8	1,188	0.9	7	24.7	20,809	130.0	0.3	133,860
Arizona	262	1.4	1,392	1.1	5	31.4	22,532	127.8	0.3	132,996
Rhode Island	73	0.4	475	0.4	7	13.2	27,863	124.2	0.3	308,065
Nebraska	72	0.4	2,811	2.2	39	48.1	17,115	118.1	0.3	126,939
Hawaii	109	0.6	596	0.5	5	12.9	21,713	94.3	0.2	179,257
Utah	88	0.5	763	0.6	9	14.1	18,509	64.7	0.1	174,816
Arkansas	91	0.5	645	0.5	7	9.4	14,600	45.4	0.1	111,326
New Mexico	96	0.5	419	0.3	4	6.6	15,730	32.9	0.1	128,480
West Virginia	37	0.2	232	0.2	6	4.1	17,595	29.9	0.1	170,914
Montana	35	0.2	305	0.2	9	4.0	13,269	22.9	0.0	104,872
Alaska	29	0.2	134	0.1	5	3.2	24,201	20.3	0.0	184,882
Minnesota	329	1.7	3,399	2.6	10	105.5	31,043	(D)	-	-
Maryland	267	1.4	1,467	1.1	5	43.2	29,459	(D)	-	-
Connecticut	226	1.2	2,134	1.6	9	67.1	31,466	(D)	-	-
Kentucky	159	0.8	1,062	0.8	7	23.5	22,122	(D)	-	-
Louisiana	143	0.8	673	0.5	5	14.0	20,825	(D)	-	-
Kansas	138	0.7	932	0.7	7	19.7	21,171	(D)	-	-
Nevada	93	0.5	792	0.6	9	16.7	21,047	(D)	-	-
Mississippi	81	0.4	570	0.4	7	9.0	15,721	(D)	-	-
New Hampshire	63	0.3	263	0.2	4	8.1	30,852	(D)	-	-
Maine	60	0.3	947	0.7	16	23.8	25,148	(D)	-	-
Idaho	46	0.2	385	0.3	8	8.0	20,831	(D)	-	-
Vermont	41	0.2	189	0.1	5	3.9	20,841	(D)	-	-
Delaware	36	0.2	183	0.1	5	4.6	25,115	(D)	-	-
D.C.	33	0.2	171	0.1	5	4.8	28,287	(D)	-	-
North Dakota	25	0.1	175	0.1	7	2.7	15,411	(D)	-	-
South Dakota	25	0.1	155	0.1	6	3.6	22,994	(D)	-	-
Wyoming	17	0.1	49	0.0	3	0.7	14,857	(D)	-	-

Source: *County Business Patterns, 1995* and *Economic Census of the U.S., 1992*. Data are sorted by 1992 revenues and, if revenues are unavailable, by establishments in 1995. The symbol (D) indicates that data are withheld by the source to avoid disclosure of competitive information. A dash (-) indicates that data are not available or undisclosed because they do not meet statistical validity standards. Shaded *states* on the state map indicate those states which have proportionately greater representation in the industry than would be indicated by the state's population; the ratio is based on total revenues or number of establishments. Shaded *regions* indicate where the industry is regionally most concentrated.

5211 - LUMBER AND OTHER BUILDING MATERIALS

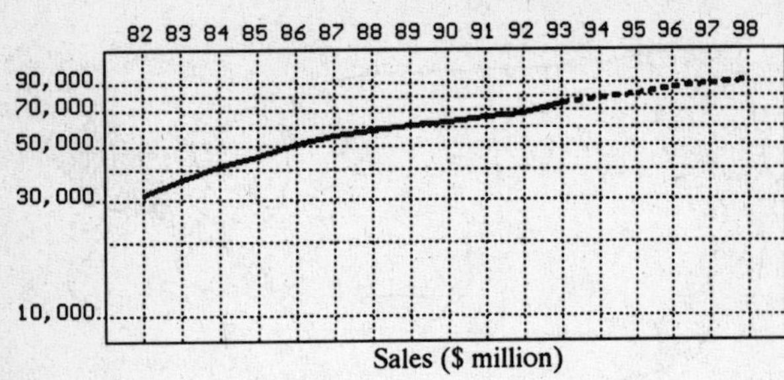

Sales ($ million)

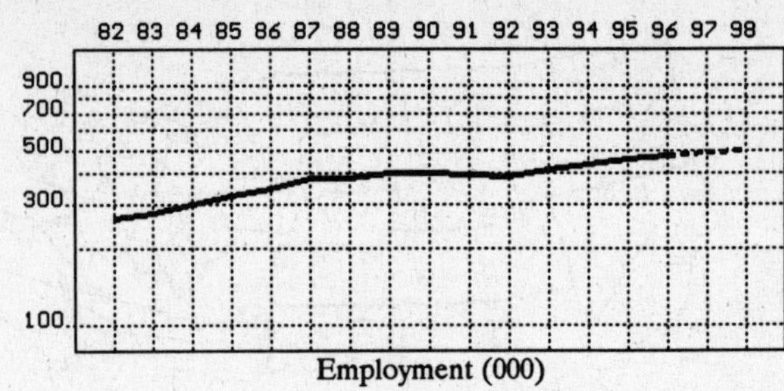

Employment (000)

GENERAL STATISTICS

Year	Establishments (number)	Employment (number)	Payroll ($ million)	Sales ($ million)	Employees per Establishment (number)	Sales per Establishment ($)	Payroll per Employee ($)
1982	26,187	264,849	3,662.7	31,451.2	10	1,201,023	13,830
1983	25,930	276,789	4,144.4	36,217.7e	11	-	14,973
1984	26,060	302,993	4,709.1	40,984.3e	12	-	15,542
1985	26,295	322,241	5,170.6	45,750.8e	12	-	16,046
1986	26,916	347,130	5,815.3	50,517.4e	13	-	16,752
1987	27,497	379,984	6,156.9	55,284.0	14	2,010,545	16,203
1988	27,077	385,580	6,831.5	57,887.3e	14	-	17,717
1989	27,025	402,369	7,287.8	60,490.6e	15	-	18,112
1990	27,518	403,174	7,503.0	63,094.0e	15	-	18,610
1991	27,362	393,825	7,584.0	65,697.3e	14	-	19,257
1992	25,401	386,260	7,519.5	68,300.7	15	2,688,896	19,467
1993	25,850	411,323	8,397.7	74,443.8p	16	-	20,416
1994	26,064	438,677	9,116.9	78,128.8p	17	-	20,783
1995	24,020	454,837	9,529.3	81,813.7p	19	-	20,951
1996	25,834p	468,083p	9,870.3p	85,498.6p	-	-	-
1997	25,762p	481,255p	10,296.6p	89,183.6p	-	-	-
1998	25,691p	494,428p	10,722.8p	92,868.5p	-	-	-

Sources: *Economic Census of the United States*, 1982, 1987, and 1992. Establishment counts, employment, and payroll are from *County Business Patterns* for non-Census years. Values followed by a 'p' are projections by the editors. Sales and expense data for non-Census years are extrapolations, marked by 'e'. Industries reclassified in 1987 will not have data for prior years. Data are the most recent available at this level of detail.

INDICES OF CHANGE

Year	Establishments (number)	Employment (number)	Payroll ($ million)	Sales ($ million)	Employees per Establishment (number)	Sales per Establishment ($)	Payroll per Employee ($)
1982	103.1	68.6	48.7	46.0	66.7	44.7	71.0
1983	102.1	71.7	55.1	53.0e	73.3	-	76.9
1984	102.6	78.4	62.6	60.0e	80.0	-	79.8
1985	103.5	83.4	68.8	67.0e	80.0	-	82.4
1986	106.0	89.9	77.3	74.0e	86.7	-	86.1
1987	108.3	98.4	81.9	80.9	93.3	74.8	83.2
1988	106.6	99.8	90.9	84.8e	93.3	-	91.0
1989	106.4	104.2	96.9	88.6e	100.0	-	93.0
1990	108.3	104.4	99.8	92.4e	100.0	-	95.6
1991	107.7	102.0	100.9	96.2e	93.3	-	98.9
1992	100.0	100.0	100.0	100.0	100.0	100.0	100.0
1993	101.8	106.5	111.7	109.0p	106.1	-	104.9
1994	102.6	113.6	121.2	114.4p	112.2	-	106.8
1995	94.6	117.8	126.7	119.8p	126.2	-	107.6
1996	101.7p	121.2p	131.3p	125.2p	-	-	-
1997	101.4p	124.6p	136.9p	130.6p	-	-	-
1998	101.1p	128.0p	142.6p	136.0p	-	-	-

Sources: Same as General Statistics. The values shown reflect change from the base year, 1992. Values above 100 mean greater than 1992, values below 100 mean less than 1992, and a value of 100 in the 1982-91 or 1993-98 period means same as 1992. Values followed by a 'p' are projections by the editors; 'e' stands for extrapolation. Data are the most recent available at this level of detail.

SELECTED RATIOS

For 1992	Avg. of All Retail	Analyzed Industry	Index	For 1992	Avg. of All Retail	Analyzed Industry	Index
Employees per Establishment	12	15	126	Sales per Employee	102,941	176,826	172
Payroll per Establishment	146,026	296,032	203	Sales per Establishment	1,241,555	2,688,898	217
Payroll per Employee	12,107	19,467	161	Expenses per Establishment	na	na	na

Sources: Same as General Statistics. The 'Average of All Manufacturing' column represents the average of all manufacturing industries reported for the most recent complete year available. The Index shows the relationship between the Average and the Analyzed Industry. For example, 100 means that they are equal; 500 that the Analyzed Industry is five times the average; 50 means that the Analyzed Industry is half the national average. The abbreviation 'na' is used to show that data are 'not available'.

LEADING COMPANIES
Number shown: **50** Total sales ($ mil): **77,730** Total employment (000): **514.9**

Company Name	Address				CEO Name	Phone	Co. Type	Sales ($ mil)	Empl. (000)
Kmart Corp.	3100 W Big Beaver	Troy	MI	48084	Floyd Hall	810-643-1000	P	31,437	265.0
Home Depot Inc.	2727 Paces Ferry	Atlanta	GA	30339	Bernard Marcus	404-433-8211	P	19,535	80.8
Lowe's Companies Inc.	PO Box 1111	N. Wilkesboro	NC	28656	Robert L Tillman	910-651-4000	P	10,136	54.0
84 Lumber Co.	Rte 519, Box 8484	Eighty Four	PA	15384	Joseph A Hardy	412-228-8820	R	1,600	4.5
Hechinger Co.	1801 McCormick	Largo	MD	20774	Anthony Perillo Jr	301-341-1000	R	1,360	28.0
Carolina Builders Corp.	3227 Wellington Ct	Raleigh	NC	27615	Fenton Hord	919-828-7471	S	1,200	4.0
Menard Inc.	4777 Menard Dr	Eau Claire	WI	54703	John Menard	715-876-5911	R	1,100	18.0
Wickes Lumber Co.	706 N Deerpath Dr	Vernon Hills	IL	60061	J Steven Wilson	847-367-3400	P	849	3.4
Lanoga Corp.	PO Box 97040	Redmond	WA	98073	Daryl D Nagel	425-883-4125	S	841 •	3.6
Harrisons and Crosfield	900 Market St	Wilmington	DE	19801	Mark L Barocas	302-888-1748	S	800	3.0
Eagle Hardware and Garden	981 Powell Ave SW	Renton	WA	98055	D J Heerensperger	206-227-5740	P	761	4.6
Orchard Supply Hardware Corp.	PO Box 49027	San Jose	CA	95161	Jerry Post	408-281-3500	S	641 •	6.0
BMC West Corp.	PO Box 8008	Boise	ID	83707	D S Hendrickson	208-338-4300	P	630	2.9
PNP Prime Corp.	1209 S Central	Kent	WA	98064	John Markley	206-854-5450	P	498	2.7
Wolohan Lumber Co.	PO Box 3235	Saginaw	MI	48605	James L Wolohan	517-793-4532	P	425	1.5
Pelican Companies Inc.	PO Box 260001	Conway	SC	29526	Ben Phillips	803-347-4235	R	420 •	1.7
United Building Centers	PO Box 5550	Winona	MN	55987	Dale Kukowski	507-452-2361	D	400	3.2
Grossman's Inc.	45 Dan Rd	Canton	MA	02021	Seymour Kroll	617-830-4000	P	386	1.4
McCoy Corp.	PO Box 1028	San Marcos	TX	78667	Brian McCoy	512-353-5400	R	370 •	1.3
Erb Lumber Co.	375 S Eton Rd	Birmingham	MI	48008	Fred A Erb	313-644-5300	R	320 •	2.0
Carter-Jones Lumber Co.	601 Tallmadge Rd	Kent	OH	44240	Bryan Carter	330-673-6100	R	290 •	4.0
West Lumber Company Inc.	5775 Glenridge Dr	Atlanta	GA	30328	Vincent West	404-847-7801	R	290 •	1.8
Anderson Lumber Co.	PO Box 9459	Ogden	UT	84409	James C Beardall	801-479-3400	R	285	1.6
Lumbermen's of Washington	PO Box 3406	Olympia	WA	98503	MD Dittmer	360-456-1880	D	220	0.7
Foxworth-Galbraith Lumber Co.	17111 Waterview	Dallas	TX	75252	Walter Foxworth	214-437-6100	R	190 •	1.2
National Home Centers Inc.	PO Box 789	Springdale	AR	72765	Dwain A Newman	501-756-1700	P	177	0.7
Copeland Lumber Yard Inc.	901 NE Glisan St	Portland	OR	97232	Helen J Whitsell	503-232-7181	R	175	1.0
Idaho Forest Industries Inc.	PO Box 6600	Coeur D'Alene	ID	83816	James M English	208-765-1414	R	175 •	0.6
DeGeorge Financial Corp.	99 Realty Dr	Cheshire	CT	06410	Peter R DeGeorge	203-699-3400	P	168	0.4
Seigle's Home and Building	1331 Davis Rd	Elgin	IL	60123	M Seigle	708-742-2000	R	151	0.7
Dixieline Lumber Co.	3250 Sports Arena	San Diego	CA	92110	William S Cowling II	619-224-4120	R	150	0.7
Strober Organization Inc.	550 Hamilton Ave	Brooklyn	NY	11232	Robert J Gaites	718-832-1212	P	126	0.3
Stambaugh-Thompson Co.	3745 Hendricks Rd	Youngstown	OH	44515	Philip F Thompson	216-792-9071	R	113	1.6
Scherer Brothers Lumber Co.	9110 83rd Ave	Brooklyn Park	MN	55445	Peter L Scherer	612-379-9633	R	110	0.4
Lampert Yards Inc.	1850 Como Ave	St. Paul	MN	55108	Daniel L Fesler	612-645-8155	R	105	0.5
Fagen's Inc.	9000 Brooktree Rd	Wexford	PA	15090	Jack Fagen	412-935-3700	R	100	0.5
Builderway Inc.	PO Drawer 27107	Greenville	SC	29616	Newell LaVoy	803-297-6266	R	98 •	0.4
Brookharts Inc.	704 S Sierra Madre	Co Springs	CO	80907	TW Watt	719-471-4500	R	96 •	0.4
Sunbelt Companies Inc.	PO Box 27169	Greenville	SC	29616	J Thomas Mills	803-244-4137	S	94	0.4
Leeds Building Products Inc.	1395 S Marietta	Marietta	GA	30067	Jack Stone	404-421-2950	R	92	0.8
A.C. Houston Lumber Co.	125 N Market St	Wichita	KS	67202	Bob Houston	316-262-8491	R	90	0.4
Hill Behan Lumber Co.	6515 Page Blvd	St. Louis	MO	63133	Patrick J Behan	314-725-1111	R	90	0.4
Gerrity Company Inc.	90 Oak St	Newton Up. Fls	MA	02164	James F Gerrity III	617-244-1400	S	87	0.3
Great Plains Supply Inc.	PO Box 64557	St. Paul	MN	55164	Michael R Wigley	612-635-9271	R	86	0.6
Church's Lumber Yards	PO Box 189005	Utica	MI	48318	W Church	313-731-2050	R	84	0.5
Alexander Lumber Co.	515 Redwood Dr	Aurora	IL	60507	Walter Alexander	708-844-5123	R	82 •	0.5
Vaughan and Sons Inc.	PO Box 17258	San Antonio	TX	78217	Curtis Vaughan III	210-352-1300	R	78 •	0.3
Babbitt Brothers Trading Co.	PO Box 1328	Flagstaff	AZ	86002	David Chambers	602-774-8711	R	75	0.6
Charles C. Meek Lumber Co.	PO Box 1746	Springfield	MO	65801	Terry O Meek	417-862-7001	R	73 •	0.5
Star Lumber and Supply	PO Box 7712	Wichita	KS	67277	CJ Goebel	316-942-2221	R	73	0.6

Source: *Ward's Business Directory of U.S. Private and Public Companies*, 1998. The company type code used is as follows: P - Public, R - Private, S - Subsidiary, D - Division, J - Joint Venture, A - Affiliate, G - Group. Sales are in millions of dollars, employees are in thousands. An asterisk (*) indicates an estimated sales volume. The symbol < stands for 'less than'.

OCCUPATIONS EMPLOYED BY SIC 521 - LUMBER AND OTHER BUILDING MATERIALS

Occupation	% of Total 1996	Change to 2006	Occupation	% of Total 1996	Change to 2006
Salespersons, retail	24.7	7.5	Industrial truck & tractor operators	2.5	12.2
Stock clerks	8.8	72.2	General office clerks	2.4	-3.5
Truck drivers light & heavy	8.7	-10.3	Freight, stock, & material movers, hand	2.4	0.9
Cashiers	8.7	13.5	Traffic, shipping, receiving clerks	2.4	12.2
Sales & related workers nec	5.7	23.4	Assemblers, fabricators, hand workers nec	1.5	12.2
Marketing & sales worker supervisors	5.1	12.2	Carpenters	1.4	-9.3
General managers & top executives	4.7	8.7	Helpers, laborers nec	1.3	12.2
Bookkeeping, accounting, & auditing clerks	3.0	-10.3	Wood machinists	1.0	-43.9

Source: *Industry-Occupation Matrix*, Bureau of Labor Statistics. These data relate to one or more 3-digit SIC industry groups rather than to a single 4-digit SIC. The change reported for each occupation to the year 2006 is a percent of growth or decline as estimated by the Bureau of Labor Statistics. The abbreviation nec stands for 'not elsewhere classified'.

STATE AND REGIONAL CONCENTRATION

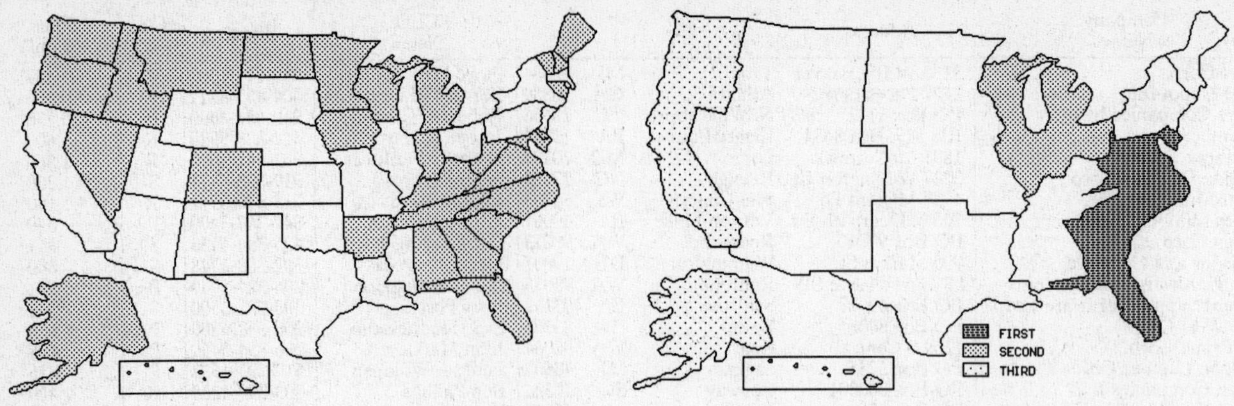

INDUSTRY DATA BY STATE

State	Establishments - 1995 Total (number)	Establishments - 1995 % of U.S.	Employment - 1995 Total (number)	Employment - 1995 % of U.S.	Employment - 1995 Per Estab.	Payroll - 1995 Total ($ mil.)	Payroll - 1995 Per Empl. ($)	Sales - 1992 Total ($ mil.)	Sales - 1992 % of U.S.	Sales - 1992 Per Estab ($)
California	1,901	7.9	45,418	10.0	24	1,010.3	22,244	7,651.1	11.4	180,022
Florida	1,109	4.6	28,828	6.3	26	538.9	18,693	4,024.6	6.0	154,124
New York	1,478	6.2	25,094	5.5	17	539.6	21,505	3,835.0	5.7	175,530
Texas	1,402	5.8	26,141	5.7	19	524.0	20,044	3,818.3	5.7	172,276
Pennsylvania	1,144	4.8	20,703	4.6	18	418.5	20,213	2,875.4	4.3	170,688
Ohio	1,009	4.2	20,442	4.5	20	415.4	20,321	2,783.8	4.1	173,210
Illinois	1,053	4.4	21,401	4.7	20	438.3	20,482	2,736.9	4.1	165,354
Michigan	996	4.1	18,113	4.0	18	410.3	22,654	2,587.7	3.8	187,336
North Carolina	753	3.1	15,560	3.4	21	319.1	20,505	2,438.6	3.6	186,479
New Jersey	631	2.6	12,192	2.7	19	316.8	25,986	2,054.4	3.1	197,867
Georgia	569	2.4	13,304	2.9	23	301.9	22,694	1,949.4	2.9	188,441
Virginia	495	2.1	12,293	2.7	25	234.0	19,038	1,893.7	2.8	171,036
Wisconsin	592	2.5	9,375	2.1	16	205.0	21,872	1,866.0	2.8	198,908
Minnesota	617	2.6	8,866	1.9	14	183.7	20,725	1,769.5	2.6	189,572
Massachusetts	470	2.0	9,339	2.1	20	236.2	25,293	1,592.3	2.4	195,062
Indiana	623	2.6	12,770	2.8	20	245.5	19,221	1,560.9	2.3	165,211
Washington	464	1.9	8,835	1.9	19	204.7	23,172	1,470.4	2.2	193,931
Tennessee	551	2.3	9,764	2.1	18	212.3	21,740	1,445.4	2.1	181,854
Maryland	341	1.4	9,189	2.0	27	183.9	20,011	1,366.5	2.0	182,806
Missouri	671	2.8	9,951	2.2	15	197.3	19,825	1,353.0	2.0	163,307
Colorado	373	1.6	8,088	1.8	22	182.0	22,506	1,161.5	1.7	190,885
Alabama	434	1.8	7,782	1.7	18	148.3	19,058	1,155.9	1.7	164,705
South Carolina	361	1.5	6,223	1.4	17	131.7	21,166	1,071.8	1.6	186,750
Kentucky	427	1.8	6,797	1.5	16	128.8	18,943	1,062.7	1.6	174,294
Connecticut	287	1.2	5,664	1.2	20	159.6	28,187	1,055.2	1.6	211,798
Arizona	226	0.9	6,246	1.4	28	123.6	19,795	944.5	1.4	187,846
Oregon	368	1.5	5,870	1.3	16	130.3	22,194	919.1	1.4	201,194
Iowa	503	2.1	6,688	1.5	13	125.5	18,770	888.6	1.3	167,410
Arkansas	322	1.3	5,562	1.2	17	104.2	18,733	733.3	1.1	166,400
Oklahoma	384	1.6	5,317	1.2	14	94.8	17,835	653.9	1.0	141,994
Kansas	331	1.4	4,778	1.1	14	85.9	17,988	608.7	0.9	147,701
West Virginia	248	1.0	3,625	0.8	15	68.6	18,916	572.5	0.9	164,478
Mississippi	290	1.2	4,317	0.9	15	74.3	17,222	549.3	0.8	149,749
New Hampshire	154	0.6	3,113	0.7	20	75.2	24,141	501.9	0.7	177,523
Utah	181	0.8	3,906	0.9	22	81.0	20,742	482.8	0.7	187,560
Maine	185	0.8	2,139	0.5	12	47.2	22,073	415.9	0.6	214,062
Nevada	112	0.5	2,839	0.6	25	59.4	20,929	408.1	0.6	173,818
New Mexico	161	0.7	3,218	0.7	20	61.5	19,106	387.1	0.6	168,145
Nebraska	290	1.2	3,609	0.8	12	65.3	18,089	380.7	0.6	137,126
Idaho	183	0.8	2,577	0.6	14	51.7	20,061	332.5	0.5	181,596
Montana	166	0.7	1,808	0.4	11	34.5	19,076	274.8	0.4	213,693
Delaware	80	0.3	1,434	0.3	18	29.5	20,559	261.8	0.4	183,178
Vermont	96	0.4	1,137	0.2	12	28.9	25,451	243.8	0.4	203,497
Hawaii	54	0.2	1,245	0.3	23	26.2	21,035	223.8	0.3	168,938
North Dakota	147	0.6	1,549	0.3	11	27.0	17,445	221.6	0.3	172,029
Alaska	70	0.3	1,189	0.3	17	38.8	32,664	221.5	0.3	236,369
Rhode Island	70	0.3	1,079	0.2	15	25.9	24,024	205.2	0.3	171,734
South Dakota	162	0.7	1,631	0.4	10	27.0	16,584	190.3	0.3	174,430
Wyoming	72	0.3	699	0.2	10	16.0	22,877	100.2	0.1	167,916
Louisiana	400	1.7	6,832	1.5	17	135.9	19,888	(D)	-	-
D.C.	14	0.1	298	0.1	21	4.7	15,698	(D)	-	-

Source: County Business Patterns, 1995 and *Economic Census of the U.S., 1992*. Data are sorted by 1992 revenues and, if revenues are unavailable, by establishments in 1995. The symbol (D) indicates that data are withheld by the source to avoid disclosure of competitive information. A dash (-) indicates that data are not available or undisclosed because they do not meet statistical validity standards. Shaded *states* on the state map indicate those states which have proportionately greater representation in the industry than would be indicated by the state's population; the ratio is based on total revenues or number of establishments. Shaded *regions* indicate where the industry is regionally most concentrated.

5231 - PAINT, GLASS, AND WALLPAPER STORES

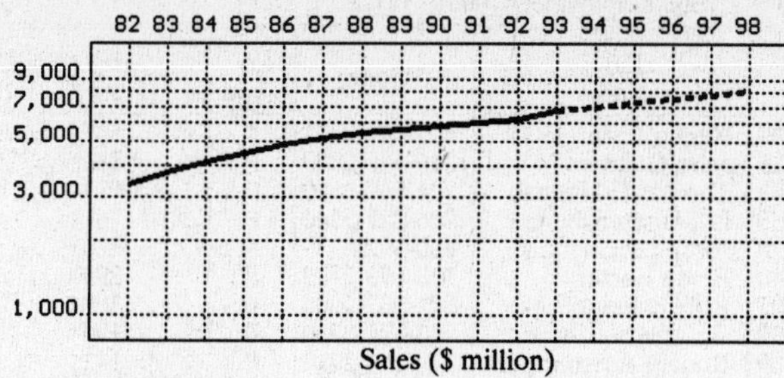

Sales ($ million)

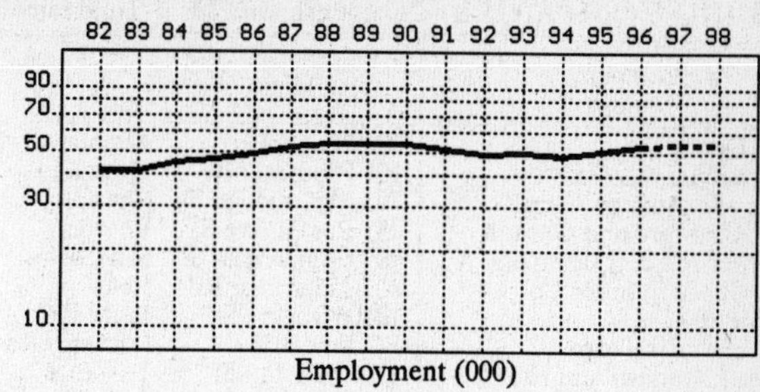

Employment (000)

GENERAL STATISTICS

Year	Establishments (number)	Employment (number)	Payroll ($ million)	Sales ($ million)	Employees per Establishment (number)	Sales per Establishment ($)	Payroll per Employee ($)
1982	9,519	41,808	515.9	3,375.4	4	354,592	12,340
1983	9,267	41,880	562.9	3,748.6e	5	-	13,440
1984	9,264	44,575	623.2	4,121.8e	5	-	13,980
1985	9,263	46,482	680.1	4,495.0e	5	-	14,632
1986	9,522	48,586	737.4	4,868.2e	5	-	15,177
1987	10,504	51,748	772.2	5,241.5	5	498,997	14,922
1988	10,199	53,389	867.4	5,433.3e	5	-	16,247
1989	10,008	54,114	907.6	5,625.1e	5	-	16,771
1990	10,182	54,015	948.3	5,816.9e	5	-	17,557
1991	10,261	51,488	930.7	6,008.8e	5	-	18,075
1992	10,188	48,944	903.0	6,200.6	5	608,616	18,451
1993	10,190	49,243	941.1	6,689.2p	5	-	19,111
1994	10,081	47,939	968.4	6,971.8p	5	-	20,200
1995	9,860	50,277	1,034.7	7,254.3p	5	-	20,581
1996	10,386p	53,145p	1,096.7p	7,536.8p	-	-	-
1997	10,453p	53,712p	1,134.4p	7,819.3p	-	-	-
1998	10,521p	54,279p	1,172.1p	8,101.9p	-	-	-

Sources: *Economic Census of the United States*, 1982, 1987, and 1992. Establishment counts, employment, and payroll are from *County Business Patterns* for non-Census years. Values followed by a 'p' are projections by the editors. Sales and expense data for non-Census years are extrapolations, marked by 'e'. Industries reclassified in 1987 will not have data for prior years. Data are the most recent available at this level of detail.

INDICES OF CHANGE

Year	Establishments (number)	Employment (number)	Payroll ($ million)	Sales ($ million)	Employees per Establishment (number)	Sales per Establishment ($)	Payroll per Employee ($)
1982	93.4	85.4	57.1	54.4	80.0	58.3	66.9
1983	91.0	85.6	62.3	60.5e	100.0	-	72.8
1984	90.9	91.1	69.0	66.5e	100.0	-	75.8
1985	90.9	95.0	75.3	72.5e	100.0	-	79.3
1986	93.5	99.3	81.7	78.5e	100.0	-	82.3
1987	103.1	105.7	85.5	84.5	100.0	82.0	80.9
1988	100.1	109.1	96.1	87.6e	100.0	-	88.1
1989	98.2	110.6	100.5	90.7e	100.0	-	90.9
1990	99.9	110.4	105.0	93.8e	100.0	-	95.2
1991	100.7	105.2	103.1	96.9e	100.0	-	98.0
1992	100.0	100.0	100.0	100.0	100.0	100.0	100.0
1993	100.0	100.6	104.2	107.9p	96.6	-	103.6
1994	98.9	97.9	107.2	112.4p	95.1	-	109.5
1995	96.8	102.7	114.6	117.0p	102.0	-	111.5
1996	101.9p	108.6p	121.4p	121.5p	-	-	-
1997	102.6p	109.7p	125.6p	126.1p	-	-	-
1998	103.3p	110.9p	129.8p	130.7p	-	-	-

Sources: Same as General Statistics. The values shown reflect change from the base year, 1992. Values above 100 mean greater than 1992, values below 100 mean less than 1992, and a value of 100 in the 1982-91 or 1993-98 period means same as 1992. Values followed by a 'p' are projections by the editors; 'e' stands for extrapolation. Data are the most recent available at this level of detail.

SELECTED RATIOS

For 1992	Avg. of All Retail	Analyzed Industry	Index	For 1992	Avg. of All Retail	Analyzed Industry	Index
Employees per Establishment	12	5	40	Sales per Employee	102,941	126,688	123
Payroll per Establishment	146,026	88,634	61	Sales per Establishment	1,241,555	608,618	49
Payroll per Employee	12,107	18,450	152	Expenses per Establishment	na	na	na

Sources: Same as General Statistics. The 'Average of All Manufacturing' column represents the average of all manufacturing industries reported for the most recent complete year available. The Index shows the relationship between the Average and the Analyzed Industry. For example, 100 means that they are equal; 500 that the Analyzed Industry is five times the average; 50 means that the Analyzed Industry is half the national average. The abbreviation 'na' is used to show that data are 'not available'.

LEADING COMPANIES

Number shown: **33** Total sales ($ mil): **28,653** Total employment (000): **141.7**

Company Name	Address				CEO Name	Phone	Co. Type	Sales ($ mil)	Empl. (000)
Home Depot Inc.	2727 Paces Ferry	Atlanta	GA	30339	Bernard Marcus	404-433-8211	P	19,535	80.8
Sherwin-Williams Co.	101 Prospect NW	Cleveland	OH	44115	John G Breen	216-566-2000	P	4,881	25.0
Collins and Aikman Corp.	701 McCullough Dr	Charlotte	NC	28262	Thomas E Hannah	704-547-8500	P	1,629	16.5
Eagle Hardware and Garden	981 Powell Ave SW	Renton	WA	98055	D J Heerensperger	206-227-5740	P	761	4.6
Kelly-Moore Paint Company	987 Commercial St	San Carlos	CA	94070	Joseph P Cristiano	650-592-8337	R	320 *	2.0
Carter-Jones Lumber Co.	601 Tallmadge Rd	Kent	OH	44240	Bryan Carter	330-673-6100	R	290 *	4.0
Duron Inc.	10406 Tucker St	Beltsville	MD	20705	Robert Feinberg	301-937-4600	R	200	1.2
Dunn Edwards Corp.	PO Box 30389	Los Angeles	CA	90030	George Matthew	213-771-3330	R	196 *	1.5
Standard Brands Paint Co.	4300 W 190th St	Torrance	CA	90509	Ronald A Scharman	310-214-2411	P	112	0.9
Fuller-O'Brien Paints Inc.	395 Oyster Pt Blvd	S San Francisco	CA	94080	Jerome J Crowley Jr	415-871-6060	R	90	0.6
W.E. Aubuchon Company Inc.	95 Aubuchon Dr	Westminster	MA	01473	W E Aubuchon Jr	508-874-0521	R	80	0.8
Hirshfield's Inc.	725 2nd Ave N	Minneapolis	MN	55405	Frank Hirshfield	612-377-3910	R	62	0.2
Martin Paint Stores	182-20 Liberty Ave	Jamaica	NY	11412	Michael Lurie	718-454-5100	R	43 *	0.5
Kay and Kay Tile Depot	28237 Orchard Lk	Farmington Hls	MI	48334	Steve Katzman	313-489-0500	R	41 *	0.3
N. Siperstein Inc.	415 Montgomery St	Jersey City	NJ	07302	Oscar Siperstein	201-333-2215	R	40	0.3
Pritchard Paint and Glass Co.	PO Box 30547	Charlotte	NC	28230	Donald R Beard	704-376-8561	R	39 *	0.2
Iowa Paint Manufacturing	PO Box 1417	Des Moines	IA	50305	Thomas Goldman	515-283-1501	R	30	0.2
Diamond Products Co.	POBox 8001	Marshalltown	IA	50158	Blair Vogel	515-753-6617	D	28	0.1
All American Home Center	7201 E Firestone	Downey	CA	90241	Leonard Gertler	310-927-8666	R	27	0.3
Rockler Cos.	4365 Willow Dr	Medina	MN	55340	Anne R Jackson	612-478-8201	R	27 *	0.3
J.C. Licht Company Inc.	45 N Brandon Dr	Glendale H.	IL	60139	Gregory Licht	708-351-0400	R	25	0.3
M.L. McDonald Sales Company	50 Oakland St	Watertown	MA	02172	Alan Kasow	617-923-0900	R	24	0.2
Volco Inc.	PO Box 448	Jerome	ID	83338	Victor E Camozzi	208-324-8161	R	21	0.2
Jones Paint and Glass Inc.	PO Box 1403	Provo	UT	84603	Harold Jones	801-373-3131	R	20 *	0.2
Wallpaper Atlanta/Dwoskins	PO Box 2327	Norcross	GA	30091	Bobby Williams	404-449-5180	S	20	0.1
Preservative Paint Company	5410 Airport Way S	Seattle	WA	98108	Richard E Wittig	206-763-0300	R	19	0.1
Mercury Paint Company Inc.	14300 Schaefer Hwy	Detroit	MI	48227	Charles A Soberman	313-491-5650	R	18	0.1
Saxon Paint and Home	3840 W Fullerton	Chicago	IL	60647	Alan Saks	312-252-8100	R	18 *	0.2
Ponderosa Paint Manufacturing	4631 Aeronca	Boise	ID	83705	AB Ellis	208-344-8683	R	17	0.1
Courtaulds Coatings Inc.	3658 Lawrenceville	Tucker	GA	30084	Tom Grant	404-938-4600	D	15 *	<0.1
Barker Lumber Co.	327 S 7th St	Delavan	WI	53115	Wayne J Hilbelink	414-728-9191	R	12	<0.1
Construction Supply	PO Box 1080	Farmington	NM	87499	Brien King	505-325-2871	R	12	<0.1
Paint America Co.	720 Leo St	Dayton	OH	45404	Thomas A Bruder Jr	513-223-3323	D	1 *	<0.1

Source: *Ward's Business Directory of U.S. Private and Public Companies*, 1998. The company type code used is as follows: P - Public, R - Private, S - Subsidiary, D - Division, J - Joint Venture, A - Affiliate, G - Group. Sales are in millions of dollars, employees are in thousands. An asterisk (*) indicates an estimated sales volume. The symbol < stands for 'less than'.

OCCUPATIONS EMPLOYED BY SIC 523 - PAINT, GLASS, AND WALLPAPER STORES

Occupation	% of Total 1996	Change to 2006	Occupation	% of Total 1996	Change to 2006
Salespersons, retail	35.1	6.5	General office clerks	3.0	-4.4
Glaziers	9.7	-26.1	Interior designers	2.4	11.1
Marketing & sales worker supervisors	9.5	11.1	Cashiers	2.0	12.4
General managers & top executives	8.0	7.6	Automotive body & related repairers	1.7	11.1
Stock clerks	5.6	37.1	Traffic, shipping, receiving clerks	1.3	11.1
Sales & related workers nec	5.5	22.2	Secretaries, except legal & medical	1.3	-11.9
Bookkeeping, accounting, & auditing clerks	4.7	-11.1	Painters & paperhangers	1.1	16.1

Source: *Industry-Occupation Matrix*, Bureau of Labor Statistics. These data relate to one or more 3-digit SIC industry groups rather than to a single 4-digit SIC. The change reported for each occupation to the year 2006 is a percent of growth or decline as estimated by the Bureau of Labor Statistics. The abbreviation nec stands for 'not elsewhere classified'.

STATE AND REGIONAL CONCENTRATION

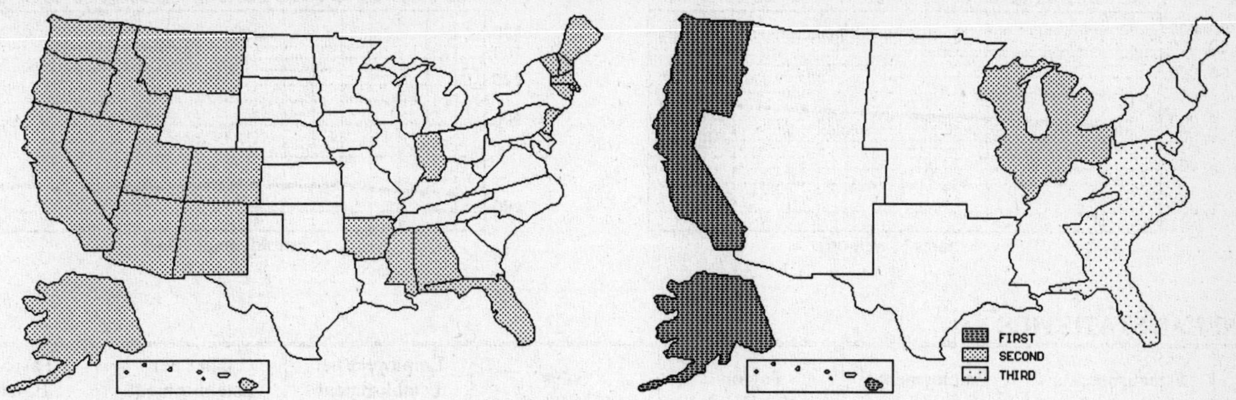

INDUSTRY DATA BY STATE

State	Establishments - 1995 Total (number)	Establishments - 1995 % of U.S.	Employment - 1995 Total (number)	Employment - 1995 % of U.S.	Employment - 1995 Per Estab.	Payroll - 1995 Total ($ mil.)	Payroll - 1995 Per Empl. ($)	Sales - 1992 Total ($ mil.)	Sales - 1992 % of U.S.	Sales - 1992 Per Estab ($)
California	1,037	10.5	5,856	11.7	6	140.5	23,989	1,005.0	16.5	137,592
Texas	623	6.3	3,505	7.0	6	73.4	20,935	418.3	6.9	147,597
New York	497	5.0	2,380	4.8	5	49.6	20,840	351.9	5.8	130,862
Florida	635	6.4	2,743	5.5	4	56.5	20,594	349.2	5.7	128,474
Illinois	396	4.0	2,246	4.5	6	46.2	20,585	264.2	4.3	109,846
Pennsylvania	400	4.1	1,741	3.5	4	33.0	18,978	252.6	4.1	128,685
Ohio	508	5.2	2,431	4.9	5	40.3	16,585	235.9	3.9	114,239
Michigan	295	3.0	1,635	3.3	6	31.8	19,457	204.6	3.4	119,975
New Jersey	278	2.8	1,515	3.0	5	36.0	23,760	191.2	3.1	137,284
Massachusetts	241	2.4	1,306	2.6	5	28.9	22,166	157.2	2.6	113,846
Indiana	268	2.7	1,399	2.8	5	27.0	19,291	151.0	2.5	109,961
Georgia	278	2.8	1,315	2.6	5	24.8	18,849	150.0	2.5	119,727
North Carolina	280	2.8	1,351	2.7	5	25.9	19,201	148.7	2.4	118,214
Washington	192	1.9	1,024	2.0	5	23.3	22,778	135.4	2.2	129,054
Tennessee	215	2.2	944	1.9	4	18.9	20,048	113.0	1.9	121,769
Arizona	120	1.2	653	1.3	5	14.3	21,832	109.4	1.8	154,907
Virginia	206	2.1	1,050	2.1	5	20.4	19,422	107.7	1.8	119,765
Colorado	178	1.8	1,060	2.1	6	22.3	21,008	107.3	1.8	133,257
Minnesota	177	1.8	1,129	2.3	6	18.7	16,530	104.7	1.7	117,934
Alabama	192	1.9	907	1.8	5	18.4	20,247	102.4	1.7	124,441
Wisconsin	191	1.9	938	1.9	5	18.0	19,215	102.0	1.7	124,660
Oregon	131	1.3	701	1.4	5	15.6	22,234	93.9	1.5	135,730
Missouri	212	2.2	953	1.9	4	18.6	19,518	90.6	1.5	106,830
Connecticut	153	1.6	670	1.3	4	16.4	24,524	90.0	1.5	122,683
Kentucky	213	2.2	881	1.8	4	15.9	18,057	85.0	1.4	110,371
South Carolina	153	1.6	722	1.4	5	13.5	18,688	76.2	1.3	103,267
Maryland	119	1.2	668	1.3	6	13.8	20,684	76.1	1.2	108,711
Utah	92	0.9	606	1.2	7	12.0	19,884	67.5	1.1	139,136
Iowa	139	1.4	660	1.3	5	12.7	19,245	66.3	1.1	114,138
Oklahoma	133	1.3	676	1.4	5	12.1	17,932	65.6	1.1	109,400
Mississippi	118	1.2	624	1.2	5	11.7	18,747	64.5	1.1	133,275
Arkansas	137	1.4	559	1.1	4	10.6	19,000	59.3	1.0	135,751
Kansas	111	1.1	579	1.2	5	11.4	19,769	53.8	0.9	116,707
Nevada	60	0.6	398	0.8	7	10.1	25,259	48.6	0.8	140,916
New Mexico	82	0.8	425	0.8	5	9.1	21,315	43.0	0.7	131,758
Idaho	75	0.8	372	0.7	5	7.4	20,005	41.0	0.7	141,990
New Hampshire	72	0.7	362	0.7	5	8.8	24,309	38.8	0.6	134,384
Maine	76	0.8	362	0.7	5	7.9	21,743	38.2	0.6	126,135
Nebraska	77	0.8	376	0.8	5	6.5	17,335	31.9	0.5	97,357
Hawaii	22	0.2	147	0.3	7	3.9	26,517	31.3	0.5	164,868
Montana	62	0.6	246	0.5	4	4.9	19,870	29.5	0.5	138,723
Rhode Island	47	0.5	181	0.4	4	3.8	21,127	25.8	0.4	116,570
West Virginia	59	0.6	304	0.6	5	5.5	17,931	25.7	0.4	109,323
Vermont	36	0.4	157	0.3	4	3.2	20,236	19.3	0.3	144,000
Alaska	18	0.2	139	0.3	8	4.5	32,597	19.1	0.3	139,146
South Dakota	28	0.3	100-249	-	-	(D)	-	14.6	0.2	130,714
Delaware	18	0.2	20-99	-	-	(D)	-	14.0	0.2	148,904
Wyoming	37	0.4	162	0.3	4	3.1	19,370	11.4	0.2	105,407
North Dakota	20	0.2	81	0.2	4	1.2	14,691	6.8	0.1	124,200
Louisiana	146	1.5	869	1.7	6	16.4	18,871	(D)	-	-
D.C.	7	0.1	20-99	-	-	(D)	-	(D)	-	-

Source: *County Business Patterns, 1995* and *Economic Census of the U.S., 1992*. Data are sorted by 1992 revenues and, if revenues are unavailable, by establishments in 1995. The symbol (D) indicates that data are withheld by the source to avoid disclosure of competitive information. A dash (-) indicates that data are not available or undisclosed because they do not meet statistical validity standards. Shaded *states* on the state map indicate those states which have proportionately greater representation in the industry than would be indicated by the state's population; the ratio is based on total revenues or number of establishments. Shaded *regions* indicate where the industry is regionally most concentrated.

5251 - HARDWARE STORES

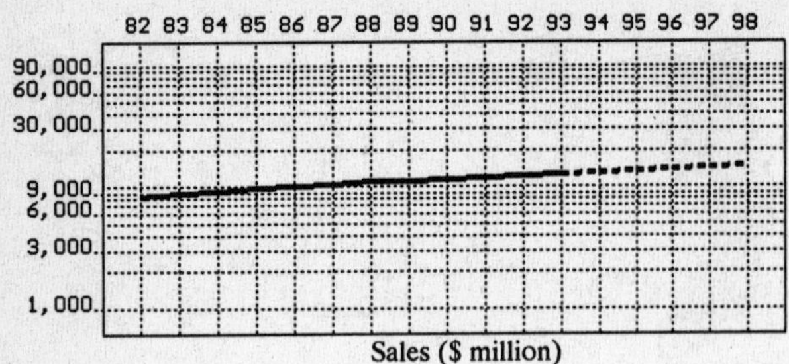

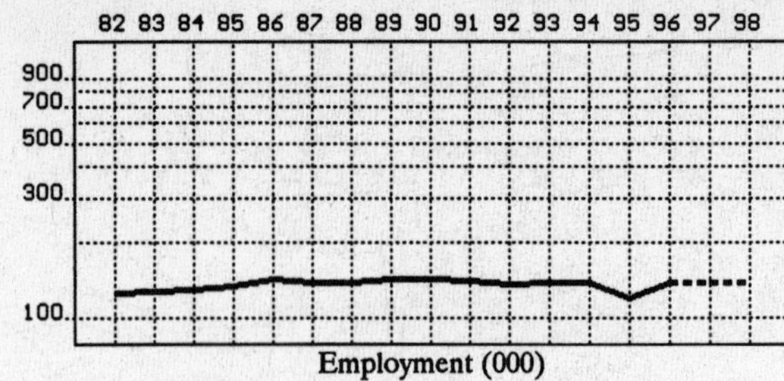

GENERAL STATISTICS

Year	Establishments (number)	Employment (number)	Payroll ($ million)	Sales ($ million)	Employees per Establishment (number)	Sales per Establishment ($)	Payroll per Employee ($)
1982	20,922	126,959	1,250.0	8,335.1	6	398,389	9,846
1983	20,376	127,591	1,330.9	8,775.1*e*	6	-	10,431
1984	19,856	129,319	1,408.4	9,215.0*e*	7	-	10,891
1985	19,515	133,660	1,500.1	9,655.0*e*	7	-	11,223
1986	19,482	142,590	1,561.3	10,095.0*e*	7	-	10,950
1987	20,059	137,860	1,564.1	10,534.9	7	525,197	11,346
1988	19,127	139,742	1,729.0	10,886.1*e*	7	-	12,373
1989	19,271	142,366	1,799.4	11,237.3*e*	7	-	12,639
1990	18,980	143,348	1,876.9	11,588.5*e*	8	-	13,093
1991	18,922	141,446	1,923.0	11,939.7*e*	7	-	13,595
1992	18,984	136,230	1,871.4	12,290.9	7	647,436	13,737
1993	18,645	138,051	1,947.2	12,787.4*p*	7	-	14,105
1994	18,227	140,019	2,042.5	13,183.0*p*	8	-	14,587
1995	13,915	120,072	1,701.7	13,578.5*p*	9	-	14,172
1996	16,791*p*	138,251*p*	2,074.0*p*	13,974.1*p*	-	-	-
1997	16,494*p*	138,596*p*	2,126.7*p*	14,369.7*p*	-	-	-
1998	16,196*p*	138,942*p*	2,179.4*p*	14,765.3*p*	-	-	-

Sources: Economic Census of the United States, 1982, 1987, and 1992. Establishment counts, employment, and payroll are from *County Business Patterns* for non-Census years. Values followed by a 'p' are projections by the editors. Sales and expense data for non-Census years are extrapolations, marked by 'e'. Industries reclassified in 1987 will not have data for prior years. Data are the most recent available at this level of detail.

INDICES OF CHANGE

Year	Establishments (number)	Employment (number)	Payroll ($ million)	Sales ($ million)	Employees per Establishment (number)	Sales per Establishment ($)	Payroll per Employee ($)
1982	110.2	93.2	66.8	67.8	85.7	61.5	71.7
1983	107.3	93.7	71.1	71.4*e*	85.7	-	75.9
1984	104.6	94.9	75.3	75.0*e*	100.0	-	79.3
1985	102.8	98.1	80.2	78.6*e*	100.0	-	81.7
1986	102.6	104.7	83.4	82.1*e*	100.0	-	79.7
1987	105.7	101.2	83.6	85.7	100.0	81.1	82.6
1988	100.8	102.6	92.4	88.6*e*	100.0	-	90.1
1989	101.5	104.5	96.2	91.4*e*	100.0	-	92.0
1990	100.0	105.2	100.3	94.3*e*	114.3	-	95.3
1991	99.7	103.8	102.8	97.1*e*	100.0	-	99.0
1992	100.0	100.0	100.0	100.0	100.0	100.0	100.0
1993	98.2	101.3	104.1	104.0*p*	105.8	-	102.7
1994	96.0	102.8	109.1	107.3*p*	109.7	-	106.2
1995	73.3	88.1	90.9	110.5*p*	123.3	-	103.2
1996	88.4*p*	101.5*p*	110.8*p*	113.7*p*	-	-	-
1997	86.9*p*	101.7*p*	113.6*p*	116.9*p*	-	-	-
1998	85.3*p*	102.0*p*	116.5*p*	120.1*p*	-	-	-

Sources: Same as General Statistics. The values shown reflect change from the base year, 1992. Values above 100 mean greater than 1992, values below 100 mean less than 1992, and a value of 100 in the 1982-91 or 1993-98 period means same as 1992. Values followed by a 'p' are projections by the editors; 'e' stands for extrapolation. Data are the most recent available at this level of detail.

SELECTED RATIOS

For 1992	Avg. of All Retail	Analyzed Industry	Index	For 1992	Avg. of All Retail	Analyzed Industry	Index
Employees per Establishment	12	7	60	Sales per Employee	102,941	90,222	88
Payroll per Establishment	146,026	98,578	68	Sales per Establishment	1,241,555	647,435	52
Payroll per Employee	12,107	13,737	113	Expenses per Establishment	na	na	na

Sources: Same as General Statistics. The 'Average of All Manufacturing' column represents the average of all manufacturing industries reported for the most recent complete year available. The Index shows the relationship between the Average and the Analyzed Industry. For example, 100 means that they are equal; 500 that the Analyzed Industry is five times the average; 50 means that the Analyzed Industry is half the national average. The abbreviation 'na' is used to show that data are 'not available'.

LEADING COMPANIES

Number shown: **50** Total sales ($ mil): **27,723** Total employment (000): **155.9**

Company Name	Address				CEO Name	Phone	Co. Type	Sales ($ mil)	Empl. (000)
Home Depot Inc.	2727 Paces Ferry	Atlanta	GA	30339	Bernard Marcus	404-433-8211	P	19,535	80.8
Hechinger Co.	1801 McCormick	Largo	MD	20774	Anthony Perillo Jr	301-341-1000	R	1,360	28.0
Andersons Inc.	480 W Dussel Dr	Maumee	OH	43537	Richard P Anderson	419-893-5050	P	1,155	3.0
Eagle Hardware and Garden	981 Powell Ave SW	Renton	WA	98055	D J Heerensperger	206-227-5740	P	761	4.6
Scotty's Inc.	5300 N Recker Hwy	Winter Haven	FL	33882	Tom Morris	941-299-1111	R	650	5.5
Ernst Home Center Inc.	1511 6th Ave	Seattle	WA	98101	Hal Smith	206-621-6700	P	572	5.2
Orchard Supply Hardware Stores	PO Box 49027	San Jose	CA	95161	Jerry Post	408-281-3500	S	532	4.9
PNP Prime Corp.	1209 S Central	Kent	WA	98064	John Markley	206-854-5450	P	498	2.7
Carter-Jones Lumber Co.	601 Tallmadge Rd	Kent	OH	44240	Bryan Carter	330-673-6100	R	290 •	4.0
Trend-Lines Inc.	135 Am Legion	Revere	MA	02151	Stanley D Black	617-853-0900	P	209	1.2
Westlake Hardware Inc.	15501 W 99th St	Lenexa	KS	66219	Howard Elsberry	913-888-0808	R	153	1.5
Lumbermen's Building Centers	3773 Martin Way E	Olympia	WA	98506	M David Dittmer	360-456-1880	S	150 •	1.0
Orscheln Farm & Home Supply	101 W Coates St	Moberly	MO	65270	Terry Shoenberger	816-263-4335	R	130 •	0.8
Stambaugh-Thompson Co.	3745 Hendricks Rd	Youngstown	OH	44515	Philip F Thompson	216-792-9071	R	113	1.6
Lampert Yards Inc.	1850 Como Ave	St. Paul	MN	55108	Daniel L Fesler	612-645-8155	R	105	0.5
Hill Behan Lumber Co.	6515 Page Blvd	St. Louis	MO	63133	Patrick J Behan	314-725-1111	R	90	0.4
W.E. Aubuchon Company Inc.	95 Aubuchon Dr	Westminster	MA	01473	W E Aubuchon Jr	508-874-0521	R	80	0.8
Scheels Hardwares Sport Shop	1331 S University	Fargo	ND	58103	Steve D Scheel	701-232-3665	R	75 •	0.9
Covington Foods Inc.	PO Box 206	Covington	IN	47932	Robert J Blagg	765-793-2470	R	65	0.5
Growers Cooperative Inc.	PO Box 2196	Terre Haute	IN	47802	Keith C Bowers	812-235-8123	R	63 •	<0.1
Welcome Home Inc.	309-D Raleigh St	Wilmington	NC	28412	Thomas H Quinn	910-791-4312	P	63	0.8
Agri Cooperative Inc.	310 Logan Rd	Holdrege	NE	68949	Ron Jurgens	308-995-8626	R	60 •	0.1
Bellevue Builders Supply Inc.	500 Duanesburg Rd	Schenectady	NY	12306	Joseph Lucarelli	518-355-7190	R	55	0.2
NHD Stores Inc.	PO Box 9113	Stoughton	MA	02072	Sheldon M Woolf	617-341-1810	P	52	0.5
A.L. Ross and Sons Inc.	1900 Hoyt Ave	Muncie	IN	47302	Donald A Ross	317-284-1441	R	50	0.5
Fleet Supply Inc.	1900 E North St	Kokomo	IN	46901	Dale Johanning	317-452-4038	R	50	0.6
Woodcraft Supply Corp.	PO Box 1686	Parkersburg	WV	26102	Bryan J Katchur	304-422-5412	R	50	0.3
Mine and Mill Supply Co.	2500 S Combee Rd	Lakeland	FL	33801	Robert Tidwell	941-665-5601	R	48 •	<0.1
Busy Beaver Building Centers	3130 W Pitt	Pittsburgh	PA	15238	Charles Bender	412-828-2323	R	46	0.4
Jacob Levy and Brothers Inc.	1126 Breckenridge	Louisville	KY	40210	Steven H Levy	502-583-5341	R	41 •	0.3
Atwood Distributing Inc.	2717 N Van Buren	Enid	OK	73701	G Atwood	405-233-3702	R	40	0.4
McLendon Hardware Inc.	710 S 2nd St	Renton	WA	98055	GR Baer	206-235-3555	R	37	0.2
A.L. Damman Co.	29235ephenson	Madison H.	MI	48071	Richard E Damman	313-399-5080	R	35	0.4
Roberts Oxygen Company Inc.	PO Box 5507	Rockville	MD	20855	Bob Roberts	301-948-8100	R	35	0.2
Dan Incorporated Oregon	PO Box 5490	Oregon City	OR	97045	Craig T Danielson	503-655-9141	R	32	0.4
Jerry's Home Improvement	PO Box 2611	Eugene	OR	97402	Dennis Orem	503-689-1911	R	32 •	0.2
Travers Tool Co.	128-15 26th Ave	Flushing	NY	11354	Barry Zolot	718-886-7200	R	32	0.2
Van Lott Inc.	3464 Sunset Blvd	West Columbia	SC	29169	Van Lott III	803-794-9340	R	32	<0.1
Wholesale Supply Group Inc.	PO Box 4080	Cleveland	TN	37320	Lloyd D Rogers	423-478-1191	R	31 •	0.2
Buttery Hardware Company	201 W Main	Llano	TX	78643	H Buttery	915-247-4141	R	30	0.1
Ellsworth Builders Supply Inc.	State St	Ellsworth	ME	04605	Austin Goodyear	207-667-7134	R	30	0.2
H.C. Shaw Co.	PO Box 31510	Stockton	CA	95212	Karen Simon	209-983-8484	R	30	0.2
Lincoln Big Three Inc.	PO Box 3274	Baton Rouge	LA	70821	C Hodges	504-357-4331	S	30	0.1
Wilson Lumber Company Inc.	4818 Meridian St N	Huntsville	AL	35811	Ken J Wilson	205-852-7411	R	30	0.2
Tri Valley Cooperative	PO Box 227	St. Edward	NE	68660	Larry Taylor	402-678-2251	R	29	<0.1
Elliott's Ace Hardware	15340 Water	Elm Grove	WI	53122	Stewart Elliott	414-782-3728	R	28	0.3
Imperial Hardware Co.	355 Olive St	El Centro	CA	92243	Phillip P Heald	760-353-1120	R	28	0.2
J.T.'s Home&Building Centers	PO Box 484	Newport	RI	02840	JT O'Reilly	401-846-2000	R	28 •	0.1
All American Home Center	7201 E Firestone	Downey	CA	90241	Leonard Gertler	310-927-8666	R	27	0.3
Rockler Cos.	4365 Willow Dr	Medina	MN	55340	Anne R Jackson	612-478-8201	R	27 •	0.3

Source: Ward's Business Directory of U.S. Private and Public Companies, 1998. The company type code used is as follows: P - Public, R - Private, S - Subsidiary, D - Division, J - Joint Venture, A - Affiliate, G - Group. Sales are in millions of dollars, employees are in thousands. An asterisk (•) indicates an estimated sales volume. The symbol < stands for 'less than'.

OCCUPATIONS EMPLOYED BY SIC 525 - HARDWARE STORES

Occupation	% of Total 1996	Change to 2006	Occupation	% of Total 1996	Change to 2006
Salespersons, retail	37.5	6.6	Purchasing managers	1.9	0.0
Cashiers	13.9	12.5	Sales & related workers nec	1.8	22.3
Stock clerks	12.1	4.1	Wholesale & retail buyers, except farm products	1.8	-8.0
General managers & top executives	7.0	7.7	Traffic, shipping, receiving clerks	1.5	11.1
Marketing & sales worker supervisors	6.2	11.1	Small engine specialists	1.4	2.4
Bookkeeping, accounting, & auditing clerks	3.8	-11.1	Counter & rental clerks	1.1	11.1
General office clerks	2.3	-4.4			

Source: Industry-Occupation Matrix, Bureau of Labor Statistics. These data relate to one or more 3-digit SIC industry groups rather than to a single 4-digit SIC. The change reported for each occupation to the year 2006 is a percent of growth or decline as estimated by the Bureau of Labor Statistics. The abbreviation nec stands for 'not elsewhere classified'.

STATE AND REGIONAL CONCENTRATION

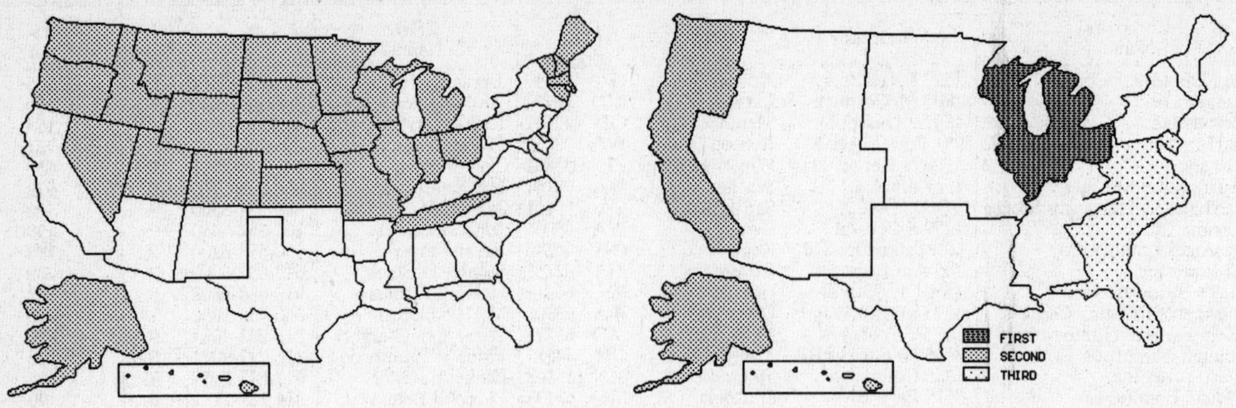

INDUSTRY DATA BY STATE

State	Establishments - 1995 Total (number)	Establishments - 1995 % of U.S.	Employment - 1995 Total (number)	Employment - 1995 % of U.S.	Employment - 1995 Per Estab.	Payroll - 1995 Total ($ mil.)	Payroll - 1995 Per Empl. ($)	Sales - 1992 Total ($ mil.)	Sales - 1992 % of U.S.	Sales - 1992 Per Estab ($)
California	1,006	7.2	12,241	10.2	12	194.3	15,871	1,468.0	12.1	105,209
New York	1,049	7.5	5,884	4.9	6	98.9	16,813	758.3	6.3	99,607
Illinois	680	4.9	7,789	6.5	11	99.1	12,718	712.1	5.9	77,195
Michigan	713	5.1	6,217	5.2	9	87.2	14,027	599.7	4.9	87,571
Washington	289	2.1	4,229	3.5	15	63.3	14,957	574.7	4.7	137,860
Texas	614	4.4	5,465	4.6	9	84.4	15,438	533.1	4.4	92,405
Ohio	580	4.2	5,465	4.6	9	67.6	12,363	531.2	4.4	76,400
Pennsylvania	659	4.7	5,244	4.4	8	66.3	12,635	499.9	4.1	89,081
Florida	605	4.3	4,587	3.8	8	66.3	14,450	457.4	3.8	76,504
Wisconsin	423	3.0	4,733	3.9	11	56.5	11,931	376.0	3.1	73,797
Indiana	377	2.7	4,153	3.5	11	49.0	11,804	342.7	2.8	73,029
Minnesota	473	3.4	4,107	3.4	9	48.4	11,774	340.9	2.8	80,305
Missouri	297	2.1	3,097	2.6	10	41.3	13,329	323.3	2.7	89,028
Georgia	401	2.9	2,864	2.4	7	43.6	15,219	306.3	2.5	90,713
North Carolina	413	3.0	2,923	2.4	7	42.4	14,497	305.4	2.5	85,081
Massachusetts	344	2.5	2,740	2.3	8	44.6	16,291	294.9	2.4	96,126
Tennessee	267	1.9	2,174	1.8	8	32.2	14,822	254.6	2.1	91,778
New Jersey	336	2.4	1,884	1.6	6	34.6	18,380	237.1	2.0	103,278
Kentucky	230	1.7	1,879	1.6	8	23.4	12,464	178.9	1.5	90,240
Iowa	292	2.1	2,012	1.7	7	22.3	11,060	176.6	1.5	74,364
Colorado	177	1.3	2,210	1.8	12	33.2	15,009	175.8	1.4	83,932
Maryland	175	1.3	1,628	1.4	9	23.9	14,706	173.8	1.4	84,688
Oregon	173	1.2	1,634	1.4	9	22.8	13,931	171.4	1.4	102,053
Virginia	261	1.9	2,020	1.7	8	27.1	13,404	167.7	1.4	76,442
Connecticut	182	1.3	1,243	1.0	7	25.5	20,504	163.8	1.4	107,810
South Carolina	237	1.7	1,656	1.4	7	24.5	14,778	158.6	1.3	85,475
Arizona	165	1.2	1,849	1.5	11	28.2	15,256	149.1	1.2	88,583
Alabama	226	1.6	1,224	1.0	5	17.8	14,576	143.4	1.2	92,012
Kansas	200	1.4	1,542	1.3	8	17.9	11,635	124.4	1.0	79,935
Idaho	92	0.7	1,159	1.0	13	16.8	14,500	118.1	1.0	115,606
Maine	171	1.2	1,103	0.9	6	15.8	14,328	114.7	0.9	92,695
Utah	59	0.4	1,148	1.0	19	15.4	13,380	106.8	0.9	104,428
Montana	127	0.9	910	0.8	7	11.9	13,049	99.8	0.8	108,846
Nebraska	173	1.2	1,002	0.8	6	11.1	11,116	88.4	0.7	83,990
New Hampshire	114	0.8	813	0.7	7	12.8	15,695	81.6	0.7	90,930
Arkansas	123	0.9	701	0.6	6	9.9	14,158	79.6	0.7	99,754
Oklahoma	130	0.9	775	0.6	6	9.2	11,903	77.6	0.6	78,447
Mississippi	137	1.0	724	0.6	5	10.6	14,652	73.3	0.6	86,780
New Mexico	56	0.4	491	0.4	9	7.1	14,369	71.3	0.6	108,899
West Virginia	120	0.9	653	0.5	5	9.0	13,744	68.2	0.6	84,791
Nevada	44	0.3	592	0.5	13	9.2	15,520	67.9	0.6	111,380
Vermont	95	0.7	584	0.5	6	9.2	15,670	66.5	0.5	100,607
Hawaii	38	0.3	467	0.4	12	9.4	20,126	60.4	0.5	123,963
South Dakota	96	0.7	638	0.5	7	6.9	10,826	54.7	0.5	82,009
Rhode Island	55	0.4	399	0.3	7	5.6	13,997	46.8	0.4	92,502
Alaska	31	0.2	301	0.3	10	7.4	24,688	42.8	0.4	169,360
North Dakota	100	0.7	507	0.4	5	5.9	11,702	42.2	0.3	80,490
Wyoming	54	0.4	553	0.5	10	7.4	13,342	41.0	0.3	92,510
Delaware	32	0.2	311	0.3	10	3.9	12,527	29.0	0.2	69,607
Louisiana	216	1.6	1,472	1.2	7	19.0	12,903	(D)	-	-
D.C.	8	0.1	76	0.1	10	1.9	25,553	(D)	-	-

Source: County Business Patterns, 1995 and *Economic Census of the U.S., 1992*. Data are sorted by 1992 revenues and, if revenues are unavailable, by establishments in 1995. The symbol (D) indicates that data are withheld by the source to avoid disclosure of competitive information. A dash (-) indicates that data are not available or undisclosed because they do not meet statistical validity standards. Shaded *states* on the state map indicate those states which have proportionately greater representation in the industry than would be indicated by the state's population; the ratio is based on total revenues or number of establishments. Shaded *regions* indicate where the industry is regionally most concentrated.

5261 - RETAIL NURSERIES AND GARDEN STORES

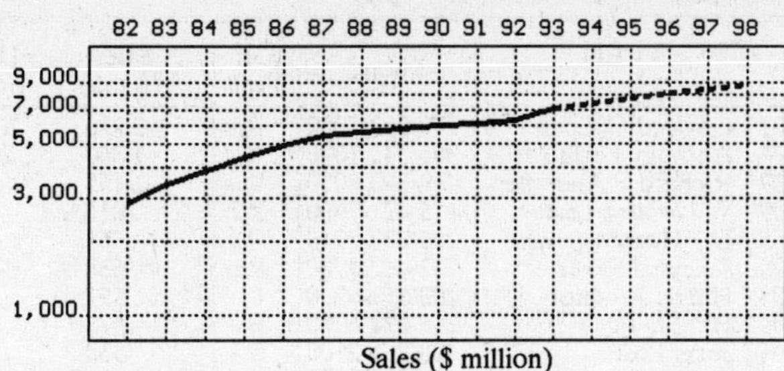

Sales ($ million)

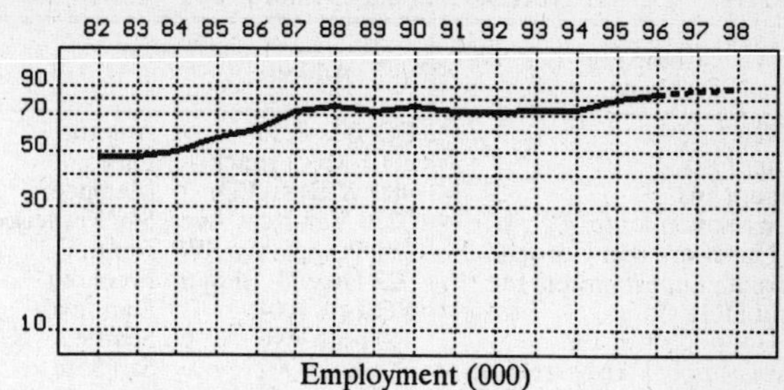

Employment (000)

GENERAL STATISTICS

Year	Establishments (number)	Employment (number)	Payroll ($ million)	Sales ($ million)	Employees per Establishment (number)	Sales per Establishment ($)	Payroll per Employee ($)
1982	8,333	46,776	455.8	2,873.4	6	344,818	9,744
1983	8,192	47,340	502.3	3,380.8*e*	6	-	10,610
1984	8,257	49,567	574.6	3,888.3*e*	6	-	11,592
1985	8,566	56,074	656.9	4,395.8*e*	7	-	11,714
1986	8,827	60,878	724.7	4,903.3*e*	7	-	11,905
1987	10,692	71,370	822.1	5,410.8	7	506,058	11,518
1988	10,427	75,942	946.9	5,594.2*e*	7	-	12,468
1989	9,904	72,378	964.0	5,777.6*e*	7	-	13,318
1990	10,141	75,515	1,029.2	5,961.0*e*	7	-	13,630
1991	10,205	72,301	1,041.9	6,144.4*e*	7	-	14,411
1992	10,857	71,499	1,017.7	6,327.8	7	582,836	14,234
1993	11,060	72,966	1,094.2	7,041.6*p*	7	-	14,996
1994	11,017	72,757	1,155.2	7,387.0*p*	7	-	15,878
1995	11,666	80,639	1,278.3	7,732.4*p*	7	-	15,852
1996	11,852*p*	84,347*p*	1,326.0*p*	8,077.9*p*	-	-	-
1997	12,116*p*	86,774*p*	1,386.0*p*	8,423.3*p*	-	-	-
1998	12,381*p*	89,201*p*	1,446.0*p*	8,768.8*p*	-	-	-

Sources: Economic Census of the United States, 1982, 1987, and 1992. Establishment counts, employment, and payroll are from *County Business Patterns* for non-Census years. Values followed by a 'p' are projections by the editors. Sales and expense data for non-Census years are extrapolations, marked by 'e'. Industries reclassified in 1987 will not have data for prior years. Data are the most recent available at this level of detail.

INDICES OF CHANGE

Year	Establishments (number)	Employment (number)	Payroll ($ million)	Sales ($ million)	Employees per Establishment (number)	Sales per Establishment ($)	Payroll per Employee ($)
1982	76.8	65.4	44.8	45.4	85.7	59.2	68.5
1983	75.5	66.2	49.4	53.4*e*	85.7	-	74.5
1984	76.1	69.3	56.5	61.4*e*	85.7	-	81.4
1985	78.9	78.4	64.5	69.5*e*	100.0	-	82.3
1986	81.3	85.1	71.2	77.5*e*	100.0	-	83.6
1987	98.5	99.8	80.8	85.5	100.0	86.8	80.9
1988	96.0	106.2	93.0	88.4*e*	100.0	-	87.6
1989	91.2	101.2	94.7	91.3*e*	100.0	-	93.6
1990	93.4	105.6	101.1	94.2*e*	100.0	-	95.8
1991	94.0	101.1	102.4	97.1*e*	100.0	-	101.2
1992	100.0	100.0	100.0	100.0	100.0	100.0	100.0
1993	101.9	102.1	107.5	111.3*p*	94.2	-	105.4
1994	101.5	101.8	113.5	116.7*p*	94.3	-	111.5
1995	107.5	112.8	125.6	122.2*p*	98.7	-	111.4
1996	109.2*p*	118.0*p*	130.3*p*	127.7*p*	-	-	-
1997	111.6*p*	121.4*p*	136.2*p*	133.1*p*	-	-	-
1998	114.0*p*	124.8*p*	142.1*p*	138.6*p*	-	-	-

Sources: Same as General Statistics. The values shown reflect change from the base year, 1992. Values above 100 mean greater than 1992, values below 100 mean less than 1992, and a value of 100 in the 1982-91 or 1993-98 period means same as 1992. Values followed by a 'p' are projections by the editors; 'e' stands for extrapolation. Data are the most recent available at this level of detail.

SELECTED RATIOS

For 1992	Avg. of All Retail	Analyzed Industry	Index	For 1992	Avg. of All Retail	Analyzed Industry	Index
Employees per Establishment	12	7	55	Sales per Employee	102,941	88,502	86
Payroll per Establishment	146,026	93,737	64	Sales per Establishment	1,241,555	582,831	47
Payroll per Employee	12,107	14,234	118	Expenses per Establishment	na	na	na

Sources: Same as General Statistics. The 'Average of All Manufacturing' column represents the average of all manufacturing industries reported for the most recent complete year available. The Index shows the relationship between the Average and the Analyzed Industry. For example, 100 means that they are equal; 500 that the Analyzed Industry is five times the average; 50 means that the Analyzed Industry is half the national average. The abbreviation 'na' is used to show that data are 'not available'.

LEADING COMPANIES

Number shown: **50** Total sales ($ mil): **11,154** Total employment (000): **103.8**

Company Name	Address				CEO Name	Phone	Co. Type	Sales ($ mil)	Empl. (000)
Gold Kist Inc.	PO Box 2210	Atlanta	GA	30301	Gaylord O Coan	770-393-5000	R	2,250 *	18.0
Hechinger Co.	1801 McCormick	Largo	MD	20774	Anthony Perillo Jr	301-341-1000	R	1,360	28.0
Andersons Inc.	480 W Dussel Dr	Maumee	OH	43537	Richard P Anderson	419-893-5050	P	1,155	3.0
Williams-Sonoma Inc.	3250 Van Ness Ave	San Francisco	CA	94109	W Howard Lester	415-421-7900	P	812	8.7
Eagle Hardware and Garden	981 Powell Ave SW	Renton	WA	98055	D J Heerensperger	206-227-5740	P	761	4.6
Foodarama Supermarkets Inc.	922 Hwy 33, Bldg 6	Freehold	NJ	07728	Joseph J Saker	732-462-4700	P	638	4.0
General Host Corp.	PO Box 10045	Stamford	CT	06904	Harris J Ashton	203-357-9900	P	597	7.2
Ernst Home Center Inc.	1511 6th Ave	Seattle	WA	98101	Hal Smith	206-621-6700	P	572	5.2
Orchard Supply Hardware Stores	PO Box 49027	San Jose	CA	95161	Jerry Post	408-281-3500	S	532	4.9
Frank's Nursery and Crafts Inc.	1175 Long Lake	Troy	MI	48098	Joseph Baczko	313-366-8400	S	530	7.0
Tractor Supply Co.	320 Plus Park Blvd	Nashville	TN	37217	Joseph H Scarlett Jr	615-366-4600	P	509	2.7
Sunbelt Nursery Group Inc.	500 Terminal	Fort Worth	TX	76106	Timothy Duoos	817-624-7253	P	96	1.4
Crop Production Services Inc.	PO Box 707500	Tulsa	OK	74170	Joe Lee	918-491-0500	R	87 *	1.0
Earl May Seed and Nursery L.P.	208 N Elm St	Shenandoah	IA	51603	Betty J Shaw	712-246-1020	R	75 *	0.8
Smith and Hawken Inc.	117 E Strawberry	Mill Valley	CA	94941	Kathy Tierney	415-383-4415	S	75	0.3
Gore Brothers Inc.	PO Box 1000	Comanche	TX	76442	JT Gore	915-356-5221	S	70	0.3
S.K.H. Management Co.	PO Box 1500	Lititz	PA	17543	Paul W Stauffer	717-626-4771	R	59	0.9
Ray-Carroll County Grain	PO Box 158	Richmond	MO	64085	A Kipping	816-776-2291	R	55 *	0.1
Fleet Supply Inc.	1900 E North St	Kokomo	IN	46901	Dale Johanning	317-452-4038	R	50	0.6
Harvest Land Cooperative Inc.	PO Box 516	Richmond	IN	47375	Marlin Larsen	317-962-1527	R	50	0.2
Busy Beaver Building Centers	3130 W Pitt	Pittsburgh	PA	15238	Charles Bender	412-828-2323	R	46	0.4
George W. Park Seed Company	PO Box 31	Greenwood	SC	29648	Leonard Park	803-223-8555	R	40	0.3
Goodland Co-op and Exchange	PO Box 99	Bird City	KS	67731	Steve Everett	913-734-2331	D	40	<0.1
Midland Co-Op Inc.	PO Box 560	Danville	IN	46122	Kevin Still	317-745-4491	R	40	0.1
Oakville Feed and Grain Inc.	PO Box 68	Oakville	IA	52646	Robert McCulley	319-766-4411	R	40	<0.1
Stein Garden and Gifts	5400 S 27th St	Milwaukee	WI	53221	Jack Stein	414-281-8400	R	40	0.8
Mid-Wood Inc.	12818 Gypsy Ln	Bowling Green	OH	43402	Tom Dorman	419-352-5231	R	38 *	<0.1
Rangen Inc.	PO Box 706	Buhl	ID	83316	Chris Rangen	208-543-6421	R	38 *	0.2
Wilco Farmers Inc.	PO Box 258	Mount Angel	OR	97362	Joseph Kirchner	503-845-6122	R	37	0.2
Z.V. Pate Inc.	PO Box 157	Laurel Hill	NC	28351	David L Burns	910-462-2122	R	35	0.9
Stanislaus Farm Supply Co.	624 E Service Rd	Modesto	CA	95358	A Bettencourt	209-538-7070	R	34 *	<0.1
Top Ag Inc.	PO Box 284	Tipton	IN	46072	James L Rice	317-675-8736	R	30	<0.1
All American Home Center	7201 E Firestone	Downey	CA	90241	Leonard Gertler	310-927-8666	R	27	0.3
Calloway's Nursery Inc.	4200 Airport Fwy	Fort Worth	TX	76117	James C Estill	817-222-1122	P	26	0.2
Wolfkill Feed&Fertilizer Corp.	PO Box 578	Monroe	WA	98272	RV Wolfkill	206-794-7065	R	25	0.1
Bengal Chemical Co.	PO Box 40487	Baton Rouge	LA	70835	Brian Leblanc	504-753-1313	R	23	<0.1
Shipman Elevator Co.	PO Box 349	Shipman	IL	62685	Brad Huette	618-836-5568	R	23	<0.1
Gibson Farmers Cooperative	PO Box 497	Trenton	TN	38382	Tommy Townsend	901-855-1891	R	22 *	<0.1
Automatic Rain Co.	4060 Campbell Ave	Menlo Park	CA	94025	Willard Hayes	415-323-5161	R	20	<0.1
Heritage F.S. Inc.	PO Box 339	Gilman	IL	60938	Steve Swearingen	815-265-4751	S	20 *	<0.1
Plow and Hearth	PO Box 5000	Madison	VA	22727	Peter Rice	703-948-2272	R	20	0.1
Alderman-Cave Feeds	PO Box 217	Winters	TX	79567	Murray Edwards	915-754-4546	R	18	0.1
Kettle-Lakes Cooperative	PO Box 305	Random Lake	WI	53075	Thomas A Rysavy	414-994-4316	R	18 *	<0.1
Producers Cooperative	1800 N Hwy 6	Bryan	TX	77806	Bobby Kurten	409-778-6000	R	18 *	<0.1
Rexius Forest By-Products Inc.	750 Chamber St	Eugene	OR	97402	Marvin L Rexius	503-342-1835	R	18	0.1
Stuppy Inc.	120 E 12th Ave	N. Kansas City	MO	64116	Jim Stuppy	816-842-3071	R	18	0.1
Arcadian Gardens Inc.	204 Gr E Neck	West Babylon	NY	11704	Steve Harris	516-669-5700	R	17 *	0.2
Mahoney's Garden Center	242 Cambridge St	Winchester	MA	01890	Paul Mahoney	617-729-5900	R	17	0.2
Recycled Wood Products	PO Box 3517	Montebello	CA	90640	Chris Kiralla	213-727-7211	R	17 *	<0.1
Pursley Turf & Garden Centers	9049 59th Cir E	Bradenton	FL	34202	Walter L Pursley	813-756-8441	R	16	0.2

Source: *Ward's Business Directory of U.S. Private and Public Companies*, 1998. The company type code used is as follows: P - Public, R - Private, S - Subsidiary, D - Division, J - Joint Venture, A - Affiliate, G - Group. Sales are in millions of dollars, employees are in thousands. An asterisk (*) indicates an estimated sales volume. The symbol < stands for 'less than'.

OCCUPATIONS EMPLOYED BY SIC 526 - RETAIL NURSERIES AND GARDEN STORES

Occupation	% of Total 1996	Change to 2006	Occupation	% of Total 1996	Change to 2006
Salespersons, retail	23.4	5.3	General office clerks	2.0	-5.5
Gardeners, nursery workers	22.4	31.8	Sales & related workers nec	2.0	20.8
Cashiers	8.5	11.1	Helpers, laborers nec	2.0	9.8
Stock clerks	7.5	18.3	Purchasing managers	1.4	-1.1
General managers & top executives	6.4	6.4	Designers, except interior designers	1.4	20.8
Marketing & sales worker supervisors	5.6	9.8	Maintenance repairers, general utility	1.2	2.3
Truck drivers light & heavy	4.0	9.8	Wholesale & retail buyers, except farm products	1.1	-9.1
Bookkeeping, accounting, & auditing clerks	3.2	-12.2			

Source: *Industry-Occupation Matrix*, Bureau of Labor Statistics. These data relate to one or more 3-digit SIC industry groups rather than to a single 4-digit SIC. The change reported for each occupation to the year 2006 is a percent of growth or decline as estimated by the Bureau of Labor Statistics. The abbreviation nec stands for 'not elsewhere classified'.

STATE AND REGIONAL CONCENTRATION

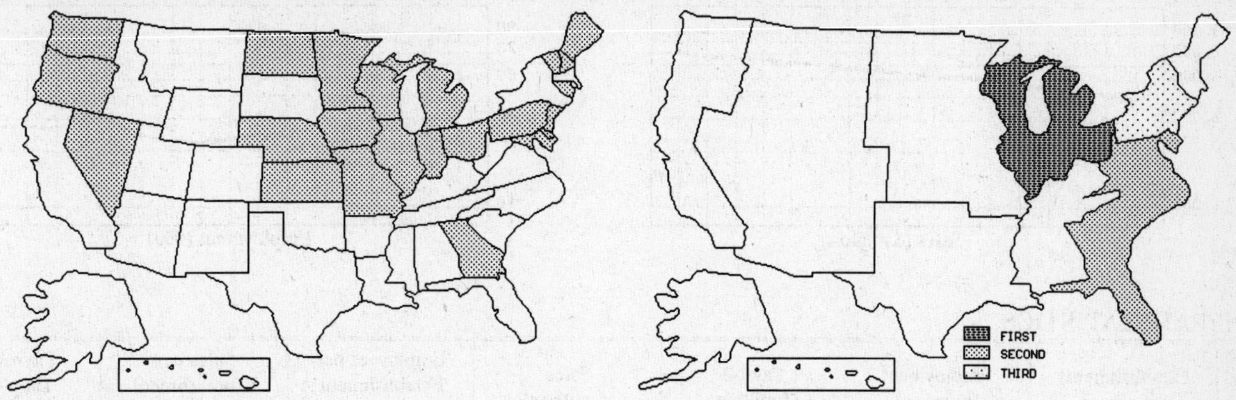

INDUSTRY DATA BY STATE

State	Establishments - 1995 Total (number)	Establishments - 1995 % of U.S.	Employment - 1995 Total (number)	Employment - 1995 % of U.S.	Employment - 1995 Per Estab.	Payroll - 1995 Total ($ mil.)	Payroll - 1995 Per Empl. ($)	Sales - 1992 Total ($ mil.)	Sales - 1992 % of U.S.	Sales - 1992 Per Estab ($)
California	922	7.9	6,557	8.1	7	112.4	17,140	583.8	9.5	84,793
Texas	781	6.7	6,298	7.8	8	78.8	12,518	412.7	6.7	69,750
New York	631	5.4	3,800	4.7	6	76.9	20,240	397.0	6.5	102,615
Michigan	449	3.8	3,695	4.6	8	65.6	17,745	386.5	6.3	109,077
Ohio	592	5.1	4,341	5.4	7	70.8	16,312	360.2	5.9	91,091
Pennsylvania	646	5.5	4,017	5.0	6	69.0	17,168	348.0	5.7	102,671
Illinois	478	4.1	4,077	5.1	9	67.4	16,536	343.5	5.6	93,468
Florida	648	5.6	3,784	4.7	6	55.2	14,594	315.6	5.2	79,026
Indiana	398	3.4	2,468	3.1	6	38.3	15,531	212.0	3.5	97,935
New Jersey	362	3.1	2,301	2.9	6	47.3	20,568	205.0	3.3	106,608
Georgia	367	3.1	2,354	2.9	6	34.1	14,475	167.3	2.7	84,008
North Carolina	394	3.4	2,037	2.5	5	29.3	14,398	152.4	2.5	88,182
Washington	276	2.4	2,211	2.7	8	38.8	17,527	152.1	2.5	86,612
Virginia	298	2.6	2,364	2.9	8	37.9	16,022	149.0	2.4	71,841
Wisconsin	231	2.0	2,062	2.6	9	29.0	14,065	148.3	2.4	84,397
Minnesota	248	2.1	1,725	2.1	7	27.2	15,773	147.4	2.4	107,358
Missouri	264	2.3	1,860	2.3	7	28.2	15,152	147.2	2.4	88,603
Maryland	215	1.8	1,795	2.2	8	28.6	15,952	146.8	2.4	72,673
Connecticut	206	1.8	1,662	2.1	8	32.3	19,421	135.1	2.2	100,700
Iowa	189	1.6	1,290	1.6	7	18.6	14,427	107.4	1.8	100,291
Tennessee	225	1.9	1,676	2.1	7	22.2	13,260	103.7	1.7	76,312
Oregon	192	1.6	1,181	1.5	6	19.1	16,176	85.7	1.4	87,496
Kentucky	180	1.5	1,226	1.5	7	15.0	12,241	71.6	1.2	72,551
Oklahoma	154	1.3	1,024	1.3	7	12.5	12,193	70.6	1.2	88,553
Arizona	147	1.3	1,459	1.8	10	21.0	14,367	65.7	1.1	77,595
South Carolina	210	1.8	943	1.2	4	13.0	13,777	65.4	1.1	88,929
Kansas	127	1.1	980	1.2	8	14.1	14,419	64.4	1.1	74,826
Alabama	181	1.6	1,131	1.4	6	14.4	12,722	62.9	1.0	78,118
Nebraska	102	0.9	828	1.0	8	12.4	15,025	53.5	0.9	96,409
Colorado	113	1.0	729	0.9	6	13.0	17,885	52.2	0.9	91,101
Mississippi	140	1.2	781	1.0	6	9.3	11,924	47.4	0.8	72,960
New Hampshire	74	0.6	392	0.5	5	8.2	20,895	41.8	0.7	137,934
Maine	87	0.7	427	0.5	5	7.7	17,934	39.4	0.6	104,523
Nevada	44	0.4	460	0.6	10	8.0	17,354	37.0	0.6	100,097
Utah	66	0.6	624	0.8	9	7.7	12,316	33.7	0.6	70,533
Arkansas	123	1.1	518	0.6	4	6.2	12,062	31.8	0.5	73,212
Delaware	42	0.4	311	0.4	7	5.8	18,711	29.3	0.5	111,240
Idaho	62	0.5	568	0.7	9	7.8	13,667	23.9	0.4	56,672
West Virginia	69	0.6	322	0.4	5	4.3	13,363	23.5	0.4	88,623
North Dakota	35	0.3	289	0.4	8	3.6	12,457	19.5	0.3	134,607
New Mexico	48	0.4	288	0.4	6	3.8	13,118	16.9	0.3	90,257
Vermont	46	0.4	167	0.2	4	3.1	18,347	14.9	0.2	127,120
South Dakota	38	0.3	169	0.2	4	3.0	17,899	14.6	0.2	117,758
Montana	38	0.3	235	0.3	6	2.9	12,460	12.7	0.2	113,054
Hawaii	24	0.2	139	0.2	6	2.2	15,705	12.4	0.2	103,575
Rhode Island	38	0.3	117	0.1	3	2.4	20,658	12.3	0.2	83,904
Wyoming	20	0.2	20-99	-	-	(D)	-	4.3	0.1	42,223
Massachusetts	255	2.2	1,601	2.0	6	32.8	20,499	(D)	-	-
Louisiana	175	1.5	1,231	1.5	7	14.9	12,119	(D)	-	-
Alaska	15	0.1	20-99	-	-	(D)	-	(D)	-	-
D.C.	1	0.0	0-19	-	-	(D)	-	(D)	-	-

Source: County Business Patterns, 1995 and *Economic Census of the U.S., 1992*. Data are sorted by 1992 revenues and, if revenues are unavailable, by establishments in 1995. The symbol (D) indicates that data are withheld by the source to avoid disclosure of competitive information. A dash (-) indicates that data are not available or undisclosed because they do not meet statistical validity standards. Shaded *states* on the state map indicate those states which have proportionately greater representation in the industry than would be indicated by the state's population; the ratio is based on total revenues or number of establishments. Shaded *regions* indicate where the industry is regionally most concentrated.

5271 - MOBILE HOME DEALERS

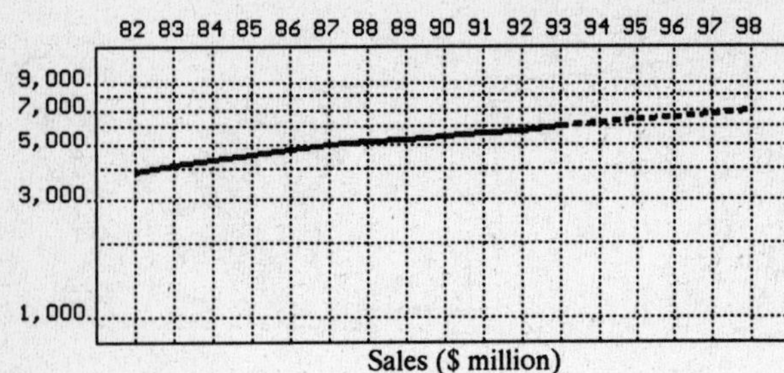

Sales ($ million)

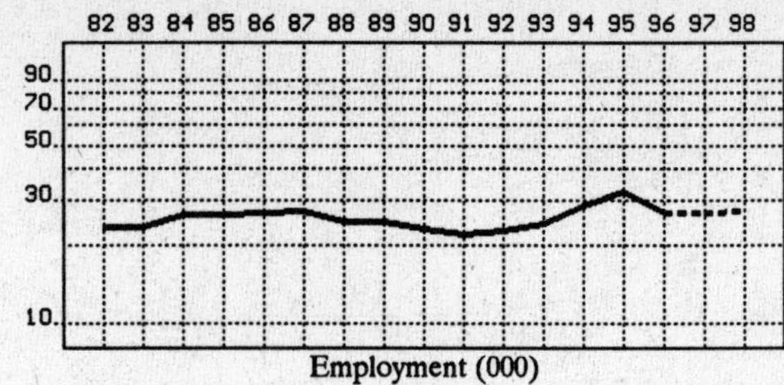

Employment (000)

GENERAL STATISTICS

Year	Establishments (number)	Employment (number)	Payroll ($ million)	Sales ($ million)	Employees per Establishment (number)	Sales per Establishment ($)	Payroll per Employee ($)
1982	5,049	23,765	336.4	3,904.3	5	773,276	14,156
1983	4,943	23,742	388.1	4,126.5e	5	-	16,346
1984	5,004	26,684	430.3	4,348.7e	5	-	16,127
1985	4,892	26,689	434.7	4,571.0e	5	-	16,289
1986	4,770	26,881	433.0	4,793.2e	6	-	16,108
1987	5,053	27,486	445.1	5,015.4	5	992,563	16,195
1988	4,545	24,711	456.0	5,154.8e	5	-	18,455
1989	4,404	24,717	447.5	5,294.1e	6	-	18,105
1990	4,162	23,053	445.7	5,433.5e	6	-	19,336
1991	4,054	22,197	420.0	5,572.8e	5	-	18,923
1992	4,053	22,814	478.2	5,712.1	6	1,409,362	20,962
1993	4,146	24,561	605.4	5,987.1p	6	-	24,647
1994	4,294	28,632	785.7	6,167.9p	7	-	27,441
1995	4,501	32,584	911.5	6,348.7p	7	-	27,974
1996	3,998p	27,017p	726.4p	6,529.5p	-	-	-
1997	3,922p	27,205p	756.4p	6,710.3p	-	-	-
1998	3,847p	27,393p	786.4p	6,891.1p	-	-	-

Sources: *Economic Census of the United States*, 1982, 1987, and 1992. Establishment counts, employment, and payroll are from *County Business Patterns* for non-Census years. Values followed by a 'p' are projections by the editors. Sales and expense data for non-Census years are extrapolations, marked by 'e'. Industries reclassified in 1987 will not have data for prior years. Data are the most recent available at this level of detail.

INDICES OF CHANGE

Year	Establishments (number)	Employment (number)	Payroll ($ million)	Sales ($ million)	Employees per Establishment (number)	Sales per Establishment ($)	Payroll per Employee ($)
1982	124.6	104.2	70.3	68.4	83.3	54.9	67.5
1983	122.0	104.1	81.2	72.2e	83.3	-	78.0
1984	123.5	117.0	90.0	76.1e	83.3	-	76.9
1985	120.7	117.0	90.9	80.0e	83.3	-	77.7
1986	117.7	117.8	90.5	83.9e	100.0	-	76.8
1987	124.7	120.5	93.1	87.8	83.3	70.4	77.3
1988	112.1	108.3	95.4	90.2e	83.3	-	88.0
1989	108.7	108.3	93.6	92.7e	100.0	-	86.4
1990	102.7	101.0	93.2	95.1e	100.0	-	92.2
1991	100.0	97.3	87.8	97.6e	83.3	-	90.3
1992	100.0	100.0	100.0	100.0	100.0	100.0	100.0
1993	102.3	107.7	126.6	104.8p	98.7	-	117.6
1994	105.9	125.5	164.3	108.0p	111.1	-	130.9
1995	111.1	142.8	190.6	111.1p	120.7	-	133.5
1996	98.6p	118.4p	151.9p	114.3p	-	-	-
1997	96.8p	119.2p	158.2p	117.5p	-	-	-
1998	94.9p	120.1p	164.5p	120.6p	-	-	-

Sources: Same as General Statistics. The values shown reflect change from the base year, 1992. Values above 100 mean greater than 1992, values below 100 mean less than 1992, and a value of 100 in the 1982-91 or 1993-98 period means same as 1992. Values followed by a 'p' are projections by the editors; 'e' stands for extrapolation. Data are the most recent available at this level of detail.

SELECTED RATIOS

For 1992	Avg. of All Retail	Analyzed Industry	Index	For 1992	Avg. of All Retail	Analyzed Industry	Index
Employees per Establishment	12	6	47	Sales per Employee	102,941	250,377	243
Payroll per Establishment	146,026	117,987	81	Sales per Establishment	1,241,555	1,409,351	114
Payroll per Employee	12,107	20,961	173	Expenses per Establishment	na	na	na

Sources: Same as General Statistics. The 'Average of All Manufacturing' column represents the average of all manufacturing industries reported for the most recent complete year available. The Index shows the relationship between the Average and the Analyzed Industry. For example, 100 means that they are equal; 500 that the Analyzed Industry is five times the average; 50 means that the Analyzed Industry is half the national average. The abbreviation 'na' is used to show that data are 'not available'.

LEADING COMPANIES

Number shown: **10** Total sales ($ mil): **1,467** Total employment (000): **10.9**

Company Name	Address				CEO Name	Phone	Co. Type	Sales ($ mil)	Empl. (000)
Oakwood Homes Corp.	PO Box 27081	Greensboro	NC	27425	Nicholas J St George	336-664-2400	P	953	7.6
American Homestar Corp.	PO Box 580484	Houston	TX	77258	Finis F Teeter	281-334-9700	P	340	2.7
Newco Homes Inc.	14901 Quorum Dr	Dallas	TX	75240	Scott Chaney	214-661-3400	R	47*	0.1
Steenberg Homes Inc.	PO Box 1257	Fond du Lac	WI	54936	WD Steenberg	414-922-3166	R	42	0.2
Bropfs Manufactured Homes	PO Box 857	St. Charles	MO	63302	Robert W Bross	314-946-6484	R	17*	<0.1
Whitworth Management Inc.	700 Smithridge Dr	Reno	NV	89502	Eugene Whitworth	702-829-1390	R	16	<0.1
Prestige Home Centers Inc.	3741 SW 7th St	Ocala	FL	34474	Thomas W Trexler	352-732-5157	S	14*	<0.1
South Atlantic Manuf Homes	1939 Gordon Hwy	Augusta	GA	30909	Ray Sollie	706-738-8531	R	14	<0.1
Dave Walters Inc.	PO Box 946	Bemidji	MN	56601	WR Fankhanel	218-751-5655	R	12	<0.1
George R. Pierce Inc.	PO Box 30777	Billings	MT	59107	William D Pierce	406-252-9313	R	12	<0.1

Source: *Ward's Business Directory of U.S. Private and Public Companies*, 1998. The company type code used is as follows: P - Public, R - Private, S - Subsidiary, D - Division, J - Joint Venture, A - Affiliate, G - Group. Sales are in millions of dollars, employees are in thousands. An asterisk (*) indicates an estimated sales volume. The symbol < stands for 'less than'.

OCCUPATIONS EMPLOYED BY SIC 527 - BOAT AND MISCELLANEOUS VEHICLE DEALERS

Occupation	% of Total 1996	Change to 2006	Occupation	% of Total 1996	Change to 2006
Salespersons, retail	20.7	19.4	Secretaries, except legal & medical	3.2	-11.1
Mechanics, installers, & repairers nec	10.5	23.3	Maintenance repairers, general utility	3.0	4.5
Sales & related workers nec	9.6	45.7	Vehicle washers & equipment cleaners	2.3	12.0
General managers & top executives	9.3	8.6	Automotive mechanics	2.1	12.0
Motorcycle repairers	6.1	0.9	Cashiers	1.7	13.4
Small engine specialists	5.3	3.3	Janitors & cleaners, maids	1.7	-10.3
Bookkeeping, accounting, & auditing clerks	4.8	-10.3	Marketing, advertising, PR managers	1.5	23.3
Marketing & sales worker supervisors	4.5	12.1	Stock clerks	1.3	147.5
General office clerks	3.9	-3.6	Clerical supervisors & managers	1.3	12.1

Source: *Industry-Occupation Matrix*, Bureau of Labor Statistics. These data relate to one or more 3-digit SIC industry groups rather than to a single 4-digit SIC. The change reported for each occupation to the year 2006 is a percent of growth or decline as estimated by the Bureau of Labor Statistics. The abbreviation nec stands for 'not elsewhere classified'.

STATE AND REGIONAL CONCENTRATION

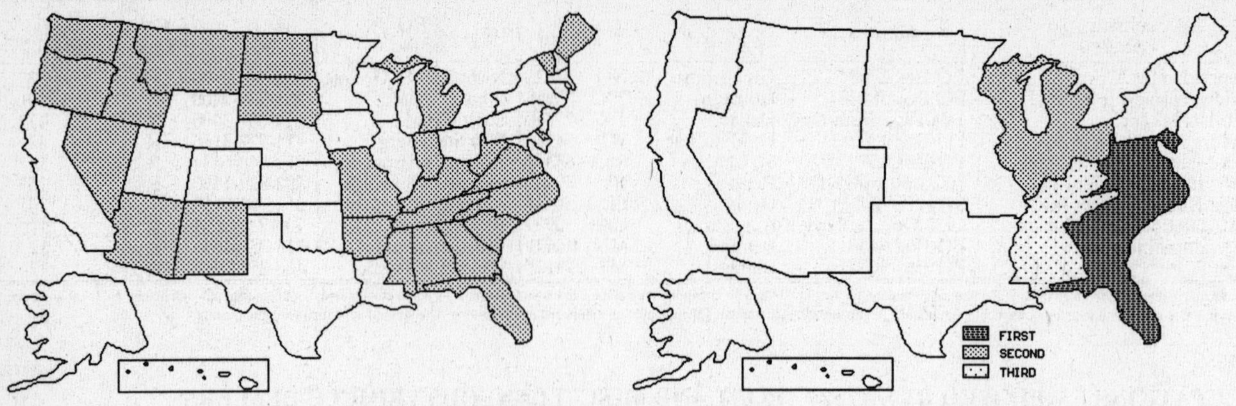

INDUSTRY DATA BY STATE

State	Establishments - 1995 Total (number)	Establishments - 1995 % of U.S.	Employment - 1995 Total (number)	Employment - 1995 % of U.S.	Employment - 1995 Per Estab.	Payroll - 1995 Total ($ mil.)	Payroll - 1995 Per Empl. ($)	Sales - 1992 Total ($ mil.)	Sales - 1992 % of U.S.	Sales - 1992 Per Estab ($)
North Carolina	380	8.4	2,705	8.3	7	85.4	31,583	491.6	8.6	260,670
Florida	293	6.5	1,714	5.3	6	39.6	23,090	377.1	6.6	239,748
Texas	309	6.9	2,564	7.9	8	82.3	32,080	312.9	5.5	273,526
South Carolina	210	4.7	1,593	4.9	8	45.9	28,795	300.0	5.3	268,071
Michigan	162	3.6	1,256	3.9	8	34.2	27,222	274.6	4.8	287,573
California	191	4.2	807	2.5	4	17.2	21,284	248.7	4.4	261,786
Tennessee	145	3.2	1,188	3.7	8	43.7	36,819	231.5	4.1	255,246
Washington	139	3.1	1,197	3.7	9	36.1	30,125	227.9	4.0	270,365
Georgia	182	4.0	1,263	3.9	7	36.4	28,800	218.4	3.8	281,766
Pennsylvania	160	3.6	1,189	3.7	7	28.2	23,712	212.4	3.7	190,449
New York	127	2.8	818	2.5	6	19.4	23,754	196.1	3.4	235,438
Oregon	98	2.2	996	3.1	10	30.2	30,370	194.8	3.4	293,845
Kentucky	130	2.9	1,037	3.2	8	29.0	27,992	190.0	3.3	231,429
Ohio	128	2.8	1,032	3.2	8	25.5	24,753	189.6	3.3	234,968
Indiana	123	2.7	840	2.6	7	23.5	27,927	178.5	3.1	247,983
Alabama	162	3.6	911	2.8	6	27.4	30,105	162.1	2.8	332,217
Virginia	124	2.8	878	2.7	7	22.1	25,213	149.4	2.6	204,048
Arizona	117	2.6	902	2.8	8	25.2	27,919	132.3	2.3	257,325
Missouri	125	2.8	940	2.9	8	25.7	27,383	127.2	2.2	229,933
Mississippi	94	2.1	712	2.2	8	18.6	26,077	100.8	1.8	214,068
Wisconsin	69	1.5	550	1.7	8	16.8	30,595	93.3	1.6	208,297
New Mexico	68	1.5	533	1.6	8	18.0	33,822	89.6	1.6	284,432
Louisiana	63	1.4	479	1.5	8	14.8	30,866	76.6	1.3	310,138
Nevada	62	1.4	360	1.1	6	11.1	30,872	76.5	1.3	274,079
Illinois	95	2.1	510	1.6	5	11.2	21,959	76.0	1.3	199,346
Arkansas	78	1.7	485	1.5	6	13.4	27,546	72.1	1.3	317,740
West Virginia	66	1.5	583	1.8	9	12.4	21,290	68.2	1.2	184,713
Idaho	40	0.9	439	1.3	11	12.3	27,907	63.6	1.1	299,778
Colorado	70	1.6	845	2.6	12	18.3	21,657	61.2	1.1	214,716
Minnesota	52	1.2	317	1.0	6	9.5	30,022	59.3	1.0	271,968
Kansas	56	1.2	350	1.1	6	9.9	28,383	56.7	1.0	234,405
Maine	43	1.0	290	0.9	7	6.2	21,214	54.4	1.0	277,612
Iowa	41	0.9	287	0.9	7	9.9	34,411	53.0	0.9	240,955
Delaware	31	0.7	180	0.6	6	4.0	22,406	49.0	0.9	219,655
Oklahoma	45	1.0	355	1.1	8	9.8	27,577	42.2	0.7	258,957
Montana	30	0.7	253	0.8	8	6.6	25,929	40.3	0.7	300,791
South Dakota	26	0.6	271	0.8	10	7.4	27,269	32.8	0.6	275,941
Maryland	31	0.7	169	0.5	5	3.8	22,391	27.0	0.5	174,245
Nebraska	29	0.6	176	0.5	6	4.3	24,489	22.7	0.4	180,421
North Dakota	19	0.4	130	0.4	7	2.6	19,662	16.9	0.3	198,682
Vermont	15	0.3	84	0.3	6	2.0	24,214	15.9	0.3	248,188
Utah	13	0.3	136	0.4	10	2.9	21,603	15.5	0.3	254,475
New Hampshire	21	0.5	66	0.2	3	1.8	26,742	13.6	0.2	203,075
Connecticut	8	0.2	74	0.2	9	3.4	45,608	5.8	0.1	140,488
New Jersey	9	0.2	44	0.1	5	0.9	21,091	5.3	0.1	239,409
Wyoming	11	0.2	20-99	-	-	(D)	-	3.2	0.1	210,267
Massachusetts	8	0.2	34	0.1	4	1.4	40,471	(D)	-	-
Alaska	3	0.1	0-19	-	-	(D)	-	(D)	-	-

Source: County Business Patterns, 1995 and *Economic Census of the U.S., 1992*. Data are sorted by 1992 revenues and, if revenues are unavailable, by establishments in 1995. The symbol (D) indicates that data are withheld by the source to avoid disclosure of competitive information. A dash (-) indicates that data are not available or undisclosed because they do not meet statistical validity standards. Shaded *states* on the state map indicate those states which have proportionately greater representation in the industry than would be indicated by the state's population; the ratio is based on total revenues or number of establishments. Shaded *regions* indicate where the industry is regionally most concentrated.

5311 - DEPARTMENT STORES

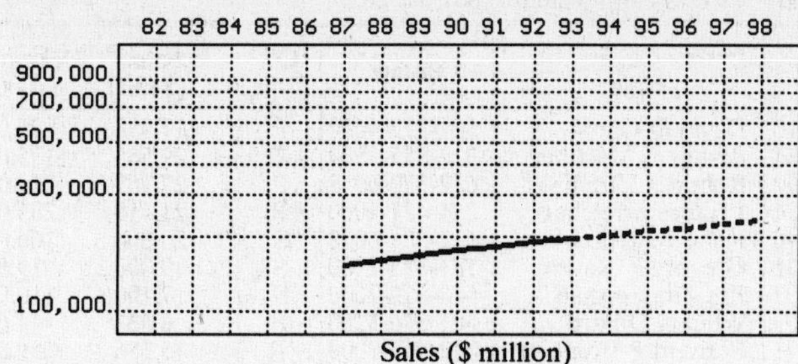

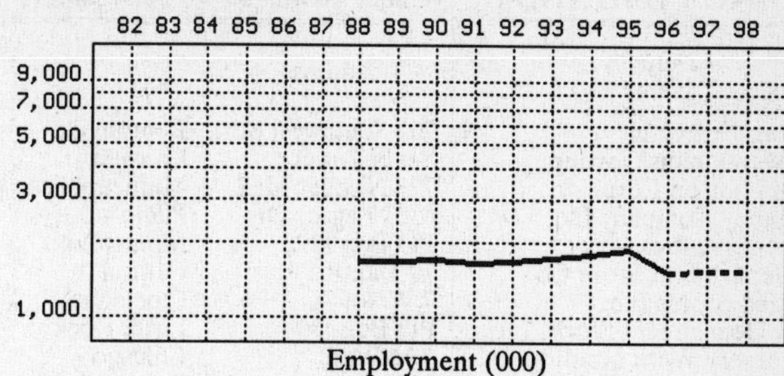

GENERAL STATISTICS

Year	Establishments (number)	Employment (number)	Payroll ($ million)	Sales ($ million)	Employees per Establishment (number)	Sales per Establishment ($)	Payroll per Employee ($)
1982	-	-	-	-	-	-	-
1983	-	-	-	-	-	-	-
1984	-	-	-	-	-	-	-
1985	-	-	-	-	-	-	-
1986	-	-	-	-	-	-	-
1987	10,041	-	-	153,679.1	-	15,305,160	-
1988	9,967	1,686,665	16,376.9	161,100.3e	169	-	9,710
1989	10,124	1,674,852	17,716.6	168,521.4e	165	-	10,578
1990	10,141	1,709,639	18,287.1	175,942.6e	169	-	10,696
1991	10,199	1,646,390	18,412.3	183,363.8e	161	-	11,183
1992	11,001	-	-	190,784.9	-	17,342,508	-
1993	10,647	1,738,595	20,613.5	198,206.1p	163	-	11,856
1994	10,758	1,786,158	21,699.1	205,627.3p	166	-	12,148
1995	10,781	1,873,865	23,643.2	213,048.4p	174	-	12,617
1996	11,010p	1,530,989p	20,272.7p	220,469.6p	-	-	-
1997	11,130p	1,534,648p	20,979.2p	227,890.8p	-	-	-
1998	11,251p	1,538,308p	21,685.6p	235,311.9p	-	-	-

Sources: Economic Census of the United States, 1982, 1987, and 1992. Establishment counts, employment, and payroll are from *County Business Patterns* for non-Census years. Values followed by a 'p' are projections by the editors. Sales and expense data for non-Census years are extrapolations, marked by 'e'. Industries reclassified in 1987 will not have data for prior years. Data are the most recent available at this level of detail.

INDICES OF CHANGE

Year	Establishments (number)	Employment (number)	Payroll ($ million)	Sales ($ million)	Employees per Establishment (number)	Sales per Establishment ($)	Payroll per Employee ($)
1982	-	-	-	-	-	-	-
1983	-	-	-	-	-	-	-
1984	-	-	-	-	-	-	-
1985	-	-	-	-	-	-	-
1986	-	-	-	-	-	-	-
1987	91.3	-	-	80.6	-	88.3	-
1988	90.6	-	-	84.4e	-	-	-
1989	92.0	-	-	88.3e	-	-	-
1990	92.2	-	-	92.2e	-	-	-
1991	92.7	-	-	96.1e	-	-	-
1992	100.0	-	-	100.0	-	100.0	-
1993	96.8	-	-	103.9p	-	-	-
1994	97.8	-	-	107.8p	-	-	-
1995	98.0	-	-	111.7p	-	-	-
1996	100.1p	-	-	115.6p	-	-	-
1997	101.2p	-	-	119.4p	-	-	-
1998	102.3p	-	-	123.3p	-	-	-

Sources: Same as General Statistics. The values shown reflect change from the base year, 1992. Values above 100 mean greater than 1992, values below 100 mean less than 1992, and a value of 100 in the 1982-91 or 1993-98 period means same as 1992. Values followed by a 'p' are projections by the editors; 'e' stands for extrapolation. Data are the most recent available at this level of detail.

SELECTED RATIOS

For 1992	Avg. of All Retail	Analyzed Industry	Index	For 1992	Avg. of All Retail	Analyzed Industry	Index
Employees per Establishment	12	0	0	Sales per Employee	102,941	0	0
Payroll per Establishment	146,026	0	0	Sales per Establishment	1,241,555	17,342,505	1,397
Payroll per Employee	12,107	0	0	Expenses per Establishment	na	na	na

Sources: Same as General Statistics. The 'Average of All Manufacturing' column represents the average of all manufacturing industries reported for the most recent complete year available. The Index shows the relationship between the Average and the Analyzed Industry. For example, 100 means that they are equal; 500 that the Analyzed Industry is five times the average; 50 means that the Analyzed Industry is half the national average. The abbreviation 'na' is used to show that data are 'not available'.

LEADING COMPANIES

Number shown: **50** Total sales ($ mil): **325,353** Total employment (000): **2,388.2**

Company Name	Address				CEO Name	Phone	Co. Type	Sales ($ mil)	Empl. (000)
Wal-Mart Stores Inc.	702 Southwest 8th	Bentonville	AR	72716	David D Glass	501-273-4000	P	117,958	825.0
Sears Merchandise Group	Sears Tower	Chicago	IL	60684	Arthur C Martinez	312-875-2500	D	29,565	175.0
Dayton Hudson Corp.	777 Nicollet Mall	Minneapolis	MN	55402	Robert J Ulrich	612-370-6948	P	27,757	218.0
J.C. Penney Company Inc.	6501 Legacy Dr	Plano	TX	75024	J E Oesterreicher	214-431-1000	P	21,419	205.0
Target Stores Inc.	PO Box 1392	Minneapolis	MN	55440	Robert J Ulrich	612-304-6073	S	20,300	166.0
Hills Department Store Co.	15 Dan Rd	Canton	MA	02021	Gregory K Raven	781-821-1000	S	19,000	19.5
Federated Stores Inc.	7 W 7th St	Cincinnati	OH	45202	Jim Zimmerman	513-579-7000	S	7,100 *	110.0
Dillard Department Stores Inc.	PO Box 486	Little Rock	AR	72203	William Dillard	501-376-5200	P	6,631	44.6
Montgomery Ward Holding	1 M Ward	Chicago	IL	60671	Bernard F Brennan	312-467-2000	R	5,386	59.0
Nordstrom Inc.	1501 5th Ave	Seattle	WA	98101	John J Whitacre	206-628-2111	P	4,852	41.0
Mervyn's	22301 Foothill Blvd	Hayward	CA	94541	Bart Butzer	510-727-3000	S	4,223	32.0
Harcourt General Inc.	27 Boylston St	Chestnut Hill	MA	02167	Richard A Smith	617-232-8200	P	3,692	18.5
Proffitt's Inc.	PO Box 9388	Alcoa	TN	37701	R Brad Martin	423-983-7000	P	3,544	14.0
Mercantile Stores Company	9450 Seward Rd	Fairfield	OH	45014	David L Nichols	513-881-8000	P	2,944	30.0
Belk Brothers Co.	PO Box 31660	Charlotte	NC	28231	John H Penenell	704-377-4251	R	2,842 *	29.0
Caldor Corp.	20 Glover Ave	Norwalk	CT	06856	Warren D Feldberg	203-846-1641	P	2,602	22.0
ShopKo Stores Inc.	PO Box 19060	Green Bay	WI	54307	Dale P Kramer	920-497-2211	P	2,448	20.0
Kohl's Corp.	17000 Ridgewood	Menomonee Fls	WI	53051	William S Kellogg	414-783-5800	P	2,388	25.5
Rich's Inc.	223 Perimeter Ctr	Atlanta	GA	30346	Russell Stravitz	770-913-4000	S	2,328 *	20.0
Hecht's	685 N Glebe Rd	Arlington	VA	22203	Irwin Zazulia	703-558-1200	D	2,300	15.0
Ames Department Stores Inc.	2418 Main St	Rocky Hill	CT	06067	Joseph R Ettore	860-257-2000	P	2,233	20.5
Neiman Marcus Group Inc.	PO Box 9187	Chestnut Hill	MA	02167	Richard A Smith	617-232-0760	P	2,210	11.3
Macy's East Inc.	151 W 34th St	New York	NY	10001	Harold D Kahn	212-695-4400	S	1,873 *	14.0
Foley's	PO Box 1971	Houston	TX	77002	Thomas J Hogan	713-651-7038	D	1,801	17.0
Parisian Inc.	750 Lkshore Pkwy	Birmingham	AL	35211	Jim Adams	205-940-4000	D	1,700 *	7.0
Robinsons-May	6160 Laurel Canyon	N. Hollywood	CA	91606	David P Mullen	818-508-5226	D	1,643 *	11.0
Bradlees Inc.	PO Box 859051	Braintree	MA	02185	Peter Thorner	617-380-8000	P	1,562	10.5
Venture Stores, Inc.	2001 E Terra Lane	O'Fallon	MO	63366	Julian M Seeherman	314-281-5500	P	1,486	12.6
Macy's California Inc.	170 O'Farrell	San Francisco	CA	94102	Michael Steingberg	415-397-3333	S	1,460 *	15.4
Schottenstein Stores Corp.	1800 Moler Rd	Columbus	OH	43207	Jay Schottenstein	614-221-9200	R	1,400	15.0
Neiman Marcus Co.	1618 Main St	Dallas	TX	75201	Burton M Tansky	214-741-6911	S	1,399	10.1
Kaufmann's	400 5th Ave	Pittsburgh	PA	15219	Richard Bennet	412-232-2000	D	1,303	8.0
Burdines Inc.	22 E Flagler St	Miami	FL	33131	Howard Socol	305-835-5151	P	1,259	11.8
Macy's South Inc.	180 Peachtree NW	Atlanta	GA	30303	Harold Kahn	404-221-7221	S	1,210	11.1
Filene's	426 Washington St	Boston	MA	02108	Joseph M Melvin	617-357-2100	D	1,162	6.0
Carson Pirie Scott and Co.	331 W Wisconsin	Milwaukee	WI	53203	Stanton J Bluestone	414-347-4141	P	1,103	12.0
Truckstops of America Inc.	24601 Ctr Ridge Rd	Westlake	OH	44145	Ed Kuhn	440-808-9100	S	1,067 *	5.0
Strawbridge and Clothier	801 Market St	Philadelphia	PA	19107	Peter S Strawbridge	215-629-6000	P	1,007	12.1
Bon Inc.	1601 3rd Ave	Seattle	WA	98181	Daniel H Edelaman	206-344-2121	S	977	7.3
Value City Department Stores	3241 Westerville Rd	Columbus	OH	43224	Jay L Schottenstein	614-471-4722	P	954	12.7
Famous-Barr	601 Olive St	St. Louis	MO	63101	J Kent McHose	314-444-3111	D	947	5.0
Woodward and Lothrop Inc.	20800 Eisenhower	Alexandria	VA	22314	Arnold Aronson	703-329-5450	S	900	14.0
Stern's Inc.	Rte 4, Bergen Mall	Paramus	NJ	07652	Matthew D Serra	201-845-5500	S	889	6.1
Stein Mart Inc.	1200 Riverplace	Jacksonville	FL	32207	Jay Stein	904-346-1500	P	793	9.1
Jamesway Corp.	40 Hartz Way	Secaucus	NJ	07096	Herbert Douglas	201-330-6000	P	681	5.9
Bon-Ton Stores Inc.	PO Box 2821	York	PA	17405	H. L Wilansky	717-757-7660	P	627	7.6
Fedco Inc.	9300 Santa Fe Spgs	Santa Fe Sprgs	CA	90670	E L Butterworth	310-946-2511	R	625	5.5
Filene's Basement Corp.	40 Walnut St	Wellesley	MA	02181	Samuel J Gerson	617-348-7000	P	608	3.9
Younkers Inc.	PO Box 1495	Des Moines	IA	50397	W Thomas Gould	515-244-1112	P	599	7.0
Smitty's Super Valu Inc.	PO Box 30550	Salt Lake City	UT	84130	David Green	801-801-1000	S	598	4.6

Source: *Ward's Business Directory of U.S. Private and Public Companies*, 1998. The company type code used is as follows: P - Public, R - Private, S - Subsidiary, D - Division, J - Joint Venture, A - Affiliate, G - Group. Sales are in millions of dollars, employees are in thousands. An asterisk (*) indicates an estimated sales volume. The symbol < stands for 'less than'.

OCCUPATIONS EMPLOYED BY SIC 531 - DEPARTMENT STORES

Occupation	% of Total 1996	Change to 2006	Occupation	% of Total 1996	Change to 2006
Salespersons, retail	43.9	15.1	General office clerks	2.9	-15.4
Stock clerks	8.2	-1.7	Hairdressers & cosmetologists	1.6	18.0
Cashiers	8.0	-0.5	General managers & top executives	1.3	-4.7
Sales & related workers nec	3.8	8.2	Adjustment clerks	1.2	-36.1
Marketing & sales worker supervisors	3.7	6.0	Home appliance/power tool repairers	1.0	-11.5
Traffic, shipping, receiving clerks	3.4	8.2	Professional workers nec	1.0	18.0

Source: *Industry-Occupation Matrix*, Bureau of Labor Statistics. These data relate to one or more 3-digit SIC industry groups rather than to a single 4-digit SIC. The change reported for each occupation to the year 2006 is a percent of growth or decline as estimated by the Bureau of Labor Statistics. The abbreviation nec stands for 'not elsewhere classified'.

STATE AND REGIONAL CONCENTRATION

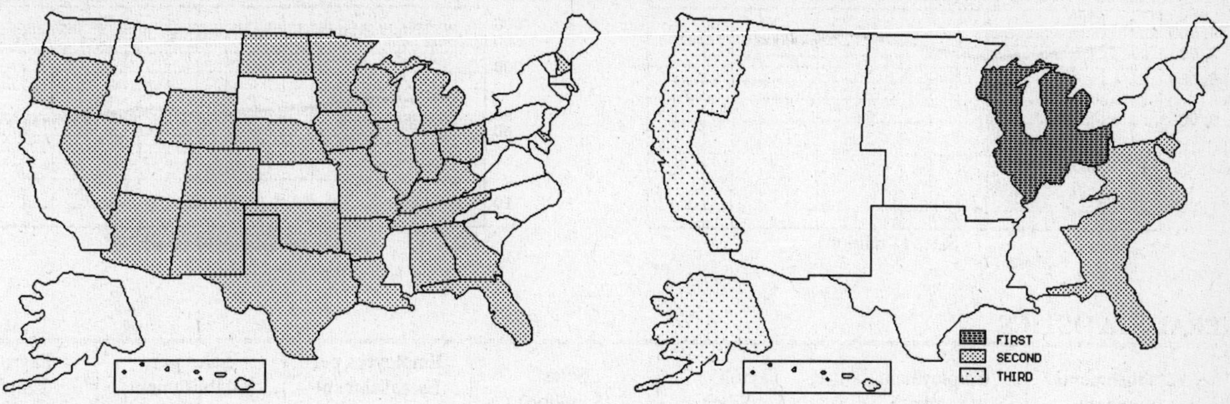

INDUSTRY DATA BY STATE

State	Establishments - 1995		Employment - 1995			Payroll - 1995		Sales - 1992		
	Total (number)	% of U.S.	Total (number)	% of U.S.	Per Estab.	Total ($ mil.)	Per Empl. ($)	Total ($ mil.)	% of U.S.	Per Estab ($)
California	949	8.8	181,344	9.7	191	2,331.2	12,855	19,448.5	10.3	-
Texas	786	7.3	141,790	7.6	180	1,867.7	13,172	14,849.7	7.9	-
Florida	613	5.7	105,066	5.6	171	1,398.5	13,311	10,525.3	5.6	-
Michigan	405	3.8	95,779	5.1	236	1,195.7	12,484	10,344.0	5.5	-
New York	493	4.6	90,440	4.8	183	1,304.2	14,421	9,466.2	5.0	-
Ohio	508	4.7	87,924	4.7	173	1,072.2	12,194	8,948.2	4.8	-
Illinois	512	4.7	94,326	5.0	184	1,128.5	11,964	8,857.0	4.7	-
Pennsylvania	548	5.1	86,324	4.6	158	1,038.5	12,030	8,546.4	4.5	-
Georgia	302	2.8	51,539	2.8	171	631.1	12,245	5,288.4	2.8	-
New Jersey	237	2.2	46,792	2.5	197	613.2	13,105	5,267.6	2.8	-
Missouri	263	2.4	50,806	2.7	193	648.7	12,769	4,975.1	2.6	-
Indiana	314	2.9	56,206	3.0	179	659.8	11,738	4,937.5	2.6	-
North Carolina	358	3.3	50,383	2.7	141	583.2	11,575	4,715.1	2.5	-
Virginia	270	2.5	44,030	2.3	163	526.1	11,949	4,296.3	2.3	-
Tennessee	247	2.3	42,812	2.3	173	546.2	12,757	4,213.1	2.2	-
Wisconsin	282	2.6	42,555	2.3	151	469.9	11,041	3,988.7	2.1	-
Minnesota	217	2.0	40,417	2.2	186	459.1	11,358	3,899.1	2.1	-
Washington	189	1.8	31,701	1.7	168	484.5	15,282	3,779.6	2.0	-
Massachusetts	220	2.0	33,305	1.8	151	471.2	14,148	3,563.9	1.9	-
Louisiana	185	1.7	33,789	1.8	183	414.1	12,254	3,475.2	1.8	-
Maryland	182	1.7	33,328	1.8	183	392.7	11,783	3,297.8	1.8	-
Alabama	184	1.7	31,983	1.7	174	410.5	12,834	3,174.7	1.7	-
Kentucky	177	1.6	31,368	1.7	177	379.1	12,087	3,007.4	1.6	-
Arizona	167	1.5	29,522	1.6	177	371.0	12,566	2,908.7	1.5	-
Colorado	163	1.5	27,846	1.5	171	336.9	12,100	2,790.3	1.5	-
Oregon	137	1.3	23,665	1.3	173	338.4	14,299	2,766.7	1.5	-
Oklahoma	155	1.4	25,581	1.4	165	329.1	12,865	2,731.6	1.5	-
South Carolina	161	1.5	24,958	1.3	155	294.9	11,816	2,417.1	1.3	-
Connecticut	133	1.2	19,453	1.0	146	260.7	13,403	2,360.0	1.3	-
Iowa	169	1.6	23,059	1.2	136	262.6	11,389	2,343.7	1.2	-
Arkansas	121	1.1	23,434	1.3	194	297.0	12,676	2,340.0	1.2	-
Mississippi	116	1.1	19,821	1.1	171	238.9	12,052	1,911.4	1.0	-
West Virginia	100	0.9	13,522	0.7	135	158.2	11,699	1,305.1	0.7	-
Utah	95	0.9	14,796	0.8	156	168.5	11,386	1,273.0	0.7	-
Nebraska	80	0.7	12,963	0.7	162	148.8	11,476	1,219.6	0.6	-
New Mexico	65	0.6	10,922	0.6	168	139.7	12,791	1,190.2	0.6	-
Nevada	55	0.5	9,997	0.5	182	143.9	14,394	1,151.9	0.6	-
New Hampshire	74	0.7	9,341	0.5	126	119.9	12,837	1,004.0	0.5	-
Delaware	35	0.3	6,882	0.4	197	81.1	11,784	703.9	0.4	-
Idaho	52	0.5	7,135	0.4	137	85.3	11,956	670.8	0.4	-
Maine	73	0.7	7,681	0.4	105	94.6	12,313	655.2	0.3	-
North Dakota	38	0.4	5,802	0.3	153	63.7	10,986	626.5	0.3	-
South Dakota	41	0.4	5,680	0.3	139	63.9	11,254	533.1	0.3	-
Montana	48	0.4	5,679	0.3	118	66.4	11,700	528.1	0.3	-
Rhode Island	32	0.3	5,169	0.3	162	71.3	13,791	527.1	0.3	-
Wyoming	27	0.3	3,337	0.2	124	39.4	11,820	363.3	0.2	-
Alaska	19	0.2	4,076	0.2	215	72.6	17,808	311.1	0.2	-
Vermont	25	0.2	1,958	0.1	78	23.2	11,848	251.9	0.1	-
D.C.	4	0.0	1,439	0.1	360	21.8	15,158	180.4	0.1	-
Kansas	127	1.2	20,493	1.1	161	251.7	12,282	(D)	-	-
Hawaii	28	0.3	5,647	0.3	202	73.9	13,089	(D)	-	-

Source: County Business Patterns, 1995 and *Economic Census of the U.S., 1992*. Data are sorted by 1992 revenues and, if revenues are unavailable, by establishments in 1995. The symbol (D) indicates that data are withheld by the source to avoid disclosure of competitive information. A dash (-) indicates that data are not available or undisclosed because they do not meet statistical validity standards. Shaded *states* on the state map indicate those states which have proportionately greater representation in the industry than would be indicated by the state's population; the ratio is based on total revenues or number of establishments. Shaded *regions* indicate where the industry is regionally most concentrated.

5331 - VARIETY STORES

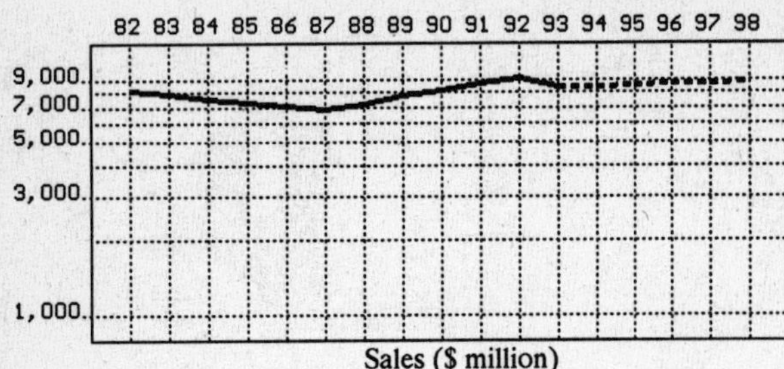

Sales ($ million)

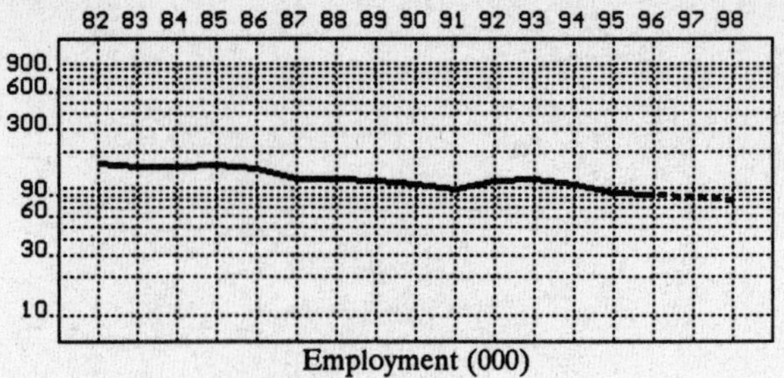

Employment (000)

GENERAL STATISTICS

Year	Establishments (number)	Employment (number)	Payroll ($ million)	Sales ($ million)	Employees per Establishment (number)	Sales per Establishment ($)	Payroll per Employee ($)
1982	11,703	160,565	1,085.3	8,090.2	14	691,294	6,759
1983	11,187	147,352	1,061.1	7,824.6e	13	-	7,201
1984	10,912	150,301	1,105.0	7,559.0e	14	-	7,352
1985	10,657	152,633	1,120.9	7,293.4e	14	-	7,344
1986	10,453	143,839	1,123.1	7,027.8e	14	-	7,808
1987	10,424	120,684	926.0	6,762.2	12	648,710	7,673
1988	10,150	118,075	943.9	7,221.1e	12	-	7,994
1989	10,069	115,985	951.1	7,680.0e	12	-	8,200
1990	9,951	109,000	976.1	8,139.0e	11	-	8,955
1991	9,861	98,740	943.3	8,597.9e	10	-	9,553
1992	12,561	115,861	1,088.5	9,056.8	9	721,027	9,395
1993	12,860	118,998	1,148.5	8,330.1p	9	-	9,651
1994	13,197	106,709	1,041.6	8,426.8p	8	-	9,761
1995	10,535	92,519	919.4	8,523.5p	9	-	9,938
1996	11,586p	89,923p	982.4p	8,620.1p	-	-	-
1997	11,660p	85,235p	975.9p	8,716.8p	-	-	-
1998	11,733p	80,546p	969.4p	8,813.4p	-	-	-

Sources: *Economic Census of the United States*, 1982, 1987, and 1992. Establishment counts, employment, and payroll are from *County Business Patterns* for non-Census years. Values followed by a 'p' are projections by the editors. Sales and expense data for non-Census years are extrapolations, marked by 'e'. Industries reclassified in 1987 will not have data for prior years. Data are the most recent available at this level of detail.

INDICES OF CHANGE

Year	Establishments (number)	Employment (number)	Payroll ($ million)	Sales ($ million)	Employees per Establishment (number)	Sales per Establishment ($)	Payroll per Employee ($)
1982	93.2	138.6	99.7	89.3	155.6	95.9	71.9
1983	89.1	127.2	97.5	86.4e	144.4	-	76.6
1984	86.9	129.7	101.5	83.5e	155.6	-	78.3
1985	84.8	131.7	103.0	80.5e	155.6	-	78.2
1986	83.2	124.1	103.2	77.6e	155.6	-	83.1
1987	83.0	104.2	85.1	74.7	133.3	90.0	81.7
1988	80.8	101.9	86.7	79.7e	133.3	-	85.1
1989	80.2	100.1	87.4	84.8e	133.3	-	87.3
1990	79.2	94.1	89.7	89.9e	122.2	-	95.3
1991	78.5	85.2	86.7	94.9e	111.1	-	101.7
1992	100.0	100.0	100.0	100.0	100.0	100.0	100.0
1993	102.4	102.7	105.5	92.0p	102.8	-	102.7
1994	105.1	92.1	95.7	93.0p	89.8	-	103.9
1995	83.9	79.9	84.5	94.1p	97.6	-	105.8
1996	92.2p	77.6p	90.3p	95.2p	-	-	-
1997	92.8p	73.6p	89.7p	96.2p	-	-	-
1998	93.4p	69.5p	89.1p	97.3p	-	-	-

Sources: Same as General Statistics. The values shown reflect change from the base year, 1992. Values above 100 mean greater than 1992, values below 100 mean less than 1992, and a value of 100 in the 1982-91 or 1993-98 period means same as 1992. Values followed by a 'p' are projections by the editors; 'e' stands for extrapolation. Data are the most recent available at this level of detail.

SELECTED RATIOS

For 1992	Avg. of All Retail	Analyzed Industry	Index	For 1992	Avg. of All Retail	Analyzed Industry	Index
Employees per Establishment	12	9	76	Sales per Employee	102,941	78,170	76
Payroll per Establishment	146,026	86,657	59	Sales per Establishment	1,241,555	721,025	58
Payroll per Employee	12,107	9,395	78	Expenses per Establishment	na	na	na

Sources: Same as General Statistics. The 'Average of All Manufacturing' column represents the average of all manufacturing industries reported for the most recent complete year available. The Index shows the relationship between the Average and the Analyzed Industry. For example, 100 means that they are equal; 500 that the Analyzed Industry is five times the average; 50 means that the Analyzed Industry is half the national average. The abbreviation 'na' is used to show that data are 'not available'.

LEADING COMPANIES

Number shown: **35** Total sales ($ mil): **163,338** Total employment (000): **1,266.7**

Company Name	Address				CEO Name	Phone	Co. Type	Sales ($ mil)	Empl. (000)
Wal-Mart Stores Inc.	702 Southwest 8th	Bentonville	AR	72716	David D Glass	501-273-4000	P	117,958	825.0
Kmart Corp.	3100 W Big Beaver	Troy	MI	48084	Floyd Hall	810-643-1000	P	31,437	265.0
Consolidated Stores Corp.	PO Box 28512	Columbus	OH	43228	William G Kelley	614-278-6800	P	2,647	38.0
Dollar General Corp.	104 Woodmont	Nashville	TN	37205	Cal Turner Jr	615-783-2000	P	2,134	25.4
F.W. Woolworth Co.	233 Broadway	New York	NY	10279	Paul T Davies	212-553-2000	S	2,080 *	32.0
Family Dollar Stores Inc.	PO Box 1017	Charlotte	NC	28201	Leon Levine	704-847-6961	P	1,995	22.5
Mac Frugal's Bargains	2430 E Del Amo	Dominguez	CA	90220	Philip L Carter	310-537-9220	P	705	7.3
McCrory Corp.	667 Madison Ave	New York	NY	10021	Meshulam Riklis	212-735-9500	R	580 *	8.0
Dollar Tree Stores Inc.	PO Box 2500	Norfolk	VA	23501	Macon F Brock Jr	757-321-5000	P	493	11.0
Value Merchants Inc.	710 N Plankinton	Milwaukee	WI	53203		414-274-2575	P	363	4.8
Sathers Inc.	PO Box 28	Round Lake	MN	56167	Bill Bradfield	507-945-8181	S	360 *	1.5
Ben Franklin Crafts Inc.	500 E North Ave	Carol Stream	IL	60188	Bob Kendig	708-462-6100	S	350	0.2
Duckwall-Alco Stores Inc.	401 Cottage St	Abilene	KS	67410	Glen Shank	785-263-3350	P	323	4.8
J.J. Newberry Co.	2955 E Market St	York	PA	17402	Meshulam Riklis	717-757-8181	S	300	2.7
Tuesday Morning Corp.	14621 Inwood Rd	Dallas	TX	75244	Jerry M Smith	972-387-3562	P	257	3.4
Bill's Dollar Stores Inc.	PO Box 9407	Jackson	MS	39286	MacDonnel Roehm	601-981-7171	R	250	2.5
Easter's Enterprises Inc.	PO Box 1351	Des Moines	IA	50305	Dennis Easter	515-265-1116	R	210	1.7
McCurdy and Company Inc.	Midtown Plz	Rochester	NY	14645	GK McCurdy	716-232-1000	R	150 *	1.6
TPI Inc. (Woodridge, Illinois)	2500 International	Woodridge	IL	60517	Pamela Alper	708-972-3000	R	120 *	1.3
Pharmhouse Corp.	860 Broadway	New York	NY	10003	Kenneth A Davis	212-477-9400	P	98	1.0
Universal International Inc.	5000 Winnetka N	New Hope	MN	55428	Mark H Ravich	612-533-1169	P	88	1.2
Cornet Stores Inc.	411 S Arroyo Pkwy	Pasadena	CA	91105	Joseph Cornet	818-796-5123	R	79	0.9
Babbitt Brothers Trading Co.	PO Box 1328	Flagstaff	AZ	86002	David Chambers	602-774-8711	R	75	0.6
Perry Brothers Inc.	107 W Lufkin Ave	Lufkin	TX	75901	Jack Simpson	409-634-6686	R	48	1.2
P.M. Place Stores Company	PO Box 555	Bethany	MO	64424	Charles Place	816-425-6301	R	48	0.5
Step Ahead Investments Inc.	3222 Winona Way	N. Highlands	CA	95660	Gary Cino	916-348-9898	R	48	0.5
Val Corp.	PO Box 670	New Castle	IN	47362	Gene R Hawkins	317-529-9770	R	33	0.4
Pechin Shopping Village	PO Box 340	Dunbar	PA	15431	Sullivan D'Amico	412-277-4251	R	30	0.4
E.B. Mott Co.	3015 Hansboro Ave	Dallas	TX	75233	John McNeil	214-339-5113	R	20	0.5
Thomas-Walker-Lacey Inc.	PO Box 1625	Canton	MS	39046	Toxey Hall III	601-859-1421	R	19	0.3
Supplee Enterprises Inc.	State 7 &ate 101	Minnetonka	MN	55345	Richard W Gibson	612-474-5266	R	13	0.1
Dollar Wholesale Company Inc.	PO Box 32	Weldon	NC	27890	William H Hand Jr	919-536-2143	R	11	0.2
Village Green Bookstore Inc.	766 Monroe Ave	Rochester	NY	14607	Raymond C Sparks	716-442-1151	P	10	0.1
Barrett Grocery Company Inc.	531 W Main St	Denison	TX	75020	Charles Kirklan	903-465-8225	R	5	<0.1
Masotta Variety and Deli	307 Main St	Woburn	MA	01801	Mararette Masotta	617-935-2648	R	1 *	<0.1

Source: *Ward's Business Directory of U.S. Private and Public Companies*, 1998. The company type code used is as follows: P - Public, R - Private, S - Subsidiary, D - Division, J - Joint Venture, A - Affiliate, G - Group. Sales are in millions of dollars, employees are in thousands. An asterisk (*) indicates an estimated sales volume. The symbol < stands for 'less than'.

OCCUPATIONS EMPLOYED BY SIC 533 - GENERAL MERCHANDISE STORES, NEC

Occupation	% of Total 1996	Change to 2006	Occupation	% of Total 1996	Change to 2006
Salespersons, retail	29.2	-36.1	Sales & related workers nec	1.9	-34.0
Cashiers	21.5	-39.3	Traffic, shipping, receiving clerks	1.6	-40.0
Stock clerks	13.4	-50.3	General office clerks	1.6	-48.4
Marketing & sales worker supervisors	9.4	-40.0	Bookkeeping, accounting, & auditing clerks	1.5	-52.0
General managers & top executives	3.7	-41.9	Freight, stock, & material movers, hand	1.1	-46.0

Source: *Industry-Occupation Matrix*, Bureau of Labor Statistics. These data relate to one or more 3-digit SIC industry groups rather than to a single 4-digit SIC. The change reported for each occupation to the year 2006 is a percent of growth or decline as estimated by the Bureau of Labor Statistics. The abbreviation nec stands for 'not elsewhere classified'.

STATE AND REGIONAL CONCENTRATION

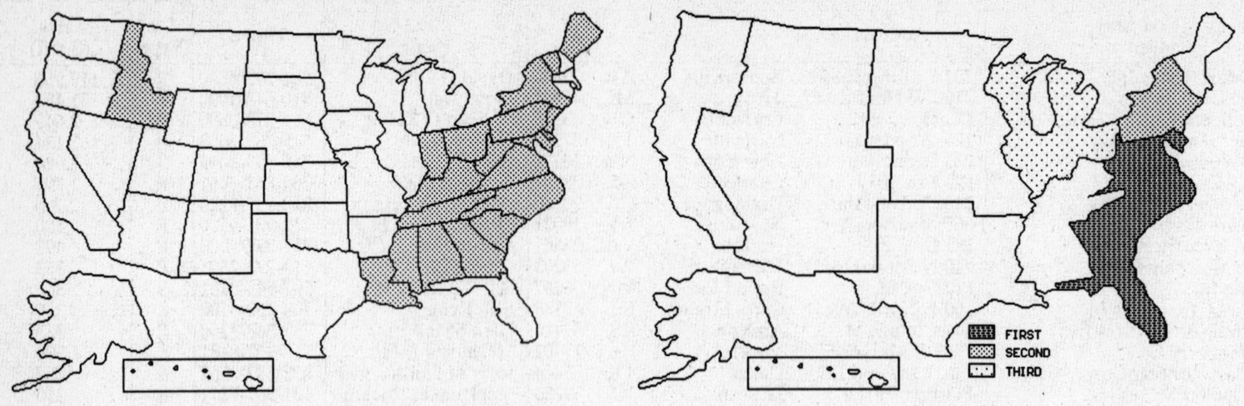

INDUSTRY DATA BY STATE

State	Establishments - 1995 Total (number)	Establishments - 1995 % of U.S.	Employment - 1995 Total (number)	Employment - 1995 % of U.S.	Employment - 1995 Per Estab.	Payroll - 1995 Total ($ mil.)	Payroll - 1995 Per Empl. ($)	Sales - 1992 Total ($ mil.)	Sales - 1992 % of U.S.	Sales - 1992 Per Estab ($)
New York	795	7.5	7,926	8.6	10	93.1	11,742	829.7	9.4	80,992
Ohio	540	5.1	6,270	6.8	12	61.5	9,803	562.2	6.4	80,438
Pennsylvania	588	5.6	5,976	6.5	10	60.8	10,173	545.5	6.2	72,966
California	444	4.2	4,486	4.9	10	49.9	11,124	543.1	6.2	75,064
Texas	713	6.8	4,584	5.0	6	42.3	9,217	519.4	5.9	68,682
Florida	575	5.5	5,715	6.2	10	55.4	9,702	460.2	5.2	83,000
North Carolina	541	5.1	4,138	4.5	8	38.4	9,291	360.4	4.1	76,787
Illinois	361	3.4	3,193	3.5	9	30.9	9,681	334.8	3.8	72,570
Georgia	415	3.9	3,613	3.9	9	34.4	9,529	333.9	3.8	83,653
Michigan	394	3.7	3,801	4.1	10	34.1	8,972	323.0	3.7	72,174
New Jersey	315	3.0	3,002	3.3	10	36.5	12,157	317.0	3.6	84,380
Virginia	350	3.3	3,445	3.7	10	36.9	10,720	302.1	3.4	78,413
Tennessee	277	2.6	2,327	2.5	8	22.3	9,596	270.9	3.1	84,387
Indiana	248	2.4	2,929	3.2	12	25.2	8,615	253.2	2.9	78,352
Kentucky	203	1.9	1,872	2.0	9	18.1	9,647	233.0	2.6	90,899
Maryland	193	1.8	2,247	2.4	12	21.0	9,354	224.3	2.5	77,506
Alabama	346	3.3	2,452	2.7	7	22.7	9,266	220.4	2.5	96,133
South Carolina	293	2.8	2,310	2.5	8	20.8	9,023	195.3	2.2	76,798
Louisiana	251	2.4	1,834	2.0	7	16.7	9,118	193.3	2.2	84,908
Missouri	188	1.8	1,522	1.7	8	14.4	9,482	171.3	1.9	77,041
Massachusetts	255	2.4	1,577	1.7	6	18.5	11,717	159.2	1.8	76,876
West Virginia	155	1.5	1,464	1.6	9	13.4	9,180	154.1	1.7	85,109
Mississippi	241	2.3	1,552	1.7	6	13.0	8,387	143.8	1.6	86,049
Wisconsin	167	1.6	1,548	1.7	9	13.4	8,647	116.7	1.3	64,180
Minnesota	149	1.4	964	1.0	6	7.7	8,023	94.2	1.1	65,958
Oklahoma	121	1.1	679	0.7	6	6.0	8,862	88.8	1.0	77,059
Washington	98	0.9	835	0.9	9	8.7	10,435	88.0	1.0	84,905
Connecticut	119	1.1	747	0.8	6	8.7	11,677	73.6	0.8	81,347
Arkansas	117	1.1	558	0.6	5	5.1	9,086	69.5	0.8	84,698
Maine	155	1.5	857	0.9	6	7.5	8,700	69.1	0.8	80,075
Oregon	56	0.5	453	0.5	8	4.3	9,585	67.2	0.8	73,667
Iowa	115	1.1	757	0.8	7	6.1	7,992	65.3	0.7	66,057
Colorado	64	0.6	564	0.6	9	5.5	9,778	59.3	0.7	72,007
Idaho	36	0.3	465	0.5	13	3.9	8,368	48.6	0.6	85,334
Arizona	72	0.7	462	0.5	6	3.9	8,372	47.6	0.5	70,016
Delaware	43	0.4	439	0.5	10	4.8	10,841	46.2	0.5	75,179
Vermont	40	0.4	441	0.5	11	4.5	10,261	35.3	0.4	75,230
New Mexico	42	0.4	357	0.4	9	3.8	10,597	28.7	0.3	81,455
Montana	32	0.3	190	0.2	6	1.7	8,700	27.6	0.3	69,808
New Hampshire	55	0.5	210	0.2	4	2.2	10,524	27.0	0.3	94,427
Utah	36	0.3	363	0.4	10	2.9	8,077	23.8	0.3	58,903
Nebraska	64	0.6	402	0.4	6	3.0	7,403	22.9	0.3	63,777
Rhode Island	37	0.4	218	0.2	6	2.1	9,628	18.8	0.2	88,948
North Dakota	39	0.4	224	0.2	6	1.7	7,509	17.6	0.2	57,695
Alaska	15	0.1	161	0.2	11	2.9	17,720	15.8	0.2	103,444
South Dakota	38	0.4	133	0.1	4	1.1	8,278	9.4	0.1	59,804
Wyoming	13	0.1	20-99	-	-	(D)	-	4.6	0.1	57,862
Kansas	71	0.7	542	0.6	8	5.8	10,731	(D)	-	-
Hawaii	32	0.3	1,216	1.3	38	15.2	12,504	(D)	-	-
Nevada	15	0.1	250-499	-	-	(D)	-	(D)	-	-
D.C.	13	0.1	100-249	-	-	(D)	-	(D)	-	-

Source: County Business Patterns, 1995 and *Economic Census of the U.S., 1992*. Data are sorted by 1992 revenues and, if revenues are unavailable, by establishments in 1995. The symbol (D) indicates that data are withheld by the source to avoid disclosure of competitive information. A dash (-) indicates that data are not available or undisclosed because they do not meet statistical validity standards. Shaded *states* on the state map indicate those states which have proportionately greater representation in the industry than would be indicated by the state's population; the ratio is based on total revenues or number of establishments. Shaded *regions* indicate where the industry is regionally most concentrated.

5399 - MISC. GENERAL MERCHANDISE STORES

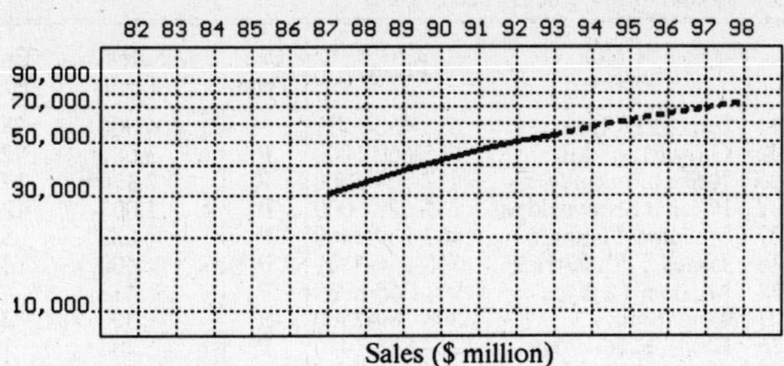

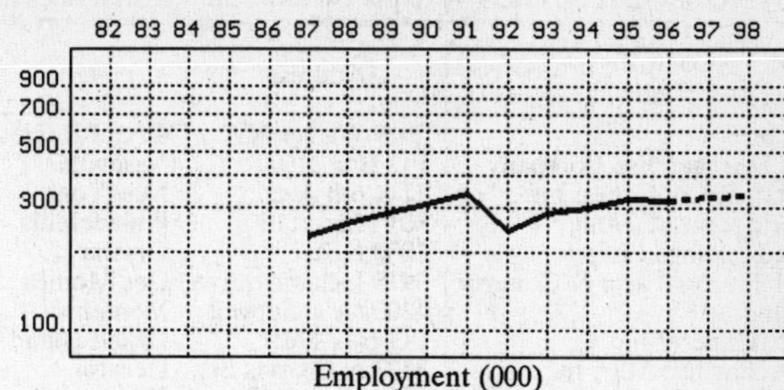

GENERAL STATISTICS

Year	Establishments (number)	Employment (number)	Payroll ($ million)	Sales ($ million)	Employees per Establishment (number)	Sales per Establishment ($)	Payroll per Employee ($)
1982	-	-	-	-	-	-	-
1983	-	-	-	-	-	-	-
1984	-	-	-	-	-	-	-
1985	-	-	-	-	-	-	-
1986	-	-	-	-	-	-	-
1987	14,969	231,032	2,294.2	30,368.1	15	2,028,736	9,930
1988	14,609	260,784	2,768.5	34,264.6e	18	-	10,616
1989	14,801	287,675	3,175.9	38,161.0e	19	-	11,040
1990	15,035	310,444	3,584.7	42,057.4e	21	-	11,547
1991	15,592	342,047	4,012.3	45,953.8e	22	-	11,730
1992	11,044	243,393	3,278.5	49,850.2	22	4,513,782	13,470
1993	12,051	284,277	3,914.3	53,746.6p	24	-	13,769
1994	12,414	302,152	4,209.9	57,643.0p	24	-	13,933
1995	14,320	322,614	4,540.2	61,539.4p	23	-	14,073
1996	12,315p	321,873p	4,737.5p	65,435.9p	-	-	-
1997	12,003p	328,816p	4,978.8p	69,332.3p	-	-	-
1998	11,692p	335,759p	5,220.1p	73,228.7p	-	-	-

Sources: Economic Census of the United States, 1982, 1987, and 1992. Establishment counts, employment, and payroll are from *County Business Patterns* for non-Census years. Values followed by a 'p' are projections by the editors. Sales and expense data for non-Census years are extrapolations, marked by 'e'. Industries reclassified in 1987 will not have data for prior years. Data are the most recent available at this level of detail.

INDICES OF CHANGE

Year	Establishments (number)	Employment (number)	Payroll ($ million)	Sales ($ million)	Employees per Establishment (number)	Sales per Establishment ($)	Payroll per Employee ($)
1982	-	-	-	-	-	-	-
1983	-	-	-	-	-	-	-
1984	-	-	-	-	-	-	-
1985	-	-	-	-	-	-	-
1986	-	-	-	-	-	-	-
1987	135.5	94.9	70.0	60.9	68.2	44.9	73.7
1988	132.3	107.1	84.4	68.7e	81.8	-	78.8
1989	134.0	118.2	96.9	76.6e	86.4	-	82.0
1990	136.1	127.5	109.3	84.4e	95.5	-	85.7
1991	141.2	140.5	122.4	92.2e	100.0	-	87.1
1992	100.0	100.0	100.0	100.0	100.0	100.0	100.0
1993	109.1	116.8	119.4	107.8p	107.2	-	102.2
1994	112.4	124.1	128.4	115.6p	110.6	-	103.4
1995	129.7	132.5	138.5	123.4p	102.4	-	104.5
1996	111.5p	132.2p	144.5p	131.3p	-	-	-
1997	108.7p	135.1p	151.9p	139.1p	-	-	-
1998	105.9p	137.9p	159.2p	146.9p	-	-	-

Sources: Same as General Statistics. The values shown reflect change from the base year, 1992. Values above 100 mean greater than 1992, values below 100 mean less than 1992, and a value of 100 in the 1982-91 or 1993-98 period means same as 1992. Values followed by a 'p' are projections by the editors; 'e' stands for extrapolation. Data are the most recent available at this level of detail.

SELECTED RATIOS

For 1992	Avg. of All Retail	Analyzed Industry	Index	For 1992	Avg. of All Retail	Analyzed Industry	Index
Employees per Establishment	12	22	183	Sales per Employee	102,941	204,814	199
Payroll per Establishment	146,026	296,858	203	Sales per Establishment	1,241,555	4,513,781	364
Payroll per Employee	12,107	13,470	111	Expenses per Establishment	na	na	na

Sources: Same as General Statistics. The 'Average of All Manufacturing' column represents the average of all manufacturing industries reported for the most recent complete year available. The Index shows the relationship between the Average and the Analyzed Industry. For example, 100 means that they are equal; 500 that the Analyzed Industry is five times the average; 50 means that the Analyzed Industry is half the national average. The abbreviation 'na' is used to show that data are 'not available'.

LEADING COMPANIES

Number shown: **50** Total sales ($ mil): **17,525** Total employment (000): **183.7**

Company Name	Address				CEO Name	Phone	Co. Type	Sales ($ mil)	Empl. (000)
Meijer Inc.	2929 Walker NW	Grand Rapids	MI	49544	Earl D Holton	616-453-6711	R	6,000 *	73.0
Service Merchandise Company	PO Box 24600	Nashville	TN	37202	Gary M Witkin	615-660-6000	P	3,662	42.7
American Retail Group Inc.	1114 6th Ave	New York	NY	10036	R Brenninkmeyer	212-704-5300	R	2,120 *	17.0
Strawbridge and Clothier	801 Market St	Philadelphia	PA	19107	Peter S Strawbridge	215-629-6000	P	1,007	12.1
Pamida Holdings Corp.	8800 F St	Omaha	NE	68127	Steven S Fishman	402-339-2400	P	633	5.7
Central Tractor Farm & Country	3915 Delaware Ave	Des Moines	IA	50316	James T McKitrick	515-266-3101	P	600	4.5
Fred's Inc.	4300 New Getwell	Memphis	TN	38118	Michael J Hayes	901-365-8880	P	418	4.2
Country General Inc.	PO Box 4905	Grand Island	NE	68802	Tony Seitz	308-389-2500	S	300	2.0
K's Merchandise Mart Inc.	3103 N Charles St	Decatur	IL	62526	David K Eldridge	217-875-1440	R	288 *	1.8
Garden Ridge Pottery Inc.	19411 Atrium Pl	Houston	TX	77084	Armand Shapiro	281-579-7901	S	225	2.9
Sharper Image Corp.	650 Davis St	San Francisco	CA	94111	Richard Thalheimer	415-445-6000	P	204	1.2
Knott's Berry Farm Foods Inc.	8039 Beach Blvd	Buena Park	CA	90620	Jack Falfas	714-827-1776	S	200	3.0
Mazel Stores Inc.	31000 Aurora Rd	Solon	OH	44139	Reuven Dessler	216-248-5200	P	180	0.9
L. Luria and Son Inc.	5770 Miami Lks Dr	Miami Lakes	FL	33014	Rachmil Lekach	305-557-9000	P	173	1.7
Gramex Corp.	11966 Charles Rock	Bridgeton	MO	63044	Tom W Holley	314-739-8300	R	170 *	1.4
G.I. Joe's Inc.	9805 Boeckman Rd	Wilsonville	OR	97070	David E Orkney	503-682-2242	R	145	1.1
Basic Living Products Inc.	1321 67th St	Emeryville	CA	94608	Gene Farb	510-428-0859	R	100 *	0.5
Pharmhouse Corp.	860 Broadway	New York	NY	10003	Kenneth A Davis	212-477-9400	P	98	1.0
Ammar's Inc.	S College Ave	Bluefield	VA	24605	Keleel A Ammar Jr	540-322-4686	R	75	0.8
Joseph B. Dahlkemper Company	PO Box 3400	Erie	PA	16508	E H Dahlkemper	814-864-4063	R	70	0.4
Grand Piano and Furniture Co.	4235 Electric SW	Roanoke	VA	24026	G B Cartledge Jr	703-343-1707	R	64	0.6
Growers Cooperative Inc.	PO Box 2196	Terre Haute	IN	47802	Keith C Bowers	812-235-8123	R	63 *	<0.1
Kugler Oil Co.	PO Box 1748	McCook	NE	69001	John Kugler	308-345-2280	R	62 *	0.2
Odd Job Trading Corp.	66 W 48th St	New York	NY	10036	Reuven Dessler	212-575-0477	S	60	0.6
University Book Store Inc.	4326 University	Seattle	WA	98105	RH Cross	206-634-3400	R	49	0.3
Marden Discount Store Inc.	184 College Ave	Waterville	ME	04901	H Marden	207-873-6111	R	48	0.5
Atwood Distributing Inc.	2717 N Van Buren	Enid	OK	73701	G Atwood	405-233-3702	R	40	0.4
Fort Recovery Equity	2351 Walbash St	Fort Recovery	OH	45846	M. Muhlenkemp	419-375-4119	R	40	<0.1
Thruway Food Market	78 Oak St	Walden	NY	12586	Arthur Concors	914-778-3535	R	39	0.4
Mid-Wood Inc.	12818 Gypsy Ln	Bowling Green	OH	43402	Tom Dorman	419-352-5231	R	38 *	<0.1
Z.V. Pate Inc.	PO Box 157	Laurel Hill	NC	28351	David L Burns	910-462-2122	R	35	0.9
Farmers Union Cooperative	PO Box 148	Britton	SD	57430	David A Andresen	605-448-2231	R	28	<0.1
Sutton Cooperative Grain Co.	Railroad & Sanders	Sutton	NE	68979	Earl Holtman	402-773-5531	R	25	<0.1
Big Blue Stores Inc.	150 N Jackson Pk	Seymour	IN	47274	M Robert Lonowski	812-522-8857	R	24	0.3
Mazer's Discount Home Centers	PO Box 321546	Birmingham	AL	35232	JB Mazer	205-591-6565	R	24 *	0.2
Rockingham Cooperative	101 Grace St	Harrisonburg	VA	22801	CM Wright	703-434-3856	R	22	0.2
Berwick Bay Oil Company Inc.	PO Box 2708	Morgan City	LA	70381	John O'Neill	504-384-1610	R	20	0.1
Gebo Distributing Company	PO Box 850	Plainview	TX	79073	Brent T Gebo	806-293-4212	R	20 *	0.2
Rippey Farmers Cooperative	403 Perseville St	Rippey	IA	50235	Mike Mace	515-436-7411	R	18	<0.1
University Cooperative Society	2246 Guadalupe	Austin	TX	78705	George Mitchell	512-476-7211	R	18	0.2
Schaeperkoetter Store Inc.	PO Box 37	Mount Sterling	MO	65062	I R Schaeperkoetter	314-943-6321	R	15	<0.1
Smith Brothers of Dudley Inc.	PO Box 10	Dudley	NC	28333	William H Smith	919-735-2764	R	15	<0.1
Danco Prairie FS Cooperative	5371 Farmco Dr	Madison	WI	53718	John Cullen	608-241-4181	R	14	<0.1
Kane Industries Corp.	753 Calle Plano	Camarillo	CA	93012	Alan S Gordon	805-388-8687	R	13 *	<0.1
Carco International Inc.	2721 Midland Blvd	Fort Smith	AR	72904	Carl M Corley	501-441-3270	R	12	<0.1
Richards Brothers Supermarket	PO Box 866	Mtn Grove	MO	65711	Wells E Richards	417-926-4168	R	12	<0.1
Waller Brothers Inc.	PO Box 6288	Mobile	AL	36660	Terrence J Silva	205-479-8621	S	12 *	0.1
Scriveners Inc.	8502 Broadway	San Antonio	TX	78217	Ernest Scrivener	210-824-2353	R	11 *	<0.1
New Cooperative Company Inc.	PO Box 607	Dillonvale	OH	43917	John Pastre	614-769-2331	R	9 *	0.1
Belk Jones Co.	Central Mall, #73	Texarkana	TX	75503	Jack Parry	903-832-1551	S	6 *	<0.1

Source: *Ward's Business Directory of U.S. Private and Public Companies*, 1998. The company type code used is as follows: P - Public, R - Private, S - Subsidiary, D - Division, J - Joint Venture, A - Affiliate, G - Group. Sales are in millions of dollars, employees are in thousands. An asterisk (*) indicates an estimated sales volume. The symbol < stands for 'less than'.

OCCUPATIONS EMPLOYED BY SIC 539 - GENERAL MERCHANDISE STORES, NEC

Occupation	% of Total 1996	Change to 2006	Occupation	% of Total 1996	Change to 2006
Salespersons, retail	29.2	-36.1	Sales & related workers nec	1.9	-34.0
Cashiers	21.5	-39.3	Traffic, shipping, receiving clerks	1.6	-40.0
Stock clerks	13.4	-50.3	General office clerks	1.6	-48.4
Marketing & sales worker supervisors	9.4	-40.0	Bookkeeping, accounting, & auditing clerks	1.5	-52.0
General managers & top executives	3.7	-41.9	Freight, stock, & material movers, hand	1.1	-46.0

Source: *Industry-Occupation Matrix*, Bureau of Labor Statistics. These data relate to one or more 3-digit SIC industry groups rather than to a single 4-digit SIC. The change reported for each occupation to the year 2006 is a percent of growth or decline as estimated by the Bureau of Labor Statistics. The abbreviation nec stands for 'not elsewhere classified'.

STATE AND REGIONAL CONCENTRATION

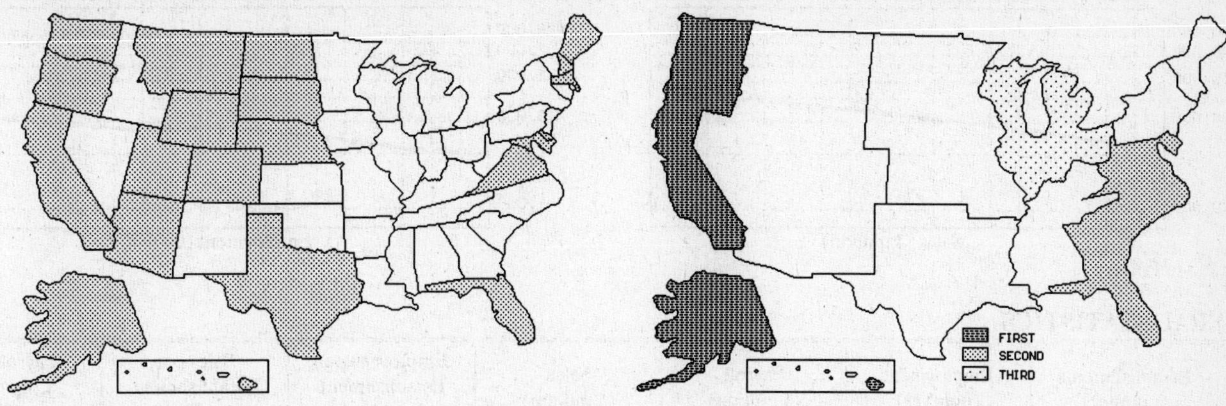

INDUSTRY DATA BY STATE

State	Establishments - 1995 Total (number)	Establishments - 1995 % of U.S.	Employment - 1995 Total (number)	Employment - 1995 % of U.S.	Employment - 1995 Per Estab.	Payroll - 1995 Total ($ mil.)	Payroll - 1995 Per Empl. ($)	Sales - 1992 Total ($ mil.)	Sales - 1992 % of U.S.	Sales - 1992 Per Estab ($)
California	1,128	7.9	36,407	11.3	32	665.3	18,275	9,182.7	18.5	289,539
Texas	1,038	7.2	23,492	7.3	23	289.3	12,313	3,829.0	7.7	220,414
Florida	702	4.9	19,000	5.9	27	277.9	14,627	3,374.3	6.8	226,739
New York	879	6.1	18,195	5.7	21	268.1	14,736	2,131.0	4.3	162,065
Washington	203	1.4	6,680	2.1	33	148.1	22,167	1,672.6	3.4	302,625
Illinois	618	4.3	13,219	4.1	21	161.0	12,179	1,669.0	3.4	175,164
Ohio	482	3.4	14,994	4.7	31	169.0	11,268	1,517.7	3.1	161,457
Pennsylvania	515	3.6	10,923	3.4	21	133.6	12,234	1,331.4	2.7	162,881
Michigan	312	2.2	9,031	2.8	29	110.6	12,250	1,289.4	2.6	198,191
Massachusetts	255	1.8	9,055	2.8	36	145.9	16,118	1,277.3	2.6	182,244
Virginia	467	3.3	9,768	3.0	21	140.2	14,350	1,275.4	2.6	204,253
Oregon	166	1.2	5,256	1.6	32	108.4	20,621	1,187.7	2.4	245,401
New Jersey	302	2.1	7,468	2.3	25	129.7	17,367	1,176.3	2.4	203,099
Hawaii	96	0.7	3,796	1.2	40	76.7	20,218	1,103.0	2.2	372,506
Georgia	384	2.7	7,045	2.2	18	84.4	11,978	1,098.0	2.2	215,809
Arizona	191	1.3	5,148	1.6	27	81.3	15,792	986.0	2.0	245,693
Maryland	215	1.5	6,438	2.0	30	88.9	13,811	970.0	2.0	194,535
Wisconsin	232	1.6	6,602	2.1	28	91.2	13,810	920.1	1.9	173,600
North Carolina	487	3.4	7,875	2.5	16	95.3	12,100	914.7	1.8	149,147
Tennessee	422	2.9	8,716	2.7	21	102.3	11,733	832.8	1.7	179,255
Indiana	356	2.5	7,406	2.3	21	83.4	11,261	827.9	1.7	168,062
Colorado	182	1.3	5,317	1.7	29	74.0	13,924	815.5	1.6	175,190
Minnesota	262	1.8	5,501	1.7	21	76.4	13,881	784.4	1.6	166,996
Louisiana	272	1.9	4,824	1.5	18	54.3	11,247	744.4	1.5	184,618
Missouri	387	2.7	5,864	1.8	15	68.7	11,715	720.2	1.5	182,598
Connecticut	105	0.7	3,096	1.0	29	52.7	17,025	599.4	1.2	185,855
Alabama	320	2.2	4,119	1.3	13	49.3	11,967	565.7	1.1	205,625
Oklahoma	257	1.8	3,979	1.2	15	44.6	11,208	524.3	1.1	188,445
New Hampshire	130	0.9	3,479	1.1	27	54.3	15,621	490.1	1.0	178,756
Kentucky	341	2.4	4,425	1.4	13	46.1	10,417	440.1	0.9	159,702
Kansas	222	1.6	3,985	1.2	18	41.4	10,397	438.3	0.9	157,563
Iowa	246	1.7	4,417	1.4	18	46.3	10,483	424.5	0.9	128,339
South Carolina	194	1.4	3,009	0.9	16	38.4	12,772	416.3	0.8	163,247
Mississippi	302	2.1	3,991	1.2	13	41.5	10,400	398.6	0.8	148,675
Utah	80	0.6	2,132	0.7	27	34.7	16,279	378.8	0.8	198,550
Alaska	118	0.8	1,766	0.6	15	35.1	19,873	378.5	0.8	292,919
Arkansas	241	1.7	3,103	1.0	13	33.2	10,696	374.9	0.8	166,020
Nebraska	156	1.1	3,322	1.0	21	33.9	10,215	354.6	0.7	132,169
Maine	165	1.2	2,850	0.9	17	35.1	12,322	352.4	0.7	158,583
New Mexico	108	0.8	2,095	0.7	19	27.3	13,039	285.8	0.6	181,479
Delaware	48	0.3	1,349	0.4	28	17.0	12,596	230.4	0.5	197,413
West Virginia	181	1.3	2,012	0.6	11	24.9	12,397	196.9	0.4	144,586
Idaho	85	0.6	1,764	0.5	21	27.2	15,446	196.3	0.4	190,755
Montana	71	0.5	1,836	0.6	26	27.7	15,084	195.0	0.4	183,996
Rhode Island	33	0.2	1,251	0.4	38	17.7	14,149	185.4	0.4	189,040
South Dakota	81	0.6	1,323	0.4	16	13.1	9,873	151.4	0.3	127,529
North Dakota	49	0.3	1,387	0.4	28	15.3	11,009	131.0	0.3	125,847
Wyoming	61	0.4	1,120	0.3	18	12.6	11,212	105.2	0.2	128,133
Vermont	96	0.7	941	0.3	10	12.6	13,402	59.0	0.1	129,002
Nevada	58	0.4	1000-2499	-	-	(D)	-	(D)	-	-
D.C.	19	0.1	100-249	-	-	(D)	-	(D)	-	-

Source: County Business Patterns, 1995 and *Economic Census of the U.S., 1992*. Data are sorted by 1992 revenues and, if revenues are unavailable, by establishments in 1995. The symbol (D) indicates that data are withheld by the source to avoid disclosure of competitive information. A dash (-) indicates that data are not available or undisclosed because they do not meet statistical validity standards. Shaded *states* on the state map indicate those states which have proportionately greater representation in the industry than would be indicated by the state's population; the ratio is based on total revenues or number of establishments. Shaded *regions* indicate where the industry is regionally most concentrated.

5411 - GROCERY STORES

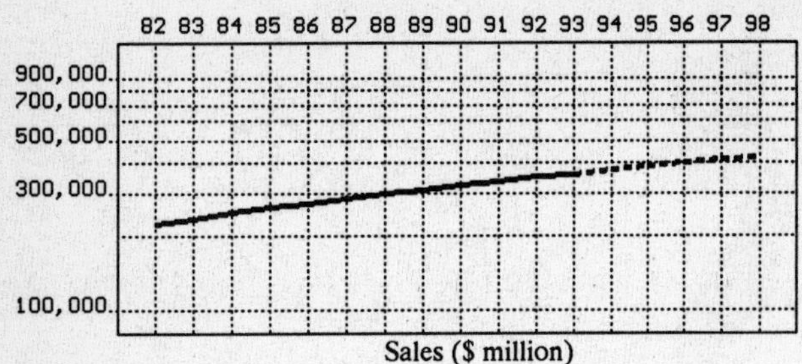

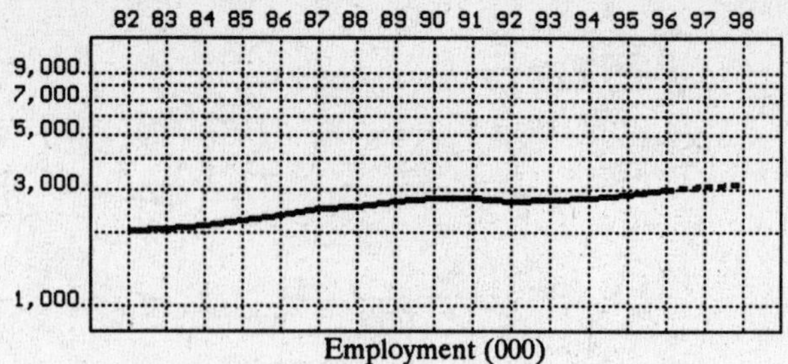

GENERAL STATISTICS

Year	Establishments (number)	Employment (number)	Payroll ($ million)	Sales ($ million)	Employees per Establishment (number)	Sales per Establishment ($)	Payroll per Employee ($)
1982	137,905	2,031,453	21,363.7	226,609.1	15	1,643,226	10,516
1983	135,292	2,059,832	22,705.8	238,383.5*e*	15	-	11,023
1984	132,929	2,148,899	23,821.2	250,157.9*e*	16	-	11,085
1985	130,286	2,241,331	25,011.6	261,932.3*e*	17	-	11,159
1986	133,159	2,357,853	26,442.7	273,706.7*e*	18	-	11,215
1987	137,584	2,502,468	27,084.0	285,481.1	18	2,074,959	10,823
1988	132,331	2,543,815	28,668.2	298,896.5*e*	19	-	11,270
1989	132,759	2,661,158	30,483.1	312,311.9*e*	20	-	11,455
1990	132,516	2,756,718	32,360.7	325,727.4*e*	21	-	11,739
1991	133,272	2,747,755	33,744.6	339,142.8*e*	21	-	12,281
1992	133,263	2,682,153	34,425.3	352,558.2	20	2,645,582	12,835
1993	133,035	2,728,594	35,159.1	363,288.3*p*	21	-	12,885
1994	131,707	2,784,784	36,348.5	375,883.2*p*	21	-	13,053
1995	130,825	2,871,354	37,985.9	388,478.1*p*	22	-	13,229
1996	131,305*p*	3,003,371*p*	39,382.4*p*	401,073.0*p*	-	-	-
1997	131,033*p*	3,069,362*p*	40,675.3*p*	413,667.9*p*	-	-	-
1998	130,761*p*	3,135,353*p*	41,968.1*p*	426,262.8*p*	-	-	-

Sources: Economic Census of the United States, 1982, 1987, and 1992. Establishment counts, employment, and payroll are from *County Business Patterns* for non-Census years. Values followed by a 'p' are projections by the editors. Sales and expense data for non-Census years are extrapolations, marked by 'e'. Industries reclassified in 1987 will not have data for prior years. Data are the most recent available at this level of detail.

INDICES OF CHANGE

Year	Establishments (number)	Employment (number)	Payroll ($ million)	Sales ($ million)	Employees per Establishment (number)	Sales per Establishment ($)	Payroll per Employee ($)
1982	103.5	75.7	62.1	64.3	75.0	62.1	81.9
1983	101.5	76.8	66.0	67.6*e*	75.0	-	85.9
1984	99.7	80.1	69.2	71.0*e*	80.0	-	86.4
1985	97.8	83.6	72.7	74.3*e*	85.0	-	86.9
1986	99.9	87.9	76.8	77.6*e*	90.0	-	87.4
1987	103.2	93.3	78.7	81.0	90.0	78.4	84.3
1988	99.3	94.8	83.3	84.8*e*	95.0	-	87.8
1989	99.6	99.2	88.5	88.6*e*	100.0	-	89.2
1990	99.4	102.8	94.0	92.4*e*	105.0	-	91.5
1991	100.0	102.4	98.0	96.2*e*	105.0	-	95.7
1992	100.0	100.0	100.0	100.0	100.0	100.0	100.0
1993	99.8	101.7	102.1	103.0*p*	102.6	-	100.4
1994	98.8	103.8	105.6	106.6*p*	105.7	-	101.7
1995	98.2	107.1	110.3	110.2*p*	109.7	-	103.1
1996	98.5*p*	112.0*p*	114.4*p*	113.8*p*	-	-	-
1997	98.3*p*	114.4*p*	118.2*p*	117.3*p*	-	-	-
1998	98.1*p*	116.9*p*	121.9*p*	120.9*p*	-	-	-

Sources: Same as General Statistics. The values shown reflect change from the base year, 1992. Values above 100 mean greater than 1992, values below 100 mean less than 1992, and a value of 100 in the 1982-91 or 1993-98 period means same as 1992. Values followed by a 'p' are projections by the editors; 'e' stands for extrapolation. Data are the most recent available at this level of detail.

SELECTED RATIOS

For 1992	Avg. of All Retail	Analyzed Industry	Index	For 1992	Avg. of All Retail	Analyzed Industry	Index
Employees per Establishment	12	20	167	Sales per Employee	102,941	131,446	128
Payroll per Establishment	146,026	258,326	177	Sales per Establishment	1,241,555	2,645,582	213
Payroll per Employee	12,107	12,835	106	Expenses per Establishment	na	na	na

Sources: Same as General Statistics. The 'Average of All Manufacturing' column represents the average of all manufacturing industries reported for the most recent complete year available. The Index shows the relationship between the Average and the Analyzed Industry. For example, 100 means that they are equal; 500 that the Analyzed Industry is five times the average; 50 means that the Analyzed Industry is half the national average. The abbreviation 'na' is used to show that data are 'not available'.

LEADING COMPANIES

Number shown: **49** Total sales ($ mil): **500,007** Total employment (000): **3,015.1**

Company Name	Address				CEO Name	Phone	Co. Type	Sales ($ mil)	Empl. (000)
Wal-Mart Stores Inc.	702 Southwest 8th	Bentonville	AR	72716	David D Glass	501-273-4000	P	117,958	825.0
Ralphs Grocery Co.	1100 W Artesia	Compton	CA	90220	George Golleher	310-884-9000	S	55,000	25.0
Kmart Corp.	3100 W Big Beaver	Troy	MI	48084	Floyd Hall	810-643-1000	P	31,437	265.0
Kroger Co.	1014 Vine St	Cincinnati	OH	45202	Joseph A Pichler	513-762-4000	P	25,171	212.0
Safeway Inc.	5918oneridge Mall	Pleasanton	CA	94588	Steven A Burd	510-467-3000	P	22,483	119.0
American Stores Co.	709 E S Temple	Salt Lake City	UT	84102	Victor L Lund	801-539-0112	P	18,678	127.0
SUPERVALU Inc.	PO Box 990	Eden Prairie	MN	55440	Michael W Wright	612-828-4000	P	16,552	44.8
Fleming Companies Inc.	PO Box 26647	Oklahoma City	OK	73126	Robert E Stauth	405-840-7200	P	16,487	41.2
Albertson's Inc.	PO Box 20	Boise	ID	83726	Gary G Michael	208-395-6200	P	14,690	94.0
Ahold USA Inc.	950 E Paces Ferry	Atlanta	GA	30326	Robert Zwartendijk	404-262-6050	S	14,000	100.0
Winn-Dixie Stores Inc.	5050 Edgewood	Jacksonville	FL	32254	A Dano Davis	904-783-5000	P	13,219	136.0
Publix Super Markets Inc.	1936 Jenkins	Lakeland	FL	33802	Howard M Jenkins	941-688-1188	R	13,100 •	100.0
Great Atlantic and Pacific Tea	PO Box 418	Montvale	NJ	07645	James Wood	201-573-9700	P	10,089	84.0
Food Lion Inc.	PO Box 1330	Salisbury	NC	28145	Tom E Smith	704-633-8250	P	9,006	73.2
Southland Corp.	PO Box 711	Dallas	TX	75221	Clark J Matthews II	214-828-7011	P	7,060	29.5
Meijer Inc.	2929 Walker NW	Grand Rapids	MI	49544	Earl D Holton	616-453-6711	R	6,000 •	73.0
Dillon Companies Inc.	PO Box 1266	Hutchinson	KS	67504	Warren F Bryant	316-663-6801	S	5,610 •	47.3
Food 4 Less Holdings Inc.	777 S Harbor Blvd	La Habra	CA	90631	George Golleher	714-738-2000	R	5,519	27.3
Emro Marketing Co.	PO Box 1500	Springfield	OH	45501	Riad N Yammine	513-864-3000	S	5,143 •	24.0
Vons Companies Inc.	618 Michillinda Ave	Arcadia	CA	91007	Richard Goodspeed	818-821-7000	S	5,071	30.0
Stop and Shop Supermarket Co.	PO Box 1942	Boston	MA	02105	William Grize	781-380-8000	S	5,052 •	40.0
H.E. Butt Grocery Co.	646 S Main St	San Antonio	TX	78204	Fully Clingman	210-938-8000	R	5,000 •	40.0
Nash Finch Co.	PO Box 355	Minneapolis	MN	55440	Alfred N Flaten	612-832-0534	P	4,392	12.2
Pathmark Stores Inc.	200 Milik Street	Carteret	NJ	07008	Jim Donald	732-499-3000	R	4,000	30.0
Yucaipa Cos.	10000 Santa Monica	Los Angeles	CA	90067	Ronald W Burkle	310-789-7200	R	3,930 •	30.0
Giant Food Inc.	6300 Sheriff Rd	Landover	MD	20785	Pete L Manos	301-341-4100	P	3,881	27.0
Fred Meyer Inc.	PO Box 42121	Portland	OR	97242	Robert G Miller	503-232-8844	P	3,725	28.0
Cub Foods	PO Box 9	Stillwater	MN	55082	John Hooley	612-439-7200	S	3,688 •	10.0
Circle K Stores Inc.	PO Box 52084	Phoenix	AZ	85072	John F Antioco	602-253-9600	S	3,563	20.5
Penn Traffic Co.	PO Box 4737	Syracuse	NY	13221	Gary D Hirsch	315-453-7284	P	3,297	27.3
Hannaford Brothers Co.	145 Pleasant Hill	Scarborough	ME	04074	Hugh G Farrington	207-883-2911	P	3,226	7.5
Tops Markets Inc.	PO Box 1027	Buffalo	NY	14240	Steve Odland	716-635-5000	S	3,135 •	24.0
Malone and Hyde Inc.	1991 Corporate Ave	Memphis	TN	38132	Bob Harris	901-367-8200	S	3,119	4.0
Giant Food Stores Inc.	PO Box 249	Carlisle	PA	17013	Anthony Schiano	717-249-4000	S	3,000	3.0
Hy-Vee Food Stores Inc.	5820 Westown	W. Des Moines	IA	50266	Ron Pearson	515-267-2800	R	3,000	40.0
Bruno's Inc.	PO Box 2486	Birmingham	AL	35201	William J Bolton	205-940-9400	P	2,899	25.0
BI-LO Inc.	PO Drawer 99	Mauldin	SC	29662	Marshall J Collins	864-234-1600	S	2,700	2.3
Dominick's Supermarkets Inc.	505 Railroad Ave	Northlake	IL	60164	Robert A Mariano	708-562-1000	P	2,585	19.4
Roundy's Inc.	23000 Roundy Dr	Pewaukee	WI	53072	Jerry Lestina	414-547-7999	R	2,500	5.0
Acme Markets Inc.	75 Val Stream Pkwy	Malvern	PA	19355	Jim Horn	610-889-4000	D	2,340 •	19.0
Randall's Food Markets Inc.	PO Box 4506	Houston	TX	77210	Randall Onstead Jr	713-268-3500	R	2,300	17.0
Ruddick Corp.	2000 Two 1st Union	Charlotte	NC	28282	Thomas W Dickson	704-372-5404	P	2,300	19.7
Golub Corp.	501 Duanesburg Rd	Schenectady	NY	12306	Lewis Golub	518-355-5000	R	2,220 •	17.0
Raley's	PO Box 15618	Sacramento	CA	95852	Charles L Collings	916-373-3333	R	2,103 •	12.0
Shaw's Supermarkets Inc.	PO Box 600	E. Bridgewater	MA	02333	Philip Francis	508-378-3020	S	2,100 •	17.8
Pilot Corp.	PO Box 10146	Knoxville	TN	37939	James A Haslam III	423-588-7487	R	2,000	6.8
Harris Teeter Inc.	PO Box 33129	Charlotte	NC	28233	F J Morganthall II	704-845-3100	S	1,931	16.1
King Soopers Inc.	65 Tejon St	Denver	CO	80223	John Burgon	303-778-3100	S	1,895 •	14.5
Super Rite Corp.	PO Box 2261	Harrisburg	PA	17105	John Stokely	717-232-6821	S	1,854 •	2.8

Source: *Ward's Business Directory of U.S. Private and Public Companies*, 1998. The company type code used is as follows: P - Public, R - Private, S - Subsidiary, D - Division, J - Joint Venture, A - Affiliate, G - Group. Sales are in millions of dollars, employees are in thousands. An asterisk (*) indicates an estimated sales volume. The symbol < stands for 'less than'.

OCCUPATIONS EMPLOYED BY SIC 541 - GROCERY STORES

Occupation	% of Total 1996	Change to 2006	Occupation	% of Total 1996	Change to 2006
Cashiers	33.3	17.6	Food preparation workers	3.7	33.0
Stock clerks	19.3	-12.7	Food counter, fountain workers	3.5	27.7
Hand packers & packagers	9.9	23.0	General managers & top executives	2.5	12.6
Marketing & sales worker supervisors	6.9	27.8	Bakers, bread & pastry	2.3	39.5
Salespersons, retail	5.7	11.4	General office clerks	1.2	-0.0
Butchers & meatcutters	4.2	-8.9			

Source: *Industry-Occupation Matrix*, Bureau of Labor Statistics. These data relate to one or more 3-digit SIC industry groups rather than to a single 4-digit SIC. The change reported for each occupation to the year 2006 is a percent of growth or decline as estimated by the Bureau of Labor Statistics. The abbreviation nec stands for 'not elsewhere classified'.

STATE AND REGIONAL CONCENTRATION

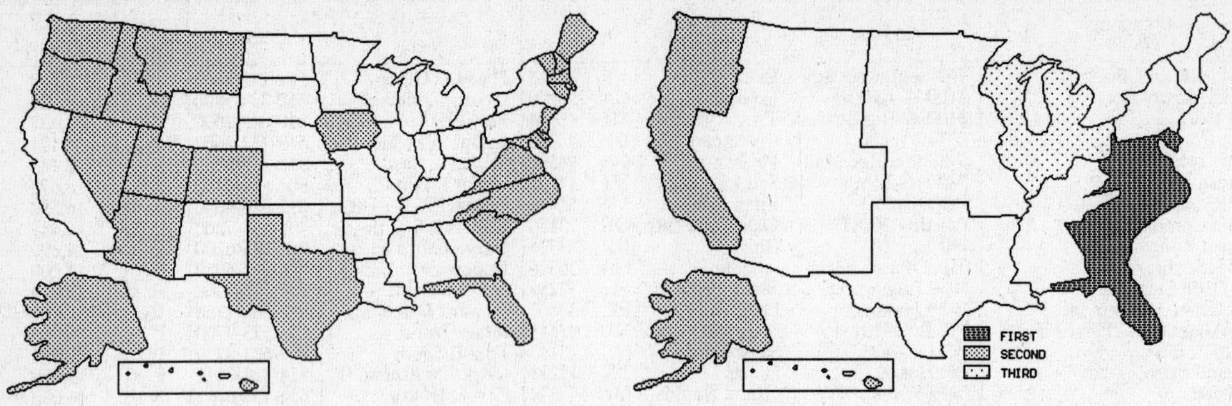

INDUSTRY DATA BY STATE

State	Establishments - 1995 Total (number)	% of U.S.	Employment - 1995 Total (number)	% of U.S.	Per Estab.	Payroll - 1995 Total ($ mil.)	Per Empl. ($)	Sales - 1992 Total ($ mil.)	% of U.S.	Per Estab ($)
California	11,196	8.6	241,180	8.4	22	4,971.2	20,612	42,733.1	12.1	173,843
Texas	10,481	8.0	215,585	7.5	21	2,576.0	11,949	25,652.8	7.3	128,568
New York	10,869	8.3	170,396	5.9	16	2,340.5	13,735	22,086.5	6.3	131,334
Florida	7,024	5.4	192,492	6.7	27	2,264.8	11,765	20,270.2	5.7	116,296
Pennsylvania	5,377	4.1	140,034	4.9	26	1,710.9	12,218	16,497.9	4.7	121,032
Ohio	5,050	3.9	126,482	4.4	25	1,500.3	11,862	14,367.5	4.1	122,194
Illinois	4,462	3.4	112,522	3.9	25	1,470.0	13,064	14,064.2	4.0	128,798
New Jersey	4,176	3.2	84,918	3.0	20	1,427.9	16,815	12,199.1	3.5	144,171
Michigan	4,921	3.8	91,715	3.2	19	1,120.5	12,217	10,433.2	3.0	121,090
Virginia	4,014	3.1	78,017	2.7	19	1,023.1	13,114	9,629.4	2.7	131,254
North Carolina	4,406	3.4	90,376	3.1	21	966.5	10,694	9,620.7	2.7	131,926
Georgia	4,086	3.1	109,944	3.8	27	1,007.9	9,168	9,094.9	2.6	115,280
Massachusetts	2,707	2.1	75,176	2.6	28	973.6	12,951	8,701.6	2.5	118,095
Washington	2,577	2.0	55,379	1.9	21	943.4	17,035	7,924.7	2.2	149,625
Maryland	2,240	1.7	52,656	1.8	24	926.9	17,603	7,351.7	2.1	144,497
Indiana	2,133	1.6	61,121	2.1	29	729.5	11,936	7,073.6	2.0	122,667
Tennessee	3,531	2.7	70,280	2.4	20	681.7	9,699	6,889.1	2.0	114,111
Missouri	2,406	1.8	52,621	1.8	22	669.8	12,729	6,711.3	1.9	128,371
Wisconsin	1,776	1.4	56,292	2.0	32	643.7	11,435	6,579.6	1.9	121,643
Arizona	1,611	1.2	45,933	1.6	29	746.1	16,244	6,016.6	1.7	139,269
Louisiana	3,018	2.3	54,825	1.9	18	557.4	10,168	5,961.0	1.7	119,590
Minnesota	1,724	1.3	47,329	1.6	27	592.9	12,526	5,781.8	1.6	128,050
Alabama	2,747	2.1	63,081	2.2	23	535.5	8,489	5,577.6	1.6	125,738
Colorado	1,198	0.9	40,846	1.4	34	747.3	18,295	5,454.6	1.5	151,572
Kentucky	2,464	1.9	45,482	1.6	18	475.6	10,457	5,164.8	1.5	123,615
Connecticut	1,474	1.1	39,726	1.4	27	610.9	15,378	5,151.9	1.5	132,907
South Carolina	2,335	1.8	50,318	1.8	22	508.3	10,101	5,072.4	1.4	119,522
Oregon	1,744	1.3	31,370	1.1	18	473.6	15,098	4,210.5	1.2	136,181
Oklahoma	2,103	1.6	32,317	1.1	15	380.6	11,777	4,102.3	1.2	135,212
Iowa	1,421	1.1	39,912	1.4	28	439.8	11,018	3,983.5	1.1	108,015
Mississippi	2,168	1.7	31,037	1.1	14	327.1	10,541	3,372.5	1.0	114,684
Kansas	1,102	0.8	27,334	1.0	25	344.8	12,614	3,286.3	0.9	130,295
Arkansas	1,614	1.2	24,884	0.9	15	274.8	11,044	3,005.4	0.9	114,128
Utah	637	0.5	20,282	0.7	32	280.7	13,841	2,671.0	0.8	137,532
West Virginia	1,308	1.0	21,249	0.7	16	240.9	11,337	2,500.8	0.7	123,168
New Hampshire	797	0.6	17,218	0.6	22	216.3	12,565	2,318.8	0.7	140,456
Nevada	637	0.5	15,844	0.6	25	292.3	18,449	2,294.3	0.7	170,477
Maine	1,139	0.9	17,152	0.6	15	206.4	12,036	2,236.9	0.6	131,923
New Mexico	681	0.5	14,962	0.5	22	232.3	15,528	2,141.2	0.6	148,182
Nebraska	810	0.6	21,390	0.7	26	225.3	10,535	2,097.4	0.6	104,933
Hawaii	593	0.5	11,345	0.4	19	205.4	18,102	1,942.4	0.6	157,961
Idaho	518	0.4	11,400	0.4	22	163.7	14,363	1,604.5	0.5	144,376
Rhode Island	442	0.3	9,969	0.3	23	133.9	13,431	1,296.8	0.4	129,271
Montana	509	0.4	9,300	0.3	18	124.0	13,333	1,248.3	0.4	126,235
Alaska	313	0.2	7,454	0.3	24	147.4	19,776	1,126.0	0.3	149,413
Delaware	357	0.3	8,258	0.3	23	125.0	15,139	1,100.1	0.3	146,043
Vermont	652	0.5	8,635	0.3	13	105.7	12,246	1,085.4	0.3	130,814
South Dakota	423	0.3	9,534	0.3	23	96.3	10,105	881.2	0.2	101,002
North Dakota	355	0.3	7,227	0.3	20	73.3	10,147	758.9	0.2	108,366
Wyoming	195	0.1	4,818	0.2	25	71.6	14,865	665.6	0.2	129,314
D.C.	304	0.2	3,737	0.1	12	82.2	22,005	566.0	0.2	138,757

Source: *County Business Patterns, 1995* and *Economic Census of the U.S., 1992*. Data are sorted by 1992 revenues and, if revenues are unavailable, by establishments in 1995. The symbol (D) indicates that data are withheld by the source to avoid disclosure of competitive information. A dash (-) indicates that data are not available or undisclosed because they do not meet statistical validity standards. Shaded *states* on the state map indicate those states which have proportionately greater representation in the industry than would be indicated by the state's population; the ratio is based on total revenues or number of establishments. Shaded *regions* indicate where the industry is regionally most concentrated.

5421 - MEAT AND FISH MARKETS

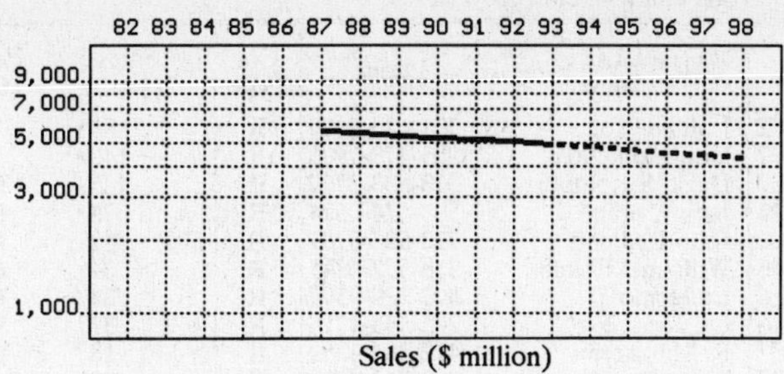

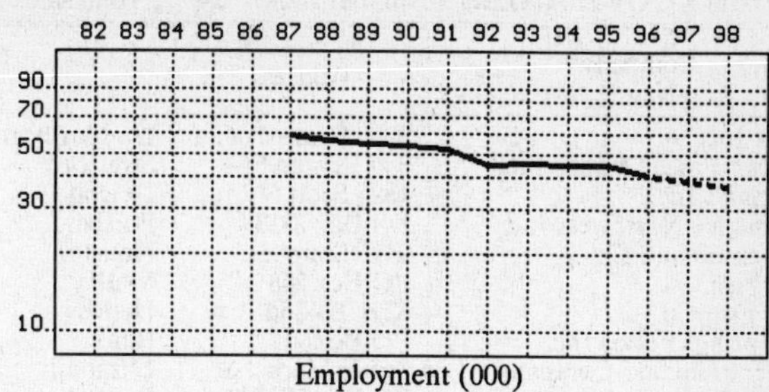

GENERAL STATISTICS

Year	Establishments (number)	Employment (number)	Payroll ($ million)	Sales ($ million)	Employees per Establishment (number)	Sales per Establishment ($)	Payroll per Employee ($)
1982	-	-	-	-	-	-	-
1983	-	-	-	-	-	-	-
1984	-	-	-	-	-	-	-
1985	-	-	-	-	-	-	-
1986	-	-	-	-	-	-	-
1987	11,364	59,044	605.7	5,616.3	5	494,215	10,259
1988	10,284	56,947	635.5	5,501.2e	6	-	11,160
1989	9,691	54,668	628.9	5,386.1e	6	-	11,503
1990	9,279	53,585	642.5	5,271.0e	6	-	11,990
1991	9,179	52,134	651.7	5,156.0e	6	-	12,500
1992	8,941	45,139	555.7	5,040.9	5	563,796	12,310
1993	8,828	45,548	584.7	4,925.8p	5	-	12,837
1994	8,480	44,536	598.8	4,810.8p	5	-	13,445
1995	8,151	45,113	613.2	4,695.7p	6	-	13,592
1996	7,661p	40,776p	591.7p	4,580.6p	-	-	-
1997	7,322p	38,782p	587.4p	4,465.5p	-	-	-
1998	6,984p	36,788p	583.2p	4,350.5p	-	-	-

Sources: *Economic Census of the United States*, 1982, 1987, and 1992. Establishment counts, employment, and payroll are from *County Business Patterns* for non-Census years. Values followed by a 'p' are projections by the editors. Sales and expense data for non-Census years are extrapolations, marked by 'e'. Industries reclassified in 1987 will not have data for prior years. Data are the most recent available at this level of detail.

INDICES OF CHANGE

Year	Establishments (number)	Employment (number)	Payroll ($ million)	Sales ($ million)	Employees per Establishment (number)	Sales per Establishment ($)	Payroll per Employee ($)
1982	-	-	-	-	-	-	-
1983	-	-	-	-	-	-	-
1984	-	-	-	-	-	-	-
1985	-	-	-	-	-	-	-
1986	-	-	-	-	-	-	-
1987	127.1	130.8	109.0	111.4	100.0	87.7	83.3
1988	115.0	126.2	114.4	109.1e	120.0	-	90.7
1989	108.4	121.1	113.2	106.8e	120.0	-	93.4
1990	103.8	118.7	115.6	104.6e	120.0	-	97.4
1991	102.7	115.5	117.3	102.3e	120.0	-	101.5
1992	100.0	100.0	100.0	100.0	100.0	100.0	100.0
1993	98.7	100.9	105.2	97.7p	103.2	-	104.3
1994	94.8	98.7	107.8	95.4p	105.0	-	109.2
1995	91.2	99.9	110.3	93.2p	110.7	-	110.4
1996	85.7p	90.3p	106.5p	90.9p	-	-	-
1997	81.9p	85.9p	105.7p	88.6p	-	-	-
1998	78.1p	81.5p	104.9p	86.3p	-	-	-

Sources: Same as General Statistics. The values shown reflect change from the base year, 1992. Values above 100 mean greater than 1992, values below 100 mean less than 1992, and a value of 100 in the 1982-91 or 1993-98 period means same as 1992. Values followed by a 'p' are projections by the editors; 'e' stands for extrapolation. Data are the most recent available at this level of detail.

SELECTED RATIOS

For 1992	Avg. of All Retail	Analyzed Industry	Index	For 1992	Avg. of All Retail	Analyzed Industry	Index
Employees per Establishment	12	5	42	Sales per Employee	102,941	111,675	108
Payroll per Establishment	146,026	62,152	43	Sales per Establishment	1,241,555	563,796	45
Payroll per Employee	12,107	12,311	102	Expenses per Establishment	na	na	na

Sources: Same as General Statistics. The 'Average of All Manufacturing' column represents the average of all manufacturing industries reported for the most recent complete year available. The Index shows the relationship between the Average and the Analyzed Industry. For example, 100 means that they are equal; 500 that the Analyzed Industry is five times the average; 50 means that the Analyzed Industry is half the national average. The abbreviation 'na' is used to show that data are 'not available'.

LEADING COMPANIES

Number shown: **24** Total sales ($ mil): **758** Total employment (000): **4.7**

Company Name	Address				CEO Name	Phone	Co. Type	Sales ($ mil)	Empl. (000)
Murry's Inc.	8300 Pennsylvania	Up Marlboro	MD	20772	I Mendelson	301-420-6400	R	180 *	1.5
American Frozen Foods Inc.	355 Benton St	Stratford	CT	06497	Don Monjello	203-378-7900	R	140 *	1.1
Cattleman's Inc.	1825 Scott St	Detroit	MI	48207	David S Rohtbart	313-833-2700	P	125	0.3
Performance Northwest Inc.	PO Box 23139	Portland	OR	97224	Jack Wynne	503-624-0624	R	78 *	0.2
C.B. Jackson and Co.	2410 Smith St	Houston	TX	77006	John Rydman	713-526-8787	R	40	0.2
Morey Fish Co.	PO Box 248	Motley	MN	56466	William J Frank	218-352-6345	R	34	0.1
Seattle Fish Co.	6211 E 42nd Ave	Denver	CO	80216	Ed Iacino	303-329-9595	R	34	0.1
Clear Springs Foods Inc.	PO Box 712	Buhl	ID	83316	L Cope	208-543-4316	R	32	0.4
M. Marraccini and Company	3rd & Market St	Elizabeth	PA	15037	R. Marraccini	412-384-4250	R	18	0.2
Associated Morris Brothers	PO Box 372730	Denver	CO	80237	Larry Floodquist	303-752-0030	R	13 *	0.1
Bazley and Junedale Markets	1458 Grand Rvr	Williamston	MI	48895	Robert L Schmidt	517-655-2185	R	12 *	0.1
Thompson's Finer Foods Inc.	901 W Touhy Ave	Park Ridge	IL	60068	RE Thompson	708-825-2177	R	12	0.2
Daniel Weaver Co.	PO Box 525	Lebanon	PA	17042	Robert Trider	717-274-6100	R	9 *	<0.1
Collins Benford and Gray	245 E Watkins St	Phoenix	AZ	85004	Rex Collins	602-253-5752	R	6 *	<0.1
L.D. Amory and Company Inc.	101 S King St	Hampton	VA	23669	CR Amory	804-722-1915	R	6	<0.1
Barney Summers Sales Company	6226 Prospect Ave	Kansas City	MO	64130	Barney Summers	816-444-3474	R	5	<0.1
Walters Meat Co.	8901 Wattsburg Rd	Erie	PA	16509	H Wagner	814-825-4857	R	4	<0.1
Mount Pleasant Seafood Co.	1 Seafood Dr	Mount Pleasant	SC	29464	Rial Fitch	803-884-4122	R	3	<0.1
Smith-Hubbard and Associates	PO Box 39986	Denver	CO	80239	Bud Hubbard	303-344-9754	R	3 *	<0.1
Byrne Sales Co.	825 Greenbay Rd	Wilmette	IL	60091	Thomas M Byrne	847-251-7722	R	2 *	<0.1
Horton's Downeast Foods Inc.	PO Box 430	Waterboro	ME	04087	Jean Horton	207-247-6900	R	1	<0.1
YS and CH Enterprises Inc.	PO Box 17223	Honolulu	HI	96817	Ronald L Kim	808-845-0447	R	1	<0.1
Martin Brothers Seafood Inc.	PO Box 219	Westwego	LA	70094	William P Martin	504-341-2251	R	0	<0.1
Coastal Marketing Associates	PO Box 67	Campbell	CA	95009	Gary Spakowsky	408-866-5775	R	0 *	<0.1

Source: *Ward's Business Directory of U.S. Private and Public Companies*, 1998. The company type code used is as follows: P - Public, R - Private, S - Subsidiary, D - Division, J - Joint Venture, A - Affiliate, G - Group. Sales are in millions of dollars, employees are in thousands. An asterisk (*) indicates an estimated sales volume. The symbol < stands for 'less than'.

OCCUPATIONS EMPLOYED BY SIC 542 - MEAT AND FISH MARKETS

Occupation	% of Total 1996	Change to 2006	Occupation	% of Total 1996	Change to 2006
Butchers & meatcutters	21.1	-1.5	Marketing & sales worker supervisors	5.1	-1.5
Salespersons, retail	21.0	-5.6	Truck drivers light & heavy	2.6	-1.6
Cashiers	11.9	-0.3	Cooks, short order & fast food	2.4	-1.6
Food counter, fountain workers	6.6	-8.3	Hand packers & packagers	2.0	-1.5
General managers & top executives	6.1	-4.6	Purchasing managers	1.8	-11.4
Stock clerks	5.9	-12.8	General office clerks	1.3	-15.4
Food preparation workers	5.1	-6.1	Wholesale & retail buyers, except farm products	1.1	-18.5

Source: *Industry-Occupation Matrix*, Bureau of Labor Statistics. These data relate to one or more 3-digit SIC industry groups rather than to a single 4-digit SIC. The change reported for each occupation to the year 2006 is a percent of growth or decline as estimated by the Bureau of Labor Statistics. The abbreviation nec stands for 'not elsewhere classified'.

STATE AND REGIONAL CONCENTRATION

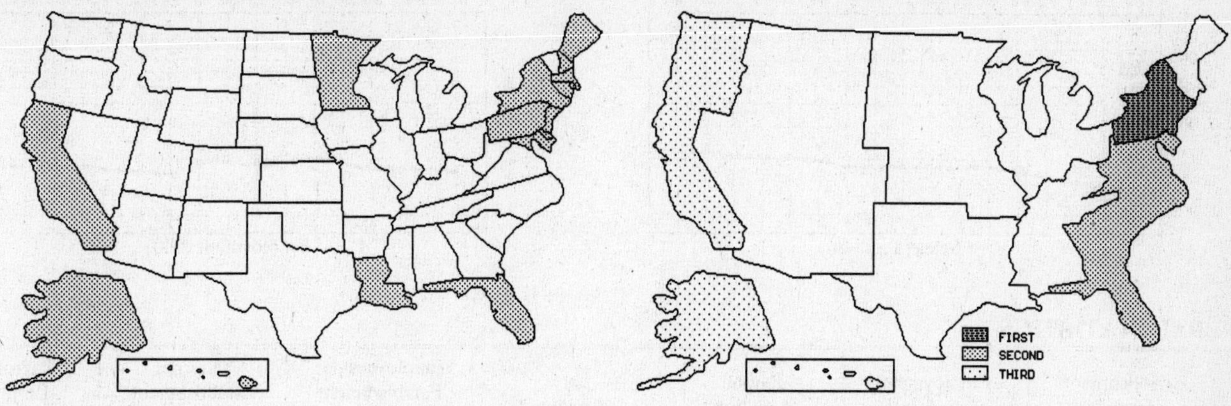

INDUSTRY DATA BY STATE

State	Establishments - 1995 Total (number)	% of U.S.	Employment - 1995 Total (number)	% of U.S.	Per Estab.	Payroll - 1995 Total ($ mil.)	Per Empl. ($)	Sales - 1992 Total ($ mil.)	% of U.S.	Per Estab ($)
New York	1,259	15.4	5,203	11.5	4	78.3	15,057	818.1	16.2	139,583
California	824	10.1	5,007	11.1	6	69.4	13,851	639.2	12.7	131,595
Pennsylvania	547	6.7	3,205	7.1	6	39.8	12,415	378.1	7.5	112,458
Florida	483	5.9	2,792	6.2	6	37.1	13,295	331.3	6.6	116,507
Texas	448	5.5	2,642	5.9	6	32.4	12,282	263.8	5.2	106,377
New Jersey	385	4.7	1,617	3.6	4	25.9	16,035	242.9	4.8	131,390
Ohio	350	4.3	2,136	4.7	6	29.2	13,669	213.5	4.2	93,979
Illinois	336	4.1	1,930	4.3	6	27.7	14,332	210.1	4.2	110,135
Massachusetts	246	3.0	1,433	3.2	6	20.5	14,296	191.6	3.8	113,065
Michigan	262	3.2	1,449	3.2	6	18.7	12,873	180.2	3.6	106,639
Maryland	215	2.6	1,488	3.3	7	20.3	13,642	175.1	3.5	106,577
Louisiana	190	2.3	1,351	3.0	7	12.7	9,371	94.5	1.9	89,113
Minnesota	173	2.1	1,119	2.5	6	14.1	12,559	92.0	1.8	90,671
Virginia	152	1.9	699	1.5	5	8.4	12,059	89.3	1.8	122,513
Wisconsin	162	2.0	1,203	2.7	7	14.8	12,279	85.4	1.7	77,739
Connecticut	93	1.1	1,566	3.5	17	29.8	19,027	72.3	1.4	136,458
North Carolina	161	2.0	723	1.6	4	8.6	11,844	71.2	1.4	87,029
Georgia	158	1.9	651	1.4	4	7.9	12,066	70.9	1.4	92,695
Indiana	119	1.5	828	1.8	7	9.8	11,849	67.3	1.3	74,244
Washington	120	1.5	562	1.2	5	12.5	22,171	52.6	1.0	98,054
Missouri	117	1.4	644	1.4	6	8.0	12,368	51.9	1.0	80,017
D.C.	26	0.3	302	0.7	12	5.2	17,169	49.4	1.0	137,189
South Carolina	101	1.2	440	1.0	4	4.5	10,152	42.9	0.9	85,677
Alabama	96	1.2	282	0.6	3	3.2	11,344	39.8	0.8	112,663
Maine	57	0.7	264	0.6	5	3.5	13,167	39.0	0.8	213,311
Hawaii	54	0.7	343	0.8	6	5.5	15,991	38.1	0.8	118,320
Iowa	97	1.2	528	1.2	5	6.9	12,981	35.5	0.7	68,965
Kentucky	66	0.8	457	1.0	7	5.6	12,265	31.7	0.6	88,436
Rhode Island	47	0.6	298	0.7	6	3.4	11,336	31.6	0.6	119,328
New Hampshire	22	0.3	224	0.5	10	3.1	13,795	29.2	0.6	100,140
Oregon	73	0.9	294	0.7	4	4.0	13,565	27.1	0.5	107,261
Delaware	35	0.4	241	0.5	7	3.0	12,440	26.3	0.5	96,381
Tennessee	68	0.8	247	0.5	4	3.1	12,688	24.0	0.5	93,859
Colorado	62	0.8	342	0.8	6	6.2	17,985	23.1	0.5	85,478
Kansas	69	0.8	309	0.7	4	3.8	12,434	22.9	0.5	78,674
Arkansas	62	0.8	223	0.5	4	2.3	10,323	20.1	0.4	84,391
Arizona	33	0.4	172	0.4	5	2.4	14,000	20.0	0.4	113,085
Oklahoma	46	0.6	285	0.6	6	3.1	10,751	19.2	0.4	101,582
Mississippi	52	0.6	188	0.4	4	2.0	10,739	18.9	0.4	91,246
Nebraska	57	0.7	297	0.7	5	3.1	10,340	16.2	0.3	58,645
Alaska	12	0.1	68	0.2	6	1.5	22,015	14.9	0.3	206,264
New Mexico	21	0.3	140	0.3	7	1.0	7,186	12.3	0.2	103,261
Montana	27	0.3	86	0.2	3	1.2	13,721	12.1	0.2	102,153
North Dakota	31	0.4	130	0.3	4	1.4	10,923	9.6	0.2	86,891
Nevada	10	0.1	122	0.3	12	2.7	21,730	8.8	0.2	96,198
South Dakota	40	0.5	186	0.4	5	1.6	8,833	8.2	0.2	52,127
Vermont	12	0.1	58	0.1	5	0.8	13,000	7.2	0.1	136,226
West Virginia	20	0.2	100	0.2	5	1.0	10,210	7.2	0.1	72,727
Idaho	23	0.3	90	0.2	4	1.1	12,633	6.4	0.1	79,650
Utah	21	0.3	120	0.3	6	1.2	9,675	5.9	0.1	91,859
Wyoming	11	0.1	29	0.1	3	0.4	12,517	1.9	0.0	68,286

Source: County Business Patterns, 1995 and *Economic Census of the U.S., 1992*. Data are sorted by 1992 revenues and, if revenues are unavailable, by establishments in 1995. The symbol (D) indicates that data are withheld by the source to avoid disclosure of competitive information. A dash (-) indicates that data are not available or undisclosed because they do not meet statistical validity standards. Shaded *states* on the state map indicate those states which have proportionately greater representation in the industry than would be indicated by the state's population; the ratio is based on total revenues or number of establishments. Shaded *regions* indicate where the industry is regionally most concentrated.

5431 - FRUIT AND VEGETABLE MARKETS

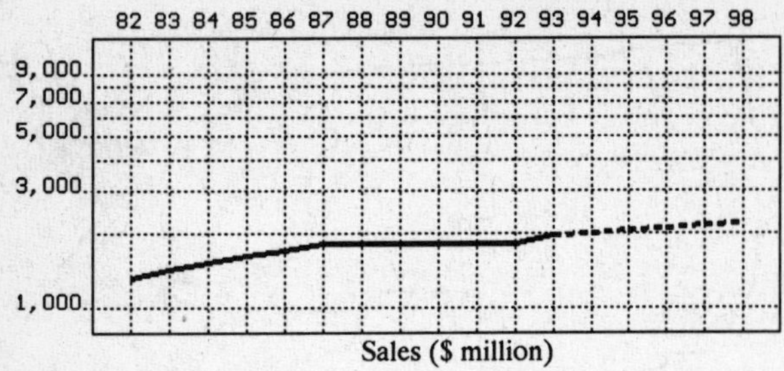

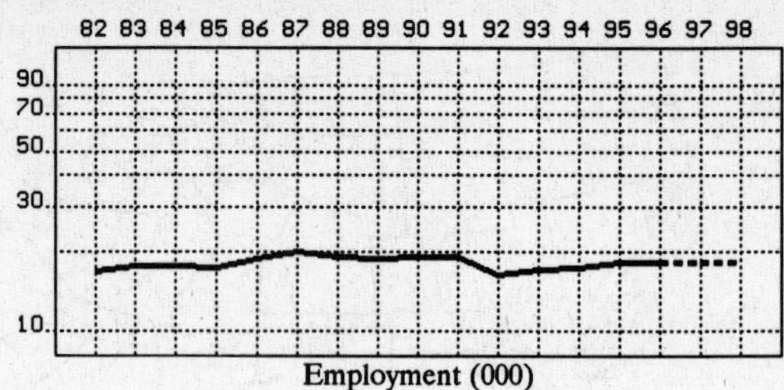

GENERAL STATISTICS

Year	Establishments (number)	Employment (number)	Payroll ($ million)	Sales ($ million)	Employees per Establishment (number)	Sales per Establishment ($)	Payroll per Employee ($)
1982	3,234	16,789	134.8	1,329.6	5	411,143	8,026
1983	3,184	17,687	156.7	1,424.2*e*	6	-	8,862
1984	3,095	17,581	157.6	1,518.7*e*	6	-	8,962
1985	2,907	17,359	169.3	1,613.2*e*	6	-	9,755
1986	2,943	18,784	189.2	1,707.7*e*	6	-	10,070
1987	3,271	20,013	185.9	1,802.2	6	550,970	9,291
1988	3,001	19,290	199.0	1,803.6*e*	6	-	10,316
1989	2,854	18,948	206.5	1,805.0*e*	7	-	10,897
1990	2,942	19,312	223.3	1,806.5*e*	7	-	11,561
1991	3,145	19,076	243.7	1,807.9*e*	6	-	12,778
1992	2,971	16,258	198.5	1,809.3	5	608,983	12,210
1993	3,092	17,166	233.1	1,963.1*p*	6	-	13,582
1994	3,108	17,268	228.9	2,011.0*p*	6	-	13,256
1995	3,103	18,227	249.5	2,059.0*p*	6	-	13,686
1996	3,024*p*	18,153*p*	257.0*p*	2,106.9*p*	-	-	-
1997	3,019*p*	18,157*p*	264.8*p*	2,154.9*p*	-	-	-
1998	3,014*p*	18,160*p*	272.6*p*	2,202.9*p*	-	-	-

Sources: *Economic Census of the United States*, 1982, 1987, and 1992. Establishment counts, employment, and payroll are from *County Business Patterns* for non-Census years. Values followed by a 'p' are projections by the editors. Sales and expense data for non-Census years are extrapolations, marked by 'e'. Industries reclassified in 1987 will not have data for prior years. Data are the most recent available at this level of detail.

INDICES OF CHANGE

Year	Establishments (number)	Employment (number)	Payroll ($ million)	Sales ($ million)	Employees per Establishment (number)	Sales per Establishment ($)	Payroll per Employee ($)
1982	108.9	103.3	67.9	73.5	100.0	67.5	65.7
1983	107.2	108.8	78.9	78.7*e*	120.0	-	72.6
1984	104.2	108.1	79.4	83.9*e*	120.0	-	73.4
1985	97.8	106.8	85.3	89.2*e*	120.0	-	79.9
1986	99.1	115.5	95.3	94.4*e*	120.0	-	82.5
1987	110.1	123.1	93.7	99.6	120.0	90.5	76.1
1988	101.0	118.6	100.3	99.7*e*	120.0	-	84.5
1989	96.1	116.5	104.0	99.8*e*	140.0	-	89.2
1990	99.0	118.8	112.5	99.8*e*	140.0	-	94.7
1991	105.9	117.3	122.8	99.9*e*	120.0	-	104.7
1992	100.0	100.0	100.0	100.0	100.0	100.0	100.0
1993	104.1	105.6	117.5	108.5*p*	111.0	-	111.2
1994	104.6	106.2	115.3	111.1*p*	111.1	-	108.6
1995	104.4	112.1	125.7	113.8*p*	117.5	-	112.1
1996	101.8*p*	111.7*p*	129.5*p*	116.4*p*	-	-	-
1997	101.6*p*	111.7*p*	133.4*p*	119.1*p*	-	-	-
1998	101.4*p*	111.7*p*	137.4*p*	121.8*p*	-	-	-

Sources: Same as General Statistics. The values shown reflect change from the base year, 1992. Values above 100 mean greater than 1992, values below 100 mean less than 1992, and a value of 100 in the 1982-91 or 1993-98 period means same as 1992. Values followed by a 'p' are projections by the editors; 'e' stands for extrapolation. Data are the most recent available at this level of detail.

SELECTED RATIOS

For 1992	Avg. of All Retail	Analyzed Industry	Index	For 1992	Avg. of All Retail	Analyzed Industry	Index
Employees per Establishment	12	5	45	Sales per Employee	102,941	111,287	108
Payroll per Establishment	146,026	66,813	46	Sales per Establishment	1,241,555	608,987	49
Payroll per Employee	12,107	12,209	101	Expenses per Establishment	na	na	na

Sources: Same as General Statistics. The 'Average of All Manufacturing' column represents the average of all manufacturing industries reported for the most recent complete year available. The Index shows the relationship between the Average and the Analyzed Industry. For example, 100 means that they are equal; 500 that the Analyzed Industry is five times the average; 50 means that the Analyzed Industry is half the national average. The abbreviation 'na' is used to show that data are 'not available'.

LEADING COMPANIES

Number shown: 9 Total sales ($ mil): **4,956** Total employment (000): **15.1**

Company Name	Address				CEO Name	Phone	Co. Type	Sales ($ mil)	Empl. (000)
Nash Finch Co.	PO Box 355	Minneapolis	MN	55440	Alfred N Flaten	612-832-0534	P	4,392	12.2
Fresh America Corp.	5400 LBJ Frwy	Dallas	TX	75240	David I Sheinfeld	972-774-0575	P	239	1.0
Harry and David	2518 S Pacific Hwy	Medford	OR	97501	William H Williams	541-776-2121	D	150	1.2
Cattleman's Inc.	1825 Scott St	Detroit	MI	48207	David S Rohtbart	313-833-2700	P	125	0.3
Earth Brothers Ltd.	PO Box 188	Proctorsville	VT	05153	Steve Birge	802-226-7480	R	21*	<0.1
Bazley and Junedale Markets	1458 Grand Rvr	Williamston	MI	48895	Robert L Schmidt	517-655-2185	R	12*	0.1
Kansas City Salad Company	5252 Speaker Rd	Kansas City	KS	66106	John Guarino	913-371-4466	R	9*	0.1
Mixon Fruit Farms Inc.	PO Box 25200	Bradenton	FL	34206	WP Mixon Jr	941-748-5829	R	6*	0.1
Capitol Foods Inc.	555 Beale St	Memphis	TN	38103	Kenneth Porter	901-526-9300	R	2	<0.1

Source: *Ward's Business Directory of U.S. Private and Public Companies*, 1998. The company type code used is as follows: P - Public, R - Private, S - Subsidiary, D - Division, J - Joint Venture, A - Affiliate, G - Group. Sales are in millions of dollars, employees are in thousands. An asterisk (*) indicates an estimated sales volume. The symbol < stands for 'less than'.

OCCUPATIONS EMPLOYED BY SIC 543 - FOOD STORES, NEC

Occupation	% of Total 1996	Change to 2006	Occupation	% of Total 1996	Change to 2006
Salespersons, retail	34.2	18.7	Truck drivers light & heavy	1.5	23.8
Cashiers	15.5	25.3	Wholesale & retail buyers, except farm products	1.5	2.5
Stock clerks	10.3	-3.7	Bookkeeping, accounting, & auditing clerks	1.4	-1.0
Food counter, fountain workers	9.2	18.5	Hand packers & packagers	1.2	23.8
Marketing & sales worker supervisors	8.0	23.8	Purchasing managers	1.2	11.4
General managers & top executives	5.2	19.9	Bakers, bread & pastry	1.2	23.7
Food preparation workers	2.9	18.0			

Source: *Industry-Occupation Matrix*, Bureau of Labor Statistics. These data relate to one or more 3-digit SIC industry groups rather than to a single 4-digit SIC. The change reported for each occupation to the year 2006 is a percent of growth or decline as estimated by the Bureau of Labor Statistics. The abbreviation nec stands for 'not elsewhere classified'.

STATE AND REGIONAL CONCENTRATION

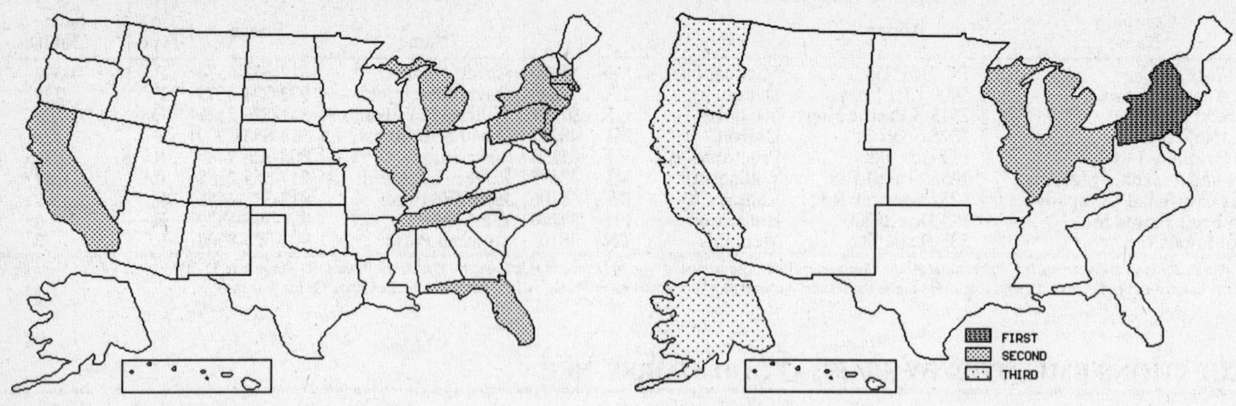

INDUSTRY DATA BY STATE

State	Establishments - 1995 Total (number)	% of U.S.	Employment - 1995 Total (number)	% of U.S.	Per Estab.	Payroll - 1995 Total ($ mil.)	Per Empl. ($)	Sales - 1992 Total ($ mil.)	% of U.S.	Per Estab ($)
New York	580	18.7	2,116	11.6	4	33.1	15,661	285.3	15.9	141,497
California	326	10.5	2,064	11.3	6	28.9	13,987	253.2	14.1	136,259
Michigan	137	4.4	1,875	10.3	14	23.8	12,678	184.3	10.3	102,593
Florida	263	8.5	1,569	8.6	6	17.9	11,395	137.3	7.7	92,212
Illinois	123	4.0	1,043	5.7	8	14.8	14,193	115.0	6.4	116,604
Pennsylvania	202	6.5	1,117	6.1	6	12.9	11,557	114.5	6.4	97,347
Massachusetts	102	3.3	1,248	6.9	12	19.1	15,334	96.3	5.4	99,413
New Jersey	173	5.6	813	4.5	5	14.4	17,772	76.8	4.3	117,755
Ohio	111	3.6	807	4.4	7	10.3	12,815	65.5	3.7	98,193
Texas	94	3.0	502	2.8	5	6.9	13,823	59.8	3.3	132,548
Tennessee	74	2.4	456	2.5	6	5.0	10,904	38.5	2.1	114,228
Indiana	60	1.9	358	2.0	6	4.5	12,472	34.9	1.9	106,798
Maryland	70	2.3	395	2.2	6	6.3	16,020	30.6	1.7	103,321
Washington	66	2.1	235	1.3	4	4.2	17,668	28.4	1.6	144,776
Connecticut	48	1.5	212	1.2	4	3.2	14,925	26.0	1.4	119,147
Georgia	39	1.3	507	2.8	13	6.8	13,410	21.8	1.2	116,989
Kentucky	41	1.3	253	1.4	6	2.6	10,419	21.3	1.2	102,144
Virginia	55	1.8	187	1.0	3	2.4	12,743	20.8	1.2	101,224
North Carolina	69	2.2	160	0.9	2	2.6	16,231	19.6	1.1	110,729
Wisconsin	30	1.0	223	1.2	7	2.8	12,695	18.3	1.0	92,904
Oregon	28	0.9	188	1.0	7	2.8	15,043	18.3	1.0	99,370
Missouri	35	1.1	105	0.6	3	1.4	13,314	13.6	0.8	95,014
Rhode Island	23	0.7	252	1.4	11	3.0	11,929	13.5	0.8	103,092
South Carolina	41	1.3	94	0.5	2	1.2	12,436	12.6	0.7	83,833
Alabama	42	1.4	148	0.8	4	1.9	12,811	10.4	0.6	106,061
New Mexico	26	0.8	153	0.8	6	2.4	15,758	10.0	0.6	97,495
Delaware	13	0.4	100	0.5	8	1.4	14,370	8.9	0.5	141,746
Hawaii	23	0.7	77	0.4	3	1.0	12,377	8.3	0.5	77,514
West Virginia	15	0.5	111	0.6	7	1.4	12,297	8.0	0.4	81,888
Louisiana	26	0.8	174	1.0	7	1.9	10,741	7.1	0.4	51,635
Arizona	22	0.7	105	0.6	5	1.1	10,905	6.8	0.4	81,369
Minnesota	14	0.5	52	0.3	4	0.8	15,577	6.7	0.4	118,786
Colorado	15	0.5	65	0.4	4	1.5	23,523	5.6	0.3	78,197
Iowa	10	0.3	87	0.5	9	0.6	6,586	4.2	0.2	58,014
Mississippi	17	0.5	44	0.2	3	0.4	9,705	3.6	0.2	77,652
Arkansas	7	0.2	22	0.1	3	0.2	11,273	3.1	0.2	87,971
Oklahoma	8	0.3	31	0.2	4	0.3	8,613	1.4	0.1	110,923
Vermont	8	0.3	7	0.0	1	0.2	24,857	1.3	0.1	266,000
Nebraska	5	0.2	6	0.0	1	0.0	7,833	0.7	0.0	83,625
Maine	13	0.4	68	0.4	5	0.8	11,559	(D)	-	-
Idaho	9	0.3	24	0.1	3	0.3	12,208	(D)	-	-
Montana	8	0.3	44	0.2	6	0.3	7,227	(D)	-	-
Kansas	7	0.2	18	0.1	3	0.2	9,889	(D)	-	-
New Hampshire	7	0.2	71	0.4	10	1.2	17,507	(D)	-	-
Utah	6	0.2	8	0.0	1	0.1	14,625	(D)	-	-
Alaska	4	0.1	12	0.1	3	0.1	7,750	(D)	-	-
Nevada	4	0.1	0-19	-	-	(D)	-	(D)	-	-
D.C.	2	0.1	0-19	-	-	(D)	-	(D)	-	-
North Dakota	1	0.0	0-19	-	-	(D)	-	-	-	-
South Dakota	1	0.0	0-19	-	-	(D)	-	(D)	-	-

Source: *County Business Patterns, 1995* and *Economic Census of the U.S., 1992*. Data are sorted by 1992 revenues and, if revenues are unavailable, by establishments in 1995. The symbol (D) indicates that data are withheld by the source to avoid disclosure of competitive information. A dash (-) indicates that data are not available or undisclosed because they do not meet statistical validity standards. Shaded *states* on the state map indicate those states which have proportionately greater representation in the industry than would be indicated by the state's population; the ratio is based on total revenues or number of establishments. Shaded *regions* indicate where the industry is regionally most concentrated.

5441 - CANDY, NUT, AND CONFECTIONERY STORES

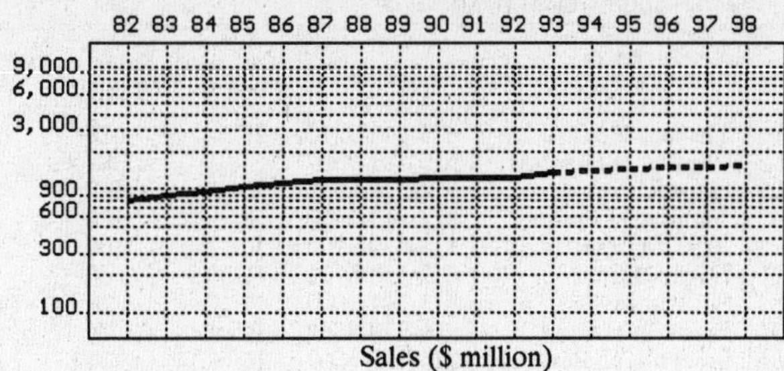

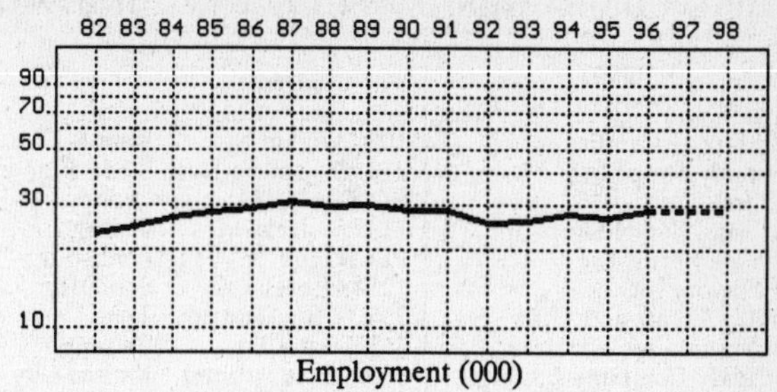

GENERAL STATISTICS

Year	Establishments (number)	Employment (number)	Payroll ($ million)	Sales ($ million)	Employees per Establishment (number)	Sales per Establishment ($)	Payroll per Employee ($)
1982	5,457	23,154	129.5	800.7	4	146,722	5,593
1983	5,400	24,900	149.6	877.0e	5	-	6,006
1984	5,595	27,059	173.0	953.3e	5	-	6,392
1985	5,519	28,112	177.4	1,029.6e	5	-	6,312
1986	5,736	29,114	190.1	1,105.9e	5	-	6,530
1987	6,124	30,767	199.3	1,182.2	5	193,050	6,479
1988	5,530	29,595	203.2	1,190.5e	5	-	6,866
1989	5,274	30,196	206.7	1,198.8e	6	-	6,845
1990	5,407	28,559	221.0	1,207.1e	5	-	7,740
1991	5,257	28,851	225.9	1,215.3e	5	-	7,831
1992	5,029	25,504	209.1	1,223.6	5	243,308	8,200
1993	5,055	26,089	222.6	1,343.2p	5	-	8,533
1994	4,940	27,829	233.5	1,385.5p	6	-	8,390
1995	4,843	26,971	240.3	1,427.8p	6	-	8,909
1996	4,938p	28,405p	252.7p	1,470.1p	-	-	-
1997	4,881p	28,509p	259.9p	1,512.4p	-	-	-
1998	4,823p	28,614p	267.1p	1,554.7p	-	-	-

Sources: *Economic Census of the United States*, 1982, 1987, and 1992. Establishment counts, employment, and payroll are from *County Business Patterns* for non-Census years. Values followed by a 'p' are projections by the editors. Sales and expense data for non-Census years are extrapolations, marked by 'e'. Industries reclassified in 1987 will not have data for prior years. Data are the most recent available at this level of detail.

INDICES OF CHANGE

Year	Establishments (number)	Employment (number)	Payroll ($ million)	Sales ($ million)	Employees per Establishment (number)	Sales per Establishment ($)	Payroll per Employee ($)
1982	108.5	90.8	61.9	65.4	80.0	60.3	68.2
1983	107.4	97.6	71.5	71.7e	100.0	-	73.2
1984	111.3	106.1	82.7	77.9e	100.0	-	78.0
1985	109.7	110.2	84.8	84.1e	100.0	-	77.0
1986	114.1	114.2	90.9	90.4e	100.0	-	79.6
1987	121.8	120.6	95.3	96.6	100.0	79.3	79.0
1988	110.0	116.0	97.2	97.3e	100.0	-	83.7
1989	104.9	118.4	98.9	98.0e	120.0	-	83.5
1990	107.5	112.0	105.7	98.7e	100.0	-	94.4
1991	104.5	113.1	108.0	99.3e	100.0	-	95.5
1992	100.0	100.0	100.0	100.0	100.0	100.0	100.0
1993	100.5	102.3	106.5	109.8p	103.2	-	104.1
1994	98.2	109.1	111.7	113.2p	112.7	-	102.3
1995	96.3	105.8	114.9	116.7p	111.4	-	108.6
1996	98.2p	111.4p	120.9p	120.1p	-	-	-
1997	97.1p	111.8p	124.3p	123.6p	-	-	-
1998	95.9p	112.2p	127.8p	127.1p	-	-	-

Sources: Same as General Statistics. The values shown reflect change from the base year, 1992. Values above 100 mean greater than 1992, values below 100 mean less than 1992, and a value of 100 in the 1982-91 or 1993-98 period means same as 1992. Values followed by a 'p' are projections by the editors; 'e' stands for extrapolation. Data are the most recent available at this level of detail.

SELECTED RATIOS

For 1992	Avg. of All Retail	Analyzed Industry	Index	For 1992	Avg. of All Retail	Analyzed Industry	Index
Employees per Establishment	12	5	42	Sales per Employee	102,941	47,977	47
Payroll per Establishment	146,026	41,579	28	Sales per Establishment	1,241,555	243,309	20
Payroll per Employee	12,107	8,199	68	Expenses per Establishment	na	na	na

Sources: Same as General Statistics. The 'Average of All Manufacturing' column represents the average of all manufacturing industries reported for the most recent complete year available. The Index shows the relationship between the Average and the Analyzed Industry. For example, 100 means that they are equal; 500 that the Analyzed Industry is five times the average; 50 means that the Analyzed Industry is half the national average. The abbreviation 'na' is used to show that data are 'not available'.

LEADING COMPANIES

Number shown: **23** Total sales ($ mil): **1,561** Total employment (000): **17.3**

Company Name	Address				CEO Name	Phone	Co. Type	Sales ($ mil)	Empl. (000)
Russell Stover Candies Inc.	1000 Walnut St	Kansas City	MO	64106	Thomas S Ward	816-842-9240	R	610 *	6.0
See's Candy Shops Inc.	210 El Camino Real	S San Francisco	CA	94080	Charles N Huggins	650-583-7307	S	389 *	2.0
Kirlins Inc.	PO Box 3097	Quincy	IL	62305	Gary Kirlin	217-224-8953	R	167 *	2.0
Fannie May Candy Shops Inc.	1137 W Jackson	Chicago	IL	60607	Thomas H Quinn	312-243-2700	S	120	3.0
Cherrydale Farms Inc.	PO Box 40	Pennsburg	PA	18073	Ross Cherry	215-679-6200	R	100 *	1.0
Sweet Factory Inc.	10343 Roselle St	San Diego	CA	92121	Edgar Berner	619-558-6771	R	60 *	1.1
Mr. Bulky Treats and Gifts	755 W Big Beaver	Troy	MI	48084	Sid Rubin	313-244-9000	R	28 *	0.4
Rocky Mountain Chocolate	265 Turner Dr	Durango	CO	81301	Franklin E Crail	970-259-0554	P	24	0.4
Price Candy Company L.L.C.	8300 Underground	Kansas City	MO	64161	Steven Hendley	816-455-6000	R	14 *	0.2
Bucks County Coffee Co.	2250 W Cabot Blvd	Langhorne	PA	19047	Rodger Owen	215-741-1855	R	11 *	0.4
Home of the Hebert Candies	575 Hartford Tpk	Shrewsbury	MA	01545	Ronald Hebert	508-845-8051	R	10	0.2
Gardner Candies Inc.	PO Box E	Tyrone	PA	16686	David J Black	814-684-3925	R	6 *	0.3
Munson's Candy Kitchen Inc.	PO Box 9217	Bolton	CT	06043	RB Munson	203-649-4332	R	6	0.2
Van Duyn Chocolates	PO Box 10384	Portland	OR	97296	Sean Gilronan	503-227-1927	D	6 *	<0.1
Lammes Candies Since 1885	PO Box 1885	Austin	TX	78767	Pam Teich	512-835-6791	R	4 *	<0.1
Glauber's Fine Candies Inc.	1020 Register Ave	Baltimore	MD	21239	Kenneth R Glauber	410-377-6800	R	2	<0.1
Baker Candy Company Inc.	12534 Lake City	Seattle	WA	98125	NL Prevele	206-363-5227	R	1	<0.1
AM Candies Inc.	929 Penn St	Reading	PA	19601	Eugene Marfuggi	610-376-7489	S	1	<0.1
Candy Express Franchising Inc.	10480 Patuxent	Columbia	MD	21044	Joel Rosenberg	410-964-5500	R	1 *	<0.1
Ternus and Company Inc.	1297 W Palmetto	Boca Raton	FL	33486	Thomas P Ternus Sr	561-395-8402	R	1	<0.1
Parkside Candy Co.	3208 Main St	Buffalo	NY	14214	Phillip Buffamonte	716-833-7540	R	0	<0.1
Baum's Candy	2147 Van Giesen St	Richland	WA	99352	Kathryn Baumgarten	509-943-5830	R	0	<0.1
Northern Chocolate Co.	2034 ML King	Milwaukee	WI	53212	James Fetzer	414-372-1885	R	0 *	<0.1

Source: *Ward's Business Directory of U.S. Private and Public Companies*, 1998. The company type code used is as follows: P - Public, R - Private, S - Subsidiary, D - Division, J - Joint Venture, A - Affiliate, G - Group. Sales are in millions of dollars, employees are in thousands. An asterisk (*) indicates an estimated sales volume. The symbol < stands for 'less than'.

OCCUPATIONS EMPLOYED BY SIC 544 - FOOD STORES, NEC

Occupation	% of Total 1996	Change to 2006	Occupation	% of Total 1996	Change to 2006
Salespersons, retail	34.2	18.7	Truck drivers light & heavy	1.5	23.8
Cashiers	15.5	25.3	Wholesale & retail buyers, except farm products	1.5	2.5
Stock clerks	10.3	-3.7	Bookkeeping, accounting, & auditing clerks	1.4	-1.0
Food counter, fountain workers	9.2	18.5	Hand packers & packagers	1.2	23.8
Marketing & sales worker supervisors	8.0	23.8	Purchasing managers	1.2	11.4
General managers & top executives	5.2	19.9	Bakers, bread & pastry	1.2	23.7
Food preparation workers	2.9	18.0			

Source: Industry-Occupation Matrix, Bureau of Labor Statistics. These data relate to one or more 3-digit SIC industry groups rather than to a single 4-digit SIC. The change reported for each occupation to the year 2006 is a percent of growth or decline as estimated by the Bureau of Labor Statistics. The abbreviation nec stands for 'not elsewhere classified'.

STATE AND REGIONAL CONCENTRATION

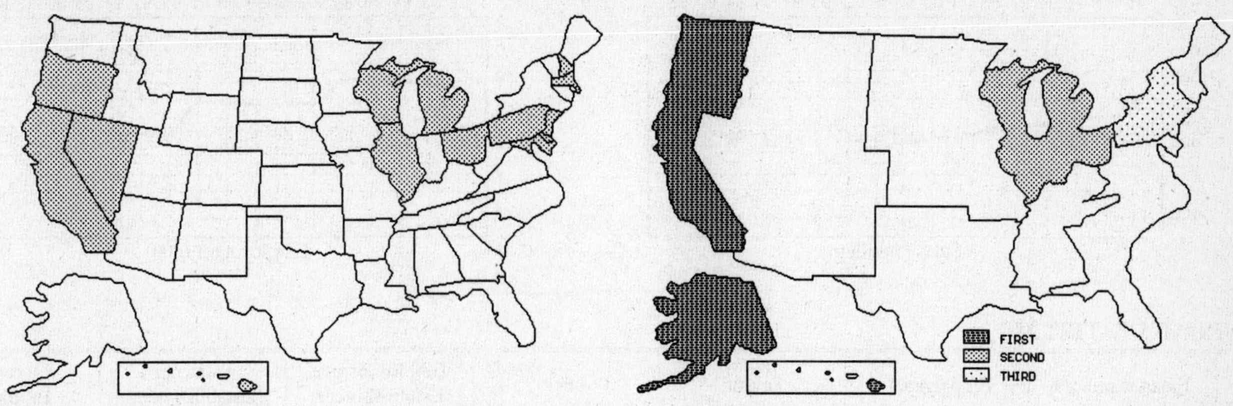

INDUSTRY DATA BY STATE

State	Establishments - 1995 Total (number)	Establishments - 1995 % of U.S.	Employment - 1995 Total (number)	Employment - 1995 % of U.S.	Employment - 1995 Per Estab.	Payroll - 1995 Total ($ mil.)	Payroll - 1995 Per Empl. ($)	Sales - 1992 Total ($ mil.)	Sales - 1992 % of U.S.	Sales - 1992 Per Estab ($)
California	604	12.5	3,387	12.6	6	39.7	11,727	244.2	20.1	78,814
Illinois	356	7.4	2,185	8.1	6	16.7	7,649	92.8	7.6	45,909
New York	382	7.9	1,484	5.5	4	13.6	9,173	82.4	6.8	50,379
Pennsylvania	329	6.8	2,044	7.6	6	14.2	6,968	69.0	5.7	36,826
Ohio	287	5.9	1,861	6.9	6	13.1	7,013	68.1	5.6	36,511
New Jersey	199	4.1	1,170	4.3	6	11.4	9,722	66.6	5.5	61,117
Michigan	182	3.8	1,048	3.9	6	11.2	10,648	59.9	4.9	49,168
Florida	192	4.0	1,000	3.7	5	8.4	8,421	41.0	3.4	42,668
Massachusetts	148	3.1	971	3.6	7	8.3	8,543	37.8	3.1	47,856
Texas	187	3.9	1,055	3.9	6	8.2	7,736	33.8	2.8	39,406
Wisconsin	126	2.6	704	2.6	6	6.3	8,950	29.5	2.4	41,669
Maryland	97	2.0	540	2.0	6	6.0	11,037	26.7	2.2	48,171
Indiana	119	2.5	687	2.6	6	5.7	8,297	26.4	2.2	37,652
Nevada	53	1.1	356	1.3	7	4.3	12,211	24.0	2.0	82,529
Washington	102	2.1	529	2.0	5	5.8	11,002	23.4	1.9	55,281
Missouri	127	2.6	735	2.7	6	5.9	7,988	21.4	1.8	40,908
Virginia	78	1.6	478	1.8	6	3.7	7,684	20.4	1.7	40,912
Tennessee	70	1.4	396	1.5	6	5.1	12,876	18.1	1.5	35,867
Minnesota	108	2.2	532	2.0	5	3.9	7,288	17.9	1.5	31,365
Hawaii	35	0.7	243	0.9	7	2.8	11,638	15.7	1.3	71,249
Colorado	96	2.0	480	1.8	5	3.7	7,804	15.7	1.3	44,487
Oregon	71	1.5	379	1.4	5	3.1	8,198	15.6	1.3	50,377
Connecticut	61	1.3	363	1.3	6	2.4	6,499	14.5	1.2	38,113
Arizona	59	1.2	284	1.1	5	2.6	9,120	14.3	1.2	64,432
Georgia	61	1.3	282	1.0	5	3.2	11,482	12.7	1.0	43,927
North Carolina	76	1.6	324	1.2	4	2.8	8,627	12.4	1.0	30,719
Louisiana	45	0.9	322	1.2	7	3.0	9,425	11.7	1.0	42,471
South Carolina	38	0.8	214	0.8	6	1.7	8,098	9.7	0.8	39,153
Kansas	33	0.7	192	0.7	6	1.4	7,193	9.3	0.8	42,315
Oklahoma	48	1.0	234	0.9	5	1.9	8,291	7.5	0.6	32,877
New Hampshire	41	0.8	188	0.7	5	1.7	9,059	7.5	0.6	42,369
Iowa	47	1.0	239	0.9	5	1.7	7,042	7.3	0.6	25,873
Utah	34	0.7	236	0.9	7	2.1	8,733	7.2	0.6	40,534
Kentucky	38	0.8	208	0.8	5	1.6	7,587	6.5	0.5	25,565
Maine	23	0.5	272	1.0	12	2.3	8,467	5.9	0.5	70,798
Nebraska	32	0.7	167	0.6	5	1.0	6,060	5.2	0.4	30,946
Delaware	21	0.4	97	0.4	5	1.7	17,629	5.1	0.4	57,371
Alabama	28	0.6	125	0.5	4	0.7	5,984	5.0	0.4	39,677
New Mexico	24	0.5	118	0.4	5	0.8	6,780	3.9	0.3	33,280
D.C.	12	0.2	61	0.2	5	0.7	11,951	3.5	0.3	49,111
Arkansas	31	0.6	97	0.4	3	0.8	7,866	2.9	0.2	29,354
Idaho	20	0.4	85	0.3	4	0.7	8,282	2.7	0.2	48,589
Rhode Island	19	0.4	90	0.3	5	0.6	7,100	2.7	0.2	48,107
Montana	14	0.3	64	0.2	5	0.4	6,406	2.2	0.2	44,792
South Dakota	13	0.3	51	0.2	4	0.4	8,333	2.1	0.2	36,155
Mississippi	25	0.5	93	0.3	4	0.7	7,140	2.1	0.2	36,070
Alaska	10	0.2	42	0.2	4	0.5	11,857	1.2	0.1	34,324
Vermont	6	0.1	20-99	-	-	(D)	-	1.1	0.1	40,321
West Virginia	17	0.4	72	0.3	4	0.5	7,319	(D)	-	-
North Dakota	11	0.2	119	0.4	11	0.7	5,765	(D)	-	-
Wyoming	8	0.2	20-99	-	-	(D)	-	(D)	-	-

Source: County Business Patterns, 1995 and *Economic Census of the U.S., 1992*. Data are sorted by 1992 revenues and, if revenues are unavailable, by establishments in 1995. The symbol (D) indicates that data are withheld by the source to avoid disclosure of competitive information. A dash (-) indicates that data are not available or undisclosed because they do not meet statistical validity standards. Shaded *states* on the state map indicate those states which have proportionately greater representation in the industry than would be indicated by the state's population; the ratio is based on total revenues or number of establishments. Shaded *regions* indicate where the industry is regionally most concentrated.

5451 - DAIRY PRODUCTS STORES

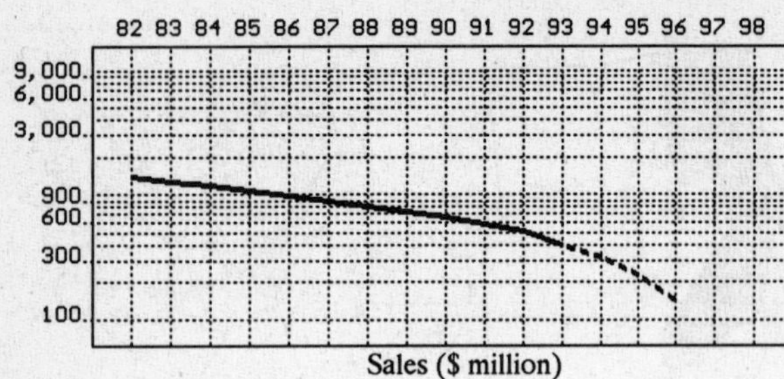

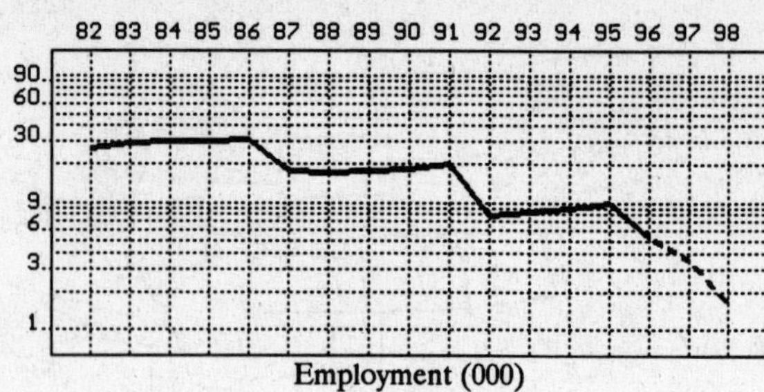

GENERAL STATISTICS

Year	Establishments (number)	Employment (number)	Payroll ($ million)	Sales ($ million)	Employees per Establishment (number)	Sales per Establishment ($)	Payroll per Employee ($)
1982	5,212	27,223	162.5	1,375.0	5	263,811	5,971
1983	5,337	29,764	185.0	1,276.0*e*	6	-	6,217
1984	5,185	30,006	187.2	1,177.0*e*	6	-	6,239
1985	5,075	30,316	200.4	1,078.1*e*	6	-	6,610
1986	5,163	30,959	217.9	979.1*e*	6	-	7,038
1987	3,302	17,377	106.0	880.1	5	266,548	6,100
1988	3,135	17,370	114.3	807.0*e*	6	-	6,582
1989	2,932	17,388	113.8	733.9*e*	6	-	6,545
1990	3,423	18,124	123.7	660.8*e*	5	-	6,823
1991	3,632	19,640	145.4	587.7*e*	5	-	7,403
1992	2,340	7,879	62.3	514.6	3	219,933	7,903
1993	2,270	8,433	74.1	399.2*p*	4	-	8,791
1994	2,338	8,967	79.1	313.2*p*	4	-	8,821
1995	2,340	9,964	85.9	227.1*p*	4	-	8,624
1996	1,661*p*	5,375*p*	59.3*p*	141.1*p*	-	-	-
1997	1,390*p*	3,488*p*	49.5*p*	-	-	-	-
1998	1,119*p*	1,601*p*	39.7*p*	-	-	-	-

Sources: Economic Census of the United States, 1982, 1987, and 1992. Establishment counts, employment, and payroll are from *County Business Patterns* for non-Census years. Values followed by a 'p' are projections by the editors. Sales and expense data for non-Census years are extrapolations, marked by 'e'. Industries reclassified in 1987 will not have data for prior years. Data are the most recent available at this level of detail.

INDICES OF CHANGE

Year	Establishments (number)	Employment (number)	Payroll ($ million)	Sales ($ million)	Employees per Establishment (number)	Sales per Establishment ($)	Payroll per Employee ($)
1982	222.7	345.5	260.8	267.2	166.7	120.0	75.6
1983	228.1	377.8	297.0	248.0*e*	200.0	-	78.7
1984	221.6	380.8	300.5	228.7*e*	200.0	-	78.9
1985	216.9	384.8	321.7	209.5*e*	200.0	-	83.6
1986	220.6	392.9	349.8	190.3*e*	200.0	-	89.1
1987	141.1	220.5	170.1	171.0	166.7	121.2	77.2
1988	134.0	220.5	183.5	156.8*e*	200.0	-	83.3
1989	125.3	220.7	182.7	142.6*e*	200.0	-	82.8
1990	146.3	230.0	198.6	128.4*e*	166.7	-	86.3
1991	155.2	249.3	233.4	114.2*e*	166.7	-	93.7
1992	100.0	100.0	100.0	100.0	100.0	100.0	100.0
1993	97.0	107.0	119.0	77.6*p*	123.8	-	111.2
1994	99.9	113.8	127.0	60.9*p*	127.8	-	111.6
1995	100.0	126.5	137.9	44.1*p*	141.9	-	109.1
1996	71.0*p*	68.2*p*	95.1*p*	27.4*p*	-	-	-
1997	59.4*p*	44.3*p*	79.4*p*	-	-	-	-
1998	47.8*p*	20.3*p*	63.7*p*	-	-	-	-

Sources: Same as General Statistics. The values shown reflect change from the base year, 1992. Values above 100 mean greater than 1992, values below 100 mean less than 1992, and a value of 100 in the 1982-91 or 1993-98 period means same as 1992. Values followed by a 'p' are projections by the editors; 'e' stands for extrapolation. Data are the most recent available at this level of detail.

SELECTED RATIOS

For 1992	Avg. of All Retail	Analyzed Industry	Index	For 1992	Avg. of All Retail	Analyzed Industry	Index
Employees per Establishment	12	3	28	Sales per Employee	102,941	65,313	63
Payroll per Establishment	146,026	26,624	18	Sales per Establishment	1,241,555	219,915	18
Payroll per Employee	12,107	7,907	65	Expenses per Establishment	na	na	na

Sources: Same as General Statistics. The 'Average of All Manufacturing' column represents the average of all manufacturing industries reported for the most recent complete year available. The Index shows the relationship between the Average and the Analyzed Industry. For example, 100 means that they are equal; 500 that the Analyzed Industry is five times the average; 50 means that the Analyzed Industry is half the national average. The abbreviation 'na' is used to show that data are 'not available'.

LEADING COMPANIES Number shown: 16 Total sales ($ mil): 914 Total employment (000): 11.4

Company Name	Address				CEO Name	Phone	Co. Type	Sales ($ mil)	Empl. (000)
W.H. Braum Inc.	PO Box 25429	Oklahoma City	OK	73125	William Braum	405-475-2460	R	350 •	7.9
Farm Stores	5800 NW 74th Ave	Miami	FL	33166	Jose Bared Sr	305-592-3100	R	150 •	1.5
Bresler's Industries Inc.	4811 Emerson Ave	Palatine	IL	60067	Stan White	847-298-1100	R	90 •	<0.1
Gold Standard Enterprises Inc.	5100 W Dempster	Skokie	IL	60077	Michael Binstein	847-674-4200	R	60	0.3
Goshen Dairy Inc.	1026 Cookson SE	New Philad.	OH	44663	William Bichsel Jr	216-339-1959	R	51 •	0.2
Yogurt Ventures USA Inc.	2849 Paces Ferry	Atlanta	GA	30339	John Stern	770-433-0983	R	45	<0.1
Oberweis Dairy Inc.	951 Ice Cream Dr	North Aurora	IL	60542	Elaine Oberweis	630-801-6100	R	31	0.2
Zack's Famous Frozen Yogurt	4400 Silas Creek	Winston-Salem	NC	27104	CH McMahan	910-768-9446	S	26 •	0.3
Heritage Dairy Stores Inc.	PO Box 158	Thorofare	NJ	08086	Harold R Heritage	609-845-2855	R	24 •	0.4
Dairy Maid Dairy Inc.	706 Vernon Ave	Frederick	MD	21701	Joseph Vona	301-663-5114	R	20	<0.1
Dixie Dairy Co.	1200 W 15th Ave	Gary	IN	46407	Thomas T Eskilson	219-885-6101	R	19 •	<0.1
Homestead Dairies Inc.	PO Box 428	Massena	NY	13662	Robert B Squires	315-769-2456	R	17 •	<0.1
Penguin Place Yogurt Shops	999 E Touhy Ave	Des Plaines	IL	60018	David E Lasky	708-298-1100	S	15	<0.1
Thompson's Finer Foods Inc.	901 W Touhy Ave	Park Ridge	IL	60068	RE Thompson	708-825-2177	R	12	0.2
Dairy Gold Foods Co.	909 E 21st St	Cheyenne	WY	82001	Robert McClusky	307-634-4433	R	4	<0.1
Baker's Dairy Co.	1808 34th St	Moline	IL	61265	Jim Baker	309-764-2451	R	0 •	<0.1

Source: *Ward's Business Directory of U.S. Private and Public Companies*, 1998. The company type code used is as follows: P - Public, R - Private, S - Subsidiary, D - Division, J - Joint Venture, A - Affiliate, G - Group. Sales are in millions of dollars, employees are in thousands. An asterisk (•) indicates an estimated sales volume. The symbol < stands for 'less than'.

OCCUPATIONS EMPLOYED BY SIC 545 - FOOD STORES, NEC

Occupation	% of Total 1996	Change to 2006	Occupation	% of Total 1996	Change to 2006
Salespersons, retail	34.2	18.7	Truck drivers light & heavy	1.5	23.8
Cashiers	15.5	25.3	Wholesale & retail buyers, except farm products	1.5	2.5
Stock clerks	10.3	-3.7	Bookkeeping, accounting, & auditing clerks	1.4	-1.0
Food counter, fountain workers	9.2	18.5	Hand packers & packagers	1.2	23.8
Marketing & sales worker supervisors	8.0	23.8	Purchasing managers	1.2	11.4
General managers & top executives	5.2	19.9	Bakers, bread & pastry	1.2	23.7
Food preparation workers	2.9	18.0			

Source: *Industry-Occupation Matrix*, Bureau of Labor Statistics. These data relate to one or more 3-digit SIC industry groups rather than to a single 4-digit SIC. The change reported for each occupation to the year 2006 is a percent of growth or decline as estimated by the Bureau of Labor Statistics. The abbreviation nec stands for 'not elsewhere classified'.

STATE AND REGIONAL CONCENTRATION

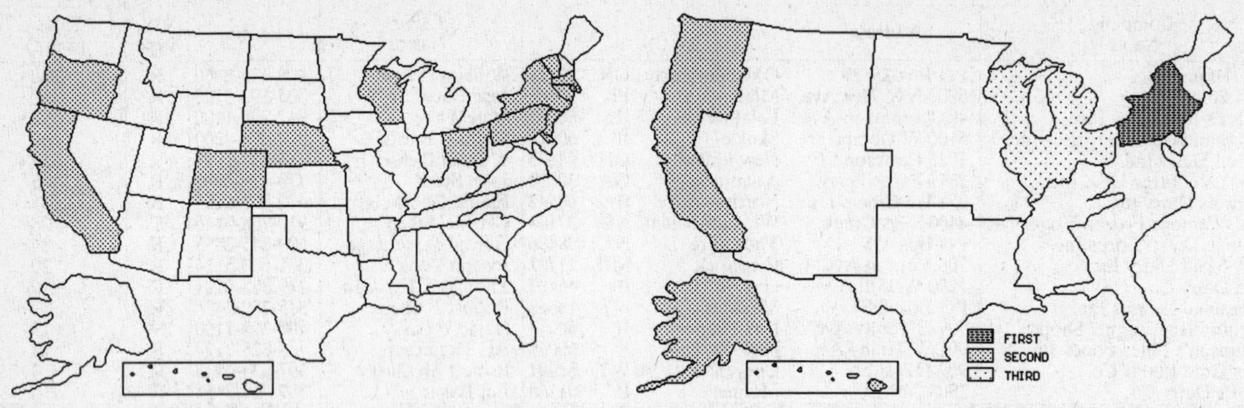

INDUSTRY DATA BY STATE

State	Establishments - 1995		Employment - 1995			Payroll - 1995		Sales - 1992		
	Total (number)	% of U.S.	Total (number)	% of U.S.	Per Estab.	Total ($ mil.)	Per Empl. ($)	Total ($ mil.)	% of U.S.	Per Estab ($)
New York	356	15.2	1,373	13.9	4	14.8	10,771	126.8	25.2	95,695
California	294	12.6	1,543	15.6	5	10.4	6,713	78.5	15.6	64,183
Pennsylvania	162	6.9	734	7.4	5	5.1	7,011	38.9	7.7	64,236
Ohio	115	4.9	644	6.5	6	7.2	11,230	36.3	7.2	67,774
New Jersey	96	4.1	263	2.7	3	2.7	10,186	21.0	4.2	74,698
Illinois	141	6.0	666	6.7	5	5.7	8,485	20.8	4.1	35,603
Wisconsin	76	3.2	389	3.9	5	4.0	10,391	18.3	3.6	52,234
Florida	96	4.1	318	3.2	3	2.3	7,094	13.9	2.8	49,063
Massachusetts	58	2.5	207	2.1	4	2.0	9,768	13.4	2.7	57,767
Texas	75	3.2	204	2.1	3	1.3	6,186	11.7	2.3	81,264
Michigan	87	3.7	221	2.2	3	1.5	6,715	9.8	1.9	60,882
Oregon	48	2.1	185	1.9	4	1.5	8,184	9.8	1.9	52,575
Connecticut	37	1.6	125	1.3	3	0.9	7,432	8.0	1.6	79,683
Colorado	39	1.7	108	1.1	3	1.0	9,185	7.5	1.5	60,699
Washington	48	2.1	214	2.2	4	2.1	9,682	7.4	1.5	58,417
Missouri	50	2.1	179	1.8	4	1.6	9,106	7.2	1.4	59,254
Maryland	36	1.5	129	1.3	4	1.0	7,605	6.7	1.3	82,852
Indiana	45	1.9	209	2.1	5	1.5	7,191	6.3	1.2	47,195
North Carolina	19	0.8	90	0.9	5	1.4	15,722	5.9	1.2	120,816
Nebraska	30	1.3	154	1.6	5	0.9	6,104	5.6	1.1	25,817
Minnesota	34	1.5	138	1.4	4	1.3	9,399	5.5	1.1	64,200
Arizona	33	1.4	250	2.5	8	1.7	6,748	4.5	0.9	37,875
Rhode Island	11	0.5	54	0.5	5	0.5	9,981	4.3	0.8	125,088
Georgia	47	2.0	150	1.5	3	1.0	6,560	4.2	0.8	35,017
Virginia	35	1.5	326	3.3	9	2.5	7,564	4.1	0.8	38,692
South Carolina	14	0.6	66	0.7	5	1.2	18,909	4.0	0.8	154,462
Iowa	28	1.2	89	0.9	3	0.7	7,820	2.8	0.6	32,291
Tennessee	24	1.0	80	0.8	3	0.5	6,275	2.6	0.5	90,276
New Mexico	11	0.5	60	0.6	5	0.6	9,500	2.6	0.5	102,280
Delaware	5	0.2	21	0.2	4	0.2	9,905	2.5	0.5	66,676
Alabama	18	0.8	65	0.7	4	0.4	5,523	2.3	0.5	51,689
Oklahoma	17	0.7	26	0.3	2	0.3	9,731	1.8	0.4	167,182
Kentucky	16	0.7	131	1.3	8	0.9	6,695	1.8	0.4	53,824
Hawaii	7	0.3	58	0.6	8	0.5	9,155	1.6	0.3	57,964
Arkansas	11	0.5	27	0.3	2	0.2	6,074	1.3	0.3	53,708
Vermont	6	0.3	0-19	-	-	(D)	-	1.3	0.3	157,250
Mississippi	10	0.4	24	0.2	2	0.2	6,917	1.0	0.2	62,188
Louisiana	12	0.5	76	0.8	6	0.5	7,039	0.6	0.1	47,385
Kansas	18	0.8	51	0.5	3	0.3	6,176	(D)	-	-
Nevada	10	0.4	80	0.8	8	1.3	16,213	(D)	-	-
New Hampshire	10	0.4	0-19	-	-	(D)	-	(D)	-	-
Utah	10	0.4	28	0.3	3	0.2	8,500	(D)	-	-
West Virginia	9	0.4	30	0.3	3	0.3	9,100	(D)	-	-
Maine	8	0.3	27	0.3	3	0.3	9,815	(D)	-	-
Idaho	7	0.3	28	0.3	4	0.4	15,214	(D)	-	-
Montana	7	0.3	32	0.3	5	0.3	8,156	(D)	-	-
North Dakota	7	0.3	20-99	-	-	(D)	-	(D)	-	-
D.C.	4	0.2	15	0.2	4	0.2	11,000	(D)	-	-
South Dakota	3	0.1	20-99	-	-	(D)	-	(D)	-	-

Source: *County Business Patterns, 1995* and *Economic Census of the U.S., 1992*. Data are sorted by 1992 revenues and, if revenues are unavailable, by establishments in 1995. The symbol (D) indicates that data are withheld by the source to avoid disclosure of competitive information. A dash (-) indicates that data are not available or undisclosed because they do not meet statistical validity standards. Shaded *states* on the state map indicate those states which have proportionately greater representation in the industry than would be indicated by the state's population; the ratio is based on total revenues or number of establishments. Shaded *regions* indicate where the industry is regionally most concentrated.

5461 - RETAIL BAKERIES

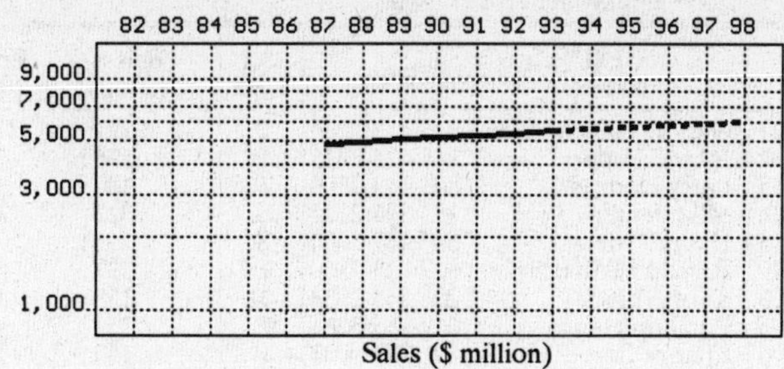

Sales ($ million)

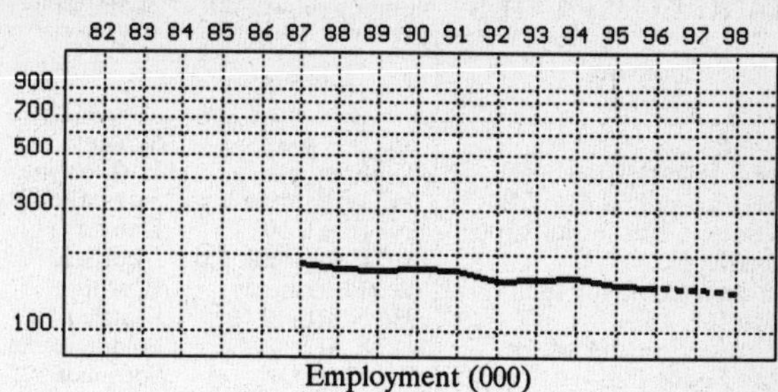

Employment (000)

GENERAL STATISTICS

Year	Establishments (number)	Employment (number)	Payroll ($ million)	Sales ($ million)	Employees per Establishment (number)	Sales per Establishment ($)	Payroll per Employee ($)
1982	-	-	-	-	-	-	-
1983	-	-	-	-	-	-	-
1984	-	-	-	-	-	-	-
1985	-	-	-	-	-	-	-
1986	-	-	-	-	-	-	-
1987	21,790	185,396	1,353.1	4,870.8	9	223,532	7,299
1988	20,389	177,776	1,431.0	4,974.0e	9	-	8,049
1989	20,119	174,667	1,458.0	5,077.2e	9	-	8,347
1990	19,897	176,392	1,543.1	5,180.4e	9	-	8,748
1991	20,757	174,842	1,623.3	5,283.7e	8	-	9,285
1992	20,418	157,136	1,407.1	5,386.9	8	263,831	8,955
1993	20,683	160,656	1,551.8	5,490.1p	8	-	9,659
1994	21,301	162,433	1,691.2	5,593.3p	8	-	10,411
1995	20,248	153,456	1,556.7	5,696.6p	8	-	10,144
1996	20,474p	150,773p	1,650.0p	5,799.8p	-	-	-
1997	20,444p	147,088p	1,677.4p	5,903.0p	-	-	-
1998	20,414p	143,404p	1,704.9p	6,006.2p	-	-	-

Sources: *Economic Census of the United States*, 1982, 1987, and 1992. Establishment counts, employment, and payroll are from *County Business Patterns* for non-Census years. Values followed by a 'p' are projections by the editors. Sales and expense data for non-Census years are extrapolations, marked by 'e'. Industries reclassified in 1987 will not have data for prior years. Data are the most recent available at this level of detail.

INDICES OF CHANGE

Year	Establishments (number)	Employment (number)	Payroll ($ million)	Sales ($ million)	Employees per Establishment (number)	Sales per Establishment ($)	Payroll per Employee ($)
1982	-	-	-	-	-	-	-
1983	-	-	-	-	-	-	-
1984	-	-	-	-	-	-	-
1985	-	-	-	-	-	-	-
1986	-	-	-	-	-	-	-
1987	106.7	118.0	96.2	90.4	112.5	84.7	81.5
1988	99.9	113.1	101.7	92.3e	112.5	-	89.9
1989	98.5	111.2	103.6	94.3e	112.5	-	93.2
1990	97.4	112.3	109.7	96.2e	112.5	-	97.7
1991	101.7	111.3	115.4	98.1e	100.0	-	103.7
1992	100.0	100.0	100.0	100.0	100.0	100.0	100.0
1993	101.3	102.2	110.3	101.9p	97.1	-	107.9
1994	104.3	103.4	120.2	103.8p	95.3	-	116.3
1995	99.2	97.7	110.6	105.7p	94.7	-	113.3
1996	100.3p	96.0p	117.3p	107.7p	-	-	-
1997	100.1p	93.6p	119.2p	109.6p	-	-	-
1998	100.0p	91.3p	121.2p	111.5p	-	-	-

Sources: Same as General Statistics. The values shown reflect change from the base year, 1992. Values above 100 mean greater than 1992, values below 100 mean less than 1992, and a value of 100 in the 1982-91 or 1993-98 period means same as 1992. Values followed by a 'p' are projections by the editors; 'e' stands for extrapolation. Data are the most recent available at this level of detail.

SELECTED RATIOS

For 1992	Avg. of All Retail	Analyzed Industry	Index	For 1992	Avg. of All Retail	Analyzed Industry	Index
Employees per Establishment	12	8	64	Sales per Employee	102,941	34,282	33
Payroll per Establishment	146,026	68,915	47	Sales per Establishment	1,241,555	263,831	21
Payroll per Employee	12,107	8,955	74	Expenses per Establishment	na	na	na

Sources: Same as General Statistics. The 'Average of All Manufacturing' column represents the average of all manufacturing industries reported for the most recent complete year available. The Index shows the relationship between the Average and the Analyzed Industry. For example, 100 means that they are equal; 500 that the Analyzed Industry is five times the average; 50 means that the Analyzed Industry is half the national average. The abbreviation 'na' is used to show that data are 'not available'.

LEADING COMPANIES

Number shown: **36** Total sales ($ mil): **6,438** Total employment (000): **84.6**

Company Name	Address				CEO Name	Phone	Co. Type	Sales ($ mil)	Empl. (000)
Penn Traffic Co.	PO Box 4737	Syracuse	NY	13221	Gary D Hirsch	315-453-7284	P	3,297	27.3
Perfection Bakeries Inc.	350 Pearl St	Fort Wayne	IN	46802	John F Popp	219-424-8245	R	696*	1.5
Mrs. Field's Original Cookies	462 W Bearcat Dr	Salt Lake City	UT	84115	Larry Hodges	801-463-2000	R	400*	6.5
Bakers Square Restaurants Inc.	PO Box 16601	Denver	CO	80216	Mike Jenkins	303-296-2121	S	325	12.0
Metz Baking Co.	520 Lake Cook Rd	Deerfield	IL	60015	Henry J Metz	847-267-3000	S	261*	7.0
Au Bon Pain Company Inc.	19 Fid Kennedy	Boston	MA	02210	Ronald M Shaich	617-423-2100	P	237	6.7
Cinnabon Inc.	936 N 34th St	Seattle	WA	98103	Kern GIllette	206-548-1032	R	155*	4.5
Chart House Enterprises Inc.	115 S Acacia Ave	Solana Beach	CA	92075	F Phillip Handy	619-755-8281	P	151	4.3
Signature Foods Inc.	400 Plaza Dr	Secaucus	NJ	07094	Charles Loccisiano	201-319-9003	P	140	1.5
Bristol Farms Inc.	880 Apollo St, #100	El Segundo	CA	90245	Kevin Davis	310-726-1300	R	120*	1.7
Saint Louis Bread Company	7930 Big Bend	Westgrove	MO	63146	Richard C Postle	314-918-7779	S	116*	3.0
Winchell's Donut Houses	1800 E 16th St	Santa Ana	CA	92701	E Thomas Dowling	714-565-1800	R	94	2.0
Bess Eaton Bakery	79 Tom Harvey Rd	Westerly	RI	02891	Louis A Gencarelli	401-596-0171	R	71*	0.7
Il Fornaio America Corp.	1000 Sansome St	San Francisco	CA	94111	Laurence B Mindel	415-986-1505	P	60	1.7
Java City Inc.	717 W Del Paso Rd	Sacramento	CA	95834	Tom Weborg	916-565-5500	D	43	0.8
C.B. Jackson and Co.	2410 Smith St	Houston	TX	77006	John Rydman	713-526-8787	R	40	0.2
Seattle Fish Co.	6211 E 42nd Ave	Denver	CO	80216	Ed Iacino	303-329-9595	R	34	0.1
Collin Street Bakery Inc.	401 W 7th Ave	Corsicana	TX	75110	Jr, LW McNutt	903-872-8111	R	30	<0.1
McKenzie's Pastry Shoppes	3847 Desire Pkwy	New Orleans	LA	70126	Donald D Entringer	504-944-8771	R	23	0.4
Quality Bakery Products Inc.	888 Las Olas Blvd	Ft Lauderdale	FL	33301	Harold Hink	954-779-3663	R	23	0.3
Clear Lake Bakery Inc.	PO Box 87	Clear Lake	IA	50428	Jim McQuaid	515-357-5264	R	15	0.2
Just Desserts Inc.	1970 Carroll Ave	San Francisco	CA	94124	Elliott Hoffman	415-330-3600	R	14	0.4
Cheryl and Co.	646 McCorkle Blvd	Westerville	OH	43082	Cheryl Krueger	614-891-8822	R	13	0.2
Thompson's Finer Foods Inc.	901 W Touhy Ave	Park Ridge	IL	60068	RE Thompson	708-825-2177	R	12	0.2
Northwest Markets Inc.	2858 Willamette St	Eugene	OR	97405	G Michael Webb	541-342-5779	R	11	<0.1
Bavarian Soft Pretzels Inc.	PO Box 7005	Lancaster	PA	17604	Robert Puccio	717-299-0968	S	11*	0.5
Byrnes and Kiefer Company	131 Kline Ave	Callery	PA	16024	EG Byrnes Jr	412-321-1900	R	11	<0.1
Grebe's Bakeries Inc.	5132 W Lincoln	West Allis	WI	53219	JW Grebe	414-543-7001	R	9	0.2
Gold Medal Bakery Inc.	21 Penn St	Fall River	MA	02724	John LeCompe	508-674-5766	R	8*	0.3
Middle East Bakery Inc.	1111 Riverside Dr	Methuen	MA	01844	Johnny Boghos	508-688-2221	R	8*	<0.1
William Greenberg Jr	533 W 47th St	New York	NY	10036	Maria Marfuggi	212-586-2826	P	3	<0.1
Rogers Bakery Inc.	33 Whiting St	Plainville	CT	06062	M Rogers	203-747-1686	R	2*	<0.1
Stahl's Bakery	51021 Washington	New Baltimore	MI	48047	Max Plant	810-725-6990	R	2*	<0.1
MGW Group Inc.	6757 Arapaho Rd	Dallas	TX	75248	Gwen Willhite	214-239-7474	R	1	<0.1
Winrock Bakery Inc.	3320 2nd St NW	Albuquerque	NM	87107	Harry Pastian	505-345-7773	R	1	<0.1
Mrs. Barry's Kona Cookies	75-5744 Alii Dr	Kailua Kona	HI	96740	Han Sung Barry	808-329-6055	R	0	<0.1

Source: *Ward's Business Directory of U.S. Private and Public Companies*, 1998. The company type code used is as follows: P - Public, R - Private, S - Subsidiary, D - Division, J - Joint Venture, A - Affiliate, G - Group. Sales are in millions of dollars, employees are in thousands. An asterisk (*) indicates an estimated sales volume. The symbol < stands for 'less than'.

OCCUPATIONS EMPLOYED BY SIC 546 - RETAIL BAKERIES

Occupation	% of Total 1996	Change to 2006	Occupation	% of Total 1996	Change to 2006
Bakers, bread & pastry	20.5	7.2	General managers & top executives	3.8	15.4
Salespersons, retail	20.1	14.2	Waiters & waitresses	3.0	32.5
Food counter, fountain workers	18.2	16.4	Driver/sales workers	2.1	19.1
Cashiers	12.0	20.5	Stock clerks	2.0	-10.3
Marketing & sales worker supervisors	5.0	19.1	Janitors & cleaners, maids	2.0	-4.7
Food preparation workers	4.4	13.5	Truck drivers light & heavy	1.4	19.1

Source: *Industry-Occupation Matrix*, Bureau of Labor Statistics. These data relate to one or more 3-digit SIC industry groups rather than to a single 4-digit SIC. The change reported for each occupation to the year 2006 is a percent of growth or decline as estimated by the Bureau of Labor Statistics. The abbreviation nec stands for 'not elsewhere classified'.

STATE AND REGIONAL CONCENTRATION

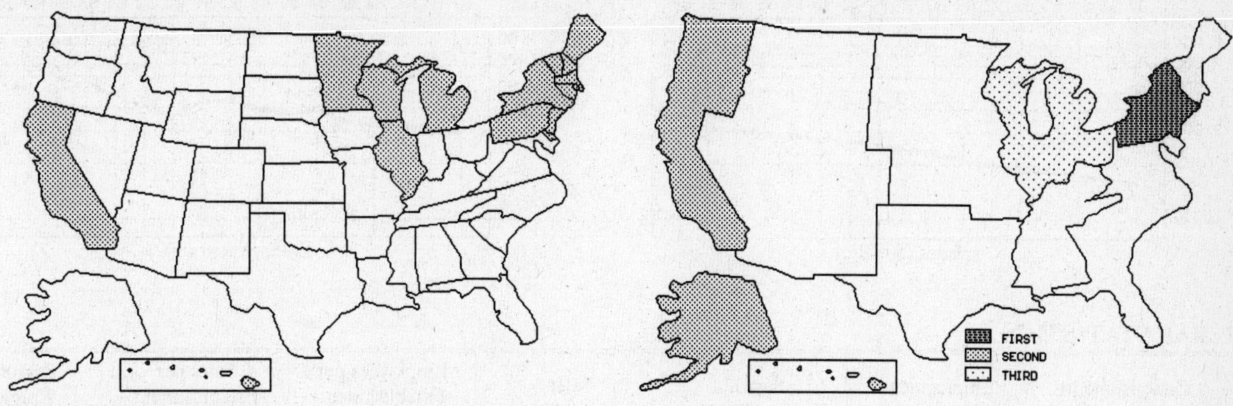

INDUSTRY DATA BY STATE

State	Establishments - 1995 Total (number)	Establishments - 1995 % of U.S.	Employment - 1995 Total (number)	Employment - 1995 % of U.S.	Employment - 1995 Per Estab.	Payroll - 1995 Total ($ mil.)	Payroll - 1995 Per Empl. ($)	Sales - 1992 Total ($ mil.)	Sales - 1992 % of U.S.	Sales - 1992 Per Estab ($)
California	3,200	15.8	19,797	12.9	6	225.3	11,381	860.8	16.0	37,062
New York	2,290	11.3	15,646	10.2	7	173.7	11,099	656.3	12.2	42,325
Massachusetts	979	4.8	11,727	7.6	12	116.4	9,925	336.6	6.2	36,404
New Jersey	1,075	5.3	8,193	5.3	8	95.8	11,688	324.4	6.0	40,810
Illinois	951	4.7	7,713	5.0	8	85.9	11,136	309.4	5.7	36,512
Pennsylvania	956	4.7	8,406	5.5	9	74.2	8,832	265.4	4.9	30,028
Texas	1,118	5.5	6,415	4.2	6	61.0	9,511	218.4	4.1	32,928
Florida	848	4.2	5,998	3.9	7	58.6	9,764	213.0	4.0	35,620
Michigan	832	4.1	5,920	3.9	7	52.6	8,888	207.5	3.9	31,989
Ohio	786	3.9	6,578	4.3	8	61.3	9,316	201.1	3.7	31,142
Connecticut	403	2.0	4,314	2.8	11	52.9	12,260	146.9	2.7	39,592
Minnesota	428	2.1	3,457	2.3	8	34.6	10,018	129.1	2.4	34,341
Wisconsin	380	1.9	3,289	2.1	9	30.4	9,237	114.1	2.1	28,140
Maryland	288	1.4	2,448	1.6	9	26.7	10,919	92.9	1.7	31,917
Washington	364	1.8	2,680	1.7	7	28.5	10,634	90.5	1.7	29,433
Indiana	355	1.8	2,864	1.9	8	27.0	9,420	82.9	1.5	28,546
Missouri	358	1.8	2,928	1.9	8	27.8	9,490	82.5	1.5	30,059
Georgia	263	1.3	2,327	1.5	9	24.1	10,341	75.0	1.4	36,246
Virginia	337	1.7	2,962	1.9	9	30.8	10,401	74.3	1.4	34,418
Rhode Island	210	1.0	2,176	1.4	10	21.8	10,001	61.3	1.1	35,053
Louisiana	258	1.3	1,946	1.3	8	16.1	8,276	60.5	1.1	29,973
Colorado	250	1.2	1,678	1.1	7	15.2	9,055	58.6	1.1	23,860
Arizona	174	0.9	1,230	0.8	7	10.6	8,640	58.3	1.1	35,252
North Carolina	244	1.2	1,988	1.3	8	18.1	9,130	54.8	1.0	29,800
Hawaii	127	0.6	1,129	0.7	9	13.2	11,708	50.8	0.9	33,384
Kentucky	165	0.8	1,364	0.9	8	12.9	9,446	42.0	0.8	30,558
Oregon	159	0.8	1,132	0.7	7	11.9	10,505	41.0	0.8	29,717
Tennessee	194	1.0	1,485	1.0	8	14.3	9,627	39.0	0.7	31,333
New Hampshire	133	0.7	1,548	1.0	12	14.8	9,568	36.2	0.7	37,455
Iowa	172	0.8	1,266	0.8	7	9.9	7,811	35.2	0.7	25,883
Oklahoma	228	1.1	1,013	0.7	4	8.1	7,973	32.7	0.6	23,869
Utah	117	0.6	1,119	0.7	10	9.4	8,408	28.8	0.5	25,401
Alabama	142	0.7	945	0.6	7	8.2	8,685	28.3	0.5	29,253
Kansas	190	0.9	1,223	0.8	6	9.6	7,870	28.3	0.5	23,704
Maine	116	0.6	1,045	0.7	9	10.0	9,572	27.7	0.5	32,440
South Carolina	115	0.6	864	0.6	8	7.7	8,855	23.7	0.4	29,352
Delaware	63	0.3	583	0.4	9	6.1	10,528	21.0	0.4	33,753
Arkansas	129	0.6	682	0.4	5	6.3	9,255	20.4	0.4	34,923
Nebraska	154	0.8	879	0.6	6	6.9	7,892	20.3	0.4	22,558
New Mexico	97	0.5	706	0.5	7	6.3	8,856	19.2	0.4	23,770
Nevada	68	0.3	385	0.3	6	4.3	11,270	15.4	0.3	24,906
West Virginia	77	0.4	474	0.3	6	3.9	8,302	15.0	0.3	25,801
Vermont	82	0.4	754	0.5	9	5.7	7,582	14.6	0.3	32,653
Mississippi	85	0.4	592	0.4	7	4.1	6,971	14.3	0.3	29,752
D.C.	40	0.2	259	0.2	6	3.2	12,259	12.7	0.2	36,977
Idaho	52	0.3	304	0.2	6	2.5	8,072	10.5	0.2	24,563
North Dakota	55	0.3	330	0.2	6	2.5	7,433	8.2	0.2	23,924
Montana	44	0.2	250	0.2	6	1.9	7,452	7.9	0.1	27,231
South Dakota	48	0.2	220	0.1	5	1.6	7,345	7.8	0.1	25,807
Alaska	24	0.1	95	0.1	4	1.1	11,221	7.1	0.1	44,631
Wyoming	25	0.1	130	0.1	5	1.0	7,708	3.7	0.1	26,268

Source: County Business Patterns, 1995 and *Economic Census of the U.S., 1992*. Data are sorted by 1992 revenues and, if revenues are unavailable, by establishments in 1995. The symbol (D) indicates that data are withheld by the source to avoid disclosure of competitive information. A dash (-) indicates that data are not available or undisclosed because they do not meet statistical validity standards. Shaded *states* on the state map indicate those states which have proportionately greater representation in the industry than would be indicated by the state's population; the ratio is based on total revenues or number of establishments. Shaded *regions* indicate where the industry is regionally most concentrated.

5499 - MISCELLANEOUS FOOD STORES

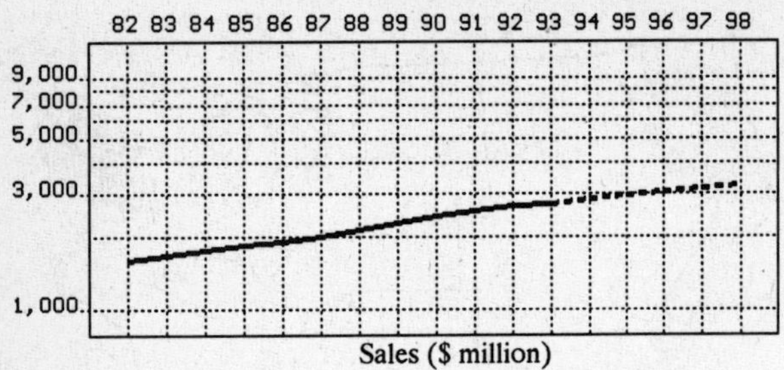

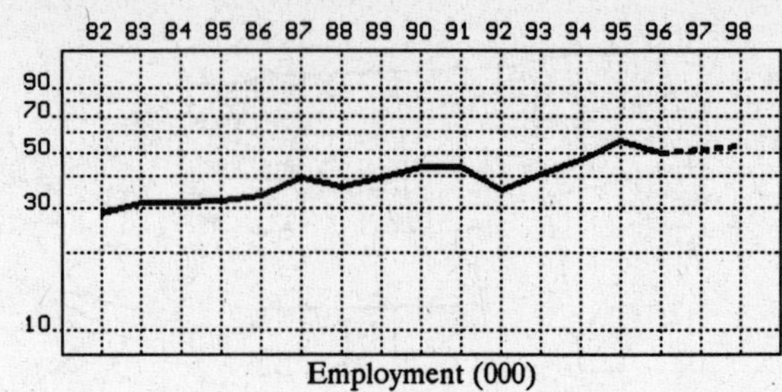

GENERAL STATISTICS

Year	Establishments (number)	Employment (number)	Payroll ($ million)	Sales ($ million)	Employees per Establishment (number)	Sales per Establishment ($)	Payroll per Employee ($)
1982	6,835	28,520	198.0	1,588.6	4	232,417	6,942
1983	6,711	31,387	239.0	1,673.7e	5	-	7,616
1984	6,708	31,563	304.6	1,758.8e	5	-	9,649
1985	6,650	32,217	260.5	1,843.9e	5	-	8,087
1986	6,674	33,519	301.8	1,929.0e	5	-	9,003
1987	7,271	39,608	284.6	2,014.1	5	277,000	7,186
1988	7,109	36,669	370.7	2,144.3e	5	-	10,111
1989	6,946	39,637	408.7	2,274.5e	6	-	10,312
1990	7,457	43,588	479.7	2,404.7e	6	-	11,006
1991	7,595	43,975	504.2	2,534.9e	6	-	11,466
1992	7,606	35,248	369.7	2,665.1	5	350,391	10,490
1993	8,546	40,654	467.9	2,721.5p	5	-	11,509
1994	9,316	46,362	546.1	2,829.1p	5	-	11,780
1995	10,063	55,569	674.5	2,936.8p	6	-	12,139
1996	9,164p	49,783p	608.0p	3,044.4p	-	-	-
1997	9,381p	51,292p	637.6p	3,152.1p	-	-	-
1998	9,599p	52,801p	667.1p	3,259.7p	-	-	-

Sources: Economic Census of the United States, 1982, 1987, and 1992. Establishment counts, employment, and payroll are from *County Business Patterns* for non-Census years. Values followed by a 'p' are projections by the editors. Sales and expense data for non-Census years are extrapolations, marked by 'e'. Industries reclassified in 1987 will not have data for prior years. Data are the most recent available at this level of detail.

INDICES OF CHANGE

Year	Establishments (number)	Employment (number)	Payroll ($ million)	Sales ($ million)	Employees per Establishment (number)	Sales per Establishment ($)	Payroll per Employee ($)
1982	89.9	80.9	53.6	59.6	80.0	66.3	66.2
1983	88.2	89.0	64.6	62.8e	100.0	-	72.6
1984	88.2	89.5	82.4	66.0e	100.0	-	92.0
1985	87.4	91.4	70.5	69.2e	100.0	-	77.1
1986	87.7	95.1	81.6	72.4e	100.0	-	85.8
1987	95.6	112.4	77.0	75.6	100.0	79.1	68.5
1988	93.5	104.0	100.3	80.5e	100.0	-	96.4
1989	91.3	112.5	110.5	85.3e	120.0	-	98.3
1990	98.0	123.7	129.8	90.2e	120.0	-	104.9
1991	99.9	124.8	136.4	95.1e	120.0	-	109.3
1992	100.0	100.0	100.0	100.0	100.0	100.0	100.0
1993	112.4	115.3	126.6	102.1p	95.1	-	109.7
1994	122.5	131.5	147.7	106.2p	99.5	-	112.3
1995	132.3	157.7	182.5	110.2p	110.4	-	115.7
1996	120.5p	141.2p	164.5p	114.2p	-	-	-
1997	123.3p	145.5p	172.5p	118.3p	-	-	-
1998	126.2p	149.8p	180.4p	122.3p	-	-	-

Sources: Same as General Statistics. The values shown reflect change from the base year, 1992. Values above 100 mean greater than 1992, values below 100 mean less than 1992, and a value of 100 in the 1982-91 or 1993-98 period means same as 1992. Values followed by a 'p' are projections by the editors; 'e' stands for extrapolation. Data are the most recent available at this level of detail.

SELECTED RATIOS

For 1992	Avg. of All Retail	Analyzed Industry	Index	For 1992	Avg. of All Retail	Analyzed Industry	Index
Employees per Establishment	12	5	38	Sales per Employee	102,941	75,610	73
Payroll per Establishment	146,026	48,606	33	Sales per Establishment	1,241,555	350,394	28
Payroll per Employee	12,107	10,489	87	Expenses per Establishment	na	na	na

Sources: Same as General Statistics. The 'Average of All Manufacturing' column represents the average of all manufacturing industries reported for the most recent complete year available. The Index shows the relationship between the Average and the Analyzed Industry. For example, 100 means that they are equal; 500 that the Analyzed Industry is five times the average; 50 means that the Analyzed Industry is half the national average. The abbreviation 'na' is used to show that data are 'not available'.

LEADING COMPANIES Number shown: **47** Total sales ($ mil): **5,552** Total employment (000): **59.7**

Company Name	Address				CEO Name	Phone	Co. Type	Sales ($ mil)	Empl. (000)
Whole Foods Market Inc.	601 N Lamar Blvd	Austin	TX	78703	John Mackey	512-477-4455	P	1,117	11.0
General Nutrition Companies	921 Penn Ave	Pittsburgh	PA	15222	William E Watts	412-288-4600	P	991	9.6
Starbucks Corp.	PO Box 34067	Seattle	WA	98124	Howard Schultz	206-447-1575	P	967	16.6
Herbalife International Inc.	1800 Century Pk E	Los Angeles	CA	90067	Mark Hughes	310-410-9600	P	783	1.5
Cost Plus Imports Inc.	PO Box 23350	Oakland	CA	94623	Ralph Dillon	510-893-7300	S	200•	2.8
Bread and Circus Inc.	17 Lincoln St	Newton Hghlds	MA	02161	AC Gallo	617-332-2400	S	163•	2.3
Hickory Farms Inc.	PO Box 219	Maumee	OH	43537	Ike Herb	419-893-7611	R	160	2.3
Sutton Place Gourmet Inc.	6903 Rockledge Dr	Bethesda	MD	20817	Tom Johnston	301-564-6006	R	120•	1.6
Wild Oats Markets Inc.	1645 Broadway	Boulder	CO	80301	Michael C Gilliland	303-440-5220	P	98	2.9
Schierl Cos.	2201 Madison St	Stevens Point	WI	54481	William Schierl	715-345-5060	R	95•	0.4
Cain's Coffee Co.	PO Box 25009	Oklahoma City	OK	73125	Thomas Donnell	405-751-7221	S	92	0.5
Brother's Gourmet Coffees Inc.	2255 Glades Rd	Boca Raton	FL	33431	donald Breen	561-995-2600	P	83	0.1
Fresh Market Inc.	802 Green Val Rd	Greensboro	NC	27408	Ray Berry	336-272-1338	R	75	1.2
Nature Food Centers Inc.	1 Natures Way	Wilmington	MA	01887	Ronald L Rossetti	978-657-5000	R	72	0.7
Bess Eaton Bakery	79 Tom Harvey Rd	Westerly	RI	02891	Louis A Gencarelli	401-596-0171	R	71•	0.7
Gold Standard Enterprises Inc.	5100 W Dempster	Skokie	IL	60077	Michael Binstein	847-674-4200	R	60	0.3
Miller and Holmes Inc.	501 Lafayette Rd	St. Paul	MN	55101	GT Peterson	612-224-5874	R	56•	0.3
Green Mountain Coffee Inc.	33 Coffee Ln	Waterbury	VT	05676	Robert P Stiller	802-244-5621	P	48	0.4
Goodland Cooperative	PO Box 998	Goodland	KS	67735	Steve Evert	913-899-3681	R	40	<0.1
Barnie's Coffee and Tea	340 N Primrose Dr	Orlando	FL	32803	Phil Jones	407-894-1416	R	35	0.5
Mr. Bulky Treats and Gifts	755 W Big Beaver	Troy	MI	48084	Sid Rubin	313-244-9000	R	28•	0.4
Belmont Springs Water	PO Box 3	Lexington	MA	02173	David Hill	617-674-7800	S	24	0.2
Bread	798 S Winchester	San Jose	CA	95128	Frank Ashton	408-371-5000	R	21	0.2
Diedrich Coffee Inc.	2144 Michelson Dr	Irvine	CA	92612	Lawrence Goelman	714-260-1600	P	17	0.9
HealthRite Inc.	11445 Cronhill Dr	Owings Mills	MD	21117	B T MacDonald	410-581-8042	P	16	0.2
Diaz Foods Inc.	5500 Bucknell SW	Atlanta	GA	30336	Rene Diaz	404-355-4508	R	15	<0.1
Living Foods Inc.	224 Greenfield Ave	San Anselmo	CA	94960	Jan Rubenstein	415-457-4317	R	13	0.1
Race Street Foods Inc.	PO Box 28385	San Jose	CA	95159	G Barsanti	408-294-6161	R	13•	0.1
Bucks County Coffee Co.	2250 W Cabot Blvd	Langhorne	PA	19047	Rodger Owen	215-741-1855	R	11•	0.4
Primetime Foods Inc.	2092 Farragut Ave	Bristol	PA	19007	AJ Passanante	215-536-3533	R	11•	0.2
New World Coffee Inc.	379 W Broadway	New York	NY	10012	Gwenn M Cagann	212-343-0552	P	10	0.2
Culligan	PO Box 2170	Olathe	KS	66061	Al Cerne	913-782-4141	D	6	<0.1
Vitamin Specialties Corp.	8160 Ogontz Ave	Wyncote	PA	19095	Bill Evans	215-572-0142	S	6•	0.2
Turner Shellfish New Zealand	PO Box 8919	Newport Beach	CA	92658	Noel Turner	714-717-5070	R	5	<0.1
Culligan Water Conditioning	1200 Arden Way	Sacramento	CA	95815	Don G Felton	916-927-5005	R	5	<0.1
Capricorn Coffees Inc.	353 10th St	San Francisco	CA	94103	Craig Edwards	415-621-8500	S	4•	<0.1
Victor Allen's Coffee and Tea	713 Post Rd	Madison	WI	53713	Victor Mondry	608-274-4666	R	4	0.1
E. Kayser Corp.	3890 La Cumbrez	Santa Barbara	CA	93105	Terry Staten	805-563-2007	R	3	<0.1
Gourmet Regency Coffee Inc.	5500 Cottonwood	Prior Lake	MN	55372	Robert A Paschke	612-226-4100	R	3	<0.1
United Noodles Inc.	2015 E 24th St	Minneapolis	MN	55404	Ted Wong	612-721-6677	R	3•	<0.1
Water Warehouse, Etc.	PO Box 123	Matawan	NJ	07747	Kenneth Siebenberg	908-739-4848	R	3	<0.1
Specialty World Foods Inc.	84 Montgomery St	Albany	NY	12207	Joseph R Messina	518-436-7603	R	2	<0.1
Scottie MacBean Inc.	660 High St	Worthington	OH	43085	Ronald M Kellogg	614-888-3494	R	2	<0.1
City Bottling Company Inc.	1820 5th Ave	Arnold	PA	15068	Louis Lombardo	412-335-3350	R	1•	<0.1
Rocky Mountain International	3418 N Ocean Blvd	Ft Lauderdale	FL	33308	Michael A Puhr	954-565-8894	P	1	0.6
Masotta Variety and Deli	307 Main St	Woburn	MA	01801	Mararette Masotta	617-935-2648	R	1•	<0.1
Cameron's Coffee Direct Inc.	PO Box 884	Hayward	WI	54843	Beth Heitmann	715-634-7706	S	0•	<0.1

Source: *Ward's Business Directory of U.S. Private and Public Companies*, 1998. The company type code used is as follows: P - Public, R - Private, S - Subsidiary, D - Division, J - Joint Venture, A - Affiliate, G - Group. Sales are in millions of dollars, employees are in thousands. An asterisk (•) indicates an estimated sales volume. The symbol < stands for 'less than'.

OCCUPATIONS EMPLOYED BY SIC 549 - FOOD STORES, NEC

Occupation	% of Total 1996	Change to 2006	Occupation	% of Total 1996	Change to 2006
Salespersons, retail	34.2	18.7	Truck drivers light & heavy	1.5	23.8
Cashiers	15.5	25.3	Wholesale & retail buyers, except farm products	1.5	2.5
Stock clerks	10.3	-3.7	Bookkeeping, accounting, & auditing clerks	1.4	-1.0
Food counter, fountain workers	9.2	18.5	Hand packers & packagers	1.2	23.8
Marketing & sales worker supervisors	8.0	23.8	Purchasing managers	1.2	11.4
General managers & top executives	5.2	19.9	Bakers, bread & pastry	1.2	23.7
Food preparation workers	2.9	18.0			

Source: *Industry-Occupation Matrix*, Bureau of Labor Statistics. These data relate to one or more 3-digit SIC industry groups rather than to a single 4-digit SIC. The change reported for each occupation to the year 2006 is a percent of growth or decline as estimated by the Bureau of Labor Statistics. The abbreviation nec stands for 'not elsewhere classified'.

STATE AND REGIONAL CONCENTRATION

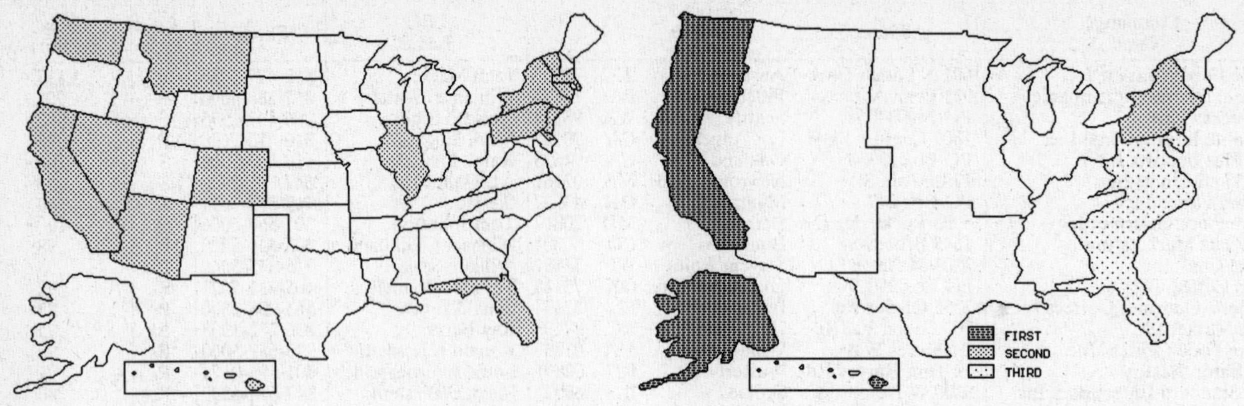

INDUSTRY DATA BY STATE

State	Establishments - 1995 Total (number)	Establishments - 1995 % of U.S.	Employment - 1995 Total (number)	Employment - 1995 % of U.S.	Employment - 1995 Per Estab.	Payroll - 1995 Total ($ mil.)	Payroll - 1995 Per Empl. ($)	Sales - 1992 Total ($ mil.)	Sales - 1992 % of U.S.	Sales - 1992 Per Estab ($)
California	1,570	15.6	10,424	18.8	7	132.5	12,709	541.2	20.3	77,661
New York	955	9.5	5,113	9.2	5	70.2	13,737	303.4	11.4	93,485
Florida	715	7.1	3,871	7.0	5	48.8	12,614	188.4	7.1	82,710
Pennsylvania	453	4.5	2,261	4.1	5	26.3	11,626	136.7	5.1	75,690
Texas	609	6.1	2,650	4.8	4	32.4	12,213	122.5	4.6	78,046
Illinois	396	3.9	2,737	4.9	7	32.5	11,867	122.1	4.6	71,253
New Jersey	374	3.7	1,698	3.1	5	24.7	14,531	113.7	4.3	99,434
Ohio	358	3.6	1,967	3.5	5	20.7	10,543	95.5	3.6	69,688
Michigan	237	2.4	1,284	2.3	5	13.4	10,400	92.9	3.5	82,898
Washington	314	3.1	2,111	3.8	7	26.9	12,724	66.0	2.5	63,236
Massachusetts	224	2.2	1,301	2.3	6	15.9	12,188	65.3	2.5	74,633
Arizona	224	2.2	1,246	2.2	6	14.9	11,949	55.6	2.1	78,929
Georgia	286	2.8	1,404	2.5	5	20.9	14,915	51.8	1.9	87,529
Virginia	228	2.3	1,320	2.4	6	13.4	10,174	46.5	1.7	65,912
Maryland	165	1.6	947	1.7	6	11.4	12,041	46.4	1.7	69,825
North Carolina	216	2.1	967	1.7	4	10.2	10,512	44.4	1.7	64,323
Connecticut	143	1.4	1,007	1.8	7	14.2	14,121	42.9	1.6	84,478
Wisconsin	145	1.4	890	1.6	6	9.4	10,608	40.8	1.5	62,353
Colorado	216	2.1	1,451	2.6	7	19.8	13,675	38.1	1.4	80,282
Minnesota	149	1.5	932	1.7	6	8.5	9,103	33.5	1.3	70,421
Oregon	197	2.0	1,073	1.9	5	10.9	10,181	30.5	1.1	49,956
Louisiana	121	1.2	723	1.3	6	7.7	10,714	30.4	1.1	59,633
Indiana	120	1.2	623	1.1	5	7.2	11,510	28.1	1.1	58,284
Missouri	146	1.5	576	1.0	4	5.7	9,891	27.6	1.0	69,278
Hawaii	78	0.8	406	0.7	5	5.1	12,458	22.0	0.8	90,769
Tennessee	122	1.2	431	0.8	4	4.0	9,183	20.2	0.8	56,851
Oklahoma	80	0.8	437	0.8	5	5.4	12,291	18.6	0.7	77,679
Alabama	106	1.1	484	0.9	5	6.0	12,469	18.2	0.7	72,498
Kansas	82	0.8	394	0.7	5	3.8	9,680	18.0	0.7	59,320
Iowa	69	0.7	312	0.6	5	2.8	8,936	15.2	0.6	51,765
Nevada	83	0.8	374	0.7	5	5.7	15,209	14.3	0.5	86,957
South Carolina	91	0.9	422	0.8	5	4.2	9,986	14.1	0.5	59,092
Utah	68	0.7	364	0.7	5	3.6	9,838	13.2	0.5	56,251
New Mexico	57	0.6	224	0.4	4	2.9	12,795	12.9	0.5	63,601
Kentucky	65	0.6	374	0.7	6	3.3	8,941	12.4	0.5	49,783
Maine	49	0.5	202	0.4	4	2.4	11,802	11.1	0.4	78,709
Mississippi	50	0.5	181	0.3	4	1.8	9,696	10.7	0.4	54,790
Nebraska	54	0.5	270	0.5	5	2.3	8,604	10.6	0.4	62,206
New Hampshire	51	0.5	153	0.3	3	1.8	11,797	10.5	0.4	62,976
Arkansas	53	0.5	164	0.3	3	1.9	11,756	9.7	0.4	71,485
Montana	51	0.5	321	0.6	6	3.0	9,193	9.4	0.4	58,627
Delaware	34	0.3	160	0.3	5	1.8	11,269	9.1	0.3	81,856
Idaho	47	0.5	194	0.3	4	1.7	8,918	8.6	0.3	65,931
Rhode Island	38	0.4	127	0.2	3	1.6	12,449	8.0	0.3	69,198
Vermont	31	0.3	212	0.4	7	2.4	11,269	8.0	0.3	70,325
D.C.	31	0.3	339	0.6	11	4.5	13,395	7.1	0.3	62,770
Alaska	29	0.3	127	0.2	4	1.9	14,732	5.6	0.2	71,359
West Virginia	28	0.3	131	0.2	5	0.9	7,221	5.1	0.2	54,989
North Dakota	24	0.2	88	0.2	4	0.6	6,500	3.8	0.1	48,244
South Dakota	16	0.2	51	0.1	3	0.5	8,882	3.0	0.1	64,413
Wyoming	15	0.1	51	0.1	3	0.3	5,706	1.5	0.1	73,095

Source: County Business Patterns, 1995 and *Economic Census of the U.S., 1992.* Data are sorted by 1992 revenues and, if revenues are unavailable, by establishments in 1995. The symbol (D) indicates that data are withheld by the source to avoid disclosure of competitive information. A dash (-) indicates that data are not available or undisclosed because they do not meet statistical validity standards. Shaded *states* on the state map indicate those states which have proportionately greater representation in the industry than would be indicated by the state's population; the ratio is based on total revenues or number of establishments. Shaded *regions* indicate where the industry is regionally most concentrated.

5511 - NEW AND USED CAR DEALERS

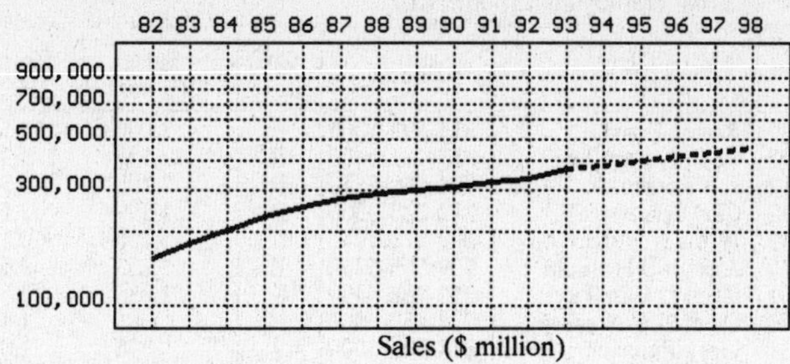

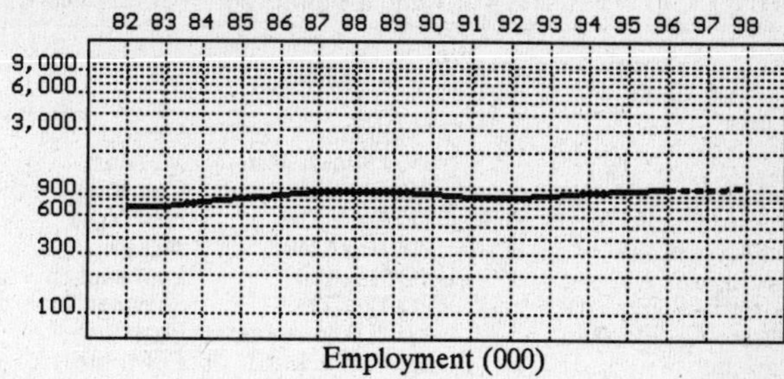

GENERAL STATISTICS

Year	Establishments (number)	Employment (number)	Payroll ($ million)	Sales ($ million)	Employees per Establishment (number)	Sales per Establishment ($)	Payroll per Employee ($)
1982	27,910	698,569	12,309.5	154,726.5	25	5,543,766	17,621
1983	27,033	708,718	14,195.5	179,887.0*e*	26	-	20,030
1984	26,572	788,840	17,601.4	205,047.6*e*	30	-	22,313
1985	26,149	838,755	19,650.3	230,208.1*e*	32	-	23,428
1986	26,267	884,069	21,332.6	255,368.7*e*	34	-	24,130
1987	28,320	939,929	22,205.0	280,529.2	33	9,905,694	23,624
1988	27,382	952,524	24,463.7	291,183.7*e*	35	-	25,683
1989	26,745	959,731	24,076.4	301,838.1*e*	36	-	25,087
1990	26,132	917,207	23,919.1	312,492.5*e*	35	-	26,078
1991	25,785	865,341	23,059.7	323,146.9*e*	34	-	26,648
1992	24,380	860,139	24,421.3	333,801.4	35	13,691,607	28,392
1993	24,561	898,983	27,563.7	368,193.1*p*	37	-	30,661
1994	24,130	949,438	30,685.7	386,100.6*p*	39	-	32,320
1995	24,230	990,767	32,425.3	404,008.1*p*	41	-	32,728
1996	24,138*p*	997,735*p*	32,257.5*p*	421,915.6*p*	-	-	-
1997	23,875*p*	1,014,071*p*	33,530.8*p*	439,823.1*p*	-	-	-
1998	23,611*p*	1,030,407*p*	34,804.1*p*	457,730.6*p*	-	-	-

Sources: Economic Census of the United States, 1982, 1987, and 1992. Establishment counts, employment, and payroll are from *County Business Patterns* for non-Census years. Values followed by a 'p' are projections by the editors. Sales and expense data for non-Census years are extrapolations, marked by 'e'. Industries reclassified in 1987 will not have data for prior years. Data are the most recent available at this level of detail.

INDICES OF CHANGE

Year	Establishments (number)	Employment (number)	Payroll ($ million)	Sales ($ million)	Employees per Establishment (number)	Sales per Establishment ($)	Payroll per Employee ($)
1982	114.5	81.2	50.4	46.4	71.4	40.5	62.1
1983	110.9	82.4	58.1	53.9*e*	74.3	-	70.5
1984	109.0	91.7	72.1	61.4*e*	85.7	-	78.6
1985	107.3	97.5	80.5	69.0*e*	91.4	-	82.5
1986	107.7	102.8	87.4	76.5*e*	97.1	-	85.0
1987	116.2	109.3	90.9	84.0	94.3	72.3	83.2
1988	112.3	110.7	100.2	87.2*e*	100.0	-	90.5
1989	109.7	111.6	98.6	90.4*e*	102.9	-	88.4
1990	107.2	106.6	97.9	93.6*e*	100.0	-	91.8
1991	105.8	100.6	94.4	96.8*e*	97.1	-	93.9
1992	100.0	100.0	100.0	100.0	100.0	100.0	100.0
1993	100.7	104.5	112.9	110.3*p*	104.6	-	108.0
1994	99.0	110.4	125.7	115.7*p*	112.4	-	113.8
1995	99.4	115.2	132.8	121.0*p*	116.8	-	115.3
1996	99.0*p*	116.0*p*	132.1*p*	126.4*p*	-	-	-
1997	97.9*p*	117.9*p*	137.3*p*	131.8*p*	-	-	-
1998	96.8*p*	119.8*p*	142.5*p*	137.1*p*	-	-	-

Sources: Same as General Statistics. The values shown reflect change from the base year, 1992. Values above 100 mean greater than 1992, values below 100 mean less than 1992, and a value of 100 in the 1982-91 or 1993-98 period means same as 1992. Values followed by a 'p' are projections by the editors; 'e' stands for extrapolation. Data are the most recent available at this level of detail.

SELECTED RATIOS

For 1992	Avg. of All Retail	Analyzed Industry	Index	For 1992	Avg. of All Retail	Analyzed Industry	Index
Employees per Establishment	12	35	293	Sales per Employee	102,941	388,078	377
Payroll per Establishment	146,026	1,001,694	686	Sales per Establishment	1,241,555	13,691,608	1,103
Payroll per Employee	12,107	28,392	235	Expenses per Establishment	na	na	na

Sources: Same as General Statistics. The 'Average of All Manufacturing' column represents the average of all manufacturing industries reported for the most recent complete year available. The Index shows the relationship between the Average and the Analyzed Industry. For example, 100 means that they are equal; 500 that the Analyzed Industry is five times the average; 50 means that the Analyzed Industry is half the national average. The abbreviation 'na' is used to show that data are 'not available'.

LEADING COMPANIES

Number shown: **50** Total sales ($ mil): **30,723** Total employment (000): **62.1**

Company Name	Address				CEO Name	Phone	Co. Type	Sales ($ mil)	Empl. (000)
Penske Corp.	13400 Outer Dr W	Detroit	MI	48239	Roger Penske	313-592-5000	R	3,000 •	11.5
V.T. Inc.	8500 Shawn Msn	Merriam	KS	66202	Cecil L Van Tuyl	913-432-6400	R	2,558 •	5.3
Hendrick Automotive Group	PO Box 18649	Charlotte	NC	28212	Jim Perkins	704-568-5550	R	2,200	4.5
United Auto Group Inc.	375 Park Ave	New York	NY	10152	Carl Spielvogel	212-223-3300	P	1,599	2.1
Prospect Motors Inc.	PO Box 1360	Jackson	CA	95642	William Halverson	209-223-1740	R	1,200	<0.1
Holman Enterprises	PO Box 1400	Pennsauken	NJ	08109	Joseph S Holman	609-663-5200	R	1,153 •	2.6
Van Enterprises Inc.	PO Box 795	Shawnee Msn	KS	66201	Cecil L Van Tuyl	913-432-6400	S	1,088	2.5
Don Massey Cadillac Inc.	40475 Ann Arbor	Plymouth	MI	48170	Donald E Massey	734-453-7500	R	886	1.4
D. Longo Inc.	3534 N Peck Rd	El Monte	CA	91731	Greg Penske	818-580-6000	S	836 •	1.0
Geneva Management	1550 Wilson Blvd	Arlington	VA	22209	Robert M Rosenthal	703-522-2300	R	805	2.0
Frank Consolidated Enterprises	666 Garland Pl	Des Plaines	IL	60016	James Frank	847-699-7000	R	730	1.3
Larry H. Miller Group	5650 S State St	Murray	UT	84107	Karen G Miller	801-264-3100	R	703	1.4
Ricart Ford Inc.	PO Box 27130	Columbus	OH	43227	Rhett Ricart	614-836-5321	R	608	1.0
Brown Automotive Group	10287 Lee Hwy	Fairfax	VA	22030	Frank Cuteri	703-352-5555	R	606	0.8
Jim Koons Management Co.	2000 Chain Bridge	Vienna	VA	22182	James E Koons	703-448-7000	R	560 •	1.1
Mel Farr Automotive Group	24750 Greenfield	Oak Park	MI	48237	Mel Farr Sr	248-967-3700	R	535 •	0.9
Galpin Motors Inc.	15505 Roscoe Blvd	North Hills	CA	91343	Bert Boeckmann	818-787-3800	R	533	0.7
Warnock Automotive Group	175 Rte 10 E	East Hanover	NJ	07936	Peter Jarvis	973-884-2100	R	530 •	0.4
Tuttle-Click Dealerships	9601 Wilshire Blvd	Beverly Hills	CA	90210	Robert H Tuttle	310-278-4411	R	510 •	1.4
AIMG Corp.	PO Box 2414	Round Rock	TX	78680	Donald J Tamburro	512-246-2412	R	500	1.0
Ourisman Chevrolet Company	4400 Branch Ave	Marlow H.	MD	20748	Mandell J Ourisman	301-423-4000	R	485	1.0
Coggin Automotive Corp.	4306 Pablo Oaks Ct	Jacksonville	FL	32224	Luther Coggin	904-992-4110	R	450	1.0
Ferman Motor Car Co.	PO Box 1321	Tampa	FL	33601	James L Ferman Jr	813-253-0681	R	450	0.9
Ancira Enterprises Inc.	PO Box 29719	San Antonio	TX	78229	Ernesto Ancira Jr	210-681-4900	R	412	0.5
Tasha Inc.	43285 Auto Mall	Fremont	CA	94538	Hank Khachaturian	510-252-5050	R	400 •	0.8
Lithia Motors Inc.	360 E Jackson St	Medford	OR	97501	S B Deboer	541-776-6401	R	394 •	0.9
Servco Pacific Inc.	PO Box 2788	Honolulu	HI	96803	Mark H Fukunaga	808-521-6511	R	361	0.9
Automotive Investment Group	PO Box 16460	Phoenix	AZ	85011	Larry Van Tuyl	602-230-1051	R	360 •	1.0
Lucas Dealership Group Inc.	19330evens Creek	Cupertino	CA	95014	Donald L Lucas	408-255-6400	R	350 •	0.8
Nalley Cos.	87 W Paces Ferry	Atlanta	GA	30305	CV Nalley III	404-261-3130	R	350	0.6
Rush Enterprises Inc.	PO Box 34630	San Antonio	TX	78265	W Marvin Rush	210-661-4511	P	344	0.7
Young Automotive Group Ltd.	3210 E 96th St	Indianapolis	IN	46240	Dan E Young	317-846-6666	R	331	0.5
Reedman Corporation	US Rte 1	Langhorne	PA	19047	S E Reedman Sr	215-757-4961	R	328	0.5
Cross-Continent Auto Retailers	PO Box 750	Amarillo	TX	79105	Bill A Gilliland	806-374-8653	P	322	0.7
Cutter Automotive Team Inc.	1311 Kapiolana	Honolulu	HI	96814	Nick Cutter	808-592-5401	R	320 •	0.9
Automanage Inc.	5670 Dixie Hwy	Fairfield	OH	45014	Mike Dever	513-870-5000	R	300	0.7
Avalon Ford Inc.	21212 S Avalon	Carson	CA	90745	Margret Kott	310-518-5770	R	300	0.4
Curtis C. Gunn Inc.	227 Broadway St	San Antonio	TX	78205	Robert Bomer	210-824-3208	R	300 •	0.9
Superior Automotive Group	8300 Shawn Msn	Merriam	KS	66202	Charles Oglesby	913-384-1550	R	290 •	0.8
Emich Oldsmobile Inc.	16400 W Colfax	Golden	CO	80401	Fred F Emich III	303-278-4433	R	275 •	0.4
Gillco Inc.	7611 Bellaire Blvd	Houston	TX	77036	Ramsay H Gillman	713-776-7000	R	275	0.9
Midway Ford Truck Center Inc.	PO Box 12656	Kansas City	MO	64116	Donald C Ahnger	816-455-3000	R	260	0.3
John Sullivan Dealerships	700 Automall Dr	Roseville	CA	95661	John Sullivan	916-782-1243	R	250	0.4
S and C Motors Inc.	2001 Market St	San Francisco	CA	94114	Ray P Siotto	415-861-6000	R	250	0.2
Toresco Enterprises Inc.	170 Rte 22 E	Springfield	NJ	07081	Donald Toresco	973-467-2900	R	250	0.5
Carlisle Motors Inc.	2085 Gulf to Bay	Clearwater	FL	34625	Dan Carlisle	813-461-3535	R	249	0.5
Guaranty Chevrolet	PO Box 279	Junction City	OR	97448	Herb Nill	541-998-2333	R	240	0.5
Geo. Byers Sons Inc.	PO Box 16513	Columbus	OH	43216	George W Byers III	614-228-5111	R	237	0.5
Sonny Hill Motors Inc.	PO Box 2420	Platte City	MO	64079	Don Haugland	816-431-2144	R	227	0.5
Capital Ford Inc.	4900 Capital Blvd	Raleigh	NC	27604	Tim Michaels	919-790-4600	R	224	0.3

Source: *Ward's Business Directory of U.S. Private and Public Companies*, 1998. The company type code used is as follows: P - Public, R - Private, S - Subsidiary, D - Division, J - Joint Venture, A - Affiliate, G - Group. Sales are in millions of dollars, employees are in thousands. An asterisk (*) indicates an estimated sales volume. The symbol < stands for 'less than'.

OCCUPATIONS EMPLOYED BY SIC 551 - MOTOR VEHICLE DEALERS

Occupation	% of Total 1996	Change to 2006	Occupation	% of Total 1996	Change to 2006
Salespersons, retail	22.4	8.3	Cashiers	2.3	2.9
Automotive mechanics	18.7	-8.5	Marketing, advertising, PR managers	2.2	-8.5
Sales & related workers nec	6.6	32.2	Truck drivers light & heavy	2.2	1.7
Vehicle washers & equipment cleaners	6.5	11.8	Clerical supervisors & managers	2.1	1.7
Marketing & sales worker supervisors	5.4	1.7	Secretaries, except legal & medical	1.7	-19.4
Automotive body & related repairers	5.0	1.7	Janitors & cleaners, maids	1.3	-18.7
General managers & top executives	4.4	-1.5	Stock clerks	1.2	135.0
General office clerks	4.4	-12.5	Billing, cost, & rate clerks	1.1	-8.5
Bookkeeping, accounting, & auditing clerks	4.2	-18.7	Dispatchers, ex police, fire, ambulance	1.1	1.7
Helpers, laborers nec	2.9	1.7			

Source: *Industry-Occupation Matrix*, Bureau of Labor Statistics. These data relate to one or more 3-digit SIC industry groups rather than to a single 4-digit SIC. The change reported for each occupation to the year 2006 is a percent of growth or decline as estimated by the Bureau of Labor Statistics. The abbreviation nec stands for 'not elsewhere classified'.

STATE AND REGIONAL CONCENTRATION

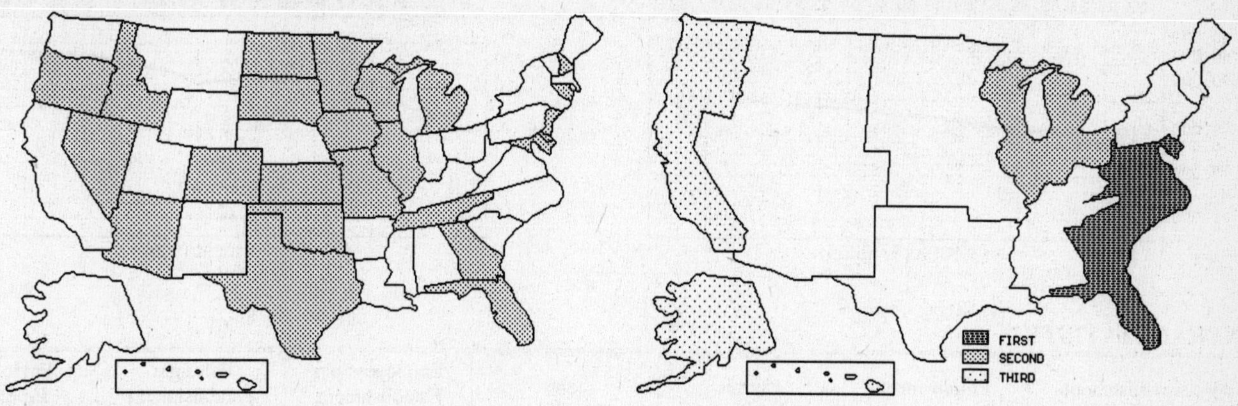

INDUSTRY DATA BY STATE

State	Establishments - 1995 Total (number)	Establishments - 1995 % of U.S.	Employment - 1995 Total (number)	Employment - 1995 % of U.S.	Employment - 1995 Per Estab.	Payroll - 1995 Total ($ mil.)	Payroll - 1995 Per Empl. ($)	Sales - 1992 Total ($ mil.)	Sales - 1992 % of U.S.	Sales - 1992 Per Estab ($)
California	2,012	8.3	98,199	9.9	49	3,642.6	37,094	36,420.2	10.9	402,936
Florida	1,044	4.3	62,194	6.3	60	2,139.1	34,394	25,324.1	7.6	487,350
Texas	1,391	5.7	72,757	7.3	52	2,529.1	34,760	25,086.1	7.5	412,960
New York	1,350	5.6	46,741	4.7	35	1,485.9	31,790	16,567.0	5.0	392,081
Illinois	1,202	5.0	45,238	4.6	38	1,522.5	33,656	16,283.0	4.9	405,241
Pennsylvania	1,476	6.1	50,662	5.1	34	1,438.2	28,388	15,587.5	4.7	341,846
Michigan	877	3.6	38,485	3.9	44	1,437.2	37,344	14,250.2	4.3	427,459
Ohio	1,101	4.5	45,330	4.6	41	1,362.5	30,057	14,218.7	4.3	363,734
New Jersey	764	3.2	29,764	3.0	39	1,058.5	35,562	11,726.9	3.5	453,443
Georgia	673	2.8	28,070	2.8	42	974.2	34,707	9,307.0	2.8	406,439
North Carolina	777	3.2	27,422	2.8	35	927.5	33,824	8,712.2	2.6	373,932
Virginia	598	2.5	28,721	2.9	48	911.8	31,746	8,304.4	2.5	346,621
Massachusetts	602	2.5	21,837	2.2	36	678.8	31,086	7,405.8	2.2	398,418
Indiana	586	2.4	22,398	2.3	38	683.2	30,503	7,268.5	2.2	372,918
Tennessee	485	2.0	21,849	2.2	45	743.0	34,006	7,250.7	2.2	398,937
Missouri	648	2.7	21,752	2.2	34	694.2	31,913	7,149.8	2.1	380,089
Wisconsin	635	2.6	21,893	2.2	34	609.2	27,825	6,998.1	2.1	358,087
Maryland	376	1.6	23,906	2.4	64	744.2	31,129	6,744.0	2.0	338,146
Minnesota	517	2.1	17,515	1.8	34	535.3	30,562	6,364.5	1.9	401,849
Washington	426	1.8	19,504	2.0	46	660.9	33,884	6,239.2	1.9	363,635
Arizona	260	1.1	17,514	1.8	67	625.0	35,687	5,148.3	1.5	372,039
Colorado	284	1.2	14,815	1.5	52	533.5	36,009	5,024.5	1.5	401,863
Louisiana	335	1.4	16,401	1.7	49	520.2	31,720	4,952.0	1.5	345,690
Alabama	386	1.6	14,426	1.5	37	445.1	30,851	4,929.1	1.5	390,205
Oklahoma	382	1.6	13,555	1.4	35	378.6	27,929	4,462.2	1.3	387,075
Connecticut	364	1.5	13,585	1.4	37	467.4	34,402	4,405.3	1.3	377,817
South Carolina	368	1.5	12,757	1.3	35	426.2	33,410	4,143.0	1.2	368,040
Oregon	315	1.3	12,969	1.3	41	425.9	32,837	4,022.5	1.2	356,798
Kentucky	416	1.7	14,342	1.4	34	390.2	27,205	4,011.7	1.2	329,202
Iowa	470	1.9	12,379	1.2	26	335.8	27,123	3,758.5	1.1	328,541
Kansas	335	1.4	10,637	1.1	32	320.6	30,136	3,366.1	1.0	362,331
Arkansas	310	1.3	8,320	0.8	27	239.9	28,829	3,047.9	0.9	406,933
Mississippi	253	1.0	8,166	0.8	32	258.8	31,688	2,457.4	0.7	339,331
Utah	178	0.7	7,190	0.7	40	221.2	30,760	2,154.4	0.6	360,637
Nebraska	239	1.0	6,183	0.6	26	181.0	29,268	1,992.8	0.6	335,658
West Virginia	240	1.0	6,965	0.7	29	170.1	24,428	1,962.8	0.6	309,256
Nevada	84	0.3	5,608	0.6	67	222.7	39,707	1,862.4	0.6	419,376
New Mexico	159	0.7	6,520	0.7	41	192.5	29,525	1,859.8	0.6	322,100
New Hampshire	176	0.7	5,894	0.6	33	187.7	31,853	1,763.5	0.5	360,714
Idaho	131	0.5	4,742	0.5	36	144.9	30,557	1,447.0	0.4	357,550
Maine	164	0.7	5,204	0.5	32	138.5	26,609	1,430.3	0.4	335,288
Hawaii	73	0.3	3,718	0.4	51	124.0	33,356	1,289.8	0.4	369,041
Montana	134	0.6	3,720	0.4	28	94.9	25,501	1,112.3	0.3	344,786
Delaware	71	0.3	3,685	0.4	52	111.1	30,143	1,061.7	0.3	345,703
South Dakota	121	0.5	3,689	0.4	30	96.1	26,040	995.5	0.3	340,456
North Dakota	121	0.5	3,380	0.3	28	86.6	25,630	967.2	0.3	332,949
Rhode Island	88	0.4	2,813	0.3	32	80.7	28,694	882.6	0.3	350,246
Vermont	102	0.4	2,650	0.3	26	69.9	26,369	760.5	0.2	331,936
Wyoming	80	0.3	2,215	0.2	28	60.7	27,412	622.3	0.2	316,215
Alaska	42	0.2	2,056	0.2	49	85.3	41,499	608.2	0.2	332,510
D.C.	9	0.0	432	0.0	48	12.8	29,572	91.5	0.0	205,256

Source: *County Business Patterns, 1995* and *Economic Census of the U.S., 1992*. Data are sorted by 1992 revenues and, if revenues are unavailable, by establishments in 1995. The symbol (D) indicates that data are withheld by the source to avoid disclosure of competitive information. A dash (-) indicates that data are not available or undisclosed because they do not meet statistical validity standards. Shaded *states* on the state map indicate those states which have proportionately greater representation in the industry than would be indicated by the state's population; the ratio is based on total revenues or number of establishments. Shaded *regions* indicate where the industry is regionally most concentrated.

5521 - USED CAR DEALERS

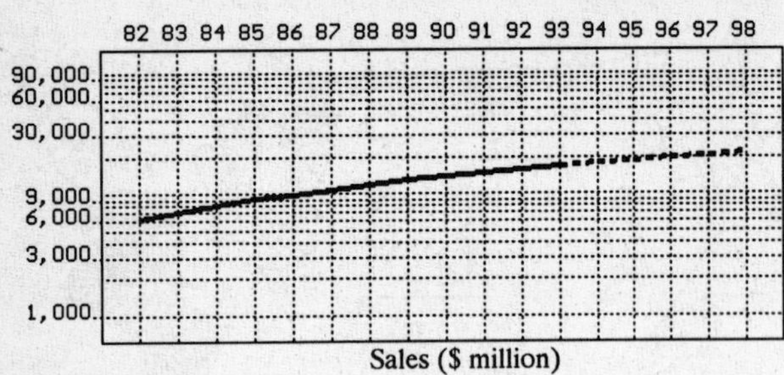

Sales ($ million)

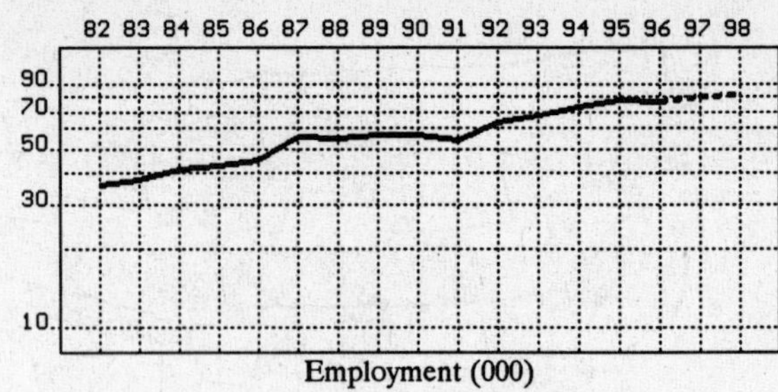

Employment (000)

GENERAL STATISTICS

Year	Establishments (number)	Employment (number)	Payroll ($ million)	Sales ($ million)	Employees per Establishment (number)	Sales per Establishment ($)	Payroll per Employee ($)
1982	12,299	36,103	449.6	6,273.1	3	510,046	12,453
1983	11,889	37,848	506.6	7,188.2*e*	3	-	13,385
1984	11,879	41,724	579.9	8,103.3*e*	4	-	13,898
1985	11,494	42,954	617.2	9,018.4*e*	4	-	14,370
1986	11,626	44,808	679.3	9,933.6*e*	4	-	15,160
1987	14,948	55,494	808.8	10,848.7	4	725,763	14,574
1988	13,781	54,407	899.4	11,885.2*e*	4	-	16,531
1989	14,819	56,888	950.0	12,921.8*e*	4	-	16,700
1990	14,283	56,125	968.9	13,958.3*e*	4	-	17,263
1991	14,656	53,952	962.1	14,994.8*e*	4	-	17,832
1992	18,672	62,793	1,131.8	16,031.3	3	858,577	18,025
1993	19,281	67,392	1,319.0	16,869.2*p*	3	-	19,572
1994	19,569	72,847	1,504.7	17,845.1*p*	4	-	20,656
1995	19,656	78,303	1,676.5	18,820.9*p*	4	-	21,411
1996	20,047*p*	76,714*p*	1,577.4*p*	19,796.7*p*	-	-	-
1997	20,731*p*	79,689*p*	1,663.4*p*	20,772.5*p*	-	-	-
1998	21,415*p*	82,664*p*	1,749.4*p*	21,748.4*p*	-	-	-

Sources: *Economic Census of the United States*, 1982, 1987, and 1992. Establishment counts, employment, and payroll are from *County Business Patterns* for non-Census years. Values followed by a 'p' are projections by the editors. Sales and expense data for non-Census years are extrapolations, marked by 'e'. Industries reclassified in 1987 will not have data for prior years. Data are the most recent available at this level of detail.

INDICES OF CHANGE

Year	Establishments (number)	Employment (number)	Payroll ($ million)	Sales ($ million)	Employees per Establishment (number)	Sales per Establishment ($)	Payroll per Employee ($)
1982	65.9	57.5	39.7	39.1	100.0	59.4	69.1
1983	63.7	60.3	44.8	44.8*e*	100.0	-	74.3
1984	63.6	66.4	51.2	50.5*e*	133.3	-	77.1
1985	61.6	68.4	54.5	56.3*e*	133.3	-	79.7
1986	62.3	71.4	60.0	62.0*e*	133.3	-	84.1
1987	80.1	88.4	71.5	67.7	133.3	84.5	80.9
1988	73.8	86.6	79.5	74.1*e*	133.3	-	91.7
1989	79.4	90.6	83.9	80.6*e*	133.3	-	92.6
1990	76.5	89.4	85.6	87.1*e*	133.3	-	95.8
1991	78.5	85.9	85.0	93.5*e*	133.3	-	98.9
1992	100.0	100.0	100.0	100.0	100.0	100.0	100.0
1993	103.3	107.3	116.5	105.2*p*	116.5	-	108.6
1994	104.8	116.0	133.0	111.3*p*	124.1	-	114.6
1995	105.3	124.7	148.1	117.4*p*	132.8	-	118.8
1996	107.4*p*	122.2*p*	139.4*p*	123.5*p*	-	-	-
1997	111.0*p*	126.9*p*	147.0*p*	129.6*p*	-	-	-
1998	114.7*p*	131.6*p*	154.6*p*	135.7*p*	-	-	-

Sources: Same as General Statistics. The values shown reflect change from the base year, 1992. Values above 100 mean greater than 1992, values below 100 mean less than 1992, and a value of 100 in the 1982-91 or 1993-98 period means same as 1992. Values followed by a 'p' are projections by the editors; 'e' stands for extrapolation. Data are the most recent available at this level of detail.

SELECTED RATIOS

For 1992	Avg. of All Retail	Analyzed Industry	Index	For 1992	Avg. of All Retail	Analyzed Industry	Index
Employees per Establishment	12	3	28	Sales per Employee	102,941	255,304	248
Payroll per Establishment	146,026	60,615	42	Sales per Establishment	1,241,555	858,574	69
Payroll per Employee	12,107	18,024	149	Expenses per Establishment	na	na	na

Sources: Same as General Statistics. The 'Average of All Manufacturing' column represents the average of all manufacturing industries reported for the most recent complete year available. The Index shows the relationship between the Average and the Analyzed Industry. For example, 100 means that they are equal; 500 that the Analyzed Industry is five times the average; 50 means that the Analyzed Industry is half the national average. The abbreviation 'na' is used to show that data are 'not available'.

LEADING COMPANIES

Number shown: **9** Total sales ($ mil): **962** Total employment (000): **3.2**

Company Name	Address				CEO Name	Phone	Co. Type	Sales ($ mil)	Empl. (000)
National Auto Credit Inc.	30000 Aurora Rd	Solon	OH	44139	Robert J Bronchetti	216-349-1000	P	452	0.4
Insurance Auto Auctions Inc.	850 E Algonquin	Axhaumburg	IL	60173	James P Alampi	84783939339	P	259	0.7
CarMax Inc.	4212 Pkace Court	Glen Allen	VA	23058	Austin Ligon	804-747-0422	P	66	1.7
David Taylor Cadillac Co.	PO Box 36428	Houston	TX	77236	David W Taylor	713-777-7151	R	61 *	0.2
Alan Young Buick-GMC Truck	7724 East Loop	Fort Worth	TX	76180	Alan J Young	817-589-3300	R	42	<0.1
Charles Clark Chevrolet Co.	PO Box 938	McAllen	TX	78502	Kirk A Clark	210-686-5441	R	33	0.1
Harvey Cadillac Co.	2600 28th St SE	Grand Rapids	MI	49512	HA Duthler	616-949-1140	R	28	<0.1
Elliff Motors Inc.	1307 W Harrison St	Harlingen	TX	78550	Larry Elliff	210-423-3434	R	11	<0.1
Edwin L. Cox Co.	2200 Ross Ave	Dallas	TX	75201	J Oliver McGonigle	214-220-3636	R	10 *	<0.1

Source: *Ward's Business Directory of U.S. Private and Public Companies*, 1998. The company type code used is as follows: P - Public, R - Private, S - Subsidiary, D - Division, J - Joint Venture, A - Affiliate, G - Group. Sales are in millions of dollars, employees are in thousands. An asterisk (*) indicates an estimated sales volume. The symbol < stands for 'less than'.

OCCUPATIONS EMPLOYED BY SIC 552 - MOTOR VEHICLE DEALERS

Occupation	% of Total 1996	Change to 2006	Occupation	% of Total 1996	Change to 2006
Salespersons, retail	22.4	8.3	Cashiers	2.3	2.9
Automotive mechanics	18.7	-8.5	Marketing, advertising, PR managers	2.2	-8.5
Sales & related workers nec	6.6	32.2	Truck drivers light & heavy	2.2	1.7
Vehicle washers & equipment cleaners	6.5	11.8	Clerical supervisors & managers	2.1	1.7
Marketing & sales worker supervisors	5.4	1.7	Secretaries, except legal & medical	1.7	-19.4
Automotive body & related repairers	5.0	1.7	Janitors & cleaners, maids	1.3	-18.7
General managers & top executives	4.4	-1.5	Stock clerks	1.2	135.0
General office clerks	4.4	-12.5	Billing, cost, & rate clerks	1.1	-8.5
Bookkeeping, accounting, & auditing clerks	4.2	-18.7	Dispatchers, ex police, fire, ambulance	1.1	1.7
Helpers, laborers nec	2.9	1.7			

Source: *Industry-Occupation Matrix*, Bureau of Labor Statistics. These data relate to one or more 3-digit SIC industry groups rather than to a single 4-digit SIC. The change reported for each occupation to the year 2006 is a percent of growth or decline as estimated by the Bureau of Labor Statistics. The abbreviation nec stands for 'not elsewhere classified'.

STATE AND REGIONAL CONCENTRATION

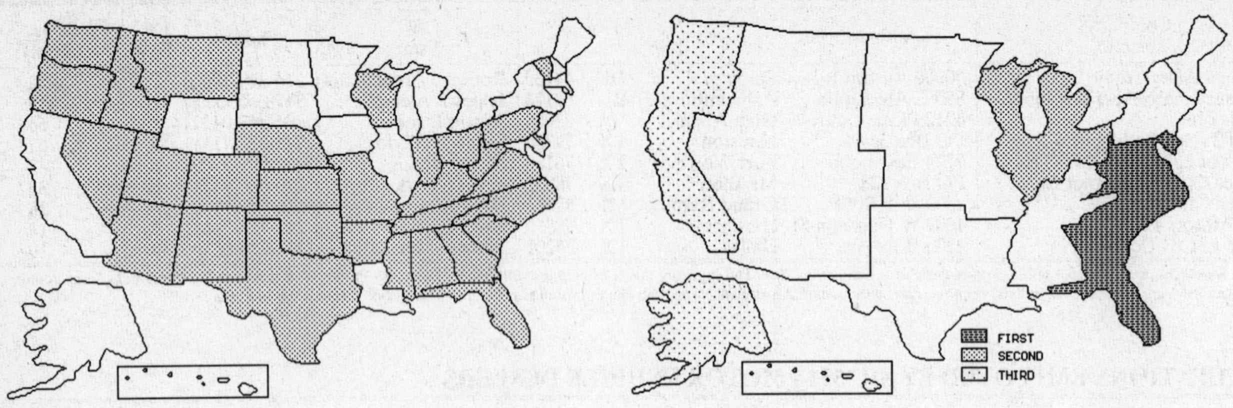

INDUSTRY DATA BY STATE

State	Establishments - 1995 Total (number)	Establishments - 1995 % of U.S.	Employment - 1995 Total (number)	Employment - 1995 % of U.S.	Employment - 1995 Per Estab.	Payroll - 1995 Total ($ mil.)	Payroll - 1995 Per Empl. ($)	Sales - 1992 Total ($ mil.)	Sales - 1992 % of U.S.	Sales - 1992 Per Estab ($)
Florida	1,340	6.8	5,847	7.5	4	131.5	22,490	1,402.0	8.8	278,391
Texas	1,671	8.5	6,839	8.7	4	147.4	21,555	1,327.9	8.4	235,491
California	1,018	5.2	4,690	6.0	5	109.8	23,404	1,133.4	7.1	295,923
Pennsylvania	877	4.5	3,436	4.4	4	70.1	20,404	768.1	4.8	258,892
Ohio	858	4.4	3,718	4.8	4	78.5	21,123	696.5	4.4	250,981
North Carolina	932	4.7	3,163	4.0	3	67.1	21,213	633.6	4.0	242,763
New York	892	4.5	2,624	3.4	3	52.7	20,096	629.8	4.0	260,240
Illinois	658	3.3	2,895	3.7	4	68.3	23,589	595.2	3.7	258,882
Indiana	721	3.7	2,906	3.7	4	57.7	19,853	507.8	3.2	258,168
Tennessee	664	3.4	2,176	2.8	3	43.1	19,806	493.0	3.1	282,662
Virginia	593	3.0	2,769	3.5	5	58.7	21,216	460.3	2.9	213,287
Michigan	497	2.5	1,876	2.4	4	40.5	21,594	451.0	2.8	283,479
Georgia	681	3.5	2,782	3.6	4	59.1	21,230	447.3	2.8	235,165
Missouri	551	2.8	2,048	2.6	4	44.2	21,595	401.6	2.5	272,274
Alabama	616	3.1	2,056	2.6	3	39.5	19,206	397.9	2.5	265,281
Wisconsin	488	2.5	1,919	2.5	4	38.1	19,847	384.8	2.4	249,194
Washington	406	2.1	1,826	2.3	4	45.7	25,033	373.7	2.4	231,706
Kentucky	402	2.0	1,833	2.3	5	33.1	18,061	351.2	2.2	243,349
Arizona	238	1.2	1,572	2.0	7	40.9	26,005	309.0	1.9	208,500
New Jersey	371	1.9	1,146	1.5	3	29.2	25,503	294.6	1.9	318,458
Colorado	294	1.5	1,513	1.9	5	38.1	25,167	281.4	1.8	249,434
Massachusetts	341	1.7	1,174	1.5	3	27.5	23,439	273.3	1.7	269,536
South Carolina	415	2.1	1,368	1.7	3	25.4	18,601	259.9	1.6	228,014
Arkansas	361	1.8	1,305	1.7	4	25.3	19,376	250.9	1.6	241,524
Oregon	210	1.1	999	1.3	5	25.5	25,545	241.7	1.5	297,627
Minnesota	241	1.2	897	1.1	4	18.5	20,672	215.5	1.4	297,223
Oklahoma	278	1.4	996	1.3	4	19.4	19,493	209.6	1.3	267,291
Kansas	237	1.2	969	1.2	4	20.5	21,128	196.3	1.2	260,676
Mississippi	331	1.7	1,040	1.3	3	18.3	17,563	193.8	1.2	240,126
Utah	148	0.8	1,169	1.5	8	26.4	22,550	188.7	1.2	325,907
Iowa	278	1.4	933	1.2	3	15.9	17,043	158.2	1.0	219,786
Maryland	203	1.0	772	1.0	4	16.8	21,780	157.5	1.0	232,708
Nebraska	186	0.9	790	1.0	4	15.2	19,247	146.8	0.9	242,666
Connecticut	165	0.8	642	0.8	4	17.6	27,403	135.4	0.9	236,300
Idaho	107	0.5	496	0.6	5	11.0	22,274	128.4	0.8	285,340
West Virginia	215	1.1	662	0.8	3	9.5	14,356	119.4	0.8	252,338
New Mexico	145	0.7	532	0.7	4	10.2	19,180	106.1	0.7	229,595
Nevada	96	0.5	504	0.6	5	11.5	22,861	87.3	0.5	217,082
Maine	130	0.7	421	0.5	3	7.3	17,349	71.0	0.4	224,835
New Hampshire	106	0.5	409	0.5	4	9.4	22,902	66.6	0.4	247,483
Montana	81	0.4	365	0.5	5	5.9	16,099	63.6	0.4	217,894
Delaware	61	0.3	336	0.4	6	9.3	27,670	48.6	0.3	184,227
Rhode Island	82	0.4	191	0.2	2	3.9	20,518	43.9	0.3	255,081
South Dakota	58	0.3	232	0.3	4	4.8	20,517	42.9	0.3	248,162
Vermont	67	0.3	251	0.3	4	5.1	20,163	42.4	0.3	191,796
North Dakota	49	0.2	206	0.3	4	3.3	15,816	29.7	0.2	233,953
Hawaii	19	0.1	106	0.1	6	3.3	31,453	26.5	0.2	215,325
Wyoming	31	0.2	20-99	-	-	(D)	-	14.1	0.1	230,852
Alaska	14	0.1	45	0.1	3	1.8	41,067	13.2	0.1	307,907
Louisiana	219	1.1	757	1.0	3	12.8	16,863	(D)	-	-
D.C.	14	0.1	20-99	-	-	(D)	-	(D)	-	-

Source: County Business Patterns, 1995 and *Economic Census of the U.S., 1992*. Data are sorted by 1992 revenues and, if revenues are unavailable, by establishments in 1995. The symbol (D) indicates that data are withheld by the source to avoid disclosure of competitive information. A dash (-) indicates that data are not available or undisclosed because they do not meet statistical validity standards. Shaded *states* on the state map indicate those states which have proportionately greater representation in the industry than would be indicated by the state's population; the ratio is based on total revenues or number of establishments. Shaded *regions* indicate where the industry is regionally most concentrated.

5531 - AUTO AND HOME SUPPLY STORES

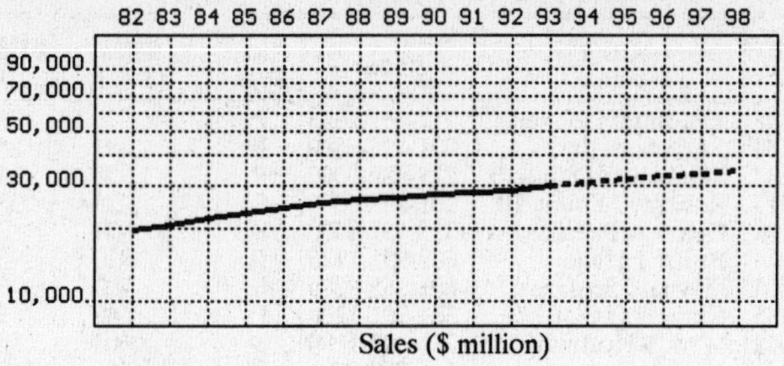

Sales ($ million)

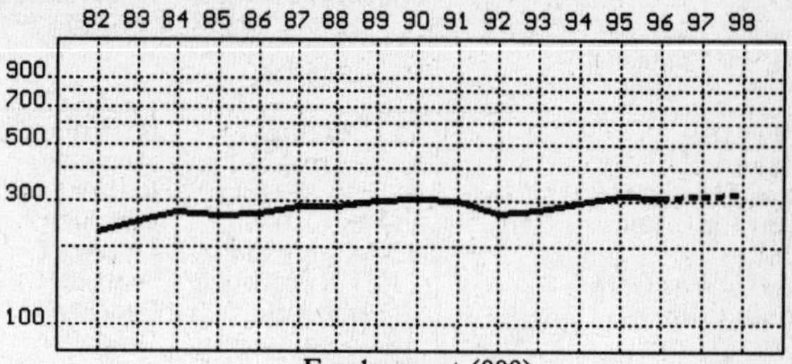

Employment (000)

GENERAL STATISTICS

Year	Establishments (number)	Employment (number)	Payroll ($ million)	Sales ($ million)	Employees per Establishment (number)	Sales per Establishment ($)	Payroll per Employee ($)
1982	40,896	229,139	3,072.3	19,638.2	6	480,200	13,408
1983	43,361	250,663	3,575.1	20,802.6e	6	-	14,263
1984	43,796	273,498	3,891.3	21,967.1e	6	-	14,228
1985	41,232	263,692	3,892.6	23,131.5e	6	-	14,762
1986	41,985	271,328	4,236.8	24,295.9e	6	-	15,615
1987	46,207	286,155	4,151.9	25,460.3	6	551,005	14,509
1988	44,157	286,940	4,482.7	26,081.3e	7	-	15,623
1989	44,240	297,531	4,868.7	26,702.3e	7	-	16,364
1990	43,370	304,567	5,143.1	27,323.3e	7	-	16,886
1991	43,684	298,668	5,237.7	27,944.3e	7	-	17,537
1992	41,308	269,069	4,683.1	28,565.3	7	691,520	17,405
1993	41,059	275,576	5,021.1	30,075.5p	7	-	18,220
1994	41,338	294,733	5,468.7	30,968.2p	7	-	18,555
1995	42,634	317,952	6,056.7	31,860.9p	7	-	19,049
1996	42,414p	311,254p	5,935.4p	32,753.6p	-	-	-
1997	42,362p	315,426p	6,119.3p	33,646.3p	-	-	-
1998	42,310p	319,598p	6,303.3p	34,539.0p	-	-	-

Sources: *Economic Census of the United States*, 1982, 1987, and 1992. Establishment counts, employment, and payroll are from *County Business Patterns* for non-Census years. Values followed by a 'p' are projections by the editors. Sales and expense data for non-Census years are extrapolations, marked by 'e'. Industries reclassified in 1987 will not have data for prior years. Data are the most recent available at this level of detail.

INDICES OF CHANGE

Year	Establishments (number)	Employment (number)	Payroll ($ million)	Sales ($ million)	Employees per Establishment (number)	Sales per Establishment ($)	Payroll per Employee ($)
1982	99.0	85.2	65.6	68.7	85.7	69.4	77.0
1983	105.0	93.2	76.3	72.8e	85.7	-	81.9
1984	106.0	101.6	83.1	76.9e	85.7	-	81.7
1985	99.8	98.0	83.1	81.0e	85.7	-	84.8
1986	101.6	100.8	90.5	85.1e	85.7	-	89.7
1987	111.9	106.4	88.7	89.1	85.7	79.7	83.4
1988	106.9	106.6	95.7	91.3e	100.0	-	89.8
1989	107.1	110.6	104.0	93.5e	100.0	-	94.0
1990	105.0	113.2	109.8	95.7e	100.0	-	97.0
1991	105.8	111.0	111.8	97.8e	100.0	-	100.8
1992	100.0	100.0	100.0	100.0	100.0	100.0	100.0
1993	99.4	102.4	107.2	105.3p	95.9	-	104.7
1994	100.1	109.5	116.8	108.4p	101.9	-	106.6
1995	103.2	118.2	129.3	111.5p	106.5	-	109.4
1996	102.7p	115.7p	126.7p	114.7p	-	-	-
1997	102.6p	117.2p	130.7p	117.8p	-	-	-
1998	102.4p	118.8p	134.6p	120.9p	-	-	-

Sources: Same as General Statistics. The values shown reflect change from the base year, 1992. Values above 100 mean greater than 1992, values below 100 mean less than 1992, and a value of 100 in the 1982-91 or 1993-98 period means same as 1992. Values followed by a 'p' are projections by the editors; 'e' stands for extrapolation. Data are the most recent available at this level of detail.

SELECTED RATIOS

For 1992	Avg. of All Retail	Analyzed Industry	Index	For 1992	Avg. of All Retail	Analyzed Industry	Index
Employees per Establishment	12	7	54	Sales per Employee	102,941	106,163	103
Payroll per Establishment	146,026	113,370	78	Sales per Establishment	1,241,555	691,520	56
Payroll per Employee	12,107	17,405	144	Expenses per Establishment	na	na	na

Sources: Same as General Statistics. The 'Average of All Manufacturing' column represents the average of all manufacturing industries reported for the most recent complete year available. The Index shows the relationship between the Average and the Analyzed Industry. For example, 100 means that they are equal; 500 that the Analyzed Industry is five times the average; 50 means that the Analyzed Industry is half the national average. The abbreviation 'na' is used to show that data are 'not available'.

LEADING COMPANIES

Number shown: **50** Total sales ($ mil): **23,870** Total employment (000): **218.8**

Company Name	Address				CEO Name	Phone	Co. Type	Sales ($ mil)	Empl. (000)
Rite Aid Corp.	PO Box 3165	Harrisburg	PA	17105	Timothy J Noonan	717-761-2633	P	6,970	73.0
AutoZone Inc.	123 S Front St	Memphis	TN	38103	J C Adams Jr	901-495-6500	P	2,691	28.7
Pep Boys-Manny, Moe and Jack	3111 W Allegheny	Philadelphia	PA	19132	Mitchell G Leibovitz	215-229-9000	P	1,828	17.6
Arkansas Best Holdings Corp.	PO Box 10048	Fort Smith	AR	72917	Robert A Young III	501-785-6000	S	1,225 •	13.1
Fay's Inc.	7245 Henry Clay	Liverpool	NY	13088	Henry A Panasci Jr	315-451-8000	S	974	9.0
Reinalt-Thomas Corp.	14631 N Scottsdale	Scottsdale	AZ	85254	Bruce T Halle	602-951-1938	R	810 •	5.0
CSK Auto Corp.	PO Box 6030	Phoenix	AZ	85005	Maynard Jenkins	602-265-9200	S	793	9.6
Dart Group Corp.	3300 75th Ave	Landover	MD	20785	Herbert H Haft	301-731-1200	P	668	7.3
A.P.S. Inc.	15710 J F Kennedy	Houston	TX	77032	Mark S Hoffman	713-507-1100	S	604	6.8
Quality Stores Inc.	PO Box 3315	Muskegon	MI	49443	Al Fansler	616-798-8787	R	556 •	3.3
Chief Auto Parts Inc.	5400 LBJ Fwy	Dallas	TX	75240	David Eisenberg	972-404-1114	R	500	5.5
Carlos R. Leffler Inc.	PO Box 278	Richland	PA	17087	Patrick Castagna	717-866-2105	R	450 •	1.0
Discount Auto Parts Inc.	4900 Frontage Rd S	Lakeland	FL	33815	Peter J Fontaine	941-687-9226	P	405	3.7
Les Schwab Warehouse Center	PO Box 667	Prineville	OR	97754	G Phil Wick	503-447-4136	R	352	2.2
Cutter Automotive Team Inc.	1311 Kapiolana	Honolulu	HI	96814	Nick Cutter	808-592-5401	R	320 •	0.9
Dunlap and Kyle Company Inc.	PO Box 720	Batesville	MS	38606	Robert H Dunlap	601-563-7601	R	280	0.7
Brad Ragan Inc.	PO 240587	Charlotte	NC	28224	Michael R Thomann	704-521-2100	P	252	1.8
Advance Stores Company Inc.	PO Box 2710	Roanoke	VA	24001	Garnett Smith	703-345-4911	R	250 •	4.0
Merchants Inc.	9073 Euclid Ave	Manassas	VA	20110	James L Matthews	703-368-3171	R	250	1.8
Hi-Lo Automotive Inc.	2575 W Bellfort	Houston	TX	77054	T Michael Young	713-663-6700	P	249	2.6
Rao Corp.	6031 Joy Rd	Detroit	MI	48204	Duane T Rao	313-895-1200	R	225	0.5
O'Reilly Automotive Inc.	233 S Patterson	Springfield	MO	65802	David E O'Reilly	417-862-6708	P	201	2.6
PACCAR Automotive Inc.	1400 N 4th St	Renton	WA	98055	Marc Graham	425-251-7600	S	186	2.1
Treadco Inc.	PO Box 48	Fort Smith	AR	72901	John R Meyers	501-785-6000	P	161	0.9
Ewald Automotive Group Inc.	2201 N Mayfair Rd	Milwaukee	WI	53226	Craig A Ewald	414-258-5000	R	150	0.3
Oliver and Winston Inc.	900 W Alameda	Burbank	CA	91506	Thomas J Bonburg	818-843-7311	R	150	1.5
Linox Gas Tech Inc.	12000 Roosevelt Rd	Hillside	IL	60162	Carl Kock	708-449-9300	R	130	0.1
Schuck's Auto Supply	2402 R St, NW	Auburn	WA	98001	Tim Goddard	253-833-1115	D	130	1.2
Terry Schulte Automotive Inc.	PO Drawer P	Sioux Falls	SD	57101	Terry Schulte	605-336-1700	R	130	0.2
WSR Corp.	9A Brick Plant Rd	South River	NJ	08882	Terry Patterson	908-390-9000	R	130 •	1.2
Tyler Corp.	2121 San Jacinto St	Dallas	TX	75201	Bruce W Wilkinson	214-754-7800	P	128	1.1
District Petroleum Products	1832 Milan Ave	Sandusky	OH	44870	Scott Stipp	419-625-8373	R	120 •	0.3
Warshawsky and Co.	1104 S Wabash Ave	Chicago	IL	60605	Gary Revansek	312-431-6000	R	120 •	0.7
Strafco Inc.	PO Box 600	San Antonio	TX	78292	Jack D Trawick	210-226-0101	R	113	1.1
Replacement Parts Inc.	1901 E Roosevelt	Little Rock	AR	72206	Bill Kuykendall	501-375-1215	R	103	0.5
ADAP Inc.	660 Bodwell St	Avon	MA	02322	Wayne Yodzio	508-587-8400	S	100 •	1.0
Champion Auto Stores Inc.	9353 Jefferson Hwy	Maple Grove	MN	55369	Gary D Bebeau	612-391-6655	R	100	0.9
GCR Truck Tire Centers Inc.	500 Capital Texas	Austin	TX	78746	EC Wagner	512-328-3446	S	100	0.4
Martin Cadillac Company Inc.	12101 W Olympic	Los Angeles	CA	90064	Dana R Martin	310-820-3611	R	98	0.2
Schierl Cos.	2201 Madison St	Stevens Point	WI	54481	William Schierl	715-345-5060	R	95 •	0.4
Somerset Tire Service Inc.	400 W Main St	Bound Brook	NJ	08805	JE Hannon	908-356-8500	R	95	0.5
Autoworks Inc.	415 W Main St	Rochester	NY	14608	Mike Futerman	716-235-1595	S	94	1.4
Dick Strauss Ford Inc.	10601 Midlothian	Richmond	VA	23235	Richard E Strauss	804-794-0500	R	88	0.2
Capitol Chevrolet Inc.	711 Eastern Blvd	Montgomery	AL	36117	F E McGough Jr	205-272-8700	R	80	0.2
T.O. Haas Tire Company Inc.	PO Box 81067	Lincoln	NE	68501	Randall Haas	402-473-1415	S	80	0.3
Frank Hurling Chevrolet Inc.	2449 Fulton Ave	Sacramento	CA	95825	M D Daugherty	916-482-1600	R	72	0.2
Gwatney Chevrolet Inc.	2000 Covington Pk	Memphis	TN	38128	Russell Gwatney	901-387-2000	S	67 •	0.1
Peerless Tyre Co.	4705 Paris St	Denver	CO	80239	Samuel E Forbes	303-371-4300	R	66	0.3
Big 10 Tire Co.	1000 Hillcrest Rd	Mobile	AL	36695	Donald Kennemer	205-639-0692	R	65 •	0.6
Big Wheel-Rossi Auto Stores	2300 Pilot Knob Rd	Mendota H.	MN	55120	Richard Shaller	612-452-7484	R	65 •	0.6

Source: *Ward's Business Directory of U.S. Private and Public Companies*, 1998. The company type code used is as follows: P - Public, R - Private, S - Subsidiary, D - Division, J - Joint Venture, A - Affiliate, G - Group. Sales are in millions of dollars, employees are in thousands. An asterisk (*) indicates an estimated sales volume. The symbol < stands for 'less than'.

OCCUPATIONS EMPLOYED BY SIC 553 - AUTO AND HOME SUPPLY STORES

Occupation	% of Total 1996	Change to 2006	Occupation	% of Total 1996	Change to 2006
Sales & related workers nec	18.9	24.1	Truck drivers light & heavy	5.3	24.1
Automotive mechanics	14.9	14.6	Bookkeeping, accounting, & auditing clerks	3.1	-23.6
Tire repairers & changers	14.2	5.0	Blue collar worker supervisors	2.6	-7.8
Salespersons, retail	9.7	1.7	Stock clerks	2.4	116.6
Marketing & sales worker supervisors	8.4	-4.5	General office clerks	2.2	-17.8
General managers & top executives	6.6	-7.5	Clerical supervisors & managers	1.1	-4.5
Cashiers	5.5	-3.4			

Source: *Industry-Occupation Matrix*, Bureau of Labor Statistics. These data relate to one or more 3-digit SIC industry groups rather than to a single 4-digit SIC. The change reported for each occupation to the year 2006 is a percent of growth or decline as estimated by the Bureau of Labor Statistics. The abbreviation nec stands for 'not elsewhere classified'.

STATE AND REGIONAL CONCENTRATION

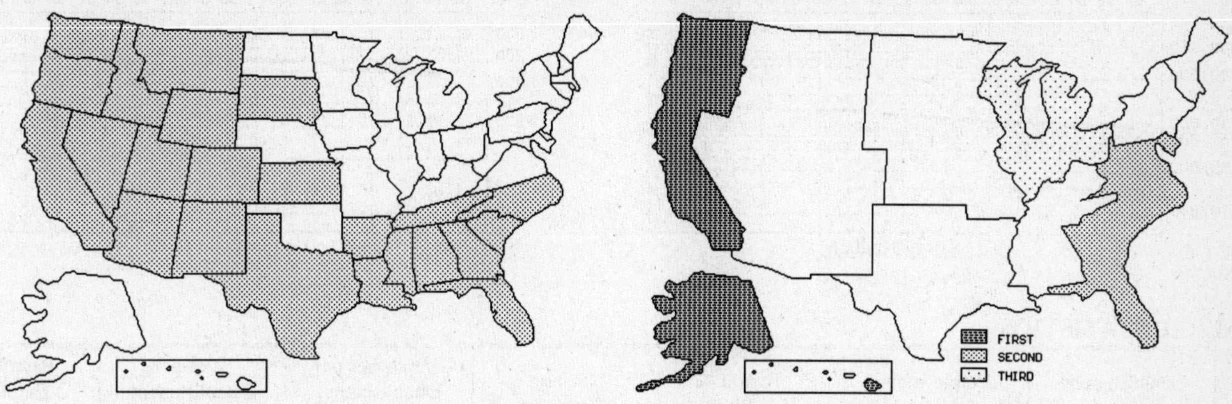

INDUSTRY DATA BY STATE

State	Establishments - 1995		Employment - 1995			Payroll - 1995		Sales - 1992		
	Total (number)	% of U.S.	Total (number)	% of U.S.	Per Estab.	Total ($ mil.)	Per Empl. ($)	Total ($ mil.)	% of U.S.	Per Estab ($)
California	4,708	11.0	38,822	12.2	8	722.2	18,602	3,940.5	13.8	113,959
Texas	3,580	8.4	28,393	8.9	8	514.1	18,108	2,559.1	9.0	103,525
Florida	2,563	6.0	17,775	5.6	7	345.8	19,455	1,628.4	5.7	102,533
Ohio	1,735	4.1	12,818	4.0	7	245.2	19,130	1,144.3	4.0	105,866
New York	1,591	3.7	11,326	3.6	7	228.6	20,182	1,136.3	4.0	112,842
Michigan	1,396	3.3	10,494	3.3	8	206.4	19,668	1,035.8	3.6	109,462
Illinois	1,358	3.2	11,369	3.6	8	213.8	18,808	1,018.9	3.6	109,305
Pennsylvania	1,537	3.6	13,986	4.4	9	261.6	18,702	1,005.9	3.5	108,169
North Carolina	1,631	3.8	11,586	3.6	7	217.2	18,743	939.3	3.3	97,121
Georgia	1,610	3.8	11,488	3.6	7	227.3	19,784	914.7	3.2	104,979
Washington	1,020	2.4	7,609	2.4	7	171.5	22,543	773.5	2.7	113,012
Tennessee	1,104	2.6	7,628	2.4	7	146.9	19,258	678.2	2.4	106,336
Virginia	1,088	2.6	8,240	2.6	8	153.0	18,567	671.9	2.4	96,418
New Jersey	869	2.0	6,379	2.0	7	140.9	22,089	659.3	2.3	113,037
Alabama	1,192	2.8	7,696	2.4	6	139.3	18,104	615.7	2.2	99,668
Indiana	987	2.3	7,278	2.3	7	137.5	18,899	609.3	2.1	93,703
Arizona	725	1.7	6,719	2.1	9	124.4	18,507	579.1	2.0	105,310
Missouri	988	2.3	6,687	2.1	7	122.6	18,338	528.9	1.9	95,375
Louisiana	776	1.8	5,492	1.7	7	99.5	18,125	496.8	1.7	96,654
Oregon	574	1.3	4,871	1.5	8	112.2	23,025	476.3	1.7	121,590
Maryland	608	1.4	5,118	1.6	8	99.4	19,423	473.4	1.7	100,694
South Carolina	858	2.0	5,597	1.8	7	98.3	17,558	467.0	1.6	95,335
Wisconsin	502	1.2	5,115	1.6	10	88.2	17,247	458.5	1.6	123,442
Colorado	685	1.6	5,191	1.6	8	106.4	20,503	440.6	1.5	106,672
Massachusetts	603	1.4	4,360	1.4	7	91.1	20,898	428.1	1.5	113,895
Kentucky	869	2.0	5,218	1.6	6	90.2	17,279	419.3	1.5	97,252
Minnesota	634	1.5	4,764	1.5	8	90.0	18,894	386.4	1.4	97,020
Mississippi	762	1.8	4,537	1.4	6	78.8	17,359	374.6	1.3	101,136
Oklahoma	707	1.7	4,157	1.3	6	74.0	17,799	355.3	1.2	92,849
Connecticut	403	0.9	2,829	0.9	7	68.2	24,123	321.7	1.1	121,436
Iowa	518	1.2	3,469	1.1	7	63.5	18,295	289.7	1.0	100,816
Kansas	529	1.2	3,337	1.0	6	61.7	18,490	287.1	1.0	99,118
Arkansas	596	1.4	3,290	1.0	6	56.1	17,053	277.9	1.0	102,733
Utah	316	0.7	2,758	0.9	9	49.2	17,835	232.9	0.8	101,477
New Mexico	325	0.8	2,604	0.8	8	45.6	17,495	229.4	0.8	101,711
Idaho	275	0.6	1,977	0.6	7	40.8	20,616	195.0	0.7	121,254
West Virginia	373	0.9	2,354	0.7	6	37.2	15,801	181.5	0.6	106,397
Nevada	230	0.5	2,082	0.7	9	40.7	19,529	177.5	0.6	124,741
Nebraska	316	0.7	2,017	0.6	6	36.3	17,998	157.1	0.5	96,711
Maine	202	0.5	1,364	0.4	7	24.7	18,085	134.8	0.5	121,307
Hawaii	158	0.4	1,071	0.3	7	27.2	25,414	131.4	0.5	122,083
Montana	220	0.5	1,433	0.5	7	27.1	18,913	108.5	0.4	119,609
New Hampshire	142	0.3	1,073	0.3	8	23.1	21,525	98.3	0.3	124,690
South Dakota	152	0.4	970	0.3	6	18.9	19,444	89.2	0.3	125,102
Rhode Island	121	0.3	1,050	0.3	9	17.5	16,624	88.9	0.3	98,768
Delaware	86	0.2	746	0.2	9	15.0	20,131	79.7	0.3	121,306
North Dakota	111	0.3	832	0.3	7	15.6	18,748	69.8	0.2	100,572
Wyoming	128	0.3	780	0.2	6	14.8	18,912	67.1	0.2	106,979
Alaska	71	0.2	551	0.2	8	14.7	26,664	65.4	0.2	127,902
Vermont	82	0.2	465	0.1	6	9.7	20,798	44.8	0.2	110,362
D.C.	20	0.0	187	0.1	9	3.1	16,449	22.2	0.1	79,211

Source: County Business Patterns, 1995 and *Economic Census of the U.S., 1992*. Data are sorted by 1992 revenues and, if revenues are unavailable, by establishments in 1995. The symbol (D) indicates that data are withheld by the source to avoid disclosure of competitive information. A dash (-) indicates that data are not available or undisclosed because they do not meet statistical validity standards. Shaded *states* on the state map indicate those states which have proportionately greater representation in the industry than would be indicated by the state's population; the ratio is based on total revenues or number of establishments. Shaded *regions* indicate where the industry is regionally most concentrated.

5541 - GASOLINE SERVICE STATIONS

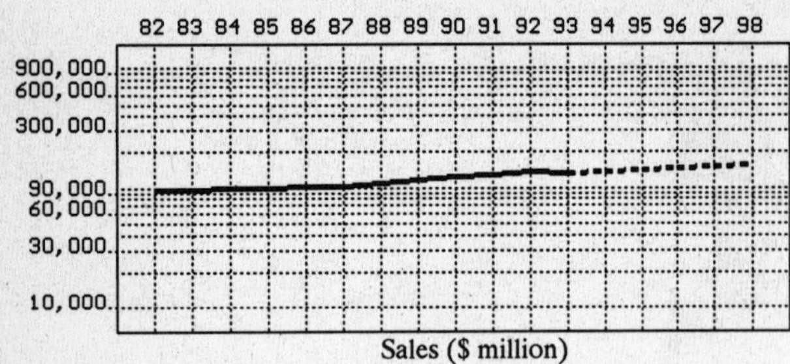

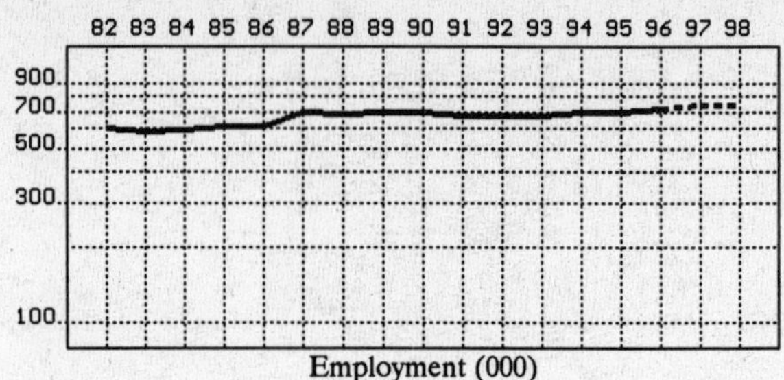

GENERAL STATISTICS

Year	Establishments (number)	Employment (number)	Payroll ($ million)	Sales ($ million)	Employees per Establishment (number)	Sales per Establishment ($)	Payroll per Employee ($)
1982	126,688	603,886	4,768.5	94,718.7	5	747,653	7,896
1983	118,445	575,574	5,006.7	96,174.4 *e*	5	-	8,699
1984	111,950	589,743	5,286.4	97,630.2 *e*	5	-	8,964
1985	105,787	608,794	5,655.8	99,085.9 *e*	6	-	9,290
1986	103,936	613,672	5,932.0	100,541.7 *e*	6	-	9,666
1987	114,748	701,690	6,413.7	101,997.4	6	888,882	9,140
1988	108,107	683,416	7,001.9	108,539.0 *e*	6	-	10,245
1989	105,767	699,348	7,274.8	115,080.6 *e*	7	-	10,402
1990	104,801	700,756	7,510.1	121,622.2 *e*	7	-	10,717
1991	101,894	674,035	7,492.9	128,163.8 *e*	7	-	11,116
1992	105,334	675,080	7,569.1	134,705.4	6	1,278,840	11,212
1993	101,383	671,870	7,887.3	132,924.7 *p*	7	-	11,739
1994	99,250	692,240	8,271.7	136,923.3 *p*	7	-	11,949
1995	97,448	701,917	8,673.0	140,922.0 *p*	7	-	12,356
1996	95,474 *p*	723,757 *p*	8,990.1 *p*	144,920.7 *p*	-	-	-
1997	93,865 *p*	732,715 *p*	9,286.5 *p*	148,919.4 *p*	-	-	-
1998	92,256 *p*	741,672 *p*	9,582.8 *p*	152,918.0 *p*	-	-	-

Sources: *Economic Census of the United States*, 1982, 1987, and 1992. Establishment counts, employment, and payroll are from *County Business Patterns* for non-Census years. Values followed by a 'p' are projections by the editors. Sales and expense data for non-Census years are extrapolations, marked by 'e'. Industries reclassified in 1987 will not have data for prior years. Data are the most recent available at this level of detail.

INDICES OF CHANGE

Year	Establishments (number)	Employment (number)	Payroll ($ million)	Sales ($ million)	Employees per Establishment (number)	Sales per Establishment ($)	Payroll per Employee ($)
1982	120.3	89.5	63.0	70.3	83.3	58.5	70.4
1983	112.4	85.3	66.1	71.4 *e*	83.3	-	77.6
1984	106.3	87.4	69.8	72.5 *e*	83.3	-	80.0
1985	100.4	90.2	74.7	73.6 *e*	100.0	-	82.9
1986	98.7	90.9	78.4	74.6 *e*	100.0	-	86.2
1987	108.9	103.9	84.7	75.7	100.0	69.5	81.5
1988	102.6	101.2	92.5	80.6 *e*	100.0	-	91.4
1989	100.4	103.6	96.1	85.4 *e*	116.7	-	92.8
1990	99.5	103.8	99.2	90.3 *e*	116.7	-	95.6
1991	96.7	99.8	99.0	95.1 *e*	116.7	-	99.1
1992	100.0	100.0	100.0	100.0	100.0	100.0	100.0
1993	96.2	99.5	104.2	98.7 *p*	110.5	-	104.7
1994	94.2	102.5	109.3	101.6 *p*	116.2	-	106.6
1995	92.5	104.0	114.6	104.6 *p*	120.0	-	110.2
1996	90.6 *p*	107.2 *p*	118.8 *p*	107.6 *p*	-	-	-
1997	89.1 *p*	108.5 *p*	122.7 *p*	110.6 *p*	-	-	-
1998	87.6 *p*	109.9 *p*	126.6 *p*	113.5 *p*	-	-	-

Sources: Same as General Statistics. The values shown reflect change from the base year, 1992. Values above 100 mean greater than 1992, values below 100 mean less than 1992, and a value of 100 in the 1982-91 or 1993-98 period means same as 1992. Values followed by a 'p' are projections by the editors; 'e' stands for extrapolation. Data are the most recent available at this level of detail.

SELECTED RATIOS

For 1992	Avg. of All Retail	Analyzed Industry	Index	For 1992	Avg. of All Retail	Analyzed Industry	Index
Employees per Establishment	12	6	53	Sales per Employee	102,941	199,540	194
Payroll per Establishment	146,026	71,858	49	Sales per Establishment	1,241,555	1,278,841	103
Payroll per Employee	12,107	11,212	93	Expenses per Establishment	na	na	na

Sources: Same as General Statistics. The 'Average of All Manufacturing' column represents the average of all manufacturing industries reported for the most recent complete year available. The Index shows the relationship between the Average and the Analyzed Industry. For example, 100 means that they are equal; 500 that the Analyzed Industry is five times the average; 50 means that the Analyzed Industry is half the national average. The abbreviation 'na' is used to show that data are 'not available'.

LEADING COMPANIES

Number shown: **50** Total sales ($ mil): **187,528** Total employment (000): **319.1**

Company Name	Address				CEO Name	Phone	Co. Type	Sales ($ mil)	Empl. (000)
Texaco Inc.	2000 Westchester	White Plains	NY	10650	Peter I Bijur	914-253-4000	P	46,667	29.3
Amoco Co.	200 E Randolph St	Chicago	IL	60601	Frederick S Addy	312-856-3200	S	25,698	38.6
Mobil Oil Corp. U.S.	3225 Gallows Rd	Fairfax	VA	22037	JL Cooper	703-849-3000	D	14,041	11.1
USX-Marathon Group	PO Box 3128	Houston	TX	77253	Victor G Beghini	713-629-6600	P	13,871	20.5
CITGO Petroleum Corp.	PO Box 3758	Tulsa	OK	74102	David J Tippeconnic	918-495-4000	S	13,645	5.2
BP America Inc.	200 Public Sq	Cleveland	OH	44114	Steve Percy	216-586-4141	S	11,550 •	12.7
Ultramar Diamond Shamrock	6000 N Loop 1604	San Antonio	TX	78249	R R Hemminghaus	210-592-2000	P	10,882	23.0
Tosco Corp.	72 Cummings Pt Rd	Stamford	CT	06902	Thomas D O'Malley	203-977-1000	P	9,923	24.3
ARCO Products Co.	333 S Hope St	Los Angeles	CA	90071	Roger E Truitt	213-486-3511	D	6,856	3.1
Emro Marketing Co.	PO Box 1500	Springfield	OH	45501	Riad N Yammine	513-864-3000	S	5,143 •	24.0
Circle K Corp.	PO Box 52084	Phoenix	AZ	85072	John F Antioco	602-437-0600	S	3,563	20.5
Pilot Corp.	PO Box 10146	Knoxville	TN	37939	James A Haslam III	423-588-7487	R	2,000	6.8
Crown Central Petroleum Corp.	PO Box 1168	Baltimore	MD	21203	H A Rosenberg Jr	410-539-7400	P	1,603	2.9
Racetrac Petroleum Inc.	300 Technology Ct	Smyrna	GA	30082	Carl E Bolch Jr	770-431-7600	R	1,600	3.0
Cumberland Farms Inc.	777 Dedham St	Canton	MA	02021	Lilly H Bentas	718-828-4900	R	1,469	7.1
Ultramar Inc.	111 W Ocean Blvd	Long Beach	CA	90802	Joel Mascitelli	310-495-5300	S	1,258	1.9
Jitney-Jungle Stores of America	4315 Industrial Dr	Jackson	MS	39209	Ronald E Johnson	601-965-8600	R	1,228	10.6
Casey's General Stores Inc.	1 Convenience Blvd	Ankeny	IA	50021	Ronald M Lamb	515-965-6100	P	1,114	9.5
Truckstops of America Inc.	24601 Ctr Ridge Rd	Westlake	OH	44145	Ed Kuhn	440-808-9100	S	1,067 •	5.0
Flying J Inc.	PO Box 678	Brigham City	UT	84302	J Phillip Adams	801-734-6400	R	1,030 •	7.0
Valvoline Co.	PO Box 14000	Lexington	KY	40512	James J O'Brien	606-357-7777	D	1,001	3.5
United Refining Co.	15 Bradley St	Warren	PA	16365	John A Catsimatidis	814-723-1500	R	871	1.7
E-Z Serve Corp.	2550 N Loop West	Houston	TX	77092	Neil H McLaurin	713-684-4300	P	744	3.6
Thrifty Oil Co.	10000 Lakewood	Downey	CA	90240	Ted Orden	310-923-9876	R	710	1.0
Kiel Brothers Oil Company Inc.	PO Box 344	Columbus	IN	47202	T Kiel	812-372-3751	R	640 •	1.3
Petro Stopping Centers L.P.	PO Box 26808	El Paso	TX	79926	James Cardwell Sr	915-779-4711	R	640 •	3.0
Dairy Mart Convenience Stores	210 Broadway E	Cuyahoga Falls	OH	44222	Robert B Stein Jr	330-923-0421	P	586	4.1
Collingwood Grain Inc.	PO Box 2150	Hutchinson	KS	67504	Lowell Downey	316-663-7121	S	580 •	0.7
Victory Markets Inc.	PO Box 4200	Utica	NY	13504	Darryl Gregson	315-734-1145	S	550	3.5
Giant Industries Inc.	23733 N Scottsdale	Scottsdale	AZ	85255	James E Acridge	602-585-8888	P	535	2.5
Emro Marketing Co.	PO Box 162	Hazel Crest	IL	60429	Michael Mittleman	708-335-0600	D	500	2.4
World Oil Co.	9302 S Garfield Ave	South Gate	CA	90280	Bernard B Roth	310-928-0100	R	480	0.3
Carlos R. Leffler Inc.	PO Box 278	Richland	PA	17087	Patrick Castagna	717-866-2105	R	450 •	1.0
Colonial Oil Industries Inc.	PO Box 576	Savannah	GA	31402	Robert Demere Jr	912-236-1331	S	450 •	0.4
Love's Country Stores Inc.	PO Box 26210	Oklahoma City	OK	73126	Greg Love	405-751-9000	R	435	2.0
U.S. Oil Company Inc.	425 S Washington	Comb. Locks	WI	54113	Tom Schmidt	414-739-6101	R	400	1.0
FFP Operating Partners L.P.	2801 Glenda Ave	Fort Worth	TX	76117	John H Harvison	817-838-4700	S	371 •	1.3
Uni-Marts Inc.	477 E Beaver Ave	State College	PA	16801	Henry D Sahakian	814-234-6000	P	352	2.8
A.T. Williams Oil Co.	PO Box 7287	Winston-Salem	NC	27109	Arthur T Williams Jr	910-767-6280	R	320 •	1.5
Dairy Mart-Conna Corp.	10300 Linn Station	Louisville	KY	40223	Robert D Stein Jr	502-339-0330	D	320 •	2.5
E-Z Serve Convenience Stores	PO Box 922021	Houston	TX	77292	Neil H McLaurin	713-684-4300	S	316	3.6
Maverik Country Stores Inc.	PO Box 8008	Afton	WY	83110	William Call	307-886-3861	R	300 •	1.4
Burns Bros. Inc.	516 SE Morrison St	Portland	OR	97214	Bruce Burns	503-238-7393	R	280	1.4
Time Oil Co.	PO Box 24447	Seattle	WA	98124	H Roger Holliday	206-285-2400	R	270 •	0.2
Gate Petroleum Co.	PO Box 23627	Jacksonville	FL	32241	Herbert Peyton	904-737-7220	R	220 •	2.0
Keystops Inc.	PO Box 2809	Franklin	KY	42135	Lester Key	502-586-8283	R	218	0.2
Englefield Oil Co.	447 James Pkwy	Newark	OH	43055	F W Englefield III	614-522-1310	R	210	1.2
Christy's Market Inc.	22 Christy's Dr	Brockton	MA	02401	Christy P Mihos	508-586-0474	R	200	1.6
Kwik Shop Inc.	PO Box 1927	Hutchinson	KS	67504	Steve Smith	316-669-8504	S	200	1.4
Watonwan Farm Services Co.	PO Box 26	St. James	MN	56081	Don Gales	507-375-3355	R	170	0.2

Source: *Ward's Business Directory of U.S. Private and Public Companies*, 1998. The company type code used is as follows: P - Public, R - Private, S - Subsidiary, D - Division, J - Joint Venture, A - Affiliate, G - Group. Sales are in millions of dollars, employees are in thousands. An asterisk (*) indicates an estimated sales volume. The symbol < stands for 'less than'.

OCCUPATIONS EMPLOYED BY SIC 554 - GASOLINE SERVICE STATIONS

Occupation	% of Total 1996	Change to 2006	Occupation	% of Total 1996	Change to 2006
Cashiers	44.3	18.6	Bookkeeping, accounting, & auditing clerks	2.4	-17.5
Service station attendants	15.4	-33.0	Waiters & waitresses	1.9	14.7
Marketing & sales worker supervisors	7.7	3.1	Food preparation workers	1.6	-1.7
Automotive mechanics	7.0	-17.5	Cooks, short order & fast food	1.5	3.1
General managers & top executives	4.3	-0.1	General office clerks	1.2	-11.3
Salespersons, retail	4.2	9.9			

Source: *Industry-Occupation Matrix*, Bureau of Labor Statistics. These data relate to one or more 3-digit SIC industry groups rather than to a single 4-digit SIC. The change reported for each occupation to the year 2006 is a percent of growth or decline as estimated by the Bureau of Labor Statistics. The abbreviation nec stands for 'not elsewhere classified'.

STATE AND REGIONAL CONCENTRATION

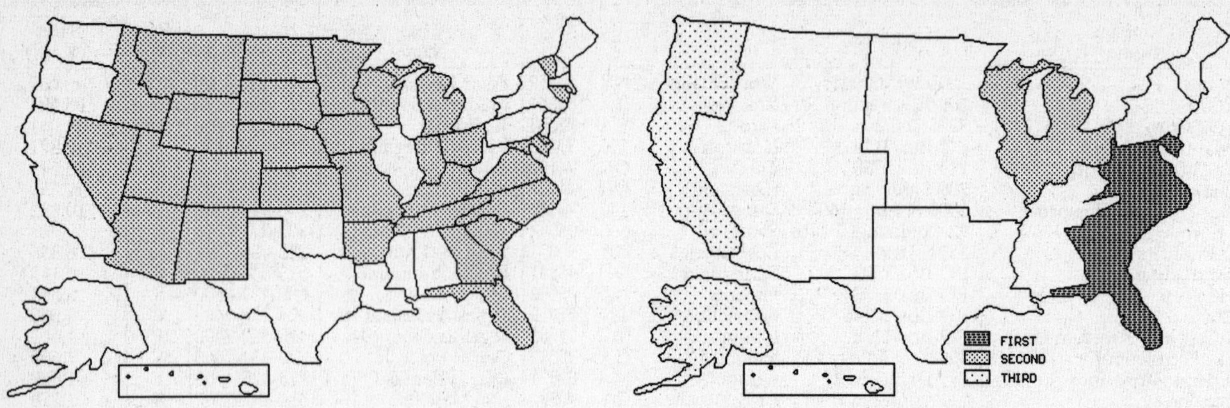

INDUSTRY DATA BY STATE

State	Establishments - 1995 Total (number)	Establishments - 1995 % of U.S.	Employment - 1995 Total (number)	Employment - 1995 % of U.S.	Employment - 1995 Per Estab.	Payroll - 1995 Total ($ mil.)	Payroll - 1995 Per Empl. ($)	Sales - 1992 Total ($ mil.)	Sales - 1992 % of U.S.	Sales - 1992 Per Estab ($)
California	7,713	7.9	59,013	8.4	8	759.0	12,862	14,696.8	10.9	249,903
Texas	6,713	6.9	41,491	5.9	6	533.5	12,859	9,066.7	6.7	225,624
Florida	5,013	5.1	33,370	4.8	7	425.5	12,751	7,463.1	5.5	219,103
New York	5,156	5.3	26,893	3.8	5	359.4	13,365	6,503.4	4.8	239,034
Ohio	4,312	4.4	32,268	4.6	7	366.3	11,350	6,254.2	4.6	192,034
Illinois	3,941	4.0	29,337	4.2	7	353.7	12,057	5,947.9	4.4	206,511
Pennsylvania	4,308	4.4	30,576	4.4	7	365.6	11,957	5,568.2	4.1	180,745
Michigan	3,801	3.9	27,203	3.9	7	311.8	11,460	5,411.3	4.0	187,567
Georgia	2,974	3.1	20,932	3.0	7	273.2	13,050	3,922.9	2.9	198,618
New Jersey	3,168	3.3	17,550	2.5	6	254.3	14,490	3,838.4	2.8	228,286
Indiana	2,531	2.6	21,920	3.1	9	252.1	11,499	3,682.1	2.7	189,945
North Carolina	3,251	3.3	19,613	2.8	6	255.2	13,014	3,674.3	2.7	197,382
Virginia	2,477	2.5	20,561	2.9	8	279.8	13,607	3,557.3	2.6	189,068
Missouri	2,625	2.7	20,269	2.9	8	242.5	11,963	3,383.3	2.5	183,657
Wisconsin	2,430	2.5	20,331	2.9	8	220.9	10,866	3,188.0	2.4	170,701
Minnesota	2,243	2.3	21,922	3.1	10	245.6	11,202	3,010.1	2.2	152,474
Massachusetts	2,412	2.5	13,701	2.0	6	201.2	14,687	2,982.9	2.2	218,236
Tennessee	2,238	2.3	15,416	2.2	7	195.5	12,679	2,937.6	2.2	194,455
Washington	1,432	1.5	12,291	1.8	9	156.0	12,688	2,665.7	2.0	230,195
Maryland	1,554	1.6	12,999	1.9	8	188.6	14,509	2,629.0	2.0	200,018
Kentucky	1,800	1.8	13,742	2.0	8	148.6	10,816	2,289.7	1.7	171,208
Arizona	1,102	1.1	11,550	1.6	10	145.8	12,626	2,194.1	1.6	215,045
Alabama	1,902	2.0	12,529	1.8	7	139.1	11,105	2,137.5	1.6	185,481
South Carolina	1,672	1.7	11,476	1.6	7	139.6	12,162	2,075.0	1.5	190,141
Louisiana	1,621	1.7	12,210	1.7	8	135.6	11,104	2,064.4	1.5	187,910
Colorado	1,396	1.4	10,096	1.4	7	129.9	12,865	1,961.0	1.5	213,086
Connecticut	1,362	1.4	8,184	1.2	6	130.4	15,937	1,908.3	1.4	230,078
Iowa	1,612	1.7	12,658	1.8	8	143.0	11,298	1,836.2	1.4	147,426
Oklahoma	1,441	1.5	8,905	1.3	6	102.7	11,535	1,574.3	1.2	184,371
Oregon	983	1.0	10,273	1.5	10	116.0	11,297	1,524.5	1.1	174,704
Kansas	1,296	1.3	8,683	1.2	7	99.4	11,446	1,401.2	1.0	164,397
Arkansas	1,227	1.3	8,741	1.2	7	92.1	10,539	1,360.3	1.0	164,386
Mississippi	1,138	1.2	7,409	1.1	7	86.6	11,692	1,089.4	0.8	159,612
New Mexico	672	0.7	5,491	0.8	8	67.1	12,215	1,014.1	0.8	205,823
Utah	752	0.8	6,540	0.9	9	67.4	10,306	979.3	0.7	157,900
Nebraska	931	1.0	6,950	1.0	7	78.4	11,286	972.9	0.7	147,658
West Virginia	872	0.9	5,977	0.9	7	63.6	10,643	966.8	0.7	175,518
Nevada	372	0.4	4,665	0.7	13	65.7	14,079	767.5	0.6	201,703
Maine	618	0.6	4,212	0.6	7	50.9	12,084	659.2	0.5	153,293
Idaho	525	0.5	4,427	0.6	8	48.4	10,936	650.7	0.5	168,223
New Hampshire	509	0.5	3,113	0.4	6	42.6	13,691	600.6	0.4	195,385
Hawaii	304	0.3	3,304	0.5	11	51.4	15,564	550.2	0.4	148,420
Montana	460	0.5	3,835	0.5	8	43.9	11,442	521.8	0.4	169,364
Rhode Island	429	0.4	2,361	0.3	6	33.2	14,055	514.3	0.4	235,811
South Dakota	486	0.5	3,727	0.5	8	39.3	10,542	509.1	0.4	145,196
Wyoming	366	0.4	3,090	0.4	8	36.6	11,829	494.9	0.4	173,822
North Dakota	407	0.4	3,435	0.5	8	40.8	11,891	440.0	0.3	169,872
Delaware	279	0.3	2,058	0.3	7	27.1	13,163	429.5	0.3	213,277
Vermont	317	0.3	2,320	0.3	7	28.6	12,329	342.6	0.3	175,332
Alaska	190	0.2	1,408	0.2	7	25.6	18,180	286.3	0.2	226,898
D.C.	115	0.1	892	0.1	8	13.9	15,599	206.6	0.2	253,514

Source: County Business Patterns, 1995 and *Economic Census of the U.S., 1992.* Data are sorted by 1992 revenues and, if revenues are unavailable, by establishments in 1995. The symbol (D) indicates that data are withheld by the source to avoid disclosure of competitive information. A dash (-) indicates that data are not available or undisclosed because they do not meet statistical validity standards. Shaded *states* on the state map indicate those states which have proportionately greater representation in the industry than would be indicated by the state's population; the ratio is based on total revenues or number of establishments. Shaded *regions* indicate where the industry is regionally most concentrated.

5551 - BOAT DEALERS

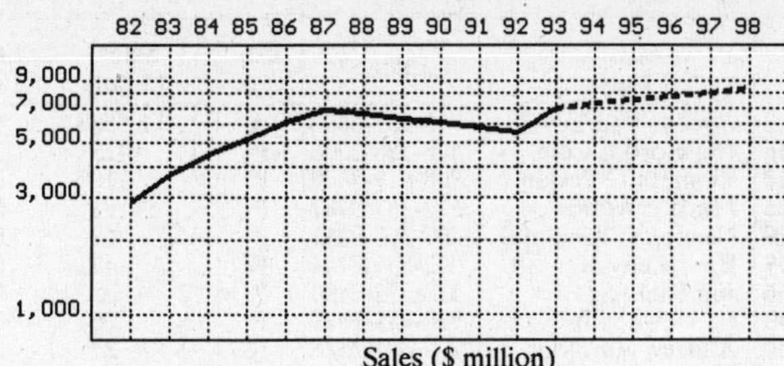

Sales ($ million)

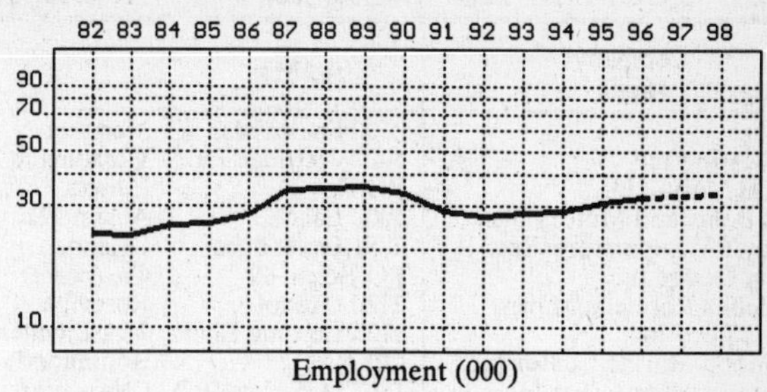

Employment (000)

GENERAL STATISTICS

Year	Establishments (number)	Employment (number)	Payroll ($ million)	Sales ($ million)	Employees per Establishment (number)	Sales per Establishment ($)	Payroll per Employee ($)
1982	4,365	23,000	304.5	2,870.3	5	657,578	13,239
1983	4,233	22,837	346.3	3,661.1e	5	-	15,165
1984	4,164	25,385	396.8	4,451.9e	6	-	15,630
1985	4,066	25,878	433.1	5,242.6e	6	-	16,736
1986	4,080	27,879	491.5	6,033.4e	7	-	17,631
1987	5,174	34,875	620.3	6,824.2	7	1,318,932	17,786
1988	4,862	35,653	689.8	6,566.7e	7	-	19,348
1989	4,631	35,756	673.0	6,309.3e	8	-	18,822
1990	4,645	33,696	629.0	6,051.9e	7	-	18,666
1991	4,541	28,573	564.7	5,794.5e	6	-	19,764
1992	4,773	27,282	558.0	5,537.1	6	1,160,095	20,452
1993	4,758	28,162	599.0	6,994.9p	6	-	21,270
1994	4,778	28,925	664.3	7,261.6p	6	-	22,966
1995	4,775	31,240	713.8	7,528.3p	7	-	22,848
1996	4,925p	32,669p	744.8p	7,795.0p	-	-	-
1997	4,973p	33,128p	770.9p	8,061.6p	-	-	-
1998	5,022p	33,587p	797.1p	8,328.3p	-	-	-

Sources: *Economic Census of the United States*, 1982, 1987, and 1992. Establishment counts, employment, and payroll are from *County Business Patterns* for non-Census years. Values followed by a 'p' are projections by the editors. Sales and expense data for non-Census years are extrapolations, marked by 'e'. Industries reclassified in 1987 will not have data for prior years. Data are the most recent available at this level of detail.

INDICES OF CHANGE

Year	Establishments (number)	Employment (number)	Payroll ($ million)	Sales ($ million)	Employees per Establishment (number)	Sales per Establishment ($)	Payroll per Employee ($)
1982	91.5	84.3	54.6	51.8	83.3	56.7	64.7
1983	88.7	83.7	62.1	66.1e	83.3	-	74.1
1984	87.2	93.0	71.1	80.4e	100.0	-	76.4
1985	85.2	94.9	77.6	94.7e	100.0	-	81.8
1986	85.5	102.2	88.1	109.0e	116.7	-	86.2
1987	108.4	127.8	111.2	123.2	116.7	113.7	87.0
1988	101.9	130.7	123.6	118.6e	116.7	-	94.6
1989	97.0	131.1	120.6	113.9e	133.3	-	92.0
1990	97.3	123.5	112.7	109.3e	116.7	-	91.3
1991	95.1	104.7	101.2	104.6e	100.0	-	96.6
1992	100.0	100.0	100.0	100.0	100.0	100.0	100.0
1993	99.7	103.2	107.3	126.3p	98.6	-	104.0
1994	100.1	106.0	119.0	131.1p	100.9	-	112.3
1995	100.0	114.5	127.9	136.0p	109.0	-	111.7
1996	103.2p	119.7p	133.5p	140.8p	-	-	-
1997	104.2p	121.4p	138.2p	145.6p	-	-	-
1998	105.2p	123.1p	142.8p	150.4p	-	-	-

Sources: Same as General Statistics. The values shown reflect change from the base year, 1992. Values above 100 mean greater than 1992, values below 100 mean less than 1992, and a value of 100 in the 1982-91 or 1993-98 period means same as 1992. Values followed by a 'p' are projections by the editors; 'e' stands for extrapolation. Data are the most recent available at this level of detail.

SELECTED RATIOS

For 1992	Avg. of All Retail	Analyzed Industry	Index	For 1992	Avg. of All Retail	Analyzed Industry	Index
Employees per Establishment	12	6	47	Sales per Employee	102,941	202,958	197
Payroll per Establishment	146,026	116,908	80	Sales per Establishment	1,241,555	1,160,088	93
Payroll per Employee	12,107	20,453	169	Expenses per Establishment	na	na	na

Sources: Same as General Statistics. The 'Average of All Manufacturing' column represents the average of all manufacturing industries reported for the most recent complete year available. The Index shows the relationship between the Average and the Analyzed Industry. For example, 100 means that they are equal; 500 that the Analyzed Industry is five times the average; 50 means that the Analyzed Industry is half the national average. The abbreviation 'na' is used to show that data are 'not available'.

LEADING COMPANIES

Number shown: **21** Total sales ($ mil): **3,500** Total employment (000): **10.7**

Company Name	Address				CEO Name	Phone	Co. Type	Sales ($ mil)	Empl. (000)
V.T. Inc.	8500 Shawn Msn	Merriam	KS	66202	Cecil L Van Tuyl	913-432-6400	R	2,558 *	5.3
West Marine Inc.	500 Westridge Dr	Watsonville	CA	95076	Crawford L Cole	408-728-2700	P	415	3.1
E and B Marine Inc.	PO Box 747	Edison	NJ	08818	Kenneth G Peskin	908-819-7400	P	110	0.8
Travis Boats and Motors Inc.	5000 Lake	Austin	TX	78746	Mark T Walton	512-347-8787	P	91	0.4
Holiday RV Superstores Inc.	7851 Greenbriar	Orlando	FL	32819	Newton C Kindlund	407-363-9211	P	68	0.2
Kenyon Dodge Inc.	PO Box 4580	Clearwater	FL	34618	Brad Kenyon	813-539-7444	R	43	0.1
Jim Riehl's Roseville Marine	2520 Gratiot	Roseville	MI	48066	Jim Riehl Sr	313-772-0800	R	38 *	0.1
Sanders Ford Inc.	1135 Lejeune Blvd	Jacksonville	NC	28540	BJ Downey Jr	910-455-1911	R	26	<0.1
Robinhood Marine Center Inc.	Off Rte 127	Robinhood	ME	04530	Andrew Varolotis	207-371-2525	R	23	<0.1
Outboarder of Sarasota Inc.	18025 US Hwy 19 N	Clearwater	FL	34624	William H McGill	813-536-9489	R	20 *	<0.1
D and R Boats Inc.	271 Rte 22	Green Brook	NJ	08812	Dominic J Barone	908-968-2600	R	17 *	<0.1
Stoltzfus Trailer Sales Inc.	1335 Wilmington	West Chester	PA	19382	Earl Stoltzfus	610-399-0628	R	16	<0.1
Manset Marine Supply Co.	PO Box 709	Rockland	ME	04841	Dale Landrith	207-596-6464	R	14 *	<0.1
Spencer Boat Company Inc.	4200 Poinsettia Ave	W. Palm Beach	FL	33407	Edward Bronstein	407-844-1800	R	14	0.2
Boat Sales Inc.	8202 US 31 S	Indianapolis	IN	46227	Michael Hoffman	317-887-2628	R	12	<0.1
Jefferson Beach Marina Inc.	24400 E Jefferson	St. Clair Shores	MI	48080	Alvin Wagner	313-778-7600	R	11 *	<0.1
Minnetonka Boat Works Inc.	294 E Grove Ln	Wayzata	MN	55391	Dennis Keating	612-473-7305	S	10 *	<0.1
Stuart Hatteras Ltd.	110 N Federal Hwy	Stuart	FL	34994	Bill Deery	407-692-1122	J	7 *	<0.1
West Marine Corp.	120 Allied Dr	Dedham	MA	02026	Randy Repass	617-329-2430	S	3	<0.1
Zidell Inc.	3121 SW Moody	Portland	OR	97201	Emery N Zidell	503-228-8691	R	3	<0.1
Boulder Outdoor Center Inc.	2510 N 47th St	Boulder	CO	80301	Eric Bader	303-444-8420	R	1	<0.1

Source: *Ward's Business Directory of U.S. Private and Public Companies*, 1998. The company type code used is as follows: P - Public, R - Private, S - Subsidiary, D - Division, J - Joint Venture, A - Affiliate, G - Group. Sales are in millions of dollars, employees are in thousands. An asterisk (*) indicates an estimated sales volume. The symbol < stands for 'less than'.

OCCUPATIONS EMPLOYED BY SIC 555 - BOAT AND MISCELLANEOUS VEHICLE DEALERS

Occupation	% of Total 1996	Change to 2006	Occupation	% of Total 1996	Change to 2006
Salespersons, retail	20.7	19.4	Secretaries, except legal & medical	3.2	-11.1
Mechanics, installers, & repairers nec	10.5	23.3	Maintenance repairers, general utility	3.0	4.5
Sales & related workers nec	9.6	45.7	Vehicle washers & equipment cleaners	2.3	12.0
General managers & top executives	9.3	8.6	Automotive mechanics	2.1	12.0
Motorcycle repairers	6.1	0.9	Cashiers	1.7	13.4
Small engine specialists	5.3	3.3	Janitors & cleaners, maids	1.7	-10.3
Bookkeeping, accounting, & auditing clerks	4.8	-10.3	Marketing, advertising, PR managers	1.5	23.3
Marketing & sales worker supervisors	4.5	12.1	Stock clerks	1.3	147.5
General office clerks	3.9	-3.6	Clerical supervisors & managers	1.3	12.1

Source: *Industry-Occupation Matrix*, Bureau of Labor Statistics. These data relate to one or more 3-digit SIC industry groups rather than to a single 4-digit SIC. The change reported for each occupation to the year 2006 is a percent of growth or decline as estimated by the Bureau of Labor Statistics. The abbreviation nec stands for 'not elsewhere classified'.

STATE AND REGIONAL CONCENTRATION

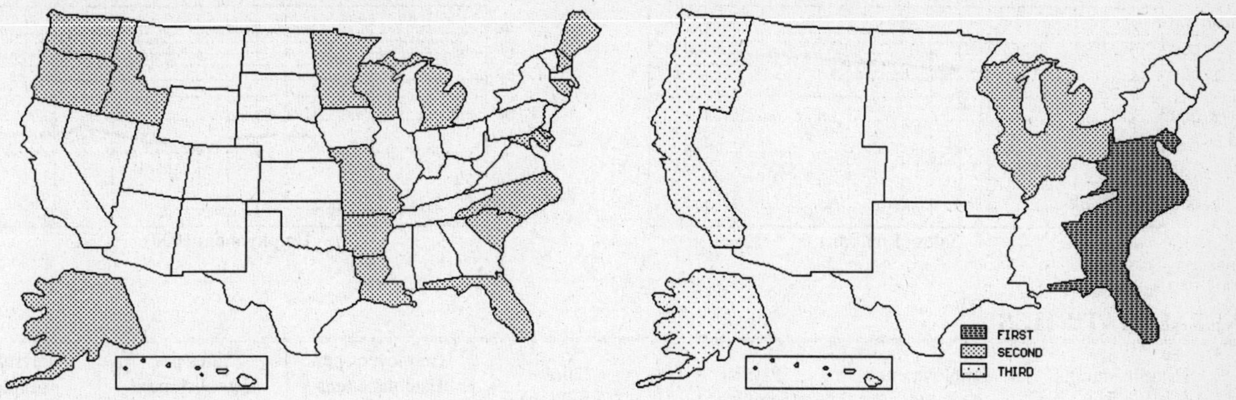

INDUSTRY DATA BY STATE

State	Establishments - 1995		Employment - 1995			Payroll - 1995		Sales - 1992		
	Total (number)	% of U.S.	Total (number)	% of U.S.	Per Estab.	Total ($ mil.)	Per Empl. ($)	Total ($ mil.)	% of U.S.	Per Estab ($)
Florida	667	14.0	4,427	14.2	7	97.3	21,988	813.8	14.9	215,114
Michigan	211	4.4	1,735	5.6	8	44.5	25,635	389.1	7.1	239,616
California	313	6.6	2,022	6.5	6	48.5	23,966	384.8	7.1	208,685
Texas	258	5.4	1,826	5.9	7	42.8	23,448	303.8	5.6	190,443
New York	243	5.1	1,330	4.3	5	31.5	23,660	280.9	5.1	201,091
Washington	189	4.0	1,129	3.6	6	27.8	24,603	255.3	4.7	227,771
Wisconsin	154	3.2	1,133	3.6	7	26.7	23,579	194.8	3.6	208,554
Maryland	139	2.9	944	3.0	7	21.5	22,798	182.1	3.3	216,245
Minnesota	111	2.3	935	3.0	8	21.5	22,945	166.9	3.1	209,351
Illinois	126	2.6	898	2.9	7	20.3	22,648	157.9	2.9	198,425
North Carolina	142	3.0	951	3.0	7	21.2	22,259	155.9	2.9	207,352
New Jersey	130	2.7	883	2.8	7	21.8	24,710	153.6	2.8	218,159
Ohio	152	3.2	963	3.1	6	22.0	22,801	150.6	2.8	194,382
Missouri	122	2.6	910	2.9	7	20.4	22,400	149.3	2.7	220,566
Indiana	88	1.8	758	2.4	9	18.3	24,148	120.8	2.2	182,769
Virginia	105	2.2	856	2.7	8	22.8	26,655	118.0	2.2	160,148
Georgia	107	2.2	610	2.0	6	13.3	21,808	103.7	1.9	211,580
Tennessee	96	2.0	499	1.6	5	11.9	23,756	103.6	1.9	238,271
Louisiana	106	2.2	733	2.4	7	14.2	19,321	102.9	1.9	187,443
South Carolina	113	2.4	672	2.2	6	14.6	21,732	98.1	1.8	178,996
Massachusetts	96	2.0	611	2.0	6	15.1	24,759	98.0	1.8	184,906
Pennsylvania	97	2.0	627	2.0	6	12.3	19,628	94.3	1.7	180,057
Oregon	67	1.4	442	1.4	7	10.9	24,731	88.4	1.6	211,426
Alabama	98	2.1	546	1.8	6	9.9	18,216	82.6	1.5	188,559
Connecticut	70	1.5	374	1.2	5	10.3	27,596	76.0	1.4	204,801
Oklahoma	55	1.2	326	1.0	6	5.7	17,543	58.8	1.1	206,337
Kentucky	63	1.3	336	1.1	5	6.7	19,836	57.2	1.0	214,876
Arkansas	60	1.3	345	1.1	6	6.1	17,681	56.1	1.0	196,297
Iowa	63	1.3	271	0.9	4	6.0	22,240	46.5	0.9	180,097
Alaska	42	0.9	198	0.6	5	6.0	30,449	46.1	0.8	260,412
Arizona	44	0.9	309	1.0	7	7.0	22,786	40.5	0.7	168,183
New Hampshire	34	0.7	235	0.8	7	6.4	27,166	39.3	0.7	213,826
Utah	28	0.6	212	0.7	8	5.1	23,910	37.6	0.7	241,179
Maine	56	1.2	270	0.9	5	5.8	21,448	35.4	0.6	151,970
Idaho	34	0.7	238	0.8	7	4.6	19,382	32.9	0.6	150,155
Colorado	30	0.6	194	0.6	6	3.9	20,263	31.3	0.6	182,169
Nevada	20	0.4	198	0.6	10	4.8	24,359	28.8	0.5	146,964
Mississippi	33	0.7	141	0.5	4	2.2	15,851	24.7	0.5	113,664
Delaware	19	0.4	201	0.6	11	4.0	20,104	22.4	0.4	131,269
Kansas	29	0.6	120	0.4	4	2.4	20,367	22.0	0.4	156,800
Montana	16	0.3	90	0.3	6	1.4	15,300	17.3	0.3	171,059
North Dakota	13	0.3	60	0.2	5	1.2	19,650	13.4	0.2	197,338
Vermont	15	0.3	47	0.2	3	1.0	22,255	8.7	0.2	185,702
South Dakota	11	0.2	47	0.2	4	0.8	16,723	8.0	0.1	172,848
New Mexico	10	0.2	32	0.1	3	0.6	18,844	5.3	0.1	314,647
Rhode Island	31	0.6	165	0.5	5	3.3	19,788	(D)	-	-
Nebraska	23	0.5	119	0.4	5	2.5	20,992	(D)	-	-
West Virginia	21	0.4	127	0.4	6	2.0	16,110	(D)	-	-
Hawaii	16	0.3	89	0.3	6	1.7	19,618	(D)	-	-
Wyoming	8	0.2	20-99	-	-	(D)	-	(D)	-	-
D.C.	1	0.0	0-19	-	-	(D)	-	(D)	-	-

Source: *County Business Patterns, 1995* and *Economic Census of the U.S., 1992*. Data are sorted by 1992 revenues and, if revenues are unavailable, by establishments in 1995. The symbol (D) indicates that data are withheld by the source to avoid disclosure of competitive information. A dash (-) indicates that data are not available or undisclosed because they do not meet statistical validity standards. Shaded *states* on the state map indicate those states which have proportionately greater representation in the industry than would be indicated by the state's population; the ratio is based on total revenues or number of establishments. Shaded *regions* indicate where the industry is regionally most concentrated.

5561 - RECREATIONAL VEHICLE DEALERS

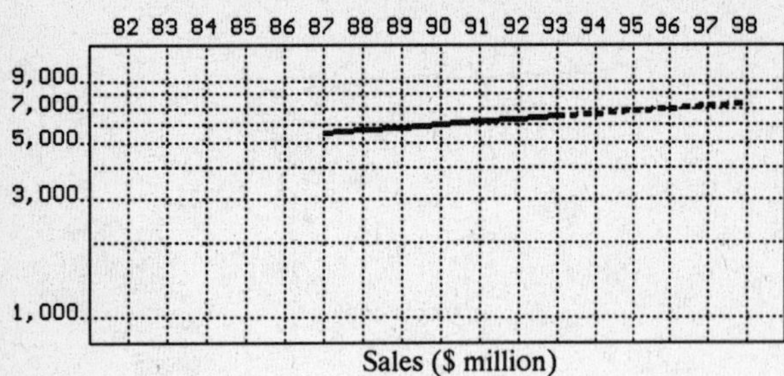

Sales ($ million)

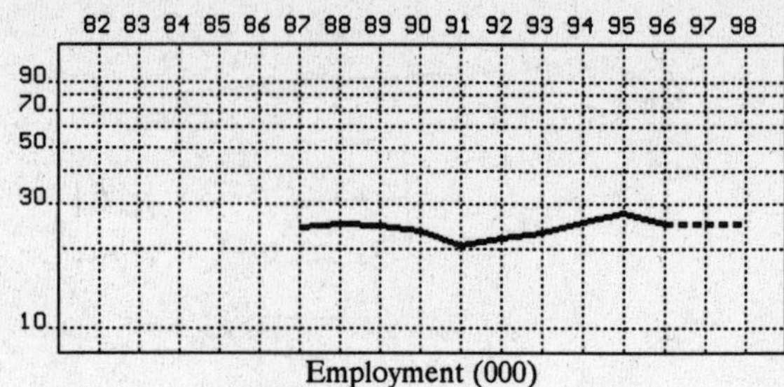

Employment (000)

GENERAL STATISTICS

Year	Establishments (number)	Employment (number)	Payroll ($ million)	Sales ($ million)	Employees per Establishment (number)	Sales per Establishment ($)	Payroll per Employee ($)
1982	-	-	-	-	-	-	-
1983	-	-	-	-	-	-	-
1984	-	-	-	-	-	-	-
1985	-	-	-	-	-	-	-
1986	-	-	-	-	-	-	-
1987	3,006	24,621	437.4	5,538.5	8	1,842,472	17,765
1988	2,815	24,991	497.4	5,693.5e	9	-	19,901
1989	2,700	24,742	483.5	5,848.6e	9	-	19,541
1990	2,711	23,523	480.1	6,003.7e	9	-	20,410
1991	2,656	20,718	458.5	6,158.7e	8	-	22,128
1992	2,826	22,304	514.3	6,313.8	8	2,234,189	23,057
1993	2,840	23,028	571.2	6,468.9p	8	-	24,805
1994	2,850	25,593	662.4	6,624.0p	9	-	25,882
1995	2,867	27,923	714.3	6,779.0p	10	-	25,580
1996	2,803p	25,024p	686.5p	6,934.1p	-	-	-
1997	2,802p	25,197p	716.7p	7,089.2p	-	-	-
1998	2,801p	25,370p	746.9p	7,244.2p	-	-	-

Sources: Economic Census of the United States, 1982, 1987, and 1992. Establishment counts, employment, and payroll are from *County Business Patterns* for non-Census years. Values followed by a 'p' are projections by the editors. Sales and expense data for non-Census years are extrapolations, marked by 'e'. Industries reclassified in 1987 will not have data for prior years. Data are the most recent available at this level of detail.

INDICES OF CHANGE

Year	Establishments (number)	Employment (number)	Payroll ($ million)	Sales ($ million)	Employees per Establishment (number)	Sales per Establishment ($)	Payroll per Employee ($)
1982	-	-	-	-	-	-	-
1983	-	-	-	-	-	-	-
1984	-	-	-	-	-	-	-
1985	-	-	-	-	-	-	-
1986	-	-	-	-	-	-	-
1987	106.4	110.4	85.0	87.7	100.0	82.5	77.0
1988	99.6	112.0	96.7	90.2e	112.5	-	86.3
1989	95.5	110.9	94.0	92.6e	112.5	-	84.8
1990	95.9	105.5	93.4	95.1e	112.5	-	88.5
1991	94.0	92.9	89.2	97.5e	100.0	-	96.0
1992	100.0	100.0	100.0	100.0	100.0	100.0	100.0
1993	100.5	103.2	111.1	102.5p	101.4	-	107.6
1994	100.8	114.7	128.8	104.9p	112.2	-	112.3
1995	101.5	125.2	138.9	107.4p	121.7	-	110.9
1996	99.2p	112.2p	133.5p	109.8p	-	-	-
1997	99.2p	113.0p	139.3p	112.3p	-	-	-
1998	99.1p	113.7p	145.2p	114.7p	-	-	-

Sources: Same as General Statistics. The values shown reflect change from the base year, 1992. Values above 100 mean greater than 1992, values below 100 mean less than 1992, and a value of 100 in the 1982-91 or 1993-98 period means same as 1992. Values followed by a 'p' are projections by the editors; 'e' stands for extrapolation. Data are the most recent available at this level of detail.

SELECTED RATIOS

For 1992	Avg. of All Retail	Analyzed Industry	Index	For 1992	Avg. of All Retail	Analyzed Industry	Index
Employees per Establishment	12	8	65	Sales per Employee	102,941	283,079	275
Payroll per Establishment	146,026	181,989	125	Sales per Establishment	1,241,555	2,234,183	180
Payroll per Employee	12,107	23,059	190	Expenses per Establishment	na	na	na

Sources: Same as General Statistics. The 'Average of All Manufacturing' column represents the average of all manufacturing industries reported for the most recent complete year available. The Index shows the relationship between the Average and the Analyzed Industry. For example, 100 means that they are equal; 500 that the Analyzed Industry is five times the average; 50 means that the Analyzed Industry is half the national average. The abbreviation 'na' is used to show that data are 'not available'.

LEADING COMPANIES Number shown: **28** Total sales ($ mil): **3,944** Total employment (000): **28.8**

Company Name	Address				CEO Name	Phone	Co. Type	Sales ($ mil)	Empl. (000)
Budget Group Inc.	125 Basin St, #210	Daytona Beach	FL	32114	Sanford Miller	904-238-7035	P	2,700	24.5
Camping World Inc.	PO Box 90018	Bowling Green	KY	42102	Tad Donnelly	502-781-2718	S	200	1.3
Cruise America Inc.	11 W Hampton Ave	Mesa	AZ	85210	Randall S Smalley	602-464-7300	S	96	0.4
Courtesy Chevrolet	PO Box 7709	Phoenix	AZ	85011	EJ Fitzgerald	602-279-3232	R	79	0.2
Biddulph Oldsmobile Inc.	4611 W Glendale	Glendale	AZ	85301	Kemp Biddulph	602-934-5211	R	76	0.2
Iten Chevrolet Co.	6701 Brooklyn Blvd	Minneapolis	MN	55429	Joseph M Iten	612-561-9220	R	76	0.2
Frank Hurling Chevrolet Inc.	2449 Fulton Ave	Sacramento	CA	95825	M D Daugherty	916-482-1600	R	72	0.2
Leif Johnson Ford Inc.	501 E Koenig Ln	Austin	TX	78765	Robert Johnson	512-454-3711	R	71	0.2
Holiday RV Superstores Inc.	7851 Greenbriar	Orlando	FL	32819	Newton C Kindlund	407-363-9211	P	68	0.2
Van Boxtel Ford Inc.	PO Box 11567	Green Bay	WI	54307	Edwin A Van Boxtel	414-499-3131	R	65	0.1
Roy Robinson Chevrolet	PO Box 168	Marysville	WA	98270	Roy Robinson	206-659-6236	R	52	0.1
Hansel Ford	PO Box 610	Santa Rosa	CA	95402	Henry Hansel	707-542-0620	R	48	0.1
Bernard Chevrolet Inc.	1001 S Milwaukee	Libertyville	IL	60048	Craig Bernard	708-362-1400	R	40 *	<0.1
McClain's RV Inc.	PO Box 969	Lake Dallas	TX	75065	Larry McClain	817-497-3300	R	40	0.1
Jim Riehl's Roseville Marine	2520 Gratiot	Roseville	MI	48066	Jim Riehl Sr	313-772-0800	R	38 *	0.1
La Mesa RV Center Inc.	7601 Alvarado Rd	La Mesa	CA	91941	Jim R Kimbrell	619-462-5660	R	32	0.1
Tom Raper Inc.	PO Box 1365	Richmond	IN	47375	Tom R Raper	317-966-8361	R	30	0.2
Robert Crist and Co.	2025 E Main St	Mesa	AZ	85213	Paul Skogebo	602-834-9410	R	20	<0.1
RV Corral Inc.	6828 Federal Blvd	Lemon Grove	CA	92045	Ludger Camp	619-582-1900	R	20 *	<0.1
Omnicor Inc. Richfield Center	2636 Brecksville Rd	Richfield	OH	44286	Jerome Stanoch	330-659-9311	D	18 *	<0.1
Stoltzfus Trailer Sales Inc.	1335 Wilmington	West Chester	PA	19382	Earl Stoltzfus	610-399-0628	R	16	<0.1
Venture Out	300 Orchard City	Campbell	CA	95008	G Lee Fitzgerald	408-378-8150	R	15 *	<0.1
Tom Stinnett Holiday R.V. Inc.	560 Kopp Ln	Clarksville	IN	47129	Tom Stinnett	812-282-7718	R	15	<0.1
Ron Hoover Co.	PO Box 747	Rockport	TX	78382	Ron Hoover	512-729-9695	R	14 *	<0.1
Blaine Jensen and Sons	5501 S 320 W	Murray	UT	84107	Craig Jensen	801-261-0481	R	12	<0.1
Stier's Leisure Vehicles Inc.	500 S Union Ave	Bakersfield	CA	93307	Mike Stier	805-323-8000	R	12	<0.1
Dean's RV Superstore Inc.	9955 E 21st St	Tulsa	OK	74129	Randy Coy	918-664-3333	R	10	<0.1
Holiday World Inc.	4630 Hwy 67 E	Mesquite	TX	75150	James E Cafmeyer	214-328-4151	S	10	<0.1

Source: *Ward's Business Directory of U.S. Private and Public Companies*, 1998. The company type code used is as follows: P - Public, R - Private, S - Subsidiary, D - Division, J - Joint Venture, A - Affiliate, G - Group. Sales are in millions of dollars, employees are in thousands. An asterisk (*) indicates an estimated sales volume. The symbol < stands for 'less than'.

OCCUPATIONS EMPLOYED BY SIC 556 - BOAT AND MISCELLANEOUS VEHICLE DEALERS

Occupation	% of Total 1996	Change to 2006	Occupation	% of Total 1996	Change to 2006
Salespersons, retail	20.7	19.4	Secretaries, except legal & medical	3.2	-11.1
Mechanics, installers, & repairers nec	10.5	23.3	Maintenance repairers, general utility	3.0	4.5
Sales & related workers nec	9.6	45.7	Vehicle washers & equipment cleaners	2.3	12.0
General managers & top executives	9.3	8.6	Automotive mechanics	2.1	12.0
Motorcycle repairers	6.1	0.9	Cashiers	1.7	13.4
Small engine specialists	5.3	3.3	Janitors & cleaners, maids	1.7	-10.3
Bookkeeping, accounting, & auditing clerks	4.8	-10.3	Marketing, advertising, PR managers	1.5	23.3
Marketing & sales worker supervisors	4.5	12.1	Stock clerks	1.3	147.5
General office clerks	3.9	-3.6	Clerical supervisors & managers	1.3	12.1

Source: *Industry-Occupation Matrix*, Bureau of Labor Statistics. These data relate to one or more 3-digit SIC industry groups rather than to a single 4-digit SIC. The change reported for each occupation to the year 2006 is a percent of growth or decline as estimated by the Bureau of Labor Statistics. The abbreviation nec stands for 'not elsewhere classified'.

STATE AND REGIONAL CONCENTRATION

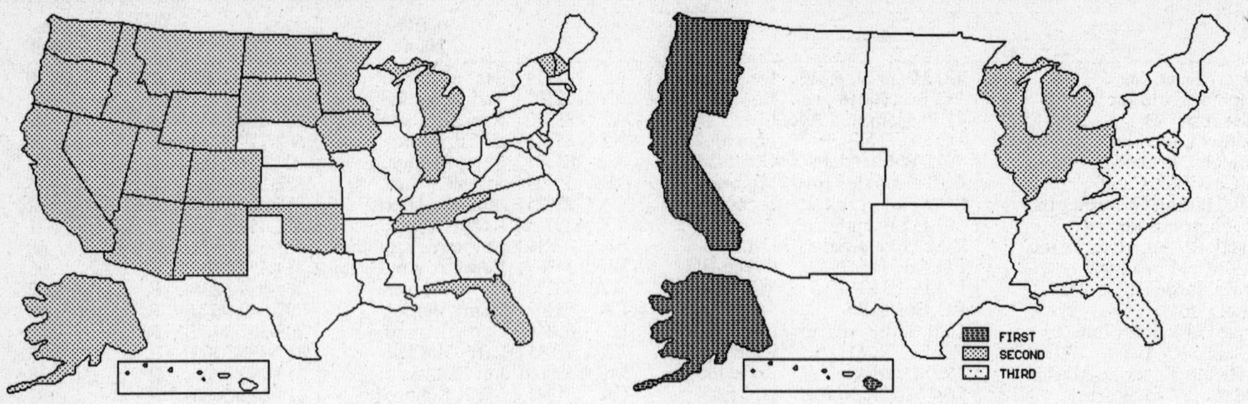

INDUSTRY DATA BY STATE

State	Establishments - 1995 Total (number)	Establishments - 1995 % of U.S.	Employment - 1995 Total (number)	Employment - 1995 % of U.S.	Employment - 1995 Per Estab.	Payroll - 1995 Total ($ mil.)	Payroll - 1995 Per Empl. ($)	Sales - 1992 Total ($ mil.)	Sales - 1992 % of U.S.	Sales - 1992 Per Estab ($)
California	336	11.7	4,038	14.5	12	107.8	26,705	960.7	15.6	254,147
Florida	176	6.1	1,998	7.2	11	49.9	24,965	550.1	8.9	336,059
Texas	193	6.7	1,758	6.3	9	45.1	25,636	389.8	6.3	288,501
Oregon	110	3.8	1,181	4.2	11	38.3	32,432	363.7	5.9	346,675
Washington	117	4.1	1,544	5.5	13	43.3	28,016	310.5	5.0	318,167
Michigan	130	4.5	1,186	4.3	9	33.3	28,067	281.6	4.6	313,884
Indiana	91	3.2	873	3.1	10	25.3	28,931	221.0	3.6	295,080
Ohio	101	3.5	945	3.4	9	24.1	25,455	214.7	3.5	271,455
Arizona	91	3.2	1,150	4.1	13	28.2	24,530	206.7	3.4	217,621
Tennessee	45	1.6	583	2.1	13	19.5	33,463	199.0	3.2	477,197
Pennsylvania	115	4.0	855	3.1	7	21.7	25,354	197.4	3.2	249,885
New York	108	3.8	812	2.9	8	20.8	25,670	184.0	3.0	235,926
Colorado	59	2.1	625	2.2	11	17.4	27,818	142.4	2.3	329,660
Illinois	83	2.9	585	2.1	7	13.0	22,183	131.6	2.1	269,652
Wisconsin	79	2.8	609	2.2	8	12.8	20,954	115.1	1.9	254,108
Oklahoma	35	1.2	398	1.4	11	8.1	20,354	112.1	1.8	335,704
Minnesota	70	2.4	555	2.0	8	13.1	23,546	111.9	1.8	289,243
Missouri	68	2.4	473	1.7	7	11.9	25,224	104.7	1.7	269,203
North Carolina	61	2.1	511	1.8	8	11.2	21,973	87.9	1.4	281,670
Nevada	27	0.9	438	1.6	16	12.2	27,854	85.6	1.4	264,191
Alabama	46	1.6	383	1.4	8	8.4	21,836	83.7	1.4	314,639
Utah	43	1.5	391	1.4	9	10.0	25,514	82.0	1.3	300,531
Iowa	43	1.5	326	1.2	8	7.0	21,328	82.0	1.3	304,877
Idaho	43	1.5	414	1.5	10	9.4	22,771	79.6	1.3	277,477
Louisiana	32	1.1	250	0.9	8	6.0	23,940	77.9	1.3	385,441
New Mexico	38	1.3	457	1.6	12	8.9	19,578	70.9	1.1	228,571
Georgia	42	1.5	481	1.7	11	10.1	21,052	70.6	1.1	240,187
South Carolina	30	1.0	334	1.2	11	7.3	21,913	62.3	1.0	257,554
Virginia	48	1.7	363	1.3	8	8.3	22,909	59.3	1.0	204,541
Arkansas	33	1.2	255	0.9	8	4.8	18,839	52.7	0.9	270,456
Montana	23	0.8	227	0.8	10	5.5	24,242	52.5	0.9	308,647
Maryland	27	0.9	302	1.1	11	5.5	18,248	46.3	0.7	199,353
New Hampshire	24	0.8	202	0.7	8	7.1	35,252	44.2	0.7	267,873
Kansas	35	1.2	224	0.8	6	4.5	20,112	41.1	0.7	253,698
Kentucky	32	1.1	261	0.9	8	5.4	20,858	40.6	0.7	210,378
Nebraska	21	0.7	180	0.6	9	3.5	19,672	30.7	0.5	224,343
Maine	29	1.0	135	0.5	5	2.9	21,452	29.9	0.5	301,929
West Virginia	14	0.5	125	0.4	9	3.1	24,752	28.8	0.5	246,145
South Dakota	22	0.8	148	0.5	7	3.8	25,486	27.4	0.4	266,068
North Dakota	14	0.5	121	0.4	9	2.5	20,496	26.0	0.4	337,818
Connecticut	15	0.5	140	0.5	9	3.2	23,129	24.8	0.4	269,728
Alaska	9	0.3	84	0.3	9	3.1	37,012	20.8	0.3	281,419
Wyoming	15	0.5	80	0.3	5	1.8	22,300	16.8	0.3	254,500
Mississippi	18	0.6	114	0.4	6	2.5	22,360	16.1	0.3	247,754
Delaware	8	0.3	20-99	-	-	(D)	-	15.3	0.2	255,500
Vermont	9	0.3	75	0.3	8	1.9	25,253	14.8	0.2	242,787
New Jersey	28	1.0	324	1.2	12	10.0	31,015	(D)	-	-
Massachusetts	26	0.9	299	1.1	11	7.2	24,057	(D)	-	-
Rhode Island	4	0.1	45	0.2	11	1.8	39,756	(D)	-	-
Hawaii	1	0.0	0-19	-	-	(D)	-	(D)	-	-

Source: County Business Patterns, 1995 and *Economic Census of the U.S., 1992*. Data are sorted by 1992 revenues and, if revenues are unavailable, by establishments in 1995. The symbol (D) indicates that data are withheld by the source to avoid disclosure of competitive information. A dash (-) indicates that data are not available or undisclosed because they do not meet statistical validity standards. Shaded *states* on the state map indicate those states which have proportionately greater representation in the industry than would be indicated by the state's population; the ratio is based on total revenues or number of establishments. Shaded *regions* indicate where the industry is regionally most concentrated.

5571 - MOTORCYCLE DEALERS

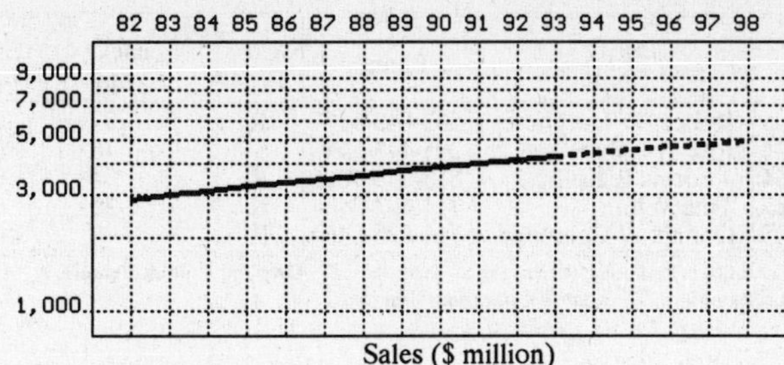

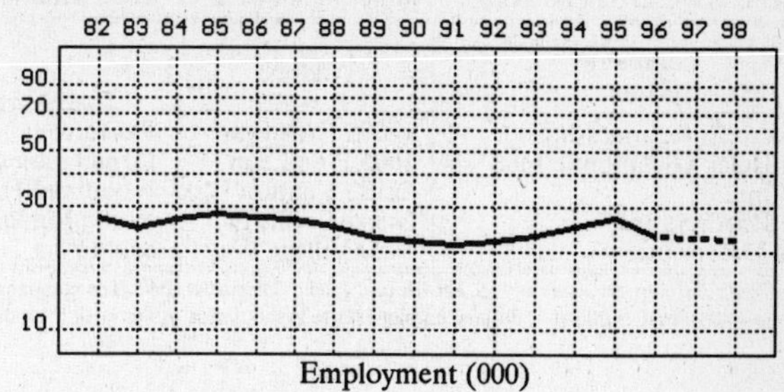

GENERAL STATISTICS

Year	Establishments (number)	Employment (number)	Payroll ($ million)	Sales ($ million)	Employees per Establishment (number)	Sales per Establishment ($)	Payroll per Employee ($)
1982	4,933	27,314	308.2	2,876.7	6	583,146	11,283
1983	4,562	24,866	320.2	2,996.4*e*	5	-	12,876
1984	4,388	27,067	369.2	3,116.2*e*	6	-	13,639
1985	4,157	28,199	393.3	3,235.9*e*	7	-	13,948
1986	4,007	27,341	396.4	3,355.6*e*	7	-	14,499
1987	4,197	27,070	381.8	3,475.4	6	828,065	14,105
1988	3,835	24,941	388.8	3,612.8*e*	7	-	15,590
1989	3,527	22,949	379.6	3,750.3*e*	7	-	16,542
1990	3,457	22,283	392.1	3,887.8*e*	6	-	17,597
1991	3,386	21,349	405.1	4,025.2*e*	6	-	18,977
1992	3,585	22,184	427.2	4,162.7	6	1,161,139	19,255
1993	3,601	23,212	482.4	4,271.2*p*	6	-	20,782
1994	3,605	24,984	547.4	4,399.8*p*	7	-	21,909
1995	3,622	27,322	623.6	4,528.4*p*	8	-	22,823
1996	3,189*p*	23,071*p*	545.9*p*	4,657.0*p*	-	-	-
1997	3,091*p*	22,803*p*	563.3*p*	4,785.6*p*	-	-	-
1998	2,994*p*	22,536*p*	580.7*p*	4,914.2*p*	-	-	-

Sources: Economic Census of the United States, 1982, 1987, and 1992. Establishment counts, employment, and payroll are from *County Business Patterns* for non-Census years. Values followed by a 'p' are projections by the editors. Sales and expense data for non-Census years are extrapolations, marked by 'e'. Industries reclassified in 1987 will not have data for prior years. Data are the most recent available at this level of detail.

INDICES OF CHANGE

Year	Establishments (number)	Employment (number)	Payroll ($ million)	Sales ($ million)	Employees per Establishment (number)	Sales per Establishment ($)	Payroll per Employee ($)
1982	137.6	123.1	72.1	69.1	100.0	50.2	58.6
1983	127.3	112.1	75.0	72.0*e*	83.3	-	66.9
1984	122.4	122.0	86.4	74.9*e*	100.0	-	70.8
1985	116.0	127.1	92.1	77.7*e*	116.7	-	72.4
1986	111.8	123.2	92.8	80.6*e*	116.7	-	75.3
1987	117.1	122.0	89.4	83.5	100.0	71.3	73.3
1988	107.0	112.4	91.0	86.8*e*	116.7	-	81.0
1989	98.4	103.4	88.9	90.1*e*	116.7	-	85.9
1990	96.4	100.4	91.8	93.4*e*	100.0	-	91.4
1991	94.4	96.2	94.8	96.7*e*	100.0	-	98.6
1992	100.0	100.0	100.0	100.0	100.0	100.0	100.0
1993	100.4	104.6	112.9	102.6*p*	107.4	-	107.9
1994	100.6	112.6	128.1	105.7*p*	115.5	-	113.8
1995	101.0	123.2	146.0	108.8*p*	125.7	-	118.5
1996	88.9*p*	104.0*p*	127.8*p*	111.9*p*	-	-	-
1997	86.2*p*	102.8*p*	131.9*p*	115.0*p*	-	-	-
1998	83.5*p*	101.6*p*	135.9*p*	118.1*p*	-	-	-

Sources: Same as General Statistics. The values shown reflect change from the base year, 1992. Values above 100 mean greater than 1992, values below 100 mean less than 1992, and a value of 100 in the 1982-91 or 1993-98 period means same as 1992. Values followed by a 'p' are projections by the editors; 'e' stands for extrapolation. Data are the most recent available at this level of detail.

SELECTED RATIOS

For 1992	Avg. of All Retail	Analyzed Industry	Index	For 1992	Avg. of All Retail	Analyzed Industry	Index
Employees per Establishment	12	6	51	Sales per Employee	102,941	187,644	182
Payroll per Establishment	146,026	119,163	82	Sales per Establishment	1,241,555	1,161,144	94
Payroll per Employee	12,107	19,257	159	Expenses per Establishment	na	na	na

Sources: Same as General Statistics. The 'Average of All Manufacturing' column represents the average of all manufacturing industries reported for the most recent complete year available. The Index shows the relationship between the Average and the Analyzed Industry. For example, 100 means that they are equal; 500 that the Analyzed Industry is five times the average; 50 means that the Analyzed Industry is half the national average. The abbreviation 'na' is used to show that data are 'not available'.

LEADING COMPANIES

Number shown: **5** Total sales ($ mil): **198** Total employment (000): **0.7**

Company Name	Address				CEO Name	Phone	Co. Type	Sales ($ mil)	Empl. (000)
Lanphere Enterprises Inc.	12505 Broadway	Beaverton	OR	97005	Robert D Lanphere	503-643-5577	R	97 *	0.4
Angel Buick Oldsmobile Inc.	1505 P de Leon	Coral Gables	FL	33134	Jose A Calvo	305-445-5550	S	40 *	<0.1
Kolbe Inc.	22123 Ventura Blvd	Woodland Hills	CA	91364	Andrew R Kolbe	818-348-7865	R	34 *	<0.1
White Brothers Inc.	24845 Corbit Pl	Yorba Linda	CA	92687	Tom White	714-692-3404	R	20 *	0.1
Bikers Dream Inc.	1420 Village Way	Santa Ana	CA	92705	Dennis W Campbell	714-835-8464	P	8	<0.1

Source: *Ward's Business Directory of U.S. Private and Public Companies*, 1998. The company type code used is as follows: P - Public, R - Private, S - Subsidiary, D - Division, J - Joint Venture, A - Affiliate, G - Group. Sales are in millions of dollars, employees are in thousands. An asterisk (*) indicates an estimated sales volume. The symbol < stands for 'less than'.

OCCUPATIONS EMPLOYED BY SIC 557 - BOAT AND MISCELLANEOUS VEHICLE DEALERS

Occupation	% of Total 1996	Change to 2006	Occupation	% of Total 1996	Change to 2006
Salespersons, retail	20.7	19.4	Secretaries, except legal & medical	3.2	-11.1
Mechanics, installers, & repairers nec	10.5	23.3	Maintenance repairers, general utility	3.0	4.5
Sales & related workers nec	9.6	45.7	Vehicle washers & equipment cleaners	2.3	12.0
General managers & top executives	9.3	8.6	Automotive mechanics	2.1	12.0
Motorcycle repairers	6.1	0.9	Cashiers	1.7	13.4
Small engine specialists	5.3	3.3	Janitors & cleaners, maids	1.7	-10.3
Bookkeeping, accounting, & auditing clerks	4.8	-10.3	Marketing, advertising, PR managers	1.5	23.3
Marketing & sales worker supervisors	4.5	12.1	Stock clerks	1.3	147.5
General office clerks	3.9	-3.6	Clerical supervisors & managers	1.3	12.1

Source: *Industry-Occupation Matrix*, Bureau of Labor Statistics. These data relate to one or more 3-digit SIC industry groups rather than to a single 4-digit SIC. The change reported for each occupation to the year 2006 is a percent of growth or decline as estimated by the Bureau of Labor Statistics. The abbreviation nec stands for 'not elsewhere classified'.

STATE AND REGIONAL CONCENTRATION

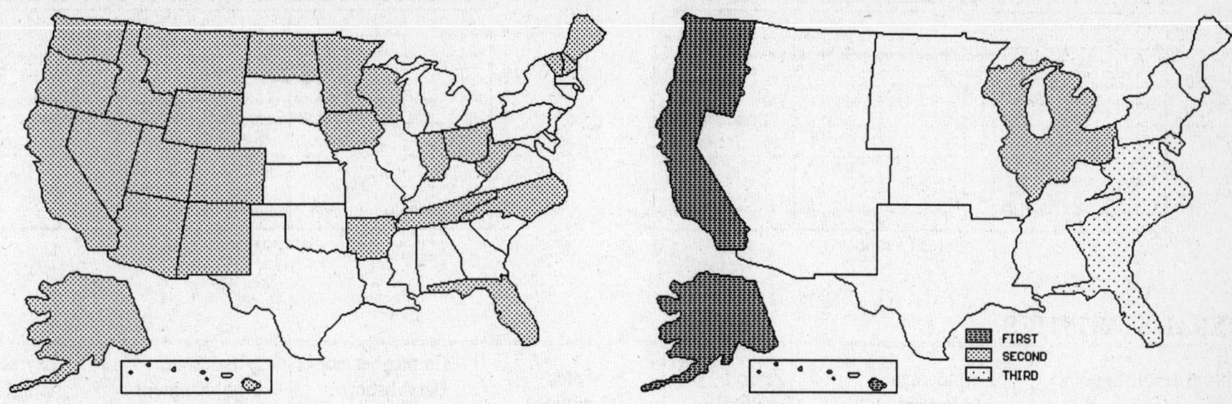

INDUSTRY DATA BY STATE

State	Establishments - 1995 Total (number)	Establishments - 1995 % of U.S.	Employment - 1995 Total (number)	Employment - 1995 % of U.S.	Employment - 1995 Per Estab.	Payroll - 1995 Total ($ mil.)	Payroll - 1995 Per Empl. ($)	Sales - 1992 Total ($ mil.)	Sales - 1992 % of U.S.	Sales - 1992 Per Estab ($)
California	428	11.8	3,245	11.9	8	79.1	24,378	587.6	14.3	186,313
Florida	171	4.7	1,297	4.7	8	30.9	23,827	241.3	5.9	245,428
Texas	194	5.4	1,514	5.5	8	37.0	24,409	226.8	5.5	186,982
Ohio	149	4.1	1,255	4.6	8	25.6	20,425	186.1	4.5	179,811
Illinois	157	4.3	1,237	4.5	8	27.0	21,822	177.8	4.3	187,709
Pennsylvania	175	4.8	1,320	4.8	8	25.8	19,572	176.3	4.3	177,169
New York	156	4.3	844	3.1	5	19.4	23,011	165.7	4.0	205,860
Michigan	105	2.9	938	3.4	9	23.6	25,133	136.5	3.3	208,731
North Carolina	127	3.5	986	3.6	8	23.1	23,471	130.4	3.2	170,624
Wisconsin	97	2.7	792	2.9	8	20.4	25,723	125.1	3.0	185,067
Washington	100	2.8	728	2.7	7	17.6	24,166	124.4	3.0	189,995
Indiana	104	2.9	724	2.6	7	14.8	20,478	100.2	2.4	176,713
Tennessee	79	2.2	620	2.3	8	14.3	23,123	96.2	2.3	206,524
Georgia	85	2.3	692	2.5	8	15.0	21,653	93.9	2.3	181,656
Minnesota	56	1.5	574	2.1	10	12.6	21,925	93.1	2.3	208,253
Virginia	82	2.3	710	2.6	9	17.3	24,432	90.6	2.2	161,813
New Jersey	66	1.8	467	1.7	7	12.9	27,585	86.6	2.1	220,893
Colorado	77	2.1	645	2.4	8	15.7	24,326	86.5	2.1	177,969
Arizona	72	2.0	560	2.0	8	13.9	24,750	83.7	2.0	173,213
Missouri	97	2.7	662	2.4	7	13.5	20,358	82.7	2.0	165,302
Massachusetts	62	1.7	492	1.8	8	12.1	24,551	67.1	1.6	222,993
Iowa	68	1.9	508	1.9	7	9.0	17,671	66.7	1.6	175,052
Maryland	41	1.1	430	1.6	10	11.2	25,951	66.2	1.6	157,545
Alabama	58	1.6	416	1.5	7	8.1	19,423	61.6	1.5	184,359
Arkansas	49	1.4	306	1.1	6	6.8	22,216	60.0	1.5	244,694
Connecticut	44	1.2	313	1.1	7	10.4	33,361	53.3	1.3	182,017
Louisiana	50	1.4	465	1.7	9	8.9	19,239	52.8	1.3	153,584
Oregon	60	1.7	430	1.6	7	7.9	18,344	51.7	1.3	171,053
Oklahoma	46	1.3	313	1.1	7	5.8	18,396	44.7	1.1	174,093
South Carolina	51	1.4	323	1.2	6	7.7	23,706	44.1	1.1	160,527
Kentucky	53	1.5	285	1.0	5	5.3	18,740	39.2	1.0	170,626
New Hampshire	31	0.9	292	1.1	9	7.5	25,702	35.6	0.9	177,950
West Virginia	33	0.9	228	0.8	7	4.5	19,746	33.8	0.8	175,264
Idaho	35	1.0	216	0.8	6	4.0	18,542	32.8	0.8	199,933
Kansas	40	1.1	214	0.8	5	4.7	22,159	32.1	0.8	163,724
New Mexico	36	1.0	234	0.9	7	5.8	24,863	31.6	0.8	194,944
Nevada	29	0.8	231	0.8	8	6.0	26,186	31.5	0.8	196,613
Mississippi	32	0.9	207	0.8	6	4.4	21,382	31.3	0.8	191,085
Utah	31	0.9	308	1.1	10	6.6	21,425	30.7	0.7	159,114
Maine	22	0.6	153	0.6	7	3.5	23,072	28.5	0.7	199,112
Hawaii	18	0.5	176	0.6	10	3.8	21,756	28.0	0.7	190,354
Montana	25	0.7	124	0.5	5	2.0	16,129	23.9	0.6	204,462
Alaska	11	0.3	94	0.3	9	2.6	27,649	21.3	0.5	304,129
Nebraska	32	0.9	157	0.6	5	2.9	18,236	21.0	0.5	153,095
Wyoming	15	0.4	87	0.3	6	1.2	14,092	11.4	0.3	189,600
North Dakota	17	0.5	81	0.3	5	1.8	22,790	10.8	0.3	144,013
Vermont	16	0.4	74	0.3	5	1.6	21,946	10.5	0.3	209,840
South Dakota	20	0.6	166	0.6	8	3.4	20,277	(D)	-	-
Delaware	12	0.3	133	0.5	11	2.7	20,098	(D)	-	-
Rhode Island	8	0.2	56	0.2	7	1.7	30,571	(D)	-	-

Source: *County Business Patterns, 1995* and *Economic Census of the U.S., 1992*. Data are sorted by 1992 revenues and, if revenues are unavailable, by establishments in 1995. The symbol (D) indicates that data are withheld by the source to avoid disclosure of competitive information. A dash (-) indicates that data are not available or undisclosed because they do not meet statistical validity standards. Shaded *states* on the state map indicate those states which have proportionately greater representation in the industry than would be indicated by the state's population; the ratio is based on total revenues or number of establishments. Shaded *regions* indicate where the industry is regionally most concentrated.

5599 - AUTOMOTIVE DEALERS, NEC

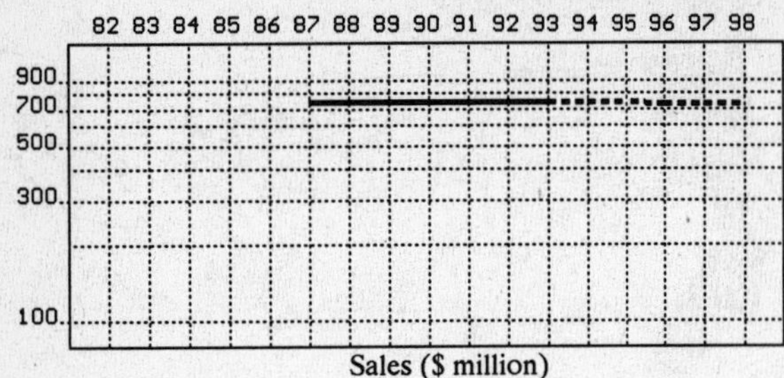

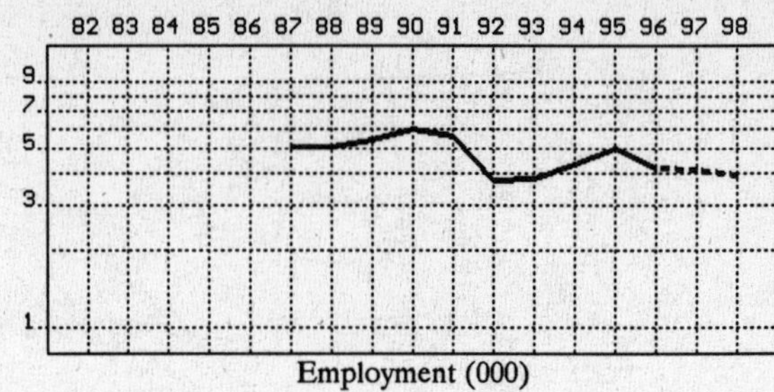

GENERAL STATISTICS

Year	Establishments (number)	Employment (number)	Payroll ($ million)	Sales ($ million)	Employees per Establishment (number)	Sales per Establishment ($)	Payroll per Employee ($)
1982	-	-	-	-	-	-	-
1983	-	-	-	-	-	-	-
1984	-	-	-	-	-	-	-
1985	-	-	-	-	-	-	-
1986	-	-	-	-	-	-	-
1987	852	5,094	82.7	743.7	6	872,942	16,227
1988	822	5,105	100.4	742.2e	6	-	19,663
1989	813	5,441	109.0	740.7e	7	-	20,025
1990	890	5,922	117.9	739.2e	7	-	19,903
1991	906	5,636	113.4	737.7e	6	-	20,120
1992	829	3,762	71.5	736.2	5	888,075	19,016
1993	869	3,811	78.0	734.7p	4	-	20,478
1994	936	4,357	95.0	733.2p	5	-	21,812
1995	1,005	4,982	111.6	731.7p	5	-	22,403
1996	964p	4,225p	97.0p	730.2p	-	-	-
1997	981p	4,090p	96.9p	728.7p	-	-	-
1998	997p	3,955p	96.7p	727.2p	-	-	-

Sources: Economic Census of the United States, 1982, 1987, and 1992. Establishment counts, employment, and payroll are from *County Business Patterns* for non-Census years. Values followed by a 'p' are projections by the editors. Sales and expense data for non-Census years are extrapolations, marked by 'e'. Industries reclassified in 1987 will not have data for prior years. Data are the most recent available at this level of detail.

INDICES OF CHANGE

Year	Establishments (number)	Employment (number)	Payroll ($ million)	Sales ($ million)	Employees per Establishment (number)	Sales per Establishment ($)	Payroll per Employee ($)
1982	-	-	-	-	-	-	-
1983	-	-	-	-	-	-	-
1984	-	-	-	-	-	-	-
1985	-	-	-	-	-	-	-
1986	-	-	-	-	-	-	-
1987	102.8	135.4	115.7	101.0	120.0	98.3	85.3
1988	99.2	135.7	140.4	100.8e	120.0	-	103.4
1989	98.1	144.6	152.4	100.6e	140.0	-	105.3
1990	107.4	157.4	164.9	100.4e	140.0	-	104.7
1991	109.3	149.8	158.6	100.2e	120.0	-	105.8
1992	100.0	100.0	100.0	100.0	100.0	100.0	100.0
1993	104.8	101.3	109.1	99.8p	87.7	-	107.7
1994	112.9	115.8	132.9	99.6p	93.1	-	114.7
1995	121.2	132.4	156.1	99.4p	99.1	-	117.8
1996	116.3p	112.3p	135.7p	99.2p	-	-	-
1997	118.3p	108.7p	135.5p	99.0p	-	-	-
1998	120.3p	105.1p	135.3p	98.8p	-	-	-

Sources: Same as General Statistics. The values shown reflect change from the base year, 1992. Values above 100 mean greater than 1992, values below 100 mean less than 1992, and a value of 100 in the 1982-91 or 1993-98 period means same as 1992. Values followed by a 'p' are projections by the editors; 'e' stands for extrapolation. Data are the most recent available at this level of detail.

SELECTED RATIOS

For 1992	Avg. of All Retail	Analyzed Industry	Index	For 1992	Avg. of All Retail	Analyzed Industry	Index
Employees per Establishment	12	5	38	Sales per Employee	102,941	195,694	190
Payroll per Establishment	146,026	86,248	59	Sales per Establishment	1,241,555	888,058	72
Payroll per Employee	12,107	19,006	157	Expenses per Establishment	na	na	na

Sources: Same as General Statistics. The 'Average of All Manufacturing' column represents the average of all manufacturing industries reported for the most recent complete year available. The Index shows the relationship between the Average and the Analyzed Industry. For example, 100 means that they are equal; 500 that the Analyzed Industry is five times the average; 50 means that the Analyzed Industry is half the national average. The abbreviation 'na' is used to show that data are 'not available'.

LEADING COMPANIES

Number shown: **30** Total sales ($ mil): **886** Total employment (000): **3.8**

Company Name	Address				CEO Name	Phone	Co. Type	Sales ($ mil)	Empl. (000)
Hitchcock Automotive Resources	PO Box 8610	City of Industry	CA	91748	F Hitchcock Jr	818-839-8400	R	120•	0.5
Stevens Aviation Inc.	PO Box 12349	Greenville	SC	29612	Kurt Herwald	803-879-6000	R	87	0.7
Tenco Tractor Inc.	PO Box X	Sacramento	CA	95813	Gordon Beatie	916-991-8200	R	70	0.3
Van Boxtel Ford Inc.	PO Box 11567	Green Bay	WI	54307	Edwin A Van Boxtel	414-499-3131	R	65	0.1
Corporate Fleet Services	5400 Airport Dr	Charlotte	NC	28208	Tom McClune	704-359-0007	R	50	<0.1
Cutter Flying Service Inc.	PO Box 274	Albuquerque	NM	87103	William R Cutter	505-842-4184	R	49•	0.2
Cutter Aviation Inc.	2802 Old Tower Rd	Phoenix	AZ	85034	William W Cutter	602-273-1237	S	33	<0.1
La Pine Truck Sales Inc.	3131 E Royalton	Cleveland	OH	44147	Mel Morris	216-526-6363	R	32	0.1
Meridian Jet Prop Inc.	3796 Vest Mill Rd	Winston-Salem	NC	27103	William D Gardner	919-765-5454	R	25	<0.1
Luke Potter Dodge Inc.	1050 N Orlando	Winter Park	FL	32789	Michael L Potter	407-644-1919	R	21•	<0.1
Turbo West Inc.	10656 W 120th Ave	Broomfield	CO	80021	Christopher Finnoff	303-469-6671	R	21•	<0.1
Austin Jet Corp.	PO Box 13063	Austin	TX	78711	Kirk Hays	512-472-8739	R	20	<0.1
C.B. Hoober and Son Inc.	3452 Phil Pike	Intercourse	PA	17534	J Charles B Hoober	717-768-8231	R	20	0.1
E and J Truck Sales Inc.	PO Box 10107	Augusta	GA	30913	Edwin L Douglass Jr	706-823-8700	R	20	<0.1
Hy-Tek Material Handling Inc.	2222 Curtis LeMay	Columbus	OH	43217	William J Miller	614-497-2500	R	20	0.1
M and L Industries Inc.	1210 St Charles St	Houma	LA	70360	MV Marmade	504-876-2280	R	20	0.1
Thurston Aviation Inc.	PO Box 19032	Charlotte	NC	28219	Ben Hughes	704-359-8670	S	20•	0.1
Utility Trailer Sales of Arizona	1402 N 22nd Ave	Phoenix	AZ	85009	Robert B Cravens	602-254-7213	R	20	<0.1
Crescent Airways Corp.	3555 Trotters Dr	Alpharetta	GA	30201	Jack R Hereth	770-663-8322	P	18	0.1
Woodland Aviation Inc.	PO Box 1157	Woodland	CA	95776	Bruce Watts	530-662-9631	R	18	<0.1
Wiggins Airways Inc. Parts East	PO Box 250	Norwood	MA	02062	David Ladd	617-762-5690	R	18•	0.1
Central Flying Service Inc.	1501 Bond St	Little Rock	AR	72202	Richard N Holbert	501-375-3245	R	17	0.2
Aviation Methods Inc.	SF In'l Airp	San Francisco	CA	94128	Roger N McMullin	415-875-1700	R	16•	0.2
Muncie Aviation Co.	PO Box 1169	Muncie	IN	47308	Otto Arrington	765-289-7141	D	15	<0.1
Jersey Shore Peterbilt Inc.	PO Box 729	Clarksburg	NJ	08510	William Demidowitz	609-259-5950	R	14	<0.1
Mike Berger Aircraft	4230 La Paloma Dr	Tucson	AZ	85718	Mike Berger	602-299-8626	R	14	<0.1
Thompson Lift Truck Co.	2222 Pinson Hwy	Birmingham	AL	35217	Mike Thompson	205-849-3658	R	14•	<0.1
JetCorp	18152 Edison Ave	Chesterfield	MO	63005	D R McCollum	314-530-7000	R	13•	0.2
Reliable Tractor Inc.	PO Box 808	Tifton	GA	31793	DN Stafford III	912-382-4400	R	12•	<0.1
Intern. Aircraft Support L.P.	821 Industrial Rd	San Carlos	CA	94070	Fred von Husen	415-595-5666	R	5•	<0.1

Source: *Ward's Business Directory of U.S. Private and Public Companies*, 1998. The company type code used is as follows: P - Public, R - Private, S - Subsidiary, D - Division, J - Joint Venture, A - Affiliate, G - Group. Sales are in millions of dollars, employees are in thousands. An asterisk (*) indicates an estimated sales volume. The symbol < stands for 'less than'.

OCCUPATIONS EMPLOYED BY SIC 559 - BOAT AND MISCELLANEOUS VEHICLE DEALERS

Occupation	% of Total 1996	Change to 2006	Occupation	% of Total 1996	Change to 2006
Salespersons, retail	20.7	19.4	Secretaries, except legal & medical	3.2	-11.1
Mechanics, installers, & repairers nec	10.5	23.3	Maintenance repairers, general utility	3.0	4.5
Sales & related workers nec	9.6	45.7	Vehicle washers & equipment cleaners	2.3	12.0
General managers & top executives	9.3	8.6	Automotive mechanics	2.1	12.0
Motorcycle repairers	6.1	0.9	Cashiers	1.7	13.4
Small engine specialists	5.3	3.3	Janitors & cleaners, maids	1.7	-10.3
Bookkeeping, accounting, & auditing clerks	4.8	-10.3	Marketing, advertising, PR managers	1.5	23.3
Marketing & sales worker supervisors	4.5	12.1	Stock clerks	1.3	147.5
General office clerks	3.9	-3.6	Clerical supervisors & managers	1.3	12.1

Source: *Industry-Occupation Matrix*, Bureau of Labor Statistics. These data relate to one or more 3-digit SIC industry groups rather than to a single 4-digit SIC. The change reported for each occupation to the year 2006 is a percent of growth or decline as estimated by the Bureau of Labor Statistics. The abbreviation nec stands for 'not elsewhere classified'.

STATE AND REGIONAL CONCENTRATION

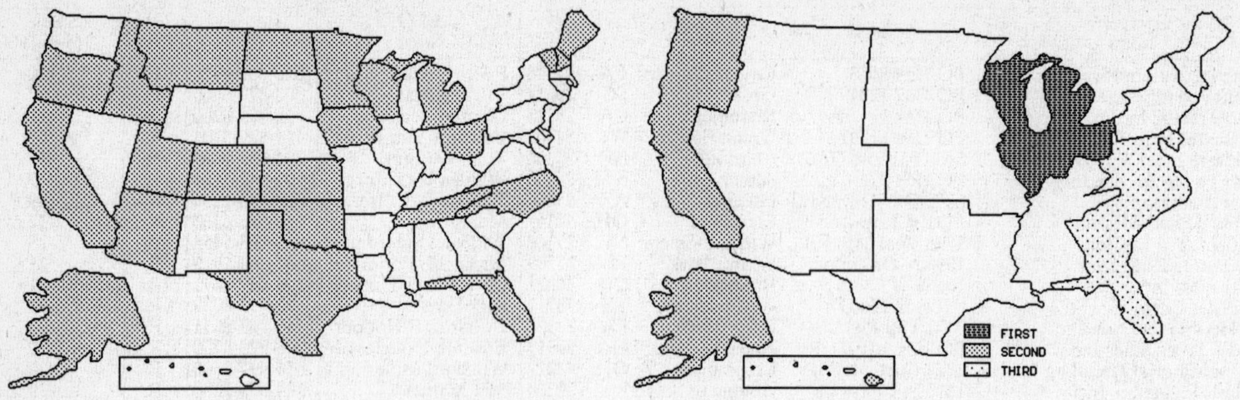

INDUSTRY DATA BY STATE

State	Establishments - 1995 Total (number)	Establishments - 1995 % of U.S.	Employment - 1995 Total (number)	Employment - 1995 % of U.S.	Employment - 1995 Per Estab.	Payroll - 1995 Total ($ mil.)	Payroll - 1995 Per Empl. ($)	Sales - 1992 Total ($ mil.)	Sales - 1992 % of U.S.	Sales - 1992 Per Estab ($)
California	84	8.4	360	7.3	4	8.8	24,375	104.0	14.6	187,344
Texas	99	9.9	502	10.1	5	13.8	27,514	88.9	12.5	228,465
Florida	91	9.1	600	12.1	7	16.2	26,965	69.6	9.8	188,200
Ohio	34	3.4	166	3.3	5	3.9	23,488	48.8	6.9	331,728
Michigan	33	3.3	199	4.0	6	4.2	21,181	43.6	6.1	231,910
Minnesota	49	4.9	234	4.7	5	4.2	17,902	30.3	4.3	187,117
Illinois	40	4.0	225	4.5	6	4.4	19,724	24.4	3.4	143,776
North Carolina	14	1.4	79	1.6	6	1.8	22,253	21.6	3.0	224,760
Oklahoma	20	2.0	126	2.5	6	2.4	18,659	19.4	2.7	175,216
Tennessee	25	2.5	88	1.8	4	1.9	22,125	17.0	2.4	207,244
Wisconsin	35	3.5	185	3.7	5	3.7	20,114	15.4	2.2	160,771
Iowa	16	1.6	77	1.6	5	1.3	16,961	15.2	2.1	187,383
Indiana	15	1.5	50	1.0	3	0.8	15,120	12.7	1.8	374,412
Missouri	16	1.6	68	1.4	4	1.2	18,206	12.4	1.7	213,879
Arizona	21	2.1	134	2.7	6	2.6	19,567	12.2	1.7	166,507
Colorado	23	2.3	131	2.6	6	2.3	17,611	11.9	1.7	146,877
Maine	17	1.7	52	1.0	3	0.9	17,115	11.7	1.6	164,718
Oregon	23	2.3	138	2.8	6	3.5	25,601	11.6	1.6	210,327
Pennsylvania	25	2.5	149	3.0	6	3.6	24,074	11.2	1.6	154,875
Idaho	14	1.4	94	1.9	7	2.5	26,766	9.9	1.4	290,206
Washington	25	2.5	132	2.7	5	4.0	30,280	9.4	1.3	156,650
Georgia	31	3.1	285	5.7	9	3.8	13,400	9.4	1.3	106,614
Alaska	13	1.3	44	0.9	3	0.9	21,364	9.2	1.3	366,760
Kansas	19	1.9	116	2.3	6	1.8	15,845	8.3	1.2	154,278
South Carolina	15	1.5	26	0.5	2	0.4	14,308	8.2	1.1	302,630
Kentucky	6	0.6	20	0.4	3	0.7	32,950	7.9	1.1	441,556
New York	28	2.8	62	1.2	2	1.5	23,968	7.9	1.1	263,900
Maryland	13	1.3	53	1.1	4	1.2	23,302	7.8	1.1	153,706
Utah	13	1.3	73	1.5	6	1.5	20,096	6.9	1.0	85,938
North Dakota	9	0.9	42	0.8	5	0.6	14,357	6.9	1.0	195,743
Mississippi	9	0.9	34	0.7	4	0.7	21,971	6.4	0.9	187,794
Vermont	11	1.1	38	0.8	3	1.0	25,658	5.2	0.7	322,250
New Hampshire	7	0.7	11	0.2	2	0.1	10,455	4.7	0.7	131,194
Alabama	10	1.0	23	0.5	2	0.5	20,174	4.3	0.6	149,828
Arkansas	14	1.4	34	0.7	2	0.8	23,941	4.3	0.6	224,421
Nevada	6	0.6	22	0.4	4	0.4	17,636	3.0	0.4	246,833
Virginia	9	0.9	34	0.7	4	0.9	27,324	2.7	0.4	144,421
Connecticut	5	0.5	20	0.4	4	0.7	36,900	2.7	0.4	99,519
Montana	17	1.7	37	0.7	2	0.5	12,757	2.4	0.3	264,889
New Mexico	3	0.3	8	0.2	3	0.3	33,375	2.2	0.3	126,706
Massachusetts	10	1.0	37	0.7	4	0.8	22,378	(D)	-	-
New Jersey	10	1.0	70	1.4	7	2.4	33,829	(D)	-	-
Louisiana	8	0.8	59	1.2	7	1.3	21,644	(D)	-	-
Delaware	5	0.5	19	0.4	4	0.4	20,105	(D)	-	-
South Dakota	5	0.5	7	0.1	1	0.1	15,857	(D)	-	-
Nebraska	3	0.3	0-19	-	-	(D)	-	(D)	-	-
Wyoming	3	0.3	2	0.0	1	0.0	17,500	(D)	-	-
Rhode Island	2	0.2	0-19	-	-	(D)	-	(D)	-	-
West Virginia	2	0.2	0-19	-	-	(D)	-	(D)	-	-

Source: County Business Patterns, 1995 and *Economic Census of the U.S., 1992*. Data are sorted by 1992 revenues and, if revenues are unavailable, by establishments in 1995. The symbol (D) indicates that data are withheld by the source to avoid disclosure of competitive information. A dash (-) indicates that data are not available or undisclosed because they do not meet statistical validity standards. Shaded *states* on the state map indicate those states which have proportionately greater representation in the industry than would be indicated by the state's population; the ratio is based on total revenues or number of establishments. Shaded *regions* indicate where the industry is regionally most concentrated.

5611 - MEN'S & BOYS' CLOTHING STORES

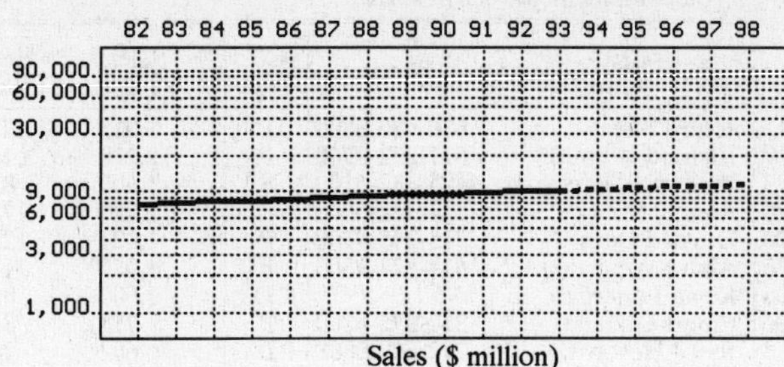

Sales ($ million)

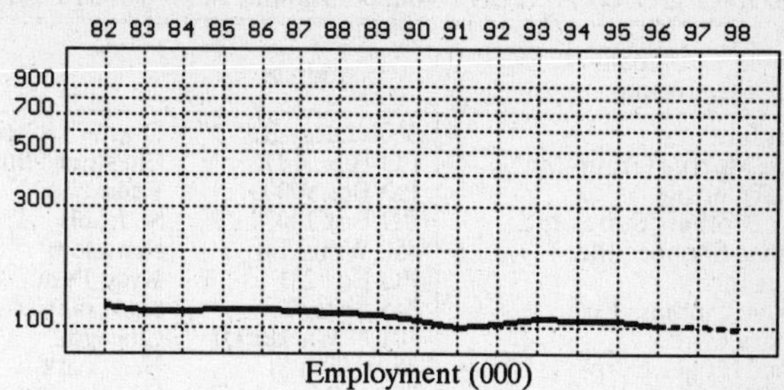

Employment (000)

GENERAL STATISTICS

Year	Establishments (number)	Employment (number)	Payroll ($ million)	Sales ($ million)	Employees per Establishment (number)	Sales per Establishment ($)	Payroll per Employee ($)
1982	18,617	123,136	1,223.6	7,734.5	7	415,455	9,937
1983	17,408	116,850	1,255.9	7,961.4e	7	-	10,748
1984	16,675	115,490	1,303.1	8,188.2e	7	-	11,283
1985	15,941	118,367	1,435.5	8,415.1e	7	-	12,127
1986	15,435	117,435	1,379.0	8,642.0e	8	-	11,743
1987	16,507	115,169	1,360.7	8,868.8	7	537,276	11,815
1988	15,420	114,967	1,485.0	9,097.8e	7	-	12,917
1989	14,986	112,560	1,523.8	9,326.7e	8	-	13,538
1990	14,677	107,805	1,496.1	9,555.7e	7	-	13,878
1991	13,979	100,567	1,416.8	9,784.7e	7	-	14,089
1992	15,566	104,520	1,439.9	10,013.6	7	643,302	13,777
1993	14,692	109,031	1,423.1	10,239.2p	7	-	13,052
1994	14,646	106,542	1,449.6	10,467.1p	7	-	13,606
1995	13,905	107,132	1,470.0	10,695.0p	8	-	13,721
1996	13,538p	102,464p	1,521.1p	10,922.9p	-	-	-
1997	13,263p	101,177p	1,536.7p	11,150.8p	-	-	-
1998	12,987p	99,891p	1,552.2p	11,378.7p	-	-	-

Sources: Economic Census of the United States, 1982, 1987, and 1992. Establishment counts, employment, and payroll are from *County Business Patterns* for non-Census years. Values followed by a 'p' are projections by the editors. Sales and expense data for non-Census years are extrapolations, marked by 'e'. Industries reclassified in 1987 will not have data for prior years. Data are the most recent available at this level of detail.

INDICES OF CHANGE

Year	Establishments (number)	Employment (number)	Payroll ($ million)	Sales ($ million)	Employees per Establishment (number)	Sales per Establishment ($)	Payroll per Employee ($)
1982	119.6	117.8	85.0	77.2	100.0	64.6	72.1
1983	111.8	111.8	87.2	79.5e	100.0	-	78.0
1984	107.1	110.5	90.5	81.8e	100.0	-	81.9
1985	102.4	113.2	99.7	84.0e	100.0	-	88.0
1986	99.2	112.4	95.8	86.3e	114.3	-	85.2
1987	106.0	110.2	94.5	88.6	100.0	83.5	85.8
1988	99.1	110.0	103.1	90.9e	100.0	-	93.8
1989	96.3	107.7	105.8	93.1e	114.3	-	98.3
1990	94.3	103.1	103.9	95.4e	100.0	-	100.7
1991	89.8	96.2	98.4	97.7e	100.0	-	102.3
1992	100.0	100.0	100.0	100.0	100.0	100.0	100.0
1993	94.4	104.3	98.8	102.3p	106.0	-	94.7
1994	94.1	101.9	100.7	104.5p	103.9	-	98.8
1995	89.3	102.5	102.1	106.8p	110.1	-	99.6
1996	87.0p	98.0p	105.6p	109.1p	-	-	-
1997	85.2p	96.8p	106.7p	111.4p	-	-	-
1998	83.4p	95.6p	107.8p	113.6p	-	-	-

Sources: Same as General Statistics. The values shown reflect change from the base year, 1992. Values above 100 mean greater than 1992, values below 100 mean less than 1992, and a value of 100 in the 1982-91 or 1993-98 period means same as 1992. Values followed by a 'p' are projections by the editors; 'e' stands for extrapolation. Data are the most recent available at this level of detail.

SELECTED RATIOS

For 1992	Avg. of All Retail	Analyzed Industry	Index	For 1992	Avg. of All Retail	Analyzed Industry	Index
Employees per Establishment	12	7	56	Sales per Employee	102,941	95,806	93
Payroll per Establishment	146,026	92,503	63	Sales per Establishment	1,241,555	643,299	52
Payroll per Employee	12,107	13,776	114	Expenses per Establishment	na	na	na

Sources: Same as General Statistics. The 'Average of All Manufacturing' column represents the average of all manufacturing industries reported for the most recent complete year available. The Index shows the relationship between the Average and the Analyzed Industry. For example, 100 means that they are equal; 500 that the Analyzed Industry is five times the average; 50 means that the Analyzed Industry is half the national average. The abbreviation 'na' is used to show that data are 'not available'.

LEADING COMPANIES

Number shown: **50** Total sales ($ mil): **17,951** Total employment (000): **151.8**

Company Name	Address				CEO Name	Phone	Co. Type	Sales ($ mil)	Empl. (000)
Spiegel Inc.	3500 Lacey Rd	Downers Grove	IL	60515	John J Shea	630-986-8800	P	3,015	13.4
Neiman Marcus Group Inc.	PO Box 9187	Chestnut Hill	MA	02167	Richard A Smith	617-232-0760	P	2,210	11.3
Eddie Bauer Inc.	PO Box 97000	Redmond	WA	98073	Richard T Fersch	425-882-6100	S	1,600	8.0
Edison Brothers Stores Inc.	PO Box 14020	St. Louis	MO	63178	Alan D Miller	314-331-6000	P	1,090	17.7
Charming Shoppes Inc.	450 Winks Ln	Bensalem	PA	19020	Dorrit J Bern	215-245-9100	P	1,024	12.1
J. Baker Inc.	PO Box 231	Hyde Park	MA	02136	Alan I Weinstein	617-828-9300	P	1,020	11.6
Old Navy Clothing Co.	345 Spear St	San Francisco	CA	94105	Kevin Lonergan	--	D	1,000	8.0
Hartmarx Corp.	101 N Wacker Dr	Chicago	IL	60606	Elbert O Hand	312-372-6300	P	718	8.1
Tommy Hilfiger Corp.	25 W 39th St	New York	NY	10018	Joel J Horowitz	212-840-8888	P	662	1.6
Men's Wearhouse Inc.	5803 Glenmont Dr	Houston	TX	77081	George Zimmer	713-295-7200	P	631	4.9
Nautica Enterprises Inc.	40 West 57th St	New York	NY	10019	Harvey Sanders	212-541-5990	P	387	1.3
American Eagle Outfitters Inc.	PO Box 788	Warrendale	PA	15095	Jay L Schottenstein	412-776-4857	P	326	5.4
Farah Inc.	PO Box 13800	El Paso	TX	79902	Richard C Allender	915-593-4444	P	274	4.0
Buckle Inc.	2407 West 24th St	Kearney	NE	68847	Dennis H Nelson	308-236-8491	P	268	4.0
Today's Man Inc.	835 Lancer Dr	Morrestown	NJ	08057	David Feld	609-235-5656	P	263	1.7
Abercrombie and Fitch Co.	4 Limited Pkwy	Reynoldsburg	OH	43068	Michael S Jeffries	614-577-6500	P	236	3.8
Bergdorf Goodman Inc.	754 5th Ave	New York	NY	10019	Stephen C Elkin	212-753-7300	S	235 *	1.2
Pacific Sunwear of California	5200 E La Palma	Anaheim	CA	92807	Greg H Weaver	714-693-8066	P	227	3.2
Casual Male Inc.	65 Sprague St	Hyde Park	MA	02136	Larry I Kelley	617-361-2000	S	214	2.3
Deb Shops Inc.	9401 Blue Grass Rd	Philadelphia	PA	19114	Marvin Rounick	215-676-6000	P	205	2.6
HSSI Inc.	222 N Lasalle 1500	Chicago	IL	60601	Harvey Weinberger	312-629-8800	R	200 *	2.5
Maurices Inc.	105 W Superior St	Duluth	MN	55802	R Brenninkmeyer	218-727-8431	R	170 *	2.2
Britches of Georgetowne Inc.	PO Box 1189	Herndon	VA	22070	Dan Finkelstein	703-471-7900	S	160 *	2.1
Urban Outfitters Inc.	1809 Walnut St	Philadelphia	PA	19103	Richard A Hayne	215-564-2313	P	156	2.2
Jos. A. Bank Clothiers Inc.	500 Hanover Pike	Hampstead	MD	21074	Timothy Finley	410-239-2700	P	155	1.4
S and K Famous Brands Inc.	PO Box 31800	Richmond	VA	23294	Stuart C Siegel	804-346-2500	P	145	1.7
Hot Topic	3410 Pomona Blvd	Pomona	CA	91768	Orv Madden	909-869-6373		122 *	1.5
Mossimo Inc.	15320 Barranca	Irvine	CA	92718	Mossimo Giannulli	714-453-1300	P	109	0.3
Harold's Stores Inc.	P O Drawer 2970	Norman	OK	73070	Rebecca P Casey	405-329-4045	P	108	1.3
Conway Stores Inc.	1 Penn Plz, 38th Fl	New York	NY	10119	Richard Cowen	212-967-0897	R	97 *	1.2
Humphrey's Inc.	2009 W Hastings St	Chicago	IL	60608	Sheldon Young	312-997-2358	R	95	0.7
Tom James Co.	PO Box 1469	Brentwood	TN	37024	J McEachern	615-771-1122	R	90	1.3
K and G Men's Center Inc.	1225 Chattah	Atlanta	GA	30318	S H Greenspan	404-351-7987	P	88	0.4
Mark Shale Co.	500 Joliet Rd	Willowbrook	IL	60522	Scott Baskin	708-789-0130	R	80	1.0
Jay Jacobs Inc.	1530 5th Ave	Seattle	WA	98101	Rex Loren Steffey	206-622-5400	P	73	0.6
Barney's Inc.	106 7th Ave	New York	NY	10011	Gene Pressman	212-593-7800	R	58 *	0.9
Bigsby and Kruthers Inc.	1750 N Clark St	Chicago	IL	60614	Gene Silverberg	312-440-1700	R	50	0.3
Fine's Men's Shops Inc.	1164 Azalea Grdn	Norfolk	VA	23502	Barry Fine	804-857-6013	S	48	0.6
Rochester Big and Tall Clothing	2660 Harrison St	San Francisco	CA	94110	Robert L Sockolov	415-550-4777	R	48 *	0.3
Paul Stuart Inc.	Madison & 45th St	New York	NY	10017	Clifford Grodd	212-682-0320	R	34	0.2
Edison Menswear Group	501 N Broadway	St. Louis	MO	63102	Karl Metchner	314-331-6000	D	32 *	0.4
H.C. Shaw Co.	PO Box 31510	Stockton	CA	95212	Karen Simon	209-983-8484	R	30	0.2
Lansons Inc.	15675 NW 15th Ave	Miami	FL	33169	A Jay Kaiser	305-621-3191	R	30 *	0.4
Gucci America Inc.	50 Hartz Way	Secaucus	NJ	07094	Domenico Desole	201-867-8800	R	28	0.5
Gentlemen's Wear-House Inc.	194 Riverside Ave	New Bedford	MA	02746	John Walsh	508-997-4508	S	26	0.2
Dick Bruhn Inc.	PO Box 81600	Salinas	CA	93912	RL Bruhn	408-758-4684	R	24	0.5
Eagleson's Big and Tall Inc.	125-B Vineland	City of Industry	CA	91746	Ira Fulten	818-855-4300	R	24	0.2
Maurice L. Rothschild and Co.	7450 Skokie Blvd	Skokie	IL	60077	Clarence Permut	708-673-7450	R	24	0.4
Long Rap Inc.	1420 Wisconsin NW	Washington	DC	20007	Chuck Rendelman	202-337-6610	R	22 *	0.2
Cavalier Mens Shop of F Street	1345 University E	Langley Park	MD	20783	Norman Orleans	301-431-1800	R	20 *	0.3

Source: *Ward's Business Directory of U.S. Private and Public Companies*, 1998. The company type code used is as follows: P - Public, R - Private, S - Subsidiary, D - Division, J - Joint Venture, A - Affiliate, G - Group. Sales are in millions of dollars, employees are in thousands. An asterisk (*) indicates an estimated sales volume. The symbol < stands for 'less than'.

OCCUPATIONS EMPLOYED BY SIC 561 - CLOTHING AND ACCESORIES STORES

Occupation	% of Total 1996	Change to 2006	Occupation	% of Total 1996	Change to 2006
Salespersons, retail	56.2	-9.3	Custom tailors & sewers	2.0	-44.7
Marketing & sales worker supervisors	12.0	-14.9	Traffic, shipping, receiving clerks	1.3	-14.9
Cashiers	6.3	-13.9	Wholesale & retail buyers, except farm products	1.1	-29.5
Stock clerks	5.2	-25.8	Bookkeeping, accounting, & auditing clerks	1.0	-31.9
General managers & top executives	3.9	-17.5			

Source: *Industry-Occupation Matrix*, Bureau of Labor Statistics. These data relate to one or more 3-digit SIC industry groups rather than to a single 4-digit SIC. The change reported for each occupation to the year 2006 is a percent of growth or decline as estimated by the Bureau of Labor Statistics. The abbreviation nec stands for 'not elsewhere classified'.

STATE AND REGIONAL CONCENTRATION

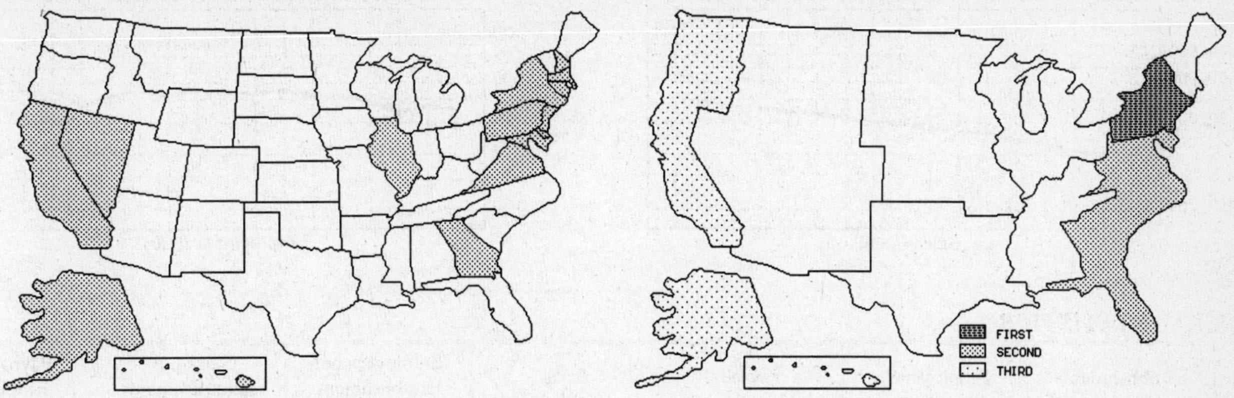

INDUSTRY DATA BY STATE

State	Establishments - 1995 Total (number)	Establishments - 1995 % of U.S.	Employment - 1995 Total (number)	Employment - 1995 % of U.S.	Employment - 1995 Per Estab.	Payroll - 1995 Total ($ mil.)	Payroll - 1995 Per Empl. ($)	Sales - 1992 Total ($ mil.)	Sales - 1992 % of U.S.	Sales - 1992 Per Estab ($)
California	1,640	11.8	12,809	12.0	8	203.7	15,904	1,330.2	13.3	99,694
New York	1,297	9.3	9,958	9.3	8	185.8	18,662	1,163.9	11.6	113,297
Texas	814	5.9	6,083	5.7	7	84.5	13,892	601.8	6.0	94,883
Illinois	717	5.2	5,357	5.0	7	73.5	13,723	540.4	5.4	98,857
Florida	860	6.2	6,122	5.7	7	78.4	12,812	508.0	5.1	97,506
New Jersey	576	4.1	4,236	4.0	7	59.3	14,002	495.2	4.9	107,404
Pennsylvania	615	4.4	5,466	5.1	9	70.4	12,874	488.8	4.9	96,906
Michigan	459	3.3	3,665	3.4	8	49.1	13,404	367.1	3.7	99,682
Ohio	500	3.6	3,957	3.7	8	45.3	11,458	337.3	3.4	79,679
Virginia	405	2.9	4,129	3.9	10	51.9	12,574	331.3	3.3	97,461
Massachusetts	356	2.6	3,121	2.9	9	45.2	14,473	319.5	3.2	101,447
Georgia	464	3.3	3,667	3.4	8	45.2	12,317	268.6	2.7	89,550
Maryland	299	2.2	2,717	2.5	9	34.3	12,626	248.4	2.5	84,016
North Carolina	356	2.6	2,655	2.5	7	32.2	12,120	214.5	2.1	82,208
Tennessee	301	2.2	2,299	2.1	8	30.4	13,210	186.8	1.9	93,855
Connecticut	195	1.4	1,678	1.6	9	24.5	14,577	170.4	1.7	103,984
Missouri	296	2.1	2,113	2.0	7	27.1	12,805	167.4	1.7	88,948
Indiana	260	1.9	2,082	1.9	8	21.9	10,541	166.2	1.7	82,226
Minnesota	231	1.7	1,703	1.6	7	21.5	12,608	152.5	1.5	87,090
Wisconsin	232	1.7	1,416	1.3	6	17.2	12,169	143.6	1.4	81,198
Louisiana	227	1.6	1,701	1.6	7	20.7	12,159	142.2	1.4	84,401
Washington	204	1.5	1,685	1.6	8	22.2	13,153	140.2	1.4	81,759
Colorado	190	1.4	1,503	1.4	8	18.8	12,485	117.7	1.2	106,848
South Carolina	204	1.5	1,352	1.3	7	14.2	10,522	105.9	1.1	88,191
Arizona	182	1.3	1,369	1.3	8	16.8	12,237	98.7	1.0	88,752
Iowa	191	1.4	1,272	1.2	7	14.4	11,347	94.1	0.9	78,299
Alabama	185	1.3	1,230	1.1	7	16.7	13,544	91.4	0.9	86,260
Hawaii	84	0.6	611	0.6	7	8.2	13,448	79.4	0.8	94,023
Kentucky	126	0.9	862	0.8	7	9.2	10,684	68.8	0.7	92,204
Kansas	116	0.8	839	0.8	7	8.5	10,079	64.4	0.6	83,986
D.C.	53	0.4	513	0.5	10	8.8	17,105	64.3	0.6	130,736
Oregon	118	0.8	790	0.7	7	10.7	13,522	62.3	0.6	83,282
Oklahoma	111	0.8	662	0.6	6	8.1	12,305	61.1	0.6	91,311
Nevada	87	0.6	673	0.6	8	12.3	18,257	60.3	0.6	109,865
Mississippi	138	1.0	817	0.8	6	7.9	9,667	55.7	0.6	80,582
New Hampshire	73	0.5	683	0.6	9	6.6	9,630	48.6	0.5	98,720
Maine	60	0.4	493	0.5	8	5.0	10,225	46.5	0.5	113,102
Nebraska	84	0.6	582	0.5	7	7.8	13,323	45.0	0.4	80,411
Arkansas	96	0.7	514	0.5	5	6.1	11,807	44.2	0.4	87,789
Utah	73	0.5	642	0.6	9	7.5	11,688	42.6	0.4	92,182
Rhode Island	51	0.4	299	0.3	6	3.5	11,609	36.8	0.4	97,687
West Virginia	55	0.4	418	0.4	8	4.7	11,158	32.1	0.3	68,976
Alaska	30	0.2	170	0.2	6	3.9	22,812	30.7	0.3	136,653
Delaware	48	0.3	459	0.4	10	4.8	10,423	30.6	0.3	87,579
South Dakota	41	0.3	286	0.3	7	3.5	12,140	25.8	0.3	76,674
Idaho	42	0.3	305	0.3	7	3.3	10,816	25.8	0.3	99,173
North Dakota	38	0.3	279	0.3	7	3.5	12,631	24.8	0.2	76,345
New Mexico	43	0.3	356	0.3	8	4.6	13,045	22.5	0.2	82,238
Vermont	38	0.3	286	0.3	8	3.2	11,115	21.2	0.2	84,311
Montana	30	0.2	158	0.1	5	1.9	11,804	17.9	0.2	95,663
Wyoming	14	0.1	90	0.1	6	1.5	16,300	10.2	0.1	114,584

Source: *County Business Patterns, 1995* and *Economic Census of the U.S., 1992*. Data are sorted by 1992 revenues and, if revenues are unavailable, by establishments in 1995. The symbol (D) indicates that data are withheld by the source to avoid disclosure of competitive information. A dash (-) indicates that data are not available or undisclosed because they do not meet statistical validity standards. Shaded *states* on the state map indicate those states which have proportionately greater representation in the industry than would be indicated by the state's population; the ratio is based on total revenues or number of establishments. Shaded *regions* indicate where the industry is regionally most concentrated.

5621 - WOMEN'S CLOTHING STORES

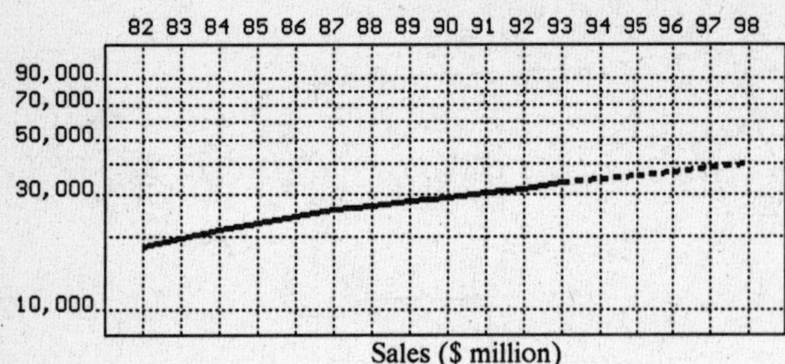

Sales ($ million)

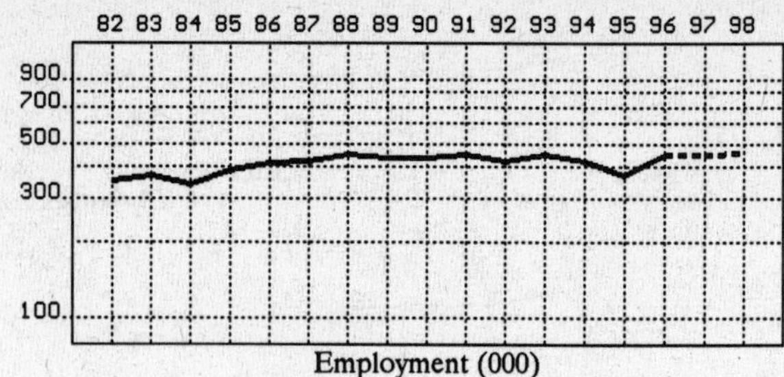

Employment (000)

GENERAL STATISTICS

Year	Establishments (number)	Employment (number)	Payroll ($ million)	Sales ($ million)	Employees per Establishment (number)	Sales per Establishment ($)	Payroll per Employee ($)
1982	45,146	351,277	2,383.4	18,002.1	8	398,753	6,785
1983	45,697	367,450	2,716.8	19,575.2*e*	8	-	7,394
1984	45,098	343,854	2,747.2	21,148.3*e*	8	-	7,990
1985	44,443	387,498	3,082.8	22,721.4*e*	9	-	7,956
1986	45,125	413,667	3,304.3	24,294.5*e*	9	-	7,988
1987	52,304	418,972	3,150.3	25,867.6	8	494,562	7,519
1988	52,758	450,551	3,728.2	26,959.3*e*	9	-	8,275
1989	50,142	434,326	3,810.9	28,051.1*e*	9	-	8,774
1990	50,175	438,983	4,013.6	29,142.8*e*	9	-	9,143
1991	48,845	444,580	4,043.8	30,234.6*e*	9	-	9,096
1992	50,174	423,022	3,690.3	31,326.3	8	624,354	8,724
1993	50,236	448,696	4,193.1	33,205.8*p*	9	-	9,345
1994	47,715	419,793	4,124.8	34,538.2*p*	9	-	9,826
1995	42,204	369,816	3,547.9	35,870.6*p*	9	-	9,594
1996	49,179*p*	444,420*p*	4,361.4*p*	37,203.0*p*	-	-	-
1997	49,354*p*	449,272*p*	4,480.6*p*	38,535.4*p*	-	-	-
1998	49,530*p*	454,123*p*	4,599.9*p*	39,867.9*p*	-	-	-

Sources: Economic Census of the United States, 1982, 1987, and 1992. Establishment counts, employment, and payroll are from *County Business Patterns* for non-Census years. Values followed by a 'p' are projections by the editors. Sales and expense data for non-Census years are extrapolations, marked by 'e'. Industries reclassified in 1987 will not have data for prior years. Data are the most recent available at this level of detail.

INDICES OF CHANGE

Year	Establishments (number)	Employment (number)	Payroll ($ million)	Sales ($ million)	Employees per Establishment (number)	Sales per Establishment ($)	Payroll per Employee ($)
1982	90.0	83.0	64.6	57.5	100.0	63.9	77.8
1983	91.1	86.9	73.6	62.5*e*	100.0	-	84.8
1984	89.9	81.3	74.4	67.5*e*	100.0	-	91.6
1985	88.6	91.6	83.5	72.5*e*	112.5	-	91.2
1986	89.9	97.8	89.5	77.6*e*	112.5	-	91.6
1987	104.2	99.0	85.4	82.6	100.0	79.2	86.2
1988	105.2	106.5	101.0	86.1*e*	112.5	-	94.9
1989	99.9	102.7	103.3	89.5*e*	112.5	-	100.6
1990	100.0	103.8	108.8	93.0*e*	112.5	-	104.8
1991	97.4	105.1	109.6	96.5*e*	112.5	-	104.3
1992	100.0	100.0	100.0	100.0	100.0	100.0	100.0
1993	100.1	106.1	113.6	106.0*p*	111.6	-	107.1
1994	95.1	99.2	111.8	110.3*p*	110.0	-	112.6
1995	84.1	87.4	96.1	114.5*p*	109.5	-	110.0
1996	98.0*p*	105.1*p*	118.2*p*	118.8*p*	-	-	-
1997	98.4*p*	106.2*p*	121.4*p*	123.0*p*	-	-	-
1998	98.7*p*	107.4*p*	124.6*p*	127.3*p*	-	-	-

Sources: Same as General Statistics. The values shown reflect change from the base year, 1992. Values above 100 mean greater than 1992, values below 100 mean less than 1992, and a value of 100 in the 1982-91 or 1993-98 period means same as 1992. Values followed by a 'p' are projections by the editors; 'e' stands for extrapolation. Data are the most recent available at this level of detail.

SELECTED RATIOS

For 1992	Avg. of All Retail	Analyzed Industry	Index	For 1992	Avg. of All Retail	Analyzed Industry	Index
Employees per Establishment	12	8	70	Sales per Employee	102,941	74,054	72
Payroll per Establishment	146,026	73,550	50	Sales per Establishment	1,241,555	624,353	50
Payroll per Employee	12,107	8,724	72	Expenses per Establishment	na	na	na

Sources: Same as General Statistics. The 'Average of All Manufacturing' column represents the average of all manufacturing industries reported for the most recent complete year available. The Index shows the relationship between the Average and the Analyzed Industry. For example, 100 means that they are equal; 500 that the Analyzed Industry is five times the average; 50 means that the Analyzed Industry is half the national average. The abbreviation 'na' is used to show that data are 'not available'.

LEADING COMPANIES

Number shown: **50** Total sales ($ mil): **30,158** Total employment (000): **318.0**

Company Name	Address				CEO Name	Phone	Co. Type	Sales ($ mil)	Empl. (000)
Limited Inc.	PO Box 16000	Columbus	OH	43216	Leslie H Wexner	614-479-7000	P	7,881	105.6
Spiegel Holdings Inc.	3500 Lacey Rd	Downers Grove	IL	60515	John Irving	630-986-8800	R	3,015 *	13.4
Neiman Marcus Group Inc.	PO Box 9187	Chestnut Hill	MA	02167	Richard A Smith	617-232-0760	P	2,210	11.3
Eddie Bauer Inc.	PO Box 97000	Redmond	WA	98073	Richard T Fersch	425-882-6100	S	1,600	8.0
Lerner New York Inc.	460 W 33rd St	New York	NY	10001	Richard P Crystal	212-736-1222	S	1,400 *	14.0
Edison Brothers Stores Inc.	PO Box 14020	St. Louis	MO	63178	Alan D Miller	314-331-6000	P	1,090	17.7
Talbots Inc.	175 Beal St	Hingham	MA	02043	Arnold Zetcher	781-749-7600	P	1,054	7.2
Charming Shoppes Inc.	450 Winks Ln	Bensalem	PA	19020	Dorrit J Bern	215-245-9100	P	1,024	12.1
Old Navy Clothing Co.	345 Spear St	San Francisco	CA	94105	Kevin Lonergan	--	D	1,000	8.0
Limited Express	1 Limited Pkwy	Columbus	OH	43230	Michael A Wiess	614-479-7000	D	740	10.0
AnnTaylor Stores Corp.	142 W 57th St	New York	NY	10019	Patricia DeRosa	212-541-3300	P	731	6.0
Dress Barn Inc.	30 Dunnigan Dr	Suffern	NY	10901	Elliot S Jaffe	914-369-4500	P	501	7.0
Cato Corp.	PO Box 34216	Charlotte	NC	28234	Wayland H Cato Jr	704-554-8510	P	492	6.8
Hit or Miss Inc.	100 Campanelli	Stoughton	MA	02072	Nesim Avigdor	781-344-0800	R	393 *	2.0
Loehmann's Inc.	2500 Halsey St	Bronx	NY	10461	Robert N Friedman	718-409-2000	P	386	2.6
United Retail Group Inc.	365 W Passaic St	Rochelle Park	NJ	07662	Raphael Benaroya	201-845-0880	P	363	5.5
Big M Inc.	12 Vreeland Ave	Totowa	NJ	07512	Larry Mandelbaum	201-890-0021	R	340 *	4.3
Lane Bryant Inc.	5 Limited Pkwy E	Reynoldsburg	OH	43068	Jill Dean	614-577-4000	S	340 *	5.0
Laura Ashley Inc.	1300 MacArthur	Mahwah	NJ	07430	Ann Iverson	201-934-3000	S	330 *	4.2
American Eagle Outfitters Inc.	PO Box 788	Warrendale	PA	15095	Jay L Schottenstein	412-776-4857	P	326	5.4
Clothestime Inc.	5325 E Hunter Ave	Anaheim	CA	92807	John Ortega II	714-779-5881	P	308	4.7
One Price Clothing Stores Inc.	PO Box 2487	Spartanburg	SC	29304	Henry D Jacobs Jr	803-433-8888	P	299	4.1
Catherines Stores Corp.	3742 Lamar Ave	Memphis	TN	38118	Bernard J Wein	901-363-3900	P	277	2.6
Buckle Inc.	2407 West 24th St	Kearney	NE	68847	Dennis H Nelson	308-236-8491	P	268	4.0
Wet Seal Inc.	64 Fairbanks	Irvine	CA	92718	Kathy Bronstein	714-583-9029	P	267	4.6
Mothers Work Inc.	456 N 5th St	Philadelphia	PA	19123	Dan W Matthias	215-873-2200	P	247	1.7
Abercrombie and Fitch Co.	4 Limited Pkwy	Reynoldsburg	OH	43068	Michael S Jeffries	614-577-6500	P	236	3.8
Bergdorf Goodman Inc.	754 5th Ave	New York	NY	10019	Stephen C Elkin	212-753-7300	S	235 *	1.2
Pacific Sunwear of California	5200 E La Palma	Anaheim	CA	92807	Greg H Weaver	714-693-8066	P	227	3.2
Deb Shops Inc.	9401 Blue Grass Rd	Philadelphia	PA	19114	Marvin Rounick	215-676-6000	P	205	2.6
HSSI Inc.	222 N Lasalle 1500	Chicago	IL	60601	Harvey Weinberger	312-629-8800	R	200 *	2.5
Paul Harris Stores Inc.	6003 Guion Rd	Indianapolis	IN	46254	Charlotte G Fischer	317-293-3900	P	190	2.5
Seifert's Inc.	1035 33rd Ave SW	Cedar Rapids	IA	52404	C Dudley Brown	319-366-7302	S	190 *	2.5
Gantos Inc.	3260 Patterson SE	Grand Rapids	MI	49512	L Douglas Gantos	616-949-7000	P	184	2.3
Maurices Inc.	105 W Superior St	Duluth	MN	55802	R Brenninkmeyer	218-727-8431	R	170 *	2.2
Urban Outfitters Inc.	1809 Walnut St	Philadelphia	PA	19103	Richard A Hayne	215-564-2313	P	156	2.2
Winkelman Stores Inc.	45000 Helm St	Plymouth	MI	48170	Daniel Maresca	313-451-5000	S	150 *	2.0
Cache Inc.	1460 Broadway	New York	NY	10036	Andrew Saul	212-575-3200	P	136	1.3
Harold's Stores Inc.	P O Drawer 2970	Norman	OK	73070	Rebecca P Casey	405-329-4045	P	108	1.3
CWT Specialty Stores Inc.	505 Collins St	S. Attleboro	MA	02703	E. S Finkelstein	508-399-6000	R	100	1.3
Vogue Shops Inc.	6225 Powers Ave	Jacksonville	FL	32217	Ronnie Rosenbaum	904-737-0811	S	99 *	1.3
Braun's Fashions Corp.	2400 Xenium Ln N	Plymouth	MN	55441	Nicholas H Cook	612-551-5000	P	96	1.5
Vanity Shop of Grand Forks	PO Box 547	Fargo	ND	58107	Emery Jahnke	701-237-3330	R	90	1.3
Evans Inc.	36 S State St	Chicago	IL	60603	Patrick J Regan	312-855-2000	P	83	0.9
Mark Shale Co.	500 Joliet Rd	Willowbrook	IL	60522	Scott Baskin	708-789-0130	R	80	1.0
Joyce Leslie Inc.	202 Washington	Carlstadt	NJ	07072	JH Gewirtz	201-804-7800	R	79 *	1.0
Jay Jacobs Inc.	1530 5th Ave	Seattle	WA	98101	Rex Loren Steffey	206-622-5400	P	73	0.6
Bedford Fair Industries	51 Weaver St, #2	Greenwich	CT	06831	Alan Glazer	203-629-2020	R	71 *	0.4
Chico's FAS Inc.	11215 Metro Pkwy	Fort Myers	FL	33912	Marvin J Gralnick	941-277-6200	P	60	0.5
Barney's Inc.	106 7th Ave	New York	NY	10011	Gene Pressman	212-593-7800	R	58 *	0.9

Source: *Ward's Business Directory of U.S. Private and Public Companies*, 1998. The company type code used is as follows: P - Public, R - Private, S - Subsidiary, D - Division, J - Joint Venture, A - Affiliate, G - Group. Sales are in millions of dollars, employees are in thousands. An asterisk (*) indicates an estimated sales volume. The symbol < stands for 'less than'.

OCCUPATIONS EMPLOYED BY SIC 562 - CLOTHING AND ACCESORIES STORES

Occupation	% of Total 1996	Change to 2006	Occupation	% of Total 1996	Change to 2006
Salespersons, retail	56.2	-9.3	Custom tailors & sewers	2.0	-44.7
Marketing & sales worker supervisors	12.0	-14.9	Traffic, shipping, receiving clerks	1.3	-14.9
Cashiers	6.3	-13.9	Wholesale & retail buyers, except farm products	1.1	-29.5
Stock clerks	5.2	-25.8	Bookkeeping, accounting, & auditing clerks	1.0	-31.9
General managers & top executives	3.9	-17.5			

Source: *Industry-Occupation Matrix*, Bureau of Labor Statistics. These data relate to one or more 3-digit SIC industry groups rather than to a single 4-digit SIC. The change reported for each occupation to the year 2006 is a percent of growth or decline as estimated by the Bureau of Labor Statistics. The abbreviation nec stands for 'not elsewhere classified'.

STATE AND REGIONAL CONCENTRATION

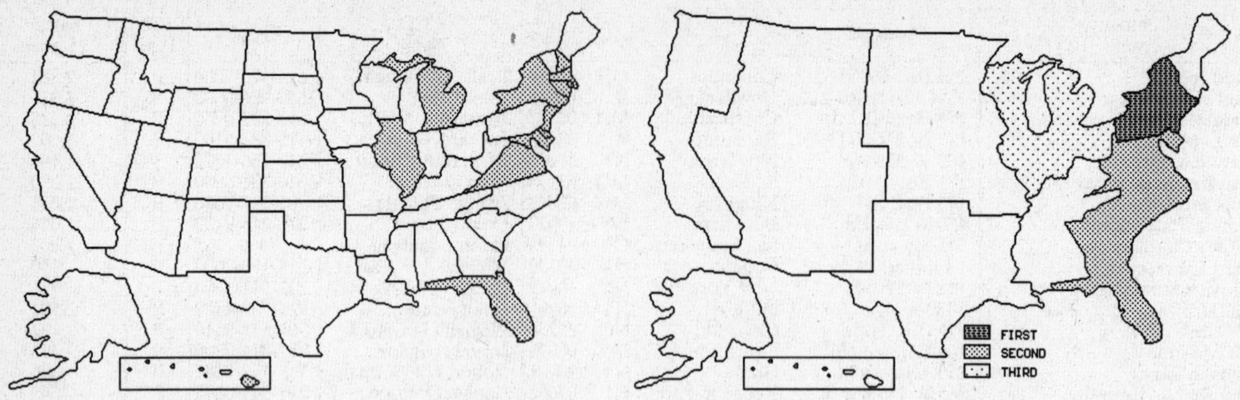

INDUSTRY DATA BY STATE

State	Establishments - 1995		Employment - 1995			Payroll - 1995		Sales - 1992		
	Total (number)	% of U.S.	Total (number)	% of U.S.	Per Estab.	Total ($ mil.)	Per Empl. ($)	Total ($ mil.)	% of U.S.	Per Estab ($)
California	4,432	10.5	35,937	9.7	8	391.6	10,898	3,418.2	10.9	74,804
New York	3,260	7.7	31,124	8.4	10	378.0	12,145	3,180.6	10.2	89,765
Texas	2,882	6.8	24,955	6.7	9	250.6	10,041	2,163.2	6.9	75,968
Florida	2,841	6.7	23,040	6.2	8	240.0	10,416	2,061.9	6.6	76,943
New Jersey	1,598	3.8	16,437	4.4	10	165.7	10,081	1,606.5	5.1	81,354
Illinois	1,866	4.4	19,341	5.2	10	179.1	9,261	1,604.3	5.1	69,236
Pennsylvania	1,891	4.5	18,175	4.9	10	173.8	9,564	1,458.9	4.7	73,554
Michigan	1,477	3.5	16,116	4.4	11	148.0	9,186	1,306.9	4.2	76,924
Ohio	1,573	3.7	15,636	4.2	10	123.7	7,913	1,182.7	3.8	67,415
Massachusetts	1,088	2.6	11,791	3.2	11	113.5	9,623	1,040.4	3.3	83,586
Virginia	1,106	2.6	10,368	2.8	9	91.6	8,835	832.1	2.7	75,545
Georgia	1,318	3.1	10,554	2.9	8	101.9	9,655	812.2	2.6	73,579
North Carolina	1,360	3.2	10,768	2.9	8	92.3	8,570	791.6	2.5	68,189
Maryland	753	1.8	8,097	2.2	11	77.1	9,526	692.3	2.2	71,768
Tennessee	921	2.2	7,365	2.0	8	63.8	8,656	568.0	1.8	74,109
Missouri	774	1.8	7,309	2.0	9	62.9	8,602	557.0	1.8	64,221
Indiana	900	2.1	8,201	2.2	9	60.8	7,415	556.7	1.8	61,627
Minnesota	765	1.8	6,975	1.9	9	57.2	8,202	544.5	1.7	65,594
Connecticut	570	1.4	5,738	1.6	10	58.7	10,231	529.4	1.7	77,076
Wisconsin	801	1.9	6,735	1.8	8	50.8	7,548	493.2	1.6	60,430
South Carolina	769	1.8	5,683	1.5	7	49.5	8,703	435.8	1.4	71,791
Louisiana	679	1.6	5,352	1.4	8	46.5	8,697	417.1	1.3	70,429
Alabama	684	1.6	4,993	1.4	7	43.3	8,675	372.1	1.2	68,946
Colorado	541	1.3	4,261	1.2	8	43.8	10,281	368.3	1.2	77,923
Arizona	533	1.3	4,472	1.2	8	41.2	9,220	346.2	1.1	71,780
Washington	637	1.5	4,258	1.2	7	38.5	9,044	340.4	1.1	67,747
Kentucky	497	1.2	4,503	1.2	9	35.1	7,802	317.8	1.0	70,691
Iowa	558	1.3	4,000	1.1	7	30.0	7,503	277.7	0.9	57,816
Oklahoma	442	1.0	2,995	0.8	7	28.1	9,397	241.1	0.8	66,795
Hawaii	290	0.7	2,243	0.6	8	28.3	12,621	237.3	0.8	82,758
Oregon	376	0.9	2,712	0.7	7	26.0	9,596	222.5	0.7	62,764
Mississippi	498	1.2	2,887	0.8	6	24.9	8,637	210.1	0.7	66,298
Kansas	377	0.9	2,872	0.8	8	21.4	7,464	205.9	0.7	62,372
Arkansas	420	1.0	2,571	0.7	6	22.9	8,892	205.6	0.7	72,498
New Hampshire	209	0.5	1,976	0.5	9	16.2	8,199	166.4	0.5	76,065
Nevada	195	0.5	2,012	0.5	10	25.5	12,682	164.0	0.5	80,808
Rhode Island	162	0.4	1,489	0.4	9	14.0	9,377	139.7	0.4	80,963
Nebraska	286	0.7	2,161	0.6	8	16.2	7,490	136.0	0.4	60,776
D.C.	102	0.2	1,418	0.4	14	15.8	11,164	134.9	0.4	85,141
West Virginia	210	0.5	1,586	0.4	8	12.1	7,645	132.8	0.4	68,835
Utah	219	0.5	1,792	0.5	8	12.8	7,160	122.9	0.4	63,011
New Mexico	265	0.6	1,573	0.4	6	15.3	9,711	119.8	0.4	66,061
Maine	166	0.4	1,205	0.3	7	9.9	8,221	112.6	0.4	80,004
Delaware	127	0.3	1,215	0.3	10	10.5	8,630	97.2	0.3	73,516
South Dakota	126	0.3	864	0.2	7	6.6	7,618	70.6	0.2	62,647
Vermont	111	0.3	844	0.2	8	7.3	8,611	69.6	0.2	78,292
North Dakota	126	0.3	878	0.2	7	6.1	6,935	69.5	0.2	58,686
Idaho	134	0.3	903	0.2	7	6.8	7,513	67.7	0.2	73,314
Montana	151	0.4	787	0.2	5	6.1	7,748	62.2	0.2	62,987
Alaska	66	0.2	318	0.1	5	3.6	11,239	37.6	0.1	59,632
Wyoming	72	0.2	331	0.1	5	2.3	6,858	24.3	0.1	67,955

Source: County Business Patterns, 1995 and *Economic Census of the U.S., 1992*. Data are sorted by 1992 revenues and, if revenues are unavailable, by establishments in 1995. The symbol (D) indicates that data are withheld by the source to avoid disclosure of competitive information. A dash (-) indicates that data are not available or undisclosed because they do not meet statistical validity standards. Shaded *states* on the state map indicate those states which have proportionately greater representation in the industry than would be indicated by the state's population; the ratio is based on total revenues or number of establishments. Shaded *regions* indicate where the industry is regionally most concentrated.

5632 - WOMEN'S ACCESSORY & SPECIALTY STORES

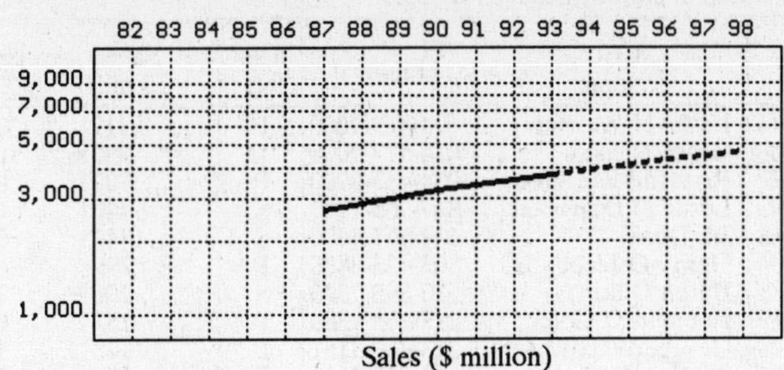

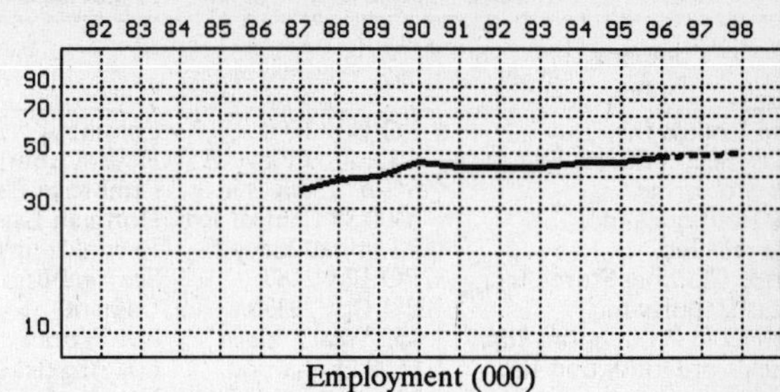

GENERAL STATISTICS

Year	Establishments (number)	Employment (number)	Payroll ($ million)	Sales ($ million)	Employees per Establishment (number)	Sales per Establishment ($)	Payroll per Employee ($)
1982	-	-	-	-	-	-	-
1983	-	-	-	-	-	-	-
1984	-	-	-	-	-	-	-
1985	-	-	-	-	-	-	-
1986	-	-	-	-	-	-	-
1987	7,490	35,640	368.4	2,663.2	5	355,574	10,337
1988	7,059	38,846	416.3	2,847.7e	6	-	10,716
1989	7,173	40,429	446.3	3,032.2e	6	-	11,039
1990	7,736	46,105	472.1	3,216.7e	6	-	10,240
1991	7,906	43,564	459.2	3,401.2e	6	-	10,542
1992	8,796	43,919	479.5	3,585.7	5	407,647	10,918
1993	8,560	43,303	505.9	3,770.1p	5	-	11,682
1994	8,291	45,485	523.8	3,954.6p	5	-	11,516
1995	7,992	45,596	524.6	4,139.1p	6	-	11,505
1996	8,684p	47,818p	555.7p	4,323.6p	-	-	-
1997	8,843p	48,873p	573.6p	4,508.1p	-	-	-
1998	9,002p	49,928p	591.5p	4,692.6p	-	-	-

Sources: Economic Census of the United States, 1982, 1987, and 1992. Establishment counts, employment, and payroll are from *County Business Patterns* for non-Census years. Values followed by a 'p' are projections by the editors. Sales and expense data for non-Census years are extrapolations, marked by 'e'. Industries reclassified in 1987 will not have data for prior years. Data are the most recent available at this level of detail.

INDICES OF CHANGE

Year	Establishments (number)	Employment (number)	Payroll ($ million)	Sales ($ million)	Employees per Establishment (number)	Sales per Establishment ($)	Payroll per Employee ($)
1982	-	-	-	-	-	-	-
1983	-	-	-	-	-	-	-
1984	-	-	-	-	-	-	-
1985	-	-	-	-	-	-	-
1986	-	-	-	-	-	-	-
1987	85.2	81.1	76.8	74.3	100.0	87.2	94.7
1988	80.3	88.4	86.8	79.4e	120.0	-	98.1
1989	81.5	92.1	93.1	84.6e	120.0	-	101.1
1990	87.9	105.0	98.5	89.7e	120.0	-	93.8
1991	89.9	99.2	95.8	94.9e	120.0	-	96.6
1992	100.0	100.0	100.0	100.0	100.0	100.0	100.0
1993	97.3	98.6	105.5	105.1p	101.2	-	107.0
1994	94.3	103.6	109.2	110.3p	109.7	-	105.5
1995	90.9	103.8	109.4	115.4p	114.1	-	105.4
1996	98.7p	108.9p	115.9p	120.6p	-	-	-
1997	100.5p	111.3p	119.6p	125.7p	-	-	-
1998	102.3p	113.7p	123.4p	130.9p	-	-	-

Sources: Same as General Statistics. The values shown reflect change from the base year, 1992. Values above 100 mean greater than 1992, values below 100 mean less than 1992, and a value of 100 in the 1982-91 or 1993-98 period means same as 1992. Values followed by a 'p' are projections by the editors; 'e' stands for extrapolation. Data are the most recent available at this level of detail.

SELECTED RATIOS

For 1992	Avg. of All Retail	Analyzed Industry	Index	For 1992	Avg. of All Retail	Analyzed Industry	Index
Employees per Establishment	12	5	41	Sales per Employee	102,941	81,643	79
Payroll per Establishment	146,026	54,513	37	Sales per Establishment	1,241,555	407,651	33
Payroll per Employee	12,107	10,918	90	Expenses per Establishment	na	na	na

Sources: Same as General Statistics. The 'Average of All Manufacturing' column represents the average of all manufacturing industries reported for the most recent complete year available. The Index shows the relationship between the Average and the Analyzed Industry. For example, 100 means that they are equal; 500 that the Analyzed Industry is five times the average; 50 means that the Analyzed Industry is half the national average. The abbreviation 'na' is used to show that data are 'not available'.

LEADING COMPANIES

Number shown: **33** Total sales ($ mil): **6,652** Total employment (000): **83.6**

Company Name	Address				CEO Name	Phone	Co. Type	Sales ($ mil)	Empl. (000)
Intimate Brands Inc.	PO Box 1600	Columbus	OH	43216	Leslie H Wexner	614-479-7000	P	2,517	30.8
Victoria's Secret Stores Div.	4 Limited Pkwy E	Reynoldsburg	OH	43068	Grace Nichols	614-577-7000	D	950 *	10.0
Claire's Stores Inc.	3 SW 129th Ave	Pembroke Pines	FL	33027	Rowland Schaefer	954-433-3900	P	500	8.5
Claire's Boutiques Inc.	2400 W Central Rd	Hoffman Est	IL	60193	Leslie D Dunavant	847-765-1100	S	440	6.5
Lane Bryant Inc.	5 Limited Pkwy E	Reynoldsburg	OH	43068	Jill Dean	614-577-4000	S	340 *	5.0
One Price Clothing Stores Inc.	PO Box 2487	Spartanburg	SC	29304	Henry D Jacobs Jr	803-433-8888	P	299	4.1
Cost Plus Imports Inc.	PO Box 23350	Oakland	CA	94623	Ralph Dillon	510-893-7300	S	200 *	2.8
Kenneth Cole Productions Inc.	152 West 57th St	New York	NY	10019	Kenneth D Cole	212-265-1500	P	152	0.6
Frederick's of Hollywood Inc.	6608 Hollywood	Los Angeles	CA	90028	George W Townson	213-466-5151	P	148	1.6
Cache Inc.	1460 Broadway	New York	NY	10036	Andrew Saul	212-575-3200	P	136	1.3
Hot Topic	3410 Pomona Blvd	Pomona	CA	91768	Orv Madden	909-869-6373		122 *	1.5
Louis Vuitton N.A. Inc.	130 E 59th St	New York	NY	10022	Thomas O'Neal	212-572-9700	S	100 *	0.4
Vogue Shops Inc.	6225 Powers Ave	Jacksonville	FL	32217	Ronnie Rosenbaum	904-737-0811	S	99 *	1.3
Conway Stores Inc.	1 Penn Plz, 38th Fl	New York	NY	10119	Richard Cowen	212-967-0897	R	97 *	1.2
Vanity Shop of Grand Forks	PO Box 547	Fargo	ND	58107	Emery Jahnke	701-237-3330	R	90	1.3
A and E Stores Inc.	1000 Huyler St	Teterboro	NJ	07608	Alan A Ades	201-393-0600	R	83 *	1.0
Evans Inc.	36 S State St	Chicago	IL	60603	Patrick J Regan	312-855-2000	P	83	0.9
Accessory Place Inc.	600 Willow Tree Rd	Leonia	NJ	07605	R H Wechsler	201-592-0400	R	40	1.0
Parklane Hosiery Company Inc.	31 E 28th St, 9th Fl	New York	NY	10016	Herbert N Somekh	212-683-1447	R	35	0.8
Gucci America Inc.	50 Hartz Way	Secaucus	NJ	07094	Domenico Desole	201-867-8800	R	28	0.5
Behr Stores Inc.	PO Box 99605	Louisville	KY	40299	Claus Behr	502-267-4411	R	25	0.4
Image Inc.	165 Chubb Ave	Lyndhurst	NJ	07071	YJ Kim	201-507-5300	R	22 *	0.4
Long Rap Inc.	1420 Wisconsin NW	Washington	DC	20007	Chuck Rendelman	202-337-6610	R	22 *	0.2
Weiss and Neuman Shoe Co.	1209 Washington	St. Louis	MO	63103	SW Weiss	314-231-5125	R	20	0.5
Flemington Fur Co.	8 Spring St	Flemington	NJ	08822	Robert Benjamin	908-782-2212	R	17 *	0.1
Walter Switzer Inc.	25 E Adams St	Phoenix	AZ	85004	Frank C Switzer	602-252-6161	R	17	0.2
McClures Stores Inc.	1052 Madison Sq	Madison	TN	37115	James D Andrews	615-868-1370	R	16	0.3
Saks Inc.	5510 Wisconsin Ave	Chevy Chase	MD	20815	Ernest Marx	301-652-2250	R	16 *	0.1
Peacock Papers Inc.	273 Summer St	Boston	MA	02109	Sharon P Whiteley	617-523-4777	R	14 *	0.1
Yarings Inc.	506 Congress Ave	Austin	TX	78701	Robert M Schmidt	512-476-6511	R	13	0.3
Gaytime Fashion Inc.	336 Pearl St	New Albany	IN	47150	CB Benjamin	812-948-1113	R	11	<0.1
Amanda Scott Publishing	700 Madison Ave	Covington	KY	41011	Donna Salyers	606-291-3300	R	1	<0.1
Pohlad Cos.	60 S 6th St, #3700	Minneapolis	MN	55402	Robert Pohlad	612-661-3700	R	1 *	<0.1

Source: *Ward's Business Directory of U.S. Private and Public Companies*, 1998. The company type code used is as follows: P - Public, R - Private, S - Subsidiary, D - Division, J - Joint Venture, A - Affiliate, G - Group. Sales are in millions of dollars, employees are in thousands. An asterisk (*) indicates an estimated sales volume. The symbol < stands for 'less than'.

OCCUPATIONS EMPLOYED BY SIC 563 - CLOTHING AND ACCESORIES STORES

Occupation	% of Total 1996	Change to 2006	Occupation	% of Total 1996	Change to 2006
Salespersons, retail	56.2	-9.3	Custom tailors & sewers	2.0	-44.7
Marketing & sales worker supervisors	12.0	-14.9	Traffic, shipping, receiving clerks	1.3	-14.9
Cashiers	6.3	-13.9	Wholesale & retail buyers, except farm products	1.1	-29.5
Stock clerks	5.2	-25.8	Bookkeeping, accounting, & auditing clerks	1.0	-31.9
General managers & top executives	3.9	-17.5			

Source: *Industry-Occupation Matrix*, Bureau of Labor Statistics. These data relate to one or more 3-digit SIC industry groups rather than to a single 4-digit SIC. The change reported for each occupation to the year 2006 is a percent of growth or decline as estimated by the Bureau of Labor Statistics. The abbreviation nec stands for 'not elsewhere classified'.

STATE AND REGIONAL CONCENTRATION

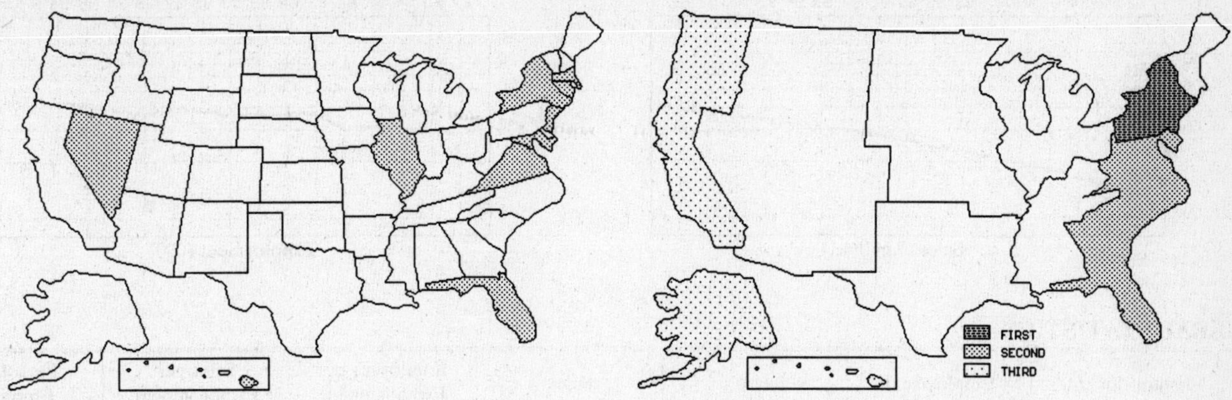

INDUSTRY DATA BY STATE

State	Establishments - 1995 Total (number)	Establishments - 1995 % of U.S.	Employment - 1995 Total (number)	Employment - 1995 % of U.S.	Employment - 1995 Per Estab.	Payroll - 1995 Total ($ mil.)	Payroll - 1995 Per Empl. ($)	Sales - 1992 Total ($ mil.)	Sales - 1992 % of U.S.	Sales - 1992 Per Estab ($)
New York	795	9.9	4,235	9.3	5	69.6	16,440	469.0	13.1	105,828
California	859	10.7	4,900	10.7	6	57.9	11,823	368.3	10.3	80,229
Florida	584	7.3	3,315	7.3	6	35.4	10,666	260.7	7.3	79,337
Texas	532	6.7	3,114	6.8	6	34.0	10,917	230.1	6.4	74,167
New Jersey	332	4.2	2,049	4.5	6	25.5	12,458	201.4	5.6	85,290
Illinois	401	5.0	2,406	5.3	6	27.7	11,505	180.9	5.0	81,576
Pennsylvania	394	4.9	2,119	4.6	5	22.1	10,415	165.9	4.6	76,394
Hawaii	67	0.8	458	1.0	7	8.8	19,269	159.4	4.4	275,339
Ohio	317	4.0	2,046	4.5	6	20.5	10,034	143.7	4.0	74,307
Michigan	278	3.5	1,501	3.3	5	17.9	11,940	121.5	3.4	72,251
Massachusetts	185	2.3	1,477	3.2	8	16.3	11,065	107.3	3.0	85,011
Virginia	217	2.7	1,347	3.0	6	14.6	10,854	103.0	2.9	75,033
Maryland	170	2.1	1,085	2.4	6	12.0	11,041	88.0	2.5	81,223
Georgia	198	2.5	1,101	2.4	6	12.7	11,547	82.3	2.3	83,632
Connecticut	132	1.7	717	1.6	5	10.2	14,180	67.9	1.9	94,507
North Carolina	197	2.5	1,081	2.4	5	10.8	9,981	65.7	1.8	71,654
Missouri	155	1.9	825	1.8	5	9.0	10,943	53.1	1.5	64,456
Tennessee	148	1.9	749	1.6	5	7.9	10,570	53.1	1.5	67,400
Colorado	118	1.5	670	1.5	6	7.2	10,803	48.5	1.4	76,574
Indiana	136	1.7	810	1.8	6	7.6	9,436	44.3	1.2	72,215
Minnesota	109	1.4	768	1.7	7	7.1	9,203	41.1	1.1	64,894
Wisconsin	122	1.5	656	1.4	5	6.6	10,012	40.6	1.1	58,786
Louisiana	97	1.2	607	1.3	6	5.5	9,138	40.2	1.1	68,641
Arizona	109	1.4	602	1.3	6	6.0	9,949	39.0	1.1	77,242
South Carolina	122	1.5	622	1.4	5	6.4	10,370	36.2	1.0	63,489
Washington	118	1.5	565	1.2	5	5.3	9,354	33.6	0.9	71,563
Alabama	99	1.2	667	1.5	7	7.0	10,435	30.8	0.9	65,991
Oregon	79	1.0	389	0.9	5	4.3	10,967	24.8	0.7	75,021
Kansas	67	0.8	402	0.9	6	4.2	10,413	23.4	0.7	65,232
Oklahoma	73	0.9	321	0.7	4	2.9	8,935	22.1	0.6	68,018
Kentucky	71	0.9	434	1.0	6	4.8	11,044	21.8	0.6	64,408
D.C.	28	0.4	231	0.5	8	2.9	12,580	21.3	0.6	96,357
Nevada	45	0.6	249	0.5	6	2.9	11,639	19.4	0.5	114,200
Iowa	88	1.1	398	0.9	5	3.6	8,975	18.4	0.5	62,969
Arkansas	57	0.7	261	0.6	5	2.8	10,693	15.7	0.4	67,322
New Hampshire	51	0.6	269	0.6	5	2.7	10,193	15.5	0.4	68,493
Maine	27	0.3	127	0.3	5	2.3	18,346	14.8	0.4	96,331
Utah	52	0.7	240	0.5	5	2.4	10,017	14.3	0.4	66,227
Nebraska	46	0.6	251	0.6	5	1.9	7,570	13.8	0.4	61,518
Mississippi	46	0.6	214	0.5	5	1.7	8,173	11.1	0.3	65,845
Rhode Island	28	0.4	138	0.3	5	1.9	13,964	10.8	0.3	74,729
West Virginia	37	0.5	211	0.5	6	1.8	8,469	10.7	0.3	47,835
New Mexico	38	0.5	164	0.4	4	1.8	11,037	10.0	0.3	74,575
Delaware	25	0.3	122	0.3	5	1.2	9,918	8.1	0.2	81,606
Vermont	22	0.3	141	0.3	6	1.5	10,830	7.6	0.2	54,921
Alaska	20	0.3	104	0.2	5	1.7	16,154	7.6	0.2	128,407
Idaho	30	0.4	129	0.3	4	1.2	9,519	6.9	0.2	53,512
South Dakota	20	0.3	90	0.2	5	0.8	8,933	4.5	0.1	34,977
North Dakota	18	0.2	86	0.2	5	0.6	6,593	4.3	0.1	64,224
Montana	18	0.2	82	0.2	5	0.6	7,073	2.1	0.1	51,561
Wyoming	15	0.2	51	0.1	3	0.3	5,686	1.4	0.0	48,714

Source: County Business Patterns, 1995 and *Economic Census of the U.S., 1992*. Data are sorted by 1992 revenues and, if revenues are unavailable, by establishments in 1995. The symbol (D) indicates that data are withheld by the source to avoid disclosure of competitive information. A dash (-) indicates that data are not available or undisclosed because they do not meet statistical validity standards. Shaded *states* on the state map indicate those states which have proportionately greater representation in the industry than would be indicated by the state's population; the ratio is based on total revenues or number of establishments. Shaded *regions* indicate where the industry is regionally most concentrated.

5641 - CHILDREN'S AND INFANTS' WEAR STORES

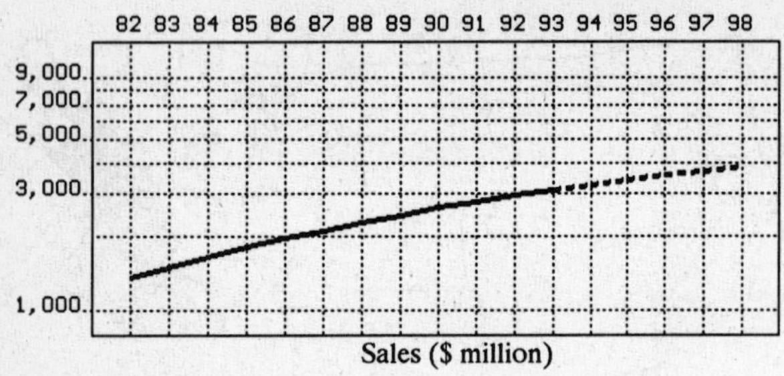

Sales ($ million)

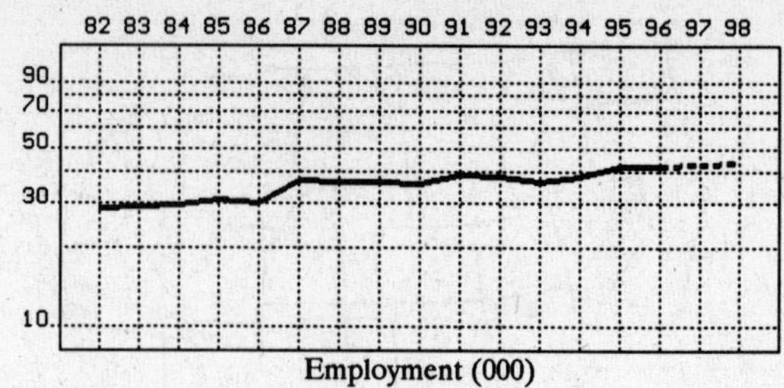

Employment (000)

GENERAL STATISTICS

Year	Establishments (number)	Employment (number)	Payroll ($ million)	Sales ($ million)	Employees per Establishment (number)	Sales per Establishment ($)	Payroll per Employee ($)
1982	5,767	28,388	172.3	1,356.0	5	235,136	6,070
1983	5,639	29,428	187.5	1,505.1e	5	-	6,372
1984	5,527	29,804	198.7	1,654.2e	5	-	6,668
1985	5,289	30,794	212.9	1,803.3e	6	-	6,915
1986	5,243	30,064	215.3	1,952.4e	6	-	7,160
1987	6,146	37,284	244.9	2,101.5	6	341,925	6,569
1988	5,786	36,566	272.7	2,272.5e	6	-	7,457
1989	5,528	36,702	288.3	2,443.6e	7	-	7,854
1990	5,592	35,867	306.0	2,614.6e	6	-	8,530
1991	5,694	38,881	324.5	2,785.6e	7	-	8,346
1992	5,637	38,509	323.0	2,956.7	7	524,513	8,389
1993	5,377	36,558	335.1	3,091.8p	7	-	9,167
1994	5,264	38,368	359.6	3,251.9p	7	-	9,373
1995	5,125	42,125	392.5	3,411.9p	8	-	9,318
1996	5,362p	42,068p	397.4p	3,572.0p	-	-	-
1997	5,337p	43,017p	413.9p	3,732.1p	-	-	-
1998	5,313p	43,966p	430.4p	3,892.1p	-	-	-

Sources: Economic Census of the United States, 1982, 1987, and 1992. Establishment counts, employment, and payroll are from *County Business Patterns* for non-Census years. Values followed by a 'p' are projections by the editors. Sales and expense data for non-Census years are extrapolations, marked by 'e'. Industries reclassified in 1987 will not have data for prior years. Data are the most recent available at this level of detail.

INDICES OF CHANGE

Year	Establishments (number)	Employment (number)	Payroll ($ million)	Sales ($ million)	Employees per Establishment (number)	Sales per Establishment ($)	Payroll per Employee ($)
1982	102.3	73.7	53.3	45.9	71.4	44.8	72.4
1983	100.0	76.4	58.0	50.9e	71.4	-	76.0
1984	98.0	77.4	61.5	55.9e	71.4	-	79.5
1985	93.8	80.0	65.9	61.0e	85.7	-	82.4
1986	93.0	78.1	66.7	66.0e	85.7	-	85.3
1987	109.0	96.8	75.8	71.1	85.7	65.2	78.3
1988	102.6	95.0	84.4	76.9e	85.7	-	88.9
1989	98.1	95.3	89.3	82.6e	100.0	-	93.6
1990	99.2	93.1	94.7	88.4e	85.7	-	101.7
1991	101.0	101.0	100.5	94.2e	100.0	-	99.5
1992	100.0	100.0	100.0	100.0	100.0	100.0	100.0
1993	95.4	94.9	103.7	104.6p	97.1	-	109.3
1994	93.4	99.6	111.3	110.0p	104.1	-	111.7
1995	90.9	109.4	121.5	115.4p	117.4	-	111.1
1996	95.1p	109.2p	123.0p	120.8p	-	-	-
1997	94.7p	111.7p	128.1p	126.2p	-	-	-
1998	94.3p	114.2p	133.2p	131.6p	-	-	-

Sources: Same as General Statistics. The values shown reflect change from the base year, 1992. Values above 100 mean greater than 1992, values below 100 mean less than 1992, and a value of 100 in the 1982-91 or 1993-98 period means same as 1992. Values followed by a 'p' are projections by the editors; 'e' stands for extrapolation. Data are the most recent available at this level of detail.

SELECTED RATIOS

For 1992	Avg. of All Retail	Analyzed Industry	Index	For 1992	Avg. of All Retail	Analyzed Industry	Index
Employees per Establishment	12	7	57	Sales per Employee	102,941	76,779	75
Payroll per Establishment	146,026	57,300	39	Sales per Establishment	1,241,555	524,517	42
Payroll per Employee	12,107	8,388	69	Expenses per Establishment	na	na	na

Sources: Same as General Statistics. The 'Average of All Manufacturing' column represents the average of all manufacturing industries reported for the most recent complete year available. The Index shows the relationship between the Average and the Analyzed Industry. For example, 100 means that they are equal; 500 that the Analyzed Industry is five times the average; 50 means that the Analyzed Industry is half the national average. The abbreviation 'na' is used to show that data are 'not available'.

LEADING COMPANIES

Number shown: **14** Total sales ($ mil): **14,068** Total employment (000): **110.2**

Company Name	Address				CEO Name	Phone	Co. Type	Sales ($ mil)	Empl. (000)
Toys R Us Inc.	461 From Rd	Paramus	NJ	07652	Michael Goldstein	201-262-7800	P	9,932	58.0
GapKids	1 Harrison street	San Francisco	CA	94105	Mickey Drexler	415-427-2000	D	1,627 *	20.3
Charming Shoppes Inc.	450 Winks Ln	Bensalem	PA	19020	Dorrit J Bern	215-245-9100	P	1,024	12.1
OshKosh B'Gosh Inc.	112 Otter Ave	Oshkosh	WI	54901	Douglas W Hyde	414-231-8800	P	445	4.7
Gymboree Corp.	700 Airport Blvd	Burlingame	CA	94010	Nancy J Pedot	650-579-0600	P	374	6.0
One Price Clothing Stores Inc.	PO Box 2487	Spartanburg	SC	29304	Henry D Jacobs Jr	803-433-8888	P	299	4.1
Children's Place Retail Stores	1 Dodge Dr	West Caldwell	NJ	07006	Ezra Dabah	201-227-8900	P	144	1.3
Kids Mart Inc.	801 Sentous Ave	City of Industry	CA	91784	Bernard Tessler	818-854-3166	P	88	2.1
InterPacific Hawaii Retail Group	PO Box 2480	Honolulu	HI	96804	Lawrence Kyman	808-971-4200	R	50 *	0.6
S.S. Retail Stores Corp.	30020 Ahern Ave	Union City	CA	94587	Donald Cohn	510-429-1515	R	32	0.3
Sealfons Inc.	257 E Ridgewood	Ridgewood	NJ	07450	Bert Model	201-652-2100	R	23 *	0.3
Watumull Brothers Ltd.	307 Lewers St	Honolulu	HI	96815	G Watumull	808-973-0010	R	16	0.2
Kenwin Shops Inc.	4747 Granite Dr	Tucker	GA	30084	Robert Schwartz	770-938-0451	P	15	0.3
Rollic Inc.	400 E Main St	Patchogue	NY	11772	Louis A Pfeifle	516-475-1630	R	0 *	<0.1

Source: *Ward's Business Directory of U.S. Private and Public Companies*, 1998. The company type code used is as follows: P - Public, R - Private, S - Subsidiary, D - Division, J - Joint Venture, A - Affiliate, G - Group. Sales are in millions of dollars, employees are in thousands. An asterisk (*) indicates an estimated sales volume. The symbol < stands for 'less than'.

OCCUPATIONS EMPLOYED BY SIC 564 - CLOTHING AND ACCESORIES STORES

Occupation	% of Total 1996	Change to 2006	Occupation	% of Total 1996	Change to 2006
Salespersons, retail	56.2	-9.3	Custom tailors & sewers	2.0	-44.7
Marketing & sales worker supervisors	12.0	-14.9	Traffic, shipping, receiving clerks	1.3	-14.9
Cashiers	6.3	-13.9	Wholesale & retail buyers, except farm products	1.1	-29.5
Stock clerks	5.2	-25.8	Bookkeeping, accounting, & auditing clerks	1.0	-31.9
General managers & top executives	3.9	-17.5			

Source: *Industry-Occupation Matrix*, Bureau of Labor Statistics. These data relate to one or more 3-digit SIC industry groups rather than to a single 4-digit SIC. The change reported for each occupation to the year 2006 is a percent of growth or decline as estimated by the Bureau of Labor Statistics. The abbreviation nec stands for 'not elsewhere classified'.

STATE AND REGIONAL CONCENTRATION

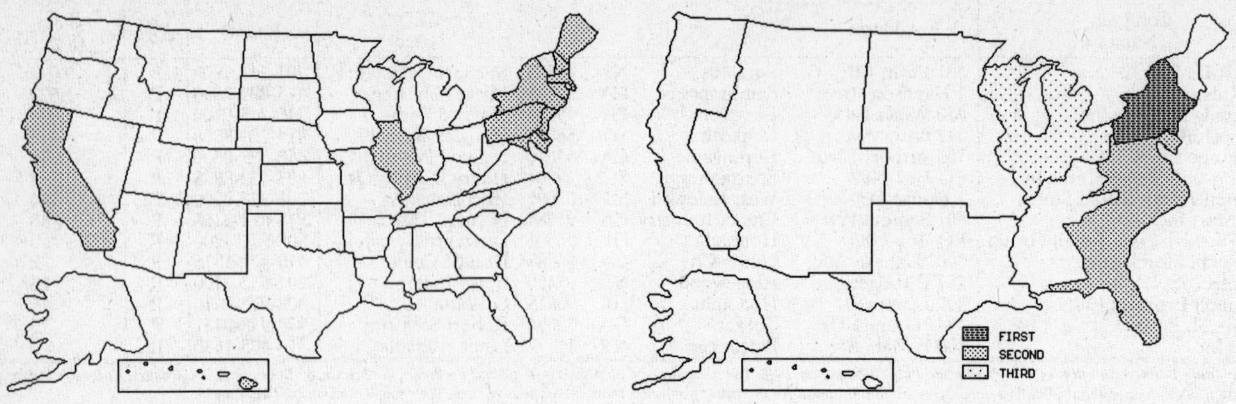

INDUSTRY DATA BY STATE

State	Establishments - 1995 Total (number)	% of U.S.	Employment - 1995 Total (number)	% of U.S.	Per Estab.	Payroll - 1995 Total ($ mil.)	Per Empl. ($)	Sales - 1992 Total ($ mil.)	% of U.S.	Per Estab ($)
New York	495	9.7	5,979	14.2	12	63.3	10,581	458.8	15.5	90,458
California	683	13.3	4,630	11.0	7	45.9	9,921	381.4	12.9	75,696
New Jersey	270	5.3	3,002	7.1	11	30.3	10,078	249.6	8.4	93,493
Pennsylvania	235	4.6	2,141	5.1	9	18.8	8,762	170.1	5.8	74,826
Illinois	249	4.9	2,151	5.1	9	18.4	8,573	169.5	5.7	78,640
Florida	302	5.9	2,371	5.6	8	24.5	10,321	146.9	5.0	79,228
Texas	327	6.4	2,458	5.8	8	23.0	9,358	135.0	4.6	69,515
Massachusetts	157	3.1	1,659	3.9	11	14.4	8,696	115.3	3.9	78,297
Michigan	146	2.8	1,339	3.2	9	11.0	8,184	105.6	3.6	77,460
Ohio	145	2.8	1,375	3.3	9	11.2	8,172	100.8	3.4	86,452
Maryland	122	2.4	1,379	3.3	11	13.1	9,505	91.4	3.1	79,728
Virginia	117	2.3	1,221	2.9	10	10.2	8,314	73.0	2.5	65,112
Connecticut	82	1.6	800	1.9	10	7.0	8,693	62.4	2.1	87,858
Georgia	130	2.5	968	2.3	7	9.6	9,898	57.0	1.9	76,767
Indiana	82	1.6	604	1.4	7	4.8	8,007	47.1	1.6	72,258
North Carolina	130	2.5	797	1.9	6	5.6	7,046	41.9	1.4	57,645
Missouri	89	1.7	631	1.5	7	4.9	7,807	41.1	1.4	64,184
Minnesota	74	1.4	631	1.5	9	4.9	7,746	38.3	1.3	72,308
Tennessee	117	2.3	681	1.6	6	5.9	8,598	35.3	1.2	61,708
Louisiana	89	1.7	484	1.1	5	4.4	9,157	34.1	1.2	61,745
Arizona	48	0.9	432	1.0	9	3.8	8,912	28.6	1.0	68,573
Wisconsin	61	1.2	371	0.9	6	3.2	8,520	28.2	1.0	66,903
South Carolina	73	1.4	393	0.9	5	3.7	9,397	24.0	0.8	68,629
Hawaii	35	0.7	239	0.6	7	2.2	9,318	20.1	0.7	64,906
Oklahoma	63	1.2	420	1.0	7	3.4	8,160	20.1	0.7	59,694
New Hampshire	36	0.7	259	0.6	7	2.5	9,529	19.9	0.7	77,863
Alabama	75	1.5	418	1.0	6	3.6	8,658	19.6	0.7	61,519
Washington	74	1.4	497	1.2	7	4.2	8,392	19.1	0.6	60,123
Utah	38	0.7	322	0.8	8	2.5	7,851	19.1	0.6	78,078
Kentucky	67	1.3	283	0.7	4	2.1	7,375	18.8	0.6	61,895
Oregon	46	0.9	480	1.1	10	7.3	15,177	17.7	0.6	68,258
Colorado	54	1.1	425	1.0	8	3.5	8,139	17.4	0.6	62,902
Delaware	24	0.5	207	0.5	9	2.6	12,454	16.5	0.6	82,295
Maine	22	0.4	160	0.4	7	1.3	8,156	15.3	0.5	91,557
Kansas	36	0.7	195	0.5	5	1.3	6,810	14.3	0.5	62,069
Arkansas	57	1.1	214	0.5	4	1.6	7,481	13.7	0.5	55,780
Mississippi	48	0.9	187	0.4	4	1.2	6,182	12.9	0.4	58,204
Iowa	46	0.9	284	0.7	6	2.3	8,155	12.2	0.4	44,768
Rhode Island	20	0.4	134	0.3	7	1.3	10,037	10.5	0.4	95,045
Nebraska	21	0.4	129	0.3	6	0.9	6,767	9.0	0.3	58,614
Nevada	20	0.4	154	0.4	8	1.7	11,013	8.4	0.3	69,570
New Mexico	20	0.4	122	0.3	6	1.0	8,049	6.5	0.2	55,154
D.C.	12	0.2	84	0.2	7	0.9	10,321	6.4	0.2	81,354
Vermont	14	0.3	66	0.2	5	0.5	7,636	5.6	0.2	68,500
West Virginia	16	0.3	83	0.2	5	0.7	8,940	4.5	0.2	57,418
South Dakota	12	0.2	67	0.2	6	0.4	6,701	4.0	0.1	68,305
Alaska	9	0.2	36	0.1	4	0.6	16,167	3.9	0.1	77,780
Idaho	16	0.3	88	0.2	6	0.6	7,216	2.6	0.1	67,744
Montana	8	0.2	19	0.0	2	0.1	5,105	1.9	0.1	43,465
North Dakota	9	0.2	46	0.1	5	0.3	7,391	0.9	0.0	49,211
Wyoming	4	0.1	10	0.0	3	0.1	5,500	0.6	0.0	46,333

Source: County Business Patterns, 1995 and *Economic Census of the U.S., 1992*. Data are sorted by 1992 revenues and, if revenues are unavailable, by establishments in 1995. The symbol (D) indicates that data are withheld by the source to avoid disclosure of competitive information. A dash (-) indicates that data are not available or undisclosed because they do not meet statistical validity standards. Shaded *states* on the state map indicate those states which have proportionately greater representation in the industry than would be indicated by the state's population; the ratio is based on total revenues or number of establishments. Shaded *regions* indicate where the industry is regionally most concentrated.

5651 - FAMILY CLOTHING STORES

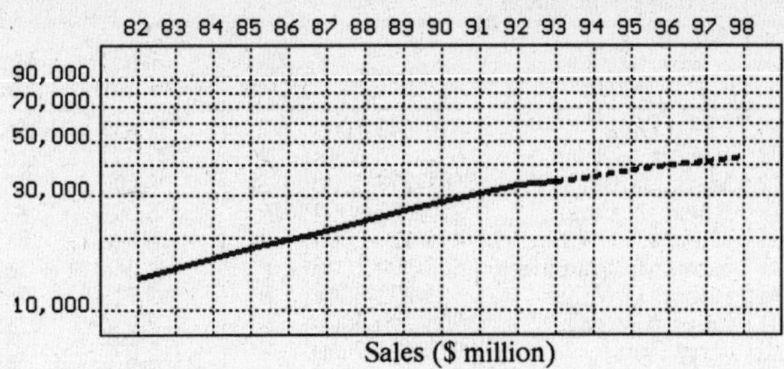

Sales ($ million)

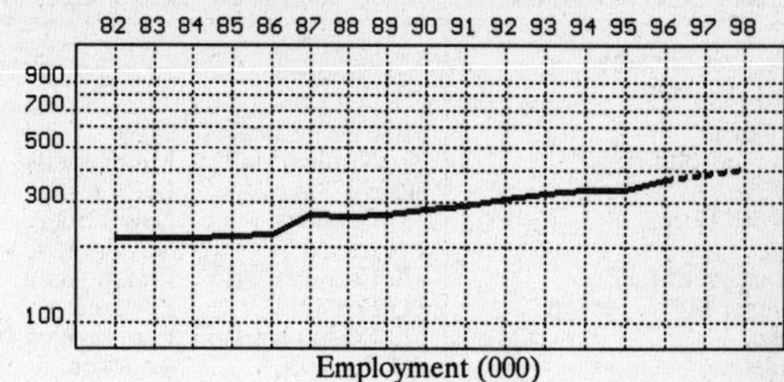

Employment (000)

GENERAL STATISTICS

Year	Establishments (number)	Employment (number)	Payroll ($ million)	Sales ($ million)	Employees per Establishment (number)	Sales per Establishment ($)	Payroll per Employee ($)
1982	19,159	218,932	1,671.1	13,451.0	11	702,072	7,633
1983	-	-	-	14,984.2*e*	-	-	-
1984	17,476	217,695	1,844.1	16,517.5*e*	12	-	8,471
1985	16,643	221,057	1,942.7	18,050.7*e*	13	-	8,788
1986	15,852	225,551	1,968.7	19,583.9*e*	14	-	8,728
1987	18,443	267,719	2,362.4	21,117.1	15	1,144,995	8,824
1988	17,786	265,267	2,498.1	23,451.1*e*	15	-	9,417
1989	17,288	269,490	2,714.6	25,785.1*e*	16	-	10,073
1990	17,796	282,608	2,954.6	28,119.1*e*	16	-	10,455
1991	17,955	292,890	3,038.3	30,453.1*e*	16	-	10,374
1992	19,452	309,516	3,468.9	32,787.1	16	1,685,540	11,207
1993	19,417	325,123	3,626.0	33,810.8*p*	17	-	11,153
1994	19,522	338,331	3,924.2	35,744.4*p*	17	-	11,599
1995	19,044	336,476	3,974.1	37,678.0*p*	18	-	11,811
1996	21,105*p*	374,080*p*	4,337.0*p*	39,611.6*p*	-	-	-
1997	21,673*p*	389,951*p*	4,572.6*p*	41,545.2*p*	-	-	-
1998	22,242*p*	405,822*p*	4,808.1*p*	43,478.8*p*	-	-	-

Sources: *Economic Census of the United States*, 1982, 1987, and 1992. Establishment counts, employment, and payroll are from *County Business Patterns* for non-Census years. Values followed by a 'p' are projections by the editors. Sales and expense data for non-Census years are extrapolations, marked by 'e'. Industries reclassified in 1987 will not have data for prior years. Data are the most recent available at this level of detail.

INDICES OF CHANGE

Year	Establishments (number)	Employment (number)	Payroll ($ million)	Sales ($ million)	Employees per Establishment (number)	Sales per Establishment ($)	Payroll per Employee ($)
1982	98.5	70.7	48.2	41.0	68.8	41.7	68.1
1983	-	-	-	45.7*e*	-	-	-
1984	89.8	70.3	53.2	50.4*e*	75.0	-	75.6
1985	85.6	71.4	56.0	55.1*e*	81.3	-	78.4
1986	81.5	72.9	56.8	59.7*e*	87.5	-	77.9
1987	94.8	86.5	68.1	64.4	93.8	67.9	78.7
1988	91.4	85.7	72.0	71.5*e*	93.8	-	84.0
1989	88.9	87.1	78.3	78.6*e*	100.0	-	89.9
1990	91.5	91.3	85.2	85.8*e*	100.0	-	93.3
1991	92.3	94.6	87.6	92.9*e*	100.0	-	92.6
1992	100.0	100.0	100.0	100.0	100.0	100.0	100.0
1993	99.8	105.0	104.5	103.1*p*	104.7	-	99.5
1994	100.4	109.3	113.1	109.0*p*	108.3	-	103.5
1995	97.9	108.7	114.6	114.9*p*	110.4	-	105.4
1996	108.5*p*	120.9*p*	125.0*p*	120.8*p*	-	-	-
1997	111.4*p*	126.0*p*	131.8*p*	126.7*p*	-	-	-
1998	114.3*p*	131.1*p*	138.6*p*	132.6*p*	-	-	-

Sources: Same as General Statistics. The values shown reflect change from the base year, 1992. Values above 100 mean greater than 1992, values below 100 mean less than 1992, and a value of 100 in the 1982-91 or 1993-98 period means same as 1992. Values followed by a 'p' are projections by the editors; 'e' stands for extrapolation. Data are the most recent available at this level of detail.

SELECTED RATIOS

For 1992	Avg. of All Retail	Analyzed Industry	Index	For 1992	Avg. of All Retail	Analyzed Industry	Index
Employees per Establishment	12	16	132	Sales per Employee	102,941	105,930	103
Payroll per Establishment	146,026	178,331	122	Sales per Establishment	1,241,555	1,685,539	136
Payroll per Employee	12,107	11,207	93	Expenses per Establishment	na	na	na

Sources: Same as General Statistics. The 'Average of All Manufacturing' column represents the average of all manufacturing industries reported for the most recent complete year available. The Index shows the relationship between the Average and the Analyzed Industry. For example, 100 means that they are equal; 500 that the Analyzed Industry is five times the average; 50 means that the Analyzed Industry is half the national average. The abbreviation 'na' is used to show that data are 'not available'.

LEADING COMPANIES

Number shown: **50** Total sales ($ mil): **125,560** Total employment (000): **988.5**

Company Name	Address				CEO Name	Phone	Co. Type	Sales ($ mil)	Empl. (000)
Kmart Corp.	3100 W Big Beaver	Troy	MI	48084	Floyd Hall	810-643-1000	P	31,437	265.0
Dayton Hudson Corp.	777 Nicollet Mall	Minneapolis	MN	55402	Robert J Ulrich	612-370-6948	P	27,757	218.0
Sam's Club	608 SW 8th St	Bentonville	AR	72712	Mark Hansen	501-277-7000	D	20,000	28.8
Woolworth Corp.	233 Broadway	New York	NY	10279	Roger N Farah	212-553-2000	P	8,092	82.0
Gap Inc.	1 Harrison St	San Francisco	CA	94105	Millard S Drexler	415-427-2000	P	6,508	81.0
TJX Companies Inc.	770 Cochituate Rd	Framingham	MA	01701	Bernard Cammarata	508-390-1000	P	4,448	58.0
Fred Meyer Inc.	PO Box 42121	Portland	OR	97242	Robert G Miller	503-232-8844	P	3,725	28.0
T.J. Maxx	770 Cochituate Rd	Framingham	MA	01701	Peter A Maich	508-390-3000	S	2,930 •	28.0
Marshalls	PO Box 9030	Andover	MA	01810	Jerry Rossi	978-474-7000	S	2,670 •	22.0
Kmart Fashions	7373 Westside Ave	North Bergen	NJ	07047	Don Keeble	201-861-9100	D	2,220 •	25.0
Dollar General Corp.	104 Woodmont	Nashville	TN	37205	Cal Turner Jr	615-783-2000	P	2,134	25.4
Ross Stores Inc.	8333 Central Ave	Newark	CA	94560	Norman A Ferber	510-505-4400	P	1,989	14.9
Burlington Coat Factory	1830 Rte 130 N	Burlington	NJ	08016	Monroe G Milstein	609-387-7800	P	1,777	17.6
Saks and Co.	12 E 49th St	New York	NY	10017	Philip B Miller	212-753-4000	S	1,687	12.6
Specialty Retailers Inc.	10201 Main St	Houston	TX	77025	Carl E Tooker	713-667-5601	P	1,000	10.0
Goody's Family Clothing Inc.	400 Goody's Lane	Knoxville	TN	37922	R M Goodfriend	615-966-2000	P	972	6.1
Pier 1 Imports Inc.	301 Commerce St	Fort Worth	TX	76102	Clark A Johnson	817-878-8000	P	947	11.3
Polo Ralph Lauren Corp.	650 Madison Ave	New York	NY	10022	Ralph Lauren	212-318-7000	R	910 •	4.0
Banana Republic	1 Harrison St	San Francisco	CA	94105	Jeanne Jackson	415-777-0250	D	781 •	9.7
Recreational Equipment Inc.	6750 S 228th St	Kent	WA	98032	Wally Smith	253-395-3780	R	485	5.1
Syms Corp.	Syms Way	Secaucus	NJ	07094	Sy Syms	201-902-9600	P	347	2.2
Brooks Brothers	346 Madison Ave	New York	NY	10017	Joseph R Gromek	212-682-8800	S	300 •	3.5
Weiner's Stores Inc.	PO Box 2612	Houston	TX	77252	Sol Weiner	713-688-1331	R	300	4.0
Designs Inc.	66 B St	Needham	MA	02194	Joel H Reichman	617-444-7222	P	290	2.1
Hamrick's Inc.	742 Peachoid Rd	Gaffney	SC	29341	Barry Hamrick	803-489-6095	R	220	2.5
Lamonts Apparel Inc.	12413 Willows Rd	Kirkland	WA	98034	Alan R Schlesinger	425-814-5700	P	204	1.5
Duck Head Apparel Co.	89 E Athens St	Winder	GA	30680	Irwin Maddrey	404-867-3111	D	200 •	4.0
Gadzooks Inc.	4121 International	Carrollton	TX	75007	G R Szczepanski	972-307-5555	P	172	2.4
D and L Venture Corp.	227 Main St	New Britain	CT	06050	George Rubin	203-223-3655	R	150 •	1.8
Palais Royal Inc.	PO Box 35167	Houston	TX	77235	Bernard Fuchs	713-667-5601	S	140	2.0
DRS Apparel Inc.	315 E 62nd St	New York	NY	10021	John A Selzer	212-980-9670	S	97	1.4
General Textiles Corp.	4000 Ruffin Rd	San Diego	CA	92123	B Chris Schwartz	619-627-1800	S	97	1.4
Smith and Hawken Inc.	117 E Strawberry	Mill Valley	CA	94941	Kathy Tierney	415-383-4415	S	75	0.3
Chun Kim Chow Ltd.	PO Box 1578	Honolulu	HI	96806	Paul Chun	808-532-5725	R	70	1.0
Barney's Inc.	106 7th Ave	New York	NY	10011	Gene Pressman	212-593-7800	R	58 •	0.9
Cignal	3300 Fashion Way	Joppa	MD	21085	Frank Tworecke	410-538-1000	D	52 •	0.8
Cooper's Inc.	11205 Montgomery	Albuquerque	NM	87111	Donald Midkiff	505-296-8344	R	44	0.5
Rogers Department Store Inc.	PO Box 9280	Wyoming	MI	49509	HY Berkowitz	616-538-6000	R	38	0.6
Cheyenne Outfitters Inc.	PO Box 12013	Cheyenne	WY	82003	Frederick Wojcik	307-775-7500	R	25 •	0.2
Dick Bruhn Inc.	PO Box 81600	Salinas	CA	93912	RL Bruhn	408-758-4684	R	24	0.5
Retail Specialists Inc.	2268 Westbrook Dr	Columbus	OH	43228	Mark R Mendelson	614-771-6670	R	24 •	0.3
David Harris Sons Company	Rte 6	Archbald	PA	18403	Phillip Harris	717-876-3157	R	22 •	0.3
Renberg's Inc.	1860 Utica Sq	Tulsa	OK	74114	Robert Renberg	918-585-5601	R	21	0.5
Mimbres Valley Farmers	811 S Platinum St	Deming	NM	88030	Garry S Carter	505-546-2769	R	19	0.2
Charivari Holding Corp.	2315 Broadway	New York	NY	10024	Selma Weiser	212-362-1212	R	19 •	0.2
Abdalla's Lafayette Inc.	PO Box 51348	Lafayette	LA	70505	Herbert Abdalla	318-262-7100	R	18	0.3
Domsey Fiber Corp.	431 Kent Ave	Brooklyn	NY	11211	Arthur Salm	718-384-6000	R	18	0.4
Dancer's Inc.	PO Box 100	Mason	MI	48854	Douglas Dancer	517-676-4474	R	17	0.3
Dunn's Inc.	1 Madison Ave	Grand Junction	TN	38039	John Meador III	901-764-6901	R	17 •	<0.1
Gallo Clothing Inc.	7713 Eastern Ave	Baltimore	MD	21224	Thomas Pappagallo	410-675-7272	R	17 •	0.2

Source: Ward's Business Directory of U.S. Private and Public Companies, 1998. The company type code used is as follows: P - Public, R - Private, S - Subsidiary, D - Division, J - Joint Venture, A - Affiliate, G - Group. Sales are in millions of dollars, employees are in thousands. An asterisk (*) indicates an estimated sales volume. The symbol < stands for 'less than'.

OCCUPATIONS EMPLOYED BY SIC 565 - CLOTHING AND ACCESORIES STORES

Occupation	% of Total 1996	Change to 2006	Occupation	% of Total 1996	Change to 2006
Salespersons, retail	56.2	-9.3	Custom tailors & sewers	2.0	-44.7
Marketing & sales worker supervisors	12.0	-14.9	Traffic, shipping, receiving clerks	1.3	-14.9
Cashiers	6.3	-13.9	Wholesale & retail buyers, except farm products	1.1	-29.5
Stock clerks	5.2	-25.8	Bookkeeping, accounting, & auditing clerks	1.0	-31.9
General managers & top executives	3.9	-17.5			

Source: Industry-Occupation Matrix, Bureau of Labor Statistics. These data relate to one or more 3-digit SIC industry groups rather than to a single 4-digit SIC. The change reported for each occupation to the year 2006 is a percent of growth or decline as estimated by the Bureau of Labor Statistics. The abbreviation nec stands for 'not elsewhere classified'.

STATE AND REGIONAL CONCENTRATION

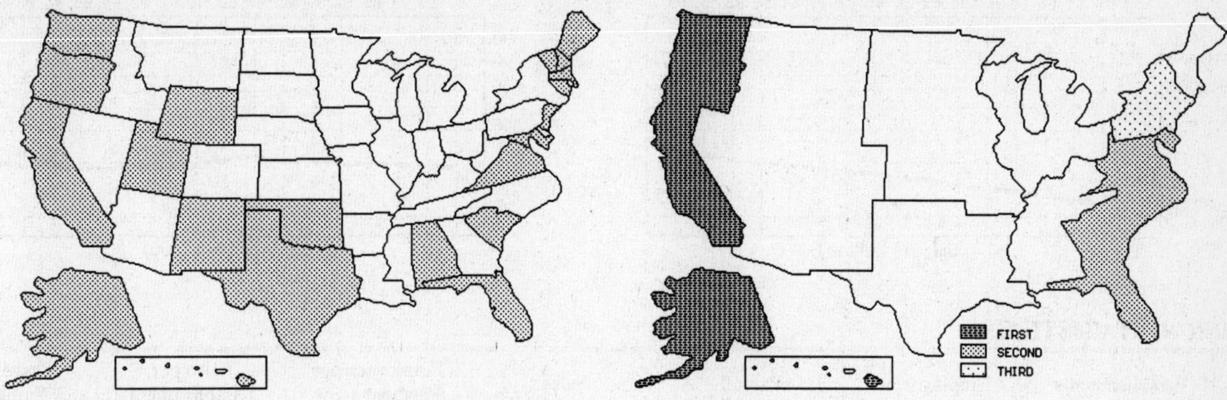

INDUSTRY DATA BY STATE

State	Establishments - 1995 Total (number)	Establishments - 1995 % of U.S.	Employment - 1995 Total (number)	Employment - 1995 % of U.S.	Employment - 1995 Per Estab.	Payroll - 1995 Total ($ mil.)	Payroll - 1995 Per Empl. ($)	Sales - 1992 Total ($ mil.)	Sales - 1992 % of U.S.	Sales - 1992 Per Estab ($)
California	1,900	10.0	47,367	14.1	25	638.5	13,480	4,818.0	14.7	118,942
Texas	1,511	7.9	25,411	7.6	17	260.6	10,254	2,411.2	7.4	99,759
New York	1,261	6.6	21,147	6.3	17	279.9	13,236	2,271.9	6.9	110,280
Florida	1,217	6.4	18,423	5.5	15	223.5	12,130	2,056.4	6.3	107,338
Illinois	754	4.0	15,209	4.5	20	183.2	12,049	1,437.4	4.4	100,498
Massachusetts	529	2.8	10,486	3.1	20	137.7	13,128	1,343.8	4.1	121,187
New Jersey	542	2.8	10,919	3.2	20	154.6	14,160	1,238.8	3.8	122,863
Pennsylvania	667	3.5	11,814	3.5	18	131.2	11,102	1,206.5	3.7	106,741
Washington	384	2.0	12,065	3.6	31	161.0	13,346	1,181.1	3.6	125,192
Michigan	586	3.1	9,708	2.9	17	105.5	10,871	893.2	2.7	94,842
Virginia	465	2.4	9,888	2.9	21	118.0	11,934	884.1	2.7	105,654
Georgia	491	2.6	9,637	2.9	20	106.2	11,017	852.0	2.6	102,239
North Carolina	580	3.0	9,558	2.8	16	97.3	10,177	794.8	2.4	90,354
Ohio	537	2.8	8,574	2.5	16	85.5	9,971	744.3	2.3	99,453
Alabama	319	1.7	6,657	2.0	21	80.5	12,092	696.1	2.1	105,291
Connecticut	265	1.4	5,771	1.7	22	73.7	12,774	676.9	2.1	124,594
Maryland	354	1.9	7,027	2.1	20	90.6	12,898	662.4	2.0	106,508
Oregon	265	1.4	6,627	2.0	25	83.2	12,550	618.9	1.9	115,926
Tennessee	386	2.0	6,608	2.0	17	69.1	10,451	566.3	1.7	103,354
Minnesota	355	1.9	5,986	1.8	17	65.6	10,966	503.2	1.5	102,970
South Carolina	364	1.9	5,495	1.6	15	60.4	10,997	477.7	1.5	86,404
Arizona	311	1.6	4,601	1.4	15	44.8	9,729	455.3	1.4	102,661
Oklahoma	341	1.8	4,438	1.3	13	44.0	9,916	418.9	1.3	88,395
Missouri	365	1.9	4,712	1.4	13	45.3	9,618	400.9	1.2	95,927
Indiana	299	1.6	4,553	1.4	15	52.0	11,423	392.4	1.2	100,041
Kentucky	250	1.3	4,001	1.2	16	41.2	10,300	369.9	1.1	92,820
Wisconsin	310	1.6	3,950	1.2	13	39.1	9,896	369.5	1.1	91,502
Louisiana	312	1.6	4,542	1.3	15	45.7	10,054	362.8	1.1	85,365
Colorado	337	1.8	3,875	1.2	11	43.1	11,117	339.3	1.0	96,301
Maine	144	0.8	2,368	0.7	16	33.4	14,097	288.6	0.9	127,513
Utah	152	0.8	3,361	1.0	22	36.3	10,796	248.6	0.8	115,584
Hawaii	221	1.2	2,421	0.7	11	38.5	15,892	237.6	0.7	100,786
New Hampshire	142	0.7	2,198	0.7	15	24.8	11,267	237.2	0.7	104,766
Kansas	211	1.1	2,565	0.8	12	23.4	9,128	233.1	0.7	80,763
New Mexico	179	0.9	2,407	0.7	13	23.9	9,941	208.4	0.6	99,722
Mississippi	205	1.1	2,744	0.8	13	24.3	8,849	208.1	0.6	83,457
Arkansas	230	1.2	2,780	0.8	12	24.6	8,862	197.6	0.6	83,155
Nebraska	142	0.7	1,759	0.5	12	18.0	10,206	186.1	0.6	79,989
Iowa	187	1.0	2,390	0.7	13	21.1	8,826	175.1	0.5	87,390
Nevada	116	0.6	1,724	0.5	15	19.7	11,412	147.8	0.5	126,874
Alaska	46	0.2	1,094	0.3	24	15.8	14,405	136.6	0.4	144,882
West Virginia	106	0.6	1,634	0.5	15	17.8	10,917	136.5	0.4	90,288
Idaho	129	0.7	1,563	0.5	12	16.3	10,413	115.1	0.4	94,276
Rhode Island	63	0.3	901	0.3	14	10.9	12,087	105.0	0.3	143,110
Montana	132	0.7	1,007	0.3	8	11.4	11,303	88.4	0.3	99,678
Delaware	52	0.3	737	0.2	14	7.9	10,664	78.4	0.2	97,090
Vermont	66	0.3	1,148	0.3	17	17.0	14,794	77.5	0.2	105,337
D.C.	65	0.3	660	0.2	10	9.7	14,702	68.4	0.2	98,149
Wyoming	82	0.4	711	0.2	9	7.3	10,210	67.8	0.2	94,999
South Dakota	71	0.4	810	0.2	11	7.4	9,154	63.0	0.2	76,062
North Dakota	46	0.2	445	0.1	10	4.0	8,969	38.3	0.1	86,029

Source: County Business Patterns, 1995 and *Economic Census of the U.S., 1992*. Data are sorted by 1992 revenues and, if revenues are unavailable, by establishments in 1995. The symbol (D) indicates that data are withheld by the source to avoid disclosure of competitive information. A dash (-) indicates that data are not available or undisclosed because they do not meet statistical validity standards. Shaded *states* on the state map indicate those states which have proportionately greater representation in the industry than would be indicated by the state's population; the ratio is based on total revenues or number of establishments. Shaded *regions* indicate where the industry is regionally most concentrated.

5661 - SHOE STORES

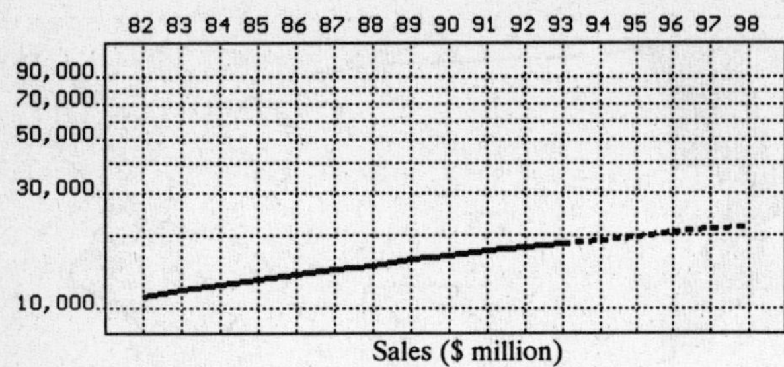

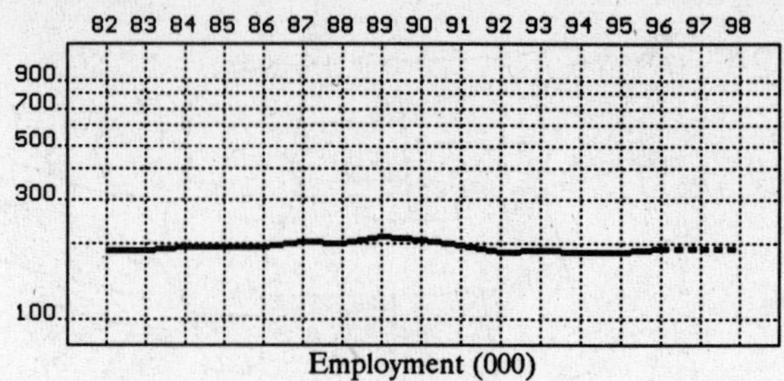

GENERAL STATISTICS

Year	Establishments (number)	Employment (number)	Payroll ($ million)	Sales ($ million)	Employees per Establishment (number)	Sales per Establishment ($)	Payroll per Employee ($)
1982	38,506	188,719	1,571.3	11,275.4	5	292,822	8,326
1983	37,511	186,402	1,638.8	11,902.5*e*	5	-	8,792
1984	37,734	194,344	1,738.2	12,529.6*e*	5	-	8,944
1985	37,343	194,243	1,819.5	13,156.6*e*	5	-	9,367
1986	37,433	194,620	1,845.5	13,783.7*e*	5	-	9,482
1987	39,488	205,237	1,880.5	14,410.8	5	364,941	9,162
1988	38,525	203,202	2,035.3	15,105.3*e*	5	-	10,016
1989	38,350	212,868	2,078.3	15,799.8*e*	6	-	9,763
1990	37,450	206,199	2,152.4	16,494.3*e*	6	-	10,438
1991	36,479	196,250	2,111.7	17,188.9*e*	5	-	10,760
1992	37,206	184,415	2,184.5	17,883.4	5	480,658	11,846
1993	35,224	186,227	2,184.0	18,467.5*p*	5	-	11,727
1994	34,795	184,533	2,236.2	19,128.3*p*	5	-	12,118
1995	33,049	184,833	2,207.3	19,789.1*p*	6	-	11,942
1996	34,846*p*	191,267*p*	2,366.3*p*	20,449.9*p*	-	-	-
1997	34,548*p*	190,844*p*	2,418.2*p*	21,110.7*p*	-	-	-
1998	34,251*p*	190,422*p*	2,470.1*p*	21,771.5*p*	-	-	-

Sources: *Economic Census of the United States*, 1982, 1987, and 1992. Establishment counts, employment, and payroll are from *County Business Patterns* for non-Census years. Values followed by a 'p' are projections by the editors. Sales and expense data for non-Census years are extrapolations, marked by 'e'. Industries reclassified in 1987 will not have data for prior years. Data are the most recent available at this level of detail.

INDICES OF CHANGE

Year	Establishments (number)	Employment (number)	Payroll ($ million)	Sales ($ million)	Employees per Establishment (number)	Sales per Establishment ($)	Payroll per Employee ($)
1982	103.5	102.3	71.9	63.0	100.0	60.9	70.3
1983	100.8	101.1	75.0	66.6*e*	100.0	-	74.2
1984	101.4	105.4	79.6	70.1*e*	100.0	-	75.5
1985	100.4	105.3	83.3	73.6*e*	100.0	-	79.1
1986	100.6	105.5	84.5	77.1*e*	100.0	-	80.0
1987	106.1	111.3	86.1	80.6	100.0	75.9	77.3
1988	103.5	110.2	93.2	84.5*e*	100.0	-	84.6
1989	103.1	115.4	95.1	88.3*e*	120.0	-	82.4
1990	100.7	111.8	98.5	92.2*e*	120.0	-	88.1
1991	98.0	106.4	96.7	96.1*e*	100.0	-	90.8
1992	100.0	100.0	100.0	100.0	100.0	100.0	100.0
1993	94.7	101.0	100.0	103.3*p*	105.7	-	99.0
1994	93.5	100.1	102.4	107.0*p*	106.1	-	102.3
1995	88.8	100.2	101.0	110.7*p*	111.9	-	100.8
1996	93.7*p*	103.7*p*	108.3*p*	114.4*p*	-	-	-
1997	92.9*p*	103.5*p*	110.7*p*	118.0*p*	-	-	-
1998	92.1*p*	103.3*p*	113.1*p*	121.7*p*	-	-	-

Sources: Same as General Statistics. The values shown reflect change from the base year, 1992. Values above 100 mean greater than 1992, values below 100 mean less than 1992, and a value of 100 in the 1982-91 or 1993-98 period means same as 1992. Values followed by a 'p' are projections by the editors; 'e' stands for extrapolation. Data are the most recent available at this level of detail.

SELECTED RATIOS

For 1992	Avg. of All Retail	Analyzed Industry	Index	For 1992	Avg. of All Retail	Analyzed Industry	Index
Employees per Establishment	12	5	41	Sales per Employee	102,941	96,974	94
Payroll per Establishment	146,026	58,714	40	Sales per Establishment	1,241,555	480,659	39
Payroll per Employee	12,107	11,846	98	Expenses per Establishment	na	na	na

Sources: Same as General Statistics. The 'Average of All Manufacturing' column represents the average of all manufacturing industries reported for the most recent complete year available. The Index shows the relationship between the Average and the Analyzed Industry. For example, 100 means that they are equal; 500 that the Analyzed Industry is five times the average; 50 means that the Analyzed Industry is half the national average. The abbreviation 'na' is used to show that data are 'not available'.

LEADING COMPANIES

Number shown: **50** Total sales ($ mil): **24,136** Total employment (000): **228.2**

Company Name	Address				CEO Name	Phone	Co. Type	Sales ($ mil)	Empl. (000)
Woolworth Corp.	233 Broadway	New York	NY	10279	Roger N Farah	212-553-2000	P	8,092	82.0
Payless ShoeSource Inc.	3231 E 6th St	Topeka	KS	66607	Steven J Douglass	913-233-5171	P	2,330	24.0
Nine West Group Inc.	9 W Broad St	Stamford	CT	06902	Vincent Camuto	914-640-6400	P	1,603	13.1
Eddie Bauer Inc.	PO Box 97000	Redmond	WA	98073	Richard T Fersch	425-882-6100	S	1,600	8.0
Brown Group Inc.	PO Box 29	St. Louis	MO	63166	BA Bridgewater Jr	314-854-4000	P	1,525	11.5
Meldisco H.C. Inc.	933 MacArthur	Mahwah	NJ	07430	John M Robinson	201-934-2000	S	1,191	8.2
J. Baker Inc.	PO Box 231	Hyde Park	MA	02136	Alan I Weinstein	617-828-9300	P	1,020	11.6
Famous Footwear	208 E Olin Ave	Madison	WI	53708	Brian C Cook	608-256-7007	D	741	8.0
Footaction U.S.A. Inc.	7880 Bent Branch	Irving	TX	75063	Ralph T Parks	972-501-5000	S	694*	7.2
Elder-Beerman Stores Corp.	3155 El-Bee Rd	Dayton	OH	45439	Frederick J Mershad	937-296-2700	R	597	7.3
Genesco Inc.	PO Box 731	Nashville	TN	37202	Ben T Harris	615-367-7000	P	536	4.3
Stride Rite Corp.	PO Box 9191	Lexington	MA	02173	Robert C Siegel	617-824-6000	P	516	2.9
Finish Line Inc.	3308 N Mitthoeffer	Indianapolis	IN	46236	Alan H Cohen	317-899-1022	P	332	5.5
Bakers-Leeds Div.	PO Box 14020	St. Louis	MO	63178	Les Wagner	314-331-6000	D	310*	3.5
Pic 'N Pay Stores Inc.	PO Box 34000	Charlotte	NC	28261	BB Tuley	704-847-8871	P	310	3.5
Athlete's Foot Group Inc.	1950 Vaughn Rd	Kennesaw	GA	30144	Pierre Seralta	770-514-4500	R	250	3.2
Florsheim Shoe Co.	130 S Canal St	Chicago	IL	60606	Charles J Campbell	312-559-2500	P	245	2.8
Shoe Carnival Inc.	8233 Baumgart Rd	Evansville	IN	47711	Mark L Lemond	812-867-6471	P	228	2.0
C and J Clark America Inc.	156 Oak St	Newton Falls	MA	02164	Bob Infantino	617-243-4100	S	200	2.5
Sneaker Stadium Inc.	55 Carter Dr	Edison	NJ	08817	Dave Bloom	908-777-9777	R	186*	1.0
Vans Inc.	15700 Shoemaker	Sante Fe Sprgs	CA	90670	Gary H Schoenfeld	562-565-8267	P	159	1.3
Kenneth Cole Productions Inc.	152 West 57th St	New York	NY	10019	Kenneth D Cole	212-265-1500	P	152	0.6
Butler Group Inc.	PO Box 105535	Atlanta	GA	30348	Elliot Lubin	404-801-1200	R	100*	1.2
Nunn Bush Shoe Co.	PO Box 2047	Milwaukee	WI	53201	Peter S Grossman	414-263-8800	S	98	0.5
Chernin Shoe Inc.	1001 S Clinton St	Chicago	IL	60607	Steve Larrick	312-922-5900	R	90*	0.9
Endicott Johnson	780 Harry L Dr	Johnson City	NY	13790	Burt Stricker	607-770-6500	D	71*	0.8
Chun Kim Chow Ltd.	PO Box 1578	Honolulu	HI	96806	Paul Chun	808-532-5725	R	70	1.0
Shonac Corp.	1675 Watkins Rd	Columbus	OH	43207	Steven Nacht	614-497-1199	R	66	0.6
Bee-Gee Shoe Corp.	3055 Kettering Blvd	Dayton	OH	45439	Donald Harrington	513-223-4241	D	62	1.3
Eurostar Inc.	13425 S Figueroa St	Los Angeles	CA	90061	Eric Alon	310-354-1387	R	62	0.3
Bally Retail Inc.	1 Bally Pl	New Rochelle	NY	10801	Merle Sloss	914-632-4444	R	54*	0.6
R and R Uniforms Inc.	3410 H Vardel	Charlotte	NC	28217	Bill Burns	704-333-6681	D	51*	0.5
Charles David of California Inc.	5731 Buckingham	Culver City	CA	90230	Charles Malka	310-348-5050	R	50	0.2
Hush Puppies Co.	9341 Courtland Dr	Rockford	MI	49351	Louis A Dubrow	616-866-5500	D	45*	<0.1
Shore Enterprises Inc.	6330 Newtown Rd	Virginia Beach	VA	23462	Aubrey L Layne Jr	804-461-2440	R	45*	0.7
Cooper's Inc.	11205 Montgomery	Albuquerque	NM	87111	Donald Midkiff	505-296-8344	R	44	0.5
Just for Feet Inc.	153 Cahaba Valley	Pelham	AL	35124	Harold Ruttenberg	205-987-3450	P	38	0.3
Knapp Shoes Inc.	1 Knapp Ctr	Brockton	MA	02401	John Schlueter	508-588-9000	R	36	0.6
Mason Shoe Manufacturing	1251 1st Ave	Chippewa Falls	WI	54729	John Lubs	715-723-1871	R	35	0.7
B.B. Walker Co.	PO Drawer 1167	Asheboro	NC	27204	Kent T Anderson	910-625-1380	P	33	0.4
Lichterman Shoe Co.	PO Box 94	Memphis	TN	38101	Barry Litchterman	901-774-8920	R	31	0.4
Cowtown Boot Company Inc.	PO Box 26428	El Paso	TX	79926	Paul Calcaterra	915-593-2565	R	30*	0.4
Tradehome Shoe Stores Inc.	429 Prior Ave N	St. Paul	MN	55104	DA Mains	612-646-1345	R	29	0.2
Gucci America Inc.	50 Hartz Way	Secaucus	NJ	07094	Domenico Desole	201-867-8800	R	28	0.5
Sibley's Shoes Inc.	100 Rennaisance	Detroit	MI	48243	NH Rosenfeld	313-259-1900	R	28	0.3
Cavender's Boot City	232 Rusk St	Pittsburg	TX	75686	James Cavender	903-856-5369	R	27*	0.3
Steve's Shoes Inc.	11333 Stangline Rd	Lenexa	KS	66215	Michael G Yeager	913-469-5535	R	25*	0.4
Marc Paul Inc.	1500 Botelho Dr	Walnut Creek	CA	94596	Marc P Kaplan	510-947-0311	R	25*	0.3
Overland Management Corp.	239 Littleton Rd	Westford	MA	01886	Daniel P Bazinet	508-692-4801	R	22	0.1
Shtofman Company Inc.	PO Box 4758	Tyler	TX	75712	Norman Shtofman	903-592-0861	R	22	0.3

Source: *Ward's Business Directory of U.S. Private and Public Companies*, 1998. The company type code used is as follows: P - Public, R - Private, S - Subsidiary, D - Division, J - Joint Venture, A - Affiliate, G - Group. Sales are in millions of dollars, employees are in thousands. An asterisk (*) indicates an estimated sales volume. The symbol < stands for 'less than'.

OCCUPATIONS EMPLOYED BY SIC 566 - SHOE STORES

Occupation	% of Total 1996	Change to 2006	Occupation	% of Total 1996	Change to 2006
Salespersons, retail	59.0	-5.4	General managers & top executives	5.0	-13.9
Marketing & sales worker supervisors	16.5	-11.2	Cashiers	3.9	-10.1
Stock clerks	6.5	-28.2	Freight, stock, & material movers, hand	1.4	-20.0

Source: *Industry-Occupation Matrix*, Bureau of Labor Statistics. These data relate to one or more 3-digit SIC industry groups rather than to a single 4-digit SIC. The change reported for each occupation to the year 2006 is a percent of growth or decline as estimated by the Bureau of Labor Statistics. The abbreviation nec stands for 'not elsewhere classified'.

STATE AND REGIONAL CONCENTRATION

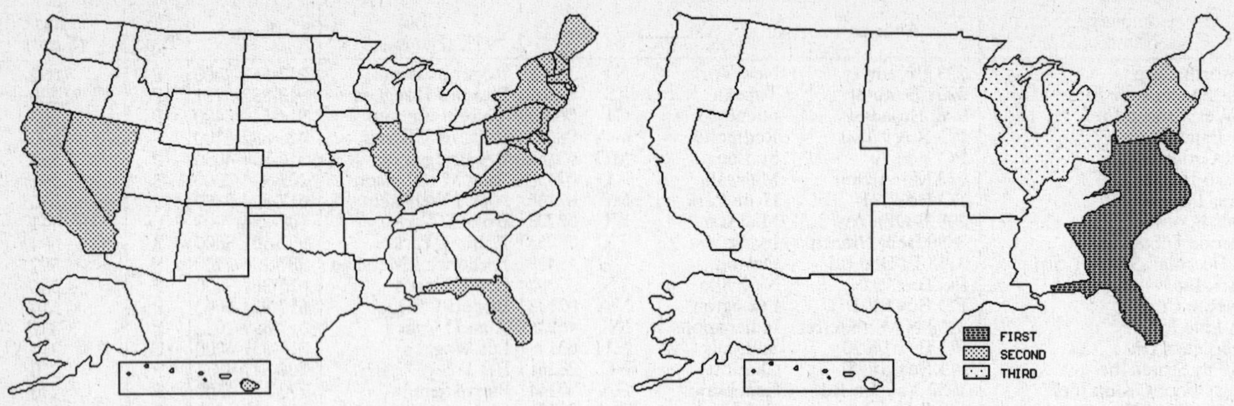

INDUSTRY DATA BY STATE

State	Establishments - 1995 Total (number)	Establishments - 1995 % of U.S.	Employment - 1995 Total (number)	Employment - 1995 % of U.S.	Employment - 1995 Per Estab.	Payroll - 1995 Total ($ mil.)	Payroll - 1995 Per Empl. ($)	Sales - 1992 Total ($ mil.)	Sales - 1992 % of U.S.	Sales - 1992 Per Estab ($)
California	3,499	10.6	19,246	10.4	6	255.3	13,266	2,171.5	12.1	105,424
New York	2,697	8.2	14,900	8.1	6	203.1	13,631	1,578.3	8.8	112,081
Texas	2,081	6.3	11,411	6.2	5	139.9	12,260	1,214.5	6.8	99,886
Florida	2,165	6.6	11,515	6.2	5	139.6	12,122	1,144.4	6.4	101,222
Pennsylvania	1,748	5.3	9,037	4.9	5	104.3	11,547	926.5	5.2	97,230
Illinois	1,543	4.7	9,397	5.1	6	119.2	12,683	888.0	5.0	95,248
New Jersey	1,253	3.8	7,366	4.0	6	95.1	12,917	782.5	4.4	106,213
Ohio	1,395	4.2	8,102	4.4	6	82.4	10,165	682.3	3.8	86,680
Michigan	1,175	3.6	6,739	3.6	6	80.0	11,873	658.4	3.7	97,765
North Carolina	1,031	3.1	6,315	3.4	6	60.3	9,546	475.3	2.7	81,344
Georgia	974	2.9	5,807	3.1	6	67.4	11,604	460.8	2.6	92,881
Massachusetts	856	2.6	4,640	2.5	5	60.4	13,022	458.6	2.6	105,240
Virginia	873	2.6	4,954	2.7	6	53.4	10,788	452.3	2.5	90,235
Maryland	743	2.2	4,578	2.5	6	53.1	11,592	437.4	2.4	90,284
Indiana	651	2.0	3,899	2.1	6	42.8	10,986	349.9	2.0	83,384
Tennessee	766	2.3	4,288	2.3	6	47.1	10,975	346.7	1.9	90,417
Wisconsin	607	1.8	3,563	1.9	6	38.1	10,694	318.2	1.8	90,539
Missouri	653	2.0	3,623	2.0	6	40.7	11,226	307.0	1.7	83,337
Washington	463	1.4	2,296	1.2	5	29.3	12,772	270.8	1.5	111,862
Louisiana	496	1.5	2,738	1.5	6	30.1	10,989	258.3	1.4	86,392
Minnesota	504	1.5	2,854	1.5	6	30.2	10,587	251.8	1.4	87,565
Arizona	449	1.4	2,220	1.2	5	27.7	12,456	244.4	1.4	101,534
Connecticut	425	1.3	2,220	1.2	5	29.5	13,299	239.9	1.3	100,089
Alabama	520	1.6	3,139	1.7	6	32.9	10,491	238.5	1.3	87,438
Colorado	425	1.3	2,375	1.3	6	29.1	12,272	221.7	1.2	95,517
South Carolina	488	1.5	2,839	1.5	6	28.8	10,150	218.1	1.2	83,077
Kentucky	445	1.3	2,330	1.3	5	25.4	10,921	203.4	1.1	88,894
Oregon	273	0.8	1,566	0.8	6	18.7	11,920	152.1	0.9	108,775
Iowa	343	1.0	1,906	1.0	6	19.0	9,992	149.3	0.8	76,612
Hawaii	141	0.4	1,366	0.7	10	20.9	15,324	144.5	0.8	108,867
Oklahoma	327	1.0	1,566	0.8	5	17.0	10,839	144.1	0.8	82,467
Kansas	283	0.9	1,745	0.9	6	20.9	11,962	140.0	0.8	86,609
New Hampshire	217	0.7	1,233	0.7	6	14.1	11,408	120.6	0.7	106,898
Mississippi	304	0.9	1,522	0.8	5	15.1	9,889	115.5	0.6	74,240
Maine	177	0.5	996	0.5	6	12.2	12,251	110.0	0.6	126,319
Nevada	164	0.5	1,034	0.6	6	15.7	15,162	109.1	0.6	129,687
Arkansas	245	0.7	1,183	0.6	5	13.0	10,980	104.3	0.6	84,610
Utah	218	0.7	1,061	0.6	5	12.4	11,729	104.3	0.6	101,175
New Mexico	162	0.5	828	0.4	5	10.5	12,687	87.8	0.5	95,309
West Virginia	220	0.7	953	0.5	4	10.4	10,890	85.8	0.5	89,261
Nebraska	212	0.6	1,158	0.6	5	11.4	9,874	85.3	0.5	77,296
Rhode Island	101	0.3	541	0.3	5	7.3	13,512	57.3	0.3	107,236
Delaware	110	0.3	694	0.4	6	7.4	10,684	56.6	0.3	104,017
D.C.	88	0.3	423	0.2	5	6.0	14,170	56.0	0.3	99,448
Idaho	115	0.3	602	0.3	5	6.3	10,435	55.4	0.3	101,199
Montana	86	0.3	427	0.2	5	4.6	10,815	45.7	0.3	92,376
Vermont	84	0.3	445	0.2	5	5.0	11,240	44.7	0.2	113,447
North Dakota	74	0.2	357	0.2	5	4.3	12,000	33.6	0.2	84,803
South Dakota	90	0.3	408	0.2	5	4.4	10,902	33.4	0.2	80,681
Alaska	40	0.1	227	0.1	6	2.9	12,687	30.0	0.2	88,454
Wyoming	50	0.2	201	0.1	4	2.5	12,328	18.5	0.1	78,889

Source: County Business Patterns, 1995 and *Economic Census of the U.S., 1992*. Data are sorted by 1992 revenues and, if revenues are unavailable, by establishments in 1995. The symbol (D) indicates that data are withheld by the source to avoid disclosure of competitive information. A dash (-) indicates that data are not available or undisclosed because they do not meet statistical validity standards. Shaded *states* on the state map indicate those states which have proportionately greater representation in the industry than would be indicated by the state's population; the ratio is based on total revenues or number of establishments. Shaded *regions* indicate where the industry is regionally most concentrated.

5699 - MISC. APPAREL & ACCESSORY STORES

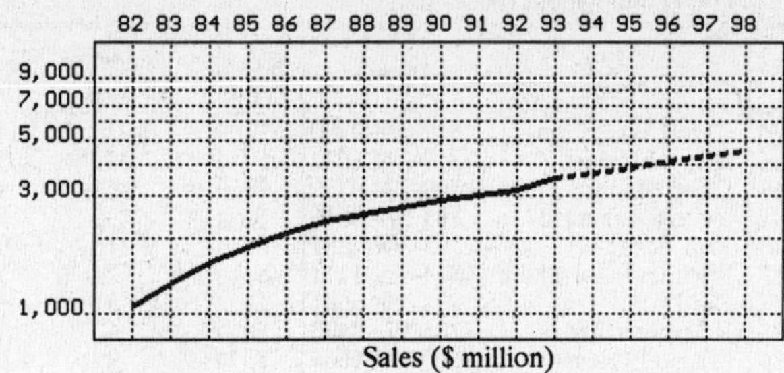

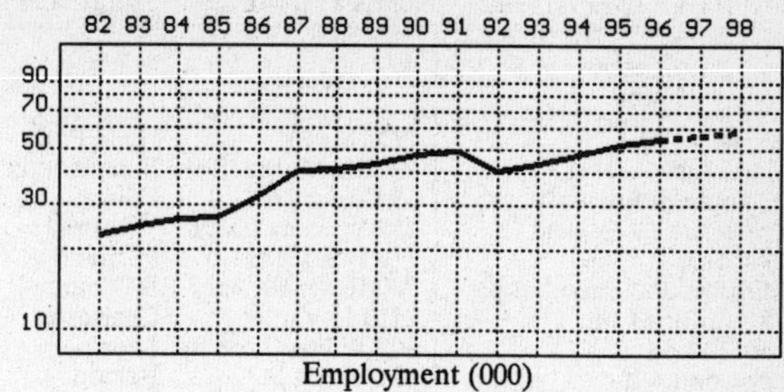

GENERAL STATISTICS

Year	Establishments (number)	Employment (number)	Payroll ($ million)	Sales ($ million)	Employees per Establishment (number)	Sales per Establishment ($)	Payroll per Employee ($)
1982	6,869	22,913	167.0	1,062.8	3	154,724	7,289
1983	6,626	24,784	209.0	1,322.6*e*	4	-	8,432
1984	6,591	26,486	215.5	1,582.4*e*	4	-	8,137
1985	6,477	27,102	238.8	1,842.1*e*	4	-	8,810
1986	7,018	32,593	290.0	2,101.9*e*	5	-	8,897
1987	9,057	40,990	357.5	2,361.7	5	260,759	8,722
1988	8,051	41,565	431.6	2,521.7*e*	5	-	10,383
1989	8,200	43,884	472.6	2,681.7*e*	5	-	10,770
1990	9,126	47,063	506.7	2,841.7*e*	5	-	10,767
1991	9,292	48,302	517.3	3,001.6*e*	5	-	10,709
1992	8,659	40,686	452.4	3,161.6	5	365,127	11,119
1993	9,177	43,168	504.0	3,484.9*p*	5	-	11,676
1994	9,458	47,451	573.2	3,694.8*p*	5	-	12,079
1995	9,603	51,730	635.7	3,904.7*p*	5	-	12,288
1996	10,085*p*	54,440*p*	658.6*p*	4,114.6*p*	-	-	-
1997	10,343*p*	56,568*p*	693.4*p*	4,324.5*p*	-	-	-
1998	10,600*p*	58,696*p*	728.2*p*	4,534.3*p*	-	-	-

Sources: Economic Census of the United States, 1982, 1987, and 1992. Establishment counts, employment, and payroll are from *County Business Patterns* for non-Census years. Values followed by a 'p' are projections by the editors. Sales and expense data for non-Census years are extrapolations, marked by 'e'. Industries reclassified in 1987 will not have data for prior years. Data are the most recent available at this level of detail.

INDICES OF CHANGE

Year	Establishments (number)	Employment (number)	Payroll ($ million)	Sales ($ million)	Employees per Establishment (number)	Sales per Establishment ($)	Payroll per Employee ($)
1982	79.3	56.3	36.9	33.6	60.0	42.4	65.6
1983	76.5	60.9	46.2	41.8*e*	80.0	-	75.8
1984	76.1	65.1	47.6	50.1*e*	80.0	-	73.2
1985	74.8	66.6	52.8	58.3*e*	80.0	-	79.2
1986	81.0	80.1	64.1	66.5*e*	100.0	-	80.0
1987	104.6	100.7	79.0	74.7	100.0	71.4	78.4
1988	93.0	102.2	95.4	79.8*e*	100.0	-	93.4
1989	94.7	107.9	104.5	84.8*e*	100.0	-	96.9
1990	105.4	115.7	112.0	89.9*e*	100.0	-	96.8
1991	107.3	118.7	114.3	94.9*e*	100.0	-	96.3
1992	100.0	100.0	100.0	100.0	100.0	100.0	100.0
1993	106.0	106.1	111.4	110.2*p*	94.1	-	105.0
1994	109.2	116.6	126.7	116.9*p*	100.3	-	108.6
1995	110.9	127.1	140.5	123.5*p*	107.7	-	110.5
1996	116.5*p*	133.8*p*	145.6*p*	130.1*p*	-	-	-
1997	119.4*p*	139.0*p*	153.3*p*	136.8*p*	-	-	-
1998	122.4*p*	144.3*p*	161.0*p*	143.4*p*	-	-	-

Sources: Same as General Statistics. The values shown reflect change from the base year, 1992. Values above 100 mean greater than 1992, values below 100 mean less than 1992, and a value of 100 in the 1982-91 or 1993-98 period means same as 1992. Values followed by a 'p' are projections by the editors; 'e' stands for extrapolation. Data are the most recent available at this level of detail.

SELECTED RATIOS

For 1992	Avg. of All Retail	Analyzed Industry	Index	For 1992	Avg. of All Retail	Analyzed Industry	Index
Employees per Establishment	12	5	39	Sales per Employee	102,941	77,707	75
Payroll per Establishment	146,026	52,246	36	Sales per Establishment	1,241,555	365,123	29
Payroll per Employee	12,107	11,119	92	Expenses per Establishment	na	na	na

Sources: Same as General Statistics. The 'Average of All Manufacturing' column represents the average of all manufacturing industries reported for the most recent complete year available. The Index shows the relationship between the Average and the Analyzed Industry. For example, 100 means that they are equal; 500 that the Analyzed Industry is five times the average; 50 means that the Analyzed Industry is half the national average. The abbreviation 'na' is used to show that data are 'not available'.

LEADING COMPANIES

Number shown: **25** Total sales ($ mil): **2,269** Total employment (000): **25.7**

Company Name	Address				CEO Name	Phone	Co. Type	Sales ($ mil)	Empl. (000)
J. Baker Inc.	PO Box 231	Hyde Park	MA	02136	Alan I Weinstein	617-828-9300	P	1,020	11.6
Finish Line Inc.	3308 N Mitthoeffer	Indianapolis	IN	46236	Alan H Cohen	317-899-1022	P	332	5.5
Sneaker Stadium Inc.	55 Carter Dr	Edison	NJ	08817	Dave Bloom	908-777-9777	R	186 *	1.0
Lost Arrow Inc.	259 W Santa Clara	Ventura	CA	93001	Yvon Chouinard	805-643-8616	R	130	0.6
Rentrak Corp.	PO Box 18888	Portland	OR	97218	Ron Berger	503-284-7581	P	116	0.2
Life Uniforms and Shoe Shops	700 Rosedale Ave	St. Louis	MO	63112	Michael E Burnham	314-889-1111	S	76	1.3
R and R Uniforms Inc.	3410 H Vardel	Charlotte	NC	28217	Bill Burns	704-333-6681	D	51 *	0.5
Accessory Place Inc.	600 Willow Tree Rd	Leonia	NJ	07605	R H Wechsler	201-592-0400	R	40	1.0
Newbury Comics Inc.	38 Everett St	Boston	MA	02134	Michael Dreese	617-254-1666	R	29 *	0.2
Cavender's Boot City	232 Rusk St	Pittsburg	TX	75686	James Cavender	903-856-5369	R	27 *	0.3
Crazy Shirts Inc.	99-969 Iwaena St	Aiea	HI	96701	R Ralston	808-487-9919	R	25 *	0.4
Special Tee Golf of Florida Inc.		Altamonte Sp	FL	32701	Jack Hazen	407-834-1000	R	25	0.2
Mitchell's Management Corp.	4030-Ceasantdale	Atlanta	GA	30340	Robert G Beaty	404-448-8381	R	23 *	0.5
Nationwide Formalwear Inc.	PO Box 2444	West Chester	PA	19380	William Galah Sr	215-692-6624	R	23 *	0.5
Long Rap Inc.	1420 Wisconsin NW	Washington	DC	20007	Chuck Rendelman	202-337-6610	R	22 *	0.2
Dennis Uniform Mfg. Co.	135 SE Hawthorne	Portland	OR	97214	Douglas W Donaca	503-238-7123	R	21 *	0.3
Water Wear Inc.	1349 3rd Ave	New York	NY	10021	D Winderbaum	212-570-6606	R	19 *	0.2
Domsey Fiber Corp.	431 Kent Ave	Brooklyn	NY	11211	Arthur Salm	718-384-6000	R	18	0.4
Queens City Distributing Co.	1320 Manor Dr	Pittsburgh	PA	15241	David Neft	412-741-1930	R	17 *	<0.1
Island Water Sports Inc.	1985 NE 2nd St	Deerfield Bch	FL	33441	Kirk G Cottrell	305-427-5665	R	16	0.2
McClures Stores Inc.	1052 Madison Sq	Madison	TN	37115	James D Andrews	615-868-1370	R	16	0.3
Norcostco Inc.	3203 N Hwy 100	Minneapolis	MN	55422	James T Scott	612-533-2791	R	12	0.2
Retail Star Inc.	6131 Bradley	St. Louis	MO	63129	Tom Noblitt	314-487-9816	R	12	0.3
Lithgow Industries Inc.	461 4th Ave	Louisville	KY	40202	Eldon Crouch	502-584-3112	R	11 *	0.2
Pro Dive	801 Seabreeze Blvd	Ft Lauderdale	FL	33316	Greg McKay	305-761-3413	R	1 *	<0.1

Source: *Ward's Business Directory of U.S. Private and Public Companies*, 1998. The company type code used is as follows: P - Public, R - Private, S - Subsidiary, D - Division, J - Joint Venture, A - Affiliate, G - Group. Sales are in millions of dollars, employees are in thousands. An asterisk (*) indicates an estimated sales volume. The symbol < stands for 'less than'.

OCCUPATIONS EMPLOYED BY SIC 569 - MISCELLANEOUS APPAREL AND ACCESSORY STORES

Occupation	% of Total 1996	Change to 2006	Occupation	% of Total 1996	Change to 2006
Salespersons, retail	51.3	40.6	Bookkeeping, accounting, & auditing clerks	2.1	5.6
Marketing & sales worker supervisors	8.8	32.0	Purchasing managers	2.0	18.8
General managers & top executives	7.9	27.9	Wholesale & retail buyers, except farm products	1.3	9.3
Stock clerks	4.8	23.8	Assemblers, fabricators, hand workers nec	1.3	31.9
Cashiers	4.0	33.6	Clerical supervisors & managers	1.2	32.1
Custom tailors & sewers	3.0	-14.2	General office clerks	1.2	13.6
Traffic, shipping, receiving clerks	2.3	32.0	Sales & related workers nec	1.0	45.1

Source: *Industry-Occupation Matrix*, Bureau of Labor Statistics. These data relate to one or more 3-digit SIC industry groups rather than to a single 4-digit SIC. The change reported for each occupation to the year 2006 is a percent of growth or decline as estimated by the Bureau of Labor Statistics. The abbreviation nec stands for 'not elsewhere classified'.

STATE AND REGIONAL CONCENTRATION

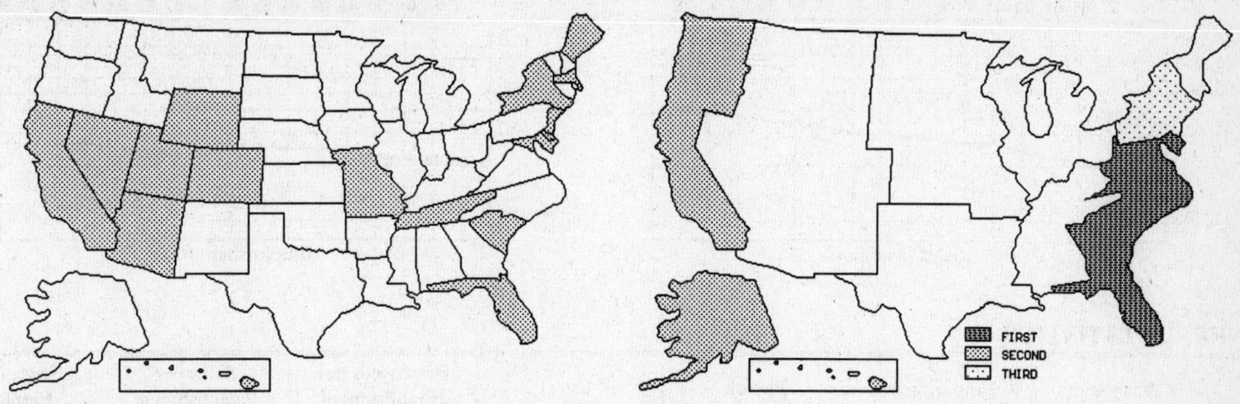

INDUSTRY DATA BY STATE

State	Establishments - 1995 Total (number)	Establishments - 1995 % of U.S.	Employment - 1995 Total (number)	Employment - 1995 % of U.S.	Employment - 1995 Per Estab.	Payroll - 1995 Total ($ mil.)	Payroll - 1995 Per Empl. ($)	Sales - 1992 Total ($ mil.)	Sales - 1992 % of U.S.	Sales - 1992 Per Estab ($)
California	1,104	11.5	6,077	11.7	6	78.4	12,895	436.2	13.8	80,662
Florida	835	8.7	4,432	8.6	5	56.9	12,828	327.8	10.4	83,667
New York	666	6.9	4,011	7.8	6	56.3	14,026	265.4	8.4	92,428
Texas	695	7.2	3,658	7.1	5	40.0	10,936	204.2	6.5	73,361
Pennsylvania	381	4.0	2,291	4.4	6	26.9	11,753	124.3	3.9	84,996
Illinois	380	4.0	2,275	4.4	6	27.8	12,226	117.3	3.7	67,234
New Jersey	352	3.7	1,745	3.4	5	21.7	12,456	114.8	3.6	95,468
Colorado	293	3.1	1,683	3.3	6	20.8	12,377	89.4	2.8	76,239
Hawaii	142	1.5	1,142	2.2	8	14.8	12,938	88.6	2.8	86,636
South Carolina	174	1.8	1,055	2.0	6	13.7	13,029	84.5	2.7	100,242
Georgia	225	2.3	1,161	2.2	5	14.0	12,070	82.1	2.6	84,481
Michigan	262	2.7	1,485	2.9	6	15.3	10,336	81.6	2.6	69,657
Massachusetts	220	2.3	1,166	2.3	5	17.4	14,963	81.0	2.6	86,803
Ohio	317	3.3	1,426	2.8	4	16.9	11,855	72.7	2.3	66,847
Missouri	217	2.3	1,212	2.3	6	14.4	11,847	69.3	2.2	77,099
Maryland	206	2.1	1,125	2.2	5	16.5	14,699	67.3	2.1	86,056
Tennessee	205	2.1	983	1.9	5	11.6	11,842	63.7	2.0	57,516
Virginia	223	2.3	1,115	2.2	5	12.9	11,601	61.3	1.9	71,656
North Carolina	211	2.2	927	1.8	4	10.1	10,926	60.7	1.9	81,458
Washington	159	1.7	743	1.4	5	8.8	11,832	55.8	1.8	76,714
Arizona	197	2.1	993	1.9	5	10.6	10,717	48.4	1.5	63,691
Indiana	183	1.9	1,006	1.9	5	11.8	11,724	40.2	1.3	53,962
Wisconsin	152	1.6	753	1.5	5	8.3	11,061	38.1	1.2	72,405
Minnesota	113	1.2	762	1.5	7	11.0	14,387	38.1	1.2	70,635
Connecticut	97	1.0	413	0.8	4	6.0	14,424	34.1	1.1	90,299
Louisiana	137	1.4	742	1.4	5	7.8	10,524	32.7	1.0	69,459
Alabama	109	1.1	657	1.3	6	8.2	12,429	30.6	1.0	77,275
Utah	99	1.0	684	1.3	7	6.1	8,864	30.2	1.0	62,852
Oregon	100	1.0	489	0.9	5	6.3	12,971	28.7	0.9	78,499
Oklahoma	87	0.9	481	0.9	6	5.5	11,370	28.1	0.9	66,104
Kansas	91	0.9	540	1.0	6	6.2	11,531	25.4	0.8	57,133
Nevada	81	0.8	405	0.8	5	6.1	14,963	23.2	0.7	88,546
Kentucky	103	1.1	405	0.8	4	3.8	9,452	22.5	0.7	60,281
Iowa	76	0.8	444	0.9	6	5.1	11,414	21.3	0.7	55,523
Delaware	39	0.4	179	0.3	5	2.2	12,486	17.1	0.5	84,723
Nebraska	51	0.5	316	0.6	6	3.4	10,617	17.1	0.5	66,229
Maine	51	0.5	176	0.3	3	3.4	19,290	16.2	0.5	108,490
New Mexico	76	0.8	339	0.7	4	3.6	10,723	15.1	0.5	66,661
West Virginia	44	0.5	285	0.6	6	4.0	14,204	14.2	0.5	76,554
Idaho	50	0.5	327	0.6	7	3.6	10,869	12.9	0.4	48,346
Arkansas	75	0.8	344	0.7	5	3.2	9,160	11.7	0.4	68,444
Rhode Island	42	0.4	162	0.3	4	2.1	12,710	10.5	0.3	77,257
Mississippi	64	0.7	278	0.5	4	2.7	9,647	10.4	0.3	60,214
New Hampshire	43	0.4	165	0.3	4	1.9	11,527	8.6	0.3	86,060
D.C.	24	0.2	73	0.1	3	1.4	18,603	8.2	0.3	72,469
Vermont	28	0.3	144	0.3	5	1.7	11,986	7.0	0.2	73,333
Wyoming	22	0.2	109	0.2	5	1.4	12,835	6.9	0.2	71,072
Montana	41	0.4	142	0.3	3	1.0	7,317	5.6	0.2	78,873
Alaska	16	0.2	47	0.1	3	0.8	16,894	3.9	0.1	64,213
North Dakota	18	0.2	61	0.1	3	0.6	9,148	3.6	0.1	53,806
South Dakota	27	0.3	97	0.2	4	0.6	6,619	3.2	0.1	55,404

Source: County Business Patterns, 1995 and *Economic Census of the U.S., 1992*. Data are sorted by 1992 revenues and, if revenues are unavailable, by establishments in 1995. The symbol (D) indicates that data are withheld by the source to avoid disclosure of competitive information. A dash (-) indicates that data are not available or undisclosed because they do not meet statistical validity standards. Shaded *states* on the state map indicate those states which have proportionately greater representation in the industry than would be indicated by the state's population; the ratio is based on total revenues or number of establishments. Shaded *regions* indicate where the industry is regionally most concentrated.

5712 - FURNITURE STORES

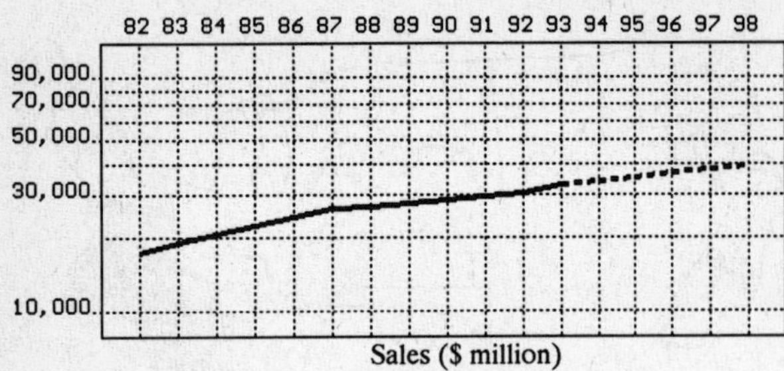

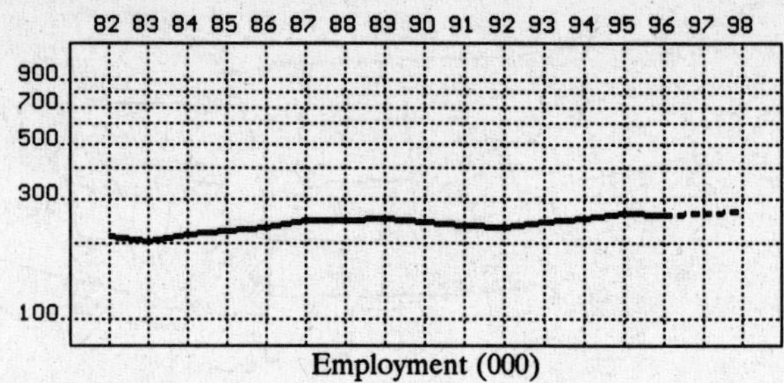

GENERAL STATISTICS

Year	Establishments (number)	Employment (number)	Payroll ($ million)	Sales ($ million)	Employees per Establishment (number)	Sales per Establishment ($)	Payroll per Employee ($)
1982	31,647	213,875	2,608.0	17,223.4	7	544,234	12,194
1983	30,510	205,303	2,810.4	18,978.1*e*	7	-	13,689
1984	29,996	218,807	3,125.2	20,732.7*e*	7	-	14,283
1985	29,331	224,708	3,336.1	22,487.4*e*	8	-	14,847
1986	29,740	230,491	3,528.6	24,242.1*e*	8	-	15,309
1987	32,763	246,772	3,827.8	25,996.8	8	793,481	15,511
1988	31,267	246,537	4,157.9	26,880.7*e*	8	-	16,865
1989	30,999	248,444	4,269.8	27,764.5*e*	8	-	17,186
1990	30,822	244,915	4,295.7	28,648.4*e*	8	-	17,539
1991	31,361	236,513	4,241.6	29,532.3*e*	8	-	17,934
1992	32,478	232,668	4,354.7	30,416.1	7	936,515	18,717
1993	32,912	245,371	4,740.2	32,725.0*p*	7	-	19,319
1994	32,828	252,493	5,001.4	34,044.2*p*	8	-	19,808
1995	32,875	263,960	5,296.4	35,363.5*p*	8	-	20,065
1996	32,907*p*	261,074*p*	5,385.2*p*	36,682.8*p*	-	-	-
1997	33,109*p*	264,352*p*	5,573.8*p*	38,002.1*p*	-	-	-
1998	33,311*p*	267,630*p*	5,762.3*p*	39,321.3*p*	-	-	-

Sources: *Economic Census of the United States*, 1982, 1987, and 1992. Establishment counts, employment, and payroll are from *County Business Patterns* for non-Census years. Values followed by a 'p' are projections by the editors. Sales and expense data for non-Census years are extrapolations, marked by 'e'. Industries reclassified in 1987 will not have data for prior years. Data are the most recent available at this level of detail.

INDICES OF CHANGE

Year	Establishments (number)	Employment (number)	Payroll ($ million)	Sales ($ million)	Employees per Establishment (number)	Sales per Establishment ($)	Payroll per Employee ($)
1982	97.4	91.9	59.9	56.6	100.0	58.1	65.1
1983	93.9	88.2	64.5	62.4*e*	100.0	-	73.1
1984	92.4	94.0	71.8	68.2*e*	100.0	-	76.3
1985	90.3	96.6	76.6	73.9*e*	114.3	-	79.3
1986	91.6	99.1	81.0	79.7*e*	114.3	-	81.8
1987	100.9	106.1	87.9	85.5	114.3	84.7	82.9
1988	96.3	106.0	95.5	88.4*e*	114.3	-	90.1
1989	95.4	106.8	98.1	91.3*e*	114.3	-	91.8
1990	94.9	105.3	98.6	94.2*e*	114.3	-	93.7
1991	96.6	101.7	97.4	97.1*e*	114.3	-	95.8
1992	100.0	100.0	100.0	100.0	100.0	100.0	100.0
1993	101.3	105.5	108.9	107.6*p*	106.5	-	103.2
1994	101.1	108.5	114.9	111.9*p*	109.9	-	105.8
1995	101.2	113.4	121.6	116.3*p*	114.7	-	107.2
1996	101.3*p*	112.2*p*	123.7*p*	120.6*p*	-	-	-
1997	101.9*p*	113.6*p*	128.0*p*	124.9*p*	-	-	-
1998	102.6*p*	115.0*p*	132.3*p*	129.3*p*	-	-	-

Sources: Same as General Statistics. The values shown reflect change from the base year, 1992. Values above 100 mean greater than 1992, values below 100 mean less than 1992, and a value of 100 in the 1982-91 or 1993-98 period means same as 1992. Values followed by a 'p' are projections by the editors; 'e' stands for extrapolation. Data are the most recent available at this level of detail.

SELECTED RATIOS

For 1992	Avg. of All Retail	Analyzed Industry	Index	For 1992	Avg. of All Retail	Analyzed Industry	Index
Employees per Establishment	12	7	59	Sales per Employee	102,941	130,727	127
Payroll per Establishment	146,026	134,082	92	Sales per Establishment	1,241,555	936,514	75
Payroll per Employee	12,107	18,716	155	Expenses per Establishment	na	na	na

Sources: Same as General Statistics. The 'Average of All Manufacturing' column represents the average of all manufacturing industries reported for the most recent complete year available. The Index shows the relationship between the Average and the Analyzed Industry. For example, 100 means that they are equal; 500 that the Analyzed Industry is five times the average; 50 means that the Analyzed Industry is half the national average. The abbreviation 'na' is used to show that data are 'not available'.

LEADING COMPANIES

Number shown: **50** Total sales ($ mil): **24,827** Total employment (000): **178.7**

Company Name	Address				CEO Name	Phone	Co. Type	Sales ($ mil)	Empl. (000)
Office Depot Inc.	2200 GermanTown	Delray Beach	FL	33445	David I Fuente	561-278-4800	P	6,069	32.0
Staples Inc.	PO Box 9328	Framingham	MA	01701	Thomas G Stemberg	508-370-8500	P	3,968	25.0
OfficeMax Inc.	PO Box 22500	Cleveland	OH	44122	Michael Feuer	216-921-6900	P	2,542	19.3
Levitz Furniture Inc.	6111 Broken Sound	Boca Raton	FL	33487	Michael Bozic	561-994-6006	P	967	5.0
Heilig-Meyers Co.	2235 Staples Mill	Richmond	VA	23230	William C DeRusha	804-359-9171	P	956	12.5
Pier 1 Imports Inc.	301 Commerce St	Fort Worth	TX	76102	Clark A Johnson	817-878-8000	P	947	11.3
Elder-Beerman Stores Corp.	3155 El-Bee Rd	Dayton	OH	45439	Frederick J Mershad	937-296-2700	R	597	7.3
Ethan Allen Inc.	Ethan Allen Dr	Danbury	CT	06811	M Farooq Kathwari	203-743-8000	S	572	5.9
Haverty Furniture Companies	866 Peachtree	Atlanta	GA	30308	John E Slater Jr	404-881-1911	P	490	3.1
W.S. Badcock Corp.	PO Box 497	Mulberry	FL	33860	Ben Badcock	941-425-4921	R	450 *	1.5
Rhodes Inc.	4370 Peachtree NE	Atlanta	GA	30319	Irwin L Lowenstein	404-264-4600	P	430	2.7
Value City Furniture Div.	1800 Moler Rd	Columbus	OH	43207	David Thompson	614-221-9200	D	425	4.0
Euromarket Design Inc.	725 Landwehr Rd	Northbrook	IL	60062	Gordon Segal	847-272-2888	R	400	4.2
Roberds Inc.	1100 E Central Ave	Dayton	OH	45449	Kenneth W Fletcher	937-859-5127	P	342	2.1
Bombay Company Inc.	550 Bailey Ave	Fort Worth	TX	76107	Carson R Thompson	817-347-8200	P	336	5.0
Aaron Rents Inc.	309 E Paces Ferry	Atlanta	GA	30305	RC Loudermilk	404-231-0011	P	311	2.5
IKEA U.S. Inc.	Plym Commons	Plym. Meeting	PA	19462	Jan Kjellman	610-834-0180	S	305 *	2.6
CORT Furniture Rental Corp.	4401 Fair Lks Court	Fairfax	VA	22033	Paul N Arnold	703-968-8500	S	287	2.5
Atlantic American Corp.	PO Box 190720	Atlanta	GA	30319	Hilton H Howell Jr	404-266-5500	P	272	0.2
Warehouse Home Furnishing	PO Box 1140	Dublin	GA	31040	Ron Payne	912-275-3150	R	270 *	1.4
Cost Plus Inc.	PO Box 23350	Oakland	CA	94607	Ralph D Dillon	510-893-7300	P	260	1.6
Amer Television & Appliance	2404 W Beltline	Madison	WI	53713	Doug Reuhl	608-271-1000	R	260	1.4
R.C. Willey Home Furnishings	2301 S 300 West	Salt Lake City	UT	84115	William H Child	801-461-3900	S	260	1.4
Seaman Furniture Company	300 Crossways Pk	Woodbury	NY	11797	Allan Rosenberg	516-496-9560	P	251	1.1
Wickes Furniture Company Inc.	351 W Dundee Rd	Wheeling	IL	60090	John Klein	708-541-0100	R	250 *	2.5
Tandycrafts Inc.	1400 Everman Pkwy	Fort Worth	TX	76140	Michael J Walsh	817-551-9600	P	245	3.7
Art Van Furniture Inc.	6500 N 14 Mile Rd	Warren	MI	48092	Art Van Elslander	810-939-2100	R	230 *	2.0
IKEA U.S. Inc. West Div.	20700 Avalon Blvd	Carson	CA	90746	Johnny Anderson	310-217-8005	D	150 *	0.9
Krause's Sofa Factory	200 N Berry St	Brea	CA	92621	Thomas M DeLitto	714-990-3100	S	122	1.0
Farmers Furniture Company	1851 Telefair	Dublin	GA	31021	Sherwin Glass	912-275-3150	S	120 *	0.2
Leath Furniture Inc.	4370 Peachtree NE	Atlanta	GA	30319	Ronald D Phillips	404-848-0880	R	120	0.8
Huffman-Koos Inc.	Rte 4 and Main St	River Edge	NJ	07661	Fred Berk	201-343-4300	S	119	0.6
Lacks Stores Inc.	200 S Ben Jordon	Victoria	TX	77902	M Lack	512-578-3571	R	117 *	1.0
Krause's Furniture Inc.	200 N Berry St	Brea	CA	92821	Philip M Hawley	714-990-3100	P	113	1.0
B.T. Miller Office Products	2230 Avenue J	Arlington	TX	76006	James B Miller	817-649-1313	S	110 *	0.6
Reliable Stores Inc.	6301 Stevens Forest	Columbia	MD	21046	Richard M Barnett	410-381-9650	R	110	1.0
Jordan Furniture Co.	100 Stockwell Dr	Avon	MA	02322	Barry Tatelman	508-580-4900	R	99	0.6
Ivan Allen Co.	PO Box 1712	Atlanta	GA	30301	Thomas L Bolton	404-332-3000	R	96	0.8
Big Sur Waterbeds Inc.	13300 E 38th St	Denver	CO	80239	Barney Visser	303-371-8560	S	94 *	0.8
Star Furniture Co.	16666 Barker Spgs	Houston	TX	77084	Melvyn Wolff	713-492-6661	R	80	0.5
Schewel Furniture Company	PO Box 1600	Lynchburg	VA	24505	Marc A Schewel	804-522-0200	R	79	0.6
Marlo Furniture Company Inc.	5650 Washington	Alexandria	VA	22312	Louis Glickfield	703-941-0800	R	76 *	0.7
Corporate Express	2010 North 1st St	San Jose	CA	95131	Steve Van Guelpen	408-000-0000	S	70	0.3
John M. Smyth's Homemakers	1013 Butterfield Rd	Downers Grove	IL	60515	Ken C Curtis	630-852-6880	R	70	0.6
TJB Inc.	9822 Sallard Ct	Up Marlboro	MD	20772	Warren Teitelbaum	301-856-6755	R	70 *	0.7
Dameron-Pierson	PO Box 61350	New Orleans	LA	70161	Jack L Becker Jr	504-525-1203	S	66 *	0.3
Central Furniture Inc.	5480 Ferguson Dr	Commerce	CA	90022	Gary Cypress	213-720-8600	R	65	0.4
Grand Piano and Furniture Co.	4235 Electric SW	Roanoke	VA	24026	G B Cartledge Jr	703-343-1707	R	64	0.6
Welcome Home Inc.	309-D Raleigh St	Wilmington	NC	28412	Thomas H Quinn	910-791-4312	P	63	0.8
Good's Furniture Inc.	2501 Oregon Pike	Lancaster	PA	17601	Richard W Good	717-560-6555	S	62 *	0.4

Source: *Ward's Business Directory of U.S. Private and Public Companies*, 1998. The company type code used is as follows: P - Public, R - Private, S - Subsidiary, D - Division, J - Joint Venture, A - Affiliate, G - Group. Sales are in millions of dollars, employees are in thousands. An asterisk (*) indicates an estimated sales volume. The symbol < stands for 'less than'.

OCCUPATIONS EMPLOYED BY SIC 571 - FURNITURE AND HOMEFURNISHINGS STORES

Occupation	% of Total 1996	Change to 2006	Occupation	% of Total 1996	Change to 2006
Salespersons, retail	32.0	14.5	Cashiers	2.9	8.8
General managers & top executives	7.2	4.1	Traffic, shipping, receiving clerks	2.2	7.5
Stock clerks	7.2	49.6	Sales & related workers nec	2.2	18.2
Truck drivers light & heavy	6.4	-3.3	Carpet installers	2.0	-14.0
Marketing & sales worker supervisors	5.5	7.5	Clerical supervisors & managers	1.4	7.5
General office clerks	4.2	-7.5	Secretaries, except legal & medical	1.4	-14.7
Bookkeeping, accounting, & auditing clerks	3.8	-14.0	Purchasing managers	1.3	-3.3
Freight, stock, & material movers, hand	3.4	-3.3	Wholesale & retail buyers, except farm products	1.2	-11.0
Interior designers	3.1	18.2	Janitors & cleaners, maids	1.1	-14.0

Source: *Industry-Occupation Matrix*, Bureau of Labor Statistics. These data relate to one or more 3-digit SIC industry groups rather than to a single 4-digit SIC. The change reported for each occupation to the year 2006 is a percent of growth or decline as estimated by the Bureau of Labor Statistics. The abbreviation nec stands for 'not elsewhere classified'.

STATE AND REGIONAL CONCENTRATION

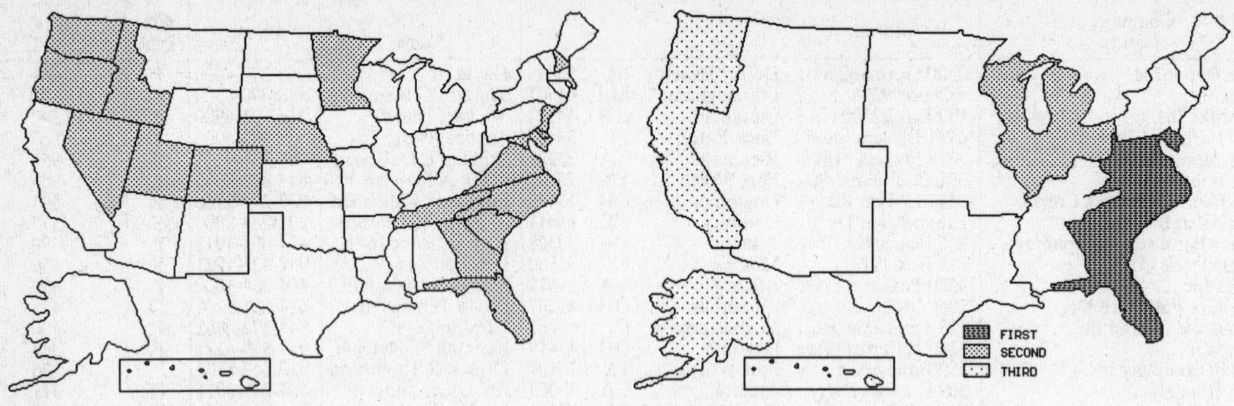

INDUSTRY DATA BY STATE

State	Establishments - 1995 Total (number)	Establishments - 1995 % of U.S.	Employment - 1995 Total (number)	Employment - 1995 % of U.S.	Employment - 1995 Per Estab.	Payroll - 1995 Total ($ mil.)	Payroll - 1995 Per Empl. ($)	Sales - 1992 Total ($ mil.)	Sales - 1992 % of U.S.	Sales - 1992 Per Estab ($)
California	2,980	9.1	21,414	8.1	7	457.2	21,348	3,138.3	10.3	142,681
Florida	2,559	7.8	18,174	6.9	7	362.9	19,966	2,212.8	7.3	138,022
New York	2,001	6.1	13,652	5.2	7	286.2	20,964	1,972.2	6.5	145,359
Texas	1,925	5.9	17,205	6.5	9	358.4	20,831	1,889.1	6.2	130,148
Illinois	1,308	4.0	11,437	4.3	9	231.0	20,195	1,342.4	4.4	131,438
Ohio	1,264	3.8	12,155	4.6	10	240.2	19,760	1,279.8	4.2	133,008
Pennsylvania	1,333	4.1	10,930	4.1	8	208.3	19,054	1,253.1	4.1	127,830
North Carolina	1,425	4.3	11,349	4.3	8	223.9	19,732	1,184.1	3.9	121,524
Michigan	898	2.7	9,425	3.6	10	205.5	21,808	1,083.5	3.6	130,384
New Jersey	990	3.0	7,483	2.8	8	172.4	23,033	1,079.5	3.5	164,687
Georgia	1,202	3.7	10,508	4.0	9	192.2	18,288	1,008.8	3.3	124,217
Virginia	1,003	3.1	9,001	3.4	9	168.8	18,748	971.2	3.2	111,365
Washington	700	2.1	5,243	2.0	7	105.4	20,111	645.2	2.1	133,175
Massachusetts	599	1.8	4,755	1.8	8	103.6	21,782	640.4	2.1	143,067
Tennessee	773	2.4	6,210	2.4	8	122.7	19,758	631.3	2.1	126,213
Minnesota	599	1.8	5,551	2.1	9	113.3	20,410	597.7	2.0	135,319
Maryland	536	1.6	5,137	1.9	10	102.5	19,962	592.9	1.9	129,474
Indiana	707	2.2	6,090	2.3	9	117.3	19,257	573.2	1.9	116,550
Wisconsin	620	1.9	4,941	1.9	8	97.3	19,682	552.8	1.8	127,573
Missouri	709	2.2	5,018	1.9	7	99.2	19,773	515.6	1.7	119,285
Alabama	743	2.3	5,395	2.0	7	92.5	17,148	494.9	1.6	105,144
South Carolina	702	2.1	4,857	1.8	7	89.9	18,504	468.1	1.5	103,279
Colorado	554	1.7	4,443	1.7	8	100.3	22,585	448.0	1.5	154,525
Louisiana	509	1.5	4,431	1.7	9	83.7	18,884	443.6	1.5	118,934
Arizona	558	1.7	4,709	1.8	8	95.7	20,312	442.0	1.5	132,481
Kentucky	526	1.6	4,395	1.7	8	76.3	17,355	439.2	1.4	126,271
Oregon	430	1.3	3,314	1.3	8	66.2	19,969	429.8	1.4	148,754
Connecticut	420	1.3	2,998	1.1	7	73.8	24,602	388.7	1.3	127,367
Utah	219	0.7	3,365	1.3	15	77.3	22,979	328.4	1.1	138,603
Nebraska	165	0.5	1,913	0.7	12	35.1	18,339	323.1	1.1	157,151
Iowa	381	1.2	2,859	1.1	8	49.8	17,431	305.4	1.0	117,379
Oklahoma	328	1.0	2,454	0.9	7	46.1	18,801	290.4	1.0	125,808
Kansas	339	1.0	2,386	0.9	7	44.8	18,776	260.0	0.9	117,360
Mississippi	429	1.3	2,885	1.1	7	52.1	18,052	257.7	0.8	102,833
Arkansas	446	1.4	2,606	1.0	6	47.0	18,050	254.3	0.8	111,690
New Mexico	198	0.6	1,903	0.7	10	41.5	21,797	177.7	0.6	118,308
West Virginia	259	0.8	2,001	0.8	8	32.5	16,238	175.0	0.6	103,633
Nevada	182	0.6	1,492	0.6	8	34.6	23,188	174.5	0.6	141,734
New Hampshire	144	0.4	1,198	0.5	8	23.8	19,901	149.2	0.5	141,293
Delaware	103	0.3	913	0.3	9	18.5	20,307	136.9	0.5	152,319
Idaho	207	0.6	1,548	0.6	7	27.3	17,620	135.8	0.4	118,006
Hawaii	85	0.3	519	0.2	6	12.7	24,382	119.9	0.4	165,664
Maine	136	0.4	926	0.4	7	16.9	18,260	96.9	0.3	109,595
Montana	145	0.4	1,030	0.4	7	18.4	17,877	95.4	0.3	118,559
South Dakota	106	0.3	897	0.3	8	15.9	17,688	83.9	0.3	103,957
Rhode Island	86	0.3	561	0.2	7	10.5	18,631	82.8	0.3	128,969
North Dakota	95	0.3	717	0.3	8	11.5	15,997	67.0	0.2	95,205
Vermont	88	0.3	462	0.2	5	8.1	17,526	52.8	0.2	105,070
Alaska	50	0.2	465	0.2	9	12.0	25,763	52.8	0.2	135,853
D.C.	44	0.1	292	0.1	7	7.1	24,260	40.9	0.1	144,060
Wyoming	67	0.2	348	0.1	5	6.6	18,945	37.2	0.1	105,969

Source: County Business Patterns, 1995 and *Economic Census of the U.S., 1992*. Data are sorted by 1992 revenues and, if revenues are unavailable, by establishments in 1995. The symbol (D) indicates that data are withheld by the source to avoid disclosure of competitive information. A dash (-) indicates that data are not available or undisclosed because they do not meet statistical validity standards. Shaded *states* on the state map indicate those states which have proportionately greater representation in the industry than would be indicated by the state's population; the ratio is based on total revenues or number of establishments. Shaded *regions* indicate where the industry is regionally most concentrated.

5713 - FLOOR COVERING STORES

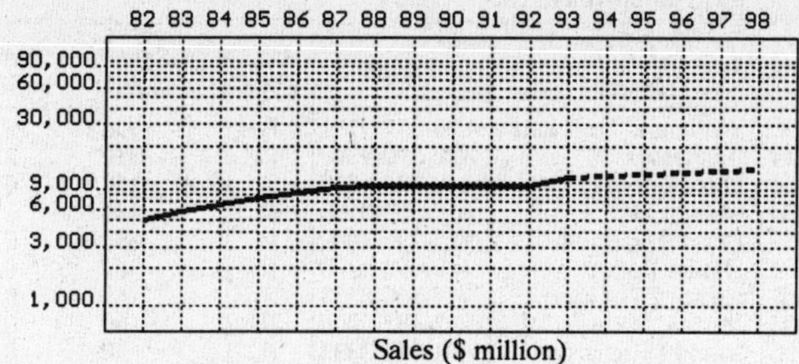

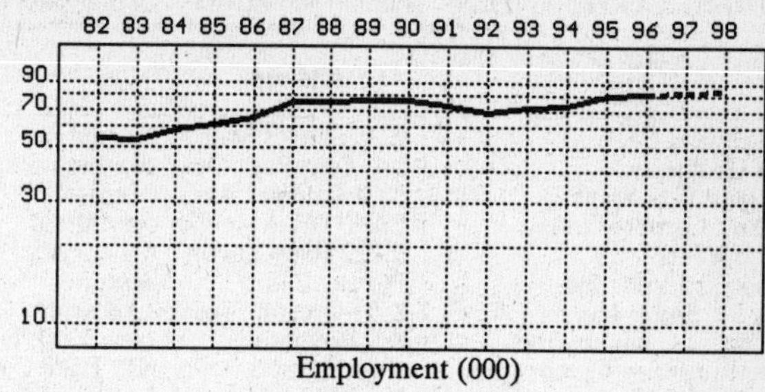

GENERAL STATISTICS

Year	Establishments (number)	Employment (number)	Payroll ($ million)	Sales ($ million)	Employees per Establishment (number)	Sales per Establishment ($)	Payroll per Employee ($)
1982	11,864	53,612	721.4	5,015.5	5	422,749	13,456
1983	11,469	52,735	800.2	5,857.6*e*	5	-	15,175
1984	11,533	58,725	923.1	6,699.7*e*	5	-	15,718
1985	11,248	60,974	1,014.8	7,541.8*e*	5	-	16,644
1986	11,766	64,784	1,127.5	8,383.9*e*	6	-	17,404
1987	13,752	75,373	1,324.6	9,225.9	5	670,880	17,574
1988	13,005	75,741	1,447.7	9,303.9*e*	6	-	19,114
1989	12,728	76,838	1,502.9	9,381.8*e*	6	-	19,559
1990	13,167	76,593	1,540.5	9,459.8*e*	6	-	20,113
1991	13,476	72,784	1,482.2	9,537.7*e*	5	-	20,364
1992	13,648	68,643	1,381.8	9,615.7	5	704,550	20,130
1993	13,945	72,047	1,472.1	10,944.1*p*	5	-	20,432
1994	14,165	72,792	1,585.1	11,404.1*p*	5	-	21,776
1995	14,562	80,210	1,798.7	11,864.1*p*	6	-	22,424
1996	14,690*p*	81,639*p*	1,832.2*p*	12,324.1*p*	-	-	-
1997	14,931*p*	83,364*p*	1,903.9*p*	12,784.1*p*	-	-	-
1998	15,172*p*	85,088*p*	1,975.6*p*	13,244.2*p*	-	-	-

Sources: Economic Census of the United States, 1982, 1987, and 1992. Establishment counts, employment, and payroll are from *County Business Patterns* for non-Census years. Values followed by a 'p' are projections by the editors. Sales and expense data for non-Census years are extrapolations, marked by 'e'. Industries reclassified in 1987 will not have data for prior years. Data are the most recent available at this level of detail.

INDICES OF CHANGE

Year	Establishments (number)	Employment (number)	Payroll ($ million)	Sales ($ million)	Employees per Establishment (number)	Sales per Establishment ($)	Payroll per Employee ($)
1982	86.9	78.1	52.2	52.2	100.0	60.0	66.8
1983	84.0	76.8	57.9	60.9*e*	100.0	-	75.4
1984	84.5	85.6	66.8	69.7*e*	100.0	-	78.1
1985	82.4	88.8	73.4	78.4*e*	100.0	-	82.7
1986	86.2	94.4	81.6	87.2*e*	120.0	-	86.5
1987	100.8	109.8	95.9	95.9	100.0	95.2	87.3
1988	95.3	110.3	104.8	96.8*e*	120.0	-	95.0
1989	93.3	111.9	108.8	97.6*e*	120.0	-	97.2
1990	96.5	111.6	111.5	98.4*e*	120.0	-	99.9
1991	98.7	106.0	107.3	99.2*e*	100.0	-	101.2
1992	100.0	100.0	100.0	100.0	100.0	100.0	100.0
1993	102.2	105.0	106.5	113.8*p*	103.3	-	101.5
1994	103.8	106.0	114.7	118.6*p*	102.8	-	108.2
1995	106.7	116.9	130.2	123.4*p*	110.2	-	111.4
1996	107.6*p*	118.9*p*	132.6*p*	128.2*p*	-	-	-
1997	109.4*p*	121.4*p*	137.8*p*	133.0*p*	-	-	-
1998	111.2*p*	124.0*p*	143.0*p*	137.7*p*	-	-	-

Sources: Same as General Statistics. The values shown reflect change from the base year, 1992. Values above 100 mean greater than 1992, values below 100 mean less than 1992, and a value of 100 in the 1982-91 or 1993-98 period means same as 1992. Values followed by a 'p' are projections by the editors; 'e' stands for extrapolation. Data are the most recent available at this level of detail.

SELECTED RATIOS

For 1992	Avg. of All Retail	Analyzed Industry	Index	For 1992	Avg. of All Retail	Analyzed Industry	Index
Employees per Establishment	12	5	42	Sales per Employee	102,941	140,083	136
Payroll per Establishment	146,026	101,246	69	Sales per Establishment	1,241,555	704,550	57
Payroll per Employee	12,107	20,130	166	Expenses per Establishment	na	na	na

Sources: Same as General Statistics. The 'Average of All Manufacturing' column represents the average of all manufacturing industries reported for the most recent complete year available. The Index shows the relationship between the Average and the Analyzed Industry. For example, 100 means that they are equal; 500 that the Analyzed Industry is five times the average; 50 means that the Analyzed Industry is half the national average. The abbreviation 'na' is used to show that data are 'not available'.

LEADING COMPANIES

Number shown: **33** Total sales ($ mil): **2,410** Total employment (000): **22.2**

Company Name	Address				CEO Name	Phone	Co. Type	Sales ($ mil)	Empl. (000)
Heilig-Meyers Co.	2235 Staples Mill	Richmond	VA	23230	William C DeRusha	804-359-9171	P	956	12.5
Maxim Group Inc.	210 TownPark Dr	Kennesaw	GA	30144	AJ Nassar	770-590-9369	P	310	2.4
Carpetland U.S.A. Inc.	8201 Calumet Ave	Munster	IN	46321	Peter Collaros	219-836-5628	S	170•	0.6
New York Carpet World	23840 W 8 Mile Rd	Southfield	MI	48034	Marvin Berlin	810-353-0180	R	140•	1.0
Carpeteria Inc.	25322 Rye Canyon	Valencia	CA	91355	Bryan Haserjian	805-295-1000	R	82	0.3
Tate Access Floors Inc.	PO Box 278	Jessup	MD	20794	Daniel Baker	410-799-4200	R	67	0.4
Good's Furniture Inc.	2501 Oregon Pike	Lancaster	PA	17601	Richard W Good	717-560-6555	S	62•	0.4
ABC Carpet Company Inc.	888 Broadway	New York	NY	10003	Jerome Weinrib	212-473-3000	R	60	0.5
Granite Furniture Company	1050 E 21st S	Salt Lake City	UT	84106	John D Richards	801-486-3333	R	58•	0.4
Carpet Barn Inc.	105 W Charleston	Las Vegas	NV	89102	Terry Williams	702-384-8551	S	43	<0.1
Martin Paint Stores	182-20 Liberty Ave	Jamaica	NY	11412	Michael Lurie	718-454-5100	R	43•	0.5
Self-Service Furniture Inc.	5401 E Sprague	Spokane	WA	99212	TW Griner	509-535-7717	R	43	0.3
Giant Carpet Inc.	120 Moonachie Ave	Moonachie	NJ	07074	Sam Rosenberg	201-507-0035	R	36•	0.3
Steinhafels Inc.	PO Box 5166	New Berlin	WI	53151	James Steinhafel	414-784-0500	R	33	0.3
Buddy's Carpet Inc.	4007 E 2nd St	Franklin	OH	45005	Lee Rozin	513-743-7700	R	29•	0.2
Plunkett Furniture Co.	2500 W Golf Rd	Hoffman Est	IL	60194	Hugh Plunkett	708-843-9000	R	29•	0.3
Nelson Brothers Furniture Corp.	2750 W Grand Ave	Chicago	IL	60612	James F Blinder	312-489-3333	R	25	0.2
Rotman's	725 Southbridge St	Worcester	MA	01610	S Rotman	508-755-5276	R	24	0.2
Cadillac Carpet Corp.	3147 Midl Cntry	Lake Grove	NY	11755	Stan Korey	516-467-7500	R	23	0.2
Hagopian and Sons Inc.	14000 W 8 Mile Rd	Oak Park	MI	48237	Edmond Hagopian	248-646-7847	R	21•	0.2
Miller's Furniture Industries	500 W Basin Rd	New Castle	DE	19720	Andrew L Miller	302-322-5451	R	15•	0.1
MMM Carpets Unlimited Inc.	3100 Molinaro St	Santa Clara	CA	95054	Victor Molinaro	408-988-4661	R	15	0.2
Vartan Pedian and Sons	6535 N Lincoln Ave	Chicago	IL	60645	H Pedian	708-675-9111	R	15	0.1
Brandon House Furniture Co.	1100 S University	Little Rock	AR	72204	Benton Brandon	501-663-1400	R	14	0.1
Donald E. McNabb Co.	PO Box 448	Milford	MI	48381	Doug McNabb	810-437-8146	R	14	0.1
O'Krent Floor Covering Co.	300 San Pedro Ave	San Antonio	TX	78212	Theodore J O'Krent	210-227-7387	R	14•	0.1
St. Paul Linoleum&Carpet Co.	1505 University Ave	St. Paul	MN	55104	Clement J Commers	612-645-4601	R	13	<0.1
Carpet King Inc.	8225 Hwy 7	St. Louis Park	MN	55426	Dennis McGraw	612-933-2181	R	12•	<0.1
Ed Marling Stores Inc.	2950 McClure Rd	Topeka	KS	66614	Mark Marling	913-273-6970	R	12	0.1
Grossman's Kensington	200 Tilton Rd	Northfield	NJ	08225	MJ Grossman	609-641-4800	R	12•	<0.1
Miller's Interiors Inc.	PO Box 1116	Lynnwood	WA	98046	William W Miller	206-743-3213	R	12•	<0.1
A.B. Closson Jr. Co.	401 Race St	Cincinnati	OH	45202	Stuart B Sutphin III	513-762-5500	R	6	<0.1
Carpetile-Plano Inc.	8-10 W Main St	Plano	IL	60545	N Michael Turner	708-552-3400	S	1	<0.1

Source: Ward's Business Directory of U.S. Private and Public Companies, 1998. The company type code used is as follows: P - Public, R - Private, S - Subsidiary, D - Division, J - Joint Venture, A - Affiliate, G - Group. Sales are in millions of dollars, employees are in thousands. An asterisk (*) indicates an estimated sales volume. The symbol < stands for 'less than'.

OCCUPATIONS EMPLOYED BY SIC 571 - FURNITURE AND HOMEFURNISHINGS STORES

Occupation	% of Total 1996	Change to 2006	Occupation	% of Total 1996	Change to 2006
Salespersons, retail	32.0	14.5	Cashiers	2.9	8.8
General managers & top executives	7.2	4.1	Traffic, shipping, receiving clerks	2.2	7.5
Stock clerks	7.2	49.6	Sales & related workers nec	2.2	18.2
Truck drivers light & heavy	6.4	-3.3	Carpet installers	2.0	-14.0
Marketing & sales worker supervisors	5.5	7.5	Clerical supervisors & managers	1.4	7.5
General office clerks	4.2	-7.5	Secretaries, except legal & medical	1.4	-14.7
Bookkeeping, accounting, & auditing clerks	3.8	-14.0	Purchasing managers	1.3	-3.3
Freight, stock, & material movers, hand	3.4	-3.3	Wholesale & retail buyers, except farm products	1.2	-11.0
Interior designers	3.1	18.2	Janitors & cleaners, maids	1.1	-14.0

Source: Industry-Occupation Matrix, Bureau of Labor Statistics. These data relate to one or more 3-digit SIC industry groups rather than to a single 4-digit SIC. The change reported for each occupation to the year 2006 is a percent of growth or decline as estimated by the Bureau of Labor Statistics. The abbreviation nec stands for 'not elsewhere classified'.

STATE AND REGIONAL CONCENTRATION

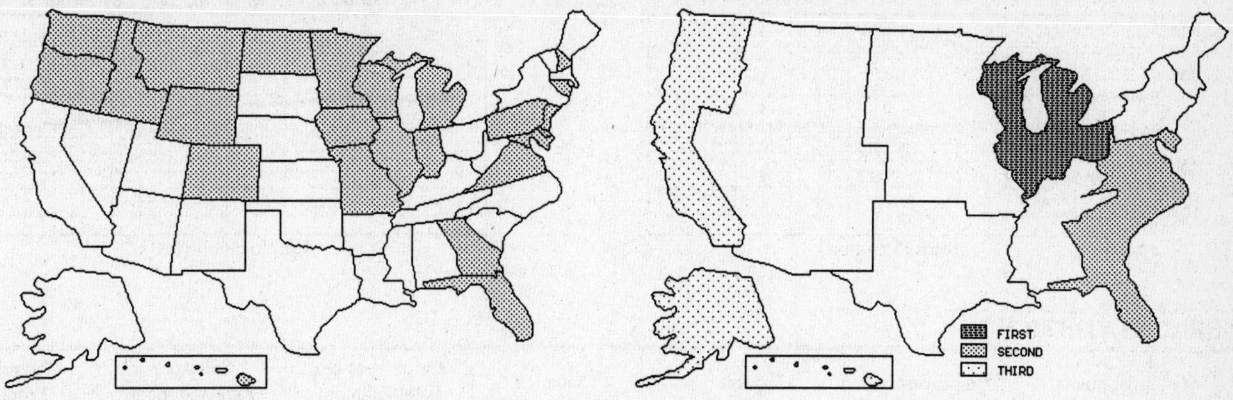

INDUSTRY DATA BY STATE

	Establishments - 1995		Employment - 1995			Payroll - 1995		Sales - 1992		
State	Total (number)	% of U.S.	Total (number)	% of U.S.	Per Estab.	Total ($ mil.)	Per Empl. ($)	Total ($ mil.)	% of U.S.	Per Estab ($)
California	1,461	10.0	8,711	10.9	6	206.8	23,737	1,162.7	12.1	129,374
New York	916	6.3	5,232	6.5	6	125.0	23,887	620.8	6.5	131,656
Florida	940	6.5	4,669	5.8	5	95.4	20,428	596.6	6.2	142,376
Illinois	641	4.4	4,207	5.3	7	103.8	24,663	517.5	5.4	145,123
Michigan	523	3.6	3,848	4.8	7	90.0	23,378	482.7	5.0	141,417
Pennsylvania	655	4.5	3,654	4.6	6	80.8	22,114	460.5	4.8	130,240
Texas	717	4.9	3,614	4.5	5	80.0	22,129	446.9	4.6	162,082
Ohio	629	4.3	3,506	4.4	6	77.3	22,062	402.6	4.2	137,746
New Jersey	473	3.2	2,345	2.9	5	59.0	25,162	367.9	3.8	166,544
Georgia	418	2.9	2,408	3.0	6	54.8	22,762	269.4	2.8	168,796
Virginia	404	2.8	2,106	2.6	5	44.6	21,201	264.6	2.8	136,332
Maryland	348	2.4	1,903	2.4	5	49.2	25,855	243.2	2.5	151,461
Washington	336	2.3	1,754	2.2	5	38.6	21,984	239.4	2.5	126,248
North Carolina	446	3.1	2,322	2.9	5	48.0	20,673	234.5	2.4	139,668
Indiana	372	2.6	2,200	2.8	6	44.7	20,298	231.4	2.4	133,930
Wisconsin	332	2.3	1,839	2.3	6	43.4	23,611	214.9	2.2	138,320
Missouri	346	2.4	1,876	2.3	5	41.0	21,834	204.7	2.1	129,961
Massachusetts	353	2.4	1,718	2.1	5	39.3	22,894	202.0	2.1	143,388
Minnesota	264	1.8	1,430	1.8	5	34.4	24,051	179.4	1.9	158,763
Colorado	268	1.8	1,386	1.7	5	37.8	27,306	178.4	1.9	174,036
Tennessee	272	1.9	1,351	1.7	5	30.6	22,626	156.2	1.6	159,995
Oregon	223	1.5	1,445	1.8	6	30.2	20,916	148.9	1.5	134,135
Kentucky	234	1.6	1,253	1.6	5	21.2	16,898	142.6	1.5	151,044
Alabama	240	1.6	1,303	1.6	5	26.6	20,451	133.5	1.4	132,708
Connecticut	205	1.4	888	1.1	4	20.9	23,521	125.9	1.3	138,217
South Carolina	233	1.6	1,041	1.3	4	20.3	19,526	123.3	1.3	141,398
Iowa	193	1.3	1,029	1.3	5	22.3	21,708	111.6	1.2	136,128
Arizona	228	1.6	1,334	1.7	6	27.9	20,891	104.5	1.1	116,799
Louisiana	183	1.3	990	1.2	5	20.3	20,511	102.0	1.1	139,475
Kansas	164	1.1	786	1.0	5	16.5	21,047	89.7	0.9	117,275
Oklahoma	185	1.3	930	1.2	5	17.3	18,551	83.6	0.9	142,148
Arkansas	127	0.9	484	0.6	4	9.8	20,341	66.0	0.7	164,216
Idaho	96	0.7	483	0.6	5	10.8	22,400	57.5	0.6	146,707
Utah	103	0.7	497	0.6	5	10.9	21,996	57.0	0.6	164,343
New Mexico	76	0.5	570	0.7	8	12.5	21,947	54.1	0.6	148,657
Mississippi	115	0.8	560	0.7	5	9.7	17,366	53.0	0.6	126,107
Nebraska	80	0.5	480	0.6	6	8.9	18,529	51.3	0.5	130,768
West Virginia	115	0.8	586	0.7	5	10.0	17,106	49.1	0.5	99,212
Nevada	63	0.4	550	0.7	9	13.5	24,589	46.1	0.5	106,734
Hawaii	37	0.3	276	0.3	7	7.8	28,290	45.7	0.5	154,861
New Hampshire	80	0.5	371	0.5	5	8.0	21,623	43.5	0.5	150,090
Montana	72	0.5	389	0.5	5	8.6	22,064	41.6	0.4	177,611
Delaware	56	0.4	315	0.4	6	6.7	21,337	36.4	0.4	135,739
Rhode Island	58	0.4	238	0.3	4	5.0	21,185	31.3	0.3	138,978
North Dakota	45	0.3	338	0.4	8	7.2	21,222	28.6	0.3	133,158
Maine	65	0.4	226	0.3	3	4.5	19,792	27.4	0.3	125,459
Wyoming	41	0.3	192	0.2	5	4.1	21,104	22.3	0.2	149,517
Alaska	35	0.2	169	0.2	5	4.5	26,704	19.9	0.2	160,653
South Dakota	40	0.3	187	0.2	5	3.5	18,963	17.6	0.2	155,894
Vermont	46	0.3	100-249	-	-	(D)	-	16.7	0.2	127,756
D.C.	10	0.1	20-99	-	-	(D)	-	8.8	0.1	104,452

Source: County Business Patterns, 1995 and *Economic Census of the U.S., 1992.* Data are sorted by 1992 revenues and, if revenues are unavailable, by establishments in 1995. The symbol (D) indicates that data are withheld by the source to avoid disclosure of competitive information. A dash (-) indicates that data are not available or undisclosed because they do not meet statistical validity standards. Shaded *states* on the state map indicate those states which have proportionately greater representation in the industry than would be indicated by the state's population; the ratio is based on total revenues or number of establishments. Shaded *regions* indicate where the industry is regionally most concentrated.

5714 - DRAPERY AND UPHOLSTERY STORES

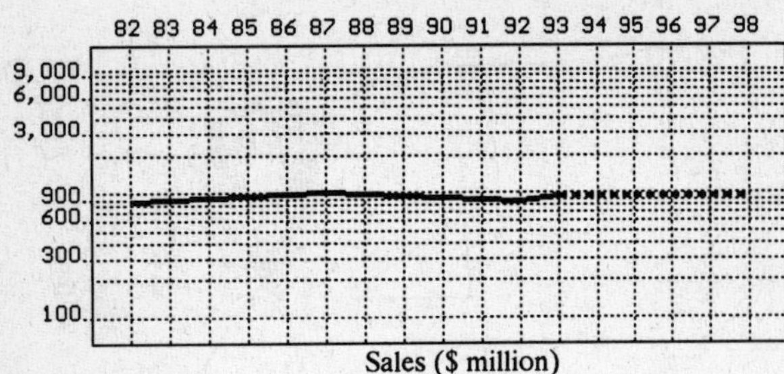

Sales ($ million)

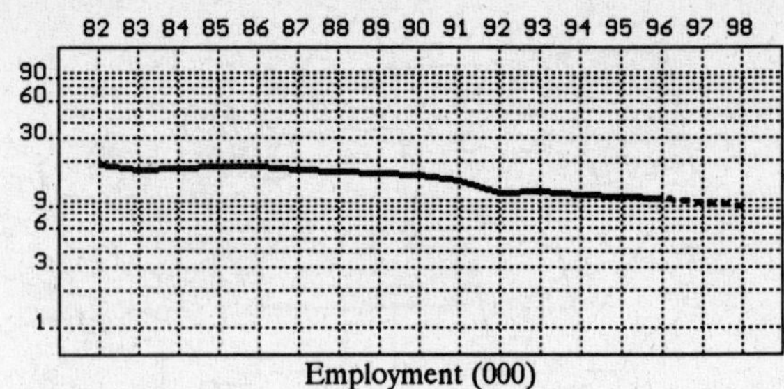

Employment (000)

GENERAL STATISTICS

Year	Establishments (number)	Employment (number)	Payroll ($ million)	Sales ($ million)	Employees per Establishment (number)	Sales per Establishment ($)	Payroll per Employee ($)
1982	4,341	18,798	168.0	858.1	4	197,670	8,935
1983	4,034	17,250	176.5	891.8*e*	4	-	10,234
1984	3,866	17,874	191.8	925.5*e*	5	-	10,731
1985	3,677	18,015	202.3	959.2*e*	5	-	11,229
1986	3,592	18,135	213.6	993.0*e*	5	-	11,777
1987	3,856	17,182	191.9	1,026.7	4	266,252	11,168
1988	3,499	16,545	200.3	993.6*e*	5	-	12,106
1989	3,309	15,971	201.3	960.6*e*	5	-	12,607
1990	3,375	15,648	203.6	927.6*e*	5	-	13,009
1991	3,281	14,058	189.4	894.6*e*	4	-	13,473
1992	2,877	11,403	153.8	861.5	4	299,458	13,487
1993	2,789	11,416	159.1	937.7*p*	4	-	13,937
1994	2,670	10,867	158.8	938.1*p*	4	-	14,611
1995	2,630	10,636	160.4	938.4*p*	4	-	15,083
1996	2,495*p*	10,223*p*	166.9*p*	938.8*p*	-	-	-
1997	2,373*p*	9,549*p*	164.7*p*	939.1*p*	-	-	-
1998	2,250*p*	8,876*p*	162.5*p*	939.5*p*	-	-	-

Sources: *Economic Census of the United States*, 1982, 1987, and 1992. Establishment counts, employment, and payroll are from *County Business Patterns* for non-Census years. Values followed by a 'p' are projections by the editors. Sales and expense data for non-Census years are extrapolations, marked by 'e'. Industries reclassified in 1987 will not have data for prior years. Data are the most recent available at this level of detail.

INDICES OF CHANGE

Year	Establishments (number)	Employment (number)	Payroll ($ million)	Sales ($ million)	Employees per Establishment (number)	Sales per Establishment ($)	Payroll per Employee ($)
1982	150.9	164.9	109.2	99.6	100.0	66.0	66.2
1983	140.2	151.3	114.8	103.5*e*	100.0	-	75.9
1984	134.4	156.7	124.7	107.4*e*	125.0	-	79.6
1985	127.8	158.0	131.5	111.3*e*	125.0	-	83.3
1986	124.9	159.0	138.9	115.3*e*	125.0	-	87.3
1987	134.0	150.7	124.8	119.2	100.0	88.9	82.8
1988	121.6	145.1	130.2	115.3*e*	125.0	-	89.8
1989	115.0	140.1	130.9	111.5*e*	125.0	-	93.5
1990	117.3	137.2	132.4	107.7*e*	125.0	-	96.5
1991	114.0	123.3	123.1	103.8*e*	100.0	-	99.9
1992	100.0	100.0	100.0	100.0	100.0	100.0	100.0
1993	96.9	100.1	103.4	108.8*p*	102.3	-	103.3
1994	92.8	95.3	103.2	108.9*p*	101.8	-	108.3
1995	91.4	93.3	104.3	108.9*p*	101.1	-	111.8
1996	86.7*p*	89.6*p*	108.5*p*	109.0*p*	-	-	-
1997	82.5*p*	83.7*p*	107.1*p*	109.0*p*	-	-	-
1998	78.2*p*	77.8*p*	105.7*p*	109.0*p*	-	-	-

Sources: Same as General Statistics. The values shown reflect change from the base year, 1992. Values above 100 mean greater than 1992, values below 100 mean less than 1992, and a value of 100 in the 1982-91 or 1993-98 period means same as 1992. Values followed by a 'p' are projections by the editors; 'e' stands for extrapolation. Data are the most recent available at this level of detail.

SELECTED RATIOS

For 1992	Avg. of All Retail	Analyzed Industry	Index	For 1992	Avg. of All Retail	Analyzed Industry	Index
Employees per Establishment	12	4	33	Sales per Employee	102,941	75,550	73
Payroll per Establishment	146,026	53,458	37	Sales per Establishment	1,241,555	299,444	24
Payroll per Employee	12,107	13,488	111	Expenses per Establishment	na	na	na

Sources: Same as General Statistics. The 'Average of All Manufacturing' column represents the average of all manufacturing industries reported for the most recent complete year available. The Index shows the relationship between the Average and the Analyzed Industry. For example, 100 means that they are equal; 500 that the Analyzed Industry is five times the average; 50 means that the Analyzed Industry is half the national average. The abbreviation 'na' is used to show that data are 'not available'.

LEADING COMPANIES Number shown: 9 Total sales ($ mil): 242 Total employment (000): 2.4

Company Name	Address				CEO Name	Phone	Co. Type	Sales ($ mil)	Empl. (000)
Granite Furniture Company	1050 E 21st S	Salt Lake City	UT	84106	John D Richards	801-486-3333	R	58 •	0.4
Three D Departments Inc.	PO Box 19773	Irvine	CA	92713	Bernard Abrams	714-662-0818	P	48	0.4
Curtains and Home Inc.	1600 Old Country	Plainview	NY	11803	Arthur Berkell	516-756-1800	R	45	0.6
Fabric Place	136 Howard St	Framingham	MA	01701	Ron Isaacson	508-872-4888	R	42 •	0.5
O'Krent Floor Covering Co.	300 San Pedro Ave	San Antonio	TX	78212	Theodore J O'Krent	210-227-7387	R	14 •	0.1
Reiters Inc.	2460 W George St	Chicago	IL	60618	David Reiter	312-267-8849	R	13 •	0.1
Allied Realty Co.	PO Box 1700	Huntington	WV	25717	L Polan	304-525-9125	R	12	0.1
Sunshine Drapery Co.	11660 Page Service	St. Louis	MO	63146	Lester Finkelstein	314-569-2980	R	9 •	<0.1
Aero Drapery Corp.	PO Box 419	Westfield	IN	46074	Ed Mullins	317-896-2521	R	1	<0.1

Source: *Ward's Business Directory of U.S. Private and Public Companies*, 1998. The company type code used is as follows: P - Public, R - Private, S - Subsidiary, D - Division, J - Joint Venture, A - Affiliate, G - Group. Sales are in millions of dollars, employees are in thousands. An asterisk (•) indicates an estimated sales volume. The symbol < stands for 'less than'.

OCCUPATIONS EMPLOYED BY SIC 571 - FURNITURE AND HOMEFURNISHINGS STORES

Occupation	% of Total 1996	Change to 2006	Occupation	% of Total 1996	Change to 2006
Salespersons, retail	32.0	14.5	Cashiers	2.9	8.8
General managers & top executives	7.2	4.1	Traffic, shipping, receiving clerks	2.2	7.5
Stock clerks	7.2	49.6	Sales & related workers nec	2.2	18.2
Truck drivers light & heavy	6.4	-3.3	Carpet installers	2.0	-14.0
Marketing & sales worker supervisors	5.5	7.5	Clerical supervisors & managers	1.4	7.5
General office clerks	4.2	-7.5	Secretaries, except legal & medical	1.4	-14.7
Bookkeeping, accounting, & auditing clerks	3.8	-14.0	Purchasing managers	1.3	-3.3
Freight, stock, & material movers, hand	3.4	-3.3	Wholesale & retail buyers, except farm products	1.2	-11.0
Interior designers	3.1	18.2	Janitors & cleaners, maids	1.1	-14.0

Source: *Industry-Occupation Matrix*, Bureau of Labor Statistics. These data relate to one or more 3-digit SIC industry groups rather than to a single 4-digit SIC. The change reported for each occupation to the year 2006 is a percent of growth or decline as estimated by the Bureau of Labor Statistics. The abbreviation nec stands for 'not elsewhere classified'.

STATE AND REGIONAL CONCENTRATION

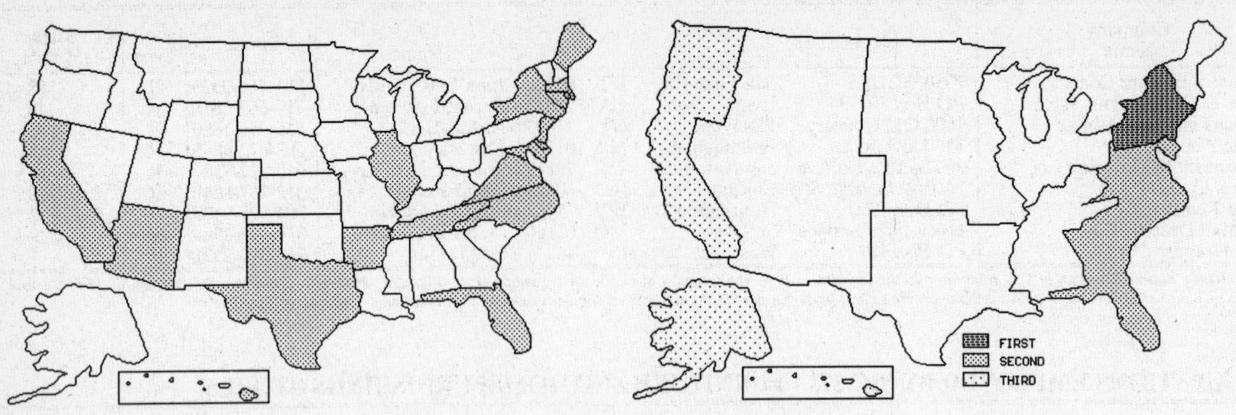

INDUSTRY DATA BY STATE

State	Establishments - 1995 Total (number)	Establishments - 1995 % of U.S.	Employment - 1995 Total (number)	Employment - 1995 % of U.S.	Employment - 1995 Per Estab.	Payroll - 1995 Total ($ mil.)	Payroll - 1995 Per Empl. ($)	Sales - 1992 Total ($ mil.)	Sales - 1992 % of U.S.	Sales - 1992 Per Estab ($)
California	275	10.5	1,080	10.2	4	18.7	17,308	106.2	12.3	80,919
New York	173	6.6	628	5.9	4	9.5	15,102	79.0	9.2	85,452
Texas	173	6.6	843	7.9	5	15.9	18,919	61.1	7.1	93,718
New Jersey	115	4.4	695	6.5	6	10.7	15,459	60.0	7.0	85,706
Florida	204	7.8	792	7.5	4	11.9	15,015	58.8	6.8	72,507
Illinois	133	5.1	509	4.8	4	8.1	15,823	43.6	5.1	82,901
Massachusetts	82	3.1	455	4.3	6	7.3	15,978	39.7	4.6	76,731
Pennsylvania	102	3.9	342	3.2	3	4.1	11,982	32.5	3.8	74,660
Ohio	89	3.4	425	4.0	5	5.7	13,442	28.8	3.3	63,607
Michigan	85	3.2	408	3.8	5	5.2	12,816	28.8	3.3	71,035
North Carolina	105	4.0	337	3.2	3	4.1	12,113	24.6	2.9	65,311
Virginia	73	2.8	349	3.3	5	4.2	12,066	23.8	2.8	60,545
Georgia	63	2.4	277	2.6	4	4.1	14,755	22.8	2.6	85,526
Maryland	54	2.1	240	2.3	4	4.1	17,133	21.3	2.5	72,047
Arizona	38	1.4	233	2.2	6	3.8	16,399	18.5	2.1	94,667
Tennessee	60	2.3	240	2.3	4	3.7	15,454	18.4	2.1	70,950
Connecticut	36	1.4	165	1.6	5	2.5	15,285	16.5	1.9	83,293
Indiana	72	2.7	307	2.9	4	3.8	12,498	15.3	1.8	54,598
Washington	46	1.7	161	1.5	4	2.6	15,857	12.2	1.4	67,470
Missouri	57	2.2	190	1.8	3	2.5	13,368	10.7	1.2	70,105
Maine	15	0.6	90	0.8	6	1.6	17,489	10.7	1.2	98,769
Wisconsin	51	1.9	186	1.8	4	2.3	12,511	9.5	1.1	55,017
South Carolina	37	1.4	92	0.9	2	1.5	16,087	8.9	1.0	67,595
Arkansas	35	1.3	114	1.1	3	1.6	14,333	8.7	1.0	67,442
Alabama	31	1.2	114	1.1	4	1.6	14,140	8.4	1.0	51,528
Minnesota	35	1.3	102	1.0	3	1.4	13,539	7.0	0.8	67,115
Kentucky	20	0.8	76	0.7	4	0.8	11,092	6.7	0.8	54,260
Iowa	47	1.8	149	1.4	3	1.6	10,926	6.5	0.8	60,269
Oregon	27	1.0	77	0.7	3	1.1	14,208	6.3	0.7	67,957
Nebraska	20	0.8	75	0.7	4	1.2	16,400	5.4	0.6	65,458
Louisiana	29	1.1	106	1.0	4	1.2	11,208	5.1	0.6	55,870
Hawaii	10	0.4	44	0.4	4	0.8	19,000	5.1	0.6	78,662
Kansas	25	1.0	87	0.8	3	0.9	10,908	4.9	0.6	57,430
Colorado	24	0.9	61	0.6	3	1.0	16,754	4.4	0.5	100,841
New Mexico	11	0.4	38	0.4	3	0.9	22,737	4.4	0.5	99,909
Mississippi	19	0.7	49	0.5	3	0.4	8,673	4.3	0.5	76,298
Oklahoma	32	1.2	110	1.0	3	2.0	18,518	3.9	0.5	61,619
Nevada	13	0.5	44	0.4	3	0.8	18,545	3.8	0.4	86,091
New Hampshire	17	0.6	45	0.4	3	0.7	14,667	3.7	0.4	82,467
Utah	19	0.7	48	0.5	3	0.7	13,708	3.7	0.4	85,465
Rhode Island	7	0.3	29	0.3	4	0.4	12,103	3.6	0.4	43,735
Delaware	11	0.4	46	0.4	4	0.8	17,935	3.1	0.4	122,760
West Virginia	12	0.5	58	0.5	5	0.8	14,534	2.4	0.3	67,972
Idaho	9	0.3	30	0.3	3	0.4	12,333	1.7	0.2	73,000
Vermont	7	0.3	0-19	-	-	(D)	-	1.2	0.1	93,462
South Dakota	8	0.3	21	0.2	3	0.2	10,762	1.2	0.1	47,000
D.C.	4	0.2	0-19	-	-	(D)	-	1.1	0.1	143,750
North Dakota	8	0.3	18	0.2	2	0.1	6,167	0.9	0.1	52,444
Montana	6	0.2	11	0.1	2	0.1	9,545	0.9	0.1	62,600
Wyoming	3	0.1	7	0.1	2	0.2	24,714	0.7	0.1	45,687
Alaska	3	0.1	14	0.1	5	0.3	23,000	0.6	0.1	63,556

Source: County Business Patterns, 1995 and *Economic Census of the U.S., 1992*. Data are sorted by 1992 revenues and, if revenues are unavailable, by establishments in 1995. The symbol (D) indicates that data are withheld by the source to avoid disclosure of competitive information. A dash (-) indicates that data are not available or undisclosed because they do not meet statistical validity standards. Shaded *states* on the state map indicate those states which have proportionately greater representation in the industry than would be indicated by the state's population; the ratio is based on total revenues or number of establishments. Shaded *regions* indicate where the industry is regionally most concentrated.

5719 - MISC. HOMEFURNISHINGS STORES

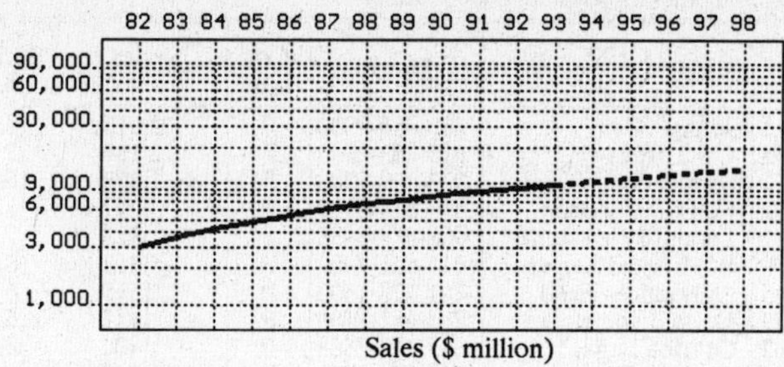

Sales ($ million)

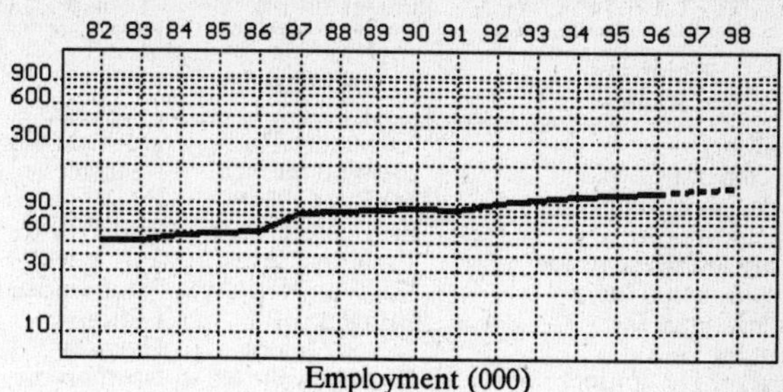

Employment (000)

GENERAL STATISTICS

Year	Establishments (number)	Employment (number)	Payroll ($ million)	Sales ($ million)	Employees per Establishment (number)	Sales per Establishment ($)	Payroll per Employee ($)
1982	10,300	51,474	430.7	2,974.7	5	288,805	8,367
1983	9,967	52,138	488.4	3,603.9e	5	-	9,368
1984	9,973	56,835	551.8	4,233.2e	6	-	9,709
1985	9,705	58,933	623.7	4,862.5e	6	-	10,583
1986	10,028	60,789	648.1	5,491.7e	6	-	10,662
1987	14,378	83,261	872.9	6,121.0	6	425,717	10,484
1988	13,427	87,423	1,006.1	6,750.9e	7	-	11,508
1989	13,024	89,716	1,068.3	7,380.8e	7	-	11,908
1990	13,314	91,715	1,138.8	8,010.7e	7	-	12,417
1991	13,593	89,392	1,145.4	8,640.6e	7	-	12,813
1992	16,492	100,658	1,299.5	9,270.5	6	562,121	12,910
1993	16,516	107,924	1,411.4	9,899.3p	7	-	13,078
1994	16,813	114,772	1,555.1	10,528.9p	7	-	13,550
1995	16,672	119,761	1,648.3	11,158.5p	7	-	13,763
1996	17,752p	124,396p	1,707.0p	11,788.1p	-	-	-
1997	18,365p	129,889p	1,802.4p	12,417.7p	-	-	-
1998	18,978p	135,382p	1,897.7p	13,047.2p	-	-	-

Sources: Economic Census of the United States, 1982, 1987, and 1992. Establishment counts, employment, and payroll are from *County Business Patterns* for non-Census years. Values followed by a 'p' are projections by the editors. Sales and expense data for non-Census years are extrapolations, marked by 'e'. Industries reclassified in 1987 will not have data for prior years. Data are the most recent available at this level of detail.

INDICES OF CHANGE

Year	Establishments (number)	Employment (number)	Payroll ($ million)	Sales ($ million)	Employees per Establishment (number)	Sales per Establishment ($)	Payroll per Employee ($)
1982	62.5	51.1	33.1	32.1	83.3	51.4	64.8
1983	60.4	51.8	37.6	38.9e	83.3	-	72.6
1984	60.5	56.5	42.5	45.7e	100.0	-	75.2
1985	58.8	58.5	48.0	52.5e	100.0	-	82.0
1986	60.8	60.4	49.9	59.2e	100.0	-	82.6
1987	87.2	82.7	67.2	66.0	100.0	75.7	81.2
1988	81.4	86.9	77.4	72.8e	116.7	-	89.1
1989	79.0	89.1	82.2	79.6e	116.7	-	92.2
1990	80.7	91.1	87.6	86.4e	116.7	-	96.2
1991	82.4	88.8	88.1	93.2e	116.7	-	99.2
1992	100.0	100.0	100.0	100.0	100.0	100.0	100.0
1993	100.1	107.2	108.6	106.8p	108.9	-	101.3
1994	101.9	114.0	119.7	113.6p	113.8	-	105.0
1995	101.1	119.0	126.8	120.4p	119.7	-	106.6
1996	107.6p	123.6p	131.4p	127.2p	-	-	-
1997	111.4p	129.0p	138.7p	133.9p	-	-	-
1998	115.1p	134.5p	146.0p	140.7p	-	-	-

Sources: Same as General Statistics. The values shown reflect change from the base year, 1992. Values above 100 mean greater than 1992, values below 100 mean less than 1992, and a value of 100 in the 1982-91 or 1993-98 period means same as 1992. Values followed by a 'p' are projections by the editors; 'e' stands for extrapolation. Data are the most recent available at this level of detail.

SELECTED RATIOS

For 1992	Avg. of All Retail	Analyzed Industry	Index	For 1992	Avg. of All Retail	Analyzed Industry	Index
Employees per Establishment	12	6	51	Sales per Employee	102,941	92,099	89
Payroll per Establishment	146,026	78,796	54	Sales per Establishment	1,241,555	562,121	45
Payroll per Employee	12,107	12,910	107	Expenses per Establishment	na	na	na

Sources: Same as General Statistics. The 'Average of All Manufacturing' column represents the average of all manufacturing industries reported for the most recent complete year available. The Index shows the relationship between the Average and the Analyzed Industry. For example, 100 means that they are equal; 500 that the Analyzed Industry is five times the average; 50 means that the Analyzed Industry is half the national average. The abbreviation 'na' is used to show that data are 'not available'.

LEADING COMPANIES

Number shown: **50** Total sales ($ mil): **13,813** Total employment (000): **132.3**

Company Name	Address				CEO Name	Phone	Co. Type	Sales ($ mil)	Empl. (000)
Spiegel Inc.	3500 Lacey Rd	Downers Grove	IL	60515	John J Shea	630-986-8800	P	3,015	13.4
Dollar General Corp.	104 Woodmont	Nashville	TN	37205	Cal Turner Jr	615-783-2000	P	2,134	25.4
Michaels Stores Inc.	PO Box 619566	DFW	TX	75261	Sam Wyly	972-409-1300	P	1,378	16.5
Pier 1 Imports Inc.	301 Commerce St	Fort Worth	TX	76102	Clark A Johnson	817-878-8000	P	947	11.3
Bed, Bath and Beyond Inc.	715 Morris Ave	Springfield	NJ	07081	Leonard Feinstein	908-688-0888	P	823	7.0
Williams-Sonoma Inc.	3250 Van Ness Ave	San Francisco	CA	94109	W Howard Lester	415-421-7900	P	812	8.7
Linens 'n Things Inc.	6 Brighton Rd	Clifton	NJ	07015	Norman Axelrod	201-778-1300	P	555	5.9
Lechters Inc.	1 Cape May St	Harrison	NJ	07029	Donald Jonas	201-481-1100	P	441	6.4
Euromarket Design Inc.	725 Landwehr Rd	Northbrook	IL	60062	Gordon Segal	847-272-2888	R	400	4.2
Mikasa Inc.	PO Box 6239	Carson	CA	90749	Alfred J Blake	310-886-3700	P	363	2.8
Laura Ashley Inc.	1300 MacArthur	Mahwah	NJ	07430	Ann Iverson	201-934-3000	S	330 •	4.2
Pergament Home Centers Inc.	101 Marcus Dr	Melville	NY	11747	Robert Tammero	516-694-9300	R	230 •	2.8
Garden Ridge Pottery Inc.	19411 Atrium Pl	Houston	TX	77084	Armand Shapiro	281-579-7901	S	225	2.9
Strouds	780 S Nogales St	City of Industry	CA	91748	Charles Chinni	818-912-2866	S	210	1.8
Cost Plus Imports Inc.	PO Box 23350	Oakland	CA	94623	Ralph Dillon	510-893-7300	S	200 •	2.8
Fortunoff Fine Jewelry	70 Lindbergh	Uniondale	NY	11553	Alan Fortunoff	516-832-9000	R	180 •	1.8
Waccamaw Corp.	3200 Pottery Dr	Myrtle Beach	SC	29577	Greg Johnson	803-236-4606	R	170 •	2.1
Container Store	2000 Valwood Pkwy	Dallas	TX	75234	Garrett Boone	214-654-2000	R	104 •	1.2
Kitchen Collection Inc.	71 E Water St	Chillicothe	OH	45601	Randall D Lynch	614-773-9150	S	89 •	1.0
Lights Fantastic Inc.	6825 Tennyson Dr	McLean	VA	22101	Armin M Bruning	703-356-2285	R	86	<0.1
Lamps Plus Inc.	20250 Plumber St	Chatsworth	CA	91311	Dennis Swanson	818-886-5267	R	84 •	1.0
Carpeteria Inc.	25322 Rye Canyon	Valencia	CA	91355	Bryan Haserjian	805-295-1000	R	82	0.3
Chun Kim Chow Ltd.	PO Box 1578	Honolulu	HI	96806	Paul Chun	808-532-5725	R	70	1.0
3 Day Blinds Inc.	2220 E Cerritos	Anaheim	CA	92806	Art Schumann	714-634-4600	R	69 •	0.8
Welcome Home Inc.	309-D Raleigh St	Wilmington	NC	28412	Thomas H Quinn	910-791-4312	P	63	0.8
Pacific Linen Inc.	15511 Redmond Rd	Woodinville	WA	98072	Leo Rosenberger	206-481-2221	R	50 •	0.5
Three D Departments Inc.	PO Box 19773	Irvine	CA	92713	Bernard Abrams	714-662-0818	P	48	0.4
Ostrow Textile L.L.C.	PO Box 10550	Rock Hill	SC	29731	Joel J Ostrow	803-324-4284	R	46 •	0.5
Curtains and Home Inc.	1600 Old Country	Plainview	NY	11803	Arthur Berkell	516-756-1800	R	45	0.6
Kay and Kay Tile Depot	28237 Orchard Lk	Farmington Hls	MI	48334	Steve Katzman	313-489-0500	R	41 •	0.3
C.W. Acquisitions Inc.	515 W 24th St	New York	NY	10011	J Leonard Silver	212-924-7300	R	40	0.4
Janovic Plaza Inc.	30-35 Thomson Ave	Long Island C.	NY	11101	Evan Janovic	718-786-4444	R	40	0.3
Seattle Lighting Fixtures Co.	222 2nd Ave	Seattle	WA	98104	J R Scarborough	206-622-1962	S	40 •	0.2
Villeroy&Boch Tableware Ltd.	5 Fawn DR, #303	Princeton	NJ	08540	Safford Sweatt	609-734-7800	R	40 •	<0.1
Gallery of Gift Shoppes Inc.	PO Box 1560	N. Hampton	NH	03862	Allan Coviello	603-929-1137	R	32	0.2
Market Antiques	1227 Slocum St	Dallas	TX	75207	JT Campbell	214-748-0472	R	32	0.2
Benny's Inc.	340 Waterman Ave	Esmond	RI	02917	Malcolm Bromberg	401-231-1000	R	27 •	0.3
Homemaker Shops Inc.	25899 W 12 Mile	Southfield	MI	48034	Sidney Freedland	313-353-0404	R	26	0.5
Arnold Furniture Inc.	4750 Kearny Mesa	San Diego	CA	92111	Jack Eiseman	619-268-3336	R	25	0.3
Function Junction Inc.	306 Delaware St	Kansas City	MO	64105	Steve Eberman	816-471-6000	R	25 •	0.1
Progressive Lighting Inc.	640 Southwest Hwy	Riverdale	GA	30274	Fred Lee	404-997-8564	R	25 •	0.1
Skinner Corp.	1009 N Lanier Ave	Lanett	AL	36863		205-644-2136	R	25	0.4
Carolina Pottery Retail Group	I-95 Industrial Park	Smithfield	NC	27577	Tim Marsh	919-934-0309	R	20	0.2
Plow and Hearth	PO Box 5000	Madison	VA	22727	Peter Rice	703-948-2272	R	20	0.1
Standale Lumber and Supply	4046 Lake Michigan	Grand Rapids	MI	49504	K L Holtvluwer	616-453-8201	R	20	<0.1
Vermont Country Store	PO Box 1103	Manchester Ctr	VT	05255	Lyman Norton	802-362-2400	R	19 •	0.1
Bering Home Center Inc.	6102 Westheimer	Houston	TX	77057	August C Bering IV	713-785-6400	R	18	0.2
Saxon Paint and Home Care	3840 W Fullerton	Chicago	IL	60647	Alan Saks	312-252-8100	R	18 •	0.2
Altmeyer Home Stores Inc.	PO Box 710	New Kensington	PA	15068	Rod Altmeyer Sr	412-339-6628	R	16 •	0.2
Better Living Inc.	PO Box 7627	Charlottesville	VA	22906	Richard L Nunley	804-973-4333	R	16 •	0.1

Source: *Ward's Business Directory of U.S. Private and Public Companies*, 1998. The company type code used is as follows: P - Public, R - Private, S - Subsidiary, D - Division, J - Joint Venture, A - Affiliate, G - Group. Sales are in millions of dollars, employees are in thousands. An asterisk (*) indicates an estimated sales volume. The symbol < stands for 'less than'.

OCCUPATIONS EMPLOYED BY SIC 571 - FURNITURE AND HOMEFURNISHINGS STORES

Occupation	% of Total 1996	Change to 2006	Occupation	% of Total 1996	Change to 2006
Salespersons, retail	32.0	14.5	Cashiers	2.9	8.8
General managers & top executives	7.2	4.1	Traffic, shipping, receiving clerks	2.2	7.5
Stock clerks	7.2	49.6	Sales & related workers nec	2.2	18.2
Truck drivers light & heavy	6.4	-3.3	Carpet installers	2.0	-14.0
Marketing & sales worker supervisors	5.5	7.5	Clerical supervisors & managers	1.4	7.5
General office clerks	4.2	-7.5	Secretaries, except legal & medical	1.4	-14.7
Bookkeeping, accounting, & auditing clerks	3.8	-14.0	Purchasing managers	1.3	-3.3
Freight, stock, & material movers, hand	3.4	-3.3	Wholesale & retail buyers, except farm products	1.2	-11.0
Interior designers	3.1	18.2	Janitors & cleaners, maids	1.1	-14.0

Source: *Industry-Occupation Matrix*, Bureau of Labor Statistics. These data relate to one or more 3-digit SIC industry groups rather than to a single 4-digit SIC. The change reported for each occupation to the year 2006 is a percent of growth or decline as estimated by the Bureau of Labor Statistics. The abbreviation nec stands for 'not elsewhere classified'.

STATE AND REGIONAL CONCENTRATION

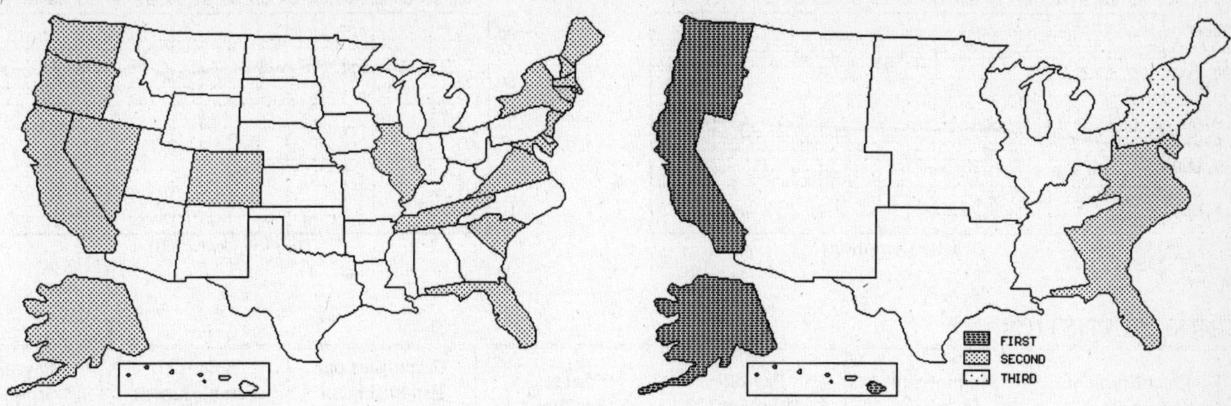

INDUSTRY DATA BY STATE

State	Establishments - 1995 Total (number)	Establishments - 1995 % of U.S.	Employment - 1995 Total (number)	Employment - 1995 % of U.S.	Employment - 1995 Per Estab.	Payroll - 1995 Total ($ mil.)	Payroll - 1995 Per Empl. ($)	Sales - 1992 Total ($ mil.)	Sales - 1992 % of U.S.	Sales - 1992 Per Estab ($)
California	2,077	12.5	15,215	12.7	7	220.7	14,509	1,505.5	16.2	106,889
New York	1,121	6.7	8,776	7.3	8	139.8	15,927	798.2	8.6	105,155
Florida	1,248	7.5	8,009	6.7	6	108.4	13,541	615.3	6.6	96,546
Texas	956	5.7	8,183	6.8	9	115.8	14,146	574.3	6.2	84,675
New Jersey	611	3.7	5,537	4.6	9	83.4	15,071	505.7	5.5	115,804
Illinois	692	4.2	5,869	4.9	8	78.5	13,373	451.8	4.9	85,879
Virginia	518	3.1	4,491	3.7	9	60.4	13,442	360.7	3.9	92,696
Massachusetts	450	2.7	3,778	3.2	8	53.7	14,215	357.9	3.9	104,958
Pennsylvania	640	3.8	4,062	3.4	6	50.1	12,322	296.7	3.2	85,762
Michigan	507	3.0	3,493	2.9	7	47.2	13,517	285.5	3.1	85,473
Ohio	625	3.7	4,496	3.8	7	55.3	12,291	277.9	3.0	83,934
Georgia	502	3.0	3,873	3.2	8	50.7	13,084	228.0	2.5	86,326
North Carolina	511	3.1	3,278	2.7	6	42.3	12,899	213.1	2.3	81,491
Washington	420	2.5	2,660	2.2	6	41.5	15,585	213.0	2.3	89,902
Tennessee	341	2.0	2,657	2.2	8	34.1	12,834	197.4	2.1	79,482
Maryland	332	2.0	2,668	2.2	8	33.8	12,663	185.3	2.0	84,682
South Carolina	280	1.7	1,636	1.4	6	20.9	12,789	154.4	1.7	90,531
Connecticut	287	1.7	2,060	1.7	7	29.7	14,399	152.2	1.6	106,335
Colorado	369	2.2	2,528	2.1	7	34.3	13,573	145.0	1.6	81,992
Missouri	313	1.9	2,070	1.7	7	28.7	13,886	130.0	1.4	77,248
Minnesota	299	1.8	2,141	1.8	7	27.6	12,891	126.3	1.4	82,191
Arizona	300	1.8	2,010	1.7	7	30.3	15,059	123.3	1.3	105,209
Indiana	306	1.8	1,701	1.4	6	21.8	12,792	120.1	1.3	73,373
Oregon	260	1.6	1,545	1.3	6	20.7	13,390	113.5	1.2	80,231
Alabama	233	1.4	1,825	1.5	8	21.4	11,725	111.7	1.2	81,247
Wisconsin	263	1.6	1,678	1.4	6	21.4	12,732	103.1	1.1	72,269
Louisiana	205	1.2	1,347	1.1	7	15.8	11,736	91.1	1.0	79,735
Kentucky	166	1.0	1,072	0.9	6	12.3	11,453	65.2	0.7	72,866
Maine	99	0.6	545	0.5	6	7.8	14,262	59.9	0.6	112,212
Nevada	91	0.5	620	0.5	7	9.1	14,611	58.0	0.6	126,814
New Hampshire	121	0.7	880	0.7	7	12.7	14,391	57.9	0.6	101,091
Rhode Island	57	0.3	544	0.5	10	8.3	15,217	56.6	0.6	113,703
Oklahoma	146	0.9	908	0.8	6	10.6	11,718	55.8	0.6	73,115
Kansas	149	0.9	804	0.7	5	9.4	11,687	55.5	0.6	75,610
New Mexico	128	0.8	598	0.5	5	9.0	15,015	43.6	0.5	79,626
Utah	106	0.6	686	0.6	6	8.3	12,124	38.6	0.4	76,300
Iowa	109	0.7	583	0.5	5	6.9	11,883	38.4	0.4	62,771
Hawaii	68	0.4	445	0.4	7	7.3	16,499	36.3	0.4	69,506
Arkansas	98	0.6	687	0.6	7	7.8	11,403	33.9	0.4	71,263
D.C.	46	0.3	387	0.3	8	5.5	14,323	26.8	0.3	90,685
Mississippi	99	0.6	501	0.4	5	5.6	11,269	26.1	0.3	54,811
West Virginia	60	0.4	387	0.3	6	5.2	13,421	25.8	0.3	68,182
Nebraska	74	0.4	419	0.3	6	4.8	11,434	25.5	0.3	73,636
Delaware	67	0.4	401	0.3	6	6.5	16,254	25.1	0.3	75,417
Idaho	84	0.5	411	0.3	5	4.9	11,815	24.4	0.3	90,419
Alaska	42	0.3	261	0.2	6	3.9	14,785	23.5	0.3	103,542
Vermont	65	0.4	462	0.4	7	6.6	14,201	21.5	0.2	84,078
Montana	53	0.3	206	0.2	4	2.6	12,675	12.2	0.1	76,350
North Dakota	26	0.2	179	0.1	7	2.8	15,698	9.0	0.1	71,365
South Dakota	30	0.2	113	0.1	4	1.5	12,956	7.1	0.1	59,033
Wyoming	22	0.1	76	0.1	3	0.8	11,105	6.6	0.1	72,912

Source: County Business Patterns, 1995 and *Economic Census of the U.S., 1992*. Data are sorted by 1992 revenues and, if revenues are unavailable, by establishments in 1995. The symbol (D) indicates that data are withheld by the source to avoid disclosure of competitive information. A dash (-) indicates that data are not available or undisclosed because they do not meet statistical validity standards. Shaded *states* on the state map indicate those states which have proportionately greater representation in the industry than would be indicated by the state's population; the ratio is based on total revenues or number of establishments. Shaded *regions* indicate where the industry is regionally most concentrated.

5722 - HOUSEHOLD APPLIANCE STORES

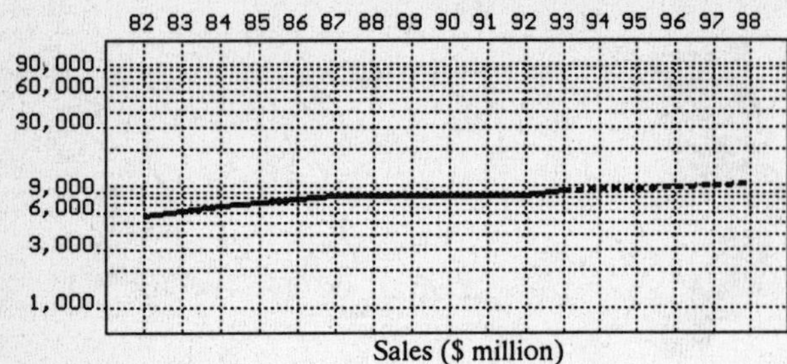

Sales ($ million)

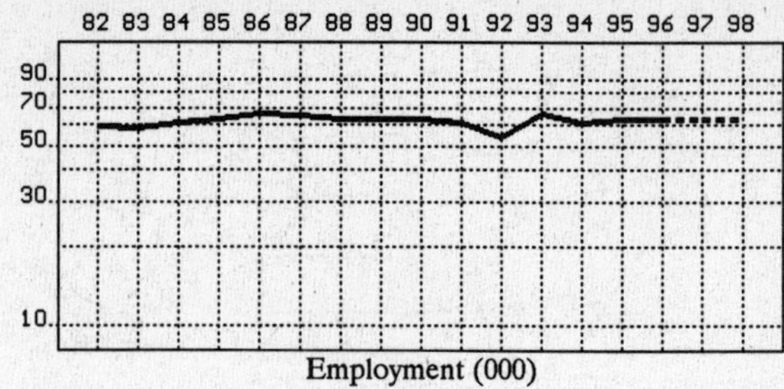

Employment (000)

GENERAL STATISTICS

Year	Establishments (number)	Employment (number)	Payroll ($ million)	Sales ($ million)	Employees per Establishment (number)	Sales per Establishment ($)	Payroll per Employee ($)
1982	11,574	59,324	696.8	5,697.3	5	492,250	11,745
1983	10,790	58,583	788.1	6,224.2e	5	-	13,452
1984	10,394	60,950	857.4	6,751.1e	6	-	14,068
1985	9,825	62,883	930.4	7,278.0e	6	-	14,796
1986	10,131	65,860	1,005.9	7,804.9e	7	-	15,274
1987	11,192	65,419	952.7	8,331.8	6	744,440	14,562
1988	10,407	62,907	1,018.0	8,296.5e	6	-	16,183
1989	9,834	62,848	1,050.2	8,261.2e	6	-	16,710
1990	10,012	63,137	1,078.1	8,226.0e	6	-	17,075
1991	10,002	61,272	1,081.0	8,190.7e	6	-	17,643
1992	9,743	53,782	964.7	8,155.4	6	837,055	17,937
1993	9,760	66,557	1,180.2	9,040.1p	7	-	17,732
1994	9,642	60,676	1,143.6	9,285.9p	6	-	18,848
1995	9,669	63,524	1,208.0	9,531.7p	7	-	19,016
1996	9,414p	62,549p	1,235.6p	9,777.5p	-	-	-
1997	9,308p	62,625p	1,267.4p	10,023.3p	-	-	-
1998	9,201p	62,701p	1,299.2p	10,269.1p	-	-	-

Sources: Economic Census of the United States, 1982, 1987, and 1992. Establishment counts, employment, and payroll are from *County Business Patterns* for non-Census years. Values followed by a 'p' are projections by the editors. Sales and expense data for non-Census years are extrapolations, marked by 'e'. Industries reclassified in 1987 will not have data for prior years. Data are the most recent available at this level of detail.

INDICES OF CHANGE

Year	Establishments (number)	Employment (number)	Payroll ($ million)	Sales ($ million)	Employees per Establishment (number)	Sales per Establishment ($)	Payroll per Employee ($)
1982	118.8	110.3	72.2	69.9	83.3	58.8	65.5
1983	110.7	108.9	81.7	76.3e	83.3	-	75.0
1984	106.7	113.3	88.9	82.8e	100.0	-	78.4
1985	100.8	116.9	96.4	89.2e	100.0	-	82.5
1986	104.0	122.5	104.3	95.7e	116.7	-	85.2
1987	114.9	121.6	98.8	102.2	100.0	88.9	81.2
1988	106.8	117.0	105.5	101.7e	100.0	-	90.2
1989	100.9	116.9	108.9	101.3e	100.0	-	93.2
1990	102.8	117.4	111.8	100.9e	100.0	-	95.2
1991	102.7	113.9	112.1	100.4e	100.0	-	98.4
1992	100.0	100.0	100.0	100.0	100.0	100.0	100.0
1993	100.2	123.8	122.3	110.8p	113.7	-	98.9
1994	99.0	112.8	118.5	113.9p	104.9	-	105.1
1995	99.2	118.1	125.2	116.9p	109.5	-	106.0
1996	96.6p	116.3p	128.1p	119.9p	-	-	-
1997	95.5p	116.4p	131.4p	122.9p	-	-	-
1998	94.4p	116.6p	134.7p	125.9p	-	-	-

Sources: Same as General Statistics. The values shown reflect change from the base year, 1992. Values above 100 mean greater than 1992, values below 100 mean less than 1992, and a value of 100 in the 1982-91 or 1993-98 period means same as 1992. Values followed by a 'p' are projections by the editors; 'e' stands for extrapolation. Data are the most recent available at this level of detail.

SELECTED RATIOS

For 1992	Avg. of All Retail	Analyzed Industry	Index	For 1992	Avg. of All Retail	Analyzed Industry	Index
Employees per Establishment	12	6	46	Sales per Employee	102,941	151,638	147
Payroll per Establishment	146,026	99,015	68	Sales per Establishment	1,241,555	837,052	67
Payroll per Employee	12,107	17,937	148	Expenses per Establishment	na	na	na

Sources: Same as General Statistics. The 'Average of All Manufacturing' column represents the average of all manufacturing industries reported for the most recent complete year available. The Index shows the relationship between the Average and the Analyzed Industry. For example, 100 means that they are equal; 500 that the Analyzed Industry is five times the average; 50 means that the Analyzed Industry is half the national average. The abbreviation 'na' is used to show that data are 'not available'.

LEADING COMPANIES

Number shown: **49** Total sales ($ mil): **21,093** Total employment (000): **108.5**

Company Name	Address				CEO Name	Phone	Co. Type	Sales ($ mil)	Empl. (000)
Best Buy Company Inc.	PO Box 9312	Minneapolis	MN	55440	Richard M Schulze	612-947-2000	P	7,771	36.3
Circuit City Stores Inc.	9950 Mayland Dr	Richmond	VA	23233	Richard L Sharp	804-527-4000	P	7,664	36.4
Heilig-Meyers Co.	2235 Staples Mill	Richmond	VA	23230	William C DeRusha	804-359-9171	P	956	12.5
Sun Television and Appliances	6600 Port Rd	Groveport	OH	43125	Robert E Oyster	614-492-5600	P	683	3.4
Fretter Inc.	12501 Grand River	Brighton	MI	48116	John B Hurley	810-220-5000	P	502	0.2
REX Stores Corp.	2875 Needmore Rd	Dayton	OH	45414	Stuart Rose	513-276-3931	P	442	1.0
Tops Appliance City Inc.	45 Brunswick Ave	Edison	NJ	08818	Robert Gross	908-248-2850	P	317	1.6
Amer Television & Appliance	2404 W Beltline	Madison	WI	53713	Doug Reuhl	608-271-1000	R	260	1.4
Brad Ragan Inc.	PO 240587	Charlotte	NC	28224	Michael R Thomann	704-521-2100	P	252	1.8
H.H. Gregg Appliances	4151 E 96th St	Indianapolis	IN	46240	Jerry Throgmartin	317-848-8710	R	240 *	1.1
Brookstone Inc.	17 Riverside St	Nashua	NH	03062	Michael Anthony	603-880-9500	P	240	2.0
Penn Fuel Gas Inc.	55 S 3rd St	Oxford	PA	19363	Terry H Hunt	610-932-2000	R	230 *	0.5
Brendle's Inc.	1919 N Bridge St	N. Carolina	NC	28621	J M McLeish Jr	910-526-5600	P	155	1.6
Conn's Appliances Inc.	2755 Liberty St	Beaumont	TX	77704	Thomas Frank	409-832-1696	R	110 *	0.7
BGE Home Products & Services	1200 67th St	Baltimore	MD	21237	Herbert D Coss	410-866-5500	S	97 *	0.6
Shipley Oil Co.	550 E King St	York	PA	17405	WS Shipley III	717-848-4100	R	80	0.4
Central Furniture Inc.	5480 Ferguson Dr	Commerce	CA	90022	Gary Cypress	213-720-8600	R	65	0.4
Grand Piano and Furniture Co.	4235 Electric SW	Roanoke	VA	24026	G B Cartledge Jr	703-343-1707	R	64	0.6
B. Olinde and Sons Company	9536 Airline Hwy	Baton Rouge	LA	70815	JB Olinde	504-926-3380	R	60 *	0.2
Tacony Corp.	1760 Gilsinn Ln	Fenton	MO	63026	Kenneth J Tacony	314-349-3000	R	60	0.2
Standard Companies Inc.	1535 Kalamazoo SE	Grand Rapids	MI	49507	T O Rottschafer	616-243-3655	R	55	0.2
Baillio's Warehouse Showroom	5301 Menaul NE	Albuquerque	NM	87110	Jack Baillio	505-883-7511	R	51 *	0.2
Furniture Distributors Inc.	PO Box 11117	Charlotte	NC	28220	Henry L Johnson	704-523-3424	R	50	0.6
Three D Departments Inc.	PO Box 19773	Irvine	CA	92713	Bernard Abrams	714-662-0818	P	48	0.4
Barbeques Galore Inc.	15041 Bake Pwky	Irvine	CA	92718	Sydney Selati	714-597-2400	R	46 *	0.3
Kimbrell Inc.	4524C South Blvd	Charlotte	NC	28209	Henry L Johnson Jr	704-523-3424	S	45 *	0.6
Dearden's Inc.	700 S Main St	Los Angeles	CA	90014	Douglas E Dearden	213-362-9600	R	44	0.4
Morris Kirschman and Company	PO Box 26427	New Orleans	LA	70186	Arnold Kirschman	504-947-6673	R	37 *	0.3
Smith's Appliance and Furniture	1450 S 10th St	Louisville	KY	40210	AK Smith	502-636-2544	R	35	0.2
Wholesale Supply Group Inc.	PO Box 4080	Cleveland	TN	37320	Lloyd D Rogers	423-478-1191	R	31 *	0.2
Badcock's Economy Furniture	512 Clematis St	W. Palm Beach	FL	33401	James C Baber III	407-659-1170	R	30	0.2
Cousins Photo and Appliance	1691 Hancock St	San Diego	CA	92101	Wally Berry	619-293-3137	R	30	0.1
Benny's Inc.	340 Waterman Ave	Esmond	RI	02917	Malcolm Bromberg	401-231-1000	R	27 *	0.3
Clark Electric Cooperative	124 N Main St	Greenwood	WI	54437	Richard Elbergen	715-267-6188	R	26 *	<0.1
Wisconsin Supply Corp.	PO Box 8124	Madison	WI	53708	Arden Hvam	608-222-7799	S	26 *	<0.1
Lappo Lumber Company Inc.	6435 Airline Rd	Fruitport	MI	49415	S Middlecamp	616-865-3121	R	25	0.1
Nelson Brothers Furniture Corp.	2750 W Grand Ave	Chicago	IL	60612	James F Blinder	312-489-3333	R	25	0.2
LFD Inc.	2321 Expwy 83 W	McAllen	TX	78503	Greg Thrash	210-686-2271	R	23	0.2
E.P. Nisbet Co.	PO Box 35367	Charlotte	NC	28235	James J White III	704-332-7755	R	23 *	<0.1
Adray Appliance & Photo Center	20219 Carlysle	Dearborn	MI	48124	D Adray-Cziraky	313-274-9500	R	20	0.1
Big Sandy Furniture Company	52 & Creek	South Point	OH	45680	John C Stewart Jr	614-894-4242	R	20 *	0.1
Royal Furniture Co.	PO Box 3784	Memphis	TN	38173	Richard Faber	901-527-6407	R	20	0.1
Dan's Fan City	300 Dunbar Ave	Oldsmar	FL	34677	Howard Christians	813-855-7384	R	17 *	0.1
Edelsteins Better Furniture Inc.	PO Box 3369	Brownsville	TX	78523	Ruben Edelstein	210-542-5605	R	17	0.3
Niederauer Inc.	1976 W San Carlos	San Jose	CA	95128	David Niederauer	408-297-2440	R	17 *	0.1
United States Water Co.	10065 E Harvard	Denver	CO	80231	Randall C Easton	303-671-4777	R	17	0.3
Blount Farmers Cooperative	1514 W Broadway	Maryville	TN	37801	Butch Loggins	615-982-2761	R	14	<0.1
Gas Inc.	77 Jefferson Pkwy	Newnan	GA	30263	Robert O Hetzler	770-502-8800	R	14 *	0.1
Maine Gas Inc.	368 Upper Maine	Fairfield	ME	04937	Bill Chase	207-453-4991	S	13	0.1

Source: *Ward's Business Directory of U.S. Private and Public Companies*, 1998. The company type code used is as follows: P - Public, R - Private, S - Subsidiary, D - Division, J - Joint Venture, A - Affiliate, G - Group. Sales are in millions of dollars, employees are in thousands. An asterisk (*) indicates an estimated sales volume. The symbol < stands for 'less than'.

OCCUPATIONS EMPLOYED BY SIC 572 - APPLIANCE, RADIO, TV, AND MUSIC STORES

Occupation	% of Total 1996	Change to 2006	Occupation	% of Total 1996	Change to 2006
Salespersons, retail	35.3	18.0	Truck drivers light & heavy	2.2	10.7
Marketing & sales worker supervisors	7.7	10.7	Home appliance/power tool repairers	1.8	-0.3
General managers & top executives	6.8	7.3	Mechanics, installers, & repairers nec	1.4	21.8
Cashiers	6.5	12.1	Traffic, shipping, receiving clerks	1.4	10.7
Sales & related workers nec	5.8	21.8	Secretaries, except legal & medical	1.1	-12.2
Stock clerks	5.4	39.3	Blue collar worker supervisors	1.0	6.9
Bookkeeping, accounting, & auditing clerks	2.6	-11.4	Purchasing managers	1.0	-0.3
General office clerks	2.5	-4.7	Wholesale & retail buyers, except farm products	1.0	-8.3
Electronic home entertainment system repairers	2.5	-28.0			

Source: *Industry-Occupation Matrix*, Bureau of Labor Statistics. These data relate to one or more 3-digit SIC industry groups rather than to a single 4-digit SIC. The change reported for each occupation to the year 2006 is a percent of growth or decline as estimated by the Bureau of Labor Statistics. The abbreviation nec stands for 'not elsewhere classified'.

STATE AND REGIONAL CONCENTRATION

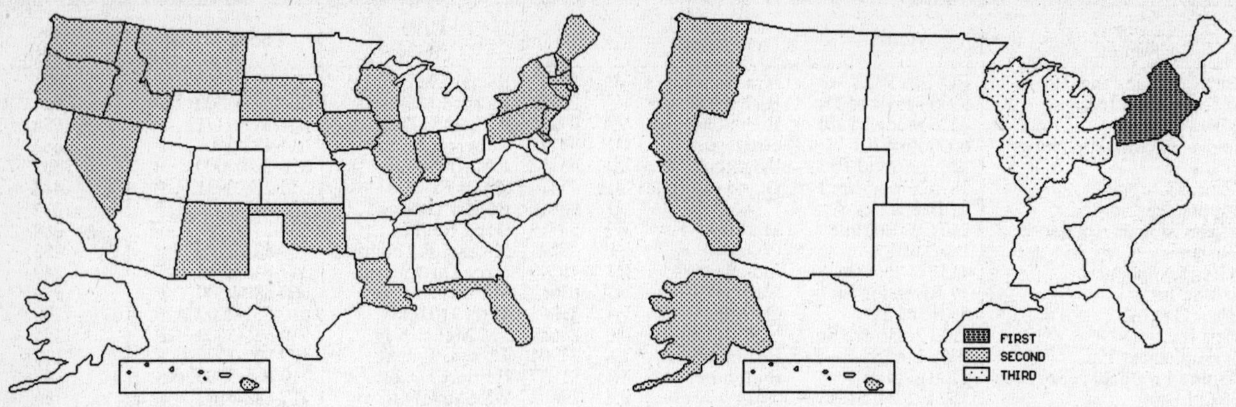

INDUSTRY DATA BY STATE

	Establishments - 1995		Employment - 1995			Payroll - 1995		Sales - 1992		
State	Total (number)	% of U.S.	Total (number)	% of U.S.	Per Estab.	Total ($ mil.)	Per Empl. ($)	Total ($ mil.)	% of U.S.	Per Estab ($)
California	818	8.5	6,790	10.7	8	131.2	19,329	959.2	11.8	175,873
New York	550	5.7	3,788	6.0	7	88.7	23,422	859.6	10.5	231,269
New Jersey	260	2.7	2,548	4.0	10	55.2	21,681	516.8	6.3	256,837
Florida	522	5.4	2,780	4.4	5	50.2	18,053	448.4	5.5	143,401
Texas	556	5.8	3,238	5.1	6	66.8	20,638	409.7	5.0	148,876
Illinois	402	4.2	2,694	4.2	7	57.1	21,182	401.5	4.9	145,640
Pennsylvania	503	5.2	4,079	6.4	8	66.3	16,248	397.2	4.9	133,466
Michigan	293	3.0	2,068	3.3	7	41.7	20,145	260.7	3.2	141,010
Indiana	254	2.6	1,868	2.9	7	35.6	19,081	249.7	3.1	159,069
Ohio	354	3.7	2,128	3.3	6	36.5	17,156	235.9	2.9	116,357
Washington	246	2.5	1,419	2.2	6	26.6	18,719	235.2	2.9	146,002
Massachusetts	202	2.1	1,229	1.9	6	26.5	21,540	229.9	2.8	184,622
Wisconsin	269	2.8	1,821	2.9	7	32.4	17,795	174.1	2.1	113,878
North Carolina	317	3.3	2,506	3.9	8	43.7	17,424	171.2	2.1	111,961
Tennessee	242	2.5	1,327	2.1	5	26.9	20,265	152.9	1.9	140,877
Louisiana	173	1.8	1,428	2.2	8	22.0	15,401	143.1	1.8	190,531
Connecticut	130	1.3	989	1.6	8	25.1	25,343	140.1	1.7	189,871
Georgia	231	2.4	1,181	1.9	5	20.5	17,319	132.3	1.6	117,524
Missouri	257	2.7	1,138	1.8	4	19.9	17,470	128.3	1.6	119,149
Maryland	163	1.7	1,307	2.1	8	42.0	32,108	128.3	1.6	154,401
Virginia	221	2.3	1,208	1.9	5	21.1	17,441	126.2	1.5	132,021
Minnesota	218	2.3	1,073	1.7	5	19.9	18,523	123.9	1.5	120,486
Oregon	146	1.5	944	1.5	6	20.4	21,600	110.6	1.4	139,812
Oklahoma	160	1.7	843	1.3	5	14.5	17,144	106.4	1.3	161,473
Alabama	160	1.7	905	1.4	6	14.1	15,614	97.3	1.2	117,355
Iowa	208	2.2	1,037	1.6	5	16.8	16,238	93.9	1.2	95,952
Kentucky	163	1.7	878	1.4	5	14.8	16,900	93.1	1.1	120,454
Arizona	113	1.2	665	1.0	6	12.8	19,272	91.3	1.1	142,146
South Carolina	148	1.5	927	1.5	6	15.6	16,845	87.5	1.1	111,318
Colorado	139	1.4	651	1.0	5	10.4	15,914	72.0	0.9	158,857
Kansas	150	1.6	646	1.0	4	10.1	15,712	66.2	0.8	114,580
New Mexico	54	0.6	388	0.6	7	7.1	18,263	55.7	0.7	123,018
Mississippi	112	1.2	599	0.9	5	9.2	15,301	55.7	0.7	120,296
Montana	71	0.7	489	0.8	7	8.3	17,020	54.1	0.7	134,796
Nevada	44	0.5	287	0.5	7	5.5	19,007	54.0	0.7	175,749
Arkansas	112	1.2	506	0.8	5	8.4	16,575	49.1	0.6	108,730
New Hampshire	50	0.5	457	0.7	9	9.3	20,245	48.4	0.6	167,464
Delaware	40	0.4	609	1.0	15	10.7	17,514	48.1	0.6	192,364
Idaho	73	0.8	1,379	2.2	19	19.2	13,928	47.2	0.6	115,281
Hawaii	48	0.5	246	0.4	5	5.3	21,740	46.9	0.6	157,758
Utah	85	0.9	511	0.8	6	8.1	15,894	45.3	0.6	116,997
Maine	67	0.7	316	0.5	5	5.6	17,601	42.9	0.5	148,343
Nebraska	104	1.1	456	0.7	4	6.6	14,546	40.9	0.5	93,235
West Virginia	65	0.7	337	0.5	5	4.9	14,531	31.1	0.4	98,914
South Dakota	49	0.5	289	0.5	6	4.4	15,370	24.9	0.3	107,000
Vermont	31	0.3	172	0.3	6	3.2	18,337	17.9	0.2	107,305
Rhode Island	26	0.3	98	0.2	4	1.7	17,286	13.6	0.2	136,960
North Dakota	35	0.4	137	0.2	4	2.4	17,277	12.6	0.2	104,339
D.C.	7	0.1	39	0.1	6	1.3	33,821	8.6	0.1	145,847
Wyoming	21	0.2	85	0.1	4	1.1	12,612	8.2	0.1	129,794
Alaska	7	0.1	21	0.0	3	0.5	25,857	7.9	0.1	148,698

Source: *County Business Patterns, 1995* and *Economic Census of the U.S., 1992*. Data are sorted by 1992 revenues and, if revenues are unavailable, by establishments in 1995. The symbol (D) indicates that data are withheld by the source to avoid disclosure of competitive information. A dash (-) indicates that data are not available or undisclosed because they do not meet statistical validity standards. Shaded *states* on the state map indicate those states which have proportionately greater representation in the industry than would be indicated by the state's population; the ratio is based on total revenues or number of establishments. Shaded *regions* indicate where the industry is regionally most concentrated.

5731 - RADIO, TV, & ELECTRONIC STORES

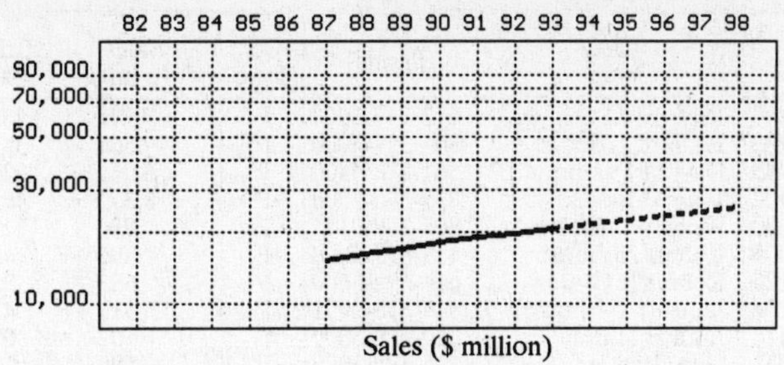

Sales ($ million)

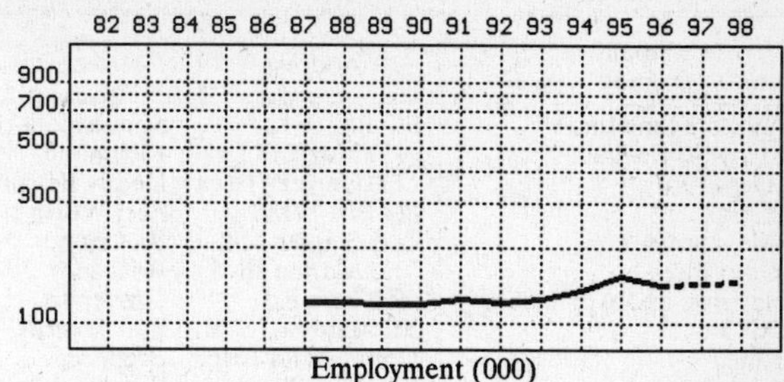

Employment (000)

GENERAL STATISTICS

Year	Establishments (number)	Employment (number)	Payroll ($ million)	Sales ($ million)	Employees per Establishment (number)	Sales per Establishment ($)	Payroll per Employee ($)
1982	-	-	-	-	-	-	-
1983	-	-	-	-	-	-	-
1984	-	-	-	-	-	-	-
1985	-	-	-	-	-	-	-
1986	-	-	-	-	-	-	-
1987	18,892	122,525	1,685.8	15,177.9	6	803,402	13,759
1988	17,835	121,825	1,988.2	16,100.5e	7	-	16,320
1989	16,433	120,191	1,964.7	17,023.2e	7	-	16,346
1990	16,483	120,165	2,059.3	17,945.9e	7	-	17,137
1991	16,925	124,891	2,233.7	18,868.6e	7	-	17,886
1992	17,324	121,115	2,111.9	19,791.2	7	1,142,417	17,437
1993	16,852	125,549	2,343.0	20,713.9p	7	-	18,662
1994	16,901	135,170	2,583.4	21,636.6p	8	-	19,112
1995	17,005	155,320	2,863.3	22,559.3p	9	-	18,435
1996	16,461p	142,657p	2,812.4p	23,481.9p	-	-	-
1997	16,316p	145,705p	2,934.2p	24,404.6p	-	-	-
1998	16,172p	148,753p	3,055.9p	25,327.3p	-	-	-

Sources: *Economic Census of the United States*, 1982, 1987, and 1992. Establishment counts, employment, and payroll are from *County Business Patterns* for non-Census years. Values followed by a 'p' are projections by the editors. Sales and expense data for non-Census years are extrapolations, marked by 'e'. Industries reclassified in 1987 will not have data for prior years. Data are the most recent available at this level of detail.

INDICES OF CHANGE

Year	Establishments (number)	Employment (number)	Payroll ($ million)	Sales ($ million)	Employees per Establishment (number)	Sales per Establishment ($)	Payroll per Employee ($)
1982	-	-	-	-	-	-	-
1983	-	-	-	-	-	-	-
1984	-	-	-	-	-	-	-
1985	-	-	-	-	-	-	-
1986	-	-	-	-	-	-	-
1987	109.1	101.2	79.8	76.7	85.7	70.3	78.9
1988	102.9	100.6	94.1	81.4e	100.0	-	93.6
1989	94.9	99.2	93.0	86.0e	100.0	-	93.7
1990	95.1	99.2	97.5	90.7e	100.0	-	98.3
1991	97.7	103.1	105.8	95.3e	100.0	-	102.6
1992	100.0	100.0	100.0	100.0	100.0	100.0	100.0
1993	97.3	103.7	110.9	104.7p	106.4	-	107.0
1994	97.6	111.6	122.3	109.3p	114.3	-	109.6
1995	98.2	128.2	135.6	114.0p	130.5	-	105.7
1996	95.0p	117.8p	133.2p	118.6p	-	-	-
1997	94.2p	120.3p	138.9p	123.3p	-	-	-
1998	93.3p	122.8p	144.7p	128.0p	-	-	-

Sources: Same as General Statistics. The values shown reflect change from the base year, 1992. Values above 100 mean greater than 1992, values below 100 mean less than 1992, and a value of 100 in the 1982-91 or 1993-98 period means same as 1992. Values followed by a 'p' are projections by the editors; 'e' stands for extrapolation. Data are the most recent available at this level of detail.

SELECTED RATIOS

For 1992	Avg. of All Retail	Analyzed Industry	Index	For 1992	Avg. of All Retail	Analyzed Industry	Index
Employees per Establishment	12	7	58	Sales per Employee	102,941	163,408	159
Payroll per Establishment	146,026	121,906	83	Sales per Establishment	1,241,555	1,142,415	92
Payroll per Employee	12,107	17,437	144	Expenses per Establishment	na	na	na

Sources: Same as General Statistics. The 'Average of All Manufacturing' column represents the average of all manufacturing industries reported for the most recent complete year available. The Index shows the relationship between the Average and the Analyzed Industry. For example, 100 means that they are equal; 500 that the Analyzed Industry is five times the average; 50 means that the Analyzed Industry is half the national average. The abbreviation 'na' is used to show that data are 'not available'.

LEADING COMPANIES

Number shown: **50** Total sales ($ mil): **34,537** Total employment (000): **193.5**

Company Name	Address				CEO Name	Phone	Co. Type	Sales ($ mil)	Empl. (000)
Best Buy Company Inc.	PO Box 9312	Minneapolis	MN	55440	Richard M Schulze	612-947-2000	P	7,771	36.3
Circuit City Stores Inc.	9950 Mayland Dr	Richmond	VA	23233	Richard L Sharp	804-527-4000	P	7,664	36.4
Office Depot Inc.	2200 GermanTown	Delray Beach	FL	33445	David I Fuente	561-278-4800	P	6,069	32.0
Tandy Corp.	PO Box 17180	Fort Worth	TX	76102	John V Roach	817-390-3700	P	5,372	44.0
Heilig-Meyers Co.	2235 Staples Mill	Richmond	VA	23230	William C DeRusha	804-359-9171	P	956	12.5
Good Guys Inc.	7000 Marina Blvd	Brisbane	CA	94005	Robert A Gunst	415-615-5000	P	890	4.2
Sun Television and Appliances	6600 Port Rd	Groveport	OH	43125	Robert E Oyster	614-492-5600	P	683	3.4
InterTAN Inc.	201 Main St	Fort Worth	TX	76102	James T Nichols	817-348-9701	P	519	4.4
Fretter Inc.	12501 Grand River	Brighton	MI	48116	John B Hurley	810-220-5000	P	502	0.2
P.C. Richard and Son Corp.	150 Price Pkwy	Farmingdale	NY	11735	Gary Richard	516-582-3800	R	500	1.5
REX Stores Corp.	2875 Needmore Rd	Dayton	OH	45414	Stuart Rose	513-276-3931	P	442	1.0
Roberds Inc.	1100 E Central Ave	Dayton	OH	45449	Kenneth W Fletcher	937-859-5127	P	342	2.1
ABC Appliance Inc.	PO Box 436001	Pontiac	MI	48343	Gordon Hartunian	810-335-4222	R	338	1.4
Tops Appliance City Inc.	45 Brunswick Ave	Edison	NJ	08818	Robert Gross	908-248-2850	P	317	1.6
Ultimate Electronics Inc.	321A W 84th Ave	Thornton	CO	80221	J Edward McEntire	303-412-2500	P	261	1.2
Amer Television & Appliance	2404 W Beltline	Madison	WI	53713	Doug Reuhl	608-271-1000	R	260	1.4
H.H. Gregg Appliances	4151 E 96th St	Indianapolis	IN	46240	Jerry Throgmartin	317-848-8710	R	240*	1.1
Sound Advice Inc.	1901 Tigertail Blvd	Dania	FL	33004	Peter Beshouri	954-922-4434	P	156	0.6
Brendle's Inc.	1919 N Bridge St	N. Carolina	NC	28621	J M McLeish Jr	910-526-5600	P	155	1.6
HiFi Buys Inc.	1200-A Wilson Way	Smyrna	GA	30080	Jeffrey Snow	770-333-9932	R	89	0.4
Ameritech Cellular Services	32255 N Western	Farmington Hls	MI	48334	Herb Hribar	248-737-6700	S	85*	0.9
Magnolia Hi-Fi Inc.	3701 7th Ave S	Seattle	WA	98134	Jim Tweten	206-623-7872	R	85	0.3
Crutchfield Corp.	1 Crutchfield Park	Charlottesville	VA	22906	W G Crutchfield	804-973-1811	R	70*	0.4
Granite Furniture Company	1050 E 21st S	Salt Lake City	UT	84106	John D Richards	801-486-3333	R	58*	0.4
Technical Industries Inc.	6000 Peachtree NE	Atlanta	GA	30341	Ed Matthews	770-455-7610	R	58*	0.2
Audio King Corp.	3501 S Hwy 100	Minneapolis	MN	55416	Henry G Thorne	612-920-0505	P	57	0.4
Baillio's Warehouse Showroom	5301 Menaul NE	Albuquerque	NM	87110	Jack Baillio	505-883-7511	R	51*	0.2
Dow Stereo/Video Inc.	7929 Arjons Dr	San Diego	CA	92126	Michael Romagnolo	619-566-9600	R	51	0.3
CWE Inc.	800 Lincoln St	Denver	CO	80203	Gregory Kinnear	303-832-1111	P	45	<0.1
Dearden's Inc.	700 S Main St	Los Angeles	CA	90014	Douglas E Dearden	213-362-9600	R	44	0.4
Cambridge SoundWorks Inc.	311 Needham St	Newton	MA	02164	Thomas J DeVesto	617-332-5936	P	44	0.3
McPhails Inc.	PO Box 950	Petaluma	CA	94953	Bruce MacPhail	707-769-9800	R	42	0.1
Cousins Photo and Appliance	1691 Hancock St	San Diego	CA	92101	Wally Berry	619-293-3137	R	30	0.1
Harvey Group Inc.	600 Secaucus Rd	Secaucus	NJ	07094	Harvey E Sampson	201-865-3418	P	25	0.1
SourceOne Wireless	1040 S Milwaukee	Wheeling	IL	60090	Dave Trop	847-465-4200	R	20*	0.1
Inkley's Inc.	2150 S State St	Salt Lake City	UT	84115	RW Inkley	801-486-5901	R	20	0.3
J.J.R. Enterprises Inc.	10491 Oldacerville	Sacramento	CA	95827	John Reilly	916-363-2666	R	20*	0.1
Hello Inc.	2315 W Broad St	Richmond	VA	23220	Charles Smith	804-353-5566	R	18*	0.1
Let's Talk Cellular and Wireless	5200 NW 77th	Miami	FL	33166	Nicolas Molina	305-477-8255	P	18	0.5
County TV & Appliance L.O.S.	2770 Summer St	Stamford	CT	06905	Lester Cohn	203-327-2630	R	17	<0.1
Edelsteins Better Furniture Inc.	PO Box 3369	Brownsville	TX	78523	Ruben Edelstein	210-542-5605	R	17	0.3
Davis Audio-Visual Inc.	1801 Federal Blvd	Denver	CO	80204		303-455-1122	R	16*	0.1
MetroCell Security Inc.	5963 E 14 Mile Rd	Sterling H.	MI	48312	Duane T Rao	810-939-4660	R	15*	0.1
Paul's TV	500 N Harbor Blvd	La Habra	CA	90631	Paul Goldenberg	562-697-6751	R	15*	0.1
Astronet Corp.	37 Skyline Dr	Lake Mary	FL	30136	Stu Sakai	407-333-4912	S	15	<0.1
Columbia Audio-Video Inc.	1741 2nd St	Highland Park	IL	60035	Norm Rozak	708-433-6010	R	15	<0.1
Home Entertainment of Texas	PO Box 25127	Houston	TX	77265	Joe L Brown Jr	713-524-1956	R	15	0.1
Orban	1525 Alvarado St	San Leandro	CA	94577	Richard Ravich	510-351-3500	D	15	<0.1
Queen City Television	85 S Service Rd	Charlotte	NC	28208	Woody Player	704-391-6000	R	15*	0.1
Racal Recorders Inc.	15375 Barranca	Irvine	CA	92718	John R Cummings	714-727-3444	S	15	<0.1

Source: *Ward's Business Directory of U.S. Private and Public Companies*, 1998. The company type code is used as follows: P - Public, R - Private, S - Subsidiary, D - Division, J - Joint Venture, A - Affiliate, G - Group. Sales are in millions of dollars, employees are in thousands. An asterisk (*) indicates an estimated sales volume. The symbol < stands for 'less than'.

OCCUPATIONS EMPLOYED BY SIC 573 - APPLIANCE, RADIO, TV, AND MUSIC STORES

Occupation	% of Total 1996	Change to 2006	Occupation	% of Total 1996	Change to 2006
Salespersons, retail	35.3	18.0	Truck drivers light & heavy	2.2	10.7
Marketing & sales worker supervisors	7.7	10.7	Home appliance/power tool repairers	1.8	-0.3
General managers & top executives	6.8	7.3	Mechanics, installers, & repairers nec	1.4	21.8
Cashiers	6.5	12.1	Traffic, shipping, receiving clerks	1.4	10.7
Sales & related workers nec	5.8	21.8	Secretaries, except legal & medical	1.1	-12.2
Stock clerks	5.4	39.3	Blue collar worker supervisors	1.0	6.9
Bookkeeping, accounting, & auditing clerks	2.6	-11.4	Purchasing managers	1.0	-0.3
General office clerks	2.5	-4.7	Wholesale & retail buyers, except farm products	1.0	-8.3
Electronic home entertainment system repairers	2.5	-28.0			

Source: *Industry-Occupation Matrix*, Bureau of Labor Statistics. These data relate to one or more 3-digit SIC industry groups rather than to a single 4-digit SIC. The change reported for each occupation to the year 2006 is a percent of growth or decline as estimated by the Bureau of Labor Statistics. The abbreviation nec stands for 'not elsewhere classified'.

STATE AND REGIONAL CONCENTRATION

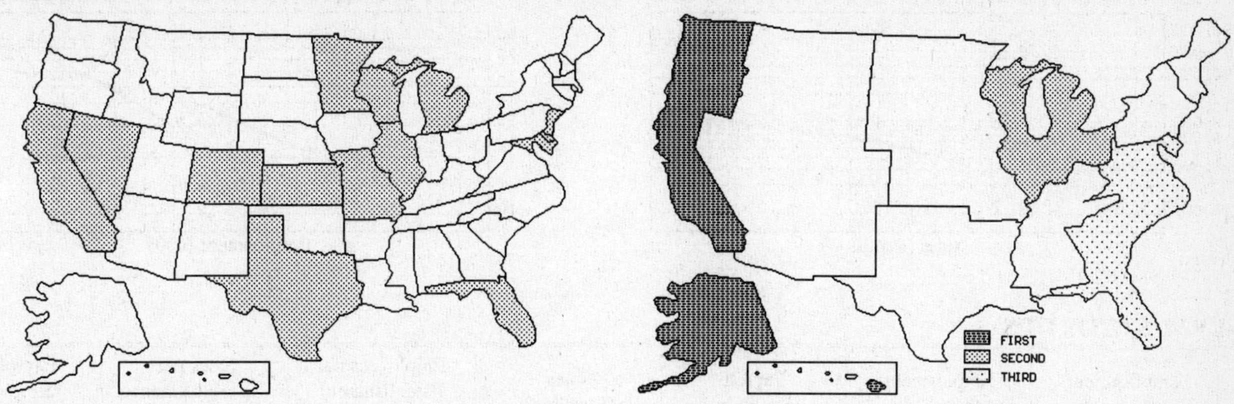

INDUSTRY DATA BY STATE

State	Establishments - 1995		Employment - 1995			Payroll - 1995		Sales - 1992		
	Total (number)	% of U.S.	Total (number)	% of U.S.	Per Estab.	Total ($ mil.)	Per Empl. ($)	Total ($ mil.)	% of U.S.	Per Estab ($)
California	2,031	11.9	22,024	14.2	11	478.6	21,733	3,314.1	16.7	168,838
Texas	1,189	7.0	12,325	8.0	10	200.2	16,245	1,563.2	7.9	171,816
Florida	1,120	6.6	9,994	6.4	9	196.3	19,643	1,417.4	7.2	189,844
New York	1,149	6.8	8,015	5.2	7	176.0	21,958	1,288.4	6.5	184,036
Illinois	790	4.6	8,682	5.6	11	135.6	15,616	1,065.9	5.4	166,474
Ohio	709	4.2	7,989	5.2	11	141.5	17,709	857.8	4.3	158,761
Michigan	546	3.2	5,373	3.5	10	92.5	17,207	779.1	3.9	166,223
Pennsylvania	669	3.9	4,782	3.1	7	84.4	17,651	752.5	3.8	163,728
New Jersey	441	2.6	3,742	2.4	8	72.4	19,343	656.2	3.3	198,237
Wisconsin	303	1.8	4,127	2.7	14	72.4	17,537	504.5	2.5	156,538
Virginia	444	2.6	4,477	2.9	10	82.4	18,409	494.5	2.5	151,785
Maryland	313	1.8	3,225	2.1	10	61.6	19,106	450.3	2.3	168,411
Missouri	353	2.1	3,703	2.4	10	63.3	17,092	419.0	2.1	156,279
Georgia	483	2.8	4,321	2.8	9	77.2	17,873	413.8	2.1	159,507
Colorado	282	1.7	2,797	1.8	10	58.3	20,834	408.7	2.1	176,710
Minnesota	276	1.6	3,768	2.4	14	55.1	14,622	391.8	2.0	164,751
Indiana	358	2.1	3,136	2.0	9	50.1	15,982	388.7	2.0	170,098
North Carolina	525	3.1	3,903	2.5	7	71.6	18,346	387.4	2.0	133,489
Washington	342	2.0	3,057	2.0	9	62.6	20,475	379.7	1.9	175,859
Tennessee	341	2.0	2,648	1.7	8	48.4	18,296	317.7	1.6	144,815
Arizona	305	1.8	3,363	2.2	11	58.1	17,273	275.9	1.4	156,963
Massachusetts	342	2.0	2,675	1.7	8	53.8	20,101	263.9	1.3	132,236
Connecticut	209	1.2	1,661	1.1	8	34.3	20,632	245.1	1.2	182,474
Alabama	302	1.8	1,923	1.2	6	34.5	17,951	238.4	1.2	147,130
Oregon	253	1.5	2,230	1.4	9	40.3	18,060	205.8	1.0	151,453
Kansas	203	1.2	1,780	1.1	9	25.9	14,544	205.0	1.0	151,175
Louisiana	227	1.3	1,774	1.1	8	30.9	17,400	201.7	1.0	143,874
Kentucky	217	1.3	1,720	1.1	8	30.6	17,804	185.2	0.9	134,567
Oklahoma	203	1.2	1,561	1.0	8	25.3	16,236	177.6	0.9	146,293
Iowa	204	1.2	1,376	0.9	7	19.2	13,948	168.6	0.9	140,410
South Carolina	241	1.4	1,814	1.2	8	29.5	16,257	161.0	0.8	120,208
Nevada	91	0.5	1,166	0.8	13	24.2	20,780	124.8	0.6	164,625
Nebraska	101	0.6	915	0.6	9	12.3	13,428	101.1	0.5	142,195
Mississippi	193	1.1	969	0.6	5	16.0	16,537	100.1	0.5	127,248
Hawaii	76	0.4	537	0.3	7	10.8	20,047	91.3	0.5	157,403
Arkansas	161	0.9	1,193	0.8	7	17.9	14,988	90.1	0.5	113,282
Utah	106	0.6	951	0.6	9	20.9	21,946	81.0	0.4	134,408
New Mexico	96	0.6	739	0.5	8	11.9	16,097	77.9	0.4	118,339
D.C.	32	0.2	100-249	-	-	(D)	-	75.2	0.4	236,443
West Virginia	112	0.7	666	0.4	6	10.7	16,122	69.0	0.3	117,555
Delaware	59	0.3	429	0.3	7	8.6	19,932	65.6	0.3	186,364
New Hampshire	108	0.6	821	0.5	8	15.6	19,044	64.1	0.3	135,495
South Dakota	56	0.3	467	0.3	8	7.9	16,970	43.6	0.2	134,633
Maine	80	0.5	380	0.2	5	6.4	16,947	39.0	0.2	122,012
Montana	71	0.4	330	0.2	5	5.6	16,927	34.3	0.2	109,287
Idaho	84	0.5	411	0.3	5	7.9	19,153	33.7	0.2	108,370
Rhode Island	48	0.3	287	0.2	6	5.1	17,704	32.9	0.2	117,778
Alaska	28	0.2	181	0.1	6	4.4	24,061	26.4	0.1	158,150
Vermont	51	0.3	215	0.1	4	3.5	16,242	23.5	0.1	114,204
North Dakota	43	0.3	330	0.2	8	5.1	15,312	20.2	0.1	105,271
Wyoming	39	0.2	100-249	-	-	(D)	-	18.5	0.1	114,296

Source: County Business Patterns, 1995 and *Economic Census of the U.S., 1992*. Data are sorted by 1992 revenues and, if revenues are unavailable, by establishments in 1995. The symbol (D) indicates that data are withheld by the source to avoid disclosure of competitive information. A dash (-) indicates that data are not available or undisclosed because they do not meet statistical validity standards. Shaded *states* on the state map indicate those states which have proportionately greater representation in the industry than would be indicated by the state's population; the ratio is based on total revenues or number of establishments. Shaded *regions* indicate where the industry is regionally most concentrated.

5734 - COMPUTER AND SOFTWARE STORES

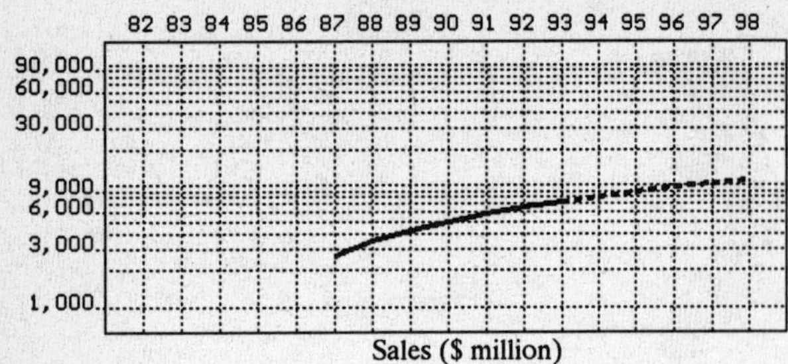

Sales ($ million)

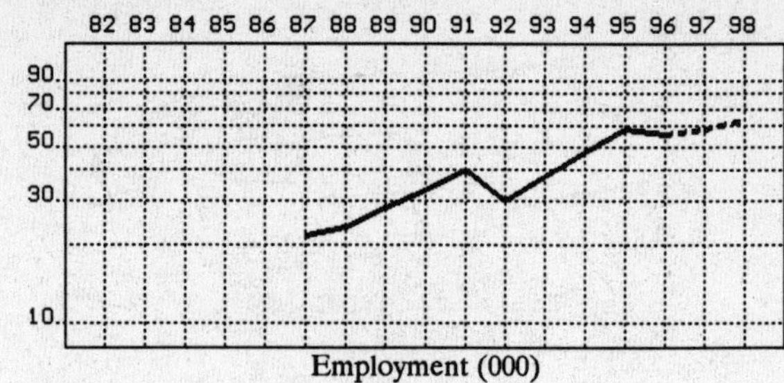

Employment (000)

GENERAL STATISTICS

Year	Establishments (number)	Employment (number)	Payroll ($ million)	Sales ($ million)	Employees per Establishment (number)	Sales per Establishment ($)	Payroll per Employee ($)
1982	-	-	-	-	-	-	-
1983	-	-	-	-	-	-	-
1984	-	-	-	-	-	-	-
1985	-	-	-	-	-	-	-
1986	-	-	-	-	-	-	-
1987	3,858	21,895	324.7	2,650.9	6	687,116	14,831
1988	3,789	23,483	475.3	3,430.8e	6	-	20,240
1989	4,177	28,168	610.4	4,210.7e	7	-	21,671
1990	5,121	33,266	753.6	4,990.6e	7	-	22,654
1991	5,980	40,393	985.9	5,770.5e	7	-	24,407
1992	5,438	29,852	607.1	6,550.4	5	1,204,567	20,337
1993	6,545	37,674	777.1	7,330.3p	6	-	20,628
1994	7,479	47,635	1,028.1	8,110.3p	6	-	21,583
1995	8,544	57,970	1,330.6	8,890.2p	7	-	22,953
1996	8,565p	54,956p	1,254.9p	9,670.1p	-	-	-
1997	9,146p	58,828p	1,352.8p	10,450.0p	-	-	-
1998	9,727p	62,701p	1,450.6p	11,229.9p	-	-	-

Sources: Economic Census of the United States, 1982, 1987, and 1992. Establishment counts, employment, and payroll are from *County Business Patterns* for non-Census years. Values followed by a 'p' are projections by the editors. Sales and expense data for non-Census years are extrapolations, marked by 'e'. Industries reclassified in 1987 will not have data for prior years. Data are the most recent available at this level of detail.

INDICES OF CHANGE

Year	Establishments (number)	Employment (number)	Payroll ($ million)	Sales ($ million)	Employees per Establishment (number)	Sales per Establishment ($)	Payroll per Employee ($)
1982	-	-	-	-	-	-	-
1983	-	-	-	-	-	-	-
1984	-	-	-	-	-	-	-
1985	-	-	-	-	-	-	-
1986	-	-	-	-	-	-	-
1987	70.9	73.3	53.5	40.5	120.0	57.0	72.9
1988	69.7	78.7	78.3	52.4e	120.0	-	99.5
1989	76.8	94.4	100.5	64.3e	140.0	-	106.6
1990	94.2	111.4	124.1	76.2e	140.0	-	111.4
1991	110.0	135.3	162.4	88.1e	140.0	-	120.0
1992	100.0	100.0	100.0	100.0	100.0	100.0	100.0
1993	120.4	126.2	128.0	111.9p	115.1	-	101.4
1994	137.5	159.6	169.3	123.8p	127.4	-	106.1
1995	157.1	194.2	219.2	135.7p	135.7	-	112.9
1996	157.5p	184.1p	206.7p	147.6p	-	-	-
1997	168.2p	197.1p	222.8p	159.5p	-	-	-
1998	178.9p	210.0p	238.9p	171.4p	-	-	-

Sources: Same as General Statistics. The values shown reflect change from the base year, 1992. Values above 100 mean greater than 1992, values below 100 mean less than 1992, and a value of 100 in the 1982-91 or 1993-98 period means same as 1992. Values followed by a 'p' are projections by the editors; 'e' stands for extrapolation. Data are the most recent available at this level of detail.

SELECTED RATIOS

For 1992	Avg. of All Retail	Analyzed Industry	Index	For 1992	Avg. of All Retail	Analyzed Industry	Index
Employees per Establishment	12	5	46	Sales per Employee	102,941	219,429	213
Payroll per Establishment	146,026	111,640	76	Sales per Establishment	1,241,555	1,204,561	97
Payroll per Employee	12,107	20,337	168	Expenses per Establishment	na	na	na

Sources: Same as General Statistics. The 'Average of All Manufacturing' column represents the average of all manufacturing industries reported for the most recent complete year available. The Index shows the relationship between the Average and the Analyzed Industry. For example, 100 means that they are equal; 500 that the Analyzed Industry is five times the average; 50 means that the Analyzed Industry is half the national average. The abbreviation 'na' is used to show that data are 'not available'.

LEADING COMPANIES

Number shown: **50** Total sales ($ mil): **18,751** Total employment (000): **83.3**

Company Name	Address				CEO Name	Phone	Co. Type	Sales ($ mil)	Empl. (000)
Office Depot Inc.	2200 GermanTown	Delray Beach	FL	33445	David I Fuente	561-278-4800	P	6,069	32.0
CompUSA Inc.	14951 N Dallas	Dallas	TX	75240	James F Halpin	972-982-4000	P	4,611	14.3
Computer City	2000 Two Tandy	Fort Worth	TX	76102	Nathan Morton	817-390-3000	D	1,904	7.0
InterTAN Inc.	201 Main St	Fort Worth	TX	76102	James T Nichols	817-348-9701	P	519	4.4
El Camino Resources	21051 Warner Ctr	Woodland Hills	CA	91367	David Harmon	818-226-6600	R	515 *	0.5
NeoStar Retail Group Inc.	10741 King William	Dallas	TX	75220	James B McCurry	214-401-9000	P	514	7.1
Micro Electronics Inc.	1555 W Lane Ave	Columbus	OH	43221	John Baker	614-481-8041	R	510 *	1.5
NECX Inc.	4 Technology Dr	Peabody	MA	01960	Henry Bertolon	978-538-8000	R	501	0.3
Wherehouse Entertainment	19701 Hamilton	Torrance	CA	90502	A. C Alvarez II	310-538-2314	R	366 *	6.0
Computer Factory Inc.	169 Main St	White Plains	NY	10601	Jay Gottlieb	212-681-6060	S	365	1.0
Egghead Inc.	22705 E Mission	Liberty Lake	WA	99019	George P Orban	509-922-7031	P	361	1.3
Elek-Tek Inc.	7350 N Linder Ave	Skokie	IL	60077	Richard Rodriguez	708-677-7660	P	338	0.9
Amer Television & Appliance	2404 W Beltline	Madison	WI	53713	Doug Reuhl	608-271-1000	R	260	1.4
Sam Ash Music Corp.	PO Box 9047	Hicksville	NY	11802	Richard Ash	516-932-6400	R	250	0.8
Software Etc. Stores Inc.	7505 Metro Blvd	Edina	MN	55439	Daniel A DeMatteo	612-893-7644	S	247	1.3
Bethco Inc.	2700 NE Expwy	Atlanta	GA	30345	Elizabeth Heddens	404-636-7330	R	150	0.3
ComputerWare	605 W California	Sunnyvale	CA	94086	Ron Dupler	408-328-1000	R	110	0.2
Basic Living Products Inc.	1321 67th St	Emeryville	CA	94608	Gene Farb	510-428-0859	R	100 *	0.5
Computer West L.L.C.	605 W California	Sunnyvale	CA	94086	Ken Krich	408-328-1000	R	90	0.2
ComputersAmerica Inc.	PO Box 9127	San Rafael	CA	94912	John R Kalleen III	415-257-1010	R	80	0.2
Champion Computer Corp.	6421 Congress Ave	Boca Raton	FL	33487	Michael Baker	407-997-2900	R	63	<0.1
Metro Business Systems Inc.	PO Box 4920	Stamford	CT	06907	Frank Pelli	203-967-3435	R	60	<0.1
Micros-to-Mainframes Inc.	614 Corporate Way	Valley Cottage	NY	10989	Steven H Rothman	914-268-5000	P	58	0.1
NCA Computer Products	1202 Kifer Rd	Sunnyvale	CA	94086	Tony Ghanma	408-739-9010	R	55 *	0.2
Baillio's Warehouse Showroom	5301 Menaul NE	Albuquerque	NM	87110	Jack Baillio	505-883-7511	R	51 *	0.2
SBI Computer Products Inc.	11369 Sunrise	R. Cordova	CA	95742	Edward Simon	916-638-8432	R	50 *	0.2
CWE Inc.	800 Lincoln St	Denver	CO	80203	Gregory Kinnear	303-832-1111	P	45	<0.1
Electronic Business Equipment	200 Bus Park Ln	Riverside	MO	64150	Kevin Fitzpatrick	913-495-5000	S	35	0.3
Resource One Computer Syst	278 N 5th St	Columbus	OH	43215	Stampp Corbin	614-241-5800	R	32	<0.1
Computerland of San Diego	5710 Ruffin Rd	San Diego	CA	92123	Brian Hammond	619-492-1400	R	30	<0.1
Central Computer Systems Inc.	3777evens Creek	Santa Clara	CA	95051	Ann Lai	408-248-5888	R	30	<0.1
Alpha Computers Inc.	14725 SW 72nd Ave	Tigard	OR	97224	Thomas Chow	503-684-1111	R	27	<0.1
Micro Marketing Group Inc.	10455 Markison Rd	Dallas	TX	75238	Jeffrey Poll	214-349-4600	R	26	0.1
HarrisData	611 N Barker Rd	Brookfield	WI	53045	AE Seyler	414-784-9099	R	26 *	<0.1
Computer Expo Inc.	11312 Westheimer	Houston	TX	77077	Wazi Ullah	713-531-0990	R	24	<0.1
JSB Corp.	108 Whisp Pine	Scotts Valley	CA	95066	Steve Jones	408-438-8300	R	24 *	<0.1
Piedmont Technology Group	830 Tyvola #104	Charlotte	NC	28217	Mitch Lemons	704-523-2400	R	23	<0.1
Technical and Scientific	2040 Houston Pkwy	Houston	TX	77043	William C Smith	713-935-1500	R	22 *	<0.1
SCH Technologies	895 Central Ave	Cincinnati	OH	45202	Edward J Bauer	513-579-0455	R	21	0.1
Creative Business Concepts Inc.	1 Technology Dr	Irvine	CA	92618	J Richard Shafer	714-727-3104	R	20 *	<0.1
CSR Computer Syst Resource	10022 Lantern Rd	Fishers	IN	46038	Robert A Annee	317-842-4777	R	20	<0.1
Computer Systems Inc.	2819 S 125th Ave	Omaha	NE	68144	Roger Able	402-330-3600	S	19 *	<0.1
Harmony Computers	1801 Flatbush Ave	Brooklyn	NY	11210	Stanley Frost	718-692-2828	R	18 *	<0.1
PC Professional Inc.	1615 Webster St	Oakland	CA	94612	Daniel Sanguinetti	510-465-5700	R	18	<0.1
ComputerLand Express	3030 S Calhoun Rd	New Berlin	WI	53151	Nizar Hemani	414-784-1850	R	17	<0.1
MPS Multimedia Inc.	379 Oyster Pt Blvd	S San Francisco	CA	94080	Steve Chen	415-583-4677	R	17 *	<0.1
Midwest Typewriter & Computer	410 W 5th St	Kansas City	MO	64105	Kendell Culbertson	816-471-3553	R	16 *	<0.1
Eakins Open Systems	67 E Evelyn Ave	Mountain View	CA	94041	Gil Eakins	415-969-5109	R	15	<0.1
Laitron Computer	1538 Montague	San Jose	CA	95131	Ming Lai	408-321-3400	R	15 *	<0.1
MacProducts USA Inc.	4544 S Lamar Blvd	Austin	TX	78745	David Goldman	512-892-4090	R	15	<0.1

Source: *Ward's Business Directory of U.S. Private and Public Companies*, 1998. The company type code used is as follows: P - Public, R - Private, S - Subsidiary, D - Division, J - Joint Venture, A - Affiliate, G - Group. Sales are in millions of dollars, employees are in thousands. An asterisk (*) indicates an estimated sales volume. The symbol < stands for 'less than'.

OCCUPATIONS EMPLOYED BY SIC 573 - APPLIANCE, RADIO, TV, AND MUSIC STORES

Occupation	% of Total 1996	Change to 2006	Occupation	% of Total 1996	Change to 2006
Salespersons, retail	35.3	18.0	Truck drivers light & heavy	2.2	10.7
Marketing & sales worker supervisors	7.7	10.7	Home appliance/power tool repairers	1.8	-0.3
General managers & top executives	6.8	7.3	Mechanics, installers, & repairers nec	1.4	21.8
Cashiers	6.5	12.1	Traffic, shipping, receiving clerks	1.4	10.7
Sales & related workers nec	5.8	21.8	Secretaries, except legal & medical	1.1	-12.2
Stock clerks	5.4	39.3	Blue collar worker supervisors	1.0	6.9
Bookkeeping, accounting, & auditing clerks	2.6	-11.4	Purchasing managers	1.0	-0.3
General office clerks	2.5	-4.7	Wholesale & retail buyers, except farm products	1.0	-8.3
Electronic home entertainment system repairers	2.5	-28.0			

Source: *Industry-Occupation Matrix*, Bureau of Labor Statistics. These data relate to one or more 3-digit SIC industry groups rather than to a single 4-digit SIC. The change reported for each occupation to the year 2006 is a percent of growth or decline as estimated by the Bureau of Labor Statistics. The abbreviation nec stands for 'not elsewhere classified'.

STATE AND REGIONAL CONCENTRATION

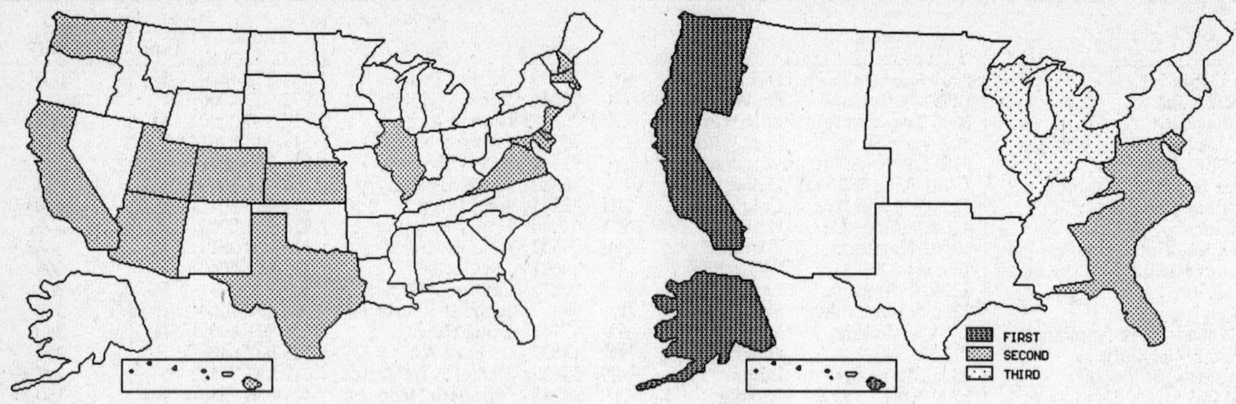

INDUSTRY DATA BY STATE

State	Establishments - 1995 Total (number)	Establishments - 1995 % of U.S.	Employment - 1995 Total (number)	Employment - 1995 % of U.S.	Employment - 1995 Per Estab.	Payroll - 1995 Total ($ mil.)	Payroll - 1995 Per Empl. ($)	Sales - 1992 Total ($ mil.)	Sales - 1992 % of U.S.	Sales - 1992 Per Estab ($)
California	1,395	16.3	11,964	20.6	9	317.3	26,519	1,598.5	24.4	259,364
Texas	596	7.0	4,579	7.9	8	104.8	22,879	626.5	9.6	235,976
Illinois	342	4.0	2,401	4.1	7	50.5	21,022	357.6	5.5	197,993
New York	442	5.2	2,618	4.5	6	55.0	21,008	337.2	5.1	248,113
Florida	552	6.5	3,006	5.2	5	63.6	21,151	323.0	4.9	214,455
Virginia	259	3.0	1,724	3.0	7	34.4	19,939	255.3	3.9	256,115
New Jersey	287	3.4	2,191	3.8	8	50.9	23,219	243.1	3.7	229,770
Michigan	203	2.4	1,690	2.9	8	35.3	20,888	223.4	3.4	207,659
Pennsylvania	297	3.5	1,966	3.4	7	39.4	20,040	219.8	3.4	245,028
Washington	240	2.8	1,816	3.1	8	40.4	22,247	200.2	3.1	209,247
Maryland	226	2.6	1,632	2.8	7	35.7	21,876	185.1	2.8	240,399
Massachusetts	219	2.6	1,853	3.2	8	51.5	27,804	162.6	2.5	227,350
Colorado	190	2.2	1,176	2.0	6	23.4	19,920	156.0	2.4	234,889
Arizona	162	1.9	899	1.6	6	21.2	23,615	135.6	2.1	216,904
Georgia	203	2.4	1,347	2.3	7	33.6	24,925	133.4	2.0	233,998
Ohio	301	3.5	2,106	3.6	7	54.4	25,828	106.8	1.6	142,192
North Carolina	236	2.8	1,326	2.3	6	28.7	21,658	95.9	1.5	170,859
Minnesota	148	1.7	1,081	1.9	7	30.8	28,458	92.8	1.4	179,214
Missouri	144	1.7	781	1.3	5	14.9	19,124	76.8	1.2	176,903
Kansas	77	0.9	498	0.9	6	10.7	21,420	75.2	1.1	205,478
Indiana	138	1.6	762	1.3	6	12.4	16,220	72.1	1.1	124,799
Connecticut	111	1.3	797	1.4	7	22.3	27,989	71.9	1.1	217,885
New Hampshire	60	0.7	496	0.9	8	12.3	24,784	68.1	1.0	298,482
Tennessee	160	1.9	773	1.3	5	17.9	23,201	64.3	1.0	169,132
Wisconsin	107	1.3	655	1.1	6	11.6	17,643	59.9	0.9	175,108
Utah	98	1.1	1,024	1.8	10	25.1	24,502	52.6	0.8	157,012
Oregon	121	1.4	688	1.2	6	14.0	20,350	52.1	0.8	160,901
Louisiana	86	1.0	583	1.0	7	11.4	19,559	49.1	0.7	183,149
Oklahoma	112	1.3	558	1.0	5	12.1	21,670	48.4	0.7	206,744
Hawaii	44	0.5	294	0.5	7	6.2	21,000	43.8	0.7	214,539
South Carolina	96	1.1	414	0.7	4	7.5	18,217	40.9	0.6	203,537
Alabama	125	1.5	524	0.9	4	8.7	16,658	38.5	0.6	177,442
Nevada	64	0.7	514	0.9	8	10.4	20,210	29.4	0.4	189,897
Idaho	45	0.5	209	0.4	5	4.3	20,646	27.3	0.4	237,322
D.C.	12	0.1	151	0.3	13	4.5	29,967	25.3	0.4	221,939
Nebraska	40	0.5	168	0.3	4	3.6	21,482	24.1	0.4	167,604
Rhode Island	28	0.3	195	0.3	7	3.3	16,903	22.2	0.3	277,850
Iowa	81	0.9	416	0.7	5	8.9	21,430	21.1	0.3	161,962
New Mexico	67	0.8	268	0.5	4	5.7	21,164	20.6	0.3	137,073
Delaware	29	0.3	247	0.4	9	4.7	19,028	18.6	0.3	201,902
Kentucky	78	0.9	275	0.5	4	4.7	17,145	17.3	0.3	119,545
Alaska	20	0.2	110	0.2	6	3.5	31,436	15.4	0.2	157,276
Arkansas	60	0.7	294	0.5	5	4.4	14,956	14.8	0.2	162,615
Mississippi	52	0.6	151	0.3	3	2.2	14,589	9.5	0.1	101,935
Montana	36	0.4	165	0.3	5	2.8	17,115	8.1	0.1	89,467
West Virginia	42	0.5	126	0.2	3	1.9	14,690	8.0	0.1	105,303
South Dakota	22	0.3	98	0.2	4	2.1	21,143	6.0	0.1	86,000
Maine	29	0.3	93	0.2	3	1.8	19,613	5.7	0.1	176,656
Wyoming	17	0.2	88	0.2	5	1.1	12,875	4.3	0.1	93,087
North Dakota	21	0.2	77	0.1	4	1.4	17,532	3.8	0.1	135,179
Vermont	24	0.3	103	0.2	4	1.5	14,340	2.8	0.0	196,929

Source: County Business Patterns, 1995 and *Economic Census of the U.S., 1992*. Data are sorted by 1992 revenues and, if revenues are unavailable, by establishments in 1995. The symbol (D) indicates that data are withheld by the source to avoid disclosure of competitive information. A dash (-) indicates that data are not available or undisclosed because they do not meet statistical validity standards. Shaded *states* on the state map indicate those states which have proportionately greater representation in the industry than would be indicated by the state's population; the ratio is based on total revenues or number of establishments. Shaded *regions* indicate where the industry is regionally most concentrated.

5735 - RECORD & PRERECORDED TAPE STORES

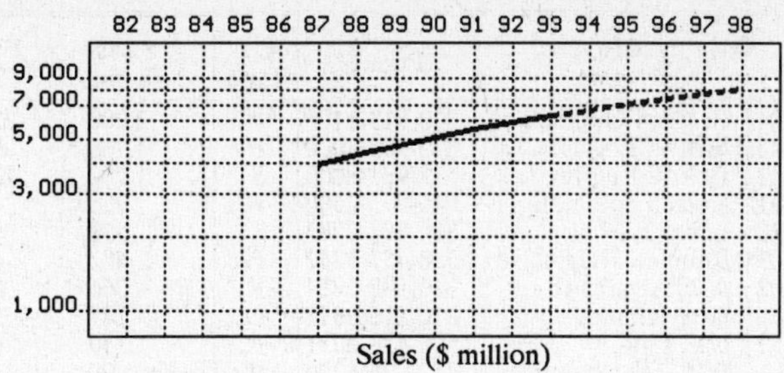

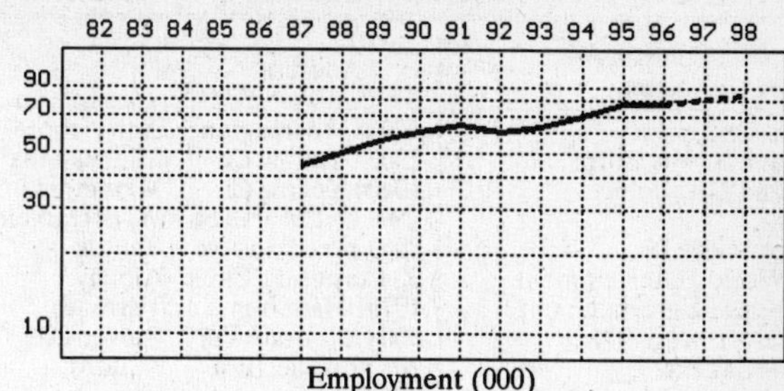

GENERAL STATISTICS

Year	Establishments (number)	Employment (number)	Payroll ($ million)	Sales ($ million)	Employees per Establishment (number)	Sales per Establishment ($)	Payroll per Employee ($)
1982	-	-	-	-	-	-	-
1983	-	-	-	-	-	-	-
1984	-	-	-	-	-	-	-
1985	-	-	-	-	-	-	-
1986	-	-	-	-	-	-	-
1987	6,272	44,408	371.7	3,930.4	7	626,659	8,370
1988	6,295	49,783	435.3	4,316.4e	8	-	8,745
1989	6,444	55,165	499.7	4,702.3e	9	-	9,059
1990	7,146	60,123	550.2	5,088.3e	8	-	9,151
1991	7,588	64,077	617.9	5,474.3e	8	-	9,643
1992	7,924	60,438	592.5	5,860.2	8	739,555	9,804
1993	8,242	62,601	643.5	6,246.2p	8	-	10,280
1994	8,714	69,209	716.9	6,632.2p	8	-	10,358
1995	8,842	77,894	774.3	7,018.1p	9	-	9,940
1996	9,322p	77,695p	810.1p	7,404.1p	-	-	-
1997	9,687p	81,152p	856.5p	7,790.1p	-	-	-
1998	10,053p	84,609p	902.9p	8,176.0p	-	-	-

Sources: *Economic Census of the United States*, 1982, 1987, and 1992. Establishment counts, employment, and payroll are from *County Business Patterns* for non-Census years. Values followed by a 'p' are projections by the editors. Sales and expense data for non-Census years are extrapolations, marked by 'e'. Industries reclassified in 1987 will not have data for prior years. Data are the most recent available at this level of detail.

INDICES OF CHANGE

Year	Establishments (number)	Employment (number)	Payroll ($ million)	Sales ($ million)	Employees per Establishment (number)	Sales per Establishment ($)	Payroll per Employee ($)
1982	-	-	-	-	-	-	-
1983	-	-	-	-	-	-	-
1984	-	-	-	-	-	-	-
1985	-	-	-	-	-	-	-
1986	-	-	-	-	-	-	-
1987	79.2	73.5	62.7	67.1	87.5	84.7	85.4
1988	79.4	82.4	73.5	73.7e	100.0	-	89.2
1989	81.3	91.3	84.3	80.2e	112.5	-	92.4
1990	90.2	99.5	92.9	86.8e	100.0	-	93.3
1991	95.8	106.0	104.3	93.4e	100.0	-	98.4
1992	100.0	100.0	100.0	100.0	100.0	100.0	100.0
1993	104.0	103.6	108.6	106.6p	94.9	-	104.9
1994	110.0	114.5	121.0	113.2p	99.3	-	105.7
1995	111.6	128.9	130.7	119.8p	110.1	-	101.4
1996	117.6p	128.6p	136.7p	126.3p	-	-	-
1997	122.3p	134.3p	144.6p	132.9p	-	-	-
1998	126.9p	140.0p	152.4p	139.5p	-	-	-

Sources: Same as General Statistics. The values shown reflect change from the base year, 1992. Values above 100 mean greater than 1992, values below 100 mean less than 1992, and a value of 100 in the 1982-91 or 1993-98 period means same as 1992. Values followed by a 'p' are projections by the editors; 'e' stands for extrapolation. Data are the most recent available at this level of detail.

SELECTED RATIOS

For 1992	Avg. of All Retail	Analyzed Industry	Index	For 1992	Avg. of All Retail	Analyzed Industry	Index
Employees per Establishment	12	8	63	Sales per Employee	102,941	96,962	94
Payroll per Establishment	146,026	74,773	51	Sales per Establishment	1,241,555	739,551	60
Payroll per Employee	12,107	9,803	81	Expenses per Establishment	na	na	na

Sources: Same as General Statistics. The 'Average of All Manufacturing' column represents the average of all manufacturing industries reported for the most recent complete year available. The Index shows the relationship between the Average and the Analyzed Industry. For example, 100 means that they are equal; 500 that the Analyzed Industry is five times the average; 50 means that the Analyzed Industry is half the national average. The abbreviation 'na' is used to show that data are 'not available'.

LEADING COMPANIES

Number shown: 37 Total sales ($ mil): 8,791 Total employment (000): 75.2

Company Name	Address				CEO Name	Phone	Co. Type	Sales ($ mil)	Empl. (000)
Borders Group Inc.	500 E Washington	Ann Arbor	MI	48104	Bruce A Quinnell	313-913-1100	P	2,000	22.8
Musicland Stores Corp.	10400 Yellow Cir	Minneapolis	MN	55343	Jack W Eugster	612-931-8000	P	1,768	9.6
Musicland Group Inc.	10400 Yellow Cir	Minnetonka	MN	55343	Jack W Eugster	612-931-8800	S	1,700	13.0
MTS Inc.	2500 Del Monte St	W. Sacramento	CA	95691	Russell Solomon	916-373-2500	R	995 *	7.0
Camelot Music Inc.	8000 Freedom Ave	Canton	OH	44720	James E Bonk	330-494-2282	S	550	5.4
Trans World Entertainment	38 Corporate Circle	Albany	NY	12203	Robert J Higgins	518-452-1242	P	482	4.0
Wherehouse Entertainment	19701 Hamilton	Torrance	CA	90502	A. C Alvarez II	310-538-2314	R	366 *	6.0
Blockbuster Music Div.	300 Corporate Pte	Culver City	CA	90230	Larry Gaines	310-216-0871	D	187 *	1.3
Strawberries Inc.	205 Fortune Blvd	Milford	MA	01757	Ivan Lipton	508-478-2031	R	140	0.1
National Record Mart Inc.	507 Forest Ave	Carnegie	PA	15106	W A Teitelbaum	412-276-6200	P	99	1.2
Spec's Music Inc.	PO Box 520248	Miami	FL	33265	Ann Lieff	305-592-7288	P	69	0.6
Kemp Mill Music Co.	11420 Baltimore Pk	Beltsville	MD	20705	Marc Applebaum	301-595-9880	R	56	0.3
Central South Music Inc.	3730 Vulcan Dr	Nashville	TN	37211	Randy Davidson	615-833-5960	R	52	0.5
Half Price Books	5915 E NW Hwy	Dallas	TX	75231	Sharon Anderson	214-360-0833	R	36 *	0.7
Schmitt Music Co.	88 S 10th St	Minneapolis	MN	55403	Tom Schmitt	612-339-4811	R	35	0.4
Peaches Entertainment Corp.	1180 E Beach	Hallandale	FL	33009	Allan Wolk	954-454-5554	S	32	0.3
URT Industries Inc.	3451 Executive Wy	Miramar	FL	33025	Allan Wolk	305-432-4200	P	32	0.3
Newbury Comics Inc.	38 Everett St	Boston	MA	02134	Michael Dreese	617-254-1666	R	29 *	0.2
Worldvision Home Video Inc.	1700 Broadway	New York	NY	10019	Bob Sigman	212-261-2900	D	27	0.1
J.R.'s Music Shops of Hawaii	710 Kakoi St	Honolulu	HI	96819	Bob Kennedy	808-837-7800	R	25 *	0.2
Palmer Corp.	1767 Morris Ave	Union	NJ	07083	Peter Balner	908-686-3030	S	23	0.4
Keystone Learning Syst Corp.	2241 Larsen Pkwy	Provo	UT	84606	G Peck	801-375-8680	R	16 *	<0.1
Poplar Tunes Record Shop Inc.	308 Poplar Ave	Memphis	TN	38103	John Novarese	901-525-6348	R	14 *	0.1
Record Exchange of Roanoke	210 S Sharon Amity	Charlotte	NC	28211	Don Rosenberg	704-364-1784	R	14 *	0.1
Transcontinents Record Sales	1762 Main St	Buffalo	NY	14208	Leonard Silver	716-883-9520	R	12	0.1
Crazy Mike's Video Inc.	1110 N 175th St	Seattle	WA	98133	Fred Rezvani	206-285-2611	R	9 *	0.1
Kingdom Tapes and Electronics	PO Box 506	Mansfield	PA	16933	Johnny Berguson	717-662-7515	D	9 *	<0.1
Time-Life Music	777 Duke St	Alexandria	VA	22314	Steven Janas	703-838-7000	D	5 *	<0.1
Educational Activities Inc.	1937 Grand Ave	Baldwin	NY	11510	Alfred S Harris	516-223-4666	R	4	<0.1
Creative Gaming Inc.	150 Morris Ave	Springfield	NJ	07081	Peter J Jegou	973-467-0266	P	2	<0.1
Intern. Film & Video Center	989 1st Ave	New York	NY	10022	B Maghsoudlou	212-826-8848	R	1	<0.1
Roadrunner Video Enterprises	819 S Floyd St	Louisville	KY	40203	Terry Schneider	502-585-1411	R	1 *	<0.1
Multimedia Replay Inc.	901 W Lake St	Minneapolis	MN	55408	Stephen A Moriarty	612-823-2205	R	1	<0.1
Biscuit Factory Publications	560 Harrison Ave	Boston	MA	02118	Kevin Sheehan	617-338-4488	S	1 *	<0.1
Laser Disc Headquarters Inc.	670 Auahi St, #A3	Honolulu	HI	96813	Val Lodholm	808-538-3472	R	1	<0.1
Circus Enterprises Inc.	4221 Beulah Rd	Richmond	VA	23237	Paul Suggs	804-275-6923	R	0 *	<0.1
Spectrum Music & Video Store	1881 Crossway	N. Bay Village	FL	33141	Angie Dwynn	305-866-3835	R	0 *	<0.1

Source: *Ward's Business Directory of U.S. Private and Public Companies*, 1998. The company type code used is as follows: P - Public, R - Private, S - Subsidiary, D - Division, J - Joint Venture, A - Affiliate, G - Group. Sales are in millions of dollars, employees are in thousands. An asterisk (*) indicates an estimated sales volume. The symbol < stands for 'less than'.

OCCUPATIONS EMPLOYED BY SIC 573 - APPLIANCE, RADIO, TV, AND MUSIC STORES

Occupation	% of Total 1996	Change to 2006	Occupation	% of Total 1996	Change to 2006
Salespersons, retail	35.3	18.0	Truck drivers light & heavy	2.2	10.7
Marketing & sales worker supervisors	7.7	10.7	Home appliance/power tool repairers	1.8	-0.3
General managers & top executives	6.8	7.3	Mechanics, installers, & repairers nec	1.4	21.8
Cashiers	6.5	12.1	Traffic, shipping, receiving clerks	1.4	10.7
Sales & related workers nec	5.8	21.8	Secretaries, except legal & medical	1.1	-12.2
Stock clerks	5.4	39.3	Blue collar worker supervisors	1.0	6.9
Bookkeeping, accounting, & auditing clerks	2.6	-11.4	Purchasing managers	1.0	-0.3
General office clerks	2.5	-4.7	Wholesale & retail buyers, except farm products	1.0	-8.3
Electronic home entertainment system repairers	2.5	-28.0			

Source: *Industry-Occupation Matrix*, Bureau of Labor Statistics. These data relate to one or more 3-digit SIC industry groups rather than to a single 4-digit SIC. The change reported for each occupation to the year 2006 is a percent of growth or decline as estimated by the Bureau of Labor Statistics. The abbreviation nec stands for 'not elsewhere classified'.

STATE AND REGIONAL CONCENTRATION

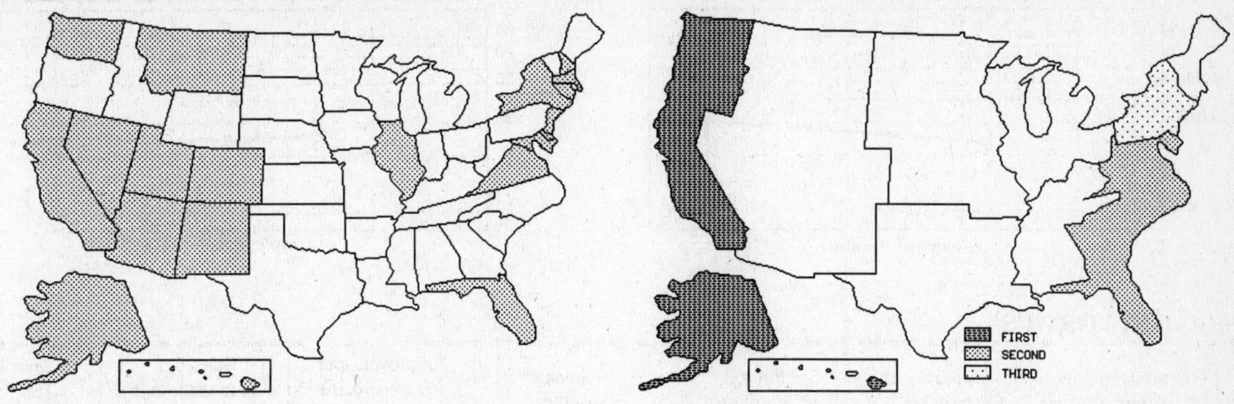

INDUSTRY DATA BY STATE

State	Establishments - 1995 Total (number)	Establishments - 1995 % of U.S.	Employment - 1995 Total (number)	Employment - 1995 % of U.S.	Employment - 1995 Per Estab.	Payroll - 1995 Total ($ mil.)	Payroll - 1995 Per Empl. ($)	Sales - 1992 Total ($ mil.)	Sales - 1992 % of U.S.	Sales - 1992 Per Estab ($)
California	1,114	12.6	14,489	18.6	13	144.8	9,997	1,148.5	20.0	89,145
New York	644	7.3	5,014	6.4	8	59.6	11,883	445.6	7.8	109,809
Texas	510	5.8	5,567	7.1	11	44.7	8,032	335.8	5.8	91,159
Florida	502	5.7	4,172	5.4	8	36.6	8,762	316.9	5.5	103,473
Illinois	416	4.7	3,238	4.2	8	31.0	9,577	294.0	5.1	95,309
Pennsylvania	426	4.8	2,890	3.7	7	27.8	9,612	243.6	4.2	107,988
Ohio	367	4.2	2,881	3.7	8	26.8	9,318	206.0	3.6	105,462
New Jersey	280	3.2	1,783	2.3	6	21.1	11,836	200.2	3.5	111,620
Michigan	299	3.4	2,194	2.8	7	21.9	9,994	184.1	3.2	103,842
Massachusetts	233	2.6	1,856	2.4	8	20.4	11,017	170.2	3.0	112,934
Virginia	243	2.7	1,909	2.5	8	19.5	10,194	158.3	2.8	101,287
Georgia	275	3.1	2,835	3.6	10	30.6	10,789	146.8	2.6	96,951
Washington	183	2.1	1,662	2.1	9	19.2	11,582	135.4	2.4	102,220
Maryland	215	2.4	1,529	2.0	7	14.8	9,700	133.4	2.3	94,487
North Carolina	251	2.8	1,875	2.4	7	16.7	8,907	110.8	1.9	89,671
Tennessee	202	2.3	1,536	2.0	8	14.8	9,614	105.8	1.8	93,740
Wisconsin	144	1.6	1,084	1.4	8	9.6	8,900	100.9	1.8	111,516
Arizona	124	1.4	1,254	1.6	10	12.5	9,935	95.2	1.7	85,801
Connecticut	138	1.6	941	1.2	7	10.7	11,362	89.1	1.6	97,307
Colorado	158	1.8	1,874	2.4	12	15.3	8,176	88.7	1.5	106,680
Indiana	211	2.4	1,319	1.7	6	15.0	11,373	87.8	1.5	95,174
Minnesota	143	1.6	1,399	1.8	10	13.9	9,956	84.0	1.5	85,856
Louisiana	105	1.2	923	1.2	9	7.6	8,195	64.1	1.1	97,342
Oregon	99	1.1	638	0.8	6	8.5	13,331	55.7	1.0	100,451
Hawaii	62	0.7	422	0.5	7	6.5	15,315	54.8	1.0	132,613
South Carolina	118	1.3	760	1.0	6	7.6	10,005	54.6	1.0	84,941
Alabama	105	1.2	675	0.9	6	6.6	9,713	50.8	0.9	98,058
Utah	84	1.0	1,246	1.6	15	16.2	13,007	47.0	0.8	85,176
Oklahoma	74	0.8	1,012	1.3	14	7.7	7,641	46.6	0.8	77,252
Kentucky	103	1.2	677	0.9	7	6.2	9,102	43.8	0.8	96,368
New Mexico	53	0.6	752	1.0	14	6.9	9,207	43.6	0.8	71,202
New Hampshire	57	0.6	330	0.4	6	4.1	12,345	41.5	0.7	131,193
Kansas	70	0.8	715	0.9	10	6.3	8,866	41.2	0.7	80,597
Iowa	98	1.1	533	0.7	5	5.0	9,311	39.3	0.7	90,076
Nevada	43	0.5	470	0.6	11	5.4	11,511	33.6	0.6	104,028
Arkansas	47	0.5	517	0.7	11	4.6	8,807	26.3	0.5	67,202
Mississippi	58	0.7	384	0.5	7	3.4	8,862	24.7	0.4	87,042
Nebraska	55	0.6	360	0.5	7	3.0	8,364	22.6	0.4	88,469
Delaware	28	0.3	229	0.3	8	2.4	10,424	22.2	0.4	108,532
Montana	28	0.3	337	0.4	12	2.8	8,442	20.8	0.4	77,578
West Virginia	47	0.5	301	0.4	6	2.9	9,668	20.5	0.4	97,209
Maine	35	0.4	154	0.2	4	1.6	10,273	19.4	0.3	117,788
Idaho	43	0.5	387	0.5	9	4.3	11,140	18.7	0.3	128,821
Rhode Island	39	0.4	177	0.2	5	2.4	13,768	17.7	0.3	104,609
Alaska	22	0.2	188	0.2	9	2.1	11,133	16.4	0.3	101,537
Vermont	25	0.3	91	0.1	4	1.3	14,000	11.2	0.2	96,655
North Dakota	26	0.3	196	0.3	8	1.6	8,255	10.9	0.2	87,072
South Dakota	26	0.3	174	0.2	7	1.7	9,632	7.8	0.1	92,988
Wyoming	18	0.2	127	0.2	7	1.0	8,039	5.4	0.1	75,639
Missouri	159	1.8	1,341	1.7	8	12.5	9,306	(D)	-	-
D.C.	37	0.4	477	0.6	13	4.7	9,864	(D)	-	-

Source: County Business Patterns, 1995 and *Economic Census of the U.S., 1992*. Data are sorted by 1992 revenues and, if revenues are unavailable, by establishments in 1995. The symbol (D) indicates that data are withheld by the source to avoid disclosure of competitive information. A dash (-) indicates that data are not available or undisclosed because they do not meet statistical validity standards. Shaded *states* on the state map indicate those states which have proportionately greater representation in the industry than would be indicated by the state's population; the ratio is based on total revenues or number of establishments. Shaded *regions* indicate where the industry is regionally most concentrated.

5736 - MUSICAL INSTRUMENT STORES

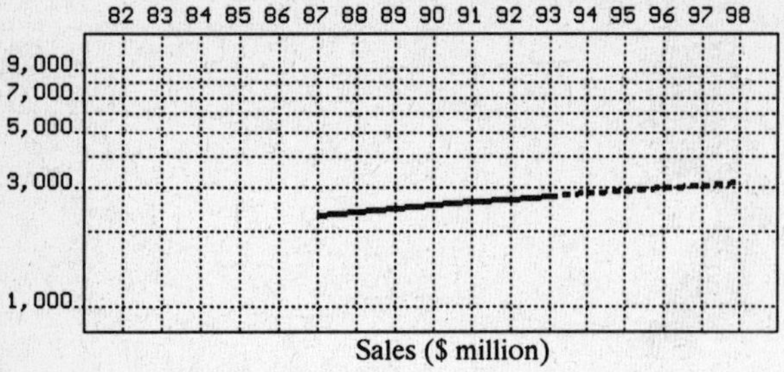

Sales ($ million)

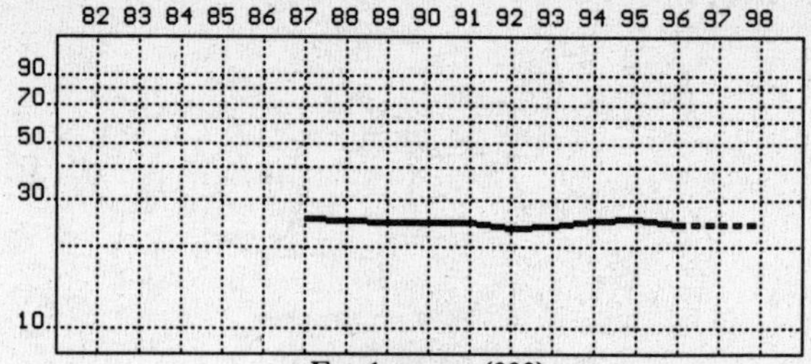

Employment (000)

GENERAL STATISTICS

Year	Establishments (number)	Employment (number)	Payroll ($ million)	Sales ($ million)	Employees per Establishment (number)	Sales per Establishment ($)	Payroll per Employee ($)
1982	-	-	-	-	-	-	-
1983	-	-	-	-	-	-	-
1984	-	-	-	-	-	-	-
1985	-	-	-	-	-	-	-
1986	-	-	-	-	-	-	-
1987	4,690	25,748	351.9	2,321.2	5	494,925	13,665
1988	4,406	25,133	383.2	2,393.9*e*	6	-	15,249
1989	4,224	24,660	386.1	2,466.7*e*	6	-	15,659
1990	4,253	24,854	404.6	2,539.4*e*	6	-	16,278
1991	4,270	24,853	410.8	2,612.1*e*	6	-	16,529
1992	4,149	23,605	402.6	2,684.8	6	647,107	17,054
1993	4,142	23,979	429.0	2,757.6*p*	6	-	17,892
1994	4,138	24,916	462.9	2,830.3*p*	6	-	18,579
1995	4,097	25,749	501.2	2,903.0*p*	6	-	19,463
1996	3,976*p*	24,562*p*	491.4*p*	2,975.8*p*	-	-	-
1997	3,919*p*	24,507*p*	506.7*p*	3,048.5*p*	-	-	-
1998	3,861*p*	24,453*p*	522.0*p*	3,121.2*p*	-	-	-

Sources: *Economic Census of the United States*, 1982, 1987, and 1992. Establishment counts, employment, and payroll are from *County Business Patterns* for non-Census years. Values followed by a 'p' are projections by the editors. Sales and expense data for non-Census years are extrapolations, marked by 'e'. Industries reclassified in 1987 will not have data for prior years. Data are the most recent available at this level of detail.

INDICES OF CHANGE

Year	Establishments (number)	Employment (number)	Payroll ($ million)	Sales ($ million)	Employees per Establishment (number)	Sales per Establishment ($)	Payroll per Employee ($)
1982	-	-	-	-	-	-	-
1983	-	-	-	-	-	-	-
1984	-	-	-	-	-	-	-
1985	-	-	-	-	-	-	-
1986	-	-	-	-	-	-	-
1987	113.0	109.1	87.4	86.5	83.3	76.5	80.1
1988	106.2	106.5	95.2	89.2*e*	100.0	-	89.4
1989	101.8	104.5	95.9	91.9*e*	100.0	-	91.8
1990	102.5	105.3	100.5	94.6*e*	100.0	-	95.4
1991	102.9	105.3	102.0	97.3*e*	100.0	-	96.9
1992	100.0	100.0	100.0	100.0	100.0	100.0	100.0
1993	99.8	101.6	106.6	102.7*p*	96.5	-	104.9
1994	99.7	105.6	115.0	105.4*p*	100.4	-	108.9
1995	98.7	109.1	124.5	108.1*p*	104.7	-	114.1
1996	95.8*p*	104.1*p*	122.0*p*	110.8*p*	-	-	-
1997	94.5*p*	103.8*p*	125.9*p*	113.5*p*	-	-	-
1998	93.1*p*	103.6*p*	129.7*p*	116.3*p*	-	-	-

Sources: Same as General Statistics. The values shown reflect change from the base year, 1992. Values above 100 mean greater than 1992, values below 100 mean less than 1992, and a value of 100 in the 1982-91 or 1993-98 period means same as 1992. Values followed by a 'p' are projections by the editors; 'e' stands for extrapolation. Data are the most recent available at this level of detail.

SELECTED RATIOS

For 1992	Avg. of All Retail	Analyzed Industry	Index	For 1992	Avg. of All Retail	Analyzed Industry	Index
Employees per Establishment	12	6	47	Sales per Employee	102,941	113,739	110
Payroll per Establishment	146,026	97,035	66	Sales per Establishment	1,241,555	647,096	52
Payroll per Employee	12,107	17,056	141	Expenses per Establishment	na	na	na

Sources: Same as General Statistics. The 'Average of All Manufacturing' column represents the average of all manufacturing industries reported for the most recent complete year available. The Index shows the relationship between the Average and the Analyzed Industry. For example, 100 means that they are equal; 500 that the Analyzed Industry is five times the average; 50 means that the Analyzed Industry is half the national average. The abbreviation 'na' is used to show that data are 'not available'.

LEADING COMPANIES

Number shown: **19** Total sales ($ mil): **864** Total employment (000): **5.0**

Company Name	Address				CEO Name	Phone	Co. Type	Sales ($ mil)	Empl. (000)
Guitar Center Inc.	5155 Clareton Dr	Agoura Hills	CA	91301	Larry Thomas	818-735-8800	P	297	1.4
Sam Ash Music Corp.	PO Box 9047	Hicksville	NY	11802	Richard Ash	516-932-6400	R	250	0.8
Waxie Maxie Quality Music Co.	205 Fortune Blvd	Milford	MA	01757	Izan Lipton	508-478-2031	S	45 *	0.3
Schmitt Music Co.	88 S 10th St	Minneapolis	MN	55403	Tom Schmitt	612-339-4811	R	35	0.4
J.R.'s Music Shops of Hawaii	710 Kakoi St	Honolulu	HI	96819	Bob Kennedy	808-837-7800	R	25 *	0.2
Fletcher Music Centers Inc.	3966 Airway Cir	Clearwater	FL	34622	John Riley	813-571-1088	R	24	0.2
Jordan-Kitt Music Inc.	9520 Baltimore	College Park	MD	20740	WJ McCormick Jr	301-474-9500	R	22	0.5
Sherman, Clay and Co.	851 Traeger Ave	San Bruno	CA	94066	Fred Concklin	415-952-2300	R	22 *	0.2
Washington Music Sales Center	11151 Viers Mill Rd	Wheaton	MD	20902	Charles L Levin	301-946-8808	R	21	<0.1
Music and Arts Center Inc.	12312 Wilkins Ave	Rockville	MD	20852	Ken O'Brien	301-881-7760	R	20	0.3
H and H Music Co.	11522 Old Katy Rd	Houston	TX	77043	Clyde W Reynolds	713-531-9222	R	16	0.1
Midco International Inc.	PO Box 748	Effingham	IL	62401	LD Samuel	217-342-9211	R	15	<0.1
Spitzer Music Management Co.	1859 Sabre St	Hayward	CA	94545	Matt Spitzer	510-785-4280	R	15	<0.1
J.W. Pepper and Son Inc.	PO Box 850	Valley Forge	PA	19482	Ron Rowe	215-648-0500	R	13 *	0.1
Mark 21 Inc.	PO Box 82838	San Diego	CA	92138	Robert Hill	619-296-0292	R	12 *	<0.1
E.E. Forbes and Sons Piano	1914 4th Ave N	Birmingham	AL	35203	French Forbes Jr	205-251-4154	R	11	<0.1
Manny's Music	156 W 48th St	New York	NY	10036	Manny Henry	212-819-0576	R	10 *	<0.1
Theodore Presser Co.	1 Presser Pl	Bryn Mawr	PA	19010	Thomas Broido	610-525-3636	R	6 *	<0.1
Paragon Music Center Inc.	2119 Hillsborough	Tampa	FL	33603	Dick Rumore	813-876-3459	R	5	<0.1

Source: *Ward's Business Directory of U.S. Private and Public Companies*, 1998. The company type code used is as follows: P - Public, R - Private, S - Subsidiary, D - Division, J - Joint Venture, A - Affiliate, G - Group. Sales are in millions of dollars, employees are in thousands. An asterisk (*) indicates an estimated sales volume. The symbol < stands for 'less than'.

OCCUPATIONS EMPLOYED BY SIC 573 - APPLIANCE, RADIO, TV, AND MUSIC STORES

Occupation	% of Total 1996	Change to 2006	Occupation	% of Total 1996	Change to 2006
Salespersons, retail	35.3	18.0	Truck drivers light & heavy	2.2	10.7
Marketing & sales worker supervisors	7.7	10.7	Home appliance/power tool repairers	1.8	-0.3
General managers & top executives	6.8	7.3	Mechanics, installers, & repairers nec	1.4	21.8
Cashiers	6.5	12.1	Traffic, shipping, receiving clerks	1.4	10.7
Sales & related workers nec	5.8	21.8	Secretaries, except legal & medical	1.1	-12.2
Stock clerks	5.4	39.3	Blue collar worker supervisors	1.0	6.9
Bookkeeping, accounting, & auditing clerks	2.6	-11.4	Purchasing managers	1.0	-0.3
General office clerks	2.5	-4.7	Wholesale & retail buyers, except farm products	1.0	-8.3
Electronic home entertainment system repairers	2.5	-28.0			

Source: *Industry-Occupation Matrix*, Bureau of Labor Statistics. These data relate to one or more 3-digit SIC industry groups rather than to a single 4-digit SIC. The change reported for each occupation to the year 2006 is a percent of growth or decline as estimated by the Bureau of Labor Statistics. The abbreviation nec stands for 'not elsewhere classified'.

STATE AND REGIONAL CONCENTRATION

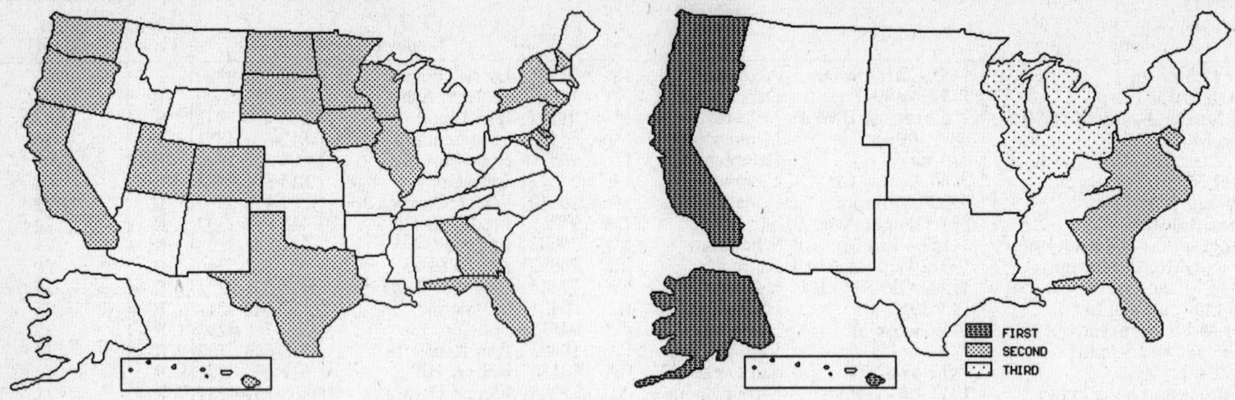

INDUSTRY DATA BY STATE

State	Establishments - 1995 Total (number)	Establishments - 1995 % of U.S.	Employment - 1995 Total (number)	Employment - 1995 % of U.S.	Employment - 1995 Per Estab.	Payroll - 1995 Total ($ mil.)	Payroll - 1995 Per Empl. ($)	Sales - 1992 Total ($ mil.)	Sales - 1992 % of U.S.	Sales - 1992 Per Estab ($)
California	486	11.9	2,742	10.7	6	51.8	18,873	381.7	14.5	131,495
New York	208	5.1	1,299	5.1	6	30.4	23,433	211.9	8.0	181,723
Texas	242	5.9	1,772	6.9	7	36.9	20,817	186.8	7.1	108,819
Florida	236	5.8	1,353	5.3	6	27.5	20,289	159.3	6.0	130,671
Illinois	191	4.7	1,291	5.0	7	23.7	18,350	131.0	5.0	112,161
Pennsylvania	177	4.3	1,088	4.2	6	24.8	22,816	99.1	3.8	109,952
Ohio	175	4.3	1,014	3.9	6	16.7	16,474	93.9	3.6	100,149
New Jersey	97	2.4	684	2.7	7	16.2	23,662	93.4	3.5	152,138
Michigan	131	3.2	1,117	4.3	9	22.1	19,803	90.0	3.4	100,285
Maryland	79	1.9	739	2.9	9	15.9	21,512	89.7	3.4	138,611
Georgia	102	2.5	583	2.3	6	13.6	23,400	76.6	2.9	141,791
Washington	135	3.3	834	3.2	6	17.3	20,753	72.5	2.8	100,296
Wisconsin	78	1.9	825	3.2	11	13.7	16,647	62.8	2.4	92,410
Minnesota	79	1.9	654	2.5	8	12.2	18,709	60.5	2.3	101,271
North Carolina	119	2.9	580	2.3	5	10.5	18,031	56.3	2.1	95,633
Massachusetts	95	2.3	508	2.0	5	10.2	20,085	51.5	2.0	104,402
Virginia	111	2.7	561	2.2	5	10.1	17,923	50.0	1.9	97,586
Indiana	95	2.3	574	2.2	6	10.2	17,800	47.5	1.8	89,019
Tennessee	106	2.6	561	2.2	5	12.1	21,631	47.5	1.8	102,484
Colorado	77	1.9	420	1.6	5	7.6	18,121	42.7	1.6	111,846
Arizona	65	1.6	381	1.5	6	8.1	21,231	39.8	1.5	124,658
Oregon	76	1.9	372	1.4	5	7.4	19,763	35.5	1.3	100,181
Connecticut	60	1.5	277	1.1	5	5.3	19,011	33.3	1.3	135,504
Iowa	56	1.4	410	1.6	7	8.5	20,680	31.1	1.2	79,023
South Carolina	58	1.4	341	1.3	6	6.0	17,727	30.4	1.2	93,006
Louisiana	50	1.2	319	1.2	6	5.9	18,461	29.4	1.1	98,782
Alabama	57	1.4	331	1.3	6	5.9	17,952	29.0	1.1	90,750
Oklahoma	52	1.3	253	1.0	5	5.0	19,870	28.4	1.1	110,623
Utah	46	1.1	368	1.4	8	6.5	17,582	28.1	1.1	101,419
Kentucky	58	1.4	334	1.3	6	5.2	15,605	27.2	1.0	99,652
Kansas	51	1.2	380	1.5	7	5.4	14,147	25.9	1.0	82,652
West Virginia	27	0.7	247	1.0	9	3.5	14,109	16.0	0.6	68,333
Hawaii	16	0.4	113	0.4	7	2.2	19,531	15.9	0.6	123,628
Nebraska	27	0.7	184	0.7	7	2.6	14,049	15.4	0.6	79,596
Arkansas	46	1.1	184	0.7	4	3.2	17,538	14.1	0.5	82,234
South Dakota	19	0.5	147	0.6	8	2.6	17,605	14.0	0.5	99,135
New Mexico	29	0.7	160	0.6	6	3.2	19,912	13.4	0.5	103,876
Nevada	19	0.5	148	0.6	8	3.5	23,730	12.8	0.5	96,429
New Hampshire	24	0.6	105	0.4	4	1.8	17,448	12.8	0.5	146,793
Mississippi	26	0.6	183	0.7	7	2.7	14,874	12.4	0.5	79,248
North Dakota	15	0.4	172	0.7	11	3.0	17,471	12.2	0.5	93,389
Maine	18	0.4	94	0.4	5	1.6	17,372	9.9	0.4	93,670
Idaho	22	0.5	114	0.4	5	1.9	16,553	9.6	0.4	107,122
Delaware	8	0.2	46	0.2	6	1.1	23,304	9.1	0.3	121,800
Montana	20	0.5	87	0.3	4	1.1	12,172	7.3	0.3	90,630
Rhode Island	13	0.3	89	0.3	7	1.3	15,000	6.9	0.3	101,162
Alaska	13	0.3	65	0.3	5	0.8	11,677	5.8	0.2	99,759
Vermont	10	0.2	42	0.2	4	1.0	24,190	3.0	0.1	89,706
Wyoming	10	0.2	20-99	-	-	(D)	-	2.4	0.1	71,471
Missouri	85	2.1	553	2.2	7	10.8	19,470	(D)	-	-
D.C.	2	0.0	0-19	-	-	(D)	-	(D)	-	-

Source: *County Business Patterns, 1995* and *Economic Census of the U.S., 1992*. Data are sorted by 1992 revenues and, if revenues are unavailable, by establishments in 1995. The symbol (D) indicates that data are withheld by the source to avoid disclosure of competitive information. A dash (-) indicates that data are not available or undisclosed because they do not meet statistical validity standards. Shaded *states* on the state map indicate those states which have proportionately greater representation in the industry than would be indicated by the state's population; the ratio is based on total revenues or number of establishments. Shaded *regions* indicate where the industry is regionally most concentrated.

5812 - EATING PLACES

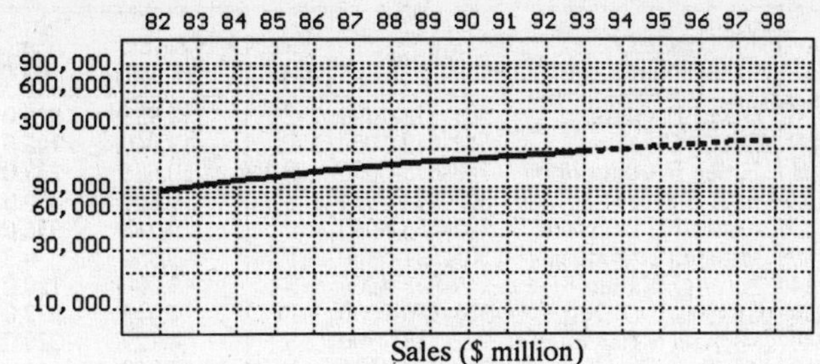

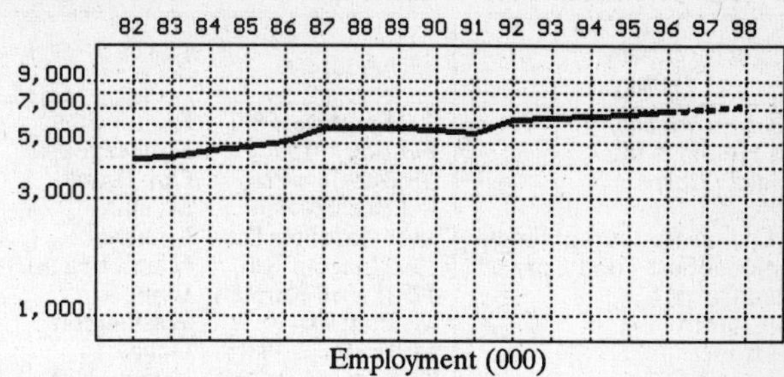

GENERAL STATISTICS

Year	Establishments (number)	Employment (number)	Payroll ($ million)	Sales ($ million)	Employees per Establishment (number)	Sales per Establishment ($)	Payroll per Employee ($)
1982	284,059	4,340,832	23,987.0	93,158.3	15	327,954	5,526
1983	282,597	4,407,936	27,342.6	102,382.9*e*	16	-	6,203
1984	282,386	4,682,469	29,963.6	111,607.6*e*	17	-	6,399
1985	281,470	4,879,026	32,443.3	120,832.3*e*	17	-	6,650
1986	289,522	5,087,460	34,428.5	130,056.9*e*	18	-	6,767
1987	332,611	5,786,889	36,632.7	139,281.6	17	418,752	6,330
1988	317,800	5,762,385	40,711.8	148,265.9*e*	18	-	7,065
1989	303,380	5,803,007	42,261.1	157,250.2*e*	19	-	7,283
1990	286,792	5,700,302	43,844.7	166,234.6*e*	20	-	7,692
1991	280,200	5,459,716	44,033.8	175,218.9*e*	19	-	8,065
1992	377,760	6,243,862	50,306.7	184,203.2	17	487,620	8,057
1993	360,212	6,345,979	53,858.3	193,580.8*p*	18	-	8,487
1994	367,205	6,476,992	56,677.6	202,685.3*p*	18	-	8,751
1995	344,854	6,568,154	58,742.0	211,789.8*p*	19	-	8,943
1996	361,385*p*	6,822,705*p*	60,634.4*p*	220,894.3*p*	-	-	-
1997	367,752*p*	6,993,875*p*	63,240.6*p*	229,998.8*p*	-	-	-
1998	374,119*p*	7,165,045*p*	65,846.8*p*	239,103.3*p*	-	-	-

Sources: *Economic Census of the United States*, 1982, 1987, and 1992. Establishment counts, employment, and payroll are from *County Business Patterns* for non-Census years. Values followed by a 'p' are projections by the editors. Sales and expense data for non-Census years are extrapolations, marked by 'e'. Industries reclassified in 1987 will not have data for prior years. Data are the most recent available at this level of detail.

INDICES OF CHANGE

Year	Establishments (number)	Employment (number)	Payroll ($ million)	Sales ($ million)	Employees per Establishment (number)	Sales per Establishment ($)	Payroll per Employee ($)
1982	75.2	69.5	47.7	50.6	88.2	67.3	68.6
1983	74.8	70.6	54.4	55.6*e*	94.1	-	77.0
1984	74.8	75.0	59.6	60.6*e*	100.0	-	79.4
1985	74.5	78.1	64.5	65.6*e*	100.0	-	82.5
1986	76.6	81.5	68.4	70.6*e*	105.9	-	84.0
1987	88.0	92.7	72.8	75.6	100.0	85.9	78.6
1988	84.1	92.3	80.9	80.5*e*	105.9	-	87.7
1989	80.3	92.9	84.0	85.4*e*	111.8	-	90.4
1990	75.9	91.3	87.2	90.2*e*	117.6	-	95.5
1991	74.2	87.4	87.5	95.1*e*	111.8	-	100.1
1992	100.0	100.0	100.0	100.0	100.0	100.0	100.0
1993	95.4	101.6	107.1	105.1*p*	103.6	-	105.3
1994	97.2	103.7	112.7	110.0*p*	103.8	-	108.6
1995	91.3	105.2	116.8	115.0*p*	112.0	-	111.0
1996	95.7*p*	109.3*p*	120.5*p*	119.9*p*	-	-	-
1997	97.4*p*	112.0*p*	125.7*p*	124.9*p*	-	-	-
1998	99.0*p*	114.8*p*	130.9*p*	129.8*p*	-	-	-

Sources: Same as General Statistics. The values shown reflect change from the base year, 1992. Values above 100 mean greater than 1992, values below 100 mean less than 1992, and a value of 100 in the 1982-91 or 1993-98 period means same as 1992. Values followed by a 'p' are projections by the editors; 'e' stands for extrapolation. Data are the most recent available at this level of detail.

SELECTED RATIOS

For 1992	Avg. of All Retail	Analyzed Industry	Index	For 1992	Avg. of All Retail	Analyzed Industry	Index
Employees per Establishment	12	17	137	Sales per Employee	102,941	29,501	29
Payroll per Establishment	146,026	133,171	91	Sales per Establishment	1,241,555	487,620	39
Payroll per Employee	12,107	8,057	67	Expenses per Establishment	na	na	na

Sources: Same as General Statistics. The 'Average of All Manufacturing' column represents the average of all manufacturing industries reported for the most recent complete year available. The Index shows the relationship between the Average and the Analyzed Industry. For example, 100 means that they are equal; 500 that the Analyzed Industry is five times the average; 50 means that the Analyzed Industry is half the national average. The abbreviation 'na' is used to show that data are 'not available'.

LEADING COMPANIES

Number shown: **50** Total sales ($ mil): **230,256** Total employment (000): **3,359.2**

Company Name	Address				CEO Name	Phone	Co. Type	Sales ($ mil)	Empl. (000)
Wal-Mart Stores Inc.	702 Southwest 8th	Bentonville	AR	72716	David D Glass	501-273-4000	P	117,958	825.0
Carlson Holdings Inc.	PO Box 59159	Minneapolis	MN	55459	Curtis Carlson	612-449-1000	R	13,040	145.0
McDonald's Corp.	McDonald's Plz	Oak Brook	IL	60521	James R Cantalupo	708-575-3000	P	10,686	237.0
Burger King Corp.	PO Box 020783	Miami	FL	33102	Paul Clayton	305-378-7011	S	9,800	300.0
Tricon Global Restaurants Inc.	1441 Gardiner Lane	Louisville	KY	40213	Andrall E Pearson	502-456-8080	P	9,738	336.0
International Fast Food Corp.	1000 Lincoln Rd	Miami Beach	FL	33139	Mitchell Rubinson	305-531-5800	P	5,351	0.3
Taco Bell Corp.	17901 Von Karman	Irvine	CA	92714	Peter C Waller	949-863-4500	S	5,000	120.0
Marriott Intern.	Marriott Dr	Washington	DC	20058	Charles P O'Dell	301-380-9000	D	4,443 *	72.0
Pizza Hut Inc.	14841 Dallas Pkwy	Dallas	TX	75240	Michael S Rawlings	972-338-7700	S	4,129	220.0
Hilton Hotels Corp.	9336 Civic Ctr Dr	Beverly Hills	CA	90210	S F Bollenbach	310-278-4321	P	3,940	65.0
GMRI Inc.	5900 Lake Ellenor	Orlando	FL	32809	Joe R Lee	407-245-4000	S	2,963	107.5
Domino's Pizza Inc.	PO Box 997	Ann Arbor	MI	48106	Thomas Monaghan	313-930-3030	R	2,400 *	20.0
Kentucky Fried Chicken Corp.	PO Box 32070	Louisville	KY	40232	Jeffrey A Moody	502-874-8300	S	2,300	66.0
Viad Corp.	1850 N Central Ave	Phoenix	AZ	85077	Robert H Bohannon	602-207-4000	P	2,263	24.8
Wendy's International Inc.	PO Box 256	Dublin	OH	43017	Gordon F Teter	614-764-3100	P	2,037	50.0
A and W Restaurants Inc.	1 A annd W Drive	Farmington	MI	48331	sid Feltenstein	248-462-2000	S	1,816	<0.1
Ogden Services Corp.	2 Penn Plz	New York	NY	10121	R Richard Ablon	212-868-6000	S	1,750	39.0
Harrah's Entertainment Inc.	1023 Cherry Rd	Memphis	TN	38117	Philip G Satre	901-762-8600	P	1,619	23.4
Brinker International Inc.	6820 LBJ Fwy	Dallas	TX	75240	R A McDougall	972-980-9917	P	1,335	47.0
Friday's Hospitality Worldwide	PO Box 809062	Dallas	TX	75380	Wallace B Doolin	972-450-5400	S	1,317	42.5
America's Favorite Chicken Co.	6 Concourse NE	Atlanta	GA	30328	Frank Velatti	770-391-9500	R	1,240 *	13.4
Stouffer Corp.	29800 Bainbridge	Solon	OH	44139	James Dintaman	216-248-3600	S	1,210	21.0
Shoney's Inc.	PO Box 1260	Nashville	TN	37202	J Michael Bodnar	615-391-5201	P	1,203	3.3
Delaware North Companies	438 Main St	Buffalo	NY	14202	Jeremy M Jacobs	716-858-5000	R	1,200	35.0
Host Marriott Services Corp.	10400 Fernwood Rd	Bethesda	MD	20817	W. M McCarten	301-380-7000	P	1,160	22.4
Little Caesar Enterprises Inc.	2211 Woodward	Detroit	MI	48201	Michael Ilitch	313-983-6000	R	1,160	86.0
Cracker Barrel Old Country	PO Box 787	Lebanon	TN	37088	Dan W Evins	615-444-5533	P	1,124	35.8
Valhi Inc.	5430 LBJ Fwy	Dallas	TX	75240	Harold C Simmons	972-233-1700	P	1,093	2.6
El Pollo Loco	PO Box 15390	Irvine	CA	92713		714-251-5000	S	1,090	2.8
Truckstops of America Inc.	24601 Ctr Ridge Rd	Westlake	OH	44145	Ed Kuhn	440-808-9100	S	1,067 *	5.0
Jack in the Box Div.	9330 Balboa Ave	San Diego	CA	92123	Robert J Nugent	619-571-2121	D	1,026	33.7
Caterair International Corp.	6550 Rock Spring	Bethesda	MD	20817	Daniel Altobello	301-897-7800	R	1,000	10.0
Metromedia Restaurant Group	12404 Pk Central	Dallas	TX	75251	Michael S Kaufman	214-404-5000	R	990 *	30.0
Outback Steakhouse Inc.	550 N Reo St, #200	Tampa	FL	33609	Chris T Sullivan	813-282-1225	P	937	23.0
Wackenhut Corp.	4200 Wackenhut Dr	P Bch Gardens	FL	33410	G R Wackenhut	407-622-5656	P	906	50.0
Bob Evans Farms Inc.	PO Box 07863	Columbus	OH	43207	Daniel E Evans	614-491-2225	P	822	27.5
Buffets Inc.	10260 Viking Dr	Eden Prairie	MN	55344	Roe H Hatlen	612-942-9760	P	809	24.8
Dobbs International Services	5100 Poplar Ave	Memphis	TN	38137	Fred J Martin	901-766-3784	S	745 *	11.8
Franchise Finance Corporation	17207 N Perimeter	Scottsdale	AZ	85255	MH Fleischer	602-585-4500	3	724 *	<0.1
Aramark Sports	1101 Market St	Philadelphia	PA	19107	Charles Gillespie	215-238-3000	S	700	7.0
Family Restaurants Inc.	18831 Von Karman	Irvine	CA	92715	Kevin Relyea	714-852-5700	R	700	25.5
Casino USA Inc.	4700 S Boyle Ave	Vernon	CA	90058	Robert J Emmons	213-589-1054	S	672	2.3
Ruby Tuesday Inc.	4721 Morrison Dr	Mobile	AL	36609	III, Sandy E Beall	334-344-3000	P	654	24.4
Friendly Ice Cream Corp.	1855 Boston Rd	Wilbraham	MA	01095	Donald Smith	413-543-2400	R	650 *	25.0
Long John Silver's Restaurants	PO Box 11988	Lexington	KY	40579	Rolf Towe	606-263-6000	R	646 *	20.0
Flagstar Enterprises Inc.	203 E Main St	Spartanburg	SC	29319	James B Adamson	803-597-8000	S	607	28.3
Ryan's Family Steak Houses	PO Box 100	Greer	SC	29652	Charles D Way	864-879-1000	P	599	18.0
CKE Restaurants Inc.	PO Box 4349	Anaheim	CA	92803	William P Foley	714-774-5796	P	588	11.1
Galpin Motors Inc.	15505 Roscoe Blvd	North Hills	CA	91343	Bert Boeckmann	818-787-3800	R	533	0.7
Applebee's International Inc.	4551 W 107th St	Overland Park	KS	66207	Lloyd L Hill	913-967-4000	P	516	18.1

Source: Ward's Business Directory of U.S. Private and Public Companies, 1998. The company type code used is as follows: P - Public, R - Private, S - Subsidiary, D - Division, J - Joint Venture, A - Affiliate, G - Group. Sales are in millions of dollars, employees are in thousands. An asterisk (*) indicates an estimated sales volume. The symbol < stands for 'less than'.

OCCUPATIONS EMPLOYED BY SIC 581 - EATING AND DRINKING PLACES

Occupation	% of Total 1996	Change to 2006	Occupation	% of Total 1996	Change to 2006
Waiters & waitresses	21.7	6.9	Dining room, bar, cafeteria attendants	3.7	9.9
Food counter, fountain workers	17.4	12.4	Food service & lodging managers	3.5	44.1
Cooks, short order & fast food	9.9	21.9	Bartenders	3.5	1.8
Food preparation workers	8.4	31.0	Hosts & hostesses, restaurant, lounge	2.5	8.1
Cooks, restaurant	7.9	19.6	General managers & top executives	2.2	16.4
Cashiers	7.5	33.3	Janitors & cleaners, maids	1.2	-3.9
Service workers nec	3.9	62.1	Driver/sales workers	1.1	20.1

Source: Industry-Occupation Matrix, Bureau of Labor Statistics. These data relate to one or more 3-digit SIC industry groups rather than to a single 4-digit SIC. The change reported for each occupation to the year 2006 is a percent of growth or decline as estimated by the Bureau of Labor Statistics. The abbreviation nec stands for 'not elsewhere classified'.

STATE AND REGIONAL CONCENTRATION

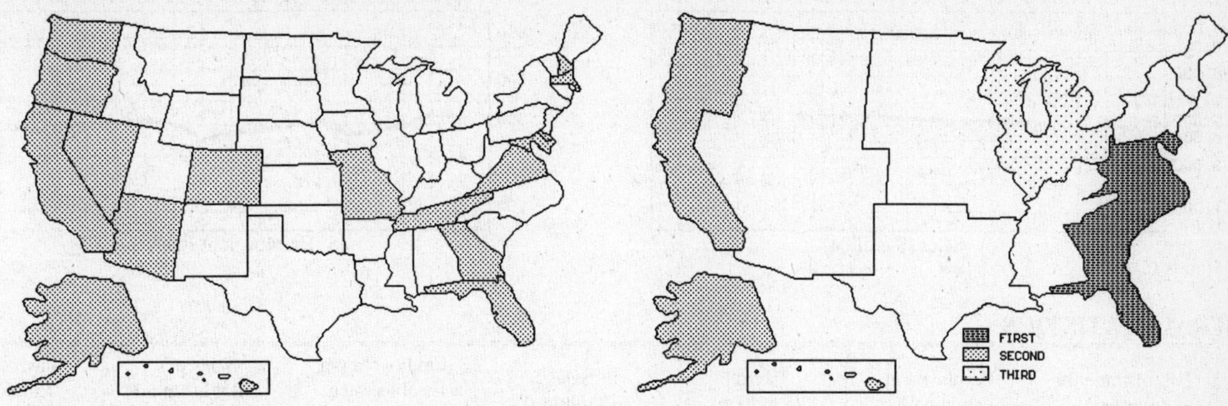

INDUSTRY DATA BY STATE

State	Establishments - 1995 Total (number)	Establishments - 1995 % of U.S.	Employment - 1995 Total (number)	Employment - 1995 % of U.S.	Employment - 1995 Per Estab.	Payroll - 1995 Total ($ mil.)	Payroll - 1995 Per Empl. ($)	Sales - 1992 Total ($ mil.)	Sales - 1992 % of U.S.	Sales - 1992 Per Estab ($)
California	42,803	12.4	745,982	11.4	17	7,220.3	9,679	24,340.8	13.2	32,205
Texas	21,244	6.2	452,689	6.9	21	4,085.7	9,025	12,701.1	6.9	30,399
New York	25,842	7.5	344,508	5.2	13	3,815.2	11,074	12,039.9	6.5	35,517
Florida	16,807	4.9	389,116	5.9	23	3,494.1	8,980	11,521.8	6.3	30,395
Illinois	15,858	4.6	298,905	4.6	19	2,709.2	9,064	8,402.4	4.6	29,260
Ohio	14,849	4.3	319,937	4.9	22	2,564.1	8,014	7,909.0	4.3	26,679
Pennsylvania	15,583	4.5	270,977	4.1	17	2,292.1	8,459	7,499.1	4.1	28,136
Michigan	11,385	3.3	244,259	3.7	21	1,997.5	8,178	6,457.7	3.5	26,811
Georgia	8,504	2.5	196,442	3.0	23	1,692.1	8,614	5,212.4	2.8	28,913
New Jersey	11,010	3.2	150,071	2.3	14	1,649.5	10,991	5,188.1	2.8	36,141
Massachusetts	8,931	2.6	151,903	2.3	17	1,600.0	10,533	5,093.2	2.8	32,819
North Carolina	8,901	2.6	189,120	2.9	21	1,594.0	8,428	4,929.6	2.7	27,868
Virginia	9,004	2.6	172,372	2.6	19	1,557.1	9,034	4,664.2	2.5	29,506
Indiana	8,068	2.3	173,844	2.6	22	1,389.8	7,994	4,092.1	2.2	26,046
Washington	8,291	2.4	144,443	2.2	17	1,356.3	9,390	4,074.8	2.2	29,677
Missouri	6,636	1.9	143,521	2.2	22	1,219.6	8,498	3,818.4	2.1	26,721
Maryland	6,403	1.9	124,452	1.9	19	1,177.5	9,461	3,715.5	2.0	31,076
Tennessee	5,989	1.7	142,023	2.2	24	1,211.0	8,527	3,688.3	2.0	29,434
Wisconsin	6,409	1.9	134,710	2.1	21	1,003.9	7,452	3,203.0	1.7	23,883
Minnesota	6,064	1.8	127,572	1.9	21	1,081.6	8,478	3,134.6	1.7	25,342
Colorado	5,307	1.5	117,551	1.8	22	1,060.9	9,025	2,886.5	1.6	27,409
Arizona	5,787	1.7	121,391	1.8	21	1,026.8	8,459	2,819.3	1.5	27,370
South Carolina	4,399	1.3	96,874	1.5	22	788.9	8,143	2,563.6	1.4	27,794
Louisiana	4,135	1.2	95,394	1.5	23	802.6	8,413	2,562.7	1.4	26,912
Kentucky	4,541	1.3	102,489	1.6	23	818.4	7,985	2,475.5	1.3	27,559
Alabama	4,304	1.2	97,789	1.5	23	722.4	7,387	2,428.9	1.3	28,203
Connecticut	4,564	1.3	67,821	1.0	15	698.3	10,297	2,349.9	1.3	33,409
Oregon	5,216	1.5	89,007	1.4	17	797.2	8,957	2,309.7	1.3	28,619
Oklahoma	4,694	1.4	84,402	1.3	18	665.4	7,884	2,096.8	1.1	27,341
Hawaii	2,117	0.6	43,559	0.7	21	537.7	12,344	1,745.6	0.9	37,683
Iowa	4,214	1.2	75,465	1.1	18	549.7	7,284	1,672.8	0.9	23,130
Kansas	3,834	1.1	72,063	1.1	19	546.2	7,579	1,658.1	0.9	25,340
Arkansas	3,115	0.9	55,712	0.8	18	411.0	7,377	1,302.1	0.7	27,504
Mississippi	2,428	0.7	50,243	0.8	21	364.0	7,244	1,184.0	0.6	26,960
New Mexico	2,387	0.7	46,667	0.7	20	387.5	8,304	1,142.9	0.6	27,837
Utah	2,566	0.7	51,664	0.8	20	402.9	7,799	1,095.4	0.6	25,385
Nevada	1,989	0.6	38,878	0.6	20	391.7	10,075	1,040.0	0.6	33,020
Nebraska	2,422	0.7	45,908	0.7	19	348.0	7,581	1,037.9	0.6	23,518
D.C.	1,308	0.4	25,233	0.4	19	350.3	13,881	982.3	0.5	39,753
West Virginia	2,183	0.6	37,635	0.6	17	294.9	7,835	914.8	0.5	27,374
New Hampshire	1,978	0.6	30,510	0.5	15	291.0	9,539	861.4	0.5	30,787
Maine	2,087	0.6	28,371	0.4	14	271.1	9,554	833.1	0.5	32,250
Rhode Island	1,727	0.5	25,203	0.4	15	237.2	9,413	704.1	0.4	31,237
Idaho	1,672	0.5	28,972	0.4	17	211.5	7,299	607.0	0.3	25,118
Delaware	1,101	0.3	21,303	0.3	19	200.2	9,399	605.8	0.3	31,382
Alaska	918	0.3	12,771	0.2	14	180.1	14,104	562.9	0.3	45,630
Montana	1,546	0.4	23,725	0.4	15	177.3	7,475	551.7	0.3	25,791
South Dakota	1,131	0.3	19,198	0.3	17	138.6	7,222	422.4	0.2	24,100
Vermont	928	0.3	14,678	0.2	16	130.1	8,864	419.7	0.2	28,259
North Dakota	919	0.3	16,885	0.3	18	116.7	6,909	352.9	0.2	22,304
Wyoming	756	0.2	13,947	0.2	18	112.7	8,083	327.2	0.2	25,800

Source: County Business Patterns, 1995 and *Economic Census of the U.S., 1992*. Data are sorted by 1992 revenues and, if revenues are unavailable, by establishments in 1995. The symbol (D) indicates that data are withheld by the source to avoid disclosure of competitive information. A dash (-) indicates that data are not available or undisclosed because they do not meet statistical validity standards. Shaded *states* on the state map indicate those states which have proportionately greater representation in the industry than would be indicated by the state's population; the ratio is based on total revenues or number of establishments. Shaded *regions* indicate where the industry is regionally most concentrated.

5813 - DRINKING PLACES

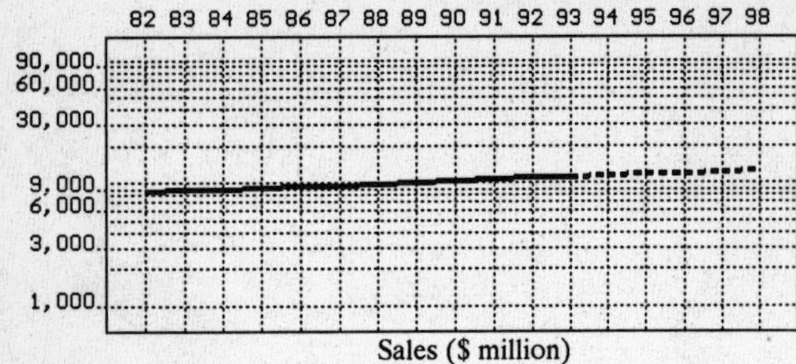

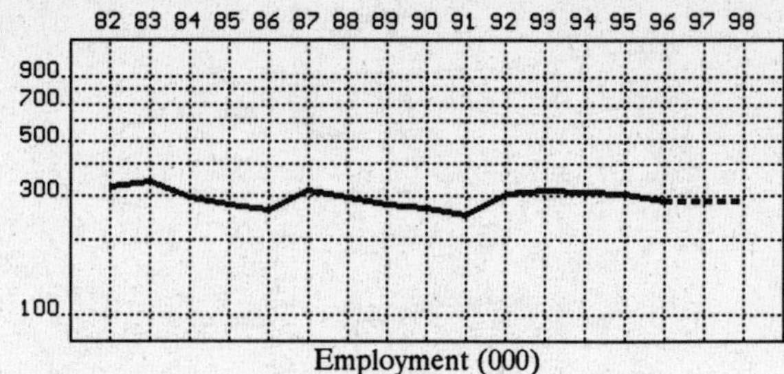

GENERAL STATISTICS

Year	Establishments (number)	Employment (number)	Payroll ($ million)	Sales ($ million)	Employees per Establishment (number)	Sales per Establishment ($)	Payroll per Employee ($)
1982	67,735	324,998	1,720.8	8,564.5	5	126,442	5,295
1983	64,884	344,127	1,998.2	8,750.6e	5	-	5,807
1984	58,109	297,249	1,746.4	8,936.7e	5	-	5,875
1985	52,624	277,418	1,704.3	9,122.7e	5	-	6,143
1986	50,205	265,808	1,693.0	9,308.8e	5	-	6,369
1987	58,692	312,831	1,949.6	9,494.9	5	161,775	6,232
1988	52,496	294,593	2,025.2	9,818.7e	6	-	6,874
1989	47,197	275,523	1,968.6	10,142.4e	6	-	7,145
1990	43,769	267,283	1,994.5	10,466.2e	6	-	7,462
1991	41,374	250,644	1,957.4	10,790.0e	6	-	7,809
1992	55,848	304,046	2,263.0	11,113.8	5	199,000	7,443
1993	52,757	314,340	2,417.7	11,212.2p	6	-	7,691
1994	52,874	310,238	2,495.5	11,467.1p	6	-	8,044
1995	47,753	304,735	2,506.1	11,722.1p	6	-	8,224
1996	44,874p	287,293p	2,477.0p	11,977.0p	-	-	-
1997	43,749p	286,133p	2,536.4p	12,231.9p	-	-	-
1998	42,625p	284,974p	2,595.9p	12,486.8p	-	-	-

Sources: *Economic Census of the United States*, 1982, 1987, and 1992. Establishment counts, employment, and payroll are from *County Business Patterns* for non-Census years. Values followed by a 'p' are projections by the editors. Sales and expense data for non-Census years are extrapolations, marked by 'e'. Industries reclassified in 1987 will not have data for prior years. Data are the most recent available at this level of detail.

INDICES OF CHANGE

Year	Establishments (number)	Employment (number)	Payroll ($ million)	Sales ($ million)	Employees per Establishment (number)	Sales per Establishment ($)	Payroll per Employee ($)
1982	121.3	106.9	76.0	77.1	100.0	63.5	71.1
1983	116.2	113.2	88.3	78.7e	100.0	-	78.0
1984	104.0	97.8	77.2	80.4e	100.0	-	78.9
1985	94.2	91.2	75.3	82.1e	100.0	-	82.5
1986	89.9	87.4	74.8	83.8e	100.0	-	85.6
1987	105.1	102.9	86.2	85.4	100.0	81.3	83.7
1988	94.0	96.9	89.5	88.3e	120.0	-	92.4
1989	84.5	90.6	87.0	91.3e	120.0	-	96.0
1990	78.4	87.9	88.1	94.2e	120.0	-	100.3
1991	74.1	82.4	86.5	97.1e	120.0	-	104.9
1992	100.0	100.0	100.0	100.0	100.0	100.0	100.0
1993	94.5	103.4	106.8	100.9p	119.2	-	103.3
1994	94.7	102.0	110.3	103.2p	117.3	-	108.1
1995	85.5	100.2	110.7	105.5p	127.6	-	110.5
1996	80.3p	94.5p	109.5p	107.8p	-	-	-
1997	78.3p	94.1p	112.1p	110.1p	-	-	-
1998	76.3p	93.7p	114.7p	112.4p	-	-	-

Sources: Same as General Statistics. The values shown reflect change from the base year, 1992. Values above 100 mean greater than 1992, values below 100 mean less than 1992, and a value of 100 in the 1982-91 or 1993-98 period means same as 1992. Values followed by a 'p' are projections by the editors; 'e' stands for extrapolation. Data are the most recent available at this level of detail.

SELECTED RATIOS

For 1992	Avg. of All Retail	Analyzed Industry	Index	For 1992	Avg. of All Retail	Analyzed Industry	Index
Employees per Establishment	12	5	45	Sales per Employee	102,941	36,553	36
Payroll per Establishment	146,026	40,521	28	Sales per Establishment	1,241,555	199,001	16
Payroll per Employee	12,107	7,443	61	Expenses per Establishment	na	na	na

Sources: Same as General Statistics. The 'Average of All Manufacturing' column represents the average of all manufacturing industries reported for the most recent complete year available. The Index shows the relationship between the Average and the Analyzed Industry. For example, 100 means that they are equal; 500 that the Analyzed Industry is five times the average; 50 means that the Analyzed Industry is half the national average. The abbreviation 'na' is used to show that data are 'not available'.

LEADING COMPANIES

Number shown: **15** Total sales ($ mil): **326** Total employment (000): **8.9**

Company Name	Address				CEO Name	Phone	Co. Type	Sales ($ mil)	Empl. (000)
Thomas and King Inc.	249 E Main St	Lexington	KY	40507	Mike Scanlon	606-254-2180	R	130 *	4.0
Chesapeake Bay Seafood House	8027 Leesburg Pike	Vienna	VA	22182	NC Hardee	703-827-0320	R	54	2.1
Grand Hotel Co.	Grand Ave	Mackinac Island	MI	49757	RD Musser	906-847-3331	R	24 *	0.5
Flanigan's Enterprises Inc.	2841 Cypress Creek	Ft Lauderdale	FL	33309	Joseph G Flanigan	305-974-9003	P	20	0.3
McMenamins Pubs&Breweries	1624 NW Glisan St	Portland	OR	97209	M. McMenamin	503-223-0109	R	19 *	0.6
Sharky's	7777 Cass St	Omaha	NE	68100	Kevin Simonson	402-390-0777	R	17	<0.1
Southern Entertainment U.S.A.	995 S Yates Rd, #C	Memphis	TN	38119	Steve Cooper	901-767-5786	R	16 *	0.5
Suburban Lodging Corp.	164 Fort Couch Rd	Pittsburgh	PA	15241	Donald F Bagnato	412-343-4600	R	15	0.5
Simpson Land Company Inc.	PO Box 1099	Solomons	MD	20688	John A Simpson Jr	410-326-6311	R	13 *	0.2
Sarasota Brewing Co.	6607 Gateway Ave	Sarasota	FL	34231	Gill Rosenberg	941-925-2337	R	8 *	<0.1
Broadway Brewing L.L.C.	2441 Broadway	Denver	CO	80205	Greg Nahm	303-292-5027	R	5 *	<0.1
First Entertainment Inc.	1380 Lawrence St	Denver	CO	80204	AB Goldberg	303-592-1234	P	2	<0.1
Mountain Valley Brewing Co.	122 Orange Ave	Suffern	NY	10901	Lisa M Cantillo	914-357-0101	R	2	<0.1
Cherryland Brewing Co.	341 N 3rd St	Sturgeon Bay	WI	54235	Tom Alberts	414-743-1945	R	1	<0.1
Skyport Lodge Inc.	Rte 3, Box 478	Grand Marais	MN	55604	Rick Ryberg	218-387-1411	R	0	<0.1

Source: *Ward's Business Directory of U.S. Private and Public Companies*, 1998. The company type code used is as follows: P - Public, R - Private, S - Subsidiary, D - Division, J - Joint Venture, A - Affiliate, G - Group. Sales are in millions of dollars, employees are in thousands. An asterisk (*) indicates an estimated sales volume. The symbol < stands for 'less than'.

OCCUPATIONS EMPLOYED BY SIC 581 - EATING AND DRINKING PLACES

Occupation	% of Total 1996	Change to 2006	Occupation	% of Total 1996	Change to 2006
Waiters & waitresses	21.7	6.9	Dining room, bar, cafeteria attendants	3.7	9.9
Food counter, fountain workers	17.4	12.4	Food service & lodging managers	3.5	44.1
Cooks, short order & fast food	9.9	21.9	Bartenders	3.5	1.8
Food preparation workers	8.4	31.0	Hosts & hostesses, restaurant, lounge	2.5	8.1
Cooks, restaurant	7.9	19.6	General managers & top executives	2.2	16.4
Cashiers	7.5	33.3	Janitors & cleaners, maids	1.2	-3.9
Service workers nec	3.9	62.1	Driver/sales workers	1.1	20.1

Source: *Industry-Occupation Matrix*, Bureau of Labor Statistics. These data relate to one or more 3-digit SIC industry groups rather than to a single 4-digit SIC. The change reported for each occupation to the year 2006 is a percent of growth or decline as estimated by the Bureau of Labor Statistics. The abbreviation nec stands for 'not elsewhere classified'.

STATE AND REGIONAL CONCENTRATION

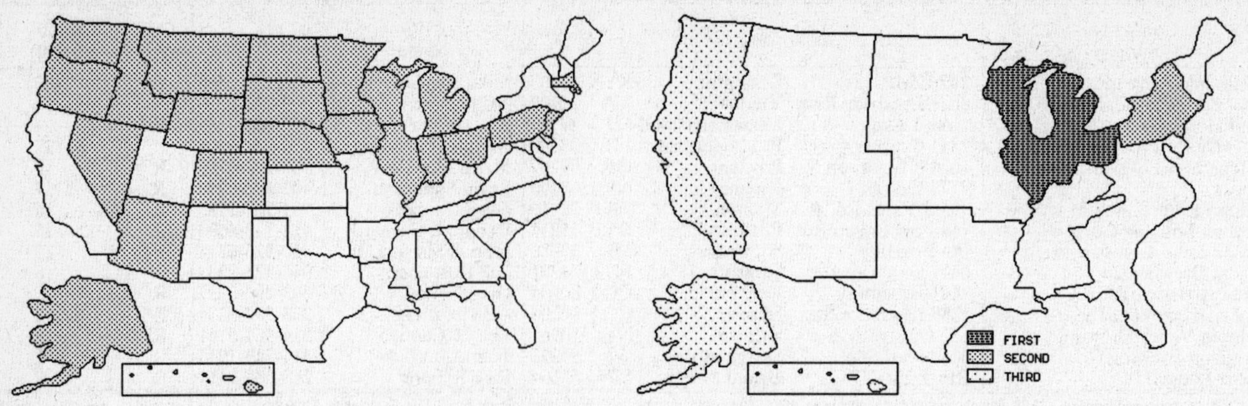

INDUSTRY DATA BY STATE

	Establishments - 1995		Employment - 1995			Payroll - 1995		Sales - 1992		
State	Total (number)	% of U.S.	Total (number)	% of U.S.	Per Estab.	Total ($ mil.)	Per Empl. ($)	Total ($ mil.)	% of U.S.	Per Estab ($)
California	4,021	8.4	28,482	9.3	7	257.5	9,042	1,118.3	10.1	35,570
Texas	2,106	4.4	22,200	7.3	11	174.9	7,880	757.9	6.8	33,470
New York	3,894	8.2	16,919	5.6	4	158.6	9,373	747.7	6.7	40,382
Pennsylvania	3,669	7.7	15,012	4.9	4	122.6	8,167	678.7	6.1	43,276
Illinois	3,308	6.9	17,162	5.6	5	146.2	8,517	654.7	5.9	38,992
Florida	1,567	3.3	13,367	4.4	9	116.3	8,699	588.7	5.3	38,992
Ohio	3,197	6.7	16,739	5.5	5	123.3	7,368	565.0	5.1	34,634
Michigan	2,118	4.4	14,540	4.8	7	111.9	7,698	496.3	4.5	35,288
Wisconsin	2,626	5.5	12,901	4.2	5	82.3	6,381	465.3	4.2	34,753
New Jersey	1,643	3.4	7,927	2.6	5	84.0	10,603	402.7	3.6	46,621
Washington	1,259	2.6	7,999	2.6	6	72.1	9,015	332.0	3.0	41,771
Massachusetts	1,171	2.5	8,337	2.7	7	77.5	9,298	317.9	2.9	32,879
Indiana	1,377	2.9	8,593	2.8	6	67.8	7,890	268.2	2.4	34,189
Minnesota	1,162	2.4	10,577	3.5	9	80.1	7,575	267.8	2.4	32,889
Colorado	778	1.6	7,880	2.6	10	63.6	8,075	213.0	1.9	30,896
Arizona	793	1.7	7,200	2.4	9	51.1	7,099	210.7	1.9	29,846
Maryland	736	1.5	4,704	1.5	6	45.7	9,722	199.3	1.8	39,600
Missouri	877	1.8	5,143	1.7	6	37.5	7,295	189.7	1.7	33,965
Iowa	1,175	2.5	5,368	1.8	5	33.4	6,226	176.4	1.6	32,205
Oregon	723	1.5	5,356	1.8	7	50.2	9,382	168.0	1.5	37,280
Georgia	426	0.9	4,674	1.5	11	43.7	9,347	163.0	1.5	36,137
Louisiana	585	1.2	4,556	1.5	8	39.1	8,575	156.8	1.4	38,992
Nevada	441	0.9	4,184	1.4	9	44.6	10,656	143.7	1.3	43,865
Nebraska	754	1.6	4,246	1.4	6	28.0	6,602	137.9	1.2	36,314
Montana	598	1.3	4,115	1.4	7	31.5	7,660	130.0	1.2	38,823
Connecticut	427	0.9	2,429	0.8	6	22.1	9,107	121.5	1.1	39,091
North Carolina	402	0.8	2,897	1.0	7	24.2	8,349	97.6	0.9	35,080
Hawaii	263	0.6	2,041	0.7	8	20.8	10,200	95.9	0.9	41,658
South Carolina	293	0.6	2,480	0.8	8	17.9	7,199	93.9	0.8	35,722
Alaska	211	0.4	1,711	0.6	8	23.2	13,531	91.6	0.8	53,259
Kentucky	397	0.8	2,705	0.9	7	20.4	7,557	84.7	0.8	32,683
Kansas	517	1.1	3,214	1.1	6	20.0	6,223	84.1	0.8	31,268
Tennessee	298	0.6	2,220	0.7	7	18.1	8,151	78.4	0.7	35,263
North Dakota	397	0.8	2,541	0.8	6	15.7	6,165	73.9	0.7	33,987
Oklahoma	395	0.8	2,549	0.8	6	17.3	6,769	69.4	0.6	33,603
Alabama	309	0.6	1,872	0.6	6	13.6	7,268	67.2	0.6	36,025
New Mexico	225	0.5	2,086	0.7	9	14.7	7,059	66.9	0.6	34,705
South Dakota	370	0.8	2,533	0.8	7	18.0	7,098	65.7	0.6	30,793
Rhode Island	277	0.6	1,513	0.5	5	13.8	9,124	64.7	0.6	44,732
Idaho	372	0.8	2,368	0.8	6	15.7	6,611	58.3	0.5	32,711
Virginia	148	0.3	1,583	0.5	11	10.1	6,349	44.3	0.4	26,270
West Virginia	359	0.8	1,357	0.4	4	8.4	6,192	40.4	0.4	35,540
Wyoming	179	0.4	1,181	0.4	7	8.3	7,005	39.8	0.4	37,578
D.C.	55	0.1	1,158	0.4	21	12.7	10,980	38.9	0.3	32,460
Utah	217	0.5	1,620	0.5	7	10.3	6,373	37.2	0.3	31,762
Maine	129	0.3	987	0.3	8	9.5	9,669	31.3	0.3	33,294
Delaware	94	0.2	698	0.2	7	7.6	10,917	28.5	0.3	36,614
Mississippi	105	0.2	737	0.2	7	5.0	6,815	26.3	0.2	28,164
Arkansas	155	0.3	758	0.2	5	5.0	6,621	24.1	0.2	33,794
Vermont	106	0.2	710	0.2	7	5.3	7,438	22.6	0.2	31,074
New Hampshire	49	0.1	606	0.2	12	4.6	7,660	16.9	0.2	29,491

Source: County Business Patterns, 1995 and *Economic Census of the U.S., 1992*. Data are sorted by 1992 revenues and, if revenues are unavailable, by establishments in 1995. The symbol (D) indicates that data are withheld by the source to avoid disclosure of competitive information. A dash (-) indicates that data are not available or undisclosed because they do not meet statistical validity standards. Shaded *states* on the state map indicate those states which have proportionately greater representation in the industry than would be indicated by the state's population; the ratio is based on total revenues or number of establishments. Shaded *regions* indicate where the industry is regionally most concentrated.

5912 - DRUG STORES AND PROPRIETARY STORES

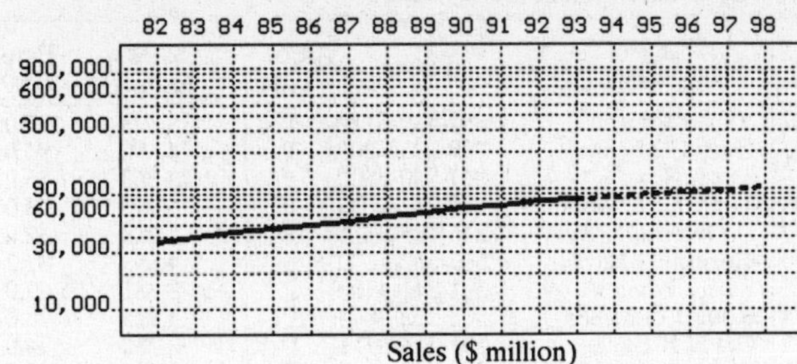

Sales ($ million)

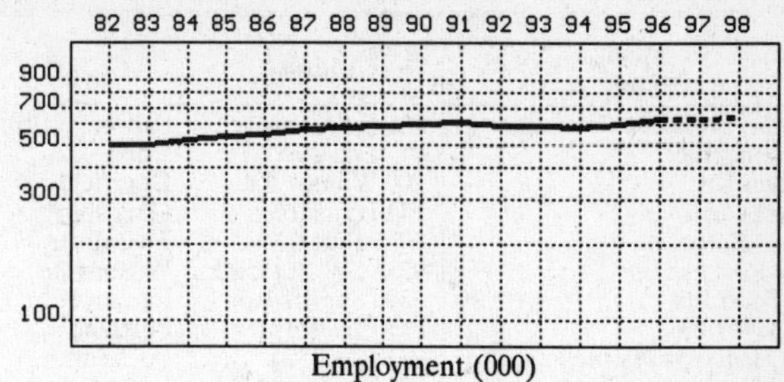

Employment (000)

GENERAL STATISTICS

Year	Establishments (number)	Employment (number)	Payroll ($ million)	Sales ($ million)	Employees per Establishment (number)	Sales per Establishment ($)	Payroll per Employee ($)
1982	51,739	496,217	4,605.4	36,242.4	10	700,485	9,281
1983	51,250	494,537	4,979.6	39,758.8e	10	-	10,069
1984	51,153	524,358	5,473.0	43,275.2e	10	-	10,438
1985	50,667	538,974	5,875.7	46,791.6e	11	-	10,902
1986	50,966	542,404	6,134.2	50,308.1e	11	-	11,309
1987	52,181	573,692	6,476.4	53,824.5	11	1,031,495	11,289
1988	50,774	576,979	7,032.7	58,557.1e	11	-	12,189
1989	50,625	587,551	7,615.2	63,289.7e	12	-	12,961
1990	49,956	593,202	8,254.3	68,022.3e	12	-	13,915
1991	49,113	609,088	8,952.0	72,755.0e	12	-	14,697
1992	48,142	587,943	9,060.3	77,487.6	12	1,609,563	15,410
1993	47,146	590,407	9,431.7	80,230.0p	13	-	15,975
1994	45,676	583,486	9,718.0	84,354.5p	13	-	16,655
1995	44,550	599,139	10,110.3	88,479.1p	13	-	16,875
1996	45,865p	624,408p	10,731.7p	92,603.6p	-	-	-
1997	45,371p	632,443p	11,174.8p	96,728.1p	-	-	-
1998	44,878p	640,479p	11,617.9p	100,852.6p	-	-	-

Sources: Economic Census of the United States, 1982, 1987, and 1992. Establishment counts, employment, and payroll are from *County Business Patterns* for non-Census years. Values followed by a 'p' are projections by the editors. Sales and expense data for non-Census years are extrapolations, marked by 'e'. Industries reclassified in 1987 will not have data for prior years. Data are the most recent available at this level of detail.

INDICES OF CHANGE

Year	Establishments (number)	Employment (number)	Payroll ($ million)	Sales ($ million)	Employees per Establishment (number)	Sales per Establishment ($)	Payroll per Employee ($)
1982	107.5	84.4	50.8	46.8	83.3	43.5	60.2
1983	106.5	84.1	55.0	51.3e	83.3	-	65.3
1984	106.3	89.2	60.4	55.8e	83.3	-	67.7
1985	105.2	91.7	64.9	60.4e	91.7	-	70.7
1986	105.9	92.3	67.7	64.9e	91.7	-	73.4
1987	108.4	97.6	71.5	69.5	91.7	64.1	73.3
1988	105.5	98.1	77.6	75.6e	91.7	-	79.1
1989	105.2	99.9	84.1	81.7e	100.0	-	84.1
1990	103.8	100.9	91.1	87.8e	100.0	-	90.3
1991	102.0	103.6	98.8	93.9e	100.0	-	95.4
1992	100.0	100.0	100.0	100.0	100.0	100.0	100.0
1993	97.9	100.4	104.1	103.5p	104.4	-	103.7
1994	94.9	99.2	107.3	108.9p	106.5	-	108.1
1995	92.5	101.9	111.6	114.2p	112.1	-	109.5
1996	95.3p	106.2p	118.4p	119.5p	-	-	-
1997	94.2p	107.6p	123.3p	124.8p	-	-	-
1998	93.2p	108.9p	128.2p	130.2p	-	-	-

Sources: Same as General Statistics. The values shown reflect change from the base year, 1992. Values above 100 mean greater than 1992, values below 100 mean less than 1992, and a value of 100 in the 1982-91 or 1993-98 period means same as 1992. Values followed by a 'p' are projections by the editors; 'e' stands for extrapolation. Data are the most recent available at this level of detail.

SELECTED RATIOS

For 1992	Avg. of All Retail	Analyzed Industry	Index	For 1992	Avg. of All Retail	Analyzed Industry	Index
Employees per Establishment	12	12	101	Sales per Employee	102,941	131,794	128
Payroll per Establishment	146,026	188,199	129	Sales per Establishment	1,241,555	1,609,563	130
Payroll per Employee	12,107	15,410	127	Expenses per Establishment	na	na	na

Sources: Same as General Statistics. The 'Average of All Manufacturing' column represents the average of all manufacturing industries reported for the most recent complete year available. The Index shows the relationship between the Average and the Analyzed Industry. For example, 100 means that they are equal; 500 that the Analyzed Industry is five times the average; 50 means that the Analyzed Industry is half the national average. The abbreviation 'na' is used to show that data are 'not available'.

LEADING COMPANIES

Number shown: **50** Total sales ($ mil): **99,225** Total employment (000): **823.3**

Company Name	Address				CEO Name	Phone	Co. Type	Sales ($ mil)	Empl. (000)
American Stores Co.	709 E S Temple	Salt Lake City	UT	84102	Victor L Lund	801-539-0112	P	18,678	127.0
Albertson's Inc.	PO Box 20	Boise	ID	83726	Gary G Michael	208-395-6200	P	14,690	94.0
Walgreen Co.	200 Wilmot Rd	Deerfield	IL	60015		847-940-2500	P	13,363	85.0
Rite Aid Corp.	PO Box 3165	Harrisburg	PA	17105	Timothy J Noonan	717-761-2633	P	6,970	73.0
Revco D.S. Inc.	1925 Enterprise	Twinsburg	OH	44087	D Dwayne Hoven	216-425-9811	P	5,088	32.0
Thrifty PayLess Inc.	9275 SW Peyton Ln	Wilsonville	OR	97070	Gordon D Barker	503-682-4100	S	4,659	31.2
Giant Food Inc.	6300 Sheriff Rd	Landover	MD	20785	Pete L Manos	301-341-4100	P	3,881	27.0
Fred Meyer Inc.	PO Box 42121	Portland	OR	97242	Robert G Miller	503-232-8844	P	3,725	28.0
Beverly Enterprises Inc.	PO Box 3324	Fort Smith	AR	72913	David R Banks	501-452-6712	P	3,230	74.0
Vencor Inc.	400 W Market St	Louisville	KY	40202	W Bruce Lunsford	502-569-7300	P	3,116	64.5
Longs Drug Stores Corp.	PO Box 5222	Walnut Creek	CA	94596	Robert M Long	510-210-6624	P	2,953	16.0
Raley's	PO Box 15618	Sacramento	CA	95852	Charles L Collings	916-373-3333	R	2,103 *	12.0
Marsh Supermarkets Inc.	9800 Crosspoint	Indianapolis	IN	46256	Don E Marsh	317-594-2100	P	1,390	12.4
Phar-Mor Inc.	20 Federal Plz W	Youngstown	OH	44501	Robert Half	330-746-6641	P	1,100	8.0
Genesis Health Ventures Inc.	148 W State St	Kennett Square	PA	19348	Michael R Walker	610-444-6350	P	1,010	43.4
J.M.	PO Box 9008	Champaign	IL	61826		217-384-2800	D	1,000 *	0.9
Fay's Inc.	7245 Henry Clay	Liverpool	NY	13088	Henry A Panasci Jr	315-451-8000	S	974	9.0
Arbor Drugs Inc.	3331 W Big Beaver	Troy	MI	48084	Eugene Applebaum	248-643-9420	P	963	7.0
Peoples Drug Stores Inc.	1 CVS Dr	Woonsocket	RI	02895	Harvey Rosenthal	401-765-1500	S	900 *	8.0
Drug Emporium Inc.	155 Hidden Ravines	Powell	OH	43065	David L Kriegel	614-548-7080	P	885	6.5
Genovese Drug Stores Inc.	80 Marcus Dr	Melville	NY	11747	Leonard Genovese	516-420-1900	P	770	5.0
Big B Inc.	PO Box 10168	Birmingham	AL	35202	Anthony J Bruno	205-424-3421	P	737	6.0
Seaway Food Town Inc.	1020 Ford St	Maumee	OH	43537	Richard B Iott	419-893-9401	P	608	5.1
Carr-Gottstein Foods Co.	6411 A St	Anchorage	AK	99518	L H Hayward	907-561-1944	P	589	3.3
Sampson Supermarkets Inc.	145 Pleasant Hill	Scarborough	ME	04074	Hugh G Farrington	207-883-2911	S	500	4.0
Stanhome Inc.	333 Western Ave	Westfield	MA	01085	HL Tower	413-562-3631	P	476	4.6
Laneco Inc.	3747 Heck Town	Palmer	PA	18043	Frank Bennen	215-253-7155	S	450 *	3.5
Fred's Inc.	4300 New Getwell	Memphis	TN	38118	Michael J Hayes	901-365-8880	P	418	4.2
Buttrey Food & Drug Stores Co.	PO Box 5008	Great Falls	MT	59403	Joseph H Fernandez	406-761-3401	P	391	2.7
Rockbottom Stores Inc.	83 Harbor Rd	P. Washington	NY	11050	Jonathan Otto	516-944-9000	R	320 *	2.0
Super Market Service Corp.	2 Paragon Dr	Montvale	NJ	07645	Paul Stillwell	201-573-9700	S	300 *	0.9
NCS HealthCare Inc.	3201 Enterprise	Beachwood	OH	44122	Kevin B Shaw	216-514-3350	P	275	2.3
Discount Drug Mart Inc.	211 Commerce Dr	Medina	OH	44256	John Wright	330-725-2340	R	220 *	2.2
Stadtlanders Drug Co.	600 Penn Ctr Blvd	Pittsburgh	PA	15235	Morris Perlis	412-824-2487	R	212 *	0.9
M and H Drugs Inc.	PO Box 757810	Memphis	TN	38175	Jerry Treece	901-367-3732	S	210 *	1.6
Super D Drugs Inc.	4895 Outland Ctr	Memphis	TN	38118	Henry Beattie III	901-366-1144	R	210 *	1.6
Duane Reade Drug Store Co.	49-29 30th Pl	Long Island C.	NY	11101	Anthony Cutie	718-391-4800	S	200 *	1.4
Kerr Drug Stores Inc.	8380 Capitol Blvd	Raleigh	NC	27604	Johnny Kerr	919-872-5710	R	200	1.8
Rosauer's Supermarkets Inc.	PO Box 9000	Spokane	WA	99209	Larry Geller	509-326-8900	R	200	1.8
Snyder Drug Stores Inc.	14525 State Hwy 7	Minnetonka	MN	55345	Michael Pan	612-935-5441	R	200	1.6
Erickson's Diversified Corp.	700 1st St	Hudson	WI	54016	Steve Erickson	715-386-9315	R	160	1.7
Happy Harry's Inc.	315 Ruthar Dr	Newark	DE	19711	Alan Levin	302-366-0335	R	140 *	1.2
Medicap Pharmacies Inc.	4700 Westown	W. Des Moines	IA	50266	William Kimball	515-224-8400	R	119 *	<0.1
Chronimed Inc.	13911 Ridgedale Dr	Minnetonka	MN	55305	Maurice R Taylor II	612-541-0239	P	117	0.3
Bartell Drug Co.	4727 Denver Ave S	Seattle	WA	98134	George D Bartell	206-763-2626	R	100	1.0
Taylor Drug Stores Inc.	PO Box 1884	Louisville	KY	40201	Sam Bouton	502-454-5642	R	97	0.8
Thrifty Drug Stores Inc.	10700 Hwy 55, #300	Minneapolis	MN	55441	Douglas A Stark	612-513-4300	R	95	1.2
Medic Drug Inc.	701 Beta Dr	Mayfield Vill.	OH	44143	Nathan Lipsyc	216-449-7722	R	90	0.6
May's Drug Stores Inc.	6705 E 81st St	Tulsa	OK	74133	Gerald Heller	918-496-9646	R	72 *	0.6
Macey's Inc.	PO Box 159	Sandy	UT	84091	Kenneth W Macey	801-561-5400	R	70 *	0.8

Source: *Ward's Business Directory of U.S. Private and Public Companies*, 1998. The company type code used is as follows: P - Public, R - Private, S - Subsidiary, D - Division, J - Joint Venture, A - Affiliate, G - Group. Sales are in millions of dollars, employees are in thousands. An asterisk (*) indicates an estimated sales volume. The symbol < stands for 'less than'.

OCCUPATIONS EMPLOYED BY SIC 591 - DRUG STORES AND PROPRIETARY STORES

Occupation	% of Total 1996	Change to 2006	Occupation	% of Total 1996	Change to 2006
Cashiers	34.4	7.4	General managers & top executives	2.6	2.8
Salespersons, retail	16.7	13.0	Bookkeeping, accounting, & auditing clerks	1.9	-15.1
Pharmacy technicians	13.2	6.1	Truck drivers light & heavy	1.8	6.1
Stock clerks	9.5	-16.1	Pharmacy assistants	1.6	6.1
Marketing & sales worker supervisors	8.3	6.1	General office clerks	1.1	-8.7

Source: *Industry-Occupation Matrix*, Bureau of Labor Statistics. These data relate to one or more 3-digit SIC industry groups rather than to a single 4-digit SIC. The change reported for each occupation to the year 2006 is a percent of growth or decline as estimated by the Bureau of Labor Statistics. The abbreviation nec stands for 'not elsewhere classified'.

STATE AND REGIONAL CONCENTRATION

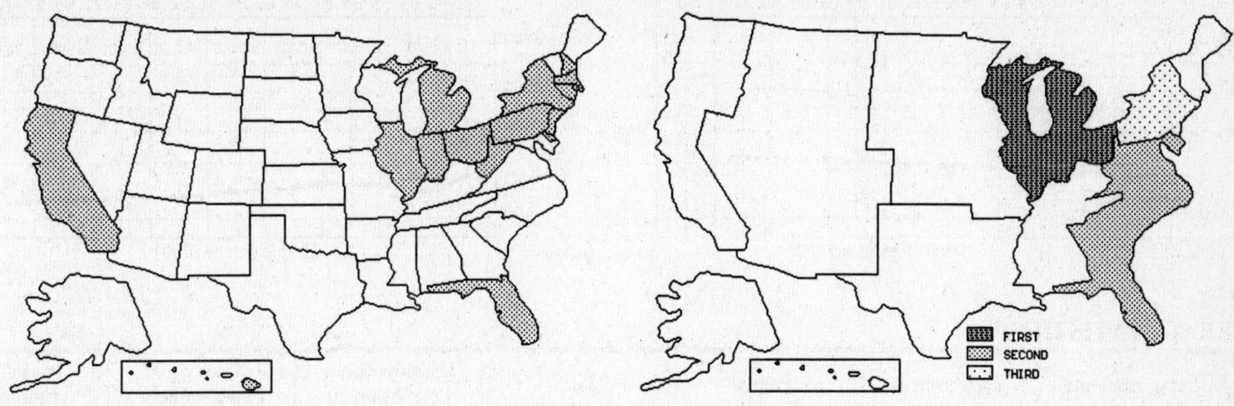

INDUSTRY DATA BY STATE

State	Establishments - 1995 Total (number)	Establishments - 1995 % of U.S.	Employment - 1995 Total (number)	Employment - 1995 % of U.S.	Employment - 1995 Per Estab.	Payroll - 1995 Total ($ mil.)	Payroll - 1995 Per Empl. ($)	Sales - 1992 Total ($ mil.)	Sales - 1992 % of U.S.	Sales - 1992 Per Estab ($)
California	3,981	8.9	68,180	11.4	17	1,420.5	20,834	9,963.7	12.9	148,029
New York	3,908	8.8	47,910	8.0	12	762.5	15,916	6,101.5	7.9	141,741
Florida	2,317	5.2	34,804	5.8	15	631.0	18,130	5,057.2	6.5	140,324
Illinois	1,820	4.1	29,022	4.8	16	505.2	17,408	4,411.4	5.7	132,497
Pennsylvania	2,705	6.1	33,418	5.6	12	520.3	15,568	4,266.8	5.5	135,035
Texas	2,490	5.6	30,540	5.1	12	508.6	16,652	3,844.0	5.0	126,707
Ohio	1,889	4.2	29,407	4.9	16	455.8	15,500	3,686.3	4.8	131,486
Michigan	1,601	3.6	23,996	4.0	15	380.5	15,858	3,054.3	3.9	130,005
New Jersey	1,691	3.8	23,578	3.9	14	371.1	15,741	2,692.9	3.5	132,957
Massachusetts	1,126	2.5	21,299	3.6	19	291.8	13,701	2,287.0	3.0	128,933
North Carolina	1,466	3.3	17,537	2.9	12	275.8	15,729	2,047.7	2.6	118,603
Indiana	1,018	2.3	14,034	2.3	14	247.8	17,658	1,983.1	2.6	132,508
Georgia	1,457	3.3	14,829	2.5	10	246.7	16,633	1,867.7	2.4	123,379
Virginia	1,089	2.4	15,006	2.5	14	235.4	15,688	1,845.4	2.4	127,198
Washington	755	1.7	11,330	1.9	15	203.6	17,974	1,517.8	2.0	129,868
Tennessee	1,056	2.4	11,215	1.9	11	208.3	18,573	1,473.6	1.9	131,774
Maryland	779	1.7	11,850	2.0	15	193.2	16,302	1,401.2	1.8	125,839
Louisiana	931	2.1	10,271	1.7	11	171.9	16,734	1,259.3	1.6	117,832
Wisconsin	763	1.7	10,583	1.8	14	177.7	16,795	1,229.6	1.6	113,644
Missouri	756	1.7	9,390	1.6	12	167.2	17,804	1,210.1	1.6	133,349
Connecticut	622	1.4	10,908	1.8	18	171.3	15,709	1,174.7	1.5	128,877
Kentucky	820	1.8	8,351	1.4	10	144.0	17,239	1,148.8	1.5	127,061
Alabama	986	2.2	10,165	1.7	10	160.3	15,771	1,132.9	1.5	123,218
Arizona	355	0.8	6,847	1.1	19	139.5	20,377	1,122.1	1.4	151,743
Minnesota	727	1.6	10,378	1.7	14	145.0	13,974	1,069.0	1.4	100,282
South Carolina	773	1.7	7,571	1.3	10	122.7	16,211	956.6	1.2	122,365
Iowa	575	1.3	6,596	1.1	11	104.8	15,887	764.7	1.0	110,736
Oklahoma	645	1.4	5,926	1.0	9	90.8	15,322	685.7	0.9	121,279
Oregon	367	0.8	4,813	0.8	13	83.9	17,429	650.9	0.8	131,025
Hawaii	135	0.3	3,636	0.6	27	70.8	19,472	648.9	0.8	194,413
West Virginia	422	0.9	5,183	0.9	12	80.7	15,577	647.5	0.8	142,036
Mississippi	638	1.4	5,328	0.9	8	84.3	15,818	612.2	0.8	115,326
Colorado	374	0.8	4,724	0.8	13	81.1	17,173	584.1	0.8	121,408
Kansas	435	1.0	4,382	0.7	10	68.5	15,639	518.9	0.7	110,626
Arkansas	570	1.3	4,020	0.7	7	67.9	16,880	467.7	0.6	117,894
Rhode Island	208	0.5	3,956	0.7	19	53.4	13,497	402.4	0.5	137,495
Nebraska	347	0.8	3,574	0.6	10	55.3	15,475	400.4	0.5	114,610
New Mexico	185	0.4	2,725	0.5	15	56.1	20,598	395.1	0.5	131,181
Nevada	117	0.3	2,072	0.3	18	40.7	19,642	370.8	0.5	141,307
New Hampshire	203	0.5	3,202	0.5	16	48.1	15,018	364.8	0.5	125,172
Maine	196	0.4	2,240	0.4	11	37.7	16,829	348.1	0.4	119,833
Delaware	133	0.3	2,082	0.3	16	28.3	13,579	265.8	0.3	124,200
Utah	165	0.4	1,873	0.3	11	30.7	16,412	231.8	0.3	108,106
D.C.	101	0.2	1,599	0.3	16	28.2	17,667	216.6	0.3	126,285
Idaho	132	0.3	1,558	0.3	12	25.7	16,510	208.3	0.3	122,250
South Dakota	155	0.3	1,819	0.3	12	24.5	13,490	184.7	0.2	108,949
Montana	152	0.3	1,266	0.2	8	19.7	15,561	172.2	0.2	130,461
Vermont	130	0.3	1,538	0.3	12	24.0	15,622	168.6	0.2	124,996
Alaska	47	0.1	673	0.1	14	17.6	26,168	154.6	0.2	179,363
North Dakota	172	0.4	1,397	0.2	8	21.3	15,240	153.0	0.2	107,259
Wyoming	65	0.1	538	0.1	8	8.1	15,099	64.8	0.1	95,865

Source: *County Business Patterns, 1995* and *Economic Census of the U.S., 1992*. Data are sorted by 1992 revenues and, if revenues are unavailable, by establishments in 1995. The symbol (D) indicates that data are withheld by the source to avoid disclosure of competitive information. A dash (-) indicates that data are not available or undisclosed because they do not meet statistical validity standards. Shaded *states* on the state map indicate those states which have proportionately greater representation in the industry than would be indicated by the state's population; the ratio is based on total revenues or number of establishments. Shaded *regions* indicate where the industry is regionally most concentrated.

5921 - LIQUOR STORES

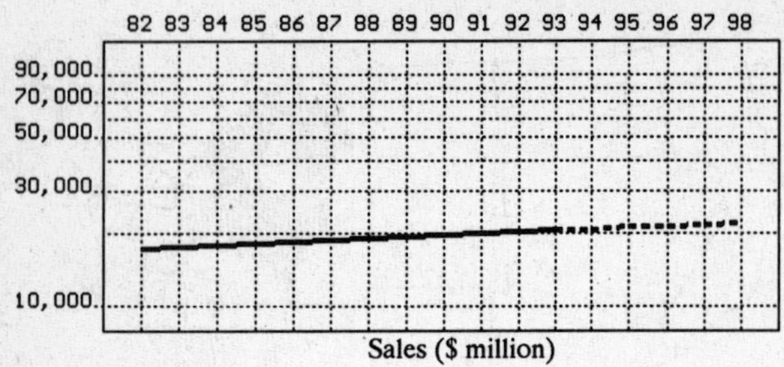

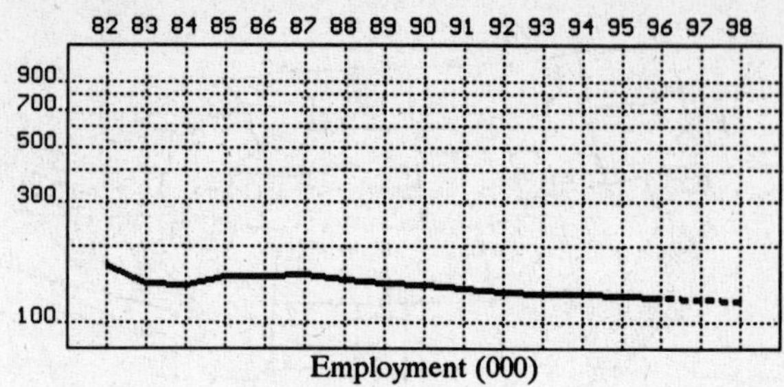

GENERAL STATISTICS

Year	Establishments (number)	Employment (number)	Payroll ($ million)	Sales ($ million)	Employees per Establishment (number)	Sales per Establishment ($)	Payroll per Employee ($)
1982	37,225	167,286	1,309.7	17,339.7	4	465,808	7,829
1983	31,897	142,246	1,139.5	17,591.2e	4	-	8,010
1984	30,360	140,603	1,162.6	17,842.6e	5	-	8,268
1985	32,529	153,528	1,436.5	18,094.1e	5	-	9,357
1986	32,492	152,832	1,447.3	18,345.5e	5	-	9,470
1987	35,194	156,519	1,454.3	18,597.0	4	528,413	9,291
1988	31,934	147,807	1,516.7	18,941.4e	5	-	10,261
1989	31,655	144,234	1,543.8	19,285.8e	5	-	10,704
1990	30,823	140,548	1,551.1	19,630.2e	5	-	11,036
1991	30,623	136,206	1,577.7	19,974.7e	4	-	11,583
1992	31,386	132,989	1,522.8	20,319.1	4	647,393	11,451
1993	30,249	129,617	1,552.9	20,511.4p	4	-	11,981
1994	29,544	128,727	1,594.5	20,809.3p	4	-	12,387
1995	28,952	127,708	1,612.9	21,107.3p	4	-	12,630
1996	29,053p	125,767p	1,690.0p	21,405.2p	-	-	-
1997	28,690p	123,480p	1,720.9p	21,703.1p	-	-	-
1998	28,327p	121,193p	1,751.7p	22,001.1p	-	-	-

Sources: Economic Census of the United States, 1982, 1987, and 1992. Establishment counts, employment, and payroll are from *County Business Patterns* for non-Census years. Values followed by a 'p' are projections by the editors. Sales and expense data for non-Census years are extrapolations, marked by 'e'. Industries reclassified in 1987 will not have data for prior years. Data are the most recent available at this level of detail.

INDICES OF CHANGE

Year	Establishments (number)	Employment (number)	Payroll ($ million)	Sales ($ million)	Employees per Establishment (number)	Sales per Establishment ($)	Payroll per Employee ($)
1982	118.6	125.8	86.0	85.3	100.0	72.0	68.4
1983	101.6	107.0	74.8	86.6e	100.0	-	70.0
1984	96.7	105.7	76.3	87.8e	125.0	-	72.2
1985	103.6	115.4	94.3	89.0e	125.0	-	81.7
1986	103.5	114.9	95.0	90.3e	125.0	-	82.7
1987	112.1	117.7	95.5	91.5	100.0	81.6	81.1
1988	101.7	111.1	99.6	93.2e	125.0	-	89.6
1989	100.9	108.5	101.4	94.9e	125.0	-	93.5
1990	98.2	105.7	101.9	96.6e	125.0	-	96.4
1991	97.6	102.4	103.6	98.3e	100.0	-	101.2
1992	100.0	100.0	100.0	100.0	100.0	100.0	100.0
1993	96.4	97.5	102.0	100.9p	107.1	-	104.6
1994	94.1	96.8	104.7	102.4p	108.9	-	108.2
1995	92.2	96.0	105.9	103.9p	110.3	-	110.3
1996	92.6p	94.6p	111.0p	105.3p	-	-	-
1997	91.4p	92.8p	113.0p	106.8p	-	-	-
1998	90.3p	91.1p	115.0p	108.3p	-	-	-

Sources: Same as General Statistics. The values shown reflect change from the base year, 1992. Values above 100 mean greater than 1992, values below 100 mean less than 1992, and a value of 100 in the 1982-91 or 1993-98 period means same as 1992. Values followed by a 'p' are projections by the editors; 'e' stands for extrapolation. Data are the most recent available at this level of detail.

SELECTED RATIOS

For 1992	Avg. of All Retail	Analyzed Industry	Index	For 1992	Avg. of All Retail	Analyzed Industry	Index
Employees per Establishment	12	4	35	Sales per Employee	102,941	152,788	148
Payroll per Establishment	146,026	48,518	33	Sales per Establishment	1,241,555	647,394	52
Payroll per Employee	12,107	11,451	95	Expenses per Establishment	na	na	na

Sources: Same as General Statistics. The 'Average of All Manufacturing' column represents the average of all manufacturing industries reported for the most recent complete year available. The Index shows the relationship between the Average and the Analyzed Industry. For example, 100 means that they are equal; 500 that the Analyzed Industry is five times the average; 50 means that the Analyzed Industry is half the national average. The abbreviation 'na' is used to show that data are 'not available'.

LEADING COMPANIES

Number shown: **30** Total sales ($ mil): **3,809** Total employment (000): **16.9**

Company Name	Address				CEO Name	Phone	Co. Type	Sales ($ mil)	Empl. (000)
Trader Joe's Co.	PO Box 3270	South Pasadena	CA	91031	John Shields	626-441-1177	R	1,800 *	4.5
Village Super Market Inc.	733 Mountain Ave	Springfield	NJ	07081	Perry Sumas	201-467-2200	P	689	3.6
Foodarama Supermarkets Inc.	922 Hwy 33, Bldg 6	Freehold	NJ	07728	Joseph J Saker	732-462-4700	P	638	4.0
ABC Liquors Inc.	PO Box 593688	Orlando	FL	32859	Charles E Bailes III	407-851-0000	R	193 *	1.7
F. Korbel and Bros. Inc.	13250 River Rd	Guerneville	CA	95446	Gary B Heck	707-887-2294	R	80	0.3
Gold Standard Enterprises Inc.	5100 W Dempster	Skokie	IL	60077	Michael Binstein	847-674-4200	R	60	0.3
David Briggs Enterprises Inc.	701 Metairie Rd	Metairie	LA	70005	David A Briggs Jr	504-831-9415	R	59 *	0.5
C.B. Jackson and Co.	2410 Smith St	Houston	TX	77006	John Rydman	713-526-8787	R	40	0.2
Flanigan's Enterprises Inc.	2841 Cypress Creek	Ft Lauderdale	FL	33309	Joseph G Flanigan	305-974-9003	P	20	0.3
Berbiglia Inc.	1101 E Bannister	Kansas City	MO	64131	Jack C Bondon	816-942-0070	R	20	0.1
S.A. Discount Liquor Inc.	4445 Walzem Rd	San Antonio	TX	78218	Johnny Gabriel	210-654-1123	R	20	<0.1
Ben Schwartz Markets Inc.	209 W McClure St	Peoria	IL	61604	Joel P Schwartz	309-682-6656	R	18 *	0.1
Vicente Foods Inc.	12027 San Vicente	Los Angeles	CA	90049	Michael Adams	310-472-5215	R	17	0.1
Goody-Goody Liquor Store	10301 Harry Hines	Dallas	TX	75220	Joe Jansen	214-350-5806	R	16 *	<0.1
Sherry-Lehmann Inc.	679 Madison Ave	New York	NY	10021	Michael Aaron	212-838-7500	R	15	<0.1
Wine Club	2110 E McFadden	Santa Ana	CA	92705	Ron Loutherback	714-835-6485	R	15	<0.1
Martin Wine Cellar Inc.	3827 Baronne St	New Orleans	LA	70115	DY Martin	504-899-7411	R	14	0.3
21st Amendments Inc.	1158 W 86th St	Indianapolis	IN	46260	James A James	317-846-1678	R	13	0.1
Kings Liquor Inc.	6659 Camp Bowie	Fort Worth	TX	76116	Jack Labovitz	817-732-8091	R	12	<0.1
Thrifty Discount Liquor & Wines	3238 Barksdale	Bossier City	LA	71112	James M Melton	318-742-3240	R	12 *	0.1
Don's and Ben's Inc.	6003 West Ave	San Antonio	TX	78213	Don Nurick	210-342-9341	R	11 *	0.1
Sav-on	21118 Bridge St	Southfield	MI	48034	Gerald Katchman	810-357-4550	S	11 *	0.1
Jordan Vineyard and Winery	PO Box 878	Healdsburg	CA	95448	Thomas N Jordan	707-431-5250	R	10	<0.1
Ralston Drug Stores Inc.	3147 Southmore	Houston	TX	77004	Rick R Zapp	713-524-3045	R	9 *	<0.1
Foss Co.	1224 Washington	Golden	CO	80401	Robert Lowry	303-279-3373	R	6	<0.1
East III Inc.	94-340 Depot	Waipahu	HI	96797	Warren Higashi	808-671-5476	R	5 *	<0.1
St. Supery Vineyards & Winery	PO Box 38	Rutherford	CA	94573	Michaela Rodeno	707-963-4507	S	3	0.1
Motts Holdings Inc.	PO Box 1675	Hartford	CT	06144	Barry P Baskind	203-289-3301	P	2	<0.1
Virtual Vineyards	3803 E Bayshore	Palo Alto	CA	94303	Robert Olson	415-938-9463	R	1 *	<0.1
Robert Denton and Company	2724 Auburn Rd	Auburn Hills	MI	48326	Robert Denton	313-299-0600	R	1	<0.1

Source: *Ward's Business Directory of U.S. Private and Public Companies*, 1998. The company type code used is as follows: P - Public, R - Private, S - Subsidiary, D - Division, J - Joint Venture, A - Affiliate, G - Group. Sales are in millions of dollars, employees are in thousands. An asterisk (*) indicates an estimated sales volume. The symbol < stands for 'less than'.

OCCUPATIONS EMPLOYED BY SIC 592 - LIQUOR STORES

Occupation	% of Total 1996	Change to 2006	Occupation	% of Total 1996	Change to 2006
Salespersons, retail	28.4	2.5	Purchasing managers	2.0	-13.4
Cashiers	27.2	-2.6	Bookkeeping, accounting, & auditing clerks	1.7	-23.0
Stock clerks	15.4	-26.7	Wholesale & retail buyers, except farm products	1.5	-20.3
Marketing & sales worker supervisors	8.3	-3.8	Bartenders	1.4	2.0
General managers & top executives	7.6	-6.7	Waiters & waitresses	1.1	7.1

Source: *Industry-Occupation Matrix*, Bureau of Labor Statistics. These data relate to one or more 3-digit SIC industry groups rather than to a single 4-digit SIC. The change reported for each occupation to the year 2006 is a percent of growth or decline as estimated by the Bureau of Labor Statistics. The abbreviation nec stands for 'not elsewhere classified'.

STATE AND REGIONAL CONCENTRATION

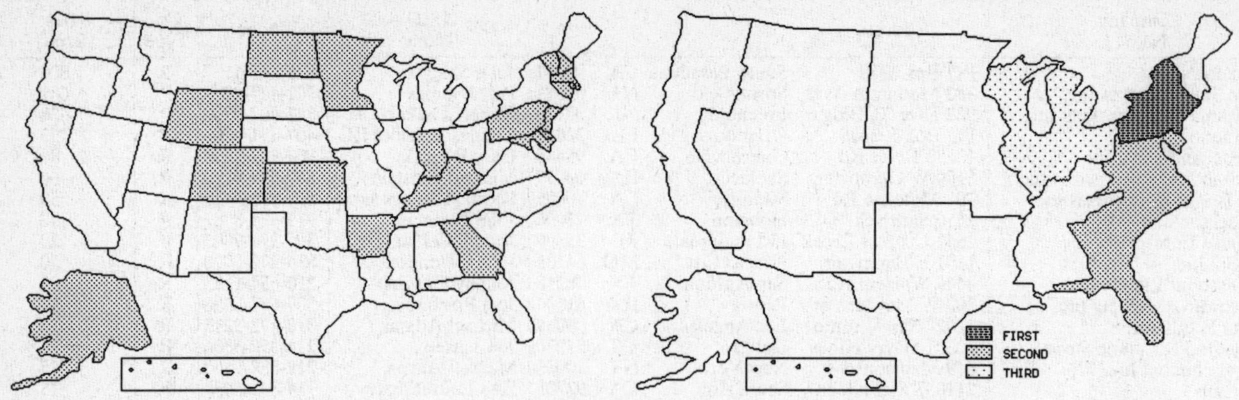

INDUSTRY DATA BY STATE

State	Establishments - 1995 Total (number)	Establishments - 1995 % of U.S.	Employment - 1995 Total (number)	Employment - 1995 % of U.S.	Employment - 1995 Per Estab.	Payroll - 1995 Total ($ mil.)	Payroll - 1995 Per Empl. ($)	Sales - 1992 Total ($ mil.)	Sales - 1992 % of U.S.	Sales - 1992 Per Estab ($)
California	3,191	11.0	10,814	8.5	3	123.1	11,385	1,909.4	9.4	148,868
New York	2,116	7.3	6,990	5.5	3	104.3	14,920	1,379.4	6.8	176,555
Pennsylvania	1,409	4.9	5,882	4.6	4	102.9	17,494	1,374.5	6.8	270,296
New Jersey	1,593	5.5	7,659	6.0	5	110.4	14,418	1,287.0	6.3	156,725
Texas	1,511	5.2	6,308	5.0	4	83.6	13,255	1,225.1	6.0	180,055
Massachusetts	1,317	4.5	8,008	6.3	6	102.2	12,763	1,193.7	5.9	143,089
Illinois	1,252	4.3	6,470	5.1	5	77.8	12,025	913.3	4.5	136,473
Florida	1,172	4.0	5,978	4.7	5	67.1	11,221	802.4	3.9	123,375
Maryland	1,065	3.7	6,326	5.0	6	78.6	12,420	778.2	3.8	116,250
Minnesota	969	3.3	7,765	6.1	8	97.3	12,532	719.9	3.5	111,838
Ohio	930	3.2	4,051	3.2	4	43.3	10,684	680.7	3.3	109,609
Georgia	825	2.8	3,277	2.6	4	44.4	13,549	616.7	3.0	182,296
Michigan	846	2.9	3,564	2.8	4	36.7	10,292	537.8	2.6	141,454
Indiana	858	3.0	4,465	3.5	5	45.8	10,262	507.8	2.5	121,041
Colorado	807	2.8	3,462	2.7	4	45.1	13,016	490.0	2.4	168,971
Connecticut	715	2.5	2,473	1.9	3	37.5	15,151	453.1	2.2	181,622
Washington	417	1.4	1,651	1.3	4	30.9	18,700	391.6	1.9	329,914
Wisconsin	511	1.8	2,485	2.0	5	23.9	9,617	362.9	1.8	135,012
North Carolina	427	1.5	1,767	1.4	4	30.2	17,110	362.6	1.8	206,957
Kentucky	469	1.6	2,257	1.8	5	24.8	10,991	320.4	1.6	137,058
Tennessee	502	1.7	1,860	1.5	4	24.1	12,939	298.8	1.5	152,229
Virginia	284	1.0	1,660	1.3	6	21.5	12,982	273.4	1.3	152,165
Alabama	296	1.0	952	0.8	3	15.0	15,770	244.8	1.2	239,293
Missouri	497	1.7	1,847	1.5	4	18.9	10,222	242.0	1.2	125,072
Kansas	576	2.0	1,845	1.5	3	12.3	6,666	231.0	1.1	125,586
Arkansas	378	1.3	1,456	1.1	4	16.5	11,329	216.4	1.1	163,421
Oregon	380	1.3	804	0.6	2	12.1	15,077	211.7	1.0	259,382
South Carolina	386	1.3	1,034	0.8	3	11.9	11,542	205.4	1.0	188,574
New Hampshire	77	0.3	500-999	-	-	(D)	-	180.8	0.9	243,995
Rhode Island	218	0.8	1,025	0.8	5	12.5	12,235	165.5	0.8	152,691
D.C.	191	0.7	876	0.7	5	15.6	17,836	162.0	0.8	159,633
Delaware	232	0.8	1,026	0.8	4	10.6	10,330	140.6	0.7	114,142
Oklahoma	300	1.0	809	0.6	3	6.3	7,800	117.0	0.6	151,298
Mississippi	280	1.0	691	0.5	2	6.5	9,421	112.7	0.6	145,588
Alaska	122	0.4	625	0.5	5	11.6	18,568	111.4	0.5	190,735
Louisiana	160	0.6	844	0.7	5	10.5	12,487	109.7	0.5	129,801
New Mexico	140	0.5	1,152	0.9	8	11.8	10,242	99.6	0.5	89,270
Nebraska	225	0.8	952	0.8	4	7.3	7,721	97.6	0.5	96,705
Utah	45	0.2	250-499	-	-	(D)	-	84.8	0.4	279,766
Arizona	195	0.7	689	0.5	4	6.6	9,578	81.8	0.4	124,562
Maine	58	0.2	264	0.2	5	4.4	16,561	81.1	0.4	203,173
North Dakota	126	0.4	709	0.6	6	6.2	8,763	78.0	0.4	102,118
Vermont	122	0.4	374	0.3	3	5.3	14,166	68.7	0.3	186,742
Wyoming	122	0.4	844	0.7	7	7.8	9,280	66.7	0.3	83,427
Nevada	62	0.2	309	0.2	5	5.8	18,654	64.0	0.3	203,943
South Dakota	153	0.5	995	0.8	7	11.5	11,513	55.4	0.3	86,756
Montana	141	0.5	289	0.2	2	3.6	12,343	55.4	0.3	183,421
Iowa	106	0.4	576	0.5	5	4.4	7,691	52.3	0.3	100,527
Idaho	64	0.2	223	0.2	3	3.6	16,049	42.8	0.2	206,700
Hawaii	61	0.2	169	0.1	3	2.6	15,189	33.2	0.2	163,512
West Virginia	53	0.2	308	0.2	6	4.1	13,234	28.0	0.1	143,764

Source: County Business Patterns, 1995 and *Economic Census of the U.S., 1992*. Data are sorted by 1992 revenues and, if revenues are unavailable, by establishments in 1995. The symbol (D) indicates that data are withheld by the source to avoid disclosure of competitive information. A dash (-) indicates that data are not available or undisclosed because they do not meet statistical validity standards. Shaded *states* on the state map indicate those states which have proportionately greater representation in the industry than would be indicated by the state's population; the ratio is based on total revenues or number of establishments. Shaded *regions* indicate where the industry is regionally most concentrated.

5932 - USED MERCHANDISE STORES

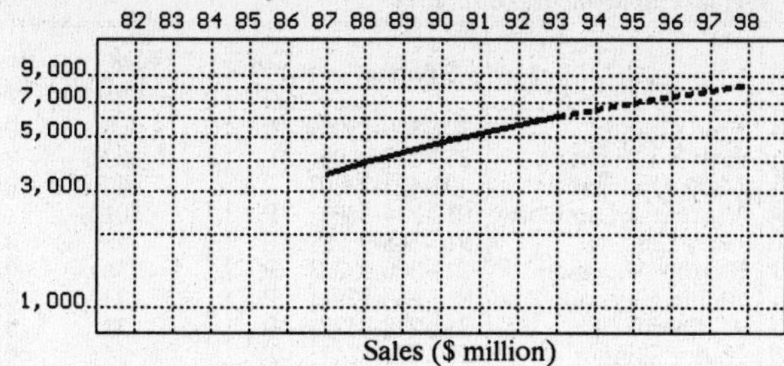

Sales ($ million)

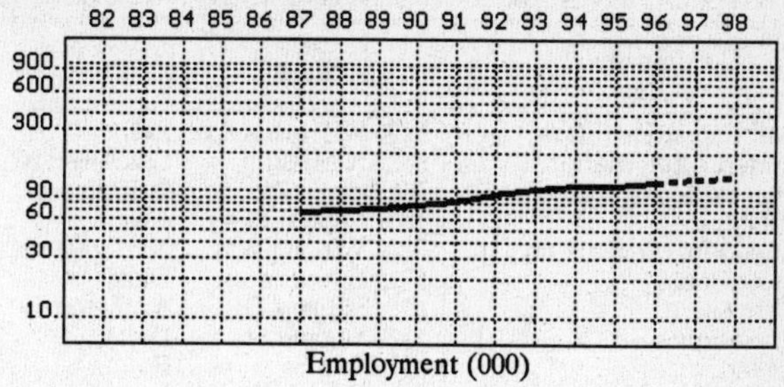

Employment (000)

GENERAL STATISTICS

Year	Establishments (number)	Employment (number)	Payroll ($ million)	Sales ($ million)	Employees per Establishment (number)	Sales per Establishment ($)	Payroll per Employee ($)
1982	-	-	-	-	-	-	-
1983	-	-	-	-	-	-	-
1984	-	-	-	-	-	-	-
1985	-	-	-	-	-	-	-
1986	-	-	-	-	-	-	-
1987	14,871	68,551	663.1	3,502.2	5	235,507	9,673
1988	13,881	70,333	772.9	3,931.9e	5	-	10,989
1989	13,756	72,832	846.7	4,361.6e	5	-	11,626
1990	14,971	78,644	934.7	4,791.2e	5	-	11,885
1991	16,316	83,462	1,031.1	5,220.9e	5	-	12,354
1992	19,826	93,267	1,124.0	5,650.6	5	285,009	12,051
1993	20,796	105,387	1,297.7	6,080.3p	5	-	12,314
1994	21,622	111,719	1,417.8	6,509.9p	5	-	12,691
1995	21,571	112,422	1,454.9	6,939.6p	5	-	12,942
1996	23,259p	120,128p	1,576.4p	7,369.3p	-	-	-
1997	24,408p	126,450p	1,679.7p	7,799.0p	-	-	-
1998	25,557p	132,773p	1,782.9p	8,228.6p	-	-	-

Sources: Economic Census of the United States, 1982, 1987, and 1992. Establishment counts, employment, and payroll are from *County Business Patterns* for non-Census years. Values followed by a 'p' are projections by the editors. Sales and expense data for non-Census years are extrapolations, marked by 'e'. Industries reclassified in 1987 will not have data for prior years. Data are the most recent available at this level of detail.

INDICES OF CHANGE

Year	Establishments (number)	Employment (number)	Payroll ($ million)	Sales ($ million)	Employees per Establishment (number)	Sales per Establishment ($)	Payroll per Employee ($)
1982	-	-	-	-	-	-	-
1983	-	-	-	-	-	-	-
1984	-	-	-	-	-	-	-
1985	-	-	-	-	-	-	-
1986	-	-	-	-	-	-	-
1987	75.0	73.5	59.0	62.0	100.0	82.6	80.3
1988	70.0	75.4	68.8	69.6e	100.0	-	91.2
1989	69.4	78.1	75.3	77.2e	100.0	-	96.5
1990	75.5	84.3	83.2	84.8e	100.0	-	98.6
1991	82.3	89.5	91.7	92.4e	100.0	-	102.5
1992	100.0	100.0	100.0	100.0	100.0	100.0	100.0
1993	104.9	113.0	115.5	107.6p	101.4	-	102.2
1994	109.1	119.8	126.1	115.2p	103.3	-	105.3
1995	108.8	120.5	129.4	122.8p	104.2	-	107.4
1996	117.3p	128.8p	140.3p	130.4p	-	-	-
1997	123.1p	135.6p	149.4p	138.0p	-	-	-
1998	128.9p	142.4p	158.6p	145.6p	-	-	-

Sources: Same as General Statistics. The values shown reflect change from the base year, 1992. Values above 100 mean greater than 1992, values below 100 mean less than 1992, and a value of 100 in the 1982-91 or 1993-98 period means same as 1992. Values followed by a 'p' are projections by the editors; 'e' stands for extrapolation. Data are the most recent available at this level of detail.

SELECTED RATIOS

For 1992	Avg. of All Retail	Analyzed Industry	Index	For 1992	Avg. of All Retail	Analyzed Industry	Index
Employees per Establishment	12	5	39	Sales per Employee	102,941	60,585	59
Payroll per Establishment	146,026	56,693	39	Sales per Establishment	1,241,555	285,010	23
Payroll per Employee	12,107	12,051	100	Expenses per Establishment	na	na	na

Sources: Same as General Statistics. The 'Average of All Manufacturing' column represents the average of all manufacturing industries reported for the most recent complete year available. The Index shows the relationship between the Average and the Analyzed Industry. For example, 100 means that they are equal; 500 that the Analyzed Industry is five times the average; 50 means that the Analyzed Industry is half the national average. The abbreviation 'na' is used to show that data are 'not available'.

LEADING COMPANIES

Number shown: **18** Total sales ($ mil): **1,796** Total employment (000): **67.4**

Company Name	Address				CEO Name	Phone	Co. Type	Sales ($ mil)	Empl. (000)
Goodwill Industries Intern.	9200 Wisconsin Ave	Bethesda	MD	20814	Fred Grandy	301-530-6500	R	1,000	60.0
Cash America International	3880 N Mission	Los Angeles	CA	90031	Jack R Daugherty	213-227-2000	P	303	2.6
Nebraska Book Company Inc.	PO Box 80529	Lincoln	NE	68501	Mark Oppegard	402-421-7300	R	160	0.6
EZCORP Inc.	1901 Capital Pkwy	Austin	TX	78746	Vincent A Lambiase	512-314-3400	P	101	1.8
Step Ahead Investments Inc.	3222 Winona Way	N. Highlands	CA	95660	Gary Cino	916-348-9898	R	48	0.5
Half Price Books	5915 E Northwest	Dallas	TX	75231	Sharon Anderson	214-360-0833	R	36•	0.7
First Cash Inc.	690 Six Flags Dr	Arlington	TX	76011	Phillip E Powell	817-633-7296	P	33	0.5
Market Antiques	1227 Slocum St	Dallas	TX	75207	JT Campbell	214-748-0472	R	32	0.2
Skinner Inc.	357 Main St	Bolton	MA	01740	Nancy Skinner	508-779-6241	R	24•	<0.1
Buffalo Exchange	209 E Helen St	Tucson	AZ	85705	Kerstin Block	520-622-2711	R	18	0.3
Federal Equipment Co.	8200 Bessemer Ave	Cleveland	OH	44127	Michael Kadis	216-271-3500	R	12	<0.1
U.S. Pawn Inc.	7215 Lowell Blvd	Westminster	CO	80030	Melvin Wedgle	303-657-3550	P	9	<0.1
A.B. Closson Jr. Co.	401 Race St	Cincinnati	OH	45202	Stuart B Sutphin III	513-762-5500	R	6	<0.1
Gallery of History Inc.	3601 W Sahara Ave	Las Vegas	NV	89102	Todd M Axelrod	702-364-1000	P	3	<0.1
Gargoyles Ltd.	512 S 3rd St	Philadelphia	PA	19147	Hadassah BenDor	215-629-1700	R	3	<0.1
Best Collateral Inc.	2447 Mission St	San Francisco	CA	94110	Ronald J Verber	415-550-6674	P	3	<0.1
Eisner Associates Inc.	516 North Ave, E	Westfield	NJ	07090	Averell Eisner	908-233-6585	R	3•	<0.1
Maverick Machinery Company	PO Box 661	Atkinson	IL	61235	WR Ellenwood	309-936-7731	R	2	<0.1

Source: *Ward's Business Directory of U.S. Private and Public Companies*, 1998. The company type code used is as follows: P - Public, R - Private, S - Subsidiary, D - Division, J - Joint Venture, A - Affiliate, G - Group. Sales are in millions of dollars, employees are in thousands. An asterisk (*) indicates an estimated sales volume. The symbol < stands for 'less than'.

OCCUPATIONS EMPLOYED BY SIC 593 - USED MERCHANDISE AND RETAIL STORES, NEC

Occupation	% of Total 1996	Change to 2006	Occupation	% of Total 1996	Change to 2006
Salespersons, retail	27.9	20.9	General office clerks	2.6	-2.3
Designers, except interior designers	9.5	24.9	Assemblers, fabricators, hand workers nec	2.1	13.5
General managers & top executives	7.0	10.0	Secretaries, except legal & medical	1.4	-9.9
Marketing & sales worker supervisors	6.1	13.5	Optical goods workers, precision	1.3	13.5
Stock clerks	5.8	8.9	Purchasing managers	1.3	2.2
Cashiers	4.8	14.9	Wholesale & retail buyers, except farm products	1.2	-6.0
Opticians, dispensing & measuring	4.5	13.5	Order fillers, wholesale & retail sales	1.2	13.5
Truck drivers light & heavy	4.3	13.5	Gardeners, nursery workers	1.1	13.5
Sales & related workers nec	2.7	24.9	Freight, stock, & material movers, hand	1.1	2.2
Bookkeeping, accounting, & auditing clerks	2.6	-9.2			

Source: *Industry-Occupation Matrix*, Bureau of Labor Statistics. These data relate to one or more 3-digit SIC industry groups rather than to a single 4-digit SIC. The change reported for each occupation to the year 2006 is a percent of growth or decline as estimated by the Bureau of Labor Statistics. The abbreviation nec stands for 'not elsewhere classified'.

STATE AND REGIONAL CONCENTRATION

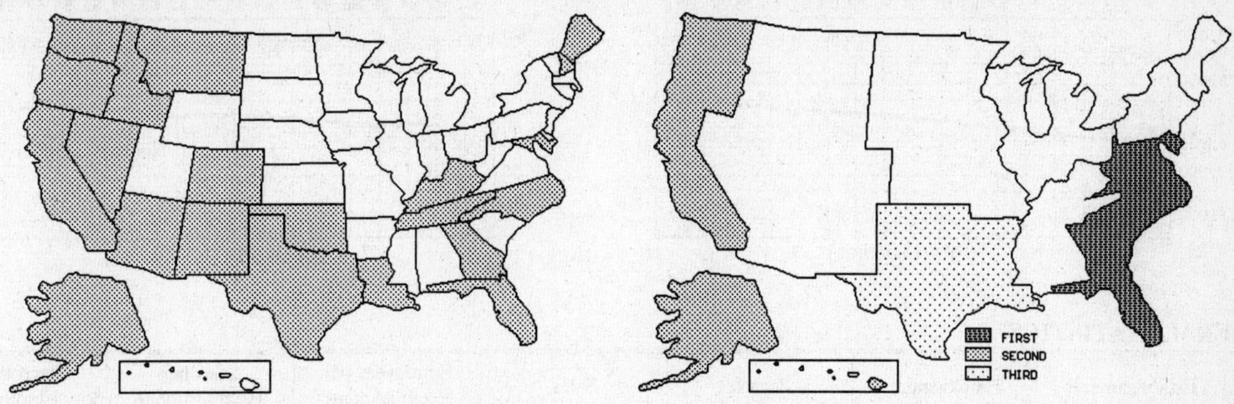

INDUSTRY DATA BY STATE

State	Establishments - 1995 Total (number)	Establishments - 1995 % of U.S.	Employment - 1995 Total (number)	Employment - 1995 % of U.S.	Employment - 1995 Per Estab.	Payroll - 1995 Total ($ mil.)	Payroll - 1995 Per Empl. ($)	Sales - 1992 Total ($ mil.)	Sales - 1992 % of U.S.	Sales - 1992 Per Estab ($)
California	1,926	8.9	13,895	12.4	7	181.7	13,079	704.4	12.5	54,857
Texas	2,161	10.0	11,274	10.0	5	168.4	14,939	654.8	11.6	71,717
Florida	1,677	7.8	6,893	6.1	4	89.6	13,001	396.2	7.0	69,587
New York	918	4.3	3,865	3.4	4	75.0	19,410	379.4	6.7	95,945
Georgia	881	4.1	3,491	3.1	4	48.6	13,910	203.0	3.6	75,030
Washington	685	3.2	3,974	3.5	6	51.0	12,834	195.7	3.5	57,247
Illinois	668	3.1	3,809	3.4	6	44.6	11,697	180.2	3.2	57,837
Pennsylvania	646	3.0	4,310	3.8	7	63.3	14,697	169.8	3.0	57,049
Ohio	647	3.0	4,059	3.6	6	44.5	10,971	158.1	2.8	51,275
North Carolina	704	3.3	3,205	2.9	5	42.6	13,295	157.7	2.8	61,546
Michigan	535	2.5	3,382	3.0	6	41.1	12,158	149.8	2.7	49,164
Virginia	558	2.6	2,947	2.6	5	35.2	11,959	122.8	2.2	51,247
Tennessee	591	2.7	2,379	2.1	4	29.7	12,490	120.3	2.1	65,421
Maryland	356	1.7	3,325	3.0	9	39.1	11,765	114.0	2.0	60,442
Colorado	492	2.3	2,726	2.4	6	34.0	12,486	112.2	2.0	54,601
Massachusetts	341	1.6	1,451	1.3	4	20.4	14,072	109.1	1.9	78,009
Oregon	371	1.7	2,220	2.0	6	25.4	11,450	102.6	1.8	56,068
Arizona	343	1.6	2,556	2.3	7	28.6	11,184	102.3	1.8	47,102
Louisiana	322	1.5	2,072	1.8	6	28.5	13,747	102.1	1.8	57,187
Missouri	543	2.5	2,196	2.0	4	26.1	11,907	98.9	1.7	49,138
New Jersey	280	1.3	1,341	1.2	5	18.9	14,087	92.8	1.6	68,975
Alabama	486	2.3	2,385	2.1	5	27.5	11,535	91.7	1.6	49,585
Oklahoma	461	2.1	1,875	1.7	4	21.5	11,445	90.4	1.6	48,162
Kentucky	382	1.8	1,541	1.4	4	18.0	11,665	88.2	1.6	60,338
Indiana	461	2.1	2,706	2.4	6	30.6	11,314	81.8	1.4	40,955
Wisconsin	358	1.7	2,072	1.8	6	19.4	9,372	76.8	1.4	47,725
South Carolina	375	1.7	1,398	1.2	4	18.9	13,549	70.9	1.3	63,374
Minnesota	309	1.4	1,488	1.3	5	17.1	11,491	68.6	1.2	55,826
Connecticut	228	1.1	873	0.8	4	13.3	15,284	66.4	1.2	89,617
Nevada	155	0.7	1,250	1.1	8	21.5	17,221	55.6	1.0	68,865
Iowa	299	1.4	1,116	1.0	4	10.0	8,963	49.2	0.9	48,079
New Mexico	182	0.8	1,076	1.0	6	13.5	12,580	47.8	0.8	55,688
Kansas	255	1.2	1,312	1.2	5	13.3	10,170	45.0	0.8	51,106
Mississippi	269	1.2	1,040	0.9	4	11.2	10,801	43.2	0.8	56,317
Arkansas	295	1.4	817	0.7	3	9.7	11,819	40.8	0.7	58,774
Idaho	132	0.6	578	0.5	4	7.6	13,176	32.2	0.6	69,052
Nebraska	137	0.6	721	0.6	5	7.8	10,853	31.7	0.6	47,039
Maine	107	0.5	351	0.3	3	4.1	11,684	29.2	0.5	99,108
New Hampshire	105	0.5	308	0.3	3	3.8	12,393	25.9	0.5	80,776
West Virginia	109	0.5	497	0.4	5	6.5	13,080	23.5	0.4	65,440
Hawaii	64	0.3	418	0.4	7	5.1	12,189	23.5	0.4	71,109
Utah	113	0.5	585	0.5	5	6.6	11,285	22.5	0.4	54,648
D.C.	57	0.3	311	0.3	5	5.0	16,203	22.0	0.4	66,423
Montana	122	0.6	469	0.4	4	5.1	10,964	20.0	0.4	53,138
South Dakota	95	0.4	363	0.3	4	4.0	11,135	15.3	0.3	53,366
Alaska	60	0.3	294	0.3	5	4.6	15,575	13.6	0.2	52,899
Delaware	58	0.3	304	0.3	5	3.1	10,329	12.6	0.2	43,297
Rhode Island	69	0.3	319	0.3	5	3.7	11,680	12.2	0.2	46,961
Vermont	74	0.3	212	0.2	3	1.9	8,792	11.0	0.2	76,257
Wyoming	55	0.3	174	0.2	3	2.1	11,793	8.2	0.1	53,627
North Dakota	54	0.3	199	0.2	4	1.5	7,784	5.0	0.1	31,823

Source: County Business Patterns, 1995 and *Economic Census of the U.S., 1992*. Data are sorted by 1992 revenues and, if revenues are unavailable, by establishments in 1995. The symbol (D) indicates that data are withheld by the source to avoid disclosure of competitive information. A dash (-) indicates that data are not available or undisclosed because they do not meet statistical validity standards. Shaded *states* on the state map indicate those states which have proportionately greater representation in the industry than would be indicated by the state's population; the ratio is based on total revenues or number of establishments. Shaded *regions* indicate where the industry is regionally most concentrated.

5941 - SPORTING GOODS AND BICYCLE SHOPS

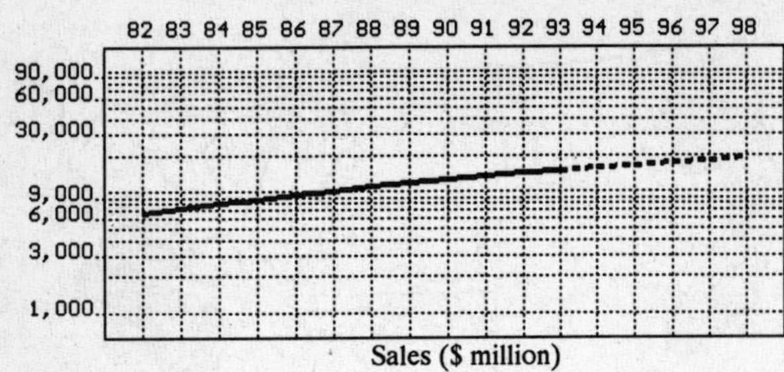

Sales ($ million)

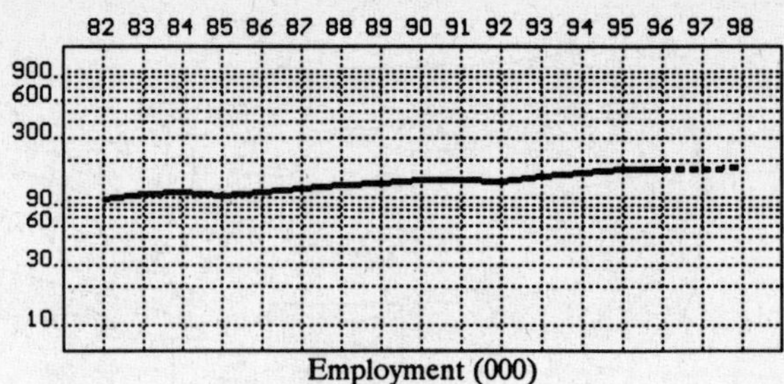

Employment (000)

GENERAL STATISTICS

Year	Establishments (number)	Employment (number)	Payroll ($ million)	Sales ($ million)	Employees per Establishment (number)	Sales per Establishment ($)	Payroll per Employee ($)
1982	19,554	97,783	843.6	6,718.5	5	343,587	8,627
1983	21,061	106,346	1,006.6	7,390.3e	5	-	9,465
1984	20,804	110,217	1,083.6	8,062.0e	5	-	9,831
1985	18,309	104,132	1,073.5	8,733.8e	6	-	10,309
1986	18,877	109,480	1,175.8	9,405.6e	6	-	10,740
1987	21,601	120,714	1,218.2	10,077.3	6	466,521	10,092
1988	20,595	127,630	1,418.4	10,954.1e	6	-	11,113
1989	20,830	132,622	1,533.9	11,830.8e	6	-	11,566
1990	21,394	138,522	1,648.7	12,707.5e	6	-	11,902
1991	22,178	139,382	1,725.7	13,584.3e	6	-	12,381
1992	23,314	137,417	1,733.1	14,461.0	6	620,271	12,612
1993	23,959	148,974	1,928.1	15,002.3p	6	-	12,943
1994	24,456	157,121	2,154.3	15,776.6p	6	-	13,711
1995	24,760	172,890	2,331.9	16,550.8p	7	-	13,488
1996	24,592p	167,121p	2,288.0p	17,325.1p	-	-	-
1997	24,997p	172,230p	2,394.3p	18,099.3p	-	-	-
1998	25,403p	177,339p	2,500.5p	18,873.6p	-	-	-

Sources: Economic Census of the United States, 1982, 1987, and 1992. Establishment counts, employment, and payroll are from *County Business Patterns* for non-Census years. Values followed by a 'p' are projections by the editors. Sales and expense data for non-Census years are extrapolations, marked by 'e'. Industries reclassified in 1987 will not have data for prior years. Data are the most recent available at this level of detail.

INDICES OF CHANGE

Year	Establishments (number)	Employment (number)	Payroll ($ million)	Sales ($ million)	Employees per Establishment (number)	Sales per Establishment ($)	Payroll per Employee ($)
1982	83.9	71.2	48.7	46.5	83.3	55.4	68.4
1983	90.3	77.4	58.1	51.1e	83.3	-	75.0
1984	89.2	80.2	62.5	55.7e	83.3	-	77.9
1985	78.5	75.8	61.9	60.4e	100.0	-	81.7
1986	81.0	79.7	67.8	65.0e	100.0	-	85.2
1987	92.7	87.8	70.3	69.7	100.0	75.2	80.0
1988	88.3	92.9	81.8	75.7e	100.0	-	88.1
1989	89.3	96.5	88.5	81.8e	100.0	-	91.7
1990	91.8	100.8	95.1	87.9e	100.0	-	94.4
1991	95.1	101.4	99.6	93.9e	100.0	-	98.2
1992	100.0	100.0	100.0	100.0	100.0	100.0	100.0
1993	102.8	108.4	111.3	103.7p	103.6	-	102.6
1994	104.9	114.3	124.3	109.1p	107.1	-	108.7
1995	106.2	125.8	134.5	114.5p	116.4	-	106.9
1996	105.5p	121.6p	132.0p	119.8p	-	-	-
1997	107.2p	125.3p	138.2p	125.2p	-	-	-
1998	109.0p	129.1p	144.3p	130.5p	-	-	-

Sources: Same as General Statistics. The values shown reflect change from the base year, 1992. Values above 100 mean greater than 1992, values below 100 mean less than 1992, and a value of 100 in the 1982-91 or 1993-98 period means same as 1992. Values followed by a 'p' are projections by the editors; 'e' stands for extrapolation. Data are the most recent available at this level of detail.

SELECTED RATIOS

For 1992	Avg. of All Retail	Analyzed Industry	Index	For 1992	Avg. of All Retail	Analyzed Industry	Index
Employees per Establishment	12	6	49	Sales per Employee	102,941	105,234	102
Payroll per Establishment	146,026	74,337	51	Sales per Establishment	1,241,555	620,271	50
Payroll per Employee	12,107	12,612	104	Expenses per Establishment	na	na	na

Sources: Same as General Statistics. The 'Average of All Manufacturing' column represents the average of all manufacturing industries reported for the most recent complete year available. The Index shows the relationship between the Average and the Analyzed Industry. For example, 100 means that they are equal; 500 that the Analyzed Industry is five times the average; 50 means that the Analyzed Industry is half the national average. The abbreviation 'na' is used to show that data are 'not available'.

LEADING COMPANIES Number shown: 49 Total sales ($ mil): 5,808 Total employment (000): 55.7

Company Name	Address				CEO Name	Phone	Co. Type	Sales ($ mil)	Empl. (000)
Sports Authority Inc.	3383 N State Rd 7	Ft Lauderdale	FL	33319	Jack A Smith	954-735-1701	P	1,049	9.0
JumboSports Inc.	4701 Hillsborough	Tampa	FL	33614	Jack E Bush	813-886-9688	P	526	5.0
Sportmart Inc.	7233 W Dempster	Niles	IL	60714	Andrew S Hochberg	847-966-1700	P	492	4.5
Recreational Equipment Inc.	6750 S 228th St	Kent	WA	98032	Wally Smith	253-395-3780	R	485	5.1
Oshman's Sporting Goods Inc.	2302 Maxwell Ln	Houston	TX	77023	Alvin N Lubetkin	713-928-3171	P	366	3.7
Herman's Sporting Goods Inc.	2 Germak Dr	Carteret	NJ	07008	Alfred F Fasola Jr	908-541-1550	R	340 *	3.0
Tops Appliance City Inc.	45 Brunswick Ave	Edison	NJ	08818	Robert Gross	908-248-2850	P	317	1.6
Trend-Lines Inc.	135 Am Legion	Revere	MA	02151	Stanley D Black	617-853-0900	P	209	1.2
Michigan Sporting Goods	3070 Shaffer SE	Grand Rapids	MI	49512	Jim Minton	616-942-2600	R	200	2.5
Dunham's Athleisure Corp.	5000 Dixie Hwy	Waterford	MI	48329	Jeffery Lynn	810-674-4991	R	180 *	2.0
Cabela's Inc.	One Cabela Dr	Sidney	NE	69160	James Cabela	308-254-5505	R	170	2.5
Gramex Corp.	11966 Charles Rock	Bridgeton	MO	63044	Tom W Holley	314-739-8300	R	170 *	1.4
Eastern Mountain Sports Inc.	1 Vose Farm Rd	Peterborough	NH	03458	Ed Howell	603-924-9571	S	150 *	1.2
Sport Chalet Inc.	920 Foothill Blvd	La Canada	CA	91011	Norbert J Olberz	818-790-2717	P	138	1.3
GRS Inc.	PO Box 128	Wilmot	WI	53192	David W Reirden	414-862-2331	S	96	1.8
All About Sports	621 Wilmer Ave	Cincinnati	OH	45226	Stan Johnson	513-533-2700	D	75	1.1
Scheels Hardwares Sport Shop	1331 S University	Fargo	ND	58103	Steve D Scheel	701-232-3665	R	75 *	0.9
Dick's Clothing	RD 2, Box 34-B	Conklin	NY	13478	Ed Stack	607-773-0165	R	74 *	0.9
Hibbett Sporting Goods Inc.	451 Industrial Ln	Birmingham	AL	35211	Michael J Newsome	205-942-4292	P	67	1.0
Koenig Sporting Goods Inc.	6675 Parkland Blvd	Solon	OH	44139	Craig W Koenig	216-248-7010	R	60	0.8
Pro Golf Discount Inc.	13405 SE 30th St	Bellevue	WA	98005	Randy Silver	206-367-3529	R	50	0.1
Score Board Inc.	1951 Old Cuthbert	Cherry Hill	NJ	08034	John F White	609-354-9000	P	43	0.2
Performance Inc.	PO Box 2741	Chapel Hill	NC	27514	Gary Snook	919-933-9113	R	37 *	0.5
Kevin Inc.	PO Box 904	Kittery	ME	03904	Gary T Adams	207-439-2700	R	34	0.3
Allied Sporting Goods Inc.	3030 NW Pkwy	Louisville	KY	40212	Sam Marks	502-778-3321	R	31	0.5
Bullrich Corp.	875 Parfet St	Lakewood	CO	80215	K Van Velkinburgh	303-237-6321	R	31	0.4
Retail Concepts Inc.	4004 Westhollow	Houston	TX	77082	Barry Goldware	713-497-7811	R	28	0.4
Special Tee Golf of Florida Inc.		Altamonte Sp	FL	32701	Jack Hazen	407-834-1000	R	25	0.2
Sound Fitness Systems Inc.	158 S Waukegan	Deerfield	IL	60015	Scott Egbert	708-470-8504	R	23	0.1
Paragon Sporting Goods Corp.	867 Broadway	New York	NY	10003	Harlin Blank	212-255-8036	R	21 *	0.3
Sports a'Foot Inc.	112 W Adams St	Jacksonville	FL	32202	John A Smith	904-731-3957	R	20	0.4
Valley Sports Co.	4450 N Brawley	Fresno	CA	93722	Dennis Makasian	209-276-6622	R	20	0.2
Detroit Pistons Basketball Co.	2 Championship Dr	Auburn Hills	MI	48326	Tom Wilson	248-377-0100	R	19 *	0.3
Any Mountain Ltd.	1600 Saratoga Ave	San Jose	CA	95129	Bud Hoffman	408-871-1001	R	18 *	0.2
Gun Parts Corp.	Williams Ln	West Hurley	NY	12491	Gregory M Jenks	914-679-2417	R	18	<0.1
Athletic Supply Inc.	PO Box C19050	Seattle	WA	98109	Mike Lambert	206-623-8972	R	16 *	0.1
B and B Group Inc.	12521 Oxnard St	N. Hollywood	CA	91606	Robert Kahn	818-985-2329	R	16	<0.1
Island Water Sports Inc.	1985 NE 2nd St	Deerfield Bch	FL	33441	Kirk G Cottrell	305-427-5665	R	16	0.2
Ron Jon Surf Shop	3850 Banana Rvr	Cocoa Beach	FL	32931	Bob Baugher	407-799-8888	R	16	0.2
United Stores Inc.	785 53rd Ave NE	Minneapolis	MN	55421	Maurice Rischall	612-572-0031	R	16	0.2
Las Vegas Discount Golf	5325 Val View	Las Vegas	NV	89118		702-798-7777	P	13	<0.1
Bicycle Exchange Inc.	4307 Wheeler Ave	Alexandria	VA	22314	Jim Bellas	703-461-9696	R	12 *	0.2
Aspen Sports Inc.	408 E Cooper Ave	Aspen	CO	81611	Ernest Frywald	970-925-6331	R	11 *	0.1
Pacific Industrial Supply	PO Box 24045	Seattle	WA	98124	Howard K Brown	206-682-2100	R	11 *	<0.1
Mel Cottons Sales and Rentals	1266 W San Carlos	San Jose	CA	95126	Mel Cotton	408-287-5995	R	9 *	0.1
Carolina Fitness Equipment	3883 Pembroke Rd	Hollywood	FL	33021	Chip Beam	305-963-2900	S	4 *	<0.1
Cole Sport Ski Shops	PO Box 3509	Park City	UT	84060	Gary E Cole	801-649-4800	R	4	<0.1
Fletcher Oil Company Inc.	PO Box 625	Bay City	MI	48707	FB Fletcher	517-684-3983	R	4	<0.1
Lady Cyana Divers Inc.	PO Box 1157	Islamorada	FL	33036	Ken Wright	305-664-8717	R	4	<0.1

Source: Ward's Business Directory of U.S. Private and Public Companies, 1998. The company type code used is as follows: P - Public, R - Private, S - Subsidiary, D - Division, J - Joint Venture, A - Affiliate, G - Group. Sales are in millions of dollars, employees are in thousands. An asterisk (*) indicates an estimated sales volume. The symbol < stands for 'less than'.

OCCUPATIONS EMPLOYED BY SIC 594 - MISCELLANEOUS SHOPPING GOODS STORES

Occupation	% of Total 1996	Change to 2006	Occupation	% of Total 1996	Change to 2006
Salespersons, retail	46.8	20.5	Bookkeeping, accounting, & auditing clerks	2.2	-9.5
Marketing & sales worker supervisors	9.3	13.1	General office clerks	1.6	-2.7
Cashiers	8.2	14.4	Wholesale & retail buyers, except farm products	1.5	-6.4
Stock clerks	7.1	6.8	Traffic, shipping, receiving clerks	1.3	13.1
General managers & top executives	5.5	9.6	Purchasing managers	1.2	1.8
Sales & related workers nec	2.5	24.4	Bicycle repairers	1.2	35.7

Source: Industry-Occupation Matrix, Bureau of Labor Statistics. These data relate to one or more 3-digit SIC industry groups rather than to a single 4-digit SIC. The change reported for each occupation to the year 2006 is a percent of growth or decline as estimated by the Bureau of Labor Statistics. The abbreviation nec stands for 'not elsewhere classified'.

STATE AND REGIONAL CONCENTRATION

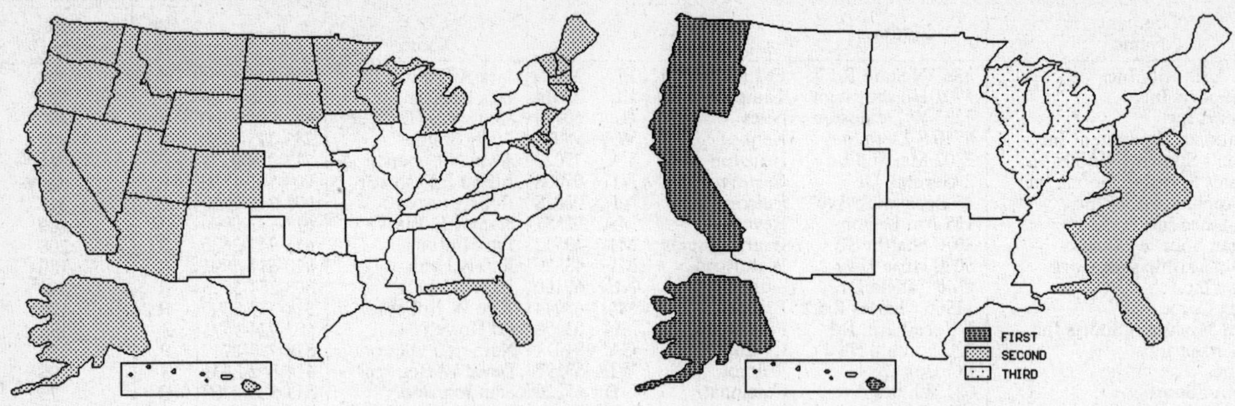

INDUSTRY DATA BY STATE

State	Establishments - 1995 Total (number)	Establishments - 1995 % of U.S.	Employment - 1995 Total (number)	Employment - 1995 % of U.S.	Employment - 1995 Per Estab.	Payroll - 1995 Total ($ mil.)	Payroll - 1995 Per Empl. ($)	Sales - 1992 Total ($ mil.)	Sales - 1992 % of U.S.	Sales - 1992 Per Estab ($)
California	2,738	11.1	23,876	13.8	9	310.3	12,995	2,203.9	15.2	107,596
New York	1,359	5.5	10,512	6.1	8	156.2	14,857	919.7	6.4	114,414
Texas	1,354	5.5	10,485	6.1	8	146.6	13,981	902.7	6.2	119,394
Florida	1,506	6.1	8,887	5.1	6	128.3	14,442	820.3	5.7	112,952
Michigan	997	4.0	6,566	3.8	7	93.7	14,277	634.3	4.4	109,064
Illinois	953	3.8	6,981	4.0	7	90.1	12,907	582.1	4.0	105,626
Pennsylvania	1,062	4.3	6,762	3.9	6	87.2	12,902	560.8	3.9	102,231
New Jersey	667	2.7	5,397	3.1	8	86.2	15,970	479.7	3.3	126,459
Ohio	953	3.8	6,024	3.5	6	81.7	13,557	476.4	3.3	99,806
Colorado	749	3.0	6,462	3.7	9	84.1	13,015	459.1	3.2	89,370
Washington	657	2.7	5,079	2.9	8	70.3	13,839	457.7	3.2	101,867
Minnesota	602	2.4	5,067	2.9	8	69.9	13,790	378.5	2.6	98,794
Massachusetts	598	2.4	4,086	2.4	7	57.3	14,022	353.4	2.4	110,122
Virginia	587	2.4	4,359	2.5	7	53.3	12,219	344.8	2.4	96,999
Wisconsin	621	2.5	3,856	2.2	6	47.7	12,368	299.0	2.1	97,410
North Carolina	649	2.6	3,486	2.0	5	46.3	13,292	285.6	2.0	99,905
Georgia	503	2.0	3,247	1.9	6	44.9	13,820	284.5	2.0	129,611
Maryland	478	1.9	3,250	1.9	7	43.5	13,378	280.9	1.9	101,930
Missouri	506	2.0	3,201	1.9	6	41.9	13,090	263.8	1.8	110,181
Arizona	413	1.7	3,289	1.9	8	40.7	12,376	235.5	1.6	97,419
Indiana	561	2.3	3,498	2.0	6	47.0	13,428	225.5	1.6	83,505
Oregon	417	1.7	2,745	1.6	7	36.4	13,277	209.4	1.4	94,570
Connecticut	357	1.4	2,317	1.3	6	33.3	14,353	192.6	1.3	123,918
Tennessee	409	1.7	2,175	1.3	5	28.2	12,947	190.4	1.3	113,524
Utah	268	1.1	2,537	1.5	9	30.3	11,963	185.7	1.3	90,173
Kentucky	311	1.3	1,574	0.9	5	20.4	12,989	138.0	1.0	104,283
Louisiana	244	1.0	1,663	1.0	7	21.3	12,793	136.6	0.9	105,393
Alabama	347	1.4	1,837	1.1	5	22.1	12,012	136.5	0.9	95,715
Hawaii	156	0.6	1,284	0.7	8	18.8	14,635	119.5	0.8	122,099
South Carolina	320	1.3	1,653	1.0	5	22.4	13,531	119.5	0.8	97,899
New Hampshire	227	0.9	1,539	0.9	7	19.7	12,812	118.7	0.8	108,597
Oklahoma	248	1.0	1,351	0.8	5	16.2	11,958	110.3	0.8	99,140
Iowa	291	1.2	1,908	1.1	7	25.5	13,367	107.0	0.7	77,385
Maine	191	0.8	1,081	0.6	6	14.9	13,802	106.3	0.7	119,248
Kansas	253	1.0	1,398	0.8	6	16.6	11,845	105.5	0.7	88,283
Idaho	243	1.0	1,533	0.9	6	17.9	11,663	104.5	0.7	93,578
Montana	205	0.8	1,283	0.7	6	16.6	12,970	100.2	0.7	96,483
Nevada	147	0.6	1,178	0.7	8	18.5	15,696	96.6	0.7	112,157
New Mexico	155	0.6	1,220	0.7	8	17.5	14,330	86.1	0.6	98,839
Nebraska	189	0.8	1,005	0.6	5	12.5	12,486	82.9	0.6	81,161
Arkansas	211	0.9	843	0.5	4	10.5	12,420	81.2	0.6	105,404
Alaska	87	0.4	703	0.4	8	12.5	17,808	73.1	0.5	125,094
Mississippi	173	0.7	950	0.5	5	11.8	12,381	68.7	0.5	109,875
Vermont	138	0.6	765	0.4	6	10.2	13,345	57.6	0.4	87,220
North Dakota	63	0.3	781	0.5	12	9.9	12,622	54.5	0.4	82,335
Rhode Island	97	0.4	507	0.3	5	6.5	12,791	44.8	0.3	125,240
Wyoming	133	0.5	582	0.3	4	7.6	13,053	43.7	0.3	80,587
South Dakota	92	0.4	686	0.4	7	9.1	13,229	43.6	0.3	91,884
Delaware	102	0.4	612	0.4	6	7.7	12,567	43.4	0.3	106,093
West Virginia	150	0.6	578	0.3	4	6.7	11,533	40.1	0.3	81,924
D.C.	23	0.1	232	0.1	10	3.4	14,573	16.0	0.1	94,353

Source: County Business Patterns, 1995 and *Economic Census of the U.S., 1992*. Data are sorted by 1992 revenues and, if revenues are unavailable, by establishments in 1995. The symbol (D) indicates that data are withheld by the source to avoid disclosure of competitive information. A dash (-) indicates that data are not available or undisclosed because they do not meet statistical validity standards. Shaded *states* on the state map indicate those states which have proportionately greater representation in the industry than would be indicated by the state's population; the ratio is based on total revenues or number of establishments. Shaded *regions* indicate where the industry is regionally most concentrated.

5942 - BOOK STORES

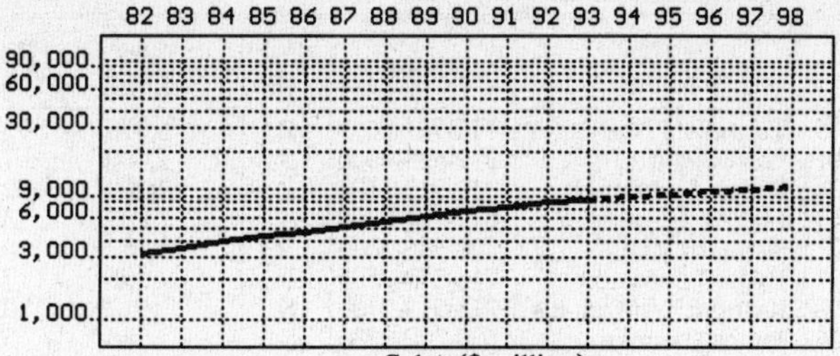

Sales ($ million)

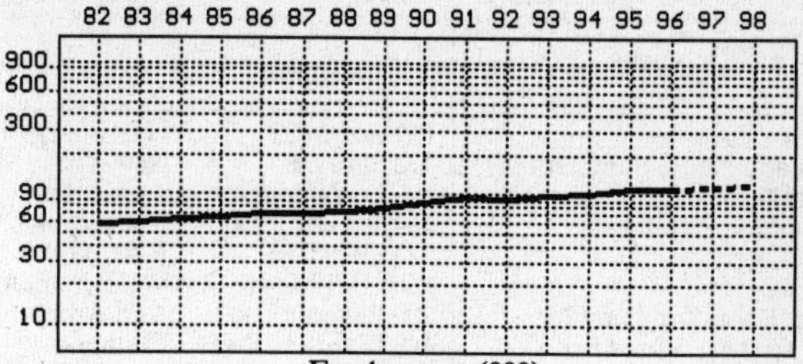

Employment (000)

GENERAL STATISTICS

Year	Establishments (number)	Employment (number)	Payroll ($ million)	Sales ($ million)	Employees per Establishment (number)	Sales per Establishment ($)	Payroll per Employee ($)
1982	9,891	58,125	400.8	3,133.0	6	316,751	6,896
1983	9,905	60,647	463.4	3,529.5*e*	6	-	7,640
1984	9,881	64,343	510.6	3,926.0*e*	7	-	7,935
1985	9,757	66,850	557.1	4,322.5*e*	7	-	8,333
1986	10,262	70,959	583.8	4,719.0*e*	7	-	8,227
1987	11,076	72,334	581.4	5,115.5	7	461,855	8,038
1988	10,628	74,705	654.9	5,695.4*e*	7	-	8,767
1989	11,529	77,716	729.3	6,275.3*e*	7	-	9,384
1990	11,722	86,077	826.3	6,855.1*e*	7	-	9,599
1991	12,272	93,696	920.3	7,435.0*e*	8	-	9,822
1992	12,887	92,480	928.0	8,014.9	7	621,936	10,035
1993	13,499	98,592	1,023.1	8,294.7*p*	7	-	10,377
1994	13,520	102,380	1,105.4	8,782.9*p*	8	-	10,797
1995	13,403	110,890	1,260.0	9,271.1*p*	8	-	11,363
1996	13,964*p*	110,215*p*	1,213.6*p*	9,759.3*p*	-	-	-
1997	14,299*p*	114,150*p*	1,275.0*p*	10,247.5*p*	-	-	-
1998	14,635*p*	118,085*p*	1,336.4*p*	10,735.7*p*	-	-	-

Sources: *Economic Census of the United States*, 1982, 1987, and 1992. Establishment counts, employment, and payroll are from *County Business Patterns* for non-Census years. Values followed by a 'p' are projections by the editors. Sales and expense data for non-Census years are extrapolations, marked by 'e'. Industries reclassified in 1987 will not have data for prior years. Data are the most recent available at this level of detail.

INDICES OF CHANGE

Year	Establishments (number)	Employment (number)	Payroll ($ million)	Sales ($ million)	Employees per Establishment (number)	Sales per Establishment ($)	Payroll per Employee ($)
1982	76.8	62.9	43.2	39.1	85.7	50.9	68.7
1983	76.9	65.6	49.9	44.0*e*	85.7	-	76.1
1984	76.7	69.6	55.0	49.0*e*	100.0	-	79.1
1985	75.7	72.3	60.0	53.9*e*	100.0	-	83.0
1986	79.6	76.7	62.9	58.9*e*	100.0	-	82.0
1987	85.9	78.2	62.7	63.8	100.0	74.3	80.1
1988	82.5	80.8	70.6	71.1*e*	100.0	-	87.4
1989	89.5	84.0	78.6	78.3*e*	100.0	-	93.5
1990	91.0	93.1	89.0	85.5*e*	100.0	-	95.7
1991	95.2	101.3	99.2	92.8*e*	114.3	-	97.9
1992	100.0	100.0	100.0	100.0	100.0	100.0	100.0
1993	104.7	106.6	110.2	103.5*p*	104.3	-	103.4
1994	104.9	110.7	119.1	109.6*p*	108.2	-	107.6
1995	104.0	119.9	135.8	115.7*p*	118.2	-	113.2
1996	108.4*p*	119.2*p*	130.8*p*	121.8*p*	-	-	-
1997	111.0*p*	123.4*p*	137.4*p*	127.9*p*	-	-	-
1998	113.6*p*	127.7*p*	144.0*p*	133.9*p*	-	-	-

Sources: Same as General Statistics. The values shown reflect change from the base year, 1992. Values above 100 mean greater than 1992, values below 100 mean less than 1992, and a value of 100 in the 1982-91 or 1993-98 period means same as 1992. Values followed by a 'p' are projections by the editors; 'e' stands for extrapolation. Data are the most recent available at this level of detail.

SELECTED RATIOS

For 1992	Avg. of All Retail	Analyzed Industry	Index	For 1992	Avg. of All Retail	Analyzed Industry	Index
Employees per Establishment	12	7	60	Sales per Employee	102,941	86,666	84
Payroll per Establishment	146,026	72,011	49	Sales per Establishment	1,241,555	621,937	50
Payroll per Employee	12,107	10,035	83	Expenses per Establishment	na	na	na

Sources: Same as General Statistics. The 'Average of All Manufacturing' column represents the average of all manufacturing industries reported for the most recent complete year available. The Index shows the relationship between the Average and the Analyzed Industry. For example, 100 means that they are equal; 500 that the Analyzed Industry is five times the average; 50 means that the Analyzed Industry is half the national average. The abbreviation 'na' is used to show that data are 'not available'.

LEADING COMPANIES

Number shown: **43** Total sales ($ mil): **18,828** Total employment (000): **168.5**

Company Name	Address				CEO Name	Phone	Co. Type	Sales ($ mil)	Empl. (000)
Rite Aid Corp.	PO Box 3165	Harrisburg	PA	17105	Timothy J Noonan	717-761-2633	P	6,970	73.0
Barnes and Noble Superstores	122 5th Ave	New York	NY	10011	Len Riggio	212-633-3300	S	2,700	7.0
Borders Group Inc.	500 E Washington	Ann Arbor	MI	48104	Bruce A Quinnell	313-913-1100	P	2,000	22.8
Musicland Group Inc.	10400 Yellow Cir	Minnetonka	MN	55343	Jack W Eugster	612-931-8800	S	1,700	13.0
Follett Corp.	2233 West St	River Grove	IL	60171	Kenneth J Hull	708-583-2000	R	1,182 •	10.2
MTS Inc.	2500 Del Monte St	W. Sacramento	CA	95691	Russell Solomon	916-373-2500	R	995 •	7.0
Walden Book Company Inc.	100 Phoenix Dr	Ann Arbor	MI	48108	Kathryn Winkelhaus	313-913-1100	S	917 •	10.0
Follett College Stores Co.	400 W Grand Ave	Elmhurst	IL	60126	James Bauman	630-279-2330	S	580	5.0
Books-A-Million Inc.	402 Industrial Ln	Birmingham	AL	35211	Clyde B Anderson	205-942-3737	P	325	4.3
Crown Books Corp.	3300 75th Ave	Landover	MD	20785	E Steve Stevens	301-731-1200	P	283	2.7
Tandycrafts Inc.	1400 Everman Pkwy	Fort Worth	TX	76140	Michael J Walsh	817-551-9600	P	245	3.7
Deb Shops Inc.	9401 Blue Grass Rd	Philadelphia	PA	19114	Marvin Rounick	215-676-6000	P	205	2.6
Brodart Co.	500 Arch St	Williamsport	PA	17705	Arthur Brody	717-326-2461	R	119 •	1.3
Little Professor Book Center	405 Little Lake Dr	Ann Arbor	MI	48103	John Glazer	734-994-1212	R	63	<0.1
Deseret Book Co.	PO Box 30178	Salt Lake City	UT	84130	R Millett	801-534-1515	S	50	0.8
University Book Store Inc.	4326 University	Seattle	WA	98105	RH Cross	206-634-3400	R	49	0.3
Baker Book House Co.	6030 E Fulton SE	Ada	MI	49301	Dwight Baker	616-676-9186	R	45	0.2
Lauriats Books Inc.	10 Pequot Way	Canton	MA	02021	Panny Gurr	617-828-8300	S	41 •	0.6
Harvard Cooperative Society	1400 Massachusetts	Cambridge	MA	02138	J P Murphy Jr	617-499-2000	R	40	<0.1
Half Price Books	5915 E NW Hwy	Dallas	TX	75231	Sharon Anderson	214-360-0833	R	36 •	0.7
Powell's Books Inc.	7 NW 9th Ave	Portland	OR	97209	Michael Powell	503-228-4651	R	35	0.4
Newbury Comics Inc.	38 Everett St	Boston	MA	02134	Michael Dreese	617-254-1666	R	29 •	0.2
Tattered Cover Book Store Inc.	1628 16th St	Denver	CO	80202	Joyce Meskis	303-322-1965	R	21 •	0.3
University Book Store	711 State St	Madison	WI	53703	Dale J Henricks	608-257-3784	R	20	0.1
Oxford Books Inc.	360 Pharr Rd NE	Atlanta	GA	30305	Rupert S LeCraw	404-262-9975	R	18 •	0.3
University Cooperative Society	2246 Guadalupe	Austin	TX	78705	George Mitchell	512-476-7211	R	18	0.2
Berean Christian Stores	8121 Hamilton Ave	Cincinnati	OH	45231	Dan Miles	513-931-4050	R	15 •	0.3
J.R. Holcomb and Co.	PO Box 94636	Cleveland	OH	44101	W. E Ferenbach	216-341-3000	R	14	0.1
Franciscan Shops	1650 Holloway Ave	San Francisco	CA	94132	Arturo Salazar	415-338-2023	R	13	0.2
Limited Ltd.	10495 Olympic Dr	Dallas	TX	75220	Michael Taylor	214-357-1700	R	13 •	0.3
Yale Cooperative Corp.	77 Broadway	New Haven	CT	06520	Harry Berkowitz	203-772-2200	R	13	0.1
Store of Knowledge	16069 Shoemaker	Cerritos	CA	90703	Michael Kaplan	562-345-1000	R	13 •	0.1
Student Book Corp.	NE 700 Thatuna St	Pullman	WA	99163	David R Cooper	509-332-2537	R	11	0.2
Wall Drug Store Inc.	510 Main St	Wall	SD	57790	Richard J Hustead	605-279-2175	R	11	0.2
Wit and Wisdom Inc.	24031 Chagrin Blvd	Beachwood	OH	44122	Joan Hulburt	216-831-5035	R	11	0.1
Christian Publications Inc.	3825 Hartzdale Dr	Camp Hill	PA	17011	K Neill Foster	717-761-7044	D	10	0.2
Moondog's Inc.	1201 Oakton St, #1	Elk Grove Vill.	IL	60007	Gary L Colabuono	708-806-6060	R	4	<0.1
Kennedy Publications Inc.	One Kennedy Pl	Fitzwilliam	NH	03447	Wayne Cooper	603-585-6544	S	3 •	<0.1
Morehouse Publishing Div.	PO Box 1321	Harrisburg	PA	17105	Kenneth H Quigley	717-541-8130	D	3	<0.1
Price Books and Forms Inc.	PO Box 9512	Azusa	CA	91702	DD Larson	818-334-0348	R	3	<0.1
Macoy Publishing	3011 Dumbarton	Richmond	VA	23228	HP Scholte IV	804-262-6551	R	3	<0.1
Voertmans Div.	1314 W Hickory	Denton	TX	76201	JD Altman	817-387-1313	D	2	<0.1
Creative Gaming Inc.	150 Morris Ave	Springfield	NJ	07081	Peter J Jegou	973-467-0266	P	2	<0.1

Source: *Ward's Business Directory of U.S. Private and Public Companies*, 1998. The company type code used is as follows: P - Public, R - Private, S - Subsidiary, D - Division, J - Joint Venture, A - Affiliate, G - Group. Sales are in millions of dollars, employees are in thousands. An asterisk (•) indicates an estimated sales volume. The symbol < stands for 'less than'.

OCCUPATIONS EMPLOYED BY SIC 594 - MISCELLANEOUS SHOPPING GOODS STORES

Occupation	% of Total 1996	Change to 2006	Occupation	% of Total 1996	Change to 2006
Salespersons, retail	46.8	20.5	Bookkeeping, accounting, & auditing clerks	2.2	-9.5
Marketing & sales worker supervisors	9.3	13.1	General office clerks	1.6	-2.7
Cashiers	8.2	14.4	Wholesale & retail buyers, except farm products	1.5	-6.4
Stock clerks	7.1	6.8	Traffic, shipping, receiving clerks	1.3	13.1
General managers & top executives	5.5	9.6	Purchasing managers	1.2	1.8
Sales & related workers nec	2.5	24.4	Bicycle repairers	1.2	35.7

Source: *Industry-Occupation Matrix*, Bureau of Labor Statistics. These data relate to one or more 3-digit SIC industry groups rather than to a single 4-digit SIC. The change reported for each occupation to the year 2006 is a percent of growth or decline as estimated by the Bureau of Labor Statistics. The abbreviation nec stands for 'not elsewhere classified'.

STATE AND REGIONAL CONCENTRATION

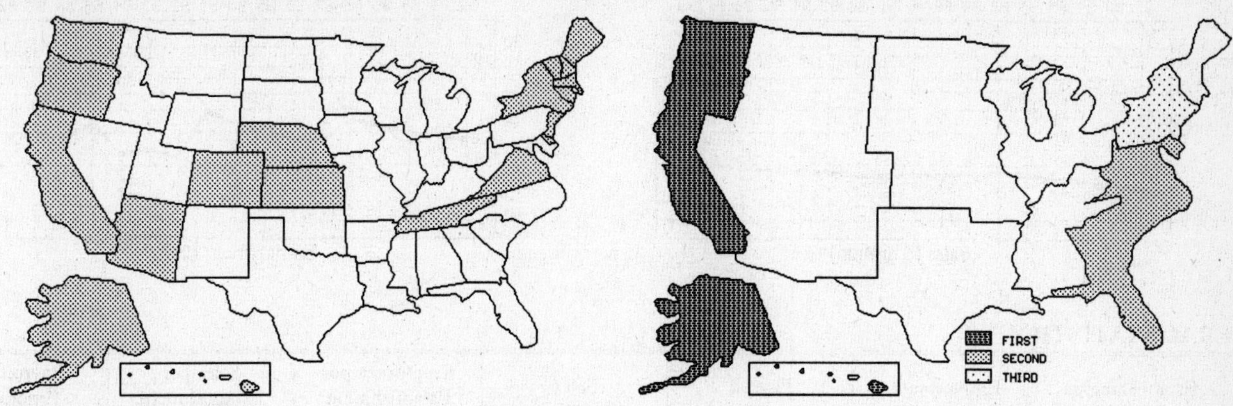

INDUSTRY DATA BY STATE

State	Establishments - 1995 Total (number)	Establishments - 1995 % of U.S.	Employment - 1995 Total (number)	Employment - 1995 % of U.S.	Employment - 1995 Per Estab.	Payroll - 1995 Total ($ mil.)	Payroll - 1995 Per Empl. ($)	Sales - 1992 Total ($ mil.)	Sales - 1992 % of U.S.	Sales - 1992 Per Estab ($)
California	1,688	12.6	16,224	14.6	10	190.4	11,736	1,229.2	15.3	86,481
New York	820	6.1	8,182	7.4	10	108.8	13,302	674.1	8.4	92,070
Texas	768	5.7	6,241	5.6	8	75.8	12,144	520.5	6.5	99,723
Illinois	554	4.1	5,285	4.8	10	57.1	10,806	363.5	4.5	91,487
Florida	689	5.1	4,884	4.4	7	55.8	11,435	356.5	4.4	90,066
Massachusetts	412	3.1	3,745	3.4	9	53.2	14,202	339.7	4.2	87,678
Pennsylvania	575	4.3	4,744	4.3	8	52.0	10,968	318.7	4.0	82,622
Ohio	501	3.7	4,877	4.4	10	47.2	9,670	292.2	3.6	77,702
Michigan	419	3.1	4,091	3.7	10	49.4	12,067	285.3	3.6	80,013
New Jersey	332	2.5	3,360	3.0	10	42.9	12,763	249.0	3.1	94,715
Virginia	384	2.9	2,979	2.7	8	31.4	10,528	224.2	2.8	89,914
Washington	413	3.1	2,919	2.6	7	34.9	11,941	221.7	2.8	89,049
North Carolina	402	3.0	2,772	2.5	7	26.7	9,640	169.2	2.1	77,777
Tennessee	355	2.6	2,729	2.5	8	31.5	11,526	159.5	2.0	84,361
Georgia	336	2.5	2,372	2.1	7	25.8	10,893	158.7	2.0	82,530
Maryland	255	1.9	2,057	1.9	8	22.6	10,997	154.8	1.9	90,446
Connecticut	194	1.4	1,709	1.5	9	19.9	11,663	152.0	1.9	90,310
Indiana	284	2.1	2,233	2.0	8	20.3	9,090	148.4	1.9	83,180
Colorado	254	1.9	1,997	1.8	8	22.6	11,323	143.6	1.8	84,987
Oregon	244	1.8	1,996	1.8	8	24.7	12,364	133.3	1.7	79,411
Arizona	240	1.8	1,707	1.5	7	20.6	12,043	124.2	1.5	90,958
Missouri	236	1.8	1,645	1.5	7	15.9	9,678	123.6	1.5	86,893
Minnesota	215	1.6	1,761	1.6	8	16.1	9,170	122.8	1.5	85,132
Wisconsin	250	1.9	1,916	1.7	8	17.8	9,295	113.7	1.4	83,575
Alabama	192	1.4	1,721	1.6	9	17.9	10,397	88.9	1.1	79,776
Kentucky	166	1.2	1,223	1.1	7	13.3	10,880	83.6	1.0	96,479
Louisiana	163	1.2	1,245	1.1	8	13.2	10,616	81.9	1.0	76,282
Kansas	131	1.0	1,241	1.1	9	12.6	10,143	81.7	1.0	74,565
South Carolina	176	1.3	1,275	1.1	7	14.1	11,057	79.6	1.0	82,367
Iowa	135	1.0	1,011	0.9	7	9.9	9,809	69.4	0.9	86,057
Oklahoma	141	1.1	888	0.8	6	8.8	9,854	62.8	0.8	78,330
D.C.	75	0.6	666	0.6	9	10.6	15,908	62.8	0.8	98,898
New Hampshire	92	0.7	748	0.7	8	8.6	11,512	55.6	0.7	90,084
Nebraska	103	0.8	804	0.7	8	5.6	6,904	52.7	0.7	83,256
Utah	107	0.8	970	0.9	9	9.7	9,957	50.0	0.6	72,570
Hawaii	67	0.5	548	0.5	8	8.5	15,429	49.8	0.6	97,472
Maine	121	0.9	711	0.6	6	7.1	10,037	46.6	0.6	79,228
New Mexico	111	0.8	711	0.6	6	8.1	11,333	45.7	0.6	83,464
Mississippi	101	0.8	578	0.5	6	5.6	9,760	36.0	0.4	89,395
Nevada	63	0.5	407	0.4	6	5.0	12,300	35.9	0.4	81,145
West Virginia	93	0.7	500	0.5	5	4.2	8,492	33.6	0.4	72,155
Arkansas	111	0.8	632	0.6	6	6.9	10,850	32.6	0.4	77,149
Rhode Island	56	0.4	369	0.3	7	4.8	13,035	32.2	0.4	83,865
Alaska	50	0.4	326	0.3	7	4.2	12,887	25.3	0.3	93,085
Montana	63	0.5	320	0.3	5	3.2	9,931	24.8	0.3	86,877
Idaho	69	0.5	452	0.4	7	3.9	8,575	24.5	0.3	70,077
Delaware	42	0.3	303	0.3	7	3.0	9,917	23.8	0.3	86,734
Vermont	56	0.4	290	0.3	5	3.2	10,862	21.7	0.3	75,902
South Dakota	37	0.3	224	0.2	6	2.0	8,719	14.0	0.2	70,833
Wyoming	42	0.3	147	0.1	4	1.5	10,184	11.1	0.1	84,333
North Dakota	20	0.1	155	0.1	8	1.3	8,503	10.1	0.1	72,107

Source: County Business Patterns, 1995 and *Economic Census of the U.S., 1992*. Data are sorted by 1992 revenues and, if revenues are unavailable, by establishments in 1995. The symbol (D) indicates that data are withheld by the source to avoid disclosure of competitive information. A dash (-) indicates that data are not available or undisclosed because they do not meet statistical validity standards. Shaded *states* on the state map indicate those states which have proportionately greater representation in the industry than would be indicated by the state's population; the ratio is based on total revenues or number of establishments. Shaded *regions* indicate where the industry is regionally most concentrated.

5943 - STATIONERY STORES

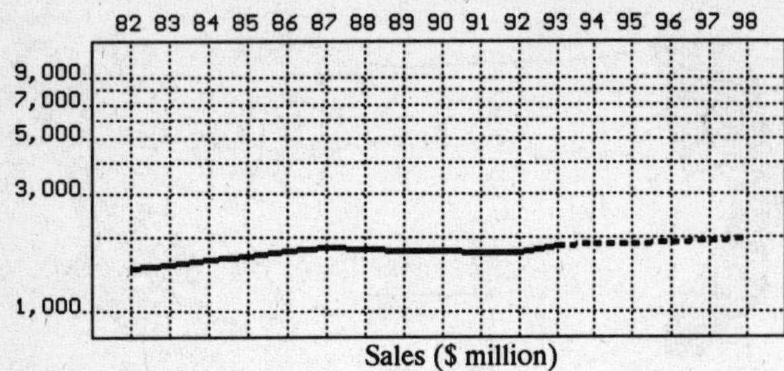

Sales ($ million)

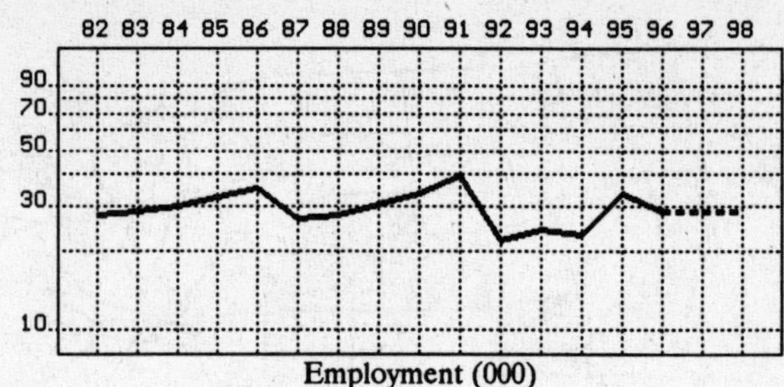

Employment (000)

GENERAL STATISTICS

Year	Establishments (number)	Employment (number)	Payroll ($ million)	Sales ($ million)	Employees per Establishment (number)	Sales per Establishment ($)	Payroll per Employee ($)
1982	5,040	27,641	257.4	1,494.8	5	296,578	9,313
1983	4,963	28,551	297.0	1,558.5e	6	-	10,403
1984	5,093	30,371	330.0	1,622.3e	6	-	10,865
1985	5,172	32,910	387.3	1,686.0e	6	-	11,768
1986	5,391	35,659	435.7	1,749.8e	7	-	12,218
1987	4,817	26,898	286.7	1,813.5	6	376,486	10,657
1988	4,621	27,993	341.4	1,795.8e	6	-	12,195
1989	4,606	30,704	377.1	1,778.2e	7	-	12,280
1990	4,821	33,888	418.7	1,760.5e	7	-	12,356
1991	5,111	39,744	537.1	1,742.8e	8	-	13,514
1992	4,344	22,228	270.0	1,725.1	5	397,121	12,146
1993	4,398	24,597	332.4	1,840.7p	6	-	13,515
1994	4,179	23,081	315.1	1,863.7p	6	-	13,653
1995	4,421	33,527	485.1	1,886.7p	8	-	14,470
1996	4,288p	28,750p	416.6p	1,909.8p	-	-	-
1997	4,221p	28,604p	423.9p	1,932.8p	-	-	-
1998	4,155p	28,458p	431.1p	1,955.8p	-	-	-

Sources: *Economic Census of the United States*, 1982, 1987, and 1992. Establishment counts, employment, and payroll are from *County Business Patterns* for non-Census years. Values followed by a 'p' are projections by the editors. Sales and expense data for non-Census years are extrapolations, marked by 'e'. Industries reclassified in 1987 will not have data for prior years. Data are the most recent available at this level of detail.

INDICES OF CHANGE

Year	Establishments (number)	Employment (number)	Payroll ($ million)	Sales ($ million)	Employees per Establishment (number)	Sales per Establishment ($)	Payroll per Employee ($)
1982	116.0	124.4	95.3	86.7	100.0	74.7	76.7
1983	114.2	128.4	110.0	90.3e	120.0	-	85.6
1984	117.2	136.6	122.2	94.0e	120.0	-	89.5
1985	119.1	148.1	143.4	97.7e	120.0	-	96.9
1986	124.1	160.4	161.4	101.4e	140.0	-	100.6
1987	110.9	121.0	106.2	105.1	120.0	94.8	87.7
1988	106.4	125.9	126.4	104.1e	120.0	-	100.4
1989	106.0	138.1	139.7	103.1e	140.0	-	101.1
1990	111.0	152.5	155.1	102.1e	140.0	-	101.7
1991	117.7	178.8	198.9	101.0e	160.0	-	111.3
1992	100.0	100.0	100.0	100.0	100.0	100.0	100.0
1993	101.2	110.7	123.1	106.7p	111.9	-	111.3
1994	96.2	103.8	116.7	108.0p	110.5	-	112.4
1995	101.8	150.8	179.7	109.4p	151.7	-	119.1
1996	98.7p	129.3p	154.3p	110.7p	-	-	-
1997	97.2p	128.7p	157.0p	112.0p	-	-	-
1998	95.7p	128.0p	159.7p	113.4p	-	-	-

Sources: Same as General Statistics. The values shown reflect change from the base year, 1992. Values above 100 mean greater than 1992, values below 100 mean less than 1992, and a value of 100 in the 1982-91 or 1993-98 period means same as 1992. Values followed by a 'p' are projections by the editors; 'e' stands for extrapolation. Data are the most recent available at this level of detail.

SELECTED RATIOS

For 1992	Avg. of All Retail	Analyzed Industry	Index	For 1992	Avg. of All Retail	Analyzed Industry	Index
Employees per Establishment	12	5	42	Sales per Employee	102,941	77,609	75
Payroll per Establishment	146,026	62,155	43	Sales per Establishment	1,241,555	397,122	32
Payroll per Employee	12,107	12,147	100	Expenses per Establishment	na	na	na

Sources: Same as General Statistics. The 'Average of All Manufacturing' column represents the average of all manufacturing industries reported for the most recent complete year available. The Index shows the relationship between the Average and the Analyzed Industry. For example, 100 means that they are equal; 500 that the Analyzed Industry is five times the average; 50 means that the Analyzed Industry is half the national average. The abbreviation 'na' is used to show that data are 'not available'.

LEADING COMPANIES

Number shown: **50** Total sales ($ mil): **16,808** Total employment (000): **111.5**

Company Name	Address				CEO Name	Phone	Co. Type	Sales ($ mil)	Empl. (000)
Office Depot Inc.	2200 GermanTown	Delray Beach	FL	33445	David I Fuente	561-278-4800	P	6,069	32.0
Staples Inc.	PO Box 9328	Framingham	MA	01701	Thomas G Stemberg	508-370-8500	P	3,968	25.0
OfficeMax Inc.	PO Box 22500	Cleveland	OH	44122	Michael Feuer	216-921-6900	P	2,542	19.3
Fay's Inc.	7245 Henry Clay	Liverpool	NY	13088	Henry A Panasci Jr	315-451-8000	S	974	9.0
Follett College Stores Co.	400 W Grand Ave	Elmhurst	IL	60126	James Bauman	630-279-2330	S	580	5.0
Franklin Covey Co.	2200 W Pkway Blvd	Salt Lake City	UT	84119	Hyrum W Smith	801-975-1776	P	433	4.7
Tandycrafts Inc.	1400 Everman Pkwy	Fort Worth	TX	76140	Michael J Walsh	817-551-9600	P	245	3.7
Nebraska Book Company Inc.	PO Box 80529	Lincoln	NE	68501	Mark Oppegard	402-421-7300	R	160	0.6
Richard Young Journal Inc.	508 S Military Tr	Deerfield Bch	FL	33442	Richard Young	954-426-8100	D	140 •	0.3
Brodart Co.	500 Arch St	Williamsport	PA	17705	Arthur Brody	717-326-2461	R	119 •	1.3
B.T. Miller Office Products	2230 Avenue J	Arlington	TX	76006	James B Miller	817-649-1313	S	110 •	0.6
Beckley-Cardy Inc.	100 Paragon Pkwy	Mansfield	OH	44903		219-589-1900	S	110 •	0.7
Seaman-Patrick Paper Co.	2000 Howard St	Detroit	MI	48216	Michael Starling	313-496-3131	S	100 •	0.1
Ivan Allen Co.	PO Box 1712	Atlanta	GA	30301	Thomas L Bolton	404-332-3000	R	96	0.8
J.L. Hammett Co.	PO Box 9057	Braintree	MA	02184	Richmond Y Holden	617-848-1000	R	80	0.5
McWhorter's Stationery Co.	621 Tully Rd	San Jose	CA	95111	Steve Andrews	408-293-7500	R	74 •	0.6
Corporate Express	2010 North 1st St	San Jose	CA	95131	Steve Van Guelpen	408-000-0000	S	70	0.3
Dameron-Pierson	PO Box 61350	New Orleans	LA	70161	Jack L Becker Jr	504-525-1203	S	66 •	0.3
Corporate Express	7700 Port Capital	Baltimore	MD	21227	Rick Nelson	410-799-7700	S	60	0.4
Silvers Inc.	151 W Fort St	Detroit	MI	48232	Ira Silver	313-963-0000	R	52	0.3
General Office Products Co.	2050 Old Hwy 8	New Brighton	MN	55112	Thomas J Reaser	612-639-4700	S	50	0.3
St. Paul Book and Stationery	1233 W County E	Arden Hills	MN	55112	Thomas Holmstrom	612-636-2250	S	49	0.5
Mills Morris Arrow	3770 Perkins Rd S	Memphis	TN	38118	William M Williams	901-362-8620	S	47	0.3
Sav-On Inc.	1400 Everman Pkwy	Fort Worth	TX	76140	George W Allen	817-568-5200	S	46	0.5
B.T. Ginn Co.	9301 Largo Dr, W	Springdale	MD	20774	Paul Christian	301-808-7136	S	44	0.5
American Trading & Production	1200 S Stafford St	Washington	MO	63090		314-239-2781	D	42 •	0.5
Harvard Cooperative Society	1400 Massachusetts	Cambridge	MA	02138	J P Murphy Jr	617-499-2000	R	40	<0.1
Macauley's Office Products	41554 Koppernick	Canton	MI	48187	Jack Macauley	313-454-9292	R	40	0.3
Office Resources Inc.	PO Box 1689	Louisville	KY	40201	Stephen Zink	502-589-5900	R	40	0.2
Arvey Paper and Office Products	3351 W Addison St	Chicago	IL	60618	Bob Smusz	773-463-6423	D	40 •	0.3
Buschart Office Products Inc.	1834 Walton Rd	St. Louis	MO	63114	Richard C Dubin	314-426-7222	S	33	0.1
Raleigh Office Supply Company	PO Box 2060	Raleigh	NC	27602	JM Ray	919-834-1601	R	27	0.1
HarrisData	611 N Barker Rd	Brookfield	WI	53045	AE Seyler	414-784-9099	R	26 •	<0.1
University Book Store	711 State St	Madison	WI	53703	Dale J Henricks	608-257-3784	R	20	0.1
Social Expressions	3393 Peachtree Rd	Atlanta	GA	30326	Al Masia	404-266-2618	R	18 •	0.2
H.A. Friend and Company Inc.	1535 Lewis Ave	Zion	IL	60099	William F Friend	708-746-1248	R	16 •	<0.1
Jacobs Gardner	5121 Buchanan St	Hyattsville	MD	20781	Daniel Grossman	301-779-3700	R	15	0.1
J.R. Holcomb and Co.	PO Box 94636	Cleveland	OH	44101	W. E Ferenbach	216-341-3000	R	14	0.1
Locke Office Products Inc.	55 Bradley Dr	Westbrook	ME	04092	William Dunlap	207-854-0011	R	14 •	0.1
Midwest Office Furniture	987 SW Temple	Salt Lake City	UT	84101	MS Lake	801-359-7681	R	14 •	<0.1
A and H Stores Inc.	1420 Maple SW	Renton	WA	98055	RB Hendrickson	206-255-7083	R	13 •	0.2
Franciscan Shops	1650 Holloway Ave	San Francisco	CA	94132	Arturo Salazar	415-338-2023	R	13	0.2
Malolo Beverages&Supply Co.	2815 Koapaka St	Honolulu	HI	96819	Sanford KJ Young	808-836-2111	R	13	<0.1
Yale Cooperative Corp.	77 Broadway	New Haven	CT	06520	Harry Berkowitz	203-772-2200	R	13	0.1
Stationers Inc.	PO Box 2167	Huntington	WV	25722	JM Aldridge	304-528-2780	S	13 •	<0.1
Antioch Co.	888 Dayton St	Yellow Springs	OH	45387	Lee Morgan	937-767-7379	R	12	0.7
Hughes-Calihan Corp.	4730 N 16th St	Phoenix	AZ	85016	PE Calihan	602-264-9631	R	12	0.1
Iowa Office Supplies Inc.	PO Box 1386	Storm Lake	IA	50588	Kirby Roberts	712-732-4801	R	12	<0.1
San Diego Office Supply	7946 Clairemont	San Diego	CA	92111	William B Sturgeon	619-565-1212	R	12 •	0.1
Waller Brothers Inc.	PO Box 6288	Mobile	AL	36660	Terrence J Silva	205-479-8621	S	12 •	0.1

Source: *Ward's Business Directory of U.S. Private and Public Companies*, 1998. The company type code used is as follows: P - Public, R - Private, S - Subsidiary, D - Division, J - Joint Venture, A - Affiliate, G - Group. Sales are in millions of dollars, employees are in thousands. An asterisk (*) indicates an estimated sales volume. The symbol < stands for 'less than'.

OCCUPATIONS EMPLOYED BY SIC 594 - MISCELLANEOUS SHOPPING GOODS STORES

Occupation	% of Total 1996	Change to 2006	Occupation	% of Total 1996	Change to 2006
Salespersons, retail	46.8	20.5	Bookkeeping, accounting, & auditing clerks	2.2	-9.5
Marketing & sales worker supervisors	9.3	13.1	General office clerks	1.6	-2.7
Cashiers	8.2	14.4	Wholesale & retail buyers, except farm products	1.5	-6.4
Stock clerks	7.1	6.8	Traffic, shipping, receiving clerks	1.3	13.1
General managers & top executives	5.5	9.6	Purchasing managers	1.2	1.8
Sales & related workers nec	2.5	24.4	Bicycle repairers	1.2	35.7

Source: *Industry-Occupation Matrix*, Bureau of Labor Statistics. These data relate to one or more 3-digit SIC industry groups rather than to a single 4-digit SIC. The change reported for each occupation to the year 2006 is a percent of growth or decline as estimated by the Bureau of Labor Statistics. The abbreviation nec stands for 'not elsewhere classified'.

STATE AND REGIONAL CONCENTRATION

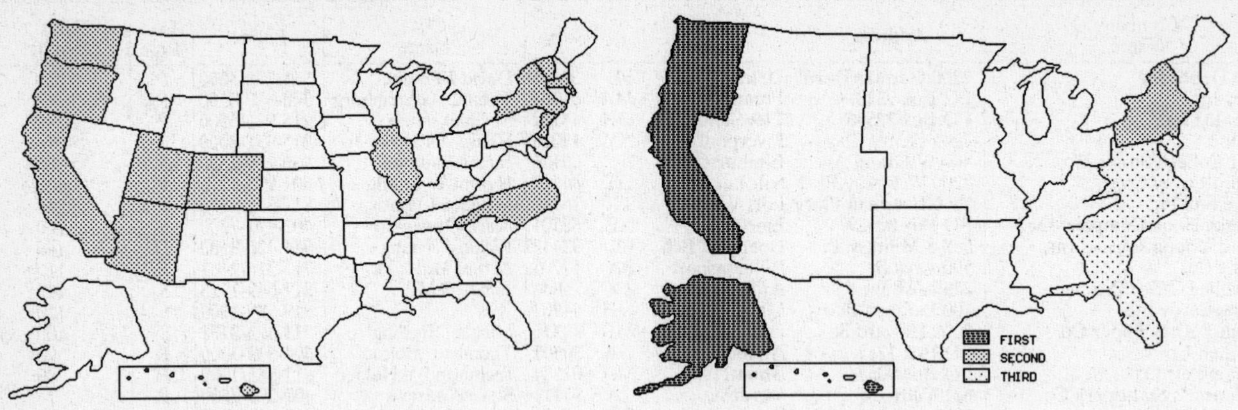

INDUSTRY DATA BY STATE

State	Establishments - 1995 Total (number)	Establishments - 1995 % of U.S.	Employment - 1995 Total (number)	Employment - 1995 % of U.S.	Employment - 1995 Per Estab.	Payroll - 1995 Total ($ mil.)	Payroll - 1995 Per Empl. ($)	Sales - 1992 Total ($ mil.)	Sales - 1992 % of U.S.	Sales - 1992 Per Estab ($)
California	721	16.3	6,087	18.2	8	83.8	13,761	341.2	20.0	75,597
New York	609	13.8	3,980	11.9	7	53.8	13,527	226.8	13.3	101,682
Texas	250	5.7	1,417	4.2	6	19.4	13,669	104.1	6.1	80,875
Illinois	177	4.0	1,165	3.5	7	17.3	14,852	83.2	4.9	76,991
Florida	224	5.1	1,530	4.6	7	22.1	14,456	77.1	4.5	76,514
New Jersey	191	4.3	1,737	5.2	9	24.2	13,928	64.6	3.8	91,956
Pennsylvania	177	4.0	1,828	5.5	10	31.9	17,473	61.6	3.6	66,884
Ohio	121	2.7	866	2.6	7	11.7	13,456	51.5	3.0	67,711
Michigan	126	2.9	894	2.7	7	16.6	18,614	51.3	3.0	82,880
North Carolina	95	2.1	452	1.4	5	6.1	13,445	47.4	2.8	66,408
Washington	101	2.3	617	1.8	6	9.8	15,867	47.4	2.8	79,724
Massachusetts	116	2.6	1,717	5.1	15	27.6	16,080	45.9	2.7	76,291
Georgia	121	2.7	824	2.5	7	13.2	16,057	44.6	2.6	78,482
Virginia	100	2.3	1,006	3.0	10	12.5	12,444	42.2	2.5	80,251
Maryland	94	2.1	1,025	3.1	11	15.7	15,358	32.9	1.9	79,187
Colorado	71	1.6	503	1.5	7	8.4	16,626	30.6	1.8	75,201
Minnesota	56	1.3	398	1.2	7	4.5	11,261	29.7	1.7	60,659
Arizona	84	1.9	650	1.9	8	9.4	14,386	28.4	1.7	59,842
Oregon	49	1.1	290	0.9	6	3.6	12,352	25.2	1.5	68,779
Tennessee	53	1.2	275	0.8	5	3.7	13,400	21.5	1.3	70,412
Louisiana	76	1.7	397	1.2	5	5.6	14,038	21.4	1.3	67,110
Connecticut	62	1.4	866	2.6	14	12.9	14,879	18.6	1.1	88,638
Missouri	55	1.2	223	0.7	4	3.2	14,202	18.3	1.1	56,972
Indiana	51	1.2	236	0.7	5	3.0	12,500	16.0	0.9	67,709
South Carolina	67	1.5	298	0.9	4	5.2	17,570	15.3	0.9	68,698
Oklahoma	43	1.0	293	0.9	7	4.5	15,427	14.1	0.8	73,702
Wisconsin	36	0.8	215	0.6	6	2.4	11,130	13.1	0.8	68,544
Utah	40	0.9	249	0.7	6	3.2	12,655	12.8	0.7	78,387
Alabama	51	1.2	263	0.8	5	2.3	8,624	12.2	0.7	71,759
Hawaii	13	0.3	92	0.3	7	2.0	21,522	11.8	0.7	91,752
Kansas	44	1.0	234	0.7	5	3.2	13,658	11.1	0.6	85,046
Arkansas	23	0.5	172	0.5	7	2.3	13,337	10.2	0.6	88,233
Vermont	15	0.3	157	0.5	10	2.7	17,255	9.5	0.6	77,803
New Mexico	19	0.4	99	0.3	5	1.9	19,343	9.4	0.6	89,619
Kentucky	23	0.5	468	1.4	20	6.8	14,489	8.4	0.5	86,163
Iowa	25	0.6	125	0.4	5	1.4	10,888	7.7	0.4	59,411
Mississippi	26	0.6	136	0.4	5	2.3	17,191	7.6	0.4	74,069
Idaho	26	0.6	182	0.5	7	2.0	11,170	7.1	0.4	60,256
New Hampshire	24	0.5	318	0.9	13	4.9	15,447	5.7	0.3	99,737
Maine	20	0.5	207	0.6	10	2.9	14,164	4.6	0.3	92,580
D.C.	17	0.4	98	0.3	6	1.6	16,153	4.5	0.3	162,357
Montana	20	0.5	125	0.4	6	1.7	13,240	4.0	0.2	66,550
Rhode Island	16	0.4	104	0.3	7	1.5	14,019	3.8	0.2	46,133
Wyoming	9	0.2	40	0.1	4	0.6	15,900	2.1	0.1	82,920
South Dakota	8	0.2	20-99	-	-	(D)	-	1.7	0.1	57,467
Nebraska	20	0.5	86	0.3	4	1.2	14,256	(D)	-	-
Alaska	16	0.4	117	0.3	7	2.4	20,188	(D)	-	-
Nevada	14	0.3	178	0.5	13	2.8	15,708	(D)	-	-
West Virginia	11	0.2	43	0.1	4	0.7	15,233	(D)	-	-
Delaware	9	0.2	195	0.6	22	2.2	11,097	(D)	-	-
North Dakota	6	0.1	20-99	-	-	(D)	-	(D)	-	-

Source: County Business Patterns, 1995 and *Economic Census of the U.S., 1992*. Data are sorted by 1992 revenues and, if revenues are unavailable, by establishments in 1995. The symbol (D) indicates that data are withheld by the source to avoid disclosure of competitive information. A dash (-) indicates that data are not available or undisclosed because they do not meet statistical validity standards. Shaded *states* on the state map indicate those states which have proportionately greater representation in the industry than would be indicated by the state's population; the ratio is based on total revenues or number of establishments. Shaded *regions* indicate where the industry is regionally most concentrated.

5944 - JEWELRY STORES

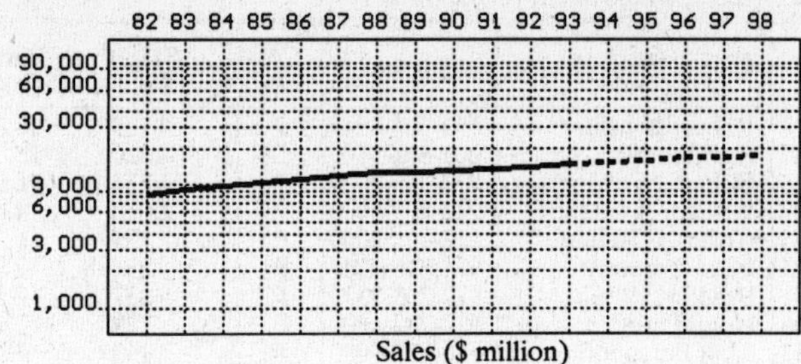

Sales ($ million)

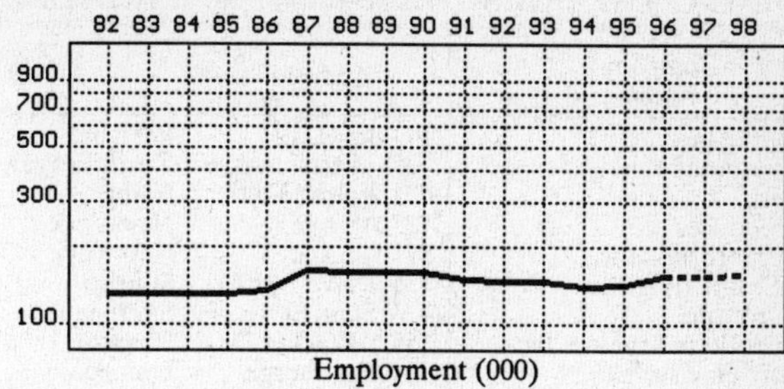

Employment (000)

GENERAL STATISTICS

Year	Establishments (number)	Employment (number)	Payroll ($ million)	Sales ($ million)	Employees per Establishment (number)	Sales per Establishment ($)	Payroll per Employee ($)
1982	24,173	132,317	1,433.3	8,352.4	5	345,528	10,833
1983	23,870	131,497	1,521.3	9,080.8*e*	6	-	11,569
1984	23,547	131,429	1,600.0	9,809.2*e*	6	-	12,174
1985	23,416	133,407	1,715.0	10,537.5*e*	6	-	12,855
1986	24,539	136,117	2,466.6	11,265.9*e*	6	-	18,121
1987	28,050	162,795	1,921.5	11,994.3	6	427,603	11,803
1988	26,951	159,650	2,162.4	12,395.8*e*	6	-	13,545
1989	27,367	159,444	2,250.2	12,797.4*e*	6	-	14,113
1990	26,583	160,811	2,322.1	13,198.9*e*	6	-	14,440
1991	26,399	150,269	2,214.6	13,600.4*e*	6	-	14,737
1992	28,077	147,888	2,224.4	14,002.0	5	498,699	15,041
1993	27,590	147,687	2,304.6	14,938.3*p*	5	-	15,605
1994	26,995	141,748	2,427.7	15,503.3*p*	5	-	17,127
1995	27,487	143,377	2,555.5	16,068.2*p*	5	-	17,824
1996	28,577*p*	154,979*p*	2,648.6*p*	16,633.2*p*	-	-	-
1997	28,910*p*	156,229*p*	2,724.4*p*	17,198.1*p*	-	-	-
1998	29,244*p*	157,479*p*	2,800.2*p*	17,763.1*p*	-	-	-

Sources: Economic Census of the United States, 1982, 1987, and 1992. Establishment counts, employment, and payroll are from *County Business Patterns* for non-Census years. Values followed by a 'p' are projections by the editors. Sales and expense data for non-Census years are extrapolations, marked by 'e'. Industries reclassified in 1987 will not have data for prior years. Data are the most recent available at this level of detail.

INDICES OF CHANGE

Year	Establishments (number)	Employment (number)	Payroll ($ million)	Sales ($ million)	Employees per Establishment (number)	Sales per Establishment ($)	Payroll per Employee ($)
1982	86.1	89.5	64.4	59.7	100.0	69.3	72.0
1983	85.0	88.9	68.4	64.9*e*	120.0	-	76.9
1984	83.9	88.9	71.9	70.1*e*	120.0	-	80.9
1985	83.4	90.2	77.1	75.3*e*	120.0	-	85.5
1986	87.4	92.0	110.9	80.5*e*	120.0	-	120.5
1987	99.9	110.1	86.4	85.7	120.0	85.7	78.5
1988	96.0	108.0	97.2	88.5*e*	120.0	-	90.1
1989	97.5	107.8	101.2	91.4*e*	120.0	-	93.8
1990	94.7	108.7	104.4	94.3*e*	120.0	-	96.0
1991	94.0	101.6	99.6	97.1*e*	120.0	-	98.0
1992	100.0	100.0	100.0	100.0	100.0	100.0	100.0
1993	98.3	99.9	103.6	106.7*p*	107.1	-	103.7
1994	96.1	95.8	109.1	110.7*p*	105.0	-	113.9
1995	97.9	96.9	114.9	114.8*p*	104.3	-	118.5
1996	101.8*p*	104.8*p*	119.1*p*	118.8*p*	-	-	-
1997	103.0*p*	105.6*p*	122.5*p*	122.8*p*	-	-	-
1998	104.2*p*	106.5*p*	125.9*p*	126.9*p*	-	-	-

Sources: Same as General Statistics. The values shown reflect change from the base year, 1992. Values above 100 mean greater than 1992, values below 100 mean less than 1992, and a value of 100 in the 1982-91 or 1993-98 period means same as 1992. Values followed by a 'p' are projections by the editors; 'e' stands for extrapolation. Data are the most recent available at this level of detail.

SELECTED RATIOS

For 1992	Avg. of All Retail	Analyzed Industry	Index	For 1992	Avg. of All Retail	Analyzed Industry	Index
Employees per Establishment	12	5	44	Sales per Employee	102,941	94,680	92
Payroll per Establishment	146,026	79,225	54	Sales per Establishment	1,241,555	498,700	40
Payroll per Employee	12,107	15,041	124	Expenses per Establishment	na	na	na

Sources: Same as General Statistics. The 'Average of All Manufacturing' column represents the average of all manufacturing industries reported for the most recent complete year available. The Index shows the relationship between the Average and the Analyzed Industry. For example, 100 means that they are equal; 500 that the Analyzed Industry is five times the average; 50 means that the Analyzed Industry is half the national average. The abbreviation 'na' is used to show that data are 'not available'.

LEADING COMPANIES Number shown: **50** Total sales ($ mil): **11,696** Total employment (000): **101.2**

Company Name	Address				CEO Name	Phone	Co. Type	Sales ($ mil)	Empl. (000)
Fred Meyer Inc.	PO Box 42121	Portland	OR	97242	Robert G Miller	503-232-8844	P	3,725	28.0
Kmart Fashions	7373 Westside Ave	North Bergen	NJ	07047	Don Keeble	201-861-9100	D	2,220 •	25.0
Zale Corp.	901 Walnut Hill	Irving	TX	75038	Robert J DiNicola	972-580-4000	P	1,254	10.0
Tiffany and Co.	727 5th Ave	New York	NY	10022	William R Chaney	212-755-8000	P	1,018	4.4
Finlay Enterprises Inc.	521 5th Ave	New York	NY	10175	Arthur E Reiner	212-808-2060	P	685	6.3
Jan Bell Marketing Inc.	13801 NW 14th St	Sunrise	FL	33323	Isaac Arguetty	954-846-2705	P	254	2.3
Friedman's Inc.	4 W State St	Savannah	GA	31401	Bradley J Stinn	912-233-9333	P	237	2.5
Marks Brothers Jewelers Inc.	155 N Wacker Dr	Chicago	IL	60606	Hugh Patinkin	312-782-6800	P	189	1.1
Fortunoff Fine Jewelry	70 C Lindbergh	Uniondale	NY	11553	Alan Fortunoff	516-832-9000	R	180 •	1.8
Piercing Pagoda Inc.	PO Box 25007	Lehigh	PA	18002	Richard H Penske	610-691-0457	P	167	3.7
Brendle's Inc.	1919 N Bridge St	N. Carolina	NC	28621	J M McLeish Jr	910-526-5600	P	155	1.6
Barry's Jewelers Inc.	111 W Lemon Ave	Monrovia	CA	91016	Robert W Bridel	818-303-4741	P	140	1.3
A.A. Friedman Company Inc.	2559 Washington	Augusta	GA	30904	Henrietta Friedman	706-731-0037	R	120 •	1.3
Reliable Stores Inc.	6301 Stevens Forest	Columbia	MD	21046	Richard M Barnett	410-381-9650	R	110	1.0
Reeds Jewelers Inc.	PO Box 2229	Wilmington	NC	28402	Alan M Zimmer	910-350-3100	P	99	0.8
Bijoux Terner L.P.	7200 NW 7th St	Miami	FL	33126	Salomon Terner	305-266-9000	R	88	0.4
Carlyle and Company Jewelers	PO Box 21768	Greensboro	NC	27420	John K Cohen	910-294-2450	R	85	0.8
Mayor's Jewelers Inc.	283 Catalonia Ave	Coral Gables	FL	33134	Samuel Getz	305-442-4233	R	80	0.4
Osterman Inc.	375 Ghent Rd	Akron	OH	44333	Nathan Light	216-668-5000	S	75	1.0
Merksamer Jewelers Inc.	2101 Hurley Way	Sacramento	CA	95825	Samuel J Merksamer	916-923-9107	R	57	0.4
Downey Designs International	2265 Executive Dr	Indianapolis	IN	46241	David G Downey	317-248-9888	R	55	0.2
Ben Bridge Jeweler Inc.	PO Box 1908	Seattle	WA	98111	RL Bridge	206-448-8800	R	53 •	0.4
J.B. Robinson Jewelers Inc.	375 Ghent Rd	Akron	OH	44333	Michael Lavington	330-633-1494	S	50	0.6
Dearden's Inc.	700 S Main St	Los Angeles	CA	90014	Douglas E Dearden	213-362-9600	R	44	0.4
Helzbergs Diamond Shops Inc.	1825 Swift	N. Kansas City	MO	64116	Jeff Comment	816-842-7780	S	44	0.8
Fox Jewelry Company Inc.	83 Monroe Ctr	Grand Rapids	MI	49503	John F Bowen	616-459-6271	R	40	0.4
Jay B. Rudolph Inc.	200 S Hoover Blvd	Tampa	FL	33609	Richard Rudolph	813-286-8888	R	40	0.3
Wedlo Inc.	3200 2nd Ave N	Birmingham	AL	35203	Robert A Keller	205-322-4444	R	40	0.4
Silverman Factory Jewelers Inc.	4605 Osborne Dr	El Paso	TX	79922	Randall McCulley	915-833-3085	R	37 •	0.3
Crescent Jewelers Inc.	315 11th St	Oakland	CA	94607	Steve Price	510-836-2810	R	35 •	0.4
Edward D. Sultan Company Ltd.	PO Box 301	Honolulu	HI	96809	Edward D Sultan III	808-923-4971	R	25	0.3
Goldstein Brothers Inc.	7956 Crestwood	Birmingham	AL	35210	Milton Goldstein	205-956-4314	R	25	0.3
Circle Fine Art Corp.	303 E Wacker Dr	Chicago	IL	60601	Jack Solomon	312-616-1300	P	20	0.2
Harry Ritchie's Jeweler Inc.	956 Willamette St	Eugene	OR	97401	Donald Ritchie	503-686-1787	R	20	0.3
Melart Jewelers Inc.	8700 Georgia Ave	Silver Spring	MD	20910	Albert Foer	301-587-6880	R	19	0.3
Shifrin Jewelers Inc.	14510 W 8 Mile Rd	Oak Park	MI	48237	W Sherman	313-968-1515	S	19 •	0.2
Trading Company of America	8900 Keystone	Indianapolis	IN	46240	Fred Klipsch	317-581-3100	R	17 •	0.1
Albert S. Smyth Company Inc.	29 Greenmeadow	Luth. Timonium	MD	21093	RL Smyth Sr	410-252-6666	R	15	0.1
Coleman E. Adler and Sons	722 Canal St	New Orleans	LA	70130	Coleman Adler II	504-523-5292	R	15	0.1
Finks Jewelers Inc.	PO Box 12906	Roanoke	VA	24029	Mark Fink	703-342-2991	R	15 •	0.2
Meyer Jewelry Co.	20500 Eureka Rd	Taylor	MI	48180	James McTevia	313-283-0900	R	15 •	0.2
Murray's Bargain Center	27207 Plymouth Rd	Detroit	MI	48239	Irving Pitt	313-937-8360	R	15 •	0.2
Raymonds Jewelry	3681 Westervill Rd	Columbus	OH	43224	Jay Schottenstein	614-471-5646	D	15	0.2
Dallas Gold and Silver Exchange	2817 Forest Ln	Dallas	TX	75234	LS Smith	214-484-3662	P	14	<0.1
Call Jewelers Inc.	8337 N 7th St	Phoenix	AZ	85020	Francis Call	602-861-2016	R	13 •	0.2
Lory's West Inc.	314 S Beverly Dr	Beverly Hills	CA	90212	Bruce Faber	310-551-1212	R	13	<0.1
Braude Jewelry Corp.	211 E Ontario St	Chicago	IL	60611	Ken Braude	312-988-4520	R	12	0.2
Dick and Jack Industries Inc.	631 S Olive St	Los Angeles	CA	90014	Jack Bouchakian	213-622-8165	R	11	0.1
Intern. Diamond & Gold Designs	4026 E 82nd St	Indianapolis	IN	46250	Julio Campins	317-578-4653	R	11	<0.1
S. Joseph and Sons Inc.	320 6th Ave	Des Moines	IA	50309	W Joseph	515-283-1961	R	11	<0.1

Source: *Ward's Business Directory of U.S. Private and Public Companies*, 1998. The company type code used is as follows: P - Public, R - Private, S - Subsidiary, D - Division, J - Joint Venture, A - Affiliate, G - Group. Sales are in millions of dollars, employees are in thousands. An asterisk (*) indicates an estimated sales volume. The symbol < stands for 'less than'.

OCCUPATIONS EMPLOYED BY SIC 594 - MISCELLANEOUS SHOPPING GOODS STORES

Occupation	% of Total 1996	Change to 2006	Occupation	% of Total 1996	Change to 2006
Salespersons, retail	46.8	20.5	Bookkeeping, accounting, & auditing clerks	2.2	-9.5
Marketing & sales worker supervisors	9.3	13.1	General office clerks	1.6	-2.7
Cashiers	8.2	14.4	Wholesale & retail buyers, except farm products	1.5	-6.4
Stock clerks	7.1	6.8	Traffic, shipping, receiving clerks	1.3	13.1
General managers & top executives	5.5	9.6	Purchasing managers	1.2	1.8
Sales & related workers nec	2.5	24.4	Bicycle repairers	1.2	35.7

Source: *Industry-Occupation Matrix*, Bureau of Labor Statistics. These data relate to one or more 3-digit SIC industry groups rather than to a single 4-digit SIC. The change reported for each occupation to the year 2006 is a percent of growth or decline as estimated by the Bureau of Labor Statistics. The abbreviation nec stands for 'not elsewhere classified'.

STATE AND REGIONAL CONCENTRATION

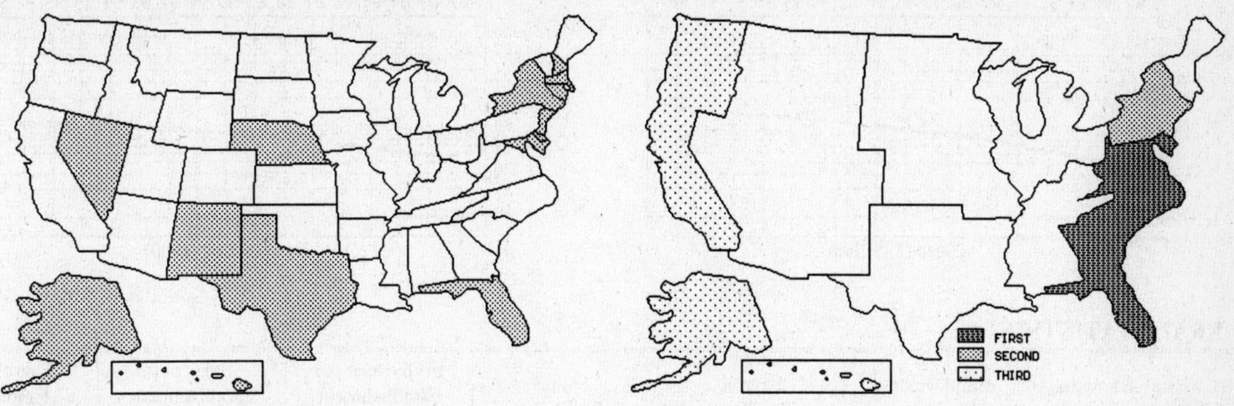

INDUSTRY DATA BY STATE

State	Establishments - 1995 Total (number)	Establishments - 1995 % of U.S.	Employment - 1995 Total (number)	Employment - 1995 % of U.S.	Employment - 1995 Per Estab.	Payroll - 1995 Total ($ mil.)	Payroll - 1995 Per Empl. ($)	Sales - 1992 Total ($ mil.)	Sales - 1992 % of U.S.	Sales - 1992 Per Estab ($)
California	2,825	10.3	12,734	8.9	5	252.0	19,789	1,642.3	11.7	104,957
New York	2,142	7.8	10,373	7.2	5	254.2	24,510	1,475.1	10.5	138,508
Texas	1,980	7.2	10,078	7.0	5	177.5	17,616	984.8	7.0	91,538
Florida	1,952	7.1	11,165	7.8	6	176.2	15,777	876.2	6.3	99,539
Illinois	1,117	4.1	6,098	4.3	5	109.2	17,908	628.1	4.5	95,928
Pennsylvania	1,325	4.8	6,431	4.5	5	101.3	15,757	582.7	4.2	85,739
Ohio	1,038	3.8	6,339	4.4	6	101.3	15,980	534.1	3.8	86,539
New Jersey	952	3.5	4,079	2.8	4	80.9	19,831	474.9	3.4	106,296
Michigan	844	3.1	4,493	3.1	5	84.6	18,823	473.3	3.4	99,284
Massachusetts	680	2.5	3,367	2.3	5	67.2	19,952	416.5	3.0	106,933
Georgia	733	2.7	4,092	2.9	6	67.5	16,500	369.0	2.6	92,033
North Carolina	881	3.2	4,787	3.3	5	73.6	15,370	344.4	2.5	77,299
Virginia	726	2.6	4,163	2.9	6	67.1	16,125	343.8	2.5	83,730
Maryland	530	1.9	3,141	2.2	6	54.9	17,492	289.4	2.1	87,875
Hawaii	380	1.4	2,044	1.4	5	42.9	20,997	273.1	2.0	116,209
Indiana	574	2.1	3,257	2.3	6	51.5	15,821	256.4	1.8	76,275
Missouri	493	1.8	2,604	1.8	5	46.2	17,749	253.0	1.8	92,939
Wisconsin	522	1.9	2,762	1.9	5	42.7	15,464	233.9	1.7	84,365
Washington	462	1.7	2,640	1.8	6	51.3	19,441	233.0	1.7	99,601
Tennessee	533	1.9	2,677	1.9	5	44.8	16,733	225.7	1.6	74,629
Connecticut	341	1.2	1,852	1.3	5	39.2	21,147	205.5	1.5	98,788
Arizona	483	1.8	2,489	1.7	5	43.6	17,515	205.0	1.5	81,439
Minnesota	425	1.5	2,299	1.6	5	39.5	17,166	204.3	1.5	89,586
Alabama	452	1.6	2,496	1.7	6	37.4	14,997	202.4	1.4	78,255
South Carolina	441	1.6	2,576	1.8	6	38.0	14,751	188.8	1.3	78,076
Colorado	415	1.5	2,237	1.6	5	39.5	17,640	184.8	1.3	88,078
Louisiana	425	1.5	2,154	1.5	5	38.9	18,082	184.8	1.3	75,604
Kentucky	380	1.4	2,014	1.4	5	29.7	14,760	156.6	1.1	80,648
Oregon	276	1.0	1,486	1.0	5	28.8	19,392	145.7	1.0	93,385
Iowa	298	1.1	1,700	1.2	6	26.0	15,294	130.1	0.9	74,868
Oklahoma	284	1.0	1,352	0.9	5	21.1	15,632	124.5	0.9	74,399
Kansas	220	0.8	1,293	0.9	6	22.0	17,027	103.8	0.7	80,362
New Mexico	215	0.8	1,074	0.7	5	17.2	16,019	99.5	0.7	85,076
Mississippi	280	1.0	1,251	0.9	4	17.8	14,237	97.0	0.7	69,351
Nevada	182	0.7	1,009	0.7	6	20.2	20,046	94.4	0.7	99,126
Nebraska	142	0.5	1,045	0.7	7	16.1	15,390	91.1	0.7	97,082
Arkansas	220	0.8	1,085	0.8	5	18.0	16,580	90.5	0.6	74,276
New Hampshire	127	0.5	683	0.5	5	12.3	18,009	67.3	0.5	98,834
Utah	150	0.5	828	0.6	6	15.6	18,832	67.3	0.5	87,026
West Virginia	170	0.6	827	0.6	5	12.1	14,670	65.8	0.5	77,243
Maine	104	0.4	534	0.4	5	9.6	18,032	46.3	0.3	89,561
Delaware	76	0.3	442	0.3	6	8.1	18,224	46.1	0.3	103,361
Rhode Island	109	0.4	589	0.4	5	10.5	17,910	45.7	0.3	90,306
Idaho	105	0.4	551	0.4	5	10.1	18,397	42.5	0.3	85,046
D.C.	63	0.2	268	0.2	4	7.2	26,840	39.6	0.3	123,738
Alaska	77	0.3	354	0.2	5	6.2	17,593	36.5	0.3	88,692
Montana	93	0.3	396	0.3	4	5.7	14,341	33.2	0.2	81,240
South Dakota	77	0.3	387	0.3	5	5.9	15,359	29.8	0.2	82,257
North Dakota	57	0.2	333	0.2	6	5.3	15,988	28.5	0.2	79,248
Vermont	61	0.2	234	0.2	4	3.2	13,791	18.9	0.1	74,271
Wyoming	50	0.2	215	0.1	4	3.4	15,693	16.1	0.1	63,711

Source: *County Business Patterns, 1995* and *Economic Census of the U.S., 1992*. Data are sorted by 1992 revenues and, if revenues are unavailable, by establishments in 1995. The symbol (D) indicates that data are withheld by the source to avoid disclosure of competitive information. A dash (-) indicates that data are not available or undisclosed because they do not meet statistical validity standards. Shaded *states* on the state map indicate those states which have proportionately greater representation in the industry than would be indicated by the state's population; the ratio is based on total revenues or number of establishments. Shaded *regions* indicate where the industry is regionally most concentrated.

5945 - HOBBY, TOY, AND GAME SHOPS

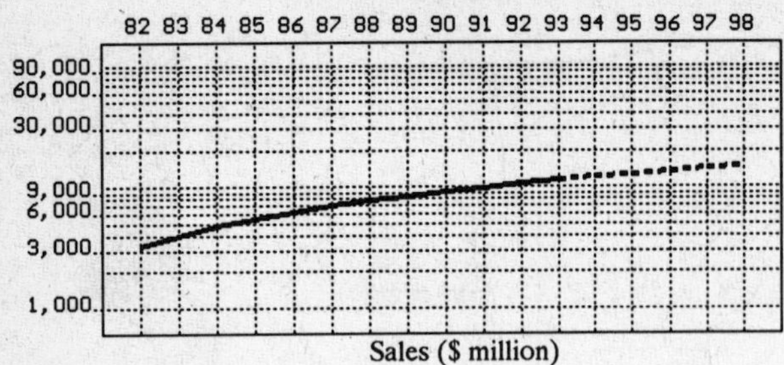

Sales ($ million)

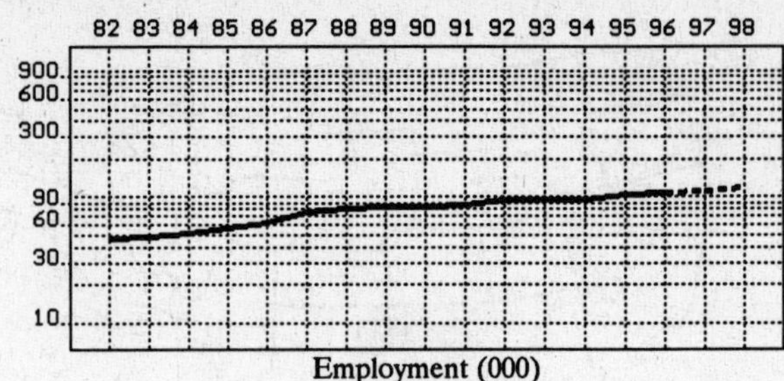

Employment (000)

GENERAL STATISTICS

Year	Establishments (number)	Employment (number)	Payroll ($ million)	Sales ($ million)	Employees per Establishment (number)	Sales per Establishment ($)	Payroll per Employee ($)
1982	8,429	46,114	325.1	3,237.6	5	384,108	7,050
1983	8,080	48,533	369.8	3,996.4*e*	6	-	7,620
1984	7,828	52,155	421.6	4,755.1*e*	7	-	8,084
1985	7,634	56,395	473.8	5,513.9*e*	7	-	8,401
1986	8,060	63,102	535.7	6,272.6*e*	8	-	8,490
1987	9,629	75,932	613.9	7,031.4	8	730,227	8,085
1988	9,213	79,867	714.8	7,750.5*e*	9	-	8,951
1989	9,036	82,830	778.5	8,469.7*e*	9	-	9,398
1990	9,378	83,121	834.0	9,188.9*e*	9	-	10,033
1991	9,629	86,947	895.9	9,908.1*e*	9	-	10,304
1992	10,860	94,804	991.9	10,627.3	9	978,570	10,462
1993	10,678	93,379	1,027.3	11,411.2*p*	9	-	11,001
1994	10,402	93,976	1,127.1	12,150.2*p*	9	-	11,993
1995	10,347	103,960	1,190.0	12,889.1*p*	10	-	11,446
1996	10,970*p*	109,346*p*	1,249.6*p*	13,628.1*p*	-	-	-
1997	11,202*p*	113,820*p*	1,318.1*p*	14,367.1*p*	-	-	-
1998	11,434*p*	118,293*p*	1,386.6*p*	15,106.0*p*	-	-	-

Sources: Economic Census of the United States, 1982, 1987, and 1992. Establishment counts, employment, and payroll are from *County Business Patterns* for non-Census years. Values followed by a 'p' are projections by the editors. Sales and expense data for non-Census years are extrapolations, marked by 'e'. Industries reclassified in 1987 will not have data for prior years. Data are the most recent available at this level of detail.

INDICES OF CHANGE

Year	Establishments (number)	Employment (number)	Payroll ($ million)	Sales ($ million)	Employees per Establishment (number)	Sales per Establishment ($)	Payroll per Employee ($)
1982	77.6	48.6	32.8	30.5	55.6	39.3	67.4
1983	74.4	51.2	37.3	37.6*e*	66.7	-	72.8
1984	72.1	55.0	42.5	44.7*e*	77.8	-	77.3
1985	70.3	59.5	47.8	51.9*e*	77.8	-	80.3
1986	74.2	66.6	54.0	59.0*e*	88.9	-	81.2
1987	88.7	80.1	61.9	66.2	88.9	74.6	77.3
1988	84.8	84.2	72.1	72.9*e*	100.0	-	85.6
1989	83.2	87.4	78.5	79.7*e*	100.0	-	89.8
1990	86.4	87.7	84.1	86.5*e*	100.0	-	95.9
1991	88.7	91.7	90.3	93.2*e*	100.0	-	98.5
1992	100.0	100.0	100.0	100.0	100.0	100.0	100.0
1993	98.3	98.5	103.6	107.4*p*	97.2	-	105.2
1994	95.8	99.1	113.6	114.3*p*	100.4	-	114.6
1995	95.3	109.7	120.0	121.3*p*	111.6	-	109.4
1996	101.0*p*	115.3*p*	126.0*p*	128.2*p*	-	-	-
1997	103.1*p*	120.1*p*	132.9*p*	135.2*p*	-	-	-
1998	105.3*p*	124.8*p*	139.8*p*	142.1*p*	-	-	-

Sources: Same as General Statistics. The values shown reflect change from the base year, 1992. Values above 100 mean greater than 1992, values below 100 mean less than 1992, and a value of 100 in the 1982-91 or 1993-98 period means same as 1992. Values followed by a 'p' are projections by the editors; 'e' stands for extrapolation. Data are the most recent available at this level of detail.

SELECTED RATIOS

For 1992	Avg. of All Retail	Analyzed Industry	Index	For 1992	Avg. of All Retail	Analyzed Industry	Index
Employees per Establishment	12	9	72	Sales per Employee	102,941	112,098	109
Payroll per Establishment	146,026	91,335	63	Sales per Establishment	1,241,555	978,573	79
Payroll per Employee	12,107	10,463	86	Expenses per Establishment	na	na	na

Sources: Same as General Statistics. The 'Average of All Manufacturing' column represents the average of all manufacturing industries reported for the most recent complete year available. The Index shows the relationship between the Average and the Analyzed Industry. For example, 100 means that they are equal; 500 that the Analyzed Industry is five times the average; 50 means that the Analyzed Industry is half the national average. The abbreviation 'na' is used to show that data are 'not available'.

LEADING COMPANIES

Number shown: 27 Total sales ($ mil): **13,990** Total employment (000): **100.8**

Company Name	Address				CEO Name	Phone	Co. Type	Sales ($ mil)	Empl. (000)
Toys R Us Inc.	461 From Rd	Paramus	NJ	07652	Michael Goldstein	201-262-7800	P	9,932	58.0
Southdate Kay-Bee Toy Inc.	100 West St	Pittsfield	MA	01201	Michael Glazer	413-496-3000	S	1,060	13.0
General Host Corp.	PO Box 10045	Stamford	CT	06904	Harris J Ashton	203-357-9900	P	597	7.2
Ben Franklin Retail Stores Inc.	PO Box 5938	Chicago	IL	60680	Robert A Kendig	708-462-6100	P	375	2.0
Value Merchants Inc.	710 N Plankinton	Milwaukee	WI	53203		414-274-2575	P	363	4.8
Ben Franklin Crafts Inc.	500 E North Ave	Carol Stream	IL	60188	Bob Kendig	708-462-6100	S	350	0.2
Brookstone Inc.	17 Riverside St	Nashua	NH	03062	Michael Anthony	603-880-9500	P	240	2.0
Brendle's Inc.	1919 N Bridge St	N. Carolina	NC	28621	J M McLeish Jr	910-526-5600	P	155	1.6
Old America Stores Inc.	PO Box 370	Howe	TX	75459	R W Tredinnick	903-532-3000	P	136	3.5
Paradies Shops Inc.	5950 Fulton Indrial	Atlanta	GA	30336	Dick Dickson	404-344-7905	R	107 *	1.4
Imaginarium Inc.	1600 Riviera Ave	Walnut Creek	CA	94596	Cynthia Cleveland	510-930-8666	R	100 *	0.9
House of Lloyd Inc.	11901 Grandview	Grandview	MO	64030	Harry Lloyd	816-966-2222	R	92	0.8
Rag Shops Inc.	111 Wagaraw Rd	Hawthorne	NJ	07506	Stanley Berenzweig	973-423-1303	P	86	1.1
Noodle Kidoodle Inc.	105 Price Pkwy	Farmingdale	NY	11735	Stanley Greenman	516-293-5300	P	81	0.9
Play Co. Toys	550 Rancheros Dr	San Marcos	CA	92069	Richard Brady	619-471-4505	R	71	0.5
Crafts Plus + Inc.	5650 Randolph	San Antonio	TX	78233	Gary Tennison	210-637-1855	R	60	0.9
Fabric Place	136 Howard St	Framingham	MA	01701	Ron Isaacson	508-872-4888	R	42 *	0.5
Amber's Stores Inc.	12092 Forestgate	Dallas	TX	75238	Neal W Stevens	214-889-1199	P	41	0.5
S and S Worldwide Inc.	PO Box 513	Colchester	CT	06415	Stephen Schwartz	203-537-3451	R	33 *	0.3
S.S. Retail Stores Corp.	30020 Ahern Ave	Union City	CA	94587	Donald Cohn	510-429-1515	R	32	0.3
Store of Knowledge	16069 Shoemaker	Cerritos	CA	90703	Michael Kaplan	562-345-1000	R	13 *	0.1
Great Train Store Partners L.P.	17101 Preston Rd	Dallas	TX	75248	James H Levi	214-733-0445	R	11 *	0.2
Building Blocks Inc.	1720 Post Rd E	Westport	CT	06880	Steven E Glass	203-256-4380	S	7	<0.1
Specialty Retail Group Inc.	477 Madison	New York	NY	10022	Steven E Glass	212-872-9684	P	3	<0.1
Creative Gaming Inc.	150 Morris Ave	Springfield	NJ	07081	Peter J Jegou	973-467-0266	P	2	<0.1
Dentt Inc.	4171 Marquis Way	Salt Lake City	UT	84124	Gale Hammond	801-277-7056	R	1	<0.1
James Page Brewing Co.	1300 Quincy St	Minneapolis	MN	55413	James Page	612-781-8247	R	1	<0.1

Source: *Ward's Business Directory of U.S. Private and Public Companies*, 1998. The company type code used is as follows: P - Public, R - Private, S - Subsidiary, D - Division, J - Joint Venture, A - Affiliate, G - Group. Sales are in millions of dollars, employees are in thousands. An asterisk (*) indicates an estimated sales volume. The symbol < stands for 'less than'.

OCCUPATIONS EMPLOYED BY SIC 594 - MISCELLANEOUS SHOPPING GOODS STORES

Occupation	% of Total 1996	Change to 2006	Occupation	% of Total 1996	Change to 2006
Salespersons, retail	46.8	20.5	Bookkeeping, accounting, & auditing clerks	2.2	-9.5
Marketing & sales worker supervisors	9.3	13.1	General office clerks	1.6	-2.7
Cashiers	8.2	14.4	Wholesale & retail buyers, except farm products	1.5	-6.4
Stock clerks	7.1	6.8	Traffic, shipping, receiving clerks	1.3	13.1
General managers & top executives	5.5	9.6	Purchasing managers	1.2	1.8
Sales & related workers nec	2.5	24.4	Bicycle repairers	1.2	35.7

Source: *Industry-Occupation Matrix*, Bureau of Labor Statistics. These data relate to one or more 3-digit SIC industry groups rather than to a single 4-digit SIC. The change reported for each occupation to the year 2006 is a percent of growth or decline as estimated by the Bureau of Labor Statistics. The abbreviation nec stands for 'not elsewhere classified'.

STATE AND REGIONAL CONCENTRATION

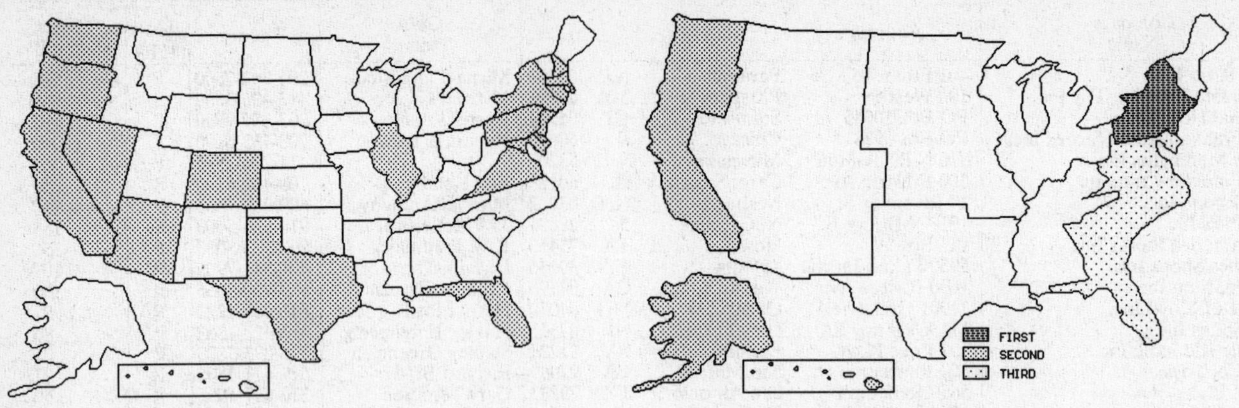

INDUSTRY DATA BY STATE

State	Establishments - 1995 Total (number)	Establishments - 1995 % of U.S.	Employment - 1995 Total (number)	Employment - 1995 % of U.S.	Employment - 1995 Per Estab.	Payroll - 1995 Total ($ mil.)	Payroll - 1995 Per Empl. ($)	Sales - 1992 Total ($ mil.)	Sales - 1992 % of U.S.	Sales - 1992 Per Estab ($)
California	1,182	11.4	13,555	13.0	11	160.4	11,830	1,528.9	14.4	123,736
New York	640	6.2	6,532	6.3	10	85.4	13,076	924.2	8.7	141,552
Texas	625	6.0	8,508	8.2	14	89.6	10,529	782.1	7.4	114,740
Florida	496	4.8	5,392	5.2	11	62.5	11,591	591.2	5.6	118,249
New Jersey	339	3.3	3,926	3.8	12	50.3	12,803	560.0	5.3	136,411
Illinois	456	4.4	4,971	4.8	11	59.5	11,969	554.3	5.2	112,694
Pennsylvania	492	4.8	4,615	4.4	9	51.4	11,145	533.5	5.0	105,776
Ohio	472	4.6	4,449	4.3	9	46.7	10,500	443.6	4.2	107,243
Michigan	330	3.2	3,228	3.1	10	36.8	11,413	337.4	3.2	107,977
Maryland	210	2.0	2,762	2.7	13	30.6	11,067	325.4	3.1	122,695
Virginia	329	3.2	3,759	3.6	11	40.9	10,891	311.1	2.9	99,515
Massachusetts	268	2.6	2,667	2.6	10	33.8	12,681	287.4	2.7	101,495
Washington	297	2.9	2,458	2.4	8	29.5	12,000	218.6	2.1	114,897
Georgia	242	2.3	2,194	2.1	9	26.3	11,966	203.8	1.9	116,087
North Carolina	310	3.0	2,476	2.4	8	28.9	11,677	197.3	1.9	95,791
Missouri	237	2.3	2,467	2.4	10	23.9	9,696	187.6	1.8	86,095
Colorado	207	2.0	2,263	2.2	11	23.1	10,227	183.5	1.7	96,497
Connecticut	153	1.5	1,488	1.4	10	20.7	13,923	174.1	1.6	122,379
Indiana	212	2.0	1,775	1.7	8	18.1	10,177	174.1	1.6	103,336
Arizona	175	1.7	1,736	1.7	10	20.7	11,929	169.8	1.6	109,113
Tennessee	184	1.8	1,466	1.4	8	17.5	11,928	156.2	1.5	109,362
Oregon	168	1.6	1,537	1.5	9	18.2	11,822	141.9	1.3	109,807
Wisconsin	231	2.2	1,799	1.7	8	18.9	10,500	141.6	1.3	93,897
Minnesota	180	1.7	1,741	1.7	10	17.2	9,867	132.2	1.2	83,434
Louisiana	126	1.2	1,444	1.4	11	16.1	11,164	128.5	1.2	97,336
Oklahoma	110	1.1	1,327	1.3	12	13.8	10,426	119.6	1.1	114,519
South Carolina	121	1.2	960	0.9	8	12.4	12,940	96.8	0.9	103,852
Alabama	108	1.0	883	0.8	8	9.8	11,117	95.0	0.9	110,775
Kansas	116	1.1	1,159	1.1	10	11.6	10,038	93.8	0.9	105,849
Kentucky	113	1.1	982	0.9	9	10.9	11,140	91.6	0.9	96,674
New Hampshire	75	0.7	691	0.7	9	7.6	11,016	81.0	0.8	104,238
Utah	116	1.1	1,263	1.2	11	12.6	10,015	76.2	0.7	81,370
Nevada	50	0.5	645	0.6	13	9.1	14,181	66.6	0.6	139,696
Iowa	142	1.4	894	0.9	6	9.3	10,375	61.0	0.6	73,048
Hawaii	52	0.5	435	0.4	8	5.3	12,292	47.5	0.4	149,804
Arkansas	75	0.7	731	0.7	10	7.8	10,689	45.9	0.4	100,214
Nebraska	74	0.7	717	0.7	10	7.2	10,057	43.9	0.4	85,155
Delaware	35	0.3	332	0.3	9	4.4	13,117	43.3	0.4	134,841
New Mexico	68	0.7	624	0.6	9	6.1	9,724	42.1	0.4	94,098
West Virginia	68	0.7	382	0.4	6	4.1	10,757	38.9	0.4	87,865
Maine	67	0.6	276	0.3	4	3.4	12,333	36.4	0.3	98,164
Mississippi	57	0.6	445	0.4	8	5.3	11,858	33.6	0.3	96,491
Rhode Island	30	0.3	211	0.2	7	2.7	12,976	26.5	0.2	103,496
Idaho	74	0.7	462	0.4	6	4.7	10,203	25.8	0.2	81,665
Montana	54	0.5	355	0.3	7	3.5	9,961	19.8	0.2	60,497
Alaska	28	0.3	246	0.2	9	3.2	12,882	14.5	0.1	99,459
South Dakota	45	0.4	278	0.3	6	3.1	11,090	10.3	0.1	60,306
North Dakota	37	0.4	156	0.2	4	1.5	9,327	9.2	0.1	54,862
Vermont	38	0.4	131	0.1	3	1.5	11,305	7.9	0.1	67,171
D.C.	12	0.1	96	0.1	8	1.2	12,354	6.8	0.1	81,500
Wyoming	21	0.2	71	0.1	3	0.7	9,944	4.9	0.0	69,557

Source: County Business Patterns, 1995 and *Economic Census of the U.S., 1992*. Data are sorted by 1992 revenues and, if revenues are unavailable, by establishments in 1995. The symbol (D) indicates that data are withheld by the source to avoid disclosure of competitive information. A dash (-) indicates that data are not available or undisclosed because they do not meet statistical validity standards. Shaded *states* on the state map indicate those states which have proportionately greater representation in the industry than would be indicated by the state's population; the ratio is based on total revenues or number of establishments. Shaded *regions* indicate where the industry is regionally most concentrated.

5946 - CAMERA & PHOTOGRAPHIC SUPPLY STORES

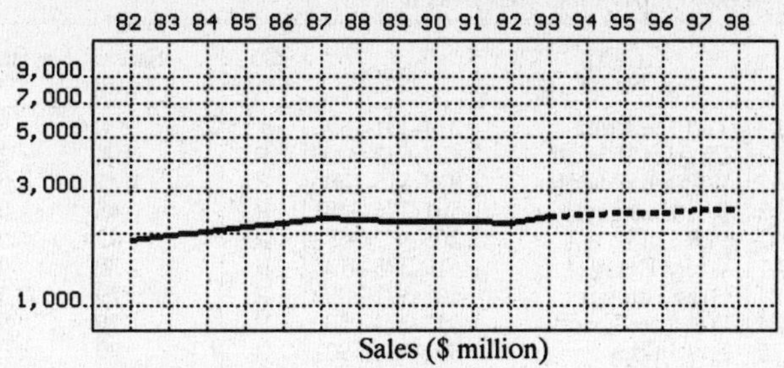

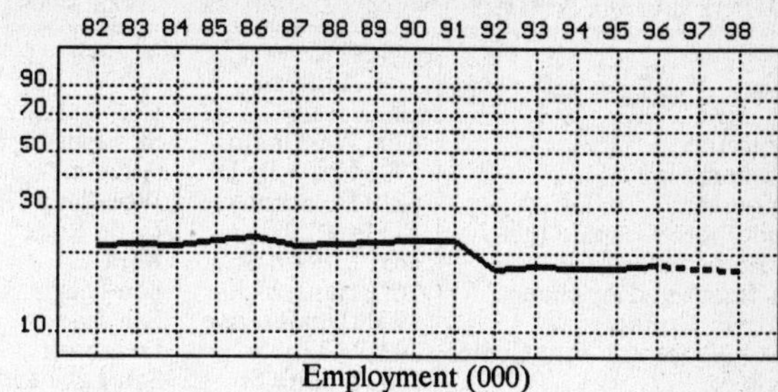

GENERAL STATISTICS

Year	Establishments (number)	Employment (number)	Payroll ($ million)	Sales ($ million)	Employees per Establishment (number)	Sales per Establishment ($)	Payroll per Employee ($)
1982	4,201	21,307	224.8	1,884.2	5	448,519	10,551
1983	4,212	21,946	249.0	1,966.2e	5	-	11,348
1984	4,026	21,533	256.2	2,048.1e	5	-	11,899
1985	3,933	22,537	285.3	2,130.1e	6	-	12,660
1986	3,921	23,031	293.2	2,212.0e	6	-	12,729
1987	3,791	21,425	276.0	2,294.0	6	605,117	12,880
1988	3,618	22,043	314.4	2,276.7e	6	-	14,263
1989	3,591	22,181	330.8	2,259.4e	6	-	14,916
1990	3,594	22,481	353.5	2,242.1e	6	-	15,724
1991	3,613	22,495	354.6	2,224.8e	6	-	15,761
1992	3,012	17,407	285.4	2,207.5	6	732,899	16,393
1993	3,035	17,965	296.8	2,352.6p	6	-	16,520
1994	2,958	17,704	297.0	2,384.9p	6	-	16,778
1995	2,935	17,792	302.2	2,417.3p	6	-	16,987
1996	2,815p	18,213p	334.7p	2,449.6p	-	-	-
1997	2,710p	17,862p	340.1p	2,481.9p	-	-	-
1998	2,605p	17,511p	345.5p	2,514.3p	-	-	-

Sources: *Economic Census of the United States*, 1982, 1987, and 1992. Establishment counts, employment, and payroll are from *County Business Patterns* for non-Census years. Values followed by a 'p' are projections by the editors. Sales and expense data for non-Census years are extrapolations, marked by 'e'. Industries reclassified in 1987 will not have data for prior years. Data are the most recent available at this level of detail.

INDICES OF CHANGE

Year	Establishments (number)	Employment (number)	Payroll ($ million)	Sales ($ million)	Employees per Establishment (number)	Sales per Establishment ($)	Payroll per Employee ($)
1982	139.5	122.4	78.8	85.4	83.3	61.2	64.4
1983	139.8	126.1	87.2	89.1e	83.3	-	69.2
1984	133.7	123.7	89.8	92.8e	83.3	-	72.6
1985	130.6	129.5	100.0	96.5e	100.0	-	77.2
1986	130.2	132.3	102.7	100.2e	100.0	-	77.6
1987	125.9	123.1	96.7	103.9	100.0	82.6	78.6
1988	120.1	126.6	110.2	103.1e	100.0	-	87.0
1989	119.2	127.4	115.9	102.4e	100.0	-	91.0
1990	119.3	129.1	123.9	101.6e	100.0	-	95.9
1991	120.0	129.2	124.2	100.8e	100.0	-	96.1
1992	100.0	100.0	100.0	100.0	100.0	100.0	100.0
1993	100.8	103.2	104.0	106.6p	98.7	-	100.8
1994	98.2	101.7	104.1	108.0p	99.8	-	102.4
1995	97.4	102.2	105.9	109.5p	101.0	-	103.6
1996	93.5p	104.6p	117.3p	111.0p	-	-	-
1997	90.0p	102.6p	119.2p	112.4p	-	-	-
1998	86.5p	100.6p	121.1p	113.9p	-	-	-

Sources: Same as General Statistics. The values shown reflect change from the base year, 1992. Values above 100 mean greater than 1992, values below 100 mean less than 1992, and a value of 100 in the 1982-91 or 1993-98 period means same as 1992. Values followed by a 'p' are projections by the editors; 'e' stands for extrapolation. Data are the most recent available at this level of detail.

SELECTED RATIOS

For 1992	Avg. of All Retail	Analyzed Industry	Index	For 1992	Avg. of All Retail	Analyzed Industry	Index
Employees per Establishment	12	6	48	Sales per Employee	102,941	126,817	123
Payroll per Establishment	146,026	94,754	65	Sales per Establishment	1,241,555	732,902	59
Payroll per Employee	12,107	16,396	135	Expenses per Establishment	na	na	na

Sources: Same as General Statistics. The 'Average of All Manufacturing' column represents the average of all manufacturing industries reported for the most recent complete year available. The Index shows the relationship between the Average and the Analyzed Industry. For example, 100 means that they are equal; 500 that the Analyzed Industry is five times the average; 50 means that the Analyzed Industry is half the national average. The abbreviation 'na' is used to show that data are 'not available'.

LEADING COMPANIES

Number shown: **25** Total sales ($ mil): **851** Total employment (000): **11.0**

Company Name	Address				CEO Name	Phone	Co. Type	Sales ($ mil)	Empl. (000)
Fox Photo Inc.	1706 Washington	St. Louis	MO	63103	Ted De Buhr	314-231-1575	S	200 *	5.0
Wolf Cameras Inc.	1706 Chantilly Dr	Atlanta	GA	30324	Charles R Wolf	404-633-9000	R	190	2.3
Panavision Inc.	6219 De Soto Ave	Woodland Hills	CA	91367	William C Scott	818-316-1000	P	125	0.8
Jungkind Photo-Graphic Inc.	PO Box 1509	Little Rock	AR	72203	R L Bumgardner	501-376-3481	R	45	0.2
Kits Cameras Inc.	6051 S 194th St	Kent	WA	98032	Phil Lalji	206-872-3688	R	42 *	0.5
Cousins Photo and Appliance	1691 Hancock St	San Diego	CA	92101	Wally Berry	619-293-3137	R	30	0.1
Photo Drive-Up Inc.	1900 Camden Ave	San Jose	CA	95124	Greg Bunker	408-371-7802	R	29 *	0.4
Adray Appliance & Photo Center	20219 Carlysle	Dearborn	MI	48124	D Adray-Cziraky	313-274-9500	R	20	0.1
Inkley's Inc.	2150 S State St	Salt Lake City	UT	84115	RW Inkley	801-486-5901	R	20	0.3
Samy's Camera Inc.	200 S La Brea Ave	Los Angeles	CA	90036	Samy Kamienowizz	213-938-2420	R	20	<0.1
Waterhouse Properties Inc.	670 Queen St	Honolulu	HI	96813	Edwin Wong	808-521-6751	R	20	0.3
Southwestern Camera	500 N Shepard	Houston	TX	77007	Gene Jones	713-880-0121	S	19	<0.1
Comgraphics Inc.	2601 E Yandell Dr	El Paso	TX	79903	James Bock	915-566-9351	R	18	0.2
Chilcote Co.	2140 Superior Ave	Cleveland	OH	44114	D Hein	216-781-6000	R	15	0.1
Camera Shop of New Britain	47 Main St	New Britain	CT	06051	Richard Tranchida	203-229-2057	R	12	0.2
Chapman/Leonard Studio	12950 Raymer St	N. Hollywood	CA	91605	Leonard Chapman	--	R	11	<0.1
Dodd Camera and Video	1120 Carnegie Ave	Cleveland	OH	44115	RL Greiner	216-771-1500	R	11	<0.1
Don McAlister Camera Co.	1454 W Lane Ave	Columbus	OH	43221	RE Longenbaker	614-488-1865	R	10 *	0.1
Alan Gordon Enterprises Inc.	1430 Cahuenga	Hollywood	CA	90028	G Loucks	213-466-3561	R	3	<0.1
Klein Camera and Hi-Fi Inc.	44 Main St	Westport	CT	06880	Rafael de Para	203-227-6980	R	3	<0.1
Hoag Enterprises Inc.	PO Box 4406	Springfield	MO	65808	Charles Hoag	417-883-8300	R	3	<0.1
Desktop Darkroom Inc.	1944 Atlantic Blvd	Jacksonville	FL	32207	Joe H Luter	904-398-9934	R	2 *	<0.1
Wright Images	3333 W Henrietta	Rochester	NY	14623	Michael Wright	716-424-3160	R	2 *	<0.1
Houston Computer Repair Ltd.	3001-C Fondren Rd	Houston	TX	77063	Charles Weems	713-780-2607	R	1	<0.1
Paulmar Industries Inc.	PO Box 638	Antioch	IL	60002	Robert F Menary	847-395-2080	R	1	<0.1

Source: *Ward's Business Directory of U.S. Private and Public Companies*, 1998. The company type code used is as follows: P - Public, R - Private, S - Subsidiary, D - Division, J - Joint Venture, A - Affiliate, G - Group. Sales are in millions of dollars, employees are in thousands. An asterisk (*) indicates an estimated sales volume. The symbol < stands for 'less than'.

OCCUPATIONS EMPLOYED BY SIC 594 - MISCELLANEOUS SHOPPING GOODS STORES

Occupation	% of Total 1996	Change to 2006	Occupation	% of Total 1996	Change to 2006
Salespersons, retail	46.8	20.5	Bookkeeping, accounting, & auditing clerks	2.2	-9.5
Marketing & sales worker supervisors	9.3	13.1	General office clerks	1.6	-2.7
Cashiers	8.2	14.4	Wholesale & retail buyers, except farm products	1.5	-6.4
Stock clerks	7.1	6.8	Traffic, shipping, receiving clerks	1.3	13.1
General managers & top executives	5.5	9.6	Purchasing managers	1.2	1.8
Sales & related workers nec	2.5	24.4	Bicycle repairers	1.2	35.7

Source: *Industry-Occupation Matrix*, Bureau of Labor Statistics. These data relate to one or more 3-digit SIC industry groups rather than to a single 4-digit SIC. The change reported for each occupation to the year 2006 is a percent of growth or decline as estimated by the Bureau of Labor Statistics. The abbreviation nec stands for 'not elsewhere classified'.

STATE AND REGIONAL CONCENTRATION

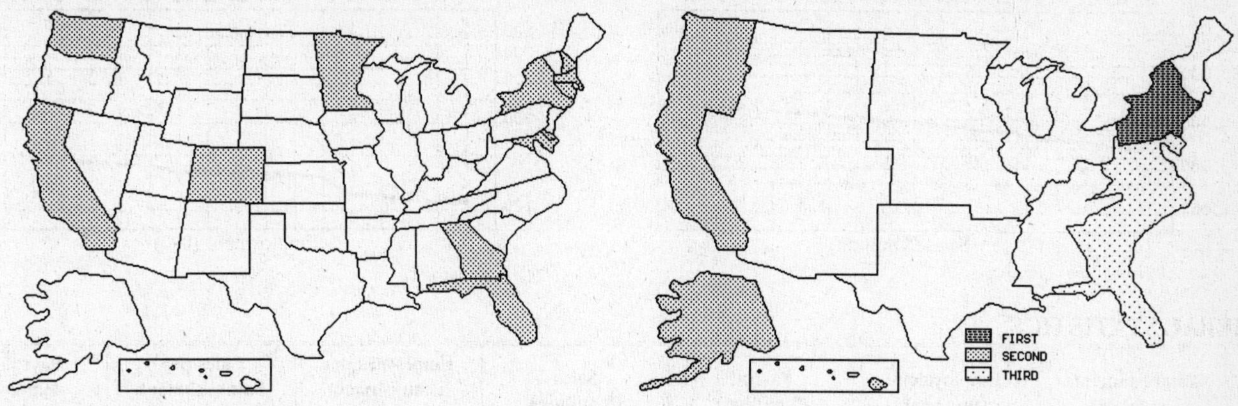

INDUSTRY DATA BY STATE

State	Establishments - 1995		Employment - 1995			Payroll - 1995		Sales - 1992		
	Total (number)	% of U.S.	Total (number)	% of U.S.	Per Estab.	Total ($ mil.)	Per Empl. ($)	Total ($ mil.)	% of U.S.	Per Estab ($)
New York	256	8.7	1,409	8.0	6	27.6	19,608	507.8	23.3	279,627
California	457	15.6	2,785	15.8	6	46.9	16,856	320.0	14.7	108,679
Florida	163	5.6	1,079	6.1	7	19.6	18,158	125.7	5.8	120,607
Pennsylvania	197	6.7	1,061	6.0	5	16.0	15,127	96.2	4.4	98,972
Ohio	123	4.2	949	5.4	8	13.9	14,681	88.1	4.0	90,276
Illinois	140	4.8	824	4.7	6	12.7	15,433	74.7	3.4	118,742
Texas	122	4.2	797	4.5	7	13.6	17,040	71.6	3.3	108,769
New Jersey	150	5.1	640	3.6	4	11.3	17,667	65.5	3.0	109,210
Georgia	73	2.5	497	2.8	7	9.5	19,197	65.0	3.0	159,644
Massachusetts	114	3.9	553	3.1	5	9.0	16,251	60.0	2.7	105,193
Colorado	32	1.1	365	2.1	11	8.3	22,696	53.5	2.5	224,828
Michigan	76	2.6	410	2.3	5	6.9	16,910	52.2	2.4	115,650
Washington	85	2.9	480	2.7	6	8.6	17,948	49.9	2.3	125,118
Maryland	57	1.9	471	2.7	8	7.0	14,964	46.6	2.1	100,620
Virginia	76	2.6	545	3.1	7	7.0	12,870	45.5	2.1	90,427
Minnesota	59	2.0	458	2.6	8	8.4	18,428	43.6	2.0	108,838
North Carolina	62	2.1	323	1.8	5	5.6	17,257	36.5	1.7	107,315
Connecticut	53	1.8	261	1.5	5	4.1	15,885	32.1	1.5	110,241
Arizona	49	1.7	257	1.5	5	4.6	17,805	28.4	1.3	115,976
Indiana	34	1.2	235	1.3	7	4.2	17,766	28.2	1.3	109,751
D.C.	22	0.7	168	1.0	8	4.2	25,185	25.1	1.2	155,950
Tennessee	40	1.4	255	1.4	6	4.6	18,208	24.4	1.1	96,352
Wisconsin	49	1.7	306	1.7	6	4.1	13,379	23.2	1.1	85,956
Missouri	35	1.2	187	1.1	5	3.5	18,604	19.9	0.9	97,828
Louisiana	25	0.9	187	1.1	7	3.1	16,342	19.1	0.9	97,198
Oregon	43	1.5	162	0.9	4	2.3	14,049	18.5	0.8	117,911
Iowa	27	0.9	189	1.1	7	2.8	14,852	13.2	0.6	77,859
Alabama	22	0.7	126	0.7	6	2.2	17,286	12.9	0.6	104,854
New Hampshire	27	0.9	161	0.9	6	2.5	15,646	12.6	0.6	88,364
Delaware	12	0.4	106	0.6	9	1.5	14,604	11.2	0.5	118,126
Kansas	13	0.4	107	0.6	8	2.4	22,430	10.8	0.5	109,081
New Mexico	15	0.5	96	0.5	6	1.9	19,865	10.6	0.5	98,785
Kentucky	19	0.6	155	0.9	8	2.5	15,903	9.1	0.4	65,848
South Carolina	35	1.2	106	0.6	3	2.1	19,915	8.7	0.4	69,416
Hawaii	12	0.4	76	0.4	6	0.9	12,487	8.2	0.4	88,129
Nebraska	8	0.3	67	0.4	8	1.1	16,836	6.7	0.3	134,580
Nevada	12	0.4	49	0.3	4	1.2	23,857	6.7	0.3	117,140
Oklahoma	15	0.5	69	0.4	5	1.3	18,971	6.4	0.3	76,298
Rhode Island	10	0.3	70	0.4	7	1.2	17,771	5.6	0.3	100,643
Maine	9	0.3	44	0.2	5	0.7	15,705	5.3	0.2	122,674
West Virginia	10	0.3	62	0.4	6	0.8	12,516	5.2	0.2	91,947
Alaska	7	0.2	20-99	-	-	(D)	-	5.2	0.2	101,510
Montana	7	0.2	20-99	-	-	(D)	-	5.0	0.2	111,778
Idaho	13	0.4	50	0.3	4	0.7	14,780	4.9	0.2	103,042
Mississippi	8	0.3	65	0.4	8	1.3	20,246	4.6	0.2	81,679
North Dakota	7	0.2	55	0.3	8	0.7	11,945	2.6	0.1	75,353
South Dakota	8	0.3	20-99	-	-	(D)	-	2.2	0.1	74,333
Vermont	5	0.2	19	0.1	4	0.2	11,368	1.9	0.1	76,600
Utah	27	0.9	217	1.2	8	3.8	17,350	(D)	-	-
Arkansas	8	0.3	65	0.4	8	1.1	17,277	(D)	-	-
Wyoming	7	0.2	40	0.2	6	0.4	10,875	(D)	-	-

Source: County Business Patterns, 1995 and *Economic Census of the U.S., 1992*. Data are sorted by 1992 revenues and, if revenues are unavailable, by establishments in 1995. The symbol (D) indicates that data are withheld by the source to avoid disclosure of competitive information. A dash (-) indicates that data are not available or undisclosed because they do not meet statistical validity standards. Shaded *states* on the state map indicate those states which have proportionately greater representation in the industry than would be indicated by the state's population; the ratio is based on total revenues or number of establishments. Shaded *regions* indicate where the industry is regionally most concentrated.

5947 - GIFT, NOVELTY, AND SOUVENIR SHOPS

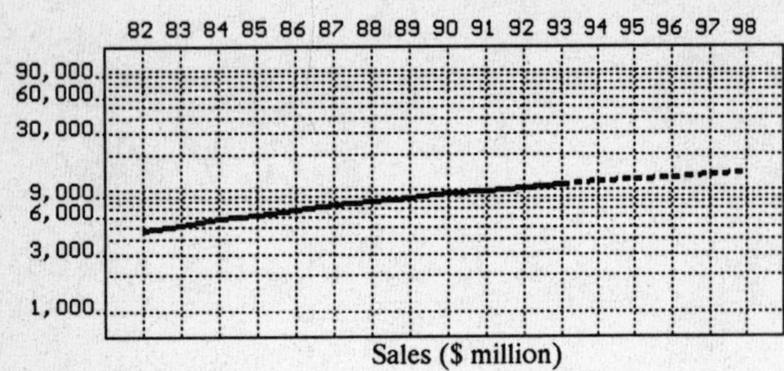

Sales ($ million)

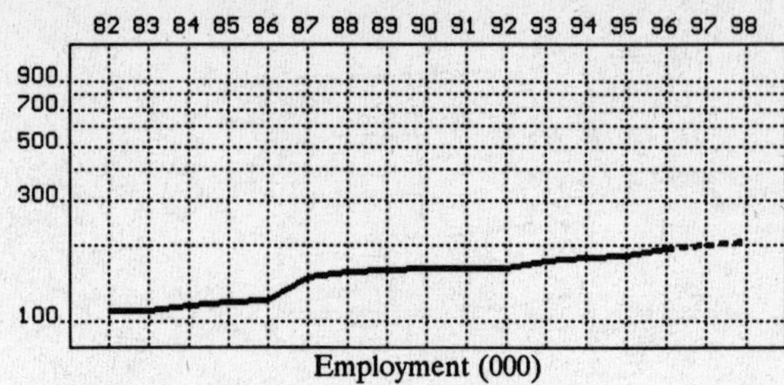

Employment (000)

GENERAL STATISTICS

Year	Establishments (number)	Employment (number)	Payroll ($ million)	Sales ($ million)	Employees per Establishment (number)	Sales per Establishment ($)	Payroll per Employee ($)
1982	23,877	109,659	693.8	4,619.8	5	193,482	6,327
1983	23,381	111,391	778.0	5,187.6e	5	-	6,984
1984	23,122	116,470	843.1	5,755.5e	5	-	7,238
1985	23,028	120,182	897.6	6,323.4e	5	-	7,469
1986	23,429	122,855	930.3	6,891.3e	5	-	7,572
1987	32,245	150,730	1,054.7	7,459.2	5	231,329	6,997
1988	30,203	157,163	1,222.8	8,078.1e	5	-	7,780
1989	28,833	159,455	1,319.4	8,696.9e	6	-	8,274
1990	29,455	164,265	1,393.7	9,315.8e	6	-	8,485
1991	29,642	163,067	1,431.2	9,934.7e	6	-	8,777
1992	34,647	164,311	1,466.9	10,553.5	5	304,601	8,927
1993	34,120	174,261	1,594.7	11,089.0p	5	-	9,151
1994	34,402	179,249	1,675.9	11,682.4p	5	-	9,349
1995	33,788	181,154	1,783.8	12,275.7p	5	-	9,847
1996	36,315p	193,469p	1,853.6p	12,869.1p	-	-	-
1997	37,308p	199,510p	1,938.0p	13,462.5p	-	-	-
1998	38,301p	205,552p	2,022.5p	14,055.9p	-	-	-

Sources: Economic Census of the United States, 1982, 1987, and 1992. Establishment counts, employment, and payroll are from *County Business Patterns* for non-Census years. Values followed by a 'p' are projections by the editors. Sales and expense data for non-Census years are extrapolations, marked by 'e'. Industries reclassified in 1987 will not have data for prior years. Data are the most recent available at this level of detail.

INDICES OF CHANGE

Year	Establishments (number)	Employment (number)	Payroll ($ million)	Sales ($ million)	Employees per Establishment (number)	Sales per Establishment ($)	Payroll per Employee ($)
1982	68.9	66.7	47.3	43.8	100.0	63.5	70.9
1983	67.5	67.8	53.0	49.2e	100.0	-	78.2
1984	66.7	70.9	57.5	54.5e	100.0	-	81.1
1985	66.5	73.1	61.2	59.9e	100.0	-	83.7
1986	67.6	74.8	63.4	65.3e	100.0	-	84.8
1987	93.1	91.7	71.9	70.7	100.0	75.9	78.4
1988	87.2	95.6	83.4	76.5e	100.0	-	87.2
1989	83.2	97.0	89.9	82.4e	120.0	-	92.7
1990	85.0	100.0	95.0	88.3e	120.0	-	95.0
1991	85.6	99.2	97.6	94.1e	120.0	-	98.3
1992	100.0	100.0	100.0	100.0	100.0	100.0	100.0
1993	98.5	106.1	108.7	105.1p	102.1	-	102.5
1994	99.3	109.1	114.2	110.7p	104.2	-	104.7
1995	97.5	110.3	121.6	116.3p	107.2	-	110.3
1996	104.8p	117.7p	126.4p	121.9p	-	-	-
1997	107.7p	121.4p	132.1p	127.6p	-	-	-
1998	110.5p	125.1p	137.9p	133.2p	-	-	-

Sources: Same as General Statistics. The values shown reflect change from the base year, 1992. Values above 100 mean greater than 1992, values below 100 mean less than 1992, and a value of 100 in the 1982-91 or 1993-98 period means same as 1992. Values followed by a 'p' are projections by the editors; 'e' stands for extrapolation. Data are the most recent available at this level of detail.

SELECTED RATIOS

For 1992	Avg. of All Retail	Analyzed Industry	Index	For 1992	Avg. of All Retail	Analyzed Industry	Index
Employees per Establishment	12	5	39	Sales per Employee	102,941	64,229	62
Payroll per Establishment	146,026	42,338	29	Sales per Establishment	1,241,555	304,601	25
Payroll per Employee	12,107	8,928	74	Expenses per Establishment	na	na	na

Sources: Same as General Statistics. The 'Average of All Manufacturing' column represents the average of all manufacturing industries reported for the most recent complete year available. The Index shows the relationship between the Average and the Analyzed Industry. For example, 100 means that they are equal; 500 that the Analyzed Industry is five times the average; 50 means that the Analyzed Industry is half the national average. The abbreviation 'na' is used to show that data are 'not available'.

LEADING COMPANIES

Number shown: **50** Total sales ($ mil): **20,299** Total employment (000): **185.1**

Company Name	Address				CEO Name	Phone	Co. Type	Sales ($ mil)	Empl. (000)
Walt Disney Co.	500 S Buena Vista	Burbank	CA	91521	Michael D Eisner	818-569-7903	P	12,112	71.0
Cole National Group Inc.	5915 Landerbrook	Mayfield H.	OH	44124	Jeffrey A Cole	216-449-4100	S	1,198	12.0
Cracker Barrel Old Country	PO Box 787	Lebanon	TN	37088	Dan W Evins	615-444-5533	P	1,124	35.8
Aramark Sports	1101 Market St	Philadelphia	PA	19107	Charles Gillespie	215-238-3000	S	700	7.0
Claire's Stores Inc.	3 SW 129th Ave	Pembroke Pines	FL	33027	Rowland Schaefer	954-433-3900	P	500	8.5
Stanhome Inc.	333 Western Ave	Westfield	MA	01085	HL Tower	413-562-3631	P	476	4.6
Discovery Communications Inc.	7700 Wisconsin Ave	Bethesda	MD	20814	John Hendricks	301-986-0444	R	475 *	1.0
Disney Store Inc.	101 N Brand Blvd	Glendale	CA	91203	Tom Heymann	818-265-3435	S	417 *	5.0
CML Group Inc.	524 Main St	Acton	MA	01720	Charles M Leighton	978-264-4155	P	341	3.1
Nature Co.	750 Hearst Ave	Berkeley	CA	94710		510-644-1337	D	261 *	2.5
CA One Services Inc.	438 Main St	Buffalo	NY	14202	Charles E Moran Jr	716-858-5000	S	254 *	2.9
Brookstone Inc.	17 Riverside St	Nashua	NH	03062	Michael Anthony	603-880-9500	P	240	2.0
Cost Plus Imports Inc.	PO Box 23350	Oakland	CA	94623	Ralph Dillon	510-893-7300	S	200 *	2.8
Carlton Cards Retail Inc.	1 American Rd	Cleveland	OH	44144	Robert Portman	216-252-7300	S	180	3.5
Kirlins Inc.	PO Box 3097	Quincy	IL	62305	Gary Kirlin	217-224-8953	R	167 *	2.0
Cole Gift Centers Inc.	5340 Evian Park	Highland H.	OH	44143	Jeffrey A Cole	216-473-2000	S	160 *	2.0
Natural Wonders Inc.	4209 Techn Dr	Fremont	CA	94538	K M Chatfield	510-252-9600	P	139	2.3
Zondervan	5300 Patterson SE	Grand Rapids	MI	49530	Bruce Ryskamp	616-698-6900	D	125	0.3
Hot Topic	3410 Pomona Blvd	Pomona	CA	91768	Orv Madden	909-869-6373		122 *	1.5
Paradies Shops Inc.	5950 Fulton Indrial	Atlanta	GA	30336	Dick Dickson	404-344-7905	R	107 *	1.4
Coach House Gifts Div.	420 E 58th Ave	Denver	CO	80216	Craig J Walker	303-292-5537	D	90 *	3.0
Ashcraft's Market Inc.	260 Oak St	Harrison	MI	48625	Daniel C Ashcraft	517-539-6001	R	78 *	0.9
Smith and Hawken Inc.	117 E Strawberry	Mill Valley	CA	94941	Kathy Tierney	415-383-4415	S	75	0.3
McWhorter's Stationery Co.	621 Tully Rd	San Jose	CA	95111	Steve Andrews	408-293-7500	R	74 *	0.6
Gorant Candies Inc.	PO Box 9068	Youngstown	OH	44513	Don Jeffcoat	216-726-8821	R	71 *	0.7
Deseret Book Co.	PO Box 30178	Salt Lake City	UT	84130	R Millett	801-534-1515	S	50	0.8
Matthews Inc.	Rte 100	Montchanin	DE	19710	JR Brinsfield	302-658-0543	R	45	1.9
Unique Industries Inc.	2400 S Weccacoe	Philadelphia	PA	19148	Everett Novak	215-336-4300	R	45	0.2
Score Board Inc.	1951 Old Cuthbert	Cherry Hill	NJ	08034	John F White	609-354-9000	P	43	0.2
C.W. Acquisitions Inc.	515 W 24th St	New York	NY	10011	J Leonard Silver	212-924-7300	R	40	0.4
DFS Group Ltd.	525 Market St	San Francisco	CA	94105	Myron Ullman	415-977-2700	R	40	0.5
Newbury Comics Inc.	38 Everett St	Boston	MA	02134	Michael Dreese	617-254-1666	R	29 *	0.2
BOWLIN Outdoor Advertising	150 Louisiana NE	Albuquerque	NM	87108	Michael L Bowlin	505-266-5985	P	25	0.3
Always Christmas Inc.	PO Box 67	Lake Orion	MI	48361	Stan Aldridge	313-391-5700	R	25 *	0.3
Goldstein Brothers Inc.	7956 Crestwood	Birmingham	AL	35210	Milton Goldstein	205-956-4314	R	25	0.3
Anthony's Fish Grotto	5232 Lovelock	San Diego	CA	92110	Anthony Ghio	619-291-7254	R	23	0.5
Bazaar Del Mundo Inc.	2754 Calhoun St	San Diego	CA	92110	Diane Powers	619-296-6301	R	23 *	0.5
Henderson Black and Greene	PO Box 589	Troy	AL	36081	SK Hendricks	205-566-4133	R	22 *	0.4
Waterhouse Properties Inc.	670 Queen St	Honolulu	HI	96813	Edwin Wong	808-521-6751	R	20	0.3
Shifrin Jewelers Inc.	14510 W 8 Mile Rd	Oak Park	MI	48237	W Sherman	313-968-1515	S	19 *	0.2
Social Expressions	3393 Peachtree Rd	Atlanta	GA	30326	Al Masia	404-266-2618	R	18 *	0.2
Discovery Channel Store Inc.	750 Hearst Ave	Berkley	CA	94710	John Hendricks	214-490-8299	D	16 *	0.2
Tuerkes-Beckers Inc.	8288 Telegraph Rd	Odenton	MD	21113	W. A Tuerke IV	410-792-7470	R	16	0.2
Hazelwood Enterprises Inc.	402 N 32nd St	Phoenix	AZ	85008	John Felix	602-275-7709	R	15 *	0.4
Index Notion Company Inc.	887 W Carmel Dr	Carmel	IN	46032	James G Sinclair	317-573-3990	R	15 *	0.2
A and H Stores Inc.	1420 Maple SW	Renton	WA	98055	RB Hendrickson	206-255-7083	R	13 *	0.2
Cheryl and Co.	646 McCorkle Blvd	Westerville	OH	43082	Cheryl Krueger	614-891-8822	R	13	0.2
Stationers Inc.	PO Box 2167	Huntington	WV	25722	JM Aldridge	304-528-2780	S	13 *	<0.1
Wall Drug Store Inc.	510 Main St	Wall	SD	57790	Richard J Hustead	605-279-2175	R	11	0.2
Pacific Card Shop Inc.	3463 Ramona Ave	Sacramento	CA	95826	C Shalz	916-456-2205	R	10	0.1

Source: Ward's Business Directory of U.S. Private and Public Companies, 1998. The company type code used is as follows: P - Public, R - Private, S - Subsidiary, D - Division, J - Joint Venture, A - Affiliate, G - Group. Sales are in millions of dollars, employees are in thousands. An asterisk (*) indicates an estimated sales volume. The symbol < stands for 'less than'.

OCCUPATIONS EMPLOYED BY SIC 594 - MISCELLANEOUS SHOPPING GOODS STORES

Occupation	% of Total 1996	Change to 2006	Occupation	% of Total 1996	Change to 2006
Salespersons, retail	46.8	20.5	Bookkeeping, accounting, & auditing clerks	2.2	-9.5
Marketing & sales worker supervisors	9.3	13.1	General office clerks	1.6	-2.7
Cashiers	8.2	14.4	Wholesale & retail buyers, except farm products	1.5	-6.4
Stock clerks	7.1	6.8	Traffic, shipping, receiving clerks	1.3	13.1
General managers & top executives	5.5	9.6	Purchasing managers	1.2	1.8
Sales & related workers nec	2.5	24.4	Bicycle repairers	1.2	35.7

Source: Industry-Occupation Matrix, Bureau of Labor Statistics. These data relate to one or more 3-digit SIC industry groups rather than to a single 4-digit SIC. The change reported for each occupation to the year 2006 is a percent of growth or decline as estimated by the Bureau of Labor Statistics. The abbreviation nec stands for 'not elsewhere classified'.

STATE AND REGIONAL CONCENTRATION

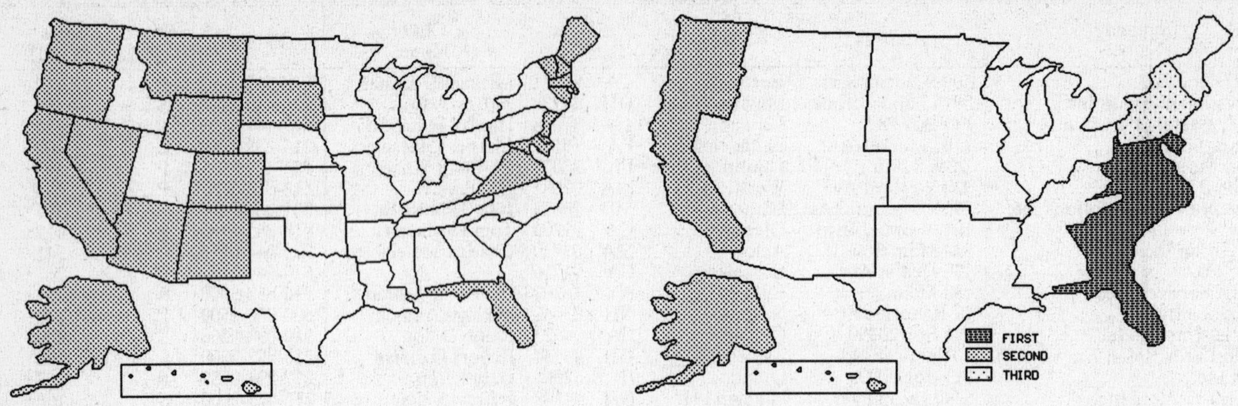

INDUSTRY DATA BY STATE

State	Establishments - 1995 Total (number)	Establishments - 1995 % of U.S.	Employment - 1995 Total (number)	Employment - 1995 % of U.S.	Employment - 1995 Per Estab.	Payroll - 1995 Total ($ mil.)	Payroll - 1995 Per Empl. ($)	Sales - 1992 Total ($ mil.)	Sales - 1992 % of U.S.	Sales - 1992 Per Estab ($)
California	3,432	10.2	19,507	10.8	6	200.4	10,276	1,328.7	12.6	70,649
Florida	2,178	6.4	12,351	6.8	6	130.0	10,525	813.3	7.7	73,128
New York	2,152	6.4	9,879	5.5	5	114.3	11,565	745.8	7.1	78,469
Texas	2,024	6.0	10,469	5.8	5	98.3	9,393	586.1	5.6	65,009
Pennsylvania	1,548	4.6	8,923	4.9	6	79.9	8,951	494.2	4.7	56,597
Illinois	1,383	4.1	8,101	4.5	6	70.2	8,668	408.4	3.9	58,420
New Jersey	1,057	3.1	5,483	3.0	5	63.1	11,504	402.5	3.8	75,176
Michigan	1,164	3.4	6,880	3.8	6	67.2	9,765	384.8	3.6	59,179
Ohio	1,211	3.6	7,338	4.1	6	61.9	8,430	373.8	3.5	52,937
Massachusetts	843	2.5	4,487	2.5	5	50.9	11,348	300.7	2.8	71,945
Virginia	927	2.7	4,878	2.7	5	44.9	9,210	266.6	2.5	58,945
Washington	825	2.4	3,921	2.2	5	39.5	10,074	258.7	2.5	66,717
North Carolina	912	2.7	4,319	2.4	5	43.2	9,993	228.5	2.2	63,922
Georgia	795	2.4	4,434	2.4	6	41.9	9,461	225.2	2.1	59,535
Maryland	589	1.7	3,825	2.1	6	36.9	9,657	212.8	2.0	56,197
Colorado	728	2.2	3,573	2.0	5	37.7	10,553	211.2	2.0	71,613
Arizona	648	1.9	3,665	2.0	6	37.2	10,151	198.0	1.9	64,011
Missouri	670	2.0	4,006	2.2	6	40.6	10,145	194.9	1.8	55,235
Indiana	778	2.3	4,432	2.4	6	35.9	8,093	189.5	1.8	52,794
Minnesota	726	2.1	4,035	2.2	6	35.4	8,766	185.7	1.8	57,282
Connecticut	409	1.2	2,455	1.4	6	25.1	10,244	182.7	1.7	69,709
Wisconsin	723	2.1	3,698	2.0	5	29.5	7,989	182.1	1.7	58,745
Nevada	264	0.8	2,382	1.3	9	28.1	11,804	166.7	1.6	77,774
Tennessee	694	2.1	3,409	1.9	5	35.7	10,483	154.4	1.5	60,749
Hawaii	322	1.0	1,835	1.0	6	26.4	14,389	151.9	1.4	94,653
Oregon	475	1.4	2,328	1.3	5	23.1	9,929	130.7	1.2	67,366
Louisiana	444	1.3	2,353	1.3	5	20.3	8,609	122.2	1.2	54,007
South Carolina	481	1.4	2,153	1.2	4	22.0	10,229	114.5	1.1	55,502
Kentucky	385	1.1	2,269	1.3	6	19.8	8,719	104.3	1.0	56,209
Iowa	455	1.3	2,403	1.3	5	18.2	7,590	98.5	0.9	47,539
Oklahoma	368	1.1	1,937	1.1	5	16.6	8,581	93.3	0.9	57,480
Alabama	407	1.2	1,722	1.0	4	14.7	8,537	88.7	0.8	52,129
New Mexico	265	0.8	1,502	0.8	6	16.0	10,668	86.4	0.8	65,362
New Hampshire	268	0.8	1,382	0.8	5	14.1	10,198	80.5	0.8	62,418
Kansas	378	1.1	1,955	1.1	5	15.7	8,054	78.6	0.7	47,704
Alaska	195	0.6	633	0.3	3	11.9	18,768	67.6	0.6	120,092
Utah	251	0.7	1,433	0.8	6	13.4	9,322	67.3	0.6	55,294
Maine	293	0.9	888	0.5	3	11.6	13,039	63.6	0.6	84,952
Nebraska	225	0.7	1,541	0.9	7	12.3	7,983	62.1	0.6	49,036
Arkansas	304	0.9	1,264	0.7	4	10.9	8,584	56.9	0.5	58,581
D.C.	87	0.3	666	0.4	8	10.3	15,393	49.8	0.5	72,919
South Dakota	144	0.4	623	0.3	4	5.7	9,175	40.7	0.4	69,019
West Virginia	186	0.6	813	0.4	4	6.3	7,796	39.6	0.4	59,244
Mississippi	219	0.6	1,026	0.6	5	8.1	7,932	39.4	0.4	45,613
Montana	197	0.6	763	0.4	4	8.0	10,549	38.5	0.4	63,625
Rhode Island	131	0.4	566	0.3	4	6.2	10,878	36.5	0.3	56,029
Delaware	121	0.4	602	0.3	5	6.2	10,291	35.6	0.3	64,980
Vermont	154	0.5	531	0.3	3	5.2	9,768	35.4	0.3	65,465
Idaho	142	0.4	596	0.3	4	4.7	7,940	27.5	0.3	50,605
Wyoming	105	0.3	378	0.2	4	3.9	10,376	24.8	0.2	75,042
North Dakota	106	0.3	542	0.3	5	4.2	7,694	23.3	0.2	44,985

Source: County Business Patterns, 1995 and *Economic Census of the U.S., 1992*. Data are sorted by 1992 revenues and, if revenues are unavailable, by establishments in 1995. The symbol (D) indicates that data are withheld by the source to avoid disclosure of competitive information. A dash (-) indicates that data are not available or undisclosed because they do not meet statistical validity standards. Shaded *states* on the state map indicate those states which have proportionately greater representation in the industry than would be indicated by the state's population; the ratio is based on total revenues or number of establishments. Shaded *regions* indicate where the industry is regionally most concentrated.

5948 - LUGGAGE AND LEATHER GOODS STORES

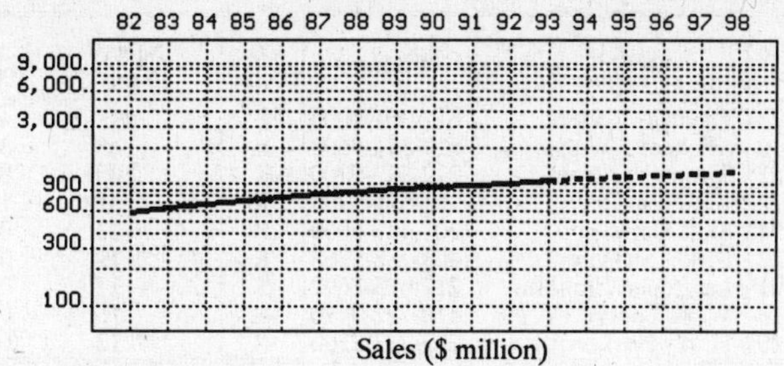

Sales ($ million)

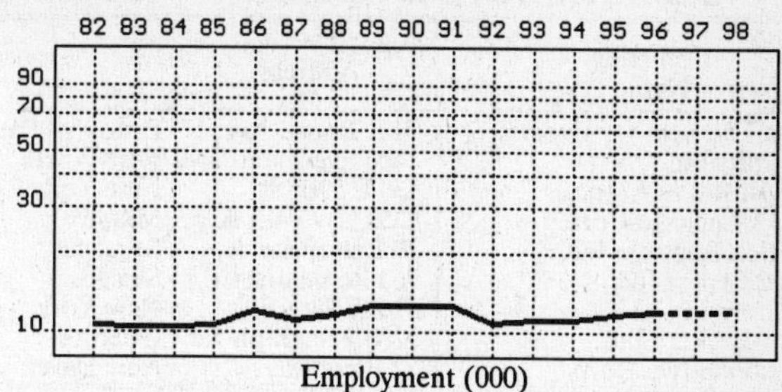

Employment (000)

GENERAL STATISTICS

Year	Establishments (number)	Employment (number)	Payroll ($ million)	Sales ($ million)	Employees per Establishment (number)	Sales per Establishment ($)	Payroll per Employee ($)
1982	1,987	10,592	94.4	589.4	5	296,624	8,913
1983	1,955	10,516	104.5	639.3e	5	-	9,933
1984	1,929	10,393	112.5	689.3e	5	-	10,822
1985	1,882	10,640	124.5	739.2e	6	-	11,701
1986	1,903	11,921	124.9	789.2e	6	-	10,474
1987	2,009	11,033	122.4	839.1	5	417,666	11,096
1988	2,010	11,659	147.4	872.8e	6	-	12,643
1989	2,005	12,644	159.7	906.6e	6	-	12,634
1990	2,054	12,524	164.5	940.3e	6	-	13,137
1991	2,157	12,666	164.9	974.1e	6	-	13,017
1992	1,907	10,684	146.9	1,007.9	6	528,501	13,754
1993	1,901	11,106	157.3	1,068.1p	6	-	14,165
1994	1,921	11,031	165.0	1,109.9p	6	-	14,954
1995	1,944	11,568	179.2	1,151.8p	6	-	15,492
1996	1,975p	11,920p	184.5p	1,193.6p	-	-	-
1997	1,976p	11,996p	190.4p	1,235.5p	-	-	-
1998	1,977p	12,071p	196.2p	1,277.3p	-	-	-

Sources: *Economic Census of the United States*, 1982, 1987, and 1992. Establishment counts, employment, and payroll are from *County Business Patterns* for non-Census years. Values followed by a 'p' are projections by the editors. Sales and expense data for non-Census years are extrapolations, marked by 'e'. Industries reclassified in 1987 will not have data for prior years. Data are the most recent available at this level of detail.

INDICES OF CHANGE

Year	Establishments (number)	Employment (number)	Payroll ($ million)	Sales ($ million)	Employees per Establishment (number)	Sales per Establishment ($)	Payroll per Employee ($)
1982	104.2	99.1	64.3	58.5	83.3	56.1	64.8
1983	102.5	98.4	71.1	63.4e	83.3	-	72.2
1984	101.2	97.3	76.6	68.4e	83.3	-	78.7
1985	98.7	99.6	84.8	73.3e	100.0	-	85.1
1986	99.8	111.6	85.0	78.3e	100.0	-	76.2
1987	105.3	103.3	83.3	83.3	83.3	79.0	80.7
1988	105.4	109.1	100.3	86.6e	100.0	-	91.9
1989	105.1	118.3	108.7	89.9e	100.0	-	91.9
1990	107.7	117.2	112.0	93.3e	100.0	-	95.5
1991	113.1	118.6	112.3	96.6e	100.0	-	94.6
1992	100.0	100.0	100.0	100.0	100.0	100.0	100.0
1993	99.7	103.9	107.1	106.0p	97.4	-	103.0
1994	100.7	103.2	112.3	110.1p	95.7	-	108.7
1995	101.9	108.3	122.0	114.3p	99.2	-	112.6
1996	103.6p	111.6p	125.6p	118.4p	-	-	-
1997	103.6p	112.3p	129.6p	122.6p	-	-	-
1998	103.7p	113.0p	133.6p	126.7p	-	-	-

Sources: Same as General Statistics. The values shown reflect change from the base year, 1992. Values above 100 mean greater than 1992, values below 100 mean less than 1992, and a value of 100 in the 1982-91 or 1993-98 period means same as 1992. Values followed by a 'p' are projections by the editors; 'e' stands for extrapolation. Data are the most recent available at this level of detail.

SELECTED RATIOS

For 1992	Avg. of All Retail	Analyzed Industry	Index	For 1992	Avg. of All Retail	Analyzed Industry	Index
Employees per Establishment	12	6	46	Sales per Employee	102,941	94,337	92
Payroll per Establishment	146,026	77,032	53	Sales per Establishment	1,241,555	528,526	43
Payroll per Employee	12,107	13,750	114	Expenses per Establishment	na	na	na

Sources: Same as General Statistics. The 'Average of All Manufacturing' column represents the average of all manufacturing industries reported for the most recent complete year available. The Index shows the relationship between the Average and the Analyzed Industry. For example, 100 means that they are equal; 500 that the Analyzed Industry is five times the average; 50 means that the Analyzed Industry is half the national average. The abbreviation 'na' is used to show that data are 'not available'.

LEADING COMPANIES

Number shown: **9** Total sales ($ mil): **934** Total employment (000): **10.1**

Company Name	Address				CEO Name	Phone	Co. Type	Sales ($ mil)	Empl. (000)
Wilsons The Leather Experts	7401 Boone Ave, N	Brooklyn Park	MN	55428	David L Rogers	612-391-4000	P	418	4.0
Tandycrafts Inc.	1400 Everman Pkwy	Fort Worth	TX	76140	Michael J Walsh	817-551-9600	P	245	3.7
Louis Vuitton N.A. Inc.	130 E 59th St	New York	NY	10022	Thomas O'Neal	212-572-9700	S	100 *	0.4
Bentley's Luggage Corp.	3353 NW 74th Ave	Miami	FL	33122	Ken Young	305-591-9700	R	84 *	1.0
Innovation Luggage Inc.	20 Enterprise Ave	Secaucus	NJ	07094	Stan Schwarz	201-487-6000	R	22	0.3
Luggage Center Inc.	960 Remillard Ct	San Jose	CA	95122	Sandy Swayne	408-288-5363	R	19	0.2
Mark Cross Inc.	516 W 34th St	New York	NY	10001	Lawrence Franklin	212-695-8692	S	17	0.2
Turkes-Beckers Inc.	8288 Telegraph Rd	Odenton	MD	21113	W. A Tuerke IV	410-792-7470	R	16	0.2
Yale Cooperative Corp.	77 Broadway	New Haven	CT	06520	Harry Berkowitz	203-772-2200	R	13	0.1

Source: *Ward's Business Directory of U.S. Private and Public Companies*, 1998. The company type code used is as follows: P - Public, R - Private, S - Subsidiary, D - Division, J - Joint Venture, A - Affiliate, G - Group. Sales are in millions of dollars, employees are in thousands. An asterisk (*) indicates an estimated sales volume. The symbol < stands for 'less than'.

OCCUPATIONS EMPLOYED BY SIC 594 - MISCELLANEOUS SHOPPING GOODS STORES

Occupation	% of Total 1996	Change to 2006	Occupation	% of Total 1996	Change to 2006
Salespersons, retail	46.8	20.5	Bookkeeping, accounting, & auditing clerks	2.2	-9.5
Marketing & sales worker supervisors	9.3	13.1	General office clerks	1.6	-2.7
Cashiers	8.2	14.4	Wholesale & retail buyers, except farm products	1.5	-6.4
Stock clerks	7.1	6.8	Traffic, shipping, receiving clerks	1.3	13.1
General managers & top executives	5.5	9.6	Purchasing managers	1.2	1.8
Sales & related workers nec	2.5	24.4	Bicycle repairers	1.2	35.7

Source: Industry-Occupation Matrix, Bureau of Labor Statistics. These data relate to one or more 3-digit SIC industry groups rather than to a single 4-digit SIC. The change reported for each occupation to the year 2006 is a percent of growth or decline as estimated by the Bureau of Labor Statistics. The abbreviation nec stands for 'not elsewhere classified'.

STATE AND REGIONAL CONCENTRATION

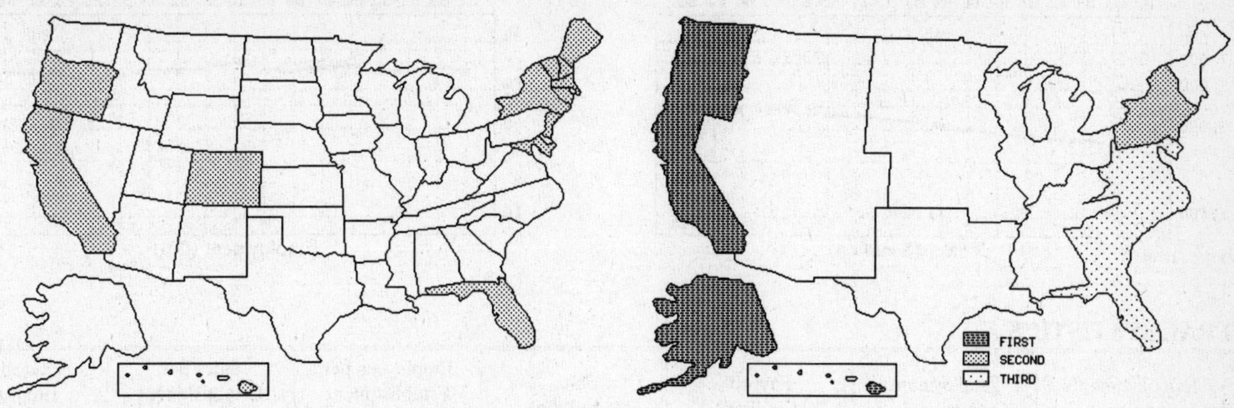

INDUSTRY DATA BY STATE

State	Establishments - 1995 Total (number)	Establishments - 1995 % of U.S.	Employment - 1995 Total (number)	Employment - 1995 % of U.S.	Employment - 1995 Per Estab.	Payroll - 1995 Total ($ mil.)	Payroll - 1995 Per Empl. ($)	Sales - 1992 Total ($ mil.)	Sales - 1992 % of U.S.	Sales - 1992 Per Estab ($)
California	280	14.4	1,690	14.7	6	31.9	18,851	205.6	21.0	119,796
New York	177	9.1	968	8.4	5	20.0	20,702	135.0	13.8	141,525
Florida	146	7.5	799	6.9	5	10.6	13,328	79.0	8.1	108,305
Texas	100	5.1	692	6.0	7	9.6	13,809	48.6	5.0	91,404
Pennsylvania	105	5.4	590	5.1	6	8.2	13,841	43.3	4.4	80,373
Illinois	73	3.8	403	3.5	6	6.1	15,256	37.5	3.8	86,304
New Jersey	65	3.3	559	4.9	9	10.5	18,826	36.9	3.8	116,075
Hawaii	29	1.5	367	3.2	13	11.1	30,125	35.4	3.6	133,592
Massachusetts	52	2.7	263	2.3	5	5.2	19,654	27.6	2.8	92,909
Michigan	74	3.8	368	3.2	5	4.6	12,530	25.9	2.6	69,408
Georgia	53	2.7	288	2.5	5	4.4	15,243	22.8	2.3	89,736
Virginia	56	2.9	292	2.5	5	3.5	12,038	22.6	2.3	71,268
Maryland	41	2.1	250	2.2	6	3.1	12,544	22.2	2.3	67,574
Ohio	46	2.4	315	2.7	7	4.3	13,765	18.9	1.9	63,443
Washington	38	2.0	265	2.3	7	3.4	12,694	18.7	1.9	84,855
North Carolina	43	2.2	298	2.6	7	3.1	10,540	17.8	1.8	61,709
Colorado	39	2.0	253	2.2	6	3.3	13,202	16.4	1.7	78,262
Connecticut	22	1.1	127	1.1	6	1.5	12,181	15.3	1.6	77,862
Missouri	42	2.2	225	2.0	5	2.4	10,756	14.6	1.5	73,768
Tennessee	33	1.7	178	1.5	5	2.2	12,478	13.9	1.4	96,583
Arizona	37	1.9	179	1.6	5	2.5	13,698	13.5	1.4	63,521
Oregon	33	1.7	162	1.4	5	3.1	18,926	11.6	1.2	68,598
Indiana	25	1.3	124	1.1	5	1.4	11,258	8.3	0.8	96,047
Minnesota	29	1.5	190	1.6	7	1.8	9,605	7.8	0.8	62,222
Wisconsin	27	1.4	162	1.4	6	1.8	10,932	7.5	0.8	56,917
Louisiana	18	0.9	117	1.0	7	1.6	13,615	7.4	0.8	80,620
Alabama	15	0.8	70	0.6	5	0.8	11,357	6.8	0.7	71,632
South Carolina	20	1.0	92	0.8	5	1.1	12,304	6.4	0.7	53,275
Kansas	9	0.5	96	0.8	11	0.8	8,073	5.9	0.6	62,904
New Hampshire	19	1.0	110	1.0	6	1.0	8,882	5.8	0.6	71,185
D.C.	13	0.7	53	0.5	4	0.9	17,415	5.5	0.6	87,698
Maine	11	0.6	46	0.4	4	0.6	12,261	5.0	0.5	96,904
New Mexico	17	0.9	92	0.8	5	1.3	13,924	4.6	0.5	94,184
Kentucky	16	0.8	127	1.1	8	1.1	8,866	4.6	0.5	53,753
Iowa	15	0.8	94	0.8	6	0.8	9,000	4.5	0.5	47,670
Oklahoma	15	0.8	62	0.5	4	0.7	11,306	4.0	0.4	73,944
Vermont	9	0.5	41	0.4	5	0.6	14,902	3.1	0.3	113,037
Rhode Island	11	0.6	36	0.3	3	0.3	9,194	2.9	0.3	58,780
Mississippi	5	0.3	25	0.2	5	0.4	14,080	1.9	0.2	55,029
Montana	3	0.2	0-19	-	-	(D)	-	1.7	0.2	57,379
Idaho	8	0.4	31	0.3	4	0.3	10,452	1.4	0.1	62,696
South Dakota	3	0.2	20-99	-	-	(D)	-	1.4	0.1	44,129
Nevada	27	1.4	160	1.4	6	3.6	22,744	(D)	-	-
Utah	10	0.5	115	1.0	11	1.5	13,017	(D)	-	-
Arkansas	9	0.5	41	0.4	5	0.3	8,488	(D)	-	-
West Virginia	8	0.4	26	0.2	3	0.3	9,731	(D)	-	-
Delaware	6	0.3	30	0.3	5	0.4	13,967	(D)	-	-
Nebraska	6	0.3	27	0.2	5	0.3	11,407	(D)	-	-
Wyoming	3	0.2	27	0.2	9	0.2	8,963	(D)	-	-
Alaska	2	0.1	0-19	-	-	(D)	-	(D)	-	-
North Dakota	1	0.1	0-19	-	-	(D)	-	(D)	-	-

Source: *County Business Patterns, 1995* and *Economic Census of the U.S., 1992*. Data are sorted by 1992 revenues and, if revenues are unavailable, by establishments in 1995. The symbol (D) indicates that data are withheld by the source to avoid disclosure of competitive information. A dash (-) indicates that data are not available or undisclosed because they do not meet statistical validity standards. Shaded *states* on the state map indicate those states which have proportionately greater representation in the industry than would be indicated by the state's population; the ratio is based on total revenues or number of establishments. Shaded *regions* indicate where the industry is regionally most concentrated.

5949 - SEWING, NEEDLEWORK, AND PIECE GOODS

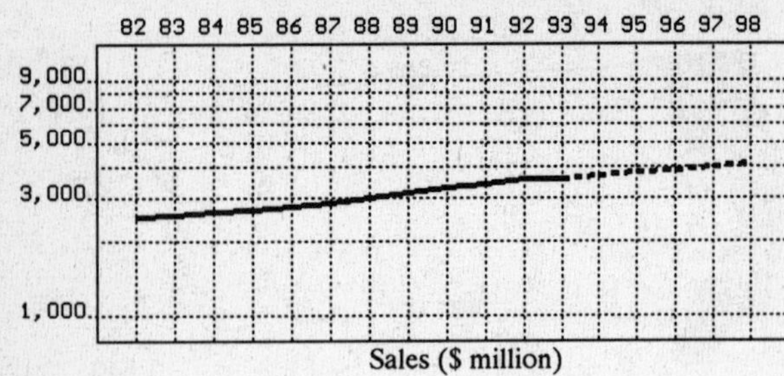

Sales ($ million)

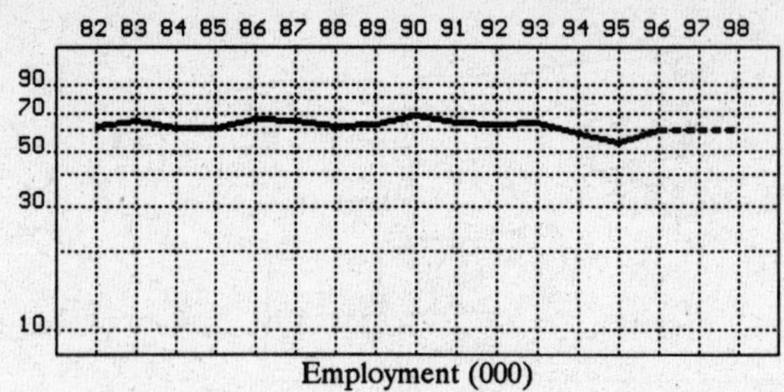

Employment (000)

GENERAL STATISTICS

Year	Establishments (number)	Employment (number)	Payroll ($ million)	Sales ($ million)	Employees per Establishment (number)	Sales per Establishment ($)	Payroll per Employee ($)
1982	10,494	62,368	350.1	2,494.7	6	237,724	5,613
1983	10,122	64,991	374.4	2,562.9e	6	-	5,762
1984	9,818	61,616	377.2	2,631.1e	6	-	6,122
1985	9,295	61,120	397.7	2,699.2e	7	-	6,508
1986	9,039	65,780	404.9	2,767.4e	7	-	6,156
1987	9,632	64,502	406.3	2,835.6	7	294,395	6,298
1988	8,790	62,227	438.3	2,983.8e	7	-	7,043
1989	8,416	63,318	476.9	3,131.9e	8	-	7,532
1990	8,180	68,193	503.7	3,280.0e	8	-	7,387
1991	8,201	64,347	546.9	3,428.2e	8	-	8,499
1992	8,264	62,728	516.0	3,576.3	8	432,759	8,225
1993	8,019	64,099	518.6	3,593.6p	8	-	8,091
1994	7,497	58,579	497.0	3,701.8p	8	-	8,484
1995	7,009	54,270	480.9	3,810.0p	8	-	8,861
1996	7,014p	60,463p	551.2p	3,918.1p	-	-	-
1997	6,780p	60,161p	564.8p	4,026.3p	-	-	-
1998	6,546p	59,859p	578.4p	4,134.4p	-	-	-

Sources: Economic Census of the United States, 1982, 1987, and 1992. Establishment counts, employment, and payroll are from *County Business Patterns* for non-Census years. Values followed by a 'p' are projections by the editors. Sales and expense data for non-Census years are extrapolations, marked by 'e'. Industries reclassified in 1987 will not have data for prior years. Data are the most recent available at this level of detail.

INDICES OF CHANGE

Year	Establishments (number)	Employment (number)	Payroll ($ million)	Sales ($ million)	Employees per Establishment (number)	Sales per Establishment ($)	Payroll per Employee ($)
1982	127.0	99.4	67.8	69.8	75.0	54.9	68.2
1983	122.5	103.6	72.6	71.7e	75.0	-	70.1
1984	118.8	98.2	73.1	73.6e	75.0	-	74.4
1985	112.5	97.4	77.1	75.5e	87.5	-	79.1
1986	109.4	104.9	78.5	77.4e	87.5	-	74.8
1987	116.6	102.8	78.7	79.3	87.5	68.0	76.6
1988	106.4	99.2	84.9	83.4e	87.5	-	85.6
1989	101.8	100.9	92.4	87.6e	100.0	-	91.6
1990	99.0	108.7	97.6	91.7e	100.0	-	89.8
1991	99.2	102.6	106.0	95.9e	100.0	-	103.3
1992	100.0	100.0	100.0	100.0	100.0	100.0	100.0
1993	97.0	102.2	100.5	100.5p	99.9	-	98.4
1994	90.7	93.4	96.3	103.5p	97.7	-	103.1
1995	84.8	86.5	93.2	106.5p	96.8	-	107.7
1996	84.9p	96.4p	106.8p	109.6p	-	-	-
1997	82.0p	95.9p	109.5p	112.6p	-	-	-
1998	79.2p	95.4p	112.1p	115.6p	-	-	-

Sources: Same as General Statistics. The values shown reflect change from the base year, 1992. Values above 100 mean greater than 1992, values below 100 mean less than 1992, and a value of 100 in the 1982-91 or 1993-98 period means same as 1992. Values followed by a 'p' are projections by the editors; 'e' stands for extrapolation. Data are the most recent available at this level of detail.

SELECTED RATIOS

For 1992	Avg. of All Retail	Analyzed Industry	Index	For 1992	Avg. of All Retail	Analyzed Industry	Index
Employees per Establishment	12	8	63	Sales per Employee	102,941	57,013	55
Payroll per Establishment	146,026	62,439	43	Sales per Establishment	1,241,555	432,757	35
Payroll per Employee	12,107	8,226	68	Expenses per Establishment	na	na	na

Sources: Same as General Statistics. The 'Average of All Manufacturing' column represents the average of all manufacturing industries reported for the most recent complete year available. The Index shows the relationship between the Average and the Analyzed Industry. For example, 100 means that they are equal; 500 that the Analyzed Industry is five times the average; 50 means that the Analyzed Industry is half the national average. The abbreviation 'na' is used to show that data are 'not available'.

LEADING COMPANIES

Number shown: **12** Total sales ($ mil): **1,995** Total employment (000): **22.5**

Company Name	Address				CEO Name	Phone	Co. Type	Sales ($ mil)	Empl. (000)
FCA of Ohio Inc.	5555 Darrow Rd	Hudson	OH	44236	Alan Rosskamm	216-656-2600	S	530 *	0.1
Hancock Fabrics Inc.	PO Box 2400	Tupelo	MS	38803	Larry G Kirk	601-842-2834	P	378	6.5
House of Fabrics Inc.	13400 Riverside Dr	Sherman Oaks	CA	91423	Gary L Larkins	818-995-7000	P	333	4.9
Liberty Fabrics Inc.	295 5th Ave	New York	NY	10016	Matthew Williams	212-684-3100	S	180 *	1.4
Old America Stores Inc.	PO Box 370	Howe	TX	75459	R W Tredinnick	903-532-3000	P	136	3.5
Piece Goods Shop L.P.	280 Charlois Blvd	Winston-Salem	NC	27103	Gary Cohen	910-768-3930	R	108 *	2.2
Everfast Inc.	203 Gale Ln	Kennett Square	PA	19348	Bert G Kerstetter	610-444-9700	R	100 *	1.2
Rag Shops Inc.	111 Wagaraw Rd	Hawthorne	NJ	07506	Stanley Berenzweig	973-423-1303	P	86	1.1
Mobile Fabrics Inc.	111 Wagaraw Rd	Hawthorne	NJ	07506	Donald Hunt	201-423-1303	S	46 *	1.0
Fabric Place	136 Howard St	Framingham	MA	01701	Ron Isaacson	508-872-4888	R	42 *	0.5
Beckenstein Men's Fabrics Inc.	121 Orchard St	New York	NY	10002	Neal Boyarsky	212-475-6666	R	29	<0.1
Mary Maxim Inc.	PO Box 5019	Port Huron	MI	48061	WM McPhedrain	810-987-2000	R	25	0.1

Source: *Ward's Business Directory of U.S. Private and Public Companies*, 1998. The company type code used is as follows: P - Public, R - Private, S - Subsidiary, D - Division, J - Joint Venture, A - Affiliate, G - Group. Sales are in millions of dollars, employees are in thousands. An asterisk (*) indicates an estimated sales volume. The symbol < stands for 'less than'.

OCCUPATIONS EMPLOYED BY SIC 594 - MISCELLANEOUS SHOPPING GOODS STORES

Occupation	% of Total 1996	Change to 2006	Occupation	% of Total 1996	Change to 2006
Salespersons, retail	46.8	20.5	Bookkeeping, accounting, & auditing clerks	2.2	-9.5
Marketing & sales worker supervisors	9.3	13.1	General office clerks	1.6	-2.7
Cashiers	8.2	14.4	Wholesale & retail buyers, except farm products	1.5	-6.4
Stock clerks	7.1	6.8	Traffic, shipping, receiving clerks	1.3	13.1
General managers & top executives	5.5	9.6	Purchasing managers	1.2	1.8
Sales & related workers nec	2.5	24.4	Bicycle repairers	1.2	35.7

Source: *Industry-Occupation Matrix*, Bureau of Labor Statistics. These data relate to one or more 3-digit SIC industry groups rather than to a single 4-digit SIC. The change reported for each occupation to the year 2006 is a percent of growth or decline as estimated by the Bureau of Labor Statistics. The abbreviation nec stands for 'not elsewhere classified'.

STATE AND REGIONAL CONCENTRATION

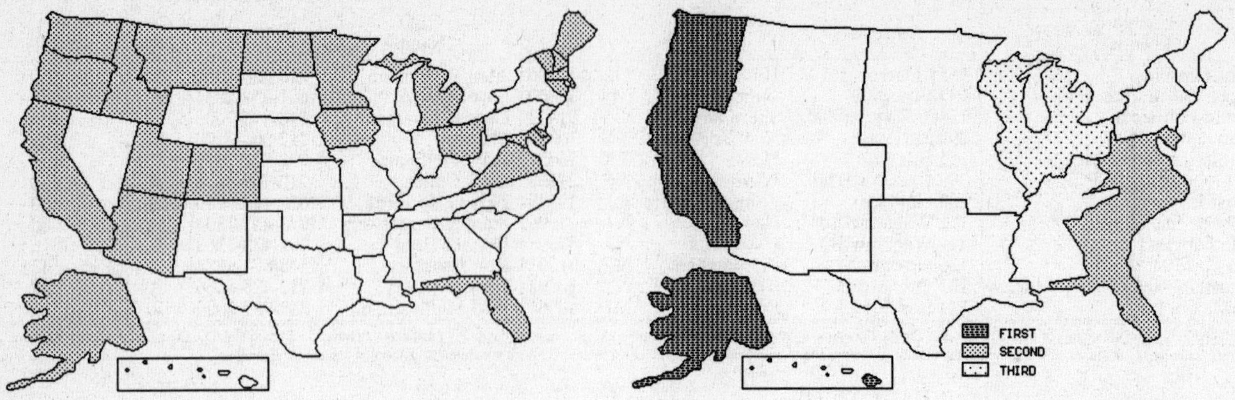

INDUSTRY DATA BY STATE

State	Establishments - 1995 Total (number)	Establishments - 1995 % of U.S.	Employment - 1995 Total (number)	Employment - 1995 % of U.S.	Employment - 1995 Per Estab.	Payroll - 1995 Total ($ mil.)	Payroll - 1995 Per Empl. ($)	Sales - 1992 Total ($ mil.)	Sales - 1992 % of U.S.	Sales - 1992 Per Estab ($)
California	751	10.7	6,901	12.7	9	68.5	9,929	533.0	14.9	60,172
Texas	452	6.4	3,430	6.3	8	30.4	8,850	232.5	6.5	61,448
Florida	406	5.8	3,021	5.6	7	27.0	8,935	202.9	5.7	59,110
New York	420	6.0	2,420	4.5	6	26.4	10,924	197.7	5.5	71,822
Ohio	313	4.5	2,605	4.8	8	18.0	6,921	158.6	4.4	56,552
Pennsylvania	270	3.9	2,384	4.4	9	20.3	8,530	147.8	4.1	56,878
Illinois	255	3.6	2,243	4.1	9	20.0	8,903	147.7	4.1	54,736
Michigan	252	3.6	2,399	4.4	10	17.9	7,462	147.5	4.1	55,910
Washington	205	2.9	1,968	3.6	10	16.6	8,454	132.9	3.7	56,378
Virginia	207	3.0	1,671	3.1	8	12.8	7,680	103.2	2.9	55,832
Massachusetts	170	2.4	1,756	3.2	10	19.5	11,108	101.3	2.8	57,307
North Carolina	234	3.3	1,413	2.6	6	14.6	10,348	89.4	2.5	63,642
Maryland	123	1.8	1,403	2.6	11	13.2	9,401	87.7	2.5	54,999
Minnesota	138	2.0	1,336	2.5	10	10.5	7,873	79.4	2.2	53,838
Georgia	186	2.7	1,287	2.4	7	12.7	9,897	73.1	2.0	54,854
Indiana	162	2.3	1,248	2.3	8	8.2	6,594	73.0	2.0	49,861
New Jersey	152	2.2	1,113	2.1	7	12.1	10,898	70.2	2.0	62,884
Wisconsin	150	2.1	935	1.7	6	7.0	7,539	66.7	1.9	51,284
Oregon	128	1.8	999	1.8	8	8.2	8,255	62.5	1.7	52,173
Missouri	128	1.8	1,022	1.9	8	8.1	7,916	57.8	1.6	46,442
Connecticut	101	1.4	863	1.6	9	8.6	10,009	56.5	1.6	56,562
Arizona	104	1.5	930	1.7	9	7.9	8,501	56.5	1.6	53,623
Tennessee	147	2.1	895	1.6	6	8.6	9,664	55.9	1.6	60,992
Colorado	102	1.5	912	1.7	9	7.2	7,914	54.0	1.5	52,096
Louisiana	103	1.5	707	1.3	7	6.4	8,986	47.3	1.3	57,035
Alabama	128	1.8	634	1.2	5	5.5	8,748	42.1	1.2	57,679
Iowa	98	1.4	533	1.0	5	3.6	6,737	41.0	1.1	48,274
Utah	80	1.1	799	1.5	10	5.5	6,921	38.7	1.1	45,048
Kentucky	72	1.0	513	0.9	7	4.5	8,844	35.0	1.0	58,384
South Carolina	115	1.6	603	1.1	5	5.5	9,088	34.9	1.0	54,245
Oklahoma	82	1.2	650	1.2	8	7.1	10,980	32.2	0.9	48,129
Kansas	91	1.3	512	0.9	6	3.4	6,570	30.4	0.9	48,063
New Hampshire	46	0.7	472	0.9	10	3.8	7,953	25.7	0.7	53,424
Nebraska	50	0.7	255	0.5	5	1.7	6,510	21.3	0.6	44,025
Mississippi	81	1.2	315	0.6	4	2.9	9,343	20.7	0.6	54,802
Maine	41	0.6	253	0.5	6	2.3	9,158	20.2	0.6	60,415
Idaho	45	0.6	327	0.6	7	2.2	6,865	18.2	0.5	45,042
Nevada	36	0.5	280	0.5	8	2.7	9,782	18.1	0.5	54,009
Arkansas	73	1.0	334	0.6	5	2.6	7,716	17.6	0.5	55,031
West Virginia	46	0.7	255	0.5	6	2.1	8,365	16.8	0.5	60,971
Montana	47	0.7	256	0.5	5	1.7	6,484	16.8	0.5	53,933
Hawaii	21	0.3	120	0.2	6	1.5	12,442	16.2	0.5	68,325
Alaska	32	0.5	202	0.4	6	1.5	7,609	15.5	0.4	66,184
New Mexico	31	0.4	249	0.5	8	2.1	8,446	14.4	0.4	54,423
Rhode Island	23	0.3	246	0.5	11	2.1	8,390	14.4	0.4	54,411
Delaware	22	0.3	179	0.3	8	1.5	8,547	12.7	0.4	67,674
North Dakota	20	0.3	85	0.2	4	0.6	6,894	11.6	0.3	52,027
South Dakota	20	0.3	104	0.2	5	1.0	9,154	9.0	0.3	47,693
Vermont	22	0.3	145	0.3	7	1.4	9,910	8.7	0.2	57,417
Wyoming	21	0.3	61	0.1	3	0.5	7,803	5.9	0.2	41,299
D.C.	7	0.1	27	0.0	4	0.4	14,889	3.6	0.1	114,935

Source: *County Business Patterns, 1995* and *Economic Census of the U.S., 1992*. Data are sorted by 1992 revenues and, if revenues are unavailable, by establishments in 1995. The symbol (D) indicates that data are withheld by the source to avoid disclosure of competitive information. A dash (-) indicates that data are not available or undisclosed because they do not meet statistical validity standards. Shaded *states* on the state map indicate those states which have proportionately greater representation in the industry than would be indicated by the state's population; the ratio is based on total revenues or number of establishments. Shaded *regions* indicate where the industry is regionally most concentrated.

5961 - CATALOG AND MAIL-ORDER HOUSES

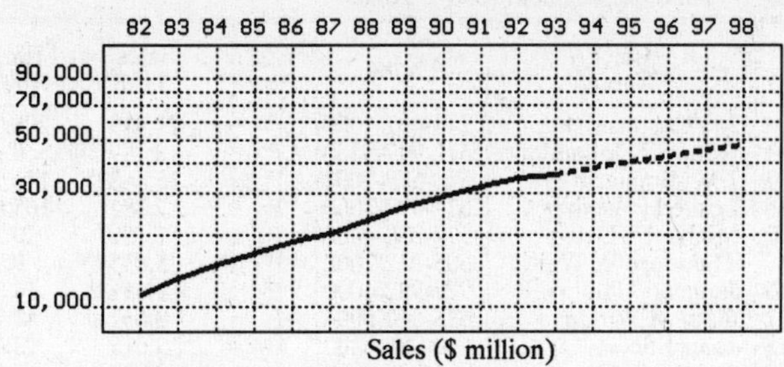

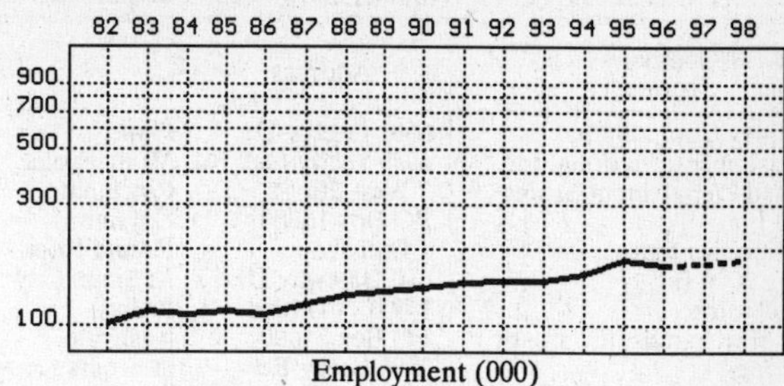

GENERAL STATISTICS

Year	Establishments (number)	Employment (number)	Payroll ($ million)	Sales ($ million)	Employees per Establishment (number)	Sales per Establishment ($)	Payroll per Employee ($)
1982	7,933	102,574	1,193.5	11,213.7	13	1,413,552	11,636
1983	8,026	114,270	1,462.9	13,040.3e	14	-	12,802
1984	7,573	109,885	1,544.9	14,866.9e	15	-	14,060
1985	7,148	113,937	1,568.6	16,693.5e	16	-	13,768
1986	6,176	110,713	1,667.4	18,520.1e	18	-	15,060
1987	7,227	123,195	1,931.6	20,346.6	17	2,815,365	15,679
1988	6,948	131,586	2,215.3	23,193.2e	19	-	16,835
1989	6,885	136,563	2,426.2	26,039.8e	20	-	17,766
1990	7,158	140,891	2,639.9	28,886.4e	20	-	18,737
1991	7,444	148,473	2,826.9	31,733.0e	20	-	19,040
1992	7,773	150,089	3,079.1	34,579.6	19	4,448,685	20,515
1993	7,396	149,927	3,024.5	35,757.1p	20	-	20,173
1994	6,422	160,462	3,427.9	38,093.7p	25	-	21,363
1995	7,217	180,773	3,920.7	40,430.3p	25	-	21,689
1996	6,939p	173,123p	3,820.7p	42,766.9p	-	-	-
1997	6,899p	178,365p	4,016.5p	45,103.5p	-	-	-
1998	6,860p	183,607p	4,212.3p	47,440.1p	-	-	-

Sources: *Economic Census of the United States*, 1982, 1987, and 1992. Establishment counts, employment, and payroll are from *County Business Patterns* for non-Census years. Values followed by a 'p' are projections by the editors. Sales and expense data for non-Census years are extrapolations, marked by 'e'. Industries reclassified in 1987 will not have data for prior years. Data are the most recent available at this level of detail.

INDICES OF CHANGE

Year	Establishments (number)	Employment (number)	Payroll ($ million)	Sales ($ million)	Employees per Establishment (number)	Sales per Establishment ($)	Payroll per Employee ($)
1982	102.1	68.3	38.8	32.4	68.4	31.8	56.7
1983	103.3	76.1	47.5	37.7e	73.7	-	62.4
1984	97.4	73.2	50.2	43.0e	78.9	-	68.5
1985	92.0	75.9	50.9	48.3e	84.2	-	67.1
1986	79.5	73.8	54.2	53.6e	94.7	-	73.4
1987	93.0	82.1	62.7	58.8	89.5	63.3	76.4
1988	89.4	87.7	71.9	67.1e	100.0	-	82.1
1989	88.6	91.0	78.8	75.3e	105.3	-	86.6
1990	92.1	93.9	85.7	83.5e	105.3	-	91.3
1991	95.8	98.9	91.8	91.8e	105.3	-	92.8
1992	100.0	100.0	100.0	100.0	100.0	100.0	100.0
1993	95.1	99.9	98.2	103.4p	106.7	-	98.3
1994	82.6	106.9	111.3	110.2p	131.5	-	104.1
1995	92.8	120.4	127.3	116.9p	131.8	-	105.7
1996	89.3p	115.3p	124.1p	123.7p	-	-	-
1997	88.8p	118.8p	130.4p	130.4p	-	-	-
1998	88.2p	122.3p	136.8p	137.2p	-	-	-

Sources: Same as General Statistics. The values shown reflect change from the base year, 1992. Values above 100 mean greater than 1992, values below 100 mean less than 1992, and a value of 100 in the 1982-91 or 1993-98 period means same as 1992. Values followed by a 'p' are projections by the editors; 'e' stands for extrapolation. Data are the most recent available at this level of detail.

SELECTED RATIOS

For 1992	Avg. of All Retail	Analyzed Industry	Index	For 1992	Avg. of All Retail	Analyzed Industry	Index
Employees per Establishment	12	19	160	Sales per Employee	102,941	230,394	224
Payroll per Establishment	146,026	396,128	271	Sales per Establishment	1,241,555	4,448,681	358
Payroll per Employee	12,107	20,515	169	Expenses per Establishment	na	na	na

Sources: Same as General Statistics. The 'Average of All Manufacturing' column represents the average of all manufacturing industries reported for the most recent complete year available. The Index shows the relationship between the Average and the Analyzed Industry. For example, 100 means that they are equal; 500 that the Analyzed Industry is five times the average; 50 means that the Analyzed Industry is half the national average. The abbreviation 'na' is used to show that data are 'not available'.

LEADING COMPANIES

Number shown: **50** Total sales ($ mil): **120,273** Total employment (000): **678.6**

Company Name	Address				CEO Name	Phone	Co. Type	Sales ($ mil)	Empl. (000)
J.C. Penney Company Inc.	6501 Legacy Dr	Plano	TX	75024	J E Oesterreicher	214-431-1000	P	21,419	205.0
ValueVision International Inc.	6740 Shady Oak Rd	Minneapolis	MN	55344	Robert L Johander	612-947-5200	P	18,189	<0.1
Federated Department Stores	7 West 7th St	Cincinnati	OH	45202	J M Zimmerman	513-579-7000	P	15,668	114.7
Limited Inc.	PO Box 16000	Columbus	OH	43216	Leslie H Wexner	614-479-7000	P	7,881	105.6
Dell Computer Corp.	1 Dell Way	Round Rock	TX	78682	Michael S Dell	512-338-4400	P	7,759	10.3
Gateway 2000 Inc.	610 Gateway Dr	N. Sioux City	SD	57049	Theodore W Waitt	605-232-2000	P	5,035	9.7
CompUSA Inc.	14951 N Dallas	Dallas	TX	75240	James F Halpin	972-982-4000	P	4,611	14.3
Service Merchandise Company	PO Box 24600	Nashville	TN	37202	Gary M Witkin	615-660-6000	P	3,662	42.7
Spiegel Inc.	3500 Lacey Rd	Downers Grove	IL	60515	John J Shea	630-986-8800	P	3,015	13.4
Reader's Digest Association	Reader's Digest Rd	Pleasantville	NY	10570	George V Grune	914-238-1000	P	2,839	6.0
Micro Warehouse Inc.	535 Connecticut	Norwalk	CT	06854	Peter Godfrey	203-899-4000	P	2,126	3.5
Barnes and Noble Inc.	122 5th Ave	New York	NY	10011	Leonard Riggio	212-633-3300	P	1,977	20.0
Fingerhut Companies Inc.	4400 Baker Rd	Minnetonka	MN	55343	Theodore Deikel	612-932-3100	P	1,799	9.5
Eddie Bauer Inc.	PO Box 97000	Redmond	WA	98073	Richard T Fersch	425-882-6100	S	1,600	8.0
QVC Inc.	Goshen Coporate	West Chester	PA	19380	Barry Diller	610-701-1000	S	1,488	4.7
CDW Computer Centers Inc.	1020 E Lake Cook	Buffalo Grove	IL	60089	Michael P Krasny	708-465-6000	P	1,277	1.0
Lands' End Inc.	1 Lands' End Ln	Dodgeville	WI	53595	Michael J Smith	608-935-9341	P	1,264	10.0
Home Shopping Network Inc.	PO Box 9090	Clearwater	FL	34618	James G Held	813-572-8585	S	1,098 *	4.1
Talbots Inc.	175 Beal St	Hingham	MA	02043	Arnold Zetcher	781-749-7600	P	1,054	7.2
HSN Inc.	2501 118th Ave, N	St. Petersburg	FL	33716	Barry Diller	813-572-8585	P	1,015	4.8
L.L. Bean Inc.	Casco St	Freeport	ME	04033	Leon A Gorman	207-865-4761	R	1,000	3.5
Fay's Inc.	7245 Henry Clay	Liverpool	NY	13088	Henry A Panasci Jr	315-451-8000	S	974	9.0
Williams-Sonoma Inc.	3250 Van Ness Ave	San Francisco	CA	94109	W Howard Lester	415-421-7900	P	812	8.7
Express Scripts Inc.	14000 Riverport Dr	Maryland H.	MO	63043	Barrett A Toan	314-770-1666	P	774	1.5
J. Crew Group Inc.	625 6th Ave	New York	NY	10011	Arthur Cinader	212-886-2500	R	750	5.0
Brylane L.P.	463 Seventh Ave	New York	NY	10018	Peter J Canzone	212-613-9500	P	705	5.1
Elcom International Inc.	10 Oceana Way	Norwood	MA	02062	Robert J Crowell	617-440-3333	P	620	0.8
Damark International Inc.	7101 Winnetka N	Brooklyn Park	MN	55428	Mark A Cohn	612-531-0066	P	595	2.0
Standex International Corp.	6 Manor Pkwy	Salem	NH	03079	Edward J Trainor	603-893-9701	P	565	4.8
Catalink Direct Inc.	111 Sinclaire St	Bristol	PA	19007	Dave King	215-788-8330	S	560	0.7
Hanover Direct Inc.	1500 Harbor Blvd	Weehawken	NJ	07087	Rakesh K Kaul	201-863-7300	P	558	2.7
Chadwick's of Boston	35 United Dr	W. Bridgewater	MA	02379	Dan Rao	508-583-8110	D	534 *	3.0
Williams-Sonoma Stores Inc.	100 N Point St	San Francisco	CA	94133	W Howard Lester	415-421-7900	S	529	6.9
Blair Corp.	220 Hickory St	Warren	PA	16366	Murray K McComas	814-723-3600	P	487	2.2
Insight Enterprises Inc.	6820 S Harl Ave	Tempe	AZ	85283	Eric J Crown	602-902-1001	P	485	0.9
Recreational Equipment Inc.	6750 S 228th St	Kent	WA	98032	Wally Smith	253-395-3780	R	485	5.1
Stanhome Inc.	333 Western Ave	Westfield	MA	01085	HL Tower	413-562-3631	P	476	4.6
Creative Computers Inc.	2645 Maricopa St	Torrance	CA	90503	Frank F Khulusi	310-787-4500	P	445	0.5
Sid Tool Company Inc.	151 Sunnyside Blvd	Plainview	NY	11803	Mitchell Jacobson	516-349-7100	S	430 *	2.0
West Marine Inc.	500 Westridge Dr	Watsonville	CA	95076	Crawford L Cole	408-728-2700	P	415	3.1
Egghead Inc.	22705 E Mission	Liberty Lake	WA	99019	George P Orban	509-922-7031	P	361	1.3
National Media Corp.	11 Penn Center	Philadelphia	PA	19103	Mark P Hershhorn	215-988-4600	P	358	0.5
TigerDirect Inc.	8700 W Flagler St	Miami	FL	33174	Gilbert Florentino	305-229-1119	S	356	0.3
Retired Persons Services Inc.	500 Montgomery St	Alexandria	VA	22314	Brian S Frid	703-684-0244	R	350 *	2.0
CML Group Inc.	524 Main St	Acton	MA	01720	Charles M Leighton	978-264-4155	P	341	3.1
Bear Creek Corp.	PO Box 299	Medford	OR	97501	Bill Williams	541-776-2362	S	330 *	1.6
Newport News Inc.	711 3rd Ave, 4th Fl	New York	NY	10017	George D Ittner	212-986-2585	S	305	1.2
Doubleday Direct Inc.	401 Franklin Ave	Garden City	NY	11530	Markus Wilhelm	516-873-4561	S	300	0.7
Multiple Zones International	707 Grady Way	Renton	WA	98055	Victor Kabani	206-603-2400	R	300 *	0.6
Pleasant Co.	PO Box 620998	Middleton	WI	53562	Pleasant Rowland	608-836-4848	R	300	0.7

Source: *Ward's Business Directory of U.S. Private and Public Companies*, 1998. The company type code used is as follows: P - Public, R - Private, S - Subsidiary, D - Division, J - Joint Venture, A - Affiliate, G - Group. Sales are in millions of dollars, employees are in thousands. An asterisk (*) indicates an estimated sales volume. The symbol < stands for 'less than'.

OCCUPATIONS EMPLOYED BY SIC 596 - NONSTORE RETAILERS

Occupation	% of Total 1996	Change to 2006	Occupation	% of Total 1996	Change to 2006
Sales & related workers nec	14.0	14.3	Stock clerks	2.3	92.0
Order clerks	10.3	-6.5	Truck drivers light & heavy	2.3	3.9
Driver/sales workers	6.5	-6.5	Food preparation workers	2.1	-0.9
Adjustment clerks	6.2	40.3	Food counter, fountain workers	2.1	-0.3
Coin & vending machine servicers & repairers	3.7	-16.9	Clerical supervisors & managers	1.6	3.9
Salespersons, retail	3.7	10.7	Hand packers & packagers	1.5	3.9
General office clerks	3.5	-10.6	Bookkeeping, accounting, & auditing clerks	1.5	-16.9
General managers & top executives	3.4	0.7	Freight, stock, & material movers, hand	1.2	-6.5
Traffic, shipping, receiving clerks	3.4	3.9	Secretaries, except legal & medical	1.2	-17.6
Order fillers, wholesale & retail sales	3.2	-6.5	Data entry keyers, except composing	1.2	-16.9
Marketing & sales worker supervisors	2.8	3.9	Cashiers	1.0	5.2

Source: *Industry-Occupation Matrix*, Bureau of Labor Statistics. These data relate to one or more 3-digit SIC industry groups rather than to a single 4-digit SIC. The change reported for each occupation to the year 2006 is a percent of growth or decline as estimated by the Bureau of Labor Statistics. The abbreviation nec stands for 'not elsewhere classified'.

STATE AND REGIONAL CONCENTRATION

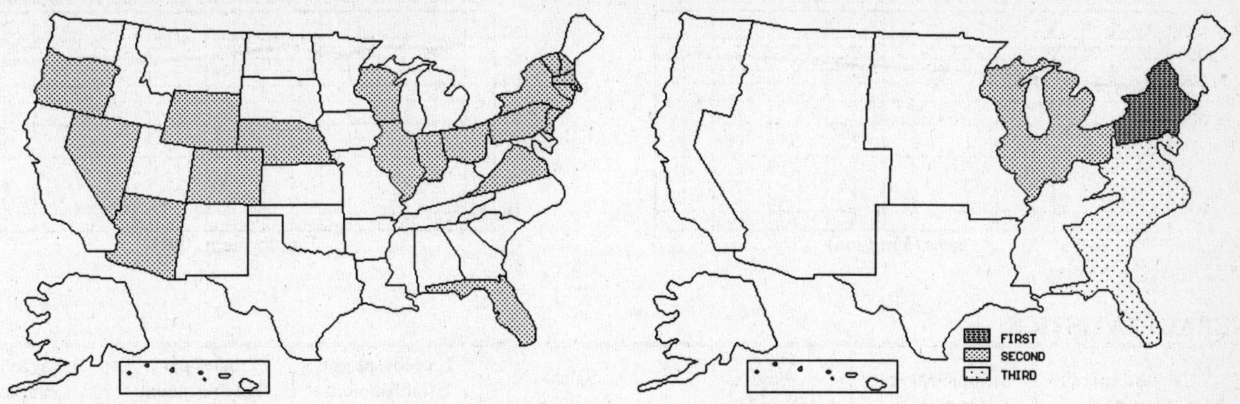

INDUSTRY DATA BY STATE

State	Establishments - 1995 Total (number)	Establishments - 1995 % of U.S.	Employment - 1995 Total (number)	Employment - 1995 % of U.S.	Employment - 1995 Per Estab.	Payroll - 1995 Total ($ mil.)	Payroll - 1995 Per Empl. ($)	Sales - 1992 Total ($ mil.)	Sales - 1992 % of U.S.	Sales - 1992 Per Estab ($)
Pennsylvania	267	3.7	11,061	6.1	41	317.0	28,662	3,971.9	12.2	316,208
New York	633	8.8	10,731	5.9	17	273.2	25,459	2,811.9	8.6	338,951
Florida	395	5.5	10,448	5.8	26	256.9	24,588	2,667.8	8.2	270,673
Illinois	351	4.9	7,862	4.3	22	211.0	26,840	2,339.0	7.2	267,656
California	889	12.3	11,318	6.3	13	266.4	23,534	2,308.9	7.1	250,911
Wisconsin	177	2.5	8,739	4.8	49	179.5	20,537	1,744.3	5.3	162,654
Ohio	284	3.9	12,096	6.7	43	235.0	19,429	1,743.7	5.3	199,441
Indiana	143	2.0	8,338	4.6	58	159.8	19,170	1,581.1	4.8	268,127
Texas	354	4.9	7,269	4.0	21	139.8	19,232	1,453.0	4.5	283,958
Connecticut	140	1.9	6,200	3.4	44	155.4	25,070	1,253.0	3.8	290,853
Virginia	183	2.5	5,869	3.2	32	120.8	20,583	1,244.1	3.8	261,593
New Jersey	253	3.5	7,225	4.0	29	194.7	26,953	1,064.7	3.3	221,224
Massachusetts	191	2.6	7,614	4.2	40	161.7	21,235	1,034.7	3.2	166,783
Washington	186	2.6	2,714	1.5	15	56.9	20,950	563.0	1.7	317,196
North Carolina	161	2.2	4,385	2.4	27	86.3	19,671	556.3	1.7	175,158
Arizona	147	2.0	2,762	1.5	19	45.6	16,508	551.7	1.7	273,772
Colorado	168	2.3	2,457	1.4	15	47.5	19,313	550.5	1.7	182,344
Oregon	126	1.7	1,480	0.8	12	36.1	24,391	474.6	1.5	271,525
Georgia	194	2.7	4,814	2.7	25	91.5	19,013	454.7	1.4	117,585
Nevada	59	0.8	2,004	1.1	34	53.9	26,910	432.6	1.3	253,293
Nebraska	53	0.7	2,973	1.6	56	51.5	17,317	414.2	1.3	186,149
Missouri	164	2.3	2,614	1.4	16	57.1	21,846	414.1	1.3	179,953
Michigan	175	2.4	2,535	1.4	14	45.9	18,124	338.4	1.0	141,542
New Hampshire	60	0.8	2,404	1.3	40	59.6	24,804	314.4	1.0	243,568
Tennessee	124	1.7	3,814	2.1	31	65.1	17,073	274.0	0.8	193,248
Alabama	68	0.9	1,164	0.6	17	21.0	18,074	222.4	0.7	211,784
Kansas	64	0.9	2,380	1.3	37	41.6	17,489	220.1	0.7	100,743
Rhode Island	35	0.5	700	0.4	20	18.1	25,814	194.2	0.6	255,805
New Mexico	60	0.8	927	0.5	15	21.1	22,728	187.4	0.6	283,086
Maryland	131	1.8	958	0.5	7	24.8	25,859	155.6	0.5	206,398
Iowa	86	1.2	973	0.5	11	16.5	16,991	146.3	0.4	70,046
Kentucky	73	1.0	635	0.4	9	13.3	20,992	121.4	0.4	143,501
Vermont	50	0.7	819	0.5	16	18.4	22,458	104.7	0.3	161,106
South Carolina	52	0.7	896	0.5	17	14.0	15,664	86.1	0.3	89,225
Wyoming	25	0.3	591	0.3	24	11.1	18,838	85.1	0.3	163,671
South Dakota	31	0.4	718	0.4	23	8.0	11,170	85.1	0.3	81,082
Arkansas	51	0.7	335	0.2	7	4.5	13,370	70.6	0.2	156,230
Louisiana	65	0.9	457	0.3	7	8.6	18,794	54.0	0.2	126,648
Oklahoma	56	0.8	257	0.1	5	4.4	17,284	45.8	0.1	158,401
Mississippi	34	0.5	243	0.1	7	4.3	17,642	42.7	0.1	123,379
Utah	65	0.9	528	0.3	8	9.1	17,218	41.3	0.1	128,230
Montana	29	0.4	225	0.1	8	3.2	14,342	39.7	0.1	147,989
Delaware	20	0.3	247	0.1	12	4.8	19,563	38.3	0.1	226,799
Idaho	30	0.4	352	0.2	12	8.6	24,364	37.6	0.1	201,064
North Dakota	16	0.2	154	0.1	10	2.6	16,961	25.0	0.1	146,409
D.C.	17	0.2	109	0.1	6	2.8	25,358	22.4	0.1	187,975
West Virginia	27	0.4	113	0.1	4	1.6	14,469	18.9	0.1	140,281
Hawaii	9	0.1	74	0.0	8	1.5	20,851	7.8	0.0	124,444
Alaska	10	0.1	55	0.0	6	1.0	18,673	4.9	0.0	132,135
Minnesota	182	2.5	15,499	8.6	85	253.5	16,358	(D)	-	-
Maine	54	0.7	1,638	0.9	30	33.8	20,649	(D)	-	-

Source: County Business Patterns, 1995 and *Economic Census of the U.S., 1992*. Data are sorted by 1992 revenues and, if revenues are unavailable, by establishments in 1995. The symbol (D) indicates that data are withheld by the source to avoid disclosure of competitive information. A dash (-) indicates that data are not available or undisclosed because they do not meet statistical validity standards. Shaded *states* on the state map indicate those states which have proportionately greater representation in the industry than would be indicated by the state's population; the ratio is based on total revenues or number of establishments. Shaded *regions* indicate where the industry is regionally most concentrated.

5962 - MERCHANDISING MACHINE OPERATORS

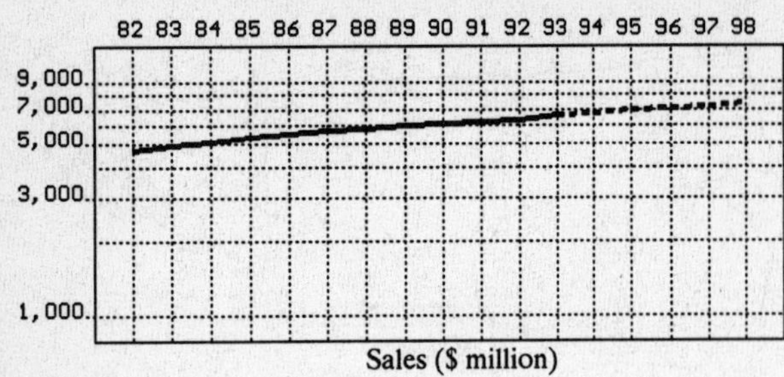

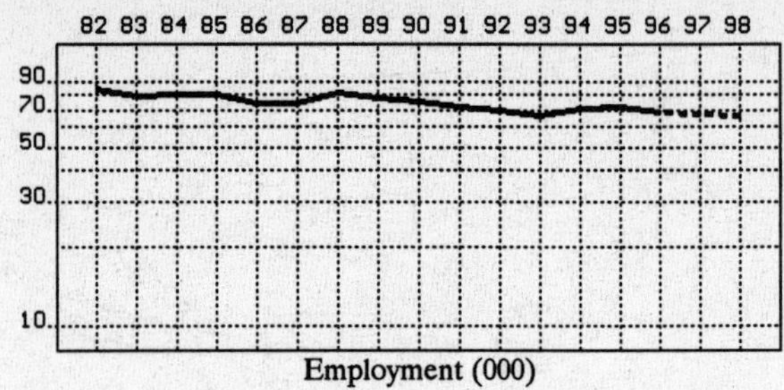

GENERAL STATISTICS

Year	Establishments (number)	Employment (number)	Payroll ($ million)	Sales ($ million)	Employees per Establishment (number)	Sales per Establishment ($)	Payroll per Employee ($)
1982	5,956	83,560	934.9	4,726.6	14	793,588	11,188
1983	5,426	78,849	940.6	4,919.7e	15	-	11,929
1984	5,322	80,029	1,018.3	5,112.9e	15	-	12,724
1985	5,010	81,040	1,055.5	5,306.0e	16	-	13,025
1986	4,838	74,271	1,078.2	5,499.2e	15	-	14,518
1987	5,302	73,652	1,090.2	5,692.3	14	1,073,612	14,802
1988	4,983	81,739	1,232.3	5,819.8e	16	-	15,076
1989	4,873	77,537	1,250.6	5,947.4e	16	-	16,129
1990	5,144	76,130	1,258.9	6,075.0e	15	-	16,536
1991	5,298	72,526	1,242.2	6,202.5e	14	-	17,127
1992	6,391	69,628	1,232.0	6,330.1	11	990,468	17,694
1993	5,881	66,651	1,227.1	6,564.9p	11	-	18,411
1994	5,975	71,046	1,323.9	6,725.3p	12	-	18,634
1995	6,124	72,054	1,378.1	6,885.6p	12	-	19,126
1996	5,872p	68,350p	1,399.6p	7,046.0p	-	-	-
1997	5,926p	67,380p	1,431.3p	7,206.3p	-	-	-
1998	5,980p	66,411p	1,463.0p	7,366.7p	-	-	-

Sources: *Economic Census of the United States*, 1982, 1987, and 1992. Establishment counts, employment, and payroll are from *County Business Patterns* for non-Census years. Values followed by a 'p' are projections by the editors. Sales and expense data for non-Census years are extrapolations, marked by 'e'. Industries reclassified in 1987 will not have data for prior years. Data are the most recent available at this level of detail.

INDICES OF CHANGE

Year	Establishments (number)	Employment (number)	Payroll ($ million)	Sales ($ million)	Employees per Establishment (number)	Sales per Establishment ($)	Payroll per Employee ($)
1982	93.2	120.0	75.9	74.7	127.3	80.1	63.2
1983	84.9	113.2	76.3	77.7e	136.4	-	67.4
1984	83.3	114.9	82.7	80.8e	136.4	-	71.9
1985	78.4	116.4	85.7	83.8e	145.5	-	73.6
1986	75.7	106.7	87.5	86.9e	136.4	-	82.1
1987	83.0	105.8	88.5	89.9	127.3	108.4	83.7
1988	78.0	117.4	100.0	91.9e	145.5	-	85.2
1989	76.2	111.4	101.5	94.0e	145.5	-	91.2
1990	80.5	109.3	102.2	96.0e	136.4	-	93.5
1991	82.9	104.2	100.8	98.0e	127.3	-	96.8
1992	100.0	100.0	100.0	100.0	100.0	100.0	100.0
1993	92.0	95.7	99.6	103.7p	103.0	-	104.0
1994	93.5	102.0	107.5	106.2p	108.1	-	105.3
1995	95.8	103.5	111.9	108.8p	107.0	-	108.1
1996	91.9p	98.2p	113.6p	111.3p	-	-	-
1997	92.7p	96.8p	116.2p	113.8p	-	-	-
1998	93.6p	95.4p	118.8p	116.4p	-	-	-

Sources: Same as General Statistics. The values shown reflect change from the base year, 1992. Values above 100 mean greater than 1992, values below 100 mean less than 1992, and a value of 100 in the 1982-91 or 1993-98 period means same as 1992. Values followed by a 'p' are projections by the editors; 'e' stands for extrapolation. Data are the most recent available at this level of detail.

SELECTED RATIOS

For 1992	Avg. of All Retail	Analyzed Industry	Index	For 1992	Avg. of All Retail	Analyzed Industry	Index
Employees per Establishment	12	11	90	Sales per Employee	102,941	90,913	88
Payroll per Establishment	146,026	192,771	132	Sales per Establishment	1,241,555	990,471	80
Payroll per Employee	12,107	17,694	146	Expenses per Establishment	na	na	na

Sources: Same as General Statistics. The 'Average of All Manufacturing' column represents the average of all manufacturing industries reported for the most recent complete year available. The Index shows the relationship between the Average and the Analyzed Industry. For example, 100 means that they are equal; 500 that the Analyzed Industry is five times the average; 50 means that the Analyzed Industry is half the national average. The abbreviation 'na' is used to show that data are 'not available'.

LEADING COMPANIES

Number shown: **22**　Total sales ($ mil): **463**　Total employment (000): **6.1**

Company Name	Address				CEO Name	Phone	Co. Type	Sales ($ mil)	Empl. (000)
Glacier Water Services Inc.	2261 Cosmos Court	Carlsbad	CA	92009	Jerry A Gordon	760-930-2420	P	46	0.3
Ace Coffee Bar Inc.	30W626 Rte 20	Elgin	IL	60120	Bernard Cavitt	847-931-2600	R	46 *	0.6
Canteen Service Co.	2139 Kalamazoo	Grand Rapids	MI	49507	FR Tiggleman	616-243-8614	R	40	0.7
Patton Music Company Inc.	811 Kearney Ave	Modesto	CA	95350	James B Reed	209-529-6500	R	33 *	0.1
Versatile Holding Corp.	80 Etna Ln	Freeville	NY	13068	Kevin Deans	607-347-6712	R	33	0.6
RE Services Inc.	PO Box 1467	La Fayette	GA	30728	Steve Ledbetter	706-638-3366	R	29 *	0.4
Pickett Industries	2627 Midway	Shreveport	LA	71108	John B Waters	318-632-8000	R	27	0.3
CulinArt Inc.	1979 Marcus Ave	Lake Success	NY	11042	Joseph Pacifico	516-437-2700	R	26	0.5
C.L. Swanson Corp.	4501 Femrite Dr	Madison	WI	53716	CL Swanson	608-221-7640	R	24 *	0.4
Calderon Brothers Vending	PO Box 29099	Indianapolis	IN	46229	Steven Calderon	317-899-1234	R	24 *	0.2
Zaug's Inc.	PO Box 2335	Appleton	WI	54913	Allen Zaug	920-734-9881	R	21	0.2
Konop Vending Machine Inc.	1725 Industrial Dr	Green Bay	WI	54302	Thomas J Konop	414-468-8517	R	18	0.2
Modern Vending Inc.	3910 Industrial Blvd	Indianapolis	IN	46254	Elliot Nelson	317-298-7000	R	15	0.2
Parina Enterprises Inc.	6777 Embarcadero	Stockton	CA	95219	Anthony E Parina	209-956-9000	R	15	<0.1
Rowe Inc.	15 Blackstone Val	Lincoln	RI	02865	George Simpson Jr	401-333-3333	R	15	0.2
Farmers Cooperative Elevator	302 W 1st St	Halstead	KS	67056	Dale Dick	316-835-2261	R	15	<0.1
Compass Group USA Div.	2400 Yorkmount	Charlotte	NC	28217	Mike Bailey	704-329-4000	S	13 *	0.3
University Auxillary Services	99 Fuller Rd	Albany	NY	12203	EN Zahm	518-442-5950	R	12	0.8
New England Variety	PO Box 804	Niantic	CT	06357	Bruce Engelman	203-739-6291	R	7	<0.1
Terminal Investment Co.	301 W Clinton Ave	Oaklyn	NJ	08107	George Hamilton Jr	609-854-2100	R	4	<0.1
P-N-L Vending Inc.	155 McNeilly Rd	Pittsburgh	PA	15226	Nancy Manolios	412-344-8530	R	1	<0.1
Siegrest Enterprises Inc.	2020 N 25th Dr	Phoenix	AZ	85009	David Siegrest	602-233-1676	R	1	<0.1

Source: *Ward's Business Directory of U.S. Private and Public Companies*, 1998. The company type code used is as follows: P - Public, R - Private, S - Subsidiary, D - Division, J - Joint Venture, A - Affiliate, G - Group. Sales are in millions of dollars, employees are in thousands. An asterisk (*) indicates an estimated sales volume. The symbol < stands for 'less than'.

OCCUPATIONS EMPLOYED BY SIC 596 - NONSTORE RETAILERS

Occupation	% of Total 1996	Change to 2006	Occupation	% of Total 1996	Change to 2006
Sales & related workers nec	14.0	14.3	Stock clerks	2.3	92.0
Order clerks	10.3	-6.5	Truck drivers light & heavy	2.3	3.9
Driver/sales workers	6.5	-6.5	Food preparation workers	2.1	-0.9
Adjustment clerks	6.2	40.3	Food counter, fountain workers	2.1	-0.3
Coin & vending machine servicers & repairers	3.7	-16.9	Clerical supervisors & managers	1.6	3.9
Salespersons, retail	3.7	10.7	Hand packers & packagers	1.5	3.9
General office clerks	3.5	-10.6	Bookkeeping, accounting, & auditing clerks	1.5	-16.9
General managers & top executives	3.4	0.7	Freight, stock, & material movers, hand	1.2	-6.5
Traffic, shipping, receiving clerks	3.4	3.9	Secretaries, except legal & medical	1.2	-17.6
Order fillers, wholesale & retail sales	3.2	-6.5	Data entry keyers, except composing	1.2	-16.9
Marketing & sales worker supervisors	2.8	3.9	Cashiers	1.0	5.2

Source: *Industry-Occupation Matrix*, Bureau of Labor Statistics. These data relate to one or more 3-digit SIC industry groups rather than to a single 4-digit SIC. The change reported for each occupation to the year 2006 is a percent of growth or decline as estimated by the Bureau of Labor Statistics. The abbreviation nec stands for 'not elsewhere classified'.

STATE AND REGIONAL CONCENTRATION

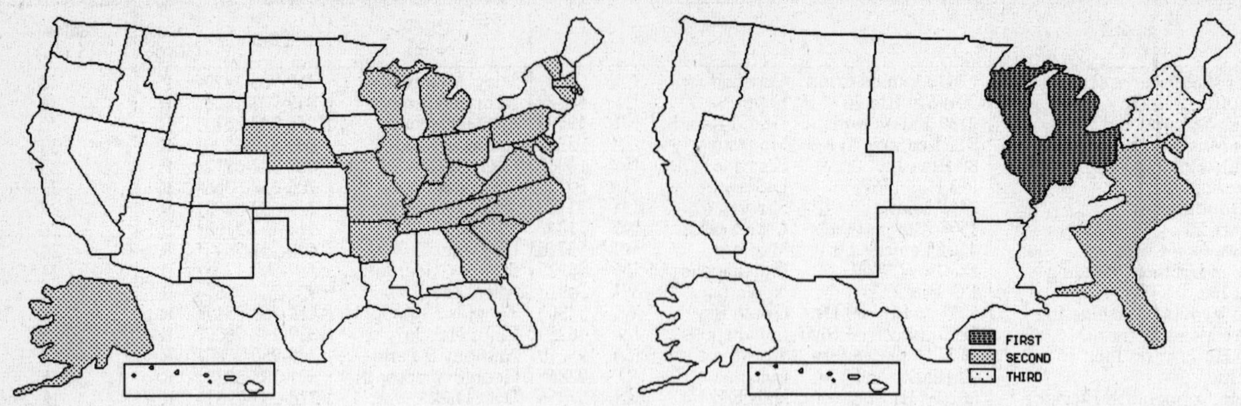

INDUSTRY DATA BY STATE

	Establishments - 1995		Employment - 1995			Payroll - 1995		Sales - 1992		
State	Total (number)	% of U.S.	Total (number)	% of U.S.	Per Estab.	Total ($ mil.)	Per Empl. ($)	Total ($ mil.)	% of U.S.	Per Estab ($)
California	427	7.0	3,745	5.2	9	87.9	23,472	467.7	7.8	115,588
Ohio	322	5.3	7,794	10.8	24	127.4	16,343	464.9	7.7	71,736
Pennsylvania	299	4.9	5,774	8.0	19	104.0	18,014	398.2	6.6	78,220
Illinois	341	5.6	3,846	5.3	11	84.6	22,000	378.7	6.3	95,134
Texas	392	6.4	3,177	4.4	8	68.8	21,658	373.5	6.2	97,449
New York	403	6.6	3,317	4.6	8	67.2	20,270	345.6	5.7	95,295
North Carolina	180	2.9	3,843	5.3	21	69.5	18,089	262.4	4.4	78,998
Michigan	234	3.8	2,749	3.8	12	57.8	21,021	255.9	4.2	98,753
Georgia	186	3.0	2,909	4.0	16	57.8	19,858	222.8	3.7	78,689
Indiana	173	2.8	2,290	3.2	13	45.8	20,016	214.3	3.6	97,968
Massachusetts	168	2.7	1,917	2.7	11	40.2	20,981	196.9	3.3	98,836
Tennessee	216	3.5	2,765	3.8	13	48.1	17,397	194.5	3.2	82,397
Wisconsin	134	2.2	2,116	2.9	16	43.8	20,702	192.9	3.2	94,654
Florida	333	5.4	1,795	2.5	5	35.6	19,820	184.4	3.1	118,868
New Jersey	164	2.7	1,448	2.0	9	33.1	22,835	179.3	3.0	110,315
Virginia	127	2.1	1,932	2.7	15	35.0	18,110	161.0	2.7	79,336
Maryland	117	1.9	1,415	2.0	12	32.9	23,226	160.2	2.7	117,044
Missouri	161	2.6	1,566	2.2	10	30.4	19,385	143.7	2.4	98,850
Kentucky	101	1.6	1,382	1.9	14	22.9	16,599	127.1	2.1	98,460
South Carolina	81	1.3	1,525	2.1	19	24.9	16,338	107.7	1.8	64,124
Alabama	117	1.9	1,316	1.8	11	22.0	16,682	98.5	1.6	80,283
Connecticut	84	1.4	601	0.8	7	13.8	22,962	88.1	1.5	120,894
Washington	92	1.5	668	0.9	7	15.3	22,873	78.5	1.3	113,247
Colorado	124	2.0	1,047	1.5	8	17.4	16,616	76.3	1.3	84,640
Arkansas	65	1.1	1,185	1.6	18	16.4	13,799	74.7	1.2	65,568
Oregon	74	1.2	649	0.9	9	14.1	21,775	64.7	1.1	108,347
Iowa	86	1.4	1,009	1.4	12	15.1	14,977	63.6	1.1	76,225
Kansas	63	1.0	601	0.8	10	10.8	18,007	59.2	1.0	95,917
Arizona	101	1.6	532	0.7	5	10.3	19,310	51.7	0.9	127,953
Oklahoma	76	1.2	570	0.8	8	9.1	15,986	47.5	0.8	92,021
Mississippi	52	0.8	899	1.2	17	14.2	15,813	47.0	0.8	63,694
Nebraska	38	0.6	522	0.7	14	8.7	16,640	39.7	0.7	88,672
Utah	34	0.6	274	0.4	8	4.9	17,996	26.1	0.4	110,470
New Hampshire	41	0.7	245	0.3	6	4.6	18,694	25.5	0.4	84,973
Rhode Island	22	0.4	96	0.1	4	1.5	15,469	25.3	0.4	118,192
Delaware	12	0.2	157	0.2	13	3.9	24,879	22.4	0.4	104,888
Alaska	17	0.3	133	0.2	8	3.4	25,549	19.9	0.3	140,338
West Virginia	54	0.9	356	0.5	7	5.0	13,989	19.1	0.3	101,431
New Mexico	26	0.4	180	0.2	7	3.2	17,644	15.2	0.3	79,832
Vermont	12	0.2	105	0.1	9	2.2	21,390	14.4	0.2	99,861
Idaho	28	0.5	152	0.2	5	2.1	13,829	11.2	0.2	128,241
South Dakota	17	0.3	108	0.1	6	2.8	25,602	7.2	0.1	126,649
North Dakota	14	0.2	76	0.1	5	1.0	13,632	6.0	0.1	133,133
Montana	16	0.3	85	0.1	5	1.1	13,094	5.3	0.1	112,830
Hawaii	14	0.2	65	0.1	5	1.1	16,354	4.8	0.1	75,524
D.C.	7	0.1	31	0.0	4	0.6	17,871	4.1	0.1	103,425
Wyoming	10	0.2	46	0.1	5	0.6	12,630	4.1	0.1	83,204
Minnesota	133	2.2	1,477	2.0	11	27.7	18,731	(D)	-	-
Louisiana	79	1.3	810	1.1	10	14.1	17,431	(D)	-	-
Nevada	31	0.5	251	0.3	8	5.4	21,566	(D)	-	-
Maine	26	0.4	503	0.7	19	8.2	16,247	(D)	-	-

Source: *County Business Patterns, 1995* and *Economic Census of the U.S., 1992*. Data are sorted by 1992 revenues and, if revenues are unavailable, by establishments in 1995. The symbol (D) indicates that data are withheld by the source to avoid disclosure of competitive information. A dash (-) indicates that data are not available or undisclosed because they do not meet statistical validity standards. Shaded *states* on the state map indicate those states which have proportionately greater representation in the industry than would be indicated by the state's population; the ratio is based on total revenues or number of establishments. Shaded *regions* indicate where the industry is regionally most concentrated.

5963 - DIRECT SELLING ESTABLISHMENTS

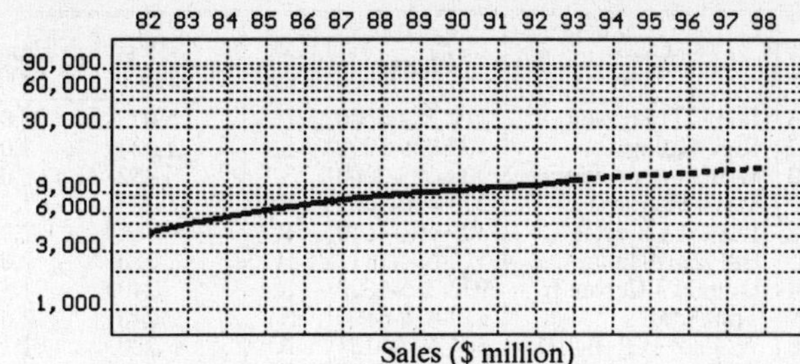

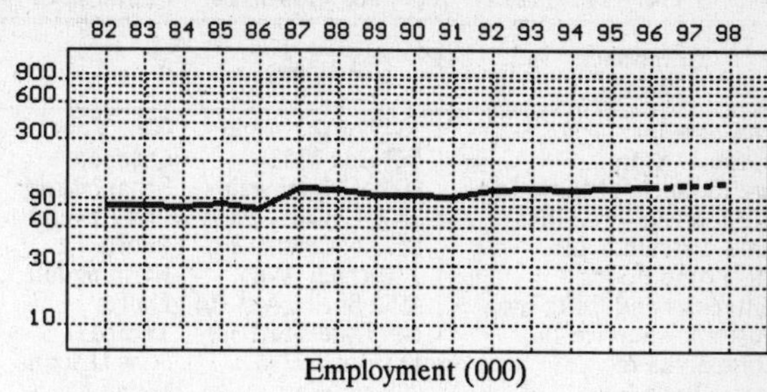

GENERAL STATISTICS

Year	Establishments (number)	Employment (number)	Payroll ($ million)	Sales ($ million)	Employees per Establishment (number)	Sales per Establishment ($)	Payroll per Employee ($)
1982	9,352	87,795	813.5	4,175.1	9	446,437	9,265
1983	8,852	88,166	873.2	4,911.0e	10	-	9,904
1984	8,251	87,500	935.2	5,646.9e	11	-	10,688
1985	7,778	91,246	997.7	6,382.8e	12	-	10,934
1986	7,370	83,151	1,003.4	7,118.8e	11	-	12,068
1987	10,535	121,125	1,501.0	7,854.7	11	745,581	12,392
1988	9,343	120,547	1,612.2	8,317.8e	13	-	13,374
1989	8,934	107,110	1,606.0	8,780.9e	12	-	14,994
1990	8,820	106,863	1,655.0	9,244.0e	12	-	15,487
1991	8,650	103,905	1,603.7	9,707.2e	12	-	15,435
1992	13,641	119,417	1,969.3	10,170.3	9	745,567	16,491
1993	13,279	121,357	2,122.1	11,079.8p	9	-	17,487
1994	13,207	119,526	2,220.9	11,679.3p	9	-	18,581
1995	13,388	122,904	2,274.4	12,278.9p	9	-	18,505
1996	13,191p	128,024p	2,416.0p	12,878.4p	-	-	-
1997	13,603p	130,993p	2,536.3p	13,477.9p	-	-	-
1998	14,015p	133,962p	2,656.7p	14,077.4p	-	-	-

Sources: *Economic Census of the United States*, 1982, 1987, and 1992. Establishment counts, employment, and payroll are from *County Business Patterns* for non-Census years. Values followed by a 'p' are projections by the editors. Sales and expense data for non-Census years are extrapolations, marked by 'e'. Industries reclassified in 1987 will not have data for prior years. Data are the most recent available at this level of detail.

INDICES OF CHANGE

Year	Establishments (number)	Employment (number)	Payroll ($ million)	Sales ($ million)	Employees per Establishment (number)	Sales per Establishment ($)	Payroll per Employee ($)
1982	68.6	73.5	41.3	41.1	100.0	59.9	56.2
1983	64.9	73.8	44.3	48.3e	111.1	-	60.1
1984	60.5	73.3	47.5	55.5e	122.2	-	64.8
1985	57.0	76.4	50.7	62.8e	133.3	-	66.3
1986	54.0	69.6	51.0	70.0e	122.2	-	73.2
1987	77.2	101.4	76.2	77.2	122.2	100.0	75.1
1988	68.5	100.9	81.9	81.8e	144.4	-	81.1
1989	65.5	89.7	81.6	86.3e	133.3	-	90.9
1990	64.7	89.5	84.0	90.9e	133.3	-	93.9
1991	63.4	87.0	81.4	95.4e	133.3	-	93.6
1992	100.0	100.0	100.0	100.0	100.0	100.0	100.0
1993	97.3	101.6	107.8	108.9p	101.5	-	106.0
1994	96.8	100.1	112.8	114.8p	100.6	-	112.7
1995	98.1	102.9	115.5	120.7p	102.0	-	112.2
1996	96.7p	107.2p	122.7p	126.6p	-	-	-
1997	99.7p	109.7p	128.8p	132.5p	-	-	-
1998	102.7p	112.2p	134.9p	138.4p	-	-	-

Sources: Same as General Statistics. The values shown reflect change from the base year, 1992. Values above 100 mean greater than 1992, values below 100 mean less than 1992, and a value of 100 in the 1982-91 or 1993-98 period means same as 1992. Values followed by a 'p' are projections by the editors; 'e' stands for extrapolation. Data are the most recent available at this level of detail.

SELECTED RATIOS

For 1992	Avg. of All Retail	Analyzed Industry	Index	For 1992	Avg. of All Retail	Analyzed Industry	Index
Employees per Establishment	12	9	73	Sales per Employee	102,941	85,166	83
Payroll per Establishment	146,026	144,366	99	Sales per Establishment	1,241,555	745,569	60
Payroll per Employee	12,107	16,491	136	Expenses per Establishment	na	na	na

Sources: Same as General Statistics. The 'Average of All Manufacturing' column represents the average of all manufacturing industries reported for the most recent complete year available. The Index shows the relationship between the Average and the Analyzed Industry. For example, 100 means that they are equal; 500 that the Analyzed Industry is five times the average; 50 means that the Analyzed Industry is half the national average. The abbreviation 'na' is used to show that data are 'not available'.

LEADING COMPANIES

Number shown: **26** Total sales ($ mil): **9,842** Total employment (000): **63.8**

Company Name	Address				CEO Name	Phone	Co. Type	Sales ($ mil)	Empl. (000)
Avon Products Inc.	1345 of the Amer	New York	NY	10105	James E Preston	212-282-5000	P	5,079	35.0
Tupperware U.S. Inc.	PO Box 2353	Orlando	FL	32802	Rick Goings	407-826-5050	S	1,034	7.0
Signature Financial/Marketing	200 N Martingale	Schaumburg	IL	60173	Worthington Linen	708-605-3000	S	852	8.0
Herbalife International Inc.	1800 Century Pk E	Los Angeles	CA	90067	Mark Hughes	310-410-9600	P	783	1.5
Foster and Gallagher Inc.	6523 N Galena Rd	Peoria	IL	61632	Robert Ostertag	309-691-4610	R	460 *	2.8
Colorado Prime Foods	1 Michael Ave	Farmingdale	NY	11735	Bill Dordelman	516-694-1111	R	350	2.0
Home Interiors and Gifts Inc.	4550 Spring Val Rd	Dallas	TX	75244	Donald J Carter Jr	972-386-1000	R	240 *	1.5
Time Customer Service Inc.	1 N Dale Mayberry	Tampa	FL	33609	Tim Adams	813-878-6100	S	240	2.0
Reily Companies Inc.	PO Box 60296	New Orleans	LA	70160	William B Reily III	504-524-6131	R	230 *	1.1
UndercoverWear Inc.	007 UCWay	Wilmington	MA	01887	Walter J James	781-938-0007	R	100 *	0.1
Veratex Group	PO Box 4031	Troy	MI	48007	James H Devlin	313-588-2970	S	97 *	0.5
Lens Express Inc.	350 Southwest 12th	Deerfield Bch	FL	33442	Mendo Akdag	305-421-5800	R	68	0.4
Princess House Inc.	470 Milesandish	Taunton	MA	02780	James Northrop	508-823-0713	R	67 *	0.6
Rena-Ware Distributors Inc.	PO Box 97050	Redmond	WA	98073	Russel Zylstra	425-881-6171	R	61	0.1
Sunlight Foods Inc.	3550 NW 112th St	Miami	FL	33167	Arthur Green	305-688-5400	R	33 *	<0.1
Geerlings and Wade Inc.	960 Turnpike St	Canton	MA	02021	Jay Essa	617-821-4152	P	30	<0.1
Belmont Springs Water	PO Box 3	Lexington	MA	02173	David Hill	617-674-7800	S	24	0.2
Artistic Impressions Inc.	240 Cortland Ave	Lombard	IL	60148	Bart Breighner	708-916-0050	R	20	0.1
Delivery Concepts Inc.	2658 Holcomb	Alpharetta	GA	30201	Bob Cotman	404-552-1424	R	16 *	0.1
Waiters on Wheels Inc.	425 Divisadero St	San Francisco	CA	94117	Takis Zarikas	415-252-1470	R	16	0.2
Crystal Bottled Waters	3302 W Earl Dr	Phoenix	AZ	85107	Chris Govorcin	602-279-7825	S	14	0.2
Industrial Catering Inc.	225 Idlewild Rd	Grand Prairie	TX	75051	JD Stephan	214-264-6191	R	14 *	0.2
Courtesy Products Co.	10630 Midwest	St. Louis	MO	63132	Matt Schwarz	314-423-3833	S	10	<0.1
E.V.G. Investments Company	6795 SW 111th St	Beaverton	OR	97005	Lester Beckman	503-643-3697	R	3	<0.1
R.J. Lindquist Company Inc.	2419 West 9th St	Los Angeles	CA	90006	Kristofer J Lindquist	213-382-1268	R	1 *	<0.1
ML Direct Inc.	300 Park Ave	New York	NY	10022	James M Lawless	212-572-6209	P	1	<0.1

Source: *Ward's Business Directory of U.S. Private and Public Companies*, 1998. The company type code used is as follows: P - Public, R - Private, S - Subsidiary, D - Division, J - Joint Venture, A - Affiliate, G - Group. Sales are in millions of dollars, employees are in thousands. An asterisk (*) indicates an estimated sales volume. The symbol < stands for 'less than'.

OCCUPATIONS EMPLOYED BY SIC 596 - NONSTORE RETAILERS

Occupation	% of Total 1996	Change to 2006	Occupation	% of Total 1996	Change to 2006
Sales & related workers nec	14.0	14.3	Stock clerks	2.3	92.0
Order clerks	10.3	-6.5	Truck drivers light & heavy	2.3	3.9
Driver/sales workers	6.5	-6.5	Food preparation workers	2.1	-0.9
Adjustment clerks	6.2	40.3	Food counter, fountain workers	2.1	-0.3
Coin & vending machine servicers & repairers	3.7	-16.9	Clerical supervisors & managers	1.6	3.9
Salespersons, retail	3.7	10.7	Hand packers & packagers	1.5	3.9
General office clerks	3.5	-10.6	Bookkeeping, accounting, & auditing clerks	1.5	-16.9
General managers & top executives	3.4	0.7	Freight, stock, & material movers, hand	1.2	-6.5
Traffic, shipping, receiving clerks	3.4	3.9	Secretaries, except legal & medical	1.2	-17.6
Order fillers, wholesale & retail sales	3.2	-6.5	Data entry keyers, except composing	1.2	-16.9
Marketing & sales worker supervisors	2.8	3.9	Cashiers	1.0	5.2

Source: *Industry-Occupation Matrix*, Bureau of Labor Statistics. These data relate to one or more 3-digit SIC industry groups rather than to a single 4-digit SIC. The change reported for each occupation to the year 2006 is a percent of growth or decline as estimated by the Bureau of Labor Statistics. The abbreviation nec stands for 'not elsewhere classified'.

STATE AND REGIONAL CONCENTRATION

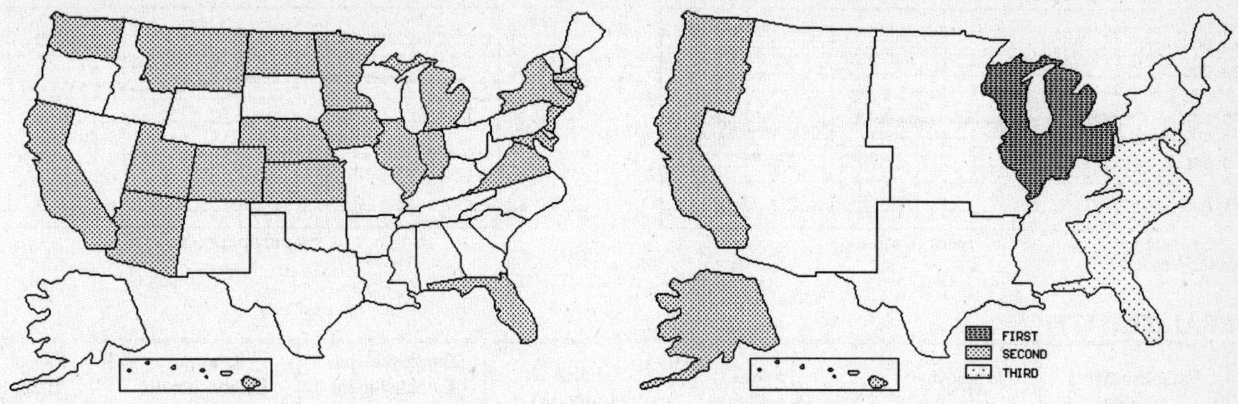

INDUSTRY DATA BY STATE

State	Establishments - 1995 Total (number)	Establishments - 1995 % of U.S.	Employment - 1995 Total (number)	Employment - 1995 % of U.S.	Employment - 1995 Per Estab.	Payroll - 1995 Total ($ mil.)	Payroll - 1995 Per Empl. ($)	Sales - 1992 Total ($ mil.)	Sales - 1992 % of U.S.	Sales - 1992 Per Estab ($)
California	1,349	10.1	14,548	11.8	11	277.7	19,086	1,314.4	13.3	88,623
New York	880	6.6	7,475	6.1	8	141.3	18,906	743.5	7.5	99,814
Illinois	595	4.4	7,628	6.2	13	150.0	19,664	644.0	6.5	94,405
Florida	830	6.2	7,247	5.9	9	124.9	17,233	591.1	6.0	82,386
Texas	751	5.6	6,282	5.1	8	117.5	18,699	569.9	5.8	100,035
Michigan	436	3.3	3,667	3.0	8	68.7	18,738	403.3	4.1	96,216
Ohio	538	4.0	5,468	4.4	10	93.5	17,096	393.4	4.0	64,677
Pennsylvania	532	4.0	6,465	5.3	12	107.4	16,614	389.7	4.0	69,832
New Jersey	429	3.2	3,161	2.6	7	60.6	19,176	347.6	3.5	99,848
Massachusetts	267	2.0	3,149	2.6	12	74.0	23,501	295.8	3.0	112,829
Washington	414	3.1	3,432	2.8	8	60.4	17,614	278.2	2.8	84,751
North Carolina	349	2.6	3,089	2.5	9	70.9	22,963	265.7	2.7	98,331
Virginia	396	3.0	3,765	3.1	10	69.1	18,350	258.2	2.6	77,740
Minnesota	311	2.3	2,611	2.1	8	58.7	22,489	250.4	2.5	100,108
Georgia	339	2.5	3,878	3.2	11	57.8	14,910	244.0	2.5	72,849
Indiana	354	2.6	2,577	2.1	7	52.2	20,255	233.5	2.4	78,455
Colorado	297	2.2	3,107	2.5	10	55.3	17,783	206.5	2.1	98,056
Maryland	377	2.8	3,322	2.7	9	66.0	19,854	201.4	2.0	72,307
Missouri	361	2.7	2,593	2.1	7	50.2	19,375	189.1	1.9	70,736
Tennessee	232	1.7	2,281	1.9	10	39.2	17,167	181.2	1.8	78,896
Wisconsin	304	2.3	2,262	1.8	7	38.4	16,993	178.7	1.8	81,419
Iowa	206	1.5	1,889	1.5	9	38.0	20,120	158.8	1.6	97,667
Arizona	208	1.6	2,459	2.0	12	47.5	19,326	150.0	1.5	54,065
Connecticut	193	1.4	1,531	1.2	8	34.9	22,784	142.9	1.4	94,901
Kansas	145	1.1	936	0.8	6	19.9	21,302	110.4	1.1	93,970
Utah	113	0.8	1,136	0.9	10	21.8	19,160	99.0	1.0	96,934
Oklahoma	140	1.0	1,375	1.1	10	23.1	16,789	94.3	1.0	61,766
Oregon	204	1.5	1,204	1.0	6	19.6	16,319	94.0	1.0	80,577
Kentucky	146	1.1	1,239	1.0	8	19.3	15,584	93.8	1.0	77,434
Alabama	170	1.3	1,178	1.0	7	18.1	15,341	86.5	0.9	77,443
South Carolina	159	1.2	1,252	1.0	8	17.5	13,999	72.1	0.7	67,727
Nebraska	98	0.7	1,215	1.0	12	17.9	14,773	72.0	0.7	70,982
Arkansas	110	0.8	683	0.6	6	11.2	16,422	55.2	0.6	85,686
Hawaii	79	0.6	498	0.4	6	7.7	15,538	53.8	0.5	72,564
Montana	69	0.5	343	0.3	5	6.5	18,988	53.2	0.5	108,765
New Hampshire	82	0.6	510	0.4	6	8.2	16,149	42.9	0.4	84,012
New Mexico	67	0.5	516	0.4	8	9.8	18,983	41.0	0.4	89,423
Mississippi	77	0.6	716	0.6	9	10.6	14,813	39.6	0.4	67,479
West Virginia	56	0.4	376	0.3	7	6.5	17,327	33.9	0.3	81,993
Rhode Island	60	0.4	648	0.5	11	9.5	14,681	33.6	0.3	67,421
Idaho	68	0.5	366	0.3	5	6.4	17,571	33.3	0.3	102,633
North Dakota	46	0.3	311	0.3	7	5.7	18,264	27.8	0.3	84,136
South Dakota	64	0.5	280	0.2	4	5.5	19,589	27.7	0.3	90,908
Vermont	50	0.4	227	0.2	5	3.8	16,630	22.1	0.2	88,584
Wyoming	34	0.3	155	0.1	5	3.1	20,006	16.0	0.2	95,766
Delaware	31	0.2	156	0.1	5	2.9	18,359	15.9	0.2	85,870
D.C.	30	0.2	262	0.2	9	3.2	12,340	9.3	0.1	38,434
Alaska	27	0.2	187	0.2	7	2.1	11,422	6.4	0.1	91,214
Louisiana	157	1.2	1,864	1.5	12	31.0	16,630	(D)	-	-
Nevada	82	0.6	928	0.8	11	20.6	22,217	(D)	-	-
Maine	76	0.6	457	0.4	6	8.4	18,429	(D)	-	-

Source: County Business Patterns, 1995 and *Economic Census of the U.S., 1992*. Data are sorted by 1992 revenues and, if revenues are unavailable, by establishments in 1995. The symbol (D) indicates that data are withheld by the source to avoid disclosure of competitive information. A dash (-) indicates that data are not available or undisclosed because they do not meet statistical validity standards. Shaded *states* on the state map indicate those states which have proportionately greater representation in the industry than would be indicated by the state's population; the ratio is based on total revenues or number of establishments. Shaded *regions* indicate where the industry is regionally most concentrated.

5983 - FUEL OIL DEALERS

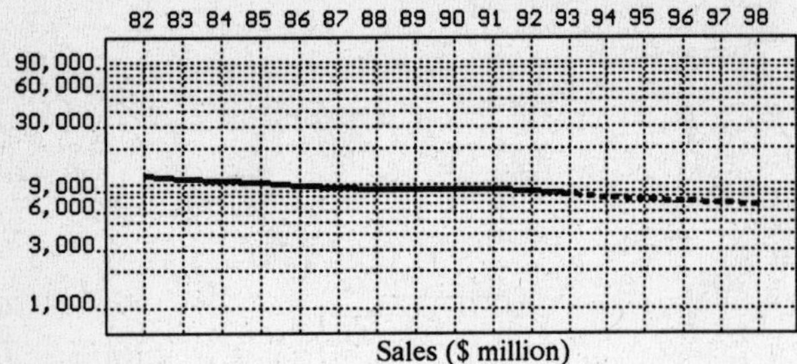

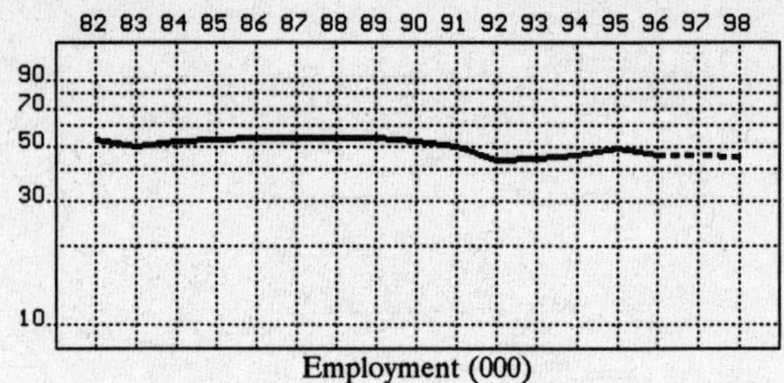

GENERAL STATISTICS

Year	Establishments (number)	Employment (number)	Payroll ($ million)	Sales ($ million)	Employees per Establishment (number)	Sales per Establishment ($)	Payroll per Employee ($)
1982	6,368	52,754	830.1	11,754.3	8	1,845,833	15,736
1983	6,056	49,920	842.4	11,262.2e	8	-	16,875
1984	5,918	52,515	936.4	10,770.2e	9	-	17,831
1985	5,714	52,886	997.8	10,278.2e	9	-	18,866
1986	5,600	53,855	1,109.6	9,786.1e	10	-	20,604
1987	5,816	54,035	1,059.0	9,294.1	9	1,598,025	19,599
1988	5,558	53,665	1,245.9	9,224.1e	10	-	23,216
1989	5,369	54,011	1,264.5	9,154.1e	10	-	23,412
1990	5,257	51,919	1,245.9	9,084.1e	10	-	23,998
1991	5,073	49,354	1,212.0	9,014.2e	10	-	24,557
1992	5,025	43,946	1,147.8	8,944.2	9	1,779,932	26,119
1993	4,924	44,395	1,181.4	8,183.6p	9	-	26,611
1994	4,859	45,632	1,258.9	7,902.5p	9	-	27,588
1995	5,073	48,548	1,298.4	7,621.5p	10	-	26,745
1996	4,676p	46,146p	1,363.9p	7,340.5p	-	-	-
1997	4,570p	45,562p	1,396.9p	7,059.5p	-	-	-
1998	4,464p	44,977p	1,430.0p	6,778.5p	-	-	-

Sources: Economic Census of the United States, 1982, 1987, and 1992. Establishment counts, employment, and payroll are from *County Business Patterns* for non-Census years. Values followed by a 'p' are projections by the editors. Sales and expense data for non-Census years are extrapolations, marked by 'e'. Industries reclassified in 1987 will not have data for prior years. Data are the most recent available at this level of detail.

INDICES OF CHANGE

Year	Establishments (number)	Employment (number)	Payroll ($ million)	Sales ($ million)	Employees per Establishment (number)	Sales per Establishment ($)	Payroll per Employee ($)
1982	126.7	120.0	72.3	131.4	88.9	103.7	60.2
1983	120.5	113.6	73.4	125.9e	88.9	-	64.6
1984	117.8	119.5	81.6	120.4e	100.0	-	68.3
1985	113.7	120.3	86.9	114.9e	100.0	-	72.2
1986	111.4	122.5	96.7	109.4e	111.1	-	78.9
1987	115.7	123.0	92.3	103.9	100.0	89.8	75.0
1988	110.6	122.1	108.5	103.1e	111.1	-	88.9
1989	106.8	122.9	110.2	102.3e	111.1	-	89.6
1990	104.6	118.1	108.5	101.6e	111.1	-	91.9
1991	101.0	112.3	105.6	100.8e	111.1	-	94.0
1992	100.0	100.0	100.0	100.0	100.0	100.0	100.0
1993	98.0	101.0	102.9	91.5p	100.2	-	101.9
1994	96.7	103.8	109.7	88.4p	104.3	-	105.6
1995	101.0	110.5	113.1	85.2p	106.3	-	102.4
1996	93.1p	105.0p	118.8p	82.1p	-	-	-
1997	91.0p	103.7p	121.7p	78.9p	-	-	-
1998	88.8p	102.3p	124.6p	75.8p	-	-	-

Sources: Same as General Statistics. The values shown reflect change from the base year, 1992. Values above 100 mean greater than 1992, values below 100 mean less than 1992, and a value of 100 in the 1982-91 or 1993-98 period means same as 1992. Values followed by a 'p' are projections by the editors; 'e' stands for extrapolation. Data are the most recent available at this level of detail.

SELECTED RATIOS

For 1992	Avg. of All Retail	Analyzed Industry	Index	For 1992	Avg. of All Retail	Analyzed Industry	Index
Employees per Establishment	12	9	73	Sales per Employee	102,941	203,527	198
Payroll per Establishment	146,026	228,418	156	Sales per Establishment	1,241,555	1,779,940	143
Payroll per Employee	12,107	26,118	216	Expenses per Establishment	na	na	na

Sources: Same as General Statistics. The 'Average of All Manufacturing' column represents the average of all manufacturing industries reported for the most recent complete year available. The Index shows the relationship between the Average and the Analyzed Industry. For example, 100 means that they are equal; 500 that the Analyzed Industry is five times the average; 50 means that the Analyzed Industry is half the national average. The abbreviation 'na' is used to show that data are 'not available'.

LEADING COMPANIES

Number shown: **50** Total sales ($ mil): **5,375** Total employment (000): **14.7**

Company Name	Address				CEO Name	Phone	Co. Type	Sales ($ mil)	Empl. (000)
Coastal Fuels Marketing Inc.	PO Box 025500	Miami	FL	33102	Dan Hill	305-551-5200	S	600	<0.1
Petroleum Heat and Power	PO Box 1457	Stamford	CT	06904	Irik P Sevin	203-325-5400	P	548	2.2
Warren Equities Inc.	375 Park Ave	New York	NY	10152	Herbert Kaplan	212-751-8100	R	480 *	1.6
Webber Oil Co.	PO Box 929	Bangor	ME	04402	Larry Mahaney	207-942-5501	R	390 *	0.8
Petro Inc.	PO Box 1457	Stamford	CT	06904	Irik Sevin	203-323-2121	S	280 *	1.5
Griffith Consumers Co.	2510 Schuster Dr	Cheverly	MD	20781	H B Schlosberg	301-322-3111	S	273	1.0
Petroleum World Inc.	PO Box 307	Cliffside	NC	28024	Michael J Frost	704-482-0438	R	200	0.4
Sico Co.	15 Mount Joy St	Mount Joy	PA	17552	Franklin R Eichler	717-653-1411	R	190 *	0.4
Meenan Oil Company L.P.	6900 Jericho Tpk	Syosset	NY	11791	Paul A Vermylen Jr	516-364-9030	R	180	0.8
River City Petroleum Inc.	840 Delta Ln	W. Sacramento	CA	95691	L. D Robinson	916-371-4960	R	180 *	0.2
Petroleum Marketers Inc.	PO Box 12203	Roanoke	VA	24023	Terry M Phelps	703-362-4900	R	151	0.7
Castle Oil Corp.	500 Mamaroneck	Harrison	NY	10528	Mauro C Romita	914-381-6500	R	130 *	0.3
Iowa Oil Co.	PO Box 712	Dubuque	IA	52001	Ronald P Enke	319-583-3563	R	100 *	0.2
Santa Fuel Inc.	154 Admiral St	Bridgeport	CT	06601	John S Santa	203-367-3661	R	97	0.2
Schierl Cos.	2201 Madison St	Stevens Point	WI	54481	William Schierl	715-345-5060	R	95 *	0.4
J.H. Williams Oil Company Inc.	PO Box 439	Tampa	FL	33601	J Hulon Williams III	813-228-7776	R	92 *	0.3
Petroleum Sales and Service	300 Ohio St	Buffalo	NY	14204	Bernard Kieffer	716-856-8675	R	88 *	<0.1
Global Petroleum Corp.	800 South St	Waltham	MA	02154	Alfred Slifka	617-894-8800	R	86 *	0.2
Jacobus Co.	2323 N Mayfair Rd	Milwaukee	WI	53226	CD Jacobus	414-476-0701	R	80 *	0.2
Quality Oil Company L.P.	PO Box 2736	Winston-Salem	NC	27102	James K Glenn Jr	910-722-3441	R	80	0.3
Shipley Oil Co.	550 E King St	York	PA	17405	WS Shipley III	717-848-4100	R	80	0.4
Kugler Oil Co.	PO Box 1748	McCook	NE	69001	John Kugler	308-345-2280	R	62 *	0.2
LaForgia Fuel Oil Co.	1640 McDonald	Brooklyn	NY	11230	Frank LaForgia	718-627-5100	R	62 *	0.1
Kingston Oil Supply Corp.	N Broadway	Port Ewen	NY	12466	Leo Lebowitz	914-331-0770	S	60	0.2
Fred M. Schildwachter and Sons	1400 Ferris Pl	Bronx	NY	10461	D A Schildwacter Jr	212-828-2500	R	57	0.2
Forward Corp.	PO Box 549	Standish	MI	48658	Terry D McTaggart	517-846-4501	R	56	0.5
AC and T Company Inc.	PO Box 4217	Hagerstown	MD	21740	AB Fulton	301-582-2700	R	45	<0.1
Union Oil Company of Maine	PO Box 2528	South Portland	ME	04106	Bernard D Shapiro	207-799-1521	R	45 *	<0.1
Johnson Oil of Gaylord	507 Otesgo Rd	Gaylord	MI	49735	Dale E Johnson	517-732-2451	R	44 *	<0.1
Patterson Oil Co.	PO Box 898	Torrington	CT	06790	Barry Patterson	860-489-1198	R	44 *	<0.1
Clarks Petroleum Service Inc.	PO Box 802	Canastota	NY	13032	RK Clark	315-697-2278	R	36	<0.1
Fuel South Company Inc.	PO Box 572	Hazlehurst	GA	31539	Jimmy Walker	912-285-4011	R	34	<0.1
L.S. Riggins Oil Co.	3938 S Main Rd	Vineland	NJ	08360	R Paul Riggins	609-825-7600	R	34 *	<0.1
Schmuckal Oil Co.	1516 Barlow	Traverse City	MI	49686	Arthur Schmuckal	616-946-2800	R	34	0.2
Hometown Inc.	1518 E North Ave	Milwaukee	WI	53202	DW Day	414-276-9311	R	30	0.1
Norbert E. Mitchell Company	7 Federal Rd	Danbury	CT	06810	Norbert E Mitchell	203-744-0600	R	30 *	<0.1
Robison Oil Corp.	500 Executive Blvd	Elmsford	NY	10523	Fran Singer	914-345-5700	R	30	0.2
Farmers Elevator Co.	434 1st St	Chappell	NE	69129	Mike Pollnow	308-874-2245	R	25	<0.1
Northeast Cooperative	445 S Main St	West Point	NE	68788	Rich Brahmer	402-372-5303	R	25	<0.1
Bedford Valley Petroleum Corp.	PO Box 120	Everett	PA	15537	RG Salathe Jr	814-623-5151	R	24 *	<0.1
E.P. Nisbet Co.	PO Box 35367	Charlotte	NC	28235	James J White III	704-332-7755	R	23 *	<0.1
Mauston Farmers Cooperative	310 Prairie St	Mauston	WI	53948	Ken Wilcox	608-847-5679	R	23	<0.1
Amos Post Co.	1 Amos Post Rd	Catskill	NY	12414	D Motzkin	518-943-3500	D	22	<0.1
S.W. Rawls Inc.	PO Box 777	Franklin	VA	23851	WE Whitfield	757-562-3115	R	22	<0.1
Pickering-Oil-Colony Inc.	295 Eastern Ave	Chelsea	MA	02150	Gary Nadeau	617-884-9350	S	21	0.1
Dahl Oil Co.	PO Box 431	Norwich	CT	06360	Fred Bryant	860-887-3525	S	19 *	<0.1
Halstead Energy Corp.	PO Box 660	Mount Kisco	NY	10549	Claire E Tarricone	914-666-3200	P	19	<0.1
New Horizons Supply	770 Lincoln Ave	Fennimore	WI	53809	Dean Roth	608-822-3217	R	18	<0.1
Star Oil Company Inc.	PO Box 610867	Port Huron	MI	48061	CA Kellerman	810-985-9586	R	16	<0.1
Agri-Tech F.S. Inc.	16119 Hwy 81 W	Darlington	WI	53530	William Hanson	608-776-4600	S	15	<0.1

Source: *Ward's Business Directory of U.S. Private and Public Companies*, 1998. The company type code used is as follows: P - Public, R - Private, S - Subsidiary, D - Division, J - Joint Venture, A - Affiliate, G - Group. Sales are in millions of dollars, employees are in thousands. An asterisk (*) indicates an estimated sales volume. The symbol < stands for 'less than'.

OCCUPATIONS EMPLOYED BY SIC 598 - FUEL DEALERS

Occupation	% of Total 1996	Change to 2006	Occupation	% of Total 1996	Change to 2006
Truck drivers light & heavy	25.2	-5.8	Salespersons, retail	3.6	0.4
Heat, air conditioning, refrigeration mechanics	13.4	13.0	Cashiers	3.4	-4.7
General managers & top executives	8.3	-8.7	Service station attendants	2.8	-5.8
General office clerks	7.8	-19.0	Sales & related workers nec	2.4	3.7
Bookkeeping, accounting, & auditing clerks	5.7	-24.6	Maintenance repairers, general utility	1.6	-12.2
Home appliance/power tool repairers	5.3	-5.8	Automotive mechanics	1.3	-5.8
Marketing & sales worker supervisors	4.5	-5.8	Billing, cost, & rate clerks	1.1	-15.2
Driver/sales workers	4.3	-5.8			

Source: *Industry-Occupation Matrix*, Bureau of Labor Statistics. These data relate to one or more 3-digit SIC industry groups rather than to a single 4-digit SIC. The change reported for each occupation to the year 2006 is a percent of growth or decline as estimated by the Bureau of Labor Statistics. The abbreviation nec stands for 'not elsewhere classified'.

STATE AND REGIONAL CONCENTRATION

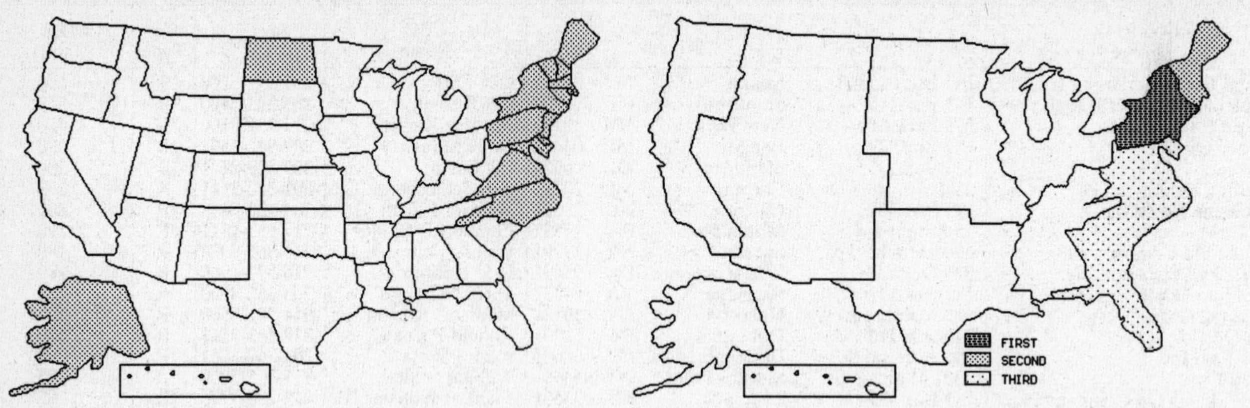

INDUSTRY DATA BY STATE

	Establishments - 1995		Employment - 1995			Payroll - 1995		Sales - 1992		
State	Total (number)	% of U.S.	Total (number)	% of U.S.	Per Estab.	Total ($ mil.)	Per Empl. ($)	Total ($ mil.)	% of U.S.	Per Estab ($)
New York	860	17.0	9,404	19.9	11	291.0	30,942	2,032.4	24.5	216,402
Pennsylvania	593	11.7	6,770	14.3	11	158.1	23,357	1,213.1	14.6	196,829
Massachusetts	620	12.2	5,246	11.1	8	159.2	30,355	997.1	12.0	200,254
New Jersey	398	7.8	4,189	8.8	11	129.6	30,938	817.1	9.8	205,761
Connecticut	374	7.4	3,868	8.2	10	127.4	32,928	782.0	9.4	203,658
Maine	217	4.3	2,493	5.3	11	52.7	21,142	382.5	4.6	175,300
Maryland	119	2.3	1,612	3.4	14	43.2	26,783	277.3	3.3	194,065
New Hampshire	120	2.4	1,404	3.0	12	34.8	24,767	271.3	3.3	197,307
North Carolina	204	4.0	1,546	3.3	8	33.5	21,688	232.1	2.8	199,071
Virginia	170	3.4	1,540	3.3	9	35.3	22,905	230.8	2.8	168,702
Vermont	90	1.8	1,058	2.2	12	25.6	24,222	197.5	2.4	210,138
Rhode Island	127	2.5	1,091	2.3	9	24.3	22,235	182.1	2.2	173,973
Delaware	35	0.7	308	0.7	9	8.2	26,591	136.5	1.6	470,862
Washington	61	1.2	1,256	2.7	21	42.1	33,541	106.7	1.3	167,838
Minnesota	81	1.6	607	1.3	7	11.7	19,275	91.1	1.1	230,678
Alaska	47	0.9	323	0.7	7	9.3	28,672	71.5	0.9	284,777
Florida	62	1.2	364	0.8	6	8.9	24,415	52.9	0.6	145,445
Oregon	26	0.5	217	0.5	8	5.3	24,608	32.5	0.4	146,437
Kentucky	28	0.6	133	0.3	5	1.8	13,293	26.9	0.3	251,393
California	22	0.4	194	0.4	9	4.1	21,361	25.7	0.3	213,833
Texas	26	0.5	114	0.2	4	1.4	12,298	24.5	0.3	148,764
North Dakota	31	0.6	100-249	-	-	(D)	-	23.4	0.3	240,742
Illinois	33	0.7	164	0.3	5	3.7	22,835	20.8	0.3	231,322
South Dakota	21	0.4	112	0.2	5	1.8	16,187	13.2	0.2	243,611
Nevada	5	0.1	20-99	-	-	(D)	-	10.0	0.1	156,484
Tennessee	12	0.2	65	0.1	5	1.2	18,831	9.6	0.1	300,813
Nebraska	14	0.3	64	0.1	5	0.8	13,188	8.7	0.1	160,722
Colorado	8	0.2	28	0.1	4	0.5	18,286	7.6	0.1	764,900
Kansas	19	0.4	20-99	-	-	(D)	-	7.5	0.1	171,114
New Mexico	7	0.1	0-19	-	-	(D)	-	6.1	0.1	322,421
Idaho	12	0.2	20-99	-	-	(D)	-	5.0	0.1	277,667
Ohio	142	2.8	962	2.0	7	18.6	19,315	(D)	-	-
Wisconsin	130	2.6	711	1.5	5	14.0	19,626	(D)	-	-
Michigan	109	2.1	650	1.4	6	15.4	23,628	(D)	-	-
South Carolina	59	1.2	337	0.7	6	6.2	18,380	(D)	-	-
Indiana	56	1.1	250-499	-	-	(D)	-	(D)	-	-
Iowa	26	0.5	100-249	-	-	(D)	-	(D)	-	-
Missouri	20	0.4	146	0.3	7	2.0	13,555	(D)	-	-
West Virginia	16	0.3	125	0.3	8	1.9	15,384	(D)	-	-
Georgia	13	0.3	106	0.2	8	1.7	16,104	(D)	-	-
Arkansas	12	0.2	100-249	-	-	(D)	-	(D)	-	-
Mississippi	11	0.2	80	0.2	7	2.6	32,713	(D)	-	-
Oklahoma	11	0.2	20-99	-	-	(D)	-	(D)	-	-
Alabama	4	0.1	0-19	-	-	(D)	-	(D)	-	-
Arizona	4	0.1	20-99	-	-	(D)	-	(D)	-	-
D.C.	4	0.1	20-99	-	-	(D)	-	(D)	-	-
Louisiana	4	0.1	20-99	-	-	(D)	-	(D)	-	-
Montana	4	0.1	20-99	-	-	(D)	-	(D)	-	-
Utah	3	0.1	54	0.1	18	0.7	13,426	(D)	-	-
Wyoming	3	0.1	20-99	-	-	(D)	-	(D)	-	-

Source: County Business Patterns, 1995 and *Economic Census of the U.S., 1992.* Data are sorted by 1992 revenues and, if revenues are unavailable, by establishments in 1995. The symbol (D) indicates that data are withheld by the source to avoid disclosure of competitive information. A dash (-) indicates that data are not available or undisclosed because they do not meet statistical validity standards. Shaded *states* on the state map indicate those states which have proportionately greater representation in the industry than would be indicated by the state's population; the ratio is based on total revenues or number of establishments. Shaded *regions* indicate where the industry is regionally most concentrated.

5984 - LIQUEFIED PETROLEUM GAS DEALERS

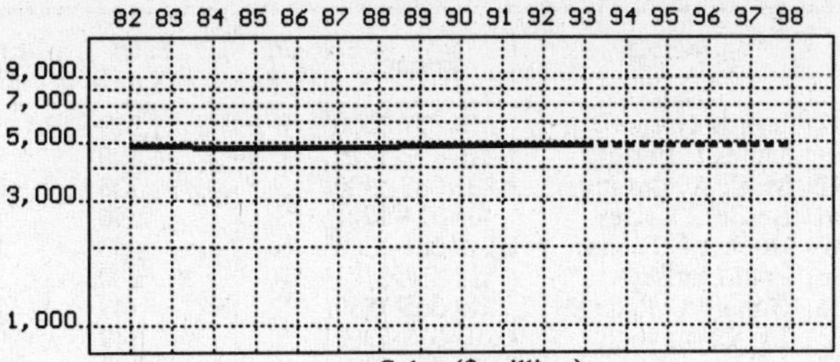

Sales ($ million)

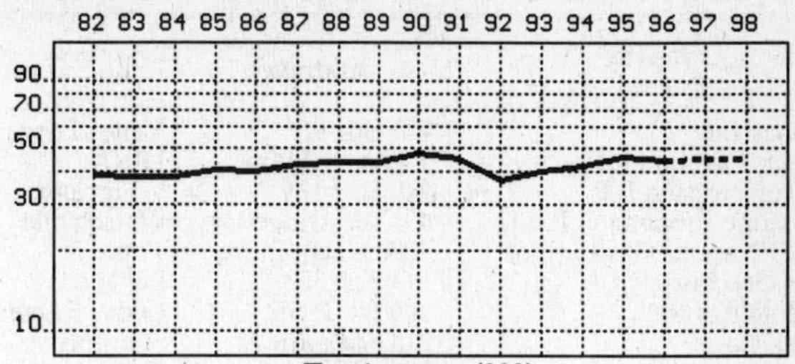

Employment (000)

GENERAL STATISTICS

Year	Establishments (number)	Employment (number)	Payroll ($ million)	Sales ($ million)	Employees per Establishment (number)	Sales per Establishment ($)	Payroll per Employee ($)
1982	6,155	39,292	543.9	4,804.5	6	780,588	13,843
1983	6,084	38,301	567.2	4,797.5*e*	6	-	14,808
1984	6,114	38,336	601.9	4,790.4*e*	6	-	15,702
1985	6,119	40,681	661.0	4,783.4*e*	7	-	16,249
1986	5,985	40,221	678.8	4,776.4*e*	7	-	16,876
1987	6,378	43,045	746.0	4,769.3	7	747,775	17,330
1988	6,297	43,938	860.4	4,788.9*e*	7	-	19,583
1989	6,170	43,547	843.2	4,808.4*e*	7	-	19,362
1990	6,272	46,768	886.1	4,828.0*e*	7	-	18,947
1991	6,224	44,708	906.8	4,847.5*e*	7	-	20,282
1992	5,651	36,841	771.2	4,867.0	7	861,272	20,934
1993	5,755	40,440	856.2	4,843.1*p*	7	-	21,172
1994	5,940	42,705	961.2	4,849.3*p*	7	-	22,509
1995	6,061	45,641	1,008.4	4,855.6*p*	8	-	22,094
1996	5,945*p*	44,323*p*	1,024.9*p*	4,861.8*p*	-	-	-
1997	5,926*p*	44,666*p*	1,057.8*p*	4,868.1*p*	-	-	-
1998	5,907*p*	45,010*p*	1,090.7*p*	4,874.3*p*	-	-	-

Sources: Economic Census of the United States, 1982, 1987, and 1992. Establishment counts, employment, and payroll are from *County Business Patterns* for non-Census years. Values followed by a 'p' are projections by the editors. Sales and expense data for non-Census years are extrapolations, marked by 'e'. Industries reclassified in 1987 will not have data for prior years. Data are the most recent available at this level of detail.

INDICES OF CHANGE

Year	Establishments (number)	Employment (number)	Payroll ($ million)	Sales ($ million)	Employees per Establishment (number)	Sales per Establishment ($)	Payroll per Employee ($)
1982	108.9	106.7	70.5	98.7	85.7	90.6	66.1
1983	107.7	104.0	73.5	98.6*e*	85.7	-	70.7
1984	108.2	104.1	78.0	98.4*e*	85.7	-	75.0
1985	108.3	110.4	85.7	98.3*e*	100.0	-	77.6
1986	105.9	109.2	88.0	98.1*e*	100.0	-	80.6
1987	112.9	116.8	96.7	98.0	100.0	86.8	82.8
1988	111.4	119.3	111.6	98.4*e*	100.0	-	93.5
1989	109.2	118.2	109.3	98.8*e*	100.0	-	92.5
1990	111.0	126.9	114.9	99.2*e*	100.0	-	90.5
1991	110.1	121.4	117.6	99.6*e*	100.0	-	96.9
1992	100.0	100.0	100.0	100.0	100.0	100.0	100.0
1993	101.8	109.8	111.0	99.5*p*	100.4	-	101.1
1994	105.1	115.9	124.6	99.6*p*	102.7	-	107.5
1995	107.3	123.9	130.8	99.8*p*	107.6	-	105.5
1996	105.2*p*	120.3*p*	132.9*p*	99.9*p*	-	-	-
1997	104.9*p*	121.2*p*	137.2*p*	100.0*p*	-	-	-
1998	104.5*p*	122.2*p*	141.4*p*	100.2*p*	-	-	-

Sources: Same as General Statistics. The values shown reflect change from the base year, 1992. Values above 100 mean greater than 1992, values below 100 mean less than 1992, and a value of 100 in the 1982-91 or 1993-98 period means same as 1992. Values followed by a 'p' are projections by the editors; 'e' stands for extrapolation. Data are the most recent available at this level of detail.

SELECTED RATIOS

For 1992	Avg. of All Retail	Analyzed Industry	Index	For 1992	Avg. of All Retail	Analyzed Industry	Index
Employees per Establishment	12	7	54	Sales per Employee	102,941	132,108	128
Payroll per Establishment	146,026	136,471	93	Sales per Establishment	1,241,555	861,263	69
Payroll per Employee	12,107	20,933	173	Expenses per Establishment	na	na	na

Sources: Same as General Statistics. The 'Average of All Manufacturing' column represents the average of all manufacturing industries reported for the most recent complete year available. The Index shows the relationship between the Average and the Analyzed Industry. For example, 100 means that they are equal; 500 that the Analyzed Industry is five times the average; 50 means that the Analyzed Industry is half the national average. The abbreviation 'na' is used to show that data are 'not available'.

LEADING COMPANIES

Number shown: **50** Total sales ($ mil): **5,864** Total employment (000): **22.4**

Company Name	Address				CEO Name	Phone	Co. Type	Sales ($ mil)	Empl. (000)
AmeriGas Inc.	PO Box 965	Valley Forge	PA	19482	Lon R Greenberg	610-337-1000	P	1,319	5.1
Ferrellgas Partners L.P.	1 Liberty Plaza	Liberty	MO	64068	James E Ferrell	816-792-1600	P	1,200	3.4
Suburban Propane L.P.	240 Rt 10 W	Whippany	NJ	07981	Mark A Alexander	201-887-5300	S	708	3.4
Cornerstone Propane G.P. Inc.	432 Westridge Dr	Watsonville	CA	95076	Keith G Baxter	408-724-1921	S	596	1.7
MAPCO Natural Gas Liquids	1800 S Baltimore	Tulsa	OK	74119	Robert G Sachse	918-581-1800	S	453	1.5
Empire Gas Corp.	PO Box 303	Lebanon	MO	65536	Paul Lindsey	417-532-3103	R	200 *	1.5
NPC Holdings Inc.	200 1st St SE	Cedar Rapids	IA	52401	Ronald D Paliughi	319-365-1550	S	149	1.0
Star Gas Corp.	2187 Atlantic St	Stamford	CT	06902	Joe Cavanaugh	203-328-7300	S	149	0.6
Heritage Operating L.P.	8801 S Yale Ave	Tulsa	OK	74137	J E Bertelsmeyer	918-492-7272	S	132	0.8
Prax Air Distribution Inc.	2301 SE Creekview	Ankeny	IA	50021	Rich Matthes	515-964-5535	R	100 *	0.8
Connecticut Airgas Corp.	PO Box 330219	West Hartford	CT	06133	Howard Wolf	203-792-2533	R	67 *	<0.1
Como Oil Company Inc.	PO Box 16108	Duluth	MN	55816	Robert M Hall	218-722-6666	R	65 *	0.1
Roanoke Gas Co.	519 Kimball Ave	Roanoke	VA	24016	Frank A Farmer Jr	540-983-3800	P	63	0.2
Ray-Carroll County Grain	PO Box 158	Richmond	MO	64085	A Kipping	816-776-2291	R	55 *	0.1
Farmers Cooperative Business	PO Box 38	Shelby	NE	68662	Roland From	402-527-5511	R	50	<0.1
Patterson Oil Co.	PO Box 898	Torrington	CT	06790	Barry Patterson	860-489-1198	R	44 *	<0.1
Energy West Inc.	PO Box 2229	Great Falls	MT	59403	Larry D Geske	406-791-7500	P	43	0.1
Midland Co-Op Inc.	PO Box 560	Danville	IN	46122	Kevin Still	317-745-4491	R	40	0.1
Jenkins Gas and Oil Company	PO Box 156	Pollocksville	NC	28573	Robert Mattocks II	919-224-8911	R	33	0.2
United Co-op Rushmore	PO Box 158	Rushmore	MN	56168	Larry Stamer	507-478-4166	R	30	<0.1
Cooperative Agricultural Services	411 W 2nd	Oakley	KS	67748	William Kuhlman	913-672-3300	R	25	<0.1
F.L. Roberts and Company Inc.	93 W Broad St	Springfield	MA	01105	Steven Roberts	413-781-7444	R	24 *	<0.1
Monte Vista Cooperative Inc.	E Hwy 160	Monte Vista	CO	81144	G Palmgren	719-852-5181	R	18	<0.1
Sharp Energy Inc.	PO Box 518	Pocomoke City	MD	21851	Jerry West	410-957-0422	S	18	0.1
Benson Farmers Cooperative	PO Box 407	Benson	IL	61516	Dean Backer	309-394-2293	R	17	<0.1
Carolane Propane Gas Inc.	339 S Main St	Lexington	NC	27292	CH Timberlake III	910-249-8981	R	17	0.1
Agland Cooperative	PO Box 125	Oakland	NE	68045	Maurice Mederow	402-685-5613	R	15	<0.1
Agri-Tech F.S. Inc.	16119 Hwy 81 W	Darlington	WI	53530	William Hanson	608-776-4600	S	15	<0.1
Mer-Roc F.S. Inc.	PO Box 129	Aledo	IL	61231	Dana Robinson	309-582-7271	R	15	<0.1
Gresham Petroleum Co.	PO Box 690	Indianola	MS	38751	WW Gresham Jr	601-887-2160	R	14	<0.1
Home Oil Co.	PO Box 608	Osceola	AR	72370	Don Hayes	501-563-6573	R	14 *	<0.1
Gas Inc.	77 Jefferson Pkwy	Newnan	GA	30263	Robert O Hetzler	770-502-8800	R	14 *	0.1
Columbia Propane Corp.	PO Box 35800	Richmond	VA	23235	A Mason Brent	804-323-5300	S	13	0.1
Litter Industries Inc.	PO Box 297	Chillicothe	OH	45601	Robert E Litter	614-773-2196	R	13 *	0.1
Maine Gas Inc.	368 Upper Maine	Fairfield	ME	04937	Bill Chase	207-453-4991	S	13	0.1
Farmers Elevator and Supply	E Market St	Morrison	IL	61270	Doug Vandermyde	815-772-4029	R	12 *	<0.1
Mutual Liquid Gas & Equipment	17117 S Broadway	Gardena	CA	90248	MS Moore	213-321-3771	R	12 *	<0.1
Central Oil of Virginia Corp.	PO Box 587	Rocky Mount	VA	24151	Don Thacker	703-483-5342	R	11	<0.1
Green Mountain Propane	PO Box 779	Richmond	VT	05477	Bob Sayers	802-434-6200	S	10 *	<0.1
Midland 66 Oil Company Inc.	1612 Garden City	Midland	TX	79701	Kenneth A Peeler	915-682-9404	R	9	<0.1
Pickelner Fuel Company Inc.	210 Locust St	Williamsport	PA	17701	William Pickelner	717-323-9488	R	9	<0.1
Southern L.P. Gas Inc.	PO Box 1010	De Queen	AR	71832	Ron Moore	501-642-2234	S	9 *	<0.1
Farmers Cooperative Oil Co.	PO Box 38	Sheldon	IA	51201	Charles Getting	712-324-3455	R	8 *	<0.1
Farmers Union Oil Co.	Hwy 75 S	Breckenridge	MN	56520	Terry Dohman	218-643-2651	R	8	<0.1
Hocon Gas Inc.	33 Rockland Rd	Norwalk	CT	06854	David Gable	203-324-6512	R	8	<0.1
United Pride Inc.	PO Box 84107	Sioux Falls	SD	57118	Wayne Krumvieda	605-336-1558	R	7 *	<0.1
Patterson Brothers Oil and Gas	141 S Pine St	Williamsville	IL	62693	George W Patterson	217-566-3328	R	6	<0.1
TriCounty Farm Service Inc.	County Rd E	Jerseyville	IL	62052	Ross Prough	618-498-5534	R	6 *	<0.1
CAP Propane Plus Inc.	PO Box 38	Kettle River	MN	55757	Mike Wayrynen	218-273-4850	R	5	<0.1
Community Co-op	PO Box 508	Marcus	IA	51035	Larry Fields	712-546-4412	R	5 *	<0.1

Source: *Ward's Business Directory of U.S. Private and Public Companies*, 1998. The company type code used is as follows: P - Public, R - Private, S - Subsidiary, D - Division, J - Joint Venture, A - Affiliate, G - Group. Sales are in millions of dollars, employees are in thousands. An asterisk (*) indicates an estimated sales volume. The symbol < stands for 'less than'.

OCCUPATIONS EMPLOYED BY SIC 598 - FUEL DEALERS

Occupation	% of Total 1996	Change to 2006	Occupation	% of Total 1996	Change to 2006
Truck drivers light & heavy	25.2	-5.8	Salespersons, retail	3.6	0.4
Heat, air conditioning, refrigeration mechanics	13.4	13.0	Cashiers	3.4	-4.7
General managers & top executives	8.3	-8.7	Service station attendants	2.8	-5.8
General office clerks	7.8	-19.0	Sales & related workers nec	2.4	3.7
Bookkeeping, accounting, & auditing clerks	5.7	-24.6	Maintenance repairers, general utility	1.6	-12.2
Home appliance/power tool repairers	5.3	-5.8	Automotive mechanics	1.3	-5.8
Marketing & sales worker supervisors	4.5	-5.8	Billing, cost, & rate clerks	1.1	-15.2
Driver/sales workers	4.3	-5.8			

Source: *Industry-Occupation Matrix*, Bureau of Labor Statistics. These data relate to one or more 3-digit SIC industry groups rather than to a single 4-digit SIC. The change reported for each occupation to the year 2006 is a percent of growth or decline as estimated by the Bureau of Labor Statistics. The abbreviation nec stands for 'not elsewhere classified'.

STATE AND REGIONAL CONCENTRATION

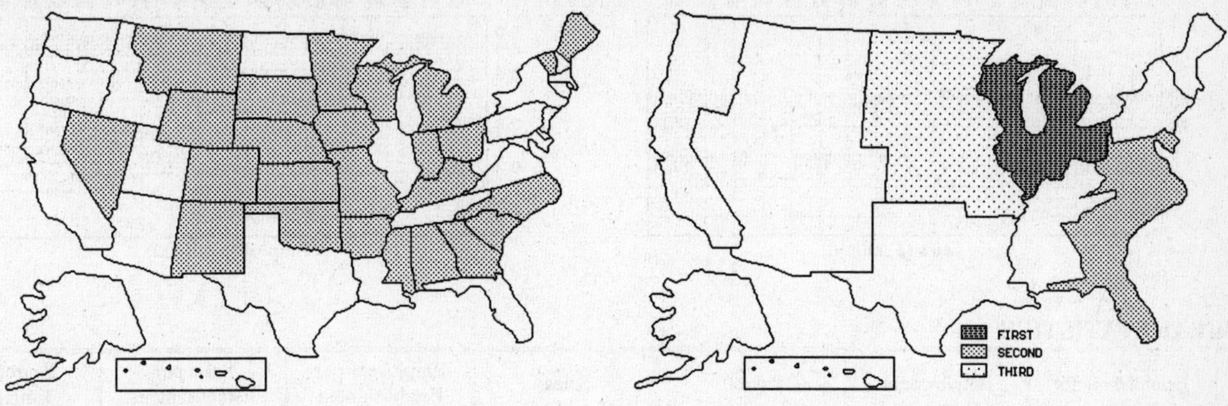

INDUSTRY DATA BY STATE

State	Establishments - 1995 Total (number)	% of U.S.	Employment - 1995 Total (number)	% of U.S.	Per Estab.	Payroll - 1995 Total ($ mil.)	Per Empl. ($)	Sales - 1992 Total ($ mil.)	% of U.S.	Per Estab ($)
Michigan	238	3.9	1,926	4.4	8	46.8	24,301	297.1	6.4	183,724
California	315	5.2	2,702	6.2	9	66.5	24,627	294.4	6.3	147,635
Texas	490	8.1	3,002	6.9	6	59.1	19,694	281.9	6.1	102,272
New York	199	3.3	1,929	4.4	10	52.1	27,020	257.5	5.5	147,206
Missouri	404	6.7	2,085	4.8	5	37.3	17,907	219.4	4.7	120,071
Georgia	290	4.8	2,425	5.6	8	50.1	20,674	218.6	4.7	119,791
Ohio	152	2.5	1,699	3.9	11	44.7	26,305	203.9	4.4	155,855
Florida	271	4.5	2,414	5.5	9	50.5	20,918	201.7	4.3	103,314
North Carolina	245	4.0	2,217	5.1	9	48.5	21,870	191.2	4.1	130,426
Alabama	237	3.9	1,766	4.1	7	37.1	20,980	172.7	3.7	110,777
Mississippi	177	2.9	1,411	3.2	8	28.3	20,046	156.9	3.4	117,716
Wisconsin	191	3.2	1,241	2.9	6	26.5	21,326	155.7	3.3	132,403
Indiana	174	2.9	1,252	2.9	7	29.7	23,745	149.4	3.2	143,475
Pennsylvania	155	2.6	1,229	2.8	8	31.1	25,327	145.6	3.1	170,940
Illinois	182	3.0	1,103	2.5	6	27.1	24,561	138.9	3.0	146,879
Minnesota	160	2.6	1,065	2.4	7	20.9	19,665	118.5	2.5	147,801
Arkansas	161	2.7	947	2.2	6	16.6	17,552	101.4	2.2	116,506
Kentucky	117	1.9	870	2.0	7	18.3	21,066	95.3	2.0	132,209
Virginia	91	1.5	1,056	2.4	12	25.6	24,285	94.8	2.0	145,199
South Carolina	123	2.0	1,137	2.6	9	22.7	19,975	94.0	2.0	105,453
Iowa	122	2.0	635	1.5	5	11.7	18,362	91.2	2.0	156,417
Tennessee	136	2.2	1,040	2.4	8	21.5	20,630	90.7	1.9	144,019
Massachusetts	71	1.2	500-999	-	-	(D)	-	86.6	1.9	149,302
Oklahoma	171	2.8	818	1.9	5	13.1	15,989	81.1	1.7	106,595
Colorado	106	1.7	671	1.5	6	14.1	21,043	80.7	1.7	142,407
Maryland	53	0.9	618	1.4	12	15.5	25,047	79.0	1.7	137,417
New Mexico	89	1.5	548	1.3	6	9.5	17,301	74.5	1.6	109,461
New Jersey	52	0.9	500-999	-	-	(D)	-	74.2	1.6	144,949
Vermont	46	0.8	250-499	-	-	(D)	-	57.3	1.2	136,510
Arizona	70	1.2	646	1.5	9	13.2	20,358	50.9	1.1	115,485
Kansas	87	1.4	494	1.1	6	10.3	20,870	49.1	1.1	141,484
Louisiana	89	1.5	549	1.3	6	10.9	19,920	40.5	0.9	96,090
Nebraska	54	0.9	229	0.5	4	4.1	17,808	30.7	0.7	131,406
Maine	45	0.7	343	0.8	8	7.1	20,790	29.3	0.6	165,593
Nevada	40	0.7	266	0.6	7	6.7	25,222	28.0	0.6	140,608
Wyoming	29	0.5	196	0.5	7	3.9	19,959	25.7	0.6	152,095
South Dakota	41	0.7	212	0.5	5	3.7	17,656	23.8	0.5	131,354
Montana	55	0.9	235	0.5	4	4.8	20,268	20.0	0.4	131,625
West Virginia	26	0.4	251	0.6	10	4.7	18,653	19.5	0.4	115,160
Idaho	42	0.7	322	0.7	8	6.6	20,478	14.6	0.3	120,057
Utah	26	0.4	184	0.4	7	3.6	19,772	14.0	0.3	137,010
North Dakota	25	0.4	163	0.4	7	2.7	16,417	7.4	0.2	96,169
Washington	54	0.9	504	1.2	9	14.0	27,708	(D)	-	-
Connecticut	39	0.6	421	1.0	11	12.8	30,406	(D)	-	-
New Hampshire	36	0.6	412	0.9	11	11.3	27,325	(D)	-	-
Oregon	29	0.5	212	0.5	7	4.8	22,575	(D)	-	-
Alaska	22	0.4	92	0.2	4	2.3	24,783	(D)	-	-
Delaware	18	0.3	100-249	-	-	(D)	-	(D)	-	-
Rhode Island	12	0.2	100-249	-	-	(D)	-	(D)	-	-
Hawaii	4	0.1	0-19	-	-	(D)	-	(D)	-	-

Source: *County Business Patterns, 1995* and *Economic Census of the U.S., 1992*. Data are sorted by 1992 revenues and, if revenues are unavailable, by establishments in 1995. The symbol (D) indicates that data are withheld by the source to avoid disclosure of competitive information. A dash (-) indicates that data are not available or undisclosed because they do not meet statistical validity standards. Shaded *states* on the state map indicate those states which have proportionately greater representation in the industry than would be indicated by the state's population; the ratio is based on total revenues or number of establishments. Shaded *regions* indicate where the industry is regionally most concentrated.

5989 - FUEL DEALERS, NEC

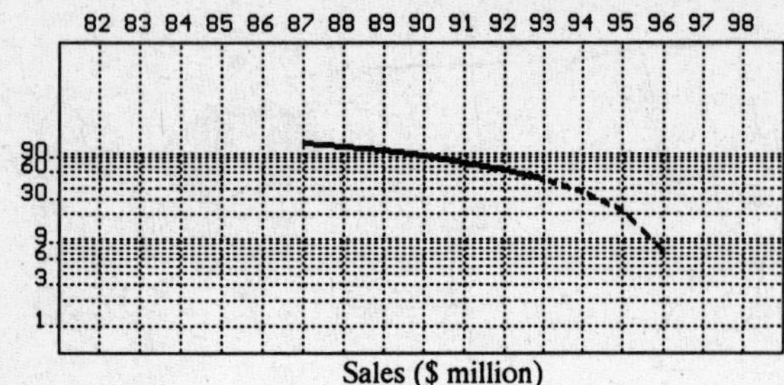

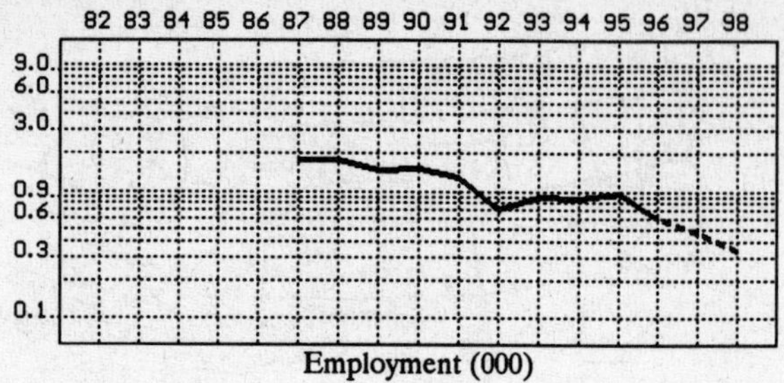

GENERAL STATISTICS

Year	Establishments (number)	Employment (number)	Payroll ($ million)	Sales ($ million)	Employees per Establishment (number)	Sales per Establishment ($)	Payroll per Employee ($)
1982	-	-	-	-	-	-	-
1983	-	-	-	-	-	-	-
1984	-	-	-	-	-	-	-
1985	-	-	-	-	-	-	-
1986	-	-	-	-	-	-	-
1987	549	1,762	18.8	134.8	3	245,548	10,672
1988	497	1,770	26.0	120.6e	4	-	14,707
1989	427	1,437	21.4	106.5e	3	-	14,910
1990	397	1,520	21.3	92.3e	4	-	14,014
1991	394	1,277	19.9	78.2e	3	-	15,618
1992	297	719	9.0	64.0	2	215,556	12,473
1993	311	899	14.4	49.9p	3	-	15,962
1994	309	876	15.1	35.7p	3	-	17,210
1995	278	961	17.2	21.5p	3	-	17,873
1996	219p	600p	12.6p	7.4p	-	-	-
1997	186p	470p	11.5p	-	-	-	-
1998	153p	341p	10.5p	-	-	-	-

Sources: Economic Census of the United States, 1982, 1987, and 1992. Establishment counts, employment, and payroll are from *County Business Patterns* for non-Census years. Values followed by a 'p' are projections by the editors. Sales and expense data for non-Census years are extrapolations, marked by 'e'. Industries reclassified in 1987 will not have data for prior years. Data are the most recent available at this level of detail.

INDICES OF CHANGE

Year	Establishments (number)	Employment (number)	Payroll ($ million)	Sales ($ million)	Employees per Establishment (number)	Sales per Establishment ($)	Payroll per Employee ($)
1982	-	-	-	-	-	-	-
1983	-	-	-	-	-	-	-
1984	-	-	-	-	-	-	-
1985	-	-	-	-	-	-	-
1986	-	-	-	-	-	-	-
1987	184.8	245.1	208.9	210.6	150.0	113.9	85.6
1988	167.3	246.2	288.9	188.4e	200.0	-	117.9
1989	143.8	199.9	237.8	166.4e	150.0	-	119.5
1990	133.7	211.4	236.7	144.2e	200.0	-	112.4
1991	132.7	177.6	221.1	122.2e	150.0	-	125.2
1992	100.0	100.0	100.0	100.0	100.0	100.0	100.0
1993	104.7	125.0	159.4	78.0p	144.5	-	128.0
1994	104.0	121.8	167.5	55.8p	141.7	-	138.0
1995	93.6	133.7	190.8	33.6p	172.8	-	143.3
1996	73.8p	83.4p	140.4p	11.6p	-	-	-
1997	62.7p	65.4p	128.3p	-	-	-	-
1998	51.6p	47.4p	116.1p	-	-	-	-

Sources: Same as General Statistics. The values shown reflect change from the base year, 1992. Values above 100 mean greater than 1992, values below 100 mean less than 1992, and a value of 100 in the 1982-91 or 1993-98 period means same as 1992. Values followed by a 'p' are projections by the editors; 'e' stands for extrapolation. Data are the most recent available at this level of detail.

SELECTED RATIOS

For 1992	Avg. of All Retail	Analyzed Industry	Index	For 1992	Avg. of All Retail	Analyzed Industry	Index
Employees per Establishment	12	2	20	Sales per Employee	102,941	89,013	86
Payroll per Establishment	146,026	30,303	21	Sales per Establishment	1,241,555	215,488	17
Payroll per Employee	12,107	12,517	103	Expenses per Establishment	na	na	na

Sources: Same as General Statistics. The 'Average of All Manufacturing' column represents the average of all manufacturing industries reported for the most recent complete year available. The Index shows the relationship between the Average and the Analyzed Industry. For example, 100 means that they are equal; 500 that the Analyzed Industry is five times the average; 50 means that the Analyzed Industry is half the national average. The abbreviation 'na' is used to show that data are 'not available'.

LEADING COMPANIES Number shown: 9 Total sales ($ mil): 939 Total employment (000): 2.8

Company Name	Address				CEO Name	Phone	Co. Type	Sales ($ mil)	Empl. (000)
Petroleum Heat and Power	PO Box 1457	Stamford	CT	06904	Irik P Sevin	203-325-5400	P	548	2.2
Time Oil Co.	PO Box 24447	Seattle	WA	98124	H Roger Holliday	206-285-2400	R	270 *	0.2
Goodland Co-op and Exchange	PO Box 99	Bird City	KS	67731	Steve Everett	913-734-2331	D	40	<0.1
Fuel South Company Inc.	PO Box 572	Hazlehurst	GA	31539	Jimmy Walker	912-285-4011	R	34	<0.1
CYR Oil Corp.	100 Water St	Lawrence	MA	01841	Gregory Bruett	508-683-2775	R	27 *	0.2
Nobles County Oil Co.	PO Box 278	Worthington	MN	56187	Lowell Nystrom	507-376-3104	R	7	<0.1
Western Cooperative Co.	PO Drawer H	Alliance	NE	69301	Mark Thompson	308-762-3112	R	6 *	<0.1
Beard Oil Pipeline Supply Inc.	PO Box 485	Mount Pleasant	MI	48804	Leo Beard	517-773-9957	R	6	<0.1
Do-All Gas Co.	3667 US 13 S	Goldsboro	NC	27530	Don Casey	919-689-2298	R	1	<0.1

Source: *Ward's Business Directory of U.S. Private and Public Companies*, 1998. The company type code used is as follows: P - Public, R - Private, S - Subsidiary, D - Division, J - Joint Venture, A - Affiliate, G - Group. Sales are in millions of dollars, employees are in thousands. An asterisk (*) indicates an estimated sales volume. The symbol < stands for 'less than'.

OCCUPATIONS EMPLOYED BY SIC 598 - FUEL DEALERS

Occupation	% of Total 1996	Change to 2006	Occupation	% of Total 1996	Change to 2006
Truck drivers light & heavy	25.2	-5.8	Salespersons, retail	3.6	0.4
Heat, air conditioning, refrigeration mechanics	13.4	13.0	Cashiers	3.4	-4.7
General managers & top executives	8.3	-8.7	Service station attendants	2.8	-5.8
General office clerks	7.8	-19.0	Sales & related workers nec	2.4	3.7
Bookkeeping, accounting, & auditing clerks	5.7	-24.6	Maintenance repairers, general utility	1.6	-12.2
Home appliance/power tool repairers	5.3	-5.8	Automotive mechanics	1.3	-5.8
Marketing & sales worker supervisors	4.5	-5.8	Billing, cost, & rate clerks	1.1	-15.2
Driver/sales workers	4.3	-5.8			

Source: *Industry-Occupation Matrix*, Bureau of Labor Statistics. These data relate to one or more 3-digit SIC industry groups rather than to a single 4-digit SIC. The change reported for each occupation to the year 2006 is a percent of growth or decline as estimated by the Bureau of Labor Statistics. The abbreviation nec stands for 'not elsewhere classified'.

STATE AND REGIONAL CONCENTRATION

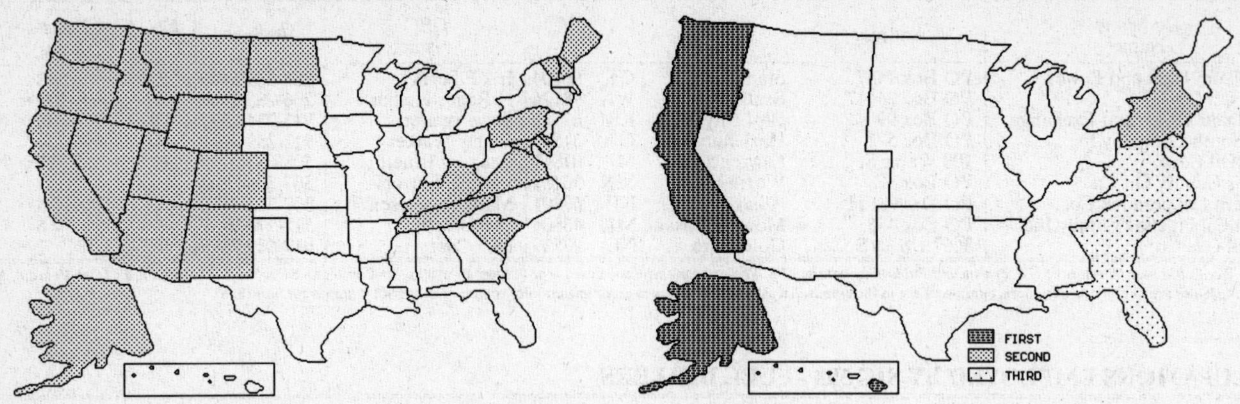

INDUSTRY DATA BY STATE

State	Establishments - 1995		Employment - 1995			Payroll - 1995		Sales - 1992		
	Total (number)	% of U.S.	Total (number)	% of U.S.	Per Estab.	Total ($ mil.)	Per Empl. ($)	Total ($ mil.)	% of U.S.	Per Estab ($)
California	45	16.2	163	21.9	4	3.0	18,485	11.2	24.8	87,015
Pennsylvania	39	14.0	105	14.1	3	1.6	15,714	10.2	22.6	135,933
New York	19	6.8	99	13.3	5	2.5	24,838	3.8	8.5	127,833
Texas	9	3.2	29	3.9	3	0.6	21,207	2.9	6.4	75,579
Kentucky	5	1.8	15	2.0	3	0.4	23,600	2.2	4.8	64,265
New Jersey	4	1.4	0-19	-	-	(D)	-	2.0	4.3	122,125
Massachusetts	6	2.2	0-19	-	-	(D)	-	1.8	4.0	112,500
Virginia	13	4.7	49	6.6	4	0.5	9,388	1.7	3.7	67,320
Maine	8	2.9	21	2.8	3	0.2	11,667	1.2	2.7	61,650
Maryland	6	2.2	25	3.4	4	0.3	10,840	1.1	2.5	59,474
Tennessee	6	2.2	19	2.6	3	0.2	8,895	1.0	2.3	43,625
Colorado	5	1.8	8	1.1	2	0.1	8,750	1.0	2.3	207,800
Illinois	5	1.8	20-99	-	-	(D)	-	0.8	1.9	93,556
Idaho	6	2.2	0-19	-	-	(D)	-	0.8	1.8	80,500
North Carolina	1	0.4	0-19	-	-	(D)	-	0.8	1.7	84,444
Nevada	4	1.4	0-19	-	-	(D)	-	0.6	1.4	79,000
Vermont	2	0.7	0-19	-	-	(D)	-	0.5	1.2	108,600
New Mexico	4	1.4	9	1.2	2	0.1	11,222	0.4	1.0	33,615
Minnesota	3	1.1	20-99	-	-	(D)	-	0.4	0.9	35,273
Florida	5	1.8	11	1.5	2	0.2	14,636	0.3	0.8	69,200
North Dakota	3	1.1	20-99	-	-	(D)	-	0.2	0.5	59,500
Michigan	10	3.6	23	3.1	2	0.3	13,000	(D)	-	-
Arizona	8	2.9	0-19	-	-	(D)	-	(D)	-	-
Washington	8	2.9	36	4.8	5	0.6	16,000	(D)	-	-
Oregon	7	2.5	33	4.4	5	0.3	10,030	(D)	-	-
South Carolina	6	2.2	22	3.0	4	0.2	10,364	(D)	-	-
Georgia	4	1.4	8	1.1	2	0.2	24,375	(D)	-	-
New Hampshire	4	1.4	7	0.9	2	0.1	10,714	(D)	-	-
Ohio	4	1.4	24	3.2	6	0.2	9,083	(D)	-	-
Alaska	3	1.1	19	2.6	6	0.5	24,842	(D)	-	-
Connecticut	3	1.1	6	0.8	2	0.1	16,833	(D)	-	-
Utah	3	1.1	12	1.6	4	0.2	20,500	(D)	-	-
Wyoming	3	1.1	0-19	-	-	(D)	-	(D)	-	-
Alabama	2	0.7	0-19	-	-	(D)	-	(D)	-	-
Indiana	2	0.7	0-19	-	-	(D)	-	(D)	-	-
Louisiana	2	0.7	0-19	-	-	(D)	-	(D)	-	-
Montana	2	0.7	0-19	-	-	(D)	-	(D)	-	-
Wisconsin	2	0.7	0-19	-	-	(D)	-	(D)	-	-
Arkansas	1	0.4	0-19	-	-	(D)	-	(D)	-	-
Delaware	1	0.4	0-19	-	-	(D)	-	(D)	-	-
Iowa	1	0.4	0-19	-	-	(D)	-	(D)	-	-
Kansas	1	0.4	0-19	-	-	(D)	-	-	-	-
Oklahoma	1	0.4	0-19	-	-	(D)	-	(D)	-	-
Rhode Island	1	0.4	0-19	-	-	(D)	-	(D)	-	-
West Virginia	1	0.4	0-19	-	-	(D)	-	(D)	-	-

Source: County Business Patterns, 1995 and *Economic Census of the U.S., 1992*. Data are sorted by 1992 revenues and, if revenues are unavailable, by establishments in 1995. The symbol (D) indicates that data are withheld by the source to avoid disclosure of competitive information. A dash (-) indicates that data are not available or undisclosed because they do not meet statistical validity standards. Shaded *states* on the state map indicate those states which have proportionately greater representation in the industry than would be indicated by the state's population; the ratio is based on total revenues or number of establishments, Shaded *regions* indicate where the industry is regionally most concentrated.

5992 - FLORISTS

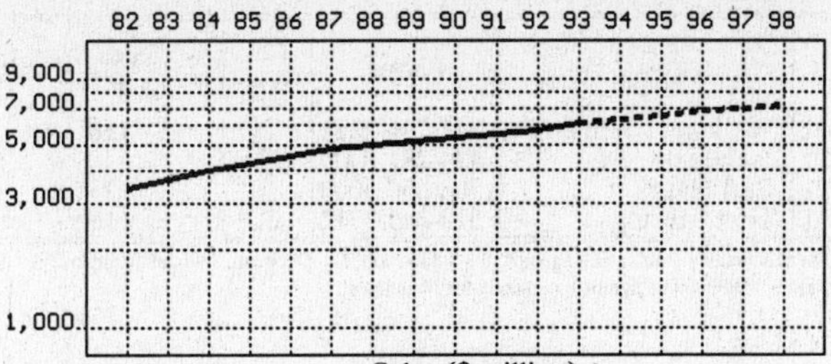

Sales ($ million)

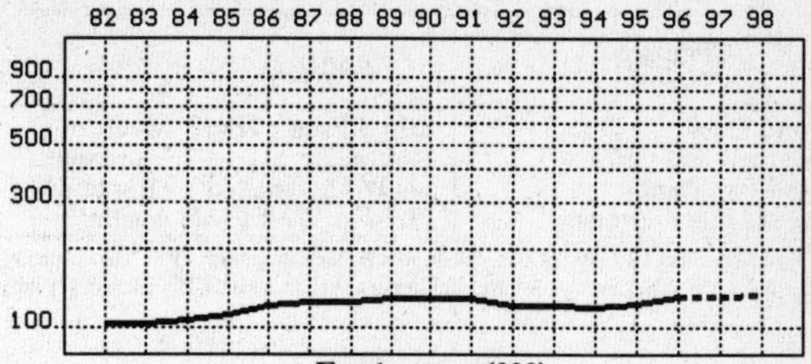

Employment (000)

GENERAL STATISTICS

Year	Establishments (number)	Employment (number)	Payroll ($ million)	Sales ($ million)	Employees per Establishment (number)	Sales per Establishment ($)	Payroll per Employee ($)
1982	24,074	103,804	710.8	3,416.0	4	141,897	6,848
1983	23,642	103,424	769.3	3,694.9*e*	4	-	7,438
1984	23,577	107,817	837.3	3,973.8*e*	5	-	7,766
1985	23,459	113,707	912.2	4,252.6*e*	5	-	8,022
1986	24,457	121,295	990.1	4,531.5*e*	5	-	8,163
1987	26,683	125,048	1,019.3	4,810.4	5	180,278	8,151
1988	25,284	124,874	1,110.3	4,992.1*e*	5	-	8,892
1989	25,859	128,691	1,173.6	5,173.9*e*	5	-	9,120
1990	25,784	130,936	1,219.0	5,355.7*e*	5	-	9,310
1991	26,537	128,547	1,222.7	5,537.5*e*	5	-	9,512
1992	27,341	122,114	1,207.3	5,719.2	4	209,182	9,887
1993	27,204	122,083	1,236.8	6,059.9*p*	4	-	10,130
1994	26,757	120,354	1,270.8	6,290.2*p*	4	-	10,559
1995	26,403	123,628	1,321.1	6,520.5*p*	5	-	10,686
1996	27,691*p*	131,093*p*	1,416.6*p*	6,750.8*p*	-	-	-
1997	27,982*p*	132,607*p*	1,462.6*p*	6,981.2*p*	-	-	-
1998	28,274*p*	134,121*p*	1,508.6*p*	7,211.5*p*	-	-	-

Sources: *Economic Census of the United States*, 1982, 1987, and 1992. Establishment counts, employment, and payroll are from *County Business Patterns* for non-Census years. Values followed by a 'p' are projections by the editors. Sales and expense data for non-Census years are extrapolations, marked by 'e'. Industries reclassified in 1987 will not have data for prior years. Data are the most recent available at this level of detail.

INDICES OF CHANGE

Year	Establishments (number)	Employment (number)	Payroll ($ million)	Sales ($ million)	Employees per Establishment (number)	Sales per Establishment ($)	Payroll per Employee ($)
1982	88.1	85.0	58.9	59.7	100.0	67.8	69.3
1983	86.5	84.7	63.7	64.6*e*	100.0	-	75.2
1984	86.2	88.3	69.4	69.5*e*	125.0	-	78.5
1985	85.8	93.1	75.6	74.4*e*	125.0	-	81.1
1986	89.5	99.3	82.0	79.2*e*	125.0	-	82.6
1987	97.6	102.4	84.4	84.1	125.0	86.2	82.4
1988	92.5	102.3	92.0	87.3*e*	125.0	-	89.9
1989	94.6	105.4	97.2	90.5*e*	125.0	-	92.2
1990	94.3	107.2	101.0	93.6*e*	125.0	-	94.2
1991	97.1	105.3	101.3	96.8*e*	125.0	-	96.2
1992	100.0	100.0	100.0	100.0	100.0	100.0	100.0
1993	99.5	100.0	102.4	106.0*p*	112.2	-	102.5
1994	97.9	98.6	105.3	110.0*p*	112.5	-	106.8
1995	96.6	101.2	109.4	114.0*p*	117.1	-	108.1
1996	101.3*p*	107.4*p*	117.3*p*	118.0*p*	-	-	-
1997	102.3*p*	108.6*p*	121.1*p*	122.1*p*	-	-	-
1998	103.4*p*	109.8*p*	125.0*p*	126.1*p*	-	-	-

Sources: Same as General Statistics. The values shown reflect change from the base year, 1992. Values above 100 mean greater than 1992, values below 100 mean less than 1992, and a value of 100 in the 1982-91 or 1993-98 period means same as 1992. Values followed by a 'p' are projections by the editors; 'e' stands for extrapolation. Data are the most recent available at this level of detail.

SELECTED RATIOS

For 1992	Avg. of All Retail	Analyzed Industry	Index	For 1992	Avg. of All Retail	Analyzed Industry	Index
Employees per Establishment	12	4	37	Sales per Employee	102,941	46,835	45
Payroll per Establishment	146,026	44,157	30	Sales per Establishment	1,241,555	209,180	17
Payroll per Employee	12,107	9,887	82	Expenses per Establishment	na	na	na

Sources: Same as General Statistics. The 'Average of All Manufacturing' column represents the average of all manufacturing industries reported for the most recent complete year available. The Index shows the relationship between the Average and the Analyzed Industry. For example, 100 means that they are equal; 500 that the Analyzed Industry is five times the average; 50 means that the Analyzed Industry is half the national average. The abbreviation 'na' is used to show that data are 'not available'.

LEADING COMPANIES Number shown: 4 Total sales ($ mil): 218 Total employment (000): 2.5

Company Name	Address				CEO Name	Phone	Co. Type	Sales ($ mil)	Empl. (000)
Harry and David	2518 S Pacific Hwy	Medford	OR	97501	William H Williams	541-776-2121	D	150	1.2
Stein Garden and Gifts	5400 S 27th St	Milwaukee	WI	53221	Jack Stein	414-281-8400	R	40	0.8
Amlings Flowerland	540 W Ogden Ave	Hinsdale	IL	60521	Carl Hayes	708-850-5000	R	25*	0.5
Northwest Hills Pharmacy	3910 Far West Blvd	Austin	TX	78731	Tom Sansing	512-345-3712	R	3*	<0.1

Source: *Ward's Business Directory of U.S. Private and Public Companies*, 1998. The company type code used is as follows: P - Public, R - Private, S - Subsidiary, D - Division, J - Joint Venture, A - Affiliate, G - Group. Sales are in millions of dollars, employees are in thousands. An asterisk (*) indicates an estimated sales volume. The symbol < stands for 'less than'.

OCCUPATIONS EMPLOYED BY SIC 599 - USED MERCHANDISE AND RETAIL STORES, NEC

Occupation	% of Total 1996	Change to 2006	Occupation	% of Total 1996	Change to 2006
Salespersons, retail	27.9	20.9	General office clerks	2.6	-2.3
Designers, except interior designers	9.5	24.9	Assemblers, fabricators, hand workers nec	2.1	13.5
General managers & top executives	7.0	10.0	Secretaries, except legal & medical	1.4	-9.9
Marketing & sales worker supervisors	6.1	13.5	Optical goods workers, precision	1.3	13.5
Stock clerks	5.8	8.9	Purchasing managers	1.3	2.2
Cashiers	4.8	14.9	Wholesale & retail buyers, except farm products	1.2	-6.0
Opticians, dispensing & measuring	4.5	13.5	Order fillers, wholesale & retail sales	1.2	13.5
Truck drivers light & heavy	4.3	13.5	Gardeners, nursery workers	1.1	13.5
Sales & related workers nec	2.7	24.9	Freight, stock, & material movers, hand	1.1	2.2
Bookkeeping, accounting, & auditing clerks	2.6	-9.2			

Source: *Industry-Occupation Matrix*, Bureau of Labor Statistics. These data relate to one or more 3-digit SIC industry groups rather than to a single 4-digit SIC. The change reported for each occupation to the year 2006 is a percent of growth or decline as estimated by the Bureau of Labor Statistics. The abbreviation nec stands for 'not elsewhere classified'.

STATE AND REGIONAL CONCENTRATION

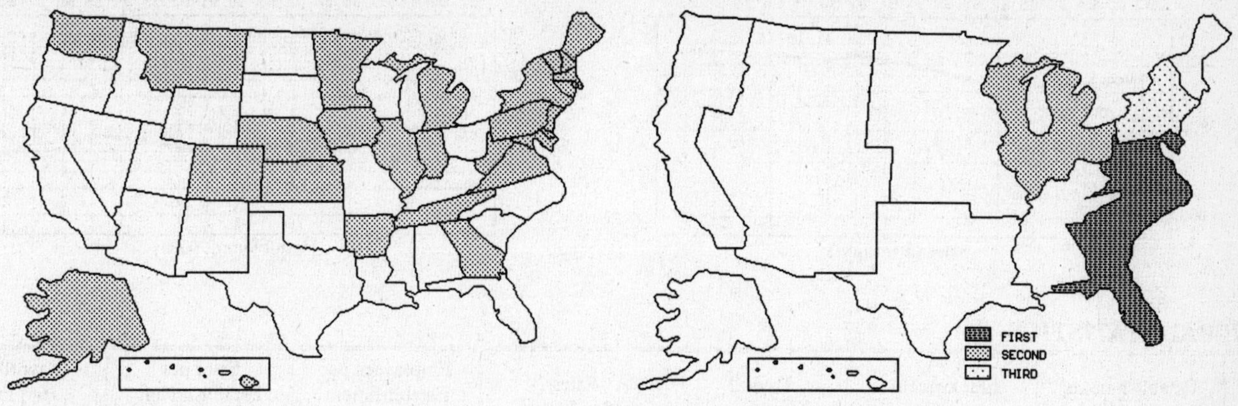

INDUSTRY DATA BY STATE

State	Establishments - 1995 Total (number)	Establishments - 1995 % of U.S.	Employment - 1995 Total (number)	Employment - 1995 % of U.S.	Employment - 1995 Per Estab.	Payroll - 1995 Total ($ mil.)	Payroll - 1995 Per Empl. ($)	Sales - 1992 Total ($ mil.)	Sales - 1992 % of U.S.	Sales - 1992 Per Estab ($)
California	2,431	9.2	11,240	9.1	5	118.4	10,531	616.8	10.8	48,559
New York	1,578	6.0	6,276	5.1	4	87.6	13,953	416.7	7.3	61,818
Texas	1,734	6.6	7,308	5.9	4	77.3	10,577	333.2	5.8	46,381
Pennsylvania	1,285	4.9	6,435	5.2	5	68.8	10,685	301.0	5.3	46,480
Florida	1,462	5.5	6,614	5.3	5	73.0	11,042	298.2	5.2	49,597
Illinois	1,108	4.2	6,092	4.9	5	68.7	11,272	284.3	5.0	47,485
Ohio	1,107	4.2	5,789	4.7	5	56.9	9,828	240.5	4.2	42,269
Michigan	916	3.5	5,432	4.4	6	57.4	10,576	223.0	3.9	44,699
New Jersey	880	3.3	3,773	3.1	4	52.0	13,778	219.0	3.8	59,331
Georgia	818	3.1	3,261	2.6	4	35.6	10,926	157.7	2.8	47,386
Massachusetts	630	2.4	2,674	2.2	4	35.5	13,263	151.0	2.6	57,771
Virginia	717	2.7	3,557	2.9	5	39.6	11,145	150.2	2.6	43,440
North Carolina	838	3.2	3,176	2.6	4	34.7	10,924	144.7	2.5	46,299
Indiana	635	2.4	3,583	2.9	6	35.1	9,806	135.3	2.4	40,338
Washington	525	2.0	2,819	2.3	5	28.7	10,181	127.4	2.2	43,285
Minnesota	496	1.9	2,923	2.4	6	28.1	9,609	125.1	2.2	44,733
Tennessee	588	2.2	2,710	2.2	5	29.3	10,803	119.1	2.1	47,875
Maryland	415	1.6	2,742	2.2	7	32.7	11,929	116.7	2.0	40,125
Missouri	608	2.3	2,421	2.0	4	25.4	10,499	109.6	1.9	44,022
Wisconsin	485	1.8	2,647	2.1	5	23.5	8,892	97.5	1.7	39,530
Connecticut	333	1.3	1,575	1.3	5	20.9	13,274	91.7	1.6	58,213
Kentucky	460	1.7	1,902	1.5	4	19.1	10,063	84.4	1.5	45,819
Alabama	496	1.9	1,889	1.5	4	17.4	9,208	83.7	1.5	42,624
Colorado	377	1.4	2,097	1.7	6	20.3	9,683	80.3	1.4	50,509
Arizona	306	1.2	1,858	1.5	6	18.7	10,044	71.0	1.2	44,281
Louisiana	402	1.5	1,736	1.4	4	16.8	9,676	70.1	1.2	41,840
Iowa	375	1.4	1,761	1.4	5	14.7	8,346	68.1	1.2	36,372
Oklahoma	383	1.5	1,535	1.2	4	14.0	9,100	67.2	1.2	42,703
South Carolina	423	1.6	1,420	1.1	3	14.4	10,108	65.9	1.2	47,626
Kansas	332	1.3	1,622	1.3	5	13.7	8,453	63.8	1.1	40,473
Oregon	340	1.3	1,566	1.3	5	13.6	8,708	59.9	1.0	40,607
Arkansas	338	1.3	1,322	1.1	4	12.1	9,122	55.4	1.0	43,887
West Virginia	265	1.0	1,142	0.9	4	10.6	9,280	47.8	0.8	40,931
Mississippi	332	1.3	1,156	0.9	3	11.0	9,542	45.9	0.8	41,013
Nebraska	209	0.8	946	0.8	5	7.4	7,780	37.1	0.6	38,475
Hawaii	147	0.6	658	0.5	4	7.9	11,953	35.9	0.6	54,100
New Hampshire	144	0.5	645	0.5	4	7.9	12,265	30.8	0.5	49,456
Utah	165	0.6	1,091	0.9	7	8.3	7,647	29.5	0.5	36,031
Maine	144	0.5	629	0.5	4	6.5	10,315	28.4	0.5	42,243
New Mexico	150	0.6	631	0.5	4	5.9	9,384	28.0	0.5	43,911
Nevada	121	0.5	559	0.5	5	7.2	12,869	27.0	0.5	47,989
D.C.	48	0.2	342	0.3	7	7.0	20,509	25.1	0.4	71,173
Rhode Island	125	0.5	483	0.4	4	6.2	12,758	24.6	0.4	56,618
Idaho	136	0.5	720	0.6	5	5.1	7,014	21.6	0.4	34,804
Montana	123	0.5	608	0.5	5	4.9	8,135	21.0	0.4	41,587
Delaware	75	0.3	472	0.4	6	5.2	11,025	17.9	0.3	42,226
South Dakota	107	0.4	510	0.4	5	3.8	7,439	16.5	0.3	33,014
Alaska	61	0.2	251	0.2	4	3.1	12,267	14.8	0.3	62,784
Vermont	77	0.3	360	0.3	5	3.7	10,181	14.4	0.3	46,987
North Dakota	86	0.3	395	0.3	5	3.1	7,775	14.3	0.3	34,083
Wyoming	67	0.3	275	0.2	4	2.4	8,807	10.2	0.2	40,672

Source: County Business Patterns, 1995 and *Economic Census of the U.S., 1992*. Data are sorted by 1992 revenues and, if revenues are unavailable, by establishments in 1995. The symbol (D) indicates that data are withheld by the source to avoid disclosure of competitive information. A dash (-) indicates that data are not available or undisclosed because they do not meet statistical validity standards. Shaded *states* on the state map indicate those states which have proportionately greater representation in the industry than would be indicated by the state's population; the ratio is based on total revenues or number of establishments. Shaded *regions* indicate where the industry is regionally most concentrated.

5993 - TOBACCO STORES AND STANDS

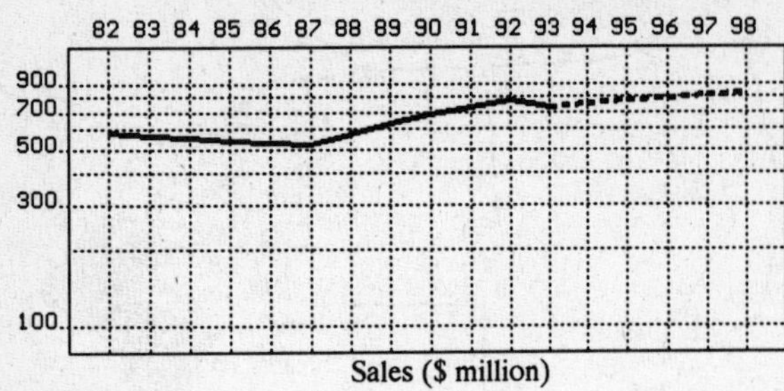

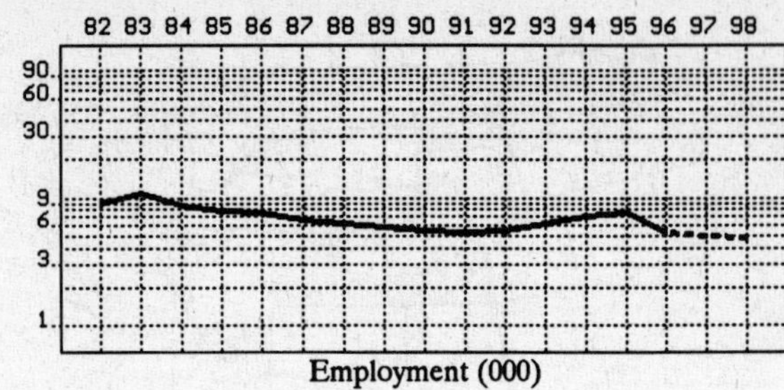

GENERAL STATISTICS

Year	Establishments (number)	Employment (number)	Payroll ($ million)	Sales ($ million)	Employees per Establishment (number)	Sales per Establishment ($)	Payroll per Employee ($)
1982	2,538	8,980	67.9	576.5	4	227,131	7,566
1983	2,691	10,745	95.4	564.8e	4	-	8,880
1984	2,284	8,736	73.3	553.1e	4	-	8,389
1985	2,094	7,922	69.4	541.5e	4	-	8,765
1986	1,903	7,526	67.7	529.8e	4	-	8,990
1987	1,948	6,736	57.2	518.1	3	265,989	8,487
1988	1,683	6,175	57.6	570.9e	4	-	9,330
1989	1,515	5,913	55.4	623.6e	4	-	9,369
1990	1,440	5,484	55.4	676.4e	4	-	10,095
1991	1,388	5,343	58.7	729.1e	4	-	10,983
1992	1,477	5,530	61.8	781.8	4	529,334	11,176
1993	1,551	6,296	77.3	729.2p	4	-	12,285
1994	1,655	7,146	91.5	749.7p	4	-	12,811
1995	1,840	7,536	106.8	770.3p	4	-	14,176
1996	1,270p	5,302p	77.6p	790.8p	-	-	-
1997	1,192p	5,055p	78.5p	811.3p	-	-	-
1998	1,113p	4,809p	79.3p	831.9p	-	-	-

Sources: Economic Census of the United States, 1982, 1987, and 1992. Establishment counts, employment, and payroll are from *County Business Patterns* for non-Census years. Values followed by a 'p' are projections by the editors. Sales and expense data for non-Census years are extrapolations, marked by 'e'. Industries reclassified in 1987 will not have data for prior years. Data are the most recent available at this level of detail.

INDICES OF CHANGE

Year	Establishments (number)	Employment (number)	Payroll ($ million)	Sales ($ million)	Employees per Establishment (number)	Sales per Establishment ($)	Payroll per Employee ($)
1982	171.8	162.4	109.9	73.7	100.0	42.9	67.7
1983	182.2	194.3	154.4	72.2e	100.0	-	79.5
1984	154.6	158.0	118.6	70.7e	100.0	-	75.1
1985	141.8	143.3	112.3	69.3e	100.0	-	78.4
1986	128.8	136.1	109.5	67.8e	100.0	-	80.4
1987	131.9	121.8	92.6	66.3	75.0	50.2	75.9
1988	113.9	111.7	93.2	73.0e	100.0	-	83.5
1989	102.6	106.9	89.6	79.8e	100.0	-	83.8
1990	97.5	99.2	89.6	86.5e	100.0	-	90.3
1991	94.0	96.6	95.0	93.3e	100.0	-	98.3
1992	100.0	100.0	100.0	100.0	100.0	100.0	100.0
1993	105.0	113.9	125.2	93.3p	101.5	-	109.9
1994	112.1	129.2	148.1	95.9p	107.9	-	114.6
1995	124.6	136.3	172.9	98.5p	102.4	-	126.8
1996	86.0p	95.9p	125.6p	101.2p	-	-	-
1997	80.7p	91.4p	127.0p	103.8p	-	-	-
1998	75.4p	87.0p	128.4p	106.4p	-	-	-

Sources: Same as General Statistics. The values shown reflect change from the base year, 1992. Values above 100 mean greater than 1992, values below 100 mean less than 1992, and a value of 100 in the 1982-91 or 1993-98 period means same as 1992. Values followed by a 'p' are projections by the editors; 'e' stands for extrapolation. Data are the most recent available at this level of detail.

SELECTED RATIOS

For 1992	Avg. of All Retail	Analyzed Industry	Index	For 1992	Avg. of All Retail	Analyzed Industry	Index
Employees per Establishment	12	4	31	Sales per Employee	102,941	141,374	137
Payroll per Establishment	146,026	41,842	29	Sales per Establishment	1,241,555	529,316	43
Payroll per Employee	12,107	11,175	92	Expenses per Establishment	na	na	na

Sources: Same as General Statistics. The 'Average of All Manufacturing' column represents the average of all manufacturing industries reported for the most recent complete year available. The Index shows the relationship between the Average and the Analyzed Industry. For example, 100 means that they are equal; 500 that the Analyzed Industry is five times the average; 50 means that the Analyzed Industry is half the national average. The abbreviation 'na' is used to show that data are 'not available'.

LEADING COMPANIES Number shown: 4 Total sales ($ mil): 291 Total employment (000): 0.3

Company Name	Address				CEO Name	Phone	Co. Type	Sales ($ mil)	Empl. (000)
Burley Tobacco Growers	620 S Broadway	Lexington	KY	40508	Danny McKinney	606-252-3561	R	240	<0.1
Patton Music Company Inc.	811 Kearney Ave	Modesto	CA	95350	James B Reed	209-529-6500	R	33 *	0.1
Alfred Dunhill of London Inc.	450 Park Ave	New York	NY	10022	David Salz	212-888-4000	S	17	<0.1
Caribbean Cigar Co.	6265 SW 8th St	Miami	FL	33144	Kevin Doyle	305-267-3911	P	1	<0.1

Source: *Ward's Business Directory of U.S. Private and Public Companies*, 1998. The company type code used is as follows: P - Public, R - Private, S - Subsidiary, D - Division, J - Joint Venture, A - Affiliate, G - Group. Sales are in millions of dollars, employees are in thousands. An asterisk (*) indicates an estimated sales volume. The symbol < stands for 'less than'.

OCCUPATIONS EMPLOYED BY SIC 599 - USED MERCHANDISE AND RETAIL STORES, NEC

Occupation	% of Total 1996	Change to 2006	Occupation	% of Total 1996	Change to 2006
Salespersons, retail	27.9	20.9	General office clerks	2.6	-2.3
Designers, except interior designers	9.5	24.9	Assemblers, fabricators, hand workers nec	2.1	13.5
General managers & top executives	7.0	10.0	Secretaries, except legal & medical	1.4	-9.9
Marketing & sales worker supervisors	6.1	13.5	Optical goods workers, precision	1.3	13.5
Stock clerks	5.8	8.9	Purchasing managers	1.3	2.2
Cashiers	4.8	14.9	Wholesale & retail buyers, except farm products	1.2	-6.0
Opticians, dispensing & measuring	4.5	13.5	Order fillers, wholesale & retail sales	1.2	13.5
Truck drivers light & heavy	4.3	13.5	Gardeners, nursery workers	1.1	13.5
Sales & related workers nec	2.7	24.9	Freight, stock, & material movers, hand	1.1	2.2
Bookkeeping, accounting, & auditing clerks	2.6	-9.2			

Source: *Industry-Occupation Matrix*, Bureau of Labor Statistics. These data relate to one or more 3-digit SIC industry groups rather than to a single 4-digit SIC. The change reported for each occupation to the year 2006 is a percent of growth or decline as estimated by the Bureau of Labor Statistics. The abbreviation nec stands for 'not elsewhere classified'.

STATE AND REGIONAL CONCENTRATION

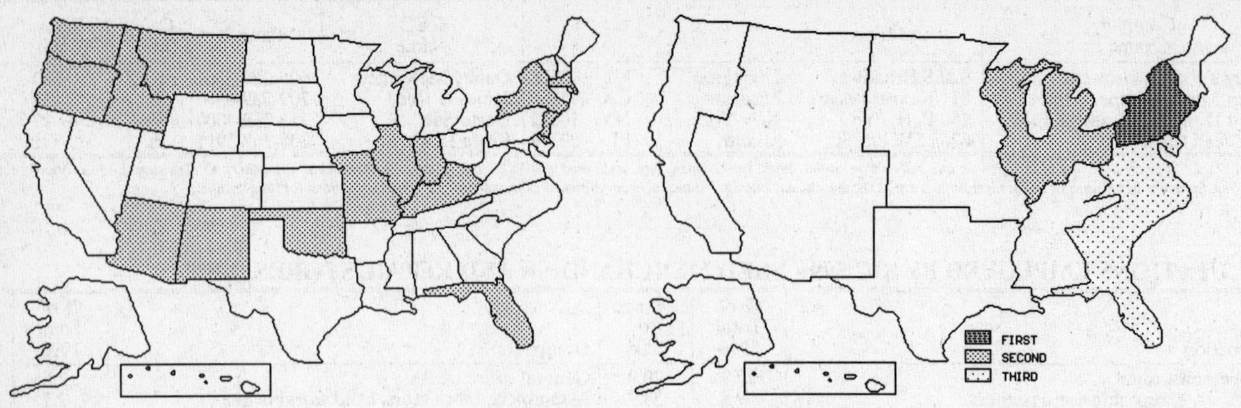

INDUSTRY DATA BY STATE

	Establishments - 1995		Employment - 1995			Payroll - 1995		Sales - 1992		
State	Total (number)	% of U.S.	Total (number)	% of U.S.	Per Estab.	Total ($ mil.)	Per Empl. ($)	Total ($ mil.)	% of U.S.	Per Estab ($)
New York	176	9.6	677	9.1	4	11.0	16,233	129.2	16.9	213,892
California	125	6.8	489	6.5	4	6.5	13,344	60.5	7.9	111,217
Illinois	86	4.7	400	5.4	5	5.2	13,088	54.4	7.1	177,332
Arizona	39	2.1	272	3.6	7	4.0	14,860	48.8	6.4	209,515
Oklahoma	85	4.6	464	6.2	5	4.6	9,970	45.9	6.0	236,768
Florida	92	5.0	393	5.3	4	5.9	14,906	45.9	6.0	136,476
Pennsylvania	82	4.5	304	4.1	4	4.0	13,161	35.5	4.6	105,223
Indiana	58	3.2	297	4.0	5	3.7	12,461	28.5	3.7	162,994
New Jersey	66	3.6	337	4.5	5	5.8	17,119	26.7	3.5	121,717
Washington	36	2.0	202	2.7	6	4.3	21,441	25.5	3.3	138,793
Massachusetts	58	3.2	199	2.7	3	2.9	14,472	23.3	3.0	105,380
Texas	83	4.5	287	3.8	3	5.4	18,676	23.3	3.0	116,869
Michigan	68	3.7	165	2.2	2	2.4	14,776	21.9	2.9	130,280
Missouri	60	3.3	227	3.0	4	3.1	13,586	19.0	2.5	163,621
Ohio	64	3.5	137	1.8	2	1.6	11,898	17.8	2.3	81,118
Virginia	29	1.6	129	1.7	4	1.8	14,202	17.7	2.3	123,476
Kentucky	45	2.4	226	3.0	5	2.3	10,208	15.4	2.0	131,521
Oregon	28	1.5	118	1.6	4	2.4	20,237	13.2	1.7	137,000
North Carolina	31	1.7	185	2.5	6	2.5	13,454	12.0	1.6	71,254
Maryland	20	1.1	61	0.8	3	0.9	15,082	9.2	1.2	97,168
Louisiana	72	3.9	315	4.2	4	3.1	9,987	8.5	1.1	243,343
Minnesota	16	0.9	72	1.0	5	0.8	11,264	7.8	1.0	243,187
Delaware	21	1.1	124	1.7	6	1.7	13,677	7.3	1.0	106,522
Connecticut	22	1.2	52	0.7	2	0.8	14,615	6.2	0.8	104,407
Wisconsin	14	0.8	87	1.2	6	1.4	15,920	6.0	0.8	143,500
Kansas	15	0.8	85	1.1	6	1.1	13,271	5.6	0.7	297,105
Colorado	27	1.5	124	1.7	5	2.0	15,903	5.4	0.7	90,083
New Mexico	12	0.7	33	0.4	3	0.5	15,182	4.9	0.6	234,905
Idaho	12	0.7	67	0.9	6	0.9	13,627	4.9	0.6	167,655
Montana	6	0.3	31	0.4	5	0.3	10,258	4.4	0.6	138,563
Georgia	24	1.3	90	1.2	4	1.5	17,133	3.7	0.5	88,881
Tennessee	54	2.9	206	2.8	4	3.0	14,379	3.7	0.5	63,931
D.C.	5	0.3	37	0.5	7	0.7	19,243	3.2	0.4	92,657
Rhode Island	7	0.4	24	0.3	3	0.3	10,958	2.9	0.4	112,423
New Hampshire	6	0.3	0-19	-	-	(D)	-	2.8	0.4	141,100
Mississippi	50	2.7	124	1.7	2	1.6	12,742	2.8	0.4	275,400
West Virginia	9	0.5	49	0.7	5	0.5	10,531	2.5	0.3	276,222
Iowa	8	0.4	29	0.4	4	0.2	7,103	2.0	0.3	59,235
Maine	4	0.2	12	0.2	3	0.1	7,167	2.0	0.3	182,091
Alabama	15	0.8	33	0.4	2	0.4	12,970	1.6	0.2	78,571
Arkansas	66	3.6	69	0.9	1	1.4	20,478	1.5	0.2	136,545
Nebraska	4	0.2	20	0.3	5	0.2	11,250	1.0	0.1	32,581
South Carolina	9	0.5	30	0.4	3	0.4	11,900	0.8	0.1	46,556
Nevada	18	1.0	192	2.6	11	2.5	13,271	(D)	-	-
South Dakota	3	0.2	0-19	-	-	(D)	-	-	-	-
Vermont	3	0.2	20-99	-	-	(D)	-	(D)	-	-
Wyoming	3	0.2	0-19	-	-	(D)	-	(D)	-	-
Alaska	2	0.1	0-19	-	-	(D)	-	(D)	-	-
North Dakota	1	0.1	0-19	-	-	(D)	-	(D)	-	-
Utah	1	0.1	0-19	-	-	(D)	-	(D)	-	-

Source: County Business Patterns, 1995 and *Economic Census of the U.S., 1992*. Data are sorted by 1992 revenues and, if revenues are unavailable, by establishments in 1995. The symbol (D) indicates that data are withheld by the source to avoid disclosure of competitive information. A dash (-) indicates that data are not available or undisclosed because they do not meet statistical validity standards. Shaded *states* on the state map indicate those states which have proportionately greater representation in the industry than would be indicated by the state's population; the ratio is based on total revenues or number of establishments. Shaded *regions* indicate where the industry is regionally most concentrated.

5994 - NEWS DEALERS AND NEWSSTANDS

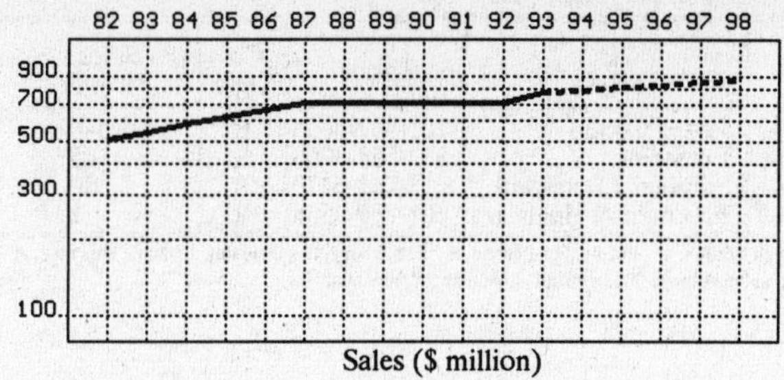

Sales ($ million)

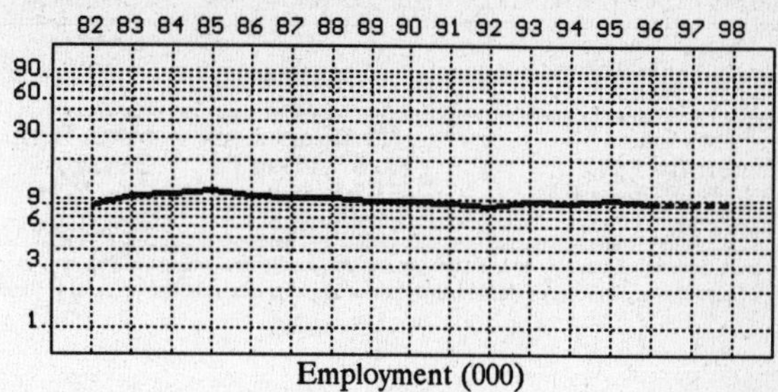

Employment (000)

GENERAL STATISTICS

Year	Establishments (number)	Employment (number)	Payroll ($ million)	Sales ($ million)	Employees per Establishment (number)	Sales per Establishment ($)	Payroll per Employee ($)
1982	2,130	8,629	60.3	500.3	4	234,901	6,991
1983	2,158	10,434	79.5	540.9e	5	-	7,619
1984	2,074	10,804	87.0	581.5e	5	-	8,049
1985	2,002	11,763	101.4	622.0e	6	-	8,623
1986	1,915	10,348	91.7	662.6e	5	-	8,864
1987	2,198	10,149	90.2	703.2	5	319,907	8,890
1988	2,078	10,252	93.6	703.4e	5	-	9,126
1989	1,967	9,718	90.4	703.6e	5	-	9,297
1990	1,982	9,663	95.5	703.8e	5	-	9,881
1991	2,022	9,208	94.2	704.1e	5	-	10,226
1992	2,260	8,696	91.1	704.3	4	311,631	10,475
1993	2,362	9,490	100.8	770.5p	4	-	10,621
1994	2,310	9,247	102.7	790.9p	4	-	11,104
1995	2,286	9,911	117.5	811.3p	4	-	11,859
1996	2,254p	9,263p	110.3p	831.7p	-	-	-
1997	2,272p	9,181p	112.7p	852.1p	-	-	-
1998	2,289p	9,099p	115.0p	872.5p	-	-	-

Sources: Economic Census of the United States, 1982, 1987, and 1992. Establishment counts, employment, and payroll are from *County Business Patterns* for non-Census years. Values followed by a 'p' are projections by the editors. Sales and expense data for non-Census years are extrapolations, marked by 'e'. Industries reclassified in 1987 will not have data for prior years. Data are the most recent available at this level of detail.

INDICES OF CHANGE

Year	Establishments (number)	Employment (number)	Payroll ($ million)	Sales ($ million)	Employees per Establishment (number)	Sales per Establishment ($)	Payroll per Employee ($)
1982	94.2	99.2	66.2	71.0	100.0	75.4	66.7
1983	95.5	120.0	87.3	76.8e	125.0	-	72.7
1984	91.8	124.2	95.5	82.6e	125.0	-	76.8
1985	88.6	135.3	111.3	88.3e	150.0	-	82.3
1986	84.7	119.0	100.7	94.1e	125.0	-	84.6
1987	97.3	116.7	99.0	99.8	125.0	102.7	84.9
1988	91.9	117.9	102.7	99.9e	125.0	-	87.1
1989	87.0	111.8	99.2	99.9e	125.0	-	88.8
1990	87.7	111.1	104.8	99.9e	125.0	-	94.3
1991	89.5	105.9	103.4	100.0e	125.0	-	97.6
1992	100.0	100.0	100.0	100.0	100.0	100.0	100.0
1993	104.5	109.1	110.6	109.4p	100.4	-	101.4
1994	102.2	106.3	112.7	112.3p	100.1	-	106.0
1995	101.2	114.0	129.0	115.2p	108.4	-	113.2
1996	99.8p	106.5p	121.1p	118.1p	-	-	-
1997	100.5p	105.6p	123.7p	121.0p	-	-	-
1998	101.3p	104.6p	126.3p	123.9p	-	-	-

Sources: Same as General Statistics. The values shown reflect change from the base year, 1992. Values above 100 mean greater than 1992, values below 100 mean less than 1992, and a value of 100 in the 1982-91 or 1993-98 period means same as 1992. Values followed by a 'p' are projections by the editors; 'e' stands for extrapolation. Data are the most recent available at this level of detail.

SELECTED RATIOS

For 1992	Avg. of All Retail	Analyzed Industry	Index	For 1992	Avg. of All Retail	Analyzed Industry	Index
Employees per Establishment	12	4	32	Sales per Employee	102,941	80,991	79
Payroll per Establishment	146,026	40,310	28	Sales per Establishment	1,241,555	311,637	25
Payroll per Employee	12,107	10,476	87	Expenses per Establishment	na	na	na

Sources: Same as General Statistics. The 'Average of All Manufacturing' column represents the average of all manufacturing industries reported for the most recent complete year available. The Index shows the relationship between the Average and the Analyzed Industry. For example, 100 means that they are equal; 500 that the Analyzed Industry is five times the average; 50 means that the Analyzed Industry is half the national average. The abbreviation 'na' is used to show that data are 'not available'.

LEADING COMPANIES

Number shown: **4** Total sales ($ mil): **456** Total employment (000): **3.0**

Company Name	Address				CEO Name	Phone	Co. Type	Sales ($ mil)	Empl. (000)
Hudson News Co.	1305 Patersonank	North Bergen	NJ	07047	James Cohen	201-867-3600	R	340 *	1.4
Faber Enterprises Inc.	100 S Wacker Dr	Chicago	IL	60606	Ed Steiner	312-558-8900	S	65 *	1.1
Eastern Lobby Shops L.P.	363 7th Ave	New York	NY	10001	Stephen J Browand	212-268-6470	R	50	0.5
Healy News Store Inc.	PO Box 504	Wakefield	RI	02880	Freeman A Healy Jr	401-789-9566	R	1	<0.1

Source: *Ward's Business Directory of U.S. Private and Public Companies*, 1998. The company type code used is as follows: P - Public, R - Private, S - Subsidiary, D - Division, J - Joint Venture, A - Affiliate, G - Group. Sales are in millions of dollars, employees are in thousands. An asterisk (*) indicates an estimated sales volume. The symbol < stands for 'less than'.

OCCUPATIONS EMPLOYED BY SIC 599 - USED MERCHANDISE AND RETAIL STORES, NEC

Occupation	% of Total 1996	Change to 2006	Occupation	% of Total 1996	Change to 2006
Salespersons, retail	27.9	20.9	General office clerks	2.6	-2.3
Designers, except interior designers	9.5	24.9	Assemblers, fabricators, hand workers nec	2.1	13.5
General managers & top executives	7.0	10.0	Secretaries, except legal & medical	1.4	-9.9
Marketing & sales worker supervisors	6.1	13.5	Optical goods workers, precision	1.3	13.5
Stock clerks	5.8	8.9	Purchasing managers	1.3	2.2
Cashiers	4.8	14.9	Wholesale & retail buyers, except farm products	1.2	-6.0
Opticians, dispensing & measuring	4.5	13.5	Order fillers, wholesale & retail sales	1.2	13.5
Truck drivers light & heavy	4.3	13.5	Gardeners, nursery workers	1.1	13.5
Sales & related workers nec	2.7	24.9	Freight, stock, & material movers, hand	1.1	2.2
Bookkeeping, accounting, & auditing clerks	2.6	-9.2			

Source: *Industry-Occupation Matrix*, Bureau of Labor Statistics. These data relate to one or more 3-digit SIC industry groups rather than to a single 4-digit SIC. The change reported for each occupation to the year 2006 is a percent of growth or decline as estimated by the Bureau of Labor Statistics. The abbreviation nec stands for 'not elsewhere classified'.

STATE AND REGIONAL CONCENTRATION

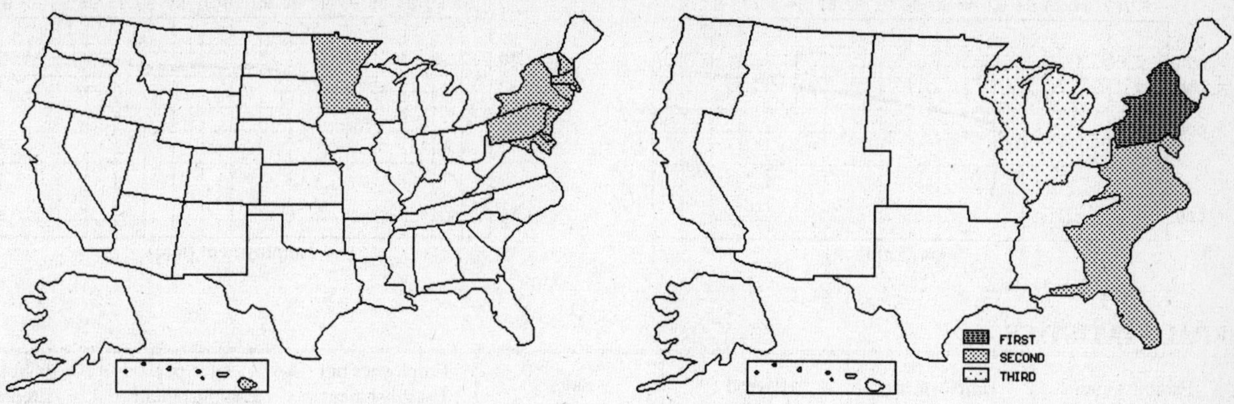

INDUSTRY DATA BY STATE

State	Establishments - 1995 Total (number)	Establishments - 1995 % of U.S.	Employment - 1995 Total (number)	Employment - 1995 % of U.S.	Employment - 1995 Per Estab.	Payroll - 1995 Total ($ mil.)	Payroll - 1995 Per Empl. ($)	Sales - 1992 Total ($ mil.)	Sales - 1992 % of U.S.	Sales - 1992 Per Estab ($)
New York	623	27.3	2,103	21.4	3	26.1	12,405	189.0	27.2	99,690
California	168	7.3	881	9.0	5	9.5	10,754	65.8	9.5	78,259
Pennsylvania	223	9.8	793	8.1	4	7.2	9,035	64.8	9.3	76,966
New Jersey	156	6.8	653	6.6	4	10.4	15,856	46.5	6.7	89,699
Massachusetts	68	3.0	393	4.0	6	4.7	11,906	37.7	5.4	87,674
Illinois	102	4.5	343	3.5	3	3.5	10,271	27.3	3.9	83,125
Florida	78	3.4	499	5.1	6	6.2	12,521	26.9	3.9	54,906
Ohio	89	3.9	377	3.8	4	3.5	9,369	25.4	3.7	59,310
Texas	74	3.2	469	4.8	6	5.8	12,335	20.2	2.9	68,544
Maryland	58	2.5	328	3.3	6	3.0	9,110	17.0	2.5	63,798
Minnesota	20	0.9	156	1.6	8	1.9	12,205	16.2	2.3	97,530
Connecticut	39	1.7	119	1.2	3	1.8	14,815	15.7	2.3	79,523
Michigan	32	1.4	135	1.4	4	2.0	14,526	15.3	2.2	105,234
North Carolina	53	2.3	247	2.5	5	2.6	10,429	11.3	1.6	68,677
Indiana	44	1.9	150	1.5	3	1.3	8,987	8.7	1.3	61,745
Washington	28	1.2	198	2.0	7	2.5	12,672	6.7	1.0	81,866
Virginia	45	2.0	158	1.6	4	1.8	11,177	6.3	0.9	72,253
Delaware	16	0.7	83	0.8	5	0.9	10,892	6.3	0.9	61,921
Arizona	11	0.5	49	0.5	4	0.6	11,735	6.2	0.9	111,393
Georgia	28	1.2	124	1.3	4	2.2	18,105	6.0	0.9	71,464
Tennessee	13	0.6	57	0.6	4	0.7	12,175	6.0	0.9	76,321
Missouri	25	1.1	124	1.3	5	1.6	12,798	5.9	0.8	72,531
Colorado	16	0.7	59	0.6	4	0.9	14,695	5.8	0.8	119,833
Wisconsin	21	0.9	101	1.0	5	1.1	10,535	5.4	0.8	85,762
South Carolina	25	1.1	90	0.9	4	0.8	8,856	5.3	0.8	71,959
Hawaii	5	0.2	84	0.9	17	1.7	19,917	5.2	0.8	65,238
New Hampshire	10	0.4	20-99	-	-	(D)	-	4.9	0.7	90,704
West Virginia	18	0.8	71	0.7	4	0.6	8,169	4.4	0.6	55,575
Louisiana	20	0.9	53	0.5	3	0.7	12,358	4.2	0.6	122,088
Oregon	16	0.7	46	0.5	3	0.6	13,674	3.9	0.6	80,479
New Mexico	10	0.4	71	0.7	7	0.7	10,408	3.2	0.5	46,559
Arkansas	6	0.3	77	0.8	13	0.8	11,000	3.0	0.4	104,034
Iowa	23	1.0	100	1.0	4	0.9	8,870	2.9	0.4	61,298
Kentucky	14	0.6	54	0.5	4	0.7	13,463	2.8	0.4	73,051
Nebraska	7	0.3	61	0.6	9	0.4	6,902	2.5	0.4	85,034
Maine	7	0.3	49	0.5	7	0.6	12,469	2.3	0.3	67,588
Rhode Island	6	0.3	14	0.1	2	0.2	12,071	1.5	0.2	85,765
Kansas	10	0.4	45	0.5	5	0.4	9,356	1.4	0.2	55,600
Oklahoma	9	0.4	48	0.5	5	0.5	10,688	1.2	0.2	110,909
Montana	7	0.3	147	1.5	21	1.5	10,082	1.1	0.2	89,000
Mississippi	6	0.3	13	0.1	2	0.2	11,615	0.9	0.1	44,250
Vermont	6	0.3	20-99	-	-	(D)	-	0.8	0.1	31,222
Alabama	8	0.3	21	0.2	3	0.3	15,143	0.7	0.1	60,083
North Dakota	4	0.2	0-19	-	-	(D)	-	0.6	0.1	90,571
Nevada	13	0.6	100	1.0	8	2.5	25,010	(D)	-	-
D.C.	12	0.5	30	0.3	3	0.4	11,867	(D)	-	-
Idaho	4	0.2	10	0.1	3	0.1	10,000	(D)	-	-
South Dakota	4	0.2	24	0.2	6	0.3	13,125	(D)	-	-
Utah	4	0.2	15	0.2	4	0.1	7,467	(D)	-	-
Alaska	1	0.0	0-19	-	-	(D)	-	(D)	-	-
Wyoming	1	0.0	0-19	-	-	(D)	-	(D)	-	-

Source: *County Business Patterns, 1995* and *Economic Census of the U.S., 1992*. Data are sorted by 1992 revenues and, if revenues are unavailable, by establishments in 1995. The symbol (D) indicates that data are withheld by the source to avoid disclosure of competitive information. A dash (-) indicates that data are not available or undisclosed because they do not meet statistical validity standards. Shaded *states* on the state map indicate those states which have proportionately greater representation in the industry than would be indicated by the state's population; the ratio is based on total revenues or number of establishments. Shaded *regions* indicate where the industry is regionally most concentrated.

5995 - OPTICAL GOODS STORES

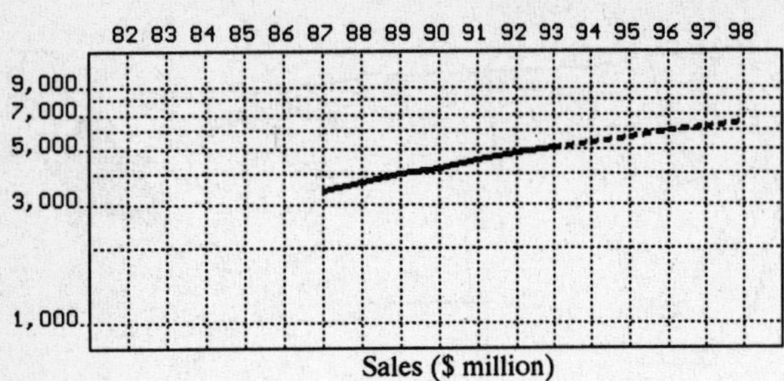

Sales ($ million)

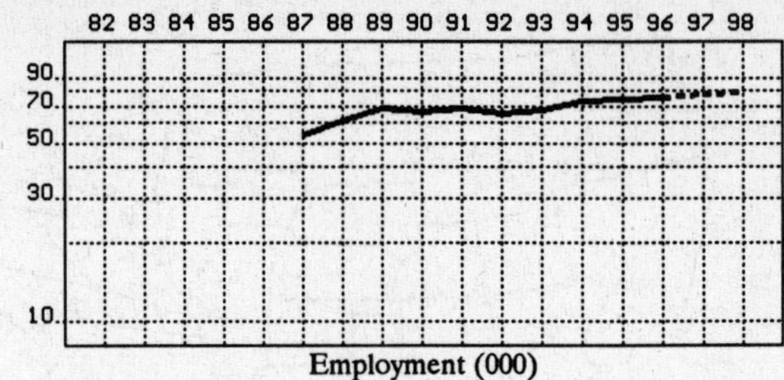

Employment (000)

GENERAL STATISTICS

Year	Establishments (number)	Employment (number)	Payroll ($ million)	Sales ($ million)	Employees per Establishment (number)	Sales per Establishment ($)	Payroll per Employee ($)
1982	-	-	-	-	-	-	-
1983	-	-	-	-	-	-	-
1984	-	-	-	-	-	-	-
1985	-	-	-	-	-	-	-
1986	-	-	-	-	-	-	-
1987	13,580	54,312	810.8	3,415.1	4	251,480	14,928
1988	13,672	61,393	976.0	3,693.3e	4	-	15,897
1989	13,397	68,744	1,048.1	3,971.5e	5	-	15,246
1990	13,214	66,041	1,111.4	4,249.8e	5	-	16,829
1991	13,691	68,526	1,126.8	4,528.0e	5	-	16,444
1992	14,160	64,986	1,114.2	4,806.2	5	339,420	17,145
1993	13,805	67,297	1,160.8	5,084.4p	5	-	17,249
1994	14,318	73,120	1,255.5	5,362.6p	5	-	17,170
1995	14,475	73,429	1,344.5	5,640.8p	5	-	18,310
1996	14,419p	75,403p	1,372.1p	5,919.0p	-	-	-
1997	14,540p	77,198p	1,425.5p	6,197.2p	-	-	-
1998	14,662p	78,993p	1,478.8p	6,475.5p	-	-	-

Sources: *Economic Census of the United States*, 1982, 1987, and 1992. Establishment counts, employment, and payroll are from *County Business Patterns* for non-Census years. Values followed by a 'p' are projections by the editors. Sales and expense data for non-Census years are extrapolations, marked by 'e'. Industries reclassified in 1987 will not have data for prior years. Data are the most recent available at this level of detail.

INDICES OF CHANGE

Year	Establishments (number)	Employment (number)	Payroll ($ million)	Sales ($ million)	Employees per Establishment (number)	Sales per Establishment ($)	Payroll per Employee ($)
1982	-	-	-	-	-	-	-
1983	-	-	-	-	-	-	-
1984	-	-	-	-	-	-	-
1985	-	-	-	-	-	-	-
1986	-	-	-	-	-	-	-
1987	95.9	83.6	72.8	71.1	80.0	74.1	87.1
1988	96.6	94.5	87.6	76.8e	80.0	-	92.7
1989	94.6	105.8	94.1	82.6e	100.0	-	88.9
1990	93.3	101.6	99.7	88.4e	100.0	-	98.2
1991	96.7	105.4	101.1	94.2e	100.0	-	95.9
1992	100.0	100.0	100.0	100.0	100.0	100.0	100.0
1993	97.5	103.6	104.2	105.8p	97.5	-	100.6
1994	101.1	112.5	112.7	111.6p	102.1	-	100.1
1995	102.2	113.0	120.7	117.4p	101.5	-	106.8
1996	101.8p	116.0p	123.1p	123.2p	-	-	-
1997	102.7p	118.8p	127.9p	128.9p	-	-	-
1998	103.5p	121.6p	132.7p	134.7p	-	-	-

Sources: Same as General Statistics. The values shown reflect change from the base year, 1992. Values above 100 mean greater than 1992, values below 100 mean less than 1992, and a value of 100 in the 1982-91 or 1993-98 period means same as 1992. Values followed by a 'p' are projections by the editors; 'e' stands for extrapolation. Data are the most recent available at this level of detail.

SELECTED RATIOS

For 1992	Avg. of All Retail	Analyzed Industry	Index	For 1992	Avg. of All Retail	Analyzed Industry	Index
Employees per Establishment	12	5	38	Sales per Employee	102,941	73,957	72
Payroll per Establishment	146,026	78,686	54	Sales per Establishment	1,241,555	339,421	27
Payroll per Employee	12,107	17,145	142	Expenses per Establishment	na	na	na

Sources: Same as General Statistics. The 'Average of All Manufacturing' column represents the average of all manufacturing industries reported for the most recent complete year available. The Index shows the relationship between the Average and the Analyzed Industry. For example, 100 means that they are equal; 500 that the Analyzed Industry is five times the average; 50 means that the Analyzed Industry is half the national average. The abbreviation 'na' is used to show that data are 'not available'.

LEADING COMPANIES

Number shown: 22 Total sales ($ mil): 4,732 Total employment (000): 50.7

Company Name	Address				CEO Name	Phone	Co. Type	Sales ($ mil)	Empl. (000)
Cole National Group Inc.	5915 Landerbrook	Mayfield H.	OH	44124	Jeffrey A Cole	216-449-4100	S	1,198	12.0
LensCrafters Inc.	8650 Gov's Hill	Cincinnati	OH	45249	David M Browne	513-583-6000	S	1,102	14.0
Pearle Vision Inc.	2534 Royal Ln	Dallas	TX	75229	David Hardie	214-277-5000	S	850 *	4.9
Cole Vision Corp.	18903 S Miles Rd	Warrensville H.	OH	44128	J David Pierson	216-475-8925	S	370 *	4.5
Benson Eyecare Corp.	555 T Fremd	Rye	NY	10580	Martin E Franklin	914-967-9400	S	301	2.5
National Vision Associates Ltd.	296 Grayson Hwy	Lawrenceville	GA	30245	James W Krause	770-822-3600	P	186	2.0
U.S. Vision Inc.	PO Box 124	Glendora	NJ	08029	GT Schanbaum	609-228-1000	R	146	3.6
Eye Care Centers of America	11103 West Ave	San Antonio	TX	78213	Bernard W Andrews	210-524-6504	R	100 *	1.3
Opti-World Inc.	1820 The Exchange	Atlanta	GA	30339	Don Chapman	404-916-2020	R	90 *	1.1
Spectera Inc.	2811 Baltimore	Baltimore	MD	21244	Larry Manchio	410-265-6033	R	64	0.7
Carrera Eyewear Corp.	35 Maple St	Norwood	NJ	07648	G Waldschutz	201-767-3820	S	63	0.3
New West Eyeworks Inc.	2104 W Southern	Tempe	AZ	85282	Barry Feld	602-438-1330	P	49	0.6
Sunsations Sunglass Co.	255 Alhambra Cir	Coral Gables	FL	33134	Bruce A Olson	305-255-5915	S	47	1.1
Duling Optical Company Inc.	PO Box 37410	Louisville	KY	40233	Larry Joel	502-459-6722	R	41	0.5
Sight Resource Corp.	67 S Bedford St	Burlington	MA	01803	W G McLendon	617-229-1100	P	30	0.5
Sterling Vision Inc.	1500 Hempstead	East Meadow	NY	11554	Robert B Greenberg	516-887-2100	P	29	0.5
Cohen's Fashion Optical Inc.	15 Bryant Ave	Roslyn	NY	11576	Robert Cohen	516-621-6200	R	16 *	0.2
Sea Vision USA	4399 35th N	St. Petersburg	FL	33714	Charlie Duffy	813-525-6906	R	16 *	0.2
T.K.C. Inc.	401 Pearl St	Sioux City	IA	51102	Steve Conley	712-252-1519	R	10 *	0.1
Franklin Ophthalmic Instruments	1265 Naperville Dr	Romeoville	IL	60446	Michael J Carroll	630-759-7666	P	10	<0.1
Rosin Optical Co.	6233 W Cermak Rd	Berwyn	IL	60402	Sorrel Rosin	708-749-2020	R	8	<0.1
Western Optical Corp.	1200 Mercer St	Seattle	WA	98109	John C D'Amico Jr	206-622-7627	R	6 *	<0.1

Source: *Ward's Business Directory of U.S. Private and Public Companies*, 1998. The company type code used is as follows: P - Public, R - Private, S - Subsidiary, D - Division, J - Joint Venture, A - Affiliate, G - Group. Sales are in millions of dollars, employees are in thousands. An asterisk (*) indicates an estimated sales volume. The symbol < stands for 'less than'.

OCCUPATIONS EMPLOYED BY SIC 599 - USED MERCHANDISE AND RETAIL STORES, NEC

Occupation	% of Total 1996	Change to 2006	Occupation	% of Total 1996	Change to 2006
Salespersons, retail	27.9	20.9	General office clerks	2.6	-2.3
Designers, except interior designers	9.5	24.9	Assemblers, fabricators, hand workers nec	2.1	13.5
General managers & top executives	7.0	10.0	Secretaries, except legal & medical	1.4	-9.9
Marketing & sales worker supervisors	6.1	13.5	Optical goods workers, precision	1.3	13.5
Stock clerks	5.8	8.9	Purchasing managers	1.3	2.2
Cashiers	4.8	14.9	Wholesale & retail buyers, except farm products	1.2	-6.0
Opticians, dispensing & measuring	4.5	13.5	Order fillers, wholesale & retail sales	1.2	13.5
Truck drivers light & heavy	4.3	13.5	Gardeners, nursery workers	1.1	13.5
Sales & related workers nec	2.7	24.9	Freight, stock, & material movers, hand	1.1	2.2
Bookkeeping, accounting, & auditing clerks	2.6	-9.2			

Source: *Industry-Occupation Matrix*, Bureau of Labor Statistics. These data relate to one or more 3-digit SIC industry groups rather than to a single 4-digit SIC. The change reported for each occupation to the year 2006 is a percent of growth or decline as estimated by the Bureau of Labor Statistics. The abbreviation nec stands for 'not elsewhere classified'.

STATE AND REGIONAL CONCENTRATION

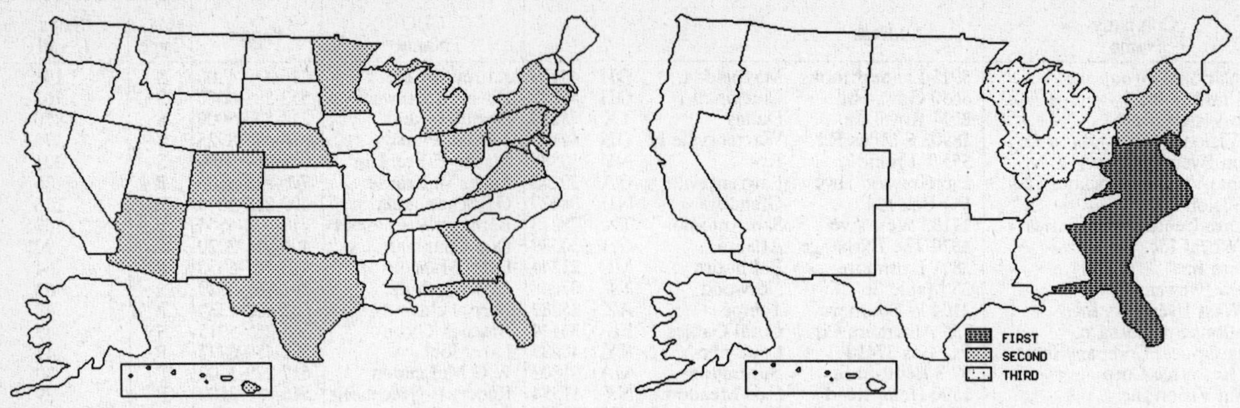

INDUSTRY DATA BY STATE

State	Establishments - 1995 Total (number)	% of U.S.	Employment - 1995 Total (number)	% of U.S.	Per Estab.	Payroll - 1995 Total ($ mil.)	Per Empl. ($)	Sales - 1992 Total ($ mil.)	% of U.S.	Per Estab ($)
California	1,162	8.0	6,305	8.6	5	112.1	17,783	454.7	9.5	73,228
New York	1,278	8.8	6,883	9.4	5	150.7	21,900	441.8	9.2	78,852
Florida	1,138	7.9	5,924	8.1	5	97.9	16,520	370.4	7.7	73,997
Texas	1,062	7.3	5,504	7.5	5	88.6	16,089	337.8	7.0	72,392
Pennsylvania	747	5.2	3,548	4.8	5	63.4	17,877	242.8	5.1	75,136
Michigan	523	3.6	2,717	3.7	5	59.0	21,705	224.3	4.7	89,595
Ohio	696	4.8	3,337	4.6	5	59.5	17,820	218.6	4.5	79,332
Illinois	548	3.8	3,311	4.5	6	61.3	18,499	211.4	4.4	73,208
New Jersey	516	3.6	2,285	3.1	4	47.8	20,915	176.2	3.7	84,014
Georgia	396	2.7	2,227	3.0	6	39.3	17,662	131.6	2.7	71,737
Virginia	411	2.8	1,887	2.6	5	35.7	18,927	131.5	2.7	70,561
Maryland	373	2.6	1,763	2.4	5	35.5	20,119	119.8	2.5	71,935
Minnesota	328	2.3	1,738	2.4	5	31.3	18,002	115.0	2.4	78,952
Massachusetts	357	2.5	1,767	2.4	5	34.4	19,492	111.7	2.3	82,085
Missouri	305	2.1	1,527	2.1	5	29.4	19,270	94.8	2.0	65,960
Indiana	256	1.8	1,439	2.0	6	23.7	16,470	93.7	2.0	61,824
Washington	313	2.2	1,528	2.1	5	30.6	20,056	93.6	1.9	77,202
Colorado	313	2.2	1,413	1.9	5	24.6	17,442	85.1	1.8	77,851
North Carolina	308	2.1	1,539	2.1	5	24.9	16,160	84.2	1.8	66,651
Wisconsin	259	1.8	1,522	2.1	6	26.6	17,485	81.1	1.7	65,123
Arizona	254	1.8	1,187	1.6	5	20.4	17,221	80.6	1.7	67,559
Tennessee	229	1.6	1,247	1.7	5	22.6	18,156	78.5	1.6	69,013
Connecticut	197	1.4	990	1.4	5	22.4	22,590	77.1	1.6	85,530
Louisiana	213	1.5	1,167	1.6	5	18.6	15,916	70.8	1.5	70,060
Kentucky	146	1.0	754	1.0	5	14.3	18,960	60.5	1.3	71,337
Alabama	183	1.3	936	1.3	5	15.0	16,059	59.6	1.2	67,506
South Carolina	199	1.4	1,011	1.4	5	15.7	15,564	53.4	1.1	63,175
Iowa	152	1.1	737	1.0	5	11.8	15,961	49.2	1.0	70,938
Oregon	180	1.2	794	1.1	4	15.8	19,845	45.8	1.0	68,224
Oklahoma	126	0.9	711	1.0	6	10.9	15,357	38.8	0.8	66,668
Nebraska	83	0.6	440	0.6	5	8.0	18,180	36.7	0.8	67,575
Utah	101	0.7	452	0.6	4	8.4	18,498	33.0	0.7	70,074
Kansas	125	0.9	497	0.7	4	8.3	16,650	31.2	0.6	67,400
Hawaii	80	0.6	421	0.6	5	7.2	17,121	28.1	0.6	78,997
West Virginia	95	0.7	386	0.5	4	6.4	16,692	25.2	0.5	64,432
Mississippi	91	0.6	435	0.6	5	7.5	17,154	24.8	0.5	59,435
New Mexico	98	0.7	373	0.5	4	5.7	15,335	21.5	0.4	71,620
New Hampshire	77	0.5	423	0.6	5	8.0	18,825	21.0	0.4	64,180
D.C.	45	0.3	171	0.2	4	4.4	25,854	18.7	0.4	101,587
Nevada	61	0.4	353	0.5	6	6.6	18,623	17.4	0.4	87,307
Arkansas	62	0.4	295	0.4	5	4.8	16,302	16.2	0.3	59,607
Delaware	50	0.3	211	0.3	4	4.0	18,981	15.3	0.3	71,009
Idaho	54	0.4	231	0.3	4	2.7	11,654	11.7	0.2	65,413
Alaska	37	0.3	100-249	-	-	(D)	-	11.3	0.2	95,932
Maine	46	0.3	169	0.2	4	3.0	17,740	10.8	0.2	67,194
South Dakota	40	0.3	183	0.2	5	2.7	14,514	9.8	0.2	61,491
Vermont	31	0.2	125	0.2	4	2.8	22,408	9.1	0.2	78,224
North Dakota	31	0.2	113	0.2	4	1.9	17,150	9.0	0.2	63,169
Rhode Island	42	0.3	128	0.2	3	2.4	18,727	8.9	0.2	70,880
Montana	38	0.3	126	0.2	3	2.0	16,175	8.2	0.2	71,509
Wyoming	20	0.1	20-99	-	-	(D)	-	3.8	0.1	66,667

Source: County Business Patterns, 1995 and *Economic Census of the U.S., 1992.* Data are sorted by 1992 revenues and, if revenues are unavailable, by establishments in 1995. The symbol (D) indicates that data are withheld by the source to avoid disclosure of competitive information. A dash (-) indicates that data are not available or undisclosed because they do not meet statistical validity standards. Shaded *states* on the state map indicate those states which have proportionately greater representation in the industry than would be indicated by the state's population; the ratio is based on total revenues or number of establishments. Shaded *regions* indicate where the industry is regionally most concentrated.

5999 - MISCELLANEOUS RETAIL STORES, NEC

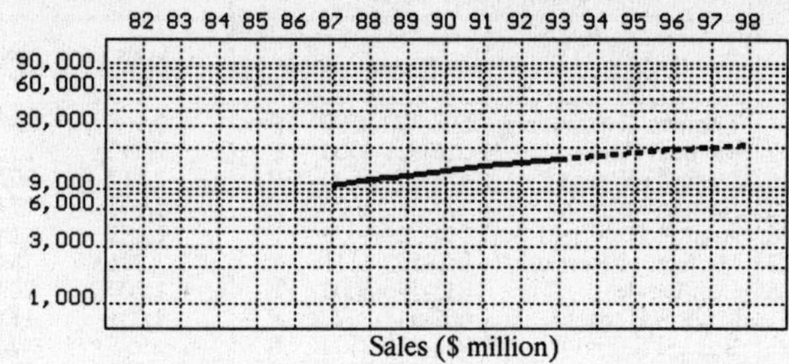

Sales ($ million)

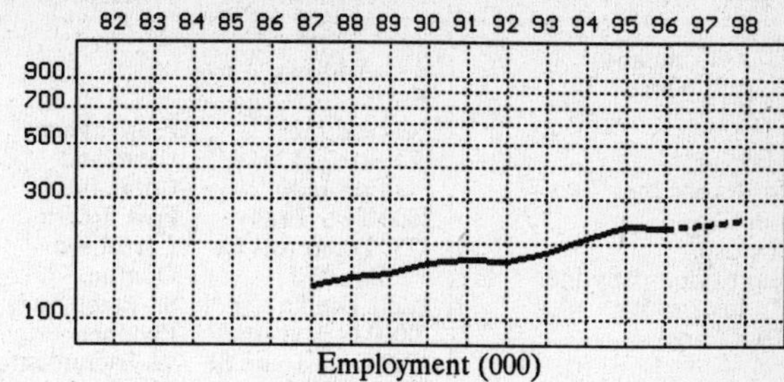

Employment (000)

GENERAL STATISTICS

Year	Establishments (number)	Employment (number)	Payroll ($ million)	Sales ($ million)	Employees per Establishment (number)	Sales per Establishment ($)	Payroll per Employee ($)
1982	-	-	-	-	-	-	-
1983	-	-	-	-	-	-	-
1984	-	-	-	-	-	-	-
1985	-	-	-	-	-	-	-
1986	-	-	-	-	-	-	-
1987	30,493	137,214	1,672.0	9,538.7	5	312,817	12,185
1988	29,006	146,380	2,020.2	10,596.9e	5	-	13,801
1989	30,122	152,582	2,226.2	11,655.1e	5	-	14,590
1990	33,467	167,413	2,460.6	12,713.3e	5	-	14,698
1991	36,848	174,081	2,598.2	13,771.5e	5	-	14,925
1992	39,998	170,475	2,542.0	14,829.6	4	370,759	14,911
1993	42,038	185,650	2,905.8	15,887.8p	4	-	15,652
1994	44,558	210,825	3,278.9	16,946.0p	5	-	15,553
1995	47,272	235,251	3,786.8	18,004.2p	5	-	16,097
1996	49,100p	230,098p	3,749.7p	19,062.4p	-	-	-
1997	51,503p	241,009p	3,977.7p	20,120.6p	-	-	-
1998	53,905p	251,921p	4,205.6p	21,178.8p	-	-	-

Sources: Economic Census of the United States, 1982, 1987, and 1992. Establishment counts, employment, and payroll are from *County Business Patterns* for non-Census years. Values followed by a 'p' are projections by the editors. Sales and expense data for non-Census years are extrapolations, marked by 'e'. Industries reclassified in 1987 will not have data for prior years. Data are the most recent available at this level of detail.

INDICES OF CHANGE

Year	Establishments (number)	Employment (number)	Payroll ($ million)	Sales ($ million)	Employees per Establishment (number)	Sales per Establishment ($)	Payroll per Employee ($)
1982	-	-	-	-	-	-	-
1983	-	-	-	-	-	-	-
1984	-	-	-	-	-	-	-
1985	-	-	-	-	-	-	-
1986	-	-	-	-	-	-	-
1987	76.2	80.5	65.8	64.3	125.0	84.4	81.7
1988	72.5	85.9	79.5	71.5e	125.0	-	92.6
1989	75.3	89.5	87.6	78.6e	125.0	-	97.8
1990	83.7	98.2	96.8	85.7e	125.0	-	98.6
1991	92.1	102.1	102.2	92.9e	125.0	-	100.1
1992	100.0	100.0	100.0	100.0	100.0	100.0	100.0
1993	105.1	108.9	114.3	107.1p	110.4	-	105.0
1994	111.4	123.7	129.0	114.3p	118.3	-	104.3
1995	118.2	138.0	149.0	121.4p	124.4	-	108.0
1996	122.8p	135.0p	147.5p	128.5p	-	-	-
1997	128.8p	141.4p	156.5p	135.7p	-	-	-
1998	134.8p	147.8p	165.4p	142.8p	-	-	-

Sources: Same as General Statistics. The values shown reflect change from the base year, 1992. Values above 100 mean greater than 1992, values below 100 mean less than 1992, and a value of 100 in the 1982-91 or 1993-98 period means same as 1992. Values followed by a 'p' are projections by the editors; 'e' stands for extrapolation. Data are the most recent available at this level of detail.

SELECTED RATIOS

For 1992	Avg. of All Retail	Analyzed Industry	Index	For 1992	Avg. of All Retail	Analyzed Industry	Index
Employees per Establishment	12	4	35	Sales per Employee	102,941	86,990	85
Payroll per Establishment	146,026	63,553	44	Sales per Establishment	1,241,555	370,759	30
Payroll per Employee	12,107	14,911	123	Expenses per Establishment	na	na	na

Sources: Same as General Statistics. The 'Average of All Manufacturing' column represents the average of all manufacturing industries reported for the most recent complete year available. The Index shows the relationship between the Average and the Analyzed Industry. For example, 100 means that they are equal; 500 that the Analyzed Industry is five times the average; 50 means that the Analyzed Industry is half the national average. The abbreviation 'na' is used to show that data are 'not available'.

LEADING COMPANIES

Number shown: **50** Total sales ($ mil): **25,724** Total employment (000): **207.1**

Company Name	Address				CEO Name	Phone	Co. Type	Sales ($ mil)	Empl. (000)
Staples Inc.	PO Box 9328	Framingham	MA	01701	Thomas G Stemberg	508-370-8500	P	3,968	25.0
OfficeMax Inc.	PO Box 22500	Cleveland	OH	44122	Michael Feuer	216-921-6900	P	2,542	19.3
Intimate Brands Inc.	PO Box 1600	Columbus	OH	43216	Leslie H Wexner	614-479-7000	P	2,517	30.8
Computer City	2000 Two Tandy	Fort Worth	TX	76102	Nathan Morton	817-390-3000	D	1,904	7.0
CellStar Corp.	1730 Briercroft Ct	Carrollton	TX	75006	Alan H Goldfield	214-323-0600	P	1,483	1.0
Sally Beauty Company Inc.	PO Box 490	Denton	TX	76202	Michael H Renzulli	940-565-1111	S	1,291 *	8.0
Danka Industries Inc.	11201 Danka Cir N	St. Petersburg	FL	33716	Dan Doyle	813-576-6003	P	1,200	20.0
PETsMART Inc.	10000 N 31st Ave	Phoenix	AZ	85051	Mark S Hansen	602-944-7070	P	1,031	11.0
MTS Inc.	2500 Del Monte St	W. Sacramento	CA	95691	Russell Solomon	916-373-2500	R	995 *	7.0
Forever Living Products Intern.	PO Box 29041	Phoenix	AZ	85038	Rex Maughan	602-998-8888	R	939 *	0.9
General Host Corp.	PO Box 10045	Stamford	CT	06904	Harris J Ashton	203-357-9900	P	597	7.2
Sunglass Hut International Inc.	255 Alhambra Cir	Coral Gables	FL	33134	John X Watson	305-461-6100	P	582	8.1
Follett College Stores Co.	400 W Grand Ave	Elmhurst	IL	60126	James Bauman	630-279-2330	S	580	5.0
Petroleum Heat and Power	PO Box 1457	Stamford	CT	06904	Irik P Sevin	203-325-5400	P	548	2.2
Claire's Stores Inc.	3 SW 129th Ave	Pembroke Pines	FL	33027	Rowland Schaefer	954-433-3900	P	500	8.5
CPI Corp.	1706 Washington	St. Louis	MO	63103	Alyn V Essman	314-231-1575	P	467	7.9
Sotheby's Holdings Inc.	500 N Woodward	Bloomfield Hills	MI	48304	Diana D Brooks	810-646-2400	P	337	1.7
Nextel Communications Inc.	1505 Farm Credit	McLean	VA	22102	Daniel F Akerson	703-394-3000	P	333	3.6
Blyth Industries Inc.	100 Field Point Rd	Greenwich	CT	06830	Robert B Goergen	203-661-1926	P	331	2.1
MG Industries	3 Great Val Pkwy	Malvern	PA	19355	James Doerr	610-695-7400	S	300 *	1.2
Petco Animal Supplies Inc.	9125 Rehco Rd	San Diego	CA	92121	Brian K Devine	619-453-7845	P	270	4.0
Southwestern Bell Telecom	1000 Des Peres Rd	St. Louis	MO	63131	Dick Moore	314-822-6900	S	240 *	0.9
Veterinary Centers of America	3420 Ocean Pk Blvd	Santa Monica	CA	90405	Robert L Antin	310-392-9599	P	182	2.4
Leslie's Poolmart Inc.	20222 Plummer St	Chatsworth	CA	91311	Brian P McDermott	818-993-4212	P	163	1.4
Sound Advice Inc.	1901 Tigertail Blvd	Dania	FL	33004	Peter Beshouri	954-922-4434	P	156	0.6
UETA Inc.	3407 Northeast	San Antonio	TX	78212	Ramon Bosquez	210-828-8382	S	145	0.6
Cosmetic Center Inc.	8839 Greenwood Pl	Savage	MD	20763	Mark S Weinstein	301-497-6800	P	132	1.7
Orscheln Farm & Home Supply	101 W Coates St	Moberly	MO	65270	Terry Shoenberger	816-263-4335	R	130 *	0.8
Hot Topic	3410 Pomona Blvd	Pomona	CA	91768	Orv Madden	909-869-6373		122 *	1.5
Funco Inc.	10120 West 76th St	Minneapolis	MN	55344	David R Pomije	612-946-8883	P	121	0.9
Garden Botanika Inc.	8624 154th Ave NE	Redmond	WA	98052	Michael W Luse	206-881-9603	P	115	2.5
Standard Brands Paint Co.	4300 W 190th St	Torrance	CA	90509	Ronald A Scharman	310-214-2411	P	112	0.9
Yankee Candle Company Inc.	PO Box 110	S. Deerfield	MA	01373	Michael Perry	413-665-8306	R	110 *	1.3
B.J. Alan Co.	555 ML King	Youngstown	OH	44502	Bruce Zoldan	216-746-1064	R	110	0.3
Miles Farm Supply Inc.	2760 Keller Rd	Owensboro	KY	42301	Billy J Miles	502-926-2420	R	109	0.5
AMMEX Tax & Duty Free	63 Copps Hill Rd	Ridgefield	CT	06877	Al Carfora	203-431-6057	S	100 *	0.4
Fenton Hill American Ltd.	JFK Int Airport	Jamaica	NY	11430	Carl Reimerdes	718-656-3000	S	100 *	0.4
Magnifique Parfumes	11701 NW 101st Rd	Miami	FL	33178	Marc Finer	305-889-1600	S	93	1.1
Dupey Management Corp.	9015 Sterling St	Irving	TX	75063	Michael Dupey	214-929-8595	R	85	1.7
Ashcraft's Market Inc.	260 Oak St	Harrison	MI	48625	Daniel C Ashcraft	517-539-6001	R	78 *	0.9
Butterfield and Butterfield	220 San Bruno Ave	San Francisco	CA	94103	Bernard Osher	415-861-7500	R	70	0.2
Calico Corners	203 Gale Ln	Kennett Square	PA	19348	Bert Kerstetter	215-444-9700	D	67 *	0.6
Charrette Corp.	31 Olympia Ave	Woburn	MA	01888	Lionel Spiro	617-935-6000	R	65	0.7
Faber Enterprises Inc.	100 S Wacker Dr	Chicago	IL	60606	Ed Steiner	312-558-8900	S	65 *	1.1
Hickory Tech Corp.	PO Box 3248	Mankato	MN	56002	Robert D Alton Jr	507-387-3355	P	63	0.4
H.H. West Co.	505 N 22nd St	Milwaukee	WI	53233	Marvin Cooper	414-344-1000	S	58	0.3
Woodworker's Supply Inc.	1108 N Glenn Rd	Casper	WY	82601	John Wirth Jr	307-237-5528	R	56 *	0.2
Successories Inc.	2520 Diehl Rd	Aurora	IL	60504	Arnold M Anderson	630-820-7200	P	56	0.6
Freeman Gas and Electric	PO Box 4366	Spartanburg	SC	29305	James R Freeman Jr	803-582-5475	R	55 *	0.1
Love Store	4 E 62nd St	New York	NY	10021	Marvin Putter	212-486-0700	R	55	0.8

Source: *Ward's Business Directory of U.S. Private and Public Companies*, 1998. The company type code used is as follows: P - Public, R - Private, S - Subsidiary, D - Division, J - Joint Venture, A - Affiliate, G - Group. Sales are in millions of dollars, employees are in thousands. An asterisk (*) indicates an estimated sales volume. The symbol < stands for 'less than'.

OCCUPATIONS EMPLOYED BY SIC 599 - USED MERCHANDISE AND RETAIL STORES, NEC

Occupation	% of Total 1996	Change to 2006	Occupation	% of Total 1996	Change to 2006
Salespersons, retail	27.9	20.9	General office clerks	2.6	-2.3
Designers, except interior designers	9.5	24.9	Assemblers, fabricators, hand workers nec	2.1	13.5
General managers & top executives	7.0	10.0	Secretaries, except legal & medical	1.4	-9.9
Marketing & sales worker supervisors	6.1	13.5	Optical goods workers, precision	1.3	13.5
Stock clerks	5.8	8.9	Purchasing managers	1.3	2.2
Cashiers	4.8	14.9	Wholesale & retail buyers, except farm products	1.2	-6.0
Opticians, dispensing & measuring	4.5	13.5	Order fillers, wholesale & retail sales	1.2	13.5
Truck drivers light & heavy	4.3	13.5	Gardeners, nursery workers	1.1	13.5
Sales & related workers nec	2.7	24.9	Freight, stock, & material movers, hand	1.1	2.2
Bookkeeping, accounting, & auditing clerks	2.6	-9.2			

Source: *Industry-Occupation Matrix*, Bureau of Labor Statistics. These data relate to one or more 3-digit SIC industry groups rather than to a single 4-digit SIC. The change reported for each occupation to the year 2006 is a percent of growth or decline as estimated by the Bureau of Labor Statistics. The abbreviation nec stands for 'not elsewhere classified'.

STATE AND REGIONAL CONCENTRATION

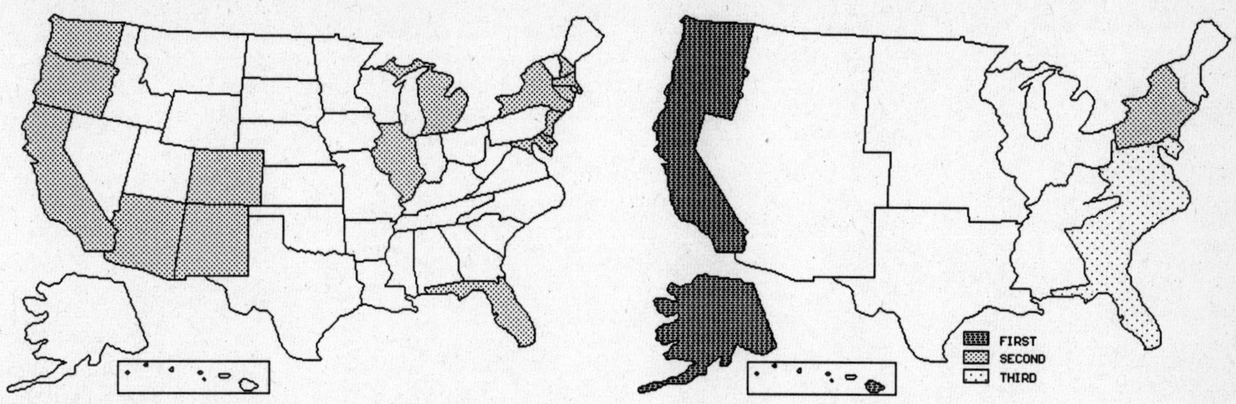

INDUSTRY DATA BY STATE

State	Establishments - 1995		Employment - 1995			Payroll - 1995		Sales - 1992		
	Total (number)	% of U.S.	Total (number)	% of U.S.	Per Estab.	Total ($ mil.)	Per Empl. ($)	Total ($ mil.)	% of U.S.	Per Estab ($)
California	5,615	11.9	29,169	12.4	5	482.3	16,535	2,169.2	15.1	92,838
New York	3,119	6.6	15,020	6.4	5	309.0	20,571	1,510.7	10.5	138,023
Florida	3,753	7.9	17,819	7.6	5	281.8	15,817	1,030.9	7.2	86,781
Texas	3,102	6.6	16,586	7.1	5	257.6	15,534	962.9	6.7	90,270
Illinois	2,108	4.5	12,461	5.3	6	206.4	16,561	716.1	5.0	85,940
Pennsylvania	1,967	4.2	10,085	4.3	5	165.6	16,422	627.2	4.4	79,683
Michigan	1,523	3.2	9,273	3.9	6	154.3	16,640	557.7	3.9	83,541
Ohio	1,929	4.1	10,051	4.3	5	154.5	15,368	555.7	3.9	76,122
New Jersey	1,387	2.9	7,147	3.0	5	128.1	17,917	502.9	3.5	97,269
Massachusetts	1,020	2.2	4,775	2.0	5	89.0	18,630	369.0	2.6	93,015
Arizona	944	2.0	4,759	2.0	5	76.7	16,113	340.0	2.4	102,585
Georgia	1,213	2.6	5,868	2.5	5	89.6	15,261	334.4	2.3	84,841
Washington	1,053	2.2	5,369	2.3	5	83.9	15,623	326.4	2.3	78,187
Colorado	1,053	2.2	4,740	2.0	5	77.1	16,256	305.4	2.1	93,435
Maryland	955	2.0	5,772	2.5	6	88.9	15,397	291.5	2.0	67,597
Virginia	1,065	2.3	5,698	2.4	5	80.8	14,188	269.9	1.9	68,112
Missouri	965	2.0	4,649	2.0	5	70.3	15,132	259.7	1.8	73,236
Indiana	991	2.1	4,756	2.0	5	66.1	13,894	243.3	1.7	71,244
Wisconsin	857	1.8	4,540	1.9	5	70.1	15,448	239.5	1.7	71,727
North Carolina	1,199	2.5	5,063	2.2	4	71.3	14,076	236.6	1.6	68,113
Minnesota	825	1.7	4,537	1.9	5	64.4	14,203	221.0	1.5	71,154
Tennessee	927	2.0	3,744	1.6	4	58.9	15,730	199.0	1.4	77,165
Connecticut	588	1.2	3,104	1.3	5	57.8	18,626	198.0	1.4	100,638
Louisiana	639	1.4	2,767	1.2	4	41.1	14,870	185.5	1.3	80,685
Oregon	613	1.3	3,010	1.3	5	45.0	14,935	185.0	1.3	80,347
New Mexico	505	1.1	2,043	0.9	4	33.0	16,167	170.6	1.2	126,175
Oklahoma	530	1.1	2,592	1.1	5	37.5	14,487	152.0	1.1	78,009
Alabama	655	1.4	2,873	1.2	4	39.3	13,675	147.8	1.0	68,442
South Carolina	627	1.3	2,563	1.1	4	37.0	14,435	145.5	1.0	74,901
Kentucky	542	1.1	2,509	1.1	5	34.9	13,906	128.6	0.9	74,658
Iowa	485	1.0	2,131	0.9	4	29.9	14,034	112.4	0.8	67,328
Kansas	478	1.0	2,370	1.0	5	32.5	13,719	106.9	0.7	73,194
Utah	346	0.7	1,911	0.8	6	26.7	13,993	75.4	0.5	68,118
New Hampshire	257	0.5	1,187	0.5	5	21.0	17,656	74.6	0.5	88,713
Arkansas	368	0.8	1,319	0.6	4	18.5	14,001	66.8	0.5	66,552
Mississippi	340	0.7	1,299	0.6	4	16.8	12,946	65.5	0.5	63,472
Nebraska	266	0.6	1,121	0.5	4	14.4	12,872	64.6	0.4	65,943
West Virginia	238	0.5	942	0.4	4	13.5	14,340	53.1	0.4	61,700
Maine	259	0.5	797	0.3	3	12.0	15,036	52.4	0.4	86,118
Delaware	150	0.3	766	0.3	5	14.5	18,932	51.8	0.4	90,157
Rhode Island	139	0.3	619	0.3	4	10.4	16,800	41.4	0.3	82,214
Montana	217	0.5	702	0.3	3	10.0	14,278	37.2	0.3	73,100
Wyoming	118	0.2	348	0.1	3	4.7	13,618	23.2	0.2	82,266
Nevada	299	0.6	1,794	0.8	6	31.6	17,601	(D)	-	-
Hawaii	235	0.5	1,346	0.6	6	24.4	18,125	(D)	-	-
Idaho	222	0.5	921	0.4	4	12.5	13,529	(D)	-	-
Vermont	134	0.3	478	0.2	4	8.7	18,282	(D)	-	-
Alaska	121	0.3	421	0.2	3	8.3	19,663	(D)	-	-
South Dakota	116	0.2	371	0.2	3	5.3	14,162	(D)	-	-
North Dakota	110	0.2	543	0.2	5	8.2	15,182	(D)	-	-
D.C.	105	0.2	523	0.2	5	10.6	20,258	(D)	-	-

Source: County Business Patterns, 1995 and *Economic Census of the U.S., 1992*. Data are sorted by 1992 revenues and, if revenues are unavailable, by establishments in 1995. The symbol (D) indicates that data are withheld by the source to avoid disclosure of competitive information. A dash (-) indicates that data are not available or undisclosed because they do not meet statistical validity standards. Shaded *states* on the state map indicate those states which have proportionately greater representation in the industry than would be indicated by the state's population; the ratio is based on total revenues or number of establishments. Shaded *regions* indicate where the industry is regionally most concentrated.

Part II

METROPOLITAN AREA DATA

ABILENE, TX MSA

Wholesale and Retail Trade USA	Establishments		Employment		Emp / Est	Pay / Employee		Annual Payroll ($ 000)	
	1994	1995	1994	1995	1995	1994	1995	1994	1995
50 – Wholesale trade	-	270	-	2,359	9	-	21,911	-	53,643
5012 Automobiles and other vehicles	-	4	-	66	17	-	27,515	-	1,854
5013 Motor vehicle supplies and new parts	-	18	-	78	4	-	18,308	-	1,416
5015 Motor vehicle parts, used	-	9	-	39	4	-	13,641	-	547
5020 Furniture and homefurnishings	-	4	-	23	6	-	18,261	-	405
5039 Construction materials, nec	-	3	-	33	11	-	26,788	-	746
5044 Office equipment	-	9	-	66	7	-	17,212	-	1,030
5045 Computers, peripherals, & software	-	11	-	85	8	-	30,871	-	3,130
5046 Commercial equipment, nec	-	4	-	39	10	-	14,872	-	544
5047 Medical and hospital equipment	-	5	-	62	12	-	25,097	-	1,434
5063 Electrical apparatus and equipment	-	7	-	58	8	-	24,138	-	1,700
5074 Plumbing & hydronic heating supplies	-	5	-	45	9	-	25,244	-	1,028
5075 Warm air heating & air conditioning	-	4	-	40	10	-	14,100	-	627
5082 Construction and mining machinery	-	7	-	91	13	-	31,648	-	2,935
5083 Farm and garden machinery	-	8	-	64	8	-	20,750	-	1,486
5084 Industrial machinery and equipment	-	34	-	154	5	-	23,870	-	3,898
5085 Industrial supplies	-	5	-	33	7	-	22,061	-	632
5087 Service establishment equipment	-	8	-	77	10	-	14,494	-	1,111
5090 Miscellaneous durable goods	-	9	-	146	16	-	19,205	-	2,736
5120 Drugs, proprietaries, and sundries	-	5	-	26	5	-	41,846	-	1,094
5130 Apparel, piece goods, and notions	-	4	-	33	8	-	15,394	-	735
5149 Groceries and related products, nec	-	5	-	167	33	-	23,521	-	4,415
5154 Livestock	-	4	-	65	16	-	8,062	-	462
5169 Chemicals & allied products, nec	-	7	-	55	8	-	21,964	-	1,318
5171 Petroleum bulk stations & terminals	-	10	-	102	10	-	32,902	-	3,183
5172 Petroleum products, nec	-	11	-	95	9	-	23,621	-	2,525
5180 Beer, wine, and distilled beverages	-	3	-	64	21	-	24,250	-	1,431
5190 Misc., nondurable goods	-	12	-	110	9	-	20,655	-	2,387
52 – Retail trade	-	879	-	10,674	12	-	12,747	-	145,461
5210 Lumber and other building materials	-	17	-	233	14	-	20,773	-	6,557
5230 Paint, glass, and wallpaper stores	-	5	-	42	8	-	19,429	-	860
5260 Retail nurseries and garden stores	-	5	-	65	13	-	9,723	-	708
5310 Department stores	-	8	-	1,223	153	-	12,500	-	15,551
5330 Variety stores	-	5	-	24	5	-	8,167	-	247
5390 Misc. general merchandise stores	-	12	-	284	24	-	14,887	-	3,999
5410 Grocery stores	-	63	-	1,169	19	-	13,896	-	18,280
5460 Retail bakeries	-	12	-	71	6	-	8,676	-	672
5510 New and used car dealers	-	12	-	552	46	-	32,471	-	20,160
5520 Used car dealers	-	26	-	126	5	-	19,714	-	2,782
5530 Auto and home supply stores	-	26	-	214	8	-	16,822	-	3,678
5540 Gasoline service stations	-	85	-	482	6	-	11,851	-	5,693
5550 Boat dealers	-	4	-	27	7	-	15,111	-	484
5610 Men's & boys' clothing stores	-	4	-	29	7	-	10,345	-	283
5620 Women's clothing stores	-	28	-	210	8	-	7,219	-	1,481
5630 Women's accessory & specialty stores	-	4	-	15	4	-	6,133	-	104
5640 Children's and infants' wear stores	-	4	-	16	4	-	6,750	-	111
5650 Family clothing stores	-	12	-	148	12	-	9,676	-	1,418
5660 Shoe stores	-	14	-	72	5	-	12,444	-	921
5690 Misc. apparel & accessory stores	-	3	-	17	6	-	9,647	-	150
5712 Furniture stores	-	15	-	133	9	-	20,331	-	2,757
5713 Floor covering stores	-	12	-	58	5	-	18,069	-	1,143
5719 Misc. homefurnishings stores	-	6	-	34	6	-	14,353	-	449
5720 Household appliance stores	-	4	-	17	4	-	22,353	-	369
5731 Radio, TV, & electronic stores	-	15	-	54	4	-	16,963	-	829
5735 Record & prerecorded tape stores	-	5	-	75	15	-	8,320	-	574
5812 Eating places	-	174	-	3,469	20	-	8,071	-	29,686
5813 Drinking places	-	17	-	193	11	-	6,010	-	1,226
5910 Drug stores and proprietary stores	-	22	-	249	11	-	15,229	-	3,459
5920 Liquor stores	-	11	-	139	13	-	15,309	-	2,182
5930 Used merchandise stores	-	23	-	87	4	-	10,115	-	912
5941 Sporting goods and bicycle shops	-	19	-	100	5	-	18,600	-	1,627
5944 Jewelry stores	-	14	-	83	6	-	17,976	-	1,389
5945 Hobby, toy, and game shops	-	11	-	88	8	-	10,364	-	990
5947 Gift, novelty, and souvenir shops	-	16	-	66	4	-	7,455	-	537
5949 Sewing, needlework, and piece goods	-	3	-	23	8	-	9,043	-	195
5963 Direct selling establishments	-	10	-	31	3	-	25,548	-	938
5992 Florists	-	13	-	39	3	-	7,897	-	321
5995 Optical goods stores	-	12	-	63	5	-	13,397	-	940
5999 Miscellaneous retail stores, nec	-	33	-	147	4	-	11,129	-	1,896

Source: County Business Patterns 1994/95, CBP-94/95, U.S. Department of Commerce, Washington DC, November 1997. The employment column represents mid-March employment in the year. Pay per employee is calculated by dividing 1st Quarter payroll, annualized, by mid-March employment. The column headed 'Emp / Est' shows 'employees per establishment'. A dash (-) means that data are unavailable or cannot be calculated. nec means not elsewhere classified. *Notes:* 1. 1994 data incomplete; unavailable or withheld. 2. 1995 data incomplete; unavailable or withheld. 3. 1994 and 1995 data incomplete; unavailable or withheld.

AKRON, OH PMSA

Wholesale and Retail Trade USA	Establishments		Employment		Emp / Est	Pay / Employee		Annual Payroll ($ 000)	
	1994	1995	1994	1995	1995	1994	1995	1994	1995
50- Wholesale trade	1,326	1,366	18,510	19,765	14	31,479	33,526	624,747	690,569
5012 Automobiles and other vehicles	15	17	362	333	20	15,249	22,030	6,252	7,370
5013 Motor vehicle supplies and new parts	69	65	634	601	9	24,000	25,231	16,338	15,139
5014 Tires and tubes	25	19	467	376	20	39,632	55,074	18,684	19,421
5015 Motor vehicle parts, used	18	22	123	185	8	23,805	20,843	3,204	3,929
5021 Furniture	18	22	373	204	9	22,660	26,216	9,870	7,141
5023 Homefurnishings [3]	14	13	189	181	14	22,265	24,530	4,766	5,561
5031 Lumber, plywood, and millwork	20	16	269	222	14	30,706	33,766	8,023	6,549
5032 Brick, stone, & related materials	11	18	62	119	7	24,581	22,353	1,840	2,872
5033 Roofing, siding, & insulation [3]	12	19	192	256	13	29,729	36,922	6,680	10,594
5039 Construction materials, nec	15	14	61	92	7	20,656	25,087	1,827	2,586
5044 Office equipment	21	20	164	193	10	20,390	23,233	4,589	6,163
5045 Computers, peripherals, & software	39	35	300	280	8	53,627	55,700	14,383	14,726
5046 Commercial equipment, nec [3]	13	14	116	134	10	25,207	26,478	3,027	3,776
5047 Medical and hospital equipment	46	39	520	501	13	39,431	38,786	21,534	20,955
5051 Metals service centers and offices	54	52	805	834	16	32,651	37,986	29,063	31,891
5063 Electrical apparatus and equipment	57	45	528	422	9	32,992	35,185	17,499	14,695
5064 Electrical appliances, TV & radios [3]	8	7	278	283	40	28,460	32,057	9,353	10,899
5065 Electronic parts and equipment	43	53	379	443	8	26,776	32,262	13,111	17,048
5072 Hardware [3]	24	23	185	185	8	24,519	36,627	6,068	8,596
5074 Plumbing & hydronic heating supplies	23	25	167	161	6	28,719	30,683	5,614	5,709
5075 Warm air heating & air conditioning	11	11	71	60	5	26,761	30,000	1,928	1,890
5078 Refrigeration equipment and supplies [3]	4	4	16	15	4	27,000	36,267	529	569
5082 Construction and mining machinery [2]	-	15	-	203	14	-	33,399	-	8,174
5083 Farm and garden machinery	-	7	-	56	8	-	28,357	-	1,802
5084 Industrial machinery and equipment	-	143	-	1,628	11	-	33,283	-	59,216
5085 Industrial supplies	-	70	-	694	10	-	33,452	-	25,320
5087 Service establishment equipment	-	16	-	241	15	-	23,618	-	6,161
5088 Transportation equipment & supplies	-	6	-	9	2	-	21,333	-	216
5091 Sporting & recreational goods	-	19	-	186	10	-	23,677	-	4,866
5092 Toys and hobby goods and supplies	-	7	-	66	9	-	21,758	-	1,342
5093 Scrap and waste materials	-	31	-	754	24	-	30,838	-	23,987
5094 Jewelry & precious stones	-	9	-	35	4	-	20,686	-	908
5099 Durable goods, nec [2]	-	46	-	126	3	-	18,190	-	2,712
5111 Printing and writing paper	-	7	-	50	7	-	49,200	-	2,924
5112 Stationery and office supplies	-	20	-	549	27	-	20,459	-	11,342
5113 Industrial & personal service paper	-	10	-	82	8	-	26,293	-	2,090
5120 Drugs, proprietaries, and sundries [2]	-	8	-	115	14	-	30,191	-	3,224
5131 Piece goods & notions [2]	-	9	-	92	10	-	37,174	-	3,138
5136 Men's and boys' clothing [2]	-	10	-	33	3	-	17,939	-	836
5137 Women's and children's clothing [2]	-	6	-	12	2	-	11,667	-	297
5141 Groceries, general line [2]	-	11	-	379	34	-	21,045	-	8,548
5142 Packaged frozen food [2]	-	4	-	269	67	-	27,703	-	7,494
5144 Poultry and poultry products [2]	-	4	-	361	90	-	20,222	-	7,908
5145 Confectionery [2]	-	9	-	185	21	-	22,659	-	4,233
5148 Fresh fruits and vegetables	-	13	-	224	17	-	19,571	-	4,681
5149 Groceries and related products, nec [2]	-	19	-	487	26	-	23,170	-	12,563
5162 Plastics materials & basic shapes	-	27	-	322	12	-	36,497	-	12,554
5169 Chemicals & allied products, nec	-	53	-	797	15	-	56,893	-	46,095
5171 Petroleum bulk stations & terminals	-	11	-	129	12	-	36,806	-	4,498
5172 Petroleum products, nec	-	8	-	45	6	-	32,178	-	1,033
5180 Beer, wine, and distilled beverages	-	6	-	203	34	-	40,946	-	10,206
5191 Farm supplies	-	17	-	81	5	-	16,938	-	1,923
5192 Books, periodicals, & newspapers	-	11	-	237	22	-	11,544	-	2,980
5193 Flowers & florists' supplies [2]	-	8	-	71	9	-	17,972	-	1,408
5198 Paints, varnishes, and supplies	-	7	-	39	6	-	29,231	-	1,317
5199 Nondurable goods, nec	-	63	-	548	9	-	18,847	-	10,718
52- Retail trade	3,896	3,892	62,716	62,401	16	12,034	13,405	838,515	877,340
5210 Lumber and other building materials	72	57	2,979	1,435	25	19,872	21,305	59,281	32,940
5230 Paint, glass, and wallpaper stores	28	26	102	107	4	15,373	17,234	1,759	2,070
5250 Hardware stores	39	28	393	312	11	10,198	11,538	4,652	3,752
5260 Retail nurseries and garden stores	24	26	185	188	7	10,422	13,383	3,302	3,589
5310 Department stores [1]	25	27	4,503	4,151	154	9,767	12,556	48,274	56,475
5330 Variety stores	37	31	308	323	10	8,870	9,139	3,123	3,211
5390 Misc. general merchandise stores	18	21	787	778	37	11,024	12,756	10,380	9,269
5410 Grocery stores	247	247	7,702	7,067	29	13,355	14,832	110,859	102,665
5420 Meat and fish markets	18	16	91	89	6	11,912	12,764	1,279	1,240
5430 Fruit and vegetable markets	8	8	20	24	3	9,800	11,500	849	892
5440 Candy, nut, and confectionery stores	23	19	119	113	6	7,126	6,761	884	731
5450 Dairy products stores	8	7	24	16	2	4,167	5,500	100	101
5460 Retail bakeries	52	51	385	396	8	8,197	8,010	3,294	3,448

Continued on next page.

AKRON, OH PMSA - [continued]

Wholesale and Retail Trade USA	Establishments		Employment		Emp / Est	Pay / Employee		Annual Payroll ($ 000)	
	1994	1995	1994	1995	1995	1994	1995	1994	1995
5490 Miscellaneous food stores	17	16	143	160	10	8,392	8,925	1,383	1,451
5510 New and used car dealers	61	63	2,641	2,798	44	25,443	27,385	77,986	82,969
5520 Used car dealers	48	50	228	280	6	17,772	19,271	5,278	6,576
5530 Auto and home supply stores	113	113	855	868	8	18,250	19,733	17,195	17,776
5540 Gasoline service stations	258	251	1,897	1,793	7	9,246	10,985	18,630	20,832
5550 Boat dealers	8	9	30	32	4	11,733	13,500	483	621
5560 Recreational vehicle dealers	10	10	113	124	12	19,788	21,548	2,978	3,280
5570 Motorcycle dealers	5	6	20	23	4	17,600	17,739	401	602
5610 Men's & boys' clothing stores	36	36	273	312	9	10,198	10,795	3,213	3,487
5620 Women's clothing stores	117	101	1,098	971	10	7,228	7,073	8,589	7,350
5630 Women's accessory & specialty stores	18	16	99	103	6	7,556	8,233	839	875
5640 Children's and infants' wear stores	12	9	96	79	9	6,792	8,000	695	593
5650 Family clothing stores	35	36	455	523	15	8,782	9,920	4,417	5,312
5660 Shoe stores	96	90	557	517	6	10,786	10,329	6,207	5,286
5690 Misc. apparel & accessory stores	21	22	57	74	3	8,772	9,027	699	1,066
5712 Furniture stores	77	82	646	764	9	16,718	17,393	12,071	14,045
5713 Floor covering stores	33	34	155	167	5	18,529	19,737	3,321	3,742
5714 Drapery and upholstery stores	9	9	36	37	4	12,111	13,405	480	522
5719 Misc. homefurnishings stores	48	42	298	183	4	13,128	14,142	3,074	2,471
5720 Household appliance stores	21	20	112	114	6	18,607	20,667	2,382	2,342
5731 Radio, TV, & electronic stores	31	35	358	395	11	18,480	18,623	4,921	7,585
5734 Computer and software stores	12	15	63	49	3	19,302	20,408	1,636	1,117
5735 Record & prerecorded tape stores[3]	14	16	95	109	7	8,211	9,908	938	1,010
5736 Musical instrument stores	13	13	130	142	11	16,154	17,324	2,413	2,887
5812 Eating places	953	903	21,449	21,583	24	7,115	7,400	168,343	168,486
5813 Drinking places	221	205	1,053	954	5	6,443	7,027	7,078	6,779
5910 Drug stores and proprietary stores	111	111	1,806	1,901	17	13,037	13,738	26,033	28,214
5920 Liquor stores	57	54	246	218	4	9,740	11,211	2,353	2,472
5930 Used merchandise stores	43	42	330	298	7	8,242	8,711	2,910	3,455
5941 Sporting goods and bicycle shops	54	55	314	364	7	11,363	11,308	4,430	5,318
5942 Book stores	33	29	255	265	9	7,200	8,528	1,913	2,622
5943 Stationery stores	5	5	10	12	2	6,400	12,333	78	118
5944 Jewelry stores	68	66	537	542	8	14,853	15,749	8,277	8,503
5945 Hobby, toy, and game shops	28	29	260	277	10	9,200	9,069	3,351	2,896
5946 Camera & photographic supply stores	10	8	51	47	6	13,412	15,489	723	766
5947 Gift, novelty, and souvenir shops	84	85	514	515	6	7,175	7,619	4,056	4,458
5949 Sewing, needlework, and piece goods	25	18	194	155	9	6,082	6,426	1,044	1,063
5961 Catalog and mail-order houses	18	23	629	1,099	48	26,970	25,343	18,410	28,631
5962 Merchandising machine operators	21	25	408	412	16	12,461	13,350	5,310	5,672
5963 Direct selling establishments	39	41	250	257	6	12,528	13,556	4,060	3,702
5980 Fuel dealers	8	9	65	76	8	24,677	26,000	1,518	1,838
5992 Florists	69	71	278	336	5	8,748	9,143	2,598	3,106
5993 Tobacco stores and stands[2]	-	3	-	10	3	-	4,000	-	83
5995 Optical goods stores	41	38	207	199	5	15,343	16,020	3,331	3,214
5999 Miscellaneous retail stores, nec	103	126	534	614	5	12,240	12,684	8,113	8,808

Source: County Business Patterns 1994/95, CBP-94/95, U.S. Department of Commerce, Washington DC, November 1997. The employment column represents mid-March employment in the year. Pay per employee is calculated by dividing 1st Quarter payroll, annualized, by mid-March employment. The column headed 'Emp / Est' shows 'employees per establishment'. A dash (-) means that data are unavailable or cannot be calculated. nec means not elsewhere classified. *Notes:* 1. 1994 data incomplete; unavailable or withheld. 2. 1995 data incomplete; unavailable or withheld. 3. 1994 and 1995 data incomplete; unavailable or withheld.

ALBANY, GA MSA

Wholesale and Retail Trade USA	Establishments		Employment		Emp / Est	Pay / Employee		Annual Payroll ($ 000)	
	1994	1995	1994	1995	1995	1994	1995	1994	1995
50- Wholesale trade	261	260	2,800	2,885	11	23,380	25,432	70,480	79,714
5012 Automobiles and other vehicles[3]	6	6	224	223	37	16,500	18,314	3,939	4,297
5013 Motor vehicle supplies and new parts	27	24	167	184	8	24,886	21,239	4,064	4,228
5031 Lumber, plywood, and millwork[2]	-	5	-	47	9	-	21,787	-	1,026
5044 Office equipment[3]	9	12	49	107	9	26,531	31,252	1,338	3,360
5045 Computers, peripherals, & software[3]	7	4	48	48	12	26,167	27,333	1,486	1,800
5046 Commercial equipment, nec[3]	5	5	67	80	16	24,119	23,900	2,220	3,213
5047 Medical and hospital equipment[3]	4	4	23	22	6	29,739	28,909	749	640
5063 Electrical apparatus and equipment[3]	8	8	60	71	9	28,400	37,239	1,873	2,482
5064 Electrical appliances, TV & radios[1]	3	-	13	-	-	12,000	-	117	-
5065 Electronic parts and equipment[1]	6	-	20	-	-	24,600	-	521	-
5075 Warm air heating & air conditioning[3]	5	5	28	29	6	27,000	25,655	749	840
5082 Construction and mining machinery[3]	4	6	167	192	32	31,018	34,979	5,835	8,143
5083 Farm and garden machinery	9	7	72	60	9	22,389	28,867	1,533	1,612
5084 Industrial machinery and equipment[3]	16	16	182	174	11	26,088	30,690	5,270	5,759

Continued on next page.

ALBANY, GA MSA - [continued]

Wholesale and Retail Trade USA	Establishments		Employment		Emp / Est	Pay / Employee		Annual Payroll ($ 000)	
	1994	1995	1994	1995	1995	1994	1995	1994	1995
5085 Industrial supplies[3]	17	16	120	120	8	24,000	26,767	3,500	3,580
5087 Service establishment equipment[3]	5	6	20	18	3	11,200	11,333	329	383
5091 Sporting & recreational goods[3]	3	4	20	21	5	19,000	21,714	508	551
5093 Scrap and waste materials[1]	4	-	4	-	-	9,000	-	49	-
5110 Paper and paper products[3]	7	6	104	71	12	29,346	35,718	2,902	2,310
5120 Drugs, proprietaries, and sundries[1]	4	-	11	-	-	15,273	-	250	-
5149 Groceries and related products, nec[3]	6	5	179	180	36	18,726	21,578	3,559	4,016
5159 Farm-product raw materials, nec[1]	3	-	21	-	-	55,810	-	1,346	-
5160 Chemicals and allied products[3]	8	9	67	73	8	21,731	20,493	1,527	1,822
5170 Petroleum and petroleum products	11	11	98	99	9	24,000	24,202	2,114	2,140
5181 Beer and ale[3]	3	3	136	131	44	21,912	24,794	3,462	3,536
5182 Wine and distilled beverages[3]	4	4	114	120	30	28,386	29,533	3,243	3,567
5191 Farm supplies	12	13	81	103	8	24,247	22,524	2,143	2,551
5193 Flowers & florists' supplies[3]	3	4	36	30	8	16,000	19,600	617	467
5199 Nondurable goods, nec[1]	6	7	80	40	6	8,750	17,500	738	758
52- Retail trade	773	750	10,320	10,614	14	10,734	11,682	120,667	129,284
5210 Lumber and other building materials[1]	14	13	280	252	19	18,943	23,810	5,966	6,588
5230 Paint, glass, and wallpaper stores[1]	7	-	39	-	-	17,333	-	753	-
5260 Retail nurseries and garden stores	7	7	43	65	9	9,674	13,292	585	794
5270 Mobile home dealers[2]	-	6	-	58	10	-	17,586	-	937
5310 Department stores[3]	8	8	1,331	1,251	156	10,431	11,853	14,415	15,100
5410 Grocery stores	70	68	1,681	1,482	22	9,218	10,896	15,585	17,224
5460 Retail bakeries[3]	8	5	27	21	4	7,259	10,667	235	307
5490 Miscellaneous food stores[3]	3	4	15	8	2	7,467	12,500	106	111
5510 New and used car dealers[3]	10	10	396	406	41	26,970	27,951	11,385	12,628
5520 Used car dealers[1]	19	20	79	87	4	14,380	13,011	1,212	1,294
5530 Auto and home supply stores	20	24	165	247	10	14,497	18,510	2,506	4,614
5540 Gasoline service stations	54	52	314	303	6	9,401	10,469	3,104	3,504
5570 Motorcycle dealers[3]	3	3	29	27	9	16,138	18,815	558	600
5610 Men's & boys' clothing stores[3]	4	4	19	17	4	6,526	12,471	130	196
5620 Women's clothing stores	43	37	359	313	8	10,830	11,463	4,220	3,898
5650 Family clothing stores[3]	4	4	40	104	26	7,100	9,615	712	955
5660 Shoe stores[3]	28	27	126	146	5	10,444	10,904	1,587	1,697
5690 Misc. apparel & accessory stores	4	4	6	4	1	9,333	15,000	53	56
5712 Furniture stores[3]	22	20	220	242	12	16,691	19,405	4,295	4,302
5713 Floor covering stores	10	9	31	34	4	19,097	21,294	667	720
5719 Misc. homefurnishings stores[3]	10	11	45	85	8	12,711	13,412	586	968
5720 Household appliance stores[3]	3	3	33	37	12	15,030	18,162	590	668
5731 Radio, TV, & electronic stores	12	12	62	58	5	19,677	21,034	1,193	1,153
5734 Computer and software stores[2]	-	5	-	29	6	-	16,138	-	444
5735 Record & prerecorded tape stores[3]	4	5	12	18	4	16,667	14,444	207	272
5736 Musical instrument stores[2]	-	3	-	15	5	-	19,200	-	322
5812 Eating places	140	127	3,072	3,356	26	7,109	6,865	23,860	24,002
5813 Drinking places[3]	13	10	76	66	7	6,947	7,939	533	508
5910 Drug stores and proprietary stores	28	25	244	284	11	15,361	14,211	4,058	3,978
5920 Liquor stores[3]	16	19	95	87	5	12,084	12,690	1,501	1,714
5930 Used merchandise stores[3]	20	18	77	67	4	11,688	11,463	938	829
5941 Sporting goods and bicycle shops[2]	9	7	82	86	12	11,366	11,860	1,002	1,006
5942 Book stores[3]	7	6	40	26	4	6,700	6,769	250	295
5943 Stationery stores[3]	9	7	28	35	5	13,286	11,771	370	457
5944 Jewelry stores[3]	14	16	87	93	6	12,782	15,871	1,095	1,171
5945 Hobby, toy, and game shops[3]	4	4	39	40	10	10,769	11,700	547	586
5947 Gift, novelty, and souvenir shops[3]	11	11	64	57	5	5,375	6,596	431	526
5949 Sewing, needlework, and piece goods[3]	5	5	37	35	7	6,919	8,114	255	278
5963 Direct selling establishments[1]	6	-	8	-	-	10,000	-	153	-
5980 Fuel dealers	6	6	42	48	8	31,619	22,083	1,132	951
5992 Florists	18	15	55	45	3	8,145	8,800	418	390
5995 Optical goods stores[3]	7	7	38	32	5	15,053	18,375	621	637
5999 Miscellaneous retail stores, nec	17	20	52	52	3	9,692	10,077	509	585

Source: County Business Patterns 1994/95, CBP-94/95, U.S. Department of Commerce, Washington DC, November 1997. The employment column represents mid-March employment in the year. Pay per employee is calculated by dividing 1st Quarter payroll, annualized, by mid-March employment. The column headed 'Emp / Est' shows 'employees per establishment'. A dash (-) means that data are unavailable or cannot be calculated. nec means not elsewhere classified. *Notes:* 1. 1994 data incomplete; unavailable or withheld. 2. 1995 data incomplete; unavailable or withheld. 3. 1994 and 1995 data incomplete; unavailable or withheld.

ALBANY - SCHENECTADY - TROY, NY MSA

Wholesale and Retail Trade USA	Establishments		Employment		Emp / Est	Pay / Employee		Annual Payroll ($ 000)	
	1994	1995	1994	1995	1995	1994	1995	1994	1995
50 - Wholesale trade	1,337	1,322	18,039	18,782	14	30,984	32,975	585,705	629,194
5012 Automobiles and other vehicles [3]	35	37	485	561	15	20,882	22,203	10,592	13,082
5013 Motor vehicle supplies and new parts	93	85	939	859	10	21,555	24,745	21,776	20,290
5014 Tires and tubes [3]	11	9	54	52	6	27,704	24,923	1,529	1,749
5015 Motor vehicle parts, used [3]	17	19	59	104	5	17,288	17,885	1,123	1,992
5021 Furniture [3]	24	22	114	109	5	25,158	25,394	3,114	2,754
5023 Homefurnishings [3]	21	19	233	198	10	31,725	31,535	9,241	7,103
5031 Lumber, plywood, and millwork [3]	25	25	389	288	12	25,614	28,111	11,692	8,272
5032 Brick, stone, & related materials [1]	15	17	79	108	6	32,810	40,111	2,921	4,636
5033 Roofing, siding, & insulation [3]	15	14	107	112	8	32,411	36,571	4,270	4,500
5039 Construction materials, nec [3]	15	25	42	248	10	18,190	28,919	1,300	7,959
5044 Office equipment [3]	35	37	586	649	18	31,945	33,972	19,214	20,435
5045 Computers, peripherals, & software [3]	63	52	806	664	13	59,290	63,590	40,734	36,253
5046 Commercial equipment, nec [2]	-	17	-	50	3	-	23,040	-	1,262
5047 Medical and hospital equipment [3]	24	23	172	161	7	33,047	35,752	5,668	5,475
5049 Professional equipment, nec [3]	5	8	83	86	11	33,349	38,233	3,325	3,615
5051 Metals service centers and offices [3]	27	29	308	352	12	29,065	30,909	9,734	11,307
5063 Electrical apparatus and equipment	56	47	529	424	9	30,284	34,358	16,543	14,403
5064 Electrical appliances, TV & radios [3]	10	11	73	63	6	31,836	29,714	2,262	1,799
5065 Electronic parts and equipment	49	51	550	810	16	44,000	42,988	23,665	32,858
5072 Hardware [3]	18	21	174	178	8	30,943	35,618	5,283	6,443
5074 Plumbing & hydronic heating supplies [3]	40	35	280	172	5	30,643	39,070	9,339	6,591
5075 Warm air heating & air conditioning [3]	22	22	196	118	5	27,347	28,542	6,499	4,297
5078 Refrigeration equipment and supplies [3]	8	8	21	33	4	31,048	29,576	750	1,077
5082 Construction and mining machinery [3]	11	10	175	178	18	36,983	38,629	7,114	7,028
5083 Farm and garden machinery [3]	17	16	91	221	14	25,451	26,624	2,907	5,422
5084 Industrial machinery and equipment [3]	70	75	562	647	9	34,406	36,841	20,817	24,502
5085 Industrial supplies [3]	53	49	411	418	9	37,937	39,742	15,952	16,199
5087 Service establishment equipment [3]	21	23	91	101	4	21,099	19,168	1,979	2,005
5091 Sporting & recreational goods [3]	11	12	120	106	9	31,000	37,585	4,113	4,416
5092 Toys and hobby goods and supplies [3]	8	11	13	59	5	17,231	25,831	239	1,716
5093 Scrap and waste materials [1]	28	27	353	358	13	21,144	21,799	8,646	9,147
5094 Jewelry & precious stones [3]	10	8	14	8	1	15,429	18,000	219	207
5099 Durable goods, nec [3]	18	18	409	411	23	26,523	30,355	11,700	13,786
5111 Printing and writing paper [3]	6	7	95	85	12	30,568	33,976	3,015	2,976
5112 Stationery and office supplies [3]	34	32	353	292	9	20,147	23,178	7,364	6,401
5113 Industrial & personal service paper [3]	11	14	70	42	3	31,143	21,143	1,433	728
5120 Drugs, proprietaries, and sundries [3]	13	12	33	62	5	14,061	20,065	469	1,203
5130 Apparel, piece goods, and notions [3]	17	13	48	49	4	44,750	49,714	2,308	2,520
5141 Groceries, general line [3]	25	27	745	787	29	28,655	33,657	22,418	26,946
5142 Packaged frozen food [3]	12	10	111	125	13	38,991	28,064	4,684	4,088
5147 Meats and meat products [3]	12	12	145	123	10	41,572	42,927	5,984	5,119
5148 Fresh fruits and vegetables [3]	14	14	109	108	8	21,321	21,556	3,328	3,335
5149 Groceries and related products, nec [1]	54	49	1,633	1,865	38	29,661	30,662	50,210	59,077
5150 Farm-product raw materials [2]	-	6	-	23	4	-	39,478	-	1,057
5162 Plastics materials & basic shapes [3]	8	8	76	64	8	34,053	33,063	2,649	2,103
5169 Chemicals & allied products, nec [3]	28	27	135	170	6	32,681	32,847	4,499	4,842
5171 Petroleum bulk stations & terminals [1]	22	-	25	-	-	38,720	-	1,050	-
5181 Beer and ale [3]	12	10	109	53	5	35,486	27,396	3,127	1,604
5182 Wine and distilled beverages [3]	9	8	303	301	38	41,056	39,375	14,095	12,775
5191 Farm supplies [3]	33	25	142	70	3	22,000	22,743	3,259	1,677
5192 Books, periodicals, & newspapers [1]	11	-	234	-	-	63,521	-	13,854	-
5193 Flowers & florists' supplies [1]	8	-	43	-	-	14,047	-	655	-
5194 Tobacco and tobacco products [3]	4	4	78	70	18	19,949	23,029	1,678	1,635
5198 Paints, varnishes, and supplies [2]	-	5	-	22	4	-	20,364	-	423
5199 Nondurable goods, nec	35	42	83	110	3	20,964	28,909	1,966	2,698
52 - Retail trade	5,458	5,413	67,385	70,607	13	12,770	13,635	972,043	996,980
5210 Lumber and other building materials	82	82	1,576	1,562	19	19,543	21,521	35,204	34,690
5230 Paint, glass, and wallpaper stores [2]	29	26	136	93	4	17,176	18,323	2,600	1,839
5250 Hardware stores	58	43	509	415	10	14,138	14,159	7,785	6,061
5260 Retail nurseries and garden stores	41	48	219	195	4	13,297	13,682	4,260	3,472
5270 Mobile home dealers [3]	14	11	43	45	4	18,419	21,956	1,258	1,164
5310 Department stores	44	44	5,254	5,981	136	10,555	12,116	64,076	76,258
5330 Variety stores	49	42	322	309	7	11,267	9,256	3,526	3,102
5390 Misc. general merchandise stores [1]	45	38	876	1,119	29	12,548	13,576	14,579	15,618
5410 Grocery stores [3]	460	471	11,485	10,688	23	11,541	11,310	137,171	125,465
5420 Meat and fish markets	34	29	111	118	4	13,045	12,203	1,546	1,477
5430 Fruit and vegetable markets [3]	7	8	34	38	5	13,765	12,421	612	569
5440 Candy, nut, and confectionery stores [3]	17	14	88	49	4	5,227	6,286	457	323
5450 Dairy products stores [3]	17	19	30	42	2	10,533	9,333	375	401
5460 Retail bakeries [3]	81	78	973	1,000	13	8,333	9,368	8,898	10,130

Continued on next page.

ALBANY-SCHENECTADY-TROY, NY MSA - [continued]

Wholesale and Retail Trade USA	Establishments		Employment		Emp / Est	Pay / Employee		Annual Payroll ($ 000)	
	1994	1995	1994	1995	1995	1994	1995	1994	1995
5490 Miscellaneous food stores[3]	43	46	115	175	4	9,113	9,211	1,161	1,733
5510 New and used car dealers	100	91	3,765	3,673	40	25,951	28,158	119,895	110,961
5520 Used car dealers	49	53	135	163	3	15,733	17,742	2,563	3,575
5530 Auto and home supply stores	93	94	551	635	7	19,158	19,622	11,896	13,706
5540 Gasoline service stations	273	256	1,632	1,684	7	12,841	12,888	21,800	22,072
5550 Boat dealers[3]	7	7	10	15	2	22,000	22,933	255	267
5560 Recreational vehicle dealers[3]	7	7	33	37	5	22,788	24,973	1,001	1,290
5570 Motorcycle dealers[3]	11	11	23	27	2	17,391	15,111	418	689
5610 Men's & boys' clothing stores[3]	48	47	408	412	9	10,490	11,243	4,573	4,576
5620 Women's clothing stores	183	166	1,807	1,716	10	7,830	7,590	15,122	13,022
5630 Women's accessory & specialty stores[3]	30	26	136	150	6	8,765	8,880	1,351	1,300
5640 Children's and infants' wear stores[3]	17	15	138	144	10	6,928	6,750	1,046	996
5650 Family clothing stores	83	84	1,414	1,272	15	8,702	11,770	13,932	15,238
5660 Shoe stores	133	120	614	563	5	10,567	11,815	7,085	6,539
5690 Misc. apparel & accessory stores[3]	25	25	97	120	5	11,093	10,233	1,221	1,465
5712 Furniture stores	87	81	679	764	9	19,323	19,796	13,782	14,472
5713 Floor covering stores[2]	45	45	168	197	4	15,619	22,802	3,114	4,855
5714 Drapery and upholstery stores[3]	7	5	44	11	2	7,455	10,545	351	95
5719 Misc. homefurnishings stores[3]	44	39	308	69	2	12,584	15,014	4,093	1,008
5720 Household appliance stores	48	45	155	180	4	17,703	16,622	2,916	3,156
5731 Radio, TV, & electronic stores	46	49	218	260	5	18,312	16,708	3,965	4,128
5734 Computer and software stores[3]	17	21	47	180	9	9,021	10,400	485	2,541
5735 Record & prerecorded tape stores[3]	44	46	235	339	7	8,749	10,077	2,760	3,225
5736 Musical instrument stores[3]	22	23	106	123	5	21,774	19,480	2,123	2,489
5812 Eating places	1,420	1,343	18,350	19,727	15	7,977	8,273	169,932	172,184
5813 Drinking places	256	228	853	861	4	8,230	8,655	7,586	7,709
5910 Drug stores and proprietary stores	161	162	2,566	2,777	17	12,675	13,020	35,507	38,092
5920 Liquor stores	114	111	436	442	4	10,229	10,443	4,982	5,184
5930 Used merchandise stores	31	32	79	127	4	8,658	7,402	744	1,207
5941 Sporting goods and bicycle shops	78	84	344	627	7	11,837	12,332	4,880	7,748
5942 Book stores[3]	58	57	556	563	10	7,576	8,490	4,259	4,775
5943 Stationery stores[3]	12	12	59	55	5	7,119	11,200	749	624
5944 Jewelry stores[3]	88	92	466	447	5	14,464	16,662	7,372	7,946
5945 Hobby, toy, and game shops[3]	41	42	305	390	9	11,318	10,800	4,700	5,207
5946 Camera & photographic supply stores[2]	-	12	-	17	1	-	13,176	-	228
5947 Gift, novelty, and souvenir shops	123	115	698	679	6	7,530	8,772	5,671	6,626
5949 Sewing, needlework, and piece goods[3]	18	16	128	108	7	7,688	8,481	1,066	911
5961 Catalog and mail-order houses[3]	24	26	384	430	17	20,667	22,521	9,819	11,841
5962 Merchandising machine operators[3]	27	27	259	335	12	16,927	13,719	4,652	4,515
5963 Direct selling establishments	27	33	246	252	8	18,699	19,079	5,359	5,337
5983 Fuel oil dealers[3]	64	66	241	262	4	29,577	25,725	7,179	6,875
5984 Liquefied petroleum gas dealers	15	14	67	46	3	29,313	19,739	2,096	1,041
5992 Florists	88	91	319	321	4	10,031	12,449	3,887	4,931
5994 News dealers and newsstands[3]	20	20	19	19	1	12,211	13,263	242	228
5995 Optical goods stores	68	66	383	403	6	20,846	20,139	8,286	8,471
5999 Miscellaneous retail stores, nec	149	154	664	688	4	13,892	14,174	10,788	11,287

Source: County Business Patterns 1994/95, CBP-94/95, U.S. Department of Commerce, Washington DC, November 1997. The employment column represents mid-March employment in the year. Pay per employee is calculated by dividing 1st Quarter payroll, annualized, by mid-March employment. The column headed 'Emp / Est' shows 'employees per establishment'. A dash (-) means that data are unavailable or cannot be calculated. nec means not elsewhere classified. *Notes:* 1. 1994 data incomplete; unavailable or withheld. 2. 1995 data incomplete; unavailable or withheld. 3. 1994 and 1995 data incomplete; unavailable or withheld.

ALBUQUERQUE, NM MSA

Wholesale and Retail Trade USA	Establishments		Employment		Emp / Est	Pay / Employee		Annual Payroll ($ 000)	
	1994	1995	1994	1995	1995	1994	1995	1994	1995
50- Wholesale trade	1,327	1,341	15,457	16,356	12	24,995	26,654	427,159	457,949
5012 Automobiles and other vehicles[3]	18	20	322	318	16	22,720	26,428	7,404	8,478
5013 Motor vehicle supplies and new parts	75	64	802	771	12	19,586	20,965	17,466	16,553
5014 Tires and tubes[3]	16	13	141	127	10	26,241	30,394	3,910	3,811
5015 Motor vehicle parts, used[3]	23	29	137	209	7	15,912	15,062	2,220	3,251
5021 Furniture[3]	18	20	282	275	14	20,596	24,625	7,327	8,107
5023 Homefurnishings[3]	28	27	271	298	11	18,111	19,369	5,780	6,369
5031 Lumber, plywood, and millwork	31	33	674	635	19	25,685	30,117	19,707	19,402
5032 Brick, stone, & related materials[3]	16	15	103	194	13	22,641	31,464	4,274	6,507
5033 Roofing, siding, & insulation[3]	14	12	135	125	10	22,311	22,656	4,053	3,188
5039 Construction materials, nec[3]	18	39	224	354	9	23,536	22,576	6,067	10,745
5044 Office equipment[3]	39	42	626	645	15	29,610	35,181	19,887	21,208
5045 Computers, peripherals, & software	67	65	869	754	12	35,613	43,767	31,832	31,894
5046 Commercial equipment, nec[2]	-	17	-	252	15	-	22,413	-	6,283

Continued on next page.

ALBUQUERQUE, NM MSA - [continued]

Wholesale and Retail Trade USA	Establishments		Employment		Emp / Est	Pay / Employee		Annual Payroll ($ 000)	
	1994	1995	1994	1995	1995	1994	1995	1994	1995
5047 Medical and hospital equipment [3]	34	29	341	195	7	31,543	45,682	10,916	8,702
5051 Metals service centers and offices [3]	21	21	173	195	9	25,087	25,313	4,884	4,994
5063 Electrical apparatus and equipment [3]	71	69	719	745	11	34,370	37,482	27,602	26,550
5064 Electrical appliances, TV & radios [1]	11	-	49	-	-	27,184	-	1,290	-
5065 Electronic parts and equipment	-	69	-	486	7	-	31,992	-	16,346
5072 Hardware [3]	12	14	141	153	11	20,681	26,118	4,301	4,985
5074 Plumbing & hydronic heating supplies [3]	40	37	320	259	7	28,575	34,440	9,539	8,676
5075 Warm air heating & air conditioning [3]	17	17	118	125	7	25,288	28,064	3,680	4,117
5078 Refrigeration equipment and supplies [3]	5	5	19	20	4	22,105	22,800	455	466
5082 Construction and mining machinery [3]	18	15	391	363	24	37,545	49,576	16,056	16,677
5083 Farm and garden machinery [3]	9	9	93	114	13	20,602	21,018	2,454	2,675
5084 Industrial machinery and equipment	57	58	454	474	8	26,934	30,557	13,287	14,523
5085 Industrial supplies	24	27	153	180	7	26,876	25,644	4,972	5,612
5087 Service establishment equipment [3]	31	29	220	239	8	25,291	26,862	6,151	6,513
5088 Transportation equipment & supplies [3]	5	4	12	13	3	23,333	24,000	262	370
5091 Sporting & recreational goods [3]	11	10	87	78	8	18,943	23,538	1,722	1,688
5092 Toys and hobby goods and supplies [3]	6	6	39	41	7	12,821	14,829	681	819
5093 Scrap and waste materials [3]	11	13	122	138	11	30,721	31,449	3,875	4,116
5094 Jewelry & precious stones	57	55	505	471	9	16,507	16,875	8,902	8,729
5099 Durable goods, nec [2]	13	12	47	106	9	13,617	23,434	977	2,427
5111 Printing and writing paper [3]	8	9	116	121	13	23,655	26,876	3,113	3,226
5112 Stationery and office supplies [3]	34	29	460	391	13	18,035	20,583	9,335	8,307
5113 Industrial & personal service paper [1]	15	-	162	-	-	23,086	-	4,269	-
5120 Drugs, proprietaries, and sundries [3]	16	20	260	283	14	26,277	34,064	8,844	11,427
5131 Piece goods & notions [3]	5	5	41	42	8	10,829	10,762	514	591
5136 Men's and boys' clothing [3]	6	7	67	113	16	12,896	14,372	1,016	1,860
5137 Women's and children's clothing [1]	7	-	26	-	-	11,385	-	362	-
5141 Groceries, general line [2]	27	24	956	1,046	44	27,226	24,382	28,748	27,276
5142 Packaged frozen food [1]	10	-	136	-	-	15,706	-	2,491	-
5145 Confectionery [3]	8	8	185	203	25	24,476	23,271	4,612	5,096
5147 Meats and meat products [3]	6	6	69	62	10	19,420	22,065	1,537	1,546
5148 Fresh fruits and vegetables [3]	7	6	168	169	28	21,548	23,314	4,204	4,573
5149 Groceries and related products, nec [3]	42	40	747	786	20	21,837	20,285	16,489	16,606
5150 Farm-product raw materials	7	7	26	29	4	9,538	10,069	310	290
5162 Plastics materials & basic shapes [3]	9	8	50	58	7	18,480	16,000	1,048	956
5169 Chemicals & allied products, nec [3]	32	32	263	273	9	26,738	28,396	7,786	8,478
5171 Petroleum bulk stations & terminals [3]	16	15	255	213	14	21,678	24,169	5,780	5,117
5172 Petroleum products, nec [2]	9	6	28	24	4	21,714	20,500	721	575
5181 Beer and ale [3]	3	3	216	239	80	26,167	26,929	6,818	7,951
5182 Wine and distilled beverages [3]	7	7	344	344	49	28,453	27,686	9,607	10,146
5191 Farm supplies [2]	14	12	67	59	5	17,015	19,051	1,147	1,155
5192 Books, periodicals, & newspapers [3]	8	10	92	102	10	22,261	21,882	1,942	2,002
5193 Flowers & florists' supplies [2]	-	10	-	95	10	-	13,600	-	1,412
5198 Paints, varnishes, and supplies [1]	8	-	58	-	-	25,034	-	1,603	-
5199 Nondurable goods, nec	40	49	169	219	4	15,361	14,082	2,816	3,406
52 - Retail trade	3,571	3,574	56,805	58,110	16	12,262	13,534	770,387	815,110
5210 Lumber and other building materials	48	55	1,318	1,706	31	15,381	19,611	24,784	32,351
5230 Paint, glass, and wallpaper stores [3]	26	29	146	182	6	17,562	21,165	2,732	4,082
5250 Hardware stores [2]	25	7	202	80	11	14,198	12,550	3,303	1,058
5260 Retail nurseries and garden stores	14	15	54	70	5	10,000	10,457	585	792
5270 Mobile home dealers [3]	28	27	224	211	8	23,375	31,829	7,969	8,927
5310 Department stores [3]	21	21	4,082	4,352	207	11,681	13,370	52,356	57,810
5330 Variety stores [3]	7	7	47	38	5	10,128	11,053	477	427
5390 Misc. general merchandise stores	31	26	877	819	32	13,076	15,668	12,907	13,088
5410 Grocery stores [1]	169	172	4,853	5,140	30	14,896	16,977	79,580	86,216
5420 Meat and fish markets [3]	12	9	43	36	4	8,651	8,778	385	342
5430 Fruit and vegetable markets [3]	14	15	106	125	8	10,943	12,384	1,503	1,829
5440 Candy, nut, and confectionery stores [3]	8	9	53	54	6	7,170	7,185	436	392
5450 Dairy products stores [3]	6	7	25	38	5	5,600	5,684	152	381
5460 Retail bakeries	48	39	462	370	9	9,524	9,330	4,744	3,672
5490 Miscellaneous food stores [1]	15	16	79	72	5	11,949	14,444	1,101	1,212
5510 New and used car dealers	48	51	3,082	3,153	62	28,945	29,834	96,066	99,943
5520 Used car dealers	46	48	239	164	3	16,335	21,098	4,174	3,399
5530 Auto and home supply stores	100	99	819	793	8	14,598	17,846	13,428	15,092
5540 Gasoline service stations	171	172	1,353	1,561	9	12,438	14,206	18,767	22,095
5560 Recreational vehicle dealers [3]	12	12	182	223	19	22,396	22,457	5,214	4,714
5570 Motorcycle dealers	14	14	131	151	11	22,137	27,788	3,335	4,252
5610 Men's & boys' clothing stores [3]	22	23	212	219	10	10,189	11,489	2,418	2,546
5620 Women's clothing stores	103	94	782	696	7	9,335	8,833	7,478	6,027
5630 Women's accessory & specialty stores [1]	18	17	96	72	4	8,833	9,444	895	705
5640 Children's and infants' wear stores [3]	9	9	59	68	8	7,797	8,000	478	574

Continued on next page.

ALBUQUERQUE, NM MSA - [continued]

Wholesale and Retail Trade USA	Establishments		Employment		Emp / Est	Pay / Employee		Annual Payroll ($ 000)	
	1994	1995	1994	1995	1995	1994	1995	1994	1995
5650 Family clothing stores	53	54	739	891	17	9,748	8,943	7,960	8,562
5660 Shoe stores	58	56	336	291	5	13,571	15,519	4,061	4,011
5690 Misc. apparel & accessory stores [3]	25	25	104	121	5	9,615	10,479	1,181	1,295
5712 Furniture stores	65	66	923	933	14	17,551	20,086	18,317	20,016
5713 Floor covering stores [3]	24	27	191	286	11	24,209	22,615	4,973	6,933
5719 Misc. homefurnishings stores [2]	58	59	220	210	4	10,036	11,410	2,410	2,484
5720 Household appliance stores [3]	16	16	223	238	15	16,448	18,555	3,790	4,311
5731 Radio, TV, & electronic stores [1]	34	33	336	389	12	16,690	16,298	5,824	6,249
5734 Computer and software stores [3]	35	42	150	174	4	16,800	19,287	2,977	3,456
5735 Record & prerecorded tape stores [3]	27	24	239	365	15	9,741	8,986	2,822	3,090
5736 Musical instrument stores [3]	16	16	83	104	7	18,265	19,654	1,529	2,238
5812 Eating places	1,010	949	21,868	21,066	22	7,466	8,041	178,872	178,473
5813 Drinking places	104	94	1,319	1,220	13	6,975	7,098	9,261	8,585
5910 Drug stores and proprietary stores	76	72	1,493	1,449	20	18,553	20,265	32,486	32,799
5920 Liquor stores	40	36	420	395	11	9,476	10,147	4,282	4,774
5930 Used merchandise stores [1]	61	61	541	563	9	10,455	11,211	6,319	6,462
5941 Sporting goods and bicycle shops [2]	66	65	661	716	11	13,174	14,726	11,075	12,218
5942 Book stores [2]	42	40	303	350	9	11,485	12,377	3,946	4,809
5943 Stationery stores [3]	6	7	40	41	6	16,600	15,415	852	1,086
5944 Jewelry stores	78	71	423	392	6	17,721	20,408	6,556	6,723
5945 Hobby, toy, and game shops [3]	29	28	324	327	12	10,358	8,404	3,646	3,148
5946 Camera & photographic supply stores [3]	7	7	53	51	7	16,604	18,039	1,053	1,113
5947 Gift, novelty, and souvenir shops	102	95	631	673	7	9,521	9,064	6,615	6,701
5948 Luggage and leather goods stores [3]	7	7	40	35	5	13,400	16,914	539	557
5949 Sewing, needlework, and piece goods [3]	19	15	153	139	9	7,843	7,252	1,115	984
5961 Catalog and mail-order houses [3]	22	25	517	809	32	17,571	21,167	12,198	19,060
5962 Merchandising machine operators [3]	15	14	98	100	7	20,898	21,640	1,965	2,149
5963 Direct selling establishments	38	32	324	343	11	16,593	15,872	5,519	5,789
5984 Liquefied petroleum gas dealers	15	14	92	89	6	16,609	16,674	1,655	1,385
5992 Florists	44	52	184	168	3	10,848	10,643	2,055	1,885
5993 Tobacco stores and stands [3]	6	6	16	17	3	7,000	12,000	144	233
5994 News dealers and newsstands [3]	7	6	49	50	8	7,429	7,920	457	533
5995 Optical goods stores [1]	46	47	180	187	4	14,156	14,353	2,570	2,827
5999 Miscellaneous retail stores, nec	162	179	951	1,025	6	12,320	14,412	14,213	15,418

Source: County Business Patterns 1994/95, CBP-94/95, U.S. Department of Commerce, Washington DC, November 1997. The employment column represents mid-March employment in the year. Pay per employee is calculated by dividing 1st Quarter payroll, annualized, by mid-March employment. The column headed 'Emp / Est' shows 'employees per establishment'. A dash (-) means that data are unavailable or cannot be calculated. nec means not elsewhere classified. *Notes:* 1. 1994 data incomplete; unavailable or withheld. 2. 1995 data incomplete; unavailable or withheld. 3. 1994 and 1995 data incomplete; unavailable or withheld.

ALEXANDRIA, LA MSA

Wholesale and Retail Trade USA	Establishments		Employment		Emp / Est	Pay / Employee		Annual Payroll ($ 000)	
	1994	1995	1994	1995	1995	1994	1995	1994	1995
50 - Wholesale trade	230	226	2,111	2,170	10	20,942	20,700	47,684	50,038
5012 Automobiles and other vehicles	5	-	44	-	-	35,727	-	1,284	-
5013 Motor vehicle supplies and new parts	15	17	100	91	5	20,360	21,363	2,295	2,453
5014 Tires and tubes	4	-	83	-	-	17,976	-	1,833	-
5015 Motor vehicle parts, used	3	3	14	14	5	7,429	6,857	102	102
5021 Furniture	-	3	-	16	5	-	16,500	-	132
5031 Lumber, plywood, and millwork	4	5	39	38	8	37,641	32,737	1,133	954
5032 Brick, stone, & related materials	-	3	-	11	4	-	20,364	-	295
5033 Roofing, siding, & insulation	3	-	30	-	-	16,800	-	524	-
5039 Construction materials, nec	3	-	18	-	-	19,111	-	428	-
5044 Office equipment	11	10	46	46	5	21,826	22,000	1,047	1,071
5045 Computers, peripherals, & software	11	8	78	83	10	20,051	23,711	2,459	3,078
5047 Medical and hospital equipment	7	7	40	39	6	20,100	22,564	918	912
5063 Electrical apparatus and equipment	5	6	81	84	14	31,457	33,714	2,314	2,592
5074 Plumbing & hydronic heating supplies	4	6	58	65	11	23,517	21,415	1,405	1,497
5075 Warm air heating & air conditioning	8	9	20	22	2	17,200	19,091	424	614
5083 Farm and garden machinery	5	5	51	54	11	17,333	17,333	1,022	1,128
5084 Industrial machinery and equipment	11	9	71	53	6	22,197	27,396	1,638	2,468
5085 Industrial supplies	7	5	61	64	13	21,180	21,875	1,473	1,646
5093 Scrap and waste materials	-	4	-	62	16	-	18,774	-	2,066
5112 Stationery and office supplies	9	-	75	-	-	21,867	-	1,940	-
5120 Drugs, proprietaries, and sundries	8	6	48	53	9	18,250	17,208	921	1,021
5149 Groceries and related products, nec	8	8	173	169	21	18,220	15,763	3,416	2,842
5153 Grain and field beans	3	-	11	-	-	10,909	-	221	-
5160 Chemicals and allied products	5	5	78	77	15	20,103	20,416	1,762	1,933
5171 Petroleum bulk stations & terminals	-	5	-	25	5	-	19,040	-	498

Continued on next page.

ALEXANDRIA, LA MSA - [continued]

Wholesale and Retail Trade USA	Establishments		Employment		Emp / Est	Pay / Employee		Annual Payroll ($ 000)	
	1994	1995	1994	1995	1995	1994	1995	1994	1995
5181 Beer and ale	4	4	120	148	37	23,333	22,541	2,813	2,635
5191 Farm supplies	12	11	80	93	8	18,150	16,172	1,634	1,715
5192 Books, periodicals, & newspapers	3	3	41	52	17	10,537	11,000	528	553
5193 Flowers & florists' supplies	-	4	-	33	8	-	18,667	-	664
5198 Paints, varnishes, and supplies	-	3	-	39	13	-	16,923	-	665
5199 Nondurable goods, nec	3	3	8	3	1	8,500	9,333	48	25
52 - Retail trade	735	729	9,693	10,150	14	10,930	11,297	114,332	118,044
5210 Lumber and other building materials	13	13	249	223	17	17,076	18,386	4,253	4,514
5230 Paint, glass, and wallpaper stores	5	4	56	35	9	15,571	17,143	944	624
5250 Hardware stores	12	7	75	48	7	9,973	11,333	784	586
5260 Retail nurseries and garden stores	8	7	34	21	3	8,941	10,095	295	218
5270 Mobile home dealers	5	4	18	27	7	24,222	21,333	555	806
5310 Department stores	10	11	1,461	1,469	134	10,784	11,897	17,137	16,692
5330 Variety stores	10	10	49	43	4	10,694	12,000	519	454
5390 Misc. general merchandise stores	8	8	203	219	27	11,448	12,858	2,535	2,538
5410 Grocery stores	85	85	1,381	1,948	23	10,639	9,704	15,394	18,981
5420 Meat and fish markets	-	4	-	15	4	-	14,933	-	234
5440 Candy, nut, and confectionery stores	-	4	-	17	4	-	4,471	-	77
5460 Retail bakeries	8	7	57	68	10	9,754	8,176	550	571
5490 Miscellaneous food stores	5	4	20	22	6	7,400	7,273	159	167
5510 New and used car dealers	15	14	600	468	33	23,227	24,034	15,916	13,436
5520 Used car dealers	4	6	39	39	7	9,744	13,538	431	618
5530 Auto and home supply stores	18	20	127	114	6	16,252	18,175	2,186	2,122
5540 Gasoline service stations	56	56	383	320	6	9,452	11,300	3,717	4,136
5550 Boat dealers	5	5	29	38	8	13,103	16,632	437	586
5610 Men's & boys' clothing stores	11	10	86	83	8	9,116	9,783	713	727
5620 Women's clothing stores	26	24	207	185	8	6,976	6,508	1,513	1,249
5630 Women's accessory & specialty stores	4	3	22	12	4	9,636	12,333	177	196
5640 Children's and infants' wear stores	4	-	14	-	-	7,429	-	107	-
5650 Family clothing stores	8	7	195	200	29	9,867	8,960	1,855	1,702
5660 Shoe stores	19	20	116	141	7	10,414	9,901	1,315	1,441
5690 Misc. apparel & accessory stores	3	-	26	-	-	7,077	-	208	-
5712 Furniture stores	14	15	137	142	9	20,117	21,887	2,749	2,760
5713 Floor covering stores	4	4	24	25	6	26,000	28,640	599	622
5719 Misc. homefurnishings stores	5	5	21	27	5	8,571	8,148	227	224
5720 Household appliance stores	5	5	62	71	14	11,419	14,310	786	834
5731 Radio, TV, & electronic stores	15	12	63	49	4	16,381	17,143	1,103	999
5734 Computer and software stores	3	4	7	9	2	15,429	14,667	123	348
5735 Record & prerecorded tape stores	4	4	21	21	5	7,810	12,571	242	236
5736 Musical instrument stores	4	3	20	17	6	8,800	8,941	178	167
5812 Eating places	142	123	2,652	2,570	21	6,843	7,458	19,298	19,825
5813 Drinking places	14	14	113	100	7	5,770	6,600	633	653
5910 Drug stores and proprietary stores	22	23	249	316	14	15,598	18,354	5,439	5,769
5920 Liquor stores	4	-	16	-	-	11,750	-	194	-
5930 Used merchandise stores	11	11	34	48	4	12,235	8,667	321	413
5941 Sporting goods and bicycle shops	4	3	30	28	9	13,867	14,714	481	472
5942 Book stores	7	-	41	-	-	8,488	-	352	-
5944 Jewelry stores	16	19	95	106	6	12,884	13,736	1,130	1,280
5945 Hobby, toy, and game shops	9	8	77	88	11	12,156	12,091	1,138	1,272
5947 Gift, novelty, and souvenir shops	13	12	90	72	6	5,467	7,278	514	546
5949 Sewing, needlework, and piece goods	4	4	29	28	7	6,345	6,000	189	185
5962 Merchandising machine operators	4	-	54	-	-	15,630	-	812	-
5963 Direct selling establishments	-	7	-	43	6	-	16,465	-	657
5992 Florists	15	13	61	55	4	7,803	10,764	480	458
5999 Miscellaneous retail stores, nec	15	17	45	52	3	12,089	12,462	587	715

Source: County Business Patterns 1994/95, CBP-94/95, U.S. Department of Commerce, Washington DC, November 1997. The employment column represents mid-March employment in the year. Pay per employee is calculated by dividing 1st Quarter payroll, annualized, by mid-March employment. The column headed 'Emp / Est' shows 'employees per establishment'. A dash (-) means that data are unavailable or cannot be calculated. nec means not elsewhere classified. *Notes:* 1. 1994 data incomplete; unavailable or withheld. 2. 1995 data incomplete; unavailable or withheld. 3. 1994 and 1995 data incomplete; unavailable or withheld.

ALLENTOWN - BETHLEHEM - EASTON, PA MSA

Wholesale and Retail Trade USA	Establishments		Employment		Emp / Est	Pay / Employee		Annual Payroll ($ 000)	
	1994	1995	1994	1995	1995	1994	1995	1994	1995
50 - Wholesale trade	-	1,039	-	13,079	13	-	31,559	-	415,949
5012 Automobiles and other vehicles	-	23	-	391	17	-	31,591	-	11,878
5013 Motor vehicle supplies and new parts	-	54	-	525	10	-	21,684	-	11,586
5014 Tires and tubes [2]	-	6	-	54	9	-	23,037	-	1,206
5015 Motor vehicle parts, used	-	23	-	89	4	-	17,933	-	1,694

Continued on next page.

ALLENTOWN – BETHLEHEM – EASTON, PA MSA - [continued]

Wholesale and Retail Trade USA	Establishments		Employment		Emp / Est	Pay / Employee		Annual Payroll ($ 000)	
	1994	1995	1994	1995	1995	1994	1995	1994	1995
5021 Furniture[2]	-	10	-	98	10	-	36,571	-	3,249
5023 Homefurnishings[2]	-	12	-	84	7	-	21,286	-	1,706
5031 Lumber, plywood, and millwork	-	15	-	348	23	-	38,552	-	12,664
5032 Brick, stone, & related materials[2]	-	7	-	40	6	-	40,400	-	1,406
5033 Roofing, siding, & insulation[2]	-	11	-	119	11	-	35,227	-	4,030
5039 Construction materials, nec[2]	-	20	-	139	7	-	29,496	-	4,047
5044 Office equipment	-	26	-	392	15	-	29,041	-	11,743
5045 Computers, peripherals, & software	-	34	-	338	10	-	45,811	-	15,512
5046 Commercial equipment, nec[2]	-	7	-	38	5	-	33,053	-	1,533
5047 Medical and hospital equipment	-	18	-	214	12	-	37,664	-	8,588
5049 Professional equipment, nec[2]	-	6	-	132	22	-	39,061	-	4,861
5051 Metals service centers and offices[2]	-	23	-	139	6	-	31,396	-	4,536
5063 Electrical apparatus and equipment[2]	-	34	-	642	19	-	43,745	-	25,761
5064 Electrical appliances, TV & radios[2]	-	6	-	33	6	-	36,000	-	1,237
5065 Electronic parts and equipment[2]	-	31	-	439	14	-	40,310	-	15,950
5072 Hardware[2]	-	14	-	356	25	-	25,213	-	9,232
5074 Plumbing & hydronic heating supplies	-	21	-	198	9	-	29,758	-	6,410
5082 Construction and mining machinery[2]	-	12	-	54	5	-	30,815	-	2,096
5083 Farm and garden machinery[2]	-	11	-	113	10	-	22,513	-	2,638
5084 Industrial machinery and equipment	-	71	-	769	11	-	35,339	-	29,242
5085 Industrial supplies	-	45	-	408	9	-	34,461	-	16,134
5087 Service establishment equipment	-	22	-	159	7	-	17,987	-	3,126
5088 Transportation equipment & supplies[2]	-	4	-	30	8	-	33,200	-	1,075
5091 Sporting & recreational goods	-	12	-	149	12	-	18,443	-	3,089
5092 Toys and hobby goods and supplies[2]	-	7	-	79	11	-	19,291	-	1,191
5093 Scrap and waste materials	-	23	-	394	17	-	23,371	-	10,642
5094 Jewelry & precious stones[2]	-	6	-	7	1	-	5,714	-	48
5111 Printing and writing paper[2]	-	6	-	50	8	-	29,840	-	1,407
5112 Stationery and office supplies[2]	-	12	-	102	9	-	29,373	-	2,870
5113 Industrial & personal service paper[2]	-	9	-	48	5	-	31,083	-	1,493
5120 Drugs, proprietaries, and sundries[2]	-	18	-	319	18	-	49,317	-	10,686
5131 Piece goods & notions[2]	-	21	-	259	12	-	17,143	-	4,843
5136 Men's and boys' clothing[2]	-	7	-	49	7	-	26,041	-	1,289
5137 Women's and children's clothing[2]	-	18	-	289	16	-	25,398	-	7,495
5141 Groceries, general line[2]	-	8	-	248	31	-	24,871	-	6,247
5143 Dairy products, exc. dried or canned	-	10	-	89	9	-	24,854	-	2,453
5145 Confectionery[2]	-	8	-	30	4	-	23,200	-	788
5147 Meats and meat products[2]	-	12	-	218	18	-	22,000	-	5,227
5148 Fresh fruits and vegetables[2]	-	9	-	129	14	-	20,992	-	3,705
5149 Groceries and related products, nec[2]	-	35	-	455	13	-	24,211	-	13,608
5153 Grain and field beans[2]	-	5	-	12	2	-	15,000	-	359
5162 Plastics materials & basic shapes	-	9	-	167	19	-	28,623	-	5,087
5169 Chemicals & allied products, nec	-	33	-	713	22	-	48,381	-	35,072
5171 Petroleum bulk stations & terminals	-	12	-	72	6	-	40,444	-	2,795
5181 Beer and ale[2]	-	13	-	13	1	-	10,769	-	131
5191 Farm supplies[2]	-	9	-	52	6	-	30,538	-	1,596
5192 Books, periodicals, & newspapers[2]	-	8	-	114	14	-	22,561	-	2,503
5193 Flowers & florists' supplies	-	9	-	35	4	-	19,429	-	868
5198 Paints, varnishes, and supplies[2]	-	8	-	52	7	-	23,692	-	1,310
5199 Nondurable goods, nec	-	42	-	258	6	-	22,465	-	6,737
52 – Retail trade	-	3,548	-	46,263	13	-	13,146	-	640,560
5210 Lumber and other building materials	-	60	-	1,324	22	-	19,927	-	27,664
5230 Paint, glass, and wallpaper stores[2]	-	22	-	66	3	-	19,455	-	1,263
5250 Hardware stores	-	36	-	354	10	-	12,531	-	4,202
5260 Retail nurseries and garden stores	-	32	-	175	5	-	12,023	-	2,997
5270 Mobile home dealers	-	9	-	59	7	-	18,780	-	1,323
5310 Department stores[2]	-	28	-	4,284	153	-	11,641	-	53,040
5330 Variety stores	-	27	-	234	9	-	8,906	-	2,312
5390 Misc. general merchandise stores	-	19	-	482	25	-	13,145	-	7,002
5410 Grocery stores	-	255	-	6,604	26	-	12,909	-	88,821
5420 Meat and fish markets	-	27	-	38	1	-	10,947	-	464
5430 Fruit and vegetable markets[2]	-	5	-	14	3	-	12,571	-	191
5440 Candy, nut, and confectionery stores[2]	-	11	-	62	6	-	9,161	-	431
5460 Retail bakeries	-	49	-	460	9	-	11,696	-	5,080
5490 Miscellaneous food stores[2]	-	21	-	85	4	-	8,141	-	800
5510 New and used car dealers	-	78	-	2,657	34	-	27,589	-	78,761
5520 Used car dealers	-	37	-	124	3	-	20,871	-	2,574
5530 Auto and home supply stores	-	72	-	434	6	-	18,147	-	8,101
5540 Gasoline service stations	-	228	-	1,459	6	-	12,003	-	18,331
5550 Boat dealers[2]	-	6	-	50	8	-	22,560	-	1,197
5560 Recreational vehicle dealers[2]	-	5	-	46	9	-	24,696	-	1,226

Continued on next page.

ALLENTOWN - BETHLEHEM - EASTON, PA MSA - [continued]

Wholesale and Retail Trade USA	Establishments		Employment		Emp / Est	Pay / Employee		Annual Payroll ($ 000)	
	1994	1995	1994	1995	1995	1994	1995	1994	1995
5570 Motorcycle dealers	-	13	-	85	7	-	17,318	-	1,757
5610 Men's & boys' clothing stores [2]	-	21	-	206	10	-	12,078	-	2,330
5620 Women's clothing stores	-	80	-	776	10	-	8,201	-	6,206
5630 Women's accessory & specialty stores [2]	-	20	-	93	5	-	9,806	-	911
5640 Children's and infants' wear stores [2]	-	7	-	63	9	-	9,016	-	560
5650 Family clothing stores [2]	-	18	-	276	15	-	9,116	-	2,683
5660 Shoe stores	-	91	-	389	4	-	10,828	-	4,142
5690 Misc. apparel & accessory stores	-	19	-	146	8	-	10,904	-	1,585
5712 Furniture stores	-	58	-	421	7	-	22,128	-	9,799
5713 Floor covering stores	-	26	-	162	6	-	21,407	-	3,732
5719 Misc. homefurnishings stores [2]	-	33	-	5	-	-	13,600	-	210
5720 Household appliance stores	-	33	-	143	4	-	14,909	-	2,348
5731 Radio, TV, & electronic stores	-	36	-	271	8	-	18,613	-	5,380
5734 Computer and software stores	-	11	-	51	5	-	18,353	-	966
5735 Record & prerecorded tape stores	-	18	-	104	6	-	9,769	-	1,002
5736 Musical instrument stores [2]	-	12	-	41	3	-	16,000	-	691
5812 Eating places	-	823	-	13,734	17	-	8,540	-	122,842
5813 Drinking places	-	139	-	606	4	-	8,211	-	5,128
5910 Drug stores and proprietary stores	-	117	-	1,778	15	-	14,418	-	24,890
5920 Liquor stores	-	72	-	307	4	-	16,078	-	5,363
5930 Used merchandise stores	-	28	-	279	10	-	12,043	-	2,587
5941 Sporting goods and bicycle shops	-	44	-	374	9	-	11,850	-	4,631
5942 Book stores [2]	-	29	-	187	6	-	11,316	-	2,402
5943 Stationery stores	-	8	-	11	1	-	5,818	-	62
5944 Jewelry stores	-	103	-	514	5	-	15,323	-	7,949
5945 Hobby, toy, and game shops [2]	-	29	-	263	9	-	11,133	-	3,100
5946 Camera & photographic supply stores [2]	-	9	-	79	9	-	15,139	-	1,278
5947 Gift, novelty, and souvenir shops	-	89	-	455	5	-	7,956	-	4,200
5948 Luggage and leather goods stores [2]	-	6	-	39	7	-	8,000	-	351
5961 Catalog and mail-order houses [2]	-	17	-	252	15	-	24,857	-	5,295
5962 Merchandising machine operators	-	16	-	433	27	-	11,584	-	5,332
5963 Direct selling establishments	-	33	-	256	8	-	15,203	-	5,294
5983 Fuel oil dealers [2]	-	51	-	341	7	-	27,390	-	9,588
5992 Florists	-	64	-	315	5	-	10,743	-	3,460
5994 News dealers and newsstands	-	8	-	19	2	-	8,632	-	173
5995 Optical goods stores	-	34	-	153	5	-	18,405	-	2,952
5999 Miscellaneous retail stores, nec	-	96	-	446	5	-	16,099	-	7,623

Source: County Business Patterns 1994/95, CBP-94/95, U.S. Department of Commerce, Washington DC, November 1997. The employment column represents mid-March employment in the year. Pay per employee is calculated by dividing 1st Quarter payroll, annualized, by mid-March employment. The column headed 'Emp / Est' shows 'employees per establishment'. A dash (-) means that data are unavailable or cannot be calculated. nec means not elsewhere classified. *Notes:* 1. 1994 data incomplete; unavailable or withheld. 2. 1995 data incomplete; unavailable or withheld. 3. 1994 and 1995 data incomplete; unavailable or withheld.

ALTOONA, PA MSA

Wholesale and Retail Trade USA	Establishments		Employment		Emp / Est	Pay / Employee		Annual Payroll ($ 000)	
	1994	1995	1994	1995	1995	1994	1995	1994	1995
50- Wholesale trade	-	213	-	3,956	19	-	23,554	-	99,965
5012 Automobiles and other vehicles	-	9	-	103	11	-	19,961	-	1,902
5013 Motor vehicle supplies and new parts	-	18	-	158	9	-	19,013	-	3,188
5031 Lumber, plywood, and millwork	-	6	-	93	16	-	17,720	-	1,718
5046 Commercial equipment, nec	-	3	-	29	10	-	16,552	-	515
5063 Electrical apparatus and equipment	-	8	-	145	18	-	27,117	-	3,738
5065 Electronic parts and equipment	-	6	-	65	11	-	14,831	-	1,155
5072 Hardware	-	3	-	7	2	-	14,286	-	123
5074 Plumbing & hydronic heating supplies	-	10	-	103	10	-	25,320	-	1,914
5084 Industrial machinery and equipment	-	7	-	97	14	-	23,918	-	2,390
5085 Industrial supplies	-	9	-	342	38	-	24,316	-	9,176
5087 Service establishment equipment	-	12	-	76	6	-	21,579	-	1,769
5093 Scrap and waste materials	-	6	-	50	8	-	18,080	-	993
5112 Stationery and office supplies	-	3	-	10	3	-	30,400	-	260
5120 Drugs, proprietaries, and sundries	-	3	-	86	29	-	32,791	-	2,559
5130 Apparel, piece goods, and notions	-	4	-	142	36	-	42,113	-	9,149
5149 Groceries and related products, nec	-	9	-	243	27	-	23,358	-	5,737
5154 Livestock	-	3	-	22	7	-	6,182	-	128
5169 Chemicals & allied products, nec	-	5	-	51	10	-	27,216	-	1,431
5170 Petroleum and petroleum products	-	7	-	60	9	-	31,800	-	1,827
5181 Beer and ale	-	5	-	56	11	-	18,143	-	1,479
5191 Farm supplies	-	6	-	41	7	-	22,537	-	1,307
52- Retail trade	-	851	-	11,917	14	-	12,283	-	155,143

Continued on next page.

ALTOONA, PA MSA - [continued]

Wholesale and Retail Trade USA	Establishments		Employment		Emp / Est	Pay / Employee		Annual Payroll ($ 000)	
	1994	1995	1994	1995	1995	1994	1995	1994	1995
5210 Lumber and other building materials	-	14	-	376	27	-	18,734	-	6,882
5250 Hardware stores	-	9	-	73	8	-	13,589	-	1,199
5270 Mobile home dealers	-	5	-	53	11	-	22,943	-	1,677
5310 Department stores	-	6	-	1,323	221	-	11,471	-	14,869
5330 Variety stores	-	10	-	47	5	-	8,851	-	487
5390 Misc. general merchandise stores	-	13	-	297	23	-	11,205	-	3,204
5410 Grocery stores	-	59	-	1,599	27	-	10,937	-	17,617
5420 Meat and fish markets	-	7	-	43	6	-	12,186	-	546
5440 Candy, nut, and confectionery stores	-	6	-	51	9	-	5,961	-	307
5460 Retail bakeries	-	10	-	56	6	-	7,071	-	462
5510 New and used car dealers	-	23	-	744	32	-	22,371	-	18,753
5520 Used car dealers	-	18	-	67	4	-	22,567	-	1,521
5530 Auto and home supply stores	-	22	-	98	4	-	13,959	-	1,415
5540 Gasoline service stations	-	60	-	852	14	-	16,239	-	14,854
5610 Men's & boys' clothing stores	-	5	-	24	5	-	10,333	-	279
5620 Women's clothing stores	-	23	-	190	8	-	8,295	-	1,532
5650 Family clothing stores	-	5	-	68	14	-	11,353	-	693
5660 Shoe stores	-	19	-	109	6	-	10,128	-	1,124
5690 Misc. apparel & accessory stores	-	5	-	18	4	-	8,222	-	200
5712 Furniture stores	-	15	-	161	11	-	24,919	-	4,031
5713 Floor covering stores	-	10	-	34	3	-	14,353	-	495
5720 Household appliance stores	-	9	-	57	6	-	16,982	-	1,066
5731 Radio, TV, & electronic stores	-	11	-	57	5	-	22,175	-	1,292
5735 Record & prerecorded tape stores	-	5	-	33	7	-	8,970	-	331
5812 Eating places	-	168	-	3,223	19	-	7,098	-	24,857
5813 Drinking places	-	41	-	144	4	-	6,361	-	974
5910 Drug stores and proprietary stores	-	34	-	392	12	-	16,867	-	6,781
5920 Liquor stores	-	15	-	61	4	-	13,836	-	796
5930 Used merchandise stores	-	8	-	41	5	-	6,341	-	302
5941 Sporting goods and bicycle shops	-	16	-	59	4	-	9,966	-	633
5942 Book stores	-	7	-	32	5	-	13,625	-	503
5944 Jewelry stores	-	15	-	74	5	-	15,297	-	1,262
5945 Hobby, toy, and game shops	-	9	-	100	11	-	9,160	-	1,045
5947 Gift, novelty, and souvenir shops	-	16	-	70	4	-	6,800	-	505
5963 Direct selling establishments	-	6	-	40	7	-	12,500	-	494
5983 Fuel oil dealers	-	6	-	85	14	-	16,753	-	1,312
5984 Liquefied petroleum gas dealers	-	3	-	26	9	-	19,692	-	581
5992 Florists	-	12	-	73	6	-	8,164	-	630
5995 Optical goods stores	-	5	-	20	4	-	14,800	-	234
5999 Miscellaneous retail stores, nec	-	31	-	96	3	-	9,750	-	1,878

Source: County Business Patterns 1994/95, CBP-94/95, U.S. Department of Commerce, Washington DC, November 1997. The employment column represents mid-March employment in the year. Pay per employee is calculated by dividing 1st Quarter payroll, annualized, by mid-March employment. The column headed 'Emp / Est' shows 'employees per establishment'. A dash (-) means that data are unavailable or cannot be calculated. nec means not elsewhere classified. *Notes:* 1. 1994 data incomplete; unavailable or withheld. 2. 1995 data incomplete; unavailable or withheld. 3. 1994 and 1995 data incomplete; unavailable or withheld.

AMARILLO, TX MSA

Wholesale and Retail Trade USA	Establishments		Employment		Emp / Est	Pay / Employee		Annual Payroll ($ 000)	
	1994	1995	1994	1995	1995	1994	1995	1994	1995
50- Wholesale trade	-	437	-	6,286	14	-	25,615	-	169,244
5012 Automobiles and other vehicles	-	17	-	281	17	-	27,573	-	8,139
5013 Motor vehicle supplies and new parts	-	24	-	263	11	-	21,354	-	5,866
5021 Furniture	-	7	-	83	12	-	18,265	-	1,515
5023 Homefurnishings	-	5	-	26	5	-	18,000	-	465
5031 Lumber, plywood, and millwork	-	10	-	50	5	-	16,800	-	1,007
5032 Brick, stone, & related materials	-	6	-	40	7	-	21,600	-	868
5044 Office equipment [2]	-	13	-	137	11	-	27,650	-	4,036
5045 Computers, peripherals, & software	-	12	-	110	9	-	37,891	-	3,530
5046 Commercial equipment, nec	-	5	-	53	11	-	24,604	-	1,295
5047 Medical and hospital equipment	-	9	-	27	3	-	21,185	-	472
5050 Metals and minerals, except petroleum	-	8	-	98	12	-	25,102	-	3,411
5063 Electrical apparatus and equipment	-	21	-	115	5	-	38,017	-	4,107
5072 Hardware	-	11	-	184	17	-	28,783	-	5,271
5075 Warm air heating & air conditioning [2]	-	8	-	89	11	-	21,303	-	2,012
5082 Construction and mining machinery [2]	-	7	-	143	20	-	36,028	-	5,133
5083 Farm and garden machinery	-	9	-	43	5	-	22,884	-	1,116
5084 Industrial machinery and equipment	-	23	-	214	9	-	32,766	-	7,412
5085 Industrial supplies	-	21	-	173	8	-	30,335	-	6,298
5087 Service establishment equipment	-	8	-	74	9	-	32,486	-	2,620

Continued on next page.

AMARILLO, TX MSA - [continued]

Wholesale and Retail Trade USA	Establishments		Employment		Emp / Est	Pay / Employee		Annual Payroll ($ 000)	
	1994	1995	1994	1995	1995	1994	1995	1994	1995
5093 Scrap and waste materials	-	12	-	79	7	-	15,241	-	1,586
5112 Stationery and office supplies	-	10	-	100	10	-	21,280	-	2,315
5149 Groceries and related products, nec	-	10	-	169	17	-	22,249	-	4,415
5153 Grain and field beans	-	15	-	146	10	-	32,822	-	5,072
5169 Chemicals & allied products, nec	-	10	-	69	7	-	26,957	-	1,951
5171 Petroleum bulk stations & terminals	-	5	-	49	10	-	23,592	-	1,238
5172 Petroleum products, nec [2]	-	6	-	63	11	-	26,921	-	2,060
5180 Beer, wine, and distilled beverages	-	6	-	167	28	-	32,719	-	6,323
5191 Farm supplies	-	18	-	155	9	-	31,277	-	5,450
5193 Flowers & florists' supplies [2]	-	4	-	26	7	-	14,462	-	367
5199 Nondurable goods, nec	-	16	-	42	3	-	14,476	-	625
52- Retail trade	-	1,369	-	19,112	14	-	13,195	-	259,664
5210 Lumber and other building materials	-	15	-	350	23	-	19,794	-	6,363
5230 Paint, glass, and wallpaper stores	-	8	-	49	6	-	21,878	-	1,142
5270 Mobile home dealers	-	8	-	29	4	-	30,207	-	1,110
5310 Department stores	-	14	-	2,444	175	-	12,591	-	30,807
5330 Variety stores	-	7	-	3	-	-	5,333	-	16
5390 Misc. general merchandise stores [2]	-	18	-	101	6	-	10,733	-	1,235
5410 Grocery stores	-	116	-	1,867	16	-	13,828	-	25,547
5440 Candy, nut, and confectionery stores [2]	-	4	-	2	1	-	12,000	-	17
5460 Retail bakeries	-	15	-	67	4	-	8,896	-	1,164
5490 Miscellaneous food stores	-	9	-	26	3	-	8,769	-	291
5510 New and used car dealers	-	19	-	999	53	-	39,171	-	37,304
5520 Used car dealers	-	28	-	98	4	-	16,939	-	2,050
5530 Auto and home supply stores	-	41	-	291	7	-	16,976	-	5,586
5540 Gasoline service stations	-	71	-	756	11	-	11,677	-	9,359
5570 Motorcycle dealers	-	4	-	16	4	-	18,750	-	307
5610 Men's & boys' clothing stores	-	9	-	57	6	-	11,298	-	606
5620 Women's clothing stores	-	40	-	285	7	-	9,347	-	2,592
5630 Women's accessory & specialty stores	-	5	-	11	2	-	10,545	-	180
5640 Children's and infants' wear stores	-	6	-	10	2	-	6,800	-	75
5650 Family clothing stores	-	23	-	393	17	-	12,743	-	6,103
5660 Shoe stores	-	31	-	143	5	-	12,056	-	1,771
5690 Misc. apparel & accessory stores	-	10	-	30	3	-	10,267	-	272
5712 Furniture stores	-	31	-	256	8	-	16,906	-	4,550
5719 Misc. homefurnishings stores	-	21	-	86	4	-	10,326	-	1,046
5720 Household appliance stores	-	10	-	102	10	-	18,196	-	1,885
5731 Radio, TV, & electronic stores	-	18	-	220	12	-	13,345	-	3,197
5812 Eating places	-	282	-	6,527	23	-	8,127	-	56,627
5813 Drinking places	-	35	-	196	6	-	6,633	-	1,326
5910 Drug stores and proprietary stores	-	33	-	450	14	-	18,222	-	8,125
5920 Liquor stores	-	24	-	81	3	-	9,728	-	759
5930 Used merchandise stores	-	30	-	123	4	-	8,618	-	1,214
5941 Sporting goods and bicycle shops	-	26	-	188	7	-	9,851	-	2,161
5942 Book stores	-	12	-	71	6	-	11,380	-	846
5944 Jewelry stores	-	18	-	106	6	-	17,509	-	1,980
5945 Hobby, toy, and game shops	-	13	-	150	12	-	8,533	-	1,533
5947 Gift, novelty, and souvenir shops	-	27	-	80	3	-	8,950	-	874
5949 Sewing, needlework, and piece goods	-	6	-	26	4	-	7,231	-	193
5961 Catalog and mail-order houses	-	6	-	35	6	-	14,400	-	542
5962 Merchandising machine operators	-	7	-	43	6	-	20,279	-	899
5963 Direct selling establishments	-	20	-	100	5	-	19,200	-	1,916
5992 Florists	-	21	-	109	5	-	12,000	-	1,322
5995 Optical goods stores	-	17	-	83	5	-	12,627	-	1,034
5999 Miscellaneous retail stores, nec	-	46	-	286	6	-	13,664	-	4,095

Source: County Business Patterns 1994/95, CBP-94/95, U.S. Department of Commerce, Washington DC, November 1997. The employment column represents mid-March employment in the year. Pay per employee is calculated by dividing 1st Quarter payroll, annualized, by mid-March employment. The column headed 'Emp / Est' shows 'employees per establishment'. A dash (-) means that data are unavailable or cannot be calculated. nec means not elsewhere classified. *Notes:* 1. 1994 data incomplete; unavailable or withheld. 2. 1995 data incomplete; unavailable or withheld. 3. 1994 and 1995 data incomplete; unavailable or withheld.

ANCHORAGE, AK MSA

Wholesale and Retail Trade USA	Establishments		Employment		Emp / Est	Pay / Employee		Annual Payroll ($ 000)	
	1994	1995	1994	1995	1995	1994	1995	1994	1995
50- Wholesale trade	-	538	-	6,271	12	-	34,511	-	226,738
5013 Motor vehicle supplies and new parts	-	27	-	374	14	-	26,706	-	11,082
5015 Motor vehicle parts, used	-	3	-	45	15	-	25,956	-	1,548
5030 Lumber and construction materials	-	27	-	174	6	-	33,586	-	7,522
5044 Office equipment	-	13	-	298	23	-	48,174	-	13,220

Continued on next page.

ANCHORAGE, AK MSA - [continued]

Wholesale and Retail Trade USA	Establishments		Employment		Emp / Est	Pay / Employee		Annual Payroll ($ 000)	
	1994	1995	1994	1995	1995	1994	1995	1994	1995
5046 Commercial equipment, nec	-	6	-	39	7	-	27,590	-	1,100
5047 Medical and hospital equipment	-	5	-	46	9	-	34,000	-	1,364
5051 Metals service centers and offices	-	8	-	71	9	-	33,634	-	2,849
5063 Electrical apparatus and equipment	-	30	-	269	9	-	34,513	-	9,571
5074 Plumbing & hydronic heating supplies	-	19	-	200	11	-	38,320	-	7,786
5082 Construction and mining machinery	-	13	-	243	19	-	44,395	-	12,783
5084 Industrial machinery and equipment	-	46	-	293	6	-	41,870	-	12,410
5085 Industrial supplies	-	18	-	130	7	-	40,123	-	4,959
5088 Transportation equipment & supplies	-	7	-	53	8	-	34,415	-	1,950
5091 Sporting & recreational goods	-	8	-	70	9	-	24,514	-	1,840
5099 Durable goods, nec	-	11	-	77	7	-	28,416	-	1,816
5110 Paper and paper products	-	11	-	235	21	-	31,030	-	8,795
5141 Groceries, general line	-	16	-	575	36	-	37,426	-	23,077
5142 Packaged frozen food	-	6	-	74	12	-	29,351	-	2,295
5146 Fish and seafoods	-	14	-	198	14	-	17,960	-	2,413
5147 Meats and meat products	-	5	-	42	8	-	25,619	-	1,411
5149 Groceries and related products, nec	-	15	-	442	29	-	35,819	-	14,813
5169 Chemicals & allied products, nec	-	18	-	145	8	-	38,510	-	5,614
5170 Petroleum and petroleum products	-	15	-	133	9	-	49,474	-	6,731
5192 Books, periodicals, & newspapers	-	5	-	82	16	-	21,463	-	1,423
5199 Nondurable goods, nec	-	18	-	97	5	-	23,423	-	2,656
52 - Retail trade	1,549	1,530	22,539	23,006	15	16,587	17,490	424,122	437,628
5210 Lumber and other building materials	21	20	546	551	28	33,128	31,652	18,438	18,365
5230 Paint, glass, and wallpaper stores	7	6	88	96	16	28,273	26,542	2,700	2,994
5250 Hardware stores	8	7	85	67	10	21,412	20,597	1,958	1,556
5310 Department stores	9	9	2,346	2,267	252	11,722	15,384	35,242	39,516
5410 Grocery stores	67	75	2,514	2,654	35	19,373	19,528	50,933	52,620
5420 Meat and fish markets	7	5	44	41	8	22,545	24,488	1,122	1,152
5440 Candy, nut, and confectionery stores	-	6	-	33	6	-	10,545	-	339
5460 Retail bakeries	19	16	90	83	5	11,867	9,687	1,175	904
5490 Miscellaneous food stores	-	12	-	57	5	-	15,439	-	926
5510 New and used car dealers	17	15	1,138	1,144	76	32,921	34,647	43,012	47,398
5520 Used car dealers	5	8	20	22	3	21,800	39,818	644	923
5530 Auto and home supply stores	25	26	232	251	10	21,069	21,307	6,596	6,441
5540 Gasoline service stations	61	60	479	496	8	17,294	17,968	9,197	9,603
5550 Boat dealers	11	11	61	69	6	25,311	23,826	1,842	1,974
5560 Recreational vehicle dealers	7	6	66	65	11	23,879	24,062	2,468	2,674
5570 Motorcycle dealers	4	4	40	51	13	29,300	29,176	1,327	1,561
5590 Automotive dealers, nec	-	7	-	21	3	-	20,381	-	482
5610 Men's & boys' clothing stores	18	17	103	101	6	15,262	16,000	2,039	2,177
5620 Women's clothing stores	47	38	244	205	5	11,279	11,239	2,702	2,186
5630 Women's accessory & specialty stores	10	11	55	70	6	22,691	19,886	1,451	1,405
5640 Children's and infants' wear stores	4	-	22	-	-	8,909	-	187	-
5650 Family clothing stores	11	13	741	752	58	15,001	14,543	11,537	11,455
5660 Shoe stores	26	27	150	157	6	12,747	13,911	2,040	2,031
5690 Misc. apparel & accessory stores	4	6	9	15	3	14,222	11,733	142	177
5712 Furniture stores	24	23	283	284	12	23,067	28,296	7,584	8,068
5713 Floor covering stores	18	18	75	80	4	21,440	24,000	2,049	2,217
5714 Drapery and upholstery stores	4	3	26	14	5	16,923	23,143	426	322
5719 Misc. homefurnishings stores	23	22	153	181	8	13,830	14,188	2,480	2,720
5720 Household appliance stores	5	-	16	-	-	23,250	-	378	-
5731 Radio, TV, & electronic stores	8	8	96	102	13	22,833	24,980	2,530	2,661
5734 Computer and software stores	13	11	69	62	6	24,348	26,194	1,816	1,872
5735 Record & prerecorded tape stores	13	11	114	97	9	8,912	9,979	1,161	1,118
5736 Musical instrument stores	6	6	31	41	7	12,000	11,707	483	515
5812 Eating places	442	414	7,381	7,676	19	11,834	12,773	105,489	108,509
5813 Drinking places	68	64	727	813	13	13,249	12,871	10,806	10,881
5910 Drug stores and proprietary stores	24	17	707	336	20	19,904	24,357	13,915	8,291
5920 Liquor stores	44	39	201	217	6	19,463	19,521	4,133	4,411
5930 Used merchandise stores	26	27	134	136	5	14,119	15,647	2,216	2,565
5941 Sporting goods and bicycle shops	37	38	459	480	13	14,597	15,583	7,868	8,145
5942 Book stores	20	20	133	193	10	11,038	11,378	1,644	2,534
5943 Stationery stores	-	3	-	48	16	-	24,417	-	1,176
5944 Jewelry stores	34	37	160	186	5	15,425	14,645	2,577	2,859
5945 Hobby, toy, and game shops	16	15	154	202	13	12,338	12,139	2,446	2,696
5946 Camera & photographic supply stores	-	4	-	24	6	-	19,000	-	490
5947 Gift, novelty, and souvenir shops	62	57	345	341	6	11,026	13,853	5,607	5,799
5949 Sewing, needlework, and piece goods	14	12	175	111	9	6,354	8,072	1,046	830
5961 Catalog and mail-order houses	7	6	33	28	5	12,000	15,286	398	431
5962 Merchandising machine operators	8	7	79	71	10	25,367	26,028	2,016	1,963
5963 Direct selling establishments	14	12	80	152	13	7,950	10,342	835	1,532

Continued on next page.

ANCHORAGE, AK MSA - [continued]

Wholesale and Retail Trade USA	Establishments		Employment		Emp / Est	Pay / Employee		Annual Payroll ($ 000)	
	1994	1995	1994	1995	1995	1994	1995	1994	1995
5984 Liquefied petroleum gas dealers	4	3	16	22	7	18,250	17,818	212	460
5995 Optical goods stores	24	23	71	91	4	21,465	22,989	2,068	1,978
5999 Miscellaneous retail stores, nec	57	58	206	211	4	17,922	18,787	4,151	4,740

Source: County Business Patterns 1994/95, CBP-94/95, U.S. Department of Commerce, Washington DC, November 1997. The employment column represents mid-March employment in the year. Pay per employee is calculated by dividing 1st Quarter payroll, annualized, by mid-March employment. The column headed 'Emp / Est' shows 'employees per establishment'. A dash (-) means that data are unavailable or cannot be calculated. nec means not elsewhere classified. *Notes:* 1. 1994 data incomplete; unavailable or withheld. 2. 1995 data incomplete; unavailable or withheld. 3. 1994 and 1995 data incomplete; unavailable or withheld.

ANN ARBOR, MI PMSA

Wholesale and Retail Trade USA	Establishments		Employment		Emp / Est	Pay / Employee		Annual Payroll ($ 000)	
	1994	1995	1994	1995	1995	1994	1995	1994	1995
50 - Wholesale trade	802	811	7,672	8,498	10	28,638	32,125	253,255	287,172
5012 Automobiles and other vehicles[1]	11	12	54	67	6	17,185	19,701	1,064	1,374
5013 Motor vehicle supplies and new parts	59	54	649	616	11	26,977	33,260	21,486	20,665
5015 Motor vehicle parts, used	15	14	65	71	5	16,185	19,042	1,134	1,440
5021 Furniture[3]	10	11	122	137	12	18,787	18,307	2,513	2,559
5023 Homefurnishings[3]	10	12	44	85	7	12,727	12,047	934	1,425
5031 Lumber, plywood, and millwork	14	12	139	85	7	28,317	22,259	5,587	2,147
5033 Roofing, siding, & insulation[3]	6	6	32	14	2	29,250	25,714	872	489
5039 Construction materials, nec[2]	7	14	32	32	2	25,625	33,375	969	1,108
5044 Office equipment[3]	10	8	90	107	13	35,689	42,654	3,112	3,758
5045 Computers, peripherals, & software[1]	47	42	309	483	12	32,000	37,101	13,184	20,986
5046 Commercial equipment, nec[3]	6	6	41	58	10	20,976	25,103	1,230	1,700
5047 Medical and hospital equipment	18	18	117	149	8	39,214	32,161	5,001	4,616
5049 Professional equipment, nec[1]	8	7	47	37	5	26,128	35,351	1,443	1,402
5051 Metals service centers and offices	19	18	50	161	9	38,560	34,435	3,663	5,934
5063 Electrical apparatus and equipment	32	29	296	313	11	37,649	40,243	13,048	13,916
5064 Electrical appliances, TV & radios[3]	5	6	17	21	4	18,588	23,810	417	558
5065 Electronic parts and equipment	29	30	325	432	14	28,431	30,852	10,877	15,590
5072 Hardware	13	15	140	135	9	33,000	38,459	4,814	5,585
5074 Plumbing & hydronic heating supplies	18	19	176	239	13	24,000	23,665	4,261	5,706
5075 Warm air heating & air conditioning	8	9	82	98	11	31,561	33,102	2,874	3,508
5083 Farm and garden machinery	17	18	111	111	6	25,405	28,613	2,869	3,121
5084 Industrial machinery and equipment	54	57	225	338	6	37,227	39,373	11,468	14,281
5085 Industrial supplies	20	22	107	134	6	37,308	32,806	4,184	3,949
5087 Service establishment equipment	12	11	76	75	7	25,316	26,080	2,338	2,082
5091 Sporting & recreational goods	17	17	169	150	9	19,763	25,493	3,662	3,750
5093 Scrap and waste materials	-	11	-	55	5	-	17,018	-	1,174
5099 Durable goods, nec[3]	16	16	27	30	2	21,778	21,733	816	754
5111 Printing and writing paper[3]	3	5	8	13	3	39,000	31,385	317	486
5112 Stationery and office supplies	11	8	133	104	13	14,466	11,846	2,161	1,201
5113 Industrial & personal service paper[3]	8	8	56	41	5	35,929	43,220	2,235	1,398
5120 Drugs, proprietaries, and sundries	11	11	20	37	3	19,600	15,568	459	618
5130 Apparel, piece goods, and notions	13	16	43	74	5	16,465	14,270	947	1,209
5143 Dairy products, exc. dried or canned[3]	6	6	60	85	14	28,867	34,494	2,403	2,990
5149 Groceries and related products, nec[3]	23	23	440	468	20	29,036	29,795	13,935	14,742
5150 Farm-product raw materials	17	14	117	118	8	17,231	15,525	2,242	1,915
5162 Plastics materials & basic shapes[3]	8	9	11	9	1	100,000	119,556	1,177	1,269
5169 Chemicals & allied products, nec	18	18	77	79	4	38,909	40,405	3,605	3,875
5171 Petroleum bulk stations & terminals	11	8	47	46	6	24,085	24,957	1,149	1,040
5181 Beer and ale[3]	5	4	139	111	28	23,971	29,622	3,477	3,710
5182 Wine and distilled beverages	7	7	70	75	11	31,657	31,840	2,385	2,554
5191 Farm supplies	30	25	224	189	8	22,321	26,349	5,530	5,364
5192 Books, periodicals, & newspapers[3]	14	10	342	53	5	25,287	79,094	8,697	3,046
5198 Paints, varnishes, and supplies[2]	-	4	-	47	12	-	32,000	-	1,957
5199 Nondurable goods, nec	20	22	179	174	8	26,480	28,437	5,206	6,241
52 - Retail trade	2,839	2,848	43,907	46,487	16	11,625	13,153	592,912	674,212
5210 Lumber and other building materials	56	53	822	970	18	22,311	23,625	24,091	24,952
5230 Paint, glass, and wallpaper stores	20	19	83	96	5	18,651	20,292	1,774	2,108
5250 Hardware stores	44	37	436	386	10	13,046	12,674	6,384	5,452
5260 Retail nurseries and garden stores	32	28	170	207	7	10,776	12,386	2,641	3,321
5270 Mobile home dealers[2]	7	7	23	23	3	18,609	26,783	473	635
5310 Department stores	21	21	5,308	5,712	272	10,639	11,436	64,642	70,500
5330 Variety stores	11	10	96	97	10	8,292	8,742	901	936
5390 Misc. general merchandise stores	19	18	599	655	36	9,950	12,000	7,474	8,077
5410 Grocery stores	205	212	4,355	4,534	21	11,626	12,520	55,951	61,006
5420 Meat and fish markets	18	17	81	112	7	14,272	10,929	1,284	1,368
5430 Fruit and vegetable markets[3]	6	6	34	19	3	9,647	8,842	333	281

Continued on next page.

ANN ARBOR, MI PMSA - [continued]

Wholesale and Retail Trade USA	Establishments		Employment		Emp / Est	Pay / Employee		Annual Payroll ($ 000)	
	1994	1995	1994	1995	1995	1994	1995	1994	1995
5440 Candy, nut, and confectionery stores	7	7	27	30	4	6,815	6,800	183	249
5460 Retail bakeries	42	40	442	333	8	6,507	6,967	3,138	2,666
5490 Miscellaneous food stores	14	13	56	95	7	11,500	9,558	767	985
5510 New and used car dealers	59	59	2,732	3,001	51	32,362	33,313	112,308	120,829
5520 Used car dealers	17	15	70	75	5	17,657	19,467	1,460	1,659
5530 Auto and home supply stores	67	69	531	490	7	16,844	18,147	9,885	10,120
5540 Gasoline service stations	183	186	1,733	1,660	9	9,918	11,265	18,747	19,381
5550 Boat dealers	8	8	55	65	8	16,073	18,277	1,498	1,697
5560 Recreational vehicle dealers	7	8	57	66	8	16,281	19,455	1,652	2,303
5610 Men's & boys' clothing stores	24	23	133	108	5	15,008	20,074	1,805	1,981
5620 Women's clothing stores	69	60	658	596	10	7,702	6,819	5,514	4,426
5630 Women's accessory & specialty stores	13	10	68	60	6	9,765	10,133	709	606
5640 Children's and infants' wear stores[3]	7	8	55	59	7	6,764	7,119	384	397
5650 Family clothing stores	21	24	365	348	15	8,964	9,931	3,522	3,398
5660 Shoe stores	54	51	274	263	5	12,438	15,194	3,637	3,881
5690 Misc. apparel & accessory stores	18	19	93	86	5	8,860	10,651	992	879
5712 Furniture stores	42	39	400	379	10	19,770	21,847	8,899	9,141
5713 Floor covering stores	26	25	137	145	6	20,526	20,855	3,462	3,443
5719 Misc. homefurnishings stores[1]	33	30	37	264	9	13,297	12,045	567	3,308
5720 Household appliance stores	13	15	168	199	13	16,690	18,653	3,142	3,962
5731 Radio, TV, & electronic stores	30	28	249	257	9	13,976	16,218	4,012	4,258
5734 Computer and software stores	15	15	86	73	5	15,163	17,808	1,443	1,471
5735 Record & prerecorded tape stores	20	19	154	152	8	10,442	11,421	1,583	1,741
5736 Musical instrument stores[3]	9	9	81	79	9	14,963	16,000	2,109	1,311
5812 Eating places	690	638	15,469	15,309	24	7,048	7,818	122,957	126,372
5813 Drinking places	69	65	793	836	13	5,851	6,541	5,199	5,489
5910 Drug stores and proprietary stores	84	79	1,137	1,245	16	13,798	15,120	16,075	19,800
5920 Liquor stores	39	36	216	210	6	9,593	9,600	2,186	2,185
5930 Used merchandise stores	48	45	234	260	6	10,496	10,492	2,747	2,886
5941 Sporting goods and bicycle shops	61	67	431	426	6	10,060	10,977	4,974	5,440
5942 Book stores	36	36	617	625	17	11,968	13,190	7,171	8,479
5944 Jewelry stores	47	48	234	215	4	16,274	18,493	4,087	3,993
5945 Hobby, toy, and game shops	12	11	97	131	12	10,144	9,282	1,258	1,614
5947 Gift, novelty, and souvenir shops	73	71	414	396	6	7,314	8,293	3,163	3,419
5948 Luggage and leather goods stores[2]	-	6	-	30	5	-	14,667	-	373
5949 Sewing, needlework, and piece goods	13	12	109	95	8	6,165	6,147	783	570
5961 Catalog and mail-order houses[3]	7	9	74	81	9	29,297	39,062	2,167	2,612
5962 Merchandising machine operators	12	13	161	169	13	16,944	17,728	3,215	3,539
5963 Direct selling establishments	19	21	84	88	4	23,476	21,682	1,674	1,933
5983 Fuel oil dealers[1]	6	8	26	30	4	23,692	21,067	675	819
5984 Liquefied petroleum gas dealers	13	12	52	59	5	28,615	24,271	1,276	1,341
5992 Florists[3]	60	52	119	146	3	7,361	7,479	1,064	1,101
5995 Optical goods stores	24	22	126	109	5	21,175	20,991	2,813	2,390
5999 Miscellaneous retail stores, nec	87	85	256	376	4	14,391	13,319	4,141	5,484

Source: County Business Patterns 1994/95, CBP-94/95, U.S. Department of Commerce, Washington DC, November 1997. The employment column represents mid-March employment in the year. Pay per employee is calculated by dividing 1st Quarter payroll, annualized, by mid-March employment. The column headed 'Emp / Est' shows 'employees per establishment'. A dash (-) means that data are unavailable or cannot be calculated. nec means not elsewhere classified. *Notes:* 1. 1994 data incomplete; unavailable or withheld. 2. 1995 data incomplete; unavailable or withheld. 3. 1994 and 1995 data incomplete; unavailable or withheld.

ANNISTON, AL MSA

Wholesale and Retail Trade USA	Establishments		Employment		Emp / Est	Pay / Employee		Annual Payroll ($ 000)	
	1994	1995	1994	1995	1995	1994	1995	1994	1995
50- Wholesale trade	154	151	2,283	2,261	15	22,474	26,243	54,312	58,090
5012 Automobiles and other vehicles	-	3	-	8	3	-	13,500	-	98
5013 Motor vehicle supplies and new parts	12	12	94	95	8	14,426	14,316	1,675	1,415
5015 Motor vehicle parts, used	5	6	20	23	4	13,200	15,130	302	320
5031 Lumber, plywood, and millwork	6	-	15	-	-	197,867	-	1,620	-
5045 Computers, peripherals, & software	3	-	18	-	-	21,333	-	410	-
5051 Metals service centers and offices	9	9	62	59	7	15,355	18,915	1,091	1,264
5074 Plumbing & hydronic heating supplies	-	5	-	41	8	-	18,049	-	853
5082 Construction and mining machinery	3	3	71	72	24	38,479	41,889	2,747	3,102
5083 Farm and garden machinery	-	3	-	27	9	-	20,889	-	887
5084 Industrial machinery and equipment	7	6	54	62	10	26,222	33,290	1,474	1,661
5085 Industrial supplies	7	6	42	41	7	21,619	27,317	945	1,271
5087 Service establishment equipment	3	3	16	16	5	9,000	11,000	159	189
5091 Sporting & recreational goods	3	-	23	-	-	7,478	-	173	-
5093 Scrap and waste materials	8	10	252	262	26	19,730	21,893	5,707	5,992
5110 Paper and paper products	4	5	52	57	11	21,077	23,018	1,011	1,275

Continued on next page.

ANNISTON, AL MSA - [continued]

Wholesale and Retail Trade USA	Establishments		Employment		Emp / Est	Pay / Employee		Annual Payroll ($ 000)	
	1994	1995	1994	1995	1995	1994	1995	1994	1995
5130 Apparel, piece goods, and notions	-	5	-	96	19	-	10,500	-	1,200
5140 Groceries and related products	10	9	526	514	57	30,221	30,163	16,224	16,455
5171 Petroleum bulk stations & terminals	7	6	105	110	18	15,429	17,818	2,109	2,429
5181 Beer and ale	-	3	-	49	16	-	22,694	-	1,706
5190 Misc., nondurable goods	-	8	-	37	5	-	18,378	-	538
52 – Retail trade	714	732	8,861	9,576	13	10,539	10,962	100,597	108,811
5210 Lumber and other building materials	14	10	256	198	20	14,578	18,000	4,165	3,925
5230 Paint, glass, and wallpaper stores	7	8	40	38	5	10,900	13,789	356	517
5250 Hardware stores	4	-	6	-	-	6,000	-	72	-
5260 Retail nurseries and garden stores	5	-	16	-	-	9,000	-	209	-
5270 Mobile home dealers	7	7	25	35	5	18,720	25,714	713	1,022
5310 Department stores	7	7	1,128	1,123	160	10,316	12,684	12,605	13,511
5330 Variety stores	10	10	60	96	10	6,933	7,083	595	810
5390 Misc. general merchandise stores	8	-	68	-	-	10,059	-	749	-
5410 Grocery stores	61	65	1,223	1,374	21	9,547	9,310	12,487	12,859
5460 Retail bakeries	5	6	8	24	4	7,500	7,167	163	196
5490 Miscellaneous food stores	-	3	-	9	3	-	18,222	-	231
5510 New and used car dealers	11	13	419	429	33	27,542	30,853	12,114	13,459
5520 Used car dealers	29	31	105	104	3	16,800	19,538	1,889	2,041
5530 Auto and home supply stores	37	40	198	242	6	12,586	14,975	2,873	3,756
5540 Gasoline service stations	80	72	420	445	6	10,857	11,119	4,624	4,886
5610 Men's & boys' clothing stores	6	5	21	21	4	10,476	11,048	254	239
5620 Women's clothing stores	13	9	105	64	7	8,533	8,688	917	593
5630 Women's accessory & specialty stores	3	3	10	11	4	7,600	6,545	70	73
5640 Children's and infants' wear stores	3	4	26	21	5	6,615	8,190	198	205
5660 Shoe stores	7	-	42	-	-	9,143	-	436	-
5690 Misc. apparel & accessory stores	3	4	13	18	5	8,923	12,222	127	192
5712 Furniture stores	21	22	139	130	6	14,561	14,523	2,056	2,136
5713 Floor covering stores	5	-	10	-	-	10,000	-	145	-
5720 Household appliance stores	-	4	-	14	4	-	4,000	-	96
5731 Radio, TV, & electronic stores	11	12	46	55	5	21,826	20,436	985	1,148
5735 Record & prerecorded tape stores	4	-	15	-	-	8,533	-	184	-
5812 Eating places	119	110	2,905	3,250	30	6,915	6,650	21,125	22,878
5813 Drinking places	7	6	44	26	4	5,818	6,308	245	158
5910 Drug stores and proprietary stores	29	27	259	273	10	14,672	14,725	4,447	4,270
5930 Used merchandise stores	32	31	72	78	3	10,556	10,872	782	869
5941 Sporting goods and bicycle shops	13	12	97	110	9	8,082	6,364	812	525
5942 Book stores	7	7	72	81	12	8,667	9,531	700	1,152
5944 Jewelry stores	11	11	88	87	8	13,818	16,276	1,134	1,241
5949 Sewing, needlework, and piece goods	-	3	-	11	4	-	12,727	-	116
5960 Nonstore retailers	9	10	162	153	15	14,025	14,824	2,266	2,451
5984 Liquefied petroleum gas dealers	-	5	-	29	6	-	23,172	-	595
5992 Florists	15	18	39	38	2	7,795	7,579	285	309
5995 Optical goods stores	8	8	28	28	4	14,857	13,286	404	413
5999 Miscellaneous retail stores, nec	20	23	89	106	5	14,876	14,792	1,707	2,057

Source: County Business Patterns 1994/95, CBP-94/95, U.S. Department of Commerce, Washington DC, November 1997. The employment column represents mid-March employment in the year. Pay per employee is calculated by dividing 1st Quarter payroll, annualized, by mid-March employment. The column headed 'Emp / Est' shows 'employees per establishment'. A dash (-) means that data are unavailable or cannot be calculated. nec means not elsewhere classified. *Notes:* 1. 1994 data incomplete; unavailable or withheld. 2. 1995 data incomplete; unavailable or withheld. 3. 1994 and 1995 data incomplete; unavailable or withheld.

APPLETON – OSHKOSH – NEENAH, WI MSA

Wholesale and Retail Trade USA	Establishments		Employment		Emp / Est	Pay / Employee		Annual Payroll ($ 000)	
	1994	1995	1994	1995	1995	1994	1995	1994	1995
50 – Wholesale trade	-	609	-	10,825	18	-	31,830	-	348,908
5012 Automobiles and other vehicles	-	12	-	205	17	-	30,829	-	8,609
5013 Motor vehicle supplies and new parts	-	31	-	434	14	-	20,387	-	9,600
5023 Homefurnishings [2]	-	8	-	23	3	-	20,522	-	542
5031 Lumber, plywood, and millwork [2]	-	7	-	125	18	-	27,264	-	3,289
5039 Construction materials, nec [2]	-	11	-	135	12	-	22,607	-	3,100
5044 Office equipment [2]	-	12	-	202	17	-	48,356	-	8,830
5045 Computers, peripherals, & software	-	12	-	214	18	-	28,093	-	6,739
5051 Metals service centers and offices [2]	-	11	-	277	25	-	28,274	-	8,941
5063 Electrical apparatus and equipment	-	26	-	491	19	-	39,202	-	20,408
5065 Electronic parts and equipment	-	21	-	237	11	-	34,414	-	8,232
5072 Hardware [2]	-	11	-	128	12	-	35,594	-	4,215
5074 Plumbing & hydronic heating supplies [2]	-	20	-	305	15	-	27,580	-	9,183
5082 Construction and mining machinery [2]	-	6	-	40	7	-	37,600	-	1,474
5083 Farm and garden machinery [2]	-	35	-	166	5	-	22,651	-	4,276

Continued on next page.

APPLETON - OSHKOSH - NEENAH, WI MSA - [continued]

Wholesale and Retail Trade USA	Establishments		Employment		Emp / Est	Pay / Employee		Annual Payroll ($ 000)	
	1994	1995	1994	1995	1995	1994	1995	1994	1995
5084 Industrial machinery and equipment	-	36	-	258	7	-	42,558	-	11,508
5085 Industrial supplies[2]	-	24	-	289	12	-	31,031	-	9,251
5092 Toys and hobby goods and supplies[2]	-	6	-	7	1	-	47,429	-	315
5093 Scrap and waste materials	-	12	-	103	9	-	14,680	-	1,844
5099 Durable goods, nec[2]	-	6	-	34	6	-	32,471	-	1,431
5111 Printing and writing paper[2]	-	7	-	126	18	-	44,159	-	6,806
5130 Apparel, piece goods, and notions[2]	-	12	-	17	1	-	11,765	-	152
5143 Dairy products, exc. dried or canned	-	11	-	47	4	-	13,957	-	970
5146 Fish and seafoods[2]	-	4	-	16	4	-	13,500	-	268
5149 Groceries and related products, nec	-	14	-	243	17	-	25,992	-	6,851
5150 Farm-product raw materials	-	7	-	33	5	-	8,606	-	487
5162 Plastics materials & basic shapes[2]	-	8	-	44	6	-	23,364	-	1,239
5169 Chemicals & allied products, nec[2]	-	13	-	130	10	-	37,846	-	5,289
5171 Petroleum bulk stations & terminals[2]	-	18	-	13	1	-	23,077	-	312
5180 Beer, wine, and distilled beverages[2]	-	7	-	167	24	-	21,772	-	4,204
5191 Farm supplies	-	26	-	253	10	-	18,814	-	5,324
5192 Books, periodicals, & newspapers[2]	-	4	-	18	5	-	16,667	-	346
5198 Paints, varnishes, and supplies[2]	-	6	-	37	6	-	20,432	-	803
5199 Nondurable goods, nec[2]	-	12	-	163	14	-	28,859	-	3,922
52 - Retail trade	-	2,071	-	30,865	15	-	11,266	-	375,774
5210 Lumber and other building materials	-	35	-	668	19	-	22,545	-	14,810
5230 Paint, glass, and wallpaper stores	-	15	-	19	1	-	24,211	-	479
5250 Hardware stores	-	22	-	323	15	-	12,074	-	4,209
5260 Retail nurseries and garden stores	-	15	-	147	10	-	10,503	-	2,150
5310 Department stores[2]	-	20	-	2,818	141	-	11,062	-	31,985
5330 Variety stores[2]	-	11	-	109	10	-	9,284	-	922
5390 Misc. general merchandise stores	-	13	-	614	47	-	14,586	-	9,640
5410 Grocery stores	-	73	-	3,593	49	-	10,814	-	41,005
5420 Meat and fish markets[2]	-	5	-	61	12	-	8,197	-	504
5440 Candy, nut, and confectionery stores[2]	-	9	-	30	3	-	6,133	-	178
5460 Retail bakeries	-	33	-	353	11	-	8,453	-	3,099
5490 Miscellaneous food stores[2]	-	11	-	37	3	-	10,811	-	421
5510 New and used car dealers	-	39	-	1,360	35	-	25,976	-	39,362
5520 Used car dealers	-	50	-	215	4	-	21,098	-	5,301
5530 Auto and home supply stores	-	43	-	388	9	-	15,000	-	6,714
5540 Gasoline service stations	-	144	-	1,155	8	-	10,341	-	12,542
5550 Boat dealers[2]	-	13	-	127	10	-	16,378	-	2,799
5570 Motorcycle dealers[2]	-	7	-	38	5	-	16,211	-	894
5610 Men's & boys' clothing stores[2]	-	25	-	178	7	-	10,315	-	1,771
5620 Women's clothing stores	-	73	-	659	9	-	7,114	-	4,875
5630 Women's accessory & specialty stores	-	6	-	13	2	-	9,846	-	113
5640 Children's and infants' wear stores[2]	-	7	-	55	8	-	7,855	-	447
5650 Family clothing stores	-	30	-	350	12	-	9,177	-	3,614
5660 Shoe stores	-	47	-	276	6	-	9,362	-	2,814
5690 Misc. apparel & accessory stores[2]	-	15	-	58	4	-	7,586	-	549
5712 Furniture stores	-	39	-	311	8	-	16,257	-	5,423
5713 Floor covering stores[2]	-	21	-	104	5	-	24,538	-	2,752
5719 Misc. homefurnishings stores	-	18	-	102	6	-	8,588	-	1,035
5720 Household appliance stores	-	23	-	175	8	-	17,280	-	3,150
5731 Radio, TV, & electronic stores	-	17	-	345	20	-	16,649	-	6,316
5735 Record & prerecorded tape stores	-	12	-	147	12	-	8,735	-	1,312
5812 Eating places	-	384	-	9,408	25	-	6,935	-	68,554
5813 Drinking places	-	167	-	781	5	-	5,782	-	4,596
5910 Drug stores and proprietary stores	-	38	-	528	14	-	18,121	-	9,869
5920 Liquor stores[2]	-	18	-	67	4	-	8,597	-	639
5930 Used merchandise stores[2]	-	23	-	223	10	-	10,637	-	2,700
5941 Sporting goods and bicycle shops	-	50	-	419	8	-	12,143	-	5,546
5942 Book stores[2]	-	23	-	189	8	-	7,407	-	1,571
5944 Jewelry stores	-	40	-	200	5	-	17,620	-	3,520
5945 Hobby, toy, and game shops	-	19	-	112	6	-	10,679	-	1,320
5947 Gift, novelty, and souvenir shops	-	54	-	313	6	-	7,003	-	2,591
5948 Luggage and leather goods stores[2]	-	4	-	15	4	-	10,933	-	168
5949 Sewing, needlework, and piece goods	-	11	-	35	3	-	4,800	-	166
5963 Direct selling establishments	-	18	-	83	5	-	12,964	-	1,104
5980 Fuel dealers	-	11	-	62	6	-	25,806	-	1,528
5992 Florists	-	16	-	147	9	-	10,259	-	1,704
5995 Optical goods stores	-	21	-	90	4	-	13,600	-	1,230
5999 Miscellaneous retail stores, nec	-	61	-	337	6	-	13,175	-	4,976

Source: County Business Patterns 1994/95, CBP-94/95, U.S. Department of Commerce, Washington DC, November 1997. The employment column represents mid-March employment in the year. Pay per employee is calculated by dividing 1st Quarter payroll, annualized, by mid-March employment. The column headed 'Emp / Est' shows 'employees per establishment'. A dash (-) means that data are unavailable or cannot be calculated. nec means not elsewhere classified. *Notes:* 1. 1994 data incomplete; unavailable or withheld. 2. 1995 data incomplete; unavailable or withheld. 3. 1994 and 1995 data incomplete; unavailable or withheld.

ASHEVILLE, NC MSA

Wholesale and Retail Trade USA	Establishments		Employment		Emp / Est	Pay / Employee		Annual Payroll ($ 000)	
	1994	1995	1994	1995	1995	1994	1995	1994	1995
50 - Wholesale trade	393	396	4,468	4,551	11	24,145	25,926	117,141	129,896
5012 Automobiles and other vehicles [3]	5	6	81	87	15	19,506	20,782	1,609	1,699
5013 Motor vehicle supplies and new parts [3]	17	14	179	142	10	14,168	18,366	2,828	2,808
5014 Tires and tubes [3]	4	3	66	39	13	31,212	27,795	1,865	1,285
5015 Motor vehicle parts, used [3]	8	8	34	34	4	19,412	21,647	757	822
5020 Furniture and homefurnishings [3]	9	10	25	23	2	19,040	17,913	475	490
5031 Lumber, plywood, and millwork [2]	11	12	133	115	10	21,564	21,843	2,955	2,940
5039 Construction materials, nec [3]	6	8	53	79	10	19,698	21,468	1,291	3,036
5044 Office equipment [3]	11	9	103	103	11	24,621	29,010	2,901	3,245
5045 Computers, peripherals, & software [3]	10	8	130	119	15	42,646	48,639	5,788	6,208
5047 Medical and hospital equipment [3]	7	8	55	66	8	33,527	34,909	2,168	2,607
5051 Metals service centers and offices [3]	3	3	21	29	10	22,286	27,448	629	1,029
5063 Electrical apparatus and equipment [3]	12	11	126	134	12	30,032	30,836	3,607	4,183
5072 Hardware [3]	8	8	63	70	9	22,349	25,200	1,677	1,932
5074 Plumbing & hydronic heating supplies [3]	9	10	86	98	10	28,930	29,673	2,332	2,772
5082 Construction and mining machinery [3]	14	14	163	175	13	29,448	34,423	4,895	5,793
5084 Industrial machinery and equipment [1]	19	17	152	176	10	29,079	35,068	5,971	7,398
5085 Industrial supplies [3]	18	20	164	183	9	24,415	28,568	4,836	5,557
5087 Service establishment equipment [3]	11	12	83	92	8	24,675	23,130	2,087	2,319
5093 Scrap and waste materials	14	13	176	200	15	18,909	20,420	4,284	6,277
5099 Durable goods, nec	7	5	20	25	5	11,200	13,280	309	336
5112 Stationery and office supplies [3]	11	11	153	181	16	17,255	17,834	2,803	3,156
5120 Drugs, proprietaries, and sundries [1]	4	-	56	-	-	47,071	-	1,648	-
5131 Piece goods & notions	-	5	-	9	2	-	30,667	-	390
5137 Women's and children's clothing [3]	4	4	9	22	6	6,222	2,909	79	68
5141 Groceries, general line [3]	8	7	742	725	104	22,566	25,181	18,841	19,460
5143 Dairy products, exc. dried or canned	6	-	71	-	-	25,915	-	1,679	-
5148 Fresh fruits and vegetables	5	-	30	-	-	12,533	-	368	-
5149 Groceries and related products, nec [3]	12	12	324	328	27	21,790	23,524	7,580	8,236
5159 Farm-product raw materials, nec [1]	5	-	28	-	-	11,429	-	169	-
5162 Plastics materials & basic shapes [3]	4	4	5	6	2	64,000	44,000	386	610
5169 Chemicals & allied products, nec [3]	7	8	45	43	5	27,556	37,767	1,283	1,662
5171 Petroleum bulk stations & terminals	-	7	-	94	13	-	23,362	-	2,731
5172 Petroleum products, nec [2]	-	3	-	33	11	-	12,606	-	470
5180 Beer, wine, and distilled beverages [3]	7	7	228	244	35	22,789	21,344	5,907	5,922
5191 Farm supplies [3]	10	11	67	61	6	15,821	16,590	1,105	1,040
5193 Flowers & florists' supplies [3]	5	4	23	23	6	17,217	19,130	416	476
5199 Nondurable goods, nec [3]	12	14	76	94	7	18,842	22,170	2,013	2,508
52 - Retail trade	1,513	1,511	19,666	20,494	14	10,990	11,943	241,723	264,214
5210 Lumber and other building materials	28	22	621	563	26	16,238	22,202	11,460	12,066
5230 Paint, glass, and wallpaper stores [3]	9	9	44	57	6	14,636	14,807	719	940
5250 Hardware stores [3]	10	8	77	70	9	12,104	11,600	1,015	885
5260 Retail nurseries and garden stores	9	11	29	44	4	13,793	12,000	536	676
5270 Mobile home dealers [3]	12	12	118	114	10	24,271	23,123	3,465	3,203
5310 Department stores [3]	17	16	2,100	2,161	135	9,850	12,063	23,195	26,066
5330 Variety stores	10	-	42	-	-	7,905	-	456	-
5390 Misc. general merchandise stores	14	-	419	-	-	11,332	-	4,628	-
5410 Grocery stores	129	129	2,489	2,551	20	10,033	10,321	25,751	27,176
5430 Fruit and vegetable markets [1]	3	-	1	-	-	4,000	-	42	-
5440 Candy, nut, and confectionery stores [2]	-	5	-	14	3	-	6,286	-	272
5460 Retail bakeries [3]	10	8	71	81	10	6,479	10,667	617	1,055
5490 Miscellaneous food stores [3]	13	14	81	132	9	11,556	11,818	1,242	1,629
5510 New and used car dealers	20	18	647	602	33	26,331	29,860	18,642	19,687
5520 Used car dealers	35	34	113	112	3	16,920	18,821	2,288	2,725
5530 Auto and home supply stores	54	54	350	385	7	15,589	17,319	5,740	6,962
5540 Gasoline service stations	95	96	587	676	7	12,150	12,929	8,666	9,359
5610 Men's & boys' clothing stores [3]	11	10	75	83	8	8,213	6,747	640	572
5620 Women's clothing stores	50	44	443	400	9	7,214	7,050	3,449	2,922
5630 Women's accessory & specialty stores [3]	11	12	59	64	5	9,356	10,438	602	662
5640 Children's and infants' wear stores [2]	-	3	-	18	6	-	4,444	-	128
5650 Family clothing stores	23	23	232	252	11	9,293	10,381	2,204	2,592
5660 Shoe stores [2]	44	37	225	232	6	15,236	12,966	3,436	3,451
5690 Misc. apparel & accessory stores [2]	-	6	-	28	5	-	8,429	-	226
5712 Furniture stores	34	34	299	308	9	16,829	18,429	5,892	6,145
5713 Floor covering stores [3]	13	14	76	92	7	18,053	16,522	1,666	1,768
5714 Drapery and upholstery stores [3]	5	3	5	4	1	13,600	3,000	59	52
5719 Misc. homefurnishings stores [3]	26	19	99	97	5	10,828	10,474	1,179	1,083
5720 Household appliance stores [3]	8	7	67	62	9	17,970	18,258	1,267	1,237
5731 Radio, TV, & electronic stores [3]	12	12	107	110	9	17,196	18,509	2,040	2,261
5734 Computer and software stores [3]	6	7	24	19	3	14,833	17,474	357	393
5735 Record & prerecorded tape stores [3]	14	14	50	64	5	10,480	11,125	629	729

Continued on next page.

ASHEVILLE, NC MSA - [continued]

Wholesale and Retail Trade USA	Establishments		Employment		Emp / Est	Pay / Employee		Annual Payroll ($ 000)	
	1994	1995	1994	1995	1995	1994	1995	1994	1995
5736 Musical instrument stores[3]	3	3	27	25	8	13,185	15,840	468	440
5812 Eating places	313	298	6,706	6,857	23	7,513	8,060	57,564	60,874
5813 Drinking places[3]	11	6	46	45	8	6,522	7,467	338	362
5910 Drug stores and proprietary stores	46	42	483	467	11	14,783	15,640	7,854	8,121
5920 Liquor stores[2]	15	14	50	56	4	19,120	18,000	1,027	1,030
5930 Used merchandise stores[3]	28	25	103	120	5	9,864	12,433	1,229	1,441
5941 Sporting goods and bicycle shops	22	21	73	93	4	12,110	12,043	1,066	1,258
5942 Book stores	22	22	141	167	8	10,355	10,491	1,571	1,762
5944 Jewelry stores[3]	25	27	123	139	5	15,122	15,482	2,201	2,327
5945 Hobby, toy, and game shops[3]	26	27	156	172	6	11,692	12,372	2,284	2,522
5947 Gift, novelty, and souvenir shops[1]	43	46	258	266	6	10,388	10,737	2,748	3,186
5949 Sewing, needlework, and piece goods	9	8	48	44	6	8,500	7,636	402	332
5961 Catalog and mail-order houses	-	11	-	407	37	-	13,474	-	5,835
5962 Merchandising machine operators[3]	6	6	164	195	33	13,341	14,441	2,654	3,106
5963 Direct selling establishments[2]	-	13	-	62	5	-	19,226	-	1,176
5980 Fuel dealers	14	14	97	100	7	20,577	18,840	1,943	1,802
5992 Florists	30	-	101	-	-	8,871	-	1,038	-
5995 Optical goods stores[2]	-	12	-	71	6	-	15,268	-	1,216
5999 Miscellaneous retail stores, nec[3]	41	48	127	157	3	13,291	13,911	1,959	2,354

Source: County Business Patterns 1994/95, CBP-94/95, U.S. Department of Commerce, Washington DC, November 1997. The employment column represents mid-March employment in the year. Pay per employee is calculated by dividing 1st Quarter payroll, annualized, by mid-March employment. The column headed 'Emp / Est' shows 'employees per establishment'. A dash (-) means that data are unavailable or cannot be calculated. nec means not elsewhere classified. *Notes:* 1. 1994 data incomplete; unavailable or withheld. 2. 1995 data incomplete; unavailable or withheld. 3. 1994 and 1995 data incomplete; unavailable or withheld.

ATHENS, GA MSA

Wholesale and Retail Trade USA	Establishments		Employment		Emp / Est	Pay / Employee		Annual Payroll ($ 000)	
	1994	1995	1994	1995	1995	1994	1995	1994	1995
50- Wholesale trade[3]	194	194	2,521	2,772	14	24,985	25,672	68,764	77,492
5010 Motor vehicles, parts, and supplies[3]	22	19	169	157	8	18,012	17,936	3,655	3,022
5032 Brick, stone, & related materials[2]	-	4	-	13	3	-	31,692	-	425
5045 Computers, peripherals, & software[3]	6	6	38	39	7	21,895	26,154	876	1,043
5047 Medical and hospital equipment[1]	4	-	24	-	-	30,000	-	1,143	-
5063 Electrical apparatus and equipment[3]	11	10	84	79	8	28,333	30,582	2,318	2,249
5064 Electrical appliances, TV & radios[1]	4	-	54	-	-	20,741	-	1,285	-
5065 Electronic parts and equipment[1]	4	-	13	-	-	13,846	-	160	-
5075 Warm air heating & air conditioning[3]	10	10	59	62	6	22,712	22,387	1,317	1,479
5084 Industrial machinery and equipment[3]	10	9	65	56	6	20,554	29,071	1,955	1,805
5087 Service establishment equipment[3]	5	5	57	81	16	26,807	22,963	2,875	3,409
5110 Paper and paper products[3]	10	8	99	90	11	21,010	25,378	1,934	2,284
5130 Apparel, piece goods, and notions[3]	5	5	13	9	2	12,923	12,444	138	183
5149 Groceries and related products, nec[3]	3	3	141	156	52	30,610	29,436	4,263	4,518
5171 Petroleum bulk stations & terminals[3]	7	7	31	27	4	30,065	34,222	1,074	1,136
5172 Petroleum products, nec[3]	4	4	40	62	16	18,200	13,871	861	915
5181 Beer and ale[3]	3	3	207	209	70	30,338	32,995	7,073	7,681
5191 Farm supplies[1]	5	-	21	-	-	17,905	-	416	-
5199 Nondurable goods, nec[3]	10	13	71	127	10	21,352	24,189	1,835	3,265
52- Retail trade[3]	894	897	12,559	13,728	15	10,472	10,536	140,141	151,390
5210 Lumber and other building materials[3]	14	10	323	254	25	15,938	19,386	5,608	5,360
5230 Paint, glass, and wallpaper stores[3]	6	6	35	30	5	10,743	13,067	373	383
5250 Hardware stores[3]	15	15	67	74	5	13,313	13,568	1,015	1,037
5260 Retail nurseries and garden stores[3]	5	7	38	39	6	11,263	10,974	411	446
5270 Mobile home dealers[3]	4	4	19	20	5	24,000	34,800	623	844
5310 Department stores[3]	9	8	1,365	1,421	178	9,582	10,334	13,417	13,594
5330 Variety stores[2]	-	5	-	78	16	-	7,641	-	680
5390 Misc. general merchandise stores[2]	-	6	-	27	5	-	4,889	-	138
5410 Grocery stores[3]	58	59	1,594	2,067	35	9,945	8,702	15,888	18,651
5440 Candy, nut, and confectionery stores[3]	5	5	17	6	1	7,059	10,000	111	53
5460 Retail bakeries[1]	7	-	64	-	-	6,938	-	423	-
5490 Miscellaneous food stores[2]	-	7	-	19	3	-	7,789	-	215
5510 New and used car dealers[3]	12	11	483	517	47	30,692	30,940	16,256	17,917
5520 Used car dealers[1]	15	-	10	-	-	13,200	-	145	-
5530 Auto and home supply stores[3]	30	30	236	255	9	17,186	19,137	4,680	5,400
5540 Gasoline service stations[3]	79	74	496	479	6	11,024	12,184	5,746	5,971
5610 Men's & boys' clothing stores[3]	10	9	73	74	8	10,082	10,757	783	790
5620 Women's clothing stores[3]	39	35	284	246	7	7,380	7,512	2,299	2,045
5630 Women's accessory & specialty stores[3]	3	3	32	26	9	5,375	8,000	198	204
5650 Family clothing stores[3]	13	13	233	225	17	7,039	8,213	1,834	2,012
5660 Shoe stores[3]	27	25	171	144	6	10,246	10,694	1,689	1,596

Continued on next page.

ATHENS, GA MSA - [continued]

Wholesale and Retail Trade USA	Establishments		Employment		Emp / Est	Pay / Employee		Annual Payroll ($ 000)	
	1994	1995	1994	1995	1995	1994	1995	1994	1995
5690 Misc. apparel & accessory stores [3]	7	7	16	21	3	5,750	6,476	121	81
5712 Furniture stores [3]	23	24	112	130	5	15,071	17,231	1,920	2,479
5713 Floor covering stores [3]	7	5	25	18	4	16,000	17,778	400	359
5719 Misc. homefurnishings stores [3]	4	5	16	20	4	8,750	9,400	160	186
5720 Household appliance stores [3]	6	8	17	23	3	17,412	16,174	322	346
5731 Radio, TV, & electronic stores [3]	14	13	64	166	13	22,000	15,446	1,913	2,249
5735 Record & prerecorded tape stores [3]	4	4	36	43	11	8,667	8,000	309	318
5812 Eating places [3]	165	162	3,789	4,071	25	7,158	7,217	28,009	30,469
5813 Drinking places [3]	15	14	93	95	7	6,882	7,326	642	720
5910 Drug stores and proprietary stores [3]	26	24	214	251	10	14,355	15,681	3,613	4,082
5920 Liquor stores [3]	22	22	103	101	5	9,010	9,584	923	1,081
5930 Used merchandise stores [3]	21	24	78	140	6	14,718	9,686	1,193	1,340
5941 Sporting goods and bicycle shops [3]	13	15	117	120	8	8,342	10,000	1,144	1,319
5942 Book stores [3]	11	10	77	90	9	7,481	10,978	725	996
5943 Stationery stores [1]	3	-	45	-	-	8,978	-	294	-
5944 Jewelry stores [3]	18	17	94	116	7	15,787	13,483	1,529	1,582
5945 Hobby, toy, and game shops [3]	5	5	63	75	15	9,968	8,587	803	809
5947 Gift, novelty, and souvenir shops [3]	19	17	75	83	5	6,453	4,964	513	476
5949 Sewing, needlework, and piece goods [3]	7	6	46	50	8	9,565	8,720	443	492
5960 Nonstore retailers [3]	13	11	528	658	60	8,697	7,629	4,829	4,940
5992 Florists [2]	-	18	-	12	1	-	8,333	-	89
5995 Optical goods stores [3]	11	9	58	54	6	10,966	18,444	710	898
5999 Miscellaneous retail stores, nec [3]	26	26	111	121	5	9,766	11,339	1,146	1,455

Source: County Business Patterns 1994/95, CBP-94/95, U.S. Department of Commerce, Washington DC, November 1997. The employment column represents mid-March employment in the year. Pay per employee is calculated by dividing 1st Quarter payroll, annualized, by mid-March employment. The column headed 'Emp / Est' shows 'employees per establishment'. A dash (-) means that data are unavailable or cannot be calculated. nec means not elsewhere classified. *Notes:* 1. 1994 data incomplete; unavailable or withheld. 2. 1995 data incomplete; unavailable or withheld. 3. 1994 and 1995 data incomplete; unavailable or withheld.

ATLANTA, GA MSA

Wholesale and Retail Trade USA	Establishments		Employment		Emp / Est	Pay / Employee		Annual Payroll ($ 000)	
	1994	1995	1994	1995	1995	1994	1995	1994	1995
50 – Wholesale trade [3]	9,920	10,205	144,752	156,285	15	35,885	38,673	5,363,316	6,120,405
5012 Automobiles and other vehicles [3]	156	160	3,208	3,210	20	34,404	41,230	112,208	127,586
5013 Motor vehicle supplies and new parts [3]	417	381	5,512	5,134	13	30,837	31,169	181,642	163,971
5014 Tires and tubes [3]	57	57	937	904	16	35,261	40,558	33,819	34,490
5015 Motor vehicle parts, used [3]	105	116	532	610	5	18,000	21,908	11,164	13,994
5021 Furniture [3]	221	236	1,988	1,996	8	30,960	32,996	66,754	70,155
5023 Homefurnishings [3]	258	263	1,770	1,873	7	30,158	31,949	59,256	61,885
5031 Lumber, plywood, and millwork [3]	183	169	2,738	2,817	17	29,097	34,089	90,283	100,904
5032 Brick, stone, & related materials [3]	108	94	716	577	6	27,291	30,253	22,616	19,290
5033 Roofing, siding, & insulation [3]	63	63	667	632	10	33,907	36,310	24,431	24,289
5039 Construction materials, nec [3]	81	152	1,197	2,145	14	27,656	30,945	37,924	74,652
5043 Photographic equipment & supplies [3]	39	41	422	370	9	47,147	54,238	20,687	20,278
5044 Office equipment [3]	128	148	4,196	4,083	28	40,258	40,156	180,401	167,470
5045 Computers, peripherals, & software [3]	584	597	11,323	11,052	19	54,077	57,024	601,219	602,095
5046 Commercial equipment, nec [3]	123	129	1,121	1,166	9	29,670	34,103	37,218	41,549
5047 Medical and hospital equipment [3]	279	265	4,021	4,088	15	42,318	47,590	170,202	196,745
5048 Ophthalmic goods [3]	33	33	192	255	8	28,688	28,831	6,055	7,204
5049 Professional equipment, nec [3]	68	66	945	980	15	32,834	34,922	33,040	36,312
5051 Metals service centers and offices [3]	239	228	1,765	1,228	5	31,855	35,964	61,181	45,099
5052 Coal and other minerals and ores [1]	7	-	11	-	-	49,455	-	503	-
5063 Electrical apparatus and equipment [3]	397	348	4,898	4,660	13	34,980	39,335	185,061	189,532
5064 Electrical appliances, TV & radios [3]	81	83	1,471	1,520	18	37,458	43,434	57,578	71,303
5065 Electronic parts and equipment [3]	413	436	5,328	7,107	16	48,088	52,015	256,267	352,511
5072 Hardware [3]	182	195	1,858	2,023	10	27,470	28,759	56,123	61,384
5074 Plumbing & hydronic heating supplies [3]	163	160	1,501	1,468	9	31,726	33,665	50,814	52,324
5075 Warm air heating & air conditioning [3]	122	131	1,203	1,316	10	32,755	35,252	43,695	53,043
5078 Refrigeration equipment and supplies [3]	37	35	172	205	6	38,907	41,463	6,659	8,254
5082 Construction and mining machinery [3]	89	85	1,433	1,404	17	40,103	45,558	59,016	65,121
5083 Farm and garden machinery [3]	86	78	725	561	7	33,545	39,444	25,902	22,720
5084 Industrial machinery and equipment [3]	684	720	6,584	7,188	10	39,832	41,953	287,707	320,459
5085 Industrial supplies [3]	304	313	2,983	3,064	10	33,420	36,504	106,030	120,415
5087 Service establishment equipment [3]	139	137	1,256	1,281	9	29,548	29,158	40,980	41,373
5088 Transportation equipment & supplies [3]	60	59	475	600	10	36,177	35,480	18,366	22,368
5091 Sporting & recreational goods [3]	116	114	1,094	1,100	10	30,457	36,444	35,078	38,322
5092 Toys and hobby goods and supplies [3]	34	34	162	197	6	30,000	28,102	5,924	6,850
5093 Scrap and waste materials [3]	149	151	1,317	1,563	10	27,016	30,316	41,703	51,944
5094 Jewelry & precious stones [3]	149	157	929	900	6	20,934	23,560	23,129	22,740

Continued on next page.

ATLANTA, GA MSA - [continued]

Wholesale and Retail Trade USA	Establishments		Employment		Emp / Est	Pay / Employee		Annual Payroll ($ 000)	
	1994	1995	1994	1995	1995	1994	1995	1994	1995
5099 Durable goods, nec[3]	170	179	1,085	1,317	7	27,539	26,891	32,428	40,672
5111 Printing and writing paper[3]	70	72	1,283	1,401	19	46,438	52,443	60,227	69,582
5112 Stationery and office supplies[3]	263	228	7,524	9,362	41	15,315	13,457	123,399	116,295
5113 Industrial & personal service paper[3]	109	121	1,521	1,874	15	43,821	46,019	68,366	91,703
5120 Drugs, proprietaries, and sundries[3]	132	147	4,818	5,350	36	43,391	52,626	203,625	275,218
5131 Piece goods & notions[3]	125	135	929	1,089	8	41,925	40,514	34,491	36,862
5136 Men's and boys' clothing[3]	110	107	1,181	1,065	10	25,006	29,559	31,839	32,409
5137 Women's and children's clothing[3]	158	148	599	607	4	23,426	23,196	16,155	15,865
5139 Footwear[3]	21	27	108	113	4	27,259	20,850	3,294	2,823
5141 Groceries, general line[3]	74	70	2,596	2,246	32	27,066	31,295	75,529	72,567
5142 Packaged frozen food[3]	68	56	1,611	1,607	29	31,166	34,019	57,001	59,521
5143 Dairy products, exc. dried or canned[3]	27	28	417	387	14	28,508	31,897	12,312	13,896
5144 Poultry and poultry products[3]	20	17	36	29	2	45,667	36,414	1,951	1,735
5145 Confectionery[3]	35	35	469	352	10	49,834	42,034	14,953	15,253
5146 Fish and seafoods[3]	19	20	234	290	15	25,573	24,014	6,292	7,462
5147 Meats and meat products[3]	48	47	1,217	1,148	24	27,908	32,125	36,517	36,280
5148 Fresh fruits and vegetables[3]	62	65	1,995	2,148	33	19,270	19,138	39,870	44,220
5149 Groceries and related products, nec[3]	197	194	4,070	3,718	19	31,972	35,055	135,869	144,872
5153 Grain and field beans[3]	9	9	20	21	2	38,400	36,190	771	597
5159 Farm-product raw materials, nec[2]	-	16	-	21	1	-	16,762	-	338
5162 Plastics materials & basic shapes[3]	109	109	707	797	7	45,935	49,862	32,836	36,414
5169 Chemicals & allied products, nec[3]	301	311	3,562	3,768	12	43,626	46,465	156,546	175,694
5171 Petroleum bulk stations & terminals[3]	82	75	629	589	8	33,469	36,054	23,736	23,594
5172 Petroleum products, nec[3]	52	58	472	435	8	51,847	48,359	20,458	21,471
5181 Beer and ale[3]	15	16	402	532	33	29,692	28,429	13,249	16,581
5182 Wine and distilled beverages[3]	29	32	947	1,033	32	40,748	37,832	44,418	39,399
5191 Farm supplies[3]	87	88	448	512	6	32,696	39,336	17,223	20,368
5192 Books, periodicals, & newspapers[3]	81	85	1,165	1,199	14	35,032	39,807	39,746	43,727
5193 Flowers & florists' supplies[3]	82	67	668	626	9	20,527	23,029	15,187	15,417
5194 Tobacco and tobacco products[3]	13	13	94	91	7	32,426	37,846	3,393	3,537
5198 Paints, varnishes, and supplies[3]	133	131	908	927	7	29,837	29,066	27,651	27,457
5199 Nondurable goods, nec[3]	400	407	2,837	3,210	8	26,448	29,792	84,132	96,420
52 - Retail trade[3]	20,000	20,409	325,605	353,798	17	13,173	13,938	4,609,410	5,118,651
5210 Lumber and other building materials[3]	222	210	6,181	6,773	32	20,476	23,585	145,470	168,972
5230 Paint, glass, and wallpaper stores[3]	138	127	393	556	4	18,860	19,518	8,237	11,407
5250 Hardware stores[3]	176	143	1,276	1,010	7	14,925	14,859	21,241	16,404
5260 Retail nurseries and garden stores[3]	163	164	1,293	1,334	8	11,814	13,046	18,593	19,687
5270 Mobile home dealers[3]	28	29	13	4	-	13,846	14,000	193	144
5310 Department stores[3]	141	149	22,302	24,269	163	11,823	12,594	293,159	306,517
5330 Variety stores[3]	141	121	1,241	1,162	10	9,280	9,398	13,029	11,773
5390 Misc. general merchandise stores[3]	120	129	3,035	2,983	23	12,992	14,140	40,545	39,036
5410 Grocery stores[3]	1,462	1,504	43,487	57,806	38	10,513	8,686	477,810	515,886
5420 Meat and fish markets[3]	54	48	207	142	3	14,783	10,620	3,673	1,508
5430 Fruit and vegetable markets[3]	21	19	329	425	22	10,359	13,186	4,097	5,621
5440 Candy, nut, and confectionery stores[3]	25	25	231	148	6	8,139	7,784	1,535	1,156
5450 Dairy products stores[3]	24	28	42	57	2	5,143	6,246	332	370
5460 Retail bakeries[3]	164	170	1,410	1,476	9	9,662	10,249	16,102	16,000
5490 Miscellaneous food stores[3]	159	195	693	1,023	5	16,947	15,288	12,001	16,914
5510 New and used car dealers[3]	236	251	13,719	14,555	58	31,943	35,055	491,675	559,338
5520 Used car dealers[3]	242	253	798	1,105	4	21,905	23,052	19,335	28,103
5530 Auto and home supply stores[3]	629	676	4,919	5,446	8	18,910	20,261	103,689	118,789
5540 Gasoline service stations[3]	1,155	1,147	8,549	8,220	7	12,688	13,884	115,277	118,688
5550 Boat dealers[3]	34	35	96	90	3	20,167	16,978	2,192	2,113
5560 Recreational vehicle dealers[3]	18	17	94	113	7	23,872	27,080	2,540	3,193
5570 Motorcycle dealers[3]	32	32	156	151	5	17,744	19,444	3,235	3,301
5590 Automotive dealers, nec[3]	16	18	204	86	5	21,608	21,256	4,662	1,396
5610 Men's & boys' clothing stores[3]	220	215	1,762	1,830	9	13,228	14,505	24,067	26,328
5620 Women's clothing stores[3]	655	596	6,302	5,608	9	9,532	9,702	64,256	57,415
5630 Women's accessory & specialty stores[3]	124	112	618	647	6	12,045	12,216	8,205	8,336
5640 Children's and infants' wear stores[3]	65	69	601	637	9	7,141	8,496	4,999	6,277
5650 Family clothing stores[3]	206	209	5,006	5,180	25	10,395	11,222	58,162	59,826
5660 Shoe stores[3]	495	488	3,130	3,113	6	11,913	12,946	39,204	39,785
5690 Misc. apparel & accessory stores[3]	135	128	572	567	4	10,734	11,711	6,582	6,917
5712 Furniture stores[3]	487	508	4,082	4,635	9	18,801	19,315	78,282	93,823
5713 Floor covering stores[3]	175	187	579	832	4	22,494	23,880	18,054	20,791
5714 Drapery and upholstery stores[3]	37	38	123	156	4	15,415	14,538	2,293	2,604
5719 Misc. homefurnishings stores[3]	280	283	2,278	2,582	9	11,117	13,123	30,677	34,878
5720 Household appliance stores[3]	100	94	431	419	4	16,882	18,673	7,488	7,608
5731 Radio, TV, & electronic stores[3]	201	224	2,212	2,515	11	18,470	18,788	42,141	49,246
5734 Computer and software stores[3]	134	137	780	1,048	8	22,518	24,901	21,247	28,064
5735 Record & prerecorded tape stores[3]	159	154	1,479	2,071	13	16,535	13,039	22,778	23,959

Continued on next page.

ATLANTA, GA MSA - [continued]

Wholesale and Retail Trade USA	Establishments		Employment		Emp / Est	Pay / Employee		Annual Payroll ($ 000)	
	1994	1995	1994	1995	1995	1994	1995	1994	1995
5736 Musical instrument stores[3]	62	56	248	261	5	21,919	24,092	6,630	7,155
5812 Eating places[3]	4,923	4,588	112,655	111,937	24	8,392	9,006	1,002,615	1,032,982
5813 Drinking places[3]	232	194	3,339	2,949	15	9,797	10,479	32,694	30,497
5910 Drug stores and proprietary stores[3]	569	589	6,579	6,926	12	14,673	16,192	104,013	116,135
5920 Liquor stores[3]	348	349	1,617	1,530	4	13,358	14,350	23,814	23,699
5930 Used merchandise stores[3]	419	424	1,876	2,018	5	14,269	14,266	28,357	29,509
5941 Sporting goods and bicycle shops[3]	239	254	1,713	2,070	8	12,985	13,617	25,253	30,019
5942 Book stores[3]	199	186	1,537	1,534	8	9,780	11,134	16,256	17,789
5943 Stationery stores[3]	60	62	442	445	7	18,561	17,483	7,225	7,903
5944 Jewelry stores[3]	329	325	1,752	1,852	6	18,055	19,328	32,327	35,859
5945 Hobby, toy, and game shops[3]	117	123	1,205	1,314	11	9,749	9,522	14,326	15,504
5946 Camera & photographic supply stores[3]	51	52	152	228	4	18,974	22,772	3,360	4,809
5947 Gift, novelty, and souvenir shops[3]	394	394	2,562	2,653	7	8,660	9,642	24,234	26,954
5948 Luggage and leather goods stores[3]	24	25	69	82	3	16,464	16,488	1,261	1,412
5949 Sewing, needlework, and piece goods[3]	104	95	653	622	7	11,712	10,836	7,649	7,049
5961 Catalog and mail-order houses[3]	105	120	898	1,289	11	21,114	22,542	23,252	31,870
5962 Merchandising machine operators[3]	100	105	830	923	9	21,489	24,126	20,154	23,046
5963 Direct selling establishments[3]	190	199	2,346	2,346	12	15,059	17,127	38,888	38,309
5984 Liquefied petroleum gas dealers[3]	53	55	208	210	4	29,442	24,648	4,862	4,557
5992 Florists[3]	339	328	990	1,302	4	12,202	12,424	13,080	16,455
5993 Tobacco stores and stands[2]	-	11	-	12	1	-	23,000	-	384
5994 News dealers and newsstands[3]	15	15	32	51	3	9,750	22,353	655	1,497
5995 Optical goods stores[3]	227	232	1,487	1,338	6	14,685	17,175	22,739	23,480
5999 Miscellaneous retail stores, nec[3]	665	710	3,524	3,768	5	12,941	13,903	50,977	57,621

Source: County Business Patterns 1994/95, CBP-94/95, U.S. Department of Commerce, Washington DC, November 1997. The employment column represents mid-March employment in the year. Pay per employee is calculated by dividing 1st Quarter payroll, annualized, by mid-March employment. The column headed 'Emp / Est' shows 'employees per establishment'. A dash (-) means that data are unavailable or cannot be calculated. nec means not elsewhere classified. *Notes:* 1. 1994 data incomplete; unavailable or withheld. 2. 1995 data incomplete; unavailable or withheld. 3. 1994 and 1995 data incomplete; unavailable or withheld.

ATLANTIC – CAPE MAY, NJ PMSA

Wholesale and Retail Trade USA	Establishments		Employment		Emp / Est	Pay / Employee		Annual Payroll ($ 000)	
	1994	1995	1994	1995	1995	1994	1995	1994	1995
50- Wholesale trade[3]	400	382	3,813	4,216	11	26,827	27,011	120,981	124,969
5012 Automobiles and other vehicles[1]	4	-	9	-	-	16,000	-	151	-
5013 Motor vehicle supplies and new parts[3]	27	24	164	158	7	18,488	20,152	3,528	3,302
5015 Motor vehicle parts, used[3]	7	6	44	40	7	21,909	23,800	997	932
5021 Furniture[3]	4	5	26	30	6	28,462	31,733	695	847
5023 Homefurnishings[3]	8	7	76	102	15	44,211	50,549	2,232	3,969
5033 Roofing, siding, & insulation[3]	8	8	197	229	29	28,020	27,109	7,915	8,384
5039 Construction materials, nec[2]	-	6	-	14	2	-	22,857	-	342
5044 Office equipment[3]	9	11	91	111	10	30,505	27,099	2,956	2,983
5046 Commercial equipment, nec[3]	8	7	28	25	4	22,857	25,440	665	668
5047 Medical and hospital equipment[2]	-	6	-	6	1	-	9,333	-	92
5063 Electrical apparatus and equipment[3]	14	9	113	83	9	27,965	33,446	3,578	2,688
5065 Electronic parts and equipment[3]	12	12	58	33	3	32,690	39,394	2,153	1,236
5074 Plumbing & hydronic heating supplies[3]	17	17	92	100	6	29,870	28,760	3,089	2,863
5083 Farm and garden machinery[3]	4	5	32	46	9	23,875	27,130	1,007	1,350
5084 Industrial machinery and equipment[3]	11	11	40	43	4	37,800	46,419	1,934	2,184
5085 Industrial supplies[3]	6	7	6	12	2	18,000	26,000	175	326
5087 Service establishment equipment[3]	8	7	28	27	4	21,571	22,963	565	549
5088 Transportation equipment & supplies[3]	7	7	30	36	5	35,067	28,889	1,204	1,139
5091 Sporting & recreational goods[3]	5	4	79	83	21	27,595	28,675	2,336	2,516
5093 Scrap and waste materials[3]	7	7	49	56	8	17,796	19,857	981	1,173
5112 Stationery and office supplies[3]	10	10	40	26	3	19,800	21,385	805	680
5113 Industrial & personal service paper[3]	6	7	53	61	9	24,830	25,967	1,687	1,867
5130 Apparel, piece goods, and notions[3]	8	11	59	63	6	30,034	33,079	2,123	2,272
5142 Packaged frozen food[2]	-	6	-	12	2	-	23,000	-	342
5143 Dairy products, exc. dried or canned[3]	5	5	80	83	17	31,550	31,807	2,983	3,194
5145 Confectionery[3]	5	5	99	89	18	22,707	28,000	2,487	2,531
5146 Fish and seafoods[3]	5	6	115	452	75	20,383	7,372	3,534	3,546
5147 Meats and meat products[3]	6	5	39	36	7	30,974	31,222	1,219	1,019
5148 Fresh fruits and vegetables[3]	26	23	314	186	8	19,694	25,871	6,869	6,448
5149 Groceries and related products, nec[3]	17	18	294	277	15	30,272	33,791	9,626	9,868
5169 Chemicals & allied products, nec[1]	8	-	6	-	-	13,333	-	105	-
5171 Petroleum bulk stations & terminals[2]	-	6	-	51	9	-	39,451	-	1,920
5180 Beer, wine, and distilled beverages[3]	10	9	295	298	33	40,163	41,329	15,782	15,181
5191 Farm supplies[2]	-	6	-	28	5	-	24,143	-	772
5193 Flowers & florists' supplies[1]	3	-	9	-	-	13,778	-	326	-

Continued on next page.

ATLANTIC - CAPE MAY, NJ PMSA - [continued]

Wholesale and Retail Trade USA	Establishments		Employment		Emp / Est	Pay / Employee		Annual Payroll ($ 000)	
	1994	1995	1994	1995	1995	1994	1995	1994	1995
5199 Nondurable goods, nec 3	17	12	92	53	4	19,565	19,623	2,488	1,241
52 - Retail trade 3	3,143	3,145	26,698	28,460	9	13,357	13,954	447,518	473,761
5210 Lumber and other building materials 3	42	38	298	370	10	24,644	25,816	8,212	9,572
5230 Paint, glass, and wallpaper stores 3	17	20	28	28	1	27,143	27,857	785	780
5250 Hardware stores 3	33	23	166	168	7	14,602	17,024	2,937	3,328
5260 Retail nurseries and garden stores 3	17	23	76	77	3	12,053	12,312	1,462	1,727
5310 Department stores 3	13	14	1,554	2,008	143	12,435	11,918	22,748	25,707
5330 Variety stores 3	41	38	168	140	4	10,452	11,086	1,967	1,999
5390 Misc. general merchandise stores 3	26	22	542	549	25	13,063	13,763	8,352	8,030
5410 Grocery stores 3	239	256	3,938	4,257	17	17,249	16,398	71,680	75,841
5420 Meat and fish markets 3	22	19	91	66	3	11,692	13,697	1,265	1,294
5430 Fruit and vegetable markets 3	17	19	54	77	4	8,519	8,052	1,015	1,130
5440 Candy, nut, and confectionery stores 3	45	46	252	285	6	8,302	8,126	3,621	3,494
5460 Retail bakeries 3	53	52	305	266	5	8,026	8,827	3,284	3,295
5490 Miscellaneous food stores 3	15	16	41	47	3	9,951	10,723	502	569
5510 New and used car dealers 3	37	37	1,445	1,527	41	26,375	27,725	44,582	44,364
5520 Used car dealers 3	12	8	41	40	5	20,390	21,200	978	837
5530 Auto and home supply stores 3	29	30	299	285	10	16,736	17,698	5,839	5,259
5540 Gasoline service stations 3	150	142	869	826	6	12,437	13,656	11,946	11,753
5550 Boat dealers 3	19	17	135	143	8	21,511	26,434	4,195	4,596
5570 Motorcycle dealers 3	5	5	35	41	8	20,229	26,244	961	1,063
5610 Men's & boys' clothing stores 3	39	33	152	127	4	18,184	17,953	2,778	2,394
5620 Women's clothing stores 3	110	101	711	602	6	9,525	10,100	8,337	7,173
5630 Women's accessory & specialty stores 3	21	19	90	64	3	12,844	15,438	1,170	1,052
5640 Children's and infants' wear stores 3	12	12	35	35	3	8,914	10,400	383	512
5650 Family clothing stores 3	50	51	454	387	8	9,498	11,018	6,420	6,055
5660 Shoe stores 3	72	66	354	349	5	11,887	12,539	5,098	4,681
5690 Misc. apparel & accessory stores 3	48	40	108	74	2	10,074	12,757	2,350	1,819
5712 Furniture stores 3	45	40	341	349	9	21,056	21,284	7,934	8,287
5713 Floor covering stores 2	-	14	-	14	1	-	16,000	-	272
5719 Misc. homefurnishings stores 3	33	32	131	158	5	16,000	17,570	2,976	3,095
5720 Household appliance stores 3	18	16	103	62	4	17,126	23,226	2,140	1,379
5731 Radio, TV, & electronic stores 3	27	25	162	177	7	15,901	15,322	2,834	2,867
5734 Computer and software stores 3	8	11	30	25	2	16,667	22,240	535	735
5735 Record & prerecorded tape stores 3	18	16	65	79	5	9,723	10,278	766	878
5736 Musical instrument stores 3	5	4	10	11	3	14,000	12,000	127	154
5812 Eating places 3	897	849	8,401	9,177	11	8,570	9,194	113,029	120,204
5813 Drinking places 3	133	119	758	643	5	9,541	10,532	10,459	10,001
5910 Drug stores and proprietary stores 3	80	82	913	1,082	13	15,882	15,227	16,401	18,243
5920 Liquor stores 3	96	99	649	617	6	13,442	15,637	10,506	10,483
5930 Used merchandise stores 3	17	15	90	49	3	4,222	9,551	512	522
5941 Sporting goods and bicycle shops 3	48	51	108	121	2	14,259	13,785	2,514	2,559
5942 Book stores 3	14	15	65	80	5	9,538	9,900	685	787
5944 Jewelry stores 3	64	68	187	201	3	18,460	20,080	3,462	4,972
5945 Hobby, toy, and game shops 3	16	16	168	143	9	11,833	14,909	2,153	2,124
5946 Camera & photographic supply stores 3	6	6	20	23	4	15,600	15,304	406	432
5947 Gift, novelty, and souvenir shops 3	140	132	485	483	4	9,155	10,369	7,506	8,069
5949 Sewing, needlework, and piece goods 3	8	9	32	31	3	6,875	8,129	256	268
5962 Merchandising machine operators 3	10	7	62	59	8	14,645	17,017	1,170	1,237
5963 Direct selling establishments 3	12	12	4	3	-	6,000	8,000	206	189
5983 Fuel oil dealers 1	17	-	5	-	-	16,000	-	85	-
5984 Liquefied petroleum gas dealers 1	6	-	32	-	-	33,000	-	979	-
5992 Florists 3	38	37	171	200	5	11,626	12,120	2,400	2,470
5993 Tobacco stores and stands 2	-	3	-	27	9	-	13,778	-	390
5995 Optical goods stores 3	38	34	135	120	4	15,230	18,000	1,956	2,232
5999 Miscellaneous retail stores, nec 3	61	67	192	217	3	12,729	13,088	3,221	3,643

Source: County Business Patterns 1994/95, CBP-94/95, U.S. Department of Commerce, Washington DC, November 1997. The employment column represents mid-March employment in the year. Pay per employee is calculated by dividing 1st Quarter payroll, annualized, by mid-March employment. The column headed 'Emp / Est' shows 'employees per establishment'. A dash (-) means that data are unavailable or cannot be calculated. nec means not elsewhere classified. *Notes:* 1. 1994 data incomplete; unavailable or withheld. 2. 1995 data incomplete; unavailable or withheld. 3. 1994 and 1995 data incomplete; unavailable or withheld.

AUGUSTA - AIKEN MSA (GA PART)

Wholesale and Retail Trade USA	Establishments		Employment		Emp / Est	Pay / Employee		Annual Payroll ($ 000)	
	1994	1995	1994	1995	1995	1994	1995	1994	1995
50 - Wholesale trade 3	402	411	4,155	4,204	10	25,427	26,955	115,279	118,533
5012 Automobiles and other vehicles 3	10	10	174	141	14	16,989	15,461	3,573	1,965
5013 Motor vehicle supplies and new parts 3	26	23	143	146	6	20,671	24,493	3,332	3,581
5014 Tires and tubes 3	6	6	84	82	14	19,762	21,317	1,728	1,759

Continued on next page.

AUGUSTA - AIKEN MSA (GA PART) - [continued]

Wholesale and Retail Trade USA	Establishments 1994	Establishments 1995	Employment 1994	Employment 1995	Emp / Est 1995	Pay / Employee 1994	Pay / Employee 1995	Annual Payroll ($ 000) 1994	Annual Payroll ($ 000) 1995
5015 Motor vehicle parts, used[3]	7	8	39	30	4	16,000	20,400	624	654
5021 Furniture	-	6	-	37	6	-	20,757	-	887
5031 Lumber, plywood, and millwork[3]	23	21	149	152	7	35,383	36,553	5,672	6,113
5033 Roofing, siding, & insulation[3]	4	5	37	40	8	25,081	30,800	1,081	1,162
5044 Office equipment[3]	9	8	83	94	12	29,783	32,255	2,797	2,959
5045 Computers, peripherals, & software	9	-	55	-	-	39,055	-	2,048	-
5046 Commercial equipment, nec	-	7	-	21	3	-	22,667	-	563
5047 Medical and hospital equipment[3]	12	15	334	365	24	34,503	38,871	12,246	15,189
5063 Electrical apparatus and equipment[3]	15	18	141	151	8	27,972	31,073	4,368	4,746
5065 Electronic parts and equipment[3]	9	9	39	38	4	30,667	32,211	1,202	1,273
5074 Plumbing & hydronic heating supplies[2]	9	10	64	68	7	20,750	21,353	1,486	1,616
5075 Warm air heating & air conditioning	-	8	-	64	8	-	28,000	-	1,985
5082 Construction and mining machinery[1]	10	10	99	147	15	26,828	30,286	3,001	4,694
5083 Farm and garden machinery	8	6	33	26	4	16,848	18,154	718	527
5084 Industrial machinery and equipment[3]	10	13	79	102	8	24,759	24,784	1,920	2,654
5085 Industrial supplies	29	29	214	240	8	29,065	32,367	6,539	8,144
5087 Service establishment equipment	8	8	54	58	7	17,556	18,690	1,035	1,099
5088 Transportation equipment & supplies[2]	4	3	4	9	3	41,000	41,333	246	458
5093 Scrap and waste materials[3]	14	15	131	145	10	19,267	19,917	2,735	3,126
5112 Stationery and office supplies[3]	11	10	129	144	14	22,698	25,194	3,354	3,598
5113 Industrial & personal service paper[3]	8	10	83	94	9	30,313	30,511	2,695	3,276
5130 Apparel, piece goods, and notions	6	-	18	-	-	21,111	-	495	-
5148 Fresh fruits and vegetables[1]	3	-	6	-	-	9,333	-	101	-
5150 Farm-product raw materials	-	5	-	11	2	-	13,455	-	171
5169 Chemicals & allied products, nec	16	10	127	98	10	38,835	35,959	5,259	3,553
5171 Petroleum bulk stations & terminals	5	6	29	65	11	18,897	25,846	508	1,685
5172 Petroleum products, nec[1]	7	-	94	-	-	24,596	-	2,986	-
5180 Beer, wine, and distilled beverages	9	9	184	193	21	20,478	20,746	3,994	4,178
5191 Farm supplies[2]	-	7	-	37	5	-	18,595	-	764
5193 Flowers & florists' supplies[3]	3	3	35	31	10	20,343	19,742	791	744
5199 Nondurable goods, nec	10	13	50	62	5	19,760	21,806	1,257	1,356
52- Retail trade[3]	1,745	1,724	26,480	26,708	15	10,997	11,741	312,875	329,890
5210 Lumber and other building materials[3]	30	25	889	738	30	18,601	23,073	17,217	16,812
5230 Paint, glass, and wallpaper stores[3]	11	12	54	53	4	13,778	17,358	708	931
5250 Hardware stores[3]	12	7	36	14	2	11,889	12,571	455	178
5260 Retail nurseries and garden stores	9	12	47	83	7	9,872	13,349	539	1,121
5270 Mobile home dealers[3]	19	18	114	138	8	18,877	21,768	2,836	3,855
5310 Department stores[3]	16	14	2,562	2,458	176	10,902	12,529	29,376	30,082
5330 Variety stores[3]	23	15	135	132	9	9,333	8,061	1,453	1,239
5390 Misc. general merchandise stores[1]	16	16	330	352	22	12,994	13,023	4,330	4,394
5410 Grocery stores[3]	123	121	2,674	2,779	23	9,487	10,104	27,163	29,730
5420 Meat and fish markets[3]	6	6	22	14	2	11,455	15,143	281	224
5460 Retail bakeries	7	5	102	88	18	7,804	8,318	874	713
5490 Miscellaneous food stores[1]	5	6	19	22	4	9,474	10,000	185	243
5510 New and used car dealers[3]	27	27	1,361	1,371	51	26,551	28,934	40,337	43,890
5520 Used car dealers[3]	30	28	145	140	5	23,559	29,143	3,746	3,685
5530 Auto and home supply stores[3]	60	60	559	539	9	15,599	16,445	9,239	9,466
5540 Gasoline service stations[3]	110	114	882	912	8	9,596	10,588	9,528	10,229
5550 Boat dealers	4	4	13	11	3	25,231	32,727	285	276
5610 Men's & boys' clothing stores[3]	27	27	149	135	5	9,557	10,519	1,475	1,441
5620 Women's clothing stores[3]	72	58	513	447	8	8,250	7,785	4,444	3,787
5630 Women's accessory & specialty stores	9	8	38	39	5	8,526	10,051	377	384
5640 Children's and infants' wear stores[3]	4	4	34	35	9	6,471	7,429	264	316
5650 Family clothing stores[3]	21	20	288	278	14	8,903	9,885	2,793	3,005
5660 Shoe stores[3]	50	47	266	268	6	10,647	10,791	3,056	2,980
5690 Misc. apparel & accessory stores	10	10	63	56	6	15,429	18,214	1,241	1,288
5712 Furniture stores[3]	49	48	444	521	11	16,459	17,006	8,086	9,663
5713 Floor covering stores[3]	19	19	97	98	5	20,948	20,980	2,338	2,212
5720 Household appliance stores[3]	10	9	37	35	4	17,838	19,886	764	796
5731 Radio, TV, & electronic stores[3]	22	21	264	250	12	13,652	13,664	3,380	3,260
5734 Computer and software stores	7	7	32	63	9	16,375	15,810	386	904
5735 Record & prerecorded tape stores[2]	11	11	69	74	7	7,652	7,243	556	517
5736 Musical instrument stores[3]	5	4	28	28	7	16,143	15,714	444	401
5812 Eating places[3]	350	328	8,759	8,855	27	7,056	7,167	65,128	65,549
5813 Drinking places	43	36	208	159	4	5,865	7,648	1,348	1,289
5910 Drug stores and proprietary stores[3]	51	52	541	536	10	13,331	15,672	8,147	8,982
5920 Liquor stores[3]	53	48	156	147	3	9,205	9,878	1,540	1,570
5930 Used merchandise stores[3]	38	42	106	135	3	11,698	11,881	1,571	1,677
5941 Sporting goods and bicycle shops[3]	26	24	62	33	1	11,419	8,485	920	368
5942 Book stores	17	15	91	113	8	8,132	8,956	703	1,023
5943 Stationery stores	6	6	11	23	4	8,727	5,565	87	71

Continued on next page.

AUGUSTA - AIKEN MSA (GA PART) - [continued]

Wholesale and Retail Trade USA	Establishments		Employment		Emp / Est	Pay / Employee		Annual Payroll ($ 000)	
	1994	1995	1994	1995	1995	1994	1995	1994	1995
5944 Jewelry stores [3]	34	35	212	228	7	15,302	16,211	3,127	3,396
5945 Hobby, toy, and game shops [1]	9	10	74	121	12	8,108	7,702	917	1,185
5946 Camera & photographic supply stores	-	5	-	18	4	-	16,000	-	329
5947 Gift, novelty, and souvenir shops [3]	37	39	176	168	4	5,773	5,952	1,112	1,123
5949 Sewing, needlework, and piece goods	11	11	72	41	4	7,667	9,366	570	398
5963 Direct selling establishments	15	16	15	16	1	15,733	24,250	340	370
5984 Liquefied petroleum gas dealers	5	5	32	40	8	28,125	26,200	688	829
5992 Florists [3]	25	28	92	118	4	12,348	10,576	1,209	1,293
5993 Tobacco stores and stands	-	7	-	9	1	-	11,556	-	117
5995 Optical goods stores	21	21	118	105	5	14,271	16,000	1,647	1,546
5999 Miscellaneous retail stores, nec [1]	56	49	277	202	4	13,083	14,554	3,599	3,283

Source: County Business Patterns 1994/95, CBP-94/95, U.S. Department of Commerce, Washington DC, November 1997. The employment column represents mid-March employment in the year. Pay per employee is calculated by dividing 1st Quarter payroll, annualized, by mid-March employment. The column headed 'Emp / Est' shows 'employees per establishment'. A dash (-) means that data are unavailable or cannot be calculated. nec means not elsewhere classified. *Notes:* 1. 1994 data incomplete; unavailable or withheld. 2. 1995 data incomplete; unavailable or withheld. 3. 1994 and 1995 data incomplete; unavailable or withheld.

AUGUSTA - AIKEN MSA (SC PART)

Wholesale and Retail Trade USA	Establishments		Employment		Emp / Est	Pay / Employee		Annual Payroll ($ 000)	
	1994	1995	1994	1995	1995	1994	1995	1994	1995
50- Wholesale trade [2]	-	127	-	775	6	-	24,717	-	18,720
5012 Automobiles and other vehicles [2]	-	6	-	25	4	-	25,440	-	625
5013 Motor vehicle supplies and new parts [2]	-	14	-	68	5	-	21,882	-	1,433
5015 Motor vehicle parts, used [2]	-	6	-	19	3	-	9,895	-	174
5048 Ophthalmic goods [2]	-	3	-	11	4	-	20,000	-	250
5070 Hardware, plumbing & heating equipment [2]	-	7	-	33	5	-	19,879	-	692
5083 Farm and garden machinery [2]	-	4	-	35	9	-	15,429	-	502
5087 Service establishment equipment [2]	-	4	-	12	3	-	27,000	-	355
5090 Miscellaneous durable goods [2]	-	3	-	20	7	-	15,800	-	395
5130 Apparel, piece goods, and notions [2]	-	4	-	56	14	-	30,857	-	1,615
5149 Groceries and related products, nec [2]	-	4	-	82	21	-	27,024	-	1,773
5160 Chemicals and allied products [2]	-	6	-	4	1	-	12,000	-	93
5171 Petroleum bulk stations & terminals [2]	-	9	-	11	1	-	23,636	-	287
5181 Beer and ale [2]	-	3	-	72	24	-	28,056	-	2,176
5191 Farm supplies [2]	-	6	-	22	4	-	17,818	-	424
52- Retail trade [2]	-	806	-	10,525	13	-	10,948	-	119,679
5210 Lumber and other building materials [2]	-	12	-	162	14	-	17,877	-	2,846
5230 Paint, glass, and wallpaper stores [2]	-	4	-	14	4	-	20,000	-	290
5250 Hardware stores [2]	-	10	-	38	4	-	10,316	-	386
5260 Retail nurseries and garden stores [2]	-	10	-	33	3	-	9,091	-	371
5270 Mobile home dealers [2]	-	10	-	80	8	-	19,250	-	2,558
5310 Department stores [2]	-	7	-	1,044	149	-	12,866	-	13,342
5330 Variety stores [2]	-	11	-	65	6	-	9,538	-	677
5390 Misc. general merchandise stores [2]	-	6	-	63	11	-	8,952	-	588
5410 Grocery stores [2]	-	83	-	2,316	28	-	9,563	-	22,062
5420 Meat and fish markets [2]	-	4	-	23	6	-	10,957	-	245
5490 Miscellaneous food stores [2]	-	4	-	4	1	-	10,000	-	53
5510 New and used car dealers [2]	-	14	-	428	31	-	30,159	-	13,517
5520 Used car dealers [2]	-	14	-	33	2	-	14,545	-	537
5530 Auto and home supply stores [2]	-	30	-	226	8	-	14,938	-	3,576
5540 Gasoline service stations [2]	-	78	-	474	6	-	12,354	-	6,957
5550 Boat dealers [2]	-	6	-	19	3	-	15,368	-	271
5610 Men's & boys' clothing stores [2]	-	5	-	16	3	-	17,500	-	261
5620 Women's clothing stores [2]	-	18	-	221	12	-	10,190	-	2,171
5630 Women's accessory & specialty stores [2]	-	3	-	8	3	-	8,500	-	80
5650 Family clothing stores [2]	-	10	-	229	23	-	10,655	-	2,270
5660 Shoe stores [2]	-	16	-	69	4	-	10,319	-	652
5712 Furniture stores [2]	-	15	-	92	6	-	16,609	-	1,610
5731 Radio, TV, & electronic stores [2]	-	10	-	31	3	-	18,968	-	499
5734 Computer and software stores [2]	-	5	-	15	3	-	9,600	-	209
5735 Record & prerecorded tape stores [2]	-	4	-	12	3	-	8,000	-	120
5812 Eating places [2]	-	144	-	3,187	22	-	6,604	-	21,835
5813 Drinking places [2]	-	7	-	27	4	-	10,519	-	181
5910 Drug stores and proprietary stores [2]	-	27	-	262	10	-	14,137	-	3,776
5920 Liquor stores [2]	-	18	-	57	3	-	8,491	-	465
5930 Used merchandise stores [2]	-	10	-	14	1	-	10,571	-	170
5941 Sporting goods and bicycle shops [2]	-	15	-	61	4	-	7,410	-	541
5942 Book stores [2]	-	3	-	10	3	-	10,400	-	87
5943 Stationery stores [2]	-	4	-	34	9	-	19,882	-	623

Continued on next page.

AUGUSTA-AIKEN MSA (SC PART) - [continued]

Wholesale and Retail Trade USA	Establishments		Employment		Emp / Est	Pay / Employee		Annual Payroll ($ 000)	
	1994	1995	1994	1995	1995	1994	1995	1994	1995
5944 Jewelry stores [2]	-	14	-	70	5	-	12,171	-	888
5947 Gift, novelty, and souvenir shops [2]	-	8	-	36	5	-	6,667	-	274
5949 Sewing, needlework, and piece goods [2]	-	4	-	19	5	-	5,684	-	116
5961 Catalog and mail-order houses [2]	-	5	-	68	14	-	13,412	-	824
5962 Merchandising machine operators [2]	-	7	-	38	5	-	16,737	-	605
5963 Direct selling establishments [2]	-	3	-	5	2	-	20,800	-	183
5984 Liquefied petroleum gas dealers [2]	-	7	-	29	4	-	22,345	-	719
5992 Florists [2]	-	19	-	66	3	-	8,848	-	586
5999 Miscellaneous retail stores, nec [2]	-	17	-	58	3	-	12,828	-	606

Source: County Business Patterns 1994/95, CBP-94/95, U.S. Department of Commerce, Washington DC, November 1997. The employment column represents mid-March employment in the year. Pay per employee is calculated by dividing 1st Quarter payroll, annualized, by mid-March employment. The column headed 'Emp / Est' shows 'employees per establishment'. A dash (-) means that data are unavailable or cannot be calculated. nec means not elsewhere classified. *Notes:* 1. 1994 data incomplete; unavailable or withheld. 2. 1995 data incomplete; unavailable or withheld. 3. 1994 and 1995 data incomplete; unavailable or withheld.

AUGUSTA-AIKEN, GA-SC MSA

Wholesale and Retail Trade USA	Establishments		Employment		Emp / Est	Pay / Employee		Annual Payroll ($ 000)	
	1994	1995	1994	1995	1995	1994	1995	1994	1995
50- Wholesale trade [1]	402	538	4,155	4,979	9	25,427	26,607	115,279	137,253
5012 Automobiles and other vehicles [3]	10	16	174	166	10	16,989	16,964	3,573	2,590
5013 Motor vehicle supplies and new parts [1]	26	37	143	214	6	20,671	23,664	3,332	5,014
5014 Tires and tubes [3]	6	8	84	82	10	19,762	21,317	1,728	1,759
5015 Motor vehicle parts, used [3]	7	14	39	49	4	16,000	16,327	624	828
5021 Furniture [2]	-	7	-	37	5	-	20,757	-	887
5031 Lumber, plywood, and millwork [3]	23	22	149	152	7	35,383	36,553	5,672	6,113
5033 Roofing, siding, & insulation [3]	4	7	37	40	6	25,081	30,800	1,081	1,162
5044 Office equipment [3]	9	8	83	94	12	29,783	32,255	2,797	2,959
5045 Computers, peripherals, & software [1]	9	-	55	-	-	39,055	-	2,048	-
5046 Commercial equipment, nec [2]	-	8	-	21	3	-	22,667	-	563
5047 Medical and hospital equipment [3]	12	15	334	365	24	34,503	38,871	12,246	15,189
5048 Ophthalmic goods [2]	-	6	-	11	2	-	20,000	-	250
5063 Electrical apparatus and equipment [3]	15	19	141	151	8	27,972	31,073	4,368	4,746
5065 Electronic parts and equipment [3]	9	10	39	38	4	30,667	32,211	1,202	1,273
5074 Plumbing & hydronic heating supplies [3]	9	15	64	68	5	20,750	21,353	1,486	1,616
5075 Warm air heating & air conditioning [2]	-	10	-	64	6	-	28,000	-	1,985
5082 Construction and mining machinery [3]	10	10	99	147	15	26,828	30,286	3,001	4,694
5083 Farm and garden machinery [3]	8	10	33	61	6	16,848	16,590	718	1,029
5084 Industrial machinery and equipment [3]	10	14	79	102	7	24,759	24,784	1,920	2,654
5085 Industrial supplies [3]	29	33	214	240	7	29,065	32,367	6,539	8,144
5087 Service establishment equipment [3]	8	12	54	70	6	17,556	20,114	1,035	1,454
5088 Transportation equipment & supplies [3]	4	4	4	9	2	41,000	41,333	246	458
5093 Scrap and waste materials [3]	14	16	131	145	9	19,267	19,917	2,735	3,126
5112 Stationery and office supplies [3]	11	11	129	144	13	22,698	25,194	3,354	3,598
5113 Industrial & personal service paper [3]	8	10	83	94	9	30,313	30,511	2,695	3,276
5130 Apparel, piece goods, and notions [3]	6	10	18	56	6	21,111	30,857	495	1,615
5148 Fresh fruits and vegetables [1]	3	-	6	-	-	9,333	-	101	-
5149 Groceries and related products, nec [2]	-	8	-	82	10	-	27,024	-	1,773
5150 Farm-product raw materials [2]	-	8	-	11	1	-	13,455	-	171
5169 Chemicals & allied products, nec [3]	16	14	127	98	7	38,835	35,959	5,259	3,553
5171 Petroleum bulk stations & terminals [3]	5	15	29	76	5	18,897	25,526	508	1,972
5172 Petroleum products, nec [1]	7	-	94	-	-	24,596	-	2,986	-
5181 Beer and ale [2]	-	6	-	72	12	-	28,056	-	2,176
5191 Farm supplies	-	13	-	59	5	-	18,305	-	1,188
5193 Flowers & florists' supplies [3]	3	3	35	31	10	20,343	19,742	791	744
5199 Nondurable goods, nec [3]	10	14	50	62	4	19,760	21,806	1,257	1,356
52- Retail trade [1]	1,745	2,530	26,480	37,233	15	10,997	11,517	312,875	449,569
5210 Lumber and other building materials [1]	30	37	889	900	24	18,601	22,138	17,217	19,658
5230 Paint, glass, and wallpaper stores [3]	11	16	54	67	4	13,778	17,910	708	1,221
5250 Hardware stores [1]	12	17	36	52	3	11,889	10,923	455	564
5260 Retail nurseries and garden stores [3]	9	22	47	116	5	9,872	12,138	539	1,492
5270 Mobile home dealers [3]	19	28	114	218	8	18,877	20,844	2,836	6,413
5310 Department stores [3]	16	21	2,562	3,502	167	10,902	12,629	29,376	43,424
5330 Variety stores [1]	23	26	135	197	8	9,333	8,548	1,453	1,916
5390 Misc. general merchandise stores [3]	16	22	330	415	19	12,994	12,405	4,330	4,982
5410 Grocery stores [3]	123	204	2,674	5,095	25	9,487	9,858	27,163	51,792
5420 Meat and fish markets [3]	6	10	22	37	4	11,455	12,541	281	469
5460 Retail bakeries [3]	7	7	102	88	13	7,804	8,318	874	713
5490 Miscellaneous food stores [3]	5	10	19	26	3	9,474	10,000	185	296
5510 New and used car dealers [1]	27	41	1,361	1,799	44	26,551	29,225	40,337	57,407

Continued on next page.

AUGUSTA - AIKEN, GA - SC MSA - [continued]

Wholesale and Retail Trade USA	Establishments		Employment		Emp / Est	Pay / Employee		Annual Payroll ($ 000)	
	1994	1995	1994	1995	1995	1994	1995	1994	1995
5520 Used car dealers [1]	30	42	145	173	4	23,559	26,358	3,746	4,222
5530 Auto and home supply stores [1]	60	90	559	765	9	15,599	16,000	9,239	13,042
5540 Gasoline service stations [1]	110	192	882	1,386	7	9,596	11,192	9,528	17,186
5550 Boat dealers [3]	4	10	13	30	3	25,231	21,733	285	547
5610 Men's & boys' clothing stores [1]	27	32	149	151	5	9,557	11,258	1,475	1,702
5620 Women's clothing stores [1]	72	76	513	668	9	8,250	8,581	4,444	5,958
5630 Women's accessory & specialty stores [3]	9	11	38	47	4	8,526	9,787	377	464
5640 Children's and infants' wear stores [3]	4	6	34	35	6	6,471	7,429	264	316
5650 Family clothing stores [1]	21	30	288	507	17	8,903	10,233	2,793	5,275
5660 Shoe stores [3]	50	63	266	337	5	10,647	10,694	3,056	3,632
5690 Misc. apparel & accessory stores [3]	10	11	63	56	5	15,429	18,214	1,241	1,288
5712 Furniture stores [1]	49	63	444	613	10	16,459	16,946	8,086	11,273
5713 Floor covering stores [3]	19	27	97	98	4	20,948	20,980	2,338	2,212
5720 Household appliance stores [3]	10	16	37	35	2	17,838	19,886	764	796
5731 Radio, TV, & electronic stores [3]	22	31	264	281	9	13,652	14,249	3,380	3,759
5734 Computer and software stores [3]	7	12	32	78	7	16,375	14,615	386	1,113
5735 Record & prerecorded tape stores [3]	11	15	69	86	6	7,652	7,349	556	637
5736 Musical instrument stores [3]	5	5	28	28	6	16,143	15,714	444	401
5812 Eating places [1]	350	472	8,759	12,042	26	7,056	7,018	65,128	87,384
5813 Drinking places [3]	43	43	208	186	4	5,865	8,065	1,348	1,470
5910 Drug stores and proprietary stores [1]	51	79	541	798	10	13,331	15,168	8,147	12,758
5920 Liquor stores [1]	53	66	156	204	3	9,205	9,490	1,540	2,035
5930 Used merchandise stores [1]	38	52	106	149	3	11,698	11,758	1,571	1,847
5941 Sporting goods and bicycle shops [1]	26	39	62	94	2	11,419	7,787	920	909
5942 Book stores [3]	17	18	91	123	7	8,132	9,073	703	1,110
5943 Stationery stores [3]	6	10	11	57	6	8,727	14,105	87	694
5944 Jewelry stores [1]	34	49	212	298	6	15,302	15,262	3,127	4,284
5945 Hobby, toy, and game shops [3]	9	12	74	121	10	8,108	7,702	917	1,185
5946 Camera & photographic supply stores [2]	-	5	-	18	4	-	16,000	-	329
5947 Gift, novelty, and souvenir shops [1]	37	47	176	204	4	5,773	6,078	1,112	1,397
5949 Sewing, needlework, and piece goods [3]	11	15	72	60	4	7,667	8,200	570	514
5961 Catalog and mail-order houses [2]	-	7	-	68	10	-	13,412	-	824
5962 Merchandising machine operators [2]	-	15	-	38	3	-	16,737	-	605
5963 Direct selling establishments [3]	15	19	15	21	1	15,733	23,429	340	553
5984 Liquefied petroleum gas dealers [3]	5	12	32	69	6	28,125	24,580	688	1,548
5992 Florists [1]	25	47	92	184	4	12,348	9,957	1,209	1,879
5993 Tobacco stores and stands [2]	-	8	-	9	1	-	11,556	-	117
5995 Optical goods stores [3]	21	22	118	105	5	14,271	16,000	1,647	1,546
5999 Miscellaneous retail stores, nec [3]	56	66	277	260	4	13,083	14,169	3,599	3,889

Source: County Business Patterns 1994/95, CBP-94/95, U.S. Department of Commerce, Washington DC, November 1997. The employment column represents mid-March employment in the year. Pay per employee is calculated by dividing 1st Quarter payroll, annualized, by mid-March employment. The column headed 'Emp / Est' shows 'employees per establishment'. A dash (-) means that data are unavailable or cannot be calculated. nec means not elsewhere classified. *Notes:* 1. 1994 data incomplete; unavailable or withheld. 2. 1995 data incomplete; unavailable or withheld. 3. 1994 and 1995 data incomplete; unavailable or withheld.

AUSTIN - SAN MARCOS, TX MSA

Wholesale and Retail Trade USA	Establishments		Employment		Emp / Est	Pay / Employee		Annual Payroll ($ 000)	
	1994	1995	1994	1995	1995	1994	1995	1994	1995
50- Wholesale trade	-	1,713	-	23,093	13	-	34,104	-	855,836
5012 Automobiles and other vehicles [2]	-	24	-	313	13	-	23,962	-	8,450
5013 Motor vehicle supplies and new parts [2]	-	57	-	1,116	20	-	23,366	-	26,881
5014 Tires and tubes [2]	-	10	-	53	5	-	23,321	-	1,276
5015 Motor vehicle parts, used	-	24	-	130	5	-	18,523	-	2,560
5021 Furniture [2]	-	23	-	297	13	-	28,296	-	9,479
5023 Homefurnishings [2]	-	37	-	239	6	-	20,301	-	5,171
5031 Lumber, plywood, and millwork [2]	-	33	-	555	17	-	25,787	-	15,850
5032 Brick, stone, & related materials [2]	-	20	-	91	5	-	29,275	-	3,772
5033 Roofing, siding, & insulation [2]	-	11	-	139	13	-	25,410	-	3,796
5039 Construction materials, nec [2]	-	17	-	230	14	-	26,939	-	6,640
5044 Office equipment [2]	-	46	-	777	17	-	42,533	-	30,091
5045 Computers, peripherals, & software [2]	-	149	-	2,248	15	-	57,488	-	136,967
5046 Commercial equipment, nec [2]	-	22	-	227	10	-	29,022	-	7,209
5047 Medical and hospital equipment [2]	-	35	-	289	8	-	35,474	-	11,690
5049 Professional equipment, nec [2]	-	15	-	110	7	-	21,127	-	2,559
5051 Metals service centers and offices [2]	-	23	-	175	8	-	28,114	-	6,031
5063 Electrical apparatus and equipment [2]	-	64	-	942	15	-	34,960	-	34,073
5064 Electrical appliances, TV & radios [2]	-	11	-	88	8	-	26,818	-	2,715
5065 Electronic parts and equipment [2]	-	144	-	1,544	11	-	52,150	-	88,556
5072 Hardware [2]	-	19	-	174	9	-	29,885	-	5,601

Continued on next page.

AUSTIN - SAN MARCOS, TX MSA - [continued]

Wholesale and Retail Trade USA	Establishments		Employment		Emp / Est	Pay / Employee		Annual Payroll ($ 000)	
	1994	1995	1994	1995	1995	1994	1995	1994	1995
5074 Plumbing & hydronic heating supplies [2]	-	33	-	302	9	-	24,252	-	8,001
5075 Warm air heating & air conditioning [2]	-	27	-	170	6	-	26,824	-	4,962
5078 Refrigeration equipment and supplies [2]	-	7	-	29	4	-	18,897	-	615
5082 Construction and mining machinery [2]	-	18	-	180	10	-	36,733	-	6,821
5083 Farm and garden machinery [2]	-	19	-	146	8	-	23,096	-	4,068
5084 Industrial machinery and equipment	-	90	-	840	9	-	32,814	-	34,592
5085 Industrial supplies	-	28	-	207	7	-	32,618	-	8,843
5087 Service establishment equipment [2]	-	27	-	185	7	-	23,632	-	4,479
5088 Transportation equipment & supplies	-	13	-	82	6	-	55,122	-	4,750
5091 Sporting & recreational goods [2]	-	21	-	478	23	-	22,402	-	16,809
5092 Toys and hobby goods and supplies [2]	-	4	-	4	1	-	15,000	-	50
5093 Scrap and waste materials	-	27	-	147	5	-	20,381	-	3,330
5094 Jewelry & precious stones [2]	-	21	-	99	5	-	36,081	-	4,221
5099 Durable goods, nec [2]	-	30	-	157	5	-	29,197	-	5,313
5111 Printing and writing paper [2]	-	9	-	80	9	-	28,900	-	1,663
5112 Stationery and office supplies [2]	-	46	-	635	14	-	22,350	-	14,039
5113 Industrial & personal service paper [2]	-	7	-	71	10	-	30,085	-	2,222
5120 Drugs, proprietaries, and sundries [2]	-	20	-	124	6	-	33,258	-	4,369
5136 Men's and boys' clothing [2]	-	7	-	64	9	-	28,250	-	1,998
5137 Women's and children's clothing [2]	-	12	-	53	4	-	16,604	-	808
5141 Groceries, general line [2]	-	11	-	365	33	-	35,485	-	11,622
5143 Dairy products, exc. dried or canned [2]	-	9	-	166	18	-	27,349	-	4,768
5145 Confectionery [2]	-	7	-	533	76	-	20,300	-	11,349
5146 Fish and seafoods [2]	-	3	-	28	9	-	17,857	-	522
5147 Meats and meat products [2]	-	6	-	113	19	-	29,204	-	3,137
5148 Fresh fruits and vegetables [2]	-	8	-	209	26	-	20,402	-	4,878
5149 Groceries and related products, nec [2]	-	41	-	419	10	-	26,444	-	11,688
5153 Grain and field beans [2]	-	6	-	26	4	-	17,077	-	535
5154 Livestock	-	11	-	115	10	-	6,957	-	807
5159 Farm-product raw materials, nec [2]	-	10	-	4	-	-	7,000	-	32
5162 Plastics materials & basic shapes [2]	-	10	-	51	5	-	25,569	-	1,519
5169 Chemicals & allied products, nec [2]	-	30	-	280	9	-	34,129	-	9,928
5171 Petroleum bulk stations & terminals [2]	-	23	-	182	8	-	26,527	-	5,636
5172 Petroleum products, nec [2]	-	22	-	103	5	-	23,573	-	2,788
5181 Beer and ale [2]	-	14	-	555	40	-	26,285	-	15,014
5182 Wine and distilled beverages [2]	-	4	-	112	28	-	33,071	-	3,847
5191 Farm supplies	-	40	-	174	4	-	16,644	-	3,099
5192 Books, periodicals, & newspapers [2]	-	13	-	274	21	-	36,365	-	12,955
5193 Flowers & florists' supplies [2]	-	16	-	171	11	-	21,754	-	3,746
5198 Paints, varnishes, and supplies [2]	-	20	-	120	6	-	22,133	-	3,246
5199 Nondurable goods, nec [2]	-	54	-	430	8	-	19,247	-	9,409
52- Retail trade	-	5,753	-	90,120	16	-	12,877	-	1,249,615
5210 Lumber and other building materials	-	60	-	1,689	28	-	17,286	-	31,008
5230 Paint, glass, and wallpaper stores [2]	-	31	-	237	8	-	22,532	-	5,418
5250 Hardware stores	-	34	-	167	5	-	14,587	-	3,196
5260 Retail nurseries and garden stores	-	58	-	562	10	-	11,032	-	7,382
5270 Mobile home dealers [2]	-	11	-	102	9	-	38,980	-	4,590
5310 Department stores [2]	-	34	-	5,455	160	-	13,663	-	79,178
5330 Variety stores	-	25	-	66	3	-	12,061	-	836
5390 Misc. general merchandise stores	-	31	-	1,029	33	-	13,703	-	13,663
5410 Grocery stores [2]	-	468	-	12,660	27	-	12,797	-	161,176
5420 Meat and fish markets [2]	-	13	-	61	5	-	14,164	-	957
5440 Candy, nut, and confectionery stores [2]	-	10	-	63	6	-	9,206	-	614
5460 Retail bakeries [2]	-	56	-	576	10	-	11,076	-	6,760
5490 Miscellaneous food stores [2]	-	39	-	152	4	-	9,895	-	2,127
5510 New and used car dealers	-	62	-	4,296	69	-	32,734	-	162,269
5520 Used car dealers	-	63	-	255	4	-	24,549	-	6,055
5530 Auto and home supply stores	-	127	-	1,242	10	-	18,576	-	24,079
5540 Gasoline service stations	-	311	-	2,156	7	-	13,512	-	31,153
5550 Boat dealers [2]	-	16	-	133	8	-	23,609	-	4,073
5570 Motorcycle dealers [2]	-	9	-	102	11	-	20,275	-	3,333
5590 Automotive dealers, nec [2]	-	6	-	43	7	-	33,488	-	1,634
5610 Men's & boys' clothing stores [2]	-	55	-	327	6	-	13,125	-	4,215
5620 Women's clothing stores	-	155	-	1,460	9	-	9,605	-	14,349
5630 Women's accessory & specialty stores [2]	-	35	-	155	4	-	10,039	-	1,506
5640 Children's and infants' wear stores [2]	-	17	-	150	9	-	8,507	-	1,368
5650 Family clothing stores	-	80	-	1,814	23	-	8,913	-	16,774
5660 Shoe stores [2]	-	109	-	699	6	-	12,681	-	8,962
5690 Misc. apparel & accessory stores	-	46	-	301	7	-	9,807	-	3,167
5712 Furniture stores	-	109	-	851	8	-	20,719	-	19,887
5713 Floor covering stores [2]	-	30	-	190	6	-	23,032	-	4,664

Continued on next page.

AUSTIN – SAN MARCOS, TX MSA - [continued]

Wholesale and Retail Trade USA	Establishments		Employment		Emp / Est	Pay / Employee		Annual Payroll ($ 000)	
	1994	1995	1994	1995	1995	1994	1995	1994	1995
5714 Drapery and upholstery stores [2]	-	9	-	34	4	-	14,471	-	447
5719 Misc. homefurnishings stores [2]	-	66	-	532	8	-	12,895	-	8,112
5720 Household appliance stores [2]	-	24	-	193	8	-	20,041	-	4,611
5731 Radio, TV, & electronic stores [2]	-	73	-	783	11	-	17,405	-	13,308
5734 Computer and software stores [2]	-	61	-	494	8	-	21,943	-	11,514
5735 Record & prerecorded tape stores [2]	-	38	-	482	13	-	7,801	-	3,972
5736 Musical instrument stores [2]	-	19	-	145	8	-	20,910	-	3,128
5812 Eating places	-	1,304	-	30,788	24	-	8,762	-	283,562
5813 Drinking places [2]	-	129	-	2,811	22	-	7,863	-	22,407
5910 Drug stores and proprietary stores	-	128	-	1,702	13	-	15,993	-	29,415
5920 Liquor stores	-	90	-	361	4	-	12,920	-	5,278
5930 Used merchandise stores	-	154	-	1,018	7	-	15,493	-	15,875
5941 Sporting goods and bicycle shops [2]	-	103	-	966	9	-	11,830	-	13,140
5942 Book stores [2]	-	71	-	758	11	-	13,098	-	10,523
5943 Stationery stores [2]	-	17	-	83	5	-	15,036	-	1,169
5944 Jewelry stores	-	85	-	465	5	-	15,604	-	7,550
5945 Hobby, toy, and game shops [2]	-	47	-	608	13	-	8,809	-	6,130
5946 Camera & photographic supply stores [2]	-	5	-	37	7	-	18,811	-	697
5947 Gift, novelty, and souvenir shops	-	131	-	698	5	-	8,934	-	7,268
5948 Luggage and leather goods stores [2]	-	9	-	46	5	-	10,435	-	501
5949 Sewing, needlework, and piece goods [2]	-	22	-	204	9	-	8,471	-	1,666
5961 Catalog and mail-order houses [2]	-	31	-	568	18	-	17,000	-	10,646
5962 Merchandising machine operators [2]	-	23	-	103	4	-	17,864	-	2,114
5963 Direct selling establishments [2]	-	50	-	561	11	-	14,645	-	9,534
5984 Liquefied petroleum gas dealers	-	31	-	135	4	-	24,504	-	2,723
5992 Florists	-	85	-	343	4	-	12,898	-	4,446
5993 Tobacco stores and stands [2]	-	6	-	32	5	-	13,375	-	468
5995 Optical goods stores [2]	-	53	-	272	5	-	15,603	-	3,783
5999 Miscellaneous retail stores, nec	-	203	-	1,071	5	-	12,766	-	16,172

Source: County Business Patterns 1994/95, CBP-94/95, U.S. Department of Commerce, Washington DC, November 1997. The employment column represents mid-March employment in the year. Pay per employee is calculated by dividing 1st Quarter payroll, annualized, by mid-March employment. The column headed 'Emp / Est' shows 'employees per establishment'. A dash (-) means that data are unavailable or cannot be calculated. nec means not elsewhere classified. *Notes:* 1. 1994 data incomplete; unavailable or withheld. 2. 1995 data incomplete; unavailable or withheld. 3. 1994 and 1995 data incomplete; unavailable or withheld.

BAKERSFIELD, CA MSA

Wholesale and Retail Trade USA	Establishments		Employment		Emp / Est	Pay / Employee		Annual Payroll ($ 000)	
	1994	1995	1994	1995	1995	1994	1995	1994	1995
50 – Wholesale trade	783	807	10,671	10,636	13	26,158	27,235	296,974	307,308
5012 Automobiles and other vehicles	10	9	165	170	19	28,097	30,188	5,299	5,665
5013 Motor vehicle supplies and new parts	38	49	522	529	11	24,575	21,089	13,464	11,861
5014 Tires and tubes	9	9	91	82	9	22,418	24,683	2,772	2,604
5015 Motor vehicle parts, used	16	19	95	108	6	14,063	17,111	1,467	1,997
5021 Furniture	5	5	47	41	8	21,617	26,537	1,688	1,487
5023 Homefurnishings	7	8	30	27	3	12,400	14,370	466	470
5031 Lumber, plywood, and millwork	6	3	112	9	3	18,929	24,000	1,901	226
5032 Brick, stone, & related materials	3	6	16	79	13	32,000	20,000	472	1,533
5033 Roofing, siding, & insulation	5	4	28	20	5	21,714	24,000	628	647
5039 Construction materials, nec	5	8	71	104	13	34,986	33,000	2,489	3,104
5044 Office equipment	16	18	197	183	10	25,178	25,661	4,986	4,645
5045 Computers, peripherals, & software	17	13	157	112	9	26,675	30,643	4,294	4,491
5047 Medical and hospital equipment	10	10	128	147	15	25,625	24,435	3,441	3,669
5051 Metals service centers and offices	13	12	213	260	22	35,343	33,492	8,663	10,122
5063 Electrical apparatus and equipment	27	27	322	189	7	37,913	33,524	15,514	6,821
5064 Electrical appliances, TV & radios	4	4	50	51	13	20,080	21,647	1,100	1,155
5065 Electronic parts and equipment	9	10	43	43	4	38,977	36,837	1,509	1,524
5072 Hardware	9	9	117	121	13	21,949	23,405	2,822	3,074
5074 Plumbing & hydronic heating supplies	15	14	121	99	7	26,215	29,374	3,226	2,685
5075 Warm air heating & air conditioning	9	9	58	47	5	21,034	23,915	1,234	1,317
5078 Refrigeration equipment and supplies	3	3	11	10	3	26,545	29,200	332	330
5082 Construction and mining machinery	6	5	99	100	20	37,980	36,840	3,579	3,871
5083 Farm and garden machinery	35	35	479	482	14	25,445	29,959	14,994	16,165
5084 Industrial machinery and equipment	113	114	889	942	8	32,337	32,344	32,118	32,904
5085 Industrial supplies	34	40	289	301	8	28,886	31,575	8,958	9,759
5087 Service establishment equipment	11	9	87	65	7	15,402	17,415	1,428	1,218
5088 Transportation equipment & supplies	3	3	12	20	7	14,667	31,000	106	599
5091 Sporting & recreational goods	-	3	-	26	9	-	19,385	-	498
5093 Scrap and waste materials	21	21	231	228	11	18,130	20,667	4,468	4,957
5099 Durable goods, nec	6	-	25	-	-	21,760	-	673	-

Continued on next page.

BAKERSFIELD, CA MSA - [continued]

Wholesale and Retail Trade USA	Establishments		Employment		Emp / Est	Pay / Employee		Annual Payroll ($ 000)	
	1994	1995	1994	1995	1995	1994	1995	1994	1995
5111 Printing and writing paper	3	3	9	12	4	36,444	39,000	423	597
5112 Stationery and office supplies	15	18	205	289	16	17,015	19,253	3,392	5,192
5120 Drugs, proprietaries, and sundries	4	4	39	28	7	23,795	27,286	1,067	963
5130 Apparel, piece goods, and notions	-	3	-	24	8	-	27,333	-	647
5141 Groceries, general line	8	8	64	68	9	22,188	21,412	1,408	1,696
5143 Dairy products, exc. dried or canned	6	5	66	50	10	36,424	30,080	2,085	1,776
5145 Confectionery	5	5	182	183	37	27,538	32,066	5,568	6,934
5147 Meats and meat products	6	6	77	77	13	44,000	30,649	4,270	3,544
5148 Fresh fruits and vegetables	42	40	2,403	2,323	58	18,489	21,422	42,710	45,122
5149 Groceries and related products, nec	18	18	226	219	12	25,876	22,539	6,176	5,520
5153 Grain and field beans	4	3	19	18	6	18,316	28,222	532	630
5154 Livestock	6	4	44	41	10	13,636	13,951	496	477
5159 Farm-product raw materials, nec	8	-	186	-	-	36,430	-	7,173	-
5160 Chemicals and allied products	23	27	288	303	11	37,722	36,832	10,311	11,266
5171 Petroleum bulk stations & terminals	30	28	338	363	13	40,793	35,769	12,193	13,297
5172 Petroleum products, nec	17	15	409	347	23	25,946	33,452	10,772	11,027
5180 Beer, wine, and distilled beverages	5	4	210	198	50	31,714	31,697	7,564	6,709
5191 Farm supplies	47	47	453	463	10	25,642	27,283	13,565	14,456
5192 Books, periodicals, & newspapers	3	3	59	63	21	17,763	16,825	1,295	1,259
5199 Nondurable goods, nec	12	14	51	45	3	17,725	28,000	863	1,312
52 - Retail trade	2,802	2,738	34,320	33,532	12	12,359	13,263	453,461	463,550
5210 Lumber and other building materials	33	29	900	892	31	17,022	19,220	15,922	16,382
5230 Paint, glass, and wallpaper stores	15	18	118	112	6	21,864	18,786	2,607	2,038
5250 Hardware stores	33	25	256	251	10	12,234	13,179	3,763	3,314
5260 Retail nurseries and garden stores	20	18	101	97	5	11,050	12,454	1,326	1,320
5270 Mobile home dealers	5	5	29	19	4	21,241	17,684	608	361
5310 Department stores	25	25	3,712	3,845	154	10,203	11,783	42,735	45,790
5330 Variety stores	17	11	100	65	6	8,320	9,169	810	605
5390 Misc. general merchandise stores	21	20	496	397	20	15,089	18,529	7,329	7,542
5410 Grocery stores	330	342	4,750	4,855	14	17,058	17,234	84,769	87,777
5420 Meat and fish markets	22	22	82	86	4	10,293	9,535	898	857
5430 Fruit and vegetable markets	6	6	7	6	1	9,143	10,667	62	36
5440 Candy, nut, and confectionery stores	9	8	43	33	4	7,535	10,061	355	307
5460 Retail bakeries	51	50	198	182	4	6,263	7,824	1,640	1,467
5490 Miscellaneous food stores	16	15	68	82	5	15,529	10,585	1,392	1,019
5510 New and used car dealers	33	33	1,619	1,615	49	27,120	29,484	47,107	51,688
5520 Used car dealers	22	23	91	116	5	21,802	21,207	2,308	2,680
5530 Auto and home supply stores	129	130	793	817	6	14,613	15,863	12,311	13,495
5540 Gasoline service stations	172	162	1,650	1,505	9	11,692	12,035	20,528	19,422
5550 Boat dealers	5	5	22	28	6	22,364	20,143	489	574
5560 Recreational vehicle dealers	7	7	157	103	15	17,580	23,417	2,944	2,911
5570 Motorcycle dealers	8	8	38	41	5	20,211	18,829	946	983
5610 Men's & boys' clothing stores	18	20	107	123	6	11,140	10,992	1,254	1,453
5620 Women's clothing stores	73	61	562	408	7	8,363	7,608	4,991	3,131
5630 Women's accessory & specialty stores	7	7	48	40	6	6,417	9,200	345	370
5640 Children's and infants' wear stores	11	9	33	32	4	8,485	8,625	284	260
5650 Family clothing stores	32	25	306	332	13	11,229	10,494	3,539	3,460
5660 Shoe stores	57	51	269	279	5	11,465	11,427	3,309	3,222
5690 Misc. apparel & accessory stores	8	9	47	53	6	9,787	11,245	566	592
5712 Furniture stores	56	51	463	435	9	17,270	16,754	8,042	7,848
5713 Floor covering stores	27	28	159	166	6	20,881	25,133	3,755	4,149
5720 Household appliance stores	14	12	100	102	9	22,560	22,980	2,308	2,338
5731 Radio, TV, & electronic stores	31	31	243	283	9	20,658	17,710	5,153	5,620
5734 Computer and software stores	11	13	33	50	4	11,636	13,040	418	601
5735 Record & prerecorded tape stores	15	15	137	180	12	8,701	9,533	1,068	1,697
5736 Musical instrument stores	4	4	22	26	7	23,273	19,692	424	432
5812 Eating places	777	715	12,021	11,052	15	7,345	8,009	94,469	92,934
5813 Drinking places	101	84	317	333	4	7,571	7,520	2,479	2,646
5910 Drug stores and proprietary stores	71	70	1,235	1,382	20	20,236	19,601	26,213	27,508
5920 Liquor stores	57	50	273	309	6	12,747	14,939	3,535	2,414
5930 Used merchandise stores	32	37	222	224	6	8,847	9,661	2,128	2,164
5941 Sporting goods and bicycle shops	45	46	224	231	5	11,411	11,117	2,705	2,814
5942 Book stores	13	13	74	79	6	6,378	7,443	511	650
5943 Stationery stores	9	9	31	41	5	10,065	9,659	329	424
5944 Jewelry stores	52	47	313	214	5	14,850	18,168	4,742	3,882
5945 Hobby, toy, and game shops	13	14	126	147	11	10,159	9,333	1,587	1,638
5946 Camera & photographic supply stores	-	4	-	32	8	-	16,250	-	534
5947 Gift, novelty, and souvenir shops	30	28	187	179	6	7,722	7,821	1,587	1,536
5949 Sewing, needlework, and piece goods	14	12	149	122	10	6,309	7,967	878	947
5961 Catalog and mail-order houses	-	3	-	14	5	-	8,000	-	187
5962 Merchandising machine operators	-	6	-	42	7	-	16,000	-	645

Continued on next page.

BAKERSFIELD, CA MSA - [continued]

Wholesale and Retail Trade USA	Establishments		Employment		Emp / Est	Pay / Employee		Annual Payroll ($ 000)	
	1994	1995	1994	1995	1995	1994	1995	1994	1995
5963 Direct selling establishments	22	22	194	190	9	17,134	17,474	3,484	3,100
5980 Fuel dealers	14	14	90	96	7	22,311	20,042	1,908	2,128
5992 Florists	41	40	207	191	5	10,686	11,204	2,212	2,099
5993 Tobacco stores and stands	-	4	-	7	2	-	10,857	-	96
5995 Optical goods stores	-	23	-	101	4	-	13,743	-	1,463
5999 Miscellaneous retail stores, nec	67	74	348	354	5	14,747	14,463	6,091	5,867

Source: County Business Patterns 1994/95, CBP-94/95, U.S. Department of Commerce, Washington DC, November 1997. The employment column represents mid-March employment in the year. Pay per employee is calculated by dividing 1st Quarter payroll, annualized, by mid-March employment. The column headed 'Emp / Est' shows 'employees per establishment'. A dash (-) means that data are unavailable or cannot be calculated. nec means not elsewhere classified. *Notes:* 1. 1994 data incomplete; unavailable or withheld. 2. 1995 data incomplete; unavailable or withheld. 3. 1994 and 1995 data incomplete; unavailable or withheld.

BALTIMORE, MD PMSA

Wholesale and Retail Trade USA	Establishments		Employment		Emp / Est	Pay / Employee		Annual Payroll ($ 000)	
	1994	1995	1994	1995	1995	1994	1995	1994	1995
50- Wholesale trade	4,074	4,101	60,453	62,052	15	30,509	33,155	1,974,912	2,128,961
5012 Automobiles and other vehicles[3]	56	58	1,208	1,357	23	31,583	32,961	41,596	46,143
5013 Motor vehicle supplies and new parts	219	203	2,185	2,237	11	22,792	24,662	56,264	56,738
5014 Tires and tubes	28	24	284	246	10	30,070	27,496	8,831	6,987
5015 Motor vehicle parts, used	38	40	169	203	5	17,728	19,172	3,324	4,085
5021 Furniture	61	62	980	1,062	17	28,910	30,546	30,240	34,540
5023 Homefurnishings	95	81	1,228	1,124	14	29,860	30,609	36,757	35,216
5031 Lumber, plywood, and millwork[3]	86	88	1,564	1,461	17	27,079	28,531	47,853	41,913
5032 Brick, stone, & related materials[3]	34	35	314	301	9	29,197	29,927	10,407	9,926
5033 Roofing, siding, & insulation[3]	36	35	249	318	9	30,763	32,906	8,868	10,402
5039 Construction materials, nec[1]	42	72	416	763	11	26,183	31,266	11,267	24,527
5043 Photographic equipment & supplies[2]	-	13	-	27	2	-	47,852	-	1,320
5044 Office equipment	87	91	1,686	1,553	17	30,951	36,683	52,478	52,767
5045 Computers, peripherals, & software[3]	180	177	2,482	2,520	14	45,657	49,060	117,232	126,364
5046 Commercial equipment, nec	56	60	699	756	13	31,514	34,053	24,215	26,944
5047 Medical and hospital equipment[3]	124	120	2,468	2,546	21	38,280	42,419	94,974	107,732
5048 Ophthalmic goods[3]	19	17	207	225	13	24,676	19,982	5,377	5,098
5049 Professional equipment, nec[3]	30	36	253	363	10	31,526	35,802	9,479	14,171
5051 Metals service centers and offices[3]	84	77	896	970	13	32,799	35,134	32,837	34,131
5052 Coal and other minerals and ores[3]	8	11	123	177	16	46,341	55,345	6,187	10,523
5063 Electrical apparatus and equipment[3]	172	144	1,322	1,380	10	37,746	42,603	52,367	57,119
5064 Electrical appliances, TV & radios[3]	33	30	279	262	9	39,470	37,206	11,833	10,909
5065 Electronic parts and equipment	165	178	2,083	2,419	14	46,758	44,870	94,206	104,311
5072 Hardware[1]	65	67	600	758	11	25,027	28,929	17,313	24,779
5074 Plumbing & hydronic heating supplies	95	102	994	1,082	11	28,600	30,100	30,551	34,248
5075 Warm air heating & air conditioning	61	62	535	463	7	33,914	36,501	22,553	18,247
5078 Refrigeration equipment and supplies[3]	12	11	18	5	-	47,333	40,000	1,050	255
5082 Construction and mining machinery[3]	53	50	804	898	18	40,060	38,717	34,007	37,131
5083 Farm and garden machinery[3]	22	24	73	255	11	19,507	22,651	1,879	6,557
5084 Industrial machinery and equipment	217	219	2,342	2,486	11	33,296	36,631	83,598	98,232
5085 Industrial supplies	118	118	944	997	8	33,008	35,302	33,066	35,796
5087 Service establishment equipment	74	72	480	535	7	26,817	32,538	16,037	17,700
5088 Transportation equipment & supplies[3]	25	26	51	40	2	30,980	31,200	1,630	1,492
5091 Sporting & recreational goods[3]	44	40	294	186	5	30,599	36,559	9,449	6,418
5092 Toys and hobby goods and supplies[3]	20	19	97	103	5	21,031	25,670	2,325	2,772
5093 Scrap and waste materials	75	82	818	986	12	21,384	25,586	21,080	29,689
5094 Jewelry & precious stones[1]	24	26	84	62	2	16,571	17,677	1,625	1,230
5099 Durable goods, nec	60	71	770	951	13	25,777	24,109	21,635	24,414
5111 Printing and writing paper[3]	21	21	387	516	25	35,370	42,202	14,513	21,669
5112 Stationery and office supplies	108	91	1,617	1,477	16	23,814	28,558	40,580	41,616
5113 Industrial & personal service paper[3]	58	60	695	1,002	17	29,790	31,824	23,659	36,463
5120 Drugs, proprietaries, and sundries[2]	52	59	1,486	1,632	28	25,109	38,581	36,827	62,716
5131 Piece goods & notions[3]	26	26	204	106	4	28,078	40,038	5,670	3,796
5136 Men's and boys' clothing[3]	35	35	487	540	15	28,961	30,185	14,510	14,686
5137 Women's and children's clothing[3]	25	23	201	266	12	15,463	19,173	4,344	5,608
5139 Footwear[3]	16	16	78	77	5	35,333	35,065	3,319	2,870
5141 Groceries, general line[3]	41	39	2,277	2,487	64	27,506	29,610	73,112	79,867
5142 Packaged frozen food[3]	32	31	484	581	19	29,620	27,442	14,641	16,727
5143 Dairy products, exc. dried or canned[3]	23	18	437	355	20	28,384	30,051	14,132	10,232
5144 Poultry and poultry products[1]	7	-	134	-	-	20,716	-	3,584	-
5145 Confectionery[3]	26	23	724	760	33	26,586	30,458	19,986	23,634
5146 Fish and seafoods[3]	39	40	384	316	8	24,135	26,532	10,849	10,291
5147 Meats and meat products[3]	23	19	410	228	12	26,537	25,930	11,201	5,171
5148 Fresh fruits and vegetables[3]	51	49	847	830	17	24,978	30,005	25,854	29,028

Continued on next page.

BALTIMORE, MD PMSA - [continued]

Wholesale and Retail Trade USA	Establishments		Employment		Emp / Est	Pay / Employee		Annual Payroll ($ 000)	
	1994	1995	1994	1995	1995	1994	1995	1994	1995
5149 Groceries and related products, nec [2]	146	144	4,719	4,758	33	26,779	28,398	132,214	134,269
5150 Farm-product raw materials	16	13	90	99	8	20,711	22,909	1,771	1,978
5162 Plastics materials & basic shapes [3]	19	21	133	194	9	26,286	25,876	3,521	5,484
5169 Chemicals & allied products, nec [3]	86	89	519	788	9	36,224	36,371	19,413	31,843
5171 Petroleum bulk stations & terminals [3]	38	37	518	520	14	38,394	34,615	18,475	16,249
5172 Petroleum products, nec [3]	16	16	196	164	10	35,898	43,976	7,251	8,019
5181 Beer and ale [1]	17	-	18	-	-	26,667	-	635	-
5191 Farm supplies	63	54	550	449	8	19,287	22,085	12,342	10,535
5192 Books, periodicals, & newspapers	38	48	800	692	14	21,405	26,376	18,768	19,320
5193 Flowers & florists' supplies [1]	31	28	300	252	9	21,213	22,365	7,358	6,490
5194 Tobacco and tobacco products [3]	10	12	499	466	39	24,377	22,970	12,187	11,679
5198 Paints, varnishes, and supplies [2]	61	50	474	375	8	24,008	25,077	12,977	11,241
5199 Nondurable goods, nec [3]	148	150	798	799	5	24,346	26,518	20,669	23,151
52 – Retail trade	14,155	14,053	192,591	201,173	14	12,900	13,822	2,766,898	2,932,179
5210 Lumber and other building materials	183	139	3,903	3,821	27	18,390	19,337	78,374	78,070
5230 Paint, glass, and wallpaper stores	55	52	296	327	6	16,054	19,095	4,976	6,510
5250 Hardware stores	139	93	943	928	10	12,602	13,694	13,884	13,420
5260 Retail nurseries and garden stores	108	107	923	925	9	11,463	14,011	14,362	15,017
5270 Mobile home dealers [3]	14	15	41	76	5	19,610	20,053	1,042	2,019
5310 Department stores [3]	84	85	13,839	15,338	180	10,380	11,441	163,800	180,979
5330 Variety stores	111	89	1,233	984	11	9,135	9,362	11,343	9,544
5390 Misc. general merchandise stores [3]	90	95	2,411	2,775	29	12,851	14,693	36,082	40,377
5410 Grocery stores	1,118	1,098	25,498	25,732	23	15,899	16,184	416,976	431,666
5420 Meat and fish markets	134	124	787	766	6	11,619	11,990	10,269	10,013
5430 Fruit and vegetable markets	44	49	164	170	3	15,195	18,471	3,132	3,669
5440 Candy, nut, and confectionery stores	50	49	266	274	6	7,444	7,927	2,012	2,281
5450 Dairy products stores [3]	17	19	45	57	3	8,533	5,965	277	401
5460 Retail bakeries	155	147	1,602	1,415	10	8,851	9,563	16,245	14,400
5490 Miscellaneous food stores [1]	87	84	502	548	7	8,558	11,102	5,396	6,820
5510 New and used car dealers	165	167	9,854	10,735	64	26,138	27,449	304,023	323,096
5520 Used car dealers	99	96	327	319	3	18,544	21,028	6,438	7,603
5530 Auto and home supply stores	280	290	2,462	2,432	8	18,232	19,563	49,271	50,207
5540 Gasoline service stations	656	658	5,529	5,317	8	12,616	13,921	74,189	74,617
5550 Boat dealers [3]	84	84	525	583	7	18,850	19,190	13,531	13,742
5560 Recreational vehicle dealers [3]	11	11	44	45	4	15,818	16,000	896	951
5570 Motorcycle dealers [3]	18	17	138	140	8	19,391	23,286	3,465	3,757
5610 Men's & boys' clothing stores	188	156	1,507	1,375	9	11,297	11,820	17,089	17,385
5620 Women's clothing stores	404	352	4,464	3,758	11	8,468	8,846	41,755	34,104
5630 Women's accessory & specialty stores	98	91	537	541	6	9,937	10,233	5,714	5,655
5640 Children's and infants' wear stores [3]	64	61	603	777	13	7,788	9,133	5,448	7,376
5650 Family clothing stores	189	172	3,731	3,518	20	10,107	12,373	45,719	47,927
5660 Shoe stores	404	380	2,181	2,255	6	12,963	12,286	32,126	28,340
5690 Misc. apparel & accessory stores	92	95	429	542	6	9,287	10,613	5,349	6,822
5712 Furniture stores	267	246	2,228	2,387	10	18,408	20,218	43,832	47,358
5713 Floor covering stores	138	145	728	908	6	23,923	26,093	18,265	23,840
5714 Drapery and upholstery stores [3]	33	31	101	108	3	16,990	16,741	1,848	1,918
5719 Misc. homefurnishings stores	175	173	1,330	1,454	8	12,039	11,884	17,298	17,045
5720 Household appliance stores [2]	76	75	324	368	5	26,728	26,989	8,358	10,029
5731 Radio, TV, & electronic stores	144	142	1,044	1,462	10	17,264	18,309	20,597	26,664
5734 Computer and software stores [1]	99	102	629	771	8	17,984	18,791	13,024	14,452
5735 Record & prerecorded tape stores [3]	106	105	823	719	7	9,740	10,709	8,287	7,345
5736 Musical instrument stores [3]	40	34	165	159	5	19,467	23,497	3,461	3,647
5812 Eating places	3,310	3,115	61,591	62,800	20	7,917	8,620	556,081	575,266
5813 Drinking places	548	518	2,980	3,110	6	8,272	8,923	26,992	28,874
5910 Drug stores and proprietary stores	417	420	5,373	6,248	15	15,041	15,937	87,470	102,559
5920 Liquor stores	572	582	3,122	3,078	5	11,440	11,897	38,334	38,270
5930 Used merchandise stores	180	169	1,761	1,678	10	8,520	9,931	17,027	17,687
5941 Sporting goods and bicycle shops	230	248	1,336	1,619	7	12,494	12,941	21,820	22,112
5942 Book stores	132	136	924	1,115	8	9,996	10,665	9,562	12,705
5943 Stationery stores [3]	41	50	137	405	8	13,489	13,580	2,745	5,985
5944 Jewelry stores	242	245	1,542	1,546	6	16,257	17,708	28,734	28,935
5945 Hobby, toy, and game shops	114	119	1,169	1,356	11	8,749	8,855	13,601	14,123
5946 Camera & photographic supply stores [3]	36	35	228	133	4	12,877	13,173	3,088	1,805
5947 Gift, novelty, and souvenir shops	307	296	2,203	2,188	7	7,147	8,033	18,853	20,137
5948 Luggage and leather goods stores	21	22	73	82	4	10,685	11,415	796	913
5949 Sewing, needlework, and piece goods [3]	60	60	577	549	9	6,711	7,869	4,272	4,647
5961 Catalog and mail-order houses	56	62	381	360	6	15,087	20,589	6,295	8,673
5962 Merchandising machine operators	81	72	454	489	7	19,304	19,501	9,754	10,700
5963 Direct selling establishments	159	177	1,712	2,035	11	19,161	20,564	35,094	43,839
5983 Fuel oil dealers [3]	58	57	399	396	7	33,203	30,152	12,002	11,216
5984 Liquefied petroleum gas dealers	21	22	108	52	2	27,741	24,308	2,982	1,210

Continued on next page.

BALTIMORE, MD PMSA - [continued]

Wholesale and Retail Trade USA	Establishments		Employment		Emp / Est	Pay / Employee		Annual Payroll ($ 000)	
	1994	1995	1994	1995	1995	1994	1995	1994	1995
5992 Florists[2]	220	220	1,597	1,549	7	10,397	11,047	19,021	18,643
5993 Tobacco stores and stands[3]	14	13	42	38	3	13,238	14,526	659	618
5994 News dealers and newsstands[2]	27	29	95	104	4	9,768	9,962	1,064	1,114
5995 Optical goods stores[3]	193	203	829	870	4	17,636	19,186	15,255	17,016
5999 Miscellaneous retail stores, nec	463	482	2,757	3,061	6	12,791	13,882	41,329	46,476

Source: County Business Patterns 1994/95, CBP-94/95, U.S. Department of Commerce, Washington DC, November 1997. The employment column represents mid-March employment in the year. Pay per employee is calculated by dividing 1st Quarter payroll, annualized, by mid-March employment. The column headed 'Emp / Est' shows 'employees per establishment'. A dash (-) means that data are unavailable or cannot be calculated. nec means not elsewhere classified. *Notes:* 1. 1994 data incomplete; unavailable or withheld. 2. 1995 data incomplete; unavailable or withheld. 3. 1994 and 1995 data incomplete; unavailable or withheld.

BATON ROUGE, LA MSA

Wholesale and Retail Trade USA	Establishments		Employment		Emp / Est	Pay / Employee		Annual Payroll ($ 000)	
	1994	1995	1994	1995	1995	1994	1995	1994	1995
50- Wholesale trade	1,082	1,090	12,872	12,796	12	26,611	28,579	364,327	378,187
5012 Automobiles and other vehicles[3]	16	17	271	237	14	23,911	25,232	7,290	6,025
5013 Motor vehicle supplies and new parts[3]	68	54	524	434	8	18,023	22,977	9,868	10,717
5014 Tires and tubes[3]	6	5	115	112	22	20,696	28,500	3,147	3,032
5015 Motor vehicle parts, used[3]	13	16	60	74	5	15,400	16,919	994	1,520
5021 Furniture[3]	18	18	175	188	10	25,783	29,894	4,516	6,262
5023 Homefurnishings[3]	11	11	126	127	12	22,190	28,724	3,300	3,877
5031 Lumber, plywood, and millwork[3]	19	17	173	145	9	22,012	21,986	3,877	3,435
5032 Brick, stone, & related materials[1]	15	14	85	115	8	32,753	24,452	2,724	3,808
5033 Roofing, siding, & insulation[3]	9	9	54	37	4	22,889	36,000	1,783	1,226
5039 Construction materials, nec[3]	17	21	167	163	8	21,677	24,025	5,214	3,963
5043 Photographic equipment & supplies[3]	3	3	43	46	15	18,047	19,217	815	960
5044 Office equipment[3]	19	19	412	408	21	35,291	40,618	16,012	16,704
5045 Computers, peripherals, & software[3]	34	31	332	302	10	37,566	47,907	12,729	12,557
5046 Commercial equipment, nec[3]	9	10	49	56	6	22,449	20,643	1,032	1,263
5047 Medical and hospital equipment[3]	20	15	86	91	6	31,953	33,363	3,474	3,414
5048 Ophthalmic goods[3]	6	5	19	18	4	13,895	13,333	260	292
5049 Professional equipment, nec[3]	11	15	86	92	6	29,256	25,000	2,730	2,091
5051 Metals service centers and offices	31	32	419	434	14	29,823	32,341	13,726	14,213
5063 Electrical apparatus and equipment[3]	58	56	507	492	9	30,438	35,341	15,537	15,261
5064 Electrical appliances, TV & radios[1]	3	-	43	-	-	28,744	-	1,302	-
5065 Electronic parts and equipment[3]	25	25	249	258	10	41,815	44,620	9,781	10,669
5072 Hardware[3]	13	16	252	258	16	23,286	24,419	6,636	6,802
5074 Plumbing & hydronic heating supplies[1]	20	21	233	252	12	29,425	40,508	7,831	7,882
5082 Construction and mining machinery[3]	10	11	298	301	27	37,463	42,419	11,456	12,748
5083 Farm and garden machinery[3]	17	16	143	96	6	23,105	29,333	3,769	2,919
5084 Industrial machinery and equipment	98	102	747	859	8	31,165	31,925	24,967	29,214
5085 Industrial supplies	107	109	1,247	1,206	11	35,564	37,662	44,714	46,498
5087 Service establishment equipment[2]	26	27	260	228	8	14,692	16,947	3,921	4,250
5091 Sporting & recreational goods[3]	5	5	135	149	30	14,637	15,570	2,305	2,351
5092 Toys and hobby goods and supplies[3]	4	4	16	17	4	16,250	16,941	296	296
5093 Scrap and waste materials	14	16	143	98	6	26,070	25,347	3,820	2,814
5094 Jewelry & precious stones[3]	5	5	12	24	5	13,667	14,333	236	245
5099 Durable goods, nec[2]	20	21	125	129	6	16,032	19,752	2,186	2,663
5112 Stationery and office supplies[3]	25	23	353	364	16	18,232	20,297	7,231	7,473
5120 Drugs, proprietaries, and sundries[3]	14	15	101	125	8	17,782	19,072	2,286	2,662
5131 Piece goods & notions[1]	5	-	14	-	-	14,286	-	222	-
5136 Men's and boys' clothing[2]	-	4	-	47	12	-	14,043	-	726
5142 Packaged frozen food[3]	4	4	104	69	17	25,731	29,333	2,911	2,300
5146 Fish and seafoods[3]	7	6	64	53	9	7,063	6,340	604	639
5147 Meats and meat products[3]	5	5	86	90	18	16,512	16,889	1,934	1,968
5148 Fresh fruits and vegetables[3]	3	3	128	147	49	16,563	15,293	2,248	2,377
5149 Groceries and related products, nec[3]	23	25	249	268	11	22,747	22,582	5,924	6,706
5162 Plastics materials & basic shapes[3]	7	8	60	55	7	26,333	23,273	1,493	1,247
5169 Chemicals & allied products, nec[3]	39	41	230	305	7	39,843	39,344	10,527	13,177
5171 Petroleum bulk stations & terminals[1]	31	29	328	404	14	29,305	21,347	9,862	10,647
5172 Petroleum products, nec[3]	5	6	14	14	2	16,571	17,714	229	339
5181 Beer and ale[3]	4	4	250	254	64	21,536	23,071	5,943	6,511
5182 Wine and distilled beverages[3]	3	3	108	107	36	28,074	19,364	3,318	1,639
5191 Farm supplies	18	14	131	71	5	20,763	20,563	3,468	1,556
5192 Books, periodicals, & newspapers[1]	6	-	56	-	-	10,357	-	696	-
5193 Flowers & florists' supplies[3]	9	5	60	41	8	16,000	15,415	995	679
5198 Paints, varnishes, and supplies[3]	8	9	59	59	7	26,034	27,458	1,457	1,618
5199 Nondurable goods, nec[2]	-	23	-	69	3	-	15,884	-	1,124
52- Retail trade	3,020	3,030	44,821	47,368	16	10,758	11,688	519,647	588,669

Continued on next page.

BATON ROUGE, LA MSA - [continued]

Wholesale and Retail Trade USA	Establishments		Employment		Emp / Est	Pay / Employee		Annual Payroll ($ 000)	
	1994	1995	1994	1995	1995	1994	1995	1994	1995
5210 Lumber and other building materials	49	46	750	1,012	22	17,344	20,202	12,642	21,117
5230 Paint, glass, and wallpaper stores [2]	28	30	143	194	6	18,098	18,536	2,686	3,373
5250 Hardware stores	48	34	350	269	8	13,726	12,312	4,959	3,299
5260 Retail nurseries and garden stores [3]	27	29	41	259	9	10,146	10,363	522	3,116
5270 Mobile home dealers [3]	8	8	32	43	5	31,625	29,209	1,184	1,449
5310 Department stores [3]	26	26	3,830	4,430	170	10,980	12,308	46,481	53,683
5330 Variety stores	32	23	179	178	8	8,514	9,393	1,688	1,320
5390 Misc. general merchandise stores	14	22	443	461	21	12,036	13,944	5,910	6,345
5410 Grocery stores	382	373	8,189	7,705	21	8,430	9,477	70,876	73,562
5420 Meat and fish markets	23	22	113	175	8	21,027	13,509	2,651	2,590
5430 Fruit and vegetable markets [1]	7	9	72	83	9	9,556	8,386	727	784
5460 Retail bakeries [3]	23	26	180	237	9	9,844	7,629	1,750	1,812
5490 Miscellaneous food stores [3]	10	12	37	80	7	7,784	13,350	296	1,227
5510 New and used car dealers [3]	35	38	2,309	2,341	62	26,084	28,668	66,391	81,728
5520 Used car dealers	23	21	83	57	3	13,349	13,895	932	802
5530 Auto and home supply stores	89	100	834	888	9	15,127	17,167	13,955	16,545
5540 Gasoline service stations	196	206	1,525	1,665	8	11,239	12,738	18,255	21,991
5550 Boat dealers [3]	10	9	51	56	6	16,941	18,143	1,038	1,029
5560 Recreational vehicle dealers [3]	8	6	66	52	9	18,424	19,462	1,345	1,172
5570 Motorcycle dealers [3]	9	9	57	68	8	15,719	16,235	1,000	1,124
5610 Men's & boys' clothing stores [3]	36	37	298	335	9	10,040	9,421	3,076	3,173
5620 Women's clothing stores [3]	113	97	847	679	7	8,043	7,788	7,551	5,818
5630 Women's accessory & specialty stores [3]	12	12	76	80	7	8,684	8,250	689	661
5640 Children's and infants' wear stores [3]	10	14	51	75	5	31,059	8,427	1,662	702
5650 Family clothing stores [3]	36	40	505	636	16	9,473	10,289	5,730	6,640
5660 Shoe stores [3]	66	63	364	382	6	10,264	10,534	3,828	4,038
5690 Misc. apparel & accessory stores [3]	19	18	86	86	5	10,093	9,256	868	792
5712 Furniture stores	83	80	671	671	8	15,911	16,250	12,096	12,660
5713 Floor covering stores [3]	26	31	151	179	6	19,099	21,318	3,255	3,880
5714 Drapery and upholstery stores [1]	4	-	1	-	-	8,000	-	67	-
5719 Misc. homefurnishings stores [3]	39	41	235	258	6	9,055	10,822	2,254	2,899
5720 Household appliance stores [1]	16	19	129	161	8	17,953	19,255	2,523	2,671
5731 Radio, TV, & electronic stores [3]	38	38	356	320	8	15,674	18,525	5,711	5,830
5734 Computer and software stores [3]	11	12	54	47	4	13,704	14,043	667	770
5735 Record & prerecorded tape stores [3]	17	15	103	154	10	9,670	6,857	1,028	1,068
5736 Musical instrument stores [3]	6	7	30	46	7	14,400	14,000	426	732
5812 Eating places	616	553	13,701	14,118	26	7,429	7,791	109,878	115,551
5813 Drinking places	79	63	596	575	9	6,336	7,784	4,410	4,802
5910 Drug stores and proprietary stores	92	93	1,133	1,384	15	13,991	15,408	17,211	22,414
5920 Liquor stores [3]	11	9	39	40	4	9,641	9,600	433	414
5930 Used merchandise stores [3]	40	35	203	188	5	12,256	12,894	2,796	2,764
5941 Sporting goods and bicycle shops	47	48	294	309	6	11,320	11,625	3,618	3,912
5942 Book stores [3]	23	24	199	217	9	9,407	9,235	1,951	2,125
5944 Jewelry stores [3]	46	40	261	228	6	17,487	19,982	4,282	4,275
5945 Hobby, toy, and game shops [3]	13	11	197	187	17	7,371	8,193	1,809	1,791
5947 Gift, novelty, and souvenir shops	47	47	292	300	6	5,438	5,853	1,855	1,916
5949 Sewing, needlework, and piece goods [3]	16	14	105	103	7	12,076	11,534	1,161	1,128
5961 Catalog and mail-order houses [3]	6	11	20	32	3	11,000	9,500	267	441
5962 Merchandising machine operators [3]	11	10	105	103	10	14,400	15,612	1,579	1,530
5963 Direct selling establishments [3]	29	25	172	162	6	18,837	16,765	3,373	2,941
5992 Florists	46	43	269	277	6	9,353	10,296	2,918	3,286
5993 Tobacco stores and stands [2]	-	16	-	84	5	-	9,333	-	788
5995 Optical goods stores [3]	28	29	179	159	5	14,503	15,296	2,611	2,434
5999 Miscellaneous retail stores, nec [3]	92	91	460	447	5	11,443	12,260	5,872	6,459

Source: County Business Patterns 1994/95, CBP-94/95, U.S. Department of Commerce, Washington DC, November 1997. The employment column represents mid-March employment in the year. Pay per employee is calculated by dividing 1st Quarter payroll, annualized, by mid-March employment. The column headed 'Emp / Est' shows 'employees per establishment'. A dash (-) means that data are unavailable or cannot be calculated. nec means not elsewhere classified. *Notes:* 1. 1994 data incomplete; unavailable or withheld. 2. 1995 data incomplete; unavailable or withheld. 3. 1994 and 1995 data incomplete; unavailable or withheld.

BEAUMONT - PORT ARTHUR, TX MSA

Wholesale and Retail Trade USA	Establishments		Employment		Emp / Est	Pay / Employee		Annual Payroll ($ 000)	
	1994	1995	1994	1995	1995	1994	1995	1994	1995
50- Wholesale trade	-	584	-	6,780	12	-	27,897	-	196,880
5013 Motor vehicle supplies and new parts	-	23	-	109	5	-	17,394	-	1,788
5015 Motor vehicle parts, used	-	11	-	75	7	-	23,680	-	1,976
5020 Furniture and homefurnishings	-	13	-	123	9	-	18,146	-	2,368
5031 Lumber, plywood, and millwork [2]	-	7	-	28	4	-	35,714	-	1,045
5032 Brick, stone, & related materials [2]	-	9	-	82	9	-	10,293	-	911

Continued on next page.

BEAUMONT - PORT ARTHUR, TX MSA - [continued]

Wholesale and Retail Trade USA	Establishments		Employment		Emp / Est	Pay / Employee		Annual Payroll ($ 000)	
	1994	1995	1994	1995	1995	1994	1995	1994	1995
5033 Roofing, siding, & insulation [2]	-	5	-	62	12	-	22,387	-	1,664
5039 Construction materials, nec [2]	-	5	-	308	62	-	23,156	-	2,716
5044 Office equipment [2]	-	15	-	139	9	-	28,201	-	4,045
5045 Computers, peripherals, & software [2]	-	13	-	145	11	-	34,538	-	4,551
5047 Medical and hospital equipment [2]	-	22	-	352	16	-	22,250	-	10,424
5051 Metals service centers and offices [2]	-	11	-	112	10	-	35,357	-	4,509
5063 Electrical apparatus and equipment	-	26	-	204	8	-	36,039	-	6,748
5064 Electrical appliances, TV & radios [2]	-	5	-	37	7	-	17,622	-	593
5065 Electronic parts and equipment [2]	-	15	-	62	4	-	27,097	-	1,644
5072 Hardware	-	13	-	82	6	-	18,683	-	1,494
5074 Plumbing & hydronic heating supplies [2]	-	13	-	77	6	-	22,026	-	1,721
5075 Warm air heating & air conditioning [2]	-	8	-	24	3	-	27,000	-	701
5082 Construction and mining machinery [2]	-	9	-	55	6	-	30,255	-	1,767
5083 Farm and garden machinery [2]	-	7	-	47	7	-	22,894	-	995
5084 Industrial machinery and equipment	-	59	-	516	9	-	36,899	-	20,726
5085 Industrial supplies [2]	-	44	-	488	11	-	27,549	-	14,402
5087 Service establishment equipment [2]	-	11	-	67	6	-	23,104	-	1,707
5088 Transportation equipment & supplies [2]	-	4	-	11	3	-	20,000	-	233
5093 Scrap and waste materials	-	22	-	216	10	-	27,370	-	6,510
5099 Durable goods, nec	-	8	-	46	6	-	20,609	-	972
5110 Paper and paper products [2]	-	15	-	156	10	-	17,103	-	2,731
5120 Drugs, proprietaries, and sundries [2]	-	10	-	64	6	-	20,938	-	1,559
5146 Fish and seafoods [2]	-	5	-	129	26	-	9,085	-	1,651
5147 Meats and meat products [2]	-	4	-	28	7	-	20,429	-	577
5149 Groceries and related products, nec	-	14	-	278	20	-	28,216	-	8,360
5150 Farm-product raw materials [2]	-	5	-	66	13	-	27,758	-	1,771
5162 Plastics materials & basic shapes [2]	-	5	-	65	13	-	26,400	-	2,098
5169 Chemicals & allied products, nec	-	16	-	190	12	-	34,337	-	7,617
5171 Petroleum bulk stations & terminals	-	26	-	307	12	-	33,915	-	12,658
5172 Petroleum products, nec [2]	-	11	-	185	17	-	40,043	-	7,720
5180 Beer, wine, and distilled beverages [2]	-	4	-	222	56	-	29,550	-	8,097
5191 Farm supplies	-	11	-	6	1	-	10,667	-	57
5192 Books, periodicals, & newspapers [2]	-	3	-	24	8	-	15,000	-	702
5193 Flowers & florists' supplies [2]	-	4	-	73	18	-	15,781	-	1,219
5198 Paints, varnishes, and supplies [2]	-	5	-	11	2	-	24,727	-	224
5199 Nondurable goods, nec [2]	-	8	-	9	1	-	13,778	-	101
52- Retail trade	-	2,071	-	27,845	13	-	12,479	-	356,364
5210 Lumber and other building materials	-	36	-	589	16	-	17,467	-	11,315
5230 Paint, glass, and wallpaper stores	-	26	-	122	5	-	22,426	-	2,523
5250 Hardware stores	-	12	-	126	11	-	12,571	-	1,818
5260 Retail nurseries and garden stores [2]	-	17	-	98	6	-	11,020	-	1,287
5270 Mobile home dealers [2]	-	12	-	90	8	-	36,978	-	2,552
5310 Department stores [2]	-	19	-	2,633	139	-	11,982	-	30,602
5330 Variety stores	-	13	-	55	4	-	8,364	-	542
5390 Misc. general merchandise stores	-	17	-	354	21	-	13,876	-	4,572
5410 Grocery stores	-	251	-	3,814	15	-	11,616	-	44,342
5420 Meat and fish markets	-	11	-	33	3	-	13,091	-	453
5440 Candy, nut, and confectionery stores [2]	-	4	-	21	5	-	6,476	-	136
5460 Retail bakeries	-	19	-	61	3	-	9,377	-	624
5490 Miscellaneous food stores [2]	-	9	-	32	4	-	8,500	-	290
5510 New and used car dealers	-	29	-	1,542	53	-	31,017	-	47,815
5520 Used car dealers	-	43	-	184	4	-	17,609	-	3,472
5530 Auto and home supply stores	-	68	-	570	8	-	17,712	-	10,743
5540 Gasoline service stations	-	181	-	1,133	6	-	12,021	-	14,646
5550 Boat dealers [2]	-	7	-	72	10	-	21,278	-	1,838
5560 Recreational vehicle dealers [2]	-	7	-	29	4	-	16,414	-	439
5570 Motorcycle dealers	-	7	-	36	5	-	15,111	-	554
5610 Men's & boys' clothing stores [2]	-	14	-	72	5	-	11,056	-	978
5620 Women's clothing stores	-	55	-	456	8	-	9,088	-	3,864
5630 Women's accessory & specialty stores [2]	-	10	-	42	4	-	9,048	-	382
5640 Children's and infants' wear stores [2]	-	5	-	22	4	-	8,182	-	175
5650 Family clothing stores	-	32	-	624	20	-	10,487	-	6,279
5660 Shoe stores	-	44	-	176	4	-	12,659	-	2,055
5690 Misc. apparel & accessory stores [2]	-	8	-	28	4	-	9,714	-	302
5712 Furniture stores	-	37	-	280	8	-	17,214	-	4,986
5713 Floor covering stores	-	19	-	113	6	-	20,991	-	2,740
5719 Misc. homefurnishings stores [2]	-	13	-	48	4	-	11,167	-	695
5720 Household appliance stores [2]	-	18	-	95	5	-	23,832	-	3,101
5731 Radio, TV, & electronic stores [2]	-	22	-	245	11	-	16,490	-	4,231
5734 Computer and software stores	-	8	-	32	4	-	11,875	-	391
5735 Record & prerecorded tape stores [2]	-	12	-	51	4	-	10,196	-	510

Continued on next page.

BEAUMONT – PORT ARTHUR, TX MSA - [continued]

Wholesale and Retail Trade USA	Establishments		Employment		Emp / Est	Pay / Employee		Annual Payroll ($ 000)	
	1994	1995	1994	1995	1995	1994	1995	1994	1995
5736 Musical instrument stores [2]	-	7	-	49	7	-	21,224	-	1,258
5812 Eating places	-	378	-	8,428	22	-	7,680	-	67,078
5813 Drinking places	-	45	-	404	9	-	6,099	-	2,274
5910 Drug stores and proprietary stores	-	66	-	755	11	-	15,396	-	11,836
5920 Liquor stores	-	30	-	152	5	-	12,237	-	2,038
5930 Used merchandise stores	-	32	-	172	5	-	14,047	-	2,429
5941 Sporting goods and bicycle shops [2]	-	24	-	217	9	-	11,263	-	2,499
5942 Book stores [2]	-	7	-	43	6	-	8,372	-	428
5944 Jewelry stores	-	37	-	237	6	-	13,350	-	3,429
5945 Hobby, toy, and game shops [2]	-	10	-	126	13	-	9,714	-	1,377
5947 Gift, novelty, and souvenir shops	-	30	-	164	5	-	9,195	-	1,583
5949 Sewing, needlework, and piece goods [2]	-	12	-	76	6	-	9,526	-	740
5961 Catalog and mail-order houses [2]	-	3	-	11	4	-	10,182	-	168
5962 Merchandising machine operators [2]	-	4	-	7	2	-	8,000	-	49
5963 Direct selling establishments	-	21	-	131	6	-	13,191	-	1,797
5984 Liquefied petroleum gas dealers	-	9	-	20	2	-	23,200	-	416
5992 Florists	-	43	-	136	3	-	8,206	-	1,108
5994 News dealers and newsstands [2]	-	3	-	4	1	-	13,000	-	64
5995 Optical goods stores	-	22	-	176	8	-	16,318	-	3,020
5999 Miscellaneous retail stores, nec	-	62	-	270	4	-	14,978	-	4,679

Source: County Business Patterns 1994/95, CBP-94/95, U.S. Department of Commerce, Washington DC, November 1997. The employment column represents mid-March employment in the year. Pay per employee is calculated by dividing 1st Quarter payroll, annualized, by mid-March employment. The column headed 'Emp / Est' shows 'employees per establishment'. A dash (-) means that data are unavailable or cannot be calculated. nec means not elsewhere classified. *Notes:* 1. 1994 data incomplete; unavailable or withheld. 2. 1995 data incomplete; unavailable or withheld. 3. 1994 and 1995 data incomplete; unavailable or withheld.

BELLINGHAM, WA MSA

Wholesale and Retail Trade USA	Establishments		Employment		Emp / Est	Pay / Employee		Annual Payroll ($ 000)	
	1994	1995	1994	1995	1995	1994	1995	1994	1995
50– Wholesale trade	-	356	-	3,071	9	-	24,061	-	81,102
5012 Automobiles and other vehicles	-	4	-	35	9	-	21,486	-	1,073
5013 Motor vehicle supplies and new parts	-	10	-	57	6	-	20,491	-	1,424
5023 Homefurnishings	-	6	-	17	3	-	22,118	-	471
5031 Lumber, plywood, and millwork	-	15	-	97	6	-	21,196	-	2,370
5032 Brick, stone, & related materials	-	4	-	29	7	-	38,483	-	1,277
5039 Construction materials, nec	-	8	-	71	9	-	29,127	-	1,893
5044 Office equipment	-	10	-	65	7	-	24,123	-	1,636
5045 Computers, peripherals, & software	-	12	-	110	9	-	23,345	-	3,470
5047 Medical and hospital equipment	-	4	-	12	3	-	32,333	-	306
5049 Professional equipment, nec	-	3	-	5	2	-	25,600	-	126
5051 Metals service centers and offices	-	3	-	33	11	-	27,758	-	879
5065 Electronic parts and equipment	-	9	-	59	7	-	33,288	-	1,818
5072 Hardware	-	6	-	73	12	-	29,753	-	1,906
5074 Plumbing & hydronic heating supplies	-	6	-	73	12	-	28,000	-	1,990
5083 Farm and garden machinery	-	9	-	143	16	-	28,308	-	4,618
5084 Industrial machinery and equipment	-	17	-	163	10	-	22,601	-	4,384
5085 Industrial supplies	-	9	-	48	5	-	25,417	-	1,411
5088 Transportation equipment & supplies	-	4	-	61	15	-	31,279	-	2,101
5091 Sporting & recreational goods	-	7	-	49	7	-	24,490	-	1,410
5092 Toys and hobby goods and supplies	-	5	-	17	3	-	10,118	-	224
5093 Scrap and waste materials	-	10	-	128	13	-	28,781	-	3,458
5094 Jewelry & precious stones	-	6	-	23	4	-	9,739	-	218
5099 Durable goods, nec	-	9	-	55	6	-	18,182	-	1,268
5112 Stationery and office supplies	-	6	-	75	13	-	16,373	-	1,032
5120 Drugs, proprietaries, and sundries	-	5	-	76	15	-	18,316	-	1,740
5131 Piece goods & notions	-	5	-	18	4	-	21,778	-	771
5143 Dairy products, exc. dried or canned	-	3	-	10	3	-	19,200	-	189
5145 Confectionery	-	3	-	25	8	-	19,680	-	296
5146 Fish and seafoods	-	15	-	153	10	-	19,739	-	3,843
5149 Groceries and related products, nec	-	8	-	168	21	-	25,810	-	4,739
5171 Petroleum bulk stations & terminals	-	10	-	69	7	-	27,304	-	2,270
5172 Petroleum products, nec	-	4	-	58	15	-	19,517	-	1,253
5180 Beer, wine, and distilled beverages	-	6	-	126	21	-	23,206	-	2,916
5191 Farm supplies	-	19	-	258	14	-	27,597	-	7,466
5193 Flowers & florists' supplies	-	5	-	50	10	-	11,200	-	483
5194 Tobacco and tobacco products	-	3	-	18	6	-	15,556	-	191
5198 Paints, varnishes, and supplies	-	3	-	11	4	-	31,273	-	313
5199 Nondurable goods, nec	-	9	-	37	4	-	18,162	-	678
52– Retail trade	-	1,157	-	15,013	13	-	12,653	-	200,218

Continued on next page.

BELLINGHAM, WA MSA - [continued]

Wholesale and Retail Trade USA	Establishments		Employment		Emp / Est	Pay / Employee		Annual Payroll ($ 000)	
	1994	1995	1994	1995	1995	1994	1995	1994	1995
5210 Lumber and other building materials	-	20	-	311	16	-	20,785	-	6,761
5230 Paint, glass, and wallpaper stores	-	7	-	56	8	-	17,857	-	1,099
5250 Hardware stores	-	11	-	150	14	-	17,467	-	2,746
5260 Retail nurseries and garden stores	-	14	-	94	7	-	9,319	-	1,165
5270 Mobile home dealers	-	5	-	43	9	-	20,651	-	981
5310 Department stores	-	7	-	1,042	149	-	13,931	-	16,405
5330 Variety stores	-	3	-	8	3	-	10,000	-	123
5410 Grocery stores	-	74	-	1,734	23	-	14,401	-	27,598
5420 Meat and fish markets	-	3	-	20	7	-	9,000	-	304
5440 Candy, nut, and confectionery stores	-	3	-	2	1	-	8,000	-	89
5460 Retail bakeries	-	14	-	96	7	-	6,708	-	643
5490 Miscellaneous food stores	-	6	-	20	3	-	12,000	-	321
5510 New and used car dealers	-	11	-	515	47	-	25,763	-	13,988
5520 Used car dealers	-	10	-	39	4	-	15,692	-	568
5530 Auto and home supply stores	-	22	-	207	9	-	22,222	-	4,371
5540 Gasoline service stations	-	77	-	686	9	-	10,787	-	7,506
5550 Boat dealers	-	15	-	75	5	-	24,427	-	1,825
5560 Recreational vehicle dealers	-	6	-	46	8	-	22,609	-	1,185
5570 Motorcycle dealers	-	6	-	22	4	-	17,091	-	410
5610 Men's & boys' clothing stores	-	12	-	81	7	-	12,395	-	943
5620 Women's clothing stores	-	26	-	209	8	-	6,354	-	1,270
5630 Women's accessory & specialty stores	-	8	-	56	7	-	9,286	-	521
5640 Children's and infants' wear stores	-	8	-	35	4	-	7,314	-	235
5650 Family clothing stores	-	20	-	298	15	-	9,799	-	2,764
5660 Shoe stores	-	29	-	178	6	-	9,955	-	1,873
5690 Misc. apparel & accessory stores	-	8	-	42	5	-	13,619	-	471
5712 Furniture stores	-	21	-	300	14	-	17,800	-	5,441
5713 Floor covering stores	-	11	-	55	5	-	17,091	-	941
5714 Drapery and upholstery stores	-	3	-	8	3	-	8,500	-	72
5719 Misc. homefurnishings stores	-	24	-	152	6	-	9,684	-	1,684
5720 Household appliance stores	-	9	-	133	15	-	20,962	-	2,152
5731 Radio, TV, & electronic stores	-	16	-	187	12	-	15,508	-	3,097
5734 Computer and software stores	-	5	-	49	10	-	23,020	-	1,219
5735 Record & prerecorded tape stores	-	5	-	40	8	-	8,300	-	312
5812 Eating places	-	273	-	5,166	19	-	7,534	-	41,831
5813 Drinking places	-	39	-	338	9	-	7,728	-	2,614
5910 Drug stores and proprietary stores	-	23	-	373	16	-	17,501	-	6,311
5920 Liquor stores	-	23	-	174	8	-	20,989	-	3,762
5930 Used merchandise stores	-	19	-	82	4	-	12,244	-	1,032
5941 Sporting goods and bicycle shops	-	20	-	172	9	-	11,186	-	2,303
5942 Book stores	-	18	-	103	6	-	12,155	-	1,244
5943 Stationery stores	-	3	-	13	4	-	11,692	-	180
5944 Jewelry stores	-	14	-	57	4	-	14,947	-	870
5945 Hobby, toy, and game shops	-	14	-	102	7	-	12,549	-	1,449
5947 Gift, novelty, and souvenir shops	-	29	-	148	5	-	5,351	-	851
5949 Sewing, needlework, and piece goods	-	6	-	64	11	-	6,688	-	458
5963 Direct selling establishments	-	10	-	59	6	-	28,678	-	1,570
5980 Fuel dealers	-	6	-	38	6	-	30,737	-	1,117
5992 Florists	-	17	-	68	4	-	8,176	-	581
5995 Optical goods stores	-	13	-	61	5	-	16,262	-	918
5999 Miscellaneous retail stores, nec	-	31	-	223	7	-	14,709	-	3,508

Source: County Business Patterns 1994/95, CBP-94/95, U.S. Department of Commerce, Washington DC, November 1997. The employment column represents mid-March employment in the year. Pay per employee is calculated by dividing 1st Quarter payroll, annualized, by mid-March employment. The column headed 'Emp / Est' shows 'employees per establishment'. A dash (-) means that data are unavailable or cannot be calculated. nec means not elsewhere classified. *Notes:* 1. 1994 data incomplete; unavailable or withheld. 2. 1995 data incomplete; unavailable or withheld. 3. 1994 and 1995 data incomplete; unavailable or withheld.

BENTON HARBOR, MI MSA

Wholesale and Retail Trade USA	Establishments		Employment		Emp / Est	Pay / Employee		Annual Payroll ($ 000)	
	1994	1995	1994	1995	1995	1994	1995	1994	1995
50- Wholesale trade	233	239	2,700	2,617	11	29,833	33,102	86,827	94,744
5012 Automobiles and other vehicles	-	3	-	16	5	-	20,250	-	406
5013 Motor vehicle supplies and new parts	20	18	148	141	8	18,811	19,546	2,940	2,883
5015 Motor vehicle parts, used	9	9	130	148	16	16,985	18,703	2,813	3,179
5021 Furniture	3	3	22	24	8	26,727	29,667	858	984
5023 Homefurnishings	3	-	13	-	-	14,769	-	213	-
5039 Construction materials, nec	-	5	-	35	7	-	20,914	-	741
5044 Office equipment	4	4	43	39	10	18,605	22,974	855	900
5045 Computers, peripherals, & software	-	8	-	149	19	-	69,611	-	9,240

Continued on next page.

BENTON HARBOR, MI MSA - [continued]

Wholesale and Retail Trade USA	Establishments		Employment		Emp / Est	Pay / Employee		Annual Payroll ($ 000)	
	1994	1995	1994	1995	1995	1994	1995	1994	1995
5051 Metals service centers and offices	12	11	116	104	9	33,207	37,038	4,488	4,501
5063 Electrical apparatus and equipment	-	5	-	58	12	-	26,414	-	1,550
5065 Electronic parts and equipment	11	-	70	-	-	17,657	-	1,246	-
5072 Hardware	4	4	101	104	26	22,733	23,308	2,210	2,252
5083 Farm and garden machinery	5	6	37	45	8	20,108	18,578	908	964
5084 Industrial machinery and equipment	8	9	59	52	6	28,610	32,385	1,795	1,704
5085 Industrial supplies	11	12	105	120	10	32,876	37,933	3,433	4,243
5091 Sporting & recreational goods	4	-	21	-	-	9,333	-	512	-
5093 Scrap and waste materials	-	7	-	29	4	-	93,931	-	2,803
5112 Stationery and office supplies	-	4	-	30	8	-	32,667	-	1,022
5113 Industrial & personal service paper	6	6	93	116	19	20,430	20,655	3,088	3,168
5130 Apparel, piece goods, and notions	4	3	22	29	10	7,091	7,448	219	268
5148 Fresh fruits and vegetables	8	9	30	44	5	14,533	12,364	709	1,212
5149 Groceries and related products, nec	8	6	142	113	19	28,873	37,239	4,398	4,637
5171 Petroleum bulk stations & terminals	10	7	94	62	9	26,128	31,871	2,616	2,102
5180 Beer, wine, and distilled beverages	6	6	102	93	16	23,569	26,538	2,783	2,721
5191 Farm supplies	11	9	56	38	4	14,357	17,579	1,016	796
5192 Books, periodicals, & newspapers	3	3	27	41	14	10,370	11,317	578	589
5199 Nondurable goods, nec	6	7	70	58	8	19,714	24,000	1,775	3,001
52- Retail trade	988	990	12,551	12,718	13	10,191	10,875	146,303	152,279
5210 Lumber and other building materials	28	26	335	425	16	15,212	19,313	6,174	8,732
5230 Paint, glass, and wallpaper stores	10	9	53	33	4	15,019	18,303	1,015	643
5250 Hardware stores	19	15	134	114	8	12,955	11,719	1,992	1,289
5260 Retail nurseries and garden stores	-	13	-	48	4	-	11,500	-	672
5310 Department stores	9	9	1,766	1,731	192	10,757	11,254	21,577	21,147
5330 Variety stores	12	13	118	128	10	8,542	8,938	1,179	1,276
5390 Misc. general merchandise stores	4	5	58	66	13	15,586	13,697	1,006	853
5410 Grocery stores	76	73	1,789	1,856	25	9,997	9,140	19,163	18,884
5420 Meat and fish markets	6	4	28	21	5	6,714	7,619	243	154
5440 Candy, nut, and confectionery stores	4	4	17	6	2	4,235	4,667	72	58
5460 Retail bakeries	17	19	112	113	6	6,750	6,867	1,136	1,076
5510 New and used car dealers	17	17	508	536	32	24,843	26,097	14,890	14,260
5520 Used car dealers	10	10	40	40	4	13,000	12,500	575	630
5530 Auto and home supply stores	30	30	192	186	6	17,188	19,075	3,579	3,733
5540 Gasoline service stations	81	79	740	700	9	8,827	10,257	7,045	7,501
5550 Boat dealers	8	8	63	74	9	14,603	13,676	1,289	1,417
5610 Men's & boys' clothing stores	7	6	47	46	8	9,617	10,435	497	444
5620 Women's clothing stores	28	23	199	140	6	8,101	7,200	1,794	1,125
5630 Women's accessory & specialty stores	6	6	30	36	6	7,733	8,556	275	301
5650 Family clothing stores	6	7	54	49	7	11,111	11,673	580	639
5660 Shoe stores	18	15	95	100	7	9,263	8,480	972	804
5712 Furniture stores	16	14	96	92	7	14,542	16,652	1,465	1,593
5719 Misc. homefurnishings stores	4	4	10	15	4	14,000	9,600	160	177
5720 Household appliance stores	10	10	61	65	7	32,262	25,477	1,463	1,331
5731 Radio, TV, & electronic stores	-	12	-	46	4	-	16,087	-	688
5735 Record & prerecorded tape stores	6	-	35	-	-	8,914	-	355	-
5812 Eating places	249	236	4,239	4,167	18	6,338	7,111	32,530	33,854
5813 Drinking places	38	36	205	211	6	7,863	7,886	1,799	1,644
5910 Drug stores and proprietary stores	27	28	331	335	12	16,145	16,239	5,517	5,807
5920 Liquor stores	17	17	95	81	5	7,116	8,148	791	854
5930 Used merchandise stores	10	10	26	32	3	6,615	6,625	207	232
5941 Sporting goods and bicycle shops	16	15	62	62	4	10,258	10,258	781	729
5944 Jewelry stores	10	12	48	52	4	11,500	12,077	581	657
5945 Hobby, toy, and game shops	5	5	16	17	3	8,500	10,118	164	192
5947 Gift, novelty, and souvenir shops	16	16	84	89	6	5,190	5,034	515	467
5949 Sewing, needlework, and piece goods	3	-	22	-	-	5,818	-	141	-
5961 Catalog and mail-order houses	3	-	11	-	-	7,273	-	131	-
5962 Merchandising machine operators	5	5	99	119	24	20,000	20,571	2,149	2,471
5963 Direct selling establishments	9	-	72	-	-	12,778	-	1,104	-
5983 Fuel oil dealers	-	5	-	25	5	-	23,840	-	553
5992 Florists	13	16	80	81	5	8,000	8,494	680	749
5995 Optical goods stores	8	6	35	34	6	21,486	21,294	818	774
5999 Miscellaneous retail stores, nec	18	19	66	71	4	5,515	7,324	630	976

Source: County Business Patterns 1994/95, CBP-94/95, U.S. Department of Commerce, Washington DC, November 1997. The employment column represents mid-March employment in the year. Pay per employee is calculated by dividing 1st Quarter payroll, annualized, by mid-March employment. The column headed 'Emp / Est' shows 'employees per establishment'. A dash (-) means that data are unavailable or cannot be calculated. nec means not elsewhere classified. *Notes:* 1. 1994 data incomplete; unavailable or withheld. 2. 1995 data incomplete; unavailable or withheld. 3. 1994 and 1995 data incomplete; unavailable or withheld.

BERGEN – PASSAIC, NJ PMSA

Wholesale and Retail Trade USA	Establishments		Employment		Emp / Est	Pay / Employee		Annual Payroll ($ 000)	
	1994	1995	1994	1995	1995	1994	1995	1994	1995
50 – Wholesale trade	5,181	5,311	75,693	78,098	15	37,889	41,242	3,127,444	3,371,817
5012 Automobiles and other vehicles	66	64	1,440	1,415	22	55,489	60,201	82,208	71,544
5013 Motor vehicle supplies and new parts	182	166	2,016	2,550	15	28,813	37,514	65,319	97,430
5014 Tires and tubes	25	25	324	297	12	32,519	34,357	12,058	10,196
5015 Motor vehicle parts, used	21	22	91	127	6	19,165	20,094	1,952	2,710
5021 Furniture	68	63	466	525	8	39,185	39,962	18,777	20,938
5023 Homefurnishings	109	105	1,884	2,175	21	29,701	29,477	64,192	71,334
5031 Lumber, plywood, and millwork	39	30	385	253	8	34,608	38,941	15,476	9,585
5032 Brick, stone, & related materials	29	25	151	164	7	28,318	29,024	5,170	5,745
5033 Roofing, siding, & insulation	21	21	360	381	18	33,244	34,205	14,696	14,220
5039 Construction materials, nec	28	51	290	660	13	25,434	31,758	8,804	21,770
5043 Photographic equipment & supplies [3]	32	31	970	812	26	41,645	47,650	43,893	41,470
5044 Office equipment	64	66	1,132	1,086	16	37,452	42,608	40,549	43,209
5045 Computers, peripherals, & software	209	206	2,099	2,296	11	47,259	49,871	108,765	119,476
5046 Commercial equipment, nec [3]	53	62	284	432	7	34,746	35,648	13,166	17,351
5047 Medical and hospital equipment	107	101	2,344	2,057	20	42,645	45,301	113,970	100,570
5048 Ophthalmic goods	26	29	1,498	1,915	66	32,171	27,522	49,887	57,177
5049 Professional equipment, nec	40	35	625	556	16	44,198	43,755	29,014	25,796
5051 Metals service centers and offices [2]	114	120	1,150	912	8	44,845	49,329	57,484	49,768
5052 Coal and other minerals and ores	-	8	-	37	5	-	68,973	-	2,137
5063 Electrical apparatus and equipment	151	126	1,628	1,314	10	36,189	41,738	63,700	56,266
5064 Electrical appliances, TV & radios	71	74	2,538	2,618	35	43,666	47,713	126,082	137,708
5065 Electronic parts and equipment	200	207	2,856	2,921	14	46,639	50,031	137,132	148,918
5072 Hardware	104	107	1,519	1,529	14	33,056	38,195	68,388	80,023
5074 Plumbing & hydronic heating supplies	65	67	883	797	12	33,445	34,986	31,767	29,548
5075 Warm air heating & air conditioning	36	37	267	296	8	32,479	36,608	10,763	11,311
5078 Refrigeration equipment and supplies [2]	7	7	32	49	7	36,000	30,122	1,492	1,753
5082 Construction and mining machinery	18	17	117	122	7	37,128	43,082	5,151	6,032
5083 Farm and garden machinery	19	17	162	193	11	44,420	41,948	9,354	9,918
5084 Industrial machinery and equipment	298	299	3,086	3,129	10	42,297	46,879	136,800	152,940
5085 Industrial supplies	121	124	1,099	1,185	10	38,136	38,704	40,298	44,625
5087 Service establishment equipment	60	60	562	505	8	31,872	37,093	19,486	17,789
5088 Transportation equipment & supplies	39	38	337	354	9	39,537	44,621	17,533	18,139
5091 Sporting & recreational goods	66	64	694	695	11	29,810	32,184	24,434	30,422
5092 Toys and hobby goods and supplies	39	44	1,219	971	22	35,803	34,896	39,812	37,609
5093 Scrap and waste materials	85	90	617	828	9	26,431	29,039	20,131	30,282
5094 Jewelry & precious stones	65	64	665	688	11	43,501	49,773	30,697	31,292
5099 Durable goods, nec	105	118	851	854	7	35,732	43,222	32,878	37,726
5111 Printing and writing paper	32	31	390	375	12	52,010	60,085	22,136	26,209
5112 Stationery and office supplies	111	100	5,631	4,949	49	13,357	14,498	79,334	65,334
5113 Industrial & personal service paper	122	127	1,228	1,259	10	42,345	59,387	55,382	90,272
5120 Drugs, proprietaries, and sundries	146	156	2,816	3,895	25	43,078	51,525	136,794	193,061
5131 Piece goods & notions	154	149	1,690	1,458	10	32,483	34,066	56,793	49,442
5136 Men's and boys' clothing	91	97	2,049	2,454	25	38,671	43,219	88,183	110,961
5137 Women's and children's clothing	137	143	2,624	2,605	18	35,082	35,694	102,902	99,817
5139 Footwear	42	43	784	498	12	56,434	46,731	35,876	24,170
5141 Groceries, general line	59	55	1,307	1,465	27	30,849	30,678	41,978	49,928
5142 Packaged frozen food	36	35	473	479	14	40,203	46,480	22,327	23,280
5143 Dairy products, exc. dried or canned	50	54	922	935	17	42,490	46,353	43,260	45,646
5145 Confectionery	32	29	586	628	22	39,420	33,968	24,657	21,344
5146 Fish and seafoods	19	17	78	66	4	26,667	34,061	2,374	2,518
5147 Meats and meat products	67	63	284	273	4	31,887	30,945	9,240	8,958
5148 Fresh fruits and vegetables	44	42	288	305	7	28,639	31,095	9,954	10,244
5149 Groceries and related products, nec	220	222	3,523	3,372	15	36,704	38,076	140,026	132,831
5153 Grain and field beans [3]	7	5	49	53	11	35,918	26,717	2,287	1,726
5154 Livestock [3]	3	3	9	9	3	44,000	63,556	408	495
5159 Farm-product raw materials, nec [3]	12	9	87	106	12	37,885	42,792	2,813	3,062
5162 Plastics materials & basic shapes	76	71	586	684	10	39,529	40,450	26,158	29,792
5169 Chemicals & allied products, nec	191	192	2,267	2,416	13	51,180	51,916	126,005	135,686
5171 Petroleum bulk stations & terminals	21	17	380	334	20	37,684	39,880	14,924	12,551
5172 Petroleum products, nec	27	22	128	127	6	56,500	66,299	8,624	9,328
5181 Beer and ale [3]	5	5	269	284	57	30,736	33,662	11,242	12,369
5182 Wine and distilled beverages [3]	16	20	346	339	17	44,890	51,799	17,709	19,104
5191 Farm supplies	28	25	271	454	18	29,948	39,700	12,265	18,188
5192 Books, periodicals, & newspapers	63	68	2,142	1,779	26	31,714	33,358	68,626	51,762
5193 Flowers & florists' supplies	44	35	507	468	13	27,053	31,000	15,685	15,770
5194 Tobacco and tobacco products	15	13	178	172	13	37,438	34,395	6,349	6,090
5198 Paints, varnishes, and supplies	34	30	315	493	16	29,663	46,580	13,437	22,659
5199 Nondurable goods, nec	217	226	1,553	1,642	7	37,084	34,821	67,453	64,963
52 – Retail trade	8,774	8,815	106,109	109,690	12	17,694	19,286	2,077,339	2,202,163
5210 Lumber and other building materials	112	97	1,576	2,164	22	24,203	26,375	47,432	58,518

Continued on next page.

BERGEN – PASSAIC, NJ PMSA - [continued]

Wholesale and Retail Trade USA	Establishments		Employment		Emp / Est	Pay / Employee		Annual Payroll ($ 000)	
	1994	1995	1994	1995	1995	1994	1995	1994	1995
5230 Paint, glass, and wallpaper stores	46	45	229	236	5	23,371	23,983	5,851	5,738
5250 Hardware stores	87	59	344	290	5	22,326	24,359	8,356	6,853
5260 Retail nurseries and garden stores	53	54	356	367	7	14,135	16,360	8,036	8,931
5310 Department stores	30	30	7,960	8,322	277	13,109	14,125	116,913	119,314
5330 Variety stores	52	41	643	521	13	12,491	10,749	8,279	6,245
5390 Misc. general merchandise stores	53	52	1,220	1,358	26	16,203	20,454	23,487	28,919
5410 Grocery stores	682	661	13,980	14,438	22	16,560	17,086	245,481	253,085
5420 Meat and fish markets	71	75	214	223	3	19,402	19,928	4,464	4,656
5430 Fruit and vegetable markets	31	36	197	205	6	9,909	10,771	2,447	2,727
5440 Candy, nut, and confectionery stores	31	29	223	233	8	8,143	7,279	1,847	1,632
5450 Dairy products stores	27	26	106	87	3	6,604	5,793	762	753
5460 Retail bakeries	235	236	1,606	1,515	6	10,919	10,867	18,958	17,504
5490 Miscellaneous food stores	67	74	200	261	4	13,080	12,736	3,572	3,984
5510 New and used car dealers	141	139	4,880	5,149	37	33,230	35,638	197,823	197,995
5520 Used car dealers	78	72	163	159	2	21,840	22,792	3,885	3,982
5530 Auto and home supply stores	127	133	816	851	6	22,917	22,703	20,267	20,204
5540 Gasoline service stations	616	599	2,579	2,632	4	14,916	15,570	41,026	41,041
5550 Boat dealers	10	8	39	35	4	14,667	14,857	786	697
5570 Motorcycle dealers	11	10	40	48	5	25,200	26,083	1,451	1,573
5610 Men's & boys' clothing stores	108	103	870	742	7	15,862	16,911	14,150	11,809
5620 Women's clothing stores	351	330	3,918	3,692	11	10,613	11,041	44,512	40,781
5630 Women's accessory & specialty stores	67	61	416	388	6	11,615	12,412	5,266	4,768
5640 Children's and infants' wear stores	63	59	603	662	11	10,600	10,580	7,304	7,500
5650 Family clothing stores	94	94	2,843	2,760	29	13,778	14,891	43,811	43,721
5660 Shoe stores	240	244	1,342	1,405	6	14,039	14,354	20,465	20,239
5690 Misc. apparel & accessory stores	49	54	269	277	5	11,286	13,025	3,366	3,598
5712 Furniture stores	180	182	1,201	1,160	6	24,846	25,910	31,182	31,706
5713 Floor covering stores	83	86	378	409	5	25,429	27,560	11,396	12,465
5714 Drapery and upholstery stores	23	23	145	186	8	16,221	15,462	2,724	2,983
5719 Misc. homefurnishings stores	121	112	1,336	1,303	12	14,859	15,318	22,056	21,331
5720 Household appliance stores	36	34	268	278	8	21,985	27,309	6,571	7,596
5731 Radio, TV, & electronic stores	79	78	650	576	7	21,735	22,361	13,258	12,214
5734 Computer and software stores	53	56	551	585	10	23,158	26,974	13,807	16,211
5735 Record & prerecorded tape stores[3]	45	40	229	192	5	10,183	11,708	2,292	2,374
5736 Musical instrument stores	15	16	110	131	8	32,436	33,252	4,078	4,388
5812 Eating places	1,950	1,868	24,835	25,249	14	10,223	10,789	278,437	283,757
5813 Drinking places	242	237	949	952	4	10,301	10,315	9,997	10,776
5910 Drug stores and proprietary stores	342	312	3,724	4,155	13	16,400	15,735	65,794	69,189
5920 Liquor stores	283	292	988	1,059	4	13,955	16,453	14,847	18,287
5930 Used merchandise stores	43	40	239	194	5	11,364	13,320	3,077	3,072
5941 Sporting goods and bicycle shops	106	100	878	986	10	15,021	15,290	14,701	17,470
5942 Book stores	49	53	462	781	15	11,108	12,410	5,729	13,471
5943 Stationery stores	51	50	155	358	7	14,142	13,698	2,104	4,782
5944 Jewelry stores	196	191	853	816	4	19,226	20,676	17,103	17,459
5945 Hobby, toy, and game shops	57	59	647	733	12	10,572	11,132	8,722	9,396
5946 Camera & photographic supply stores	35	35	132	150	4	18,485	19,227	2,811	2,898
5947 Gift, novelty, and souvenir shops	157	161	960	971	6	11,621	12,375	12,742	12,952
5948 Luggage and leather goods stores	20	18	42	81	5	15,048	12,049	710	1,035
5949 Sewing, needlework, and piece goods	29	27	181	185	7	10,475	11,178	2,166	2,440
5961 Catalog and mail-order houses	54	52	3,293	1,981	38	18,949	25,074	73,121	50,734
5962 Merchandising machine operators	31	30	202	199	7	22,634	23,196	4,788	4,505
5963 Direct selling establishments	91	90	838	691	8	15,422	20,625	14,819	14,519
5983 Fuel oil dealers[3]	51	53	298	298	6	37,409	34,819	10,282	9,350
5984 Liquefied petroleum gas dealers	6	6	25	23	4	27,040	15,130	642	420
5992 Florists	150	158	608	631	4	13,941	14,910	9,368	10,199
5993 Tobacco stores and stands	12	11	16	22	2	21,750	19,455	367	454
5994 News dealers and newsstands	21	26	67	128	5	16,119	18,781	1,419	4,274
5995 Optical goods stores	94	94	451	462	5	20,346	21,524	9,840	10,133
5999 Miscellaneous retail stores, nec	256	255	1,263	1,434	6	16,656	18,569	26,103	28,820

Source: County Business Patterns 1994/95, CBP-94/95, U.S. Department of Commerce, Washington DC, November 1997. The employment column represents mid-March employment in the year. Pay per employee is calculated by dividing 1st Quarter payroll, annualized, by mid-March employment. The column headed 'Emp / Est' shows 'employees per establishment'. A dash (-) means that data are unavailable or cannot be calculated. nec means not elsewhere classified. *Notes:* 1. 1994 data incomplete; unavailable or withheld. 2. 1995 data incomplete; unavailable or withheld. 3. 1994 and 1995 data incomplete; unavailable or withheld.

BILLINGS, MT MSA

Wholesale and Retail Trade USA	Establishments		Employment		Emp / Est	Pay / Employee		Annual Payroll ($ 000)	
	1994	1995	1994	1995	1995	1994	1995	1994	1995
50- Wholesale trade	451	454	5,792	6,053	13	25,103	26,217	153,666	161,447
5012 Automobiles and other vehicles	13	14	323	394	28	21,028	20,345	6,818	7,737
5013 Motor vehicle supplies and new parts	32	26	494	378	15	22,947	23,757	11,053	8,615
5014 Tires and tubes	10	14	98	142	10	22,490	19,915	2,563	3,447
5015 Motor vehicle parts, used	7	8	58	65	8	14,069	15,446	881	1,092
5021 Furniture	4	-	44	-	-	26,000	-	1,370	-
5023 Homefurnishings	4	-	31	-	-	22,194	-	753	-
5031 Lumber, plywood, and millwork	14	11	196	173	16	28,714	29,064	6,142	5,247
5039 Construction materials, nec	5	7	55	53	8	22,400	26,415	958	1,503
5044 Office equipment	8	9	72	66	7	26,611	26,061	1,743	1,656
5045 Computers, peripherals, & software	16	15	146	144	10	30,630	29,417	3,781	3,822
5047 Medical and hospital equipment	10	-	46	-	-	28,522	-	1,580	-
5049 Professional equipment, nec	3	3	50	47	16	17,840	20,000	985	1,140
5050 Metals and minerals, except petroleum	6	8	106	126	16	16,075	16,127	1,727	2,235
5063 Electrical apparatus and equipment	16	17	134	143	8	34,537	33,203	5,098	5,067
5072 Hardware	6	6	62	72	12	25,484	23,500	1,730	1,200
5074 Plumbing & hydronic heating supplies	8	7	156	161	23	27,872	29,689	4,016	4,265
5082 Construction and mining machinery	11	12	301	308	26	31,030	35,234	9,673	10,226
5083 Farm and garden machinery	12	12	125	133	11	24,320	25,774	3,643	3,666
5084 Industrial machinery and equipment	28	27	161	170	6	24,795	27,412	4,322	4,500
5085 Industrial supplies	13	14	137	169	12	29,635	28,686	4,037	4,857
5087 Service establishment equipment	11	9	112	92	10	23,571	22,130	2,879	2,021
5091 Sporting & recreational goods	-	4	-	75	19	-	20,587	-	1,633
5092 Toys and hobby goods and supplies	3	-	12	-	-	20,333	-	229	-
5093 Scrap and waste materials	5	-	49	-	-	22,694	-	1,144	-
5099 Durable goods, nec	-	5	-	47	9	-	35,574	-	2,099
5112 Stationery and office supplies	6	-	26	-	-	20,308	-	589	-
5120 Drugs, proprietaries, and sundries	5	-	84	-	-	31,000	-	2,188	-
5130 Apparel, piece goods, and notions	8	7	125	121	17	16,480	16,793	2,212	2,157
5141 Groceries, general line	12	12	798	793	66	29,579	28,580	24,152	23,502
5147 Meats and meat products	-	4	-	18	5	-	31,778	-	355
5149 Groceries and related products, nec	15	13	206	235	18	25,262	37,481	6,156	6,600
5150 Farm-product raw materials	11	10	103	101	10	17,087	19,446	1,839	2,122
5160 Chemicals and allied products	16	16	85	96	6	30,259	28,292	3,092	3,210
5171 Petroleum bulk stations & terminals	13	11	119	96	9	21,983	23,000	2,703	2,165
5172 Petroleum products, nec	7	7	110	124	18	17,382	20,774	1,985	2,189
5181 Beer and ale	4	4	97	94	24	24,495	28,511	2,866	3,092
5191 Farm supplies	25	29	205	381	13	27,141	28,220	6,743	9,149
5199 Nondurable goods, nec	4	-	66	-	-	12,061	-	771	-
52- Retail trade	962	996	12,989	13,791	14	12,163	12,454	167,488	178,645
5210 Lumber and other building materials	17	20	253	407	20	15,668	18,221	4,604	7,188
5230 Paint, glass, and wallpaper stores	9	11	46	58	5	22,783	27,310	887	1,423
5250 Hardware stores	12	10	147	109	11	10,912	12,073	1,941	1,271
5260 Retail nurseries and garden stores	3	3	26	24	8	9,692	12,000	266	281
5270 Mobile home dealers	8	9	110	107	12	36,836	31,252	3,999	3,175
5310 Department stores	10	10	1,179	1,312	131	11,260	10,567	14,517	15,092
5330 Variety stores	-	3	-	30	10	-	7,333	-	272
5390 Misc. general merchandise stores	6	5	453	498	100	14,446	17,141	7,806	8,416
5410 Grocery stores	62	57	1,368	1,338	23	13,275	13,578	19,544	18,616
5420 Meat and fish markets	-	3	-	5	2	-	7,200	-	114
5440 Candy, nut, and confectionery stores	3	3	20	16	5	7,200	4,500	113	79
5460 Retail bakeries	10	6	98	37	6	6,204	5,189	691	226
5490 Miscellaneous food stores	10	12	48	82	7	8,333	9,268	555	900
5510 New and used car dealers	15	20	816	966	48	29,397	26,497	22,857	25,881
5520 Used car dealers	12	14	44	53	4	9,727	7,321	435	539
5530 Auto and home supply stores	29	24	214	232	10	15,196	19,776	3,752	4,939
5540 Gasoline service stations	52	53	397	449	8	11,184	10,993	4,486	5,100
5610 Men's & boys' clothing stores	11	10	76	55	6	11,421	11,273	682	582
5620 Women's clothing stores	30	27	243	184	7	8,000	7,500	2,085	1,388
5630 Women's accessory & specialty stores	-	5	-	21	4	-	7,429	-	167
5650 Family clothing stores	19	21	198	187	9	10,828	10,930	2,031	1,912
5660 Shoe stores	22	22	107	116	5	11,888	12,069	1,316	1,297
5690 Misc. apparel & accessory stores	7	8	31	33	4	4,645	5,818	164	181
5712 Furniture stores	26	27	300	284	11	16,133	17,761	4,978	4,994
5713 Floor covering stores	5	8	80	99	12	32,600	29,172	2,442	2,653
5719 Misc. homefurnishings stores	-	10	-	41	4	-	10,634	-	472
5720 Household appliance stores	6	6	59	65	11	20,068	19,138	1,148	1,151
5731 Radio, TV, & electronic stores	11	11	76	78	7	17,263	18,256	1,309	1,426
5734 Computer and software stores	6	-	23	-	-	15,826	-	440	-
5736 Musical instrument stores	-	3	-	14	5	-	10,857	-	155
5812 Eating places	212	200	4,174	4,384	22	7,561	7,594	34,257	35,515

Continued on next page.

BILLINGS, MT MSA - [continued]

Wholesale and Retail Trade USA	Establishments		Employment		Emp / Est	Pay / Employee		Annual Payroll ($ 000)	
	1994	1995	1994	1995	1995	1994	1995	1994	1995
5813 Drinking places	58	57	641	599	11	8,243	8,955	5,819	5,522
5910 Drug stores and proprietary stores	16	15	150	148	10	17,440	17,649	2,707	2,764
5930 Used merchandise stores	30	30	125	143	5	12,480	13,483	1,705	2,041
5941 Sporting goods and bicycle shops	26	25	211	224	9	13,081	12,446	2,860	3,075
5942 Book stores	8	-	53	-	-	9,509	-	544	-
5943 Stationery stores	3	-	19	-	-	13,263	-	268	-
5944 Jewelry stores	13	15	83	89	6	14,747	15,910	1,141	1,226
5945 Hobby, toy, and game shops	12	11	108	118	11	8,074	8,373	1,041	1,068
5947 Gift, novelty, and souvenir shops	13	15	77	70	5	8,312	6,800	659	713
5949 Sewing, needlework, and piece goods	7	5	62	19	4	6,065	8,421	414	165
5960 Nonstore retailers	19	20	78	98	5	15,897	13,061	1,254	1,324
5980 Fuel dealers	4	4	15	16	4	24,800	24,000	361	373
5992 Florists	10	10	119	136	14	11,563	11,500	1,557	1,711
5995 Optical goods stores	10	9	39	38	4	16,000	17,895	668	570
5999 Miscellaneous retail stores, nec	46	53	174	182	3	13,310	14,264	2,467	2,749

Source: County Business Patterns 1994/95, CBP-94/95, U.S. Department of Commerce, Washington DC, November 1997. The employment column represents mid-March employment in the year. Pay per employee is calculated by dividing 1st Quarter payroll, annualized, by mid-March employment. The column headed 'Emp / Est' shows 'employees per establishment'. A dash (-) means that data are unavailable or cannot be calculated. nec means not elsewhere classified. *Notes:* 1. 1994 data incomplete; unavailable or withheld. 2. 1995 data incomplete; unavailable or withheld. 3. 1994 and 1995 data incomplete; unavailable or withheld.

BILOXI - GULFPORT - PASCAGOULA, MS MSA

Wholesale and Retail Trade USA	Establishments		Employment		Emp / Est	Pay / Employee		Annual Payroll ($ 000)	
	1994	1995	1994	1995	1995	1994	1995	1994	1995
50- Wholesale trade	347	366	3,278	3,400	9	19,407	20,625	73,076	75,530
5012 Automobiles and other vehicles[3]	6	9	26	91	10	18,154	10,681	618	1,114
5013 Motor vehicle supplies and new parts	26	22	129	90	4	26,667	21,600	3,787	2,183
5014 Tires and tubes[3]	3	4	47	50	13	22,809	23,040	1,200	1,246
5015 Motor vehicle parts, used[3]	13	15	44	45	3	11,818	12,622	575	641
5020 Furniture and homefurnishings[3]	7	7	64	67	10	22,063	19,284	1,502	1,231
5031 Lumber, plywood, and millwork[3]	6	6	114	130	22	25,333	25,600	3,242	3,431
5032 Brick, stone, & related materials[3]	5	6	21	36	6	21,714	20,889	573	1,379
5044 Office equipment[3]	8	7	82	85	12	24,341	26,353	2,350	2,662
5046 Commercial equipment, nec[2]	-	4	-	29	7	-	17,793	-	523
5047 Medical and hospital equipment[3]	3	3	31	28	9	17,935	22,857	624	383
5063 Electrical apparatus and equipment[3]	7	8	53	56	7	39,321	35,000	1,674	1,492
5072 Hardware[3]	7	7	27	19	3	15,111	20,000	486	430
5074 Plumbing & hydronic heating supplies	8	11	34	21	2	20,000	20,190	745	403
5075 Warm air heating & air conditioning[2]	-	7	-	35	5	-	19,771	-	631
5082 Construction and mining machinery[3]	6	7	44	38	5	35,455	31,579	1,405	1,225
5084 Industrial machinery and equipment[3]	13	14	36	38	3	21,556	21,263	815	912
5085 Industrial supplies	17	16	149	157	10	22,550	23,541	3,797	4,260
5087 Service establishment equipment[3]	7	9	52	58	6	16,462	19,931	934	1,305
5093 Scrap and waste materials	11	11	46	33	3	20,957	25,939	962	900
5099 Durable goods, nec	6	9	14	19	2	19,429	21,474	308	435
5112 Stationery and office supplies[3]	6	6	30	73	12	11,200	15,945	712	1,077
5142 Packaged frozen food[3]	5	6	119	156	26	25,210	20,103	3,774	3,826
5146 Fish and seafoods	30	29	267	264	9	8,419	11,318	3,408	3,545
5148 Fresh fruits and vegetables[1]	4	-	36	-	-	19,111	-	729	-
5149 Groceries and related products, nec	8	9	103	112	12	23,883	22,464	2,622	2,691
5160 Chemicals and allied products[3]	4	4	42	49	12	19,048	21,143	1,006	1,161
5171 Petroleum bulk stations & terminals[1]	7	-	64	-	-	21,063	-	1,470	-
5172 Petroleum products, nec[1]	6	-	50	-	-	18,560	-	809	-
5181 Beer and ale[3]	4	4	232	271	68	18,931	20,251	5,693	5,841
5199 Nondurable goods, nec[1]	5	6	28	21	4	20,143	19,429	590	789
52- Retail trade	1,959	1,988	24,535	25,823	13	10,105	10,869	274,697	294,512
5210 Lumber and other building materials	34	33	816	794	24	15,270	16,322	14,012	13,525
5230 Paint, glass, and wallpaper stores	18	20	67	85	4	15,642	16,706	1,150	1,585
5250 Hardware stores	28	21	85	53	3	12,188	12,226	1,132	659
5260 Retail nurseries and garden stores	20	21	42	71	3	8,762	8,563	495	758
5270 Mobile home dealers[3]	10	11	70	97	9	37,371	32,330	2,265	2,701
5310 Department stores[3]	19	19	2,726	2,965	156	9,580	12,154	29,233	35,101
5330 Variety stores	26	15	146	77	5	7,397	9,039	1,189	719
5390 Misc. general merchandise stores	17	27	408	518	19	11,784	11,236	5,303	5,435
5410 Grocery stores[3]	202	205	3,600	3,587	17	9,088	9,356	34,074	34,866
5420 Meat and fish markets	12	11	49	54	5	9,224	9,926	492	547
5440 Candy, nut, and confectionery stores[3]	4	6	11	17	3	6,545	4,941	84	120
5460 Retail bakeries[3]	11	10	81	51	5	8,000	6,588	740	178
5490 Miscellaneous food stores[3]	9	9	40	53	6	7,300	8,679	345	519

Continued on next page.

BILOXI – GULFPORT – PASCAGOULA, MS MSA - [continued]

Wholesale and Retail Trade USA	Establishments		Employment		Emp / Est	Pay / Employee		Annual Payroll ($ 000)	
	1994	1995	1994	1995	1995	1994	1995	1994	1995
5510 New and used car dealers	24	24	968	1,007	42	26,574	27,225	29,780	31,718
5520 Used car dealers	44	43	140	131	3	14,514	15,389	2,301	2,259
5530 Auto and home supply stores	75	80	523	556	7	14,241	15,827	8,593	9,118
5540 Gasoline service stations	138	135	977	1,029	8	10,612	12,327	10,989	12,552
5550 Boat dealers	-	13	-	57	4	-	12,491	-	792
5560 Recreational vehicle dealers [2]	-	4	-	18	5	-	15,333	-	291
5570 Motorcycle dealers [3]	5	6	22	25	4	11,818	14,400	365	428
5610 Men's & boys' clothing stores	15	20	79	90	5	8,962	9,333	815	883
5620 Women's clothing stores	63	54	387	318	6	9,385	9,031	3,788	2,856
5630 Women's accessory & specialty stores [3]	8	10	36	31	3	8,333	10,839	325	332
5640 Children's and infants' wear stores	6	7	5	6	1	3,200	3,333	17	41
5650 Family clothing stores [3]	7	10	29	101	10	7,172	7,129	277	794
5660 Shoe stores	37	38	162	162	4	8,519	9,827	1,573	1,670
5690 Misc. apparel & accessory stores [1]	9	12	29	27	2	8,138	8,593	257	278
5712 Furniture stores [1]	44	42	242	249	6	14,810	14,956	4,001	4,198
5713 Floor covering stores	19	21	87	112	5	20,138	18,179	2,295	2,255
5719 Misc. homefurnishings stores	13	16	67	54	3	8,716	11,778	806	759
5720 Household appliance stores	13	13	84	93	7	15,714	20,559	1,389	1,502
5731 Radio, TV, & electronic stores [1]	21	20	123	143	7	18,211	19,357	2,391	2,769
5734 Computer and software stores [3]	6	7	5	12	2	11,200	8,000	71	120
5735 Record & prerecorded tape stores [2]	-	8	-	50	6	-	9,520	-	460
5812 Eating places	382	358	8,123	8,445	24	6,930	6,981	61,263	62,552
5813 Drinking places	60	39	299	268	7	6,528	7,418	2,246	2,528
5910 Drug stores and proprietary stores	64	63	597	598	9	14,238	15,886	9,170	9,549
5920 Liquor stores	45	48	127	118	2	6,835	7,763	914	965
5930 Used merchandise stores	48	49	266	331	7	8,902	9,184	3,037	3,407
5941 Sporting goods and bicycle shops	27	30	118	160	5	10,271	9,250	1,437	1,613
5942 Book stores	14	13	71	63	5	7,324	9,333	610	610
5944 Jewelry stores [1]	32	36	138	142	4	13,942	15,127	1,987	2,211
5945 Hobby, toy, and game shops	16	15	67	65	4	7,224	7,692	593	645
5947 Gift, novelty, and souvenir shops	50	46	311	248	5	5,711	7,435	2,290	2,197
5949 Sewing, needlework, and piece goods	10	-	37	-	-	7,676	-	296	-
5963 Direct selling establishments	10	-	22	-	-	18,000	-	399	-
5992 Florists	36	41	148	142	3	8,270	9,408	1,549	1,580
5993 Tobacco stores and stands [3]	8	9	20	25	3	9,800	12,640	187	348
5995 Optical goods stores	17	17	61	27	2	17,705	21,185	1,207	576
5999 Miscellaneous retail stores, nec	47	50	168	152	3	9,595	12,026	1,878	1,916

Source: County Business Patterns 1994/95, CBP-94/95, U.S. Department of Commerce, Washington DC, November 1997. The employment column represents mid-March employment in the year. Pay per employee is calculated by dividing 1st Quarter payroll, annualized, by mid-March employment. The column headed 'Emp / Est' shows 'employees per establishment'. A dash (-) means that data are unavailable or cannot be calculated. nec means not elsewhere classified. *Notes:* 1. 1994 data incomplete; unavailable or withheld. 2. 1995 data incomplete; unavailable or withheld. 3. 1994 and 1995 data incomplete; unavailable or withheld.

BINGHAMTON, NY MSA

Wholesale and Retail Trade USA	Establishments		Employment		Emp / Est	Pay / Employee		Annual Payroll ($ 000)	
	1994	1995	1994	1995	1995	1994	1995	1994	1995
50 – Wholesale trade	396	371	5,530	5,749	15	25,849	27,246	148,727	163,621
5012 Automobiles and other vehicles [2]	12	12	90	88	7	19,467	20,409	2,014	1,986
5013 Motor vehicle supplies and new parts	26	23	211	199	9	17,820	17,789	4,181	3,756
5014 Tires and tubes	6	4	27	22	6	17,037	18,182	527	417
5015 Motor vehicle parts, used	5	5	66	68	14	25,091	24,000	1,756	1,839
5021 Furniture [1]	3	-	5	-	-	20,800	-	51	-
5031 Lumber, plywood, and millwork [2]	10	10	152	143	14	22,842	24,979	4,023	3,666
5033 Roofing, siding, & insulation [1]	4	-	39	-	-	23,077	-	1,153	-
5039 Construction materials, nec	-	5	-	33	7	-	20,121	-	789
5043 Photographic equipment & supplies [3]	3	3	34	36	12	18,706	20,667	784	794
5044 Office equipment	18	16	143	125	8	20,587	19,488	2,917	2,470
5045 Computers, peripherals, & software [3]	11	10	117	116	12	45,744	41,552	4,993	5,149
5046 Commercial equipment, nec [3]	5	4	42	37	9	25,810	29,297	1,092	1,220
5051 Metals service centers and offices	-	9	-	175	19	-	22,171	-	3,945
5065 Electronic parts and equipment	18	22	138	224	10	28,928	28,018	5,114	7,023
5072 Hardware [1]	7	9	68	69	8	17,882	21,043	1,416	1,600
5074 Plumbing & hydronic heating supplies [3]	13	10	95	80	8	26,358	29,500	2,707	2,559
5075 Warm air heating & air conditioning	5	5	9	20	4	20,889	18,800	258	384
5078 Refrigeration equipment and supplies [3]	3	3	27	24	8	22,667	28,667	767	766
5082 Construction and mining machinery	9	9	91	90	10	27,516	29,556	2,528	2,620
5083 Farm and garden machinery	9	7	137	63	9	14,015	15,937	2,350	927
5084 Industrial machinery and equipment	18	18	112	122	7	27,893	28,328	3,049	3,471
5087 Service establishment equipment [3]	5	5	75	86	17	23,733	27,209	2,069	2,653

Continued on next page.

BINGHAMTON, NY MSA - [continued]

Wholesale and Retail Trade USA	Establishments		Employment		Emp / Est	Pay / Employee		Annual Payroll ($ 000)	
	1994	1995	1994	1995	1995	1994	1995	1994	1995
5093 Scrap and waste materials	10	11	516	487	44	21,349	22,817	11,239	13,805
5099 Durable goods, nec [1]	5	7	15	17	2	14,667	14,118	333	559
5112 Stationery and office supplies	16	12	123	78	7	19,967	16,564	2,297	1,392
5141 Groceries, general line [1]	5	-	153	-	-	22,797	-	3,885	-
5143 Dairy products, exc. dried or canned [3]	4	5	76	87	17	46,737	44,828	3,589	3,967
5147 Meats and meat products [3]	4	4	32	34	9	16,125	16,471	643	679
5149 Groceries and related products, nec	13	13	284	356	27	27,507	25,787	7,892	9,545
5169 Chemicals & allied products, nec [1]	5	-	28	-	-	26,143	-	926	-
5171 Petroleum bulk stations & terminals [3]	7	7	40	42	6	48,600	48,476	1,878	1,979
5172 Petroleum products, nec [3]	5	5	30	30	6	41,333	46,933	1,288	1,346
5180 Beer, wine, and distilled beverages [3]	6	6	115	89	15	21,496	26,697	3,047	2,846
5191 Farm supplies	10	-	77	-	-	32,000	-	2,306	-
5193 Flowers & florists' supplies [1]	3	4	47	40	10	18,383	20,900	807	786
5198 Paints, varnishes, and supplies [3]	6	4	38	37	9	20,632	24,973	829	1,259
5199 Nondurable goods, nec	6	4	4	3	1	8,000	8,000	54	23
52- Retail trade	1,541	1,478	19,535	19,162	13	10,979	11,466	231,548	225,791
5210 Lumber and other building materials	37	31	320	312	10	18,250	18,372	7,963	6,131
5230 Paint, glass, and wallpaper stores	9	9	33	40	4	15,030	20,000	483	845
5250 Hardware stores	9	8	56	51	6	12,286	11,529	760	637
5260 Retail nurseries and garden stores	8	10	64	58	6	12,813	13,310	1,015	918
5270 Mobile home dealers	9	9	44	33	4	19,091	21,939	905	886
5310 Department stores [3]	16	16	2,109	2,128	133	9,369	11,009	22,159	23,258
5330 Variety stores	8	8	43	47	6	7,349	7,574	374	398
5390 Misc. general merchandise stores	10	8	260	290	36	11,185	12,510	3,351	3,403
5410 Grocery stores	116	108	3,214	3,044	28	11,232	10,945	36,734	33,211
5440 Candy, nut, and confectionery stores [2]	-	4	-	24	6	-	8,167	-	189
5450 Dairy products stores [3]	4	3	18	6	2	4,222	6,000	111	46
5460 Retail bakeries	18	23	163	213	9	6,528	7,117	1,216	1,573
5490 Miscellaneous food stores [3]	5	7	48	38	5	11,750	9,053	545	372
5510 New and used car dealers	24	24	886	822	34	23,440	25,766	22,530	21,795
5520 Used car dealers	28	25	102	107	4	13,882	16,075	1,650	1,817
5530 Auto and home supply stores	39	34	275	327	10	19,316	19,890	5,784	6,917
5540 Gasoline service stations	105	94	705	672	7	10,661	10,857	7,812	7,768
5570 Motorcycle dealers [3]	4	5	21	22	4	18,857	23,273	600	605
5610 Men's & boys' clothing stores	14	11	112	107	10	8,429	7,477	896	820
5620 Women's clothing stores	54	47	426	354	8	6,901	6,531	3,030	2,403
5640 Children's and infants' wear stores	8	8	51	70	9	6,353	7,714	369	537
5650 Family clothing stores	13	12	127	131	11	10,551	9,832	1,287	1,363
5660 Shoe stores	39	35	172	157	4	9,674	10,013	1,724	1,555
5712 Furniture stores	25	26	350	346	13	14,103	16,289	5,130	5,612
5713 Floor covering stores	17	18	92	95	5	19,217	17,600	1,863	1,870
5720 Household appliance stores	8	7	17	17	2	12,235	12,471	214	213
5731 Radio, TV, & electronic stores [3]	12	10	58	72	7	18,759	17,056	1,013	1,243
5734 Computer and software stores [3]	3	4	17	14	4	15,059	11,714	199	159
5735 Record & prerecorded tape stores	9	9	43	41	5	9,767	10,732	478	470
5736 Musical instrument stores [3]	5	4	19	16	4	13,684	16,000	267	275
5812 Eating places	375	352	5,935	5,822	17	7,507	7,775	49,162	47,707
5813 Drinking places	113	101	373	358	4	7,807	8,223	3,030	2,915
5910 Drug stores and proprietary stores	54	49	781	769	16	12,609	13,295	10,298	10,766
5920 Liquor stores	26	25	90	95	4	10,400	9,811	1,053	1,044
5930 Used merchandise stores	13	12	86	65	5	8,744	8,308	761	575
5941 Sporting goods and bicycle shops	24	19	244	208	11	8,426	8,096	2,117	2,007
5942 Book stores	14	13	168	142	11	8,881	10,056	1,553	1,532
5944 Jewelry stores	24	21	151	135	6	13,748	15,200	2,090	2,444
5945 Hobby, toy, and game shops	10	11	126	124	11	10,413	11,032	1,466	1,425
5946 Camera & photographic supply stores [3]	5	5	20	18	4	15,400	18,000	314	315
5947 Gift, novelty, and souvenir shops	29	25	141	142	6	6,865	6,732	1,090	1,166
5949 Sewing, needlework, and piece goods	7	-	44	-	-	5,545	-	277	-
5963 Direct selling establishments	17	18	121	119	7	16,727	14,790	1,962	1,728
5983 Fuel oil dealers	9	9	98	110	12	23,061	19,200	2,471	1,917
5984 Liquefied petroleum gas dealers	5	6	54	51	9	19,407	16,157	1,117	925
5992 Florists	21	19	102	110	6	10,863	9,964	1,265	1,265
5995 Optical goods stores [3]	20	18	96	105	6	19,375	20,305	1,769	1,681
5999 Miscellaneous retail stores, nec	42	44	152	223	5	12,316	10,906	2,629	3,078

Source: County Business Patterns 1994/95, CBP-94/95, U.S. Department of Commerce, Washington DC, November 1997. The employment column represents mid-March employment in the year. Pay per employee is calculated by dividing 1st Quarter payroll, annualized, by mid-March employment. The column headed 'Emp / Est' shows 'employees per establishment'. A dash (-) means that data are unavailable or cannot be calculated. nec means not elsewhere classified. *Notes:* 1. 1994 data incomplete; unavailable or withheld. 2. 1995 data incomplete; unavailable or withheld. 3. 1994 and 1995 data incomplete; unavailable or withheld.

BIRMINGHAM, AL MSA

Wholesale and Retail Trade USA	Establishments		Employment		Emp / Est	Pay / Employee		Annual Payroll ($ 000)	
	1994	1995	1994	1995	1995	1994	1995	1994	1995
50- Wholesale trade	2,173	2,219	30,613	33,380	15	29,301	31,705	967,016	1,103,100
5012 Automobiles and other vehicles[3]	48	54	651	661	12	26,777	33,132	20,430	23,353
5013 Motor vehicle supplies and new parts	106	101	1,312	1,279	13	24,817	27,515	37,480	38,269
5014 Tires and tubes[3]	25	18	245	224	12	26,596	29,643	7,588	7,691
5015 Motor vehicle parts, used	24	29	134	139	5	22,179	23,799	3,582	3,619
5021 Furniture	42	42	319	395	9	24,476	26,066	9,228	12,823
5023 Homefurnishings[3]	27	24	327	274	11	22,716	26,672	8,222	7,421
5031 Lumber, plywood, and millwork[3]	50	55	731	840	15	31,152	35,524	24,653	29,123
5032 Brick, stone, & related materials[3]	24	18	221	128	7	30,624	36,875	7,086	4,440
5033 Roofing, siding, & insulation[3]	12	14	117	109	8	29,607	33,725	3,696	3,847
5039 Construction materials, nec[3]	17	29	175	259	9	26,194	28,556	5,532	8,571
5043 Photographic equipment & supplies[3]	4	5	8	9	2	23,000	32,444	173	307
5044 Office equipment[3]	43	48	820	961	20	30,449	41,886	25,829	37,904
5045 Computers, peripherals, & software[2]	69	70	874	814	12	49,693	51,405	38,918	40,098
5046 Commercial equipment, nec[3]	21	22	337	333	15	24,309	25,694	9,743	9,751
5047 Medical and hospital equipment	76	73	898	905	12	35,180	39,854	32,899	38,106
5048 Ophthalmic goods[3]	5	5	48	51	10	19,333	25,882	1,010	1,126
5049 Professional equipment, nec[3]	8	10	200	357	36	23,780	24,291	5,370	9,766
5051 Metals service centers and offices	100	100	2,487	2,408	24	30,684	32,365	85,311	85,902
5052 Coal and other minerals and ores[3]	17	15	79	85	6	31,747	32,282	2,652	3,690
5063 Electrical apparatus and equipment[3]	109	100	1,343	1,180	12	31,217	40,393	43,287	44,542
5064 Electrical appliances, TV & radios[3]	14	17	114	238	14	22,421	20,807	2,698	5,090
5065 Electronic parts and equipment[1]	50	59	496	596	10	41,121	40,779	19,762	22,702
5072 Hardware[3]	59	64	680	706	11	27,106	28,618	19,736	22,916
5074 Plumbing & hydronic heating supplies[3]	41	40	293	286	7	26,799	29,860	9,351	9,383
5075 Warm air heating & air conditioning[3]	43	48	414	439	9	29,575	30,743	13,301	14,528
5078 Refrigeration equipment and supplies[3]	9	9	147	152	17	32,299	36,474	5,475	6,351
5082 Construction and mining machinery	37	38	1,004	1,139	30	38,275	40,660	37,949	43,910
5083 Farm and garden machinery	25	22	287	295	13	17,408	27,797	6,972	8,152
5084 Industrial machinery and equipment	202	200	1,679	1,860	9	32,000	35,228	61,517	73,200
5085 Industrial supplies	128	123	1,134	1,055	9	29,291	31,666	37,436	37,128
5087 Service establishment equipment[3]	32	34	274	362	11	26,394	23,613	8,036	9,918
5088 Transportation equipment & supplies[3]	9	7	103	104	15	32,350	34,077	3,745	3,679
5091 Sporting & recreational goods[3]	22	22	164	252	11	30,024	25,000	7,195	8,169
5092 Toys and hobby goods and supplies[3]	4	5	7	25	5	19,429	13,600	217	438
5093 Scrap and waste materials[2]	52	55	622	696	13	27,929	38,891	18,909	25,265
5094 Jewelry & precious stones[3]	15	15	122	113	8	31,934	31,646	4,342	3,968
5099 Durable goods, nec[3]	30	30	139	139	5	22,216	21,324	3,308	3,488
5111 Printing and writing paper[3]	14	13	265	247	19	29,660	34,850	8,040	9,566
5112 Stationery and office supplies[3]	55	46	821	576	13	22,943	24,521	19,370	13,501
5113 Industrial & personal service paper[3]	17	22	299	370	17	27,371	28,519	8,745	11,512
5120 Drugs, proprietaries, and sundries[3]	30	32	777	955	30	39,326	45,847	30,814	41,393
5131 Piece goods & notions[3]	14	14	117	114	8	27,009	27,439	3,193	3,107
5136 Men's and boys' clothing[2]	-	6	-	73	12	-	24,822	-	1,773
5137 Women's and children's clothing[3]	12	10	72	160	16	21,167	19,850	2,193	4,031
5139 Footwear[2]	-	4	-	18	5	-	31,333	-	616
5141 Groceries, general line[3]	20	21	1,068	1,163	55	22,532	25,183	27,886	30,506
5142 Packaged frozen food[3]	8	8	171	194	24	31,509	33,546	6,087	6,932
5145 Confectionery[3]	11	11	567	574	52	29,136	26,787	16,861	17,175
5147 Meats and meat products[3]	7	7	294	318	45	22,095	22,113	6,829	7,217
5148 Fresh fruits and vegetables[3]	17	16	426	903	56	21,371	15,181	11,616	17,372
5149 Groceries and related products, nec[3]	36	35	1,034	1,243	36	26,197	26,845	29,610	35,212
5150 Farm-product raw materials[3]	5	5	40	43	9	37,500	34,884	2,039	2,386
5162 Plastics materials & basic shapes[3]	13	14	68	73	5	21,588	22,247	1,536	1,780
5169 Chemicals & allied products, nec[3]	47	47	537	533	11	35,292	47,054	20,418	25,870
5171 Petroleum bulk stations & terminals[3]	29	29	349	456	16	23,851	19,860	8,957	9,701
5172 Petroleum products, nec[3]	15	13	74	98	8	29,622	26,980	2,750	3,313
5181 Beer and ale[3]	3	4	309	411	103	22,356	26,102	7,499	10,240
5182 Wine and distilled beverages[3]	7	8	97	169	21	24,000	25,254	2,240	4,541
5191 Farm supplies	22	22	97	118	5	17,361	23,763	1,838	2,829
5192 Books, periodicals, & newspapers[3]	14	14	253	331	24	26,008	24,810	7,322	9,181
5193 Flowers & florists' supplies	21	18	167	132	7	16,934	19,212	3,107	2,609
5194 Tobacco and tobacco products[1]	5	-	306	-	-	17,346	-	5,834	-
5198 Paints, varnishes, and supplies[3]	17	15	81	79	5	29,136	29,013	2,636	2,499
5199 Nondurable goods, nec[3]	58	62	327	411	7	16,245	17,547	6,912	8,573
52- Retail trade	5,153	5,177	73,855	86,940	17	12,431	12,511	982,658	1,057,395
5210 Lumber and other building materials	74	77	1,710	1,788	23	16,671	18,664	31,201	33,619
5230 Paint, glass, and wallpaper stores[3]	37	33	229	161	5	19,266	24,944	4,511	3,944
5250 Hardware stores	58	45	257	245	5	15,704	14,645	4,792	3,954
5260 Retail nurseries and garden stores	30	31	192	310	10	10,313	12,400	2,629	4,405
5270 Mobile home dealers[3]	16	20	50	62	3	17,440	18,323	1,166	1,318

Continued on next page.

BIRMINGHAM, AL MSA - [continued]

Wholesale and Retail Trade USA	Establishments		Employment		Emp / Est	Pay / Employee		Annual Payroll ($ 000)	
	1994	1995	1994	1995	1995	1994	1995	1994	1995
5310 Department stores[3]	40	40	6,127	6,007	150	10,639	12,455	70,513	75,305
5330 Variety stores	59	52	444	417	8	8,505	8,403	3,949	3,948
5390 Misc. general merchandise stores	38	46	745	726	16	12,376	14,006	9,973	9,538
5410 Grocery stores[3]	495	495	10,546	20,792	42	9,448	10,494	109,258	136,484
5420 Meat and fish markets[3]	12	14	51	62	4	14,980	11,032	896	1,008
5450 Dairy products stores[2]	-	5	-	18	4	-	4,889	-	104
5460 Retail bakeries[2]	36	39	363	316	8	9,025	9,013	3,466	3,230
5490 Miscellaneous food stores[3]	23	26	170	178	7	7,412	8,427	1,521	1,622
5510 New and used car dealers	64	64	3,481	3,540	55	30,367	32,435	114,571	123,903
5520 Used car dealers	103	112	378	390	3	17,661	19,405	7,451	8,999
5530 Auto and home supply stores	203	205	1,543	1,437	7	17,929	19,836	30,523	30,079
5540 Gasoline service stations	339	322	2,157	2,077	6	11,303	11,775	25,585	26,504
5550 Boat dealers[3]	13	13	61	62	5	18,689	20,258	1,198	1,350
5560 Recreational vehicle dealers[3]	15	14	117	96	7	20,137	25,750	3,022	2,598
5570 Motorcycle dealers	10	9	35	37	4	15,314	18,054	728	788
5590 Automotive dealers, nec[3]	4	4	6	8	2	16,667	22,500	306	285
5610 Men's & boys' clothing stores[3]	40	39	331	297	8	13,196	14,990	4,408	4,378
5620 Women's clothing stores	178	145	1,778	1,557	11	9,467	9,654	17,799	14,979
5630 Women's accessory & specialty stores[3]	23	23	140	129	6	10,257	15,287	1,459	1,724
5640 Children's and infants' wear stores[3]	18	17	131	147	9	6,137	7,483	1,012	1,115
5650 Family clothing stores[3]	59	62	1,860	1,812	29	11,953	13,181	24,701	23,908
5660 Shoe stores	132	125	728	731	6	11,505	11,639	9,229	9,182
5690 Misc. apparel & accessory stores[3]	33	31	167	144	5	9,102	10,583	1,605	1,569
5712 Furniture stores	153	149	1,234	1,142	8	17,387	18,977	23,392	22,896
5713 Floor covering stores[3]	42	42	168	188	4	16,976	20,319	3,723	4,083
5714 Drapery and upholstery stores[3]	12	12	57	62	5	10,316	11,677	645	760
5719 Misc. homefurnishings stores[3]	63	63	543	604	10	9,215	9,536	5,714	6,810
5720 Household appliance stores[3]	29	29	376	212	7	15,011	13,472	5,779	2,949
5731 Radio, TV, & electronic stores[1]	58	57	410	465	8	18,420	18,581	8,386	9,292
5734 Computer and software stores[3]	27	29	131	210	7	18,595	16,190	3,353	3,786
5735 Record & prerecorded tape stores[3]	29	28	181	230	8	9,768	9,252	1,873	2,115
5736 Musical instrument stores[3]	8	8	64	77	10	20,500	17,922	1,477	1,645
5812 Eating places	1,056	1,006	20,381	21,856	22	7,739	7,882	169,397	182,911
5813 Drinking places	76	60	474	401	7	7,654	7,731	3,659	3,105
5910 Drug stores and proprietary stores	207	202	2,449	2,493	12	16,114	15,434	39,530	38,551
5920 Liquor stores[3]	65	62	191	184	3	18,325	15,174	3,506	2,991
5930 Used merchandise stores	103	108	908	995	9	9,282	10,143	9,062	11,545
5941 Sporting goods and bicycle shops[3]	78	77	540	593	8	13,422	13,828	8,527	8,680
5942 Book stores[3]	43	41	306	439	11	9,529	9,130	3,196	3,908
5943 Stationery stores[3]	18	15	65	75	5	10,954	7,253	643	579
5944 Jewelry stores	83	85	417	470	6	14,811	16,043	6,766	7,689
5945 Hobby, toy, and game shops[3]	27	29	243	313	11	12,675	11,553	3,182	3,569
5947 Gift, novelty, and souvenir shops[3]	100	104	523	556	5	7,098	8,633	4,286	5,167
5949 Sewing, needlework, and piece goods[3]	23	24	151	158	7	10,887	10,506	1,782	1,684
5961 Catalog and mail-order houses[3]	8	9	531	447	50	19,299	19,293	10,044	8,022
5962 Merchandising machine operators[3]	23	26	331	318	12	16,725	17,673	6,002	6,152
5963 Direct selling establishments[2]	44	38	249	269	7	14,972	16,030	4,419	4,949
5984 Liquefied petroleum gas dealers	28	29	132	128	4	19,758	20,750	2,534	2,518
5992 Florists	96	95	372	373	4	9,613	9,555	3,772	3,684
5993 Tobacco stores and stands[3]	4	3	11	13	4	12,364	12,000	145	186
5994 News dealers and newsstands[2]	-	3	-	8	3	-	16,500	-	144
5995 Optical goods stores	55	52	316	285	5	14,025	15,509	4,824	4,661
5999 Miscellaneous retail stores, nec	147	164	672	776	5	11,905	13,634	8,774	11,792

Source: County Business Patterns 1994/95, CBP-94/95, U.S. Department of Commerce, Washington DC, November 1997. The employment column represents mid-March employment in the year. Pay per employee is calculated by dividing 1st Quarter payroll, annualized, by mid-March employment. The column headed 'Emp / Est' shows 'employees per establishment'. A dash (-) means that data are unavailable or cannot be calculated. nec means not elsewhere classified. *Notes:* 1. 1994 data incomplete; unavailable or withheld. 2. 1995 data incomplete; unavailable or withheld. 3. 1994 and 1995 data incomplete; unavailable or withheld.

BISMARCK, ND MSA

Wholesale and Retail Trade USA	Establishments		Employment		Emp / Est	Pay / Employee		Annual Payroll ($ 000)	
	1994	1995	1994	1995	1995	1994	1995	1994	1995
50– Wholesale trade	240	238	2,495	2,453	10	21,052	22,704	56,466	60,123
5012 Automobiles and other vehicles	7	7	53	55	8	24,906	26,618	1,506	1,660
5013 Motor vehicle supplies and new parts	9	9	121	73	8	19,570	21,315	2,678	1,631
5014 Tires and tubes	6	5	45	35	7	17,511	19,543	733	683
5015 Motor vehicle parts, used	7	7	18	15	2	17,556	16,533	315	272
5031 Lumber, plywood, and millwork[1]	6	-	52	-	-	14,385	-	1,005	-
5044 Office equipment	7	6	78	72	12	19,026	19,222	1,733	1,758

Continued on next page.

BISMARCK, ND MSA - [continued]

Wholesale and Retail Trade USA	Establishments		Employment		Emp / Est	Pay / Employee		Annual Payroll ($ 000)	
	1994	1995	1994	1995	1995	1994	1995	1994	1995
5045 Computers, peripherals, & software [2]	6	7	50	60	9	27,680	29,067	1,402	2,585
5049 Professional equipment, nec [3]	6	5	30	33	7	19,600	18,061	622	653
5063 Electrical apparatus and equipment	7	7	48	45	6	28,250	34,844	1,571	1,667
5072 Hardware [2]	-	4	-	39	10	-	10,974	-	569
5074 Plumbing & hydronic heating supplies	6	-	46	-	-	33,652	-	1,654	-
5082 Construction and mining machinery	9	8	99	103	13	33,253	37,903	3,325	3,672
5083 Farm and garden machinery	15	15	107	87	6	19,664	19,816	2,533	1,990
5084 Industrial machinery and equipment	9	9	93	68	8	25,204	28,765	2,701	2,056
5087 Service establishment equipment	-	10	-	51	5	-	22,039	-	927
5091 Sporting & recreational goods [3]	4	4	33	28	7	19,030	36,286	685	895
5093 Scrap and waste materials	5	5	20	22	4	10,200	10,545	322	415
5110 Paper and paper products [3]	8	5	40	26	5	25,500	37,692	968	881
5140 Groceries and related products	18	18	571	525	29	25,051	25,905	14,523	13,884
5150 Farm-product raw materials	14	14	188	174	12	11,085	12,529	2,290	2,311
5171 Petroleum bulk stations & terminals	11	10	156	165	17	11,821	12,121	1,975	2,046
5172 Petroleum products, nec	4	4	10	12	3	21,600	29,000	252	439
5180 Beer, wine, and distilled beverages [3]	4	4	74	78	20	22,541	23,231	2,047	2,001
5199 Nondurable goods, nec [2]	-	5	-	41	8	-	12,780	-	766
52- Retail trade	607	620	8,954	8,957	14	10,597	11,348	105,881	109,651
5210 Lumber and other building materials	17	17	197	235	14	16,183	18,451	3,822	4,223
5230 Paint, glass, and wallpaper stores [1]	3	-	7	-	-	14,857	-	102	-
5250 Hardware stores	7	6	81	59	10	11,753	13,898	997	868
5270 Mobile home dealers	5	5	17	15	3	9,647	12,000	224	218
5310 Department stores [3]	9	8	1,151	1,190	149	10,210	11,318	12,948	13,805
5410 Grocery stores	23	23	970	934	41	9,625	11,370	10,483	11,521
5460 Retail bakeries	6	8	30	30	4	7,467	7,467	242	250
5490 Miscellaneous food stores [3]	5	7	19	14	2	4,632	6,857	81	102
5510 New and used car dealers	11	11	567	591	54	23,979	23,418	15,509	16,187
5520 Used car dealers	10	11	47	57	5	15,830	12,912	794	835
5530 Auto and home supply stores	13	13	88	79	6	16,045	18,329	1,592	1,676
5540 Gasoline service stations	44	45	401	426	9	13,526	14,347	5,649	6,104
5610 Men's & boys' clothing stores [3]	7	6	37	41	7	9,622	9,366	371	340
5620 Women's clothing stores [3]	23	20	169	130	7	7,740	7,631	1,540	962
5630 Women's accessory & specialty stores [2]	-	3	-	12	4	-	8,000	-	93
5650 Family clothing stores [2]	-	5	-	28	6	-	9,571	-	269
5660 Shoe stores	13	12	54	49	4	11,481	11,755	652	497
5712 Furniture stores	12	13	128	94	7	14,500	17,574	2,171	1,618
5713 Floor covering stores	7	8	98	107	13	18,857	20,860	2,757	2,686
5720 Household appliance stores	7	7	21	21	3	20,571	24,381	404	445
5731 Radio, TV, & electronic stores [2]	-	4	-	30	8	-	13,867	-	505
5735 Record & prerecorded tape stores [2]	-	5	-	26	5	-	9,692	-	224
5812 Eating places	125	115	2,816	2,778	24	6,991	7,070	20,655	20,834
5813 Drinking places	32	30	259	265	9	4,911	5,328	1,438	1,432
5910 Drug stores and proprietary stores	22	19	215	217	11	15,051	16,055	3,475	3,444
5920 Liquor stores	14	13	63	78	6	7,619	7,385	479	646
5930 Used merchandise stores	8	8	48	49	6	6,417	7,265	361	393
5941 Sporting goods and bicycle shops [3]	9	9	128	132	15	10,531	15,394	1,401	1,698
5944 Jewelry stores	11	10	64	62	6	12,375	14,516	819	918
5945 Hobby, toy, and game shops	4	6	11	9	2	9,455	11,111	124	120
5947 Gift, novelty, and souvenir shops	17	22	87	102	5	7,080	6,431	730	771
5949 Sewing, needlework, and piece goods [3]	5	4	43	21	5	5,767	6,667	269	135
5960 Nonstore retailers	6	5	36	29	6	13,111	14,897	444	455
5992 Florists	7	9	60	59	7	5,533	7,525	342	503
5995 Optical goods stores [1]	9	-	34	-	-	15,647	-	573	-
5999 Miscellaneous retail stores, nec	25	27	126	116	4	10,413	13,448	1,664	1,813

Source: County Business Patterns 1994/95, CBP-94/95, U.S. Department of Commerce, Washington DC, November 1997. The employment column represents mid-March employment in the year. Pay per employee is calculated by dividing 1st Quarter payroll, annualized, by mid-March employment. The column headed 'Emp / Est' shows 'employees per establishment'. A dash (-) means that data are unavailable or cannot be calculated. nec means not elsewhere classified. *Notes:* 1. 1994 data incomplete; unavailable or withheld. 2. 1995 data incomplete; unavailable or withheld. 3. 1994 and 1995 data incomplete; unavailable or withheld.

BLOOMINGTON, IN MSA

Wholesale and Retail Trade USA	Establishments		Employment		Emp / Est	Pay / Employee		Annual Payroll ($ 000)	
	1994	1995	1994	1995	1995	1994	1995	1994	1995
50- Wholesale trade	127	138	1,552	1,408	10	24,977	21,730	40,971	33,058
5013 Motor vehicle supplies and new parts	8	8	45	53	7	16,267	21,057	773	1,080
5021 Furniture	4	5	30	44	9	21,200	22,909	641	1,188
5023 Homefurnishings	3	4	18	18	5	16,444	19,111	329	457
5039 Construction materials, nec	-	4	-	25	6	-	14,880	-	421

Continued on next page.

BLOOMINGTON, IN MSA - [continued]

Wholesale and Retail Trade USA	Establishments		Employment		Emp / Est	Pay / Employee		Annual Payroll ($ 000)	
	1994	1995	1994	1995	1995	1994	1995	1994	1995
5044 Office equipment	4	4	66	69	17	18,364	21,275	1,495	1,530
5045 Computers, peripherals, & software	-	13	-	69	5	-	23,130	-	1,944
5046 Commercial equipment, nec	3	3	14	15	5	26,857	26,133	371	425
5051 Metals service centers and offices	3	3	12	16	5	19,667	17,500	342	498
5065 Electronic parts and equipment	9	9	74	65	7	27,297	31,815	1,825	2,129
5070 Hardware, plumbing & heating equipment	7	8	56	80	10	21,571	24,300	1,364	1,892
5083 Farm and garden machinery	3	-	4	-	-	9,000	-	51	-
5085 Industrial supplies	4	5	10	19	4	37,200	25,684	450	534
5099 Durable goods, nec	4	4	5	10	3	16,000	31,200	238	463
5110 Paper and paper products	4	-	20	-	-	21,800	-	470	-
5149 Groceries and related products, nec	4	5	238	326	65	27,782	27,472	7,075	9,048
5170 Petroleum and petroleum products	7	7	43	52	7	12,651	13,769	639	804
5192 Books, periodicals, & newspapers	-	3	-	100	33	-	13,520	-	1,441
5199 Nondurable goods, nec	4	4	31	24	6	13,290	16,500	515	476
52 - Retail trade	732	730	12,029	12,412	17	9,301	10,291	122,871	133,928
5210 Lumber and other building materials	10	8	186	268	34	16,989	16,030	3,446	3,946
5230 Paint, glass, and wallpaper stores	4	4	28	23	6	13,571	15,826	496	530
5250 Hardware stores	4	3	59	61	20	14,508	13,443	902	858
5260 Retail nurseries and garden stores	7	8	47	54	7	11,234	12,222	750	843
5270 Mobile home dealers	4	4	11	14	4	16,000	20,571	304	388
5310 Department stores	8	8	1,113	1,124	141	8,305	9,562	10,413	11,278
5410 Grocery stores	38	38	1,335	1,234	32	11,446	12,911	15,143	16,013
5460 Retail bakeries	5	6	15	32	5	4,267	6,375	220	362
5490 Miscellaneous food stores	4	3	19	11	4	6,947	6,182	132	78
5510 New and used car dealers	8	8	319	366	46	25,592	27,672	9,253	11,172
5520 Used car dealers	8	9	21	18	2	14,476	15,778	389	287
5530 Auto and home supply stores	11	12	82	100	8	19,854	21,320	1,757	2,176
5540 Gasoline service stations	37	39	298	302	8	10,752	12,066	3,479	3,925
5570 Motorcycle dealers	4	4	27	35	9	14,519	14,171	489	539
5610 Men's & boys' clothing stores	4	3	31	26	9	10,581	9,231	305	167
5620 Women's clothing stores	25	21	270	184	9	6,148	7,500	1,761	1,281
5630 Women's accessory & specialty stores	5	4	28	38	10	7,429	7,053	238	276
5650 Family clothing stores	9	10	74	74	7	7,351	9,730	548	675
5660 Shoe stores	14	13	117	118	9	8,479	9,458	1,062	1,036
5690 Misc. apparel & accessory stores	6	5	10	18	4	5,600	7,333	101	158
5712 Furniture stores	15	18	80	99	6	14,300	17,657	1,493	1,723
5713 Floor covering stores	-	7	-	42	6	-	17,905	-	895
5719 Misc. homefurnishings stores	11	9	43	47	5	11,442	10,043	488	523
5720 Household appliance stores	7	4	51	50	13	19,216	19,440	1,041	1,061
5731 Radio, TV, & electronic stores	7	7	36	27	4	10,778	15,111	397	377
5734 Computer and software stores	6	8	23	24	3	7,826	13,833	248	386
5735 Record & prerecorded tape stores	9	9	65	51	6	6,954	9,725	506	535
5736 Musical instrument stores	5	6	56	55	9	7,643	8,582	439	486
5812 Eating places	192	182	4,887	5,183	28	6,320	6,714	34,396	37,094
5813 Drinking places	18	14	273	272	19	5,832	6,412	1,688	1,676
5910 Drug stores and proprietary stores	16	17	204	177	10	14,627	17,695	3,254	3,281
5920 Liquor stores	16	15	101	110	7	8,119	8,109	833	888
5930 Used merchandise stores	11	12	84	83	7	8,857	11,277	846	977
5941 Sporting goods and bicycle shops	17	18	101	111	6	7,525	9,477	872	1,013
5942 Book stores	18	18	181	190	11	12,000	12,084	2,417	2,187
5944 Jewelry stores	16	17	97	92	5	9,979	10,696	1,024	1,083
5945 Hobby, toy, and game shops	5	5	13	15	3	12,923	12,533	215	245
5947 Gift, novelty, and souvenir shops	24	21	144	139	7	5,333	5,554	834	853
5962 Merchandising machine operators	-	3	-	5	2	-	7,200	-	42
5984 Liquefied petroleum gas dealers	4	-	25	-	-	20,000	-	493	-
5992 Florists	11	9	66	74	8	8,303	8,919	562	635
5995 Optical goods stores	6	-	46	-	-	10,261	-	478	-
5999 Miscellaneous retail stores, nec	23	30	89	102	3	8,360	9,098	812	1,107

Source: County Business Patterns 1994/95, CBP-94/95, U.S. Department of Commerce, Washington DC, November 1997. The employment column represents mid-March employment in the year. Pay per employee is calculated by dividing 1st Quarter payroll, annualized, by mid-March employment. The column headed 'Emp / Est' shows 'employees per establishment'. A dash (-) means that data are unavailable or cannot be calculated. nec means not elsewhere classified. *Notes:* 1. 1994 data incomplete; unavailable or withheld. 2. 1995 data incomplete; unavailable or withheld. 3. 1994 and 1995 data incomplete; unavailable or withheld.

BLOOMINGTON - NORMAL, IL MSA

Wholesale and Retail Trade USA	Establishments		Employment		Emp / Est	Pay / Employee		Annual Payroll ($ 000)	
	1994	1995	1994	1995	1995	1994	1995	1994	1995
50 - Wholesale trade	259	261	3,432	3,453	13	30,735	35,662	113,910	121,201
5012 Automobiles and other vehicles	5	7	144	149	21	25,750	29,584	4,113	4,569

Continued on next page.

BLOOMINGTON – NORMAL, IL MSA - [continued]

Wholesale and Retail Trade USA	Establishments		Employment		Emp / Est	Pay / Employee		Annual Payroll ($ 000)	
	1994	1995	1994	1995	1995	1994	1995	1994	1995
5013 Motor vehicle supplies and new parts	18	15	243	201	13	25,728	30,766	6,010	5,306
5021 Furniture	4	-	36	-	-	21,444	-	845	-
5023 Homefurnishings	3	-	14	-	-	10,571	-	220	-
5039 Construction materials, nec	-	3	-	28	9	-	22,571	-	780
5044 Office equipment	4	-	22	-	-	22,182	-	565	-
5045 Computers, peripherals, & software	12	12	206	184	15	45,068	79,630	10,298	11,781
5047 Medical and hospital equipment	5	3	41	17	6	42,341	21,647	1,752	489
5051 Metals service centers and offices	-	3	-	10	3	-	23,600	-	303
5063 Electrical apparatus and equipment	-	6	-	76	13	-	30,789	-	2,228
5072 Hardware	-	3	-	26	9	-	15,231	-	426
5074 Plumbing & hydronic heating supplies	4	4	45	41	10	19,644	23,902	978	963
5075 Warm air heating & air conditioning	5	5	51	88	18	20,078	19,000	1,269	1,771
5083 Farm and garden machinery	4	5	47	45	9	21,362	27,200	1,153	1,445
5084 Industrial machinery and equipment	9	9	57	58	6	27,158	32,000	1,659	2,002
5087 Service establishment equipment	6	-	47	-	-	25,106	-	1,324	-
5093 Scrap and waste materials	4	5	64	87	17	18,688	21,793	1,543	2,282
5110 Paper and paper products	8	7	100	88	13	29,400	30,318	3,771	2,875
5130 Apparel, piece goods, and notions	4	4	20	27	7	12,600	14,519	237	410
5144 Poultry and poultry products	-	3	-	27	9	-	12,148	-	342
5149 Groceries and related products, nec	7	7	73	74	11	30,685	30,108	2,337	2,311
5153 Grain and field beans	25	25	137	190	8	21,401	21,979	3,541	5,329
5169 Chemicals & allied products, nec	-	3	-	12	4	-	43,667	-	358
5171 Petroleum bulk stations & terminals	9	8	74	80	10	19,568	19,250	1,470	1,536
5172 Petroleum products, nec	4	4	29	22	6	28,966	37,273	634	690
5191 Farm supplies	29	28	267	211	8	27,221	32,417	7,287	6,016
5192 Books, periodicals, & newspapers	3	-	45	-	-	17,156	-	787	-
5193 Flowers & florists' supplies	5	3	89	88	29	16,225	15,727	1,522	1,688
5199 Nondurable goods, nec	-	5	-	14	3	-	62,571	-	544
52 – Retail trade	873	896	14,211	14,613	16	10,040	11,008	160,051	169,377
5210 Lumber and other building materials	18	16	369	426	27	17,366	18,535	7,955	8,747
5230 Paint, glass, and wallpaper stores	6	8	48	52	7	19,250	17,000	945	829
5260 Retail nurseries and garden stores	10	12	51	78	7	12,784	13,179	1,057	1,264
5310 Department stores	7	7	1,121	1,149	164	9,616	11,715	11,857	13,167
5410 Grocery stores	37	36	1,237	1,235	34	11,654	12,418	15,557	15,815
5420 Meat and fish markets	3	3	13	14	5	10,462	11,143	150	163
5440 Candy, nut, and confectionery stores	3	3	42	21	7	4,000	7,238	184	158
5460 Retail bakeries	8	6	88	68	11	8,227	8,471	744	602
5490 Miscellaneous food stores	6	5	34	53	11	7,882	6,943	321	347
5510 New and used car dealers	16	18	568	604	34	26,789	28,040	17,535	17,925
5520 Used car dealers	7	8	33	34	4	23,636	22,235	819	878
5530 Auto and home supply stores	10	12	186	227	19	12,602	14,819	2,636	3,463
5540 Gasoline service stations	73	68	803	801	12	10,869	11,361	9,162	9,353
5570 Motorcycle dealers	4	4	39	43	11	21,026	21,116	858	923
5610 Men's & boys' clothing stores	14	13	86	80	6	7,721	9,950	699	714
5620 Women's clothing stores	33	31	300	243	8	6,480	6,782	2,124	1,801
5630 Women's accessory & specialty stores	6	5	26	30	6	10,000	8,533	252	261
5640 Children's and infants' wear stores	-	4	-	11	3	-	6,545	-	122
5650 Family clothing stores	11	10	384	364	36	10,469	12,462	4,503	4,591
5660 Shoe stores	23	24	148	160	7	9,541	10,200	1,680	1,820
5690 Misc. apparel & accessory stores	4	5	24	18	4	11,000	12,000	255	172
5712 Furniture stores	20	20	155	156	8	14,968	14,821	2,622	2,592
5713 Floor covering stores	9	9	100	144	16	21,920	25,056	3,183	4,082
5714 Drapery and upholstery stores	-	3	-	7	2	-	4,000	-	39
5719 Misc. homefurnishings stores	-	14	-	63	5	-	10,794	-	774
5720 Household appliance stores	6	6	29	29	5	16,000	19,448	609	602
5731 Radio, TV, & electronic stores	11	11	118	182	17	10,373	10,967	1,176	1,851
5734 Computer and software stores	-	7	-	49	7	-	11,673	-	683
5735 Record & prerecorded tape stores	4	-	33	-	-	7,273	-	249	-
5812 Eating places	228	223	5,697	5,675	25	6,459	7,016	40,963	41,938
5813 Drinking places	37	34	132	169	5	5,879	6,935	1,065	1,269
5910 Drug stores and proprietary stores	15	15	276	263	18	13,986	16,015	4,360	4,474
5920 Liquor stores	-	6	-	43	7	-	10,698	-	472
5930 Used merchandise stores	10	12	44	43	4	8,818	10,884	514	589
5941 Sporting goods and bicycle shops	19	17	107	102	6	8,972	9,569	1,130	1,098
5942 Book stores	11	12	169	200	17	7,645	8,660	1,352	1,698
5944 Jewelry stores	9	10	78	78	8	12,513	14,103	1,052	1,081
5945 Hobby, toy, and game shops	8	9	98	107	12	8,735	9,458	985	1,355
5947 Gift, novelty, and souvenir shops	27	25	159	125	5	5,962	6,496	1,054	968
5949 Sewing, needlework, and piece goods	-	9	-	45	5	-	9,333	-	387
5961 Catalog and mail-order houses	7	7	207	245	35	7,826	8,522	1,626	1,889
5962 Merchandising machine operators	5	5	135	123	25	18,637	18,179	2,609	2,465

Continued on next page.

BLOOMINGTON – NORMAL, IL MSA - [continued]

Wholesale and Retail Trade USA	Establishments		Employment		Emp / Est	Pay / Employee		Annual Payroll ($ 000)	
	1994	1995	1994	1995	1995	1994	1995	1994	1995
5963 Direct selling establishments	12	10	46	37	4	10,522	9,514	560	381
5984 Liquefied petroleum gas dealers	-	4	-	33	8	-	18,061	-	691
5992 Florists	-	10	-	77	8	-	10,649	-	866
5995 Optical goods stores	13	13	75	80	6	18,987	18,900	1,466	1,529
5999 Miscellaneous retail stores, nec	30	33	137	148	4	9,810	9,189	1,481	1,636

Source: County Business Patterns 1994/95, CBP-94/95, U.S. Department of Commerce, Washington DC, November 1997. The employment column represents mid-March employment in the year. Pay per employee is calculated by dividing 1st Quarter payroll, annualized, by mid-March employment. The column headed 'Emp / Est' shows 'employees per establishment'. A dash (-) means that data are unavailable or cannot be calculated. nec means not elsewhere classified. *Notes:* 1. 1994 data incomplete; unavailable or withheld. 2. 1995 data incomplete; unavailable or withheld. 3. 1994 and 1995 data incomplete; unavailable or withheld.

BOISE CITY, ID MSA

Wholesale and Retail Trade USA	Establishments		Employment		Emp / Est	Pay / Employee		Annual Payroll ($ 000)	
	1994	1995	1994	1995	1995	1994	1995	1994	1995
50 - Wholesale trade	827	878	9,810	10,172	12	25,660	27,886	264,285	376,992
5012 Automobiles and other vehicles	22	22	349	406	18	21,330	23,488	8,251	9,277
5013 Motor vehicle supplies and new parts	56	51	576	488	10	19,826	21,139	11,849	10,463
5014 Tires and tubes	9	9	92	103	11	25,870	26,485	2,367	2,727
5015 Motor vehicle parts, used	11	12	85	89	7	16,941	18,292	1,523	1,559
5021 Furniture	8	8	78	95	12	26,359	33,263	2,164	2,601
5023 Homefurnishings [3]	14	15	130	123	8	18,277	22,114	2,561	2,993
5031 Lumber, plywood, and millwork	40	34	629	368	11	27,421	31,891	17,928	11,618
5032 Brick, stone, & related materials [1]	9	13	90	110	8	21,156	21,491	2,197	2,789
5033 Roofing, siding, & insulation [3]	11	9	167	76	8	22,180	27,316	3,595	2,221
5039 Construction materials, nec	9	20	52	203	10	18,308	24,020	1,170	5,216
5044 Office equipment	15	15	201	211	14	31,383	32,929	6,512	6,162
5045 Computers, peripherals, & software [3]	28	30	279	441	15	50,437	55,120	12,432	19,225
5046 Commercial equipment, nec [3]	7	7	58	64	9	16,483	21,063	1,196	1,514
5047 Medical and hospital equipment [3]	15	17	89	104	6	33,798	32,692	3,673	4,429
5051 Metals service centers and offices	8	10	120	126	13	24,367	24,476	3,135	3,344
5063 Electrical apparatus and equipment	31	28	208	200	7	35,173	46,400	7,041	7,857
5065 Electronic parts and equipment	32	-	180	-	-	32,289	-	6,561	-
5072 Hardware	16	22	92	116	5	21,261	21,034	2,246	2,711
5074 Plumbing & hydronic heating supplies	14	15	156	174	12	28,821	30,736	4,392	4,744
5075 Warm air heating & air conditioning	14	15	80	101	7	30,950	32,396	2,773	3,384
5078 Refrigeration equipment and supplies [3]	4	4	38	27	7	21,684	22,222	789	743
5082 Construction and mining machinery	13	14	256	235	17	27,984	39,421	9,396	9,952
5083 Farm and garden machinery	26	29	290	302	10	21,586	21,536	7,510	7,885
5084 Industrial machinery and equipment	40	40	278	299	7	27,813	30,140	8,830	11,002
5085 Industrial supplies	24	26	234	267	10	33,726	35,326	7,263	8,669
5087 Service establishment equipment [3]	10	10	171	150	15	15,298	19,093	2,781	3,040
5091 Sporting & recreational goods [3]	4	5	72	99	20	15,056	14,061	1,217	1,423
5093 Scrap and waste materials	13	14	135	119	9	20,207	22,588	2,765	2,400
5094 Jewelry & precious stones [2]	-	3	-	14	5	-	11,429	-	152
5099 Durable goods, nec	-	8	-	13	2	-	10,769	-	165
5112 Stationery and office supplies	24	-	285	-	-	17,053	-	5,190	-
5120 Drugs, proprietaries, and sundries	12	15	64	90	6	26,375	24,844	2,238	3,451
5130 Apparel, piece goods, and notions	9	8	20	20	3	14,200	8,200	118	178
5141 Groceries, general line	11	14	344	359	26	26,407	26,730	10,060	9,825
5142 Packaged frozen food [3]	8	8	113	125	16	34,372	35,968	4,037	4,925
5145 Confectionery [3]	4	3	63	68	23	22,540	23,353	1,493	1,621
5147 Meats and meat products	8	8	98	124	16	16,163	17,613	1,836	2,893
5148 Fresh fruits and vegetables	11	10	194	215	22	12,371	12,502	3,015	2,613
5149 Groceries and related products, nec	29	31	555	610	20	25,859	26,295	15,745	17,229
5153 Grain and field beans	5	8	110	129	16	25,709	33,271	2,760	4,331
5160 Chemicals and allied products	16	16	89	80	5	37,124	37,600	3,679	3,515
5171 Petroleum bulk stations & terminals	25	23	306	344	15	16,745	20,349	4,745	6,384
5172 Petroleum products, nec [3]	3	3	44	50	17	26,455	36,720	1,537	2,202
5180 Beer, wine, and distilled beverages [3]	9	9	270	287	32	23,570	24,488	7,060	7,668
5191 Farm supplies	43	47	519	573	12	21,588	23,958	12,382	15,019
5192 Books, periodicals, & newspapers [1]	4	-	32	-	-	23,875	-	754	-
5193 Flowers & florists' supplies [1]	9	-	57	-	-	12,070	-	995	-
5194 Tobacco and tobacco products [3]	3	3	59	56	19	16,949	19,000	1,327	1,568
5198 Paints, varnishes, and supplies [1]	5	-	25	-	-	22,560	-	612	-
5199 Nondurable goods, nec	11	14	76	151	11	26,579	21,616	2,473	3,662
52 - Retail trade	2,163	2,272	32,911	33,952	15	13,462	14,141	466,639	508,093
5210 Lumber and other building materials	51	48	693	983	20	20,935	21,978	16,639	21,584
5230 Paint, glass, and wallpaper stores [1]	26	23	66	50	2	19,939	17,120	1,313	935
5250 Hardware stores	23	16	259	182	11	14,734	12,330	4,714	2,344

Continued on next page.

BOISE CITY, ID MSA - [continued]

Wholesale and Retail Trade USA	Establishments		Employment		Emp / Est	Pay / Employee		Annual Payroll ($ 000)	
	1994	1995	1994	1995	1995	1994	1995	1994	1995
5260 Retail nurseries and garden stores	19	21	172	258	12	10,628	10,419	2,824	3,854
5310 Department stores	16	16	2,296	2,577	161	11,510	12,581	30,705	33,463
5330 Variety stores	9	8	87	89	11	6,575	11,685	719	932
5390 Misc. general merchandise stores[3]	11	16	278	267	17	17,899	23,326	5,862	6,961
5410 Grocery stores	92	91	3,094	2,920	32	13,982	15,792	44,583	46,788
5420 Meat and fish markets	9	6	11	28	5	11,636	19,714	176	426
5440 Candy, nut, and confectionery stores	9	9	46	46	5	7,565	9,478	438	438
5460 Retail bakeries	22	20	192	122	6	8,854	10,689	1,716	1,195
5490 Miscellaneous food stores	-	15	-	71	5	-	8,000	-	642
5510 New and used car dealers	28	30	1,532	1,568	52	30,601	29,487	49,650	52,329
5520 Used car dealers	37	35	235	198	6	21,770	24,404	5,342	5,320
5530 Auto and home supply stores	67	71	558	564	8	18,337	20,191	11,658	12,361
5540 Gasoline service stations	140	143	1,247	1,393	10	11,047	10,685	14,822	15,826
5550 Boat dealers	11	10	54	53	5	19,407	19,321	1,114	1,260
5560 Recreational vehicle dealers	15	15	154	160	11	18,286	20,250	3,939	4,254
5570 Motorcycle dealers	-	10	-	75	8	-	18,080	-	1,517
5610 Men's & boys' clothing stores	18	16	88	100	6	10,682	11,160	1,160	1,043
5620 Women's clothing stores	59	51	452	421	8	8,257	7,259	4,074	3,179
5630 Women's accessory & specialty stores	7	8	24	27	3	11,333	10,815	301	311
5640 Children's and infants' wear stores[3]	5	4	39	41	10	10,872	11,415	430	354
5650 Family clothing stores	30	30	491	478	16	10,273	10,661	5,201	5,049
5660 Shoe stores	44	39	231	229	6	10,667	11,336	2,420	2,576
5690 Misc. apparel & accessory stores	17	17	58	66	4	12,552	12,121	776	860
5712 Furniture stores	60	60	575	630	11	20,292	20,133	11,987	11,788
5713 Floor covering stores	31	36	170	166	5	24,094	21,711	3,876	3,990
5714 Drapery and upholstery stores	4	4	2	12	3	6,000	13,000	82	151
5719 Misc. homefurnishings stores	25	28	123	157	6	9,821	9,197	1,417	1,565
5720 Household appliance stores[3]	18	17	12	20	1	8,667	10,600	215	201
5731 Radio, TV, & electronic stores	24	26	112	160	6	19,536	17,675	2,152	3,613
5734 Computer and software stores	8	10	75	89	9	19,893	22,022	1,935	2,432
5735 Record & prerecorded tape stores	16	20	203	177	9	9,911	11,819	2,001	2,165
5812 Eating places	520	530	11,660	11,409	22	6,786	7,271	83,201	88,605
5813 Drinking places	94	82	622	799	10	7,389	7,074	5,091	5,429
5910 Drug stores and proprietary stores	34	32	521	494	15	15,370	18,113	7,858	8,506
5920 Liquor stores	-	17	-	53	3	-	15,774	-	972
5930 Used merchandise stores	52	50	232	250	5	13,103	13,040	3,372	4,025
5941 Sporting goods and bicycle shops	63	64	576	669	10	11,063	10,774	6,841	7,507
5942 Book stores	24	25	130	152	6	10,123	10,605	1,359	1,492
5943 Stationery stores	-	6	-	9	2	-	18,222	-	134
5944 Jewelry stores	35	33	184	216	7	21,348	19,704	4,030	4,230
5945 Hobby, toy, and game shops	21	24	199	168	7	8,884	9,548	1,977	1,939
5947 Gift, novelty, and souvenir shops	43	50	200	214	4	7,080	7,028	1,625	1,642
5949 Sewing, needlework, and piece goods	13	16	135	120	8	6,193	6,867	823	804
5961 Catalog and mail-order houses	9	9	49	33	4	8,898	18,182	531	855
5962 Merchandising machine operators[1]	7	9	55	46	5	14,909	19,304	905	953
5963 Direct selling establishments	25	24	134	129	5	14,448	13,271	2,098	1,948
5980 Fuel dealers	10	10	63	75	8	18,540	17,547	1,155	1,361
5992 Florists	37	38	157	173	5	8,280	8,532	1,422	1,492
5995 Optical goods stores	-	15	-	119	8	-	11,866	-	1,244
5999 Miscellaneous retail stores, nec	65	69	304	332	5	12,895	12,422	4,543	4,822

Source: County Business Patterns 1994/95, CBP-94/95, U.S. Department of Commerce, Washington DC, November 1997. The employment column represents mid-March employment in the year. Pay per employee is calculated by dividing 1st Quarter payroll, annualized, by mid-March employment. The column headed 'Emp / Est' shows 'employees per establishment'. A dash (-) means that data are unavailable or cannot be calculated. nec means not elsewhere classified. *Notes:* 1. 1994 data incomplete; unavailable or withheld. 2. 1995 data incomplete; unavailable or withheld. 3. 1994 and 1995 data incomplete; unavailable or withheld.

BOULDER - LONGMONT, CO PMSA

Wholesale and Retail Trade USA	Establishments		Employment		Emp / Est	Pay / Employee		Annual Payroll ($ 000)	
	1994	1995	1994	1995	1995	1994	1995	1994	1995
50 - Wholesale trade	593	603	5,854	5,401	9	32,839	33,469	216,820	196,280
5013 Motor vehicle supplies and new parts	22	15	147	131	9	24,327	24,427	3,826	3,403
5015 Motor vehicle parts, used	3	3	9	10	3	20,000	22,800	172	214
5021 Furniture	7	7	58	50	7	27,379	42,320	1,671	1,994
5023 Homefurnishings	9	9	43	32	4	25,488	26,750	1,078	982
5031 Lumber, plywood, and millwork	9	7	65	66	9	27,138	27,939	2,904	2,116
5032 Brick, stone, & related materials	6	4	56	25	6	30,000	20,960	1,484	603
5033 Roofing, siding, & insulation	3	4	11	28	7	36,364	42,143	644	1,368
5039 Construction materials, nec	4	6	32	35	6	29,625	29,714	1,469	1,120
5044 Office equipment	9	10	119	170	17	21,378	31,435	3,627	5,155

Continued on next page.

BOULDER - LONGMONT, CO PMSA - [continued]

Wholesale and Retail Trade USA	Establishments		Employment		Emp / Est	Pay / Employee		Annual Payroll ($ 000)	
	1994	1995	1994	1995	1995	1994	1995	1994	1995
5045 Computers, peripherals, & software	74	68	1,768	1,180	17	40,127	39,627	83,113	50,674
5046 Commercial equipment, nec	8	8	86	69	9	22,140	36,058	2,394	3,073
5047 Medical and hospital equipment	17	16	121	131	8	65,388	67,359	8,161	9,080
5049 Professional equipment, nec	4	-	14	-	-	45,429	-	723	-
5050 Metals and minerals, except petroleum	5	5	78	71	14	27,077	29,915	2,041	2,048
5063 Electrical apparatus and equipment	19	13	126	120	9	25,587	24,333	3,720	3,565
5064 Electrical appliances, TV & radios	4	5	13	16	3	17,538	14,500	247	400
5065 Electronic parts and equipment	44	49	225	186	4	46,364	48,237	11,770	11,081
5074 Plumbing & hydronic heating supplies	-	10	-	57	6	-	25,684	-	2,063
5082 Construction and mining machinery	3	3	9	3	1	28,000	80,000	276	310
5083 Farm and garden machinery	7	6	63	42	7	20,508	22,476	1,655	1,230
5084 Industrial machinery and equipment	24	24	133	142	6	35,519	42,056	5,853	7,764
5085 Industrial supplies	7	-	34	-	-	26,235	-	1,024	-
5087 Service establishment equipment	3	4	12	11	3	30,000	30,182	406	454
5088 Transportation equipment & supplies	4	4	19	21	5	26,737	34,857	801	870
5091 Sporting & recreational goods	33	35	354	309	9	30,701	33,126	10,543	10,691
5092 Toys and hobby goods and supplies	6	8	43	46	6	15,256	18,522	791	1,176
5093 Scrap and waste materials	5	6	86	81	14	16,884	18,519	1,491	1,697
5094 Jewelry & precious stones	13	12	36	35	3	13,778	14,629	638	610
5099 Durable goods, nec	7	12	23	31	3	22,261	21,161	678	967
5112 Stationery and office supplies	20	13	210	193	15	13,810	18,093	2,594	3,296
5113 Industrial & personal service paper	3	4	14	17	4	25,714	25,882	460	614
5120 Drugs, proprietaries, and sundries	9	11	86	204	19	16,651	21,275	3,139	4,555
5131 Piece goods & notions	5	8	45	54	7	14,844	21,111	825	1,259
5136 Men's and boys' clothing	12	14	56	88	6	29,643	27,500	2,218	2,590
5137 Women's and children's clothing	-	10	-	53	5	-	19,623	-	1,115
5141 Groceries, general line	-	3	-	4	1	-	31,000	-	118
5149 Groceries and related products, nec	17	16	181	208	13	15,492	16,365	3,117	3,550
5153 Grain and field beans	5	6	17	15	3	27,765	20,800	520	489
5159 Farm-product raw materials, nec	-	3	-	45	15	-	20,800	-	1,034
5162 Plastics materials & basic shapes	4	4	20	26	7	31,800	24,923	737	745
5169 Chemicals & allied products, nec	5	5	14	13	3	20,000	26,462	329	357
5170 Petroleum and petroleum products	5	5	26	23	5	27,231	21,217	520	490
5181 Beer and ale	-	3	-	82	27	-	28,293	-	2,587
5182 Wine and distilled beverages	-	4	-	4	1	-	10,000	-	121
5191 Farm supplies	11	8	130	135	17	28,123	27,259	3,268	3,316
5192 Books, periodicals, & newspapers	10	10	60	66	7	27,867	29,212	1,547	1,704
5193 Flowers & florists' supplies	-	5	-	47	9	-	14,298	-	945
5199 Nondurable goods, nec	29	29	142	130	4	17,127	17,569	3,006	2,970
52- Retail trade	1,809	1,823	26,687	28,752	16	12,268	13,222	373,257	414,731
5210 Lumber and other building materials	25	21	449	483	23	23,439	26,468	11,753	12,121
5230 Paint, glass, and wallpaper stores	20	21	97	131	6	21,031	21,191	2,432	3,141
5250 Hardware stores	12	12	406	437	36	15,478	16,650	6,849	7,251
5260 Retail nurseries and garden stores	11	12	42	51	4	8,857	9,569	566	594
5270 Mobile home dealers	3	3	16	13	4	23,000	10,154	635	200
5310 Department stores	13	15	1,780	2,221	148	10,488	10,680	20,987	24,617
5390 Misc. general merchandise stores	-	9	-	336	37	-	11,655	-	4,042
5410 Grocery stores	63	64	3,747	3,096	48	15,943	17,176	64,388	56,722
5440 Candy, nut, and confectionery stores	3	-	21	-	-	6,476	-	198	-
5460 Retail bakeries	24	23	134	192	8	9,433	8,146	1,607	1,631
5490 Miscellaneous food stores	19	25	258	304	12	14,558	16,250	4,545	5,227
5510 New and used car dealers	25	23	1,209	1,176	51	28,020	30,003	40,279	43,450
5520 Used car dealers	26	22	149	154	7	21,315	25,143	4,145	4,153
5530 Auto and home supply stores	42	46	380	380	8	18,000	19,821	7,447	8,183
5540 Gasoline service stations	76	77	576	656	9	11,542	11,494	6,634	7,525
5560 Recreational vehicle dealers	-	7	-	15	2	-	11,467	-	421
5570 Motorcycle dealers	6	6	51	53	9	17,961	21,509	1,219	1,364
5610 Men's & boys' clothing stores	12	13	100	97	7	10,120	11,258	954	1,118
5620 Women's clothing stores	51	41	413	382	9	9,259	8,681	4,167	3,029
5630 Women's accessory & specialty stores	9	7	56	79	11	8,429	6,177	499	501
5640 Children's and infants' wear stores	4	5	12	31	6	7,667	9,161	200	282
5650 Family clothing stores	20	24	218	233	10	9,596	10,129	2,375	2,802
5660 Shoe stores	39	38	201	217	6	10,209	11,023	2,356	2,333
5690 Misc. apparel & accessory stores	18	17	132	121	7	8,091	11,140	1,353	1,578
5712 Furniture stores	39	39	174	200	5	17,954	20,960	3,713	4,681
5713 Floor covering stores	17	21	96	100	5	21,833	24,480	2,400	2,768
5714 Drapery and upholstery stores	3	3	9	10	3	18,222	20,400	195	211
5719 Misc. homefurnishings stores	35	39	215	237	6	12,986	13,181	3,405	3,744
5720 Household appliance stores	9	9	42	31	3	25,905	17,419	889	676
5731 Radio, TV, & electronic stores	23	19	153	200	11	20,183	23,220	3,485	4,434
5734 Computer and software stores	19	25	90	121	5	19,867	31,471	2,022	3,082

Continued on next page.

BOULDER - LONGMONT, CO PMSA - [continued]

Wholesale and Retail Trade USA	Establishments		Employment		Emp / Est	Pay / Employee		Annual Payroll ($ 000)	
	1994	1995	1994	1995	1995	1994	1995	1994	1995
5735 Record & prerecorded tape stores	14	18	173	227	13	11,029	10,273	2,012	2,241
5736 Musical instrument stores	9	10	38	43	4	12,632	13,953	618	659
5812 Eating places	430	386	9,631	9,568	25	7,606	8,520	89,644	87,159
5813 Drinking places	34	31	355	410	13	7,786	8,312	3,201	3,685
5910 Drug stores and proprietary stores	20	21	291	293	14	15,780	17,297	4,724	5,149
5920 Liquor stores	54	54	304	340	6	12,000	12,835	4,122	4,549
5930 Used merchandise stores	36	39	168	180	5	9,619	10,467	1,890	1,941
5941 Sporting goods and bicycle shops	58	62	497	580	9	12,040	12,469	6,767	6,879
5942 Book stores	20	20	232	242	12	9,586	9,851	2,453	2,571
5943 Stationery stores	8	6	219	80	13	28,584	13,700	3,810	1,219
5944 Jewelry stores	34	32	177	177	6	12,068	12,429	2,248	2,483
5945 Hobby, toy, and game shops	16	15	159	178	12	9,107	8,764	1,694	1,792
5947 Gift, novelty, and souvenir shops	47	44	221	242	6	6,914	7,818	1,740	2,001
5961 Catalog and mail-order houses	26	28	431	581	21	18,914	22,334	10,038	15,242
5984 Liquefied petroleum gas dealers	5	5	23	22	4	19,652	22,000	451	438
5992 Florists	29	29	210	207	7	9,257	10,628	2,289	2,508
5994 News dealers and newsstands	-	3	-	20	7	-	10,800	-	232
5995 Optical goods stores	25	27	98	96	4	11,918	14,042	1,454	1,446
5999 Miscellaneous retail stores, nec	96	93	548	565	6	12,825	14,442	7,588	8,197

Source: County Business Patterns 1994/95, CBP-94/95, U.S. Department of Commerce, Washington DC, November 1997. The employment column represents mid-March employment in the year. Pay per employee is calculated by dividing 1st Quarter payroll, annualized, by mid-March employment. The column headed 'Emp / Est' shows 'employees per establishment'. A dash (-) means that data are unavailable or cannot be calculated. nec means not elsewhere classified. *Notes:* 1. 1994 data incomplete; unavailable or withheld. 2. 1995 data incomplete; unavailable or withheld. 3. 1994 and 1995 data incomplete; unavailable or withheld.

BRAZORIA, TX PMSA

Wholesale and Retail Trade USA	Establishments		Employment		Emp / Est	Pay / Employee		Annual Payroll ($ 000)	
	1994	1995	1994	1995	1995	1994	1995	1994	1995
50- Wholesale trade	-	242	-	2,530	10	-	28,617	-	75,220
5013 Motor vehicle supplies and new parts	-	7	-	35	5	-	20,800	-	798
5015 Motor vehicle parts, used	-	6	-	5	1	-	23,200	-	139
5032 Brick, stone, & related materials	-	8	-	186	23	-	19,032	-	3,645
5045 Computers, peripherals, & software	-	7	-	19	3	-	18,737	-	388
5051 Metals service centers and offices	-	8	-	97	12	-	22,845	-	2,515
5063 Electrical apparatus and equipment	-	10	-	116	12	-	32,897	-	4,202
5065 Electronic parts and equipment	-	5	-	55	11	-	34,400	-	1,926
5072 Hardware	-	7	-	44	6	-	26,636	-	990
5074 Plumbing & hydronic heating supplies	-	4	-	13	3	-	23,077	-	286
5075 Warm air heating & air conditioning	-	4	-	21	5	-	19,238	-	403
5082 Construction and mining machinery	-	3	-	43	14	-	29,302	-	1,360
5084 Industrial machinery and equipment	-	26	-	480	18	-	31,333	-	15,282
5085 Industrial supplies	-	29	-	416	14	-	32,452	-	13,180
5087 Service establishment equipment	-	7	-	45	6	-	19,289	-	935
5088 Transportation equipment & supplies	-	4	-	14	4	-	34,571	-	587
5093 Scrap and waste materials	-	5	-	60	12	-	22,133	-	1,781
5110 Paper and paper products	-	5	-	44	9	-	23,364	-	1,014
5140 Groceries and related products	-	10	-	214	21	-	31,551	-	6,940
5160 Chemicals and allied products	-	19	-	170	9	-	28,259	-	4,650
5171 Petroleum bulk stations & terminals	-	11	-	139	13	-	33,986	-	5,251
5172 Petroleum products, nec	-	4	-	26	7	-	24,769	-	657
5199 Nondurable goods, nec	-	7	-	24	3	-	12,333	-	286
52- Retail trade	-	872	-	12,328	14	-	12,076	-	155,875
5210 Lumber and other building materials	-	22	-	287	13	-	19,359	-	6,772
5250 Hardware stores	-	4	-	13	3	-	12,308	-	153
5260 Retail nurseries and garden stores	-	9	-	60	7	-	6,733	-	365
5310 Department stores	-	10	-	1,886	189	-	13,039	-	23,611
5330 Variety stores	-	8	-	43	5	-	7,907	-	331
5390 Misc. general merchandise stores	-	7	-	181	26	-	9,768	-	1,684
5410 Grocery stores	-	121	-	2,694	22	-	9,142	-	26,029
5420 Meat and fish markets	-	3	-	4	1	-	12,000	-	49
5460 Retail bakeries	-	10	-	35	4	-	7,314	-	268
5490 Miscellaneous food stores	-	4	-	13	3	-	5,538	-	93
5510 New and used car dealers	-	15	-	900	60	-	29,004	-	28,236
5520 Used car dealers	-	13	-	33	3	-	20,364	-	725
5530 Auto and home supply stores	-	26	-	233	9	-	16,773	-	4,062
5540 Gasoline service stations	-	50	-	403	8	-	9,658	-	4,407
5550 Boat dealers	-	3	-	12	4	-	26,333	-	342
5610 Men's & boys' clothing stores	-	3	-	21	7	-	8,190	-	151
5620 Women's clothing stores	-	21	-	122	6	-	7,639	-	870

Continued on next page.

BRAZORIA, TX PMSA - [continued]

Wholesale and Retail Trade USA	Establishments		Employment		Emp / Est	Pay / Employee		Annual Payroll ($ 000)	
	1994	1995	1994	1995	1995	1994	1995	1994	1995
5630 Women's accessory & specialty stores	-	3	-	13	4	-	6,769	-	80
5650 Family clothing stores	-	17	-	249	15	-	9,269	-	2,234
5660 Shoe stores	-	14	-	70	5	-	11,771	-	788
5690 Misc. apparel & accessory stores	-	6	-	9	2	-	9,778	-	115
5712 Furniture stores	-	21	-	141	7	-	15,262	-	2,422
5719 Misc. homefurnishings stores	-	5	-	37	7	-	12,865	-	499
5720 Household appliance stores	-	6	-	29	5	-	19,724	-	565
5731 Radio, TV, & electronic stores	-	7	-	29	4	-	12,690	-	362
5735 Record & prerecorded tape stores	-	4	-	52	13	-	9,538	-	435
5812 Eating places	-	178	-	3,054	17	-	8,386	-	26,589
5813 Drinking places	-	17	-	59	3	-	7,797	-	371
5910 Drug stores and proprietary stores	-	24	-	260	11	-	17,277	-	4,788
5920 Liquor stores	-	7	-	26	4	-	10,769	-	314
5930 Used merchandise stores	-	19	-	62	3	-	15,355	-	1,005
5941 Sporting goods and bicycle shops	-	11	-	147	13	-	9,850	-	1,699
5942 Book stores	-	6	-	32	5	-	14,750	-	429
5944 Jewelry stores	-	13	-	70	5	-	13,143	-	917
5945 Hobby, toy, and game shops	-	5	-	30	6	-	10,533	-	398
5947 Gift, novelty, and souvenir shops	-	18	-	85	5	-	10,024	-	897
5960 Nonstore retailers	-	9	-	141	16	-	20,454	-	2,857
5980 Fuel dealers	-	9	-	59	7	-	19,525	-	1,107
5992 Florists	-	22	-	104	5	-	6,885	-	834
5995 Optical goods stores	-	9	-	64	7	-	13,750	-	900
5999 Miscellaneous retail stores, nec	-	17	-	44	3	-	10,727	-	611

Source: County Business Patterns 1994/95, CBP-94/95, U.S. Department of Commerce, Washington DC, November 1997. The employment column represents mid-March employment in the year. Pay per employee is calculated by dividing 1st Quarter payroll, annualized, by mid-March employment. The column headed 'Emp / Est' shows 'employees per establishment'. A dash (-) means that data are unavailable or cannot be calculated. nec means not elsewhere classified. *Notes:* 1. 1994 data incomplete; unavailable or withheld. 2. 1995 data incomplete; unavailable or withheld. 3. 1994 and 1995 data incomplete; unavailable or withheld.

BREMERTON, WA PMSA

Wholesale and Retail Trade USA	Establishments		Employment		Emp / Est	Pay / Employee		Annual Payroll ($ 000)	
	1994	1995	1994	1995	1995	1994	1995	1994	1995
50- Wholesale trade	-	182	-	1,261	7	-	26,830	-	35,188
5013 Motor vehicle supplies and new parts	-	7	-	64	9	-	19,813	-	1,316
5015 Motor vehicle parts, used	-	4	-	23	6	-	19,304	-	458
5021 Furniture	-	6	-	49	8	-	21,959	-	973
5023 Homefurnishings	-	8	-	30	4	-	24,800	-	756
5031 Lumber, plywood, and millwork	-	4	-	108	27	-	24,000	-	2,708
5039 Construction materials, nec	-	7	-	41	6	-	28,390	-	1,154
5044 Office equipment	-	7	-	31	4	-	26,710	-	791
5045 Computers, peripherals, & software	-	5	-	21	4	-	26,857	-	499
5047 Medical and hospital equipment	-	5	-	19	4	-	30,105	-	505
5060 Electrical goods	-	9	-	74	8	-	43,622	-	3,309
5070 Hardware, plumbing & heating equipment	-	6	-	53	9	-	25,434	-	1,424
5084 Industrial machinery and equipment	-	5	-	17	3	-	25,882	-	409
5085 Industrial supplies	-	7	-	22	3	-	35,818	-	844
5087 Service establishment equipment	-	3	-	8	3	-	9,000	-	60
5099 Durable goods, nec	-	4	-	23	6	-	17,043	-	472
5112 Stationery and office supplies	-	6	-	61	10	-	16,721	-	820
5131 Piece goods & notions	-	4	-	6	2	-	8,000	-	49
5136 Men's and boys' clothing	-	4	-	46	12	-	20,435	-	1,042
5149 Groceries and related products, nec	-	7	-	116	17	-	33,931	-	4,081
5181 Beer and ale	-	4	-	89	22	-	37,753	-	3,409
5191 Farm supplies	-	6	-	41	7	-	12,293	-	546
5193 Flowers & florists' supplies	-	3	-	28	9	-	22,714	-	1,485
5198 Paints, varnishes, and supplies	-	3	-	11	4	-	25,091	-	261
5199 Nondurable goods, nec	-	8	-	16	2	-	23,750	-	456
52- Retail trade	-	1,125	-	14,881	13	-	13,909	-	215,359
5210 Lumber and other building materials	-	15	-	453	30	-	19,779	-	9,899
5230 Paint, glass, and wallpaper stores	-	6	-	23	4	-	18,435	-	463
5250 Hardware stores	-	6	-	110	18	-	15,964	-	1,662
5260 Retail nurseries and garden stores	-	12	-	82	7	-	11,463	-	1,366
5270 Mobile home dealers	-	5	-	42	8	-	29,238	-	1,269
5310 Department stores	-	9	-	1,373	153	-	13,212	-	19,833
5330 Variety stores	-	6	-	33	6	-	11,152	-	412
5390 Misc. general merchandise stores	-	4	-	214	54	-	24,523	-	6,100
5410 Grocery stores	-	85	-	1,917	23	-	18,001	-	34,588
5420 Meat and fish markets	-	3	-	10	3	-	12,800	-	127

Continued on next page.

BREMERTON, WA PMSA - [continued]

Wholesale and Retail Trade USA	Establishments		Employment		Emp / Est	Pay / Employee		Annual Payroll ($ 000)	
	1994	1995	1994	1995	1995	1994	1995	1994	1995
5440 Candy, nut, and confectionery stores	-	4	-	18	5	-	7,778	-	151
5460 Retail bakeries	-	12	-	85	7	-	9,694	-	902
5490 Miscellaneous food stores	-	8	-	44	6	-	9,636	-	511
5510 New and used car dealers	-	16	-	924	58	-	29,372	-	25,400
5520 Used car dealers	-	11	-	77	7	-	25,610	-	1,926
5530 Auto and home supply stores	-	38	-	319	8	-	21,643	-	8,176
5540 Gasoline service stations	-	35	-	310	9	-	11,135	-	3,891
5550 Boat dealers	-	6	-	39	7	-	12,821	-	497
5560 Recreational vehicle dealers	-	7	-	211	30	-	29,820	-	7,255
5610 Men's & boys' clothing stores	-	6	-	34	6	-	14,706	-	456
5620 Women's clothing stores	-	28	-	157	6	-	7,032	-	1,035
5630 Women's accessory & specialty stores	-	6	-	21	4	-	9,524	-	194
5640 Children's and infants' wear stores	-	4	-	10	3	-	4,400	-	31
5650 Family clothing stores	-	12	-	191	16	-	9,654	-	1,863
5660 Shoe stores	-	20	-	87	4	-	10,897	-	958
5690 Misc. apparel & accessory stores	-	4	-	25	6	-	8,800	-	241
5712 Furniture stores	-	27	-	190	7	-	20,989	-	3,499
5719 Misc. homefurnishings stores	-	10	-	75	8	-	14,773	-	1,372
5720 Household appliance stores	-	8	-	79	10	-	16,709	-	1,492
5731 Radio, TV, & electronic stores	-	19	-	202	11	-	15,743	-	3,124
5734 Computer and software stores	-	11	-	39	4	-	18,564	-	616
5735 Record & prerecorded tape stores	-	8	-	59	7	-	14,305	-	709
5736 Musical instrument stores	-	7	-	28	4	-	10,429	-	350
5812 Eating places	-	265	-	5,054	19	-	8,062	-	42,118
5813 Drinking places	-	45	-	271	6	-	7,661	-	1,987
5910 Drug stores and proprietary stores	-	28	-	350	13	-	17,749	-	6,256
5930 Used merchandise stores	-	25	-	102	4	-	10,941	-	1,152
5941 Sporting goods and bicycle shops	-	25	-	138	6	-	12,899	-	2,091
5942 Book stores	-	10	-	55	6	-	9,309	-	526
5944 Jewelry stores	-	17	-	76	4	-	15,895	-	1,171
5945 Hobby, toy, and game shops	-	8	-	114	14	-	9,860	-	1,311
5947 Gift, novelty, and souvenir shops	-	29	-	163	6	-	8,859	-	1,467
5949 Sewing, needlework, and piece goods	-	10	-	83	8	-	7,663	-	703
5963 Direct selling establishments	-	13	-	103	8	-	16,350	-	1,692
5980 Fuel dealers	-	5	-	61	12	-	30,295	-	1,294
5992 Florists	-	18	-	98	5	-	10,490	-	1,050
5995 Optical goods stores	-	13	-	58	4	-	19,655	-	1,184
5999 Miscellaneous retail stores, nec	-	46	-	195	4	-	11,856	-	2,363

Source: County Business Patterns 1994/95, CBP-94/95, U.S. Department of Commerce, Washington DC, November 1997. The employment column represents mid-March employment in the year. Pay per employee is calculated by dividing 1st Quarter payroll, annualized, by mid-March employment. The column headed 'Emp / Est' shows 'employees per establishment'. A dash (-) means that data are unavailable or cannot be calculated. nec means not elsewhere classified. *Notes:* 1. 1994 data incomplete; unavailable or withheld. 2. 1995 data incomplete; unavailable or withheld. 3. 1994 and 1995 data incomplete; unavailable or withheld.

BROWNSVILLE – HARLINGEN – SAN BENITO, TX MSA

Wholesale and Retail Trade USA	Establishments		Employment		Emp / Est	Pay / Employee		Annual Payroll ($ 000)	
	1994	1995	1994	1995	1995	1994	1995	1994	1995
50 - Wholesale trade	-	453	-	4,305	10	-	18,959	-	83,263
5012 Automobiles and other vehicles	-	3	-	7	2	-	16,000	-	55
5013 Motor vehicle supplies and new parts	-	26	-	212	8	-	17,377	-	3,789
5014 Tires and tubes	-	4	-	34	9	-	14,941	-	492
5015 Motor vehicle parts, used	-	7	-	11	2	-	9,091	-	104
5023 Homefurnishings	-	6	-	38	6	-	15,053	-	550
5031 Lumber, plywood, and millwork	-	6	-	53	9	-	26,264	-	1,389
5032 Brick, stone, & related materials	-	6	-	16	3	-	31,000	-	513
5044 Office equipment	-	11	-	97	9	-	20,742	-	1,928
5045 Computers, peripherals, & software	-	7	-	22	3	-	14,545	-	247
5050 Metals and minerals, except petroleum	-	8	-	33	4	-	26,303	-	1,097
5063 Electrical apparatus and equipment	-	15	-	144	10	-	21,833	-	2,800
5064 Electrical appliances, TV & radios	-	6	-	29	5	-	20,828	-	524
5065 Electronic parts and equipment	-	14	-	70	5	-	22,686	-	1,682
5072 Hardware	-	8	-	85	11	-	19,200	-	1,747
5074 Plumbing & hydronic heating supplies	-	6	-	49	8	-	14,612	-	703
5075 Warm air heating & air conditioning	-	8	-	41	5	-	18,049	-	820
5083 Farm and garden machinery	-	5	-	76	15	-	25,737	-	1,927
5084 Industrial machinery and equipment	-	39	-	118	3	-	19,966	-	2,572
5085 Industrial supplies	-	19	-	116	6	-	20,793	-	2,381
5087 Service establishment equipment	-	5	-	37	7	-	11,351	-	403
5088 Transportation equipment & supplies	-	3	-	29	10	-	19,172	-	553

Continued on next page.

BROWNSVILLE – HARLINGEN – SAN BENITO, TX MSA - [continued]

Wholesale and Retail Trade USA	Establishments		Employment		Emp / Est	Pay / Employee		Annual Payroll ($ 000)	
	1994	1995	1994	1995	1995	1994	1995	1994	1995
5091 Sporting & recreational goods	-	3	-	28	9	-	17,857	-	504
5093 Scrap and waste materials	-	17	-	476	28	-	11,513	-	6,348
5099 Durable goods, nec	-	10	-	30	3	-	19,467	-	454
5112 Stationery and office supplies	-	6	-	76	13	-	23,579	-	1,684
5131 Piece goods & notions	-	3	-	36	12	-	24,778	-	857
5137 Women's and children's clothing	-	8	-	44	6	-	11,182	-	603
5141 Groceries, general line	-	8	-	207	26	-	11,575	-	2,658
5142 Packaged frozen food	-	9	-	80	9	-	24,050	-	1,984
5146 Fish and seafoods	-	13	-	82	6	-	22,341	-	1,594
5147 Meats and meat products	-	4	-	48	12	-	16,583	-	626
5148 Fresh fruits and vegetables	-	5	-	97	19	-	12,165	-	1,238
5149 Groceries and related products, nec	-	11	-	285	26	-	22,947	-	6,399
5153 Grain and field beans	-	5	-	51	10	-	17,176	-	942
5162 Plastics materials & basic shapes	-	6	-	17	3	-	29,176	-	734
5169 Chemicals & allied products, nec	-	7	-	49	7	-	29,878	-	1,499
5171 Petroleum bulk stations & terminals	-	9	-	88	10	-	26,682	-	2,341
5172 Petroleum products, nec	-	6	-	99	17	-	23,919	-	2,487
5181 Beer and ale	-	3	-	137	46	-	25,080	-	3,533
5182 Wine and distilled beverages	-	3	-	15	5	-	11,200	-	182
5191 Farm supplies	-	8	-	46	6	-	25,913	-	1,015
5193 Flowers & florists' supplies	-	8	-	60	8	-	12,867	-	727
5199 Nondurable goods, nec	-	16	-	98	6	-	16,041	-	1,602
52 – Retail trade	-	1,610	-	20,513	13	-	11,098	-	228,164
5210 Lumber and other building materials	-	23	-	491	21	-	14,876	-	7,475
5230 Paint, glass, and wallpaper stores	-	7	-	57	8	-	15,789	-	913
5250 Hardware stores	-	10	-	112	11	-	11,714	-	1,346
5260 Retail nurseries and garden stores	-	9	-	45	5	-	11,822	-	475
5270 Mobile home dealers	-	6	-	26	4	-	13,231	-	352
5310 Department stores	-	18	-	2,621	146	-	12,752	-	32,184
5330 Variety stores	-	10	-	124	12	-	7,871	-	918
5390 Misc. general merchandise stores	-	28	-	431	15	-	12,093	-	4,771
5410 Grocery stores	-	153	-	2,931	19	-	11,461	-	33,852
5420 Meat and fish markets	-	5	-	16	3	-	13,000	-	270
5460 Retail bakeries	-	22	-	77	4	-	7,844	-	602
5490 Miscellaneous food stores	-	10	-	31	3	-	12,258	-	413
5510 New and used car dealers	-	16	-	669	42	-	24,562	-	17,787
5520 Used car dealers	-	29	-	102	4	-	12,667	-	1,433
5530 Auto and home supply stores	-	51	-	424	8	-	14,755	-	6,582
5540 Gasoline service stations	-	90	-	511	6	-	11,609	-	6,183
5550 Boat dealers	-	8	-	42	5	-	15,048	-	669
5560 Recreational vehicle dealers	-	3	-	38	13	-	17,368	-	601
5570 Motorcycle dealers	-	3	-	11	4	-	11,273	-	135
5610 Men's & boys' clothing stores	-	17	-	71	4	-	8,113	-	539
5620 Women's clothing stores	-	72	-	1,003	14	-	8,435	-	8,881
5630 Women's accessory & specialty stores	-	15	-	40	3	-	9,000	-	347
5640 Children's and infants' wear stores	-	5	-	17	3	-	7,059	-	117
5650 Family clothing stores	-	32	-	446	14	-	9,749	-	4,169
5660 Shoe stores	-	57	-	282	5	-	11,177	-	3,013
5690 Misc. apparel & accessory stores	-	17	-	104	6	-	5,885	-	705
5712 Furniture stores	-	33	-	324	10	-	16,173	-	4,859
5713 Floor covering stores	-	7	-	48	7	-	10,333	-	463
5714 Drapery and upholstery stores	-	4	-	8	2	-	7,000	-	52
5719 Misc. homefurnishings stores	-	8	-	43	5	-	15,070	-	671
5720 Household appliance stores	-	6	-	60	10	-	17,400	-	1,099
5731 Radio, TV, & electronic stores	-	21	-	143	7	-	15,552	-	2,101
5734 Computer and software stores	-	3	-	7	2	-	17,714	-	122
5812 Eating places	-	312	-	5,991	19	-	7,782	-	46,203
5813 Drinking places	-	43	-	621	14	-	6,158	-	3,079
5910 Drug stores and proprietary stores	-	38	-	326	9	-	15,215	-	5,049
5920 Liquor stores	-	15	-	65	4	-	14,646	-	870
5930 Used merchandise stores	-	47	-	247	5	-	13,231	-	3,125
5941 Sporting goods and bicycle shops	-	15	-	68	5	-	12,118	-	763
5942 Book stores	-	7	-	47	7	-	9,277	-	453
5944 Jewelry stores	-	31	-	171	6	-	12,702	-	2,161
5945 Hobby, toy, and game shops	-	13	-	109	8	-	7,963	-	1,011
5947 Gift, novelty, and souvenir shops	-	40	-	177	4	-	8,271	-	1,323
5949 Sewing, needlework, and piece goods	-	25	-	82	3	-	9,512	-	742
5963 Direct selling establishments	-	8	-	57	7	-	16,281	-	907
5983 Fuel oil dealers	-	3	-	16	5	-	10,250	-	165
5984 Liquefied petroleum gas dealers	-	6	-	43	7	-	19,256	-	777
5992 Florists	-	19	-	73	4	-	7,562	-	525

Continued on next page.

BROWNSVILLE – HARLINGEN – SAN BENITO, TX MSA - [continued]

Wholesale and Retail Trade USA	Establishments		Employment		Emp / Est	Pay / Employee		Annual Payroll ($ 000)	
	1994	1995	1994	1995	1995	1994	1995	1994	1995
5995 Optical goods stores	-	18	-	108	6	-	13,926	-	1,480
5999 Miscellaneous retail stores, nec	-	31	-	102	3	-	11,843	-	958

Source: County Business Patterns 1994/95, CBP-94/95, U.S. Department of Commerce, Washington DC, November 1997. The employment column represents mid-March employment in the year. Pay per employee is calculated by dividing 1st Quarter payroll, annualized, by mid-March employment. The column headed 'Emp / Est' shows 'employees per establishment'. A dash (-) means that data are unavailable or cannot be calculated. nec means not elsewhere classified. *Notes:* 1. 1994 data incomplete; unavailable or withheld. 2. 1995 data incomplete; unavailable or withheld. 3. 1994 and 1995 data incomplete; unavailable or withheld.

BRYAN – COLLEGE STATION, TX MSA

Wholesale and Retail Trade USA	Establishments		Employment		Emp / Est	Pay / Employee		Annual Payroll ($ 000)	
	1994	1995	1994	1995	1995	1994	1995	1994	1995
50 – Wholesale trade	-	172	-	2,050	12	-	22,529	-	46,666
5013 Motor vehicle supplies and new parts	-	5	-	24	5	-	17,167	-	580
5030 Lumber and construction materials	-	5	-	57	11	-	21,684	-	1,091
5044 Office equipment	-	8	-	104	13	-	23,808	-	2,091
5045 Computers, peripherals, & software	-	15	-	111	7	-	20,937	-	2,518
5060 Electrical goods	-	7	-	79	11	-	29,671	-	2,444
5075 Warm air heating & air conditioning	-	3	-	15	5	-	20,267	-	334
5084 Industrial machinery and equipment	-	11	-	78	7	-	27,436	-	2,375
5085 Industrial supplies	-	6	-	58	10	-	23,724	-	1,386
5091 Sporting & recreational goods	-	3	-	8	3	-	22,000	-	185
5099 Durable goods, nec	-	4	-	11	3	-	9,818	-	109
5110 Paper and paper products	-	6	-	38	6	-	18,526	-	746
5147 Meats and meat products	-	3	-	158	53	-	16,177	-	2,505
5149 Groceries and related products, nec	-	5	-	150	30	-	20,373	-	4,080
5150 Farm-product raw materials	-	6	-	64	11	-	23,375	-	1,448
5169 Chemicals & allied products, nec	-	6	-	103	17	-	36,427	-	2,984
5171 Petroleum bulk stations & terminals	-	7	-	81	12	-	28,790	-	2,260
5181 Beer and ale	-	4	-	102	26	-	37,490	-	3,020
5191 Farm supplies	-	7	-	114	16	-	17,579	-	2,606
5199 Nondurable goods, nec	-	5	-	22	4	-	9,636	-	284
52 – Retail trade	-	760	-	11,982	16	-	10,777	-	135,218
5210 Lumber and other building materials	-	8	-	204	26	-	18,471	-	3,469
5230 Paint, glass, and wallpaper stores	-	7	-	57	8	-	18,947	-	1,193
5250 Hardware stores	-	3	-	13	4	-	15,692	-	226
5260 Retail nurseries and garden stores	-	3	-	36	12	-	8,778	-	214
5270 Mobile home dealers	-	5	-	46	9	-	14,696	-	807
5310 Department stores	-	8	-	1,466	183	-	12,431	-	18,289
5410 Grocery stores	-	66	-	1,498	23	-	10,454	-	15,822
5460 Retail bakeries	-	4	-	46	12	-	8,174	-	434
5490 Miscellaneous food stores	-	6	-	17	3	-	11,529	-	248
5510 New and used car dealers	-	13	-	507	39	-	29,893	-	16,259
5520 Used car dealers	-	8	-	30	4	-	20,800	-	829
5530 Auto and home supply stores	-	17	-	179	11	-	15,508	-	2,809
5540 Gasoline service stations	-	47	-	257	5	-	13,323	-	3,930
5610 Men's & boys' clothing stores	-	8	-	66	8	-	8,000	-	529
5620 Women's clothing stores	-	23	-	223	10	-	6,673	-	1,359
5630 Women's accessory & specialty stores	-	5	-	51	10	-	5,020	-	250
5640 Children's and infants' wear stores	-	4	-	10	3	-	9,600	-	92
5650 Family clothing stores	-	12	-	192	16	-	8,917	-	1,763
5660 Shoe stores	-	18	-	99	6	-	10,828	-	1,100
5690 Misc. apparel & accessory stores	-	4	-	28	7	-	8,571	-	246
5712 Furniture stores	-	11	-	91	8	-	21,407	-	1,867
5713 Floor covering stores	-	7	-	25	4	-	32,000	-	849
5719 Misc. homefurnishings stores	-	8	-	57	7	-	16,211	-	993
5731 Radio, TV, & electronic stores	-	8	-	51	6	-	18,353	-	1,182
5735 Record & prerecorded tape stores	-	6	-	92	15	-	9,087	-	894
5736 Musical instrument stores	-	4	-	8	2	-	5,000	-	49
5812 Eating places	-	165	-	4,306	26	-	6,979	-	31,281
5813 Drinking places	-	18	-	339	19	-	6,277	-	2,627
5910 Drug stores and proprietary stores	-	13	-	120	9	-	14,433	-	1,883
5920 Liquor stores	-	9	-	59	7	-	8,610	-	515
5930 Used merchandise stores	-	24	-	124	5	-	12,516	-	1,538
5941 Sporting goods and bicycle shops	-	23	-	198	9	-	14,444	-	3,456
5942 Book stores	-	17	-	251	15	-	10,215	-	3,251
5943 Stationery stores	-	3	-	12	4	-	10,000	-	130
5944 Jewelry stores	-	16	-	75	5	-	17,387	-	1,093
5945 Hobby, toy, and game shops	-	5	-	76	15	-	9,895	-	882
5947 Gift, novelty, and souvenir shops	-	17	-	79	5	-	7,342	-	620

Continued on next page.

BRYAN – COLLEGE STATION, TX MSA - [continued]

Wholesale and Retail Trade USA	Establishments		Employment		Emp / Est	Pay / Employee		Annual Payroll ($ 000)	
	1994	1995	1994	1995	1995	1994	1995	1994	1995
5949 Sewing, needlework, and piece goods	-	9	-	47	5	-	7,319	-	332
5961 Catalog and mail-order houses	-	6	-	31	5	-	20,903	-	701
5963 Direct selling establishments	-	6	-	24	4	-	20,500	-	550
5984 Liquefied petroleum gas dealers	-	3	-	18	6	-	20,444	-	328
5992 Florists	-	10	-	53	5	-	9,283	-	464
5995 Optical goods stores	-	9	-	43	5	-	13,674	-	583
5999 Miscellaneous retail stores, nec	-	19	-	130	7	-	8,646	-	1,250

Source: County Business Patterns 1994/95, CBP-94/95, U.S. Department of Commerce, Washington DC, November 1997. The employment column represents mid-March employment in the year. Pay per employee is calculated by dividing 1st Quarter payroll, annualized, by mid-March employment. The column headed 'Emp / Est' shows 'employees per establishment'. A dash (-) means that data are unavailable or cannot be calculated. nec means not elsewhere classified. *Notes:* 1. 1994 data incomplete; unavailable or withheld. 2. 1995 data incomplete; unavailable or withheld. 3. 1994 and 1995 data incomplete; unavailable or withheld.

BUFFALO – NIAGARA FALLS, NY MSA

Wholesale and Retail Trade USA	Establishments		Employment		Emp / Est	Pay / Employee		Annual Payroll ($ 000)	
	1994	1995	1994	1995	1995	1994	1995	1994	1995
50 - Wholesale trade	2,178	2,180	28,139	28,840	13	26,784	28,704	795,774	855,785
5012 Automobiles and other vehicles	32	37	755	838	23	20,339	22,067	17,988	19,742
5013 Motor vehicle supplies and new parts	160	155	1,579	1,523	10	20,998	22,616	35,457	35,271
5014 Tires and tubes	17	16	185	164	10	21,622	26,878	4,705	4,862
5015 Motor vehicle parts, used	37	41	306	371	9	18,379	21,930	6,168	8,046
5021 Furniture [3]	27	35	241	329	9	25,925	25,629	6,720	8,637
5023 Homefurnishings	34	33	265	284	9	26,294	28,394	7,434	8,344
5031 Lumber, plywood, and millwork	42	43	568	544	13	25,556	26,897	15,593	15,252
5032 Brick, stone, & related materials	15	14	117	128	9	32,821	32,781	5,954	6,041
5033 Roofing, siding, & insulation [2]	19	14	260	225	16	29,523	33,067	7,508	6,313
5039 Construction materials, nec	25	32	99	303	9	24,404	20,422	2,822	7,187
5043 Photographic equipment & supplies	7	6	35	25	4	25,257	33,120	916	723
5044 Office equipment	42	40	628	616	15	29,866	34,565	19,450	19,325
5045 Computers, peripherals, & software	51	55	1,130	1,624	30	36,832	33,973	41,662	56,923
5046 Commercial equipment, nec	28	27	157	159	6	19,898	22,491	3,665	3,647
5047 Medical and hospital equipment	62	53	713	670	13	35,916	40,955	28,785	28,578
5048 Ophthalmic goods [2]	9	8	183	181	23	27,541	23,757	5,429	5,085
5049 Professional equipment, nec	17	15	244	247	16	49,852	42,089	8,445	7,706
5051 Metals service centers and offices	-	64	-	689	11	-	33,010	-	23,874
5052 Coal and other minerals and ores	-	4	-	9	2	-	57,778	-	554
5063 Electrical apparatus and equipment	95	80	1,022	866	11	29,483	33,843	30,556	28,455
5064 Electrical appliances, TV & radios	17	17	205	223	13	21,815	22,081	4,640	5,359
5065 Electronic parts and equipment	70	73	678	888	12	33,316	35,694	22,571	31,449
5072 Hardware	35	39	493	502	13	31,245	34,072	16,486	17,637
5074 Plumbing & hydronic heating supplies	58	59	540	587	10	28,096	29,492	16,730	17,855
5075 Warm air heating & air conditioning	25	26	164	171	7	28,829	32,374	5,777	7,005
5078 Refrigeration equipment and supplies [3]	6	6	38	40	7	27,368	29,600	1,101	1,200
5082 Construction and mining machinery	19	19	188	196	10	32,043	42,939	7,259	7,900
5083 Farm and garden machinery	18	16	155	115	7	21,755	21,878	3,753	2,567
5084 Industrial machinery and equipment	201	211	1,842	1,886	9	30,056	32,677	59,742	67,940
5085 Industrial supplies	100	100	1,036	1,062	11	30,633	32,942	34,105	37,476
5087 Service establishment equipment	37	43	352	366	9	26,057	25,213	9,184	9,771
5088 Transportation equipment & supplies	8	7	83	77	11	24,482	25,922	2,268	2,457
5091 Sporting & recreational goods	21	20	133	139	7	31,398	31,050	4,544	4,864
5092 Toys and hobby goods and supplies [3]	10	8	83	70	9	19,566	26,171	1,834	1,844
5093 Scrap and waste materials	63	65	666	742	11	19,886	24,658	16,187	20,265
5094 Jewelry & precious stones	29	26	185	185	7	24,454	25,816	4,879	4,875
5099 Durable goods, nec	33	30	206	241	8	16,757	19,104	3,860	4,622
5111 Printing and writing paper [3]	13	12	134	114	10	40,239	39,088	5,555	4,131
5112 Stationery and office supplies	53	48	894	773	16	25,664	27,772	20,122	17,778
5113 Industrial & personal service paper	26	26	676	612	24	29,527	34,484	20,724	21,058
5120 Drugs, proprietaries, and sundries	20	20	596	521	26	24,805	26,656	15,021	13,472
5131 Piece goods & notions	10	9	42	23	3	11,619	15,652	457	411
5136 Men's and boys' clothing [3]	14	15	164	209	14	22,927	13,033	4,005	2,603
5137 Women's and children's clothing [2]	-	5	-	29	6	-	13,379	-	605
5139 Footwear [3]	5	4	35	14	4	27,771	26,857	866	399
5141 Groceries, general line	27	26	1,159	999	38	27,517	32,064	32,798	34,327
5142 Packaged frozen food	22	18	222	216	12	25,135	28,000	6,142	6,381
5143 Dairy products, exc. dried or canned	12	13	45	120	9	22,400	29,167	969	3,681
5145 Confectionery	18	17	389	438	26	22,231	22,566	9,301	10,933
5146 Fish and seafoods	9	9	72	44	5	20,833	29,000	1,389	1,096
5147 Meats and meat products [3]	22	18	185	164	9	16,670	18,439	3,389	3,198
5148 Fresh fruits and vegetables	29	26	294	310	12	29,156	25,329	7,806	7,972

Continued on next page.

BUFFALO - NIAGARA FALLS, NY MSA - [continued]

Wholesale and Retail Trade USA	Establishments		Employment		Emp / Est	Pay / Employee		Annual Payroll ($ 000)	
	1994	1995	1994	1995	1995	1994	1995	1994	1995
5149 Groceries and related products, nec	56	56	863	846	15	23,305	24,232	21,538	21,373
5150 Farm-product raw materials [3]	9	9	132	125	14	24,152	24,160	3,083	3,109
5162 Plastics materials & basic shapes	15	20	88	150	8	32,455	29,493	3,596	4,923
5169 Chemicals & allied products, nec	42	41	436	513	13	28,872	31,064	15,680	17,918
5171 Petroleum bulk stations & terminals	16	11	362	278	25	27,392	32,777	9,226	9,390
5172 Petroleum products, nec [2]	15	13	91	90	7	23,824	26,978	2,477	2,887
5181 Beer and ale	8	9	566	571	63	25,739	27,489	15,843	16,684
5182 Wine and distilled beverages [3]	6	5	354	352	70	24,588	27,943	10,663	10,757
5191 Farm supplies	27	17	151	87	5	19,788	22,805	3,244	2,077
5192 Books, periodicals, & newspapers	20	20	617	643	32	25,945	23,894	13,764	14,671
5193 Flowers & florists' supplies [2]	12	12	99	102	9	19,273	19,725	2,368	2,539
5194 Tobacco and tobacco products	12	13	493	487	37	23,221	23,088	11,723	11,548
5198 Paints, varnishes, and supplies	14	11	157	130	12	28,994	31,938	4,212	3,905
5199 Nondurable goods, nec [3]	59	58	566	607	10	22,042	22,036	12,796	15,018
52 - Retail trade	7,467	7,361	102,914	101,272	14	11,175	11,554	1,241,638	1,241,620
5210 Lumber and other building materials	138	128	2,346	2,334	18	14,321	16,045	39,074	43,155
5250 Hardware stores	82	59	464	359	6	12,000	12,178	6,266	4,652
5260 Retail nurseries and garden stores	54	58	483	502	9	13,052	13,131	8,302	8,567
5310 Department stores	57	63	9,362	8,526	135	9,073	11,334	86,897	100,521
5330 Variety stores	56	49	589	522	11	9,168	8,613	5,491	4,744
5390 Misc. general merchandise stores	27	28	1,188	1,148	41	10,731	12,443	13,975	16,979
5410 Grocery stores	532	540	16,919	16,136	30	9,838	10,192	178,358	172,820
5420 Meat and fish markets	56	52	355	348	7	15,808	14,977	5,403	5,167
5430 Fruit and vegetable markets	11	12	51	63	5	8,000	8,762	618	740
5440 Candy, nut, and confectionery stores	35	38	195	170	4	6,503	6,871	1,310	1,210
5450 Dairy products stores	13	12	84	78	7	12,905	13,641	1,164	1,089
5460 Retail bakeries	125	111	1,068	1,051	9	9,120	8,441	9,915	8,860
5490 Miscellaneous food stores	46	40	186	202	5	9,269	9,663	1,982	2,094
5510 New and used car dealers	109	109	4,619	4,828	44	24,887	27,012	133,415	139,646
5520 Used car dealers	72	76	188	239	3	16,128	15,598	3,534	3,989
5530 Auto and home supply stores	132	131	931	1,071	8	17,856	18,999	19,579	21,834
5540 Gasoline service stations	395	369	2,442	2,519	7	11,590	11,976	29,139	30,183
5550 Boat dealers	19	20	150	180	9	16,987	16,200	3,463	3,588
5560 Recreational vehicle dealers	10	10	61	60	6	13,246	14,267	1,233	1,090
5570 Motorcycle dealers	14	13	75	96	7	17,867	16,208	1,864	2,068
5610 Men's & boys' clothing stores	78	84	713	734	9	10,496	11,488	8,079	8,284
5620 Women's clothing stores	211	185	2,356	2,019	11	7,384	6,996	19,270	15,004
5630 Women's accessory & specialty stores	36	40	198	254	6	10,020	9,134	2,156	2,552
5640 Children's and infants' wear stores	19	16	200	176	11	6,840	8,091	1,439	1,397
5650 Family clothing stores	95	95	1,348	1,206	13	8,849	10,129	12,144	12,496
5660 Shoe stores	244	215	1,187	977	5	11,060	11,554	13,059	11,065
5690 Misc. apparel & accessory stores	46	45	290	301	7	11,434	11,429	3,865	3,830
5712 Furniture stores	122	114	976	1,024	9	16,926	17,418	18,031	18,920
5713 Floor covering stores	83	85	340	402	5	17,176	19,572	6,635	8,469
5714 Drapery and upholstery stores [2]	10	9	34	20	2	12,941	10,400	429	239
5719 Misc. homefurnishings stores	83	73	714	556	8	8,751	11,022	6,624	6,217
5720 Household appliance stores	52	47	320	311	7	19,425	19,125	6,643	6,319
5731 Radio, TV, & electronic stores	64	67	581	839	13	15,422	15,375	8,764	13,053
5734 Computer and software stores	23	24	163	184	8	13,521	14,304	2,373	2,627
5735 Record & prerecorded tape stores	50	44	638	558	13	6,809	10,301	5,461	5,070
5736 Musical instrument stores	17	17	54	69	4	13,630	12,870	848	932
5812 Eating places	2,015	1,913	32,070	32,631	17	6,833	7,261	244,602	251,098
5813 Drinking places	495	431	2,218	1,984	5	6,404	6,774	14,489	13,458
5910 Drug stores and proprietary stores	254	243	3,787	4,330	18	12,617	13,373	52,473	60,446
5920 Liquor stores	129	126	777	594	5	9,508	10,175	8,281	6,954
5930 Used merchandise stores	58	55	294	224	4	9,946	10,161	3,301	2,373
5941 Sporting goods and bicycle shops	114	110	867	886	8	10,764	10,790	9,909	11,297
5942 Book stores	50	41	445	416	10	9,169	10,433	4,079	4,449
5943 Stationery stores	12	13	105	139	11	10,057	13,583	1,240	2,091
5944 Jewelry stores	130	131	683	652	5	12,293	14,166	8,561	8,788
5945 Hobby, toy, and game shops	61	58	458	526	9	10,227	9,703	5,678	6,440
5946 Camera & photographic supply stores	-	13	-	5	-	-	10,400	-	47
5947 Gift, novelty, and souvenir shops	134	130	810	763	6	6,909	7,644	6,705	6,641
5949 Sewing, needlework, and piece goods	29	29	220	209	7	6,327	7,483	1,535	1,644
5961 Catalog and mail-order houses	19	26	145	207	8	22,014	21,043	3,104	4,287
5962 Merchandising machine operators	35	37	427	452	12	13,920	14,425	5,866	6,785
5963 Direct selling establishments	89	85	1,015	1,000	12	15,121	14,824	17,063	15,037
5983 Fuel oil dealers	5	7	75	85	12	23,787	24,424	1,749	2,043
5984 Liquefied petroleum gas dealers	6	8	30	35	4	21,600	22,971	669	819
5989 Fuel dealers, nec [2]	-	3	-	4	1	-	17,000	-	266
5992 Florists	97	88	415	415	5	9,687	10,198	4,453	4,656

Continued on next page.

BUFFALO - NIAGARA FALLS, NY MSA - [continued]

Wholesale and Retail Trade USA	Establishments		Employment		Emp / Est	Pay / Employee		Annual Payroll ($ 000)	
	1994	1995	1994	1995	1995	1994	1995	1994	1995
5993 Tobacco stores and stands [3]	13	17	21	15	1	16,762	16,533	266	304
5994 News dealers and newsstands [3]	8	11	23	20	2	10,087	10,400	235	246
5995 Optical goods stores	114	113	589	541	5	17,508	19,490	10,710	11,339
5999 Miscellaneous retail stores, nec	170	172	882	998	6	11,696	12,200	13,514	15,520

Source: County Business Patterns 1994/95, CBP-94/95, U.S. Department of Commerce, Washington DC, November 1997. The employment column represents mid-March employment in the year. Pay per employee is calculated by dividing 1st Quarter payroll, annualized, by mid-March employment. The column headed 'Emp / Est' shows 'employees per establishment'. A dash (-) means that data are unavailable or cannot be calculated. nec means not elsewhere classified. *Notes:* 1. 1994 data incomplete; unavailable or withheld. 2. 1995 data incomplete; unavailable or withheld. 3. 1994 and 1995 data incomplete; unavailable or withheld.

CANTON - MASSILLON, OH MSA

Wholesale and Retail Trade USA	Establishments		Employment		Emp / Est	Pay / Employee		Annual Payroll ($ 000)	
	1994	1995	1994	1995	1995	1994	1995	1994	1995
50- Wholesale trade	627	643	9,065	9,905	15	25,082	27,777	243,640	291,198
5012 Automobiles and other vehicles [3]	17	14	198	229	16	30,242	28,629	6,462	7,169
5013 Motor vehicle supplies and new parts	49	46	375	351	8	18,955	19,009	7,494	7,057
5014 Tires and tubes [2]	10	8	152	163	20	30,263	30,552	4,285	4,735
5015 Motor vehicle parts, used	13	13	47	54	4	18,468	18,815	1,096	1,316
5021 Furniture	8	9	29	42	5	29,931	19,238	1,022	840
5023 Homefurnishings [3]	8	8	90	78	10	24,044	28,000	2,406	2,572
5031 Lumber, plywood, and millwork	14	10	279	186	19	20,014	21,183	7,449	4,796
5032 Brick, stone, & related materials [3]	11	7	96	51	7	32,917	48,314	3,275	1,714
5033 Roofing, siding, & insulation [3]	9	8	75	49	6	25,173	26,449	1,571	1,416
5039 Construction materials, nec [3]	4	15	42	207	14	14,667	21,797	926	5,267
5044 Office equipment [3]	18	19	840	910	48	34,571	37,130	29,295	35,952
5045 Computers, peripherals, & software [3]	14	13	194	170	13	23,402	23,200	4,625	4,995
5046 Commercial equipment, nec [3]	4	6	32	37	6	12,625	14,811	522	605
5047 Medical and hospital equipment	8	10	34	30	3	18,353	24,000	696	619
5050 Metals and minerals, except petroleum [3]	22	26	170	516	20	25,012	40,039	5,603	22,774
5063 Electrical apparatus and equipment [3]	23	21	207	231	11	26,763	33,247	5,368	7,022
5065 Electronic parts and equipment [1]	9	-	146	-	-	26,301	-	4,040	-
5072 Hardware [2]	-	11	-	182	17	-	18,593	-	3,703
5074 Plumbing & hydronic heating supplies [1]	13	-	164	-	-	21,268	-	4,051	-
5082 Construction and mining machinery [2]	-	9	-	107	12	-	32,935	-	3,568
5083 Farm and garden machinery	-	10	-	178	18	-	25,191	-	4,823
5084 Industrial machinery and equipment [2]	-	53	-	493	9	-	30,385	-	16,469
5085 Industrial supplies [2]	-	24	-	203	8	-	27,744	-	5,970
5087 Service establishment equipment [2]	-	8	-	61	8	-	29,049	-	1,523
5091 Sporting & recreational goods	-	15	-	252	17	-	23,635	-	6,296
5093 Scrap and waste materials	-	23	-	486	21	-	25,169	-	13,004
5112 Stationery and office supplies [2]	-	10	-	294	29	-	37,714	-	9,996
5113 Industrial & personal service paper [2]	-	12	-	295	25	-	27,742	-	8,596
5120 Drugs, proprietaries, and sundries [2]	-	8	-	207	26	-	25,990	-	5,114
5141 Groceries, general line [2]	-	7	-	503	72	-	29,901	-	19,509
5147 Meats and meat products [2]	-	7	-	496	71	-	25,282	-	10,844
5148 Fresh fruits and vegetables [2]	-	6	-	55	9	-	29,673	-	1,916
5149 Groceries and related products, nec [2]	-	15	-	363	24	-	24,342	-	7,617
5162 Plastics materials & basic shapes	-	10	-	96	10	-	41,333	-	4,124
5169 Chemicals & allied products, nec	-	16	-	192	12	-	25,500	-	5,801
5171 Petroleum bulk stations & terminals	-	9	-	214	24	-	24,224	-	4,826
5172 Petroleum products, nec [2]	-	7	-	16	2	-	29,750	-	594
5180 Beer, wine, and distilled beverages [2]	-	6	-	230	38	-	27,757	-	7,351
5191 Farm supplies	-	14	-	61	4	-	11,607	-	779
5192 Books, periodicals, & newspapers [2]	-	4	-	76	19	-	18,789	-	1,133
5193 Flowers & florists' supplies [2]	-	5	-	246	49	-	16,195	-	4,986
5194 Tobacco and tobacco products [2]	-	4	-	99	25	-	24,162	-	2,630
5198 Paints, varnishes, and supplies [2]	-	6	-	58	10	-	24,138	-	1,510
5199 Nondurable goods, nec	-	23	-	153	7	-	19,007	-	3,605
52- Retail trade	2,430	2,450	34,671	35,650	15	10,514	11,424	404,274	429,857
5210 Lumber and other building materials	43	48	740	828	17	13,703	18,599	13,180	16,259
5230 Paint, glass, and wallpaper stores	22	24	85	114	5	13,365	15,193	1,301	1,916
5250 Hardware stores	27	17	332	252	15	10,434	13,286	4,304	3,901
5260 Retail nurseries and garden stores [3]	18	21	111	149	7	11,532	11,624	2,093	2,443
5270 Mobile home dealers [3]	4	4	42	46	12	26,000	28,000	1,127	1,206
5310 Department stores	16	17	2,374	2,175	128	10,704	12,999	27,811	30,238
5330 Variety stores	33	28	301	312	11	8,638	8,577	2,990	2,806
5390 Misc. general merchandise stores [2]	13	11	390	359	33	11,856	13,738	4,583	4,865
5410 Grocery stores [3]	181	172	4,511	4,284	25	11,710	12,991	55,794	55,914
5420 Meat and fish markets [3]	15	15	91	85	6	10,725	10,965	1,011	1,016

Continued on next page.

CANTON – MASSILLON, OH MSA - [continued]

Wholesale and Retail Trade USA	Establishments		Employment		Emp / Est	Pay / Employee		Annual Payroll ($ 000)	
	1994	1995	1994	1995	1995	1994	1995	1994	1995
5440 Candy, nut, and confectionery stores[3]	10	12	124	116	10	7,419	8,517	1,120	1,211
5450 Dairy products stores[1]	5	-	22	-	-	5,091	-	141	-
5460 Retail bakeries	30	31	199	192	6	7,296	7,875	1,631	1,556
5490 Miscellaneous food stores[3]	12	12	99	80	7	7,919	8,900	754	728
5510 New and used car dealers	43	44	1,666	1,643	37	22,341	25,057	43,774	46,816
5520 Used car dealers	32	35	122	117	3	14,820	16,752	2,049	2,382
5530 Auto and home supply stores	70	70	444	574	8	16,396	18,390	9,608	10,340
5540 Gasoline service stations	170	164	1,191	1,102	7	9,014	10,457	11,286	11,920
5550 Boat dealers	8	9	41	42	5	11,805	14,000	685	741
5560 Recreational vehicle dealers[3]	5	4	64	62	16	19,688	21,548	1,538	1,506
5570 Motorcycle dealers[3]	6	6	57	67	11	19,088	25,552	1,506	1,810
5610 Men's & boys' clothing stores[3]	18	23	162	172	7	8,716	8,047	1,424	1,658
5620 Women's clothing stores	64	58	709	607	10	7,289	6,959	5,474	4,236
5630 Women's accessory & specialty stores[3]	14	15	94	96	6	6,809	7,250	706	773
5640 Children's and infants' wear stores[2]	7	5	65	58	12	6,892	9,103	516	523
5650 Family clothing stores[3]	23	23	400	463	20	8,470	9,330	4,053	4,617
5660 Shoe stores	60	57	319	252	4	10,245	11,413	3,252	3,520
5690 Misc. apparel & accessory stores[3]	12	16	42	42	3	7,905	7,524	353	448
5712 Furniture stores	41	44	258	273	6	17,643	15,692	4,460	4,640
5713 Floor covering stores	32	29	170	167	6	19,647	23,449	3,864	4,338
5714 Drapery and upholstery stores[3]	3	3	20	22	7	14,400	14,545	315	302
5719 Misc. homefurnishings stores[3]	29	32	129	126	4	9,426	11,143	1,289	1,541
5720 Household appliance stores	18	20	89	171	9	17,079	11,345	1,679	2,145
5731 Radio, TV, & electronic stores[3]	26	27	193	361	13	19,378	16,166	3,126	5,461
5734 Computer and software stores	6	9	51	92	10	25,020	24,478	1,325	2,484
5735 Record & prerecorded tape stores[3]	9	10	97	123	12	12,041	11,057	1,356	1,459
5736 Musical instrument stores[3]	6	8	29	31	4	12,552	13,806	397	444
5812 Eating places	608	570	11,708	11,984	21	6,673	6,826	85,771	86,953
5813 Drinking places	120	112	501	543	5	6,539	6,858	3,724	3,744
5910 Drug stores and proprietary stores	78	84	1,197	1,453	17	12,030	13,335	16,417	19,979
5920 Liquor stores[3]	31	35	123	133	4	11,642	10,977	1,518	1,560
5930 Used merchandise stores[3]	15	16	85	87	5	11,059	11,172	906	954
5941 Sporting goods and bicycle shops[3]	46	48	242	274	6	10,149	10,248	3,024	3,418
5942 Book stores	20	16	221	297	19	6,606	6,263	1,616	1,986
5943 Stationery stores[2]	5	4	30	31	8	10,667	10,581	319	322
5944 Jewelry stores[3]	39	40	244	250	6	25,607	25,712	4,601	5,011
5945 Hobby, toy, and game shops[3]	22	22	194	214	10	9,196	8,654	2,103	2,186
5947 Gift, novelty, and souvenir shops[3]	37	39	300	386	10	6,000	4,912	2,127	2,360
5949 Sewing, needlework, and piece goods[3]	13	12	104	100	8	5,346	7,040	665	653
5962 Merchandising machine operators[3]	12	14	499	526	38	10,749	12,266	6,001	6,681
5983 Fuel oil dealers[3]	5	5	24	23	5	15,833	16,174	313	406
5984 Liquefied petroleum gas dealers[3]	3	3	21	22	7	22,476	22,182	557	582
5992 Florists	51	48	232	248	5	8,276	8,532	2,197	2,307
5995 Optical goods stores[3]	18	19	108	103	5	16,519	17,709	1,948	1,862
5999 Miscellaneous retail stores, nec[3]	71	77	356	415	5	10,921	12,482	4,735	5,418

Source: County Business Patterns 1994/95, CBP-94/95, U.S. Department of Commerce, Washington DC, November 1997. The employment column represents mid-March employment in the year. Pay per employee is calculated by dividing 1st Quarter payroll, annualized, by mid-March employment. The column headed 'Emp / Est' shows 'employees per establishment'. A dash (-) means that data are unavailable or cannot be calculated. nec means not elsewhere classified. *Notes:* 1. 1994 data incomplete; unavailable or withheld. 2. 1995 data incomplete; unavailable or withheld. 3. 1994 and 1995 data incomplete; unavailable or withheld.

CASPER, WY MSA

Wholesale and Retail Trade USA	Establishments		Employment		Emp / Est	Pay / Employee		Annual Payroll ($ 000)	
	1994	1995	1994	1995	1995	1994	1995	1994	1995
50 – Wholesale trade	-	262	-	2,234	9	-	29,522	-	68,095
5013 Motor vehicle supplies and new parts	-	12	-	90	8	-	22,044	-	2,034
5033 Roofing, siding, & insulation	-	3	-	6	2	-	28,000	-	136
5039 Construction materials, nec	-	4	-	42	11	-	30,667	-	1,323
5040 Professional & commercial equipment	-	13	-	97	7	-	26,474	-	2,288
5051 Metals service centers and offices	-	12	-	104	9	-	22,038	-	2,715
5063 Electrical apparatus and equipment	-	12	-	89	7	-	28,135	-	2,371
5065 Electronic parts and equipment	-	4	-	12	3	-	14,000	-	200
5075 Warm air heating & air conditioning	-	3	-	15	5	-	22,667	-	409
5082 Construction and mining machinery	-	12	-	283	24	-	38,431	-	11,408
5083 Farm and garden machinery	-	3	-	34	11	-	25,176	-	1,072
5084 Industrial machinery and equipment	-	63	-	407	6	-	42,486	-	16,757
5085 Industrial supplies	-	10	-	134	13	-	26,776	-	3,774
5087 Service establishment equipment	-	3	-	12	4	-	19,667	-	245
5093 Scrap and waste materials	-	4	-	14	4	-	12,000	-	231

Continued on next page.

CASPER, WY MSA - [continued]

Wholesale and Retail Trade USA	Establishments		Employment		Emp / Est	Pay / Employee		Annual Payroll ($ 000)	
	1994	1995	1994	1995	1995	1994	1995	1994	1995
5120 Drugs, proprietaries, and sundries	-	3	-	25	8	-	15,200	-	391
5140 Groceries and related products	-	9	-	85	9	-	27,247	-	2,442
5169 Chemicals & allied products, nec	-	14	-	90	6	-	29,511	-	2,908
5171 Petroleum bulk stations & terminals	-	9	-	85	9	-	26,353	-	2,581
5172 Petroleum products, nec	-	7	-	60	9	-	33,667	-	2,080
5180 Beer, wine, and distilled beverages	-	8	-	69	9	-	30,435	-	2,414
5190 Misc., nondurable goods	-	12	-	88	7	-	14,045	-	1,322
52 - Retail trade	-	543	-	6,159	11	-	12,253	-	79,926
5210 Lumber and other building materials	-	8	-	117	15	-	19,932	-	2,417
5230 Paint, glass, and wallpaper stores	-	6	-	28	5	-	16,714	-	483
5310 Department stores	-	6	-	737	123	-	11,533	-	8,397
5390 Misc. general merchandise stores	-	5	-	174	35	-	11,149	-	1,802
5410 Grocery stores	-	22	-	552	25	-	16,978	-	9,818
5460 Retail bakeries	-	5	-	41	8	-	8,390	-	382
5490 Miscellaneous food stores	-	3	-	11	4	-	8,000	-	55
5510 New and used car dealers	-	11	-	407	37	-	24,619	-	11,808
5520 Used car dealers	-	6	-	16	3	-	23,500	-	389
5530 Auto and home supply stores	-	15	-	134	9	-	18,179	-	2,532
5540 Gasoline service stations	-	35	-	269	8	-	11,063	-	2,994
5550 Boat dealers	-	4	-	16	4	-	11,500	-	184
5560 Recreational vehicle dealers	-	4	-	42	11	-	19,619	-	899
5570 Motorcycle dealers	-	3	-	25	8	-	8,960	-	332
5610 Men's & boys' clothing stores	-	3	-	29	10	-	21,241	-	419
5620 Women's clothing stores	-	11	-	49	4	-	7,510	-	368
5630 Women's accessory & specialty stores	-	8	-	34	4	-	5,176	-	193
5650 Family clothing stores	-	9	-	65	7	-	12,369	-	737
5660 Shoe stores	-	9	-	39	4	-	13,436	-	534
5690 Misc. apparel & accessory stores	-	3	-	29	10	-	14,345	-	414
5712 Furniture stores	-	7	-	59	8	-	18,847	-	1,183
5720 Household appliance stores	-	4	-	17	4	-	12,235	-	227
5731 Radio, TV, & electronic stores	-	8	-	30	4	-	16,667	-	523
5734 Computer and software stores	-	4	-	15	4	-	14,133	-	279
5812 Eating places	-	101	-	1,880	19	-	7,443	-	14,434
5813 Drinking places	-	15	-	99	7	-	7,556	-	719
5910 Drug stores and proprietary stores	-	5	-	51	10	-	15,294	-	867
5920 Liquor stores	-	16	-	109	7	-	8,991	-	1,033
5930 Used merchandise stores	-	16	-	48	3	-	8,333	-	456
5941 Sporting goods and bicycle shops	-	14	-	71	5	-	8,901	-	639
5942 Book stores	-	9	-	35	4	-	8,571	-	317
5944 Jewelry stores	-	9	-	53	6	-	15,019	-	845
5945 Hobby, toy, and game shops	-	7	-	25	4	-	8,160	-	219
5947 Gift, novelty, and souvenir shops	-	13	-	50	4	-	6,080	-	352
5961 Catalog and mail-order houses	-	5	-	87	17	-	19,908	-	1,674
5992 Florists	-	10	-	46	5	-	11,826	-	579
5995 Optical goods stores	-	6	-	29	5	-	11,310	-	393
5999 Miscellaneous retail stores, nec	-	22	-	66	3	-	10,788	-	686

Source: County Business Patterns 1994/95, CBP-94/95, U.S. Department of Commerce, Washington DC, November 1997. The employment column represents mid-March employment in the year. Pay per employee is calculated by dividing 1st Quarter payroll, annualized, by mid-March employment. The column headed 'Emp / Est' shows 'employees per establishment'. A dash (-) means that data are unavailable or cannot be calculated. nec means not elsewhere classified. *Notes:* 1. 1994 data incomplete; unavailable or withheld. 2. 1995 data incomplete; unavailable or withheld. 3. 1994 and 1995 data incomplete; unavailable or withheld.

CEDAR RAPIDS, IA MSA

Wholesale and Retail Trade USA	Establishments		Employment		Emp / Est	Pay / Employee		Annual Payroll ($ 000)	
	1994	1995	1994	1995	1995	1994	1995	1994	1995
50 - Wholesale trade	444	439	5,412	5,553	13	27,147	29,923	158,374	172,759
5012 Automobiles and other vehicles	7	9	361	347	39	22,914	28,012	8,899	9,091
5013 Motor vehicle supplies and new parts	31	24	275	281	12	21,178	21,808	5,898	6,456
5014 Tires and tubes	-	3	-	50	17	-	26,400	-	1,390
5015 Motor vehicle parts, used	-	3	-	34	11	-	12,824	-	414
5020 Furniture and homefurnishings	11	11	125	133	12	27,776	26,376	3,619	3,803
5031 Lumber, plywood, and millwork	-	5	-	68	14	-	31,235	-	2,042
5033 Roofing, siding, & insulation	-	3	-	11	4	-	16,364	-	218
5044 Office equipment	13	12	163	178	15	30,331	32,539	5,313	5,651
5045 Computers, peripherals, & software	15	18	234	210	12	54,444	57,829	9,720	9,427
5046 Commercial equipment, nec	6	-	56	-	-	24,429	-	1,691	-
5047 Medical and hospital equipment	-	5	-	15	3	-	29,333	-	376
5051 Metals service centers and offices	12	13	154	180	14	28,623	28,933	4,759	5,865
5063 Electrical apparatus and equipment	19	19	208	218	11	35,519	41,835	7,327	8,271

Continued on next page.

CEDAR RAPIDS, IA MSA - [continued]

Wholesale and Retail Trade USA	Establishments 1994	Establishments 1995	Employment 1994	Employment 1995	Emp / Est 1995	Pay / Employee 1994	Pay / Employee 1995	Annual Payroll ($ 000) 1994	Annual Payroll ($ 000) 1995
5064 Electrical appliances, TV & radios	3	3	41	32	11	34,927	54,125	1,143	1,354
5065 Electronic parts and equipment	40	38	265	257	7	32,408	33,167	10,207	10,184
5072 Hardware	-	7	-	33	5	-	36,727	-	1,222
5074 Plumbing & hydronic heating supplies	6	6	86	96	16	32,977	45,542	4,069	4,476
5082 Construction and mining machinery	8	8	165	171	21	39,079	45,708	6,803	7,440
5083 Farm and garden machinery	8	8	76	74	9	28,842	28,324	2,221	2,171
5084 Industrial machinery and equipment	30	28	248	279	10	27,435	28,401	7,583	8,851
5085 Industrial supplies	32	31	415	494	16	26,496	29,725	12,074	15,520
5092 Toys and hobby goods and supplies	-	3	-	22	7	-	15,455	-	891
5093 Scrap and waste materials	9	11	120	127	12	14,500	15,717	2,022	2,177
5099 Durable goods, nec	4	-	15	-	-	17,067	-	468	-
5111 Printing and writing paper	4	5	63	53	11	25,778	39,321	1,522	2,279
5130 Apparel, piece goods, and notions	4	-	113	-	-	12,389	-	1,420	-
5149 Groceries and related products, nec	10	11	147	146	13	31,320	31,151	4,698	5,702
5153 Grain and field beans	17	16	122	93	6	26,230	31,613	3,272	3,275
5169 Chemicals & allied products, nec	11	-	33	-	-	18,424	-	658	-
5171 Petroleum bulk stations & terminals	5	4	23	10	3	15,652	26,800	347	274
5172 Petroleum products, nec	5	4	77	75	19	28,675	33,333	3,332	3,623
5181 Beer and ale	6	6	163	171	29	22,233	24,164	4,432	4,785
5191 Farm supplies	13	12	80	87	7	26,000	22,299	2,462	2,291
5198 Paints, varnishes, and supplies	4	4	69	90	23	17,623	16,356	1,323	1,483
5199 Nondurable goods, nec	8	9	69	68	8	18,087	19,941	1,367	1,437
52 - Retail trade	1,201	1,181	18,328	18,913	16	10,801	11,713	217,607	233,040
5210 Lumber and other building materials	23	23	455	393	17	20,422	21,812	10,374	8,627
5230 Paint, glass, and wallpaper stores	11	8	47	74	9	19,319	21,243	1,049	1,922
5250 Hardware stores	11	10	97	99	10	9,649	9,697	967	957
5260 Retail nurseries and garden stores	13	13	104	120	9	11,923	12,267	1,753	1,833
5270 Mobile home dealers	3	4	64	42	11	20,563	43,524	1,944	2,342
5310 Department stores	14	15	1,995	2,176	145	10,544	11,717	22,472	25,869
5390 Misc. general merchandise stores	-	5	-	294	59	-	10,830	-	3,160
5410 Grocery stores	48	46	2,690	2,820	61	9,429	10,282	27,501	30,839
5420 Meat and fish markets	7	6	35	28	5	11,543	16,714	415	439
5440 Candy, nut, and confectionery stores	-	5	-	19	4	-	7,789	-	147
5460 Retail bakeries	14	15	175	149	10	7,794	7,490	1,439	1,067
5490 Miscellaneous food stores	5	6	20	24	4	8,600	9,500	188	299
5510 New and used car dealers	23	21	927	1,035	49	23,594	24,661	26,413	28,538
5520 Used car dealers	25	23	73	77	3	14,466	18,130	1,199	1,589
5530 Auto and home supply stores	23	26	205	257	10	14,380	15,735	3,453	4,436
5540 Gasoline service stations	69	73	554	618	8	10,614	10,764	6,507	7,463
5550 Boat dealers	3	4	9	11	3	15,556	18,545	224	258
5560 Recreational vehicle dealers	3	-	28	-	-	15,000	-	719	-
5570 Motorcycle dealers	4	3	31	33	11	10,065	12,606	466	476
5610 Men's & boys' clothing stores	10	10	71	68	7	15,324	15,824	1,099	1,030
5620 Women's clothing stores	46	39	408	321	8	8,304	8,012	3,370	2,506
5630 Women's accessory & specialty stores	11	11	37	38	3	8,973	8,000	295	284
5640 Children's and infants' wear stores	-	3	-	11	4	-	6,545	-	78
5650 Family clothing stores	13	13	121	159	12	8,198	9,333	1,234	1,479
5660 Shoe stores	28	22	183	171	8	7,825	8,491	1,546	1,485
5690 Misc. apparel & accessory stores	5	5	54	64	13	8,741	8,063	476	774
5712 Furniture stores	22	19	296	298	16	18,122	19,235	5,933	6,329
5713 Floor covering stores	10	11	56	51	5	23,286	24,157	1,385	1,318
5720 Household appliance stores	9	8	50	33	4	10,880	17,212	600	629
5731 Radio, TV, & electronic stores	11	11	130	153	14	14,492	13,176	1,788	2,027
5734 Computer and software stores	10	9	49	106	12	16,408	28,189	1,882	3,159
5735 Record & prerecorded tape stores	11	11	77	81	7	8,987	9,877	777	811
5736 Musical instrument stores	4	4	36	34	9	15,333	20,235	619	693
5812 Eating places	299	277	5,980	5,944	21	7,106	7,680	45,988	47,816
5813 Drinking places	83	75	487	488	7	6,283	6,557	3,261	3,254
5910 Drug stores and proprietary stores	32	33	508	540	16	15,220	15,363	8,257	8,328
5920 Liquor stores	3	3	21	18	6	8,762	10,667	191	192
5930 Used merchandise stores	29	30	155	158	5	6,787	6,886	1,161	1,194
5941 Sporting goods and bicycle shops	22	23	317	344	15	24,429	24,221	7,455	7,830
5942 Book stores	10	10	56	107	11	7,786	9,645	561	954
5944 Jewelry stores	19	24	162	170	7	17,679	18,353	2,660	2,731
5945 Hobby, toy, and game shops	11	10	90	98	10	9,111	8,367	971	1,037
5946 Camera & photographic supply stores	6	6	41	44	7	18,634	17,091	721	720
5947 Gift, novelty, and souvenir shops	26	27	155	129	5	5,652	7,504	1,027	993
5948 Luggage and leather goods stores	4	3	13	19	6	12,308	11,158	159	181
5949 Sewing, needlework, and piece goods	8	5	62	26	5	7,419	6,615	472	169
5963 Direct selling establishments	27	23	165	141	6	18,036	20,965	2,850	2,830
5980 Fuel dealers	6	6	55	59	10	20,945	21,153	1,260	1,335

Continued on next page.

CEDAR RAPIDS, IA MSA - [continued]

Wholesale and Retail Trade USA	Establishments		Employment		Emp / Est	Pay / Employee		Annual Payroll ($ 000)	
	1994	1995	1994	1995	1995	1994	1995	1994	1995
5992 Florists	-	14	-	93	7	-	9,419	-	869
5995 Optical goods stores	13	12	84	71	6	11,810	14,592	935	1,034
5999 Miscellaneous retail stores, nec	37	37	155	152	4	9,832	12,342	1,634	1,890

Source: County Business Patterns 1994/95, CBP-94/95, U.S. Department of Commerce, Washington DC, November 1997. The employment column represents mid-March employment in the year. Pay per employee is calculated by dividing 1st Quarter payroll, annualized, by mid-March employment. The column headed 'Emp / Est' shows 'employees per establishment'. A dash (-) means that data are unavailable or cannot be calculated. nec means not elsewhere classified. *Notes:* 1. 1994 data incomplete; unavailable or withheld. 2. 1995 data incomplete; unavailable or withheld. 3. 1994 and 1995 data incomplete; unavailable or withheld.

CHAMPAIGN – URBANA, IL MSA

Wholesale and Retail Trade USA	Establishments		Employment		Emp / Est	Pay / Employee		Annual Payroll ($ 000)	
	1994	1995	1994	1995	1995	1994	1995	1994	1995
50 – Wholesale trade	246	249	4,303	4,757	19	25,341	25,775	117,620	130,960
5013 Motor vehicle supplies and new parts	13	9	92	68	8	13,522	15,059	1,168	1,059
5014 Tires and tubes	-	3	-	25	8	-	20,960	-	534
5015 Motor vehicle parts, used	3	-	38	-	-	16,526	-	689	-
5021 Furniture	3	3	26	28	9	23,846	24,286	645	570
5023 Homefurnishings	4	3	12	10	3	17,000	19,200	136	260
5031 Lumber, plywood, and millwork	-	5	-	67	13	-	24,179	-	1,566
5033 Roofing, siding, & insulation	3	-	30	-	-	37,467	-	984	-
5044 Office equipment	8	7	107	90	13	28,486	24,889	2,387	2,450
5045 Computers, peripherals, & software	9	10	245	301	30	24,245	24,718	5,893	7,375
5046 Commercial equipment, nec	3	4	8	17	4	25,500	23,294	320	419
5063 Electrical apparatus and equipment	4	4	69	74	19	37,623	29,189	2,739	2,291
5072 Hardware	3	3	15	22	7	24,267	21,455	427	505
5082 Construction and mining machinery	3	4	56	53	13	41,571	39,774	2,170	2,078
5083 Farm and garden machinery	10	10	170	163	16	23,176	25,914	4,628	4,615
5084 Industrial machinery and equipment	-	4	-	20	5	-	22,800	-	522
5085 Industrial supplies	6	6	34	51	9	30,353	28,392	1,307	1,654
5087 Service establishment equipment	7	8	51	55	7	19,922	19,782	1,087	1,193
5093 Scrap and waste materials	6	-	39	-	-	11,385	-	521	-
5099 Durable goods, nec	4	-	11	-	-	18,545	-	220	-
5110 Paper and paper products	11	7	53	70	10	21,434	25,257	1,089	1,623
5130 Apparel, piece goods, and notions	6	5	203	270	54	14,227	12,830	3,283	3,626
5149 Groceries and related products, nec	8	7	74	85	12	27,892	26,965	2,134	2,369
5150 Farm-product raw materials	28	29	175	231	8	23,566	23,931	4,864	7,077
5160 Chemicals and allied products	5	-	38	-	-	30,737	-	1,166	-
5171 Petroleum bulk stations & terminals	-	6	-	35	6	-	24,914	-	998
5180 Beer, wine, and distilled beverages	6	6	84	89	15	28,619	28,270	2,442	2,320
5191 Farm supplies	15	13	336	299	23	21,524	20,803	12,256	7,831
52 – Retail trade	1,026	1,047	16,650	18,067	17	10,107	10,823	184,710	202,980
5210 Lumber and other building materials	23	19	385	452	24	17,132	17,354	7,472	7,908
5230 Paint, glass, and wallpaper stores	7	7	52	39	6	16,385	22,872	885	924
5250 Hardware stores	11	8	113	97	12	11,080	11,588	1,438	1,213
5260 Retail nurseries and garden stores	5	6	152	166	28	11,184	13,831	2,125	2,248
5270 Mobile home dealers	3	5	27	33	7	25,481	28,121	708	957
5310 Department stores	11	12	1,660	2,388	199	9,087	10,251	17,696	24,717
5330 Variety stores	9	6	76	44	7	7,895	9,182	614	497
5390 Misc. general merchandise stores	4	6	452	432	72	9,345	10,963	4,624	4,722
5410 Grocery stores	53	51	1,843	2,178	43	10,915	11,225	21,127	23,584
5420 Meat and fish markets	3	-	20	-	-	9,600	-	210	-
5440 Candy, nut, and confectionery stores	5	-	34	-	-	6,941	-	216	-
5460 Retail bakeries	6	8	51	62	8	7,059	10,258	412	692
5510 New and used car dealers	15	15	739	759	51	28,184	29,481	23,147	23,916
5520 Used car dealers	13	11	67	64	6	12,955	15,750	955	1,102
5530 Auto and home supply stores	19	18	178	161	9	13,685	14,783	2,661	2,434
5540 Gasoline service stations	71	73	452	438	6	9,664	10,767	4,595	5,073
5570 Motorcycle dealers	4	-	22	-	-	15,455	-	463	-
5610 Men's & boys' clothing stores	11	11	88	90	8	12,045	11,867	1,126	1,062
5620 Women's clothing stores	36	34	353	324	10	6,448	6,765	2,473	2,265
5630 Women's accessory & specialty stores	4	4	33	29	7	7,636	9,517	246	242
5640 Children's and infants' wear stores	4	3	33	42	14	5,697	5,429	200	232
5650 Family clothing stores	13	13	140	134	10	7,571	9,075	1,216	1,122
5660 Shoe stores	31	28	166	158	6	10,578	11,190	1,710	1,836
5690 Misc. apparel & accessory stores	8	8	74	71	9	8,919	10,028	655	637
5712 Furniture stores	19	19	191	186	10	14,681	16,581	2,890	3,274
5713 Floor covering stores	7	7	59	61	9	16,678	15,475	1,119	1,362
5714 Drapery and upholstery stores	3	3	7	7	2	12,000	13,143	111	80
5719 Misc. homefurnishings stores	9	11	40	47	4	8,700	9,957	416	493

Continued on next page.

CHAMPAIGN - URBANA, IL MSA - [continued]

Wholesale and Retail Trade USA	Establishments		Employment		Emp / Est	Pay / Employee		Annual Payroll ($ 000)	
	1994	1995	1994	1995	1995	1994	1995	1994	1995
5720 Household appliance stores	7	8	43	39	5	13,395	12,615	707	450
5731 Radio, TV, & electronic stores	13	14	183	207	15	17,552	16,058	2,923	3,926
5734 Computer and software stores	7	7	48	70	10	10,167	13,600	549	869
5735 Record & prerecorded tape stores	13	12	118	98	8	7,932	8,286	945	798
5736 Musical instrument stores	7	7	23	20	3	11,304	12,000	222	231
5812 Eating places	271	266	6,216	6,219	23	6,859	7,239	46,890	47,398
5813 Drinking places	48	46	624	613	13	5,795	5,892	3,776	3,830
5910 Drug stores and proprietary stores	19	20	285	313	16	14,344	18,607	4,568	6,041
5920 Liquor stores	13	16	127	132	8	10,142	10,000	1,324	1,343
5930 Used merchandise stores	16	18	38	52	3	8,947	7,000	390	375
5941 Sporting goods and bicycle shops	18	16	94	97	6	12,723	17,402	1,501	1,580
5942 Book stores	11	14	220	259	19	10,018	9,730	2,522	2,702
5944 Jewelry stores	19	19	119	128	7	12,840	13,500	1,511	1,622
5945 Hobby, toy, and game shops	9	9	58	58	6	9,379	8,138	577	526
5947 Gift, novelty, and souvenir shops	18	21	125	142	7	6,688	6,648	1,027	1,137
5963 Direct selling establishments	-	9	-	80	9	-	16,200	-	1,330
5984 Liquefied petroleum gas dealers	-	5	-	17	3	-	19,529	-	339
5992 Florists	22	21	113	105	5	8,248	8,533	927	916
5995 Optical goods stores	13	10	79	69	7	15,949	16,696	1,179	1,077
5999 Miscellaneous retail stores, nec	26	31	151	169	5	12,291	12,710	2,126	2,475

Source: County Business Patterns 1994/95, CBP-94/95, U.S. Department of Commerce, Washington DC, November 1997. The employment column represents mid-March employment in the year. Pay per employee is calculated by dividing 1st Quarter payroll, annualized, by mid-March employment. The column headed 'Emp / Est' shows 'employees per establishment'. A dash (-) means that data are unavailable or cannot be calculated. nec means not elsewhere classified. *Notes:* 1. 1994 data incomplete; unavailable or withheld. 2. 1995 data incomplete; unavailable or withheld. 3. 1994 and 1995 data incomplete; unavailable or withheld.

CHARLESTON - NORTH CHARLESTON, SC MSA

Wholesale and Retail Trade USA	Establishments		Employment		Emp / Est	Pay / Employee		Annual Payroll ($ 000)	
	1994	1995	1994	1995	1995	1994	1995	1994	1995
50 - Wholesale trade	-	710	-	8,115	11	-	27,785	-	231,134
5012 Automobiles and other vehicles [2]	-	11	-	86	8	-	28,884	-	2,972
5013 Motor vehicle supplies and new parts	-	48	-	422	9	-	18,000	-	7,897
5014 Tires and tubes [2]	-	9	-	60	7	-	23,933	-	1,565
5015 Motor vehicle parts, used	-	18	-	31	2	-	13,290	-	428
5021 Furniture	-	11	-	57	5	-	20,491	-	1,583
5023 Homefurnishings [2]	-	15	-	292	19	-	30,151	-	8,996
5031 Lumber, plywood, and millwork [2]	-	14	-	156	11	-	27,974	-	4,227
5032 Brick, stone, & related materials [2]	-	9	-	37	4	-	20,432	-	843
5033 Roofing, siding, & insulation [2]	-	10	-	79	8	-	24,557	-	2,192
5039 Construction materials, nec	-	9	-	79	9	-	24,354	-	2,139
5044 Office equipment [2]	-	21	-	238	11	-	29,462	-	6,960
5045 Computers, peripherals, & software [2]	-	18	-	151	8	-	22,755	-	3,225
5046 Commercial equipment, nec [2]	-	9	-	60	7	-	24,467	-	1,433
5047 Medical and hospital equipment [2]	-	21	-	142	7	-	38,761	-	5,742
5051 Metals service centers and offices	-	11	-	70	6	-	28,971	-	1,956
5063 Electrical apparatus and equipment	-	30	-	246	8	-	32,829	-	7,965
5072 Hardware [2]	-	9	-	106	12	-	23,283	-	2,856
5074 Plumbing & hydronic heating supplies [2]	-	10	-	113	11	-	23,717	-	3,042
5075 Warm air heating & air conditioning	-	19	-	147	8	-	26,476	-	4,226
5078 Refrigeration equipment and supplies [2]	-	3	-	13	4	-	17,538	-	260
5082 Construction and mining machinery	-	12	-	66	6	-	29,333	-	2,090
5083 Farm and garden machinery [2]	-	5	-	36	7	-	21,667	-	806
5084 Industrial machinery and equipment	-	28	-	256	9	-	32,672	-	8,716
5085 Industrial supplies	-	33	-	375	11	-	26,272	-	9,849
5087 Service establishment equipment [2]	-	8	-	69	9	-	20,638	-	1,659
5088 Transportation equipment & supplies [2]	-	4	-	19	5	-	20,000	-	347
5093 Scrap and waste materials	-	17	-	176	10	-	23,727	-	4,347
5094 Jewelry & precious stones [2]	-	6	-	49	8	-	48,163	-	1,645
5099 Durable goods, nec	-	17	-	110	6	-	25,491	-	3,313
5112 Stationery and office supplies [2]	-	14	-	232	17	-	17,931	-	4,149
5120 Drugs, proprietaries, and sundries [2]	-	7	-	119	17	-	23,092	-	2,864
5136 Men's and boys' clothing [2]	-	4	-	29	7	-	16,138	-	496
5141 Groceries, general line [2]	-	10	-	126	13	-	26,063	-	3,725
5143 Dairy products, exc. dried or canned [2]	-	4	-	17	4	-	23,765	-	397
5145 Confectionery [2]	-	5	-	9	2	-	10,667	-	108
5146 Fish and seafoods [2]	-	12	-	135	11	-	20,889	-	3,198
5148 Fresh fruits and vegetables [2]	-	4	-	60	15	-	15,067	-	1,075
5149 Groceries and related products, nec	-	24	-	545	23	-	27,905	-	15,208
5169 Chemicals & allied products, nec	-	19	-	191	10	-	41,005	-	8,286

Continued on next page.

CHARLESTON - NORTH CHARLESTON, SC MSA - [continued]

Wholesale and Retail Trade USA	Establishments		Employment		Emp / Est	Pay / Employee		Annual Payroll ($ 000)	
	1994	1995	1994	1995	1995	1994	1995	1994	1995
5171 Petroleum bulk stations & terminals	-	15	-	158	11	-	29,570	-	4,575
5172 Petroleum products, nec [2]	-	9	-	137	15	-	24,730	-	3,358
5180 Beer, wine, and distilled beverages [2]	-	6	-	136	23	-	33,441	-	4,309
5191 Farm supplies	-	13	-	59	5	-	24,271	-	1,563
5192 Books, periodicals, & newspapers [2]	-	9	-	74	8	-	18,703	-	1,399
5193 Flowers & florists' supplies [2]	-	5	-	47	9	-	15,830	-	822
5198 Paints, varnishes, and supplies [2]	-	9	-	48	5	-	28,250	-	1,309
5199 Nondurable goods, nec	-	18	-	26	1	-	17,692	-	617
52 - Retail trade	-	3,318	-	43,924	13	-	11,715	-	546,386
5210 Lumber and other building materials	-	44	-	831	19	-	20,804	-	17,762
5230 Paint, glass, and wallpaper stores	-	21	-	94	4	-	15,915	-	1,489
5250 Hardware stores	-	24	-	223	9	-	14,457	-	3,466
5260 Retail nurseries and garden stores	-	29	-	168	6	-	12,619	-	2,290
5270 Mobile home dealers	-	17	-	140	8	-	21,657	-	3,619
5310 Department stores [2]	-	20	-	2,504	125	-	12,513	-	30,112
5330 Variety stores	-	31	-	283	9	-	8,212	-	2,544
5390 Misc. general merchandise stores	-	30	-	486	16	-	12,765	-	6,902
5410 Grocery stores	-	220	-	6,666	30	-	10,771	-	76,031
5420 Meat and fish markets	-	20	-	61	3	-	10,361	-	750
5440 Candy, nut, and confectionery stores [2]	-	8	-	57	7	-	8,281	-	263
5460 Retail bakeries [2]	-	18	-	142	8	-	10,620	-	1,506
5490 Miscellaneous food stores	-	19	-	124	7	-	8,323	-	1,136
5510 New and used car dealers	-	45	-	2,207	49	-	32,034	-	78,667
5520 Used car dealers	-	46	-	146	3	-	19,562	-	2,965
5530 Auto and home supply stores	-	95	-	732	8	-	17,393	-	14,038
5540 Gasoline service stations	-	187	-	1,387	7	-	10,336	-	15,470
5550 Boat dealers	-	27	-	149	6	-	18,980	-	3,701
5560 Recreational vehicle dealers [2]	-	4	-	39	10	-	18,256	-	764
5570 Motorcycle dealers [2]	-	5	-	40	8	-	20,800	-	915
5610 Men's & boys' clothing stores [2]	-	26	-	161	6	-	14,634	-	2,240
5620 Women's clothing stores	-	127	-	1,004	8	-	8,506	-	9,028
5630 Women's accessory & specialty stores [2]	-	24	-	123	5	-	8,813	-	1,313
5640 Children's and infants' wear stores [2]	-	10	-	61	6	-	9,246	-	516
5650 Family clothing stores	-	51	-	621	12	-	11,498	-	7,346
5660 Shoe stores	-	74	-	362	5	-	13,171	-	4,371
5690 Misc. apparel & accessory stores [2]	-	19	-	59	3	-	9,017	-	627
5712 Furniture stores	-	84	-	674	8	-	18,849	-	12,145
5713 Floor covering stores	-	29	-	118	4	-	20,373	-	2,594
5714 Drapery and upholstery stores	-	5	-	11	2	-	11,636	-	136
5719 Misc. homefurnishings stores	-	52	-	263	5	-	11,848	-	3,124
5720 Household appliance stores [2]	-	16	-	104	7	-	17,269	-	1,872
5731 Radio, TV, & electronic stores	-	36	-	243	7	-	18,008	-	4,393
5734 Computer and software stores [2]	-	17	-	97	6	-	16,206	-	1,520
5735 Record & prerecorded tape stores	-	24	-	185	8	-	9,686	-	1,641
5736 Musical instrument stores [2]	-	5	-	27	5	-	18,667	-	620
5812 Eating places	-	607	-	14,919	25	-	7,797	-	122,396
5813 Drinking places	-	64	-	433	7	-	7,381	-	3,311
5910 Drug stores and proprietary stores	-	93	-	967	10	-	15,636	-	16,302
5920 Liquor stores	-	55	-	143	3	-	11,497	-	1,842
5930 Used merchandise stores	-	75	-	284	4	-	14,056	-	4,195
5941 Sporting goods and bicycle shops	-	51	-	333	7	-	12,300	-	4,164
5942 Book stores	-	38	-	191	5	-	9,487	-	1,878
5943 Stationery stores [2]	-	13	-	62	5	-	13,935	-	1,049
5944 Jewelry stores	-	55	-	297	5	-	18,734	-	5,237
5945 Hobby, toy, and game shops	-	25	-	178	7	-	8,921	-	2,055
5947 Gift, novelty, and souvenir shops	-	105	-	503	5	-	8,724	-	5,055
5949 Sewing, needlework, and piece goods [2]	-	14	-	106	8	-	10,377	-	1,078
5961 Catalog and mail-order houses [2]	-	7	-	25	4	-	23,360	-	826
5962 Merchandising machine operators	-	9	-	34	4	-	14,000	-	481
5963 Direct selling establishments	-	35	-	233	7	-	11,605	-	2,947
5984 Liquefied petroleum gas dealers	-	10	-	61	6	-	17,377	-	1,067
5992 Florists	-	53	-	175	3	-	10,080	-	1,768
5995 Optical goods stores	-	36	-	180	5	-	15,467	-	2,825
5999 Miscellaneous retail stores, nec	-	118	-	469	4	-	12,776	-	6,585

Source: County Business Patterns 1994/95, CBP-94/95, U.S. Department of Commerce, Washington DC, November 1997. The employment column represents mid-March employment in the year. Pay per employee is calculated by dividing 1st Quarter payroll, annualized, by mid-March employment. The column headed 'Emp / Est' shows 'employees per establishment'. A dash (-) means that data are unavailable or cannot be calculated. nec means not elsewhere classified. *Notes:* 1. 1994 data incomplete; unavailable or withheld. 2. 1995 data incomplete; unavailable or withheld. 3. 1994 and 1995 data incomplete; unavailable or withheld.

CHARLESTON, WV MSA

Wholesale and Retail Trade USA	Establishments		Employment		Emp / Est	Pay / Employee		Annual Payroll ($ 000)	
	1994	1995	1994	1995	1995	1994	1995	1994	1995
50- Wholesale trade	-	552	-	7,241	13	-	29,981	-	224,396
5012 Automobiles and other vehicles [2]	-	8	-	134	17	-	22,657	-	3,539
5013 Motor vehicle supplies and new parts	-	43	-	411	10	-	25,976	-	9,968
5014 Tires and tubes	-	8	-	148	19	-	21,027	-	3,090
5015 Motor vehicle parts, used	-	6	-	55	9	-	16,582	-	973
5021 Furniture	-	8	-	142	18	-	20,845	-	3,516
5023 Homefurnishings	-	7	-	55	8	-	23,636	-	1,367
5033 Roofing, siding, & insulation	-	5	-	15	3	-	37,067	-	498
5039 Construction materials, nec	-	11	-	33	3	-	21,091	-	775
5044 Office equipment	-	21	-	384	18	-	33,958	-	12,784
5045 Computers, peripherals, & software [2]	-	23	-	216	9	-	56,352	-	10,353
5047 Medical and hospital equipment	-	12	-	84	7	-	41,714	-	3,379
5051 Metals service centers and offices	-	10	-	73	7	-	24,438	-	1,972
5052 Coal and other minerals and ores [2]	-	9	-	53	6	-	48,453	-	2,912
5063 Electrical apparatus and equipment	-	27	-	234	9	-	28,376	-	7,126
5072 Hardware [2]	-	9	-	63	7	-	27,683	-	1,844
5074 Plumbing & hydronic heating supplies	-	8	-	51	6	-	31,373	-	1,622
5075 Warm air heating & air conditioning	-	11	-	88	8	-	26,273	-	2,665
5078 Refrigeration equipment and supplies [2]	-	3	-	14	5	-	15,429	-	220
5082 Construction and mining machinery	-	23	-	770	33	-	38,021	-	29,466
5084 Industrial machinery and equipment	-	47	-	659	14	-	33,062	-	22,614
5085 Industrial supplies	-	34	-	422	12	-	27,943	-	13,418
5087 Service establishment equipment [2]	-	14	-	66	5	-	20,788	-	1,619
5091 Sporting & recreational goods	-	4	-	7	2	-	10,286	-	110
5093 Scrap and waste materials	-	9	-	144	16	-	22,667	-	3,458
5110 Paper and paper products	-	18	-	96	5	-	19,208	-	2,047
5120 Drugs, proprietaries, and sundries [2]	-	5	-	40	8	-	47,500	-	2,240
5130 Apparel, piece goods, and notions [2]	-	5	-	31	6	-	12,258	-	346
5141 Groceries, general line	-	5	-	19	4	-	24,000	-	346
5143 Dairy products, exc. dried or canned [2]	-	3	-	23	8	-	21,565	-	346
5145 Confectionery [2]	-	4	-	20	5	-	15,200	-	331
5149 Groceries and related products, nec	-	9	-	100	11	-	18,680	-	1,933
5169 Chemicals & allied products, nec [2]	-	18	-	12	1	-	36,667	-	448
5171 Petroleum bulk stations & terminals	-	9	-	87	10	-	28,782	-	2,649
5180 Beer, wine, and distilled beverages [2]	-	5	-	107	21	-	28,449	-	3,407
5191 Farm supplies	-	6	-	30	5	-	11,600	-	507
5192 Books, periodicals, & newspapers	-	6	-	18	3	-	18,667	-	324
5198 Paints, varnishes, and supplies [2]	-	4	-	26	7	-	57,385	-	823
5199 Nondurable goods, nec	-	8	-	20	3	-	9,600	-	254
52- Retail trade	-	1,628	-	24,116	15	-	11,870	-	306,089
5210 Lumber and other building materials	-	35	-	656	19	-	20,073	-	12,833
5230 Paint, glass, and wallpaper stores [2]	-	9	-	59	7	-	17,763	-	1,276
5250 Hardware stores	-	19	-	115	6	-	11,617	-	1,645
5260 Retail nurseries and garden stores	-	13	-	45	3	-	8,978	-	544
5270 Mobile home dealers	-	7	-	64	9	-	19,688	-	2,035
5310 Department stores [2]	-	17	-	2,542	150	-	11,369	-	29,302
5330 Variety stores	-	18	-	125	7	-	7,872	-	1,163
5390 Misc. general merchandise stores	-	15	-	370	25	-	12,032	-	4,877
5410 Grocery stores [2]	-	149	-	2,921	20	-	10,569	-	31,976
5440 Candy, nut, and confectionery stores [2]	-	4	-	21	5	-	7,048	-	157
5460 Retail bakeries	-	11	-	90	8	-	8,533	-	791
5490 Miscellaneous food stores [2]	-	5	-	48	10	-	4,583	-	202
5510 New and used car dealers	-	25	-	1,407	56	-	24,335	-	40,681
5520 Used car dealers	-	17	-	92	5	-	13,565	-	1,278
5530 Auto and home supply stores	-	50	-	319	6	-	14,483	-	4,845
5540 Gasoline service stations	-	121	-	964	8	-	10,336	-	11,021
5550 Boat dealers [2]	-	5	-	29	6	-	15,448	-	463
5570 Motorcycle dealers	-	5	-	36	7	-	18,111	-	772
5610 Men's & boys' clothing stores [2]	-	10	-	87	9	-	18,575	-	1,482
5620 Women's clothing stores	-	42	-	309	7	-	7,184	-	2,204
5630 Women's accessory & specialty stores	-	11	-	65	6	-	7,754	-	524
5640 Children's and infants' wear stores	-	6	-	21	4	-	7,429	-	154
5650 Family clothing stores [2]	-	15	-	382	25	-	10,817	-	4,371
5660 Shoe stores	-	41	-	177	4	-	12,384	-	2,136
5690 Misc. apparel & accessory stores	-	10	-	78	8	-	24,256	-	1,288
5712 Furniture stores	-	31	-	203	7	-	19,310	-	4,387
5713 Floor covering stores	-	25	-	120	5	-	14,867	-	2,260
5714 Drapery and upholstery stores [2]	-	4	-	15	4	-	11,733	-	187
5719 Misc. homefurnishings stores	-	17	-	77	5	-	11,429	-	913
5720 Household appliance stores	-	11	-	40	4	-	18,100	-	714
5731 Radio, TV, & electronic stores	-	15	-	83	6	-	16,145	-	1,255

Continued on next page.

CHARLESTON, WV MSA - [continued]

Wholesale and Retail Trade USA	Establishments		Employment		Emp / Est	Pay / Employee		Annual Payroll ($ 000)	
	1994	1995	1994	1995	1995	1994	1995	1994	1995
5734 Computer and software stores[2]	-	9	-	29	3	-	14,621	-	496
5735 Record & prerecorded tape stores[2]	-	7	-	55	8	-	11,200	-	665
5736 Musical instrument stores[2]	-	3	-	21	7	-	14,095	-	301
5812 Eating places	-	370	-	7,042	19	-	7,834	-	58,886
5813 Drinking places	-	39	-	176	5	-	7,295	-	1,432
5910 Drug stores and proprietary stores	-	53	-	968	18	-	11,649	-	12,331
5930 Used merchandise stores	-	23	-	154	7	-	13,818	-	2,546
5941 Sporting goods and bicycle shops	-	25	-	171	7	-	10,269	-	1,847
5942 Book stores	-	16	-	68	4	-	10,294	-	722
5944 Jewelry stores	-	25	-	154	6	-	20,104	-	2,768
5945 Hobby, toy, and game shops[2]	-	16	-	85	5	-	10,729	-	1,026
5947 Gift, novelty, and souvenir shops	-	31	-	167	5	-	6,563	-	1,259
5949 Sewing, needlework, and piece goods	-	8	-	63	8	-	7,238	-	476
5962 Merchandising machine operators	-	12	-	124	10	-	13,645	-	1,636
5963 Direct selling establishments	-	11	-	76	7	-	17,789	-	1,215
5992 Florists	-	42	-	216	5	-	9,407	-	1,996
5995 Optical goods stores	-	20	-	83	4	-	15,904	-	1,288
5999 Miscellaneous retail stores, nec	-	47	-	226	5	-	13,204	-	3,271

Source: County Business Patterns 1994/95, CBP-94/95, U.S. Department of Commerce, Washington DC, November 1997. The employment column represents mid-March employment in the year. Pay per employee is calculated by dividing 1st Quarter payroll, annualized, by mid-March employment. The column headed 'Emp / Est' shows 'employees per establishment'. A dash (-) means that data are unavailable or cannot be calculated. nec means not elsewhere classified. *Notes:* 1. 1994 data incomplete; unavailable or withheld. 2. 1995 data incomplete; unavailable or withheld. 3. 1994 and 1995 data incomplete; unavailable or withheld.

CHARLOTTE - GASTONIA - ROCK HILL MSA (NC PART)

Wholesale and Retail Trade USA	Establishments		Employment		Emp / Est	Pay / Employee		Annual Payroll ($ 000)	
	1994	1995	1994	1995	1995	1994	1995	1994	1995
50 - Wholesale trade	3,726	3,828	47,259	49,745	13	32,287	34,762	1,618,180	1,795,443
5012 Automobiles and other vehicles[2]	49	48	760	987	21	33,095	35,959	26,260	36,758
5013 Motor vehicle supplies and new parts	165	156	1,597	1,700	11	26,337	29,024	45,659	51,396
5014 Tires and tubes[2]	42	40	436	405	10	28,862	36,899	12,403	15,361
5015 Motor vehicle parts, used[3]	38	40	186	181	5	17,161	20,530	3,339	3,917
5021 Furniture[1]	63	60	490	533	9	29,020	32,293	16,680	17,751
5023 Homefurnishings[2]	65	66	439	427	6	32,938	32,806	15,349	15,781
5031 Lumber, plywood, and millwork[3]	56	64	923	901	14	25,686	26,824	26,015	26,658
5032 Brick, stone, & related materials[3]	30	27	139	148	5	26,129	30,189	4,205	4,471
5033 Roofing, siding, & insulation[1]	33	34	230	212	6	30,400	32,151	8,342	6,742
5039 Construction materials, nec[3]	28	52	207	391	8	35,324	32,000	6,917	14,096
5043 Photographic equipment & supplies[3]	13	13	243	251	19	47,358	58,614	10,865	13,048
5044 Office equipment[3]	57	60	928	932	16	32,897	36,953	30,715	34,761
5045 Computers, peripherals, & software	100	102	1,318	1,265	12	50,786	58,046	64,184	64,197
5046 Commercial equipment, nec[3]	44	46	367	366	8	28,469	33,563	11,424	12,672
5047 Medical and hospital equipment[3]	68	66	1,020	958	15	36,271	42,401	38,641	39,237
5048 Ophthalmic goods[3]	13	13	69	62	5	21,217	24,258	1,535	1,554
5049 Professional equipment, nec[3]	17	16	147	196	12	26,068	32,837	3,322	6,646
5051 Metals service centers and offices[1]	93	97	76	1,224	13	31,579	37,261	2,384	49,046
5063 Electrical apparatus and equipment	178	164	1,824	1,921	12	37,044	38,911	69,347	76,226
5064 Electrical appliances, TV & radios[3]	19	22	178	180	8	42,337	43,600	8,093	8,940
5065 Electronic parts and equipment[1]	87	102	758	1,022	10	36,375	36,466	28,865	39,314
5072 Hardware[3]	80	82	978	1,191	15	24,937	24,366	28,790	34,969
5074 Plumbing & hydronic heating supplies[2]	80	80	690	677	8	34,742	39,888	26,229	26,251
5075 Warm air heating & air conditioning[2]	60	61	437	474	8	38,792	45,232	17,057	21,596
5078 Refrigeration equipment and supplies[3]	9	6	25	46	8	41,760	31,739	1,000	1,829
5082 Construction and mining machinery[3]	34	35	763	800	23	38,716	43,295	28,249	32,786
5083 Farm and garden machinery[3]	33	37	330	442	12	27,964	29,638	10,817	15,050
5084 Industrial machinery and equipment	493	501	5,969	6,136	12	38,378	40,881	241,940	265,385
5085 Industrial supplies	169	179	1,746	1,723	10	32,674	36,713	63,546	66,340
5087 Service establishment equipment[3]	52	50	557	585	12	27,246	29,162	16,823	18,327
5088 Transportation equipment & supplies[3]	16	15	68	76	5	34,000	30,737	2,298	2,605
5091 Sporting & recreational goods[3]	33	36	202	197	5	18,158	20,284	4,010	4,061
5092 Toys and hobby goods and supplies[3]	15	16	30	15	1	37,733	61,333	928	1,026
5093 Scrap and waste materials	67	73	975	1,173	16	26,749	27,308	32,227	35,531
5094 Jewelry & precious stones[3]	25	28	95	107	4	29,095	29,271	3,073	3,180
5099 Durable goods, nec[3]	47	57	855	898	16	14,568	18,018	15,346	18,016
5111 Printing and writing paper[3]	12	12	149	176	15	39,973	40,750	5,186	7,467
5112 Stationery and office supplies[3]	69	69	1,003	1,083	16	25,731	26,164	26,450	29,855
5113 Industrial & personal service paper[3]	58	57	704	797	14	36,244	37,897	26,622	31,822
5120 Drugs, proprietaries, and sundries[3]	32	37	394	501	14	31,624	35,481	12,979	18,764
5131 Piece goods & notions	79	83	335	340	4	24,287	26,918	9,584	11,126

Continued on next page.

CHARLOTTE – GASTONIA – ROCK HILL MSA (NC PART) - [continued]

Wholesale and Retail Trade USA	Establishments		Employment		Emp / Est	Pay / Employee		Annual Payroll ($ 000)	
	1994	1995	1994	1995	1995	1994	1995	1994	1995
5136 Men's and boys' clothing	35	34	262	221	7	32,824	29,629	8,277	6,583
5137 Women's and children's clothing[3]	52	47	208	183	4	21,308	35,344	5,784	6,937
5139 Footwear[3]	14	15	27	47	3	100,148	49,787	2,771	3,307
5141 Groceries, general line[3]	23	26	2,280	2,587	100	27,130	30,465	68,852	80,818
5142 Packaged frozen food[3]	22	18	856	916	51	32,411	33,297	31,449	33,440
5143 Dairy products, exc. dried or canned[3]	20	18	352	301	17	42,875	34,472	16,863	12,083
5144 Poultry and poultry products[3]	7	5	251	156	31	19,952	26,359	6,273	4,956
5145 Confectionery[3]	11	11	458	500	45	29,843	28,152	13,620	15,990
5147 Meats and meat products[3]	11	10	84	72	7	23,619	17,389	1,858	1,341
5149 Groceries and related products, nec[3]	70	69	1,684	1,801	26	28,753	36,340	50,933	67,779
5150 Farm-product raw materials[2]	18	16	70	64	4	24,800	28,375	1,960	2,089
5162 Plastics materials & basic shapes[3]	43	40	365	334	8	38,049	41,988	14,037	13,842
5169 Chemicals & allied products, nec[3]	148	149	2,008	2,091	14	36,588	36,865	75,285	79,495
5171 Petroleum bulk stations & terminals	49	46	282	225	5	23,234	29,191	7,264	7,102
5172 Petroleum products, nec	27	26	176	183	7	40,295	39,016	6,971	7,185
5181 Beer and ale[3]	10	10	256	281	28	29,719	29,395	8,832	8,429
5182 Wine and distilled beverages[3]	11	12	165	207	17	25,406	22,667	4,403	5,409
5191 Farm supplies	49	42	261	270	6	23,693	26,148	6,220	7,156
5192 Books, periodicals, & newspapers[3]	24	22	245	314	14	33,404	28,127	7,481	9,289
5193 Flowers & florists' supplies[3]	35	30	215	207	7	19,498	20,599	4,195	4,176
5198 Paints, varnishes, and supplies[3]	39	32	174	174	5	29,517	30,782	4,899	4,522
5199 Nondurable goods, nec	167	177	934	1,004	6	24,642	25,980	27,007	31,129
52 – Retail trade	6,855	6,989	102,616	110,159	16	13,657	14,412	1,510,397	1,659,453
5210 Lumber and other building materials	125	110	2,736	2,479	23	17,270	20,032	52,416	52,465
5230 Paint, glass, and wallpaper stores	41	40	177	171	4	17,492	19,930	3,438	3,626
5250 Hardware stores	75	51	583	450	9	16,597	18,027	10,063	7,673
5260 Retail nurseries and garden stores	50	51	268	285	6	12,522	12,112	4,161	4,199
5270 Mobile home dealers	32	34	138	184	5	33,130	30,674	5,296	7,615
5310 Department stores[2]	57	57	8,537	8,651	152	10,453	12,006	100,394	103,867
5330 Variety stores	77	65	446	510	8	8,780	8,824	4,412	5,146
5390 Misc. general merchandise stores[1]	39	52	698	1,132	22	14,166	12,435	9,695	14,871
5410 Grocery stores[3]	573	575	14,044	15,158	26	9,612	10,742	143,125	165,932
5420 Meat and fish markets[3]	15	12	18	24	2	13,556	11,667	262	350
5440 Candy, nut, and confectionery stores[3]	14	16	52	42	3	5,538	5,619	254	248
5460 Retail bakeries[3]	33	33	224	220	7	9,679	10,364	2,159	2,394
5490 Miscellaneous food stores	34	37	128	139	4	10,406	11,482	1,460	1,805
5510 New and used car dealers	117	114	4,885	5,192	46	31,122	33,774	175,703	201,030
5520 Used car dealers	105	109	363	409	4	21,609	22,220	8,540	9,655
5530 Auto and home supply stores	203	208	1,629	1,611	8	17,024	18,826	30,218	32,212
5540 Gasoline service stations	411	416	2,715	2,766	7	12,172	13,048	36,859	37,864
5550 Boat dealers	18	19	71	98	5	17,296	18,612	1,457	2,080
5560 Recreational vehicle dealers[3]	7	9	33	32	4	17,333	23,250	742	895
5570 Motorcycle dealers	18	19	101	118	6	15,683	16,712	1,982	2,345
5610 Men's & boys' clothing stores[3]	56	54	412	400	7	14,816	16,150	5,925	6,110
5620 Women's clothing stores	254	230	2,160	1,981	9	8,665	8,872	20,150	17,104
5630 Women's accessory & specialty stores[3]	51	46	207	229	5	9,643	10,603	2,171	2,166
5640 Children's and infants' wear stores[3]	21	17	128	166	10	7,469	6,916	1,107	1,165
5650 Family clothing stores	74	80	1,584	1,661	21	8,273	9,320	14,807	16,201
5660 Shoe stores	192	180	1,149	1,226	7	10,030	9,886	12,586	11,689
5690 Misc. apparel & accessory stores[3]	22	28	104	102	4	9,538	10,471	1,080	1,161
5712 Furniture stores	198	202	1,505	1,510	7	18,512	20,254	29,814	32,695
5713 Floor covering stores	61	67	210	233	3	19,352	22,850	4,584	6,070
5714 Drapery and upholstery stores[3]	15	17	32	46	3	14,125	13,043	462	549
5719 Misc. homefurnishings stores	105	106	806	774	7	11,697	13,323	10,349	10,687
5720 Household appliance stores	47	51	242	290	6	25,554	24,414	5,032	5,784
5731 Radio, TV, & electronic stores[1]	81	80	602	951	12	19,316	17,237	13,878	16,727
5734 Computer and software stores[3]	38	46	373	406	9	19,753	23,419	8,423	10,169
5735 Record & prerecorded tape stores	38	44	201	407	9	11,025	9,376	3,244	3,752
5736 Musical instrument stores[3]	19	19	115	124	7	20,557	23,581	2,271	2,633
5812 Eating places	1,540	1,477	31,405	32,410	22	8,170	8,547	274,173	289,995
5813 Drinking places	82	70	593	562	8	9,619	11,302	5,464	5,787
5910 Drug stores and proprietary stores	219	217	2,786	3,006	14	13,925	14,176	43,523	46,027
5920 Liquor stores	44	44	196	213	5	18,939	18,948	3,932	5,713
5930 Used merchandise stores	109	109	541	618	6	10,240	11,320	6,423	7,288
5941 Sporting goods and bicycle shops	92	102	608	659	6	14,270	13,147	8,775	9,486
5942 Book stores	62	63	400	470	7	9,750	10,443	4,091	4,893
5943 Stationery stores[3]	23	21	110	85	4	10,509	10,306	936	860
5944 Jewelry stores	145	155	773	801	5	16,223	16,779	13,320	13,894
5945 Hobby, toy, and game shops	43	44	437	509	12	8,714	8,330	4,670	5,096
5946 Camera & photographic supply stores[3]	17	17	128	121	7	16,938	20,231	2,342	2,385
5947 Gift, novelty, and souvenir shops	119	121	740	860	7	7,957	9,116	6,697	8,671

Continued on next page.

CHARLOTTE - GASTONIA - ROCK HILL MSA (NC PART) - [continued]

Wholesale and Retail Trade USA	Establishments		Employment		Emp / Est	Pay / Employee		Annual Payroll ($ 000)	
	1994	1995	1994	1995	1995	1994	1995	1994	1995
5948 Luggage and leather goods stores[3]	11	11	74	79	7	9,189	8,810	750	872
5949 Sewing, needlework, and piece goods	42	46	191	373	8	9,424	11,517	1,886	4,643
5961 Catalog and mail-order houses[1]	19	24	66	93	4	18,242	17,935	1,230	1,678
5962 Merchandising machine operators	45	45	665	668	15	15,970	16,689	11,624	12,203
5963 Direct selling establishments	72	76	421	592	8	29,910	28,270	14,330	18,055
5983 Fuel oil dealers	33	31	88	90	3	23,409	25,067	2,435	2,576
5984 Liquefied petroleum gas dealers	18	17	79	61	4	29,570	28,787	2,131	1,742
5992 Florists	114	111	313	416	4	11,412	11,173	3,844	4,777
5994 News dealers and newsstands[1]	9	-	30	-	-	6,933	-	223	-
5995 Optical goods stores[2]	54	56	312	359	6	15,295	17,315	4,588	5,681
5999 Miscellaneous retail stores, nec[3]	202	210	1,006	1,092	5	12,592	13,132	14,333	15,988

Source: County Business Patterns 1994/95, CBP-94/95, U.S. Department of Commerce, Washington DC, November 1997. The employment column represents mid-March employment in the year. Pay per employee is calculated by dividing 1st Quarter payroll, annualized, by mid-March employment. The column headed 'Emp / Est' shows 'employees per establishment'. A dash (-) means that data are unavailable or cannot be calculated. nec means not elsewhere classified. *Notes:* 1. 1994 data incomplete; unavailable or withheld. 2. 1995 data incomplete; unavailable or withheld. 3. 1994 and 1995 data incomplete; unavailable or withheld.

CHARLOTTE - GASTONIA - ROCK HILL MSA (SC PART)

Wholesale and Retail Trade USA	Establishments		Employment		Emp / Est	Pay / Employee		Annual Payroll ($ 000)	
	1994	1995	1994	1995	1995	1994	1995	1994	1995
50- Wholesale trade	-	280	-	2,561	9	-	30,752	-	81,044
5013 Motor vehicle supplies and new parts	-	7	-	28	4	-	16,000	-	405
5015 Motor vehicle parts, used	-	4	-	18	5	-	18,889	-	350
5020 Furniture and homefurnishings	-	8	-	148	19	-	15,595	-	2,650
5039 Construction materials, nec	-	4	-	59	15	-	24,949	-	1,690
5045 Computers, peripherals, & software	-	3	-	4	1	-	25,000	-	141
5047 Medical and hospital equipment	-	6	-	35	6	-	79,543	-	2,641
5051 Metals service centers and offices	-	10	-	40	4	-	57,500	-	2,124
5063 Electrical apparatus and equipment	-	8	-	52	7	-	28,231	-	1,568
5074 Plumbing & hydronic heating supplies	-	6	-	31	5	-	28,903	-	774
5075 Warm air heating & air conditioning	-	3	-	12	4	-	31,000	-	286
5084 Industrial machinery and equipment	-	43	-	367	9	-	38,845	-	16,759
5085 Industrial supplies	-	14	-	115	8	-	24,139	-	3,423
5087 Service establishment equipment	-	5	-	132	26	-	30,667	-	4,177
5088 Transportation equipment & supplies	-	5	-	26	5	-	29,385	-	884
5093 Scrap and waste materials	-	10	-	85	9	-	48,518	-	4,049
5099 Durable goods, nec	-	8	-	26	3	-	19,231	-	547
5110 Paper and paper products	-	4	-	9	2	-	22,222	-	353
5131 Piece goods & notions	-	11	-	210	19	-	32,552	-	5,334
5149 Groceries and related products, nec	-	3	-	40	13	-	29,600	-	1,233
5160 Chemicals and allied products	-	17	-	133	8	-	25,744	-	3,267
5170 Petroleum and petroleum products	-	7	-	27	4	-	29,481	-	773
5181 Beer and ale	-	3	-	95	32	-	28,884	-	3,045
5191 Farm supplies	-	5	-	50	10	-	17,840	-	903
5199 Nondurable goods, nec	-	11	-	209	19	-	34,220	-	5,809
52- Retail trade	-	788	-	10,249	13	-	12,022	-	132,192
5210 Lumber and other building materials	-	16	-	229	14	-	19,633	-	5,016
5230 Paint, glass, and wallpaper stores	-	4	-	10	3	-	16,800	-	152
5250 Hardware stores	-	10	-	60	6	-	12,000	-	776
5260 Retail nurseries and garden stores	-	4	-	25	6	-	9,280	-	305
5270 Mobile home dealers	-	8	-	58	7	-	28,690	-	2,180
5310 Department stores	-	5	-	706	141	-	12,368	-	8,427
5330 Variety stores	-	9	-	69	8	-	7,420	-	570
5390 Misc. general merchandise stores	-	6	-	47	8	-	7,915	-	625
5410 Grocery stores	-	79	-	1,946	25	-	10,298	-	19,829
5460 Retail bakeries	-	3	-	10	3	-	11,200	-	77
5510 New and used car dealers	-	18	-	572	32	-	30,538	-	19,266
5520 Used car dealers	-	14	-	55	4	-	25,455	-	1,419
5530 Auto and home supply stores	-	29	-	213	7	-	19,455	-	4,493
5540 Gasoline service stations	-	61	-	457	7	-	11,764	-	5,579
5550 Boat dealers	-	4	-	44	11	-	23,182	-	1,135
5610 Men's & boys' clothing stores	-	6	-	38	6	-	7,368	-	311
5620 Women's clothing stores	-	22	-	125	6	-	8,800	-	1,053
5630 Women's accessory & specialty stores	-	4	-	9	2	-	8,000	-	66
5650 Family clothing stores	-	7	-	198	28	-	10,222	-	1,900
5660 Shoe stores	-	19	-	198	10	-	8,081	-	1,495
5690 Misc. apparel & accessory stores	-	3	-	5	2	-	8,800	-	61
5712 Furniture stores	-	24	-	138	6	-	19,101	-	2,975
5719 Misc. homefurnishings stores	-	10	-	159	16	-	10,541	-	1,582

Continued on next page.

CHARLOTTE - GASTONIA - ROCK HILL MSA (SC PART) - [continued]

Wholesale and Retail Trade USA	Establishments		Employment		Emp / Est	Pay / Employee		Annual Payroll ($ 000)	
	1994	1995	1994	1995	1995	1994	1995	1994	1995
5720 Household appliance stores	-	3	-	19	6	-	24,000	-	409
5734 Computer and software stores	-	3	-	2	1	-	10,000	-	32
5736 Musical instrument stores	-	4	-	14	4	-	11,429	-	162
5812 Eating places	-	151	-	3,397	22	-	7,411	-	26,749
5813 Drinking places	-	11	-	57	5	-	9,333	-	409
5910 Drug stores and proprietary stores	-	27	-	321	12	-	14,542	-	4,964
5920 Liquor stores	-	10	-	40	4	-	12,900	-	540
5930 Used merchandise stores	-	13	-	47	4	-	11,319	-	567
5941 Sporting goods and bicycle shops	-	7	-	25	4	-	16,960	-	436
5942 Book stores	-	4	-	26	7	-	10,769	-	329
5944 Jewelry stores	-	16	-	79	5	-	15,848	-	1,180
5947 Gift, novelty, and souvenir shops	-	12	-	71	6	-	4,056	-	362
5949 Sewing, needlework, and piece goods	-	5	-	29	6	-	9,103	-	256
5963 Direct selling establishments	-	12	-	57	5	-	18,807	-	1,215
5983 Fuel oil dealers	-	3	-	10	3	-	22,400	-	238
5984 Liquefied petroleum gas dealers	-	4	-	26	7	-	21,385	-	553
5992 Florists	-	14	-	54	4	-	8,444	-	490
5999 Miscellaneous retail stores, nec	-	21	-	72	3	-	12,833	-	1,021

Source: County Business Patterns 1994/95, CBP-94/95, U.S. Department of Commerce, Washington DC, November 1997. The employment column represents mid-March employment in the year. Pay per employee is calculated by dividing 1st Quarter payroll, annualized, by mid-March employment. The column headed 'Emp / Est' shows 'employees per establishment'. A dash (-) means that data are unavailable or cannot be calculated. nec means not elsewhere classified. *Notes:* 1. 1994 data incomplete; unavailable or withheld. 2. 1995 data incomplete; unavailable or withheld. 3. 1994 and 1995 data incomplete; unavailable or withheld.

CHARLOTTE - GASTONIA - ROCK HILL, NC - SC MSA

Wholesale and Retail Trade USA	Establishments		Employment		Emp / Est	Pay / Employee		Annual Payroll ($ 000)	
	1994	1995	1994	1995	1995	1994	1995	1994	1995
50 - Wholesale trade [1]	3,726	4,108	47,259	52,306	13	32,287	34,566	1,618,180	1,876,487
5012 Automobiles and other vehicles [3]	49	48	760	987	21	33,095	35,959	26,260	36,758
5013 Motor vehicle supplies and new parts [1]	165	163	1,597	1,728	11	26,337	28,813	45,659	51,801
5014 Tires and tubes [3]	42	40	436	405	10	28,862	36,899	12,403	15,361
5015 Motor vehicle parts, used [3]	38	44	186	199	5	17,161	20,382	3,339	4,267
5021 Furniture [1]	63	63	490	533	8	29,020	32,293	16,680	17,751
5023 Homefurnishings [3]	65	71	439	427	6	32,938	32,806	15,349	15,781
5031 Lumber, plywood, and millwork [3]	56	66	923	901	14	25,686	26,824	26,015	26,658
5032 Brick, stone, & related materials [3]	30	28	139	148	5	26,129	30,189	4,205	4,471
5033 Roofing, siding, & insulation [3]	33	34	230	212	6	30,400	32,151	8,342	6,742
5039 Construction materials, nec [3]	28	56	207	450	8	35,324	31,076	6,917	15,786
5043 Photographic equipment & supplies [3]	13	14	243	251	18	47,358	58,614	10,865	13,048
5044 Office equipment [3]	57	63	928	932	15	32,897	36,953	30,715	34,761
5045 Computers, peripherals, & software [1]	100	105	1,318	1,269	12	50,786	57,942	64,184	64,338
5046 Commercial equipment, nec [3]	44	48	367	366	8	28,469	33,563	11,424	12,672
5047 Medical and hospital equipment [3]	68	72	1,020	993	14	36,271	43,710	38,641	41,878
5048 Ophthalmic goods [3]	13	13	69	62	5	21,217	24,258	1,535	1,554
5049 Professional equipment, nec [3]	17	18	147	196	11	26,068	32,837	3,322	6,646
5051 Metals service centers and offices [1]	93	107	76	1,264	12	31,579	37,902	2,384	51,170
5063 Electrical apparatus and equipment [1]	178	172	1,824	1,973	11	37,044	38,629	69,347	77,794
5064 Electrical appliances, TV & radios [3]	19	24	178	180	8	42,337	43,600	8,093	8,940
5065 Electronic parts and equipment [1]	87	105	758	1,022	10	36,375	36,466	28,865	39,314
5072 Hardware [3]	80	87	978	1,191	14	24,937	24,366	28,790	34,969
5074 Plumbing & hydronic heating supplies [3]	80	86	690	708	8	34,742	39,407	26,229	27,025
5075 Warm air heating & air conditioning [3]	60	64	437	486	8	38,792	44,881	17,057	21,882
5078 Refrigeration equipment and supplies [3]	9	7	25	46	7	41,760	31,739	1,000	1,829
5082 Construction and mining machinery [3]	34	39	763	800	21	38,716	43,295	28,249	32,786
5083 Farm and garden machinery [3]	33	39	330	442	11	27,964	29,638	10,817	15,050
5084 Industrial machinery and equipment [1]	493	544	5,969	6,503	12	38,378	40,766	241,940	282,144
5085 Industrial supplies [1]	169	193	1,746	1,838	10	32,674	35,926	63,546	69,763
5087 Service establishment equipment [3]	52	55	557	717	13	27,246	29,439	16,823	22,504
5088 Transportation equipment & supplies [3]	16	20	68	102	5	34,000	30,392	2,298	3,489
5091 Sporting & recreational goods [3]	33	37	202	197	5	18,158	20,284	4,010	4,061
5092 Toys and hobby goods and supplies [3]	15	17	30	15	1	37,733	61,333	928	1,026
5093 Scrap and waste materials [1]	67	83	975	1,258	15	26,749	28,741	32,227	39,580
5094 Jewelry & precious stones [3]	25	29	95	107	4	29,095	29,271	3,073	3,180
5099 Durable goods, nec [3]	47	65	855	924	14	14,568	18,052	15,346	18,563
5111 Printing and writing paper [3]	12	12	149	176	15	39,973	40,750	5,186	7,467
5112 Stationery and office supplies [3]	69	72	1,003	1,083	15	25,731	26,164	26,450	29,855
5113 Industrial & personal service paper [3]	58	58	704	797	14	36,244	37,897	26,622	31,822
5120 Drugs, proprietaries, and sundries [3]	32	39	394	501	13	31,624	35,481	12,979	18,764
5131 Piece goods & notions [1]	79	94	335	550	6	24,287	29,069	9,584	16,460

Continued on next page.

CHARLOTTE - GASTONIA - ROCK HILL, NC - SC MSA - [continued]

Wholesale and Retail Trade USA	Establishments		Employment		Emp / Est	Pay / Employee		Annual Payroll ($ 000)	
	1994	1995	1994	1995	1995	1994	1995	1994	1995
5136 Men's and boys' clothing [1]	35	35	262	221	6	32,824	29,629	8,277	6,583
5137 Women's and children's clothing [3]	52	53	208	183	3	21,308	35,344	5,784	6,937
5139 Footwear [3]	14	15	27	47	3	100,148	49,787	2,771	3,307
5141 Groceries, general line [3]	23	27	2,280	2,587	96	27,130	30,465	68,852	80,818
5142 Packaged frozen food [3]	22	19	856	916	48	32,411	33,297	31,449	33,440
5143 Dairy products, exc. dried or canned [3]	20	18	352	301	17	42,875	34,472	16,863	12,083
5144 Poultry and poultry products [3]	7	6	251	156	26	19,952	26,359	6,273	4,956
5145 Confectionery [3]	11	12	458	500	42	29,843	28,152	13,620	15,990
5147 Meats and meat products [3]	11	12	84	72	6	23,619	17,389	1,858	1,341
5149 Groceries and related products, nec [3]	70	72	1,684	1,841	26	28,753	36,193	50,933	69,012
5150 Farm-product raw materials [3]	18	20	70	64	3	24,800	28,375	1,960	2,089
5162 Plastics materials & basic shapes [3]	43	41	365	334	8	38,049	41,988	14,037	13,842
5169 Chemicals & allied products, nec [3]	148	165	2,008	2,091	13	36,588	36,865	75,285	79,495
5171 Petroleum bulk stations & terminals [1]	49	48	282	225	5	23,234	29,191	7,264	7,102
5172 Petroleum products, nec [1]	27	31	176	183	6	40,295	39,016	6,971	7,185
5181 Beer and ale [3]	10	13	256	376	29	29,719	29,266	8,832	11,474
5182 Wine and distilled beverages [3]	11	12	165	207	17	25,406	22,667	4,403	5,409
5191 Farm supplies [1]	49	47	261	320	7	23,693	24,850	6,220	8,059
5192 Books, periodicals, & newspapers [3]	24	23	245	314	14	33,404	28,127	7,481	9,289
5193 Flowers & florists' supplies [3]	35	33	215	207	6	19,498	20,599	4,195	4,176
5198 Paints, varnishes, and supplies [3]	39	34	174	174	5	29,517	30,782	4,899	4,522
5199 Nondurable goods, nec [1]	167	188	934	1,213	6	24,642	27,400	27,007	36,938
52 - Retail trade [1]	6,855	7,777	102,616	120,408	15	13,657	14,209	1,510,397	1,791,645
5210 Lumber and other building materials [1]	125	126	2,736	2,708	21	17,270	19,999	52,416	57,481
5230 Paint, glass, and wallpaper stores [1]	41	44	177	181	4	17,492	19,757	3,438	3,778
5250 Hardware stores [1]	75	61	583	510	8	16,597	17,318	10,063	8,449
5260 Retail nurseries and garden stores [1]	50	55	268	310	6	12,522	11,884	4,161	4,504
5270 Mobile home dealers [1]	32	42	138	242	6	33,130	30,198	5,296	9,795
5310 Department stores [3]	57	62	8,537	9,357	151	10,453	12,033	100,394	112,294
5330 Variety stores [1]	77	74	446	579	8	8,780	8,656	4,412	5,716
5390 Misc. general merchandise stores [1]	39	58	698	1,179	20	14,166	12,254	9,695	15,496
5410 Grocery stores [3]	573	654	14,044	17,104	26	9,612	10,692	143,125	185,761
5420 Meat and fish markets [3]	15	14	18	24	2	13,556	11,667	262	350
5440 Candy, nut, and confectionery stores [3]	14	16	52	42	3	5,538	5,619	254	248
5460 Retail bakeries [3]	33	36	224	230	6	9,679	10,400	2,159	2,471
5490 Miscellaneous food stores [1]	34	38	128	139	4	10,406	11,482	1,460	1,805
5510 New and used car dealers [1]	117	132	4,885	5,764	44	31,122	33,453	175,703	220,296
5520 Used car dealers [1]	105	123	363	464	4	21,609	22,603	8,540	11,074
5530 Auto and home supply stores [1]	203	237	1,629	1,824	8	17,024	18,899	30,218	36,705
5540 Gasoline service stations [1]	411	477	2,715	3,223	7	12,172	12,866	36,859	43,443
5550 Boat dealers [1]	18	23	71	142	6	17,296	20,028	1,457	3,215
5560 Recreational vehicle dealers [3]	7	10	33	32	3	17,333	23,250	742	895
5570 Motorcycle dealers [1]	18	21	101	118	6	15,683	16,712	1,982	2,345
5610 Men's & boys' clothing stores [3]	56	60	412	438	7	14,816	15,388	5,925	6,421
5620 Women's clothing stores [1]	254	252	2,160	2,106	8	8,665	8,868	20,150	18,157
5630 Women's accessory & specialty stores [3]	51	50	207	238	5	9,643	10,504	2,171	2,232
5640 Children's and infants' wear stores [3]	21	18	128	166	9	7,469	6,916	1,107	1,165
5650 Family clothing stores [1]	74	87	1,584	1,859	21	8,273	9,416	14,807	18,101
5660 Shoe stores [1]	192	199	1,149	1,424	7	10,030	9,635	12,586	13,184
5690 Misc. apparel & accessory stores [3]	22	31	104	107	3	9,538	10,393	1,080	1,222
5712 Furniture stores [1]	198	226	1,505	1,648	7	18,512	20,158	29,814	35,670
5713 Floor covering stores [1]	61	76	210	233	3	19,352	22,850	4,584	6,070
5714 Drapery and upholstery stores [3]	15	18	32	46	3	14,125	13,043	462	549
5719 Misc. homefurnishings stores [1]	105	116	806	933	8	11,697	12,849	10,349	12,269
5720 Household appliance stores [1]	47	54	242	309	6	25,554	24,388	5,032	6,193
5731 Radio, TV, & electronic stores [1]	81	88	602	951	11	19,316	17,237	13,878	16,727
5734 Computer and software stores [3]	38	49	373	408	8	19,753	23,353	8,423	10,201
5735 Record & prerecorded tape stores [1]	38	47	201	407	9	11,025	9,376	3,244	3,752
5736 Musical instrument stores [3]	19	23	115	138	6	20,557	22,348	2,271	2,795
5812 Eating places [1]	1,540	1,628	31,405	35,807	22	8,170	8,439	274,173	316,744
5813 Drinking places [1]	82	81	593	619	8	9,619	11,121	5,464	6,196
5910 Drug stores and proprietary stores [1]	219	244	2,786	3,327	14	13,925	14,211	43,523	50,991
5920 Liquor stores [1]	44	54	196	253	5	18,939	17,992	3,932	6,253
5930 Used merchandise stores [1]	109	122	541	665	5	10,240	11,320	6,423	7,855
5941 Sporting goods and bicycle shops [1]	92	109	608	684	6	14,270	13,287	8,775	9,922
5942 Book stores [1]	62	67	400	496	7	9,750	10,460	4,091	5,222
5943 Stationery stores [3]	23	21	110	85	4	10,509	10,306	936	860
5944 Jewelry stores [1]	145	171	773	880	5	16,223	16,695	13,320	15,074
5945 Hobby, toy, and game shops [1]	43	46	437	509	11	8,714	8,330	4,670	5,096
5946 Camera & photographic supply stores [3]	17	17	128	121	7	16,938	20,231	2,342	2,385
5947 Gift, novelty, and souvenir shops [1]	119	133	740	931	7	7,957	8,730	6,697	9,033

Continued on next page.

CHARLOTTE - GASTONIA - ROCK HILL, NC - SC MSA - [continued]

Wholesale and Retail Trade USA	Establishments		Employment		Emp / Est	Pay / Employee		Annual Payroll ($ 000)	
	1994	1995	1994	1995	1995	1994	1995	1994	1995
5948 Luggage and leather goods stores [3]	11	12	74	79	7	9,189	8,810	750	872
5949 Sewing, needlework, and piece goods [1]	42	51	191	402	8	9,424	11,343	1,886	4,899
5961 Catalog and mail-order houses [1]	19	26	66	93	4	18,242	17,935	1,230	1,678
5962 Merchandising machine operators [1]	45	46	665	668	15	15,970	16,689	11,624	12,203
5963 Direct selling establishments [1]	72	88	421	649	7	29,910	27,439	14,330	19,270
5983 Fuel oil dealers [1]	33	34	88	100	3	23,409	24,800	2,435	2,814
5984 Liquefied petroleum gas dealers [1]	18	21	79	87	4	29,570	26,575	2,131	2,295
5992 Florists [1]	114	125	313	470	4	11,412	10,860	3,844	5,267
5994 News dealers and newsstands [1]	9	-	30	-	-	6,933	-	223	-
5995 Optical goods stores [3]	54	64	312	359	6	15,295	17,315	4,588	5,681
5999 Miscellaneous retail stores, nec [3]	202	231	1,006	1,164	5	12,592	13,113	14,333	17,009

Source: County Business Patterns 1994/95, CBP-94/95, U.S. Department of Commerce, Washington DC, November 1997. The employment column represents mid-March employment in the year. Pay per employee is calculated by dividing 1st Quarter payroll, annualized, by mid-March employment. The column headed 'Emp / Est' shows 'employees per establishment'. A dash (-) means that data are unavailable or cannot be calculated. nec means not elsewhere classified. *Notes:* 1. 1994 data incomplete; unavailable or withheld. 2. 1995 data incomplete; unavailable or withheld. 3. 1994 and 1995 data incomplete; unavailable or withheld.

CHARLOTTESVILLE, VA MSA

Wholesale and Retail Trade USA	Establishments		Employment		Emp / Est	Pay / Employee		Annual Payroll ($ 000)	
	1994	1995	1994	1995	1995	1994	1995	1994	1995
50 - Wholesale trade	-	178	-	1,843	10	-	26,728	-	53,410
5013 Motor vehicle supplies and new parts [2]	-	11	-	91	8	-	16,747	-	1,565
5020 Furniture and homefurnishings [2]	-	4	-	54	14	-	25,704	-	2,360
5044 Office equipment [2]	-	8	-	55	7	-	22,691	-	1,637
5045 Computers, peripherals, & software [2]	-	10	-	70	7	-	50,229	-	3,252
5063 Electrical apparatus and equipment [2]	-	9	-	75	8	-	45,547	-	3,423
5070 Hardware, plumbing & heating equipment [2]	-	11	-	83	8	-	27,373	-	2,499
5085 Industrial supplies [2]	-	5	-	12	2	-	27,667	-	364
5099 Durable goods, nec [2]	-	5	-	26	5	-	26,154	-	801
5112 Stationery and office supplies [2]	-	3	-	37	12	-	22,486	-	713
5120 Drugs, proprietaries, and sundries [2]	-	3	-	13	4	-	17,846	-	179
5149 Groceries and related products, nec [2]	-	5	-	60	12	-	24,867	-	1,547
5169 Chemicals & allied products, nec [2]	-	6	-	58	10	-	32,276	-	1,934
5181 Beer and ale [2]	-	3	-	130	43	-	22,523	-	3,161
5182 Wine and distilled beverages [2]	-	3	-	43	14	-	23,349	-	1,034
5199 Nondurable goods, nec [2]	-	10	-	58	6	-	18,897	-	1,202
52 - Retail trade	-	991	-	13,472	14	-	12,506	-	176,259
5210 Lumber and other building materials [2]	-	11	-	240	22	-	21,600	-	5,542
5250 Hardware stores [2]	-	6	-	50	8	-	22,160	-	1,077
5260 Retail nurseries and garden stores	-	8	-	22	3	-	10,727	-	325
5310 Department stores [2]	-	7	-	1,015	145	-	11,673	-	11,890
5390 Misc. general merchandise stores [2]	-	12	-	76	6	-	10,158	-	829
5410 Grocery stores	-	115	-	1,706	15	-	12,110	-	21,444
5460 Retail bakeries [2]	-	9	-	41	5	-	11,317	-	494
5490 Miscellaneous food stores [2]	-	5	-	32	6	-	10,125	-	361
5510 New and used car dealers [2]	-	16	-	509	32	-	29,297	-	15,430
5520 Used car dealers [2]	-	5	-	31	6	-	19,355	-	618
5530 Auto and home supply stores	-	26	-	144	6	-	18,972	-	2,870
5540 Gasoline service stations	-	43	-	358	8	-	12,123	-	4,624
5610 Men's & boys' clothing stores [2]	-	10	-	85	9	-	12,706	-	1,099
5620 Women's clothing stores [2]	-	32	-	277	9	-	6,946	-	2,047
5650 Family clothing stores [2]	-	13	-	271	21	-	8,531	-	2,385
5660 Shoe stores [2]	-	19	-	101	5	-	10,455	-	1,095
5690 Misc. apparel & accessory stores [2]	-	9	-	44	5	-	9,636	-	403
5712 Furniture stores [2]	-	24	-	168	7	-	17,095	-	3,185
5713 Floor covering stores [2]	-	10	-	61	6	-	22,295	-	1,410
5719 Misc. homefurnishings stores [2]	-	16	-	105	7	-	13,333	-	1,411
5731 Radio, TV, & electronic stores [2]	-	11	-	91	8	-	13,407	-	1,570
5734 Computer and software stores [2]	-	7	-	13	2	-	19,385	-	363
5736 Musical instrument stores [2]	-	4	-	10	3	-	20,800	-	241
5812 Eating places	-	217	-	4,828	22	-	8,766	-	44,000
5910 Drug stores and proprietary stores	-	19	-	247	13	-	17,150	-	4,166
5920 Liquor stores [2]	-	9	-	56	6	-	14,571	-	694
5930 Used merchandise stores [2]	-	19	-	49	3	-	15,020	-	845
5941 Sporting goods and bicycle shops [2]	-	22	-	93	4	-	13,376	-	1,538
5942 Book stores [2]	-	15	-	112	7	-	7,964	-	872
5943 Stationery stores [2]	-	7	-	44	6	-	13,455	-	546
5944 Jewelry stores [2]	-	14	-	84	6	-	14,000	-	1,239
5945 Hobby, toy, and game shops [2]	-	11	-	118	11	-	9,186	-	1,164

Continued on next page.

CHARLOTTESVILLE, VA MSA - [continued]

Wholesale and Retail Trade USA	Establishments		Employment		Emp / Est	Pay / Employee		Annual Payroll ($ 000)	
	1994	1995	1994	1995	1995	1994	1995	1994	1995
5946 Camera & photographic supply stores [2]	-	4	-	30	8	-	13,333	-	427
5947 Gift, novelty, and souvenir shops [2]	-	23	-	132	6	-	9,727	-	1,530
5963 Direct selling establishments [2]	-	14	-	66	5	-	17,939	-	1,708
5980 Fuel dealers [2]	-	10	-	68	7	-	21,765	-	1,466
5992 Florists	-	24	-	38	2	-	11,474	-	426
5995 Optical goods stores [2]	-	8	-	33	4	-	18,424	-	528
5999 Miscellaneous retail stores, nec [2]	-	31	-	177	6	-	10,237	-	1,820

Source: County Business Patterns 1994/95, CBP-94/95, U.S. Department of Commerce, Washington DC, November 1997. The employment column represents mid-March employment in the year. Pay per employee is calculated by dividing 1st Quarter payroll, annualized, by mid-March employment. The column headed 'Emp / Est' shows 'employees per establishment'. A dash (-) means that data are unavailable or cannot be calculated. nec means not elsewhere classified. *Notes:* 1. 1994 data incomplete; unavailable or withheld. 2. 1995 data incomplete; unavailable or withheld. 3. 1994 and 1995 data incomplete; unavailable or withheld.

CHATTANOOGA MSA (GA PART)

Wholesale and Retail Trade USA	Establishments		Employment		Emp / Est	Pay / Employee		Annual Payroll ($ 000)	
	1994	1995	1994	1995	1995	1994	1995	1994	1995
50- Wholesale trade	118	121	1,398	1,331	11	19,479	21,815	29,136	30,011
5013 Motor vehicle supplies and new parts [2]	9	10	27	49	5	17,185	18,939	456	1,048
5015 Motor vehicle parts, used	6	-	8	-	-	13,000	-	136	-
5020 Furniture and homefurnishings [3]	9	7	429	399	57	22,070	24,341	9,614	9,875
5040 Professional & commercial equipment [3]	9	9	75	83	9	21,333	26,072	1,888	2,031
5060 Electrical goods	-	5	-	16	3	-	21,750	-	368
5085 Industrial supplies [3]	4	4	60	58	15	16,200	25,862	999	1,541
5090 Miscellaneous durable goods [3]	12	13	96	126	10	13,208	15,175	1,587	1,837
5113 Industrial & personal service paper [2]	-	3	-	25	8	-	11,200	-	485
5130 Apparel, piece goods, and notions	7	6	44	66	11	11,000	13,273	780	956
5171 Petroleum bulk stations & terminals [2]	-	5	-	29	6	-	24,690	-	981
5191 Farm supplies [1]	3	-	12	-	-	12,333	-	160	-
5199 Nondurable goods, nec [2]	-	7	-	18	3	-	17,111	-	325
52- Retail trade	501	494	6,341	6,703	14	10,164	11,119	70,982	81,691
5210 Lumber and other building materials	9	7	95	106	15	15,789	15,245	1,576	1,708
5250 Hardware stores	10	8	31	32	4	12,129	12,375	399	444
5260 Retail nurseries and garden stores	-	6	-	18	3	-	3,778	-	103
5270 Mobile home dealers [3]	4	4	5	17	4	23,200	14,118	122	257
5390 Misc. general merchandise stores [1]	3	5	18	25	5	21,333	9,440	266	266
5410 Grocery stores [3]	65	70	464	511	7	10,431	10,591	5,618	5,956
5510 New and used car dealers [3]	10	10	161	177	18	18,907	19,955	4,055	4,385
5520 Used car dealers [3]	15	14	19	30	2	11,579	16,400	216	479
5530 Auto and home supply stores	21	26	89	109	4	15,775	14,972	1,367	1,691
5540 Gasoline service stations	63	59	413	512	9	11,458	13,008	5,692	8,061
5620 Women's clothing stores [2]	-	4	-	23	6	-	7,652	-	176
5660 Shoe stores	10	8	68	17	2	7,118	8,000	771	134
5712 Furniture stores [1]	13	16	62	159	10	11,419	16,830	856	3,162
5731 Radio, TV, & electronic stores [3]	4	5	21	23	5	16,000	14,435	302	294
5812 Eating places	89	82	1,777	1,767	22	6,717	7,450	12,374	14,392
5910 Drug stores and proprietary stores	26	25	176	173	7	15,727	16,971	3,025	3,096
5930 Used merchandise stores	-	13	-	31	2	-	8,000	-	345
5941 Sporting goods and bicycle shops [2]	-	6	-	11	2	-	17,091	-	226
5944 Jewelry stores [3]	10	10	20	17	2	20,600	20,235	372	280
5947 Gift, novelty, and souvenir shops	10	9	28	28	3	7,000	8,857	237	269
5963 Direct selling establishments [1]	4	-	9	-	-	13,333	-	122	-
5984 Liquefied petroleum gas dealers [3]	3	4	11	15	4	23,636	28,000	264	332
5992 Florists	13	12	64	18	2	10,375	10,444	879	170
5999 Miscellaneous retail stores, nec [3]	7	5	13	15	3	9,538	6,933	117	111

Source: County Business Patterns 1994/95, CBP-94/95, U.S. Department of Commerce, Washington DC, November 1997. The employment column represents mid-March employment in the year. Pay per employee is calculated by dividing 1st Quarter payroll, annualized, by mid-March employment. The column headed 'Emp / Est' shows 'employees per establishment'. A dash (-) means that data are unavailable or cannot be calculated. nec means not elsewhere classified. *Notes:* 1. 1994 data incomplete; unavailable or withheld. 2. 1995 data incomplete; unavailable or withheld. 3. 1994 and 1995 data incomplete; unavailable or withheld.

CHATTANOOGA MSA (TN PART)

Wholesale and Retail Trade USA	Establishments		Employment		Emp / Est	Pay / Employee		Annual Payroll ($ 000)	
	1994	1995	1994	1995	1995	1994	1995	1994	1995
50- Wholesale trade	-	836	-	10,276	12	-	26,561	-	297,799
5012 Automobiles and other vehicles [2]	-	17	-	253	15	-	29,676	-	9,603
5013 Motor vehicle supplies and new parts	-	38	-	494	13	-	22,591	-	11,860
5014 Tires and tubes [2]	-	10	-	98	10	-	33,633	-	3,204

Continued on next page.

CHATTANOOGA MSA (TN PART) - [continued]

Wholesale and Retail Trade USA	Establishments		Employment		Emp / Est	Pay / Employee		Annual Payroll ($ 000)	
	1994	1995	1994	1995	1995	1994	1995	1994	1995
5015 Motor vehicle parts, used [2]	-	9	-	34	4	-	15,294	-	543
5021 Furniture [2]	-	14	-	134	10	-	26,358	-	4,063
5023 Homefurnishings [2]	-	18	-	171	10	-	20,959	-	3,953
5031 Lumber, plywood, and millwork	-	15	-	258	17	-	22,186	-	5,837
5032 Brick, stone, & related materials	-	8	-	75	9	-	24,747	-	2,385
5033 Roofing, siding, & insulation [2]	-	10	-	78	8	-	20,923	-	1,898
5039 Construction materials, nec [2]	-	9	-	114	13	-	30,000	-	3,194
5044 Office equipment [2]	-	19	-	285	15	-	29,530	-	7,858
5045 Computers, peripherals, & software [2]	-	28	-	277	10	-	41,848	-	11,295
5046 Commercial equipment, nec [2]	-	12	-	79	7	-	30,937	-	2,482
5047 Medical and hospital equipment [2]	-	17	-	244	14	-	28,131	-	7,331
5051 Metals service centers and offices [2]	-	17	-	610	36	-	30,675	-	21,415
5052 Coal and other minerals and ores [2]	-	5	-	18	4	-	37,333	-	768
5063 Electrical apparatus and equipment [2]	-	39	-	354	9	-	31,616	-	11,718
5064 Electrical appliances, TV & radios [2]	-	8	-	111	14	-	22,595	-	2,869
5065 Electronic parts and equipment	-	23	-	211	9	-	24,171	-	5,710
5072 Hardware	-	18	-	150	8	-	27,627	-	4,683
5075 Warm air heating & air conditioning [2]	-	17	-	166	10	-	33,133	-	5,217
5082 Construction and mining machinery [2]	-	10	-	132	13	-	30,000	-	4,259
5083 Farm and garden machinery [2]	-	7	-	56	8	-	23,500	-	1,461
5084 Industrial machinery and equipment [2]	-	46	-	454	10	-	23,304	-	11,825
5085 Industrial supplies [2]	-	57	-	656	12	-	33,939	-	23,102
5087 Service establishment equipment [2]	-	13	-	109	8	-	25,284	-	3,106
5091 Sporting & recreational goods [2]	-	9	-	152	17	-	23,921	-	3,141
5092 Toys and hobby goods and supplies	-	7	-	24	3	-	13,500	-	354
5093 Scrap and waste materials	-	14	-	328	23	-	21,134	-	10,047
5094 Jewelry & precious stones [2]	-	7	-	99	14	-	28,606	-	2,015
5099 Durable goods, nec	-	15	-	43	3	-	19,256	-	929
5111 Printing and writing paper [2]	-	7	-	61	9	-	34,492	-	2,300
5112 Stationery and office supplies [2]	-	19	-	188	10	-	26,957	-	4,592
5113 Industrial & personal service paper [2]	-	14	-	146	10	-	26,274	-	4,369
5120 Drugs, proprietaries, and sundries [2]	-	9	-	228	25	-	25,298	-	5,804
5131 Piece goods & notions [2]	-	12	-	49	4	-	31,510	-	1,587
5136 Men's and boys' clothing [2]	-	7	-	49	7	-	29,959	-	4,441
5137 Women's and children's clothing [2]	-	9	-	40	4	-	20,100	-	949
5141 Groceries, general line [2]	-	6	-	212	35	-	22,491	-	4,684
5142 Packaged frozen food [2]	-	4	-	64	16	-	25,938	-	1,873
5145 Confectionery	-	10	-	418	42	-	15,120	-	6,337
5148 Fresh fruits and vegetables [2]	-	9	-	115	13	-	20,383	-	2,754
5149 Groceries and related products, nec	-	10	-	294	29	-	29,864	-	8,450
5162 Plastics materials & basic shapes [2]	-	4	-	8	2	-	38,500	-	509
5169 Chemicals & allied products, nec [2]	-	40	-	409	10	-	34,729	-	16,654
5171 Petroleum bulk stations & terminals	-	16	-	149	9	-	27,758	-	5,036
5172 Petroleum products, nec [2]	-	8	-	104	13	-	32,423	-	3,831
5180 Beer, wine, and distilled beverages [2]	-	7	-	219	31	-	32,037	-	8,429
5193 Flowers & florists' supplies [2]	-	3	-	53	18	-	17,962	-	947
5198 Paints, varnishes, and supplies [2]	-	6	-	31	5	-	22,452	-	734
5199 Nondurable goods, nec	-	39	-	165	4	-	22,303	-	4,073
52 – Retail trade	-	2,263	-	33,514	15	-	12,385	-	451,752
5210 Lumber and other building materials	-	42	-	706	17	-	21,314	-	15,593
5230 Paint, glass, and wallpaper stores	-	21	-	83	4	-	17,976	-	1,573
5250 Hardware stores	-	19	-	183	10	-	13,574	-	2,953
5260 Retail nurseries and garden stores [2]	-	12	-	122	10	-	7,311	-	1,265
5270 Mobile home dealers	-	6	-	39	7	-	26,667	-	1,584
5310 Department stores [2]	-	20	-	3,290	165	-	11,431	-	38,267
5330 Variety stores	-	16	-	113	7	-	8,991	-	1,163
5390 Misc. general merchandise stores	-	19	-	463	24	-	12,916	-	5,523
5410 Grocery stores	-	178	-	4,374	25	-	9,681	-	47,328
5420 Meat and fish markets [2]	-	5	-	18	4	-	13,556	-	287
5440 Candy, nut, and confectionery stores [2]	-	6	-	16	3	-	19,250	-	373
5460 Retail bakeries [2]	-	19	-	165	9	-	8,194	-	1,412
5490 Miscellaneous food stores [2]	-	8	-	21	3	-	14,286	-	293
5510 New and used car dealers	-	25	-	1,414	57	-	28,775	-	50,316
5520 Used car dealers [2]	-	29	-	116	4	-	23,552	-	3,690
5530 Auto and home supply stores	-	67	-	588	9	-	18,905	-	12,875
5540 Gasoline service stations	-	161	-	908	6	-	13,018	-	15,024
5550 Boat dealers [2]	-	11	-	37	3	-	28,324	-	1,098
5570 Motorcycle dealers [2]	-	5	-	37	7	-	16,216	-	793
5590 Automotive dealers, nec [2]	-	3	-	21	7	-	15,619	-	386
5610 Men's & boys' clothing stores [2]	-	29	-	238	8	-	10,437	-	2,422
5620 Women's clothing stores	-	60	-	474	8	-	7,511	-	3,586

Continued on next page.

CHATTANOOGA MSA (TN PART) - [continued]

Wholesale and Retail Trade USA	Establishments		Employment		Emp / Est	Pay / Employee		Annual Payroll ($ 000)	
	1994	1995	1994	1995	1995	1994	1995	1994	1995
5630 Women's accessory & specialty stores [2]	-	13	-	62	5	-	8,839	-	621
5640 Children's and infants' wear stores	-	9	-	49	5	-	9,143	-	344
5650 Family clothing stores	-	29	-	729	25	-	10,332	-	7,967
5660 Shoe stores	-	58	-	334	6	-	10,216	-	3,116
5690 Misc. apparel & accessory stores	-	16	-	67	4	-	11,104	-	734
5712 Furniture stores	-	40	-	397	10	-	17,814	-	8,120
5713 Floor covering stores [2]	-	15	-	36	2	-	18,778	-	774
5719 Misc. homefurnishings stores [2]	-	35	-	234	7	-	11,641	-	3,059
5720 Household appliance stores	-	17	-	73	4	-	20,164	-	1,583
5731 Radio, TV, & electronic stores	-	23	-	174	8	-	17,241	-	2,829
5734 Computer and software stores [2]	-	12	-	84	7	-	20,476	-	1,899
5735 Record & prerecorded tape stores [2]	-	14	-	107	8	-	7,963	-	803
5736 Musical instrument stores [2]	-	11	-	28	3	-	9,714	-	344
5812 Eating places	-	492	-	11,545	23	-	8,000	-	97,921
5813 Drinking places [2]	-	28	-	199	7	-	10,754	-	1,500
5910 Drug stores and proprietary stores	-	73	-	797	11	-	16,949	-	17,094
5920 Liquor stores	-	38	-	116	3	-	10,586	-	1,218
5930 Used merchandise stores	-	44	-	141	3	-	11,376	-	1,898
5941 Sporting goods and bicycle shops [2]	-	33	-	228	7	-	11,123	-	2,808
5942 Book stores [2]	-	25	-	203	8	-	9,498	-	2,074
5943 Stationery stores [2]	-	5	-	57	11	-	20,702	-	1,285
5944 Jewelry stores	-	44	-	274	6	-	30,234	-	5,390
5945 Hobby, toy, and game shops	-	16	-	135	8	-	10,163	-	1,679
5947 Gift, novelty, and souvenir shops	-	47	-	216	5	-	8,148	-	1,896
5949 Sewing, needlework, and piece goods	-	15	-	62	4	-	11,613	-	713
5962 Merchandising machine operators	-	14	-	243	17	-	16,477	-	4,282
5980 Fuel dealers [2]	-	6	-	27	5	-	21,185	-	505
5992 Florists	-	28	-	180	6	-	9,467	-	1,741
5995 Optical goods stores [2]	-	29	-	132	5	-	18,939	-	2,617
5999 Miscellaneous retail stores, nec	-	76	-	393	5	-	15,359	-	6,764

Source: County Business Patterns 1994/95, CBP-94/95, U.S. Department of Commerce, Washington DC, November 1997. The employment column represents mid-March employment in the year. Pay per employee is calculated by dividing 1st Quarter payroll, annualized, by mid-March employment. The column headed 'Emp / Est' shows 'employees per establishment'. A dash (-) means that data are unavailable or cannot be calculated. nec means not elsewhere classified. *Notes:* 1. 1994 data incomplete; unavailable or withheld. 2. 1995 data incomplete; unavailable or withheld. 3. 1994 and 1995 data incomplete; unavailable or withheld.

CHATTANOOGA, TN - GA MSA

Wholesale and Retail Trade USA	Establishments		Employment		Emp / Est	Pay / Employee		Annual Payroll ($ 000)	
	1994	1995	1994	1995	1995	1994	1995	1994	1995
50- Wholesale trade [1]	118	957	1,398	11,607	12	19,479	26,017	29,136	327,810
5012 Automobiles and other vehicles [2]	-	20	-	253	13	-	29,676	-	9,603
5013 Motor vehicle supplies and new parts [3]	9	48	27	543	11	17,185	22,262	456	12,908
5014 Tires and tubes [2]	-	11	-	98	9	-	33,633	-	3,204
5015 Motor vehicle parts, used [3]	6	15	8	34	2	13,000	15,294	136	543
5021 Furniture [2]	-	15	-	134	9	-	26,358	-	4,063
5023 Homefurnishings [2]	-	24	-	171	7	-	20,959	-	3,953
5031 Lumber, plywood, and millwork [2]	-	17	-	258	15	-	22,186	-	5,837
5032 Brick, stone, & related materials [2]	-	8	-	75	9	-	24,747	-	2,385
5033 Roofing, siding, & insulation [2]	-	11	-	78	7	-	20,923	-	1,898
5039 Construction materials, nec [2]	-	12	-	114	10	-	30,000	-	3,194
5044 Office equipment [2]	-	20	-	285	14	-	29,530	-	7,858
5045 Computers, peripherals, & software [2]	-	32	-	277	9	-	41,848	-	11,295
5046 Commercial equipment, nec [2]	-	13	-	79	6	-	30,937	-	2,482
5047 Medical and hospital equipment [2]	-	20	-	244	12	-	28,131	-	7,331
5051 Metals service centers and offices [2]	-	19	-	610	32	-	30,675	-	21,415
5052 Coal and other minerals and ores [2]	-	5	-	18	4	-	37,333	-	768
5063 Electrical apparatus and equipment [2]	-	42	-	354	8	-	31,616	-	11,718
5064 Electrical appliances, TV & radios [2]	-	8	-	111	14	-	22,595	-	2,869
5065 Electronic parts and equipment [2]	-	25	-	211	8	-	24,171	-	5,710
5072 Hardware [2]	-	18	-	150	8	-	27,627	-	4,683
5075 Warm air heating & air conditioning [2]	-	18	-	166	9	-	33,133	-	5,217
5082 Construction and mining machinery [2]	-	13	-	132	10	-	30,000	-	4,259
5083 Farm and garden machinery [2]	-	8	-	56	7	-	23,500	-	1,461
5084 Industrial machinery and equipment [2]	-	52	-	454	9	-	23,304	-	11,825
5085 Industrial supplies [3]	4	61	60	714	12	16,200	33,283	999	24,643
5087 Service establishment equipment [2]	-	14	-	109	8	-	25,284	-	3,106
5091 Sporting & recreational goods [2]	-	11	-	152	14	-	23,921	-	3,141
5092 Toys and hobby goods and supplies [2]	-	8	-	24	3	-	13,500	-	354
5093 Scrap and waste materials [2]	-	23	-	328	14	-	21,134	-	10,047

Continued on next page.

CHATTANOOGA, TN - GA MSA - [continued]

Wholesale and Retail Trade USA	Establishments		Employment		Emp / Est	Pay / Employee		Annual Payroll ($ 000)	
	1994	1995	1994	1995	1995	1994	1995	1994	1995
5094 Jewelry & precious stones [2]	-	7	-	99	14	-	28,606	-	2,015
5099 Durable goods, nec [2]	-	16	-	43	3	-	19,256	-	929
5111 Printing and writing paper [2]	-	8	-	61	8	-	34,492	-	2,300
5112 Stationery and office supplies [2]	-	22	-	188	9	-	26,957	-	4,592
5113 Industrial & personal service paper [2]	-	17	-	171	10	-	24,070	-	4,854
5120 Drugs, proprietaries, and sundries [2]	-	9	-	228	25	-	25,298	-	5,804
5131 Piece goods & notions [2]	-	15	-	49	3	-	31,510	-	1,587
5136 Men's and boys' clothing [2]	-	7	-	49	7	-	29,959	-	4,441
5137 Women's and children's clothing [2]	-	9	-	40	4	-	20,100	-	949
5141 Groceries, general line [2]	-	6	-	212	35	-	22,491	-	4,684
5142 Packaged frozen food [2]	-	4	-	64	16	-	25,938	-	1,873
5145 Confectionery [2]	-	10	-	418	42	-	15,120	-	6,337
5148 Fresh fruits and vegetables [2]	-	10	-	115	12	-	20,383	-	2,754
5149 Groceries and related products, nec [2]	-	11	-	294	27	-	29,864	-	8,450
5162 Plastics materials & basic shapes [2]	-	5	-	8	2	-	38,500	-	509
5169 Chemicals & allied products, nec [2]	-	44	-	409	9	-	34,729	-	16,654
5171 Petroleum bulk stations & terminals [2]	-	21	-	178	8	-	27,258	-	6,017
5172 Petroleum products, nec [2]	-	9	-	104	12	-	32,423	-	3,831
5180 Beer, wine, and distilled beverages [2]	-	7	-	219	31	-	32,037	-	8,429
5191 Farm supplies [1]	3	-	12	-	-	12,333	-	160	-
5193 Flowers & florists' supplies [2]	-	8	-	53	7	-	17,962	-	947
5198 Paints, varnishes, and supplies [2]	-	6	-	31	5	-	22,452	-	734
5199 Nondurable goods, nec [2]	-	46	-	183	4	-	21,792	-	4,398
52- Retail trade [1]	501	2,757	6,341	40,217	15	10,164	12,174	70,982	533,443
5210 Lumber and other building materials [1]	9	49	95	812	17	15,789	20,522	1,576	17,301
5230 Paint, glass, and wallpaper stores [2]	-	23	-	83	4	-	17,976	-	1,573
5250 Hardware stores [1]	10	27	31	215	8	12,129	13,395	399	3,397
5260 Retail nurseries and garden stores [2]	-	18	-	140	8	-	6,857	-	1,368
5270 Mobile home dealers [3]	4	10	5	56	6	23,200	22,857	122	1,841
5310 Department stores [2]	-	23	-	3,290	143	-	11,431	-	38,267
5330 Variety stores	-	28	-	113	4	-	8,991	-	1,163
5390 Misc. general merchandise stores [1]	3	24	18	488	20	21,333	12,738	266	5,789
5410 Grocery stores [3]	65	248	464	4,885	20	10,431	9,776	5,618	53,284
5420 Meat and fish markets [2]	-	6	-	18	3	-	13,556	-	287
5440 Candy, nut, and confectionery stores [2]	-	7	-	16	2	-	19,250	-	373
5460 Retail bakeries [2]	-	22	-	165	8	-	8,194	-	1,412
5490 Miscellaneous food stores [2]	-	13	-	21	2	-	14,286	-	293
5510 New and used car dealers [3]	10	35	161	1,591	45	18,907	27,794	4,055	54,701
5520 Used car dealers [3]	15	43	19	146	3	11,579	22,082	216	4,169
5530 Auto and home supply stores [1]	21	93	89	697	7	15,775	18,290	1,367	14,566
5540 Gasoline service stations [1]	63	220	413	1,420	6	11,458	13,014	5,692	23,085
5550 Boat dealers [2]	-	12	-	37	3	-	28,324	-	1,098
5570 Motorcycle dealers [2]	-	6	-	37	6	-	16,216	-	793
5590 Automotive dealers, nec [2]	-	3	-	21	7	-	15,619	-	386
5610 Men's & boys' clothing stores [2]	-	30	-	238	8	-	10,437	-	2,422
5620 Women's clothing stores [2]	-	64	-	497	8	-	7,517	-	3,762
5630 Women's accessory & specialty stores [2]	-	13	-	62	5	-	8,839	-	621
5640 Children's and infants' wear stores [2]	-	9	-	49	5	-	9,143	-	344
5650 Family clothing stores [2]	-	30	-	729	24	-	10,332	-	7,967
5660 Shoe stores [1]	10	66	68	351	5	7,118	10,108	771	3,250
5690 Misc. apparel & accessory stores [2]	-	19	-	67	4	-	11,104	-	734
5712 Furniture stores [1]	13	56	62	556	10	11,419	17,532	856	11,282
5713 Floor covering stores [2]	-	20	-	36	2	-	18,778	-	774
5719 Misc. homefurnishings stores [2]	-	39	-	234	6	-	11,641	-	3,059
5720 Household appliance stores [2]	-	19	-	73	4	-	20,164	-	1,583
5731 Radio, TV, & electronic stores [3]	4	28	21	197	7	16,000	16,914	302	3,123
5734 Computer and software stores [2]	-	13	-	84	6	-	20,476	-	1,899
5735 Record & prerecorded tape stores [2]	-	14	-	107	8	-	7,963	-	803
5736 Musical instrument stores [2]	-	11	-	28	3	-	9,714	-	344
5812 Eating places [1]	89	574	1,777	13,312	23	6,717	7,927	12,374	112,313
5813 Drinking places [2]	-	28	-	199	7	-	10,754	-	1,500
5910 Drug stores and proprietary stores [1]	26	98	176	970	10	15,727	16,953	3,025	20,190
5920 Liquor stores [2]	-	40	-	116	3	-	10,586	-	1,218
5930 Used merchandise stores	-	57	-	172	3	-	10,767	-	2,243
5941 Sporting goods and bicycle shops [2]	-	39	-	239	6	-	11,397	-	3,034
5942 Book stores [2]	-	28	-	203	7	-	9,498	-	2,074
5943 Stationery stores [2]	-	5	-	57	11	-	20,702	-	1,285
5944 Jewelry stores [3]	10	54	20	291	5	20,600	29,649	372	5,670
5945 Hobby, toy, and game shops [2]	-	17	-	135	8	-	10,163	-	1,679
5947 Gift, novelty, and souvenir shops [1]	10	56	28	244	4	7,000	8,230	237	2,165
5949 Sewing, needlework, and piece goods [2]	-	16	-	62	4	-	11,613	-	713

Continued on next page.

CHATTANOOGA, TN – GA MSA - [continued]

Wholesale and Retail Trade USA	Establishments		Employment		Emp / Est	Pay / Employee		Annual Payroll ($ 000)	
	1994	1995	1994	1995	1995	1994	1995	1994	1995
5962 Merchandising machine operators [2]	-	16	-	243	15	-	16,477	-	4,282
5963 Direct selling establishments [1]	4	-	9	-	-	13,333	-	122	-
5984 Liquefied petroleum gas dealers [3]	3	9	11	15	2	23,636	28,000	264	332
5992 Florists [1]	13	40	64	198	5	10,375	9,556	879	1,911
5995 Optical goods stores [2]	-	30	-	132	4	-	18,939	-	2,617
5999 Miscellaneous retail stores, nec [3]	7	81	13	408	5	9,538	15,049	117	6,875

Source: County Business Patterns 1994/95, CBP-94/95, U.S. Department of Commerce, Washington DC, November 1997. The employment column represents mid-March employment in the year. Pay per employee is calculated by dividing 1st Quarter payroll, annualized, by mid-March employment. The column headed 'Emp / Est' shows 'employees per establishment'. A dash (-) means that data are unavailable or cannot be calculated. nec means not elsewhere classified. *Notes:* 1. 1994 data incomplete; unavailable or withheld. 2. 1995 data incomplete; unavailable or withheld. 3. 1994 and 1995 data incomplete; unavailable or withheld.

CHEYENNE, WY MSA

Wholesale and Retail Trade USA	Establishments		Employment		Emp / Est	Pay / Employee		Annual Payroll ($ 000)	
	1994	1995	1994	1995	1995	1994	1995	1994	1995
50- Wholesale trade	-	104	-	871	8	-	23,463	-	22,894
5010 Motor vehicles, parts, and supplies	-	7	-	79	11	-	18,430	-	1,448
5031 Lumber, plywood, and millwork	-	5	-	45	9	-	39,911	-	2,021
5039 Construction materials, nec	-	3	-	23	8	-	29,565	-	864
5044 Office equipment	-	6	-	91	15	-	23,648	-	2,207
5060 Electrical goods	-	8	-	33	4	-	30,788	-	1,089
5070 Hardware, plumbing & heating equipment	-	4	-	17	4	-	21,882	-	391
5087 Service establishment equipment	-	3	-	36	12	-	20,556	-	818
5112 Stationery and office supplies	-	5	-	21	4	-	25,333	-	542
5149 Groceries and related products, nec	-	4	-	54	14	-	20,963	-	1,612
5169 Chemicals & allied products, nec	-	4	-	17	4	-	27,529	-	486
5170 Petroleum and petroleum products	-	8	-	64	8	-	27,750	-	2,116
5191 Farm supplies	-	5	-	36	7	-	20,222	-	755
52- Retail trade	-	476	-	7,418	16	-	12,404	-	98,819
5210 Lumber and other building materials	-	6	-	69	12	-	26,957	-	1,826
5270 Mobile home dealers	-	6	-	7	1	-	25,714	-	234
5310 Department stores	-	7	-	839	120	-	11,523	-	9,792
5410 Grocery stores	-	16	-	581	36	-	13,652	-	8,347
5490 Miscellaneous food stores	-	4	-	7	2	-	9,714	-	83
5510 New and used car dealers	-	7	-	427	61	-	26,473	-	12,416
5520 Used car dealers	-	8	-	20	3	-	16,000	-	399
5530 Auto and home supply stores	-	13	-	107	8	-	18,579	-	2,192
5540 Gasoline service stations	-	43	-	405	9	-	12,385	-	5,510
5560 Recreational vehicle dealers	-	3	-	13	4	-	24,308	-	377
5570 Motorcycle dealers	-	3	-	14	5	-	17,714	-	291
5620 Women's clothing stores	-	9	-	55	6	-	7,273	-	409
5650 Family clothing stores	-	12	-	124	10	-	9,452	-	1,108
5660 Shoe stores	-	9	-	33	4	-	9,939	-	346
5712 Furniture stores	-	5	-	30	6	-	20,800	-	711
5719 Misc. homefurnishings stores	-	8	-	45	6	-	9,511	-	437
5720 Household appliance stores	-	3	-	28	9	-	15,714	-	513
5731 Radio, TV, & electronic stores	-	6	-	36	6	-	9,889	-	447
5812 Eating places	-	94	-	2,662	28	-	7,800	-	22,632
5813 Drinking places	-	14	-	112	8	-	6,786	-	807
5910 Drug stores and proprietary stores	-	5	-	66	13	-	19,394	-	1,294
5920 Liquor stores	-	12	-	125	10	-	10,016	-	1,375
5930 Used merchandise stores	-	8	-	46	6	-	12,696	-	586
5941 Sporting goods and bicycle shops	-	8	-	44	6	-	9,455	-	470
5942 Book stores	-	5	-	22	4	-	7,273	-	159
5944 Jewelry stores	-	8	-	45	6	-	16,711	-	741
5945 Hobby, toy, and game shops	-	4	-	15	4	-	8,533	-	138
5947 Gift, novelty, and souvenir shops	-	9	-	35	4	-	5,714	-	207
5961 Catalog and mail-order houses	-	3	-	424	141	-	17,792	-	8,627
5992 Florists	-	8	-	42	5	-	7,905	-	310
5995 Optical goods stores	-	7	-	27	4	-	14,370	-	410
5999 Miscellaneous retail stores, nec	-	20	-	99	5	-	10,505	-	1,128

Source: County Business Patterns 1994/95, CBP-94/95, U.S. Department of Commerce, Washington DC, November 1997. The employment column represents mid-March employment in the year. Pay per employee is calculated by dividing 1st Quarter payroll, annualized, by mid-March employment. The column headed 'Emp / Est' shows 'employees per establishment'. A dash (-) means that data are unavailable or cannot be calculated. nec means not elsewhere classified. *Notes:* 1. 1994 data incomplete; unavailable or withheld. 2. 1995 data incomplete; unavailable or withheld. 3. 1994 and 1995 data incomplete; unavailable or withheld.

CHICAGO, IL PMSA

Wholesale and Retail Trade USA	Establishments		Employment		Emp / Est	Pay / Employee		Annual Payroll ($ 000)	
	1994	1995	1994	1995	1995	1994	1995	1994	1995
50- Wholesale trade	17,928	18,207	284,233	296,836	16	37,996	40,218	11,412,157	12,294,669
5012 Automobiles and other vehicles[3]	172	172	4,252	4,472	26	36,683	40,124	165,273	177,918
5013 Motor vehicle supplies and new parts	689	626	9,493	10,094	16	28,496	34,146	295,892	349,239
5014 Tires and tubes[3]	86	81	1,323	1,201	15	28,587	33,229	41,573	42,007
5015 Motor vehicle parts, used[3]	108	129	1,158	1,276	10	24,190	23,480	29,533	31,047
5021 Furniture[3]	349	348	2,786	2,916	8	36,639	38,870	113,776	127,488
5023 Homefurnishings[3]	351	347	4,888	5,110	15	32,606	36,410	169,914	189,102
5031 Lumber, plywood, and millwork	264	246	2,888	3,152	13	32,568	36,027	107,634	116,057
5032 Brick, stone, & related materials[3]	137	123	1,115	1,073	9	30,709	33,297	42,927	39,726
5033 Roofing, siding, & insulation[3]	102	92	907	910	10	35,563	37,424	38,206	38,688
5039 Construction materials, nec[3]	137	196	1,910	2,204	11	31,644	34,361	66,629	81,564
5043 Photographic equipment & supplies[3]	83	88	2,290	2,228	25	42,817	47,318	95,772	100,197
5044 Office equipment	266	282	5,699	6,031	21	36,032	39,054	216,193	232,436
5045 Computers, peripherals, & software[3]	651	643	15,249	14,686	23	55,842	57,864	868,166	895,157
5046 Commercial equipment, nec[3]	219	228	3,025	3,277	14	31,422	34,898	107,012	122,121
5047 Medical and hospital equipment[3]	421	437	8,472	9,398	22	46,464	49,053	372,070	443,579
5048 Ophthalmic goods[3]	57	52	523	585	11	25,866	23,897	15,504	13,721
5049 Professional equipment, nec[3]	115	119	2,279	2,297	19	34,085	36,796	79,298	86,717
5051 Metals service centers and offices[3]	696	689	13,950	14,307	21	36,137	40,835	545,756	588,066
5052 Coal and other minerals and ores[3]	20	15	216	75	5	52,222	55,520	13,415	5,230
5063 Electrical apparatus and equipment[3]	781	679	8,858	7,696	11	35,638	41,270	341,247	323,190
5064 Electrical appliances, TV & radios[3]	153	151	1,997	2,135	14	39,631	41,430	85,283	94,305
5065 Electronic parts and equipment[3]	802	853	15,011	15,787	19	46,189	48,265	701,897	806,835
5072 Hardware[3]	472	501	5,415	5,832	12	31,023	35,377	194,607	214,945
5074 Plumbing & hydronic heating supplies	259	253	3,218	3,395	13	36,574	39,257	132,888	137,097
5075 Warm air heating & air conditioning[3]	165	170	1,742	1,714	10	39,401	44,439	72,090	74,110
5078 Refrigeration equipment and supplies[3]	53	52	416	440	8	34,885	37,091	15,757	18,392
5082 Construction and mining machinery[3]	117	117	1,497	1,589	14	40,644	44,496	64,924	70,442
5083 Farm and garden machinery	99	91	1,234	1,179	13	29,219	29,350	41,301	37,658
5084 Industrial machinery and equipment[3]	1,471	1,496	16,397	17,558	12	41,326	45,117	753,085	843,348
5085 Industrial supplies	637	650	7,418	8,227	13	37,115	40,374	303,172	342,181
5087 Service establishment equipment[3]	258	256	2,200	2,374	9	29,104	30,721	72,517	77,617
5088 Transportation equipment & supplies[3]	99	104	962	1,415	14	34,823	40,447	38,400	60,938
5091 Sporting & recreational goods[3]	198	203	2,079	2,285	11	32,610	33,822	80,720	89,158
5092 Toys and hobby goods and supplies[3]	117	115	1,203	1,290	11	33,486	33,296	51,919	50,267
5093 Scrap and waste materials[3]	329	337	3,929	4,299	13	26,032	30,833	119,909	150,959
5094 Jewelry & precious stones[3]	274	273	2,535	2,239	8	23,940	30,353	65,537	68,255
5099 Durable goods, nec[1]	417	423	2,649	3,055	7	35,473	36,203	100,966	108,457
5111 Printing and writing paper[3]	145	148	2,066	2,086	14	43,772	49,267	100,355	113,046
5112 Stationery and office supplies[3]	500	461	11,222	10,766	23	21,948	22,719	262,096	261,503
5113 Industrial & personal service paper[3]	348	355	3,628	3,807	11	43,656	48,187	171,180	192,515
5120 Drugs, proprietaries, and sundries[3]	234	241	8,574	9,906	41	43,088	44,621	367,057	449,406
5131 Piece goods & notions[3]	165	172	1,565	1,598	9	31,312	33,935	53,825	56,286
5136 Men's and boys' clothing[3]	159	144	1,990	2,071	14	30,022	31,075	65,400	69,500
5137 Women's and children's clothing[3]	226	217	1,322	1,253	6	26,893	28,466	40,564	40,970
5139 Footwear[3]	38	38	230	245	6	25,061	28,522	8,494	8,822
5141 Groceries, general line[3]	197	190	4,997	5,346	28	35,559	37,176	192,308	205,635
5142 Packaged frozen food[3]	125	121	2,823	2,949	24	31,741	31,414	107,319	105,535
5143 Dairy products, exc. dried or canned[3]	134	123	2,189	1,868	15	46,977	32,919	90,200	66,117
5144 Poultry and poultry products[3]	31	28	635	647	23	25,720	27,073	19,866	18,154
5145 Confectionery[3]	92	92	2,658	2,764	30	30,077	30,067	87,494	83,207
5146 Fish and seafoods[3]	49	52	590	543	10	29,749	25,297	20,180	16,742
5147 Meats and meat products[3]	224	222	4,335	4,463	20	26,469	28,389	125,300	129,298
5148 Fresh fruits and vegetables[3]	157	147	1,561	1,410	10	37,432	38,417	60,218	64,071
5149 Groceries and related products, nec[3]	448	455	10,343	10,504	23	40,444	31,432	404,822	351,882
5153 Grain and field beans[2]	62	61	398	339	6	30,241	32,330	14,871	12,009
5154 Livestock[1]	7	-	12	-	-	10,667	-	176	-
5159 Farm-product raw materials, nec[3]	15	14	25	25	2	60,640	58,880	1,691	2,165
5162 Plastics materials & basic shapes[3]	198	213	2,247	2,471	12	40,265	41,789	96,761	112,999
5169 Chemicals & allied products, nec[3]	445	451	5,509	5,792	13	42,801	44,356	242,468	262,415
5171 Petroleum bulk stations & terminals[3]	106	102	1,293	1,382	14	36,959	39,809	52,505	61,350
5172 Petroleum products, nec[2]	101	99	775	761	8	39,979	32,825	33,262	25,818
5181 Beer and ale[3]	52	53	1,805	2,101	40	31,262	32,611	66,588	74,767
5182 Wine and distilled beverages[3]	58	60	2,797	2,631	44	37,084	39,409	104,780	105,297
5191 Farm supplies[2]	150	139	1,605	1,525	11	34,358	41,527	58,361	66,261
5192 Books, periodicals, & newspapers[3]	196	198	5,009	5,665	29	31,471	30,794	155,684	176,585
5193 Flowers & florists' supplies[3]	122	110	2,136	2,090	19	24,189	26,869	56,818	61,454
5194 Tobacco and tobacco products[3]	33	32	665	688	22	31,549	33,105	23,618	24,904
5198 Paints, varnishes, and supplies[3]	125	117	856	918	8	29,944	37,333	27,232	35,032
5199 Nondurable goods, nec	726	747	6,485	6,763	9	30,048	34,330	207,101	232,548
52- Retail trade	41,489	41,332	619,808	633,997	15	14,039	15,292	9,503,437	10,080,880

Continued on next page.

CHICAGO, IL PMSA - [continued]

Wholesale and Retail Trade USA	Establishments		Employment		Emp / Est	Pay / Employee		Annual Payroll ($ 000)	
	1994	1995	1994	1995	1995	1994	1995	1994	1995
5210 Lumber and other building materials	562	521	11,945	12,861	25	17,844	19,899	254,738	274,722
5230 Paint, glass, and wallpaper stores [3]	240	245	1,158	1,436	6	18,387	18,404	23,813	30,335
5250 Hardware stores	516	382	6,159	5,252	14	13,138	13,236	90,172	69,163
5260 Retail nurseries and garden stores	227	233	2,304	2,674	11	12,648	12,489	44,763	46,739
5270 Mobile home dealers [3]	16	18	27	35	2	25,037	20,686	708	757
5310 Department stores [3]	281	283	57,252	59,775	211	10,391	11,741	679,148	730,024
5330 Variety stores [3]	236	201	2,023	1,795	9	9,772	9,348	20,205	18,324
5390 Misc. general merchandise stores [2]	325	331	6,969	7,424	22	12,037	13,766	97,174	100,296
5410 Grocery stores	2,849	2,865	69,980	73,642	26	13,152	13,680	954,399	1,002,541
5420 Meat and fish markets [3]	219	212	1,187	1,143	5	14,147	14,565	17,930	18,171
5430 Fruit and vegetable markets [3]	92	93	773	848	9	11,172	12,349	10,890	12,353
5440 Candy, nut, and confectionery stores [3]	288	281	1,840	1,656	6	6,498	7,812	13,014	13,292
5450 Dairy products stores [3]	102	102	452	509	5	4,779	6,798	2,926	4,528
5460 Retail bakeries	761	720	6,363	5,952	8	10,542	11,025	76,448	71,435
5490 Miscellaneous food stores [3]	290	297	1,819	2,144	7	10,769	11,295	21,145	26,016
5510 New and used car dealers	579	578	27,439	28,791	50	30,619	32,781	1,012,891	1,055,895
5520 Used car dealers	309	304	1,431	1,565	5	21,154	22,668	39,129	42,342
5530 Auto and home supply stores	749	741	5,920	6,383	9	18,552	19,385	121,444	129,064
5540 Gasoline service stations	2,083	2,017	15,532	14,840	7	11,825	12,800	192,738	197,401
5550 Boat dealers [3]	53	57	443	475	8	19,955	19,739	11,883	12,233
5560 Recreational vehicle dealers [3]	33	31	108	200	6	17,444	18,400	2,522	4,667
5570 Motorcycle dealers [3]	60	60	462	504	8	18,554	19,190	11,424	11,957
5590 Automotive dealers, nec [3]	17	16	84	71	4	18,286	25,803	1,446	1,444
5610 Men's & boys' clothing stores	589	543	4,353	4,303	8	13,556	14,517	63,629	62,405
5620 Women's clothing stores	1,363	1,252	16,227	14,777	12	9,233	9,598	164,852	145,908
5630 Women's accessory & specialty stores [3]	311	301	1,851	1,936	6	12,458	12,603	24,204	23,473
5640 Children's and infants' wear stores [3]	200	187	1,737	1,833	10	8,021	8,517	15,318	16,145
5650 Family clothing stores [3]	544	520	10,740	11,783	23	10,728	12,315	123,890	148,378
5660 Shoe stores [3]	1,149	1,085	7,191	6,997	6	11,910	13,383	92,875	94,208
5690 Misc. apparel & accessory stores [1]	254	257	1,508	1,650	6	11,302	12,616	18,833	21,531
5712 Furniture stores	791	792	6,948	7,211	9	19,508	20,863	154,184	161,514
5713 Floor covering stores	404	391	2,508	2,642	7	23,207	24,544	65,786	69,628
5714 Drapery and upholstery stores [3]	99	94	406	412	4	15,340	15,398	6,783	6,971
5719 Misc. homefurnishings stores	555	537	5,044	5,121	10	11,627	12,850	66,542	69,845
5720 Household appliance stores [3]	151	152	1,062	1,222	8	20,761	22,710	27,573	31,659
5731 Radio, TV, & electronic stores [3]	524	506	5,545	6,197	12	15,911	15,493	90,580	97,373
5734 Computer and software stores [3]	218	245	1,542	1,854	8	18,724	21,219	32,679	42,651
5735 Record & prerecorded tape stores [3]	331	308	2,600	2,524	8	9,409	9,805	25,177	24,693
5736 Musical instrument stores [3]	124	117	799	852	7	20,290	19,202	15,433	17,539
5812 Eating places	10,793	10,318	196,141	195,815	19	8,429	9,276	1,850,158	1,945,966
5813 Drinking places	1,760	1,657	9,349	9,751	6	8,403	8,992	85,238	93,057
5910 Drug stores and proprietary stores	1,185	1,122	21,226	20,792	19	15,727	17,386	348,364	358,472
5920 Liquor stores	874	847	4,373	4,344	5	11,723	11,924	56,617	57,286
5930 Used merchandise stores [2]	384	373	2,834	2,699	7	11,092	12,138	35,247	34,847
5941 Sporting goods and bicycle shops	579	608	4,625	5,437	9	11,582	12,166	65,749	72,107
5942 Book stores [3]	368	380	3,215	3,906	10	11,308	11,062	38,000	44,690
5943 Stationery stores [3]	136	138	775	775	6	14,142	14,679	11,912	11,793
5944 Jewelry stores [3]	732	763	3,944	3,988	5	18,254	19,408	75,998	81,623
5945 Hobby, toy, and game shops [3]	280	277	3,504	3,766	14	10,148	10,376	44,318	47,650
5946 Camera & photographic supply stores [3]	117	113	644	679	6	15,124	15,340	10,361	10,584
5947 Gift, novelty, and souvenir shops	893	881	5,608	5,512	6	7,859	8,669	48,735	50,813
5948 Luggage and leather goods stores [3]	59	63	328	312	5	15,683	16,731	5,117	5,387
5949 Sewing, needlework, and piece goods	159	139	1,811	1,526	11	7,980	9,476	15,164	14,786
5961 Catalog and mail-order houses [3]	230	260	6,802	6,674	26	25,384	30,773	174,571	189,505
5962 Merchandising machine operators [3]	198	202	2,488	2,551	13	20,453	22,049	55,957	59,600
5963 Direct selling establishments	384	380	5,100	5,579	15	18,215	19,568	106,321	112,764
5983 Fuel oil dealers [1]	11	-	37	-	-	23,459	-	987	-
5984 Liquefied petroleum gas dealers [3]	23	21	120	90	4	24,767	27,956	3,545	2,601
5989 Fuel dealers, nec [1]	5	-	3	-	-	8,000	-	29	-
5992 Florists	617	600	3,497	3,610	6	12,222	12,111	45,504	46,045
5993 Tobacco stores and stands [3]	67	71	283	322	5	11,901	12,050	3,762	4,450
5994 News dealers and newsstands [3]	75	71	191	219	3	9,445	10,922	2,017	2,364
5995 Optical goods stores [3]	384	375	2,341	2,303	6	15,927	17,134	40,090	42,413
5999 Miscellaneous retail stores, nec	1,350	1,441	8,419	9,450	7	14,836	16,355	147,711	164,700

Source: County Business Patterns 1994/95, CBP-94/95, U.S. Department of Commerce, Washington DC, November 1997. The employment column represents mid-March employment in the year. Pay per employee is calculated by dividing 1st Quarter payroll, annualized, by mid-March employment. The column headed 'Emp / Est' shows 'employees per establishment'. A dash (-) means that data are unavailable or cannot be calculated. nec means not elsewhere classified. *Notes:* 1. 1994 data incomplete; unavailable or withheld. 2. 1995 data incomplete; unavailable or withheld. 3. 1994 and 1995 data incomplete; unavailable or withheld.

CHICO – PARADISE, CA MSA

Wholesale and Retail Trade USA	Establishments		Employment		Emp / Est	Pay / Employee		Annual Payroll ($ 000)	
	1994	1995	1994	1995	1995	1994	1995	1994	1995
50 – Wholesale trade	242	250	2,476	2,646	11	22,465	23,426	63,600	70,150
5013 Motor vehicle supplies and new parts	7	8	65	71	9	18,338	17,014	1,266	1,331
5015 Motor vehicle parts, used	4	4	18	20	5	14,000	15,400	293	295
5031 Lumber, plywood, and millwork	9	10	86	78	8	28,093	26,615	2,554	2,864
5044 Office equipment	11	10	110	112	11	19,200	23,607	2,335	2,654
5045 Computers, peripherals, & software	6	7	59	68	10	19,525	21,647	1,270	1,409
5047 Medical and hospital equipment	-	3	-	15	5	-	16,533	-	266
5051 Metals service centers and offices	3	3	36	35	12	18,111	19,429	636	738
5063 Electrical apparatus and equipment	6	6	45	51	9	23,822	26,118	1,125	1,185
5072 Hardware	6	8	83	122	15	24,048	28,033	2,233	4,023
5074 Plumbing & hydronic heating supplies	-	7	-	54	8	-	22,889	-	1,379
5082 Construction and mining machinery	4	4	73	69	17	29,534	28,406	2,178	2,268
5083 Farm and garden machinery	5	5	54	60	12	23,852	22,200	1,297	1,339
5084 Industrial machinery and equipment	9	9	49	40	4	25,714	24,100	1,390	914
5085 Industrial supplies	4	4	22	18	5	17,455	24,222	464	507
5087 Service establishment equipment	-	5	-	31	6	-	25,419	-	853
5091 Sporting & recreational goods	7	-	60	-	-	19,067	-	1,381	-
5092 Toys and hobby goods and supplies	3	3	4	3	1	21,000	20,000	114	85
5093 Scrap and waste materials	5	8	31	40	5	11,355	12,700	424	913
5094 Jewelry & precious stones	-	3	-	12	4	-	4,333	-	96
5130 Apparel, piece goods, and notions	3	-	3	-	-	18,667	-	32	-
5148 Fresh fruits and vegetables	5	5	122	148	30	21,344	22,757	3,449	4,127
5149 Groceries and related products, nec	15	15	173	145	10	22,150	26,593	3,704	3,796
5150 Farm-product raw materials	6	6	116	124	21	30,276	29,161	3,951	3,992
5169 Chemicals & allied products, nec	6	7	55	68	10	44,800	26,588	1,792	2,109
5171 Petroleum bulk stations & terminals	14	12	62	52	4	24,129	23,000	1,552	1,518
5181 Beer and ale	3	3	84	101	34	25,000	26,574	2,431	3,148
5191 Farm supplies	20	18	138	152	8	27,913	31,026	5,124	5,262
5192 Books, periodicals, & newspapers	4	-	39	-	-	24,000	-	810	-
5199 Nondurable goods, nec	-	6	-	16	3	-	10,250	-	159
52 – Retail trade	1,108	1,096	14,024	14,169	13	11,531	12,192	173,917	179,753
5210 Lumber and other building materials	20	19	300	287	15	19,227	20,125	6,224	6,085
5230 Paint, glass, and wallpaper stores	10	9	44	44	5	19,455	19,727	935	941
5250 Hardware stores	15	11	133	104	9	13,083	12,885	1,531	1,399
5260 Retail nurseries and garden stores	9	8	63	70	9	13,016	11,486	831	884
5270 Mobile home dealers	7	7	29	33	5	23,724	18,545	848	821
5310 Department stores	10	11	1,465	1,546	141	10,067	12,290	17,502	18,861
5410 Grocery stores	93	85	1,753	1,718	20	17,134	18,563	31,216	32,187
5420 Meat and fish markets	8	6	28	24	4	9,857	12,167	332	304
5450 Dairy products stores	3	3	10	18	6	4,800	4,222	69	93
5460 Retail bakeries	12	17	88	92	5	5,318	5,783	545	487
5490 Miscellaneous food stores	9	8	72	64	8	5,889	7,375	499	447
5510 New and used car dealers	14	13	650	653	50	23,385	26,646	17,669	18,380
5520 Used car dealers	10	10	48	43	4	15,333	16,837	759	716
5530 Auto and home supply stores	36	32	235	247	8	16,800	17,862	4,485	4,504
5540 Gasoline service stations	53	54	346	397	7	8,474	8,071	2,989	3,364
5550 Boat dealers	4	4	14	13	3	10,571	12,000	211	208
5560 Recreational vehicle dealers	7	6	63	64	11	16,444	17,500	1,238	1,470
5570 Motorcycle dealers	9	9	48	41	5	15,250	15,317	719	727
5610 Men's & boys' clothing stores	6	6	37	32	5	14,270	18,500	506	535
5620 Women's clothing stores	33	26	234	160	6	7,402	7,775	1,951	1,214
5630 Women's accessory & specialty stores	6	7	23	29	4	9,565	7,034	219	256
5650 Family clothing stores	9	10	134	144	14	8,328	9,083	1,249	1,401
5660 Shoe stores	19	19	86	77	4	10,558	12,104	896	819
5690 Misc. apparel & accessory stores	9	9	34	31	3	5,176	3,742	182	168
5712 Furniture stores	17	16	133	102	6	15,218	19,608	2,027	1,902
5713 Floor covering stores	12	13	70	68	5	23,714	25,706	1,931	1,752
5719 Misc. homefurnishings stores	13	13	61	90	7	10,885	9,911	795	907
5720 Household appliance stores	12	11	95	90	8	17,389	14,400	1,631	1,301
5731 Radio, TV, & electronic stores	19	18	139	209	12	12,806	13,474	2,098	2,863
5735 Record & prerecorded tape stores	11	9	92	89	10	8,000	8,090	813	726
5812 Eating places	263	260	4,780	4,836	19	6,675	6,802	32,954	34,256
5813 Drinking places	42	38	372	356	9	4,839	4,989	1,859	1,761
5910 Drug stores and proprietary stores	33	31	555	530	17	20,519	20,875	11,646	11,005
5920 Liquor stores	16	16	90	76	5	6,356	7,895	616	564
5930 Used merchandise stores	19	15	92	83	6	8,957	8,819	868	723
5941 Sporting goods and bicycle shops	28	24	197	162	7	10,863	12,667	2,302	2,218
5942 Book stores	14	13	98	89	7	7,673	9,708	782	811
5943 Stationery stores	4	-	32	-	-	14,625	-	405	-
5944 Jewelry stores	16	14	75	79	6	17,547	16,203	1,420	1,115
5945 Hobby, toy, and game shops	11	12	99	134	11	11,152	9,194	1,258	1,372

Continued on next page.

CHICO – PARADISE, CA MSA - [continued]

Wholesale and Retail Trade USA	Establishments		Employment		Emp / Est	Pay / Employee		Annual Payroll ($ 000)	
	1994	1995	1994	1995	1995	1994	1995	1994	1995
5946 Camera & photographic supply stores	3	-	12	-	-	9,667	-	125	-
5947 Gift, novelty, and souvenir shops	24	21	132	122	6	6,182	6,000	818	794
5949 Sewing, needlework, and piece goods	7	8	58	43	5	6,414	6,884	337	296
5963 Direct selling establishments	14	11	61	56	5	12,721	15,143	781	867
5984 Liquefied petroleum gas dealers	6	6	46	51	9	22,957	21,647	1,012	1,166
5992 Florists	17	17	46	58	3	8,000	7,172	402	424
5995 Optical goods stores	-	9	-	40	4	-	11,100	-	649
5999 Miscellaneous retail stores, nec	26	30	120	103	3	8,967	9,786	1,021	1,042

Source: County Business Patterns 1994/95, CBP-94/95, U.S. Department of Commerce, Washington DC, November 1997. The employment column represents mid-March employment in the year. Pay per employee is calculated by dividing 1st Quarter payroll, annualized, by mid-March employment. The column headed 'Emp / Est' shows 'employees per establishment'. A dash (-) means that data are unavailable or cannot be calculated. nec means not elsewhere classified. *Notes:* 1. 1994 data incomplete; unavailable or withheld. 2. 1995 data incomplete; unavailable or withheld. 3. 1994 and 1995 data incomplete; unavailable or withheld.

CINCINNATI PMSA (IN PART)

Wholesale and Retail Trade USA	Establishments		Employment		Emp / Est	Pay / Employee		Annual Payroll ($ 000)	
	1994	1995	1994	1995	1995	1994	1995	1994	1995
50 – Wholesale trade	51	51	333	343	7	20,757	22,134	7,561	7,845
5010 Motor vehicles, parts, and supplies[3]	6	5	60	56	11	18,467	20,500	1,184	998
5040 Professional & commercial equipment[3]	4	3	44	48	16	13,909	15,500	708	805
5060 Electrical goods[3]	4	4	29	32	8	20,828	21,500	681	801
5080 Machinery, equipment, and supplies[3]	5	6	35	41	7	24,914	25,756	967	1,081
5090 Miscellaneous durable goods[3]	3	4	2	5	1	14,000	20,000	24	123
5140 Groceries and related products[3]	3	3	8	10	3	14,000	18,000	152	142
5170 Petroleum and petroleum products[3]	4	4	25	14	4	34,560	52,286	627	511
5191 Farm supplies	-	7	-	45	6	-	17,511	-	993
52 – Retail trade	237	243	2,675	2,934	12	9,927	10,958	30,981	34,486
5210 Lumber and other building materials	-	6	-	58	10	-	17,724	-	1,159
5250 Hardware stores[1]	5	-	22	-	-	7,818	-	191	-
5260 Retail nurseries and garden stores	6	7	7	11	2	6,286	6,545	75	85
5300 General merchandise stores	8	7	295	335	48	9,993	11,821	3,418	3,700
5410 Grocery stores	22	23	506	551	24	9,510	10,243	5,339	5,746
5460 Retail bakeries[1]	4	-	21	-	-	5,524	-	140	-
5510 New and used car dealers[3]	7	7	193	209	30	25,658	26,909	5,908	6,601
5530 Auto and home supply stores	9	12	30	42	4	18,533	17,619	654	956
5540 Gasoline service stations[3]	17	17	135	120	7	8,267	9,667	1,215	1,286
5620 Women's clothing stores[1]	3	4	35	33	8	5,829	7,030	223	216
5710 Furniture and homefurnishings stores[3]	6	6	33	34	6	12,485	12,000	457	411
5720 Household appliance stores[3]	4	4	22	22	6	8,727	8,909	222	205
5731 Radio, TV, & electronic stores[2]	-	3	-	15	5	-	11,733	-	177
5812 Eating places	49	50	756	840	17	6,127	6,781	5,476	6,166
5813 Drinking places	18	16	67	53	3	5,612	5,736	375	298
5910 Drug stores and proprietary stores	6	6	88	78	13	15,136	18,000	1,597	1,661
5930 Used merchandise stores[1]	5	-	37	-	-	3,243	-	153	-
5941 Sporting goods and bicycle shops[3]	3	3	6	7	2	12,667	10,857	94	101
5999 Miscellaneous retail stores, nec[3]	6	6	11	8	1	9,818	9,500	152	94

Source: County Business Patterns 1994/95, CBP-94/95, U.S. Department of Commerce, Washington DC, November 1997. The employment column represents mid-March employment in the year. Pay per employee is calculated by dividing 1st Quarter payroll, annualized, by mid-March employment. The column headed 'Emp / Est' shows 'employees per establishment'. A dash (-) means that data are unavailable or cannot be calculated. nec means not elsewhere classified. *Notes:* 1. 1994 data incomplete; unavailable or withheld. 2. 1995 data incomplete; unavailable or withheld. 3. 1994 and 1995 data incomplete; unavailable or withheld.

CINCINNATI PMSA (KY PART)

Wholesale and Retail Trade USA	Establishments		Employment		Emp / Est	Pay / Employee		Annual Payroll ($ 000)	
	1994	1995	1994	1995	1995	1994	1995	1994	1995
50 – Wholesale trade[1]	456	478	7,101	6,300	13	32,929	32,325	250,660	208,446
5013 Motor vehicle supplies and new parts[3]	24	28	155	157	6	19,639	20,204	3,355	3,425
5015 Motor vehicle parts, used[1]	15	-	62	-	-	13,613	-	999	-
5020 Furniture and homefurnishings[3]	11	12	86	213	18	12,233	24,357	1,212	5,787
5031 Lumber, plywood, and millwork[3]	10	10	89	137	14	32,000	29,956	3,091	4,212
5032 Brick, stone, & related materials[2]	-	8	-	28	4	-	28,286	-	592
5039 Construction materials, nec[3]	4	11	5	73	7	23,200	32,822	126	2,204
5045 Computers, peripherals, & software[3]	9	11	60	53	5	48,933	37,358	2,217	2,331
5047 Medical and hospital equipment[3]	11	11	72	56	5	32,167	47,929	2,378	1,947
5051 Metals service centers and offices[3]	15	15	78	85	6	33,949	42,776	3,447	4,089
5052 Coal and other minerals and ores[2]	-	8	-	7	1	-	57,143	-	370
5063 Electrical apparatus and equipment[3]	22	17	364	232	14	29,352	32,500	11,242	7,894

Continued on next page.

CINCINNATI PMSA (KY PART) - [continued]

Wholesale and Retail Trade USA	Establishments		Employment		Emp / Est	Pay / Employee		Annual Payroll ($ 000)	
	1994	1995	1994	1995	1995	1994	1995	1994	1995
5065 Electronic parts and equipment [3]	10	11	6	75	7	78,667	52,853	550	3,848
5070 Hardware, plumbing & heating equipment [3]	16	18	126	142	8	26,889	26,845	3,816	3,914
5082 Construction and mining machinery [1]	7	-	56	-	-	32,143	-	2,130	-
5083 Farm and garden machinery [2]	-	5	-	16	3	-	22,000	-	543
5084 Industrial machinery and equipment [3]	37	40	741	390	10	58,910	44,800	48,769	18,471
5085 Industrial supplies [3]	20	19	110	147	8	26,873	29,905	3,750	6,152
5087 Service establishment equipment [1]	5	-	12	-	-	21,000	-	222	-
5090 Miscellaneous durable goods [3]	21	24	179	191	8	27,017	29,340	4,836	6,354
5112 Stationery and office supplies [2]	-	16	-	66	4	-	12,970	-	921
5113 Industrial & personal service paper [3]	7	6	65	68	11	42,954	40,941	2,633	2,460
5120 Drugs, proprietaries, and sundries [3]	7	6	189	96	16	46,519	75,458	6,600	4,874
5141 Groceries, general line [3]	6	7	7	9	1	34,286	24,889	565	755
5145 Confectionery [1]	3	-	19	-	-	21,684	-	395	-
5149 Groceries and related products, nec [3]	11	12	169	169	14	33,302	36,308	6,138	6,275
5162 Plastics materials & basic shapes [3]	5	5	59	63	13	22,983	22,540	1,603	1,532
5169 Chemicals & allied products, nec [1]	9	-	57	-	-	28,982	-	1,777	-
5170 Petroleum and petroleum products [2]	-	9	-	41	5	-	22,634	-	1,206
5180 Beer, wine, and distilled beverages [3]	9	10	156	165	17	26,410	28,170	4,725	4,963
5199 Nondurable goods, nec [3]	17	15	42	138	9	22,762	23,304	1,115	2,631
52- Retail trade	1,842	1,901	30,116	32,430	17	11,100	11,929	378,047	407,058
5210 Lumber and other building materials [3]	37	29	664	520	18	16,982	18,185	13,462	9,649
5230 Paint, glass, and wallpaper stores [3]	15	13	52	44	3	16,615	19,455	1,006	904
5250 Hardware stores [3]	19	15	140	66	4	13,714	14,848	1,445	1,079
5260 Retail nurseries and garden stores [3]	17	16	92	93	6	9,130	10,409	1,189	1,380
5270 Mobile home dealers [3]	6	6	36	42	7	34,444	33,238	1,666	2,018
5310 Department stores [3]	16	14	2,194	2,076	148	9,493	11,509	24,179	25,168
5330 Variety stores [2]	17	11	101	46	4	8,752	9,304	1,084	520
5390 Misc. general merchandise stores [2]	-	18	-	228	13	-	14,807	-	3,127
5410 Grocery stores	167	179	4,489	5,049	28	10,341	11,965	51,233	53,028
5420 Meat and fish markets [3]	11	13	62	77	6	11,742	9,766	722	829
5430 Fruit and vegetable markets [1]	4	-	13	-	-	7,692	-	131	-
5440 Candy, nut, and confectionery stores [3]	11	9	40	43	5	5,700	6,698	231	298
5460 Retail bakeries [3]	21	23	195	201	9	10,338	10,746	1,884	1,853
5490 Miscellaneous food stores [2]	-	6	-	10	2	-	7,600	-	90
5510 New and used car dealers [3]	28	33	1,069	1,107	34	24,430	25,492	31,502	32,780
5520 Used car dealers [3]	37	34	65	32	1	21,292	13,625	1,621	442
5530 Auto and home supply stores [3]	39	37	268	275	7	15,925	19,549	4,967	5,532
5540 Gasoline service stations	127	130	1,361	1,347	10	10,292	10,818	14,570	14,586
5610 Men's & boys' clothing stores [3]	13	13	56	59	5	7,214	8,881	570	647
5620 Women's clothing stores [3]	39	36	441	311	9	6,485	6,842	3,068	2,212
5630 Women's accessory & specialty stores [3]	6	6	37	44	7	7,892	9,000	339	385
5640 Children's and infants' wear stores [2]	-	5	-	24	5	-	7,333	-	217
5650 Family clothing stores [3]	17	20	94	104	5	7,702	9,308	743	1,082
5660 Shoe stores [3]	49	44	304	240	5	10,000	12,233	3,177	3,134
5690 Misc. apparel & accessory stores [2]	-	15	-	27	2	-	7,259	-	240
5712 Furniture stores [3]	26	27	205	195	7	22,556	24,041	4,660	4,442
5713 Floor covering stores [3]	13	17	65	110	6	20,985	21,455	1,466	2,389
5719 Misc. homefurnishings stores [3]	23	19	31	215	11	14,452	11,163	505	2,573
5720 Household appliance stores [3]	11	10	17	46	5	17,647	16,522	404	831
5731 Radio, TV, & electronic stores [3]	19	21	187	244	12	20,000	18,574	3,824	4,867
5734 Computer and software stores [3]	7	10	27	29	3	15,407	14,759	421	545
5735 Record & prerecorded tape stores [3]	13	11	48	104	9	9,333	9,846	597	787
5736 Musical instrument stores [3]	10	10	49	53	5	16,735	17,434	916	920
5812 Eating places	463	452	10,955	12,027	27	8,009	8,223	98,659	106,244
5813 Drinking places	115	105	454	502	5	7,392	7,139	3,765	4,163
5910 Drug stores and proprietary stores	60	60	764	759	13	15,356	16,390	12,763	13,182
5920 Liquor stores	52	47	246	231	5	13,545	13,818	3,880	3,774
5930 Used merchandise stores [3]	20	21	122	146	7	9,967	10,849	1,583	1,817
5941 Sporting goods and bicycle shops [3]	25	27	112	153	6	11,679	12,418	1,471	2,669
5942 Book stores [1]	7	-	29	-	-	6,069	-	187	-
5944 Jewelry stores [3]	23	23	151	161	7	12,609	15,155	2,057	2,333
5945 Hobby, toy, and game shops [3]	8	9	70	96	11	10,057	7,958	898	977
5947 Gift, novelty, and souvenir shops [3]	32	35	207	270	8	7,884	8,207	2,060	2,288
5949 Sewing, needlework, and piece goods [1]	6	-	29	-	-	4,966	-	147	-
5963 Direct selling establishments [2]	-	9	-	5	1	-	3,200	-	49
5984 Liquefied petroleum gas dealers [2]	-	10	-	22	2	-	14,182	-	359
5992 Florists [3]	28	29	161	129	4	7,950	10,419	1,474	1,453
5995 Optical goods stores [3]	18	20	86	85	4	16,279	18,212	1,508	1,791
5999 Miscellaneous retail stores, nec [3]	48	47	226	338	7	10,301	13,160	4,602	5,336

Source: County Business Patterns 1994/95, CBP-94/95, U.S. Department of Commerce, Washington DC, November 1997. The employment column represents mid-March employment in the year. Pay per employee is calculated by dividing 1st Quarter payroll, annualized, by mid-March employment. The column headed 'Emp / Est' shows 'employees per establishment'. A dash (-) means that data are unavailable or cannot be calculated. nec means not elsewhere classified. *Notes:* 1. 1994 data incomplete; unavailable or withheld. 2. 1995 data incomplete; unavailable or withheld. 3. 1994 and 1995 data incomplete; unavailable or withheld.

CINCINNATI PMSA (OH PART)

Wholesale and Retail Trade USA	Establishments		Employment		Emp / Est	Pay / Employee		Annual Payroll ($ 000)	
	1994	1995	1994	1995	1995	1994	1995	1994	1995
50 - Wholesale trade	2,725	2,769	52,593	54,358	20	32,176	37,096	1,802,948	2,051,028
5012 Automobiles and other vehicles [3]	32	31	734	778	25	33,308	40,828	25,912	30,678
5013 Motor vehicle supplies and new parts [2]	119	109	1,461	1,457	13	22,672	25,216	37,584	39,627
5014 Tires and tubes [3]	11	12	138	140	12	44,290	41,657	5,616	5,262
5015 Motor vehicle parts, used	24	26	156	174	7	19,128	22,989	3,746	4,419
5021 Furniture [3]	37	35	615	438	13	24,982	34,712	14,441	14,997
5023 Homefurnishings [3]	47	50	853	796	16	37,205	45,864	32,360	32,063
5031 Lumber, plywood, and millwork [3]	48	41	451	521	13	31,512	26,027	17,030	14,590
5032 Brick, stone, & related materials [3]	24	24	207	239	10	26,647	28,452	6,818	7,607
5033 Roofing, siding, & insulation [3]	24	22	287	277	13	36,711	39,336	11,174	9,891
5039 Construction materials, nec [3]	26	40	222	514	13	25,964	32,109	5,958	17,710
5043 Photographic equipment & supplies [3]	10	8	107	108	14	34,168	37,889	3,695	4,045
5044 Office equipment [3]	50	47	1,138	1,102	23	35,047	38,802	38,480	39,465
5045 Computers, peripherals, & software	112	127	2,136	2,361	19	49,429	51,307	98,802	111,310
5046 Commercial equipment, nec [3]	32	33	620	697	21	23,323	24,138	16,812	20,114
5047 Medical and hospital equipment [3]	79	70	938	774	11	38,657	40,889	40,233	34,327
5048 Ophthalmic goods [3]	10	9	159	123	14	20,151	22,146	3,138	3,094
5049 Professional equipment, nec [3]	15	17	170	191	11	39,671	39,979	6,461	6,953
5051 Metals service centers and offices	87	85	1,073	1,107	13	34,531	38,157	39,731	43,081
5052 Coal and other minerals and ores [3]	13	7	57	39	6	39,649	37,436	2,267	1,526
5063 Electrical apparatus and equipment [3]	135	128	1,388	1,301	10	37,478	43,634	53,236	53,162
5064 Electrical appliances, TV & radios [3]	23	21	147	208	10	29,497	51,558	4,565	11,136
5065 Electronic parts and equipment [3]	81	81	925	1,024	13	34,551	36,320	33,629	38,640
5072 Hardware [3]	47	51	628	701	14	25,739	27,504	17,867	20,111
5074 Plumbing & hydronic heating supplies [1]	46	47	317	343	7	27,533	30,472	9,713	10,955
5075 Warm air heating & air conditioning [3]	37	37	357	433	12	31,395	32,028	13,403	14,575
5078 Refrigeration equipment and supplies [3]	12	11	147	152	14	29,007	33,263	5,160	6,453
5082 Construction and mining machinery [2]	-	18	-	258	14	-	39,287	-	10,483
5083 Farm and garden machinery	-	16	-	144	9	-	22,556	-	3,138
5084 Industrial machinery and equipment [2]	-	289	-	2,520	9	-	39,530	-	111,451
5085 Industrial supplies [2]	-	141	-	2,088	15	-	38,090	-	80,261
5087 Service establishment equipment [2]	-	40	-	495	12	-	27,782	-	16,556
5088 Transportation equipment & supplies [2]	-	21	-	161	8	-	37,590	-	7,543
5091 Sporting & recreational goods [2]	-	23	-	87	4	-	25,931	-	2,380
5092 Toys and hobby goods and supplies [2]	-	16	-	615	38	-	45,268	-	26,275
5093 Scrap and waste materials [2]	-	35	-	605	17	-	23,154	-	15,586
5094 Jewelry & precious stones [2]	-	25	-	452	18	-	20,416	-	9,227
5099 Durable goods, nec	-	68	-	532	8	-	35,767	-	19,212
5111 Printing and writing paper [2]	-	24	-	425	18	-	46,522	-	19,459
5112 Stationery and office supplies [2]	-	73	-	5,402	74	-	11,713	-	61,659
5113 Industrial & personal service paper [2]	-	48	-	677	14	-	34,854	-	24,263
5120 Drugs, proprietaries, and sundries [2]	-	34	-	782	23	-	28,737	-	21,913
5131 Piece goods & notions [2]	-	16	-	90	6	-	34,000	-	3,283
5136 Men's and boys' clothing [2]	-	17	-	286	17	-	41,469	-	8,392
5137 Women's and children's clothing [2]	-	14	-	88	6	-	18,818	-	1,683
5139 Footwear [2]	-	10	-	50	5	-	21,200	-	7,534
5141 Groceries, general line [2]	-	21	-	1,146	55	-	28,723	-	33,241
5142 Packaged frozen food [2]	-	15	-	620	41	-	29,168	-	20,812
5145 Confectionery [2]	-	19	-	1,048	55	-	22,935	-	24,577
5147 Meats and meat products [2]	-	17	-	321	19	-	22,953	-	8,295
5148 Fresh fruits and vegetables [2]	-	23	-	1,122	49	-	28,866	-	31,446
5149 Groceries and related products, nec [2]	-	78	-	1,985	25	-	29,916	-	62,352
5153 Grain and field beans [2]	-	7	-	100	14	-	34,040	-	3,270
5159 Farm-product raw materials, nec [2]	-	8	-	70	9	-	6,743	-	330
5162 Plastics materials & basic shapes [2]	-	32	-	204	6	-	37,863	-	7,569
5169 Chemicals & allied products, nec [2]	-	79	-	1,771	22	-	61,317	-	101,366
5171 Petroleum bulk stations & terminals [2]	-	17	-	364	21	-	36,989	-	13,732
5172 Petroleum products, nec [2]	-	15	-	114	8	-	42,842	-	5,383
5181 Beer and ale [2]	-	12	-	446	37	-	27,668	-	14,897
5191 Farm supplies	-	23	-	116	5	-	18,552	-	2,593
5192 Books, periodicals, & newspapers [2]	-	19	-	260	14	-	21,585	-	5,330
5193 Flowers & florists' supplies [2]	-	29	-	245	8	-	16,963	-	4,329
5198 Paints, varnishes, and supplies [2]	-	18	-	133	7	-	32,060	-	5,154
5199 Nondurable goods, nec	-	86	-	656	8	-	24,012	-	19,154
52 - Retail trade	7,346	7,323	123,380	129,560	18	13,365	14,914	1,789,014	1,909,560
5210 Lumber and other building materials	101	83	2,571	2,330	28	21,781	22,996	57,408	50,955
5230 Paint, glass, and wallpaper stores [3]	55	56	243	324	6	16,626	19,062	4,433	6,472
5250 Hardware stores	79	53	908	534	10	14,824	12,614	10,331	6,960
5260 Retail nurseries and garden stores	66	69	539	603	9	10,664	12,093	8,254	9,831
5270 Mobile home dealers [3]	11	12	52	27	2	23,462	20,296	1,284	584
5310 Department stores [3]	56	52	10,816	11,098	213	10,609	12,749	155,984	133,550

Continued on next page.

CINCINNATI PMSA (OH PART) - [continued]

Wholesale and Retail Trade USA	Establishments		Employment		Emp / Est	Pay / Employee		Annual Payroll ($ 000)	
	1994	1995	1994	1995	1995	1994	1995	1994	1995
5330 Variety stores	50	48	548	532	11	8,759	9,098	5,699	5,360
5390 Misc. general merchandise stores[1]	42	50	1,152	1,273	25	11,135	12,220	13,549	14,798
5410 Grocery stores[3]	597	575	16,097	16,561	29	11,086	13,144	195,328	168,577
5420 Meat and fish markets[3]	63	61	338	261	4	14,580	14,375	5,332	4,201
5430 Fruit and vegetable markets[3]	18	17	231	243	14	8,156	8,198	2,340	2,363
5440 Candy, nut, and confectionery stores[3]	33	30	225	198	7	5,600	6,828	1,488	1,475
5450 Dairy products stores	22	-	144	-	-	12,667	-	2,654	-
5460 Retail bakeries	123	113	1,213	1,075	10	10,084	8,841	12,479	10,184
5490 Miscellaneous food stores[3]	54	54	326	371	7	8,380	8,884	2,925	3,560
5510 New and used car dealers	100	101	5,090	5,258	52	26,340	28,602	151,563	166,209
5520 Used car dealers	59	61	224	191	3	19,054	21,864	4,743	4,461
5530 Auto and home supply stores	145	160	1,269	1,307	8	17,529	20,964	25,288	28,677
5540 Gasoline service stations	408	399	3,007	2,932	7	10,526	11,854	34,112	35,534
5550 Boat dealers[3]	11	13	93	112	9	21,591	22,393	2,587	2,975
5560 Recreational vehicle dealers[2]	-	5	-	23	5	-	30,435	-	751
5570 Motorcycle dealers[3]	15	14	55	56	4	17,964	19,286	1,154	1,230
5610 Men's & boys' clothing stores[3]	74	71	599	587	8	10,992	11,448	6,945	6,667
5620 Women's clothing stores	241	214	2,717	2,321	11	8,149	8,591	23,347	19,939
5630 Women's accessory & specialty stores[3]	56	50	335	341	7	9,457	9,666	3,348	3,306
5640 Children's and infants' wear stores[3]	21	21	172	182	9	7,093	7,121	1,372	1,198
5650 Family clothing stores[3]	70	73	1,139	1,426	20	10,283	11,170	12,637	15,196
5660 Shoe stores[2]	190	174	1,132	1,251	7	10,297	10,158	12,625	12,504
5690 Misc. apparel & accessory stores[3]	53	43	211	188	4	9,555	13,021	2,515	3,064
5712 Furniture stores	128	136	1,133	1,186	9	20,635	21,997	24,728	25,593
5713 Floor covering stores	60	63	218	285	5	22,404	26,091	6,041	7,737
5714 Drapery and upholstery stores[3]	9	10	62	78	8	14,581	18,410	972	1,370
5719 Misc. homefurnishings stores[2]	107	109	832	855	8	9,971	11,135	9,821	10,151
5720 Household appliance stores[3]	19	22	268	269	12	17,448	20,907	5,410	5,951
5731 Radio, TV, & electronic stores	85	93	864	1,064	11	18,315	18,778	18,181	21,452
5734 Computer and software stores[3]	38	46	438	533	12	29,132	32,360	14,147	18,580
5735 Record & prerecorded tape stores[3]	58	62	372	574	9	8,151	8,369	3,559	4,319
5736 Musical instrument stores[3]	21	23	70	86	4	19,943	21,907	1,299	1,447
5812 Eating places	1,789	1,698	38,412	40,165	24	7,675	8,065	325,114	348,908
5813 Drinking places	377	344	3,036	2,926	9	8,207	8,372	26,525	25,049
5910 Drug stores and proprietary stores	197	186	3,270	2,924	16	15,750	17,725	57,376	57,699
5920 Liquor stores	88	77	407	324	4	9,622	10,358	4,159	3,565
5930 Used merchandise stores[3]	98	98	671	646	7	9,037	9,300	6,870	7,063
5941 Sporting goods and bicycle shops	106	116	726	888	8	10,176	10,721	9,023	12,160
5942 Book stores[3]	56	61	368	515	8	8,500	10,478	3,266	5,817
5943 Stationery stores[3]	11	12	85	189	16	8,329	11,831	775	2,016
5944 Jewelry stores[3]	135	145	878	990	7	13,130	14,339	12,397	14,111
5945 Hobby, toy, and game shops[3]	63	71	648	709	10	9,679	10,161	6,738	7,967
5946 Camera & photographic supply stores[3]	10	10	88	82	8	15,818	18,244	1,609	1,557
5947 Gift, novelty, and souvenir shops	159	160	1,048	977	6	6,103	7,984	7,114	8,337
5948 Luggage and leather goods stores[3]	8	8	66	67	8	12,545	12,119	862	867
5949 Sewing, needlework, and piece goods[3]	35	34	314	304	9	5,860	6,553	1,869	2,029
5961 Catalog and mail-order houses[3]	24	26	61	72	3	14,557	18,778	1,126	1,566
5962 Merchandising machine operators[1]	33	34	719	690	20	16,490	17,797	13,121	12,772
5963 Direct selling establishments[3]	64	60	937	836	14	14,391	15,608	15,437	14,233
5983 Fuel oil dealers	18	19	34	32	2	21,059	19,375	591	500
5984 Liquefied petroleum gas dealers	13	12	279	284	24	33,907	33,296	8,375	8,444
5992 Florists	102	105	510	528	5	11,247	12,242	6,204	6,604
5993 Tobacco stores and stands[3]	3	3	8	8	3	14,500	17,500	131	148
5994 News dealers and newsstands[3]	5	8	28	24	3	9,429	10,333	268	242
5995 Optical goods stores[3]	100	95	518	488	5	12,826	15,311	7,905	7,741
5999 Miscellaneous retail stores, nec	214	241	1,216	1,386	6	12,878	16,283	17,965	23,653

Source: County Business Patterns 1994/95, CBP-94/95, U.S. Department of Commerce, Washington DC, November 1997. The employment column represents mid-March employment in the year. Pay per employee is calculated by dividing 1st Quarter payroll, annualized, by mid-March employment. The column headed 'Emp / Est' shows 'employees per establishment'. A dash (-) means that data are unavailable or cannot be calculated. nec means not elsewhere classified. *Notes:* 1. 1994 data incomplete; unavailable or withheld. 2. 1995 data incomplete; unavailable or withheld. 3. 1994 and 1995 data incomplete; unavailable or withheld.

CINCINNATI, OH-KY-IN PMSA

Wholesale and Retail Trade USA	Establishments		Employment		Emp / Est	Pay / Employee		Annual Payroll ($ 000)	
	1994	1995	1994	1995	1995	1994	1995	1994	1995
50- Wholesale trade[1]	3,232	3,298	60,027	61,001	18	32,202	36,519	2,061,169	2,267,319
5012 Automobiles and other vehicles[3]	43	42	734	778	19	33,308	40,828	25,912	30,678
5013 Motor vehicle supplies and new parts[3]	147	140	1,616	1,614	12	22,381	24,729	40,939	43,052
5014 Tires and tubes[3]	13	14	138	140	10	44,290	41,657	5,616	5,262

Continued on next page.

CINCINNATI, OH - KY - IN PMSA - [continued]

Wholesale and Retail Trade USA	Establishments		Employment		Emp / Est	Pay / Employee		Annual Payroll ($ 000)	
	1994	1995	1994	1995	1995	1994	1995	1994	1995
5015 Motor vehicle parts, used[3]	39	40	218	174	4	17,560	22,989	4,745	4,419
5021 Furniture[3]	41	40	615	438	11	24,982	34,712	14,441	14,997
5023 Homefurnishings[3]	54	58	853	796	14	37,205	45,864	32,360	32,063
5031 Lumber, plywood, and millwork[3]	60	52	540	658	13	31,593	26,845	20,121	18,802
5032 Brick, stone, & related materials[3]	29	32	207	267	8	26,647	28,434	6,818	8,199
5033 Roofing, siding, & insulation[3]	26	25	287	277	11	36,711	39,336	11,174	9,891
5039 Construction materials, nec[3]	30	52	227	587	11	25,903	32,198	6,084	19,914
5043 Photographic equipment & supplies[3]	12	10	107	108	11	34,168	37,889	3,695	4,045
5044 Office equipment[3]	57	54	1,138	1,102	20	35,047	38,802	38,480	39,465
5045 Computers, peripherals, & software[3]	123	139	2,196	2,414	17	49,415	51,001	101,019	113,641
5046 Commercial equipment, nec[3]	34	35	620	697	20	23,323	24,138	16,812	20,114
5047 Medical and hospital equipment[3]	90	81	1,010	830	10	38,194	41,364	42,611	36,274
5048 Ophthalmic goods[3]	10	9	159	123	14	20,151	22,146	3,138	3,094
5049 Professional equipment, nec[3]	16	18	170	191	11	39,671	39,979	6,461	6,953
5051 Metals service centers and offices[3]	102	100	1,151	1,192	12	34,492	38,487	43,178	47,170
5052 Coal and other minerals and ores[3]	22	15	57	46	3	39,649	40,435	2,267	1,896
5063 Electrical apparatus and equipment[3]	160	148	1,752	1,533	10	35,790	41,949	64,478	61,056
5064 Electrical appliances, TV & radios[3]	24	22	147	208	9	29,497	51,558	4,565	11,136
5065 Electronic parts and equipment[3]	92	93	931	1,099	12	34,836	37,449	34,179	42,488
5072 Hardware[3]	51	55	628	701	13	25,739	27,504	17,867	20,111
5074 Plumbing & hydronic heating supplies[3]	55	57	317	343	6	27,533	30,472	9,713	10,955
5075 Warm air heating & air conditioning[3]	42	43	357	433	10	31,395	32,028	13,403	14,575
5078 Refrigeration equipment and supplies[3]	12	11	147	152	14	29,007	33,263	5,160	6,453
5082 Construction and mining machinery[3]	7	25	56	258	10	32,143	39,287	2,130	10,483
5083 Farm and garden machinery[2]	-	23	-	160	7	-	22,500	-	3,681
5084 Industrial machinery and equipment[3]	40	332	741	2,910	9	58,910	40,236	48,769	129,922
5085 Industrial supplies[3]	21	161	110	2,235	14	26,873	37,552	3,750	86,413
5087 Service establishment equipment[3]	5	44	12	495	11	21,000	27,782	222	16,556
5088 Transportation equipment & supplies[2]	-	22	-	161	7	-	37,590	-	7,543
5091 Sporting & recreational goods[2]	-	25	-	87	3	-	25,931	-	2,380
5092 Toys and hobby goods and supplies[2]	-	17	-	615	36	-	45,268	-	26,275
5093 Scrap and waste materials[2]	-	48	-	605	13	-	23,154	-	15,586
5094 Jewelry & precious stones[2]	-	28	-	452	16	-	20,416	-	9,227
5099 Durable goods, nec[2]	-	77	-	532	7	-	35,767	-	19,212
5111 Printing and writing paper[2]	-	26	-	425	16	-	46,522	-	19,459
5112 Stationery and office supplies[2]	-	90	-	5,468	61	-	11,729	-	62,580
5113 Industrial & personal service paper[3]	7	55	65	745	14	42,954	35,409	2,633	26,723
5120 Drugs, proprietaries, and sundries[3]	7	40	189	878	22	46,519	33,845	6,600	26,787
5131 Piece goods & notions[2]	-	17	-	90	5	-	34,000	-	3,283
5136 Men's and boys' clothing[2]	-	19	-	286	15	-	41,469	-	8,392
5137 Women's and children's clothing[2]	-	15	-	88	6	-	18,818	-	1,683
5139 Footwear[2]	-	12	-	50	4	-	21,200	-	7,534
5141 Groceries, general line[3]	6	28	7	1,155	41	34,286	28,693	565	33,996
5142 Packaged frozen food[2]	-	18	-	620	34	-	29,168	-	20,812
5145 Confectionery[3]	3	22	19	1,048	48	21,684	22,935	395	24,577
5147 Meats and meat products[2]	-	22	-	321	15	-	22,953	-	8,295
5148 Fresh fruits and vegetables[2]	-	28	-	1,122	40	-	28,866	-	31,446
5149 Groceries and related products, nec[3]	11	90	169	2,154	24	33,302	30,418	6,138	68,627
5153 Grain and field beans[2]	-	11	-	100	9	-	34,040	-	3,270
5159 Farm-product raw materials, nec[2]	-	9	-	70	8	-	6,743	-	330
5162 Plastics materials & basic shapes[3]	5	37	59	267	7	22,983	34,247	1,603	9,101
5169 Chemicals & allied products, nec[3]	10	91	57	1,771	19	28,982	61,317	1,777	101,366
5171 Petroleum bulk stations & terminals[2]	-	25	-	364	15	-	36,989	-	13,732
5172 Petroleum products, nec[2]	-	19	-	114	6	-	42,842	-	5,383
5181 Beer and ale[2]	-	18	-	446	25	-	27,668	-	14,897
5191 Farm supplies	-	39	-	161	4	-	18,261	-	3,586
5192 Books, periodicals, & newspapers[2]	-	21	-	260	12	-	21,585	-	5,330
5193 Flowers & florists' supplies[2]	-	32	-	245	8	-	16,963	-	4,329
5198 Paints, varnishes, and supplies[2]	-	20	-	133	7	-	32,060	-	5,154
5199 Nondurable goods, nec[3]	19	102	42	794	8	22,762	23,889	1,115	21,785
52- Retail trade	9,425	9,467	156,171	164,924	17	12,870	14,257	2,198,042	2,351,104
5210 Lumber and other building materials[3]	141	118	3,235	2,908	25	20,796	22,030	70,870	61,763
5230 Paint, glass, and wallpaper stores[3]	71	70	295	368	5	16,624	19,109	5,439	7,376
5250 Hardware stores[3]	103	71	1,070	600	8	14,535	12,860	11,967	8,039
5260 Retail nurseries and garden stores[3]	89	92	638	707	8	10,395	11,785	9,518	11,296
5270 Mobile home dealers[3]	18	19	88	69	4	27,955	28,174	2,950	2,602
5310 Department stores[3]	73	67	13,010	13,174	197	10,421	12,554	180,163	158,718
5330 Variety stores[2]	70	61	649	578	9	8,758	9,114	6,783	5,880
5390 Misc. general merchandise stores[3]	57	72	1,152	1,501	21	11,135	12,613	13,549	17,925
5410 Grocery stores[3]	786	777	21,092	22,161	29	10,889	12,803	251,900	227,351
5420 Meat and fish markets[3]	76	76	400	338	4	14,140	13,325	6,054	5,030

Continued on next page.

CINCINNATI, OH – KY – IN PMSA - [continued]

Wholesale and Retail Trade USA	Establishments		Employment		Emp / Est	Pay / Employee		Annual Payroll ($ 000)	
	1994	1995	1994	1995	1995	1994	1995	1994	1995
5430 Fruit and vegetable markets[3]	23	20	244	243	12	8,131	8,198	2,471	2,363
5440 Candy, nut, and confectionery stores[3]	44	39	265	241	6	5,615	6,805	1,719	1,773
5450 Dairy products stores[1]	22	-	144	-	-	12,667	-	2,654	-
5460 Retail bakeries[3]	148	138	1,429	1,276	9	10,052	9,141	14,503	12,037
5490 Miscellaneous food stores[3]	61	61	326	381	6	8,380	8,850	2,925	3,650
5510 New and used car dealers[3]	135	141	6,352	6,574	47	25,998	28,024	188,973	205,590
5520 Used car dealers[3]	102	100	289	223	2	19,557	20,682	6,364	4,903
5530 Auto and home supply stores[3]	193	209	1,567	1,624	8	17,274	20,638	30,909	35,165
5540 Gasoline service stations[3]	552	546	4,503	4,399	8	10,388	11,477	49,897	51,406
5550 Boat dealers[3]	16	17	93	112	7	21,591	22,393	2,587	2,975
5560 Recreational vehicle dealers[2]	-	6	-	23	4	-	30,435	-	751
5570 Motorcycle dealers[3]	18	18	55	56	3	17,964	19,286	1,154	1,230
5610 Men's & boys' clothing stores[3]	88	85	655	646	8	10,669	11,214	7,515	7,314
5620 Women's clothing stores[3]	283	254	3,193	2,665	10	7,894	8,368	26,638	22,367
5630 Women's accessory & specialty stores[3]	62	56	372	385	7	9,301	9,590	3,687	3,691
5640 Children's and infants' wear stores[3]	25	27	172	206	8	7,093	7,146	1,372	1,415
5650 Family clothing stores[3]	89	95	1,233	1,530	16	10,086	11,043	13,380	16,278
5660 Shoe stores[3]	241	220	1,436	1,491	7	10,234	10,492	15,802	15,638
5690 Misc. apparel & accessory stores[3]	66	58	211	215	4	9,555	12,298	2,515	3,304
5712 Furniture stores[3]	157	166	1,338	1,381	8	20,930	22,285	29,388	30,035
5713 Floor covering stores[3]	76	83	283	395	5	22,078	24,800	7,507	10,126
5714 Drapery and upholstery stores[3]	9	10	62	78	8	14,581	18,410	972	1,370
5719 Misc. homefurnishings stores[3]	130	128	863	1,070	8	10,132	11,140	10,326	12,724
5720 Household appliance stores[3]	34	36	307	337	9	16,834	19,525	6,036	6,987
5731 Radio, TV, & electronic stores[3]	107	117	1,051	1,323	11	18,615	18,661	22,005	26,496
5734 Computer and software stores[3]	46	56	465	562	10	28,335	31,452	14,568	19,125
5735 Record & prerecorded tape stores[3]	71	73	420	678	9	8,286	8,596	4,156	5,106
5736 Musical instrument stores[3]	31	33	119	139	4	18,622	20,201	2,215	2,367
5812 Eating places	2,301	2,200	50,123	53,032	24	7,725	8,080	429,249	461,318
5813 Drinking places	510	465	3,557	3,481	7	8,054	8,154	30,665	29,510
5910 Drug stores and proprietary stores	263	252	4,122	3,761	15	15,664	17,461	71,736	72,542
5920 Liquor stores[3]	151	134	653	555	4	11,100	11,798	8,039	7,339
5930 Used merchandise stores[3]	123	123	830	792	6	8,916	9,586	8,606	8,880
5941 Sporting goods and bicycle shops[3]	134	146	844	1,048	7	10,393	10,969	10,588	14,930
5942 Book stores[3]	64	69	397	515	7	8,322	10,478	3,453	5,817
5943 Stationery stores[3]	12	16	85	189	12	8,329	11,831	775	2,016
5944 Jewelry stores[3]	160	170	1,029	1,151	7	13,053	14,454	14,454	16,444
5945 Hobby, toy, and game shops[3]	71	80	718	805	10	9,716	9,898	7,636	8,944
5946 Camera & photographic supply stores[3]	12	12	88	82	7	15,818	18,244	1,609	1,557
5947 Gift, novelty, and souvenir shops[3]	192	197	1,255	1,247	6	6,397	8,032	9,174	10,625
5948 Luggage and leather goods stores[3]	10	10	66	67	7	12,545	12,119	862	867
5949 Sewing, needlework, and piece goods[3]	41	39	343	304	8	5,784	6,553	2,016	2,029
5961 Catalog and mail-order houses[3]	29	32	61	72	2	14,557	18,778	1,126	1,566
5962 Merchandising machine operators[3]	37	40	719	690	17	16,490	17,797	13,121	12,772
5963 Direct selling establishments[3]	73	71	937	841	12	14,391	15,534	15,437	14,282
5983 Fuel oil dealers[3]	26	26	34	32	1	21,059	19,375	591	500
5984 Liquefied petroleum gas dealers[3]	21	22	279	306	14	33,907	31,922	8,375	8,803
5992 Florists[3]	136	139	671	657	5	10,456	11,884	7,678	8,057
5993 Tobacco stores and stands[3]	4	4	8	8	2	14,500	17,500	131	148
5994 News dealers and newsstands[3]	6	9	28	24	3	9,429	10,333	268	242
5995 Optical goods stores[3]	120	117	604	573	5	13,318	15,742	9,413	9,532
5999 Miscellaneous retail stores, nec[3]	268	294	1,453	1,732	6	12,454	15,642	22,719	29,083

Source: County Business Patterns 1994/95, CBP-94/95, U.S. Department of Commerce, Washington DC, November 1997. The employment column represents mid-March employment in the year. Pay per employee is calculated by dividing 1st Quarter payroll, annualized, by mid-March employment. The column headed 'Emp / Est' shows 'employees per establishment'. A dash (-) means that data are unavailable or cannot be calculated. nec means not elsewhere classified. *Notes:* 1. 1994 data incomplete; unavailable or withheld. 2. 1995 data incomplete; unavailable or withheld. 3. 1994 and 1995 data incomplete; unavailable or withheld.

CLARKSVILLE – HOPKINSVILLE MSA (KY PART)

Wholesale and Retail Trade USA	Establishments		Employment		Emp / Est	Pay / Employee		Annual Payroll ($ 000)	
	1994	1995	1994	1995	1995	1994	1995	1994	1995
50 – Wholesale trade	99	98	1,246	1,478	15	19,063	20,135	27,628	30,505
5013 Motor vehicle supplies and new parts	7	7	43	43	6	14,512	13,860	679	622
5015 Motor vehicle parts, used	4	4	18	23	6	10,667	10,087	225	237
5030 Lumber and construction materials	5	5	48	58	12	19,167	21,655	1,417	1,507
5040 Professional & commercial equipment	3	-	19	-	-	17,263	-	348	-
5070 Hardware, plumbing & heating equipment	-	3	-	49	16	-	21,469	-	1,239
5083 Farm and garden machinery	7	7	103	104	15	19,767	22,038	2,550	2,433
5084 Industrial machinery and equipment	7	7	200	227	32	26,300	30,643	6,188	7,135

Continued on next page.

CLARKSVILLE - HOPKINSVILLE MSA (KY PART) - [continued]

Wholesale and Retail Trade USA	Establishments		Employment		Emp / Est	Pay / Employee		Annual Payroll ($ 000)	
	1994	1995	1994	1995	1995	1994	1995	1994	1995
5093 Scrap and waste materials	-	4	-	20	5	-	12,600	-	295
5140 Groceries and related products	5	3	95	108	36	26,147	25,963	2,665	2,998
5153 Grain and field beans	4	4	61	68	17	17,049	17,176	1,325	1,454
5154 Livestock	3	3	48	41	14	12,167	11,707	533	510
5159 Farm-product raw materials, nec	8	8	97	129	16	8,495	6,760	531	423
5180 Beer, wine, and distilled beverages	3	3	47	67	22	28,426	21,015	1,319	1,379
5191 Farm supplies	8	7	102	95	14	16,392	19,158	1,949	1,825
52- Retail trade	373	380	4,366	4,591	12	9,914	10,396	47,507	51,922
5210 Lumber and other building materials	7	8	83	98	12	16,048	15,837	1,592	1,645
5230 Paint, glass, and wallpaper stores	30	35	198	230	7	9,273	12,730	2,590	3,392
5260 Retail nurseries and garden stores	6	-	2	-	-	12,000	-	71	-
5300 General merchandise stores	8	9	349	368	41	9,169	12,717	3,665	5,122
5410 Grocery stores	32	32	649	761	24	9,455	8,173	6,340	6,342
5510 New and used car dealers	8	8	222	208	26	20,180	24,077	5,059	5,510
5520 Used car dealers	4	4	8	6	2	12,000	12,667	87	72
5530 Auto and home supply stores	11	12	77	80	7	13,247	15,500	1,205	1,325
5540 Gasoline service stations	22	25	209	185	7	11,024	10,811	2,300	2,083
5620 Women's clothing stores	12	12	89	80	7	9,213	8,650	950	691
5660 Shoe stores	8	8	31	27	3	10,194	9,481	323	261
5712 Furniture stores	7	9	52	52	6	13,692	17,231	792	1,299
5720 Household appliance stores	4	4	24	22	6	9,833	11,818	361	332
5730 Radio, television, & computer stores	6	5	42	48	10	15,810	16,583	672	700
5812 Eating places	77	74	1,652	1,727	23	7,097	6,879	12,215	12,624
5813 Drinking places	4	3	4	6	2	8,000	4,000	48	28
5910 Drug stores and proprietary stores	12	11	93	95	9	19,097	19,747	1,966	2,049
5920 Liquor stores	23	19	75	66	3	9,653	10,000	734	667
5930 Used merchandise stores	12	13	54	61	5	10,667	9,639	568	616
5941 Sporting goods and bicycle shops	7	4	10	10	3	12,000	11,600	134	128
5942 Book stores	4	-	9	-	-	7,556	-	62	-
5944 Jewelry stores	6	6	35	32	5	13,943	15,375	481	443
5947 Gift, novelty, and souvenir shops	-	3	-	13	4	-	5,538	-	80
5960 Nonstore retailers	7	6	66	65	11	9,758	11,262	824	830
5984 Liquefied petroleum gas dealers	3	4	16	22	6	21,500	17,455	301	384
5992 Florists	7	8	49	48	6	9,796	10,333	485	515

Source: County Business Patterns 1994/95, CBP-94/95, U.S. Department of Commerce, Washington DC, November 1997. The employment column represents mid-March employment in the year. Pay per employee is calculated by dividing 1st Quarter payroll, annualized, by mid-March employment. The column headed 'Emp / Est' shows 'employees per establishment'. A dash (-) means that data are unavailable or cannot be calculated. nec means not elsewhere classified. *Notes:* 1. 1994 data incomplete; unavailable or withheld. 2. 1995 data incomplete; unavailable or withheld. 3. 1994 and 1995 data incomplete; unavailable or withheld.

CLARKSVILLE - HOPKINSVILLE MSA (TN PART)

Wholesale and Retail Trade USA	Establishments		Employment		Emp / Est	Pay / Employee		Annual Payroll ($ 000)	
	1994	1995	1994	1995	1995	1994	1995	1994	1995
50- Wholesale trade	-	112	-	821	7	-	19,206	-	19,246
5013 Motor vehicle supplies and new parts	-	9	-	37	4	-	15,027	-	557
5015 Motor vehicle parts, used	-	4	-	6	2	-	10,000	-	100
5020 Furniture and homefurnishings	-	3	-	2	1	-	8,000	-	155
5039 Construction materials, nec	-	3	-	12	4	-	16,333	-	250
5044 Office equipment	-	5	-	30	6	-	17,467	-	604
5051 Metals service centers and offices	-	4	-	34	9	-	22,941	-	1,390
5065 Electronic parts and equipment	-	3	-	6	2	-	15,333	-	128
5070 Hardware, plumbing & heating equipment	-	6	-	35	6	-	25,943	-	937
5085 Industrial supplies	-	5	-	28	6	-	29,571	-	834
5093 Scrap and waste materials	-	4	-	17	4	-	16,941	-	324
5110 Paper and paper products	-	3	-	51	17	-	11,216	-	502
5149 Groceries and related products, nec	-	3	-	49	16	-	25,469	-	1,283
5171 Petroleum bulk stations & terminals	-	5	-	66	13	-	18,970	-	1,491
5181 Beer and ale	-	3	-	101	34	-	25,901	-	4,065
5191 Farm supplies	-	7	-	78	11	-	18,769	-	1,619
52- Retail trade	-	706	-	9,986	14	-	11,353	-	125,141
5210 Lumber and other building materials	-	7	-	286	41	-	21,105	-	9,303
5230 Paint, glass, and wallpaper stores	-	4	-	14	4	-	22,000	-	312
5270 Mobile home dealers	-	3	-	21	7	-	26,286	-	806
5310 Department stores	-	9	-	1,634	182	-	11,985	-	19,109
5330 Variety stores	-	7	-	70	10	-	7,714	-	623
5390 Misc. general merchandise stores	-	9	-	102	11	-	11,961	-	1,455
5410 Grocery stores	-	57	-	1,189	21	-	9,881	-	12,075
5460 Retail bakeries	-	6	-	48	8	-	8,833	-	409
5510 New and used car dealers	-	10	-	662	66	-	26,332	-	20,364

Continued on next page.

CLARKSVILLE – HOPKINSVILLE MSA (TN PART) - [continued]

Wholesale and Retail Trade USA	Establishments		Employment		Emp / Est	Pay / Employee		Annual Payroll ($ 000)	
	1994	1995	1994	1995	1995	1994	1995	1994	1995
5520 Used car dealers	-	32	-	131	4	-	20,672	-	2,887
5530 Auto and home supply stores	-	21	-	172	8	-	16,233	-	2,946
5540 Gasoline service stations	-	49	-	283	6	-	12,028	-	3,623
5560 Recreational vehicle dealers	-	3	-	11	4	-	25,455	-	270
5570 Motorcycle dealers	-	3	-	27	9	-	17,630	-	558
5610 Men's & boys' clothing stores	-	5	-	25	5	-	11,360	-	273
5620 Women's clothing stores	-	19	-	143	8	-	6,769	-	992
5630 Women's accessory & specialty stores	-	5	-	20	4	-	11,000	-	219
5650 Family clothing stores	-	8	-	153	19	-	8,366	-	1,599
5660 Shoe stores	-	20	-	115	6	-	10,365	-	1,254
5690 Misc. apparel & accessory stores	-	6	-	31	5	-	6,710	-	232
5712 Furniture stores	-	24	-	189	8	-	15,894	-	3,085
5713 Floor covering stores	-	6	-	30	5	-	15,467	-	802
5731 Radio, TV, & electronic stores	-	8	-	62	8	-	20,774	-	1,294
5734 Computer and software stores	-	5	-	13	3	-	10,462	-	173
5812 Eating places	-	138	-	3,423	25	-	7,093	-	25,621
5813 Drinking places	-	16	-	74	5	-	5,676	-	664
5910 Drug stores and proprietary stores	-	10	-	91	9	-	21,670	-	2,087
5920 Liquor stores	-	10	-	24	2	-	6,833	-	222
5930 Used merchandise stores	-	17	-	53	3	-	10,943	-	605
5941 Sporting goods and bicycle shops	-	8	-	37	5	-	6,595	-	297
5942 Book stores	-	6	-	64	11	-	6,938	-	480
5944 Jewelry stores	-	12	-	90	8	-	13,289	-	1,243
5945 Hobby, toy, and game shops	-	7	-	44	6	-	10,364	-	794
5947 Gift, novelty, and souvenir shops	-	8	-	34	4	-	6,824	-	264
5949 Sewing, needlework, and piece goods	-	4	-	31	8	-	7,097	-	222
5962 Merchandising machine operators	-	6	-	7	1	-	10,857	-	81
5992 Florists	-	13	-	53	4	-	7,849	-	404
5999 Miscellaneous retail stores, nec	-	17	-	75	4	-	12,267	-	920

Source: County Business Patterns 1994/95, CBP-94/95, U.S. Department of Commerce, Washington DC, November 1997. The employment column represents mid-March employment in the year. Pay per employee is calculated by dividing 1st Quarter payroll, annualized, by mid-March employment. The column headed 'Emp / Est' shows 'employees per establishment'. A dash (-) means that data are unavailable or cannot be calculated, nec means not elsewhere classified. *Notes:* 1. 1994 data incomplete; unavailable or withheld. 2. 1995 data incomplete; unavailable or withheld. 3. 1994 and 1995 data incomplete; unavailable or withheld.

CLARKSVILLE – HOPKINSVILLE, TN – KY MSA

Wholesale and Retail Trade USA	Establishments		Employment		Emp / Est	Pay / Employee		Annual Payroll ($ 000)	
	1994	1995	1994	1995	1995	1994	1995	1994	1995
50- Wholesale trade [1]	99	210	1,246	2,299	11	19,063	19,803	27,628	49,751
5013 Motor vehicle supplies and new parts [1]	7	16	43	80	5	14,512	14,400	679	1,179
5015 Motor vehicle parts, used [1]	4	8	18	29	4	10,667	10,069	225	337
5020 Furniture and homefurnishings	-	4	-	2	1	-	8,000	-	155
5039 Construction materials, nec	-	4	-	12	3	-	16,333	-	250
5044 Office equipment	-	6	-	30	5	-	17,467	-	604
5051 Metals service centers and offices [2]	-	4	-	34	9	-	22,941	-	1,390
5065 Electronic parts and equipment	-	4	-	6	2	-	15,333	-	128
5070 Hardware, plumbing & heating equipment	-	9	-	84	9	-	23,333	-	2,176
5083 Farm and garden machinery [1]	7	11	103	104	9	19,767	22,038	2,550	2,433
5084 Industrial machinery and equipment [1]	7	8	200	227	28	26,300	30,643	6,188	7,135
5085 Industrial supplies	-	8	-	28	4	-	29,571	-	834
5093 Scrap and waste materials	-	8	-	37	5	-	14,595	-	619
5110 Paper and paper products	-	4	-	51	13	-	11,216	-	502
5149 Groceries and related products, nec	-	5	-	49	10	-	25,469	-	1,283
5153 Grain and field beans [3]	4	4	61	68	17	17,049	17,176	1,325	1,454
5154 Livestock [3]	3	3	48	41	14	12,167	11,707	533	510
5159 Farm-product raw materials, nec [1]	8	9	97	129	14	8,495	6,760	531	423
5171 Petroleum bulk stations & terminals [2]	-	9	-	66	7	-	18,970	-	1,491
5181 Beer and ale	-	5	-	101	20	-	25,901	-	4,065
5191 Farm supplies [1]	8	14	102	173	12	16,392	18,983	1,949	3,444
52- Retail trade [1]	373	1,086	4,366	14,577	13	9,914	11,051	47,507	177,063
5210 Lumber and other building materials [1]	7	15	83	384	26	16,048	19,760	1,592	10,948
5230 Paint, glass, and wallpaper stores [1]	30	39	198	244	6	9,273	13,262	2,590	3,704
5260 Retail nurseries and garden stores [1]	6	-	2	-	-	12,000	-	71	-
5270 Mobile home dealers	-	5	-	21	4	-	26,286	-	806
5310 Department stores [2]	-	11	-	1,634	149	-	11,985	-	19,109
5330 Variety stores	-	11	-	70	6	-	7,714	-	623
5390 Misc. general merchandise stores	-	12	-	102	9	-	11,961	-	1,455
5410 Grocery stores [1]	32	89	649	1,950	22	9,455	9,214	6,340	18,417
5460 Retail bakeries [2]	-	6	-	48	8	-	8,833	-	409

Continued on next page.

CLARKSVILLE - HOPKINSVILLE, TN - KY MSA - [continued]

Wholesale and Retail Trade USA	Establishments		Employment		Emp / Est	Pay / Employee		Annual Payroll ($ 000)	
	1994	1995	1994	1995	1995	1994	1995	1994	1995
5510 New and used car dealers [1]	8	18	222	870	48	20,180	25,793	5,059	25,874
5520 Used car dealers [1]	4	36	8	137	4	12,000	20,321	87	2,959
5530 Auto and home supply stores [1]	11	33	77	252	8	13,247	16,000	1,205	4,271
5540 Gasoline service stations [1]	22	74	209	468	6	11,024	11,547	2,300	5,706
5560 Recreational vehicle dealers [2]	-	3	-	11	4	-	25,455	-	270
5570 Motorcycle dealers	-	4	-	27	7	-	17,630	-	558
5610 Men's & boys' clothing stores	-	6	-	25	4	-	11,360	-	273
5620 Women's clothing stores [1]	12	31	89	223	7	9,213	7,444	950	1,683
5630 Women's accessory & specialty stores	-	6	-	20	3	-	11,000	-	219
5650 Family clothing stores	-	10	-	153	15	-	8,366	-	1,599
5660 Shoe stores [1]	8	28	31	142	5	10,194	10,197	323	1,515
5690 Misc. apparel & accessory stores	-	7	-	31	4	-	6,710	-	232
5712 Furniture stores [1]	7	33	52	241	7	13,692	16,183	792	4,384
5713 Floor covering stores	-	13	-	30	2	-	15,467	-	802
5720 Household appliance stores [1]	4	10	24	22	2	9,833	11,818	361	332
5731 Radio, TV, & electronic stores	-	10	-	62	6	-	20,774	-	1,294
5734 Computer and software stores	-	6	-	13	2	-	10,462	-	173
5812 Eating places [1]	77	212	1,652	5,150	24	7,097	7,021	12,215	38,245
5813 Drinking places [1]	4	19	4	80	4	8,000	5,550	48	692
5910 Drug stores and proprietary stores [1]	12	21	93	186	9	19,097	20,688	1,966	4,136
5920 Liquor stores [1]	23	29	75	90	3	9,653	9,156	734	889
5930 Used merchandise stores [1]	12	30	54	114	4	10,667	10,246	568	1,221
5941 Sporting goods and bicycle shops [1]	7	12	10	47	4	12,000	7,660	134	425
5942 Book stores [1]	4	9	9	64	7	7,556	6,938	62	480
5944 Jewelry stores [1]	6	18	35	122	7	13,943	13,836	481	1,686
5945 Hobby, toy, and game shops	-	10	-	44	4	-	10,364	-	794
5947 Gift, novelty, and souvenir shops	-	11	-	47	4	-	6,468	-	344
5949 Sewing, needlework, and piece goods	-	6	-	31	5	-	7,097	-	222
5962 Merchandising machine operators	-	8	-	7	1	-	10,857	-	81
5984 Liquefied petroleum gas dealers [1]	3	6	16	22	4	21,500	17,455	301	384
5992 Florists [1]	7	21	49	101	5	9,796	9,030	485	919
5999 Miscellaneous retail stores, nec	-	25	-	75	3	-	12,267	-	920

Source: County Business Patterns 1994/95, CBP-94/95, U.S. Department of Commerce, Washington DC, November 1997. The employment column represents mid-March employment in the year. Pay per employee is calculated by dividing 1st Quarter payroll, annualized, by mid-March employment. The column headed 'Emp / Est' shows 'employees per establishment'. A dash (-) means that data are unavailable or cannot be calculated. nec means not elsewhere classified. *Notes:* 1. 1994 data incomplete; unavailable or withheld. 2. 1995 data incomplete; unavailable or withheld. 3. 1994 and 1995 data incomplete; unavailable or withheld.

CLEVELAND - LORAIN - ELYRIA, OH PMSA

Wholesale and Retail Trade USA	Establishments		Employment		Emp / Est	Pay / Employee		Annual Payroll ($ 000)	
	1994	1995	1994	1995	1995	1994	1995	1994	1995
50 - Wholesale trade	5,026	5,094	71,754	73,960	15	31,521	33,614	2,400,532	2,580,661
5012 Automobiles and other vehicles	44	50	548	523	10	26,715	27,946	16,253	16,119
5013 Motor vehicle supplies and new parts	271	242	4,076	3,475	14	29,528	34,371	120,310	117,573
5014 Tires and tubes [3]	26	23	344	260	11	28,872	33,800	9,890	9,274
5015 Motor vehicle parts, used	50	62	318	371	6	16,994	20,464	6,039	7,920
5021 Furniture [3]	61	58	482	476	8	27,427	29,202	14,139	14,885
5023 Homefurnishings [3]	69	63	609	596	9	28,420	29,094	18,227	18,472
5031 Lumber, plywood, and millwork [2]	75	59	762	567	10	28,866	35,640	28,132	22,030
5032 Brick, stone, & related materials [3]	47	48	388	393	8	30,258	31,949	15,534	16,161
5033 Roofing, siding, & insulation [1]	41	46	422	630	14	40,227	42,133	16,985	27,281
5039 Construction materials, nec [3]	25	61	208	1,022	17	20,385	21,331	5,195	24,855
5043 Photographic equipment & supplies [3]	17	18	345	353	20	37,936	43,331	12,369	13,825
5044 Office equipment [1]	83	81	2,059	1,956	24	32,515	34,757	66,517	64,991
5045 Computers, peripherals, & software	202	195	2,805	2,418	12	44,913	52,017	118,256	116,936
5046 Commercial equipment, nec [3]	54	50	654	620	12	25,584	27,806	20,026	19,065
5047 Medical and hospital equipment	119	117	1,534	1,440	12	37,799	41,767	61,400	62,240
5048 Ophthalmic goods [3]	14	14	176	195	14	17,341	19,856	3,414	4,345
5049 Professional equipment, nec [3]	29	24	428	239	10	35,243	43,682	14,657	9,153
5051 Metals service centers and offices	273	274	3,906	4,240	15	36,794	41,704	161,396	179,014
5052 Coal and other minerals and ores [3]	17	18	130	139	8	41,231	40,777	5,693	5,554
5063 Electrical apparatus and equipment	226	209	2,733	2,488	12	36,563	40,069	106,013	99,745
5064 Electrical appliances, TV & radios [3]	35	32	428	433	14	33,243	36,231	15,067	16,300
5065 Electronic parts and equipment	194	205	2,344	2,807	14	39,503	39,833	99,393	121,047
5072 Hardware [3]	127	134	2,996	3,245	24	24,505	27,180	82,766	91,497
5074 Plumbing & hydronic heating supplies	103	111	1,130	1,304	12	27,161	27,561	34,361	40,035
5075 Warm air heating & air conditioning [3]	57	55	440	411	7	30,173	37,528	14,393	16,779
5078 Refrigeration equipment and supplies [3]	4	4	77	79	20	48,831	46,481	3,709	3,718
5082 Construction and mining machinery [2]	-	43	-	710	17	-	41,645	-	28,642

Continued on next page.

CLEVELAND - LORAIN - ELYRIA, OH PMSA - [continued]

Wholesale and Retail Trade USA	Establishments		Employment		Emp / Est	Pay / Employee		Annual Payroll ($ 000)	
	1994	1995	1994	1995	1995	1994	1995	1994	1995
5083 Farm and garden machinery	-	36	-	477	13	-	20,847	-	12,432
5084 Industrial machinery and equipment	-	543	-	4,437	8	-	38,042	-	186,526
5085 Industrial supplies	-	269	-	3,594	13	-	35,557	-	132,974
5087 Service establishment equipment	-	68	-	649	10	-	25,861	-	18,595
5088 Transportation equipment & supplies	-	27	-	186	7	-	29,097	-	6,302
5091 Sporting & recreational goods [2]	-	40	-	240	6	-	22,650	-	5,834
5092 Toys and hobby goods and supplies [2]	-	20	-	343	17	-	27,475	-	13,593
5093 Scrap and waste materials	-	132	-	1,478	11	-	34,931	-	54,904
5094 Jewelry & precious stones [2]	-	38	-	232	6	-	27,207	-	7,281
5099 Durable goods, nec	-	121	-	489	4	-	32,581	-	17,585
5111 Printing and writing paper [2]	-	26	-	427	16	-	40,356	-	16,998
5112 Stationery and office supplies	-	112	-	3,750	33	-	15,613	-	61,495
5113 Industrial & personal service paper	-	68	-	1,066	16	-	29,872	-	36,539
5120 Drugs, proprietaries, and sundries [2]	-	56	-	1,412	25	-	30,201	-	44,908
5131 Piece goods & notions [2]	-	29	-	133	5	-	35,609	-	4,519
5136 Men's and boys' clothing [2]	-	25	-	233	9	-	25,494	-	6,774
5137 Women's and children's clothing [2]	-	19	-	90	5	-	46,489	-	4,075
5139 Footwear [2]	-	3	-	14	5	-	18,000	-	104
5141 Groceries, general line	-	36	-	2,213	61	-	28,125	-	67,064
5142 Packaged frozen food [2]	-	22	-	446	20	-	32,978	-	12,542
5143 Dairy products, exc. dried or canned [2]	-	12	-	139	12	-	33,295	-	5,031
5144 Poultry and poultry products [2]	-	4	-	91	23	-	21,714	-	2,361
5145 Confectionery [2]	-	28	-	436	16	-	27,202	-	12,161
5146 Fish and seafoods [2]	-	8	-	99	12	-	18,465	-	2,030
5147 Meats and meat products [2]	-	20	-	136	7	-	20,588	-	3,101
5148 Fresh fruits and vegetables [2]	-	29	-	446	15	-	40,404	-	15,968
5149 Groceries and related products, nec	-	97	-	1,850	19	-	29,565	-	58,805
5162 Plastics materials & basic shapes	-	58	-	639	11	-	47,737	-	28,977
5169 Chemicals & allied products, nec	-	164	-	2,791	17	-	35,546	-	108,402
5171 Petroleum bulk stations & terminals [2]	-	32	-	326	10	-	36,785	-	12,418
5172 Petroleum products, nec [2]	-	28	-	203	7	-	30,877	-	7,731
5181 Beer and ale [2]	-	19	-	693	36	-	28,208	-	22,275
5182 Wine and distilled beverages [2]	-	16	-	177	11	-	42,305	-	6,505
5191 Farm supplies	-	50	-	431	9	-	27,397	-	12,121
5192 Books, periodicals, & newspapers [2]	-	42	-	549	13	-	31,060	-	18,992
5193 Flowers & florists' supplies [2]	-	35	-	441	13	-	19,791	-	9,208
5194 Tobacco and tobacco products [2]	-	13	-	239	18	-	25,105	-	7,835
5198 Paints, varnishes, and supplies [2]	-	43	-	2,098	49	-	40,446	-	72,657
5199 Nondurable goods, nec	-	166	-	1,473	9	-	20,956	-	34,597
52 - Retail trade	13,202	13,100	181,503	186,059	14	11,643	12,889	2,336,518	2,522,539
5210 Lumber and other building materials	177	165	3,211	3,554	22	16,245	19,167	64,133	72,904
5230 Paint, glass, and wallpaper stores [3]	91	90	95	111	1	14,568	16,505	1,535	2,065
5250 Hardware stores	150	108	1,262	1,053	10	11,861	12,201	17,335	13,037
5260 Retail nurseries and garden stores	126	132	857	933	7	12,135	12,669	16,101	16,710
5310 Department stores [3]	76	79	14,396	12,867	163	9,762	12,461	157,566	171,124
5330 Variety stores	113	92	1,059	980	11	8,952	8,665	10,428	9,286
5390 Misc. general merchandise stores	73	75	2,168	1,950	26	11,279	10,706	25,977	21,217
5410 Grocery stores	1,077	1,062	21,871	22,841	22	12,689	13,387	295,012	311,218
5420 Meat and fish markets	101	101	486	481	5	12,584	13,514	6,658	6,755
5430 Fruit and vegetable markets [3]	28	25	213	178	7	13,540	15,798	3,509	3,435
5440 Candy, nut, and confectionery stores	103	94	735	624	7	5,649	6,353	4,412	4,171
5450 Dairy products stores [2]	31	24	105	92	4	5,676	6,565	704	739
5460 Retail bakeries	221	211	1,627	1,635	8	7,995	8,377	14,337	14,140
5490 Miscellaneous food stores [1]	74	78	328	342	4	8,841	10,152	3,292	3,849
5510 New and used car dealers	192	193	8,460	8,495	44	27,207	29,455	269,364	279,744
5520 Used car dealers	138	140	435	466	3	18,593	19,708	9,463	10,050
5530 Auto and home supply stores	297	300	2,035	2,165	7	16,763	17,709	37,989	41,222
5540 Gasoline service stations	818	803	6,449	5,972	7	10,211	11,415	68,071	69,957
5550 Boat dealers [3]	29	28	125	153	5	17,600	17,778	3,057	3,156
5560 Recreational vehicle dealers [2]	16	17	64	89	5	15,188	18,202	1,194	1,930
5570 Motorcycle dealers [3]	21	22	138	145	7	17,710	19,200	3,027	3,132
5610 Men's & boys' clothing stores [3]	131	127	1,043	943	7	12,506	12,314	13,803	12,048
5620 Women's clothing stores	412	365	4,398	3,818	10	8,420	8,546	40,419	32,990
5630 Women's accessory & specialty stores [3]	77	75	672	539	7	10,321	12,186	6,652	6,495
5640 Children's and infants' wear stores [1]	34	39	278	336	9	7,151	8,369	2,324	2,865
5650 Family clothing stores	110	108	2,388	1,957	18	9,446	10,351	24,225	19,646
5660 Shoe stores	319	288	1,851	1,747	6	10,083	10,908	19,284	18,865
5690 Misc. apparel & accessory stores	59	54	188	290	5	11,553	10,414	2,462	3,362
5712 Furniture stores	281	280	2,377	2,700	10	18,595	18,813	46,826	55,605
5713 Floor covering stores	126	126	612	672	5	19,163	21,875	13,907	15,981
5714 Drapery and upholstery stores [3]	29	31	110	114	4	10,073	10,281	1,127	1,190

Continued on next page.

CLEVELAND - LORAIN - ELYRIA, OH PMSA - [continued]

Wholesale and Retail Trade USA	Establishments		Employment		Emp / Est	Pay / Employee		Annual Payroll ($ 000)	
	1994	1995	1994	1995	1995	1994	1995	1994	1995
5719 Misc. homefurnishings stores [2]	149	141	1,125	992	7	9,611	13,218	12,029	12,931
5720 Household appliance stores	56	54	290	245	5	16,014	17,176	4,835	4,439
5731 Radio, TV, & electronic stores	120	119	1,283	1,731	15	18,956	17,174	20,370	29,669
5734 Computer and software stores [2]	65	75	364	363	5	20,374	21,333	8,729	8,363
5735 Record & prerecorded tape stores	81	91	512	559	6	9,438	11,270	5,345	6,557
5736 Musical instrument stores [3]	36	35	130	143	4	14,215	15,413	2,027	2,239
5812 Eating places	3,125	2,963	59,088	61,335	21	7,176	7,508	474,693	490,983
5813 Drinking places	808	717	3,571	3,477	5	6,716	7,246	25,923	25,784
5910 Drug stores and proprietary stores	399	377	8,411	8,764	23	12,029	13,015	112,172	119,811
5920 Liquor stores	197	182	649	659	4	14,163	12,437	8,608	8,324
5930 Used merchandise stores	113	104	894	825	8	9,235	9,227	8,981	8,172
5941 Sporting goods and bicycle shops	196	199	1,157	1,202	6	11,125	11,930	15,460	17,420
5942 Book stores	108	101	993	1,287	13	9,208	8,476	9,230	10,615
5943 Stationery stores [2]	-	23	-	19	1	-	12,842	-	236
5944 Jewelry stores	228	232	1,247	1,241	5	15,929	16,342	20,465	20,146
5945 Hobby, toy, and game shops	93	95	1,093	1,173	12	10,005	9,234	13,635	11,817
5946 Camera & photographic supply stores [2]	41	40	201	163	4	13,333	14,160	2,686	2,195
5947 Gift, novelty, and souvenir shops	237	221	1,378	1,429	6	7,440	8,202	11,375	12,449
5949 Sewing, needlework, and piece goods	56	58	404	395	7	7,020	7,433	2,823	3,110
5961 Catalog and mail-order houses	46	58	913	983	17	15,010	17,457	16,223	17,935
5962 Merchandising machine operators [3]	63	66	963	977	15	15,003	15,746	15,473	16,087
5963 Direct selling establishments [3]	113	115	1,097	1,232	11	16,011	14,935	18,423	18,573
5980 Fuel dealers	26	29	287	344	12	20,070	24,593	6,457	8,447
5992 Florists [3]	209	204	872	921	5	9,220	9,299	8,748	9,101
5993 Tobacco stores and stands [3]	18	20	47	32	2	11,064	12,750	536	396
5994 News dealers and newsstands [3]	12	15	26	23	2	13,692	12,870	364	306
5995 Optical goods stores	185	179	962	874	5	17,688	19,867	17,099	16,347
5999 Miscellaneous retail stores, nec	363	399	1,884	2,069	5	11,183	12,321	24,280	28,923

Source: County Business Patterns 1994/95, CBP-94/95, U.S. Department of Commerce, Washington DC, November 1997. The employment column represents mid-March employment in the year. Pay per employee is calculated by dividing 1st Quarter payroll, annualized, by mid-March employment. The column headed 'Emp / Est' shows 'employees per establishment'. A dash (-) means that data are unavailable or cannot be calculated. nec means not elsewhere classified. *Notes:* 1. 1994 data incomplete; unavailable or withheld. 2. 1995 data incomplete; unavailable or withheld. 3. 1994 and 1995 data incomplete; unavailable or withheld.

COLORADO SPRINGS, CO MSA

Wholesale and Retail Trade USA	Establishments		Employment		Emp / Est	Pay / Employee		Annual Payroll ($ 000)	
	1994	1995	1994	1995	1995	1994	1995	1994	1995
50- Wholesale trade	599	623	6,293	6,902	11	24,287	27,758	166,825	208,601
5012 Automobiles and other vehicles	15	15	182	173	12	15,714	18,821	3,147	3,506
5013 Motor vehicle supplies and new parts	39	40	296	244	6	16,932	21,705	5,339	5,451
5014 Tires and tubes	7	7	53	56	8	28,981	27,214	1,640	1,476
5015 Motor vehicle parts, used	19	22	98	99	5	14,122	15,556	1,517	1,481
5021 Furniture	12	10	113	64	6	21,947	22,188	2,251	1,536
5023 Homefurnishings	13	9	77	59	7	28,208	29,220	2,301	1,834
5031 Lumber, plywood, and millwork	12	14	70	125	9	30,629	28,224	2,593	4,474
5032 Brick, stone, & related materials	-	7	-	75	11	-	21,867	-	1,833
5033 Roofing, siding, & insulation	-	5	-	59	12	-	21,898	-	1,359
5039 Construction materials, nec	9	10	89	73	7	30,472	32,055	3,425	2,541
5044 Office equipment	12	12	170	160	13	27,247	30,150	4,613	4,684
5045 Computers, peripherals, & software	36	35	540	1,466	42	50,059	42,207	26,953	63,430
5046 Commercial equipment, nec	11	13	78	100	8	24,667	25,120	2,338	2,758
5047 Medical and hospital equipment	12	13	45	59	5	24,444	27,186	1,271	2,212
5048 Ophthalmic goods	4	4	19	22	6	32,000	32,182	778	766
5049 Professional equipment, nec	5	6	71	79	13	20,113	24,456	2,516	2,724
5050 Metals and minerals, except petroleum	8	8	68	90	11	31,353	19,467	2,069	1,837
5063 Electrical apparatus and equipment	23	20	286	218	11	35,874	30,734	12,536	7,980
5064 Electrical appliances, TV & radios	4	5	36	62	12	18,889	14,129	892	938
5065 Electronic parts and equipment	34	33	350	305	9	31,166	35,108	10,375	10,807
5072 Hardware	-	15	-	53	4	-	25,962	-	1,794
5074 Plumbing & hydronic heating supplies	13	14	154	221	16	27,039	27,928	5,801	7,591
5075 Warm air heating & air conditioning	9	10	87	92	9	32,598	30,130	2,630	2,856
5083 Farm and garden machinery	-	9	-	53	6	-	17,509	-	1,084
5084 Industrial machinery and equipment	19	20	109	159	8	20,037	24,931	2,434	4,779
5085 Industrial supplies	18	17	557	144	8	12,819	21,472	5,708	3,541
5087 Service establishment equipment	15	17	69	86	5	20,232	16,651	1,351	1,764
5088 Transportation equipment & supplies	3	-	4	-	-	19,000	-	163	-
5091 Sporting & recreational goods	-	10	-	11	1	-	21,091	-	648
5093 Scrap and waste materials	9	8	53	81	10	20,830	18,864	1,535	1,815
5094 Jewelry & precious stones	11	-	39	-	-	15,692	-	656	-

Continued on next page.

COLORADO SPRINGS, CO MSA - [continued]

Wholesale and Retail Trade USA	Establishments		Employment		Emp / Est	Pay / Employee		Annual Payroll ($ 000)	
	1994	1995	1994	1995	1995	1994	1995	1994	1995
5099 Durable goods, nec	10	11	132	172	16	21,970	28,163	3,777	5,533
5111 Printing and writing paper	3	-	45	-	-	23,644	-	794	-
5112 Stationery and office supplies	22	28	261	283	10	14,743	18,671	4,039	5,528
5113 Industrial & personal service paper	5	-	23	-	-	16,174	-	476	-
5120 Drugs, proprietaries, and sundries	8	7	43	26	4	18,977	23,385	909	733
5130 Apparel, piece goods, and notions	9	-	40	-	-	14,400	-	597	-
5148 Fresh fruits and vegetables	4	4	226	231	58	18,248	16,814	4,117	4,026
5149 Groceries and related products, nec	14	17	192	216	13	23,833	25,241	4,873	5,531
5162 Plastics materials & basic shapes	3	3	12	15	5	15,000	16,267	293	369
5169 Chemicals & allied products, nec	8	8	52	54	7	24,308	26,444	1,543	1,554
5170 Petroleum and petroleum products	13	11	625	543	49	19,354	22,401	15,264	14,135
5180 Beer, wine, and distilled beverages	7	8	244	179	22	26,951	32,045	6,728	6,685
5191 Farm supplies	11	9	39	43	5	13,641	13,767	685	619
5192 Books, periodicals, & newspapers	9	11	105	120	11	15,276	15,500	1,609	2,099
5193 Flowers & florists' supplies	5	4	55	51	13	17,673	12,471	1,129	897
5198 Paints, varnishes, and supplies	6	4	37	20	5	24,324	35,000	976	643
5199 Nondurable goods, nec	20	21	57	74	4	20,561	19,351	1,312	1,358
52 – Retail trade	2,595	2,634	35,237	36,700	14	11,960	12,913	479,653	519,742
5210 Lumber and other building materials	35	30	849	1,025	34	18,393	19,017	18,659	21,923
5230 Paint, glass, and wallpaper stores	21	22	148	172	8	20,595	20,047	3,513	3,739
5250 Hardware stores	15	9	146	121	13	10,685	10,347	1,453	1,333
5260 Retail nurseries and garden stores	14	15	61	67	4	5,705	6,448	762	932
5270 Mobile home dealers	9	10	71	77	8	13,352	17,247	1,939	1,875
5310 Department stores	19	21	3,138	3,599	171	11,154	12,403	39,572	46,059
5330 Variety stores	6	7	51	54	8	9,725	8,963	479	534
5390 Misc. general merchandise stores	16	16	475	480	30	12,573	14,117	6,178	6,414
5410 Grocery stores	111	112	3,539	3,767	34	18,021	17,808	67,544	70,080
5440 Candy, nut, and confectionery stores	12	13	55	64	5	8,364	8,000	516	572
5450 Dairy products stores	5	4	19	6	2	5,684	12,000	110	51
5460 Retail bakeries	33	26	373	206	8	7,239	7,709	2,925	1,730
5490 Miscellaneous food stores	25	27	99	139	5	7,192	7,770	810	1,424
5510 New and used car dealers	26	29	1,829	1,897	65	30,261	33,223	67,960	71,454
5520 Used car dealers	39	43	170	214	5	22,635	24,710	4,182	5,228
5530 Auto and home supply stores	73	75	579	662	9	16,981	19,644	11,821	13,723
5540 Gasoline service stations	145	143	930	981	7	11,243	12,049	11,227	12,072
5550 Boat dealers	4	5	26	41	8	13,077	13,756	461	645
5560 Recreational vehicle dealers	9	8	83	82	10	25,639	30,585	2,559	2,817
5570 Motorcycle dealers	12	13	108	112	9	17,074	17,321	2,153	2,806
5610 Men's & boys' clothing stores	14	15	74	84	6	12,649	12,381	937	1,051
5620 Women's clothing stores	69	56	587	460	8	9,083	9,183	5,482	4,232
5630 Women's accessory & specialty stores	10	10	42	42	4	8,857	10,476	411	393
5640 Children's and infants' wear stores	6	5	16	32	6	7,750	7,125	201	264
5650 Family clothing stores	27	25	384	403	16	10,250	10,362	4,306	4,730
5660 Shoe stores	50	49	251	231	5	9,912	11,844	2,762	2,921
5690 Misc. apparel & accessory stores	15	17	74	91	5	11,297	8,352	1,071	1,160
5712 Furniture stores	48	47	434	476	10	21,078	20,857	9,992	10,776
5713 Floor covering stores	27	31	147	152	5	21,714	27,079	3,738	4,647
5714 Drapery and upholstery stores	3	3	12	12	4	17,000	16,667	212	259
5719 Misc. homefurnishings stores	33	31	216	216	7	10,481	11,296	2,343	2,640
5720 Household appliance stores	9	10	54	111	11	12,148	6,450	937	930
5731 Radio, TV, & electronic stores	37	36	362	402	11	16,309	16,796	6,122	7,829
5734 Computer and software stores	15	20	73	107	5	12,603	14,467	1,053	1,491
5735 Record & prerecorded tape stores	19	18	222	238	13	9,820	8,824	2,081	2,033
5736 Musical instrument stores	9	7	48	35	5	20,833	28,343	812	633
5812 Eating places	593	555	12,757	12,846	23	6,880	7,515	103,194	108,653
5813 Drinking places	102	87	772	700	8	6,793	7,526	5,402	5,273
5910 Drug stores and proprietary stores	30	34	483	530	16	17,681	19,245	8,997	11,343
5920 Liquor stores	78	75	320	340	5	13,250	13,259	3,779	4,316
5930 Used merchandise stores	95	87	530	512	6	10,060	11,203	5,630	6,180
5941 Sporting goods and bicycle shops	65	66	560	514	8	11,357	10,739	6,590	6,534
5942 Book stores	22	25	152	171	7	11,632	12,444	2,110	2,446
5943 Stationery stores	7	7	39	42	6	13,128	13,429	570	587
5944 Jewelry stores	42	42	242	245	6	13,570	14,465	4,171	4,736
5945 Hobby, toy, and game shops	28	30	320	320	11	7,788	8,450	2,878	3,231
5946 Camera & photographic supply stores	4	4	49	33	8	18,857	24,485	1,411	707
5947 Gift, novelty, and souvenir shops	83	87	416	404	5	6,760	7,861	3,971	4,104
5949 Sewing, needlework, and piece goods	19	15	154	105	7	7,740	7,771	1,389	917
5961 Catalog and mail-order houses	20	27	513	529	20	16,452	17,308	9,136	10,310
5962 Merchandising machine operators	11	10	36	39	4	12,667	12,923	490	507
5963 Direct selling establishments	34	31	257	211	7	16,700	20,171	4,062	4,146
5984 Liquefied petroleum gas dealers	5	5	47	62	12	21,106	20,387	1,164	1,465

Continued on next page.

COLORADO SPRINGS, CO MSA - [continued]

Wholesale and Retail Trade USA	Establishments		Employment		Emp / Est	Pay / Employee		Annual Payroll ($ 000)	
	1994	1995	1994	1995	1995	1994	1995	1994	1995
5992 Florists	-	49	-	213	4	-	9,427	-	2,376
5995 Optical goods stores	39	41	187	203	5	13,027	16,374	2,554	3,303
5999 Miscellaneous retail stores, nec	108	123	486	564	5	12,774	13,475	7,254	8,553

Source: County Business Patterns 1994/95, CBP-94/95, U.S. Department of Commerce, Washington DC, November 1997. The employment column represents mid-March employment in the year. Pay per employee is calculated by dividing 1st Quarter payroll, annualized, by mid-March employment. The column headed 'Emp / Est' shows 'employees per establishment'. A dash (-) means that data are unavailable or cannot be calculated. nec means not elsewhere classified. *Notes:* 1. 1994 data incomplete; unavailable or withheld. 2. 1995 data incomplete; unavailable or withheld. 3. 1994 and 1995 data incomplete; unavailable or withheld.

COLUMBIA, MO MSA

Wholesale and Retail Trade USA	Establishments		Employment		Emp / Est	Pay / Employee		Annual Payroll ($ 000)	
	1994	1995	1994	1995	1995	1994	1995	1994	1995
50 – Wholesale trade	194	191	2,718	2,900	15	24,144	25,589	75,607	82,325
5012 Automobiles and other vehicles	6	-	95	-	-	8,926	-	868	-
5013 Motor vehicle supplies and new parts	12	15	104	167	11	15,385	18,443	1,596	3,580
5014 Tires and tubes	5	3	84	40	13	19,857	17,900	1,895	800
5015 Motor vehicle parts, used	3	-	15	-	-	15,733	-	244	-
5020 Furniture and homefurnishings	5	4	20	22	6	17,600	18,000	401	435
5031 Lumber, plywood, and millwork	3	-	90	-	-	22,933	-	2,114	-
5044 Office equipment	8	9	94	98	11	20,766	25,388	2,253	2,214
5045 Computers, peripherals, & software	9	8	242	324	41	29,124	26,210	12,302	12,971
5051 Metals service centers and offices	4	4	31	43	11	22,065	22,512	893	1,153
5063 Electrical apparatus and equipment	5	5	59	53	11	32,271	27,396	1,943	1,533
5072 Hardware	3	3	10	8	3	22,000	34,000	238	269
5074 Plumbing & hydronic heating supplies	4	-	78	-	-	27,590	-	2,165	-
5075 Warm air heating & air conditioning	-	7	-	26	4	-	23,385	-	685
5082 Construction and mining machinery	4	4	24	25	6	25,667	33,760	697	768
5083 Farm and garden machinery	6	5	50	65	13	21,440	31,200	1,720	1,810
5087 Service establishment equipment	4	4	35	40	10	22,629	21,700	843	922
5091 Sporting & recreational goods	4	-	19	-	-	22,316	-	429	-
5093 Scrap and waste materials	-	3	-	36	12	-	12,556	-	503
5110 Paper and paper products	4	3	60	41	14	14,200	16,878	649	618
5147 Meats and meat products	3	3	36	33	11	17,111	18,061	692	720
5149 Groceries and related products, nec	8	7	134	128	18	23,612	25,688	3,218	3,479
5169 Chemicals & allied products, nec	3	-	18	-	-	19,333	-	385	-
5170 Petroleum and petroleum products	7	6	28	42	7	15,857	13,048	470	523
5180 Beer, wine, and distilled beverages	5	6	101	115	19	27,327	27,478	2,935	3,355
5191 Farm supplies	8	8	56	52	7	21,571	20,154	1,350	1,156
52 – Retail trade	790	814	12,769	13,002	16	10,205	11,200	145,475	156,399
5210 Lumber and other building materials	17	20	320	359	18	15,763	16,223	6,419	6,448
5230 Paint, glass, and wallpaper stores	-	4	-	40	10	-	21,100	-	963
5250 Hardware stores	-	5	-	72	14	-	13,222	-	1,057
5260 Retail nurseries and garden stores	9	7	45	40	6	7,200	9,000	509	494
5270 Mobile home dealers	6	6	85	89	15	23,153	28,270	2,175	3,213
5310 Department stores	9	9	1,509	1,617	180	9,347	10,961	16,078	17,716
5410 Grocery stores	47	47	1,364	1,457	31	11,132	10,852	16,944	17,422
5440 Candy, nut, and confectionery stores	3	-	28	-	-	6,857	-	219	-
5460 Retail bakeries	5	7	45	95	14	7,467	8,632	430	860
5490 Miscellaneous food stores	5	4	19	26	7	4,632	6,308	131	172
5510 New and used car dealers	16	16	619	627	39	26,520	27,509	19,863	20,998
5520 Used car dealers	8	9	57	57	6	17,895	15,018	1,014	1,022
5530 Auto and home supply stores	12	12	94	115	10	16,511	18,817	1,642	2,518
5540 Gasoline service stations	62	64	546	580	9	10,403	12,938	6,344	6,889
5570 Motorcycle dealers	-	3	-	37	12	-	15,243	-	727
5610 Men's & boys' clothing stores	8	-	56	-	-	7,286	-	439	-
5620 Women's clothing stores	31	24	325	237	10	7,040	7,426	2,263	1,896
5630 Women's accessory & specialty stores	-	8	-	27	3	-	7,407	-	233
5650 Family clothing stores	9	10	144	175	18	7,583	9,394	1,269	1,370
5660 Shoe stores	20	19	108	107	6	11,815	11,888	1,272	1,214
5690 Misc. apparel & accessory stores	11	13	75	69	5	8,267	10,087	683	722
5712 Furniture stores	21	23	134	143	6	16,567	16,615	2,384	2,651
5719 Misc. homefurnishings stores	7	8	51	44	6	11,686	14,545	606	627
5720 Household appliance stores	6	5	35	36	7	17,029	19,222	723	772
5731 Radio, TV, & electronic stores	13	11	163	219	20	14,479	11,836	2,462	2,546
5734 Computer and software stores	6	9	47	63	7	11,404	13,333	590	936
5735 Record & prerecorded tape stores	7	9	53	61	7	8,075	9,377	450	541
5736 Musical instrument stores	6	6	39	42	7	8,821	10,000	364	451
5812 Eating places	167	156	4,385	3,989	26	6,679	7,489	31,335	32,291
5813 Drinking places	17	15	269	283	19	4,268	4,749	1,227	1,344

Continued on next page.

COLUMBIA, MO MSA - [continued]

Wholesale and Retail Trade USA	Establishments		Employment		Emp / Est	Pay / Employee		Annual Payroll ($ 000)	
	1994	1995	1994	1995	1995	1994	1995	1994	1995
5910 Drug stores and proprietary stores	13	11	152	163	15	16,816	17,693	2,590	2,717
5930 Used merchandise stores	16	-	39	-	-	8,923	-	440	-
5941 Sporting goods and bicycle shops	18	21	127	150	7	10,047	9,573	1,597	1,758
5942 Book stores	6	-	39	-	-	8,513	-	375	-
5944 Jewelry stores	13	14	81	84	6	14,025	16,524	1,183	1,462
5945 Hobby, toy, and game shops	8	8	73	106	13	9,534	7,585	857	1,014
5947 Gift, novelty, and souvenir shops	20	22	74	80	4	7,838	7,150	809	737
5949 Sewing, needlework, and piece goods	4	3	34	43	14	7,176	6,047	235	261
5963 Direct selling establishments	9	-	87	-	-	19,310	-	1,601	-
5980 Fuel dealers	-	5	-	20	4	-	17,200	-	358
5992 Florists	11	11	69	71	6	21,507	21,803	972	1,011
5995 Optical goods stores	10	10	43	44	4	16,744	17,000	766	721
5999 Miscellaneous retail stores, nec	27	32	160	167	5	9,100	9,557	1,580	1,739

Source: County Business Patterns 1994/95, CBP-94/95, U.S. Department of Commerce, Washington DC, November 1997. The employment column represents mid-March employment in the year. Pay per employee is calculated by dividing 1st Quarter payroll, annualized, by mid-March employment. The column headed 'Emp / Est' shows 'employees per establishment'. A dash (-) means that data are unavailable or cannot be calculated. nec means not elsewhere classified. *Notes:* 1. 1994 data incomplete; unavailable or withheld. 2. 1995 data incomplete; unavailable or withheld. 3. 1994 and 1995 data incomplete; unavailable or withheld.

COLUMBIA, SC MSA

Wholesale and Retail Trade USA	Establishments		Employment		Emp / Est	Pay / Employee		Annual Payroll ($ 000)	
	1994	1995	1994	1995	1995	1994	1995	1994	1995
50- Wholesale trade	-	1,025	-	14,074	14	-	28,790	-	423,622
5012 Automobiles and other vehicles	-	28	-	327	12	-	22,618	-	8,180
5013 Motor vehicle supplies and new parts	-	54	-	555	10	-	21,348	-	12,533
5014 Tires and tubes	-	9	-	107	12	-	25,121	-	2,659
5015 Motor vehicle parts, used	-	12	-	66	6	-	14,424	-	1,114
5021 Furniture	-	16	-	169	11	-	20,781	-	4,246
5023 Homefurnishings	-	16	-	74	5	-	23,514	-	1,875
5031 Lumber, plywood, and millwork	-	20	-	537	27	-	24,521	-	15,041
5032 Brick, stone, & related materials	-	6	-	48	8	-	49,000	-	1,930
5033 Roofing, siding, & insulation	-	12	-	84	7	-	30,524	-	2,407
5039 Construction materials, nec	-	22	-	304	14	-	28,461	-	6,869
5044 Office equipment	-	37	-	488	13	-	33,975	-	14,934
5045 Computers, peripherals, & software	-	31	-	362	12	-	58,519	-	20,172
5046 Commercial equipment, nec	-	18	-	65	4	-	29,723	-	2,111
5047 Medical and hospital equipment	-	37	-	298	8	-	33,812	-	10,933
5048 Ophthalmic goods	-	9	-	65	7	-	14,585	-	1,356
5051 Metals service centers and offices [2]	-	14	-	78	6	-	32,308	-	2,244
5063 Electrical apparatus and equipment	-	39	-	418	11	-	33,703	-	13,498
5064 Electrical appliances, TV & radios	-	6	-	9	2	-	23,111	-	220
5065 Electronic parts and equipment	-	31	-	300	10	-	37,467	-	11,344
5072 Hardware	-	13	-	150	12	-	29,787	-	5,125
5074 Plumbing & hydronic heating supplies	-	12	-	127	11	-	27,654	-	3,900
5075 Warm air heating & air conditioning	-	21	-	252	12	-	37,587	-	10,372
5078 Refrigeration equipment and supplies	-	4	-	20	5	-	38,400	-	791
5082 Construction and mining machinery	-	16	-	459	29	-	31,861	-	16,526
5083 Farm and garden machinery	-	15	-	192	13	-	18,896	-	3,696
5084 Industrial machinery and equipment	-	59	-	559	9	-	28,107	-	17,695
5085 Industrial supplies	-	37	-	367	10	-	29,809	-	11,382
5087 Service establishment equipment	-	22	-	187	9	-	25,412	-	5,410
5091 Sporting & recreational goods	-	15	-	526	35	-	30,798	-	14,042
5093 Scrap and waste materials	-	15	-	189	13	-	20,127	-	5,048
5099 Durable goods, nec	-	26	-	205	8	-	24,254	-	5,058
5112 Stationery and office supplies	-	22	-	221	10	-	21,140	-	5,310
5120 Drugs, proprietaries, and sundries	-	13	-	215	17	-	28,353	-	6,699
5131 Piece goods & notions	-	13	-	85	7	-	31,059	-	2,477
5136 Men's and boys' clothing	-	10	-	208	21	-	23,942	-	5,457
5137 Women's and children's clothing [2]	-	7	-	19	3	-	31,158	-	567
5142 Packaged frozen food [2]	-	6	-	23	4	-	13,913	-	499
5143 Dairy products, exc. dried or canned	-	6	-	45	8	-	25,867	-	1,217
5145 Confectionery	-	5	-	102	20	-	17,137	-	1,278
5146 Fish and seafoods [2]	-	4	-	12	3	-	14,000	-	207
5147 Meats and meat products	-	4	-	33	8	-	19,030	-	633
5148 Fresh fruits and vegetables	-	19	-	186	10	-	22,731	-	5,833
5149 Groceries and related products, nec	-	23	-	815	35	-	27,789	-	26,451
5162 Plastics materials & basic shapes	-	10	-	149	15	-	23,705	-	3,714
5169 Chemicals & allied products, nec	-	29	-	250	9	-	32,256	-	8,349
5171 Petroleum bulk stations & terminals	-	12	-	70	6	-	21,257	-	1,691

Continued on next page.

COLUMBIA, SC MSA - [continued]

Wholesale and Retail Trade USA	Establishments		Employment		Emp / Est	Pay / Employee		Annual Payroll ($ 000)	
	1994	1995	1994	1995	1995	1994	1995	1994	1995
5181 Beer and ale [2]	-	5	-	226	45	-	28,018	-	6,982
5182 Wine and distilled beverages [2]	-	8	-	489	61	-	30,618	-	14,625
5191 Farm supplies	-	15	-	142	9	-	22,056	-	3,140
5193 Flowers & florists' supplies [2]	-	6	-	22	4	-	14,000	-	329
5198 Paints, varnishes, and supplies	-	11	-	60	5	-	28,067	-	1,384
5199 Nondurable goods, nec	-	26	-	150	6	-	24,480	-	3,417
52- Retail trade	-	3,100	-	46,231	15	-	11,590	-	563,789
5210 Lumber and other building materials	-	41	-	1,085	26	-	18,573	-	20,684
5230 Paint, glass, and wallpaper stores	-	21	-	85	4	-	16,847	-	1,501
5250 Hardware stores	-	22	-	179	8	-	15,464	-	2,761
5260 Retail nurseries and garden stores	-	17	-	81	5	-	11,556	-	1,122
5270 Mobile home dealers	-	20	-	118	6	-	25,186	-	4,511
5310 Department stores	-	29	-	4,540	157	-	12,082	-	56,442
5330 Variety stores	-	24	-	123	5	-	7,122	-	1,014
5390 Misc. general merchandise stores	-	14	-	344	25	-	13,686	-	4,264
5410 Grocery stores	-	242	-	7,002	29	-	9,006	-	64,572
5420 Meat and fish markets	-	19	-	84	4	-	12,286	-	1,110
5430 Fruit and vegetable markets	-	5	-	6	1	-	5,333	-	52
5460 Retail bakeries	-	20	-	171	9	-	6,573	-	1,282
5490 Miscellaneous food stores	-	15	-	128	9	-	9,281	-	1,219
5510 New and used car dealers	-	42	-	2,146	51	-	33,390	-	80,016
5520 Used car dealers	-	36	-	143	4	-	20,196	-	3,257
5530 Auto and home supply stores	-	96	-	797	8	-	17,802	-	15,218
5540 Gasoline service stations	-	196	-	1,620	8	-	12,153	-	20,885
5550 Boat dealers	-	10	-	52	5	-	41,077	-	1,704
5560 Recreational vehicle dealers	-	5	-	16	3	-	27,000	-	428
5570 Motorcycle dealers	-	9	-	58	6	-	20,759	-	1,686
5610 Men's & boys' clothing stores	-	30	-	222	7	-	9,730	-	2,326
5620 Women's clothing stores	-	121	-	1,208	10	-	8,596	-	9,994
5630 Women's accessory & specialty stores [2]	-	20	-	123	6	-	8,683	-	1,109
5640 Children's and infants' wear stores	-	11	-	73	7	-	8,658	-	640
5650 Family clothing stores	-	29	-	570	20	-	11,053	-	6,238
5660 Shoe stores	-	77	-	443	6	-	9,941	-	4,223
5690 Misc. apparel & accessory stores	-	11	-	51	5	-	8,078	-	381
5712 Furniture stores	-	83	-	661	8	-	18,179	-	12,960
5713 Floor covering stores	-	33	-	143	4	-	20,056	-	3,105
5714 Drapery and upholstery stores [2]	-	7	-	20	3	-	18,400	-	378
5719 Misc. homefurnishings stores	-	51	-	327	6	-	13,480	-	4,920
5720 Household appliance stores	-	20	-	105	5	-	20,076	-	2,388
5731 Radio, TV, & electronic stores	-	39	-	462	12	-	13,758	-	6,235
5734 Computer and software stores	-	21	-	85	4	-	20,235	-	1,862
5735 Record & prerecorded tape stores	-	24	-	186	8	-	12,151	-	2,338
5736 Musical instrument stores	-	13	-	88	7	-	19,000	-	1,689
5812 Eating places	-	615	-	14,935	24	-	7,532	-	117,391
5813 Drinking places	-	36	-	293	8	-	7,290	-	2,010
5910 Drug stores and proprietary stores	-	89	-	972	11	-	13,914	-	14,876
5920 Liquor stores	-	56	-	145	3	-	11,283	-	1,742
5930 Used merchandise stores	-	57	-	219	4	-	13,242	-	2,937
5941 Sporting goods and bicycle shops	-	53	-	382	7	-	12,743	-	4,814
5942 Book stores	-	33	-	351	11	-	10,667	-	3,878
5943 Stationery stores	-	16	-	55	3	-	11,782	-	874
5944 Jewelry stores	-	60	-	436	7	-	15,963	-	7,092
5945 Hobby, toy, and game shops	-	18	-	235	13	-	8,528	-	2,449
5946 Camera & photographic supply stores	-	7	-	46	7	-	14,609	-	711
5947 Gift, novelty, and souvenir shops	-	60	-	257	4	-	8,467	-	2,269
5948 Luggage and leather goods stores [2]	-	4	-	24	6	-	10,667	-	281
5949 Sewing, needlework, and piece goods	-	14	-	105	8	-	7,048	-	766
5961 Catalog and mail-order houses	-	11	-	167	15	-	14,036	-	2,593
5962 Merchandising machine operators [2]	-	7	-	132	19	-	14,000	-	1,960
5963 Direct selling establishments	-	26	-	241	9	-	11,004	-	2,457
5980 Fuel dealers	-	13	-	123	9	-	21,268	-	2,277
5992 Florists [2]	-	54	-	64	1	-	9,438	-	635
5995 Optical goods stores	-	37	-	201	5	-	16,279	-	3,251
5999 Miscellaneous retail stores, nec	-	95	-	434	5	-	18,175	-	7,512

Source: County Business Patterns 1994/95, CBP-94/95, U.S. Department of Commerce, Washington DC, November 1997. The employment column represents mid-March employment in the year. Pay per employee is calculated by dividing 1st Quarter payroll, annualized, by mid-March employment. The column headed 'Emp / Est' shows 'employees per establishment'. A dash (-) means that data are unavailable or cannot be calculated. nec means not elsewhere classified. *Notes:* 1. 1994 data incomplete; unavailable or withheld. 2. 1995 data incomplete; unavailable or withheld. 3. 1994 and 1995 data incomplete; unavailable or withheld.

COLUMBUS MSA (AL PART)

Wholesale and Retail Trade USA	Establishments		Employment		Emp / Est	Pay / Employee		Annual Payroll ($ 000)	
	1994	1995	1994	1995	1995	1994	1995	1994	1995
50- Wholesale trade	37	32	189	240	8	22,561	20,217	5,313	5,434
5010 Motor vehicles, parts, and supplies	4	4	7	10	3	22,286	16,400	167	253
5030 Lumber and construction materials	4	-	47	-	-	24,170	-	1,316	-
5080 Machinery, equipment, and supplies	4	4	11	9	2	34,909	24,000	405	354
5190 Misc., nondurable goods	6	3	17	5	2	8,471	21,600	171	69
52- Retail trade	221	233	2,440	2,610	11	10,057	10,506	26,108	27,730
5210 Lumber and other building materials	4	6	25	45	8	13,920	12,178	392	690
5250 Hardware stores	3	4	27	22	6	10,519	12,545	310	303
5260 Retail nurseries and garden stores	3	3	21	15	5	6,286	7,467	168	154
5300 General merchandise stores	7	8	429	454	57	10,312	12,626	4,893	5,463
5400 Food stores	43	43	692	615	14	8,798	10,660	6,488	6,575
5520 Used car dealers	12	12	33	31	3	10,909	20,387	482	614
5530 Auto and home supply stores	12	14	77	99	7	15,013	14,263	1,226	1,485
5540 Gasoline service stations	15	14	73	83	6	8,384	9,928	730	807
5620 Women's clothing stores	7	6	41	25	4	9,561	8,800	381	220
5713 Floor covering stores	3	-	21	-	-	15,619	-	363	-
5731 Radio, TV, & electronic stores	3	-	8	-	-	18,500	-	136	-
5812 Eating places	44	45	688	860	19	7,622	6,367	5,597	5,650
5813 Drinking places	-	3	-	6	2	-	6,667	-	39
5910 Drug stores and proprietary stores	11	9	91	74	8	21,055	22,162	1,808	1,612
5930 Used merchandise stores	4	4	3	10	3	10,667	12,400	45	144
5941 Sporting goods and bicycle shops	5	7	19	22	3	17,895	17,818	376	374
5999 Miscellaneous retail stores, nec	-	3	-	8	3	-	7,500	-	40

Source: County Business Patterns 1994/95, CBP-94/95, U.S. Department of Commerce, Washington DC, November 1997. The employment column represents mid-March employment in the year. Pay per employee is calculated by dividing 1st Quarter payroll, annualized, by mid-March employment. The column headed 'Emp / Est' shows 'employees per establishment'. A dash (-) means that data are unavailable or cannot be calculated. nec means not elsewhere classified. *Notes:* 1. 1994 data incomplete; unavailable or withheld. 2. 1995 data incomplete; unavailable or withheld. 3. 1994 and 1995 data incomplete; unavailable or withheld.

COLUMBUS MSA (GA PART)

Wholesale and Retail Trade USA	Establishments		Employment		Emp / Est	Pay / Employee		Annual Payroll ($ 000)	
	1994	1995	1994	1995	1995	1994	1995	1994	1995
50- Wholesale trade[1]	264	262	3,302	3,593	14	28,219	32,710	96,173	113,472
5012 Automobiles and other vehicles[3]	4	3	40	30	10	16,800	14,800	552	509
5013 Motor vehicle supplies and new parts[3]	22	17	177	142	8	19,819	17,831	3,830	2,363
5015 Motor vehicle parts, used[2]	-	5	-	19	4	-	16,421	-	296
5020 Furniture and homefurnishings[3]	8	10	197	199	20	44,690	49,789	9,328	10,692
5031 Lumber, plywood, and millwork[3]	5	3	51	17	6	21,176	23,529	1,212	227
5039 Construction materials, nec[2]	-	5	-	24	5	-	22,333	-	573
5044 Office equipment[3]	10	10	170	181	18	22,847	22,564	4,123	4,199
5045 Computers, peripherals, & software[3]	6	7	65	45	6	59,385	88,622	3,003	2,598
5046 Commercial equipment, nec[2]	-	4	-	28	7	-	16,857	-	551
5047 Medical and hospital equipment[3]	5	3	19	14	5	39,158	52,000	635	765
5063 Electrical apparatus and equipment[3]	9	8	109	131	16	25,284	25,313	3,064	3,689
5064 Electrical appliances, TV & radios[3]	4	4	36	39	10	28,444	28,513	1,297	1,381
5065 Electronic parts and equipment[3]	6	7	24	26	4	33,500	34,000	787	825
5072 Hardware[2]	-	3	-	18	6	-	22,444	-	415
5074 Plumbing & hydronic heating supplies[1]	4	-	45	-	-	24,711	-	1,226	-
5075 Warm air heating & air conditioning[3]	5	5	56	56	11	27,571	28,929	1,401	1,528
5083 Farm and garden machinery[1]	6	-	19	-	-	14,947	-	329	-
5084 Industrial machinery and equipment[3]	12	11	64	49	4	24,313	34,776	1,770	1,842
5085 Industrial supplies[3]	15	13	109	94	7	22,972	28,170	2,663	2,678
5087 Service establishment equipment[3]	7	7	52	63	9	19,077	19,619	1,376	1,482
5093 Scrap and waste materials[3]	7	7	106	114	16	12,075	14,807	1,557	2,077
5113 Industrial & personal service paper[3]	3	3	58	64	21	33,310	33,250	1,957	2,144
5130 Apparel, piece goods, and notions[2]	-	6	-	354	59	-	27,435	-	11,125
5141 Groceries, general line[3]	5	3	180	83	28	20,689	27,855	3,774	2,265
5143 Dairy products, exc. dried or canned[3]	3	3	24	22	7	12,833	15,273	386	425
5169 Chemicals & allied products, nec[3]	8	7	73	84	12	29,808	66,143	2,228	4,133
5170 Petroleum and petroleum products[3]	11	10	81	41	4	21,136	26,341	1,604	1,203
5180 Beer, wine, and distilled beverages[3]	4	4	124	175	44	23,516	39,429	3,389	7,225
5193 Flowers & florists' supplies[3]	7	5	43	29	6	11,628	14,207	565	441
5199 Nondurable goods, nec[3]	8	9	43	31	3	16,279	18,065	653	638
52- Retail trade	1,293	1,291	16,995	18,352	14	11,612	12,555	217,893	241,533
5210 Lumber and other building materials[3]	13	10	441	406	41	15,392	18,709	7,853	8,394
5230 Paint, glass, and wallpaper stores[3]	8	7	59	60	9	19,864	19,000	1,303	1,330
5250 Hardware stores[3]	10	8	55	54	7	12,873	14,370	802	847
5260 Retail nurseries and garden stores[1]	8	-	54	-	-	10,000	-	612	-
5270 Mobile home dealers[1]	4	-	24	-	-	17,833	-	609	-

Continued on next page.

COLUMBUS MSA (GA PART) - [continued]

Wholesale and Retail Trade USA	Establishments		Employment		Emp / Est	Pay / Employee		Annual Payroll ($ 000)	
	1994	1995	1994	1995	1995	1994	1995	1994	1995
5310 Department stores [3]	9	9	1,423	1,568	174	11,123	12,781	17,967	19,722
5330 Variety stores [3]	16	15	106	123	8	9,698	10,114	1,220	1,246
5390 Misc. general merchandise stores [3]	15	13	353	264	20	12,136	13,788	4,275	3,332
5410 Grocery stores	86	94	1,844	2,232	24	8,976	9,283	18,959	22,070
5420 Meat and fish markets [3]	3	3	6	9	3	16,000	12,444	143	116
5430 Fruit and vegetable markets [3]	4	5	9	9	2	6,222	8,444	68	79
5460 Retail bakeries [3]	7	7	82	72	10	7,951	10,611	722	770
5490 Miscellaneous food stores [3]	6	6	17	14	2	8,000	12,000	151	211
5510 New and used car dealers [3]	19	20	1,086	1,157	58	29,319	35,136	34,693	41,902
5520 Used car dealers [3]	18	22	127	124	6	21,008	22,452	2,750	2,804
5530 Auto and home supply stores [3]	49	47	368	415	9	17,272	17,966	7,129	8,017
5540 Gasoline service stations [3]	73	76	492	531	7	12,846	12,994	6,998	8,518
5570 Motorcycle dealers [3]	4	3	21	17	6	15,238	19,059	438	402
5610 Men's & boys' clothing stores [3]	17	17	164	182	11	9,512	8,615	1,615	1,498
5620 Women's clothing stores [3]	54	45	497	435	10	8,748	8,524	4,482	3,929
5630 Women's accessory & specialty stores [2]	-	6	-	31	5	-	8,129	-	244
5650 Family clothing stores [3]	10	10	291	262	26	11,230	12,565	3,662	3,348
5660 Shoe stores [3]	35	29	159	152	5	9,836	11,026	1,633	1,801
5690 Misc. apparel & accessory stores [3]	7	7	51	59	8	6,980	10,983	416	732
5712 Furniture stores [3]	39	42	397	423	10	14,196	15,726	6,594	6,660
5713 Floor covering stores [3]	10	11	60	63	6	15,333	16,254	1,042	1,110
5714 Drapery and upholstery stores [3]	4	5	13	9	2	8,615	9,778	103	97
5719 Misc. homefurnishings stores [3]	18	19	123	111	6	7,447	10,126	989	1,251
5720 Household appliance stores [3]	9	8	41	37	5	16,585	19,135	732	793
5731 Radio, TV, & electronic stores [3]	15	15	146	159	11	17,589	16,604	2,779	2,620
5735 Record & prerecorded tape stores [3]	9	9	38	61	7	13,368	9,836	561	656
5812 Eating places	263	245	5,383	5,836	24	7,365	7,705	42,351	48,256
5813 Drinking places [3]	43	34	290	188	6	6,731	8,362	1,938	1,562
5910 Drug stores and proprietary stores [3]	40	38	455	393	10	15,279	16,641	6,793	6,689
5920 Liquor stores [3]	36	37	187	209	6	10,203	9,569	2,054	2,170
5930 Used merchandise stores [3]	36	36	124	139	4	13,290	14,043	1,870	2,037
5941 Sporting goods and bicycle shops [3]	13	12	19	35	3	11,789	14,400	320	631
5942 Book stores [3]	8	6	66	60	10	6,606	8,133	480	567
5943 Stationery stores [3]	3	3	3	11	4	8,000	14,545	87	173
5944 Jewelry stores [3]	34	33	169	181	5	15,006	15,602	2,693	2,715
5945 Hobby, toy, and game shops [3]	10	9	73	70	8	7,945	9,029	758	790
5947 Gift, novelty, and souvenir shops [3]	22	21	86	112	5	7,116	6,679	741	758
5949 Sewing, needlework, and piece goods [3]	8	7	50	46	7	8,800	8,957	423	407
5961 Catalog and mail-order houses [3]	9	8	106	139	17	18,000	21,007	2,051	2,591
5962 Merchandising machine operators [3]	8	8	194	209	26	14,495	15,789	3,513	3,224
5963 Direct selling establishments [3]	14	13	91	99	8	17,187	18,222	1,903	1,830
5992 Florists [3]	33	30	98	92	3	9,714	11,348	1,032	1,028
5995 Optical goods stores [3]	14	13	96	85	7	14,458	16,847	1,424	1,424
5999 Miscellaneous retail stores, nec [3]	30	39	114	157	4	15,439	15,541	1,991	2,740

Source: County Business Patterns 1994/95, CBP-94/95, U.S. Department of Commerce, Washington DC, November 1997. The employment column represents mid-March employment in the year. Pay per employee is calculated by dividing 1st Quarter payroll, annualized, by mid-March employment. The column headed 'Emp / Est' shows 'employees per establishment'. A dash (-) means that data are unavailable or cannot be calculated. nec means not elsewhere classified. *Notes:* 1. 1994 data incomplete; unavailable or withheld. 2. 1995 data incomplete; unavailable or withheld. 3. 1994 and 1995 data incomplete; unavailable or withheld.

COLUMBUS, GA - AL MSA

Wholesale and Retail Trade USA	Establishments		Employment		Emp / Est	Pay / Employee		Annual Payroll ($ 000)	
	1994	1995	1994	1995	1995	1994	1995	1994	1995
50 - Wholesale trade [1]	301	294	3,491	3,833	13	27,913	31,928	101,486	118,906
5012 Automobiles and other vehicles [3]	4	4	40	30	8	16,800	14,800	552	509
5013 Motor vehicle supplies and new parts [3]	24	18	177	142	8	19,819	17,831	3,830	2,363
5015 Motor vehicle parts, used [2]	-	7	-	19	3	-	16,421	-	296
5020 Furniture and homefurnishings [3]	10	12	197	199	17	44,690	49,789	9,328	10,692
5031 Lumber, plywood, and millwork [3]	5	3	51	17	6	21,176	23,529	1,212	227
5039 Construction materials, nec [2]	-	5	-	24	5	-	22,333	-	573
5044 Office equipment [3]	11	11	170	181	16	22,847	22,564	4,123	4,199
5045 Computers, peripherals, & software [3]	6	7	65	45	6	59,385	88,622	3,003	2,598
5046 Commercial equipment, nec [2]	-	4	-	28	7	-	16,857	-	551
5047 Medical and hospital equipment [3]	5	3	19	14	5	39,158	52,000	635	765
5063 Electrical apparatus and equipment [3]	10	9	109	131	15	25,284	25,313	3,064	3,689
5064 Electrical appliances, TV & radios [3]	4	4	36	39	10	28,444	28,513	1,297	1,381
5065 Electronic parts and equipment [3]	6	8	24	26	3	33,500	34,000	787	825
5072 Hardware [2]	-	3	-	18	6	-	22,444	-	415
5074 Plumbing & hydronic heating supplies [1]	5	-	45	-	-	24,711	-	1,226	-

Continued on next page.

COLUMBUS, GA-AL MSA - [continued]

Wholesale and Retail Trade USA	Establishments		Employment		Emp / Est	Pay / Employee		Annual Payroll ($ 000)	
	1994	1995	1994	1995	1995	1994	1995	1994	1995
5075 Warm air heating & air conditioning[3]	5	5	56	56	11	27,571	28,929	1,401	1,528
5083 Farm and garden machinery[1]	6	-	19	-	-	14,947	-	329	-
5084 Industrial machinery and equipment[3]	13	12	64	49	4	24,313	34,776	1,770	1,842
5085 Industrial supplies[3]	15	13	109	94	7	22,972	28,170	2,663	2,678
5087 Service establishment equipment[3]	8	8	52	63	8	19,077	19,619	1,376	1,482
5093 Scrap and waste materials[3]	7	7	106	114	16	12,075	14,807	1,557	2,077
5113 Industrial & personal service paper[3]	3	3	58	64	21	33,310	33,250	1,957	2,144
5130 Apparel, piece goods, and notions[2]	-	7	-	354	51	-	27,435	-	11,125
5141 Groceries, general line[3]	5	3	180	83	28	20,689	27,855	3,774	2,265
5143 Dairy products, exc. dried or canned[3]	3	3	24	22	7	12,833	15,273	386	425
5169 Chemicals & allied products, nec[3]	8	8	73	84	11	29,808	66,143	2,228	4,133
5170 Petroleum and petroleum products[3]	13	10	81	41	4	21,136	26,341	1,604	1,203
5180 Beer, wine, and distilled beverages[3]	5	5	124	175	35	23,516	39,429	3,389	7,225
5193 Flowers & florists' supplies[3]	7	5	43	29	6	11,628	14,207	565	441
5199 Nondurable goods, nec[3]	10	9	43	31	3	16,279	18,065	653	638
52- Retail trade	1,514	1,524	19,435	20,962	14	11,417	12,300	244,001	269,263
5210 Lumber and other building materials[3]	17	16	466	451	28	15,313	18,058	8,245	9,084
5230 Paint, glass, and wallpaper stores[3]	9	8	59	60	8	19,864	19,000	1,303	1,330
5250 Hardware stores[3]	13	12	82	76	6	12,098	13,842	1,112	1,150
5260 Retail nurseries and garden stores[3]	11	10	75	15	2	8,960	7,467	780	154
5270 Mobile home dealers[1]	6	-	24	-	-	17,833	-	609	-
5310 Department stores[3]	11	11	1,423	1,568	143	11,123	12,781	17,967	19,722
5330 Variety stores[3]	20	19	106	123	6	9,698	10,114	1,220	1,246
5390 Misc. general merchandise stores[3]	16	15	353	264	18	12,136	13,788	4,275	3,332
5410 Grocery stores[3]	128	135	1,844	2,232	17	8,976	9,283	18,959	22,070
5420 Meat and fish markets[3]	3	3	6	9	3	16,000	12,444	143	116
5430 Fruit and vegetable markets[3]	4	5	9	9	2	6,222	8,444	68	79
5460 Retail bakeries[3]	8	8	82	72	9	7,951	10,611	722	770
5490 Miscellaneous food stores[3]	6	7	17	14	2	8,000	12,000	151	211
5510 New and used car dealers[3]	20	22	1,086	1,157	53	29,319	35,136	34,693	41,902
5520 Used car dealers[3]	30	34	160	155	5	18,925	22,039	3,232	3,418
5530 Auto and home supply stores[3]	61	61	445	514	8	16,881	17,253	8,355	9,502
5540 Gasoline service stations[3]	88	90	565	614	7	12,269	12,580	7,728	9,325
5570 Motorcycle dealers[3]	5	4	21	17	4	15,238	19,059	438	402
5610 Men's & boys' clothing stores[3]	17	17	164	182	11	9,512	8,615	1,615	1,498
5620 Women's clothing stores[3]	61	51	538	460	9	8,810	8,539	4,863	4,149
5630 Women's accessory & specialty stores[2]	-	6	-	31	5	-	8,129	-	244
5650 Family clothing stores[3]	10	10	291	262	26	11,230	12,565	3,662	3,348
5660 Shoe stores[3]	38	32	159	152	5	9,836	11,026	1,633	1,801
5690 Misc. apparel & accessory stores[3]	9	9	51	59	7	6,980	10,983	416	732
5712 Furniture stores[3]	42	45	397	423	9	14,196	15,726	6,594	6,660
5713 Floor covering stores[3]	13	14	81	63	5	15,407	16,254	1,405	1,110
5714 Drapery and upholstery stores[3]	4	5	13	9	2	8,615	9,778	103	97
5719 Misc. homefurnishings stores[3]	18	19	123	111	6	7,447	10,126	989	1,251
5720 Household appliance stores[3]	9	8	41	37	5	16,585	19,135	732	793
5731 Radio, TV, & electronic stores[3]	18	19	154	159	8	17,636	16,604	2,915	2,620
5735 Record & prerecorded tape stores[3]	9	9	38	61	7	13,368	9,836	561	656
5812 Eating places	307	290	6,071	6,696	23	7,394	7,533	47,948	53,906
5813 Drinking places[3]	45	37	290	194	5	6,731	8,309	1,938	1,601
5910 Drug stores and proprietary stores[3]	51	47	546	467	10	16,242	17,516	8,601	8,301
5920 Liquor stores[3]	37	38	187	209	6	10,203	9,569	2,054	2,170
5930 Used merchandise stores[3]	40	40	127	149	4	13,228	13,933	1,915	2,181
5941 Sporting goods and bicycle shops[3]	18	19	38	57	3	14,842	15,719	696	1,005
5942 Book stores[3]	8	6	66	60	10	6,606	8,133	480	567
5943 Stationery stores[3]	3	3	3	11	4	8,000	14,545	87	173
5944 Jewelry stores[3]	36	35	169	181	5	15,006	15,602	2,693	2,715
5945 Hobby, toy, and game shops[3]	10	9	73	70	8	7,945	9,029	758	790
5947 Gift, novelty, and souvenir shops[3]	24	22	86	112	5	7,116	6,679	741	758
5949 Sewing, needlework, and piece goods[3]	8	7	50	46	7	8,800	8,957	423	407
5961 Catalog and mail-order houses[3]	9	8	106	139	17	18,000	21,007	2,051	2,591
5962 Merchandising machine operators[3]	8	8	194	209	26	14,495	15,789	3,513	3,224
5963 Direct selling establishments[3]	17	15	91	99	7	17,187	18,222	1,903	1,830
5992 Florists[3]	39	36	98	92	3	9,714	11,348	1,032	1,028
5995 Optical goods stores[3]	14	13	96	85	7	14,458	16,847	1,424	1,424
5999 Miscellaneous retail stores, nec[3]	34	42	114	165	4	15,439	15,152	1,991	2,780

Source: County Business Patterns 1994/95, CBP-94/95, U.S. Department of Commerce, Washington DC, November 1997. The employment column represents mid-March employment in the year. Pay per employee is calculated by dividing 1st Quarter payroll, annualized, by mid-March employment. The column headed 'Emp / Est' shows 'employees per establishment'. A dash (-) means that data are unavailable or cannot be calculated. nec means not elsewhere classified. *Notes:* 1. 1994 data incomplete; unavailable or withheld. 2. 1995 data incomplete; unavailable or withheld. 3. 1994 and 1995 data incomplete; unavailable or withheld.

COLUMBUS, OH MSA

Wholesale and Retail Trade USA	Establishments		Employment		Emp / Est	Pay / Employee		Annual Payroll ($ 000)	
	1994	1995	1994	1995	1995	1994	1995	1994	1995
50- Wholesale trade	2,674	2,705	42,470	45,139	17	31,388	34,142	1,425,981	1,616,928
5012 Automobiles and other vehicles[3]	47	51	841	1,664	33	22,102	20,050	20,328	31,674
5013 Motor vehicle supplies and new parts[3]	135	121	1,624	1,600	13	24,786	26,998	43,973	45,811
5014 Tires and tubes[3]	21	22	179	213	10	27,039	26,854	4,947	5,932
5015 Motor vehicle parts, used	31	35	183	209	6	18,536	22,029	3,914	5,212
5021 Furniture[3]	36	39	825	688	18	25,290	33,610	23,247	24,877
5023 Homefurnishings[3]	36	34	325	307	9	32,775	34,189	10,875	10,842
5031 Lumber, plywood, and millwork[3]	57	54	706	609	11	29,241	31,468	22,562	18,381
5032 Brick, stone, & related materials[3]	18	16	184	140	9	25,000	26,371	6,068	5,225
5033 Roofing, siding, & insulation[3]	23	20	324	181	9	25,296	31,867	9,783	5,528
5039 Construction materials, nec[3]	26	43	183	460	11	27,913	30,652	6,164	15,761
5043 Photographic equipment & supplies[3]	10	11	40	45	4	23,700	21,956	1,096	1,208
5044 Office equipment[3]	56	60	997	1,037	17	35,944	39,337	33,894	38,493
5045 Computers, peripherals, & software[3]	112	123	2,176	1,976	16	48,616	53,289	100,864	98,665
5046 Commercial equipment, nec[3]	41	40	590	611	15	30,251	31,372	18,854	20,715
5047 Medical and hospital equipment	85	76	970	910	12	34,037	36,668	34,584	32,523
5048 Ophthalmic goods[3]	6	5	93	107	21	21,290	22,355	2,641	3,025
5049 Professional equipment, nec[3]	12	13	256	259	20	23,219	24,958	6,879	7,522
5051 Metals service centers and offices[3]	48	46	12	184	4	20,000	16,413	327	3,514
5063 Electrical apparatus and equipment[3]	115	103	1,230	1,210	12	31,106	37,752	39,361	41,220
5064 Electrical appliances TV & radios[3]	19	19	302	256	13	29,510	30,109	10,683	8,938
5065 Electronic parts and equipment[3]	87	106	855	1,071	10	39,457	40,370	36,581	45,133
5072 Hardware[3]	56	61	483	515	8	27,429	29,957	15,129	18,275
5074 Plumbing & hydronic heating supplies[3]	56	54	572	619	11	26,552	29,118	18,107	19,579
5075 Warm air heating & air conditioning[3]	47	47	696	732	16	37,701	39,257	27,178	29,256
5078 Refrigeration equipment and supplies[3]	14	13	105	135	10	25,829	22,430	3,020	3,297
5082 Construction and mining machinery[2]	-	33	-	656	20	-	35,488	-	25,419
5083 Farm and garden machinery	-	42	-	961	23	-	31,359	-	31,641
5084 Industrial machinery and equipment	-	167	-	1,854	11	-	38,496	-	74,542
5085 Industrial supplies[2]	-	95	-	1,099	12	-	32,066	-	36,016
5087 Service establishment equipment[2]	-	39	-	374	10	-	27,551	-	10,484
5088 Transportation equipment & supplies[2]	-	11	-	216	20	-	25,722	-	6,147
5091 Sporting & recreational goods[2]	-	35	-	499	14	-	20,970	-	12,488
5092 Toys and hobby goods and supplies[2]	-	13	-	135	10	-	27,200	-	4,130
5093 Scrap and waste materials[2]	-	43	-	548	13	-	26,489	-	16,632
5094 Jewelry & precious stones[2]	-	21	-	166	8	-	17,614	-	3,015
5099 Durable goods, nec[2]	-	59	-	659	11	-	20,182	-	14,788
5111 Printing and writing paper[2]	-	21	-	188	9	-	40,638	-	7,261
5112 Stationery and office supplies[2]	-	62	-	796	13	-	28,588	-	23,355
5113 Industrial & personal service paper[2]	-	29	-	789	27	-	35,554	-	26,983
5120 Drugs, proprietaries, and sundries[2]	-	31	-	1,364	44	-	49,114	-	76,944
5131 Piece goods & notions[2]	-	10	-	62	6	-	26,516	-	1,932
5136 Men's and boys' clothing[2]	-	23	-	244	11	-	21,754	-	5,756
5137 Women's and children's clothing[2]	-	15	-	138	9	-	22,087	-	3,099
5139 Footwear[2]	-	4	-	11	3	-	22,545	-	186
5141 Groceries, general line[2]	-	21	-	1,333	63	-	33,962	-	40,941
5142 Packaged frozen food[2]	-	12	-	383	32	-	29,358	-	11,769
5145 Confectionery[2]	-	18	-	424	24	-	24,330	-	11,597
5147 Meats and meat products[2]	-	13	-	428	33	-	30,224	-	15,169
5149 Groceries and related products, nec[2]	-	54	-	1,398	26	-	29,413	-	42,469
5153 Grain and field beans[2]	-	20	-	50	3	-	18,480	-	960
5162 Plastics materials & basic shapes[2]	-	28	-	290	10	-	29,200	-	8,943
5169 Chemicals & allied products, nec[2]	-	65	-	444	7	-	37,342	-	19,525
5171 Petroleum bulk stations & terminals	-	29	-	246	8	-	32,065	-	9,288
5172 Petroleum products, nec[2]	-	18	-	77	4	-	39,584	-	3,006
5181 Beer and ale[2]	-	6	-	346	58	-	27,040	-	9,815
5182 Wine and distilled beverages[2]	-	13	-	483	37	-	28,671	-	14,231
5191 Farm supplies[2]	-	55	-	283	5	-	22,148	-	5,904
5192 Books, periodicals, & newspapers[2]	-	32	-	805	25	-	20,964	-	16,625
5193 Flowers & florists' supplies[2]	-	15	-	166	11	-	19,157	-	3,950
5194 Tobacco and tobacco products[2]	-	10	-	210	21	-	20,743	-	4,773
5198 Paints, varnishes, and supplies[2]	-	20	-	252	13	-	29,683	-	7,917
5199 Nondurable goods, nec	-	110	-	896	8	-	28,897	-	28,941
52- Retail trade	8,282	8,298	152,159	161,163	19	13,751	15,028	2,291,812	2,518,521
5210 Lumber and other building materials	125	123	2,532	2,721	22	17,300	20,989	50,649	58,899
5230 Paint, glass, and wallpaper stores	82	82	575	561	7	10,963	12,913	6,902	7,314
5250 Hardware stores	70	51	793	597	12	13,367	11,692	9,446	7,134
5260 Retail nurseries and garden stores	65	65	533	571	9	13,043	14,207	9,733	10,778
5270 Mobile home dealers[2]	18	17	100	114	7	15,080	16,281	1,894	2,090
5310 Department stores[3]	65	67	12,881	13,409	200	10,377	11,584	153,566	165,270
5330 Variety stores	66	60	702	577	10	9,926	9,899	7,740	6,287

Continued on next page.

COLUMBUS, OH MSA - [continued]

Wholesale and Retail Trade USA	Establishments		Employment		Emp / Est	Pay / Employee		Annual Payroll ($ 000)	
	1994	1995	1994	1995	1995	1994	1995	1994	1995
5390 Misc. general merchandise stores [1]	52	53	2,155	2,246	42	10,613	12,812	25,957	28,281
5410 Grocery stores [1]	588	565	15,528	16,199	29	10,908	11,593	180,299	202,765
5420 Meat and fish markets [3]	22	18	175	166	9	13,349	13,542	2,657	2,423
5430 Fruit and vegetable markets [1]	13	13	15	24	2	13,067	9,167	308	320
5440 Candy, nut, and confectionery stores [3]	47	45	283	263	6	5,965	7,468	1,948	2,035
5450 Dairy products stores [3]	15	15	60	56	4	9,800	9,857	677	662
5460 Retail bakeries	104	95	1,035	1,046	11	10,195	10,608	12,191	11,067
5490 Miscellaneous food stores [1]	49	58	290	356	6	11,462	11,640	3,865	4,375
5510 New and used car dealers	118	117	6,803	7,203	62	28,130	30,935	221,263	237,586
5520 Used car dealers	98	94	472	468	5	24,619	25,521	12,567	13,209
5530 Auto and home supply stores	196	204	1,706	1,626	8	17,615	19,565	33,457	33,333
5540 Gasoline service stations	485	483	4,309	4,115	9	11,007	12,248	49,584	53,099
5550 Boat dealers [3]	8	7	57	78	11	20,561	22,000	1,562	2,062
5560 Recreational vehicle dealers [3]	11	10	94	96	10	20,043	23,042	2,973	2,923
5570 Motorcycle dealers [3]	13	13	102	120	9	17,255	18,200	2,335	3,047
5590 Automotive dealers, nec [3]	5	5	63	74	15	24,127	33,027	1,935	2,324
5610 Men's & boys' clothing stores [3]	59	57	615	641	11	11,473	11,020	7,198	7,097
5620 Women's clothing stores	211	187	2,452	2,085	11	7,783	7,824	20,173	16,207
5630 Women's accessory & specialty stores [3]	53	52	366	343	7	9,191	10,181	3,463	3,474
5640 Children's and infants' wear stores [3]	19	20	238	260	13	8,252	8,538	2,168	2,219
5650 Family clothing stores [3]	71	66	1,081	1,045	16	9,095	10,251	10,508	10,469
5660 Shoe stores	194	182	1,104	1,131	6	11,101	9,708	13,283	11,256
5690 Misc. apparel & accessory stores [3]	53	55	291	273	5	10,763	11,487	3,299	3,261
5712 Furniture stores	151	159	1,354	1,580	10	19,368	18,995	27,661	31,168
5713 Floor covering stores	67	73	406	497	7	20,256	21,111	9,462	12,139
5714 Drapery and upholstery stores [3]	13	11	77	46	4	15,117	18,870	1,436	910
5719 Misc. homefurnishings stores [3]	99	92	641	556	6	9,548	11,719	7,143	6,855
5720 Household appliance stores [3]	39	40	145	145	4	16,166	17,517	2,678	2,836
5731 Radio, TV, & electronic stores [3]	97	100	1,053	1,492	15	20,323	18,933	49,349	26,312
5734 Computer and software stores [3]	36	45	304	404	9	20,329	22,752	7,580	11,123
5735 Record & prerecorded tape stores [3]	48	49	512	537	11	8,305	9,318	4,606	4,536
5736 Musical instrument stores [3]	23	25	163	143	6	18,969	17,874	2,901	2,535
5812 Eating places	2,075	2,011	45,543	48,007	24	7,848	8,331	393,886	423,323
5813 Drinking places	403	360	2,216	2,252	6	6,912	7,353	16,413	16,796
5910 Drug stores and proprietary stores [1]	221	218	2,740	2,756	13	13,790	16,276	39,437	46,576
5920 Liquor stores	138	130	541	497	4	11,645	12,394	6,383	6,066
5930 Used merchandise stores [1]	103	102	646	690	7	10,947	11,965	8,114	9,338
5941 Sporting goods and bicycle shops	141	137	960	1,249	9	12,354	12,583	14,398	16,526
5942 Book stores [3]	85	82	735	787	10	12,332	13,103	9,781	10,340
5943 Stationery stores	26	28	173	203	7	11,422	13,084	1,583	2,757
5944 Jewelry stores [3]	105	98	781	754	8	19,052	22,239	13,724	14,483
5945 Hobby, toy, and game shops [3]	61	57	623	640	11	8,571	9,119	6,522	6,626
5946 Camera & photographic supply stores [3]	30	30	230	273	9	10,730	12,454	2,670	3,751
5947 Gift, novelty, and souvenir shops	174	162	1,155	1,030	6	7,602	8,280	9,874	9,448
5948 Luggage and leather goods stores [3]	7	8	56	59	7	9,429	12,881	678	801
5949 Sewing, needlework, and piece goods [2]	45	43	455	336	8	6,031	7,107	2,802	2,290
5961 Catalog and mail-order houses	38	40	6,578	6,513	163	17,815	17,545	115,831	123,391
5962 Merchandising machine operators [3]	50	44	1,536	1,581	36	13,448	15,079	22,678	23,988
5963 Direct selling establishments [1]	80	77	843	813	11	16,413	19,011	14,926	16,178
5983 Fuel oil dealers [3]	7	10	24	36	4	24,667	32,444	717	1,253
5984 Liquefied petroleum gas dealers [3]	11	11	51	47	4	26,275	22,553	1,580	1,308
5992 Florists	133	136	757	826	6	10,071	9,341	8,303	8,573
5993 Tobacco stores and stands [3]	6	9	12	18	2	14,333	11,111	166	251
5994 News dealers and newsstands [3]	10	8	50	51	6	10,800	11,608	560	663
5995 Optical goods stores [3]	114	110	593	561	5	17,410	19,237	11,414	11,234
5999 Miscellaneous retail stores, nec	267	285	1,687	1,662	6	12,749	16,212	25,127	28,558

Source: County Business Patterns 1994/95, CBP-94/95, U.S. Department of Commerce, Washington DC, November 1997. The employment column represents mid-March employment in the year. Pay per employee is calculated by dividing 1st Quarter payroll, annualized, by mid-March employment. The column headed 'Emp / Est' shows 'employees per establishment'. A dash (-) means that data are unavailable or cannot be calculated. nec means not elsewhere classified. *Notes:* 1. 1994 data incomplete; unavailable or withheld. 2. 1995 data incomplete; unavailable or withheld. 3. 1994 and 1995 data incomplete; unavailable or withheld.

CORPUS CHRISTI, TX MSA

Wholesale and Retail Trade USA	Establishments		Employment		Emp / Est	Pay / Employee		Annual Payroll ($ 000)	
	1994	1995	1994	1995	1995	1994	1995	1994	1995
50 – Wholesale trade	-	659	-	6,423	10	-	26,295	-	179,036
5012 Automobiles and other vehicles [2]	-	8	-	109	14	-	23,560	-	2,821
5013 Motor vehicle supplies and new parts	-	31	-	254	8	-	22,315	-	6,131
5015 Motor vehicle parts, used [2]	-	14	-	57	4	-	12,842	-	687

Continued on next page.

CORPUS CHRISTI, TX MSA - [continued]

Wholesale and Retail Trade USA	Establishments		Employment		Emp / Est	Pay / Employee		Annual Payroll ($ 000)	
	1994	1995	1994	1995	1995	1994	1995	1994	1995
5021 Furniture [2]	-	5	-	63	13	-	15,492	-	940
5023 Homefurnishings [2]	-	8	-	79	10	-	18,937	-	1,617
5031 Lumber, plywood, and millwork [2]	-	5	-	26	5	-	18,154	-	405
5032 Brick, stone, & related materials [2]	-	6	-	29	5	-	23,172	-	733
5033 Roofing, siding, & insulation [2]	-	3	-	64	21	-	23,125	-	1,556
5039 Construction materials, nec [2]	-	9	-	195	22	-	21,149	-	4,142
5044 Office equipment	-	14	-	230	16	-	24,783	-	5,564
5045 Computers, peripherals, & software	-	18	-	121	7	-	37,455	-	4,315
5046 Commercial equipment, nec [2]	-	3	-	25	8	-	30,240	-	603
5047 Medical and hospital equipment [2]	-	15	-	166	11	-	28,964	-	5,245
5050 Metals and minerals, except petroleum [2]	-	23	-	309	13	-	32,673	-	10,896
5063 Electrical apparatus and equipment	-	27	-	220	8	-	34,491	-	7,390
5064 Electrical appliances, TV & radios [2]	-	3	-	19	6	-	28,421	-	566
5065 Electronic parts and equipment [2]	-	18	-	86	5	-	27,721	-	2,440
5072 Hardware	-	13	-	83	6	-	22,843	-	2,326
5074 Plumbing & hydronic heating supplies [2]	-	7	-	61	9	-	23,738	-	1,752
5075 Warm air heating & air conditioning [2]	-	12	-	98	8	-	29,959	-	3,127
5078 Refrigeration equipment and supplies [2]	-	4	-	26	7	-	18,923	-	628
5082 Construction and mining machinery [2]	-	8	-	107	13	-	31,963	-	3,296
5083 Farm and garden machinery	-	12	-	188	16	-	30,447	-	5,593
5084 Industrial machinery and equipment	-	89	-	588	7	-	31,898	-	19,777
5085 Industrial supplies	-	44	-	402	9	-	27,970	-	12,547
5087 Service establishment equipment [2]	-	14	-	144	10	-	21,194	-	3,150
5093 Scrap and waste materials [2]	-	6	-	104	17	-	21,846	-	2,948
5094 Jewelry & precious stones [2]	-	3	-	14	5	-	16,857	-	221
5099 Durable goods, nec	-	13	-	61	5	-	13,180	-	833
5110 Paper and paper products	-	14	-	237	17	-	21,114	-	4,789
5148 Fresh fruits and vegetables [2]	-	3	-	45	15	-	17,778	-	900
5149 Groceries and related products, nec [2]	-	13	-	349	27	-	24,516	-	8,470
5150 Farm-product raw materials	-	24	-	164	7	-	16,585	-	3,353
5169 Chemicals & allied products, nec	-	34	-	367	11	-	32,872	-	12,050
5171 Petroleum bulk stations & terminals	-	16	-	168	11	-	25,762	-	4,344
5172 Petroleum products, nec [2]	-	16	-	124	8	-	23,839	-	3,182
5181 Beer and ale [2]	-	3	-	210	70	-	31,486	-	9,970
5182 Wine and distilled beverages [2]	-	3	-	129	43	-	37,333	-	3,806
5191 Farm supplies	-	18	-	61	3	-	21,902	-	1,456
5193 Flowers & florists' supplies [2]	-	3	-	33	11	-	14,061	-	486
5199 Nondurable goods, nec	-	14	-	63	5	-	12,698	-	994
52- Retail trade	-	2,225	-	29,647	13	-	12,204	-	378,955
5210 Lumber and other building materials	-	23	-	426	19	-	16,094	-	7,465
5230 Paint, glass, and wallpaper stores	-	12	-	62	5	-	21,097	-	1,318
5250 Hardware stores	-	8	-	49	6	-	13,306	-	644
5260 Retail nurseries and garden stores	-	11	-	130	12	-	13,908	-	1,826
5270 Mobile home dealers	-	5	-	28	6	-	24,429	-	809
5310 Department stores [2]	-	15	-	2,755	184	-	13,138	-	35,025
5330 Variety stores	-	14	-	79	6	-	7,443	-	659
5390 Misc. general merchandise stores	-	18	-	472	26	-	12,237	-	5,565
5410 Grocery stores	-	236	-	4,470	19	-	13,220	-	59,852
5420 Meat and fish markets	-	13	-	40	3	-	11,100	-	439
5460 Retail bakeries	-	33	-	149	5	-	7,597	-	1,361
5490 Miscellaneous food stores [2]	-	7	-	12	2	-	10,000	-	144
5510 New and used car dealers	-	33	-	1,516	46	-	27,559	-	45,275
5520 Used car dealers	-	36	-	141	4	-	20,113	-	2,756
5530 Auto and home supply stores	-	61	-	515	8	-	16,730	-	9,230
5540 Gasoline service stations	-	121	-	774	6	-	13,044	-	10,692
5550 Boat dealers	-	10	-	63	6	-	16,698	-	1,149
5560 Recreational vehicle dealers	-	7	-	43	6	-	21,488	-	917
5570 Motorcycle dealers [2]	-	5	-	48	10	-	15,500	-	1,015
5610 Men's & boys' clothing stores [2]	-	11	-	79	7	-	12,962	-	929
5620 Women's clothing stores	-	49	-	391	8	-	8,624	-	3,376
5630 Women's accessory & specialty stores [2]	-	11	-	54	5	-	8,889	-	476
5640 Children's and infants' wear stores [2]	-	5	-	36	7	-	9,556	-	323
5650 Family clothing stores	-	36	-	633	18	-	9,428	-	5,686
5660 Shoe stores	-	46	-	188	4	-	12,021	-	2,132
5690 Misc. apparel & accessory stores	-	18	-	87	5	-	8,966	-	768
5712 Furniture stores	-	50	-	437	9	-	17,153	-	7,979
5713 Floor covering stores	-	17	-	80	5	-	17,050	-	1,470
5714 Drapery and upholstery stores [2]	-	3	-	9	3	-	8,000	-	70
5719 Misc. homefurnishings stores [2]	-	15	-	114	8	-	10,772	-	1,320
5720 Household appliance stores [2]	-	8	-	76	10	-	18,842	-	1,510
5731 Radio, TV, & electronic stores	-	18	-	231	13	-	13,333	-	3,316

Continued on next page.

CORPUS CHRISTI, TX MSA - [continued]

Wholesale and Retail Trade USA	Establishments		Employment		Emp / Est	Pay / Employee		Annual Payroll ($ 000)	
	1994	1995	1994	1995	1995	1994	1995	1994	1995
5734 Computer and software stores [2]	-	10	-	72	7	-	14,500	-	1,062
5735 Record & prerecorded tape stores [2]	-	11	-	79	7	-	9,418	-	747
5736 Musical instrument stores [2]	-	5	-	27	5	-	19,556	-	609
5812 Eating places	-	486	-	9,795	20	-	7,827	-	80,579
5813 Drinking places	-	62	-	679	11	-	6,297	-	4,163
5910 Drug stores and proprietary stores	-	48	-	491	10	-	15,438	-	8,137
5920 Liquor stores	-	38	-	139	4	-	11,482	-	1,640
5930 Used merchandise stores	-	48	-	269	6	-	13,680	-	3,780
5941 Sporting goods and bicycle shops	-	40	-	265	7	-	11,185	-	3,626
5942 Book stores [2]	-	13	-	118	9	-	11,220	-	1,481
5944 Jewelry stores	-	44	-	180	4	-	13,756	-	2,598
5945 Hobby, toy, and game shops [2]	-	12	-	170	14	-	9,647	-	1,981
5947 Gift, novelty, and souvenir shops	-	61	-	314	5	-	6,803	-	2,521
5963 Direct selling establishments	-	17	-	86	5	-	19,442	-	1,679
5984 Liquefied petroleum gas dealers	-	8	-	18	2	-	21,111	-	424
5992 Florists	-	32	-	115	4	-	9,983	-	1,227
5993 Tobacco stores and stands [2]	-	3	-	3	1	-	10,667	-	57
5994 News dealers and newsstands [2]	-	3	-	3	1	-	8,000	-	27
5995 Optical goods stores	-	33	-	159	5	-	16,906	-	2,702
5999 Miscellaneous retail stores, nec	-	64	-	298	5	-	13,705	-	4,547

Source: County Business Patterns 1994/95, CBP-94/95, U.S. Department of Commerce, Washington DC, November 1997. The employment column represents mid-March employment in the year. Pay per employee is calculated by dividing 1st Quarter payroll, annualized, by mid-March employment. The column headed 'Emp / Est' shows 'employees per establishment'. A dash (-) means that data are unavailable or cannot be calculated. nec means not elsewhere classified. *Notes:* 1. 1994 data incomplete; unavailable or withheld. 2. 1995 data incomplete; unavailable or withheld. 3. 1994 and 1995 data incomplete; unavailable or withheld.

CUMBERLAND MSA (MD PART)

Wholesale and Retail Trade USA	Establishments		Employment		Emp / Est	Pay / Employee		Annual Payroll ($ 000)	
	1994	1995	1994	1995	1995	1994	1995	1994	1995
50- Wholesale trade	99	95	1,524	1,249	13	36,619	33,179	56,320	42,120
5010 Motor vehicles, parts, and supplies	18	16	233	149	9	39,983	21,154	9,878	3,289
5030 Lumber and construction materials	5	6	70	36	6	19,657	17,667	1,945	624
5044 Office equipment	4	-	46	-	-	21,130	-	615	-
5063 Electrical apparatus and equipment	3	3	12	11	4	18,333	21,091	251	238
5065 Electronic parts and equipment	-	3	-	35	12	-	20,343	-	691
5074 Plumbing & hydronic heating supplies	3	-	28	-	-	22,571	-	576	-
5075 Warm air heating & air conditioning	5	-	40	-	-	21,500	-	1,063	-
5085 Industrial supplies	3	3	23	22	7	20,696	23,636	554	582
5090 Miscellaneous durable goods	3	-	20	-	-	16,600	-	419	-
5112 Stationery and office supplies	7	6	59	39	7	17,695	13,333	1,222	624
5145 Confectionery	3	3	16	16	5	15,500	12,250	233	254
5149 Groceries and related products, nec	8	7	159	126	18	22,792	27,365	3,598	3,069
5170 Petroleum and petroleum products	5	3	60	54	18	22,400	21,852	1,212	1,166
5181 Beer and ale	3	-	40	-	-	20,000	-	991	-
5190 Misc., nondurable goods	-	4	-	23	6	-	22,435	-	528
52- Retail trade	571	556	6,710	6,997	13	9,331	10,142	70,645	75,379
5210 Lumber and other building materials	10	9	119	155	17	16,202	19,613	2,106	3,622
5230 Paint, glass, and wallpaper stores	4	-	15	-	-	15,467	-	257	-
5250 Hardware stores	10	9	61	77	9	10,689	11,377	720	937
5310 Department stores	7	7	932	979	140	9,300	11,322	10,158	11,056
5410 Grocery stores	41	41	876	909	22	10,840	10,667	9,933	10,029
5440 Candy, nut, and confectionery stores	3	3	9	14	5	3,111	2,571	30	38
5460 Retail bakeries	4	3	29	28	9	8,138	8,429	219	227
5510 New and used car dealers	9	9	269	283	31	20,059	20,919	6,492	6,612
5520 Used car dealers	7	7	28	37	5	14,143	16,973	534	619
5530 Auto and home supply stores	19	19	113	116	6	14,690	16,414	1,894	1,908
5540 Gasoline service stations	41	37	240	262	7	9,167	8,947	2,309	2,509
5570 Motorcycle dealers	4	4	13	13	3	10,154	8,923	147	134
5610 Men's & boys' clothing stores	5	4	34	24	6	8,941	8,833	348	298
5620 Women's clothing stores	19	18	134	120	7	7,403	7,033	1,237	888
5650 Family clothing stores	4	4	94	99	25	7,064	9,616	913	933
5660 Shoe stores	17	14	90	93	7	10,356	9,505	907	922
5712 Furniture stores	16	16	83	81	5	11,614	15,407	1,190	1,260
5713 Floor covering stores	4	5	16	16	3	13,750	15,500	259	293
5719 Misc. homefurnishings stores	3	-	8	-	-	7,500	-	48	-
5731 Radio, TV, & electronic stores	-	5	-	42	8	-	24,286	-	981
5735 Record & prerecorded tape stores	5	6	26	23	4	8,462	8,870	184	188
5812 Eating places	129	123	2,235	2,285	19	6,137	6,432	15,742	15,883
5813 Drinking places	27	26	106	96	4	5,094	5,875	541	613

Continued on next page.

CUMBERLAND MSA (MD PART) - [continued]

Wholesale and Retail Trade USA	Establishments		Employment		Emp / Est	Pay / Employee		Annual Payroll ($ 000)	
	1994	1995	1994	1995	1995	1994	1995	1994	1995
5910 Drug stores and proprietary stores	24	24	243	272	11	15,062	14,779	4,059	4,243
5920 Liquor stores	21	20	73	66	3	9,315	9,212	751	713
5941 Sporting goods and bicycle shops	10	12	12	15	1	7,667	7,467	120	156
5942 Book stores	4	3	31	24	8	5,290	6,000	158	155
5944 Jewelry stores	14	13	94	80	6	10,979	11,850	1,074	1,023
5945 Hobby, toy, and game shops	5	4	36	35	9	5,889	5,943	241	232
5947 Gift, novelty, and souvenir shops	6	6	50	61	10	6,720	7,475	432	549
5960 Nonstore retailers	7	10	60	97	10	12,133	15,175	756	1,535
5992 Florists	9	8	58	60	8	7,517	8,667	503	530
5995 Optical goods stores	7	-	29	-	-	16,138	-	574	-
5999 Miscellaneous retail stores, nec	18	18	78	91	5	8,821	10,154	833	976

Source: County Business Patterns 1994/95, CBP-94/95, U.S. Department of Commerce, Washington DC, November 1997. The employment column represents mid-March employment in the year. Pay per employee is calculated by dividing 1st Quarter payroll, annualized, by mid-March employment. The column headed 'Emp / Est' shows 'employees per establishment'. A dash (-) means that data are unavailable or cannot be calculated. nec means not elsewhere classified. *Notes:* 1. 1994 data incomplete; unavailable or withheld. 2. 1995 data incomplete; unavailable or withheld. 3. 1994 and 1995 data incomplete; unavailable or withheld.

CUMBERLAND MSA (WV PART)

Wholesale and Retail Trade USA	Establishments		Employment		Emp / Est	Pay / Employee		Annual Payroll ($ 000)	
	1994	1995	1994	1995	1995	1994	1995	1994	1995
50- Wholesale trade	-	17	-	252	15	-	16,460	-	4,223
5010 Motor vehicles, parts, and supplies	-	6	-	13	2	-	12,615	-	175
5100 Wholesale trade-nondurable goods	-	4	-	31	8	-	15,742	-	490
52- Retail trade	-	148	-	1,187	8	-	9,368	-	11,987
5210 Lumber and other building materials	-	6	-	36	6	-	10,556	-	531
5300 General merchandise stores	-	4	-	82	21	-	8,829	-	787
5400 Food stores	-	17	-	197	12	-	9,076	-	1,929
5510 New and used car dealers	-	4	-	52	13	-	19,231	-	922
5520 Used car dealers	-	5	-	15	3	-	13,067	-	213
5540 Gasoline service stations	-	10	-	60	6	-	10,200	-	639
5600 Apparel and accessory stores	-	6	-	31	5	-	7,871	-	241
5710 Furniture and homefurnishings stores	-	5	-	21	4	-	13,714	-	319
5720 Household appliance stores	-	3	-	8	3	-	10,000	-	88
5730 Radio, television, & computer stores	-	6	-	34	6	-	10,824	-	435
5812 Eating places	-	31	-	404	13	-	6,406	-	2,698
5813 Drinking places	-	7	-	25	4	-	7,200	-	176
5910 Drug stores and proprietary stores	-	7	-	55	8	-	14,691	-	939
5942 Book stores	-	3	-	3	1	-	4,000	-	14
5947 Gift, novelty, and souvenir shops	-	7	-	15	2	-	3,733	-	78
5990 Retail stores, nec	-	5	-	9	2	-	5,333	-	57

Source: County Business Patterns 1994/95, CBP-94/95, U.S. Department of Commerce, Washington DC, November 1997. The employment column represents mid-March employment in the year. Pay per employee is calculated by dividing 1st Quarter payroll, annualized, by mid-March employment. The column headed 'Emp / Est' shows 'employees per establishment'. A dash (-) means that data are unavailable or cannot be calculated. nec means not elsewhere classified. *Notes:* 1. 1994 data incomplete; unavailable or withheld. 2. 1995 data incomplete; unavailable or withheld. 3. 1994 and 1995 data incomplete; unavailable or withheld.

CUMBERLAND, MD-WV MSA

Wholesale and Retail Trade USA	Establishments		Employment		Emp / Est	Pay / Employee		Annual Payroll ($ 000)	
	1994	1995	1994	1995	1995	1994	1995	1994	1995
50- Wholesale trade [1]	99	112	1,524	1,501	13	36,619	30,372	56,320	46,343
5010 Motor vehicles, parts, and supplies [1]	18	22	233	162	7	39,983	20,469	9,878	3,464
5030 Lumber and construction materials [1]	5	7	70	36	5	19,657	17,667	1,945	624
5044 Office equipment [1]	4	-	46	-	-	21,130	-	615	-
5063 Electrical apparatus and equipment [3]	3	3	12	11	4	18,333	21,091	251	238
5065 Electronic parts and equipment [2]	-	3	-	35	12	-	20,343	-	691
5074 Plumbing & hydronic heating supplies [1]	3	-	28	-	-	22,571	-	576	-
5075 Warm air heating & air conditioning [1]	5	-	40	-	-	21,500	-	1,063	-
5085 Industrial supplies [3]	3	3	23	22	7	20,696	23,636	554	582
5090 Miscellaneous durable goods [1]	3	-	20	-	-	16,600	-	419	-
5112 Stationery and office supplies [3]	7	6	59	39	7	17,695	13,333	1,222	624
5145 Confectionery [3]	3	3	16	16	5	15,500	12,250	233	254
5149 Groceries and related products, nec [3]	8	7	159	126	18	22,792	27,365	3,598	3,069
5170 Petroleum and petroleum products [1]	5	4	60	54	14	22,400	21,852	1,212	1,166
5181 Beer and ale [1]	3	-	40	-	-	20,000	-	991	-
5190 Misc., nondurable goods	-	5	-	23	5	-	22,435	-	528
52- Retail trade [1]	571	704	6,710	8,184	12	9,331	10,030	70,645	87,366
5210 Lumber and other building materials [1]	10	15	119	191	13	16,202	17,906	2,106	4,153

Continued on next page.

CUMBERLAND, MD – WV MSA - [continued]

Wholesale and Retail Trade USA	Establishments		Employment		Emp / Est	Pay / Employee		Annual Payroll ($ 000)	
	1994	1995	1994	1995	1995	1994	1995	1994	1995
5230 Paint, glass, and wallpaper stores [1]	4	-	15	-	-	15,467	-	257	-
5250 Hardware stores [1]	10	12	61	77	6	10,689	11,377	720	937
5310 Department stores [1]	7	8	932	979	122	9,300	11,322	10,158	11,056
5410 Grocery stores [3]	41	57	876	909	16	10,840	10,667	9,933	10,029
5440 Candy, nut, and confectionery stores [3]	3	3	9	14	5	3,111	2,571	30	38
5460 Retail bakeries [3]	4	3	29	28	9	8,138	8,429	219	227
5510 New and used car dealers [1]	9	13	269	335	26	20,059	20,657	6,492	7,534
5520 Used car dealers [1]	7	12	28	52	4	14,143	15,846	534	832
5530 Auto and home supply stores [1]	19	22	113	116	5	14,690	16,414	1,894	1,908
5540 Gasoline service stations [1]	41	47	240	322	7	9,167	9,180	2,309	3,148
5570 Motorcycle dealers [1]	4	5	13	13	3	10,154	8,923	147	134
5610 Men's & boys' clothing stores [3]	5	4	34	24	6	8,941	8,833	348	298
5620 Women's clothing stores [1]	19	20	134	120	6	7,403	7,033	1,237	888
5650 Family clothing stores [1]	4	6	94	99	17	7,064	9,616	913	933
5660 Shoe stores [1]	17	16	90	93	6	10,356	9,505	907	922
5712 Furniture stores [1]	16	19	83	81	4	11,614	15,407	1,190	1,260
5713 Floor covering stores [1]	4	7	16	16	2	13,750	15,500	259	293
5719 Misc. homefurnishings stores [1]	3	-	8	-	-	7,500	-	48	-
5720 Household appliance stores	-	10	-	8	1	-	10,000	-	88
5731 Radio, TV, & electronic stores	-	9	-	42	5	-	24,286	-	981
5735 Record & prerecorded tape stores [1]	5	7	26	23	3	8,462	8,870	184	188
5812 Eating places [1]	129	154	2,235	2,689	17	6,137	6,428	15,742	18,581
5813 Drinking places [1]	27	33	106	121	4	5,094	6,149	541	789
5910 Drug stores and proprietary stores [1]	24	31	243	327	11	15,062	14,765	4,059	5,182
5920 Liquor stores [1]	21	21	73	66	3	9,315	9,212	751	713
5941 Sporting goods and bicycle shops [1]	10	13	12	15	1	7,667	7,467	120	156
5942 Book stores [1]	4	6	31	27	5	5,290	5,778	158	169
5944 Jewelry stores [1]	14	15	94	80	5	10,979	11,850	1,074	1,023
5945 Hobby, toy, and game shops [3]	5	4	36	35	9	5,889	5,943	241	232
5947 Gift, novelty, and souvenir shops [1]	6	13	50	76	6	6,720	6,737	432	627
5960 Nonstore retailers [1]	7	11	60	97	9	12,133	15,175	756	1,535
5992 Florists [1]	9	11	58	60	5	7,517	8,667	503	530
5995 Optical goods stores [1]	7	-	29	-	-	16,138	-	574	-
5999 Miscellaneous retail stores, nec [1]	18	19	78	91	5	8,821	10,154	833	976

Source: County Business Patterns 1994/95, CBP-94/95, U.S. Department of Commerce, Washington DC, November 1997. The employment column represents mid-March employment in the year. Pay per employee is calculated by dividing 1st Quarter payroll, annualized, by mid-March employment. The column headed 'Emp / Est' shows 'employees per establishment'. A dash (-) means that data are unavailable or cannot be calculated. nec means not elsewhere classified. *Notes:* 1. 1994 data incomplete; unavailable or withheld. 2. 1995 data incomplete; unavailable or withheld. 3. 1994 and 1995 data incomplete; unavailable or withheld.

DALLAS, TX PMSA

Wholesale and Retail Trade USA	Establishments		Employment		Emp / Est	Pay / Employee		Annual Payroll ($ 000)	
	1994	1995	1994	1995	1995	1994	1995	1994	1995
50- Wholesale trade	-	8,545	-	134,051	16	-	38,613	-	5,318,866
5012 Automobiles and other vehicles [2]	-	121	-	2,842	23	-	32,395	-	96,234
5013 Motor vehicle supplies and new parts	-	265	-	5,156	19	-	33,458	-	177,756
5014 Tires and tubes [2]	-	50	-	627	13	-	32,823	-	21,001
5015 Motor vehicle parts, used	-	106	-	800	8	-	20,675	-	17,368
5021 Furniture [2]	-	221	-	1,945	9	-	34,597	-	67,432
5023 Homefurnishings	-	239	-	3,014	13	-	29,213	-	95,059
5031 Lumber, plywood, and millwork [2]	-	94	-	1,480	16	-	37,100	-	54,291
5032 Brick, stone, & related materials [2]	-	75	-	662	9	-	29,535	-	21,182
5033 Roofing, siding, & insulation [2]	-	41	-	638	16	-	47,335	-	28,551
5039 Construction materials, nec [2]	-	98	-	1,307	13	-	31,624	-	43,279
5043 Photographic equipment & supplies [2]	-	29	-	774	27	-	57,199	-	38,495
5044 Office equipment [2]	-	144	-	3,270	23	-	39,853	-	126,758
5045 Computers, peripherals, & software	-	518	-	10,728	21	-	56,723	-	589,932
5046 Commercial equipment, nec [2]	-	115	-	1,018	9	-	35,528	-	38,809
5047 Medical and hospital equipment [2]	-	183	-	2,512	14	-	44,123	-	114,608
5048 Ophthalmic goods [2]	-	31	-	1,933	62	-	26,783	-	51,202
5049 Professional equipment, nec [2]	-	38	-	352	9	-	25,489	-	10,120
5051 Metals service centers and offices	-	179	-	2,465	14	-	32,131	-	88,959
5052 Coal and other minerals and ores [2]	-	4	-	28	7	-	44,143	-	1,537
5063 Electrical apparatus and equipment [2]	-	308	-	3,618	12	-	40,928	-	155,945
5064 Electrical appliances, TV & radios [2]	-	92	-	1,178	13	-	44,302	-	54,305
5065 Electronic parts and equipment [2]	-	608	-	11,591	19	-	51,219	-	610,411
5072 Hardware [2]	-	140	-	1,468	10	-	30,444	-	48,893
5074 Plumbing & hydronic heating supplies	-	123	-	982	8	-	33,279	-	32,496
5075 Warm air heating & air conditioning [2]	-	108	-	1,749	16	-	45,859	-	79,136

Continued on next page.

DALLAS, TX PMSA - [continued]

Wholesale and Retail Trade USA	Establishments		Employment		Emp / Est	Pay / Employee		Annual Payroll ($ 000)	
	1994	1995	1994	1995	1995	1994	1995	1994	1995
5078 Refrigeration equipment and supplies [2]	-	25	-	369	15	-	30,515	-	11,979
5082 Construction and mining machinery [2]	-	57	-	881	15	-	40,232	-	38,078
5083 Farm and garden machinery	-	67	-	933	14	-	34,199	-	34,696
5084 Industrial machinery and equipment [2]	-	482	-	4,585	10	-	40,015	-	189,749
5085 Industrial supplies	-	224	-	2,582	12	-	37,902	-	104,714
5087 Service establishment equipment [2]	-	125	-	935	7	-	26,785	-	27,098
5088 Transportation equipment & supplies [2]	-	99	-	1,106	11	-	42,821	-	47,747
5091 Sporting & recreational goods [2]	-	102	-	1,141	11	-	20,417	-	31,294
5092 Toys and hobby goods and supplies [2]	-	55	-	633	12	-	31,374	-	22,433
5093 Scrap and waste materials	-	97	-	1,629	17	-	27,244	-	44,386
5094 Jewelry & precious stones [2]	-	185	-	1,452	8	-	25,818	-	38,820
5099 Durable goods, nec [2]	-	160	-	1,922	12	-	24,110	-	48,484
5111 Printing and writing paper [2]	-	72	-	764	11	-	40,487	-	32,325
5112 Stationery and office supplies [2]	-	194	-	5,518	28	-	19,849	-	111,252
5113 Industrial & personal service paper [2]	-	96	-	1,009	11	-	39,282	-	40,297
5120 Drugs, proprietaries, and sundries [2]	-	148	-	3,160	21	-	54,811	-	171,147
5131 Piece goods & notions [2]	-	105	-	982	9	-	25,943	-	26,846
5136 Men's and boys' clothing [2]	-	100	-	607	6	-	38,741	-	22,893
5137 Women's and children's clothing [2]	-	218	-	1,516	7	-	24,525	-	39,852
5139 Footwear [2]	-	25	-	117	5	-	43,385	-	5,165
5141 Groceries, general line [2]	-	40	-	2,885	72	-	29,880	-	85,979
5142 Packaged frozen food [2]	-	30	-	1,635	55	-	26,547	-	45,063
5143 Dairy products, exc. dried or canned [2]	-	17	-	394	23	-	30,508	-	13,309
5144 Poultry and poultry products [2]	-	12	-	98	8	-	44,245	-	4,872
5145 Confectionery [2]	-	32	-	841	26	-	32,181	-	28,690
5146 Fish and seafoods [2]	-	11	-	300	27	-	31,200	-	9,781
5147 Meats and meat products [2]	-	41	-	813	20	-	26,755	-	23,459
5148 Fresh fruits and vegetables [2]	-	59	-	1,360	23	-	29,500	-	41,539
5149 Groceries and related products, nec [2]	-	162	-	3,934	24	-	39,245	-	163,010
5154 Livestock [2]	-	9	-	35	4	-	5,486	-	195
5159 Farm-product raw materials, nec [2]	-	23	-	259	11	-	30,950	-	9,659
5162 Plastics materials & basic shapes [2]	-	64	-	841	13	-	46,673	-	38,128
5169 Chemicals & allied products, nec [2]	-	168	-	2,090	12	-	36,810	-	86,440
5171 Petroleum bulk stations & terminals [2]	-	44	-	326	7	-	37,460	-	12,206
5172 Petroleum products, nec [2]	-	61	-	742	12	-	67,143	-	54,283
5181 Beer and ale [2]	-	17	-	690	41	-	35,293	-	37,347
5182 Wine and distilled beverages [2]	-	20	-	623	31	-	50,395	-	27,505
5191 Farm supplies	-	94	-	746	8	-	27,812	-	20,626
5192 Books, periodicals, & newspapers [2]	-	72	-	743	10	-	45,217	-	32,446
5193 Flowers & florists' supplies [2]	-	61	-	1,005	16	-	18,933	-	19,364
5194 Tobacco and tobacco products [2]	-	10	-	295	30	-	21,464	-	7,122
5198 Paints, varnishes, and supplies [2]	-	85	-	580	7	-	31,614	-	19,758
5199 Nondurable goods, nec	-	320	-	2,286	7	-	28,154	-	68,887
52- Retail trade	-	16,898	-	275,739	16	-	16,846	-	4,718,951
5210 Lumber and other building materials	-	159	-	4,074	26	-	19,833	-	92,430
5230 Paint, glass, and wallpaper stores	-	96	-	412	4	-	20,874	-	9,041
5250 Hardware stores	-	89	-	761	9	-	17,193	-	13,707
5260 Retail nurseries and garden stores	-	136	-	1,070	8	-	11,746	-	14,526
5270 Mobile home dealers [2]	-	31	-	197	6	-	24,041	-	5,993
5310 Department stores [2]	-	119	-	21,150	178	-	13,983	-	302,323
5330 Variety stores [2]	-	72	-	485	7	-	10,433	-	5,119
5390 Misc. general merchandise stores [2]	-	122	-	3,917	32	-	14,746	-	56,444
5410 Grocery stores	-	1,308	-	34,409	26	-	13,048	-	457,130
5420 Meat and fish markets [2]	-	38	-	144	4	-	20,833	-	2,803
5430 Fruit and vegetable markets [2]	-	12	-	77	6	-	9,247	-	969
5440 Candy, nut, and confectionery stores [2]	-	35	-	297	8	-	7,596	-	2,409
5450 Dairy products stores [2]	-	14	-	38	3	-	4,316	-	178
5460 Retail bakeries	-	160	-	730	5	-	9,912	-	7,672
5490 Miscellaneous food stores	-	126	-	665	5	-	10,502	-	7,175
5510 New and used car dealers	-	178	-	13,279	75	-	34,161	-	528,324
5520 Used car dealers	-	235	-	1,024	4	-	21,930	-	24,440
5530 Auto and home supply stores	-	515	-	4,885	9	-	18,870	-	96,553
5540 Gasoline service stations	-	961	-	6,551	7	-	13,787	-	92,978
5550 Boat dealers [2]	-	33	-	257	8	-	25,759	-	7,461
5560 Recreational vehicle dealers [2]	-	29	-	234	8	-	26,034	-	7,643
5570 Motorcycle dealers [2]	-	32	-	210	7	-	24,362	-	5,753
5590 Automotive dealers, nec [2]	-	18	-	39	2	-	25,128	-	1,004
5610 Men's & boys' clothing stores [2]	-	158	-	1,512	10	-	15,889	-	24,213
5620 Women's clothing stores [2]	-	457	-	4,371	10	-	12,471	-	54,506
5630 Women's accessory & specialty stores [2]	-	93	-	774	8	-	13,876	-	10,899
5640 Children's and infants' wear stores [2]	-	63	-	654	10	-	10,049	-	6,562

Continued on next page.

DALLAS, TX PMSA - [continued]

Wholesale and Retail Trade USA	Establishments		Employment		Emp / Est	Pay / Employee		Annual Payroll ($ 000)	
	1994	1995	1994	1995	1995	1994	1995	1994	1995
5650 Family clothing stores	-	190	-	3,562	19	-	10,978	-	39,878
5660 Shoe stores [2]	-	351	-	1,901	5	-	13,134	-	25,504
5690 Misc. apparel & accessory stores [2]	-	124	-	786	6	-	11,934	-	9,862
5712 Furniture stores	-	288	-	3,360	12	-	23,624	-	78,790
5713 Floor covering stores [2]	-	136	-	674	5	-	23,015	-	17,108
5714 Drapery and upholstery stores [2]	-	29	-	138	5	-	16,435	-	3,177
5719 Misc. homefurnishings stores [2]	-	199	-	2,082	10	-	13,927	-	28,112
5720 Household appliance stores	-	88	-	565	6	-	17,437	-	10,536
5731 Radio, TV, & electronic stores	-	200	-	2,572	13	-	15,698	-	44,678
5734 Computer and software stores [2]	-	136	-	1,559	11	-	23,628	-	40,115
5735 Record & prerecorded tape stores [2]	-	96	-	1,043	11	-	6,017	-	6,109
5736 Musical instrument stores [2]	-	35	-	279	8	-	23,828	-	6,675
5812 Eating places	-	3,660	-	82,873	23	-	9,611	-	813,865
5813 Drinking places	-	262	-	4,300	16	-	8,766	-	41,336
5910 Drug stores and proprietary stores	-	327	-	5,727	18	-	15,255	-	90,399
5920 Liquor stores	-	305	-	1,483	5	-	15,633	-	25,379
5930 Used merchandise stores	-	345	-	1,894	5	-	15,848	-	31,731
5941 Sporting goods and bicycle shops [2]	-	222	-	2,021	9	-	14,943	-	29,201
5942 Book stores	-	145	-	1,419	10	-	13,116	-	19,370
5943 Stationery stores [2]	-	44	-	170	4	-	17,459	-	2,921
5944 Jewelry stores	-	462	-	2,431	5	-	25,195	-	60,103
5945 Hobby, toy, and game shops [2]	-	101	-	1,885	19	-	9,152	-	20,669
5946 Camera & photographic supply stores [2]	-	35	-	186	5	-	21,290	-	3,512
5947 Gift, novelty, and souvenir shops	-	368	-	2,183	6	-	9,343	-	24,012
5948 Luggage and leather goods stores [2]	-	25	-	112	4	-	15,179	-	1,856
5949 Sewing, needlework, and piece goods [2]	-	65	-	627	10	-	9,671	-	6,095
5961 Catalog and mail-order houses [2]	-	85	-	2,652	31	-	18,229	-	55,402
5962 Merchandising machine operators [2]	-	75	-	693	9	-	22,701	-	16,238
5963 Direct selling establishments [2]	-	136	-	1,299	10	-	26,285	-	32,613
5984 Liquefied petroleum gas dealers	-	34	-	192	6	-	21,688	-	3,931
5992 Florists	-	267	-	1,386	5	-	12,606	-	17,330
5993 Tobacco stores and stands [2]	-	22	-	103	5	-	17,748	-	2,117
5994 News dealers and newsstands [2]	-	19	-	91	5	-	15,560	-	1,705
5995 Optical goods stores [2]	-	186	-	963	5	-	16,519	-	16,405
5999 Miscellaneous retail stores, nec	-	636	-	3,961	6	-	17,323	-	74,327

Source: County Business Patterns 1994/95, CBP-94/95, U.S. Department of Commerce, Washington DC, November 1997. The employment column represents mid-March employment in the year. Pay per employee is calculated by dividing 1st Quarter payroll, annualized, by mid-March employment. The column headed 'Emp / Est' shows 'employees per establishment'. A dash (-) means that data are unavailable or cannot be calculated. nec means not elsewhere classified. *Notes:* 1. 1994 data incomplete; unavailable or withheld. 2. 1995 data incomplete; unavailable or withheld. 3. 1994 and 1995 data incomplete; unavailable or withheld.

DANVILLE, VA MSA

Wholesale and Retail Trade USA	Establishments		Employment		Emp / Est	Pay / Employee		Annual Payroll ($ 000)	
	1994	1995	1994	1995	1995	1994	1995	1994	1995
50– Wholesale trade	-	141	-	1,666	12	-	19,666	-	33,314
5013 Motor vehicle supplies and new parts	-	10	-	36	4	-	22,778	-	870
5040 Professional & commercial equipment	-	11	-	81	7	-	20,296	-	1,507
5063 Electrical apparatus and equipment	-	7	-	69	10	-	18,667	-	1,489
5065 Electronic parts and equipment	-	5	-	7	1	-	21,714	-	187
5075 Warm air heating & air conditioning	-	5	-	8	2	-	28,500	-	225
5083 Farm and garden machinery	-	6	-	39	7	-	19,487	-	957
5085 Industrial supplies	-	5	-	14	3	-	32,286	-	451
5090 Miscellaneous durable goods	-	9	-	66	7	-	16,848	-	1,219
5140 Groceries and related products	-	14	-	254	18	-	24,283	-	5,358
5159 Farm-product raw materials, nec	-	6	-	7	1	-	7,429	-	420
5171 Petroleum bulk stations & terminals	-	6	-	62	10	-	22,645	-	1,293
5191 Farm supplies	-	7	-	37	5	-	13,730	-	439
52– Retail trade	-	648	-	7,954	12	-	12,012	-	98,457
5210 Lumber and other building materials	-	11	-	208	19	-	18,231	-	3,875
5250 Hardware stores	-	5	-	13	3	-	9,231	-	127
5260 Retail nurseries and garden stores	-	5	-	10	2	-	12,800	-	143
5270 Mobile home dealers [2]	-	5	-	36	7	-	21,333	-	1,151
5310 Department stores [2]	-	8	-	1,154	144	-	16,118	-	15,574
5410 Grocery stores [2]	-	86	-	1,005	12	-	10,710	-	11,275
5460 Retail bakeries [2]	-	4	-	21	5	-	7,048	-	162
5510 New and used car dealers	-	17	-	451	27	-	24,639	-	12,123
5520 Used car dealers	-	16	-	41	3	-	12,683	-	462
5530 Auto and home supply stores	-	22	-	189	9	-	15,767	-	3,333
5540 Gasoline service stations	-	55	-	334	6	-	11,281	-	3,917

Continued on next page.

DANVILLE, VA MSA - [continued]

Wholesale and Retail Trade USA	Establishments		Employment		Emp / Est	Pay / Employee		Annual Payroll ($ 000)	
	1994	1995	1994	1995	1995	1994	1995	1994	1995
5610 Men's & boys' clothing stores	-	7	-	23	3	-	9,913	-	233
5620 Women's clothing stores	-	21	-	124	6	-	9,161	-	1,204
5660 Shoe stores [2]	-	15	-	81	5	-	11,309	-	864
5712 Furniture stores	-	16	-	149	9	-	11,893	-	1,970
5720 Household appliance stores [2]	-	3	-	10	3	-	16,800	-	131
5735 Record & prerecorded tape stores [2]	-	3	-	18	6	-	9,778	-	188
5736 Musical instrument stores	-	5	-	11	2	-	17,455	-	213
5812 Eating places	-	137	-	2,283	17	-	7,814	-	18,926
5910 Drug stores and proprietary stores	-	22	-	253	12	-	15,304	-	4,447
5930 Used merchandise stores	-	7	-	21	3	-	8,571	-	249
5941 Sporting goods and bicycle shops	-	6	-	11	2	-	7,636	-	113
5944 Jewelry stores	-	11	-	90	8	-	14,044	-	1,337
5945 Hobby, toy, and game shops	-	5	-	8	2	-	10,000	-	232
5947 Gift, novelty, and souvenir shops	-	7	-	21	3	-	8,000	-	185
5962 Merchandising machine operators	-	5	-	22	4	-	18,727	-	446
5992 Florists	-	16	-	61	4	-	9,377	-	560
5999 Miscellaneous retail stores, nec	-	15	-	59	4	-	11,661	-	791

Source: County Business Patterns 1994/95, CBP-94/95, U.S. Department of Commerce, Washington DC, November 1997. The employment column represents mid-March employment in the year. Pay per employee is calculated by dividing 1st Quarter payroll, annualized, by mid-March employment. The column headed 'Emp / Est' shows 'employees per establishment'. A dash (-) means that data are unavailable or cannot be calculated. nec means not elsewhere classified. *Notes:* 1. 1994 data incomplete; unavailable or withheld. 2. 1995 data incomplete; unavailable or withheld. 3. 1994 and 1995 data incomplete; unavailable or withheld.

DAVENPORT – MOLINE – ROCK ISLAND MSA (IL PART)

Wholesale and Retail Trade USA	Establishments		Employment		Emp / Est	Pay / Employee		Annual Payroll ($ 000)	
	1994	1995	1994	1995	1995	1994	1995	1994	1995
50 – Wholesale trade	385	396	5,217	5,703	14	27,534	27,953	152,490	179,018
5012 Automobiles and other vehicles	5	5	231	131	26	23,134	25,038	7,523	3,352
5013 Motor vehicle supplies and new parts	30	31	148	228	7	19,730	24,123	4,443	6,009
5015 Motor vehicle parts, used	-	10	-	107	11	-	25,009	-	2,382
5021 Furniture [3]	3	3	10	13	4	9,600	8,000	91	106
5023 Homefurnishings [3]	5	5	72	67	13	27,167	31,045	1,872	1,939
5031 Lumber, plywood, and millwork [3]	5	3	150	97	32	33,200	36,495	4,696	3,613
5033 Roofing, siding, & insulation	-	4	-	22	6	-	21,455	-	526
5044 Office equipment [3]	11	11	131	139	13	21,954	23,626	3,561	3,716
5045 Computers, peripherals, & software [3]	3	4	360	349	87	69,722	65,077	20,334	22,278
5047 Medical and hospital equipment [3]	5	5	66	77	15	21,394	21,662	1,934	1,956
5051 Metals service centers and offices	10	9	112	122	14	31,393	33,738	3,223	3,538
5063 Electrical apparatus and equipment	9	6	60	53	9	27,200	45,509	1,664	1,762
5065 Electronic parts and equipment	7	9	37	51	6	40,000	30,667	1,359	5,280
5072 Hardware [3]	5	5	260	304	61	20,231	20,474	6,707	7,124
5074 Plumbing & hydronic heating supplies [1]	7	6	110	39	7	27,164	29,949	3,277	1,088
5082 Construction and mining machinery	8	8	83	86	11	46,024	49,860	4,193	4,869
5083 Farm and garden machinery	18	20	254	256	13	32,567	32,766	8,865	9,331
5084 Industrial machinery and equipment	40	39	341	350	9	28,152	30,766	10,054	11,040
5085 Industrial supplies	18	19	160	232	12	28,725	29,017	4,932	6,794
5093 Scrap and waste materials	16	14	162	285	20	17,728	24,196	3,240	9,845
5099 Durable goods, nec	7	7	86	96	14	12,698	10,458	1,420	1,116
5112 Stationery and office supplies [1]	4	-	11	-	-	28,000	-	315	-
5143 Dairy products, exc. dried or canned	4	-	30	-	-	16,933	-	549	-
5149 Groceries and related products, nec	7	10	43	137	14	25,395	27,562	1,184	3,970
5153 Grain and field beans	14	15	158	216	14	19,038	21,815	4,037	7,125
5154 Livestock	10	11	100	70	6	14,720	15,371	1,425	954
5162 Plastics materials & basic shapes [3]	3	4	45	60	15	24,622	24,667	1,146	1,992
5169 Chemicals & allied products, nec [3]	3	3	34	31	10	28,000	32,903	1,092	1,123
5171 Petroleum bulk stations & terminals	-	12	-	21	2	-	25,905	-	581
5180 Beer, wine, and distilled beverages	6	6	76	80	13	25,684	25,450	2,355	2,865
5191 Farm supplies	24	27	325	301	11	22,572	22,219	8,882	7,944
5198 Paints, varnishes, and supplies	4	-	15	-	-	14,667	-	258	-
5199 Nondurable goods, nec	-	9	-	20	2	-	15,600	-	359
52 – Retail trade	1,281	1,287	17,056	16,922	13	12,129	12,420	228,819	226,153
5210 Lumber and other building materials	21	19	439	460	24	16,847	17,904	8,145	8,190
5250 Hardware stores	18	17	129	131	8	9,860	11,359	1,507	1,583
5260 Retail nurseries and garden stores	13	12	58	39	3	6,897	10,154	608	508
5310 Department stores [3]	10	11	1,127	1,173	107	10,335	11,086	13,514	13,720
5410 Grocery stores	74	77	2,206	2,113	27	11,652	12,167	27,088	27,473
5420 Meat and fish markets [2]	-	7	-	38	5	-	12,316	-	442
5440 Candy, nut, and confectionery stores [3]	4	6	17	28	5	7,529	7,429	155	184
5450 Dairy products stores	-	5	-	16	3	-	11,000	-	166

Continued on next page.

DAVENPORT – MOLINE – ROCK ISLAND MSA (IL PART) - [continued]

Wholesale and Retail Trade USA	Establishments		Employment		Emp / Est	Pay / Employee		Annual Payroll ($ 000)	
	1994	1995	1994	1995	1995	1994	1995	1994	1995
5460 Retail bakeries	19	17	153	136	8	5,961	7,324	1,121	985
5490 Miscellaneous food stores [3]	7	6	38	26	4	11,263	17,231	343	311
5510 New and used car dealers	29	28	964	951	34	26,017	27,487	28,933	29,346
5520 Used car dealers	14	15	59	67	4	19,051	22,209	1,183	1,406
5530 Auto and home supply stores	26	25	173	154	6	16,902	18,649	3,334	3,248
5540 Gasoline service stations	95	96	644	706	7	9,130	9,127	6,706	7,324
5550 Boat dealers [3]	3	3	30	38	13	18,400	19,368	813	895
5560 Recreational vehicle dealers	4	4	16	16	4	14,000	16,000	415	408
5570 Motorcycle dealers	5	-	3	-	-	12,000	-	120	-
5610 Men's & boys' clothing stores [3]	10	10	84	61	6	9,095	10,557	679	614
5620 Women's clothing stores	35	32	284	196	6	7,366	7,265	2,221	1,361
5650 Family clothing stores	12	12	232	228	19	11,828	13,596	2,865	2,849
5660 Shoe stores	26	25	125	135	5	8,928	9,570	1,469	1,346
5690 Misc. apparel & accessory stores [3]	10	11	42	54	5	11,429	10,963	544	1,045
5712 Furniture stores	21	21	269	282	13	14,454	15,418	4,227	4,444
5713 Floor covering stores	11	14	73	101	7	20,000	20,238	1,753	2,272
5719 Misc. homefurnishings stores	-	9	-	36	4	-	9,444	-	346
5720 Household appliance stores	13	12	4	41	3	9,000	14,537	25	742
5731 Radio, TV, & electronic stores	10	10	101	107	11	12,792	12,897	1,219	1,239
5734 Computer and software stores [3]	5	7	42	61	9	15,714	15,934	779	1,030
5735 Record & prerecorded tape stores [3]	7	7	36	33	5	9,000	10,182	323	306
5736 Musical instrument stores [3]	6	8	42	54	7	6,667	9,111	289	470
5812 Eating places	307	291	5,520	5,362	18	6,854	7,100	41,170	41,782
5813 Drinking places	113	101	577	517	5	6,558	6,917	3,952	3,676
5910 Drug stores and proprietary stores	28	27	456	449	17	15,070	15,920	7,216	7,425
5920 Liquor stores	19	18	153	106	6	6,588	6,830	975	603
5930 Used merchandise stores	-	12	-	41	3	-	7,024	-	292
5941 Sporting goods and bicycle shops	22	19	98	78	4	9,143	9,282	1,098	830
5942 Book stores	6	5	35	34	7	6,514	9,647	249	340
5944 Jewelry stores	22	23	123	116	5	18,667	15,138	1,885	1,904
5945 Hobby, toy, and game shops	11	11	80	79	7	9,150	9,468	775	780
5946 Camera & photographic supply stores [1]	4	-	14	-	-	8,571	-	134	-
5947 Gift, novelty, and souvenir shops	31	27	157	151	6	5,707	6,146	966	951
5962 Merchandising machine operators	8	8	84	85	11	17,667	18,118	1,712	1,758
5963 Direct selling establishments	-	11	-	14	1	-	28,286	-	449
5980 Fuel dealers	5	5	11	12	2	21,455	20,000	238	155
5992 Florists [3]	36	33	54	50	2	5,185	5,840	296	300
5995 Optical goods stores [3]	11	12	80	72	6	16,100	16,444	1,184	1,253
5999 Miscellaneous retail stores, nec	38	42	191	237	6	11,393	12,743	3,068	3,913

Source: County Business Patterns 1994/95, CBP-94/95, U.S. Department of Commerce, Washington DC, November 1997. The employment column represents mid-March employment in the year. Pay per employee is calculated by dividing 1st Quarter payroll, annualized, by mid-March employment. The column headed 'Emp / Est' shows 'employees per establishment'. A dash (-) means that data are unavailable or cannot be calculated. nec means not elsewhere classified. *Notes:* 1. 1994 data incomplete; unavailable or withheld. 2. 1995 data incomplete; unavailable or withheld. 3. 1994 and 1995 data incomplete; unavailable or withheld.

DAVENPORT – MOLINE – ROCK ISLAND MSA (IA PART)

Wholesale and Retail Trade USA	Establishments		Employment		Emp / Est	Pay / Employee		Annual Payroll ($ 000)	
	1994	1995	1994	1995	1995	1994	1995	1994	1995
50 - Wholesale trade	452	451	5,266	5,815	13	27,929	29,653	162,412	181,035
5012 Automobiles and other vehicles	10	14	240	392	28	27,150	30,337	7,524	14,067
5013 Motor vehicle supplies and new parts	27	22	351	217	10	27,681	22,120	11,637	5,126
5014 Tires and tubes	4	5	39	78	16	28,410	24,154	1,224	2,063
5015 Motor vehicle parts, used	5	5	32	32	6	13,375	13,625	473	495
5021 Furniture	7	7	48	53	8	23,083	28,604	1,241	1,492
5023 Homefurnishings	9	8	101	58	7	24,634	22,897	2,612	1,468
5031 Lumber, plywood, and millwork	-	9	-	69	8	-	28,522	-	1,736
5032 Brick, stone, & related materials	6	5	120	125	25	62,333	71,648	4,178	4,727
5033 Roofing, siding, & insulation	8	7	96	107	15	18,583	21,383	2,240	2,507
5039 Construction materials, nec	-	8	-	211	26	-	17,555	-	4,312
5044 Office equipment	10	10	186	180	18	36,086	43,956	6,658	7,087
5045 Computers, peripherals, & software	15	17	98	134	8	32,776	34,627	3,904	4,786
5046 Commercial equipment, nec	5	5	32	27	5	28,125	27,111	899	841
5047 Medical and hospital equipment	7	8	30	28	4	33,067	33,857	1,101	1,077
5051 Metals service centers and offices	16	14	141	166	12	28,255	28,964	4,680	5,365
5063 Electrical apparatus and equipment	17	16	275	297	19	36,785	38,721	9,734	11,653
5064 Electrical appliances, TV & radios	6	6	45	84	14	31,200	32,810	1,456	2,201
5065 Electronic parts and equipment	6	7	41	66	9	29,756	30,121	1,528	2,399
5072 Hardware	8	8	73	83	10	31,342	33,108	2,479	3,122
5074 Plumbing & hydronic heating supplies	9	9	69	108	12	33,333	34,741	2,027	3,188

Continued on next page.

DAVENPORT – MOLINE – ROCK ISLAND MSA (IA PART) - [continued]

Wholesale and Retail Trade USA	Establishments		Employment		Emp / Est	Pay / Employee		Annual Payroll ($ 000)	
	1994	1995	1994	1995	1995	1994	1995	1994	1995
5075 Warm air heating & air conditioning	8	-	46	-	-	38,522	-	2,059	-
5078 Refrigeration equipment and supplies	3	-	46	-	-	24,435	-	1,556	-
5082 Construction and mining machinery	9	7	120	131	19	29,900	32,153	3,698	3,935
5083 Farm and garden machinery	8	8	98	99	12	21,755	26,869	2,432	2,885
5084 Industrial machinery and equipment	32	33	364	450	14	32,923	33,467	13,237	16,062
5085 Industrial supplies	28	30	226	245	8	31,717	32,245	7,922	9,276
5087 Service establishment equipment	-	13	-	59	5	-	18,712	-	1,187
5093 Scrap and waste materials	8	9	116	134	15	24,586	27,224	3,904	4,258
5099 Durable goods, nec	5	5	24	14	3	4,833	7,143	135	103
5112 Stationery and office supplies	13	10	125	114	11	17,248	19,018	2,393	2,205
5141 Groceries, general line	6	7	454	441	63	28,846	31,066	14,223	14,600
5142 Packaged frozen food	3	-	25	-	-	17,280	-	399	-
5143 Dairy products, exc. dried or canned	4	4	51	53	13	37,882	40,000	2,225	2,290
5147 Meats and meat products	-	3	-	36	12	-	24,111	-	1,016
5149 Groceries and related products, nec	12	11	247	258	23	25,781	26,558	6,730	6,917
5150 Farm-product raw materials	13	13	128	148	11	24,438	29,568	3,943	5,897
5160 Chemicals and allied products	12	13	110	123	9	30,073	30,472	3,417	3,665
5171 Petroleum bulk stations & terminals	7	6	59	50	8	20,814	25,920	1,295	1,360
5172 Petroleum products, nec	3	4	17	38	10	28,000	20,842	553	822
5180 Beer, wine, and distilled beverages	7	6	137	151	25	25,314	26,066	4,027	4,404
5191 Farm supplies	10	10	68	41	4	24,765	23,220	3,472	1,023
5192 Books, periodicals, & newspapers	4	4	88	98	25	26,182	23,551	2,242	2,410
5199 Nondurable goods, nec	11	10	22	34	3	19,091	11,765	466	465
52 – Retail trade	1,033	1,055	16,620	17,523	17	11,305	12,272	208,809	225,565
5210 Lumber and other building materials	21	17	381	530	31	17,218	18,015	7,393	9,346
5230 Paint, glass, and wallpaper stores	7	7	48	48	7	13,167	14,667	753	730
5250 Hardware stores	8	-	174	-	-	9,816	-	1,949	-
5260 Retail nurseries and garden stores	9	12	86	99	8	13,116	19,434	1,504	1,706
5310 Department stores	14	14	1,869	1,923	137	10,179	11,777	22,123	22,748
5330 Variety stores	6	5	30	39	8	9,467	8,718	356	367
5390 Misc. general merchandise stores	5	7	289	333	48	9,495	10,787	3,410	3,602
5410 Grocery stores	57	56	2,062	2,040	36	11,038	11,647	24,598	25,658
5420 Meat and fish markets	7	7	28	24	3	11,571	15,333	421	455
5440 Candy, nut, and confectionery stores	6	6	26	23	4	4,615	5,391	141	127
5460 Retail bakeries	12	11	75	97	9	6,667	8,948	605	928
5490 Miscellaneous food stores	5	7	21	32	5	8,000	6,875	164	244
5510 New and used car dealers	11	11	738	803	73	27,897	27,158	24,087	24,235
5520 Used car dealers	18	17	44	44	3	13,455	15,455	705	677
5530 Auto and home supply stores	15	19	156	174	9	20,256	19,057	3,380	3,586
5540 Gasoline service stations	79	78	773	814	10	12,678	15,076	10,664	13,783
5550 Boat dealers	5	5	20	18	4	15,000	16,222	387	342
5570 Motorcycle dealers	5	4	44	45	11	15,182	19,111	918	1,105
5610 Men's & boys' clothing stores	13	13	86	95	7	13,070	13,516	1,299	1,356
5620 Women's clothing stores	40	36	365	339	9	7,288	6,678	2,755	2,217
5630 Women's accessory & specialty stores	8	-	37	-	-	9,081	-	404	-
5650 Family clothing stores	9	11	138	138	13	8,232	9,362	1,294	1,479
5660 Shoe stores	25	22	138	136	6	8,812	9,559	1,359	1,327
5690 Misc. apparel & accessory stores	7	-	11	-	-	12,727	-	164	-
5712 Furniture stores	20	21	253	231	11	13,897	14,753	3,890	3,783
5713 Floor covering stores	8	9	127	117	13	19,244	23,350	2,717	2,907
5714 Drapery and upholstery stores	5	6	29	23	4	6,621	9,391	246	267
5719 Misc. homefurnishings stores	12	14	79	81	6	13,418	11,062	982	959
5720 Household appliance stores	6	8	43	44	6	17,116	18,000	837	766
5731 Radio, TV, & electronic stores	13	13	126	150	12	13,587	13,600	1,731	2,265
5734 Computer and software stores	-	5	-	44	9	-	30,545	-	1,611
5735 Record & prerecorded tape stores	6	7	40	43	6	11,400	13,395	425	492
5736 Musical instrument stores	-	5	-	55	11	-	17,455	-	1,054
5812 Eating places	232	224	5,522	5,994	27	7,336	7,794	45,113	50,721
5813 Drinking places	77	69	408	431	6	6,745	7,007	3,029	3,499
5910 Drug stores and proprietary stores	23	24	373	358	15	15,024	17,676	5,872	6,470
5920 Liquor stores	3	3	15	14	5	11,733	9,143	153	129
5930 Used merchandise stores	17	19	89	78	4	7,865	7,590	795	743
5941 Sporting goods and bicycle shops	24	23	93	178	8	10,667	11,258	1,234	2,105
5942 Book stores	5	5	62	43	9	5,742	8,744	358	433
5944 Jewelry stores	19	20	141	136	7	16,113	18,059	2,450	2,548
5945 Hobby, toy, and game shops	13	12	137	134	11	8,350	9,284	1,343	1,371
5947 Gift, novelty, and souvenir shops	28	27	160	149	6	5,875	7,705	1,074	1,082
5949 Sewing, needlework, and piece goods	4	3	49	35	12	8,490	7,200	417	243
5961 Catalog and mail-order houses	7	10	190	212	21	28,926	28,057	4,851	4,778
5962 Merchandising machine operators	6	5	23	23	5	12,870	17,739	351	408
5963 Direct selling establishments	13	13	48	49	4	10,583	12,735	579	590

Continued on next page.

DAVENPORT - MOLINE - ROCK ISLAND MSA (IA PART) - [continued]

Wholesale and Retail Trade USA	Establishments		Employment		Emp / Est	Pay / Employee		Annual Payroll ($ 000)	
	1994	1995	1994	1995	1995	1994	1995	1994	1995
5984 Liquefied petroleum gas dealers	3	3	9	10	3	19,111	22,000	207	248
5992 Florists	21	19	84	85	4	6,571	6,024	519	495
5995 Optical goods stores	13	14	85	89	6	12,329	10,697	1,022	1,153
5999 Miscellaneous retail stores, nec	30	35	166	207	6	11,566	11,188	2,206	2,522

Source: County Business Patterns 1994/95, CBP-94/95, U.S. Department of Commerce, Washington DC, November 1997. The employment column represents mid-March employment in the year. Pay per employee is calculated by dividing 1st Quarter payroll, annualized, by mid-March employment. The column headed 'Emp / Est' shows 'employees per establishment'. A dash (-) means that data are unavailable or cannot be calculated. nec means not elsewhere classified. *Notes:* 1. 1994 data incomplete; unavailable or withheld. 2. 1995 data incomplete; unavailable or withheld. 3. 1994 and 1995 data incomplete; unavailable or withheld.

DAVENPORT - MOLINE - ROCK ISLAND, IA - IL MSA

Wholesale and Retail Trade USA	Establishments		Employment		Emp / Est	Pay / Employee		Annual Payroll ($ 000)	
	1994	1995	1994	1995	1995	1994	1995	1994	1995
50 - Wholesale trade	837	847	10,483	11,518	14	27,733	28,811	314,902	360,053
5012 Automobiles and other vehicles	15	19	471	523	28	25,180	29,010	15,047	17,419
5013 Motor vehicle supplies and new parts	57	53	499	445	8	25,323	23,146	16,080	11,135
5014 Tires and tubes [3]	6	5	39	78	16	28,410	24,154	1,224	2,063
5015 Motor vehicle parts, used	14	15	32	139	9	13,375	22,388	473	2,877
5021 Furniture [3]	10	10	58	66	7	20,759	24,545	1,332	1,598
5023 Homefurnishings [3]	14	13	173	125	10	25,688	27,264	4,484	3,407
5031 Lumber, plywood, and millwork [3]	13	12	150	166	14	33,200	33,181	4,696	5,349
5032 Brick, stone, & related materials [3]	7	7	120	125	18	62,333	71,648	4,178	4,727
5033 Roofing, siding, & insulation [1]	11	11	96	129	12	18,583	21,395	2,240	3,033
5039 Construction materials, nec [2]	-	12	-	211	18	-	17,555	-	4,312
5044 Office equipment [3]	21	21	317	319	15	30,246	35,097	10,219	10,803
5045 Computers, peripherals, & software [3]	18	21	458	483	23	61,817	56,629	24,238	27,064
5046 Commercial equipment, nec [3]	6	6	32	27	5	28,125	27,111	899	841
5047 Medical and hospital equipment [3]	12	13	96	105	8	25,042	24,914	3,035	3,033
5051 Metals service centers and offices	26	23	253	288	13	29,644	30,986	7,903	8,903
5063 Electrical apparatus and equipment	26	22	335	350	16	35,069	39,749	11,398	13,415
5064 Electrical appliances, TV & radios [3]	6	6	45	84	14	31,200	32,810	1,456	2,201
5065 Electronic parts and equipment	13	16	78	117	7	34,615	30,359	2,887	7,679
5072 Hardware [3]	13	13	333	387	30	22,667	23,183	9,186	10,246
5074 Plumbing & hydronic heating supplies [1]	16	15	179	147	10	29,542	33,469	5,304	4,276
5075 Warm air heating & air conditioning [1]	10	-	46	-	-	38,522	-	2,059	-
5078 Refrigeration equipment and supplies [1]	4	-	46	-	-	24,435	-	1,556	-
5082 Construction and mining machinery	17	15	203	217	14	36,493	39,171	7,891	8,804
5083 Farm and garden machinery	26	28	352	355	13	29,557	31,121	11,297	12,216
5084 Industrial machinery and equipment	72	72	705	800	11	30,616	32,285	23,291	27,102
5085 Industrial supplies	46	49	386	477	10	30,477	30,675	12,854	16,070
5087 Service establishment equipment	-	16	-	59	4	-	18,712	-	1,187
5093 Scrap and waste materials	24	23	278	419	18	20,590	25,165	7,144	14,103
5099 Durable goods, nec	12	12	110	110	9	10,982	10,036	1,555	1,219
5112 Stationery and office supplies [3]	17	14	136	114	8	18,118	19,018	2,708	2,205
5141 Groceries, general line	9	10	454	441	44	28,846	31,066	14,223	14,600
5142 Packaged frozen food [1]	6	-	25	-	-	17,280	-	399	-
5143 Dairy products, exc. dried or canned	8	7	81	53	8	30,123	40,000	2,774	2,290
5147 Meats and meat products	-	5	-	36	7	-	24,111	-	1,016
5149 Groceries and related products, nec	19	21	290	395	19	25,724	26,906	7,914	10,887
5153 Grain and field beans [3]	24	25	158	216	9	19,038	21,815	4,037	7,125
5154 Livestock [3]	10	11	100	70	6	14,720	15,371	1,425	954
5162 Plastics materials & basic shapes [3]	4	5	45	60	12	24,622	24,667	1,146	1,992
5169 Chemicals & allied products, nec [3]	14	15	34	31	2	28,000	32,903	1,092	1,123
5171 Petroleum bulk stations & terminals	20	18	59	71	4	20,814	25,915	1,295	1,941
5172 Petroleum products, nec [3]	4	5	17	38	8	28,000	20,842	553	822
5180 Beer, wine, and distilled beverages	13	12	213	231	19	25,446	25,853	6,382	7,269
5191 Farm supplies	34	37	393	342	9	22,952	22,339	12,354	8,967
5192 Books, periodicals, & newspapers [3]	6	7	88	98	14	26,182	23,551	2,242	2,410
5198 Paints, varnishes, and supplies	8	-	15	-	-	14,667	-	258	-
5199 Nondurable goods, nec	19	19	22	54	3	19,091	13,185	466	824
52 - Retail trade	2,314	2,342	33,676	34,445	15	11,722	12,345	437,628	451,718
5210 Lumber and other building materials	42	36	820	990	28	17,020	17,964	15,538	17,536
5230 Paint, glass, and wallpaper stores	13	13	48	48	4	13,167	14,667	753	730
5250 Hardware stores	26	22	303	131	6	9,835	11,359	3,456	1,583
5260 Retail nurseries and garden stores	22	24	144	138	6	10,611	16,812	2,112	2,214
5310 Department stores [3]	24	25	2,996	3,096	124	10,238	11,516	35,637	36,468
5330 Variety stores	12	10	30	39	4	9,467	8,718	356	367
5390 Misc. general merchandise stores [3]	14	17	289	333	20	9,495	10,787	3,410	3,602
5410 Grocery stores	131	133	4,268	4,153	31	11,355	11,911	51,686	53,131

Continued on next page.

DAVENPORT - MOLINE - ROCK ISLAND, IA - IL MSA - [continued]

Wholesale and Retail Trade USA	Establishments		Employment		Emp / Est	Pay / Employee		Annual Payroll ($ 000)	
	1994	1995	1994	1995	1995	1994	1995	1994	1995
5420 Meat and fish markets [3]	15	14	28	62	4	11,571	13,484	421	897
5440 Candy, nut, and confectionery stores [3]	10	12	43	51	4	5,767	6,510	296	311
5450 Dairy products stores	-	6	-	16	3	-	11,000	-	166
5460 Retail bakeries	31	28	228	233	8	6,193	8,000	1,726	1,913
5490 Miscellaneous food stores [3]	12	13	59	58	4	10,102	11,517	507	555
5510 New and used car dealers	40	39	1,702	1,754	45	26,832	27,336	53,020	53,581
5520 Used car dealers	32	32	103	111	3	16,660	19,532	1,888	2,083
5530 Auto and home supply stores	41	44	329	328	7	18,492	18,866	6,714	6,834
5540 Gasoline service stations	174	174	1,417	1,520	9	11,066	12,313	17,370	21,107
5550 Boat dealers [3]	8	8	50	56	7	17,040	18,357	1,200	1,237
5560 Recreational vehicle dealers	6	6	16	16	3	14,000	16,000	415	408
5570 Motorcycle dealers	10	8	47	45	6	14,979	19,111	1,038	1,105
5610 Men's & boys' clothing stores [3]	23	23	170	156	7	11,106	12,359	1,978	1,970
5620 Women's clothing stores	75	68	649	535	8	7,322	6,893	4,976	3,578
5630 Women's accessory & specialty stores [1]	12	-	37	-	-	9,081	-	404	-
5650 Family clothing stores	21	23	370	366	16	10,486	12,000	4,159	4,328
5660 Shoe stores	51	47	263	271	6	8,867	9,565	2,828	2,673
5690 Misc. apparel & accessory stores [3]	17	18	53	54	3	11,698	10,963	708	1,045
5712 Furniture stores	41	42	522	513	12	14,184	15,119	8,117	8,227
5713 Floor covering stores	19	23	200	218	9	19,520	21,908	4,470	5,179
5714 Drapery and upholstery stores	8	9	29	23	3	6,621	9,391	246	267
5719 Misc. homefurnishings stores	20	23	79	117	5	13,418	10,564	982	1,305
5720 Household appliance stores	19	20	47	85	4	16,426	16,329	862	1,508
5731 Radio, TV, & electronic stores	23	23	227	257	11	13,233	13,307	2,950	3,504
5734 Computer and software stores [3]	9	12	42	105	9	15,714	22,057	779	2,641
5735 Record & prerecorded tape stores [3]	13	14	76	76	5	10,263	12,000	748	798
5736 Musical instrument stores [3]	10	13	42	109	8	6,667	13,321	289	1,524
5812 Eating places	539	515	11,042	11,356	22	7,095	7,467	86,283	92,503
5813 Drinking places	190	170	985	948	6	6,636	6,958	6,981	7,175
5910 Drug stores and proprietary stores	51	51	829	807	16	15,049	16,699	13,088	13,895
5920 Liquor stores	22	21	168	120	6	7,048	7,100	1,128	732
5930 Used merchandise stores	27	31	89	119	4	7,865	7,395	795	1,035
5941 Sporting goods and bicycle shops	46	42	191	256	6	9,885	10,656	2,332	2,935
5942 Book stores	11	10	97	77	8	6,021	9,143	607	773
5944 Jewelry stores	41	43	264	252	6	17,303	16,714	4,335	4,452
5945 Hobby, toy, and game shops	24	23	217	213	9	8,645	9,352	2,118	2,151
5946 Camera & photographic supply stores [1]	6	-	14	-	-	8,571	-	134	-
5947 Gift, novelty, and souvenir shops	59	54	317	300	6	5,792	6,920	2,040	2,033
5949 Sewing, needlework, and piece goods	10	8	49	35	4	8,490	7,200	417	243
5961 Catalog and mail-order houses	10	13	190	212	16	28,926	28,057	4,851	4,778
5962 Merchandising machine operators	14	13	107	108	8	16,636	18,037	2,063	2,166
5963 Direct selling establishments	24	24	48	63	3	10,583	16,190	579	1,039
5984 Liquefied petroleum gas dealers	7	7	9	10	1	19,111	22,000	207	248
5992 Florists [3]	57	52	138	135	3	6,029	5,956	815	795
5995 Optical goods stores [3]	24	26	165	161	6	14,158	13,267	2,206	2,406
5999 Miscellaneous retail stores, nec	68	77	357	444	6	11,473	12,018	5,274	6,435

Source: County Business Patterns 1994/95, CBP-94/95, U.S. Department of Commerce, Washington DC, November 1997. The employment column represents mid-March employment in the year. Pay per employee is calculated by dividing 1st Quarter payroll, annualized, by mid-March employment. The column headed 'Emp / Est' shows 'employees per establishment'. A dash (-) means that data are unavailable or cannot be calculated. nec means not elsewhere classified. *Notes:* 1. 1994 data incomplete; unavailable or withheld. 2. 1995 data incomplete; unavailable or withheld. 3. 1994 and 1995 data incomplete; unavailable or withheld.

DAYTON - SPRINGFIELD, OH MSA

Wholesale and Retail Trade USA	Establishments		Employment		Emp / Est	Pay / Employee		Annual Payroll ($ 000)	
	1994	1995	1994	1995	1995	1994	1995	1994	1995
50 - Wholesale trade	1,488	1,477	19,274	20,341	14	31,314	33,178	628,544	704,113
5012 Automobiles and other vehicles [3]	11	12	202	239	20	30,376	32,218	7,107	7,566
5013 Motor vehicle supplies and new parts	90	89	813	862	10	23,109	27,754	21,189	22,947
5014 Tires and tubes [3]	9	8	94	107	13	23,064	24,075	2,556	2,820
5015 Motor vehicle parts, used	27	28	67	74	3	14,209	15,081	1,381	1,628
5021 Furniture [3]	17	17	212	220	13	21,434	22,273	4,658	5,160
5023 Homefurnishings [1]	15	15	37	28	2	16,324	14,857	617	421
5031 Lumber, plywood, and millwork	19	16	198	199	12	28,404	29,628	6,331	5,765
5032 Brick, stone, & related materials [1]	13	12	87	85	7	19,172	21,694	1,938	1,771
5033 Roofing, siding, & insulation [3]	10	10	119	142	14	26,891	29,437	3,787	4,248
5039 Construction materials, nec [3]	10	22	36	136	6	26,667	24,676	991	3,772
5044 Office equipment	28	30	446	411	14	34,637	37,810	13,796	14,332
5045 Computers, peripherals, & software [3]	71	60	1,045	882	15	52,299	54,902	52,392	64,442
5046 Commercial equipment, nec [3]	14	12	160	171	14	26,950	30,667	4,602	5,164

Continued on next page.

DAYTON – SPRINGFIELD, OH MSA - [continued]

Wholesale and Retail Trade USA	Establishments		Employment		Emp / Est	Pay / Employee		Annual Payroll ($ 000)	
	1994	1995	1994	1995	1995	1994	1995	1994	1995
5047 Medical and hospital equipment[2]	22	15	194	143	10	25,753	32,587	5,480	4,791
5049 Professional equipment, nec[3]	14	14	187	208	15	64,214	69,308	8,016	10,063
5051 Metals service centers and offices[3]	47	47	372	431	9	28,849	29,578	11,916	13,490
5063 Electrical apparatus and equipment	75	66	710	662	10	30,175	34,073	23,224	22,230
5064 Electrical appliances, TV & radios[3]	13	14	170	154	11	35,576	41,662	6,205	6,353
5065 Electronic parts and equipment[1]	99	107	1,207	1,266	12	36,278	41,096	46,745	56,970
5072 Hardware	29	27	171	187	7	23,439	40,706	4,539	8,194
5074 Plumbing & hydronic heating supplies	34	39	317	394	10	44,555	44,914	11,263	13,583
5075 Warm air heating & air conditioning[3]	17	18	115	126	7	31,200	32,667	3,591	3,732
5078 Refrigeration equipment and supplies[3]	6	6	68	71	12	25,706	29,239	2,220	2,512
5082 Construction and mining machinery	-	15	-	87	6	-	38,621	-	3,651
5083 Farm and garden machinery	-	18	-	142	8	-	22,563	-	3,632
5084 Industrial machinery and equipment	-	130	-	1,300	10	-	34,631	-	48,367
5085 Industrial supplies	-	74	-	1,181	16	-	35,461	-	43,940
5087 Service establishment equipment	-	21	-	150	7	-	21,040	-	3,120
5088 Transportation equipment & supplies[2]	-	7	-	43	6	-	32,930	-	1,403
5091 Sporting & recreational goods[2]	-	12	-	262	22	-	25,038	-	6,473
5092 Toys and hobby goods and supplies	-	7	-	46	7	-	16,435	-	903
5093 Scrap and waste materials	-	27	-	405	15	-	28,909	-	14,809
5094 Jewelry & precious stones[2]	-	11	-	17	2	-	17,882	-	359
5099 Durable goods, nec	-	29	-	157	5	-	29,376	-	4,233
5111 Printing and writing paper[2]	-	16	-	400	25	-	44,540	-	14,051
5112 Stationery and office supplies	-	49	-	412	8	-	28,175	-	12,571
5113 Industrial & personal service paper	-	22	-	249	11	-	24,145	-	6,752
5120 Drugs, proprietaries, and sundries	-	11	-	161	15	-	20,969	-	3,369
5136 Men's and boys' clothing[2]	-	13	-	222	17	-	26,595	-	6,405
5137 Women's and children's clothing[2]	-	4	-	9	2	-	8,000	-	127
5141 Groceries, general line[2]	-	10	-	205	21	-	29,073	-	5,100
5142 Packaged frozen food[2]	-	5	-	104	21	-	30,308	-	3,158
5147 Meats and meat products[2]	-	5	-	46	9	-	19,652	-	958
5148 Fresh fruits and vegetables[2]	-	8	-	74	9	-	24,811	-	2,094
5149 Groceries and related products, nec[2]	-	20	-	403	20	-	28,387	-	12,581
5153 Grain and field beans	-	16	-	59	4	-	21,356	-	1,410
5159 Farm-product raw materials, nec[2]	-	4	-	18	5	-	21,111	-	397
5162 Plastics materials & basic shapes[2]	-	14	-	146	10	-	33,945	-	4,486
5169 Chemicals & allied products, nec	-	31	-	273	9	-	41,099	-	11,635
5171 Petroleum bulk stations & terminals	-	18	-	201	11	-	31,522	-	6,553
5172 Petroleum products, nec[2]	-	9	-	43	5	-	42,605	-	2,231
5181 Beer and ale[2]	-	7	-	290	41	-	28,303	-	10,229
5191 Farm supplies	-	19	-	74	4	-	19,622	-	1,527
5193 Flowers & florists' supplies[2]	-	11	-	67	6	-	22,149	-	1,955
5198 Paints, varnishes, and supplies[2]	-	8	-	68	9	-	19,824	-	1,306
5199 Nondurable goods, nec	-	42	-	259	6	-	22,409	-	7,432
52- Retail trade	5,372	5,324	87,801	91,066	17	11,042	11,851	1,070,486	1,138,738
5210 Lumber and other building materials	64	76	1,307	2,009	26	18,568	18,134	30,587	35,521
5230 Paint, glass, and wallpaper stores[1]	51	49	96	52	1	16,167	15,615	1,703	868
5250 Hardware stores	58	40	567	390	10	9,199	9,682	5,692	3,575
5260 Retail nurseries and garden stores	56	57	491	415	7	13,515	11,441	6,110	5,868
5310 Department stores	58	59	12,372	12,861	218	9,300	10,665	132,478	144,047
5330 Variety stores	53	43	458	421	10	8,445	8,494	4,407	4,008
5390 Misc. general merchandise stores	29	34	962	924	27	10,212	11,416	9,908	10,503
5410 Grocery stores	353	332	9,573	9,837	30	10,449	9,933	101,033	103,209
5420 Meat and fish markets[3]	22	21	151	146	7	10,755	11,260	1,769	1,647
5430 Fruit and vegetable markets[3]	6	4	8	5	1	8,000	8,800	106	67
5440 Candy, nut, and confectionery stores	18	21	87	63	3	4,690	6,921	500	436
5450 Dairy products stores[2]	-	7	-	21	3	-	6,476	-	137
5460 Retail bakeries	67	63	634	529	8	8,221	8,968	5,901	4,463
5490 Miscellaneous food stores	30	35	156	199	6	10,026	8,925	1,789	2,037
5510 New and used car dealers	85	81	4,217	4,332	53	25,383	26,994	124,276	130,315
5520 Used car dealers	53	55	223	258	5	18,906	20,667	5,176	5,867
5530 Auto and home supply stores	141	145	1,367	1,206	8	15,865	19,698	24,013	24,079
5540 Gasoline service stations	322	328	2,821	2,466	8	8,750	10,795	25,854	27,522
5550 Boat dealers[3]	11	10	63	74	7	16,508	18,054	1,547	1,729
5560 Recreational vehicle dealers[3]	5	5	25	24	5	18,240	21,000	587	600
5570 Motorcycle dealers[3]	17	14	205	192	14	11,941	14,271	3,240	3,249
5590 Automotive dealers, nec[2]	-	5	-	14	3	-	12,857	-	315
5610 Men's & boys' clothing stores	43	43	309	344	8	10,084	10,116	3,545	3,614
5620 Women's clothing stores	175	148	1,810	1,438	10	8,164	7,352	16,185	10,810
5630 Women's accessory & specialty stores	27	26	170	136	5	8,024	8,794	1,482	1,229
5640 Children's and infants' wear stores[3]	16	16	147	174	11	7,728	8,966	1,172	1,547
5650 Family clothing stores	38	40	460	743	19	8,635	10,127	4,400	7,312

Continued on next page.

DAYTON - SPRINGFIELD, OH MSA - [continued]

Wholesale and Retail Trade USA	Establishments		Employment		Emp / Est	Pay / Employee		Annual Payroll ($ 000)	
	1994	1995	1994	1995	1995	1994	1995	1994	1995
5660 Shoe stores	139	136	742	878	6	11,811	9,613	9,072	8,567
5690 Misc. apparel & accessory stores	31	31	134	127	4	8,090	10,583	1,306	1,412
5712 Furniture stores	89	94	1,360	1,508	16	18,968	20,114	28,503	30,157
5713 Floor covering stores	57	62	274	307	5	17,708	20,169	5,715	6,483
5719 Misc. homefurnishings stores	55	47	288	284	6	9,750	10,859	3,103	3,330
5720 Household appliance stores	32	31	168	180	6	12,214	12,289	2,228	2,413
5731 Radio, TV, & electronic stores	62	62	350	701	11	20,606	16,057	8,148	10,730
5734 Computer and software stores	28	34	181	200	6	14,895	17,460	3,115	3,899
5735 Record & prerecorded tape stores	30	33	193	209	6	10,010	10,565	2,115	2,288
5736 Musical instrument stores	16	14	67	83	6	18,627	16,578	1,312	1,462
5812 Eating places	1,334	1,270	29,895	30,471	24	7,194	7,705	236,169	246,209
5813 Drinking places	278	254	1,380	1,463	6	7,046	7,114	10,443	10,435
5910 Drug stores and proprietary stores	166	163	2,069	2,116	13	15,254	15,790	33,316	35,027
5920 Liquor stores	121	119	649	678	6	10,743	10,437	7,387	7,081
5930 Used merchandise stores	70	61	413	398	7	9,743	11,849	4,411	5,059
5941 Sporting goods and bicycle shops	96	102	399	468	5	11,479	11,667	5,455	6,983
5942 Book stores	52	59	399	480	8	8,632	9,583	3,493	4,720
5943 Stationery stores [3]	13	10	79	46	5	14,987	17,913	979	893
5944 Jewelry stores	105	110	671	686	6	14,307	15,102	10,302	10,183
5945 Hobby, toy, and game shops	37	34	296	322	9	7,811	7,677	2,994	2,732
5947 Gift, novelty, and souvenir shops	115	113	773	766	7	7,477	8,475	6,127	6,570
5949 Sewing, needlework, and piece goods	28	27	274	254	9	6,015	6,378	1,811	1,748
5961 Catalog and mail-order houses	20	23	265	297	13	15,789	16,094	4,468	4,972
5962 Merchandising machine operators [3]	31	31	467	440	14	14,801	16,736	7,392	7,718
5963 Direct selling establishments	47	45	377	332	7	13,740	16,325	5,836	6,073
5983 Fuel oil dealers	11	13	22	37	3	19,636	21,514	424	826
5984 Liquefied petroleum gas dealers	9	10	64	61	6	28,313	29,639	2,026	1,837
5992 Florists	87	88	464	442	5	10,724	10,688	5,495	5,203
5995 Optical goods stores	66	65	289	287	4	13,827	15,986	4,226	4,717
5999 Miscellaneous retail stores, nec	131	143	935	1,214	8	13,566	12,764	14,832	18,878

Source: County Business Patterns 1994/95, CBP-94/95, U.S. Department of Commerce, Washington DC, November 1997. The employment column represents mid-March employment in the year. Pay per employee is calculated by dividing 1st Quarter payroll, annualized, by mid-March employment. The column headed 'Emp / Est' shows 'employees per establishment'. A dash (-) means that data are unavailable or cannot be calculated. nec means not elsewhere classified. *Notes:* 1. 1994 data incomplete; unavailable or withheld. 2. 1995 data incomplete; unavailable or withheld. 3. 1994 and 1995 data incomplete; unavailable or withheld.

DAYTONA BEACH, FL MSA

Wholesale and Retail Trade USA	Establishments		Employment		Emp / Est	Pay / Employee		Annual Payroll ($ 000)	
	1994	1995	1994	1995	1995	1994	1995	1994	1995
50- Wholesale trade	578	593	4,684	5,017	8	20,182	21,055	104,474	106,511
5012 Automobiles and other vehicles [3]	25	22	261	360	16	12,015	10,900	3,404	4,080
5013 Motor vehicle supplies and new parts [2]	40	34	194	186	5	14,928	16,667	3,578	3,603
5014 Tires and tubes [3]	7	4	69	64	16	25,159	28,813	2,263	2,526
5015 Motor vehicle parts, used	15	18	45	82	5	12,978	13,512	695	1,115
5021 Furniture [3]	8	10	35	41	4	30,171	28,780	1,293	1,676
5023 Homefurnishings [1]	14	12	69	51	4	20,696	18,980	1,571	1,004
5031 Lumber, plywood, and millwork	9	13	32	69	5	22,875	22,899	880	1,669
5032 Brick, stone, & related materials [3]	6	6	126	131	22	22,825	25,924	4,300	3,741
5033 Roofing, siding, & insulation [3]	4	3	25	17	6	24,160	29,176	685	706
5039 Construction materials, nec [1]	3	11	17	119	11	29,176	27,429	507	2,886
5044 Office equipment [3]	15	16	125	137	9	22,304	22,832	2,912	3,227
5045 Computers, peripherals, & software [1]	21	21	87	93	4	21,793	22,194	2,072	2,398
5046 Commercial equipment, nec [3]	8	9	42	40	4	16,476	18,300	832	913
5047 Medical and hospital equipment [3]	14	13	147	107	8	17,959	25,832	3,405	2,875
5051 Metals service centers and offices	7	9	35	39	4	17,600	18,872	642	660
5063 Electrical apparatus and equipment	21	21	125	128	6	23,456	26,906	3,233	3,286
5065 Electronic parts and equipment	15	14	71	92	7	19,324	19,000	1,606	1,734
5072 Hardware [3]	6	7	59	59	8	18,305	22,034	1,259	1,303
5074 Plumbing & hydronic heating supplies [3]	11	13	87	102	8	24,414	23,294	2,042	2,409
5082 Construction and mining machinery [3]	4	3	11	23	8	17,455	25,217	334	605
5083 Farm and garden machinery	11	10	60	57	6	16,000	20,772	1,210	1,169
5084 Industrial machinery and equipment	18	16	84	108	7	23,238	26,593	2,446	3,073
5085 Industrial supplies [1]	10	11	187	46	4	30,888	23,043	6,100	995
5087 Service establishment equipment	12	10	43	73	7	13,023	7,945	599	552
5088 Transportation equipment & supplies	4	6	19	24	4	13,053	15,167	326	419
5091 Sporting & recreational goods [1]	7	8	22	30	4	12,000	18,667	270	576
5092 Toys and hobby goods and supplies [2]	-	3	-	12	4	-	14,667	-	84
5093 Scrap and waste materials [3]	10	8	72	55	7	22,778	26,255	1,680	1,688
5094 Jewelry & precious stones	-	6	-	7	1	-	17,714	-	110

Continued on next page.

DAYTONA BEACH, FL MSA - [continued]

Wholesale and Retail Trade USA	Establishments		Employment		Emp / Est	Pay / Employee		Annual Payroll ($ 000)	
	1994	1995	1994	1995	1995	1994	1995	1994	1995
5099 Durable goods, nec	14	16	31	51	3	17,419	16,784	721	808
5112 Stationery and office supplies[3]	15	13	180	118	9	15,778	17,119	3,102	1,824
5113 Industrial & personal service paper[3]	3	4	15	12	3	45,067	26,667	454	319
5120 Drugs, proprietaries, and sundries	14	13	113	130	10	21,664	23,723	2,860	3,222
5136 Men's and boys' clothing[3]	7	7	37	45	6	26,162	26,400	1,134	1,236
5142 Packaged frozen food[3]	5	5	203	212	42	18,424	19,358	3,900	3,807
5146 Fish and seafoods[3]	7	7	21	20	3	8,952	9,600	199	201
5147 Meats and meat products[3]	3	4	7	8	2	13,714	13,000	112	129
5148 Fresh fruits and vegetables	-	4	-	70	18	-	8,057	-	531
5149 Groceries and related products, nec	12	10	186	164	16	27,914	31,171	5,405	5,686
5150 Farm-product raw materials[1]	3	-	17	-	-	12,941	-	260	-
5162 Plastics materials & basic shapes[3]	5	8	89	127	16	27,685	27,244	2,944	3,631
5169 Chemicals & allied products, nec[3]	8	8	27	25	3	18,074	18,400	505	500
5171 Petroleum bulk stations & terminals	9	8	65	83	10	16,677	15,373	1,119	1,301
5172 Petroleum products, nec[3]	4	5	25	25	5	42,080	40,000	1,143	1,069
5181 Beer and ale[3]	5	5	200	205	41	27,200	27,532	5,845	4,704
5191 Farm supplies	16	13	66	74	6	29,879	19,351	1,468	1,455
5192 Books, periodicals, & newspapers[3]	4	4	32	40	10	19,250	55,600	614	1,377
5193 Flowers & florists' supplies[3]	16	14	259	239	17	6,873	6,544	1,330	1,405
5198 Paints, varnishes, and supplies	5	4	19	21	5	20,842	24,190	648	571
5199 Nondurable goods, nec	20	24	73	95	4	14,849	13,011	1,359	1,246
52- Retail trade	2,780	2,799	37,737	38,298	14	11,123	11,940	438,486	461,409
5210 Lumber and other building materials	45	33	855	759	23	15,251	15,499	14,793	12,303
5230 Paint, glass, and wallpaper stores[3]	11	11	99	93	8	19,192	21,376	2,147	2,082
5250 Hardware stores	35	26	200	153	6	10,020	10,222	2,042	1,664
5260 Retail nurseries and garden stores	34	27	131	124	5	11,878	12,323	1,649	1,604
5270 Mobile home dealers[3]	7	5	61	68	14	14,820	14,529	987	904
5310 Department stores[3]	22	23	3,073	3,397	148	11,348	13,108	37,423	42,780
5330 Variety stores[3]	21	15	214	175	12	8,748	9,006	1,996	1,650
5390 Misc. general merchandise stores[3]	22	27	567	487	18	10,935	12,485	6,593	5,132
5410 Grocery stores	202	199	6,673	6,794	34	10,388	11,558	70,924	77,792
5420 Meat and fish markets	15	15	81	72	5	11,407	11,889	908	842
5430 Fruit and vegetable markets	11	11	23	25	2	10,783	9,760	247	265
5440 Candy, nut, and confectionery stores	11	6	43	13	2	5,860	6,769	173	83
5450 Dairy products stores[2]	5	5	17	16	3	4,706	5,750	99	97
5460 Retail bakeries	19	20	189	205	10	9,122	9,054	1,770	1,800
5490 Miscellaneous food stores	20	18	62	66	4	9,032	11,091	597	759
5510 New and used car dealers	38	41	1,682	1,707	42	31,888	33,256	58,683	61,382
5520 Used car dealers	57	56	277	236	4	18,614	21,831	5,318	5,351
5530 Auto and home supply stores	79	87	463	530	6	16,976	17,268	8,377	9,680
5540 Gasoline service stations	184	181	1,069	1,114	6	12,157	11,899	13,062	13,806
5550 Boat dealers[3]	15	16	82	93	6	13,415	15,269	1,355	1,608
5560 Recreational vehicle dealers[3]	5	7	47	56	8	23,830	26,429	1,578	1,684
5570 Motorcycle dealers[3]	11	12	95	142	12	19,789	22,169	2,079	2,869
5610 Men's & boys' clothing stores[3]	16	12	75	45	4	9,547	10,133	653	459
5620 Women's clothing stores	68	51	442	301	6	8,407	8,146	3,541	2,348
5630 Women's accessory & specialty stores[3]	13	14	75	81	6	6,827	7,506	591	561
5640 Children's and infants' wear stores[1]	3	-	8	-	-	7,500	-	33	-
5650 Family clothing stores	36	36	622	630	18	8,650	9,454	6,138	6,402
5660 Shoe stores	62	58	255	257	4	10,620	10,786	2,784	2,715
5690 Misc. apparel & accessory stores[3]	29	29	111	93	3	9,153	12,000	1,068	1,145
5712 Furniture stores	73	68	514	471	7	16,607	17,308	8,969	8,530
5713 Floor covering stores	28	27	92	88	3	17,087	23,273	2,091	2,067
5714 Drapery and upholstery stores[3]	5	6	17	20	3	12,000	10,200	222	186
5719 Misc. homefurnishings stores	24	26	172	173	7	10,837	12,116	2,062	2,217
5720 Household appliance stores	21	22	92	106	5	17,609	18,642	1,834	2,126
5731 Radio, TV, & electronic stores	23	25	171	181	7	16,468	16,818	2,835	3,647
5734 Computer and software stores[3]	13	18	27	53	3	11,407	14,264	448	787
5735 Record & prerecorded tape stores[3]	8	9	86	95	11	9,116	9,642	776	745
5736 Musical instrument stores[3]	9	8	66	76	10	26,485	20,421	2,174	1,784
5812 Eating places	621	583	13,468	13,366	23	7,675	8,095	102,547	102,885
5813 Drinking places	92	84	720	682	8	6,628	7,525	4,632	4,948
5910 Drug stores and proprietary stores	62	58	1,022	1,015	18	15,597	16,650	17,712	19,014
5920 Liquor stores	33	36	169	161	4	9,633	9,988	1,726	1,706
5930 Used merchandise stores	53	49	178	179	4	12,584	11,888	2,517	2,371
5941 Sporting goods and bicycle shops[1]	46	44	144	127	3	9,667	10,866	1,592	1,577
5942 Book stores[1]	24	23	114	116	5	9,649	10,207	1,150	1,209
5944 Jewelry stores	47	47	174	184	4	13,678	14,152	2,417	2,533
5945 Hobby, toy, and game shops[3]	12	12	110	112	9	10,364	12,964	1,339	1,343
5946 Camera & photographic supply stores[2]	-	5	-	36	7	-	16,333	-	571
5947 Gift, novelty, and souvenir shops	108	109	538	546	5	8,149	7,993	4,150	4,291

Continued on next page.

DAYTONA BEACH, FL MSA - [continued]

Wholesale and Retail Trade USA	Establishments		Employment		Emp / Est	Pay / Employee		Annual Payroll ($ 000)	
	1994	1995	1994	1995	1995	1994	1995	1994	1995
5949 Sewing, needlework, and piece goods	15	12	98	106	9	6,653	7,321	673	789
5963 Direct selling establishments	26	28	140	168	6	27,429	25,952	3,515	3,825
5980 Fuel dealers	11	12	98	105	9	25,184	25,143	2,376	2,540
5992 Florists	50	54	197	205	4	8,934	9,327	1,881	1,878
5995 Optical goods stores	31	32	130	117	4	14,985	16,308	2,022	1,959
5999 Miscellaneous retail stores, nec	86	100	323	396	4	11,666	12,758	4,340	5,787

Source: County Business Patterns 1994/95, CBP-94/95, U.S. Department of Commerce, Washington DC, November 1997. The employment column represents mid-March employment in the year. Pay per employee is calculated by dividing 1st Quarter payroll, annualized, by mid-March employment. The column headed 'Emp / Est' shows 'employees per establishment'. A dash (-) means that data are unavailable or cannot be calculated. nec means not elsewhere classified. *Notes:* 1. 1994 data incomplete; unavailable or withheld. 2. 1995 data incomplete; unavailable or withheld. 3. 1994 and 1995 data incomplete; unavailable or withheld.

DECATUR, AL MSA

Wholesale and Retail Trade USA	Establishments		Employment		Emp / Est	Pay / Employee		Annual Payroll ($ 000)	
	1994	1995	1994	1995	1995	1994	1995	1994	1995
50- Wholesale trade	248	247	2,392	2,436	10	21,559	22,773	59,516	60,174
5012 Automobiles and other vehicles [3]	5	4	75	72	18	35,307	33,389	2,286	2,267
5013 Motor vehicle supplies and new parts	15	9	85	85	9	19,576	23,059	1,903	2,209
5020 Furniture and homefurnishings [3]	7	10	118	177	18	16,000	15,164	2,261	3,069
5031 Lumber, plywood, and millwork [3]	9	7	158	112	16	17,316	22,179	3,289	2,792
5039 Construction materials, nec [2]	-	4	-	33	8	-	27,758	-	967
5044 Office equipment [1]	4	-	17	-	-	15,294	-	279	-
5045 Computers, peripherals, & software [3]	7	7	34	32	5	15,176	14,750	576	554
5047 Medical and hospital equipment [3]	7	6	20	46	8	13,200	14,348	600	841
5049 Professional equipment, nec [2]	-	4	-	10	3	-	23,600	-	390
5051 Metals service centers and offices [3]	6	6	83	88	15	49,446	41,409	3,235	3,119
5063 Electrical apparatus and equipment	11	13	102	82	6	25,333	31,951	3,766	2,496
5072 Hardware [1]	6	-	51	-	-	16,235	-	870	-
5075 Warm air heating & air conditioning [2]	-	4	-	57	14	-	21,333	-	1,193
5083 Farm and garden machinery	-	8	-	13	2	-	13,846	-	219
5084 Industrial machinery and equipment [3]	15	16	72	94	6	29,833	28,894	2,593	3,357
5085 Industrial supplies [3]	21	22	180	134	6	26,622	27,791	4,562	4,063
5087 Service establishment equipment [3]	9	8	63	66	8	19,365	22,788	1,473	1,711
5093 Scrap and waste materials [3]	7	9	121	140	16	19,835	29,343	2,650	3,321
5099 Durable goods, nec [3]	6	7	14	11	2	19,143	19,273	255	253
5112 Stationery and office supplies [1]	3	-	19	-	-	10,737	-	206	-
5120 Drugs, proprietaries, and sundries [2]	-	4	-	42	11	-	22,381	-	929
5149 Groceries and related products, nec [3]	3	4	141	153	38	23,291	22,536	4,166	4,301
5150 Farm-product raw materials	5	5	36	39	8	8,667	9,333	357	418
5169 Chemicals & allied products, nec	4	4	14	18	5	107,714	77,778	1,401	1,461
5171 Petroleum bulk stations & terminals	13	-	29	-	-	16,276	-	501	-
5191 Farm supplies	15	14	354	327	23	12,441	14,850	7,674	6,296
52- Retail trade	832	839	9,239	9,898	12	10,600	10,907	108,883	115,230
5210 Lumber and other building materials	17	18	269	312	17	16,550	16,936	4,774	5,575
5230 Paint, glass, and wallpaper stores	10	11	35	29	3	11,543	14,897	433	506
5250 Hardware stores	12	7	20	9	1	14,000	11,111	310	123
5260 Retail nurseries and garden stores [3]	6	7	40	46	7	8,800	10,000	484	379
5270 Mobile home dealers [3]	5	5	23	25	5	19,478	20,960	480	623
5310 Department stores	8	8	1,025	982	123	10,053	12,200	11,119	11,933
5330 Variety stores	12	9	51	28	3	9,098	9,857	490	310
5390 Misc. general merchandise stores	12	12	82	103	9	8,976	9,126	861	1,038
5410 Grocery stores [3]	101	100	1,205	1,494	15	9,856	7,944	12,855	12,498
5460 Retail bakeries [3]	4	3	10	13	4	8,400	7,077	100	105
5490 Miscellaneous food stores [3]	4	4	9	6	2	8,444	12,667	76	59
5510 New and used car dealers	14	16	491	515	32	25,727	27,635	15,944	16,903
5520 Used car dealers	12	12	37	28	2	18,162	21,714	674	630
5530 Auto and home supply stores	36	39	212	246	6	15,943	16,520	3,609	4,215
5540 Gasoline service stations	65	63	349	316	5	10,430	10,861	4,173	3,608
5620 Women's clothing stores	20	18	87	72	4	8,920	7,833	786	646
5640 Children's and infants' wear stores [2]	-	4	-	2	1	-	4,000	-	17
5650 Family clothing stores	8	8	269	253	32	10,364	11,557	3,075	2,929
5660 Shoe stores [3]	15	14	68	62	4	9,294	12,387	694	742
5690 Misc. apparel & accessory stores [3]	5	4	15	19	5	6,133	5,474	143	124
5712 Furniture stores	26	25	141	148	6	12,624	14,054	1,983	2,193
5713 Floor covering stores [3]	10	10	47	49	5	12,085	13,388	679	717
5719 Misc. homefurnishings stores	8	9	42	40	4	10,286	9,700	473	337
5720 Household appliance stores [3]	5	5	17	18	4	17,412	14,889	299	297
5731 Radio, TV, & electronic stores	12	13	47	53	4	16,851	16,679	737	879
5734 Computer and software stores [2]	-	4	-	15	4	-	7,733	-	153

Continued on next page.

DECATUR, AL MSA - [continued]

Wholesale and Retail Trade USA	Establishments		Employment		Emp / Est	Pay / Employee		Annual Payroll ($ 000)	
	1994	1995	1994	1995	1995	1994	1995	1994	1995
5735 Record & prerecorded tape stores [2]	-	3	-	14	5	-	10,000	-	127
5736 Musical instrument stores [3]	3	3	25	23	8	9,600	11,130	269	254
5812 Eating places [1]	154	138	2,643	3,052	22	6,956	6,987	19,355	22,260
5813 Drinking places [2]	11	11	80	84	8	9,400	10,048	837	880
5910 Drug stores and proprietary stores	38	34	311	314	9	16,502	15,631	5,438	5,262
5920 Liquor stores	10	10	47	45	5	12,170	13,778	666	695
5930 Used merchandise stores	12	13	29	31	2	10,069	11,742	337	397
5941 Sporting goods and bicycle shops [3]	10	10	52	37	4	9,077	8,541	437	394
5942 Book stores	7	6	15	12	2	8,000	11,667	150	142
5944 Jewelry stores	22	21	126	116	6	12,413	14,000	1,671	1,738
5945 Hobby, toy, and game shops [3]	7	7	19	23	3	9,895	9,217	240	259
5947 Gift, novelty, and souvenir shops [1]	12	14	40	40	3	7,200	6,900	320	324
5949 Sewing, needlework, and piece goods [3]	4	3	16	18	6	11,000	9,778	190	168
5961 Catalog and mail-order houses [2]	-	3	-	7	2	-	9,143	-	81
5984 Liquefied petroleum gas dealers	-	5	-	20	4	-	20,400	-	411
5992 Florists	16	16	40	43	3	6,400	6,140	294	275
5993 Tobacco stores and stands [2]	-	4	-	5	1	-	9,600	-	40
5995 Optical goods stores	7	8	30	33	4	14,000	12,848	399	424
5999 Miscellaneous retail stores, nec	20	23	41	67	3	8,293	8,657	407	606

Source: County Business Patterns 1994/95, CBP-94/95, U.S. Department of Commerce, Washington DC, November 1997. The employment column represents mid-March employment in the year. Pay per employee is calculated by dividing 1st Quarter payroll, annualized, by mid-March employment. The column headed 'Emp / Est' shows 'employees per establishment'. A dash (-) means that data are unavailable or cannot be calculated. nec means not elsewhere classified. *Notes:* 1. 1994 data incomplete; unavailable or withheld. 2. 1995 data incomplete; unavailable or withheld. 3. 1994 and 1995 data incomplete; unavailable or withheld.

DECATUR, IL MSA

Wholesale and Retail Trade USA	Establishments		Employment		Emp / Est	Pay / Employee		Annual Payroll ($ 000)	
	1994	1995	1994	1995	1995	1994	1995	1994	1995
50- Wholesale trade	199	206	2,183	2,206	11	24,590	27,258	57,822	63,990
5012 Automobiles and other vehicles	5	4	138	142	36	13,217	13,549	2,178	2,344
5013 Motor vehicle supplies and new parts	12	12	68	72	6	16,529	19,611	1,233	1,403
5014 Tires and tubes	4	-	37	-	-	19,351	-	735	-
5015 Motor vehicle parts, used	3	-	33	-	-	14,909	-	575	-
5020 Furniture and homefurnishings	4	-	58	-	-	18,138	-	1,408	-
5031 Lumber, plywood, and millwork	-	3	-	79	26	-	26,886	-	2,090
5039 Construction materials, nec	-	3	-	45	15	-	19,111	-	1,009
5044 Office equipment	5	5	26	32	6	35,077	33,750	1,121	1,156
5045 Computers, peripherals, & software	6	4	39	16	4	22,872	24,750	812	390
5046 Commercial equipment, nec	4	3	58	51	17	23,241	24,157	1,644	1,381
5047 Medical and hospital equipment	5	4	30	30	8	43,333	34,267	1,321	1,522
5050 Metals and minerals, except petroleum	4	-	73	-	-	28,603	-	2,820	-
5063 Electrical apparatus and equipment	9	8	121	111	14	27,438	47,712	4,262	4,813
5072 Hardware	-	7	-	68	10	-	22,235	-	1,828
5074 Plumbing & hydronic heating supplies	9	8	48	53	7	36,417	36,755	1,465	1,748
5075 Warm air heating & air conditioning	4	-	18	-	-	33,778	-	644	-
5083 Farm and garden machinery	5	5	64	85	17	26,563	25,035	2,461	3,133
5084 Industrial machinery and equipment	10	10	89	84	8	28,404	36,048	2,824	3,161
5085 Industrial supplies	9	8	79	64	8	29,671	34,000	2,401	2,104
5087 Service establishment equipment	-	4	-	145	36	-	13,821	-	1,749
5093 Scrap and waste materials	4	5	62	56	11	14,516	16,143	1,254	1,653
5110 Paper and paper products	8	7	108	95	14	24,185	26,905	2,314	2,550
5130 Apparel, piece goods, and notions	-	3	-	12	4	-	13,667	-	141
5147 Meats and meat products	4	4	33	36	9	17,939	16,778	654	630
5149 Groceries and related products, nec	5	7	85	120	17	26,165	26,933	2,232	3,279
5153 Grain and field beans	11	-	91	-	-	40,176	-	3,974	-
5169 Chemicals & allied products, nec	5	-	32	-	-	31,750	-	1,011	-
5170 Petroleum and petroleum products	5	5	45	50	10	39,911	42,720	1,502	1,653
5180 Beer, wine, and distilled beverages	3	-	51	-	-	27,843	-	1,693	-
5191 Farm supplies	12	13	81	82	6	25,877	29,561	2,171	2,431
5198 Paints, varnishes, and supplies	3	4	18	22	6	17,778	26,364	319	635
52- Retail trade	709	691	10,577	10,334	15	11,519	12,511	132,758	131,407
5210 Lumber and other building materials	23	18	418	325	18	15,770	19,495	7,482	6,856
5230 Paint, glass, and wallpaper stores	6	-	25	-	-	20,800	-	545	-
5250 Hardware stores	5	-	66	-	-	8,485	-	621	-
5260 Retail nurseries and garden stores	7	7	25	28	4	13,600	11,143	409	360
5310 Department stores	9	8	1,174	1,124	141	9,543	11,541	12,260	13,307
5330 Variety stores	8	5	45	59	12	7,644	8,068	535	547
5390 Misc. general merchandise stores	4	7	317	320	46	10,057	11,350	3,491	3,640
5410 Grocery stores	35	37	1,034	961	26	12,565	14,356	13,260	13,099

Continued on next page.

DECATUR, IL MSA - [continued]

Wholesale and Retail Trade USA	Establishments 1994	Establishments 1995	Employment 1994	Employment 1995	Emp / Est 1995	Pay / Employee 1994	Pay / Employee 1995	Annual Payroll ($ 000) 1994	Annual Payroll ($ 000) 1995
5440 Candy, nut, and confectionery stores	5	6	36	37	6	5,667	5,622	226	223
5460 Retail bakeries	3	3	42	37	12	4,286	6,162	232	232
5490 Miscellaneous food stores	4	4	38	36	9	12,316	8,111	370	241
5510 New and used car dealers	17	16	560	536	34	26,414	26,769	16,004	14,319
5530 Auto and home supply stores	16	16	199	208	13	14,171	14,808	3,130	3,336
5540 Gasoline service stations	40	38	360	314	8	8,389	10,140	3,235	3,262
5560 Recreational vehicle dealers	5	4	38	36	9	14,211	12,333	635	593
5570 Motorcycle dealers	4	4	19	20	5	24,211	17,400	432	335
5610 Men's & boys' clothing stores	15	12	82	61	5	11,171	11,475	862	468
5620 Women's clothing stores	26	21	241	172	8	7,270	7,651	1,805	1,219
5660 Shoe stores	20	18	95	92	5	9,516	9,739	897	816
5690 Misc. apparel & accessory stores	5	4	13	19	5	7,692	10,316	151	193
5712 Furniture stores	11	12	67	62	5	15,940	18,581	1,252	1,463
5713 Floor covering stores	5	6	25	50	8	21,440	19,680	592	1,180
5719 Misc. homefurnishings stores	5	4	10	11	3	6,000	6,182	84	42
5720 Household appliance stores	8	8	47	44	6	17,447	21,091	830	758
5731 Radio, TV, & electronic stores	10	10	90	92	9	20,622	22,000	2,124	2,182
5734 Computer and software stores	-	3	-	15	5	-	24,267	-	320
5735 Record & prerecorded tape stores	5	5	24	23	5	11,833	12,348	303	303
5736 Musical instrument stores	-	3	-	13	4	-	16,615	-	218
5812 Eating places	164	154	3,209	3,433	22	6,926	7,375	24,267	26,712
5813 Drinking places	37	35	286	234	7	7,105	8,034	2,052	2,067
5910 Drug stores and proprietary stores	13	15	247	277	18	17,312	18,830	4,628	5,479
5920 Liquor stores	17	18	108	91	5	9,259	9,890	1,001	986
5930 Used merchandise stores	9	8	35	35	4	7,314	7,657	268	290
5941 Sporting goods and bicycle shops	11	12	45	35	3	10,489	9,257	524	387
5942 Book stores	9	10	48	48	5	7,667	7,583	367	412
5944 Jewelry stores	10	10	62	60	6	16,129	18,533	1,159	1,183
5945 Hobby, toy, and game shops	-	9	-	30	3	-	7,467	-	241
5947 Gift, novelty, and souvenir shops	17	17	113	105	6	7,894	6,781	831	795
5960 Nonstore retailers	13	11	246	234	21	24,732	26,513	8,374	5,909
5980 Fuel dealers	6	6	34	35	6	22,118	21,257	810	821
5992 Florists	14	11	70	62	6	9,314	10,387	703	680
5995 Optical goods stores	8	7	40	38	5	19,100	18,000	701	689
5999 Miscellaneous retail stores, nec	21	23	96	105	5	11,458	11,962	1,346	1,252

Source: County Business Patterns 1994/95, CBP-94/95, U.S. Department of Commerce, Washington DC, November 1997. The employment column represents mid-March employment in the year. Pay per employee is calculated by dividing 1st Quarter payroll, annualized, by mid-March employment. The column headed 'Emp / Est' shows 'employees per establishment'. A dash (-) means that data are unavailable or cannot be calculated. nec means not elsewhere classified. *Notes:* 1. 1994 data incomplete; unavailable or withheld. 2. 1995 data incomplete; unavailable or withheld. 3. 1994 and 1995 data incomplete; unavailable or withheld.

DENVER, CO PMSA

Wholesale and Retail Trade USA	Establishments 1994	Establishments 1995	Employment 1994	Employment 1995	Emp / Est 1995	Pay / Employee 1994	Pay / Employee 1995	Annual Payroll ($ 000) 1994	Annual Payroll ($ 000) 1995
50- Wholesale trade	5,002	5,056	67,405	71,072	14	32,867	35,407	2,326,049	2,545,638
5012 Automobiles and other vehicles	90	94	1,819	2,075	22	30,012	33,400	59,630	68,837
5013 Motor vehicle supplies and new parts	187	175	2,502	2,357	13	25,496	26,637	67,831	63,413
5014 Tires and tubes	40	33	512	387	12	29,805	32,227	16,485	12,971
5015 Motor vehicle parts, used	60	70	306	385	6	16,026	18,577	5,451	8,090
5021 Furniture	119	124	1,061	1,208	10	27,947	31,272	31,773	39,057
5023 Homefurnishings	105	97	1,203	1,175	12	25,210	24,786	34,036	32,481
5031 Lumber, plywood, and millwork	88	83	1,761	1,604	19	28,663	31,975	55,602	53,702
5032 Brick, stone, & related materials [2]	40	40	521	300	8	34,534	34,973	19,427	11,035
5033 Roofing, siding, & insulation [3]	34	36	365	424	12	27,375	29,151	13,527	15,533
5039 Construction materials, nec	61	90	607	1,039	12	28,112	32,805	19,206	32,774
5043 Photographic equipment & supplies [3]	18	20	121	150	8	22,942	28,053	2,938	4,128
5044 Office equipment	92	92	1,953	1,989	22	34,536	40,080	68,561	73,803
5045 Computers, peripherals, & software	286	274	4,915	5,213	19	43,460	48,734	223,967	264,640
5046 Commercial equipment, nec	68	69	553	594	9	26,821	27,623	16,891	17,244
5047 Medical and hospital equipment	158	154	1,743	1,553	10	35,128	40,561	60,770	62,092
5048 Ophthalmic goods [3]	16	13	48	32	2	19,000	28,625	871	915
5049 Professional equipment, nec	38	39	395	450	12	31,899	36,836	17,782	19,055
5050 Metals and minerals, except petroleum	91	99	1,283	1,331	13	32,209	32,544	45,633	46,741
5063 Electrical apparatus and equipment [3]	198	182	1,845	1,979	11	38,539	41,439	73,915	82,632
5064 Electrical appliances, TV & radios	49	49	391	363	7	36,481	37,752	13,794	13,956
5065 Electronic parts and equipment	324	317	4,400	5,036	16	49,511	51,657	206,450	238,627
5072 Hardware [3]	97	101	1,085	1,193	12	27,746	29,100	33,031	35,751
5074 Plumbing & hydronic heating supplies [1]	118	109	1,194	1,211	11	30,901	33,093	43,396	42,368
5075 Warm air heating & air conditioning [3]	47	51	614	564	11	33,616	38,092	22,685	23,213

Continued on next page.

DENVER, CO PMSA - [continued]

Wholesale and Retail Trade USA	Establishments		Employment		Emp / Est	Pay / Employee		Annual Payroll ($ 000)	
	1994	1995	1994	1995	1995	1994	1995	1994	1995
5078 Refrigeration equipment and supplies [2]	13	13	125	130	10	33,696	32,123	3,978	5,523
5082 Construction and mining machinery	67	71	1,292	1,440	20	39,211	35,375	51,436	52,892
5083 Farm and garden machinery	35	38	279	397	10	27,828	27,416	9,297	12,217
5084 Industrial machinery and equipment	345	350	2,571	2,823	8	34,261	35,972	96,942	111,868
5085 Industrial supplies	140	147	1,276	1,377	9	31,034	34,649	43,638	50,869
5087 Service establishment equipment	90	95	862	940	10	26,116	27,796	24,803	27,504
5088 Transportation equipment & supplies	25	22	102	116	5	29,490	32,586	3,772	3,842
5091 Sporting & recreational goods	95	87	931	894	10	22,569	25,369	23,147	23,887
5092 Toys and hobby goods and supplies	26	31	246	311	10	16,764	16,823	5,168	5,789
5093 Scrap and waste materials [1]	43	52	552	606	12	21,167	22,607	13,650	15,103
5094 Jewelry & precious stones	56	47	184	182	4	20,304	21,670	4,480	4,300
5099 Durable goods, nec	106	107	784	866	8	25,878	20,037	23,264	20,796
5111 Printing and writing paper [3]	25	21	592	574	27	30,595	43,937	16,635	25,050
5112 Stationery and office supplies	125	114	1,836	1,613	14	20,190	23,645	40,486	36,424
5113 Industrial & personal service paper	51	53	244	262	5	36,623	39,313	9,116	9,821
5120 Drugs, proprietaries, and sundries [2]	70	73	898	911	12	33,265	30,889	33,166	28,972
5131 Piece goods & notions	38	43	378	389	9	19,672	21,871	8,230	8,717
5136 Men's and boys' clothing [2]	37	34	275	303	9	23,840	27,406	7,742	8,560
5137 Women's and children's clothing [3]	55	50	602	566	11	22,439	24,622	15,125	14,968
5139 Footwear [2]	-	7	-	4	1	-	34,000	-	141
5141 Groceries, general line [3]	45	47	2,198	1,835	39	30,708	33,275	70,974	62,928
5142 Packaged frozen food [3]	23	22	1,120	1,192	54	29,957	29,010	36,246	39,422
5143 Dairy products, exc. dried or canned [3]	16	16	373	339	21	21,437	24,602	8,691	8,801
5145 Confectionery [3]	38	34	524	686	20	29,443	29,726	16,779	21,132
5146 Fish and seafoods [3]	8	9	176	193	21	21,205	23,150	4,270	5,054
5147 Meats and meat products	46	43	617	573	13	27,203	30,422	18,202	17,288
5148 Fresh fruits and vegetables [3]	23	22	453	460	21	23,117	20,600	11,431	11,484
5149 Groceries and related products, nec	131	137	2,099	2,317	17	30,340	29,621	68,386	69,484
5153 Grain and field beans	13	12	7	7	1	29,143	32,000	206	239
5162 Plastics materials & basic shapes	37	36	350	358	10	29,851	35,017	11,922	12,332
5169 Chemicals & allied products, nec	100	103	1,261	1,237	12	32,501	38,015	45,001	48,828
5171 Petroleum bulk stations & terminals [3]	34	35	750	772	22	36,651	38,751	28,506	32,243
5172 Petroleum products, nec	35	36	229	240	7	51,197	60,167	9,971	10,640
5181 Beer and ale [3]	15	15	45	54	4	35,644	35,185	1,743	2,174
5182 Wine and distilled beverages [1]	21	-	49	-	-	46,612	-	1,769	-
5191 Farm supplies [1]	53	47	271	593	13	24,782	25,450	7,967	17,605
5192 Books, periodicals, & newspapers	38	37	892	1,153	31	23,323	21,429	21,061	25,167
5193 Flowers & florists' supplies	47	42	575	592	14	18,323	19,014	11,889	11,590
5194 Tobacco and tobacco products [2]	-	8	-	88	11	-	18,909	-	799
5198 Paints, varnishes, and supplies	47	38	376	311	8	25,787	26,740	10,214	8,995
5199 Nondurable goods, nec	166	184	938	978	5	18,776	21,022	20,296	22,667
52- Retail trade	10,856	11,134	167,916	171,790	15	14,017	14,733	2,515,719	2,663,687
5210 Lumber and other building materials	147	139	3,680	3,809	27	18,760	21,691	82,595	85,934
5230 Paint, glass, and wallpaper stores	69	67	275	410	6	18,124	18,546	5,780	8,085
5250 Hardware stores	87	59	819	684	12	13,944	14,655	13,224	10,219
5260 Retail nurseries and garden stores	45	53	347	376	7	12,392	12,862	6,097	7,106
5270 Mobile home dealers	19	20	309	512	26	23,741	15,063	11,997	9,107
5310 Department stores [3]	75	74	12,233	13,357	181	11,215	11,654	155,392	159,861
5330 Variety stores [3]	24	29	115	279	10	10,330	9,219	1,304	2,888
5390 Misc. general merchandise stores [3]	60	62	2,125	2,306	37	24,572	17,226	38,652	35,234
5410 Grocery stores	478	476	24,772	20,605	43	17,324	18,378	395,489	396,418
5420 Meat and fish markets [3]	30	32	193	202	6	16,332	19,644	3,801	3,953
5430 Fruit and vegetable markets [3]	5	5	14	16	3	10,000	10,250	181	184
5440 Candy, nut, and confectionery stores [2]	36	42	174	202	5	6,276	7,941	1,221	1,638
5450 Dairy products stores [3]	21	23	69	66	3	8,928	8,242	615	646
5460 Retail bakeries	128	107	859	707	7	9,355	8,832	8,802	6,772
5490 Miscellaneous food stores	83	94	445	676	7	11,946	12,959	5,972	9,518
5510 New and used car dealers	103	106	7,563	7,894	74	30,200	33,220	271,511	294,763
5520 Used car dealers	124	125	619	644	5	20,620	24,547	14,894	19,071
5530 Auto and home supply stores	296	316	2,350	2,514	8	16,931	19,613	46,149	54,603
5540 Gasoline service stations	577	584	4,314	4,358	7	12,938	13,679	61,239	60,873
5550 Boat dealers	14	16	47	45	3	13,957	14,667	1,036	983
5560 Recreational vehicle dealers [3]	22	20	252	246	12	26,984	30,699	7,928	7,532
5570 Motorcycle dealers	23	25	198	205	8	18,303	22,888	5,237	5,230
5590 Automotive dealers, nec	-	11	-	33	3	-	22,788	-	771
5610 Men's & boys' clothing stores	99	101	810	835	8	12,928	14,055	11,730	12,099
5620 Women's clothing stores	259	234	2,782	2,216	9	10,855	12,309	31,681	25,290
5630 Women's accessory & specialty stores	60	58	315	327	6	10,654	11,021	3,662	3,691
5640 Children's and infants' wear stores	20	20	157	228	11	9,452	7,526	1,425	1,809
5650 Family clothing stores	107	105	1,829	1,732	16	9,677	10,536	18,947	18,686
5660 Shoe stores	220	207	1,200	1,264	6	11,270	11,642	14,599	17,084

Continued on next page.

DENVER, CO PMSA - [continued]

Wholesale and Retail Trade USA	Establishments		Employment		Emp / Est	Pay / Employee		Annual Payroll ($ 000)	
	1994	1995	1994	1995	1995	1994	1995	1994	1995
5690 Misc. apparel & accessory stores	90	96	411	492	5	9,528	10,846	4,416	5,726
5712 Furniture stores	235	249	2,261	2,455	10	21,509	22,697	51,187	57,942
5713 Floor covering stores	109	114	642	600	5	26,037	28,547	18,711	18,659
5714 Drapery and upholstery stores[3]	11	9	10	9	1	12,000	32,444	294	200
5719 Misc. homefurnishings stores	167	173	1,170	1,523	9	10,489	11,777	14,955	18,952
5720 Household appliance stores	63	64	258	282	4	17,054	17,035	5,066	5,148
5731 Radio, TV, & electronic stores	134	142	1,556	1,630	11	18,738	19,593	31,665	36,910
5734 Computer and software stores	78	98	597	797	8	19,430	20,698	12,704	15,742
5735 Record & prerecorded tape stores	71	78	673	948	12	8,957	7,131	6,387	6,949
5736 Musical instrument stores	36	35	260	222	6	19,692	19,514	5,209	4,687
5812 Eating places	2,579	2,383	55,780	56,025	24	8,348	9,184	520,006	540,211
5813 Drinking places	388	358	4,063	4,257	12	7,972	8,416	34,250	37,419
5910 Drug stores and proprietary stores	160	160	2,187	2,206	14	16,234	16,578	37,484	38,918
5920 Liquor stores	370	380	1,537	1,622	4	11,802	12,819	21,030	22,535
5930 Used merchandise stores	215	214	1,556	1,508	7	11,450	12,422	19,894	20,288
5941 Sporting goods and bicycle shops	244	257	1,952	2,275	9	12,645	13,874	29,269	31,775
5942 Book stores	132	123	1,177	1,127	9	10,104	11,642	14,139	13,025
5943 Stationery stores[2]	37	34	102	230	7	11,373	15,774	1,311	4,200
5944 Jewelry stores	175	179	1,004	1,032	6	17,016	18,674	17,914	19,652
5945 Hobby, toy, and game shops	102	93	1,212	1,320	14	9,053	8,742	12,728	13,357
5946 Camera & photographic supply stores	12	-	37	-	-	20,541	-	779	-
5947 Gift, novelty, and souvenir shops	275	277	1,663	1,763	6	8,815	9,078	16,073	18,305
5948 Luggage and leather goods stores[3]	19	18	126	41	2	12,444	11,512	1,728	553
5949 Sewing, needlework, and piece goods	51	47	493	498	11	8,957	8,217	4,211	4,002
5961 Catalog and mail-order houses	50	58	336	355	6	17,440	20,552	5,519	8,293
5962 Merchandising machine operators	73	74	659	800	11	16,455	16,515	12,716	13,828
5963 Direct selling establishments[2]	147	158	1,682	1,804	11	14,433	12,803	25,323	25,070
5984 Liquefied petroleum gas dealers[2]	-	14	-	72	5	-	18,111	-	1,390
5992 Florists	165	162	727	928	6	10,316	10,194	8,222	9,146
5993 Tobacco stores and stands[1]	12	17	11	10	1	12,364	8,800	212	131
5994 News dealers and newsstands[2]	-	10	-	11	1	-	9,455	-	156
5995 Optical goods stores	168	169	760	752	4	14,895	18,303	12,378	13,922
5999 Miscellaneous retail stores, nec	487	505	2,170	2,365	5	14,446	15,410	36,237	41,536

Source: County Business Patterns 1994/95, CBP-94/95, U.S. Department of Commerce, Washington DC, November 1997. The employment column represents mid-March employment in the year. Pay per employee is calculated by dividing 1st Quarter payroll, annualized, by mid-March employment. The column headed 'Emp / Est' shows 'employees per establishment'. A dash (-) means that data are unavailable or cannot be calculated. nec means not elsewhere classified. *Notes:* 1. 1994 data incomplete; unavailable or withheld. 2. 1995 data incomplete; unavailable or withheld. 3. 1994 and 1995 data incomplete; unavailable or withheld.

DES MOINES, IA MSA

Wholesale and Retail Trade USA	Establishments		Employment		Emp / Est	Pay / Employee		Annual Payroll ($ 000)	
	1994	1995	1994	1995	1995	1994	1995	1994	1995
50- Wholesale trade	1,168	1,208	17,743	18,922	16	28,722	33,390	543,274	659,383
5012 Automobiles and other vehicles[2]	30	27	579	610	23	27,710	30,393	18,200	20,763
5013 Motor vehicle supplies and new parts	78	75	758	814	11	23,858	24,246	19,061	19,259
5014 Tires and tubes[3]	14	12	147	106	9	29,306	30,830	8,088	3,221
5015 Motor vehicle parts, used[3]	16	18	113	149	8	21,416	21,584	2,549	3,388
5021 Furniture[3]	9	10	159	295	30	26,340	27,376	5,147	9,001
5023 Homefurnishings[3]	21	20	257	267	13	27,440	28,524	7,790	7,182
5031 Lumber, plywood, and millwork[3]	21	20	482	423	21	30,631	35,877	14,079	12,476
5032 Brick, stone, & related materials[3]	11	11	77	93	8	33,039	33,548	2,687	3,217
5033 Roofing, siding, & insulation[3]	13	17	211	204	12	23,507	35,196	5,402	5,751
5039 Construction materials, nec[3]	16	27	174	238	9	26,920	28,756	5,249	7,639
5043 Photographic equipment & supplies[1]	5	-	41	-	-	28,098	-	1,159	-
5044 Office equipment[3]	33	29	534	508	18	32,457	37,512	18,409	18,041
5045 Computers, peripherals, & software	37	43	520	569	13	31,446	35,220	17,989	20,909
5046 Commercial equipment, nec[3]	16	14	142	121	9	24,563	23,934	4,079	3,556
5047 Medical and hospital equipment	38	35	409	515	15	25,829	35,083	11,686	18,430
5048 Ophthalmic goods[3]	7	7	53	54	8	21,057	23,407	1,152	1,304
5049 Professional equipment, nec[1]	3	-	15	-	-	24,267	-	420	-
5051 Metals service centers and offices[3]	19	20	332	356	18	27,639	28,831	10,152	10,797
5063 Electrical apparatus and equipment[3]	46	46	389	423	9	38,961	42,704	14,112	17,066
5064 Electrical appliances, TV & radios[3]	8	10	70	66	7	26,286	32,303	1,732	1,980
5065 Electronic parts and equipment[3]	30	26	342	374	14	38,409	35,594	16,323	16,796
5072 Hardware[3]	22	24	236	257	11	25,864	28,031	7,378	8,053
5074 Plumbing & hydronic heating supplies[1]	27	26	286	290	11	33,189	36,428	10,330	11,136
5075 Warm air heating & air conditioning[3]	17	19	85	144	8	34,541	37,056	3,101	5,617
5078 Refrigeration equipment and supplies[3]	7	7	220	221	32	37,691	41,900	9,015	9,879
5082 Construction and mining machinery[3]	22	23	424	460	20	34,755	36,287	16,153	16,796

Continued on next page.

DES MOINES, IA MSA - [continued]

Wholesale and Retail Trade USA	Establishments		Employment		Emp / Est	Pay / Employee		Annual Payroll ($ 000)	
	1994	1995	1994	1995	1995	1994	1995	1994	1995
5083 Farm and garden machinery[1]	23	22	32	196	9	20,875	25,265	729	5,436
5084 Industrial machinery and equipment	57	63	661	736	12	28,974	31,201	20,537	23,768
5085 Industrial supplies[3]	30	29	323	342	12	29,548	31,099	10,148	11,027
5087 Service establishment equipment[3]	21	21	212	228	11	25,264	25,368	5,641	6,129
5091 Sporting & recreational goods	14	15	76	81	5	18,368	18,222	1,909	1,902
5092 Toys and hobby goods and supplies[3]	4	4	21	16	4	13,333	19,500	296	280
5093 Scrap and waste materials[2]	16	17	114	150	9	22,491	22,400	2,936	3,710
5094 Jewelry & precious stones[3]	11	11	42	39	4	48,857	52,205	1,390	1,474
5099 Durable goods, nec[3]	18	17	90	96	6	17,644	17,750	1,845	1,772
5111 Printing and writing paper[3]	8	9	235	265	29	32,085	35,577	7,673	10,570
5112 Stationery and office supplies	38	33	735	409	12	29,192	25,663	20,514	10,412
5113 Industrial & personal service paper[3]	16	14	236	162	12	40,322	32,617	9,449	6,671
5120 Drugs, proprietaries, and sundries[3]	10	13	176	251	19	46,250	53,833	9,527	12,051
5131 Piece goods & notions[3]	5	5	81	96	19	26,321	20,875	2,170	1,729
5136 Men's and boys' clothing[2]	-	3	-	42	14	-	20,571	-	940
5137 Women's and children's clothing[2]	-	5	-	46	9	-	16,174	-	464
5141 Groceries, general line[3]	14	11	1,347	1,176	107	35,819	31,320	44,557	38,000
5142 Packaged frozen food[3]	6	6	127	146	24	24,063	31,671	3,130	6,239
5145 Confectionery[3]	8	6	214	147	25	24,617	30,694	5,370	5,034
5147 Meats and meat products	11	11	84	70	6	20,952	23,143	2,076	1,866
5148 Fresh fruits and vegetables	10	9	110	124	14	28,909	30,226	4,474	4,691
5149 Groceries and related products, nec[3]	26	26	295	425	16	22,373	27,746	6,542	12,343
5153 Grain and field beans[3]	26	29	64	67	2	20,375	22,090	1,581	1,586
5162 Plastics materials & basic shapes[3]	5	6	64	67	11	27,688	32,358	1,877	2,413
5169 Chemicals & allied products, nec	33	34	382	348	10	41,623	40,218	16,452	15,394
5171 Petroleum bulk stations & terminals	22	17	128	94	6	22,969	30,043	3,248	3,078
5172 Petroleum products, nec[1]	12	12	85	58	5	31,059	25,586	2,184	1,712
5181 Beer and ale[3]	5	5	177	194	39	29,175	30,969	5,747	6,291
5182 Wine and distilled beverages[3]	8	8	120	130	16	18,667	21,446	2,251	2,968
5191 Farm supplies	47	44	783	738	17	33,676	35,154	30,491	24,741
5192 Books, periodicals, & newspapers[3]	10	9	161	175	19	23,056	23,931	4,143	4,595
5193 Flowers & florists' supplies[3]	7	5	149	100	20	13,423	17,480	2,198	1,782
5199 Nondurable goods, nec[3]	28	29	326	334	12	13,718	16,395	5,177	7,315
52- Retail trade	2,798	2,767	46,562	46,477	17	12,548	13,194	639,797	650,452
5210 Lumber and other building materials	43	39	1,025	1,160	30	18,802	20,155	24,584	24,151
5230 Paint, glass, and wallpaper stores[3]	18	16	91	84	5	16,835	18,000	1,668	1,712
5250 Hardware stores	31	32	254	274	9	11,748	12,350	3,560	3,890
5260 Retail nurseries and garden stores	25	28	172	229	8	12,512	13,467	2,967	4,073
5270 Mobile home dealers[3]	4	4	12	14	4	30,000	30,571	459	482
5310 Department stores[3]	27	27	4,337	4,301	159	9,979	11,957	48,298	51,742
5330 Variety stores[3]	11	10	58	52	5	9,517	7,923	593	475
5390 Misc. general merchandise stores	23	23	474	527	23	12,051	11,810	5,788	5,788
5410 Grocery stores[3]	180	178	6,421	6,356	36	11,539	11,944	78,120	81,402
5420 Meat and fish markets[1]	10	-	102	-	-	8,824	-	1,197	-
5440 Candy, nut, and confectionery stores[2]	-	9	-	53	6	-	7,774	-	367
5450 Dairy products stores[1]	5	-	26	-	-	3,231	-	84	-
5460 Retail bakeries	26	24	138	166	7	6,841	8,193	1,091	1,357
5490 Miscellaneous food stores[3]	13	15	104	84	6	7,923	8,238	833	964
5510 New and used car dealers	40	43	1,899	1,842	43	28,731	30,686	61,958	67,139
5520 Used car dealers	36	34	89	111	3	17,843	18,595	2,005	2,323
5530 Auto and home supply stores	60	55	449	441	8	16,588	19,093	8,231	9,312
5540 Gasoline service stations	184	170	1,521	1,482	9	11,692	12,435	19,508	19,658
5550 Boat dealers[3]	4	4	43	29	7	15,535	19,862	762	739
5560 Recreational vehicle dealers[3]	11	10	58	59	6	13,310	13,898	1,141	1,010
5570 Motorcycle dealers[3]	7	8	34	33	4	17,765	14,667	740	657
5610 Men's & boys' clothing stores	34	35	269	261	7	15,420	14,483	4,322	4,010
5620 Women's clothing stores[3]	89	81	915	749	9	7,515	8,101	7,346	6,063
5630 Women's accessory & specialty stores[3]	16	12	91	75	6	8,044	9,013	734	657
5640 Children's and infants' wear stores[3]	8	7	69	79	11	5,449	7,443	528	624
5650 Family clothing stores[3]	25	25	408	548	22	7,990	8,073	3,509	4,475
5660 Shoe stores	58	56	326	350	6	10,589	10,869	3,793	3,859
5690 Misc. apparel & accessory stores[3]	17	18	83	90	5	8,771	13,378	736	1,262
5712 Furniture stores	49	49	422	424	9	18,635	20,783	8,796	9,144
5713 Floor covering stores[3]	23	26	126	148	6	20,381	23,081	3,031	4,629
5714 Drapery and upholstery stores[3]	4	5	43	38	8	16,651	17,368	713	685
5719 Misc. homefurnishings stores[3]	22	23	137	127	6	16,964	21,386	1,909	1,778
5720 Household appliance stores[3]	20	20	152	121	6	16,158	17,157	2,747	2,185
5731 Radio, TV, & electronic stores	33	31	346	395	13	15,595	15,089	5,088	5,541
5735 Record & prerecorded tape stores[3]	21	17	113	91	5	8,319	11,824	869	881
5812 Eating places	710	674	13,876	13,547	20	7,622	7,956	114,426	114,557
5813 Drinking places	161	139	758	822	6	7,404	7,212	5,795	6,111

Continued on next page.

DES MOINES, IA MSA - [continued]

Wholesale and Retail Trade USA	Establishments		Employment		Emp / Est	Pay / Employee		Annual Payroll ($ 000)	
	1994	1995	1994	1995	1995	1994	1995	1994	1995
5910 Drug stores and proprietary stores	75	77	1,002	1,015	13	15,082	16,323	15,968	17,150
5920 Liquor stores [3]	10	9	37	114	13	10,486	7,614	538	695
5930 Used merchandise stores	46	42	180	172	4	9,422	9,535	1,828	1,797
5941 Sporting goods and bicycle shops [1]	47	49	289	384	8	10,768	11,094	4,177	4,681
5942 Book stores [3]	24	23	248	215	9	7,581	9,916	2,153	2,417
5944 Jewelry stores	44	47	309	255	5	18,265	20,894	5,721	4,931
5945 Hobby, toy, and game shops [3]	24	22	213	222	10	9,333	9,351	2,405	2,382
5946 Camera & photographic supply stores [3]	8	8	49	54	7	13,633	13,407	698	776
5947 Gift, novelty, and souvenir shops	76	71	521	535	8	7,163	7,843	4,010	4,465
5949 Sewing, needlework, and piece goods [3]	19	15	152	98	7	6,842	7,714	1,054	776
5961 Catalog and mail-order houses [2]	-	9	-	63	7	-	12,571	-	817
5962 Merchandising machine operators [2]	-	30	-	332	11	-	11,783	-	4,223
5963 Direct selling establishments	38	36	569	612	17	17,237	18,183	9,674	10,944
5980 Fuel dealers	-	6	-	31	5	-	21,548	-	653
5992 Florists	-	44	-	249	6	-	10,988	-	3,031
5994 News dealers and newsstands [2]	-	3	-	6	2	-	4,000	-	32
5995 Optical goods stores [3]	38	44	211	205	5	14,654	16,293	3,679	3,935
5999 Miscellaneous retail stores, nec	85	86	450	449	5	14,196	15,359	7,203	7,314

Source: County Business Patterns 1994/95, CBP-94/95, U.S. Department of Commerce, Washington DC, November 1997. The employment column represents mid-March employment in the year. Pay per employee is calculated by dividing 1st Quarter payroll, annualized, by mid-March employment. The column headed 'Emp / Est' shows 'employees per establishment'. A dash (-) means that data are unavailable or cannot be calculated. nec means not elsewhere classified. *Notes:* 1. 1994 data incomplete; unavailable or withheld. 2. 1995 data incomplete; unavailable or withheld. 3. 1994 and 1995 data incomplete; unavailable or withheld.

DETROIT, MI PMSA

Wholesale and Retail Trade USA	Establishments		Employment		Emp / Est	Pay / Employee		Annual Payroll ($ 000)	
	1994	1995	1994	1995	1995	1994	1995	1994	1995
50- Wholesale trade	7,810	7,932	108,667	114,946	14	35,863	40,172	4,296,801	4,874,551
5012 Automobiles and other vehicles [3]	122	126	2,247	2,695	21	48,781	54,713	107,494	136,142
5013 Motor vehicle supplies and new parts	744	709	12,510	15,924	22	39,583	44,486	542,522	741,962
5014 Tires and tubes [3]	44	47	400	453	10	32,340	32,574	13,783	14,233
5015 Motor vehicle parts, used	76	93	503	797	9	21,113	21,671	12,492	17,968
5021 Furniture [3]	90	85	955	941	11	33,466	36,060	34,889	42,342
5023 Homefurnishings [3]	101	91	833	1,276	14	26,761	25,382	31,109	34,928
5031 Lumber, plywood, and millwork	115	112	1,394	1,456	13	31,225	32,830	56,452	56,664
5032 Brick, stone, & related materials	74	68	590	573	8	30,061	37,145	22,439	23,823
5033 Roofing, siding, & insulation [3]	56	51	603	632	12	37,015	40,354	25,062	25,627
5039 Construction materials, nec [1]	52	85	459	797	9	29,743	33,797	16,521	30,706
5043 Photographic equipment & supplies [3]	13	14	123	143	10	34,114	29,399	4,792	4,354
5044 Office equipment	96	90	2,108	2,136	24	35,332	40,367	75,671	81,682
5045 Computers, peripherals, & software [3]	279	263	5,898	4,796	18	50,808	62,065	274,663	266,914
5046 Commercial equipment, nec [3]	93	93	657	726	8	28,298	29,267	20,642	22,472
5047 Medical and hospital equipment	172	173	2,693	2,421	14	32,186	37,735	100,229	100,226
5048 Ophthalmic goods [3]	26	25	187	182	7	22,096	25,055	4,703	4,997
5049 Professional equipment, nec [3]	30	30	313	341	11	29,917	26,991	9,785	10,184
5051 Metals service centers and offices [3]	381	375	2,701	2,819	8	46,380	50,306	137,376	151,624
5063 Electrical apparatus and equipment [1]	285	254	3,866	4,245	17	41,310	46,327	176,662	194,439
5064 Electrical appliances, TV & radios [3]	58	59	630	616	10	33,638	40,714	22,991	27,036
5065 Electronic parts and equipment [3]	229	264	2,366	3,037	12	44,904	46,560	111,238	141,340
5072 Hardware	182	197	1,796	1,931	10	31,403	34,086	67,199	80,984
5074 Plumbing & hydronic heating supplies	127	118	1,146	1,287	11	32,890	32,528	41,755	45,786
5075 Warm air heating & air conditioning [3]	90	92	784	839	9	36,209	40,362	34,082	38,817
5078 Refrigeration equipment and supplies [3]	15	14	108	77	6	28,296	32,935	4,499	3,453
5082 Construction and mining machinery [3]	43	41	670	608	15	36,203	42,092	27,373	31,458
5083 Farm and garden machinery	48	41	542	482	12	26,768	30,407	18,200	17,019
5084 Industrial machinery and equipment	748	748	7,692	8,453	11	38,768	43,727	356,890	400,834
5085 Industrial supplies	335	335	3,896	4,336	13	37,152	40,093	167,558	190,690
5087 Service establishment equipment [3]	109	110	1,236	1,257	11	24,663	26,253	35,842	43,265
5088 Transportation equipment & supplies [3]	42	39	276	243	6	29,217	30,551	9,674	10,119
5091 Sporting & recreational goods	73	72	474	477	7	23,080	24,562	16,072	15,160
5092 Toys and hobby goods and supplies [1]	29	32	266	178	6	19,308	24,539	5,690	5,357
5093 Scrap and waste materials	167	172	1,804	2,054	12	29,463	31,470	67,769	86,250
5094 Jewelry & precious stones [3]	78	80	668	625	8	35,503	36,358	20,039	20,132
5099 Durable goods, nec [1]	155	164	585	691	4	31,487	37,001	22,928	31,510
5111 Printing and writing paper [3]	43	45	550	599	13	42,851	54,411	23,612	32,686
5112 Stationery and office supplies [2]	193	174	2,969	2,562	15	22,782	25,048	73,418	70,439
5113 Industrial & personal service paper [3]	75	75	1,036	924	12	37,220	42,087	40,929	45,661
5120 Drugs, proprietaries, and sundries [3]	65	71	1,874	1,842	26	31,127	33,878	63,115	68,133
5131 Piece goods & notions [3]	51	53	373	394	7	34,241	43,990	14,885	16,722

Continued on next page.

DETROIT, MI PMSA - [continued]

Wholesale and Retail Trade USA	Establishments		Employment		Emp / Est	Pay / Employee		Annual Payroll ($ 000)	
	1994	1995	1994	1995	1995	1994	1995	1994	1995
5136 Men's and boys' clothing[3]	36	34	632	724	21	26,576	28,254	22,083	25,719
5137 Women's and children's clothing[3]	32	29	122	134	5	22,066	39,612	3,288	3,478
5141 Groceries, general line[1]	62	62	3,080	2,968	48	29,422	30,760	98,912	93,937
5142 Packaged frozen food[3]	51	49	839	950	19	30,741	27,844	29,575	31,166
5143 Dairy products, exc. dried or canned[3]	50	46	1,024	1,042	23	31,320	33,263	36,292	36,893
5144 Poultry and poultry products[3]	11	10	72	74	7	28,111	30,324	2,425	2,571
5145 Confectionery[3]	37	41	947	945	23	24,139	27,450	24,030	28,731
5146 Fish and seafoods[3]	16	16	235	229	14	22,519	23,738	6,337	6,474
5147 Meats and meat products	75	75	1,400	1,442	19	23,634	25,110	39,489	38,968
5148 Fresh fruits and vegetables[2]	70	68	891	841	12	25,625	28,951	30,580	30,375
5149 Groceries and related products, nec[3]	191	185	5,667	5,414	29	25,651	30,777	166,334	177,122
5153 Grain and field beans	-	15	-	46	3	-	20,957	-	1,177
5159 Farm-product raw materials, nec[3]	7	8	28	30	4	16,286	13,333	692	637
5162 Plastics materials & basic shapes[3]	112	112	1,291	1,316	12	48,998	52,933	71,787	71,351
5169 Chemicals & allied products, nec[3]	169	169	2,023	2,214	13	48,734	53,615	104,917	123,946
5171 Petroleum bulk stations & terminals[2]	57	52	1,019	1,006	19	37,574	40,171	41,572	42,524
5172 Petroleum products, nec[3]	26	22	200	187	9	34,240	33,647	7,467	6,649
5181 Beer and ale[3]	22	24	1,058	1,059	44	32,601	35,120	40,175	43,092
5182 Wine and distilled beverages[3]	38	34	1,110	1,166	34	40,404	43,033	46,126	50,650
5191 Farm supplies	47	42	313	291	7	25,917	31,725	8,795	10,371
5192 Books, periodicals, & newspapers	63	60	939	894	15	32,341	35,007	33,486	33,218
5193 Flowers & florists' supplies[3]	48	45	550	592	13	18,713	19,676	12,311	12,845
5194 Tobacco and tobacco products[3]	19	19	356	311	16	19,719	25,916	8,320	8,349
5198 Paints, varnishes, and supplies[3]	58	70	516	608	9	37,031	36,230	20,171	21,731
5199 Nondurable goods, nec[2]	205	207	1,076	1,247	6	26,301	30,310	36,646	42,495
52 – Retail trade	23,771	23,629	353,048	359,289	15	12,863	14,039	5,116,278	5,468,146
5210 Lumber and other building materials	325	297	6,405	7,342	25	19,166	21,937	141,973	173,392
5230 Paint, glass, and wallpaper stores	121	114	653	592	5	16,227	16,081	11,584	11,120
5250 Hardware stores	319	249	2,803	2,538	10	13,751	14,380	43,026	36,432
5260 Retail nurseries and garden stores	173	175	1,639	1,755	10	13,335	13,908	31,273	33,463
5270 Mobile home dealers[3]	38	36	231	318	9	22,719	23,509	7,816	10,042
5310 Department stores[3]	163	161	39,876	41,306	257	10,748	11,695	477,668	522,726
5330 Variety stores	148	128	1,247	1,425	11	8,616	8,067	11,533	12,968
5390 Misc. general merchandise stores[1]	101	94	3,275	3,441	37	11,844	13,383	42,695	43,503
5410 Grocery stores	2,153	2,105	33,562	36,301	17	13,774	13,807	491,018	525,462
5420 Meat and fish markets	152	137	850	760	6	12,169	13,000	12,652	11,058
5430 Fruit and vegetable markets	59	60	1,279	1,403	23	9,780	10,178	15,350	18,189
5440 Candy, nut, and confectionery stores[3]	81	82	581	563	7	8,227	14,231	5,777	6,336
5450 Dairy products stores	45	46	99	138	3	5,212	4,667	660	861
5460 Retail bakeries	451	432	3,479	3,188	7	9,380	9,108	35,627	30,404
5490 Miscellaneous food stores	132	117	682	686	6	9,959	9,708	7,248	7,324
5510 New and used car dealers	293	298	16,647	17,650	59	31,798	35,121	706,398	756,826
5520 Used car dealers	163	162	505	552	3	20,523	23,254	11,863	14,085
5530 Auto and home supply stores	532	552	4,301	4,341	8	16,795	17,884	78,601	90,023
5540 Gasoline service stations	1,592	1,624	10,082	9,495	6	10,388	11,482	108,464	110,700
5550 Boat dealers	65	60	484	511	9	17,752	20,008	13,101	14,679
5560 Recreational vehicle dealers[3]	31	29	307	321	11	24,599	22,143	9,919	9,779
5570 Motorcycle dealers[3]	29	29	192	228	8	18,792	21,175	5,276	6,241
5590 Automotive dealers, nec[3]	12	9	85	83	9	21,600	23,277	2,160	2,249
5610 Men's & boys' clothing stores[2]	273	245	2,141	1,872	8	13,943	15,274	31,791	28,829
5620 Women's clothing stores	796	717	10,814	9,275	13	9,531	9,994	113,878	94,241
5630 Women's accessory & specialty stores[3]	150	145	902	826	6	10,785	11,927	11,080	10,948
5640 Children's and infants' wear stores[3]	67	70	678	712	10	7,298	8,006	5,708	6,051
5650 Family clothing stores	227	222	3,994	3,940	18	9,915	10,999	43,472	44,762
5660 Shoe stores	660	594	3,637	3,617	6	11,679	12,431	46,042	44,535
5690 Misc. apparel & accessory stores[3]	115	116	668	676	6	9,162	10,237	7,034	7,153
5712 Furniture stores	363	368	3,961	4,182	11	20,271	21,999	91,896	97,681
5713 Floor covering stores	210	211	1,453	1,622	8	21,401	23,028	35,539	41,306
5714 Drapery and upholstery stores[3]	54	47	258	256	5	12,202	13,375	3,502	3,685
5719 Misc. homefurnishings stores[1]	254	244	2,170	1,887	8	11,928	13,384	28,122	26,688
5720 Household appliance stores	90	88	454	426	5	21,295	25,906	9,873	10,620
5731 Radio, TV, & electronic stores	225	218	2,462	2,704	12	15,724	16,697	43,732	45,979
5734 Computer and software stores[1]	87	103	974	1,096	11	18,033	20,690	20,615	24,507
5735 Record & prerecorded tape stores[3]	138	145	1,062	1,224	8	9,168	9,212	10,379	11,782
5736 Musical instrument stores[3]	62	66	398	469	7	19,206	20,247	8,815	10,511
5812 Eating places	5,418	4,989	113,640	110,727	22	7,719	8,314	952,131	969,802
5813 Drinking places	901	798	5,931	5,624	7	7,922	8,433	49,323	48,551
5910 Drug stores and proprietary stores	772	743	12,506	12,897	17	13,198	15,343	163,581	205,729
5920 Liquor stores	532	533	2,036	1,986	4	10,314	10,588	22,035	22,733
5930 Used merchandise stores	194	197	1,707	1,681	9	11,890	12,366	23,409	23,493
5941 Sporting goods and bicycle shops	351	360	2,776	2,876	8	12,640	13,579	41,047	43,964

Continued on next page.

DETROIT, MI PMSA - [continued]

Wholesale and Retail Trade USA	Establishments		Employment		Emp / Est	Pay / Employee		Annual Payroll ($ 000)	
	1994	1995	1994	1995	1995	1994	1995	1994	1995
5942 Book stores	172	166	1,335	1,462	9	9,127	10,613	12,750	15,927
5943 Stationery stores[3]	60	65	281	469	7	12,726	19,386	3,543	9,908
5944 Jewelry stores	428	432	2,410	2,373	5	18,425	21,116	50,152	50,145
5945 Hobby, toy, and game shops	146	139	1,678	1,815	13	9,640	9,060	19,355	20,428
5946 Camera & photographic supply stores[3]	33	32	176	163	5	16,068	17,325	3,168	3,231
5947 Gift, novelty, and souvenir shops	423	417	3,013	3,069	7	7,531	8,438	25,984	29,509
5948 Luggage and leather goods stores[3]	33	38	120	172	5	13,233	13,884	1,782	2,315
5949 Sewing, needlework, and piece goods	101	95	1,238	980	10	6,194	7,029	7,756	7,375
5961 Catalog and mail-order houses	54	69	551	650	9	17,619	20,572	10,227	14,011
5962 Merchandising machine operators[1]	99	115	1,247	1,224	11	18,050	19,261	24,475	25,239
5963 Direct selling establishments	194	192	1,972	1,798	9	17,087	19,497	37,487	36,422
5983 Fuel oil dealers	18	19	64	64	3	26,625	26,813	1,444	1,742
5984 Liquefied petroleum gas dealers	20	17	77	55	3	27,169	23,564	1,971	1,320
5992 Florists	358	344	2,142	2,194	6	10,627	11,263	24,906	26,050
5993 Tobacco stores and stands[3]	34	46	152	114	2	12,526	15,754	1,574	1,900
5994 News dealers and newsstands[3]	17	14	51	52	4	13,020	12,692	705	792
5995 Optical goods stores[1]	263	260	1,454	1,323	5	19,755	21,457	30,619	30,084
5999 Miscellaneous retail stores, nec	698	761	4,282	5,125	7	15,889	16,297	77,000	91,481

Source: County Business Patterns 1994/95, CBP-94/95, U.S. Department of Commerce, Washington DC, November 1997. The employment column represents mid-March employment in the year. Pay per employee is calculated by dividing 1st Quarter payroll, annualized, by mid-March employment. The column headed 'Emp / Est' shows 'employees per establishment'. A dash (-) means that data are unavailable or cannot be calculated. nec means not elsewhere classified. *Notes:* 1. 1994 data incomplete; unavailable or withheld. 2. 1995 data incomplete; unavailable or withheld. 3. 1994 and 1995 data incomplete; unavailable or withheld.

DOTHAN, AL MSA

Wholesale and Retail Trade USA	Establishments		Employment		Emp / Est	Pay / Employee		Annual Payroll ($ 000)	
	1994	1995	1994	1995	1995	1994	1995	1994	1995
50- Wholesale trade	302	308	3,776	3,588	12	19,612	21,685	77,814	81,104
5012 Automobiles and other vehicles	16	15	367	405	27	21,493	25,748	8,505	10,273
5013 Motor vehicle supplies and new parts	25	18	191	166	9	18,010	18,386	3,753	3,345
5021 Furniture	-	5	-	34	7	-	19,294	-	648
5023 Homefurnishings[2]	-	4	-	94	24	-	19,830	-	1,962
5039 Construction materials, nec	-	4	-	48	12	-	16,250	-	800
5044 Office equipment[3]	8	11	65	76	7	20,246	22,053	1,544	1,719
5045 Computers, peripherals, & software	6	-	12	-	-	29,667	-	471	-
5046 Commercial equipment, nec[3]	5	6	25	28	5	26,720	24,143	656	748
5047 Medical and hospital equipment[3]	5	3	86	51	17	14,419	14,980	1,000	744
5051 Metals service centers and offices[3]	3	3	46	39	13	17,217	22,667	857	832
5063 Electrical apparatus and equipment	10	12	260	204	17	25,138	26,961	5,222	5,913
5072 Hardware[3]	5	5	43	44	9	26,698	27,364	1,252	1,292
5074 Plumbing & hydronic heating supplies[3]	4	3	99	100	33	20,525	22,400	2,561	2,626
5075 Warm air heating & air conditioning	6	7	28	37	5	27,857	19,243	761	868
5083 Farm and garden machinery	11	11	90	98	9	19,867	20,122	2,117	2,350
5084 Industrial machinery and equipment[3]	11	11	54	65	6	20,963	22,031	1,268	1,770
5085 Industrial supplies[3]	13	13	104	122	9	23,808	29,902	2,701	3,200
5087 Service establishment equipment[3]	5	5	25	21	4	20,160	21,714	505	497
5094 Jewelry & precious stones[2]	-	3	-	14	5	-	21,429	-	242
5112 Stationery and office supplies	14	10	104	106	11	18,000	16,528	1,882	1,837
5113 Industrial & personal service paper[3]	4	4	69	58	15	27,304	28,207	2,009	1,442
5149 Groceries and related products, nec	12	12	214	221	18	17,458	19,023	4,312	4,301
5150 Farm-product raw materials	12	12	58	58	5	9,379	16,345	580	1,009
5160 Chemicals and allied products[2]	-	7	-	47	7	-	22,723	-	1,068
5170 Petroleum and petroleum products	6	6	53	33	6	26,113	25,333	1,357	854
5180 Beer, wine, and distilled beverages[3]	5	4	71	71	18	29,070	28,563	2,124	2,154
5191 Farm supplies	24	25	181	192	8	15,448	16,813	3,515	3,534
5192 Books, periodicals, & newspapers	-	5	-	26	5	-	15,231	-	653
5199 Nondurable goods, nec	-	6	-	15	3	-	15,733	-	292
52- Retail trade	970	965	11,095	11,645	12	10,985	11,578	131,055	140,938
5210 Lumber and other building materials	24	17	380	317	19	15,737	18,625	6,614	6,752
5230 Paint, glass, and wallpaper stores	9	8	78	66	8	19,385	20,000	1,574	1,406
5250 Hardware stores	8	-	38	-	-	11,474	-	457	-
5260 Retail nurseries and garden stores[1]	5	-	30	-	-	10,933	-	332	-
5270 Mobile home dealers[3]	11	10	113	96	10	14,690	20,250	2,101	2,010
5310 Department stores[3]	10	10	1,234	1,185	119	11,018	13,303	14,514	15,312
5330 Variety stores	-	12	-	21	2	-	9,143	-	204
5410 Grocery stores	114	114	1,680	1,719	15	8,231	9,315	15,246	17,061
5460 Retail bakeries	8	8	43	32	4	7,163	8,125	303	273
5510 New and used car dealers[2]	13	13	453	471	36	28,512	31,847	13,657	14,673
5520 Used car dealers	24	20	99	66	3	29,818	29,455	1,897	1,892

Continued on next page.

DOTHAN, AL MSA - [continued]

Wholesale and Retail Trade USA	Establishments		Employment		Emp / Est	Pay / Employee		Annual Payroll ($ 000)	
	1994	1995	1994	1995	1995	1994	1995	1994	1995
5530 Auto and home supply stores	36	43	196	252	6	14,061	15,048	3,366	4,470
5540 Gasoline service stations	64	61	305	354	6	9,207	8,215	3,230	3,411
5550 Boat dealers	5	4	31	14	4	12,129	11,429	436	177
5570 Motorcycle dealers	6	6	25	25	4	15,840	20,000	518	764
5610 Men's & boys' clothing stores	9	11	56	54	5	6,571	7,037	332	390
5620 Women's clothing stores	31	26	232	193	7	6,914	7,067	1,754	1,402
5650 Family clothing stores	13	12	222	200	17	13,099	14,560	3,165	2,940
5660 Shoe stores	23	22	113	89	4	10,867	11,596	1,272	1,001
5690 Misc. apparel & accessory stores [2]	5	4	10	20	5	11,200	10,800	137	216
5712 Furniture stores	25	26	108	121	5	15,852	15,207	1,957	2,139
5713 Floor covering stores	12	12	63	60	5	18,540	22,000	1,260	1,415
5720 Household appliance stores	10	11	39	44	4	12,923	13,545	524	580
5731 Radio, TV, & electronic stores	12	15	53	57	4	17,057	16,351	950	1,387
5734 Computer and software stores [1]	4	5	18	13	3	6,222	10,462	102	154
5735 Record & prerecorded tape stores [2]	-	3	-	28	9	-	7,429	-	225
5736 Musical instrument stores [2]	-	5	-	21	4	-	9,905	-	203
5812 Eating places	168	159	3,232	3,549	22	7,410	7,052	25,559	25,590
5813 Drinking places	20	18	119	124	7	6,185	8,194	797	768
5910 Drug stores and proprietary stores	30	27	230	246	9	19,913	18,813	4,586	4,368
5920 Liquor stores	8	8	17	23	3	14,118	10,957	228	271
5930 Used merchandise stores	17	20	59	63	3	7,932	9,778	522	634
5941 Sporting goods and bicycle shops	14	14	31	7	1	12,000	6,857	433	58
5942 Book stores [3]	5	8	27	30	4	7,407	7,067	210	318
5943 Stationery stores [1]	3	-	11	-	-	4,727	-	84	-
5944 Jewelry stores	16	19	122	156	8	16,885	14,154	2,207	2,306
5945 Hobby, toy, and game shops	6	6	36	47	8	10,889	9,702	535	598
5947 Gift, novelty, and souvenir shops	16	17	85	71	4	7,765	9,296	649	547
5949 Sewing, needlework, and piece goods	7	7	37	32	5	8,757	9,750	308	299
5963 Direct selling establishments [3]	13	11	106	92	8	13,623	15,000	1,422	1,522
5984 Liquefied petroleum gas dealers	4	-	11	-	-	15,273	-	249	-
5992 Florists	26	22	93	80	4	7,398	8,200	723	682
5995 Optical goods stores	7	6	3	4	1	32,000	31,000	115	111
5999 Miscellaneous retail stores, nec	34	35	90	142	4	12,356	12,028	1,301	1,826

Source: County Business Patterns 1994/95, CBP-94/95, U.S. Department of Commerce, Washington DC, November 1997. The employment column represents mid-March employment in the year. Pay per employee is calculated by dividing 1st Quarter payroll, annualized, by mid-March employment. The column headed 'Emp / Est' shows 'employees per establishment'. A dash (-) means that data are unavailable or cannot be calculated. nec means not elsewhere classified. *Notes:* 1. 1994 data incomplete; unavailable or withheld. 2. 1995 data incomplete; unavailable or withheld. 3. 1994 and 1995 data incomplete; unavailable or withheld.

DOVER, DE MSA

Wholesale and Retail Trade USA	Establishments		Employment		Emp / Est	Pay / Employee		Annual Payroll ($ 000)	
	1994	1995	1994	1995	1995	1994	1995	1994	1995
50- Wholesale trade	167	159	1,285	1,310	8	23,421	24,021	32,770	32,271
5012 Automobiles and other vehicles	3	3	13	12	4	19,692	31,333	284	433
5013 Motor vehicle supplies and new parts	16	15	80	86	6	20,750	19,581	1,791	2,012
5023 Homefurnishings	4	-	23	-	-	17,043	-	463	-
5030 Lumber and construction materials	8	7	73	56	8	21,973	24,071	2,091	1,415
5040 Professional & commercial equipment	15	14	63	39	3	19,683	25,641	1,422	1,120
5060 Electrical goods	11	11	101	104	9	27,010	26,500	3,024	3,064
5072 Hardware	4	-	13	-	-	22,769	-	307	-
5074 Plumbing & hydronic heating supplies	7	5	31	36	7	21,032	22,000	730	744
5083 Farm and garden machinery	8	7	54	54	8	21,111	20,667	1,433	1,363
5084 Industrial machinery and equipment	6	5	8	6	1	20,500	19,333	199	100
5093 Scrap and waste materials	8	7	28	43	6	15,571	13,953	966	695
5099 Durable goods, nec	4	4	43	31	8	10,326	14,968	534	532
5112 Stationery and office supplies	4	4	60	52	13	16,267	18,462	952	975
5113 Industrial & personal service paper	3	4	34	37	9	16,118	17,838	665	788
5148 Fresh fruits and vegetables	3	-	3	-	-	21,333	-	68	-
5149 Groceries and related products, nec	5	5	72	87	17	15,611	25,287	1,483	2,463
5170 Petroleum and petroleum products	-	4	-	21	5	-	33,714	-	768
5191 Farm supplies	10	11	77	80	7	20,623	21,200	1,703	1,728
52- Retail trade	768	770	10,454	10,775	14	11,333	12,157	134,894	135,880
5210 Lumber and other building materials	15	17	404	408	24	16,554	18,706	7,231	8,453
5260 Retail nurseries and garden stores	9	11	66	100	9	19,758	16,280	1,775	1,808
5270 Mobile home dealers	12	-	152	-	-	20,211	-	4,275	-
5390 Misc. general merchandise stores	3	6	250	285	48	13,984	13,839	3,486	3,732
5410 Grocery stores	70	66	1,199	1,151	17	12,554	13,439	14,775	15,495
5420 Meat and fish markets	4	3	13	16	5	10,769	9,750	196	216
5460 Retail bakeries	7	5	60	44	9	15,467	10,000	971	444

Continued on next page.

DOVER, DE MSA - [continued]

Wholesale and Retail Trade USA	Establishments		Employment		Emp / Est	Pay / Employee		Annual Payroll ($ 000)	
	1994	1995	1994	1995	1995	1994	1995	1994	1995
5510 New and used car dealers	19	17	654	712	42	21,670	23,000	17,830	17,546
5520 Used car dealers	15	16	79	71	4	22,177	26,028	2,705	3,212
5530 Auto and home supply stores	12	12	107	105	9	15,664	17,333	1,859	1,879
5540 Gasoline service stations	46	46	306	328	7	10,327	10,598	3,525	3,417
5560 Recreational vehicle dealers	3	-	19	-	-	14,947	-	361	-
5610 Men's & boys' clothing stores	10	10	66	69	7	7,939	8,406	568	562
5620 Women's clothing stores	20	15	235	194	13	7,098	6,804	1,890	1,289
5630 Women's accessory & specialty stores	4	4	24	23	6	7,167	9,043	216	184
5650 Family clothing stores	8	7	87	77	11	7,954	8,883	783	742
5660 Shoe stores	15	13	80	75	6	12,400	10,880	1,104	864
5712 Furniture stores	14	16	145	151	9	17,159	19,364	2,762	2,766
5719 Misc. homefurnishings stores	-	7	-	31	4	-	8,000	-	224
5720 Household appliance stores	6	6	27	33	6	9,333	10,424	309	322
5731 Radio, TV, & electronic stores	9	9	44	39	4	15,364	15,385	632	531
5734 Computer and software stores	4	-	17	-	-	10,824	-	224	-
5812 Eating places	175	162	3,440	3,356	21	6,707	7,361	26,792	23,951
5813 Drinking places	13	14	135	114	8	6,163	8,737	874	950
5910 Drug stores and proprietary stores	20	19	217	247	13	15,853	14,186	3,621	3,800
5920 Liquor stores	33	35	152	147	4	7,500	7,429	1,172	1,165
5930 Used merchandise stores	10	11	66	64	6	10,545	10,625	734	771
5941 Sporting goods and bicycle shops	10	12	18	23	2	10,667	9,913	233	286
5942 Book stores	-	7	-	28	4	-	7,000	-	240
5944 Jewelry stores	10	11	56	69	6	15,929	16,174	991	1,101
5945 Hobby, toy, and game shops	5	5	49	53	11	10,041	10,792	649	695
5947 Gift, novelty, and souvenir shops	11	12	60	63	5	3,867	5,206	391	620
5949 Sewing, needlework, and piece goods	8	-	55	-	-	6,182	-	346	-
5960 Nonstore retailers	11	11	121	120	11	16,727	17,967	2,233	2,265
5983 Fuel oil dealers	9	8	53	54	7	16,679	13,333	928	765
5984 Liquefied petroleum gas dealers	7	7	73	85	12	24,877	16,847	1,603	1,452
5992 Florists	11	12	92	108	9	10,435	10,222	1,102	1,101
5999 Miscellaneous retail stores, nec	24	23	95	96	4	15,200	15,083	1,983	1,971

Source: County Business Patterns 1994/95, CBP-94/95, U.S. Department of Commerce, Washington DC, November 1997. The employment column represents mid-March employment in the year. Pay per employee is calculated by dividing 1st Quarter payroll, annualized, by mid-March employment. The column headed 'Emp / Est' shows 'employees per establishment'. A dash (-) means that data are unavailable or cannot be calculated. nec means not elsewhere classified. *Notes:* 1. 1994 data incomplete; unavailable or withheld. 2. 1995 data incomplete; unavailable or withheld. 3. 1994 and 1995 data incomplete; unavailable or withheld.

DUBUQUE, IA MSA

Wholesale and Retail Trade USA	Establishments		Employment		Emp / Est	Pay / Employee		Annual Payroll ($ 000)	
	1994	1995	1994	1995	1995	1994	1995	1994	1995
50- Wholesale trade	214	209	2,194	2,163	10	20,873	22,273	52,515	53,162
5013 Motor vehicle supplies and new parts	10	-	123	-	-	19,772	-	2,246	-
5015 Motor vehicle parts, used	3	4	20	66	17	20,600	20,182	447	1,461
5031 Lumber, plywood, and millwork	4	-	128	-	-	19,188	-	3,694	-
5032 Brick, stone, & related materials	6	4	30	18	5	12,667	15,333	494	384
5044 Office equipment	10	10	50	52	5	20,080	25,385	1,344	1,419
5045 Computers, peripherals, & software	8	8	33	51	6	27,879	23,843	1,069	1,460
5046 Commercial equipment, nec	3	3	13	12	4	19,385	17,667	243	158
5063 Electrical apparatus and equipment	9	7	73	77	11	26,027	27,325	2,154	2,212
5065 Electronic parts and equipment	-	3	-	5	2	-	30,400	-	159
5074 Plumbing & hydronic heating supplies	4	3	39	39	13	26,051	25,949	1,148	1,075
5075 Warm air heating & air conditioning	3	3	31	36	12	24,387	23,222	774	889
5083 Farm and garden machinery	12	15	133	139	9	19,850	20,863	3,284	3,358
5084 Industrial machinery and equipment	5	6	68	73	12	29,765	29,205	1,974	2,194
5085 Industrial supplies	7	5	30	31	6	23,333	28,645	733	836
5093 Scrap and waste materials	8	-	66	-	-	13,333	-	1,189	-
5099 Durable goods, nec	-	6	-	54	9	-	21,259	-	1,075
5112 Stationery and office supplies	-	4	-	19	5	-	20,842	-	410
5113 Industrial & personal service paper	-	3	-	32	11	-	31,000	-	1,259
5120 Drugs, proprietaries, and sundries	3	-	26	-	-	26,462	-	798	-
5143 Dairy products, exc. dried or canned	4	-	21	-	-	12,571	-	323	-
5149 Groceries and related products, nec	5	5	74	83	17	19,568	20,337	1,650	1,822
5150 Farm-product raw materials	6	6	48	59	10	16,583	15,458	1,094	1,261
5160 Chemicals and allied products	4	3	13	15	5	17,538	15,467	227	238
5170 Petroleum and petroleum products	16	16	164	181	11	18,415	19,403	3,348	3,808
5181 Beer and ale	4	4	75	88	22	21,493	21,000	1,985	2,014
5191 Farm supplies	27	31	191	194	6	19,288	18,392	4,261	4,493
52- Retail trade	701	687	9,128	9,372	14	10,587	11,490	105,337	112,150
5210 Lumber and other building materials	21	18	267	316	18	22,157	23,633	5,717	7,267

Continued on next page.

DUBUQUE, IA MSA - [continued]

Wholesale and Retail Trade USA	Establishments		Employment		Emp / Est	Pay / Employee		Annual Payroll ($ 000)	
	1994	1995	1994	1995	1995	1994	1995	1994	1995
5230 Paint, glass, and wallpaper stores	-	6	-	21	4	-	24,571	-	466
5250 Hardware stores	9	8	102	102	13	13,176	14,196	1,332	1,335
5260 Retail nurseries and garden stores	6	6	60	60	10	15,333	15,733	1,090	1,258
5310 Department stores	8	8	1,220	1,209	151	9,000	10,422	12,343	12,859
5330 Variety stores	5	3	15	20	7	8,533	7,200	161	192
5390 Misc. general merchandise stores	3	3	87	76	25	10,943	12,368	955	910
5410 Grocery stores	43	39	1,169	1,194	31	10,214	10,931	13,206	13,982
5460 Retail bakeries	8	5	36	32	6	8,556	8,750	312	281
5510 New and used car dealers	14	13	381	316	24	23,906	25,696	11,045	8,695
5520 Used car dealers	9	9	24	27	3	17,833	16,296	488	445
5530 Auto and home supply stores	10	14	110	152	11	17,345	17,395	2,134	3,076
5540 Gasoline service stations	53	48	407	402	8	8,226	8,547	3,524	3,501
5550 Boat dealers	-	3	-	2	1	-	8,000	-	69
5570 Motorcycle dealers	3	3	34	37	12	11,882	12,649	539	639
5590 Automotive dealers, nec	-	3	-	11	4	-	11,636	-	204
5610 Men's & boys' clothing stores	4	4	29	31	8	11,724	9,806	312	293
5620 Women's clothing stores	26	22	184	168	8	7,957	7,381	1,873	1,713
5630 Women's accessory & specialty stores	5	5	28	24	5	16,714	15,000	368	324
5650 Family clothing stores	5	4	37	36	9	6,486	7,667	284	241
5660 Shoe stores	15	16	106	106	7	8,566	8,755	943	972
5712 Furniture stores	19	17	118	129	8	15,763	15,690	2,131	2,222
5713 Floor covering stores	7	10	52	68	7	16,923	17,294	1,239	1,414
5720 Household appliance stores	5	7	30	41	6	15,067	15,610	491	721
5731 Radio, TV, & electronic stores	8	9	34	37	4	22,941	30,378	735	779
5736 Musical instrument stores	4	3	32	28	9	13,250	12,000	358	315
5812 Eating places	149	145	2,861	2,906	20	6,371	6,602	19,974	20,359
5813 Drinking places	46	36	129	115	3	5,519	5,878	755	681
5910 Drug stores and proprietary stores	19	19	248	268	14	15,032	15,060	3,806	4,101
5920 Liquor stores	6	7	62	70	10	5,548	7,714	397	547
5930 Used merchandise stores	-	9	-	31	3	-	6,839	-	275
5941 Sporting goods and bicycle shops	12	11	63	75	7	6,857	6,507	679	644
5942 Book stores	5	5	30	29	6	5,600	6,759	168	202
5944 Jewelry stores	10	12	53	73	6	13,736	13,041	768	993
5945 Hobby, toy, and game shops	9	8	54	56	7	10,593	10,929	644	683
5947 Gift, novelty, and souvenir shops	27	26	151	142	5	6,225	7,437	1,235	1,232
5949 Sewing, needlework, and piece goods	3	-	40	-	-	4,400	-	177	-
5961 Catalog and mail-order houses	-	3	-	19	6	-	17,053	-	439
5962 Merchandising machine operators	3	3	169	169	56	16,355	16,331	3,076	3,167
5963 Direct selling establishments	-	9	-	98	11	-	8,327	-	942
5992 Florists	13	11	75	86	8	6,613	8,093	648	759
5995 Optical goods stores	6	7	32	38	5	17,875	18,947	643	689
5999 Miscellaneous retail stores, nec	22	23	102	138	6	11,451	12,609	1,716	1,992

Source: County Business Patterns 1994/95, CBP-94/95, U.S. Department of Commerce, Washington DC, November 1997. The employment column represents mid-March employment in the year. Pay per employee is calculated by dividing 1st Quarter payroll, annualized, by mid-March employment. The column headed 'Emp / Est' shows 'employees per establishment'. A dash (-) means that data are unavailable or cannot be calculated. nec means not elsewhere classified. *Notes:* 1. 1994 data incomplete; unavailable or withheld. 2. 1995 data incomplete; unavailable or withheld. 3. 1994 and 1995 data incomplete; unavailable or withheld.

DULUTH – SUPERIOR MSA (MN PART)

Wholesale and Retail Trade USA	Establishments		Employment		Emp / Est	Pay / Employee		Annual Payroll ($ 000)	
	1994	1995	1994	1995	1995	1994	1995	1994	1995
50– Wholesale trade	351	351	3,588	3,639	10	26,550	26,472	100,291	100,457
5012 Automobiles and other vehicles	6	5	81	69	14	26,963	29,275	2,250	2,028
5013 Motor vehicle supplies and new parts	26	23	199	187	8	19,136	21,540	4,025	4,109
5014 Tires and tubes	6	5	43	48	10	23,442	23,250	1,882	2,598
5015 Motor vehicle parts, used	7	7	40	40	6	11,800	12,900	513	557
5021 Furniture	4	-	31	-	-	21,548	-	718	-
5023 Homefurnishings	4	-	7	-	-	18,286	-	206	-
5031 Lumber, plywood, and millwork	10	7	135	101	14	28,267	31,881	4,580	2,705
5032 Brick, stone, & related materials	4	7	33	37	5	41,333	38,270	1,514	1,761
5044 Office equipment	8	10	110	125	13	22,545	23,264	2,487	4,228
5045 Computers, peripherals, & software	-	8	-	83	10	-	20,337	-	1,640
5047 Medical and hospital equipment	5	-	18	-	-	24,667	-	493	-
5050 Metals and minerals, except petroleum	6	6	36	38	6	23,889	24,211	918	971
5063 Electrical apparatus and equipment	13	15	84	129	9	34,905	33,953	2,736	4,373
5065 Electronic parts and equipment	-	7	-	20	3	-	34,800	-	708
5072 Hardware	6	6	64	70	12	23,500	24,229	2,028	2,068
5074 Plumbing & hydronic heating supplies	5	6	70	59	10	26,343	29,898	1,924	1,661
5082 Construction and mining machinery	28	29	308	335	12	35,234	36,788	11,656	12,775

Continued on next page.

DULUTH – SUPERIOR MSA (MN PART) - [continued]

Wholesale and Retail Trade USA	Establishments		Employment		Emp / Est	Pay / Employee		Annual Payroll ($ 000)	
	1994	1995	1994	1995	1995	1994	1995	1994	1995
5084 Industrial machinery and equipment	20	19	156	169	9	26,436	27,243	4,711	4,984
5085 Industrial supplies	26	23	152	154	7	28,184	33,065	4,464	5,218
5091 Sporting & recreational goods	6	6	55	52	9	12,873	16,308	844	780
5092 Toys and hobby goods and supplies	3	-	8	-	-	10,000	-	103	-
5093 Scrap and waste materials	14	14	113	134	10	19,186	20,687	2,762	3,184
5099 Durable goods, nec	-	5	-	15	3	-	16,267	-	364
5112 Stationery and office supplies	11	10	129	99	10	16,837	20,202	2,245	2,349
5113 Industrial & personal service paper	8	8	62	52	7	22,968	30,692	1,500	1,748
5130 Apparel, piece goods, and notions	4	-	20	-	-	60,400	-	621	-
5142 Packaged frozen food	3	-	38	-	-	16,105	-	731	-
5143 Dairy products, exc. dried or canned	6	5	16	12	2	24,750	18,333	325	237
5149 Groceries and related products, nec	12	11	181	209	19	24,133	24,842	4,855	5,490
5150 Farm-product raw materials	4	4	90	84	21	18,578	21,333	2,348	2,202
5160 Chemicals and allied products	-	5	-	37	7	-	78,811	-	2,845
5170 Petroleum and petroleum products	13	14	281	310	22	16,954	17,045	5,436	5,814
5181 Beer and ale	5	5	67	64	13	20,060	27,813	1,882	1,739
5182 Wine and distilled beverages	3	3	52	54	18	49,154	52,148	1,667	1,746
5190 Misc., nondurable goods	9	9	144	138	15	21,139	20,957	3,501	3,303
52- Retail trade	1,519	1,528	18,749	19,375	13	10,927	11,480	223,440	234,698
5210 Lumber and other building materials	42	34	579	542	16	16,829	17,269	10,497	9,542
5230 Paint, glass, and wallpaper stores	10	9	75	69	8	20,320	23,710	1,689	1,757
5250 Hardware stores	27	20	202	153	8	11,129	12,157	2,559	2,025
5310 Department stores	14	14	2,298	2,126	152	9,704	11,153	24,420	25,314
5330 Variety stores	3	-	23	-	-	8,348	-	155	-
5390 Misc. general merchandise stores	17	-	323	-	-	8,755	-	3,125	-
5410 Grocery stores	101	97	1,711	1,857	19	12,168	11,285	21,912	25,201
5420 Meat and fish markets	3	4	25	21	5	13,920	15,810	359	349
5440 Candy, nut, and confectionery stores	9	12	61	55	5	4,459	5,236	323	358
5460 Retail bakeries	21	20	185	129	6	8,346	10,326	1,714	1,387
5490 Miscellaneous food stores	7	8	34	37	5	8,235	7,568	296	319
5510 New and used car dealers	22	21	650	699	33	25,877	26,678	19,522	20,269
5520 Used car dealers	9	10	45	46	5	12,000	12,261	604	581
5530 Auto and home supply stores	30	32	181	184	6	14,829	15,717	3,082	3,490
5540 Gasoline service stations	132	123	1,051	1,068	9	8,696	9,146	9,955	10,197
5550 Boat dealers	10	9	59	53	6	13,424	15,396	921	975
5610 Men's & boys' clothing stores	17	18	100	98	5	9,280	9,551	954	966
5620 Women's clothing stores	56	52	425	361	7	7,586	6,748	3,612	2,514
5630 Women's accessory & specialty stores	4	4	19	16	4	8,632	10,250	170	173
5650 Family clothing stores	18	18	178	223	12	8,854	8,502	1,927	2,123
5660 Shoe stores	28	28	115	126	5	8,487	11,302	1,176	1,192
5690 Misc. apparel & accessory stores	6	4	31	27	7	9,032	9,333	302	265
5712 Furniture stores	27	26	233	214	8	16,481	18,561	4,271	4,180
5713 Floor covering stores	8	9	61	49	5	11,541	18,694	900	774
5714 Drapery and upholstery stores	-	3	-	3	1	-	12,000	-	48
5719 Misc. homefurnishings stores	-	9	-	63	7	-	13,524	-	896
5720 Household appliance stores	11	11	76	79	7	15,263	15,646	1,181	1,337
5731 Radio, TV, & electronic stores	13	13	130	161	12	13,723	13,292	1,945	2,261
5734 Computer and software stores	4	5	17	15	3	7,529	10,400	139	201
5735 Record & prerecorded tape stores	5	8	47	44	6	10,468	11,727	558	629
5736 Musical instrument stores	5	5	36	33	7	11,778	12,121	475	430
5812 Eating places	315	307	5,149	5,442	18	6,615	6,914	38,461	37,589
5813 Drinking places	102	101	663	683	7	6,842	6,946	4,727	5,645
5910 Drug stores and proprietary stores	42	41	510	476	12	13,035	14,824	7,313	6,984
5920 Liquor stores	49	55	257	293	5	8,576	8,232	2,489	2,576
5930 Used merchandise stores	17	14	62	63	5	6,258	8,000	434	435
5941 Sporting goods and bicycle shops	44	43	297	298	7	8,660	9,557	2,988	3,208
5944 Jewelry stores	18	17	104	108	6	15,923	18,593	1,790	1,836
5945 Hobby, toy, and game shops	17	14	71	120	9	9,127	7,567	872	1,051
5947 Gift, novelty, and souvenir shops	38	36	190	172	5	5,621	6,907	1,350	1,302
5949 Sewing, needlework, and piece goods	10	8	100	82	10	6,880	6,439	633	542
5961 Catalog and mail-order houses	8	12	704	907	76	8,176	9,499	6,325	9,021
5962 Merchandising machine operators	5	6	53	68	11	14,943	13,412	933	976
5963 Direct selling establishments	19	17	101	78	5	16,673	14,205	1,753	1,323
5983 Fuel oil dealers	10	10	98	106	11	22,245	23,585	2,728	2,978
5984 Liquefied petroleum gas dealers	10	10	67	69	7	23,164	24,464	1,566	1,597
5995 Optical goods stores	24	24	104	98	4	13,500	16,245	1,484	1,751
5999 Miscellaneous retail stores, nec	34	40	196	218	5	13,388	15,156	3,156	3,794

Source: County Business Patterns 1994/95, CBP-94/95, U.S. Department of Commerce, Washington DC, November 1997. The employment column represents mid-March employment in the year. Pay per employee is calculated by dividing 1st Quarter payroll, annualized, by mid-March employment. The column headed 'Emp / Est' shows 'employees per establishment'. A dash (-) means that data are unavailable or cannot be calculated. nec means not elsewhere classified. *Notes:* 1. 1994 data incomplete; unavailable or withheld. 2. 1995 data incomplete; unavailable or withheld. 3. 1994 and 1995 data incomplete; unavailable or withheld.

DULUTH – SUPERIOR MSA (WI PART)

Wholesale and Retail Trade USA	Establishments		Employment		Emp / Est	Pay / Employee		Annual Payroll ($ 000)	
	1994	1995	1994	1995	1995	1994	1995	1994	1995
50 – Wholesale trade	-	62	-	876	14	-	30,137	-	27,893
5010 Motor vehicles, parts, and supplies	-	6	-	42	7	-	13,333	-	634
5030 Lumber and construction materials	-	4	-	82	21	-	36,049	-	2,981
5040 Professional & commercial equipment	-	5	-	50	10	-	19,040	-	977
5060 Electrical goods	-	5	-	22	4	-	18,727	-	503
5080 Machinery, equipment, and supplies	-	7	-	43	6	-	27,163	-	1,135
5093 Scrap and waste materials	-	3	-	15	5	-	22,933	-	362
5170 Petroleum and petroleum products	-	7	-	57	8	-	30,596	-	2,011
5180 Beer, wine, and distilled beverages	-	7	-	110	16	-	31,527	-	3,525
52 – Retail trade	-	331	-	3,703	11	-	10,279	-	39,678
5210 Lumber and other building materials	-	6	-	56	9	-	21,786	-	1,801
5250 Hardware stores	-	5	-	59	12	-	10,915	-	615
5310 Department stores	-	3	-	309	103	-	12,660	-	4,006
5410 Grocery stores	-	17	-	313	18	-	13,252	-	4,226
5460 Retail bakeries	-	6	-	33	6	-	9,091	-	282
5510 New and used car dealers	-	6	-	191	32	-	29,634	-	5,717
5530 Auto and home supply stores	-	4	-	30	8	-	15,467	-	537
5540 Gasoline service stations	-	34	-	215	6	-	9,488	-	1,960
5620 Women's clothing stores	-	4	-	16	4	-	10,250	-	172
5660 Shoe stores	-	6	-	19	3	-	7,368	-	170
5712 Furniture stores	-	3	-	20	7	-	14,600	-	296
5730 Radio, television, & computer stores	-	5	-	17	3	-	10,118	-	167
5812 Eating places	-	68	-	1,305	19	-	6,360	-	8,544
5813 Drinking places	-	54	-	284	5	-	5,070	-	1,542
5910 Drug stores and proprietary stores	-	8	-	124	16	-	13,194	-	1,615
5920 Liquor stores	-	13	-	194	15	-	9,938	-	2,049
5930 Used merchandise stores	-	3	-	17	6	-	7,765	-	148
5941 Sporting goods and bicycle shops	-	6	-	46	8	-	14,000	-	655
5960 Nonstore retailers	-	3	-	3	1	-	6,667	-	18
5980 Fuel dealers	-	8	-	53	7	-	25,962	-	1,175
5995 Optical goods stores	-	3	-	4	1	-	14,000	-	58

Source: County Business Patterns 1994/95, CBP-94/95, U.S. Department of Commerce, Washington DC, November 1997. The employment column represents mid-March employment in the year. Pay per employee is calculated by dividing 1st Quarter payroll, annualized, by mid-March employment. The column headed 'Emp / Est' shows 'employees per establishment'. A dash (-) means that data are unavailable or cannot be calculated. nec means not elsewhere classified. *Notes:* 1. 1994 data incomplete; unavailable or withheld. 2. 1995 data incomplete; unavailable or withheld. 3. 1994 and 1995 data incomplete; unavailable or withheld.

DULUTH – SUPERIOR, MN – WI MSA

Wholesale and Retail Trade USA	Establishments		Employment		Emp / Est	Pay / Employee		Annual Payroll ($ 000)	
	1994	1995	1994	1995	1995	1994	1995	1994	1995
50 – Wholesale trade [1]	351	413	3,588	4,515	11	26,550	27,183	100,291	128,350
5012 Automobiles and other vehicles [3]	6	5	81	69	14	26,963	29,275	2,250	2,028
5013 Motor vehicle supplies and new parts [1]	26	28	199	187	7	19,136	21,540	4,025	4,109
5014 Tires and tubes [3]	6	5	43	48	10	23,442	23,250	1,882	2,598
5015 Motor vehicle parts, used [1]	7	8	40	40	5	11,800	12,900	513	557
5021 Furniture [1]	4	-	31	-	-	21,548	-	718	-
5023 Homefurnishings [1]	4	-	7	-	-	18,286	-	206	-
5031 Lumber, plywood, and millwork [1]	10	9	135	101	11	28,267	31,881	4,580	2,705
5032 Brick, stone, & related materials [1]	4	8	33	37	5	41,333	38,270	1,514	1,761
5044 Office equipment [1]	8	11	110	125	11	22,545	23,264	2,487	4,228
5045 Computers, peripherals, & software	-	10	-	83	8	-	20,337	-	1,640
5047 Medical and hospital equipment [1]	5	-	18	-	-	24,667	-	493	-
5050 Metals and minerals, except petroleum [1]	6	8	36	38	5	23,889	24,211	918	971
5063 Electrical apparatus and equipment [1]	13	17	84	129	8	34,905	33,953	2,736	4,373
5065 Electronic parts and equipment	-	10	-	20	2	-	34,800	-	708
5072 Hardware [1]	6	7	64	70	10	23,500	24,229	2,028	2,068
5074 Plumbing & hydronic heating supplies [1]	5	7	70	59	8	26,343	29,898	1,924	1,661
5082 Construction and mining machinery [1]	28	31	308	335	11	35,234	36,788	11,656	12,775
5084 Industrial machinery and equipment [1]	20	21	156	169	8	26,436	27,243	4,711	4,984
5085 Industrial supplies [1]	26	24	152	154	6	28,184	33,065	4,464	5,218
5091 Sporting & recreational goods [1]	6	7	55	52	7	12,873	16,308	844	780
5092 Toys and hobby goods and supplies [1]	3	-	8	-	-	10,000	-	103	-
5093 Scrap and waste materials [1]	14	17	113	149	9	19,186	20,913	2,762	3,546
5099 Durable goods, nec	-	6	-	15	3	-	16,267	-	364
5112 Stationery and office supplies [3]	11	10	129	99	10	16,837	20,202	2,245	2,349
5113 Industrial & personal service paper [3]	8	8	62	52	7	22,968	30,692	1,500	1,748
5130 Apparel, piece goods, and notions [1]	4	-	20	-	-	60,400	-	621	-
5142 Packaged frozen food [1]	3	-	38	-	-	16,105	-	731	-
5143 Dairy products, exc. dried or canned [1]	6	6	16	12	2	24,750	18,333	325	237

Continued on next page.

DULUTH – SUPERIOR, MN – WI MSA - [continued]

Wholesale and Retail Trade USA	Establishments		Employment		Emp / Est	Pay / Employee		Annual Payroll ($ 000)	
	1994	1995	1994	1995	1995	1994	1995	1994	1995
5149 Groceries and related products, nec[1]	12	12	181	209	17	24,133	24,842	4,855	5,490
5150 Farm-product raw materials[3]	4	7	90	84	12	18,578	21,333	2,348	2,202
5160 Chemicals and allied products	-	7	-	37	5	-	78,811	-	2,845
5170 Petroleum and petroleum products[1]	13	21	281	367	17	16,954	19,150	5,436	7,825
5181 Beer and ale[1]	5	10	67	64	6	20,060	27,813	1,882	1,739
5182 Wine and distilled beverages[1]	3	4	52	54	14	49,154	52,148	1,667	1,746
5190 Misc., nondurable goods[1]	9	10	144	138	14	21,139	20,957	3,501	3,303
52 – Retail trade[1]	1,519	1,859	18,749	23,078	12	10,927	11,287	223,440	274,376
5210 Lumber and other building materials[1]	42	40	579	598	15	16,829	17,692	10,497	11,343
5230 Paint, glass, and wallpaper stores[1]	10	11	75	69	6	20,320	23,710	1,689	1,757
5250 Hardware stores[1]	27	25	202	212	8	11,129	11,811	2,559	2,640
5310 Department stores[1]	14	17	2,298	2,435	143	9,704	11,345	24,420	29,320
5330 Variety stores[1]	3	-	23	-	-	8,348	-	155	-
5390 Misc. general merchandise stores[1]	17	-	323	-	-	8,755	-	3,125	-
5410 Grocery stores[1]	101	114	1,711	2,170	19	12,168	11,569	21,912	29,427
5420 Meat and fish markets[3]	3	4	25	21	5	13,920	15,810	359	349
5440 Candy, nut, and confectionery stores[1]	9	14	61	55	4	4,459	5,236	323	358
5460 Retail bakeries[1]	21	26	185	162	6	8,346	10,074	1,714	1,669
5490 Miscellaneous food stores[1]	7	9	34	37	4	8,235	7,568	296	319
5510 New and used car dealers[1]	22	27	650	890	33	25,877	27,312	19,522	25,986
5520 Used car dealers[1]	9	11	45	46	4	12,000	12,261	604	581
5530 Auto and home supply stores[1]	30	36	181	214	6	14,829	15,682	3,082	4,027
5540 Gasoline service stations[1]	132	157	1,051	1,283	8	8,696	9,203	9,955	12,157
5550 Boat dealers[1]	10	11	59	53	5	13,424	15,396	921	975
5610 Men's & boys' clothing stores[3]	17	18	100	98	5	9,280	9,551	954	966
5620 Women's clothing stores[1]	56	56	425	377	7	7,586	6,897	3,612	2,686
5630 Women's accessory & specialty stores[1]	4	5	19	16	3	8,632	10,250	170	173
5650 Family clothing stores[1]	18	19	178	223	12	8,854	8,502	1,927	2,123
5660 Shoe stores[1]	28	34	115	145	4	8,487	10,786	1,176	1,362
5690 Misc. apparel & accessory stores[1]	6	6	31	27	5	9,032	9,333	302	265
5712 Furniture stores[1]	27	29	233	234	8	16,481	18,222	4,271	4,476
5713 Floor covering stores[1]	8	11	61	49	4	11,541	18,694	900	774
5714 Drapery and upholstery stores[2]	-	3	-	3	1	-	12,000	-	48
5719 Misc. homefurnishings stores	-	10	-	63	6	-	13,524	-	896
5720 Household appliance stores[1]	11	12	76	79	7	15,263	15,646	1,181	1,337
5731 Radio, TV, & electronic stores[1]	13	16	130	161	10	13,723	13,292	1,945	2,261
5734 Computer and software stores[3]	4	5	17	15	3	7,529	10,400	139	201
5735 Record & prerecorded tape stores[1]	5	9	47	44	5	10,468	11,727	558	629
5736 Musical instrument stores[1]	5	6	36	33	6	11,778	12,121	475	430
5812 Eating places[1]	315	375	5,149	6,747	18	6,615	6,807	38,461	46,133
5813 Drinking places[1]	102	155	663	967	6	6,842	6,395	4,727	7,187
5910 Drug stores and proprietary stores[1]	42	49	510	600	12	13,035	14,487	7,313	8,599
5920 Liquor stores[1]	49	68	257	487	7	8,576	8,912	2,489	4,625
5930 Used merchandise stores[1]	17	17	62	80	5	6,258	7,950	434	583
5941 Sporting goods and bicycle shops[1]	44	49	297	344	7	8,660	10,151	2,988	3,863
5944 Jewelry stores[1]	18	19	104	108	6	15,923	18,593	1,790	1,836
5945 Hobby, toy, and game shops[1]	17	15	71	120	8	9,127	7,567	872	1,051
5947 Gift, novelty, and souvenir shops[3]	38	36	190	172	5	5,621	6,907	1,350	1,302
5949 Sewing, needlework, and piece goods[3]	10	8	100	82	10	6,880	6,439	633	542
5961 Catalog and mail-order houses[1]	8	13	704	907	70	8,176	9,499	6,325	9,021
5962 Merchandising machine operators[1]	5	7	53	68	10	14,943	13,412	933	976
5963 Direct selling establishments[1]	19	18	101	78	4	16,673	14,205	1,753	1,323
5983 Fuel oil dealers[1]	10	13	98	106	8	22,245	23,585	2,728	2,978
5984 Liquefied petroleum gas dealers[1]	10	15	67	69	5	23,164	24,464	1,566	1,597
5995 Optical goods stores[1]	24	27	104	102	4	13,500	16,157	1,484	1,809
5999 Miscellaneous retail stores, nec[1]	34	43	196	218	5	13,388	15,156	3,156	3,794

Source: County Business Patterns 1994/95, CBP-94/95, U.S. Department of Commerce, Washington DC, November 1997. The employment column represents mid-March employment in the year. Pay per employee is calculated by dividing 1st Quarter payroll, annualized, by mid-March employment. The column headed 'Emp / Est' shows 'employees per establishment'. A dash (-) means that data are unavailable or cannot be calculated. nec means not elsewhere classified. *Notes:* 1. 1994 data incomplete; unavailable or withheld. 2. 1995 data incomplete; unavailable or withheld. 3. 1994 and 1995 data incomplete; unavailable or withheld.

DUTCHESS COUNTY, NY PMSA

Wholesale and Retail Trade USA	Establishments		Employment		Emp / Est	Pay / Employee		Annual Payroll ($ 000)	
	1994	1995	1994	1995	1995	1994	1995	1994	1995
50 – Wholesale trade	315	314	2,362	2,762	9	32,787	37,959	86,310	117,553
5012 Automobiles and other vehicles	9	7	68	66	9	25,059	28,000	1,918	1,867
5013 Motor vehicle supplies and new parts	25	23	131	141	6	19,817	20,738	2,845	3,096
5021 Furniture	4	4	34	30	8	19,882	27,600	822	885

Continued on next page.

DUTCHESS COUNTY, NY PMSA - [continued]

Wholesale and Retail Trade USA	Establishments		Employment		Emp / Est	Pay / Employee		Annual Payroll ($ 000)	
	1994	1995	1994	1995	1995	1994	1995	1994	1995
5023 Homefurnishings	4	-	24	-	-	7,500	-	215	-
5031 Lumber, plywood, and millwork	9	7	80	49	7	36,100	36,163	3,630	2,764
5032 Brick, stone, & related materials	3	4	61	44	11	26,820	26,091	2,320	1,528
5033 Roofing, siding, & insulation	-	4	-	28	7	-	22,857	-	786
5039 Construction materials, nec	-	4	-	14	4	-	20,857	-	275
5044 Office equipment	7	7	63	65	9	27,111	29,415	1,728	1,947
5047 Medical and hospital equipment	7	-	132	-	-	43,091	-	5,651	-
5050 Metals and minerals, except petroleum	3	3	13	13	4	21,846	24,308	348	365
5063 Electrical apparatus and equipment	-	9	-	137	15	-	26,949	-	3,809
5065 Electronic parts and equipment	39	40	254	252	6	64,189	65,667	17,489	17,933
5072 Hardware	5	4	52	49	12	21,846	27,918	1,308	1,413
5074 Plumbing & hydronic heating supplies	12	14	128	133	10	29,219	32,090	3,646	3,880
5075 Warm air heating & air conditioning	-	7	-	15	2	-	38,933	-	459
5083 Farm and garden machinery	8	6	55	34	6	16,509	19,176	1,048	759
5084 Industrial machinery and equipment	15	14	88	86	6	29,636	33,163	4,687	4,678
5085 Industrial supplies	-	6	-	25	4	-	32,480	-	773
5087 Service establishment equipment	6	6	27	53	9	16,444	28,075	519	1,547
5091 Sporting & recreational goods	3	4	19	15	4	11,368	13,600	172	215
5093 Scrap and waste materials	9	9	39	46	5	19,795	22,000	954	1,172
5110 Paper and paper products	9	5	90	56	11	16,133	12,929	1,640	774
5120 Drugs, proprietaries, and sundries	-	5	-	51	10	-	17,490	-	833
5130 Apparel, piece goods, and notions	-	5	-	7	1	-	44,571	-	547
5149 Groceries and related products, nec	14	14	73	58	4	17,534	23,103	1,495	1,529
5172 Petroleum products, nec	-	4	-	19	5	-	26,526	-	465
5180 Beer, wine, and distilled beverages	4	4	118	99	25	25,492	31,273	3,789	3,492
5191 Farm supplies	8	7	38	20	3	21,263	27,400	1,065	552
5192 Books, periodicals, & newspapers	8	8	54	54	7	31,407	35,556	2,195	1,968
5198 Paints, varnishes, and supplies	4	3	30	11	4	23,600	17,818	818	212
5199 Nondurable goods, nec	5	6	13	12	2	10,769	24,667	154	189
52 - Retail trade	1,651	1,649	17,925	18,491	11	12,379	12,977	244,495	256,012
5210 Lumber and other building materials	36	31	571	581	19	20,378	21,260	12,772	13,037
5230 Paint, glass, and wallpaper stores	-	10	-	60	6	-	23,600	-	1,365
5250 Hardware stores	16	10	96	62	6	15,875	11,161	1,565	716
5260 Retail nurseries and garden stores	19	17	124	136	8	12,419	14,412	2,147	2,332
5310 Department stores	16	16	1,793	1,844	115	10,945	12,078	22,559	23,904
5330 Variety stores	9	8	60	55	7	9,600	8,800	552	555
5390 Misc. general merchandise stores	13	12	604	587	49	12,444	12,934	8,048	7,654
5410 Grocery stores	178	159	3,431	3,269	21	13,717	14,176	46,799	47,249
5420 Meat and fish markets	9	8	58	68	9	8,966	9,765	699	735
5450 Dairy products stores	-	6	-	10	2	-	6,000	-	128
5460 Retail bakeries	32	31	230	183	6	8,104	8,590	2,140	1,772
5490 Miscellaneous food stores	20	17	70	77	5	9,943	9,870	771	740
5510 New and used car dealers	31	34	818	825	24	27,389	30,366	26,785	27,517
5520 Used car dealers	17	20	39	39	2	20,308	19,385	869	786
5530 Auto and home supply stores	29	29	189	197	7	17,651	19,431	3,555	4,017
5540 Gasoline service stations	81	86	407	428	5	12,806	13,383	5,724	5,894
5610 Men's & boys' clothing stores	16	12	127	133	11	8,346	7,489	1,176	982
5620 Women's clothing stores	54	46	447	384	8	7,758	8,000	3,698	2,979
5630 Women's accessory & specialty stores	9	9	58	55	6	9,103	10,473	581	585
5640 Children's and infants' wear stores	8	7	80	87	12	6,550	7,080	545	632
5650 Family clothing stores	24	24	505	510	21	9,323	9,922	5,414	5,376
5660 Shoe stores	44	40	240	229	6	7,983	9,223	2,106	2,100
5690 Misc. apparel & accessory stores	7	8	65	60	8	8,738	9,933	590	589
5712 Furniture stores	33	26	236	213	8	15,492	18,610	4,008	3,975
5713 Floor covering stores	13	12	67	73	6	23,642	25,808	1,681	1,732
5720 Household appliance stores	4	5	25	23	5	14,720	16,870	391	413
5731 Radio, TV, & electronic stores	10	-	43	-	-	14,884	-	649	-
5734 Computer and software stores	7	6	30	17	3	6,933	9,412	212	235
5735 Record & prerecorded tape stores	12	13	62	122	9	9,419	9,934	909	1,097
5736 Musical instrument stores	3	-	22	-	-	19,455	-	446	-
5812 Eating places	404	398	4,704	5,100	13	8,046	8,390	44,213	47,230
5813 Drinking places	32	30	94	86	3	7,872	9,721	827	801
5910 Drug stores and proprietary stores	51	53	648	688	13	14,636	14,192	9,993	10,724
5920 Liquor stores	38	41	119	126	3	13,311	13,270	1,849	1,894
5930 Used merchandise stores	11	13	37	42	3	11,676	11,714	521	544
5941 Sporting goods and bicycle shops	25	25	89	98	4	11,685	13,469	1,224	1,613
5942 Book stores	20	18	194	181	10	9,814	10,851	1,957	2,053
5943 Stationery stores	4	6	35	60	10	9,714	10,467	365	623
5944 Jewelry stores	26	25	158	141	6	14,456	15,489	2,263	2,022
5945 Hobby, toy, and game shops	10	9	111	96	11	9,153	9,667	1,191	1,068
5947 Gift, novelty, and souvenir shops	37	36	132	144	4	7,758	7,500	1,155	1,175

Continued on next page.

DUTCHESS COUNTY, NY PMSA - [continued]

Wholesale and Retail Trade USA	Establishments		Employment		Emp / Est	Pay / Employee		Annual Payroll ($ 000)	
	1994	1995	1994	1995	1995	1994	1995	1994	1995
5949 Sewing, needlework, and piece goods	5	6	31	38	6	8,903	9,263	321	362
5961 Catalog and mail-order houses	11	12	45	46	4	14,044	13,304	585	778
5962 Merchandising machine operators	8	8	43	18	2	12,465	16,889	680	326
5963 Direct selling establishments	14	15	57	66	4	15,088	16,606	1,077	1,359
5983 Fuel oil dealers	25	25	242	310	12	32,000	31,510	8,354	10,932
5984 Liquefied petroleum gas dealers	11	11	81	77	7	26,074	21,714	2,012	1,776
5992 Florists	22	23	62	78	3	12,387	10,051	766	889
5994 News dealers and newsstands	4	3	12	9	3	12,333	12,889	158	117
5995 Optical goods stores	15	15	94	81	5	16,851	17,728	1,549	1,391
5999 Miscellaneous retail stores, nec	55	56	208	241	4	9,788	10,871	2,465	3,217

Source: County Business Patterns 1994/95, CBP-94/95, U.S. Department of Commerce, Washington DC, November 1997. The employment column represents mid-March employment in the year. Pay per employee is calculated by dividing 1st Quarter payroll, annualized, by mid-March employment. The column headed 'Emp / Est' shows 'employees per establishment'. A dash (-) means that data are unavailable or cannot be calculated. nec means not elsewhere classified. *Notes:* 1. 1994 data incomplete; unavailable or withheld. 2. 1995 data incomplete; unavailable or withheld. 3. 1994 and 1995 data incomplete; unavailable or withheld.

EAU CLAIRE, WI MSA

Wholesale and Retail Trade USA	Establishments		Employment		Emp / Est	Pay / Employee		Annual Payroll ($ 000)	
	1994	1995	1994	1995	1995	1994	1995	1994	1995
50- Wholesale trade	-	255	-	2,775	11	-	26,164	-	74,825
5012 Automobiles and other vehicles	-	4	-	173	43	-	25,988	-	4,541
5013 Motor vehicle supplies and new parts	-	20	-	235	12	-	19,030	-	4,753
5030 Lumber and construction materials	-	12	-	155	13	-	22,452	-	4,196
5044 Office equipment	-	8	-	64	8	-	31,375	-	2,046
5045 Computers, peripherals, & software [2]	-	6	-	100	17	-	27,000	-	3,002
5047 Medical and hospital equipment [2]	-	8	-	23	3	-	23,826	-	696
5063 Electrical apparatus and equipment	-	4	-	86	22	-	31,302	-	3,063
5065 Electronic parts and equipment [2]	-	6	-	16	3	-	26,750	-	441
5072 Hardware	-	4	-	34	9	-	20,118	-	741
5075 Warm air heating & air conditioning [2]	-	3	-	28	9	-	26,714	-	840
5082 Construction and mining machinery [2]	-	6	-	68	11	-	30,235	-	2,005
5083 Farm and garden machinery	-	17	-	91	5	-	16,220	-	1,661
5084 Industrial machinery and equipment	-	8	-	81	10	-	39,309	-	3,172
5085 Industrial supplies [2]	-	3	-	23	8	-	22,609	-	580
5093 Scrap and waste materials	-	5	-	76	15	-	27,316	-	2,209
5110 Paper and paper products	-	10	-	26	3	-	28,000	-	784
5120 Drugs, proprietaries, and sundries	-	5	-	21	4	-	27,619	-	681
5130 Apparel, piece goods, and notions [2]	-	3	-	8	3	-	9,000	-	56
5149 Groceries and related products, nec	-	5	-	124	25	-	29,774	-	3,722
5169 Chemicals & allied products, nec	-	6	-	29	5	-	31,862	-	1,475
5170 Petroleum and petroleum products	-	12	-	110	9	-	22,982	-	2,705
5180 Beer, wine, and distilled beverages [2]	-	5	-	137	27	-	27,066	-	4,989
5191 Farm supplies	-	20	-	71	4	-	21,408	-	1,220
52- Retail trade	-	981	-	15,631	16	-	11,038	-	189,609
5210 Lumber and other building materials	-	20	-	382	19	-	20,492	-	7,810
5230 Paint, glass, and wallpaper stores	-	6	-	32	5	-	15,875	-	549
5250 Hardware stores	-	11	-	79	7	-	8,101	-	656
5310 Department stores	-	12	-	1,605	134	-	10,383	-	16,938
5410 Grocery stores	-	41	-	1,709	42	-	8,873	-	16,022
5460 Retail bakeries	-	13	-	77	6	-	6,961	-	582
5490 Miscellaneous food stores	-	6	-	18	3	-	8,444	-	201
5510 New and used car dealers	-	16	-	574	36	-	24,690	-	14,464
5520 Used car dealers	-	20	-	80	4	-	16,250	-	1,423
5530 Auto and home supply stores	-	21	-	292	14	-	14,630	-	4,572
5540 Gasoline service stations	-	82	-	816	10	-	8,147	-	7,222
5560 Recreational vehicle dealers	-	9	-	51	6	-	16,000	-	1,105
5620 Women's clothing stores	-	29	-	260	9	-	6,954	-	1,960
5630 Women's accessory & specialty stores [2]	-	4	-	29	7	-	8,966	-	255
5650 Family clothing stores	-	13	-	299	23	-	9,431	-	2,050
5660 Shoe stores	-	21	-	130	6	-	9,877	-	1,204
5712 Furniture stores	-	20	-	138	7	-	16,667	-	2,082
5713 Floor covering stores	-	7	-	37	5	-	19,892	-	776
5720 Household appliance stores	-	7	-	39	6	-	15,179	-	1,062
5731 Radio, TV, & electronic stores	-	10	-	134	13	-	13,224	-	1,617
5734 Computer and software stores [2]	-	4	-	79	20	-	15,595	-	1,223
5812 Eating places	-	192	-	4,731	25	-	6,202	-	29,523
5813 Drinking places	-	92	-	626	7	-	5,559	-	3,447
5910 Drug stores and proprietary stores	-	20	-	256	13	-	17,469	-	4,135
5920 Liquor stores	-	5	-	17	3	-	3,294	-	55

Continued on next page.

EAU CLAIRE, WI MSA - [continued]

Wholesale and Retail Trade USA	Establishments		Employment		Emp / Est	Pay / Employee		Annual Payroll ($ 000)	
	1994	1995	1994	1995	1995	1994	1995	1994	1995
5930 Used merchandise stores	-	6	-	28	5	-	6,714	-	208
5941 Sporting goods and bicycle shops	-	21	-	113	5	-	14,372	-	1,936
5944 Jewelry stores	-	17	-	105	6	-	15,848	-	1,758
5945 Hobby, toy, and game shops	-	9	-	48	5	-	11,167	-	779
5947 Gift, novelty, and souvenir shops	-	17	-	94	6	-	5,319	-	677
5949 Sewing, needlework, and piece goods [2]	-	3	-	9	3	-	14,222	-	97
5963 Direct selling establishments [2]	-	18	-	27	2	-	7,704	-	196
5980 Fuel dealers [2]	-	6	-	65	11	-	15,692	-	878
5992 Florists	-	9	-	31	3	-	11,742	-	255
5995 Optical goods stores	-	6	-	27	5	-	17,630	-	453
5999 Miscellaneous retail stores, nec	-	35	-	128	4	-	13,844	-	1,725

Source: County Business Patterns 1994/95, CBP-94/95, U.S. Department of Commerce, Washington DC, November 1997. The employment column represents mid-March employment in the year. Pay per employee is calculated by dividing 1st Quarter payroll, annualized, by mid-March employment. The column headed 'Emp / Est' shows 'employees per establishment'. A dash (-) means that data are unavailable or cannot be calculated. nec means not elsewhere classified. *Notes:* 1. 1994 data incomplete; unavailable or withheld. 2. 1995 data incomplete; unavailable or withheld. 3. 1994 and 1995 data incomplete; unavailable or withheld.

EL PASO, TX MSA

Wholesale and Retail Trade USA	Establishments		Employment		Emp / Est	Pay / Employee		Annual Payroll ($ 000)	
	1994	1995	1994	1995	1995	1994	1995	1994	1995
50- Wholesale trade	-	1,152	-	12,002	10	-	23,438	-	281,404
5012 Automobiles and other vehicles	-	21	-	266	13	-	25,504	-	8,279
5013 Motor vehicle supplies and new parts	-	48	-	435	9	-	21,591	-	9,618
5014 Tires and tubes	-	6	-	125	21	-	24,672	-	3,429
5015 Motor vehicle parts, used	-	22	-	37	2	-	14,054	-	657
5021 Furniture	-	16	-	247	15	-	16,567	-	5,280
5023 Homefurnishings	-	22	-	220	10	-	19,182	-	4,651
5031 Lumber, plywood, and millwork	-	25	-	208	8	-	22,500	-	4,637
5032 Brick, stone, & related materials	-	7	-	81	12	-	17,333	-	1,378
5033 Roofing, siding, & insulation	-	5	-	25	5	-	14,720	-	583
5039 Construction materials, nec	-	22	-	116	5	-	26,828	-	4,771
5043 Photographic equipment & supplies	-	3	-	3	1	-	10,667	-	57
5044 Office equipment	-	25	-	300	12	-	25,467	-	7,390
5045 Computers, peripherals, & software	-	32	-	253	8	-	33,628	-	7,907
5046 Commercial equipment, nec	-	7	-	154	22	-	23,273	-	3,752
5047 Medical and hospital equipment	-	24	-	145	6	-	20,248	-	3,194
5051 Metals service centers and offices	-	25	-	215	9	-	18,084	-	4,265
5063 Electrical apparatus and equipment	-	42	-	426	10	-	31,230	-	12,143
5064 Electrical appliances, TV & radios	-	11	-	815	74	-	34,375	-	15,317
5065 Electronic parts and equipment	-	37	-	231	6	-	30,615	-	7,795
5072 Hardware	-	22	-	130	6	-	23,077	-	3,113
5074 Plumbing & hydronic heating supplies	-	21	-	182	9	-	21,011	-	4,205
5075 Warm air heating & air conditioning	-	18	-	171	10	-	23,018	-	4,378
5082 Construction and mining machinery	-	15	-	232	15	-	30,931	-	7,793
5083 Farm and garden machinery	-	6	-	56	9	-	19,357	-	1,086
5084 Industrial machinery and equipment	-	82	-	592	7	-	26,196	-	16,347
5085 Industrial supplies	-	35	-	286	8	-	24,881	-	7,459
5087 Service establishment equipment	-	23	-	165	7	-	24,048	-	3,900
5088 Transportation equipment & supplies	-	7	-	45	6	-	20,089	-	957
5093 Scrap and waste materials	-	24	-	325	14	-	14,991	-	5,220
5094 Jewelry & precious stones	-	19	-	104	5	-	15,808	-	2,053
5099 Durable goods, nec	-	26	-	95	4	-	14,905	-	1,517
5111 Printing and writing paper	-	7	-	38	5	-	23,684	-	951
5112 Stationery and office supplies	-	17	-	278	16	-	20,345	-	5,455
5113 Industrial & personal service paper	-	16	-	224	14	-	25,518	-	6,158
5120 Drugs, proprietaries, and sundries	-	13	-	76	6	-	21,000	-	1,588
5131 Piece goods & notions	-	17	-	102	6	-	25,686	-	2,602
5136 Men's and boys' clothing	-	17	-	364	21	-	15,835	-	5,750
5137 Women's and children's clothing	-	28	-	143	5	-	13,538	-	1,948
5139 Footwear	-	10	-	64	6	-	15,750	-	851
5141 Groceries, general line	-	13	-	560	43	-	29,793	-	16,450
5142 Packaged frozen food	-	5	-	34	7	-	23,882	-	794
5144 Poultry and poultry products	-	7	-	50	7	-	14,880	-	785
5145 Confectionery	-	11	-	373	34	-	26,917	-	11,030
5147 Meats and meat products	-	17	-	135	8	-	22,993	-	3,314
5148 Fresh fruits and vegetables	-	20	-	131	7	-	19,450	-	2,476
5149 Groceries and related products, nec	-	27	-	498	18	-	19,880	-	10,954
5153 Grain and field beans	-	4	-	9	2	-	16,889	-	160
5154 Livestock	-	4	-	7	2	-	22,286	-	159

Continued on next page.

EL PASO, TX MSA - [continued]

Wholesale and Retail Trade USA	Establishments		Employment		Emp / Est	Pay / Employee		Annual Payroll ($ 000)	
	1994	1995	1994	1995	1995	1994	1995	1994	1995
5159 Farm-product raw materials, nec	-	6	-	114	19	-	21,368	-	2,589
5162 Plastics materials & basic shapes	-	6	-	50	8	-	34,400	-	1,577
5169 Chemicals & allied products, nec	-	17	-	131	8	-	18,656	-	2,472
5171 Petroleum bulk stations & terminals	-	7	-	193	28	-	22,943	-	4,734
5172 Petroleum products, nec	-	5	-	55	11	-	20,800	-	1,705
5181 Beer and ale	-	5	-	367	73	-	21,668	-	8,652
5182 Wine and distilled beverages	-	7	-	87	12	-	29,195	-	3,215
5191 Farm supplies	-	13	-	76	6	-	16,895	-	1,510
5192 Books, periodicals, & newspapers	-	4	-	32	8	-	18,375	-	596
5193 Flowers & florists' supplies	-	7	-	79	11	-	13,165	-	1,041
5194 Tobacco and tobacco products	-	3	-	51	17	-	17,804	-	945
5198 Paints, varnishes, and supplies	-	6	-	34	6	-	17,765	-	623
5199 Nondurable goods, nec	-	48	-	483	10	-	18,609	-	7,680
52- Retail trade	-	3,177	-	43,788	14	-	12,115	-	553,251
5210 Lumber and other building materials	-	45	-	1,095	24	-	16,416	-	19,795
5230 Paint, glass, and wallpaper stores	-	20	-	98	5	-	20,653	-	1,999
5250 Hardware stores	-	13	-	138	11	-	13,652	-	2,012
5260 Retail nurseries and garden stores	-	8	-	97	12	-	9,856	-	990
5270 Mobile home dealers	-	10	-	85	9	-	21,035	-	1,978
5310 Department stores	-	29	-	5,291	182	-	12,424	-	65,813
5330 Variety stores	-	24	-	182	8	-	8,418	-	1,724
5390 Misc. general merchandise stores	-	36	-	1,401	39	-	12,899	-	16,337
5410 Grocery stores	-	208	-	5,130	25	-	13,769	-	71,500
5420 Meat and fish markets	-	8	-	92	12	-	8,913	-	1,248
5430 Fruit and vegetable markets	-	8	-	43	5	-	12,279	-	628
5440 Candy, nut, and confectionery stores	-	5	-	21	4	-	7,619	-	128
5460 Retail bakeries	-	47	-	286	6	-	8,224	-	2,417
5490 Miscellaneous food stores	-	15	-	51	3	-	9,569	-	560
5510 New and used car dealers	-	26	-	2,058	79	-	25,685	-	60,830
5520 Used car dealers	-	69	-	243	4	-	14,650	-	3,953
5530 Auto and home supply stores	-	117	-	1,029	9	-	14,888	-	16,049
5540 Gasoline service stations	-	184	-	1,448	8	-	12,541	-	18,793
5560 Recreational vehicle dealers	-	3	-	27	9	-	19,852	-	571
5570 Motorcycle dealers	-	6	-	40	7	-	15,700	-	819
5610 Men's & boys' clothing stores	-	37	-	253	7	-	11,194	-	2,576
5620 Women's clothing stores	-	138	-	909	7	-	8,968	-	7,502
5630 Women's accessory & specialty stores	-	25	-	106	4	-	8,453	-	857
5640 Children's and infants' wear stores	-	9	-	75	8	-	8,213	-	784
5650 Family clothing stores	-	51	-	788	15	-	8,888	-	6,984
5660 Shoe stores	-	104	-	512	5	-	12,063	-	5,988
5690 Misc. apparel & accessory stores	-	24	-	173	7	-	9,295	-	1,991
5712 Furniture stores	-	69	-	707	10	-	18,297	-	14,707
5713 Floor covering stores	-	10	-	64	6	-	12,938	-	809
5714 Drapery and upholstery stores	-	10	-	35	4	-	13,829	-	425
5719 Misc. homefurnishings stores	-	24	-	136	6	-	11,765	-	1,809
5720 Household appliance stores	-	13	-	70	5	-	14,686	-	1,012
5731 Radio, TV, & electronic stores	-	50	-	582	12	-	14,838	-	8,130
5734 Computer and software stores	-	17	-	125	7	-	15,392	-	1,968
5735 Record & prerecorded tape stores	-	18	-	148	8	-	9,811	-	1,392
5736 Musical instrument stores	-	8	-	73	9	-	18,356	-	1,536
5812 Eating places	-	662	-	13,467	20	-	8,243	-	114,313
5813 Drinking places	-	143	-	878	6	-	6,966	-	6,158
5910 Drug stores and proprietary stores	-	52	-	743	14	-	17,378	-	13,877
5920 Liquor stores	-	36	-	142	4	-	9,155	-	1,243
5930 Used merchandise stores	-	62	-	301	5	-	14,020	-	4,302
5941 Sporting goods and bicycle shops	-	36	-	184	5	-	10,761	-	2,063
5942 Book stores	-	27	-	161	6	-	10,186	-	1,654
5944 Jewelry stores	-	71	-	366	5	-	17,727	-	6,086
5945 Hobby, toy, and game shops	-	17	-	188	11	-	7,936	-	2,185
5947 Gift, novelty, and souvenir shops	-	59	-	235	4	-	7,370	-	1,866
5948 Luggage and leather goods stores	-	5	-	163	33	-	11,681	-	2,015
5949 Sewing, needlework, and piece goods	-	13	-	97	7	-	7,835	-	800
5961 Catalog and mail-order houses	-	3	-	18	6	-	7,778	-	112
5962 Merchandising machine operators	-	10	-	86	9	-	18,279	-	1,717
5963 Direct selling establishments	-	16	-	155	10	-	16,052	-	3,373
5980 Fuel dealers	-	9	-	69	8	-	16,232	-	1,089
5992 Florists	-	47	-	194	4	-	9,340	-	1,835
5995 Optical goods stores	-	40	-	239	6	-	12,703	-	3,058
5999 Miscellaneous retail stores, nec	-	87	-	546	6	-	12,117	-	6,864

Source: County Business Patterns 1994/95, CBP-94/95, U.S. Department of Commerce, Washington DC, November 1997. The employment column represents mid-March employment in the year. Pay per employee is calculated by dividing 1st Quarter payroll, annualized, by mid-March employment. The column headed 'Emp / Est' shows 'employees per establishment'. A dash (-) means that data are unavailable or cannot be calculated. nec means not elsewhere classified. *Notes:* 1. 1994 data incomplete; unavailable or withheld. 2. 1995 data incomplete; unavailable or withheld. 3. 1994 and 1995 data incomplete; unavailable or withheld.

ELKHART-GOSHEN, IN MSA

Wholesale and Retail Trade USA	Establishments		Employment		Emp / Est	Pay / Employee		Annual Payroll ($ 000)	
	1994	1995	1994	1995	1995	1994	1995	1994	1995
50- Wholesale trade	452	480	5,831	6,283	13	26,542	29,451	172,307	190,822
5012 Automobiles and other vehicles	26	27	477	493	18	23,807	27,521	13,165	13,555
5013 Motor vehicle supplies and new parts	57	54	655	646	12	20,000	22,105	15,422	14,706
5014 Tires and tubes	6	6	82	83	14	19,805	21,060	1,934	1,934
5015 Motor vehicle parts, used	3	4	11	13	3	13,091	21,231	157	373
5021 Furniture	4	4	56	71	18	26,500	22,761	1,589	1,733
5023 Homefurnishings	11	11	150	129	12	31,440	42,574	4,326	5,526
5031 Lumber, plywood, and millwork	22	26	577	608	23	27,258	27,355	16,738	16,508
5032 Brick, stone, & related materials	4	-	9	-	-	21,333	-	207	-
5033 Roofing, siding, & insulation	4	-	45	-	-	33,422	-	1,693	-
5039 Construction materials, nec	12	15	215	302	20	33,563	36,609	8,429	11,791
5044 Office equipment	6	5	43	51	10	21,395	22,824	985	1,234
5045 Computers, peripherals, & software	6	6	20	26	4	25,200	23,538	520	710
5051 Metals service centers and offices	18	21	345	375	18	20,174	24,587	7,923	9,378
5063 Electrical apparatus and equipment	15	14	315	228	16	31,225	33,825	10,418	7,220
5072 Hardware	23	26	387	443	17	24,796	27,865	11,223	12,729
5074 Plumbing & hydronic heating supplies	10	11	240	277	25	25,733	43,134	6,776	11,029
5083 Farm and garden machinery	14	15	95	101	7	16,716	17,307	1,768	2,124
5084 Industrial machinery and equipment	27	27	291	332	12	31,340	35,181	9,320	11,642
5085 Industrial supplies	15	13	124	104	8	25,677	35,462	3,826	3,673
5087 Service establishment equipment	4	5	14	15	3	17,143	17,867	268	292
5091 Sporting & recreational goods	7	7	68	76	11	24,941	23,000	1,997	1,845
5093 Scrap and waste materials	5	7	88	109	16	24,364	25,578	2,490	3,392
5099 Durable goods, nec	10	-	18	-	-	28,667	-	971	-
5112 Stationery and office supplies	6	4	48	50	13	18,250	18,480	878	926
5113 Industrial & personal service paper	3	3	54	60	20	25,185	25,467	1,867	2,913
5131 Piece goods & notions	-	9	-	79	9	-	20,506	-	1,658
5149 Groceries and related products, nec	-	6	-	42	7	-	11,429	-	805
5162 Plastics materials & basic shapes	11	11	192	213	19	27,792	26,761	6,090	6,172
5169 Chemicals & allied products, nec	8	10	48	69	7	29,750	35,768	1,855	2,696
5171 Petroleum bulk stations & terminals	-	8	-	135	17	-	25,333	-	3,665
5172 Petroleum products, nec	-	3	-	7	2	-	22,857	-	171
5191 Farm supplies	16	16	167	166	10	21,341	20,578	3,857	3,452
5192 Books, periodicals, & newspapers	3	-	7	-	-	16,000	-	108	-
5198 Paints, varnishes, and supplies	3	4	33	56	14	30,424	26,571	1,219	1,641
5199 Nondurable goods, nec	13	13	29	32	2	29,655	17,375	668	584
52- Retail trade	1,024	1,034	14,235	15,354	15	10,509	11,475	169,185	190,433
5210 Lumber and other building materials	25	19	245	465	24	19,543	17,901	7,210	8,468
5230 Paint, glass, and wallpaper stores	8	6	139	111	19	22,504	26,054	3,638	3,505
5250 Hardware stores	19	17	204	192	11	10,451	11,000	2,423	2,231
5260 Retail nurseries and garden stores	10	11	60	74	7	15,600	15,730	1,387	1,527
5270 Mobile home dealers	12	12	87	74	6	22,943	24,811	2,087	2,497
5310 Department stores	9	10	1,396	2,215	222	10,756	10,333	15,403	23,696
5330 Variety stores	-	10	-	156	16	-	8,487	-	1,329
5390 Misc. general merchandise stores	-	8	-	175	22	-	11,771	-	1,966
5410 Grocery stores	43	44	1,765	1,685	38	11,263	12,809	20,569	22,149
5420 Meat and fish markets	6	5	69	57	11	10,319	11,439	705	723
5440 Candy, nut, and confectionery stores	-	3	-	8	3	-	11,000	-	97
5460 Retail bakeries	12	14	105	99	7	7,810	7,556	946	790
5510 New and used car dealers	18	20	509	559	28	27,505	27,621	17,087	17,581
5520 Used car dealers	32	31	129	147	5	19,039	21,769	2,838	3,543
5530 Auto and home supply stores	31	31	290	272	9	15,793	18,750	4,581	5,248
5540 Gasoline service stations	76	70	634	624	9	9,836	10,955	6,797	7,868
5560 Recreational vehicle dealers	18	21	140	129	6	19,000	20,682	3,342	3,727
5570 Motorcycle dealers	-	3	-	38	13	-	38,000	-	1,309
5610 Men's & boys' clothing stores	5	6	32	35	6	13,250	14,057	464	473
5620 Women's clothing stores	24	19	229	166	9	6,952	7,036	1,696	1,194
5630 Women's accessory & specialty stores	6	4	26	24	6	5,846	5,333	142	132
5650 Family clothing stores	5	5	37	60	12	7,568	10,400	357	658
5660 Shoe stores	21	20	107	98	5	9,720	11,796	1,119	1,115
5690 Misc. apparel & accessory stores	4	5	19	16	3	9,263	12,500	232	210
5712 Furniture stores	29	30	252	297	10	15,429	16,458	4,752	5,298
5713 Floor covering stores	9	-	25	-	-	18,880	-	512	-
5714 Drapery and upholstery stores	3	-	4	-	-	5,000	-	21	-
5719 Misc. homefurnishings stores	5	4	12	10	3	24,333	27,600	292	270
5720 Household appliance stores	9	9	40	44	5	12,100	12,636	518	539
5731 Radio, TV, & electronic stores	12	12	51	58	5	14,039	15,103	820	786
5734 Computer and software stores	6	4	22	20	5	11,636	20,400	287	399
5735 Record & prerecorded tape stores	-	6	-	37	6	-	8,541	-	317
5812 Eating places	262	254	5,260	5,221	21	6,542	7,229	40,141	42,265
5813 Drinking places	31	30	192	189	6	6,688	7,534	1,381	1,466

Continued on next page.

ELKHART - GOSHEN, IN MSA - [continued]

Wholesale and Retail Trade USA	Establishments		Employment		Emp / Est	Pay / Employee		Annual Payroll ($ 000)	
	1994	1995	1994	1995	1995	1994	1995	1994	1995
5910 Drug stores and proprietary stores	30	34	514	529	16	13,331	14,389	7,625	8,140
5920 Liquor stores	17	19	81	95	5	9,383	9,726	873	928
5930 Used merchandise stores	22	21	85	88	4	8,094	9,727	732	848
5941 Sporting goods and bicycle shops	19	17	86	95	6	9,442	9,053	918	941
5942 Book stores	11	8	68	56	7	6,294	7,071	339	391
5944 Jewelry stores	14	17	96	106	6	12,792	14,264	1,222	1,491
5947 Gift, novelty, and souvenir shops	23	25	93	92	4	4,516	6,739	551	681
5949 Sewing, needlework, and piece goods	11	8	51	51	6	8,078	6,667	378	357
5961 Catalog and mail-order houses	-	4	-	6	2	-	8,667	-	38
5962 Merchandising machine operators	-	4	-	12	3	-	23,000	-	345
5963 Direct selling establishments	5	6	102	112	19	18,039	19,143	2,027	2,171
5992 Florists	12	14	112	111	8	11,679	12,396	1,353	1,440
5995 Optical goods stores	8	8	42	34	4	10,571	15,647	529	601
5999 Miscellaneous retail stores, nec	22	21	70	106	5	11,657	10,792	1,142	1,338

Source: County Business Patterns 1994/95, CBP-94/95, U.S. Department of Commerce, Washington DC, November 1997. The employment column represents mid-March employment in the year. Pay per employee is calculated by dividing 1st Quarter payroll, annualized, by mid-March employment. The column headed 'Emp / Est' shows 'employees per establishment'. A dash (-) means that data are unavailable or cannot be calculated. nec means not elsewhere classified. *Notes:* 1. 1994 data incomplete; unavailable or withheld. 2. 1995 data incomplete; unavailable or withheld. 3. 1994 and 1995 data incomplete; unavailable or withheld.

ELMIRA, NY MSA

Wholesale and Retail Trade USA	Establishments		Employment		Emp / Est	Pay / Employee		Annual Payroll ($ 000)	
	1994	1995	1994	1995	1995	1994	1995	1994	1995
50- Wholesale trade	140	136	2,281	2,248	17	22,408	25,101	55,327	57,457
5013 Motor vehicle supplies and new parts	11	9	74	62	7	17,892	18,452	1,396	1,315
5014 Tires and tubes	3	3	29	51	17	20,828	16,627	811	912
5044 Office equipment	7	6	61	60	10	26,689	27,067	1,706	1,795
5046 Commercial equipment, nec	3	3	18	17	6	18,667	21,882	366	373
5063 Electrical apparatus and equipment	5	5	66	62	12	24,667	27,742	1,738	1,861
5065 Electronic parts and equipment	5	-	20	-	-	18,400	-	406	-
5074 Plumbing & hydronic heating supplies	5	4	82	79	20	24,049	25,873	1,959	2,002
5084 Industrial machinery and equipment	4	4	31	80	20	18,968	13,700	781	918
5085 Industrial supplies	8	8	73	87	11	27,123	30,667	2,054	2,385
5087 Service establishment equipment	5	5	49	48	10	26,367	27,250	1,541	1,397
5093 Scrap and waste materials	3	3	61	57	19	18,754	28,281	1,748	2,250
5110 Paper and paper products	4	-	44	-	-	20,000	-	1,016	-
5149 Groceries and related products, nec	8	9	159	199	22	19,899	22,513	3,494	4,642
5169 Chemicals & allied products, nec	4	4	139	126	32	23,827	28,476	3,685	4,047
5170 Petroleum and petroleum products	6	5	91	68	14	24,000	22,824	2,289	1,562
5199 Nondurable goods, nec	3	-	17	-	-	11,765	-	181	-
52- Retail trade	645	616	7,599	7,429	12	10,130	10,967	86,089	85,362
5210 Lumber and other building materials	10	9	175	168	19	22,834	22,810	3,926	3,824
5250 Hardware stores	-	3	-	15	5	-	17,067	-	250
5260 Retail nurseries and garden stores	7	7	43	48	7	12,000	11,583	668	737
5310 Department stores	8	7	1,076	910	130	10,052	12,207	13,040	11,907
5410 Grocery stores	35	39	781	720	18	10,658	10,411	8,494	7,747
5420 Meat and fish markets	3	3	6	6	2	10,000	10,667	60	65
5440 Candy, nut, and confectionery stores	4	3	17	14	5	4,941	4,286	74	59
5460 Retail bakeries	6	5	77	66	13	9,091	8,424	766	580
5490 Miscellaneous food stores	4	4	11	9	2	10,182	11,111	98	104
5510 New and used car dealers	8	8	298	312	39	21,409	23,103	7,540	7,692
5530 Auto and home supply stores	20	15	97	103	7	18,103	15,806	2,073	1,805
5540 Gasoline service stations	37	36	216	222	6	9,648	10,468	2,328	2,302
5610 Men's & boys' clothing stores	6	6	39	50	8	8,308	12,560	447	527
5620 Women's clothing stores	20	18	210	184	10	6,610	6,848	1,533	1,329
5650 Family clothing stores	7	5	44	37	7	9,545	9,622	415	375
5660 Shoe stores	14	13	104	90	7	7,962	8,800	938	804
5690 Misc. apparel & accessory stores	6	4	29	27	7	8,690	9,481	266	244
5712 Furniture stores	8	8	51	72	9	12,863	12,944	723	957
5713 Floor covering stores	-	4	-	21	5	-	17,905	-	425
5719 Misc. homefurnishings stores	5	5	17	22	4	10,824	9,273	204	222
5720 Household appliance stores	4	3	22	15	5	18,727	19,467	369	307
5731 Radio, TV, & electronic stores	7	-	48	-	-	16,833	-	706	-
5735 Record & prerecorded tape stores	-	5	-	24	5	-	8,833	-	223
5736 Musical instrument stores	5	5	13	14	3	11,385	10,857	154	164
5812 Eating places	159	146	2,290	2,407	16	7,380	7,731	19,099	19,268
5813 Drinking places	44	42	145	117	3	7,200	7,077	1,044	957
5910 Drug stores and proprietary stores	18	15	298	289	19	13,128	13,564	4,683	4,792
5920 Liquor stores	11	12	46	47	4	9,913	10,723	534	531

Continued on next page.

ELMIRA, NY MSA - [continued]

Wholesale and Retail Trade USA	Establishments		Employment		Emp / Est	Pay / Employee		Annual Payroll ($ 000)	
	1994	1995	1994	1995	1995	1994	1995	1994	1995
5930 Used merchandise stores	4	5	28	34	7	11,143	11,059	350	403
5941 Sporting goods and bicycle shops	10	10	183	139	14	8,699	11,338	1,722	1,747
5942 Book stores	5	5	40	31	6	6,200	6,839	241	224
5944 Jewelry stores	13	17	95	96	6	11,032	11,833	1,073	1,258
5945 Hobby, toy, and game shops	10	10	60	89	9	8,267	11,011	848	1,071
5947 Gift, novelty, and souvenir shops	19	17	77	88	5	7,013	5,773	614	608
5949 Sewing, needlework, and piece goods	4	3	49	33	11	4,898	6,061	239	202
5962 Merchandising machine operators	3	3	38	38	13	20,211	19,053	861	826
5963 Direct selling establishments	8	8	92	45	6	9,522	16,889	798	771
5980 Fuel dealers	4	4	32	42	11	25,125	15,810	881	715
5995 Optical goods stores	10	9	85	55	6	10,400	22,545	932	914
5999 Miscellaneous retail stores, nec	16	14	74	78	6	8,324	8,821	768	746

Source: County Business Patterns 1994/95, CBP-94/95, U.S. Department of Commerce, Washington DC, November 1997. The employment column represents mid-March employment in the year. Pay per employee is calculated by dividing 1st Quarter payroll, annualized, by mid-March employment. The column headed 'Emp / Est' shows 'employees per establishment'. A dash (-) means that data are unavailable or cannot be calculated. nec means not elsewhere classified. *Notes:* 1. 1994 data incomplete; unavailable or withheld. 2. 1995 data incomplete; unavailable or withheld. 3. 1994 and 1995 data incomplete; unavailable or withheld.

ENID, OK MSA

Wholesale and Retail Trade USA	Establishments		Employment		Emp / Est	Pay / Employee		Annual Payroll ($ 000)	
	1994	1995	1994	1995	1995	1994	1995	1994	1995
50- Wholesale trade	-	146	-	1,920	13	-	22,513	-	45,726
5012 Automobiles and other vehicles	-	4	-	75	19	-	22,240	-	1,252
5013 Motor vehicle supplies and new parts	-	7	-	69	10	-	17,275	-	1,201
5030 Lumber and construction materials	-	3	-	26	9	-	16,308	-	442
5040 Professional & commercial equipment	-	4	-	48	12	-	24,333	-	1,420
5063 Electrical apparatus and equipment	-	4	-	18	5	-	22,667	-	478
5065 Electronic parts and equipment	-	3	-	47	16	-	20,000	-	1,122
5074 Plumbing & hydronic heating supplies	-	4	-	20	5	-	26,400	-	445
5082 Construction and mining machinery	-	4	-	19	5	-	34,316	-	681
5083 Farm and garden machinery	-	7	-	75	11	-	22,187	-	1,729
5084 Industrial machinery and equipment	-	19	-	152	8	-	24,553	-	4,038
5085 Industrial supplies	-	5	-	12	2	-	17,333	-	202
5087 Service establishment equipment	-	4	-	18	5	-	20,444	-	337
5149 Groceries and related products, nec	-	4	-	58	15	-	25,103	-	1,483
5153 Grain and field beans	-	15	-	149	10	-	25,315	-	3,671
5160 Chemicals and allied products	-	7	-	40	6	-	18,200	-	814
5170 Petroleum and petroleum products	-	9	-	67	7	-	26,687	-	1,713
5190 Misc., nondurable goods	-	8	-	48	6	-	35,500	-	1,884
52- Retail trade	-	426	-	4,994	12	-	11,071	-	57,478
5210 Lumber and other building materials	-	8	-	92	12	-	18,826	-	1,562
5260 Retail nurseries and garden stores	-	4	-	24	6	-	10,333	-	265
5310 Department stores	-	5	-	663	133	-	12,555	-	8,098
5410 Grocery stores	-	33	-	633	19	-	11,090	-	7,274
5460 Retail bakeries	-	4	-	23	6	-	8,348	-	175
5510 New and used car dealers	-	9	-	268	30	-	23,134	-	6,713
5520 Used car dealers	-	6	-	17	3	-	13,412	-	234
5530 Auto and home supply stores	-	12	-	78	7	-	16,718	-	1,451
5540 Gasoline service stations	-	29	-	125	4	-	11,328	-	1,528
5620 Women's clothing stores	-	15	-	77	5	-	9,455	-	711
5650 Family clothing stores	-	10	-	101	10	-	8,950	-	891
5660 Shoe stores	-	9	-	33	4	-	10,303	-	311
5712 Furniture stores	-	5	-	27	5	-	16,444	-	453
5713 Floor covering stores	-	4	-	26	7	-	16,769	-	485
5720 Household appliance stores	-	7	-	47	7	-	12,851	-	697
5735 Record & prerecorded tape stores	-	4	-	58	15	-	8,069	-	422
5812 Eating places	-	90	-	1,647	18	-	7,150	-	12,260
5813 Drinking places	-	11	-	50	5	-	6,320	-	260
5910 Drug stores and proprietary stores	-	11	-	116	11	-	15,241	-	2,246
5920 Liquor stores	-	5	-	14	3	-	6,857	-	104
5930 Used merchandise stores	-	6	-	17	3	-	12,706	-	237
5941 Sporting goods and bicycle shops	-	5	-	16	3	-	9,000	-	118
5942 Book stores	-	6	-	27	5	-	9,037	-	290
5944 Jewelry stores	-	9	-	43	5	-	16,093	-	525
5947 Gift, novelty, and souvenir shops	-	14	-	51	4	-	8,706	-	438
5992 Florists	-	8	-	51	6	-	7,451	-	400
5995 Optical goods stores	-	6	-	26	4	-	11,385	-	297
5999 Miscellaneous retail stores, nec	-	12	-	49	4	-	13,633	-	689

Source: County Business Patterns 1994/95, CBP-94/95, U.S. Department of Commerce, Washington DC, November 1997. The employment column represents mid-March employment in the year. Pay per employee is calculated by dividing 1st Quarter payroll, annualized, by mid-March employment. The column headed 'Emp / Est' shows 'employees per establishment'. A dash (-) means that data are unavailable or cannot be calculated. nec means not elsewhere classified. *Notes:* 1. 1994 data incomplete; unavailable or withheld. 2. 1995 data incomplete; unavailable or withheld. 3. 1994 and 1995 data incomplete; unavailable or withheld.

ERIE, PA MSA

Wholesale and Retail Trade USA	Establishments		Employment		Emp / Est	Pay / Employee		Annual Payroll ($ 000)	
	1994	1995	1994	1995	1995	1994	1995	1994	1995
50- Wholesale trade	-	424	-	4,864	11	-	26,427	-	135,471
5012 Automobiles and other vehicles	-	4	-	164	41	-	17,512	-	3,097
5013 Motor vehicle supplies and new parts	-	24	-	166	7	-	15,614	-	2,846
5021 Furniture	-	6	-	68	11	-	24,235	-	1,631
5023 Homefurnishings	-	5	-	50	10	-	23,040	-	1,190
5031 Lumber, plywood, and millwork	-	10	-	110	11	-	25,964	-	2,991
5033 Roofing, siding, & insulation	-	6	-	67	11	-	30,090	-	2,231
5044 Office equipment	-	11	-	128	12	-	29,000	-	3,600
5045 Computers, peripherals, & software	-	12	-	108	9	-	40,444	-	3,953
5046 Commercial equipment, nec	-	8	-	67	8	-	15,582	-	1,091
5047 Medical and hospital equipment	-	6	-	44	7	-	27,545	-	1,307
5051 Metals service centers and offices	-	14	-	187	13	-	33,754	-	7,647
5063 Electrical apparatus and equipment	-	16	-	356	22	-	28,169	-	11,481
5064 Electrical appliances, TV & radios	-	3	-	18	6	-	18,889	-	322
5065 Electronic parts and equipment	-	7	-	31	4	-	19,097	-	649
5072 Hardware	-	6	-	117	20	-	41,094	-	5,192
5074 Plumbing & hydronic heating supplies	-	11	-	107	10	-	25,047	-	2,531
5075 Warm air heating & air conditioning	-	3	-	26	9	-	42,615	-	630
5082 Construction and mining machinery	-	12	-	108	9	-	35,037	-	4,122
5083 Farm and garden machinery	-	4	-	35	9	-	17,371	-	628
5084 Industrial machinery and equipment	-	32	-	276	9	-	37,696	-	10,371
5085 Industrial supplies	-	34	-	372	11	-	27,677	-	10,831
5087 Service establishment equipment	-	11	-	246	22	-	25,236	-	6,057
5091 Sporting & recreational goods	-	4	-	21	5	-	15,048	-	330
5093 Scrap and waste materials	-	13	-	244	19	-	28,246	-	7,765
5099 Durable goods, nec	-	5	-	19	4	-	20,421	-	397
5112 Stationery and office supplies	-	10	-	81	8	-	18,321	-	2,534
5142 Packaged frozen food	-	4	-	33	8	-	22,667	-	588
5147 Meats and meat products	-	4	-	51	13	-	20,392	-	1,197
5148 Fresh fruits and vegetables	-	4	-	42	11	-	16,762	-	786
5149 Groceries and related products, nec	-	12	-	367	31	-	28,272	-	8,721
5162 Plastics materials & basic shapes	-	6	-	74	12	-	23,838	-	2,093
5169 Chemicals & allied products, nec	-	4	-	45	11	-	26,756	-	1,861
5170 Petroleum and petroleum products	-	7	-	147	21	-	22,231	-	3,189
5181 Beer and ale	-	9	-	176	20	-	25,841	-	4,881
5191 Farm supplies	-	9	-	61	7	-	20,459	-	1,241
5199 Nondurable goods, nec	-	14	-	52	4	-	16,538	-	1,378
52- Retail trade	-	1,735	-	22,816	13	-	10,793	-	268,280
5210 Lumber and other building materials	-	35	-	596	17	-	15,805	-	9,644
5230 Paint, glass, and wallpaper stores	-	11	-	68	6	-	14,176	-	1,076
5250 Hardware stores	-	15	-	77	5	-	10,390	-	845
5260 Retail nurseries and garden stores	-	23	-	106	5	-	11,057	-	1,446
5270 Mobile home dealers	-	5	-	64	13	-	11,250	-	969
5310 Department stores	-	15	-	2,139	143	-	11,306	-	26,920
5330 Variety stores	-	20	-	190	10	-	9,263	-	1,830
5390 Misc. general merchandise stores	-	15	-	420	28	-	11,457	-	4,529
5410 Grocery stores	-	127	-	3,400	27	-	10,600	-	40,183
5420 Meat and fish markets	-	13	-	88	7	-	9,455	-	916
5450 Dairy products stores	-	3	-	6	2	-	13,333	-	89
5460 Retail bakeries	-	25	-	233	9	-	6,867	-	1,651
5490 Miscellaneous food stores	-	7	-	35	5	-	12,800	-	495
5510 New and used car dealers	-	37	-	1,316	36	-	26,009	-	38,052
5520 Used car dealers	-	28	-	110	4	-	14,436	-	1,720
5530 Auto and home supply stores	-	47	-	306	7	-	15,882	-	5,294
5540 Gasoline service stations	-	105	-	740	7	-	10,535	-	8,019
5570 Motorcycle dealers	-	6	-	80	13	-	14,200	-	1,408
5610 Men's & boys' clothing stores	-	17	-	132	8	-	10,061	-	1,419
5620 Women's clothing stores	-	44	-	349	8	-	7,060	-	2,559
5630 Women's accessory & specialty stores	-	4	-	34	9	-	7,647	-	265
5640 Children's and infants' wear stores	-	7	-	72	10	-	6,333	-	480
5650 Family clothing stores	-	16	-	206	13	-	10,816	-	2,290
5660 Shoe stores	-	42	-	181	4	-	11,757	-	2,076
5690 Misc. apparel & accessory stores	-	7	-	27	4	-	9,333	-	376
5712 Furniture stores	-	31	-	291	9	-	17,017	-	5,657
5713 Floor covering stores	-	15	-	158	11	-	17,696	-	2,914
5720 Household appliance stores	-	12	-	56	5	-	19,071	-	1,007
5731 Radio, TV, & electronic stores	-	23	-	219	10	-	18,740	-	3,672
5734 Computer and software stores	-	11	-	44	4	-	13,818	-	604
5735 Record & prerecorded tape stores	-	13	-	188	14	-	10,596	-	1,493
5736 Musical instrument stores	-	6	-	30	5	-	10,533	-	445
5812 Eating places	-	363	-	7,175	20	-	6,329	-	48,875

Continued on next page.

ERIE, PA MSA - [continued]

Wholesale and Retail Trade USA	Establishments		Employment		Emp / Est	Pay / Employee		Annual Payroll ($ 000)	
	1994	1995	1994	1995	1995	1994	1995	1994	1995
5813 Drinking places	-	126	-	654	5	-	7,388	-	4,922
5910 Drug stores and proprietary stores	-	50	-	653	13	-	15,136	-	10,131
5920 Liquor stores	-	44	-	166	4	-	13,855	-	2,360
5930 Used merchandise stores	-	15	-	47	3	-	8,170	-	453
5941 Sporting goods and bicycle shops	-	35	-	283	8	-	10,926	-	3,313
5942 Book stores	-	14	-	149	11	-	8,940	-	1,284
5944 Jewelry stores	-	29	-	144	5	-	11,667	-	1,744
5945 Hobby, toy, and game shops	-	8	-	91	11	-	9,802	-	1,005
5947 Gift, novelty, and souvenir shops	-	29	-	121	4	-	9,124	-	1,266
5949 Sewing, needlework, and piece goods	-	6	-	62	10	-	5,613	-	369
5961 Catalog and mail-order houses	-	9	-	58	6	-	13,586	-	1,108
5962 Merchandising machine operators	-	7	-	165	24	-	13,600	-	2,400
5963 Direct selling establishments	-	12	-	73	6	-	20,384	-	1,462
5980 Fuel dealers	-	3	-	36	12	-	18,889	-	864
5992 Florists	-	38	-	173	5	-	7,283	-	1,362
5993 Tobacco stores and stands	-	3	-	20	7	-	9,000	-	201
5994 News dealers and newsstands	-	3	-	19	6	-	7,158	-	139
5995 Optical goods stores	-	17	-	115	7	-	14,470	-	1,745
5999 Miscellaneous retail stores, nec	-	45	-	204	5	-	11,647	-	2,867

Source: County Business Patterns 1994/95, CBP-94/95, U.S. Department of Commerce, Washington DC, November 1997. The employment column represents mid-March employment in the year. Pay per employee is calculated by dividing 1st Quarter payroll, annualized, by mid-March employment. The column headed 'Emp / Est' shows 'employees per establishment'. A dash (-) means that data are unavailable or cannot be calculated. nec means not elsewhere classified. *Notes:* 1. 1994 data incomplete; unavailable or withheld. 2. 1995 data incomplete; unavailable or withheld. 3. 1994 and 1995 data incomplete; unavailable or withheld.

EUGENE – SPRINGFIELD, OR MSA

Wholesale and Retail Trade USA	Establishments		Employment		Emp / Est	Pay / Employee		Annual Payroll ($ 000)	
	1994	1995	1994	1995	1995	1994	1995	1994	1995
50– Wholesale trade	-	607	-	7,244	12	-	25,191	-	194,973
5012 Automobiles and other vehicles	-	6	-	162	27	-	23,827	-	3,728
5013 Motor vehicle supplies and new parts	-	28	-	262	9	-	25,176	-	6,718
5014 Tires and tubes	-	6	-	82	14	-	21,561	-	2,064
5015 Motor vehicle parts, used	-	11	-	70	6	-	19,600	-	1,543
5023 Homefurnishings	-	6	-	122	20	-	21,213	-	2,767
5031 Lumber, plywood, and millwork	-	57	-	577	10	-	32,513	-	20,182
5039 Construction materials, nec	-	9	-	270	30	-	24,696	-	7,258
5044 Office equipment	-	17	-	185	11	-	32,735	-	5,328
5045 Computers, peripherals, & software	-	29	-	212	7	-	27,585	-	6,101
5046 Commercial equipment, nec	-	5	-	59	12	-	38,983	-	3,136
5047 Medical and hospital equipment	-	6	-	66	11	-	30,788	-	2,117
5051 Metals service centers and offices	-	8	-	299	37	-	20,254	-	10,243
5063 Electrical apparatus and equipment	-	23	-	212	9	-	33,358	-	6,845
5072 Hardware	-	9	-	273	30	-	19,985	-	6,019
5074 Plumbing & hydronic heating supplies	-	12	-	146	12	-	23,370	-	3,154
5082 Construction and mining machinery	-	16	-	453	28	-	30,834	-	16,059
5083 Farm and garden machinery	-	12	-	148	12	-	25,270	-	3,389
5084 Industrial machinery and equipment	-	32	-	225	7	-	31,787	-	7,035
5085 Industrial supplies	-	31	-	362	12	-	28,939	-	11,077
5087 Service establishment equipment	-	13	-	104	8	-	23,192	-	2,692
5088 Transportation equipment & supplies	-	4	-	31	8	-	38,452	-	1,131
5091 Sporting & recreational goods	-	8	-	83	10	-	15,036	-	1,326
5093 Scrap and waste materials	-	11	-	130	12	-	21,908	-	3,101
5099 Durable goods, nec	-	23	-	171	7	-	23,649	-	4,263
5112 Stationery and office supplies	-	20	-	195	10	-	19,590	-	3,613
5143 Dairy products, exc. dried or canned	-	4	-	25	6	-	32,480	-	840
5145 Confectionery	-	5	-	34	7	-	12,824	-	408
5147 Meats and meat products	-	4	-	85	21	-	20,188	-	1,305
5148 Fresh fruits and vegetables	-	7	-	92	13	-	18,652	-	1,921
5149 Groceries and related products, nec	-	13	-	134	10	-	24,567	-	3,663
5150 Farm-product raw materials	-	5	-	50	10	-	5,200	-	288
5160 Chemicals and allied products	-	11	-	55	5	-	33,091	-	2,017
5170 Petroleum and petroleum products	-	14	-	313	22	-	18,888	-	6,076
5181 Beer and ale	-	5	-	132	26	-	27,030	-	3,903
5182 Wine and distilled beverages	-	4	-	50	13	-	21,280	-	1,284
5191 Farm supplies	-	12	-	132	11	-	22,545	-	3,139
5192 Books, periodicals, & newspapers	-	7	-	192	27	-	16,646	-	3,162
5193 Flowers & florists' supplies	-	8	-	60	8	-	14,867	-	926
5199 Nondurable goods, nec	-	18	-	189	11	-	18,836	-	3,754
52– Retail trade	-	2,049	-	26,784	13	-	13,727	-	390,544

Continued on next page.

EUGENE – SPRINGFIELD, OR MSA - [continued]

Wholesale and Retail Trade USA	Establishments		Employment		Emp / Est	Pay / Employee		Annual Payroll ($ 000)	
	1994	1995	1994	1995	1995	1994	1995	1994	1995
5210 Lumber and other building materials	-	28	-	657	23	-	23,275	-	15,396
5230 Paint, glass, and wallpaper stores	-	10	-	55	6	-	16,291	-	1,007
5250 Hardware stores	-	14	-	87	6	-	14,943	-	1,309
5260 Retail nurseries and garden stores	-	20	-	132	7	-	12,545	-	1,919
5270 Mobile home dealers	-	12	-	136	11	-	21,500	-	3,309
5310 Department stores	-	13	-	2,040	157	-	13,614	-	29,108
5330 Variety stores	-	7	-	34	5	-	8,000	-	283
5390 Misc. general merchandise stores	-	18	-	643	36	-	20,068	-	13,161
5410 Grocery stores	-	186	-	3,238	17	-	14,483	-	48,626
5420 Meat and fish markets	-	8	-	53	7	-	8,755	-	577
5440 Candy, nut, and confectionery stores	-	4	-	15	4	-	6,133	-	133
5460 Retail bakeries	-	21	-	205	10	-	8,351	-	1,812
5490 Miscellaneous food stores	-	18	-	119	7	-	7,496	-	849
5510 New and used car dealers	-	29	-	1,459	50	-	28,455	-	48,245
5520 Used car dealers	-	17	-	58	3	-	23,724	-	1,664
5530 Auto and home supply stores	-	50	-	537	11	-	21,698	-	11,554
5540 Gasoline service stations	-	79	-	831	11	-	10,960	-	9,720
5550 Boat dealers	-	4	-	87	22	-	25,287	-	2,428
5560 Recreational vehicle dealers	-	16	-	203	13	-	31,586	-	9,578
5570 Motorcycle dealers	-	9	-	33	4	-	20,727	-	637
5590 Automotive dealers, nec	-	3	-	5	2	-	25,600	-	118
5610 Men's & boys' clothing stores	-	10	-	64	6	-	10,500	-	696
5620 Women's clothing stores	-	41	-	346	8	-	9,630	-	3,194
5630 Women's accessory & specialty stores	-	10	-	61	6	-	9,443	-	554
5650 Family clothing stores	-	23	-	441	19	-	10,975	-	5,205
5660 Shoe stores	-	32	-	156	5	-	11,795	-	1,811
5690 Misc. apparel & accessory stores	-	8	-	31	4	-	12,387	-	483
5712 Furniture stores	-	41	-	285	7	-	22,807	-	6,554
5713 Floor covering stores	-	26	-	125	5	-	23,296	-	3,770
5720 Household appliance stores	-	13	-	81	6	-	17,679	-	1,613
5731 Radio, TV, & electronic stores	-	27	-	164	6	-	16,902	-	2,811
5734 Computer and software stores	-	17	-	74	4	-	15,568	-	1,131
5735 Record & prerecorded tape stores	-	15	-	94	6	-	12,511	-	1,344
5736 Musical instrument stores	-	8	-	26	3	-	15,692	-	456
5812 Eating places	-	517	-	8,684	17	-	8,070	-	75,058
5813 Drinking places	-	55	-	417	8	-	9,679	-	4,255
5910 Drug stores and proprietary stores	-	31	-	417	13	-	18,302	-	7,492
5920 Liquor stores	-	27	-	83	3	-	12,434	-	1,141
5930 Used merchandise stores	-	49	-	328	7	-	9,524	-	3,389
5941 Sporting goods and bicycle shops	-	37	-	299	8	-	13,217	-	4,374
5942 Book stores	-	31	-	352	11	-	11,705	-	4,207
5943 Stationery stores	-	6	-	44	7	-	12,636	-	424
5944 Jewelry stores	-	26	-	137	5	-	26,891	-	2,781
5945 Hobby, toy, and game shops	-	19	-	183	10	-	9,552	-	2,020
5946 Camera & photographic supply stores	-	7	-	27	4	-	10,519	-	278
5947 Gift, novelty, and souvenir shops	-	43	-	249	6	-	9,671	-	2,578
5948 Luggage and leather goods stores	-	5	-	18	4	-	9,556	-	236
5949 Sewing, needlework, and piece goods	-	18	-	99	6	-	8,566	-	885
5961 Catalog and mail-order houses	-	11	-	70	6	-	18,114	-	1,198
5962 Merchandising machine operators	-	8	-	61	8	-	22,098	-	1,314
5963 Direct selling establishments	-	33	-	193	6	-	12,352	-	2,758
5980 Fuel dealers	-	5	-	35	7	-	24,000	-	788
5992 Florists	-	33	-	158	5	-	7,975	-	1,309
5995 Optical goods stores	-	22	-	122	6	-	19,410	-	2,668
5999 Miscellaneous retail stores, nec	-	71	-	372	5	-	11,720	-	4,960

Source: County Business Patterns 1994/95, CBP-94/95, U.S. Department of Commerce, Washington DC, November 1997. The employment column represents mid-March employment in the year. Pay per employee is calculated by dividing 1st Quarter payroll, annualized, by mid-March employment. The column headed 'Emp / Est' shows 'employees per establishment'. A dash (-) means that data are unavailable or cannot be calculated. nec means not elsewhere classified. *Notes:* 1. 1994 data incomplete; unavailable or withheld. 2. 1995 data incomplete; unavailable or withheld. 3. 1994 and 1995 data incomplete; unavailable or withheld.

EVANSVILLE – HENDERSON MSA (IN PART)

Wholesale and Retail Trade USA	Establishments		Employment		Emp / Est	Pay / Employee		Annual Payroll ($ 000)	
	1994	1995	1994	1995	1995	1994	1995	1994	1995
50 – Wholesale trade	533	512	6,504	6,727	13	25,231	26,303	178,137	186,643
5012 Automobiles and other vehicles [3]	6	6	276	234	39	15,507	21,966	4,965	5,384
5013 Motor vehicle supplies and new parts [3]	36	29	362	306	11	18,144	18,510	7,198	6,234
5014 Tires and tubes [2]	-	5	-	99	20	-	30,061	-	3,344
5015 Motor vehicle parts, used [2]	-	6	-	56	9	-	16,000	-	931

Continued on next page.

EVANSVILLE – HENDERSON MSA (IN PART) - [continued]

Wholesale and Retail Trade USA	Establishments		Employment		Emp / Est	Pay / Employee		Annual Payroll ($ 000)	
	1994	1995	1994	1995	1995	1994	1995	1994	1995
5021 Furniture [3]	4	3	44	88	29	22,727	16,818	1,169	1,452
5023 Homefurnishings [3]	6	3	26	13	4	19,385	11,077	441	142
5031 Lumber, plywood, and millwork [3]	15	12	344	284	24	19,581	21,944	8,077	6,526
5032 Brick, stone, & related materials	6	5	37	52	10	18,486	15,769	1,333	934
5033 Roofing, siding, & insulation	8	6	115	73	12	25,391	25,151	4,024	1,895
5039 Construction materials, nec [3]	4	8	17	113	14	8,471	30,053	271	3,886
5044 Office equipment [3]	12	11	144	154	14	22,417	24,104	3,727	4,001
5045 Computers, peripherals, & software [3]	16	13	134	143	11	44,776	57,986	5,455	6,310
5046 Commercial equipment, nec [3]	5	5	50	50	10	19,920	23,840	1,233	1,319
5047 Medical and hospital equipment [1]	8	-	32	-	-	17,625	-	511	-
5048 Ophthalmic goods [2]	-	5	-	23	5	-	20,696	-	448
5049 Professional equipment, nec [1]	3	-	7	-	-	12,000	-	151	-
5050 Metals and minerals, except petroleum [3]	11	11	108	114	10	26,556	32,316	3,111	3,830
5063 Electrical apparatus and equipment [3]	18	16	236	238	15	28,712	35,025	6,542	7,451
5072 Hardware [3]	13	12	158	126	11	31,013	20,413	4,103	2,814
5074 Plumbing & hydronic heating supplies [3]	10	11	148	136	12	23,730	26,588	3,842	3,805
5075 Warm air heating & air conditioning [3]	16	17	96	122	7	23,292	20,852	2,325	2,565
5078 Refrigeration equipment and supplies [3]	3	3	13	16	5	51,077	37,250	658	565
5082 Construction and mining machinery [3]	14	14	250	320	23	39,648	37,050	11,093	12,214
5084 Industrial machinery and equipment	36	31	597	630	20	27,899	30,724	19,492	20,600
5085 Industrial supplies	25	26	251	305	12	25,355	24,407	7,161	8,091
5087 Service establishment equipment [3]	11	10	88	73	7	14,409	17,479	1,397	1,204
5093 Scrap and waste materials [1]	12	16	170	155	10	25,647	25,574	4,579	4,890
5112 Stationery and office supplies [3]	12	14	158	164	12	17,215	20,317	2,787	3,199
5120 Drugs, proprietaries, and sundries [3]	6	6	164	146	24	26,366	24,877	5,529	5,593
5130 Apparel, piece goods, and notions [3]	5	5	7	9	2	8,000	10,222	159	89
5142 Packaged frozen food [3]	4	4	126	156	39	24,317	18,564	3,694	3,137
5145 Confectionery [3]	4	4	46	59	15	16,870	19,864	1,328	1,364
5149 Groceries and related products, nec [3]	19	21	340	351	17	26,012	25,584	10,571	10,378
5153 Grain and field beans	7	8	89	103	13	25,573	25,515	2,503	3,641
5162 Plastics materials & basic shapes [1]	11	13	140	142	11	61,314	37,831	5,538	5,322
5169 Chemicals & allied products, nec [3]	5	5	35	49	10	31,200	35,755	1,247	1,713
5171 Petroleum bulk stations & terminals	15	15	157	142	9	17,070	19,155	2,975	2,977
5172 Petroleum products, nec [3]	3	3	16	11	4	29,250	34,545	530	253
5180 Beer, wine, and distilled beverages [3]	6	6	173	123	21	27,838	32,423	5,060	4,416
5191 Farm supplies	19	19	156	237	12	26,718	28,658	4,441	6,222
5192 Books, periodicals, & newspapers [3]	5	4	44	52	13	16,364	14,000	764	791
5198 Paints, varnishes, and supplies [3]	7	6	63	41	7	19,429	22,049	1,199	915
5199 Nondurable goods, nec [3]	16	15	22	20	1	21,818	24,200	539	497
52 – Retail trade	1,590	1,583	25,105	26,126	17	10,568	11,381	297,802	310,347
5210 Lumber and other building materials	26	36	496	735	20	15,484	19,004	9,979	13,637
5230 Paint, glass, and wallpaper stores	17	21	47	99	5	15,319	14,828	730	1,338
5250 Hardware stores	16	10	182	39	4	11,538	11,692	2,537	490
5260 Retail nurseries and garden stores	17	19	144	167	9	9,778	11,401	1,745	2,160
5270 Mobile home dealers [1]	4	5	16	9	2	22,000	43,111	432	443
5310 Department stores [3]	15	13	2,485	2,465	190	9,962	10,668	26,617	26,713
5330 Variety stores [2]	14	7	85	70	10	7,388	7,029	760	502
5390 Misc. general merchandise stores [1]	6	14	256	311	22	11,625	12,116	3,131	3,445
5410 Grocery stores	96	88	2,955	2,967	34	9,369	10,090	29,685	32,048
5420 Meat and fish markets [3]	6	7	58	66	9	11,379	15,091	784	1,076
5440 Candy, nut, and confectionery stores [2]	-	6	-	69	12	-	9,739	-	706
5460 Retail bakeries [3]	17	18	209	234	13	8,593	9,470	2,319	2,304
5510 New and used car dealers	24	21	982	1,039	49	22,566	23,442	25,536	24,728
5520 Used car dealers	40	44	88	118	3	15,045	14,644	1,589	1,911
5530 Auto and home supply stores	44	42	308	364	9	15,156	16,484	5,265	6,246
5540 Gasoline service stations	104	101	821	819	8	9,208	10,276	8,269	8,846
5550 Boat dealers [3]	6	6	18	19	3	26,222	23,579	531	511
5560 Recreational vehicle dealers [3]	6	5	47	56	11	16,851	19,571	1,031	1,188
5570 Motorcycle dealers [3]	7	5	39	53	11	17,128	16,830	1,005	1,220
5610 Men's & boys' clothing stores [3]	21	21	196	209	10	11,531	10,718	2,440	2,018
5620 Women's clothing stores	54	45	685	536	12	7,982	8,201	5,510	4,664
5630 Women's accessory & specialty stores [3]	7	6	46	38	6	6,870	9,263	329	346
5640 Children's and infants' wear stores [2]	-	4	-	53	13	-	6,717	-	342
5650 Family clothing stores [3]	12	12	131	136	11	10,931	11,529	1,534	1,519
5660 Shoe stores	25	23	222	178	8	9,586	12,584	2,345	2,360
5690 Misc. apparel & accessory stores [3]	8	8	35	31	4	6,629	7,355	269	219
5712 Furniture stores	35	35	293	342	10	16,573	16,211	5,558	5,876
5713 Floor covering stores	16	20	89	118	6	20,270	20,814	2,153	2,450
5719 Misc. homefurnishings stores	18	17	118	121	7	8,441	8,926	1,101	1,077
5720 Household appliance stores [3]	10	9	118	136	15	15,763	15,824	2,357	2,247
5731 Radio, TV, & electronic stores	17	15	202	249	17	15,743	14,088	3,355	3,607

Continued on next page.

EVANSVILLE - HENDERSON MSA (IN PART) - [continued]

Wholesale and Retail Trade USA	Establishments		Employment		Emp / Est	Pay / Employee		Annual Payroll ($ 000)	
	1994	1995	1994	1995	1995	1994	1995	1994	1995
5734 Computer and software stores[3]	5	8	27	32	4	17,333	19,375	693	851
5735 Record & prerecorded tape stores[3]	9	9	46	65	7	11,043	9,662	520	567
5736 Musical instrument stores[3]	6	5	97	90	18	14,722	18,089	1,591	1,565
5812 Eating places	390	369	8,007	8,629	23	7,012	7,615	63,218	69,517
5813 Drinking places	66	54	298	257	5	6,604	6,848	2,050	1,913
5910 Drug stores and proprietary stores	41	44	527	510	12	15,028	17,082	8,999	9,128
5920 Liquor stores	26	25	89	91	4	8,899	11,648	929	984
5930 Used merchandise stores	33	31	151	136	4	9,934	10,176	1,740	1,531
5941 Sporting goods and bicycle shops	31	32	216	201	6	8,574	9,831	2,375	2,395
5942 Book stores[3]	14	15	96	113	8	6,583	8,708	658	1,012
5944 Jewelry stores	33	32	292	271	8	15,315	15,867	4,339	4,294
5945 Hobby, toy, and game shops[3]	15	14	153	184	13	8,471	8,283	1,641	1,579
5947 Gift, novelty, and souvenir shops	30	32	153	199	6	6,222	7,136	1,234	1,610
5949 Sewing, needlework, and piece goods[3]	10	10	7	7	1	2,857	2,857	22	23
5961 Catalog and mail-order houses[3]	7	6	21	18	3	14,476	16,222	314	201
5962 Merchandising machine operators[3]	14	13	168	148	11	16,190	17,676	2,887	2,741
5963 Direct selling establishments[3]	20	20	107	125	6	17,832	16,320	2,050	2,388
5992 Florists	26	27	179	181	7	9,832	11,028	2,037	1,975
5994 News dealers and newsstands[3]	5	5	21	19	4	7,048	9,684	161	197
5995 Optical goods stores[3]	6	7	62	66	9	14,516	14,606	881	922
5999 Miscellaneous retail stores, nec[2]	50	54	234	284	5	14,342	13,000	3,542	4,046

Source: County Business Patterns 1994/95, CBP-94/95, U.S. Department of Commerce, Washington DC, November 1997. The employment column represents mid-March employment in the year. Pay per employee is calculated by dividing 1st Quarter payroll, annualized, by mid-March employment. The column headed 'Emp / Est' shows 'employees per establishment'. A dash (-) means that data are unavailable or cannot be calculated. nec means not elsewhere classified. *Notes:* 1. 1994 data incomplete; unavailable or withheld. 2. 1995 data incomplete; unavailable or withheld. 3. 1994 and 1995 data incomplete; unavailable or withheld.

EVANSVILLE - HENDERSON MSA (KY PART)

Wholesale and Retail Trade USA	Establishments		Employment		Emp / Est	Pay / Employee		Annual Payroll ($ 000)	
	1994	1995	1994	1995	1995	1994	1995	1994	1995
50- Wholesale trade	82	83	905	875	11	23,558	26,651	23,027	23,898
5013 Motor vehicle supplies and new parts	3	-	12	-	-	16,333	-	194	-
5040 Professional & commercial equipment	6	5	65	58	12	17,538	18,759	1,211	1,119
5060 Electrical goods	5	5	12	11	2	16,667	13,455	173	188
5084 Industrial machinery and equipment	9	10	98	105	11	26,122	26,971	3,270	3,136
5150 Farm-product raw materials	5	6	36	48	8	23,000	25,500	1,174	1,381
5171 Petroleum bulk stations & terminals	6	6	54	49	8	13,333	15,755	852	919
5191 Farm supplies	4	-	32	-	-	22,250	-	802	-
5199 Nondurable goods, nec	3	3	16	16	5	19,750	22,000	331	333
52- Retail trade	272	269	3,375	3,423	13	11,095	11,368	40,911	41,725
5210 Lumber and other building materials	7	6	39	43	7	18,564	22,977	715	892
5230 Paint, glass, and wallpaper stores	5	-	21	-	-	15,619	-	397	-
5250 Hardware stores	3	-	13	-	-	14,462	-	244	-
5390 Misc. general merchandise stores	4	4	65	71	18	9,785	9,070	670	687
5400 Food stores	29	33	497	526	16	8,885	8,829	4,597	4,841
5510 New and used car dealers	4	4	242	225	56	30,314	31,929	8,947	8,243
5520 Used car dealers	8	7	39	25	4	13,026	19,360	555	567
5530 Auto and home supply stores	8	8	50	46	6	18,640	18,609	1,043	923
5540 Gasoline service stations	31	26	367	258	10	10,627	11,550	3,192	3,112
5620 Women's clothing stores	10	8	80	62	8	7,250	6,129	636	371
5660 Shoe stores	4	5	30	29	6	17,067	17,103	619	600
5712 Furniture stores	-	7	-	56	8	-	14,571	-	845
5713 Floor covering stores	4	-	33	-	-	18,061	-	743	-
5812 Eating places	59	58	1,067	1,187	20	6,812	6,881	8,341	9,052
5813 Drinking places	4	5	27	41	8	7,259	7,220	230	339
5910 Drug stores and proprietary stores	11	10	79	98	10	15,544	16,776	1,394	1,730
5920 Liquor stores	9	8	80	39	5	13,600	9,744	1,169	381
5930 Used merchandise stores	5	5	13	10	2	5,231	8,000	76	82
5941 Sporting goods and bicycle shops	3	-	15	-	-	9,067	-	167	-
5944 Jewelry stores	5	5	37	48	10	12,432	11,500	471	650
5963 Direct selling establishments	5	4	6	7	2	56,667	42,857	143	153
5992 Florists	-	7	-	37	5	-	11,892	-	474
5999 Miscellaneous retail stores, nec	5	4	12	7	2	7,333	7,429	85	75

Source: County Business Patterns 1994/95, CBP-94/95, U.S. Department of Commerce, Washington DC, November 1997. The employment column represents mid-March employment in the year. Pay per employee is calculated by dividing 1st Quarter payroll, annualized, by mid-March employment. The column headed 'Emp / Est' shows 'employees per establishment'. A dash (-) means that data are unavailable or cannot be calculated. nec means not elsewhere classified. *Notes:* 1. 1994 data incomplete; unavailable or withheld. 2. 1995 data incomplete; unavailable or withheld. 3. 1994 and 1995 data incomplete; unavailable or withheld.

EVANSVILLE – HENDERSON, IN – KY MSA

Wholesale and Retail Trade USA	Establishments		Employment		Emp / Est	Pay / Employee		Annual Payroll ($ 000)	
	1994	1995	1994	1995	1995	1994	1995	1994	1995
50 – Wholesale trade	615	595	7,409	7,602	13	25,026	26,343	201,164	210,541
5012 Automobiles and other vehicles[3]	7	7	276	234	33	15,507	21,966	4,965	5,384
5013 Motor vehicle supplies and new parts[3]	39	33	374	306	9	18,086	18,510	7,392	6,234
5014 Tires and tubes[2]	-	6	-	99	17	-	30,061	-	3,344
5015 Motor vehicle parts, used[2]	-	6	-	56	9	-	16,000	-	931
5021 Furniture[3]	5	5	44	88	18	22,727	16,818	1,169	1,452
5023 Homefurnishings[3]	6	3	26	13	4	19,385	11,077	441	142
5031 Lumber, plywood, and millwork[3]	15	12	344	284	24	19,581	21,944	8,077	6,526
5032 Brick, stone, & related materials	7	6	37	52	9	18,486	15,769	1,333	934
5033 Roofing, siding, & insulation[3]	8	6	115	73	12	25,391	25,151	4,024	1,895
5039 Construction materials, nec[3]	5	8	17	113	14	8,471	30,053	271	3,886
5044 Office equipment[3]	15	13	144	154	12	22,417	24,104	3,727	4,001
5045 Computers, peripherals, & software[3]	16	13	134	143	11	44,776	57,986	5,455	6,310
5046 Commercial equipment, nec[3]	5	5	50	50	10	19,920	23,840	1,233	1,319
5047 Medical and hospital equipment[1]	9	-	32	-	-	17,625	-	511	-
5048 Ophthalmic goods[2]	-	5	-	23	5	-	20,696	-	448
5049 Professional equipment, nec[1]	4	-	7	-	-	12,000	-	151	-
5050 Metals and minerals, except petroleum[3]	16	15	108	114	8	26,556	32,316	3,111	3,830
5063 Electrical apparatus and equipment[3]	22	19	236	238	13	28,712	35,025	6,542	7,451
5072 Hardware[3]	14	13	158	126	10	31,013	20,413	4,103	2,814
5074 Plumbing & hydronic heating supplies[3]	10	12	148	136	11	23,730	26,588	3,842	3,805
5075 Warm air heating & air conditioning[3]	16	17	96	122	7	23,292	20,852	2,325	2,565
5078 Refrigeration equipment and supplies[3]	3	3	13	16	5	51,077	37,250	658	565
5082 Construction and mining machinery[3]	16	16	250	320	20	39,648	37,050	11,093	12,214
5084 Industrial machinery and equipment	45	41	695	735	18	27,649	30,188	22,762	23,736
5085 Industrial supplies	29	30	251	305	10	25,355	24,407	7,161	8,091
5087 Service establishment equipment[3]	11	10	88	73	7	14,409	17,479	1,397	1,204
5093 Scrap and waste materials[1]	14	19	170	155	8	25,647	25,574	4,579	4,890
5112 Stationery and office supplies[3]	15	16	158	164	10	17,215	20,317	2,787	3,199
5120 Drugs, proprietaries, and sundries[3]	7	8	164	146	18	26,366	24,877	5,529	5,593
5130 Apparel, piece goods, and notions[3]	6	6	7	9	2	8,000	10,222	159	89
5142 Packaged frozen food[3]	4	4	126	156	39	24,317	18,564	3,694	3,137
5145 Confectionery[3]	4	4	46	59	15	16,870	19,864	1,328	1,364
5149 Groceries and related products, nec[3]	20	22	340	351	16	26,012	25,584	10,571	10,378
5153 Grain and field beans	10	12	89	103	9	25,573	25,515	2,503	3,641
5162 Plastics materials & basic shapes[3]	11	13	140	142	11	61,314	37,831	5,538	5,322
5169 Chemicals & allied products, nec[3]	9	9	35	49	5	31,200	35,755	1,247	1,713
5171 Petroleum bulk stations & terminals	21	21	211	191	9	16,114	18,283	3,827	3,896
5172 Petroleum products, nec[3]	3	3	16	11	4	29,250	34,545	530	253
5180 Beer, wine, and distilled beverages[3]	8	8	173	123	15	27,838	32,423	5,060	4,416
5191 Farm supplies	23	23	188	237	10	25,957	28,658	5,243	6,222
5192 Books, periodicals, & newspapers[3]	5	4	44	52	13	16,364	14,000	764	791
5198 Paints, varnishes, and supplies[3]	9	7	63	41	6	19,429	22,049	1,199	915
5199 Nondurable goods, nec[3]	19	18	38	36	2	20,947	23,222	870	830
52 – Retail trade	1,862	1,852	28,480	29,549	16	10,631	11,379	338,713	352,072
5210 Lumber and other building materials	33	42	535	778	19	15,708	19,224	10,694	14,529
5230 Paint, glass, and wallpaper stores	22	26	68	99	4	15,412	14,828	1,127	1,338
5250 Hardware stores	19	11	195	39	4	11,733	11,692	2,781	490
5260 Retail nurseries and garden stores	19	20	144	167	8	9,778	11,401	1,745	2,160
5270 Mobile home dealers[3]	5	5	16	9	2	22,000	43,111	432	443
5310 Department stores[3]	17	15	2,485	2,465	164	9,962	10,668	26,617	26,713
5330 Variety stores[2]	18	11	85	70	6	7,388	7,029	760	502
5390 Misc. general merchandise stores[1]	10	18	321	382	21	11,252	11,550	3,801	4,132
5410 Grocery stores[3]	121	117	2,955	2,967	25	9,369	10,090	29,685	32,048
5420 Meat and fish markets[3]	6	7	58	66	9	11,379	15,091	784	1,076
5440 Candy, nut, and confectionery stores[2]	-	6	-	69	12	-	9,739	-	706
5460 Retail bakeries[3]	20	21	209	234	11	8,593	9,470	2,319	2,304
5510 New and used car dealers	28	25	1,224	1,264	51	24,098	24,953	34,483	32,971
5520 Used car dealers	48	51	127	143	3	14,425	15,469	2,144	2,478
5530 Auto and home supply stores	52	50	358	410	8	15,642	16,722	6,308	7,169
5540 Gasoline service stations	135	127	1,188	1,077	8	9,646	10,581	11,461	11,958
5550 Boat dealers[3]	6	6	18	19	3	26,222	23,579	531	511
5560 Recreational vehicle dealers[3]	6	5	47	56	11	16,851	19,571	1,031	1,188
5570 Motorcycle dealers[3]	7	5	39	53	11	17,128	16,830	1,005	1,220
5610 Men's & boys' clothing stores[3]	22	22	196	209	10	11,531	10,718	2,440	2,018
5620 Women's clothing stores	64	53	765	598	11	7,906	7,987	6,146	5,035
5630 Women's accessory & specialty stores[3]	8	7	46	38	5	6,870	9,263	329	346
5640 Children's and infants' wear stores[2]	-	5	-	53	11	-	6,717	-	342
5650 Family clothing stores[3]	14	14	131	136	10	10,931	11,529	1,534	1,519
5660 Shoe stores	29	28	252	207	7	10,476	13,217	2,964	2,960
5690 Misc. apparel & accessory stores[3]	8	8	35	31	4	6,629	7,355	269	219

Continued on next page.

EVANSVILLE – HENDERSON, IN – KY MSA - [continued]

Wholesale and Retail Trade USA	Establishments		Employment		Emp / Est	Pay / Employee		Annual Payroll ($ 000)	
	1994	1995	1994	1995	1995	1994	1995	1994	1995
5712 Furniture stores	41	42	293	398	9	16,573	15,980	5,558	6,721
5713 Floor covering stores	20	23	122	118	5	19,672	20,814	2,896	2,450
5719 Misc. homefurnishings stores	20	19	118	121	6	8,441	8,926	1,101	1,077
5720 Household appliance stores [3]	11	11	118	136	12	15,763	15,824	2,357	2,247
5731 Radio, TV, & electronic stores	18	16	202	249	16	15,743	14,088	3,355	3,607
5734 Computer and software stores [3]	6	9	27	32	4	17,333	19,375	693	851
5735 Record & prerecorded tape stores [3]	10	10	46	65	7	11,043	9,662	520	567
5736 Musical instrument stores [3]	6	5	97	90	18	14,722	18,089	1,591	1,565
5812 Eating places	449	427	9,074	9,816	23	6,988	7,526	71,559	78,569
5813 Drinking places	70	59	325	298	5	6,658	6,899	2,280	2,252
5910 Drug stores and proprietary stores	52	54	606	608	11	15,096	17,033	10,393	10,858
5920 Liquor stores	35	33	169	130	4	11,124	11,077	2,098	1,365
5930 Used merchandise stores	38	36	164	146	4	9,561	10,027	1,816	1,613
5941 Sporting goods and bicycle shops	34	35	231	201	6	8,606	9,831	2,542	2,395
5942 Book stores [3]	15	16	96	113	7	6,583	8,708	658	1,012
5944 Jewelry stores	38	37	329	319	9	14,991	15,210	4,810	4,944
5945 Hobby, toy, and game shops [3]	16	14	153	184	13	8,471	8,283	1,641	1,579
5947 Gift, novelty, and souvenir shops	32	34	153	199	6	6,222	7,136	1,234	1,610
5949 Sewing, needlework, and piece goods [3]	10	10	7	7	1	2,857	2,857	22	23
5961 Catalog and mail-order houses [3]	8	8	21	18	2	14,476	16,222	314	201
5962 Merchandising machine operators [3]	16	14	168	148	11	16,190	17,676	2,887	2,741
5963 Direct selling establishments [3]	25	24	113	132	6	19,894	17,727	2,193	2,541
5992 Florists	32	34	179	218	6	9,832	11,174	2,037	2,449
5994 News dealers and newsstands [3]	6	6	21	19	3	7,048	9,684	161	197
5995 Optical goods stores [3]	6	7	62	66	9	14,516	14,606	881	922
5999 Miscellaneous retail stores, nec [2]	55	58	246	291	5	14,000	12,866	3,627	4,121

Source: County Business Patterns 1994/95, CBP-94/95, U.S. Department of Commerce, Washington DC, November 1997. The employment column represents mid-March employment in the year. Pay per employee is calculated by dividing 1st Quarter payroll, annualized, by mid-March employment. The column headed 'Emp / Est' shows 'employees per establishment'. A dash (-) means that data are unavailable or cannot be calculated. nec means not elsewhere classified. *Notes:* 1. 1994 data incomplete; unavailable or withheld. 2. 1995 data incomplete; unavailable or withheld. 3. 1994 and 1995 data incomplete; unavailable or withheld.

FARGO – MOORHEAD MSA (MN PART)

Wholesale and Retail Trade USA	Establishments		Employment		Emp / Est	Pay / Employee		Annual Payroll ($ 000)	
	1994	1995	1994	1995	1995	1994	1995	1994	1995
50 – Wholesale trade	82	81	671	712	9	23,004	23,388	15,157	16,295
5013 Motor vehicle supplies and new parts	4	4	42	45	11	25,429	26,933	1,048	1,150
5030 Lumber and construction materials	3	4	20	12	3	11,600	11,333	361	272
5040 Professional & commercial equipment	-	4	-	43	11	-	22,698	-	1,063
5060 Electrical goods	5	5	23	30	6	30,261	36,533	677	955
5080 Machinery, equipment, and supplies	8	8	106	119	15	25,434	27,697	2,748	3,139
5112 Stationery and office supplies	3	-	57	-	-	27,579	-	984	-
5153 Grain and field beans	14	13	64	74	6	26,375	25,730	1,936	1,940
5171 Petroleum bulk stations & terminals	7	7	72	69	10	16,778	16,000	1,332	1,134
5191 Farm supplies	10	13	68	113	9	19,588	14,159	1,423	1,939
52 – Retail trade	294	285	4,049	4,017	14	9,892	10,147	42,737	44,193
5210 Lumber and other building materials	7	6	64	40	7	18,438	21,000	1,263	998
5230 Paint, glass, and wallpaper stores	-	3	-	10	3	-	14,400	-	150
5250 Hardware stores	4	-	22	-	-	8,364	-	217	-
5260 Retail nurseries and garden stores	4	4	26	29	7	8,923	6,621	325	307
5300 General merchandise stores	8	8	648	636	80	9,574	11,019	6,847	7,275
5410 Grocery stores	16	17	563	590	35	9,741	9,478	5,812	6,288
5460 Retail bakeries	-	3	-	8	3	-	11,000	-	73
5490 Miscellaneous food stores	-	3	-	4	1	-	6,000	-	33
5510 New and used car dealers	4	4	145	155	39	23,917	22,942	4,092	4,691
5530 Auto and home supply stores	-	6	-	61	10	-	14,361	-	945
5540 Gasoline service stations	25	23	212	229	10	10,585	10,655	2,358	2,503
5620 Women's clothing stores	12	9	85	50	6	7,671	8,160	651	439
5660 Shoe stores	4	4	22	20	5	8,000	9,000	217	176
5710 Furniture and homefurnishings stores	8	8	76	110	14	15,526	16,982	1,222	1,726
5720 Household appliance stores	4	4	60	55	14	17,533	19,345	1,328	1,373
5730 Radio, television, & computer stores	3	5	27	31	6	19,259	19,097	583	642
5812 Eating places	71	66	1,313	1,303	20	6,541	6,530	9,319	8,823
5813 Drinking places	14	15	118	106	7	4,610	4,906	541	539
5910 Drug stores and proprietary stores	9	8	98	92	12	12,694	14,739	1,292	1,320
5920 Liquor stores	11	10	60	54	5	6,933	7,630	437	439
5941 Sporting goods and bicycle shops	9	9	83	100	11	23,518	10,480	1,452	1,217
5944 Jewelry stores	5	3	13	14	5	6,154	5,714	89	90
5945 Hobby, toy, and game shops	3	-	23	-	-	5,913	-	130	-

Continued on next page.

FARGO – MOORHEAD MSA (MN PART) - [continued]

Wholesale and Retail Trade USA	Establishments		Employment		Emp / Est	Pay / Employee		Annual Payroll ($ 000)	
	1994	1995	1994	1995	1995	1994	1995	1994	1995
5947 Gift, novelty, and souvenir shops	8	8	40	26	3	3,900	6,462	160	165
5963 Direct selling establishments	-	6	-	15	3	-	32,533	-	479
5992 Florists	5	-	50	-	-	7,360	-	385	-
5995 Optical goods stores	6	4	24	18	5	13,333	15,111	299	282
5999 Miscellaneous retail stores, nec	10	9	34	33	4	8,471	8,000	308	271

Source: County Business Patterns 1994/95, CBP-94/95, U.S. Department of Commerce, Washington DC, November 1997. The employment column represents mid-March employment in the year. Pay per employee is calculated by dividing 1st Quarter payroll, annualized, by mid-March employment. The column headed 'Emp / Est' shows 'employees per establishment'. A dash (-) means that data are unavailable or cannot be calculated. nec means not elsewhere classified. *Notes:* 1. 1994 data incomplete; unavailable or withheld. 2. 1995 data incomplete; unavailable or withheld. 3. 1994 and 1995 data incomplete; unavailable or withheld.

FARGO – MOORHEAD MSA (ND PART)

Wholesale and Retail Trade USA	Establishments		Employment		Emp / Est	Pay / Employee		Annual Payroll ($ 000)	
	1994	1995	1994	1995	1995	1994	1995	1994	1995
50- Wholesale trade	448	453	6,615	6,762	15	27,010	29,398	192,398	208,075
5012 Automobiles and other vehicles	11	11	303	313	28	24,436	27,361	8,117	8,926
5013 Motor vehicle supplies and new parts	31	31	455	446	14	24,316	26,170	11,716	12,246
5021 Furniture	-	6	-	58	10	-	25,931	-	1,848
5031 Lumber, plywood, and millwork	10	9	288	253	28	30,319	34,087	8,303	7,621
5039 Construction materials, nec	8	10	87	125	13	24,046	27,264	2,728	3,937
5044 Office equipment	11	12	143	147	12	27,692	29,469	4,008	4,688
5045 Computers, peripherals, & software	17	17	273	280	16	32,147	36,843	9,378	10,042
5048 Ophthalmic goods	4	-	25	-	-	16,960	-	443	-
5049 Professional equipment, nec	5	5	101	113	23	24,158	22,796	2,528	2,624
5063 Electrical apparatus and equipment	19	19	218	196	10	31,725	39,898	6,947	7,384
5074 Plumbing & hydronic heating supplies	8	6	84	76	13	25,143	32,789	2,250	2,311
5075 Warm air heating & air conditioning	4	4	19	23	6	24,842	23,130	537	680
5082 Construction and mining machinery	8	9	188	239	27	31,532	33,021	6,973	8,525
5083 Farm and garden machinery	33	33	323	335	10	20,533	24,143	8,317	8,743
5084 Industrial machinery and equipment	17	19	200	237	12	27,020	32,017	6,213	7,721
5085 Industrial supplies	8	9	58	68	8	35,034	39,000	2,157	2,489
5091 Sporting & recreational goods	3	3	32	36	12	17,375	24,222	878	831
5093 Scrap and waste materials	5	5	62	61	12	19,806	20,590	1,463	1,612
5112 Stationery and office supplies	6	-	80	-	-	16,150	-	1,129	-
5141 Groceries, general line	10	9	696	707	79	29,885	29,211	21,739	22,100
5153 Grain and field beans	26	25	244	278	11	23,066	22,705	6,480	8,041
5160 Chemicals and allied products	13	12	56	65	5	25,714	26,708	1,892	2,157
5171 Petroleum bulk stations & terminals	14	11	134	95	9	21,821	22,905	2,815	2,044
5172 Petroleum products, nec	5	7	15	22	3	33,600	34,727	563	704
5180 Beer, wine, and distilled beverages	5	5	202	152	30	22,139	23,053	4,673	4,362
5191 Farm supplies	16	15	232	241	16	26,914	37,261	8,243	11,169
5192 Books, periodicals, & newspapers	3	-	21	-	-	12,190	-	296	-
5198 Paints, varnishes, and supplies	-	3	-	38	13	-	23,368	-	854
5199 Nondurable goods, nec	9	10	78	94	9	14,821	15,021	1,330	1,391
52- Retail trade	754	772	13,081	14,740	19	10,479	11,072	150,520	168,153
5210 Lumber and other building materials	25	21	457	495	24	16,595	17,430	7,797	7,665
5230 Paint, glass, and wallpaper stores	-	5	-	36	7	-	14,889	-	567
5250 Hardware stores	7	7	66	53	8	14,545	12,151	1,005	794
5260 Retail nurseries and garden stores	4	-	32	-	-	11,875	-	522	-
5310 Department stores	8	8	1,407	1,627	203	10,209	10,136	16,609	17,435
5330 Variety stores	3	-	66	-	-	7,818	-	464	-
5390 Misc. general merchandise stores	5	-	263	-	-	14,677	-	4,053	-
5410 Grocery stores	48	47	1,418	1,545	33	8,728	9,258	13,236	14,972
5440 Candy, nut, and confectionery stores	3	-	21	-	-	7,238	-	188	-
5460 Retail bakeries	10	7	114	77	11	8,175	8,000	834	646
5490 Miscellaneous food stores	5	5	24	30	6	5,667	5,067	199	174
5510 New and used car dealers	12	12	595	667	56	27,066	27,172	16,748	18,119
5520 Used car dealers	11	11	29	47	4	16,552	16,085	537	745
5530 Auto and home supply stores	20	18	142	220	12	16,648	17,182	2,556	4,112
5540 Gasoline service stations	53	52	480	726	14	10,792	9,548	5,372	7,360
5610 Men's & boys' clothing stores	10	10	84	92	9	18,286	16,870	1,748	1,571
5620 Women's clothing stores	24	20	255	233	12	7,953	7,193	2,164	1,560
5630 Women's accessory & specialty stores	5	-	20	-	-	8,000	-	175	-
5640 Children's and infants' wear stores	4	4	14	37	9	4,286	7,243	185	291
5650 Family clothing stores	5	6	81	94	16	7,901	8,511	752	873
5660 Shoe stores	17	17	82	85	5	10,780	11,200	977	888
5712 Furniture stores	18	20	188	208	10	13,617	14,558	3,185	3,143
5713 Floor covering stores	7	8	43	60	8	24,837	27,000	1,210	1,677
5731 Radio, TV, & electronic stores	6	8	100	148	19	12,320	13,432	1,286	1,887

Continued on next page.

FARGO - MOORHEAD MSA (ND PART) - [continued]

Wholesale and Retail Trade USA	Establishments		Employment		Emp / Est	Pay / Employee		Annual Payroll ($ 000)	
	1994	1995	1994	1995	1995	1994	1995	1994	1995
5734 Computer and software stores	6	-	21	-	-	10,476	-	221	-
5735 Record & prerecorded tape stores	-	6	-	93	16	-	7,570	-	677
5736 Musical instrument stores	-	4	-	28	7	-	10,286	-	279
5812 Eating places	155	158	4,233	4,324	27	6,185	6,651	28,917	30,378
5813 Drinking places	37	37	544	604	16	6,882	6,914	4,010	4,214
5910 Drug stores and proprietary stores	24	22	209	208	9	15,215	17,692	3,432	3,657
5920 Liquor stores	18	18	136	136	8	9,971	8,588	1,444	1,357
5930 Used merchandise stores	7	6	31	32	5	6,323	6,250	206	203
5941 Sporting goods and bicycle shops	17	15	330	311	21	12,158	13,685	3,501	3,870
5942 Book stores	5	-	51	-	-	8,784	-	513	-
5944 Jewelry stores	9	10	106	109	11	21,283	23,303	2,090	2,288
5945 Hobby, toy, and game shops	8	9	32	37	4	7,500	7,243	281	655
5947 Gift, novelty, and souvenir shops	25	21	155	161	8	6,452	6,211	1,113	1,132
5963 Direct selling establishments	12	14	147	161	12	11,184	11,925	1,536	1,746
5980 Fuel dealers	-	8	-	57	7	-	17,123	-	992
5992 Florists	9	8	80	66	8	9,200	11,576	857	828
5999 Miscellaneous retail stores, nec	21	27	141	210	8	15,433	15,676	2,542	3,929

Source: County Business Patterns 1994/95, CBP-94/95, U.S. Department of Commerce, Washington DC, November 1997. The employment column represents mid-March employment in the year. Pay per employee is calculated by dividing 1st Quarter payroll, annualized, by mid-March employment. The column headed 'Emp / Est' shows 'employees per establishment'. A dash (-) means that data are unavailable or cannot be calculated. nec means not elsewhere classified. *Notes:* 1. 1994 data incomplete; unavailable or withheld. 2. 1995 data incomplete; unavailable or withheld. 3. 1994 and 1995 data incomplete; unavailable or withheld.

FARGO - MOORHEAD, ND - MN MSA

Wholesale and Retail Trade USA	Establishments		Employment		Emp / Est	Pay / Employee		Annual Payroll ($ 000)	
	1994	1995	1994	1995	1995	1994	1995	1994	1995
50- Wholesale trade	530	534	7,286	7,474	14	26,641	28,826	207,555	224,370
5012 Automobiles and other vehicles	13	13	303	313	24	24,436	27,361	8,117	8,926
5013 Motor vehicle supplies and new parts	35	35	497	491	14	24,410	26,240	12,764	13,396
5021 Furniture	-	8	-	58	7	-	25,931	-	1,848
5031 Lumber, plywood, and millwork	11	10	288	253	25	30,319	34,087	8,303	7,621
5039 Construction materials, nec[1]	8	12	87	125	10	24,046	27,264	2,728	3,937
5044 Office equipment[1]	11	13	143	147	11	27,692	29,469	4,008	4,688
5045 Computers, peripherals, & software	18	18	273	280	16	32,147	36,843	9,378	10,042
5048 Ophthalmic goods[1]	4	-	25	-	-	16,960	-	443	-
5049 Professional equipment, nec	6	6	101	113	19	24,158	22,796	2,528	2,624
5063 Electrical apparatus and equipment	22	22	218	196	9	31,725	39,898	6,947	7,384
5074 Plumbing & hydronic heating supplies[3]	8	6	84	76	13	25,143	32,789	2,250	2,311
5075 Warm air heating & air conditioning	5	5	19	23	5	24,842	23,130	537	680
5082 Construction and mining machinery[3]	8	9	188	239	27	31,532	33,021	6,973	8,525
5083 Farm and garden machinery	38	38	323	335	9	20,533	24,143	8,317	8,743
5084 Industrial machinery and equipment	18	20	200	237	12	27,020	32,017	6,213	7,721
5085 Industrial supplies[3]	8	9	58	68	8	35,034	39,000	2,157	2,489
5091 Sporting & recreational goods	4	4	32	36	9	17,375	24,222	878	831
5093 Scrap and waste materials	6	6	62	61	10	19,806	20,590	1,463	1,612
5112 Stationery and office supplies	9	-	137	-	-	20,905	-	2,113	-
5141 Groceries, general line[3]	10	9	696	707	79	29,885	29,211	21,739	22,100
5153 Grain and field beans	40	38	308	352	9	23,753	23,341	8,416	9,981
5160 Chemicals and allied products	14	13	56	65	5	25,714	26,708	1,892	2,157
5171 Petroleum bulk stations & terminals	21	18	206	164	9	20,058	20,000	4,147	3,178
5172 Petroleum products, nec[3]	5	7	15	22	3	33,600	34,727	563	704
5180 Beer, wine, and distilled beverages	7	7	202	152	22	22,139	23,053	4,673	4,362
5191 Farm supplies	26	28	300	354	13	25,253	29,887	9,666	13,108
5192 Books, periodicals, & newspapers	5	-	21	-	-	12,190	-	296	-
5198 Paints, varnishes, and supplies[2]	-	3	-	38	13	-	23,368	-	854
5199 Nondurable goods, nec	11	12	78	94	8	14,821	15,021	1,330	1,391
52- Retail trade	1,048	1,057	17,130	18,757	18	10,340	10,874	193,257	212,346
5210 Lumber and other building materials	32	27	521	535	20	16,821	17,697	9,060	8,663
5230 Paint, glass, and wallpaper stores	-	8	-	46	6	-	14,783	-	717
5250 Hardware stores	11	9	88	53	6	13,000	12,151	1,222	794
5260 Retail nurseries and garden stores	8	8	58	29	4	10,552	6,621	847	307
5310 Department stores[3]	12	12	1,407	1,627	136	10,209	10,136	16,609	17,435
5330 Variety stores	6	-	66	-	-	7,818	-	464	-
5390 Misc. general merchandise stores	6	-	263	-	-	14,677	-	4,053	-
5410 Grocery stores	64	64	1,981	2,135	33	9,016	9,319	19,048	21,260
5440 Candy, nut, and confectionery stores[1]	3	-	21	-	-	7,238	-	188	-
5460 Retail bakeries	14	10	114	85	9	8,175	8,282	834	719
5490 Miscellaneous food stores	7	8	24	34	4	5,667	5,176	199	207
5510 New and used car dealers	16	16	740	822	51	26,449	26,375	20,840	22,810

Continued on next page.

FARGO-MOORHEAD, ND-MN MSA - [continued]

Wholesale and Retail Trade USA	Establishments		Employment		Emp / Est	Pay / Employee		Annual Payroll ($ 000)	
	1994	1995	1994	1995	1995	1994	1995	1994	1995
5520 Used car dealers	13	13	29	47	4	16,552	16,085	537	745
5530 Auto and home supply stores	26	24	142	281	12	16,648	16,569	2,556	5,057
5540 Gasoline service stations	78	75	692	955	13	10,728	9,814	7,730	9,863
5610 Men's & boys' clothing stores	12	11	84	92	8	18,286	16,870	1,748	1,571
5620 Women's clothing stores	36	29	340	283	10	7,882	7,364	2,815	1,999
5630 Women's accessory & specialty stores	7	-	20	-	-	8,000	-	175	-
5640 Children's and infants' wear stores [3]	4	4	14	37	9	4,286	7,243	185	291
5650 Family clothing stores	6	7	81	94	13	7,901	8,511	752	873
5660 Shoe stores	21	21	104	105	5	10,192	10,781	1,194	1,064
5712 Furniture stores	25	26	188	208	8	13,617	14,558	3,185	3,143
5713 Floor covering stores	8	10	43	60	6	24,837	27,000	1,210	1,677
5720 Household appliance stores	5	7	60	55	8	17,533	19,345	1,328	1,373
5731 Radio, TV, & electronic stores	7	10	100	148	15	12,320	13,432	1,286	1,887
5734 Computer and software stores [1]	6	-	21	-	-	10,476	-	221	-
5735 Record & prerecorded tape stores	-	8	-	93	12	-	7,570	-	677
5736 Musical instrument stores	-	5	-	28	6	-	10,286	-	279
5812 Eating places	226	224	5,546	5,627	25	6,269	6,623	38,236	39,201
5813 Drinking places	51	52	662	710	14	6,477	6,614	4,551	4,753
5910 Drug stores and proprietary stores	33	30	307	300	10	14,410	16,787	4,724	4,977
5920 Liquor stores	29	28	196	190	7	9,041	8,316	1,881	1,796
5930 Used merchandise stores	9	8	31	32	4	6,323	6,250	206	203
5941 Sporting goods and bicycle shops	26	24	413	411	17	14,441	12,905	4,953	5,087
5942 Book stores	6	-	51	-	-	8,784	-	513	-
5944 Jewelry stores	14	13	119	123	9	19,630	21,301	2,179	2,378
5945 Hobby, toy, and game shops	11	13	55	37	3	6,836	7,243	411	655
5947 Gift, novelty, and souvenir shops	33	29	195	187	6	5,928	6,246	1,273	1,297
5963 Direct selling establishments	17	20	147	176	9	11,184	13,682	1,536	2,225
5980 Fuel dealers	-	9	-	57	6	-	17,123	-	992
5992 Florists	14	12	130	66	6	8,492	11,576	1,242	828
5995 Optical goods stores	12	11	24	18	2	13,333	15,111	299	282
5999 Miscellaneous retail stores, nec	31	36	175	243	7	14,080	14,634	2,850	4,200

Source: County Business Patterns 1994/95, CBP-94/95, U.S. Department of Commerce, Washington DC, November 1997. The employment column represents mid-March employment in the year. Pay per employee is calculated by dividing 1st Quarter payroll, annualized, by mid-March employment. The column headed 'Emp / Est' shows 'employees per establishment'. A dash (-) means that data are unavailable or cannot be calculated. nec means not elsewhere classified. *Notes:* 1. 1994 data incomplete; unavailable or withheld. 2. 1995 data incomplete; unavailable or withheld. 3. 1994 and 1995 data incomplete; unavailable or withheld.

FAYETTEVILLE, NC MSA

Wholesale and Retail Trade USA	Establishments		Employment		Emp / Est	Pay / Employee		Annual Payroll ($ 000)	
	1994	1995	1994	1995	1995	1994	1995	1994	1995
50- Wholesale trade	270	275	3,149	3,302	12	22,726	23,600	78,064	80,255
5012 Automobiles and other vehicles	-	7	-	10	1	-	24,000	-	310
5013 Motor vehicle supplies and new parts	30	25	197	174	7	19,980	22,805	3,664	3,422
5014 Tires and tubes	5	5	73	71	14	18,959	21,239	1,622	1,576
5015 Motor vehicle parts, used	8	7	38	35	5	16,105	16,571	619	608
5020 Furniture and homefurnishings	8	8	62	111	14	25,677	20,468	1,836	1,395
5031 Lumber, plywood, and millwork	4	5	114	238	48	22,702	20,353	2,734	5,628
5032 Brick, stone, & related materials	5	5	42	44	9	21,714	23,364	1,083	1,197
5033 Roofing, siding, & insulation	-	3	-	44	15	-	20,182	-	970
5039 Construction materials, nec	5	5	53	87	17	31,774	29,563	1,568	2,392
5044 Office equipment	12	14	132	150	11	22,697	23,760	2,771	3,473
5045 Computers, peripherals, & software	7	6	82	61	10	24,293	26,361	1,983	1,440
5046 Commercial equipment, nec	3	-	32	-	-	28,375	-	1,064	-
5063 Electrical apparatus and equipment	9	11	78	88	8	27,897	29,364	1,968	2,397
5065 Electronic parts and equipment	8	8	152	163	20	27,500	34,209	4,799	5,345
5074 Plumbing & hydronic heating supplies	5	6	63	80	13	21,524	25,650	1,800	2,563
5075 Warm air heating & air conditioning	7	8	52	56	7	31,077	28,929	1,350	1,380
5082 Construction and mining machinery	5	5	84	70	14	25,143	37,543	2,331	2,418
5083 Farm and garden machinery	3	3	47	45	15	28,085	33,956	1,707	1,707
5084 Industrial machinery and equipment	10	11	93	98	9	23,871	25,020	2,599	2,925
5085 Industrial supplies	11	14	87	80	6	24,920	29,700	2,375	2,564
5087 Service establishment equipment	4	4	11	12	3	16,000	15,333	157	163
5093 Scrap and waste materials	7	7	101	134	19	23,287	23,075	2,713	3,273
5099 Durable goods, nec	-	3	-	21	7	-	29,905	-	602
5112 Stationery and office supplies	6	5	80	52	10	13,700	10,615	1,197	697
5143 Dairy products, exc. dried or canned	4	3	38	26	9	26,211	30,615	918	713
5147 Meats and meat products	6	6	66	61	10	18,606	18,623	1,328	1,184
5149 Groceries and related products, nec	6	8	257	274	34	23,533	21,956	6,310	6,610
5160 Chemicals and allied products	7	6	61	64	11	20,787	25,438	1,472	1,624

Continued on next page.

FAYETTEVILLE, NC MSA - [continued]

Wholesale and Retail Trade USA	Establishments		Employment		Emp / Est	Pay / Employee		Annual Payroll ($ 000)	
	1994	1995	1994	1995	1995	1994	1995	1994	1995
5171 Petroleum bulk stations & terminals	-	5	-	52	10	-	24,692	-	2,064
5180 Beer, wine, and distilled beverages	6	6	285	222	37	20,800	22,901	7,548	5,334
5191 Farm supplies	5	-	13	-	-	16,000	-	255	-
5193 Flowers & florists' supplies	3	4	11	15	4	13,091	12,533	146	187
5199 Nondurable goods, nec	8	11	56	66	6	16,929	16,848	948	1,214
52- Retail trade	1,534	1,541	22,461	23,889	16	11,599	12,109	278,250	305,408
5210 Lumber and other building materials	20	18	712	440	24	18,028	24,091	13,584	9,991
5230 Paint, glass, and wallpaper stores	9	5	59	42	8	18,305	19,238	1,073	894
5250 Hardware stores	11	7	48	36	5	12,000	13,444	578	465
5260 Retail nurseries and garden stores	9	8	49	38	5	10,041	14,947	617	693
5270 Mobile home dealers	13	15	68	80	5	29,235	27,750	2,287	2,863
5310 Department stores	13	14	2,454	2,478	177	9,821	10,746	25,434	27,805
5330 Variety stores	18	16	191	173	11	7,225	8,046	1,632	1,583
5390 Misc. general merchandise stores	11	13	377	407	31	12,552	12,275	4,805	4,934
5410 Grocery stores	125	129	2,437	2,994	23	10,436	10,931	27,626	31,491
5420 Meat and fish markets	7	5	26	19	4	10,000	9,895	317	184
5430 Fruit and vegetable markets	4	4	8	14	4	10,000	9,429	186	205
5460 Retail bakeries	9	7	81	79	11	7,358	7,443	613	475
5490 Miscellaneous food stores	9	11	17	30	3	8,000	7,867	181	302
5510 New and used car dealers	21	19	1,214	1,324	70	32,896	34,157	40,354	45,805
5520 Used car dealers	48	54	192	169	3	16,458	19,598	3,187	3,397
5530 Auto and home supply stores	62	64	580	571	9	15,193	17,366	9,650	10,725
5540 Gasoline service stations	113	109	685	669	6	9,834	11,031	7,314	7,668
5560 Recreational vehicle dealers	3	4	37	36	9	17,730	19,000	712	759
5570 Motorcycle dealers	6	6	66	61	10	18,424	19,738	1,498	1,636
5610 Men's & boys' clothing stores	14	14	114	116	8	11,649	12,483	1,460	1,381
5620 Women's clothing stores	47	42	431	366	9	7,759	7,268	3,461	2,883
5630 Women's accessory & specialty stores	6	6	26	32	5	9,231	10,375	271	315
5640 Children's and infants' wear stores	3	4	33	34	9	8,121	8,353	300	295
5650 Family clothing stores	10	10	236	193	19	7,797	8,477	1,843	1,646
5660 Shoe stores	37	36	242	240	7	9,752	9,650	2,441	2,356
5690 Misc. apparel & accessory stores	13	14	89	92	7	8,944	8,217	932	824
5712 Furniture stores	43	44	483	488	11	15,694	16,156	8,913	9,113
5713 Floor covering stores	10	13	57	63	5	17,825	19,175	1,132	1,676
5714 Drapery and upholstery stores	-	4	-	11	3	-	9,091	-	88
5719 Misc. homefurnishings stores	-	18	-	85	5	-	11,153	-	1,237
5720 Household appliance stores	3	-	53	-	-	16,755	-	960	-
5731 Radio, TV, & electronic stores	22	23	236	241	10	18,475	18,456	4,634	4,748
5734 Computer and software stores	4	4	20	23	6	13,800	13,043	294	181
5735 Record & prerecorded tape stores	12	11	82	95	9	9,951	9,474	885	930
5736 Musical instrument stores	3	4	21	11	3	14,095	30,182	487	196
5812 Eating places	347	323	7,637	8,477	26	6,824	7,048	56,112	64,769
5813 Drinking places	48	42	241	221	5	5,693	6,389	1,448	1,324
5910 Drug stores and proprietary stores	35	33	417	446	14	14,456	14,027	6,467	6,683
5930 Used merchandise stores	45	44	274	313	7	14,511	15,578	4,808	5,406
5941 Sporting goods and bicycle shops	12	16	100	101	6	9,440	10,851	1,062	1,176
5942 Book stores	9	8	58	54	7	10,690	12,222	611	602
5944 Jewelry stores	31	35	190	199	6	13,074	14,854	2,735	2,924
5945 Hobby, toy, and game shops	8	5	79	75	15	7,342	9,653	792	855
5947 Gift, novelty, and souvenir shops	20	18	105	96	5	7,276	8,292	857	979
5949 Sewing, needlework, and piece goods	8	7	41	42	6	7,707	8,381	326	368
5963 Direct selling establishments	16	17	129	127	7	15,194	12,598	2,064	1,540
5983 Fuel oil dealers	6	7	27	36	5	13,037	16,667	369	616
5984 Liquefied petroleum gas dealers	5	6	53	63	11	20,830	21,778	1,130	1,556
5992 Florists	27	25	137	111	4	9,810	11,171	1,223	1,208
5995 Optical goods stores	15	18	85	96	5	15,718	16,083	1,327	1,744
5999 Miscellaneous retail stores, nec	39	41	165	166	4	9,673	10,313	1,715	1,908

Source: County Business Patterns 1994/95, CBP-94/95, U.S. Department of Commerce, Washington DC, November 1997. The employment column represents mid-March employment in the year. Pay per employee is calculated by dividing 1st Quarter payroll, annualized, by mid-March employment. The column headed 'Emp / Est' shows 'employees per establishment'. A dash (-) means that data are unavailable or cannot be calculated. nec means not elsewhere classified. *Notes:* 1. 1994 data incomplete; unavailable or withheld. 2. 1995 data incomplete; unavailable or withheld. 3. 1994 and 1995 data incomplete; unavailable or withheld.

FAYETTEVILLE – SPRINGDALE – ROGERS, AR MSA

Wholesale and Retail Trade USA	Establishments		Employment		Emp / Est	Pay / Employee		Annual Payroll ($ 000)	
	1994	1995	1994	1995	1995	1994	1995	1994	1995
50- Wholesale trade	484	506	5,183	5,659	11	25,702	27,920	144,689	157,882
5012 Automobiles and other vehicles	21	22	404	418	19	26,842	29,502	11,110	12,214
5013 Motor vehicle supplies and new parts	30	24	190	164	7	16,989	22,634	3,485	3,325

Continued on next page.

FAYETTEVILLE - SPRINGDALE - ROGERS, AR MSA - [continued]

Wholesale and Retail Trade USA	Establishments		Employment		Emp / Est	Pay / Employee		Annual Payroll ($ 000)	
	1994	1995	1994	1995	1995	1994	1995	1994	1995
5015 Motor vehicle parts, used	12	15	11	40	3	10,182	15,800	119	680
5021 Furniture	-	4	-	2	1	-	14,000	-	32
5023 Homefurnishings	-	6	-	25	4	-	34,080	-	731
5031 Lumber, plywood, and millwork	9	11	135	144	13	17,600	17,139	2,361	2,692
5033 Roofing, siding, & insulation	-	5	-	61	12	-	21,836	-	1,094
5039 Construction materials, nec	6	-	28	-	-	20,143	-	569	-
5044 Office equipment	15	12	56	104	9	23,429	24,038	1,290	2,463
5045 Computers, peripherals, & software	20	16	337	320	20	52,059	65,425	18,061	16,622
5046 Commercial equipment, nec[3]	5	6	20	25	4	18,800	15,680	420	487
5047 Medical and hospital equipment	-	13	-	20	2	-	18,200	-	385
5051 Metals service centers and offices	6	7	48	78	11	18,083	24,872	927	1,757
5063 Electrical apparatus and equipment	14	18	83	81	5	40,096	46,667	2,758	2,922
5074 Plumbing & hydronic heating supplies	13	16	58	84	5	24,828	25,381	1,657	2,194
5075 Warm air heating & air conditioning	7	8	12	22	3	12,000	20,000	166	470
5082 Construction and mining machinery	7	7	64	44	6	30,688	47,636	2,092	1,739
5083 Farm and garden machinery	15	17	114	131	8	18,632	20,916	3,288	3,856
5084 Industrial machinery and equipment	23	25	223	217	9	18,762	22,783	4,880	5,686
5085 Industrial supplies	20	18	121	129	7	27,868	33,302	3,665	3,761
5087 Service establishment equipment	6	6	14	16	3	12,286	13,500	192	160
5088 Transportation equipment & supplies[1]	3	-	3	-	-	16,000	-	52	-
5091 Sporting & recreational goods	8	-	10	-	-	35,200	-	660	-
5093 Scrap and waste materials	5	6	38	43	7	9,263	10,326	392	535
5112 Stationery and office supplies	-	9	-	30	3	-	28,800	-	1,049
5130 Apparel, piece goods, and notions	9	10	194	237	24	20,041	12,506	3,565	3,576
5144 Poultry and poultry products	12	11	482	550	50	16,282	19,498	9,475	12,266
5148 Fresh fruits and vegetables	7	7	83	102	15	78,458	75,216	3,466	4,158
5149 Groceries and related products, nec	16	16	214	241	15	23,738	28,647	5,744	7,329
5154 Livestock	5	-	52	-	-	3,538	-	155	-
5160 Chemicals and allied products	14	15	123	250	17	57,626	48,800	7,348	11,452
5170 Petroleum and petroleum products	13	13	136	130	10	29,235	31,385	4,012	4,108
5181 Beer and ale[2]	-	3	-	57	19	-	27,719	-	1,907
5191 Farm supplies	40	37	342	346	9	25,778	24,775	9,736	9,108
5193 Flowers & florists' supplies[2]	-	3	-	2	1	-	2,000	-	15
5199 Nondurable goods, nec	7	-	18	-	-	22,222	-	592	-
52- Retail trade	1,701	1,789	26,362	28,607	16	16,394	18,639	477,242	521,848
5210 Lumber and other building materials	45	38	890	825	22	17,411	18,676	17,331	16,546
5230 Paint, glass, and wallpaper stores	15	21	42	50	2	17,429	18,960	817	985
5250 Hardware stores	17	11	141	70	6	15,348	14,286	2,678	1,114
5260 Retail nurseries and garden stores	15	15	29	100	7	15,724	11,960	531	1,283
5270 Mobile home dealers	7	8	25	14	2	14,720	21,714	432	408
5310 Department stores[3]	11	12	1,825	2,074	173	11,176	14,293	24,623	27,701
5410 Grocery stores	101	106	1,983	2,088	20	10,540	11,454	22,848	25,187
5420 Meat and fish markets	6	7	9	22	3	12,444	12,727	117	311
5460 Retail bakeries	14	14	76	51	4	7,211	6,353	593	368
5490 Miscellaneous food stores	4	4	10	7	2	17,600	6,286	230	63
5510 New and used car dealers	33	36	1,152	1,173	33	24,875	25,282	32,354	34,891
5520 Used car dealers	46	48	155	165	3	17,084	18,036	2,825	3,176
5530 Auto and home supply stores	44	50	253	267	5	13,043	15,341	3,859	4,521
5540 Gasoline service stations	105	102	771	735	7	9,914	10,095	7,922	7,704
5570 Motorcycle dealers	7	7	38	47	7	12,316	12,766	630	732
5610 Men's & boys' clothing stores	12	13	37	66	5	10,703	10,606	432	669
5620 Women's clothing stores	43	40	251	228	6	8,207	7,912	2,171	1,856
5630 Women's accessory & specialty stores	7	7	16	30	4	12,250	6,000	157	145
5650 Family clothing stores	27	29	324	274	9	7,086	8,978	2,497	2,621
5660 Shoe stores	29	33	117	152	5	8,308	9,737	1,039	1,549
5690 Misc. apparel & accessory stores	9	10	21	21	2	8,190	8,000	236	173
5712 Furniture stores	43	46	248	320	7	16,516	17,138	4,753	6,016
5713 Floor covering stores	-	13	-	85	7	-	16,188	-	1,849
5719 Misc. homefurnishings stores	8	7	24	25	4	7,500	9,920	210	281
5720 Household appliance stores	17	16	25	30	2	13,440	13,733	362	426
5731 Radio, TV, & electronic stores	15	15	82	81	5	25,366	20,593	2,237	1,704
5734 Computer and software stores	4	5	34	50	10	10,588	13,920	442	701
5735 Record & prerecorded tape stores	7	8	71	77	10	8,958	9,766	577	694
5736 Musical instrument stores	6	6	17	14	2	20,000	23,143	320	313
5812 Eating places	364	337	6,346	6,458	19	7,160	7,804	51,435	53,080
5813 Drinking places	20	18	160	115	6	5,100	6,539	885	873
5910 Drug stores and proprietary stores	39	37	260	246	7	17,477	19,073	5,098	4,870
5920 Liquor stores	31	32	179	170	5	9,877	11,200	1,975	2,113
5930 Used merchandise stores	38	38	125	72	2	9,984	9,833	1,285	802
5941 Sporting goods and bicycle shops	31	29	143	161	6	8,895	9,043	1,522	1,761
5942 Book stores	21	20	189	197	10	9,778	10,355	2,097	2,257

Continued on next page.

FAYETTEVILLE - SPRINGDALE - ROGERS, AR MSA - [continued]

Wholesale and Retail Trade USA	Establishments		Employment		Emp / Est	Pay / Employee		Annual Payroll ($ 000)	
	1994	1995	1994	1995	1995	1994	1995	1994	1995
5944 Jewelry stores	25	28	81	142	5	19,457	16,761	1,631	2,377
5945 Hobby, toy, and game shops	11	13	109	116	9	10,018	10,690	1,235	1,431
5947 Gift, novelty, and souvenir shops	35	35	146	178	5	6,685	6,719	1,074	1,254
5949 Sewing, needlework, and piece goods	8	7	43	47	7	8,651	6,979	357	334
5962 Merchandising machine operators	5	7	282	294	42	12,284	12,571	3,798	3,833
5963 Direct selling establishments	17	-	14	-	-	12,286	-	216	-
5984 Liquefied petroleum gas dealers	11	11	73	36	3	18,740	20,111	1,422	718
5992 Florists	-	33	-	144	4	-	8,417	-	1,234
5995 Optical goods stores	6	-	130	-	-	16,092	-	1,920	-
5999 Miscellaneous retail stores, nec	45	51	116	202	4	10,138	10,673	1,589	2,479

Source: County Business Patterns 1994/95, CBP-94/95, U.S. Department of Commerce, Washington DC, November 1997. The employment column represents mid-March employment in the year. Pay per employee is calculated by dividing 1st Quarter payroll, annualized, by mid-March employment. The column headed 'Emp / Est' shows 'employees per establishment'. A dash (-) means that data are unavailable or cannot be calculated. nec means not elsewhere classified. *Notes:* 1. 1994 data incomplete; unavailable or withheld. 2. 1995 data incomplete; unavailable or withheld. 3. 1994 and 1995 data incomplete; unavailable or withheld.

FLINT, MI PMSA

Wholesale and Retail Trade USA	Establishments		Employment		Emp / Est	Pay / Employee		Annual Payroll ($ 000)	
	1994	1995	1994	1995	1995	1994	1995	1994	1995
50 - Wholesale trade	509	507	6,740	7,051	14	29,222	32,415	211,096	228,564
5012 Automobiles and other vehicles	25	26	456	502	19	17,500	14,701	10,215	7,717
5013 Motor vehicle supplies and new parts	29	23	259	208	9	20,510	25,481	6,555	6,460
5014 Tires and tubes	4	4	68	71	18	20,647	21,634	1,587	1,729
5015 Motor vehicle parts, used	17	19	154	152	8	16,182	17,605	2,904	2,837
5021 Furniture	5	7	47	56	8	31,149	31,643	1,571	1,706
5023 Homefurnishings	8	6	77	79	13	22,805	22,937	1,883	1,948
5031 Lumber, plywood, and millwork	7	10	47	97	10	23,745	29,897	1,277	3,117
5033 Roofing, siding, & insulation	3	-	34	-	-	27,529	-	1,592	-
5039 Construction materials, nec	-	8	-	120	15	-	27,200	-	3,723
5044 Office equipment	15	15	154	171	11	29,558	32,421	4,694	5,355
5045 Computers, peripherals, & software	22	20	107	130	7	34,280	45,969	4,601	5,048
5046 Commercial equipment, nec	-	6	-	62	10	-	19,484	-	2,137
5047 Medical and hospital equipment	15	14	190	200	14	18,989	20,400	3,370	3,868
5049 Professional equipment, nec	3	-	27	-	-	14,222	-	556	-
5051 Metals service centers and offices	8	10	138	169	17	26,174	26,840	3,930	4,920
5063 Electrical apparatus and equipment	21	19	273	294	15	31,414	41,265	8,386	11,096
5072 Hardware	8	8	79	94	12	28,608	29,277	3,280	3,458
5074 Plumbing & hydronic heating supplies	17	17	119	171	10	25,714	25,708	3,416	5,049
5075 Warm air heating & air conditioning	10	10	95	98	10	31,326	33,184	3,764	4,304
5083 Farm and garden machinery	6	5	32	28	6	20,875	22,429	1,017	985
5084 Industrial machinery and equipment	40	36	368	373	10	32,587	37,158	11,364	12,536
5085 Industrial supplies	24	23	245	251	11	34,890	40,382	10,814	11,830
5087 Service establishment equipment	12	12	75	81	7	21,333	24,296	1,777	2,143
5091 Sporting & recreational goods	10	11	228	223	20	19,368	28,305	6,056	6,218
5093 Scrap and waste materials	17	15	122	97	6	16,459	22,598	2,702	2,993
5112 Stationery and office supplies	-	13	-	187	14	-	18,781	-	3,722
5113 Industrial & personal service paper	-	3	-	5	2	-	31,200	-	417
5141 Groceries, general line	4	4	215	251	63	21,619	20,781	4,740	5,424
5142 Packaged frozen food	7	7	121	125	18	14,711	16,352	2,169	2,217
5147 Meats and meat products	3	3	60	66	22	28,933	26,121	1,713	1,927
5149 Groceries and related products, nec	20	20	472	429	21	22,254	26,704	11,291	11,955
5162 Plastics materials & basic shapes	3	3	44	54	18	24,545	25,185	1,401	1,657
5169 Chemicals & allied products, nec	6	6	17	25	4	15,765	18,720	292	541
5170 Petroleum and petroleum products	7	7	57	65	9	33,333	26,523	1,870	1,968
5180 Beer, wine, and distilled beverages	4	4	221	219	55	32,090	33,607	7,523	7,923
5192 Books, periodicals, & newspapers	6	6	54	63	11	24,074	22,349	1,374	1,461
5193 Flowers & florists' supplies	5	4	81	75	19	16,543	18,240	2,126	1,368
5198 Paints, varnishes, and supplies	5	5	15	28	6	16,267	18,429	305	593
5199 Nondurable goods, nec	9	12	53	79	7	12,075	14,835	1,104	1,788
52 - Retail trade	2,499	2,524	36,174	37,004	15	11,306	12,335	470,946	489,172
5210 Lumber and other building materials	54	45	842	700	16	19,297	20,234	19,589	15,124
5230 Paint, glass, and wallpaper stores	11	9	76	73	8	15,000	14,192	1,436	1,242
5250 Hardware stores	35	33	317	322	10	12,530	12,261	4,528	4,545
5260 Retail nurseries and garden stores	19	19	168	173	9	11,762	13,110	2,930	3,181
5270 Mobile home dealers	11	9	140	123	14	18,257	26,439	2,837	2,906
5310 Department stores	19	21	4,787	4,686	223	10,461	11,548	55,513	62,231
5330 Variety stores	23	25	223	240	10	8,000	7,633	1,994	2,131
5390 Misc. general merchandise stores	17	12	691	700	58	12,805	13,749	9,531	9,476
5410 Grocery stores	246	234	3,998	3,902	17	10,138	10,922	41,932	43,500

Continued on next page.

FLINT, MI PMSA - [continued]

Wholesale and Retail Trade USA	Establishments		Employment		Emp / Est	Pay / Employee		Annual Payroll ($ 000)	
	1994	1995	1994	1995	1995	1994	1995	1994	1995
5420 Meat and fish markets	11	9	47	33	4	10,128	12,485	504	380
5430 Fruit and vegetable markets	6	7	73	62	9	8,767	8,774	787	536
5440 Candy, nut, and confectionery stores	5	5	27	28	6	5,037	6,286	124	207
5460 Retail bakeries	42	37	227	262	7	7,753	7,771	1,974	2,179
5490 Miscellaneous food stores	8	9	45	33	4	9,422	11,273	433	431
5510 New and used car dealers	30	31	1,791	1,892	61	29,215	32,175	59,362	65,417
5520 Used car dealers	20	20	64	68	3	20,000	23,941	1,448	1,755
5530 Auto and home supply stores	63	67	565	684	10	16,991	19,170	11,172	14,030
5540 Gasoline service stations	196	197	1,526	1,482	8	10,459	11,889	34,220	19,203
5550 Boat dealers	7	9	45	49	5	18,222	20,163	1,244	1,468
5560 Recreational vehicle dealers	10	10	54	54	5	18,593	20,074	1,417	1,326
5570 Motorcycle dealers	6	7	50	43	6	16,720	22,791	1,218	1,322
5610 Men's & boys' clothing stores	26	21	170	149	7	9,835	12,510	2,229	2,031
5620 Women's clothing stores	75	72	790	693	10	7,686	7,665	6,911	5,637
5630 Women's accessory & specialty stores	17	16	114	94	6	8,702	10,936	1,037	1,020
5640 Children's and infants' wear stores	7	7	49	71	10	6,939	6,648	463	493
5650 Family clothing stores	30	30	516	521	17	8,395	9,812	4,911	5,139
5660 Shoe stores	67	63	377	308	5	9,687	11,532	3,795	3,417
5690 Misc. apparel & accessory stores	13	13	97	86	7	7,959	9,488	788	697
5712 Furniture stores	35	34	410	500	15	22,907	22,288	10,573	11,363
5713 Floor covering stores	18	21	185	208	10	19,784	21,731	5,015	5,829
5719 Misc. homefurnishings stores	18	19	140	126	7	9,857	12,190	1,536	1,791
5720 Household appliance stores	8	7	92	48	7	10,870	18,250	908	837
5731 Radio, TV, & electronic stores	35	36	342	360	10	16,012	18,133	6,228	6,374
5734 Computer and software stores	7	7	21	26	4	12,190	10,000	241	379
5735 Record & prerecorded tape stores	16	15	72	78	5	8,278	10,821	665	797
5736 Musical instrument stores	4	4	22	23	6	17,091	21,913	434	421
5812 Eating places	508	483	10,978	11,165	23	7,037	7,279	83,884	84,878
5813 Drinking places	130	121	977	958	8	6,796	7,027	6,771	6,775
5910 Drug stores and proprietary stores	80	82	1,093	1,208	15	13,852	14,940	15,813	18,631
5920 Liquor stores	28	26	118	101	4	8,169	9,149	1,011	935
5930 Used merchandise stores	27	28	120	123	4	12,967	12,748	1,753	1,759
5941 Sporting goods and bicycle shops	41	39	264	274	7	13,909	14,949	4,370	4,686
5942 Book stores	13	16	96	102	6	9,375	11,608	964	1,159
5943 Stationery stores	-	3	-	12	4	-	4,000	-	53
5944 Jewelry stores	40	44	246	265	6	15,122	17,177	4,456	4,834
5945 Hobby, toy, and game shops	17	20	118	169	8	8,915	8,876	1,320	1,787
5947 Gift, novelty, and souvenir shops	42	39	206	207	5	6,621	6,918	1,582	1,750
5949 Sewing, needlework, and piece goods	19	20	144	140	7	6,306	8,286	1,096	1,401
5961 Catalog and mail-order houses	4	6	23	123	21	12,870	10,829	637	1,588
5962 Merchandising machine operators	16	15	191	278	19	18,262	14,950	3,448	3,966
5963 Direct selling establishments	22	22	136	153	7	16,029	15,869	2,709	2,843
5984 Liquefied petroleum gas dealers	-	8	-	130	16	-	29,385	-	3,304
5992 Florists	47	46	228	231	5	10,035	11,394	2,604	2,931
5993 Tobacco stores and stands	-	5	-	9	2	-	15,556	-	131
5994 News dealers and newsstands	-	3	-	2	1	-	14,000	-	24
5995 Optical goods stores	22	20	178	168	8	19,573	17,286	3,783	3,110
5999 Miscellaneous retail stores, nec	66	69	545	568	8	12,484	14,768	7,948	9,225

Source: County Business Patterns 1994/95, CBP-94/95, U.S. Department of Commerce, Washington DC, November 1997. The employment column represents mid-March employment in the year. Pay per employee is calculated by dividing 1st Quarter payroll, annualized, by mid-March employment. The column headed 'Emp / Est' shows 'employees per establishment'. A dash (-) means that data are unavailable or cannot be calculated. nec means not elsewhere classified. *Notes:* 1. 1994 data incomplete; unavailable or withheld. 2. 1995 data incomplete; unavailable or withheld. 3. 1994 and 1995 data incomplete; unavailable or withheld.

FLORENCE, AL MSA

Wholesale and Retail Trade USA	Establishments		Employment		Emp / Est	Pay / Employee		Annual Payroll ($ 000)	
	1994	1995	1994	1995	1995	1994	1995	1994	1995
50 - Wholesale trade	248	245	2,744	3,083	13	20,362	23,045	63,027	75,088
5012 Automobiles and other vehicles	7	6	95	85	14	21,137	24,000	2,665	2,372
5013 Motor vehicle supplies and new parts	12	11	188	185	17	13,979	15,892	2,980	3,231
5015 Motor vehicle parts, used	7	9	37	55	6	14,054	17,382	628	931
5030 Lumber and construction materials	13	12	189	176	15	23,132	30,182	5,101	5,697
5044 Office equipment	7	7	40	33	5	17,700	23,273	753	775
5045 Computers, peripherals, & software [3]	3	6	31	31	5	20,129	24,516	691	812
5051 Metals service centers and offices [1]	6	6	57	46	8	25,193	25,217	1,478	1,281
5063 Electrical apparatus and equipment	9	9	69	84	9	20,116	21,190	1,633	1,850
5065 Electronic parts and equipment	6	5	33	26	5	24,000	25,538	858	578
5072 Hardware	7	10	18	95	10	13,556	20,463	252	2,030
5084 Industrial machinery and equipment	10	8	96	81	10	22,083	24,198	2,329	2,112

Continued on next page.

FLORENCE, AL MSA - [continued]

Wholesale and Retail Trade USA	Establishments		Employment		Emp / Est	Pay / Employee		Annual Payroll ($ 000)	
	1994	1995	1994	1995	1995	1994	1995	1994	1995
5085 Industrial supplies	14	12	120	120	10	22,100	25,533	2,971	3,267
5087 Service establishment equipment	4	4	17	12	3	13,176	6,667	210	149
5091 Sporting & recreational goods	4	4	12	8	2	6,333	11,000	89	86
5092 Toys and hobby goods and supplies	7	6	343	592	99	24,058	22,270	7,740	13,812
5093 Scrap and waste materials	8	8	44	69	9	19,455	18,841	954	1,628
5099 Durable goods, nec	6	4	17	16	4	14,824	10,000	268	180
5112 Stationery and office supplies	5	-	18	-	-	22,667	-	380	-
5131 Piece goods & notions	-	5	-	12	2	-	18,667	-	317
5147 Meats and meat products	4	4	34	30	8	12,588	15,867	580	581
5149 Groceries and related products, nec	8	7	151	120	17	26,437	26,200	4,371	3,445
5169 Chemicals & allied products, nec[2]	5	4	21	20	5	29,524	33,200	580	658
5171 Petroleum bulk stations & terminals	9	8	86	70	9	15,163	13,543	1,639	1,096
5172 Petroleum products, nec[3]	3	3	30	35	12	21,467	16,686	931	1,046
5180 Beer, wine, and distilled beverages[2]	-	3	-	44	15	-	28,636	-	1,424
5191 Farm supplies	9	11	25	103	9	9,120	21,942	385	2,229
5193 Flowers & florists' supplies[2]	6	4	5	8	2	7,200	13,500	83	110
5199 Nondurable goods, nec	6	6	18	18	3	5,556	6,889	92	91
52 – Retail trade	932	950	10,547	11,101	12	10,275	10,967	120,514	132,594
5210 Lumber and other building materials	21	22	350	312	14	15,966	18,449	6,067	5,852
5230 Paint, glass, and wallpaper stores	6	8	15	48	6	13,600	15,667	224	774
5250 Hardware stores	7	6	25	20	3	7,840	10,600	213	214
5260 Retail nurseries and garden stores	6	7	41	40	6	11,122	12,700	517	472
5270 Mobile home dealers	7	8	22	35	4	17,818	23,771	649	1,129
5310 Department stores	9	9	1,479	1,494	166	10,540	12,169	16,677	19,698
5330 Variety stores	16	11	66	66	6	7,576	8,545	594	634
5390 Misc. general merchandise stores	7	10	176	161	16	12,068	14,137	2,291	2,210
5410 Grocery stores	99	98	1,757	1,718	18	8,503	9,108	16,451	17,373
5420 Meat and fish markets	5	6	6	19	3	7,333	9,474	45	208
5490 Miscellaneous food stores	6	7	5	19	3	7,200	7,789	89	182
5510 New and used car dealers	14	14	472	588	42	27,780	25,782	14,803	16,619
5520 Used car dealers	24	28	38	75	3	12,211	13,760	665	1,239
5530 Auto and home supply stores	32	32	153	182	6	15,503	13,956	2,544	2,992
5540 Gasoline service stations	60	56	288	288	5	9,972	11,486	3,343	3,285
5550 Boat dealers	-	5	-	24	5	-	18,167	-	573
5560 Recreational vehicle dealers[3]	3	3	10	16	5	19,200	20,000	267	359
5610 Men's & boys' clothing stores	5	5	14	13	3	6,000	8,923	80	118
5620 Women's clothing stores	33	24	183	140	6	8,787	8,029	1,646	1,086
5640 Children's and infants' wear stores	6	-	14	-	-	7,143	-	104	-
5650 Family clothing stores	6	8	353	329	41	9,552	11,027	3,708	3,712
5660 Shoe stores	22	16	81	104	7	10,272	7,269	960	820
5690 Misc. apparel & accessory stores	9	7	31	28	4	10,581	13,286	374	330
5712 Furniture stores	16	21	104	91	4	12,231	11,297	1,425	1,042
5713 Floor covering stores	8	9	18	18	2	13,556	16,667	228	432
5720 Household appliance stores	8	-	27	-	-	18,667	-	768	-
5731 Radio, TV, & electronic stores	10	9	44	37	4	20,545	25,730	815	826
5812 Eating places	182	167	3,151	3,214	19	6,936	7,024	23,725	23,445
5813 Drinking places	11	10	80	75	8	5,900	6,773	505	492
5910 Drug stores and proprietary stores	46	43	281	275	6	14,505	16,611	4,534	5,102
5920 Liquor stores	22	25	74	85	3	12,108	11,435	931	1,058
5930 Used merchandise stores	15	15	29	30	2	11,034	11,600	392	406
5941 Sporting goods and bicycle shops	17	19	66	75	4	10,182	10,187	728	771
5942 Book stores	11	11	113	171	16	10,230	13,380	1,468	2,801
5944 Jewelry stores	16	18	74	82	5	11,946	12,927	1,073	1,213
5947 Gift, novelty, and souvenir shops	19	19	75	3	-	6,293	6,667	478	33
5949 Sewing, needlework, and piece goods[2]	-	6	-	30	5	-	9,333	-	245
5963 Direct selling establishments	-	6	-	24	4	-	13,167	-	355
5984 Liquefied petroleum gas dealers	5	5	23	28	6	16,000	16,143	382	462
5995 Optical goods stores	-	4	-	26	7	-	22,154	-	749
5999 Miscellaneous retail stores, nec	23	27	98	88	3	11,878	12,318	1,225	1,330

Source: County Business Patterns 1994/95, CBP-94/95, U.S. Department of Commerce, Washington DC, November 1997. The employment column represents mid-March employment in the year. Pay per employee is calculated by dividing 1st Quarter payroll, annualized, by mid-March employment. The column headed 'Emp / Est' shows 'employees per establishment'. A dash (-) means that data are unavailable or cannot be calculated. nec means not elsewhere classified. *Notes:* 1. 1994 data incomplete; unavailable or withheld. 2. 1995 data incomplete; unavailable or withheld. 3. 1994 and 1995 data incomplete; unavailable or withheld.

FLORENCE, SC MSA

Wholesale and Retail Trade USA	Establishments		Employment		Emp / Est	Pay / Employee		Annual Payroll ($ 000)	
	1994	1995	1994	1995	1995	1994	1995	1994	1995
50– Wholesale trade	-	263	-	3,414	13	-	24,296	-	89,856
5012 Automobiles and other vehicles	-	13	-	104	8	-	33,385	-	3,540
5013 Motor vehicle supplies and new parts	-	22	-	173	8	-	19,329	-	3,549
5014 Tires and tubes	-	4	-	108	27	-	19,630	-	2,301
5015 Motor vehicle parts, used	-	5	-	25	5	-	16,320	-	419
5020 Furniture and homefurnishings	-	5	-	37	7	-	24,324	-	956
5032 Brick, stone, & related materials	-	3	-	15	5	-	22,133	-	511
5044 Office equipment	-	9	-	48	5	-	20,833	-	864
5045 Computers, peripherals, & software	-	3	-	34	11	-	32,000	-	1,045
5046 Commercial equipment, nec	-	4	-	24	6	-	19,333	-	499
5047 Medical and hospital equipment	-	6	-	54	9	-	29,852	-	1,422
5063 Electrical apparatus and equipment	-	8	-	81	10	-	26,617	-	2,244
5072 Hardware	-	3	-	114	38	-	25,333	-	3,234
5074 Plumbing & hydronic heating supplies	-	6	-	181	30	-	35,514	-	6,465
5075 Warm air heating & air conditioning	-	4	-	45	11	-	28,889	-	1,144
5082 Construction and mining machinery	-	5	-	77	15	-	25,506	-	2,364
5083 Farm and garden machinery	-	4	-	95	24	-	18,695	-	1,812
5084 Industrial machinery and equipment	-	12	-	121	10	-	29,190	-	3,515
5085 Industrial supplies	-	12	-	129	11	-	29,116	-	3,915
5087 Service establishment equipment	-	4	-	37	9	-	19,568	-	648
5091 Sporting & recreational goods	-	3	-	28	9	-	15,571	-	443
5099 Durable goods, nec	-	9	-	57	6	-	34,105	-	1,888
5112 Stationery and office supplies	-	7	-	77	11	-	33,195	-	3,157
5120 Drugs, proprietaries, and sundries	-	4	-	51	13	-	25,804	-	1,442
5130 Apparel, piece goods, and notions	-	5	-	23	5	-	27,478	-	614
5140 Groceries and related products	-	10	-	571	57	-	23,664	-	14,768
5153 Grain and field beans	-	3	-	12	4	-	10,667	-	141
5160 Chemicals and allied products	-	4	-	31	8	-	33,161	-	1,086
5170 Petroleum and petroleum products	-	16	-	141	9	-	20,057	-	2,964
5181 Beer and ale	-	3	-	112	37	-	24,786	-	3,992
5191 Farm supplies	-	12	-	103	9	-	16,699	-	1,886
5198 Paints, varnishes, and supplies	-	4	-	30	8	-	15,067	-	479
52– Retail trade	-	898	-	10,961	12	-	11,749	-	139,503
5210 Lumber and other building materials	-	15	-	314	21	-	19,516	-	6,381
5230 Paint, glass, and wallpaper stores	-	7	-	41	6	-	17,171	-	790
5250 Hardware stores	-	8	-	76	10	-	12,632	-	1,045
5260 Retail nurseries and garden stores	-	7	-	19	3	-	13,684	-	337
5270 Mobile home dealers	-	23	-	285	12	-	15,705	-	6,559
5310 Department stores	-	8	-	1,345	168	-	10,834	-	14,014
5330 Variety stores	-	10	-	88	9	-	8,682	-	842
5390 Misc. general merchandise stores	-	10	-	90	9	-	11,644	-	2,250
5410 Grocery stores	-	103	-	1,722	17	-	10,086	-	18,086
5420 Meat and fish markets	-	3	-	13	4	-	8,000	-	103
5440 Candy, nut, and confectionery stores	-	4	-	16	4	-	7,000	-	144
5460 Retail bakeries	-	6	-	62	10	-	8,645	-	615
5510 New and used car dealers	-	18	-	544	30	-	27,676	-	17,188
5520 Used car dealers	-	25	-	89	4	-	14,831	-	1,507
5530 Auto and home supply stores	-	25	-	174	7	-	16,345	-	2,970
5540 Gasoline service stations	-	76	-	646	9	-	11,845	-	7,444
5550 Boat dealers	-	7	-	51	7	-	13,490	-	1,063
5570 Motorcycle dealers	-	3	-	24	8	-	18,167	-	543
5610 Men's & boys' clothing stores	-	10	-	56	6	-	9,357	-	571
5620 Women's clothing stores	-	31	-	340	11	-	6,988	-	2,482
5630 Women's accessory & specialty stores	-	4	-	29	7	-	6,207	-	182
5650 Family clothing stores	-	12	-	114	10	-	9,333	-	1,299
5660 Shoe stores	-	24	-	169	7	-	10,225	-	1,756
5690 Misc. apparel & accessory stores	-	4	-	15	4	-	10,933	-	188
5712 Furniture stores	-	24	-	157	7	-	20,408	-	3,751
5713 Floor covering stores	-	12	-	57	5	-	21,754	-	1,335
5720 Household appliance stores	-	7	-	92	13	-	12,609	-	1,251
5734 Computer and software stores	-	7	-	35	5	-	13,714	-	437
5736 Musical instrument stores	-	4	-	18	5	-	13,111	-	225
5812 Eating places	-	125	-	2,786	22	-	7,378	-	21,340
5813 Drinking places	-	3	-	4	1	-	6,000	-	18
5910 Drug stores and proprietary stores	-	30	-	296	10	-	16,014	-	5,255
5920 Liquor stores	-	9	-	24	3	-	10,000	-	239
5930 Used merchandise stores	-	12	-	26	2	-	14,769	-	441
5941 Sporting goods and bicycle shops	-	14	-	32	2	-	10,000	-	330
5942 Book stores	-	7	-	49	7	-	11,020	-	760
5944 Jewelry stores	-	15	-	121	8	-	12,562	-	1,489
5945 Hobby, toy, and game shops	-	5	-	43	9	-	10,326	-	553

Continued on next page.

FLORENCE, SC MSA - [continued]

Wholesale and Retail Trade USA	Establishments		Employment		Emp / Est	Pay / Employee		Annual Payroll ($ 000)	
	1994	1995	1994	1995	1995	1994	1995	1994	1995
5947 Gift, novelty, and souvenir shops	-	18	-	49	3	-	9,633	-	490
5949 Sewing, needlework, and piece goods	-	3	-	24	8	-	8,000	-	183
5960 Nonstore retailers	-	12	-	100	8	-	16,280	-	1,552
5980 Fuel dealers	-	5	-	47	9	-	18,213	-	1,064
5992 Florists	-	15	-	67	4	-	8,657	-	586
5995 Optical goods stores	-	10	-	43	4	-	15,256	-	695
5999 Miscellaneous retail stores, nec	-	25	-	108	4	-	17,481	-	2,106

Source: County Business Patterns 1994/95, CBP-94/95, U.S. Department of Commerce, Washington DC, November 1997. The employment column represents mid-March employment in the year. Pay per employee is calculated by dividing 1st Quarter payroll, annualized, by mid-March employment. The column headed 'Emp / Est' shows 'employees per establishment'. A dash (-) means that data are unavailable or cannot be calculated. nec means not elsewhere classified. *Notes:* 1. 1994 data incomplete; unavailable or withheld. 2. 1995 data incomplete; unavailable or withheld. 3. 1994 and 1995 data incomplete; unavailable or withheld.

FORT COLLINS - LOVELAND, CO MSA

Wholesale and Retail Trade USA	Establishments		Employment		Emp / Est	Pay / Employee		Annual Payroll ($ 000)	
	1994	1995	1994	1995	1995	1994	1995	1994	1995
50- Wholesale trade	350	358	2,835	3,066	9	23,414	24,896	75,188	80,111
5013 Motor vehicle supplies and new parts	20	15	197	170	11	16,223	17,388	3,422	2,874
5015 Motor vehicle parts, used	3	4	10	9	2	16,400	16,444	147	146
5021 Furniture	-	6	-	12	2	-	19,000	-	190
5023 Homefurnishings	-	3	-	9	3	-	12,444	-	162
5031 Lumber, plywood, and millwork	10	13	152	228	18	20,026	20,281	3,607	5,105
5044 Office equipment	9	9	87	83	9	23,862	29,880	2,608	2,753
5045 Computers, peripherals, & software	25	20	243	265	13	33,778	29,917	8,403	8,609
5046 Commercial equipment, nec	6	4	10	10	3	21,600	26,000	164	167
5047 Medical and hospital equipment	10	6	29	54	9	25,655	43,037	816	2,293
5049 Professional equipment, nec	4	6	73	74	12	34,137	38,811	2,708	2,894
5051 Metals service centers and offices	-	6	-	61	10	-	19,803	-	1,512
5063 Electrical apparatus and equipment	12	12	155	106	9	26,684	27,623	4,444	3,052
5072 Hardware	4	6	10	25	4	22,800	25,760	283	677
5074 Plumbing & hydronic heating supplies	9	9	57	66	7	16,351	22,000	1,182	1,701
5075 Warm air heating & air conditioning	4	4	10	13	3	32,400	36,923	349	359
5082 Construction and mining machinery	4	4	21	22	6	24,381	26,545	571	600
5083 Farm and garden machinery	-	11	-	48	4	-	21,500	-	1,248
5084 Industrial machinery and equipment	14	16	190	208	13	24,063	27,635	5,333	6,466
5085 Industrial supplies	11	10	192	191	19	30,813	40,838	6,749	7,094
5087 Service establishment equipment	9	7	30	31	4	23,067	28,516	832	802
5091 Sporting & recreational goods	-	7	-	4	1	-	18,000	-	171
5093 Scrap and waste materials	5	-	21	-	-	19,619	-	481	-
5094 Jewelry & precious stones	6	6	35	31	5	9,029	12,516	410	445
5099 Durable goods, nec	9	9	13	11	1	17,538	14,545	201	187
5112 Stationery and office supplies	10	9	101	101	11	15,802	18,931	1,705	1,655
5120 Drugs, proprietaries, and sundries	5	6	61	86	14	26,295	29,860	2,041	3,124
5131 Piece goods & notions	3	3	16	23	8	19,500	18,609	371	429
5137 Women's and children's clothing	3	-	14	-	-	7,143	-	120	-
5147 Meats and meat products	-	3	-	60	20	-	20,400	-	1,320
5150 Farm-product raw materials	7	7	81	84	12	20,593	19,857	1,814	1,654
5169 Chemicals & allied products, nec	-	5	-	11	2	-	41,091	-	480
5170 Petroleum and petroleum products	6	5	65	52	10	26,031	19,923	1,976	1,124
5191 Farm supplies	-	9	-	30	3	-	18,533	-	666
5192 Books, periodicals, & newspapers	5	5	109	92	18	20,257	26,913	2,381	2,576
5193 Flowers & florists' supplies	4	4	25	23	6	9,920	5,739	265	208
5199 Nondurable goods, nec	13	17	121	152	9	22,017	20,816	3,008	3,104
52- Retail trade	1,487	1,541	19,364	21,756	14	11,528	11,910	265,958	283,539
5210 Lumber and other building materials	27	21	700	643	31	20,131	22,974	17,542	16,292
5230 Paint, glass, and wallpaper stores	15	13	62	65	5	15,806	17,354	1,208	1,265
5250 Hardware stores	8	5	63	60	12	12,190	12,267	802	742
5260 Retail nurseries and garden stores	-	3	-	16	5	-	10,000	-	203
5270 Mobile home dealers	-	7	-	36	5	-	23,333	-	1,011
5310 Department stores	12	12	1,712	1,699	142	9,645	11,348	18,339	19,286
5390 Misc. general merchandise stores	10	13	582	630	48	12,103	13,390	8,571	9,047
5410 Grocery stores	50	47	1,992	2,128	45	16,145	15,938	40,924	36,606
5440 Candy, nut, and confectionery stores	11	-	35	-	-	5,714	-	389	-
5460 Retail bakeries	20	20	133	124	6	6,526	6,065	1,143	818
5490 Miscellaneous food stores	-	12	-	61	5	-	6,033	-	520
5510 New and used car dealers	15	15	822	837	56	30,044	33,051	28,374	31,591
5520 Used car dealers	12	15	72	64	4	13,222	16,000	1,063	1,226
5530 Auto and home supply stores	26	28	196	222	8	16,367	15,495	3,508	3,888
5540 Gasoline service stations	80	81	558	583	7	10,968	11,314	6,327	6,699

Continued on next page.

FORT COLLINS - LOVELAND, CO MSA - [continued]

Wholesale and Retail Trade USA	Establishments		Employment		Emp / Est	Pay / Employee		Annual Payroll ($ 000)	
	1994	1995	1994	1995	1995	1994	1995	1994	1995
5560 Recreational vehicle dealers	6	5	41	61	12	25,366	19,869	1,335	1,463
5570 Motorcycle dealers	10	10	61	80	8	14,557	16,900	1,283	1,743
5610 Men's & boys' clothing stores	13	17	90	178	10	8,756	7,438	1,123	1,437
5620 Women's clothing stores	44	47	335	326	7	7,057	7,595	2,760	2,704
5630 Women's accessory & specialty stores	9	10	40	57	6	7,600	6,877	329	456
5640 Children's and infants' wear stores	-	3	-	6	2	-	6,000	-	42
5650 Family clothing stores	31	34	261	360	11	9,916	8,878	2,803	3,327
5660 Shoe stores	28	29	127	152	5	10,394	9,842	1,688	1,746
5690 Misc. apparel & accessory stores	19	20	49	83	4	8,653	8,627	745	1,120
5712 Furniture stores	35	36	307	348	10	18,319	20,931	6,183	7,802
5713 Floor covering stores	16	15	94	103	7	20,468	22,447	2,179	2,808
5719 Misc. homefurnishings stores	27	30	111	168	6	10,883	10,881	1,563	2,013
5720 Household appliance stores	9	11	31	39	4	13,548	15,385	510	518
5731 Radio, TV, & electronic stores	16	20	204	254	13	15,471	14,000	3,297	3,576
5734 Computer and software stores	7	9	34	21	2	10,235	13,524	316	311
5735 Record & prerecorded tape stores	7	6	77	66	11	5,662	5,091	467	364
5736 Musical instrument stores	6	6	37	34	6	15,568	12,000	572	446
5812 Eating places	320	302	6,541	7,061	23	6,843	7,108	54,087	55,033
5813 Drinking places	36	29	375	428	15	6,955	6,168	2,752	2,575
5910 Drug stores and proprietary stores	21	19	251	302	16	17,673	21,430	4,149	5,379
5920 Liquor stores	37	40	149	194	5	10,846	13,278	2,056	2,616
5930 Used merchandise stores	30	27	105	140	5	8,533	8,857	1,073	1,382
5941 Sporting goods and bicycle shops	55	54	302	354	7	11,020	10,621	4,352	4,401
5942 Book stores	18	21	123	122	6	10,016	11,016	1,381	1,527
5943 Stationery stores	-	3	-	25	8	-	14,400	-	351
5944 Jewelry stores	30	31	176	168	5	10,955	11,500	2,023	2,096
5945 Hobby, toy, and game shops	15	16	139	162	10	8,978	8,222	1,426	1,622
5947 Gift, novelty, and souvenir shops	71	64	299	317	5	10,020	10,259	3,540	3,920
5948 Luggage and leather goods stores	3	-	13	-	-	9,846	-	132	-
5949 Sewing, needlework, and piece goods	8	6	56	44	7	8,857	7,364	473	326
5961 Catalog and mail-order houses	10	11	46	78	7	17,391	15,385	1,110	1,476
5962 Merchandising machine operators	3	5	12	8	2	18,333	26,500	221	204
5963 Direct selling establishments	19	22	54	90	4	20,963	15,467	1,249	1,427
5984 Liquefied petroleum gas dealers	7	6	42	53	9	19,429	19,396	953	1,144
5992 Florists	20	17	168	172	10	6,548	6,721	1,139	1,215
5995 Optical goods stores	11	11	63	69	6	13,524	12,928	804	937
5999 Miscellaneous retail stores, nec	71	77	353	332	4	11,275	11,217	4,057	4,190

Source: County Business Patterns 1994/95, CBP-94/95, U.S. Department of Commerce, Washington DC, November 1997. The employment column represents mid-March employment in the year. Pay per employee is calculated by dividing 1st Quarter payroll, annualized, by mid-March employment. The column headed 'Emp / Est' shows 'employees per establishment'. A dash (-) means that data are unavailable or cannot be calculated. nec means not elsewhere classified. *Notes:* 1. 1994 data incomplete; unavailable or withheld. 2. 1995 data incomplete; unavailable or withheld. 3. 1994 and 1995 data incomplete; unavailable or withheld.

FORT LAUDERDALE, FL PMSA

Wholesale and Retail Trade USA	Establishments		Employment		Emp / Est	Pay / Employee		Annual Payroll ($ 000)	
	1994	1995	1994	1995	1995	1994	1995	1994	1995
50 - Wholesale trade	4,232	4,380	39,870	40,141	9	29,570	32,784	1,260,399	1,359,763
5012 Automobiles and other vehicles	63	65	573	655	10	45,208	44,598	26,000	30,241
5013 Motor vehicle supplies and new parts	207	181	1,683	1,581	9	25,459	28,397	47,469	44,319
5014 Tires and tubes	24	23	126	162	7	21,619	23,778	3,106	4,337
5015 Motor vehicle parts, used	32	42	188	269	6	16,745	20,565	3,591	6,022
5021 Furniture	115	103	1,039	925	9	25,143	29,565	27,103	28,589
5023 Homefurnishings	118	116	712	711	6	22,489	24,709	16,987	17,434
5031 Lumber, plywood, and millwork	40	40	459	591	15	27,102	33,245	11,828	19,418
5032 Brick, stone, & related materials	53	48	473	641	13	26,833	28,730	14,906	20,088
5033 Roofing, siding, & insulation	19	17	165	226	13	29,285	22,850	4,970	4,998
5039 Construction materials, nec	36	63	263	562	9	32,776	30,036	9,009	17,717
5043 Photographic equipment & supplies	17	17	111	83	5	30,378	32,771	3,052	2,686
5044 Office equipment	66	68	1,227	787	12	30,575	27,268	37,920	23,093
5045 Computers, peripherals, & software	175	171	1,411	1,518	9	41,191	45,979	62,432	71,659
5046 Commercial equipment, nec	64	62	615	549	9	30,504	31,417	18,151	17,246
5047 Medical and hospital equipment	126	120	900	887	7	36,493	37,425	34,417	36,911
5048 Ophthalmic goods	19	19	111	116	6	19,315	21,310	2,723	2,916
5049 Professional equipment, nec	24	26	309	378	15	29,877	30,952	9,682	11,790
5051 Metals service centers and offices	60	64	558	612	10	29,183	34,980	18,682	23,214
5063 Electrical apparatus and equipment	166	143	1,642	1,333	9	32,794	35,442	56,964	47,169
5064 Electrical appliances, TV & radios	40	47	271	330	7	35,129	32,400	10,421	11,369
5065 Electronic parts and equipment	217	223	2,805	2,779	12	43,529	43,015	130,017	120,176
5072 Hardware	60	65	403	455	7	28,794	27,807	11,574	13,396

Continued on next page.

FORT LAUDERDALE, FL PMSA - [continued]

Wholesale and Retail Trade USA	Establishments		Employment		Emp / Est	Pay / Employee		Annual Payroll ($ 000)	
	1994	1995	1994	1995	1995	1994	1995	1994	1995
5074 Plumbing & hydronic heating supplies	62	53	453	484	9	31,497	29,802	15,185	15,951
5075 Warm air heating & air conditioning	41	43	380	412	10	28,200	30,437	12,002	13,018
5078 Refrigeration equipment and supplies	14	11	43	37	3	24,279	24,541	1,239	1,249
5082 Construction and mining machinery	20	21	227	266	13	29,797	33,023	7,942	9,820
5083 Farm and garden machinery	26	26	205	226	9	27,805	29,752	6,201	6,248
5084 Industrial machinery and equipment	149	149	800	828	6	27,655	30,908	24,480	25,879
5085 Industrial supplies	61	61	356	366	6	29,978	30,754	11,306	12,517
5087 Service establishment equipment	66	65	328	428	7	28,378	29,150	9,296	11,519
5088 Transportation equipment & supplies	137	138	1,320	1,387	10	35,494	41,699	48,615	56,734
5091 Sporting & recreational goods	70	68	484	508	7	30,702	31,425	17,236	19,296
5092 Toys and hobby goods and supplies	23	23	92	105	5	22,957	22,971	2,240	2,453
5093 Scrap and waste materials	30	29	333	310	11	16,565	21,045	6,147	6,321
5094 Jewelry & precious stones	99	105	1,170	970	9	25,268	32,478	34,775	30,900
5099 Durable goods, nec	99	120	260	267	2	16,615	21,423	4,919	6,065
5111 Printing and writing paper	16	16	146	186	12	38,219	38,624	5,779	7,196
5112 Stationery and office supplies	96	82	1,604	1,473	18	18,022	20,630	30,628	31,574
5113 Industrial & personal service paper	37	39	433	469	12	39,621	46,866	16,284	18,966
5120 Drugs, proprietaries, and sundries	92	105	1,427	1,537	15	28,008	31,209	45,061	55,871
5131 Piece goods & notions	67	63	505	535	8	20,554	25,787	11,632	13,701
5136 Men's and boys' clothing	34	33	208	216	7	17,808	16,426	4,098	3,800
5137 Women's and children's clothing	80	79	557	584	7	21,515	23,890	15,451	16,264
5139 Footwear	11	13	41	34	3	21,561	29,529	653	1,345
5141 Groceries, general line	26	28	384	341	12	22,844	26,628	9,591	9,863
5142 Packaged frozen food	34	32	301	283	9	31,628	35,180	9,970	10,445
5143 Dairy products, exc. dried or canned	19	16	327	278	17	31,890	36,360	11,068	9,670
5144 Poultry and poultry products	3	-	59	-	-	16,814	-	1,216	-
5145 Confectionery	12	13	325	318	24	24,086	27,660	8,262	7,978
5146 Fish and seafoods	32	37	295	277	7	22,631	24,029	7,060	6,878
5147 Meats and meat products	34	30	434	276	9	27,760	29,522	10,560	8,378
5148 Fresh fruits and vegetables	81	77	694	640	8	29,700	30,256	20,368	19,859
5149 Groceries and related products, nec	121	114	2,121	2,536	22	29,492	26,043	67,685	68,652
5159 Farm-product raw materials, nec	3	-	10	-	-	10,400	-	93	-
5162 Plastics materials & basic shapes	19	24	71	145	6	28,845	27,117	2,141	3,615
5169 Chemicals & allied products, nec	79	82	809	805	10	28,183	30,281	25,014	25,958
5171 Petroleum bulk stations & terminals	30	28	465	496	18	37,884	38,347	17,604	19,670
5172 Petroleum products, nec	18	17	182	110	6	39,538	26,327	6,306	3,073
5181 Beer and ale	5	6	654	577	96	29,853	34,198	19,368	19,079
5182 Wine and distilled beverages	13	16	642	706	44	42,399	43,581	24,495	26,541
5191 Farm supplies	37	25	1,671	159	6	14,030	33,711	25,435	5,284
5192 Books, periodicals, & newspapers	34	31	490	516	17	25,167	30,225	14,782	17,439
5193 Flowers & florists' supplies	41	37	191	179	5	22,681	22,190	4,653	4,357
5194 Tobacco and tobacco products	7	6	20	18	3	21,800	15,333	444	253
5198 Paints, varnishes, and supplies	44	39	259	210	5	21,081	21,962	6,176	4,343
5199 Nondurable goods, nec	208	204	804	835	4	19,990	21,533	19,479	18,911
52- Retail trade	9,739	9,739	130,341	132,736	14	13,840	14,791	1,900,384	1,974,511
5210 Lumber and other building materials	105	81	3,291	2,619	32	18,194	20,472	68,399	54,523
5230 Paint, glass, and wallpaper stores	68	63	290	310	5	20,483	21,884	6,227	6,853
5250 Hardware stores	62	40	315	244	6	16,241	15,246	5,535	3,765
5260 Retail nurseries and garden stores	49	48	160	204	4	21,325	16,314	3,261	3,597
5270 Mobile home dealers	8	7	12	15	2	23,000	20,800	358	346
5310 Department stores	51	51	9,115	10,199	200	12,192	13,097	120,686	135,008
5330 Variety stores	81	60	535	517	9	9,279	8,418	5,440	4,476
5390 Misc. general merchandise stores	63	64	2,173	2,302	36	14,303	16,646	34,014	37,909
5410 Grocery stores	626	612	18,364	18,805	31	12,149	12,638	226,535	237,194
5420 Meat and fish markets	62	61	492	338	6	12,748	13,598	6,929	4,988
5430 Fruit and vegetable markets	24	24	226	132	6	9,469	14,273	2,422	1,985
5440 Candy, nut, and confectionery stores	33	31	158	147	5	7,165	8,218	1,142	1,252
5450 Dairy products stores	6	7	15	15	2	5,333	5,600	86	129
5460 Retail bakeries	102	93	839	868	9	8,200	10,000	7,260	6,621
5490 Miscellaneous food stores	96	98	431	578	6	11,981	11,882	5,880	7,656
5510 New and used car dealers	87	89	7,525	7,846	88	35,502	36,101	290,045	293,752
5520 Used car dealers	123	113	554	439	4	22,000	26,733	12,419	11,934
5530 Auto and home supply stores	254	247	1,623	1,784	7	19,670	19,800	32,854	36,510
5540 Gasoline service stations	418	431	2,777	2,804	7	12,903	13,805	38,525	39,772
5550 Boat dealers	125	120	571	649	5	22,816	23,599	14,941	16,279
5560 Recreational vehicle dealers	13	12	66	59	5	24,364	29,017	1,807	1,898
5570 Motorcycle dealers	21	17	73	73	4	18,247	18,575	1,956	1,647
5590 Automotive dealers, nec	11	14	30	25	2	19,333	22,560	576	584
5610 Men's & boys' clothing stores	111	106	743	771	7	13,475	14,495	10,349	11,537
5620 Women's clothing stores	361	303	2,795	2,345	8	10,068	10,412	28,253	23,867
5630 Women's accessory & specialty stores	89	82	510	509	6	10,000	10,381	5,345	5,189

Continued on next page.

FORT LAUDERDALE, FL PMSA - [continued]

Wholesale and Retail Trade USA	Establishments		Employment		Emp / Est	Pay / Employee		Annual Payroll ($ 000)	
	1994	1995	1994	1995	1995	1994	1995	1994	1995
5640 Children's and infants' wear stores	39	39	288	337	9	9,292	11,442	2,907	3,722
5650 Family clothing stores	118	121	2,151	2,200	18	11,477	12,995	26,828	28,271
5660 Shoe stores	251	230	1,404	1,270	6	11,909	12,391	17,529	15,021
5690 Misc. apparel & accessory stores	104	101	447	486	5	10,166	12,041	5,564	6,034
5712 Furniture stores	280	268	1,885	1,739	6	21,776	22,279	41,395	38,207
5713 Floor covering stores	108	117	402	499	4	18,080	18,870	7,556	9,975
5714 Drapery and upholstery stores	18	21	82	98	5	18,780	17,265	1,518	1,568
5719 Misc. homefurnishings stores	155	156	1,176	1,159	7	14,687	15,037	17,281	17,614
5720 Household appliance stores	43	41	137	147	4	16,496	17,578	2,430	2,576
5731 Radio, TV, & electronic stores	112	120	985	1,327	11	18,104	19,445	19,710	27,094
5734 Computer and software stores	44	54	240	270	5	18,283	20,044	5,202	6,448
5735 Record & prerecorded tape stores	43	55	460	632	11	8,600	8,152	4,229	5,126
5736 Musical instrument stores	22	23	151	139	6	16,344	19,597	2,776	2,911
5812 Eating places	2,027	1,863	41,041	41,378	22	9,259	10,166	377,483	398,000
5813 Drinking places	210	176	1,909	1,689	10	9,982	9,873	17,965	15,419
5910 Drug stores and proprietary stores	257	245	4,183	4,085	17	16,104	19,158	73,924	78,030
5920 Liquor stores	107	101	618	646	6	11,909	13,133	7,194	8,163
5930 Used merchandise stores	181	168	796	784	5	13,633	15,061	11,902	12,382
5941 Sporting goods and bicycle shops	178	167	1,300	1,417	8	14,335	15,486	20,360	22,096
5942 Book stores	70	59	326	363	6	13,252	13,785	4,441	5,230
5943 Stationery stores	29	28	133	134	5	14,316	15,701	2,083	1,991
5944 Jewelry stores	226	232	3,273	819	4	10,343	17,011	36,554	14,148
5945 Hobby, toy, and game shops	50	56	498	648	12	11,574	10,537	7,312	8,466
5946 Camera & photographic supply stores	28	28	134	157	6	15,821	15,592	2,129	2,352
5947 Gift, novelty, and souvenir shops	203	190	1,047	1,024	5	9,043	10,371	10,588	10,745
5948 Luggage and leather goods stores	15	14	94	86	6	11,702	14,791	1,111	1,229
5949 Sewing, needlework, and piece goods	38	37	233	228	6	10,386	11,140	2,471	2,563
5961 Catalog and mail-order houses	59	71	660	683	10	17,212	19,924	14,094	15,673
5962 Merchandising machine operators	52	53	305	273	5	22,295	21,333	7,301	5,961
5963 Direct selling establishments	107	111	1,084	907	8	17,354	19,361	20,373	17,962
5983 Fuel oil dealers	3	4	10	10	3	12,000	25,600	208	253
5984 Liquefied petroleum gas dealers	11	11	95	97	9	21,853	23,464	2,202	2,441
5992 Florists	118	112	450	538	5	13,076	12,721	6,147	6,942
5993 Tobacco stores and stands	18	14	112	101	7	10,179	11,564	1,400	1,275
5994 News dealers and newsstands	9	9	12	13	1	9,667	10,462	201	193
5995 Optical goods stores	156	156	685	737	5	17,296	17,764	12,372	12,467
5999 Miscellaneous retail stores, nec	463	463	2,162	2,369	5	14,368	15,436	36,934	39,724

Source: County Business Patterns 1994/95, CBP-94/95, U.S. Department of Commerce, Washington DC, November 1997. The employment column represents mid-March employment in the year. Pay per employee is calculated by dividing 1st Quarter payroll, annualized, by mid-March employment. The column headed 'Emp / Est' shows 'employees per establishment'. A dash (-) means that data are unavailable or cannot be calculated. nec means not elsewhere classified. *Notes:* 1. 1994 data incomplete; unavailable or withheld. 2. 1995 data incomplete; unavailable or withheld. 3. 1994 and 1995 data incomplete; unavailable or withheld.

FORT MYERS - CAPE CORAL, FL MSA

Wholesale and Retail Trade USA	Establishments		Employment		Emp / Est	Pay / Employee		Annual Payroll ($ 000)	
	1994	1995	1994	1995	1995	1994	1995	1994	1995
50 - Wholesale trade	602	621	4,912	5,061	8	24,827	26,528	129,983	138,222
5012 Automobiles and other vehicles	17	15	124	185	12	25,161	17,686	3,353	3,754
5013 Motor vehicle supplies and new parts	42	35	389	348	10	19,075	19,023	7,508	6,789
5014 Tires and tubes	4	4	33	41	10	27,030	29,463	947	1,245
5015 Motor vehicle parts, used	6	10	39	64	6	19,692	20,813	789	1,425
5021 Furniture	9	9	61	71	8	19,344	24,789	1,353	1,686
5023 Homefurnishings	14	13	82	81	6	20,780	22,914	2,099	2,034
5031 Lumber, plywood, and millwork	15	16	166	165	10	26,313	30,255	4,444	4,741
5032 Brick, stone, & related materials	15	13	82	121	9	22,829	24,926	2,074	3,245
5033 Roofing, siding, & insulation	7	4	47	24	6	16,936	23,833	1,020	794
5039 Construction materials, nec	6	20	61	168	8	35,475	29,952	2,454	5,188
5044 Office equipment	16	17	169	148	9	21,538	24,595	3,848	3,636
5045 Computers, peripherals, & software	13	13	121	139	11	32,694	33,813	4,190	5,022
5046 Commercial equipment, nec	10	10	73	67	7	17,589	18,030	1,198	1,275
5047 Medical and hospital equipment	21	17	103	88	5	22,408	24,318	2,729	2,271
5051 Metals service centers and offices	-	12	-	91	8	-	25,626	-	2,549
5063 Electrical apparatus and equipment	23	25	194	240	10	27,072	29,350	5,533	6,855
5064 Electrical appliances, TV & radios	6	6	88	99	17	28,818	31,394	2,779	2,993
5065 Electronic parts and equipment	12	13	125	146	11	28,768	31,205	4,028	5,153
5072 Hardware	9	10	90	92	9	26,889	31,174	2,160	2,600
5074 Plumbing & hydronic heating supplies	15	17	112	124	7	31,143	28,935	3,389	3,651
5075 Warm air heating & air conditioning	13	-	86	-	-	27,256	-	2,486	-
5082 Construction and mining machinery	7	10	123	130	13	30,341	39,323	4,030	4,655

Continued on next page.

FORT MYERS – CAPE CORAL, FL MSA - [continued]

Wholesale and Retail Trade USA	Establishments		Employment		Emp / Est	Pay / Employee		Annual Payroll ($ 000)	
	1994	1995	1994	1995	1995	1994	1995	1994	1995
5083 Farm and garden machinery	16	13	100	83	6	20,800	22,169	2,284	2,104
5084 Industrial machinery and equipment	29	29	141	156	5	27,149	32,256	4,204	5,023
5085 Industrial supplies	5	6	61	71	12	34,033	42,366	2,137	2,403
5087 Service establishment equipment	10	10	79	71	7	22,734	25,296	2,004	2,027
5088 Transportation equipment & supplies	11	10	82	52	5	23,122	22,769	2,294	1,258
5091 Sporting & recreational goods	-	7	-	41	6	-	17,171	-	745
5093 Scrap and waste materials	9	10	69	74	7	13,043	17,568	1,034	1,530
5094 Jewelry & precious stones	4	-	20	-	-	10,400	-	334	-
5099 Durable goods, nec	14	13	60	63	5	25,067	26,476	2,065	2,212
5112 Stationery and office supplies	8	7	137	146	21	19,416	21,068	2,814	3,013
5120 Drugs, proprietaries, and sundries	6	-	34	-	-	19,294	-	703	-
5137 Women's and children's clothing	5	4	26	27	7	11,692	13,185	311	324
5141 Groceries, general line	6	6	32	25	4	22,875	18,400	827	424
5145 Confectionery	-	3	-	5	2	-	8,000	-	93
5146 Fish and seafoods	11	10	57	85	9	15,719	13,835	1,080	1,144
5147 Meats and meat products	-	4	-	14	4	-	19,429	-	113
5148 Fresh fruits and vegetables	10	11	91	93	8	30,286	32,774	3,026	3,018
5149 Groceries and related products, nec	18	16	219	259	16	29,772	25,266	6,984	6,491
5162 Plastics materials & basic shapes	-	4	-	32	8	-	50,625	-	2,743
5169 Chemicals & allied products, nec	10	11	51	59	5	33,176	34,237	1,853	2,015
5171 Petroleum bulk stations & terminals	4	3	60	67	22	32,000	30,090	2,251	2,343
5172 Petroleum products, nec	3	3	16	27	9	28,250	20,148	459	576
5180 Beer, wine, and distilled beverages	5	6	329	285	48	27,915	31,228	9,535	8,494
5191 Farm supplies	9	10	33	36	4	22,667	21,111	776	815
5192 Books, periodicals, & newspapers	6	6	38	36	6	16,105	17,556	632	667
5193 Flowers & florists' supplies	15	13	77	70	5	37,662	39,600	2,353	2,580
5198 Paints, varnishes, and supplies	6	5	229	21	4	15,319	22,476	1,963	432
5199 Nondurable goods, nec	24	24	107	108	5	21,383	21,185	2,508	2,465
52- Retail trade	2,628	2,549	35,575	36,743	14	13,090	13,714	466,509	486,040
5210 Lumber and other building materials	47	35	1,212	1,216	35	20,129	20,566	26,312	25,311
5230 Paint, glass, and wallpaper stores	25	23	71	78	3	26,141	25,846	1,542	1,808
5250 Hardware stores	28	19	254	221	12	13,496	13,828	3,872	3,086
5260 Retail nurseries and garden stores	16	17	106	134	8	12,717	13,194	1,500	1,837
5270 Mobile home dealers	9	7	151	26	4	11,788	17,846	2,026	601
5310 Department stores	19	19	3,035	3,674	193	12,345	13,404	39,019	48,815
5330 Variety stores	22	16	123	131	8	9,951	9,618	1,479	1,273
5390 Misc. general merchandise stores	13	20	416	447	22	13,385	13,315	5,712	5,536
5410 Grocery stores	168	163	6,116	6,274	38	11,566	12,166	68,807	72,771
5420 Meat and fish markets	9	4	32	14	4	12,500	16,286	317	146
5430 Fruit and vegetable markets	10	8	35	43	5	13,029	13,302	397	554
5440 Candy, nut, and confectionery stores	6	5	23	25	5	6,609	6,080	168	172
5450 Dairy products stores	4	4	10	14	4	12,000	10,286	134	154
5460 Retail bakeries	21	15	135	152	10	11,111	9,711	1,687	1,183
5490 Miscellaneous food stores	20	20	61	68	3	11,016	10,824	694	835
5510 New and used car dealers	22	26	1,581	1,791	69	33,574	29,289	54,054	56,518
5520 Used car dealers	42	39	208	231	6	21,885	24,797	4,722	6,251
5530 Auto and home supply stores	51	52	354	394	8	20,034	20,091	7,630	8,447
5540 Gasoline service stations	126	118	1,252	936	8	11,262	13,308	13,894	12,298
5550 Boat dealers	41	45	259	275	6	20,927	20,713	5,746	5,614
5560 Recreational vehicle dealers	10	11	166	157	14	18,747	23,312	2,908	2,928
5570 Motorcycle dealers	6	4	46	45	11	19,130	20,889	942	1,027
5590 Automotive dealers, nec	-	3	-	9	3	-	24,444	-	215
5610 Men's & boys' clothing stores	20	21	84	115	5	12,810	11,026	1,188	1,160
5620 Women's clothing stores	138	117	792	692	6	9,278	9,584	7,377	6,331
5630 Women's accessory & specialty stores	18	15	80	82	5	9,800	10,341	840	773
5640 Children's and infants' wear stores	10	9	48	56	6	8,333	8,571	391	428
5650 Family clothing stores	46	51	539	614	12	10,033	10,801	5,597	6,486
5660 Shoe stores	55	52	312	334	6	10,987	10,862	3,312	3,155
5690 Misc. apparel & accessory stores	46	42	209	186	4	13,818	11,828	2,955	2,048
5712 Furniture stores	85	86	689	708	8	21,550	23,056	15,587	16,435
5713 Floor covering stores	31	25	152	105	4	15,395	20,952	2,348	2,359
5714 Drapery and upholstery stores	7	6	31	30	5	17,161	17,067	539	700
5719 Misc. homefurnishings stores	43	45	204	241	5	13,196	13,378	2,797	3,026
5720 Household appliance stores	20	21	85	88	4	18,729	19,909	1,515	1,567
5731 Radio, TV, & electronic stores	26	28	191	244	9	22,743	22,508	4,300	5,177
5734 Computer and software stores	9	8	47	61	8	22,553	21,902	1,221	1,310
5735 Record & prerecorded tape stores	11	12	79	85	7	11,747	11,482	1,002	1,010
5736 Musical instrument stores	9	8	47	40	5	18,979	44,700	1,022	1,241
5812 Eating places	507	441	11,196	10,532	24	9,293	9,794	95,009	92,302
5813 Drinking places	39	39	289	271	7	8,304	8,930	2,229	1,896
5910 Drug stores and proprietary stores	60	57	973	993	17	16,580	18,127	16,958	17,158

Continued on next page.

FORT MYERS – CAPE CORAL, FL MSA - [continued]

Wholesale and Retail Trade USA	Establishments		Employment		Emp / Est	Pay / Employee		Annual Payroll ($ 000)	
	1994	1995	1994	1995	1995	1994	1995	1994	1995
5920 Liquor stores	36	33	170	174	5	10,965	10,529	1,882	1,844
5930 Used merchandise stores	50	52	132	180	3	11,091	12,356	1,643	2,317
5941 Sporting goods and bicycle shops	52	56	247	303	5	13,036	11,512	3,552	3,881
5942 Book stores	26	21	120	142	7	11,433	14,620	1,911	2,222
5943 Stationery stores	8	4	25	23	6	12,480	6,957	270	188
5944 Jewelry stores	41	36	196	199	6	18,551	20,905	4,125	4,714
5945 Hobby, toy, and game shops	20	18	206	202	11	12,252	12,871	2,539	2,313
5946 Camera & photographic supply stores	5	-	24	-	-	17,000	-	379	-
5947 Gift, novelty, and souvenir shops	83	77	533	513	7	9,058	9,918	5,128	5,166
5948 Luggage and leather goods stores	4	4	22	20	5	11,091	14,800	256	278
5961 Catalog and mail-order houses	10	6	59	62	10	17,966	18,645	990	1,110
5962 Merchandising machine operators	7	9	70	62	7	11,486	14,194	900	811
5963 Direct selling establishments	28	23	148	141	6	16,000	16,965	2,673	2,488
5980 Fuel dealers	9	7	85	100	14	39,388	62,880	2,944	3,396
5995 Optical goods stores	26	27	146	156	6	14,329	15,692	1,998	2,355
5999 Miscellaneous retail stores, nec	97	111	354	538	5	13,932	12,944	5,591	7,521

Source: County Business Patterns 1994/95, CBP-94/95, U.S. Department of Commerce, Washington DC, November 1997. The employment column represents mid-March employment in the year. Pay per employee is calculated by dividing 1st Quarter payroll, annualized, by mid-March employment. The column headed 'Emp / Est' shows 'employees per establishment'. A dash (-) means that data are unavailable or cannot be calculated. nec means not elsewhere classified. *Notes:* 1. 1994 data incomplete; unavailable or withheld. 2. 1995 data incomplete; unavailable or withheld. 3. 1994 and 1995 data incomplete; unavailable or withheld.

FORT PIERCE – PORT ST. LUCIE, FL MSA

Wholesale and Retail Trade USA	Establishments		Employment		Emp / Est	Pay / Employee		Annual Payroll ($ 000)	
	1994	1995	1994	1995	1995	1994	1995	1994	1995
50 - Wholesale trade	413	414	3,385	3,619	9	24,735	27,087	84,566	88,708
5012 Automobiles and other vehicles	8	-	40	-	-	12,100	-	453	-
5013 Motor vehicle supplies and new parts	25	26	233	256	10	19,966	19,641	6,182	6,180
5015 Motor vehicle parts, used	5	7	43	41	6	9,209	10,146	471	338
5020 Furniture and homefurnishings	12	8	20	27	3	23,600	18,074	556	450
5031 Lumber, plywood, and millwork	11	10	109	48	5	22,716	27,167	2,800	1,488
5032 Brick, stone, & related materials	13	11	31	43	4	26,452	22,791	892	987
5039 Construction materials, nec	6	10	17	62	6	17,647	31,484	138	1,910
5044 Office equipment	5	5	44	47	9	28,818	29,787	1,295	1,260
5045 Computers, peripherals, & software	13	13	31	182	14	362,323	74,066	4,777	5,597
5047 Medical and hospital equipment	9	6	59	8	1	18,983	21,000	1,303	73
5063 Electrical apparatus and equipment	14	12	44	87	7	20,636	30,437	1,006	2,376
5065 Electronic parts and equipment	8	8	61	37	5	19,541	16,973	1,575	595
5072 Hardware	9	9	26	25	3	20,000	21,600	605	698
5074 Plumbing & hydronic heating supplies	14	13	86	72	6	25,163	28,889	2,369	2,100
5075 Warm air heating & air conditioning	9	9	35	32	4	18,629	27,250	790	965
5078 Refrigeration equipment and supplies[1]	3	-	12	-	-	25,000	-	270	-
5083 Farm and garden machinery	11	11	89	94	9	23,146	23,872	2,187	2,138
5084 Industrial machinery and equipment	11	9	55	75	8	25,382	25,120	1,635	2,015
5085 Industrial supplies	10	10	39	56	6	21,436	27,786	922	1,532
5087 Service establishment equipment	6	-	20	-	-	16,200	-	398	-
5088 Transportation equipment & supplies[1]	6	5	16	15	3	14,750	25,867	390	393
5091 Sporting & recreational goods	-	14	-	39	3	-	33,128	-	1,756
5093 Scrap and waste materials	7	8	100	121	15	17,840	20,562	1,690	2,172
5099 Durable goods, nec	12	14	61	60	4	30,689	45,067	3,066	2,898
5112 Stationery and office supplies	9	8	111	81	10	14,162	20,691	1,687	1,508
5113 Industrial & personal service paper[1]	3	-	30	-	-	23,600	-	781	-
5130 Apparel, piece goods, and notions	-	6	-	24	4	-	18,000	-	451
5141 Groceries, general line	6	5	16	8	2	27,250	46,500	400	339
5146 Fish and seafoods	4	-	32	-	-	10,875	-	314	-
5148 Fresh fruits and vegetables	28	30	709	693	23	19,171	22,776	11,660	12,173
5149 Groceries and related products, nec	8	-	85	-	-	28,847	-	2,439	-
5160 Chemicals and allied products	9	-	21	-	-	16,000	-	583	-
5171 Petroleum bulk stations & terminals	-	9	-	40	4	-	38,200	-	1,468
5181 Beer and ale[3]	3	3	176	160	53	26,659	27,925	4,703	4,681
5191 Farm supplies	12	13	86	88	7	28,093	29,500	2,947	2,889
5193 Flowers & florists' supplies	8	6	29	21	4	16,690	22,286	496	484
5199 Nondurable goods, nec	16	17	83	92	5	24,000	20,130	1,845	2,077
52 - Retail trade	1,761	1,720	21,278	21,872	13	12,898	13,753	286,073	298,963
5210 Lumber and other building materials	36	28	717	784	28	16,753	17,888	12,875	14,139
5230 Paint, glass, and wallpaper stores	20	21	73	67	3	16,548	19,224	1,294	1,452
5250 Hardware stores	14	10	90	87	9	12,356	12,552	1,324	1,089
5260 Retail nurseries and garden stores	12	13	32	48	4	18,625	14,833	561	773
5270 Mobile home dealers[3]	3	3	7	6	2	12,000	13,333	91	102

Continued on next page.

FORT PIERCE - PORT ST. LUCIE, FL MSA - [continued]

Wholesale and Retail Trade USA	Establishments		Employment		Emp / Est	Pay / Employee		Annual Payroll ($ 000)	
	1994	1995	1994	1995	1995	1994	1995	1994	1995
5310 Department stores	15	15	2,301	2,319	155	10,757	12,181	25,993	27,958
5330 Variety stores	8	5	4	30	6	31,000	9,600	94	296
5390 Misc. general merchandise stores [2]	8	11	228	108	10	13,930	11,963	3,203	1,150
5410 Grocery stores	145	133	3,798	3,861	29	12,400	12,944	47,091	49,058
5420 Meat and fish markets	12	11	63	58	5	14,095	14,345	904	891
5430 Fruit and vegetable markets	8	8	14	24	3	11,143	11,167	116	222
5440 Candy, nut, and confectionery stores	7	-	26	-	-	4,923	-	105	-
5450 Dairy products stores	4	4	37	16	4	2,811	5,000	108	88
5460 Retail bakeries	20	15	111	96	6	9,405	8,292	1,121	570
5490 Miscellaneous food stores	9	13	63	58	4	8,190	34,069	647	1,191
5510 New and used car dealers	27	23	1,309	1,335	58	31,141	32,249	42,334	44,832
5520 Used car dealers	25	27	109	128	5	19,853	27,969	2,649	3,791
5530 Auto and home supply stores	49	51	289	314	6	20,055	20,497	6,169	6,610
5540 Gasoline service stations	103	96	661	571	6	10,651	13,226	7,411	7,315
5550 Boat dealers	35	35	210	238	7	16,305	16,235	3,898	3,590
5560 Recreational vehicle dealers	5	5	22	46	9	20,000	21,652	675	1,158
5570 Motorcycle dealers	-	5	-	15	3	-	19,733	-	266
5610 Men's & boys' clothing stores	18	19	91	90	5	10,769	9,378	910	782
5620 Women's clothing stores	70	52	401	316	6	9,895	10,013	3,864	2,746
5630 Women's accessory & specialty stores	7	9	36	37	4	9,778	8,865	332	318
5650 Family clothing stores	25	23	352	335	15	8,545	9,839	3,308	3,403
5660 Shoe stores	44	39	165	158	4	11,418	11,949	1,929	1,706
5690 Misc. apparel & accessory stores	14	14	65	69	5	11,446	11,652	764	769
5712 Furniture stores	67	59	438	409	7	15,105	17,203	6,695	6,086
5713 Floor covering stores	22	-	80	-	-	17,650	-	1,300	-
5719 Misc. homefurnishings stores	33	33	83	179	5	15,373	13,475	1,440	2,499
5720 Household appliance stores	17	18	121	116	6	20,893	20,931	2,640	2,401
5731 Radio, TV, & electronic stores	21	22	90	94	4	21,244	20,596	1,741	1,835
5734 Computer and software stores	6	6	16	17	3	22,500	30,118	471	577
5735 Record & prerecorded tape stores	10	11	7	14	1	13,143	11,143	107	130
5736 Musical instrument stores	6	-	14	-	-	16,000	-	216	-
5812 Eating places	328	299	5,895	5,925	20	9,035	9,199	50,457	50,803
5813 Drinking places	25	22	208	174	8	10,000	9,793	1,892	1,810
5910 Drug stores and proprietary stores	51	49	747	759	15	17,414	19,262	13,969	14,577
5920 Liquor stores	19	16	28	73	5	11,857	10,356	297	658
5930 Used merchandise stores	34	28	97	96	3	11,216	13,458	1,234	1,197
5941 Sporting goods and bicycle shops	38	41	147	158	4	11,782	12,177	1,861	2,141
5942 Book stores	11	10	40	38	4	6,800	8,737	291	330
5944 Jewelry stores	22	25	108	116	5	16,259	14,759	1,766	1,681
5945 Hobby, toy, and game shops	10	9	97	114	13	10,268	9,439	1,200	1,178
5947 Gift, novelty, and souvenir shops	40	41	136	148	4	8,088	8,541	1,159	1,331
5948 Luggage and leather goods stores	4	4	13	13	3	12,308	11,692	169	161
5949 Sewing, needlework, and piece goods	10	7	78	59	8	6,359	9,288	518	550
5961 Catalog and mail-order houses [2]	5	8	8	11	1	10,000	8,364	87	77
5962 Merchandising machine operators	-	6	-	7	1	-	12,571	-	88
5963 Direct selling establishments	-	15	-	69	5	-	17,913	-	1,309
5984 Liquefied petroleum gas dealers	5	5	49	49	10	26,449	28,245	1,550	1,681
5992 Florists	33	28	96	107	4	9,833	11,028	970	1,127
5995 Optical goods stores	16	17	20	56	3	16,800	16,857	351	1,126
5999 Miscellaneous retail stores, nec	62	63	196	298	5	15,020	16,376	3,215	5,348

Source: County Business Patterns 1994/95, CBP-94/95, U.S. Department of Commerce, Washington DC, November 1997. The employment column represents mid-March employment in the year. Pay per employee is calculated by dividing 1st Quarter payroll, annualized, by mid-March employment. The column headed 'Emp / Est' shows 'employees per establishment'. A dash (-) means that data are unavailable or cannot be calculated. nec means not elsewhere classified. *Notes:* 1. 1994 data incomplete; unavailable or withheld. 2. 1995 data incomplete; unavailable or withheld. 3. 1994 and 1995 data incomplete; unavailable or withheld.

FORT SMITH MSA (AR PART)

Wholesale and Retail Trade USA	Establishments		Employment		Emp / Est	Pay / Employee		Annual Payroll ($ 000)	
	1994	1995	1994	1995	1995	1994	1995	1994	1995
50- Wholesale trade	381	372	3,148	3,453	9	22,062	23,174	76,245	81,272
5012 Automobiles and other vehicles	7	7	110	110	16	26,327	29,345	3,065	3,381
5013 Motor vehicle supplies and new parts	27	28	238	253	9	22,504	21,755	5,440	5,548
5014 Tires and tubes [2]	-	4	-	9	2	-	12,444	-	146
5020 Furniture and homefurnishings	12	11	91	72	7	17,363	18,000	1,873	1,528
5031 Lumber, plywood, and millwork	6	-	54	-	-	18,074	-	1,104	-
5032 Brick, stone, & related materials	8	-	34	-	-	22,941	-	881	-
5044 Office equipment	13	12	88	103	9	20,000	23,223	2,021	2,217
5045 Computers, peripherals, & software [3]	9	10	58	71	7	29,793	19,268	1,573	1,317
5046 Commercial equipment, nec [2]	-	6	-	65	11	-	19,138	-	1,164

Continued on next page.

FORT SMITH MSA (AR PART) - [continued]

Wholesale and Retail Trade USA	Establishments		Employment		Emp / Est	Pay / Employee		Annual Payroll ($ 000)	
	1994	1995	1994	1995	1995	1994	1995	1994	1995
5047 Medical and hospital equipment [1]	7	-	63	-	-	20,254	-	1,379	-
5050 Metals and minerals, except petroleum [3]	6	7	86	102	15	23,070	26,431	2,287	2,866
5063 Electrical apparatus and equipment	13	9	132	98	11	24,697	34,857	3,333	2,923
5072 Hardware [3]	11	13	118	112	9	19,864	26,214	2,470	2,655
5074 Plumbing & hydronic heating supplies	5	7	87	101	14	20,782	25,624	1,991	2,432
5082 Construction and mining machinery	9	9	96	83	9	27,042	34,120	2,843	2,649
5083 Farm and garden machinery	7	4	98	21	5	16,367	30,476	1,783	702
5084 Industrial machinery and equipment	40	44	202	335	8	28,198	26,054	7,445	9,235
5085 Industrial supplies	19	17	92	97	6	27,696	25,938	2,615	2,591
5087 Service establishment equipment	12	10	47	45	5	19,660	20,533	997	1,094
5090 Miscellaneous durable goods	16	13	102	121	9	14,941	15,669	2,047	2,237
5112 Stationery and office supplies	-	10	-	35	4	-	25,943	-	953
5113 Industrial & personal service paper [3]	7	6	85	124	21	21,271	17,000	2,073	2,344
5130 Apparel, piece goods, and notions	7	5	20	15	3	15,400	12,000	278	187
5149 Groceries and related products, nec	-	5	-	27	5	-	19,704	-	571
5169 Chemicals & allied products, nec	10	11	13	14	1	28,615	23,143	395	343
5171 Petroleum bulk stations & terminals	10	10	86	87	9	16,837	19,494	2,017	2,078
5172 Petroleum products, nec	8	8	59	42	5	17,492	16,476	1,259	766
5180 Beer, wine, and distilled beverages [1]	5	-	97	-	-	41,814	-	2,852	-
5191 Farm supplies	11	11	63	58	5	21,651	21,793	1,249	1,242
5198 Paints, varnishes, and supplies	5	-	10	-	-	29,200	-	257	-
5199 Nondurable goods, nec	6	7	11	12	2	26,909	23,000	235	257
52- Retail trade	1,055	1,051	12,657	13,114	12	10,906	11,649	158,490	163,684
5210 Lumber and other building materials	26	20	412	359	18	19,612	19,744	10,145	7,763
5230 Paint, glass, and wallpaper stores	8	-	36	-	-	15,222	-	661	-
5250 Hardware stores	6	-	43	-	-	10,419	-	347	-
5260 Retail nurseries and garden stores	7	7	30	33	5	9,067	9,212	345	377
5270 Mobile home dealers [3]	6	6	17	24	4	24,235	23,000	771	882
5310 Department stores [3]	12	11	1,718	1,616	147	10,563	13,163	19,738	20,456
5330 Variety stores	12	9	49	22	2	5,469	6,727	348	199
5390 Misc. general merchandise stores	6	16	247	302	19	12,227	13,285	3,190	3,774
5410 Grocery stores	89	97	1,542	1,291	13	10,444	11,331	18,500	16,236
5420 Meat and fish markets [1]	3	-	11	-	-	7,636	-	115	-
5440 Candy, nut, and confectionery stores [2]	-	5	-	9	2	-	8,889	-	90
5460 Retail bakeries	9	9	44	44	5	7,727	7,818	405	390
5490 Miscellaneous food stores	4	4	12	21	5	10,333	9,905	152	215
5510 New and used car dealers	16	17	544	564	33	22,449	25,071	15,847	16,518
5520 Used car dealers	-	21	-	48	2	-	19,750	-	1,003
5530 Auto and home supply stores	36	33	232	247	7	15,672	16,470	4,027	4,381
5540 Gasoline service stations	74	71	429	428	6	9,259	9,224	4,450	4,193
5550 Boat dealers [3]	5	6	59	76	13	9,966	9,789	676	833
5570 Motorcycle dealers [3]	6	6	32	39	7	15,875	14,769	711	883
5610 Men's & boys' clothing stores	8	8	27	30	4	11,556	10,933	341	298
5620 Women's clothing stores	35	30	238	246	8	7,798	7,610	1,934	1,736
5630 Women's accessory & specialty stores [2]	-	7	-	22	3	-	8,000	-	203
5640 Children's and infants' wear stores	-	4	-	5	1	-	7,200	-	41
5650 Family clothing stores [3]	10	10	96	125	13	8,583	6,400	843	929
5660 Shoe stores [3]	21	19	82	88	5	11,610	13,955	997	1,178
5690 Misc. apparel & accessory stores	8	7	63	97	14	11,873	9,608	811	788
5712 Furniture stores	23	24	144	160	7	15,389	16,650	2,560	2,819
5713 Floor covering stores	-	9	-	35	4	-	19,543	-	1,000
5719 Misc. homefurnishings stores	6	8	139	223	28	9,871	7,300	1,522	1,625
5720 Household appliance stores [3]	5	5	27	21	4	16,148	17,714	415	378
5731 Radio, TV, & electronic stores	11	10	97	116	12	12,866	10,828	1,234	1,290
5734 Computer and software stores [2]	-	6	-	20	3	-	17,600	-	328
5736 Musical instrument stores [1]	5	-	32	-	-	20,125	-	695	-
5812 Eating places	256	221	3,987	4,297	19	7,343	7,874	32,449	35,533
5813 Drinking places	25	21	59	77	4	5,559	6,338	440	487
5910 Drug stores and proprietary stores	36	33	302	312	9	14,411	15,551	5,077	5,449
5920 Liquor stores [3]	19	18	79	84	5	8,101	8,000	708	711
5930 Used merchandise stores	28	28	71	68	2	11,775	13,647	903	936
5941 Sporting goods and bicycle shops	14	17	29	40	2	10,897	10,800	403	473
5942 Book stores [3]	6	8	36	34	4	10,333	10,588	354	373
5944 Jewelry stores	23	22	93	86	4	16,172	15,860	1,531	1,452
5945 Hobby, toy, and game shops [3]	11	9	82	110	12	9,561	9,709	1,145	1,222
5947 Gift, novelty, and souvenir shops	19	17	68	68	4	5,529	7,824	439	540
5949 Sewing, needlework, and piece goods [3]	3	3	21	30	10	9,524	6,800	188	183
5962 Merchandising machine operators	8	9	138	142	16	11,565	11,662	1,707	1,173
5984 Liquefied petroleum gas dealers	-	5	-	31	6	-	13,161	-	341

Continued on next page.

FORT SMITH MSA (AR PART) - [continued]

Wholesale and Retail Trade USA	Establishments		Employment		Emp / Est	Pay / Employee		Annual Payroll ($ 000)	
	1994	1995	1994	1995	1995	1994	1995	1994	1995
5992 Florists	20	23	96	109	5	9,542	9,321	975	1,080
5995 Optical goods stores[3]	5	5	15	23	5	14,133	13,565	315	330
5999 Miscellaneous retail stores, nec	20	24	101	102	4	11,683	12,000	1,418	1,237

Source: County Business Patterns 1994/95, CBP-94/95, U.S. Department of Commerce, Washington DC, November 1997. The employment column represents mid-March employment in the year. Pay per employee is calculated by dividing 1st Quarter payroll, annualized, by mid-March employment. The column headed 'Emp / Est' shows 'employees per establishment'. A dash (-) means that data are unavailable or cannot be calculated. nec means not elsewhere classified. *Notes:* 1. 1994 data incomplete; unavailable or withheld. 2. 1995 data incomplete; unavailable or withheld. 3. 1994 and 1995 data incomplete; unavailable or withheld.

FORT SMITH MSA (OK PART)

Wholesale and Retail Trade USA	Establishments		Employment		Emp / Est	Pay / Employee		Annual Payroll ($ 000)	
	1994	1995	1994	1995	1995	1994	1995	1994	1995
50- Wholesale trade	-	21	-	138	7	-	12,696	-	2,078
5015 Motor vehicle parts, used	-	3	-	25	8	-	11,360	-	319
5100 Wholesale trade-nondurable goods	-	9	-	86	10	-	12,047	-	1,170
52- Retail trade	-	201	-	1,885	9	-	9,821	-	20,231
5200 Building materials & garden supplies	-	9	-	65	7	-	16,123	-	1,499
5410 Grocery stores	-	47	-	633	13	-	9,017	-	5,958
5510 New and used car dealers	-	3	-	45	15	-	23,200	-	1,252
5520 Used car dealers	-	4	-	15	4	-	15,467	-	253
5540 Gasoline service stations	-	19	-	152	8	-	9,000	-	1,479
5600 Apparel and accessory stores	-	4	-	27	7	-	8,593	-	224
5710 Furniture and homefurnishings stores	-	5	-	15	3	-	15,467	-	197
5812 Eating places	-	42	-	569	14	-	6,587	-	4,081
5910 Drug stores and proprietary stores	-	9	-	41	5	-	13,366	-	606
5920 Liquor stores	-	4	-	8	2	-	6,500	-	47
5930 Used merchandise stores	-	5	-	13	3	-	6,769	-	102
5940 Miscellaneous shopping goods stores	-	5	-	18	4	-	14,667	-	263
5960 Nonstore retailers	-	3	-	13	4	-	16,615	-	207
5993 Tobacco stores and stands	-	4	-	12	3	-	10,333	-	78

Source: County Business Patterns 1994/95, CBP-94/95, U.S. Department of Commerce, Washington DC, November 1997. The employment column represents mid-March employment in the year. Pay per employee is calculated by dividing 1st Quarter payroll, annualized, by mid-March employment. The column headed 'Emp / Est' shows 'employees per establishment'. A dash (-) means that data are unavailable or cannot be calculated. nec means not elsewhere classified. *Notes:* 1. 1994 data incomplete; unavailable or withheld. 2. 1995 data incomplete; unavailable or withheld. 3. 1994 and 1995 data incomplete; unavailable or withheld.

FORT SMITH, AR-OK MSA

Wholesale and Retail Trade USA	Establishments		Employment		Emp / Est	Pay / Employee		Annual Payroll ($ 000)	
	1994	1995	1994	1995	1995	1994	1995	1994	1995
50- Wholesale trade[1]	381	393	3,148	3,591	9	22,062	22,771	76,245	83,350
5012 Automobiles and other vehicles[1]	7	8	110	110	14	26,327	29,345	3,065	3,381
5013 Motor vehicle supplies and new parts[1]	27	30	238	253	8	22,504	21,755	5,440	5,548
5014 Tires and tubes[2]	-	4	-	9	2	-	12,444	-	146
5015 Motor vehicle parts, used	-	8	-	25	3	-	11,360	-	319
5020 Furniture and homefurnishings[3]	12	11	91	72	7	17,363	18,000	1,873	1,528
5031 Lumber, plywood, and millwork[1]	6	-	54	-	-	18,074	-	1,104	-
5032 Brick, stone, & related materials[1]	8	-	34	-	-	22,941	-	881	-
5044 Office equipment[3]	13	12	88	103	9	20,000	23,223	2,021	2,217
5045 Computers, peripherals, & software[3]	9	10	58	71	7	29,793	19,268	1,573	1,317
5046 Commercial equipment, nec[2]	-	7	-	65	9	-	19,138	-	1,164
5047 Medical and hospital equipment[1]	7	-	63	-	-	20,254	-	1,379	-
5050 Metals and minerals, except petroleum[3]	6	7	86	102	15	23,070	26,431	2,287	2,866
5063 Electrical apparatus and equipment[1]	13	10	132	98	10	24,697	34,857	3,333	2,923
5072 Hardware[3]	11	14	118	112	8	19,864	26,214	2,470	2,655
5074 Plumbing & hydronic heating supplies[3]	5	7	87	101	14	20,782	25,624	1,991	2,432
5082 Construction and mining machinery[3]	9	9	96	83	9	27,042	34,120	2,843	2,649
5083 Farm and garden machinery[1]	7	5	98	21	4	16,367	30,476	1,783	702
5084 Industrial machinery and equipment[3]	40	44	202	335	8	28,198	26,054	7,445	9,235
5085 Industrial supplies[3]	19	17	92	97	6	27,696	25,938	2,615	2,591
5087 Service establishment equipment[3]	12	10	47	45	5	19,660	20,533	997	1,094
5090 Miscellaneous durable goods[3]	16	13	102	121	9	14,941	15,669	2,047	2,237
5112 Stationery and office supplies	-	11	-	35	3	-	25,943	-	953
5113 Industrial & personal service paper[3]	7	6	85	124	21	21,271	17,000	2,073	2,344
5130 Apparel, piece goods, and notions[3]	7	5	20	15	3	15,400	12,000	278	187
5149 Groceries and related products, nec	-	6	-	27	5	-	19,704	-	571
5169 Chemicals & allied products, nec[3]	10	11	13	14	1	28,615	23,143	395	343
5171 Petroleum bulk stations & terminals[1]	10	11	86	87	8	16,837	19,494	2,017	2,078

Continued on next page.

FORT SMITH, AR-OK MSA - [continued]

Wholesale and Retail Trade USA	Establishments		Employment		Emp / Est	Pay / Employee		Annual Payroll ($ 000)	
	1994	1995	1994	1995	1995	1994	1995	1994	1995
5172 Petroleum products, nec[1]	8	9	59	42	5	17,492	16,476	1,259	766
5180 Beer, wine, and distilled beverages[1]	5	-	97	-	-	41,814	-	2,852	-
5191 Farm supplies[1]	11	14	63	58	4	21,651	21,793	1,249	1,242
5198 Paints, varnishes, and supplies[1]	5	-	10	-	-	29,200	-	257	-
5199 Nondurable goods, nec[3]	6	7	11	12	2	26,909	23,000	235	257
52- Retail trade[1]	1,055	1,252	12,657	14,999	12	10,906	11,419	158,490	183,915
5210 Lumber and other building materials[1]	26	23	412	359	16	19,612	19,744	10,145	7,763
5230 Paint, glass, and wallpaper stores[1]	8	-	36	-	-	15,222	-	661	-
5250 Hardware stores[1]	6	-	43	-	-	10,419	-	347	-
5260 Retail nurseries and garden stores[3]	7	7	30	33	5	9,067	9,212	345	377
5270 Mobile home dealers[3]	6	7	17	24	3	24,235	23,000	771	882
5310 Department stores[3]	12	12	1,718	1,616	135	10,563	13,163	19,738	20,456
5330 Variety stores[3]	12	9	49	22	2	5,469	6,727	348	199
5390 Misc. general merchandise stores[1]	6	20	247	302	15	12,227	13,285	3,190	3,774
5410 Grocery stores[1]	89	144	1,542	1,924	13	10,444	10,570	18,500	22,194
5420 Meat and fish markets[1]	3	-	11	-	-	7,636	-	115	-
5440 Candy, nut, and confectionery stores[2]	-	5	-	9	2	-	8,889	-	90
5460 Retail bakeries[1]	9	11	44	44	4	7,727	7,818	405	390
5490 Miscellaneous food stores[3]	4	4	12	21	5	10,333	9,905	152	215
5510 New and used car dealers[1]	16	20	544	609	30	22,449	24,933	15,847	17,770
5520 Used car dealers	-	25	-	63	3	-	18,730	-	1,256
5530 Auto and home supply stores[1]	36	45	232	247	5	15,672	16,470	4,027	4,381
5540 Gasoline service stations[1]	74	90	429	580	6	9,259	9,166	4,450	5,672
5550 Boat dealers[3]	5	7	59	76	11	9,966	9,789	676	833
5570 Motorcycle dealers[3]	6	6	32	39	7	15,875	14,769	711	883
5610 Men's & boys' clothing stores[3]	8	8	27	30	4	11,556	10,933	341	298
5620 Women's clothing stores[1]	35	31	238	246	8	7,798	7,610	1,934	1,736
5630 Women's accessory & specialty stores[2]	-	7	-	22	3	-	8,000	-	203
5640 Children's and infants' wear stores[2]	-	4	-	5	1	-	7,200	-	41
5650 Family clothing stores[3]	10	12	96	125	10	8,583	6,400	843	929
5660 Shoe stores[3]	21	20	82	88	4	11,610	13,955	997	1,178
5690 Misc. apparel & accessory stores[3]	8	7	63	97	14	11,873	9,608	811	788
5712 Furniture stores[1]	23	28	144	160	6	15,389	16,650	2,560	2,819
5713 Floor covering stores	-	10	-	35	4	-	19,543	-	1,000
5719 Misc. homefurnishings stores[3]	6	8	139	223	28	9,871	7,300	1,522	1,625
5720 Household appliance stores[3]	5	5	27	21	4	16,148	17,714	415	378
5731 Radio, TV, & electronic stores[3]	11	10	97	116	12	12,866	10,828	1,234	1,290
5734 Computer and software stores[2]	-	6	-	20	3	-	17,600	-	328
5736 Musical instrument stores[1]	5	-	32	-	-	20,125	-	695	-
5812 Eating places[1]	256	263	3,987	4,866	19	7,343	7,724	32,449	39,614
5813 Drinking places[1]	25	23	59	77	3	5,559	6,338	440	487
5910 Drug stores and proprietary stores[1]	36	42	302	353	8	14,411	15,297	5,077	6,055
5920 Liquor stores[3]	19	22	79	92	4	8,101	7,870	708	758
5930 Used merchandise stores[1]	28	33	71	81	2	11,775	12,543	903	1,038
5941 Sporting goods and bicycle shops[1]	14	19	29	40	2	10,897	10,800	403	473
5942 Book stores[3]	6	8	36	34	4	10,333	10,588	354	373
5944 Jewelry stores[3]	23	22	93	86	4	16,172	15,860	1,531	1,452
5945 Hobby, toy, and game shops[3]	11	10	82	110	11	9,561	9,709	1,145	1,222
5947 Gift, novelty, and souvenir shops[1]	19	19	68	68	4	5,529	7,824	439	540
5949 Sewing, needlework, and piece goods[3]	3	3	21	30	10	9,524	6,800	188	183
5962 Merchandising machine operators[1]	8	10	138	142	14	11,565	11,662	1,707	1,173
5984 Liquefied petroleum gas dealers	-	7	-	31	4	-	13,161	-	341
5992 Florists[1]	20	26	96	109	4	9,542	9,321	975	1,080
5993 Tobacco stores and stands	-	6	-	12	2	-	10,333	-	78
5995 Optical goods stores[3]	5	5	15	23	5	14,133	13,565	315	330
5999 Miscellaneous retail stores, nec[1]	20	25	101	102	4	11,683	12,000	1,418	1,237

Source: County Business Patterns 1994/95, CBP-94/95, U.S. Department of Commerce, Washington DC, November 1997. The employment column represents mid-March employment in the year. Pay per employee is calculated by dividing 1st Quarter payroll, annualized, by mid-March employment. The column headed 'Emp / Est' shows 'employees per establishment'. A dash (-) means that data are unavailable or cannot be calculated. nec means not elsewhere classified. *Notes:* 1. 1994 data incomplete; unavailable or withheld. 2. 1995 data incomplete; unavailable or withheld. 3. 1994 and 1995 data incomplete; unavailable or withheld.

FORT WALTON BEACH, FL MSA

Wholesale and Retail Trade USA	Establishments		Employment		Emp / Est	Pay / Employee		Annual Payroll ($ 000)	
	1994	1995	1994	1995	1995	1994	1995	1994	1995
50- Wholesale trade	170	168	1,145	1,088	6	19,231	18,985	24,274	22,052
5012 Automobiles and other vehicles	4	-	9	-	-	13,333	-	107	-
5013 Motor vehicle supplies and new parts	12	11	60	46	4	26,000	15,217	1,620	819
5015 Motor vehicle parts, used	3	3	12	14	5	13,333	14,286	254	406

Continued on next page.

FORT WALTON BEACH, FL MSA - [continued]

Wholesale and Retail Trade USA	Establishments		Employment		Emp / Est	Pay / Employee		Annual Payroll ($ 000)	
	1994	1995	1994	1995	1995	1994	1995	1994	1995
5023 Homefurnishings	4	4	25	16	4	21,440	20,000	560	333
5031 Lumber, plywood, and millwork	3	-	22	-	-	18,000	-	378	-
5032 Brick, stone, & related materials	-	3	-	12	4	-	18,000	-	213
5039 Construction materials, nec	-	5	-	17	3	-	19,765	-	347
5044 Office equipment	6	6	32	36	6	23,625	23,778	774	847
5047 Medical and hospital equipment	6	-	25	-	-	20,000	-	437	-
5063 Electrical apparatus and equipment	6	7	57	67	10	28,281	28,955	1,782	2,036
5065 Electronic parts and equipment	8	9	26	29	3	28,000	26,621	768	828
5074 Plumbing & hydronic heating supplies	7	6	41	44	7	19,122	21,909	771	823
5088 Transportation equipment & supplies	3	4	3	6	2	13,333	20,000	91	143
5091 Sporting & recreational goods	4	-	12	-	-	12,667	-	199	-
5093 Scrap and waste materials	4	3	19	18	6	14,526	18,222	331	420
5112 Stationery and office supplies	6	6	59	55	9	11,254	16,582	675	750
5120 Drugs, proprietaries, and sundries	7	7	70	124	18	10,514	9,161	866	1,221
5137 Women's and children's clothing	5	-	24	-	-	7,000	-	171	-
5146 Fish and seafoods	6	5	17	12	2	13,882	15,333	295	253
5149 Groceries and related products, nec	-	6	-	71	12	-	22,592	-	1,760
5171 Petroleum bulk stations & terminals	7	-	54	-	-	18,741	-	1,045	-
5181 Beer and ale	3	3	60	63	21	20,933	25,778	1,448	1,681
5190 Misc., nondurable goods	-	7	-	11	2	-	12,727	-	174
52 - Retail trade	1,275	1,283	15,603	16,783	13	10,105	11,285	183,319	204,765
5210 Lumber and other building materials	19	22	431	470	21	14,200	16,460	6,471	8,306
5230 Paint, glass, and wallpaper stores	16	12	81	59	5	13,630	17,627	1,158	1,106
5250 Hardware stores	9	8	68	93	12	11,588	11,570	1,053	1,219
5310 Department stores	10	11	1,736	1,782	162	10,774	13,118	20,558	23,918
5410 Grocery stores	71	70	1,645	1,735	25	9,717	10,877	17,321	19,083
5420 Meat and fish markets	-	3	-	13	4	-	13,846	-	211
5430 Fruit and vegetable markets	6	6	13	22	4	6,769	8,364	108	124
5440 Candy, nut, and confectionery stores	3	4	4	16	4	6,000	5,750	78	134
5460 Retail bakeries	12	13	82	149	11	5,902	6,550	733	1,129
5490 Miscellaneous food stores	9	8	16	29	4	17,000	12,414	370	410
5510 New and used car dealers	14	16	650	678	42	27,803	28,578	20,867	23,824
5520 Used car dealers	18	20	66	74	4	14,182	15,243	1,022	1,340
5530 Auto and home supply stores	42	41	262	260	6	12,092	14,969	3,731	4,171
5540 Gasoline service stations	77	74	539	630	9	9,492	8,660	5,732	5,765
5550 Boat dealers	8	8	100	146	18	17,280	17,616	2,500	3,077
5570 Motorcycle dealers	5	5	26	29	6	19,538	21,241	735	926
5610 Men's & boys' clothing stores	13	15	84	100	7	9,619	58,560	907	2,142
5620 Women's clothing stores	59	49	335	318	6	9,576	9,220	3,595	3,066
5630 Women's accessory & specialty stores	7	7	20	38	5	10,200	10,211	339	395
5640 Children's and infants' wear stores	4	5	16	22	4	8,500	7,818	148	173
5650 Family clothing stores	14	15	135	125	8	9,807	11,424	1,474	1,666
5660 Shoe stores	31	31	143	182	6	8,224	10,176	1,385	1,875
5690 Misc. apparel & accessory stores	23	19	94	100	5	6,894	8,080	1,048	1,118
5712 Furniture stores	38	35	237	248	7	15,781	16,903	4,013	4,645
5713 Floor covering stores	-	14	-	73	5	-	23,616	-	1,849
5719 Misc. homefurnishings stores	22	-	133	-	-	11,338	-	1,475	-
5720 Household appliance stores	9	9	44	50	6	15,545	16,640	691	847
5731 Radio, TV, & electronic stores	12	12	107	104	9	14,654	15,731	1,613	1,777
5734 Computer and software stores	6	9	20	33	4	10,000	14,545	248	581
5735 Record & prerecorded tape stores	7	7	40	38	5	11,100	11,053	453	421
5736 Musical instrument stores	4	4	26	21	5	9,692	12,381	285	276
5812 Eating places	254	242	5,743	6,098	25	6,551	7,195	47,319	50,222
5813 Drinking places	26	28	253	284	10	6,245	5,887	1,785	1,654
5910 Drug stores and proprietary stores	22	21	298	278	13	14,416	13,827	4,367	4,108
5920 Liquor stores	22	20	175	154	8	7,794	6,857	1,635	1,122
5930 Used merchandise stores	33	29	69	73	3	11,362	11,836	1,031	940
5941 Sporting goods and bicycle shops	26	26	105	105	4	11,429	12,724	1,385	1,414
5942 Book stores	15	13	67	70	5	6,388	6,686	481	487
5944 Jewelry stores	27	26	87	121	5	14,667	13,455	1,403	1,721
5945 Hobby, toy, and game shops	4	5	18	18	4	6,000	9,111	164	201
5947 Gift, novelty, and souvenir shops	40	40	186	158	4	7,548	7,468	1,570	1,393
5949 Sewing, needlework, and piece goods	9	11	49	44	4	5,796	6,545	321	286
5960 Nonstore retailers	9	10	114	108	11	20,877	24,778	2,669	3,184
5992 Florists	23	-	126	-	-	7,524	-	1,019	-
5994 News dealers and newsstands	3	-	9	-	-	9,778	-	236	-
5995 Optical goods stores	10	10	60	67	7	15,200	17,373	953	1,185
5999 Miscellaneous retail stores, nec	51	47	168	239	5	12,238	13,272	2,290	3,480

Source: County Business Patterns 1994/95, CBP-94/95, U.S. Department of Commerce, Washington DC, November 1997. The employment column represents mid-March employment in the year. Pay per employee is calculated by dividing 1st Quarter payroll, annualized, by mid-March employment. The column headed 'Emp / Est' shows 'employees per establishment'. A dash (-) means that data are unavailable or cannot be calculated. nec means not elsewhere classified. *Notes:* 1. 1994 data incomplete; unavailable or withheld. 2. 1995 data incomplete; unavailable or withheld. 3. 1994 and 1995 data incomplete; unavailable or withheld.

FORT WAYNE, IN MSA

Wholesale and Retail Trade USA	Establishments		Employment		Emp / Est	Pay / Employee		Annual Payroll ($ 000)	
	1994	1995	1994	1995	1995	1994	1995	1994	1995
50- Wholesale trade	1,043	1,030	14,288	15,708	15	26,558	26,953	406,644	431,826
5012 Automobiles and other vehicles[3]	30	31	862	998	32	25,698	28,481	23,485	27,246
5013 Motor vehicle supplies and new parts	70	65	611	1,074	17	21,473	21,069	14,059	20,876
5014 Tires and tubes[3]	7	7	64	62	9	23,813	24,258	1,625	1,615
5015 Motor vehicle parts, used[3]	9	9	27	30	3	18,370	16,133	500	526
5021 Furniture[3]	7	11	91	151	14	24,176	28,503	2,385	4,091
5023 Homefurnishings[3]	15	15	84	72	5	18,143	21,389	1,795	1,592
5031 Lumber, plywood, and millwork[3]	16	14	527	602	43	28,038	28,246	21,746	17,880
5032 Brick, stone, & related materials[3]	10	10	74	43	4	32,541	29,581	2,721	1,601
5033 Roofing, siding, & insulation[3]	13	11	53	63	6	26,792	23,238	1,381	1,468
5039 Construction materials, nec[3]	6	8	46	68	9	27,391	22,588	1,265	1,460
5044 Office equipment[3]	28	26	354	342	13	30,802	32,035	10,670	11,138
5045 Computers, peripherals, & software[3]	33	30	199	215	7	42,794	53,526	8,442	9,237
5046 Commercial equipment, nec[3]	13	13	150	163	13	23,013	30,405	3,999	4,704
5047 Medical and hospital equipment[3]	12	12	93	107	9	32,903	38,617	3,106	4,045
5049 Professional equipment, nec[3]	9	8	88	79	10	20,955	21,266	1,718	1,707
5051 Metals service centers and offices[3]	21	23	269	311	14	32,580	34,971	9,549	11,333
5063 Electrical apparatus and equipment[3]	33	28	267	247	9	29,124	32,955	8,537	8,436
5064 Electrical appliances, TV & radios[3]	5	4	58	55	14	26,207	28,945	1,619	1,714
5065 Electronic parts and equipment[3]	45	49	280	408	8	33,929	35,647	10,598	15,371
5072 Hardware[3]	23	24	231	291	12	31,152	28,027	6,708	8,032
5074 Plumbing & hydronic heating supplies[3]	14	13	126	78	6	26,667	37,641	3,309	2,526
5075 Warm air heating & air conditioning[3]	14	14	113	117	8	33,310	34,598	3,808	3,959
5082 Construction and mining machinery[3]	15	13	150	142	11	30,507	35,070	5,071	5,101
5083 Farm and garden machinery[3]	25	24	153	143	6	16,941	16,839	2,845	2,625
5084 Industrial machinery and equipment[3]	67	67	530	666	10	28,317	28,511	16,762	20,371
5085 Industrial supplies[3]	48	53	553	636	12	33,678	34,358	18,618	21,188
5087 Service establishment equipment[3]	19	18	159	134	7	21,434	28,478	3,922	3,812
5088 Transportation equipment & supplies[3]	5	5	16	19	4	31,250	28,211	656	584
5091 Sporting & recreational goods[3]	12	12	97	78	7	34,557	33,385	2,723	2,687
5093 Scrap and waste materials[3]	21	18	427	482	27	26,248	29,054	12,028	16,965
5099 Durable goods, nec[3]	18	18	160	158	9	27,625	30,203	4,847	5,113
5111 Printing and writing paper[3]	5	5	105	126	25	25,143	28,889	2,280	3,070
5112 Stationery and office supplies[3]	20	17	229	181	11	20,157	22,961	4,445	4,243
5113 Industrial & personal service paper[3]	13	12	147	138	12	20,082	20,551	3,073	3,155
5120 Drugs, proprietaries, and sundries[3]	8	8	111	80	10	20,793	26,100	1,890	1,959
5136 Men's and boys' clothing[3]	6	5	36	35	7	18,000	21,029	812	818
5141 Groceries, general line[3]	12	11	1,348	1,477	134	35,318	28,097	49,640	42,445
5145 Confectionery[3]	6	5	36	12	2	11,111	16,333	456	204
5147 Meats and meat products[1]	5	-	41	-	-	19,317	-	847	-
5149 Groceries and related products, nec[3]	25	25	607	638	26	26,056	26,132	17,375	18,183
5153 Grain and field beans	31	32	91	146	5	29,143	32,164	2,486	4,395
5154 Livestock	-	14	-	9	1	-	18,222	-	169
5162 Plastics materials & basic shapes[3]	8	8	184	172	22	27,609	27,419	5,612	5,380
5169 Chemicals & allied products, nec[3]	33	33	368	382	12	27,326	30,356	11,254	12,769
5171 Petroleum bulk stations & terminals	36	34	116	124	4	26,483	24,258	3,245	3,399
5172 Petroleum products, nec[3]	10	10	112	77	8	25,429	25,610	2,902	2,029
5180 Beer, wine, and distilled beverages[3]	8	8	119	123	15	25,580	24,585	3,178	3,124
5191 Farm supplies[1]	42	35	271	160	5	34,244	22,600	9,817	4,162
5198 Paints, varnishes, and supplies[3]	10	10	57	54	5	25,614	28,741	1,721	1,551
5199 Nondurable goods, nec[3]	19	23	64	53	2	17,063	22,566	1,118	1,218
52- Retail trade	2,888	2,924	46,262	47,159	16	10,627	11,706	562,853	583,217
5210 Lumber and other building materials	47	51	801	1,082	21	20,155	20,721	18,101	22,156
5230 Paint, glass, and wallpaper stores[3]	21	21	79	113	5	14,127	21,204	1,444	2,674
5250 Hardware stores	42	37	462	375	10	10,632	9,952	5,692	4,077
5260 Retail nurseries and garden stores	36	38	190	228	6	15,221	16,316	3,367	3,987
5270 Mobile home dealers[3]	10	11	51	68	6	20,078	22,118	1,231	1,731
5310 Department stores[3]	29	31	3,435	5,450	176	9,506	9,778	45,429	56,953
5330 Variety stores[2]	26	22	133	298	14	8,842	6,913	1,333	1,732
5390 Misc. general merchandise stores[1]	23	30	400	452	15	10,280	10,230	4,455	4,138
5410 Grocery stores[2]	154	152	7,772	5,225	34	8,278	10,967	80,125	59,413
5420 Meat and fish markets[1]	15	18	68	99	6	11,412	11,556	879	1,286
5430 Fruit and vegetable markets[3]	4	4	31	29	7	7,226	7,448	402	383
5440 Candy, nut, and confectionery stores[3]	5	7	15	69	10	5,067	10,899	81	689
5460 Retail bakeries[3]	30	29	227	237	8	7,930	7,747	1,976	2,010
5490 Miscellaneous food stores[3]	15	15	54	38	3	10,148	10,105	524	398
5510 New and used car dealers	50	52	2,142	2,219	43	26,564	27,760	66,675	70,404
5520 Used car dealers	67	66	161	197	3	16,795	19,127	3,160	4,089
5530 Auto and home supply stores	72	75	629	689	9	17,138	19,762	12,189	13,859
5540 Gasoline service stations	185	180	1,594	1,631	9	9,380	10,506	16,362	17,921
5560 Recreational vehicle dealers[3]	6	6	12	17	3	22,667	18,588	302	349

Continued on next page.

FORT WAYNE, IN MSA - [continued]

Wholesale and Retail Trade USA	Establishments		Employment		Emp / Est	Pay / Employee		Annual Payroll ($ 000)	
	1994	1995	1994	1995	1995	1994	1995	1994	1995
5570 Motorcycle dealers [3]	12	14	75	73	5	18,453	19,014	1,561	1,591
5610 Men's & boys' clothing stores [3]	21	19	125	135	7	9,984	12,059	1,517	1,600
5620 Women's clothing stores	87	83	807	708	9	6,032	6,412	5,330	4,724
5630 Women's accessory & specialty stores [3]	12	12	76	66	6	9,368	10,485	665	672
5640 Children's and infants' wear stores [3]	11	12	58	91	8	8,828	8,220	605	778
5650 Family clothing stores [3]	22	21	222	233	11	7,802	8,240	2,021	2,001
5660 Shoe stores [3]	53	45	285	262	6	10,821	12,229	3,233	3,223
5690 Misc. apparel & accessory stores [3]	20	18	79	91	5	9,215	9,714	873	913
5712 Furniture stores	63	62	436	493	8	19,294	21,452	9,029	10,145
5713 Floor covering stores	35	35	171	197	6	19,088	20,345	3,685	4,308
5714 Drapery and upholstery stores [3]	6	7	24	28	4	10,500	10,286	297	272
5719 Misc. homefurnishings stores [3]	30	29	164	166	6	10,951	13,301	2,041	2,223
5720 Household appliance stores	24	24	127	147	6	19,969	20,381	2,626	3,215
5731 Radio, TV, & electronic stores	31	36	237	302	8	15,831	13,576	4,047	4,583
5734 Computer and software stores [3]	7	8	25	29	4	18,880	17,241	517	587
5735 Record & prerecorded tape stores [3]	15	20	72	91	5	7,611	8,440	568	791
5736 Musical instrument stores [3]	11	10	23	24	2	20,522	21,167	521	545
5812 Eating places	724	687	15,482	15,208	22	6,943	7,716	117,514	122,415
5813 Drinking places	129	124	963	983	8	7,198	7,626	7,513	7,789
5910 Drug stores and proprietary stores	79	79	1,158	1,158	15	15,534	15,589	18,858	17,937
5920 Liquor stores	55	55	383	412	7	8,752	9,330	3,999	4,239
5930 Used merchandise stores [3]	34	32	182	188	6	10,022	11,340	1,963	2,411
5941 Sporting goods and bicycle shops	59	57	236	295	5	11,407	12,407	2,963	4,190
5942 Book stores [2]	25	24	185	183	8	6,249	7,213	1,304	1,446
5944 Jewelry stores	47	46	267	250	5	15,700	18,192	4,264	4,341
5945 Hobby, toy, and game shops [3]	18	16	130	143	9	8,985	7,916	1,357	1,375
5947 Gift, novelty, and souvenir shops [3]	54	48	274	280	6	7,007	6,657	2,051	2,150
5949 Sewing, needlework, and piece goods [3]	14	15	113	78	5	5,947	6,359	720	524
5961 Catalog and mail-order houses [3]	13	16	44	67	4	15,000	21,493	802	1,386
5962 Merchandising machine operators [3]	16	16	168	140	9	17,333	18,914	3,187	2,804
5963 Direct selling establishments	38	44	235	217	5	13,634	15,760	3,680	4,152
5984 Liquefied petroleum gas dealers	12	11	25	24	2	25,120	24,667	541	555
5992 Florists	54	51	360	355	7	8,656	9,059	3,493	3,418
5995 Optical goods stores [3]	19	20	168	158	8	16,119	19,899	2,883	3,113
5999 Miscellaneous retail stores, nec [3]	90	93	378	502	5	14,138	13,307	6,275	7,667

Source: County Business Patterns 1994/95, CBP-94/95, U.S. Department of Commerce, Washington DC, November 1997. The employment column represents mid-March employment in the year. Pay per employee is calculated by dividing 1st Quarter payroll, annualized, by mid-March employment. The column headed 'Emp / Est' shows 'employees per establishment'. A dash (-) means that data are unavailable or cannot be calculated. nec means not elsewhere classified. *Notes:* 1. 1994 data incomplete; unavailable or withheld. 2. 1995 data incomplete; unavailable or withheld. 3. 1994 and 1995 data incomplete; unavailable or withheld.

FORT WORTH - ARLINGTON, TX PMSA

Wholesale and Retail Trade USA	Establishments		Employment		Emp / Est	Pay / Employee		Annual Payroll ($ 000)	
	1994	1995	1994	1995	1995	1994	1995	1994	1995
50- Wholesale trade	-	2,734	-	36,018	13	-	30,884	-	1,187,630
5012 Automobiles and other vehicles	-	43	-	775	18	-	26,725	-	19,596
5013 Motor vehicle supplies and new parts [2]	-	139	-	2,392	17	-	33,856	-	90,404
5014 Tires and tubes [2]	-	17	-	151	9	-	26,093	-	4,099
5015 Motor vehicle parts, used [2]	-	60	-	599	10	-	22,063	-	14,010
5021 Furniture [2]	-	35	-	417	12	-	33,976	-	14,359
5023 Homefurnishings [2]	-	37	-	369	10	-	23,848	-	9,606
5031 Lumber, plywood, and millwork [2]	-	53	-	1,125	21	-	34,613	-	39,028
5032 Brick, stone, & related materials [2]	-	25	-	228	9	-	29,526	-	7,521
5033 Roofing, siding, & insulation [2]	-	19	-	198	10	-	32,707	-	13,117
5039 Construction materials, nec [2]	-	53	-	821	15	-	27,313	-	23,979
5043 Photographic equipment & supplies [2]	-	6	-	79	13	-	31,949	-	2,581
5044 Office equipment [2]	-	44	-	1,253	28	-	43,090	-	57,464
5045 Computers, peripherals, & software [2]	-	88	-	719	8	-	44,078	-	33,721
5046 Commercial equipment, nec [2]	-	29	-	186	6	-	24,559	-	5,361
5047 Medical and hospital equipment [2]	-	63	-	771	12	-	47,077	-	37,907
5048 Ophthalmic goods [2]	-	6	-	29	5	-	14,069	-	362
5049 Professional equipment, nec [2]	-	18	-	265	15	-	19,804	-	5,347
5051 Metals service centers and offices	-	80	-	874	11	-	32,929	-	31,173
5063 Electrical apparatus and equipment	-	88	-	980	11	-	35,804	-	35,996
5064 Electrical appliances, TV & radios [2]	-	33	-	655	20	-	33,240	-	25,449
5065 Electronic parts and equipment	-	114	-	1,859	16	-	38,421	-	80,490
5072 Hardware [2]	-	92	-	1,036	11	-	29,992	-	34,003
5074 Plumbing & hydronic heating supplies	-	60	-	466	8	-	26,464	-	17,935
5075 Warm air heating & air conditioning [2]	-	37	-	286	8	-	22,979	-	7,265

Continued on next page.

FORT WORTH – ARLINGTON, TX PMSA - [continued]

Wholesale and Retail Trade USA	Establishments		Employment		Emp / Est	Pay / Employee		Annual Payroll ($ 000)	
	1994	1995	1994	1995	1995	1994	1995	1994	1995
5078 Refrigeration equipment and supplies[2]	-	10	-	44	4	-	32,364	-	1,706
5082 Construction and mining machinery[2]	-	15	-	348	23	-	48,023	-	16,758
5083 Farm and garden machinery	-	26	-	276	11	-	23,913	-	6,664
5084 Industrial machinery and equipment	-	186	-	1,671	9	-	33,522	-	59,591
5085 Industrial supplies[2]	-	97	-	1,032	11	-	33,163	-	36,036
5087 Service establishment equipment	-	59	-	426	7	-	24,507	-	11,478
5088 Transportation equipment & supplies	-	71	-	465	7	-	46,417	-	18,274
5091 Sporting & recreational goods[2]	-	38	-	399	11	-	25,694	-	10,226
5092 Toys and hobby goods and supplies[2]	-	13	-	156	12	-	14,795	-	3,124
5093 Scrap and waste materials	-	41	-	391	10	-	21,729	-	10,017
5094 Jewelry & precious stones[2]	-	22	-	190	9	-	16,126	-	3,456
5099 Durable goods, nec	-	64	-	529	8	-	22,057	-	15,356
5111 Printing and writing paper[2]	-	18	-	357	20	-	23,104	-	8,335
5112 Stationery and office supplies[2]	-	68	-	1,282	19	-	25,051	-	31,097
5113 Industrial & personal service paper[2]	-	30	-	283	9	-	34,883	-	9,626
5120 Drugs, proprietaries, and sundries	-	45	-	588	13	-	30,878	-	17,474
5131 Piece goods & notions[2]	-	25	-	291	12	-	21,113	-	5,980
5136 Men's and boys' clothing[2]	-	17	-	124	7	-	19,581	-	3,321
5137 Women's and children's clothing[2]	-	17	-	199	12	-	20,382	-	3,947
5139 Footwear[2]	-	5	-	160	32	-	62,925	-	9,155
5141 Groceries, general line[2]	-	12	-	483	40	-	27,776	-	15,706
5142 Packaged frozen food[2]	-	9	-	223	25	-	29,794	-	7,354
5143 Dairy products, exc. dried or canned[2]	-	5	-	134	27	-	30,328	-	4,169
5144 Poultry and poultry products[2]	-	5	-	180	36	-	25,467	-	4,719
5145 Confectionery[2]	-	9	-	607	67	-	21,041	-	14,057
5147 Meats and meat products[2]	-	16	-	288	18	-	20,819	-	7,167
5148 Fresh fruits and vegetables[2]	-	7	-	280	40	-	19,443	-	4,276
5149 Groceries and related products, nec	-	48	-	1,198	25	-	28,868	-	36,091
5153 Grain and field beans[2]	-	9	-	57	6	-	24,842	-	1,458
5154 Livestock[2]	-	10	-	37	4	-	41,405	-	2,124
5159 Farm-product raw materials, nec[2]	-	4	-	95	24	-	21,516	-	2,596
5162 Plastics materials & basic shapes[2]	-	26	-	227	9	-	36,388	-	9,801
5169 Chemicals & allied products, nec[2]	-	56	-	366	7	-	41,301	-	13,834
5171 Petroleum bulk stations & terminals	-	41	-	391	10	-	38,803	-	14,987
5172 Petroleum products, nec[2]	-	24	-	436	18	-	20,798	-	8,118
5181 Beer and ale[2]	-	6	-	612	102	-	30,595	-	22,714
5182 Wine and distilled beverages[2]	-	8	-	390	49	-	37,405	-	13,573
5191 Farm supplies	-	48	-	311	6	-	15,588	-	5,293
5192 Books, periodicals, & newspapers[2]	-	24	-	343	14	-	24,455	-	8,559
5193 Flowers & florists' supplies[2]	-	14	-	75	5	-	18,347	-	1,761
5194 Tobacco and tobacco products[2]	-	4	-	160	40	-	19,425	-	2,599
5198 Paints, varnishes, and supplies[2]	-	22	-	182	8	-	26,066	-	5,534
5199 Nondurable goods, nec	-	96	-	767	8	-	23,312	-	19,371
52 – Retail trade	-	8,115	-	128,137	16	-	14,540	-	1,935,789
5210 Lumber and other building materials	-	86	-	2,103	24	-	19,718	-	45,792
5230 Paint, glass, and wallpaper stores[2]	-	52	-	288	6	-	23,889	-	7,401
5250 Hardware stores	-	44	-	483	11	-	20,041	-	8,832
5260 Retail nurseries and garden stores	-	65	-	704	11	-	10,943	-	8,356
5270 Mobile home dealers[2]	-	25	-	234	9	-	21,915	-	6,741
5310 Department stores[2]	-	69	-	10,766	156	-	13,645	-	150,701
5330 Variety stores	-	50	-	217	4	-	8,258	-	1,892
5390 Misc. general merchandise stores	-	63	-	1,463	23	-	13,610	-	18,528
5410 Grocery stores	-	691	-	16,161	23	-	12,399	-	201,723
5420 Meat and fish markets	-	16	-	117	7	-	12,000	-	1,345
5430 Fruit and vegetable markets	-	13	-	30	2	-	12,267	-	575
5440 Candy, nut, and confectionery stores[2]	-	19	-	63	3	-	8,571	-	560
5460 Retail bakeries	-	98	-	507	5	-	9,594	-	4,999
5490 Miscellaneous food stores	-	57	-	238	4	-	9,563	-	2,883
5510 New and used car dealers	-	82	-	5,750	70	-	31,366	-	220,563
5520 Used car dealers	-	164	-	813	5	-	23,911	-	21,797
5530 Auto and home supply stores	-	309	-	2,728	9	-	16,828	-	49,567
5540 Gasoline service stations	-	480	-	3,094	6	-	12,403	-	39,695
5550 Boat dealers[2]	-	14	-	70	5	-	17,657	-	1,551
5560 Recreational vehicle dealers[2]	-	19	-	153	8	-	26,065	-	5,029
5570 Motorcycle dealers[2]	-	21	-	152	7	-	21,211	-	3,436
5590 Automotive dealers, nec[2]	-	12	-	80	7	-	25,000	-	2,412
5610 Men's & boys' clothing stores[2]	-	66	-	449	7	-	14,726	-	6,538
5620 Women's clothing stores	-	191	-	1,504	8	-	8,356	-	12,864
5630 Women's accessory & specialty stores[2]	-	46	-	299	7	-	10,876	-	3,150
5640 Children's and infants' wear stores[2]	-	29	-	258	9	-	8,140	-	1,980
5650 Family clothing stores	-	94	-	1,477	16	-	10,218	-	15,221

Continued on next page.

FORT WORTH – ARLINGTON, TX PMSA - [continued]

Wholesale and Retail Trade USA	Establishments		Employment		Emp / Est	Pay / Employee		Annual Payroll ($ 000)	
	1994	1995	1994	1995	1995	1994	1995	1994	1995
5660 Shoe stores	-	167	-	960	6	-	13,942	-	13,388
5690 Misc. apparel & accessory stores [2]	-	55	-	297	5	-	10,074	-	3,088
5712 Furniture stores	-	147	-	1,111	8	-	20,504	-	23,957
5713 Floor covering stores	-	65	-	290	4	-	23,324	-	7,080
5714 Drapery and upholstery stores [2]	-	9	-	26	3	-	13,538	-	347
5719 Misc. homefurnishings stores	-	100	-	849	8	-	14,097	-	11,921
5720 Household appliance stores [2]	-	30	-	178	6	-	22,067	-	4,232
5731 Radio, TV, & electronic stores	-	96	-	1,328	14	-	16,054	-	20,899
5734 Computer and software stores	-	41	-	328	8	-	18,024	-	7,556
5735 Record & prerecorded tape stores [2]	-	43	-	401	9	-	7,481	-	2,974
5736 Musical instrument stores [2]	-	20	-	130	7	-	18,985	-	2,965
5812 Eating places	-	1,705	-	41,483	24	-	8,816	-	381,286
5813 Drinking places [2]	-	139	-	1,985	14	-	7,252	-	14,893
5910 Drug stores and proprietary stores	-	176	-	2,654	15	-	15,546	-	42,225
5920 Liquor stores	-	82	-	368	4	-	13,217	-	5,549
5930 Used merchandise stores	-	166	-	844	5	-	16,370	-	14,434
5941 Sporting goods and bicycle shops	-	129	-	962	7	-	13,027	-	14,318
5942 Book stores	-	63	-	608	10	-	11,901	-	7,049
5943 Stationery stores [2]	-	15	-	108	7	-	10,963	-	1,289
5944 Jewelry stores	-	138	-	709	5	-	15,385	-	11,559
5945 Hobby, toy, and game shops	-	58	-	730	13	-	8,351	-	8,238
5946 Camera & photographic supply stores [2]	-	14	-	86	6	-	20,698	-	1,841
5947 Gift, novelty, and souvenir shops	-	161	-	934	6	-	8,150	-	8,473
5949 Sewing, needlework, and piece goods [2]	-	38	-	277	7	-	10,195	-	2,994
5961 Catalog and mail-order houses	-	41	-	1,195	29	-	23,290	-	33,381
5962 Merchandising machine operators [2]	-	35	-	291	8	-	25,251	-	8,416
5963 Direct selling establishments [2]	-	53	-	294	6	-	19,864	-	5,683
5984 Liquefied petroleum gas dealers [2]	-	28	-	89	3	-	22,067	-	1,943
5992 Florists	-	117	-	620	5	-	11,226	-	7,009
5993 Tobacco stores and stands [2]	-	10	-	25	3	-	17,440	-	518
5994 News dealers and newsstands [2]	-	6	-	168	28	-	5,524	-	1,036
5995 Optical goods stores	-	99	-	438	4	-	15,324	-	6,869
5999 Miscellaneous retail stores, nec	-	282	-	1,614	6	-	12,714	-	21,967

Source: County Business Patterns 1994/95, CBP-94/95, U.S. Department of Commerce, Washington DC, November 1997. The employment column represents mid-March employment in the year. Pay per employee is calculated by dividing 1st Quarter payroll, annualized, by mid-March employment. The column headed 'Emp / Est' shows 'employees per establishment'. A dash (-) means that data are unavailable or cannot be calculated. nec means not elsewhere classified. *Notes:* 1. 1994 data incomplete; unavailable or withheld. 2. 1995 data incomplete; unavailable or withheld. 3. 1994 and 1995 data incomplete; unavailable or withheld.

FRESNO, CA MSA

Wholesale and Retail Trade USA	Establishments		Employment		Emp / Est	Pay / Employee		Annual Payroll ($ 000)	
	1994	1995	1994	1995	1995	1994	1995	1994	1995
50 – Wholesale trade	1,271	1,269	15,878	15,850	12	27,146	29,087	477,153	489,149
5012 Automobiles and other vehicles	25	24	484	447	19	25,455	27,060	13,216	13,251
5013 Motor vehicle supplies and new parts	83	77	911	813	11	21,572	23,911	21,581	18,854
5014 Tires and tubes	22	17	202	180	11	23,188	24,911	5,655	5,054
5015 Motor vehicle parts, used	27	27	244	257	10	17,393	17,167	4,780	5,032
5021 Furniture	11	12	214	294	25	18,710	17,265	4,504	5,183
5023 Homefurnishings [3]	11	9	132	146	16	24,576	24,110	3,349	3,573
5031 Lumber, plywood, and millwork	25	26	225	193	7	30,044	31,917	7,086	6,368
5032 Brick, stone, & related materials	9	10	110	104	10	21,200	21,000	3,557	3,006
5033 Roofing, siding, & insulation	7	8	76	133	17	23,789	32,180	2,133	4,490
5039 Construction materials, nec [2]	12	18	200	157	9	31,180	25,350	6,869	4,208
5043 Photographic equipment & supplies [1]	3	-	8	-	-	53,000	-	425	-
5044 Office equipment	31	32	397	413	13	30,005	33,075	12,517	13,796
5045 Computers, peripherals, & software [1]	23	23	151	169	7	36,927	39,266	5,283	6,126
5046 Commercial equipment, nec [3]	9	10	61	56	6	24,721	30,714	1,666	1,652
5047 Medical and hospital equipment [3]	16	16	270	239	15	23,259	24,184	6,476	6,038
5048 Ophthalmic goods [1]	4	-	18	-	-	20,000	-	352	-
5049 Professional equipment, nec [3]	3	5	59	119	24	20,678	18,622	1,297	2,286
5050 Metals and minerals, except petroleum	17	19	282	274	14	27,163	27,387	8,783	8,061
5063 Electrical apparatus and equipment	36	38	317	294	8	33,249	37,333	10,119	11,215
5064 Electrical appliances, TV & radios [3]	7	7	53	50	7	26,491	24,720	1,377	1,351
5065 Electronic parts and equipment [3]	21	20	188	159	8	32,362	30,591	4,718	5,030
5072 Hardware	20	18	218	184	10	35,505	39,804	8,523	7,655
5074 Plumbing & hydronic heating supplies [3]	16	14	216	223	16	28,204	28,753	6,476	6,442
5075 Warm air heating & air conditioning [3]	18	15	122	122	8	30,852	29,770	4,097	3,688
5078 Refrigeration equipment and supplies [3]	8	9	71	79	9	32,225	34,177	2,565	2,678
5082 Construction and mining machinery	14	14	255	282	20	35,592	35,773	9,711	10,880

Continued on next page.

FRESNO, CA MSA - [continued]

Wholesale and Retail Trade USA	Establishments		Employment		Emp / Est	Pay / Employee		Annual Payroll ($ 000)	
	1994	1995	1994	1995	1995	1994	1995	1994	1995
5083 Farm and garden machinery	57	54	699	672	12	27,628	29,589	20,975	20,807
5084 Industrial machinery and equipment	58	59	433	469	8	28,028	27,804	14,270	13,779
5085 Industrial supplies	33	32	343	377	12	27,044	28,435	10,706	11,271
5087 Service establishment equipment [2]	24	22	215	217	10	21,358	21,917	4,882	4,986
5088 Transportation equipment & supplies [3]	6	5	52	54	11	23,769	23,556	1,402	1,331
5091 Sporting & recreational goods	11	11	71	73	7	18,141	17,753	1,311	1,076
5093 Scrap and waste materials	33	36	461	492	14	14,030	17,317	7,108	8,671
5094 Jewelry & precious stones	5	-	18	-	-	5,778	-	116	-
5111 Printing and writing paper [2]	-	6	-	39	7	-	39,897	-	1,425
5112 Stationery and office supplies [2]	29	27	470	428	16	18,528	21,206	9,014	9,169
5113 Industrial & personal service paper [3]	5	6	67	77	13	64,299	78,026	3,316	4,066
5120 Drugs, proprietaries, and sundries	16	20	376	369	18	21,191	23,794	9,102	8,879
5131 Piece goods & notions [3]	4	5	21	20	4	18,476	24,000	453	476
5136 Men's and boys' clothing [1]	5	-	36	-	-	18,111	-	665	-
5141 Groceries, general line	11	12	112	129	11	23,036	21,891	2,810	3,213
5142 Packaged frozen food [3]	5	5	60	52	10	24,867	26,154	1,527	992
5143 Dairy products, exc. dried or canned	17	16	121	189	12	29,421	26,836	4,152	4,460
5145 Confectionery [1]	11	9	237	250	28	30,970	28,064	8,030	7,683
5147 Meats and meat products [3]	13	14	205	211	15	22,380	22,009	5,431	5,724
5148 Fresh fruits and vegetables	79	75	1,220	1,351	18	34,148	35,233	51,394	54,240
5149 Groceries and related products, nec	48	48	1,355	1,343	28	30,456	33,513	48,745	50,059
5153 Grain and field beans	11	11	98	91	8	19,184	26,945	2,873	3,399
5154 Livestock	6	6	42	13	2	6,000	15,077	215	225
5159 Farm-product raw materials, nec	18	17	281	126	7	24,712	47,873	10,042	7,738
5162 Plastics materials & basic shapes	8	8	39	60	8	22,564	21,533	975	1,323
5169 Chemicals & allied products, nec	24	24	204	205	9	31,882	35,902	7,163	7,678
5171 Petroleum bulk stations & terminals	32	25	263	187	7	22,875	25,604	6,053	5,322
5172 Petroleum products, nec [3]	8	8	80	86	11	25,450	26,047	2,573	2,712
5180 Beer, wine, and distilled beverages [3]	6	5	157	156	31	25,656	27,923	4,278	4,803
5191 Farm supplies	81	85	1,061	1,049	12	37,127	39,520	40,229	41,874
5193 Flowers & florists' supplies	14	14	76	75	5	12,158	12,373	1,166	989
5198 Paints, varnishes, and supplies [3]	9	8	104	87	11	28,923	37,057	2,731	2,846
5199 Nondurable goods, nec	35	39	292	301	8	17,562	18,445	5,884	5,883
52 - Retail trade	4,105	4,056	51,587	51,890	13	12,341	12,944	688,687	707,845
5210 Lumber and other building materials	79	63	1,230	1,205	19	18,345	20,226	23,525	24,389
5230 Paint, glass, and wallpaper stores	21	25	126	192	8	22,794	25,521	2,975	4,974
5250 Hardware stores	52	44	558	416	9	13,219	13,019	8,324	5,779
5260 Retail nurseries and garden stores	26	28	136	171	6	15,000	14,246	2,186	2,355
5270 Mobile home dealers	6	6	17	29	5	17,882	18,345	340	620
5310 Department stores	30	27	5,153	4,708	174	10,403	12,002	62,714	59,632
5330 Variety stores	23	19	124	135	7	7,355	7,970	876	871
5390 Misc. general merchandise stores	32	30	524	559	19	19,237	20,837	10,574	11,366
5410 Grocery stores	475	490	6,247	7,143	15	16,993	16,390	111,156	119,974
5420 Meat and fish markets	17	13	91	89	7	9,451	10,157	892	978
5430 Fruit and vegetable markets	6	-	21	-	-	4,381	-	84	-
5440 Candy, nut, and confectionery stores	14	13	86	68	5	10,930	11,118	1,030	877
5450 Dairy products stores [3]	4	5	40	20	4	1,900	10,400	185	213
5460 Retail bakeries	76	73	317	246	3	9,779	8,033	2,773	2,107
5490 Miscellaneous food stores	20	22	121	104	5	6,512	9,769	900	941
5510 New and used car dealers	59	61	2,399	2,550	42	30,073	31,158	81,046	87,383
5520 Used car dealers	44	44	137	168	4	19,445	17,833	3,355	3,795
5530 Auto and home supply stores	174	176	1,277	1,300	7	15,233	17,108	22,709	23,585
5540 Gasoline service stations	234	229	1,595	1,545	7	10,969	11,627	18,613	18,230
5550 Boat dealers	4	4	41	48	12	12,195	15,417	787	841
5560 Recreational vehicle dealers [3]	9	9	176	192	21	29,909	30,479	6,051	6,787
5570 Motorcycle dealers	9	9	34	38	4	21,176	22,000	822	990
5610 Men's & boys' clothing stores	35	36	189	186	5	14,540	15,570	2,728	2,631
5620 Women's clothing stores	99	84	807	610	7	8,560	8,643	7,180	5,548
5630 Women's accessory & specialty stores [3]	11	15	61	49	3	7,541	9,796	457	539
5640 Children's and infants' wear stores	13	13	81	79	6	7,062	6,633	617	564
5650 Family clothing stores	46	42	616	582	14	9,500	9,704	6,336	5,788
5660 Shoe stores	84	87	402	442	5	11,114	11,186	4,577	4,947
5690 Misc. apparel & accessory stores	19	22	81	69	3	11,704	14,551	1,030	1,058
5712 Furniture stores	82	81	648	524	6	17,691	18,878	12,325	12,722
5713 Floor covering stores	37	30	151	163	5	16,689	17,816	2,886	2,819
5714 Drapery and upholstery stores	6	5	9	3	1	17,333	18,667	160	132
5719 Misc. homefurnishings stores	38	39	196	210	5	11,959	12,229	2,751	2,911
5720 Household appliance stores	19	17	50	48	3	12,880	15,667	737	699
5731 Radio, TV, & electronic stores	43	43	381	407	9	18,383	17,818	7,319	7,769
5734 Computer and software stores	23	24	162	132	6	21,704	18,727	3,126	2,709
5735 Record & prerecorded tape stores	22	21	192	187	9	9,438	10,396	1,855	1,793

Continued on next page.

FRESNO, CA MSA - [continued]

Wholesale and Retail Trade USA	Establishments		Employment		Emp / Est	Pay / Employee		Annual Payroll ($ 000)	
	1994	1995	1994	1995	1995	1994	1995	1994	1995
5736 Musical instrument stores	12	13	60	54	4	10,867	11,111	650	639
5812 Eating places	1,078	1,014	18,373	18,079	18	6,778	7,217	132,522	136,974
5813 Drinking places	112	98	591	653	7	7,168	6,836	4,512	4,642
5910 Drug stores and proprietary stores	122	118	1,963	1,997	17	20,385	19,593	40,822	39,241
5920 Liquor stores	102	99	338	317	3	8,888	8,517	3,242	2,838
5930 Used merchandise stores	47	40	244	267	7	10,361	9,813	2,729	2,927
5941 Sporting goods and bicycle shops	61	59	478	406	7	11,021	13,015	5,883	5,539
5942 Book stores	23	23	307	355	15	9,590	8,946	2,988	3,073
5943 Stationery stores [2]	10	7	47	36	5	7,915	8,556	356	311
5944 Jewelry stores	70	62	364	366	6	16,066	15,639	5,775	5,318
5945 Hobby, toy, and game shops [3]	19	20	206	200	10	10,136	10,200	2,675	2,702
5946 Camera & photographic supply stores	-	5	-	35	7	-	21,600	-	799
5947 Gift, novelty, and souvenir shops	66	58	268	271	5	8,134	8,458	2,462	2,486
5948 Luggage and leather goods stores [3]	5	4	17	21	5	10,118	8,571	202	192
5949 Sewing, needlework, and piece goods	17	14	149	135	10	8,617	10,193	1,285	1,416
5961 Catalog and mail-order houses [3]	5	5	84	75	15	8,571	9,227	850	812
5962 Merchandising machine operators [3]	10	12	124	157	13	21,484	18,828	2,905	3,341
5963 Direct selling establishments [2]	38	38	436	445	12	17,266	19,398	8,170	8,013
5984 Liquefied petroleum gas dealers	20	21	201	152	7	21,811	19,579	4,305	3,457
5992 Florists	66	64	305	299	5	11,292	11,666	3,324	3,349
5993 Tobacco stores and stands [2]	-	5	-	3	1	-	16,000	-	122
5995 Optical goods stores	19	22	9	111	5	18,222	10,883	166	1,715
5999 Miscellaneous retail stores, nec	111	115	747	769	7	12,129	13,342	9,836	11,184

Source: County Business Patterns 1994/95, CBP-94/95, U.S. Department of Commerce, Washington DC, November 1997. The employment column represents mid-March employment in the year. Pay per employee is calculated by dividing 1st Quarter payroll, annualized, by mid-March employment. The column headed 'Emp / Est' shows 'employees per establishment'. A dash (-) means that data are unavailable or cannot be calculated. nec means not elsewhere classified. *Notes:* 1. 1994 data incomplete; unavailable or withheld. 2. 1995 data incomplete; unavailable or withheld. 3. 1994 and 1995 data incomplete; unavailable or withheld.

GADSDEN, AL MSA

Wholesale and Retail Trade USA	Establishments		Employment		Emp / Est	Pay / Employee		Annual Payroll ($ 000)	
	1994	1995	1994	1995	1995	1994	1995	1994	1995
50 - Wholesale trade	146	142	1,667	1,733	12	20,034	22,943	38,167	45,653
5012 Automobiles and other vehicles	7	7	70	102	15	24,800	15,725	1,823	1,938
5015 Motor vehicle parts, used	9	8	20	35	4	11,400	13,257	358	488
5020 Furniture and homefurnishings	4	4	59	65	16	15,797	16,862	809	1,072
5030 Lumber and construction materials	4	4	68	68	17	29,529	32,118	2,201	2,122
5044 Office equipment	4	4	22	21	5	17,636	17,714	365	342
5050 Metals and minerals, except petroleum	8	8	117	123	15	25,231	22,179	2,974	2,847
5063 Electrical apparatus and equipment	3	3	18	26	9	34,222	23,846	600	697
5070 Hardware, plumbing & heating equipment	4	4	85	25	6	7,200	21,920	671	646
5085 Industrial supplies	7	6	67	58	10	26,269	27,586	1,857	1,696
5087 Service establishment equipment	3	3	14	17	6	15,143	11,765	199	218
5093 Scrap and waste materials	12	12	204	235	20	25,529	25,770	5,650	6,035
5110 Paper and paper products	4	-	139	-	-	11,655	-	2,027	-
5120 Drugs, proprietaries, and sundries	3	3	24	25	8	22,000	25,280	573	709
5141 Groceries, general line	4	4	121	124	31	27,901	29,613	3,339	3,405
5169 Chemicals & allied products, nec	5	5	60	41	8	23,467	29,561	1,611	1,187
5171 Petroleum bulk stations & terminals	3	3	36	33	11	25,444	27,758	1,076	1,071
5172 Petroleum products, nec	6	5	29	28	6	21,241	21,571	570	553
5191 Farm supplies	5	-	29	-	-	11,862	-	377	-
5199 Nondurable goods, nec	5	5	19	22	4	10,947	12,545	238	265
52 - Retail trade	590	601	7,275	7,862	13	10,250	10,601	80,935	87,993
5210 Lumber and other building materials	13	12	247	210	18	14,494	17,695	3,780	3,975
5230 Paint, glass, and wallpaper stores	5	5	34	30	6	13,176	15,067	467	459
5260 Retail nurseries and garden stores	5	-	24	-	-	9,000	-	271	-
5310 Department stores	7	7	939	981	140	10,245	12,367	10,434	11,877
5330 Variety stores	12	9	86	72	8	8,186	8,111	838	687
5390 Misc. general merchandise stores	5	8	70	87	11	8,343	7,356	615	648
5410 Grocery stores	46	51	1,004	1,103	22	9,602	9,578	10,825	10,706
5450 Dairy products stores	3	-	14	-	-	5,429	-	79	-
5460 Retail bakeries	9	8	25	37	5	7,200	6,270	174	266
5490 Miscellaneous food stores	4	5	10	12	2	11,600	12,333	121	138
5510 New and used car dealers	5	6	233	231	39	22,352	22,649	4,850	5,530
5520 Used car dealers	15	17	60	56	3	17,400	19,071	875	863
5530 Auto and home supply stores	27	27	224	381	14	12,643	15,192	4,873	7,001
5540 Gasoline service stations	50	49	252	238	5	10,079	10,487	2,507	2,533
5620 Women's clothing stores	15	15	120	69	5	9,000	9,333	1,050	545
5630 Women's accessory & specialty stores	6	6	28	21	4	5,286	7,619	155	143

Continued on next page.

GADSDEN, AL MSA - [continued]

Wholesale and Retail Trade USA	Establishments		Employment		Emp / Est	Pay / Employee		Annual Payroll ($ 000)	
	1994	1995	1994	1995	1995	1994	1995	1994	1995
5650 Family clothing stores	5	6	198	195	33	8,222	8,185	1,734	1,750
5660 Shoe stores	17	15	65	66	4	9,169	8,727	642	584
5712 Furniture stores	16	15	95	102	7	13,263	15,216	1,403	1,708
5713 Floor covering stores	5	5	71	77	15	18,197	21,870	1,481	1,949
5720 Household appliance stores	3	3	4	4	1	13,000	13,000	49	40
5731 Radio, TV, & electronic stores	11	12	69	60	5	19,826	20,667	1,228	1,197
5734 Computer and software stores	-	6	-	26	4	-	10,308	-	314
5812 Eating places	119	108	2,483	2,667	25	6,785	6,587	17,811	18,429
5813 Drinking places	9	9	39	28	3	6,872	7,857	257	251
5910 Drug stores and proprietary stores	26	26	204	208	8	16,275	15,288	3,567	3,468
5920 Liquor stores	8	9	23	25	3	20,870	18,560	480	452
5930 Used merchandise stores	11	12	30	32	3	9,467	10,750	319	319
5941 Sporting goods and bicycle shops	5	5	11	18	4	13,818	8,889	170	186
5942 Book stores	6	6	31	27	5	7,742	9,037	276	269
5944 Jewelry stores	12	15	73	82	5	16,767	15,415	1,179	1,287
5945 Hobby, toy, and game shops	4	-	7	-	-	12,571	-	114	-
5947 Gift, novelty, and souvenir shops	10	9	19	29	3	7,579	6,759	159	210
5960 Nonstore retailers	5	6	20	34	6	17,000	14,706	424	437
5984 Liquefied petroleum gas dealers	5	6	35	40	7	21,371	21,100	707	738
5992 Florists	10	-	37	-	-	9,946	-	409	-
5995 Optical goods stores	-	6	-	26	4	-	19,385	-	546
5999 Miscellaneous retail stores, nec	18	18	53	69	4	10,113	10,087	797	958

Source: County Business Patterns 1994/95, CBP-94/95, U.S. Department of Commerce, Washington DC, November 1997. The employment column represents mid-March employment in the year. Pay per employee is calculated by dividing 1st Quarter payroll, annualized, by mid-March employment. The column headed 'Emp / Est' shows 'employees per establishment'. A dash (-) means that data are unavailable or cannot be calculated. nec means not elsewhere classified. *Notes:* 1. 1994 data incomplete; unavailable or withheld. 2. 1995 data incomplete; unavailable or withheld. 3. 1994 and 1995 data incomplete; unavailable or withheld.

GAINESVILLE, FL MSA

Wholesale and Retail Trade USA	Establishments		Employment		Emp / Est	Pay / Employee		Annual Payroll ($ 000)	
	1994	1995	1994	1995	1995	1994	1995	1994	1995
50 - Wholesale trade	264	251	2,264	2,248	9	21,813	24,719	51,947	56,082
5013 Motor vehicle supplies and new parts	15	13	139	175	13	17,122	17,326	2,575	2,420
5021 Furniture	10	8	72	65	8	19,000	22,400	1,475	1,510
5023 Homefurnishings	6	6	17	25	4	20,941	17,760	380	495
5031 Lumber, plywood, and millwork	-	4	-	36	9	-	27,444	-	948
5032 Brick, stone, & related materials	3	-	82	-	-	25,512	-	2,291	-
5039 Construction materials, nec	-	3	-	8	3	-	37,000	-	263
5044 Office equipment	11	12	75	80	7	21,653	23,950	1,730	1,966
5045 Computers, peripherals, & software	11	11	77	76	7	31,325	46,526	2,504	2,580
5047 Medical and hospital equipment	7	10	61	86	9	27,148	28,558	1,878	2,777
5051 Metals service centers and offices	4	4	11	11	3	16,364	24,364	252	247
5063 Electrical apparatus and equipment	9	9	119	127	14	45,513	50,047	4,488	5,154
5065 Electronic parts and equipment	9	8	39	41	5	17,128	18,829	718	774
5072 Hardware	6	6	31	38	6	31,355	37,368	1,047	1,307
5074 Plumbing & hydronic heating supplies	8	7	59	56	8	28,814	30,571	1,642	1,621
5075 Warm air heating & air conditioning	4	4	31	29	7	24,258	22,069	764	761
5083 Farm and garden machinery	7	6	62	52	9	21,097	22,538	1,449	1,073
5084 Industrial machinery and equipment	9	6	20	19	3	32,000	42,737	810	815
5085 Industrial supplies	4	4	27	24	6	20,741	22,500	584	575
5094 Jewelry & precious stones	6	-	28	-	-	16,143	-	544	-
5099 Durable goods, nec	8	8	88	113	14	17,318	17,805	1,881	2,119
5110 Paper and paper products	7	6	107	87	15	10,093	14,483	1,092	1,169
5136 Men's and boys' clothing	3	3	44	19	6	13,273	17,263	626	282
5137 Women's and children's clothing	3	3	5	4	1	11,200	17,000	54	58
5146 Fish and seafoods	3	3	39	52	17	7,282	9,538	382	521
5148 Fresh fruits and vegetables	-	3	-	52	17	-	22,231	-	1,207
5149 Groceries and related products, nec	12	11	218	176	16	21,651	27,136	4,882	5,527
5150 Farm-product raw materials	-	3	-	44	15	-	10,273	-	450
5160 Chemicals and allied products	5	6	25	37	6	41,600	34,054	1,265	1,643
5171 Petroleum bulk stations & terminals	6	4	84	43	11	17,667	20,279	1,766	988
5191 Farm supplies	16	15	82	80	5	16,829	17,150	1,301	1,312
5199 Nondurable goods, nec	13	-	50	-	-	18,160	-	962	-
52 - Retail trade	1,265	1,281	18,833	20,251	16	10,564	10,822	213,635	228,935
5210 Lumber and other building materials	13	13	518	489	38	15,421	18,307	8,648	9,631
5230 Paint, glass, and wallpaper stores	-	10	-	34	3	-	20,824	-	785
5250 Hardware stores	19	14	100	87	6	11,000	9,701	1,080	907
5260 Retail nurseries and garden stores	8	11	55	84	8	11,564	14,286	683	1,325
5270 Mobile home dealers	-	3	-	32	11	-	10,375	-	88

Continued on next page.

GAINESVILLE, FL MSA - [continued]

Wholesale and Retail Trade USA	Establishments		Employment		Emp / Est	Pay / Employee		Annual Payroll ($ 000)	
	1994	1995	1994	1995	1995	1994	1995	1994	1995
5310 Department stores	10	10	1,790	1,764	176	10,588	11,866	20,073	20,612
5330 Variety stores	10	7	84	95	14	5,286	6,232	680	642
5390 Misc. general merchandise stores	12	14	557	468	33	11,181	14,188	6,587	6,053
5410 Grocery stores	101	95	3,095	3,077	32	9,824	10,697	32,395	33,911
5420 Meat and fish markets	3	4	46	43	11	4,957	5,953	226	264
5460 Retail bakeries	9	11	69	84	8	8,116	7,810	542	525
5490 Miscellaneous food stores	8	8	52	67	8	13,154	11,821	784	819
5510 New and used car dealers	17	17	871	861	51	28,473	29,157	26,626	26,995
5520 Used car dealers	18	17	62	75	4	20,516	16,640	1,287	1,217
5530 Auto and home supply stores	29	35	251	280	8	18,151	18,314	4,997	5,882
5540 Gasoline service stations	74	75	487	559	7	11,179	11,721	5,789	6,695
5550 Boat dealers	5	5	14	16	3	15,143	14,000	256	242
5610 Men's & boys' clothing stores	11	9	101	90	10	5,861	5,822	578	471
5620 Women's clothing stores	37	34	328	319	9	7,427	6,345	2,555	2,207
5630 Women's accessory & specialty stores	6	6	42	45	8	7,619	6,933	323	312
5650 Family clothing stores	9	13	122	151	12	7,869	9,113	1,138	1,788
5660 Shoe stores	34	32	162	167	5	11,160	13,078	1,903	2,035
5690 Misc. apparel & accessory stores	10	9	53	68	8	10,491	8,824	624	680
5712 Furniture stores	35	34	220	213	6	14,073	13,559	3,509	3,211
5713 Floor covering stores	-	16	-	63	4	-	16,571	-	1,225
5719 Misc. homefurnishings stores	12	11	74	65	6	10,162	12,738	858	1,081
5720 Household appliance stores	9	12	56	165	14	18,286	7,830	1,091	2,005
5731 Radio, TV, & electronic stores	16	17	141	162	10	17,730	16,790	2,609	2,786
5734 Computer and software stores	11	11	61	87	8	17,705	15,080	1,253	1,450
5735 Record & prerecorded tape stores	11	11	125	159	14	9,184	7,648	1,146	1,062
5736 Musical instrument stores	6	4	38	25	6	12,632	14,560	568	415
5812 Eating places	288	274	6,266	7,091	26	7,335	7,461	48,951	54,163
5813 Drinking places	30	23	301	232	10	6,299	7,690	1,937	1,766
5910 Drug stores and proprietary stores	28	26	364	343	13	13,033	13,469	5,097	5,315
5920 Liquor stores	20	18	130	159	9	9,138	7,874	1,257	1,335
5930 Used merchandise stores	24	23	90	124	5	8,489	7,484	886	1,067
5941 Sporting goods and bicycle shops	24	27	112	112	4	10,464	10,500	1,306	1,571
5942 Book stores	18	17	189	211	12	10,561	9,896	2,184	2,351
5943 Stationery stores	7	6	65	30	5	10,892	11,867	644	190
5944 Jewelry stores	28	33	154	170	5	10,234	11,694	1,730	2,047
5945 Hobby, toy, and game shops	11	11	91	102	9	7,604	8,588	971	970
5947 Gift, novelty, and souvenir shops	21	22	127	118	5	7,433	8,678	1,089	1,105
5949 Sewing, needlework, and piece goods	6	6	49	48	8	5,306	7,417	302	349
5961 Catalog and mail-order houses	13	11	122	173	16	17,082	14,012	2,155	2,377
5980 Fuel dealers	7	8	59	63	8	18,780	20,127	1,081	1,335
5992 Florists	16	16	84	127	8	9,762	9,102	897	1,285
5995 Optical goods stores	21	23	113	121	5	14,195	15,074	1,717	1,873
5999 Miscellaneous retail stores, nec	42	41	174	215	5	10,966	10,419	2,155	2,521

Source: County Business Patterns 1994/95, CBP-94/95, U.S. Department of Commerce, Washington DC, November 1997. The employment column represents mid-March employment in the year. Pay per employee is calculated by dividing 1st Quarter payroll, annualized, by mid-March employment. The column headed 'Emp / Est' shows 'employees per establishment'. A dash (-) means that data are unavailable or cannot be calculated. nec means not elsewhere classified. *Notes:* 1. 1994 data incomplete; unavailable or withheld. 2. 1995 data incomplete; unavailable or withheld. 3. 1994 and 1995 data incomplete; unavailable or withheld.

GALVESTON - TEXAS CITY, TX PMSA

Wholesale and Retail Trade USA	Establishments		Employment		Emp / Est	Pay / Employee		Annual Payroll ($ 000)	
	1994	1995	1994	1995	1995	1994	1995	1994	1995
50- Wholesale trade	-	216	-	1,840	9	-	25,157	-	49,742
5013 Motor vehicle supplies and new parts	-	9	-	50	6	-	19,600	-	1,053
5031 Lumber, plywood, and millwork	-	6	-	78	13	-	18,564	-	1,460
5032 Brick, stone, & related materials	-	4	-	13	3	-	28,000	-	389
5044 Office equipment	-	6	-	31	5	-	19,355	-	645
5046 Commercial equipment, nec	-	3	-	7	2	-	11,429	-	71
5047 Medical and hospital equipment	-	4	-	10	3	-	31,600	-	346
5051 Metals service centers and offices	-	6	-	118	20	-	26,983	-	4,025
5063 Electrical apparatus and equipment	-	5	-	61	12	-	26,426	-	1,770
5065 Electronic parts and equipment	-	8	-	91	11	-	45,538	-	4,433
5074 Plumbing & hydronic heating supplies	-	9	-	52	6	-	18,923	-	1,098
5075 Warm air heating & air conditioning	-	6	-	13	2	-	27,077	-	393
5084 Industrial machinery and equipment	-	17	-	161	9	-	31,702	-	4,769
5085 Industrial supplies	-	13	-	80	6	-	30,700	-	2,581
5087 Service establishment equipment	-	3	-	12	4	-	15,333	-	196
5088 Transportation equipment & supplies	-	5	-	40	8	-	16,700	-	753
5093 Scrap and waste materials	-	5	-	39	8	-	40,205	-	1,591

Continued on next page.

GALVESTON – TEXAS CITY, TX PMSA - [continued]

Wholesale and Retail Trade USA	Establishments		Employment		Emp / Est	Pay / Employee		Annual Payroll ($ 000)	
	1994	1995	1994	1995	1995	1994	1995	1994	1995
5130 Apparel, piece goods, and notions	-	9	-	116	13	-	15,138	-	2,100
5146 Fish and seafoods	-	8	-	120	15	-	7,600	-	1,039
5169 Chemicals & allied products, nec	-	8	-	68	9	-	40,941	-	2,690
5171 Petroleum bulk stations & terminals	-	6	-	88	15	-	17,591	-	2,113
5172 Petroleum products, nec	-	6	-	53	9	-	31,094	-	1,479
5181 Beer and ale	-	3	-	175	58	-	30,903	-	5,639
5191 Farm supplies	-	7	-	34	5	-	11,294	-	418
5199 Nondurable goods, nec	-	4	-	14	4	-	15,429	-	313
52 - Retail trade	-	1,381	-	18,871	14	-	11,366	-	228,055
5210 Lumber and other building materials	-	17	-	188	11	-	18,234	-	5,505
5230 Paint, glass, and wallpaper stores	-	15	-	63	4	-	21,587	-	1,185
5250 Hardware stores	-	7	-	52	7	-	13,615	-	803
5260 Retail nurseries and garden stores	-	6	-	50	8	-	8,560	-	480
5310 Department stores	-	9	-	1,437	160	-	13,055	-	20,372
5410 Grocery stores	-	160	-	3,599	22	-	9,094	-	33,963
5420 Meat and fish markets	-	11	-	178	16	-	6,652	-	1,164
5440 Candy, nut, and confectionery stores	-	4	-	34	9	-	8,353	-	256
5460 Retail bakeries	-	15	-	83	6	-	9,253	-	723
5490 Miscellaneous food stores	-	6	-	23	4	-	10,783	-	257
5510 New and used car dealers	-	12	-	699	58	-	31,308	-	24,006
5520 Used car dealers	-	8	-	49	6	-	20,735	-	1,193
5530 Auto and home supply stores	-	35	-	300	9	-	16,787	-	5,357
5540 Gasoline service stations	-	59	-	287	5	-	12,502	-	3,815
5550 Boat dealers	-	16	-	115	7	-	29,635	-	3,286
5570 Motorcycle dealers	-	3	-	19	6	-	11,789	-	270
5610 Men's & boys' clothing stores	-	18	-	164	9	-	9,634	-	1,532
5620 Women's clothing stores	-	53	-	422	8	-	7,697	-	3,276
5630 Women's accessory & specialty stores	-	5	-	38	8	-	9,789	-	275
5640 Children's and infants' wear stores	-	5	-	46	9	-	7,391	-	348
5650 Family clothing stores	-	25	-	304	12	-	9,724	-	3,023
5660 Shoe stores	-	32	-	225	7	-	10,524	-	2,384
5690 Misc. apparel & accessory stores	-	15	-	111	7	-	7,063	-	907
5712 Furniture stores	-	14	-	61	4	-	21,377	-	1,671
5719 Misc. homefurnishings stores	-	20	-	95	5	-	12,337	-	1,301
5720 Household appliance stores	-	7	-	22	3	-	19,273	-	483
5731 Radio, TV, & electronic stores	-	12	-	48	4	-	18,833	-	719
5735 Record & prerecorded tape stores	-	7	-	37	5	-	12,000	-	349
5812 Eating places	-	284	-	6,898	24	-	8,879	-	64,909
5813 Drinking places	-	49	-	305	6	-	8,669	-	2,681
5910 Drug stores and proprietary stores	-	34	-	463	14	-	14,877	-	7,193
5920 Liquor stores	-	26	-	70	3	-	13,143	-	839
5930 Used merchandise stores	-	20	-	117	6	-	15,692	-	1,786
5941 Sporting goods and bicycle shops	-	23	-	145	6	-	12,414	-	2,215
5942 Book stores	-	8	-	43	5	-	10,233	-	433
5944 Jewelry stores	-	30	-	155	5	-	16,800	-	2,500
5945 Hobby, toy, and game shops	-	8	-	55	7	-	9,600	-	674
5947 Gift, novelty, and souvenir shops	-	41	-	233	6	-	7,622	-	1,986
5949 Sewing, needlework, and piece goods	-	4	-	36	9	-	6,667	-	252
5963 Direct selling establishments	-	7	-	34	5	-	8,941	-	288
5984 Liquefied petroleum gas dealers	-	4	-	16	4	-	15,250	-	269
5992 Florists	-	22	-	117	5	-	10,496	-	1,240
5995 Optical goods stores	-	18	-	112	6	-	13,857	-	1,649
5999 Miscellaneous retail stores, nec	-	42	-	190	5	-	16,421	-	3,224

Source: County Business Patterns 1994/95, CBP-94/95, U.S. Department of Commerce, Washington DC, November 1997. The employment column represents mid-March employment in the year. Pay per employee is calculated by dividing 1st Quarter payroll, annualized, by mid-March employment. The column headed 'Emp / Est' shows 'employees per establishment'. A dash (-) means that data are unavailable or cannot be calculated. nec means not elsewhere classified. *Notes:* 1. 1994 data incomplete; unavailable or withheld. 2. 1995 data incomplete; unavailable or withheld. 3. 1994 and 1995 data incomplete; unavailable or withheld.

GARY, IN PMSA

Wholesale and Retail Trade USA	Establishments		Employment		Emp / Est	Pay / Employee		Annual Payroll ($ 000)	
	1994	1995	1994	1995	1995	1994	1995	1994	1995
50 - Wholesale trade	807	808	9,226	9,869	12	27,543	29,660	275,794	305,127
5012 Automobiles and other vehicles	21	19	290	269	14	24,579	27,941	7,691	7,373
5013 Motor vehicle supplies and new parts	34	29	302	280	10	21,669	22,729	7,224	6,957
5014 Tires and tubes[3]	5	5	54	71	14	32,444	28,845	2,022	2,187
5015 Motor vehicle parts, used	16	18	257	293	16	12,700	14,922	3,846	5,150
5021 Furniture	5	5	29	24	5	17,655	21,833	534	529
5023 Homefurnishings	9	8	25	30	4	16,640	11,467	411	269

Continued on next page.

GARY, IN PMSA - [continued]

Wholesale and Retail Trade USA	Establishments		Employment		Emp / Est	Pay / Employee		Annual Payroll ($ 000)	
	1994	1995	1994	1995	1995	1994	1995	1994	1995
5031 Lumber, plywood, and millwork	10	13	56	129	10	19,143	29,302	1,435	3,487
5032 Brick, stone, & related materials	9	9	49	47	5	25,388	20,511	1,557	1,120
5033 Roofing, siding, & insulation	10	11	112	120	11	15,893	21,533	2,984	3,044
5039 Construction materials, nec[2]	7	8	46	41	5	20,000	26,732	1,282	960
5043 Photographic equipment & supplies[2]	-	3	-	10	3	-	23,200	-	197
5044 Office equipment[1]	12	15	137	130	9	22,686	21,662	2,920	2,930
5046 Commercial equipment, nec[1]	4	-	20	-	-	13,000	-	285	-
5047 Medical and hospital equipment	12	11	71	50	5	31,718	38,720	1,824	1,823
5049 Professional equipment, nec[3]	5	6	59	67	11	11,051	10,746	686	814
5050 Metals and minerals, except petroleum	55	63	1,137	1,345	21	34,030	35,390	39,306	44,212
5063 Electrical apparatus and equipment	34	26	259	231	9	30,965	45,818	8,332	8,633
5065 Electronic parts and equipment[3]	25	24	42	39	2	31,810	38,564	1,534	1,677
5072 Hardware	14	15	109	123	8	22,862	23,902	3,175	3,491
5074 Plumbing & hydronic heating supplies	15	13	159	130	10	27,069	31,323	5,056	4,181
5078 Refrigeration equipment and supplies	4	4	19	27	7	29,263	28,148	752	964
5082 Construction and mining machinery	6	6	92	101	17	42,826	45,743	3,795	4,228
5083 Farm and garden machinery	8	6	28	22	4	15,000	15,636	491	376
5084 Industrial machinery and equipment	66	70	490	545	8	31,045	32,462	16,342	19,202
5085 Industrial supplies	51	46	428	435	9	29,159	32,782	13,116	14,386
5087 Service establishment equipment	23	22	166	161	7	15,976	17,540	2,984	3,071
5088 Transportation equipment & supplies[3]	3	3	41	44	15	20,976	24,273	981	1,220
5091 Sporting & recreational goods	6	6	39	52	9	27,282	25,846	989	1,123
5092 Toys and hobby goods and supplies	5	7	8	13	2	13,500	14,154	145	141
5093 Scrap and waste materials	46	46	1,033	1,126	24	36,515	34,437	39,360	42,469
5094 Jewelry & precious stones	6	5	8	11	2	16,500	10,182	123	108
5099 Durable goods, nec	18	22	59	126	6	18,983	36,190	2,433	6,192
5112 Stationery and office supplies	9	7	144	98	14	16,250	18,408	3,344	1,949
5113 Industrial & personal service paper	10	-	56	-	-	23,286	-	1,291	-
5120 Drugs, proprietaries, and sundries	8	8	132	82	10	28,394	36,488	2,844	2,770
5136 Men's and boys' clothing[2]	-	5	-	39	8	-	14,154	-	591
5137 Women's and children's clothing	5	5	6	10	2	10,667	12,800	99	127
5147 Meats and meat products	10	8	76	65	8	18,316	18,769	1,599	1,266
5148 Fresh fruits and vegetables[3]	3	3	80	79	26	22,550	25,468	2,142	2,356
5149 Groceries and related products, nec	20	22	451	622	28	25,357	28,701	13,681	19,655
5153 Grain and field beans	-	8	-	29	4	-	22,483	-	795
5160 Chemicals and allied products	21	22	207	201	9	37,005	39,502	9,098	9,615
5171 Petroleum bulk stations & terminals	20	19	251	235	12	28,303	34,928	7,717	8,654
5172 Petroleum products, nec	19	19	303	307	16	30,759	33,967	10,756	11,892
5180 Beer, wine, and distilled beverages[3]	5	5	109	106	21	19,450	21,547	2,354	2,439
5191 Farm supplies[2]	12	9	34	24	3	14,000	19,667	1,181	547
5192 Books, periodicals, & newspapers[3]	3	3	2	4	1	90,000	22,000	115	103
5193 Flowers & florists' supplies	9	10	59	48	5	17,017	15,417	1,173	813
5194 Tobacco and tobacco products	5	5	118	85	17	20,102	24,941	2,237	1,862
5198 Paints, varnishes, and supplies[1]	8	7	37	34	5	19,784	25,647	798	791
5199 Nondurable goods, nec	13	17	142	167	10	14,704	15,186	2,052	2,882
52 - Retail trade	3,288	3,285	48,300	48,730	15	10,735	11,807	575,735	608,352
5210 Lumber and other building materials	56	57	1,282	1,362	24	17,354	17,947	26,381	27,982
5230 Paint, glass, and wallpaper stores[3]	27	26	21	22	1	12,381	17,455	307	414
5250 Hardware stores	50	38	495	434	11	10,271	10,728	5,242	4,658
5260 Retail nurseries and garden stores	28	30	181	274	9	12,508	12,511	3,535	4,422
5270 Mobile home dealers	-	4	-	11	3	-	16,364	-	171
5310 Department stores[3]	24	24	3,308	3,693	154	10,629	11,701	40,323	45,132
5330 Variety stores	28	24	292	260	11	7,425	8,708	2,587	2,329
5390 Misc. general merchandise stores	14	14	335	456	33	13,588	11,342	4,701	4,875
5410 Grocery stores	166	167	6,188	6,618	40	11,800	12,416	77,154	82,469
5420 Meat and fish markets	21	17	145	134	8	11,366	11,552	1,714	1,579
5430 Fruit and vegetable markets	12	10	77	64	6	8,000	9,375	956	940
5440 Candy, nut, and confectionery stores	17	18	120	91	5	6,633	9,143	1,138	1,173
5460 Retail bakeries	45	45	566	515	11	7,859	8,311	4,547	4,473
5490 Miscellaneous food stores	8	9	23	27	3	8,522	7,556	204	214
5510 New and used car dealers	54	53	2,210	2,401	45	27,330	28,195	70,723	74,326
5520 Used car dealers	65	60	200	224	4	17,400	17,661	3,927	4,065
5530 Auto and home supply stores	88	84	715	708	8	16,006	17,186	13,032	13,535
5540 Gasoline service stations	283	268	2,948	2,814	11	9,585	10,867	30,117	32,292
5560 Recreational vehicle dealers[3]	4	4	60	55	14	21,933	24,873	1,735	1,706
5570 Motorcycle dealers	-	11	-	116	11	-	14,828	-	2,083
5610 Men's & boys' clothing stores	27	26	239	192	7	10,025	11,667	2,529	2,350
5620 Women's clothing stores	96	89	1,007	761	9	7,297	7,059	8,088	5,704
5630 Women's accessory & specialty stores	12	11	47	48	4	10,298	10,167	494	497
5640 Children's and infants' wear stores[3]	10	11	85	104	9	5,882	6,308	638	736
5650 Family clothing stores	32	28	605	494	18	8,740	9,927	5,315	4,967

Continued on next page.

GARY, IN PMSA - [continued]

Wholesale and Retail Trade USA	Establishments		Employment		Emp / Est	Pay / Employee		Annual Payroll ($ 000)	
	1994	1995	1994	1995	1995	1994	1995	1994	1995
5660 Shoe stores	73	70	402	428	6	11,463	12,196	5,077	5,223
5690 Misc. apparel & accessory stores	15	14	70	74	5	7,886	7,784	581	603
5712 Furniture stores	49	52	553	688	13	18,676	20,105	11,199	14,652
5713 Floor covering stores	27	29	199	229	8	20,402	21,432	4,575	4,949
5714 Drapery and upholstery stores [1]	4	-	22	-	-	16,182	-	249	-
5719 Misc. homefurnishings stores	19	23	85	14	1	12,235	10,571	1,343	212
5720 Household appliance stores	18	18	89	85	5	15,775	17,318	1,517	1,550
5731 Radio, TV, & electronic stores	32	32	310	346	11	15,135	15,896	4,918	5,643
5734 Computer and software stores	8	6	6	15	3	12,000	18,400	212	284
5735 Record & prerecorded tape stores	18	18	77	85	5	8,831	10,965	786	845
5812 Eating places	863	811	17,005	16,220	20	6,322	7,087	120,343	123,431
5813 Drinking places	163	165	741	784	5	6,845	7,046	5,455	5,450
5910 Drug stores and proprietary stores	106	103	1,893	1,817	18	17,177	18,743	33,799	34,732
5920 Liquor stores	107	101	465	451	4	9,144	9,588	4,675	4,573
5930 Used merchandise stores	26	28	202	203	7	9,564	10,660	2,207	2,087
5941 Sporting goods and bicycle shops	51	50	318	325	7	11,082	10,954	3,957	4,155
5942 Book stores	26	28	171	204	7	7,836	9,275	1,474	2,067
5943 Stationery stores [3]	6	6	57	48	8	9,123	11,583	508	529
5944 Jewelry stores	44	40	282	283	7	16,582	18,106	4,627	5,028
5945 Hobby, toy, and game shops	20	20	125	138	7	9,792	9,362	1,689	1,654
5946 Camera & photographic supply stores [3]	4	4	25	24	6	15,200	17,500	450	468
5947 Gift, novelty, and souvenir shops	63	66	388	410	6	7,392	6,985	3,113	3,218
5949 Sewing, needlework, and piece goods	13	15	136	107	7	5,882	7,439	828	740
5961 Catalog and mail-order houses	-	13	-	220	17	-	12,473	-	3,067
5962 Merchandising machine operators	-	16	-	64	4	-	15,750	-	1,177
5963 Direct selling establishments	28	28	288	262	9	10,667	12,229	3,263	3,374
5980 Fuel dealers	8	8	46	40	5	17,391	23,700	1,001	1,130
5992 Florists	60	59	230	239	4	9,235	9,339	2,195	2,280
5993 Tobacco stores and stands [3]	11	12	85	70	6	7,435	9,429	693	781
5994 News dealers and newsstands [2]	-	3	-	26	9	-	7,077	-	162
5995 Optical goods stores	27	26	134	132	5	13,015	14,697	1,968	1,892
5999 Miscellaneous retail stores, nec	97	106	453	525	5	9,898	10,530	5,536	6,404

Source: County Business Patterns 1994/95, CBP-94/95, U.S. Department of Commerce, Washington DC, November 1997. The employment column represents mid-March employment in the year. Pay per employee is calculated by dividing 1st Quarter payroll, annualized, by mid-March employment. The column headed 'Emp / Est' shows 'employees per establishment'. A dash (-) means that data are unavailable or cannot be calculated. nec means not elsewhere classified. *Notes:* 1. 1994 data incomplete; unavailable or withheld. 2. 1995 data incomplete; unavailable or withheld. 3. 1994 and 1995 data incomplete; unavailable or withheld.

GLENS FALLS, NY MSA

Wholesale and Retail Trade USA	Establishments		Employment		Emp / Est	Pay / Employee		Annual Payroll ($ 000)	
	1994	1995	1994	1995	1995	1994	1995	1994	1995
50- Wholesale trade	167	155	1,726	1,609	10	21,126	22,327	41,064	38,124
5013 Motor vehicle supplies and new parts	17	10	75	48	5	17,013	18,917	1,274	868
5030 Lumber and construction materials	11	12	120	57	5	24,000	18,175	3,832	1,611
5044 Office equipment	4	4	39	34	9	21,333	22,941	781	604
5063 Electrical apparatus and equipment	7	6	83	80	13	24,048	23,100	2,454	2,157
5074 Plumbing & hydronic heating supplies [3]	5	5	93	85	17	30,624	29,224	2,906	2,328
5084 Industrial machinery and equipment	7	6	25	26	4	43,520	34,769	959	836
5085 Industrial supplies [3]	8	8	33	30	4	31,515	37,867	1,142	1,231
5093 Scrap and waste materials	-	8	-	77	10	-	22,649	-	1,834
5110 Paper and paper products	6	-	22	-	-	23,091	-	566	-
5149 Groceries and related products, nec	7	7	155	131	19	23,794	22,412	3,934	3,257
5150 Farm-product raw materials [3]	5	5	46	42	8	6,957	8,286	370	342
5160 Chemicals and allied products	5	4	8	3	1	23,000	26,667	186	76
5191 Farm supplies [3]	12	9	120	82	9	13,500	18,146	1,858	1,803
52- Retail trade	1,017	1,021	9,066	9,685	9	12,086	12,370	126,072	130,511
5210 Lumber and other building materials	15	14	164	176	13	21,878	22,409	4,159	4,115
5230 Paint, glass, and wallpaper stores	-	5	-	9	2	-	21,333	-	200
5250 Hardware stores	19	21	113	111	5	15,575	15,640	1,909	1,950
5260 Retail nurseries and garden stores	-	8	-	58	7	-	15,172	-	1,050
5310 Department stores [3]	6	7	314	297	42	11,554	11,758	3,975	5,005
5330 Variety stores	6	-	25	-	-	8,640	-	154	-
5390 Misc. general merchandise stores	9	9	180	101	11	12,111	10,772	2,091	1,166
5410 Grocery stores	103	105	1,571	2,024	19	12,303	11,547	21,915	25,119
5440 Candy, nut, and confectionery stores [3]	5	4	13	6	2	7,077	4,667	104	53
5460 Retail bakeries	7	8	41	50	6	7,220	13,200	383	704
5510 New and used car dealers	19	19	478	494	26	25,556	26,656	13,967	13,536
5520 Used car dealers	9	8	15	44	6	15,200	25,727	244	969
5530 Auto and home supply stores	26	24	180	215	9	21,911	21,581	4,267	4,960

Continued on next page.

GLENS FALLS, NY MSA - [continued]

Wholesale and Retail Trade USA	Establishments		Employment		Emp / Est	Pay / Employee		Annual Payroll ($ 000)	
	1994	1995	1994	1995	1995	1994	1995	1994	1995
5540 Gasoline service stations	53	51	314	311	6	11,898	12,707	4,144	4,053
5550 Boat dealers [3]	6	6	36	43	7	20,111	18,419	1,028	1,106
5610 Men's & boys' clothing stores	13	13	84	100	8	9,381	9,440	997	980
5620 Women's clothing stores [2]	24	22	133	161	7	8,180	7,056	1,397	1,226
5630 Women's accessory & specialty stores [3]	5	6	20	29	5	10,400	9,517	234	299
5640 Children's and infants' wear stores [3]	4	4	27	42	11	7,111	5,619	220	284
5650 Family clothing stores	20	17	166	152	9	7,157	7,947	1,771	1,463
5660 Shoe stores	27	24	141	320	13	7,262	9,750	1,380	1,816
5690 Misc. apparel & accessory stores	7	7	30	30	4	9,333	11,733	315	314
5712 Furniture stores	12	13	39	28	2	19,077	23,143	714	658
5719 Misc. homefurnishings stores [3]	17	17	94	108	6	9,660	9,926	1,067	1,280
5731 Radio, TV, & electronic stores	11	9	47	40	4	19,915	20,000	897	655
5735 Record & prerecorded tape stores	5	5	36	20	4	7,222	12,600	246	254
5812 Eating places	280	262	2,593	2,538	10	8,517	8,506	27,446	25,952
5813 Drinking places	47	44	121	104	2	9,223	8,038	1,082	989
5910 Drug stores and proprietary stores	29	27	303	304	11	13,215	14,408	3,952	4,767
5920 Liquor stores	21	20	50	61	3	12,640	12,066	727	791
5930 Used merchandise stores	9	8	33	30	4	9,939	9,067	333	301
5941 Sporting goods and bicycle shops	13	16	112	78	5	12,821	14,513	1,192	963
5942 Book stores	6	7	41	35	5	10,732	13,486	428	463
5944 Jewelry stores	9	9	47	34	4	20,170	19,294	731	635
5947 Gift, novelty, and souvenir shops	37	38	92	79	2	9,043	11,595	1,429	1,355
5949 Sewing, needlework, and piece goods	5	6	25	25	4	7,040	7,200	206	231
5962 Merchandising machine operators	-	6	-	80	13	-	18,050	-	1,412
5980 Fuel dealers	18	19	107	124	7	22,467	24,355	2,701	2,943
5992 Florists	15	-	11	-	-	7,636	-	82	-
5995 Optical goods stores	9	10	123	45	5	6,179	20,978	831	957
5999 Miscellaneous retail stores, nec	16	17	53	30	2	12,075	17,600	609	456

Source: County Business Patterns 1994/95, CBP-94/95, U.S. Department of Commerce, Washington DC, November 1997. The employment column represents mid-March employment in the year. Pay per employee is calculated by dividing 1st Quarter payroll, annualized, by mid-March employment. The column headed 'Emp / Est' shows 'employees per establishment'. A dash (-) means that data are unavailable or cannot be calculated. nec means not elsewhere classified. *Notes:* 1. 1994 data incomplete; unavailable or withheld. 2. 1995 data incomplete; unavailable or withheld. 3. 1994 and 1995 data incomplete; unavailable or withheld.

GOLDSBORO, NC MSA

Wholesale and Retail Trade USA	Establishments		Employment		Emp / Est	Pay / Employee		Annual Payroll ($ 000)	
	1994	1995	1994	1995	1995	1994	1995	1994	1995
50- Wholesale trade	189	185	2,481	2,522	14	22,555	23,489	60,896	63,423
5013 Motor vehicle supplies and new parts	12	12	120	115	10	19,800	18,887	2,290	2,346
5015 Motor vehicle parts, used	7	7	74	70	10	16,486	17,257	1,275	1,286
5023 Homefurnishings	-	5	-	47	9	-	48,766	-	2,399
5031 Lumber, plywood, and millwork	3	-	23	-	-	26,783	-	445	-
5033 Roofing, siding, & insulation	-	5	-	35	7	-	30,400	-	2,281
5040 Professional & commercial equipment	9	9	56	66	7	15,500	22,970	1,521	1,665
5060 Electrical goods	11	9	71	72	8	38,197	29,944	2,468	2,241
5072 Hardware	7	7	217	232	33	23,724	27,017	5,984	6,543
5074 Plumbing & hydronic heating supplies	-	4	-	36	9	-	29,000	-	1,226
5075 Warm air heating & air conditioning	3	-	16	-	-	31,500	-	459	-
5083 Farm and garden machinery	11	10	208	235	24	25,442	26,485	5,554	5,212
5084 Industrial machinery and equipment	7	7	61	69	10	24,393	27,188	1,584	2,108
5085 Industrial supplies	4	3	30	32	11	20,133	21,125	605	636
5093 Scrap and waste materials	3	3	100	93	31	19,400	22,323	2,026	2,162
5110 Paper and paper products	3	3	34	30	10	15,765	16,267	512	491
5130 Apparel, piece goods, and notions	6	6	111	109	18	12,252	12,734	1,565	1,409
5147 Meats and meat products	4	4	121	120	30	16,826	18,733	2,101	2,165
5149 Groceries and related products, nec	7	7	165	158	23	28,582	31,013	4,754	4,547
5153 Grain and field beans	6	-	73	-	-	15,014	-	1,277	-
5159 Farm-product raw materials, nec	-	4	-	12	3	-	48,333	-	940
5171 Petroleum bulk stations & terminals	-	7	-	117	17	-	22,325	-	2,939
5172 Petroleum products, nec	-	4	-	62	16	-	22,516	-	1,426
5191 Farm supplies	21	20	182	141	7	15,407	17,050	2,872	2,503
52- Retail trade	643	654	7,670	8,071	12	10,079	11,021	84,726	93,508
5210 Lumber and other building materials	12	11	242	250	23	18,446	22,128	4,488	5,231
5230 Paint, glass, and wallpaper stores	6	4	24	21	5	14,000	14,095	338	309
5250 Hardware stores	6	7	30	42	6	12,533	14,000	448	527
5260 Retail nurseries and garden stores	5	5	18	18	4	9,778	10,667	193	206
5270 Mobile home dealers	14	17	66	89	5	19,879	22,067	1,743	2,521
5310 Department stores	6	8	795	869	109	9,977	11,728	7,561	9,499
5330 Variety stores	9	9	58	60	7	6,828	7,733	428	460

Continued on next page.

GOLDSBORO, NC MSA - [continued]

Wholesale and Retail Trade USA	Establishments		Employment		Emp / Est	Pay / Employee		Annual Payroll ($ 000)	
	1994	1995	1994	1995	1995	1994	1995	1994	1995
5390 Misc. general merchandise stores	10	8	272	265	33	10,794	11,109	2,857	2,795
5410 Grocery stores	57	52	1,133	1,137	22	8,420	9,274	10,222	11,049
5420 Meat and fish markets	7	8	81	89	11	12,691	13,393	1,129	1,259
5460 Retail bakeries	4	-	68	-	-	6,176	-	546	-
5490 Miscellaneous food stores	3	3	15	9	3	6,133	10,667	126	116
5510 New and used car dealers	18	16	316	295	18	22,342	23,064	8,125	7,382
5520 Used car dealers	25	26	69	86	3	14,551	17,953	1,208	2,402
5530 Auto and home supply stores	21	22	151	134	6	12,874	16,358	2,127	2,327
5540 Gasoline service stations	56	58	346	397	7	10,405	11,013	3,749	4,173
5610 Men's & boys' clothing stores	-	5	-	21	4	-	13,524	-	287
5620 Women's clothing stores	25	25	173	190	8	7,815	6,295	1,458	1,530
5640 Children's and infants' wear stores	3	3	8	7	2	9,000	8,000	68	62
5650 Family clothing stores	5	5	148	127	25	8,135	10,394	1,275	1,285
5660 Shoe stores	17	14	85	90	6	9,835	9,289	927	954
5690 Misc. apparel & accessory stores	4	-	7	-	-	4,571	-	44	-
5712 Furniture stores	23	25	169	191	8	14,627	17,969	2,814	3,083
5713 Floor covering stores	7	7	44	49	7	15,818	17,224	773	903
5714 Drapery and upholstery stores	3	-	8	-	-	11,500	-	97	-
5719 Misc. homefurnishings stores	3	3	4	11	4	16,000	18,545	200	251
5720 Household appliance stores	10	10	60	126	13	11,800	7,397	723	914
5731 Radio, TV, & electronic stores	11	10	43	61	6	17,581	19,148	843	997
5812 Eating places	105	97	2,096	2,188	23	6,490	6,976	14,992	16,120
5813 Drinking places	5	4	54	45	11	6,222	7,200	388	351
5910 Drug stores and proprietary stores	17	18	191	211	12	13,822	14,844	3,007	3,384
5930 Used merchandise stores	11	11	82	76	7	13,366	13,105	1,604	997
5941 Sporting goods and bicycle shops	4	5	38	37	7	13,368	14,703	539	635
5944 Jewelry stores	12	14	75	98	7	14,987	13,755	1,329	1,514
5945 Hobby, toy, and game shops	3	3	12	11	4	10,333	10,909	151	158
5947 Gift, novelty, and souvenir shops	11	14	41	49	4	5,854	8,000	294	433
5949 Sewing, needlework, and piece goods	5	4	47	35	9	5,957	8,000	298	322
5960 Nonstore retailers	5	6	20	19	3	12,800	14,737	201	344
5980 Fuel dealers	8	9	82	79	9	15,805	16,506	1,357	1,306
5999 Miscellaneous retail stores, nec	20	20	83	88	4	11,904	12,636	1,225	1,408

Source: County Business Patterns 1994/95, CBP-94/95, U.S. Department of Commerce, Washington DC, November 1997. The employment column represents mid-March employment in the year. Pay per employee is calculated by dividing 1st Quarter payroll, annualized, by mid-March employment. The column headed 'Emp / Est' shows 'employees per establishment'. A dash (-) means that data are unavailable or cannot be calculated. nec means not elsewhere classified. *Notes:* 1. 1994 data incomplete; unavailable or withheld. 2. 1995 data incomplete; unavailable or withheld. 3. 1994 and 1995 data incomplete; unavailable or withheld.

GRAND FORKS MSA (MN PART)

Wholesale and Retail Trade USA	Establishments		Employment		Emp / Est	Pay / Employee		Annual Payroll ($ 000)	
	1994	1995	1994	1995	1995	1994	1995	1994	1995
50 - Wholesale trade	86	81	683	754	9	21,066	23,220	17,347	18,608
5010 Motor vehicles, parts, and supplies	7	7	35	31	4	16,114	16,387	586	549
5083 Farm and garden machinery	9	-	93	-	-	18,280	-	2,326	-
5140 Groceries and related products	7	6	204	221	37	24,490	25,158	5,763	5,957
5150 Farm-product raw materials	17	17	96	133	8	22,375	18,406	2,240	2,704
5171 Petroleum bulk stations & terminals	-	9	-	82	9	-	17,561	-	1,520
5191 Farm supplies	17	-	91	-	-	18,374	-	2,490	-
52 - Retail trade	203	207	2,212	2,241	11	8,743	9,505	21,432	22,787
5210 Lumber and other building materials	6	8	73	107	13	23,233	22,916	1,801	2,017
5300 General merchandise stores	8	7	100	107	15	10,040	10,131	1,109	1,108
5400 Food stores	21	21	387	400	19	8,258	9,300	3,732	4,100
5510 New and used car dealers	5	5	94	96	19	19,191	18,667	1,971	1,955
5520 Used car dealers	4	-	9	-	-	11,556	-	117	-
5530 Auto and home supply stores	-	6	-	38	6	-	21,789	-	925
5540 Gasoline service stations	18	21	93	112	5	9,892	9,643	962	1,165
5610 Men's & boys' clothing stores	3	-	12	-	-	8,667	-	110	-
5620 Women's clothing stores	-	3	-	5	2	-	8,000	-	62
5712 Furniture stores	-	3	-	15	5	-	12,000	-	171
5812 Eating places	50	48	884	844	18	5,769	6,052	5,538	5,596
5813 Drinking places	9	8	100	70	9	4,000	4,171	433	287
5910 Drug stores and proprietary stores	8	9	69	71	8	9,739	10,423	821	976
5920 Liquor stores	6	6	88	92	15	7,636	7,739	707	735
5940 Miscellaneous shopping goods stores	6	7	30	29	4	10,933	11,034	342	337
5960 Nonstore retailers	8	7	33	31	4	12,000	11,871	356	345
5992 Florists	5	5	25	25	5	6,400	5,920	174	172
5995 Optical goods stores	5	5	17	14	3	11,529	14,286	171	167

Source: County Business Patterns 1994/95, CBP-94/95, U.S. Department of Commerce, Washington DC, November 1997. The employment column represents mid-March employment in the year. Pay per employee is calculated by dividing 1st Quarter payroll, annualized, by mid-March employment. The column headed 'Emp / Est' shows 'employees per establishment'. A dash (-) means that data are unavailable or cannot be calculated. nec means not elsewhere classified. *Notes:* 1. 1994 data incomplete; unavailable or withheld. 2. 1995 data incomplete; unavailable or withheld. 3. 1994 and 1995 data incomplete; unavailable or withheld.

GRAND FORKS MSA (ND PART)

Wholesale and Retail Trade USA	Establishments		Employment		Emp / Est	Pay / Employee		Annual Payroll ($ 000)	
	1994	1995	1994	1995	1995	1994	1995	1994	1995
50 - Wholesale trade	157	158	1,585	1,673	11	22,943	24,557	39,289	42,175
5013 Motor vehicle supplies and new parts	-	12	-	93	8	-	19,914	-	1,838
5020 Furniture and homefurnishings	3	3	69	80	27	19,594	23,300	1,609	1,897
5040 Professional & commercial equipment	7	6	67	64	11	22,627	21,938	1,648	1,631
5063 Electrical apparatus and equipment	-	3	-	60	20	-	38,333	-	2,125
5065 Electronic parts and equipment	-	5	-	11	2	-	33,091	-	405
5083 Farm and garden machinery	13	12	143	149	12	22,182	22,738	3,846	3,787
5084 Industrial machinery and equipment	5	6	27	29	5	24,296	24,414	768	839
5087 Service establishment equipment	5	5	51	64	13	38,039	21,125	1,509	1,541
5092 Toys and hobby goods and supplies	3	3	9	10	3	15,111	15,200	261	246
5110 Paper and paper products	-	3	-	13	4	-	34,154	-	525
5140 Groceries and related products	11	11	233	218	20	14,094	16,679	3,735	3,820
5153 Grain and field beans	18	-	120	-	-	30,067	-	3,357	-
5170 Petroleum and petroleum products	14	10	91	74	7	15,648	16,486	1,749	1,426
5180 Beer, wine, and distilled beverages	6	6	60	66	11	20,333	23,636	1,859	2,105
5191 Farm supplies	13	15	85	96	6	53,318	67,167	3,453	4,277
5199 Nondurable goods, nec	4	-	21	-	-	10,857	-	264	-
52 - Retail trade	481	469	8,143	8,223	18	10,149	10,311	89,081	91,246
5210 Lumber and other building materials	8	11	227	233	21	21,850	21,150	4,607	4,663
5250 Hardware stores	3	-	24	-	-	5,000	-	154	-
5260 Retail nurseries and garden stores	7	-	78	-	-	8,462	-	962	-
5310 Department stores	6	6	1,079	1,070	178	9,427	10,329	11,204	11,664
5410 Grocery stores	22	23	811	879	38	8,178	8,819	8,046	8,950
5460 Retail bakeries	4	-	42	-	-	8,190	-	366	-
5490 Miscellaneous food stores	4	5	21	23	5	6,095	6,261	129	153
5510 New and used car dealers	9	10	474	466	47	24,793	23,974	13,223	12,634
5520 Used car dealers	6	5	29	46	9	18,345	16,783	818	1,041
5530 Auto and home supply stores	8	7	92	78	11	16,348	19,744	1,609	1,728
5540 Gasoline service stations	34	38	321	405	11	11,227	10,015	3,827	4,450
5550 Boat dealers	3	-	19	-	-	13,053	-	308	-
5610 Men's & boys' clothing stores	6	5	74	62	12	11,892	11,548	664	784
5620 Women's clothing stores	25	21	233	139	7	6,747	7,799	1,730	1,140
5630 Women's accessory & specialty stores	4	-	18	-	-	8,444	-	136	-
5650 Family clothing stores	6	6	80	90	15	7,350	8,133	679	739
5660 Shoe stores	15	12	90	83	7	9,867	11,614	957	1,084
5712 Furniture stores	9	7	45	44	6	16,000	15,364	741	611
5713 Floor covering stores	4	3	21	28	9	14,286	12,143	356	396
5719 Misc. homefurnishings stores	9	9	64	65	7	13,125	17,046	1,036	1,177
5720 Household appliance stores	4	4	16	20	5	20,250	16,000	343	363
5735 Record & prerecorded tape stores	5	5	44	32	6	7,455	9,125	315	266
5812 Eating places	102	94	2,532	2,554	27	6,269	6,224	17,368	17,479
5813 Drinking places	29	28	273	331	12	6,125	6,127	1,874	1,862
5910 Drug stores and proprietary stores	10	10	80	88	9	16,900	17,864	1,584	1,824
5920 Liquor stores	10	10	112	116	12	9,607	9,069	1,183	1,244
5930 Used merchandise stores	8	8	25	25	3	7,840	8,640	228	232
5941 Sporting goods and bicycle shops	9	8	162	144	18	13,827	10,917	1,835	1,652
5944 Jewelry stores	11	11	72	70	6	12,111	13,257	879	934
5945 Hobby, toy, and game shops	6	4	45	31	8	5,244	7,613	284	269
5947 Gift, novelty, and souvenir shops	16	18	119	96	5	5,681	6,917	909	975
5949 Sewing, needlework, and piece goods	4	3	49	17	6	6,041	6,824	327	128
5963 Direct selling establishments	3	3	10	8	3	2,400	2,000	98	74
5992 Florists	9	-	50	-	-	7,200	-	364	-
5999 Miscellaneous retail stores, nec	11	14	93	105	8	9,462	8,990	903	739

Source: County Business Patterns 1994/95, CBP-94/95, U.S. Department of Commerce, Washington DC, November 1997. The employment column represents mid-March employment in the year. Pay per employee is calculated by dividing 1st Quarter payroll, annualized, by mid-March employment. The column headed 'Emp / Est' shows 'employees per establishment'. A dash (-) means that data are unavailable or cannot be calculated. nec means not elsewhere classified. *Notes:* 1. 1994 data incomplete; unavailable or withheld. 2. 1995 data incomplete; unavailable or withheld. 3. 1994 and 1995 data incomplete; unavailable or withheld.

GRAND FORKS, ND - MN MSA

Wholesale and Retail Trade USA	Establishments		Employment		Emp / Est	Pay / Employee		Annual Payroll ($ 000)	
	1994	1995	1994	1995	1995	1994	1995	1994	1995
50 - Wholesale trade	243	239	2,268	2,427	10	22,377	24,142	56,636	60,783
5013 Motor vehicle supplies and new parts	-	18	-	93	5	-	19,914	-	1,838
5020 Furniture and homefurnishings[3]	3	3	69	80	27	19,594	23,300	1,609	1,897
5040 Professional & commercial equipment	9	8	67	64	8	22,627	21,938	1,648	1,631
5063 Electrical apparatus and equipment	-	4	-	60	15	-	38,333	-	2,125
5065 Electronic parts and equipment	-	7	-	11	2	-	33,091	-	405
5083 Farm and garden machinery[2]	22	20	236	149	7	20,644	22,738	6,172	3,787

Continued on next page.

GRAND FORKS, ND - MN MSA - [continued]

Wholesale and Retail Trade USA	Establishments		Employment		Emp / Est	Pay / Employee		Annual Payroll ($ 000)	
	1994	1995	1994	1995	1995	1994	1995	1994	1995
5084 Industrial machinery and equipment[3]	5	6	27	29	5	24,296	24,414	768	839
5087 Service establishment equipment	7	7	51	64	9	38,039	21,125	1,509	1,541
5092 Toys and hobby goods and supplies[2]	4	3	9	10	3	15,111	15,200	261	246
5110 Paper and paper products	-	6	-	13	2	-	34,154	-	525
5140 Groceries and related products	18	17	437	439	26	18,947	20,948	9,498	9,777
5153 Grain and field beans	34	-	120	-	-	30,067	-	3,357	-
5171 Petroleum bulk stations & terminals	-	17	-	82	5	-	17,561	-	1,520
5180 Beer, wine, and distilled beverages	8	8	60	66	8	20,333	23,636	1,859	2,105
5191 Farm supplies[2]	30	31	176	96	3	35,250	67,167	5,943	4,277
5199 Nondurable goods, nec[1]	4	-	21	-	-	10,857	-	264	-
52- Retail trade	684	676	10,355	10,464	15	9,849	10,138	110,513	114,033
5210 Lumber and other building materials	14	19	300	340	18	22,187	21,706	6,408	6,680
5250 Hardware stores	9	-	24	-	-	5,000	-	154	-
5260 Retail nurseries and garden stores	9	-	78	-	-	8,462	-	962	-
5310 Department stores[3]	6	6	1,079	1,070	178	9,427	10,329	11,204	11,664
5410 Grocery stores[3]	40	42	811	879	21	8,178	8,819	8,046	8,950
5460 Retail bakeries	5	-	42	-	-	8,190	-	366	-
5490 Miscellaneous food stores[3]	4	5	21	23	5	6,095	6,261	129	153
5510 New and used car dealers	14	15	568	562	37	23,866	23,068	15,194	14,589
5520 Used car dealers	10	9	38	46	5	16,737	16,783	935	1,041
5530 Auto and home supply stores	13	13	92	116	9	16,348	20,414	1,609	2,653
5540 Gasoline service stations	52	59	414	517	9	10,928	9,934	4,789	5,615
5550 Boat dealers	4	-	19	-	-	13,053	-	308	-
5610 Men's & boys' clothing stores	9	8	86	62	8	11,442	11,548	774	784
5620 Women's clothing stores	27	24	233	144	6	6,747	7,806	1,730	1,202
5630 Women's accessory & specialty stores[1]	4	-	18	-	-	8,444	-	136	-
5650 Family clothing stores	7	7	80	90	13	7,350	8,133	679	739
5660 Shoe stores[3]	15	12	90	83	7	9,867	11,614	957	1,084
5712 Furniture stores	13	10	45	59	6	16,000	14,508	741	782
5713 Floor covering stores	8	6	21	28	5	14,286	12,143	356	396
5719 Misc. homefurnishings stores	10	10	64	65	7	13,125	17,046	1,036	1,177
5720 Household appliance stores	6	7	16	20	3	20,250	16,000	343	363
5735 Record & prerecorded tape stores	7	7	44	32	5	7,455	9,125	315	266
5812 Eating places	152	142	3,416	3,398	24	6,139	6,181	22,906	23,075
5813 Drinking places	38	36	373	401	11	5,555	5,786	2,307	2,149
5910 Drug stores and proprietary stores	18	19	149	159	8	13,584	14,541	2,405	2,800
5920 Liquor stores	16	16	200	208	13	8,740	8,481	1,890	1,979
5930 Used merchandise stores	10	10	25	25	3	7,840	8,640	228	232
5941 Sporting goods and bicycle shops	10	9	162	144	16	13,827	10,917	1,835	1,652
5944 Jewelry stores	13	13	72	70	5	12,111	13,257	879	934
5945 Hobby, toy, and game shops[3]	6	4	45	31	8	5,244	7,613	284	269
5947 Gift, novelty, and souvenir shops	18	21	119	96	5	5,681	6,917	909	975
5949 Sewing, needlework, and piece goods[3]	4	3	49	17	6	6,041	6,824	327	128
5963 Direct selling establishments	8	6	10	8	1	2,400	2,000	98	74
5992 Florists	14	13	75	25	2	6,933	5,920	538	172
5995 Optical goods stores	12	11	17	14	1	11,529	14,286	171	167
5999 Miscellaneous retail stores, nec[3]	11	14	93	105	8	9,462	8,990	903	739

Source: County Business Patterns 1994/95, CBP-94/95, U.S. Department of Commerce, Washington DC, November 1997. The employment column represents mid-March employment in the year. Pay per employee is calculated by dividing 1st Quarter payroll, annualized, by mid-March employment. The column headed 'Emp / Est' shows 'employees per establishment'. A dash (-) means that data are unavailable or cannot be calculated. nec means not elsewhere classified. *Notes:* 1. 1994 data incomplete; unavailable or withheld. 2. 1995 data incomplete; unavailable or withheld. 3. 1994 and 1995 data incomplete; unavailable or withheld.

GRAND RAPIDS - MUSKEGON - HOLLAND, MI MSA

Wholesale and Retail Trade USA	Establishments		Employment		Emp / Est	Pay / Employee		Annual Payroll ($ 000)	
	1994	1995	1994	1995	1995	1994	1995	1994	1995
50- Wholesale trade	2,095	2,146	35,962	38,448	18	28,197	30,858	1,134,860	1,254,246
5012 Automobiles and other vehicles	40	45	979	1,209	27	33,446	36,321	36,462	43,102
5013 Motor vehicle supplies and new parts	132	123	1,626	1,843	15	24,920	26,843	49,363	56,217
5014 Tires and tubes[3]	15	11	137	133	12	22,102	24,782	3,573	3,636
5015 Motor vehicle parts, used	23	32	91	171	5	20,703	20,912	2,134	3,749
5021 Furniture	40	38	682	702	18	39,150	44,353	32,201	31,532
5023 Homefurnishings[3]	26	29	235	244	8	27,609	29,426	7,275	7,896
5031 Lumber, plywood, and millwork	46	44	956	776	18	35,795	37,175	33,726	28,203
5032 Brick, stone, & related materials[3]	16	20	134	162	8	27,612	26,099	4,601	4,750
5033 Roofing, siding, & insulation[3]	22	19	290	251	13	25,710	27,952	10,257	9,138
5039 Construction materials, nec	17	39	66	532	14	20,909	33,256	1,960	14,987
5043 Photographic equipment & supplies[1]	8	-	8	-	-	16,500	-	149	-
5044 Office equipment[3]	30	34	539	546	16	31,161	33,912	16,862	17,318

Continued on next page.

GRAND RAPIDS – MUSKEGON – HOLLAND, MI MSA - [continued]

Wholesale and Retail Trade USA	Establishments		Employment		Emp / Est	Pay / Employee		Annual Payroll ($ 000)	
	1994	1995	1994	1995	1995	1994	1995	1994	1995
5045 Computers, peripherals, & software [3]	50	54	476	514	10	44,059	50,778	23,120	25,252
5046 Commercial equipment, nec [3]	24	27	193	200	7	22,653	30,340	5,723	6,937
5047 Medical and hospital equipment	30	28	312	299	11	45,949	48,013	12,059	12,101
5048 Ophthalmic goods [3]	7	9	290	303	34	18,731	21,043	6,176	7,464
5049 Professional equipment, nec [1]	10	-	38	-	-	18,211	-	703	-
5051 Metals service centers and offices	62	65	1,265	1,480	23	31,181	32,854	44,643	50,835
5063 Electrical apparatus and equipment [1]	82	76	753	978	13	35,633	38,106	28,676	36,256
5064 Electrical appliances, TV & radios [3]	11	8	58	61	8	27,931	28,131	1,987	1,893
5065 Electronic parts and equipment	56	66	425	488	7	33,751	33,992	15,507	16,623
5072 Hardware [3]	43	46	1,041	1,131	25	27,785	27,742	33,465	35,916
5074 Plumbing & hydronic heating supplies	42	39	521	565	14	27,378	28,368	15,748	17,373
5075 Warm air heating & air conditioning [3]	33	30	72	84	3	22,500	23,619	1,876	2,295
5082 Construction and mining machinery	21	20	343	297	15	37,516	43,219	14,537	13,887
5083 Farm and garden machinery	31	27	465	413	15	27,054	33,443	14,975	14,913
5084 Industrial machinery and equipment	184	183	1,848	2,122	12	33,944	37,698	71,996	87,935
5085 Industrial supplies	99	103	838	941	9	35,594	38,087	34,338	41,781
5087 Service establishment equipment [1]	33	36	400	412	11	27,090	26,922	11,830	13,550
5088 Transportation equipment & supplies [1]	10	10	156	133	13	22,282	21,143	3,784	3,178
5091 Sporting & recreational goods	27	27	121	128	5	22,645	23,531	3,710	4,346
5092 Toys and hobby goods and supplies [1]	6	-	16	-	-	7,750	-	141	-
5093 Scrap and waste materials	37	34	439	410	12	29,813	30,507	15,389	15,220
5094 Jewelry & precious stones [1]	7	-	24	-	-	20,333	-	861	-
5099 Durable goods, nec	57	57	912	786	14	21,522	23,293	20,534	18,871
5111 Printing and writing paper [3]	10	11	180	193	18	38,489	44,622	7,740	8,636
5112 Stationery and office supplies	50	42	757	762	18	19,081	23,822	16,887	19,709
5113 Industrial & personal service paper [2]	18	18	203	232	13	29,419	36,086	6,754	8,641
5120 Drugs, proprietaries, and sundries [3]	12	14	82	100	7	29,854	30,320	2,753	3,338
5131 Piece goods & notions [3]	16	14	497	251	18	14,889	31,920	7,315	7,857
5141 Groceries, general line	29	31	2,900	3,401	110	24,709	25,997	75,944	92,968
5142 Packaged frozen food [3]	18	18	627	677	38	30,922	33,235	19,727	22,518
5145 Confectionery [3]	19	19	327	304	16	20,012	24,289	7,929	8,779
5147 Meats and meat products	14	14	78	93	7	21,179	25,204	1,969	2,256
5148 Fresh fruits and vegetables	34	35	667	785	22	23,928	22,726	18,955	20,402
5149 Groceries and related products, nec	43	44	3,144	3,017	69	28,000	30,088	97,134	98,132
5153 Grain and field beans [1]	7	-	32	-	-	14,750	-	406	-
5154 Livestock [1]	7	-	32	-	-	2,500	-	80	-
5162 Plastics materials & basic shapes [1]	30	31	183	196	6	28,372	34,796	6,305	6,957
5169 Chemicals & allied products, nec	39	45	500	603	13	36,264	37,897	20,006	24,336
5171 Petroleum bulk stations & terminals [3]	28	26	115	117	5	27,478	29,094	3,628	3,945
5172 Petroleum products, nec [3]	10	9	36	41	5	31,222	28,780	1,489	1,698
5181 Beer and ale	13	13	268	275	21	28,269	28,349	9,519	12,287
5182 Wine and distilled beverages	7	7	95	92	13	26,021	27,565	2,648	2,769
5191 Farm supplies	41	35	333	308	9	21,309	23,636	7,838	8,363
5192 Books, periodicals, & newspapers [3]	16	15	333	410	27	26,859	30,068	9,352	12,530
5193 Flowers & florists' supplies [2]	-	13	-	30	2	-	28,800	-	1,118
5198 Paints, varnishes, and supplies [3]	17	13	215	141	11	32,707	36,652	7,403	5,594
5199 Nondurable goods, nec	59	61	493	573	9	24,535	30,960	9,617	12,447
52 – Retail trade	5,330	5,308	85,925	90,109	17	12,195	13,016	1,170,951	1,272,475
5210 Lumber and other building materials	110	99	1,951	2,257	23	21,841	22,857	50,848	51,826
5230 Paint, glass, and wallpaper stores	31	31	188	185	6	18,596	20,670	3,824	4,192
5250 Hardware stores	80	66	714	606	9	13,899	12,607	11,140	8,507
5260 Retail nurseries and garden stores	41	40	341	359	9	13,537	14,930	6,322	6,535
5270 Mobile home dealers	23	26	126	168	6	15,206	22,405	2,801	5,075
5310 Department stores [3]	41	41	10,562	11,264	275	10,516	10,973	126,885	139,649
5330 Variety stores	32	30	253	228	8	7,494	7,754	2,193	2,009
5390 Misc. general merchandise stores [3]	40	40	1,422	1,458	36	11,494	12,250	17,322	16,891
5410 Grocery stores	385	368	9,982	10,196	28	9,803	9,930	103,510	105,840
5420 Meat and fish markets [3]	23	24	135	128	5	8,741	9,469	1,268	1,398
5430 Fruit and vegetable markets	10	9	55	48	5	9,164	10,167	657	593
5440 Candy, nut, and confectionery stores	20	18	93	86	5	7,742	9,581	873	890
5460 Retail bakeries	88	81	557	502	6	6,564	6,940	3,891	3,636
5490 Miscellaneous food stores [3]	23	18	124	93	5	9,000	10,624	1,294	1,311
5510 New and used car dealers	94	93	3,776	3,985	43	28,925	30,333	127,469	135,346
5520 Used car dealers	89	90	254	287	3	18,630	18,969	5,654	5,929
5530 Auto and home supply stores	137	145	963	1,048	7	16,042	18,073	17,457	20,176
5540 Gasoline service stations	317	299	2,893	2,816	9	9,716	10,845	30,331	32,441
5550 Boat dealers	31	32	239	353	11	15,816	15,241	6,666	7,528
5560 Recreational vehicle dealers	26	26	174	193	7	23,747	26,280	5,620	6,420
5570 Motorcycle dealers [3]	12	11	85	102	9	21,271	23,373	2,066	2,342
5610 Men's & boys' clothing stores	37	36	467	425	12	11,246	12,904	5,509	4,207
5620 Women's clothing stores	148	134	1,761	1,600	12	8,261	7,828	15,416	12,624

Continued on next page.

GRAND RAPIDS – MUSKEGON – HOLLAND, MI MSA - [continued]

Wholesale and Retail Trade USA	Establishments		Employment		Emp / Est	Pay / Employee		Annual Payroll ($ 000)	
	1994	1995	1994	1995	1995	1994	1995	1994	1995
5630 Women's accessory & specialty stores	27	27	134	121	4	8,776	10,810	1,276	1,304
5640 Children's and infants' wear stores[3]	14	17	89	152	9	6,022	7,079	610	1,055
5650 Family clothing stores	65	59	1,383	1,275	22	11,948	12,668	15,650	15,876
5660 Shoe stores	115	112	673	659	6	11,596	12,734	8,374	8,149
5690 Misc. apparel & accessory stores	21	21	95	114	5	8,800	10,211	1,129	1,353
5712 Furniture stores	105	108	1,149	1,270	12	19,979	21,890	24,112	29,662
5713 Floor covering stores	60	60	485	524	9	21,674	23,779	11,507	12,316
5714 Drapery and upholstery stores[3]	7	10	22	26	3	10,909	12,154	309	389
5719 Misc. homefurnishings stores	68	65	412	445	7	11,369	12,072	5,368	5,983
5720 Household appliance stores	38	39	395	401	10	18,096	20,479	8,729	9,003
5731 Radio, TV, & electronic stores	60	58	514	601	10	19,315	17,344	10,695	10,184
5734 Computer and software stores[2]	25	25	83	130	5	17,398	18,985	1,706	2,804
5735 Record & prerecorded tape stores	22	25	119	153	6	10,151	9,516	1,251	1,685
5736 Musical instrument stores[3]	18	18	145	160	9	15,614	17,050	2,505	2,757
5812 Eating places	1,172	1,097	24,989	25,360	23	6,804	7,318	191,321	197,796
5813 Drinking places	164	156	1,318	1,305	8	7,457	7,617	10,446	10,460
5910 Drug stores and proprietary stores	152	144	1,994	2,117	15	13,751	14,182	28,763	32,334
5920 Liquor stores	67	65	360	327	5	7,378	8,024	2,833	2,947
5930 Used merchandise stores	64	61	281	275	5	9,779	9,004	3,049	2,508
5941 Sporting goods and bicycle shops	110	123	691	791	6	13,569	13,613	9,761	11,300
5942 Book stores	53	48	689	712	15	14,775	15,309	10,431	11,425
5943 Stationery stores[3]	10	13	30	79	6	9,200	9,418	269	777
5944 Jewelry stores	70	72	438	446	6	15,169	15,937	6,994	7,359
5945 Hobby, toy, and game shops	38	41	292	297	7	9,205	10,613	3,241	3,825
5946 Camera & photographic supply stores[3]	11	11	40	50	5	16,600	15,760	656	822
5947 Gift, novelty, and souvenir shops	125	116	652	635	5	6,939	7,376	5,782	5,690
5948 Luggage and leather goods stores[3]	9	10	45	49	5	10,933	9,878	462	491
5949 Sewing, needlework, and piece goods[1]	34	31	441	327	11	6,295	7,193	2,810	2,421
5961 Catalog and mail-order houses[3]	19	24	826	997	42	16,160	16,124	12,715	17,382
5962 Merchandising machine operators[3]	20	21	296	304	14	20,973	20,250	6,848	7,909
5963 Direct selling establishments	51	54	311	389	7	13,994	13,789	5,407	5,764
5984 Liquefied petroleum gas dealers	20	-	25	-	-	30,560	-	707	-
5992 Florists	87	83	709	736	9	10,336	11,647	7,881	8,580
5995 Optical goods stores	72	75	324	321	4	20,235	20,312	6,899	7,387
5999 Miscellaneous retail stores, nec	160	163	850	942	6	12,489	13,762	13,403	14,942

Source: County Business Patterns 1994/95, CBP-94/95, U.S. Department of Commerce, Washington DC, November 1997. The employment column represents mid-March employment in the year. Pay per employee is calculated by dividing 1st Quarter payroll, annualized, by mid-March employment. The column headed 'Emp / Est' shows 'employees per establishment'. A dash (-) means that data are unavailable or cannot be calculated. nec means not elsewhere classified. *Notes:* 1. 1994 data incomplete; unavailable or withheld. 2. 1995 data incomplete; unavailable or withheld. 3. 1994 and 1995 data incomplete; unavailable or withheld.

GREAT FALLS, MT MSA

Wholesale and Retail Trade USA	Establishments		Employment		Emp / Est	Pay / Employee		Annual Payroll ($ 000)	
	1994	1995	1994	1995	1995	1994	1995	1994	1995
50 – Wholesale trade	188	187	1,917	1,895	10	22,416	24,000	46,020	47,636
5012 Automobiles and other vehicles	7	6	57	59	10	23,649	25,085	1,453	1,615
5013 Motor vehicle supplies and new parts	12	8	124	92	12	19,806	20,000	2,515	1,898
5020 Furniture and homefurnishings	7	-	46	-	-	16,435	-	928	-
5031 Lumber, plywood, and millwork	4	-	90	-	-	26,978	-	2,383	-
5044 Office equipment	5	5	48	48	10	18,917	20,167	944	1,005
5045 Computers, peripherals, & software	4	4	51	50	13	25,961	30,560	1,339	1,561
5049 Professional equipment, nec	-	3	-	45	15	-	27,733	-	1,006
5063 Electrical apparatus and equipment	4	-	38	-	-	22,842	-	766	-
5075 Warm air heating & air conditioning	-	4	-	16	4	-	35,250	-	696
5082 Construction and mining machinery	6	7	78	84	12	30,615	32,286	2,898	2,754
5083 Farm and garden machinery	7	6	68	70	12	20,824	17,086	1,441	1,396
5084 Industrial machinery and equipment	4	-	16	-	-	19,500	-	396	-
5087 Service establishment equipment	-	5	-	24	5	-	19,833	-	474
5093 Scrap and waste materials	7	7	149	147	21	21,208	22,857	3,078	4,301
5112 Stationery and office supplies	3	-	15	-	-	22,133	-	362	-
5149 Groceries and related products, nec	6	-	87	-	-	20,644	-	1,950	-
5150 Farm-product raw materials	10	10	85	95	10	20,941	30,526	2,032	2,572
5170 Petroleum and petroleum products	9	9	86	81	9	19,163	19,605	1,682	1,740
5181 Beer and ale	4	4	85	78	20	22,824	24,513	2,072	1,974
5191 Farm supplies	14	15	123	112	7	23,610	27,500	2,902	2,990
5199 Nondurable goods, nec	-	3	-	6	2	-	8,667	-	55
52 – Retail trade	630	642	7,640	8,151	13	12,071	11,654	98,229	103,464
5210 Lumber and other building materials	7	8	41	215	27	35,707	18,195	1,437	4,084
5230 Paint, glass, and wallpaper stores	5	4	31	14	4	17,677	21,143	455	289

Continued on next page.

GREAT FALLS, MT MSA - [continued]

Wholesale and Retail Trade USA	Establishments		Employment		Emp / Est	Pay / Employee		Annual Payroll ($ 000)	
	1994	1995	1994	1995	1995	1994	1995	1994	1995
5250 Hardware stores	7	4	66	58	15	14,545	13,241	1,072	767
5310 Department stores	8	8	922	936	117	9,462	10,611	9,581	10,426
5410 Grocery stores	30	32	729	745	23	13,454	14,078	10,892	10,961
5460 Retail bakeries	7	5	26	25	5	10,308	10,400	285	250
5490 Miscellaneous food stores	5	-	12	-	-	7,000	-	91	-
5510 New and used car dealers	9	6	419	339	57	25,699	26,985	10,672	9,177
5520 Used car dealers	16	16	88	99	6	21,364	16,364	1,713	1,647
5530 Auto and home supply stores	17	19	122	141	7	15,639	16,312	2,079	2,503
5540 Gasoline service stations	37	38	247	277	7	10,283	10,022	2,689	2,862
5570 Motorcycle dealers	4	4	27	28	7	10,667	11,286	333	349
5620 Women's clothing stores	15	14	128	102	7	8,906	7,569	1,265	852
5650 Family clothing stores	6	8	83	72	9	14,120	14,500	1,096	1,130
5660 Shoe stores	13	12	72	63	5	10,333	11,111	708	672
5690 Misc. apparel & accessory stores	5	5	8	10	2	8,000	8,000	93	80
5712 Furniture stores	17	16	129	122	8	13,147	14,000	1,846	1,704
5713 Floor covering stores	6	8	40	61	8	19,900	19,541	878	1,505
5720 Household appliance stores	7	6	62	72	12	16,710	16,667	1,078	1,137
5731 Radio, TV, & electronic stores	7	9	32	28	3	25,625	21,857	918	708
5735 Record & prerecorded tape stores	5	5	67	56	11	8,955	10,000	572	550
5812 Eating places	157	146	2,339	2,480	17	7,384	7,558	18,845	19,777
5813 Drinking places	68	61	511	534	9	7,601	7,648	4,323	4,405
5910 Drug stores and proprietary stores	9	8	138	165	21	12,377	11,709	2,012	2,395
5930 Used merchandise stores	13	12	67	58	5	12,776	13,793	884	750
5941 Sporting goods and bicycle shops	16	15	114	123	8	11,684	12,358	1,452	1,465
5942 Book stores	-	3	-	16	5	-	7,750	-	125
5943 Stationery stores	-	3	-	21	7	-	15,238	-	337
5944 Jewelry stores	8	11	41	47	4	14,146	16,426	562	660
5945 Hobby, toy, and game shops	9	8	43	44	6	9,767	10,455	472	490
5947 Gift, novelty, and souvenir shops	18	18	60	69	4	5,400	5,449	456	477
5949 Sewing, needlework, and piece goods	5	-	33	-	-	7,273	-	304	-
5960 Nonstore retailers	12	11	68	62	6	20,412	21,935	1,509	1,211
5992 Florists	8	10	62	54	5	6,903	8,815	460	440
5999 Miscellaneous retail stores, nec	16	21	56	89	4	11,214	9,708	649	948

Source: County Business Patterns 1994/95, CBP-94/95, U.S. Department of Commerce, Washington DC, November 1997. The employment column represents mid-March employment in the year. Pay per employee is calculated by dividing 1st Quarter payroll, annualized, by mid-March employment. The column headed 'Emp / Est' shows 'employees per establishment'. A dash (-) means that data are unavailable or cannot be calculated. nec means not elsewhere classified. *Notes:* 1. 1994 data incomplete; unavailable or withheld. 2. 1995 data incomplete; unavailable or withheld. 3. 1994 and 1995 data incomplete; unavailable or withheld.

GREELEY, CO PMSA

Wholesale and Retail Trade USA	Establishments		Employment		Emp / Est	Pay / Employee		Annual Payroll ($ 000)	
	1994	1995	1994	1995	1995	1994	1995	1994	1995
50- Wholesale trade	272	285	2,873	3,178	11	23,659	24,491	75,477	82,484
5012 Automobiles and other vehicles	10	8	73	79	10	29,370	27,848	1,968	2,038
5013 Motor vehicle supplies and new parts	16	16	110	133	8	15,527	17,323	1,873	2,438
5014 Tires and tubes	5	5	43	51	10	19,535	33,725	1,185	1,304
5015 Motor vehicle parts, used	9	10	40	42	4	21,200	20,286	915	895
5020 Furniture and homefurnishings	5	6	31	33	6	18,194	20,000	568	687
5039 Construction materials, nec	-	3	-	26	9	-	22,615	-	751
5044 Office equipment	-	5	-	38	8	-	19,158	-	891
5047 Medical and hospital equipment	5	-	15	-	-	21,600	-	528	-
5050 Metals and minerals, except petroleum	5	-	116	-	-	24,517	-	3,351	-
5060 Electrical goods	7	5	56	46	9	16,500	20,087	1,021	1,039
5072 Hardware	6	6	26	30	5	14,615	16,800	468	551
5083 Farm and garden machinery	23	25	262	300	12	27,985	28,960	7,042	8,033
5084 Industrial machinery and equipment	-	16	-	71	4	-	27,268	-	1,730
5085 Industrial supplies	8	8	66	75	9	34,909	39,893	2,204	2,522
5091 Sporting & recreational goods	4	4	45	47	12	4,889	7,149	288	360
5093 Scrap and waste materials	8	9	63	80	9	22,921	20,350	1,603	1,936
5110 Paper and paper products	7	9	97	98	11	20,742	21,633	2,352	2,760
5147 Meats and meat products	3	3	34	43	14	24,941	22,419	880	1,207
5148 Fresh fruits and vegetables	7	8	107	90	11	17,981	20,667	2,941	2,847
5149 Groceries and related products, nec	4	4	132	134	34	26,091	26,478	3,313	3,540
5153 Grain and field beans	21	21	175	219	10	22,331	18,941	4,524	4,444
5154 Livestock	-	4	-	45	11	-	15,467	-	783
5159 Farm-product raw materials, nec	-	3	-	7	2	-	21,714	-	170
5169 Chemicals & allied products, nec	7	7	55	67	10	21,818	19,284	1,422	1,397
5171 Petroleum bulk stations & terminals	10	9	97	110	12	19,876	19,745	2,108	2,264
5172 Petroleum products, nec	3	3	12	19	6	52,000	31,789	738	712

Continued on next page.

GREELEY, CO PMSA - [continued]

Wholesale and Retail Trade USA	Establishments		Employment		Emp / Est	Pay / Employee		Annual Payroll ($ 000)	
	1994	1995	1994	1995	1995	1994	1995	1994	1995
5181 Beer and ale	4	4	57	71	18	28,140	26,423	1,798	1,337
5190 Misc., nondurable goods	31	30	740	756	25	24,627	27,614	21,079	22,700
52- Retail trade	691	718	9,101	9,648	13	11,266	11,960	112,959	121,338
5210 Lumber and other building materials	11	9	203	227	25	13,695	19,665	3,568	4,175
5230 Paint, glass, and wallpaper stores	6	-	25	-	-	21,280	-	602	-
5250 Hardware stores	5	6	41	51	9	14,049	11,686	668	666
5260 Retail nurseries and garden stores	4	-	16	-	-	7,500	-	193	-
5270 Mobile home dealers	4	6	18	24	4	24,889	21,500	695	886
5300 General merchandise stores	11	9	989	1,072	119	11,304	12,201	13,258	12,941
5410 Grocery stores	43	47	1,195	1,579	34	15,635	15,184	21,071	23,905
5460 Retail bakeries	9	7	56	46	7	9,857	10,696	589	493
5490 Miscellaneous food stores	-	5	-	13	3	-	8,923	-	122
5510 New and used car dealers	16	16	594	521	33	24,673	26,987	15,820	15,445
5520 Used car dealers	15	15	39	42	3	23,590	18,190	941	932
5530 Auto and home supply stores	20	19	130	139	7	18,185	18,475	2,400	2,562
5540 Gasoline service stations	50	51	336	365	7	10,036	9,721	3,639	4,073
5560 Recreational vehicle dealers	-	7	-	106	15	-	20,755	-	2,612
5570 Motorcycle dealers	3	3	20	24	8	15,000	14,500	476	564
5610 Men's & boys' clothing stores	-	3	-	15	5	-	8,000	-	122
5620 Women's clothing stores	13	11	119	97	9	8,571	6,598	1,100	683
5650 Family clothing stores	-	5	-	35	7	-	5,829	-	296
5660 Shoe stores	13	14	59	65	5	9,898	9,600	589	633
5690 Misc. apparel & accessory stores	3	3	8	5	2	4,500	8,800	38	37
5712 Furniture stores	12	12	78	65	5	14,359	20,369	1,373	1,750
5713 Floor covering stores	11	10	37	51	5	15,892	20,471	936	949
5719 Misc. homefurnishings stores	8	8	59	55	7	11,119	12,582	857	803
5720 Household appliance stores	6	5	29	24	5	15,586	19,333	456	479
5731 Radio, TV, & electronic stores	8	8	56	51	6	15,214	17,490	842	958
5735 Record & prerecorded tape stores	3	-	9	-	-	10,667	-	149	-
5736 Musical instrument stores	-	3	-	5	2	-	12,000	-	81
5812 Eating places	170	168	3,429	3,354	20	6,941	7,194	24,588	24,768
5813 Drinking places	35	30	213	160	5	5,052	6,100	1,070	1,010
5910 Drug stores and proprietary stores	11	11	141	124	11	12,993	15,419	1,778	1,938
5920 Liquor stores	25	26	120	115	4	7,833	8,696	1,083	1,062
5930 Used merchandise stores	10	10	61	42	4	10,426	12,286	712	603
5941 Sporting goods and bicycle shops	18	17	98	102	6	9,918	10,667	1,152	1,251
5942 Book stores	5	6	35	32	5	7,314	7,875	246	282
5944 Jewelry stores	6	7	32	41	6	23,875	19,902	676	741
5945 Hobby, toy, and game shops	5	4	16	51	13	10,500	9,882	245	522
5947 Gift, novelty, and souvenir shops	11	10	75	75	8	8,053	8,320	678	586
5949 Sewing, needlework, and piece goods	-	3	-	28	9	-	5,714	-	164
5962 Merchandising machine operators	5	6	105	110	18	11,848	13,018	1,465	1,617
5984 Liquefied petroleum gas dealers	4	4	15	19	5	11,200	10,947	175	188
5992 Florists	-	10	-	59	6	-	8,542	-	485
5995 Optical goods stores	6	7	17	26	4	16,706	17,692	360	521
5999 Miscellaneous retail stores, nec	25	28	87	160	6	10,943	12,300	1,178	2,105

Source: County Business Patterns 1994/95, CBP-94/95, U.S. Department of Commerce, Washington DC, November 1997. The employment column represents mid-March employment in the year. Pay per employee is calculated by dividing 1st Quarter payroll, annualized, by mid-March employment. The column headed 'Emp / Est' shows 'employees per establishment'. A dash (-) means that data are unavailable or cannot be calculated. nec means not elsewhere classified. *Notes:* 1. 1994 data incomplete; unavailable or withheld. 2. 1995 data incomplete; unavailable or withheld. 3. 1994 and 1995 data incomplete; unavailable or withheld.

GREEN BAY, WI MSA

Wholesale and Retail Trade USA	Establishments		Employment		Emp / Est	Pay / Employee		Annual Payroll ($ 000)	
	1994	1995	1994	1995	1995	1994	1995	1994	1995
50- Wholesale trade	-	537	-	7,879	15	-	29,696	-	239,804
5012 Automobiles and other vehicles	-	10	-	416	42	-	28,721	-	12,597
5013 Motor vehicle supplies and new parts	-	25	-	240	10	-	21,767	-	5,344
5021 Furniture	-	8	-	44	6	-	23,364	-	1,344
5023 Homefurnishings	-	10	-	92	9	-	20,435	-	1,811
5031 Lumber, plywood, and millwork	-	13	-	283	22	-	24,028	-	7,466
5032 Brick, stone, & related materials	-	4	-	32	8	-	30,500	-	1,174
5033 Roofing, siding, & insulation	-	7	-	248	35	-	46,903	-	11,490
5039 Construction materials, nec	-	11	-	102	9	-	27,804	-	3,587
5044 Office equipment	-	11	-	78	7	-	28,051	-	2,974
5045 Computers, peripherals, & software	-	14	-	255	18	-	61,051	-	11,369
5047 Medical and hospital equipment	-	9	-	116	13	-	33,138	-	3,435
5048 Ophthalmic goods	-	5	-	197	39	-	17,665	-	3,778
5051 Metals service centers and offices	-	8	-	84	11	-	49,952	-	3,404

Continued on next page.

GREEN BAY, WI MSA - [continued]

Wholesale and Retail Trade USA	Establishments		Employment		Emp / Est	Pay / Employee		Annual Payroll ($ 000)	
	1994	1995	1994	1995	1995	1994	1995	1994	1995
5052 Coal and other minerals and ores	-	3	-	24	8	-	32,833	-	779
5063 Electrical apparatus and equipment	-	29	-	368	13	-	33,924	-	11,713
5072 Hardware	-	9	-	344	38	-	28,570	-	10,376
5074 Plumbing & hydronic heating supplies	-	11	-	98	9	-	26,776	-	2,937
5075 Warm air heating & air conditioning	-	3	-	58	19	-	45,655	-	2,565
5078 Refrigeration equipment and supplies	-	5	-	61	12	-	26,230	-	1,750
5082 Construction and mining machinery	-	6	-	87	15	-	35,632	-	3,216
5083 Farm and garden machinery	-	10	-	95	10	-	24,126	-	2,455
5084 Industrial machinery and equipment	-	54	-	801	15	-	34,662	-	29,475
5085 Industrial supplies	-	17	-	182	11	-	38,945	-	7,384
5087 Service establishment equipment	-	15	-	96	6	-	22,708	-	2,414
5088 Transportation equipment & supplies	-	4	-	32	8	-	24,000	-	793
5091 Sporting & recreational goods	-	9	-	88	10	-	36,955	-	3,849
5093 Scrap and waste materials	-	17	-	274	16	-	24,978	-	7,478
5112 Stationery and office supplies	-	10	-	428	43	-	25,374	-	10,037
5136 Men's and boys' clothing	-	4	-	55	14	-	13,527	-	716
5142 Packaged frozen food	-	4	-	38	10	-	23,684	-	976
5143 Dairy products, exc. dried or canned	-	8	-	273	34	-	15,927	-	4,235
5146 Fish and seafoods	-	3	-	19	6	-	24,632	-	516
5147 Meats and meat products	-	3	-	79	26	-	25,823	-	2,241
5149 Groceries and related products, nec	-	15	-	332	22	-	28,048	-	10,783
5150 Farm-product raw materials	-	5	-	17	3	-	20,235	-	351
5160 Chemicals and allied products	-	10	-	69	7	-	36,290	-	2,575
5171 Petroleum bulk stations & terminals	-	13	-	137	11	-	25,343	-	3,830
5172 Petroleum products, nec	-	4	-	19	5	-	13,474	-	148
5181 Beer and ale	-	4	-	133	33	-	33,744	-	5,278
5191 Farm supplies	-	21	-	219	10	-	21,699	-	4,933
5193 Flowers & florists' supplies	-	4	-	27	7	-	18,074	-	557
5198 Paints, varnishes, and supplies	-	4	-	21	5	-	20,762	-	520
5199 Nondurable goods, nec	-	11	-	86	8	-	16,884	-	1,740
52 – Retail trade	-	1,339	-	22,534	17	-	13,028	-	307,290
5210 Lumber and other building materials	-	24	-	735	31	-	27,010	-	20,281
5230 Paint, glass, and wallpaper stores	-	14	-	69	5	-	16,754	-	1,226
5250 Hardware stores	-	10	-	100	10	-	14,600	-	1,527
5260 Retail nurseries and garden stores	-	6	-	91	15	-	9,538	-	947
5270 Mobile home dealers	-	5	-	34	7	-	19,059	-	1,208
5310 Department stores	-	19	-	2,940	155	-	11,476	-	33,721
5330 Variety stores	-	3	-	47	16	-	8,000	-	422
5390 Misc. general merchandise stores	-	4	-	354	89	-	20,893	-	8,002
5410 Grocery stores	-	50	-	2,306	46	-	10,134	-	24,993
5420 Meat and fish markets	-	9	-	53	6	-	10,868	-	699
5440 Candy, nut, and confectionery stores	-	6	-	59	10	-	12,678	-	924
5460 Retail bakeries	-	21	-	182	9	-	7,341	-	1,401
5490 Miscellaneous food stores	-	8	-	31	4	-	15,355	-	479
5510 New and used car dealers	-	19	-	1,175	62	-	28,347	-	36,975
5520 Used car dealers	-	32	-	117	4	-	17,368	-	2,207
5530 Auto and home supply stores	-	16	-	215	13	-	16,205	-	3,961
5540 Gasoline service stations	-	77	-	824	11	-	9,442	-	8,451
5550 Boat dealers	-	10	-	61	6	-	18,230	-	1,381
5560 Recreational vehicle dealers	-	3	-	18	6	-	17,778	-	344
5570 Motorcycle dealers	-	4	-	64	16	-	20,938	-	1,530
5610 Men's & boys' clothing stores	-	10	-	45	5	-	13,600	-	576
5620 Women's clothing stores	-	36	-	373	10	-	6,488	-	2,507
5630 Women's accessory & specialty stores	-	7	-	39	6	-	8,308	-	337
5640 Children's and infants' wear stores	-	4	-	14	4	-	8,857	-	152
5650 Family clothing stores	-	11	-	172	16	-	9,651	-	1,657
5660 Shoe stores	-	36	-	162	5	-	9,877	-	1,706
5690 Misc. apparel & accessory stores	-	10	-	69	7	-	6,261	-	490
5712 Furniture stores	-	30	-	308	10	-	20,896	-	7,131
5713 Floor covering stores	-	16	-	62	4	-	21,484	-	1,445
5714 Drapery and upholstery stores	-	3	-	4	1	-	11,000	-	65
5719 Misc. homefurnishings stores	-	13	-	71	5	-	11,324	-	979
5720 Household appliance stores	-	11	-	62	6	-	18,387	-	1,120
5731 Radio, TV, & electronic stores	-	15	-	212	14	-	17,717	-	3,271
5734 Computer and software stores	-	5	-	16	3	-	12,750	-	187
5735 Record & prerecorded tape stores	-	11	-	69	6	-	9,739	-	679
5736 Musical instrument stores	-	6	-	87	15	-	17,425	-	1,534
5812 Eating places	-	256	-	6,440	25	-	7,329	-	51,400
5813 Drinking places	-	107	-	500	5	-	6,248	-	3,283
5910 Drug stores and proprietary stores	-	19	-	271	14	-	17,299	-	4,897
5920 Liquor stores	-	32	-	159	5	-	9,283	-	1,516

Continued on next page.

GREEN BAY, WI MSA - [continued]

Wholesale and Retail Trade USA	Establishments		Employment		Emp / Est	Pay / Employee		Annual Payroll ($ 000)	
	1994	1995	1994	1995	1995	1994	1995	1994	1995
5930 Used merchandise stores	-	13	-	54	4	-	10,667	-	580
5941 Sporting goods and bicycle shops	-	34	-	308	9	-	11,545	-	3,711
5942 Book stores	-	12	-	77	6	-	7,429	-	630
5944 Jewelry stores	-	28	-	169	6	-	15,811	-	2,639
5945 Hobby, toy, and game shops	-	14	-	141	10	-	8,879	-	1,517
5947 Gift, novelty, and souvenir shops	-	35	-	222	6	-	6,414	-	1,432
5961 Catalog and mail-order houses	-	7	-	42	6	-	27,333	-	1,236
5962 Merchandising machine operators	-	4	-	85	21	-	26,306	-	2,451
5963 Direct selling establishments	-	17	-	119	7	-	18,622	-	2,366
5980 Fuel dealers	-	5	-	30	6	-	20,533	-	517
5992 Florists	-	14	-	82	6	-	9,463	-	798
5995 Optical goods stores	-	8	-	70	9	-	10,229	-	769
5999 Miscellaneous retail stores, nec	-	38	-	210	6	-	13,886	-	3,385

Source: County Business Patterns 1994/95, CBP-94/95, U.S. Department of Commerce, Washington DC, November 1997. The employment column represents mid-March employment in the year. Pay per employee is calculated by dividing 1st Quarter payroll, annualized, by mid-March employment. The column headed 'Emp / Est' shows 'employees per establishment'. A dash (-) means that data are unavailable or cannot be calculated. nec means not elsewhere classified. *Notes:* 1. 1994 data incomplete; unavailable or withheld. 2. 1995 data incomplete; unavailable or withheld. 3. 1994 and 1995 data incomplete; unavailable or withheld.

GREENSBORO – WINSTON-SALEM – HIGH POINT, NC MSA

Wholesale and Retail Trade USA	Establishments		Employment		Emp / Est	Pay / Employee		Annual Payroll ($ 000)	
	1994	1995	1994	1995	1995	1994	1995	1994	1995
50– Wholesale trade	2,768	2,820	34,274	36,036	13	28,793	31,713	1,073,194	1,180,370
5012 Automobiles and other vehicles	59	55	1,150	1,231	22	20,383	22,671	26,138	29,329
5013 Motor vehicle supplies and new parts[3]	142	129	1,220	1,362	11	22,784	24,975	30,216	35,400
5014 Tires and tubes[3]	21	20	524	468	23	23,145	24,812	13,047	11,937
5015 Motor vehicle parts, used[3]	26	31	86	155	5	17,395	17,316	1,662	2,802
5021 Furniture[3]	145	140	1,165	1,180	8	25,998	27,397	32,566	32,808
5023 Homefurnishings[3]	67	67	579	540	8	28,608	34,481	17,003	17,229
5031 Lumber, plywood, and millwork[3]	124	117	1,482	745	6	27,026	33,621	44,228	25,380
5032 Brick, stone, & related materials[3]	16	16	42	70	4	24,762	26,457	1,444	2,321
5033 Roofing, siding, & insulation[3]	18	18	167	238	13	27,808	26,538	5,921	6,820
5039 Construction materials, nec[3]	19	36	116	695	19	28,207	24,184	3,575	18,634
5044 Office equipment[3]	39	47	592	708	15	37,324	44,288	22,861	29,321
5045 Computers, peripherals, & software[3]	75	74	805	1,037	14	42,236	45,161	34,364	46,253
5046 Commercial equipment, nec[3]	24	26	171	213	8	28,398	30,272	6,149	8,031
5047 Medical and hospital equipment[3]	52	53	390	433	8	34,472	37,321	15,615	17,250
5048 Ophthalmic goods[3]	8	8	218	199	25	22,734	31,317	5,093	5,720
5051 Metals service centers and offices[3]	41	44	63	68	2	30,032	29,706	2,116	2,499
5063 Electrical apparatus and equipment[3]	94	86	928	863	10	36,082	37,136	33,703	33,015
5064 Electrical appliances, TV & radios[3]	13	13	133	123	9	24,722	30,081	3,718	3,820
5065 Electronic parts and equipment[3]	70	80	1,112	1,278	16	38,191	44,801	43,969	56,429
5072 Hardware[3]	49	51	965	1,040	20	26,491	26,731	28,875	30,526
5074 Plumbing & hydronic heating supplies[3]	41	38	352	419	11	33,705	34,406	10,138	12,548
5075 Warm air heating & air conditioning[3]	62	60	443	444	7	33,634	33,063	15,833	17,029
5078 Refrigeration equipment and supplies[3]	6	5	36	24	5	28,889	27,167	1,153	643
5082 Construction and mining machinery[3]	22	22	271	284	13	30,627	34,197	8,797	10,431
5083 Farm and garden machinery[3]	36	35	444	497	14	26,586	30,101	13,653	16,567
5084 Industrial machinery and equipment[3]	198	203	2,330	2,524	12	34,575	37,114	85,535	96,622
5085 Industrial supplies[3]	98	100	1,010	1,016	10	29,406	31,295	31,951	34,204
5087 Service establishment equipment[3]	80	81	579	543	7	22,446	25,090	14,745	14,794
5088 Transportation equipment & supplies[3]	13	13	54	51	4	43,407	39,059	2,360	2,018
5091 Sporting & recreational goods[3]	32	30	239	220	7	25,054	42,673	5,830	6,578
5092 Toys and hobby goods and supplies[3]	9	8	25	27	3	52,320	52,593	1,438	1,430
5093 Scrap and waste materials[3]	46	51	489	588	12	27,697	28,503	15,467	18,351
5094 Jewelry & precious stones[3]	11	14	88	93	7	23,227	27,269	2,443	2,760
5099 Durable goods, nec	51	52	314	279	5	22,268	32,186	7,509	8,378
5111 Printing and writing paper[3]	11	11	192	454	41	28,583	39,022	6,317	16,691
5112 Stationery and office supplies[3]	57	47	818	772	16	21,428	24,399	18,938	19,965
5113 Industrial & personal service paper[3]	44	46	69	379	8	28,290	40,253	2,224	16,256
5120 Drugs, proprietaries, and sundries[3]	20	20	380	311	16	42,800	48,887	16,843	14,835
5131 Piece goods & notions[3]	139	140	1,147	1,190	9	33,444	39,966	43,965	51,869
5136 Men's and boys' clothing[3]	26	25	261	282	11	13,594	18,099	4,327	4,863
5137 Women's and children's clothing[3]	32	32	266	176	6	20,526	20,727	6,193	2,436
5139 Footwear[3]	9	9	141	104	12	17,702	13,577	2,830	1,313
5141 Groceries, general line[3]	15	16	125	117	7	16,576	22,427	2,486	2,242
5142 Packaged frozen food[3]	12	11	525	541	49	29,112	30,529	16,239	18,435
5143 Dairy products, exc. dried or canned[3]	14	11	111	107	10	21,225	22,804	2,476	2,588
5144 Poultry and poultry products[3]	8	10	179	281	28	25,564	22,064	4,424	6,251

Continued on next page.

GREENSBORO – WINSTON-SALEM – HIGH POINT, NC MSA - [continued]

Wholesale and Retail Trade USA	Establishments		Employment		Emp / Est	Pay / Employee		Annual Payroll ($ 000)	
	1994	1995	1994	1995	1995	1994	1995	1994	1995
5145 Confectionery[3]	13	11	309	263	24	22,498	20,882	6,670	4,873
5146 Fish and seafoods[3]	5	5	23	24	5	15,304	15,833	389	432
5147 Meats and meat products[3]	12	13	14	16	1	14,857	18,000	254	268
5148 Fresh fruits and vegetables[3]	13	14	182	192	14	21,473	21,271	5,337	6,072
5149 Groceries and related products, nec[3]	37	41	508	521	13	25,575	24,691	13,257	13,243
5159 Farm-product raw materials, nec[3]	16	15	15	15	1	21,333	23,733	336	417
5162 Plastics materials & basic shapes[3]	17	17	167	227	13	33,677	31,366	8,010	9,622
5169 Chemicals & allied products, nec[3]	59	63	674	711	11	39,116	61,361	29,143	34,659
5171 Petroleum bulk stations & terminals[3]	38	36	281	284	8	32,342	32,268	9,362	9,184
5172 Petroleum products, nec[3]	11	10	68	75	8	22,471	21,653	1,605	1,688
5180 Beer, wine, and distilled beverages[3]	10	11	396	481	44	27,505	23,817	12,179	13,790
5191 Farm supplies	46	44	160	145	3	18,725	18,510	3,960	3,564
5192 Books, periodicals, & newspapers[3]	18	19	136	148	8	22,265	23,757	2,992	3,354
5193 Flowers & florists' supplies[3]	15	16	74	93	6	18,000	20,215	1,546	1,919
5194 Tobacco and tobacco products[3]	12	13	97	73	6	22,103	18,356	1,676	1,451
5198 Paints, varnishes, and supplies[3]	26	22	157	155	7	26,573	21,213	3,859	3,564
5199 Nondurable goods, nec	122	135	912	1,043	8	25,158	28,165	25,781	31,910
52- Retail trade	7,255	7,296	98,680	105,477	14	12,127	13,026	1,315,379	1,458,376
5210 Lumber and other building materials	125	123	2,458	2,751	22	18,304	20,941	47,660	57,582
5230 Paint, glass, and wallpaper stores[3]	45	47	186	206	4	17,699	19,417	3,590	4,331
5250 Hardware stores	71	55	459	346	6	13,830	13,295	7,073	4,880
5260 Retail nurseries and garden stores	66	67	291	342	5	12,385	13,275	4,345	5,178
5270 Mobile home dealers[3]	44	49	251	274	6	26,104	29,328	7,495	9,947
5310 Department stores[3]	53	52	7,789	7,868	151	10,175	11,616	82,358	88,539
5330 Variety stores	74	68	460	485	7	9,113	8,404	4,577	4,489
5390 Misc. general merchandise stores[1]	59	59	1,016	1,038	18	13,236	13,545	13,144	13,223
5410 Grocery stores[3]	594	570	11,095	13,061	23	10,398	10,558	125,438	143,557
5420 Meat and fish markets[3]	21	21	89	91	4	10,157	10,681	1,061	1,115
5430 Fruit and vegetable markets[3]	10	9	8	6	1	8,000	9,333	71	69
5440 Candy, nut, and confectionery stores[3]	15	13	37	33	3	4,757	7,515	143	351
5460 Retail bakeries[3]	60	57	498	578	10	8,321	7,370	4,488	4,678
5490 Miscellaneous food stores[3]	31	35	117	175	5	9,880	9,943	1,520	1,851
5510 New and used car dealers	114	113	4,684	5,021	44	28,865	30,612	153,912	170,099
5520 Used car dealers	148	144	437	468	3	16,348	17,855	8,282	9,021
5530 Auto and home supply stores	210	225	1,547	1,653	7	17,872	19,102	30,384	34,752
5540 Gasoline service stations	546	557	3,420	3,462	6	12,518	13,422	45,935	48,479
5550 Boat dealers[3]	13	15	48	57	4	16,083	17,404	1,127	1,291
5560 Recreational vehicle dealers[3]	12	12	91	97	8	23,648	25,773	2,644	2,905
5570 Motorcycle dealers[3]	21	22	114	121	6	14,702	17,058	2,328	2,849
5610 Men's & boys' clothing stores[3]	78	76	567	633	8	10,448	11,754	6,546	7,309
5620 Women's clothing stores	255	234	2,284	2,142	9	8,131	8,325	19,813	17,899
5630 Women's accessory & specialty stores[3]	40	41	217	242	6	8,590	9,521	2,106	2,606
5640 Children's and infants' wear stores[3]	25	23	107	168	7	7,551	6,405	933	1,083
5650 Family clothing stores	87	92	1,339	1,437	16	9,541	10,107	14,529	15,575
5660 Shoe stores[3]	192	192	1,112	1,169	6	10,597	10,269	12,537	11,707
5690 Misc. apparel & accessory stores[3]	32	32	115	142	4	9,043	9,465	1,280	1,589
5712 Furniture stores	247	242	2,353	2,450	10	19,189	21,600	50,215	56,604
5713 Floor covering stores[3]	67	68	302	338	5	20,755	21,444	6,930	8,307
5714 Drapery and upholstery stores[3]	18	16	30	26	2	13,467	10,923	360	299
5719 Misc. homefurnishings stores[3]	100	98	565	662	7	10,860	11,589	6,655	8,099
5720 Household appliance stores	62	56	1,185	1,141	20	15,946	17,125	20,431	20,368
5731 Radio, TV, & electronic stores	78	87	589	564	6	16,129	15,099	11,755	11,345
5734 Computer and software stores[3]	30	38	189	211	6	18,265	19,507	3,932	3,972
5735 Record & prerecorded tape stores[3]	42	46	251	306	7	8,319	8,301	2,550	2,795
5736 Musical instrument stores[3]	29	27	134	132	5	14,925	15,848	2,144	2,067
5812 Eating places	1,604	1,523	33,252	34,032	22	7,631	8,247	278,864	295,467
5813 Drinking places[3]	91	69	517	449	7	8,580	9,310	4,466	4,341
5910 Drug stores and proprietary stores	246	233	2,990	3,115	13	14,454	13,903	46,939	47,776
5920 Liquor stores[3]	51	48	144	159	3	19,139	18,465	2,951	3,048
5930 Used merchandise stores[2]	96	91	460	454	5	11,591	13,101	6,247	6,401
5941 Sporting goods and bicycle shops[2]	97	92	404	489	5	11,941	11,476	5,461	6,099
5942 Book stores[3]	78	75	511	563	8	8,611	9,016	5,058	5,224
5943 Stationery stores[3]	19	16	51	50	3	10,353	11,280	504	637
5944 Jewelry stores	129	134	725	768	6	18,869	20,354	12,974	14,008
5945 Hobby, toy, and game shops[3]	50	49	358	496	10	9,274	7,944	4,292	4,908
5947 Gift, novelty, and souvenir shops	109	108	613	615	6	7,093	7,889	4,894	5,474
5948 Luggage and leather goods stores[3]	12	12	32	77	6	8,750	8,364	342	819
5949 Sewing, needlework, and piece goods	50	45	264	263	6	10,136	8,715	2,874	2,345
5961 Catalog and mail-order houses[3]	29	28	1,513	1,688	60	18,633	22,121	30,935	39,399
5962 Merchandising machine operators[3]	28	27	342	423	16	16,690	16,823	6,682	7,826
5963 Direct selling establishments[3]	71	69	651	681	10	22,667	23,806	17,438	18,523

Continued on next page.

GREENSBORO – WINSTON-SALEM – HIGH POINT, NC MSA - [continued]

Wholesale and Retail Trade USA	Establishments		Employment		Emp / Est	Pay / Employee		Annual Payroll ($ 000)	
	1994	1995	1994	1995	1995	1994	1995	1994	1995
5983 Fuel oil dealers[3]	43	46	189	165	4	21,630	25,042	4,439	4,497
5984 Liquefied petroleum gas dealers[3]	15	18	35	95	5	27,657	28,168	1,603	3,091
5992 Florists	125	118	446	512	4	12,924	13,063	6,221	7,097
5993 Tobacco stores and stands[3]	7	8	9	13	2	12,889	12,308	132	154
5994 News dealers and newsstands[3]	13	12	24	31	3	8,000	8,645	216	269
5995 Optical goods stores[3]	51	54	231	260	5	16,173	19,108	3,658	4,696
5999 Miscellaneous retail stores, nec[3]	215	232	1,054	1,187	5	12,645	12,883	14,231	16,233

Source: County Business Patterns 1994/95, CBP-94/95, U.S. Department of Commerce, Washington DC, November 1997. The employment column represents mid-March employment in the year. Pay per employee is calculated by dividing 1st Quarter payroll, annualized, by mid-March employment. The column headed 'Emp / Est' shows 'employees per establishment'. A dash (-) means that data are unavailable or cannot be calculated. nec means not elsewhere classified. *Notes:* 1. 1994 data incomplete; unavailable or withheld. 2. 1995 data incomplete; unavailable or withheld. 3. 1994 and 1995 data incomplete; unavailable or withheld.

GREENVILLE, NC MSA

Wholesale and Retail Trade USA	Establishments		Employment		Emp / Est	Pay / Employee		Annual Payroll ($ 000)	
	1994	1995	1994	1995	1995	1994	1995	1994	1995
50- Wholesale trade	201	214	2,561	2,750	13	24,150	24,858	70,292	74,643
5012 Automobiles and other vehicles	9	10	88	95	10	12,636	13,432	1,260	1,389
5013 Motor vehicle supplies and new parts	6	-	30	-	-	20,133	-	582	-
5015 Motor vehicle parts, used	-	5	-	34	7	-	14,706	-	529
5031 Lumber, plywood, and millwork	3	4	28	86	22	28,857	24,140	754	2,082
5032 Brick, stone, & related materials	3	4	3	11	3	21,333	15,273	91	136
5044 Office equipment	7	5	109	111	22	27,229	26,486	3,539	3,013
5045 Computers, peripherals, & software	7	6	97	91	15	25,691	27,165	2,670	2,525
5046 Commercial equipment, nec	3	4	17	18	5	25,647	27,111	453	601
5047 Medical and hospital equipment	10	9	103	76	8	42,874	28,579	4,012	1,915
5063 Electrical apparatus and equipment	9	9	86	88	10	25,674	30,409	2,323	2,631
5065 Electronic parts and equipment	3	3	16	8	3	20,750	24,500	301	180
5072 Hardware	7	10	103	125	13	22,563	18,752	2,562	2,627
5074 Plumbing & hydronic heating supplies	4	4	54	54	14	19,481	24,815	1,177	1,611
5075 Warm air heating & air conditioning	5	4	24	9	2	16,833	36,444	315	242
5082 Construction and mining machinery	5	5	95	92	18	25,979	29,739	2,719	2,960
5083 Farm and garden machinery	3	3	58	63	21	16,483	15,810	977	1,051
5085 Industrial supplies	11	11	92	90	8	24,913	29,511	2,587	2,885
5090 Miscellaneous durable goods	5	8	30	30	4	11,467	16,667	439	508
5112 Stationery and office supplies	-	4	-	42	11	-	14,476	-	622
5149 Groceries and related products, nec	-	4	-	83	21	-	27,952	-	2,146
5150 Farm-product raw materials	15	15	498	493	33	32,249	34,661	21,029	22,746
5171 Petroleum bulk stations & terminals	5	5	47	45	9	18,043	21,333	745	768
5172 Petroleum products, nec	4	4	35	36	9	19,086	21,111	731	832
5191 Farm supplies	18	15	158	126	8	18,785	20,794	3,033	2,947
5194 Tobacco and tobacco products	3	4	16	13	3	7,750	25,846	172	341
5199 Nondurable goods, nec	8	9	82	89	10	21,073	21,303	1,787	2,045
52- Retail trade	818	819	11,247	11,770	14	10,267	10,765	124,601	136,119
5210 Lumber and other building materials	11	11	280	214	19	17,243	19,234	5,144	4,287
5230 Paint, glass, and wallpaper stores	3	4	19	24	6	18,316	16,000	376	404
5250 Hardware stores	8	6	49	27	5	12,245	9,778	661	256
5260 Retail nurseries and garden stores	4	4	24	23	6	5,833	8,174	160	142
5270 Mobile home dealers	12	11	105	113	10	24,610	21,522	2,659	2,864
5310 Department stores	6	6	827	842	140	10,268	11,240	8,093	9,250
5330 Variety stores	8	6	51	46	8	6,510	7,130	376	381
5390 Misc. general merchandise stores	7	6	98	64	11	10,857	9,875	776	741
5410 Grocery stores	80	74	1,364	1,315	18	10,293	11,024	14,859	14,638
5420 Meat and fish markets	-	6	-	13	2	-	9,231	-	124
5460 Retail bakeries	5	5	60	57	11	8,200	6,877	572	425
5490 Miscellaneous food stores	5	6	13	16	3	6,462	7,750	82	116
5510 New and used car dealers	16	15	501	528	35	24,271	25,598	14,238	15,072
5520 Used car dealers	20	21	107	111	5	29,869	36,324	3,616	4,124
5530 Auto and home supply stores	29	30	180	225	8	15,533	15,858	3,149	3,951
5540 Gasoline service stations	49	53	296	337	6	10,595	10,315	3,563	4,051
5550 Boat dealers	-	3	-	28	9	-	21,286	-	675
5610 Men's & boys' clothing stores	5	5	27	30	6	9,926	10,267	278	301
5620 Women's clothing stores	35	36	270	238	7	6,622	7,529	2,140	1,920
5630 Women's accessory & specialty stores	4	4	16	16	4	6,250	6,750	86	191
5640 Children's and infants' wear stores	4	4	13	9	2	7,385	9,778	98	96
5650 Family clothing stores	6	6	387	410	68	7,814	11,659	1,975	4,395
5660 Shoe stores	22	19	120	125	7	9,567	8,896	1,182	973
5690 Misc. apparel & accessory stores	7	5	20	20	4	7,400	6,200	142	158
5712 Furniture stores	20	26	199	233	9	15,779	14,798	3,517	4,012

Continued on next page.

GREENVILLE, NC MSA - [continued]

Wholesale and Retail Trade USA	Establishments		Employment		Emp / Est	Pay / Employee		Annual Payroll ($ 000)	
	1994	1995	1994	1995	1995	1994	1995	1994	1995
5713 Floor covering stores	-	11	-	71	6	-	14,197	-	1,067
5719 Misc. homefurnishings stores	12	-	97	-	-	8,784	-	940	-
5720 Household appliance stores	-	6	-	39	7	-	16,308	-	676
5731 Radio, TV, & electronic stores	10	8	41	30	4	13,854	14,400	735	483
5734 Computer and software stores	7	7	30	28	4	26,133	13,286	605	391
5735 Record & prerecorded tape stores	7	6	27	61	10	14,370	7,803	442	480
5736 Musical instrument stores	4	4	19	15	4	15,158	18,400	286	286
5812 Eating places	158	154	4,065	4,390	29	6,445	6,713	28,308	30,644
5813 Drinking places	13	11	115	101	9	4,278	3,446	388	318
5910 Drug stores and proprietary stores	27	27	266	284	11	14,692	15,592	4,130	5,013
5930 Used merchandise stores	16	18	59	64	4	10,102	10,438	634	699
5941 Sporting goods and bicycle shops	10	-	38	-	-	8,632	-	447	-
5942 Book stores	7	7	96	100	14	10,583	10,360	1,110	1,243
5944 Jewelry stores	16	17	85	94	6	13,224	13,064	1,153	1,270
5945 Hobby, toy, and game shops	6	6	51	58	10	8,784	8,897	589	595
5947 Gift, novelty, and souvenir shops	16	14	80	80	6	7,050	8,000	608	707
5949 Sewing, needlework, and piece goods	-	5	-	14	3	-	10,857	-	158
5963 Direct selling establishments	7	-	64	-	-	9,375	-	809	-
5980 Fuel dealers	6	6	28	34	6	20,143	19,765	580	715
5992 Florists	11	10	59	63	6	10,576	10,540	663	693
5995 Optical goods stores	10	8	44	43	5	11,636	13,488	571	644
5999 Miscellaneous retail stores, nec	15	14	83	62	4	7,181	8,903	563	631

Source: County Business Patterns 1994/95, CBP-94/95, U.S. Department of Commerce, Washington DC, November 1997. The employment column represents mid-March employment in the year. Pay per employee is calculated by dividing 1st Quarter payroll, annualized, by mid-March employment. The column headed 'Emp / Est' shows 'employees per establishment'. A dash (-) means that data are unavailable or cannot be calculated. nec means not elsewhere classified. *Notes:* 1. 1994 data incomplete; unavailable or withheld. 2. 1995 data incomplete; unavailable or withheld. 3. 1994 and 1995 data incomplete; unavailable or withheld.

GREENVILLE - SPARTANBURG - ANDERSON, SC MSA

Wholesale and Retail Trade USA	Establishments		Employment		Emp / Est	Pay / Employee		Annual Payroll ($ 000)	
	1994	1995	1994	1995	1995	1994	1995	1994	1995
50- Wholesale trade	-	1,895	-	25,904	14	-	30,879	-	836,722
5012 Automobiles and other vehicles [2]	-	58	-	537	9	-	24,216	-	14,365
5013 Motor vehicle supplies and new parts [2]	-	62	-	251	4	-	21,721	-	5,965
5015 Motor vehicle parts, used	-	31	-	130	4	-	24,492	-	3,393
5021 Furniture [2]	-	21	-	111	5	-	24,036	-	3,128
5023 Homefurnishings [2]	-	30	-	317	11	-	52,315	-	17,560
5031 Lumber, plywood, and millwork [2]	-	26	-	531	20	-	38,991	-	19,969
5032 Brick, stone, & related materials [2]	-	16	-	69	4	-	28,928	-	1,943
5033 Roofing, siding, & insulation [2]	-	23	-	126	5	-	28,667	-	3,893
5039 Construction materials, nec [2]	-	23	-	153	7	-	22,876	-	4,753
5044 Office equipment [2]	-	36	-	712	20	-	28,292	-	17,284
5045 Computers, peripherals, & software [2]	-	46	-	465	10	-	46,314	-	19,805
5046 Commercial equipment, nec [2]	-	15	-	228	15	-	30,684	-	8,243
5047 Medical and hospital equipment [2]	-	26	-	323	12	-	36,285	-	12,665
5051 Metals service centers and offices [2]	-	29	-	408	14	-	30,039	-	13,112
5052 Coal and other minerals and ores [2]	-	3	-	7	2	-	24,571	-	183
5063 Electrical apparatus and equipment	-	77	-	668	9	-	35,389	-	24,708
5065 Electronic parts and equipment [2]	-	43	-	482	11	-	41,510	-	20,477
5074 Plumbing & hydronic heating supplies	-	26	-	166	6	-	32,482	-	4,840
5075 Warm air heating & air conditioning	-	48	-	402	8	-	39,900	-	15,139
5082 Construction and mining machinery [2]	-	18	-	306	17	-	29,712	-	10,523
5083 Farm and garden machinery	-	17	-	88	5	-	20,636	-	1,984
5084 Industrial machinery and equipment	-	254	-	2,630	10	-	37,982	-	106,948
5085 Industrial supplies	-	108	-	868	8	-	32,945	-	31,106
5087 Service establishment equipment	-	44	-	277	6	-	22,469	-	6,181
5091 Sporting & recreational goods [2]	-	25	-	1,188	48	-	26,906	-	33,230
5093 Scrap and waste materials	-	48	-	638	13	-	23,655	-	15,385
5099 Durable goods, nec	-	39	-	333	9	-	24,144	-	8,933
5111 Printing and writing paper [2]	-	3	-	31	10	-	39,226	-	1,306
5112 Stationery and office supplies [2]	-	26	-	292	11	-	25,233	-	7,153
5113 Industrial & personal service paper [2]	-	23	-	348	15	-	32,954	-	12,086
5120 Drugs, proprietaries, and sundries [2]	-	15	-	17	1	-	50,353	-	836
5131 Piece goods & notions [2]	-	53	-	492	9	-	28,911	-	15,609
5137 Women's and children's clothing [2]	-	17	-	101	6	-	16,950	-	1,439
5141 Groceries, general line [2]	-	17	-	287	17	-	25,073	-	8,095
5142 Packaged frozen food [2]	-	6	-	245	41	-	33,714	-	8,729
5143 Dairy products, exc. dried or canned [2]	-	7	-	86	12	-	25,721	-	3,014
5147 Meats and meat products [2]	-	8	-	18	2	-	30,444	-	622

Continued on next page.

GREENVILLE – SPARTANBURG – ANDERSON, SC MSA - [continued]

Wholesale and Retail Trade USA	Establishments		Employment		Emp / Est	Pay / Employee		Annual Payroll ($ 000)	
	1994	1995	1994	1995	1995	1994	1995	1994	1995
5148 Fresh fruits and vegetables [2]	-	14	-	104	7	-	17,269	-	1,938
5149 Groceries and related products, nec [2]	-	24	-	882	37	-	29,551	-	25,412
5159 Farm-product raw materials, nec [2]	-	10	-	28	3	-	32,429	-	1,504
5162 Plastics materials & basic shapes [2]	-	27	-	435	16	-	26,915	-	13,036
5169 Chemicals & allied products, nec	-	80	-	700	9	-	38,651	-	28,256
5171 Petroleum bulk stations & terminals	-	34	-	184	5	-	31,674	-	5,568
5172 Petroleum products, nec [2]	-	14	-	64	5	-	43,500	-	3,040
5181 Beer and ale [2]	-	8	-	110	14	-	25,018	-	3,294
5191 Farm supplies [2]	-	23	-	81	4	-	15,259	-	1,182
5192 Books, periodicals, & newspapers [2]	-	6	-	12	2	-	19,000	-	457
5193 Flowers & florists' supplies [2]	-	11	-	46	4	-	18,174	-	842
5198 Paints, varnishes, and supplies [2]	-	19	-	151	8	-	27,868	-	4,952
5199 Nondurable goods, nec [2]	-	65	-	431	7	-	27,517	-	13,695
52- Retail trade	-	5,610	-	80,683	14	-	12,939	-	1,083,175
5210 Lumber and other building materials	-	81	-	1,658	20	-	21,841	-	38,915
5230 Paint, glass, and wallpaper stores	-	37	-	214	6	-	18,953	-	4,245
5250 Hardware stores	-	63	-	468	7	-	14,231	-	7,068
5260 Retail nurseries and garden stores	-	53	-	248	5	-	11,274	-	3,557
5270 Mobile home dealers	-	49	-	312	6	-	24,474	-	10,514
5310 Department stores [2]	-	39	-	6,473	166	-	11,996	-	74,894
5330 Variety stores	-	59	-	420	7	-	8,981	-	4,152
5390 Misc. general merchandise stores	-	35	-	805	23	-	12,959	-	10,217
5410 Grocery stores	-	509	-	11,662	23	-	9,948	-	120,380
5420 Meat and fish markets	-	13	-	48	4	-	11,000	-	477
5430 Fruit and vegetable markets [2]	-	14	-	6	-	-	13,333	-	99
5440 Candy, nut, and confectionery stores [2]	-	11	-	38	3	-	8,105	-	272
5450 Dairy products stores [2]	-	4	-	15	4	-	19,200	-	266
5460 Retail bakeries [2]	-	26	-	268	10	-	8,821	-	2,249
5490 Miscellaneous food stores [2]	-	20	-	76	4	-	9,842	-	887
5510 New and used car dealers	-	77	-	3,284	43	-	30,667	-	111,490
5520 Used car dealers	-	117	-	391	3	-	17,708	-	7,712
5530 Auto and home supply stores	-	224	-	1,336	6	-	15,320	-	21,932
5540 Gasoline service stations	-	396	-	2,408	6	-	12,150	-	30,660
5550 Boat dealers [2]	-	18	-	75	4	-	14,507	-	1,217
5560 Recreational vehicle dealers [2]	-	9	-	52	6	-	24,000	-	1,246
5570 Motorcycle dealers	-	17	-	84	5	-	16,524	-	1,856
5610 Men's & boys' clothing stores	-	46	-	366	8	-	11,071	-	4,014
5620 Women's clothing stores	-	158	-	1,035	7	-	8,359	-	8,582
5630 Women's accessory & specialty stores [2]	-	26	-	162	6	-	9,679	-	1,656
5640 Children's and infants' wear stores [2]	-	21	-	138	7	-	8,638	-	1,221
5650 Family clothing stores [2]	-	58	-	1,205	21	-	8,568	-	13,596
5660 Shoe stores	-	117	-	682	6	-	10,979	-	7,649
5690 Misc. apparel & accessory stores	-	37	-	274	7	-	7,664	-	2,463
5712 Furniture stores	-	178	-	1,088	6	-	16,912	-	19,869
5713 Floor covering stores	-	52	-	211	4	-	18,654	-	4,260
5719 Misc. homefurnishings stores	-	62	-	337	5	-	12,510	-	4,341
5720 Household appliance stores	-	33	-	242	7	-	15,554	-	4,044
5731 Radio, TV, & electronic stores	-	65	-	516	8	-	16,178	-	9,740
5734 Computer and software stores [2]	-	23	-	97	4	-	17,691	-	1,765
5735 Record & prerecorded tape stores	-	27	-	112	4	-	9,643	-	1,080
5736 Musical instrument stores	-	20	-	127	6	-	18,047	-	2,405
5812 Eating places	-	1,102	-	25,839	23	-	7,337	-	197,565
5813 Drinking places	-	61	-	407	7	-	6,251	-	2,649
5910 Drug stores and proprietary stores	-	207	-	2,106	10	-	14,053	-	33,010
5920 Liquor stores	-	61	-	121	2	-	12,066	-	1,550
5930 Used merchandise stores	-	92	-	399	4	-	13,995	-	5,660
5941 Sporting goods and bicycle shops [2]	-	59	-	349	6	-	14,659	-	4,999
5942 Book stores	-	47	-	378	8	-	11,312	-	4,576
5943 Stationery stores	-	17	-	53	3	-	15,472	-	936
5944 Jewelry stores	-	111	-	711	6	-	16,079	-	9,854
5945 Hobby, toy, and game shops [2]	-	27	-	317	12	-	9,047	-	3,523
5946 Camera & photographic supply stores	-	15	-	4	-	-	6,000	-	58
5947 Gift, novelty, and souvenir shops	-	88	-	420	5	-	9,229	-	4,419
5949 Sewing, needlework, and piece goods [2]	-	35	-	182	5	-	9,692	-	1,869
5961 Catalog and mail-order houses [2]	-	8	-	34	4	-	31,529	-	1,326
5962 Merchandising machine operators [2]	-	25	-	823	33	-	14,765	-	13,321
5963 Direct selling establishments	-	42	-	331	8	-	14,115	-	4,597
5983 Fuel oil dealers [2]	-	31	-	97	3	-	18,433	-	1,749
5984 Liquefied petroleum gas dealers [2]	-	18	-	80	4	-	22,100	-	898

Continued on next page.

GREENVILLE – SPARTANBURG – ANDERSON, SC MSA - [continued]

Wholesale and Retail Trade USA	Establishments		Employment		Emp / Est	Pay / Employee		Annual Payroll ($ 000)	
	1994	1995	1994	1995	1995	1994	1995	1994	1995
5992 Florists [2]	-	103	-	179	2	-	8,916	-	1,695
5995 Optical goods stores	-	47	-	220	5	-	15,636	-	3,162
5999 Miscellaneous retail stores, nec	-	139	-	554	4	-	14,195	-	8,159

Source: County Business Patterns 1994/95, CBP-94/95, U.S. Department of Commerce, Washington DC, November 1997. The employment column represents mid-March employment in the year. Pay per employee is calculated by dividing 1st Quarter payroll, annualized, by mid-March employment. The column headed 'Emp / Est' shows 'employees per establishment'. A dash (-) means that data are unavailable or cannot be calculated. nec means not elsewhere classified. *Notes:* 1. 1994 data incomplete; unavailable or withheld. 2. 1995 data incomplete; unavailable or withheld. 3. 1994 and 1995 data incomplete; unavailable or withheld.

HAGERSTOWN, MD PMSA

Wholesale and Retail Trade USA	Establishments		Employment		Emp / Est	Pay / Employee		Annual Payroll ($ 000)	
	1994	1995	1994	1995	1995	1994	1995	1994	1995
50– Wholesale trade	219	211	2,813	2,846	13	24,336	26,302	73,974	78,069
5012 Automobiles and other vehicles	9	10	118	134	13	22,407	22,358	3,291	3,596
5013 Motor vehicle supplies and new parts	17	15	104	109	7	17,077	17,394	2,069	1,930
5015 Motor vehicle parts, used	-	3	-	11	4	-	14,182	-	177
5020 Furniture and homefurnishings	5	4	86	87	22	17,023	14,759	1,438	1,474
5031 Lumber, plywood, and millwork	8	7	66	79	11	39,394	30,886	1,938	1,843
5039 Construction materials, nec	-	5	-	72	14	-	24,000	-	1,951
5044 Office equipment	8	9	61	57	6	17,508	19,088	1,131	1,133
5045 Computers, peripherals, & software	-	4	-	59	15	-	58,644	-	2,882
5049 Professional equipment, nec	3	-	16	-	-	8,750	-	170	-
5051 Metals service centers and offices	6	6	58	71	12	19,724	17,803	1,410	1,364
5063 Electrical apparatus and equipment	8	7	184	206	29	32,739	36,194	6,422	7,526
5075 Warm air heating & air conditioning	7	7	76	79	11	23,842	26,076	1,860	2,470
5082 Construction and mining machinery	3	3	35	34	11	26,743	27,765	1,230	1,276
5083 Farm and garden machinery	8	7	75	68	10	18,293	22,412	1,767	1,736
5084 Industrial machinery and equipment	10	10	64	69	7	22,688	28,174	1,865	2,086
5085 Industrial supplies	8	8	88	85	11	24,182	27,812	2,414	2,535
5087 Service establishment equipment	4	3	29	30	10	26,621	30,400	892	978
5093 Scrap and waste materials	-	6	-	101	17	-	26,297	-	3,346
5099 Durable goods, nec	5	-	27	-	-	38,963	-	1,133	-
5110 Paper and paper products	11	9	140	122	14	22,029	25,541	3,660	3,295
5149 Groceries and related products, nec	7	8	257	317	40	27,798	23,672	7,158	7,610
5150 Farm-product raw materials	3	3	39	27	9	13,744	39,852	380	509
5171 Petroleum bulk stations & terminals	6	5	203	190	38	26,089	28,232	5,326	5,033
5181 Beer and ale	3	3	67	53	18	23,045	24,981	1,714	1,692
5191 Farm supplies	7	7	114	106	15	23,474	25,660	3,089	2,978
5199 Nondurable goods, nec	5	-	45	-	-	10,311	-	536	-
52– Retail trade	800	804	9,974	10,592	13	11,066	12,069	125,227	131,416
5210 Lumber and other building materials	14	12	249	212	18	18,538	20,000	4,970	4,228
5230 Paint, glass, and wallpaper stores	5	5	15	16	3	14,133	14,750	240	259
5250 Hardware stores	10	-	27	-	-	13,185	-	437	-
5260 Retail nurseries and garden stores	8	7	47	54	8	10,894	13,407	738	955
5270 Mobile home dealers	3	-	11	-	-	16,364	-	218	-
5310 Department stores	7	7	993	1,052	150	10,453	12,148	11,527	12,756
5330 Variety stores	13	10	157	131	13	6,573	6,748	1,058	932
5390 Misc. general merchandise stores	7	9	167	209	23	12,263	15,234	2,638	2,854
5410 Grocery stores	63	61	1,519	1,521	25	10,668	11,016	16,185	16,607
5420 Meat and fish markets	6	6	39	42	7	14,667	19,619	548	668
5440 Candy, nut, and confectionery stores	4	4	24	18	5	4,833	5,556	107	84
5460 Retail bakeries	6	5	60	52	10	10,467	12,000	658	642
5490 Miscellaneous food stores	7	7	26	26	4	6,000	5,846	155	192
5510 New and used car dealers	15	15	664	663	44	21,645	24,097	17,383	16,546
5520 Used car dealers	8	11	24	28	3	13,833	18,143	456	588
5530 Auto and home supply stores	23	24	106	108	5	16,415	17,074	1,908	1,943
5540 Gasoline service stations	49	52	400	442	9	10,520	10,814	4,565	5,031
5560 Recreational vehicle dealers	3	3	12	13	4	20,000	23,385	334	323
5610 Men's & boys' clothing stores	4	4	25	19	5	12,000	15,158	337	293
5620 Women's clothing stores	23	21	173	136	6	7,353	7,971	1,655	1,100
5650 Family clothing stores	7	6	36	30	5	9,000	9,467	380	332
5660 Shoe stores	16	11	78	83	8	11,077	10,072	808	742
5690 Misc. apparel & accessory stores	6	-	13	-	-	10,154	-	146	-
5712 Furniture stores	19	18	129	155	9	18,481	21,058	2,714	2,819
5713 Floor covering stores	8	8	56	53	7	15,286	17,509	1,033	1,019
5719 Misc. homefurnishings stores	4	4	19	20	5	15,368	15,800	334	342
5734 Computer and software stores	6	7	28	17	2	21,571	28,941	484	470
5735 Record & prerecorded tape stores	4	4	24	28	7	8,000	7,714	220	229
5736 Musical instrument stores	6	5	31	31	6	5,032	7,226	250	236

Continued on next page.

HAGERSTOWN, MD PMSA - [continued]

Wholesale and Retail Trade USA	Establishments		Employment		Emp / Est	Pay / Employee		Annual Payroll ($ 000)	
	1994	1995	1994	1995	1995	1994	1995	1994	1995
5812 Eating places	173	162	2,781	3,191	20	6,642	7,262	23,072	24,013
5813 Drinking places	39	38	95	115	3	8,042	6,922	799	888
5910 Drug stores and proprietary stores	22	25	276	274	11	16,812	18,307	4,813	5,513
5920 Liquor stores	32	34	121	143	4	9,653	9,063	1,336	1,436
5930 Used merchandise stores	14	16	124	131	8	8,323	9,099	1,212	1,352
5941 Sporting goods and bicycle shops	10	9	42	40	4	10,190	11,500	497	538
5942 Book stores	5	7	33	38	5	5,455	9,474	206	372
5944 Jewelry stores	18	17	99	90	5	11,434	12,978	1,089	1,094
5945 Hobby, toy, and game shops	8	7	59	63	9	6,441	8,381	459	633
5947 Gift, novelty, and souvenir shops	17	16	120	98	6	6,133	8,082	818	884
5963 Direct selling establishments	-	8	-	62	8	-	17,742	-	1,196
5983 Fuel oil dealers	4	5	29	39	8	30,207	28,103	975	1,192
5984 Liquefied petroleum gas dealers	3	3	47	54	18	24,681	24,370	1,265	1,252
5992 Florists	16	16	93	96	6	9,118	12,083	1,013	1,082
5995 Optical goods stores	11	12	88	81	7	17,955	21,778	1,517	1,587
5999 Miscellaneous retail stores, nec	17	17	86	108	6	9,349	12,778	1,177	1,304

Source: County Business Patterns 1994/95, CBP-94/95, U.S. Department of Commerce, Washington DC, November 1997. The employment column represents mid-March employment in the year. Pay per employee is calculated by dividing 1st Quarter payroll, annualized, by mid-March employment. The column headed 'Emp / Est' shows 'employees per establishment'. A dash (-) means that data are unavailable or cannot be calculated. nec means not elsewhere classified. *Notes:* 1. 1994 data incomplete; unavailable or withheld. 2. 1995 data incomplete; unavailable or withheld. 3. 1994 and 1995 data incomplete; unavailable or withheld.

HAMILTON - MIDDLETOWN, OH PMSA

Wholesale and Retail Trade USA	Establishments		Employment		Emp / Est	Pay / Employee		Annual Payroll ($ 000)	
	1994	1995	1994	1995	1995	1994	1995	1994	1995
50- Wholesale trade	446	456	7,205	7,994	18	28,093	28,583	225,918	253,200
5012 Automobiles and other vehicles	9	11	247	279	25	20,065	19,484	5,426	5,984
5013 Motor vehicle supplies and new parts	24	22	233	213	10	15,142	16,563	3,886	3,794
5014 Tires and tubes	5	3	34	28	9	24,706	25,429	1,019	935
5015 Motor vehicle parts, used	8	10	24	59	6	14,333	10,508	431	610
5021 Furniture	8	9	69	70	8	21,449	16,400	1,268	1,258
5023 Homefurnishings	11	8	229	205	26	23,441	26,966	8,784	9,006
5031 Lumber, plywood, and millwork	11	12	138	174	15	29,130	25,885	4,496	4,730
5039 Construction materials, nec	8	8	72	105	13	20,000	18,438	1,761	1,950
5044 Office equipment	7	8	40	38	5	27,900	30,632	1,247	1,320
5045 Computers, peripherals, & software	10	-	53	-	-	32,302	-	1,393	-
5046 Commercial equipment, nec	8	9	48	50	6	22,917	23,040	1,059	1,160
5047 Medical and hospital equipment	9	11	62	76	7	39,484	34,158	2,885	2,904
5050 Metals and minerals, except petroleum	16	22	535	626	28	41,510	35,540	23,384	24,479
5063 Electrical apparatus and equipment	17	14	274	211	15	48,891	62,275	14,817	14,414
5065 Electronic parts and equipment	7	-	37	-	-	18,162	-	671	-
5072 Hardware	10	9	279	280	31	26,122	29,429	8,044	8,980
5074 Plumbing & hydronic heating supplies	9	10	80	89	9	29,750	29,708	2,635	2,781
5082 Construction and mining machinery	-	5	-	139	28	-	36,115	-	5,149
5083 Farm and garden machinery	-	3	-	48	16	-	16,000	-	799
5084 Industrial machinery and equipment	-	48	-	488	10	-	43,016	-	22,632
5085 Industrial supplies	-	20	-	172	9	-	36,558	-	6,235
5087 Service establishment equipment	-	7	-	63	9	-	23,873	-	1,693
5091 Sporting & recreational goods	-	5	-	56	11	-	16,214	-	1,060
5093 Scrap and waste materials	-	13	-	196	15	-	27,000	-	6,530
5099 Durable goods, nec	-	9	-	365	41	-	21,819	-	8,943
5112 Stationery and office supplies	-	11	-	312	28	-	23,679	-	8,007
5120 Drugs, proprietaries, and sundries	-	8	-	511	64	-	21,331	-	13,318
5130 Apparel, piece goods, and notions	-	6	-	241	40	-	19,519	-	5,077
5141 Groceries, general line	-	6	-	683	114	-	26,430	-	18,953
5145 Confectionery	-	3	-	49	16	-	24,000	-	1,272
5149 Groceries and related products, nec	-	13	-	575	44	-	26,052	-	17,261
5162 Plastics materials & basic shapes	-	4	-	78	20	-	30,410	-	2,896
5169 Chemicals & allied products, nec	-	18	-	361	20	-	39,601	-	15,445
5170 Petroleum and petroleum products	-	5	-	100	20	-	29,320	-	3,530
5193 Flowers & florists' supplies	-	3	-	23	8	-	33,217	-	965
5199 Nondurable goods, nec	-	9	-	87	10	-	15,770	-	1,514
52- Retail trade	1,332	1,350	20,292	21,245	16	11,981	13,518	269,197	293,116
5210 Lumber and other building materials	16	18	410	456	25	17,015	22,728	8,979	11,044
5250 Hardware stores	16	14	219	167	12	12,219	10,874	2,249	1,904
5260 Retail nurseries and garden stores	16	16	178	156	10	11,258	12,487	2,839	2,842
5310 Department stores	10	14	1,141	1,621	116	8,901	11,447	11,640	20,888
5330 Variety stores	10	-	148	-	-	9,189	-	1,651	-
5390 Misc. general merchandise stores	3	-	68	-	-	10,882	-	814	-

Continued on next page.

HAMILTON - MIDDLETOWN, OH PMSA - [continued]

Wholesale and Retail Trade USA	Establishments		Employment		Emp / Est	Pay / Employee		Annual Payroll ($ 000)	
	1994	1995	1994	1995	1995	1994	1995	1994	1995
5410 Grocery stores	125	120	3,456	3,587	30	10,554	11,524	38,962	39,341
5460 Retail bakeries	18	16	83	92	6	8,386	8,174	727	782
5490 Miscellaneous food stores	4	7	5	4	1	8,800	7,000	57	103
5510 New and used car dealers	19	19	731	804	42	25,921	27,005	21,254	22,992
5520 Used car dealers	30	29	131	154	5	16,794	17,013	2,606	2,886
5530 Auto and home supply stores	34	42	300	299	7	15,680	18,997	5,431	5,869
5540 Gasoline service stations	105	104	660	647	6	10,648	11,555	7,572	7,865
5560 Recreational vehicle dealers	3	3	18	22	7	21,111	24,000	415	622
5610 Men's & boys' clothing stores	8	-	29	-	-	9,379	-	235	-
5620 Women's clothing stores	22	17	224	140	8	7,964	6,171	1,821	895
5650 Family clothing stores	3	3	48	51	17	7,917	8,471	460	346
5660 Shoe stores	22	21	99	83	4	9,455	9,060	925	766
5690 Misc. apparel & accessory stores	-	4	-	13	3	-	9,231	-	152
5712 Furniture stores	22	20	229	234	12	20,856	23,368	5,565	6,159
5713 Floor covering stores	17	19	73	83	4	16,438	19,133	1,306	1,598
5720 Household appliance stores	-	4	-	21	5	-	19,429	-	444
5731 Radio, TV, & electronic stores	14	14	101	100	7	17,822	20,040	1,948	2,209
5734 Computer and software stores	-	5	-	32	6	-	20,500	-	911
5735 Record & prerecorded tape stores	4	4	25	38	10	9,440	6,947	262	266
5736 Musical instrument stores	-	3	-	16	5	-	17,500	-	258
5812 Eating places	351	332	8,097	7,971	24	6,734	7,542	61,706	64,505
5813 Drinking places	72	67	362	332	5	5,138	5,807	1,851	1,862
5910 Drug stores and proprietary stores	43	44	508	499	11	16,811	18,020	9,363	9,108
5920 Liquor stores	31	27	153	148	5	9,098	9,676	1,348	1,352
5930 Used merchandise stores	13	12	48	45	4	8,000	7,289	476	424
5941 Sporting goods and bicycle shops	19	17	152	168	10	14,263	16,381	2,607	3,227
5942 Book stores	9	7	52	60	9	8,385	8,200	484	481
5944 Jewelry stores	14	17	67	70	4	13,015	14,057	948	1,018
5945 Hobby, toy, and game shops	-	7	-	15	2	-	8,000	-	132
5947 Gift, novelty, and souvenir shops	19	23	92	93	4	7,391	9,935	883	954
5949 Sewing, needlework, and piece goods	8	8	63	70	9	6,603	6,629	458	485
5961 Catalog and mail-order houses	5	6	16	50	8	18,250	20,000	329	992
5962 Merchandising machine operators	8	8	57	46	6	16,211	22,348	1,305	1,032
5963 Direct selling establishments	11	10	88	78	8	19,500	21,590	1,640	1,626
5980 Fuel dealers	10	11	133	167	15	12,030	12,623	1,906	1,945
5992 Florists	26	25	111	115	5	8,468	8,904	1,081	1,136
5994 News dealers and newsstands	3	-	6	-	-	8,000	-	93	-
5995 Optical goods stores	10	9	19	15	2	14,947	17,333	363	304
5999 Miscellaneous retail stores, nec	38	41	141	122	3	12,539	12,197	1,962	1,734

Source: County Business Patterns 1994/95, CBP-94/95, U.S. Department of Commerce, Washington DC, November 1997. The employment column represents mid-March employment in the year. Pay per employee is calculated by dividing 1st Quarter payroll, annualized, by mid-March employment. The column headed 'Emp / Est' shows 'employees per establishment'. A dash (-) means that data are unavailable or cannot be calculated. nec means not elsewhere classified. *Notes:* 1. 1994 data incomplete; unavailable or withheld. 2. 1995 data incomplete; unavailable or withheld. 3. 1994 and 1995 data incomplete; unavailable or withheld.

HARRISBURG - LEBANON - CARLISLE, PA MSA

Wholesale and Retail Trade USA	Establishments		Employment		Emp / Est	Pay / Employee		Annual Payroll ($ 000)	
	1994	1995	1994	1995	1995	1994	1995	1994	1995
50- Wholesale trade	-	950	-	17,399	18	-	30,304	-	539,009
5012 Automobiles and other vehicles	-	25	-	512	20	-	25,055	-	13,742
5013 Motor vehicle supplies and new parts	-	88	-	982	11	-	23,108	-	22,226
5014 Tires and tubes [2]	-	10	-	64	6	-	25,875	-	1,495
5015 Motor vehicle parts, used [2]	-	8	-	11	1	-	18,545	-	241
5021 Furniture [2]	-	8	-	48	6	-	38,250	-	2,249
5023 Homefurnishings [2]	-	11	-	181	16	-	29,635	-	5,764
5031 Lumber, plywood, and millwork [2]	-	19	-	476	25	-	29,815	-	14,214
5033 Roofing, siding, & insulation [2]	-	12	-	65	5	-	33,108	-	2,247
5039 Construction materials, nec [2]	-	11	-	87	8	-	28,690	-	2,536
5044 Office equipment [2]	-	26	-	624	24	-	41,590	-	24,453
5045 Computers, peripherals, & software [2]	-	47	-	1,317	28	-	37,516	-	45,457
5046 Commercial equipment, nec [2]	-	10	-	98	10	-	24,122	-	2,383
5047 Medical and hospital equipment	-	20	-	90	5	-	47,378	-	5,067
5050 Metals and minerals, except petroleum [2]	-	11	-	149	14	-	31,866	-	4,501
5063 Electrical apparatus and equipment [2]	-	27	-	370	14	-	40,314	-	13,820
5064 Electrical appliances, TV & radios [2]	-	14	-	117	8	-	28,581	-	3,583
5065 Electronic parts and equipment [2]	-	22	-	392	18	-	39,500	-	15,869
5072 Hardware [2]	-	12	-	72	6	-	47,611	-	3,235
5074 Plumbing & hydronic heating supplies [2]	-	25	-	464	19	-	28,879	-	13,403
5075 Warm air heating & air conditioning	-	17	-	115	7	-	37,322	-	4,510

Continued on next page.

HARRISBURG - LEBANON - CARLISLE, PA MSA - [continued]

Wholesale and Retail Trade USA	Establishments		Employment		Emp / Est	Pay / Employee		Annual Payroll ($ 000)	
	1994	1995	1994	1995	1995	1994	1995	1994	1995
5078 Refrigeration equipment and supplies [2]	-	6	-	59	10	-	23,119	-	1,267
5082 Construction and mining machinery	-	19	-	423	22	-	38,298	-	16,124
5083 Farm and garden machinery	-	32	-	318	10	-	23,208	-	8,372
5084 Industrial machinery and equipment [2]	-	36	-	430	12	-	30,391	-	16,474
5085 Industrial supplies [2]	-	22	-	151	7	-	26,993	-	5,003
5087 Service establishment equipment [2]	-	21	-	137	7	-	23,095	-	3,737
5091 Sporting & recreational goods [2]	-	15	-	168	11	-	17,738	-	3,000
5092 Toys and hobby goods and supplies [2]	-	7	-	21	3	-	14,857	-	358
5093 Scrap and waste materials	-	16	-	123	8	-	22,211	-	3,089
5099 Durable goods, nec [2]	-	13	-	31	2	-	32,903	-	4,134
5111 Printing and writing paper [2]	-	4	-	131	33	-	40,244	-	5,220
5112 Stationery and office supplies [2]	-	21	-	97	5	-	21,196	-	2,212
5113 Industrial & personal service paper [2]	-	8	-	35	4	-	41,600	-	1,582
5120 Drugs, proprietaries, and sundries [2]	-	16	-	227	14	-	28,229	-	5,773
5130 Apparel, piece goods, and notions [2]	-	12	-	132	11	-	24,545	-	3,242
5141 Groceries, general line [2]	-	11	-	2,008	183	-	31,120	-	66,106
5143 Dairy products, exc. dried or canned [2]	-	8	-	189	24	-	28,614	-	5,955
5145 Confectionery [2]	-	8	-	79	10	-	24,405	-	2,210
5147 Meats and meat products [2]	-	4	-	32	8	-	32,750	-	1,089
5148 Fresh fruits and vegetables [2]	-	9	-	523	58	-	21,117	-	11,583
5149 Groceries and related products, nec [2]	-	28	-	525	19	-	32,046	-	18,033
5150 Farm-product raw materials	-	13	-	80	6	-	15,950	-	1,345
5162 Plastics materials & basic shapes [2]	-	4	-	45	11	-	36,356	-	1,610
5169 Chemicals & allied products, nec [2]	-	18	-	239	13	-	32,519	-	8,219
5171 Petroleum bulk stations & terminals [2]	-	20	-	124	6	-	42,484	-	4,601
5172 Petroleum products, nec [2]	-	6	-	27	5	-	62,370	-	1,951
5181 Beer and ale	-	11	-	168	15	-	38,667	-	6,769
5191 Farm supplies	-	19	-	183	10	-	30,142	-	5,488
5192 Books, periodicals, & newspapers [2]	-	10	-	346	35	-	20,231	-	8,132
5193 Flowers & florists' supplies [2]	-	9	-	72	8	-	19,111	-	1,446
5199 Nondurable goods, nec [2]	-	25	-	148	6	-	17,243	-	2,318
52- Retail trade	-	3,749	-	55,908	15	-	13,548	-	802,684
5210 Lumber and other building materials	-	47	-	1,275	27	-	19,918	-	24,432
5230 Paint, glass, and wallpaper stores [2]	-	16	-	69	4	-	22,261	-	1,612
5250 Hardware stores	-	38	-	285	8	-	11,818	-	3,500
5260 Retail nurseries and garden stores	-	41	-	362	9	-	14,320	-	6,779
5270 Mobile home dealers	-	13	-	27	2	-	23,704	-	653
5310 Department stores [2]	-	33	-	4,761	144	-	11,918	-	59,084
5330 Variety stores	-	20	-	230	12	-	8,278	-	1,979
5390 Misc. general merchandise stores	-	27	-	831	31	-	12,361	-	10,002
5410 Grocery stores [2]	-	258	-	7,113	28	-	10,137	-	74,629
5420 Meat and fish markets	-	27	-	140	5	-	11,229	-	1,595
5430 Fruit and vegetable markets	-	11	-	17	2	-	15,294	-	296
5440 Candy, nut, and confectionery stores [2]	-	21	-	195	9	-	6,523	-	1,566
5450 Dairy products stores [2]	-	8	-	15	2	-	3,733	-	38
5460 Retail bakeries [2]	-	35	-	330	9	-	7,261	-	2,349
5490 Miscellaneous food stores [2]	-	17	-	64	4	-	7,563	-	500
5510 New and used car dealers	-	82	-	3,291	40	-	27,396	-	99,634
5520 Used car dealers	-	56	-	340	6	-	21,435	-	7,588
5530 Auto and home supply stores	-	67	-	538	8	-	18,714	-	10,355
5540 Gasoline service stations	-	285	-	2,537	9	-	11,820	-	30,858
5550 Boat dealers [2]	-	8	-	29	4	-	15,862	-	612
5570 Motorcycle dealers [2]	-	10	-	42	4	-	17,048	-	795
5610 Men's & boys' clothing stores	-	32	-	243	8	-	10,107	-	2,718
5620 Women's clothing stores	-	98	-	932	10	-	6,974	-	6,530
5630 Women's accessory & specialty stores [2]	-	22	-	94	4	-	10,553	-	977
5640 Children's and infants' wear stores [2]	-	10	-	35	4	-	7,886	-	361
5650 Family clothing stores	-	36	-	501	14	-	10,331	-	5,416
5660 Shoe stores	-	88	-	411	5	-	11,416	-	4,674
5690 Misc. apparel & accessory stores [2]	-	20	-	153	8	-	13,725	-	1,659
5712 Furniture stores	-	67	-	488	7	-	18,156	-	9,492
5713 Floor covering stores	-	46	-	292	6	-	22,301	-	7,377
5714 Drapery and upholstery stores [2]	-	3	-	6	2	-	8,667	-	59
5719 Misc. homefurnishings stores [2]	-	30	-	180	6	-	10,111	-	1,956
5720 Household appliance stores	-	36	-	203	6	-	21,458	-	4,437
5731 Radio, TV, & electronic stores	-	33	-	185	6	-	22,811	-	3,641
5734 Computer and software stores [2]	-	15	-	56	4	-	11,571	-	775
5735 Record & prerecorded tape stores	-	27	-	146	5	-	8,247	-	1,299
5736 Musical instrument stores [2]	-	15	-	62	4	-	17,613	-	1,231
5812 Eating places	-	846	-	15,481	18	-	7,600	-	126,171
5813 Drinking places	-	139	-	799	6	-	8,345	-	6,715

Continued on next page.

HARRISBURG - LEBANON - CARLISLE, PA MSA - [continued]

Wholesale and Retail Trade USA	Establishments		Employment		Emp / Est	Pay / Employee		Annual Payroll ($ 000)	
	1994	1995	1994	1995	1995	1994	1995	1994	1995
5910 Drug stores and proprietary stores	-	118	-	1,516	13	-	15,821	-	24,550
5920 Liquor stores	-	62	-	287	5	-	15,415	-	4,566
5930 Used merchandise stores	-	45	-	416	9	-	8,923	-	3,153
5941 Sporting goods and bicycle shops	-	62	-	372	6	-	10,839	-	4,057
5942 Book stores [2]	-	33	-	367	11	-	11,030	-	3,809
5943 Stationery stores [2]	-	9	-	65	7	-	12,985	-	800
5944 Jewelry stores	-	75	-	368	5	-	13,739	-	4,682
5945 Hobby, toy, and game shops	-	26	-	346	13	-	16,035	-	4,377
5946 Camera & photographic supply stores [2]	-	9	-	30	3	-	14,533	-	438
5947 Gift, novelty, and souvenir shops	-	84	-	429	5	-	7,580	-	3,562
5949 Sewing, needlework, and piece goods [2]	-	16	-	218	14	-	11,798	-	2,668
5961 Catalog and mail-order houses [2]	-	16	-	41	3	-	21,463	-	952
5962 Merchandising machine operators	-	13	-	287	22	-	22,202	-	7,186
5963 Direct selling establishments [2]	-	36	-	1,099	31	-	26,180	-	23,904
5983 Fuel oil dealers [2]	-	57	-	395	7	-	22,086	-	9,760
5992 Florists	-	48	-	500	10	-	10,656	-	5,554
5994 News dealers and newsstands	-	12	-	34	3	-	8,588	-	343
5995 Optical goods stores	-	44	-	162	4	-	16,370	-	2,601
5999 Miscellaneous retail stores, nec	-	95	-	390	4	-	12,051	-	5,109

Source: County Business Patterns 1994/95, CBP-94/95, U.S. Department of Commerce, Washington DC, November 1997. The employment column represents mid-March employment in the year. Pay per employee is calculated by dividing 1st Quarter payroll, annualized, by mid-March employment. The column headed 'Emp / Est' shows 'employees per establishment'. A dash (-) means that data are unavailable or cannot be calculated. nec means not elsewhere classified. *Notes:* 1. 1994 data incomplete; unavailable or withheld. 2. 1995 data incomplete; unavailable or withheld. 3. 1994 and 1995 data incomplete; unavailable or withheld.

HICKORY - MORGANTON, NC MSA

Wholesale and Retail Trade USA	Establishments		Employment		Emp / Est	Pay / Employee		Annual Payroll ($ 000)	
	1994	1995	1994	1995	1995	1994	1995	1994	1995
50 - Wholesale trade	525	535	7,915	8,417	16	27,124	29,066	240,418	251,517
5012 Automobiles and other vehicles [3]	10	11	262	201	18	19,038	29,174	5,930	5,006
5013 Motor vehicle supplies and new parts	16	15	77	77	5	17,818	17,195	1,403	1,472
5014 Tires and tubes [3]	10	7	87	57	8	24,690	24,281	2,651	1,781
5015 Motor vehicle parts, used [3]	11	9	53	34	4	13,887	16,000	714	589
5021 Furniture [3]	34	33	145	167	5	21,655	21,533	3,686	3,817
5023 Homefurnishings [3]	7	6	30	32	5	11,600	27,375	384	962
5031 Lumber, plywood, and millwork [3]	34	33	206	209	6	27,495	30,086	6,599	6,381
5044 Office equipment [3]	13	14	59	67	5	23,322	23,164	1,439	1,560
5045 Computers, peripherals, & software [3]	9	7	141	307	44	33,135	27,648	4,690	8,780
5051 Metals service centers and offices [1]	5	-	62	-	-	29,419	-	2,447	-
5063 Electrical apparatus and equipment [3]	14	14	125	150	11	23,264	24,320	3,987	4,573
5072 Hardware [1]	15	16	82	94	6	20,780	17,957	1,964	1,850
5074 Plumbing & hydronic heating supplies [3]	8	10	64	72	7	26,563	25,167	1,730	2,035
5075 Warm air heating & air conditioning [3]	9	8	61	54	7	23,213	24,000	1,329	1,449
5083 Farm and garden machinery [2]	-	6	-	22	4	-	21,455	-	536
5084 Industrial machinery and equipment [3]	38	39	269	310	8	34,201	32,077	9,336	10,831
5085 Industrial supplies	32	32	410	414	13	20,820	23,082	9,506	10,330
5087 Service establishment equipment [3]	9	8	112	114	14	27,357	30,316	3,295	3,812
5091 Sporting & recreational goods [2]	-	5	-	9	2	-	18,667	-	193
5093 Scrap and waste materials [3]	10	9	51	49	5	19,294	21,469	1,070	1,067
5099 Durable goods, nec [3]	8	13	12	7	1	19,000	14,286	362	219
5112 Stationery and office supplies [3]	19	17	162	118	7	28,889	30,407	4,945	3,705
5113 Industrial & personal service paper [3]	4	8	35	34	4	38,286	35,059	1,299	1,572
5131 Piece goods & notions [1]	21	-	442	-	-	33,466	-	15,048	-
5137 Women's and children's clothing [3]	4	4	4	5	1	18,000	9,600	51	36
5140 Groceries and related products	17	18	1,632	1,729	96	26,770	30,487	52,707	55,914
5150 Farm-product raw materials [2]	-	4	-	17	4	-	2,588	-	45
5169 Chemicals & allied products, nec [3]	13	12	7	8	1	25,143	44,000	234	309
5171 Petroleum bulk stations & terminals [2]	12	11	65	77	7	24,308	25,662	1,590	1,980
5180 Beer, wine, and distilled beverages [3]	6	6	156	152	25	24,974	30,079	4,172	4,376
5191 Farm supplies	11	-	9	-	-	10,667	-	117	-
5198 Paints, varnishes, and supplies [1]	4	-	83	-	-	34,795	-	2,842	-
5199 Nondurable goods, nec	25	27	126	141	5	30,730	34,298	4,768	5,215
52 - Retail trade	1,940	1,948	24,309	25,642	13	10,869	11,801	287,158	317,582
5210 Lumber and other building materials	50	35	581	460	13	17,425	23,113	10,314	10,425
5230 Paint, glass, and wallpaper stores	13	14	30	24	2	18,400	16,833	615	396
5250 Hardware stores	27	22	157	90	4	11,083	12,044	1,962	1,383
5260 Retail nurseries and garden stores	18	17	91	106	6	14,242	13,283	1,547	1,634
5270 Mobile home dealers [1]	19	22	60	143	7	26,000	19,692	1,972	3,120
5310 Department stores [3]	15	13	2,707	2,140	165	8,873	11,978	25,684	23,764

Continued on next page.

HICKORY-MORGANTON, NC MSA - [continued]

Wholesale and Retail Trade USA	Establishments		Employment		Emp / Est	Pay / Employee		Annual Payroll ($ 000)	
	1994	1995	1994	1995	1995	1994	1995	1994	1995
5330 Variety stores	22	18	88	69	4	7,227	7,768	756	620
5390 Misc. general merchandise stores	10	17	261	276	16	11,862	12,058	3,088	3,313
5410 Grocery stores[3]	211	209	3,685	4,377	21	9,424	9,636	34,095	43,219
5460 Retail bakeries[3]	7	5	41	40	8	9,073	9,100	406	398
5490 Miscellaneous food stores	8	-	12	-	-	11,667	-	163	-
5510 New and used car dealers	38	39	1,073	1,146	29	26,084	28,925	31,515	37,217
5520 Used car dealers	50	51	105	127	2	22,210	25,701	3,028	3,354
5530 Auto and home supply stores	74	79	526	590	7	16,342	18,881	9,394	11,650
5540 Gasoline service stations	121	124	581	693	6	10,995	11,619	6,940	8,397
5550 Boat dealers[3]	7	8	40	50	6	21,400	20,640	1,072	1,232
5570 Motorcycle dealers[3]	8	9	20	21	2	14,200	16,381	324	415
5610 Men's & boys' clothing stores[1]	7	-	22	-	-	12,545	-	292	-
5620 Women's clothing stores	59	56	520	449	8	8,315	8,766	4,645	3,991
5630 Women's accessory & specialty stores[2]	7	6	25	24	4	7,520	8,167	192	203
5640 Children's and infants' wear stores[1]	4	-	28	-	-	6,714	-	187	-
5650 Family clothing stores[2]	21	23	273	229	10	9,846	10,166	2,800	2,629
5660 Shoe stores	41	37	160	169	5	10,925	9,941	1,704	1,725
5690 Misc. apparel & accessory stores[3]	5	6	31	23	4	5,032	9,043	164	227
5712 Furniture stores	95	102	723	747	7	18,307	20,037	14,895	16,113
5713 Floor covering stores	15	17	52	85	5	19,462	16,941	1,138	1,629
5714 Drapery and upholstery stores	11	-	8	-	-	16,000	-	124	-
5719 Misc. homefurnishings stores[3]	13	16	46	52	3	11,217	11,000	588	616
5720 Household appliance stores	14	14	56	49	4	16,000	20,245	1,009	1,063
5731 Radio, TV, & electronic stores	29	26	148	157	6	16,297	17,146	2,673	2,787
5734 Computer and software stores[2]	-	7	-	21	3	-	19,429	-	460
5735 Record & prerecorded tape stores[3]	6	7	16	94	13	13,500	9,191	362	653
5736 Musical instrument stores[2]	-	5	-	7	1	-	12,571	-	95
5812 Eating places	390	359	8,009	8,308	23	7,226	7,688	62,755	66,438
5813 Drinking places[2]	17	14	89	140	10	5,303	8,371	842	1,125
5910 Drug stores and proprietary stores	79	73	707	685	9	14,976	16,350	11,463	12,138
5930 Used merchandise stores[1]	29	31	109	117	4	8,881	8,855	1,074	1,123
5941 Sporting goods and bicycle shops	29	28	96	84	3	9,583	11,286	1,081	1,128
5942 Book stores	12	11	52	44	4	7,615	7,909	382	357
5944 Jewelry stores	44	43	158	148	3	16,684	15,216	2,526	2,259
5945 Hobby, toy, and game shops[3]	15	14	170	190	14	11,624	11,242	2,285	2,228
5947 Gift, novelty, and souvenir shops[2]	20	22	147	121	6	6,476	6,975	1,022	883
5949 Sewing, needlework, and piece goods[3]	6	6	33	37	6	10,424	8,324	364	300
5961 Catalog and mail-order houses	8	11	9	24	2	11,111	14,000	113	359
5962 Merchandising machine operators	22	18	407	474	26	20,216	18,456	8,426	9,701
5963 Direct selling establishments[3]	19	19	91	96	5	16,747	18,083	1,702	1,726
5980 Fuel dealers	20	18	73	95	5	20,986	21,263	1,543	1,924
5992 Florists	38	39	108	107	3	8,000	8,972	926	1,002
5995 Optical goods stores[3]	10	10	66	47	5	11,576	19,064	963	891
5999 Miscellaneous retail stores, nec	38	37	152	160	4	9,316	9,925	1,723	1,858

Source: County Business Patterns 1994/95, CBP-94/95, U.S. Department of Commerce, Washington DC, November 1997. The employment column represents mid-March employment in the year. Pay per employee is calculated by dividing 1st Quarter payroll, annualized, by mid-March employment. The column headed 'Emp / Est' shows 'employees per establishment'. A dash (-) means that data are unavailable or cannot be calculated. nec means not elsewhere classified. *Notes:* 1. 1994 data incomplete; unavailable or withheld. 2. 1995 data incomplete; unavailable or withheld. 3. 1994 and 1995 data incomplete; unavailable or withheld.

HONOLULU, HI MSA

Wholesale and Retail Trade USA	Establishments		Employment		Emp / Est	Pay / Employee		Annual Payroll ($ 000)	
	1994	1995	1994	1995	1995	1994	1995	1994	1995
50- Wholesale trade	1,710	1,704	18,152	18,108	11	29,225	30,985	546,292	561,642
5012 Automobiles and other vehicles	-	16	-	115	7	-	35,270	-	4,330
5013 Motor vehicle supplies and new parts	57	52	860	810	16	21,507	22,998	20,249	19,067
5020 Furniture and homefurnishings	60	64	550	679	11	27,455	28,801	16,498	19,144
5031 Lumber, plywood, and millwork	30	22	465	367	17	34,822	41,777	17,699	14,939
5032 Brick, stone, & related materials	15	14	82	69	5	31,171	32,928	2,580	1,976
5033 Roofing, siding, & insulation	15	-	123	-	-	26,309	-	2,859	-
5039 Construction materials, nec	22	35	179	205	6	29,922	37,659	5,938	7,972
5044 Office equipment	27	28	598	691	25	36,167	41,766	22,341	25,091
5045 Computers, peripherals, & software	35	36	488	464	13	52,656	63,672	24,205	26,443
5046 Commercial equipment, nec	-	22	-	195	9	-	24,349	-	4,798
5047 Medical and hospital equipment	35	32	251	218	7	31,745	36,881	8,375	8,258
5051 Metals service centers and offices	19	18	178	173	10	35,483	38,173	6,740	6,739
5063 Electrical apparatus and equipment	54	-	556	-	-	41,317	-	21,591	-
5065 Electronic parts and equipment	34	38	424	476	13	39,387	45,025	17,861	22,048
5072 Hardware	36	38	334	294	8	27,545	29,810	8,914	9,006

Continued on next page.

HONOLULU, HI MSA - [continued]

Wholesale and Retail Trade USA	Establishments		Employment		Emp / Est	Pay / Employee		Annual Payroll ($ 000)	
	1994	1995	1994	1995	1995	1994	1995	1994	1995
5075 Warm air heating & air conditioning	11	12	77	97	8	33,247	33,031	3,181	4,001
5082 Construction and mining machinery	8	8	292	284	36	46,562	45,169	11,802	11,174
5083 Farm and garden machinery	7	8	85	82	10	37,647	41,317	3,232	3,084
5084 Industrial machinery and equipment	36	34	252	248	7	32,175	32,903	8,010	7,946
5085 Industrial supplies	27	27	282	287	11	31,447	31,373	9,299	9,669
5087 Service establishment equipment	19	20	137	120	6	21,460	21,000	3,143	2,795
5088 Transportation equipment & supplies	7	7	27	35	5	20,741	19,429	584	640
5091 Sporting & recreational goods	39	-	177	-	-	26,418	-	4,996	-
5093 Scrap and waste materials	17	18	122	136	8	22,525	28,882	3,259	4,713
5099 Durable goods, nec	41	40	292	257	6	25,753	25,167	7,322	6,487
5111 Printing and writing paper	5	-	53	-	-	35,472	-	1,688	-
5112 Stationery and office supplies	42	41	505	480	12	22,970	23,917	11,857	11,702
5113 Industrial & personal service paper	22	21	514	512	24	29,012	30,883	14,252	15,751
5120 Drugs, proprietaries, and sundries	41	44	649	572	13	29,159	32,587	18,287	17,649
5131 Piece goods & notions	24	-	187	-	-	28,556	-	5,212	-
5136 Men's and boys' clothing	31	33	255	348	11	20,471	21,115	6,048	8,116
5137 Women's and children's clothing	35	36	218	348	10	22,972	21,770	6,894	8,476
5139 Footwear	16	15	55	56	4	20,509	20,429	1,242	1,187
5141 Groceries, general line	38	37	627	550	15	24,848	25,324	14,706	14,108
5142 Packaged frozen food	43	39	293	278	7	28,969	30,576	8,903	8,642
5143 Dairy products, exc. dried or canned	4	4	83	62	16	24,723	26,323	1,873	1,691
5145 Confectionery	18	20	205	210	11	20,293	22,324	5,325	5,768
5146 Fish and seafoods	34	33	319	324	10	26,019	24,728	8,307	8,669
5147 Meats and meat products	21	20	407	407	20	24,619	22,978	10,073	10,467
5148 Fresh fruits and vegetables	34	33	527	579	18	23,871	26,964	15,196	15,250
5149 Groceries and related products, nec	67	61	1,071	1,076	18	24,773	25,710	26,943	28,351
5162 Plastics materials & basic shapes	8	9	101	118	13	30,099	28,746	3,546	3,634
5169 Chemicals & allied products, nec	23	-	250	-	-	31,936	-	8,041	-
5171 Petroleum bulk stations & terminals	10	8	199	161	20	38,010	45,118	7,300	7,381
5172 Petroleum products, nec	17	16	271	302	19	48,546	46,291	12,142	12,124
5181 Beer and ale	6	-	344	-	-	37,965	-	14,090	-
5182 Wine and distilled beverages	10	-	196	-	-	32,714	-	6,739	-
5191 Farm supplies	22	18	103	101	6	19,573	20,832	2,112	2,175
5193 Flowers & florists' supplies	23	18	163	128	7	18,282	17,625	3,045	2,500
5198 Paints, varnishes, and supplies	14	11	97	77	7	22,309	26,649	2,091	2,063
5199 Nondurable goods, nec	98	96	534	511	5	20,180	20,736	11,739	11,442
52 - Retail trade	5,371	5,386	78,906	80,600	15	15,992	16,138	1,291,502	1,330,302
5210 Lumber and other building materials	38	31	1,130	958	31	18,743	19,006	20,614	19,085
5230 Paint, glass, and wallpaper stores	9	7	90	102	15	23,733	23,333	2,512	2,453
5250 Hardware stores	15	8	133	80	10	22,346	20,900	3,163	1,898
5260 Retail nurseries and garden stores	9	12	37	75	6	16,541	15,680	824	1,159
5390 Misc. general merchandise stores	40	42	2,901	3,105	74	18,683	18,851	62,201	61,677
5410 Grocery stores	376	372	7,052	6,764	18	17,807	18,270	125,241	126,343
5420 Meat and fish markets	41	43	300	308	7	14,347	14,013	4,744	4,896
5430 Fruit and vegetable markets	13	13	60	49	4	12,133	12,653	719	675
5440 Candy, nut, and confectionery stores	25	26	158	189	7	12,785	11,725	2,279	2,399
5460 Retail bakeries	96	95	1,111	879	9	11,568	11,618	13,183	10,477
5490 Miscellaneous food stores	42	52	159	220	4	11,849	10,691	2,217	2,664
5510 New and used car dealers	44	46	2,804	2,815	61	32,649	33,698	93,899	96,739
5520 Used car dealers	11	12	51	67	6	34,275	28,836	1,798	1,977
5530 Auto and home supply stores	96	104	632	762	7	24,468	24,840	16,095	19,369
5540 Gasoline service stations	203	194	2,279	2,160	11	13,839	14,341	33,724	32,320
5550 Boat dealers	-	6	-	59	10	-	22,169	-	1,252
5570 Motorcycle dealers	9	8	129	129	16	24,775	23,659	3,289	2,936
5610 Men's & boys' clothing stores	56	53	499	458	9	13,539	13,668	6,605	6,174
5620 Women's clothing stores	209	203	1,690	1,755	9	12,462	12,944	20,831	22,647
5630 Women's accessory & specialty stores	52	49	422	372	8	17,365	20,086	8,192	7,654
5640 Children's and infants' wear stores	25	24	181	188	8	8,950	8,766	1,496	1,663
5650 Family clothing stores	129	123	1,530	1,609	13	14,267	15,876	23,285	27,991
5660 Shoe stores	90	94	936	1,085	12	16,068	16,247	15,944	17,241
5690 Misc. apparel & accessory stores	80	80	752	797	10	13,819	11,960	10,292	9,934
5712 Furniture stores	56	52	359	314	6	25,170	25,325	8,868	7,912
5713 Floor covering stores	18	18	113	139	8	32,142	29,094	3,970	4,682
5714 Drapery and upholstery stores	6	6	34	29	5	22,000	22,483	770	647
5719 Misc. homefurnishings stores	46	46	295	366	8	15,675	16,404	5,389	6,256
5720 Household appliance stores	27	27	136	140	5	20,500	20,600	2,879	2,952
5731 Radio, TV, & electronic stores	49	51	385	392	8	20,177	21,633	7,649	7,830
5734 Computer and software stores	31	32	288	252	8	20,833	21,381	6,112	5,489
5735 Record & prerecorded tape stores	34	35	324	347	10	13,494	15,009	4,476	4,962
5736 Musical instrument stores	13	13	123	99	8	18,179	23,111	2,201	2,093
5812 Eating places	1,607	1,513	30,860	32,045	21	12,511	12,329	390,294	402,975

Continued on next page.

HONOLULU, HI MSA - [continued]

Wholesale and Retail Trade USA	Establishments		Employment		Emp / Est	Pay / Employee		Annual Payroll ($ 000)	
	1994	1995	1994	1995	1995	1994	1995	1994	1995
5813 Drinking places	248	211	1,928	1,668	8	11,668	11,084	21,797	17,416
5910 Drug stores and proprietary stores	94	92	2,930	2,701	29	19,618	19,591	57,403	51,684
5920 Liquor stores	45	42	125	120	3	15,104	15,967	1,988	1,926
5930 Used merchandise stores	49	45	306	287	6	12,967	12,390	4,174	3,527
5941 Sporting goods and bicycle shops	93	87	806	943	11	14,427	14,753	12,159	13,588
5942 Book stores	36	40	307	392	10	11,883	13,082	3,821	5,944
5944 Jewelry stores	253	266	1,515	1,495	6	19,398	20,621	28,793	31,644
5945 Hobby, toy, and game shops	42	38	356	360	9	19,865	11,789	5,781	4,618
5946 Camera & photographic supply stores	10	-	54	-	-	12,963	-	716	-
5947 Gift, novelty, and souvenir shops	201	197	1,117	1,201	6	13,404	14,172	16,342	17,761
5948 Luggage and leather goods stores	24	24	300	350	15	24,187	27,086	7,901	10,665
5949 Sewing, needlework, and piece goods	18	14	130	84	6	11,231	11,429	1,539	1,024
5963 Direct selling establishments	54	59	428	380	6	15,813	16,063	6,758	6,425
5992 Florists	104	102	440	481	5	11,364	11,701	5,369	5,728
5995 Optical goods stores	56	-	394	-	-	14,569	-	5,841	-
5999 Miscellaneous retail stores, nec	119	137	758	891	7	15,836	16,934	12,928	15,562

Source: County Business Patterns 1994/95, CBP-94/95, U.S. Department of Commerce, Washington DC, November 1997. The employment column represents mid-March employment in the year. Pay per employee is calculated by dividing 1st Quarter payroll, annualized, by mid-March employment. The column headed 'Emp / Est' shows 'employees per establishment'. A dash (-) means that data are unavailable or cannot be calculated. nec means not elsewhere classified. *Notes:* 1. 1994 data incomplete; unavailable or withheld. 2. 1995 data incomplete; unavailable or withheld. 3. 1994 and 1995 data incomplete; unavailable or withheld.

HOUMA, LA MSA

Wholesale and Retail Trade USA	Establishments		Employment		Emp / Est	Pay / Employee		Annual Payroll ($ 000)	
	1994	1995	1994	1995	1995	1994	1995	1994	1995
50- Wholesale trade	338	338	3,630	3,717	11	18,584	19,132	73,710	76,694
5012 Automobiles and other vehicles	5	5	139	117	23	10,532	7,624	1,786	944
5013 Motor vehicle supplies and new parts	16	12	98	92	8	20,939	25,565	2,151	2,455
5015 Motor vehicle parts, used [1]	5	6	17	18	3	9,882	11,778	179	218
5039 Construction materials, nec	-	6	-	75	13	-	25,227	-	1,690
5045 Computers, peripherals, & software	4	-	18	-	-	16,444	-	390	-
5050 Metals and minerals, except petroleum	8	8	176	62	8	25,568	24,194	4,632	1,760
5063 Electrical apparatus and equipment	12	10	68	60	6	20,647	22,133	1,656	1,608
5065 Electronic parts and equipment	9	9	13	14	2	17,846	20,286	273	317
5074 Plumbing & hydronic heating supplies	-	6	-	61	10	-	17,770	-	1,144
5075 Warm air heating & air conditioning	5	5	10	14	3	16,000	19,429	220	287
5084 Industrial machinery and equipment	52	53	493	500	9	29,225	29,856	14,935	15,327
5085 Industrial supplies	22	22	189	194	9	25,228	24,165	5,239	5,439
5088 Transportation equipment & supplies	9	9	34	49	5	26,706	23,510	1,060	1,635
5091 Sporting & recreational goods [3]	3	3	14	14	5	8,000	6,857	123	103
5112 Stationery and office supplies	9	6	54	18	3	15,852	19,556	855	376
5141 Groceries, general line	-	5	-	29	6	-	14,207	-	424
5142 Packaged frozen food	7	7	348	352	50	16,287	19,886	6,046	6,890
5146 Fish and seafoods	46	47	612	671	14	6,281	6,528	4,932	5,218
5149 Groceries and related products, nec	6	6	76	92	15	25,684	21,957	2,116	2,155
5169 Chemicals & allied products, nec	12	14	30	36	3	28,000	27,556	1,441	1,468
5171 Petroleum bulk stations & terminals	17	14	127	136	10	29,417	27,559	3,396	3,447
5172 Petroleum products, nec [3]	4	4	8	8	2	30,000	41,500	240	270
5191 Farm supplies	10	10	44	63	6	19,727	18,476	1,030	1,187
5199 Nondurable goods, nec [3]	4	4	34	43	11	15,647	14,047	552	683
52- Retail trade	1,097	1,071	12,568	13,102	12	10,736	11,256	144,753	156,677
5210 Lumber and other building materials	26	22	546	439	20	16,147	15,982	8,736	7,554
5230 Paint, glass, and wallpaper stores	6	5	19	15	3	17,684	17,333	462	298
5250 Hardware stores	24	15	101	74	5	12,950	10,595	1,395	841
5260 Retail nurseries and garden stores	11	11	51	47	4	12,000	10,723	556	619
5270 Mobile home dealers	-	4	-	27	7	-	13,037	-	542
5310 Department stores [3]	10	10	963	1,159	116	10,193	12,894	10,691	13,682
5330 Variety stores	14	8	79	71	9	8,354	8,000	722	604
5390 Misc. general merchandise stores	7	12	96	116	10	11,792	11,759	1,259	1,347
5410 Grocery stores	149	144	2,532	2,671	19	9,536	9,516	25,063	26,565
5420 Meat and fish markets	15	14	47	63	5	11,660	8,000	565	526
5460 Retail bakeries	19	20	100	121	6	6,120	7,471	728	928
5490 Miscellaneous food stores	6	-	28	-	-	8,286	-	225	-
5510 New and used car dealers	17	15	690	784	52	24,255	25,046	19,071	23,686
5520 Used car dealers	8	9	29	14	2	5,793	12,000	163	187
5530 Auto and home supply stores	42	41	228	224	5	15,281	16,946	3,803	3,900
5540 Gasoline service stations	95	94	516	588	6	9,217	9,034	5,236	5,521
5550 Boat dealers	14	12	71	81	7	15,042	15,407	1,161	1,369
5610 Men's & boys' clothing stores	9	7	35	19	3	8,571	11,368	237	198

Continued on next page.

HOUMA, LA MSA - [continued]

Wholesale and Retail Trade USA	Establishments		Employment		Emp / Est	Pay / Employee		Annual Payroll ($ 000)	
	1994	1995	1994	1995	1995	1994	1995	1994	1995
5620 Women's clothing stores	33	29	234	178	6	9,487	9,348	2,076	1,518
5640 Children's and infants' wear stores [3]	4	5	19	25	5	10,105	8,800	163	222
5650 Family clothing stores	13	13	156	147	11	9,103	8,626	1,355	1,549
5660 Shoe stores	22	21	104	97	5	9,077	11,464	1,115	1,126
5690 Misc. apparel & accessory stores	6	6	15	19	3	9,067	10,105	138	159
5712 Furniture stores	19	22	173	176	8	12,948	12,341	2,403	2,413
5720 Household appliance stores	14	14	68	65	5	11,824	12,431	817	873
5731 Radio, TV, & electronic stores	13	15	72	67	4	15,333	15,761	1,032	1,018
5812 Eating places	182	168	3,180	3,264	19	8,000	8,141	27,630	28,109
5813 Drinking places	41	32	152	140	4	6,632	6,143	1,005	809
5910 Drug stores and proprietary stores	47	42	414	448	11	14,580	15,929	6,561	7,321
5930 Used merchandise stores	8	11	39	60	5	8,308	9,133	411	552
5941 Sporting goods and bicycle shops	12	12	31	38	3	11,871	12,316	489	508
5944 Jewelry stores	19	19	85	95	5	15,106	13,516	1,298	1,355
5947 Gift, novelty, and souvenir shops	16	16	73	50	3	5,425	6,240	369	311
5949 Sewing, needlework, and piece goods [3]	4	3	24	27	9	10,333	8,444	288	261
5963 Direct selling establishments	9	7	27	16	2	19,407	9,250	467	132
5980 Fuel dealers [1]	3	-	6	-	-	18,000	-	197	-
5992 Florists	18	17	48	43	3	6,083	7,814	315	346
5995 Optical goods stores	12	10	57	50	5	14,035	14,240	731	650
5999 Miscellaneous retail stores, nec	32	34	178	131	4	9,348	13,008	1,835	1,980

Source: County Business Patterns 1994/95, CBP-94/95, U.S. Department of Commerce, Washington DC, November 1997. The employment column represents mid-March employment in the year. Pay per employee is calculated by dividing 1st Quarter payroll, annualized, by mid-March employment. The column headed 'Emp / Est' shows 'employees per establishment'. A dash (-) means that data are unavailable or cannot be calculated. nec means not elsewhere classified. *Notes:* 1. 1994 data incomplete; unavailable or withheld. 2. 1995 data incomplete; unavailable or withheld. 3. 1994 and 1995 data incomplete; unavailable or withheld.

HOUSTON, TX PMSA

Wholesale and Retail Trade USA	Establishments		Employment		Emp / Est	Pay / Employee		Annual Payroll ($ 000)	
	1994	1995	1994	1995	1995	1994	1995	1994	1995
50- Wholesale trade	-	9,230	-	121,853	13	-	37,270	-	4,719,351
5012 Automobiles and other vehicles [2]	-	98	-	1,824	19	-	23,950	-	46,302
5013 Motor vehicle supplies and new parts [2]	-	266	-	3,206	12	-	28,337	-	94,220
5014 Tires and tubes [2]	-	46	-	517	11	-	29,462	-	15,175
5015 Motor vehicle parts, used [2]	-	117	-	806	7	-	19,538	-	16,423
5021 Furniture [2]	-	136	-	1,625	12	-	30,299	-	51,622
5023 Homefurnishings [2]	-	127	-	1,514	12	-	24,240	-	42,700
5031 Lumber, plywood, and millwork [2]	-	81	-	1,807	22	-	26,864	-	51,327
5032 Brick, stone, & related materials [2]	-	106	-	928	9	-	28,250	-	28,907
5033 Roofing, siding, & insulation [2]	-	36	-	552	15	-	34,239	-	21,528
5039 Construction materials, nec [2]	-	125	-	1,454	12	-	26,366	-	42,096
5043 Photographic equipment & supplies [2]	-	21	-	208	10	-	28,135	-	5,991
5044 Office equipment [2]	-	126	-	2,573	20	-	37,172	-	93,859
5045 Computers, peripherals, & software [2]	-	383	-	5,687	15	-	53,423	-	271,620
5046 Commercial equipment, nec [2]	-	74	-	493	7	-	28,584	-	14,816
5047 Medical and hospital equipment [2]	-	182	-	1,801	10	-	35,438	-	67,336
5048 Ophthalmic goods [2]	-	15	-	179	12	-	24,000	-	3,625
5049 Professional equipment, nec [2]	-	55	-	584	11	-	37,219	-	21,677
5051 Metals service centers and offices [2]	-	424	-	5,782	14	-	39,794	-	247,104
5052 Coal and other minerals and ores [2]	-	10	-	38	4	-	49,263	-	1,934
5063 Electrical apparatus and equipment [2]	-	288	-	3,881	13	-	40,581	-	160,342
5064 Electrical appliances, TV & radios [2]	-	48	-	377	8	-	30,621	-	11,052
5065 Electronic parts and equipment	-	306	-	3,685	12	-	40,762	-	167,378
5072 Hardware [2]	-	173	-	2,336	14	-	27,003	-	67,243
5074 Plumbing & hydronic heating supplies [2]	-	140	-	1,337	10	-	31,874	-	45,065
5075 Warm air heating & air conditioning [2]	-	135	-	1,304	10	-	32,564	-	45,943
5078 Refrigeration equipment and supplies [2]	-	24	-	280	12	-	42,314	-	11,114
5082 Construction and mining machinery [2]	-	90	-	1,895	21	-	38,199	-	73,962
5083 Farm and garden machinery [2]	-	53	-	485	9	-	28,924	-	14,762
5084 Industrial machinery and equipment	-	1,206	-	11,046	9	-	39,001	-	464,353
5085 Industrial supplies	-	527	-	6,477	12	-	35,502	-	255,642
5087 Service establishment equipment [2]	-	118	-	1,044	9	-	30,625	-	32,889
5088 Transportation equipment & supplies [2]	-	81	-	671	8	-	31,028	-	23,110
5091 Sporting & recreational goods [2]	-	85	-	627	7	-	23,132	-	15,538
5092 Toys and hobby goods and supplies [2]	-	28	-	299	11	-	24,241	-	7,143
5093 Scrap and waste materials [2]	-	157	-	1,733	11	-	24,485	-	51,600
5094 Jewelry & precious stones [2]	-	131	-	512	4	-	31,445	-	14,521
5099 Durable goods, nec [2]	-	162	-	791	5	-	25,664	-	22,190
5111 Printing and writing paper [2]	-	36	-	394	11	-	29,442	-	12,386

Continued on next page.

HOUSTON, TX PMSA - [continued]

Wholesale and Retail Trade USA	Establishments		Employment		Emp / Est	Pay / Employee		Annual Payroll ($ 000)	
	1994	1995	1994	1995	1995	1994	1995	1994	1995
5112 Stationery and office supplies [2]	-	169	-	3,045	18	-	22,544	-	68,818
5113 Industrial & personal service paper [2]	-	60	-	728	12	-	32,286	-	23,588
5120 Drugs, proprietaries, and sundries [2]	-	97	-	1,370	14	-	36,879	-	55,606
5131 Piece goods & notions [2]	-	42	-	309	7	-	20,816	-	7,178
5136 Men's and boys' clothing [2]	-	40	-	408	10	-	24,569	-	11,851
5137 Women's and children's clothing [2]	-	57	-	400	7	-	15,520	-	7,071
5139 Footwear [2]	-	16	-	129	8	-	22,109	-	3,194
5141 Groceries, general line [2]	-	48	-	3,666	76	-	30,128	-	109,158
5142 Packaged frozen food [2]	-	30	-	686	23	-	24,910	-	19,290
5143 Dairy products, exc. dried or canned [2]	-	25	-	596	24	-	30,772	-	18,809
5144 Poultry and poultry products [2]	-	10	-	149	15	-	29,477	-	4,408
5145 Confectionery [2]	-	17	-	442	26	-	28,688	-	12,935
5146 Fish and seafoods [2]	-	35	-	290	8	-	19,710	-	5,612
5147 Meats and meat products [2]	-	48	-	863	18	-	25,789	-	21,161
5148 Fresh fruits and vegetables [2]	-	60	-	1,439	24	-	23,366	-	37,099
5149 Groceries and related products, nec [2]	-	160	-	2,733	17	-	31,139	-	86,943
5153 Grain and field beans [2]	-	23	-	204	9	-	37,412	-	7,776
5154 Livestock [2]	-	4	-	37	9	-	3,676	-	122
5159 Farm-product raw materials, nec [2]	-	13	-	15	1	-	25,600	-	918
5162 Plastics materials & basic shapes [2]	-	111	-	1,086	10	-	34,501	-	38,306
5169 Chemicals & allied products, nec [2]	-	403	-	5,028	12	-	55,577	-	294,816
5171 Petroleum bulk stations & terminals	-	113	-	2,120	19	-	49,930	-	120,075
5172 Petroleum products, nec [2]	-	144	-	2,490	17	-	67,634	-	163,308
5181 Beer and ale [2]	-	26	-	1,427	55	-	33,071	-	47,736
5182 Wine and distilled beverages [2]	-	18	-	957	53	-	32,949	-	34,251
5191 Farm supplies	-	96	-	729	8	-	29,674	-	19,911
5192 Books, periodicals, & newspapers [2]	-	63	-	968	15	-	30,029	-	30,418
5193 Flowers & florists' supplies [2]	-	72	-	706	10	-	16,941	-	12,261
5194 Tobacco and tobacco products [2]	-	10	-	492	49	-	21,374	-	11,363
5198 Paints, varnishes, and supplies [2]	-	82	-	726	9	-	38,948	-	28,217
5199 Nondurable goods, nec [2]	-	278	-	1,958	7	-	25,937	-	51,822
52- Retail trade	-	19,004	-	298,686	16	-	13,429	-	4,215,900
5210 Lumber and other building materials	-	153	-	5,041	33	-	19,106	-	99,243
5230 Paint, glass, and wallpaper stores [2]	-	127	-	755	6	-	21,928	-	16,908
5250 Hardware stores	-	118	-	1,264	11	-	14,972	-	19,393
5260 Retail nurseries and garden stores [2]	-	135	-	1,161	9	-	11,504	-	14,156
5270 Mobile home dealers [2]	-	55	-	460	8	-	28,000	-	16,761
5310 Department stores [2]	-	152	-	28,398	187	-	13,122	-	373,620
5330 Variety stores	-	78	-	476	6	-	9,294	-	5,076
5390 Misc. general merchandise stores	-	127	-	3,982	31	-	13,177	-	49,497
5410 Grocery stores [2]	-	2,197	-	48,832	22	-	9,999	-	512,327
5420 Meat and fish markets [2]	-	142	-	571	4	-	12,967	-	7,706
5430 Fruit and vegetable markets [2]	-	14	-	156	11	-	16,590	-	2,689
5440 Candy, nut, and confectionery stores [2]	-	35	-	171	5	-	9,427	-	1,542
5450 Dairy products stores [2]	-	19	-	50	3	-	4,400	-	225
5460 Retail bakeries [2]	-	226	-	1,513	7	-	9,420	-	14,880
5490 Miscellaneous food stores [2]	-	107	-	478	4	-	10,703	-	5,880
5510 New and used car dealers [2]	-	207	-	15,338	74	-	32,690	-	562,969
5520 Used car dealers [2]	-	268	-	1,208	5	-	22,987	-	27,198
5530 Auto and home supply stores	-	606	-	5,716	9	-	17,560	-	107,261
5540 Gasoline service stations [2]	-	1,031	-	5,640	5	-	13,167	-	79,300
5550 Boat dealers [2]	-	47	-	339	7	-	22,926	-	8,630
5560 Recreational vehicle dealers [2]	-	21	-	196	9	-	25,020	-	5,497
5570 Motorcycle dealers [2]	-	24	-	282	12	-	27,262	-	9,096
5590 Automotive dealers, nec [2]	-	20	-	93	5	-	26,710	-	3,006
5610 Men's & boys' clothing stores [2]	-	163	-	1,233	8	-	17,749	-	19,964
5620 Women's clothing stores [2]	-	518	-	5,706	11	-	10,920	-	62,098
5630 Women's accessory & specialty stores [2]	-	100	-	559	6	-	12,673	-	6,766
5640 Children's and infants' wear stores [2]	-	66	-	681	10	-	9,844	-	6,876
5650 Family clothing stores [2]	-	253	-	4,676	18	-	10,257	-	47,941
5660 Shoe stores [2]	-	428	-	2,511	6	-	12,725	-	32,327
5690 Misc. apparel & accessory stores [2]	-	135	-	595	4	-	11,738	-	7,548
5712 Furniture stores	-	293	-	2,847	10	-	23,364	-	71,079
5713 Floor covering stores [2]	-	144	-	746	5	-	21,046	-	15,572
5714 Drapery and upholstery stores [2]	-	41	-	296	7	-	16,986	-	7,104
5719 Misc. homefurnishings stores [2]	-	217	-	2,128	10	-	13,897	-	33,107
5720 Household appliance stores	-	97	-	525	5	-	23,817	-	14,997
5731 Radio, TV, & electronic stores [2]	-	197	-	2,610	13	-	16,389	-	43,435
5734 Computer and software stores [2]	-	161	-	1,224	8	-	23,582	-	30,101
5735 Record & prerecorded tape stores [2]	-	109	-	1,173	11	-	8,399	-	11,070
5736 Musical instrument stores [2]	-	48	-	403	8	-	19,821	-	9,074

Continued on next page.

HOUSTON, TX PMSA - [continued]

Wholesale and Retail Trade USA	Establishments		Employment		Emp / Est	Pay / Employee		Annual Payroll ($ 000)	
	1994	1995	1994	1995	1995	1994	1995	1994	1995
5812 Eating places	-	3,997	-	91,827	23	-	9,317	-	878,605
5813 Drinking places [2]	-	416	-	4,051	10	-	9,152	-	35,800
5910 Drug stores and proprietary stores	-	454	-	6,962	15	-	16,813	-	122,470
5920 Liquor stores	-	245	-	742	3	-	12,394	-	9,203
5930 Used merchandise stores [2]	-	415	-	2,462	6	-	15,357	-	40,353
5941 Sporting goods and bicycle shops [2]	-	283	-	2,814	10	-	12,338	-	41,911
5942 Book stores [2]	-	149	-	1,249	8	-	11,456	-	14,986
5943 Stationery stores [2]	-	44	-	318	7	-	15,220	-	4,138
5944 Jewelry stores [2]	-	396	-	1,918	5	-	17,919	-	32,921
5945 Hobby, toy, and game shops [2]	-	139	-	1,932	14	-	8,557	-	18,906
5946 Camera & photographic supply stores [2]	-	24	-	123	5	-	16,488	-	2,165
5947 Gift, novelty, and souvenir shops [2]	-	350	-	1,887	5	-	9,465	-	18,350
5948 Luggage and leather goods stores [2]	-	23	-	115	5	-	16,730	-	2,207
5949 Sewing, needlework, and piece goods [2]	-	99	-	795	8	-	8,689	-	6,780
5961 Catalog and mail-order houses [2]	-	58	-	258	4	-	18,093	-	5,798
5962 Merchandising machine operators [2]	-	94	-	670	7	-	18,746	-	13,623
5963 Direct selling establishments [2]	-	153	-	1,725	11	-	14,711	-	25,838
5984 Liquefied petroleum gas dealers [2]	-	42	-	81	2	-	20,741	-	1,885
5992 Florists [2]	-	266	-	1,076	4	-	12,052	-	13,170
5993 Tobacco stores and stands [2]	-	11	-	36	3	-	18,111	-	937
5994 News dealers and newsstands [2]	-	19	-	91	5	-	13,319	-	1,357
5995 Optical goods stores [2]	-	224	-	1,122	5	-	18,082	-	21,730
5999 Miscellaneous retail stores, nec	-	619	-	3,653	6	-	14,741	-	56,172

Source: County Business Patterns 1994/95, CBP-94/95, U.S. Department of Commerce, Washington DC, November 1997. The employment column represents mid-March employment in the year. Pay per employee is calculated by dividing 1st Quarter payroll, annualized, by mid-March employment. The column headed 'Emp / Est' shows 'employees per establishment'. A dash (-) means that data are unavailable or cannot be calculated. nec means not elsewhere classified. *Notes:* 1. 1994 data incomplete; unavailable or withheld. 2. 1995 data incomplete; unavailable or withheld. 3. 1994 and 1995 data incomplete; unavailable or withheld.

HUNTINGTON – ASHLAND MSA (KY PART)

Wholesale and Retail Trade USA	Establishments		Employment		Emp / Est	Pay / Employee		Annual Payroll ($ 000)	
	1994	1995	1994	1995	1995	1994	1995	1994	1995
50 – Wholesale trade	150	155	1,808	2,000	13	29,409	28,166	64,001	58,891
5013 Motor vehicle supplies and new parts	11	9	60	67	7	16,133	19,881	1,026	1,223
5030 Lumber and construction materials	5	6	7	11	2	10,286	9,091	125	113
5045 Computers, peripherals, & software [2]	-	4	-	7	2	-	12,571	-	97
5052 Coal and other minerals and ores [2]	-	7	-	32	5	-	22,375	-	757
5063 Electrical apparatus and equipment [2]	-	6	-	56	9	-	26,929	-	1,363
5065 Electronic parts and equipment [3]	5	6	90	100	17	35,689	35,960	3,062	3,530
5074 Plumbing & hydronic heating supplies [2]	-	5	-	22	4	-	17,636	-	413
5075 Warm air heating & air conditioning [3]	3	3	21	15	5	15,238	29,067	411	371
5084 Industrial machinery and equipment [2]	-	7	-	173	25	-	35,861	-	5,021
5085 Industrial supplies [1]	4	-	34	-	-	21,176	-	679	-
5093 Scrap and waste materials [2]	-	6	-	162	27	-	31,062	-	4,246
5110 Paper and paper products [1]	3	-	114	-	-	17,579	-	2,200	-
5140 Groceries and related products [2]	11	12	122	131	11	16,459	17,557	2,535	2,426
5171 Petroleum bulk stations & terminals	6	7	76	80	11	24,053	24,800	2,756	2,771
5172 Petroleum products, nec [1]	4	6	18	21	4	14,889	13,714	284	361
5191 Farm supplies	-	7	-	20	3	-	13,400	-	300
5194 Tobacco and tobacco products [3]	3	3	115	117	39	14,400	16,000	2,168	2,187
52 – Retail trade	691	698	8,085	8,664	12	9,808	10,322	91,858	97,180
5210 Lumber and other building materials	13	13	169	147	11	16,118	18,667	3,356	2,804
5230 Paint, glass, and wallpaper stores [1]	6	6	18	21	4	15,556	15,238	288	318
5250 Hardware stores	11	-	46	-	-	7,391	-	370	-
5270 Mobile home dealers	6	9	17	15	2	13,176	20,533	486	577
5310 Department stores [3]	7	7	768	792	113	9,448	12,545	8,494	9,655
5330 Variety stores	17	-	45	-	-	7,733	-	520	-
5390 Misc. general merchandise stores	9	-	147	-	-	12,735	-	1,642	-
5410 Grocery stores [1]	72	68	1,122	1,506	22	9,929	9,562	12,727	14,952
5460 Retail bakeries [3]	5	5	28	23	5	6,143	7,826	196	202
5510 New and used car dealers	12	14	275	318	23	19,796	21,107	7,255	8,123
5520 Used car dealers	21	25	23	20	1	9,565	16,600	242	383
5530 Auto and home supply stores	34	37	142	202	5	14,254	14,040	2,516	3,315
5540 Gasoline service stations	62	62	431	441	7	9,253	9,950	4,651	4,765
5610 Men's & boys' clothing stores [3]	5	4	8	5	1	4,500	9,600	48	44
5620 Women's clothing stores [2]	18	10	194	146	15	8,144	8,466	1,627	1,334
5630 Women's accessory & specialty stores [3]	6	6	32	36	6	6,000	5,889	186	212
5650 Family clothing stores [1]	9	9	204	187	21	7,314	8,684	1,651	1,710
5660 Shoe stores [3]	19	18	78	75	4	8,615	9,280	734	612

Continued on next page.

HUNTINGTON – ASHLAND MSA (KY PART) - [continued]

Wholesale and Retail Trade USA	Establishments		Employment		Emp / Est	Pay / Employee		Annual Payroll ($ 000)	
	1994	1995	1994	1995	1995	1994	1995	1994	1995
5712 Furniture stores	17	17	118	108	6	11,729	11,704	1,435	1,417
5713 Floor covering stores	10	9	30	40	4	9,867	11,400	366	360
5720 Household appliance stores	-	6	-	28	5	-	8,143	-	231
5731 Radio, TV, & electronic stores[3]	6	8	27	18	2	11,704	16,000	299	351
5735 Record & prerecorded tape stores[1]	3	-	20	-	-	7,200	-	162	-
5812 Eating places[1]	131	121	2,052	2,572	21	6,942	6,980	16,067	19,495
5910 Drug stores and proprietary stores	20	22	237	253	12	16,810	17,154	4,281	4,863
5920 Liquor stores[3]	6	6	47	47	8	10,128	10,723	524	541
5930 Used merchandise stores	7	8	21	21	3	5,143	6,476	182	186
5941 Sporting goods and bicycle shops[3]	7	7	8	9	1	9,500	4,444	77	55
5944 Jewelry stores[3]	12	16	64	76	5	13,063	12,895	917	1,067
5945 Hobby, toy, and game shops[3]	3	4	12	16	4	9,000	8,750	135	193
5947 Gift, novelty, and souvenir shops[3]	15	16	51	39	2	5,804	7,692	326	313
5960 Nonstore retailers[3]	7	7	63	62	9	17,016	17,484	1,038	1,116
5992 Florists	18	17	24	55	3	6,667	8,364	155	449
5993 Tobacco stores and stands[3]	5	5	18	16	3	11,556	11,500	204	185
5995 Optical goods stores[3]	5	6	18	7	1	11,111	16,000	232	143
5999 Miscellaneous retail stores, nec	26	23	76	76	3	11,526	13,316	1,216	1,076

Source: County Business Patterns 1994/95, CBP-94/95, U.S. Department of Commerce, Washington DC, November 1997. The employment column represents mid-March employment in the year. Pay per employee is calculated by dividing 1st Quarter payroll, annualized, by mid-March employment. The column headed 'Emp / Est' shows 'employees per establishment'. A dash (-) means that data are unavailable or cannot be calculated. nec means not elsewhere classified. *Notes:* 1. 1994 data incomplete; unavailable or withheld. 2. 1995 data incomplete; unavailable or withheld. 3. 1994 and 1995 data incomplete; unavailable or withheld.

HUNTINGTON – ASHLAND MSA (OH PART)

Wholesale and Retail Trade USA	Establishments		Employment		Emp / Est	Pay / Employee		Annual Payroll ($ 000)	
	1994	1995	1994	1995	1995	1994	1995	1994	1995
50- Wholesale trade	41	40	334	354	9	20,419	21,356	8,108	8,892
5013 Motor vehicle supplies and new parts	-	5	-	19	4	-	18,947	-	383
5015 Motor vehicle parts, used	4	-	9	-	-	9,333	-	98	-
5070 Hardware, plumbing & heating equipment	3	4	16	17	4	24,500	23,059	381	409
5080 Machinery, equipment, and supplies	5	-	26	-	-	24,308	-	665	-
5149 Groceries and related products, nec	-	4	-	53	13	-	18,868	-	1,168
52- Retail trade	265	276	2,983	3,375	12	10,217	10,989	34,267	38,187
5210 Lumber and other building materials	5	6	52	208	35	12,308	17,308	816	3,592
5230 Paint, glass, and wallpaper stores	-	3	-	9	3	-	14,667	-	163
5250 Hardware stores	8	-	23	-	-	10,609	-	257	-
5310 Department stores	3	3	488	561	187	9,328	11,558	5,438	5,978
5410 Grocery stores	30	34	593	567	17	9,976	10,434	6,097	6,059
5510 New and used car dealers	5	5	99	99	20	16,162	22,667	1,747	1,929
5520 Used car dealers	-	3	-	2	1	-	6,000	-	17
5530 Auto and home supply stores	11	13	69	76	6	16,928	18,895	1,421	1,770
5540 Gasoline service stations	27	26	160	190	7	11,600	11,200	2,107	2,172
5620 Women's clothing stores	-	3	-	9	3	-	5,778	-	103
5660 Shoe stores	6	-	25	-	-	8,480	-	235	-
5712 Furniture stores	-	6	-	137	23	-	14,861	-	1,972
5734 Computer and software stores	3	-	2	-	-	8,000	-	58	-
5812 Eating places	59	61	770	811	13	6,971	6,742	6,036	6,260
5813 Drinking places	9	7	23	23	3	8,174	8,174	195	191
5910 Drug stores and proprietary stores	10	10	103	160	16	17,204	10,975	2,093	1,936
5920 Liquor stores	11	9	39	42	5	9,231	7,619	381	353
5941 Sporting goods and bicycle shops	3	3	17	17	6	6,353	7,294	139	149
5944 Jewelry stores	-	3	-	12	4	-	14,667	-	263
5960 Nonstore retailers	4	4	9	8	2	7,111	11,000	69	89
5992 Florists	5	8	15	16	2	10,400	8,750	108	158
5999 Miscellaneous retail stores, nec	-	7	-	23	3	-	8,174	-	271

Source: County Business Patterns 1994/95, CBP-94/95, U.S. Department of Commerce, Washington DC, November 1997. The employment column represents mid-March employment in the year. Pay per employee is calculated by dividing 1st Quarter payroll, annualized, by mid-March employment. The column headed 'Emp / Est' shows 'employees per establishment'. A dash (-) means that data are unavailable or cannot be calculated. nec means not elsewhere classified. *Notes:* 1. 1994 data incomplete; unavailable or withheld. 2. 1995 data incomplete; unavailable or withheld. 3. 1994 and 1995 data incomplete; unavailable or withheld.

HUNTINGTON – ASHLAND MSA (WV PART)

Wholesale and Retail Trade USA	Establishments		Employment		Emp / Est	Pay / Employee		Annual Payroll ($ 000)	
	1994	1995	1994	1995	1995	1994	1995	1994	1995
50- Wholesale trade	-	254	-	3,511	14	-	24,775	-	91,093
5012 Automobiles and other vehicles	-	6	-	139	23	-	20,058	-	3,342

Continued on next page.

HUNTINGTON - ASHLAND MSA (WV PART) - [continued]

Wholesale and Retail Trade USA	Establishments		Employment		Emp / Est	Pay / Employee		Annual Payroll ($ 000)	
	1994	1995	1994	1995	1995	1994	1995	1994	1995
5013 Motor vehicle supplies and new parts	-	7	-	46	7	-	21,826	-	1,256
5014 Tires and tubes	-	4	-	33	8	-	17,333	-	591
5015 Motor vehicle parts, used	-	8	-	29	4	-	17,103	-	523
5021 Furniture	-	6	-	52	9	-	19,000	-	1,287
5030 Lumber and construction materials	-	11	-	53	5	-	31,623	-	1,543
5044 Office equipment [2]	-	4	-	61	15	-	23,344	-	1,589
5046 Commercial equipment, nec	-	4	-	27	7	-	23,407	-	628
5047 Medical and hospital equipment [2]	-	9	-	108	12	-	30,630	-	3,137
5049 Professional equipment, nec	-	4	-	11	3	-	20,727	-	229
5051 Metals service centers and offices [2]	-	4	-	28	7	-	24,857	-	713
5052 Coal and other minerals and ores [2]	-	4	-	9	2	-	30,667	-	194
5063 Electrical apparatus and equipment	-	9	-	131	15	-	24,916	-	3,389
5065 Electronic parts and equipment	-	13	-	59	5	-	23,729	-	1,627
5074 Plumbing & hydronic heating supplies	-	6	-	66	11	-	24,970	-	1,838
5075 Warm air heating & air conditioning	-	7	-	31	4	-	22,323	-	712
5082 Construction and mining machinery	-	8	-	152	19	-	28,000	-	3,714
5084 Industrial machinery and equipment	-	13	-	273	21	-	35,092	-	8,711
5085 Industrial supplies	-	19	-	176	9	-	27,386	-	5,561
5093 Scrap and waste materials	-	7	-	38	5	-	13,895	-	586
5099 Durable goods, nec [2]	-	3	-	10	3	-	12,400	-	120
5110 Paper and paper products [2]	-	8	-	180	23	-	29,178	-	4,891
5120 Drugs, proprietaries, and sundries [2]	-	5	-	60	12	-	21,533	-	1,360
5148 Fresh fruits and vegetables [2]	-	7	-	62	9	-	20,839	-	1,331
5149 Groceries and related products, nec	-	8	-	119	15	-	24,101	-	3,049
5150 Farm-product raw materials [2]	-	3	-	37	12	-	5,081	-	151
5191 Farm supplies [2]	-	3	-	17	6	-	15,294	-	254
52- Retail trade	-	938	-	12,749	14	-	10,568	-	143,582
5210 Lumber and other building materials	-	16	-	272	17	-	19,368	-	5,208
5230 Paint, glass, and wallpaper stores	-	5	-	26	5	-	16,462	-	438
5250 Hardware stores	-	11	-	78	7	-	12,000	-	1,009
5310 Department stores [2]	-	9	-	1,470	163	-	11,325	-	15,950
5330 Variety stores	-	7	-	49	7	-	8,980	-	514
5390 Misc. general merchandise stores [2]	-	12	-	150	13	-	13,360	-	4,436
5410 Grocery stores	-	67	-	1,479	22	-	10,115	-	16,455
5420 Meat and fish markets	-	4	-	19	5	-	9,474	-	231
5440 Candy, nut, and confectionery stores [2]	-	3	-	16	5	-	5,500	-	103
5460 Retail bakeries	-	8	-	40	5	-	9,000	-	352
5510 New and used car dealers	-	16	-	488	31	-	23,328	-	12,066
5520 Used car dealers	-	17	-	47	3	-	13,617	-	763
5530 Auto and home supply stores	-	39	-	267	7	-	15,116	-	4,404
5540 Gasoline service stations	-	66	-	464	7	-	9,638	-	4,777
5570 Motorcycle dealers [2]	-	4	-	29	7	-	16,000	-	602
5610 Men's & boys' clothing stores [2]	-	12	-	85	7	-	10,400	-	857
5620 Women's clothing stores	-	28	-	275	10	-	7,200	-	1,990
5630 Women's accessory & specialty stores	-	4	-	19	5	-	11,158	-	217
5650 Family clothing stores	-	7	-	70	10	-	7,829	-	584
5660 Shoe stores	-	28	-	144	5	-	10,722	-	1,812
5712 Furniture stores	-	22	-	133	6	-	16,331	-	2,332
5713 Floor covering stores	-	14	-	60	4	-	15,933	-	1,030
5719 Misc. homefurnishings stores	-	8	-	89	11	-	7,326	-	1,066
5731 Radio, TV, & electronic stores	-	10	-	76	8	-	18,316	-	1,359
5735 Record & prerecorded tape stores [2]	-	4	-	31	8	-	8,387	-	254
5736 Musical instrument stores	-	5	-	116	23	-	18,655	-	1,918
5812 Eating places	-	212	-	4,310	20	-	6,897	-	31,623
5813 Drinking places	-	45	-	189	4	-	6,307	-	1,083
5910 Drug stores and proprietary stores	-	34	-	702	21	-	9,869	-	7,753
5920 Liquor stores	-	8	-	29	4	-	6,069	-	185
5930 Used merchandise stores	-	13	-	32	2	-	10,125	-	346
5941 Sporting goods and bicycle shops	-	11	-	49	4	-	12,980	-	868
5942 Book stores [2]	-	10	-	71	7	-	9,521	-	763
5944 Jewelry stores [2]	-	16	-	91	6	-	16,396	-	1,423
5945 Hobby, toy, and game shops	-	9	-	101	11	-	8,634	-	1,067
5947 Gift, novelty, and souvenir shops	-	18	-	79	4	-	8,152	-	735
5960 Nonstore retailers	-	11	-	34	3	-	22,235	-	873
5995 Optical goods stores	-	10	-	67	7	-	18,627	-	1,289
5999 Miscellaneous retail stores, nec	-	21	-	98	5	-	12,898	-	1,446

Source: County Business Patterns 1994/95, CBP-94/95, U.S. Department of Commerce, Washington DC, November 1997. The employment column represents mid-March employment in the year. Pay per employee is calculated by dividing 1st Quarter payroll, annualized, by mid-March employment. The column headed 'Emp / Est' shows 'employees per establishment'. A dash (-) means that data are unavailable or cannot be calculated. nec means not elsewhere classified. *Notes:* 1. 1994 data incomplete; unavailable or withheld. 2. 1995 data incomplete; unavailable or withheld. 3. 1994 and 1995 data incomplete; unavailable or withheld.

HUNTINGTON - ASHLAND, WV - KY - OH MSA

Wholesale and Retail Trade USA	Establishments		Employment		Emp / Est	Pay / Employee		Annual Payroll ($ 000)	
	1994	1995	1994	1995	1995	1994	1995	1994	1995
50- Wholesale trade[1]	191	449	2,142	5,865	13	28,007	25,725	72,109	158,876
5012 Automobiles and other vehicles[2]	-	10	-	139	14	-	20,058	-	3,342
5013 Motor vehicle supplies and new parts[1]	19	21	60	132	6	16,133	20,424	1,026	2,862
5014 Tires and tubes[2]	-	5	-	33	7	-	17,333	-	591
5015 Motor vehicle parts, used[3]	6	16	9	29	2	9,333	17,103	98	523
5021 Furniture[2]	-	7	-	52	7	-	19,000	-	1,287
5030 Lumber and construction materials[1]	7	19	7	64	3	10,286	27,750	125	1,656
5044 Office equipment[2]	-	7	-	61	9	-	23,344	-	1,589
5045 Computers, peripherals, & software[2]	-	12	-	7	1	-	12,571	-	97
5046 Commercial equipment, nec[2]	-	5	-	27	5	-	23,407	-	628
5047 Medical and hospital equipment[2]	-	10	-	108	11	-	30,630	-	3,137
5049 Professional equipment, nec[2]	-	4	-	11	3	-	20,727	-	229
5051 Metals service centers and offices[2]	-	7	-	28	4	-	24,857	-	713
5052 Coal and other minerals and ores[2]	-	11	-	41	4	-	24,195	-	951
5063 Electrical apparatus and equipment[2]	-	16	-	187	12	-	25,519	-	4,752
5065 Electronic parts and equipment[3]	6	20	90	159	8	35,689	31,421	3,062	5,157
5074 Plumbing & hydronic heating supplies[2]	-	13	-	88	7	-	23,136	-	2,251
5075 Warm air heating & air conditioning[3]	4	11	21	46	4	15,238	24,522	411	1,083
5082 Construction and mining machinery[2]	-	13	-	152	12	-	28,000	-	3,714
5084 Industrial machinery and equipment[2]	-	21	-	446	21	-	35,390	-	13,732
5085 Industrial supplies[3]	4	25	34	176	7	21,176	27,386	679	5,561
5093 Scrap and waste materials[2]	-	13	-	200	15	-	27,800	-	4,832
5099 Durable goods, nec[2]	-	7	-	10	1	-	12,400	-	120
5110 Paper and paper products[3]	3	11	114	180	16	17,579	29,178	2,200	4,891
5120 Drugs, proprietaries, and sundries[2]	-	6	-	60	10	-	21,533	-	1,360
5148 Fresh fruits and vegetables[2]	-	8	-	62	8	-	20,839	-	1,331
5149 Groceries and related products, nec[2]	-	15	-	172	11	-	22,488	-	4,217
5150 Farm-product raw materials[2]	-	4	-	37	9	-	5,081	-	151
5171 Petroleum bulk stations & terminals[3]	6	9	76	80	9	24,053	24,800	2,756	2,771
5172 Petroleum products, nec[3]	4	9	18	21	2	14,889	13,714	284	361
5191 Farm supplies[2]	-	10	-	37	4	-	14,270	-	554
5194 Tobacco and tobacco products[3]	3	4	115	117	29	14,400	16,000	2,168	2,187
52- Retail trade[1]	956	1,912	11,068	24,788	13	9,918	10,539	126,125	278,949
5210 Lumber and other building materials[1]	18	35	221	627	18	15,222	18,520	4,172	11,604
5230 Paint, glass, and wallpaper stores[1]	8	14	18	56	4	15,556	15,714	288	919
5250 Hardware stores[1]	19	22	69	78	4	8,464	12,000	627	1,009
5270 Mobile home dealers[3]	7	12	17	15	1	13,176	20,533	486	577
5310 Department stores[3]	10	19	1,256	2,823	149	9,401	11,714	13,932	31,583
5330 Variety stores[1]	22	22	45	49	2	7,733	8,980	520	514
5390 Misc. general merchandise stores[3]	12	28	147	150	5	12,735	13,360	1,642	4,436
5410 Grocery stores[1]	102	169	1,715	3,552	21	9,945	9,931	18,824	37,466
5420 Meat and fish markets[2]	-	8	-	19	2	-	9,474	-	231
5440 Candy, nut, and confectionery stores[2]	-	4	-	16	4	-	5,500	-	103
5460 Retail bakeries[3]	7	14	28	63	5	6,143	8,571	196	554
5510 New and used car dealers[1]	17	35	374	905	26	18,834	22,475	9,002	22,118
5520 Used car dealers[1]	23	45	23	69	2	9,565	14,261	242	1,163
5530 Auto and home supply stores[1]	45	89	211	545	6	15,128	15,244	3,937	9,489
5540 Gasoline service stations[1]	89	154	591	1,095	7	9,888	10,035	6,758	11,714
5570 Motorcycle dealers[2]	-	5	-	29	6	-	16,000	-	602
5610 Men's & boys' clothing stores[3]	5	16	8	90	6	4,500	10,356	48	901
5620 Women's clothing stores[3]	21	41	194	430	10	8,144	7,600	1,627	3,427
5630 Women's accessory & specialty stores[3]	7	11	32	55	5	6,000	7,709	186	429
5650 Family clothing stores[3]	10	16	204	257	16	7,314	8,451	1,651	2,294
5660 Shoe stores[3]	25	52	103	219	4	8,583	10,228	969	2,424
5712 Furniture stores[1]	23	45	118	378	8	11,729	14,476	1,435	5,721
5713 Floor covering stores[1]	11	24	30	100	4	9,867	14,120	366	1,390
5719 Misc. homefurnishings stores[2]	-	12	-	89	7	-	7,326	-	1,066
5720 Household appliance stores[2]	-	11	-	28	3	-	8,143	-	231
5731 Radio, TV, & electronic stores[3]	7	18	27	94	5	11,704	17,872	299	1,710
5734 Computer and software stores[1]	5	-	2	-	-	8,000	-	58	-
5735 Record & prerecorded tape stores[3]	3	7	20	31	4	7,200	8,387	162	254
5736 Musical instrument stores[2]	-	6	-	116	19	-	18,655	-	1,918
5812 Eating places[1]	190	394	2,822	7,693	20	6,950	6,908	22,103	57,378
5813 Drinking places[3]	11	55	23	212	4	8,174	6,509	195	1,274
5910 Drug stores and proprietary stores[1]	30	66	340	1,115	17	16,929	11,681	6,374	14,552
5920 Liquor stores[3]	17	23	86	118	5	9,721	8,475	905	1,079
5930 Used merchandise stores[1]	9	23	21	53	2	5,143	8,679	182	532
5941 Sporting goods and bicycle shops[3]	10	21	25	75	4	7,360	10,667	216	1,072
5942 Book stores[2]	-	14	-	71	5	-	9,521	-	763
5944 Jewelry stores[3]	13	35	64	179	5	13,063	14,793	917	2,753
5945 Hobby, toy, and game shops[3]	4	13	12	117	9	9,000	8,650	135	1,260

Continued on next page.

HUNTINGTON - ASHLAND, WV - KY - OH MSA - [continued]

Wholesale and Retail Trade USA	Establishments		Employment		Emp / Est	Pay / Employee		Annual Payroll ($ 000)	
	1994	1995	1994	1995	1995	1994	1995	1994	1995
5947 Gift, novelty, and souvenir shops[3]	18	36	51	118	3	5,804	8,000	326	1,048
5960 Nonstore retailers[3]	11	22	72	104	5	15,778	18,538	1,107	2,078
5992 Florists[1]	23	43	39	71	2	8,103	8,451	263	607
5993 Tobacco stores and stands[3]	5	7	18	16	2	11,556	11,500	204	185
5995 Optical goods stores[3]	7	18	18	74	4	11,111	18,378	232	1,432
5999 Miscellaneous retail stores, nec[1]	32	51	76	197	4	11,526	12,508	1,216	2,793

Source: County Business Patterns 1994/95, CBP-94/95, U.S. Department of Commerce, Washington DC, November 1997. The employment column represents mid-March employment in the year. Pay per employee is calculated by dividing 1st Quarter payroll, annualized, by mid-March employment. The column headed 'Emp / Est' shows 'employees per establishment'. A dash (-) means that data are unavailable or cannot be calculated. nec means not elsewhere classified. *Notes:* 1. 1994 data incomplete; unavailable or withheld. 2. 1995 data incomplete; unavailable or withheld. 3. 1994 and 1995 data incomplete; unavailable or withheld.

HUNTSVILLE, AL MSA

Wholesale and Retail Trade USA	Establishments		Employment		Emp / Est	Pay / Employee		Annual Payroll ($ 000)	
	1994	1995	1994	1995	1995	1994	1995	1994	1995
50- Wholesale trade	571	589	6,229	6,266	11	25,231	29,064	171,254	187,000
5012 Automobiles and other vehicles	11	11	103	67	6	5,398	10,149	674	715
5013 Motor vehicle supplies and new parts	21	24	150	139	6	14,880	17,842	2,343	2,249
5014 Tires and tubes[3]	3	3	20	42	14	20,000	25,238	336	872
5015 Motor vehicle parts, used	13	13	39	39	3	9,641	11,590	350	468
5021 Furniture[3]	9	7	122	104	15	23,475	21,692	2,362	1,969
5023 Homefurnishings	8	8	74	60	8	16,649	17,867	1,246	1,290
5031 Lumber, plywood, and millwork	14	13	276	347	27	18,174	19,712	6,326	7,728
5039 Construction materials, nec[1]	4	11	28	63	6	15,143	14,095	368	1,080
5044 Office equipment[3]	7	9	72	87	10	20,000	18,207	1,445	1,592
5045 Computers, peripherals, & software	53	52	843	699	13	33,044	38,581	28,979	25,862
5046 Commercial equipment, nec[1]	4	-	10	-	-	12,800	-	153	-
5047 Medical and hospital equipment[2]	12	10	75	62	6	25,493	30,194	1,759	1,958
5049 Professional equipment, nec[2]	-	7	-	37	5	-	19,676	-	859
5051 Metals service centers and offices	7	8	29	35	4	22,897	25,371	754	1,050
5063 Electrical apparatus and equipment	33	33	295	251	8	27,878	32,542	9,156	8,719
5064 Electrical appliances, TV & radios[3]	4	5	141	168	34	27,348	27,119	4,400	5,102
5065 Electronic parts and equipment[2]	107	110	644	753	7	43,099	51,501	30,055	38,992
5072 Hardware[3]	9	9	56	69	8	24,214	20,290	1,333	1,547
5074 Plumbing & hydronic heating supplies	10	11	108	114	10	28,741	31,368	2,680	3,464
5082 Construction and mining machinery	7	10	63	85	9	27,746	26,682	2,082	2,077
5083 Farm and garden machinery	-	11	-	108	10	-	18,593	-	2,380
5084 Industrial machinery and equipment[1]	26	26	239	269	10	26,812	30,454	7,328	8,214
5085 Industrial supplies	10	9	69	58	6	22,841	24,897	1,609	1,641
5087 Service establishment equipment	6	6	31	36	6	21,290	17,889	679	655
5091 Sporting & recreational goods[2]	-	10	-	45	5	-	107,022	-	2,328
5093 Scrap and waste materials	9	11	66	70	6	18,242	20,286	1,431	1,654
5094 Jewelry & precious stones[1]	6	-	33	-	-	16,364	-	638	-
5099 Durable goods, nec[3]	10	10	66	68	7	26,485	38,118	2,353	3,221
5112 Stationery and office supplies[3]	11	12	125	126	11	18,816	19,905	2,341	2,685
5120 Drugs, proprietaries, and sundries	8	8	160	129	16	20,125	27,504	3,603	3,911
5130 Apparel, piece goods, and notions[1]	8	-	21	-	-	10,476	-	237	-
5145 Confectionery[1]	3	-	1	-	-	8,000	-	12	-
5148 Fresh fruits and vegetables[1]	3	-	25	-	-	25,280	-	468	-
5162 Plastics materials & basic shapes	5	-	37	-	-	22,162	-	890	-
5169 Chemicals & allied products, nec	9	-	47	-	-	22,383	-	1,178	-
5171 Petroleum bulk stations & terminals	9	9	79	81	9	23,696	23,358	2,036	2,109
5181 Beer and ale[3]	3	3	130	134	45	29,354	32,537	4,112	4,428
5182 Wine and distilled beverages[3]	4	4	72	77	19	19,778	18,234	1,499	1,579
5191 Farm supplies	16	10	96	21	2	16,792	17,905	2,135	411
5192 Books, periodicals, & newspapers[3]	6	7	95	159	23	21,179	18,591	1,835	3,036
5193 Flowers & florists' supplies[2]	4	3	18	14	5	12,667	15,714	244	201
5199 Nondurable goods, nec	7	8	91	79	10	19,956	23,342	1,977	1,900
52- Retail trade	1,858	1,900	26,151	27,464	14	10,965	11,477	313,830	324,967
5210 Lumber and other building materials	24	20	884	684	34	17,814	20,088	15,665	12,205
5230 Paint, glass, and wallpaper stores	14	14	47	38	3	20,340	23,684	1,201	1,261
5250 Hardware stores	17	10	64	42	4	13,688	17,429	938	758
5260 Retail nurseries and garden stores	11	12	49	65	5	9,388	12,985	633	940
5270 Mobile home dealers	7	7	27	34	5	19,852	20,941	928	796
5310 Department stores[3]	16	16	2,560	2,385	149	10,072	12,220	27,942	30,268
5330 Variety stores	14	12	74	98	8	6,865	8,449	743	931
5390 Misc. general merchandise stores	19	22	486	398	18	11,547	14,442	5,712	5,575
5410 Grocery stores[3]	173	183	3,278	4,118	23	9,308	8,648	34,618	35,379
5420 Meat and fish markets[3]	4	3	10	10	3	15,600	17,600	168	168

Continued on next page.

HUNTSVILLE, AL MSA - [continued]

Wholesale and Retail Trade USA	Establishments		Employment		Emp / Est	Pay / Employee		Annual Payroll ($ 000)	
	1994	1995	1994	1995	1995	1994	1995	1994	1995
5430 Fruit and vegetable markets	4	7	28	35	5	8,143	8,800	337	463
5460 Retail bakeries[3]	12	12	90	116	10	5,867	6,931	636	780
5490 Miscellaneous food stores[3]	8	9	46	38	4	10,783	12,526	490	545
5510 New and used car dealers	21	22	1,238	1,311	60	30,171	29,889	39,962	39,518
5520 Used car dealers	40	39	114	130	3	13,439	16,215	1,921	2,103
5530 Auto and home supply stores	71	78	557	602	8	17,867	19,601	10,689	12,275
5540 Gasoline service stations	117	110	657	653	6	11,068	11,204	7,369	7,384
5550 Boat dealers	8	9	44	61	7	11,909	14,689	748	1,017
5560 Recreational vehicle dealers[3]	7	7	69	76	11	19,710	21,105	1,553	1,649
5610 Men's & boys' clothing stores	14	13	71	80	6	6,592	7,300	612	546
5620 Women's clothing stores	55	46	441	373	8	8,562	9,083	4,007	3,717
5630 Women's accessory & specialty stores	12	12	47	43	4	8,000	8,279	384	382
5640 Children's and infants' wear stores	6	7	17	12	2	6,588	8,000	126	156
5650 Family clothing stores	23	24	691	624	26	11,786	13,481	9,242	8,066
5660 Shoe stores	46	47	226	239	5	10,000	10,259	2,433	2,496
5690 Misc. apparel & accessory stores	9	10	16	20	2	8,750	9,600	149	174
5712 Furniture stores	41	44	348	359	8	15,184	15,833	6,045	6,552
5713 Floor covering stores	23	24	122	127	5	16,852	21,512	2,153	2,541
5719 Misc. homefurnishings stores	-	23	-	152	7	-	11,368	-	2,222
5720 Household appliance stores	16	13	67	76	6	15,940	12,632	1,302	1,310
5731 Radio, TV, & electronic stores	26	26	202	205	8	18,218	18,146	4,124	4,280
5734 Computer and software stores[3]	19	21	78	73	3	15,385	13,644	1,403	1,260
5735 Record & prerecorded tape stores	15	14	58	60	4	8,759	11,733	607	614
5736 Musical instrument stores[3]	7	7	59	50	7	12,339	14,800	753	739
5812 Eating places	384	353	9,092	9,369	27	7,295	7,584	71,640	73,557
5813 Drinking places[3]	37	28	214	185	7	6,654	6,530	1,496	1,203
5910 Drug stores and proprietary stores	44	45	454	495	11	19,216	16,622	9,131	8,752
5920 Liquor stores[3]	18	18	60	65	4	17,200	15,385	1,037	1,046
5930 Used merchandise stores	39	39	97	104	3	8,825	10,000	914	1,164
5941 Sporting goods and bicycle shops	32	34	143	192	6	10,937	10,042	1,659	1,949
5942 Book stores	24	22	181	208	9	9,149	9,481	1,916	1,848
5943 Stationery stores	7	6	25	24	4	7,200	6,833	162	250
5944 Jewelry stores	40	41	177	214	5	13,492	14,150	2,572	3,058
5945 Hobby, toy, and game shops[3]	13	13	139	110	8	8,230	10,691	1,466	1,361
5947 Gift, novelty, and souvenir shops	36	34	176	148	4	5,977	6,973	1,169	1,179
5949 Sewing, needlework, and piece goods	11	13	74	79	6	8,270	7,848	609	622
5961 Catalog and mail-order houses	-	9	-	57	6	-	18,526	-	1,132
5962 Merchandising machine operators	12	14	94	116	8	16,383	16,759	1,871	2,128
5963 Direct selling establishments[2]	-	9	-	73	8	-	17,425	-	1,369
5984 Liquefied petroleum gas dealers	15	15	90	109	7	16,756	18,752	1,520	2,042
5992 Florists	34	37	163	153	4	9,448	11,033	1,747	1,819
5995 Optical goods stores	18	-	102	-	-	14,471	-	1,642	-
5999 Miscellaneous retail stores, nec	50	54	206	242	4	9,728	10,198	2,243	2,862

Source: County Business Patterns 1994/95, CBP-94/95, U.S. Department of Commerce, Washington DC, November 1997. The employment column represents mid-March employment in the year. Pay per employee is calculated by dividing 1st Quarter payroll, annualized, by mid-March employment. The column headed 'Emp / Est' shows 'employees per establishment'. A dash (-) means that data are unavailable or cannot be calculated. nec means not elsewhere classified. *Notes:* 1. 1994 data incomplete; unavailable or withheld. 2. 1995 data incomplete; unavailable or withheld. 3. 1994 and 1995 data incomplete; unavailable or withheld.

INDIANAPOLIS, IN MSA

Wholesale and Retail Trade USA	Establishments		Employment		Emp / Est	Pay / Employee		Annual Payroll ($ 000)	
	1994	1995	1994	1995	1995	1994	1995	1994	1995
50- Wholesale trade	3,408	3,468	45,636	48,366	14	31,184	34,246	1,514,645	1,718,834
5012 Automobiles and other vehicles[3]	58	57	1,658	1,728	30	18,914	23,079	37,206	43,393
5013 Motor vehicle supplies and new parts	197	168	1,803	1,676	10	25,750	28,308	47,594	47,068
5014 Tires and tubes[3]	16	15	100	102	7	23,440	24,235	1,794	2,560
5015 Motor vehicle parts, used[1]	41	43	186	183	4	13,505	19,148	2,755	3,553
5021 Furniture[3]	44	46	421	436	9	28,684	31,624	13,068	15,399
5023 Homefurnishings[3]	52	49	415	420	9	24,260	25,705	11,163	11,746
5031 Lumber, plywood, and millwork[3]	68	68	750	1,004	15	28,352	31,785	25,552	36,202
5032 Brick, stone, & related materials[3]	27	24	233	274	11	27,279	32,920	6,894	9,959
5033 Roofing, siding, & insulation[3]	31	34	329	355	10	28,742	30,276	10,816	11,641
5039 Construction materials, nec[3]	27	50	215	374	7	30,530	30,802	6,507	12,210
5043 Photographic equipment & supplies[3]	7	9	244	238	26	37,311	48,269	9,314	10,931
5044 Office equipment[3]	58	61	1,444	1,525	25	32,357	36,283	47,551	54,779
5045 Computers, peripherals, & software	131	127	1,779	1,736	14	45,608	53,671	79,828	87,202
5046 Commercial equipment, nec[3]	37	38	465	489	13	25,806	29,808	14,501	15,936
5047 Medical and hospital equipment	87	92	1,841	1,878	20	47,605	51,457	93,664	103,229
5048 Ophthalmic goods[3]	14	14	205	195	14	19,024	20,677	4,754	4,371

Continued on next page.

INDIANAPOLIS, IN MSA - [continued]

Wholesale and Retail Trade USA	Establishments		Employment		Emp / Est	Pay / Employee		Annual Payroll ($ 000)	
	1994	1995	1994	1995	1995	1994	1995	1994	1995
5049 Professional equipment, nec[3]	21	19	119	58	3	28,538	43,517	2,760	2,058
5051 Metals service centers and offices[3]	78	75	1,093	1,070	14	30,587	32,120	36,825	34,093
5052 Coal and other minerals and ores[1]	4	-	13	-	-	38,769	-	546	-
5063 Electrical apparatus and equipment[3]	154	136	1,319	1,401	10	34,284	38,370	47,646	53,943
5064 Electrical appliances, TV & radios[3]	27	27	561	620	23	57,982	57,026	32,733	35,556
5065 Electronic parts and equipment[3]	177	192	1,753	2,226	12	39,936	37,982	73,089	95,889
5072 Hardware[3]	70	72	943	863	12	25,837	32,862	26,423	28,852
5074 Plumbing & hydronic heating supplies[3]	74	77	565	648	8	38,237	40,741	22,429	25,617
5075 Warm air heating & air conditioning[3]	47	54	379	484	9	41,119	44,248	17,415	22,551
5078 Refrigeration equipment and supplies[3]	9	6	109	113	19	32,073	33,239	4,091	4,274
5082 Construction and mining machinery[3]	31	32	513	539	17	34,058	38,679	19,892	23,138
5083 Farm and garden machinery	42	36	354	330	9	23,831	25,006	10,042	9,143
5084 Industrial machinery and equipment	280	285	2,626	2,694	9	33,502	37,519	99,468	109,029
5085 Industrial supplies	134	138	1,230	1,225	9	35,109	39,429	46,053	47,243
5087 Service establishment equipment[3]	55	54	595	604	11	21,882	25,079	15,161	17,610
5088 Transportation equipment & supplies[3]	14	14	96	175	13	47,250	27,406	3,007	4,962
5091 Sporting & recreational goods[3]	37	36	725	722	20	22,141	31,269	18,119	20,495
5092 Toys and hobby goods and supplies[3]	15	14	181	41	3	12,508	19,220	1,749	1,049
5093 Scrap and waste materials[3]	55	57	730	638	11	24,389	28,696	21,447	21,462
5094 Jewelry & precious stones[3]	24	23	244	236	10	26,131	24,881	6,864	6,994
5099 Durable goods, nec	75	85	268	324	4	22,940	23,864	7,310	9,671
5111 Printing and writing paper[3]	19	19	376	314	17	30,223	36,535	11,797	16,855
5112 Stationery and office supplies[3]	77	61	1,117	1,124	18	21,572	24,463	24,709	27,930
5113 Industrial & personal service paper[3]	45	43	558	615	14	31,233	32,956	19,712	21,685
5120 Drugs, proprietaries, and sundries[3]	37	46	814	849	18	40,482	48,320	30,512	38,203
5131 Piece goods & notions[3]	18	19	127	148	8	27,559	28,703	4,009	4,136
5136 Men's and boys' clothing[3]	14	15	73	74	5	17,260	22,216	1,287	1,500
5137 Women's and children's clothing[3]	16	19	26	45	2	19,692	20,978	827	1,041
5139 Footwear[2]	-	6	-	17	3	-	66,118	-	400
5141 Groceries, general line[3]	27	29	829	916	32	30,422	30,354	26,364	28,882
5142 Packaged frozen food[3]	19	19	258	641	34	32,884	36,587	7,878	20,705
5143 Dairy products, exc. dried or canned[3]	16	16	364	467	29	40,099	36,308	14,179	16,667
5144 Poultry and poultry products[3]	5	5	53	28	6	27,321	31,429	1,726	861
5145 Confectionery[3]	23	22	130	157	7	20,246	18,268	2,717	3,895
5146 Fish and seafoods[3]	5	6	31	44	7	24,387	23,273	781	1,047
5147 Meats and meat products[3]	12	10	116	99	10	26,000	21,131	2,896	1,968
5148 Fresh fruits and vegetables[3]	28	27	967	1,024	38	24,364	25,984	25,750	28,296
5149 Groceries and related products, nec	81	87	1,230	1,203	14	27,522	28,233	36,420	35,216
5153 Grain and field beans[3]	45	43	62	61	1	21,742	22,557	1,441	1,538
5162 Plastics materials & basic shapes[3]	28	26	247	241	9	28,972	28,548	7,846	6,902
5169 Chemicals & allied products, nec[3]	92	92	1,397	1,562	17	38,216	39,775	62,208	71,252
5171 Petroleum bulk stations & terminals	49	43	458	373	9	27,537	29,126	13,192	11,743
5172 Petroleum products, nec[3]	16	18	111	92	5	23,207	33,087	2,883	3,053
5181 Beer and ale[1]	12	-	344	-	-	21,709	-	9,139	-
5182 Wine and distilled beverages[1]	8	-	487	-	-	36,838	-	15,669	-
5191 Farm supplies	88	88	831	744	8	29,646	36,156	25,533	26,649
5192 Books, periodicals, & newspapers[3]	26	24	212	202	8	24,528	29,723	5,371	6,738
5193 Flowers & florists' supplies[3]	31	22	303	237	11	15,102	21,181	5,655	5,507
5194 Tobacco and tobacco products[3]	10	10	254	263	26	22,031	24,943	10,584	9,372
5198 Paints, varnishes, and supplies[3]	29	30	141	153	5	30,043	28,471	4,419	4,425
5199 Nondurable goods, nec[3]	103	111	510	496	4	23,482	30,395	12,421	15,635
52- Retail trade	8,798	8,943	143,341	148,670	17	12,357	13,140	1,947,911	2,061,801
5210 Lumber and other building materials	140	123	3,215	3,027	25	17,407	18,575	68,626	56,915
5230 Paint, glass, and wallpaper stores[3]	74	69	213	280	4	16,526	18,714	3,551	5,506
5250 Hardware stores	89	71	1,016	743	10	12,098	10,837	10,144	7,897
5260 Retail nurseries and garden stores	86	85	529	522	6	13,376	15,019	8,158	8,391
5270 Mobile home dealers[3]	16	17	69	106	6	21,217	27,811	1,934	2,949
5310 Department stores[3]	82	84	9,730	10,878	130	10,510	11,593	121,918	135,288
5330 Variety stores[3]	79	66	500	494	7	8,112	7,870	4,909	4,236
5390 Misc. general merchandise stores[3]	46	64	757	782	12	10,732	12,205	8,747	9,039
5410 Grocery stores[1]	462	469	14,026	15,062	32	13,339	13,323	183,212	196,683
5420 Meat and fish markets[3]	21	24	52	49	2	15,385	15,918	881	727
5430 Fruit and vegetable markets[2]	-	16	-	15	1	-	10,133	-	417
5440 Candy, nut, and confectionery stores[1]	32	30	131	129	4	5,985	5,488	839	757
5450 Dairy products stores[3]	10	13	47	61	5	8,511	7,869	451	459
5460 Retail bakeries	96	98	654	717	7	9,853	10,416	7,095	7,929
5490 Miscellaneous food stores[3]	37	32	180	152	5	16,422	20,026	3,062	3,337
5510 New and used car dealers	117	120	5,897	6,249	52	28,550	30,044	196,646	210,185
5520 Used car dealers	150	152	712	893	6	17,742	18,943	15,270	18,360
5530 Auto and home supply stores	219	232	1,893	1,830	8	17,606	20,715	36,060	37,866
5540 Gasoline service stations	583	578	5,377	4,745	8	9,590	12,193	54,594	61,755

Continued on next page.

INDIANAPOLIS, IN MSA - [continued]

Wholesale and Retail Trade USA	Establishments		Employment		Emp / Est	Pay / Employee		Annual Payroll ($ 000)	
	1994	1995	1994	1995	1995	1994	1995	1994	1995
5550 Boat dealers[3]	16	16	157	209	13	22,242	21,531	4,943	5,575
5560 Recreational vehicle dealers[3]	11	11	226	245	22	25,274	26,857	7,301	7,691
5570 Motorcycle dealers[3]	15	16	73	84	5	18,137	21,286	1,661	1,854
5590 Automotive dealers, nec[2]	-	6	-	8	1	-	12,000	-	85
5610 Men's & boys' clothing stores[3]	80	75	508	519	7	13,567	12,655	7,111	6,386
5620 Women's clothing stores	273	246	2,857	2,619	11	7,178	7,423	22,604	20,647
5630 Women's accessory & specialty stores[3]	44	46	235	282	6	9,004	10,397	2,479	2,939
5640 Children's and infants' wear stores[3]	25	25	140	173	7	7,086	7,491	1,163	1,362
5650 Family clothing stores[3]	62	64	1,291	1,221	19	9,614	11,283	12,968	20,472
5660 Shoe stores	181	187	1,177	1,180	6	10,287	11,590	13,297	13,410
5690 Misc. apparel & accessory stores[3]	57	55	438	449	8	12,429	13,871	5,639	6,775
5712 Furniture stores[1]	178	179	1,358	1,562	9	21,105	21,928	29,612	34,175
5713 Floor covering stores	99	99	547	609	6	17,982	19,757	11,169	13,234
5714 Drapery and upholstery stores[3]	29	30	139	155	5	10,676	11,432	1,646	1,791
5719 Misc. homefurnishings stores[3]	105	105	648	586	6	11,691	11,782	8,012	8,233
5720 Household appliance stores	50	47	390	385	8	23,169	25,091	9,574	9,762
5731 Radio, TV, & electronic stores	98	96	1,048	1,072	11	17,405	15,940	19,022	18,332
5734 Computer and software stores[3]	47	52	406	398	8	13,350	13,116	5,785	5,332
5735 Record & prerecorded tape stores[3]	58	63	346	402	6	8,069	9,323	2,964	4,980
5736 Musical instrument stores[3]	26	26	157	160	6	23,490	26,575	3,765	4,000
5812 Eating places[1]	2,246	2,185	50,067	52,295	24	7,707	8,329	425,608	464,607
5813 Drinking places	339	312	2,528	2,490	8	7,828	8,238	20,420	22,005
5910 Drug stores and proprietary stores[2]	250	252	3,884	3,712	15	16,312	18,717	70,180	70,274
5920 Liquor stores	239	234	1,346	1,298	6	10,368	11,193	16,187	16,058
5930 Used merchandise stores	150	146	826	892	6	9,937	10,942	9,850	10,660
5941 Sporting goods and bicycle shops[3]	144	142	962	1,241	9	10,478	11,130	13,141	16,058
5942 Book stores[1]	67	73	544	486	7	7,846	9,037	4,529	4,460
5943 Stationery stores[3]	21	20	20	78	4	9,800	12,154	176	1,072
5944 Jewelry stores	168	176	919	976	6	15,321	16,709	15,645	17,574
5945 Hobby, toy, and game shops[3]	59	63	518	611	10	8,602	8,367	5,516	6,316
5946 Camera & photographic supply stores[3]	12	12	50	60	5	19,760	19,600	1,339	1,441
5947 Gift, novelty, and souvenir shops	218	220	1,234	1,378	6	7,300	7,422	10,475	11,345
5948 Luggage and leather goods stores[2]	-	9	-	40	4	-	13,400	-	566
5949 Sewing, needlework, and piece goods[3]	40	34	261	267	8	6,176	6,262	1,516	1,621
5961 Catalog and mail-order houses[1]	37	45	3,273	3,638	81	17,365	19,599	65,005	71,965
5962 Merchandising machine operators[3]	49	51	795	709	14	17,655	21,117	15,357	14,779
5963 Direct selling establishments	100	97	866	716	7	18,767	21,536	17,317	16,919
5983 Fuel oil dealers[3]	11	11	27	70	6	17,926	10,743	478	853
5984 Liquefied petroleum gas dealers[3]	16	17	34	33	2	29,059	32,970	972	1,231
5992 Florists	150	163	821	810	5	10,324	11,309	9,121	9,471
5993 Tobacco stores and stands[3]	8	15	11	21	1	13,091	9,905	166	349
5994 News dealers and newsstands[3]	12	11	13	18	2	17,231	12,889	250	323
5995 Optical goods stores[3]	89	87	432	357	4	14,278	15,384	6,518	5,394
5999 Miscellaneous retail stores, nec	283	303	1,555	1,710	6	10,814	12,622	21,477	27,586

Source: County Business Patterns 1994/95, CBP-94/95, U.S. Department of Commerce, Washington DC, November 1997. The employment column represents mid-March employment in the year. Pay per employee is calculated by dividing 1st Quarter payroll, annualized, by mid-March employment. The column headed 'Emp / Est' shows 'employees per establishment'. A dash (-) means that data are unavailable or cannot be calculated. nec means not elsewhere classified. *Notes:* 1. 1994 data incomplete; unavailable or withheld. 2. 1995 data incomplete; unavailable or withheld. 3. 1994 and 1995 data incomplete; unavailable or withheld.

IOWA CITY, IA MSA

Wholesale and Retail Trade USA	Establishments		Employment		Emp / Est	Pay / Employee		Annual Payroll ($ 000)	
	1994	1995	1994	1995	1995	1994	1995	1994	1995
50 - Wholesale trade	102	104	1,142	1,183	11	22,658	24,416	29,871	31,751
5010 Motor vehicles, parts, and supplies	9	10	66	95	10	19,636	19,200	1,336	1,756
5030 Lumber and construction materials	6	-	62	-	-	22,194	-	1,567	-
5045 Computers, peripherals, & software	5	5	24	26	5	25,000	23,231	683	717
5047 Medical and hospital equipment	4	-	65	-	-	27,323	-	2,175	-
5063 Electrical apparatus and equipment	4	4	36	48	12	36,444	35,750	1,371	1,897
5070 Hardware, plumbing & heating equipment	5	6	73	76	13	24,164	28,579	1,931	2,091
5080 Machinery, equipment, and supplies	10	10	62	59	6	19,355	20,881	1,379	1,924
5090 Miscellaneous durable goods	-	5	-	91	18	-	19,077	-	1,989
5110 Paper and paper products	-	3	-	6	2	-	11,333	-	72
5153 Grain and field beans	-	8	-	64	8	-	25,188	-	2,391
5171 Petroleum bulk stations & terminals	5	-	59	-	-	10,102	-	592	-
5180 Beer, wine, and distilled beverages	-	4	-	27	7	-	16,593	-	498
5191 Farm supplies	7	8	122	146	18	26,328	28,986	4,034	4,281
52 - Retail trade	650	658	10,412	11,197	17	10,206	10,387	115,435	122,057
5210 Lumber and other building materials	18	14	247	360	26	16,211	18,700	5,097	6,317

Continued on next page.

IOWA CITY, IA MSA - [continued]

Wholesale and Retail Trade USA	Establishments		Employment		Emp / Est	Pay / Employee		Annual Payroll ($ 000)	
	1994	1995	1994	1995	1995	1994	1995	1994	1995
5250 Hardware stores	6	5	66	65	13	12,667	12,369	858	853
5260 Retail nurseries and garden stores	5	5	63	79	16	13,206	13,367	1,286	1,426
5310 Department stores	8	8	1,011	1,026	128	9,555	11,018	10,806	11,554
5390 Misc. general merchandise stores	4	4	119	118	30	12,067	9,254	1,532	864
5410 Grocery stores	36	37	1,468	1,709	46	10,534	9,994	16,457	17,771
5460 Retail bakeries	8	5	205	81	16	7,259	5,630	1,581	500
5510 New and used car dealers	11	11	426	424	39	23,465	24,396	11,164	11,138
5520 Used car dealers	5	7	7	4	1	10,286	9,000	89	79
5530 Auto and home supply stores	10	10	62	63	6	16,903	17,968	1,196	1,237
5540 Gasoline service stations	40	39	399	385	10	10,506	11,138	4,430	4,583
5610 Men's & boys' clothing stores	4	4	32	35	9	13,375	12,114	422	414
5620 Women's clothing stores	17	14	152	118	8	7,237	6,780	1,120	792
5630 Women's accessory & specialty stores	4	4	15	25	6	6,933	8,000	144	194
5650 Family clothing stores	10	10	114	103	10	7,123	8,466	829	909
5660 Shoe stores	16	15	122	117	8	7,770	7,932	958	935
5712 Furniture stores	11	13	95	108	8	13,600	14,259	1,368	1,598
5713 Floor covering stores	8	10	49	50	5	32,000	29,280	1,538	1,648
5719 Misc. homefurnishings stores	8	5	43	50	10	8,186	10,800	324	563
5731 Radio, TV, & electronic stores	7	7	92	144	21	14,000	11,500	1,276	1,427
5734 Computer and software stores	-	7	-	25	4	-	10,560	-	231
5735 Record & prerecorded tape stores	11	13	58	59	5	10,345	10,237	601	622
5736 Musical instrument stores	-	6	-	79	13	-	28,304	-	2,030
5812 Eating places	154	150	3,334	3,723	25	6,786	6,901	24,930	27,051
5813 Drinking places	38	35	476	512	15	5,218	5,328	2,592	2,949
5910 Drug stores and proprietary stores	16	16	268	259	16	18,015	13,838	4,625	3,898
5920 Liquor stores	-	3	-	42	14	-	5,429	-	203
5930 Used merchandise stores	17	16	103	90	6	8,854	5,911	1,029	661
5941 Sporting goods and bicycle shops	12	11	103	120	11	9,204	9,400	1,144	1,221
5942 Book stores	8	8	161	123	15	8,472	11,220	1,447	1,438
5944 Jewelry stores	14	15	80	94	6	10,400	13,447	823	1,176
5945 Hobby, toy, and game shops	6	6	44	56	9	8,091	8,143	408	507
5947 Gift, novelty, and souvenir shops	14	14	97	104	7	4,907	5,846	496	849
5949 Sewing, needlework, and piece goods	5	-	62	-	-	5,806	-	287	-
5960 Nonstore retailers	17	18	162	182	10	18,074	21,275	3,324	4,371
5984 Liquefied petroleum gas dealers	-	5	-	26	5	-	16,769	-	382
5992 Florists	13	11	82	82	7	11,317	8,341	778	701
5999 Miscellaneous retail stores, nec	18	24	110	132	6	15,927	13,879	1,874	2,041

Source: County Business Patterns 1994/95, CBP-94/95, U.S. Department of Commerce, Washington DC, November 1997. The employment column represents mid-March employment in the year. Pay per employee is calculated by dividing 1st Quarter payroll, annualized, by mid-March employment. The column headed 'Emp / Est' shows 'employees per establishment'. A dash (-) means that data are unavailable or cannot be calculated. nec means not elsewhere classified. *Notes:* 1. 1994 data incomplete; unavailable or withheld. 2. 1995 data incomplete; unavailable or withheld. 3. 1994 and 1995 data incomplete; unavailable or withheld.

JACKSON, MI MSA

Wholesale and Retail Trade USA	Establishments		Employment		Emp / Est	Pay / Employee		Annual Payroll ($ 000)	
	1994	1995	1994	1995	1995	1994	1995	1994	1995
50- Wholesale trade	201	210	2,565	2,813	13	25,977	27,428	75,619	83,489
5012 Automobiles and other vehicles	6	5	71	74	15	20,056	22,595	1,547	1,663
5013 Motor vehicle supplies and new parts	13	9	79	72	8	17,975	23,611	1,814	1,736
5015 Motor vehicle parts, used	-	4	-	12	3	-	12,667	-	153
5039 Construction materials, nec	-	3	-	44	15	-	17,818	-	862
5047 Medical and hospital equipment	-	3	-	325	108	-	23,680	-	7,835
5051 Metals service centers and offices	8	7	213	223	32	38,404	43,498	9,877	10,016
5063 Electrical apparatus and equipment	5	7	55	62	9	27,927	32,645	1,671	2,042
5065 Electronic parts and equipment	3	3	42	39	13	17,429	19,692	775	971
5072 Hardware	3	-	13	-	-	17,538	-	262	-
5074 Plumbing & hydronic heating supplies	6	6	42	69	12	18,286	16,464	889	1,227
5082 Construction and mining machinery	5	-	38	-	-	28,947	-	1,505	-
5084 Industrial machinery and equipment	19	21	143	167	8	32,531	34,084	5,665	6,268
5085 Industrial supplies	14	14	155	155	11	31,252	34,839	5,422	5,854
5087 Service establishment equipment	7	8	64	70	9	17,688	19,257	1,289	1,517
5099 Durable goods, nec	4	6	40	40	7	20,600	21,800	954	877
5112 Stationery and office supplies	5	5	30	29	6	33,733	37,103	1,150	1,231
5113 Industrial & personal service paper	4	4	36	39	10	32,333	39,897	1,155	1,456
5149 Groceries and related products, nec	5	5	75	73	15	26,880	29,096	2,335	2,015
5160 Chemicals and allied products	-	3	-	15	5	-	44,533	-	505
5170 Petroleum and petroleum products	11	10	101	115	12	31,168	31,165	3,391	3,672
5180 Beer, wine, and distilled beverages	4	4	175	180	45	24,846	26,111	5,052	5,543
5191 Farm supplies	3	-	12	-	-	31,333	-	501	-

Continued on next page.

JACKSON, MI MSA - [continued]

Wholesale and Retail Trade USA	Establishments		Employment		Emp / Est	Pay / Employee		Annual Payroll ($ 000)	
	1994	1995	1994	1995	1995	1994	1995	1994	1995
5199 Nondurable goods, nec	-	3	-	8	3	-	24,500	-	231
52- Retail trade	839	813	12,049	12,494	15	11,496	12,075	155,508	162,581
5210 Lumber and other building materials	20	20	184	172	9	20,913	25,209	4,752	4,671
5230 Paint, glass, and wallpaper stores	10	6	71	40	7	18,479	23,200	1,692	1,286
5250 Hardware stores	18	15	167	129	9	12,790	12,806	2,365	1,780
5260 Retail nurseries and garden stores	7	5	38	35	7	13,158	13,829	541	582
5270 Mobile home dealers	4	5	24	31	6	16,500	15,742	533	654
5310 Department stores	10	10	2,518	2,541	254	9,951	10,859	28,437	30,556
5330 Variety stores	6	-	60	-	-	7,733	-	548	-
5390 Misc. general merchandise stores	5	-	183	-	-	10,645	-	2,083	-
5410 Grocery stores	79	72	1,111	1,121	16	9,811	10,205	11,521	12,500
5420 Meat and fish markets	5	3	14	11	4	6,857	7,273	106	109
5450 Dairy products stores	-	3	-	13	4	-	1,231	-	44
5460 Retail bakeries	9	11	82	91	8	7,220	7,604	647	744
5490 Miscellaneous food stores	6	6	27	27	5	7,556	9,037	255	348
5510 New and used car dealers	10	10	457	487	49	25,602	26,702	13,942	14,378
5520 Used car dealers	10	7	45	34	5	19,378	23,647	937	890
5530 Auto and home supply stores	22	22	177	175	8	15,638	19,040	3,081	3,516
5540 Gasoline service stations	66	68	472	464	7	9,746	12,457	5,159	5,555
5550 Boat dealers	4	4	7	10	3	31,429	25,600	276	307
5610 Men's & boys' clothing stores	6	6	80	88	15	17,600	15,045	1,406	1,123
5620 Women's clothing stores	17	15	183	141	9	7,781	6,752	1,578	1,003
5630 Women's accessory & specialty stores	3	3	13	12	4	8,000	9,000	114	111
5650 Family clothing stores	4	4	31	28	7	7,226	7,714	276	276
5660 Shoe stores	20	17	67	93	5	10,925	9,118	822	820
5690 Misc. apparel & accessory stores	5	4	12	15	4	8,000	4,267	94	73
5712 Furniture stores	9	11	109	126	11	28,220	27,175	3,126	3,459
5713 Floor covering stores	9	9	70	83	9	17,371	18,458	1,396	1,624
5719 Misc. homefurnishings stores	3	-	16	-	-	11,250	-	145	-
5720 Household appliance stores	5	6	78	79	13	18,974	20,506	1,656	1,779
5731 Radio, TV, & electronic stores	10	-	43	-	-	13,395	-	582	-
5734 Computer and software stores	4	-	29	-	-	11,310	-	389	-
5735 Record & prerecorded tape stores	-	3	-	22	7	-	9,273	-	214
5812 Eating places	173	165	3,302	3,625	22	7,220	6,918	26,378	27,060
5813 Drinking places	43	38	201	204	5	6,667	6,686	1,475	1,458
5910 Drug stores and proprietary stores	23	16	322	325	20	16,683	18,831	5,337	6,194
5920 Liquor stores	12	8	64	63	8	8,125	8,000	539	525
5930 Used merchandise stores	6	6	32	25	4	6,125	7,680	210	186
5941 Sporting goods and bicycle shops	19	17	84	98	6	11,095	10,367	1,114	1,061
5942 Book stores	7	6	55	43	7	6,909	8,558	412	433
5944 Jewelry stores	10	12	65	72	6	12,738	12,778	871	986
5945 Hobby, toy, and game shops	7	8	52	59	7	11,154	11,322	697	780
5947 Gift, novelty, and souvenir shops	18	18	105	110	6	12,952	12,982	1,603	1,610
5962 Merchandising machine operators	-	4	-	57	14	-	18,105	-	1,213
5963 Direct selling establishments	10	-	82	-	-	16,293	-	1,159	-
5984 Liquefied petroleum gas dealers	4	4	34	32	8	25,765	26,750	783	773
5992 Florists	12	-	76	-	-	8,053	-	757	-
5995 Optical goods stores	7	7	55	54	8	15,855	16,741	1,056	844
5999 Miscellaneous retail stores, nec	22	22	87	91	4	11,632	12,396	1,072	1,138

Source: County Business Patterns 1994/95, CBP-94/95, U.S. Department of Commerce, Washington DC, November 1997. The employment column represents mid-March employment in the year. Pay per employee is calculated by dividing 1st Quarter payroll, annualized, by mid-March employment. The column headed 'Emp / Est' shows 'employees per establishment'. A dash (-) means that data are unavailable or cannot be calculated. nec means not elsewhere classified. *Notes:* 1. 1994 data incomplete; unavailable or withheld. 2. 1995 data incomplete; unavailable or withheld. 3. 1994 and 1995 data incomplete; unavailable or withheld.

JACKSON, MS MSA

Wholesale and Retail Trade USA	Establishments		Employment		Emp / Est	Pay / Employee		Annual Payroll ($ 000)	
	1994	1995	1994	1995	1995	1994	1995	1994	1995
50- Wholesale trade	913	933	12,041	13,282	14	27,708	28,688	359,165	387,544
5012 Automobiles and other vehicles	24	24	482	498	21	26,539	29,124	13,221	15,475
5013 Motor vehicle supplies and new parts [1]	50	51	673	710	14	23,233	22,676	15,147	15,572
5014 Tires and tubes [1]	9	11	88	148	13	32,818	29,514	2,498	3,727
5015 Motor vehicle parts, used [1]	9	-	26	-	-	17,385	-	499	-
5021 Furniture	15	17	117	183	11	25,880	25,071	3,713	4,618
5023 Homefurnishings	9	9	56	58	6	23,571	25,517	1,464	1,594
5031 Lumber, plywood, and millwork	21	22	250	322	15	28,208	29,292	8,278	10,524
5032 Brick, stone, & related materials	-	8	-	19	2	-	22,737	-	556
5033 Roofing, siding, & insulation	10	9	18	23	3	48,889	47,130	1,066	1,261
5039 Construction materials, nec	-	10	-	92	9	-	19,348	-	2,019

Continued on next page.

JACKSON, MS MSA - [continued]

Wholesale and Retail Trade USA	Establishments		Employment		Emp / Est	Pay / Employee		Annual Payroll ($ 000)	
	1994	1995	1994	1995	1995	1994	1995	1994	1995
5044 Office equipment	20	23	129	142	6	30,047	32,451	4,013	4,529
5045 Computers, peripherals, & software	32	29	377	456	16	43,629	45,211	18,654	17,633
5046 Commercial equipment, nec[3]	13	14	143	124	9	20,615	21,903	3,509	3,244
5047 Medical and hospital equipment	27	24	565	360	15	28,297	38,200	18,093	12,945
5048 Ophthalmic goods[2]	6	5	37	49	10	27,568	16,163	1,018	816
5049 Professional equipment, nec[2]	10	7	147	125	18	36,463	39,968	7,264	6,235
5051 Metals service centers and offices	18	19	99	103	5	25,253	26,408	2,834	2,896
5063 Electrical apparatus and equipment	44	43	416	809	19	32,933	28,667	13,947	20,278
5064 Electrical appliances, TV & radios	7	8	104	103	13	24,154	30,524	3,280	3,392
5065 Electronic parts and equipment	30	27	184	276	10	30,500	29,899	5,611	9,002
5072 Hardware	22	23	190	193	8	19,958	24,021	5,642	6,660
5074 Plumbing & hydronic heating supplies	17	17	135	127	7	27,052	28,000	3,622	3,941
5075 Warm air heating & air conditioning	18	18	214	212	12	24,019	25,547	6,123	6,671
5078 Refrigeration equipment and supplies[3]	5	5	28	24	5	21,286	27,667	647	710
5082 Construction and mining machinery	16	16	296	352	22	39,311	39,489	16,278	16,111
5083 Farm and garden machinery	-	13	-	42	3	-	29,905	-	1,467
5084 Industrial machinery and equipment	51	54	386	455	8	32,394	31,411	12,053	13,939
5085 Industrial supplies[1]	30	31	292	281	9	24,329	27,374	7,972	8,191
5087 Service establishment equipment	16	14	108	99	7	19,037	22,949	2,134	2,061
5091 Sporting & recreational goods	-	8	-	32	4	-	15,125	-	521
5093 Scrap and waste materials[3]	16	17	131	147	9	20,031	20,898	3,068	3,626
5099 Durable goods, nec	25	28	136	150	5	19,588	19,547	3,293	3,334
5112 Stationery and office supplies	25	22	266	242	11	18,917	22,413	5,300	5,278
5120 Drugs, proprietaries, and sundries	10	11	178	214	19	27,079	26,449	5,245	6,367
5131 Piece goods & notions	6	-	32	-	-	15,750	-	572	-
5136 Men's and boys' clothing[3]	9	10	47	54	5	19,830	24,815	1,027	1,167
5137 Women's and children's clothing[3]	10	10	127	86	9	22,457	21,953	2,442	1,194
5141 Groceries, general line[1]	9	-	454	-	-	24,678	-	12,861	-
5142 Packaged frozen food	10	9	352	508	56	30,000	24,661	10,637	12,836
5144 Poultry and poultry products	-	7	-	32	5	-	46,875	-	1,820
5147 Meats and meat products[3]	8	8	117	124	16	22,906	22,774	2,728	2,842
5148 Fresh fruits and vegetables[3]	8	8	71	78	10	14,141	13,282	1,352	1,254
5149 Groceries and related products, nec	20	20	413	451	23	23,893	24,089	10,162	11,311
5150 Farm-product raw materials[1]	4	-	26	-	-	22,462	-	529	-
5162 Plastics materials & basic shapes	9	9	36	38	4	39,222	43,368	1,404	1,641
5169 Chemicals & allied products, nec	20	20	124	126	6	23,806	24,190	3,361	3,407
5170 Petroleum and petroleum products[3]	23	21	117	73	3	18,632	19,671	2,561	1,804
5180 Beer, wine, and distilled beverages[3]	7	7	244	243	35	26,918	27,473	6,836	6,833
5191 Farm supplies	16	15	188	143	10	20,574	20,224	4,524	3,017
5192 Books, periodicals, & newspapers[3]	4	6	22	27	5	34,000	31,259	769	914
5193 Flowers & florists' supplies[3]	6	7	55	54	8	15,345	17,185	857	916
5198 Paints, varnishes, and supplies[2]	-	5	-	36	7	-	32,667	-	1,197
5199 Nondurable goods, nec	23	22	134	52	2	23,134	31,692	3,677	1,906
52- Retail trade	2,407	2,375	34,978	36,183	15	12,436	13,181	462,574	501,295
5210 Lumber and other building materials	36	30	887	700	23	16,000	16,217	15,957	12,512
5230 Paint, glass, and wallpaper stores	16	16	140	156	10	15,829	16,077	2,806	2,941
5250 Hardware stores[2]	33	27	167	39	1	11,665	14,051	2,150	584
5260 Retail nurseries and garden stores[1]	23	24	146	321	13	9,589	10,355	1,608	3,609
5270 Mobile home dealers[3]	8	8	32	24	3	42,875	21,333	857	741
5310 Department stores[3]	17	17	3,187	2,957	174	11,034	12,850	37,228	37,974
5330 Variety stores	33	32	180	162	5	7,689	7,383	1,569	1,338
5390 Misc. general merchandise stores	29	35	607	701	20	13,160	13,255	8,120	9,164
5410 Grocery stores	224	204	4,998	4,737	23	10,153	10,924	51,879	54,303
5440 Candy, nut, and confectionery stores[3]	4	6	3	16	3	20,000	10,750	76	158
5460 Retail bakeries	18	16	105	94	6	6,057	6,128	722	614
5490 Miscellaneous food stores[3]	11	9	58	44	5	8,207	9,727	526	470
5510 New and used car dealers	37	39	2,035	2,177	56	29,834	32,009	71,171	85,186
5520 Used car dealers	32	34	110	95	3	14,909	13,053	1,821	1,465
5530 Auto and home supply stores	81	83	627	737	9	16,523	19,457	11,426	15,611
5540 Gasoline service stations	159	154	1,072	1,041	7	10,653	12,138	12,634	13,482
5570 Motorcycle dealers[2]	-	5	-	16	3	-	18,000	-	373
5610 Men's & boys' clothing stores	34	29	264	265	9	10,152	10,445	2,752	2,636
5620 Women's clothing stores	97	78	775	671	9	8,681	8,668	6,930	5,765
5630 Women's accessory & specialty stores[3]	15	12	79	86	7	8,962	8,605	650	699
5640 Children's and infants' wear stores[3]	6	8	44	57	7	6,364	6,316	333	373
5650 Family clothing stores	20	20	272	294	15	7,750	9,143	2,356	2,486
5660 Shoe stores	68	62	362	353	6	10,939	11,501	3,915	3,761
5690 Misc. apparel & accessory stores[3]	10	12	82	87	7	9,073	11,310	735	974
5712 Furniture stores	44	45	479	528	12	19,265	22,758	11,697	13,527
5719 Misc. homefurnishings stores	28	26	209	231	9	9,665	10,043	2,422	2,604
5720 Household appliance stores	16	17	90	101	6	16,133	18,416	1,617	1,715

Continued on next page.

JACKSON, MS MSA - [continued]

Wholesale and Retail Trade USA	Establishments		Employment		Emp / Est	Pay / Employee		Annual Payroll ($ 000)	
	1994	1995	1994	1995	1995	1994	1995	1994	1995
5731 Radio, TV, & electronic stores	32	32	215	218	7	21,023	18,789	4,629	3,844
5734 Computer and software stores	14	-	21	-	-	14,095	-	430	-
5735 Record & prerecorded tape stores	13	14	50	104	7	9,840	9,423	629	1,012
5812 Eating places	497	477	10,748	11,539	24	7,148	7,236	81,777	88,145
5813 Drinking places	20	16	52	67	4	7,154	7,463	444	639
5910 Drug stores and proprietary stores	84	75	1,018	993	13	14,562	14,671	15,307	14,559
5920 Liquor stores	50	43	98	98	2	9,633	10,449	1,013	1,115
5930 Used merchandise stores	45	48	205	228	5	10,166	9,632	2,278	2,442
5941 Sporting goods and bicycle shops	24	28	179	249	9	12,380	10,876	2,562	2,968
5942 Book stores	20	19	163	182	10	8,638	9,275	1,551	1,777
5944 Jewelry stores	44	52	202	236	5	23,208	21,102	3,569	4,335
5945 Hobby, toy, and game shops	14	12	157	156	13	9,503	10,487	1,614	1,854
5947 Gift, novelty, and souvenir shops	43	39	257	253	6	7,751	7,731	2,308	2,369
5949 Sewing, needlework, and piece goods	11	11	54	52	5	11,926	10,615	590	529
5961 Catalog and mail-order houses [3]	6	6	55	54	9	32,655	32,296	1,940	1,691
5962 Merchandising machine operators	8	10	22	33	3	18,182	16,727	455	519
5963 Direct selling establishments	25	26	280	333	13	15,471	13,477	4,303	4,482
5980 Fuel dealers	13	13	63	69	5	17,270	18,203	1,093	1,183
5992 Florists	46	49	147	218	4	11,401	11,284	1,796	2,595
5993 Tobacco stores and stands	12	13	22	34	3	7,091	9,647	216	437
5995 Optical goods stores	19	20	97	108	5	15,464	15,037	1,744	1,687
5999 Miscellaneous retail stores, nec	62	65	366	427	7	13,388	14,717	5,710	6,256

Source: County Business Patterns 1994/95, CBP-94/95, U.S. Department of Commerce, Washington DC, November 1997. The employment column represents mid-March employment in the year. Pay per employee is calculated by dividing 1st Quarter payroll, annualized, by mid-March employment. The column headed 'Emp / Est' shows 'employees per establishment'. A dash (-) means that data are unavailable or cannot be calculated. nec means not elsewhere classified. *Notes:* 1. 1994 data incomplete; unavailable or withheld. 2. 1995 data incomplete; unavailable or withheld. 3. 1994 and 1995 data incomplete; unavailable or withheld.

JACKSON, TN MSA

Wholesale and Retail Trade USA	Establishments		Employment		Emp / Est	Pay / Employee		Annual Payroll ($ 000)	
	1994	1995	1994	1995	1995	1994	1995	1994	1995
50 – Wholesale trade	-	180	-	2,367	13	-	24,379	-	59,129
5013 Motor vehicle supplies and new parts	-	12	-	267	22	-	16,794	-	4,904
5020 Furniture and homefurnishings	-	3	-	17	6	-	28,000	-	467
5031 Lumber, plywood, and millwork	-	5	-	75	15	-	17,280	-	1,308
5044 Office equipment	-	4	-	61	15	-	25,574	-	1,581
5051 Metals service centers and offices	-	8	-	113	14	-	37,416	-	4,059
5063 Electrical apparatus and equipment	-	8	-	163	20	-	39,583	-	5,438
5065 Electronic parts and equipment	-	6	-	34	6	-	32,706	-	1,052
5072 Hardware	-	4	-	101	25	-	20,238	-	1,951
5074 Plumbing & hydronic heating supplies	-	3	-	54	18	-	21,852	-	1,492
5082 Construction and mining machinery	-	3	-	28	9	-	31,286	-	875
5083 Farm and garden machinery	-	5	-	31	6	-	15,226	-	542
5084 Industrial machinery and equipment	-	11	-	91	8	-	30,681	-	2,935
5085 Industrial supplies	-	15	-	151	10	-	32,079	-	4,521
5093 Scrap and waste materials	-	7	-	106	15	-	19,472	-	1,803
5110 Paper and paper products	-	4	-	51	13	-	18,588	-	945
5149 Groceries and related products, nec	-	3	-	163	54	-	24,933	-	4,118
5150 Farm-product raw materials	-	3	-	11	4	-	38,909	-	278
5171 Petroleum bulk stations & terminals	-	3	-	107	36	-	16,299	-	2,451
5172 Petroleum products, nec	-	4	-	20	5	-	9,400	-	491
5191 Farm supplies	-	3	-	38	13	-	19,474	-	856
5193 Flowers & florists' supplies	-	3	-	33	11	-	15,273	-	564
52 – Retail trade	-	671	-	10,317	15	-	11,147	-	118,020
5210 Lumber and other building materials	-	12	-	241	20	-	19,801	-	4,942
5230 Paint, glass, and wallpaper stores	-	3	-	27	9	-	13,185	-	370
5270 Mobile home dealers	-	5	-	85	17	-	21,224	-	2,438
5310 Department stores	-	7	-	1,336	191	-	13,749	-	16,837
5410 Grocery stores	-	49	-	823	17	-	9,628	-	7,471
5460 Retail bakeries	-	4	-	61	15	-	5,836	-	357
5490 Miscellaneous food stores	-	4	-	16	4	-	6,750	-	122
5510 New and used car dealers	-	10	-	408	41	-	25,422	-	11,593
5520 Used car dealers	-	17	-	99	6	-	13,657	-	1,776
5530 Auto and home supply stores	-	18	-	125	7	-	20,384	-	2,580
5540 Gasoline service stations	-	44	-	489	11	-	9,252	-	4,629
5610 Men's & boys' clothing stores	-	7	-	32	5	-	10,625	-	316
5620 Women's clothing stores	-	25	-	214	9	-	6,935	-	1,637
5640 Children's and infants' wear stores	-	4	-	12	3	-	3,667	-	57
5650 Family clothing stores	-	9	-	305	34	-	9,613	-	3,146

Continued on next page.

JACKSON, TN MSA - [continued]

Wholesale and Retail Trade USA	Establishments		Employment		Emp / Est	Pay / Employee		Annual Payroll ($ 000)	
	1994	1995	1994	1995	1995	1994	1995	1994	1995
5660 Shoe stores	-	19	-	130	7	-	10,400	-	1,374
5690 Misc. apparel & accessory stores	-	5	-	28	6	-	16,429	-	484
5712 Furniture stores	-	18	-	154	9	-	17,636	-	3,097
5713 Floor covering stores	-	7	-	62	9	-	20,452	-	1,201
5720 Household appliance stores	-	4	-	34	9	-	42,824	-	904
5731 Radio, TV, & electronic stores	-	6	-	71	12	-	20,620	-	1,498
5735 Record & prerecorded tape stores	-	4	-	19	5	-	11,368	-	190
5812 Eating places	-	113	-	3,366	30	-	7,277	-	24,978
5910 Drug stores and proprietary stores	-	19	-	168	9	-	17,952	-	2,963
5920 Liquor stores	-	13	-	60	5	-	10,733	-	695
5930 Used merchandise stores	-	12	-	43	4	-	8,093	-	285
5941 Sporting goods and bicycle shops	-	13	-	45	3	-	10,311	-	458
5942 Book stores	-	8	-	54	7	-	7,778	-	425
5944 Jewelry stores	-	13	-	63	5	-	18,857	-	1,150
5945 Hobby, toy, and game shops	-	5	-	82	16	-	7,659	-	568
5947 Gift, novelty, and souvenir shops	-	45	-	431	10	-	5,930	-	3,257
5949 Sewing, needlework, and piece goods	-	3	-	28	9	-	7,571	-	213
5962 Merchandising machine operators	-	4	-	143	36	-	15,049	-	2,202
5963 Direct selling establishments	-	8	-	42	5	-	20,667	-	878
5984 Liquefied petroleum gas dealers	-	3	-	24	8	-	21,500	-	557
5992 Florists	-	12	-	60	5	-	8,067	-	567
5999 Miscellaneous retail stores, nec	-	26	-	106	4	-	13,698	-	1,510

Source: County Business Patterns 1994/95, CBP-94/95, U.S. Department of Commerce, Washington DC, November 1997. The employment column represents mid-March employment in the year. Pay per employee is calculated by dividing 1st Quarter payroll, annualized, by mid-March employment. The column headed 'Emp / Est' shows 'employees per establishment'. A dash (-) means that data are unavailable or cannot be calculated. nec means not elsewhere classified. *Notes:* 1. 1994 data incomplete; unavailable or withheld. 2. 1995 data incomplete; unavailable or withheld. 3. 1994 and 1995 data incomplete; unavailable or withheld.

JACKSONVILLE, FL MSA

Wholesale and Retail Trade USA	Establishments		Employment		Emp / Est	Pay / Employee		Annual Payroll ($ 000)	
	1994	1995	1994	1995	1995	1994	1995	1994	1995
50- Wholesale trade	1,956	1,970	25,290	26,781	14	29,984	32,344	801,867	901,995
5012 Automobiles and other vehicles	38	41	515	499	12	28,497	33,130	15,434	16,411
5013 Motor vehicle supplies and new parts	117	106	1,753	1,728	16	27,268	31,215	52,477	52,364
5014 Tires and tubes [3]	27	23	260	261	11	34,431	33,900	8,177	9,984
5015 Motor vehicle parts, used [1]	25	27	140	145	5	16,457	18,841	2,777	2,902
5021 Furniture [3]	27	26	398	387	15	25,327	29,416	10,917	11,951
5023 Homefurnishings [3]	24	24	176	170	7	22,795	26,376	4,352	4,560
5031 Lumber, plywood, and millwork [3]	42	40	590	509	13	27,708	29,564	17,119	16,479
5032 Brick, stone, & related materials [3]	22	23	188	199	9	26,064	28,523	5,364	5,288
5033 Roofing, siding, & insulation [3]	22	19	192	151	8	20,292	24,397	4,236	4,106
5039 Construction materials, nec [1]	14	38	92	392	10	28,130	29,959	2,436	11,130
5043 Photographic equipment & supplies [3]	5	6	49	26	4	15,429	13,846	454	323
5044 Office equipment [3]	51	49	874	887	18	28,371	31,278	25,320	25,250
5045 Computers, peripherals, & software [1]	73	72	642	631	9	47,215	55,848	29,806	30,811
5046 Commercial equipment, nec [3]	23	21	133	160	8	23,850	23,750	3,431	3,766
5047 Medical and hospital equipment	59	65	574	712	11	40,718	45,146	25,468	36,438
5048 Ophthalmic goods [3]	9	9	131	132	15	24,977	35,212	3,560	3,903
5049 Professional equipment, nec [3]	9	8	53	56	7	19,321	33,143	1,032	2,261
5051 Metals service centers and offices [3]	46	42	10	10	-	61,600	65,600	641	708
5063 Electrical apparatus and equipment	69	65	697	650	10	31,472	33,532	22,661	22,446
5064 Electrical appliances, TV & radios [3]	11	15	176	191	13	26,432	30,073	5,316	5,380
5065 Electronic parts and equipment	50	52	297	626	12	33,387	34,492	10,746	24,665
5072 Hardware [3]	40	39	418	460	12	25,502	29,070	11,610	12,963
5074 Plumbing & hydronic heating supplies [3]	45	46	396	373	8	28,970	31,764	11,565	11,683
5075 Warm air heating & air conditioning [3]	46	45	453	376	8	31,823	30,021	15,287	12,816
5078 Refrigeration equipment and supplies [3]	11	12	37	39	3	32,757	31,897	1,357	1,398
5082 Construction and mining machinery [3]	20	20	734	728	36	30,714	32,956	23,617	24,513
5083 Farm and garden machinery [3]	24	23	258	226	10	20,853	20,478	6,340	5,056
5084 Industrial machinery and equipment	105	104	651	707	7	30,992	32,526	23,085	24,756
5085 Industrial supplies	75	76	700	747	10	29,680	31,679	21,977	25,917
5087 Service establishment equipment [3]	34	33	307	321	10	23,036	24,698	7,896	8,520
5088 Transportation equipment & supplies [3]	20	21	87	101	5	26,759	31,802	3,831	4,966
5091 Sporting & recreational goods [1]	27	26	166	152	6	23,157	20,816	3,715	3,588
5093 Scrap and waste materials [3]	27	29	339	361	12	20,968	23,756	8,088	9,110
5099 Durable goods, nec [3]	39	38	79	75	2	22,430	23,360	1,600	1,932
5111 Printing and writing paper [3]	10	9	152	159	18	33,053	39,748	4,781	7,485
5112 Stationery and office supplies [3]	44	38	649	590	16	22,367	24,820	14,439	14,183
5113 Industrial & personal service paper [3]	37	35	394	355	10	36,721	41,161	15,867	14,019

Continued on next page.

JACKSONVILLE, FL MSA - [continued]

Wholesale and Retail Trade USA	Establishments		Employment		Emp / Est	Pay / Employee		Annual Payroll ($ 000)	
	1994	1995	1994	1995	1995	1994	1995	1994	1995
5120 Drugs, proprietaries, and sundries [2]	29	26	787	873	34	46,307	44,362	35,640	42,189
5131 Piece goods & notions [3]	8	9	24	45	5	37,667	33,867	976	1,744
5136 Men's and boys' clothing [3]	11	9	66	72	8	24,545	27,000	1,475	1,771
5137 Women's and children's clothing [3]	11	10	38	38	4	22,737	27,789	1,110	1,237
5139 Footwear [3]	5	5	15	9	2	47,200	35,556	664	296
5141 Groceries, general line [3]	19	18	441	461	26	29,406	30,586	13,570	14,765
5142 Packaged frozen food [3]	17	18	508	574	32	33,528	37,289	19,538	24,458
5143 Dairy products, exc. dried or canned [3]	7	8	92	70	9	25,435	28,971	2,180	1,940
5144 Poultry and poultry products [3]	4	4	61	73	18	15,738	14,630	1,100	1,178
5145 Confectionery [3]	6	6	258	242	40	27,674	27,636	7,016	6,946
5146 Fish and seafoods [1]	19	19	156	159	8	17,359	20,679	3,741	3,848
5147 Meats and meat products [3]	13	12	99	93	8	21,455	23,484	2,897	2,562
5148 Fresh fruits and vegetables [3]	22	19	547	524	28	20,878	23,527	12,605	13,212
5149 Groceries and related products, nec [3]	53	51	1,219	1,506	30	30,674	27,668	40,114	44,301
5150 Farm-product raw materials [3]	5	5	48	47	9	24,583	21,787	1,293	1,420
5162 Plastics materials & basic shapes [3]	16	15	137	167	11	29,518	29,509	5,016	5,957
5169 Chemicals & allied products, nec [3]	41	39	838	814	21	41,456	47,322	34,690	40,572
5171 Petroleum bulk stations & terminals [3]	30	29	354	397	14	33,412	29,531	11,011	11,602
5172 Petroleum products, nec [3]	13	12	161	240	20	31,453	29,667	5,791	6,729
5180 Beer, wine, and distilled beverages [3]	10	10	582	590	59	35,773	39,458	20,352	19,898
5191 Farm supplies	40	37	181	197	5	23,558	33,401	4,725	7,793
5192 Books, periodicals, & newspapers [2]	22	23	230	272	12	35,426	31,691	8,250	8,380
5193 Flowers & florists' supplies	21	19	148	148	8	18,351	19,459	3,044	3,070
5194 Tobacco and tobacco products [3]	5	5	402	406	81	28,398	36,502	10,872	13,331
5198 Paints, varnishes, and supplies [3]	17	21	106	131	6	24,528	24,794	2,775	3,312
5199 Nondurable goods, nec	60	58	819	740	13	19,560	22,135	17,074	16,423
52- Retail trade	6,271	6,279	87,881	90,859	14	12,766	13,046	1,185,826	1,236,757
5210 Lumber and other building materials	87	78	1,794	1,887	24	19,104	17,942	37,923	34,775
5230 Paint, glass, and wallpaper stores	48	52	165	158	3	20,436	19,544	3,733	4,851
5250 Hardware stores	57	37	479	418	11	13,528	14,134	6,952	5,578
5260 Retail nurseries and garden stores [3]	41	36	359	380	11	11,721	12,705	5,115	5,397
5270 Mobile home dealers	19	16	57	75	5	23,649	21,227	1,605	1,744
5310 Department stores [3]	45	46	6,658	6,979	152	11,402	13,057	84,149	91,774
5330 Variety stores	54	43	420	354	8	9,114	9,175	4,154	3,466
5390 Misc. general merchandise stores	47	56	1,493	1,565	28	12,766	13,748	20,265	20,465
5410 Grocery stores	551	541	12,859	13,782	25	9,971	10,628	134,923	152,837
5420 Meat and fish markets	40	42	149	171	4	14,282	14,292	2,610	2,747
5430 Fruit and vegetable markets	16	18	43	81	5	11,907	8,889	563	760
5440 Candy, nut, and confectionery stores	22	15	95	65	4	7,874	10,400	866	864
5460 Retail bakeries	56	59	409	405	7	8,538	9,481	3,728	4,156
5490 Miscellaneous food stores	41	44	197	169	4	8,975	11,858	1,651	2,060
5510 New and used car dealers	93	94	4,939	5,210	55	30,155	31,020	164,523	177,077
5520 Used car dealers	112	107	481	507	5	19,867	19,574	10,069	11,234
5530 Auto and home supply stores	206	209	1,391	1,476	7	18,096	18,930	27,716	30,329
5540 Gasoline service stations	414	385	2,767	2,752	7	11,426	12,017	34,121	35,317
5550 Boat dealers [3]	32	28	199	179	6	17,065	20,045	4,301	4,208
5560 Recreational vehicle dealers [3]	12	12	153	161	13	20,471	23,627	3,638	3,914
5570 Motorcycle dealers [3]	13	15	79	81	5	18,380	24,049	1,927	2,266
5610 Men's & boys' clothing stores [3]	67	58	615	575	10	10,673	10,574	6,726	6,416
5620 Women's clothing stores	195	178	1,675	1,535	9	8,492	8,847	15,398	13,839
5630 Women's accessory & specialty stores	36	35	191	212	6	9,906	9,566	2,092	2,037
5640 Children's and infants' wear stores	18	22	105	162	7	7,505	9,210	862	1,601
5650 Family clothing stores	53	55	979	1,098	20	11,326	13,654	13,628	15,372
5660 Shoe stores	171	160	718	718	4	10,830	12,201	8,143	10,389
5690 Misc. apparel & accessory stores	44	48	174	189	4	9,218	10,349	2,000	2,283
5712 Furniture stores	159	166	1,014	1,205	7	19,073	21,079	20,840	25,224
5713 Floor covering stores	54	53	261	219	4	20,582	23,689	5,813	4,667
5714 Drapery and upholstery stores	12	9	18	12	1	12,667	12,000	221	162
5719 Misc. homefurnishings stores	78	79	501	581	7	11,872	11,917	6,188	7,095
5720 Household appliance stores	37	38	136	141	4	16,941	15,972	2,401	2,216
5731 Radio, TV, & electronic stores	80	85	756	778	9	19,085	19,743	15,508	14,571
5734 Computer and software stores [3]	28	38	153	204	5	14,196	19,941	3,193	4,547
5735 Record & prerecorded tape stores [3]	36	35	159	276	8	9,484	6,638	1,570	1,934
5736 Musical instrument stores [3]	11	15	32	50	3	19,875	15,600	700	1,138
5812 Eating places	1,334	1,226	27,865	28,558	23	8,025	7,960	232,511	234,437
5813 Drinking places	123	104	1,100	1,102	11	8,247	8,588	9,191	9,642
5910 Drug stores and proprietary stores	128	116	1,903	1,853	16	14,796	16,473	31,258	33,433
5920 Liquor stores	86	88	523	418	5	9,583	11,215	5,414	4,973
5930 Used merchandise stores	154	156	654	698	4	10,795	12,006	7,550	8,359
5941 Sporting goods and bicycle shops	84	84	531	538	6	11,789	12,900	6,823	7,116
5942 Book stores	61	60	384	456	8	9,375	9,079	4,137	4,778

Continued on next page.

JACKSONVILLE, FL MSA - [continued]

Wholesale and Retail Trade USA	Establishments		Employment		Emp / Est	Pay / Employee		Annual Payroll ($ 000)	
	1994	1995	1994	1995	1995	1994	1995	1994	1995
5943 Stationery stores[3]	14	14	40	47	3	15,600	23,660	1,266	1,197
5944 Jewelry stores	121	119	528	561	5	15,098	16,364	8,333	8,996
5945 Hobby, toy, and game shops[3]	38	37	334	415	11	9,521	8,694	4,001	4,279
5947 Gift, novelty, and souvenir shops	133	140	698	704	5	7,553	8,290	5,932	6,578
5948 Luggage and leather goods stores[1]	8	-	16	-	-	10,750	-	181	-
5949 Sewing, needlework, and piece goods[3]	30	29	243	217	7	6,551	7,705	1,729	1,705
5961 Catalog and mail-order houses	17	16	102	164	10	21,490	18,756	2,497	3,613
5962 Merchandising machine operators[3]	31	31	354	407	13	16,102	15,499	6,032	7,782
5963 Direct selling establishments[3]	65	69	697	574	8	15,656	14,418	11,995	8,406
5984 Liquefied petroleum gas dealers	30	31	199	216	7	19,357	20,667	3,662	4,213
5992 Florists	84	91	399	467	5	11,779	11,966	4,583	5,422
5994 News dealers and newsstands[2]	-	8	-	13	2	-	9,846	-	135
5995 Optical goods stores[3]	50	55	289	301	5	16,125	17,754	4,595	5,024
5999 Miscellaneous retail stores, nec	194	207	1,365	1,301	6	11,599	12,932	16,437	18,686

Source: County Business Patterns 1994/95, CBP-94/95, U.S. Department of Commerce, Washington DC, November 1997. The employment column represents mid-March employment in the year. Pay per employee is calculated by dividing 1st Quarter payroll, annualized, by mid-March employment. The column headed 'Emp / Est' shows 'employees per establishment'. A dash (-) means that data are unavailable or cannot be calculated. nec means not elsewhere classified. *Notes:* 1. 1994 data incomplete; unavailable or withheld. 2. 1995 data incomplete; unavailable or withheld. 3. 1994 and 1995 data incomplete; unavailable or withheld.

JACKSONVILLE, NC MSA

Wholesale and Retail Trade USA	Establishments		Employment		Emp / Est	Pay / Employee		Annual Payroll ($ 000)	
	1994	1995	1994	1995	1995	1994	1995	1994	1995
50 – Wholesale trade	85	86	590	515	6	16,115	17,918	9,996	9,551
5013 Motor vehicle supplies and new parts	7	7	68	50	7	16,941	14,880	1,194	778
5020 Furniture and homefurnishings	-	3	-	8	3	-	8,000	-	78
5044 Office equipment	3	3	15	15	5	17,333	19,200	398	420
5045 Computers, peripherals, & software	3	4	25	26	7	18,720	21,231	616	568
5060 Electrical goods	6	5	41	37	7	20,878	27,459	865	897
5070 Hardware, plumbing & heating equipment	6	6	30	33	6	19,200	20,000	569	589
5084 Industrial machinery and equipment	3	3	18	20	7	17,778	20,000	356	481
5093 Scrap and waste materials	4	-	12	-	-	9,333	-	120	-
5112 Stationery and office supplies	5	-	38	-	-	10,737	-	264	-
5149 Groceries and related products, nec	3	3	6	11	4	9,333	8,727	64	130
5170 Petroleum and petroleum products	6	6	42	45	8	21,524	15,733	896	677
5180 Beer, wine, and distilled beverages	-	4	-	34	9	-	19,529	-	831
5191 Farm supplies	-	5	-	31	6	-	10,710	-	356
5199 Nondurable goods, nec	-	3	-	4	1	-	11,000	-	65
52 – Retail trade	770	765	9,785	9,929	13	10,314	11,342	107,864	119,039
5210 Lumber and other building materials	14	14	300	249	18	14,960	22,410	4,426	4,766
5230 Paint, glass, and wallpaper stores	3	5	22	40	8	19,091	19,700	477	781
5250 Hardware stores	10	7	57	51	7	8,561	9,569	617	490
5260 Retail nurseries and garden stores	3	3	13	16	5	12,923	11,500	202	220
5270 Mobile home dealers	10	10	91	101	10	14,769	18,416	1,601	2,176
5310 Department stores	9	7	1,012	968	138	10,111	12,310	10,187	11,143
5330 Variety stores	14	16	100	120	8	8,960	8,233	902	1,106
5390 Misc. general merchandise stores	4	5	61	68	14	8,852	7,412	551	599
5410 Grocery stores	49	44	1,192	1,177	27	8,611	9,451	11,161	11,570
5490 Miscellaneous food stores	3	3	8	11	4	7,500	7,636	79	95
5510 New and used car dealers	17	17	577	629	37	26,461	27,892	16,331	19,945
5520 Used car dealers	25	28	79	93	3	14,430	12,903	1,121	1,283
5530 Auto and home supply stores	36	37	245	253	7	14,824	16,000	4,149	4,038
5540 Gasoline service stations	62	60	288	321	5	9,875	9,844	3,100	3,178
5550 Boat dealers	4	4	22	24	6	14,909	14,667	407	436
5560 Recreational vehicle dealers	3	3	15	17	6	19,467	21,412	361	397
5570 Motorcycle dealers	4	-	28	-	-	19,000	-	591	-
5610 Men's & boys' clothing stores	6	8	51	54	7	9,569	10,296	452	691
5620 Women's clothing stores	24	21	172	125	6	8,279	8,992	1,511	1,512
5630 Women's accessory & specialty stores	4	-	12	-	-	7,000	-	73	-
5650 Family clothing stores	6	7	28	28	4	11,857	11,857	343	307
5660 Shoe stores	17	15	88	72	5	9,227	10,389	807	695
5690 Misc. apparel & accessory stores	8	7	28	33	5	10,429	9,697	335	400
5712 Furniture stores	18	18	322	285	16	13,963	16,168	5,217	4,957
5713 Floor covering stores	-	7	-	36	5	-	19,444	-	787
5719 Misc. homefurnishings stores	4	6	25	35	6	8,960	11,429	253	457
5731 Radio, TV, & electronic stores	11	12	54	89	7	20,370	16,764	1,082	1,425
5734 Computer and software stores	7	-	18	-	-	10,667	-	240	-
5735 Record & prerecorded tape stores	4	-	20	-	-	16,400	-	369	-
5736 Musical instrument stores	3	3	14	15	5	18,857	15,733	172	168

Continued on next page.

JACKSONVILLE, NC MSA - [continued]

Wholesale and Retail Trade USA	Establishments		Employment		Emp / Est	Pay / Employee		Annual Payroll ($ 000)	
	1994	1995	1994	1995	1995	1994	1995	1994	1995
5812 Eating places	153	137	3,566	3,589	26	6,596	7,152	25,273	27,494
5813 Drinking places	47	35	226	231	7	6,265	6,165	1,322	1,400
5910 Drug stores and proprietary stores	17	17	174	177	10	16,667	17,740	3,208	3,348
5920 Liquor stores	-	8	-	25	3	-	15,360	-	382
5930 Used merchandise stores	21	23	88	91	4	13,818	14,286	1,267	1,276
5941 Sporting goods and bicycle shops	9	12	37	30	3	8,432	9,733	377	394
5942 Book stores	-	4	-	28	7	-	7,286	-	174
5944 Jewelry stores	12	13	66	65	5	13,818	14,769	947	1,082
5945 Hobby, toy, and game shops	4	4	17	20	5	9,176	8,000	191	208
5947 Gift, novelty, and souvenir shops	11	13	38	46	4	6,632	7,565	398	381
5963 Direct selling establishments	4	-	18	-	-	23,778	-	318	-
5980 Fuel dealers	7	6	33	44	7	24,606	20,000	695	843
5992 Florists	15	14	50	57	4	8,560	7,719	401	424
5995 Optical goods stores	5	5	17	18	4	17,882	18,000	328	321
5999 Miscellaneous retail stores, nec	16	17	70	73	4	9,657	9,479	701	676

Source: County Business Patterns 1994/95, CBP-94/95, U.S. Department of Commerce, Washington DC, November 1997. The employment column represents mid-March employment in the year. Pay per employee is calculated by dividing 1st Quarter payroll, annualized, by mid-March employment. The column headed 'Emp / Est' shows 'employees per establishment'. A dash (-) means that data are unavailable or cannot be calculated. nec means not elsewhere classified. *Notes:* 1. 1994 data incomplete; unavailable or withheld. 2. 1995 data incomplete; unavailable or withheld. 3. 1994 and 1995 data incomplete; unavailable or withheld.

JAMESTOWN, NY MSA

Wholesale and Retail Trade USA	Establishments		Employment		Emp / Est	Pay / Employee		Annual Payroll ($ 000)	
	1994	1995	1994	1995	1995	1994	1995	1994	1995
50– Wholesale trade	203	196	2,424	2,341	12	21,262	23,411	56,132	59,418
5013 Motor vehicle supplies and new parts	15	13	159	155	12	15,572	15,174	2,531	2,436
5023 Homefurnishings	3	-	6	-	-	5,333	-	37	-
5031 Lumber, plywood, and millwork	3	-	17	-	-	27,529	-	478	-
5039 Construction materials, nec	-	3	-	7	2	-	7,429	-	61
5044 Office equipment	6	7	69	71	10	23,826	26,141	1,726	1,745
5045 Computers, peripherals, & software	6	7	52	47	7	26,385	26,894	1,356	1,514
5046 Commercial equipment, nec	3	-	4	-	-	42,000	-	166	-
5051 Metals service centers and offices	6	-	31	-	-	25,290	-	833	-
5063 Electrical apparatus and equipment	9	11	76	81	7	24,789	26,765	2,002	2,222
5065 Electronic parts and equipment	3	4	24	23	6	25,000	30,435	678	559
5074 Plumbing & hydronic heating supplies	4	5	24	28	6	22,000	22,714	593	680
5083 Farm and garden machinery	12	9	117	101	11	18,564	18,495	2,241	2,074
5084 Industrial machinery and equipment	10	10	43	45	5	21,116	24,000	1,075	1,072
5085 Industrial supplies	-	10	-	54	5	-	29,704	-	1,716
5087 Service establishment equipment	5	5	17	18	4	16,941	18,444	343	363
5093 Scrap and waste materials	8	7	168	192	27	25,905	24,938	4,488	5,514
5112 Stationery and office supplies	3	-	16	-	-	25,500	-	408	-
5113 Industrial & personal service paper	3	-	70	-	-	33,029	-	2,741	-
5149 Groceries and related products, nec	5	3	80	64	21	30,450	33,875	2,520	2,280
5150 Farm-product raw materials	3	4	25	30	8	9,440	9,467	262	312
5160 Chemicals and allied products	5	5	70	68	14	26,400	30,824	1,932	2,072
5171 Petroleum bulk stations & terminals	5	4	76	46	12	21,211	21,043	1,892	1,187
5172 Petroleum products, nec	6	5	83	83	17	20,289	21,880	2,051	2,304
5181 Beer and ale	3	3	67	68	23	21,731	23,235	1,624	1,699
5191 Farm supplies	14	10	98	74	7	22,286	19,892	2,344	1,469
5192 Books, periodicals, & newspapers	3	3	27	32	11	17,926	15,625	524	536
5199 Nondurable goods, nec	-	3	-	17	6	-	11,059	-	249
52– Retail trade	947	917	10,060	10,208	11	10,595	11,098	116,121	122,464
5210 Lumber and other building materials	21	20	257	264	13	14,195	15,061	4,268	4,518
5230 Paint, glass, and wallpaper stores	7	7	41	41	6	14,439	15,317	622	716
5250 Hardware stores	18	12	76	61	5	10,421	10,754	870	687
5260 Retail nurseries and garden stores	8	9	22	21	2	12,182	13,333	371	395
5270 Mobile home dealers	6	6	37	37	6	20,000	21,081	839	959
5310 Department stores	6	7	750	734	105	8,976	10,654	7,773	9,384
5330 Variety stores	9	7	49	39	6	10,939	7,897	431	310
5390 Misc. general merchandise stores	10	10	353	374	37	9,972	11,358	4,037	4,709
5410 Grocery stores	75	77	1,705	1,639	21	10,447	9,872	19,535	18,938
5430 Fruit and vegetable markets	4	-	3	-	-	4,000	-	107	-
5440 Candy, nut, and confectionery stores	4	3	17	9	3	7,059	9,333	102	110
5450 Dairy products stores	4	4	6	9	2	5,333	4,444	36	28
5460 Retail bakeries	8	6	66	63	11	10,182	6,286	770	405
5490 Miscellaneous food stores	-	3	-	9	3	-	10,222	-	89
5510 New and used car dealers	23	23	566	636	28	22,544	23,403	14,547	15,430
5520 Used car dealers	13	15	25	29	2	12,800	12,828	377	442

Continued on next page.

JAMESTOWN, NY MSA - [continued]

Wholesale and Retail Trade USA	Establishments		Employment		Emp / Est	Pay / Employee		Annual Payroll ($ 000)	
	1994	1995	1994	1995	1995	1994	1995	1994	1995
5530 Auto and home supply stores	15	18	142	133	7	12,620	14,857	2,154	2,207
5540 Gasoline service stations	55	51	317	320	6	10,322	11,088	3,604	3,587
5550 Boat dealers	6	-	31	-	-	8,645	-	421	-
5560 Recreational vehicle dealers	-	3	-	13	4	-	18,154	-	279
5620 Women's clothing stores	22	17	120	85	5	6,767	7,482	808	598
5650 Family clothing stores	11	10	98	119	12	9,347	10,655	1,195	1,254
5660 Shoe stores	21	19	84	65	3	9,762	9,354	844	636
5712 Furniture stores	13	12	70	76	6	13,657	13,842	1,089	1,147
5713 Floor covering stores	11	9	43	48	5	13,581	13,833	721	713
5719 Misc. homefurnishings stores	-	6	-	19	3	-	11,579	-	215
5720 Household appliance stores	11	12	55	56	5	16,727	16,714	999	1,021
5731 Radio, TV, & electronic stores	9	10	35	39	4	16,686	16,513	508	584
5734 Computer and software stores	3	4	9	12	3	11,111	10,333	172	125
5735 Record & prerecorded tape stores	4	4	20	28	7	11,800	8,429	227	280
5736 Musical instrument stores	4	5	12	13	3	12,667	13,538	161	177
5812 Eating places	248	231	3,091	3,207	14	6,077	6,627	21,158	22,179
5813 Drinking places	62	48	225	182	4	5,689	6,571	1,397	1,302
5910 Drug stores and proprietary stores	33	31	347	328	11	12,876	13,476	4,700	4,847
5920 Liquor stores	18	20	43	37	2	6,791	6,162	300	256
5930 Used merchandise stores	7	7	34	37	5	9,412	9,189	355	377
5941 Sporting goods and bicycle shops	19	13	67	52	4	10,149	11,385	754	699
5942 Book stores	5	4	73	63	16	7,671	8,635	519	534
5944 Jewelry stores	11	12	52	52	4	10,154	12,462	595	650
5947 Gift, novelty, and souvenir shops	15	13	50	42	3	6,160	7,238	353	397
5949 Sewing, needlework, and piece goods	9	8	50	53	7	3,920	3,849	226	203
5963 Direct selling establishments	8	7	53	56	8	24,528	25,000	1,349	1,289
5980 Fuel dealers	5	6	49	66	11	17,061	22,788	867	1,545
5992 Florists	21	19	75	70	4	8,107	8,514	647	614
5994 News dealers and newsstands	-	5	-	13	3	-	10,154	-	98
5995 Optical goods stores	8	9	27	27	3	17,037	14,370	421	398
5999 Miscellaneous retail stores, nec	22	22	63	83	4	11,492	12,627	925	1,047

Source: County Business Patterns 1994/95, CBP-94/95, U.S. Department of Commerce, Washington DC, November 1997. The employment column represents mid-March employment in the year. Pay per employee is calculated by dividing 1st Quarter payroll, annualized, by mid-March employment. The column headed 'Emp / Est' shows 'employees per establishment'. A dash (-) means that data are unavailable or cannot be calculated. nec means not elsewhere classified. *Notes:* 1. 1994 data incomplete; unavailable or withheld. 2. 1995 data incomplete; unavailable or withheld. 3. 1994 and 1995 data incomplete; unavailable or withheld.

JANESVILLE - BELOIT, WI MSA

Wholesale and Retail Trade USA	Establishments		Employment		Emp / Est	Pay / Employee		Annual Payroll ($ 000)	
	1994	1995	1994	1995	1995	1994	1995	1994	1995
50 - Wholesale trade	-	202	-	3,739	19	-	28,248	-	108,710
5012 Automobiles and other vehicles	-	4	-	52	13	-	28,538	-	1,592
5013 Motor vehicle supplies and new parts	-	13	-	495	38	-	28,808	-	15,851
5015 Motor vehicle parts, used	-	8	-	56	7	-	31,500	-	1,762
5020 Furniture and homefurnishings	-	5	-	24	5	-	29,667	-	667
5031 Lumber, plywood, and millwork	-	3	-	66	22	-	29,152	-	1,756
5033 Roofing, siding, & insulation	-	4	-	175	44	-	33,623	-	7,313
5045 Computers, peripherals, & software	-	7	-	42	6	-	19,810	-	951
5051 Metals service centers and offices	-	3	-	18	6	-	9,778	-	193
5063 Electrical apparatus and equipment	-	6	-	90	15	-	32,533	-	3,147
5074 Plumbing & hydronic heating supplies	-	3	-	77	26	-	30,338	-	2,156
5083 Farm and garden machinery	-	15	-	169	11	-	22,982	-	4,817
5085 Industrial supplies	-	9	-	776	86	-	31,206	-	22,784
5092 Toys and hobby goods and supplies	-	3	-	136	45	-	16,706	-	2,477
5130 Apparel, piece goods, and notions	-	3	-	12	4	-	8,333	-	124
5149 Groceries and related products, nec	-	4	-	98	25	-	27,143	-	3,029
5153 Grain and field beans	-	7	-	55	8	-	20,218	-	1,147
5154 Livestock	-	3	-	10	3	-	17,200	-	171
5170 Petroleum and petroleum products	-	6	-	63	11	-	14,667	-	1,054
5181 Beer and ale	-	3	-	64	21	-	27,625	-	2,277
5191 Farm supplies	-	15	-	133	9	-	26,466	-	4,022
5192 Books, periodicals, & newspapers	-	4	-	59	15	-	14,034	-	881
52 - Retail trade	-	858	-	12,474	15	-	11,195	-	151,736
5210 Lumber and other building materials	-	14	-	324	23	-	22,000	-	7,279
5250 Hardware stores	-	12	-	172	14	-	8,860	-	1,750
5260 Retail nurseries and garden stores	-	10	-	67	7	-	12,478	-	863
5310 Department stores	-	11	-	1,564	142	-	11,361	-	17,753
5410 Grocery stores	-	47	-	1,383	29	-	11,841	-	19,400
5420 Meat and fish markets	-	4	-	7	2	-	12,571	-	141

Continued on next page.

JANESVILLE – BELOIT, WI MSA - [continued]

Wholesale and Retail Trade USA	Establishments		Employment		Emp / Est	Pay / Employee		Annual Payroll ($ 000)	
	1994	1995	1994	1995	1995	1994	1995	1994	1995
5450 Dairy products stores	-	3	-	12	4	-	6,667	-	134
5460 Retail bakeries	-	8	-	76	10	-	10,474	-	868
5490 Miscellaneous food stores	-	4	-	10	3	-	7,200	-	78
5510 New and used car dealers	-	15	-	588	39	-	28,048	-	19,330
5520 Used car dealers	-	12	-	40	3	-	21,000	-	886
5530 Auto and home supply stores	-	14	-	303	22	-	14,785	-	4,833
5540 Gasoline service stations	-	74	-	769	10	-	10,705	-	8,470
5550 Boat dealers	-	3	-	11	4	-	24,000	-	330
5560 Recreational vehicle dealers	-	3	-	40	13	-	19,300	-	1,116
5570 Motorcycle dealers	-	4	-	29	7	-	17,517	-	653
5620 Women's clothing stores	-	23	-	189	8	-	8,423	-	1,537
5640 Children's and infants' wear stores	-	3	-	10	3	-	7,600	-	58
5660 Shoe stores	-	15	-	86	6	-	10,326	-	937
5712 Furniture stores	-	12	-	133	11	-	18,887	-	2,836
5713 Floor covering stores	-	7	-	52	7	-	22,615	-	1,248
5714 Drapery and upholstery stores	-	3	-	8	3	-	4,000	-	38
5719 Misc. homefurnishings stores	-	3	-	11	4	-	6,545	-	71
5720 Household appliance stores	-	10	-	89	9	-	15,236	-	1,399
5731 Radio, TV, & electronic stores	-	6	-	22	4	-	25,273	-	388
5736 Musical instrument stores	-	6	-	33	6	-	10,667	-	416
5812 Eating places	-	180	-	3,928	22	-	7,040	-	29,177
5813 Drinking places	-	74	-	413	6	-	6,964	-	2,957
5910 Drug stores and proprietary stores	-	27	-	357	13	-	16,336	-	6,279
5920 Liquor stores	-	14	-	45	3	-	9,600	-	516
5930 Used merchandise stores	-	12	-	63	5	-	8,317	-	440
5941 Sporting goods and bicycle shops	-	17	-	72	4	-	12,667	-	932
5942 Book stores	-	8	-	47	6	-	7,404	-	341
5944 Jewelry stores	-	10	-	91	9	-	15,341	-	1,476
5945 Hobby, toy, and game shops	-	8	-	63	8	-	10,159	-	710
5947 Gift, novelty, and souvenir shops	-	10	-	75	8	-	8,480	-	588
5961 Catalog and mail-order houses	-	6	-	53	9	-	11,245	-	488
5962 Merchandising machine operators	-	4	-	107	27	-	17,084	-	1,808
5963 Direct selling establishments	-	9	-	172	19	-	3,442	-	549
5983 Fuel oil dealers	-	3	-	12	4	-	11,000	-	131
5984 Liquefied petroleum gas dealers	-	5	-	50	10	-	19,520	-	905
5992 Florists	-	16	-	91	6	-	10,549	-	1,167
5995 Optical goods stores	-	7	-	56	8	-	15,357	-	1,032
5999 Miscellaneous retail stores, nec	-	20	-	90	5	-	10,222	-	1,174

Source: County Business Patterns 1994/95, CBP-94/95, U.S. Department of Commerce, Washington DC, November 1997. The employment column represents mid-March employment in the year. Pay per employee is calculated by dividing 1st Quarter payroll, annualized, by mid-March employment. The column headed 'Emp / Est' shows 'employees per establishment'. A dash (-) means that data are unavailable or cannot be calculated. nec means not elsewhere classified. *Notes:* 1. 1994 data incomplete; unavailable or withheld. 2. 1995 data incomplete; unavailable or withheld. 3. 1994 and 1995 data incomplete; unavailable or withheld.

JERSEY CITY, NJ PMSA

Wholesale and Retail Trade USA	Establishments		Employment		Emp / Est	Pay / Employee		Annual Payroll ($ 000)	
	1994	1995	1994	1995	1995	1994	1995	1994	1995
50 – Wholesale trade	1,238	1,255	27,188	27,325	22	34,763	37,282	1,016,575	1,032,335
5012 Automobiles and other vehicles	12	15	199	304	20	26,472	32,303	5,994	10,209
5013 Motor vehicle supplies and new parts	37	30	367	319	11	19,760	13,906	8,228	4,603
5014 Tires and tubes	5	6	27	31	5	28,296	27,742	1,084	1,018
5015 Motor vehicle parts, used	9	11	40	62	6	14,000	16,645	589	990
5021 Furniture	18	16	133	134	8	31,549	36,836	4,933	5,080
5023 Homefurnishings	48	46	1,141	1,115	24	26,731	31,358	34,963	40,557
5031 Lumber, plywood, and millwork	13	9	218	409	45	31,229	32,919	12,481	13,821
5032 Brick, stone, & related materials	14	-	89	-	-	35,326	-	4,372	-
5039 Construction materials, nec	-	8	-	109	14	-	29,798	-	4,066
5044 Office equipment	10	12	102	56	5	30,157	29,071	3,218	1,759
5045 Computers, peripherals, & software	21	22	157	143	7	34,318	36,364	5,935	6,038
5046 Commercial equipment, nec	13	13	82	80	6	24,585	26,750	2,159	2,224
5047 Medical and hospital equipment	13	10	247	104	10	37,619	33,885	10,068	3,294
5049 Professional equipment, nec	-	6	-	53	9	-	28,075	-	1,483
5050 Metals and minerals, except petroleum	34	35	855	863	25	39,036	41,543	34,655	35,625
5063 Electrical apparatus and equipment	28	27	528	304	11	36,500	34,408	19,695	11,076
5064 Electrical appliances, TV & radios	-	10	-	2,255	226	-	59,047	-	150,946
5065 Electronic parts and equipment	-	21	-	275	13	-	37,833	-	11,388
5072 Hardware	19	20	368	357	18	29,098	33,647	12,332	12,739
5074 Plumbing & hydronic heating supplies	19	16	155	154	10	33,290	34,104	5,941	5,653
5075 Warm air heating & air conditioning	4	4	16	17	4	47,000	53,882	847	911

Continued on next page.

JERSEY CITY, NJ PMSA - [continued]

Wholesale and Retail Trade USA	Establishments		Employment		Emp / Est	Pay / Employee		Annual Payroll ($ 000)	
	1994	1995	1994	1995	1995	1994	1995	1994	1995
5078 Refrigeration equipment and supplies	4	3	33	20	7	34,303	43,600	1,204	899
5084 Industrial machinery and equipment	46	48	338	344	7	34,059	38,744	11,823	13,344
5085 Industrial supplies	19	19	177	189	10	39,006	36,868	7,715	7,856
5087 Service establishment equipment	15	13	159	127	10	33,937	33,858	5,768	4,874
5088 Transportation equipment & supplies	8	8	96	104	13	30,667	31,500	3,286	3,343
5091 Sporting & recreational goods	7	6	144	113	19	24,694	18,088	3,744	2,002
5092 Toys and hobby goods and supplies	13	14	163	203	15	32,957	30,581	7,726	8,408
5093 Scrap and waste materials	40	46	554	704	15	27,942	29,830	18,996	23,794
5094 Jewelry & precious stones	19	20	115	163	8	20,870	18,479	2,964	3,037
5099 Durable goods, nec	17	16	200	246	15	20,820	22,520	4,568	7,200
5111 Printing and writing paper	5	4	15	13	3	57,333	60,923	1,081	940
5112 Stationery and office supplies	25	22	370	267	12	31,730	39,206	10,994	10,901
5113 Industrial & personal service paper	23	20	214	186	9	32,897	32,000	6,938	6,065
5120 Drugs, proprietaries, and sundries	32	38	1,226	1,262	33	28,519	34,162	36,633	43,416
5131 Piece goods & notions	71	71	660	635	9	28,703	30,350	21,482	20,422
5136 Men's and boys' clothing	40	33	608	583	18	37,474	39,630	26,882	21,943
5137 Women's and children's clothing	97	93	3,570	3,563	38	31,296	34,812	122,083	122,097
5139 Footwear	17	14	553	556	40	19,342	37,252	11,309	18,239
5141 Groceries, general line	19	18	751	667	37	35,569	44,882	29,043	32,288
5142 Packaged frozen food	9	9	214	242	27	32,505	44,727	8,746	11,405
5143 Dairy products, exc. dried or canned	7	8	183	136	17	32,109	36,500	7,314	4,421
5144 Poultry and poultry products	4	5	20	20	4	56,200	53,000	877	854
5145 Confectionery	8	7	223	230	33	34,762	37,896	9,159	9,060
5146 Fish and seafoods	5	5	134	126	25	14,388	18,794	1,998	2,286
5147 Meats and meat products	28	27	389	438	16	40,165	43,288	16,352	19,118
5148 Fresh fruits and vegetables	11	13	81	78	6	20,494	24,051	2,107	1,996
5149 Groceries and related products, nec	51	52	1,329	1,268	24	29,381	28,016	42,368	38,282
5159 Farm-product raw materials, nec	3	-	13	-	-	26,154	-	468	-
5162 Plastics materials & basic shapes	11	11	252	280	25	31,714	30,243	11,737	12,212
5169 Chemicals & allied products, nec	27	27	268	312	12	46,910	48,641	15,410	15,372
5171 Petroleum bulk stations & terminals	9	8	337	312	39	45,282	45,308	10,884	10,889
5172 Petroleum products, nec	14	12	143	97	8	45,846	47,835	5,481	4,505
5180 Beer, wine, and distilled beverages	9	7	499	506	72	39,655	43,834	19,303	22,254
5191 Farm supplies	7	6	24	23	4	14,333	14,783	411	400
5192 Books, periodicals, & newspapers	11	13	774	806	62	34,196	28,630	27,614	24,478
5193 Flowers & florists' supplies	7	7	51	20	3	16,627	19,200	703	346
5194 Tobacco and tobacco products	11	11	91	92	8	21,495	23,304	2,277	2,392
5198 Paints, varnishes, and supplies	12	9	124	101	11	19,806	18,020	2,032	1,759
5199 Nondurable goods, nec	52	54	439	609	11	28,811	26,851	13,023	15,037
52 - Retail trade	3,505	3,510	35,829	34,968	10	17,006	16,957	646,960	606,942
5210 Lumber and other building materials	27	27	358	504	19	20,804	24,667	9,969	13,084
5230 Paint, glass, and wallpaper stores	-	15	-	71	5	-	22,085	-	1,523
5250 Hardware stores	26	19	118	107	6	16,610	15,028	2,071	1,771
5310 Department stores	10	10	1,914	2,000	200	10,800	12,022	22,825	25,486
5330 Variety stores	38	40	331	322	8	11,420	11,019	4,020	3,634
5390 Misc. general merchandise stores	30	28	110	236	8	13,818	13,797	3,043	3,453
5410 Grocery stores	390	387	5,249	4,685	12	15,624	15,893	79,155	73,775
5420 Meat and fish markets	37	39	206	191	5	14,505	14,429	2,905	2,842
5430 Fruit and vegetable markets	12	12	26	21	2	12,462	14,476	359	372
5440 Candy, nut, and confectionery stores	17	17	60	59	3	11,200	11,593	659	572
5450 Dairy products stores	-	3	-	2	1	-	6,000	-	30
5460 Retail bakeries	83	81	637	615	8	13,093	12,650	8,682	8,183
5490 Miscellaneous food stores	-	20	-	64	3	-	13,500	-	1,041
5510 New and used car dealers	30	30	778	810	27	28,231	32,035	25,754	29,534
5520 Used car dealers	24	22	42	43	2	19,048	23,721	1,037	1,039
5530 Auto and home supply stores	51	46	295	280	6	13,871	17,843	4,488	5,488
5540 Gasoline service stations	176	171	814	807	5	14,658	15,569	12,469	12,527
5610 Men's & boys' clothing stores	75	67	470	466	7	11,974	10,936	7,672	6,076
5620 Women's clothing stores	174	155	1,813	1,576	10	9,754	10,056	19,709	16,121
5630 Women's accessory & specialty stores	41	39	305	317	8	11,305	11,748	3,668	3,512
5640 Children's and infants' wear stores	36	34	259	266	8	10,100	10,060	2,896	2,876
5650 Family clothing stores	57	52	572	533	10	12,874	13,163	8,318	7,541
5660 Shoe stores	114	121	605	707	6	12,926	12,102	8,975	9,739
5690 Misc. apparel & accessory stores	23	22	170	177	8	12,729	12,023	2,176	1,734
5712 Furniture stores	65	68	271	275	4	16,959	18,036	5,413	5,519
5713 Floor covering stores	26	27	143	158	6	19,189	20,481	3,119	3,374
5714 Drapery and upholstery stores	4	4	37	40	10	28,865	25,300	810	785
5719 Misc. homefurnishings stores	39	34	343	331	10	13,061	14,320	5,047	5,056
5720 Household appliance stores	13	13	309	288	22	21,553	19,278	7,794	6,073
5731 Radio, TV, & electronic stores	34	35	199	192	5	19,095	18,875	3,996	3,407
5734 Computer and software stores	12	15	80	99	7	26,050	26,990	2,350	2,378

Continued on next page.

JERSEY CITY, NJ PMSA - [continued]

Wholesale and Retail Trade USA	Establishments		Employment		Emp / Est	Pay / Employee		Annual Payroll ($ 000)	
	1994	1995	1994	1995	1995	1994	1995	1994	1995
5735 Record & prerecorded tape stores	-	23	-	125	5	-	8,320	-	1,138
5812 Eating places	699	679	6,827	6,955	10	10,718	11,374	79,394	81,405
5813 Drinking places	238	220	669	616	3	9,477	10,344	6,603	6,388
5910 Drug stores and proprietary stores	145	140	1,434	1,540	11	14,335	14,055	21,883	22,499
5920 Liquor stores	138	141	493	423	3	17,452	12,170	8,934	5,312
5930 Used merchandise stores	-	12	-	41	3	-	15,317	-	710
5941 Sporting goods and bicycle shops	23	23	696	704	31	13,724	15,040	12,728	11,152
5942 Book stores	10	10	74	96	10	10,378	11,458	737	1,148
5943 Stationery stores	-	12	-	111	9	-	13,081	-	1,424
5944 Jewelry stores	62	65	194	191	3	16,639	18,995	3,573	3,628
5945 Hobby, toy, and game shops	16	13	197	202	16	10,883	10,238	2,688	2,493
5946 Camera & photographic supply stores	-	5	-	25	5	-	17,440	-	458
5947 Gift, novelty, and souvenir shops	50	51	287	214	4	18,272	9,701	5,808	2,161
5948 Luggage and leather goods stores	-	8	-	228	29	-	26,491	-	6,104
5949 Sewing, needlework, and piece goods	9	9	33	33	4	20,121	24,121	979	1,059
5961 Catalog and mail-order houses	15	19	275	988	52	33,484	30,818	9,677	32,072
5962 Merchandising machine operators	12	11	78	81	7	34,359	31,407	2,718	2,529
5963 Direct selling establishments	18	13	574	251	19	30,167	13,833	19,301	3,686
5980 Fuel dealers	29	28	351	342	12	34,815	35,380	12,194	12,384
5992 Florists	44	43	154	152	4	10,701	12,053	1,786	1,987
5993 Tobacco stores and stands	4	4	7	8	2	15,429	16,500	123	142
5994 News dealers and newsstands	30	26	63	50	2	11,873	13,600	689	702
5995 Optical goods stores	28	28	113	111	4	16,389	17,910	1,980	2,161
5999 Miscellaneous retail stores, nec	60	57	226	234	4	13,558	14,667	3,665	3,717

Source: County Business Patterns 1994/95, CBP-94/95, U.S. Department of Commerce, Washington DC, November 1997. The employment column represents mid-March employment in the year. Pay per employee is calculated by dividing 1st Quarter payroll, annualized, by mid-March employment. The column headed 'Emp / Est' shows 'employees per establishment'. A dash (-) means that data are unavailable or cannot be calculated. nec means not elsewhere classified. *Notes:* 1. 1994 data incomplete; unavailable or withheld. 2. 1995 data incomplete; unavailable or withheld. 3. 1994 and 1995 data incomplete; unavailable or withheld.

JOHNSON CITY - KINGSPORT - BRISTOL MSA (TN PART)

Wholesale and Retail Trade USA	Establishments		Employment		Emp / Est	Pay / Employee		Annual Payroll ($ 000)	
	1994	1995	1994	1995	1995	1994	1995	1994	1995
50- Wholesale trade	-	554	-	6,550	12	-	26,352	-	176,295
5012 Automobiles and other vehicles [2]	-	16	-	130	8	-	16,492	-	2,544
5013 Motor vehicle supplies and new parts	-	41	-	595	15	-	21,129	-	13,562
5014 Tires and tubes [2]	-	5	-	49	10	-	21,469	-	1,050
5015 Motor vehicle parts, used [2]	-	15	-	36	2	-	16,889	-	619
5021 Furniture [2]	-	11	-	65	6	-	28,369	-	1,354
5023 Homefurnishings [2]	-	9	-	68	8	-	20,647	-	1,418
5031 Lumber, plywood, and millwork [2]	-	18	-	152	8	-	26,211	-	4,038
5032 Brick, stone, & related materials [2]	-	5	-	9	2	-	22,222	-	212
5033 Roofing, siding, & insulation [2]	-	8	-	30	4	-	20,533	-	885
5039 Construction materials, nec [2]	-	11	-	102	9	-	20,039	-	2,191
5044 Office equipment [2]	-	18	-	128	7	-	23,156	-	3,344
5045 Computers, peripherals, & software [2]	-	18	-	106	6	-	37,057	-	3,731
5046 Commercial equipment, nec [2]	-	7	-	72	10	-	26,444	-	2,160
5047 Medical and hospital equipment [2]	-	11	-	23	2	-	25,739	-	631
5050 Metals and minerals, except petroleum [2]	-	11	-	69	6	-	18,319	-	1,347
5063 Electrical apparatus and equipment [2]	-	23	-	150	7	-	28,293	-	4,220
5065 Electronic parts and equipment [2]	-	14	-	52	4	-	24,538	-	1,629
5072 Hardware [2]	-	13	-	97	7	-	22,351	-	2,314
5074 Plumbing & hydronic heating supplies [2]	-	8	-	36	5	-	20,556	-	835
5075 Warm air heating & air conditioning [2]	-	13	-	130	10	-	21,108	-	2,645
5082 Construction and mining machinery [2]	-	7	-	95	14	-	30,989	-	3,108
5083 Farm and garden machinery [2]	-	15	-	115	8	-	17,426	-	2,124
5084 Industrial machinery and equipment	-	30	-	218	7	-	25,927	-	6,070
5085 Industrial supplies [2]	-	26	-	172	7	-	29,140	-	5,175
5091 Sporting & recreational goods [2]	-	6	-	11	2	-	12,727	-	145
5093 Scrap and waste materials [2]	-	10	-	40	4	-	20,800	-	880
5094 Jewelry & precious stones [2]	-	4	-	6	2	-	3,333	-	34
5099 Durable goods, nec [2]	-	9	-	38	4	-	12,947	-	497
5113 Industrial & personal service paper [2]	-	6	-	36	6	-	19,222	-	651
5130 Apparel, piece goods, and notions [2]	-	9	-	36	4	-	16,000	-	649
5141 Groceries, general line [2]	-	7	-	70	10	-	17,771	-	959
5147 Meats and meat products [2]	-	5	-	34	7	-	16,824	-	582
5148 Fresh fruits and vegetables [2]	-	6	-	59	10	-	11,864	-	580
5149 Groceries and related products, nec [2]	-	10	-	517	52	-	28,735	-	14,568
5150 Farm-product raw materials [2]	-	4	-	41	10	-	5,854	-	347

Continued on next page.

JOHNSON CITY - KINGSPORT - BRISTOL MSA (TN PART) - [continued]

Wholesale and Retail Trade USA	Establishments		Employment		Emp / Est	Pay / Employee		Annual Payroll ($ 000)	
	1994	1995	1994	1995	1995	1994	1995	1994	1995
5169 Chemicals & allied products, nec[2]	-	17	-	29	2	-	30,897	-	934
5171 Petroleum bulk stations & terminals[2]	-	8	-	242	30	-	17,769	-	5,470
5181 Beer and ale[2]	-	3	-	139	46	-	27,482	-	4,398
5191 Farm supplies[2]	-	9	-	126	14	-	18,159	-	2,454
5192 Books, periodicals, & newspapers[2]	-	5	-	90	18	-	14,578	-	1,638
5193 Flowers & florists' supplies[2]	-	7	-	54	8	-	21,407	-	1,099
5199 Nondurable goods, nec[2]	-	12	-	19	2	-	14,316	-	225
52- Retail trade	-	2,082	-	30,331	15	-	11,255	-	357,556
5210 Lumber and other building materials	-	38	-	646	17	-	18,489	-	12,379
5230 Paint, glass, and wallpaper stores[2]	-	13	-	50	4	-	14,320	-	726
5250 Hardware stores	-	17	-	49	3	-	9,633	-	480
5260 Retail nurseries and garden stores	-	17	-	74	4	-	12,216	-	1,180
5270 Mobile home dealers[2]	-	15	-	91	6	-	23,033	-	2,326
5310 Department stores[2]	-	21	-	3,150	150	-	12,146	-	37,529
5330 Variety stores	-	20	-	95	5	-	8,463	-	900
5390 Misc. general merchandise stores[2]	-	17	-	274	16	-	14,569	-	3,613
5410 Grocery stores[2]	-	219	-	3,848	18	-	10,506	-	40,371
5430 Fruit and vegetable markets[2]	-	6	-	2	-	-	4,000	-	16
5490 Miscellaneous food stores[2]	-	12	-	32	3	-	9,875	-	396
5510 New and used car dealers[2]	-	40	-	1,498	37	-	24,139	-	40,114
5520 Used car dealers[2]	-	38	-	87	2	-	19,080	-	1,486
5530 Auto and home supply stores	-	81	-	462	6	-	15,654	-	7,599
5540 Gasoline service stations	-	169	-	1,050	6	-	10,556	-	11,498
5550 Boat dealers[2]	-	6	-	15	3	-	14,933	-	237
5560 Recreational vehicle dealers[2]	-	5	-	37	7	-	23,243	-	996
5570 Motorcycle dealers[2]	-	9	-	39	4	-	11,077	-	587
5610 Men's & boys' clothing stores[2]	-	11	-	72	7	-	9,389	-	623
5620 Women's clothing stores[2]	-	52	-	374	7	-	9,850	-	3,519
5630 Women's accessory & specialty stores[2]	-	9	-	52	6	-	5,000	-	252
5640 Children's and infants' wear stores[2]	-	5	-	16	3	-	9,750	-	160
5650 Family clothing stores[2]	-	21	-	227	11	-	9,322	-	2,477
5660 Shoe stores	-	43	-	202	5	-	9,921	-	1,793
5690 Misc. apparel & accessory stores[2]	-	14	-	57	4	-	9,474	-	504
5712 Furniture stores	-	45	-	361	8	-	16,033	-	6,537
5713 Floor covering stores[2]	-	21	-	66	3	-	16,061	-	1,234
5714 Drapery and upholstery stores[2]	-	4	-	12	3	-	11,667	-	134
5719 Misc. homefurnishings stores[2]	-	17	-	65	4	-	11,877	-	898
5720 Household appliance stores[2]	-	22	-	60	3	-	11,800	-	752
5731 Radio, TV, & electronic stores[2]	-	24	-	102	4	-	22,235	-	1,806
5734 Computer and software stores[2]	-	13	-	39	3	-	11,077	-	437
5735 Record & prerecorded tape stores[2]	-	12	-	55	5	-	10,327	-	612
5736 Musical instrument stores[2]	-	11	-	58	5	-	11,103	-	714
5812 Eating places	-	397	-	9,623	24	-	7,531	-	73,839
5813 Drinking places[2]	-	16	-	85	5	-	7,482	-	639
5910 Drug stores and proprietary stores	-	81	-	738	9	-	17,469	-	14,241
5920 Liquor stores[2]	-	36	-	154	4	-	10,390	-	1,728
5930 Used merchandise stores	-	27	-	61	2	-	7,344	-	477
5941 Sporting goods and bicycle shops[2]	-	34	-	70	2	-	12,800	-	978
5942 Book stores[2]	-	18	-	68	4	-	8,941	-	912
5944 Jewelry stores[2]	-	36	-	142	4	-	11,803	-	1,881
5945 Hobby, toy, and game shops[2]	-	16	-	81	5	-	11,160	-	1,125
5947 Gift, novelty, and souvenir shops[2]	-	41	-	137	3	-	7,270	-	1,111
5949 Sewing, needlework, and piece goods[2]	-	11	-	59	5	-	8,475	-	510
5962 Merchandising machine operators[2]	-	15	-	200	13	-	15,680	-	3,330
5980 Fuel dealers[2]	-	8	-	34	4	-	11,529	-	335
5992 Florists	-	43	-	183	4	-	9,311	-	1,881
5993 Tobacco stores and stands[2]	-	4	-	1	-	-	8,000	-	21
5999 Miscellaneous retail stores, nec[2]	-	53	-	166	3	-	11,084	-	2,104

Source: County Business Patterns 1994/95, CBP-94/95, U.S. Department of Commerce, Washington DC, November 1997. The employment column represents mid-March employment in the year. Pay per employee is calculated by dividing 1st Quarter payroll, annualized, by mid-March employment. The column headed 'Emp / Est' shows 'employees per establishment'. A dash (-) means that data are unavailable or cannot be calculated. nec means not elsewhere classified. *Notes:* 1. 1994 data incomplete; unavailable or withheld. 2. 1995 data incomplete; unavailable or withheld. 3. 1994 and 1995 data incomplete; unavailable or withheld.

JOHNSON CITY - KINGSPORT - BRISTOL MSA (VA PART)

Wholesale and Retail Trade USA	Establishments		Employment		Emp / Est	Pay / Employee		Annual Payroll ($ 000)	
	1994	1995	1994	1995	1995	1994	1995	1994	1995
50- Wholesale trade	-	143	-	2,180	15	-	22,560	-	50,791
5015 Motor vehicle parts, used[2]	-	4	-	12	3	-	14,000	-	166

Continued on next page.

JOHNSON CITY-KINGSPORT-BRISTOL MSA (VA PART) - [continued]

Wholesale and Retail Trade USA	Establishments		Employment		Emp / Est	Pay / Employee		Annual Payroll ($ 000)	
	1994	1995	1994	1995	1995	1994	1995	1994	1995
5020 Furniture and homefurnishings [2]	-	6	-	24	4	-	16,167	-	409
5040 Professional & commercial equipment [2]	-	7	-	29	4	-	21,931	-	546
5050 Metals and minerals, except petroleum [2]	-	6	-	45	8	-	25,778	-	1,316
5063 Electrical apparatus and equipment	-	9	-	28	3	-	18,000	-	476
5075 Warm air heating & air conditioning [2]	-	4	-	20	5	-	32,600	-	465
5082 Construction and mining machinery [2]	-	7	-	7	1	-	36,000	-	251
5090 Miscellaneous durable goods	-	6	-	33	6	-	9,333	-	366
5140 Groceries and related products [2]	-	10	-	639	64	-	23,424	-	15,782
5150 Farm-product raw materials [2]	-	6	-	128	21	-	6,406	-	819
5170 Petroleum and petroleum products	-	10	-	101	10	-	21,980	-	2,832
5191 Farm supplies	-	14	-	139	10	-	14,043	-	1,996
52- Retail trade	-	620	-	7,896	13	-	10,858	-	93,738
5210 Lumber and other building materials	-	11	-	219	20	-	16,201	-	4,496
5230 Paint, glass, and wallpaper stores [2]	-	5	-	5	1	-	16,000	-	79
5250 Hardware stores [2]	-	5	-	5	1	-	4,000	-	19
5260 Retail nurseries and garden stores	-	6	-	18	3	-	6,222	-	136
5270 Mobile home dealers	-	7	-	57	8	-	23,579	-	1,478
5310 Department stores [2]	-	4	-	753	188	-	9,328	-	7,828
5410 Grocery stores [2]	-	90	-	1,121	12	-	9,577	-	10,908
5510 New and used car dealers	-	7	-	221	32	-	21,593	-	5,197
5520 Used car dealers	-	18	-	39	2	-	16,205	-	670
5530 Auto and home supply stores	-	25	-	128	5	-	14,438	-	2,189
5540 Gasoline service stations	-	43	-	285	7	-	9,530	-	2,956
5620 Women's clothing stores	-	15	-	78	5	-	7,897	-	593
5650 Family clothing stores	-	6	-	57	10	-	11,018	-	647
5660 Shoe stores	-	14	-	60	4	-	14,067	-	868
5712 Furniture stores	-	15	-	97	6	-	14,186	-	1,524
5719 Misc. homefurnishings stores	-	6	-	8	1	-	14,500	-	164
5720 Household appliance stores	-	5	-	4	1	-	10,000	-	36
5731 Radio, TV, & electronic stores [2]	-	6	-	16	3	-	9,500	-	305
5812 Eating places	-	109	-	2,344	22	-	6,867	-	18,673
5910 Drug stores and proprietary stores	-	24	-	163	7	-	17,497	-	2,841
5930 Used merchandise stores	-	6	-	7	1	-	6,286	-	41
5941 Sporting goods and bicycle shops [2]	-	7	-	21	3	-	8,571	-	203
5942 Book stores [2]	-	4	-	16	4	-	7,500	-	124
5944 Jewelry stores	-	15	-	80	5	-	13,900	-	1,195
5945 Hobby, toy, and game shops [2]	-	5	-	17	3	-	8,000	-	147
5947 Gift, novelty, and souvenir shops [2]	-	9	-	91	10	-	8,879	-	875
5962 Merchandising machine operators	-	7	-	40	6	-	12,300	-	485
5963 Direct selling establishments [2]	-	7	-	23	3	-	18,435	-	400
5980 Fuel dealers	-	7	-	11	2	-	13,455	-	145
5992 Florists	-	15	-	62	4	-	9,097	-	591
5995 Optical goods stores [2]	-	6	-	22	4	-	20,182	-	433
5999 Miscellaneous retail stores, nec [2]	-	12	-	47	4	-	9,021	-	433

Source: County Business Patterns 1994/95, CBP-94/95, U.S. Department of Commerce, Washington DC, November 1997. The employment column represents mid-March employment in the year. Pay per employee is calculated by dividing 1st Quarter payroll, annualized, by mid-March employment. The column headed 'Emp / Est' shows 'employees per establishment'. A dash (-) means that data are unavailable or cannot be calculated. nec means not elsewhere classified. *Notes:* 1. 1994 data incomplete; unavailable or withheld. 2. 1995 data incomplete; unavailable or withheld. 3. 1994 and 1995 data incomplete; unavailable or withheld.

JOHNSON CITY-KINGSPORT-BRISTOL, TN-VA MSA

Wholesale and Retail Trade USA	Establishments		Employment		Emp / Est	Pay / Employee		Annual Payroll ($ 000)	
	1994	1995	1994	1995	1995	1994	1995	1994	1995
50- Wholesale trade	-	697	-	8,730	13	-	25,405	-	227,086
5012 Automobiles and other vehicles [2]	-	22	-	130	6	-	16,492	-	2,544
5013 Motor vehicle supplies and new parts [2]	-	50	-	595	12	-	21,129	-	13,562
5014 Tires and tubes [2]	-	6	-	49	8	-	21,469	-	1,050
5015 Motor vehicle parts, used [2]	-	19	-	48	3	-	16,167	-	785
5021 Furniture [2]	-	14	-	65	5	-	28,369	-	1,354
5023 Homefurnishings [2]	-	12	-	68	6	-	20,647	-	1,418
5031 Lumber, plywood, and millwork [2]	-	19	-	152	8	-	26,211	-	4,038
5032 Brick, stone, & related materials [2]	-	5	-	9	2	-	22,222	-	212
5033 Roofing, siding, & insulation [2]	-	9	-	30	3	-	20,533	-	885
5039 Construction materials, nec [2]	-	12	-	102	9	-	20,039	-	2,191
5044 Office equipment [2]	-	19	-	128	7	-	23,156	-	3,344
5045 Computers, peripherals, & software [2]	-	20	-	106	5	-	37,057	-	3,731
5046 Commercial equipment, nec [2]	-	7	-	72	10	-	26,444	-	2,160
5047 Medical and hospital equipment [2]	-	12	-	23	2	-	25,739	-	631
5050 Metals and minerals, except petroleum [2]	-	17	-	114	7	-	21,263	-	2,663

Continued on next page.

JOHNSON CITY - KINGSPORT - BRISTOL, TN - VA MSA - [continued]

Wholesale and Retail Trade USA	Establishments		Employment		Emp / Est	Pay / Employee		Annual Payroll ($ 000)	
	1994	1995	1994	1995	1995	1994	1995	1994	1995
5063 Electrical apparatus and equipment [2]	-	32	-	178	6	-	26,674	-	4,696
5065 Electronic parts and equipment [2]	-	16	-	52	3	-	24,538	-	1,629
5072 Hardware [2]	-	14	-	97	7	-	22,351	-	2,314
5074 Plumbing & hydronic heating supplies [2]	-	9	-	36	4	-	20,556	-	835
5075 Warm air heating & air conditioning [2]	-	17	-	150	9	-	22,640	-	3,110
5082 Construction and mining machinery [2]	-	14	-	102	7	-	31,333	-	3,359
5083 Farm and garden machinery [2]	-	19	-	115	6	-	17,426	-	2,124
5084 Industrial machinery and equipment [2]	-	32	-	218	7	-	25,927	-	6,070
5085 Industrial supplies [2]	-	28	-	172	6	-	29,140	-	5,175
5091 Sporting & recreational goods [2]	-	7	-	11	2	-	12,727	-	145
5093 Scrap and waste materials [2]	-	11	-	40	4	-	20,800	-	880
5094 Jewelry & precious stones [2]	-	5	-	6	1	-	3,333	-	34
5099 Durable goods, nec [2]	-	12	-	38	3	-	12,947	-	497
5113 Industrial & personal service paper [2]	-	7	-	36	5	-	19,222	-	651
5130 Apparel, piece goods, and notions [2]	-	10	-	36	4	-	16,000	-	649
5141 Groceries, general line [2]	-	9	-	70	8	-	17,771	-	959
5147 Meats and meat products [2]	-	6	-	34	6	-	16,824	-	582
5148 Fresh fruits and vegetables [2]	-	6	-	59	10	-	11,864	-	580
5149 Groceries and related products, nec [2]	-	13	-	517	40	-	28,735	-	14,568
5150 Farm-product raw materials [2]	-	10	-	169	17	-	6,272	-	1,166
5169 Chemicals & allied products, nec [2]	-	21	-	29	1	-	30,897	-	934
5171 Petroleum bulk stations & terminals [2]	-	15	-	242	16	-	17,769	-	5,470
5181 Beer and ale [2]	-	5	-	139	28	-	27,482	-	4,398
5191 Farm supplies [2]	-	23	-	265	12	-	16,000	-	4,450
5192 Books, periodicals, & newspapers [2]	-	5	-	90	18	-	14,578	-	1,638
5193 Flowers & florists' supplies [2]	-	7	-	54	8	-	21,407	-	1,099
5199 Nondurable goods, nec [2]	-	15	-	19	1	-	14,316	-	225
52 - Retail trade	-	2,702	-	38,227	14	-	11,173	-	451,294
5210 Lumber and other building materials	-	49	-	865	18	-	17,910	-	16,875
5230 Paint, glass, and wallpaper stores [2]	-	18	-	55	3	-	14,473	-	805
5250 Hardware stores [2]	-	22	-	54	2	-	9,111	-	499
5260 Retail nurseries and garden stores	-	23	-	92	4	-	11,043	-	1,316
5270 Mobile home dealers [2]	-	22	-	148	7	-	23,243	-	3,804
5310 Department stores [2]	-	25	-	3,903	156	-	11,602	-	45,357
5330 Variety stores [2]	-	24	-	95	4	-	8,463	-	900
5390 Misc. general merchandise stores [2]	-	26	-	274	11	-	14,569	-	3,613
5410 Grocery stores [2]	-	309	-	4,969	16	-	10,297	-	51,279
5430 Fruit and vegetable markets [2]	-	9	-	2	-	-	4,000	-	16
5490 Miscellaneous food stores [2]	-	17	-	32	2	-	9,875	-	396
5510 New and used car dealers [2]	-	47	-	1,719	37	-	23,812	-	45,311
5520 Used car dealers [2]	-	56	-	126	2	-	18,190	-	2,156
5530 Auto and home supply stores	-	106	-	590	6	-	15,390	-	9,788
5540 Gasoline service stations	-	212	-	1,335	6	-	10,337	-	14,454
5550 Boat dealers [2]	-	7	-	15	2	-	14,933	-	237
5560 Recreational vehicle dealers [2]	-	6	-	37	6	-	23,243	-	996
5570 Motorcycle dealers [2]	-	12	-	39	3	-	11,077	-	587
5610 Men's & boys' clothing stores [2]	-	13	-	72	6	-	9,389	-	623
5620 Women's clothing stores [2]	-	67	-	452	7	-	9,513	-	4,112
5630 Women's accessory & specialty stores [2]	-	11	-	52	5	-	5,000	-	252
5640 Children's and infants' wear stores [2]	-	6	-	16	3	-	9,750	-	160
5650 Family clothing stores [2]	-	27	-	284	11	-	9,662	-	3,124
5660 Shoe stores	-	57	-	262	5	-	10,870	-	2,661
5690 Misc. apparel & accessory stores [2]	-	15	-	57	4	-	9,474	-	504
5712 Furniture stores	-	60	-	458	8	-	15,642	-	8,061
5713 Floor covering stores [2]	-	32	-	66	2	-	16,061	-	1,234
5714 Drapery and upholstery stores [2]	-	6	-	12	2	-	11,667	-	134
5719 Misc. homefurnishings stores [2]	-	23	-	73	3	-	12,164	-	1,062
5720 Household appliance stores [2]	-	27	-	64	2	-	11,688	-	788
5731 Radio, TV, & electronic stores [2]	-	30	-	118	4	-	20,508	-	2,111
5734 Computer and software stores [2]	-	14	-	39	3	-	11,077	-	437
5735 Record & prerecorded tape stores [2]	-	18	-	55	3	-	10,327	-	612
5736 Musical instrument stores [2]	-	12	-	58	5	-	11,103	-	714
5812 Eating places	-	506	-	11,967	24	-	7,401	-	92,512
5813 Drinking places [2]	-	18	-	85	5	-	7,482	-	639
5910 Drug stores and proprietary stores	-	105	-	901	9	-	17,474	-	17,082
5920 Liquor stores [2]	-	39	-	154	4	-	10,390	-	1,728
5930 Used merchandise stores	-	33	-	68	2	-	7,235	-	518
5941 Sporting goods and bicycle shops [2]	-	41	-	91	2	-	11,824	-	1,181
5942 Book stores [2]	-	22	-	84	4	-	8,667	-	1,036
5944 Jewelry stores [2]	-	51	-	222	4	-	12,559	-	3,076
5945 Hobby, toy, and game shops [2]	-	21	-	98	5	-	10,612	-	1,272

Continued on next page.

JOHNSON CITY - KINGSPORT - BRISTOL, TN - VA MSA - [continued]

Wholesale and Retail Trade USA	Establishments		Employment		Emp / Est	Pay / Employee		Annual Payroll ($ 000)	
	1994	1995	1994	1995	1995	1994	1995	1994	1995
5947 Gift, novelty, and souvenir shops [2]	-	50	-	228	5	-	7,912	-	1,986
5949 Sewing, needlework, and piece goods [2]	-	11	-	59	5	-	8,475	-	510
5962 Merchandising machine operators [2]	-	22	-	240	11	-	15,117	-	3,815
5963 Direct selling establishments [2]	-	29	-	23	1	-	18,435	-	400
5980 Fuel dealers [2]	-	15	-	45	3	-	12,000	-	480
5992 Florists	-	58	-	245	4	-	9,257	-	2,472
5993 Tobacco stores and stands [2]	-	7	-	1	-	-	8,000	-	21
5995 Optical goods stores [2]	-	17	-	22	1	-	20,182	-	433
5999 Miscellaneous retail stores, nec [2]	-	65	-	213	3	-	10,629	-	2,537

Source: County Business Patterns 1994/95, CBP-94/95, U.S. Department of Commerce, Washington DC, November 1997. The employment column represents mid-March employment in the year. Pay per employee is calculated by dividing 1st Quarter payroll, annualized, by mid-March employment. The column headed 'Emp / Est' shows 'employees per establishment'. A dash (-) means that data are unavailable or cannot be calculated. nec means not elsewhere classified. *Notes:* 1. 1994 data incomplete; unavailable or withheld. 2. 1995 data incomplete; unavailable or withheld. 3. 1994 and 1995 data incomplete; unavailable or withheld.

JOHNSTOWN, PA MSA

Wholesale and Retail Trade USA	Establishments		Employment		Emp / Est	Pay / Employee		Annual Payroll ($ 000)	
	1994	1995	1994	1995	1995	1994	1995	1994	1995
50- Wholesale trade	-	320	-	3,323	10	-	20,678	-	74,474
5012 Automobiles and other vehicles	-	8	-	107	13	-	20,523	-	2,246
5013 Motor vehicle supplies and new parts	-	30	-	248	8	-	17,806	-	4,833
5015 Motor vehicle parts, used	-	11	-	65	6	-	16,862	-	1,308
5020 Furniture and homefurnishings [2]	-	3	-	34	11	-	23,176	-	776
5031 Lumber, plywood, and millwork	-	8	-	97	12	-	15,505	-	1,692
5039 Construction materials, nec	-	10	-	57	6	-	15,088	-	853
5044 Office equipment	-	11	-	58	5	-	21,448	-	1,379
5045 Computers, peripherals, & software	-	11	-	35	3	-	16,000	-	554
5046 Commercial equipment, nec [2]	-	4	-	12	3	-	16,000	-	187
5047 Medical and hospital equipment	-	5	-	12	2	-	19,000	-	207
5051 Metals service centers and offices [2]	-	12	-	53	4	-	21,811	-	1,164
5052 Coal and other minerals and ores	-	5	-	10	2	-	16,800	-	151
5063 Electrical apparatus and equipment	-	11	-	44	4	-	26,636	-	1,076
5065 Electronic parts and equipment	-	4	-	10	3	-	12,000	-	136
5070 Hardware, plumbing & heating equipment	-	17	-	137	8	-	25,489	-	3,154
5082 Construction and mining machinery	-	10	-	132	13	-	32,788	-	5,091
5083 Farm and garden machinery	-	9	-	43	5	-	14,605	-	681
5084 Industrial machinery and equipment	-	12	-	66	6	-	20,242	-	1,625
5085 Industrial supplies	-	12	-	73	6	-	28,329	-	1,812
5087 Service establishment equipment	-	5	-	49	10	-	21,061	-	974
5093 Scrap and waste materials	-	14	-	161	12	-	17,193	-	3,573
5110 Paper and paper products	-	6	-	30	5	-	32,533	-	724
5149 Groceries and related products, nec	-	10	-	391	39	-	18,701	-	7,488
5171 Petroleum bulk stations & terminals	-	7	-	53	8	-	28,906	-	1,618
5181 Beer and ale	-	19	-	106	6	-	21,623	-	2,720
5191 Farm supplies	-	7	-	26	4	-	25,692	-	529
5199 Nondurable goods, nec	-	4	-	14	4	-	13,714	-	277
52- Retail trade	-	1,475	-	16,494	11	-	10,383	-	185,853
5210 Lumber and other building materials	-	30	-	353	12	-	16,861	-	7,793
5250 Hardware stores	-	18	-	160	9	-	9,725	-	1,635
5260 Retail nurseries and garden stores	-	16	-	80	5	-	8,300	-	938
5310 Department stores [2]	-	10	-	1,407	141	-	10,217	-	14,996
5330 Variety stores	-	9	-	84	9	-	8,667	-	832
5390 Misc. general merchandise stores [2]	-	20	-	253	13	-	8,411	-	2,197
5410 Grocery stores	-	128	-	2,657	21	-	9,633	-	27,700
5420 Meat and fish markets	-	5	-	14	3	-	4,000	-	64
5440 Candy, nut, and confectionery stores	-	11	-	64	6	-	5,188	-	339
5460 Retail bakeries	-	11	-	88	8	-	6,273	-	573
5490 Miscellaneous food stores	-	8	-	51	6	-	8,078	-	420
5510 New and used car dealers	-	49	-	1,109	23	-	18,027	-	21,833
5520 Used car dealers	-	27	-	89	3	-	15,011	-	1,461
5530 Auto and home supply stores	-	40	-	218	5	-	13,872	-	3,148
5540 Gasoline service stations	-	104	-	805	8	-	10,102	-	8,642
5560 Recreational vehicle dealers	-	5	-	7	1	-	13,143	-	108
5570 Motorcycle dealers	-	5	-	30	6	-	11,467	-	408
5610 Men's & boys' clothing stores	-	15	-	128	9	-	8,875	-	1,141
5620 Women's clothing stores	-	40	-	239	6	-	10,226	-	2,228
5630 Women's accessory & specialty stores	-	8	-	13	2	-	7,385	-	93
5650 Family clothing stores	-	20	-	159	8	-	11,069	-	1,753
5660 Shoe stores	-	33	-	150	5	-	9,467	-	1,417

Continued on next page.

JOHNSTOWN, PA MSA - [continued]

Wholesale and Retail Trade USA	Establishments		Employment		Emp / Est	Pay / Employee		Annual Payroll ($ 000)	
	1994	1995	1994	1995	1995	1994	1995	1994	1995
5712 Furniture stores	-	23	-	102	4	-	12,275	-	1,532
5713 Floor covering stores	-	8	-	18	2	-	19,556	-	347
5719 Misc. homefurnishings stores	-	11	-	71	6	-	8,620	-	624
5720 Household appliance stores	-	15	-	50	3	-	12,560	-	725
5731 Radio, TV, & electronic stores	-	18	-	114	6	-	19,228	-	1,959
5735 Record & prerecorded tape stores [2]	-	7	-	38	5	-	8,947	-	324
5812 Eating places	-	294	-	4,537	15	-	6,789	-	33,526
5813 Drinking places	-	90	-	311	3	-	5,839	-	1,860
5910 Drug stores and proprietary stores	-	52	-	554	11	-	17,444	-	9,444
5920 Liquor stores	-	32	-	95	3	-	14,568	-	1,433
5930 Used merchandise stores	-	9	-	39	4	-	7,590	-	406
5941 Sporting goods and bicycle shops	-	18	-	64	4	-	11,688	-	695
5943 Stationery stores	-	5	-	37	7	-	13,514	-	632
5944 Jewelry stores	-	22	-	126	6	-	10,889	-	1,513
5945 Hobby, toy, and game shops	-	8	-	51	6	-	7,686	-	631
5947 Gift, novelty, and souvenir shops	-	26	-	134	5	-	9,552	-	1,348
5949 Sewing, needlework, and piece goods	-	5	-	39	8	-	6,154	-	245
5962 Merchandising machine operators	-	6	-	5	1	-	40,800	-	82
5963 Direct selling establishments	-	7	-	55	8	-	22,691	-	1,123
5983 Fuel oil dealers	-	19	-	246	13	-	15,382	-	3,775
5984 Liquefied petroleum gas dealers	-	7	-	47	7	-	22,213	-	1,131
5989 Fuel dealers, nec [2]	-	4	-	10	3	-	13,600	-	168
5992 Florists	-	26	-	80	3	-	7,100	-	556
5994 News dealers and newsstands	-	4	-	4	1	-	8,000	-	34
5999 Miscellaneous retail stores, nec	-	36	-	272	8	-	10,985	-	3,815

Source: County Business Patterns 1994/95, CBP-94/95, U.S. Department of Commerce, Washington DC, November 1997. The employment column represents mid-March employment in the year. Pay per employee is calculated by dividing 1st Quarter payroll, annualized, by mid-March employment. The column headed 'Emp / Est' shows 'employees per establishment'. A dash (-) means that data are unavailable or cannot be calculated. nec means not elsewhere classified. *Notes:* 1. 1994 data incomplete; unavailable or withheld. 2. 1995 data incomplete; unavailable or withheld. 3. 1994 and 1995 data incomplete; unavailable or withheld.

JOPLIN, MO MSA

Wholesale and Retail Trade USA	Establishments		Employment		Emp / Est	Pay / Employee		Annual Payroll ($ 000)	
	1994	1995	1994	1995	1995	1994	1995	1994	1995
50 - Wholesale trade	318	308	3,124	2,937	10	20,493	21,815	67,328	65,733
5012 Automobiles and other vehicles	12	13	217	215	17	26,544	30,400	5,545	5,972
5013 Motor vehicle supplies and new parts	27	28	207	239	9	17,913	15,816	4,071	4,078
5014 Tires and tubes	11	10	30	22	2	19,333	24,000	656	581
5015 Motor vehicle parts, used	12	9	59	41	5	15,051	16,000	866	679
5020 Furniture and homefurnishings [3]	4	4	18	13	3	18,889	23,385	400	353
5031 Lumber, plywood, and millwork	10	9	109	125	14	21,431	24,256	3,211	3,318
5044 Office equipment [3]	7	9	76	97	11	17,211	21,278	1,686	2,109
5045 Computers, peripherals, & software	9	8	37	71	9	36,000	29,915	1,356	2,023
5047 Medical and hospital equipment	5	-	26	-	-	20,000	-	545	-
5051 Metals service centers and offices [3]	6	6	41	49	8	21,171	19,673	893	1,035
5063 Electrical apparatus and equipment [1]	9	8	109	53	7	22,495	24,604	2,889	1,399
5072 Hardware [1]	5	-	19	-	-	15,368	-	337	-
5074 Plumbing & hydronic heating supplies [2]	-	7	-	97	14	-	22,722	-	2,176
5075 Warm air heating & air conditioning [1]	3	-	7	-	-	20,000	-	176	-
5082 Construction and mining machinery	6	6	51	62	10	31,843	30,452	2,440	2,608
5083 Farm and garden machinery	11	7	23	49	7	11,478	12,408	270	568
5084 Industrial machinery and equipment [1]	9	-	26	-	-	23,231	-	597	-
5085 Industrial supplies	14	14	96	110	8	26,375	25,127	2,696	2,858
5087 Service establishment equipment [3]	7	7	48	54	8	12,917	12,667	713	734
5093 Scrap and waste materials	10	12	74	90	8	18,649	19,600	1,559	1,839
5112 Stationery and office supplies [3]	6	4	94	70	18	12,681	13,257	1,213	979
5147 Meats and meat products [1]	3	-	37	-	-	16,541	-	624	-
5149 Groceries and related products, nec	8	8	301	305	38	16,239	18,793	5,231	5,637
5153 Grain and field beans [2]	-	7	-	47	7	-	15,234	-	703
5154 Livestock	9	5	86	18	4	6,279	6,444	334	119
5169 Chemicals & allied products, nec	5	-	8	-	-	19,000	-	174	-
5171 Petroleum bulk stations & terminals	6	7	49	49	7	21,633	23,510	1,169	1,298
5172 Petroleum products, nec	6	6	37	37	6	17,622	14,595	693	609
5181 Beer and ale [3]	4	4	78	79	20	34,974	38,430	3,285	3,431
5191 Farm supplies [1]	21	19	66	71	4	19,394	18,817	1,264	1,264
5193 Flowers & florists' supplies [3]	4	4	22	23	6	16,182	16,522	387	395
52 - Retail trade	986	1,003	12,605	12,925	13	10,082	11,273	142,175	152,953
5210 Lumber and other building materials	23	21	474	425	20	14,979	18,174	7,245	7,377
5230 Paint, glass, and wallpaper stores	8	9	39	35	4	15,897	16,800	672	679

Continued on next page.

JOPLIN, MO MSA - [continued]

Wholesale and Retail Trade USA	Establishments		Employment		Emp / Est	Pay / Employee		Annual Payroll ($ 000)	
	1994	1995	1994	1995	1995	1994	1995	1994	1995
5260 Retail nurseries and garden stores	11	10	55	47	5	10,036	9,362	679	522
5270 Mobile home dealers	-	6	-	11	2	-	14,182	-	258
5310 Department stores[3]	11	12	1,599	1,578	132	10,124	13,070	18,089	20,113
5410 Grocery stores	72	75	1,349	1,370	18	10,497	11,489	15,072	16,808
5440 Candy, nut, and confectionery stores[2]	-	4	-	20	5	-	6,000	-	136
5460 Retail bakeries	9	7	27	25	4	6,519	9,760	191	278
5490 Miscellaneous food stores	6	9	9	19	2	10,222	7,579	118	177
5510 New and used car dealers	22	22	604	620	28	22,192	24,116	15,856	16,749
5520 Used car dealers	34	28	87	80	3	15,034	18,500	1,478	1,292
5530 Auto and home supply stores	29	35	213	242	7	15,793	16,463	3,753	4,336
5540 Gasoline service stations	74	71	634	629	9	10,852	11,364	7,078	7,602
5570 Motorcycle dealers	-	5	-	10	2	-	14,400	-	152
5610 Men's & boys' clothing stores[2]	-	6	-	34	6	-	11,529	-	392
5620 Women's clothing stores	29	22	238	197	9	6,773	6,721	1,646	1,355
5630 Women's accessory & specialty stores[3]	3	3	22	21	7	7,818	10,095	184	201
5650 Family clothing stores	12	11	163	130	12	11,411	12,769	1,938	1,779
5660 Shoe stores	21	21	133	130	6	11,218	10,923	1,398	1,313
5690 Misc. apparel & accessory stores	8	9	20	29	3	9,400	8,690	186	243
5712 Furniture stores	27	31	114	146	5	13,684	14,712	1,918	2,357
5713 Floor covering stores	8	8	34	33	4	12,706	17,939	555	607
5719 Misc. homefurnishings stores[3]	6	7	43	46	7	12,186	11,913	670	417
5720 Household appliance stores	14	14	41	41	3	15,024	13,756	617	557
5731 Radio, TV, & electronic stores	10	11	33	33	3	20,848	20,000	653	521
5734 Computer and software stores[2]	-	4	-	46	12	-	13,826	-	655
5735 Record & prerecorded tape stores[2]	-	4	-	65	16	-	9,231	-	527
5736 Musical instrument stores	6	6	18	18	3	11,333	12,667	241	268
5812 Eating places	213	191	4,224	4,490	24	6,413	6,892	30,922	32,533
5813 Drinking places	23	18	97	77	4	5,814	6,078	500	454
5910 Drug stores and proprietary stores	18	16	152	134	8	12,947	15,522	2,281	2,152
5920 Liquor stores	20	17	73	53	3	9,315	6,868	653	361
5930 Used merchandise stores	16	24	24	69	3	8,167	8,812	256	628
5941 Sporting goods and bicycle shops	12	13	36	37	3	7,000	8,973	520	555
5942 Book stores[3]	4	4	22	16	4	6,727	8,500	165	146
5944 Jewelry stores	11	13	55	64	5	13,018	11,688	714	813
5945 Hobby, toy, and game shops	12	12	115	95	8	9,670	12,379	1,226	1,356
5947 Gift, novelty, and souvenir shops	23	24	193	196	8	9,472	12,959	2,819	3,633
5962 Merchandising machine operators[1]	7	-	34	-	-	13,765	-	527	-
5963 Direct selling establishments[3]	5	6	19	17	3	19,368	19,059	370	370
5984 Liquefied petroleum gas dealers	10	-	46	-	-	8,783	-	561	-
5992 Florists	20	23	67	75	3	7,761	8,960	559	719
5993 Tobacco stores and stands	5	4	31	17	4	12,129	10,118	432	175
5995 Optical goods stores[3]	9	9	68	47	5	11,000	14,894	737	749
5999 Miscellaneous retail stores, nec	28	30	91	120	4	13,055	12,267	1,452	1,615

Source: County Business Patterns 1994/95, CBP-94/95, U.S. Department of Commerce, Washington DC, November 1997. The employment column represents mid-March employment in the year. Pay per employee is calculated by dividing 1st Quarter payroll, annualized, by mid-March employment. The column headed 'Emp / Est' shows 'employees per establishment'. A dash (-) means that data are unavailable or cannot be calculated. nec means not elsewhere classified. *Notes:* 1. 1994 data incomplete; unavailable or withheld. 2. 1995 data incomplete; unavailable or withheld. 3. 1994 and 1995 data incomplete; unavailable or withheld.

KALAMAZOO - BATTLE CREEK, MI MSA

Wholesale and Retail Trade USA	Establishments		Employment		Emp / Est	Pay / Employee		Annual Payroll ($ 000)	
	1994	1995	1994	1995	1995	1994	1995	1994	1995
50- Wholesale trade	633	633	7,852	8,189	13	30,340	32,055	254,970	277,668
5012 Automobiles and other vehicles	12	12	114	133	11	18,667	20,451	3,091	4,454
5013 Motor vehicle supplies and new parts	34	30	593	551	18	28,263	33,140	16,105	16,841
5015 Motor vehicle parts, used	12	13	39	38	3	14,769	14,632	596	539
5021 Furniture[3]	9	8	200	172	22	30,200	31,767	6,207	6,534
5023 Homefurnishings	5	6	6	7	1	16,000	17,714	116	98
5031 Lumber, plywood, and millwork	14	12	95	72	6	22,526	37,556	2,388	1,926
5033 Roofing, siding, & insulation[1]	9	-	33	-	-	29,091	-	1,049	-
5039 Construction materials, nec[2]	-	8	-	72	9	-	38,611	-	2,913
5044 Office equipment[3]	13	13	178	163	13	33,685	28,663	5,496	5,036
5045 Computers, peripherals, & software[2]	20	16	124	136	9	41,548	45,735	5,013	6,044
5048 Ophthalmic goods[2]	-	4	-	28	7	-	12,143	-	569
5049 Professional equipment, nec[2]	6	4	58	36	9	18,483	29,333	1,159	1,182
5050 Metals and minerals, except petroleum[3]	11	12	153	170	14	31,294	29,624	5,332	5,416
5063 Electrical apparatus and equipment	33	31	340	283	9	28,706	36,057	10,738	10,254
5065 Electronic parts and equipment[3]	12	16	42	70	4	26,095	35,429	1,359	2,529
5072 Hardware[3]	11	10	186	194	19	18,323	19,526	3,960	4,183

Continued on next page.

KALAMAZOO - BATTLE CREEK, MI MSA - [continued]

Wholesale and Retail Trade USA	Establishments		Employment		Emp / Est	Pay / Employee		Annual Payroll ($ 000)	
	1994	1995	1994	1995	1995	1994	1995	1994	1995
5074 Plumbing & hydronic heating supplies [1]	11	12	86	82	7	27,070	28,585	2,582	2,682
5075 Warm air heating & air conditioning	12	12	68	70	6	28,000	31,886	2,441	2,601
5082 Construction and mining machinery [3]	6	6	58	63	11	33,448	35,302	2,328	2,601
5083 Farm and garden machinery	11	11	83	65	6	18,554	20,185	1,927	1,748
5084 Industrial machinery and equipment	45	46	408	477	10	30,029	31,614	14,352	17,393
5085 Industrial supplies	35	35	400	440	13	29,830	33,055	12,970	15,356
5087 Service establishment equipment	10	9	114	145	16	21,193	21,131	2,740	3,383
5091 Sporting & recreational goods	-	5	-	30	6	-	16,267	-	532
5093 Scrap and waste materials	15	16	158	211	13	30,734	27,147	6,284	7,203
5099 Durable goods, nec	7	-	8	-	-	16,500	-	154	-
5111 Printing and writing paper [3]	7	10	58	66	7	29,517	35,091	1,722	2,699
5112 Stationery and office supplies [2]	13	13	170	201	15	19,035	19,065	3,496	4,174
5113 Industrial & personal service paper	6	8	137	184	23	27,387	29,978	4,751	6,036
5120 Drugs, proprietaries, and sundries	7	6	44	45	8	27,000	28,622	1,252	1,330
5147 Meats and meat products [3]	5	5	57	62	12	15,719	17,097	1,029	1,195
5149 Groceries and related products, nec	24	23	379	351	15	23,609	29,162	11,576	12,753
5150 Farm-product raw materials	12	11	67	62	6	16,537	19,742	1,226	1,292
5162 Plastics materials & basic shapes	9	9	122	130	14	25,934	27,046	3,279	3,615
5169 Chemicals & allied products, nec	18	18	135	154	9	30,607	31,766	4,581	4,886
5171 Petroleum bulk stations & terminals [1]	15	12	84	80	7	26,143	26,750	2,479	2,341
5172 Petroleum products, nec [3]	5	5	21	26	5	24,762	22,154	569	526
5180 Beer, wine, and distilled beverages	10	9	223	205	23	20,933	24,468	5,670	5,237
5191 Farm supplies	21	16	70	50	3	34,400	18,080	1,831	860
5192 Books, periodicals, & newspapers [3]	4	4	49	43	11	22,531	25,767	1,151	1,410
5193 Flowers & florists' supplies	-	7	-	41	6	-	21,756	-	1,045
5199 Nondurable goods, nec [3]	12	11	50	39	4	24,880	20,615	1,442	1,080
52- Retail trade	2,577	2,552	38,242	39,637	16	11,408	11,238	462,152	480,989
5210 Lumber and other building materials	57	55	830	980	18	18,313	18,971	18,812	19,218
5230 Paint, glass, and wallpaper stores	20	20	123	135	7	17,626	17,956	2,424	2,626
5250 Hardware stores	34	32	187	171	5	9,882	10,409	2,153	2,020
5260 Retail nurseries and garden stores	22	19	169	203	11	11,337	10,384	2,731	2,810
5270 Mobile home dealers	-	9	-	58	6	-	18,138	-	809
5310 Department stores [3]	25	26	5,606	5,850	225	9,413	10,475	61,693	67,061
5330 Variety stores [3]	20	18	134	100	6	6,985	7,160	808	853
5390 Misc. general merchandise stores [3]	12	10	402	307	31	9,851	12,156	4,562	3,550
5410 Grocery stores	196	194	3,986	4,079	21	10,074	10,095	41,885	42,358
5420 Meat and fish markets	10	8	22	17	2	8,909	7,529	192	158
5440 Candy, nut, and confectionery stores [3]	8	6	37	33	6	5,405	6,788	231	272
5460 Retail bakeries	34	30	303	284	9	10,244	9,915	3,400	2,992
5490 Miscellaneous food stores [1]	11	15	56	92	6	7,357	6,522	467	703
5510 New and used car dealers	50	48	1,733	1,756	37	29,606	30,526	62,325	63,425
5520 Used car dealers	26	27	101	98	4	16,238	16,816	1,858	1,839
5530 Auto and home supply stores	70	68	541	535	8	14,780	16,082	9,183	9,343
5540 Gasoline service stations	172	166	1,611	1,717	10	9,631	10,770	16,806	20,008
5550 Boat dealers	8	8	32	35	4	16,125	18,400	775	956
5560 Recreational vehicle dealers	5	5	21	25	5	17,333	16,160	450	488
5570 Motorcycle dealers	-	8	-	6	1	-	16,667	-	114
5610 Men's & boys' clothing stores	16	15	146	136	9	11,726	11,971	1,735	1,587
5620 Women's clothing stores	79	67	750	616	9	6,992	6,519	5,468	4,481
5630 Women's accessory & specialty stores [3]	13	13	55	66	5	7,855	10,182	452	650
5640 Children's and infants' wear stores [3]	4	5	35	6	1	8,000	9,333	272	120
5650 Family clothing stores	32	31	704	569	18	52,858	9,413	14,625	5,000
5660 Shoe stores	58	52	292	318	6	13,589	13,547	3,737	3,783
5690 Misc. apparel & accessory stores	14	13	138	137	11	8,551	11,474	1,236	1,597
5712 Furniture stores	61	58	485	526	9	17,823	19,513	9,265	10,019
5713 Floor covering stores	26	25	208	224	9	17,635	18,518	4,295	4,677
5720 Household appliance stores	20	20	58	61	3	16,000	16,328	1,058	1,129
5731 Radio, TV, & electronic stores	24	22	145	174	8	16,910	20,483	2,492	4,099
5734 Computer and software stores	13	11	64	84	8	17,688	17,000	1,197	1,384
5735 Record & prerecorded tape stores [3]	13	13	80	60	5	7,850	7,867	677	579
5736 Musical instrument stores [3]	7	7	49	57	8	15,755	15,789	842	987
5812 Eating places	609	575	12,297	12,628	22	6,718	7,080	92,619	96,960
5813 Drinking places	93	90	728	773	9	6,846	7,581	5,466	5,910
5910 Drug stores and proprietary stores	71	66	886	856	13	14,397	16,556	13,573	14,506
5920 Liquor stores	29	30	162	160	5	9,630	9,100	1,666	1,612
5930 Used merchandise stores	32	32	249	229	7	7,149	7,109	1,872	1,781
5941 Sporting goods and bicycle shops	46	47	301	350	7	11,163	12,149	4,106	4,871
5942 Book stores [3]	20	23	173	164	7	11,006	14,927	1,974	2,426
5944 Jewelry stores	36	40	183	198	5	14,208	15,495	2,871	3,083
5945 Hobby, toy, and game shops	21	16	178	168	11	9,079	11,500	2,041	2,142
5947 Gift, novelty, and souvenir shops	54	52	386	363	7	5,192	6,446	2,238	2,511

Continued on next page.

KALAMAZOO – BATTLE CREEK, MI MSA - [continued]

Wholesale and Retail Trade USA	Establishments		Employment		Emp / Est	Pay / Employee		Annual Payroll ($ 000)	
	1994	1995	1994	1995	1995	1994	1995	1994	1995
5949 Sewing, needlework, and piece goods [3]	10	5	125	33	7	5,760	5,576	585	191
5961 Catalog and mail-order houses	6	8	18	21	3	21,111	22,667	467	472
5962 Merchandising machine operators	11	13	94	116	9	20,511	18,241	2,011	2,428
5963 Direct selling establishments	19	20	95	142	7	15,284	14,535	1,984	2,377
5983 Fuel oil dealers [2]	10	8	37	32	4	18,811	22,000	609	687
5984 Liquefied petroleum gas dealers	12	12	67	98	8	22,925	26,653	1,438	2,473
5992 Florists	45	49	239	286	6	8,234	8,280	2,283	2,623
5995 Optical goods stores	30	30	195	171	6	16,738	19,439	3,325	3,535
5999 Miscellaneous retail stores, nec	65	64	361	352	6	15,213	13,511	5,550	4,815

Source: County Business Patterns 1994/95, CBP-94/95, U.S. Department of Commerce, Washington DC, November 1997. The employment column represents mid-March employment in the year. Pay per employee is calculated by dividing 1st Quarter payroll, annualized, by mid-March employment. The column headed 'Emp / Est' shows 'employees per establishment'. A dash (-) means that data are unavailable or cannot be calculated. nec means not elsewhere classified. *Notes:* 1. 1994 data incomplete; unavailable or withheld. 2. 1995 data incomplete; unavailable or withheld. 3. 1994 and 1995 data incomplete; unavailable or withheld.

KANKAKEE, IL PMSA

Wholesale and Retail Trade USA	Establishments		Employment		Emp / Est	Pay / Employee		Annual Payroll ($ 000)	
	1994	1995	1994	1995	1995	1994	1995	1994	1995
50– Wholesale trade	148	145	1,931	2,062	14	21,871	23,697	47,993	51,683
5013 Motor vehicle supplies and new parts	10	11	130	129	12	21,446	23,752	3,081	3,422
5020 Furniture and homefurnishings	-	3	-	81	27	-	25,975	-	2,266
5030 Lumber and construction materials	5	6	81	79	13	22,272	22,228	2,170	2,138
5045 Computers, peripherals, & software	-	4	-	30	8	-	18,533	-	531
5063 Electrical apparatus and equipment	3	3	56	57	19	32,143	38,316	1,895	2,126
5074 Plumbing & hydronic heating supplies	8	8	82	50	6	28,293	52,960	2,614	2,106
5075 Warm air heating & air conditioning	-	3	-	4	1	-	21,000	-	461
5083 Farm and garden machinery	-	6	-	115	19	-	24,278	-	3,018
5084 Industrial machinery and equipment	7	6	20	21	4	11,600	12,762	278	264
5085 Industrial supplies	6	6	67	73	12	17,134	20,274	1,219	1,441
5090 Miscellaneous durable goods	6	8	126	159	20	19,810	25,107	3,051	4,493
5120 Drugs, proprietaries, and sundries	3	-	14	-	-	12,000	-	171	-
5130 Apparel, piece goods, and notions	-	3	-	9	3	-	3,556	-	53
5147 Meats and meat products	3	-	33	-	-	10,909	-	401	-
5149 Groceries and related products, nec	4	4	77	90	23	36,571	33,689	3,181	3,445
5153 Grain and field beans	12	11	79	66	6	29,671	27,939	2,259	1,813
5160 Chemicals and allied products	6	5	14	13	3	18,286	29,538	266	526
5170 Petroleum and petroleum products	5	4	52	50	13	19,538	18,240	1,176	1,154
5180 Beer, wine, and distilled beverages	3	-	36	-	-	28,889	-	1,047	-
5190 Misc., nondurable goods	15	18	675	759	42	18,548	20,053	15,142	14,406
52– Retail trade	585	575	8,856	8,931	16	10,953	11,528	107,084	109,936
5210 Lumber and other building materials	13	16	183	377	24	17,290	18,568	4,112	7,581
5230 Paint, glass, and wallpaper stores	5	3	8	7	2	13,000	22,857	157	161
5250 Hardware stores	-	6	-	33	6	-	15,879	-	465
5260 Retail nurseries and garden stores	4	-	18	-	-	7,778	-	98	-
5310 Department stores	8	5	1,149	724	145	11,189	12,818	14,231	9,464
5410 Grocery stores	24	21	858	1,109	53	12,844	12,700	10,618	14,437
5460 Retail bakeries	9	11	97	100	9	6,227	7,120	650	681
5510 New and used car dealers	16	16	437	450	28	28,137	29,440	13,659	13,404
5520 Used car dealers	10	9	37	32	4	17,730	23,250	833	587
5530 Auto and home supply stores	9	12	214	234	20	13,533	13,880	3,136	3,485
5540 Gasoline service stations	41	39	230	207	5	8,313	9,623	2,275	2,422
5550 Boat dealers	3	3	6	9	3	14,000	7,556	117	119
5610 Men's & boys' clothing stores	-	4	-	14	4	-	12,286	-	136
5620 Women's clothing stores	17	16	192	160	10	7,479	6,750	1,518	1,115
5630 Women's accessory & specialty stores	3	-	11	-	-	8,364	-	75	-
5650 Family clothing stores	9	9	237	231	26	6,498	7,706	1,717	1,729
5660 Shoe stores	14	12	71	56	5	9,183	11,643	673	688
5690 Misc. apparel & accessory stores	4	-	16	-	-	7,500	-	118	-
5712 Furniture stores	10	12	42	63	5	18,762	15,746	914	1,032
5713 Floor covering stores	5	5	25	18	4	15,360	17,333	410	271
5719 Misc. homefurnishings stores	5	3	23	16	5	10,609	10,500	279	160
5720 Household appliance stores	6	6	90	88	15	17,644	19,045	1,720	1,977
5731 Radio, TV, & electronic stores	5	6	27	25	4	14,963	13,440	369	410
5735 Record & prerecorded tape stores	6	6	27	33	6	8,444	8,242	254	283
5812 Eating places	161	150	2,785	2,882	19	6,591	6,444	20,039	19,789
5813 Drinking places	32	29	118	130	4	7,695	8,554	1,032	1,200
5910 Drug stores and proprietary stores	15	14	218	206	15	16,018	18,078	3,894	3,877
5920 Liquor stores	9	9	29	33	4	23,172	19,030	488	486
5930 Used merchandise stores	6	7	48	57	8	8,667	13,404	562	464

Continued on next page.

KANKAKEE, IL PMSA - [continued]

Wholesale and Retail Trade USA	Establishments		Employment		Emp / Est	Pay / Employee		Annual Payroll ($ 000)	
	1994	1995	1994	1995	1995	1994	1995	1994	1995
5941 Sporting goods and bicycle shops	9	9	28	26	3	7,857	9,692	264	313
5942 Book stores	3	3	22	20	7	3,636	4,800	91	107
5944 Jewelry stores	8	8	45	58	7	13,067	12,759	607	707
5945 Hobby, toy, and game shops	4	5	32	31	6	9,000	10,452	356	394
5947 Gift, novelty, and souvenir shops	10	9	63	64	7	6,349	7,125	440	492
5949 Sewing, needlework, and piece goods	3	-	37	-	-	4,541	-	177	-
5963 Direct selling establishments	7	7	87	55	8	20,184	23,491	2,009	1,461
5984 Liquefied petroleum gas dealers	4	-	30	-	-	29,200	-	831	-
5995 Optical goods stores	7	6	58	49	8	13,586	16,735	602	853
5999 Miscellaneous retail stores, nec	11	10	24	41	4	13,333	11,707	449	623

Source: County Business Patterns 1994/95, CBP-94/95, U.S. Department of Commerce, Washington DC, November 1997. The employment column represents mid-March employment in the year. Pay per employee is calculated by dividing 1st Quarter payroll, annualized, by mid-March employment. The column headed 'Emp / Est' shows 'employees per establishment'. A dash (-) means that data are unavailable or cannot be calculated. nec means not elsewhere classified. *Notes:* 1. 1994 data incomplete; unavailable or withheld. 2. 1995 data incomplete; unavailable or withheld. 3. 1994 and 1995 data incomplete; unavailable or withheld.

KANSAS CITY MSA (KS PART)

Wholesale and Retail Trade USA	Establishments		Employment		Emp / Est	Pay / Employee		Annual Payroll ($ 000)	
	1994	1995	1994	1995	1995	1994	1995	1994	1995
50- Wholesale trade	1,985	2,019	28,231	30,200	15	32,935	35,804	999,003	1,095,965
5012 Automobiles and other vehicles[3]	39	36	520	633	18	33,346	39,956	19,632	23,495
5013 Motor vehicle supplies and new parts	71	75	983	1,200	16	26,079	33,437	27,958	40,688
5014 Tires and tubes[3]	11	9	188	135	15	53,277	45,896	9,487	5,724
5015 Motor vehicle parts, used[3]	20	20	85	9	-	19,812	22,222	1,638	222
5021 Furniture[3]	39	35	170	147	4	28,800	29,224	5,451	5,567
5023 Homefurnishings[3]	50	53	314	309	6	26,051	28,518	9,469	9,664
5031 Lumber, plywood, and millwork[3]	30	26	590	496	19	31,525	39,137	21,590	18,632
5032 Brick, stone, & related materials[3]	18	14	126	74	5	27,492	30,919	3,704	2,518
5033 Roofing, siding, & insulation[3]	17	17	185	201	12	40,130	38,169	7,553	7,372
5039 Construction materials, nec[3]	18	27	143	78	3	23,804	33,487	3,610	2,939
5043 Photographic equipment & supplies[2]	-	10	-	422	42	-	55,782	-	21,778
5044 Office equipment[3]	37	38	935	987	26	35,807	41,986	33,204	37,586
5045 Computers, peripherals, & software[3]	105	112	1,415	1,508	13	46,751	53,446	64,272	74,898
5046 Commercial equipment, nec[1]	27	-	61	-	-	28,131	-	2,438	-
5047 Medical and hospital equipment[3]	76	72	640	663	9	38,488	41,092	25,694	28,212
5049 Professional equipment, nec[3]	10	12	260	260	22	27,831	30,646	7,770	7,999
5051 Metals service centers and offices[3]	37	36	133	165	5	29,414	30,424	5,257	6,622
5063 Electrical apparatus and equipment	101	90	667	724	8	32,360	39,552	23,232	28,944
5064 Electrical appliances, TV & radios[3]	26	24	305	263	11	36,275	38,403	11,947	11,011
5065 Electronic parts and equipment[3]	113	122	1,632	1,724	14	40,983	45,810	69,156	80,846
5072 Hardware[3]	40	42	485	602	14	29,707	33,502	15,279	20,421
5074 Plumbing & hydronic heating supplies[3]	47	49	297	367	7	27,906	30,812	9,436	12,336
5075 Warm air heating & air conditioning[3]	26	25	189	216	9	41,397	52,556	8,969	11,459
5078 Refrigeration equipment and supplies[3]	8	8	15	17	2	33,600	26,588	550	490
5082 Construction and mining machinery[3]	21	20	268	294	15	29,761	39,265	10,662	11,569
5083 Farm and garden machinery[3]	16	13	76	40	3	27,263	38,700	2,518	1,840
5084 Industrial machinery and equipment[3]	131	134	1,012	1,127	8	34,427	36,202	40,026	44,367
5085 Industrial supplies[3]	84	88	710	760	9	33,837	36,579	26,706	31,571
5087 Service establishment equipment[3]	19	16	235	151	9	23,064	31,364	6,404	4,087
5088 Transportation equipment & supplies[3]	13	12	178	195	16	26,112	31,446	5,385	7,125
5091 Sporting & recreational goods[3]	35	32	892	895	28	25,843	25,895	26,020	26,298
5092 Toys and hobby goods and supplies[3]	16	18	113	102	6	15,257	21,647	2,068	2,544
5093 Scrap and waste materials	21	23	210	231	10	26,971	25,472	5,211	5,821
5094 Jewelry & precious stones[3]	13	14	554	580	41	16,621	20,793	9,391	9,381
5099 Durable goods, nec[3]	29	34	122	121	4	24,721	29,719	3,848	5,123
5111 Printing and writing paper[3]	18	18	271	281	16	41,122	41,409	9,368	10,901
5112 Stationery and office supplies[3]	43	42	354	366	9	22,463	24,710	8,269	8,759
5113 Industrial & personal service paper[3]	20	21	109	119	6	41,028	49,748	4,605	6,004
5120 Drugs, proprietaries, and sundries[3]	15	20	649	693	35	64,302	53,962	37,568	36,449
5131 Piece goods & notions[2]	-	16	-	55	3	-	26,400	-	1,333
5136 Men's and boys' clothing[3]	17	18	94	100	6	37,106	68,640	3,697	5,053
5137 Women's and children's clothing[1]	8	-	9	-	-	38,667	-	309	-
5141 Groceries, general line[3]	19	18	728	714	40	30,209	34,230	24,713	24,815
5142 Packaged frozen food[3]	14	16	479	446	28	38,956	34,422	18,458	16,840
5145 Confectionery[3]	8	10	139	133	13	30,647	27,669	4,161	3,974
5146 Fish and seafoods[3]	4	5	12	17	3	20,333	18,118	293	347
5147 Meats and meat products[3]	13	11	279	322	29	24,387	25,329	8,499	9,771
5148 Fresh fruits and vegetables[3]	10	10	420	421	42	19,210	24,523	8,499	9,091
5149 Groceries and related products, nec	53	49	2,137	2,195	45	32,717	33,766	80,592	76,065

Continued on next page.

KANSAS CITY MSA (KS PART) - [continued]

Wholesale and Retail Trade USA	Establishments		Employment		Emp / Est	Pay / Employee		Annual Payroll ($ 000)	
	1994	1995	1994	1995	1995	1994	1995	1994	1995
5153 Grain and field beans	30	27	330	317	12	39,030	44,353	14,677	15,468
5162 Plastics materials & basic shapes [3]	14	13	94	87	7	32,638	37,057	3,496	3,302
5169 Chemicals & allied products, nec [3]	44	46	263	323	7	29,901	33,362	9,206	11,109
5171 Petroleum bulk stations & terminals	14	11	88	71	6	28,864	30,085	2,641	2,111
5172 Petroleum products, nec [3]	13	14	61	20	1	30,951	21,000	1,869	423
5180 Beer, wine, and distilled beverages	8	11	264	309	28	25,561	27,793	7,510	9,327
5191 Farm supplies	33	36	236	242	7	29,661	28,711	9,018	8,072
5192 Books, periodicals, & newspapers [3]	14	14	155	180	13	25,419	30,622	3,909	5,473
5193 Flowers & florists' supplies	11	10	29	35	4	26,345	22,971	787	700
5198 Paints, varnishes, and supplies [3]	15	14	150	121	9	20,293	20,959	3,533	3,207
5199 Nondurable goods, nec [3]	74	76	288	440	6	20,847	20,891	7,284	10,398
52 - Retail trade	3,595	3,579	57,787	59,260	17	12,223	13,253	779,011	831,043
5210 Lumber and other building materials	47	48	1,092	993	21	13,593	18,095	16,266	17,280
5230 Paint, glass, and wallpaper stores [2]	-	29	-	135	5	-	17,600	-	2,505
5250 Hardware stores	40	40	386	348	9	10,974	11,322	5,174	4,074
5260 Retail nurseries and garden stores [3]	33	36	271	312	9	13,358	15,013	4,365	5,199
5310 Department stores [3]	32	34	6,251	5,775	170	10,688	12,128	73,003	72,944
5330 Variety stores	14	-	48	-	-	8,417	-	403	-
5390 Misc. general merchandise stores [1]	19	-	22	-	-	9,091	-	184	-
5410 Grocery stores [2]	183	173	7,043	6,768	39	11,899	12,917	87,374	91,254
5420 Meat and fish markets [3]	12	11	180	75	7	5,889	15,680	1,200	1,273
5440 Candy, nut, and confectionery stores [3]	13	10	82	75	8	7,756	8,053	667	615
5450 Dairy products stores [3]	7	10	30	40	4	7,600	6,400	245	256
5460 Retail bakeries	49	49	308	500	10	10,130	8,648	3,551	4,568
5490 Miscellaneous food stores [3]	24	24	113	136	6	6,867	7,971	943	1,534
5510 New and used car dealers	60	64	3,146	3,478	54	31,167	31,029	113,489	122,616
5520 Used car dealers	36	36	115	108	3	19,374	22,111	2,730	3,462
5530 Auto and home supply stores	87	89	818	785	9	17,672	19,735	15,643	16,936
5540 Gasoline service stations	225	210	1,512	1,529	7	12,664	12,746	20,581	20,253
5570 Motorcycle dealers [3]	5	5	25	30	6	32,160	34,400	859	1,098
5590 Automotive dealers, nec [1]	3	-	19	-	-	25,263	-	562	-
5610 Men's & boys' clothing stores	33	31	250	249	8	12,064	12,369	3,061	2,977
5620 Women's clothing stores	95	80	1,042	943	12	7,781	6,906	9,298	6,637
5630 Women's accessory & specialty stores [3]	23	23	163	192	8	17,669	15,104	2,286	2,307
5640 Children's and infants' wear stores [3]	13	11	110	116	11	7,055	7,724	792	822
5650 Family clothing stores	31	30	519	504	17	7,931	8,929	4,527	4,735
5660 Shoe stores [3]	65	64	376	427	7	10,809	10,979	4,465	4,821
5690 Misc. apparel & accessory stores [3]	24	24	112	99	4	8,750	12,040	1,108	1,334
5712 Furniture stores	78	75	766	655	9	17,525	19,481	13,749	12,827
5713 Floor covering stores	43	45	250	255	6	21,024	22,808	5,854	6,538
5714 Drapery and upholstery stores [3]	10	8	21	24	3	11,429	10,333	289	234
5719 Misc. homefurnishings stores	56	54	314	331	6	10,917	12,399	3,490	4,524
5720 Household appliance stores [3]	20	19	84	107	6	16,762	16,411	1,667	1,835
5731 Radio, TV, & electronic stores	46	43	466	703	16	15,948	14,441	8,287	10,019
5734 Computer and software stores [3]	28	28	266	273	10	18,722	18,447	5,327	5,360
5735 Record & prerecorded tape stores [3]	23	21	195	229	11	8,697	7,721	1,628	1,619
5736 Musical instrument stores [3]	12	9	84	83	9	16,905	18,988	1,438	1,313
5812 Eating places	843	796	17,779	18,170	23	7,545	8,439	145,943	159,124
5813 Drinking places	112	104	670	720	7	7,200	7,672	5,164	5,185
5910 Drug stores and proprietary stores	91	88	1,276	1,349	15	13,621	14,805	18,615	19,406
5920 Liquor stores [2]	134	131	294	302	2	6,068	6,848	1,969	2,405
5930 Used merchandise stores	51	51	262	262	5	10,275	10,763	3,020	2,956
5941 Sporting goods and bicycle shops [2]	67	76	464	500	7	12,060	11,952	6,819	6,807
5942 Book stores [1]	32	34	294	294	9	7,905	10,952	2,614	3,464
5944 Jewelry stores [3]	55	58	449	490	8	20,722	22,718	9,550	10,353
5945 Hobby, toy, and game shops [1]	39	37	457	500	14	8,341	8,600	4,364	4,711
5946 Camera & photographic supply stores [3]	4	5	36	38	8	15,667	16,632	623	656
5947 Gift, novelty, and souvenir shops [2]	87	86	684	699	8	6,865	7,868	5,437	5,769
5949 Sewing, needlework, and piece goods [2]	21	16	211	135	8	8,284	7,704	1,625	1,047
5961 Catalog and mail-order houses [3]	23	24	2,023	2,078	87	15,100	16,508	36,037	37,045
5962 Merchandising machine operators [3]	20	19	123	115	6	19,089	25,148	2,910	2,600
5963 Direct selling establishments [3]	43	40	379	363	9	18,438	20,474	7,155	7,788
5984 Liquefied petroleum gas dealers [3]	8	8	114	96	12	11,649	14,583	1,606	1,769
5992 Florists	75	81	387	367	5	10,274	11,019	4,275	3,958
5993 Tobacco stores and stands [1]	5	-	25	-	-	11,200	-	339	-
5995 Optical goods stores	46	43	181	178	4	15,536	16,517	2,968	2,908
5999 Miscellaneous retail stores, nec [3]	129	137	686	793	6	12,711	13,740	10,585	12,320

Source: County Business Patterns 1994/95, CBP-94/95, U.S. Department of Commerce, Washington DC, November 1997. The employment column represents mid-March employment in the year. Pay per employee is calculated by dividing 1st Quarter payroll, annualized, by mid-March employment. The column headed 'Emp / Est' shows 'employees per establishment'. A dash (-) means that data are unavailable or cannot be calculated. nec means not elsewhere classified. *Notes:* 1. 1994 data incomplete; unavailable or withheld. 2. 1995 data incomplete; unavailable or withheld. 3. 1994 and 1995 data incomplete; unavailable or withheld.

KANSAS CITY MSA (MO PART)

Wholesale and Retail Trade USA	Establishments		Employment		Emp / Est	Pay / Employee		Annual Payroll ($ 000)	
	1994	1995	1994	1995	1995	1994	1995	1994	1995
50 – Wholesale trade	2,141	2,169	31,302	31,784	15	30,258	32,586	1,011,196	1,059,261
5012 Automobiles and other vehicles [3]	43	43	1,535	1,688	39	32,266	35,637	54,514	56,598
5013 Motor vehicle supplies and new parts [2]	142	138	1,231	1,306	9	22,301	22,328	29,229	29,915
5014 Tires and tubes [3]	20	21	173	175	8	24,578	25,349	4,605	4,919
5015 Motor vehicle parts, used [3]	39	44	154	171	4	16,104	17,170	2,802	3,209
5021 Furniture [3]	30	29	322	265	9	28,360	32,347	10,014	9,561
5023 Homefurnishings [3]	44	42	740	753	18	27,546	33,604	26,399	25,429
5031 Lumber, plywood, and millwork [3]	37	34	786	654	19	28,331	30,563	24,658	20,478
5032 Brick, stone, & related materials [3]	14	12	159	125	10	38,314	42,240	5,646	4,258
5033 Roofing, siding, & insulation [3]	14	16	204	201	13	26,373	39,403	7,893	7,862
5039 Construction materials, nec [3]	19	36	144	441	12	26,028	37,905	4,009	15,260
5043 Photographic equipment & supplies [3]	10	8	50	27	3	20,720	17,185	1,051	523
5044 Office equipment [3]	46	34	614	450	13	28,046	29,787	16,319	13,226
5045 Computers, peripherals, & software [3]	56	59	993	962	16	57,942	72,266	53,992	56,123
5046 Commercial equipment, nec [3]	25	26	142	187	7	21,662	21,711	3,151	4,545
5047 Medical and hospital equipment [3]	56	50	579	546	11	34,618	38,073	21,371	21,934
5048 Ophthalmic goods [3]	10	10	16	44	4	24,500	24,636	371	1,129
5049 Professional equipment, nec [3]	8	9	298	308	34	15,329	20,234	6,299	7,446
5051 Metals service centers and offices [3]	51	50	303	16	-	33,769	46,000	11,084	1,109
5063 Electrical apparatus and equipment [3]	78	69	823	788	11	36,156	42,162	32,171	32,335
5064 Electrical appliances, TV & radios [3]	13	15	73	97	6	22,959	27,093	3,343	4,958
5065 Electronic parts and equipment [3]	57	59	551	535	9	35,644	38,079	19,999	18,967
5072 Hardware [3]	47	48	748	757	16	26,390	30,705	21,961	24,378
5074 Plumbing & hydronic heating supplies [3]	47	45	389	349	8	35,753	33,066	14,924	12,755
5075 Warm air heating & air conditioning [3]	20	17	259	256	15	35,552	40,078	9,916	10,918
5078 Refrigeration equipment and supplies [3]	7	8	10	10	1	26,000	25,600	283	421
5082 Construction and mining machinery [3]	26	28	462	517	18	36,554	43,497	19,827	22,486
5083 Farm and garden machinery	31	28	472	543	19	39,407	34,232	19,904	20,739
5084 Industrial machinery and equipment [3]	151	162	1,753	1,816	11	36,694	37,727	68,832	72,936
5085 Industrial supplies [3]	74	73	908	991	14	29,661	30,281	28,679	30,659
5087 Service establishment equipment [3]	46	40	496	416	10	16,952	18,865	8,199	8,301
5088 Transportation equipment & supplies [3]	27	25	174	170	7	28,966	36,188	5,422	6,106
5091 Sporting & recreational goods [3]	29	29	177	279	10	25,424	24,358	8,011	10,025
5092 Toys and hobby goods and supplies [3]	15	16	35	50	3	18,743	30,240	771	1,761
5093 Scrap and waste materials [3]	30	30	363	381	13	25,543	28,241	9,911	12,319
5094 Jewelry & precious stones [3]	13	14	147	164	12	23,102	22,732	3,380	3,672
5099 Durable goods, nec [3]	36	39	87	256	7	15,310	32,891	1,653	8,225
5111 Printing and writing paper [3]	15	13	299	221	17	40,749	42,950	11,736	9,751
5112 Stationery and office supplies [3]	59	56	1,367	1,756	31	32,919	32,797	43,648	62,215
5113 Industrial & personal service paper [3]	26	27	471	517	19	30,446	30,545	15,307	17,390
5120 Drugs, proprietaries, and sundries [3]	34	35	650	508	15	37,871	25,480	23,120	14,870
5131 Piece goods & notions [3]	16	16	167	212	13	22,922	26,340	4,563	5,885
5136 Men's and boys' clothing [3]	13	13	360	387	30	21,067	22,532	8,846	9,109
5141 Groceries, general line [3]	14	12	240	86	7	30,233	16,000	7,196	923
5142 Packaged frozen food [3]	18	18	188	206	11	32,957	34,272	5,827	6,090
5143 Dairy products, exc. dried or canned [3]	11	12	175	189	16	23,977	25,503	4,928	5,655
5144 Poultry and poultry products [2]	-	8	-	46	6	-	22,261	-	1,251
5145 Confectionery [3]	18	13	511	552	42	25,057	24,587	13,148	13,203
5147 Meats and meat products [3]	15	15	163	157	10	22,675	26,166	4,067	4,456
5148 Fresh fruits and vegetables [3]	16	15	334	406	27	24,084	25,369	10,708	12,007
5149 Groceries and related products, nec [3]	44	50	406	427	9	27,103	25,845	11,345	11,967
5153 Grain and field beans	44	44	401	325	7	25,287	23,926	12,012	8,114
5154 Livestock [1]	7	-	9	-	-	21,778	-	277	-
5162 Plastics materials & basic shapes [3]	18	21	199	230	11	29,628	26,452	7,047	7,448
5169 Chemicals & allied products, nec [3]	42	44	305	286	7	28,118	31,007	8,986	9,342
5171 Petroleum bulk stations & terminals	35	35	192	207	6	30,917	31,401	6,834	7,082
5172 Petroleum products, nec [3]	7	9	26	37	4	27,846	31,459	964	1,516
5180 Beer, wine, and distilled beverages [3]	12	13	748	729	56	33,797	42,749	26,310	29,138
5191 Farm supplies	53	50	341	366	7	21,478	26,306	6,863	9,027
5192 Books, periodicals, & newspapers [3]	16	15	138	130	9	43,188	32,862	5,822	4,123
5193 Flowers & florists' supplies [3]	16	16	245	61	4	18,269	22,492	5,098	1,512
5194 Tobacco and tobacco products [1]	3	-	103	-	-	33,709	-	3,239	-
5198 Paints, varnishes, and supplies [3]	24	21	136	144	7	25,235	27,222	3,548	3,835
5199 Nondurable goods, nec [3]	62	74	472	486	7	25,085	25,358	14,138	14,197
52 – Retail trade	5,912	5,960	86,868	90,534	15	12,533	13,678	1,163,076	1,273,295
5210 Lumber and other building materials	84	81	1,803	1,824	23	16,617	18,757	35,848	33,925
5230 Paint, glass, and wallpaper stores [3]	42	38	149	132	3	16,779	18,697	2,674	2,515
5250 Hardware stores	72	57	571	535	9	12,883	13,249	7,824	6,821
5260 Retail nurseries and garden stores [3]	46	49	346	362	7	10,208	12,619	4,472	6,374
5270 Mobile home dealers [3]	11	12	25	33	3	20,640	25,576	865	1,049
5310 Department stores [3]	52	52	8,745	9,123	175	10,711	12,551	101,025	116,039

Continued on next page.

KANSAS CITY MSA (MO PART) - [continued]

Wholesale and Retail Trade USA	Establishments		Employment		Emp / Est	Pay / Employee		Annual Payroll ($ 000)	
	1994	1995	1994	1995	1995	1994	1995	1994	1995
5330 Variety stores[3]	51	34	475	299	9	9,204	11,344	4,377	3,224
5390 Misc. general merchandise stores[3]	46	58	1,011	1,129	19	12,471	12,351	13,591	13,884
5410 Grocery stores[1]	360	349	9,753	10,588	30	12,418	12,468	126,766	142,436
5420 Meat and fish markets[3]	17	18	148	76	4	6,730	16,158	1,200	1,335
5430 Fruit and vegetable markets[3]	4	4	10	9	2	10,400	7,111	223	230
5440 Candy, nut, and confectionery stores[3]	39	36	222	197	5	7,694	7,127	1,667	1,592
5450 Dairy products stores[3]	10	9	11	20	2	9,091	9,200	148	211
5460 Retail bakeries[3]	96	82	456	561	7	10,640	9,740	5,539	5,459
5490 Miscellaneous food stores[3]	26	31	124	137	4	8,516	10,277	1,154	1,425
5510 New and used car dealers	106	105	4,211	4,545	43	27,746	30,971	135,189	152,407
5520 Used car dealers[3]	91	99	352	441	4	17,875	20,109	7,554	9,294
5530 Auto and home supply stores	154	153	1,190	1,241	8	16,703	19,284	21,331	24,775
5540 Gasoline service stations	439	429	3,313	3,507	8	10,801	11,224	39,074	42,618
5550 Boat dealers[3]	10	9	33	32	4	23,515	25,250	931	1,009
5560 Recreational vehicle dealers[3]	11	10	54	58	6	16,741	17,103	1,147	1,332
5570 Motorcycle dealers[3]	16	16	71	85	5	17,465	17,412	1,772	2,070
5610 Men's & boys' clothing stores[3]	48	50	382	385	8	15,958	17,403	6,699	7,725
5620 Women's clothing stores[3]	130	118	1,306	1,271	11	8,943	8,954	12,623	11,917
5630 Women's accessory & specialty stores[3]	29	26	157	143	6	10,064	10,238	1,481	1,392
5640 Children's and infants' wear stores[3]	10	8	65	76	10	7,138	7,368	576	662
5650 Family clothing stores[3]	56	53	954	895	17	7,736	9,234	8,249	8,221
5660 Shoe stores[3]	117	120	644	665	6	10,596	11,579	7,546	7,943
5690 Misc. apparel & accessory stores[3]	37	37	251	163	4	9,355	12,000	2,546	2,062
5712 Furniture stores[2]	93	87	621	594	7	18,918	21,232	13,098	13,180
5713 Floor covering stores	65	69	331	357	5	17,233	19,854	7,234	8,186
5714 Drapery and upholstery stores[3]	4	5	5	8	2	11,200	10,500	65	83
5719 Misc. homefurnishings stores[3]	56	59	368	295	5	10,446	12,176	4,153	3,921
5720 Household appliance stores[3]	35	36	204	197	5	15,255	18,396	3,587	3,778
5731 Radio, TV, & electronic stores[3]	65	68	562	762	11	16,377	15,659	11,482	12,918
5734 Computer and software stores[3]	20	27	86	88	3	11,674	15,773	1,121	1,322
5735 Record & prerecorded tape stores[3]	30	26	249	242	9	8,498	10,992	2,329	2,374
5736 Musical instrument stores[3]	22	20	139	162	8	17,612	15,975	2,760	3,468
5812 Eating places	1,425	1,355	30,234	30,134	22	7,853	8,444	256,573	269,948
5813 Drinking places	200	182	1,311	1,256	7	7,423	7,936	10,357	10,038
5910 Drug stores and proprietary stores	161	157	2,067	2,164	14	14,918	15,601	32,186	34,303
5920 Liquor stores[3]	120	112	476	492	4	10,992	11,033	5,498	5,609
5930 Used merchandise stores[3]	112	117	689	769	7	9,782	10,767	7,829	8,715
5941 Sporting goods and bicycle shops[2]	95	100	361	407	4	11,634	10,919	4,784	5,127
5942 Book stores[3]	50	55	300	285	5	8,307	9,025	2,696	2,978
5943 Stationery stores[3]	8	11	19	20	2	11,368	12,600	254	320
5944 Jewelry stores	93	95	558	562	6	16,932	19,537	10,615	11,716
5945 Hobby, toy, and game shops[3]	54	53	523	684	13	8,635	7,965	5,871	6,438
5946 Camera & photographic supply stores[2]	-	9	-	18	2	-	17,111	-	385
5947 Gift, novelty, and souvenir shops[3]	113	99	695	625	6	7,102	8,371	5,445	5,356
5948 Luggage and leather goods stores[3]	10	10	70	76	8	8,914	7,842	594	457
5949 Sewing, needlework, and piece goods[3]	19	16	180	162	10	8,978	9,012	1,626	1,436
5961 Catalog and mail-order houses[3]	32	40	290	334	8	20,428	23,449	6,339	7,325
5962 Merchandising machine operators[3]	40	39	300	405	10	20,973	17,412	6,524	8,470
5963 Direct selling establishments[3]	57	65	501	482	7	16,942	17,137	8,919	8,208
5984 Liquefied petroleum gas dealers	26	26	62	102	4	17,871	17,569	1,127	1,836
5992 Florists	111	115	345	358	3	9,333	9,978	3,407	3,670
5993 Tobacco stores and stands[2]	-	12	-	28	2	-	17,714	-	635
5995 Optical goods stores[3]	73	77	435	393	5	16,938	18,270	7,639	7,648
5999 Miscellaneous retail stores, nec	185	189	904	952	5	12,956	14,403	14,302	14,622

Source: County Business Patterns 1994/95, CBP-94/95, U.S. Department of Commerce, Washington DC, November 1997. The employment column represents mid-March employment in the year. Pay per employee is calculated by dividing 1st Quarter payroll, annualized, by mid-March employment. The column headed 'Emp / Est' shows 'employees per establishment'. A dash (-) means that data are unavailable or cannot be calculated. nec means not elsewhere classified. *Notes:* 1. 1994 data incomplete; unavailable or withheld. 2. 1995 data incomplete; unavailable or withheld. 3. 1994 and 1995 data incomplete; unavailable or withheld.

KANSAS CITY, MO – KS MSA

Wholesale and Retail Trade USA	Establishments		Employment		Emp / Est	Pay / Employee		Annual Payroll ($ 000)	
	1994	1995	1994	1995	1995	1994	1995	1994	1995
50 – Wholesale trade	4,126	4,188	59,533	61,984	15	31,528	34,154	2,010,199	2,155,226
5012 Automobiles and other vehicles[3]	82	79	2,055	2,321	29	32,539	36,815	74,146	80,093
5013 Motor vehicle supplies and new parts[2]	213	213	2,214	2,506	12	23,978	27,647	57,187	70,603
5014 Tires and tubes[3]	31	30	361	310	10	39,524	34,297	14,092	10,643
5015 Motor vehicle parts, used[3]	59	64	239	180	3	17,423	17,422	4,440	3,431
5021 Furniture[3]	69	64	492	412	6	28,512	31,233	15,465	15,128

Continued on next page.

KANSAS CITY, MO-KS MSA - [continued]

Wholesale and Retail Trade USA	Establishments		Employment		Emp / Est	Pay / Employee		Annual Payroll ($ 000)	
	1994	1995	1994	1995	1995	1994	1995	1994	1995
5023 Homefurnishings [3]	94	95	1,054	1,062	11	27,101	32,124	35,868	35,093
5031 Lumber, plywood, and millwork [3]	67	60	1,376	1,150	19	29,701	34,261	46,248	39,110
5032 Brick, stone, & related materials [3]	32	26	285	199	8	33,530	38,030	9,350	6,776
5033 Roofing, siding, & insulation [3]	31	33	389	402	12	32,915	38,786	15,446	15,234
5039 Construction materials, nec [3]	37	63	287	519	8	24,920	37,241	7,619	18,199
5043 Photographic equipment & supplies [3]	20	18	50	449	25	20,720	53,461	1,051	22,301
5044 Office equipment [3]	83	72	1,549	1,437	20	32,731	38,166	49,523	50,812
5045 Computers, peripherals, & software [3]	161	171	2,408	2,470	14	51,365	60,776	118,264	131,021
5046 Commercial equipment, nec [3]	52	54	203	187	3	23,606	21,711	5,589	4,545
5047 Medical and hospital equipment [3]	132	122	1,219	1,209	10	36,650	39,729	47,065	50,146
5048 Ophthalmic goods [3]	13	13	16	44	3	24,500	24,636	371	1,129
5049 Professional equipment, nec [3]	18	21	558	568	27	21,154	25,000	14,069	15,445
5051 Metals service centers and offices [3]	88	86	436	181	2	32,440	31,801	16,341	7,731
5063 Electrical apparatus and equipment [3]	179	159	1,490	1,512	10	34,456	40,913	55,403	61,279
5064 Electrical appliances, TV & radios [3]	39	39	378	360	9	33,704	35,356	15,290	15,969
5065 Electronic parts and equipment [3]	170	181	2,183	2,259	12	39,635	43,979	89,155	99,813
5072 Hardware [3]	87	90	1,233	1,359	15	27,695	31,944	37,240	44,799
5074 Plumbing & hydronic heating supplies [3]	94	94	686	716	8	32,356	31,911	24,360	25,091
5075 Warm air heating & air conditioning [3]	46	42	448	472	11	38,018	45,788	18,885	22,377
5078 Refrigeration equipment and supplies [3]	15	16	25	27	2	30,560	26,222	833	911
5082 Construction and mining machinery [3]	47	48	730	811	17	34,060	41,963	30,489	34,055
5083 Farm and garden machinery [3]	47	41	548	583	14	37,723	34,539	22,422	22,579
5084 Industrial machinery and equipment [3]	282	296	2,765	2,943	10	35,864	37,143	108,858	117,303
5085 Industrial supplies [3]	158	161	1,618	1,751	11	31,493	33,014	55,385	62,230
5087 Service establishment equipment [3]	65	56	731	567	10	18,917	22,194	14,603	12,388
5088 Transportation equipment & supplies [3]	40	37	352	365	10	27,523	33,655	10,807	13,231
5091 Sporting & recreational goods [3]	64	61	1,069	1,174	19	25,774	25,530	34,031	36,323
5092 Toys and hobby goods and supplies [3]	31	34	148	152	4	16,081	24,474	2,839	4,305
5093 Scrap and waste materials [3]	51	53	573	612	12	26,066	27,196	15,122	18,140
5094 Jewelry & precious stones [3]	26	28	701	744	27	17,980	21,220	12,771	13,053
5099 Durable goods, nec [3]	65	73	209	377	5	20,804	31,873	5,501	13,348
5111 Printing and writing paper [3]	33	31	570	502	16	40,926	42,088	21,104	20,652
5112 Stationery and office supplies [3]	102	98	1,721	2,122	22	30,768	31,402	51,917	70,974
5113 Industrial & personal service paper [3]	46	48	580	636	13	32,434	34,138	19,912	23,394
5120 Drugs, proprietaries, and sundries [3]	49	55	1,299	1,201	22	51,076	41,915	60,688	51,319
5131 Piece goods & notions [3]	33	32	167	267	8	22,922	26,352	4,563	7,218
5136 Men's and boys' clothing [3]	30	31	454	487	16	24,388	32,000	12,543	14,162
5137 Women's and children's clothing [1]	22	-	9	-	-	38,667	-	309	-
5141 Groceries, general line [3]	33	30	968	800	27	30,215	32,270	31,909	25,738
5142 Packaged frozen food [3]	32	34	667	652	19	37,265	34,374	24,285	22,930
5143 Dairy products, exc. dried or canned [3]	18	16	175	189	12	23,977	25,503	4,928	5,655
5144 Poultry and poultry products [2]	-	10	-	46	5	-	22,261	-	1,251
5145 Confectionery [3]	26	23	650	685	30	26,252	25,185	17,309	17,177
5146 Fish and seafoods [3]	6	7	12	17	2	20,333	18,118	293	347
5147 Meats and meat products [3]	28	26	442	479	18	23,756	25,603	12,566	14,227
5148 Fresh fruits and vegetables [3]	26	25	754	827	33	21,369	24,938	19,207	21,098
5149 Groceries and related products, nec [3]	97	99	2,543	2,622	26	31,821	32,476	91,937	88,032
5153 Grain and field beans	74	71	731	642	9	31,491	34,012	26,689	23,582
5154 Livestock [1]	11	-	9	-	-	21,778	-	277	-
5162 Plastics materials & basic shapes [3]	32	34	293	317	9	30,594	29,363	10,543	10,750
5169 Chemicals & allied products, nec [3]	86	90	568	609	7	28,944	32,256	18,192	20,451
5171 Petroleum bulk stations & terminals	49	46	280	278	6	30,271	31,065	9,475	9,193
5172 Petroleum products, nec [3]	20	23	87	57	2	30,023	27,789	2,833	1,939
5180 Beer, wine, and distilled beverages [3]	20	24	1,012	1,038	43	31,648	38,297	33,820	38,465
5191 Farm supplies	86	86	577	608	7	24,825	27,263	15,881	17,099
5192 Books, periodicals, & newspapers [3]	30	29	293	310	11	33,788	31,561	9,731	9,596
5193 Flowers & florists' supplies [3]	27	26	274	96	4	19,124	22,667	5,885	2,212
5194 Tobacco and tobacco products [1]	5	-	103	-	-	33,709	-	3,239	-
5198 Paints, varnishes, and supplies [3]	39	35	286	265	8	22,643	24,362	7,081	7,042
5199 Nondurable goods, nec [3]	136	150	760	926	6	23,479	23,235	21,422	24,595
52- Retail trade	9,507	9,539	144,655	149,794	16	12,409	13,510	1,942,087	2,104,338
5210 Lumber and other building materials	131	129	2,895	2,817	22	15,476	18,523	52,114	51,205
5230 Paint, glass, and wallpaper stores [3]	77	67	149	267	4	16,779	18,142	2,674	5,020
5250 Hardware stores	112	97	957	883	9	12,113	12,489	12,998	10,895
5260 Retail nurseries and garden stores [3]	79	85	617	674	8	11,592	13,727	8,837	11,573
5270 Mobile home dealers [3]	17	18	25	33	2	20,640	25,576	865	1,049
5310 Department stores [3]	84	86	14,996	14,898	173	10,701	12,387	174,028	188,983
5330 Variety stores [3]	65	44	523	299	7	9,132	11,344	4,780	3,224
5390 Misc. general merchandise stores [3]	65	79	1,033	1,129	14	12,399	12,351	13,775	13,884
5410 Grocery stores [3]	543	522	16,796	17,356	33	12,201	12,643	214,140	233,690
5420 Meat and fish markets [3]	29	29	328	151	5	6,268	15,921	2,400	2,608

Continued on next page.

KANSAS CITY, MO–KS MSA - [continued]

Wholesale and Retail Trade USA	Establishments		Employment		Emp / Est	Pay / Employee		Annual Payroll ($ 000)	
	1994	1995	1994	1995	1995	1994	1995	1994	1995
5430 Fruit and vegetable markets [3]	5	5	10	9	2	10,400	7,111	223	230
5440 Candy, nut, and confectionery stores [3]	52	46	304	272	6	7,711	7,382	2,334	2,207
5450 Dairy products stores [3]	17	19	41	60	3	8,000	7,333	393	467
5460 Retail bakeries [3]	145	131	764	1,061	8	10,435	9,225	9,090	10,027
5490 Miscellaneous food stores [3]	50	55	237	273	5	7,730	9,128	2,097	2,959
5510 New and used car dealers	166	169	7,357	8,023	47	29,209	30,996	248,678	275,023
5520 Used car dealers [3]	127	135	467	549	4	18,244	20,503	10,284	12,756
5530 Auto and home supply stores	241	242	2,008	2,026	8	17,098	19,459	36,974	41,711
5540 Gasoline service stations	664	639	4,825	5,036	8	11,385	11,686	59,655	62,871
5550 Boat dealers [3]	13	12	33	32	3	23,515	25,250	931	1,009
5560 Recreational vehicle dealers [3]	13	12	54	58	5	16,741	17,103	1,147	1,332
5570 Motorcycle dealers [3]	21	21	96	115	5	21,292	21,843	2,631	3,168
5590 Automotive dealers, nec [1]	10	-	19	-	-	25,263	-	562	-
5610 Men's & boys' clothing stores [3]	81	81	632	634	8	14,418	15,426	9,760	10,702
5620 Women's clothing stores [3]	225	198	2,348	2,214	11	8,428	8,081	21,921	18,554
5630 Women's accessory & specialty stores [3]	52	49	320	335	7	13,938	13,027	3,767	3,699
5640 Children's and infants' wear stores [3]	23	19	175	192	10	7,086	7,583	1,368	1,484
5650 Family clothing stores [3]	87	83	1,473	1,399	17	7,804	9,124	12,776	12,956
5660 Shoe stores [3]	182	184	1,020	1,092	6	10,675	11,344	12,011	12,764
5690 Misc. apparel & accessory stores [3]	61	61	363	262	4	9,168	12,015	3,654	3,396
5712 Furniture stores [2]	171	162	1,387	1,249	8	18,149	20,314	26,847	26,007
5713 Floor covering stores	108	114	581	612	5	18,864	21,085	13,088	14,724
5714 Drapery and upholstery stores [3]	14	13	26	32	2	11,385	10,375	354	317
5719 Misc. homefurnishings stores [3]	112	113	682	626	6	10,663	12,294	7,643	8,445
5720 Household appliance stores [3]	55	55	288	304	6	15,694	17,697	5,254	5,613
5731 Radio, TV, & electronic stores [3]	111	111	1,028	1,465	13	16,183	15,074	19,769	22,937
5734 Computer and software stores [3]	48	55	352	361	7	17,000	17,795	6,448	6,682
5735 Record & prerecorded tape stores [3]	53	47	444	471	10	8,586	9,401	3,957	3,993
5736 Musical instrument stores [3]	34	29	223	245	8	17,345	16,996	4,198	4,781
5812 Eating places	2,268	2,151	48,013	48,304	22	7,739	8,443	402,516	429,072
5813 Drinking places	312	286	1,981	1,976	7	7,348	7,840	15,521	15,223
5910 Drug stores and proprietary stores	252	245	3,343	3,513	14	14,423	15,295	50,801	53,709
5920 Liquor stores [3]	254	243	770	794	3	9,112	9,441	7,467	8,014
5930 Used merchandise stores [3]	163	168	951	1,031	6	9,918	10,766	10,849	11,671
5941 Sporting goods and bicycle shops [2]	162	176	825	907	5	11,874	11,488	11,603	11,934
5942 Book stores [3]	82	89	594	579	7	8,108	10,003	5,310	6,442
5943 Stationery stores [3]	18	22	19	20	1	11,368	12,600	254	320
5944 Jewelry stores [3]	148	153	1,007	1,052	7	18,622	21,019	20,165	22,069
5945 Hobby, toy, and game shops [3]	93	90	980	1,184	13	8,498	8,233	10,235	11,149
5946 Camera & photographic supply stores [3]	10	14	36	56	4	15,667	16,786	623	1,041
5947 Gift, novelty, and souvenir shops [3]	200	185	1,379	1,324	7	6,985	8,106	10,882	11,125
5948 Luggage and leather goods stores [3]	12	12	70	76	6	8,914	7,842	594	457
5949 Sewing, needlework, and piece goods [3]	40	32	391	297	9	8,604	8,418	3,251	2,483
5961 Catalog and mail-order houses [3]	55	64	2,313	2,412	38	15,768	17,469	42,376	44,370
5962 Merchandising machine operators [3]	60	58	423	520	9	20,426	19,123	9,434	11,070
5963 Direct selling establishments [3]	100	105	880	845	8	17,586	18,570	16,074	15,996
5984 Liquefied petroleum gas dealers [3]	34	34	176	198	6	13,841	16,121	2,733	3,605
5992 Florists	186	196	732	725	4	9,831	10,505	7,682	7,628
5993 Tobacco stores and stands [3]	17	18	25	28	2	11,200	17,714	339	635
5995 Optical goods stores [3]	119	120	616	571	5	16,526	17,723	10,607	10,556
5999 Miscellaneous retail stores, nec [3]	314	326	1,590	1,745	5	12,850	14,102	24,887	26,942

Source: County Business Patterns 1994/95, CBP-94/95, U.S. Department of Commerce, Washington DC, November 1997. The employment column represents mid-March employment in the year. Pay per employee is calculated by dividing 1st Quarter payroll, annualized, by mid-March employment. The column headed 'Emp / Est' shows 'employees per establishment'. A dash (-) means that data are unavailable or cannot be calculated. nec means not elsewhere classified. *Notes:* 1. 1994 data incomplete; unavailable or withheld. 2. 1995 data incomplete; unavailable or withheld. 3. 1994 and 1995 data incomplete; unavailable or withheld.

KENOSHA, WI PMSA

Wholesale and Retail Trade USA	Establishments		Employment		Emp / Est	Pay / Employee		Annual Payroll ($ 000)	
	1994	1995	1994	1995	1995	1994	1995	1994	1995
50– Wholesale trade	-	145	-	3,093	21	-	37,790	-	117,045
5015 Motor vehicle parts, used	-	4	-	51	13	-	24,235	-	1,446
5030 Lumber and construction materials	-	8	-	89	11	-	26,787	-	3,686
5045 Computers, peripherals, & software	-	3	-	32	11	-	31,625	-	1,165
5070 Hardware, plumbing & heating equipment	-	8	-	168	21	-	40,286	-	6,792
5082 Construction and mining machinery	-	3	-	10	3	-	17,200	-	260
5084 Industrial machinery and equipment	-	11	-	167	15	-	45,509	-	6,978
5085 Industrial supplies	-	4	-	21	5	-	24,571	-	495
5091 Sporting & recreational goods	-	5	-	61	12	-	38,820	-	1,971

Continued on next page.

KENOSHA, WI PMSA - [continued]

Wholesale and Retail Trade USA	Establishments		Employment		Emp / Est	Pay / Employee		Annual Payroll ($ 000)	
	1994	1995	1994	1995	1995	1994	1995	1994	1995
5112 Stationery and office supplies	-	3	-	11	4	-	26,909	-	171
5113 Industrial & personal service paper	-	3	-	31	10	-	40,774	-	1,176
5143 Dairy products, exc. dried or canned	-	6	-	146	24	-	22,740	-	3,101
5149 Groceries and related products, nec	-	7	-	157	22	-	22,726	-	3,950
5169 Chemicals & allied products, nec	-	5	-	23	5	-	38,609	-	1,006
5180 Beer, wine, and distilled beverages	-	5	-	100	20	-	26,360	-	2,880
5199 Nondurable goods, nec	-	5	-	20	4	-	8,400	-	140
52 – Retail trade	-	817	-	11,730	14	-	10,442	-	126,951
5210 Lumber and other building materials	-	7	-	98	14	-	17,878	-	2,005
5230 Paint, glass, and wallpaper stores	-	3	-	9	3	-	20,000	-	192
5250 Hardware stores	-	8	-	184	23	-	8,217	-	1,567
5260 Retail nurseries and garden stores	-	5	-	28	6	-	16,143	-	464
5310 Department stores	-	6	-	972	162	-	11,160	-	10,645
5330 Variety stores	-	4	-	68	17	-	7,059	-	521
5410 Grocery stores	-	39	-	1,369	35	-	11,585	-	16,748
5460 Retail bakeries	-	12	-	90	8	-	9,067	-	875
5490 Miscellaneous food stores	-	4	-	18	5	-	7,778	-	166
5510 New and used car dealers	-	8	-	356	45	-	21,798	-	8,631
5520 Used car dealers	-	12	-	46	4	-	18,522	-	920
5530 Auto and home supply stores	-	10	-	63	6	-	20,190	-	1,344
5540 Gasoline service stations	-	61	-	499	8	-	10,389	-	5,447
5550 Boat dealers	-	6	-	60	10	-	15,667	-	1,509
5570 Motorcycle dealers	-	4	-	30	8	-	15,600	-	598
5610 Men's & boys' clothing stores	-	19	-	152	8	-	9,184	-	1,361
5620 Women's clothing stores	-	32	-	267	8	-	8,300	-	2,259
5630 Women's accessory & specialty stores	-	3	-	18	6	-	9,111	-	150
5640 Children's and infants' wear stores	-	4	-	34	9	-	8,706	-	363
5650 Family clothing stores	-	23	-	233	10	-	9,717	-	2,318
5660 Shoe stores	-	24	-	209	9	-	8,325	-	2,005
5690 Misc. apparel & accessory stores	-	9	-	55	6	-	7,345	-	571
5712 Furniture stores	-	12	-	69	6	-	23,420	-	1,622
5713 Floor covering stores	-	12	-	63	5	-	12,444	-	924
5714 Drapery and upholstery stores	-	6	-	10	2	-	9,600	-	81
5719 Misc. homefurnishings stores	-	19	-	119	6	-	9,546	-	1,319
5720 Household appliance stores	-	4	-	36	9	-	19,000	-	725
5735 Record & prerecorded tape stores	-	4	-	21	5	-	13,524	-	317
5812 Eating places	-	164	-	3,549	22	-	7,021	-	25,960
5813 Drinking places	-	76	-	324	4	-	5,790	-	1,844
5910 Drug stores and proprietary stores	-	14	-	247	18	-	15,320	-	3,928
5920 Liquor stores	-	9	-	77	9	-	7,065	-	756
5930 Used merchandise stores	-	3	-	20	7	-	8,200	-	148
5941 Sporting goods and bicycle shops	-	13	-	159	12	-	10,264	-	1,855
5944 Jewelry stores	-	6	-	39	7	-	25,333	-	763
5945 Hobby, toy, and game shops	-	7	-	37	5	-	9,514	-	335
5947 Gift, novelty, and souvenir shops	-	9	-	71	8	-	10,535	-	821
5948 Luggage and leather goods stores	-	5	-	30	6	-	10,133	-	342
5992 Florists	-	10	-	92	9	-	9,609	-	806
5999 Miscellaneous retail stores, nec	-	25	-	88	4	-	12,364	-	1,289

Source: County Business Patterns 1994/95, CBP-94/95, U.S. Department of Commerce, Washington DC, November 1997. The employment column represents mid-March employment in the year. Pay per employee is calculated by dividing 1st Quarter payroll, annualized, by mid-March employment. The column headed 'Emp / Est' shows 'employees per establishment'. A dash (-) means that data are unavailable or cannot be calculated. nec means not elsewhere classified. *Notes:* 1. 1994 data incomplete; unavailable or withheld. 2. 1995 data incomplete; unavailable or withheld. 3. 1994 and 1995 data incomplete; unavailable or withheld.

KILLEEN – TEMPLE, TX MSA

Wholesale and Retail Trade USA	Establishments		Employment		Emp / Est	Pay / Employee		Annual Payroll ($ 000)	
	1994	1995	1994	1995	1995	1994	1995	1994	1995
50 – Wholesale trade	-	196	-	3,310	17	-	28,021	-	94,342
5012 Automobiles and other vehicles [2]	-	9	-	129	14	-	20,341	-	2,545
5013 Motor vehicle supplies and new parts	-	18	-	142	8	-	19,268	-	4,543
5039 Construction materials, nec [2]	-	4	-	38	10	-	22,737	-	796
5044 Office equipment [2]	-	7	-	61	9	-	22,951	-	1,461
5051 Metals service centers and offices [2]	-	3	-	41	14	-	21,073	-	976
5063 Electrical apparatus and equipment [2]	-	5	-	47	9	-	28,511	-	1,487
5072 Hardware [2]	-	3	-	18	6	-	21,778	-	397
5075 Warm air heating & air conditioning [2]	-	4	-	17	4	-	21,176	-	425
5083 Farm and garden machinery [2]	-	4	-	68	17	-	18,765	-	1,482
5085 Industrial supplies [2]	-	5	-	24	5	-	29,333	-	744
5087 Service establishment equipment [2]	-	4	-	52	13	-	15,769	-	831

Continued on next page.

KILLEEN - TEMPLE, TX MSA - [continued]

Wholesale and Retail Trade USA	Establishments		Employment		Emp / Est	Pay / Employee		Annual Payroll ($ 000)	
	1994	1995	1994	1995	1995	1994	1995	1994	1995
5091 Sporting & recreational goods[2]	-	3	-	13	4	-	10,462	-	137
5093 Scrap and waste materials[2]	-	5	-	12	2	-	19,000	-	313
5110 Paper and paper products	-	8	-	62	8	-	18,452	-	1,409
5140 Groceries and related products[2]	-	12	-	387	32	-	31,504	-	11,262
5153 Grain and field beans[2]	-	4	-	24	6	-	11,000	-	343
5160 Chemicals and allied products	-	7	-	114	16	-	23,649	-	3,025
5170 Petroleum and petroleum products	-	9	-	54	6	-	17,556	-	1,009
5181 Beer and ale[2]	-	3	-	125	42	-	39,008	-	4,523
5190 Misc., nondurable goods	-	19	-	969	51	-	26,547	-	27,464
52- Retail trade	-	1,345	-	17,659	13	-	12,746	-	239,711
5210 Lumber and other building materials	-	20	-	280	14	-	18,314	-	6,035
5230 Paint, glass, and wallpaper stores	-	9	-	64	7	-	16,938	-	1,127
5260 Retail nurseries and garden stores	-	14	-	66	5	-	15,333	-	823
5310 Department stores[2]	-	15	-	2,030	135	-	12,841	-	25,699
5330 Variety stores	-	9	-	57	6	-	7,860	-	492
5390 Misc. general merchandise stores	-	12	-	249	21	-	13,478	-	3,572
5410 Grocery stores	-	141	-	2,286	16	-	15,111	-	36,390
5420 Meat and fish markets[2]	-	4	-	20	5	-	9,200	-	218
5460 Retail bakeries	-	11	-	54	5	-	7,852	-	486
5490 Miscellaneous food stores	-	5	-	23	5	-	7,652	-	191
5510 New and used car dealers	-	26	-	1,055	41	-	24,516	-	32,170
5520 Used car dealers	-	40	-	128	3	-	18,969	-	2,213
5530 Auto and home supply stores	-	60	-	437	7	-	15,140	-	6,973
5540 Gasoline service stations	-	98	-	612	6	-	12,464	-	7,987
5550 Boat dealers	-	5	-	40	8	-	9,400	-	418
5570 Motorcycle dealers[2]	-	5	-	29	6	-	20,000	-	807
5610 Men's & boys' clothing stores[2]	-	7	-	37	5	-	7,459	-	258
5620 Women's clothing stores	-	34	-	218	6	-	8,349	-	1,786
5630 Women's accessory & specialty stores	-	8	-	30	4	-	6,667	-	195
5650 Family clothing stores	-	16	-	202	13	-	8,594	-	1,795
5660 Shoe stores[2]	-	21	-	118	6	-	9,085	-	1,211
5712 Furniture stores	-	32	-	257	8	-	25,230	-	5,033
5713 Floor covering stores	-	10	-	35	4	-	17,714	-	691
5719 Misc. homefurnishings stores[2]	-	7	-	14	2	-	6,000	-	105
5720 Household appliance stores[2]	-	5	-	20	4	-	19,800	-	516
5731 Radio, TV, & electronic stores	-	24	-	134	6	-	18,716	-	2,911
5734 Computer and software stores	-	6	-	13	2	-	9,846	-	192
5735 Record & prerecorded tape stores	-	8	-	44	6	-	9,273	-	469
5736 Musical instrument stores[2]	-	5	-	16	3	-	17,500	-	329
5812 Eating places	-	262	-	5,373	21	-	7,507	-	41,314
5813 Drinking places	-	36	-	359	10	-	5,905	-	2,280
5910 Drug stores and proprietary stores	-	16	-	153	10	-	18,327	-	2,687
5920 Liquor stores	-	10	-	37	4	-	13,514	-	488
5930 Used merchandise stores	-	42	-	176	4	-	12,568	-	2,353
5941 Sporting goods and bicycle shops	-	16	-	43	3	-	8,930	-	476
5942 Book stores	-	12	-	51	4	-	7,843	-	471
5943 Stationery stores	-	7	-	30	4	-	13,733	-	381
5944 Jewelry stores[2]	-	20	-	153	8	-	12,261	-	1,882
5945 Hobby, toy, and game shops[2]	-	8	-	127	16	-	8,220	-	1,274
5947 Gift, novelty, and souvenir shops	-	32	-	137	4	-	8,146	-	1,231
5961 Catalog and mail-order houses[2]	-	4	-	21	5	-	7,810	-	220
5962 Merchandising machine operators[2]	-	5	-	29	6	-	12,966	-	493
5963 Direct selling establishments	-	12	-	58	5	-	16,759	-	1,037
5992 Florists	-	25	-	125	5	-	9,440	-	1,162
5995 Optical goods stores	-	25	-	153	6	-	13,882	-	2,085
5999 Miscellaneous retail stores, nec	-	28	-	74	3	-	8,973	-	735

Source: County Business Patterns 1994/95, CBP-94/95, U.S. Department of Commerce, Washington DC, November 1997. The employment column represents mid-March employment in the year. Pay per employee is calculated by dividing 1st Quarter payroll, annualized, by mid-March employment. The column headed 'Emp / Est' shows 'employees per establishment'. A dash (-) means that data are unavailable or cannot be calculated. nec means not elsewhere classified. *Notes:* 1. 1994 data incomplete; unavailable or withheld. 2. 1995 data incomplete; unavailable or withheld. 3. 1994 and 1995 data incomplete; unavailable or withheld.

KNOXVILLE, TN MSA

Wholesale and Retail Trade USA	Establishments		Employment		Emp / Est	Pay / Employee		Annual Payroll ($ 000)	
	1994	1995	1994	1995	1995	1994	1995	1994	1995
50- Wholesale trade	-	1,365	-	16,608	12	-	27,880	-	501,196
5012 Automobiles and other vehicles[2]	-	17	-	560	33	-	26,929	-	15,485
5013 Motor vehicle supplies and new parts[2]	-	77	-	713	9	-	20,011	-	15,231
5014 Tires and tubes[2]	-	19	-	140	7	-	22,943	-	3,544

Continued on next page.

KNOXVILLE, TN MSA - [continued]

Wholesale and Retail Trade USA	Establishments		Employment		Emp / Est	Pay / Employee		Annual Payroll ($ 000)	
	1994	1995	1994	1995	1995	1994	1995	1994	1995
5015 Motor vehicle parts, used [2]	-	30	-	67	2	-	18,209	-	1,619
5021 Furniture [2]	-	18	-	230	13	-	33,983	-	7,921
5031 Lumber, plywood, and millwork [2]	-	29	-	333	11	-	31,315	-	10,436
5032 Brick, stone, & related materials [2]	-	9	-	64	7	-	28,563	-	1,832
5033 Roofing, siding, & insulation [2]	-	10	-	60	6	-	29,467	-	1,880
5039 Construction materials, nec [2]	-	24	-	339	14	-	28,625	-	9,854
5043 Photographic equipment & supplies [2]	-	5	-	78	16	-	34,051	-	2,857
5044 Office equipment [2]	-	34	-	406	12	-	33,507	-	12,572
5045 Computers, peripherals, & software [2]	-	46	-	489	11	-	39,648	-	18,820
5046 Commercial equipment, nec [2]	-	15	-	104	7	-	24,423	-	3,119
5047 Medical and hospital equipment [2]	-	39	-	319	8	-	35,536	-	10,894
5048 Ophthalmic goods [2]	-	10	-	82	8	-	15,756	-	1,310
5049 Professional equipment, nec [2]	-	12	-	105	9	-	23,962	-	3,031
5051 Metals service centers and offices [2]	-	29	-	285	10	-	25,811	-	8,364
5052 Coal and other minerals and ores [2]	-	13	-	41	3	-	49,171	-	2,843
5063 Electrical apparatus and equipment [2]	-	66	-	618	9	-	36,757	-	22,477
5064 Electrical appliances, TV & radios [2]	-	12	-	164	14	-	27,098	-	4,289
5065 Electronic parts and equipment [2]	-	36	-	241	7	-	35,353	-	10,165
5072 Hardware [2]	-	20	-	282	14	-	25,305	-	8,619
5074 Plumbing & hydronic heating supplies [2]	-	24	-	298	12	-	25,329	-	8,505
5075 Warm air heating & air conditioning [2]	-	33	-	347	11	-	47,285	-	17,880
5078 Refrigeration equipment and supplies [2]	-	6	-	30	5	-	22,133	-	722
5082 Construction and mining machinery [2]	-	20	-	396	20	-	36,859	-	16,229
5083 Farm and garden machinery [2]	-	19	-	96	5	-	22,167	-	2,345
5084 Industrial machinery and equipment	-	94	-	795	8	-	31,190	-	28,885
5085 Industrial supplies [2]	-	59	-	501	8	-	27,816	-	16,252
5087 Service establishment equipment [2]	-	21	-	287	14	-	30,495	-	9,719
5088 Transportation equipment & supplies [2]	-	7	-	11	2	-	17,455	-	169
5091 Sporting & recreational goods [2]	-	18	-	113	6	-	30,407	-	3,745
5092 Toys and hobby goods and supplies [2]	-	8	-	6	1	-	16,000	-	129
5093 Scrap and waste materials [2]	-	24	-	177	7	-	29,446	-	6,366
5094 Jewelry & precious stones [2]	-	13	-	75	6	-	18,667	-	1,899
5099 Durable goods, nec [2]	-	19	-	70	4	-	14,971	-	828
5111 Printing and writing paper [2]	-	9	-	59	7	-	39,864	-	2,378
5112 Stationery and office supplies [2]	-	35	-	266	8	-	26,632	-	7,424
5113 Industrial & personal service paper [2]	-	12	-	193	16	-	29,534	-	6,030
5120 Drugs, proprietaries, and sundries [2]	-	14	-	338	24	-	23,680	-	7,798
5131 Piece goods & notions [2]	-	10	-	38	4	-	22,211	-	800
5136 Men's and boys' clothing [2]	-	10	-	52	5	-	16,692	-	977
5141 Groceries, general line [2]	-	11	-	265	24	-	24,453	-	6,183
5144 Poultry and poultry products [2]	-	3	-	56	19	-	19,714	-	1,309
5145 Confectionery [2]	-	8	-	165	21	-	29,503	-	5,310
5147 Meats and meat products [2]	-	4	-	53	13	-	17,887	-	1,218
5148 Fresh fruits and vegetables [2]	-	17	-	350	21	-	20,846	-	8,685
5149 Groceries and related products, nec [2]	-	27	-	416	15	-	35,077	-	17,465
5159 Farm-product raw materials, nec [2]	-	3	-	23	8	-	17,739	-	369
5162 Plastics materials & basic shapes [2]	-	10	-	74	7	-	22,162	-	1,766
5169 Chemicals & allied products, nec [2]	-	31	-	178	6	-	27,708	-	5,754
5171 Petroleum bulk stations & terminals	-	28	-	323	12	-	23,777	-	10,509
5172 Petroleum products, nec [2]	-	14	-	86	6	-	21,767	-	2,690
5181 Beer and ale [2]	-	5	-	280	56	-	26,043	-	8,717
5182 Wine and distilled beverages [2]	-	4	-	112	28	-	36,643	-	5,939
5191 Farm supplies	-	17	-	156	9	-	20,333	-	3,105
5192 Books, periodicals, & newspapers [2]	-	9	-	546	61	-	12,608	-	7,221
5193 Flowers & florists' supplies [2]	-	16	-	142	9	-	20,704	-	2,959
5198 Paints, varnishes, and supplies [2]	-	7	-	33	5	-	25,212	-	779
5199 Nondurable goods, nec	-	44	-	240	5	-	17,367	-	4,837
52 - Retail trade	-	4,640	-	69,676	15	-	12,721	-	966,389
5210 Lumber and other building materials [2]	-	81	-	1,650	20	-	22,361	-	38,545
5230 Paint, glass, and wallpaper stores [2]	-	34	-	122	4	-	22,951	-	3,273
5250 Hardware stores [2]	-	39	-	243	6	-	15,029	-	4,186
5260 Retail nurseries and garden stores [2]	-	33	-	262	8	-	11,756	-	4,030
5270 Mobile home dealers [2]	-	21	-	136	6	-	28,824	-	4,580
5310 Department stores [2]	-	32	-	5,022	157	-	12,428	-	62,990
5330 Variety stores [2]	-	34	-	284	8	-	8,873	-	2,878
5390 Misc. general merchandise stores [2]	-	49	-	1,146	23	-	12,635	-	13,670
5410 Grocery stores [2]	-	459	-	9,853	21	-	9,105	-	91,914
5420 Meat and fish markets [2]	-	7	-	10	1	-	11,200	-	117
5430 Fruit and vegetable markets [2]	-	19	-	81	4	-	9,630	-	971
5440 Candy, nut, and confectionery stores [2]	-	25	-	177	7	-	12,791	-	2,951
5460 Retail bakeries [2]	-	31	-	197	6	-	9,096	-	1,937

Continued on next page.

KNOXVILLE, TN MSA - [continued]

Wholesale and Retail Trade USA	Establishments 1994	Establishments 1995	Employment 1994	Employment 1995	Emp / Est 1995	Pay / Employee 1994	Pay / Employee 1995	Annual Payroll ($ 000) 1994	Annual Payroll ($ 000) 1995
5490 Miscellaneous food stores [2]	-	21	-	58	3	-	8,483	-	509
5510 New and used car dealers [2]	-	62	-	3,443	56	-	31,108	-	125,060
5520 Used car dealers	-	76	-	231	3	-	18,442	-	4,404
5530 Auto and home supply stores	-	127	-	1,018	8	-	17,827	-	19,239
5540 Gasoline service stations	-	270	-	2,256	8	-	11,410	-	27,352
5550 Boat dealers [2]	-	12	-	52	4	-	21,077	-	1,344
5560 Recreational vehicle dealers [2]	-	12	-	326	27	-	34,147	-	11,892
5570 Motorcycle dealers [2]	-	9	-	34	4	-	18,353	-	964
5610 Men's & boys' clothing stores [2]	-	43	-	416	10	-	10,481	-	4,726
5620 Women's clothing stores [2]	-	137	-	1,065	8	-	9,202	-	9,728
5630 Women's accessory & specialty stores [2]	-	27	-	130	5	-	10,892	-	1,525
5640 Children's and infants' wear stores [2]	-	17	-	99	6	-	9,899	-	971
5650 Family clothing stores	-	72	-	1,104	15	-	11,569	-	13,275
5660 Shoe stores [2]	-	105	-	687	7	-	11,592	-	7,311
5690 Misc. apparel & accessory stores [2]	-	46	-	189	4	-	10,349	-	2,493
5712 Furniture stores [2]	-	87	-	670	8	-	20,967	-	14,238
5713 Floor covering stores	-	28	-	127	5	-	27,118	-	3,937
5714 Drapery and upholstery stores [2]	-	5	-	29	6	-	14,483	-	440
5719 Misc. homefurnishings stores [2]	-	77	-	586	8	-	12,546	-	8,555
5720 Household appliance stores	-	34	-	100	3	-	17,240	-	1,940
5731 Radio, TV, & electronic stores [2]	-	57	-	493	9	-	17,712	-	9,531
5734 Computer and software stores [2]	-	22	-	97	4	-	23,299	-	2,213
5735 Record & prerecorded tape stores [2]	-	31	-	197	6	-	11,289	-	1,947
5736 Musical instrument stores [2]	-	15	-	64	4	-	17,563	-	1,266
5812 Eating places	-	849	-	21,836	26	-	8,141	-	198,088
5813 Drinking places [2]	-	35	-	280	8	-	10,186	-	2,631
5910 Drug stores and proprietary stores	-	130	-	1,471	11	-	17,523	-	28,438
5920 Liquor stores [2]	-	59	-	235	4	-	13,430	-	3,136
5930 Used merchandise stores [2]	-	68	-	433	6	-	9,589	-	4,431
5941 Sporting goods and bicycle shops [2]	-	59	-	341	6	-	12,152	-	4,485
5942 Book stores [2]	-	112	-	744	7	-	9,957	-	8,397
5943 Stationery stores [2]	-	12	-	37	3	-	8,973	-	336
5944 Jewelry stores	-	81	-	431	5	-	15,805	-	8,045
5945 Hobby, toy, and game shops [2]	-	41	-	262	6	-	9,649	-	3,096
5947 Gift, novelty, and souvenir shops	-	176	-	933	5	-	8,789	-	13,055
5948 Luggage and leather goods stores [2]	-	10	-	43	4	-	15,535	-	706
5949 Sewing, needlework, and piece goods [2]	-	28	-	148	5	-	9,405	-	1,486
5961 Catalog and mail-order houses [2]	-	16	-	311	19	-	21,878	-	6,612
5962 Merchandising machine operators [2]	-	33	-	367	11	-	16,131	-	6,417
5963 Direct selling establishments [2]	-	32	-	400	13	-	15,340	-	6,664
5984 Liquefied petroleum gas dealers [2]	-	11	-	17	2	-	27,529	-	392
5992 Florists	-	72	-	431	6	-	9,847	-	4,639
5993 Tobacco stores and stands [2]	-	6	-	11	2	-	8,727	-	110
5995 Optical goods stores [2]	-	31	-	158	5	-	15,949	-	2,606
5999 Miscellaneous retail stores, nec	-	168	-	637	4	-	12,163	-	9,856

Source: County Business Patterns 1994/95, CBP-94/95, U.S. Department of Commerce, Washington DC, November 1997. The employment column represents mid-March employment in the year. Pay per employee is calculated by dividing 1st Quarter payroll, annualized, by mid-March employment. The column headed 'Emp / Est' shows 'employees per establishment'. A dash (-) means that data are unavailable or cannot be calculated. nec means not elsewhere classified. *Notes:* 1. 1994 data incomplete; unavailable or withheld. 2. 1995 data incomplete; unavailable or withheld. 3. 1994 and 1995 data incomplete; unavailable or withheld.

KOKOMO, IN MSA

Wholesale and Retail Trade USA	Establishments 1994	Establishments 1995	Employment 1994	Employment 1995	Emp / Est 1995	Pay / Employee 1994	Pay / Employee 1995	Annual Payroll ($ 000) 1994	Annual Payroll ($ 000) 1995
50- Wholesale trade	137	148	1,045	1,268	9	24,750	28,861	29,933	40,944
5013 Motor vehicle supplies and new parts	8	8	51	46	6	16,314	16,087	827	725
5030 Lumber and construction materials [2]	-	5	-	43	9	-	29,302	-	1,603
5044 Office equipment	-	5	-	10	2	-	12,000	-	125
5045 Computers, peripherals, & software [2]	-	4	-	30	8	-	26,800	-	956
5051 Metals service centers and offices	-	7	-	56	8	-	29,786	-	1,797
5063 Electrical apparatus and equipment [2]	-	6	-	60	10	-	29,933	-	1,834
5065 Electronic parts and equipment [1]	16	20	103	111	6	47,573	53,658	5,405	6,883
5074 Plumbing & hydronic heating supplies [3]	6	4	42	41	10	18,571	23,317	852	1,025
5083 Farm and garden machinery	4	4	40	45	11	24,600	25,156	1,179	1,171
5085 Industrial supplies [3]	8	8	74	81	10	27,351	29,926	2,285	2,462
5087 Service establishment equipment [3]	6	5	34	23	5	15,882	21,391	537	523
5099 Durable goods, nec	4	4	9	8	2	8,000	8,500	80	66
5110 Paper and paper products [2]	-	3	-	4	1	-	24,000	-	104
5149 Groceries and related products, nec [3]	3	3	55	58	19	25,673	26,690	1,524	1,725

Continued on next page.

KOKOMO, IN MSA - [continued]

Wholesale and Retail Trade USA	Establishments		Employment		Emp / Est	Pay / Employee		Annual Payroll ($ 000)	
	1994	1995	1994	1995	1995	1994	1995	1994	1995
5153 Grain and field beans	11	-	71	-	-	22,197	-	1,856	-
5160 Chemicals and allied products	4	-	3	-	-	16,000	-	50	-
5191 Farm supplies	5	-	57	-	-	29,754	-	2,501	-
52- Retail trade	660	654	9,515	9,973	15	10,806	12,067	113,076	123,900
5210 Lumber and other building materials	13	15	353	328	22	14,674	18,085	5,785	5,808
5230 Paint, glass, and wallpaper stores [3]	5	4	26	19	5	16,000	16,842	440	323
5250 Hardware stores [3]	8	7	34	35	5	8,471	8,229	316	268
5260 Retail nurseries and garden stores	5	5	15	32	6	22,133	7,250	285	308
5310 Department stores [3]	9	10	1,053	1,317	132	9,751	12,106	11,876	18,516
5330 Variety stores	7	7	69	78	11	9,391	7,846	721	521
5390 Misc. general merchandise stores	10	10	214	206	21	10,224	12,233	2,373	2,353
5410 Grocery stores	44	44	1,041	1,108	25	12,984	13,206	13,093	13,848
5420 Meat and fish markets [2]	-	4	-	31	8	-	9,935	-	296
5460 Retail bakeries [3]	8	8	60	53	7	7,000	7,019	469	403
5490 Miscellaneous food stores [3]	3	3	21	11	4	4,571	9,091	93	99
5510 New and used car dealers	9	9	402	395	44	30,985	33,863	13,645	13,911
5520 Used car dealers	13	12	30	43	4	20,133	21,209	674	1,159
5530 Auto and home supply stores	21	22	144	140	6	16,167	17,943	2,495	2,560
5540 Gasoline service stations	43	44	357	308	7	8,896	11,104	3,437	3,590
5560 Recreational vehicle dealers [1]	3	-	14	-	-	8,571	-	210	-
5570 Motorcycle dealers [3]	3	3	3	9	3	20,000	19,111	89	197
5620 Women's clothing stores [3]	23	18	207	150	8	6,531	6,907	1,475	1,010
5630 Women's accessory & specialty stores [3]	4	3	13	11	4	6,462	8,000	88	82
5650 Family clothing stores [3]	4	4	71	68	17	8,507	9,529	598	713
5660 Shoe stores [3]	16	15	108	92	6	10,519	11,217	1,132	1,062
5690 Misc. apparel & accessory stores [3]	3	3	3	2	1	6,667	10,000	24	21
5712 Furniture stores	15	16	93	91	6	14,839	15,560	1,542	1,723
5713 Floor covering stores	6	5	30	36	7	16,933	21,444	716	834
5720 Household appliance stores [3]	5	5	56	61	12	22,429	21,443	1,281	1,312
5731 Radio, TV, & electronic stores [2]	-	5	-	19	4	-	13,053	-	267
5736 Musical instrument stores [1]	3	-	17	-	-	14,588	-	222	-
5812 Eating places	160	153	3,472	3,554	23	7,033	7,804	27,313	28,052
5813 Drinking places	37	31	210	256	8	6,857	6,844	1,606	1,666
5910 Drug stores and proprietary stores	17	20	240	260	13	15,150	16,631	4,071	4,580
5920 Liquor stores	17	16	86	92	6	9,209	10,000	795	1,024
5930 Used merchandise stores	-	10	-	47	5	-	7,064	-	372
5941 Sporting goods and bicycle shops [2]	6	7	10	33	5	15,600	11,152	211	364
5944 Jewelry stores [3]	11	13	83	74	6	11,470	15,459	1,078	1,259
5945 Hobby, toy, and game shops [3]	5	7	13	14	2	7,385	10,000	124	129
5947 Gift, novelty, and souvenir shops	15	13	70	65	5	6,000	6,831	479	477
5949 Sewing, needlework, and piece goods [3]	5	5	50	44	9	5,920	6,273	347	275
5960 Nonstore retailers [3]	4	4	15	94	24	21,333	20,723	1,065	2,036
5992 Florists	14	13	101	112	9	6,931	6,321	747	725
5995 Optical goods stores	9	9	37	37	4	14,919	16,108	638	605
5999 Miscellaneous retail stores, nec	24	23	71	75	3	7,944	9,280	623	740

Source: County Business Patterns 1994/95, CBP-94/95, U.S. Department of Commerce, Washington DC, November 1997. The employment column represents mid-March employment in the year. Pay per employee is calculated by dividing 1st Quarter payroll, annualized, by mid-March employment. The column headed 'Emp / Est' shows 'employees per establishment'. A dash (-) means that data are unavailable or cannot be calculated. nec means not elsewhere classified. *Notes:* 1. 1994 data incomplete; unavailable or withheld. 2. 1995 data incomplete; unavailable or withheld. 3. 1994 and 1995 data incomplete; unavailable or withheld.

LA CROSSE MSA (MN PART)

Wholesale and Retail Trade USA	Establishments		Employment		Emp / Est	Pay / Employee		Annual Payroll ($ 000)	
	1994	1995	1994	1995	1995	1994	1995	1994	1995
50- Wholesale trade	34	32	286	267	8	14,909	16,015	4,648	4,435
5010 Motor vehicles, parts, and supplies	3	-	6	-	-	19,333	-	146	-
5080 Machinery, equipment, and supplies	7	7	47	51	7	20,000	21,647	1,139	1,218
5150 Farm-product raw materials	5	4	69	48	12	14,319	15,083	958	669
5171 Petroleum bulk stations & terminals	3	-	12	-	-	16,333	-	205	-
5190 Misc., nondurable goods	8	7	97	79	11	13,113	13,367	1,423	1,100
52- Retail trade	94	102	671	728	7	8,000	8,055	5,894	6,017
5250 Hardware stores	7	6	30	28	5	4,933	6,429	171	165
5300 General merchandise stores	3	-	14	-	-	6,571	-	100	-
5400 Food stores	10	10	165	161	16	6,473	6,683	1,133	923
5510 New and used car dealers	-	3	-	41	14	-	19,220	-	816
5540 Gasoline service stations	14	14	117	125	9	11,453	11,072	1,417	1,430
5812 Eating places	22	21	170	159	8	4,588	4,453	867	770
5813 Drinking places	6	7	25	30	4	3,840	3,600	149	103
5910 Drug stores and proprietary stores	3	3	17	15	5	6,353	7,733	113	121

Continued on next page.

LA CROSSE MSA (MN PART) - [continued]

Wholesale and Retail Trade USA	Establishments		Employment		Emp / Est	Pay / Employee		Annual Payroll ($ 000)	
	1994	1995	1994	1995	1995	1994	1995	1994	1995
5920 Liquor stores	4	4	53	53	13	9,132	9,358	574	590
5940 Miscellaneous shopping goods stores	3	5	4	3	1	3,000	5,333	13	38
5992 Florists	4	4	17	18	5	4,471	4,889	88	90

Source: County Business Patterns 1994/95, CBP-94/95, U.S. Department of Commerce, Washington DC, November 1997. The employment column represents mid-March employment in the year. Pay per employee is calculated by dividing 1st Quarter payroll, annualized, by mid-March employment. The column headed 'Emp / Est' shows 'employees per establishment'. A dash (-) means that data are unavailable or cannot be calculated. nec means not elsewhere classified. *Notes:* 1. 1994 data incomplete; unavailable or withheld. 2. 1995 data incomplete; unavailable or withheld. 3. 1994 and 1995 data incomplete; unavailable or withheld.

LA CROSSE MSA (WI PART)

Wholesale and Retail Trade USA	Establishments		Employment		Emp / Est	Pay / Employee		Annual Payroll ($ 000)	
	1994	1995	1994	1995	1995	1994	1995	1994	1995
50- Wholesale trade	-	192	-	4,675	24	-	27,282	-	133,623
5012 Automobiles and other vehicles	-	7	-	181	26	-	22,541	-	4,891
5013 Motor vehicle supplies and new parts	-	9	-	131	15	-	22,809	-	3,185
5023 Homefurnishings	-	3	-	22	7	-	16,909	-	401
5031 Lumber, plywood, and millwork	-	8	-	160	20	-	32,000	-	5,304
5044 Office equipment	-	9	-	104	12	-	30,500	-	3,781
5045 Computers, peripherals, & software	-	11	-	76	7	-	27,895	-	2,218
5063 Electrical apparatus and equipment	-	4	-	120	30	-	29,400	-	3,543
5072 Hardware	-	7	-	251	36	-	15,474	-	4,062
5083 Farm and garden machinery	-	4	-	39	10	-	22,974	-	1,201
5084 Industrial machinery and equipment	-	6	-	43	7	-	34,140	-	1,611
5085 Industrial supplies	-	5	-	62	12	-	31,226	-	2,347
5093 Scrap and waste materials	-	7	-	56	8	-	19,571	-	1,473
5110 Paper and paper products	-	9	-	117	13	-	17,641	-	2,563
5130 Apparel, piece goods, and notions	-	3	-	7	2	-	7,429	-	83
5147 Meats and meat products	-	3	-	43	14	-	20,930	-	980
5149 Groceries and related products, nec	-	8	-	284	36	-	26,141	-	7,851
5160 Chemicals and allied products	-	4	-	25	6	-	34,880	-	891
5180 Beer, wine, and distilled beverages	-	8	-	285	36	-	49,628	-	13,974
5191 Farm supplies	-	12	-	151	13	-	17,987	-	3,014
5199 Nondurable goods, nec	-	8	-	32	4	-	9,375	-	355
52- Retail trade	-	770	-	13,792	18	-	11,187	-	164,886
5210 Lumber and other building materials	-	11	-	232	21	-	20,138	-	5,148
5250 Hardware stores	-	5	-	63	13	-	11,746	-	840
5300 General merchandise stores	-	18	-	1,878	104	-	10,922	-	20,418
5410 Grocery stores	-	32	-	1,458	46	-	10,609	-	16,916
5460 Retail bakeries	-	8	-	80	10	-	8,150	-	720
5490 Miscellaneous food stores	-	6	-	47	8	-	5,277	-	268
5510 New and used car dealers	-	13	-	574	44	-	22,125	-	13,986
5520 Used car dealers	-	10	-	23	2	-	10,783	-	239
5530 Auto and home supply stores	-	13	-	200	15	-	14,540	-	3,086
5540 Gasoline service stations	-	49	-	362	7	-	12,818	-	4,853
5560 Recreational vehicle dealers	-	4	-	28	7	-	15,571	-	629
5610 Men's & boys' clothing stores	-	4	-	16	4	-	9,500	-	146
5620 Women's clothing stores	-	25	-	212	8	-	6,679	-	1,403
5630 Women's accessory & specialty stores	-	5	-	22	4	-	8,727	-	191
5650 Family clothing stores	-	7	-	65	9	-	12,246	-	619
5660 Shoe stores	-	19	-	97	5	-	11,340	-	937
5690 Misc. apparel & accessory stores	-	4	-	26	7	-	7,846	-	280
5712 Furniture stores	-	15	-	129	9	-	15,194	-	2,373
5713 Floor covering stores	-	8	-	55	7	-	21,818	-	1,373
5731 Radio, TV, & electronic stores	-	7	-	126	18	-	14,508	-	1,689
5735 Record & prerecorded tape stores	-	6	-	46	8	-	7,913	-	306
5812 Eating places	-	154	-	4,417	29	-	6,096	-	28,140
5813 Drinking places	-	71	-	442	6	-	5,249	-	2,370
5910 Drug stores and proprietary stores	-	14	-	215	15	-	12,670	-	2,894
5920 Liquor stores	-	5	-	18	4	-	8,444	-	238
5930 Used merchandise stores	-	14	-	45	3	-	5,867	-	284
5941 Sporting goods and bicycle shops	-	23	-	112	5	-	8,464	-	1,029
5942 Book stores	-	10	-	74	7	-	7,784	-	578
5944 Jewelry stores	-	12	-	91	8	-	13,495	-	1,369
5945 Hobby, toy, and game shops	-	11	-	114	10	-	7,368	-	929
5947 Gift, novelty, and souvenir shops	-	14	-	77	6	-	5,922	-	515
5949 Sewing, needlework, and piece goods	-	8	-	50	6	-	7,040	-	323
5963 Direct selling establishments	-	8	-	57	7	-	25,895	-	1,425
5983 Fuel oil dealers	-	4	-	20	5	-	21,400	-	434
5984 Liquefied petroleum gas dealers	-	3	-	67	22	-	25,015	-	1,466

Continued on next page.

LA CROSSE MSA (WI PART) - [continued]

Wholesale and Retail Trade USA	Establishments		Employment		Emp / Est	Pay / Employee		Annual Payroll ($ 000)	
	1994	1995	1994	1995	1995	1994	1995	1994	1995
5992 Florists	-	12	-	99	8	-	7,960	-	820
5995 Optical goods stores	-	5	-	42	8	-	15,238	-	537
5999 Miscellaneous retail stores, nec	-	20	-	141	7	-	13,021	-	2,112

Source: County Business Patterns 1994/95, CBP-94/95, U.S. Department of Commerce, Washington DC, November 1997. The employment column represents mid-March employment in the year. Pay per employee is calculated by dividing 1st Quarter payroll, annualized, by mid-March employment. The column headed 'Emp / Est' shows 'employees per establishment'. A dash (-) means that data are unavailable or cannot be calculated. nec means not elsewhere classified. *Notes:* 1. 1994 data incomplete; unavailable or withheld. 2. 1995 data incomplete; unavailable or withheld. 3. 1994 and 1995 data incomplete; unavailable or withheld.

LA CROSSE, WI - MN MSA

Wholesale and Retail Trade USA	Establishments		Employment		Emp / Est	Pay / Employee		Annual Payroll ($ 000)	
	1994	1995	1994	1995	1995	1994	1995	1994	1995
50 - Wholesale trade [1]	34	224	286	4,942	22	14,909	26,673	4,648	138,058
5012 Automobiles and other vehicles [2]	-	7	-	181	26	-	22,541	-	4,891
5013 Motor vehicle supplies and new parts	-	12	-	131	11	-	22,809	-	3,185
5023 Homefurnishings [2]	-	3	-	22	7	-	16,909	-	401
5031 Lumber, plywood, and millwork	-	10	-	160	16	-	32,000	-	5,304
5044 Office equipment [2]	-	9	-	104	12	-	30,500	-	3,781
5045 Computers, peripherals, & software [2]	-	11	-	76	7	-	27,895	-	2,218
5063 Electrical apparatus and equipment [2]	-	4	-	120	30	-	29,400	-	3,543
5072 Hardware [2]	-	7	-	251	36	-	15,474	-	4,062
5083 Farm and garden machinery	-	9	-	39	4	-	22,974	-	1,201
5084 Industrial machinery and equipment [2]	-	6	-	43	7	-	34,140	-	1,611
5085 Industrial supplies [2]	-	5	-	62	12	-	31,226	-	2,347
5093 Scrap and waste materials [2]	-	7	-	56	8	-	19,571	-	1,473
5110 Paper and paper products [2]	-	9	-	117	13	-	17,641	-	2,563
5130 Apparel, piece goods, and notions	-	4	-	7	2	-	7,429	-	83
5147 Meats and meat products [2]	-	3	-	43	14	-	20,930	-	980
5149 Groceries and related products, nec [2]	-	8	-	284	36	-	26,141	-	7,851
5150 Farm-product raw materials [1]	5	6	69	48	8	14,319	15,083	958	669
5160 Chemicals and allied products [2]	-	4	-	25	6	-	34,880	-	891
5171 Petroleum bulk stations & terminals [1]	3	-	12	-	-	16,333	-	205	-
5180 Beer, wine, and distilled beverages [2]	-	8	-	285	36	-	49,628	-	13,974
5191 Farm supplies	-	17	-	151	9	-	17,987	-	3,014
5199 Nondurable goods, nec	-	9	-	32	4	-	9,375	-	355
52 - Retail trade [1]	94	872	671	14,520	17	8,000	11,030	5,894	170,903
5210 Lumber and other building materials	-	14	-	232	17	-	20,138	-	5,148
5250 Hardware stores [1]	7	11	30	91	8	4,933	10,110	171	1,005
5300 General merchandise stores [1]	3	21	14	1,878	89	6,571	10,922	100	20,418
5410 Grocery stores [2]	-	41	-	1,458	36	-	10,609	-	16,916
5460 Retail bakeries	-	9	-	80	9	-	8,150	-	720
5490 Miscellaneous food stores [2]	-	6	-	47	8	-	5,277	-	268
5510 New and used car dealers	-	16	-	615	38	-	21,932	-	14,802
5520 Used car dealers	-	12	-	23	2	-	10,783	-	239
5530 Auto and home supply stores	-	14	-	200	14	-	14,540	-	3,086
5540 Gasoline service stations [1]	14	63	117	487	8	11,453	12,370	1,417	6,283
5560 Recreational vehicle dealers [2]	-	4	-	28	7	-	15,571	-	629
5610 Men's & boys' clothing stores	-	5	-	16	3	-	9,500	-	146
5620 Women's clothing stores	-	26	-	212	8	-	6,679	-	1,403
5630 Women's accessory & specialty stores [2]	-	5	-	22	4	-	8,727	-	191
5650 Family clothing stores	-	8	-	65	8	-	12,246	-	619
5660 Shoe stores [2]	-	19	-	97	5	-	11,340	-	937
5690 Misc. apparel & accessory stores [2]	-	4	-	26	7	-	7,846	-	280
5712 Furniture stores [2]	-	15	-	129	9	-	15,194	-	2,373
5713 Floor covering stores [2]	-	8	-	55	7	-	21,818	-	1,373
5731 Radio, TV, & electronic stores	-	8	-	126	16	-	14,508	-	1,689
5735 Record & prerecorded tape stores [2]	-	6	-	46	8	-	7,913	-	306
5812 Eating places [1]	22	175	170	4,576	26	4,588	6,038	867	28,910
5813 Drinking places [1]	6	78	25	472	6	3,840	5,144	149	2,473
5910 Drug stores and proprietary stores [1]	3	17	17	230	14	6,353	12,348	113	3,015
5920 Liquor stores [1]	4	9	53	71	8	9,132	9,127	574	828
5930 Used merchandise stores [2]	-	14	-	45	3	-	5,867	-	284
5941 Sporting goods and bicycle shops [2]	-	23	-	112	5	-	8,464	-	1,029
5942 Book stores [2]	-	10	-	74	7	-	7,784	-	578
5944 Jewelry stores	-	14	-	91	7	-	13,495	-	1,369
5945 Hobby, toy, and game shops [2]	-	11	-	114	10	-	7,368	-	929
5947 Gift, novelty, and souvenir shops	-	17	-	77	5	-	5,922	-	515
5949 Sewing, needlework, and piece goods [2]	-	8	-	50	6	-	7,040	-	323
5963 Direct selling establishments [2]	-	8	-	57	7	-	25,895	-	1,425

Continued on next page.

LA CROSSE, WI - MN MSA - [continued]

Wholesale and Retail Trade USA	Establishments		Employment		Emp / Est	Pay / Employee		Annual Payroll ($ 000)	
	1994	1995	1994	1995	1995	1994	1995	1994	1995
5983 Fuel oil dealers	-	5	-	20	4	-	21,400	-	434
5984 Liquefied petroleum gas dealers	-	4	-	67	17	-	25,015	-	1,466
5992 Florists[1]	4	16	17	117	7	4,471	7,487	88	910
5995 Optical goods stores[2]	-	5	-	42	8	-	15,238	-	537
5999 Miscellaneous retail stores, nec[2]	-	20	-	141	7	-	13,021	-	2,112

Source: County Business Patterns 1994/95, CBP-94/95, U.S. Department of Commerce, Washington DC, November 1997. The employment column represents mid-March employment in the year. Pay per employee is calculated by dividing 1st Quarter payroll, annualized, by mid-March employment. The column headed 'Emp / Est' shows 'employees per establishment'. A dash (-) means that data are unavailable or cannot be calculated. nec means not elsewhere classified. *Notes:* 1. 1994 data incomplete; unavailable or withheld. 2. 1995 data incomplete; unavailable or withheld. 3. 1994 and 1995 data incomplete; unavailable or withheld.

LAFAYETTE, IN MSA

Wholesale and Retail Trade USA	Establishments		Employment		Emp / Est	Pay / Employee		Annual Payroll ($ 000)	
	1994	1995	1994	1995	1995	1994	1995	1994	1995
50- Wholesale trade	226	201	2,204	2,063	10	21,370	22,071	51,599	48,937
5013 Motor vehicle supplies and new parts	10	9	100	103	11	22,600	22,485	2,435	2,554
5030 Lumber and construction materials	5	6	29	38	6	21,655	18,632	732	756
5044 Office equipment[3]	4	3	37	21	7	20,865	18,476	685	377
5045 Computers, peripherals, & software	8	-	56	-	-	31,500	-	1,376	-
5049 Professional equipment, nec[3]	3	3	10	12	4	22,800	22,667	252	297
5065 Electronic parts and equipment	-	9	-	66	7	-	24,545	-	1,478
5074 Plumbing & hydronic heating supplies	9	6	78	72	12	31,333	23,667	2,392	1,842
5082 Construction and mining machinery[3]	3	3	19	18	6	32,211	38,222	739	814
5083 Farm and garden machinery	9	10	25	25	3	19,680	20,480	603	608
5084 Industrial machinery and equipment[2]	-	5	-	36	7	-	25,000	-	1,040
5085 Industrial supplies	10	-	53	-	-	16,151	-	1,022	-
5099 Durable goods, nec[3]	9	8	27	20	3	16,741	19,200	497	444
5112 Stationery and office supplies	-	7	-	102	15	-	21,725	-	2,216
5149 Groceries and related products, nec[3]	4	3	152	160	53	17,526	17,400	3,157	3,261
5153 Grain and field beans	16	15	32	27	2	23,125	27,852	708	749
5169 Chemicals & allied products, nec[3]	6	4	42	21	5	43,524	51,619	2,093	906
5171 Petroleum bulk stations & terminals	6	-	14	-	-	21,143	-	288	-
5191 Farm supplies	23	23	40	49	2	20,200	24,163	1,308	1,674
5199 Nondurable goods, nec[1]	6	6	3	4	1	12,000	22,000	45	117
52- Retail trade	940	961	15,021	15,884	17	10,053	11,041	165,536	184,934
5210 Lumber and other building materials	16	16	365	486	30	18,203	20,420	8,177	9,178
5230 Paint, glass, and wallpaper stores	-	5	-	22	4	-	16,727	-	362
5250 Hardware stores[3]	6	5	52	39	8	18,846	23,590	1,077	936
5260 Retail nurseries and garden stores	10	13	74	71	5	11,892	13,070	1,212	1,235
5270 Mobile home dealers[2]	-	3	-	40	13	-	21,900	-	1,154
5310 Department stores[3]	12	13	1,692	2,089	161	8,920	10,392	16,679	24,546
5410 Grocery stores	54	51	1,624	1,778	35	10,956	10,799	17,742	18,823
5440 Candy, nut, and confectionery stores	4	4	24	12	3	4,333	2,000	88	23
5460 Retail bakeries	10	12	76	82	7	7,211	7,659	601	648
5510 New and used car dealers	20	19	714	661	35	25,546	31,268	21,069	22,201
5520 Used car dealers	18	19	80	79	4	21,550	23,899	1,903	2,088
5530 Auto and home supply stores	17	17	163	181	11	13,840	16,199	2,558	3,140
5540 Gasoline service stations	53	51	449	373	7	8,998	11,550	4,400	4,466
5570 Motorcycle dealers[3]	3	3	32	22	7	10,250	13,636	293	313
5610 Men's & boys' clothing stores	7	8	30	42	5	10,267	7,810	363	453
5620 Women's clothing stores	35	28	327	207	7	6,459	7,208	2,115	1,556
5630 Women's accessory & specialty stores[1]	3	-	16	-	-	8,500	-	131	-
5650 Family clothing stores[3]	9	11	111	116	11	6,883	7,310	838	948
5660 Shoe stores	19	20	130	115	6	11,538	13,252	1,438	1,417
5690 Misc. apparel & accessory stores	9	8	4	44	6	5,000	4,727	22	264
5712 Furniture stores	21	19	118	158	8	17,559	16,835	2,150	2,682
5713 Floor covering stores	9	9	69	75	8	20,812	22,613	1,725	1,889
5720 Household appliance stores	6	8	43	69	9	21,023	19,478	1,005	1,322
5731 Radio, TV, & electronic stores	13	12	100	98	8	18,520	18,653	1,826	1,872
5734 Computer and software stores[3]	3	3	11	13	4	9,455	22,769	163	348
5735 Record & prerecorded tape stores[3]	8	8	53	54	7	7,472	7,556	389	381
5736 Musical instrument stores	4	4	31	28	7	16,387	18,143	549	521
5812 Eating places	242	241	5,315	5,545	23	6,826	7,279	39,566	43,089
5813 Drinking places	45	40	547	573	14	7,452	6,799	4,319	4,054
5910 Drug stores and proprietary stores	25	26	326	354	14	12,761	14,068	4,787	5,141
5920 Liquor stores	20	20	111	123	6	7,099	8,943	844	1,165
5941 Sporting goods and bicycle shops	10	13	45	53	4	10,400	12,302	551	858
5942 Book stores	15	17	292	303	18	7,493	7,868	2,343	2,445
5944 Jewelry stores	20	22	105	111	5	12,724	14,234	1,284	1,667

Continued on next page.

LAFAYETTE, IN MSA - [continued]

Wholesale and Retail Trade USA	Establishments		Employment		Emp / Est	Pay / Employee		Annual Payroll ($ 000)	
	1994	1995	1994	1995	1995	1994	1995	1994	1995
5945 Hobby, toy, and game shops[2]	11	9	76	73	8	7,421	8,219	643	706
5947 Gift, novelty, and souvenir shops	20	24	143	140	6	5,958	6,171	1,013	963
5949 Sewing, needlework, and piece goods[3]	6	4	70	60	15	6,457	5,067	405	288
5962 Merchandising machine operators	5	-	58	-	-	15,448	-	937	-
5963 Direct selling establishments	-	11	-	93	8	-	7,355	-	757
5980 Fuel dealers	8	8	38	54	7	21,053	17,407	846	923
5992 Florists	16	14	110	8	1	7,818	15,500	777	127
5994 News dealers and newsstands[1]	3	-	9	-	-	4,889	-	49	-
5995 Optical goods stores	12	13	75	68	5	10,400	13,118	863	934
5999 Miscellaneous retail stores, nec	28	35	114	115	3	7,930	12,174	1,091	1,392

Source: County Business Patterns 1994/95, CBP-94/95, U.S. Department of Commerce, Washington DC, November 1997. The employment column represents mid-March employment in the year. Pay per employee is calculated by dividing 1st Quarter payroll, annualized, by mid-March employment. The column headed 'Emp / Est' shows 'employees per establishment'. A dash (-) means that data are unavailable or cannot be calculated. nec means not elsewhere classified. *Notes:* 1. 1994 data incomplete; unavailable or withheld. 2. 1995 data incomplete; unavailable or withheld. 3. 1994 and 1995 data incomplete; unavailable or withheld.

LAFAYETTE, LA MSA

Wholesale and Retail Trade USA	Establishments		Employment		Emp / Est	Pay / Employee		Annual Payroll ($ 000)	
	1994	1995	1994	1995	1995	1994	1995	1994	1995
50- Wholesale trade	801	797	10,115	10,225	13	22,784	23,891	243,356	263,969
5012 Automobiles and other vehicles[3]	11	10	96	100	10	21,333	22,320	2,376	2,665
5013 Motor vehicle supplies and new parts	50	42	273	244	6	16,190	17,131	4,732	4,343
5014 Tires and tubes[2]	-	8	-	72	9	-	18,833	-	1,548
5015 Motor vehicle parts, used[3]	6	9	12	10	1	10,000	12,800	127	147
5021 Furniture[2]	-	3	-	9	3	-	16,444	-	158
5023 Homefurnishings[2]	-	5	-	127	25	-	12,882	-	1,702
5031 Lumber, plywood, and millwork[2]	12	10	174	47	5	16,920	39,319	3,041	1,814
5032 Brick, stone, & related materials[3]	7	9	31	50	6	22,581	21,600	808	1,046
5033 Roofing, siding, & insulation[1]	4	-	17	-	-	7,765	-	151	-
5039 Construction materials, nec[3]	7	6	202	40	7	16,495	19,800	3,735	910
5044 Office equipment[3]	16	18	149	138	8	29,181	33,884	4,309	4,253
5045 Computers, peripherals, & software[3]	10	8	62	62	8	22,645	24,387	1,622	1,522
5046 Commercial equipment, nec[3]	7	7	84	101	14	17,381	16,752	1,780	1,902
5047 Medical and hospital equipment[3]	14	16	162	175	11	30,864	31,314	5,446	5,628
5049 Professional equipment, nec[2]	-	6	-	37	6	-	16,432	-	1,264
5050 Metals and minerals, except petroleum[3]	21	23	140	164	7	33,771	34,366	4,738	6,920
5063 Electrical apparatus and equipment[3]	20	17	219	191	11	24,311	26,283	5,762	5,411
5064 Electrical appliances, TV & radios[3]	4	4	16	16	4	17,500	22,250	318	336
5065 Electronic parts and equipment[3]	10	10	77	78	8	25,714	26,000	2,150	2,018
5072 Hardware[1]	5	-	27	-	-	14,519	-	461	-
5074 Plumbing & hydronic heating supplies[3]	15	16	85	106	7	26,212	23,170	2,258	2,483
5075 Warm air heating & air conditioning[3]	12	12	67	73	6	29,254	25,260	2,051	2,225
5082 Construction and mining machinery[3]	6	8	102	121	15	31,490	33,587	3,366	4,434
5083 Farm and garden machinery	13	16	119	165	10	20,067	20,267	2,681	3,436
5084 Industrial machinery and equipment	159	157	1,682	1,819	12	34,901	32,781	59,852	63,980
5085 Industrial supplies	31	31	255	251	8	28,502	28,574	7,377	7,587
5087 Service establishment equipment[3]	17	19	167	186	10	17,796	19,290	3,391	2,976
5088 Transportation equipment & supplies[3]	7	7	15	13	2	24,533	27,385	388	334
5093 Scrap and waste materials[1]	8	-	66	-	-	10,182	-	708	-
5099 Durable goods, nec	12	10	60	50	5	21,200	19,200	1,153	1,029
5110 Paper and paper products[2]	15	14	134	210	15	15,940	20,419	2,033	4,237
5120 Drugs, proprietaries, and sundries[3]	11	10	134	123	12	25,701	24,130	2,649	2,530
5130 Apparel, piece goods, and notions[3]	4	3	23	24	8	10,957	16,000	393	446
5141 Groceries, general line[2]	-	6	-	373	62	-	27,882	-	9,503
5146 Fish and seafoods	21	23	379	227	10	7,166	12,546	2,561	2,815
5147 Meats and meat products[3]	5	5	35	41	8	18,057	18,634	672	823
5148 Fresh fruits and vegetables[2]	-	5	-	7	1	-	10,286	-	86
5149 Groceries and related products, nec[1]	12	12	217	228	19	27,244	26,930	6,166	6,569
5153 Grain and field beans[3]	16	15	87	46	3	12,046	16,261	975	805
5169 Chemicals & allied products, nec[3]	38	35	379	465	13	29,055	36,482	14,351	19,206
5171 Petroleum bulk stations & terminals[1]	34	32	66	266	8	24,727	19,880	1,928	5,693
5172 Petroleum products, nec[2]	13	10	77	80	8	28,052	36,500	1,993	2,941
5181 Beer and ale[3]	5	5	263	278	56	22,586	23,482	6,468	7,168
5182 Wine and distilled beverages[3]	4	4	175	197	49	24,251	23,675	4,597	6,020
5191 Farm supplies	31	31	228	306	10	15,526	17,451	4,078	6,074
5198 Paints, varnishes, and supplies[3]	6	6	41	40	7	29,073	25,600	1,079	1,209
5199 Nondurable goods, nec	14	14	24	27	2	13,833	15,259	521	563
52- Retail trade	2,052	2,040	27,924	28,489	14	10,341	11,352	316,609	344,820
5210 Lumber and other building materials	41	41	724	843	21	16,260	19,098	14,475	17,480

Continued on next page.

LAFAYETTE, LA MSA - [continued]

Wholesale and Retail Trade USA	Establishments		Employment		Emp / Est	Pay / Employee		Annual Payroll ($ 000)	
	1994	1995	1994	1995	1995	1994	1995	1994	1995
5230 Paint, glass, and wallpaper stores [3]	11	11	64	64	6	17,563	18,563	1,268	1,164
5250 Hardware stores	20	12	79	52	4	14,734	13,462	1,470	749
5260 Retail nurseries and garden stores [2]	16	15	126	160	11	8,952	8,575	1,421	1,612
5270 Mobile home dealers [3]	8	8	61	68	9	34,164	40,824	1,817	2,683
5310 Department stores [3]	15	14	1,920	1,850	132	10,950	12,043	23,001	22,998
5330 Variety stores	33	27	51	51	2	9,176	11,529	576	576
5390 Misc. general merchandise stores [1]	17	28	360	403	14	11,978	13,092	4,540	4,883
5410 Grocery stores	259	256	4,543	4,879	19	9,421	10,311	45,641	51,805
5420 Meat and fish markets	21	20	123	110	6	6,537	7,164	823	735
5460 Retail bakeries	23	19	172	203	11	7,209	7,271	1,300	1,454
5490 Miscellaneous food stores [2]	-	12	-	91	8	-	8,088	-	701
5510 New and used car dealers	28	29	1,369	1,430	49	25,028	26,344	39,763	44,170
5520 Used car dealers	17	16	39	32	2	17,128	18,375	583	727
5530 Auto and home supply stores	62	68	425	486	7	16,329	17,342	7,713	9,056
5540 Gasoline service stations	164	156	1,169	1,272	8	10,262	10,563	13,737	14,535
5550 Boat dealers [3]	6	6	56	59	10	16,786	17,220	1,082	1,117
5560 Recreational vehicle dealers [2]	-	4	-	26	7	-	17,231	-	593
5570 Motorcycle dealers [3]	5	5	48	54	11	21,583	29,481	879	1,116
5610 Men's & boys' clothing stores [3]	24	20	89	82	4	11,056	12,146	1,090	1,051
5620 Women's clothing stores [3]	53	47	477	362	8	6,273	6,464	3,278	2,494
5630 Women's accessory & specialty stores [3]	8	7	63	61	9	6,921	7,148	473	437
5640 Children's and infants' wear stores [3]	9	9	27	41	5	5,778	6,927	166	260
5650 Family clothing stores	36	33	640	613	19	10,438	10,506	7,166	6,965
5660 Shoe stores [3]	41	42	233	213	5	10,884	12,808	2,646	2,696
5690 Misc. apparel & accessory stores [3]	9	12	55	72	6	11,491	12,056	718	853
5712 Furniture stores	53	53	388	396	7	19,268	21,677	6,997	8,253
5713 Floor covering stores [1]	23	-	78	-	-	14,359	-	1,384	-
5719 Misc. homefurnishings stores [3]	18	18	111	121	7	10,595	10,876	1,845	1,418
5720 Household appliance stores	15	19	97	117	6	17,814	15,419	2,052	1,857
5731 Radio, TV, & electronic stores	18	17	88	164	10	17,500	14,439	1,701	2,650
5734 Computer and software stores [3]	11	10	87	110	11	16,138	18,582	1,759	2,234
5735 Record & prerecorded tape stores [3]	9	8	48	68	9	11,083	8,412	588	520
5736 Musical instrument stores [3]	3	3	30	34	11	19,067	18,706	646	699
5812 Eating places	418	358	8,877	8,103	23	6,642	7,412	62,821	61,987
5813 Drinking places	47	43	415	379	9	6,130	5,689	2,460	2,367
5910 Drug stores and proprietary stores	98	98	813	850	9	13,082	14,315	12,039	13,322
5920 Liquor stores [3]	10	10	6	30	3	7,333	7,200	46	356
5930 Used merchandise stores	13	18	47	46	3	12,766	12,000	545	652
5941 Sporting goods and bicycle shops	20	22	94	239	11	12,043	11,029	1,747	2,973
5942 Book stores [3]	9	11	63	87	8	8,444	7,908	504	729
5944 Jewelry stores	32	38	151	164	4	13,377	12,854	2,083	2,311
5945 Hobby, toy, and game shops [3]	12	10	103	218	22	7,301	4,257	1,212	1,345
5947 Gift, novelty, and souvenir shops	41	42	160	160	4	6,650	7,775	1,244	1,318
5949 Sewing, needlework, and piece goods [3]	13	14	76	76	5	7,789	7,368	539	572
5963 Direct selling establishments [3]	10	12	33	38	3	16,727	13,368	556	518
5984 Liquefied petroleum gas dealers [3]	6	6	24	24	4	19,500	19,833	565	578
5992 Florists	31	36	107	111	3	7,888	8,505	932	966
5993 Tobacco stores and stands [3]	9	9	12	16	2	7,000	9,250	107	219
5994 News dealers and newsstands [3]	3	3	8	8	3	6,000	5,000	41	35
5995 Optical goods stores [3]	20	22	119	124	6	11,866	12,806	1,496	1,698
5999 Miscellaneous retail stores, nec	51	55	222	208	4	12,216	13,365	2,889	2,926

Source: County Business Patterns 1994/95, CBP-94/95, U.S. Department of Commerce, Washington DC, November 1997. The employment column represents mid-March employment in the year. Pay per employee is calculated by dividing 1st Quarter payroll, annualized, by mid-March employment. The column headed 'Emp / Est' shows 'employees per establishment'. A dash (-) means that data are unavailable or cannot be calculated. nec means not elsewhere classified. *Notes:* 1. 1994 data incomplete; unavailable or withheld. 2. 1995 data incomplete; unavailable or withheld. 3. 1994 and 1995 data incomplete; unavailable or withheld.

LAKE CHARLES, LA MSA

Wholesale and Retail Trade USA	Establishments		Employment		Emp / Est	Pay / Employee		Annual Payroll ($ 000)	
	1994	1995	1994	1995	1995	1994	1995	1994	1995
50- Wholesale trade	301	301	3,129	3,357	11	23,429	24,108	77,264	84,776
5012 Automobiles and other vehicles	-	3	-	52	17	-	24,923	-	1,455
5013 Motor vehicle supplies and new parts	18	16	240	238	15	21,150	21,429	5,802	5,523
5015 Motor vehicle parts, used	6	-	25	-	-	10,720	-	226	-
5031 Lumber, plywood, and millwork	6	6	150	212	35	25,867	28,623	3,760	6,019
5044 Office equipment	10	11	96	119	11	26,250	25,210	2,881	2,974
5045 Computers, peripherals, & software	-	4	-	18	5	-	17,333	-	350
5049 Professional equipment, nec	3	3	11	8	3	25,091	24,000	244	292
5050 Metals and minerals, except petroleum	8	8	99	66	8	27,596	34,303	2,980	3,223

Continued on next page.

LAKE CHARLES, LA MSA - [continued]

Wholesale and Retail Trade USA	Establishments		Employment		Emp / Est	Pay / Employee		Annual Payroll ($ 000)	
	1994	1995	1994	1995	1995	1994	1995	1994	1995
5063 Electrical apparatus and equipment	14	11	111	112	10	38,450	42,964	3,626	3,714
5072 Hardware	6	8	40	46	6	15,400	17,391	657	874
5074 Plumbing & hydronic heating supplies	5	6	40	43	7	25,800	23,721	977	1,008
5075 Warm air heating & air conditioning	5	5	28	27	5	18,571	27,852	631	920
5082 Construction and mining machinery	6	7	65	58	8	25,723	28,552	1,769	1,920
5084 Industrial machinery and equipment	27	26	273	307	12	22,623	23,700	6,515	7,278
5085 Industrial supplies	25	27	234	239	9	29,846	30,745	7,230	8,011
5087 Service establishment equipment	13	13	102	109	8	27,686	22,862	2,749	2,926
5093 Scrap and waste materials	3	-	35	-	-	6,971	-	281	-
5099 Durable goods, nec	8	7	63	44	6	15,492	13,364	1,103	691
5112 Stationery and office supplies	7	5	70	60	12	21,029	20,600	1,073	1,194
5120 Drugs, proprietaries, and sundries	6	-	65	-	-	24,369	-	1,701	-
5130 Apparel, piece goods, and notions	3	-	31	-	-	8,903	-	264	-
5149 Groceries and related products, nec	5	8	117	118	15	24,342	23,559	2,963	3,121
5169 Chemicals & allied products, nec	-	12	-	81	7	-	21,580	-	2,291
5171 Petroleum bulk stations & terminals	17	17	350	319	19	19,966	24,113	7,494	7,991
5172 Petroleum products, nec	3	3	74	77	26	31,459	26,442	2,331	2,099
5181 Beer and ale	4	4	152	168	42	28,447	27,833	4,608	3,703
5191 Farm supplies	12	11	45	45	4	13,244	16,000	657	687
5193 Flowers & florists' supplies	3	-	8	-	-	10,500	-	84	-
5194 Tobacco and tobacco products	-	3	-	43	14	-	23,349	-	1,034
5199 Nondurable goods, nec	5	5	23	21	4	13,913	16,571	408	295
52- Retail trade	959	965	13,821	14,081	15	10,152	11,022	155,121	162,901
5210 Lumber and other building materials	24	22	423	384	17	13,712	15,781	6,696	7,189
5230 Paint, glass, and wallpaper stores	7	8	40	50	6	19,600	19,360	927	951
5250 Hardware stores	9	5	36	12	2	13,778	15,000	557	216
5260 Retail nurseries and garden stores	11	9	92	97	11	9,652	10,433	1,137	1,149
5270 Mobile home dealers	8	8	46	63	8	16,087	18,540	1,240	1,480
5310 Department stores	10	10	1,760	1,852	185	9,909	12,251	19,899	21,741
5330 Variety stores	18	13	106	76	6	7,094	7,421	821	562
5390 Misc. general merchandise stores	9	13	287	291	22	10,676	12,756	3,363	3,636
5410 Grocery stores	103	101	2,153	2,075	21	10,399	10,415	23,376	21,689
5420 Meat and fish markets	8	9	84	186	21	6,000	3,914	533	673
5460 Retail bakeries	-	11	-	47	4	-	5,702	-	301
5490 Miscellaneous food stores	5	4	12	13	3	14,000	15,692	207	199
5510 New and used car dealers	12	14	777	855	61	23,506	23,476	21,547	23,048
5520 Used car dealers	-	8	-	52	7	-	16,000	-	988
5530 Auto and home supply stores	31	34	227	238	7	13,709	16,487	3,458	4,179
5540 Gasoline service stations	81	82	794	857	10	9,259	8,747	7,972	7,574
5550 Boat dealers	5	3	42	34	11	19,333	22,235	871	824
5610 Men's & boys' clothing stores	7	7	44	44	6	10,818	9,000	486	405
5620 Women's clothing stores	31	30	241	210	7	7,900	8,590	2,112	1,870
5640 Children's and infants' wear stores	5	8	32	29	4	5,750	7,172	192	359
5650 Family clothing stores	16	19	186	276	15	10,473	7,870	2,201	2,386
5660 Shoe stores	25	26	124	138	5	9,903	10,290	1,419	1,502
5690 Misc. apparel & accessory stores	7	8	26	25	3	9,538	16,640	233	377
5712 Furniture stores	19	21	130	141	7	16,246	15,887	2,029	2,379
5719 Misc. homefurnishings stores	9	11	54	74	7	7,481	7,946	533	608
5720 Household appliance stores	9	9	83	97	11	16,867	17,113	1,455	1,637
5731 Radio, TV, & electronic stores	15	15	86	81	5	14,977	14,864	1,184	1,042
5734 Computer and software stores	-	5	-	20	4	-	11,600	-	462
5735 Record & prerecorded tape stores	3	-	19	-	-	11,789	-	237	-
5812 Eating places	179	159	4,206	3,947	25	6,463	7,344	29,543	30,151
5813 Drinking places	26	19	189	150	8	6,582	8,373	1,331	1,198
5910 Drug stores and proprietary stores	42	37	397	403	11	15,295	17,221	6,314	6,960
5920 Liquor stores	5	5	11	13	3	7,636	10,154	117	136
5930 Used merchandise stores	16	13	51	77	6	8,627	7,948	488	599
5941 Sporting goods and bicycle shops	7	8	24	24	3	12,667	13,500	382	443
5942 Book stores	-	4	-	35	9	-	7,543	-	266
5943 Stationery stores	5	5	16	19	4	8,750	8,421	157	203
5944 Jewelry stores	13	15	53	65	4	12,830	13,415	824	1,061
5945 Hobby, toy, and game shops	4	5	33	23	5	13,091	14,087	401	475
5947 Gift, novelty, and souvenir shops	17	19	87	71	4	7,678	7,099	667	512
5949 Sewing, needlework, and piece goods	5	-	37	-	-	7,459	-	256	-
5962 Merchandising machine operators	4	4	23	16	4	17,739	15,750	331	265
5963 Direct selling establishments	10	9	48	53	6	15,667	10,340	722	588
5984 Liquefied petroleum gas dealers	5	5	24	35	7	16,500	15,886	490	717
5992 Florists	23	22	110	117	5	9,018	9,470	1,076	1,164
5993 Tobacco stores and stands	3	4	8	12	3	9,000	8,333	85	100
5995 Optical goods stores	9	9	49	55	6	14,939	14,691	752	798
5999 Miscellaneous retail stores, nec	20	22	96	69	3	10,500	14,261	1,034	1,133

Source: County Business Patterns 1994/95, CBP-94/95, U.S. Department of Commerce, Washington DC, November 1997. The employment column represents mid-March employment in the year. Pay per employee is calculated by dividing 1st Quarter payroll, annualized, by mid-March employment. The column headed 'Emp / Est' shows 'employees per establishment'. A dash (-) means that data are unavailable or cannot be calculated. nec means not elsewhere classified. *Notes:* 1. 1994 data incomplete; unavailable or withheld. 2. 1995 data incomplete; unavailable or withheld. 3. 1994 and 1995 data incomplete; unavailable or withheld.

LAKELAND - WINTER HAVEN, FL MSA

Wholesale and Retail Trade USA	Establishments		Employment		Emp / Est	Pay / Employee		Annual Payroll ($ 000)	
	1994	1995	1994	1995	1995	1994	1995	1994	1995
50- Wholesale trade	766	754	9,968	10,959	15	21,604	23,167	227,393	250,596
5012 Automobiles and other vehicles	26	28	824	852	30	12,325	15,460	11,198	13,065
5013 Motor vehicle supplies and new parts	50	42	444	374	9	20,991	20,289	9,178	8,099
5014 Tires and tubes	9	7	79	78	11	29,823	29,436	2,132	2,064
5015 Motor vehicle parts, used	15	16	92	99	6	15,739	17,657	1,622	1,848
5021 Furniture	10	-	38	-	-	25,263	-	1,118	-
5023 Homefurnishings	19	-	131	-	-	20,702	-	2,751	-
5031 Lumber, plywood, and millwork	15	18	215	397	22	22,921	20,816	5,210	7,561
5032 Brick, stone, & related materials	10	9	60	54	6	34,133	35,185	2,175	1,687
5033 Roofing, siding, & insulation	-	3	-	65	22	-	23,262	-	1,567
5039 Construction materials, nec	12	16	52	93	6	23,308	24,731	1,428	2,282
5044 Office equipment	12	11	175	177	16	21,714	24,113	3,852	4,433
5045 Computers, peripherals, & software	10	11	57	57	5	19,158	20,982	1,186	1,439
5046 Commercial equipment, nec	6	7	49	48	7	19,020	20,417	1,011	1,114
5047 Medical and hospital equipment	4	5	18	15	3	13,556	18,667	260	243
5051 Metals service centers and offices	11	11	150	186	17	28,987	28,086	3,994	5,060
5063 Electrical apparatus and equipment	25	23	196	191	8	29,490	34,723	5,977	6,591
5065 Electronic parts and equipment	-	18	-	144	8	-	25,833	-	3,986
5072 Hardware	14	14	151	200	14	23,126	20,880	4,075	4,876
5074 Plumbing & hydronic heating supplies	12	11	137	161	15	23,708	25,068	3,731	3,963
5075 Warm air heating & air conditioning	14	13	67	73	6	18,567	20,219	1,309	1,220
5078 Refrigeration equipment and supplies	5	5	29	31	6	24,414	26,065	583	369
5082 Construction and mining machinery	12	11	54	74	7	36,000	47,135	2,816	4,009
5083 Farm and garden machinery	16	15	120	127	8	27,367	28,220	3,431	4,004
5084 Industrial machinery and equipment	65	67	473	644	10	32,524	30,863	16,786	20,138
5085 Industrial supplies	32	32	498	513	16	25,631	30,035	14,694	16,777
5087 Service establishment equipment	9	9	56	58	6	47,214	39,241	2,427	2,247
5088 Transportation equipment & supplies	10	9	52	45	5	21,923	24,889	1,179	1,013
5091 Sporting & recreational goods	5	5	16	17	3	28,250	23,294	341	378
5093 Scrap and waste materials	16	13	113	101	8	27,292	24,990	2,851	2,731
5094 Jewelry & precious stones	6	-	22	-	-	11,091	-	241	-
5099 Durable goods, nec	9	10	79	86	9	24,861	29,209	2,194	2,555
5111 Printing and writing paper	5	5	11	22	4	36,364	26,182	490	515
5112 Stationery and office supplies	16	13	190	90	7	17,621	19,822	3,344	1,679
5113 Industrial & personal service paper	7	7	14	24	3	29,143	24,000	499	487
5120 Drugs, proprietaries, and sundries	8	8	110	128	16	24,182	24,531	2,504	3,522
5130 Apparel, piece goods, and notions	5	6	10	17	3	12,800	11,765	127	196
5141 Groceries, general line	13	12	168	185	15	26,238	27,546	4,427	3,409
5142 Packaged frozen food	6	4	58	49	12	26,552	29,959	1,829	1,300
5148 Fresh fruits and vegetables	45	45	2,176	2,142	48	13,281	12,863	27,366	23,864
5149 Groceries and related products, nec	24	20	618	527	26	32,285	29,283	21,979	15,638
5150 Farm-product raw materials	5	3	37	13	4	10,703	17,538	314	172
5162 Plastics materials & basic shapes	5	5	64	71	14	22,875	28,225	1,710	2,065
5169 Chemicals & allied products, nec	20	22	140	183	8	25,686	26,098	4,030	5,194
5171 Petroleum bulk stations & terminals	12	10	257	210	21	26,335	31,390	6,771	6,539
5172 Petroleum products, nec	4	4	17	14	4	24,235	27,714	424	413
5181 Beer and ale	5	5	176	176	35	27,432	31,818	4,905	5,381
5191 Farm supplies	29	26	425	444	17	24,122	24,144	11,339	12,075
5193 Flowers & florists' supplies	9	-	59	-	-	15,322	-	986	-
5198 Paints, varnishes, and supplies	-	5	-	51	10	-	21,569	-	1,128
5199 Nondurable goods, nec	22	21	193	184	9	18,031	20,022	3,783	3,953
52- Retail trade	2,305	2,258	35,672	37,188	16	15,130	15,823	553,260	595,967
5210 Lumber and other building materials	37	27	1,070	853	32	15,607	14,757	17,797	13,204
5230 Paint, glass, and wallpaper stores	11	10	42	32	3	16,857	21,500	737	675
5250 Hardware stores	20	15	122	95	6	14,098	12,926	1,777	1,118
5260 Retail nurseries and garden stores	24	19	106	96	5	12,075	17,167	1,430	1,595
5270 Mobile home dealers	22	26	133	131	5	20,872	22,382	3,133	3,277
5310 Department stores	23	22	3,375	3,465	158	11,341	13,201	40,180	43,220
5330 Variety stores	30	20	241	210	11	8,149	8,438	2,331	1,870
5390 Misc. general merchandise stores	12	21	346	426	20	14,775	13,474	5,144	5,389
5410 Grocery stores	261	245	5,456	5,676	23	10,673	11,091	60,816	63,372
5420 Meat and fish markets	10	7	82	70	10	14,244	16,629	1,294	1,187
5430 Fruit and vegetable markets	5	6	18	14	2	10,667	11,429	143	152
5440 Candy, nut, and confectionery stores	3	3	18	17	6	5,111	8,000	112	108
5460 Retail bakeries	11	9	93	66	7	7,183	7,515	605	418
5490 Miscellaneous food stores	11	12	44	53	4	10,545	10,415	496	648
5510 New and used car dealers	36	36	1,693	1,680	47	28,940	32,514	57,028	62,026
5520 Used car dealers	49	47	177	163	3	22,644	25,423	3,843	4,124
5530 Auto and home supply stores	82	81	534	556	7	16,779	18,122	9,274	10,123
5540 Gasoline service stations	198	174	1,194	1,041	6	10,429	12,576	13,144	13,171
5550 Boat dealers	10	11	56	53	5	19,357	18,038	1,117	1,019

Continued on next page.

LAKELAND - WINTER HAVEN, FL MSA - [continued]

Wholesale and Retail Trade USA	Establishments		Employment		Emp / Est	Pay / Employee		Annual Payroll ($ 000)	
	1994	1995	1994	1995	1995	1994	1995	1994	1995
5560 Recreational vehicle dealers	5	4	29	22	6	11,448	17,091	450	469
5570 Motorcycle dealers	7	6	43	44	7	18,791	19,091	789	876
5590 Automotive dealers, nec	7	8	30	29	4	16,933	19,034	487	672
5610 Men's & boys' clothing stores	11	10	61	64	6	13,311	13,438	825	851
5620 Women's clothing stores	62	48	495	355	7	7,515	8,428	3,811	3,046
5630 Women's accessory & specialty stores	10	9	53	45	5	9,132	9,689	473	423
5640 Children's and infants' wear stores	4	3	11	11	4	8,000	8,000	85	97
5650 Family clothing stores	23	26	389	367	14	10,499	11,335	4,329	4,403
5660 Shoe stores	53	52	240	234	5	10,917	11,915	2,881	2,673
5690 Misc. apparel & accessory stores	8	7	44	48	7	10,273	10,667	538	525
5712 Furniture stores	75	70	972	582	8	19,119	17,271	19,295	10,693
5713 Floor covering stores	25	22	120	126	6	18,100	18,921	2,495	2,304
5720 Household appliance stores	20	19	135	69	4	18,104	18,841	2,540	1,267
5731 Radio, TV, & electronic stores	19	21	154	195	9	15,429	14,626	2,404	3,162
5734 Computer and software stores	8	9	47	78	9	16,085	16,308	838	1,211
5735 Record & prerecorded tape stores	9	7	63	58	8	8,571	9,379	609	527
5736 Musical instrument stores	6	6	32	35	6	13,250	15,886	517	631
5812 Eating places	424	404	8,645	9,234	23	7,794	8,133	66,896	73,227
5813 Drinking places	54	45	223	225	5	7,031	7,769	1,723	1,566
5910 Drug stores and proprietary stores	63	60	814	763	13	17,577	18,280	14,818	14,508
5920 Liquor stores	33	33	180	149	5	9,111	9,638	1,654	1,557
5930 Used merchandise stores	40	38	157	172	5	12,586	13,163	1,975	2,220
5941 Sporting goods and bicycle shops	34	33	135	141	4	10,548	12,028	1,584	1,869
5942 Book stores	18	14	92	118	8	10,217	10,407	1,034	1,170
5944 Jewelry stores	47	47	240	229	5	13,900	15,616	3,402	3,437
5945 Hobby, toy, and game shops	14	15	110	137	9	8,764	10,161	1,307	1,440
5947 Gift, novelty, and souvenir shops	37	39	175	198	5	9,280	8,848	1,764	2,043
5949 Sewing, needlework, and piece goods	15	10	94	72	7	5,532	7,944	595	604
5963 Direct selling establishments	17	17	63	68	4	20,952	19,353	1,282	1,294
5980 Fuel dealers	11	11	88	83	8	19,682	18,651	1,644	1,609
5992 Florists	51	47	210	190	4	7,962	8,568	1,672	1,658
5995 Optical goods stores	22	21	109	120	6	16,330	16,467	2,130	2,116
5999 Miscellaneous retail stores, nec	74	79	249	284	4	14,008	14,014	4,111	4,642

Source: County Business Patterns 1994/95, CBP-94/95, U.S. Department of Commerce, Washington DC, November 1997. The employment column represents mid-March employment in the year. Pay per employee is calculated by dividing 1st Quarter payroll, annualized, by mid-March employment. The column headed 'Emp / Est' shows 'employees per establishment'. A dash (-) means that data are unavailable or cannot be calculated. nec means not elsewhere classified. *Notes:* 1. 1994 data incomplete; unavailable or withheld. 2. 1995 data incomplete; unavailable or withheld. 3. 1994 and 1995 data incomplete; unavailable or withheld.

LANCASTER, PA MSA

Wholesale and Retail Trade USA	Establishments		Employment		Emp / Est	Pay / Employee		Annual Payroll ($ 000)	
	1994	1995	1994	1995	1995	1994	1995	1994	1995
50- Wholesale trade	-	781	-	13,051	17	-	26,913	-	368,496
5012 Automobiles and other vehicles	-	27	-	1,619	60	-	18,174	-	32,574
5013 Motor vehicle supplies and new parts	-	50	-	561	11	-	22,852	-	13,238
5014 Tires and tubes	-	5	-	118	24	-	28,814	-	3,138
5015 Motor vehicle parts, used	-	13	-	56	4	-	18,214	-	1,149
5021 Furniture	-	11	-	110	10	-	29,236	-	3,424
5023 Homefurnishings	-	12	-	126	11	-	23,524	-	3,163
5031 Lumber, plywood, and millwork	-	24	-	359	15	-	29,493	-	10,695
5033 Roofing, siding, & insulation	-	8	-	417	52	-	28,470	-	12,414
5044 Office equipment	-	13	-	214	16	-	31,178	-	6,717
5045 Computers, peripherals, & software	-	21	-	166	8	-	40,627	-	5,326
5046 Commercial equipment, nec	-	7	-	145	21	-	25,517	-	4,290
5047 Medical and hospital equipment	-	14	-	215	15	-	24,149	-	5,229
5050 Metals and minerals, except petroleum	-	11	-	195	18	-	33,292	-	6,980
5063 Electrical apparatus and equipment	-	12	-	96	8	-	34,708	-	3,038
5065 Electronic parts and equipment	-	13	-	172	13	-	35,023	-	5,552
5072 Hardware	-	16	-	340	21	-	31,000	-	11,223
5074 Plumbing & hydronic heating supplies	-	18	-	226	13	-	26,425	-	5,716
5082 Construction and mining machinery	-	8	-	55	7	-	32,145	-	2,105
5083 Farm and garden machinery	-	41	-	769	19	-	32,853	-	26,157
5084 Industrial machinery and equipment	-	44	-	599	14	-	32,588	-	21,647
5085 Industrial supplies	-	27	-	246	9	-	31,724	-	8,460
5087 Service establishment equipment	-	13	-	112	9	-	26,929	-	3,269
5088 Transportation equipment & supplies	-	3	-	26	9	-	18,154	-	686
5091 Sporting & recreational goods	-	7	-	141	20	-	21,390	-	2,873
5092 Toys and hobby goods and supplies	-	8	-	26	3	-	11,231	-	336
5093 Scrap and waste materials	-	14	-	113	8	-	22,619	-	3,390

Continued on next page.

LANCASTER, PA MSA - [continued]

Wholesale and Retail Trade USA	Establishments 1994	Establishments 1995	Employment 1994	Employment 1995	Emp / Est 1995	Pay / Employee 1994	Pay / Employee 1995	Annual Payroll ($ 000) 1994	Annual Payroll ($ 000) 1995
5094 Jewelry & precious stones	-	13	-	152	12	-	25,053	-	3,885
5099 Durable goods, nec	-	13	-	180	14	-	15,711	-	2,891
5112 Stationery and office supplies	-	9	-	113	13	-	29,805	-	3,491
5131 Piece goods & notions	-	3	-	6	2	-	10,000	-	65
5137 Women's and children's clothing	-	3	-	21	7	-	18,667	-	376
5142 Packaged frozen food	-	6	-	115	19	-	27,165	-	3,228
5143 Dairy products, exc. dried or canned	-	4	-	119	30	-	39,092	-	4,346
5144 Poultry and poultry products	-	11	-	184	17	-	19,652	-	3,677
5145 Confectionery	-	5	-	118	24	-	20,237	-	2,564
5147 Meats and meat products	-	3	-	16	5	-	12,000	-	218
5148 Fresh fruits and vegetables	-	13	-	333	26	-	20,144	-	8,600
5149 Groceries and related products, nec	-	20	-	839	42	-	29,378	-	26,323
5153 Grain and field beans	-	13	-	189	15	-	29,693	-	5,973
5154 Livestock	-	9	-	142	16	-	11,746	-	1,773
5159 Farm-product raw materials, nec	-	5	-	59	12	-	48,000	-	2,560
5162 Plastics materials & basic shapes	-	3	-	20	7	-	29,400	-	642
5169 Chemicals & allied products, nec	-	11	-	129	12	-	35,566	-	4,667
5170 Petroleum and petroleum products	-	8	-	133	17	-	25,143	-	3,410
5180 Beer, wine, and distilled beverages	-	6	-	87	15	-	33,287	-	3,475
5191 Farm supplies	-	39	-	762	20	-	25,276	-	20,881
5193 Flowers & florists' supplies	-	8	-	130	16	-	18,677	-	2,746
5198 Paints, varnishes, and supplies	-	6	-	102	17	-	27,843	-	2,555
5199 Nondurable goods, nec	-	36	-	273	8	-	18,330	-	5,604
52 - Retail trade	-	2,674	-	40,833	15	-	12,609	-	550,963
5210 Lumber and other building materials	-	49	-	1,263	26	-	25,960	-	29,709
5230 Paint, glass, and wallpaper stores	-	18	-	77	4	-	18,182	-	1,538
5250 Hardware stores	-	13	-	142	11	-	11,803	-	1,767
5260 Retail nurseries and garden stores	-	21	-	148	7	-	13,892	-	2,301
5270 Mobile home dealers	-	9	-	121	13	-	24,397	-	3,637
5310 Department stores	-	16	-	2,626	164	-	11,377	-	31,063
5330 Variety stores	-	10	-	147	15	-	10,313	-	1,719
5390 Misc. general merchandise stores	-	20	-	485	24	-	14,136	-	7,137
5410 Grocery stores	-	215	-	7,105	33	-	10,350	-	76,592
5420 Meat and fish markets	-	34	-	344	10	-	9,791	-	3,776
5430 Fruit and vegetable markets	-	25	-	208	8	-	8,327	-	2,083
5440 Candy, nut, and confectionery stores	-	17	-	77	5	-	6,597	-	591
5450 Dairy products stores	-	3	-	19	6	-	5,263	-	98
5460 Retail bakeries	-	53	-	393	7	-	9,059	-	3,774
5490 Miscellaneous food stores	-	26	-	95	4	-	8,632	-	964
5510 New and used car dealers	-	53	-	1,891	36	-	29,438	-	63,455
5520 Used car dealers	-	43	-	178	4	-	19,933	-	3,828
5530 Auto and home supply stores	-	46	-	329	7	-	19,234	-	6,453
5540 Gasoline service stations	-	137	-	959	7	-	11,825	-	11,465
5550 Boat dealers	-	6	-	31	5	-	20,645	-	926
5560 Recreational vehicle dealers	-	5	-	64	13	-	23,188	-	2,353
5570 Motorcycle dealers	-	9	-	71	8	-	17,521	-	1,549
5590 Automotive dealers, nec	-	6	-	42	7	-	27,143	-	1,099
5610 Men's & boys' clothing stores	-	34	-	416	12	-	10,375	-	4,343
5620 Women's clothing stores	-	56	-	648	12	-	7,796	-	5,626
5630 Women's accessory & specialty stores	-	15	-	105	7	-	11,124	-	1,396
5640 Children's and infants' wear stores	-	10	-	127	13	-	7,559	-	945
5650 Family clothing stores	-	30	-	695	23	-	12,616	-	8,215
5660 Shoe stores	-	68	-	486	7	-	9,597	-	4,871
5690 Misc. apparel & accessory stores	-	21	-	125	6	-	10,400	-	1,460
5712 Furniture stores	-	67	-	750	11	-	24,373	-	17,488
5713 Floor covering stores	-	23	-	215	9	-	22,233	-	5,239
5714 Drapery and upholstery stores	-	4	-	9	2	-	14,667	-	130
5719 Misc. homefurnishings stores	-	49	-	383	8	-	13,253	-	5,275
5720 Household appliance stores	-	22	-	298	14	-	18,013	-	5,128
5731 Radio, TV, & electronic stores	-	29	-	160	6	-	18,225	-	2,525
5734 Computer and software stores	-	10	-	41	4	-	14,341	-	624
5735 Record & prerecorded tape stores	-	11	-	83	8	-	10,795	-	783
5736 Musical instrument stores	-	11	-	42	4	-	16,667	-	696
5812 Eating places	-	543	-	11,936	22	-	7,904	-	107,310
5813 Drinking places	-	76	-	406	5	-	8,108	-	3,349
5910 Drug stores and proprietary stores	-	70	-	1,037	15	-	14,831	-	16,634
5920 Liquor stores	-	43	-	178	4	-	15,213	-	3,054
5930 Used merchandise stores	-	47	-	175	4	-	7,840	-	1,544
5941 Sporting goods and bicycle shops	-	44	-	226	5	-	12,212	-	2,946
5942 Book stores	-	21	-	334	16	-	11,222	-	3,533
5943 Stationery stores	-	5	-	72	14	-	11,222	-	923

Continued on next page.

LANCASTER, PA MSA - [continued]

Wholesale and Retail Trade USA	Establishments		Employment		Emp / Est	Pay / Employee		Annual Payroll ($ 000)	
	1994	1995	1994	1995	1995	1994	1995	1994	1995
5944 Jewelry stores	-	34	-	178	5	-	16,989	-	2,989
5945 Hobby, toy, and game shops	-	34	-	264	8	-	9,394	-	2,775
5946 Camera & photographic supply stores	-	6	-	41	7	-	14,341	-	797
5947 Gift, novelty, and souvenir shops	-	89	-	637	7	-	9,049	-	6,523
5948 Luggage and leather goods stores	-	10	-	52	5	-	11,538	-	656
5949 Sewing, needlework, and piece goods	-	21	-	124	6	-	7,806	-	934
5961 Catalog and mail-order houses	-	11	-	78	7	-	17,179	-	1,642
5962 Merchandising machine operators	-	7	-	205	29	-	19,824	-	4,183
5963 Direct selling establishments	-	25	-	234	9	-	13,385	-	3,465
5983 Fuel oil dealers	-	26	-	450	17	-	25,920	-	11,230
5992 Florists	-	36	-	215	6	-	11,758	-	2,625
5993 Tobacco stores and stands	-	4	-	16	4	-	8,750	-	145
5994 News dealers and newsstands	-	5	-	18	4	-	7,333	-	148
5995 Optical goods stores	-	19	-	135	7	-	21,452	-	2,702
5999 Miscellaneous retail stores, nec	-	79	-	607	8	-	14,379	-	9,589

Source: County Business Patterns 1994/95, CBP-94/95, U.S. Department of Commerce, Washington DC, November 1997. The employment column represents mid-March employment in the year. Pay per employee is calculated by dividing 1st Quarter payroll, annualized, by mid-March employment. The column headed 'Emp / Est' shows 'employees per establishment'. A dash (-) means that data are unavailable or cannot be calculated. nec means not elsewhere classified. *Notes:* 1. 1994 data incomplete; unavailable or withheld. 2. 1995 data incomplete; unavailable or withheld. 3. 1994 and 1995 data incomplete; unavailable or withheld.

LANSING - EAST LANSING, MI MSA

Wholesale and Retail Trade USA	Establishments		Employment		Emp / Est	Pay / Employee		Annual Payroll ($ 000)	
	1994	1995	1994	1995	1995	1994	1995	1994	1995
50- Wholesale trade	603	600	8,243	8,350	14	28,407	31,698	259,058	279,541
5012 Automobiles and other vehicles[3]	14	15	164	276	18	30,512	23,797	4,844	6,998
5013 Motor vehicle supplies and new parts	48	42	551	434	10	24,348	27,705	13,857	11,784
5021 Furniture[3]	12	10	222	209	21	25,802	29,072	5,984	6,362
5023 Homefurnishings	8	8	67	75	9	19,940	16,853	1,485	1,478
5031 Lumber, plywood, and millwork	16	14	180	124	9	33,311	35,452	6,411	4,387
5032 Brick, stone, & related materials[2]	8	12	27	62	5	32,000	28,194	1,149	2,186
5033 Roofing, siding, & insulation[3]	4	7	31	46	7	27,742	28,000	874	1,386
5039 Construction materials, nec[3]	3	3	23	18	6	19,304	21,111	609	512
5044 Office equipment[3]	15	15	462	486	32	38,779	46,091	17,304	19,719
5045 Computers, peripherals, & software	26	26	416	295	11	55,221	66,319	20,929	17,746
5047 Medical and hospital equipment[3]	11	11	327	296	27	23,927	23,176	9,038	9,735
5049 Professional equipment, nec[3]	8	8	181	248	31	22,586	24,806	4,462	6,519
5051 Metals service centers and offices	8	9	106	103	11	44,038	50,058	6,225	6,610
5063 Electrical apparatus and equipment	20	20	160	174	9	35,800	39,057	5,713	6,931
5064 Electrical appliances, TV & radios[1]	4	-	5	-	-	40,800	-	159	-
5065 Electronic parts and equipment	15	-	131	-	-	41,099	-	5,284	-
5072 Hardware[3]	7	7	33	37	5	28,242	42,270	1,357	1,775
5074 Plumbing & hydronic heating supplies[1]	5	7	50	51	7	26,080	27,608	1,455	1,602
5075 Warm air heating & air conditioning[3]	11	11	85	94	9	29,788	28,255	2,751	3,064
5082 Construction and mining machinery[3]	4	6	79	93	16	24,304	35,785	2,388	3,443
5083 Farm and garden machinery	20	18	131	183	10	20,092	22,492	3,404	4,542
5084 Industrial machinery and equipment	23	25	145	162	6	34,841	35,926	5,646	6,533
5085 Industrial supplies	25	25	168	158	6	27,833	28,810	4,969	5,356
5087 Service establishment equipment[3]	7	8	124	159	20	17,710	19,497	2,672	3,243
5091 Sporting & recreational goods[1]	3	-	15	-	-	20,800	-	490	-
5093 Scrap and waste materials	6	8	76	90	11	24,316	25,822	2,390	3,264
5094 Jewelry & precious stones[1]	4	-	3	-	-	17,333	-	52	-
5099 Durable goods, nec[2]	10	9	40	35	4	17,600	19,086	745	842
5112 Stationery and office supplies[2]	20	14	136	129	9	19,676	21,395	2,848	2,966
5141 Groceries, general line[1]	4	-	63	-	-	28,190	-	1,836	-
5143 Dairy products, exc. dried or canned	-	7	-	42	6	-	24,095	-	1,032
5145 Confectionery[3]	4	4	84	49	12	13,905	26,367	1,324	1,459
5148 Fresh fruits and vegetables[3]	6	6	49	45	8	20,327	22,844	1,521	1,149
5149 Groceries and related products, nec[3]	24	25	546	547	22	27,795	31,422	16,255	15,873
5153 Grain and field beans	19	20	163	162	8	19,828	20,889	4,589	4,963
5160 Chemicals and allied products[2]	-	8	-	68	9	-	35,294	-	2,476
5171 Petroleum bulk stations & terminals	15	10	85	68	7	26,918	27,294	2,799	2,319
5180 Beer, wine, and distilled beverages	7	7	124	151	22	24,613	21,589	3,511	3,486
5191 Farm supplies[3]	19	19	150	80	4	22,240	28,200	3,415	2,236
5192 Books, periodicals, & newspapers[3]	9	9	265	290	32	23,442	27,007	7,685	8,498
5198 Paints, varnishes, and supplies[3]	5	4	23	22	6	21,043	18,545	558	447
5199 Nondurable goods, nec	16	15	70	85	6	26,343	27,671	2,062	2,525
52- Retail trade	2,389	2,378	38,825	41,547	17	10,932	11,338	470,671	497,824
5210 Lumber and other building materials	43	43	645	717	17	22,878	25,026	17,569	18,985

Continued on next page.

LANSING - EAST LANSING, MI MSA - [continued]

Wholesale and Retail Trade USA	Establishments		Employment		Emp / Est	Pay / Employee		Annual Payroll ($ 000)	
	1994	1995	1994	1995	1995	1994	1995	1994	1995
5230 Paint, glass, and wallpaper stores	15	14	75	96	7	19,680	17,667	1,661	1,942
5250 Hardware stores	29	21	226	200	10	13,593	14,220	3,441	3,111
5260 Retail nurseries and garden stores	20	21	181	200	10	13,370	14,200	3,002	3,319
5310 Department stores[3]	24	23	5,416	5,327	232	10,324	11,027	62,501	63,246
5330 Variety stores	15	15	89	81	5	8,854	9,580	838	878
5390 Misc. general merchandise stores	11	11	311	360	33	13,608	13,511	4,677	4,659
5410 Grocery stores	195	195	4,454	5,032	26	9,849	9,681	47,083	50,600
5420 Meat and fish markets	7	-	15	-	-	6,933	-	133	-
5440 Candy, nut, and confectionery stores[1]	10	11	49	38	3	5,224	6,421	213	244
5450 Dairy products stores[3]	5	5	3	8	2	9,333	9,000	43	78
5460 Retail bakeries	24	22	223	202	9	6,709	7,762	1,802	1,505
5490 Miscellaneous food stores[1]	6	6	20	22	4	7,200	6,182	164	167
5510 New and used car dealers	38	40	1,843	1,879	47	27,184	29,652	55,177	60,228
5520 Used car dealers[3]	19	20	48	61	3	18,167	15,279	931	1,050
5530 Auto and home supply stores	55	54	365	459	9	15,759	19,259	6,791	9,274
5540 Gasoline service stations	144	152	1,381	1,328	9	10,503	11,985	15,716	16,263
5550 Boat dealers	6	-	10	-	-	10,800	-	136	-
5560 Recreational vehicle dealers[3]	6	5	17	22	4	29,882	28,727	790	748
5570 Motorcycle dealers[3]	9	8	26	27	3	19,077	18,519	582	617
5610 Men's & boys' clothing stores	31	28	260	224	8	9,308	10,732	2,494	2,429
5620 Women's clothing stores	86	75	780	754	10	7,641	7,225	6,491	5,626
5630 Women's accessory & specialty stores	15	14	64	65	5	9,375	10,031	615	647
5640 Children's and infants' wear stores[3]	9	8	69	71	9	7,884	8,169	657	579
5650 Family clothing stores	31	33	400	401	12	7,510	8,130	3,374	3,477
5660 Shoe stores	62	58	350	346	6	9,817	10,139	3,720	3,744
5690 Misc. apparel & accessory stores	24	24	94	111	5	7,574	8,252	982	994
5712 Furniture stores	43	44	410	455	10	18,927	19,288	8,660	9,045
5713 Floor covering stores	31	30	182	192	6	18,264	18,083	3,718	3,826
5719 Misc. homefurnishings stores	28	31	153	185	6	10,222	11,632	1,932	2,278
5720 Household appliance stores	13	13	65	57	4	14,031	13,684	940	847
5731 Radio, TV, & electronic stores	31	29	229	227	8	16,087	17,198	4,013	4,699
5735 Record & prerecorded tape stores[3]	17	16	105	105	7	9,219	9,333	1,021	1,004
5812 Eating places	534	508	12,073	13,329	26	6,621	6,755	89,310	95,151
5813 Drinking places	88	84	1,026	936	11	6,472	6,799	6,941	6,768
5910 Drug stores and proprietary stores	57	56	643	714	13	13,779	14,605	9,286	11,211
5920 Liquor stores	20	17	120	125	7	5,700	6,720	797	896
5930 Used merchandise stores	22	23	164	168	7	12,171	13,048	2,274	2,359
5941 Sporting goods and bicycle shops	40	37	284	283	8	12,155	12,466	3,954	3,942
5942 Book stores[3]	29	31	383	460	15	9,608	10,122	3,850	4,708
5944 Jewelry stores	37	36	201	212	6	13,632	14,604	3,018	3,001
5945 Hobby, toy, and game shops	19	18	118	166	9	9,932	8,723	1,566	1,668
5946 Camera & photographic supply stores[1]	4	-	21	-	-	17,143	-	373	-
5947 Gift, novelty, and souvenir shops	60	56	343	341	6	7,603	7,601	3,042	2,956
5949 Sewing, needlework, and piece goods	15	15	168	193	13	6,405	7,378	1,124	1,249
5961 Catalog and mail-order houses	9	9	166	205	23	19,904	19,102	3,498	3,754
5962 Merchandising machine operators	11	14	61	49	4	21,508	24,163	1,457	1,270
5963 Direct selling establishments	20	15	88	77	5	19,455	18,338	1,242	1,190
5983 Fuel oil dealers	7	8	36	40	5	29,333	31,900	1,323	1,358
5992 Florists	36	37	205	233	6	10,478	10,060	2,356	2,522
5995 Optical goods stores	27	29	172	160	6	17,302	18,300	2,978	2,970
5999 Miscellaneous retail stores, nec	70	69	464	522	8	12,034	12,414	6,131	6,813

Source: County Business Patterns 1994/95, CBP-94/95, U.S. Department of Commerce, Washington DC, November 1997. The employment column represents mid-March employment in the year. Pay per employee is calculated by dividing 1st Quarter payroll, annualized, by mid-March employment. The column headed 'Emp / Est' shows 'employees per establishment'. A dash (-) means that data are unavailable or cannot be calculated. nec means not elsewhere classified. *Notes:* 1. 1994 data incomplete; unavailable or withheld. 2. 1995 data incomplete; unavailable or withheld. 3. 1994 and 1995 data incomplete; unavailable or withheld.

LAREDO, TX MSA

Wholesale and Retail Trade USA	Establishments		Employment		Emp / Est	Pay / Employee		Annual Payroll ($ 000)	
	1994	1995	1994	1995	1995	1994	1995	1994	1995
50- Wholesale trade	-	402	-	2,891	7	-	18,442	-	53,252
5013 Motor vehicle supplies and new parts	-	18	-	128	7	-	19,906	-	2,777
5015 Motor vehicle parts, used	-	3	-	8	3	-	9,500	-	65
5021 Furniture	-	4	-	35	9	-	13,829	-	493
5023 Homefurnishings	-	7	-	110	16	-	19,745	-	2,047
5031 Lumber, plywood, and millwork	-	4	-	12	3	-	15,667	-	135
5032 Brick, stone, & related materials	-	8	-	25	3	-	18,560	-	428
5039 Construction materials, nec	-	9	-	29	3	-	20,552	-	573
5044 Office equipment	-	11	-	71	6	-	14,704	-	1,234

Continued on next page.

LAREDO, TX MSA - [continued]

Wholesale and Retail Trade USA	Establishments		Employment		Emp / Est	Pay / Employee		Annual Payroll ($ 000)	
	1994	1995	1994	1995	1995	1994	1995	1994	1995
5045 Computers, peripherals, & software	-	11	-	76	7	-	16,789	-	1,234
5047 Medical and hospital equipment	-	10	-	22	2	-	13,273	-	272
5048 Ophthalmic goods	-	3	-	5	2	-	7,200	-	36
5051 Metals service centers and offices	-	7	-	51	7	-	22,353	-	1,254
5063 Electrical apparatus and equipment	-	11	-	91	8	-	27,385	-	2,179
5064 Electrical appliances, TV & radios	-	7	-	69	10	-	23,246	-	1,478
5065 Electronic parts and equipment	-	13	-	53	4	-	20,453	-	1,051
5072 Hardware	-	5	-	77	15	-	23,377	-	1,585
5075 Warm air heating & air conditioning	-	3	-	9	3	-	18,222	-	173
5084 Industrial machinery and equipment	-	29	-	108	4	-	22,222	-	2,350
5085 Industrial supplies	-	10	-	28	3	-	16,857	-	624
5087 Service establishment equipment	-	6	-	27	5	-	20,444	-	547
5088 Transportation equipment & supplies	-	4	-	61	15	-	16,525	-	927
5091 Sporting & recreational goods	-	4	-	14	4	-	12,857	-	166
5092 Toys and hobby goods and supplies	-	5	-	39	8	-	14,154	-	607
5093 Scrap and waste materials	-	4	-	52	13	-	17,385	-	1,140
5094 Jewelry & precious stones	-	9	-	34	4	-	20,824	-	701
5099 Durable goods, nec	-	15	-	51	3	-	12,549	-	643
5112 Stationery and office supplies	-	6	-	57	10	-	12,842	-	584
5120 Drugs, proprietaries, and sundries	-	4	-	7	2	-	8,571	-	59
5131 Piece goods & notions	-	3	-	19	6	-	12,842	-	279
5136 Men's and boys' clothing	-	4	-	15	4	-	6,667	-	119
5137 Women's and children's clothing	-	9	-	45	5	-	16,800	-	662
5139 Footwear	-	7	-	71	10	-	17,070	-	606
5141 Groceries, general line	-	3	-	37	12	-	14,811	-	604
5143 Dairy products, exc. dried or canned	-	3	-	34	11	-	16,353	-	527
5148 Fresh fruits and vegetables	-	5	-	47	9	-	21,872	-	1,087
5149 Groceries and related products, nec	-	11	-	272	25	-	22,176	-	6,220
5154 Livestock	-	4	-	16	4	-	7,500	-	156
5160 Chemicals and allied products	-	6	-	37	6	-	33,514	-	1,094
5170 Petroleum and petroleum products	-	10	-	190	19	-	19,558	-	3,982
5180 Beer, wine, and distilled beverages	-	6	-	118	20	-	16,915	-	2,039
5191 Farm supplies	-	6	-	25	4	-	14,240	-	328
5198 Paints, varnishes, and supplies	-	3	-	8	3	-	15,000	-	78
5199 Nondurable goods, nec	-	31	-	239	8	-	11,130	-	2,945
52 - Retail trade	-	1,042	-	13,783	13	-	11,195	-	150,281
5210 Lumber and other building materials	-	15	-	382	25	-	14,565	-	5,432
5260 Retail nurseries and garden stores	-	5	-	51	10	-	11,294	-	644
5270 Mobile home dealers	-	7	-	64	9	-	23,250	-	1,713
5310 Department stores	-	9	-	1,723	191	-	11,603	-	18,388
5330 Variety stores	-	12	-	150	13	-	11,467	-	1,581
5390 Misc. general merchandise stores	-	17	-	530	31	-	12,589	-	5,659
5410 Grocery stores	-	87	-	1,940	22	-	12,480	-	24,061
5460 Retail bakeries	-	16	-	108	7	-	8,704	-	1,021
5490 Miscellaneous food stores	-	6	-	26	4	-	8,923	-	245
5510 New and used car dealers	-	7	-	335	48	-	26,531	-	9,289
5520 Used car dealers	-	12	-	31	3	-	18,968	-	570
5530 Auto and home supply stores	-	44	-	323	7	-	16,471	-	5,191
5540 Gasoline service stations	-	44	-	352	8	-	10,648	-	3,666
5570 Motorcycle dealers	-	5	-	35	7	-	9,829	-	278
5610 Men's & boys' clothing stores	-	19	-	155	8	-	12,413	-	1,881
5620 Women's clothing stores	-	55	-	423	8	-	9,333	-	3,494
5630 Women's accessory & specialty stores	-	11	-	60	5	-	10,000	-	571
5640 Children's and infants' wear stores	-	4	-	12	3	-	5,333	-	43
5650 Family clothing stores	-	31	-	523	17	-	11,434	-	5,817
5660 Shoe stores	-	43	-	232	5	-	10,741	-	2,269
5690 Misc. apparel & accessory stores	-	14	-	63	5	-	9,016	-	494
5712 Furniture stores	-	8	-	127	16	-	18,488	-	2,110
5719 Misc. homefurnishings stores	-	8	-	76	10	-	13,895	-	1,028
5720 Household appliance stores	-	4	-	14	4	-	8,571	-	94
5731 Radio, TV, & electronic stores	-	25	-	277	11	-	13,661	-	3,781
5734 Computer and software stores	-	3	-	8	3	-	14,000	-	101
5735 Record & prerecorded tape stores	-	7	-	37	5	-	9,297	-	285
5812 Eating places	-	171	-	3,649	21	-	7,890	-	28,793
5813 Drinking places	-	16	-	79	5	-	8,456	-	576
5910 Drug stores and proprietary stores	-	16	-	150	9	-	15,387	-	2,521
5920 Liquor stores	-	9	-	63	7	-	11,111	-	565
5930 Used merchandise stores	-	28	-	171	6	-	12,304	-	2,075
5941 Sporting goods and bicycle shops	-	14	-	78	6	-	10,872	-	796
5942 Book stores	-	6	-	24	4	-	10,667	-	346
5944 Jewelry stores	-	36	-	165	5	-	12,048	-	1,698

Continued on next page.

LAREDO, TX MSA - [continued]

Wholesale and Retail Trade USA	Establishments		Employment		Emp / Est	Pay / Employee		Annual Payroll ($ 000)	
	1994	1995	1994	1995	1995	1994	1995	1994	1995
5945 Hobby, toy, and game shops	-	14	-	135	10	-	9,126	-	1,299
5947 Gift, novelty, and souvenir shops	-	39	-	223	6	-	9,525	-	1,986
5949 Sewing, needlework, and piece goods	-	8	-	38	5	-	10,737	-	489
5962 Merchandising machine operators	-	3	-	11	4	-	13,455	-	151
5992 Florists	-	12	-	47	4	-	8,936	-	413
5995 Optical goods stores	-	12	-	50	4	-	13,680	-	644
5999 Miscellaneous retail stores, nec	-	34	-	151	4	-	10,464	-	1,579

Source: County Business Patterns 1994/95, CBP-94/95, U.S. Department of Commerce, Washington DC, November 1997. The employment column represents mid-March employment in the year. Pay per employee is calculated by dividing 1st Quarter payroll, annualized, by mid-March employment. The column headed 'Emp / Est' shows 'employees per establishment'. A dash (-) means that data are unavailable or cannot be calculated. nec means not elsewhere classified. *Notes:* 1. 1994 data incomplete; unavailable or withheld. 2. 1995 data incomplete; unavailable or withheld. 3. 1994 and 1995 data incomplete; unavailable or withheld.

LAS CRUCES, NM MSA

Wholesale and Retail Trade USA	Establishments		Employment		Emp / Est	Pay / Employee		Annual Payroll ($ 000)	
	1994	1995	1994	1995	1995	1994	1995	1994	1995
50 - Wholesale trade	169	167	1,267	1,384	8	18,750	18,671	25,689	26,721
5012 Automobiles and other vehicles	6	7	45	46	7	20,267	23,652	988	1,092
5013 Motor vehicle supplies and new parts	10	10	77	70	7	14,182	16,057	1,154	1,170
5015 Motor vehicle parts, used	6	6	21	18	3	13,905	14,667	275	239
5021 Furniture	-	3	-	16	5	-	14,750	-	259
5031 Lumber, plywood, and millwork	-	5	-	64	13	-	14,750	-	1,274
5032 Brick, stone, & related materials	-	5	-	44	9	-	22,545	-	965
5039 Construction materials, nec	-	3	-	17	6	-	26,118	-	429
5044 Office equipment	5	4	15	17	4	14,133	18,588	166	428
5045 Computers, peripherals, & software	5	6	16	37	6	21,250	18,486	485	728
5063 Electrical apparatus and equipment	4	4	33	41	10	37,212	34,439	927	1,112
5065 Electronic parts and equipment	6	6	14	18	3	21,429	18,889	372	310
5074 Plumbing & hydronic heating supplies	6	8	47	78	10	17,447	17,590	900	1,497
5083 Farm and garden machinery	7	5	60	62	12	17,600	17,548	895	580
5084 Industrial machinery and equipment	5	4	22	16	4	8,000	17,000	227	241
5085 Industrial supplies	4	5	27	26	5	14,370	14,923	376	470
5094 Jewelry & precious stones	-	3	-	6	2	-	10,000	-	75
5112 Stationery and office supplies	4	3	54	47	16	17,778	17,191	1,043	891
5130 Apparel, piece goods, and notions	-	3	-	3	1	-	6,667	-	21
5148 Fresh fruits and vegetables	7	8	19	19	2	47,579	42,316	1,083	975
5150 Farm-product raw materials	-	5	-	65	13	-	10,892	-	1,025
5169 Chemicals & allied products, nec	3	-	12	-	-	25,333	-	339	-
5171 Petroleum bulk stations & terminals	8	7	81	79	11	16,148	20,304	1,439	1,434
5172 Petroleum products, nec	3	3	17	17	6	23,294	25,647	413	428
5180 Beer, wine, and distilled beverages	5	5	84	87	17	25,619	24,782	2,377	2,390
5191 Farm supplies	8	8	86	84	11	20,047	21,667	1,741	1,744
52 - Retail trade	732	749	10,319	10,658	14	9,975	10,599	111,466	115,234
5210 Lumber and other building materials	9	11	182	218	20	22,396	19,927	3,357	3,991
5230 Paint, glass, and wallpaper stores	-	5	-	32	6	-	18,625	-	558
5250 Hardware stores	7	-	89	-	-	9,573	-	1,042	-
5270 Mobile home dealers	10	9	70	75	8	15,429	26,667	2,040	2,436
5310 Department stores	7	7	948	966	138	10,198	12,783	10,690	11,841
5410 Grocery stores	52	51	1,276	1,155	23	13,781	14,185	16,961	15,878
5440 Candy, nut, and confectionery stores	6	-	40	-	-	6,700	-	290	-
5460 Retail bakeries	10	12	47	45	4	5,702	6,489	284	291
5490 Miscellaneous food stores	4	4	19	13	3	12,211	13,846	210	221
5510 New and used car dealers	11	9	432	467	52	25,259	24,771	11,649	12,666
5520 Used car dealers	12	11	45	38	3	15,733	17,789	763	759
5530 Auto and home supply stores	23	25	204	206	8	12,686	14,544	2,948	3,325
5540 Gasoline service stations	56	53	512	409	8	8,328	10,885	4,537	3,931
5560 Recreational vehicle dealers	6	7	74	127	18	23,135	22,236	2,153	2,370
5610 Men's & boys' clothing stores	4	4	34	19	5	12,235	17,684	383	291
5620 Women's clothing stores	23	20	193	124	6	7,275	7,710	1,515	865
5630 Women's accessory & specialty stores	-	3	-	11	4	-	7,273	-	145
5640 Children's and infants' wear stores	3	3	21	19	6	6,095	6,316	149	138
5650 Family clothing stores	11	14	147	176	13	7,891	10,841	1,293	2,144
5660 Shoe stores	10	10	56	63	6	10,214	9,968	591	582
5690 Misc. apparel & accessory stores	4	5	21	19	4	7,429	5,895	153	89
5712 Furniture stores	11	12	86	60	5	14,465	18,067	1,488	1,559
5713 Floor covering stores	5	8	38	51	6	14,947	16,941	757	1,058
5714 Drapery and upholstery stores	3	3	4	3	1	9,000	13,333	42	39
5719 Misc. homefurnishings stores	4	4	18	22	6	10,222	9,091	204	247
5720 Household appliance stores	4	-	23	-	-	16,000	-	398	-

Continued on next page.

LAS CRUCES, NM MSA - [continued]

Wholesale and Retail Trade USA	Establishments		Employment		Emp / Est	Pay / Employee		Annual Payroll ($ 000)	
	1994	1995	1994	1995	1995	1994	1995	1994	1995
5731 Radio, TV, & electronic stores	12	10	76	73	7	15,421	16,658	1,220	1,016
5735 Record & prerecorded tape stores	-	4	-	51	13	-	10,275	-	531
5812 Eating places	210	197	4,198	4,309	22	6,067	6,456	27,646	28,188
5813 Drinking places	12	11	137	133	12	6,978	6,917	1,120	1,034
5910 Drug stores and proprietary stores	11	11	156	152	14	16,436	17,421	2,679	2,859
5920 Liquor stores	15	18	137	264	15	7,737	5,318	1,271	1,455
5930 Used merchandise stores	11	10	63	51	5	9,905	10,039	702	522
5941 Sporting goods and bicycle shops	7	8	44	38	5	7,545	8,316	359	359
5942 Book stores	8	8	46	38	5	7,913	10,316	419	445
5944 Jewelry stores	12	10	47	48	5	12,681	15,000	644	709
5945 Hobby, toy, and game shops	5	5	66	67	13	8,485	8,597	698	686
5947 Gift, novelty, and souvenir shops	20	21	79	92	4	7,190	7,565	720	773
5949 Sewing, needlework, and piece goods	4	-	22	-	-	6,909	-	142	-
5961 Catalog and mail-order houses	-	3	-	13	4	-	10,154	-	121
5962 Merchandising machine operators	-	3	-	5	2	-	15,200	-	68
5963 Direct selling establishments	7	7	35	47	7	23,429	22,638	874	1,019
5984 Liquefied petroleum gas dealers	4	4	24	25	6	18,833	20,640	422	430
5992 Florists	13	13	57	76	6	8,421	6,895	491	521
5995 Optical goods stores	-	8	-	44	6	-	11,909	-	569
5999 Miscellaneous retail stores, nec	23	26	98	131	5	8,571	8,031	860	1,168

Source: County Business Patterns 1994/95, CBP-94/95, U.S. Department of Commerce, Washington DC, November 1997. The employment column represents mid-March employment in the year. Pay per employee is calculated by dividing 1st Quarter payroll, annualized, by mid-March employment. The column headed 'Emp / Est' shows 'employees per establishment'. A dash (-) means that data are unavailable or cannot be calculated. nec means not elsewhere classified. *Notes:* 1. 1994 data incomplete; unavailable or withheld. 2. 1995 data incomplete; unavailable or withheld. 3. 1994 and 1995 data incomplete; unavailable or withheld.

LAS VEGAS MSA (AZ PART)

Wholesale and Retail Trade USA	Establishments		Employment		Emp / Est	Pay / Employee		Annual Payroll ($ 000)	
	1994	1995	1994	1995	1995	1994	1995	1994	1995
50– Wholesale trade	142	-	1,092	-	-	18,908	-	22,373	-
5013 Motor vehicle supplies and new parts	11	12	94	70	6	16,213	16,457	1,813	1,255
5020 Furniture and homefurnishings	5	7	32	42	6	16,625	18,095	618	735
5031 Lumber, plywood, and millwork	8	7	62	50	7	16,452	19,920	1,072	1,012
5044 Office equipment	4	5	33	38	8	13,576	15,158	477	598
5047 Medical and hospital equipment	3	-	8	-	-	14,500	-	48	-
5050 Metals and minerals, except petroleum	-	3	-	14	5	-	9,143	-	224
5063 Electrical apparatus and equipment	7	7	23	29	4	20,174	20,552	546	596
5065 Electronic parts and equipment	-	3	-	22	7	-	19,455	-	405
5074 Plumbing & hydronic heating supplies	11	8	83	69	9	21,542	20,870	1,999	1,388
5082 Construction and mining machinery	4	4	41	30	8	26,439	31,733	1,079	1,062
5084 Industrial machinery and equipment	3	4	8	10	3	25,000	24,000	253	351
5091 Sporting & recreational goods	5	5	21	17	3	9,524	18,824	252	317
5149 Groceries and related products, nec	7	9	88	79	9	21,273	24,557	2,009	1,971
5171 Petroleum bulk stations & terminals	4	4	37	34	9	13,838	21,412	531	755
5172 Petroleum products, nec	3	3	29	25	8	14,207	10,080	339	279
5180 Beer, wine, and distilled beverages	4	4	100	109	27	19,320	17,945	2,183	2,220
5199 Nondurable goods, nec	3	-	6	-	-	14,000	-	112	-
52– Retail trade	772	756	8,820	9,252	12	11,609	12,410	109,871	117,706
5210 Lumber and other building materials	24	16	219	206	13	14,466	14,990	3,593	3,261
5230 Paint, glass, and wallpaper stores	4	5	24	22	4	14,333	34,909	299	833
5250 Hardware stores	11	9	111	105	12	11,351	10,324	1,238	1,194
5260 Retail nurseries and garden stores	7	7	24	35	5	7,500	6,286	217	219
5270 Mobile home dealers	13	12	45	50	4	23,733	29,600	1,191	1,326
5300 General merchandise stores	14	18	1,106	1,160	64	9,910	12,755	12,166	14,291
5410 Grocery stores	56	55	1,390	1,391	25	15,986	16,868	21,913	23,689
5460 Retail bakeries	-	3	-	21	7	-	5,333	-	87
5490 Miscellaneous food stores	7	7	27	34	5	13,481	12,235	429	433
5510 New and used car dealers	16	17	411	479	28	22,706	23,841	10,886	11,500
5520 Used car dealers	8	8	78	86	11	16,769	15,814	1,352	1,565
5530 Auto and home supply stores	33	36	306	366	10	13,373	15,366	4,831	5,784
5540 Gasoline service stations	79	69	673	688	10	11,019	10,703	8,060	8,052
5550 Boat dealers	11	12	63	72	6	17,460	20,500	1,619	1,784
5560 Recreational vehicle dealers	4	6	39	23	4	15,179	23,130	447	544
5570 Motorcycle dealers	6	7	26	39	6	16,154	14,769	474	659
5620 Women's clothing stores	12	8	112	69	9	9,000	7,304	1,110	498
5650 Family clothing stores	13	13	164	169	13	9,951	8,876	1,564	1,516
5660 Shoe stores	12	11	51	45	4	8,941	9,422	499	445
5690 Misc. apparel & accessory stores	4	4	6	8	2	8,667	11,000	59	67
5712 Furniture stores	21	22	92	99	5	15,348	15,030	1,585	1,794

Continued on next page.

LAS VEGAS MSA (AZ PART) - [continued]

Wholesale and Retail Trade USA	Establishments		Employment		Emp / Est	Pay / Employee		Annual Payroll ($ 000)	
	1994	1995	1994	1995	1995	1994	1995	1994	1995
5713 Floor covering stores	12	15	108	101	7	13,296	17,307	1,634	1,831
5731 Radio, TV, & electronic stores	8	-	40	-	-	14,200	-	750	-
5812 Eating places	189	175	2,760	2,885	16	7,148	7,178	20,919	20,925
5813 Drinking places	35	30	140	161	5	7,629	7,453	996	1,132
5910 Drug stores and proprietary stores	16	13	213	225	17	20,169	20,498	4,462	4,664
5920 Liquor stores	8	-	52	-	-	10,154	-	552	-
5930 Used merchandise stores	11	11	34	33	3	8,941	9,576	353	309
5941 Sporting goods and bicycle shops	3	3	3	3	1	5,333	5,333	26	21
5942 Book stores	5	-	9	-	-	6,667	-	58	-
5944 Jewelry stores	11	8	47	31	4	11,574	14,581	670	494
5945 Hobby, toy, and game shops	-	3	-	10	3	-	3,600	-	34
5947 Gift, novelty, and souvenir shops	21	22	91	98	4	8,264	8,286	748	816
5963 Direct selling establishments	6	6	46	42	7	15,826	16,667	731	741
5984 Liquefied petroleum gas dealers	4	4	28	30	8	19,286	21,200	539	648
5992 Florists	8	6	27	25	4	6,519	8,320	206	209
5999 Miscellaneous retail stores, nec	23	19	59	73	4	9,288	11,726	607	921

Source: County Business Patterns 1994/95, CBP-94/95, U.S. Department of Commerce, Washington DC, November 1997. The employment column represents mid-March employment in the year. Pay per employee is calculated by dividing 1st Quarter payroll, annualized, by mid-March employment. The column headed 'Emp / Est' shows 'employees per establishment'. A dash (-) means that data are unavailable or cannot be calculated. nec means not elsewhere classified. *Notes:* 1. 1994 data incomplete; unavailable or withheld. 2. 1995 data incomplete; unavailable or withheld. 3. 1994 and 1995 data incomplete; unavailable or withheld.

LAS VEGAS MSA (NV PART)

Wholesale and Retail Trade USA	Establishments		Employment		Emp / Est	Pay / Employee		Annual Payroll ($ 000)	
	1994	1995	1994	1995	1995	1994	1995	1994	1995
50- Wholesale trade	-	1,380	-	15,852	11	-	29,731	-	491,898
5012 Automobiles and other vehicles	-	20	-	305	15	-	30,413	-	10,325
5013 Motor vehicle supplies and new parts	-	58	-	675	12	-	22,767	-	16,756
5014 Tires and tubes	-	11	-	134	12	-	22,597	-	4,530
5015 Motor vehicle parts, used [2]	-	23	-	191	8	-	18,974	-	3,908
5031 Lumber, plywood, and millwork	-	30	-	448	15	-	30,188	-	14,736
5032 Brick, stone, & related materials	-	26	-	251	10	-	25,163	-	6,633
5033 Roofing, siding, & insulation [2]	-	5	-	76	15	-	24,842	-	1,791
5039 Construction materials, nec	-	27	-	249	9	-	23,968	-	6,781
5044 Office equipment [2]	-	29	-	526	18	-	26,951	-	13,889
5045 Computers, peripherals, & software [2]	-	55	-	403	7	-	40,149	-	17,061
5046 Commercial equipment, nec [2]	-	31	-	311	10	-	26,328	-	9,649
5047 Medical and hospital equipment [2]	-	24	-	169	7	-	52,355	-	7,134
5051 Metals service centers and offices [2]	-	13	-	122	9	-	33,148	-	4,418
5063 Electrical apparatus and equipment [2]	-	65	-	818	13	-	35,878	-	30,386
5064 Electrical appliances, TV & radios [2]	-	8	-	131	16	-	25,069	-	3,124
5065 Electronic parts and equipment [2]	-	45	-	432	10	-	36,009	-	15,858
5072 Hardware [2]	-	32	-	396	12	-	27,020	-	12,155
5074 Plumbing & hydronic heating supplies	-	35	-	425	12	-	25,722	-	11,624
5075 Warm air heating & air conditioning [2]	-	21	-	214	10	-	30,542	-	7,002
5078 Refrigeration equipment and supplies [2]	-	9	-	40	4	-	30,600	-	1,101
5082 Construction and mining machinery	-	30	-	477	16	-	39,153	-	19,880
5083 Farm and garden machinery [2]	-	8	-	72	9	-	23,222	-	1,854
5084 Industrial machinery and equipment [2]	-	29	-	103	4	-	25,049	-	2,791
5085 Industrial supplies [2]	-	23	-	137	6	-	25,431	-	3,619
5087 Service establishment equipment [2]	-	34	-	292	9	-	46,589	-	10,656
5088 Transportation equipment & supplies [2]	-	5	-	28	6	-	47,143	-	1,407
5091 Sporting & recreational goods	-	22	-	145	7	-	25,738	-	4,882
5092 Toys and hobby goods and supplies [2]	-	10	-	180	18	-	27,600	-	5,232
5093 Scrap and waste materials [2]	-	9	-	178	20	-	18,404	-	3,503
5094 Jewelry & precious stones [2]	-	19	-	104	5	-	25,538	-	3,105
5099 Durable goods, nec [2]	-	25	-	382	15	-	31,016	-	12,747
5112 Stationery and office supplies	-	38	-	430	11	-	20,865	-	9,623
5120 Drugs, proprietaries, and sundries [2]	-	46	-	420	9	-	30,190	-	13,086
5136 Men's and boys' clothing [2]	-	11	-	195	18	-	30,605	-	6,425
5137 Women's and children's clothing [2]	-	13	-	126	10	-	18,698	-	4,301
5141 Groceries, general line [2]	-	31	-	657	21	-	23,933	-	16,732
5142 Packaged frozen food [2]	-	10	-	92	9	-	34,870	-	3,578
5143 Dairy products, exc. dried or canned [2]	-	7	-	56	8	-	22,857	-	2,224
5147 Meats and meat products [2]	-	10	-	140	14	-	40,343	-	6,838
5149 Groceries and related products, nec [2]	-	45	-	1,444	32	-	26,053	-	39,672
5162 Plastics materials & basic shapes [2]	-	9	-	83	9	-	26,169	-	2,599
5169 Chemicals & allied products, nec [2]	-	24	-	173	7	-	29,364	-	5,479
5171 Petroleum bulk stations & terminals	-	10	-	153	15	-	30,196	-	5,503

Continued on next page.

LAS VEGAS MSA (NV PART) - [continued]

Wholesale and Retail Trade USA	Establishments		Employment		Emp / Est	Pay / Employee		Annual Payroll ($ 000)	
	1994	1995	1994	1995	1995	1994	1995	1994	1995
5172 Petroleum products, nec	-	10	-	42	4	-	24,000	-	1,075
5180 Beer, wine, and distilled beverages 2	-	7	-	844	121	-	55,640	-	38,506
5191 Farm supplies 2	-	15	-	107	7	-	25,907	-	3,806
5192 Books, periodicals, & newspapers 2	-	15	-	172	11	-	21,233	-	3,351
5193 Flowers & florists' supplies 2	-	14	-	71	5	-	19,324	-	1,326
5199 Nondurable goods, nec 2	-	64	-	624	10	-	22,788	-	12,684
52- Retail trade	4,906	5,135	74,655	81,414	16	14,562	15,442	1,188,729	1,323,061
5210 Lumber and other building materials	52	53	1,569	1,617	31	18,669	20,928	32,868	34,194
5230 Paint, glass, and wallpaper stores 3	29	33	161	195	6	22,236	20,369	4,226	4,587
5250 Hardware stores	29	21	326	275	13	14,577	13,629	5,237	4,075
5260 Retail nurseries and garden stores	21	21	224	260	12	12,054	15,215	3,015	3,702
5270 Mobile home dealers	31	30	172	185	6	23,930	28,865	6,048	6,681
5310 Department stores 3	34	33	6,458	6,511	197	13,174	15,246	93,502	97,797
5330 Variety stores 2	-	7	-	212	30	-	13,000	-	3,216
5390 Misc. general merchandise stores	-	32	-	1,219	38	-	17,828	-	22,706
5410 Grocery stores 3	366	386	8,658	9,438	24	17,362	18,458	156,183	181,024
5440 Candy, nut, and confectionery stores 3	38	37	308	284	8	12,000	11,803	3,865	3,486
5460 Retail bakeries 2	57	49	298	275	6	11,060	11,796	3,894	3,379
5490 Miscellaneous food stores	-	57	-	264	5	-	12,803	-	4,242
5510 New and used car dealers	40	42	3,525	3,938	94	36,042	37,013	144,008	158,063
5520 Used car dealers	55	52	265	289	6	21,147	20,291	5,630	6,599
5530 Auto and home supply stores	118	125	1,212	1,296	10	15,805	16,142	22,221	23,344
5540 Gasoline service stations	198	187	2,320	2,476	13	13,138	13,090	33,175	34,969
5550 Boat dealers 3	14	13	149	163	13	19,758	21,840	3,410	3,958
5560 Recreational vehicle dealers	14	16	245	278	17	25,339	24,878	7,360	8,733
5570 Motorcycle dealers 3	16	17	120	135	8	20,767	24,474	3,158	3,936
5610 Men's & boys' clothing stores 3	69	71	582	564	8	17,828	18,582	10,486	11,039
5620 Women's clothing stores 3	154	135	1,760	1,582	12	12,139	12,961	24,621	22,033
5630 Women's accessory & specialty stores 3	34	34	221	207	6	10,136	12,715	2,322	2,412
5640 Children's and infants' wear stores 3	10	10	58	90	9	13,241	12,489	825	1,128
5650 Family clothing stores	63	68	846	1,180	17	10,099	11,478	11,670	13,792
5660 Shoe stores 3	119	117	783	778	7	14,084	15,039	11,722	12,875
5690 Misc. apparel & accessory stores 3	47	53	184	263	5	13,478	12,365	2,811	3,749
5712 Furniture stores 3	110	121	918	1,006	8	24,954	23,229	22,637	24,406
5713 Floor covering stores 3	30	32	204	360	11	19,176	18,122	5,165	8,981
5719 Misc. homefurnishings stores 3	67	64	485	495	8	12,751	13,034	6,471	7,169
5720 Household appliance stores	18	20	223	154	8	18,027	17,377	3,857	2,894
5731 Radio, TV, & electronic stores	53	59	470	848	14	19,677	17,453	11,307	16,549
5734 Computer and software stores 3	29	33	335	386	12	16,155	19,098	6,335	7,792
5735 Record & prerecorded tape stores 3	27	28	247	358	13	11,028	9,899	2,839	4,222
5736 Musical instrument stores 3	14	12	104	95	8	18,769	21,389	2,176	2,133
5812 Eating places	1,299	1,276	24,476	26,839	21	9,596	10,057	252,113	279,763
5813 Drinking places	267	256	2,922	3,144	12	10,797	11,677	34,717	35,490
5910 Drug stores and proprietary stores	72	69	1,387	1,362	20	16,934	21,175	26,000	27,033
5920 Liquor stores 2	36	36	196	189	5	15,490	16,106	3,367	3,435
5930 Used merchandise stores 2	80	88	773	821	9	15,022	16,078	13,629	14,465
5941 Sporting goods and bicycle shops	80	79	702	770	10	14,952	14,016	11,184	12,022
5942 Book stores	38	41	269	280	7	12,178	11,543	3,305	3,578
5943 Stationery stores 2	-	8	-	143	18	-	18,042	-	2,238
5944 Jewelry stores 1	114	123	673	733	6	21,177	20,126	13,692	14,760
5945 Hobby, toy, and game shops 3	36	33	372	477	14	12,849	12,906	5,253	6,899
5947 Gift, novelty, and souvenir shops	174	175	1,883	1,883	11	11,507	12,000	22,249	22,775
5948 Luggage and leather goods stores 3	20	23	129	136	6	17,736	20,941	2,443	3,406
5949 Sewing, needlework, and piece goods 3	19	20	157	175	9	10,293	9,943	1,690	1,750
5961 Catalog and mail-order houses	38	35	718	743	21	26,429	28,479	20,593	28,046
5962 Merchandising machine operators 3	14	19	166	194	10	21,012	21,402	3,826	4,304
5963 Direct selling establishments 3	48	52	484	724	14	25,702	25,122	13,283	15,812
5984 Liquefied petroleum gas dealers	11	10	33	34	3	20,364	19,294	678	734
5992 Florists	72	74	320	311	4	11,100	12,193	3,909	4,071
5993 Tobacco stores and stands 3	9	9	51	67	7	16,549	15,403	917	978
5995 Optical goods stores 3	47	43	277	259	6	13,300	18,147	4,191	4,863
5999 Miscellaneous retail stores, nec 3	194	192	1,183	1,266	7	17,238	17,738	20,902	22,718

Source: County Business Patterns 1994/95, CBP-94/95, U.S. Department of Commerce, Washington DC, November 1997. The employment column represents mid-March employment in the year. Pay per employee is calculated by dividing 1st Quarter payroll, annualized, by mid-March employment. The column headed 'Emp / Est' shows 'employees per establishment'. A dash (-) means that data are unavailable or cannot be calculated. nec means not elsewhere classified. *Notes:* 1. 1994 data incomplete; unavailable or withheld. 2. 1995 data incomplete; unavailable or withheld. 3. 1994 and 1995 data incomplete; unavailable or withheld.

LAS VEGAS, NV - AZ MSA

Wholesale and Retail Trade USA	Establishments		Employment		Emp / Est	Pay / Employee		Annual Payroll ($ 000)	
	1994	1995	1994	1995	1995	1994	1995	1994	1995
50 - Wholesale trade [3]	142	1,527	1,092	15,852	10	18,908	29,731	22,373	491,898
5012 Automobiles and other vehicles	-	21	-	305	15	-	30,413	-	10,325
5013 Motor vehicle supplies and new parts [1]	11	70	94	745	11	16,213	22,174	1,813	18,011
5014 Tires and tubes [2]	-	11	-	134	12	-	22,597	-	4,530
5015 Motor vehicle parts, used [2]	-	27	-	191	7	-	18,974	-	3,908
5020 Furniture and homefurnishings [3]	5	36	32	42	1	16,625	18,095	618	735
5031 Lumber, plywood, and millwork [1]	8	37	62	498	13	16,452	29,157	1,072	15,748
5032 Brick, stone, & related materials	-	30	-	251	8	-	25,163	-	6,633
5033 Roofing, siding, & insulation [2]	-	6	-	76	13	-	24,842	-	1,791
5039 Construction materials, nec	-	33	-	249	8	-	23,968	-	6,781
5044 Office equipment [3]	4	34	33	564	17	13,576	26,156	477	14,487
5045 Computers, peripherals, & software [2]	-	58	-	403	7	-	40,149	-	17,061
5046 Commercial equipment, nec [2]	-	34	-	311	9	-	26,328	-	9,649
5047 Medical and hospital equipment [3]	-	25	8	169	7	14,500	52,355	48	7,134
5051 Metals service centers and offices [2]	-	15	-	122	8	-	33,148	-	4,418
5063 Electrical apparatus and equipment [3]	7	72	23	847	12	20,174	35,353	546	30,982
5064 Electrical appliances, TV & radios [2]	-	8	-	131	16	-	25,069	-	3,124
5065 Electronic parts and equipment [2]	-	48	-	454	9	-	35,207	-	16,263
5072 Hardware [2]	-	35	-	396	11	-	27,020	-	12,155
5074 Plumbing & hydronic heating supplies [1]	11	43	83	494	11	21,542	25,045	1,999	13,012
5075 Warm air heating & air conditioning [2]	-	26	-	214	8	-	30,542	-	7,002
5078 Refrigeration equipment and supplies [2]	-	9	-	40	4	-	30,600	-	1,101
5082 Construction and mining machinery [1]	4	34	41	507	15	26,439	38,714	1,079	20,942
5083 Farm and garden machinery [2]	-	8	-	72	9	-	23,222	-	1,854
5084 Industrial machinery and equipment [3]	3	33	8	113	3	25,000	24,956	253	3,142
5085 Industrial supplies [2]	-	24	-	137	6	-	25,431	-	3,619
5087 Service establishment equipment [2]	-	37	-	292	8	-	46,589	-	10,656
5088 Transportation equipment & supplies [2]	-	5	-	28	6	-	47,143	-	1,407
5091 Sporting & recreational goods [1]	5	27	21	162	6	9,524	25,012	252	5,199
5092 Toys and hobby goods and supplies [2]	-	10	-	180	18	-	27,600	-	5,232
5093 Scrap and waste materials [2]	-	11	-	178	16	-	18,404	-	3,503
5094 Jewelry & precious stones [2]	-	21	-	104	5	-	25,538	-	3,105
5099 Durable goods, nec [2]	-	26	-	382	15	-	31,016	-	12,747
5112 Stationery and office supplies	-	39	-	430	11	-	20,865	-	9,623
5120 Drugs, proprietaries, and sundries [2]	-	46	-	420	9	-	30,190	-	13,086
5136 Men's and boys' clothing [2]	-	11	-	195	18	-	30,605	-	6,425
5137 Women's and children's clothing [2]	-	14	-	126	9	-	18,698	-	4,301
5141 Groceries, general line [2]	-	33	-	657	20	-	23,933	-	16,732
5142 Packaged frozen food [2]	-	11	-	92	8	-	34,870	-	3,578
5143 Dairy products, exc. dried or canned [2]	-	8	-	56	7	-	22,857	-	2,224
5147 Meats and meat products [2]	-	10	-	140	14	-	40,343	-	6,838
5149 Groceries and related products, nec [3]	7	54	88	1,523	28	21,273	25,975	2,009	41,643
5162 Plastics materials & basic shapes [2]	-	9	-	83	9	-	26,169	-	2,599
5169 Chemicals & allied products, nec [2]	-	25	-	173	7	-	29,364	-	5,479
5171 Petroleum bulk stations & terminals [1]	4	14	37	187	13	13,838	28,599	531	6,258
5172 Petroleum products, nec [1]	3	13	29	67	5	14,207	18,806	339	1,354
5180 Beer, wine, and distilled beverages [3]	4	11	100	953	87	19,320	51,328	2,183	40,726
5191 Farm supplies [2]	-	16	-	107	7	-	25,907	-	3,806
5192 Books, periodicals, & newspapers [2]	-	15	-	172	11	-	21,233	-	3,351
5193 Flowers & florists' supplies [2]	-	15	-	71	5	-	19,324	-	1,326
5199 Nondurable goods, nec [3]	3	66	6	624	9	14,000	22,788	112	12,684
52 - Retail trade	5,678	5,891	83,475	90,666	15	14,250	15,133	1,298,600	1,440,767
5210 Lumber and other building materials	76	69	1,788	1,823	26	18,154	20,257	36,461	37,455
5230 Paint, glass, and wallpaper stores [3]	33	38	185	217	6	21,211	21,843	4,525	5,420
5250 Hardware stores	40	30	437	380	13	13,757	12,716	6,475	5,269
5260 Retail nurseries and garden stores	28	28	248	295	11	11,613	14,156	3,232	3,921
5270 Mobile home dealers	44	42	217	235	6	23,889	29,021	7,239	8,007
5310 Department stores [3]	40	39	6,458	6,511	167	13,174	15,246	93,502	97,797
5330 Variety stores [2]	-	10	-	212	21	-	13,000	-	3,216
5390 Misc. general merchandise stores	-	40	-	1,219	30	-	17,828	-	22,706
5410 Grocery stores [3]	422	441	10,048	10,829	25	17,172	18,254	178,096	204,713
5440 Candy, nut, and confectionery stores [3]	39	38	308	284	7	12,000	11,803	3,865	3,486
5460 Retail bakeries [2]	59	52	298	296	6	11,060	11,338	3,894	3,466
5490 Miscellaneous food stores [1]	52	64	27	298	5	13,481	12,738	429	4,675
5510 New and used car dealers	56	59	3,936	4,417	75	34,649	35,584	154,894	169,563
5520 Used car dealers	63	60	343	375	6	20,152	19,264	6,982	8,164
5530 Auto and home supply stores	151	161	1,518	1,662	10	15,315	15,971	27,052	29,128
5540 Gasoline service stations	277	256	2,993	3,164	12	12,662	12,571	41,235	43,021
5550 Boat dealers [3]	25	25	212	235	9	19,075	21,430	5,029	5,742
5560 Recreational vehicle dealers	18	22	284	301	14	23,944	24,744	7,807	9,277
5570 Motorcycle dealers [3]	22	24	146	174	7	19,945	22,299	3,632	4,595

Continued on next page.

LAS VEGAS, NV–AZ MSA - [continued]

Wholesale and Retail Trade USA	Establishments		Employment		Emp / Est	Pay / Employee		Annual Payroll ($ 000)	
	1994	1995	1994	1995	1995	1994	1995	1994	1995
5610 Men's & boys' clothing stores [3]	71	73	582	564	8	17,828	18,582	10,486	11,039
5620 Women's clothing stores [3]	166	143	1,872	1,651	12	11,951	12,724	25,731	22,531
5630 Women's accessory & specialty stores [3]	34	36	221	207	6	10,136	12,715	2,322	2,412
5640 Children's and infants' wear stores [3]	11	11	58	90	8	13,241	12,489	825	1,128
5650 Family clothing stores	76	81	1,010	1,349	17	10,075	11,152	13,234	15,308
5660 Shoe stores [3]	131	128	834	823	6	13,770	14,731	12,221	13,320
5690 Misc. apparel & accessory stores [3]	51	57	190	271	5	13,326	12,325	2,870	3,816
5712 Furniture stores [3]	131	143	1,010	1,105	8	24,079	22,494	24,222	26,200
5713 Floor covering stores [3]	42	47	312	461	10	17,141	17,944	6,799	10,812
5719 Misc. homefurnishings stores [3]	73	68	485	495	7	12,751	13,034	6,471	7,169
5720 Household appliance stores	21	25	223	154	6	18,027	17,377	3,857	2,894
5731 Radio, TV, & electronic stores	61	68	510	848	12	19,247	17,453	12,057	16,549
5734 Computer and software stores [3]	29	34	335	386	11	16,155	19,098	6,335	7,792
5735 Record & prerecorded tape stores [3]	30	32	247	358	11	11,028	9,899	2,839	4,222
5736 Musical instrument stores [3]	16	14	104	95	7	18,769	21,389	2,176	2,133
5812 Eating places	1,488	1,451	27,236	29,724	20	9,348	9,778	273,032	300,688
5813 Drinking places	302	286	3,062	3,305	12	10,652	11,471	35,713	36,622
5910 Drug stores and proprietary stores	88	82	1,600	1,587	19	17,365	21,079	30,462	31,697
5920 Liquor stores [2]	44	43	248	189	4	14,371	16,106	3,919	3,435
5930 Used merchandise stores [2]	91	99	807	854	9	14,766	15,827	13,982	14,774
5941 Sporting goods and bicycle shops	83	82	705	773	9	14,911	13,982	11,210	12,043
5942 Book stores	43	46	278	280	6	12,000	11,543	3,363	3,578
5943 Stationery stores [2]	-	9	-	143	16	-	18,042	-	2,238
5944 Jewelry stores [1]	125	131	720	764	6	20,550	19,901	14,362	15,254
5945 Hobby, toy, and game shops [3]	38	36	372	487	14	12,849	12,715	5,253	6,933
5947 Gift, novelty, and souvenir shops	195	197	1,974	1,981	10	11,358	11,816	22,997	23,591
5948 Luggage and leather goods stores [3]	20	23	129	136	6	17,736	20,941	2,443	3,406
5949 Sewing, needlework, and piece goods [3]	21	20	157	175	9	10,293	9,943	1,690	1,750
5961 Catalog and mail-order houses	40	38	718	743	20	26,429	28,479	20,593	28,046
5962 Merchandising machine operators [3]	18	23	166	194	8	21,012	21,402	3,826	4,304
5963 Direct selling establishments [3]	54	58	530	766	13	24,845	24,658	14,014	16,553
5984 Liquefied petroleum gas dealers	15	14	61	64	5	19,869	20,188	1,217	1,382
5992 Florists	80	80	347	336	4	10,744	11,905	4,115	4,280
5993 Tobacco stores and stands [3]	10	10	51	67	7	16,549	15,403	917	978
5995 Optical goods stores [3]	55	51	277	259	5	13,300	18,147	4,191	4,863
5999 Miscellaneous retail stores, nec [3]	217	211	1,242	1,339	6	16,860	17,410	21,509	23,639

Source: County Business Patterns 1994/95, CBP-94/95, U.S. Department of Commerce, Washington DC, November 1997. The employment column represents mid-March employment in the year. Pay per employee is calculated by dividing 1st Quarter payroll, annualized, by mid-March employment. The column headed 'Emp / Est' shows 'employees per establishment'. A dash (-) means that data are unavailable or cannot be calculated. nec means not elsewhere classified. *Notes:* 1. 1994 data incomplete; unavailable or withheld. 2. 1995 data incomplete; unavailable or withheld. 3. 1994 and 1995 data incomplete; unavailable or withheld.

LAWRENCE, KS MSA

Wholesale and Retail Trade USA	Establishments		Employment		Emp / Est	Pay / Employee		Annual Payroll ($ 000)	
	1994	1995	1994	1995	1995	1994	1995	1994	1995
50- Wholesale trade	113	110	952	938	9	20,273	20,576	21,235	20,755
5013 Motor vehicle supplies and new parts	7	4	70	44	11	17,086	14,455	1,223	728
5015 Motor vehicle parts, used	4	4	22	28	7	20,364	23,286	518	325
5020 Furniture and homefurnishings	-	3	-	25	8	-	19,200	-	340
5030 Lumber and construction materials	-	3	-	58	19	-	22,966	-	1,324
5044 Office equipment	-	3	-	13	4	-	12,308	-	171
5045 Computers, peripherals, & software	8	7	71	84	12	13,014	16,905	1,603	1,757
5047 Medical and hospital equipment	5	-	43	-	-	21,023	-	1,023	-
5063 Electrical apparatus and equipment	5	-	39	-	-	23,179	-	1,006	-
5065 Electronic parts and equipment	4	-	51	-	-	26,667	-	1,218	-
5074 Plumbing & hydronic heating supplies	3	-	15	-	-	20,267	-	332	-
5083 Farm and garden machinery	4	4	73	82	21	31,014	22,585	2,347	2,305
5084 Industrial machinery and equipment	6	-	12	-	-	26,667	-	357	-
5085 Industrial supplies	4	4	19	22	6	23,579	25,818	435	486
5087 Service establishment equipment	3	-	21	-	-	23,810	-	326	-
5093 Scrap and waste materials	-	3	-	15	5	-	8,533	-	125
5094 Jewelry & precious stones	3	3	7	4	1	8,000	11,000	58	44
5140 Groceries and related products	5	5	26	26	5	13,077	18,923	377	463
5153 Grain and field beans	4	5	26	20	4	18,154	18,400	579	413
5169 Chemicals & allied products, nec	4	4	48	46	12	41,333	37,739	1,989	1,693
5170 Petroleum and petroleum products	5	5	49	53	11	12,653	12,226	912	767
5191 Farm supplies	7	8	77	60	8	20,364	18,667	1,685	1,166
52- Retail trade	582	608	8,790	9,120	15	10,188	10,779	97,518	106,251
5210 Lumber and other building materials	7	5	80	36	7	18,750	22,667	1,672	1,083

Continued on next page.

LAWRENCE, KS MSA - [continued]

Wholesale and Retail Trade USA	Establishments		Employment		Emp / Est	Pay / Employee		Annual Payroll ($ 000)	
	1994	1995	1994	1995	1995	1994	1995	1994	1995
5250 Hardware stores	7	6	88	79	13	11,000	9,367	1,074	760
5260 Retail nurseries and garden stores	4	3	34	17	6	6,235	6,118	285	160
5310 Department stores	4	5	601	617	123	9,644	11,553	6,058	9,193
5390 Misc. general merchandise stores	-	5	-	58	12	-	10,621	-	670
5410 Grocery stores	25	27	833	1,108	41	11,789	11,191	11,168	12,549
5460 Retail bakeries	5	6	60	60	10	6,667	5,267	395	294
5510 New and used car dealers	6	6	298	251	42	26,711	29,020	8,796	8,240
5530 Auto and home supply stores	10	10	82	102	10	16,439	17,294	1,441	1,873
5540 Gasoline service stations	33	29	247	244	8	9,749	9,590	2,643	2,671
5550 Boat dealers	3	3	9	8	3	14,667	16,000	233	168
5610 Men's & boys' clothing stores	-	4	-	47	12	-	5,362	-	259
5620 Women's clothing stores	18	19	160	151	8	8,875	8,980	1,425	1,538
5630 Women's accessory & specialty stores	5	-	31	-	-	9,032	-	276	-
5650 Family clothing stores	13	12	154	135	11	7,377	8,948	1,229	1,245
5660 Shoe stores	14	14	131	145	10	6,626	5,848	911	932
5690 Misc. apparel & accessory stores	8	8	48	86	11	12,917	12,186	794	1,263
5712 Furniture stores	9	-	76	-	-	12,421	-	971	-
5713 Floor covering stores	5	7	46	53	8	17,913	23,094	1,001	1,335
5714 Drapery and upholstery stores	3	-	19	-	-	15,579	-	308	-
5719 Misc. homefurnishings stores	15	16	98	108	7	10,571	10,667	1,056	1,083
5720 Household applince stores	5	5	19	21	4	14,316	10,667	266	244
5731 Radio, TV, & electronic stores	6	6	46	49	8	16,957	19,184	990	1,007
5734 Computer and software stores	5	5	37	39	8	14,595	21,846	761	559
5735 Record & prerecorded tape stores	6	6	65	82	14	8,800	6,829	498	597
5736 Musical instrument stores	5	5	37	41	8	5,946	7,415	254	257
5812 Eating places	128	127	3,045	3,138	25	6,194	6,419	21,043	22,451
5813 Drinking places	26	21	369	307	15	4,260	4,860	1,586	1,475
5910 Drug stores and proprietary stores	18	19	220	216	11	12,727	14,130	2,710	3,188
5920 Liquor stores	21	22	114	97	4	4,982	6,804	643	744
5930 Used merchandise stores	13	14	43	60	4	8,093	8,267	337	437
5941 Sporting goods and bicycle shops	8	-	46	-	-	11,565	-	641	-
5942 Book stores	9	9	205	180	20	9,522	10,778	1,903	1,883
5944 Jewelry stores	6	6	48	45	8	12,750	14,311	633	693
5945 Hobby, toy, and game shops	7	6	51	52	9	8,941	9,308	526	533
5947 Gift, novelty, and souvenir shops	11	12	53	47	4	4,906	6,043	334	355
5948 Luggage and leather goods stores	3	3	18	15	5	9,556	10,933	178	177
5949 Sewing, needlework, and piece goods	8	8	49	33	4	5,878	7,636	309	249
5961 Catalog and mail-order houses	4	3	14	13	4	14,000	10,154	276	228
5962 Merchandising machine operators	4	6	86	84	14	8,884	8,667	720	657
5963 Direct selling establishments	7	6	60	32	5	8,133	14,625	593	528
5992 Florists	9	11	79	62	6	5,367	7,742	505	513
5995 Optical goods stores	-	6	-	8	1	-	7,500	-	80
5999 Miscellaneous retail stores, nec	25	31	108	171	6	13,333	14,760	1,629	2,572

Source: County Business Patterns 1994/95, CBP-94/95, U.S. Department of Commerce, Washington DC, November 1997. The employment column represents mid-March employment in the year. Pay per employee is calculated by dividing 1st Quarter payroll, annualized, by mid-March employment. The column headed 'Emp / Est' shows 'employees per establishment'. A dash (-) means that data are unavailable or cannot be calculated. nec means not elsewhere classified. *Notes:* 1. 1994 data incomplete; unavailable or withheld. 2. 1995 data incomplete; unavailable or withheld. 3. 1994 and 1995 data incomplete; unavailable or withheld.

LAWTON, OK MSA

Wholesale and Retail Trade USA	Establishments		Employment		Emp / Est	Pay / Employee		Annual Payroll ($ 000)	
	1994	1995	1994	1995	1995	1994	1995	1994	1995
50- Wholesale trade	-	89	-	813	9	-	19,173	-	16,193
5013 Motor vehicle supplies and new parts	-	5	-	39	8	-	18,462	-	730
5015 Motor vehicle parts, used	-	6	-	33	6	-	16,121	-	695
5044 Office equipment	-	5	-	41	8	-	13,854	-	613
5065 Electronic parts and equipment	-	4	-	23	6	-	19,652	-	500
5074 Plumbing & hydronic heating supplies	-	3	-	13	4	-	18,462	-	234
5084 Industrial machinery and equipment	-	3	-	10	3	-	16,800	-	171
5090 Miscellaneous durable goods	-	4	-	10	3	-	8,400	-	105
5140 Groceries and related products	-	9	-	168	19	-	20,690	-	3,761
5170 Petroleum and petroleum products	-	5	-	37	7	-	23,135	-	872
5181 Beer and ale	-	3	-	84	28	-	21,476	-	1,970
5190 Misc., nondurable goods	-	6	-	63	11	-	15,873	-	1,075
52- Retail trade	-	638	-	8,421	13	-	10,526	-	91,239
5210 Lumber and other building materials	-	12	-	175	15	-	17,257	-	3,314
5230 Paint, glass, and wallpaper stores	-	5	-	22	4	-	16,364	-	371
5310 Department stores	-	7	-	1,111	159	-	12,587	-	13,726
5410 Grocery stores	-	68	-	865	13	-	10,469	-	9,367

Continued on next page.

LAWTON, OK MSA - [continued]

Wholesale and Retail Trade USA	Establishments		Employment		Emp / Est	Pay / Employee		Annual Payroll ($ 000)	
	1994	1995	1994	1995	1995	1994	1995	1994	1995
5420 Meat and fish markets	-	3	-	8	3	-	9,000	-	54
5460 Retail bakeries	-	8	-	46	6	-	7,130	-	423
5490 Miscellaneous food stores	-	4	-	23	6	-	5,391	-	140
5510 New and used car dealers	-	14	-	470	34	-	20,119	-	9,739
5520 Used car dealers	-	9	-	44	5	-	16,636	-	776
5530 Auto and home supply stores	-	16	-	112	7	-	20,571	-	2,238
5540 Gasoline service stations	-	29	-	181	6	-	10,077	-	1,913
5570 Motorcycle dealers	-	4	-	16	4	-	13,750	-	250
5610 Men's & boys' clothing stores	-	7	-	33	5	-	8,848	-	250
5620 Women's clothing stores	-	13	-	74	6	-	7,514	-	547
5650 Family clothing stores	-	7	-	81	12	-	8,444	-	686
5660 Shoe stores	-	12	-	44	4	-	12,545	-	598
5712 Furniture stores	-	20	-	138	7	-	12,377	-	1,709
5713 Floor covering stores	-	8	-	75	9	-	16,480	-	1,425
5720 Household appliance stores	-	6	-	31	5	-	10,839	-	472
5731 Radio, TV, & electronic stores	-	10	-	78	8	-	15,538	-	1,256
5734 Computer and software stores	-	3	-	10	3	-	10,400	-	113
5735 Record & prerecorded tape stores	-	4	-	56	14	-	10,429	-	520
5736 Musical instrument stores	-	3	-	19	6	-	13,263	-	270
5812 Eating places	-	131	-	2,886	22	-	7,380	-	22,698
5813 Drinking places	-	30	-	158	5	-	5,646	-	875
5910 Drug stores and proprietary stores	-	16	-	145	9	-	12,662	-	1,928
5920 Liquor stores	-	11	-	25	2	-	5,920	-	159
5930 Used merchandise stores	-	27	-	57	2	-	9,193	-	575
5941 Sporting goods and bicycle shops	-	7	-	42	6	-	9,524	-	444
5942 Book stores	-	8	-	50	6	-	9,280	-	509
5944 Jewelry stores	-	14	-	62	4	-	12,774	-	771
5947 Gift, novelty, and souvenir shops	-	11	-	57	5	-	8,000	-	508
5962 Merchandising machine operators	-	5	-	86	17	-	7,535	-	654
5980 Fuel dealers	-	5	-	16	3	-	12,500	-	211
5992 Florists	-	4	-	81	20	-	8,790	-	768
5993 Tobacco stores and stands	-	4	-	23	6	-	10,957	-	245
5995 Optical goods stores	-	4	-	21	5	-	11,238	-	257
5999 Miscellaneous retail stores, nec	-	15	-	33	2	-	10,303	-	353

Source: County Business Patterns 1994/95, CBP-94/95, U.S. Department of Commerce, Washington DC, November 1997. The employment column represents mid-March employment in the year. Pay per employee is calculated by dividing 1st Quarter payroll, annualized, by mid-March employment. The column headed 'Emp / Est' shows 'employees per establishment'. A dash (-) means that data are unavailable or cannot be calculated. nec means not elsewhere classified. *Notes:* 1. 1994 data incomplete; unavailable or withheld. 2. 1995 data incomplete; unavailable or withheld. 3. 1994 and 1995 data incomplete; unavailable or withheld.

LEXINGTON, KY MSA

Wholesale and Retail Trade USA	Establishments		Employment		Emp / Est	Pay / Employee		Annual Payroll ($ 000)	
	1994	1995	1994	1995	1995	1994	1995	1994	1995
50- Wholesale trade	789	802	11,246	10,678	13	28,479	27,088	325,651	303,401
5012 Automobiles and other vehicles[3]	14	14	292	340	24	16,671	18,400	5,544	6,741
5013 Motor vehicle supplies and new parts[3]	42	39	378	520	13	26,899	26,015	10,074	13,981
5014 Tires and tubes[3]	11	10	140	51	5	21,657	22,667	3,993	1,211
5015 Motor vehicle parts, used[3]	16	16	61	73	5	16,656	13,699	1,122	1,125
5021 Furniture[3]	11	11	78	61	6	19,128	26,098	1,664	1,667
5023 Homefurnishings[3]	12	10	79	56	6	20,304	25,357	1,587	1,402
5031 Lumber, plywood, and millwork[3]	20	15	231	233	16	22,632	28,635	5,588	6,141
5032 Brick, stone, & related materials[3]	6	8	89	70	9	29,303	38,000	2,880	2,507
5033 Roofing, siding, & insulation[3]	5	5	38	37	7	19,158	24,108	1,085	990
5039 Construction materials, nec[3]	6	13	58	123	9	31,448	28,553	1,930	3,329
5044 Office equipment[3]	24	24	247	267	11	27,320	29,243	7,347	8,208
5045 Computers, peripherals, & software[3]	29	35	457	558	16	40,263	48,681	16,602	25,022
5046 Commercial equipment, nec[3]	6	6	54	63	11	28,000	24,381	1,339	1,623
5047 Medical and hospital equipment[3]	15	18	214	214	12	25,327	26,075	6,003	6,111
5051 Metals service centers and offices[3]	19	20	83	88	4	25,831	31,909	2,366	2,871
5052 Coal and other minerals and ores[3]	8	13	11	26	2	63,636	49,846	754	990
5063 Electrical apparatus and equipment[3]	30	29	282	305	11	32,085	36,262	9,595	10,214
5064 Electrical appliances, TV & radios[2]	-	3	-	21	7	-	24,762	-	748
5065 Electronic parts and equipment[2]	-	30	-	134	4	-	28,627	-	4,456
5072 Hardware[3]	14	13	169	129	10	19,929	28,279	3,641	3,835
5074 Plumbing & hydronic heating supplies[3]	19	18	143	157	9	25,371	25,783	4,041	4,457
5075 Warm air heating & air conditioning[3]	12	11	235	255	23	29,668	29,380	6,327	6,877
5082 Construction and mining machinery[3]	13	12	165	175	15	30,933	32,320	4,729	5,898
5084 Industrial machinery and equipment[3]	23	23	94	120	5	19,830	18,133	1,967	2,437
5085 Industrial supplies[3]	22	27	200	233	9	28,360	31,245	6,169	7,366

Continued on next page.

LEXINGTON, KY MSA - [continued]

Wholesale and Retail Trade USA	Establishments		Employment		Emp / Est	Pay / Employee		Annual Payroll ($ 000)	
	1994	1995	1994	1995	1995	1994	1995	1994	1995
5087 Service establishment equipment [3]	23	21	363	422	20	30,248	21,194	11,038	8,154
5093 Scrap and waste materials [3]	17	16	147	149	9	15,537	18,819	3,236	3,990
5094 Jewelry & precious stones [1]	8	-	13	-	-	20,615	-	425	-
5112 Stationery and office supplies [3]	20	20	208	340	17	17,192	17,518	3,850	5,664
5120 Drugs, proprietaries, and sundries [3]	6	7	34	40	6	24,235	28,500	972	1,193
5137 Women's and children's clothing [1]	5	-	18	-	-	17,556	-	293	-
5147 Meats and meat products [3]	7	6	91	81	14	19,956	22,667	1,942	2,110
5149 Groceries and related products, nec [3]	18	16	220	222	14	24,182	25,009	5,433	6,308
5159 Farm-product raw materials, nec [3]	25	26	191	195	8	19,937	18,769	3,605	3,638
5162 Plastics materials & basic shapes [1]	6	-	3	-	-	9,333	-	79	-
5169 Chemicals & allied products, nec [1]	18	-	111	-	-	27,784	-	2,661	-
5171 Petroleum bulk stations & terminals [1]	12	-	42	-	-	24,667	-	817	-
5172 Petroleum products, nec [1]	5	-	63	-	-	27,365	-	1,770	-
5180 Beer, wine, and distilled beverages [3]	12	12	247	251	21	27,822	26,454	6,915	7,097
5191 Farm supplies	42	36	314	355	10	29,592	28,394	8,974	9,236
5192 Books, periodicals, & newspapers [3]	7	8	338	308	39	15,905	20,182	6,272	6,734
5193 Flowers & florists' supplies [1]	7	-	17	-	-	11,294	-	213	-
5198 Paints, varnishes, and supplies [3]	6	6	24	33	6	30,667	20,970	572	588
5199 Nondurable goods, nec [3]	19	22	62	64	3	19,935	20,563	1,347	1,620
52 - Retail trade	2,798	2,779	43,804	44,939	16	10,754	11,511	524,866	560,522
5210 Lumber and other building materials [3]	38	33	614	687	21	15,883	17,584	11,758	12,601
5230 Paint, glass, and wallpaper stores [3]	18	20	60	71	4	21,267	23,211	1,430	1,728
5250 Hardware stores [2]	31	24	180	179	7	10,867	11,709	2,419	2,244
5260 Retail nurseries and garden stores [1]	16	16	27	21	1	12,889	14,667	469	394
5270 Mobile home dealers [3]	8	10	29	34	3	36,276	29,412	1,383	1,547
5310 Department stores [3]	26	25	4,299	3,577	143	10,196	10,950	47,575	41,849
5330 Variety stores [2]	22	13	95	90	7	8,295	7,911	914	795
5390 Misc. general merchandise stores [1]	17	24	286	366	15	14,420	12,328	4,277	4,288
5410 Grocery stores [3]	219	209	4,855	4,859	23	9,849	10,559	47,760	52,875
5420 Meat and fish markets [3]	8	7	56	61	9	20,571	25,443	1,538	1,777
5440 Candy, nut, and confectionery stores [1]	5	-	30	-	-	7,200	-	213	-
5460 Retail bakeries [3]	31	29	241	220	8	8,183	8,782	2,090	1,976
5490 Miscellaneous food stores [3]	14	12	80	121	10	5,600	5,223	473	640
5510 New and used car dealers [3]	45	45	2,034	2,076	46	24,846	26,480	59,334	63,366
5520 Used car dealers [3]	21	23	47	65	3	14,383	15,631	986	1,217
5530 Auto and home supply stores	81	82	608	609	7	14,461	18,351	9,106	11,738
5540 Gasoline service stations	192	174	1,687	1,479	9	8,747	10,245	15,876	15,965
5570 Motorcycle dealers [2]	-	8	-	10	1	-	21,600	-	274
5610 Men's & boys' clothing stores [3]	21	22	197	188	9	9,320	10,383	1,831	1,940
5620 Women's clothing stores [2]	81	73	804	708	10	7,259	7,090	6,752	5,324
5630 Women's accessory & specialty stores [3]	11	11	89	88	8	17,978	17,955	1,578	1,723
5640 Children's and infants' wear stores [3]	5	8	41	47	6	6,732	7,489	325	446
5650 Family clothing stores [3]	29	31	674	765	25	11,828	12,308	8,778	10,482
5660 Shoe stores	75	68	382	348	5	9,822	10,655	3,974	3,709
5690 Misc. apparel & accessory stores [3]	23	23	67	87	4	9,254	9,379	720	856
5712 Furniture stores [2]	63	53	383	418	8	17,587	20,842	8,575	9,410
5713 Floor covering stores [2]	35	31	176	129	4	14,341	15,473	2,203	2,124
5714 Drapery and upholstery stores [3]	4	3	7	8	3	10,286	9,500	84	82
5719 Misc. homefurnishings stores	30	28	116	124	4	8,655	9,355	1,153	1,226
5720 Household appliance stores [1]	16	18	15	88	5	14,133	18,727	235	1,720
5731 Radio, TV, & electronic stores [3]	30	31	259	386	12	17,483	16,394	5,916	6,802
5734 Computer and software stores [1]	15	-	43	-	-	13,953	-	603	-
5735 Record & prerecorded tape stores [3]	19	19	101	93	5	9,663	9,333	944	838
5736 Musical instrument stores [3]	7	7	52	54	8	18,769	21,926	1,066	1,249
5812 Eating places	664	645	15,737	16,128	25	7,308	7,521	126,415	127,640
5813 Drinking places [3]	55	47	574	408	9	5,171	5,824	3,640	3,033
5910 Drug stores and proprietary stores	78	73	873	853	12	13,814	13,458	13,585	12,808
5920 Liquor stores [3]	78	71	345	303	4	6,910	9,135	2,733	2,980
5930 Used merchandise stores	57	48	152	136	3	8,737	7,765	1,453	1,254
5941 Sporting goods and bicycle shops [2]	60	59	383	375	6	11,457	11,659	5,224	4,997
5942 Book stores [3]	38	43	401	416	10	10,195	11,404	4,424	5,776
5944 Jewelry stores	55	57	319	308	5	13,542	14,649	4,925	4,762
5945 Hobby, toy, and game shops [3]	18	18	120	156	9	7,800	8,128	1,126	1,633
5947 Gift, novelty, and souvenir shops [3]	86	87	345	415	5	7,154	7,133	2,772	3,126
5949 Sewing, needlework, and piece goods [3]	18	14	93	75	5	6,882	7,733	676	636
5961 Catalog and mail-order houses [3]	8	14	40	56	4	14,000	19,214	642	3,668
5962 Merchandising machine operators [3]	17	17	154	147	9	16,390	18,122	2,620	2,784
5963 Direct selling establishments [3]	28	25	116	117	5	17,517	20,821	2,317	2,598
5992 Florists	49	49	185	176	4	9,968	10,614	1,956	2,044
5995 Optical goods stores [3]	31	32	158	165	5	16,658	16,703	2,618	2,829
5999 Miscellaneous retail stores, nec [1]	69	74	302	336	5	10,596	9,940	4,052	4,432

Source: County Business Patterns 1994/95, CBP-94/95, U.S. Department of Commerce, Washington DC, November 1997. The employment column represents mid-March employment in the year. Pay per employee is calculated by dividing 1st Quarter payroll, annualized, by mid-March employment. The column headed 'Emp / Est' shows 'employees per establishment'. A dash (-) means that data are unavailable or cannot be calculated. nec means not elsewhere classified. *Notes:* 1. 1994 data incomplete; unavailable or withheld. 2. 1995 data incomplete; unavailable or withheld. 3. 1994 and 1995 data incomplete; unavailable or withheld.

LIMA, OH MSA

Wholesale and Retail Trade USA	Establishments		Employment		Emp / Est	Pay / Employee		Annual Payroll ($ 000)	
	1994	1995	1994	1995	1995	1994	1995	1994	1995
50- Wholesale trade	273	280	4,187	4,183	15	23,174	26,472	112,919	118,197
5012 Automobiles and other vehicles[3]	12	12	151	207	17	24,821	24,039	4,960	5,454
5013 Motor vehicle supplies and new parts	17	17	322	352	21	21,665	22,773	8,468	8,141
5014 Tires and tubes[3]	3	3	51	63	21	25,647	23,746	1,727	1,632
5015 Motor vehicle parts, used[1]	3	4	31	33	8	15,355	14,909	494	519
5023 Homefurnishings[3]	3	3	14	16	5	17,714	16,000	275	262
5031 Lumber, plywood, and millwork	5	-	32	-	-	22,500	-	1,221	-
5039 Construction materials, nec[2]	-	7	-	129	18	-	26,171	-	3,695
5045 Computers, peripherals, & software[3]	5	4	32	35	9	27,625	26,629	869	875
5063 Electrical apparatus and equipment	11	10	108	111	11	25,815	27,351	2,811	3,387
5075 Warm air heating & air conditioning	5	5	18	19	4	24,667	28,211	530	578
5083 Farm and garden machinery	-	5	-	19	4	-	23,158	-	494
5084 Industrial machinery and equipment	-	15	-	137	9	-	16,555	-	2,591
5085 Industrial supplies[2]	-	16	-	156	10	-	24,795	-	4,250
5087 Service establishment equipment	-	7	-	78	11	-	23,333	-	1,667
5099 Durable goods, nec	-	4	-	6	2	-	6,000	-	34
5110 Paper and paper products[2]	-	11	-	93	8	-	16,129	-	1,738
5142 Packaged frozen food[2]	-	3	-	77	26	-	15,844	-	1,527
5149 Groceries and related products, nec[2]	-	8	-	615	77	-	25,424	-	16,939
5150 Farm-product raw materials	-	21	-	145	7	-	17,131	-	2,767
5171 Petroleum bulk stations & terminals	-	5	-	66	13	-	42,061	-	2,871
5172 Petroleum products, nec	-	4	-	9	2	-	18,222	-	162
5180 Beer, wine, and distilled beverages[2]	-	4	-	128	32	-	30,063	-	4,446
5191 Farm supplies	-	8	-	66	8	-	24,121	-	1,781
5199 Nondurable goods, nec[2]	-	4	-	20	5	-	9,600	-	246
52- Retail trade	1,005	1,012	14,247	14,315	14	10,459	11,439	163,521	171,326
5210 Lumber and other building materials	24	18	271	222	12	17,210	19,063	5,664	4,474
5230 Paint, glass, and wallpaper stores	5	-	23	-	-	19,478	-	485	-
5250 Hardware stores	14	11	68	102	9	9,882	10,039	747	976
5260 Retail nurseries and garden stores	11	13	79	81	6	10,228	11,012	1,041	1,126
5310 Department stores[3]	11	11	1,936	1,959	178	9,147	10,413	20,123	21,804
5330 Variety stores	11	10	124	115	12	8,774	8,800	1,164	1,080
5390 Misc. general merchandise stores	9	9	502	514	57	10,438	11,370	5,763	5,912
5410 Grocery stores	65	61	1,736	1,681	28	10,864	10,839	19,882	18,933
5450 Dairy products stores[2]	-	4	-	11	3	-	10,182	-	135
5460 Retail bakeries	11	12	41	74	6	9,561	6,703	411	476
5490 Miscellaneous food stores	-	6	-	23	4	-	9,043	-	172
5510 New and used car dealers	22	21	799	748	36	25,207	29,107	22,175	21,868
5520 Used car dealers	21	24	70	93	4	12,229	11,828	1,028	1,250
5530 Auto and home supply stores	33	36	208	219	6	14,962	17,224	3,672	3,921
5540 Gasoline service stations	83	82	605	595	7	9,197	10,454	6,062	6,438
5610 Men's & boys' clothing stores	8	5	29	14	3	16,138	19,143	325	246
5620 Women's clothing stores	33	26	299	273	11	6,689	5,407	2,155	1,553
5630 Women's accessory & specialty stores[3]	5	5	20	17	3	9,200	9,647	168	169
5650 Family clothing stores	5	6	18	30	5	9,333	9,600	230	289
5660 Shoe stores	26	26	122	134	5	10,098	10,149	1,289	1,367
5690 Misc. apparel & accessory stores	6	5	11	11	2	6,182	4,727	88	72
5712 Furniture stores	24	24	117	144	6	20,239	18,028	2,270	2,737
5713 Floor covering stores[2]	9	9	54	62	7	15,407	16,774	908	1,169
5714 Drapery and upholstery stores	6	-	23	-	-	14,261	-	328	-
5719 Misc. homefurnishings stores	5	-	10	-	-	10,000	-	114	-
5720 Household appliance stores	8	10	72	66	7	14,222	15,758	1,166	1,085
5731 Radio, TV, & electronic stores	11	16	57	132	8	16,281	17,242	963	2,279
5734 Computer and software stores[2]	-	3	-	5	2	-	9,600	-	155
5735 Record & prerecorded tape stores	5	-	27	-	-	6,963	-	190	-
5812 Eating places	230	224	4,554	4,342	19	6,928	7,593	34,359	34,604
5813 Drinking places	50	52	178	190	4	5,865	5,832	1,112	1,192
5910 Drug stores and proprietary stores	33	29	361	338	12	14,781	15,953	5,808	5,887
5920 Liquor stores	12	12	63	58	5	7,048	8,069	396	483
5930 Used merchandise stores	-	7	-	24	3	-	6,500	-	145
5941 Sporting goods and bicycle shops	9	10	33	52	5	8,364	8,385	332	467
5942 Book stores[1]	7	8	48	43	5	8,750	9,953	449	449
5944 Jewelry stores	15	17	76	99	6	22,053	24,404	1,639	1,894
5945 Hobby, toy, and game shops	9	11	61	49	4	8,328	13,469	655	913
5947 Gift, novelty, and souvenir shops	23	22	124	128	6	6,000	6,313	783	906
5949 Sewing, needlework, and piece goods	6	6	61	49	8	4,852	6,367	328	319
5963 Direct selling establishments[2]	11	10	96	91	9	20,875	22,374	2,315	2,356
5992 Florists	19	18	88	46	3	7,909	7,391	800	381
5995 Optical goods stores[2]	-	7	-	56	8	-	19,429	-	1,157
5999 Miscellaneous retail stores, nec	26	24	93	82	3	12,688	13,805	1,311	1,236

Source: County Business Patterns 1994/95, CBP-94/95, U.S. Department of Commerce, Washington DC, November 1997. The employment column represents mid-March employment in the year. Pay per employee is calculated by dividing 1st Quarter payroll, annualized, by mid-March employment. The column headed 'Emp / Est' shows 'employees per establishment'. A dash (-) means that data are unavailable or cannot be calculated. nec means not elsewhere classified. *Notes:* 1. 1994 data incomplete; unavailable or withheld. 2. 1995 data incomplete; unavailable or withheld. 3. 1994 and 1995 data incomplete; unavailable or withheld.

LINCOLN, NE MSA

Wholesale and Retail Trade USA	Establishments		Employment		Emp / Est	Pay / Employee		Annual Payroll ($ 000)	
	1994	1995	1994	1995	1995	1994	1995	1994	1995
50- Wholesale trade	392	399	5,557	5,838	15	23,053	25,017	141,317	172,655
5012 Automobiles and other vehicles	8	9	109	139	15	21,064	23,626	2,583	3,540
5013 Motor vehicle supplies and new parts	24	21	227	188	9	15,330	17,404	3,935	3,094
5014 Tires and tubes	7	7	220	175	25	24,764	27,520	6,225	5,274
5015 Motor vehicle parts, used	4	6	35	43	7	11,543	88,465	725	1,830
5021 Furniture	-	5	-	125	25	-	25,280	-	3,503
5023 Homefurnishings	-	4	-	23	6	-	17,565	-	426
5031 Lumber, plywood, and millwork	9	9	99	134	15	25,374	22,328	2,683	24,218
5033 Roofing, siding, & insulation	4	-	50	-	-	29,600	-	1,609	-
5039 Construction materials, nec	5	5	37	61	12	29,405	27,279	1,068	1,796
5044 Office equipment	15	15	152	154	10	22,895	24,883	3,198	3,431
5045 Computers, peripherals, & software	20	22	209	245	11	28,976	36,980	7,904	7,958
5047 Medical and hospital equipment	9	9	119	92	10	24,471	30,739	2,404	2,656
5049 Professional equipment, nec	-	5	-	51	10	-	13,412	-	797
5063 Electrical apparatus and equipment	20	18	187	200	11	25,583	25,960	5,098	5,498
5064 Electrical appliances, TV & radios	4	4	34	38	10	20,118	20,105	706	713
5065 Electronic parts and equipment	8	8	135	138	17	23,230	26,696	3,384	3,758
5072 Hardware	8	9	206	336	37	17,592	13,548	4,385	4,925
5074 Plumbing & hydronic heating supplies	14	11	107	94	9	20,897	21,872	2,433	2,192
5082 Construction and mining machinery	4	4	90	90	23	32,356	34,444	2,838	2,951
5083 Farm and garden machinery	10	11	111	144	13	21,982	19,278	3,236	3,550
5084 Industrial machinery and equipment	14	18	86	97	5	24,791	26,969	2,970	3,327
5085 Industrial supplies	9	9	75	79	9	26,613	27,443	2,473	2,665
5091 Sporting & recreational goods	7	6	76	79	13	13,632	16,304	1,089	1,369
5093 Scrap and waste materials	7	10	137	166	17	14,774	14,771	2,439	2,740
5099 Durable goods, nec	-	4	-	32	8	-	22,375	-	718
5110 Paper and paper products	14	12	215	176	15	17,786	24,227	4,275	4,153
5143 Dairy products, exc. dried or canned	3	3	96	97	32	24,667	25,814	2,530	2,548
5147 Meats and meat products	3	4	84	105	26	20,143	17,486	1,669	1,904
5149 Groceries and related products, nec	9	9	394	383	43	27,574	30,580	10,603	12,175
5150 Farm-product raw materials	15	16	169	187	12	17,231	27,059	3,256	5,610
5160 Chemicals and allied products	6	6	31	30	5	22,194	21,067	674	689
5171 Petroleum bulk stations & terminals	9	8	112	96	12	19,179	20,833	2,408	1,924
5172 Petroleum products, nec	6	7	35	41	6	13,829	12,683	502	580
5181 Beer and ale	4	4	90	90	23	29,911	32,133	2,867	3,025
5191 Farm supplies	23	17	311	249	15	38,405	31,952	13,170	8,155
5192 Books, periodicals, & newspapers	5	5	329	361	72	23,246	24,521	7,392	8,725
5199 Nondurable goods, nec	9	-	55	-	-	16,727	-	1,100	-
52- Retail trade	1,472	1,451	23,631	24,095	17	9,956	10,669	253,364	268,842
5210 Lumber and other building materials	29	19	582	464	24	15,608	17,267	10,891	7,286
5230 Paint, glass, and wallpaper stores	-	10	-	58	6	-	21,379	-	1,306
5250 Hardware stores	13	-	118	-	-	10,576	-	1,271	-
5260 Retail nurseries and garden stores	16	16	203	241	15	11,901	10,971	3,164	3,299
5310 Department stores	11	10	2,153	1,659	166	9,321	10,611	21,289	18,456
5330 Variety stores	8	7	85	65	9	7,624	7,631	597	541
5390 Misc. general merchandise stores	6	6	528	536	89	10,159	11,701	5,741	5,833
5410 Grocery stores	47	55	2,493	3,035	55	9,876	10,459	25,630	33,995
5440 Candy, nut, and confectionery stores	9	11	54	56	5	6,370	5,429	369	361
5460 Retail bakeries	21	19	145	131	7	7,283	7,725	1,224	1,056
5490 Miscellaneous food stores	-	6	-	42	7	-	5,810	-	299
5510 New and used car dealers	19	18	920	906	50	22,765	24,512	23,783	25,130
5520 Used car dealers	33	29	89	94	3	19,865	21,277	1,913	2,110
5530 Auto and home supply stores	24	28	211	223	8	17,289	20,018	3,769	4,356
5540 Gasoline service stations	112	110	775	839	8	10,415	10,923	8,597	9,637
5570 Motorcycle dealers	4	-	18	-	-	19,556	-	484	-
5610 Men's & boys' clothing stores	9	8	74	61	8	16,108	18,820	1,190	1,275
5620 Women's clothing stores	33	32	367	294	9	7,684	8,122	2,845	2,462
5630 Women's accessory & specialty stores	5	6	13	31	5	8,000	7,871	188	249
5650 Family clothing stores	16	16	295	331	21	8,881	9,390	2,870	2,803
5660 Shoe stores	30	29	182	179	6	8,637	9,497	1,715	1,698
5690 Misc. apparel & accessory stores	13	13	139	165	13	8,317	10,473	1,628	1,726
5712 Furniture stores	28	31	226	223	7	16,743	18,260	3,950	4,108
5713 Floor covering stores	14	14	84	87	6	17,667	19,172	1,757	1,711
5714 Drapery and upholstery stores	4	3	8	8	3	17,500	17,000	157	169
5719 Misc. homefurnishings stores	9	8	60	48	6	9,133	9,917	491	478
5720 Household appliance stores	13	12	82	95	8	16,341	14,274	1,550	1,453
5731 Radio, TV, & electronic stores	13	12	161	206	17	12,323	10,816	2,103	2,248
5735 Record & prerecorded tape stores	14	14	89	72	5	10,112	8,000	778	563
5812 Eating places	385	366	8,541	8,831	24	6,706	7,270	61,664	66,500
5813 Drinking places	79	73	855	920	13	6,241	6,757	5,760	6,402
5910 Drug stores and proprietary stores	32	30	568	508	17	14,908	16,543	8,921	8,711

Continued on next page.

LINCOLN, NE MSA - [continued]

Wholesale and Retail Trade USA	Establishments		Employment		Emp / Est	Pay / Employee		Annual Payroll ($ 000)	
	1994	1995	1994	1995	1995	1994	1995	1994	1995
5920 Liquor stores	45	42	292	263	6	6,877	6,981	1,945	1,822
5930 Used merchandise stores	20	19	112	93	5	9,036	10,065	897	868
5941 Sporting goods and bicycle shops	31	31	195	236	8	8,000	8,339	1,935	2,610
5942 Book stores	20	16	199	189	12	7,457	8,063	1,466	1,478
5943 Stationery stores	-	3	-	5	2	-	29,600	-	59
5944 Jewelry stores	20	22	149	159	7	17,664	19,472	2,682	2,996
5945 Hobby, toy, and game shops	16	15	210	169	11	10,114	12,047	2,068	2,417
5947 Gift, novelty, and souvenir shops	45	38	284	283	7	5,718	6,205	1,819	2,047
5949 Sewing, needlework, and piece goods	6	-	80	-	-	6,250	-	481	-
5961 Catalog and mail-order houses	-	8	-	693	87	-	16,271	-	11,608
5962 Merchandising machine operators	-	5	-	67	13	-	19,104	-	1,362
5963 Direct selling establishments	15	11	84	63	6	18,048	16,825	1,439	1,139
5992 Florists	-	24	-	147	6	-	9,850	-	1,398
5995 Optical goods stores	19	17	136	117	7	15,176	17,846	2,089	2,147
5999 Miscellaneous retail stores, nec	53	47	294	249	5	9,469	10,554	2,715	2,726

Source: County Business Patterns 1994/95, CBP-94/95, U.S. Department of Commerce, Washington DC, November 1997. The employment column represents mid-March employment in the year. Pay per employee is calculated by dividing 1st Quarter payroll, annualized, by mid-March employment. The column headed 'Emp / Est' shows 'employees per establishment'. A dash (-) means that data are unavailable or cannot be calculated. nec means not elsewhere classified. *Notes:* 1. 1994 data incomplete; unavailable or withheld. 2. 1995 data incomplete; unavailable or withheld. 3. 1994 and 1995 data incomplete; unavailable or withheld.

LITTLE ROCK–NORTH LITTLE ROCK, AR MSA

Wholesale and Retail Trade USA	Establishments		Employment		Emp / Est	Pay / Employee		Annual Payroll ($ 000)	
	1994	1995	1994	1995	1995	1994	1995	1994	1995
50- Wholesale trade	1,290	1,308	16,075	18,035	14	26,602	28,139	465,532	529,799
5012 Automobiles and other vehicles	24	28	454	501	18	28,573	27,968	12,763	14,812
5013 Motor vehicle supplies and new parts	92	79	1,078	967	12	21,098	22,180	24,175	22,556
5014 Tires and tubes[3]	12	11	137	111	10	20,788	24,937	3,666	3,378
5015 Motor vehicle parts, used[1]	18	29	115	188	6	14,157	17,574	1,784	3,660
5021 Furniture[3]	21	22	180	224	10	23,111	23,929	4,570	6,386
5023 Homefurnishings[3]	26	28	221	232	8	23,710	23,379	6,375	6,555
5031 Lumber, plywood, and millwork[3]	16	13	179	131	10	22,659	28,550	4,452	3,359
5032 Brick, stone, & related materials[3]	13	15	60	74	5	29,333	32,703	2,180	2,792
5033 Roofing, siding, & insulation[3]	16	12	121	133	11	25,388	31,068	3,652	4,536
5039 Construction materials, nec[3]	17	21	156	194	9	19,410	21,691	3,717	4,542
5044 Office equipment[3]	34	35	477	502	14	29,132	30,637	14,714	15,226
5045 Computers, peripherals, & software	48	43	485	465	11	41,864	48,378	20,514	22,257
5046 Commercial equipment, nec[3]	12	11	80	95	9	22,200	19,200	1,988	2,297
5047 Medical and hospital equipment[3]	41	44	338	362	8	33,444	33,116	11,740	12,846
5051 Metals service centers and offices[1]	22	-	368	-	-	27,630	-	11,794	-
5063 Electrical apparatus and equipment	62	60	710	770	13	32,975	32,790	23,588	25,790
5064 Electrical appliances, TV & radios[3]	11	11	125	160	15	38,176	35,250	5,076	6,144
5065 Electronic parts and equipment[3]	40	38	397	804	21	28,826	30,244	11,985	24,228
5072 Hardware[3]	18	19	188	198	10	28,234	31,798	5,563	6,427
5074 Plumbing & hydronic heating supplies[3]	27	26	108	150	6	26,370	30,480	3,159	4,370
5075 Warm air heating & air conditioning[3]	17	17	142	145	9	26,958	29,186	4,618	5,138
5078 Refrigeration equipment and supplies[3]	10	12	82	94	8	25,366	30,511	2,431	2,967
5082 Construction and mining machinery[3]	21	21	430	449	21	31,209	32,748	15,256	16,364
5083 Farm and garden machinery	24	21	173	205	10	27,653	26,302	5,352	6,504
5084 Industrial machinery and equipment[2]	72	78	586	626	8	27,584	29,923	18,002	20,404
5085 Industrial supplies[3]	40	43	363	396	9	27,140	30,202	10,947	12,613
5087 Service establishment equipment	27	26	184	179	7	23,391	25,408	5,128	5,182
5088 Transportation equipment & supplies[3]	6	6	24	103	17	29,167	28,078	480	2,998
5091 Sporting & recreational goods[1]	11	12	75	85	7	19,787	19,153	2,078	1,682
5092 Toys and hobby goods and supplies[3]	4	4	27	32	8	12,444	10,125	392	386
5093 Scrap and waste materials[3]	25	26	231	241	9	21,558	24,349	6,783	8,468
5094 Jewelry & precious stones[3]	12	14	56	65	5	22,857	20,923	1,500	1,610
5099 Durable goods, nec	18	22	302	452	21	23,033	20,841	7,682	8,793
5111 Printing and writing paper[3]	7	7	105	132	19	32,724	34,909	2,857	4,553
5112 Stationery and office supplies[3]	29	22	319	294	13	23,373	27,306	8,145	8,299
5113 Industrial & personal service paper[1]	13	-	87	-	-	22,529	-	2,481	-
5120 Drugs, proprietaries, and sundries[1]	19	20	314	350	18	24,242	27,749	8,504	10,004
5131 Piece goods & notions[3]	5	4	20	17	4	17,800	21,882	411	423
5136 Men's and boys' clothing[3]	7	8	76	85	11	20,421	20,753	1,650	2,130
5137 Women's and children's clothing[3]	8	8	47	21	3	10,553	16,381	485	343
5141 Groceries, general line[3]	18	18	1,180	1,280	71	27,695	28,091	34,907	36,579
5142 Packaged frozen food[3]	10	11	351	536	49	31,624	27,440	13,968	15,962
5143 Dairy products, exc. dried or canned[2]	-	4	-	22	6	-	30,000	-	612
5145 Confectionery[3]	8	8	197	202	25	28,386	27,901	5,424	6,149

Continued on next page.

LITTLE ROCK - NORTH LITTLE ROCK, AR MSA - [continued]

Wholesale and Retail Trade USA	Establishments		Employment		Emp / Est	Pay / Employee		Annual Payroll ($ 000)	
	1994	1995	1994	1995	1995	1994	1995	1994	1995
5147 Meats and meat products [1]	3	-	47	-	-	23,574	-	1,111	-
5148 Fresh fruits and vegetables [3]	5	4	44	66	17	29,455	15,818	1,435	1,076
5149 Groceries and related products, nec [3]	33	35	862	999	29	25,128	28,773	23,264	26,284
5162 Plastics materials & basic shapes [3]	9	8	49	48	6	27,837	29,167	1,690	1,743
5169 Chemicals & allied products, nec	36	36	209	224	6	24,632	24,643	5,689	6,854
5171 Petroleum bulk stations & terminals	31	27	217	160	6	31,668	30,725	6,121	4,792
5172 Petroleum products, nec [3]	13	13	60	75	6	24,400	28,213	1,883	2,471
5181 Beer and ale [3]	4	3	183	181	60	26,863	34,188	5,775	5,947
5182 Wine and distilled beverages [3]	5	5	251	254	51	28,972	30,205	7,582	8,202
5191 Farm supplies [1]	35	31	409	451	15	24,010	27,450	10,917	13,680
5192 Books, periodicals, & newspapers [3]	14	14	174	172	12	27,839	25,791	4,607	4,277
5198 Paints, varnishes, and supplies [3]	14	12	105	84	7	19,276	23,857	2,319	2,382
5199 Nondurable goods, nec	28	33	106	135	4	16,000	19,407	1,920	2,917
52- Retail trade	3,414	3,490	48,300	51,276	15	12,072	12,990	653,322	697,881
5210 Lumber and other building materials	66	57	1,754	1,585	28	14,171	18,289	28,934	30,126
5230 Paint, glass, and wallpaper stores [3]	27	26	117	105	4	18,701	20,038	2,358	2,210
5250 Hardware stores [2]	24	17	109	91	5	17,835	15,956	2,061	1,501
5260 Retail nurseries and garden stores	24	28	115	137	5	11,826	12,438	1,759	1,996
5270 Mobile home dealers	19	20	117	173	9	23,556	24,069	4,125	5,136
5310 Department stores [3]	26	26	4,535	4,662	179	10,864	12,511	55,498	58,847
5330 Variety stores	25	19	118	77	4	8,305	8,052	1,066	695
5390 Misc. general merchandise stores	23	36	755	838	23	11,698	12,811	9,854	9,469
5410 Grocery stores [2]	268	270	5,142	4,784	18	11,403	11,904	61,561	58,977
5420 Meat and fish markets [3]	10	9	24	25	3	12,167	13,120	344	377
5430 Fruit and vegetable markets [2]	-	3	-	6	2	-	12,000	-	71
5440 Candy, nut, and confectionery stores [3]	11	5	56	22	4	6,286	7,091	220	125
5450 Dairy products stores [3]	4	4	11	12	3	5,818	6,000	70	53
5460 Retail bakeries [2]	43	41	194	251	6	9,402	10,279	2,577	2,742
5490 Miscellaneous food stores	13	16	31	33	2	10,710	10,909	361	424
5510 New and used car dealers	51	54	2,409	2,552	47	27,680	29,743	80,630	85,788
5520 Used car dealers	63	69	328	396	6	21,634	19,707	8,051	8,719
5530 Auto and home supply stores	114	113	665	685	6	15,976	17,588	11,998	13,008
5540 Gasoline service stations	228	233	1,840	1,948	8	11,039	11,222	21,839	23,266
5550 Boat dealers [3]	9	7	39	33	5	16,821	16,121	688	515
5560 Recreational vehicle dealers [3]	11	10	99	104	10	15,273	17,962	1,909	2,060
5570 Motorcycle dealers [3]	10	10	55	61	6	26,836	29,902	1,803	1,941
5610 Men's & boys' clothing stores [3]	35	33	230	214	6	13,443	14,972	3,148	3,173
5620 Women's clothing stores	115	101	1,040	862	9	9,081	9,494	9,572	8,440
5630 Women's accessory & specialty stores [3]	21	19	138	136	7	12,696	12,500	1,751	1,732
5640 Children's and infants' wear stores	16	15	72	85	6	11,444	10,353	793	819
5650 Family clothing stores [2]	37	38	631	610	16	10,149	10,393	6,355	5,988
5660 Shoe stores	65	61	334	352	6	10,994	11,341	3,821	3,935
5690 Misc. apparel & accessory stores [1]	23	25	66	89	4	10,242	9,213	920	953
5712 Furniture stores	85	87	466	467	5	19,519	19,734	9,691	9,641
5713 Floor covering stores [1]	28	29	91	89	3	20,088	21,483	1,994	2,059
5714 Drapery and upholstery stores [3]	15	15	61	66	4	17,115	15,818	1,138	1,149
5719 Misc. homefurnishings stores [3]	37	35	231	231	7	12,260	14,043	3,396	3,525
5720 Household appliance stores	17	19	94	115	6	17,617	18,957	1,776	2,285
5731 Radio, TV, & electronic stores	45	44	385	564	13	17,662	14,745	8,256	8,824
5734 Computer and software stores [3]	16	22	58	123	6	15,931	15,447	1,082	1,945
5735 Record & prerecorded tape stores [3]	18	18	156	161	9	8,872	9,217	1,397	1,280
5736 Musical instrument stores [3]	9	10	36	40	4	22,333	18,800	714	783
5812 Eating places	801	772	15,993	17,116	22	6,998	7,465	120,855	131,268
5813 Drinking places [3]	29	27	149	187	7	7,356	6,353	1,193	1,105
5910 Drug stores and proprietary stores	106	107	931	977	9	14,883	14,985	14,432	16,136
5920 Liquor stores [1]	106	105	401	408	4	11,581	11,686	4,774	5,116
5930 Used merchandise stores	81	76	283	279	4	10,530	12,487	3,505	3,406
5941 Sporting goods and bicycle shops	60	66	319	321	5	12,577	12,561	4,539	4,588
5942 Book stores	33	30	163	174	6	9,571	11,494	1,466	2,215
5943 Stationery stores [3]	5	4	29	41	10	14,621	14,537	556	676
5944 Jewelry stores [3]	43	40	190	197	5	16,358	19,086	3,413	3,623
5945 Hobby, toy, and game shops [3]	25	24	233	261	11	9,202	8,352	2,500	2,719
5947 Gift, novelty, and souvenir shops	66	58	399	378	7	6,797	6,963	3,484	3,535
5949 Sewing, needlework, and piece goods [3]	19	20	105	99	5	9,295	8,646	910	849
5961 Catalog and mail-order houses [3]	8	8	42	51	6	17,524	16,235	752	1,047
5962 Merchandising machine operators [3]	16	16	235	228	14	15,200	16,684	3,772	3,955
5963 Direct selling establishments	39	39	238	274	7	16,773	17,766	4,135	4,491
5984 Liquefied petroleum gas dealers	10	10	24	40	4	23,167	20,100	610	685
5992 Florists	62	61	256	353	6	10,391	10,935	2,985	3,697
5993 Tobacco stores and stands [1]	9	20	20	20	1	8,600	10,600	245	366
5994 News dealers and newsstands [1]	4	-	25	-	-	13,920	-	447	-

Continued on next page.

LITTLE ROCK - NORTH LITTLE ROCK, AR MSA - [continued]

Wholesale and Retail Trade USA	Establishments		Employment		Emp / Est	Pay / Employee		Annual Payroll ($ 000)	
	1994	1995	1994	1995	1995	1994	1995	1994	1995
5995 Optical goods stores [1]	27	29	124	123	4	12,935	15,024	1,693	2,026
5999 Miscellaneous retail stores, nec	98	107	469	468	4	10,542	11,325	5,666	6,013

Source: County Business Patterns 1994/95, CBP-94/95, U.S. Department of Commerce, Washington DC, November 1997. The employment column represents mid-March employment in the year. Pay per employee is calculated by dividing 1st Quarter payroll, annualized, by mid-March employment. The column headed 'Emp / Est' shows 'employees per establishment'. A dash (-) means that data are unavailable or cannot be calculated. nec means not elsewhere classified. *Notes:* 1. 1994 data incomplete; unavailable or withheld. 2. 1995 data incomplete; unavailable or withheld. 3. 1994 and 1995 data incomplete; unavailable or withheld.

LONGVIEW - MARSHALL, TX MSA

Wholesale and Retail Trade USA	Establishments		Employment		Emp / Est	Pay / Employee		Annual Payroll ($ 000)	
	1994	1995	1994	1995	1995	1994	1995	1994	1995
50- Wholesale trade	-	492	-	4,886	10	-	26,204	-	139,010
5012 Automobiles and other vehicles	-	15	-	266	18	-	24,602	-	4,322
5013 Motor vehicle supplies and new parts [2]	-	33	-	226	7	-	21,699	-	5,549
5020 Furniture and homefurnishings [2]	-	5	-	17	3	-	17,647	-	311
5032 Brick, stone, & related materials [2]	-	4	-	20	5	-	15,200	-	496
5044 Office equipment [2]	-	9	-	58	6	-	25,103	-	1,558
5045 Computers, peripherals, & software [2]	-	13	-	87	7	-	24,920	-	2,351
5051 Metals service centers and offices	-	18	-	176	10	-	32,818	-	6,861
5063 Electrical apparatus and equipment	-	18	-	120	7	-	32,033	-	3,458
5065 Electronic parts and equipment [2]	-	4	-	21	5	-	15,048	-	323
5072 Hardware [2]	-	10	-	62	6	-	22,645	-	1,450
5074 Plumbing & hydronic heating supplies [2]	-	7	-	75	11	-	24,800	-	1,835
5075 Warm air heating & air conditioning [2]	-	5	-	15	3	-	24,267	-	339
5078 Refrigeration equipment and supplies [2]	-	3	-	8	3	-	20,500	-	249
5082 Construction and mining machinery [2]	-	7	-	213	30	-	35,437	-	8,472
5083 Farm and garden machinery	-	10	-	43	4	-	26,419	-	1,469
5084 Industrial machinery and equipment [2]	-	85	-	662	8	-	30,502	-	23,164
5085 Industrial supplies [2]	-	24	-	205	9	-	28,000	-	5,752
5087 Service establishment equipment [2]	-	12	-	78	7	-	18,923	-	1,716
5093 Scrap and waste materials [2]	-	9	-	91	10	-	18,022	-	1,903
5099 Durable goods, nec [2]	-	15	-	54	4	-	23,259	-	1,275
5110 Paper and paper products [2]	-	11	-	63	6	-	19,238	-	1,156
5130 Apparel, piece goods, and notions [2]	-	5	-	18	4	-	6,222	-	126
5149 Groceries and related products, nec [2]	-	10	-	184	18	-	23,761	-	4,581
5160 Chemicals and allied products [2]	-	21	-	242	12	-	30,264	-	7,799
5171 Petroleum bulk stations & terminals	-	21	-	316	15	-	39,418	-	12,525
5172 Petroleum products, nec	-	11	-	62	6	-	25,032	-	1,383
5181 Beer and ale [2]	-	3	-	106	35	-	23,585	-	2,771
5182 Wine and distilled beverages [2]	-	4	-	167	42	-	28,503	-	5,247
5191 Farm supplies	-	14	-	39	3	-	17,026	-	698
5193 Flowers & florists' supplies [2]	-	3	-	27	9	-	15,704	-	416
5199 Nondurable goods, nec [2]	-	4	-	18	5	-	18,889	-	360
52- Retail trade	-	1,382	-	16,973	12	-	12,089	-	216,563
5210 Lumber and other building materials	-	24	-	384	16	-	18,552	-	7,185
5230 Paint, glass, and wallpaper stores [2]	-	9	-	38	4	-	17,263	-	696
5260 Retail nurseries and garden stores [2]	-	8	-	75	9	-	9,227	-	726
5310 Department stores [2]	-	12	-	1,615	135	-	13,122	-	21,471
5330 Variety stores [2]	-	10	-	45	5	-	7,378	-	365
5390 Misc. general merchandise stores	-	17	-	265	16	-	13,223	-	3,383
5410 Grocery stores	-	133	-	2,345	18	-	11,468	-	28,078
5460 Retail bakeries	-	13	-	46	4	-	8,087	-	294
5510 New and used car dealers	-	23	-	701	30	-	31,817	-	26,043
5520 Used car dealers	-	32	-	117	4	-	19,590	-	2,746
5530 Auto and home supply stores	-	71	-	344	5	-	17,128	-	6,132
5540 Gasoline service stations	-	136	-	975	7	-	10,064	-	9,860
5550 Boat dealers [2]	-	4	-	29	7	-	14,621	-	514
5610 Men's & boys' clothing stores [2]	-	8	-	44	6	-	8,545	-	541
5620 Women's clothing stores [2]	-	38	-	231	6	-	8,242	-	1,892
5650 Family clothing stores	-	21	-	330	16	-	8,715	-	4,324
5660 Shoe stores [2]	-	28	-	141	5	-	10,723	-	1,512
5690 Misc. apparel & accessory stores [2]	-	8	-	33	4	-	6,545	-	282
5712 Furniture stores	-	51	-	260	5	-	18,800	-	5,448
5713 Floor covering stores [2]	-	10	-	8	1	-	14,500	-	139
5719 Misc. homefurnishings stores [2]	-	13	-	174	13	-	10,736	-	2,050
5720 Household appliance stores	-	10	-	19	2	-	14,526	-	286
5731 Radio, TV, & electronic stores	-	24	-	144	6	-	17,472	-	2,437
5735 Record & prerecorded tape stores [2]	-	5	-	55	11	-	7,564	-	396
5812 Eating places	-	236	-	4,769	20	-	7,925	-	40,283

Continued on next page.

LONGVIEW - MARSHALL, TX MSA - [continued]

Wholesale and Retail Trade USA	Establishments		Employment		Emp / Est	Pay / Employee		Annual Payroll ($ 000)	
	1994	1995	1994	1995	1995	1994	1995	1994	1995
5813 Drinking places[2]	-	30	-	478	16	-	6,653	-	2,744
5910 Drug stores and proprietary stores	-	40	-	417	10	-	16,700	-	6,667
5920 Liquor stores	-	38	-	140	4	-	13,171	-	2,290
5930 Used merchandise stores[2]	-	25	-	120	5	-	12,400	-	1,457
5941 Sporting goods and bicycle shops	-	20	-	92	5	-	9,174	-	1,034
5942 Book stores[2]	-	5	-	76	15	-	7,632	-	537
5943 Stationery stores[2]	-	4	-	17	4	-	10,118	-	174
5944 Jewelry stores[2]	-	22	-	95	4	-	13,558	-	1,319
5945 Hobby, toy, and game shops[2]	-	9	-	96	11	-	9,458	-	986
5947 Gift, novelty, and souvenir shops	-	20	-	62	3	-	7,806	-	578
5963 Direct selling establishments[2]	-	13	-	67	5	-	18,806	-	1,394
5984 Liquefied petroleum gas dealers	-	10	-	27	3	-	23,111	-	549
5992 Florists	-	23	-	85	4	-	8,894	-	821
5995 Optical goods stores[2]	-	9	-	38	4	-	16,316	-	673
5999 Miscellaneous retail stores, nec	-	28	-	106	4	-	13,170	-	1,550

Source: County Business Patterns 1994/95, CBP-94/95, U.S. Department of Commerce, Washington DC, November 1997. The employment column represents mid-March employment in the year. Pay per employee is calculated by dividing 1st Quarter payroll, annualized, by mid-March employment. The column headed 'Emp / Est' shows 'employees per establishment'. A dash (-) means that data are unavailable or cannot be calculated. nec means not elsewhere classified. *Notes:* 1. 1994 data incomplete; unavailable or withheld. 2. 1995 data incomplete; unavailable or withheld. 3. 1994 and 1995 data incomplete; unavailable or withheld.

LOS ANGELES - LONG BEACH, CA PMSA

Wholesale and Retail Trade USA	Establishments		Employment		Emp / Est	Pay / Employee		Annual Payroll ($ 000)	
	1994	1995	1994	1995	1995	1994	1995	1994	1995
50- Wholesale trade	21,406	22,237	282,983	288,275	13	33,279	34,257	9,964,796	10,246,273
5012 Automobiles and other vehicles	226	221	6,120	6,193	28	44,776	51,058	304,708	332,181
5013 Motor vehicle supplies and new parts	846	787	10,555	10,644	14	25,843	27,215	296,145	302,498
5014 Tires and tubes	90	84	1,173	1,023	12	28,126	28,766	40,981	34,155
5015 Motor vehicle parts, used	208	255	1,505	1,982	8	17,770	19,112	29,107	40,042
5021 Furniture	377	386	3,758	4,150	11	27,986	29,454	119,277	123,969
5023 Homefurnishings	512	487	6,379	6,015	12	25,401	28,390	185,202	182,041
5031 Lumber, plywood, and millwork	156	160	2,118	2,147	13	29,345	29,876	70,960	68,258
5032 Brick, stone, & related materials	131	123	1,152	1,200	10	26,910	26,323	36,330	33,600
5033 Roofing, siding, & insulation	49	39	916	685	18	31,231	29,489	32,621	25,286
5039 Construction materials, nec	96	168	1,105	1,675	10	28,076	28,743	33,976	52,738
5043 Photographic equipment & supplies	109	109	2,546	2,505	23	42,666	46,691	109,067	114,776
5044 Office equipment	228	229	5,221	5,455	24	35,747	38,733	185,006	199,129
5045 Computers, peripherals, & software	914	897	13,648	12,042	13	39,721	43,962	550,899	517,841
5046 Commercial equipment, nec	190	191	2,054	2,079	11	31,628	29,481	70,850	66,184
5047 Medical and hospital equipment	332	334	3,993	3,971	12	37,459	40,149	158,757	174,792
5048 Ophthalmic goods	108	104	1,644	1,704	16	30,063	33,622	54,310	61,251
5049 Professional equipment, nec	73	72	1,178	1,287	18	30,591	34,266	39,796	47,892
5051 Metals service centers and offices	416	412	7,080	7,209	17	34,828	37,115	275,756	297,941
5052 Coal and other minerals and ores	9	-	40	-	-	27,800	-	1,109	-
5063 Electrical apparatus and equipment	608	525	7,615	6,866	13	36,059	35,428	284,919	246,080
5064 Electrical appliances, TV & radios	287	297	4,804	5,084	17	32,865	35,618	175,056	185,364
5065 Electronic parts and equipment	892	916	12,443	13,968	15	38,632	40,120	518,015	598,481
5072 Hardware	368	378	5,347	5,716	15	27,732	29,474	164,063	174,479
5074 Plumbing & hydronic heating supplies	231	222	3,066	3,066	14	28,903	29,431	98,818	96,788
5075 Warm air heating & air conditioning	103	94	986	912	10	39,006	40,921	40,646	38,657
5078 Refrigeration equipment and supplies	48	46	666	648	14	30,625	32,401	21,725	21,882
5082 Construction and mining machinery	72	79	1,188	940	12	31,172	34,723	37,112	35,042
5083 Farm and garden machinery	64	61	819	761	12	38,427	38,392	32,416	30,444
5084 Industrial machinery and equipment	849	838	9,879	10,505	13	33,201	35,990	359,984	424,041
5085 Industrial supplies	478	466	5,461	5,589	12	32,129	33,214	181,947	191,483
5087 Service establishment equipment	208	196	2,248	2,110	11	25,737	28,506	60,624	60,661
5088 Transportation equipment & supplies	288	276	3,442	2,884	10	36,371	40,595	132,584	119,874
5091 Sporting & recreational goods	270	280	2,526	2,831	10	28,238	27,448	82,763	84,781
5092 Toys and hobby goods and supplies	283	286	3,846	3,763	13	38,503	39,567	141,273	138,508
5093 Scrap and waste materials	331	339	4,473	4,876	14	22,339	24,445	113,582	134,656
5094 Jewelry & precious stones	779	768	4,995	4,886	6	27,471	29,519	145,978	149,383
5099 Durable goods, nec	612	657	6,114	5,571	8	31,831	36,937	199,276	213,126
5111 Printing and writing paper	89	82	1,865	1,952	24	45,021	45,740	79,641	84,288
5112 Stationery and office supplies	397	318	6,795	5,221	16	24,472	27,167	171,305	147,188
5113 Industrial & personal service paper	244	246	3,617	3,695	15	31,444	34,887	125,437	141,348
5120 Drugs, proprietaries, and sundries	381	394	7,036	7,330	19	37,411	36,588	285,267	292,139
5131 Piece goods & notions	726	765	6,375	6,992	9	26,102	26,584	192,124	196,176
5136 Men's and boys' clothing	427	420	4,753	5,091	12	31,274	31,277	160,754	146,438
5137 Women's and children's clothing	1,038	969	8,955	9,259	10	25,835	25,970	259,826	250,938

Continued on next page.

LOS ANGELES – LONG BEACH, CA PMSA - [continued]

Wholesale and Retail Trade USA	Establishments		Employment		Emp / Est	Pay / Employee		Annual Payroll ($ 000)	
	1994	1995	1994	1995	1995	1994	1995	1994	1995
5139 Footwear	161	160	1,387	1,811	11	33,355	28,853	58,323	57,261
5141 Groceries, general line	275	264	7,135	7,425	28	30,019	30,395	224,713	235,358
5142 Packaged frozen food	132	128	4,642	5,077	40	26,457	26,302	129,674	142,197
5143 Dairy products, exc. dried or canned	73	77	1,690	1,797	23	32,653	33,928	56,831	62,828
5144 Poultry and poultry products	32	28	901	860	31	21,558	23,847	20,741	22,150
5145 Confectionery	89	90	1,897	2,179	24	24,506	23,009	48,315	50,617
5146 Fish and seafoods	137	143	1,899	1,814	13	25,032	25,649	48,855	49,650
5147 Meats and meat products	205	198	3,599	3,787	19	23,653	25,060	92,635	104,602
5148 Fresh fruits and vegetables	289	277	6,584	6,601	24	28,157	27,567	200,127	197,464
5149 Groceries and related products, nec	570	550	11,927	11,814	21	29,017	30,056	351,601	357,487
5153 Grain and field beans	16	16	182	192	12	19,209	23,417	4,806	5,026
5154 Livestock	4	4	8	9	2	25,000	24,000	226	297
5159 Farm-product raw materials, nec	30	31	176	169	5	28,295	32,450	7,048	6,959
5162 Plastics materials & basic shapes	156	159	1,928	2,050	13	34,710	34,496	69,515	75,268
5169 Chemicals & allied products, nec	287	296	3,842	3,865	13	37,114	38,073	146,530	154,739
5171 Petroleum bulk stations & terminals	82	79	1,814	2,017	26	38,381	38,453	77,314	82,470
5172 Petroleum products, nec	85	81	900	871	11	52,169	48,588	45,331	44,598
5181 Beer and ale	40	36	2,794	2,843	79	31,970	34,431	104,115	103,135
5182 Wine and distilled beverages	47	47	2,422	2,280	49	42,821	46,537	96,728	102,352
5191 Farm supplies	100	88	880	785	9	29,155	34,685	27,624	28,856
5192 Books, periodicals, & newspapers	185	195	2,812	3,128	16	31,697	31,532	88,911	102,247
5193 Flowers & florists' supplies	188	163	1,773	1,750	11	20,074	22,021	39,289	39,182
5194 Tobacco and tobacco products	25	24	496	501	21	27,185	28,687	15,196	16,574
5198 Paints, varnishes, and supplies	123	115	1,123	1,173	10	27,466	29,749	36,645	38,266
5199 Nondurable goods, nec	1,571	1,813	9,057	10,054	6	23,455	24,384	245,678	271,101
52 – Retail trade	42,341	42,125	565,833	584,061	14	15,297	15,789	9,279,965	9,625,483
5210 Lumber and other building materials	455	412	10,677	11,864	29	20,096	21,959	237,779	257,719
5230 Paint, glass, and wallpaper stores	246	237	1,257	1,260	5	22,396	23,695	30,239	30,958
5250 Hardware stores	290	198	2,083	1,867	9	18,274	18,627	45,961	35,874
5260 Retail nurseries and garden stores	169	169	1,298	1,264	7	15,282	15,747	21,894	21,673
5270 Mobile home dealers	19	16	73	61	4	11,836	15,541	971	1,141
5310 Department stores	193	196	40,374	44,822	229	12,863	12,865	560,281	574,469
5330 Variety stores	174	160	2,140	1,937	12	11,264	12,070	24,302	24,243
5390 Misc. general merchandise stores	333	336	9,346	9,423	28	15,224	17,287	158,055	162,301
5410 Grocery stores	2,578	2,522	61,375	61,341	24	18,922	19,767	1,205,401	1,261,352
5420 Meat and fish markets	311	304	1,713	1,821	6	11,972	12,145	21,505	24,022
5430 Fruit and vegetable markets	79	80	352	391	5	13,159	12,440	5,323	5,738
5440 Candy, nut, and confectionery stores	163	151	751	848	6	10,557	10,519	8,826	9,275
5450 Dairy products stores	107	101	399	448	4	5,634	5,473	2,620	2,512
5460 Retail bakeries	1,119	1,088	7,220	7,003	6	13,440	13,107	102,492	94,421
5490 Miscellaneous food stores	350	360	2,018	2,584	7	11,816	11,570	25,615	34,114
5510 New and used car dealers	501	492	25,946	27,176	55	33,762	34,373	969,139	1,014,295
5520 Used car dealers	242	245	1,297	1,287	5	19,692	20,848	28,487	28,609
5530 Auto and home supply stores	1,244	1,212	10,010	10,202	8	16,378	16,610	178,061	172,971
5540 Gasoline service stations	2,103	2,066	12,615	13,080	6	11,682	12,000	156,292	165,144
5550 Boat dealers	50	46	252	270	6	17,571	18,785	5,762	6,735
5560 Recreational vehicle dealers	50	43	578	509	12	23,965	24,314	15,155	13,248
5570 Motorcycle dealers	83	80	705	736	9	23,569	24,424	17,513	19,715
5590 Automotive dealers, nec	18	16	62	61	4	22,710	25,311	1,767	1,796
5610 Men's & boys' clothing stores	561	530	4,185	4,288	8	13,732	16,343	62,173	78,154
5620 Women's clothing stores	1,517	1,368	13,023	11,962	9	11,706	12,495	161,787	145,056
5630 Women's accessory & specialty stores	256	256	1,454	1,600	6	12,003	13,555	19,414	21,079
5640 Children's and infants' wear stores	241	224	1,517	1,519	7	9,793	10,670	16,646	16,698
5650 Family clothing stores	556	493	11,259	12,050	24	13,526	13,831	163,729	168,267
5660 Shoe stores	1,092	1,061	5,619	5,715	5	13,946	14,666	81,870	83,432
5690 Misc. apparel & accessory stores	302	308	1,400	1,573	5	11,714	12,531	21,273	21,186
5712 Furniture stores	788	774	5,827	6,465	8	20,128	19,376	131,195	133,945
5713 Floor covering stores	346	360	1,775	2,046	6	18,098	19,636	39,495	44,670
5714 Drapery and upholstery stores	80	70	265	277	4	19,351	20,534	5,639	6,190
5719 Misc. homefurnishings stores	553	544	4,342	4,296	8	13,397	14,948	66,774	67,552
5720 Household appliance stores	213	207	2,057	1,818	9	19,714	21,281	45,698	38,309
5731 Radio, TV, & electronic stores	552	572	5,704	7,234	13	21,720	20,137	141,806	158,044
5734 Computer and software stores	309	339	2,469	2,737	8	20,770	22,217	55,994	67,975
5735 Record & prerecorded tape stores	352	358	4,016	4,691	13	9,579	11,151	40,909	54,145
5736 Musical instrument stores	136	138	853	869	6	18,893	18,776	16,701	17,927
5812 Eating places	12,047	11,368	200,983	201,288	18	9,344	9,935	2,025,038	2,074,163
5813 Drinking places	1,004	977	7,225	6,997	7	7,905	8,333	59,985	60,636
5910 Drug stores and proprietary stores	1,277	1,242	16,222	17,487	14	21,743	20,410	388,505	358,529
5920 Liquor stores	1,097	1,047	3,235	3,094	3	10,573	10,374	36,035	33,692
5930 Used merchandise stores	466	475	3,137	3,283	7	13,827	13,885	47,963	49,217
5941 Sporting goods and bicycle shops	544	530	4,880	5,076	10	12,937	12,418	67,516	67,368

Continued on next page.

LOS ANGELES - LONG BEACH, CA PMSA - [continued]

Wholesale and Retail Trade USA	Establishments		Employment		Emp / Est	Pay / Employee		Annual Payroll ($ 000)	
	1994	1995	1994	1995	1995	1994	1995	1994	1995
5942 Book stores	455	442	4,424	4,760	11	12,131	11,634	55,637	57,323
5943 Stationery stores	209	223	1,501	2,134	10	13,018	14,388	20,068	30,120
5944 Jewelry stores	852	845	3,980	3,827	5	18,409	19,749	79,067	77,655
5945 Hobby, toy, and game shops	296	284	3,036	3,628	13	10,664	10,836	39,338	43,437
5946 Camera & photographic supply stores	128	131	742	706	5	17,892	20,606	13,910	13,996
5947 Gift, novelty, and souvenir shops	846	822	4,551	4,825	6	9,333	9,795	48,276	50,605
5948 Luggage and leather goods stores	73	72	691	481	7	16,197	19,983	12,735	11,166
5949 Sewing, needlework, and piece goods	178	165	1,508	1,485	9	12,401	11,577	18,902	17,437
5961 Catalog and mail-order houses	225	258	2,525	2,714	11	26,758	29,770	72,880	75,191
5962 Merchandising machine operators	107	108	1,097	1,151	11	24,204	23,854	27,595	36,450
5963 Direct selling establishments	312	319	4,256	4,701	15	16,442	16,739	77,147	81,729
5983 Fuel oil dealers	7	6	93	74	12	23,355	21,622	2,649	1,675
5984 Liquefied petroleum gas dealers	21	22	218	228	10	23,633	26,070	5,345	5,810
5989 Fuel dealers, nec	5	4	9	10	3	11,556	8,800	141	134
5992 Florists	603	596	3,116	3,019	5	10,375	11,412	34,387	35,197
5993 Tobacco stores and stands	23	30	98	101	3	11,796	13,545	1,204	1,551
5994 News dealers and newsstands	53	50	327	316	6	10,153	10,633	3,651	3,657
5995 Optical goods stores	309	304	1,435	1,544	5	15,744	16,943	24,898	27,875
5999 Miscellaneous retail stores, nec	1,365	1,429	7,024	7,622	5	15,584	16,633	122,253	138,119

Source: County Business Patterns 1994/95, CBP-94/95, U.S. Department of Commerce, Washington DC, November 1997. The employment column represents mid-March employment in the year. Pay per employee is calculated by dividing 1st Quarter payroll, annualized, by mid-March employment. The column headed 'Emp / Est' shows 'employees per establishment'. A dash (-) means that data are unavailable or cannot be calculated. nec means not elsewhere classified. *Notes:* 1. 1994 data incomplete; unavailable or withheld. 2. 1995 data incomplete; unavailable or withheld. 3. 1994 and 1995 data incomplete; unavailable or withheld.

LOUISVILLE MSA (IN PART)

Wholesale and Retail Trade USA	Establishments		Employment		Emp / Est	Pay / Employee		Annual Payroll ($ 000)	
	1994	1995	1994	1995	1995	1994	1995	1994	1995
50- Wholesale trade	316	314	3,099	3,279	10	21,200	21,376	74,172	75,317
5012 Automobiles and other vehicles [3]	6	6	152	227	38	25,158	23,278	4,348	5,414
5013 Motor vehicle supplies and new parts	32	25	135	116	5	13,481	14,862	2,053	1,722
5014 Tires and tubes [1]	4	-	51	-	-	23,686	-	1,450	-
5015 Motor vehicle parts, used [3]	10	10	25	20	2	11,360	11,000	269	211
5031 Lumber, plywood, and millwork	13	14	112	50	4	39,607	61,760	3,830	1,743
5046 Commercial equipment, nec [3]	5	4	49	54	14	17,388	17,259	1,090	1,068
5047 Medical and hospital equipment [3]	7	6	13	28	5	22,462	32,286	315	971
5051 Metals service centers and offices [3]	8	10	144	185	19	20,500	20,627	3,631	4,136
5065 Electronic parts and equipment [3]	11	10	66	16	2	31,394	30,750	2,177	689
5070 Hardware, plumbing & heating equipment [3]	14	13	118	81	6	22,678	23,704	2,834	1,738
5084 Industrial machinery and equipment [3]	16	17	93	101	6	21,720	23,248	2,337	2,701
5087 Service establishment equipment [3]	6	6	51	39	7	17,647	17,538	1,098	679
5099 Durable goods, nec	9	8	18	3	-	16,444	12,000	602	44
5113 Industrial & personal service paper [3]	6	9	51	62	7	18,118	20,645	1,059	1,649
5149 Groceries and related products, nec [3]	5	8	93	96	12	28,989	31,083	2,986	3,240
5169 Chemicals & allied products, nec [3]	5	6	26	24	4	30,000	21,667	746	466
5170 Petroleum and petroleum products	16	13	130	136	10	25,877	20,676	4,499	4,527
5180 Beer, wine, and distilled beverages [2]	-	5	-	41	8	-	20,098	-	899
5191 Farm supplies	17	12	54	43	4	12,370	14,605	725	731
5198 Paints, varnishes, and supplies [1]	5	-	7	-	-	21,714	-	162	-
5199 Nondurable goods, nec [3]	7	9	18	36	4	16,889	16,111	397	666
52- Retail trade	1,229	1,246	16,852	17,640	14	10,419	11,468	197,079	215,263
5210 Lumber and other building materials	20	20	623	511	26	14,844	19,194	9,906	8,902
5230 Paint, glass, and wallpaper stores [3]	11	12	71	85	7	15,493	17,882	1,307	1,757
5250 Hardware stores	20	18	45	92	5	9,422	8,870	469	1,066
5260 Retail nurseries and garden stores	12	14	80	101	7	10,800	11,010	1,207	1,389
5270 Mobile home dealers	10	10	42	47	5	22,286	28,255	1,147	1,321
5310 Department stores [3]	12	13	1,390	1,653	127	10,409	11,197	16,707	19,953
5330 Variety stores [2]	-	8	-	46	6	-	9,652	-	513
5390 Misc. general merchandise stores	-	15	-	101	7	-	11,366	-	1,243
5410 Grocery stores	97	97	2,124	2,165	22	9,844	10,688	22,466	23,689
5430 Fruit and vegetable markets [3]	6	6	20	20	3	6,400	6,800	183	197
5440 Candy, nut, and confectionery stores [2]	-	4	-	17	4	-	6,824	-	120
5450 Dairy products stores [3]	3	4	15	34	9	7,467	4,588	156	182
5460 Retail bakeries [3]	15	15	67	65	4	6,030	6,892	479	494
5490 Miscellaneous food stores [1]	6	-	13	-	-	7,385	-	95	-
5510 New and used car dealers	16	17	614	668	39	27,707	29,749	19,510	22,346
5520 Used car dealers	24	30	125	137	5	10,880	12,321	1,488	1,792
5530 Auto and home supply stores	39	43	312	248	6	15,500	17,935	4,920	4,652
5540 Gasoline service stations	101	96	903	841	9	9,475	11,006	9,233	9,863

Continued on next page.

LOUISVILLE MSA (IN PART) - [continued]

Wholesale and Retail Trade USA	Establishments		Employment		Emp / Est	Pay / Employee		Annual Payroll ($ 000)	
	1994	1995	1994	1995	1995	1994	1995	1994	1995
5550 Boat dealers [3]	6	6	57	72	12	19,860	17,833	1,636	1,885
5610 Men's & boys' clothing stores [2]	-	3	-	33	11	-	6,667	-	197
5620 Women's clothing stores [3]	26	23	236	202	9	11,220	9,921	2,158	1,376
5630 Women's accessory & specialty stores [3]	6	5	26	23	5	5,846	7,130	167	150
5650 Family clothing stores [3]	8	9	138	122	14	7,362	9,246	1,182	855
5660 Shoe stores [3]	29	29	136	140	5	10,147	10,771	1,389	1,504
5690 Misc. apparel & accessory stores [3]	7	8	15	19	2	9,333	6,316	125	127
5712 Furniture stores	22	22	207	215	10	20,773	21,805	4,269	4,900
5713 Floor covering stores	20	19	68	69	4	13,647	13,159	1,059	1,137
5719 Misc. homefurnishings stores [3]	9	9	10	15	2	7,600	7,733	117	119
5720 Household appliance stores [1]	6	7	13	14	2	14,462	12,857	197	199
5731 Radio, TV, & electronic stores [3]	12	11	67	98	9	17,373	18,122	1,576	1,933
5734 Computer and software stores [2]	-	7	-	6	1	-	13,333	-	83
5735 Record & prerecorded tape stores [3]	9	8	43	41	5	8,558	11,220	382	326
5812 Eating places	277	269	5,750	5,957	22	6,783	7,474	44,822	48,240
5813 Drinking places	37	28	170	141	5	6,588	7,177	1,168	1,003
5910 Drug stores and proprietary stores	36	37	430	475	13	14,474	15,082	6,807	7,767
5920 Liquor stores	40	38	196	208	5	8,551	7,788	1,768	1,807
5930 Used merchandise stores	20	20	43	103	5	6,605	7,728	323	805
5941 Sporting goods and bicycle shops [3]	15	19	93	92	5	9,935	11,652	1,265	1,470
5944 Jewelry stores [3]	19	20	92	82	4	14,696	14,976	1,410	1,225
5945 Hobby, toy, and game shops [3]	8	7	54	56	8	7,556	8,429	571	600
5947 Gift, novelty, and souvenir shops	32	33	101	99	3	7,248	7,192	826	882
5963 Direct selling establishments [1]	11	-	40	-	-	16,400	-	625	-
5984 Liquefied petroleum gas dealers	11	13	29	39	3	25,517	23,897	762	943
5992 Florists	23	24	104	124	5	9,808	9,613	1,156	1,266
5995 Optical goods stores [3]	7	6	51	52	9	26,667	25,154	1,390	1,720
5999 Miscellaneous retail stores, nec	39	42	117	136	3	11,487	12,265	1,592	1,965

Source: County Business Patterns 1994/95, CBP-94/95, U.S. Department of Commerce, Washington DC, November 1997. The employment column represents mid-March employment in the year. Pay per employee is calculated by dividing 1st Quarter payroll, annualized, by mid-March employment. The column headed 'Emp / Est' shows 'employees per establishment'. A dash (-) means that data are unavailable or cannot be calculated. nec means not elsewhere classified. *Notes:* 1. 1994 data incomplete; unavailable or withheld. 2. 1995 data incomplete; unavailable or withheld. 3. 1994 and 1995 data incomplete; unavailable or withheld.

LOUISVILLE MSA (KY PART)

Wholesale and Retail Trade USA	Establishments		Employment		Emp / Est	Pay / Employee		Annual Payroll ($ 000)	
	1994	1995	1994	1995	1995	1994	1995	1994	1995
50 - Wholesale trade	1,804	1,831	28,493	30,368	17	29,241	32,232	886,012	955,665
5012 Automobiles and other vehicles [3]	18	20	427	440	22	22,482	23,336	10,231	10,816
5013 Motor vehicle supplies and new parts	106	100	1,443	1,532	15	21,131	23,107	35,745	36,157
5014 Tires and tubes [3]	16	14	254	180	13	31,701	34,333	7,937	6,298
5015 Motor vehicle parts, used [3]	32	31	186	238	8	16,946	18,807	4,570	5,127
5021 Furniture [3]	28	31	284	447	14	26,070	30,148	9,552	14,798
5023 Homefurnishings [3]	26	25	235	255	10	19,319	24,549	6,005	6,226
5031 Lumber, plywood, and millwork [3]	54	46	639	548	12	32,488	34,066	23,376	20,410
5032 Brick, stone, & related materials [3]	13	11	90	87	8	25,867	41,333	2,368	2,907
5033 Roofing, siding, & insulation [3]	12	11	229	257	23	18,061	20,669	6,083	6,176
5039 Construction materials, nec [1]	22	37	308	467	13	22,740	27,143	7,330	13,036
5043 Photographic equipment & supplies [3]	4	4	102	107	27	19,176	21,720	2,503	2,636
5044 Office equipment [3]	32	33	718	712	22	31,370	37,067	23,419	25,147
5045 Computers, peripherals, & software	61	56	667	791	14	47,916	46,397	29,863	33,463
5046 Commercial equipment, nec [3]	20	22	254	310	14	29,780	33,897	8,415	10,485
5047 Medical and hospital equipment [2]	68	65	746	760	12	29,158	32,447	23,773	25,509
5048 Ophthalmic goods [3]	11	10	209	228	23	23,081	24,649	5,413	6,400
5049 Professional equipment, nec [3]	14	16	160	175	11	20,225	22,286	3,917	4,271
5050 Metals and minerals, except petroleum [3]	46	44	481	518	12	29,854	32,486	16,811	17,956
5063 Electrical apparatus and equipment	79	78	960	976	13	31,375	34,914	30,449	32,417
5064 Electrical appliances, TV & radios [3]	18	21	161	194	9	22,783	21,464	4,173	4,809
5065 Electronic parts and equipment [3]	39	48	410	541	11	28,898	27,024	12,482	14,451
5072 Hardware [3]	28	28	304	341	12	29,474	30,381	9,569	10,707
5074 Plumbing & hydronic heating supplies [1]	32	34	434	475	14	23,189	24,589	11,499	13,098
5075 Warm air heating & air conditioning [3]	33	35	381	423	12	30,436	31,811	12,833	15,106
5078 Refrigeration equipment and supplies [3]	14	14	154	173	12	27,922	28,763	6,154	7,013
5082 Construction and mining machinery [3]	30	29	885	1,040	36	37,894	38,031	34,483	38,563
5083 Farm and garden machinery [3]	20	19	211	194	10	20,550	23,938	5,422	5,304
5084 Industrial machinery and equipment	142	141	1,618	1,816	13	31,654	34,956	56,885	66,689
5085 Industrial supplies [3]	78	79	1,018	1,232	16	28,216	29,984	31,576	38,966
5087 Service establishment equipment [1]	29	32	267	242	8	19,326	19,207	5,406	4,900
5088 Transportation equipment & supplies [3]	12	11	110	127	12	27,164	27,780	3,642	4,050

Continued on next page.

LOUISVILLE MSA (KY PART) - [continued]

Wholesale and Retail Trade USA	Establishments		Employment		Emp / Est	Pay / Employee		Annual Payroll ($ 000)	
	1994	1995	1994	1995	1995	1994	1995	1994	1995
5091 Sporting & recreational goods[3]	31	25	196	190	8	19,918	22,358	4,707	4,692
5092 Toys and hobby goods and supplies[3]	8	9	32	27	3	15,500	16,593	473	472
5093 Scrap and waste materials[3]	30	32	416	495	15	25,375	26,917	13,494	14,770
5094 Jewelry & precious stones[3]	12	10	55	59	6	25,091	25,085	1,196	1,416
5099 Durable goods, nec[3]	17	17	92	101	6	33,087	33,941	2,867	3,172
5111 Printing and writing paper[3]	13	10	183	220	22	38,951	38,727	7,019	9,233
5112 Stationery and office supplies[3]	32	29	461	312	11	19,254	24,885	9,259	8,484
5113 Industrial & personal service paper[3]	20	23	213	250	11	26,873	30,960	6,577	7,680
5120 Drugs, proprietaries, and sundries[3]	20	23	809	669	29	22,571	27,001	22,377	19,804
5131 Piece goods & notions[3]	6	7	53	56	8	29,660	31,286	1,443	1,603
5136 Men's and boys' clothing[3]	14	15	90	126	8	13,289	16,921	1,593	2,320
5137 Women's and children's clothing[3]	8	8	231	232	29	13,039	18,655	4,377	6,305
5141 Groceries, general line[3]	19	21	1,220	1,332	63	25,793	26,634	33,316	36,786
5142 Packaged frozen food[3]	13	14	166	176	13	29,663	29,591	4,881	5,645
5143 Dairy products, exc. dried or canned[3]	12	13	156	139	11	24,179	25,554	4,033	3,747
5144 Poultry and poultry products[3]	3	3	55	50	17	25,091	28,400	1,611	1,676
5145 Confectionery[3]	7	7	74	87	12	47,892	28,690	2,878	2,583
5147 Meats and meat products[3]	13	12	239	237	20	17,004	18,920	4,626	4,832
5148 Fresh fruits and vegetables[3]	20	20	255	237	12	19,608	22,785	5,201	5,514
5149 Groceries and related products, nec[3]	37	37	780	958	26	31,226	30,017	26,761	31,073
5153 Grain and field beans[3]	6	6	65	65	11	26,092	24,677	2,374	1,751
5154 Livestock[3]	5	5	89	94	19	15,910	18,043	1,597	1,964
5159 Farm-product raw materials, nec[3]	6	5	22	15	3	44,000	53,067	950	667
5162 Plastics materials & basic shapes[3]	12	13	109	113	9	36,917	46,690	3,724	4,991
5169 Chemicals & allied products, nec	55	54	448	456	8	33,875	33,825	16,998	16,806
5171 Petroleum bulk stations & terminals[3]	21	19	286	226	12	34,587	36,142	8,626	7,870
5172 Petroleum products, nec	12	13	181	191	15	14,387	16,021	2,650	3,655
5181 Beer and ale[3]	3	3	396	283	94	29,293	31,703	12,509	9,999
5182 Wine and distilled beverages[3]	10	11	250	258	23	45,008	38,775	10,230	9,231
5191 Farm supplies	32	29	293	298	10	21,802	26,483	7,595	7,946
5192 Books, periodicals, & newspapers[3]	14	16	175	175	11	19,977	27,543	3,728	4,597
5198 Paints, varnishes, and supplies[3]	30	22	325	228	10	32,062	31,684	10,991	7,367
5199 Nondurable goods, nec	51	56	356	370	7	24,978	28,627	11,401	12,763
52 – Retail trade	4,763	4,705	78,921	82,449	18	12,064	12,701	1,028,736	1,097,723
5210 Lumber and other building materials[2]	61	53	1,498	1,256	24	18,011	22,436	28,800	25,315
5250 Hardware stores	54	40	495	503	13	11,758	12,787	6,815	6,530
5260 Retail nurseries and garden stores	35	37	350	455	12	11,623	10,884	5,231	5,659
5310 Department stores[3]	32	33	5,861	7,069	214	10,572	11,160	69,276	85,895
5330 Variety stores[2]	47	31	438	373	12	7,909	8,418	4,113	3,535
5390 Misc. general merchandise stores[1]	18	33	580	668	20	13,172	13,479	7,811	8,329
5410 Grocery stores[3]	322	318	7,765	7,936	25	10,661	12,058	84,420	95,838
5420 Meat and fish markets[3]	18	18	123	129	7	9,398	9,612	1,283	1,426
5430 Fruit and vegetable markets	19	15	102	124	8	9,961	8,355	1,129	1,253
5440 Candy, nut, and confectionery stores[3]	11	12	55	55	5	5,382	5,745	373	433
5450 Dairy products stores[1]	6	-	19	-	-	2,737	-	149	-
5460 Retail bakeries[3]	59	57	511	486	9	8,384	9,745	5,495	5,303
5490 Miscellaneous food stores[3]	14	17	79	131	8	8,000	7,634	1,019	1,277
5510 New and used car dealers	54	53	3,678	3,733	70	23,958	26,184	101,203	108,419
5520 Used car dealers	77	75	586	567	8	19,038	21,728	12,163	12,326
5530 Auto and home supply stores	140	148	1,127	1,075	7	14,910	17,563	19,715	19,513
5540 Gasoline service stations	288	279	2,495	2,372	9	10,002	11,553	27,963	28,878
5550 Boat dealers[3]	10	11	68	85	8	18,294	19,200	2,003	2,114
5560 Recreational vehicle dealers[3]	10	11	69	67	6	14,609	18,507	1,262	1,347
5570 Motorcycle dealers[3]	6	5	27	23	5	9,037	12,696	345	366
5610 Men's & boys' clothing stores[3]	32	32	285	288	9	10,863	11,861	3,287	3,598
5620 Women's clothing stores	126	105	1,381	1,498	14	7,493	8,521	12,371	12,816
5630 Women's accessory & specialty stores[3]	21	22	116	117	5	9,759	10,256	1,194	1,235
5640 Children's and infants' wear stores[3]	9	13	56	79	6	7,786	7,443	462	699
5650 Family clothing stores[3]	33	28	572	579	21	9,315	9,437	5,811	5,136
5660 Shoe stores[3]	107	96	584	575	6	10,795	11,402	6,687	6,685
5690 Misc. apparel & accessory stores[3]	29	27	129	145	5	10,264	10,317	1,470	1,646
5712 Furniture stores	86	85	967	1,114	13	16,620	16,596	18,551	20,014
5713 Floor covering stores[1]	49	52	319	300	6	16,514	16,867	4,844	5,363
5714 Drapery and upholstery stores[3]	8	8	48	31	4	12,583	12,258	499	381
5719 Misc. homefurnishings stores	58	56	400	399	7	10,680	12,341	4,954	5,106
5720 Household appliance stores[3]	19	18	99	94	5	32,121	31,617	2,581	2,570
5731 Radio, TV, & electronic stores[3]	39	40	509	501	13	16,864	18,116	9,411	9,903
5734 Computer and software stores[3]	19	24	71	94	4	12,732	15,447	1,176	1,682
5735 Record & prerecorded tape stores[3]	27	27	175	193	7	8,411	9,637	1,688	1,876
5736 Musical instrument stores[3]	18	19	134	154	8	12,507	13,377	1,970	2,100
5812 Eating places	1,148	1,086	27,970	28,672	26	7,337	8,043	227,613	245,186

Continued on next page.

LOUISVILLE MSA (KY PART) - [continued]

Wholesale and Retail Trade USA	Establishments		Employment		Emp / Est	Pay / Employee		Annual Payroll ($ 000)	
	1994	1995	1994	1995	1995	1994	1995	1994	1995
5813 Drinking places[3]	174	156	1,102	1,148	7	6,955	7,540	8,422	8,851
5910 Drug stores and proprietary stores	135	132	2,078	1,914	15	14,395	15,737	32,751	32,172
5920 Liquor stores[3]	130	129	627	661	5	9,410	10,451	6,550	7,553
5930 Used merchandise stores	90	97	693	681	7	11,469	13,803	9,342	9,770
5941 Sporting goods and bicycle shops	78	82	515	566	7	9,825	11,265	6,164	7,237
5942 Book stores[3]	37	42	353	395	9	10,006	10,734	3,337	4,207
5944 Jewelry stores[3]	91	93	437	485	5	17,968	20,709	8,278	9,040
5945 Hobby, toy, and game shops[3]	37	36	375	397	11	9,173	9,693	4,204	4,311
5946 Camera & photographic supply stores[3]	10	9	96	92	10	13,417	16,478	1,533	1,674
5947 Gift, novelty, and souvenir shops	92	95	646	732	8	6,935	7,820	5,503	6,475
5949 Sewing, needlework, and piece goods	20	19	212	218	11	10,396	10,679	2,200	2,286
5961 Catalog and mail-order houses[1]	14	17	227	226	13	13,515	19,575	3,722	4,816
5962 Merchandising machine operators[3]	37	36	604	541	15	13,007	16,288	8,151	9,045
5963 Direct selling establishments[3]	49	44	475	524	12	11,764	12,626	6,018	6,648
5980 Fuel dealers	9	10	67	74	7	17,851	17,730	1,181	1,375
5992 Florists	74	69	421	407	6	10,413	11,342	5,086	5,130
5993 Tobacco stores and stands[2]	-	3	-	12	4	-	9,333	-	137
5994 News dealers and newsstands[3]	3	3	19	19	6	12,000	12,000	228	235
5995 Optical goods stores[3]	47	43	320	284	7	21,038	21,282	5,801	5,780
5999 Miscellaneous retail stores, nec	147	139	738	771	6	11,198	12,296	9,624	10,531

Source: County Business Patterns 1994/95, CBP-94/95, U.S. Department of Commerce, Washington DC, November 1997. The employment column represents mid-March employment in the year. Pay per employee is calculated by dividing 1st Quarter payroll, annualized, by mid-March employment. The column headed 'Emp / Est' shows 'employees per establishment'. A dash (-) means that data are unavailable or cannot be calculated. nec means not elsewhere classified. *Notes:* 1. 1994 data incomplete; unavailable or withheld. 2. 1995 data incomplete; unavailable or withheld. 3. 1994 and 1995 data incomplete; unavailable or withheld.

LOUISVILLE, KY - IN MSA

Wholesale and Retail Trade USA	Establishments		Employment		Emp / Est	Pay / Employee		Annual Payroll ($ 000)	
	1994	1995	1994	1995	1995	1994	1995	1994	1995
50- Wholesale trade	2,120	2,145	31,592	33,647	16	28,452	31,174	960,184	1,030,982
5012 Automobiles and other vehicles[3]	24	26	579	667	26	23,185	23,316	14,579	16,230
5013 Motor vehicle supplies and new parts	138	125	1,578	1,648	13	20,477	22,527	37,798	37,879
5014 Tires and tubes[3]	20	18	305	180	10	30,361	34,333	9,387	6,298
5015 Motor vehicle parts, used[3]	42	41	211	258	6	16,284	18,202	4,839	5,338
5021 Furniture[3]	29	33	284	447	14	26,070	30,148	9,552	14,798
5023 Homefurnishings[3]	29	28	235	255	9	19,319	24,549	6,005	6,226
5031 Lumber, plywood, and millwork[3]	67	60	751	598	10	33,550	36,381	27,206	22,153
5032 Brick, stone, & related materials[3]	19	13	90	87	7	25,867	41,333	2,368	2,907
5033 Roofing, siding, & insulation[3]	14	13	229	257	20	18,061	20,669	6,083	6,176
5039 Construction materials, nec[3]	27	42	308	467	11	22,740	27,143	7,330	13,036
5043 Photographic equipment & supplies[3]	4	4	102	107	27	19,176	21,720	2,503	2,636
5044 Office equipment[3]	34	34	718	712	21	31,370	37,067	23,419	25,147
5045 Computers, peripherals, & software[3]	67	62	667	791	13	47,916	46,397	29,863	33,463
5046 Commercial equipment, nec[3]	25	26	303	364	14	27,776	31,429	9,505	11,553
5047 Medical and hospital equipment[3]	75	71	759	788	11	29,043	32,442	24,088	26,480
5048 Ophthalmic goods[3]	13	14	209	228	16	23,081	24,649	5,413	6,400
5049 Professional equipment, nec[3]	15	17	160	175	10	20,225	22,286	3,917	4,271
5051 Metals service centers and offices[3]	50	51	144	185	4	20,500	20,627	3,631	4,136
5063 Electrical apparatus and equipment[3]	81	79	960	976	12	31,375	34,914	30,449	32,417
5064 Electrical appliances, TV & radios[3]	18	22	161	194	9	22,783	21,464	4,173	4,809
5065 Electronic parts and equipment[3]	50	58	476	557	10	29,244	27,131	14,659	15,140
5072 Hardware[3]	31	33	304	341	10	29,474	30,381	9,569	10,707
5074 Plumbing & hydronic heating supplies[3]	39	38	434	475	13	23,189	24,589	11,499	13,098
5075 Warm air heating & air conditioning[3]	35	37	381	423	11	30,436	31,811	12,833	15,106
5078 Refrigeration equipment and supplies[3]	16	16	154	173	11	27,922	28,763	6,154	7,013
5082 Construction and mining machinery[3]	31	31	885	1,040	34	37,894	38,031	34,483	38,563
5083 Farm and garden machinery[3]	31	32	211	194	6	20,550	23,938	5,422	5,304
5084 Industrial machinery and equipment[3]	158	158	1,711	1,917	12	31,114	34,339	59,222	69,390
5085 Industrial supplies[3]	82	85	1,018	1,232	14	28,216	29,984	31,576	38,966
5087 Service establishment equipment[3]	35	38	318	281	7	19,057	18,975	6,504	5,579
5088 Transportation equipment & supplies[3]	15	14	110	127	9	27,164	27,780	3,642	4,050
5091 Sporting & recreational goods[3]	35	29	196	190	7	19,918	22,358	4,707	4,692
5092 Toys and hobby goods and supplies[3]	10	12	32	27	2	15,500	16,593	473	472
5093 Scrap and waste materials[3]	35	37	416	495	13	25,375	26,917	13,494	14,770
5094 Jewelry & precious stones[3]	13	11	55	59	5	25,091	25,085	1,196	1,416
5099 Durable goods, nec[3]	26	25	110	104	4	30,364	33,308	3,469	3,216
5111 Printing and writing paper[3]	16	13	183	220	17	38,951	38,727	7,019	9,233
5112 Stationery and office supplies[3]	41	36	461	312	9	19,254	24,885	9,259	8,484
5113 Industrial & personal service paper[3]	26	32	264	312	10	25,182	28,910	7,636	9,329

Continued on next page.

LOUISVILLE, KY - IN MSA - [continued]

Wholesale and Retail Trade USA	Establishments		Employment		Emp / Est	Pay / Employee		Annual Payroll ($ 000)	
	1994	1995	1994	1995	1995	1994	1995	1994	1995
5120 Drugs, proprietaries, and sundries[3]	22	25	809	669	27	22,571	27,001	22,377	19,804
5131 Piece goods & notions[3]	6	7	53	56	8	29,660	31,286	1,443	1,603
5136 Men's and boys' clothing[3]	15	16	90	126	8	13,289	16,921	1,593	2,320
5137 Women's and children's clothing[3]	9	9	231	232	26	13,039	18,655	4,377	6,305
5141 Groceries, general line[3]	22	24	1,220	1,332	56	25,793	26,634	33,316	36,786
5142 Packaged frozen food[3]	15	16	166	176	11	29,663	29,591	4,881	5,645
5143 Dairy products, exc. dried or canned[3]	15	16	156	139	9	24,179	25,554	4,033	3,747
5144 Poultry and poultry products[3]	3	3	55	50	17	25,091	28,400	1,611	1,676
5145 Confectionery[3]	9	9	74	87	10	47,892	28,690	2,878	2,583
5147 Meats and meat products[3]	17	16	239	237	15	17,004	18,920	4,626	4,832
5148 Fresh fruits and vegetables[3]	22	23	255	237	10	19,608	22,785	5,201	5,514
5149 Groceries and related products, nec[3]	42	45	873	1,054	23	30,987	30,114	29,747	34,313
5153 Grain and field beans[3]	9	8	65	65	8	26,092	24,677	2,374	1,751
5154 Livestock[3]	5	5	89	94	19	15,910	18,043	1,597	1,964
5159 Farm-product raw materials, nec[3]	7	6	22	15	3	44,000	53,067	950	667
5162 Plastics materials & basic shapes[3]	12	13	109	113	9	36,917	46,690	3,724	4,991
5169 Chemicals & allied products, nec[3]	60	60	474	480	8	33,662	33,217	17,744	17,272
5171 Petroleum bulk stations & terminals[3]	36	31	286	226	7	34,587	36,142	8,626	7,870
5172 Petroleum products, nec[3]	13	14	181	191	14	14,387	16,021	2,650	3,655
5181 Beer and ale[3]	7	7	396	283	40	29,293	31,703	12,509	9,999
5182 Wine and distilled beverages[3]	11	12	250	258	22	45,008	38,775	10,230	9,231
5191 Farm supplies	49	41	347	341	8	20,334	24,985	8,320	8,677
5192 Books, periodicals, & newspapers[3]	15	17	175	175	10	19,977	27,543	3,728	4,597
5198 Paints, varnishes, and supplies[3]	35	25	332	228	9	31,843	31,684	11,153	7,367
5199 Nondurable goods, nec[3]	58	65	374	406	6	24,588	27,517	11,798	13,429
52- Retail trade	5,992	5,951	95,773	100,089	17	11,775	12,484	1,225,815	1,312,986
5210 Lumber and other building materials[2]	81	73	2,121	1,767	24	17,081	21,499	38,706	34,217
5230 Paint, glass, and wallpaper stores[3]	57	61	71	85	1	15,493	17,882	1,307	1,757
5250 Hardware stores	74	58	540	595	10	11,563	12,182	7,284	7,596
5260 Retail nurseries and garden stores	47	51	430	556	11	11,470	10,906	6,438	7,048
5270 Mobile home dealers[3]	12	12	42	47	4	22,286	28,255	1,147	1,321
5310 Department stores[3]	44	46	7,251	8,722	190	10,541	11,167	85,983	105,848
5330 Variety stores[3]	62	39	438	419	11	7,909	8,554	4,113	4,048
5390 Misc. general merchandise stores[1]	27	48	580	769	16	13,172	13,202	7,811	9,572
5410 Grocery stores[3]	419	415	9,889	10,101	24	10,486	11,764	106,886	119,527
5420 Meat and fish markets[3]	21	21	123	129	6	9,398	9,612	1,283	1,426
5430 Fruit and vegetable markets[3]	25	21	122	144	7	9,377	8,139	1,312	1,450
5440 Candy, nut, and confectionery stores[3]	15	16	55	72	5	5,382	6,000	373	553
5450 Dairy products stores[3]	9	7	34	34	5	4,824	4,588	305	182
5460 Retail bakeries[3]	74	72	578	551	8	8,111	9,408	5,974	5,797
5490 Miscellaneous food stores[3]	20	22	92	131	6	7,913	7,634	1,114	1,277
5510 New and used car dealers	70	70	4,292	4,401	63	24,494	26,725	120,713	130,765
5520 Used car dealers	101	105	711	704	7	17,603	19,898	13,651	14,118
5530 Auto and home supply stores	179	191	1,439	1,323	7	15,038	17,633	24,635	24,165
5540 Gasoline service stations	389	375	3,398	3,213	9	9,862	11,410	37,196	38,741
5550 Boat dealers[3]	16	17	125	157	9	19,008	18,573	3,639	3,999
5560 Recreational vehicle dealers[3]	13	14	69	67	5	14,609	18,507	1,262	1,347
5570 Motorcycle dealers[3]	10	10	27	23	2	9,037	12,696	345	366
5610 Men's & boys' clothing stores[3]	35	35	285	321	9	10,863	11,327	3,287	3,795
5620 Women's clothing stores[3]	152	128	1,617	1,700	13	8,037	8,687	14,529	14,192
5630 Women's accessory & specialty stores[3]	27	27	142	140	5	9,042	9,743	1,361	1,385
5640 Children's and infants' wear stores[3]	9	14	56	79	6	7,786	7,443	462	699
5650 Family clothing stores[3]	41	37	710	701	19	8,935	9,404	6,993	5,991
5660 Shoe stores[3]	136	125	720	715	6	10,672	11,278	8,076	8,189
5690 Misc. apparel & accessory stores[3]	36	35	144	164	5	10,167	9,854	1,595	1,773
5712 Furniture stores	108	107	1,174	1,329	12	17,353	17,439	22,820	24,914
5713 Floor covering stores[1]	69	71	387	369	5	16,010	16,173	5,903	6,500
5714 Drapery and upholstery stores[3]	10	10	48	31	3	12,583	12,258	499	381
5719 Misc. homefurnishings stores[3]	67	65	410	414	6	10,605	12,174	5,071	5,225
5720 Household appliance stores[3]	25	25	112	108	4	30,071	29,185	2,778	2,769
5731 Radio, TV, & electronic stores[3]	51	51	576	599	12	16,924	18,117	10,987	11,836
5734 Computer and software stores[3]	24	31	71	100	3	12,732	15,320	1,176	1,765
5735 Record & prerecorded tape stores[3]	36	35	218	234	7	8,440	9,915	2,070	2,202
5736 Musical instrument stores[3]	24	25	134	154	6	12,507	13,377	1,970	2,100
5812 Eating places	1,425	1,355	33,720	34,629	26	7,243	7,945	272,435	293,426
5813 Drinking places[3]	211	184	1,272	1,289	7	6,906	7,500	9,590	9,854
5910 Drug stores and proprietary stores	171	169	2,508	2,389	14	14,408	15,607	39,558	39,939
5920 Liquor stores[3]	170	167	823	869	5	9,205	9,814	8,318	9,360
5930 Used merchandise stores	110	117	736	784	7	11,185	13,005	9,665	10,575
5941 Sporting goods and bicycle shops[3]	93	101	608	658	7	9,842	11,319	7,429	8,707
5942 Book stores[3]	44	48	353	395	8	10,006	10,734	3,337	4,207

Continued on next page.

LOUISVILLE, KY – IN MSA - [continued]

Wholesale and Retail Trade USA	Establishments		Employment		Emp / Est	Pay / Employee		Annual Payroll ($ 000)	
	1994	1995	1994	1995	1995	1994	1995	1994	1995
5944 Jewelry stores[3]	110	113	529	567	5	17,399	19,880	9,688	10,265
5945 Hobby, toy, and game shops[3]	45	43	429	453	11	8,970	9,536	4,775	4,911
5946 Camera & photographic supply stores[3]	11	10	96	92	9	13,417	16,478	1,533	1,674
5947 Gift, novelty, and souvenir shops	124	128	747	831	6	6,977	7,745	6,329	7,357
5949 Sewing, needlework, and piece goods[3]	26	25	212	218	9	10,396	10,679	2,200	2,286
5961 Catalog and mail-order houses[3]	15	19	227	226	12	13,515	19,575	3,722	4,816
5962 Merchandising machine operators[3]	39	39	604	541	14	13,007	16,288	8,151	9,045
5963 Direct selling establishments[3]	60	55	515	524	10	12,124	12,626	6,643	6,648
5984 Liquefied petroleum gas dealers	17	20	29	39	2	25,517	23,897	762	943
5992 Florists	97	93	525	531	6	10,293	10,938	6,242	6,396
5993 Tobacco stores and stands[2]	-	4	-	12	3	-	9,333	-	137
5994 News dealers and newsstands[3]	4	3	19	19	6	12,000	12,000	228	235
5995 Optical goods stores[3]	54	49	371	336	7	21,811	21,881	7,191	7,500
5999 Miscellaneous retail stores, nec	186	181	855	907	5	11,237	12,291	11,216	12,496

Source: County Business Patterns 1994/95, CBP-94/95, U.S. Department of Commerce, Washington DC, November 1997. The employment column represents mid-March employment in the year. Pay per employee is calculated by dividing 1st Quarter payroll, annualized, by mid-March employment. The column headed 'Emp / Est' shows 'employees per establishment'. A dash (-) means that data are unavailable or cannot be calculated. nec means not elsewhere classified. *Notes:* 1. 1994 data incomplete; unavailable or withheld. 2. 1995 data incomplete; unavailable or withheld. 3. 1994 and 1995 data incomplete; unavailable or withheld.

LUBBOCK, TX MSA

Wholesale and Retail Trade USA	Establishments		Employment		Emp / Est	Pay / Employee		Annual Payroll ($ 000)	
	1994	1995	1994	1995	1995	1994	1995	1994	1995
50 – Wholesale trade	-	606	-	7,314	12	-	26,024	-	193,731
5012 Automobiles and other vehicles	-	18	-	466	26	-	19,047	-	8,890
5013 Motor vehicle supplies and new parts	-	26	-	199	8	-	19,457	-	3,811
5014 Tires and tubes	-	7	-	50	7	-	23,520	-	1,187
5015 Motor vehicle parts, used	-	12	-	81	7	-	17,630	-	1,394
5020 Furniture and homefurnishings	-	13	-	113	9	-	22,549	-	3,344
5031 Lumber, plywood, and millwork	-	8	-	166	21	-	30,819	-	4,442
5032 Brick, stone, & related materials	-	7	-	39	6	-	19,897	-	877
5033 Roofing, siding, & insulation	-	5	-	56	11	-	32,143	-	2,200
5039 Construction materials, nec	-	7	-	25	4	-	20,160	-	605
5044 Office equipment	-	20	-	193	10	-	27,689	-	4,742
5045 Computers, peripherals, & software	-	12	-	154	13	-	36,571	-	5,600
5047 Medical and hospital equipment	-	19	-	58	3	-	36,000	-	2,693
5051 Metals service centers and offices	-	12	-	80	7	-	33,800	-	2,719
5063 Electrical apparatus and equipment	-	26	-	270	10	-	31,378	-	9,245
5064 Electrical appliances, TV & radios	-	4	-	54	14	-	21,259	-	1,061
5065 Electronic parts and equipment	-	14	-	81	6	-	29,383	-	2,420
5072 Hardware	-	7	-	108	15	-	27,963	-	2,456
5074 Plumbing & hydronic heating supplies	-	10	-	172	17	-	26,977	-	4,558
5075 Warm air heating & air conditioning	-	13	-	79	6	-	35,190	-	2,703
5078 Refrigeration equipment and supplies	-	4	-	13	3	-	28,615	-	388
5082 Construction and mining machinery	-	6	-	116	19	-	34,207	-	4,612
5083 Farm and garden machinery	-	28	-	339	12	-	26,619	-	10,038
5084 Industrial machinery and equipment	-	34	-	280	8	-	22,071	-	7,610
5085 Industrial supplies	-	16	-	139	9	-	22,964	-	3,769
5087 Service establishment equipment	-	13	-	100	8	-	16,480	-	1,760
5091 Sporting & recreational goods	-	4	-	38	10	-	15,789	-	604
5093 Scrap and waste materials	-	8	-	100	13	-	19,240	-	2,045
5099 Durable goods, nec	-	9	-	50	6	-	16,720	-	978
5112 Stationery and office supplies	-	12	-	126	11	-	20,381	-	2,425
5120 Drugs, proprietaries, and sundries	-	7	-	88	13	-	43,091	-	3,640
5130 Apparel, piece goods, and notions	-	5	-	35	7	-	15,086	-	553
5141 Groceries, general line	-	10	-	629	63	-	33,386	-	17,084
5142 Packaged frozen food	-	10	-	664	66	-	27,042	-	18,494
5147 Meats and meat products	-	4	-	22	6	-	27,636	-	478
5149 Groceries and related products, nec	-	14	-	382	27	-	26,471	-	10,467
5153 Grain and field beans	-	9	-	73	8	-	21,479	-	2,071
5159 Farm-product raw materials, nec	-	34	-	252	7	-	34,460	-	9,001
5169 Chemicals & allied products, nec	-	11	-	75	7	-	23,253	-	1,819
5171 Petroleum bulk stations & terminals	-	10	-	137	14	-	14,949	-	2,283
5172 Petroleum products, nec	-	12	-	99	8	-	28,242	-	2,913
5181 Beer and ale	-	5	-	121	24	-	24,397	-	3,044
5191 Farm supplies	-	21	-	162	8	-	22,395	-	4,044
5192 Books, periodicals, & newspapers	-	6	-	93	16	-	18,968	-	1,922
5193 Flowers & florists' supplies	-	4	-	49	12	-	17,878	-	927
5199 Nondurable goods, nec	-	9	-	47	5	-	14,723	-	867

Continued on next page.

LUBBOCK, TX MSA - [continued]

Wholesale and Retail Trade USA	Establishments		Employment		Emp / Est	Pay / Employee		Annual Payroll ($ 000)	
	1994	1995	1994	1995	1995	1994	1995	1994	1995
52- Retail trade	-	1,549	-	23,574	15	-	12,647	-	311,166
5210 Lumber and other building materials	-	22	-	428	19	-	19,654	-	8,418
5230 Paint, glass, and wallpaper stores	-	8	-	56	7	-	17,357	-	1,082
5260 Retail nurseries and garden stores	-	12	-	107	9	-	12,785	-	1,613
5310 Department stores	-	12	-	2,031	169	-	14,042	-	27,509
5330 Variety stores	-	6	-	25	4	-	10,080	-	253
5390 Misc. general merchandise stores	-	16	-	452	28	-	12,478	-	5,280
5410 Grocery stores	-	102	-	2,650	26	-	12,966	-	37,296
5420 Meat and fish markets	-	5	-	11	2	-	13,818	-	125
5440 Candy, nut, and confectionery stores	-	4	-	31	8	-	13,032	-	279
5460 Retail bakeries	-	14	-	79	6	-	8,557	-	694
5490 Miscellaneous food stores	-	15	-	128	9	-	15,219	-	2,511
5510 New and used car dealers	-	16	-	1,140	71	-	34,081	-	44,090
5520 Used car dealers	-	27	-	102	4	-	22,863	-	2,801
5530 Auto and home supply stores	-	41	-	390	10	-	16,923	-	7,482
5540 Gasoline service stations	-	94	-	612	7	-	10,190	-	6,608
5560 Recreational vehicle dealers	-	6	-	77	13	-	23,896	-	2,044
5570 Motorcycle dealers	-	7	-	41	6	-	19,707	-	1,008
5610 Men's & boys' clothing stores	-	12	-	82	7	-	11,707	-	907
5620 Women's clothing stores	-	49	-	336	7	-	8,333	-	2,625
5630 Women's accessory & specialty stores	-	12	-	70	6	-	7,886	-	658
5640 Children's and infants' wear stores	-	9	-	36	4	-	9,556	-	396
5650 Family clothing stores	-	25	-	462	18	-	13,377	-	5,817
5660 Shoe stores	-	30	-	162	5	-	12,988	-	1,908
5690 Misc. apparel & accessory stores	-	13	-	81	6	-	8,840	-	753
5712 Furniture stores	-	35	-	279	8	-	19,398	-	5,457
5713 Floor covering stores	-	8	-	53	7	-	31,472	-	2,173
5720 Household appliance stores	-	10	-	50	5	-	14,720	-	707
5731 Radio, TV, & electronic stores	-	21	-	248	12	-	14,903	-	3,987
5734 Computer and software stores	-	8	-	27	3	-	12,000	-	384
5735 Record & prerecorded tape stores	-	7	-	58	8	-	9,586	-	535
5812 Eating places	-	355	-	8,586	24	-	8,056	-	69,623
5813 Drinking places	-	33	-	442	13	-	6,769	-	2,944
5910 Drug stores and proprietary stores	-	30	-	328	11	-	16,927	-	5,454
5920 Liquor stores	-	28	-	249	9	-	9,976	-	3,097
5930 Used merchandise stores	-	35	-	195	6	-	10,379	-	2,047
5941 Sporting goods and bicycle shops	-	20	-	117	6	-	10,359	-	1,585
5942 Book stores	-	19	-	170	9	-	11,106	-	1,941
5944 Jewelry stores	-	27	-	118	4	-	19,220	-	2,283
5945 Hobby, toy, and game shops	-	10	-	155	16	-	9,239	-	1,595
5947 Gift, novelty, and souvenir shops	-	29	-	194	7	-	6,536	-	1,370
5949 Sewing, needlework, and piece goods	-	8	-	97	12	-	7,670	-	678
5961 Catalog and mail-order houses	-	3	-	6	2	-	17,333	-	140
5962 Merchandising machine operators	-	7	-	73	10	-	14,192	-	1,095
5963 Direct selling establishments	-	22	-	136	6	-	17,118	-	2,202
5980 Fuel dealers	-	4	-	10	3	-	10,000	-	92
5992 Florists	-	25	-	161	6	-	10,957	-	1,683
5993 Tobacco stores and stands	-	4	-	15	4	-	12,533	-	254
5995 Optical goods stores	-	17	-	99	6	-	14,061	-	1,400
5999 Miscellaneous retail stores, nec	-	49	-	247	5	-	13,587	-	3,475

Source: County Business Patterns 1994/95, CBP-94/95, U.S. Department of Commerce, Washington DC, November 1997. The employment column represents mid-March employment in the year. Pay per employee is calculated by dividing 1st Quarter payroll, annualized, by mid-March employment. The column headed 'Emp / Est' shows 'employees per establishment'. A dash (-) means that data are unavailable or cannot be calculated. nec means not elsewhere classified. *Notes:* 1. 1994 data incomplete; unavailable or withheld. 2. 1995 data incomplete; unavailable or withheld. 3. 1994 and 1995 data incomplete; unavailable or withheld.

LYNCHBURG, VA MSA

Wholesale and Retail Trade USA	Establishments		Employment		Emp / Est	Pay / Employee		Annual Payroll ($ 000)	
	1994	1995	1994	1995	1995	1994	1995	1994	1995
50- Wholesale trade	-	300	-	4,168	14	-	30,032	-	134,608
5013 Motor vehicle supplies and new parts	-	18	-	76	4	-	15,421	-	1,153
5015 Motor vehicle parts, used [2]	-	11	-	21	2	-	14,857	-	453
5021 Furniture [2]	-	7	-	26	4	-	16,308	-	430
5030 Lumber and construction materials [2]	-	11	-	22	2	-	18,909	-	762
5044 Office equipment [2]	-	6	-	33	6	-	18,667	-	613
5046 Commercial equipment, nec [2]	-	5	-	13	3	-	29,538	-	536
5047 Medical and hospital equipment [2]	-	5	-	51	10	-	32,000	-	1,390
5050 Metals and minerals, except petroleum [2]	-	7	-	53	8	-	28,226	-	1,535
5060 Electrical goods	-	26	-	849	33	-	52,796	-	48,641

Continued on next page.

LYNCHBURG, VA MSA - [continued]

Wholesale and Retail Trade USA	Establishments		Employment		Emp / Est	Pay / Employee		Annual Payroll ($ 000)	
	1994	1995	1994	1995	1995	1994	1995	1994	1995
5072 Hardware [2]	-	5	-	169	34	-	22,864	-	4,066
5074 Plumbing & hydronic heating supplies [2]	-	8	-	68	9	-	34,471	-	1,912
5082 Construction and mining machinery [2]	-	8	-	7	1	-	14,857	-	125
5083 Farm and garden machinery [2]	-	5	-	22	4	-	16,545	-	444
5084 Industrial machinery and equipment [2]	-	14	-	61	4	-	31,082	-	2,011
5085 Industrial supplies [2]	-	13	-	78	6	-	30,872	-	2,888
5090 Miscellaneous durable goods	-	16	-	228	14	-	17,614	-	4,004
5110 Paper and paper products [2]	-	7	-	46	7	-	43,391	-	1,887
5140 Groceries and related products	-	17	-	198	12	-	19,232	-	4,075
5160 Chemicals and allied products [2]	-	5	-	10	2	-	19,200	-	172
5171 Petroleum bulk stations & terminals [2]	-	14	-	61	4	-	19,672	-	1,180
5172 Petroleum products, nec [2]	-	4	-	27	7	-	31,556	-	855
5181 Beer and ale [2]	-	3	-	120	40	-	27,400	-	3,518
5191 Farm supplies	-	14	-	45	3	-	18,489	-	802
5199 Nondurable goods, nec [2]	-	9	-	37	4	-	22,054	-	950
52- Retail trade	-	1,220	-	15,998	13	-	12,177	-	205,801
5210 Lumber and other building materials	-	22	-	303	14	-	21,663	-	6,368
5250 Hardware stores	-	10	-	23	2	-	13,913	-	347
5260 Retail nurseries and garden stores	-	16	-	74	5	-	9,622	-	770
5270 Mobile home dealers [2]	-	11	-	53	5	-	20,755	-	1,368
5310 Department stores [2]	-	14	-	1,202	86	-	11,215	-	13,519
5390 Misc. general merchandise stores [2]	-	16	-	8	1	-	9,000	-	70
5410 Grocery stores [2]	-	138	-	1,866	14	-	9,908	-	19,322
5450 Dairy products stores [2]	-	3	-	26	9	-	3,385	-	137
5460 Retail bakeries [2]	-	13	-	112	9	-	8,464	-	1,073
5490 Miscellaneous food stores [2]	-	4	-	13	3	-	8,308	-	103
5510 New and used car dealers [2]	-	23	-	771	34	-	23,933	-	19,433
5520 Used car dealers	-	21	-	39	2	-	12,103	-	540
5530 Auto and home supply stores	-	39	-	300	8	-	16,213	-	4,991
5540 Gasoline service stations	-	85	-	584	7	-	11,322	-	7,159
5570 Motorcycle dealers [2]	-	6	-	22	4	-	12,909	-	384
5610 Men's & boys' clothing stores [2]	-	14	-	76	5	-	11,526	-	870
5620 Women's clothing stores	-	32	-	183	6	-	8,481	-	1,583
5630 Women's accessory & specialty stores [2]	-	4	-	31	8	-	8,774	-	265
5650 Family clothing stores [2]	-	9	-	94	10	-	9,489	-	887
5660 Shoe stores [2]	-	23	-	90	4	-	11,733	-	1,097
5712 Furniture stores	-	28	-	299	11	-	19,478	-	6,368
5713 Floor covering stores	-	12	-	34	3	-	18,353	-	932
5719 Misc. homefurnishings stores [2]	-	15	-	57	4	-	7,649	-	482
5720 Household appliance stores	-	12	-	17	1	-	17,647	-	325
5731 Radio, TV, & electronic stores	-	13	-	91	7	-	16,308	-	1,625
5735 Record & prerecorded tape stores [2]	-	6	-	33	6	-	8,848	-	275
5812 Eating places	-	264	-	4,709	18	-	7,282	-	37,822
5813 Drinking places [2]	-	5	-	8	2	-	6,000	-	59
5910 Drug stores and proprietary stores	-	40	-	519	13	-	15,091	-	7,904
5930 Used merchandise stores [2]	-	15	-	77	5	-	9,143	-	810
5941 Sporting goods and bicycle shops	-	16	-	30	2	-	12,800	-	448
5942 Book stores [2]	-	10	-	40	4	-	9,100	-	387
5944 Jewelry stores [2]	-	19	-	85	4	-	17,224	-	1,246
5945 Hobby, toy, and game shops [2]	-	10	-	105	11	-	8,076	-	982
5947 Gift, novelty, and souvenir shops [2]	-	18	-	85	5	-	7,200	-	672
5949 Sewing, needlework, and piece goods [2]	-	9	-	29	3	-	6,345	-	194
5962 Merchandising machine operators [2]	-	6	-	104	17	-	11,154	-	1,302
5983 Fuel oil dealers [2]	-	13	-	76	6	-	18,158	-	1,452
5992 Florists	-	29	-	91	3	-	10,593	-	985
5999 Miscellaneous retail stores, nec	-	30	-	70	2	-	13,257	-	1,114

Source: County Business Patterns 1994/95, CBP-94/95, U.S. Department of Commerce, Washington DC, November 1997. The employment column represents mid-March employment in the year. Pay per employee is calculated by dividing 1st Quarter payroll, annualized, by mid-March employment. The column headed 'Emp / Est' shows 'employees per establishment'. A dash (-) means that data are unavailable or cannot be calculated. nec means not elsewhere classified. *Notes:* 1. 1994 data incomplete; unavailable or withheld. 2. 1995 data incomplete; unavailable or withheld. 3. 1994 and 1995 data incomplete; unavailable or withheld.

MACON, GA MSA

Wholesale and Retail Trade USA	Establishments		Employment		Emp / Est	Pay / Employee		Annual Payroll ($ 000)	
	1994	1995	1994	1995	1995	1994	1995	1994	1995
50- Wholesale trade	451	455	5,372	5,621	12	25,226	26,242	145,314	157,477
5012 Automobiles and other vehicles [3]	11	12	152	171	14	27,658	26,550	4,781	5,048
5013 Motor vehicle supplies and new parts [3]	44	39	424	367	9	19,566	20,926	8,864	8,037
5014 Tires and tubes [3]	7	8	70	60	8	27,029	27,000	1,855	1,789

Continued on next page.

MACON, GA MSA - [continued]

Wholesale and Retail Trade USA	Establishments		Employment		Emp / Est	Pay / Employee		Annual Payroll ($ 000)	
	1994	1995	1994	1995	1995	1994	1995	1994	1995
5015 Motor vehicle parts, used[3]	9	9	34	39	4	15,176	15,897	592	628
5020 Furniture and homefurnishings[3]	8	11	53	103	9	24,528	23,845	1,523	2,444
5031 Lumber, plywood, and millwork[1]	9	-	109	-	-	26,018	-	2,970	-
5032 Brick, stone, & related materials[2]	-	3	-	5	2	-	22,400	-	96
5039 Construction materials, nec[3]	4	13	47	93	7	17,277	20,344	1,068	2,885
5044 Office equipment[3]	12	11	75	73	7	26,880	29,918	2,963	3,153
5045 Computers, peripherals, & software[1]	10	-	43	-	-	39,442	-	1,208	-
5046 Commercial equipment, nec[3]	4	3	25	30	10	22,240	26,400	685	899
5050 Metals and minerals, except petroleum[3]	8	8	66	91	11	30,424	33,582	1,912	3,179
5063 Electrical apparatus and equipment[3]	20	16	209	202	13	29,148	32,812	6,356	6,723
5065 Electronic parts and equipment[3]	12	14	20	30	2	39,000	34,000	923	1,237
5072 Hardware[1]	8	-	52	-	-	24,462	-	1,430	-
5074 Plumbing & hydronic heating supplies[3]	8	10	67	87	9	24,478	27,264	1,867	2,633
5075 Warm air heating & air conditioning[3]	11	10	91	85	9	29,231	31,059	2,449	2,328
5082 Construction and mining machinery[2]	-	10	-	159	16	-	28,226	-	4,678
5083 Farm and garden machinery[2]	-	11	-	43	4	-	21,116	-	1,155
5084 Industrial machinery and equipment[3]	15	15	157	161	11	27,618	28,174	4,794	5,060
5085 Industrial supplies[3]	22	21	247	263	13	28,275	31,909	7,446	8,461
5087 Service establishment equipment[3]	15	13	126	140	11	33,905	31,971	4,500	5,077
5093 Scrap and waste materials[3]	14	13	236	122	9	16,254	24,820	3,646	3,587
5094 Jewelry & precious stones[2]	-	5	-	3	1	-	48,000	-	150
5099 Durable goods, nec[1]	7	-	51	-	-	24,941	-	1,440	-
5112 Stationery and office supplies[3]	18	17	250	234	14	29,360	27,812	7,476	6,815
5113 Industrial & personal service paper[3]	6	6	84	88	15	37,190	36,227	3,167	3,060
5130 Apparel, piece goods, and notions[2]	-	9	-	51	6	-	58,431	-	3,259
5143 Dairy products, exc. dried or canned[3]	3	3	25	25	8	28,640	32,000	789	805
5149 Groceries and related products, nec[3]	10	9	262	240	27	25,053	25,117	6,906	6,351
5150 Farm-product raw materials[3]	5	6	20	18	3	13,800	15,556	321	259
5169 Chemicals & allied products, nec[1]	11	-	67	-	-	31,164	-	2,127	-
5170 Petroleum and petroleum products[3]	11	10	82	63	6	25,268	39,556	2,324	3,755
5181 Beer and ale[3]	4	4	148	150	38	27,730	29,013	5,246	5,347
5182 Wine and distilled beverages[3]	4	4	70	79	20	32,971	33,367	2,373	2,782
5191 Farm supplies[2]	15	14	62	67	5	20,516	15,642	1,763	1,288
5198 Paints, varnishes, and supplies[3]	7	5	50	24	5	17,600	19,167	694	427
5199 Nondurable goods, nec[3]	15	14	31	26	2	30,065	30,462	1,143	820
52 - Retail trade	1,887	1,892	26,023	28,087	15	11,068	11,251	311,655	320,500
5210 Lumber and other building materials[3]	27	23	688	475	21	17,070	18,181	12,939	9,161
5230 Paint, glass, and wallpaper stores[3]	14	14	52	59	4	16,615	18,305	967	1,127
5250 Hardware stores	22	17	59	108	6	9,356	8,148	631	872
5260 Retail nurseries and garden stores[3]	12	11	87	109	10	11,310	10,642	1,237	1,365
5270 Mobile home dealers[2]	-	8	-	4	1	-	15,000	-	115
5310 Department stores[3]	16	14	2,791	2,550	182	10,280	11,871	30,174	28,984
5410 Grocery stores[3]	153	155	4,043	5,064	33	8,769	8,032	39,255	37,236
5420 Meat and fish markets[3]	10	11	13	29	3	8,308	8,276	114	258
5460 Retail bakeries[3]	10	12	50	54	5	7,360	5,778	339	348
5490 Miscellaneous food stores[1]	6	-	27	-	-	9,037	-	252	-
5510 New and used car dealers[3]	31	34	1,362	1,524	45	26,185	28,407	40,174	47,665
5520 Used car dealers[3]	28	23	95	79	3	19,074	21,215	1,969	1,663
5530 Auto and home supply stores[3]	68	75	448	533	7	16,643	17,689	8,961	9,408
5540 Gasoline service stations[1]	155	158	1,103	1,116	7	10,325	11,631	11,888	13,019
5550 Boat dealers[3]	6	6	41	39	7	14,341	18,051	835	882
5610 Men's & boys' clothing stores[3]	26	27	148	159	6	22,162	19,094	2,611	2,466
5620 Women's clothing stores[3]	84	68	634	459	7	7,691	7,773	5,059	3,612
5630 Women's accessory & specialty stores[3]	8	10	40	51	5	8,600	9,098	364	487
5640 Children's and infants' wear stores[3]	5	4	10	5	1	10,000	13,600	88	98
5650 Family clothing stores[3]	21	22	261	455	21	7,464	9,275	2,515	3,894
5660 Shoe stores[3]	60	61	262	287	5	10,260	10,118	2,736	2,929
5690 Misc. apparel & accessory stores[3]	6	7	21	36	5	10,667	9,222	230	386
5712 Furniture stores[3]	46	47	443	484	10	15,946	16,413	7,943	8,105
5713 Floor covering stores[3]	14	13	80	108	8	15,950	16,444	1,524	2,113
5719 Misc. homefurnishings stores[3]	24	23	34	55	2	9,882	9,818	368	664
5720 Household appliance stores[3]	7	6	6	8	1	12,000	12,000	103	154
5731 Radio, TV, & electronic stores[3]	27	27	201	219	8	17,373	20,968	3,974	4,324
5734 Computer and software stores[2]	-	5	-	31	6	-	19,097	-	740
5735 Record & prerecorded tape stores[2]	-	11	-	25	2	-	7,680	-	409
5736 Musical instrument stores[3]	7	7	34	33	5	18,235	18,424	577	562
5812 Eating places	377	361	8,482	8,917	25	7,431	7,131	65,246	65,427
5813 Drinking places[3]	25	19	95	86	5	7,747	7,721	685	627
5910 Drug stores and proprietary stores	53	54	496	592	11	16,694	17,027	9,352	10,185
5920 Liquor stores[3]	51	53	160	161	3	11,475	11,006	1,891	1,853
5930 Used merchandise stores[3]	47	49	131	149	3	15,145	13,852	2,207	2,329

Continued on next page.

MACON, GA MSA - [continued]

Wholesale and Retail Trade USA	Establishments		Employment		Emp / Est	Pay / Employee		Annual Payroll ($ 000)	
	1994	1995	1994	1995	1995	1994	1995	1994	1995
5941 Sporting goods and bicycle shops [3]	28	27	143	151	6	7,301	9,589	1,337	1,530
5942 Book stores [3]	21	19	95	117	6	9,600	10,735	1,014	1,370
5943 Stationery stores [3]	8	7	31	34	5	13,419	14,824	465	503
5944 Jewelry stores [3]	33	38	174	185	5	14,092	16,454	2,642	2,828
5945 Hobby, toy, and game shops [3]	17	17	117	116	7	7,726	9,793	1,219	1,485
5947 Gift, novelty, and souvenir shops [3]	36	36	144	168	5	7,750	6,690	1,216	1,243
5949 Sewing, needlework, and piece goods [3]	9	9	42	41	5	9,333	8,098	372	335
5962 Merchandising machine operators [3]	4	4	18	18	5	15,111	16,667	293	316
5963 Direct selling establishments [3]	11	11	170	129	12	16,282	13,829	2,671	1,728
5984 Liquefied petroleum gas dealers [3]	8	8	24	26	3	22,333	23,231	475	497
5992 Florists [3]	36	31	148	159	5	10,189	10,138	1,726	1,611
5995 Optical goods stores [3]	22	21	107	134	6	18,654	19,463	2,307	2,776
5999 Miscellaneous retail stores, nec [3]	57	59	224	287	5	12,607	13,854	2,936	4,212

Source: County Business Patterns 1994/95, CBP-94/95, U.S. Department of Commerce, Washington DC, November 1997. The employment column represents mid-March employment in the year. Pay per employee is calculated by dividing 1st Quarter payroll, annualized, by mid-March employment. The column headed 'Emp / Est' shows 'employees per establishment'. A dash (-) means that data are unavailable or cannot be calculated. nec means not elsewhere classified. *Notes:* 1. 1994 data incomplete; unavailable or withheld. 2. 1995 data incomplete; unavailable or withheld. 3. 1994 and 1995 data incomplete; unavailable or withheld.

MADISON, WI MSA

Wholesale and Retail Trade USA	Establishments		Employment		Emp / Est	Pay / Employee		Annual Payroll ($ 000)	
	1994	1995	1994	1995	1995	1994	1995	1994	1995
50- Wholesale trade	-	806	-	11,883	15	-	29,295	-	362,862
5012 Automobiles and other vehicles	-	17	-	516	30	-	33,047	-	16,696
5013 Motor vehicle supplies and new parts	-	42	-	513	12	-	22,908	-	12,169
5014 Tires and tubes	-	6	-	85	14	-	27,624	-	2,399
5015 Motor vehicle parts, used	-	8	-	86	11	-	17,488	-	1,750
5021 Furniture	-	11	-	125	11	-	29,440	-	3,999
5023 Homefurnishings	-	16	-	208	13	-	30,000	-	6,477
5031 Lumber, plywood, and millwork	-	18	-	286	16	-	31,734	-	7,793
5032 Brick, stone, & related materials	-	9	-	32	4	-	25,500	-	731
5033 Roofing, siding, & insulation	-	8	-	65	8	-	28,492	-	2,371
5039 Construction materials, nec	-	10	-	143	14	-	22,462	-	3,633
5044 Office equipment	-	18	-	448	25	-	38,455	-	16,443
5045 Computers, peripherals, & software	-	41	-	739	18	-	43,323	-	33,342
5046 Commercial equipment, nec	-	10	-	41	4	-	19,610	-	833
5047 Medical and hospital equipment	-	17	-	142	8	-	33,915	-	5,101
5048 Ophthalmic goods	-	3	-	41	14	-	20,976	-	827
5049 Professional equipment, nec	-	4	-	95	24	-	43,368	-	3,983
5051 Metals service centers and offices	-	8	-	58	7	-	27,310	-	1,973
5063 Electrical apparatus and equipment	-	34	-	374	11	-	29,551	-	12,125
5064 Electrical appliances, TV & radios	-	5	-	62	12	-	29,161	-	2,093
5065 Electronic parts and equipment	-	26	-	234	9	-	35,778	-	8,302
5072 Hardware	-	15	-	125	8	-	28,704	-	3,702
5074 Plumbing & hydronic heating supplies	-	15	-	411	27	-	30,647	-	12,143
5075 Warm air heating & air conditioning	-	10	-	124	12	-	45,129	-	6,117
5078 Refrigeration equipment and supplies	-	4	-	59	15	-	40,881	-	2,365
5082 Construction and mining machinery	-	11	-	292	27	-	40,986	-	11,326
5083 Farm and garden machinery	-	18	-	213	12	-	30,911	-	6,489
5084 Industrial machinery and equipment	-	39	-	338	9	-	36,154	-	12,093
5085 Industrial supplies	-	14	-	306	22	-	30,562	-	9,972
5087 Service establishment equipment	-	9	-	484	54	-	10,835	-	5,856
5091 Sporting & recreational goods	-	14	-	159	11	-	18,616	-	4,377
5093 Scrap and waste materials	-	12	-	197	16	-	24,162	-	5,563
5099 Durable goods, nec	-	12	-	52	4	-	23,077	-	1,576
5112 Stationery and office supplies	-	25	-	368	15	-	22,761	-	8,889
5113 Industrial & personal service paper	-	14	-	115	8	-	40,209	-	5,315
5120 Drugs, proprietaries, and sundries	-	17	-	356	21	-	23,663	-	9,323
5131 Piece goods & notions	-	4	-	32	8	-	17,500	-	1,122
5136 Men's and boys' clothing	-	4	-	185	46	-	19,481	-	3,883
5139 Footwear	-	3	-	3	1	-	66,667	-	140
5141 Groceries, general line	-	7	-	285	41	-	22,456	-	7,050
5142 Packaged frozen food	-	4	-	50	13	-	24,240	-	1,343
5143 Dairy products, exc. dried or canned	-	11	-	62	6	-	28,129	-	1,952
5145 Confectionery	-	6	-	206	34	-	26,136	-	4,318
5147 Meats and meat products	-	4	-	172	43	-	29,814	-	7,345
5148 Fresh fruits and vegetables	-	4	-	97	24	-	22,887	-	2,111
5149 Groceries and related products, nec	-	18	-	343	19	-	29,843	-	10,282
5150 Farm-product raw materials	-	9	-	240	27	-	28,100	-	6,481

Continued on next page.

MADISON, WI MSA - [continued]

Wholesale and Retail Trade USA	Establishments		Employment		Emp / Est	Pay / Employee		Annual Payroll ($ 000)	
	1994	1995	1994	1995	1995	1994	1995	1994	1995
5162 Plastics materials & basic shapes	-	6	-	35	6	-	29,371	-	1,330
5169 Chemicals & allied products, nec	-	15	-	170	11	-	34,941	-	6,476
5171 Petroleum bulk stations & terminals	-	14	-	99	7	-	30,545	-	2,921
5172 Petroleum products, nec	-	3	-	9	3	-	28,889	-	347
5181 Beer and ale	-	6	-	168	28	-	31,048	-	5,790
5182 Wine and distilled beverages	-	6	-	240	40	-	33,800	-	8,987
5191 Farm supplies	-	36	-	311	9	-	28,167	-	9,366
5192 Books, periodicals, & newspapers	-	11	-	304	28	-	24,224	-	7,891
5193 Flowers & florists' supplies	-	7	-	78	11	-	16,154	-	1,036
5199 Nondurable goods, nec	-	31	-	107	3	-	22,355	-	2,616
52 – Retail trade	-	2,665	-	46,112	17	-	12,096	-	584,611
5210 Lumber and other building materials	-	42	-	1,039	25	-	24,947	-	24,142
5230 Paint, glass, and wallpaper stores	-	16	-	71	4	-	25,465	-	1,729
5250 Hardware stores	-	23	-	315	14	-	12,406	-	3,693
5260 Retail nurseries and garden stores	-	16	-	113	7	-	24,142	-	2,445
5270 Mobile home dealers	-	3	-	20	7	-	21,000	-	631
5310 Department stores	-	24	-	3,889	162	-	10,444	-	42,149
5330 Variety stores	-	10	-	164	16	-	8,293	-	1,286
5390 Misc. general merchandise stores	-	8	-	289	36	-	12,595	-	3,490
5410 Grocery stores	-	112	-	3,818	34	-	12,392	-	50,812
5420 Meat and fish markets	-	14	-	107	8	-	10,617	-	1,237
5450 Dairy products stores	-	8	-	76	10	-	24,158	-	1,440
5460 Retail bakeries	-	26	-	387	15	-	9,220	-	3,031
5490 Miscellaneous food stores	-	18	-	284	16	-	12,310	-	3,302
5510 New and used car dealers	-	33	-	2,135	65	-	25,473	-	58,428
5520 Used car dealers	-	19	-	83	4	-	26,940	-	2,743
5530 Auto and home supply stores	-	33	-	401	12	-	16,160	-	7,038
5540 Gasoline service stations	-	159	-	1,272	8	-	11,440	-	15,521
5550 Boat dealers	-	9	-	74	8	-	11,892	-	1,278
5560 Recreational vehicle dealers	-	8	-	108	14	-	21,519	-	2,260
5570 Motorcycle dealers	-	4	-	85	21	-	19,294	-	1,979
5610 Men's & boys' clothing stores	-	24	-	154	6	-	13,429	-	2,133
5620 Women's clothing stores	-	82	-	879	11	-	6,994	-	6,464
5630 Women's accessory & specialty stores	-	14	-	88	6	-	10,455	-	964
5640 Children's and infants' wear stores	-	6	-	53	9	-	8,226	-	516
5650 Family clothing stores	-	41	-	551	13	-	8,842	-	5,070
5660 Shoe stores	-	56	-	478	9	-	11,707	-	5,583
5690 Misc. apparel & accessory stores	-	13	-	91	7	-	17,758	-	992
5712 Furniture stores	-	55	-	461	8	-	17,380	-	8,725
5713 Floor covering stores	-	32	-	228	7	-	25,351	-	6,261
5720 Household appliance stores	-	23	-	182	8	-	20,505	-	3,862
5731 Radio, TV, & electronic stores	-	23	-	898	39	-	21,158	-	20,202
5734 Computer and software stores	-	15	-	77	5	-	19,065	-	1,739
5735 Record & prerecorded tape stores	-	18	-	177	10	-	8,429	-	1,491
5736 Musical instrument stores	-	10	-	156	16	-	16,026	-	2,905
5812 Eating places	-	560	-	14,793	26	-	6,862	-	104,806
5813 Drinking places	-	148	-	1,214	8	-	7,216	-	8,961
5910 Drug stores and proprietary stores	-	68	-	899	13	-	17,028	-	16,101
5920 Liquor stores	-	56	-	303	5	-	7,525	-	2,621
5930 Used merchandise stores	-	47	-	224	5	-	8,018	-	2,170
5941 Sporting goods and bicycle shops	-	59	-	593	10	-	10,712	-	7,444
5942 Book stores	-	34	-	421	12	-	12,475	-	5,642
5943 Stationery stores	-	5	-	29	6	-	6,897	-	224
5944 Jewelry stores	-	48	-	310	6	-	16,671	-	5,254
5945 Hobby, toy, and game shops	-	26	-	295	11	-	8,773	-	2,860
5946 Camera & photographic supply stores	-	6	-	29	5	-	18,483	-	737
5947 Gift, novelty, and souvenir shops	-	74	-	510	7	-	7,067	-	4,191
5948 Luggage and leather goods stores	-	3	-	27	9	-	8,148	-	224
5949 Sewing, needlework, and piece goods	-	16	-	108	7	-	6,963	-	799
5961 Catalog and mail-order houses	-	16	-	1,211	76	-	26,533	-	35,231
5962 Merchandising machine operators	-	15	-	171	11	-	19,930	-	3,326
5963 Direct selling establishments	-	28	-	172	6	-	12,837	-	2,830
5983 Fuel oil dealers	-	6	-	23	4	-	19,826	-	458
5984 Liquefied petroleum gas dealers	-	5	-	31	6	-	25,935	-	600
5992 Florists	-	41	-	247	6	-	8,065	-	1,889
5994 News dealers and newsstands	-	3	-	16	5	-	5,250	-	84
5995 Optical goods stores	-	22	-	129	6	-	14,853	-	2,097
5999 Miscellaneous retail stores, nec	-	103	-	576	6	-	17,806	-	10,712

Source: County Business Patterns 1994/95, CBP-94/95, U.S. Department of Commerce, Washington DC, November 1997. The employment column represents mid-March employment in the year. Pay per employee is calculated by dividing 1st Quarter payroll, annualized, by mid-March employment. The column headed 'Emp / Est' shows 'employees per establishment'. A dash (-) means that data are unavailable or cannot be calculated. nec means not elsewhere classified. *Notes:* 1. 1994 data incomplete; unavailable or withheld. 2. 1995 data incomplete; unavailable or withheld. 3. 1994 and 1995 data incomplete; unavailable or withheld.

MANSFIELD, OH MSA

Wholesale and Retail Trade USA	Establishments		Employment		Emp / Est	Pay / Employee		Annual Payroll ($ 000)	
	1994	1995	1994	1995	1995	1994	1995	1994	1995
50- Wholesale trade	280	274	3,286	3,594	13	22,222	23,495	79,795	87,596
5012 Automobiles and other vehicles	7	6	112	105	18	24,143	29,905	3,563	3,569
5013 Motor vehicle supplies and new parts	21	19	133	157	8	22,045	21,223	3,973	4,475
5015 Motor vehicle parts, used	11	12	29	63	5	16,000	20,571	444	1,527
5021 Furniture [2]	-	3	-	73	24	-	35,616	-	2,671
5031 Lumber, plywood, and millwork	-	7	-	20	3	-	62,800	-	869
5045 Computers, peripherals, & software [1]	5	-	27	-	-	20,444	-	512	-
5047 Medical and hospital equipment [2]	-	3	-	14	5	-	10,000	-	157
5051 Metals service centers and offices	10	10	115	197	20	30,817	30,112	3,819	3,840
5063 Electrical apparatus and equipment [3]	8	8	127	88	11	28,441	31,545	4,031	3,016
5065 Electronic parts and equipment	7	7	66	70	10	28,909	21,829	1,713	1,301
5072 Hardware [3]	6	6	86	85	14	31,814	32,894	2,358	2,543
5074 Plumbing & hydronic heating supplies	8	8	42	29	4	25,524	28,690	1,137	736
5075 Warm air heating & air conditioning [3]	3	3	31	32	11	21,419	23,375	714	746
5078 Refrigeration equipment and supplies	4	4	29	28	7	20,000	22,714	671	755
5084 Industrial machinery and equipment	-	13	-	166	13	-	26,819	-	4,640
5085 Industrial supplies	-	16	-	119	7	-	24,639	-	3,193
5087 Service establishment equipment	-	7	-	96	14	-	24,500	-	2,988
5091 Sporting & recreational goods	-	6	-	19	3	-	9,684	-	227
5093 Scrap and waste materials	-	14	-	169	12	-	24,213	-	4,948
5094 Jewelry & precious stones	-	4	-	7	2	-	18,286	-	127
5099 Durable goods, nec [2]	-	4	-	56	14	-	22,429	-	742
5112 Stationery and office supplies [2]	-	6	-	11	2	-	24,727	-	469
5140 Groceries and related products	-	15	-	422	28	-	17,602	-	8,021
5150 Farm-product raw materials [2]	-	7	-	100	14	-	16,560	-	1,738
5160 Chemicals and allied products [2]	-	6	-	95	16	-	14,695	-	1,399
5181 Beer and ale [2]	-	3	-	74	25	-	29,027	-	2,358
5191 Farm supplies	-	11	-	64	6	-	14,938	-	1,564
5199 Nondurable goods, nec	-	7	-	46	7	-	14,087	-	734
52- Retail trade	1,057	1,080	14,538	15,420	14	10,287	11,078	169,928	177,176
5210 Lumber and other building materials	25	24	385	449	19	17,101	18,708	7,326	9,228
5250 Hardware stores	18	16	190	128	8	9,495	9,000	2,231	1,239
5260 Retail nurseries and garden stores	10	10	64	74	7	13,375	16,865	1,419	1,388
5310 Department stores [3]	9	8	1,614	1,045	131	10,107	12,911	18,107	13,753
5330 Variety stores	15	10	101	88	9	8,911	9,500	1,037	935
5390 Misc. general merchandise stores	9	14	883	939	67	9,173	10,356	9,078	9,823
5410 Grocery stores	71	70	1,537	2,060	29	11,076	11,322	18,526	23,335
5420 Meat and fish markets	7	8	63	48	6	11,746	13,833	801	789
5460 Retail bakeries	10	9	42	30	3	7,143	8,667	289	285
5490 Miscellaneous food stores [3]	5	5	24	23	5	13,500	13,913	333	337
5510 New and used car dealers	21	21	693	745	35	21,172	22,668	17,524	15,154
5520 Used car dealers	25	25	130	141	6	20,646	21,106	2,884	2,943
5530 Auto and home supply stores	31	30	171	172	6	14,947	17,698	2,932	3,157
5540 Gasoline service stations	89	90	946	1,152	13	11,353	11,462	12,862	12,870
5570 Motorcycle dealers [2]	-	3	-	30	10	-	18,800	-	789
5610 Men's & boys' clothing stores [3]	4	4	26	22	6	7,077	11,091	261	271
5620 Women's clothing stores	30	26	266	217	8	7,008	6,654	1,980	1,468
5630 Women's accessory & specialty stores [3]	7	6	16	28	5	8,500	7,714	188	200
5650 Family clothing stores	6	5	58	51	10	7,172	9,725	476	523
5660 Shoe stores	27	24	101	108	5	9,584	10,037	974	953
5690 Misc. apparel & accessory stores	7	7	36	25	4	7,000	8,960	244	226
5712 Furniture stores	18	17	88	99	6	14,091	13,737	1,418	1,504
5731 Radio, TV, & electronic stores	13	14	88	88	6	18,455	20,545	950	1,651
5734 Computer and software stores [3]	5	6	24	56	9	12,833	12,429	356	687
5812 Eating places	244	235	4,596	4,915	21	6,508	6,848	35,810	37,179
5813 Drinking places	68	69	197	211	3	7,533	7,507	1,665	1,680
5910 Drug stores and proprietary stores	31	30	451	438	15	15,592	17,461	7,192	7,770
5920 Liquor stores	15	17	74	65	4	8,757	9,662	670	661
5930 Used merchandise stores	10	9	32	25	3	7,375	7,680	219	204
5941 Sporting goods and bicycle shops	15	16	69	71	4	8,812	8,732	612	880
5942 Book stores [2]	12	12	83	83	7	5,880	6,265	514	566
5944 Jewelry stores	18	20	102	105	5	16,000	17,676	1,834	2,055
5945 Hobby, toy, and game shops	7	8	56	56	7	8,857	10,143	589	738
5947 Gift, novelty, and souvenir shops	17	18	97	138	8	7,423	6,899	777	872
5949 Sewing, needlework, and piece goods [3]	5	5	37	35	7	5,189	7,429	231	231
5962 Merchandising machine operators [3]	5	5	153	156	31	12,314	13,179	1,931	2,134
5983 Fuel oil dealers	-	6	-	17	3	-	17,882	-	312
5992 Florists	15	17	47	55	3	10,043	9,091	543	532
5995 Optical goods stores [2]	-	8	-	50	6	-	11,760	-	581
5999 Miscellaneous retail stores, nec	24	32	86	93	3	13,302	15,226	1,429	1,774

Source: County Business Patterns 1994/95, CBP-94/95, U.S. Department of Commerce, Washington DC, November 1997. The employment column represents mid-March employment in the year. Pay per employee is calculated by dividing 1st Quarter payroll, annualized, by mid-March employment. The column headed 'Emp / Est' shows 'employees per establishment'. A dash (-) means that data are unavailable or cannot be calculated. nec means not elsewhere classified. *Notes:* 1. 1994 data incomplete; unavailable or withheld. 2. 1995 data incomplete; unavailable or withheld. 3. 1994 and 1995 data incomplete; unavailable or withheld.

MCALLEN - EDINBURG - MISSION, TX MSA

Wholesale and Retail Trade USA	Establishments		Employment		Emp / Est	Pay / Employee		Annual Payroll ($ 000)	
	1994	1995	1994	1995	1995	1994	1995	1994	1995
50- Wholesale trade	-	703	-	8,445	12	-	17,116	-	146,643
5012 Automobiles and other vehicles	-	14	-	198	14	-	17,475	-	3,691
5013 Motor vehicle supplies and new parts	-	30	-	380	13	-	19,316	-	7,608
5014 Tires and tubes	-	5	-	14	3	-	14,857	-	225
5015 Motor vehicle parts, used	-	15	-	87	6	-	14,207	-	1,542
5023 Homefurnishings	-	7	-	94	13	-	18,553	-	1,811
5032 Brick, stone, & related materials	-	11	-	55	5	-	16,509	-	1,025
5039 Construction materials, nec	-	7	-	198	28	-	16,182	-	3,547
5044 Office equipment	-	11	-	114	10	-	20,561	-	2,542
5045 Computers, peripherals, & software	-	22	-	69	3	-	24,928	-	1,740
5047 Medical and hospital equipment	-	10	-	56	6	-	21,571	-	1,240
5049 Professional equipment, nec	-	3	-	9	3	-	4,889	-	44
5051 Metals service centers and offices	-	7	-	40	6	-	25,800	-	1,380
5063 Electrical apparatus and equipment	-	14	-	147	11	-	24,163	-	3,212
5064 Electrical appliances, TV & radios	-	11	-	117	11	-	19,111	-	2,161
5065 Electronic parts and equipment	-	19	-	95	5	-	23,368	-	2,479
5072 Hardware	-	10	-	176	18	-	17,250	-	2,884
5074 Plumbing & hydronic heating supplies	-	7	-	111	16	-	21,405	-	2,529
5083 Farm and garden machinery	-	17	-	261	15	-	25,349	-	6,361
5084 Industrial machinery and equipment	-	47	-	285	6	-	22,667	-	6,292
5085 Industrial supplies	-	15	-	100	7	-	18,200	-	1,949
5087 Service establishment equipment	-	9	-	55	6	-	19,273	-	973
5088 Transportation equipment & supplies	-	5	-	14	3	-	35,714	-	463
5091 Sporting & recreational goods	-	3	-	22	7	-	7,455	-	163
5092 Toys and hobby goods and supplies	-	4	-	11	3	-	9,455	-	84
5093 Scrap and waste materials	-	12	-	112	9	-	13,964	-	1,750
5094 Jewelry & precious stones	-	13	-	71	5	-	42,817	-	2,526
5099 Durable goods, nec	-	11	-	66	6	-	35,576	-	2,454
5112 Stationery and office supplies	-	8	-	140	18	-	20,600	-	3,023
5120 Drugs, proprietaries, and sundries	-	11	-	130	12	-	22,431	-	3,450
5131 Piece goods & notions	-	3	-	8	3	-	4,500	-	27
5136 Men's and boys' clothing	-	5	-	46	9	-	9,391	-	395
5137 Women's and children's clothing	-	8	-	98	12	-	14,286	-	1,288
5139 Footwear	-	4	-	103	26	-	16,816	-	1,325
5141 Groceries, general line	-	6	-	24	4	-	12,667	-	303
5142 Packaged frozen food	-	8	-	53	7	-	30,868	-	1,635
5143 Dairy products, exc. dried or canned	-	6	-	65	11	-	18,154	-	1,233
5145 Confectionery	-	5	-	56	11	-	12,500	-	691
5147 Meats and meat products	-	10	-	51	5	-	17,176	-	882
5148 Fresh fruits and vegetables	-	75	-	2,925	39	-	11,420	-	31,079
5149 Groceries and related products, nec	-	9	-	84	9	-	9,333	-	727
5153 Grain and field beans	-	14	-	134	10	-	18,806	-	4,473
5162 Plastics materials & basic shapes	-	3	-	2	1	-	12,000	-	26
5169 Chemicals & allied products, nec	-	6	-	13	2	-	24,000	-	408
5171 Petroleum bulk stations & terminals	-	7	-	126	18	-	20,413	-	2,714
5172 Petroleum products, nec	-	8	-	70	9	-	25,371	-	1,841
5181 Beer and ale	-	4	-	228	57	-	22,842	-	5,390
5191 Farm supplies	-	35	-	312	9	-	22,487	-	6,854
5192 Books, periodicals, & newspapers	-	4	-	13	3	-	13,231	-	145
5193 Flowers & florists' supplies	-	9	-	64	7	-	14,313	-	928
5198 Paints, varnishes, and supplies	-	5	-	23	5	-	16,348	-	381
5199 Nondurable goods, nec	-	24	-	159	7	-	9,157	-	2,019
52- Retail trade	-	2,056	-	29,836	15	-	11,842	-	354,430
5210 Lumber and other building materials	-	42	-	679	16	-	14,940	-	9,656
5230 Paint, glass, and wallpaper stores	-	11	-	45	4	-	18,667	-	764
5250 Hardware stores	-	15	-	224	15	-	11,054	-	2,866
5260 Retail nurseries and garden stores	-	12	-	95	8	-	12,632	-	1,587
5270 Mobile home dealers	-	11	-	69	6	-	43,362	-	2,925
5310 Department stores	-	15	-	3,612	241	-	12,480	-	42,465
5330 Variety stores	-	22	-	200	9	-	9,020	-	1,816
5390 Misc. general merchandise stores	-	24	-	648	27	-	12,809	-	7,584
5410 Grocery stores	-	207	-	4,679	23	-	11,188	-	51,392
5420 Meat and fish markets	-	12	-	122	10	-	9,377	-	1,167
5430 Fruit and vegetable markets	-	12	-	70	6	-	7,314	-	582
5460 Retail bakeries	-	31	-	140	5	-	8,057	-	1,142
5490 Miscellaneous food stores	-	10	-	37	4	-	12,216	-	508
5510 New and used car dealers	-	25	-	1,290	52	-	25,169	-	36,813
5520 Used car dealers	-	61	-	254	4	-	13,291	-	3,416
5530 Auto and home supply stores	-	79	-	654	8	-	15,859	-	10,632
5540 Gasoline service stations	-	129	-	845	7	-	11,588	-	10,019
5560 Recreational vehicle dealers	-	13	-	139	11	-	18,647	-	1,897

Continued on next page.

MCALLEN - EDINBURG - MISSION, TX MSA - [continued]

Wholesale and Retail Trade USA	Establishments 1994	Establishments 1995	Employment 1994	Employment 1995	Emp / Est 1995	Pay / Employee 1994	Pay / Employee 1995	Annual Payroll ($ 000) 1994	Annual Payroll ($ 000) 1995
5610 Men's & boys' clothing stores	-	18	-	196	11	-	11,735	-	2,265
5620 Women's clothing stores	-	78	-	1,467	19	-	8,733	-	13,426
5630 Women's accessory & specialty stores	-	14	-	81	6	-	9,877	-	795
5640 Children's and infants' wear stores	-	6	-	39	7	-	9,538	-	403
5650 Family clothing stores	-	42	-	930	22	-	11,639	-	10,005
5660 Shoe stores	-	56	-	331	6	-	11,227	-	3,624
5690 Misc. apparel & accessory stores	-	13	-	84	6	-	7,667	-	621
5712 Furniture stores	-	46	-	623	14	-	18,453	-	10,368
5719 Misc. homefurnishings stores	-	10	-	38	4	-	13,895	-	517
5720 Household appliance stores	-	9	-	40	4	-	13,500	-	512
5731 Radio, TV, & electronic stores	-	35	-	314	9	-	12,994	-	3,872
5735 Record & prerecorded tape stores	-	5	-	63	13	-	5,143	-	304
5812 Eating places	-	375	-	7,847	21	-	7,920	-	61,306
5813 Drinking places	-	45	-	199	4	-	7,558	-	1,501
5910 Drug stores and proprietary stores	-	47	-	489	10	-	16,384	-	8,419
5920 Liquor stores	-	17	-	92	5	-	12,130	-	941
5930 Used merchandise stores	-	68	-	380	6	-	12,747	-	4,971
5941 Sporting goods and bicycle shops	-	17	-	175	10	-	12,183	-	2,230
5942 Book stores	-	8	-	23	3	-	7,652	-	224
5943 Stationery stores	-	4	-	60	15	-	12,067	-	680
5944 Jewelry stores	-	50	-	242	5	-	12,612	-	2,956
5945 Hobby, toy, and game shops	-	12	-	164	14	-	7,780	-	1,365
5947 Gift, novelty, and souvenir shops	-	26	-	182	7	-	10,857	-	1,823
5949 Sewing, needlework, and piece goods	-	12	-	106	9	-	12,679	-	1,438
5963 Direct selling establishments	-	11	-	52	5	-	10,615	-	690
5984 Liquefied petroleum gas dealers	-	10	-	45	5	-	20,356	-	810
5992 Florists	-	21	-	105	5	-	8,419	-	892
5995 Optical goods stores	-	18	-	115	6	-	13,809	-	1,538
5999 Miscellaneous retail stores, nec	-	58	-	219	4	-	12,493	-	3,406

Source: County Business Patterns 1994/95, CBP-94/95, U.S. Department of Commerce, Washington DC, November 1997. The employment column represents mid-March employment in the year. Pay per employee is calculated by dividing 1st Quarter payroll, annualized, by mid-March employment. The column headed 'Emp / Est' shows 'employees per establishment'. A dash (-) means that data are unavailable or cannot be calculated. nec means not elsewhere classified. *Notes:* 1. 1994 data incomplete; unavailable or withheld. 2. 1995 data incomplete; unavailable or withheld. 3. 1994 and 1995 data incomplete; unavailable or withheld.

MEDFORD - ASHLAND, OR MSA

Wholesale and Retail Trade USA	Establishments 1994	Establishments 1995	Employment 1994	Employment 1995	Emp / Est 1995	Pay / Employee 1994	Pay / Employee 1995	Annual Payroll ($ 000) 1994	Annual Payroll ($ 000) 1995
50- Wholesale trade	-	313	-	2,778	9	-	26,347	-	79,074
5012 Automobiles and other vehicles	-	6	-	104	17	-	26,654	-	2,798
5013 Motor vehicle supplies and new parts	-	16	-	151	9	-	23,417	-	3,610
5020 Furniture and homefurnishings	-	7	-	47	7	-	16,851	-	874
5031 Lumber, plywood, and millwork	-	29	-	186	6	-	23,462	-	4,619
5039 Construction materials, nec	-	7	-	51	7	-	25,490	-	1,364
5044 Office equipment	-	13	-	74	6	-	24,162	-	1,707
5045 Computers, peripherals, & software	-	8	-	39	5	-	25,538	-	999
5047 Medical and hospital equipment	-	8	-	34	4	-	23,647	-	1,040
5051 Metals service centers and offices	-	5	-	50	10	-	28,960	-	1,689
5063 Electrical apparatus and equipment	-	5	-	45	9	-	42,756	-	1,577
5064 Electrical appliances, TV & radios	-	3	-	21	7	-	71,810	-	1,328
5065 Electronic parts and equipment	-	6	-	33	6	-	28,121	-	918
5072 Hardware	-	8	-	61	8	-	21,705	-	1,462
5074 Plumbing & hydronic heating supplies	-	5	-	73	15	-	30,301	-	2,201
5075 Warm air heating & air conditioning	-	3	-	10	3	-	24,000	-	256
5078 Refrigeration equipment and supplies	-	3	-	7	2	-	21,714	-	189
5082 Construction and mining machinery	-	9	-	103	11	-	25,204	-	3,348
5084 Industrial machinery and equipment	-	14	-	120	9	-	35,633	-	4,289
5085 Industrial supplies	-	8	-	55	7	-	35,273	-	1,733
5087 Service establishment equipment	-	9	-	41	5	-	20,098	-	922
5099 Durable goods, nec	-	6	-	25	4	-	20,480	-	637
5112 Stationery and office supplies	-	9	-	66	7	-	17,091	-	1,758
5120 Drugs, proprietaries, and sundries	-	4	-	27	7	-	28,889	-	1,422
5148 Fresh fruits and vegetables	-	5	-	82	16	-	16,537	-	1,959
5149 Groceries and related products, nec	-	11	-	105	10	-	20,724	-	2,292
5169 Chemicals & allied products, nec	-	5	-	47	9	-	18,468	-	817
5170 Petroleum and petroleum products	-	8	-	65	8	-	27,754	-	2,464
5181 Beer and ale	-	5	-	125	25	-	29,760	-	3,709
5191 Farm supplies	-	11	-	117	11	-	15,009	-	1,829
5192 Books, periodicals, & newspapers	-	3	-	32	11	-	25,625	-	983

Continued on next page.

MEDFORD - ASHLAND, OR MSA - [continued]

Wholesale and Retail Trade USA	Establishments		Employment		Emp / Est	Pay / Employee		Annual Payroll ($ 000)	
	1994	1995	1994	1995	1995	1994	1995	1994	1995
52- Retail trade	-	1,139	-	14,017	12	-	13,131	-	200,288
5210 Lumber and other building materials	-	18	-	325	18	-	22,658	-	7,247
5230 Paint, glass, and wallpaper stores	-	8	-	56	7	-	15,429	-	891
5250 Hardware stores	-	11	-	139	13	-	14,129	-	2,084
5260 Retail nurseries and garden stores	-	8	-	32	4	-	16,125	-	616
5270 Mobile home dealers	-	11	-	74	7	-	21,730	-	1,989
5310 Department stores	-	11	-	1,560	142	-	13,015	-	22,149
5410 Grocery stores	-	84	-	1,673	20	-	14,135	-	24,130
5420 Meat and fish markets	-	6	-	17	3	-	6,353	-	155
5440 Candy, nut, and confectionery stores	-	5	-	11	2	-	8,364	-	123
5460 Retail bakeries	-	7	-	38	5	-	8,632	-	326
5490 Miscellaneous food stores	-	13	-	33	3	-	8,606	-	318
5510 New and used car dealers	-	15	-	691	46	-	29,754	-	22,634
5520 Used car dealers	-	18	-	104	6	-	27,692	-	3,166
5530 Auto and home supply stores	-	32	-	224	7	-	20,500	-	4,384
5540 Gasoline service stations	-	66	-	617	9	-	10,820	-	7,048
5550 Boat dealers	-	6	-	52	9	-	20,538	-	1,613
5560 Recreational vehicle dealers	-	7	-	93	13	-	25,290	-	3,051
5570 Motorcycle dealers	-	5	-	37	7	-	15,459	-	616
5610 Men's & boys' clothing stores	-	7	-	69	10	-	8,812	-	651
5620 Women's clothing stores	-	30	-	174	6	-	7,816	-	1,279
5630 Women's accessory & specialty stores	-	6	-	25	4	-	7,360	-	170
5650 Family clothing stores	-	13	-	169	13	-	9,775	-	1,482
5660 Shoe stores	-	21	-	107	5	-	11,028	-	1,169
5690 Misc. apparel & accessory stores	-	6	-	19	3	-	11,368	-	279
5712 Furniture stores	-	20	-	152	8	-	17,079	-	2,676
5713 Floor covering stores	-	13	-	60	5	-	20,467	-	1,225
5720 Household appliance stores	-	7	-	56	8	-	18,071	-	1,049
5731 Radio, TV, & electronic stores	-	13	-	142	11	-	17,803	-	2,438
5734 Computer and software stores	-	8	-	29	4	-	16,690	-	461
5735 Record & prerecorded tape stores	-	7	-	21	3	-	9,524	-	232
5736 Musical instrument stores	-	4	-	18	5	-	13,111	-	240
5812 Eating places	-	276	-	4,627	17	-	7,876	-	41,255
5813 Drinking places	-	34	-	279	8	-	9,419	-	2,537
5910 Drug stores and proprietary stores	-	18	-	226	13	-	17,451	-	3,742
5920 Liquor stores	-	20	-	35	2	-	14,857	-	554
5930 Used merchandise stores	-	22	-	76	3	-	10,000	-	844
5941 Sporting goods and bicycle shops	-	21	-	143	7	-	10,685	-	1,857
5942 Book stores	-	16	-	76	5	-	9,053	-	799
5944 Jewelry stores	-	18	-	98	5	-	15,755	-	1,585
5945 Hobby, toy, and game shops	-	7	-	60	9	-	11,267	-	979
5946 Camera & photographic supply stores	-	3	-	4	1	-	9,000	-	40
5947 Gift, novelty, and souvenir shops	-	23	-	138	6	-	11,478	-	1,765
5949 Sewing, needlework, and piece goods	-	7	-	45	6	-	7,022	-	310
5961 Catalog and mail-order houses	-	12	-	229	19	-	20,664	-	5,314
5992 Florists	-	14	-	52	4	-	9,846	-	467
5995 Optical goods stores	-	8	-	32	4	-	13,375	-	426
5999 Miscellaneous retail stores, nec	-	24	-	82	3	-	11,512	-	1,162

Source: County Business Patterns 1994/95, CBP-94/95, U.S. Department of Commerce, Washington DC, November 1997. The employment column represents mid-March employment in the year. Pay per employee is calculated by dividing 1st Quarter payroll, annualized, by mid-March employment. The column headed 'Emp / Est' shows 'employees per establishment'. A dash (-) means that data are unavailable or cannot be calculated. nec means not elsewhere classified. *Notes:* 1. 1994 data incomplete; unavailable or withheld. 2. 1995 data incomplete; unavailable or withheld. 3. 1994 and 1995 data incomplete; unavailable or withheld.

MELBOURNE - TITUSVILLE - PALM BAY, FL MSA

Wholesale and Retail Trade USA	Establishments		Employment		Emp / Est	Pay / Employee		Annual Payroll ($ 000)	
	1994	1995	1994	1995	1995	1994	1995	1994	1995
50- Wholesale trade	634	655	5,148	5,171	8	23,534	25,312	128,058	137,015
5012 Automobiles and other vehicles	11	12	71	77	6	18,817	19,221	1,415	1,479
5013 Motor vehicle supplies and new parts	47	44	309	322	7	22,317	22,012	7,584	7,253
5014 Tires and tubes	5	-	48	-	-	30,500	-	2,044	-
5015 Motor vehicle parts, used	10	15	54	58	4	12,222	13,655	773	806
5021 Furniture	12	10	81	75	8	21,185	22,880	1,774	1,163
5023 Homefurnishings	7	6	41	46	8	20,780	46,348	1,132	1,570
5031 Lumber, plywood, and millwork	9	13	94	99	8	20,340	22,828	2,173	2,538
5032 Brick, stone, & related materials	10	8	96	55	7	23,042	29,455	3,004	1,584
5033 Roofing, siding, & insulation	-	6	-	34	6	-	31,529	-	1,080
5039 Construction materials, nec	-	9	-	47	5	-	19,234	-	979
5044 Office equipment	18	15	349	357	24	26,029	26,241	9,502	9,690

Continued on next page.

MELBOURNE - TITUSVILLE - PALM BAY, FL MSA - [continued]

Wholesale and Retail Trade USA	Establishments		Employment		Emp / Est	Pay / Employee		Annual Payroll ($ 000)	
	1994	1995	1994	1995	1995	1994	1995	1994	1995
5045 Computers, peripherals, & software	33	37	274	321	9	37,372	39,240	10,636	13,582
5046 Commercial equipment, nec	9	8	53	56	7	25,057	23,571	1,430	1,487
5047 Medical and hospital equipment	9	9	46	37	4	36,087	24,108	1,136	792
5051 Metals service centers and offices	8	9	25	27	3	23,680	20,148	591	606
5063 Electrical apparatus and equipment	27	22	157	160	7	26,013	28,125	3,991	4,320
5065 Electronic parts and equipment	40	44	289	340	8	25,536	29,635	8,218	10,886
5072 Hardware	11	10	117	115	12	25,573	28,487	3,298	3,497
5074 Plumbing & hydronic heating supplies	17	-	127	-	-	16,787	-	2,348	-
5075 Warm air heating & air conditioning	-	17	-	83	5	-	23,470	-	2,245
5083 Farm and garden machinery	9	9	63	53	6	17,206	20,000	1,225	1,241
5084 Industrial machinery and equipment	24	24	111	165	7	30,703	31,224	4,844	6,295
5085 Industrial supplies	13	14	85	105	8	16,565	24,571	2,038	2,693
5087 Service establishment equipment	6	8	29	48	6	18,483	23,500	603	962
5088 Transportation equipment & supplies	18	18	78	88	5	24,051	21,955	1,967	2,312
5091 Sporting & recreational goods	23	22	87	101	5	19,816	17,901	1,932	1,967
5093 Scrap and waste materials	10	13	155	187	14	20,077	23,615	3,699	4,752
5099 Durable goods, nec	8	11	98	108	10	16,980	19,889	1,853	2,317
5112 Stationery and office supplies	16	11	148	123	11	13,838	16,293	2,160	1,785
5113 Industrial & personal service paper	4	3	28	18	6	21,143	27,111	725	683
5120 Drugs, proprietaries, and sundries	8	8	18	23	3	23,111	22,261	506	604
5131 Piece goods & notions	5	3	19	9	3	18,526	16,000	212	138
5136 Men's and boys' clothing	5	5	51	54	11	21,725	16,148	1,108	1,174
5137 Women's and children's clothing	5	6	14	15	3	14,857	19,733	249	357
5141 Groceries, general line	-	3	-	5	2	-	16,000	-	90
5146 Fish and seafoods	19	20	182	140	7	13,495	15,857	2,289	1,786
5148 Fresh fruits and vegetables	7	6	94	75	13	15,191	18,933	1,367	1,476
5149 Groceries and related products, nec	17	14	275	273	20	26,327	28,190	8,031	7,638
5160 Chemicals and allied products	13	11	81	76	7	17,877	20,526	2,138	1,909
5171 Petroleum bulk stations & terminals	10	9	94	91	10	26,085	28,176	2,535	2,365
5181 Beer and ale	4	4	181	201	50	30,961	30,647	5,976	6,598
5191 Farm supplies	8	9	80	65	7	13,400	18,769	1,092	1,145
5192 Books, periodicals, & newspapers	-	3	-	39	13	-	21,846	-	811
5193 Flowers & florists' supplies	6	8	48	63	8	14,750	17,270	733	1,078
5198 Paints, varnishes, and supplies	11	-	77	-	-	19,896	-	1,715	-
5199 Nondurable goods, nec	21	25	70	107	4	15,714	18,729	1,513	2,455
52- Retail trade	2,655	2,611	35,167	35,939	14	11,332	12,341	425,445	443,386
5210 Lumber and other building materials	36	33	882	907	27	16,544	16,851	15,491	15,175
5230 Paint, glass, and wallpaper stores	24	21	79	78	4	16,608	18,154	1,284	1,416
5250 Hardware stores	24	21	207	185	9	11,382	12,259	2,557	2,520
5260 Retail nurseries and garden stores	24	21	106	118	6	14,000	14,136	1,730	1,812
5270 Mobile home dealers	8	8	27	38	5	12,889	15,895	436	523
5310 Department stores	26	26	3,758	4,228	163	10,959	12,518	44,912	50,704
5330 Variety stores	25	14	193	152	11	8,456	7,947	1,773	1,287
5390 Misc. general merchandise stores	10	19	436	373	20	11,697	14,155	5,393	4,785
5410 Grocery stores	184	190	6,065	5,906	31	9,614	11,304	61,778	68,164
5420 Meat and fish markets	10	10	45	40	4	12,356	12,000	574	461
5430 Fruit and vegetable markets	4	4	4	6	2	11,000	6,667	16	28
5440 Candy, nut, and confectionery stores	5	4	22	11	3	7,818	12,364	274	251
5450 Dairy products stores	4	5	16	13	3	5,750	8,308	106	108
5460 Retail bakeries	37	39	282	258	7	6,199	6,946	1,947	1,881
5490 Miscellaneous food stores	20	16	115	108	7	10,574	12,593	1,263	1,461
5510 New and used car dealers	36	37	1,815	1,872	51	32,106	32,590	65,448	67,143
5520 Used car dealers	34	35	136	144	4	14,824	16,528	2,036	2,270
5530 Auto and home supply stores	63	71	433	480	7	17,958	18,650	8,477	9,277
5540 Gasoline service stations	188	156	1,091	999	6	11,003	12,088	12,793	12,396
5550 Boat dealers	16	18	77	74	4	18,234	17,243	1,540	1,438
5560 Recreational vehicle dealers	5	8	31	36	5	19,226	27,778	808	1,148
5570 Motorcycle dealers	7	8	30	36	5	18,667	17,556	622	673
5590 Automotive dealers, nec	4	4	6	11	3	14,667	8,000	89	105
5610 Men's & boys' clothing stores	15	13	70	53	4	10,171	12,981	707	726
5620 Women's clothing stores	61	50	489	375	8	8,082	7,637	4,263	2,844
5630 Women's accessory & specialty stores	13	12	71	55	5	7,042	8,945	508	501
5640 Children's and infants' wear stores	3	3	11	9	3	5,818	7,111	72	96
5650 Family clothing stores	22	23	312	338	15	8,962	9,692	3,186	3,248
5660 Shoe stores	45	46	181	200	4	11,691	10,700	2,080	1,979
5690 Misc. apparel & accessory stores	19	17	250	259	15	14,112	41,004	5,618	6,648
5712 Furniture stores	65	72	437	443	6	17,410	17,761	7,847	7,914
5713 Floor covering stores	32	33	148	148	4	16,081	17,892	2,805	2,768
5714 Drapery and upholstery stores	9	8	15	14	2	8,533	8,571	148	114
5719 Misc. homefurnishings stores	27	26	152	138	5	11,500	11,652	1,803	1,665
5720 Household appliance stores	14	15	54	50	3	16,000	14,320	837	681

Continued on next page.

MELBOURNE – TITUSVILLE – PALM BAY, FL MSA - [continued]

Wholesale and Retail Trade USA	Establishments		Employment		Emp / Est	Pay / Employee		Annual Payroll ($ 000)	
	1994	1995	1994	1995	1995	1994	1995	1994	1995
5731 Radio, TV, & electronic stores	38	36	253	346	10	18,957	17,006	5,124	5,379
5734 Computer and software stores	18	18	99	134	7	17,172	16,985	1,883	2,766
5735 Record & prerecorded tape stores	10	10	54	70	7	10,148	8,286	587	651
5736 Musical instrument stores	12	12	52	54	5	15,077	14,889	723	728
5812 Eating places	581	520	11,775	11,688	22	8,093	8,210	93,820	91,065
5813 Drinking places	89	77	561	569	7	8,927	9,293	5,279	5,443
5910 Drug stores and proprietary stores	57	55	991	1,007	18	16,052	17,716	17,889	18,579
5920 Liquor stores	35	32	255	189	6	8,800	9,757	2,169	1,819
5930 Used merchandise stores	54	53	178	202	4	11,843	11,743	2,239	2,308
5941 Sporting goods and bicycle shops	63	63	211	210	3	10,900	12,533	2,627	2,852
5942 Book stores	29	27	160	136	5	7,675	8,559	1,326	1,459
5943 Stationery stores	5	6	21	56	9	14,095	15,000	371	908
5944 Jewelry stores	47	56	181	213	4	15,757	16,319	3,085	3,333
5945 Hobby, toy, and game shops	16	16	149	216	14	9,074	9,111	1,691	1,873
5946 Camera & photographic supply stores	4	-	28	-	-	12,429	-	349	-
5947 Gift, novelty, and souvenir shops	67	61	350	349	6	8,160	9,238	2,989	3,223
5949 Sewing, needlework, and piece goods	15	12	104	93	8	5,846	6,925	614	547
5961 Catalog and mail-order houses	9	8	87	91	11	14,391	12,396	1,058	999
5962 Merchandising machine operators	11	12	38	48	4	20,842	19,333	862	1,014
5963 Direct selling establishments	15	10	74	48	5	13,027	15,917	1,343	745
5980 Fuel dealers	6	6	49	50	8	18,776	19,920	906	1,037
5992 Florists	65	62	236	217	4	8,763	9,770	2,065	2,078
5995 Optical goods stores	-	30	-	136	5	-	15,971	-	1,899
5999 Miscellaneous retail stores, nec	91	101	352	400	4	12,261	12,990	4,689	5,196

Source: County Business Patterns 1994/95, CBP-94/95, U.S. Department of Commerce, Washington DC, November 1997. The employment column represents mid-March employment in the year. Pay per employee is calculated by dividing 1st Quarter payroll, annualized, by mid-March employment. The column headed 'Emp / Est' shows 'employees per establishment'. A dash (-) means that data are unavailable or cannot be calculated. nec means not elsewhere classified. *Notes:* 1. 1994 data incomplete; unavailable or withheld. 2. 1995 data incomplete; unavailable or withheld. 3. 1994 and 1995 data incomplete; unavailable or withheld.

MEMPHIS MSA (AR PART)

Wholesale and Retail Trade USA	Establishments		Employment		Emp / Est	Pay / Employee		Annual Payroll ($ 000)	
	1994	1995	1994	1995	1995	1994	1995	1994	1995
50 - Wholesale trade	86	80	778	794	10	24,864	24,982	21,707	23,264
5012 Automobiles and other vehicles	-	4	-	8	2	-	9,500	-	160
5013 Motor vehicle supplies and new parts	6	3	32	23	8	19,375	20,870	766	558
5051 Metals service centers and offices	4	4	101	122	31	29,465	25,770	3,077	3,405
5083 Farm and garden machinery	13	12	118	128	11	24,780	25,156	3,531	3,634
5084 Industrial machinery and equipment	5	-	31	-	-	20,903	-	776	-
5090 Miscellaneous durable goods	4	4	11	19	5	18,545	17,263	197	241
5169 Chemicals & allied products, nec	4	3	28	24	8	28,857	24,000	763	598
5171 Petroleum bulk stations & terminals	4	3	18	13	4	18,444	22,462	327	280
5172 Petroleum products, nec	4	4	120	101	25	19,833	22,337	2,407	2,544
5181 Beer and ale	3	3	77	80	27	24,052	25,600	2,175	2,308
5191 Farm supplies	6	-	50	-	-	18,320	-	1,226	-
5199 Nondurable goods, nec	5	-	7	-	-	12,000	-	561	-
52 - Retail trade	251	247	4,362	4,888	20	13,111	13,464	60,504	66,800
5210 Lumber and other building materials	-	5	-	64	13	-	14,000	-	949
5300 General merchandise stores	10	12	324	615	51	10,383	12,442	3,952	6,621
5410 Grocery stores	29	28	463	467	17	9,114	9,987	4,550	4,480
5510 New and used car dealers	6	4	105	102	26	18,400	17,961	2,033	2,087
5520 Used car dealers	13	10	21	30	3	13,333	17,733	398	558
5530 Auto and home supply stores	14	13	94	109	8	15,745	16,514	1,673	1,855
5540 Gasoline service stations	35	33	725	710	22	9,412	9,121	7,558	6,960
5620 Women's clothing stores	8	8	41	42	5	10,244	10,857	447	456
5650 Family clothing stores	3	-	5	-	-	7,200	-	38	-
5660 Shoe stores	-	4	-	16	4	-	10,000	-	166
5712 Furniture stores	6	-	36	-	-	16,444	-	662	-
5730 Radio, television, & computer stores	-	5	-	27	5	-	21,333	-	557
5812 Eating places	50	47	1,095	1,141	24	6,820	6,556	8,090	8,160
5813 Drinking places	6	5	9	14	3	6,222	9,714	105	142
5910 Drug stores and proprietary stores	6	7	82	93	13	15,659	15,656	1,353	1,487
5920 Liquor stores	6	-	11	-	-	6,545	-	68	-
5944 Jewelry stores	-	3	-	11	4	-	5,091	-	39
5992 Florists	-	5	-	27	5	-	10,222	-	236

Source: County Business Patterns 1994/95, CBP-94/95, U.S. Department of Commerce, Washington DC, November 1997. The employment column represents mid-March employment in the year. Pay per employee is calculated by dividing 1st Quarter payroll, annualized, by mid-March employment. The column headed 'Emp / Est' shows 'employees per establishment'. A dash (-) means that data are unavailable or cannot be calculated. nec means not elsewhere classified. *Notes:* 1. 1994 data incomplete; unavailable or withheld. 2. 1995 data incomplete; unavailable or withheld. 3. 1994 and 1995 data incomplete; unavailable or withheld.

MEMPHIS MSA (MS PART)

Wholesale and Retail Trade USA	Establishments		Employment		Emp / Est	Pay / Employee		Annual Payroll ($ 000)	
	1994	1995	1994	1995	1995	1994	1995	1994	1995
50 - Wholesale trade	80	83	1,676	1,762	21	29,508	29,716	51,340	47,284
5012 Automobiles and other vehicles	-	3	-	15	5	-	18,133	-	292
5013 Motor vehicle supplies and new parts	6	6	22	21	4	17,455	21,333	446	417
5030 Lumber and construction materials	5	4	91	144	36	18,549	19,139	2,531	2,828
5040 Professional & commercial equipment	-	7	-	22	3	-	13,818	-	331
5063 Electrical apparatus and equipment	3	-	16	-	-	18,750	-	412	-
5065 Electronic parts and equipment	5	6	20	22	4	24,800	24,727	555	572
5070 Hardware, plumbing & heating equipment	6	4	27	19	5	20,148	19,368	685	342
5084 Industrial machinery and equipment	-	3	-	30	10	-	20,000	-	811
5112 Stationery and office supplies	4	5	47	50	10	19,489	21,200	1,039	1,179
5181 Beer and ale	3	3	60	73	24	24,533	25,041	1,582	1,766
52 - Retail trade	332	348	4,261	4,743	14	10,107	11,286	48,920	60,410
5210 Lumber and other building materials	5	5	39	51	10	17,744	22,039	794	1,198
5230 Paint, glass, and wallpaper stores	4	-	11	-	-	13,091	-	244	-
5260 Retail nurseries and garden stores	-	3	-	25	8	-	10,720	-	356
5300 General merchandise stores	8	9	519	539	60	9,865	13,284	5,969	6,002
5410 Grocery stores	57	56	1,178	1,195	21	9,868	10,715	12,832	16,921
5510 New and used car dealers	4	4	140	212	53	31,257	31,189	5,499	7,902
5520 Used car dealers	8	-	19	-	-	11,789	-	251	-
5530 Auto and home supply stores	16	19	102	116	6	13,961	17,552	1,634	2,127
5540 Gasoline service stations	24	25	165	172	7	9,624	11,256	1,932	2,052
5560 Recreational vehicle dealers	-	3	-	21	7	-	19,619	-	637
5620 Women's clothing stores	12	11	91	64	6	8,044	8,375	831	551
5660 Shoe stores	3	4	11	13	3	11,273	12,000	135	207
5712 Furniture stores	4	5	35	16	3	13,143	12,000	453	282
5713 Floor covering stores	3	3	14	4	1	3,143	12,000	51	61
5730 Radio, television, & computer stores	3	-	31	-	-	12,258	-	404	-
5812 Eating places	63	60	1,340	1,509	25	6,493	6,319	9,110	10,081
5813 Drinking places	3	3	24	23	8	6,000	6,783	166	182
5910 Drug stores and proprietary stores	16	15	149	168	11	17,638	18,476	2,923	3,305
5920 Liquor stores	9	8	27	18	2	10,815	19,778	377	371
5930 Used merchandise stores	7	8	13	12	2	13,846	13,667	179	172
5941 Sporting goods and bicycle shops	7	5	61	46	9	8,852	14,435	761	786
5942 Book stores	-	3	-	3	1	-	8,000	-	32
5945 Hobby, toy, and game shops	-	3	-	2	1	-	10,000	-	25
5947 Gift, novelty, and souvenir shops	10	9	9	25	3	7,111	5,920	92	121
5960 Nonstore retailers	3	3	26	27	9	12,769	10,667	381	330
5992 Florists	8	-	26	-	-	8,769	-	251	-
5999 Miscellaneous retail stores, nec	7	8	26	25	3	11,077	12,480	357	353

Source: County Business Patterns 1994/95, CBP-94/95, U.S. Department of Commerce, Washington DC, November 1997. The employment column represents mid-March employment in the year. Pay per employee is calculated by dividing 1st Quarter payroll, annualized, by mid-March employment. The column headed 'Emp / Est' shows 'employees per establishment'. A dash (-) means that data are unavailable or cannot be calculated. nec means not elsewhere classified. *Notes:* 1. 1994 data incomplete; unavailable or withheld. 2. 1995 data incomplete; unavailable or withheld. 3. 1994 and 1995 data incomplete; unavailable or withheld.

MEMPHIS MSA (TN PART)

Wholesale and Retail Trade USA	Establishments		Employment		Emp / Est	Pay / Employee		Annual Payroll ($ 000)	
	1994	1995	1994	1995	1995	1994	1995	1994	1995
50 - Wholesale trade	-	2,175	-	38,118	18	-	31,229	-	1,262,223
5012 Automobiles and other vehicles 2	-	46	-	1,173	26	-	31,707	-	42,051
5013 Motor vehicle supplies and new parts 2	-	117	-	2,166	19	-	29,455	-	68,067
5014 Tires and tubes 2	-	18	-	477	27	-	32,218	-	15,374
5015 Motor vehicle parts, used	-	34	-	121	4	-	20,959	-	2,739
5021 Furniture 2	-	28	-	185	7	-	30,054	-	6,349
5023 Homefurnishings 2	-	44	-	720	16	-	23,544	-	19,722
5031 Lumber, plywood, and millwork 2	-	42	-	764	18	-	34,466	-	24,544
5032 Brick, stone, & related materials 2	-	16	-	173	11	-	31,792	-	5,042
5033 Roofing, siding, & insulation 2	-	13	-	92	7	-	30,522	-	2,750
5039 Construction materials, nec 2	-	31	-	385	12	-	32,925	-	13,041
5043 Photographic equipment & supplies 2	-	6	-	46	8	-	31,739	-	1,548
5044 Office equipment 2	-	47	-	829	18	-	33,698	-	29,066
5045 Computers, peripherals, & software 2	-	65	-	1,087	17	-	39,812	-	47,188
5046 Commercial equipment, nec 2	-	30	-	269	9	-	31,301	-	8,177
5047 Medical and hospital equipment 2	-	62	-	914	15	-	41,698	-	42,094
5048 Ophthalmic goods 2	-	7	-	145	21	-	21,131	-	4,210
5049 Professional equipment, nec 2	-	7	-	51	7	-	22,196	-	1,214
5050 Metals and minerals, except petroleum 2	-	48	-	717	15	-	30,276	-	24,001
5063 Electrical apparatus and equipment 2	-	102	-	1,158	11	-	32,007	-	42,304
5064 Electrical appliances, TV & radios 2	-	18	-	219	12	-	40,146	-	9,455

Continued on next page.

MEMPHIS MSA (TN PART) - [continued]

Wholesale and Retail Trade USA	Establishments		Employment		Emp / Est	Pay / Employee		Annual Payroll ($ 000)	
	1994	1995	1994	1995	1995	1994	1995	1994	1995
5065 Electronic parts and equipment [2]	-	56	-	1,129	20	-	37,371	-	42,118
5072 Hardware [2]	-	49	-	1,143	23	-	34,849	-	35,621
5074 Plumbing & hydronic heating supplies [2]	-	36	-	309	9	-	32,181	-	10,164
5075 Warm air heating & air conditioning [2]	-	37	-	359	10	-	36,379	-	14,208
5078 Refrigeration equipment and supplies [2]	-	14	-	109	8	-	27,450	-	3,667
5082 Construction and mining machinery [2]	-	22	-	525	24	-	37,653	-	21,831
5083 Farm and garden machinery	-	33	-	406	12	-	32,079	-	13,554
5084 Industrial machinery and equipment [2]	-	139	-	1,921	14	-	32,179	-	69,444
5085 Industrial supplies [2]	-	92	-	1,031	11	-	36,539	-	39,957
5087 Service establishment equipment [2]	-	45	-	253	6	-	27,415	-	7,473
5088 Transportation equipment & supplies [2]	-	27	-	356	13	-	31,079	-	11,493
5091 Sporting & recreational goods [2]	-	21	-	175	8	-	23,474	-	4,534
5092 Toys and hobby goods and supplies [2]	-	6	-	95	16	-	20,547	-	1,842
5093 Scrap and waste materials [2]	-	30	-	391	13	-	22,977	-	9,922
5094 Jewelry & precious stones [2]	-	22	-	166	8	-	24,386	-	4,814
5099 Durable goods, nec [2]	-	31	-	158	5	-	27,038	-	4,748
5111 Printing and writing paper [2]	-	11	-	113	10	-	38,832	-	6,105
5112 Stationery and office supplies [2]	-	51	-	1,055	21	-	28,091	-	28,658
5113 Industrial & personal service paper [2]	-	30	-	519	17	-	35,175	-	20,925
5120 Drugs, proprietaries, and sundries [2]	-	45	-	1,701	38	-	35,344	-	60,362
5131 Piece goods & notions [2]	-	16	-	87	5	-	31,954	-	2,746
5136 Men's and boys' clothing [2]	-	12	-	118	10	-	20,407	-	2,534
5137 Women's and children's clothing [2]	-	18	-	253	14	-	17,091	-	4,435
5139 Footwear [2]	-	4	-	797	199	-	19,207	-	17,584
5141 Groceries, general line [2]	-	16	-	778	49	-	36,237	-	25,013
5142 Packaged frozen food [2]	-	20	-	545	27	-	25,761	-	15,136
5143 Dairy products, exc. dried or canned [2]	-	9	-	114	13	-	21,965	-	2,581
5144 Poultry and poultry products [2]	-	6	-	68	11	-	31,529	-	2,451
5145 Confectionery [2]	-	13	-	278	21	-	26,331	-	6,509
5146 Fish and seafoods [2]	-	6	-	40	7	-	13,700	-	580
5147 Meats and meat products [2]	-	14	-	461	33	-	27,653	-	13,009
5148 Fresh fruits and vegetables [2]	-	13	-	313	24	-	22,888	-	9,443
5149 Groceries and related products, nec [2]	-	57	-	1,315	23	-	31,915	-	41,659
5159 Farm-product raw materials, nec	-	39	-	709	18	-	35,921	-	41,442
5162 Plastics materials & basic shapes [2]	-	19	-	153	8	-	30,170	-	4,546
5169 Chemicals & allied products, nec [2]	-	47	-	662	14	-	35,686	-	23,281
5171 Petroleum bulk stations & terminals	-	20	-	187	9	-	29,262	-	6,398
5172 Petroleum products, nec [2]	-	12	-	89	7	-	25,798	-	2,522
5181 Beer and ale [2]	-	3	-	377	126	-	28,074	-	12,850
5182 Wine and distilled beverages [2]	-	6	-	327	55	-	26,067	-	8,935
5191 Farm supplies	-	40	-	314	8	-	31,376	-	11,251
5192 Books, periodicals, & newspapers [2]	-	11	-	153	14	-	15,556	-	2,414
5193 Flowers & florists' supplies [2]	-	9	-	99	11	-	17,859	-	1,849
5194 Tobacco and tobacco products [2]	-	9	-	581	65	-	34,754	-	17,597
5198 Paints, varnishes, and supplies [2]	-	14	-	421	30	-	25,169	-	10,479
5199 Nondurable goods, nec	-	55	-	519	9	-	16,609	-	9,100
52- Retail trade	-	5,147	-	82,774	16	-	14,573	-	1,235,309
5210 Lumber and other building materials	-	62	-	1,224	20	-	18,853	-	24,820
5230 Paint, glass, and wallpaper stores [2]	-	35	-	173	5	-	22,035	-	3,999
5250 Hardware stores	-	32	-	674	21	-	13,003	-	8,725
5260 Retail nurseries and garden stores	-	26	-	262	10	-	14,214	-	3,553
5270 Mobile home dealers [2]	-	6	-	41	7	-	36,195	-	1,548
5310 Department stores [2]	-	39	-	6,910	177	-	12,919	-	88,474
5330 Variety stores	-	44	-	410	9	-	8,673	-	4,191
5390 Misc. general merchandise stores	-	56	-	1,721	31	-	13,048	-	22,150
5410 Grocery stores	-	451	-	9,752	22	-	10,982	-	110,585
5420 Meat and fish markets [2]	-	26	-	117	5	-	13,231	-	1,631
5430 Fruit and vegetable markets [2]	-	14	-	191	14	-	9,445	-	2,049
5440 Candy, nut, and confectionery stores [2]	-	11	-	77	7	-	10,597	-	876
5460 Retail bakeries [2]	-	35	-	327	9	-	9,969	-	3,073
5490 Miscellaneous food stores [2]	-	18	-	80	4	-	7,400	-	606
5510 New and used car dealers	-	65	-	4,419	68	-	35,192	-	175,673
5520 Used car dealers	-	96	-	286	3	-	16,587	-	5,616
5530 Auto and home supply stores	-	149	-	1,413	9	-	18,163	-	26,786
5540 Gasoline service stations	-	314	-	2,500	8	-	11,958	-	31,428
5550 Boat dealers [2]	-	6	-	53	9	-	29,585	-	1,786
5560 Recreational vehicle dealers [2]	-	6	-	70	12	-	23,657	-	2,086
5570 Motorcycle dealers [2]	-	9	-	71	8	-	22,592	-	1,992
5590 Automotive dealers, nec [2]	-	4	-	35	9	-	14,400	-	595
5610 Men's & boys' clothing stores	-	90	-	701	8	-	15,138	-	11,609
5620 Women's clothing stores	-	209	-	2,009	10	-	8,516	-	17,263

Continued on next page.

MEMPHIS MSA (TN PART) - [continued]

Wholesale and Retail Trade USA	Establishments		Employment		Emp / Est	Pay / Employee		Annual Payroll ($ 000)	
	1994	1995	1994	1995	1995	1994	1995	1994	1995
5630 Women's accessory & specialty stores [2]	-	36	-	177	5	-	12,768	-	2,262
5640 Children's and infants' wear stores [2]	-	18	-	194	11	-	8,144	-	1,656
5650 Family clothing stores [2]	-	60	-	1,017	17	-	9,648	-	10,111
5660 Shoe stores [2]	-	152	-	921	6	-	12,261	-	11,002
5690 Misc. apparel & accessory stores [2]	-	31	-	170	5	-	9,859	-	2,183
5712 Furniture stores	-	120	-	1,137	9	-	21,136	-	26,341
5713 Floor covering stores	-	45	-	371	8	-	21,531	-	8,174
5714 Drapery and upholstery stores [2]	-	13	-	50	4	-	14,480	-	761
5719 Misc. homefurnishings stores [2]	-	74	-	714	10	-	11,938	-	8,697
5720 Household appliance stores [2]	-	22	-	105	5	-	21,600	-	2,089
5731 Radio, TV, & electronic stores [2]	-	60	-	619	10	-	21,325	-	11,704
5734 Computer and software stores [2]	-	36	-	180	5	-	22,311	-	4,295
5735 Record & prerecorded tape stores [2]	-	42	-	344	8	-	10,186	-	3,183
5736 Musical instrument stores [2]	-	12	-	98	8	-	18,776	-	2,279
5812 Eating places	-	1,023	-	25,286	25	-	8,375	-	220,175
5813 Drinking places [2]	-	54	-	611	11	-	7,974	-	4,615
5910 Drug stores and proprietary stores	-	143	-	2,338	16	-	17,341	-	42,731
5920 Liquor stores [2]	-	132	-	449	3	-	12,321	-	5,782
5930 Used merchandise stores	-	104	-	526	5	-	13,323	-	7,163
5941 Sporting goods and bicycle shops [2]	-	67	-	432	6	-	10,602	-	5,376
5942 Book stores [2]	-	49	-	435	9	-	11,384	-	5,597
5943 Stationery stores [2]	-	7	-	32	5	-	11,500	-	325
5944 Jewelry stores	-	84	-	475	6	-	17,735	-	9,607
5945 Hobby, toy, and game shops [2]	-	34	-	339	10	-	9,274	-	3,885
5946 Camera & photographic supply stores [2]	-	9	-	53	6	-	20,151	-	1,058
5947 Gift, novelty, and souvenir shops [2]	-	99	-	465	5	-	8,516	-	4,556
5948 Luggage and leather goods stores [2]	-	5	-	39	8	-	6,974	-	265
5949 Sewing, needlework, and piece goods [2]	-	23	-	176	8	-	11,000	-	2,111
5961 Catalog and mail-order houses [2]	-	21	-	251	12	-	18,996	-	4,878
5962 Merchandising machine operators [2]	-	41	-	562	14	-	17,011	-	10,112
5963 Direct selling establishments [2]	-	43	-	548	13	-	14,883	-	8,438
5984 Liquefied petroleum gas dealers	-	11	-	86	8	-	19,814	-	1,797
5992 Florists	-	89	-	457	5	-	10,985	-	5,332
5993 Tobacco stores and stands [2]	-	12	-	46	4	-	17,391	-	959
5995 Optical goods stores [2]	-	48	-	263	5	-	15,103	-	4,392
5999 Miscellaneous retail stores, nec [2]	-	164	-	805	5	-	14,211	-	12,604

Source: County Business Patterns 1994/95, CBP-94/95, U.S. Department of Commerce, Washington DC, November 1997. The employment column represents mid-March employment in the year. Pay per employee is calculated by dividing 1st Quarter payroll, annualized, by mid-March employment. The column headed 'Emp / Est' shows 'employees per establishment'. A dash (-) means that data are unavailable or cannot be calculated. nec means not elsewhere classified. *Notes:* 1. 1994 data incomplete; unavailable or withheld. 2. 1995 data incomplete; unavailable or withheld. 3. 1994 and 1995 data incomplete; unavailable or withheld.

MEMPHIS, TN-AR-MS MSA

Wholesale and Retail Trade USA	Establishments		Employment		Emp / Est	Pay / Employee		Annual Payroll ($ 000)	
	1994	1995	1994	1995	1995	1994	1995	1994	1995
50- Wholesale trade [1]	166	2,338	2,454	40,674	17	28,036	31,041	73,047	1,332,771
5012 Automobiles and other vehicles [2]	-	53	-	1,196	23	-	31,388	-	42,503
5013 Motor vehicle supplies and new parts [3]	12	126	54	2,210	18	18,593	29,289	1,212	69,042
5014 Tires and tubes [2]	-	20	-	477	24	-	32,218	-	15,374
5015 Motor vehicle parts, used	-	37	-	121	3	-	20,959	-	2,739
5021 Furniture [2]	-	30	-	185	6	-	30,054	-	6,349
5023 Homefurnishings [2]	-	48	-	720	15	-	23,544	-	19,722
5031 Lumber, plywood, and millwork [2]	-	43	-	764	18	-	34,466	-	24,544
5032 Brick, stone, & related materials [2]	-	17	-	173	10	-	31,792	-	5,042
5033 Roofing, siding, & insulation [2]	-	14	-	92	7	-	30,522	-	2,750
5039 Construction materials, nec [2]	-	34	-	385	11	-	32,925	-	13,041
5043 Photographic equipment & supplies [2]	-	6	-	46	8	-	31,739	-	1,548
5044 Office equipment [2]	-	50	-	829	17	-	33,698	-	29,066
5045 Computers, peripherals, & software [2]	-	67	-	1,087	16	-	39,812	-	47,188
5046 Commercial equipment, nec [2]	-	31	-	269	9	-	31,301	-	8,177
5047 Medical and hospital equipment [2]	-	64	-	914	14	-	41,698	-	42,094
5048 Ophthalmic goods [2]	-	7	-	145	21	-	21,131	-	4,210
5049 Professional equipment, nec [2]	-	7	-	51	7	-	22,196	-	1,214
5051 Metals service centers and offices [3]	4	50	101	122	2	29,465	25,770	3,077	3,405
5063 Electrical apparatus and equipment [3]	4	105	16	1,158	11	18,750	32,007	412	42,304
5064 Electrical appliances, TV & radios [2]	-	19	-	219	12	-	40,146	-	9,455
5065 Electronic parts and equipment [3]	6	63	20	1,151	18	24,800	37,129	555	42,690
5072 Hardware [2]	-	49	-	1,143	23	-	34,849	-	35,621
5074 Plumbing & hydronic heating supplies [2]	-	38	-	309	8	-	32,181	-	10,164

Continued on next page.

MEMPHIS, TN–AR–MS MSA - [continued]

Wholesale and Retail Trade USA	Establishments		Employment		Emp / Est	Pay / Employee		Annual Payroll ($ 000)	
	1994	1995	1994	1995	1995	1994	1995	1994	1995
5075 Warm air heating & air conditioning[2]	-	40	-	359	9	-	36,379	-	14,208
5078 Refrigeration equipment and supplies[2]	-	14	-	109	8	-	27,450	-	3,667
5082 Construction and mining machinery[2]	-	24	-	525	22	-	37,653	-	21,831
5083 Farm and garden machinery[1]	15	48	118	534	11	24,780	30,419	3,531	17,188
5084 Industrial machinery and equipment[3]	7	147	31	1,951	13	20,903	31,992	776	70,255
5085 Industrial supplies[2]	-	94	-	1,031	11	-	36,539	-	39,957
5087 Service establishment equipment[2]	-	48	-	253	5	-	27,415	-	7,473
5088 Transportation equipment & supplies[2]	-	27	-	356	13	-	31,079	-	11,493
5091 Sporting & recreational goods[2]	-	21	-	175	8	-	23,474	-	4,534
5092 Toys and hobby goods and supplies[2]	-	6	-	95	16	-	20,547	-	1,842
5093 Scrap and waste materials[2]	-	34	-	391	12	-	22,977	-	9,922
5094 Jewelry & precious stones[2]	-	22	-	166	8	-	24,386	-	4,814
5099 Durable goods, nec[2]	-	32	-	158	5	-	27,038	-	4,748
5111 Printing and writing paper[2]	-	11	-	113	10	-	38,832	-	6,105
5112 Stationery and office supplies[3]	5	57	47	1,105	19	19,489	27,779	1,039	29,837
5113 Industrial & personal service paper[2]	-	31	-	519	17	-	35,175	-	20,925
5120 Drugs, proprietaries, and sundries[2]	-	46	-	1,701	37	-	35,344	-	60,362
5131 Piece goods & notions[2]	-	16	-	87	5	-	31,954	-	2,746
5136 Men's and boys' clothing[2]	-	14	-	118	8	-	20,407	-	2,534
5137 Women's and children's clothing[2]	-	18	-	253	14	-	17,091	-	4,435
5139 Footwear[2]	-	4	-	797	199	-	19,207	-	17,584
5141 Groceries, general line[2]	-	17	-	778	46	-	36,237	-	25,013
5142 Packaged frozen food[2]	-	21	-	545	26	-	25,761	-	15,136
5143 Dairy products, exc. dried or canned[2]	-	11	-	114	10	-	21,965	-	2,581
5144 Poultry and poultry products[2]	-	6	-	68	11	-	31,529	-	2,451
5145 Confectionery[2]	-	14	-	278	20	-	26,331	-	6,509
5146 Fish and seafoods[2]	-	6	-	40	7	-	13,700	-	580
5147 Meats and meat products[2]	-	14	-	461	33	-	27,653	-	13,009
5148 Fresh fruits and vegetables[2]	-	13	-	313	24	-	22,888	-	9,443
5149 Groceries and related products, nec[2]	-	59	-	1,315	22	-	31,915	-	41,659
5159 Farm-product raw materials, nec[2]	-	41	-	709	17	-	35,921	-	41,442
5162 Plastics materials & basic shapes[2]	-	19	-	153	8	-	30,170	-	4,546
5169 Chemicals & allied products, nec[3]	5	51	28	686	13	28,857	35,277	763	23,879
5171 Petroleum bulk stations & terminals[1]	5	24	18	200	8	18,444	28,820	327	6,678
5172 Petroleum products, nec[3]	5	17	120	190	11	19,833	23,958	2,407	5,066
5181 Beer and ale[3]	6	9	137	530	59	24,263	27,283	3,757	16,924
5182 Wine and distilled beverages[2]	-	6	-	327	55	-	26,067	-	8,935
5191 Farm supplies[1]	11	52	50	314	6	18,320	31,376	1,226	11,251
5192 Books, periodicals, & newspapers[2]	-	12	-	153	13	-	15,556	-	2,414
5193 Flowers & florists' supplies[2]	-	10	-	99	10	-	17,859	-	1,849
5194 Tobacco and tobacco products[2]	-	9	-	581	65	-	34,754	-	17,597
5198 Paints, varnishes, and supplies[2]	-	14	-	421	30	-	25,169	-	10,479
5199 Nondurable goods, nec[1]	7	61	7	519	9	12,000	16,609	561	9,100
52– Retail trade[1]	583	5,742	8,623	92,405	16	11,627	14,345	109,424	1,362,519
5210 Lumber and other building materials[1]	9	72	39	1,339	19	17,744	18,742	794	26,967
5230 Paint, glass, and wallpaper stores[3]	6	43	11	173	4	13,091	22,035	244	3,999
5250 Hardware stores	-	34	-	674	20	-	13,003	-	8,725
5260 Retail nurseries and garden stores	-	30	-	287	10	-	13,909	-	3,909
5270 Mobile home dealers[2]	-	8	-	41	5	-	36,195	-	1,548
5310 Department stores[2]	-	42	-	6,910	165	-	12,919	-	88,474
5330 Variety stores	-	50	-	410	8	-	8,673	-	4,191
5390 Misc. general merchandise stores	-	68	-	1,721	25	-	13,048	-	22,150
5410 Grocery stores[1]	86	535	1,641	11,414	21	9,655	10,914	17,382	131,986
5420 Meat and fish markets[2]	-	28	-	117	4	-	13,231	-	1,631
5430 Fruit and vegetable markets[2]	-	15	-	191	13	-	9,445	-	2,049
5440 Candy, nut, and confectionery stores[2]	-	12	-	77	6	-	10,597	-	876
5460 Retail bakeries[2]	-	38	-	327	9	-	9,969	-	3,073
5490 Miscellaneous food stores[2]	-	18	-	80	4	-	7,400	-	606
5510 New and used car dealers[1]	10	73	245	4,733	65	25,747	34,641	7,532	185,662
5520 Used car dealers[1]	21	115	40	316	3	12,600	16,696	649	6,174
5530 Auto and home supply stores[1]	30	181	196	1,638	9	14,816	18,010	3,307	30,768
5540 Gasoline service stations[1]	59	372	890	3,382	9	9,452	11,327	9,490	40,440
5550 Boat dealers[2]	-	7	-	53	8	-	29,585	-	1,786
5560 Recreational vehicle dealers[2]	-	9	-	91	10	-	22,725	-	2,723
5570 Motorcycle dealers[2]	-	11	-	71	6	-	22,592	-	1,992
5590 Automotive dealers, nec[2]	-	4	-	35	9	-	14,400	-	595
5610 Men's & boys' clothing stores[2]	-	92	-	701	8	-	15,138	-	11,609
5620 Women's clothing stores[1]	20	228	132	2,115	9	8,727	8,558	1,278	18,270
5630 Women's accessory & specialty stores[2]	-	36	-	177	5	-	12,768	-	2,262
5640 Children's and infants' wear stores[2]	-	20	-	194	10	-	8,144	-	1,656
5650 Family clothing stores[3]	6	64	5	1,017	16	7,200	9,648	38	10,111

Continued on next page.

MEMPHIS, TN - AR - MS MSA - [continued]

Wholesale and Retail Trade USA	Establishments		Employment		Emp / Est	Pay / Employee		Annual Payroll ($ 000)	
	1994	1995	1994	1995	1995	1994	1995	1994	1995
5660 Shoe stores[3]	7	160	11	950	6	11,273	12,219	135	11,375
5690 Misc. apparel & accessory stores[2]	-	33	-	170	5	-	9,859	-	2,183
5712 Furniture stores[1]	10	132	71	1,153	9	14,817	21,010	1,115	26,623
5713 Floor covering stores[1]	4	49	14	375	8	3,143	21,429	51	8,235
5714 Drapery and upholstery stores[2]	-	15	-	50	3	-	14,480	-	761
5719 Misc. homefurnishings stores[2]	-	76	-	714	9	-	11,938	-	8,697
5720 Household appliance stores[2]	-	23	-	105	5	-	21,600	-	2,089
5731 Radio, TV, & electronic stores[2]	-	65	-	619	10	-	21,325	-	11,704
5734 Computer and software stores[2]	-	37	-	180	5	-	22,311	-	4,295
5735 Record & prerecorded tape stores[2]	-	43	-	344	8	-	10,186	-	3,183
5736 Musical instrument stores[2]	-	12	-	98	8	-	18,776	-	2,279
5812 Eating places[1]	113	1,130	2,435	27,936	25	6,640	8,190	17,200	238,416
5813 Drinking places[3]	9	62	33	648	10	6,061	7,969	271	4,939
5910 Drug stores and proprietary stores[1]	22	165	231	2,599	16	16,935	17,354	4,276	47,523
5920 Liquor stores[3]	15	145	38	467	3	9,579	12,608	445	6,153
5930 Used merchandise stores[1]	9	113	13	538	5	13,846	13,331	179	7,335
5941 Sporting goods and bicycle shops[3]	9	74	61	478	6	8,852	10,971	761	6,162
5942 Book stores[2]	-	53	-	438	8	-	11,361	-	5,629
5943 Stationery stores[2]	-	9	-	32	4	-	11,500	-	325
5944 Jewelry stores	-	88	-	486	6	-	17,449	-	9,646
5945 Hobby, toy, and game shops[2]	-	37	-	341	9	-	9,279	-	3,910
5946 Camera & photographic supply stores[2]	-	9	-	53	6	-	20,151	-	1,058
5947 Gift, novelty, and souvenir shops[3]	12	110	9	490	4	7,111	8,384	92	4,677
5948 Luggage and leather goods stores[2]	-	5	-	39	8	-	6,974	-	265
5949 Sewing, needlework, and piece goods[2]	-	24	-	176	7	-	11,000	-	2,111
5961 Catalog and mail-order houses[2]	-	21	-	251	12	-	18,996	-	4,878
5962 Merchandising machine operators[2]	-	42	-	562	13	-	17,011	-	10,112
5963 Direct selling establishments[2]	-	45	-	548	12	-	14,883	-	8,438
5984 Liquefied petroleum gas dealers	-	16	-	86	5	-	19,814	-	1,797
5992 Florists[1]	11	103	26	484	5	8,769	10,942	251	5,568
5993 Tobacco stores and stands[2]	-	14	-	46	3	-	17,391	-	959
5995 Optical goods stores[2]	-	49	-	263	5	-	15,103	-	4,392
5999 Miscellaneous retail stores, nec[3]	14	178	26	830	5	11,077	14,159	357	12,957

Source: County Business Patterns 1994/95, CBP-94/95, U.S. Department of Commerce, Washington DC, November 1997. The employment column represents mid-March employment in the year. Pay per employee is calculated by dividing 1st Quarter payroll, annualized, by mid-March employment. The column headed 'Emp / Est' shows 'employees per establishment'. A dash (-) means that data are unavailable or cannot be calculated. nec means not elsewhere classified. *Notes:* 1. 1994 data incomplete; unavailable or withheld. 2. 1995 data incomplete; unavailable or withheld. 3. 1994 and 1995 data incomplete; unavailable or withheld.

MERCED, CA MSA

Wholesale and Retail Trade USA	Establishments		Employment		Emp / Est	Pay / Employee		Annual Payroll ($ 000)	
	1994	1995	1994	1995	1995	1994	1995	1994	1995
50- Wholesale trade	161	162	1,893	1,929	12	23,201	24,201	51,457	53,032
5013 Motor vehicle supplies and new parts	13	11	61	69	6	16,525	16,406	1,096	1,142
5015 Motor vehicle parts, used	-	4	-	31	8	-	13,032	-	459
5030 Lumber and construction materials	-	5	-	22	4	-	37,455	-	958
5040 Professional & commercial equipment	6	5	33	35	7	19,879	19,086	728	727
5060 Electrical goods	7	7	51	57	8	25,255	28,070	1,344	1,362
5074 Plumbing & hydronic heating supplies	-	4	-	24	6	-	25,667	-	681
5083 Farm and garden machinery	13	13	171	198	15	24,444	23,939	5,229	5,893
5085 Industrial supplies	-	6	-	29	5	-	34,621	-	1,129
5087 Service establishment equipment	4	4	12	12	3	13,000	13,000	144	137
5112 Stationery and office supplies	5	4	67	69	17	15,582	17,333	1,161	1,171
5147 Meats and meat products	3	-	94	-	-	25,277	-	2,383	-
5148 Fresh fruits and vegetables	6	6	124	85	14	14,806	16,894	5,250	3,706
5149 Groceries and related products, nec	12	11	51	52	5	25,882	30,615	1,671	1,860
5154 Livestock	3	-	79	-	-	6,076	-	461	-
5170 Petroleum and petroleum products	10	10	73	75	8	22,356	23,893	2,108	2,266
5191 Farm supplies	18	16	214	179	11	25,252	31,240	6,565	6,573
52- Retail trade	779	767	8,709	8,647	11	12,056	12,425	113,043	113,390
5210 Lumber and other building materials	8	8	140	120	15	20,257	19,533	2,932	2,669
5250 Hardware stores	9	8	77	129	16	11,948	12,992	1,742	1,752
5260 Retail nurseries and garden stores	6	5	40	43	9	9,300	11,256	429	508
5310 Department stores	10	10	1,093	1,256	126	9,559	10,863	12,243	14,265
5410 Grocery stores	100	97	1,118	1,086	11	17,882	18,350	20,770	20,190
5420 Meat and fish markets	5	3	4	5	2	11,000	9,600	53	46
5460 Retail bakeries	13	13	43	45	3	6,419	6,933	313	322
5490 Miscellaneous food stores	6	7	18	11	2	6,444	9,091	118	128
5510 New and used car dealers	16	15	603	548	37	21,167	22,080	13,492	13,369

Continued on next page.

MERCED, CA MSA - [continued]

Wholesale and Retail Trade USA	Establishments		Employment		Emp / Est	Pay / Employee		Annual Payroll ($ 000)	
	1994	1995	1994	1995	1995	1994	1995	1994	1995
5520 Used car dealers	-	7	-	24	3	-	18,500	-	542
5530 Auto and home supply stores	30	28	246	259	9	13,512	14,502	3,763	4,046
5540 Gasoline service stations	61	60	475	460	8	13,128	13,122	6,711	6,426
5570 Motorcycle dealers	4	-	16	-	-	18,250	-	373	-
5610 Men's & boys' clothing stores	5	4	16	15	4	9,750	9,333	133	78
5620 Women's clothing stores	20	16	175	104	7	7,611	7,885	1,427	777
5650 Family clothing stores	8	6	101	107	18	8,594	7,626	895	875
5660 Shoe stores	13	12	59	49	4	9,424	12,571	552	558
5712 Furniture stores	13	11	83	68	6	15,084	13,647	1,419	1,431
5719 Misc. homefurnishings stores	-	5	-	8	2	-	13,000	-	72
5720 Household appliance stores	5	4	41	39	10	16,000	14,359	654	619
5731 Radio, TV, & electronic stores	10	10	112	108	11	13,679	15,037	1,661	2,083
5734 Computer and software stores	3	-	7	-	-	8,571	-	93	-
5735 Record & prerecorded tape stores	-	5	-	29	6	-	9,793	-	250
5812 Eating places	201	190	2,804	2,698	14	7,334	7,327	21,620	20,776
5813 Drinking places	27	29	103	103	4	6,524	6,990	702	758
5910 Drug stores and proprietary stores	19	17	323	314	18	20,161	20,357	6,838	6,348
5920 Liquor stores	16	12	53	51	4	8,755	7,451	476	409
5930 Used merchandise stores	9	10	56	64	6	7,929	8,438	496	579
5941 Sporting goods and bicycle shops	10	12	54	54	5	8,444	8,444	489	529
5944 Jewelry stores	16	15	51	65	4	15,451	16,738	937	1,041
5945 Hobby, toy, and game shops	9	9	41	46	5	12,195	11,478	557	713
5947 Gift, novelty, and souvenir shops	4	-	3	-	-	5,333	-	99	-
5949 Sewing, needlework, and piece goods	3	3	39	33	11	7,179	7,636	283	253
5963 Direct selling establishments	-	9	-	19	2	-	14,737	-	292
5984 Liquefied petroleum gas dealers	4	-	41	-	-	27,805	-	890	-
5992 Florists	12	11	53	48	4	9,283	8,250	487	380
5999 Miscellaneous retail stores, nec	23	23	84	78	3	10,619	11,077	1,000	973

Source: County Business Patterns 1994/95, CBP-94/95, U.S. Department of Commerce, Washington DC, November 1997. The employment column represents mid-March employment in the year. Pay per employee is calculated by dividing 1st Quarter payroll, annualized, by mid-March employment. The column headed 'Emp / Est' shows 'employees per establishment'. A dash (-) means that data are unavailable or cannot be calculated. nec means not elsewhere classified. *Notes:* 1. 1994 data incomplete; unavailable or withheld. 2. 1995 data incomplete; unavailable or withheld. 3. 1994 and 1995 data incomplete; unavailable or withheld.

MIAMI, FL PMSA

Wholesale and Retail Trade USA	Establishments		Employment		Emp / Est	Pay / Employee		Annual Payroll ($ 000)	
	1994	1995	1994	1995	1995	1994	1995	1994	1995
50 - Wholesale trade	8,804	8,992	70,888	72,888	8	26,899	28,622	2,067,558	2,205,840
5012 Automobiles and other vehicles	133	131	910	1,113	8	27,767	31,335	31,058	36,901
5013 Motor vehicle supplies and new parts	367	330	2,924	3,045	9	22,674	23,627	73,560	77,267
5014 Tires and tubes	51	48	487	435	9	25,191	30,722	12,598	13,614
5015 Motor vehicle parts, used	86	105	398	459	4	16,271	17,786	7,051	8,902
5021 Furniture	129	118	790	702	6	23,119	27,487	18,915	19,685
5023 Homefurnishings	195	181	1,617	1,532	8	24,643	28,245	41,507	42,512
5031 Lumber, plywood, and millwork	78	73	687	623	9	25,467	23,576	18,239	16,396
5032 Brick, stone, & related materials	98	94	703	640	7	23,420	23,600	17,574	17,050
5033 Roofing, siding, & insulation	23	26	255	308	12	26,165	27,195	7,536	9,594
5039 Construction materials, nec	55	77	412	497	6	19,097	22,809	9,126	11,369
5043 Photographic equipment & supplies	30	29	289	336	12	27,875	30,119	8,765	10,384
5044 Office equipment	82	84	1,060	1,619	19	34,630	35,143	35,917	59,125
5045 Computers, peripherals, & software	383	356	2,460	2,699	8	31,907	35,075	84,816	99,726
5046 Commercial equipment, nec	88	89	609	605	7	26,187	29,078	17,957	20,057
5047 Medical and hospital equipment	291	267	1,543	1,403	5	34,012	41,460	53,622	56,445
5048 Ophthalmic goods	62	61	651	713	12	29,806	37,980	18,851	22,008
5049 Professional equipment, nec	29	35	168	221	6	36,262	35,475	6,680	9,569
5051 Metals service centers and offices	-	89	-	658	7	-	28,790	-	22,969
5063 Electrical apparatus and equipment	229	206	1,765	1,760	9	27,597	31,495	56,596	57,460
5064 Electrical appliances, TV & radios	192	188	1,802	1,859	10	31,845	33,878	58,723	64,221
5065 Electronic parts and equipment	376	383	2,632	2,776	7	29,460	30,427	83,428	89,830
5072 Hardware	96	100	1,044	908	9	27,031	31,088	29,404	27,465
5074 Plumbing & hydronic heating supplies	85	77	735	613	8	25,083	27,015	20,882	20,038
5075 Warm air heating & air conditioning	58	58	687	725	13	33,438	33,964	25,492	25,986
5078 Refrigeration equipment and supplies	23	20	151	161	8	24,291	26,062	4,171	4,547
5082 Construction and mining machinery	85	81	1,168	1,154	14	29,065	33,092	38,046	39,913
5083 Farm and garden machinery	67	65	411	371	6	24,438	27,957	11,646	10,843
5084 Industrial machinery and equipment	431	429	2,273	2,363	6	27,312	28,477	65,800	73,514
5085 Industrial supplies	161	158	974	970	6	29,433	31,761	28,090	29,887
5087 Service establishment equipment	76	73	625	656	9	25,510	27,360	18,418	18,171
5088 Transportation equipment & supplies	260	258	2,313	2,155	8	28,422	29,568	72,268	70,677

Continued on next page.

MIAMI, FL PMSA - [continued]

Wholesale and Retail Trade USA	Establishments		Employment		Emp / Est	Pay / Employee		Annual Payroll ($ 000)	
	1994	1995	1994	1995	1995	1994	1995	1994	1995
5091 Sporting & recreational goods	83	72	777	797	11	24,978	27,859	22,023	22,120
5092 Toys and hobby goods and supplies	62	53	516	466	9	24,434	26,558	15,364	12,369
5093 Scrap and waste materials	88	84	766	842	10	20,157	21,967	18,462	21,623
5094 Jewelry & precious stones	266	267	1,159	1,124	4	23,538	24,413	30,531	29,641
5099 Durable goods, nec	441	460	2,312	2,715	6	22,756	25,778	61,178	76,672
5111 Printing and writing paper	25	24	424	373	16	30,123	44,064	14,847	18,420
5112 Stationery and office supplies	126	110	1,659	1,491	14	20,528	19,302	37,776	29,719
5113 Industrial & personal service paper	94	92	1,183	1,174	13	26,597	28,893	34,186	37,700
5120 Drugs, proprietaries, and sundries	215	207	2,465	2,191	11	23,366	26,649	63,215	61,959
5131 Piece goods & notions	140	141	841	842	6	22,673	22,969	21,117	20,961
5136 Men's and boys' clothing	97	96	832	933	10	22,216	25,072	28,128	29,151
5137 Women's and children's clothing	231	217	1,786	1,711	8	18,571	18,656	34,665	32,209
5139 Footwear	99	92	602	576	6	27,980	29,174	19,398	17,662
5141 Groceries, general line	88	92	2,303	2,192	24	29,495	30,732	69,177	68,444
5142 Packaged frozen food	63	58	918	893	15	26,331	27,100	25,499	24,731
5143 Dairy products, exc. dried or canned	34	28	495	317	11	22,432	25,754	9,780	8,702
5144 Poultry and poultry products	11	13	407	411	32	20,570	21,139	8,968	8,968
5145 Confectionery	30	27	242	272	10	22,843	25,147	5,941	6,550
5146 Fish and seafoods	109	102	633	664	7	22,774	25,506	18,994	17,891
5147 Meats and meat products	65	57	899	837	15	25,210	26,557	23,922	21,761
5148 Fresh fruits and vegetables	150	137	2,138	2,486	18	22,056	21,475	47,082	52,493
5149 Groceries and related products, nec	198	177	2,421	2,205	12	27,346	25,872	66,182	58,202
5153 Grain and field beans	11	10	56	42	4	35,571	29,238	3,510	1,233
5154 Livestock	-	4	-	18	5	-	10,444	-	176
5159 Farm-product raw materials, nec	17	17	77	101	6	24,519	42,376	2,136	4,809
5162 Plastics materials & basic shapes	37	40	322	332	8	24,075	25,036	8,744	9,901
5169 Chemicals & allied products, nec	130	129	845	818	6	27,328	30,494	30,382	30,339
5171 Petroleum bulk stations & terminals	31	24	497	396	17	35,581	39,162	16,723	13,840
5172 Petroleum products, nec	26	21	106	130	6	30,113	34,677	3,669	4,126
5181 Beer and ale	7	7	794	699	100	26,982	34,587	22,930	25,090
5182 Wine and distilled beverages	29	28	991	1,062	38	58,026	58,192	61,233	61,912
5191 Farm supplies	87	64	466	356	6	26,258	32,539	13,347	11,396
5192 Books, periodicals, & newspapers	48	49	599	642	13	21,509	21,826	13,193	14,349
5193 Flowers & florists' supplies	188	178	2,597	2,979	17	23,714	26,425	65,973	78,635
5194 Tobacco and tobacco products	26	27	268	270	10	23,104	23,496	7,130	7,503
5198 Paints, varnishes, and supplies	52	44	259	239	5	21,483	20,502	5,748	5,273
5199 Nondurable goods, nec	462	475	2,137	2,286	5	19,251	18,429	47,039	49,420
52- Retail trade	13,598	13,394	165,147	164,135	12	14,410	15,448	2,479,895	2,582,884
5210 Lumber and other building materials	143	120	3,452	3,321	28	17,071	19,145	63,660	63,701
5230 Paint, glass, and wallpaper stores	81	84	390	351	4	20,923	20,000	8,316	6,832
5250 Hardware stores	122	78	794	507	7	16,332	16,686	13,021	8,787
5260 Retail nurseries and garden stores	55	61	196	235	4	17,408	15,489	3,405	3,629
5270 Mobile home dealers	5	-	17	-	-	13,176	-	189	-
5310 Department stores	45	45	10,985	11,208	249	15,082	16,277	175,806	186,186
5330 Variety stores	112	92	1,151	967	11	11,006	11,177	13,123	10,631
5390 Misc. general merchandise stores	112	111	3,233	3,074	28	15,973	19,390	53,197	56,402
5410 Grocery stores	1,018	986	22,340	22,357	23	12,068	12,554	272,917	280,261
5420 Meat and fish markets	86	81	543	364	4	10,453	13,736	5,761	4,981
5430 Fruit and vegetable markets	32	33	212	209	6	14,962	14,545	2,967	3,145
5440 Candy, nut, and confectionery stores	25	21	130	94	4	9,015	11,064	1,118	1,008
5450 Dairy products stores	9	9	16	27	3	7,250	5,630	239	168
5460 Retail bakeries	233	237	1,426	1,326	6	10,864	10,154	16,354	14,911
5490 Miscellaneous food stores	100	118	377	528	4	14,207	13,977	6,125	7,861
5510 New and used car dealers	109	108	7,972	8,365	77	28,827	30,662	252,583	269,385
5520 Used car dealers	192	178	757	657	4	16,206	18,088	13,150	12,341
5530 Auto and home supply stores	431	415	2,535	2,610	6	17,499	18,665	47,916	51,064
5540 Gasoline service stations	654	653	3,657	3,558	5	12,738	13,103	47,365	47,617
5550 Boat dealers	68	69	661	615	9	18,941	21,483	13,689	13,192
5560 Recreational vehicle dealers	5	5	68	44	9	21,176	28,000	1,245	1,110
5570 Motorcycle dealers	10	10	106	91	9	21,962	25,275	2,504	2,463
5590 Automotive dealers, nec	19	15	155	160	11	19,355	23,025	3,617	4,202
5610 Men's & boys' clothing stores	222	205	1,423	1,416	7	14,994	15,469	22,364	21,750
5620 Women's clothing stores	614	527	5,243	4,922	9	11,408	11,719	62,581	58,724
5630 Women's accessory & specialty stores	142	121	711	651	5	12,512	12,952	8,826	8,756
5640 Children's and infants' wear stores	97	87	779	762	9	10,557	10,808	8,831	8,330
5650 Family clothing stores	224	207	3,002	2,779	13	11,993	13,124	37,662	38,008
5660 Shoe stores	457	435	2,455	2,535	6	14,196	14,512	36,810	36,168
5690 Misc. apparel & accessory stores	143	141	626	694	5	12,843	13,556	8,435	9,474
5712 Furniture stores	377	370	2,343	2,226	6	19,855	19,540	46,730	43,425
5713 Floor covering stores	115	106	774	664	6	16,000	20,476	13,610	14,265
5714 Drapery and upholstery stores	28	27	105	90	3	17,524	17,022	1,512	1,279

Continued on next page.

MIAMI, FL PMSA - [continued]

Wholesale and Retail Trade USA	Establishments 1994	Establishments 1995	Employment 1994	Employment 1995	Emp / Est 1995	Pay / Employee 1994	Pay / Employee 1995	Annual Payroll ($ 000) 1994	Annual Payroll ($ 000) 1995
5719 Misc. homefurnishings stores	182	163	1,067	1,115	7	15,295	16,140	16,330	17,091
5720 Household appliance stores	50	51	210	238	5	17,524	17,513	4,242	4,456
5731 Radio, TV, & electronic stores	211	214	1,996	2,018	9	17,808	19,233	36,929	40,996
5734 Computer and software stores	78	83	584	650	8	17,973	20,775	12,349	14,811
5735 Record & prerecorded tape stores	105	105	816	953	9	8,127	7,866	7,083	7,777
5736 Musical instrument stores	30	31	181	173	6	19,227	22,197	4,024	4,221
5812 Eating places	2,545	2,300	48,492	46,182	20	10,120	10,726	481,062	484,986
5813 Drinking places	155	136	1,461	1,181	9	9,692	11,191	13,782	12,257
5910 Drug stores and proprietary stores	492	488	6,669	6,364	13	15,131	17,125	107,922	110,087
5920 Liquor stores	179	174	837	713	4	13,424	14,311	11,303	10,494
5930 Used merchandise stores	195	190	918	786	4	13,007	14,636	12,332	11,620
5941 Sporting goods and bicycle shops	177	169	1,240	1,148	7	13,648	16,115	18,160	18,697
5942 Book stores	101	93	637	654	7	10,154	12,349	6,711	7,794
5943 Stationery stores	40	41	241	241	6	12,282	12,929	2,906	2,804
5944 Jewelry stores	407	411	1,522	1,518	4	17,995	18,991	30,016	30,069
5945 Hobby, toy, and game shops	64	60	704	762	13	11,102	10,457	9,852	10,185
5946 Camera & photographic supply stores	35	30	182	155	5	20,989	24,077	4,023	3,764
5947 Gift, novelty, and souvenir shops	268	248	1,563	1,823	7	10,462	11,605	17,402	21,098
5948 Luggage and leather goods stores	41	42	221	223	5	14,769	17,417	3,212	3,522
5949 Sewing, needlework, and piece goods	88	83	553	519	6	10,503	11,368	6,097	6,118
5961 Catalog and mail-order houses	46	51	812	1,187	23	18,365	20,381	29,644	39,976
5962 Merchandising machine operators	59	54	238	281	5	19,328	20,313	5,409	5,750
5963 Direct selling establishments	133	132	960	892	7	14,267	16,215	14,957	15,291
5980 Fuel dealers	18	18	265	247	14	24,196	24,907	6,410	5,592
5992 Florists	213	198	936	990	5	13,521	12,861	12,411	11,956
5993 Tobacco stores and stands	14	16	71	59	4	16,676	21,085	1,310	1,884
5994 News dealers and newsstands	14	15	253	245	16	12,980	14,449	3,110	3,484
5995 Optical goods stores	197	201	1,199	1,228	6	16,490	17,586	20,349	21,025
5999 Miscellaneous retail stores, nec	584	614	2,493	2,907	5	15,931	16,176	44,462	51,773

Source: County Business Patterns 1994/95, CBP-94/95, U.S. Department of Commerce, Washington DC, November 1997. The employment column represents mid-March employment in the year. Pay per employee is calculated by dividing 1st Quarter payroll, annualized, by mid-March employment. The column headed 'Emp / Est' shows 'employees per establishment'. A dash (-) means that data are unavailable or cannot be calculated. nec means not elsewhere classified. *Notes:* 1. 1994 data incomplete; unavailable or withheld. 2. 1995 data incomplete; unavailable or withheld. 3. 1994 and 1995 data incomplete; unavailable or withheld.

MIDDLESEX - SOMERSET - HUNTERDON, NJ PMSA

Wholesale and Retail Trade USA	Establishments 1994	Establishments 1995	Employment 1994	Employment 1995	Emp / Est 1995	Pay / Employee 1994	Pay / Employee 1995	Annual Payroll ($ 000) 1994	Annual Payroll ($ 000) 1995
50- Wholesale trade	2,844	2,880	56,253	57,414	20	40,453	43,076	2,420,539	2,547,403
5012 Automobiles and other vehicles[3]	29	36	298	315	9	32,886	36,457	11,485	11,552
5013 Motor vehicle supplies and new parts	115	110	1,511	1,568	14	27,926	30,737	44,875	47,074
5014 Tires and tubes	22	23	307	343	15	34,007	41,353	10,935	15,141
5015 Motor vehicle parts, used	26	30	179	212	7	58,860	56,528	6,959	8,038
5021 Furniture	45	42	472	478	11	36,220	38,033	18,495	17,656
5023 Homefurnishings	51	45	934	1,221	27	33,422	29,749	43,908	46,829
5031 Lumber, plywood, and millwork	38	38	655	604	16	32,049	31,437	26,925	21,101
5032 Brick, stone, & related materials	28	26	191	238	9	36,733	38,992	7,978	9,789
5033 Roofing, siding, & insulation	14	12	238	197	16	35,328	40,000	10,197	8,289
5039 Construction materials, nec[1]	16	34	82	354	10	27,220	40,554	2,685	13,781
5043 Photographic equipment & supplies[3]	10	11	213	275	25	36,075	40,335	8,044	11,652
5044 Office equipment	43	45	1,331	1,408	31	35,853	37,455	50,660	58,524
5045 Computers, peripherals, & software	205	212	3,759	4,542	21	46,121	52,351	182,635	227,656
5046 Commercial equipment, nec	27	27	262	297	11	27,939	30,424	8,396	9,342
5047 Medical and hospital equipment	67	60	3,312	2,823	47	50,296	58,225	158,867	155,941
5048 Ophthalmic goods	6	8	27	33	4	23,111	24,000	618	840
5049 Professional equipment, nec[1]	22	22	326	338	15	38,196	32,911	13,060	11,791
5051 Metals service centers and offices[1]	75	70	717	837	12	35,286	40,798	28,840	38,974
5063 Electrical apparatus and equipment	115	98	1,168	1,139	12	38,568	38,388	49,042	45,875
5064 Electrical appliances, TV & radios	41	38	854	868	23	30,183	33,581	28,294	26,957
5065 Electronic parts and equipment	134	145	2,026	1,983	14	43,192	49,598	88,716	100,596
5072 Hardware	39	39	491	494	13	36,546	38,704	18,575	20,055
5074 Plumbing & hydronic heating supplies	47	41	544	534	13	32,963	36,936	19,425	20,222
5075 Warm air heating & air conditioning	23	24	133	128	5	42,286	42,656	5,815	5,201
5078 Refrigeration equipment and supplies[3]	5	4	12	9	2	29,000	31,556	320	309
5082 Construction and mining machinery	22	23	623	713	31	41,169	44,780	30,070	32,280
5083 Farm and garden machinery	16	17	188	173	10	25,021	27,121	5,873	5,409
5084 Industrial machinery and equipment	169	178	2,598	2,922	16	39,287	41,459	115,801	126,100
5085 Industrial supplies	100	104	862	839	8	37,847	41,254	33,643	36,323
5087 Service establishment equipment	40	37	303	302	8	33,663	34,358	10,369	10,709

Continued on next page.

MIDDLESEX - SOMERSET - HUNTERDON, NJ PMSA - [continued]

Wholesale and Retail Trade USA	Establishments		Employment		Emp / Est	Pay / Employee		Annual Payroll ($ 000)	
	1994	1995	1994	1995	1995	1994	1995	1994	1995
5088 Transportation equipment & supplies	14	15	114	126	8	48,526	49,873	5,181	5,794
5091 Sporting & recreational goods	31	29	296	174	6	26,135	32,529	8,853	5,548
5092 Toys and hobby goods and supplies [3]	24	22	1,212	1,246	57	20,558	23,480	32,027	33,017
5093 Scrap and waste materials	40	39	571	540	14	25,296	31,156	17,420	17,607
5094 Jewelry & precious stones	27	25	58	56	2	31,103	25,143	1,920	2,293
5099 Durable goods, nec [1]	51	47	368	431	9	23,413	31,926	11,683	16,301
5111 Printing and writing paper [3]	19	15	135	87	6	37,867	34,115	5,103	3,134
5112 Stationery and office supplies	74	69	1,332	1,173	17	27,691	29,920	40,159	36,349
5113 Industrial & personal service paper	31	31	626	630	20	37,642	36,330	24,627	24,383
5120 Drugs, proprietaries, and sundries	72	76	8,915	8,686	114	50,179	55,883	476,755	501,407
5131 Piece goods & notions	22	25	141	141	6	27,801	29,277	4,882	4,769
5136 Men's and boys' clothing [2]	34	31	651	633	20	39,576	50,964	40,989	53,593
5137 Women's and children's clothing [2]	49	46	1,962	1,655	36	45,635	50,497	84,535	75,245
5139 Footwear [1]	25	22	841	766	35	27,605	28,731	24,142	21,515
5141 Groceries, general line [3]	24	21	1,592	1,913	91	46,264	33,311	75,055	66,387
5142 Packaged frozen food [3]	16	15	311	333	22	29,389	30,006	10,432	10,624
5143 Dairy products, exc. dried or canned	15	15	459	252	17	31,007	31,603	16,286	9,166
5146 Fish and seafoods [2]	-	12	-	43	4	-	59,256	-	1,665
5147 Meats and meat products	22	20	208	118	6	36,808	35,288	8,535	5,028
5148 Fresh fruits and vegetables	13	13	61	77	6	27,672	32,260	2,301	2,565
5149 Groceries and related products, nec	99	101	1,607	2,046	20	35,510	32,526	59,962	70,562
5162 Plastics materials & basic shapes	41	41	201	228	6	42,388	44,526	10,704	11,860
5169 Chemicals & allied products, nec	99	100	987	1,334	13	42,460	41,034	46,494	57,256
5171 Petroleum bulk stations & terminals	21	16	559	354	22	50,240	42,215	20,344	14,845
5172 Petroleum products, nec [3]	15	14	156	174	12	55,513	52,943	9,749	10,517
5180 Beer, wine, and distilled beverages	15	13	425	346	27	43,078	52,428	14,658	14,688
5191 Farm supplies	34	27	302	286	11	24,185	26,867	8,549	8,145
5192 Books, periodicals, & newspapers [3]	26	22	704	581	26	34,563	38,788	25,299	21,828
5193 Flowers & florists' supplies	24	19	383	383	20	24,501	26,089	10,814	11,143
5194 Tobacco and tobacco products [3]	7	7	203	201	29	27,271	31,761	6,099	5,789
5198 Paints, varnishes, and supplies	18	16	114	107	7	26,702	28,972	3,561	3,403
5199 Nondurable goods, nec	83	87	608	825	9	35,711	28,499	24,532	26,930
52- Retail trade	6,480	6,602	85,659	90,705	14	16,260	17,354	1,530,360	1,624,823
5210 Lumber and other building materials	91	87	1,406	2,145	25	24,276	25,223	45,138	61,389
5230 Paint, glass, and wallpaper stores	32	23	149	134	6	19,114	18,000	3,261	3,037
5250 Hardware stores	43	38	237	193	5	19,224	17,223	5,244	3,550
5260 Retail nurseries and garden stores	59	61	256	282	5	15,125	15,277	5,506	5,863
5310 Department stores	32	33	6,873	8,215	249	13,044	12,312	100,543	103,307
5330 Variety stores	37	38	224	297	8	11,661	11,704	2,932	3,605
5390 Misc. general merchandise stores [2]	40	35	1,065	990	28	16,428	17,543	19,470	17,573
5410 Grocery stores	558	562	11,636	11,417	20	15,994	16,946	188,426	197,637
5420 Meat and fish markets	28	28	115	113	4	12,278	11,965	1,481	1,379
5430 Fruit and vegetable markets	-	16	-	20	1	-	14,200	-	458
5440 Candy, nut, and confectionery stores	17	13	85	63	5	9,224	9,714	685	494
5450 Dairy products stores	15	16	33	25	2	4,606	7,040	227	204
5460 Retail bakeries	136	130	1,010	962	7	11,014	10,437	12,376	10,452
5490 Miscellaneous food stores	43	47	178	202	4	12,000	13,564	2,635	2,925
5510 New and used car dealers	107	105	4,181	4,260	41	29,656	32,217	154,583	147,878
5520 Used car dealers	31	35	85	98	3	21,506	28,531	2,656	3,283
5530 Auto and home supply stores	111	111	703	799	7	22,651	23,149	17,359	19,144
5540 Gasoline service stations	451	454	2,736	2,731	6	13,770	14,877	40,279	41,224
5550 Boat dealers	6	7	14	16	2	9,429	11,250	195	202
5570 Motorcycle dealers	7	7	49	41	6	14,041	23,610	1,138	1,354
5590 Automotive dealers, nec [3]	4	5	9	14	3	26,667	24,571	303	352
5610 Men's & boys' clothing stores	85	76	792	755	10	12,308	11,682	10,041	9,726
5620 Women's clothing stores	234	221	2,652	2,454	11	8,952	9,208	25,774	22,614
5630 Women's accessory & specialty stores	48	44	362	361	8	14,895	14,526	5,295	5,067
5640 Children's and infants' wear stores	31	27	415	399	15	7,614	7,970	3,492	3,379
5650 Family clothing stores	81	78	2,407	2,232	29	11,096	12,168	29,090	30,440
5660 Shoe stores	174	165	1,074	1,080	7	11,292	11,533	13,198	12,492
5690 Misc. apparel & accessory stores	49	47	223	316	7	10,206	10,709	2,489	3,536
5712 Furniture stores	128	130	1,105	1,198	9	23,037	23,960	27,684	29,613
5713 Floor covering stores	58	63	279	309	5	22,781	23,871	7,297	8,196
5714 Drapery and upholstery stores	12	16	75	83	5	9,547	10,265	783	947
5719 Misc. homefurnishings stores	112	113	1,094	1,221	11	15,996	14,788	18,569	18,568
5720 Household appliance stores	32	34	309	347	10	20,142	18,040	6,877	7,254
5731 Radio, TV, & electronic stores	58	59	489	668	11	20,892	20,371	11,682	13,571
5734 Computer and software stores	42	48	318	277	6	17,296	20,144	5,305	5,863
5735 Record & prerecorded tape stores	41	41	249	250	6	9,526	10,768	2,644	2,977
5736 Musical instrument stores	18	17	126	111	7	19,778	17,910	2,736	2,183
5812 Eating places	1,504	1,480	19,789	20,697	14	9,403	10,389	208,731	225,495

Continued on next page.

MIDDLESEX-SOMERSET-HUNTERDON, NJ PMSA - [continued]

Wholesale and Retail Trade USA	Establishments		Employment		Emp / Est	Pay / Employee		Annual Payroll ($ 000)	
	1994	1995	1994	1995	1995	1994	1995	1994	1995
5813 Drinking places	212	203	1,073	961	5	8,723	10,035	9,665	9,111
5910 Drug stores and proprietary stores	182	184	2,528	2,567	14	14,002	14,753	38,381	39,688
5920 Liquor stores	187	182	934	904	5	12,946	13,540	13,067	13,200
5930 Used merchandise stores	35	37	134	115	3	14,119	13,426	2,142	1,853
5941 Sporting goods and bicycle shops	84	91	589	992	11	15,681	14,294	10,676	16,223
5942 Book stores	47	48	455	589	12	8,062	9,589	4,010	5,941
5943 Stationery stores	21	26	76	212	8	13,316	12,245	1,050	2,645
5944 Jewelry stores	130	129	652	677	5	15,166	15,846	10,936	11,426
5945 Hobby, toy, and game shops	56	51	692	648	13	9,682	11,148	7,936	8,268
5946 Camera & photographic supply stores	13	14	60	53	4	19,467	23,925	1,264	1,267
5947 Gift, novelty, and souvenir shops	146	133	828	775	6	8,488	9,156	8,498	7,741
5948 Luggage and leather goods stores	8	10	43	39	4	11,163	13,641	385	471
5949 Sewing, needlework, and piece goods	23	22	205	86	4	11,824	7,070	2,292	682
5961 Catalog and mail-order houses	33	31	735	854	28	18,547	19,897	16,740	16,691
5962 Merchandising machine operators	27	25	161	161	6	20,994	18,161	3,570	2,870
5963 Direct selling establishments	45	50	341	427	9	18,804	19,382	7,461	8,743
5980 Fuel dealers	51	51	447	476	9	32,752	32,924	14,992	15,632
5992 Florists	120	122	522	512	4	12,031	14,258	7,181	7,567
5993 Tobacco stores and stands[3]	6	7	8	9	1	13,500	13,333	112	115
5994 News dealers and newsstands	16	17	39	74	4	8,718	9,784	322	755
5995 Optical goods stores	65	63	327	324	5	17,113	18,198	5,965	6,050
5999 Miscellaneous retail stores, nec	188	190	1,131	1,202	6	13,015	14,902	16,474	19,265

Source: County Business Patterns 1994/95, CBP-94/95, U.S. Department of Commerce, Washington DC, November 1997. The employment column represents mid-March employment in the year. Pay per employee is calculated by dividing 1st Quarter payroll, annualized, by mid-March employment. The column headed 'Emp / Est' shows 'employees per establishment'. A dash (-) means that data are unavailable or cannot be calculated. nec means not elsewhere classified. *Notes:* 1. 1994 data incomplete; unavailable or withheld. 2. 1995 data incomplete; unavailable or withheld. 3. 1994 and 1995 data incomplete; unavailable or withheld.

MILWAUKEE-WAUKESHA, WI PMSA

Wholesale and Retail Trade USA	Establishments		Employment		Emp / Est	Pay / Employee		Annual Payroll ($ 000)	
	1994	1995	1994	1995	1995	1994	1995	1994	1995
50- Wholesale trade	-	3,432	-	47,605	14	-	33,526	-	1,659,284
5012 Automobiles and other vehicles	-	50	-	910	18	-	36,897	-	33,914
5013 Motor vehicle supplies and new parts	-	144	-	1,697	12	-	22,282	-	40,510
5014 Tires and tubes[2]	-	12	-	159	13	-	28,604	-	4,369
5015 Motor vehicle parts, used	-	40	-	247	6	-	19,158	-	4,882
5021 Furniture[2]	-	34	-	723	21	-	35,347	-	26,124
5023 Homefurnishings	-	47	-	404	9	-	28,604	-	12,862
5031 Lumber, plywood, and millwork	-	51	-	639	13	-	36,163	-	23,404
5032 Brick, stone, & related materials	-	30	-	226	8	-	31,186	-	9,057
5033 Roofing, siding, & insulation	-	23	-	264	11	-	33,258	-	9,678
5039 Construction materials, nec	-	52	-	429	8	-	31,767	-	15,383
5043 Photographic equipment & supplies[2]	-	10	-	95	10	-	24,253	-	2,475
5044 Office equipment	-	64	-	1,139	18	-	38,500	-	41,616
5045 Computers, peripherals, & software	-	139	-	1,950	14	-	54,101	-	96,383
5046 Commercial equipment, nec	-	41	-	403	10	-	30,005	-	13,083
5047 Medical and hospital equipment[2]	-	89	-	967	11	-	48,997	-	45,988
5048 Ophthalmic goods[2]	-	7	-	121	17	-	20,926	-	2,602
5049 Professional equipment, nec	-	24	-	94	4	-	37,149	-	4,590
5051 Metals service centers and offices[2]	-	107	-	319	3	-	49,956	-	15,105
5063 Electrical apparatus and equipment	-	163	-	1,944	12	-	38,208	-	75,164
5064 Electrical appliances, TV & radios	-	17	-	186	11	-	36,688	-	6,317
5065 Electronic parts and equipment	-	129	-	1,405	11	-	39,542	-	61,206
5072 Hardware	-	75	-	1,078	14	-	31,677	-	35,581
5074 Plumbing & hydronic heating supplies	-	66	-	660	10	-	33,309	-	23,886
5075 Warm air heating & air conditioning[2]	-	36	-	424	12	-	50,453	-	19,197
5078 Refrigeration equipment and supplies[2]	-	10	-	64	6	-	39,563	-	2,348
5082 Construction and mining machinery	-	36	-	846	24	-	44,600	-	38,340
5083 Farm and garden machinery[2]	-	21	-	212	10	-	31,491	-	6,866
5084 Industrial machinery and equipment	-	379	-	4,025	11	-	39,666	-	172,236
5085 Industrial supplies	-	177	-	2,105	12	-	35,776	-	79,487
5087 Service establishment equipment	-	61	-	499	8	-	27,271	-	13,430
5088 Transportation equipment & supplies[2]	-	10	-	168	17	-	24,762	-	6,524
5091 Sporting & recreational goods	-	41	-	464	11	-	26,293	-	14,451
5092 Toys and hobby goods and supplies[2]	-	14	-	299	21	-	26,809	-	8,050
5093 Scrap and waste materials	-	68	-	1,111	16	-	28,608	-	41,776
5094 Jewelry & precious stones[2]	-	28	-	106	4	-	25,472	-	2,911
5099 Durable goods, nec	-	56	-	372	7	-	31,860	-	10,550
5111 Printing and writing paper[2]	-	21	-	291	14	-	40,330	-	11,908

Continued on next page.

MILWAUKEE - WAUKESHA, WI PMSA - [continued]

Wholesale and Retail Trade USA	Establishments		Employment		Emp / Est	Pay / Employee		Annual Payroll ($ 000)	
	1994	1995	1994	1995	1995	1994	1995	1994	1995
5112 Stationery and office supplies	-	71	-	944	13	-	23,424	-	21,966
5113 Industrial & personal service paper [2]	-	49	-	195	4	-	31,056	-	6,438
5120 Drugs, proprietaries, and sundries [2]	-	33	-	536	16	-	27,433	-	16,766
5131 Piece goods & notions	-	17	-	114	7	-	22,667	-	2,946
5136 Men's and boys' clothing [2]	-	18	-	185	10	-	26,724	-	3,635
5137 Women's and children's clothing [2]	-	9	-	49	5	-	16,571	-	1,056
5139 Footwear [2]	-	12	-	102	9	-	53,529	-	6,653
5141 Groceries, general line [2]	-	21	-	569	27	-	23,796	-	14,490
5142 Packaged frozen food	-	32	-	1,679	52	-	25,489	-	45,213
5143 Dairy products, exc. dried or canned	-	20	-	220	11	-	27,382	-	6,150
5145 Confectionery [2]	-	23	-	357	16	-	29,535	-	9,896
5146 Fish and seafoods [2]	-	7	-	58	8	-	12,000	-	1,148
5147 Meats and meat products	-	27	-	459	17	-	19,712	-	9,356
5148 Fresh fruits and vegetables	-	27	-	670	25	-	18,424	-	14,059
5149 Groceries and related products, nec [2]	-	66	-	2,410	37	-	33,027	-	77,268
5153 Grain and field beans [2]	-	5	-	60	12	-	23,800	-	1,962
5154 Livestock [2]	-	9	-	38	4	-	19,368	-	834
5159 Farm-product raw materials, nec [2]	-	5	-	18	4	-	27,778	-	585
5162 Plastics materials & basic shapes	-	35	-	802	23	-	39,641	-	31,630
5169 Chemicals & allied products, nec [2]	-	101	-	996	10	-	31,454	-	33,636
5171 Petroleum bulk stations & terminals	-	35	-	415	12	-	35,123	-	14,893
5172 Petroleum products, nec	-	19	-	54	3	-	28,963	-	1,993
5181 Beer and ale [2]	-	13	-	394	30	-	25,949	-	10,446
5182 Wine and distilled beverages [2]	-	13	-	230	18	-	29,983	-	7,012
5191 Farm supplies	-	39	-	505	13	-	21,988	-	11,624
5192 Books, periodicals, & newspapers [2]	-	23	-	356	15	-	28,292	-	12,273
5193 Flowers & florists' supplies	-	23	-	285	12	-	20,716	-	6,570
5194 Tobacco and tobacco products [2]	-	9	-	13	1	-	17,846	-	229
5198 Paints, varnishes, and supplies	-	24	-	298	12	-	22,295	-	6,280
5199 Nondurable goods, nec	-	148	-	1,174	8	-	25,465	-	32,441
52- Retail trade	-	8,120	-	129,372	16	-	12,712	-	1,725,628
5210 Lumber and other building materials	-	104	-	2,292	22	-	20,843	-	49,465
5230 Paint, glass, and wallpaper stores	-	65	-	355	5	-	18,276	-	7,546
5250 Hardware stores	-	83	-	1,274	15	-	11,281	-	15,516
5260 Retail nurseries and garden stores	-	71	-	893	13	-	10,410	-	11,384
5270 Mobile home dealers [2]	-	6	-	25	4	-	12,800	-	331
5310 Department stores [2]	-	64	-	11,692	183	-	10,462	-	128,269
5330 Variety stores [2]	-	39	-	386	10	-	8,653	-	3,440
5390 Misc. general merchandise stores	-	27	-	1,122	42	-	13,159	-	15,017
5410 Grocery stores	-	483	-	15,327	32	-	11,981	-	191,363
5420 Meat and fish markets	-	38	-	261	7	-	11,724	-	3,281
5430 Fruit and vegetable markets [2]	-	10	-	146	15	-	11,315	-	1,811
5440 Candy, nut, and confectionery stores	-	51	-	259	5	-	7,089	-	1,804
5450 Dairy products stores [2]	-	9	-	28	3	-	4,571	-	200
5460 Retail bakeries	-	103	-	937	9	-	9,392	-	9,146
5490 Miscellaneous food stores	-	43	-	282	7	-	8,397	-	2,748
5510 New and used car dealers	-	118	-	6,791	58	-	27,562	-	202,424
5520 Used car dealers	-	94	-	411	4	-	17,586	-	8,356
5530 Auto and home supply stores	-	131	-	1,288	10	-	16,161	-	22,576
5540 Gasoline service stations	-	502	-	4,355	9	-	10,464	-	48,356
5550 Boat dealers	-	23	-	175	8	-	20,800	-	4,956
5570 Motorcycle dealers	-	28	-	207	7	-	20,406	-	5,365
5610 Men's & boys' clothing stores	-	75	-	510	7	-	13,310	-	6,636
5620 Women's clothing stores	-	221	-	2,134	10	-	7,775	-	17,078
5630 Women's accessory & specialty stores [2]	-	47	-	285	6	-	9,937	-	3,011
5640 Children's and infants' wear stores	-	21	-	152	7	-	7,632	-	1,199
5650 Family clothing stores	-	67	-	985	15	-	10,400	-	10,421
5660 Shoe stores	-	179	-	1,223	7	-	11,166	-	13,763
5690 Misc. apparel & accessory stores	-	49	-	271	6	-	11,646	-	3,153
5712 Furniture stores	-	168	-	1,708	10	-	18,787	-	35,452
5713 Floor covering stores	-	91	-	604	7	-	24,523	-	15,765
5714 Drapery and upholstery stores [2]	-	14	-	49	4	-	9,551	-	582
5719 Misc. homefurnishings stores	-	91	-	619	7	-	12,439	-	8,270
5720 Household appliance stores	-	57	-	282	5	-	17,106	-	5,279
5731 Radio, TV, & electronic stores	-	83	-	1,533	18	-	16,488	-	27,663
5734 Computer and software stores	-	42	-	336	8	-	17,607	-	5,881
5735 Record & prerecorded tape stores	-	47	-	324	7	-	10,432	-	3,118
5736 Musical instrument stores	-	23	-	207	9	-	16,870	-	3,451
5812 Eating places	-	1,612	-	37,728	23	-	7,746	-	310,101
5813 Drinking places	-	547	-	3,272	6	-	6,856	-	22,190
5910 Drug stores and proprietary stores	-	222	-	4,052	18	-	17,337	-	68,653

Continued on next page.

MILWAUKEE – WAUKESHA, WI PMSA - [continued]

Wholesale and Retail Trade USA	Establishments		Employment		Emp / Est	Pay / Employee		Annual Payroll ($ 000)	
	1994	1995	1994	1995	1995	1994	1995	1994	1995
5920 Liquor stores	-	156	-	720	5	-	10,222	-	7,895
5930 Used merchandise stores	-	91	-	801	9	-	8,744	-	7,273
5941 Sporting goods and bicycle shops	-	158	-	1,195	8	-	10,711	-	15,314
5942 Book stores	-	63	-	546	9	-	8,396	-	4,687
5943 Stationery stores [2]	-	9	-	45	5	-	12,089	-	590
5944 Jewelry stores	-	167	-	959	6	-	15,937	-	15,394
5945 Hobby, toy, and game shops	-	74	-	730	10	-	12,170	-	7,898
5946 Camera & photographic supply stores [2]	-	20	-	142	7	-	12,704	-	1,693
5947 Gift, novelty, and souvenir shops	-	172	-	1,135	7	-	6,964	-	8,125
5948 Luggage and leather goods stores	-	8	-	22	3	-	8,727	-	171
5949 Sewing, needlework, and piece goods	-	39	-	369	9	-	7,675	-	3,146
5961 Catalog and mail-order houses [2]	-	46	-	2,349	51	-	18,299	-	44,950
5962 Merchandising machine operators	-	53	-	904	17	-	18,779	-	17,446
5963 Direct selling establishments	-	83	-	502	6	-	17,896	-	9,051
5980 Fuel dealers	-	33	-	197	6	-	25,645	-	5,043
5992 Florists [2]	-	144	-	484	3	-	9,727	-	4,833
5993 Tobacco stores and stands [2]	-	7	-	52	7	-	18,692	-	823
5995 Optical goods stores	-	109	-	689	6	-	19,001	-	12,881
5999 Miscellaneous retail stores, nec	-	277	-	1,967	7	-	15,471	-	32,451

Source: County Business Patterns 1994/95, CBP-94/95, U.S. Department of Commerce, Washington DC, November 1997. The employment column represents mid-March employment in the year. Pay per employee is calculated by dividing 1st Quarter payroll, annualized, by mid-March employment. The column headed 'Emp / Est' shows 'employees per establishment'. A dash (-) means that data are unavailable or cannot be calculated. nec means not elsewhere classified. *Notes:* 1. 1994 data incomplete; unavailable or withheld. 2. 1995 data incomplete; unavailable or withheld. 3. 1994 and 1995 data incomplete; unavailable or withheld.

MINNEAPOLIS – ST. PAUL MSA (MN PART)

Wholesale and Retail Trade USA	Establishments		Employment		Emp / Est	Pay / Employee		Annual Payroll ($ 000)	
	1994	1995	1994	1995	1995	1994	1995	1994	1995
50 – Wholesale trade	6,822	6,971	100,510	109,266	16	34,934	37,889	3,798,213	4,288,460
5012 Automobiles and other vehicles [3]	87	89	1,878	2,061	23	30,405	33,621	63,803	69,608
5013 Motor vehicle supplies and new parts [1]	278	267	3,502	3,334	12	26,128	28,338	98,795	96,245
5014 Tires and tubes [3]	39	37	389	424	11	32,627	31,896	13,718	13,077
5015 Motor vehicle parts, used [3]	64	61	347	361	6	18,271	20,942	7,170	8,259
5021 Furniture [3]	129	130	1,330	1,448	11	36,520	39,227	56,125	61,883
5023 Homefurnishings [3]	161	154	875	1,295	8	29,582	32,096	28,337	44,797
5031 Lumber, plywood, and millwork [3]	123	124	2,002	2,152	17	37,149	38,439	91,082	91,045
5032 Brick, stone, & related materials [3]	61	52	415	460	9	34,429	39,565	15,759	21,106
5033 Roofing, siding, & insulation [3]	43	45	376	406	9	39,713	40,739	16,028	18,356
5039 Construction materials, nec [3]	59	97	498	743	8	32,546	34,600	18,869	27,030
5043 Photographic equipment & supplies [3]	24	21	443	522	25	41,336	44,674	17,257	20,898
5044 Office equipment [3]	109	104	2,914	3,117	30	33,580	38,592	104,543	120,852
5045 Computers, peripherals, & software	445	438	7,201	7,596	17	46,172	51,147	345,190	389,046
5046 Commercial equipment, nec [3]	92	89	1,027	1,054	12	30,536	34,087	35,447	39,249
5047 Medical and hospital equipment [3]	206	206	3,476	4,129	20	43,753	52,476	155,637	212,931
5048 Ophthalmic goods [3]	17	21	345	304	14	29,380	32,184	9,635	8,947
5049 Professional equipment, nec [3]	47	50	611	565	11	29,362	33,593	18,153	19,019
5051 Metals service centers and offices [3]	125	130	384	2,235	17	36,344	40,854	15,230	89,818
5063 Electrical apparatus and equipment [3]	294	257	3,100	2,914	11	35,872	40,807	119,564	120,773
5064 Electrical appliances, TV & radios [3]	65	68	781	782	12	43,877	51,494	36,532	38,427
5065 Electronic parts and equipment [3]	366	394	3,959	4,387	11	41,009	44,987	176,161	208,182
5072 Hardware [3]	149	154	1,998	1,982	13	31,153	31,824	68,874	66,085
5074 Plumbing & hydronic heating supplies [3]	130	119	1,580	1,377	12	38,997	38,751	59,739	56,502
5075 Warm air heating & air conditioning [3]	65	69	524	589	9	33,901	35,864	20,928	24,189
5078 Refrigeration equipment and supplies [3]	23	22	195	193	9	35,836	44,041	8,516	9,217
5082 Construction and mining machinery [3]	62	60	1,155	1,250	21	36,232	41,139	46,596	51,614
5083 Farm and garden machinery [1]	87	85	1,307	1,449	17	41,500	38,921	58,663	61,677
5084 Industrial machinery and equipment	474	497	5,783	6,624	13	43,348	45,269	262,693	310,746
5085 Industrial supplies [3]	215	216	3,105	3,381	16	35,074	38,462	118,236	131,207
5087 Service establishment equipment [3]	76	78	1,074	1,323	17	29,613	33,185	34,970	46,765
5088 Transportation equipment & supplies [3]	36	34	267	257	8	32,434	31,206	9,025	8,373
5091 Sporting & recreational goods [3]	122	132	1,007	2,104	16	29,867	24,321	36,093	48,665
5092 Toys and hobby goods and supplies [3]	43	47	338	400	9	28,201	30,940	12,408	15,359
5093 Scrap and waste materials [3]	95	99	959	1,087	11	26,532	29,490	29,122	34,130
5094 Jewelry & precious stones [3]	71	76	1,319	1,327	17	10,138	13,245	14,094	16,881
5099 Durable goods, nec [3]	159	173	2,003	2,420	14	31,431	32,155	79,506	96,146
5111 Printing and writing paper [3]	47	48	1,118	1,042	22	40,894	45,931	48,209	48,726
5112 Stationery and office supplies [3]	141	137	2,116	2,244	16	25,966	27,175	55,680	61,629
5113 Industrial & personal service paper [3]	71	74	1,000	1,309	18	25,524	29,803	27,394	41,672
5120 Drugs, proprietaries, and sundries [3]	96	99	1,955	2,048	21	31,482	32,779	66,280	72,488

Continued on next page.

MINNEAPOLIS – ST. PAUL MSA (MN PART) - [continued]

Wholesale and Retail Trade USA	Establishments		Employment		Emp / Est	Pay / Employee		Annual Payroll ($ 000)	
	1994	1995	1994	1995	1995	1994	1995	1994	1995
5131 Piece goods & notions[3]	54	55	441	385	7	17,587	23,023	8,821	9,774
5136 Men's and boys' clothing[3]	59	59	450	456	8	29,973	42,377	15,896	18,564
5137 Women's and children's clothing[3]	93	87	621	571	7	28,225	27,496	19,650	16,856
5139 Footwear[3]	18	18	17	67	4	22,353	34,090	509	2,505
5141 Groceries, general line[3]	29	32	3,132	3,179	99	33,736	34,203	114,217	112,903
5142 Packaged frozen food[3]	48	45	482	509	11	29,004	31,112	16,044	18,503
5143 Dairy products, exc. dried or canned[3]	31	30	328	245	8	44,927	47,755	15,647	12,486
5144 Poultry and poultry products[3]	6	5	33	32	6	34,545	40,125	1,131	1,276
5145 Confectionery[3]	36	35	453	430	12	30,561	33,442	14,253	13,869
5146 Fish and seafoods[3]	9	10	39	37	4	31,487	35,459	1,182	1,196
5147 Meats and meat products[3]	39	37	334	331	9	30,527	33,970	11,079	12,672
5148 Fresh fruits and vegetables[3]	53	51	986	1,007	20	34,572	29,092	36,023	37,200
5149 Groceries and related products, nec[3]	146	140	2,779	2,435	17	30,650	33,046	88,537	85,754
5153 Grain and field beans[3]	61	59	175	555	9	25,349	43,942	5,774	26,207
5154 Livestock[3]	10	10	119	215	22	42,185	21,842	4,173	4,421
5159 Farm-product raw materials, nec[2]	-	4	-	21	5	-	43,048	-	747
5162 Plastics materials & basic shapes[3]	77	77	626	680	9	33,610	38,594	23,523	27,490
5169 Chemicals & allied products, nec[3]	144	150	1,365	1,597	11	35,851	39,579	55,220	66,317
5171 Petroleum bulk stations & terminals	56	52	579	640	12	29,216	30,563	18,288	19,385
5172 Petroleum products, nec[3]	33	33	257	293	9	31,626	35,986	8,816	10,280
5181 Beer and ale[3]	29	25	468	308	12	34,214	36,909	15,761	11,265
5182 Wine and distilled beverages[3]	14	15	651	152	10	33,051	42,237	19,183	5,657
5191 Farm supplies[2]	123	106	1,614	1,358	13	26,387	29,490	43,508	38,165
5192 Books, periodicals, & newspapers[3]	73	77	1,345	1,604	21	26,412	29,683	36,974	45,515
5193 Flowers & florists' supplies[3]	42	36	521	497	14	19,271	18,181	10,727	10,048
5194 Tobacco and tobacco products[3]	12	12	298	413	34	25,638	26,392	11,175	12,011
5198 Paints, varnishes, and supplies[3]	42	36	459	309	9	22,057	26,395	11,992	7,658
5199 Nondurable goods, nec[3]	253	265	1,882	2,695	10	30,446	32,561	72,146	90,025
52 – Retail trade	14,467	14,460	254,393	265,422	18	13,109	14,374	3,669,766	3,983,496
5210 Lumber and other building materials	205	189	5,167	4,778	25	20,667	21,156	118,777	101,883
5230 Paint, glass, and wallpaper stores[3]	78	84	515	700	8	18,757	15,457	11,353	11,138
5250 Hardware stores	210	164	1,963	1,868	11	11,213	10,400	25,848	22,970
5260 Retail nurseries and garden stores	122	129	1,025	1,183	9	9,752	11,334	15,843	18,752
5270 Mobile home dealers[3]	25	21	34	78	4	23,059	17,333	1,065	1,835
5310 Department stores[3]	112	116	23,203	25,814	223	10,635	11,540	268,276	298,712
5330 Variety stores[3]	62	60	218	224	4	10,073	9,054	2,334	2,120
5390 Misc. general merchandise stores[3]	81	79	1,070	1,405	18	13,712	16,256	15,346	22,250
5410 Grocery stores[3]	752	741	23,507	24,442	33	13,355	13,450	324,224	349,946
5420 Meat and fish markets[3]	70	73	537	473	6	9,616	14,334	5,676	6,924
5440 Candy, nut, and confectionery stores[3]	79	75	343	373	5	5,598	7,850	2,079	2,879
5450 Dairy products stores[3]	17	18	15	20	1	4,800	5,600	119	145
5460 Retail bakeries	268	239	2,586	1,974	8	9,502	10,766	25,959	21,984
5490 Miscellaneous food stores[3]	96	97	471	740	8	9,486	8,351	5,430	6,809
5510 New and used car dealers	193	193	9,984	10,036	52	29,081	30,093	332,932	341,406
5520 Used car dealers[3]	89	90	272	314	3	22,147	22,102	6,687	7,382
5530 Auto and home supply stores	314	315	2,605	2,765	9	16,204	17,568	47,656	55,645
5540 Gasoline service stations	1,016	982	11,226	11,790	12	11,086	11,509	129,973	141,726
5550 Boat dealers[3]	50	50	464	426	9	17,853	19,061	10,577	10,043
5560 Recreational vehicle dealers[3]	26	27	117	165	6	20,513	18,545	3,338	3,820
5570 Motorcycle dealers[3]	27	29	186	264	9	23,763	21,015	4,672	5,590
5590 Automotive dealers, nec[3]	15	18	61	75	4	22,230	20,853	1,489	1,516
5610 Men's & boys' clothing stores[3]	136	130	1,183	1,147	9	13,488	13,733	15,117	15,334
5620 Women's clothing stores[3]	474	410	5,050	4,544	11	8,642	8,616	45,960	39,561
5630 Women's accessory & specialty stores[3]	73	74	549	581	8	9,734	9,735	5,852	5,489
5640 Children's and infants' wear stores[3]	49	49	513	507	10	6,776	7,763	3,942	4,079
5650 Family clothing stores[3]	212	209	4,378	4,206	20	9,813	10,925	46,694	48,314
5660 Shoe stores[3]	309	281	1,769	1,753	6	10,469	11,459	19,921	19,344
5690 Misc. apparel & accessory stores[3]	85	76	504	526	7	12,286	13,437	7,173	8,494
5712 Furniture stores	316	317	3,051	3,573	11	20,561	21,971	66,921	80,955
5713 Floor covering stores	151	158	763	813	5	20,257	25,048	18,662	22,093
5714 Drapery and upholstery stores[3]	22	23	64	55	2	12,625	15,491	938	940
5719 Misc. homefurnishings stores[1]	210	212	1,605	1,621	8	11,940	13,229	20,667	22,145
5720 Household appliance stores[2]	97	89	419	412	5	20,974	22,767	8,002	8,358
5731 Radio, TV, & electronic stores[3]	144	151	1,899	2,725	18	15,404	15,237	35,331	40,787
5734 Computer and software stores[3]	95	109	515	832	8	21,157	30,375	13,874	26,656
5735 Record & prerecorded tape stores[3]	91	89	1,007	884	10	9,160	10,262	10,010	9,286
5736 Musical instrument stores[3]	42	47	387	463	10	19,721	19,447	8,492	9,550
5812 Eating places	3,418	3,267	81,180	80,369	25	7,851	8,742	704,486	750,362
5813 Drinking places	439	437	4,974	5,876	13	7,947	8,291	44,412	50,728
5910 Drug stores and proprietary stores	341	334	6,089	6,040	18	13,749	14,705	85,937	89,970
5920 Liquor stores	401	398	3,755	3,880	10	13,595	14,030	54,064	57,425

Continued on next page.

MINNEAPOLIS - ST. PAUL MSA (MN PART) - [continued]

Wholesale and Retail Trade USA	Establishments		Employment		Emp / Est	Pay / Employee		Annual Payroll ($ 000)	
	1994	1995	1994	1995	1995	1994	1995	1994	1995
5930 Used merchandise stores [2]	187	172	1,318	1,081	6	12,046	11,260	19,155	13,219
5941 Sporting goods and bicycle shops	318	336	2,863	3,598	11	11,999	13,008	41,816	52,392
5942 Book stores [3]	124	132	1,120	1,224	9	8,818	9,846	10,886	12,113
5943 Stationery stores [3]	46	42	215	251	6	9,470	11,618	1,916	2,780
5944 Jewelry stores [3]	241	247	1,381	1,495	6	17,767	19,460	24,575	28,195
5945 Hobby, toy, and game shops [3]	118	104	1,048	1,150	11	9,134	8,727	11,177	11,622
5946 Camera & photographic supply stores [3]	48	47	310	331	7	18,077	17,970	6,248	6,664
5947 Gift, novelty, and souvenir shops	392	394	2,516	2,588	7	7,576	8,216	22,455	24,413
5948 Luggage and leather goods stores [3]	28	25	135	124	5	10,519	9,097	1,461	1,326
5949 Sewing, needlework, and piece goods [3]	80	81	892	864	11	7,220	7,829	6,962	7,271
5961 Catalog and mail-order houses [3]	102	110	5,097	9,017	82	17,786	17,487	103,708	152,602
5962 Merchandising machine operators [3]	82	87	1,577	952	11	16,517	19,143	27,724	18,702
5963 Direct selling establishments [1]	176	181	1,589	1,734	10	21,687	23,324	37,769	40,105
5983 Fuel oil dealers [1]	15	-	19	-	-	24,421	-	699	-
5984 Liquefied petroleum gas dealers [1]	28	29	9	48	2	26,222	22,833	235	920
5992 Florists [1]	236	247	1,469	1,497	6	9,468	9,590	15,264	15,984
5995 Optical goods stores [3]	197	189	1,094	955	5	16,351	16,993	18,527	17,433
5999 Miscellaneous retail stores, nec	534	574	2,924	3,396	6	11,529	12,622	39,964	48,353

Source: County Business Patterns 1994/95, CBP-94/95, U.S. Department of Commerce, Washington DC, November 1997. The employment column represents mid-March employment in the year. Pay per employee is calculated by dividing 1st Quarter payroll, annualized, by mid-March employment. The column headed 'Emp / Est' shows 'employees per establishment'. A dash (-) means that data are unavailable or cannot be calculated. nec means not elsewhere classified. *Notes:* 1. 1994 data incomplete; unavailable or withheld. 2. 1995 data incomplete; unavailable or withheld. 3. 1994 and 1995 data incomplete; unavailable or withheld.

MINNEAPOLIS - ST. PAUL MSA (WI PART)

Wholesale and Retail Trade USA	Establishments		Employment		Emp / Est	Pay / Employee		Annual Payroll ($ 000)	
	1994	1995	1994	1995	1995	1994	1995	1994	1995
50- Wholesale trade	-	126	-	1,228	10	-	23,622	-	31,845
5013 Motor vehicle supplies and new parts	-	9	-	58	6	-	21,586	-	1,700
5030 Lumber and construction materials	-	6	-	20	3	-	17,600	-	517
5040 Professional & commercial equipment	-	8	-	91	11	-	20,571	-	2,061
5070 Hardware, plumbing & heating equipment [2]	-	4	-	21	5	-	28,190	-	630
5083 Farm and garden machinery	-	11	-	90	8	-	26,267	-	2,305
5084 Industrial machinery and equipment [2]	-	6	-	44	7	-	17,818	-	680
5090 Miscellaneous durable goods	-	12	-	57	5	-	27,789	-	2,235
5130 Apparel, piece goods, and notions [2]	-	3	-	2	1	-	22,000	-	74
5140 Groceries and related products [2]	-	6	-	49	8	-	12,735	-	786
5150 Farm-product raw materials	-	4	-	16	4	-	12,750	-	182
5171 Petroleum bulk stations & terminals	-	6	-	27	5	-	19,704	-	674
5191 Farm supplies [2]	-	20	-	121	6	-	16,364	-	2,076
52- Retail trade	-	530	-	6,510	12	-	10,443	-	71,662
5210 Lumber and other building materials	-	13	-	201	15	-	18,687	-	3,626
5250 Hardware stores	-	11	-	36	3	-	11,556	-	418
5300 General merchandise stores	-	12	-	642	54	-	11,340	-	7,674
5410 Grocery stores	-	30	-	910	30	-	10,743	-	9,506
5420 Meat and fish markets	-	5	-	9	2	-	7,556	-	81
5460 Retail bakeries	-	7	-	30	4	-	6,533	-	183
5510 New and used car dealers	-	16	-	349	22	-	25,352	-	10,278
5530 Auto and home supply stores	-	10	-	12	1	-	13,333	-	172
5540 Gasoline service stations	-	50	-	585	12	-	10,496	-	6,698
5650 Family clothing stores	-	4	-	11	3	-	5,818	-	55
5660 Shoe stores	-	5	-	8	2	-	8,000	-	78
5712 Furniture stores	-	8	-	55	7	-	15,345	-	926
5713 Floor covering stores	-	5	-	9	2	-	13,333	-	92
5719 Misc. homefurnishings stores [2]	-	3	-	3	1	-	9,333	-	34
5731 Radio, TV, & electronic stores	-	6	-	18	3	-	9,778	-	171
5812 Eating places	-	119	-	2,220	19	-	6,169	-	14,677
5813 Drinking places	-	56	-	250	4	-	5,712	-	1,542
5910 Drug stores and proprietary stores	-	16	-	155	10	-	10,194	-	1,741
5920 Liquor stores	-	16	-	77	5	-	8,416	-	642
5930 Used merchandise stores	-	4	-	7	2	-	2,857	-	17
5941 Sporting goods and bicycle shops	-	12	-	24	2	-	7,833	-	212
5944 Jewelry stores	-	7	-	19	3	-	8,000	-	155
5947 Gift, novelty, and souvenir shops	-	7	-	21	3	-	4,571	-	136
5980 Fuel dealers	-	9	-	57	6	-	17,193	-	901
5999 Miscellaneous retail stores, nec	-	10	-	33	3	-	12,848	-	658

Source: County Business Patterns 1994/95, CBP-94/95, U.S. Department of Commerce, Washington DC, November 1997. The employment column represents mid-March employment in the year. Pay per employee is calculated by dividing 1st Quarter payroll, annualized, by mid-March employment. The column headed 'Emp / Est' shows 'employees per establishment'. A dash (-) means that data are unavailable or cannot be calculated. nec means not elsewhere classified. *Notes:* 1. 1994 data incomplete; unavailable or withheld. 2. 1995 data incomplete; unavailable or withheld. 3. 1994 and 1995 data incomplete; unavailable or withheld.

MINNEAPOLIS - ST. PAUL, MN - WI MSA

Wholesale and Retail Trade USA	Establishments		Employment		Emp / Est	Pay / Employee		Annual Payroll ($ 000)	
	1994	1995	1994	1995	1995	1994	1995	1994	1995
50 - Wholesale trade [1]	6,822	7,097	100,510	110,494	16	34,934	37,730	3,798,213	4,320,305
5012 Automobiles and other vehicles [3]	87	91	1,878	2,061	23	30,405	33,621	63,803	69,608
5013 Motor vehicle supplies and new parts [1]	278	276	3,502	3,392	12	26,128	28,223	98,795	97,945
5014 Tires and tubes [3]	39	37	389	424	11	32,627	31,896	13,718	13,077
5015 Motor vehicle parts, used [3]	64	63	347	361	6	18,271	20,942	7,170	8,259
5021 Furniture [3]	129	131	1,330	1,448	11	36,520	39,227	56,125	61,883
5023 Homefurnishings [3]	161	156	875	1,295	8	29,582	32,096	28,337	44,797
5031 Lumber, plywood, and millwork [3]	123	126	2,002	2,152	17	37,149	38,439	91,082	91,045
5032 Brick, stone, & related materials [3]	61	53	415	460	9	34,429	39,565	15,759	21,106
5033 Roofing, siding, & insulation [3]	43	45	376	406	9	39,713	40,739	16,028	18,356
5039 Construction materials, nec [3]	59	100	498	743	7	32,546	34,600	18,869	27,030
5043 Photographic equipment & supplies [3]	24	22	443	522	24	41,336	44,674	17,257	20,898
5044 Office equipment [3]	109	106	2,914	3,117	29	33,580	38,592	104,543	120,852
5045 Computers, peripherals, & software [3]	445	438	7,201	7,596	17	46,172	51,147	345,190	389,046
5046 Commercial equipment, nec [3]	92	91	1,027	1,054	12	30,536	34,087	35,447	39,249
5047 Medical and hospital equipment [3]	206	207	3,476	4,129	20	43,753	52,476	155,637	212,931
5048 Ophthalmic goods [3]	17	21	345	304	14	29,380	32,184	9,635	8,947
5049 Professional equipment, nec [3]	47	52	611	565	11	29,362	33,593	18,153	19,019
5051 Metals service centers and offices [3]	125	133	384	2,235	17	36,344	40,854	15,230	89,818
5063 Electrical apparatus and equipment [3]	294	261	3,100	2,914	11	35,872	40,807	119,564	120,773
5064 Electrical appliances, TV & radios [3]	65	69	781	782	11	43,877	51,494	36,532	38,427
5065 Electronic parts and equipment [3]	366	396	3,959	4,387	11	41,009	44,987	176,161	208,182
5072 Hardware [3]	149	155	1,998	1,982	13	31,153	31,824	68,874	66,085
5074 Plumbing & hydronic heating supplies [3]	130	122	1,580	1,377	11	38,997	38,751	59,739	56,502
5075 Warm air heating & air conditioning [3]	65	69	524	589	9	33,901	35,864	20,928	24,189
5078 Refrigeration equipment and supplies [3]	23	22	195	193	9	35,836	44,041	8,516	9,217
5082 Construction and mining machinery [3]	62	60	1,155	1,250	21	36,232	41,139	46,596	51,614
5083 Farm and garden machinery [1]	87	96	1,307	1,539	16	41,500	38,181	58,663	63,982
5084 Industrial machinery and equipment [3]	474	503	5,783	6,668	13	43,348	45,088	262,693	311,426
5085 Industrial supplies [3]	215	217	3,105	3,381	16	35,074	38,462	118,236	131,207
5087 Service establishment equipment [3]	76	78	1,074	1,323	17	29,613	33,185	34,970	46,765
5088 Transportation equipment & supplies [3]	36	35	267	257	7	32,434	31,206	9,025	8,373
5091 Sporting & recreational goods [3]	122	134	1,007	2,104	16	29,867	24,321	36,093	48,665
5092 Toys and hobby goods and supplies [3]	43	49	338	400	8	28,201	30,940	12,408	15,359
5093 Scrap and waste materials [3]	95	105	959	1,087	10	26,532	29,490	29,122	34,130
5094 Jewelry & precious stones [3]	71	77	1,319	1,327	17	10,138	13,245	14,094	16,881
5099 Durable goods, nec [3]	159	174	2,003	2,420	14	31,431	32,155	79,506	96,146
5111 Printing and writing paper [3]	47	49	1,118	1,042	21	40,894	45,931	48,209	48,726
5112 Stationery and office supplies [3]	141	137	2,116	2,244	16	25,966	27,175	55,680	61,629
5113 Industrial & personal service paper [3]	71	75	1,000	1,309	17	25,524	29,803	27,394	41,672
5120 Drugs, proprietaries, and sundries [3]	96	99	1,955	2,048	21	31,482	32,779	66,280	72,488
5131 Piece goods & notions [3]	54	55	441	385	7	17,587	23,023	8,821	9,774
5136 Men's and boys' clothing [3]	59	61	450	456	7	29,973	42,377	15,896	18,564
5137 Women's and children's clothing [3]	93	88	621	571	6	28,225	27,496	19,650	16,856
5139 Footwear [3]	18	18	17	67	4	22,353	34,090	509	2,505
5141 Groceries, general line [3]	29	32	3,132	3,179	99	33,736	34,203	114,217	112,903
5142 Packaged frozen food [3]	48	45	482	509	11	29,004	31,112	16,044	18,503
5143 Dairy products, exc. dried or canned [3]	31	31	328	245	8	44,927	47,755	15,647	12,486
5144 Poultry and poultry products [3]	6	6	33	32	5	34,545	40,125	1,131	1,276
5145 Confectionery [3]	36	35	453	430	12	30,561	33,442	14,253	13,869
5146 Fish and seafoods [3]	9	10	39	37	4	31,487	35,459	1,182	1,196
5147 Meats and meat products [3]	39	38	334	331	9	30,527	33,970	11,079	12,672
5148 Fresh fruits and vegetables [3]	53	53	986	1,007	19	34,572	29,092	36,023	37,200
5149 Groceries and related products, nec [3]	146	141	2,779	2,435	17	30,650	33,046	88,537	85,754
5153 Grain and field beans [3]	61	62	175	555	9	25,349	43,942	5,774	26,207
5154 Livestock [3]	10	11	119	215	20	42,185	21,842	4,173	4,421
5159 Farm-product raw materials, nec [2]	-	4	-	21	5	-	43,048	-	747
5162 Plastics materials & basic shapes [3]	77	78	626	680	9	33,610	38,594	23,523	27,490
5169 Chemicals & allied products, nec [3]	144	151	1,365	1,597	11	35,851	39,579	55,220	66,317
5171 Petroleum bulk stations & terminals [1]	56	58	579	667	12	29,216	30,123	18,288	20,059
5172 Petroleum products, nec [3]	33	33	257	293	9	31,626	35,986	8,816	10,280
5181 Beer and ale [3]	29	26	468	308	12	34,214	36,909	15,761	11,265
5182 Wine and distilled beverages [3]	14	15	651	152	10	33,051	42,237	19,183	5,657
5191 Farm supplies [3]	123	126	1,614	1,479	12	26,387	28,416	43,508	40,241
5192 Books, periodicals, & newspapers [3]	73	77	1,345	1,604	21	26,412	29,683	36,974	45,515
5193 Flowers & florists' supplies [3]	42	36	521	497	14	19,271	18,181	10,727	10,048
5194 Tobacco and tobacco products [3]	12	12	298	413	34	25,638	26,392	11,175	12,011
5198 Paints, varnishes, and supplies [3]	42	38	459	309	8	22,057	26,395	11,992	7,658
5199 Nondurable goods, nec [3]	253	267	1,882	2,695	10	30,446	32,561	72,146	90,025
52 - Retail trade [1]	14,467	14,990	254,393	271,932	18	13,109	14,280	3,669,766	4,055,158
5210 Lumber and other building materials [1]	205	202	5,167	4,979	25	20,667	21,056	118,777	105,509

Continued on next page.

MINNEAPOLIS – ST. PAUL, MN – WI MSA - [continued]

Wholesale and Retail Trade USA	Establishments		Employment		Emp / Est	Pay / Employee		Annual Payroll ($ 000)	
	1994	1995	1994	1995	1995	1994	1995	1994	1995
5230 Paint, glass, and wallpaper stores [3]	78	85	515	700	8	18,757	15,457	11,353	11,138
5250 Hardware stores [1]	210	175	1,963	1,904	11	11,213	10,422	25,848	23,388
5260 Retail nurseries and garden stores [1]	122	131	1,025	1,183	9	9,752	11,334	15,843	18,752
5270 Mobile home dealers [3]	25	21	34	78	4	23,059	17,333	1,065	1,835
5310 Department stores [3]	112	119	23,203	25,814	217	10,635	11,540	268,276	298,712
5330 Variety stores [3]	62	62	218	224	4	10,073	9,054	2,334	2,120
5390 Misc. general merchandise stores [3]	81	86	1,070	1,405	16	13,712	16,256	15,346	22,250
5410 Grocery stores [3]	752	771	23,507	25,352	33	13,355	13,353	324,224	359,452
5420 Meat and fish markets [3]	70	78	537	482	6	9,616	14,207	5,676	7,005
5440 Candy, nut, and confectionery stores [3]	79	75	343	373	5	5,598	7,850	2,079	2,879
5450 Dairy products stores [3]	17	19	15	20	1	4,800	5,600	119	145
5460 Retail bakeries [1]	268	246	2,586	2,004	8	9,502	10,703	25,959	22,167
5490 Miscellaneous food stores [3]	96	97	471	740	8	9,486	8,351	5,430	6,809
5510 New and used car dealers [1]	193	209	9,984	10,385	50	29,081	29,934	332,932	351,684
5520 Used car dealers [3]	89	91	272	314	3	22,147	22,102	6,687	7,382
5530 Auto and home supply stores [1]	314	325	2,605	2,777	9	16,204	17,550	47,656	55,817
5540 Gasoline service stations [1]	1,016	1,032	11,226	12,375	12	11,086	11,461	129,973	148,424
5550 Boat dealers [3]	50	52	464	426	8	17,853	19,061	10,577	10,043
5560 Recreational vehicle dealers [3]	26	27	117	165	6	20,513	18,545	3,338	3,820
5570 Motorcycle dealers [3]	27	30	186	264	9	23,763	21,015	4,672	5,590
5590 Automotive dealers, nec [3]	15	18	61	75	4	22,230	20,853	1,489	1,516
5610 Men's & boys' clothing stores [3]	136	130	1,183	1,147	9	13,488	13,733	15,117	15,334
5620 Women's clothing stores [3]	474	416	5,050	4,544	11	8,642	8,616	45,960	39,561
5630 Women's accessory & specialty stores [3]	73	74	549	581	8	9,734	9,735	5,852	5,489
5640 Children's and infants' wear stores [3]	49	49	513	507	10	6,776	7,763	3,942	4,079
5650 Family clothing stores [3]	212	213	4,378	4,217	20	9,813	10,912	46,694	48,369
5660 Shoe stores [3]	309	286	1,769	1,761	6	10,469	11,443	19,921	19,422
5690 Misc. apparel & accessory stores [3]	85	78	504	526	7	12,286	13,437	7,173	8,494
5712 Furniture stores [1]	316	325	3,051	3,628	11	20,561	21,871	66,921	81,881
5713 Floor covering stores [1]	151	163	763	822	5	20,257	24,920	18,662	22,185
5714 Drapery and upholstery stores [3]	22	23	64	55	2	12,625	15,491	938	940
5719 Misc. homefurnishings stores [3]	210	215	1,605	1,624	8	11,940	13,222	20,667	22,179
5720 Household appliance stores [3]	97	92	419	412	4	20,974	22,767	8,002	8,358
5731 Radio, TV, & electronic stores [3]	144	157	1,899	2,743	17	15,404	15,201	35,331	40,958
5734 Computer and software stores [3]	95	109	515	832	8	21,157	30,375	13,874	26,656
5735 Record & prerecorded tape stores [3]	91	89	1,007	884	10	9,160	10,262	10,010	9,286
5736 Musical instrument stores [3]	42	48	387	463	10	19,721	19,447	8,492	9,550
5812 Eating places [1]	3,418	3,386	81,180	82,589	24	7,851	8,672	704,486	765,039
5813 Drinking places [1]	439	493	4,974	6,126	12	7,947	8,185	44,412	52,270
5910 Drug stores and proprietary stores [1]	341	350	6,089	6,195	18	13,749	14,592	85,937	91,711
5920 Liquor stores [1]	401	414	3,755	3,957	10	13,595	13,921	54,064	58,067
5930 Used merchandise stores [3]	187	176	1,318	1,088	6	12,046	11,206	19,155	13,236
5941 Sporting goods and bicycle shops [1]	318	348	2,863	3,622	10	11,999	12,974	41,816	52,604
5942 Book stores [3]	124	139	1,120	1,224	9	8,818	9,846	10,886	12,113
5943 Stationery stores [3]	46	43	215	251	6	9,470	11,618	1,916	2,780
5944 Jewelry stores [3]	241	254	1,381	1,514	6	17,767	19,316	24,575	28,350
5945 Hobby, toy, and game shops [3]	118	105	1,048	1,150	11	9,134	8,727	11,177	11,622
5946 Camera & photographic supply stores [3]	48	47	310	331	7	18,077	17,970	6,248	6,664
5947 Gift, novelty, and souvenir shops [1]	392	401	2,516	2,609	7	7,576	8,187	22,455	24,549
5948 Luggage and leather goods stores [3]	28	25	135	124	5	10,519	9,097	1,461	1,326
5949 Sewing, needlework, and piece goods [3]	80	82	892	864	11	7,220	7,829	6,962	7,271
5961 Catalog and mail-order houses [3]	102	113	5,097	9,017	80	17,786	17,487	103,708	152,602
5962 Merchandising machine operators [3]	82	87	1,577	952	11	16,517	19,143	27,724	18,702
5963 Direct selling establishments [1]	176	186	1,589	1,734	9	21,687	23,324	37,769	40,105
5983 Fuel oil dealers [1]	15	-	19	-	-	24,421	-	699	-
5984 Liquefied petroleum gas dealers [1]	28	34	9	48	1	26,222	22,833	235	920
5992 Florists [1]	236	257	1,469	1,497	6	9,468	9,590	15,264	15,984
5995 Optical goods stores [3]	197	191	1,094	955	5	16,351	16,993	18,527	17,433
5999 Miscellaneous retail stores, nec [1]	534	584	2,924	3,429	6	11,529	12,624	39,964	49,011

Source: County Business Patterns 1994/95, CBP-94/95, U.S. Department of Commerce, Washington DC, November 1997. The employment column represents mid-March employment in the year. Pay per employee is calculated by dividing 1st Quarter payroll, annualized, by mid-March employment. The column headed 'Emp / Est' shows 'employees per establishment'. A dash (-) means that data are unavailable or cannot be calculated. nec means not elsewhere classified. *Notes:* 1. 1994 data incomplete; unavailable or withheld. 2. 1995 data incomplete; unavailable or withheld. 3. 1994 and 1995 data incomplete; unavailable or withheld.

MOBILE, AL MSA

Wholesale and Retail Trade USA	Establishments		Employment		Emp / Est	Pay / Employee		Annual Payroll ($ 000)	
	1994	1995	1994	1995	1995	1994	1995	1994	1995
50- Wholesale trade	1,036	1,023	11,547	11,925	12	23,428	24,702	297,544	325,512
5012 Automobiles and other vehicles	19	18	201	252	14	23,960	24,444	5,264	7,072
5013 Motor vehicle supplies and new parts	57	45	556	514	11	19,647	19,907	11,925	10,394
5014 Tires and tubes[3]	9	7	76	78	11	21,789	23,385	2,080	1,922
5015 Motor vehicle parts, used	15	15	68	49	3	15,176	18,122	1,158	974
5021 Furniture	7	6	79	73	12	23,190	23,671	1,981	1,929
5023 Homefurnishings[2]	16	18	197	195	11	37,076	41,067	7,020	7,799
5031 Lumber, plywood, and millwork	28	31	381	473	15	21,533	21,209	8,783	11,241
5032 Brick, stone, & related materials	19	19	134	147	8	24,896	25,741	3,314	3,779
5033 Roofing, siding, & insulation[3]	9	10	70	82	8	24,743	28,537	2,114	2,642
5039 Construction materials, nec	6	16	16	200	13	20,000	17,420	519	4,024
5044 Office equipment	21	24	249	273	11	23,454	22,828	6,214	6,734
5045 Computers, peripherals, & software	27	25	234	193	8	31,368	33,907	7,007	6,501
5046 Commercial equipment, nec	8	-	37	-	-	18,486	-	739	-
5047 Medical and hospital equipment	26	23	260	272	12	22,892	26,074	6,286	6,886
5050 Metals and minerals, except petroleum	22	18	377	361	20	30,568	31,479	12,333	12,495
5063 Electrical apparatus and equipment	50	50	624	636	13	29,160	29,478	18,851	20,979
5064 Electrical appliances, TV & radios[3]	8	8	59	62	8	18,780	25,226	1,058	1,377
5065 Electronic parts and equipment	32	30	277	344	11	28,260	26,395	8,352	10,644
5072 Hardware	19	17	174	165	10	21,609	26,109	4,390	4,949
5075 Warm air heating & air conditioning[3]	15	15	161	175	12	26,186	31,749	5,083	5,433
5082 Construction and mining machinery	14	14	225	271	19	31,929	30,819	7,355	8,649
5083 Farm and garden machinery	9	9	55	58	6	21,964	25,103	1,528	1,477
5084 Industrial machinery and equipment	85	84	853	891	11	28,277	31,744	26,167	31,923
5085 Industrial supplies	61	67	773	750	11	34,091	36,923	27,613	29,951
5087 Service establishment equipment[1]	8	9	122	139	15	26,852	23,597	3,339	3,589
5088 Transportation equipment & supplies	10	16	158	157	10	24,329	28,713	4,736	5,323
5091 Sporting & recreational goods	8	7	57	46	7	13,895	16,087	917	851
5093 Scrap and waste materials	18	20	150	226	11	14,160	21,416	2,285	6,466
5094 Jewelry & precious stones[3]	9	9	45	59	7	16,622	13,966	828	790
5099 Durable goods, nec	21	21	112	156	7	24,821	23,667	5,559	6,098
5112 Stationery and office supplies	24	17	294	214	13	15,619	19,234	4,880	3,348
5113 Industrial & personal service paper[3]	8	9	225	229	25	24,462	25,450	6,116	5,922
5120 Drugs, proprietaries, and sundries	13	10	131	140	14	24,061	24,114	3,817	3,923
5136 Men's and boys' clothing[3]	3	4	20	24	6	16,600	14,167	393	325
5141 Groceries, general line	8	10	83	102	10	18,795	20,980	1,897	2,143
5142 Packaged frozen food	15	15	170	164	11	19,529	20,976	3,551	3,515
5143 Dairy products, exc. dried or canned[3]	5	5	78	92	18	17,846	23,652	2,017	2,247
5144 Poultry and poultry products	5	5	42	50	10	19,905	17,440	891	934
5145 Confectionery	4	5	43	29	6	15,721	23,034	875	863
5146 Fish and seafoods	54	50	787	774	15	6,379	6,698	6,096	6,114
5147 Meats and meat products[2]	-	3	-	37	12	-	23,568	-	838
5148 Fresh fruits and vegetables	6	6	25	20	3	19,200	19,000	517	417
5149 Groceries and related products, nec	23	19	323	283	15	19,257	21,216	6,916	6,595
5150 Farm-product raw materials	7	6	51	15	3	5,098	14,133	240	207
5162 Plastics materials & basic shapes	7	7	30	33	5	23,600	29,576	827	927
5169 Chemicals & allied products, nec	23	22	312	315	14	26,231	27,911	8,865	9,368
5171 Petroleum bulk stations & terminals	28	24	411	400	17	21,538	19,990	9,312	8,592
5172 Petroleum products, nec	7	7	89	27	4	25,169	25,481	2,525	822
5180 Beer, wine, and distilled beverages	10	9	362	397	44	22,895	22,912	9,377	9,989
5191 Farm supplies	21	21	98	103	5	18,082	20,000	2,137	2,262
5192 Books, periodicals, & newspapers[3]	5	5	107	36	7	15,514	15,556	1,451	675
5193 Flowers & florists' supplies	13	10	116	104	10	16,138	18,346	2,123	2,057
5198 Paints, varnishes, and supplies[3]	6	8	35	63	8	26,971	22,603	920	1,544
5199 Nondurable goods, nec	22	21	81	71	3	15,457	16,563	1,227	1,426
52- Retail trade	3,126	3,149	42,210	42,877	14	10,869	11,664	499,845	527,386
5210 Lumber and other building materials	40	41	891	879	21	16,979	18,348	17,643	17,623
5230 Paint, glass, and wallpaper stores	28	24	199	176	7	16,000	18,659	3,607	3,449
5250 Hardware stores	30	22	291	179	8	13,003	14,726	4,472	2,862
5260 Retail nurseries and garden stores	26	27	187	175	6	10,995	18,720	2,560	2,632
5270 Mobile home dealers	9	12	47	58	5	15,830	14,759	1,054	1,251
5310 Department stores	18	18	3,792	3,964	220	11,120	14,989	46,389	58,686
5330 Variety stores	52	35	378	272	8	9,492	9,500	3,896	2,696
5390 Misc. general merchandise stores	18	37	511	648	18	11,421	11,272	5,995	7,493
5410 Grocery stores	303	289	6,298	6,622	23	9,626	9,802	65,696	65,867
5420 Meat and fish markets	28	23	63	58	3	9,651	9,931	693	665
5430 Fruit and vegetable markets	8	10	29	42	4	10,069	7,524	306	374
5440 Candy, nut, and confectionery stores	-	8	-	35	4	-	6,629	-	177
5460 Retail bakeries	17	17	111	115	7	9,117	9,183	1,107	1,178
5490 Miscellaneous food stores	12	19	49	90	5	8,408	13,644	468	1,522
5510 New and used car dealers	36	36	1,871	2,004	56	24,631	26,768	51,693	61,585

Continued on next page.

MOBILE, AL MSA - [continued]

Wholesale and Retail Trade USA	Establishments 1994	Establishments 1995	Employment 1994	Employment 1995	Emp / Est 1995	Pay / Employee 1994	Pay / Employee 1995	Annual Payroll ($ 000) 1994	Annual Payroll ($ 000) 1995
5520 Used car dealers	56	57	166	211	4	15,422	16,664	2,861	3,929
5530 Auto and home supply stores	131	139	876	965	7	14,525	15,308	13,869	15,528
5540 Gasoline service stations	245	234	1,590	1,828	8	11,341	10,648	19,869	20,244
5550 Boat dealers	23	26	82	121	5	17,659	18,149	1,745	2,426
5560 Recreational vehicle dealers[3]	5	5	23	38	8	15,652	16,105	523	543
5570 Motorcycle dealers	8	8	52	58	7	16,000	17,931	962	1,077
5610 Men's & boys' clothing stores	30	31	201	240	8	10,468	11,050	2,368	5,280
5620 Women's clothing stores	111	99	798	727	7	8,451	8,902	7,130	6,471
5630 Women's accessory & specialty stores	17	18	90	94	5	8,222	7,830	780	798
5640 Children's and infants' wear stores	7	6	74	63	11	8,865	8,762	655	592
5650 Family clothing stores	36	38	615	664	17	11,480	12,012	7,802	8,047
5660 Shoe stores	68	73	489	572	8	10,323	9,776	5,537	5,835
5690 Misc. apparel & accessory stores	10	12	29	91	8	10,759	7,604	492	986
5712 Furniture stores	85	87	618	615	7	15,521	18,387	10,329	10,753
5713 Floor covering stores	25	32	146	184	6	17,616	19,196	3,168	3,877
5719 Misc. homefurnishings stores[3]	41	40	110	184	5	13,491	11,826	1,894	2,547
5720 Household appliance stores	16	17	72	71	4	14,722	14,873	1,111	1,093
5731 Radio, TV, & electronic stores	31	30	282	294	10	18,496	18,789	5,561	5,055
5734 Computer and software stores	16	19	48	51	3	16,833	14,824	1,242	786
5735 Record & prerecorded tape stores	18	15	66	75	5	9,758	14,507	611	1,267
5736 Musical instrument stores	12	10	34	38	4	14,118	15,789	527	630
5812 Eating places	594	532	12,874	12,821	24	6,874	6,955	95,288	94,718
5813 Drinking places	89	79	433	389	5	6,716	6,817	3,054	2,739
5910 Drug stores and proprietary stores	111	112	1,359	1,271	11	15,632	16,963	22,664	22,589
5920 Liquor stores	38	36	103	105	3	16,233	14,286	1,624	1,578
5930 Used merchandise stores	66	69	467	323	5	9,062	10,638	3,896	3,514
5941 Sporting goods and bicycle shops	54	54	271	285	5	10,037	10,596	3,194	3,316
5942 Book stores	20	19	131	169	9	9,252	9,751	1,605	1,749
5943 Stationery stores	-	8	-	25	3	-	9,600	-	176
5944 Jewelry stores	52	55	306	349	6	16,052	15,622	5,482	6,054
5945 Hobby, toy, and game shops	14	10	150	138	14	8,400	7,333	1,493	1,218
5947 Gift, novelty, and souvenir shops	58	57	299	281	5	6,957	8,114	2,387	2,535
5948 Luggage and leather goods stores	5	5	21	20	4	10,667	12,800	264	277
5949 Sewing, needlework, and piece goods	22	22	80	104	5	8,750	7,731	685	759
5963 Direct selling establishments	29	28	209	310	11	14,335	16,013	3,617	4,528
5984 Liquefied petroleum gas dealers	10	11	36	29	3	26,556	23,862	774	619
5992 Florists	50	49	225	241	5	8,907	10,324	2,164	2,394
5995 Optical goods stores	23	22	153	123	6	13,882	15,805	2,249	1,981
5999 Miscellaneous retail stores, nec	85	88	547	488	6	9,082	11,689	5,638	5,593

Source: County Business Patterns 1994/95, CBP-94/95, U.S. Department of Commerce, Washington DC, November 1997. The employment column represents mid-March employment in the year. Pay per employee is calculated by dividing 1st Quarter payroll, annualized, by mid-March employment. The column headed 'Emp / Est' shows 'employees per establishment'. A dash (-) means that data are unavailable or cannot be calculated. nec means not elsewhere classified. *Notes:* 1. 1994 data incomplete; unavailable or withheld. 2. 1995 data incomplete; unavailable or withheld. 3. 1994 and 1995 data incomplete; unavailable or withheld.

MODESTO, CA MSA

Wholesale and Retail Trade USA	Establishments 1994	Establishments 1995	Employment 1994	Employment 1995	Emp / Est 1995	Pay / Employee 1994	Pay / Employee 1995	Annual Payroll ($ 000) 1994	Annual Payroll ($ 000) 1995
50- Wholesale trade	539	534	6,638	6,700	13	25,517	26,190	185,682	183,354
5012 Automobiles and other vehicles	8	7	144	160	23	24,806	26,925	3,983	4,215
5013 Motor vehicle supplies and new parts	29	25	283	244	10	20,170	22,361	6,188	5,749
5014 Tires and tubes	11	9	96	99	11	26,750	25,535	2,795	2,753
5015 Motor vehicle parts, used	10	11	61	78	7	19,279	15,949	1,265	1,232
5021 Furniture	8	-	48	-	-	13,500	-	839	-
5023 Homefurnishings	4	-	30	-	-	24,000	-	763	-
5031 Lumber, plywood, and millwork	6	-	20	-	-	30,000	-	492	-
5032 Brick, stone, & related materials	8	6	56	57	10	21,000	17,053	1,184	1,346
5039 Construction materials, nec	4	8	59	126	16	32,746	29,492	2,424	3,830
5044 Office equipment	12	11	117	97	9	22,974	23,711	2,482	2,358
5045 Computers, peripherals, & software	11	12	57	65	5	24,842	24,985	1,653	1,653
5046 Commercial equipment, nec	4	4	20	16	4	18,600	27,750	413	268
5047 Medical and hospital equipment	11	9	82	69	8	29,756	30,957	2,644	2,135
5051 Metals service centers and offices	-	7	-	95	14	-	24,800	-	2,344
5063 Electrical apparatus and equipment	11	10	109	91	9	34,532	40,264	3,551	3,462
5064 Electrical appliances, TV & radios	3	4	10	11	3	23,200	29,091	274	378
5065 Electronic parts and equipment	11	13	91	94	7	29,451	31,064	2,874	3,072
5072 Hardware	8	8	55	51	6	23,564	25,098	1,509	1,394
5074 Plumbing & hydronic heating supplies	8	8	102	126	16	32,863	33,048	3,841	4,765
5075 Warm air heating & air conditioning	3	3	51	28	9	30,824	21,000	1,616	484

Continued on next page.

MODESTO, CA MSA - [continued]

Wholesale and Retail Trade USA	Establishments		Employment		Emp / Est	Pay / Employee		Annual Payroll ($ 000)	
	1994	1995	1994	1995	1995	1994	1995	1994	1995
5078 Refrigeration equipment and supplies	4	5	15	20	4	25,867	23,800	465	603
5083 Farm and garden machinery	30	31	368	372	12	24,293	26,817	10,111	10,875
5084 Industrial machinery and equipment	22	23	191	198	9	29,277	30,606	5,750	6,182
5085 Industrial supplies	23	21	183	201	10	26,820	30,826	5,493	6,333
5087 Service establishment equipment	13	13	83	93	7	22,747	23,484	2,242	2,456
5093 Scrap and waste materials	9	10	195	192	19	24,349	25,417	5,186	5,127
5094 Jewelry & precious stones	4	-	28	-	-	17,286	-	486	-
5099 Durable goods, nec	9	9	52	70	8	18,000	16,514	1,018	1,204
5112 Stationery and office supplies	8	6	94	88	15	15,617	15,682	1,407	1,236
5113 Industrial & personal service paper	7	8	42	39	5	21,048	21,436	1,052	1,052
5120 Drugs, proprietaries, and sundries	7	7	113	118	17	21,345	24,407	2,824	3,182
5141 Groceries, general line	7	6	445	443	74	36,881	34,718	16,978	15,727
5143 Dairy products, exc. dried or canned	-	3	-	28	9	-	16,000	-	537
5144 Poultry and poultry products	5	7	87	97	14	25,333	27,175	2,395	2,600
5145 Confectionery	11	7	256	90	13	24,063	20,311	6,190	1,744
5147 Meats and meat products	14	14	131	165	12	22,901	20,824	3,558	2,872
5148 Fresh fruits and vegetables	6	-	276	-	-	15,696	-	5,994	-
5149 Groceries and related products, nec	19	20	375	327	16	26,795	30,434	10,964	11,429
5153 Grain and field beans	7	8	100	79	10	17,080	19,646	1,928	1,670
5154 Livestock	6	6	55	54	9	8,218	7,630	453	420
5159 Farm-product raw materials, nec	4	5	58	57	11	22,621	23,579	1,244	1,289
5160 Chemicals and allied products	12	13	99	97	7	28,970	31,546	3,178	3,607
5171 Petroleum bulk stations & terminals	19	18	232	233	13	22,017	22,781	5,665	6,056
5172 Petroleum products, nec	3	3	40	41	14	26,700	27,805	1,070	1,061
5181 Beer and ale	4	4	101	106	27	31,762	30,981	3,767	3,697
5182 Wine and distilled beverages	4	3	139	138	46	29,986	33,623	4,570	4,769
5191 Farm supplies	46	46	633	678	15	28,215	29,617	20,058	18,996
5199 Nondurable goods, nec	18	14	87	82	6	16,368	20,195	1,530	1,714
52 – Retail trade	1,923	1,922	24,981	25,458	13	13,430	13,805	358,134	367,613
5210 Lumber and other building materials	29	29	631	602	21	18,491	20,924	13,060	12,338
5230 Paint, glass, and wallpaper stores	18	18	92	90	5	22,870	21,644	2,159	2,077
5250 Hardware stores	23	21	295	253	12	14,034	13,296	4,507	3,468
5260 Retail nurseries and garden stores	17	17	121	110	6	13,223	14,073	1,464	1,630
5270 Mobile home dealers	3	3	23	7	2	6,435	20,571	137	127
5310 Department stores	16	16	2,632	2,751	172	10,892	11,889	32,115	32,699
5330 Variety stores	14	7	90	73	10	8,222	7,068	705	604
5390 Misc. general merchandise stores	13	15	872	882	59	13,083	15,755	13,053	14,334
5410 Grocery stores	172	175	3,129	3,076	18	18,237	18,740	59,460	59,949
5420 Meat and fish markets	10	9	38	47	5	9,789	9,702	416	510
5430 Fruit and vegetable markets	4	4	17	19	5	7,765	6,737	162	173
5440 Candy, nut, and confectionery stores	8	7	36	31	4	11,222	20,516	571	716
5460 Retail bakeries	45	39	302	152	4	10,940	7,500	3,204	1,094
5490 Miscellaneous food stores	12	10	41	51	5	8,098	7,373	389	412
5510 New and used car dealers	31	33	1,063	1,109	34	31,895	32,646	35,863	38,003
5520 Used car dealers	30	29	119	155	5	25,681	24,852	3,410	4,427
5530 Auto and home supply stores	65	68	505	559	8	16,784	16,687	9,382	10,123
5540 Gasoline service stations	102	95	908	855	9	9,837	10,157	9,139	8,954
5550 Boat dealers	4	4	19	26	7	15,579	17,077	704	782
5560 Recreational vehicle dealers	3	-	94	-	-	26,340	-	2,855	-
5570 Motorcycle dealers	7	8	53	59	7	17,509	17,220	1,074	1,111
5610 Men's & boys' clothing stores	15	16	92	97	6	12,130	14,309	1,300	1,338
5620 Women's clothing stores	46	42	450	335	8	8,720	8,657	4,251	2,820
5630 Women's accessory & specialty stores	4	3	24	25	8	11,000	11,040	275	281
5640 Children's and infants' wear stores	6	7	42	54	8	7,143	6,593	342	398
5650 Family clothing stores	22	21	207	220	10	10,280	10,691	2,462	2,479
5660 Shoe stores	44	44	248	204	5	9,565	11,098	2,344	2,302
5690 Misc. apparel & accessory stores	12	8	51	53	7	9,569	8,755	516	507
5712 Furniture stores	53	51	415	373	7	19,364	19,442	8,217	7,765
5713 Floor covering stores	28	26	138	123	5	20,725	24,033	3,070	3,188
5714 Drapery and upholstery stores	5	6	21	20	3	10,857	12,200	270	252
5719 Misc. homefurnishings stores	11	13	98	87	7	10,000	10,759	1,216	1,295
5720 Household appliance stores	8	9	80	79	9	17,150	18,481	1,506	1,318
5731 Radio, TV, & electronic stores	17	19	195	213	11	22,318	21,221	4,473	4,949
5734 Computer and software stores	8	8	30	51	6	12,533	13,647	447	716
5735 Record & prerecorded tape stores	16	14	113	114	8	8,991	10,070	1,096	1,005
5736 Musical instrument stores	6	6	29	29	5	9,379	10,759	292	315
5812 Eating places	510	474	7,688	8,055	17	7,327	7,559	59,929	62,237
5813 Drinking places	52	46	305	284	6	7,554	7,310	2,183	2,021
5910 Drug stores and proprietary stores	53	51	1,081	1,159	23	19,463	19,413	21,630	22,772
5920 Liquor stores	29	31	114	133	4	8,035	8,060	1,041	1,109
5930 Used merchandise stores	26	26	151	118	5	10,331	11,424	1,692	1,417

Continued on next page.

MODESTO, CA MSA - [continued]

Wholesale and Retail Trade USA	Establishments		Employment		Emp / Est	Pay / Employee		Annual Payroll ($ 000)	
	1994	1995	1994	1995	1995	1994	1995	1994	1995
5941 Sporting goods and bicycle shops	35	33	306	341	10	9,699	8,950	3,304	3,496
5942 Book stores	16	11	94	70	6	10,851	8,686	1,029	682
5943 Stationery stores	7	9	87	105	12	18,069	16,305	1,606	1,716
5944 Jewelry stores	34	30	181	155	5	19,580	21,987	3,700	3,058
5945 Hobby, toy, and game shops	10	11	166	161	15	8,988	8,671	1,879	1,818
5947 Gift, novelty, and souvenir shops	23	21	123	131	6	9,431	9,160	1,388	1,317
5949 Sewing, needlework, and piece goods	-	9	-	93	10	-	13,118	-	1,460
5961 Catalog and mail-order houses	5	-	37	-	-	10,919	-	569	-
5962 Merchandising machine operators	5	-	85	-	-	24,471	-	2,294	-
5963 Direct selling establishments	23	22	134	116	5	16,388	18,621	2,269	2,381
5984 Liquefied petroleum gas dealers	-	4	-	27	7	-	17,778	-	509
5989 Fuel dealers, nec	4	-	8	-	-	16,500	-	89	-
5992 Florists	35	35	140	163	5	8,886	8,663	1,327	1,385
5999 Miscellaneous retail stores, nec	62	68	363	395	6	14,810	16,152	6,111	7,006

Source: County Business Patterns 1994/95, CBP-94/95, U.S. Department of Commerce, Washington DC, November 1997. The employment column represents mid-March employment in the year. Pay per employee is calculated by dividing 1st Quarter payroll, annualized, by mid-March employment. The column headed 'Emp / Est' shows 'employees per establishment'. A dash (-) means that data are unavailable or cannot be calculated. nec means not elsewhere classified. *Notes:* 1. 1994 data incomplete; unavailable or withheld. 2. 1995 data incomplete; unavailable or withheld. 3. 1994 and 1995 data incomplete; unavailable or withheld.

MONMOUTH - OCEAN, NJ PMSA

Wholesale and Retail Trade USA	Establishments		Employment		Emp / Est	Pay / Employee		Annual Payroll ($ 000)	
	1994	1995	1994	1995	1995	1994	1995	1994	1995
50- Wholesale trade	1,687	1,740	13,658	14,670	8	34,631	35,228	508,272	550,237
5012 Automobiles and other vehicles	31	32	179	201	6	26,503	28,358	6,517	6,171
5013 Motor vehicle supplies and new parts	92	79	837	860	11	23,001	24,958	21,572	22,133
5014 Tires and tubes[3]	7	4	39	39	10	19,590	22,769	934	871
5015 Motor vehicle parts, used	17	22	88	135	6	22,455	20,296	2,311	3,153
5021 Furniture	20	21	59	66	3	33,559	38,000	2,443	2,599
5023 Homefurnishings	33	31	435	477	15	37,177	30,281	17,006	17,109
5031 Lumber, plywood, and millwork	16	23	158	250	11	32,278	31,040	5,722	10,370
5032 Brick, stone, & related materials	17	15	61	38	3	19,344	28,105	1,764	1,418
5033 Roofing, siding, & insulation	12	14	162	173	12	33,531	35,954	6,202	6,910
5039 Construction materials, nec	18	20	85	128	6	27,059	32,188	2,482	3,550
5044 Office equipment	18	16	131	157	10	23,511	25,325	3,523	4,694
5045 Computers, peripherals, & software	77	82	447	464	6	41,217	43,336	20,320	20,373
5046 Commercial equipment, nec	22	22	95	110	5	20,295	26,691	3,079	3,701
5047 Medical and hospital equipment	52	51	440	457	9	34,464	33,917	16,569	16,469
5049 Professional equipment, nec	7	9	38	55	6	33,158	38,400	1,288	2,261
5051 Metals service centers and offices	29	30	61	65	2	32,393	35,569	2,405	2,692
5063 Electrical apparatus and equipment	64	53	492	403	8	34,585	42,918	18,794	18,049
5064 Electrical appliances, TV & radios	12	11	133	99	9	40,150	47,354	5,589	4,738
5065 Electronic parts and equipment	73	79	666	563	7	43,105	46,046	23,060	25,273
5072 Hardware	24	27	104	110	4	37,462	35,709	5,343	5,381
5074 Plumbing & hydronic heating supplies	34	34	357	390	11	28,459	31,067	11,617	13,017
5075 Warm air heating & air conditioning	17	16	83	87	5	35,373	39,494	3,811	4,434
5082 Construction and mining machinery	8	9	126	124	14	39,206	37,032	4,604	4,945
5083 Farm and garden machinery	4	-	7	-	-	37,143	-	469	-
5084 Industrial machinery and equipment	69	76	587	576	8	34,787	36,007	21,337	22,664
5085 Industrial supplies	46	41	261	246	6	29,088	29,821	8,855	8,518
5087 Service establishment equipment	22	24	131	144	6	20,641	26,250	3,378	4,097
5088 Transportation equipment & supplies	19	20	78	127	6	36,308	31,874	4,218	5,571
5091 Sporting & recreational goods	15	14	86	110	8	19,395	20,400	1,702	2,749
5092 Toys and hobby goods and supplies	15	16	102	117	7	22,902	24,000	2,445	3,270
5093 Scrap and waste materials	29	29	253	276	10	25,375	25,609	8,648	8,401
5094 Jewelry & precious stones	21	21	100	110	5	33,680	31,309	4,164	3,906
5099 Durable goods, nec	37	37	155	134	4	33,574	37,493	6,725	6,995
5111 Printing and writing paper[1]	8	-	31	-	-	38,452	-	819	-
5112 Stationery and office supplies[2]	40	34	316	165	5	22,532	29,406	7,703	5,639
5113 Industrial & personal service paper	33	35	141	167	5	34,950	30,778	6,456	6,827
5120 Drugs, proprietaries, and sundries	37	42	776	1,218	29	30,180	27,189	24,486	39,867
5131 Piece goods & notions	36	37	109	106	3	32,881	34,642	5,390	5,412
5136 Men's and boys' clothing	22	18	86	125	7	19,535	21,888	1,993	2,159
5137 Women's and children's clothing	30	27	94	101	4	28,043	28,911	3,253	3,144
5139 Footwear[3]	6	5	22	33	7	53,273	39,758	1,144	1,383
5141 Groceries, general line	-	16	-	92	6	-	14,087	-	1,581
5142 Packaged frozen food	16	16	112	87	5	17,393	24,276	2,898	2,963
5143 Dairy products, exc. dried or canned	12	14	158	163	12	22,076	24,957	4,040	4,655
5144 Poultry and poultry products	7	7	31	46	7	20,258	31,391	668	1,960

Continued on next page.

MONMOUTH – OCEAN, NJ PMSA - [continued]

Wholesale and Retail Trade USA	Establishments		Employment		Emp / Est	Pay / Employee		Annual Payroll ($ 000)	
	1994	1995	1994	1995	1995	1994	1995	1994	1995
5145 Confectionery[2]	6	6	74	80	13	19,622	22,100	1,542	1,798
5146 Fish and seafoods	23	21	137	184	9	15,971	17,304	2,763	3,477
5147 Meats and meat products	23	23	108	118	5	22,593	25,153	2,959	3,121
5148 Fresh fruits and vegetables	20	20	58	141	7	35,793	32,965	3,029	3,936
5149 Groceries and related products, nec	80	76	936	923	12	29,338	25,907	31,978	26,227
5162 Plastics materials & basic shapes	18	20	62	60	3	37,613	49,733	2,917	3,115
5169 Chemicals & allied products, nec	48	56	163	179	3	47,681	49,631	8,441	9,194
5171 Petroleum bulk stations & terminals[3]	9	8	105	164	21	109,410	32,098	7,300	6,333
5181 Beer and ale[3]	3	3	237	247	82	44,878	39,870	14,887	13,587
5191 Farm supplies	26	20	349	177	9	20,997	22,780	8,635	3,898
5192 Books, periodicals, & newspapers	9	13	71	94	7	25,183	25,872	2,152	2,497
5193 Flowers & florists' supplies	18	15	171	211	14	10,363	25,251	1,764	5,905
5198 Paints, varnishes, and supplies	6	4	14	15	4	27,143	28,267	347	468
5199 Nondurable goods, nec	62	68	165	296	4	27,515	23,554	5,433	8,473
52 – Retail trade	6,705	6,781	74,986	80,338	12	13,418	14,337	1,162,520	1,246,957
5210 Lumber and other building materials	98	90	1,415	1,807	20	22,505	23,134	41,888	44,313
5230 Paint, glass, and wallpaper stores	47	43	252	266	6	22,889	23,820	6,858	6,901
5250 Hardware stores	52	39	218	176	5	16,275	15,318	3,787	2,923
5260 Retail nurseries and garden stores	62	66	407	474	7	13,769	14,439	7,614	8,025
5310 Department stores	36	38	6,042	6,166	162	11,633	13,216	79,589	85,608
5330 Variety stores	38	39	418	397	10	10,402	9,935	4,520	4,371
5390 Misc. general merchandise stores	42	44	1,367	1,576	36	12,609	14,873	20,815	24,823
5410 Grocery stores	523	534	13,292	12,726	24	14,509	15,954	206,458	211,320
5420 Meat and fish markets	56	56	175	180	3	11,634	11,311	2,579	2,652
5430 Fruit and vegetable markets	22	22	127	132	6	12,252	13,152	2,476	2,757
5440 Candy, nut, and confectionery stores	21	24	129	154	6	8,682	9,948	1,563	1,787
5450 Dairy products stores	14	15	101	45	3	8,594	12,178	1,095	747
5460 Retail bakeries	146	147	1,248	1,439	10	11,487	10,941	16,382	16,674
5490 Miscellaneous food stores	49	50	200	230	5	11,440	12,278	2,604	3,134
5510 New and used car dealers	102	102	3,943	4,098	40	29,797	32,752	140,942	148,261
5520 Used car dealers	31	36	84	106	3	21,190	21,547	2,049	2,476
5530 Auto and home supply stores	126	123	925	957	8	19,814	21,250	20,213	20,538
5540 Gasoline service stations	391	400	2,594	2,605	7	11,944	12,674	33,539	33,404
5550 Boat dealers	64	64	339	352	6	19,316	19,739	8,427	9,058
5560 Recreational vehicle dealers	7	7	34	41	6	19,294	23,220	908	1,075
5570 Motorcycle dealers	8	8	38	47	6	18,105	17,447	818	1,099
5610 Men's & boys' clothing stores	73	61	608	501	8	13,211	12,814	8,902	6,803
5620 Women's clothing stores	219	198	2,320	2,105	11	8,636	8,454	23,001	19,414
5630 Women's accessory & specialty stores	36	32	216	220	7	10,519	11,127	2,426	2,551
5640 Children's and infants' wear stores	37	38	345	358	9	7,026	7,475	2,808	2,889
5650 Family clothing stores	86	83	1,969	1,971	24	10,631	11,310	24,338	24,560
5660 Shoe stores	169	150	866	890	6	10,808	11,317	9,977	10,181
5690 Misc. apparel & accessory stores	53	61	215	279	5	11,721	10,724	3,131	3,442
5712 Furniture stores	151	156	905	1,045	7	20,743	21,558	21,287	23,949
5713 Floor covering stores	88	92	296	331	4	20,568	21,450	7,290	7,559
5714 Drapery and upholstery stores	19	15	112	98	7	13,000	12,286	1,316	1,309
5719 Misc. homefurnishings stores	107	98	647	656	7	12,773	13,348	8,999	9,015
5720 Household appliance stores	35	36	326	415	12	17,301	14,843	6,712	6,827
5731 Radio, TV, & electronic stores	53	53	393	430	8	15,186	14,884	6,187	6,496
5734 Computer and software stores	35	40	289	308	8	23,197	24,325	6,835	8,219
5735 Record & prerecorded tape stores	30	34	182	180	5	10,132	11,556	2,025	2,165
5736 Musical instrument stores	14	13	71	78	6	16,282	17,436	1,230	1,380
5812 Eating places	1,638	1,585	19,332	21,290	13	8,668	8,970	211,636	220,488
5813 Drinking places	156	150	1,194	1,256	8	7,960	10,392	12,137	13,651
5910 Drug stores and proprietary stores	211	220	2,994	3,187	14	14,683	14,808	45,848	48,714
5920 Liquor stores	194	187	1,177	1,285	7	11,691	11,443	15,823	16,022
5930 Used merchandise stores	47	48	174	136	3	10,851	10,618	2,127	1,629
5941 Sporting goods and bicycle shops	101	107	477	504	5	11,950	12,571	7,659	8,258
5942 Book stores	48	42	225	278	7	9,564	10,331	2,305	2,860
5943 Stationery stores	19	22	165	228	10	13,988	14,526	2,391	3,456
5944 Jewelry stores	113	116	469	492	4	16,077	17,886	8,277	9,476
5945 Hobby, toy, and game shops	52	56	633	647	12	9,896	11,023	7,680	8,500
5946 Camera & photographic supply stores	17	16	38	39	2	14,526	17,026	595	641
5947 Gift, novelty, and souvenir shops	160	151	748	686	5	9,369	10,128	8,468	8,292
5948 Luggage and leather goods stores	8	8	38	52	7	8,842	12,462	385	616
5949 Sewing, needlework, and piece goods	21	20	162	203	10	7,827	6,562	1,306	1,423
5961 Catalog and mail-order houses[2]	25	33	298	287	9	22,309	21,631	7,161	7,165
5962 Merchandising machine operators	15	15	74	69	5	16,811	18,841	1,367	1,301
5963 Direct selling establishments	52	49	304	223	5	16,553	17,740	6,080	4,471
5983 Fuel oil dealers	38	35	409	429	12	33,976	31,888	13,389	13,163
5984 Liquefied petroleum gas dealers	11	9	48	41	5	33,250	37,463	1,444	1,539

Continued on next page.

MONMOUTH - OCEAN, NJ PMSA - [continued]

Wholesale and Retail Trade USA	Establishments		Employment		Emp / Est	Pay / Employee		Annual Payroll ($ 000)	
	1994	1995	1994	1995	1995	1994	1995	1994	1995
5992 Florists	131	125	475	492	4	11,722	11,943	6,056	6,458
5993 Tobacco stores and stands	8	7	15	13	2	13,600	14,462	188	161
5994 News dealers and newsstands	7	6	19	14	2	9,053	10,857	205	154
5995 Optical goods stores	76	77	395	337	4	18,592	20,297	8,014	6,480
5999 Miscellaneous retail stores, nec	215	229	912	1,054	5	15,123	16,209	16,063	19,087

Source: County Business Patterns 1994/95, CBP-94/95, U.S. Department of Commerce, Washington DC, November 1997. The employment column represents mid-March employment in the year. Pay per employee is calculated by dividing 1st Quarter payroll, annualized, by mid-March employment. The column headed 'Emp / Est' shows 'employees per establishment'. A dash (-) means that data are unavailable or cannot be calculated. nec means not elsewhere classified. *Notes:* 1. 1994 data incomplete; unavailable or withheld. 2. 1995 data incomplete; unavailable or withheld. 3. 1994 and 1995 data incomplete; unavailable or withheld.

MONROE, LA MSA

Wholesale and Retail Trade USA	Establishments		Employment		Emp / Est	Pay / Employee		Annual Payroll ($ 000)	
	1994	1995	1994	1995	1995	1994	1995	1994	1995
50- Wholesale trade	282	289	3,128	3,404	12	22,798	23,570	78,419	87,290
5012 Automobiles and other vehicles	6	9	75	91	10	25,227	27,824	1,869	2,436
5013 Motor vehicle supplies and new parts	25	25	313	261	10	19,859	20,398	6,672	5,454
5014 Tires and tubes	-	3	-	19	6	-	25,263	-	502
5015 Motor vehicle parts, used	-	6	-	99	17	-	22,263	-	2,294
5031 Lumber, plywood, and millwork	5	6	81	133	22	29,926	27,850	2,746	3,944
5033 Roofing, siding, & insulation	5	-	83	-	-	18,699	-	2,009	-
5039 Construction materials, nec	-	4	-	56	14	-	16,071	-	989
5044 Office equipment	10	8	110	133	17	18,291	18,316	2,265	2,602
5045 Computers, peripherals, & software	7	7	34	38	5	38,824	32,947	1,224	1,208
5046 Commercial equipment, nec	3	3	7	9	3	26,857	24,889	192	206
5047 Medical and hospital equipment	4	3	33	35	12	31,879	25,371	1,213	990
5051 Metals service centers and offices	7	7	79	95	14	24,456	25,895	2,352	2,711
5063 Electrical apparatus and equipment	9	11	113	142	13	28,991	29,746	3,753	4,734
5065 Electronic parts and equipment	-	10	-	84	8	-	27,095	-	2,105
5072 Hardware	4	4	49	56	14	19,755	19,714	1,011	1,038
5074 Plumbing & hydronic heating supplies	3	5	33	40	8	32,727	18,400	899	1,014
5082 Construction and mining machinery	5	5	206	247	49	27,359	28,826	6,520	7,532
5083 Farm and garden machinery	7	7	106	116	17	28,453	29,207	2,813	3,189
5084 Industrial machinery and equipment	10	9	55	75	8	23,055	19,840	1,495	1,748
5085 Industrial supplies	14	14	210	230	16	21,867	23,704	5,317	5,951
5093 Scrap and waste materials	4	5	53	55	11	16,679	20,873	1,002	1,316
5099 Durable goods, nec	6	6	38	56	9	19,474	17,643	1,006	1,194
5112 Stationery and office supplies	4	6	87	65	11	24,046	29,969	2,474	2,682
5120 Drugs, proprietaries, and sundries	4	4	136	119	30	18,853	21,479	2,492	2,407
5143 Dairy products, exc. dried or canned	6	7	34	34	5	10,000	12,000	341	408
5145 Confectionery	3	3	16	21	7	17,500	20,571	292	502
5149 Groceries and related products, nec	10	8	50	69	9	21,120	19,884	1,325	1,394
5162 Plastics materials & basic shapes	5	5	31	34	7	48,129	46,824	1,530	1,712
5169 Chemicals & allied products, nec	10	11	55	62	6	27,491	27,613	1,541	1,756
5171 Petroleum bulk stations & terminals	8	7	111	107	15	25,658	25,458	4,082	3,801
5172 Petroleum products, nec	4	4	8	8	2	20,500	17,500	209	210
5181 Beer and ale	6	6	210	209	35	21,657	21,990	4,486	5,143
5182 Wine and distilled beverages	3	4	47	50	13	29,106	30,720	1,224	1,377
5191 Farm supplies	7	7	120	114	16	22,467	21,509	3,325	3,365
5199 Nondurable goods, nec	3	3	10	10	3	16,800	17,600	166	165
52- Retail trade	963	971	12,909	13,996	14	10,792	11,546	152,385	174,675
5210 Lumber and other building materials	21	20	269	397	20	13,993	17,854	4,740	8,272
5230 Paint, glass, and wallpaper stores	7	6	59	53	9	16,407	15,094	1,195	958
5250 Hardware stores	6	3	40	33	11	15,000	15,273	676	455
5260 Retail nurseries and garden stores	14	12	55	44	4	7,927	10,182	507	475
5270 Mobile home dealers	4	8	36	48	6	16,889	18,000	667	1,433
5310 Department stores	10	9	1,728	1,520	169	11,120	12,574	18,876	20,980
5330 Variety stores	10	9	65	51	6	8,615	7,922	608	434
5390 Misc. general merchandise stores	8	12	286	324	27	11,259	12,617	3,438	3,689
5410 Grocery stores	93	96	1,251	1,701	18	11,357	11,243	17,947	20,049
5440 Candy, nut, and confectionery stores	3	-	19	-	-	7,368	-	147	-
5460 Retail bakeries	8	10	49	52	5	7,592	7,538	362	500
5490 Miscellaneous food stores	6	6	16	19	3	7,750	9,474	164	206
5510 New and used car dealers	10	12	661	785	65	26,064	28,504	18,886	25,299
5520 Used car dealers	23	18	101	74	4	16,040	14,649	1,493	1,017
5530 Auto and home supply stores	30	30	210	208	7	15,410	16,904	3,537	3,814
5540 Gasoline service stations	58	58	599	556	10	8,227	8,216	5,351	5,504
5550 Boat dealers	3	3	6	17	6	10,667	16,235	216	308
5560 Recreational vehicle dealers	5	4	28	24	6	15,429	17,667	501	465

Continued on next page.

MONROE, LA MSA - [continued]

Wholesale and Retail Trade USA	Establishments		Employment		Emp / Est	Pay / Employee		Annual Payroll ($ 000)	
	1994	1995	1994	1995	1995	1994	1995	1994	1995
5610 Men's & boys' clothing stores	11	11	109	123	11	10,752	11,187	1,125	1,273
5620 Women's clothing stores	41	37	348	346	9	6,667	6,497	2,540	2,367
5630 Women's accessory & specialty stores	6	6	32	31	5	8,750	8,903	287	297
5640 Children's and infants' wear stores	8	5	36	26	5	8,111	6,462	298	207
5650 Family clothing stores	9	7	101	110	16	8,752	6,545	880	893
5660 Shoe stores	28	28	169	174	6	10,627	11,333	1,746	2,142
5690 Misc. apparel & accessory stores	11	13	47	75	6	9,617	9,547	589	704
5712 Furniture stores	24	26	215	239	9	14,381	12,854	3,393	2,676
5713 Floor covering stores	13	12	56	68	6	13,500	15,412	830	1,198
5720 Household appliance stores	7	8	77	75	9	13,039	14,133	1,237	1,275
5731 Radio, TV, & electronic stores	13	10	126	124	12	15,587	17,097	1,995	1,927
5735 Record & prerecorded tape stores	5	4	20	34	9	9,400	7,294	222	251
5812 Eating places	177	174	4,158	4,219	24	6,868	7,233	30,403	32,230
5813 Drinking places	21	18	148	151	8	6,054	5,960	868	852
5910 Drug stores and proprietary stores	46	42	429	454	11	12,765	13,965	5,959	6,300
5920 Liquor stores	7	5	15	14	3	8,533	8,857	203	200
5930 Used merchandise stores	21	21	65	70	3	7,262	7,943	505	603
5941 Sporting goods and bicycle shops	15	14	77	75	5	9,195	11,627	862	897
5942 Book stores	6	8	35	39	5	8,800	7,692	292	357
5943 Stationery stores	6	6	87	88	15	17,609	19,409	1,751	1,692
5944 Jewelry stores	19	23	115	131	6	21,357	17,466	1,975	2,192
5945 Hobby, toy, and game shops	3	4	75	136	34	7,947	5,059	798	979
5947 Gift, novelty, and souvenir shops	19	19	95	93	5	6,400	7,054	718	699
5949 Sewing, needlework, and piece goods	5	4	29	29	7	9,103	8,966	257	257
5961 Catalog and mail-order houses	-	4	-	61	15	-	19,607	-	1,279
5962 Merchandising machine operators	-	4	-	33	8	-	18,061	-	578
5963 Direct selling establishments	10	9	73	61	7	14,575	13,967	980	737
5992 Florists	12	12	51	45	4	14,745	11,378	801	571
5995 Optical goods stores	-	7	-	47	7	-	12,596	-	554
5999 Miscellaneous retail stores, nec	29	35	112	158	5	8,857	10,051	1,308	1,754

Source: County Business Patterns 1994/95, CBP-94/95, U.S. Department of Commerce, Washington DC, November 1997. The employment column represents mid-March employment in the year. Pay per employee is calculated by dividing 1st Quarter payroll, annualized, by mid-March employment. The column headed 'Emp / Est' shows 'employees per establishment'. A dash (-) means that data are unavailable or cannot be calculated. nec means not elsewhere classified. *Notes:* 1. 1994 data incomplete; unavailable or withheld. 2. 1995 data incomplete; unavailable or withheld. 3. 1994 and 1995 data incomplete; unavailable or withheld.

MONTGOMERY, AL MSA

Wholesale and Retail Trade USA	Establishments		Employment		Emp / Est	Pay / Employee		Annual Payroll ($ 000)	
	1994	1995	1994	1995	1995	1994	1995	1994	1995
50 - Wholesale trade	553	547	7,032	7,032	13	24,453	25,670	187,614	188,930
5012 Automobiles and other vehicles [3]	16	16	179	200	13	23,441	23,560	4,538	4,477
5013 Motor vehicle supplies and new parts	39	38	323	319	8	19,307	16,702	6,647	5,288
5014 Tires and tubes [3]	8	6	74	74	12	28,162	27,081	2,109	2,026
5015 Motor vehicle parts, used [3]	10	10	42	42	4	18,000	19,714	799	863
5021 Furniture [3]	7	6	38	26	4	25,684	25,538	1,006	657
5023 Homefurnishings [3]	7	8	41	26	3	21,268	26,000	811	699
5031 Lumber, plywood, and millwork [1]	16	18	190	170	9	22,653	25,835	5,203	4,856
5033 Roofing, siding, & insulation [2]	-	3	-	12	4	-	25,333	-	309
5044 Office equipment [3]	18	18	261	238	13	21,410	27,143	6,009	6,725
5045 Computers, peripherals, & software [3]	17	22	245	268	12	48,327	53,597	11,097	12,028
5046 Commercial equipment, nec [3]	7	7	77	71	10	20,312	24,901	1,806	2,109
5047 Medical and hospital equipment [3]	10	9	50	38	4	21,120	20,947	1,132	850
5048 Ophthalmic goods [3]	4	4	41	36	9	19,805	22,556	875	867
5050 Metals and minerals, except petroleum [3]	9	11	198	213	19	24,747	27,643	5,517	6,213
5063 Electrical apparatus and equipment [3]	18	16	183	176	11	25,377	31,273	5,223	5,817
5072 Hardware [3]	12	14	103	100	7	25,320	27,080	3,056	2,930
5074 Plumbing & hydronic heating supplies [3]	10	8	104	94	12	22,308	24,766	2,659	2,434
5075 Warm air heating & air conditioning [3]	10	9	100	106	12	29,520	29,736	2,952	3,105
5078 Refrigeration equipment and supplies [3]	3	3	19	18	6	26,105	32,444	446	479
5082 Construction and mining machinery [3]	11	11	205	218	20	31,883	34,220	6,831	7,773
5083 Farm and garden machinery [1]	11	11	89	89	8	22,382	20,494	2,290	2,104
5084 Industrial machinery and equipment [3]	14	14	104	123	9	23,692	22,341	2,902	3,333
5085 Industrial supplies	22	21	165	164	8	32,388	34,878	5,486	5,760
5087 Service establishment equipment	15	15	100	106	7	23,440	26,189	3,446	3,073
5091 Sporting & recreational goods [1]	6	-	29	-	-	19,034	-	623	-
5093 Scrap and waste materials [2]	14	12	139	152	13	18,273	21,658	3,040	3,442
5099 Durable goods, nec	-	19	-	110	6	-	23,673	-	3,252
5112 Stationery and office supplies [3]	15	13	140	137	11	24,514	22,745	3,878	2,919
5120 Drugs, proprietaries, and sundries [3]	8	10	245	213	21	28,571	30,141	8,356	7,930

Continued on next page.

MONTGOMERY, AL MSA - [continued]

Wholesale and Retail Trade USA	Establishments		Employment		Emp / Est	Pay / Employee		Annual Payroll ($ 000)	
	1994	1995	1994	1995	1995	1994	1995	1994	1995
5136 Men's and boys' clothing[3]	3	3	19	47	16	22,316	8,936	334	614
5141 Groceries, general line[2]	-	6	-	96	16	-	19,792	-	1,700
5148 Fresh fruits and vegetables[3]	6	7	64	53	8	13,563	13,660	717	572
5149 Groceries and related products, nec	19	18	399	415	23	21,714	23,586	9,752	10,286
5159 Farm-product raw materials, nec	12	9	77	69	8	27,584	31,652	3,448	3,372
5169 Chemicals & allied products, nec[3]	7	9	34	88	10	29,176	27,727	1,061	2,378
5171 Petroleum bulk stations & terminals[3]	12	9	125	67	7	27,808	31,881	3,564	2,068
5172 Petroleum products, nec[3]	8	6	53	42	7	23,094	26,381	1,371	1,301
5180 Beer, wine, and distilled beverages[3]	5	5	262	287	57	20,870	21,017	6,158	6,502
5191 Farm supplies	15	13	113	105	8	18,726	21,638	2,286	2,324
5192 Books, periodicals, & newspapers[3]	4	3	75	4	1	17,013	34,000	990	159
5198 Paints, varnishes, and supplies[3]	6	4	24	17	4	28,000	24,471	603	440
5199 Nondurable goods, nec[3]	13	13	136	127	10	13,118	12,913	1,860	1,659
52 – Retail trade	1,872	1,887	27,195	28,191	15	11,302	11,698	328,533	342,543
5210 Lumber and other building materials	39	37	660	586	16	18,158	18,710	10,954	11,063
5230 Paint, glass, and wallpaper stores[3]	21	22	89	78	4	20,674	25,590	1,865	1,929
5250 Hardware stores	17	12	91	78	7	13,363	12,410	1,296	1,045
5260 Retail nurseries and garden stores	9	10	35	47	5	13,943	11,489	579	635
5270 Mobile home dealers	11	11	26	27	2	17,846	21,926	621	775
5310 Department stores[3]	13	13	2,008	2,101	162	11,319	13,974	24,539	30,350
5330 Variety stores	18	18	125	112	6	8,000	8,286	1,044	1,025
5390 Misc. general merchandise stores	14	15	281	333	22	13,281	12,637	4,196	4,211
5410 Grocery stores[2]	174	159	4,010	3,185	20	8,740	9,182	36,982	30,904
5420 Meat and fish markets	9	10	8	10	1	24,000	12,400	203	123
5460 Retail bakeries[3]	11	11	74	77	7	6,054	6,026	451	474
5490 Miscellaneous food stores[3]	9	9	41	52	6	8,683	13,154	434	741
5510 New and used car dealers	23	22	1,236	1,298	59	27,657	29,840	37,236	39,255
5520 Used car dealers	41	40	163	171	4	17,840	20,257	3,629	3,536
5530 Auto and home supply stores	71	71	533	713	10	16,495	18,799	9,373	13,752
5540 Gasoline service stations	185	186	1,252	1,278	7	10,578	11,252	14,070	15,747
5550 Boat dealers[3]	5	5	40	34	7	13,800	14,353	599	484
5560 Recreational vehicle dealers[3]	5	6	29	38	6	19,172	16,211	609	674
5570 Motorcycle dealers[3]	4	5	32	30	6	15,000	20,000	547	625
5610 Men's & boys' clothing stores[3]	19	19	124	127	7	11,484	12,378	1,522	1,620
5620 Women's clothing stores	63	57	498	480	8	8,080	7,683	4,211	3,794
5630 Women's accessory & specialty stores[3]	6	8	52	62	8	24,692	29,290	1,752	2,013
5640 Children's and infants' wear stores[3]	6	7	39	87	12	12,615	12,552	664	915
5650 Family clothing stores[3]	20	18	635	549	31	11,628	12,583	8,368	7,388
5660 Shoe stores	50	48	229	274	6	11,581	10,686	3,330	2,819
5690 Misc. apparel & accessory stores[3]	6	6	46	48	8	9,304	10,667	564	724
5712 Furniture stores	51	52	423	435	8	16,435	17,536	7,667	7,752
5713 Floor covering stores	14	19	69	101	5	18,609	20,594	1,774	2,626
5719 Misc. homefurnishings stores[2]	-	19	-	149	8	-	10,604	-	1,511
5720 Household appliance stores[3]	10	10	72	70	7	17,944	17,657	1,446	1,407
5731 Radio, TV, & electronic stores	20	22	210	244	11	17,733	16,918	4,291	3,950
5734 Computer and software stores[3]	7	8	36	26	3	20,000	13,846	987	393
5735 Record & prerecorded tape stores[3]	8	8	45	57	7	8,267	8,702	409	453
5736 Musical instrument stores[3]	4	4	28	31	8	12,714	13,161	463	505
5812 Eating places	352	339	8,501	9,180	27	7,042	6,920	63,646	66,731
5813 Drinking places	29	26	187	183	7	8,706	10,033	1,764	1,742
5910 Drug stores and proprietary stores	62	63	755	861	14	15,725	13,282	12,336	11,728
5920 Liquor stores	24	23	83	85	4	15,133	15,341	1,364	1,345
5930 Used merchandise stores	46	46	161	178	4	12,870	15,551	2,236	2,906
5941 Sporting goods and bicycle shops[1]	23	20	74	75	4	11,351	11,733	847	901
5942 Book stores[3]	20	20	138	190	10	7,623	7,642	1,126	1,351
5944 Jewelry stores	36	31	229	176	6	15,231	16,136	3,777	2,807
5945 Hobby, toy, and game shops[3]	16	16	106	116	7	8,226	7,966	1,094	1,125
5947 Gift, novelty, and souvenir shops	32	34	142	130	4	5,803	6,431	919	903
5949 Sewing, needlework, and piece goods	14	-	54	-	-	10,000	-	399	-
5961 Catalog and mail-order houses[3]	3	5	10	10	2	16,800	9,200	124	108
5962 Merchandising machine operators	11	12	72	61	5	15,278	16,525	1,077	1,142
5963 Direct selling establishments[3]	13	13	74	84	6	13,027	10,143	1,010	757
5984 Liquefied petroleum gas dealers[1]	11	12	80	66	6	20,150	27,636	1,710	1,704
5992 Florists[2]	34	33	122	41	1	9,934	7,707	1,237	318
5995 Optical goods stores	21	21	119	113	5	13,210	14,973	1,611	1,740
5999 Miscellaneous retail stores, nec	56	59	340	325	6	10,600	12,603	4,367	4,914

Source: County Business Patterns 1994/95, CBP-94/95, U.S. Department of Commerce, Washington DC, November 1997. The employment column represents mid-March employment in the year. Pay per employee is calculated by dividing 1st Quarter payroll, annualized, by mid-March employment. The column headed 'Emp / Est' shows 'employees per establishment'. A dash (-) means that data are unavailable or cannot be calculated. nec means not elsewhere classified. *Notes:* 1. 1994 data incomplete; unavailable or withheld. 2. 1995 data incomplete; unavailable or withheld. 3. 1994 and 1995 data incomplete; unavailable or withheld.

MUNCIE, IN MSA

Wholesale and Retail Trade USA	Establishments		Employment		Emp / Est	Pay / Employee		Annual Payroll ($ 000)	
	1994	1995	1994	1995	1995	1994	1995	1994	1995
50 - Wholesale trade	174	180	2,064	2,017	11	22,483	24,462	51,332	53,065
5012 Automobiles and other vehicles	9	8	167	146	18	19,305	20,274	3,122	3,357
5013 Motor vehicle supplies and new parts	13	11	279	219	20	24,559	33,553	8,143	7,959
5031 Lumber, plywood, and millwork	5	5	60	33	7	21,467	19,879	1,583	860
5044 Office equipment	8	8	129	104	13	21,054	25,577	2,970	3,056
5045 Computers, peripherals, & software	-	3	-	6	2	-	16,667	-	131
5051 Metals service centers and offices	-	4	-	99	25	-	19,677	-	1,832
5063 Electrical apparatus and equipment	9	9	66	80	9	25,273	26,350	1,677	2,255
5065 Electronic parts and equipment	8	8	30	35	4	17,867	17,829	476	730
5074 Plumbing & hydronic heating supplies	3	4	21	55	14	29,524	25,164	608	1,485
5083 Farm and garden machinery	5	5	50	50	10	34,720	34,800	1,950	1,915
5084 Industrial machinery and equipment	10	8	27	36	5	20,889	25,778	841	991
5085 Industrial supplies	9	11	52	52	5	30,077	36,308	1,629	1,771
5087 Service establishment equipment	4	4	18	19	5	20,000	22,105	372	383
5090 Miscellaneous durable goods	5	6	72	93	16	20,278	18,065	1,996	2,204
5112 Stationery and office supplies	6	-	40	-	-	19,200	-	794	-
5140 Groceries and related products	11	10	322	274	27	24,037	27,124	8,066	7,697
5153 Grain and field beans	3	3	34	39	13	24,706	23,487	993	1,119
5170 Petroleum and petroleum products	5	5	106	119	24	27,245	26,420	3,232	3,297
5191 Farm supplies	7	-	45	-	-	14,756	-	714	-
5199 Nondurable goods, nec	4	7	23	43	6	10,087	10,512	283	621
52 - Retail trade	727	745	10,964	11,677	16	10,162	11,112	119,488	135,131
5210 Lumber and other building materials	11	10	312	264	26	14,615	19,788	5,128	5,142
5250 Hardware stores	7	9	40	82	9	8,700	10,049	372	844
5260 Retail nurseries and garden stores	7	6	36	38	6	11,778	13,684	566	605
5310 Department stores	8	8	1,218	1,255	157	10,207	12,201	13,521	14,815
5410 Grocery stores	50	49	1,331	1,381	28	11,297	11,794	15,091	15,253
5440 Candy, nut, and confectionery stores	-	4	-	31	8	-	5,935	-	180
5460 Retail bakeries	4	3	34	35	12	9,529	9,829	409	398
5490 Miscellaneous food stores	3	3	14	11	4	5,143	7,273	80	85
5510 New and used car dealers	9	8	441	430	54	24,063	26,037	11,355	11,879
5520 Used car dealers	18	19	82	76	4	15,512	20,526	1,385	1,543
5530 Auto and home supply stores	27	27	271	243	9	13,122	18,765	4,269	4,498
5540 Gasoline service stations	51	51	627	529	10	8,466	9,905	5,896	5,475
5610 Men's & boys' clothing stores	5	8	18	81	10	10,667	6,667	189	518
5620 Women's clothing stores	23	24	223	208	9	5,848	5,731	1,425	1,346
5630 Women's accessory & specialty stores	4	3	17	14	5	7,059	8,857	133	125
5650 Family clothing stores	8	9	59	128	14	6,441	8,750	395	1,087
5660 Shoe stores	16	19	100	143	8	9,720	7,776	956	1,021
5690 Misc. apparel & accessory stores	5	4	15	28	7	4,533	6,571	103	296
5712 Furniture stores	17	16	123	141	9	14,374	15,007	2,051	2,217
5713 Floor covering stores	5	7	36	50	7	16,667	15,440	782	847
5719 Misc. homefurnishings stores	13	14	29	68	5	15,310	13,941	535	901
5720 Household appliance stores	4	-	51	-	-	23,137	-	1,233	-
5731 Radio, TV, & electronic stores	10	10	57	57	6	14,105	16,842	886	975
5734 Computer and software stores	4	3	10	12	4	17,600	18,667	104	241
5812 Eating places	160	164	4,080	4,331	26	6,276	6,833	28,126	30,923
5813 Drinking places	37	35	170	171	5	7,694	7,743	1,359	1,373
5910 Drug stores and proprietary stores	18	24	233	295	12	14,129	16,393	3,575	5,039
5920 Liquor stores	16	15	90	83	6	6,267	7,277	600	625
5930 Used merchandise stores	11	10	60	67	7	8,400	10,090	571	699
5941 Sporting goods and bicycle shops	11	11	54	59	5	7,630	8,407	529	511
5942 Book stores	8	6	76	73	12	9,579	11,068	820	890
5944 Jewelry stores	19	19	118	97	5	11,831	16,619	1,508	1,659
5945 Hobby, toy, and game shops	6	7	31	45	6	4,516	4,711	257	299
5947 Gift, novelty, and souvenir shops	21	19	122	142	7	8,623	7,775	1,107	1,020
5963 Direct selling establishments	6	6	21	21	4	14,095	14,286	346	321
5980 Fuel dealers	5	4	18	20	5	20,889	22,400	481	551
5992 Florists	12	10	56	50	5	7,071	10,160	452	489
5995 Optical goods stores	7	7	67	64	9	13,552	15,750	983	962
5999 Miscellaneous retail stores, nec	16	18	50	47	3	8,080	11,064	432	562

Source: County Business Patterns 1994/95, CBP-94/95, U.S. Department of Commerce, Washington DC, November 1997. The employment column represents mid-March employment in the year. Pay per employee is calculated by dividing 1st Quarter payroll, annualized, by mid-March employment. The column headed 'Emp / Est' shows 'employees per establishment'. A dash (-) means that data are unavailable or cannot be calculated. nec means not elsewhere classified. *Notes:* 1. 1994 data incomplete; unavailable or withheld. 2. 1995 data incomplete; unavailable or withheld. 3. 1994 and 1995 data incomplete; unavailable or withheld.

MYRTLE BEACH, SC MSA

Wholesale and Retail Trade USA	Establishments		Employment		Emp / Est	Pay / Employee		Annual Payroll ($ 000)	
	1994	1995	1994	1995	1995	1994	1995	1994	1995
50 – Wholesale trade	-	277	-	2,160	8	-	20,337	-	49,090
5013 Motor vehicle supplies and new parts	-	8	-	80	10	-	19,100	-	2,075
5020 Furniture and homefurnishings	-	5	-	27	5	-	15,407	-	436
5032 Brick, stone, & related materials	-	5	-	13	3	-	31,385	-	617
5039 Construction materials, nec	-	7	-	36	5	-	14,667	-	639
5044 Office equipment	-	8	-	54	7	-	16,074	-	1,156
5045 Computers, peripherals, & software	-	4	-	25	6	-	20,480	-	573
5050 Metals and minerals, except petroleum	-	3	-	3	1	-	36,000	-	160
5063 Electrical apparatus and equipment	-	8	-	82	10	-	19,171	-	1,544
5064 Electrical appliances, TV & radios	-	3	-	22	7	-	22,545	-	556
5065 Electronic parts and equipment	-	7	-	37	5	-	21,189	-	944
5075 Warm air heating & air conditioning	-	12	-	64	5	-	22,938	-	1,580
5082 Construction and mining machinery	-	4	-	63	16	-	20,000	-	1,446
5083 Farm and garden machinery	-	6	-	55	9	-	22,545	-	1,423
5084 Industrial machinery and equipment	-	8	-	48	6	-	22,583	-	1,248
5091 Sporting & recreational goods	-	11	-	34	3	-	12,824	-	649
5099 Durable goods, nec	-	10	-	37	4	-	28,216	-	1,085
5110 Paper and paper products	-	5	-	73	15	-	20,164	-	1,460
5136 Men's and boys' clothing	-	4	-	24	6	-	16,167	-	504
5143 Dairy products, exc. dried or canned	-	4	-	36	9	-	27,111	-	946
5146 Fish and seafoods	-	5	-	48	10	-	18,250	-	963
5149 Groceries and related products, nec	-	6	-	244	41	-	20,426	-	5,539
5159 Farm-product raw materials, nec	-	4	-	16	4	-	6,000	-	273
5160 Chemicals and allied products	-	6	-	19	3	-	25,684	-	481
5171 Petroleum bulk stations & terminals	-	7	-	140	20	-	15,057	-	1,988
5172 Petroleum products, nec	-	4	-	10	3	-	18,400	-	184
5181 Beer and ale	-	3	-	164	55	-	28,098	-	5,813
5182 Wine and distilled beverages	-	4	-	29	7	-	23,310	-	745
5191 Farm supplies	-	13	-	112	9	-	15,250	-	1,541
5193 Flowers & florists' supplies	-	5	-	34	7	-	26,353	-	909
5198 Paints, varnishes, and supplies	-	6	-	25	4	-	30,080	-	663
5199 Nondurable goods, nec	-	13	-	96	7	-	17,125	-	1,614
52 – Retail trade	-	2,090	-	24,821	12	-	10,625	-	325,798
5210 Lumber and other building materials	-	24	-	467	19	-	21,191	-	9,850
5230 Paint, glass, and wallpaper stores	-	18	-	64	4	-	19,875	-	1,375
5250 Hardware stores	-	14	-	94	7	-	12,979	-	1,494
5260 Retail nurseries and garden stores	-	12	-	35	3	-	10,857	-	513
5270 Mobile home dealers	-	13	-	88	7	-	19,955	-	2,520
5310 Department stores	-	12	-	1,638	137	-	12,481	-	19,406
5330 Variety stores	-	17	-	150	9	-	7,467	-	1,326
5390 Misc. general merchandise stores	-	19	-	470	25	-	13,030	-	5,875
5410 Grocery stores	-	122	-	2,884	24	-	9,431	-	31,606
5420 Meat and fish markets	-	9	-	22	2	-	8,909	-	300
5440 Candy, nut, and confectionery stores	-	6	-	20	3	-	11,200	-	344
5460 Retail bakeries	-	13	-	76	6	-	10,579	-	1,057
5490 Miscellaneous food stores	-	10	-	23	2	-	11,826	-	338
5510 New and used car dealers	-	28	-	778	28	-	25,707	-	25,068
5520 Used car dealers	-	16	-	47	3	-	12,851	-	719
5530 Auto and home supply stores	-	40	-	252	6	-	18,079	-	5,127
5540 Gasoline service stations	-	96	-	464	5	-	12,681	-	6,451
5550 Boat dealers	-	12	-	52	4	-	19,385	-	1,159
5560 Recreational vehicle dealers	-	4	-	40	10	-	19,900	-	937
5570 Motorcycle dealers	-	4	-	21	5	-	16,952	-	442
5590 Automotive dealers, nec	-	3	-	2	1	-	16,000	-	38
5610 Men's & boys' clothing stores	-	23	-	188	8	-	7,936	-	1,556
5620 Women's clothing stores	-	74	-	606	8	-	8,574	-	5,837
5630 Women's accessory & specialty stores	-	15	-	67	4	-	12,418	-	823
5640 Children's and infants' wear stores	-	10	-	53	5	-	11,245	-	623
5650 Family clothing stores	-	63	-	561	9	-	10,032	-	7,032
5660 Shoe stores	-	45	-	256	6	-	8,938	-	2,450
5690 Misc. apparel & accessory stores	-	74	-	481	7	-	11,360	-	7,487
5712 Furniture stores	-	42	-	337	8	-	16,439	-	6,222
5713 Floor covering stores	-	21	-	95	5	-	17,305	-	1,816
5714 Drapery and upholstery stores	-	6	-	9	2	-	15,111	-	173
5719 Misc. homefurnishings stores	-	30	-	230	8	-	10,904	-	3,105
5720 Household appliance stores	-	8	-	97	12	-	13,979	-	1,419
5731 Radio, TV, & electronic stores	-	10	-	47	5	-	17,191	-	1,119
5735 Record & prerecorded tape stores	-	10	-	71	7	-	9,465	-	662
5812 Eating places	-	459	-	9,194	20	-	7,960	-	98,602
5813 Drinking places	-	42	-	730	17	-	8,466	-	6,450
5910 Drug stores and proprietary stores	-	33	-	327	10	-	16,343	-	5,977

Continued on next page.

MYRTLE BEACH, SC MSA - [continued]

Wholesale and Retail Trade USA	Establishments		Employment		Emp / Est	Pay / Employee		Annual Payroll ($ 000)	
	1994	1995	1994	1995	1995	1994	1995	1994	1995
5920 Liquor stores	-	30	-	90	3	-	11,511	-	1,178
5930 Used merchandise stores	-	25	-	101	4	-	12,594	-	1,333
5941 Sporting goods and bicycle shops	-	34	-	144	4	-	13,500	-	2,522
5942 Book stores	-	11	-	82	7	-	9,561	-	934
5943 Stationery stores	-	3	-	14	5	-	13,143	-	198
5944 Jewelry stores	-	44	-	182	4	-	11,033	-	2,303
5945 Hobby, toy, and game shops	-	14	-	54	4	-	11,037	-	878
5947 Gift, novelty, and souvenir shops	-	65	-	238	4	-	8,639	-	3,327
5948 Luggage and leather goods stores	-	5	-	18	4	-	10,444	-	241
5949 Sewing, needlework, and piece goods	-	12	-	33	3	-	9,212	-	421
5961 Catalog and mail-order houses	-	3	-	9	3	-	8,000	-	104
5962 Merchandising machine operators	-	9	-	25	3	-	10,720	-	291
5963 Direct selling establishments	-	15	-	85	6	-	13,271	-	1,124
5980 Fuel dealers	-	5	-	41	8	-	21,171	-	916
5995 Optical goods stores	-	27	-	122	5	-	12,098	-	1,619
5999 Miscellaneous retail stores, nec	-	61	-	286	5	-	9,343	-	3,197

Source: County Business Patterns 1994/95, CBP-94/95, U.S. Department of Commerce, Washington DC, November 1997. The employment column represents mid-March employment in the year. Pay per employee is calculated by dividing 1st Quarter payroll, annualized, by mid-March employment. The column headed 'Emp / Est' shows 'employees per establishment'. A dash (-) means that data are unavailable or cannot be calculated. nec means not elsewhere classified. *Notes:* 1. 1994 data incomplete; unavailable or withheld. 2. 1995 data incomplete; unavailable or withheld. 3. 1994 and 1995 data incomplete; unavailable or withheld.

NAPLES, FL MSA

Wholesale and Retail Trade USA	Establishments		Employment		Emp / Est	Pay / Employee		Annual Payroll ($ 000)	
	1994	1995	1994	1995	1995	1994	1995	1994	1995
50 - Wholesale trade	317	341	1,956	2,273	7	21,971	25,003	49,172	60,683
5013 Motor vehicle supplies and new parts	15	15	98	96	6	18,612	19,417	2,007	2,067
5014 Tires and tubes	3	-	16	-	-	29,500	-	566	-
5021 Furniture	5	4	19	9	2	19,158	32,889	340	260
5023 Homefurnishings	16	13	106	117	9	22,981	24,308	2,744	2,779
5031 Lumber, plywood, and millwork	-	10	-	42	4	-	26,000	-	1,027
5032 Brick, stone, & related materials	7	8	26	34	4	22,308	24,118	687	851
5033 Roofing, siding, & insulation	-	4	-	23	6	-	33,565	-	651
5039 Construction materials, nec	4	6	13	33	6	24,308	23,515	503	984
5044 Office equipment	7	7	53	53	8	24,151	26,642	1,401	1,526
5045 Computers, peripherals, & software	13	16	60	46	3	23,267	45,565	1,424	3,002
5047 Medical and hospital equipment	4	-	17	-	-	29,412	-	590	-
5051 Metals service centers and offices	7	5	41	45	9	20,098	24,000	974	1,501
5063 Electrical apparatus and equipment	12	13	65	104	8	27,631	33,115	1,960	2,836
5065 Electronic parts and equipment	-	6	-	20	3	-	32,200	-	781
5072 Hardware	9	-	19	-	-	17,263	-	430	-
5074 Plumbing & hydronic heating supplies	12	12	76	73	6	26,421	33,425	1,923	2,255
5075 Warm air heating & air conditioning	-	4	-	10	3	-	24,400	-	233
5082 Construction and mining machinery	4	4	36	33	8	24,556	28,364	988	1,011
5083 Farm and garden machinery	6	6	89	89	15	15,011	16,989	1,469	1,447
5084 Industrial machinery and equipment	3	6	4	5	1	30,000	26,400	120	209
5085 Industrial supplies	-	3	-	7	2	-	23,429	-	179
5087 Service establishment equipment	3	3	4	5	2	12,000	10,400	51	46
5088 Transportation equipment & supplies	7	8	76	124	16	27,895	26,742	2,491	3,951
5091 Sporting & recreational goods	5	6	31	24	4	24,000	17,000	1,219	845
5099 Durable goods, nec	8	6	27	12	2	21,185	29,333	628	389
5112 Stationery and office supplies	8	9	119	114	13	11,966	17,404	1,426	1,777
5120 Drugs, proprietaries, and sundries	-	5	-	16	3	-	27,500	-	352
5130 Apparel, piece goods, and notions	5	7	9	39	6	23,111	11,692	203	587
5143 Dairy products, exc. dried or canned	3	-	26	-	-	34,923	-	984	-
5146 Fish and seafoods	6	5	18	12	2	14,444	17,667	178	163
5147 Meats and meat products	6	6	32	41	7	14,750	18,732	556	994
5148 Fresh fruits and vegetables	20	16	368	407	25	19,076	20,560	8,173	9,135
5149 Groceries and related products, nec	9	8	28	23	3	21,429	15,478	560	339
5162 Plastics materials & basic shapes	3	4	3	7	2	24,000	42,857	87	327
5169 Chemicals & allied products, nec	4	6	11	25	4	27,273	16,320	512	642
5171 Petroleum bulk stations & terminals	5	5	36	49	10	25,222	23,755	1,119	1,489
5191 Farm supplies	13	13	68	72	6	23,235	28,889	1,835	1,795
5193 Flowers & florists' supplies	6	4	34	37	9	33,412	15,459	1,736	590
5198 Paints, varnishes, and supplies	4	3	19	12	4	21,053	28,667	364	337
5199 Nondurable goods, nec	10	16	32	64	4	17,625	39,688	1,194	2,373
52 - Retail trade	1,665	1,665	20,267	21,472	13	13,902	14,775	277,762	299,014
5210 Lumber and other building materials	26	17	489	489	29	21,211	21,145	10,962	11,209
5230 Paint, glass, and wallpaper stores	16	15	74	88	6	21,189	20,773	1,681	1,831

Continued on next page.

NAPLES, FL MSA - [continued]

Wholesale and Retail Trade USA	Establishments		Employment		Emp / Est	Pay / Employee		Annual Payroll ($ 000)	
	1994	1995	1994	1995	1995	1994	1995	1994	1995
5250 Hardware stores	16	9	183	171	19	14,601	14,924	2,915	2,424
5260 Retail nurseries and garden stores	12	11	103	93	8	18,835	24,129	1,987	1,980
5310 Department stores	11	11	1,213	1,442	131	13,758	14,730	17,774	20,704
5330 Variety stores	8	8	44	38	5	8,091	8,737	393	359
5390 Misc. general merchandise stores	8	7	521	472	67	12,491	15,441	6,464	6,364
5410 Grocery stores	116	112	3,591	3,783	34	11,671	13,160	40,862	46,819
5420 Meat and fish markets	4	5	5	15	3	8,800	10,133	61	155
5430 Fruit and vegetable markets	7	8	53	42	5	6,340	9,619	352	379
5440 Candy, nut, and confectionery stores	4	3	17	12	4	8,471	12,333	112	107
5450 Dairy products stores	4	5	27	48	10	5,630	6,000	165	248
5460 Retail bakeries	10	6	61	43	7	11,016	12,279	593	422
5490 Miscellaneous food stores	16	16	62	66	4	11,677	21,273	1,014	1,559
5510 New and used car dealers	14	15	732	705	47	32,656	34,513	25,971	28,101
5520 Used car dealers	9	8	38	35	4	22,947	25,714	959	814
5530 Auto and home supply stores	33	34	151	193	6	19,099	20,850	3,118	3,848
5540 Gasoline service stations	57	50	514	373	7	12,802	14,702	6,494	5,358
5550 Boat dealers	12	16	125	116	7	21,536	24,483	2,522	2,695
5560 Recreational vehicle dealers	3	3	10	6	2	17,600	19,333	160	90
5590 Automotive dealers, nec	4	4	14	11	3	8,000	16,000	105	185
5610 Men's & boys' clothing stores	21	19	106	113	6	13,358	13,310	1,348	1,214
5620 Women's clothing stores	101	96	813	858	9	12,846	13,040	10,342	10,772
5630 Women's accessory & specialty stores	18	16	114	108	7	9,123	10,000	1,035	971
5640 Children's and infants' wear stores	9	9	40	45	5	8,900	8,444	359	337
5650 Family clothing stores	32	33	431	421	13	10,255	12,209	4,606	4,771
5660 Shoe stores	41	41	225	220	5	13,404	14,509	2,867	2,825
5690 Misc. apparel & accessory stores	17	16	130	112	7	11,631	14,571	1,496	1,606
5712 Furniture stores	77	79	538	533	7	24,937	26,882	13,846	13,517
5713 Floor covering stores	24	25	189	169	7	18,116	23,124	3,463	3,590
5714 Drapery and upholstery stores	12	11	37	37	3	15,351	17,297	618	532
5719 Misc. homefurnishings stores	56	56	360	388	7	15,867	17,010	5,863	6,130
5720 Household appliance stores	11	11	51	56	5	17,647	21,429	812	1,076
5731 Radio, TV, & electronic stores	21	23	96	148	6	20,792	21,243	2,592	2,953
5734 Computer and software stores	9	11	49	65	6	20,490	23,631	1,231	1,917
5735 Record & prerecorded tape stores	5	5	37	35	7	9,622	10,286	372	398
5736 Musical instrument stores	7	5	28	20	4	19,714	24,800	469	435
5812 Eating places	323	295	6,479	6,902	23	11,352	11,300	63,578	64,323
5813 Drinking places	15	13	71	63	5	9,352	9,333	572	564
5910 Drug stores and proprietary stores	35	34	468	494	15	19,231	19,822	9,242	9,320
5920 Liquor stores	15	13	90	136	10	11,422	12,412	1,329	1,648
5930 Used merchandise stores	36	33	150	149	5	11,893	13,235	1,862	1,873
5941 Sporting goods and bicycle shops	27	31	116	107	3	14,103	17,944	1,937	2,033
5942 Book stores	17	17	93	96	6	8,731	9,792	873	891
5944 Jewelry stores	43	42	163	162	4	19,411	19,975	3,085	3,173
5945 Hobby, toy, and game shops	5	5	14	21	4	14,000	9,905	237	235
5947 Gift, novelty, and souvenir shops	58	55	229	210	4	11,074	11,886	2,335	2,374
5948 Luggage and leather goods stores	3	3	20	20	7	13,600	19,200	282	402
5949 Sewing, needlework, and piece goods	-	4	-	26	7	-	10,000	-	250
5962 Merchandising machine operators	-	3	-	15	5	-	16,800	-	256
5963 Direct selling establishments	9	-	51	-	-	19,843	-	1,117	-
5984 Liquefied petroleum gas dealers	7	-	32	-	-	22,750	-	752	-
5992 Florists	25	23	101	107	5	9,901	11,252	972	1,155
5993 Tobacco stores and stands	3	4	8	6	2	12,500	11,333	89	101
5995 Optical goods stores	14	13	72	70	5	20,167	19,771	1,362	1,207
5999 Miscellaneous retail stores, nec	62	74	219	248	3	13,735	14,500	3,271	3,775

Source: County Business Patterns 1994/95, CBP-94/95, U.S. Department of Commerce, Washington DC, November 1997. The employment column represents mid-March employment in the year. Pay per employee is calculated by dividing 1st Quarter payroll, annualized, by mid-March employment. The column headed 'Emp / Est' shows 'employees per establishment'. A dash (-) means that data are unavailable or cannot be calculated. nec means not elsewhere classified. *Notes:* 1. 1994 data incomplete; unavailable or withheld. 2. 1995 data incomplete; unavailable or withheld. 3. 1994 and 1995 data incomplete; unavailable or withheld.

NASHVILLE, TN MSA

Wholesale and Retail Trade USA	Establishments		Employment		Emp / Est	Pay / Employee		Annual Payroll ($ 000)	
	1994	1995	1994	1995	1995	1994	1995	1994	1995
50- Wholesale trade	-	2,460	-	37,306	15	-	32,178	-	1,251,844
5012 Automobiles and other vehicles	-	56	-	1,338	24	-	29,719	-	45,471
5013 Motor vehicle supplies and new parts [2]	-	131	-	2,230	17	-	28,084	-	63,294
5014 Tires and tubes [2]	-	19	-	298	16	-	32,671	-	9,302
5015 Motor vehicle parts, used [2]	-	32	-	112	4	-	15,929	-	1,938
5021 Furniture [2]	-	22	-	335	15	-	35,940	-	15,015

Continued on next page.

NASHVILLE, TN MSA - [continued]

Wholesale and Retail Trade USA	Establishments		Employment		Emp / Est	Pay / Employee		Annual Payroll ($ 000)	
	1994	1995	1994	1995	1995	1994	1995	1994	1995
5023 Homefurnishings [2]	-	32	-	246	8	-	29,951	-	6,796
5031 Lumber, plywood, and millwork [2]	-	53	-	613	12	-	25,886	-	17,652
5032 Brick, stone, & related materials [2]	-	21	-	189	9	-	40,635	-	6,858
5033 Roofing, siding, & insulation [2]	-	19	-	122	6	-	39,049	-	4,674
5039 Construction materials, nec	-	40	-	338	8	-	30,260	-	12,363
5043 Photographic equipment & supplies [2]	-	10	-	150	15	-	33,440	-	5,056
5044 Office equipment [2]	-	39	-	845	22	-	41,141	-	31,720
5045 Computers, peripherals, & software [2]	-	85	-	1,067	13	-	52,761	-	48,778
5046 Commercial equipment, nec [2]	-	31	-	307	10	-	29,928	-	12,449
5047 Medical and hospital equipment [2]	-	74	-	731	10	-	38,561	-	30,154
5048 Ophthalmic goods [2]	-	7	-	187	27	-	28,578	-	4,845
5049 Professional equipment, nec [2]	-	14	-	170	12	-	26,847	-	5,100
5051 Metals service centers and offices [2]	-	62	-	1,124	18	-	33,943	-	39,796
5052 Coal and other minerals and ores [2]	-	7	-	20	3	-	84,400	-	2,220
5063 Electrical apparatus and equipment [2]	-	97	-	900	9	-	38,009	-	35,026
5064 Electrical appliances, TV & radios [2]	-	22	-	237	11	-	25,401	-	6,561
5065 Electronic parts and equipment [2]	-	84	-	819	10	-	40,156	-	33,404
5072 Hardware [2]	-	43	-	470	11	-	30,979	-	15,671
5074 Plumbing & hydronic heating supplies [2]	-	53	-	489	9	-	30,757	-	16,572
5075 Warm air heating & air conditioning [2]	-	41	-	516	13	-	31,488	-	17,840
5082 Construction and mining machinery [2]	-	26	-	444	17	-	40,378	-	19,800
5083 Farm and garden machinery	-	29	-	192	7	-	23,875	-	5,328
5084 Industrial machinery and equipment	-	159	-	1,650	10	-	36,058	-	62,757
5085 Industrial supplies [2]	-	81	-	838	10	-	32,883	-	30,489
5087 Service establishment equipment [2]	-	43	-	257	6	-	27,875	-	7,693
5088 Transportation equipment & supplies [2]	-	14	-	84	6	-	36,667	-	3,263
5091 Sporting & recreational goods [2]	-	25	-	149	6	-	30,738	-	4,809
5092 Toys and hobby goods and supplies [2]	-	19	-	55	3	-	18,109	-	1,031
5093 Scrap and waste materials [2]	-	27	-	428	16	-	26,234	-	16,440
5094 Jewelry & precious stones [2]	-	25	-	127	5	-	14,772	-	1,903
5099 Durable goods, nec [2]	-	79	-	958	12	-	28,426	-	30,996
5111 Printing and writing paper [2]	-	14	-	280	20	-	40,429	-	12,838
5112 Stationery and office supplies [2]	-	56	-	811	14	-	26,022	-	23,075
5113 Industrial & personal service paper [2]	-	24	-	110	5	-	52,618	-	4,833
5120 Drugs, proprietaries, and sundries [2]	-	34	-	509	15	-	44,322	-	17,201
5131 Piece goods & notions [2]	-	16	-	201	13	-	34,866	-	8,501
5136 Men's and boys' clothing [2]	-	13	-	242	19	-	21,223	-	5,118
5137 Women's and children's clothing [2]	-	17	-	54	3	-	18,815	-	1,091
5139 Footwear [2]	-	18	-	603	34	-	37,937	-	24,293
5141 Groceries, general line [2]	-	23	-	1,800	78	-	33,238	-	58,296
5142 Packaged frozen food [2]	-	12	-	215	18	-	30,195	-	6,381
5143 Dairy products, exc. dried or canned [2]	-	7	-	77	11	-	30,961	-	2,649
5144 Poultry and poultry products [2]	-	5	-	91	18	-	16,264	-	1,617
5147 Meats and meat products [2]	-	18	-	352	20	-	28,943	-	9,225
5148 Fresh fruits and vegetables [2]	-	25	-	592	24	-	19,385	-	13,608
5149 Groceries and related products, nec [2]	-	44	-	643	15	-	26,016	-	16,885
5154 Livestock [2]	-	9	-	15	2	-	16,000	-	233
5159 Farm-product raw materials, nec [2]	-	9	-	56	6	-	12,929	-	410
5162 Plastics materials & basic shapes [2]	-	21	-	240	11	-	31,117	-	8,594
5169 Chemicals & allied products, nec [2]	-	49	-	321	7	-	35,477	-	12,673
5171 Petroleum bulk stations & terminals	-	41	-	318	8	-	26,843	-	9,025
5181 Beer and ale [2]	-	3	-	401	134	-	34,304	-	15,204
5182 Wine and distilled beverages [2]	-	9	-	214	24	-	43,121	-	10,355
5191 Farm supplies [2]	-	51	-	230	5	-	28,174	-	7,202
5192 Books, periodicals, & newspapers [2]	-	35	-	1,679	48	-	25,844	-	45,408
5193 Flowers & florists' supplies [2]	-	18	-	99	6	-	19,758	-	2,188
5194 Tobacco and tobacco products [2]	-	6	-	17	3	-	19,059	-	442
5198 Paints, varnishes, and supplies [2]	-	20	-	84	4	-	31,571	-	2,586
5199 Nondurable goods, nec [2]	-	85	-	542	6	-	22,089	-	13,398
52 - Retail trade	-	7,051	-	120,687	17	-	13,581	-	1,750,540
5210 Lumber and other building materials	-	86	-	2,071	24	-	22,295	-	50,025
5230 Paint, glass, and wallpaper stores [2]	-	44	-	189	4	-	18,032	-	4,061
5250 Hardware stores [2]	-	50	-	343	7	-	17,085	-	6,988
5260 Retail nurseries and garden stores [2]	-	57	-	390	7	-	12,882	-	5,644
5270 Mobile home dealers [2]	-	21	-	116	6	-	34,207	-	5,102
5310 Department stores [2]	-	54	-	8,670	161	-	12,901	-	118,476
5330 Variety stores [2]	-	41	-	329	8	-	8,328	-	3,025
5390 Misc. general merchandise stores	-	69	-	2,273	33	-	13,264	-	29,347
5410 Grocery stores [2]	-	588	-	18,446	31	-	7,982	-	154,365
5420 Meat and fish markets [2]	-	11	-	13	1	-	19,077	-	230
5430 Fruit and vegetable markets [2]	-	9	-	61	7	-	7,672	-	503

Continued on next page.

NASHVILLE, TN MSA - [continued]

Wholesale and Retail Trade USA	Establishments		Employment		Emp / Est	Pay / Employee		Annual Payroll ($ 000)	
	1994	1995	1994	1995	1995	1994	1995	1994	1995
5440 Candy, nut, and confectionery stores [2]	-	16	-	75	5	-	7,680	-	568
5460 Retail bakeries [2]	-	56	-	425	8	-	11,868	-	5,322
5490 Miscellaneous food stores [2]	-	36	-	154	4	-	9,377	-	1,419
5510 New and used car dealers	-	94	-	5,417	58	-	31,990	-	191,762
5520 Used car dealers	-	144	-	596	4	-	18,544	-	12,321
5530 Auto and home supply stores	-	196	-	1,541	8	-	21,612	-	35,379
5540 Gasoline service stations	-	452	-	3,405	8	-	13,514	-	49,482
5550 Boat dealers [2]	-	17	-	108	6	-	19,370	-	2,785
5560 Recreational vehicle dealers [2]	-	7	-	68	10	-	31,294	-	2,865
5570 Motorcycle dealers [2]	-	14	-	124	9	-	20,258	-	3,331
5610 Men's & boys' clothing stores	-	82	-	599	7	-	13,075	-	7,956
5620 Women's clothing stores [2]	-	220	-	2,065	9	-	9,292	-	18,328
5630 Women's accessory & specialty stores [2]	-	42	-	232	6	-	9,483	-	2,454
5640 Children's and infants' wear stores [2]	-	36	-	246	7	-	8,179	-	2,155
5650 Family clothing stores [2]	-	77	-	1,565	20	-	11,223	-	15,592
5660 Shoe stores [2]	-	205	-	1,215	6	-	10,966	-	14,529
5690 Misc. apparel & accessory stores [2]	-	54	-	324	6	-	11,086	-	3,828
5712 Furniture stores	-	166	-	1,202	7	-	21,038	-	27,593
5713 Floor covering stores	-	67	-	326	5	-	24,429	-	9,052
5714 Drapery and upholstery stores [2]	-	17	-	39	2	-	12,718	-	564
5719 Misc. homefurnishings stores [2]	-	85	-	802	9	-	11,177	-	9,868
5720 Household appliance stores [2]	-	49	-	392	8	-	21,806	-	10,240
5731 Radio, TV, & electronic stores [2]	-	69	-	685	10	-	18,674	-	12,696
5734 Computer and software stores [2]	-	47	-	224	5	-	21,357	-	5,887
5735 Record & prerecorded tape stores [2]	-	62	-	609	10	-	8,768	-	6,146
5736 Musical instrument stores [2]	-	34	-	192	6	-	30,104	-	5,908
5812 Eating places	-	1,429	-	37,880	27	-	8,815	-	351,881
5813 Drinking places [2]	-	80	-	614	8	-	9,003	-	5,780
5910 Drug stores and proprietary stores	-	198	-	2,247	11	-	17,994	-	42,793
5920 Liquor stores [2]	-	101	-	408	4	-	13,196	-	7,143
5930 Used merchandise stores [2]	-	172	-	673	4	-	12,701	-	10,228
5941 Sporting goods and bicycle shops [2]	-	91	-	578	6	-	13,696	-	8,889
5942 Book stores [2]	-	76	-	774	10	-	11,039	-	9,257
5944 Jewelry stores	-	125	-	611	5	-	18,782	-	10,546
5945 Hobby, toy, and game shops [2]	-	43	-	374	9	-	11,123	-	4,858
5947 Gift, novelty, and souvenir shops	-	151	-	777	5	-	9,447	-	8,364
5948 Luggage and leather goods stores [2]	-	12	-	45	4	-	13,956	-	608
5949 Sewing, needlework, and piece goods [2]	-	36	-	228	6	-	8,491	-	2,152
5961 Catalog and mail-order houses [2]	-	39	-	779	20	-	23,245	-	18,447
5962 Merchandising machine operators	-	58	-	514	9	-	17,852	-	9,654
5963 Direct selling establishments [2]	-	57	-	495	9	-	17,689	-	10,970
5984 Liquefied petroleum gas dealers	-	22	-	78	4	-	24,103	-	1,891
5992 Florists	-	116	-	571	5	-	13,632	-	7,747
5993 Tobacco stores and stands [2]	-	11	-	36	3	-	11,556	-	534
5995 Optical goods stores [2]	-	67	-	368	5	-	18,533	-	7,249
5999 Miscellaneous retail stores, nec [2]	-	234	-	1,041	4	-	15,024	-	18,066

Source: County Business Patterns 1994/95, CBP-94/95, U.S. Department of Commerce, Washington DC, November 1997. The employment column represents mid-March employment in the year. Pay per employee is calculated by dividing 1st Quarter payroll, annualized, by mid-March employment. The column headed 'Emp / Est' shows 'employees per establishment'. A dash (-) means that data are unavailable or cannot be calculated. nec means not elsewhere classified. *Notes:* 1. 1994 data incomplete; unavailable or withheld. 2. 1995 data incomplete; unavailable or withheld. 3. 1994 and 1995 data incomplete; unavailable or withheld.

NASSAU - SUFFOLK, NY PMSA

Wholesale and Retail Trade USA	Establishments		Employment		Emp / Est	Pay / Employee		Annual Payroll ($ 000)	
	1994	1995	1994	1995	1995	1994	1995	1994	1995
50- Wholesale trade	8,421	8,437	86,460	89,181	11	33,042	35,646	3,172,071	3,362,562
5012 Automobiles and other vehicles	85	86	598	603	7	28,328	29,904	20,935	17,616
5013 Motor vehicle supplies and new parts	380	336	3,399	2,981	9	24,027	25,841	91,470	80,283
5014 Tires and tubes	31	31	421	403	13	25,853	29,122	11,499	12,035
5015 Motor vehicle parts, used	68	84	421	919	11	20,551	21,624	10,073	20,834
5021 Furniture	91	103	576	720	7	31,424	29,839	20,086	24,739
5023 Homefurnishings	204	201	1,860	1,860	9	29,548	28,609	63,315	62,578
5031 Lumber, plywood, and millwork	96	98	1,131	1,419	14	35,194	36,730	43,497	49,834
5032 Brick, stone, & related materials	78	68	496	375	6	28,282	29,760	17,095	14,396
5033 Roofing, siding, & insulation	27	19	327	144	8	33,235	31,972	13,396	5,601
5039 Construction materials, nec	58	88	390	777	9	30,390	31,197	13,623	25,677
5043 Photographic equipment & supplies	44	43	703	722	17	37,400	39,823	27,680	30,759
5044 Office equipment	100	99	2,395	2,803	28	40,516	41,712	103,875	111,928
5045 Computers, peripherals, & software	280	278	3,216	3,443	12	42,195	42,746	141,041	149,551

Continued on next page.

NASSAU - SUFFOLK, NY PMSA - [continued]

Wholesale and Retail Trade USA	Establishments		Employment		Emp / Est	Pay / Employee		Annual Payroll ($ 000)	
	1994	1995	1994	1995	1995	1994	1995	1994	1995
5046 Commercial equipment, nec	91	91	904	945	10	35,173	37,405	34,024	36,128
5047 Medical and hospital equipment	242	223	5,494	5,103	23	37,053	42,335	242,524	247,691
5048 Ophthalmic goods	59	61	1,448	1,440	24	29,373	30,628	50,408	53,803
5049 Professional equipment, nec	48	47	641	548	12	33,298	44,438	22,758	22,376
5051 Metals service centers and offices [3]	149	147	445	520	4	42,840	45,123	23,704	25,864
5052 Coal and other minerals and ores	-	6	-	10	2	-	33,200	-	359
5063 Electrical apparatus and equipment	273	230	2,809	2,303	10	33,935	36,394	107,387	93,704
5064 Electrical appliances, TV & radios	73	76	851	924	12	32,625	31,952	32,238	33,646
5065 Electronic parts and equipment	547	545	6,158	6,536	12	39,495	41,853	256,107	290,200
5072 Hardware	146	153	1,190	1,293	8	34,551	38,323	47,108	52,792
5074 Plumbing & hydronic heating supplies	132	124	1,004	1,005	8	35,761	40,060	36,752	38,330
5075 Warm air heating & air conditioning	63	67	445	514	8	33,699	35,276	16,299	19,386
5078 Refrigeration equipment and supplies	12	12	190	193	16	39,726	41,264	8,656	8,684
5082 Construction and mining machinery	28	28	282	287	10	32,794	35,136	9,954	9,781
5083 Farm and garden machinery	33	31	335	286	9	24,824	26,615	9,264	8,489
5084 Industrial machinery and equipment	336	331	2,832	3,120	9	37,123	39,797	116,121	135,820
5085 Industrial supplies	139	134	1,594	1,508	11	38,873	45,117	66,036	71,212
5087 Service establishment equipment	90	82	884	837	10	28,181	28,774	27,397	26,229
5088 Transportation equipment & supplies	89	90	786	750	8	37,359	38,507	31,793	30,992
5091 Sporting & recreational goods	97	99	1,202	1,357	14	24,639	28,318	37,684	40,987
5092 Toys and hobby goods and supplies	78	81	616	635	8	27,779	30,665	22,420	23,276
5093 Scrap and waste materials	92	101	889	1,114	11	26,479	28,032	29,253	35,800
5094 Jewelry & precious stones	148	143	727	757	5	23,912	27,593	22,916	23,141
5099 Durable goods, nec	166	164	1,002	1,088	7	29,381	33,099	34,839	38,035
5111 Printing and writing paper	42	43	195	205	5	39,713	43,863	8,719	9,277
5112 Stationery and office supplies	200	156	1,699	1,203	8	23,602	28,888	44,411	37,404
5113 Industrial & personal service paper	152	152	1,290	1,322	9	29,712	32,542	45,395	52,280
5120 Drugs, proprietaries, and sundries	194	195	7,448	7,296	37	25,787	30,004	203,054	225,969
5131 Piece goods & notions	190	186	1,481	1,677	9	32,818	34,753	61,346	66,487
5136 Men's and boys' clothing	77	70	609	517	7	23,475	32,201	16,940	16,522
5137 Women's and children's clothing	201	201	1,420	1,553	8	32,169	28,028	49,355	45,925
5139 Footwear	62	54	435	275	5	41,830	41,833	19,434	12,837
5141 Groceries, general line	77	75	650	680	9	26,283	29,771	20,232	22,822
5142 Packaged frozen food	47	47	1,097	1,183	25	36,751	42,046	45,663	40,520
5143 Dairy products, exc. dried or canned	67	66	659	620	9	25,979	26,445	18,919	15,928
5144 Poultry and poultry products	14	9	88	76	8	30,864	33,526	2,650	2,411
5145 Confectionery	64	57	687	666	12	24,367	26,294	17,649	18,443
5146 Fish and seafoods	84	83	564	553	7	20,461	23,067	12,005	13,225
5147 Meats and meat products	133	132	380	417	3	23,368	23,271	10,525	11,183
5148 Fresh fruits and vegetables	73	68	434	420	6	33,115	39,771	16,771	17,167
5149 Groceries and related products, nec	712	691	4,329	4,040	6	35,810	34,422	157,347	133,979
5153 Grain and field beans	8	8	31	34	4	30,452	37,412	1,024	1,328
5159 Farm-product raw materials, nec	-	17	-	68	4	-	39,471	-	2,418
5162 Plastics materials & basic shapes	72	75	596	627	8	37,483	39,502	24,132	26,009
5169 Chemicals & allied products, nec	161	153	1,187	1,204	8	41,806	45,654	54,632	57,772
5171 Petroleum bulk stations & terminals	36	34	533	719	21	40,623	41,847	21,609	28,038
5172 Petroleum products, nec	51	47	430	473	10	41,005	40,913	19,760	20,673
5181 Beer and ale	44	42	647	563	13	28,068	32,504	19,539	21,121
5182 Wine and distilled beverages	33	32	1,222	1,150	36	41,169	47,840	48,508	49,953
5191 Farm supplies	70	62	492	415	7	31,667	35,634	15,953	14,090
5192 Books, periodicals, & newspapers	102	101	1,171	1,187	12	31,798	31,006	38,115	36,630
5193 Flowers & florists' supplies	69	58	791	863	15	20,536	21,085	22,878	22,050
5194 Tobacco and tobacco products	25	25	597	578	23	33,152	27,190	16,400	15,992
5198 Paints, varnishes, and supplies	37	33	442	483	15	30,561	29,855	14,871	15,388
5199 Nondurable goods, nec	351	367	2,472	2,621	7	26,717	29,747	77,411	82,902
52 - Retail trade	19,127	19,065	201,258	208,845	11	15,168	16,164	3,396,072	3,564,933
5210 Lumber and other building materials	288	264	5,072	5,814	22	21,539	23,344	127,398	143,099
5230 Paint, glass, and wallpaper stores [1]	111	98	261	437	4	18,866	19,725	5,147	8,905
5250 Hardware stores	191	136	1,206	923	7	16,302	16,451	21,923	15,786
5260 Retail nurseries and garden stores	146	146	800	808	6	14,440	14,589	16,254	17,187
5310 Department stores	65	69	16,745	18,890	274	12,170	13,284	228,265	250,781
5330 Variety stores	89	76	921	849	11	11,201	11,647	10,273	9,056
5390 Misc. general merchandise stores	78	76	2,220	2,553	34	16,223	17,963	39,755	54,593
5410 Grocery stores	1,689	1,677	29,536	29,458	18	14,808	15,677	463,810	481,745
5420 Meat and fish markets	251	247	816	810	3	15,637	16,756	13,847	14,261
5430 Fruit and vegetable markets	65	57	314	307	5	11,248	14,072	4,915	4,947
5440 Candy, nut, and confectionery stores	73	73	319	325	4	8,476	8,258	2,888	2,926
5450 Dairy products stores	84	84	277	258	3	8,144	9,194	2,600	2,817
5460 Retail bakeries	485	459	3,034	2,838	6	10,780	10,905	36,670	32,166
5490 Miscellaneous food stores	162	176	848	975	6	13,179	13,986	12,199	14,726
5510 New and used car dealers	238	237	8,780	9,722	41	33,150	35,522	359,486	370,792

Continued on next page.

NASSAU – SUFFOLK, NY PMSA - [continued]

Wholesale and Retail Trade USA	Establishments		Employment		Emp / Est	Pay / Employee		Annual Payroll ($ 000)	
	1994	1995	1994	1995	1995	1994	1995	1994	1995
5520 Used car dealers	127	130	338	409	3	22,249	23,374	9,042	9,930
5530 Auto and home supply stores	290	283	2,040	2,053	7	20,259	22,389	44,523	46,251
5540 Gasoline service stations	1,108	1,127	4,288	4,351	4	14,689	15,157	67,450	66,020
5550 Boat dealers	93	85	420	446	5	20,914	20,843	11,249	10,804
5560 Recreational vehicle dealers	10	10	54	57	6	27,037	30,316	1,508	1,665
5570 Motorcycle dealers	23	26	140	130	5	18,886	22,646	3,400	3,960
5590 Automotive dealers, nec	7	7	13	8	1	15,385	18,000	211	209
5610 Men's & boys' clothing stores	230	201	1,748	1,618	8	15,204	14,339	27,660	22,818
5620 Women's clothing stores	669	605	5,990	5,798	10	10,021	10,475	65,863	64,949
5630 Women's accessory & specialty stores	140	135	718	658	5	11,465	11,951	9,145	9,096
5640 Children's and infants' wear stores	112	103	1,063	1,110	11	8,312	9,362	10,410	10,761
5650 Family clothing stores	200	193	5,154	4,274	22	9,943	11,597	52,977	50,102
5660 Shoe stores	433	423	2,880	2,815	7	10,922	12,207	35,658	35,749
5690 Misc. apparel & accessory stores	119	119	550	558	5	12,131	13,147	7,964	8,454
5712 Furniture stores	382	376	2,823	2,938	8	21,049	20,908	62,494	62,596
5713 Floor covering stores	181	163	969	1,026	6	20,227	22,335	22,307	24,352
5714 Drapery and upholstery stores	39	41	263	115	3	11,224	14,330	2,826	1,440
5719 Misc. homefurnishings stores	256	243	2,421	2,403	10	17,074	17,092	43,174	44,235
5720 Household appliance stores	87	92	1,005	973	11	22,886	27,597	25,192	26,875
5731 Radio, TV, & electronic stores	172	170	1,116	1,322	8	18,072	17,846	21,353	25,308
5734 Computer and software stores	88	96	484	700	7	15,760	21,097	9,753	15,529
5735 Record & prerecorded tape stores	104	103	690	637	6	11,867	13,325	8,655	8,641
5736 Musical instrument stores	39	40	246	263	7	20,894	22,586	5,676	6,771
5812 Eating places	4,300	4,023	51,530	52,718	13	9,480	10,188	561,146	580,775
5813 Drinking places	611	548	2,103	1,825	3	8,978	9,499	21,259	19,103
5910 Drug stores and proprietary stores	658	641	7,507	8,364	13	15,252	15,269	126,211	137,711
5920 Liquor stores	375	368	1,125	1,100	3	14,251	14,618	17,315	17,350
5930 Used merchandise stores	120	114	468	422	4	15,368	15,555	8,149	7,362
5941 Sporting goods and bicycle shops	321	321	2,060	2,256	7	14,342	14,179	33,482	36,943
5942 Book stores	107	120	794	1,111	9	11,335	13,149	9,050	14,223
5943 Stationery stores	175	180	535	994	6	12,636	13,179	7,078	12,908
5944 Jewelry stores	336	339	1,575	1,487	4	19,294	21,590	31,380	32,704
5945 Hobby, toy, and game shops	149	142	1,980	1,544	11	11,531	10,585	26,339	20,683
5946 Camera & photographic supply stores	55	51	295	275	5	22,075	23,433	6,913	6,443
5947 Gift, novelty, and souvenir shops	467	428	1,987	1,879	4	9,619	10,623	21,202	21,902
5948 Luggage and leather goods stores	28	30	130	131	4	16,708	15,939	2,411	2,328
5949 Sewing, needlework, and piece goods	53	50	230	222	4	11,704	12,090	3,020	2,914
5961 Catalog and mail-order houses	131	149	4,313	4,298	29	19,782	24,367	106,326	107,771
5962 Merchandising machine operators	92	92	575	616	7	22,630	23,734	13,412	15,167
5963 Direct selling establishments	210	196	1,074	1,116	6	17,709	18,767	24,608	26,551
5983 Fuel oil dealers	254	257	3,459	3,410	13	39,039	36,461	119,332	115,195
5984 Liquefied petroleum gas dealers	40	40	400	439	11	31,120	32,510	13,834	15,558
5989 Fuel dealers, nec	6	4	8	8	2	36,500	19,000	302	185
5992 Florists	326	310	1,241	1,347	4	13,679	14,091	18,853	19,689
5993 Tobacco stores and stands	41	37	115	100	3	13,287	15,960	1,720	1,653
5994 News dealers and newsstands	54	56	98	121	2	11,510	11,669	1,280	1,421
5995 Optical goods stores	260	286	1,288	1,849	6	20,661	21,488	28,375	44,559
5999 Miscellaneous retail stores, nec	564	580	2,455	3,055	5	15,596	17,394	46,002	56,469

Source: County Business Patterns 1994/95, CBP-94/95, U.S. Department of Commerce, Washington DC, November 1997. The employment column represents mid-March employment in the year. Pay per employee is calculated by dividing 1st Quarter payroll, annualized, by mid-March employment. The column headed 'Emp / Est' shows 'employees per establishment'. A dash (-) means that data are unavailable or cannot be calculated. nec means not elsewhere classified. *Notes:* 1. 1994 data incomplete; unavailable or withheld. 2. 1995 data incomplete; unavailable or withheld. 3. 1994 and 1995 data incomplete; unavailable or withheld.

NEW ORLEANS, LA MSA

Wholesale and Retail Trade USA	Establishments		Employment		Emp / Est	Pay / Employee		Annual Payroll ($ 000)	
	1994	1995	1994	1995	1995	1994	1995	1994	1995
50 - Wholesale trade	2,504	2,488	29,650	30,490	12	27,523	28,821	861,378	915,196
5012 Automobiles and other vehicles [3]	15	16	224	198	12	30,411	33,354	7,224	6,683
5013 Motor vehicle supplies and new parts [3]	102	91	906	816	9	21,956	24,525	20,565	20,575
5014 Tires and tubes [3]	17	16	155	168	11	27,303	28,952	4,644	4,253
5015 Motor vehicle parts, used [3]	23	23	90	116	5	16,089	16,862	1,746	1,973
5021 Furniture [3]	26	31	152	195	6	20,342	25,456	3,471	5,046
5023 Homefurnishings [3]	32	28	403	189	7	24,596	25,143	9,599	4,648
5031 Lumber, plywood, and millwork [3]	33	28	480	562	20	28,783	24,683	13,967	14,850
5032 Brick, stone, & related materials [1]	26	29	204	209	7	27,157	29,837	6,296	7,033
5033 Roofing, siding, & insulation [3]	12	13	113	131	10	32,389	30,473	5,444	5,474
5039 Construction materials, nec [3]	30	35	259	227	6	19,351	30,203	5,467	6,613
5044 Office equipment [3]	51	45	810	690	15	33,748	36,209	25,934	24,326

Continued on next page.

NEW ORLEANS, LA MSA - [continued]

Wholesale and Retail Trade USA	Establishments		Employment		Emp / Est	Pay / Employee		Annual Payroll ($ 000)	
	1994	1995	1994	1995	1995	1994	1995	1994	1995
5045 Computers, peripherals, & software [3]	68	62	806	826	13	41,295	40,228	30,978	28,027
5046 Commercial equipment, nec [3]	26	27	186	200	7	20,409	23,500	4,334	4,948
5047 Medical and hospital equipment [3]	86	80	550	525	7	37,084	39,040	22,476	23,140
5049 Professional equipment, nec [1]	11	-	52	-	-	24,615	-	1,670	-
5051 Metals service centers and offices [3]	63	60	453	768	13	30,322	30,406	13,679	24,162
5063 Electrical apparatus and equipment [3]	128	117	1,259	1,277	11	32,829	36,219	40,073	43,557
5064 Electrical appliances, TV & radios [3]	19	19	358	494	26	20,190	22,688	7,567	12,138
5065 Electronic parts and equipment [3]	61	64	468	527	8	35,256	36,387	18,334	20,920
5072 Hardware [3]	38	38	116	168	4	26,931	23,476	1,937	4,567
5074 Plumbing & hydronic heating supplies [3]	41	45	266	313	7	26,195	24,601	8,034	8,594
5075 Warm air heating & air conditioning [3]	48	46	293	296	6	24,137	28,081	8,843	10,201
5078 Refrigeration equipment and supplies [3]	9	9	37	38	4	23,459	25,789	1,014	1,099
5082 Construction and mining machinery [3]	24	24	194	238	10	32,351	33,361	7,327	8,571
5083 Farm and garden machinery [3]	19	18	104	116	6	26,731	26,000	3,391	3,197
5084 Industrial machinery and equipment [3]	230	244	2,081	2,335	10	32,504	34,914	74,010	87,876
5085 Industrial supplies [3]	119	117	1,059	981	8	35,569	38,279	43,637	43,308
5087 Service establishment equipment [3]	40	40	483	481	12	22,733	28,183	12,134	14,131
5088 Transportation equipment & supplies [3]	57	52	562	578	11	30,235	32,180	19,160	19,664
5091 Sporting & recreational goods [3]	25	28	229	167	6	19,004	22,036	4,977	3,888
5092 Toys and hobby goods and supplies [3]	12	11	93	71	6	13,978	17,127	1,216	1,228
5093 Scrap and waste materials [3]	23	29	342	346	12	21,848	20,682	7,188	7,843
5094 Jewelry & precious stones [3]	26	26	166	133	5	17,614	20,150	2,696	2,558
5099 Durable goods, nec [3]	37	36	98	175	5	17,633	18,217	1,987	3,565
5111 Printing and writing paper [3]	13	13	235	223	17	25,106	27,677	6,377	6,633
5112 Stationery and office supplies [3]	51	44	780	650	15	17,205	19,569	13,954	12,533
5113 Industrial & personal service paper [3]	22	22	194	156	7	25,649	31,513	5,468	5,395
5120 Drugs, proprietaries, and sundries [3]	50	53	662	745	14	29,450	34,443	21,941	25,568
5131 Piece goods & notions [3]	12	11	94	90	8	20,936	21,422	2,300	2,328
5136 Men's and boys' clothing [2]	-	13	-	79	6	-	15,747	-	1,219
5141 Groceries, general line [3]	47	44	1,179	1,324	30	25,520	24,082	31,210	33,173
5142 Packaged frozen food [3]	20	18	269	304	17	18,320	17,816	5,474	5,714
5143 Dairy products, exc. dried or canned [3]	13	10	21	27	3	26,476	26,222	657	793
5145 Confectionery [3]	12	11	228	225	20	26,421	26,756	5,874	6,232
5146 Fish and seafoods [3]	77	79	430	627	8	12,921	12,172	5,696	8,249
5147 Meats and meat products [3]	15	14	204	236	17	26,333	25,390	5,194	5,421
5148 Fresh fruits and vegetables [3]	22	25	570	625	25	19,972	20,250	13,522	14,690
5149 Groceries and related products, nec [3]	81	79	1,206	1,165	15	23,333	21,377	29,890	30,122
5150 Farm-product raw materials [3]	24	23	337	197	9	34,457	31,310	12,123	6,110
5162 Plastics materials & basic shapes [3]	13	13	125	120	9	24,704	28,500	3,786	4,096
5169 Chemicals & allied products, nec	80	79	731	647	8	32,208	33,929	23,474	22,274
5171 Petroleum bulk stations & terminals	50	46	554	549	12	32,946	31,687	19,251	18,633
5172 Petroleum products, nec [3]	32	31	346	319	10	37,064	30,270	12,015	10,674
5180 Beer, wine, and distilled beverages [3]	25	24	1,060	1,090	45	25,608	27,648	29,048	27,613
5191 Farm supplies [3]	25	25	87	94	4	14,345	13,745	1,444	1,398
5192 Books, periodicals, & newspapers [3]	19	19	138	90	5	23,275	29,600	3,426	2,525
5193 Flowers & florists' supplies [3]	12	12	32	43	4	18,875	22,698	656	970
5194 Tobacco and tobacco products [1]	11	-	311	-	-	19,743	-	7,784	-
5198 Paints, varnishes, and supplies [3]	14	15	102	103	7	28,353	33,942	2,960	3,605
5199 Nondurable goods, nec [3]	57	60	335	298	5	21,158	23,624	7,260	7,277
52 - Retail trade	7,616	7,522	115,260	116,793	16	11,526	12,230	1,407,927	1,510,949
5210 Lumber and other building materials	100	95	1,669	1,548	16	19,089	20,912	33,184	35,186
5230 Paint, glass, and wallpaper stores [3]	40	37	199	220	6	23,156	21,127	4,822	4,783
5250 Hardware stores [3]	87	68	519	468	7	12,008	12,829	7,027	6,396
5260 Retail nurseries and garden stores [3]	37	37	251	235	6	11,060	11,915	3,360	3,392
5270 Mobile home dealers [3]	4	4	11	15	4	9,818	9,333	285	292
5310 Department stores [3]	53	50	8,715	8,902	178	11,189	12,581	105,908	114,382
5330 Variety stores	59	45	609	543	12	10,049	9,893	6,207	5,715
5390 Misc. general merchandise stores [3]	46	50	1,264	1,234	25	11,117	12,097	14,862	15,202
5410 Grocery stores	859	823	18,786	18,714	23	8,804	9,771	169,867	189,322
5420 Meat and fish markets	70	68	321	437	6	11,090	10,773	3,996	4,811
5440 Candy, nut, and confectionery stores [3]	19	21	160	174	8	9,625	10,322	1,685	1,708
5450 Dairy products stores [3]	6	6	18	38	6	3,111	5,263	78	325
5460 Retail bakeries	132	122	982	933	8	8,916	9,248	8,332	8,335
5490 Miscellaneous food stores [3]	54	64	332	389	6	7,506	8,864	2,861	4,096
5510 New and used car dealers [3]	76	73	4,555	4,531	62	27,168	29,596	135,985	161,000
5520 Used car dealers [3]	38	41	92	93	2	28,304	21,720	2,273	2,760
5530 Auto and home supply stores	177	179	1,547	1,488	8	16,052	18,804	27,153	30,050
5540 Gasoline service stations	390	378	2,840	2,617	7	10,663	11,060	31,289	30,906
5550 Boat dealers [3]	37	37	130	152	4	15,662	17,368	2,336	3,114
5560 Recreational vehicle dealers [1]	7	-	6	-	-	10,667	-	56	-
5570 Motorcycle dealers [3]	13	13	43	56	4	15,349	18,500	741	1,076

Continued on next page.

NEW ORLEANS, LA MSA - [continued]

Wholesale and Retail Trade USA	Establishments		Employment		Emp / Est	Pay / Employee		Annual Payroll ($ 000)	
	1994	1995	1994	1995	1995	1994	1995	1994	1995
5610 Men's & boys' clothing stores[3]	94	93	771	734	8	13,131	14,196	10,515	10,619
5620 Women's clothing stores[3]	271	236	2,465	2,155	9	8,933	9,619	24,274	21,140
5630 Women's accessory & specialty stores[3]	58	46	332	301	7	9,386	9,037	3,147	2,778
5640 Children's and infants' wear stores[3]	28	27	173	198	7	7,075	7,798	1,492	1,829
5650 Family clothing stores[3]	96	94	1,215	1,251	13	8,658	9,049	11,029	12,274
5660 Shoe stores[3]	204	191	1,026	1,087	6	10,764	11,316	11,852	11,969
5690 Misc. apparel & accessory stores[3]	56	57	261	286	5	9,732	9,986	2,618	2,877
5712 Furniture stores[3]	121	124	1,175	1,237	10	17,539	18,622	23,183	26,996
5713 Floor covering stores[3]	44	46	211	154	3	17,877	22,857	4,941	4,814
5714 Drapery and upholstery stores[3]	11	10	20	8	1	10,400	14,000	211	130
5719 Misc. homefurnishings stores[3]	83	84	454	463	6	11,683	14,350	5,944	6,632
5720 Household appliance stores[3]	40	46	242	327	7	17,934	20,306	4,939	6,116
5731 Radio, TV, & electronic stores[3]	67	61	513	583	10	18,300	18,792	9,913	12,113
5734 Computer and software stores[3]	29	31	181	211	7	17,613	17,555	3,777	4,338
5735 Record & prerecorded tape stores[3]	45	43	402	452	11	8,010	7,717	3,352	3,614
5736 Musical instrument stores[3]	17	18	74	97	5	18,703	17,649	1,434	1,761
5812 Eating places	1,700	1,533	38,883	38,325	25	8,675	9,148	358,286	359,786
5813 Drinking places	312	283	2,566	2,547	9	9,548	10,169	24,027	25,060
5910 Drug stores and proprietary stores	235	227	3,332	3,403	15	15,264	16,554	54,131	60,316
5920 Liquor stores[3]	32	29	198	236	8	17,374	15,407	2,829	4,029
5930 Used merchandise stores[3]	133	139	1,273	1,169	8	12,063	15,104	17,480	18,354
5941 Sporting goods and bicycle shops[3]	80	73	474	533	7	11,367	11,865	6,911	6,990
5942 Book stores[3]	63	63	380	524	8	9,537	11,260	3,891	6,529
5943 Stationery stores[3]	29	34	164	136	4	10,171	11,147	1,881	1,599
5944 Jewelry stores[3]	161	163	931	907	6	18,552	21,469	17,590	19,880
5945 Hobby, toy, and game shops[3]	56	62	575	567	9	9,037	11,182	6,410	7,889
5946 Camera & photographic supply stores[3]	18	16	58	62	4	14,966	14,645	906	851
5947 Gift, novelty, and souvenir shops[3]	210	207	1,182	1,221	6	9,154	9,572	10,839	11,582
5948 Luggage and leather goods stores[3]	11	11	63	49	4	12,381	13,143	899	733
5949 Sewing, needlework, and piece goods[3]	39	38	274	287	8	9,431	8,711	2,446	2,605
5961 Catalog and mail-order houses[3]	18	23	184	182	8	16,717	22,484	3,422	4,355
5962 Merchandising machine operators[3]	28	26	311	292	11	18,174	20,151	6,076	6,142
5963 Direct selling establishments[3]	53	53	822	914	17	19,231	18,818	16,705	17,213
5992 Florists	100	108	417	492	5	10,782	10,114	4,479	5,055
5993 Tobacco stores and stands[3]	19	22	13	41	2	10,462	10,927	144	470
5994 News dealers and newsstands[2]	-	7	-	13	2	-	9,231	-	132
5995 Optical goods stores[3]	84	82	454	430	5	16,449	17,963	8,061	8,080
5999 Miscellaneous retail stores, nec[3]	222	243	1,047	1,135	5	14,258	15,330	16,427	18,816

Source: County Business Patterns 1994/95, CBP-94/95, U.S. Department of Commerce, Washington DC, November 1997. The employment column represents mid-March employment in the year. Pay per employee is calculated by dividing 1st Quarter payroll, annualized, by mid-March employment. The column headed 'Emp / Est' shows 'employees per establishment'. A dash (-) means that data are unavailable or cannot be calculated. nec means not elsewhere classified. *Notes:* 1. 1994 data incomplete; unavailable or withheld. 2. 1995 data incomplete; unavailable or withheld. 3. 1994 and 1995 data incomplete; unavailable or withheld.

NEW YORK, NY PMSA

Wholesale and Retail Trade USA	Establishments		Employment		Emp / Est	Pay / Employee		Annual Payroll ($ 000)	
	1994	1995	1994	1995	1995	1994	1995	1994	1995
50- Wholesale trade	22,911	23,245	240,445	241,580	10	40,284	43,274	10,490,732	10,711,952
5012 Automobiles and other vehicles	112	127	1,060	969	8	37,566	36,995	43,201	39,740
5013 Motor vehicle supplies and new parts	446	410	4,215	4,179	10	25,467	26,684	119,868	118,193
5014 Tires and tubes[3]	35	29	362	307	11	33,436	36,000	17,251	10,252
5015 Motor vehicle parts, used	124	143	748	938	7	25,021	25,514	19,313	23,497
5021 Furniture	341	336	3,319	3,549	11	35,717	39,896	135,848	145,478
5023 Homefurnishings[1]	744	720	6,434	6,705	9	36,500	39,436	269,559	281,311
5031 Lumber, plywood, and millwork[1]	151	146	1,653	1,568	11	31,247	31,023	58,147	55,023
5032 Brick, stone, & related materials[1]	128	111	763	638	6	29,688	32,038	27,332	23,786
5033 Roofing, siding, & insulation[3]	33	29	313	213	7	34,019	39,962	14,037	9,335
5039 Construction materials, nec[3]	74	145	372	1,180	8	24,344	31,688	11,402	39,161
5043 Photographic equipment & supplies[3]	115	116	2,027	2,020	17	42,230	48,420	86,662	95,182
5044 Office equipment	194	191	4,765	4,954	26	40,613	46,978	196,205	220,813
5045 Computers, peripherals, & software	478	483	8,306	8,342	17	66,457	74,527	519,802	547,590
5046 Commercial equipment, nec	187	196	1,235	1,320	7	27,569	30,164	38,899	43,444
5047 Medical and hospital equipment	292	263	3,298	2,955	11	46,509	40,751	167,167	129,191
5048 Ophthalmic goods[3]	74	72	678	868	12	35,150	47,217	30,644	50,762
5049 Professional equipment, nec[3]	67	61	880	978	16	41,027	34,135	43,077	47,546
5051 Metals service centers and offices[3]	284	289	3,044	3,576	12	55,551	63,698	189,139	246,222
5052 Coal and other minerals and ores[3]	45	44	286	341	8	60,909	68,645	19,508	24,329
5063 Electrical apparatus and equipment	425	390	4,893	4,222	11	34,703	38,126	187,870	166,443
5064 Electrical appliances, TV & radios[2]	208	202	1,523	1,555	8	29,190	30,832	49,301	55,015

Continued on next page.

NEW YORK, NY PMSA - [continued]

Wholesale and Retail Trade USA	Establishments		Employment		Emp / Est	Pay / Employee		Annual Payroll ($ 000)	
	1994	1995	1994	1995	1995	1994	1995	1994	1995
5065 Electronic parts and equipment	556	591	6,683	7,063	12	45,712	46,862	306,350	331,257
5072 Hardware	247	253	2,586	2,514	10	31,206	33,434	89,530	90,047
5074 Plumbing & hydronic heating supplies	283	283	2,992	2,577	9	32,282	36,034	106,575	96,745
5075 Warm air heating & air conditioning	82	87	768	788	9	49,526	52,843	40,523	43,930
5078 Refrigeration equipment and supplies[3]	33	33	341	395	12	34,827	31,565	12,440	12,895
5082 Construction and mining machinery[3]	46	46	381	455	10	29,785	32,686	12,909	15,279
5083 Farm and garden machinery[3]	26	23	187	136	6	22,396	29,529	5,378	4,651
5084 Industrial machinery and equipment	427	405	3,505	3,434	8	41,277	41,845	162,004	159,860
5085 Industrial supplies	197	200	1,532	1,601	8	33,196	35,131	59,719	65,812
5087 Service establishment equipment	179	172	1,161	1,197	7	27,104	28,414	35,827	38,082
5088 Transportation equipment & supplies	72	72	458	477	7	40,786	47,262	23,459	26,363
5091 Sporting & recreational goods[2]	88	84	702	676	8	31,613	31,195	24,665	23,146
5092 Toys and hobby goods and supplies[3]	211	205	1,374	1,535	7	45,447	44,500	65,390	66,288
5093 Scrap and waste materials	291	309	2,964	3,091	10	21,148	22,983	69,474	78,363
5094 Jewelry & precious stones[3]	2,218	2,216	13,546	14,044	6	32,702	34,418	495,662	503,362
5099 Durable goods, nec	498	486	3,109	2,787	6	52,751	47,657	160,550	136,344
5111 Printing and writing paper[3]	117	107	2,074	1,968	18	51,788	61,907	107,579	130,613
5112 Stationery and office supplies	391	316	7,724	6,633	21	18,404	20,260	147,195	136,754
5113 Industrial & personal service paper	304	307	3,679	3,774	12	34,545	36,234	149,208	160,414
5120 Drugs, proprietaries, and sundries	417	424	10,200	12,434	29	49,626	55,969	500,024	639,506
5131 Piece goods & notions	1,652	1,667	15,148	15,533	9	44,910	49,363	755,999	775,191
5136 Men's and boys' clothing[1]	782	717	7,891	7,799	11	41,852	44,140	356,563	352,529
5137 Women's and children's clothing	2,394	2,293	26,886	25,241	11	34,726	39,897	1,088,668	1,095,013
5139 Footwear[3]	272	273	2,600	2,646	10	52,392	53,887	151,190	151,232
5141 Groceries, general line	264	251	3,199	3,495	14	29,030	30,967	119,120	129,671
5142 Packaged frozen food[3]	109	103	1,120	1,348	13	27,025	29,246	34,906	36,515
5143 Dairy products, exc. dried or canned[1]	172	167	2,117	2,245	13	34,169	34,081	74,220	75,201
5144 Poultry and poultry products	49	51	558	591	12	27,104	28,643	17,825	17,537
5145 Confectionery[1]	95	100	643	604	6	37,723	34,642	23,249	22,154
5146 Fish and seafoods[3]	197	195	1,738	1,739	9	24,237	26,273	46,143	49,653
5147 Meats and meat products	319	320	3,184	3,229	10	29,373	30,507	100,776	104,232
5148 Fresh fruits and vegetables	274	272	3,521	3,737	14	30,427	31,050	122,154	130,027
5149 Groceries and related products, nec	906	903	9,998	10,148	11	32,887	34,193	352,185	363,334
5153 Grain and field beans[3]	25	20	179	119	6	61,385	63,697	12,110	9,209
5154 Livestock[3]	6	5	4	7	1	18,000	16,000	181	160
5159 Farm-product raw materials, nec[3]	81	81	342	322	4	45,427	37,925	19,155	14,425
5162 Plastics materials & basic shapes[3]	110	103	889	733	7	36,670	41,839	35,894	31,933
5169 Chemicals & allied products, nec[2]	327	317	3,605	2,761	9	51,560	59,516	195,416	166,189
5171 Petroleum bulk stations & terminals[3]	66	52	952	795	15	42,076	42,153	39,793	32,267
5172 Petroleum products, nec	90	82	2,149	2,135	26	48,551	42,559	128,869	93,385
5181 Beer and ale[3]	128	123	1,791	1,796	15	31,169	33,742	60,142	64,510
5182 Wine and distilled beverages[3]	72	67	1,898	1,963	29	78,620	82,447	127,630	129,468
5191 Farm supplies[2]	144	103	759	665	6	40,121	49,750	33,604	34,286
5192 Books, periodicals, & newspapers[2]	318	321	5,422	6,417	20	38,684	38,045	220,522	238,754
5193 Flowers & florists' supplies[1]	162	140	1,186	1,041	7	24,061	25,741	32,472	28,354
5194 Tobacco and tobacco products[3]	104	96	1,778	1,205	13	55,246	82,470	81,431	87,338
5198 Paints, varnishes, and supplies	115	102	914	812	8	30,985	32,862	31,144	29,064
5199 Nondurable goods, nec	1,372	1,342	8,174	8,125	6	38,252	43,254	373,751	373,361
52- Retail trade	48,766	49,344	428,898	449,338	9	17,293	17,818	8,067,403	8,428,204
5210 Lumber and other building materials	400	427	4,251	5,696	13	22,448	22,551	105,810	135,165
5230 Paint, glass, and wallpaper stores	210	189	913	887	5	23,338	22,931	21,892	20,935
5250 Hardware stores	619	465	2,868	2,020	4	21,428	20,077	62,583	40,286
5260 Retail nurseries and garden stores	109	119	708	820	7	16,542	18,083	15,885	19,581
5310 Department stores[3]	65	73	23,861	29,004	397	17,932	17,461	486,968	529,975
5330 Variety stores[2]	483	440	5,092	4,630	11	12,667	12,263	63,624	61,213
5390 Misc. general merchandise stores	503	500	5,701	6,331	13	13,128	14,630	82,004	96,468
5410 Grocery stores	5,566	5,634	52,417	51,721	9	14,668	15,151	792,058	800,964
5420 Meat and fish markets	856	818	3,272	3,255	4	14,689	14,844	49,674	49,739
5430 Fruit and vegetable markets	457	439	1,460	1,487	3	14,052	14,453	22,734	23,980
5440 Candy, nut, and confectionery stores	178	178	503	509	3	11,093	11,615	5,694	6,066
5450 Dairy products stores	147	150	616	623	4	8,591	9,130	5,790	6,210
5460 Retail bakeries	1,256	1,242	7,503	7,487	6	12,115	12,169	97,322	92,781
5490 Miscellaneous food stores	498	537	2,288	2,958	6	13,747	13,175	35,378	42,781
5510 New and used car dealers	262	273	10,510	11,308	41	30,231	32,157	391,165	395,196
5520 Used car dealers	249	250	469	534	2	17,851	17,745	9,599	10,776
5530 Auto and home supply stores	461	463	2,614	3,087	7	18,366	19,182	53,036	62,504
5540 Gasoline service stations	1,599	1,591	6,406	6,297	4	14,761	15,034	98,748	96,652
5550 Boat dealers[2]	29	25	185	136	5	21,600	25,647	4,995	4,083
5570 Motorcycle dealers	30	33	77	100	3	21,247	21,680	2,052	2,594
5610 Men's & boys' clothing stores[2]	779	730	5,152	5,200	7	19,844	24,140	109,771	129,718
5620 Women's clothing stores	1,735	1,611	15,380	15,666	10	14,423	14,369	240,326	237,543

Continued on next page.

NEW YORK, NY PMSA - [continued]

Wholesale and Retail Trade USA	Establishments		Employment		Emp / Est	Pay / Employee		Annual Payroll ($ 000)	
	1994	1995	1994	1995	1995	1994	1995	1994	1995
5630 Women's accessory & specialty stores	482	466	2,312	2,451	5	16,844	16,055	47,495	49,695
5640 Children's and infants' wear stores [2]	290	288	3,162	3,799	13	10,794	11,223	37,035	44,481
5650 Family clothing stores	589	555	10,134	8,773	16	16,633	14,545	189,187	146,446
5660 Shoe stores	1,321	1,306	6,894	7,325	6	15,385	15,567	114,937	116,106
5690 Misc. apparel & accessory stores	309	323	1,770	2,162	7	12,841	12,984	28,349	34,189
5712 Furniture stores	931	931	4,936	5,230	6	21,363	22,576	116,983	124,817
5713 Floor covering stores	353	347	1,784	2,210	6	21,617	23,828	45,040	57,531
5714 Drapery and upholstery stores	86	88	439	373	4	13,995	16,847	7,019	6,280
5719 Misc. homefurnishings stores	562	547	3,936	4,106	8	16,365	16,270	72,488	69,018
5720 Household appliance stores [1]	193	193	1,655	1,555	8	19,712	22,300	35,808	37,768
5731 Radio, TV, & electronic stores	601	586	3,906	4,051	7	20,748	20,570	84,485	107,881
5734 Computer and software stores	155	180	786	941	5	22,163	23,005	18,994	24,098
5735 Record & prerecorded tape stores [1]	289	286	2,222	2,205	8	12,214	13,711	30,450	31,380
5736 Musical instrument stores [3]	65	61	481	498	8	25,480	25,341	13,305	15,008
5812 Eating places	11,977	11,250	134,309	136,774	12	12,700	13,493	1,884,026	1,942,778
5813 Drinking places	1,422	1,297	6,443	6,780	5	11,343	11,219	75,649	77,922
5910 Drug stores and proprietary stores	1,956	1,965	17,309	19,306	10	15,973	16,649	303,753	332,578
5920 Liquor stores	985	966	2,980	3,020	3	15,885	16,318	52,500	53,451
5930 Used merchandise stores	478	471	2,090	2,011	4	22,243	24,125	51,637	52,077
5941 Sporting goods and bicycle shops	368	395	2,730	3,545	9	16,766	15,544	50,759	61,481
5942 Book stores	356	364	3,414	3,964	11	14,288	15,806	51,991	62,802
5943 Stationery stores	322	317	1,239	1,890	6	15,245	14,836	19,491	27,653
5944 Jewelry stores	1,173	1,170	5,285	5,612	5	28,540	31,614	159,663	172,540
5945 Hobby, toy, and game shops [2]	200	206	2,387	2,609	13	11,859	12,063	33,799	35,960
5946 Camera & photographic supply stores [3]	125	128	729	778	6	22,206	22,226	17,249	16,487
5947 Gift, novelty, and souvenir shops	938	913	3,847	3,996	4	12,277	12,788	51,153	55,361
5948 Luggage and leather goods stores [3]	114	113	504	472	4	21,992	23,356	12,737	13,300
5949 Sewing, needlework, and piece goods [3]	207	205	817	784	4	15,001	16,648	13,417	13,496
5961 Catalog and mail-order houses	277	304	3,667	4,202	14	25,498	27,715	106,265	119,947
5962 Merchandising machine operators	124	126	679	704	6	21,785	22,375	16,649	16,371
5963 Direct selling establishments	310	308	3,621	3,446	11	15,717	17,026	71,405	62,967
5983 Fuel oil dealers [3]	253	252	1,859	1,715	7	45,696	42,610	72,199	64,048
5984 Liquefied petroleum gas dealers [3]	20	21	308	254	12	27,740	28,378	8,682	7,301
5992 Florists	644	638	2,024	2,133	3	15,945	15,989	36,106	36,256
5993 Tobacco stores and stands [3]	95	85	225	207	2	16,604	19,304	4,248	4,268
5994 News dealers and newsstands [3]	455	461	1,324	1,486	3	12,157	12,423	17,018	19,309
5995 Optical goods stores [3]	459	485	2,287	2,300	5	20,819	21,894	51,898	54,047
5999 Miscellaneous retail stores, nec	1,474	1,522	6,368	7,166	5	22,576	22,721	162,891	181,023

Source: County Business Patterns 1994/95, CBP-94/95, U.S. Department of Commerce, Washington DC, November 1997. The employment column represents mid-March employment in the year. Pay per employee is calculated by dividing 1st Quarter payroll, annualized, by mid-March employment. The column headed 'Emp / Est' shows 'employees per establishment'. A dash (-) means that data are unavailable or cannot be calculated. nec means not elsewhere classified. *Notes:* 1. 1994 data incomplete; unavailable or withheld. 2. 1995 data incomplete; unavailable or withheld. 3. 1994 and 1995 data incomplete; unavailable or withheld.

NEWARK, NJ PMSA

Wholesale and Retail Trade USA	Establishments		Employment		Emp / Est	Pay / Employee		Annual Payroll ($ 000)	
	1994	1995	1994	1995	1995	1994	1995	1994	1995
50 – Wholesale trade	4,764	4,815	74,697	75,758	16	41,177	43,960	3,229,425	3,330,992
5012 Automobiles and other vehicles	52	58	1,016	1,203	21	29,425	33,912	34,731	40,510
5013 Motor vehicle supplies and new parts	210	202	2,231	2,170	11	25,008	26,339	64,313	59,348
5014 Tires and tubes [3]	26	25	222	216	9	23,730	24,852	5,820	5,636
5015 Motor vehicle parts, used	48	56	278	415	7	17,914	24,048	6,319	10,342
5021 Furniture	63	70	787	868	12	35,710	35,217	31,586	32,930
5023 Homefurnishings [3]	104	106	1,703	1,743	16	28,587	30,639	56,729	55,979
5031 Lumber, plywood, and millwork	54	55	606	535	10	31,683	34,011	21,147	18,907
5032 Brick, stone, & related materials	40	37	236	200	5	32,559	36,820	10,895	8,433
5033 Roofing, siding, & insulation	24	22	247	259	12	37,053	37,653	11,123	10,481
5039 Construction materials, nec [3]	36	48	504	783	16	41,873	41,231	23,828	32,446
5043 Photographic equipment & supplies [3]	24	24	413	451	19	45,191	47,601	20,231	22,066
5044 Office equipment	84	100	3,260	3,350	34	40,391	46,860	143,204	154,630
5045 Computers, peripherals, & software	201	199	3,094	3,146	16	67,970	66,332	193,800	181,055
5046 Commercial equipment, nec [1]	52	54	246	461	9	35,154	42,204	9,664	16,180
5047 Medical and hospital equipment	112	106	1,723	1,616	15	41,516	46,329	75,629	81,115
5048 Ophthalmic goods [3]	15	20	661	746	37	32,478	35,206	23,286	28,309
5049 Professional equipment, nec [2]	39	35	342	400	11	31,404	40,390	11,449	15,813
5051 Metals service centers and offices [3]	109	108	765	605	6	40,507	47,775	32,776	30,435
5063 Electrical apparatus and equipment	180	153	2,449	2,109	14	39,030	41,756	98,347	88,832
5064 Electrical appliances, TV & radios [3]	38	34	676	658	19	44,609	43,520	33,616	30,481
5065 Electronic parts and equipment	225	237	3,130	3,308	14	44,386	52,403	147,948	169,832

Continued on next page.

NEWARK, NJ PMSA - [continued]

Wholesale and Retail Trade USA	Establishments		Employment		Emp / Est	Pay / Employee		Annual Payroll ($ 000)	
	1994	1995	1994	1995	1995	1994	1995	1994	1995
5072 Hardware	97	97	867	824	8	30,524	33,806	31,136	30,751
5074 Plumbing & hydronic heating supplies [3]	94	99	503	547	6	36,485	37,865	19,483	21,692
5075 Warm air heating & air conditioning [3]	40	41	497	509	12	43,670	43,709	22,513	23,839
5078 Refrigeration equipment and supplies [1]	6	-	10	-	-	21,200	-	255	-
5082 Construction and mining machinery [1]	20	24	110	185	8	39,127	41,341	5,472	7,971
5083 Farm and garden machinery	21	19	188	155	8	30,660	38,271	7,547	6,558
5084 Industrial machinery and equipment	331	334	2,663	2,933	9	39,330	41,165	115,734	125,139
5085 Industrial supplies	184	179	1,748	1,862	10	36,293	38,311	70,141	77,080
5087 Service establishment equipment	82	81	752	735	9	26,149	27,287	22,393	21,866
5088 Transportation equipment & supplies [3]	24	25	182	198	8	35,165	35,798	7,100	7,701
5091 Sporting & recreational goods	37	38	227	192	5	30,767	37,479	8,233	7,291
5092 Toys and hobby goods and supplies	28	33	361	403	12	30,227	34,839	15,216	16,814
5093 Scrap and waste materials	118	113	1,703	1,878	17	25,966	28,128	55,127	59,816
5094 Jewelry & precious stones [3]	57	59	406	413	7	35,635	39,622	14,192	14,022
5099 Durable goods, nec	87	80	531	578	7	30,614	32,118	16,978	19,276
5111 Printing and writing paper [3]	32	32	769	718	22	40,744	40,685	38,632	32,152
5112 Stationery and office supplies	129	111	1,611	1,284	12	34,287	40,726	56,655	52,305
5113 Industrial & personal service paper	106	99	941	896	9	32,115	33,982	34,194	34,064
5120 Drugs, proprietaries, and sundries	126	126	11,618	10,391	82	56,332	58,529	630,656	576,332
5131 Piece goods & notions	66	63	312	341	5	42,962	41,889	17,935	17,937
5136 Men's and boys' clothing [3]	52	47	353	274	6	21,700	25,956	8,442	7,318
5137 Women's and children's clothing [3]	65	63	1,176	1,249	20	27,844	28,307	39,756	39,320
5139 Footwear [3]	15	13	61	44	3	27,082	32,727	1,794	1,239
5141 Groceries, general line [3]	32	34	366	450	13	33,858	35,547	14,125	15,081
5142 Packaged frozen food	34	29	292	354	12	28,342	27,209	10,148	9,950
5143 Dairy products, exc. dried or canned	30	30	360	411	14	39,389	34,618	13,923	14,744
5144 Poultry and poultry products [3]	5	6	49	77	13	33,388	39,688	1,809	2,793
5145 Confectionery [3]	23	22	500	470	21	28,376	31,302	15,463	15,952
5146 Fish and seafoods [3]	28	23	168	231	10	31,286	28,710	5,068	7,541
5147 Meats and meat products [3]	63	62	684	695	11	30,737	43,447	26,379	33,723
5148 Fresh fruits and vegetables [3]	28	29	637	621	21	34,650	41,881	25,617	26,033
5149 Groceries and related products, nec	166	166	2,211	2,595	16	31,848	31,505	79,378	84,558
5150 Farm-product raw materials [3]	14	14	253	295	21	28,490	23,810	7,532	6,740
5162 Plastics materials & basic shapes	63	62	906	852	14	37,934	42,005	38,277	39,570
5169 Chemicals & allied products, nec	156	153	1,615	1,682	11	44,473	49,983	72,268	85,380
5171 Petroleum bulk stations & terminals	33	32	543	546	17	42,328	47,209	24,159	26,196
5172 Petroleum products, nec [3]	20	20	265	200	10	35,034	37,620	9,979	8,327
5181 Beer and ale [3]	13	13	818	741	57	31,550	37,188	27,050	29,111
5182 Wine and distilled beverages [3]	25	24	392	524	22	44,918	41,038	18,516	20,501
5191 Farm supplies	30	30	209	299	10	29,455	39,264	6,939	10,637
5192 Books, periodicals, & newspapers [3]	29	28	294	349	12	32,327	37,845	11,029	15,395
5193 Flowers & florists' supplies	31	28	549	502	18	18,084	23,410	12,846	15,731
5194 Tobacco and tobacco products	26	24	300	292	12	25,453	26,260	8,007	7,977
5198 Paints, varnishes, and supplies [3]	24	20	130	204	10	36,708	35,490	5,956	9,122
5199 Nondurable goods, nec	155	163	1,514	1,744	11	38,108	37,252	59,195	67,203
52 - Retail trade	11,628	11,735	117,041	123,654	11	15,470	16,427	1,996,997	2,152,220
5210 Lumber and other building materials	161	151	1,647	2,297	15	25,275	25,929	51,948	63,154
5230 Paint, glass, and wallpaper stores	83	72	325	373	5	20,603	20,097	7,911	8,179
5250 Hardware stores	111	86	548	417	5	17,701	18,791	10,699	8,236
5260 Retail nurseries and garden stores	73	81	350	498	6	19,531	18,040	9,085	11,111
5310 Department stores [3]	41	42	6,444	7,137	170	12,423	13,005	91,184	95,618
5330 Variety stores	61	56	703	529	9	11,977	11,365	8,579	6,821
5390 Misc. general merchandise stores	66	65	792	1,247	19	12,273	15,929	12,285	21,776
5410 Grocery stores	948	951	18,669	17,891	19	16,243	17,460	309,294	319,237
5420 Meat and fish markets	113	107	491	481	4	15,145	15,035	8,324	7,830
5430 Fruit and vegetable markets [3]	35	36	94	93	3	11,319	16,043	1,536	1,875
5440 Candy, nut, and confectionery stores	38	34	192	174	5	8,521	9,264	1,773	1,648
5450 Dairy products stores	23	20	65	46	2	6,585	4,783	362	242
5460 Retail bakeries	273	253	2,022	1,885	7	10,615	10,814	23,839	21,637
5490 Miscellaneous food stores	89	100	512	530	5	12,906	13,102	7,191	8,400
5510 New and used car dealers	198	189	6,700	7,125	38	30,764	33,245	254,993	253,690
5520 Used car dealers	108	107	272	316	3	23,015	22,608	7,319	8,144
5530 Auto and home supply stores	201	216	1,177	1,332	6	20,353	21,895	26,531	31,056
5540 Gasoline service stations	820	791	3,812	3,755	5	14,188	14,788	57,585	57,168
5550 Boat dealers [3]	13	13	26	37	3	17,077	18,703	895	1,108
5560 Recreational vehicle dealers [3]	6	6	30	31	5	21,467	23,742	704	755
5570 Motorcycle dealers	16	17	90	82	5	23,422	27,610	2,277	2,680
5610 Men's & boys' clothing stores	144	139	898	832	6	15,350	15,327	14,824	13,162
5620 Women's clothing stores	374	324	3,484	3,116	10	10,563	10,733	42,620	34,288
5630 Women's accessory & specialty stores [2]	82	79	314	327	4	12,268	11,841	4,260	4,195
5640 Children's and infants' wear stores [3]	56	56	589	746	13	10,594	10,354	7,029	8,096

Continued on next page.

NEWARK, NJ PMSA - [continued]

Wholesale and Retail Trade USA	Establishments		Employment		Emp / Est	Pay / Employee		Annual Payroll ($ 000)	
	1994	1995	1994	1995	1995	1994	1995	1994	1995
5650 Family clothing stores	93	93	1,408	1,401	15	11,278	11,889	17,022	23,453
5660 Shoe stores	249	244	1,387	1,463	6	13,090	13,545	19,197	19,385
5690 Misc. apparel & accessory stores	72	64	466	322	5	10,987	13,019	4,930	4,509
5712 Furniture stores	246	243	1,778	2,178	9	21,057	19,216	42,675	45,463
5713 Floor covering stores	108	104	564	581	6	21,348	21,990	13,331	14,657
5714 Drapery and upholstery stores[3]	32	32	156	155	5	15,949	17,884	2,760	2,669
5719 Misc. homefurnishings stores	123	122	749	1,088	9	12,721	12,625	11,853	15,403
5720 Household appliance stores	66	65	590	644	10	20,915	20,466	13,478	14,518
5731 Radio, TV, & electronic stores	111	107	859	811	8	26,976	22,762	23,429	19,451
5734 Computer and software stores	50	62	306	419	7	18,575	21,957	6,118	9,341
5735 Record & prerecorded tape stores	59	62	307	306	5	10,085	11,673	3,118	3,527
5736 Musical instrument stores	25	24	110	124	5	21,709	24,548	2,790	3,453
5812 Eating places	2,643	2,553	33,212	34,335	13	10,372	11,139	382,772	403,143
5813 Drinking places	450	413	1,781	1,742	4	9,375	9,791	17,624	17,338
5910 Drug stores and proprietary stores	408	407	5,390	5,825	14	15,277	15,611	88,361	94,084
5920 Liquor stores	423	417	1,589	1,633	4	13,385	13,999	24,068	24,027
5930 Used merchandise stores[1]	83	71	421	397	6	12,950	13,683	6,136	6,118
5941 Sporting goods and bicycle shops	146	153	791	911	6	16,465	15,025	14,176	15,004
5942 Book stores	94	97	803	752	8	9,833	11,468	8,337	8,835
5943 Stationery stores	48	54	226	430	8	15,752	14,447	3,717	6,600
5944 Jewelry stores	225	217	992	842	4	17,714	19,663	19,102	17,941
5945 Hobby, toy, and game shops	71	78	593	656	8	10,266	11,171	7,768	8,237
5946 Camera & photographic supply stores	42	41	120	144	4	16,567	16,611	2,167	2,459
5947 Gift, novelty, and souvenir shops	203	202	1,055	1,075	5	9,084	9,838	11,012	11,800
5948 Luggage and leather goods stores[3]	12	10	29	48	5	19,586	12,500	611	566
5949 Sewing, needlework, and piece goods	42	39	213	178	5	11,944	13,371	2,787	2,330
5961 Catalog and mail-order houses	59	71	563	1,124	16	22,302	35,577	14,387	39,436
5962 Merchandising machine operators	43	44	499	518	12	23,022	23,459	12,732	12,877
5963 Direct selling establishments	121	128	503	698	5	21,400	18,716	11,826	13,485
5983 Fuel oil dealers[3]	112	104	522	407	4	32,575	31,892	15,728	14,063
5984 Liquefied petroleum gas dealers[3]	11	12	134	111	9	27,761	24,288	3,456	2,713
5992 Florists	232	225	900	947	4	12,280	13,119	12,428	13,315
5993 Tobacco stores and stands[2]	17	15	166	30	2	9,904	8,667	2,697	255
5994 News dealers and newsstands[3]	49	45	236	236	5	12,864	10,492	2,858	2,647
5995 Optical goods stores	124	123	387	454	4	21,695	22,053	9,549	11,122
5999 Miscellaneous retail stores, nec	293	322	1,184	1,615	5	15,902	17,672	22,321	32,479

Source: County Business Patterns 1994/95, CBP-94/95, U.S. Department of Commerce, Washington DC, November 1997. The employment column represents mid-March employment in the year. Pay per employee is calculated by dividing 1st Quarter payroll, annualized, by mid-March employment. The column headed 'Emp / Est' shows 'employees per establishment'. A dash (-) means that data are unavailable or cannot be calculated. nec means not elsewhere classified. *Notes:* 1. 1994 data incomplete; unavailable or withheld. 2. 1995 data incomplete; unavailable or withheld. 3. 1994 and 1995 data incomplete; unavailable or withheld.

NEWBURGH PMSA (NY PART)

Wholesale and Retail Trade USA	Establishments		Employment		Emp / Est	Pay / Employee		Annual Payroll ($ 000)	
	1994	1995	1994	1995	1995	1994	1995	1994	1995
50- Wholesale trade	503	518	6,592	6,721	13	25,318	27,020	184,535	190,871
5013 Motor vehicle supplies and new parts	31	28	367	334	12	20,327	20,323	9,566	8,179
5015 Motor vehicle parts, used	-	5	-	49	10	-	14,531	-	863
5021 Furniture	7	8	25	47	6	20,640	66,638	682	1,514
5023 Homefurnishings	12	10	94	87	9	19,064	19,034	1,988	1,828
5031 Lumber, plywood, and millwork	9	13	228	238	18	32,947	40,118	8,038	9,423
5039 Construction materials, nec	4	8	31	70	9	30,581	22,571	816	1,594
5044 Office equipment	6	6	33	33	6	25,333	25,455	984	926
5045 Computers, peripherals, & software	11	14	56	53	4	39,500	42,868	2,210	2,410
5046 Commercial equipment, nec	6	5	28	26	5	24,000	28,615	771	792
5047 Medical and hospital equipment	6	-	29	-	-	23,586	-	868	-
5049 Professional equipment, nec	-	7	-	34	5	-	26,000	-	1,191
5051 Metals service centers and offices	9	12	166	189	16	23,663	22,603	4,387	5,321
5063 Electrical apparatus and equipment	17	17	227	182	11	32,511	35,978	7,630	7,433
5064 Electrical appliances, TV & radios	3	3	5	3	1	24,000	29,333	115	133
5065 Electronic parts and equipment	14	14	68	65	5	28,529	32,615	2,080	2,180
5072 Hardware	7	-	20	-	-	18,200	-	351	-
5074 Plumbing & hydronic heating supplies	13	10	128	89	9	20,000	25,169	2,701	2,383
5083 Farm and garden machinery	5	5	42	44	9	24,095	29,727	1,193	1,259
5084 Industrial machinery and equipment	15	15	100	109	7	27,000	26,092	2,822	2,977
5085 Industrial supplies	10	10	60	63	6	35,400	39,619	2,528	3,029
5087 Service establishment equipment	7	8	59	65	8	25,288	24,185	1,608	1,661
5088 Transportation equipment & supplies	-	4	-	5	1	-	48,000	-	292
5091 Sporting & recreational goods	-	4	-	29	7	-	30,345	-	913

Continued on next page.

NEWBURGH PMSA (NY PART) - [continued]

Wholesale and Retail Trade USA	Establishments		Employment		Emp / Est	Pay / Employee		Annual Payroll ($ 000)	
	1994	1995	1994	1995	1995	1994	1995	1994	1995
5093 Scrap and waste materials	16	17	162	182	11	23,531	26,923	4,171	5,098
5094 Jewelry & precious stones	6	-	11	-	-	12,364	-	184	-
5099 Durable goods, nec	5	4	50	43	11	41,200	38,512	2,148	1,980
5111 Printing and writing paper	5	5	19	17	3	18,947	30,824	455	511
5112 Stationery and office supplies	6	5	52	58	12	19,077	23,586	1,357	1,469
5113 Industrial & personal service paper	11	11	123	131	12	40,911	42,015	5,298	5,901
5120 Drugs, proprietaries, and sundries	12	13	140	163	13	21,943	24,172	3,525	4,143
5131 Piece goods & notions	8	10	24	46	5	50,833	32,000	1,596	2,477
5136 Men's and boys' clothing	5	4	10	7	2	21,600	20,571	189	129
5137 Women's and children's clothing	13	13	236	321	25	18,305	16,885	7,248	8,864
5143 Dairy products, exc. dried or canned	7	7	97	151	22	41,402	33,086	4,113	5,446
5145 Confectionery	3	-	28	-	-	14,714	-	578	-
5146 Fish and seafoods	-	3	-	2	1	-	38,000	-	34
5147 Meats and meat products	7	9	90	110	12	22,222	21,527	2,261	2,508
5148 Fresh fruits and vegetables	7	8	82	89	11	17,171	16,764	1,915	1,964
5149 Groceries and related products, nec	31	32	562	613	19	27,103	26,636	16,911	18,476
5162 Plastics materials & basic shapes	5	4	7	12	3	51,429	36,333	539	737
5169 Chemicals & allied products, nec	15	15	152	142	9	29,711	33,887	4,752	5,131
5171 Petroleum bulk stations & terminals	7	7	168	161	23	35,500	39,429	5,730	6,202
5172 Petroleum products, nec	6	6	43	40	7	53,581	54,100	2,619	2,526
5181 Beer and ale	3	-	66	-	-	18,727	-	1,478	-
5191 Farm supplies	19	16	202	162	10	16,238	18,494	3,363	3,042
5192 Books, periodicals, & newspapers	7	8	79	134	17	20,962	20,269	1,933	2,728
5193 Flowers & florists' supplies	-	3	-	75	25	-	23,040	-	2,016
5194 Tobacco and tobacco products	3	3	95	111	37	18,147	14,955	1,829	1,758
5199 Nondurable goods, nec	18	16	95	85	5	24,716	28,047	1,788	2,546
52- Retail trade	1,960	1,950	21,056	22,869	12	13,293	13,971	313,870	334,798
5210 Lumber and other building materials	39	36	660	718	20	21,345	23,064	15,377	15,835
5250 Hardware stores	25	19	139	117	6	14,331	13,641	2,083	1,575
5260 Retail nurseries and garden stores	15	15	67	74	5	20,418	18,108	1,755	1,747
5310 Department stores	15	14	1,868	1,933	138	10,313	12,478	23,379	25,269
5330 Variety stores	15	12	119	101	8	9,244	8,911	1,169	921
5390 Misc. general merchandise stores	7	10	317	369	37	10,322	11,339	4,008	4,028
5410 Grocery stores	189	187	3,613	3,522	19	13,506	14,003	48,693	50,701
5420 Meat and fish markets	10	8	40	54	7	13,600	9,111	546	514
5430 Fruit and vegetable markets	4	-	16	-	-	5,500	-	140	-
5440 Candy, nut, and confectionery stores	6	4	17	12	3	6,353	7,000	250	69
5450 Dairy products stores	5	-	33	-	-	11,273	-	388	-
5460 Retail bakeries	34	38	187	251	7	9,797	10,614	1,960	2,742
5490 Miscellaneous food stores	12	13	46	58	4	7,478	8,828	418	522
5510 New and used car dealers	44	43	1,068	1,136	26	26,816	30,074	35,747	38,014
5520 Used car dealers	19	17	63	60	4	19,556	22,133	1,378	1,469
5530 Auto and home supply stores	45	48	306	308	6	19,712	20,221	6,372	6,498
5540 Gasoline service stations	113	110	595	583	5	13,997	15,129	9,082	8,878
5550 Boat dealers	4	4	16	28	7	17,250	13,571	571	669
5560 Recreational vehicle dealers	-	6	-	12	2	-	20,333	-	295
5570 Motorcycle dealers	5	5	42	49	10	15,524	17,714	880	1,000
5610 Men's & boys' clothing stores	26	24	199	314	13	9,869	8,280	2,333	2,873
5620 Women's clothing stores	74	73	652	636	9	9,644	10,541	7,179	7,516
5630 Women's accessory & specialty stores	12	15	74	103	7	13,027	11,495	818	1,101
5640 Children's and infants' wear stores	11	9	76	138	15	8,579	11,681	1,776	1,146
5650 Family clothing stores	30	22	457	355	16	9,479	10,952	4,867	3,810
5660 Shoe stores	50	47	315	376	8	11,086	11,574	4,092	4,750
5690 Misc. apparel & accessory stores	11	11	76	101	9	10,000	9,822	1,044	1,186
5712 Furniture stores	31	30	185	202	7	21,838	22,139	4,391	4,759
5719 Misc. homefurnishings stores	27	26	165	189	7	12,121	12,106	2,500	2,523
5720 Household appliance stores	9	10	51	62	6	18,275	18,839	1,068	1,215
5731 Radio, TV, & electronic stores	16	15	105	125	8	16,990	16,128	1,956	2,111
5734 Computer and software stores	7	10	19	28	3	7,789	10,714	245	299
5735 Record & prerecorded tape stores	13	14	61	132	9	9,770	9,152	870	1,092
5736 Musical instrument stores	3	4	10	22	6	11,200	14,727	125	377
5812 Eating places	473	442	5,036	5,794	13	7,737	8,472	45,946	52,524
5813 Drinking places	86	74	209	226	3	7,904	7,770	1,793	1,705
5910 Drug stores and proprietary stores	53	56	631	772	14	16,368	14,860	10,890	12,304
5920 Liquor stores	43	42	125	140	3	11,552	10,914	1,630	1,603
5930 Used merchandise stores	9	8	67	41	5	6,866	11,415	499	513
5941 Sporting goods and bicycle shops	17	22	157	210	10	13,885	17,238	2,933	4,150
5942 Book stores	12	11	87	87	8	11,908	13,195	1,175	1,263
5943 Stationery stores	10	9	47	61	7	11,064	10,623	552	653
5944 Jewelry stores	33	35	176	164	5	13,455	13,171	2,534	2,177
5945 Hobby, toy, and game shops	17	16	81	163	10	11,753	10,184	1,389	1,824

Continued on next page.

NEWBURGH PMSA (NY PART) - [continued]

Wholesale and Retail Trade USA	Establishments		Employment		Emp / Est	Pay / Employee		Annual Payroll ($ 000)	
	1994	1995	1994	1995	1995	1994	1995	1994	1995
5946 Camera & photographic supply stores	4	3	13	13	4	12,923	13,846	144	136
5947 Gift, novelty, and souvenir shops	47	44	220	197	4	7,436	8,589	1,796	1,809
5948 Luggage and leather goods stores	5	4	27	24	6	11,407	13,167	348	339
5949 Sewing, needlework, and piece goods	6	6	61	54	9	5,049	6,222	340	344
5961 Catalog and mail-order houses	5	5	89	84	17	13,258	15,381	1,215	1,388
5962 Merchandising machine operators	8	8	45	45	6	23,467	23,556	1,094	1,076
5963 Direct selling establishments	12	13	59	53	4	14,847	15,472	879	1,024
5983 Fuel oil dealers	22	21	211	205	10	33,156	30,127	6,761	5,795
5992 Florists	29	34	99	105	3	9,778	10,629	1,155	1,161
5995 Optical goods stores	16	17	66	74	4	18,424	18,757	1,379	1,352
5999 Miscellaneous retail stores, nec	54	62	286	310	5	12,643	13,871	4,295	5,049

Source: County Business Patterns 1994/95, CBP-94/95, U.S. Department of Commerce, Washington DC, November 1997. The employment column represents mid-March employment in the year. Pay per employee is calculated by dividing 1st Quarter payroll, annualized, by mid-March employment. The column headed 'Emp / Est' shows 'employees per establishment'. A dash (-) means that data are unavailable or cannot be calculated. nec means not elsewhere classified. *Notes:* 1. 1994 data incomplete; unavailable or withheld. 2. 1995 data incomplete; unavailable or withheld. 3. 1994 and 1995 data incomplete; unavailable or withheld.

NEWBURGH PMSA (PA PART)

Wholesale and Retail Trade USA	Establishments		Employment		Emp / Est	Pay / Employee		Annual Payroll ($ 000)	
	1994	1995	1994	1995	1995	1994	1995	1994	1995
50- Wholesale trade	-	23	-	102	4	-	29,569	-	2,475
5130 Apparel, piece goods, and notions	-	4	-	2	1	-	366,000	-	313
5190 Misc., nondurable goods	-	4	-	15	4	-	12,533	-	183
52- Retail trade	-	156	-	1,594	10	-	11,473	-	20,168
5210 Lumber and other building materials	-	7	-	108	15	-	20,259	-	2,393
5300 General merchandise stores	-	5	-	370	74	-	12,443	-	5,027
5400 Food stores	-	19	-	220	12	-	15,036	-	3,648
5540 Gasoline service stations	-	15	-	122	8	-	11,246	-	1,377
5550 Boat dealers	-	3	-	6	2	-	26,667	-	236
5660 Shoe stores	-	3	-	12	4	-	9,000	-	109
5812 Eating places	-	48	-	519	11	-	6,474	-	3,844
5813 Drinking places	-	8	-	15	2	-	6,667	-	135
5910 Drug stores and proprietary stores	-	4	-	49	12	-	16,000	-	761
5947 Gift, novelty, and souvenir shops	-	3	-	7	2	-	4,571	-	37
5990 Retail stores, nec	-	4	-	20	5	-	10,400	-	232

Source: County Business Patterns 1994/95, CBP-94/95, U.S. Department of Commerce, Washington DC, November 1997. The employment column represents mid-March employment in the year. Pay per employee is calculated by dividing 1st Quarter payroll, annualized, by mid-March employment. The column headed 'Emp / Est' shows 'employees per establishment'. A dash (-) means that data are unavailable or cannot be calculated. nec means not elsewhere classified. *Notes:* 1. 1994 data incomplete; unavailable or withheld. 2. 1995 data incomplete; unavailable or withheld. 3. 1994 and 1995 data incomplete; unavailable or withheld.

NEWBURGH, NY-PA PMSA

Wholesale and Retail Trade USA	Establishments		Employment		Emp / Est	Pay / Employee		Annual Payroll ($ 000)	
	1994	1995	1994	1995	1995	1994	1995	1994	1995
50- Wholesale trade [1]	503	541	6,592	6,823	13	25,318	27,058	184,535	193,346
5013 Motor vehicle supplies and new parts [1]	31	30	367	334	11	20,327	20,323	9,566	8,179
5015 Motor vehicle parts, used [2]	-	5	-	49	10	-	14,531	-	863
5021 Furniture [3]	7	8	25	47	6	20,640	66,638	682	1,514
5023 Homefurnishings [3]	12	10	94	87	9	19,064	19,034	1,988	1,828
5031 Lumber, plywood, and millwork [3]	9	13	228	238	18	32,947	40,118	8,038	9,423
5039 Construction materials, nec [3]	4	8	31	70	9	30,581	22,571	816	1,594
5044 Office equipment [3]	6	6	33	33	6	25,333	25,455	984	926
5045 Computers, peripherals, & software [3]	11	14	56	53	4	39,500	42,868	2,210	2,410
5046 Commercial equipment, nec [3]	6	5	28	26	5	24,000	28,615	771	792
5047 Medical and hospital equipment [1]	6	-	29	-	-	23,586	-	868	-
5049 Professional equipment, nec	-	8	-	34	4	-	26,000	-	1,191
5051 Metals service centers and offices [3]	9	12	166	189	16	23,663	22,603	4,387	5,321
5063 Electrical apparatus and equipment [1]	17	18	227	182	10	32,511	35,978	7,630	7,433
5064 Electrical appliances, TV & radios [3]	3	3	5	3	1	24,000	29,333	115	133
5065 Electronic parts and equipment [1]	14	15	68	65	4	28,529	32,615	2,080	2,180
5072 Hardware [1]	7	-	20	-	-	18,200	-	351	-
5074 Plumbing & hydronic heating supplies [3]	13	10	128	89	9	20,000	25,169	2,701	2,383
5083 Farm and garden machinery [3]	5	5	42	44	9	24,095	29,727	1,193	1,259
5084 Industrial machinery and equipment [3]	15	15	100	109	7	27,000	26,092	2,822	2,977
5085 Industrial supplies [3]	10	10	60	63	6	35,400	39,619	2,528	3,029
5087 Service establishment equipment [1]	7	10	59	65	7	25,288	24,185	1,608	1,661
5088 Transportation equipment & supplies [2]	-	4	-	5	1	-	48,000	-	292

Continued on next page.

NEWBURGH, NY - PA PMSA - [continued]

Wholesale and Retail Trade USA	Establishments		Employment		Emp / Est	Pay / Employee		Annual Payroll ($ 000)	
	1994	1995	1994	1995	1995	1994	1995	1994	1995
5091 Sporting & recreational goods [2]	-	4	-	29	7	-	30,345	-	913
5093 Scrap and waste materials [1]	16	19	162	182	10	23,531	26,923	4,171	5,098
5094 Jewelry & precious stones [1]	6	-	11	-	-	12,364	-	184	-
5099 Durable goods, nec [3]	5	4	50	43	11	41,200	38,512	2,148	1,980
5111 Printing and writing paper [3]	5	5	19	17	3	18,947	30,824	455	511
5112 Stationery and office supplies [3]	6	5	52	58	12	19,077	23,586	1,357	1,469
5113 Industrial & personal service paper [3]	11	11	123	131	12	40,911	42,015	5,298	5,901
5120 Drugs, proprietaries, and sundries [1]	12	14	140	163	12	21,943	24,172	3,525	4,143
5131 Piece goods & notions [1]	8	12	24	46	4	50,833	32,000	1,596	2,477
5136 Men's and boys' clothing [3]	5	4	10	7	2	21,600	20,571	189	129
5137 Women's and children's clothing [3]	13	13	236	321	25	18,305	16,885	7,248	8,864
5143 Dairy products, exc. dried or canned [3]	7	7	97	151	22	41,402	33,086	4,113	5,446
5145 Confectionery [1]	3	-	28	-	-	14,714	-	578	-
5146 Fish and seafoods [2]	-	3	-	2	1	-	38,000	-	34
5147 Meats and meat products [3]	7	9	90	110	12	22,222	21,527	2,261	2,508
5148 Fresh fruits and vegetables [1]	7	9	82	89	10	17,171	16,764	1,915	1,964
5149 Groceries and related products, nec [3]	31	32	562	613	19	27,103	26,636	16,911	18,476
5162 Plastics materials & basic shapes [3]	5	4	7	12	3	51,429	36,333	539	737
5169 Chemicals & allied products, nec [1]	15	16	152	142	9	29,711	33,887	4,752	5,131
5171 Petroleum bulk stations & terminals [1]	7	8	168	161	20	35,500	39,429	5,730	6,202
5172 Petroleum products, nec [1]	6	7	43	40	6	53,581	54,100	2,619	2,526
5181 Beer and ale [1]	3	-	66	-	-	18,727	-	1,478	-
5191 Farm supplies [1]	19	17	202	162	10	16,238	18,494	3,363	3,042
5192 Books, periodicals, & newspapers [3]	7	8	79	134	17	20,962	20,269	1,933	2,728
5193 Flowers & florists' supplies	-	4	-	75	19	-	23,040	-	2,016
5194 Tobacco and tobacco products [3]	3	3	95	111	37	18,147	14,955	1,829	1,758
5199 Nondurable goods, nec [1]	18	18	95	85	5	24,716	28,047	1,788	2,546
52- Retail trade [1]	1,960	2,106	21,056	24,463	12	13,293	13,808	313,870	354,966
5210 Lumber and other building materials [1]	39	43	660	826	19	21,345	22,697	15,377	18,228
5250 Hardware stores [1]	25	20	139	117	6	14,331	13,641	2,083	1,575
5260 Retail nurseries and garden stores [1]	15	17	67	74	4	20,418	18,108	1,755	1,747
5310 Department stores [3]	15	16	1,868	1,933	121	10,313	12,478	23,379	25,269
5330 Variety stores [1]	15	13	119	101	8	9,244	8,911	1,169	921
5390 Misc. general merchandise stores [1]	7	11	317	369	34	10,322	11,339	4,008	4,028
5410 Grocery stores [3]	189	204	3,613	3,522	17	13,506	14,003	48,693	50,701
5420 Meat and fish markets [3]	10	8	40	54	7	13,600	9,111	546	514
5430 Fruit and vegetable markets [1]	4	-	16	-	-	5,500	-	140	-
5440 Candy, nut, and confectionery stores [3]	6	4	17	12	3	6,353	7,000	250	69
5450 Dairy products stores [1]	5	-	33	-	-	11,273	-	388	-
5460 Retail bakeries [3]	34	38	187	251	7	9,797	10,614	1,960	2,742
5490 Miscellaneous food stores [3]	12	13	46	58	4	7,478	8,828	418	522
5510 New and used car dealers [1]	44	44	1,068	1,136	26	26,816	30,074	35,747	38,014
5520 Used car dealers [1]	19	18	63	60	3	19,556	22,133	1,378	1,469
5530 Auto and home supply stores [1]	45	50	306	308	6	19,712	20,221	6,372	6,498
5540 Gasoline service stations [1]	113	125	595	705	6	13,997	14,457	9,082	10,255
5550 Boat dealers [1]	4	7	16	34	5	17,250	15,882	571	905
5560 Recreational vehicle dealers	-	8	-	12	2	-	20,333	-	295
5570 Motorcycle dealers [3]	5	5	42	49	10	15,524	17,714	880	1,000
5610 Men's & boys' clothing stores [3]	26	24	199	314	13	9,869	8,280	2,333	2,873
5620 Women's clothing stores [1]	74	75	652	636	8	9,644	10,541	7,179	7,516
5630 Women's accessory & specialty stores [3]	12	15	74	103	7	13,027	11,495	818	1,101
5640 Children's and infants' wear stores [3]	11	9	76	138	15	8,579	11,681	1,776	1,146
5650 Family clothing stores [3]	30	22	457	355	16	9,479	10,952	4,867	3,810
5660 Shoe stores [1]	50	50	315	388	8	11,086	11,495	4,092	4,859
5690 Misc. apparel & accessory stores [3]	11	11	76	101	9	10,000	9,822	1,044	1,186
5712 Furniture stores [1]	31	34	185	202	6	21,838	22,139	4,391	4,759
5719 Misc. homefurnishings stores [3]	27	26	165	189	7	12,121	12,106	2,500	2,523
5720 Household appliance stores [3]	9	10	51	62	6	18,275	18,839	1,068	1,215
5731 Radio, TV, & electronic stores [3]	16	15	105	125	8	16,990	16,128	1,956	2,111
5734 Computer and software stores [1]	7	11	19	28	3	7,789	10,714	245	299
5735 Record & prerecorded tape stores [3]	13	14	61	132	9	9,770	9,152	870	1,092
5736 Musical instrument stores [3]	3	4	10	22	6	11,200	14,727	125	377
5812 Eating places [1]	473	490	5,036	6,313	13	7,737	8,307	45,946	56,368
5813 Drinking places [1]	86	82	209	241	3	7,904	7,701	1,793	1,840
5910 Drug stores and proprietary stores [1]	53	60	631	821	14	16,368	14,928	10,890	13,065
5920 Liquor stores [1]	43	45	125	140	3	11,552	10,914	1,630	1,603
5930 Used merchandise stores [3]	9	8	67	41	5	6,866	11,415	499	513
5941 Sporting goods and bicycle shops [1]	17	23	157	210	9	13,885	17,238	2,933	4,150
5942 Book stores [1]	12	12	87	87	7	11,908	13,195	1,175	1,263
5943 Stationery stores [1]	10	11	47	61	6	11,064	10,623	552	653
5944 Jewelry stores [1]	33	36	176	164	5	13,455	13,171	2,534	2,177

Continued on next page.

NEWBURGH, NY - PA PMSA - [continued]

Wholesale and Retail Trade USA	Establishments		Employment		Emp / Est	Pay / Employee		Annual Payroll ($ 000)	
	1994	1995	1994	1995	1995	1994	1995	1994	1995
5945 Hobby, toy, and game shops [1]	17	18	81	163	9	11,753	10,184	1,389	1,824
5946 Camera & photographic supply stores [3]	4	3	13	13	4	12,923	13,846	144	136
5947 Gift, novelty, and souvenir shops [1]	47	47	220	204	4	7,436	8,451	1,796	1,846
5948 Luggage and leather goods stores [3]	5	4	27	24	6	11,407	13,167	348	339
5949 Sewing, needlework, and piece goods [1]	6	7	61	54	8	5,049	6,222	340	344
5961 Catalog and mail-order houses [3]	5	5	89	84	17	13,258	15,381	1,215	1,388
5962 Merchandising machine operators [1]	8	9	45	45	5	23,467	23,556	1,094	1,076
5963 Direct selling establishments [3]	12	13	59	53	4	14,847	15,472	879	1,024
5983 Fuel oil dealers [1]	22	22	211	205	9	33,156	30,127	6,761	5,795
5992 Florists [1]	29	35	99	105	3	9,778	10,629	1,155	1,161
5995 Optical goods stores [1]	16	19	66	74	4	18,424	18,757	1,379	1,352
5999 Miscellaneous retail stores, nec [1]	54	63	286	310	5	12,643	13,871	4,295	5,049

Source: County Business Patterns 1994/95, CBP-94/95, U.S. Department of Commerce, Washington DC, November 1997. The employment column represents mid-March employment in the year. Pay per employee is calculated by dividing 1st Quarter payroll, annualized, by mid-March employment. The column headed 'Emp / Est' shows 'employees per establishment'. A dash (-) means that data are unavailable or cannot be calculated. nec means not elsewhere classified. *Notes:* 1. 1994 data incomplete; unavailable or withheld. 2. 1995 data incomplete; unavailable or withheld. 3. 1994 and 1995 data incomplete; unavailable or withheld.

NORFOLK - VIRGINIA BEACH - NEWPORT NEWS MSA (NC PART)

Wholesale and Retail Trade USA	Establishments		Employment		Emp / Est	Pay / Employee		Annual Payroll ($ 000)	
	1994	1995	1994	1995	1995	1994	1995	1994	1995
50- Wholesale trade	16	16	53	58	4	20,000	19,103	1,199	1,264
5190 Misc., nondurable goods	4	3	13	8	3	25,231	18,000	326	145
52- Retail trade	79	91	582	686	8	11,162	13,353	8,255	9,663
5210 Lumber and other building materials	3	-	73	-	-	26,575	-	1,749	-
5410 Grocery stores	10	12	136	139	12	8,559	12,144	1,664	1,903
5540 Gasoline service stations	7	8	47	55	7	10,128	11,127	516	634
5710 Furniture and homefurnishings stores	-	5	-	20	4	-	14,800	-	305
5812 Eating places	9	9	108	106	12	6,407	6,075	903	843
5947 Gift, novelty, and souvenir shops	7	6	36	43	7	9,889	9,023	481	418

Source: County Business Patterns 1994/95, CBP-94/95, U.S. Department of Commerce, Washington DC, November 1997. The employment column represents mid-March employment in the year. Pay per employee is calculated by dividing 1st Quarter payroll, annualized, by mid-March employment. The column headed 'Emp / Est' shows 'employees per establishment'. A dash (-) means that data are unavailable or cannot be calculated. nec means not elsewhere classified. *Notes:* 1. 1994 data incomplete; unavailable or withheld. 2. 1995 data incomplete; unavailable or withheld. 3. 1994 and 1995 data incomplete; unavailable or withheld.

NORFOLK - VIRGINIA BEACH - NEWPORT NEWS MSA (VA PART)

Wholesale and Retail Trade USA	Establishments		Employment		Emp / Est	Pay / Employee		Annual Payroll ($ 000)	
	1994	1995	1994	1995	1995	1994	1995	1994	1995
50- Wholesale trade	-	1,903	-	24,543	13	-	25,848	-	678,824
5012 Automobiles and other vehicles [2]	-	40	-	382	10	-	21,393	-	9,794
5013 Motor vehicle supplies and new parts [2]	-	131	-	911	7	-	21,247	-	21,314
5014 Tires and tubes [2]	-	13	-	150	12	-	33,013	-	3,799
5015 Motor vehicle parts, used [2]	-	43	-	159	4	-	19,094	-	3,182
5021 Furniture [2]	-	25	-	229	9	-	17,345	-	4,195
5023 Homefurnishings [2]	-	38	-	237	6	-	20,911	-	5,351
5031 Lumber, plywood, and millwork [2]	-	38	-	690	18	-	23,275	-	16,878
5032 Brick, stone, & related materials [2]	-	26	-	126	5	-	22,794	-	3,805
5033 Roofing, siding, & insulation [2]	-	20	-	231	12	-	27,931	-	6,844
5039 Construction materials, nec [2]	-	39	-	279	7	-	25,907	-	7,904
5043 Photographic equipment & supplies [2]	-	9	-	19	2	-	13,053	-	209
5044 Office equipment [2]	-	47	-	743	16	-	29,341	-	21,660
5045 Computers, peripherals, & software [2]	-	67	-	666	10	-	39,502	-	27,647
5046 Commercial equipment, nec [2]	-	16	-	111	7	-	29,622	-	3,824
5047 Medical and hospital equipment [2]	-	31	-	243	8	-	32,840	-	8,285
5048 Ophthalmic goods [2]	-	6	-	29	5	-	13,931	-	483
5051 Metals service centers and offices [2]	-	21	-	181	9	-	32,066	-	6,355
5063 Electrical apparatus and equipment [2]	-	71	-	699	10	-	32,126	-	22,440
5064 Electrical appliances, TV & radios [2]	-	14	-	20	1	-	22,200	-	408
5065 Electronic parts and equipment [2]	-	59	-	334	6	-	33,102	-	12,149
5072 Hardware [2]	-	48	-	302	6	-	22,742	-	7,259
5074 Plumbing & hydronic heating supplies [2]	-	36	-	248	7	-	29,758	-	7,579
5075 Warm air heating & air conditioning [2]	-	33	-	287	9	-	27,861	-	8,326
5078 Refrigeration equipment and supplies [2]	-	9	-	53	6	-	26,868	-	1,460
5082 Construction and mining machinery [2]	-	21	-	198	9	-	38,081	-	7,889
5083 Farm and garden machinery [2]	-	12	-	58	5	-	28,897	-	2,007
5084 Industrial machinery and equipment [2]	-	75	-	593	8	-	31,460	-	19,846

Continued on next page.

NORFOLK - VIRGINIA BEACH - NEWPORT NEWS MSA (VA PART) - [continued]

Wholesale and Retail Trade USA	Establishments		Employment		Emp / Est	Pay / Employee		Annual Payroll ($ 000)	
	1994	1995	1994	1995	1995	1994	1995	1994	1995
5085 Industrial supplies[2]	-	70	-	731	10	-	29,806	-	23,662
5087 Service establishment equipment[2]	-	25	-	175	7	-	25,874	-	4,613
5088 Transportation equipment & supplies[2]	-	20	-	181	9	-	23,271	-	5,032
5091 Sporting & recreational goods[2]	-	27	-	234	9	-	21,915	-	5,411
5092 Toys and hobby goods and supplies[2]	-	6	-	58	10	-	20,138	-	2,701
5093 Scrap and waste materials[2]	-	27	-	183	7	-	20,087	-	4,221
5094 Jewelry & precious stones[2]	-	16	-	25	2	-	25,600	-	656
5099 Durable goods, nec[2]	-	33	-	337	10	-	18,754	-	6,967
5111 Printing and writing paper[2]	-	10	-	9	1	-	36,444	-	347
5112 Stationery and office supplies[2]	-	41	-	456	11	-	20,228	-	9,566
5113 Industrial & personal service paper[2]	-	15	-	175	12	-	35,451	-	5,109
5120 Drugs, proprietaries, and sundries[2]	-	21	-	304	14	-	39,605	-	12,567
5136 Men's and boys' clothing[2]	-	26	-	248	10	-	27,194	-	5,606
5137 Women's and children's clothing[2]	-	13	-	19	1	-	11,579	-	316
5141 Groceries, general line[2]	-	23	-	79	3	-	31,848	-	2,218
5142 Packaged frozen food[2]	-	23	-	686	30	-	23,312	-	18,113
5145 Confectionery[2]	-	12	-	50	4	-	23,680	-	1,160
5146 Fish and seafoods[2]	-	44	-	200	5	-	7,500	-	2,049
5147 Meats and meat products[2]	-	19	-	248	13	-	22,355	-	6,297
5148 Fresh fruits and vegetables[2]	-	9	-	241	27	-	20,349	-	5,153
5149 Groceries and related products, nec[2]	-	47	-	2,148	46	-	19,428	-	45,102
5150 Farm-product raw materials[2]	-	21	-	159	8	-	25,258	-	3,568
5162 Plastics materials & basic shapes[2]	-	12	-	76	6	-	21,053	-	1,631
5169 Chemicals & allied products, nec[2]	-	40	-	186	5	-	31,935	-	5,147
5171 Petroleum bulk stations & terminals[2]	-	36	-	355	10	-	30,468	-	10,329
5172 Petroleum products, nec[2]	-	17	-	145	9	-	17,628	-	2,661
5191 Farm supplies[2]	-	24	-	160	7	-	24,200	-	3,861
5192 Books, periodicals, & newspapers[2]	-	14	-	107	8	-	19,065	-	2,132
5198 Paints, varnishes, and supplies[2]	-	24	-	86	4	-	25,349	-	2,439
5199 Nondurable goods, nec[2]	-	51	-	101	2	-	18,297	-	2,112
52 - Retail trade	-	8,203	-	126,086	15	-	11,979	-	1,607,487
5210 Lumber and other building materials[2]	-	80	-	2,820	35	-	16,417	-	44,816
5230 Paint, glass, and wallpaper stores[2]	-	52	-	218	4	-	20,917	-	4,919
5250 Hardware stores	-	56	-	252	5	-	10,619	-	2,990
5260 Retail nurseries and garden stores[2]	-	53	-	393	7	-	12,468	-	6,081
5310 Department stores[2]	-	64	-	9,241	144	-	11,714	-	107,397
5330 Variety stores[2]	-	83	-	1,080	13	-	12,578	-	14,466
5390 Misc. general merchandise stores[2]	-	65	-	1,480	23	-	15,586	-	22,885
5410 Grocery stores[2]	-	687	-	16,670	24	-	10,397	-	176,368
5420 Meat and fish markets[2]	-	53	-	170	3	-	10,635	-	2,255
5430 Fruit and vegetable markets[2]	-	12	-	3	-	-	6,667	-	59
5440 Candy, nut, and confectionery stores[2]	-	26	-	70	3	-	6,743	-	741
5460 Retail bakeries[2]	-	83	-	832	10	-	10,471	-	9,107
5490 Miscellaneous food stores[2]	-	41	-	94	2	-	12,426	-	1,263
5510 New and used car dealers[2]	-	103	-	6,183	60	-	28,098	-	191,467
5520 Used car dealers[2]	-	117	-	904	8	-	19,350	-	19,787
5530 Auto and home supply stores	-	233	-	1,800	8	-	16,064	-	30,647
5540 Gasoline service stations	-	460	-	3,574	8	-	12,088	-	45,203
5550 Boat dealers[2]	-	44	-	285	6	-	17,544	-	5,889
5570 Motorcycle dealers[2]	-	15	-	75	5	-	22,773	-	1,988
5610 Men's & boys' clothing stores[2]	-	112	-	1,009	9	-	10,240	-	11,322
5620 Women's clothing stores[2]	-	249	-	2,238	9	-	8,116	-	18,613
5630 Women's accessory & specialty stores[2]	-	50	-	199	4	-	13,005	-	2,561
5640 Children's and infants' wear stores[2]	-	24	-	144	6	-	8,111	-	1,008
5650 Family clothing stores[2]	-	98	-	1,668	17	-	10,209	-	18,576
5660 Shoe stores[2]	-	224	-	1,297	6	-	10,146	-	12,809
5690 Misc. apparel & accessory stores[2]	-	60	-	261	4	-	9,640	-	2,933
5712 Furniture stores[2]	-	198	-	1,917	10	-	18,865	-	37,894
5713 Floor covering stores[2]	-	65	-	361	6	-	20,720	-	7,447
5714 Drapery and upholstery stores[2]	-	15	-	23	2	-	13,565	-	282
5719 Misc. homefurnishings stores[2]	-	107	-	1,089	10	-	11,750	-	16,473
5720 Household appliance stores[2]	-	31	-	75	2	-	13,600	-	1,168
5731 Radio, TV, & electronic stores[2]	-	81	-	766	9	-	16,037	-	13,081
5734 Computer and software stores[2]	-	49	-	364	7	-	16,846	-	6,785
5735 Record & prerecorded tape stores[2]	-	57	-	299	5	-	9,324	-	3,069
5736 Musical instrument stores[2]	-	26	-	76	3	-	18,000	-	1,417
5812 Eating places	-	2,083	-	41,742	20	-	7,599	-	349,959
5813 Drinking places[2]	-	68	-	817	12	-	6,404	-	4,855
5910 Drug stores and proprietary stores	-	198	-	2,782	14	-	14,470	-	42,577
5930 Used merchandise stores[2]	-	146	-	958	7	-	11,545	-	11,718
5941 Sporting goods and bicycle shops[2]	-	130	-	886	7	-	10,501	-	9,725

Continued on next page.

NORFOLK - VIRGINIA BEACH - NEWPORT NEWS MSA (VA PART) - [continued]

Wholesale and Retail Trade USA	Establishments		Employment		Emp / Est	Pay / Employee		Annual Payroll ($ 000)	
	1994	1995	1994	1995	1995	1994	1995	1994	1995
5942 Book stores [2]	-	73	-	434	6	-	8,645	-	4,025
5943 Stationery stores [2]	-	11	-	43	4	-	8,744	-	430
5944 Jewelry stores [2]	-	166	-	891	5	-	14,923	-	13,539
5945 Hobby, toy, and game shops [2]	-	77	-	836	11	-	9,804	-	9,164
5946 Camera & photographic supply stores [2]	-	19	-	23	1	-	15,130	-	380
5947 Gift, novelty, and souvenir shops	-	233	-	1,192	5	-	8,138	-	12,347
5948 Luggage and leather goods stores [2]	-	9	-	28	3	-	8,429	-	300
5949 Sewing, needlework, and piece goods [2]	-	47	-	264	6	-	7,394	-	1,950
5961 Catalog and mail-order houses [2]	-	42	-	72	2	-	20,389	-	1,467
5962 Merchandising machine operators [2]	-	25	-	250	10	-	18,176	-	4,995
5963 Direct selling establishments [2]	-	79	-	159	2	-	20,403	-	3,549
5980 Fuel dealers [2]	-	46	-	507	11	-	21,996	-	11,229
5992 Florists [2]	-	125	-	353	3	-	10,799	-	3,869
5994 News dealers and newsstands [2]	-	8	-	13	2	-	6,769	-	88
5995 Optical goods stores [2]	-	111	-	466	4	-	16,755	-	8,617
5999 Miscellaneous retail stores, nec	-	236	-	1,255	5	-	11,069	-	15,587

Source: County Business Patterns 1994/95, CBP-94/95, U.S. Department of Commerce, Washington DC, November 1997. The employment column represents mid-March employment in the year. Pay per employee is calculated by dividing 1st Quarter payroll, annualized, by mid-March employment. The column headed 'Emp / Est' shows 'employees per establishment'. A dash (-) means that data are unavailable or cannot be calculated. nec means not elsewhere classified. *Notes:* 1. 1994 data incomplete; unavailable or withheld. 2. 1995 data incomplete; unavailable or withheld. 3. 1994 and 1995 data incomplete; unavailable or withheld.

NORFOLK - VIRGINIA BEACH - NEWPORT NEWS, VA - NC MSA

Wholesale and Retail Trade USA	Establishments		Employment		Emp / Est	Pay / Employee		Annual Payroll ($ 000)	
	1994	1995	1994	1995	1995	1994	1995	1994	1995
50- Wholesale trade [1]	16	1,919	53	24,601	13	20,000	25,832	1,199	680,088
5012 Automobiles and other vehicles [2]	-	40	-	382	10	-	21,393	-	9,794
5013 Motor vehicle supplies and new parts [2]	-	131	-	911	7	-	21,247	-	21,314
5014 Tires and tubes [2]	-	13	-	150	12	-	33,013	-	3,799
5015 Motor vehicle parts, used [2]	-	43	-	159	4	-	19,094	-	3,182
5021 Furniture [2]	-	25	-	229	9	-	17,345	-	4,195
5023 Homefurnishings [2]	-	38	-	237	6	-	20,911	-	5,351
5031 Lumber, plywood, and millwork [2]	-	39	-	690	18	-	23,275	-	16,878
5032 Brick, stone, & related materials [2]	-	26	-	126	5	-	22,794	-	3,805
5033 Roofing, siding, & insulation [2]	-	20	-	231	12	-	27,931	-	6,844
5039 Construction materials, nec [2]	-	40	-	279	7	-	25,907	-	7,904
5043 Photographic equipment & supplies [2]	-	9	-	19	2	-	13,053	-	209
5044 Office equipment [2]	-	47	-	743	16	-	29,341	-	21,660
5045 Computers, peripherals, & software [2]	-	67	-	666	10	-	39,502	-	27,647
5046 Commercial equipment, nec [2]	-	16	-	111	7	-	29,622	-	3,824
5047 Medical and hospital equipment [2]	-	31	-	243	8	-	32,840	-	8,285
5048 Ophthalmic goods [2]	-	6	-	29	5	-	13,931	-	483
5051 Metals service centers and offices [2]	-	21	-	181	9	-	32,066	-	6,355
5063 Electrical apparatus and equipment [2]	-	72	-	699	10	-	32,126	-	22,440
5064 Electrical appliances, TV & radios [2]	-	14	-	20	1	-	22,200	-	408
5065 Electronic parts and equipment [2]	-	60	-	334	6	-	33,102	-	12,149
5072 Hardware [2]	-	48	-	302	6	-	22,742	-	7,259
5074 Plumbing & hydronic heating supplies [2]	-	37	-	248	7	-	29,758	-	7,579
5075 Warm air heating & air conditioning [2]	-	33	-	287	9	-	27,861	-	8,326
5078 Refrigeration equipment and supplies [2]	-	9	-	53	6	-	26,868	-	1,460
5082 Construction and mining machinery [2]	-	21	-	198	9	-	38,081	-	7,889
5083 Farm and garden machinery [2]	-	12	-	58	5	-	28,897	-	2,007
5084 Industrial machinery and equipment [2]	-	75	-	593	8	-	31,460	-	19,846
5085 Industrial supplies [2]	-	70	-	731	10	-	29,806	-	23,662
5087 Service establishment equipment [2]	-	25	-	175	7	-	25,874	-	4,613
5088 Transportation equipment & supplies [2]	-	20	-	181	9	-	23,271	-	5,032
5091 Sporting & recreational goods [2]	-	27	-	234	9	-	21,915	-	5,411
5092 Toys and hobby goods and supplies [2]	-	6	-	58	10	-	20,138	-	2,701
5093 Scrap and waste materials [2]	-	28	-	183	7	-	20,087	-	4,221
5094 Jewelry & precious stones [2]	-	16	-	25	2	-	25,600	-	656
5099 Durable goods, nec [2]	-	34	-	337	10	-	18,754	-	6,967
5111 Printing and writing paper [2]	-	10	-	9	1	-	36,444	-	347
5112 Stationery and office supplies [2]	-	41	-	456	11	-	20,228	-	9,566
5113 Industrial & personal service paper [2]	-	15	-	175	12	-	35,451	-	5,109
5120 Drugs, proprietaries, and sundries [2]	-	21	-	304	14	-	39,605	-	12,567
5136 Men's and boys' clothing [2]	-	26	-	248	10	-	27,194	-	5,606
5137 Women's and children's clothing [2]	-	13	-	19	1	-	11,579	-	316
5141 Groceries, general line [2]	-	23	-	79	3	-	31,848	-	2,218
5142 Packaged frozen food [2]	-	23	-	686	30	-	23,312	-	18,113

Continued on next page.

NORFOLK - VIRGINIA BEACH - NEWPORT NEWS, VA - NC MSA - [continued]

Wholesale and Retail Trade USA	Establishments		Employment		Emp / Est	Pay / Employee		Annual Payroll ($ 000)	
	1994	1995	1994	1995	1995	1994	1995	1994	1995
5145 Confectionery[2]	-	12	-	50	4	-	23,680	-	1,160
5146 Fish and seafoods[2]	-	45	-	200	4	-	7,500	-	2,049
5147 Meats and meat products[2]	-	19	-	248	13	-	22,355	-	6,297
5148 Fresh fruits and vegetables[2]	-	9	-	241	27	-	20,349	-	5,153
5149 Groceries and related products, nec[2]	-	47	-	2,148	46	-	19,428	-	45,102
5150 Farm-product raw materials[2]	-	24	-	159	7	-	25,258	-	3,568
5162 Plastics materials & basic shapes[2]	-	12	-	76	6	-	21,053	-	1,631
5169 Chemicals & allied products, nec[2]	-	40	-	186	5	-	31,935	-	5,147
5171 Petroleum bulk stations & terminals[2]	-	37	-	355	10	-	30,468	-	10,329
5172 Petroleum products, nec[2]	-	17	-	145	9	-	17,628	-	2,661
5191 Farm supplies[2]	-	26	-	160	6	-	24,200	-	3,861
5192 Books, periodicals, & newspapers[2]	-	14	-	107	8	-	19,065	-	2,132
5198 Paints, varnishes, and supplies[2]	-	24	-	86	4	-	25,349	-	2,439
5199 Nondurable goods, nec[2]	-	51	-	101	2	-	18,297	-	2,112
52- Retail trade[1]	79	8,294	582	126,772	15	11,162	11,986	8,255	1,617,150
5210 Lumber and other building materials[3]	3	82	73	2,820	34	26,575	16,417	1,749	44,816
5230 Paint, glass, and wallpaper stores[2]	-	52	-	218	4	-	20,917	-	4,919
5250 Hardware stores	-	57	-	252	4	-	10,619	-	2,990
5260 Retail nurseries and garden stores[2]	-	53	-	393	7	-	12,468	-	6,081
5310 Department stores[2]	-	64	-	9,241	144	-	11,714	-	107,397
5330 Variety stores[2]	-	83	-	1,080	13	-	12,578	-	14,466
5390 Misc. general merchandise stores[2]	-	67	-	1,480	22	-	15,586	-	22,885
5410 Grocery stores[3]	10	699	136	16,809	24	8,559	10,412	1,664	178,271
5420 Meat and fish markets[2]	-	54	-	170	3	-	10,635	-	2,255
5430 Fruit and vegetable markets[2]	-	14	-	3	-	-	6,667	-	59
5440 Candy, nut, and confectionery stores[2]	-	26	-	70	3	-	6,743	-	741
5460 Retail bakeries[2]	-	84	-	832	10	-	10,471	-	9,107
5490 Miscellaneous food stores[2]	-	41	-	94	2	-	12,426	-	1,263
5510 New and used car dealers[2]	-	104	-	6,183	59	-	28,098	-	191,467
5520 Used car dealers[2]	-	119	-	904	8	-	19,350	-	19,787
5530 Auto and home supply stores	-	237	-	1,800	8	-	16,064	-	30,647
5540 Gasoline service stations[1]	7	468	47	3,629	8	10,128	12,074	516	45,837
5550 Boat dealers[2]	-	44	-	285	6	-	17,544	-	5,889
5570 Motorcycle dealers[2]	-	15	-	75	5	-	22,773	-	1,988
5610 Men's & boys' clothing stores[2]	-	112	-	1,009	9	-	10,240	-	11,322
5620 Women's clothing stores[2]	-	250	-	2,238	9	-	8,116	-	18,613
5630 Women's accessory & specialty stores[2]	-	50	-	199	4	-	13,005	-	2,561
5640 Children's and infants' wear stores[2]	-	24	-	144	6	-	8,111	-	1,008
5650 Family clothing stores[2]	-	100	-	1,668	17	-	10,209	-	18,576
5660 Shoe stores[2]	-	224	-	1,297	6	-	10,146	-	12,809
5690 Misc. apparel & accessory stores[2]	-	62	-	261	4	-	9,640	-	2,933
5712 Furniture stores[2]	-	202	-	1,917	9	-	18,865	-	37,894
5713 Floor covering stores[2]	-	66	-	361	5	-	20,720	-	7,447
5714 Drapery and upholstery stores[2]	-	15	-	23	2	-	13,565	-	282
5719 Misc. homefurnishings stores[2]	-	107	-	1,089	10	-	11,750	-	16,473
5720 Household appliance stores[2]	-	31	-	75	2	-	13,600	-	1,168
5731 Radio, TV, & electronic stores[2]	-	81	-	766	9	-	16,037	-	13,081
5734 Computer and software stores[2]	-	49	-	364	7	-	16,846	-	6,785
5735 Record & prerecorded tape stores[2]	-	57	-	299	5	-	9,324	-	3,069
5736 Musical instrument stores[2]	-	26	-	76	3	-	18,000	-	1,417
5812 Eating places[1]	9	2,092	108	41,848	20	6,407	7,595	903	350,802
5813 Drinking places[2]	-	70	-	817	12	-	6,404	-	4,855
5910 Drug stores and proprietary stores	-	199	-	2,782	14	-	14,470	-	42,577
5930 Used merchandise stores[2]	-	146	-	958	7	-	11,545	-	11,718
5941 Sporting goods and bicycle shops[2]	-	132	-	886	7	-	10,501	-	9,725
5942 Book stores[2]	-	73	-	434	6	-	8,645	-	4,025
5943 Stationery stores[2]	-	11	-	43	4	-	8,744	-	430
5944 Jewelry stores[2]	-	166	-	891	5	-	14,923	-	13,539
5945 Hobby, toy, and game shops[2]	-	79	-	836	11	-	9,804	-	9,164
5946 Camera & photographic supply stores[2]	-	19	-	23	1	-	15,130	-	380
5947 Gift, novelty, and souvenir shops[1]	7	239	36	1,235	5	9,889	8,168	481	12,765
5948 Luggage and leather goods stores[2]	-	9	-	28	3	-	8,429	-	300
5949 Sewing, needlework, and piece goods[2]	-	47	-	264	6	-	7,394	-	1,950
5961 Catalog and mail-order houses[2]	-	43	-	72	2	-	20,389	-	1,467
5962 Merchandising machine operators[2]	-	25	-	250	10	-	18,176	-	4,995
5963 Direct selling establishments[2]	-	79	-	159	2	-	20,403	-	3,549
5980 Fuel dealers[2]	-	47	-	507	11	-	21,996	-	11,229
5992 Florists[2]	-	126	-	353	3	-	10,799	-	3,869
5994 News dealers and newsstands[2]	-	8	-	13	2	-	6,769	-	88
5995 Optical goods stores[2]	-	111	-	466	4	-	16,755	-	8,617
5999 Miscellaneous retail stores, nec	-	237	-	1,255	5	-	11,069	-	15,587

Source: County Business Patterns 1994/95, CBP-94/95, U.S. Department of Commerce, Washington DC, November 1997. The employment column represents mid-March employment in the year. Pay per employee is calculated by dividing 1st Quarter payroll, annualized, by mid-March employment. The column headed 'Emp / Est' shows 'employees per establishment'. A dash (-) means that data are unavailable or cannot be calculated. nec means not elsewhere classified. *Notes:* 1. 1994 data incomplete; unavailable or withheld. 2. 1995 data incomplete; unavailable or withheld. 3. 1994 and 1995 data incomplete; unavailable or withheld.

OAKLAND, CA PMSA

Wholesale and Retail Trade USA	Establishments		Employment		Emp / Est	Pay / Employee		Annual Payroll ($ 000)	
	1994	1995	1994	1995	1995	1994	1995	1994	1995
50- Wholesale trade	4,497	4,554	64,194	66,288	15	35,233	37,799	2,383,734	2,572,004
5012 Automobiles and other vehicles	62	65	1,698	1,736	27	30,061	33,922	53,358	60,385
5013 Motor vehicle supplies and new parts	183	174	2,348	2,053	12	32,714	36,460	80,291	76,648
5014 Tires and tubes	29	25	352	365	15	41,580	34,849	13,545	15,493
5015 Motor vehicle parts, used	44	45	288	395	9	17,986	23,716	5,790	10,081
5021 Furniture	79	76	891	879	12	24,269	28,223	22,769	25,404
5023 Homefurnishings	79	72	825	660	9	23,491	29,170	22,220	21,072
5031 Lumber, plywood, and millwork	63	54	607	576	11	35,671	30,764	23,518	18,931
5032 Brick, stone, & related materials	41	39	346	285	7	35,029	35,719	13,385	10,392
5033 Roofing, siding, & insulation	24	23	350	335	15	29,189	23,284	11,058	9,532
5039 Construction materials, nec	35	58	307	540	9	35,114	32,563	12,068	18,811
5043 Photographic equipment & supplies	6	6	77	50	8	26,182	25,920	2,187	1,188
5044 Office equipment	63	67	1,512	1,430	21	35,397	41,057	56,097	56,678
5045 Computers, peripherals, & software	362	376	4,578	5,669	15	43,429	45,446	203,351	254,403
5046 Commercial equipment, nec	56	54	352	336	6	27,932	32,643	9,877	11,977
5047 Medical and hospital equipment	80	69	1,096	1,241	18	43,777	44,548	55,440	58,433
5048 Ophthalmic goods	14	13	114	102	8	31,895	32,627	3,912	4,178
5049 Professional equipment, nec	40	42	762	643	15	40,651	41,356	24,174	21,554
5051 Metals service centers and offices[3]	106	107	1,443	1,400	13	34,581	36,654	53,712	56,473
5052 Coal and other minerals and ores	4	4	9	10	3	44,000	48,000	468	502
5063 Electrical apparatus and equipment	202	189	2,239	2,219	12	37,633	43,059	88,756	107,522
5064 Electrical appliances, TV & radios	29	32	424	463	14	38,708	42,367	16,475	19,808
5065 Electronic parts and equipment	217	231	2,765	3,358	15	44,314	48,728	127,431	163,959
5072 Hardware	75	85	946	1,195	14	30,854	30,279	35,703	41,783
5074 Plumbing & hydronic heating supplies	71	66	761	754	11	37,561	38,223	30,529	29,939
5075 Warm air heating & air conditioning	23	25	230	191	8	44,226	46,576	9,843	8,981
5078 Refrigeration equipment and supplies	22	21	223	247	12	39,695	45,328	9,108	12,020
5082 Construction and mining machinery	37	39	493	567	15	44,876	46,208	22,223	27,443
5083 Farm and garden machinery	32	30	276	276	9	30,232	32,058	10,919	10,042
5084 Industrial machinery and equipment	262	254	2,440	2,734	11	39,089	43,245	104,067	127,802
5085 Industrial supplies	150	139	1,518	1,446	10	39,286	44,816	61,436	64,798
5087 Service establishment equipment	53	45	455	426	9	27,631	28,648	14,219	13,874
5088 Transportation equipment & supplies	33	31	301	272	9	34,086	34,926	11,207	10,226
5091 Sporting & recreational goods	44	39	290	250	6	20,441	22,384	6,871	5,881
5092 Toys and hobby goods and supplies	24	29	427	451	16	32,946	31,166	15,192	15,350
5093 Scrap and waste materials	96	100	1,653	1,702	17	21,614	23,288	38,435	39,961
5094 Jewelry & precious stones	34	36	178	182	5	20,292	20,879	3,714	4,065
5099 Durable goods, nec	76	86	595	515	6	26,790	28,311	20,376	20,275
5111 Printing and writing paper	29	30	451	433	14	46,554	51,788	21,674	24,179
5112 Stationery and office supplies	112	103	2,283	2,194	21	27,164	31,537	65,801	63,038
5113 Industrial & personal service paper	70	69	1,025	1,103	16	40,812	42,274	42,891	47,722
5120 Drugs, proprietaries, and sundries	66	70	1,535	1,410	20	41,313	42,851	66,302	44,425
5131 Piece goods & notions	19	22	188	116	5	16,574	28,483	3,574	4,051
5136 Men's and boys' clothing	23	22	155	199	9	35,845	37,447	7,745	9,620
5137 Women's and children's clothing	52	44	529	389	9	18,964	20,165	9,201	7,771
5139 Footwear	6	9	53	67	7	33,811	35,761	1,973	2,517
5141 Groceries, general line	78	74	3,245	3,001	41	33,222	34,682	112,169	110,185
5142 Packaged frozen food	34	29	839	761	26	32,010	35,049	27,751	30,443
5143 Dairy products, exc. dried or canned	33	30	1,016	861	29	33,189	33,779	35,585	30,692
5144 Poultry and poultry products[2]	10	8	135	129	16	23,319	26,078	4,532	5,061
5145 Confectionery	21	21	451	439	21	36,231	40,720	17,055	17,608
5146 Fish and seafoods	17	16	218	139	9	21,670	24,115	4,883	4,072
5147 Meats and meat products	43	38	489	461	12	35,452	35,028	17,104	15,037
5148 Fresh fruits and vegetables	57	50	555	536	11	33,211	37,373	19,277	21,802
5149 Groceries and related products, nec	202	195	4,475	4,682	24	34,202	35,359	165,518	170,760
5153 Grain and field beans	4	-	14	-	-	18,000	-	292	-
5159 Farm-product raw materials, nec	5	-	3	-	-	21,333	-	103	-
5162 Plastics materials & basic shapes	37	38	300	292	8	36,267	37,260	11,441	10,880
5169 Chemicals & allied products, nec[2]	101	91	1,547	687	8	41,135	38,643	64,086	24,501
5171 Petroleum bulk stations & terminals	26	26	418	497	19	37,110	37,425	15,059	18,536
5172 Petroleum products, nec	11	11	85	71	6	47,294	55,380	3,902	3,816
5181 Beer and ale	10	11	595	603	55	28,524	28,776	18,001	18,661
5182 Wine and distilled beverages	26	25	1,407	1,411	56	45,274	44,992	62,554	63,994
5191 Farm supplies	31	29	375	407	14	46,357	49,012	16,317	18,952
5192 Books, periodicals, & newspapers	40	41	789	911	22	28,041	37,862	30,238	33,144
5193 Flowers & florists' supplies	39	37	651	822	22	16,203	13,893	11,905	13,472
5194 Tobacco and tobacco products[3]	8	7	519	546	78	27,314	28,908	15,577	14,732
5198 Paints, varnishes, and supplies	36	37	334	301	8	33,952	34,618	12,169	10,438
5199 Nondurable goods, nec	224	238	1,872	1,930	8	24,739	27,445	48,834	52,136
52- Retail trade	11,163	11,070	151,796	154,455	14	16,957	18,101	2,696,676	2,841,241
5210 Lumber and other building materials	140	126	2,451	3,058	24	21,307	23,213	57,191	72,693

Continued on next page.

OAKLAND, CA PMSA - [continued]

Wholesale and Retail Trade USA	Establishments		Employment		Emp / Est	Pay / Employee		Annual Payroll ($ 000)	
	1994	1995	1994	1995	1995	1994	1995	1994	1995
5230 Paint, glass, and wallpaper stores	70	65	370	421	6	26,346	23,458	9,795	10,191
5250 Hardware stores	95	74	1,947	1,668	23	14,958	15,115	30,801	26,318
5260 Retail nurseries and garden stores	53	57	639	619	11	15,080	15,405	11,246	11,578
5310 Department stores	59	63	11,602	12,304	195	12,582	12,727	158,002	160,880
5330 Variety stores	34	25	321	252	10	9,956	10,460	3,189	2,474
5390 Misc. general merchandise stores	69	66	2,822	2,955	45	18,738	22,060	57,317	65,716
5410 Grocery stores	839	821	17,585	16,828	20	20,955	22,888	372,695	393,912
5420 Meat and fish markets	63	60	237	241	4	15,122	14,324	3,622	3,849
5430 Fruit and vegetable markets	29	29	202	230	8	21,188	20,139	4,112	4,476
5440 Candy, nut, and confectionery stores	37	40	187	208	5	11,144	10,558	2,418	2,442
5450 Dairy products stores	31	32	261	254	8	7,218	7,969	2,096	2,130
5460 Retail bakeries	213	189	1,518	1,226	6	10,311	9,987	16,244	12,437
5490 Miscellaneous food stores	112	118	801	847	7	15,171	18,767	12,748	17,071
5510 New and used car dealers	158	154	6,389	6,489	42	38,949	40,436	269,507	282,691
5520 Used car dealers	56	59	292	238	4	24,000	32,891	8,325	8,735
5530 Auto and home supply stores	283	276	2,366	2,530	9	20,833	21,853	54,841	56,158
5540 Gasoline service stations	527	516	3,851	3,918	8	13,307	13,388	53,875	54,410
5550 Boat dealers	24	23	155	151	7	23,458	22,358	4,328	4,059
5560 Recreational vehicle dealers	28	26	216	232	9	19,370	20,086	4,338	4,927
5570 Motorcycle dealers	29	22	207	174	8	24,444	25,908	5,098	4,928
5590 Automotive dealers, nec	5	7	18	18	3	26,889	29,333	505	583
5610 Men's & boys' clothing stores	92	86	703	576	7	12,791	16,236	8,890	9,118
5620 Women's clothing stores	314	278	2,556	2,278	8	9,236	9,610	24,521	19,729
5630 Women's accessory & specialty stores	54	50	328	294	6	9,366	9,946	3,345	2,997
5640 Children's and infants' wear stores	45	48	337	314	7	10,220	11,185	3,604	3,529
5650 Family clothing stores	130	121	3,848	3,876	32	12,086	12,805	50,812	50,724
5660 Shoe stores	232	212	1,235	1,127	5	13,613	13,427	16,711	15,298
5690 Misc. apparel & accessory stores	71	64	382	364	6	11,770	13,725	4,633	5,016
5712 Furniture stores	224	228	1,483	1,600	7	22,115	21,843	35,009	34,160
5713 Floor covering stores	118	110	651	619	6	19,902	20,717	14,735	15,030
5714 Drapery and upholstery stores	25	22	82	69	3	12,878	14,319	1,098	1,024
5719 Misc. homefurnishings stores	168	165	1,317	1,321	8	12,240	12,951	18,166	18,204
5720 Household appliance stores	56	61	346	361	6	22,347	22,360	8,047	8,798
5731 Radio, TV, & electronic stores	124	122	1,137	1,326	11	22,758	20,700	26,490	29,103
5734 Computer and software stores	91	113	932	1,031	9	23,069	26,371	24,868	30,613
5735 Record & prerecorded tape stores	75	69	1,029	1,197	17	9,913	9,293	11,944	12,660
5736 Musical instrument stores	47	41	241	227	6	16,382	18,643	4,225	4,546
5812 Eating places	3,228	3,026	48,114	48,012	16	9,083	9,674	464,235	481,933
5813 Drinking places	302	279	1,523	1,416	5	8,909	9,444	13,830	13,302
5910 Drug stores and proprietary stores	254	250	5,237	5,470	22	21,192	21,655	114,902	121,838
5920 Liquor stores	245	239	812	813	3	12,049	15,208	11,033	12,355
5930 Used merchandise stores	133	134	1,071	978	7	11,376	12,397	13,351	12,864
5941 Sporting goods and bicycle shops	201	206	2,056	2,063	10	13,981	13,906	29,576	27,063
5942 Book stores	154	162	1,541	1,696	10	10,188	10,361	15,579	17,110
5943 Stationery stores	39	44	224	229	5	8,304	9,485	1,910	3,351
5944 Jewelry stores	178	175	932	836	5	18,803	19,493	17,501	16,245
5945 Hobby, toy, and game shops	98	94	1,034	1,241	13	12,066	10,859	14,973	15,061
5946 Camera & photographic supply stores	49	46	308	297	6	13,909	15,219	4,577	4,249
5947 Gift, novelty, and souvenir shops	199	195	1,272	1,319	7	8,553	9,010	11,785	12,126
5948 Luggage and leather goods stores	12	12	39	16	1	17,744	18,750	701	427
5949 Sewing, needlework, and piece goods	56	55	643	535	10	8,442	10,236	5,573	5,434
5961 Catalog and mail-order houses	36	40	347	486	12	16,634	24,247	6,500	9,589
5962 Merchandising machine operators	33	32	428	380	12	22,579	22,758	10,105	8,806
5963 Direct selling establishments	100	92	933	1,055	11	18,024	17,202	18,512	19,315
5984 Liquefied petroleum gas dealers	9	9	26	27	3	26,923	24,296	655	678
5992 Florists	165	159	686	664	4	10,595	10,964	7,589	7,472
5993 Tobacco stores and stands	6	-	23	-	-	11,304	-	316	-
5994 News dealers and newsstands	10	8	33	37	5	14,788	14,486	527	569
5995 Optical goods stores	100	96	569	567	6	17,336	17,220	10,145	10,388
5999 Miscellaneous retail stores, nec	379	397	2,101	2,242	6	14,277	15,627	33,034	37,938

Source: County Business Patterns 1994/95, CBP-94/95, U.S. Department of Commerce, Washington DC, November 1997. The employment column represents mid-March employment in the year. Pay per employee is calculated by dividing 1st Quarter payroll, annualized, by mid-March employment. The column headed 'Emp / Est' shows 'employees per establishment'. A dash (-) means that data are unavailable or cannot be calculated. nec means not elsewhere classified. *Notes:* 1. 1994 data incomplete; unavailable or withheld. 2. 1995 data incomplete; unavailable or withheld. 3. 1994 and 1995 data incomplete; unavailable or withheld.

OCALA, FL MSA

Wholesale and Retail Trade USA	Establishments		Employment		Emp / Est	Pay / Employee		Annual Payroll ($ 000)	
	1994	1995	1994	1995	1995	1994	1995	1994	1995
50 – Wholesale trade	327	330	4,289	4,254	13	20,990	23,197	102,185	102,237
5012 Automobiles and other vehicles	11	11	97	114	10	18,763	20,211	2,287	2,587
5013 Motor vehicle supplies and new parts	27	21	260	245	12	19,954	21,176	5,661	5,628
5014 Tires and tubes	6	5	39	33	7	20,821	22,667	813	682
5015 Motor vehicle parts, used	5	5	24	25	5	18,667	13,600	383	359
5021 Furniture	3	3	9	9	3	58,222	68,889	559	658
5023 Homefurnishings	4	3	13	5	2	15,692	13,600	228	63
5031 Lumber, plywood, and millwork	8	9	142	176	20	19,099	17,409	2,742	2,827
5032 Brick, stone, & related materials	7	7	42	44	6	20,762	21,545	975	1,624
5033 Roofing, siding, & insulation	3	6	8	35	6	38,000	25,600	249	896
5039 Construction materials, nec	8	6	104	35	6	17,192	16,114	1,905	637
5044 Office equipment	9	8	109	96	12	19,339	18,833	2,141	1,752
5045 Computers, peripherals, & software	10	10	40	48	5	16,800	16,000	820	954
5047 Medical and hospital equipment	4	4	36	32	8	30,778	22,250	1,030	770
5050 Metals and minerals, except petroleum	7	8	35	39	5	23,086	24,103	928	774
5063 Electrical apparatus and equipment	7	7	64	70	10	25,875	29,714	1,733	1,984
5064 Electrical appliances, TV & radios	4	5	25	28	6	16,960	20,857	529	674
5065 Electronic parts and equipment	11	12	90	123	10	33,289	35,642	3,341	4,216
5072 Hardware	7	7	100	96	14	18,560	21,125	1,915	1,930
5074 Plumbing & hydronic heating supplies	10	10	113	105	11	21,912	27,695	2,541	3,102
5075 Warm air heating & air conditioning	7	7	42	42	6	20,476	21,238	1,002	944
5082 Construction and mining machinery	6	6	141	141	24	29,220	33,277	4,397	4,928
5083 Farm and garden machinery	-	6	-	42	7	-	15,619	-	704
5084 Industrial machinery and equipment	18	20	208	213	11	23,558	26,798	5,153	5,763
5085 Industrial supplies	9	10	82	68	7	20,732	20,882	1,846	1,044
5087 Service establishment equipment	5	5	22	22	4	17,091	16,545	402	395
5091 Sporting & recreational goods	-	4	-	33	8	-	24,485	-	657
5093 Scrap and waste materials	7	7	86	102	15	15,535	16,941	1,433	2,106
5099 Durable goods, nec	12	12	87	99	8	19,540	19,152	2,007	2,257
5112 Stationery and office supplies	-	3	-	47	16	-	16,511	-	791
5113 Industrial & personal service paper	5	5	77	78	16	27,792	38,667	2,279	2,651
5120 Drugs, proprietaries, and sundries	3	-	66	-	-	29,212	-	2,153	-
5136 Men's and boys' clothing	-	3	-	7	2	-	10,857	-	146
5141 Groceries, general line	4	5	92	80	16	26,739	19,150	2,304	1,972
5148 Fresh fruits and vegetables	6	6	220	237	40	7,491	8,489	1,889	2,030
5149 Groceries and related products, nec	7	7	93	82	12	30,624	30,976	2,918	2,765
5169 Chemicals & allied products, nec	3	-	20	-	-	18,400	-	449	-
5171 Petroleum bulk stations & terminals	-	6	-	75	13	-	25,120	-	1,737
5191 Farm supplies	17	-	151	-	-	14,490	-	2,310	-
52 – Retail trade	1,304	1,314	17,460	17,627	13	11,883	12,715	217,265	229,564
5210 Lumber and other building materials	23	18	562	460	26	16,911	17,730	8,327	8,257
5230 Paint, glass, and wallpaper stores	12	11	46	40	4	16,522	17,500	820	710
5250 Hardware stores	27	21	101	96	5	10,970	11,208	1,203	1,116
5260 Retail nurseries and garden stores	13	14	203	203	15	11,310	12,906	2,501	2,644
5270 Mobile home dealers	18	18	104	123	7	22,769	33,919	3,410	5,032
5310 Department stores	12	12	1,852	1,866	156	10,233	11,556	20,141	21,708
5330 Variety stores	10	7	59	76	11	6,508	7,737	749	622
5390 Misc. general merchandise stores	6	9	303	348	39	13,795	13,667	4,330	4,574
5410 Grocery stores	105	101	2,899	2,925	29	10,475	11,545	30,707	33,905
5420 Meat and fish markets	5	8	36	35	4	12,556	13,829	458	477
5430 Fruit and vegetable markets	7	5	34	27	5	8,118	9,926	267	192
5460 Retail bakeries	8	6	95	42	7	8,337	11,143	732	524
5490 Miscellaneous food stores	7	6	37	38	6	10,919	11,895	456	494
5510 New and used car dealers	11	15	786	753	50	29,628	32,467	25,887	26,315
5520 Used car dealers	33	29	131	99	3	21,038	25,333	3,038	2,947
5530 Auto and home supply stores	48	52	307	346	7	16,651	18,104	5,315	6,606
5540 Gasoline service stations	132	125	1,110	1,027	8	11,258	12,090	12,386	12,187
5550 Boat dealers	5	4	21	24	6	17,905	19,333	434	522
5560 Recreational vehicle dealers	4	5	31	37	7	16,516	23,135	480	788
5570 Motorcycle dealers	5	-	28	-	-	18,571	-	550	-
5610 Men's & boys' clothing stores	13	13	74	92	7	9,243	7,391	855	798
5620 Women's clothing stores	34	32	235	189	6	8,698	8,169	2,234	1,488
5630 Women's accessory & specialty stores	4	5	25	27	5	10,400	9,926	287	270
5640 Children's and infants' wear stores	-	3	-	3	1	-	5,333	-	20
5650 Family clothing stores	10	12	123	123	10	8,911	9,724	1,224	1,280
5660 Shoe stores	26	25	97	101	4	10,639	10,772	1,071	1,063
5690 Misc. apparel & accessory stores	6	6	19	20	3	9,684	11,400	204	234
5712 Furniture stores	38	36	285	315	9	17,151	16,444	5,091	5,020
5713 Floor covering stores	18	17	94	117	7	15,745	13,812	1,695	1,597
5714 Drapery and upholstery stores	7	6	18	23	4	15,778	13,913	272	292
5719 Misc. homefurnishings stores	12	13	53	69	5	14,642	14,087	857	951

Continued on next page.

OCALA, FL MSA - [continued]

Wholesale and Retail Trade USA	Establishments		Employment		Emp / Est	Pay / Employee		Annual Payroll ($ 000)	
	1994	1995	1994	1995	1995	1994	1995	1994	1995
5720 Household appliance stores	9	9	30	32	4	14,400	14,375	477	517
5731 Radio, TV, & electronic stores	13	14	223	336	24	20,054	22,583	6,079	8,147
5734 Computer and software stores	6	6	11	16	3	21,455	10,250	179	179
5735 Record & prerecorded tape stores	6	7	28	43	6	9,571	7,814	294	316
5736 Musical instrument stores	7	6	36	33	6	14,444	16,970	487	523
5812 Eating places	224	212	4,869	4,915	23	8,094	8,334	39,385	39,695
5813 Drinking places	26	22	174	253	12	8,368	7,051	1,665	2,249
5910 Drug stores and proprietary stores	38	33	579	474	14	16,180	19,342	10,143	9,556
5920 Liquor stores	22	21	94	87	4	9,234	8,414	883	642
5930 Used merchandise stores	22	19	79	74	4	13,316	12,595	1,145	900
5941 Sporting goods and bicycle shops	22	22	71	98	4	12,394	12,082	958	1,487
5942 Book stores	7	8	33	59	7	10,061	9,153	357	562
5943 Stationery stores	6	5	69	86	17	15,710	14,605	899	1,155
5944 Jewelry stores	19	21	114	114	5	13,754	15,789	1,604	1,875
5945 Hobby, toy, and game shops	8	8	88	86	11	11,955	12,233	1,266	805
5947 Gift, novelty, and souvenir shops	33	31	121	128	4	11,471	11,844	1,670	1,783
5949 Sewing, needlework, and piece goods	8	6	41	32	5	7,220	9,250	278	287
5963 Direct selling establishments	14	16	354	302	19	11,797	12,530	4,028	4,112
5984 Liquefied petroleum gas dealers	-	10	-	55	6	-	18,327	-	912
5992 Florists	-	17	-	86	5	-	10,930	-	940
5995 Optical goods stores	18	21	60	64	3	15,333	16,875	922	1,108
5999 Miscellaneous retail stores, nec	31	40	151	154	4	13,510	15,844	2,368	2,594

Source: County Business Patterns 1994/95, CBP-94/95, U.S. Department of Commerce, Washington DC, November 1997. The employment column represents mid-March employment in the year. Pay per employee is calculated by dividing 1st Quarter payroll, annualized, by mid-March employment. The column headed 'Emp / Est' shows 'employees per establishment'. A dash (-) means that data are unavailable or cannot be calculated. nec means not elsewhere classified. *Notes:* 1. 1994 data incomplete; unavailable or withheld. 2. 1995 data incomplete; unavailable or withheld. 3. 1994 and 1995 data incomplete; unavailable or withheld.

ODESSA - MIDLAND, TX MSA

Wholesale and Retail Trade USA	Establishments		Employment		Emp / Est	Pay / Employee		Annual Payroll ($ 000)	
	1994	1995	1994	1995	1995	1994	1995	1994	1995
50- Wholesale trade	-	748	-	7,034	9	-	29,567	-	216,984
5012 Automobiles and other vehicles	-	10	-	75	8	-	33,227	-	2,513
5013 Motor vehicle supplies and new parts	-	30	-	216	7	-	25,981	-	5,910
5014 Tires and tubes	-	4	-	76	19	-	24,474	-	2,192
5020 Furniture and homefurnishings	-	5	-	14	3	-	14,000	-	228
5032 Brick, stone, & related materials	-	7	-	75	11	-	14,293	-	858
5033 Roofing, siding, & insulation	-	8	-	30	4	-	12,933	-	418
5044 Office equipment	-	14	-	116	8	-	21,621	-	2,586
5045 Computers, peripherals, & software	-	17	-	114	7	-	36,491	-	3,597
5046 Commercial equipment, nec	-	6	-	4	1	-	25,000	-	90
5047 Medical and hospital equipment	-	9	-	34	4	-	21,294	-	798
5049 Professional equipment, nec [2]	-	3	-	33	11	-	24,364	-	822
5051 Metals service centers and offices [2]	-	27	-	109	4	-	32,477	-	3,828
5063 Electrical apparatus and equipment [2]	-	19	-	83	4	-	29,494	-	2,559
5065 Electronic parts and equipment	-	11	-	70	6	-	29,829	-	2,117
5072 Hardware	-	9	-	70	8	-	29,771	-	2,164
5074 Plumbing & hydronic heating supplies	-	11	-	87	8	-	15,724	-	1,284
5075 Warm air heating & air conditioning	-	9	-	9	1	-	34,667	-	327
5082 Construction and mining machinery	-	13	-	175	13	-	30,994	-	5,832
5084 Industrial machinery and equipment	-	246	-	2,040	8	-	32,196	-	68,556
5085 Industrial supplies	-	33	-	334	10	-	28,419	-	9,161
5087 Service establishment equipment	-	9	-	71	8	-	15,324	-	1,183
5093 Scrap and waste materials [2]	-	13	-	67	5	-	11,045	-	517
5112 Stationery and office supplies	-	9	-	21	2	-	23,048	-	499
5113 Industrial & personal service paper	-	6	-	51	9	-	31,059	-	1,518
5120 Drugs, proprietaries, and sundries	-	7	-	15	2	-	18,133	-	277
5149 Groceries and related products, nec	-	11	-	158	14	-	23,975	-	4,723
5162 Plastics materials & basic shapes	-	7	-	106	15	-	26,415	-	2,885
5169 Chemicals & allied products, nec	-	47	-	577	12	-	35,133	-	21,037
5171 Petroleum bulk stations & terminals [2]	-	19	-	212	11	-	35,698	-	8,075
5172 Petroleum products, nec	-	12	-	84	7	-	44,762	-	3,976
5180 Beer, wine, and distilled beverages	-	6	-	100	17	-	30,360	-	4,225
5191 Farm supplies	-	8	-	40	5	-	17,400	-	667
5199 Nondurable goods, nec	-	12	-	22	2	-	18,909	-	428
52- Retail trade	-	1,558	-	17,988	12	-	12,867	-	241,657
5210 Lumber and other building materials	-	20	-	189	9	-	19,153	-	5,613
5230 Paint, glass, and wallpaper stores	-	7	-	54	8	-	23,778	-	1,338
5250 Hardware stores	-	6	-	47	8	-	14,383	-	689

Continued on next page.

ODESSA - MIDLAND, TX MSA - [continued]

Wholesale and Retail Trade USA	Establishments		Employment		Emp / Est	Pay / Employee		Annual Payroll ($ 000)	
	1994	1995	1994	1995	1995	1994	1995	1994	1995
5260 Retail nurseries and garden stores	-	9	-	98	11	-	9,224	-	981
5270 Mobile home dealers	-	14	-	117	8	-	30,769	-	4,465
5310 Department stores	-	13	-	2,135	164	-	14,078	-	29,065
5390 Misc. general merchandise stores [2]	-	16	-	225	14	-	13,813	-	2,881
5410 Grocery stores	-	145	-	2,158	15	-	14,119	-	30,963
5460 Retail bakeries	-	16	-	147	9	-	6,667	-	1,229
5490 Miscellaneous food stores	-	26	-	81	3	-	10,519	-	1,044
5510 New and used car dealers	-	16	-	883	55	-	29,984	-	30,054
5520 Used car dealers	-	27	-	107	4	-	28,224	-	3,145
5530 Auto and home supply stores	-	50	-	366	7	-	17,770	-	7,278
5540 Gasoline service stations	-	100	-	645	6	-	12,248	-	8,139
5560 Recreational vehicle dealers	-	10	-	40	4	-	20,800	-	1,279
5570 Motorcycle dealers	-	6	-	23	4	-	15,652	-	414
5610 Men's & boys' clothing stores	-	9	-	44	5	-	11,636	-	414
5620 Women's clothing stores	-	50	-	303	6	-	10,191	-	2,939
5630 Women's accessory & specialty stores	-	10	-	43	4	-	7,442	-	296
5640 Children's and infants' wear stores	-	6	-	9	2	-	9,778	-	77
5650 Family clothing stores	-	17	-	240	14	-	9,567	-	2,148
5660 Shoe stores	-	33	-	157	5	-	10,471	-	1,692
5690 Misc. apparel & accessory stores	-	14	-	36	3	-	9,556	-	351
5712 Furniture stores	-	29	-	183	6	-	18,470	-	3,545
5713 Floor covering stores	-	11	-	40	4	-	22,500	-	1,002
5719 Misc. homefurnishings stores	-	12	-	44	4	-	10,455	-	495
5720 Household appliance stores	-	13	-	52	4	-	16,077	-	968
5731 Radio, TV, & electronic stores	-	22	-	219	10	-	15,836	-	3,170
5734 Computer and software stores	-	12	-	55	5	-	16,145	-	943
5735 Record & prerecorded tape stores	-	7	-	96	14	-	10,583	-	877
5736 Musical instrument stores	-	8	-	50	6	-	18,240	-	798
5812 Eating places	-	312	-	5,768	18	-	8,430	-	50,047
5813 Drinking places	-	25	-	231	9	-	6,771	-	1,379
5910 Drug stores and proprietary stores	-	25	-	323	13	-	20,173	-	7,134
5920 Liquor stores	-	23	-	127	6	-	8,756	-	1,227
5930 Used merchandise stores	-	38	-	126	3	-	12,794	-	1,930
5941 Sporting goods and bicycle shops	-	17	-	77	5	-	9,662	-	878
5942 Book stores	-	11	-	63	6	-	8,444	-	549
5943 Stationery stores	-	5	-	21	4	-	14,667	-	324
5944 Jewelry stores	-	32	-	155	5	-	12,542	-	1,855
5945 Hobby, toy, and game shops	-	10	-	175	18	-	9,417	-	1,905
5947 Gift, novelty, and souvenir shops	-	33	-	88	3	-	7,591	-	683
5949 Sewing, needlework, and piece goods	-	7	-	61	9	-	6,754	-	415
5962 Merchandising machine operators	-	5	-	55	11	-	14,982	-	762
5963 Direct selling establishments	-	14	-	19	1	-	31,789	-	587
5992 Florists	-	28	-	148	5	-	10,054	-	1,497
5993 Tobacco stores and stands	-	7	-	11	2	-	8,000	-	108
5995 Optical goods stores	-	22	-	99	5	-	13,697	-	1,328
5999 Miscellaneous retail stores, nec	-	53	-	198	4	-	13,212	-	2,752

Source: County Business Patterns 1994/95, CBP-94/95, U.S. Department of Commerce, Washington DC, November 1997. The employment column represents mid-March employment in the year. Pay per employee is calculated by dividing 1st Quarter payroll, annualized, by mid-March employment. The column headed 'Emp / Est' shows 'employees per establishment'. A dash (-) means that data are unavailable or cannot be calculated. nec means not elsewhere classified. *Notes:* 1. 1994 data incomplete; unavailable or withheld. 2. 1995 data incomplete; unavailable or withheld. 3. 1994 and 1995 data incomplete; unavailable or withheld.

OKLAHOMA CITY, OK MSA

Wholesale and Retail Trade USA	Establishments		Employment		Emp / Est	Pay / Employee		Annual Payroll ($ 000)	
	1994	1995	1994	1995	1995	1994	1995	1994	1995
50- Wholesale trade	-	2,108	-	25,965	12	-	28,342	-	751,043
5012 Automobiles and other vehicles [2]	-	42	-	982	23	-	24,134	-	23,320
5013 Motor vehicle supplies and new parts [2]	-	119	-	1,228	10	-	21,547	-	27,557
5014 Tires and tubes [2]	-	16	-	171	11	-	25,263	-	4,823
5015 Motor vehicle parts, used [2]	-	58	-	440	8	-	19,418	-	8,949
5021 Furniture [2]	-	24	-	127	5	-	21,386	-	3,438
5023 Homefurnishings [2]	-	32	-	349	11	-	21,616	-	8,180
5031 Lumber, plywood, and millwork [2]	-	27	-	424	16	-	21,500	-	9,593
5032 Brick, stone, & related materials [2]	-	19	-	118	6	-	26,746	-	3,303
5033 Roofing, siding, & insulation [2]	-	15	-	166	11	-	27,783	-	5,789
5039 Construction materials, nec [2]	-	32	-	264	8	-	21,227	-	5,974
5044 Office equipment [2]	-	49	-	770	16	-	36,369	-	25,611
5045 Computers, peripherals, & software [2]	-	68	-	771	11	-	40,249	-	29,463
5046 Commercial equipment, nec [2]	-	33	-	449	14	-	29,595	-	11,961

Continued on next page.

OKLAHOMA CITY, OK MSA - [continued]

Wholesale and Retail Trade USA	Establishments		Employment		Emp / Est	Pay / Employee		Annual Payroll ($ 000)	
	1994	1995	1994	1995	1995	1994	1995	1994	1995
5047 Medical and hospital equipment [2]	-	64	-	519	8	-	30,628	-	15,896
5049 Professional equipment, nec [2]	-	10	-	114	11	-	29,649	-	5,474
5051 Metals service centers and offices [2]	-	45	-	17	-	-	12,706	-	364
5063 Electrical apparatus and equipment [2]	-	59	-	577	10	-	31,841	-	18,293
5064 Electrical appliances, TV & radios [2]	-	15	-	100	7	-	29,960	-	3,009
5065 Electronic parts and equipment [2]	-	50	-	545	11	-	35,552	-	19,567
5072 Hardware [2]	-	34	-	329	10	-	25,167	-	8,594
5074 Plumbing & hydronic heating supplies [2]	-	43	-	387	9	-	30,026	-	10,917
5075 Warm air heating & air conditioning [2]	-	38	-	378	10	-	29,259	-	12,004
5078 Refrigeration equipment and supplies [2]	-	5	-	84	17	-	27,667	-	2,319
5082 Construction and mining machinery [2]	-	10	-	286	29	-	30,392	-	9,152
5083 Farm and garden machinery	-	28	-	128	5	-	19,031	-	2,722
5084 Industrial machinery and equipment	-	228	-	2,036	9	-	32,387	-	67,678
5085 Industrial supplies [2]	-	54	-	384	7	-	26,938	-	10,372
5087 Service establishment equipment [2]	-	39	-	227	6	-	21,921	-	5,194
5088 Transportation equipment & supplies [2]	-	23	-	659	29	-	37,997	-	26,274
5091 Sporting & recreational goods [2]	-	19	-	109	6	-	24,514	-	3,070
5093 Scrap and waste materials [2]	-	27	-	248	9	-	22,887	-	5,111
5099 Durable goods, nec [2]	-	30	-	63	2	-	13,270	-	857
5111 Printing and writing paper [2]	-	8	-	185	23	-	34,941	-	6,621
5112 Stationery and office supplies [2]	-	50	-	648	13	-	22,389	-	14,496
5113 Industrial & personal service paper [2]	-	15	-	205	14	-	29,873	-	6,125
5120 Drugs, proprietaries, and sundries [2]	-	31	-	733	24	-	23,640	-	18,889
5131 Piece goods & notions [2]	-	8	-	50	6	-	22,000	-	1,027
5136 Men's and boys' clothing [2]	-	13	-	308	24	-	14,416	-	4,841
5137 Women's and children's clothing [2]	-	9	-	68	8	-	17,647	-	1,257
5141 Groceries, general line [2]	-	23	-	935	41	-	35,114	-	32,428
5142 Packaged frozen food [2]	-	12	-	906	76	-	22,817	-	22,016
5143 Dairy products, exc. dried or canned [2]	-	9	-	117	13	-	21,846	-	2,594
5145 Confectionery [2]	-	8	-	200	25	-	20,200	-	4,372
5147 Meats and meat products [2]	-	13	-	169	13	-	21,302	-	4,202
5148 Fresh fruits and vegetables [2]	-	21	-	351	17	-	21,413	-	7,649
5149 Groceries and related products, nec [2]	-	49	-	777	16	-	22,378	-	18,768
5153 Grain and field beans [2]	-	16	-	91	6	-	26,505	-	2,282
5154 Livestock [2]	-	18	-	51	3	-	16,000	-	853
5162 Plastics materials & basic shapes [2]	-	16	-	165	10	-	33,042	-	5,447
5169 Chemicals & allied products, nec	-	69	-	498	7	-	29,092	-	15,595
5171 Petroleum bulk stations & terminals [2]	-	34	-	299	9	-	32,187	-	9,845
5172 Petroleum products, nec [2]	-	20	-	84	4	-	38,571	-	3,003
5181 Beer and ale [2]	-	10	-	266	27	-	29,218	-	8,386
5182 Wine and distilled beverages [2]	-	9	-	116	13	-	16,828	-	2,313
5191 Farm supplies	-	47	-	271	6	-	23,380	-	6,636
5192 Books, periodicals, & newspapers [2]	-	20	-	218	11	-	20,881	-	5,571
5193 Flowers & florists' supplies [2]	-	11	-	109	10	-	18,385	-	2,151
5198 Paints, varnishes, and supplies [2]	-	12	-	95	8	-	25,642	-	2,488
5199 Nondurable goods, nec [2]	-	58	-	538	9	-	20,766	-	10,798
52 - Retail trade	-	6,324	-	90,738	14	-	12,343	-	1,174,774
5210 Lumber and other building materials	-	88	-	1,862	21	-	17,132	-	31,407
5230 Paint, glass, and wallpaper stores	-	38	-	186	5	-	16,344	-	3,091
5250 Hardware stores	-	26	-	260	10	-	12,062	-	3,339
5260 Retail nurseries and garden stores	-	57	-	326	6	-	11,153	-	4,266
5270 Mobile home dealers [2]	-	14	-	115	8	-	35,617	-	4,079
5310 Department stores [2]	-	47	-	6,408	136	-	13,693	-	87,383
5330 Variety stores [2]	-	25	-	139	6	-	8,777	-	1,325
5390 Misc. general merchandise stores [2]	-	48	-	1,010	21	-	13,085	-	12,837
5410 Grocery stores [2]	-	515	-	9,314	18	-	12,166	-	114,867
5420 Meat and fish markets [2]	-	11	-	50	5	-	16,480	-	681
5430 Fruit and vegetable markets [2]	-	3	-	24	8	-	8,667	-	175
5440 Candy, nut, and confectionery stores [2]	-	20	-	97	5	-	6,763	-	774
5460 Retail bakeries	-	70	-	322	5	-	8,087	-	2,780
5490 Miscellaneous food stores [2]	-	27	-	181	7	-	14,762	-	2,822
5510 New and used car dealers	-	96	-	5,430	57	-	27,277	-	161,811
5520 Used car dealers	-	107	-	351	3	-	18,359	-	7,689
5530 Auto and home supply stores	-	181	-	1,454	8	-	17,004	-	26,844
5540 Gasoline service stations	-	402	-	2,690	7	-	10,998	-	31,799
5550 Boat dealers [2]	-	9	-	63	7	-	18,667	-	1,265
5560 Recreational vehicle dealers [2]	-	12	-	202	17	-	21,307	-	3,811
5570 Motorcycle dealers [2]	-	14	-	103	7	-	14,874	-	1,800
5590 Automotive dealers, nec [2]	-	10	-	34	3	-	17,059	-	586
5610 Men's & boys' clothing stores [2]	-	44	-	307	7	-	13,134	-	4,094
5620 Women's clothing stores [2]	-	137	-	1,207	9	-	9,130	-	11,240

Continued on next page.

OKLAHOMA CITY, OK MSA - [continued]

Wholesale and Retail Trade USA	Establishments		Employment		Emp / Est	Pay / Employee		Annual Payroll ($ 000)	
	1994	1995	1994	1995	1995	1994	1995	1994	1995
5630 Women's accessory & specialty stores [2]	-	30	-	133	4	-	10,015	-	1,323
5640 Children's and infants' wear stores [2]	-	18	-	139	8	-	8,921	-	1,245
5650 Family clothing stores	-	93	-	1,439	15	-	10,858	-	14,822
5660 Shoe stores [2]	-	120	-	616	5	-	12,026	-	6,969
5690 Misc. apparel & accessory stores [2]	-	43	-	207	5	-	10,628	-	2,516
5712 Furniture stores	-	85	-	941	11	-	19,354	-	19,314
5713 Floor covering stores [2]	-	68	-	341	5	-	16,575	-	6,610
5714 Drapery and upholstery stores [2]	-	12	-	40	3	-	12,800	-	905
5719 Misc. homefurnishings stores [2]	-	66	-	301	5	-	12,186	-	3,674
5720 Household appliance stores [2]	-	44	-	246	6	-	16,813	-	4,348
5731 Radio, TV, & electronic stores	-	72	-	681	9	-	15,236	-	10,925
5734 Computer and software stores [2]	-	42	-	263	6	-	20,259	-	6,266
5735 Record & prerecorded tape stores [2]	-	33	-	462	14	-	6,468	-	2,755
5736 Musical instrument stores [2]	-	15	-	58	4	-	20,069	-	1,415
5812 Eating places	-	1,646	-	34,119	21	-	7,761	-	281,959
5813 Drinking places	-	128	-	1,217	10	-	6,889	-	8,476
5910 Drug stores and proprietary stores	-	176	-	1,979	11	-	15,913	-	31,450
5920 Liquor stores	-	83	-	269	3	-	7,509	-	2,278
5930 Used merchandise stores [2]	-	174	-	819	5	-	11,277	-	9,424
5941 Sporting goods and bicycle shops [2]	-	94	-	530	6	-	12,423	-	7,047
5942 Book stores [2]	-	53	-	389	7	-	9,090	-	3,836
5943 Stationery stores [2]	-	13	-	80	6	-	15,650	-	1,264
5944 Jewelry stores	-	98	-	520	5	-	15,308	-	8,402
5945 Hobby, toy, and game shops [2]	-	53	-	652	12	-	8,908	-	6,915
5946 Camera & photographic supply stores [2]	-	9	-	27	3	-	17,778	-	766
5947 Gift, novelty, and souvenir shops	-	146	-	836	6	-	7,885	-	7,393
5949 Sewing, needlework, and piece goods [2]	-	28	-	211	8	-	8,550	-	1,878
5961 Catalog and mail-order houses [2]	-	14	-	85	6	-	10,918	-	919
5962 Merchandising machine operators [2]	-	32	-	238	7	-	16,605	-	4,235
5963 Direct selling establishments [2]	-	52	-	656	13	-	13,530	-	10,431
5984 Liquefied petroleum gas dealers	-	27	-	70	3	-	21,429	-	1,451
5992 Florists	-	103	-	507	5	-	10,895	-	5,491
5993 Tobacco stores and stands [2]	-	17	-	16	1	-	16,000	-	275
5994 News dealers and newsstands [2]	-	7	-	28	4	-	9,429	-	285
5995 Optical goods stores [2]	-	65	-	296	5	-	14,338	-	4,312
5999 Miscellaneous retail stores, nec	-	201	-	1,203	6	-	14,052	-	18,623

Source: County Business Patterns 1994/95, CBP-94/95, U.S. Department of Commerce, Washington DC, November 1997. The employment column represents mid-March employment in the year. Pay per employee is calculated by dividing 1st Quarter payroll, annualized, by mid-March employment. The column headed 'Emp / Est' shows 'employees per establishment'. A dash (-) means that data are unavailable or cannot be calculated. nec means not elsewhere classified. *Notes:* 1. 1994 data incomplete; unavailable or withheld. 2. 1995 data incomplete; unavailable or withheld. 3. 1994 and 1995 data incomplete; unavailable or withheld.

OLYMPIA, WA PMSA

Wholesale and Retail Trade USA	Establishments		Employment		Emp / Est	Pay / Employee		Annual Payroll ($ 000)	
	1994	1995	1994	1995	1995	1994	1995	1994	1995
50 – Wholesale trade	-	236	-	2,208	9	-	24,737	-	59,557
5012 Automobiles and other vehicles	-	4	-	29	7	-	14,345	-	510
5013 Motor vehicle supplies and new parts	-	8	-	75	9	-	16,427	-	1,153
5015 Motor vehicle parts, used	-	6	-	20	3	-	15,200	-	367
5020 Furniture and homefurnishings	-	4	-	13	3	-	25,846	-	368
5031 Lumber, plywood, and millwork	-	11	-	120	11	-	22,867	-	3,234
5039 Construction materials, nec	-	8	-	69	9	-	26,667	-	1,807
5044 Office equipment	-	6	-	99	17	-	29,091	-	3,202
5045 Computers, peripherals, & software	-	11	-	75	7	-	56,000	-	4,195
5063 Electrical apparatus and equipment	-	10	-	82	8	-	32,146	-	2,686
5065 Electronic parts and equipment	-	12	-	90	8	-	29,556	-	2,914
5074 Plumbing & hydronic heating supplies	-	4	-	57	14	-	24,211	-	1,520
5084 Industrial machinery and equipment	-	4	-	18	5	-	18,889	-	405
5085 Industrial supplies	-	4	-	18	5	-	20,000	-	367
5087 Service establishment equipment	-	5	-	75	15	-	19,840	-	1,830
5092 Toys and hobby goods and supplies	-	5	-	25	5	-	26,080	-	926
5099 Durable goods, nec	-	11	-	51	5	-	17,882	-	904
5110 Paper and paper products	-	11	-	97	9	-	18,062	-	1,776
5130 Apparel, piece goods, and notions	-	3	-	33	11	-	9,939	-	262
5145 Confectionery	-	4	-	5	1	-	22,400	-	82
5147 Meats and meat products	-	3	-	68	23	-	18,471	-	1,346
5149 Groceries and related products, nec	-	13	-	155	12	-	26,555	-	4,818
5180 Beer, wine, and distilled beverages	-	4	-	113	28	-	25,628	-	2,911
5191 Farm supplies	-	11	-	124	11	-	20,129	-	2,534

Continued on next page.

OLYMPIA, WA PMSA - [continued]

Wholesale and Retail Trade USA	Establishments		Employment		Emp / Est	Pay / Employee		Annual Payroll ($ 000)	
	1994	1995	1994	1995	1995	1994	1995	1994	1995
5192 Books, periodicals, & newspapers	-	7	-	83	12	-	25,831	-	1,931
5193 Flowers & florists' supplies	-	3	-	35	12	-	16,000	-	635
5199 Nondurable goods, nec	-	5	-	21	4	-	17,714	-	344
52 - Retail trade	-	1,070	-	14,065	13	-	14,352	-	207,942
5210 Lumber and other building materials	-	11	-	414	38	-	22,068	-	8,461
5230 Paint, glass, and wallpaper stores	-	5	-	35	7	-	16,343	-	638
5250 Hardware stores	-	6	-	123	21	-	14,699	-	1,749
5260 Retail nurseries and garden stores	-	10	-	49	5	-	18,449	-	1,248
5270 Mobile home dealers	-	6	-	54	9	-	30,444	-	1,784
5310 Department stores	-	9	-	1,352	150	-	14,213	-	20,959
5410 Grocery stores	-	81	-	1,777	22	-	16,536	-	30,788
5460 Retail bakeries	-	14	-	135	10	-	8,533	-	1,213
5490 Miscellaneous food stores	-	13	-	87	7	-	11,632	-	992
5510 New and used car dealers	-	11	-	570	52	-	34,091	-	19,657
5520 Used car dealers	-	18	-	81	5	-	18,469	-	1,534
5530 Auto and home supply stores	-	36	-	262	7	-	20,336	-	5,434
5540 Gasoline service stations	-	44	-	433	10	-	12,794	-	6,079
5550 Boat dealers	-	9	-	45	5	-	22,044	-	1,205
5560 Recreational vehicle dealers	-	6	-	33	6	-	16,000	-	655
5570 Motorcycle dealers	-	4	-	23	6	-	18,087	-	530
5610 Men's & boys' clothing stores	-	5	-	25	5	-	20,640	-	494
5620 Women's clothing stores	-	21	-	110	5	-	7,600	-	941
5630 Women's accessory & specialty stores	-	4	-	17	4	-	8,235	-	133
5650 Family clothing stores	-	10	-	124	12	-	9,323	-	1,249
5660 Shoe stores	-	15	-	83	6	-	11,181	-	931
5690 Misc. apparel & accessory stores	-	3	-	7	2	-	10,857	-	65
5712 Furniture stores	-	21	-	183	9	-	19,279	-	2,806
5713 Floor covering stores	-	17	-	116	7	-	24,897	-	2,781
5720 Household appliance stores	-	6	-	34	6	-	18,706	-	718
5731 Radio, TV, & electronic stores	-	13	-	100	8	-	22,160	-	2,559
5734 Computer and software stores	-	6	-	43	7	-	15,256	-	818
5735 Record & prerecorded tape stores	-	10	-	59	6	-	9,695	-	540
5736 Musical instrument stores	-	5	-	24	5	-	23,000	-	623
5812 Eating places	-	273	-	4,827	18	-	8,168	-	40,983
5813 Drinking places	-	31	-	220	7	-	8,818	-	2,046
5910 Drug stores and proprietary stores	-	21	-	373	18	-	16,365	-	6,387
5930 Used merchandise stores	-	24	-	108	5	-	11,407	-	1,352
5941 Sporting goods and bicycle shops	-	21	-	157	7	-	10,369	-	1,871
5942 Book stores	-	24	-	166	7	-	14,145	-	1,932
5944 Jewelry stores	-	12	-	84	7	-	24,905	-	2,165
5945 Hobby, toy, and game shops	-	9	-	193	21	-	9,057	-	1,820
5947 Gift, novelty, and souvenir shops	-	26	-	112	4	-	11,500	-	1,278
5949 Sewing, needlework, and piece goods	-	7	-	71	10	-	8,169	-	564
5963 Direct selling establishments	-	11	-	53	5	-	18,792	-	1,188
5980 Fuel dealers	-	4	-	59	15	-	20,475	-	1,183
5992 Florists	-	20	-	84	4	-	9,524	-	791
5995 Optical goods stores	-	13	-	49	4	-	14,367	-	762
5999 Miscellaneous retail stores, nec	-	33	-	199	6	-	12,925	-	2,212

Source: County Business Patterns 1994/95, CBP-94/95, U.S. Department of Commerce, Washington DC, November 1997. The employment column represents mid-March employment in the year. Pay per employee is calculated by dividing 1st Quarter payroll, annualized, by mid-March employment. The column headed 'Emp / Est' shows 'employees per establishment'. A dash (-) means that data are unavailable or cannot be calculated. nec means not elsewhere classified. *Notes:* 1. 1994 data incomplete; unavailable or withheld. 2. 1995 data incomplete; unavailable or withheld. 3. 1994 and 1995 data incomplete; unavailable or withheld.

OMAHA MSA (IA PART)

Wholesale and Retail Trade USA	Establishments		Employment		Emp / Est	Pay / Employee		Annual Payroll ($ 000)	
	1994	1995	1994	1995	1995	1994	1995	1994	1995
50 - Wholesale trade	138	131	1,489	1,521	12	23,253	25,181	37,906	40,179
5012 Automobiles and other vehicles	6	7	102	119	17	35,569	37,277	3,470	4,389
5013 Motor vehicle supplies and new parts	13	12	92	107	9	17,391	18,542	1,770	2,045
5030 Lumber and construction materials	-	5	-	38	8	-	27,053	-	1,131
5040 Professional & commercial equipment	4	3	45	14	5	21,244	21,714	1,050	347
5060 Electrical goods	6	6	121	136	23	24,364	29,118	3,962	4,308
5070 Hardware, plumbing & heating equipment	5	6	13	51	9	18,462	16,863	320	948
5083 Farm and garden machinery	9	9	101	98	11	19,287	20,694	2,428	2,407
5093 Scrap and waste materials	6	6	79	87	15	28,405	32,322	2,521	2,882
5150 Farm-product raw materials	13	11	126	128	12	20,762	23,094	2,786	3,218
5160 Chemicals and allied products	5	5	57	57	11	24,070	27,789	1,630	1,783
5170 Petroleum and petroleum products	15	11	260	244	22	24,354	24,180	6,515	5,942

Continued on next page.

OMAHA MSA (IA PART) - [continued]

Wholesale and Retail Trade USA	Establishments		Employment		Emp / Est	Pay / Employee		Annual Payroll ($ 000)	
	1994	1995	1994	1995	1995	1994	1995	1994	1995
5180 Beer, wine, and distilled beverages	4	-	53	-	-	32,906	-	1,963	-
5190 Misc., nondurable goods	28	25	314	312	12	20,102	22,205	6,463	6,949
52- Retail trade	539	509	7,416	7,464	15	10,821	11,825	87,147	92,236
5210 Lumber and other building materials	7	5	241	189	38	16,432	16,212	3,922	2,818
5250 Hardware stores	5	4	83	63	16	11,229	11,619	881	464
5260 Retail nurseries and garden stores	4	4	32	31	8	9,250	9,806	326	330
5310 Department stores	5	5	667	747	149	10,483	11,406	7,692	8,803
5410 Grocery stores	29	29	1,026	1,091	38	10,749	10,310	11,364	12,004
5440 Candy, nut, and confectionery stores	3	-	11	-	-	4,364	-	42	-
5450 Dairy products stores	3	-	5	-	-	6,400	-	37	-
5460 Retail bakeries	5	5	21	20	4	8,000	8,400	187	180
5490 Miscellaneous food stores	3	-	14	-	-	4,571	-	72	-
5510 New and used car dealers	12	12	721	732	61	22,890	25,016	17,735	19,631
5520 Used car dealers	7	6	46	28	5	15,913	20,857	687	464
5530 Auto and home supply stores	21	17	116	108	6	14,034	16,370	1,842	2,089
5540 Gasoline service stations	66	62	696	659	11	10,822	11,132	8,253	8,030
5570 Motorcycle dealers	4	4	7	8	2	10,857	12,500	109	127
5620 Women's clothing stores	18	14	190	127	9	6,737	6,551	1,341	872
5630 Women's accessory & specialty stores	4	4	18	15	4	9,111	9,067	152	138
5650 Family clothing stores	4	4	179	161	40	6,726	8,870	1,411	1,396
5660 Shoe stores	12	12	63	63	5	8,825	14,984	566	617
5713 Floor covering stores	5	5	26	21	4	16,923	16,952	442	374
5731 Radio, TV, & electronic stores	5	4	29	14	4	13,793	14,857	452	184
5735 Record & prerecorded tape stores	-	4	-	21	5	-	12,190	-	180
5812 Eating places	116	112	2,076	2,049	18	6,850	7,818	15,646	16,904
5813 Drinking places	43	38	181	160	4	6,033	6,500	1,107	980
5910 Drug stores and proprietary stores	16	15	290	290	19	14,510	14,345	4,471	4,350
5930 Used merchandise stores	13	14	64	61	4	7,063	8,328	572	563
5941 Sporting goods and bicycle shops	5	4	22	24	6	7,636	8,333	182	202
5942 Book stores	5	3	28	23	8	5,143	8,000	129	191
5944 Jewelry stores	10	12	70	91	8	12,114	13,055	1,058	1,214
5945 Hobby, toy, and game shops	-	4	-	18	5	-	10,222	-	400
5947 Gift, novelty, and souvenir shops	8	8	35	41	5	8,914	11,220	387	454
5949 Sewing, needlework, and piece goods	4	-	43	-	-	6,512	-	320	-
5961 Catalog and mail-order houses	3	4	27	62	16	14,519	20,645	419	1,358
5962 Merchandising machine operators	4	-	42	-	-	10,095	-	457	-
5963 Direct selling establishments	4	-	20	-	-	12,400	-	307	-
5992 Florists	8	-	40	-	-	10,000	-	400	-
5995 Optical goods stores	-	8	-	27	3	-	46,370	-	635
5999 Miscellaneous retail stores, nec	13	9	27	29	3	8,444	6,897	207	273

Source: County Business Patterns 1994/95, CBP-94/95, U.S. Department of Commerce, Washington DC, November 1997. The employment column represents mid-March employment in the year. Pay per employee is calculated by dividing 1st Quarter payroll, annualized, by mid-March employment. The column headed 'Emp / Est' shows 'employees per establishment'. A dash (-) means that data are unavailable or cannot be calculated. nec means not elsewhere classified. *Notes:* 1. 1994 data incomplete; unavailable or withheld. 2. 1995 data incomplete; unavailable or withheld. 3. 1994 and 1995 data incomplete; unavailable or withheld.

OMAHA MSA (NE PART)

Wholesale and Retail Trade USA	Establishments		Employment		Emp / Est	Pay / Employee		Annual Payroll ($ 000)	
	1994	1995	1994	1995	1995	1994	1995	1994	1995
50- Wholesale trade	1,347	1,350	22,184	23,261	17	25,573	28,050	622,399	664,651
5012 Automobiles and other vehicles [3]	28	27	669	717	27	25,674	35,437	17,793	22,452
5013 Motor vehicle supplies and new parts	82	79	810	855	11	21,057	22,400	19,487	20,285
5014 Tires and tubes [3]	12	11	243	184	17	22,403	26,391	6,110	5,464
5015 Motor vehicle parts, used	18	19	139	135	7	22,561	23,378	3,292	3,311
5021 Furniture [3]	10	12	251	266	22	26,151	28,060	7,371	7,880
5023 Homefurnishings [3]	19	16	212	194	12	22,491	22,495	5,733	5,598
5031 Lumber, plywood, and millwork [3]	23	18	545	275	15	28,316	29,615	17,065	6,933
5032 Brick, stone, & related materials [3]	8	11	89	111	10	30,382	30,559	2,699	3,412
5033 Roofing, siding, & insulation [3]	10	14	60	57	4	35,067	25,614	2,525	1,290
5039 Construction materials, nec [3]	11	22	106	286	13	21,434	25,413	2,558	7,880
5044 Office equipment [3]	25	25	479	475	19	32,292	39,899	15,818	16,459
5045 Computers, peripherals, & software [3]	52	57	788	1,008	18	51,010	51,925	39,061	45,461
5046 Commercial equipment, nec [3]	16	15	305	221	15	35,974	24,959	10,952	5,409
5047 Medical and hospital equipment	54	56	733	741	13	30,778	31,968	23,350	25,517
5048 Ophthalmic goods [3]	12	10	269	279	28	19,420	21,161	5,784	6,193
5051 Metals service centers and offices [3]	19	18	110	119	7	31,782	35,597	4,147	4,450
5063 Electrical apparatus and equipment [3]	61	56	565	576	10	26,676	31,563	16,073	17,472
5064 Electrical appliances, TV & radios [3]	10	9	184	206	23	18,739	21,961	3,961	4,860
5065 Electronic parts and equipment [3]	39	40	389	399	10	37,635	41,323	13,978	15,402

Continued on next page.

OMAHA MSA (NE PART) - [continued]

Wholesale and Retail Trade USA	Establishments		Employment		Emp / Est	Pay / Employee		Annual Payroll ($ 000)	
	1994	1995	1994	1995	1995	1994	1995	1994	1995
5072 Hardware [3]	26	26	601	492	19	17,830	23,382	12,049	13,094
5074 Plumbing & hydronic heating supplies [2]	-	27	-	202	7	-	28,257	-	5,975
5075 Warm air heating & air conditioning [3]	32	31	267	277	9	28,629	31,986	8,326	10,191
5078 Refrigeration equipment and supplies [2]	-	10	-	128	13	-	33,188	-	4,404
5082 Construction and mining machinery [3]	13	12	378	374	31	32,381	37,604	13,565	13,700
5083 Farm and garden machinery	22	22	200	210	10	20,880	23,295	4,843	3,828
5084 Industrial machinery and equipment	75	73	648	665	9	30,370	32,547	21,437	24,832
5085 Industrial supplies [3]	51	53	689	746	14	28,627	30,649	22,184	24,724
5087 Service establishment equipment [3]	22	24	586	625	26	23,072	24,742	14,474	16,852
5088 Transportation equipment & supplies [3]	12	10	94	47	5	26,979	30,809	2,900	2,000
5091 Sporting & recreational goods [3]	17	18	100	112	6	28,040	26,500	2,888	2,830
5093 Scrap and waste materials [3]	22	18	307	354	20	15,896	21,390	5,809	7,654
5099 Durable goods, nec [3]	21	23	195	205	9	25,621	26,790	6,076	6,231
5112 Stationery and office supplies [3]	35	28	404	354	13	20,475	23,119	9,653	8,702
5120 Drugs, proprietaries, and sundries [3]	21	22	432	514	23	19,611	19,728	10,568	10,448
5131 Piece goods & notions [1]	8	-	60	-	-	23,333	-	1,343	-
5141 Groceries, general line [3]	14	15	667	633	42	25,265	26,079	17,850	17,762
5142 Packaged frozen food [1]	13	-	204	-	-	26,941	-	6,728	-
5145 Confectionery [3]	7	7	203	220	31	25,320	24,873	5,624	6,323
5147 Meats and meat products [3]	16	16	837	849	53	24,444	26,648	23,032	23,225
5148 Fresh fruits and vegetables [3]	6	6	211	203	34	26,806	29,773	5,353	5,459
5149 Groceries and related products, nec [3]	28	29	607	679	23	28,896	29,638	19,018	21,698
5153 Grain and field beans	23	27	185	238	9	33,968	27,361	6,450	6,875
5154 Livestock [1]	15	-	83	-	-	19,759	-	1,686	-
5169 Chemicals & allied products, nec	32	-	233	-	-	27,107	-	7,713	-
5171 Petroleum bulk stations & terminals	16	-	131	-	-	24,824	-	3,763	-
5172 Petroleum products, nec [1]	8	-	144	-	-	17,083	-	2,074	-
5181 Beer and ale [3]	6	5	189	125	25	26,857	28,032	5,887	3,909
5182 Wine and distilled beverages [3]	6	6	241	260	43	29,593	29,338	7,406	7,944
5191 Farm supplies	42	42	841	696	17	25,170	31,167	25,209	24,220
5198 Paints, varnishes, and supplies [3]	10	9	58	54	6	26,759	29,556	1,540	1,635
5199 Nondurable goods, nec [3]	38	41	1,918	2,661	65	11,975	17,333	29,406	45,635
52- Retail trade	3,546	3,524	56,085	57,516	16	11,213	12,164	694,586	744,384
5210 Lumber and other building materials	44	37	941	1,156	31	16,179	20,401	16,781	23,197
5230 Paint, glass, and wallpaper stores [3]	21	21	121	124	6	15,967	16,645	2,355	2,362
5250 Hardware stores	40	30	244	223	7	10,475	11,731	3,019	2,646
5260 Retail nurseries and garden stores	37	34	190	281	8	10,758	12,797	2,803	5,044
5270 Mobile home dealers [3]	8	6	48	43	7	21,500	39,535	1,123	1,368
5310 Department stores [3]	35	33	5,356	5,678	172	10,270	11,394	58,188	65,165
5330 Variety stores [3]	16	11	93	66	6	8,473	7,152	728	600
5390 Misc. general merchandise stores [3]	19	24	357	450	19	12,874	11,787	4,574	5,259
5410 Grocery stores [3]	171	180	7,183	7,987	44	11,562	10,795	87,699	91,517
5420 Meat and fish markets [1]	14	16	90	100	6	10,133	10,800	967	1,056
5440 Candy, nut, and confectionery stores [3]	11	15	46	60	4	6,087	8,400	331	450
5450 Dairy products stores [3]	15	11	64	54	5	5,500	6,667	373	406
5460 Retail bakeries [3]	53	48	249	264	6	8,177	8,667	2,356	2,386
5490 Miscellaneous food stores [1]	25	22	140	127	6	7,143	7,118	1,113	944
5510 New and used car dealers [3]	43	46	2,197	2,223	48	26,403	27,352	68,996	75,470
5520 Used car dealers [3]	48	49	339	356	7	24,767	27,494	6,730	7,645
5530 Auto and home supply stores	94	94	696	686	7	15,552	17,971	12,546	13,198
5540 Gasoline service stations	245	234	1,852	1,788	8	11,045	12,447	22,881	22,983
5550 Boat dealers	11	11	40	44	4	20,700	21,909	976	1,030
5560 Recreational vehicle dealers [3]	9	9	38	42	5	16,526	16,286	784	846
5570 Motorcycle dealers [3]	5	5	49	46	9	14,612	18,783	882	1,023
5610 Men's & boys' clothing stores [3]	47	44	327	299	7	12,294	13,311	4,766	4,516
5620 Women's clothing stores [3]	102	99	1,063	989	10	7,955	8,291	9,112	8,051
5630 Women's accessory & specialty stores [3]	31	28	187	175	6	7,529	7,566	1,456	1,339
5640 Children's and infants' wear stores [3]	11	10	90	86	9	7,200	6,047	690	673
5650 Family clothing stores [3]	37	44	567	606	14	9,813	9,861	5,336	7,726
5660 Shoe stores [3]	95	88	555	536	6	9,996	11,343	5,433	5,467
5690 Misc. apparel & accessory stores [3]	22	24	106	92	4	7,434	10,522	911	1,078
5712 Furniture stores [3]	43	32	923	871	27	19,918	19,100	17,492	18,739
5713 Floor covering stores [2]	22	22	237	193	9	16,456	19,959	4,468	4,426
5714 Drapery and upholstery stores [3]	4	4	20	21	5	24,200	23,429	470	533
5719 Misc. homefurnishings stores [3]	44	45	261	264	6	9,732	10,485	2,789	3,296
5720 Household appliance stores	17	19	63	71	4	18,159	16,676	1,041	1,336
5731 Radio, TV, & electronic stores [3]	33	34	373	436	13	15,282	13,587	6,356	6,582
5734 Computer and software stores [3]	13	18	77	69	4	12,571	18,783	1,070	1,654
5735 Record & prerecorded tape stores [3]	26	26	155	156	6	8,955	10,205	1,438	1,447
5736 Musical instrument stores [3]	11	11	54	55	5	13,333	15,055	829	893
5812 Eating places	873	808	19,153	18,177	22	7,202	8,160	149,724	155,420

Continued on next page.

OMAHA MSA (NE PART) - [continued]

Wholesale and Retail Trade USA	Establishments		Employment		Emp / Est	Pay / Employee		Annual Payroll ($ 000)	
	1994	1995	1994	1995	1995	1994	1995	1994	1995
5813 Drinking places	268	244	1,350	1,319	5	6,741	7,478	9,626	9,837
5910 Drug stores and proprietary stores	93	94	1,263	1,309	14	13,337	14,005	18,111	19,207
5920 Liquor stores	33	33	157	159	5	10,369	12,126	1,678	1,975
5930 Used merchandise stores	56	54	412	400	7	9,728	10,950	4,570	4,836
5941 Sporting goods and bicycle shops	68	74	506	506	7	12,980	14,308	7,397	7,193
5942 Book stores [3]	46	44	360	422	10	6,322	6,237	2,604	2,670
5943 Stationery stores [2]	-	9	-	46	5	-	15,217	-	834
5944 Jewelry stores [3]	46	48	562	577	12	15,459	17,775	9,164	9,539
5945 Hobby, toy, and game shops [3]	33	32	405	433	14	7,704	8,249	3,642	4,007
5947 Gift, novelty, and souvenir shops	81	86	736	757	9	6,929	7,160	5,559	6,078
5949 Sewing, needlework, and piece goods [2]	20	16	194	111	7	7,381	8,180	1,424	825
5961 Catalog and mail-order houses [3]	13	14	350	357	26	16,491	20,941	6,450	7,639
5962 Merchandising machine operators [3]	16	21	247	273	13	16,874	16,864	4,219	4,585
5963 Direct selling establishments	32	29	772	734	25	9,378	10,332	17,861	7,554
5984 Liquefied petroleum gas dealers [2]	-	4	-	24	6	-	22,333	-	499
5992 Florists	48	45	243	211	5	9,086	9,934	2,259	2,134
5994 News dealers and newsstands [2]	-	6	-	50	8	-	5,440	-	306
5995 Optical goods stores [3]	40	46	253	245	5	15,368	17,633	4,091	4,490
5999 Miscellaneous retail stores, nec	103	108	495	569	5	10,982	10,721	5,871	7,176

Source: County Business Patterns 1994/95, CBP-94/95, U.S. Department of Commerce, Washington DC, November 1997. The employment column represents mid-March employment in the year. Pay per employee is calculated by dividing 1st Quarter payroll, annualized, by mid-March employment. The column headed 'Emp / Est' shows 'employees per establishment'. A dash (-) means that data are unavailable or cannot be calculated. nec means not elsewhere classified. *Notes:* 1. 1994 data incomplete; unavailable or withheld. 2. 1995 data incomplete; unavailable or withheld. 3. 1994 and 1995 data incomplete; unavailable or withheld.

OMAHA, NE – IA MSA

Wholesale and Retail Trade USA	Establishments		Employment		Emp / Est	Pay / Employee		Annual Payroll ($ 000)	
	1994	1995	1994	1995	1995	1994	1995	1994	1995
50- Wholesale trade	1,485	1,481	23,673	24,782	17	25,427	27,874	660,305	704,830
5012 Automobiles and other vehicles [3]	34	34	771	836	25	26,983	35,699	21,263	26,841
5013 Motor vehicle supplies and new parts	95	91	902	962	11	20,683	21,971	21,257	22,330
5014 Tires and tubes [3]	13	12	243	184	15	22,403	26,391	6,110	5,464
5015 Motor vehicle parts, used	23	24	139	135	6	22,561	23,378	3,292	3,311
5021 Furniture [3]	10	12	251	266	22	26,151	28,060	7,371	7,880
5023 Homefurnishings [3]	19	16	212	194	12	22,491	22,495	5,733	5,598
5031 Lumber, plywood, and millwork [3]	24	19	545	275	14	28,316	29,615	17,065	6,933
5032 Brick, stone, & related materials [3]	8	11	89	111	10	30,382	30,559	2,699	3,412
5033 Roofing, siding, & insulation [3]	11	15	60	57	4	35,067	25,614	2,525	1,290
5039 Construction materials, nec [3]	12	25	106	286	11	21,434	25,413	2,558	7,880
5044 Office equipment [3]	26	26	479	475	18	32,292	39,899	15,818	16,459
5045 Computers, peripherals, & software [3]	53	58	788	1,008	17	51,010	51,925	39,061	45,461
5046 Commercial equipment, nec [3]	17	16	305	221	14	35,974	24,959	10,952	5,409
5047 Medical and hospital equipment [2]	55	56	733	741	13	30,778	31,968	23,350	25,517
5048 Ophthalmic goods [3]	12	10	269	279	28	19,420	21,161	5,784	6,193
5051 Metals service centers and offices [3]	20	20	110	119	6	31,782	35,597	4,147	4,450
5063 Electrical apparatus and equipment [3]	63	58	565	576	10	26,676	31,563	16,073	17,472
5064 Electrical appliances, TV & radios [3]	10	9	184	206	23	18,739	21,961	3,961	4,860
5065 Electronic parts and equipment [3]	42	43	389	399	9	37,635	41,323	13,978	15,402
5072 Hardware [3]	28	28	601	492	18	17,830	23,382	12,049	13,094
5074 Plumbing & hydronic heating supplies [2]	-	28	-	202	7	-	28,257	-	5,975
5075 Warm air heating & air conditioning [3]	34	33	267	277	8	28,629	31,986	8,326	10,191
5078 Refrigeration equipment and supplies [2]	-	11	-	128	12	-	33,188	-	4,404
5082 Construction and mining machinery [3]	13	12	378	374	31	32,381	37,604	13,565	13,700
5083 Farm and garden machinery	31	31	301	308	10	20,346	22,468	7,271	6,235
5084 Industrial machinery and equipment	77	75	648	665	9	30,370	32,547	21,437	24,832
5085 Industrial supplies [3]	52	54	689	746	14	28,627	30,649	22,184	24,724
5087 Service establishment equipment [3]	22	24	586	625	26	23,072	24,742	14,474	16,852
5088 Transportation equipment & supplies [3]	12	10	94	47	5	26,979	30,809	2,900	2,000
5091 Sporting & recreational goods [3]	18	19	100	112	6	28,040	26,500	2,888	2,830
5093 Scrap and waste materials [3]	28	24	386	441	18	18,456	23,546	8,330	10,536
5099 Durable goods, nec [3]	23	26	195	205	8	25,621	26,790	6,076	6,231
5112 Stationery and office supplies [3]	35	28	404	354	13	20,475	23,119	9,653	8,702
5120 Drugs, proprietaries, and sundries [3]	21	22	432	514	23	19,611	19,728	10,568	10,448
5131 Piece goods & notions [1]	8	-	60	-	-	23,333	-	1,343	-
5141 Groceries, general line [3]	14	15	667	633	42	25,265	26,079	17,850	17,762
5142 Packaged frozen food [1]	13	-	204	-	-	26,941	-	6,728	-
5145 Confectionery [3]	7	7	203	220	31	25,320	24,873	5,624	6,323
5147 Meats and meat products [3]	16	16	837	849	53	24,444	26,648	23,032	23,225
5148 Fresh fruits and vegetables [3]	6	6	211	203	34	26,806	29,773	5,353	5,459

Continued on next page.

OMAHA, NE - IA MSA - [continued]

Wholesale and Retail Trade USA	Establishments		Employment		Emp / Est	Pay / Employee		Annual Payroll ($ 000)	
	1994	1995	1994	1995	1995	1994	1995	1994	1995
5149 Groceries and related products, nec [3]	29	30	607	679	23	28,896	29,638	19,018	21,698
5153 Grain and field beans [3]	34	36	185	238	7	33,968	27,361	6,450	6,875
5154 Livestock [1]	16	-	83	-	-	19,759	-	1,686	-
5169 Chemicals & allied products, nec	36	-	233	-	-	27,107	-	7,713	-
5171 Petroleum bulk stations & terminals [1]	28	-	131	-	-	24,824	-	3,763	-
5172 Petroleum products, nec [1]	11	-	144	-	-	17,083	-	2,074	-
5181 Beer and ale [3]	9	7	189	125	18	26,857	28,032	5,887	3,909
5182 Wine and distilled beverages [3]	7	7	241	260	37	29,593	29,338	7,406	7,944
5191 Farm supplies [3]	68	64	841	696	11	25,170	31,167	25,209	24,220
5198 Paints, varnishes, and supplies [3]	10	9	58	54	6	26,759	29,556	1,540	1,635
5199 Nondurable goods, nec [3]	39	42	1,918	2,661	63	11,975	17,333	29,406	45,635
52- Retail trade	4,085	4,033	63,501	64,980	16	11,167	12,125	781,733	836,620
5210 Lumber and other building materials	51	42	1,182	1,345	32	16,230	19,813	20,703	26,015
5230 Paint, glass, and wallpaper stores [3]	25	25	121	124	5	15,967	16,645	2,355	2,362
5250 Hardware stores	45	34	327	286	8	10,667	11,706	3,900	3,110
5260 Retail nurseries and garden stores	41	38	222	312	8	10,541	12,500	3,129	5,374
5270 Mobile home dealers [3]	9	7	48	43	6	21,500	39,535	1,123	1,368
5310 Department stores [3]	40	38	6,023	6,425	169	10,294	11,395	65,880	73,968
5330 Variety stores [3]	21	16	93	66	4	8,473	7,152	728	600
5390 Misc. general merchandise stores [3]	22	27	357	450	17	12,874	11,787	4,574	5,259
5410 Grocery stores [3]	200	209	8,209	9,078	43	11,460	10,736	99,063	103,521
5420 Meat and fish markets [1]	16	17	90	100	6	10,133	10,800	967	1,056
5440 Candy, nut, and confectionery stores [3]	14	15	57	60	4	5,754	8,400	373	450
5450 Dairy products stores [3]	18	13	69	54	4	5,565	6,667	410	406
5460 Retail bakeries [3]	58	53	270	284	5	8,163	8,648	2,543	2,566
5490 Miscellaneous food stores [1]	28	24	154	127	5	6,909	7,118	1,185	944
5510 New and used car dealers [3]	55	58	2,918	2,955	51	25,535	26,774	86,731	95,101
5520 Used car dealers [3]	55	55	385	384	7	23,709	27,010	7,417	8,109
5530 Auto and home supply stores	115	111	812	794	7	15,335	17,753	14,388	15,287
5540 Gasoline service stations	311	296	2,548	2,447	8	10,984	12,093	31,134	31,013
5550 Boat dealers	13	13	40	44	3	20,700	21,909	976	1,030
5560 Recreational vehicle dealers [3]	10	10	38	42	4	16,526	16,286	784	846
5570 Motorcycle dealers [3]	9	9	56	54	6	14,143	17,852	991	1,150
5610 Men's & boys' clothing stores [3]	49	46	327	299	7	12,294	13,311	4,766	4,516
5620 Women's clothing stores [3]	120	113	1,253	1,116	10	7,770	8,093	10,453	8,923
5630 Women's accessory & specialty stores [3]	35	32	205	190	6	7,668	7,684	1,608	1,477
5640 Children's and infants' wear stores [3]	12	11	90	86	8	7,200	6,047	690	673
5650 Family clothing stores [3]	41	48	746	767	16	9,072	9,653	6,747	9,122
5660 Shoe stores [3]	107	100	618	599	6	9,877	11,726	5,999	6,084
5690 Misc. apparel & accessory stores [3]	23	25	106	92	4	7,434	10,522	911	1,078
5712 Furniture stores [3]	45	34	923	871	26	19,918	19,100	17,492	18,739
5713 Floor covering stores [2]	27	27	263	214	8	16,502	19,664	4,910	4,800
5714 Drapery and upholstery stores [3]	4	4	20	21	5	24,200	23,429	470	533
5719 Misc. homefurnishings stores [3]	46	47	261	264	6	9,732	10,485	2,789	3,296
5720 Household appliance stores	20	21	63	71	3	18,159	16,676	1,041	1,336
5731 Radio, TV, & electronic stores [3]	38	38	402	450	12	15,174	13,627	6,808	6,766
5734 Computer and software stores [3]	14	20	77	69	3	12,571	18,783	1,070	1,654
5735 Record & prerecorded tape stores [3]	30	30	155	177	6	8,955	10,441	1,438	1,627
5736 Musical instrument stores [3]	12	12	54	55	5	13,333	15,055	829	893
5812 Eating places	989	920	21,229	20,226	22	7,168	8,125	165,370	172,324
5813 Drinking places	311	282	1,531	1,479	5	6,657	7,373	10,733	10,817
5910 Drug stores and proprietary stores	109	109	1,553	1,599	15	13,556	14,066	22,582	23,557
5920 Liquor stores	35	35	157	159	5	10,369	12,126	1,678	1,975
5930 Used merchandise stores	69	68	476	461	7	9,370	10,603	5,142	5,399
5941 Sporting goods and bicycle shops	73	78	528	530	7	12,758	14,038	7,579	7,395
5942 Book stores [3]	51	47	388	445	9	6,237	6,328	2,733	2,861
5943 Stationery stores [2]	-	10	-	46	5	-	15,217	-	834
5944 Jewelry stores [3]	56	60	632	668	11	15,089	17,132	10,222	10,753
5945 Hobby, toy, and game shops [3]	37	36	405	451	13	7,704	8,328	3,642	4,407
5947 Gift, novelty, and souvenir shops	89	94	771	798	8	7,019	7,368	5,946	6,532
5949 Sewing, needlework, and piece goods [2]	24	19	237	111	6	7,224	8,180	1,744	825
5961 Catalog and mail-order houses [3]	16	18	377	419	23	16,350	20,897	6,869	8,997
5962 Merchandising machine operators [3]	20	25	289	273	11	15,889	16,864	4,676	4,585
5963 Direct selling establishments	36	33	792	734	22	9,455	10,332	18,168	7,554
5984 Liquefied petroleum gas dealers [2]	-	4	-	24	6	-	22,333	-	499
5992 Florists	56	52	283	211	4	9,216	9,934	2,659	2,134
5994 News dealers and newsstands [2]	-	6	-	50	8	-	5,440	-	306
5995 Optical goods stores [3]	48	54	253	272	5	15,368	20,485	4,091	5,125
5999 Miscellaneous retail stores, nec	116	117	522	598	5	10,851	10,535	6,078	7,449

Source: County Business Patterns 1994/95, CBP-94/95, U.S. Department of Commerce, Washington DC, November 1997. The employment column represents mid-March employment in the year. Pay per employee is calculated by dividing 1st Quarter payroll, annualized, by mid-March employment. The column headed 'Emp / Est' shows 'employees per establishment'. A dash (-) means that data are unavailable or cannot be calculated. nec means not elsewhere classified. *Notes:* 1. 1994 data incomplete; unavailable or withheld. 2. 1995 data incomplete; unavailable or withheld. 3. 1994 and 1995 data incomplete; unavailable or withheld.

ORANGE COUNTY, CA PMSA

Wholesale and Retail Trade USA	Establishments		Employment		Emp / Est	Pay / Employee		Annual Payroll ($ 000)	
	1994	1995	1994	1995	1995	1994	1995	1994	1995
50- Wholesale trade	7,005	7,196	97,905	106,903	15	34,680	36,488	3,674,004	4,059,920
5012 Automobiles and other vehicles	86	90	2,881	3,125	35	46,392	47,488	129,389	141,401
5013 Motor vehicle supplies and new parts	307	281	3,491	3,597	13	27,479	27,698	104,130	105,157
5014 Tires and tubes	27	31	440	425	14	38,745	41,111	18,031	17,588
5015 Motor vehicle parts, used	42	54	264	490	9	20,833	32,098	6,409	12,436
5021 Furniture	115	121	1,044	739	6	26,720	30,620	29,390	24,160
5023 Homefurnishings	142	140	1,194	1,312	9	27,240	26,265	36,318	35,128
5031 Lumber, plywood, and millwork	87	84	1,152	942	11	30,094	33,558	38,047	34,031
5032 Brick, stone, & related materials	72	58	535	634	11	27,559	26,498	15,718	16,941
5033 Roofing, siding, & insulation	26	21	362	341	16	33,901	34,651	12,512	12,098
5039 Construction materials, nec	46	64	455	766	12	32,079	36,574	15,896	27,158
5043 Photographic equipment & supplies	27	27	613	641	24	39,582	43,944	27,300	29,175
5044 Office equipment	115	113	3,097	3,501	31	40,456	42,453	123,125	140,820
5045 Computers, peripherals, & software	580	586	10,387	10,978	19	46,524	45,743	525,212	517,208
5046 Commercial equipment, nec	71	65	579	717	11	35,413	40,932	20,654	27,085
5047 Medical and hospital equipment	189	192	2,684	3,272	17	41,590	50,660	123,199	149,520
5048 Ophthalmic goods	32	32	504	516	16	24,278	28,899	13,267	17,944
5049 Professional equipment, nec	46	44	812	1,109	25	36,138	37,032	33,480	42,964
5051 Metals service centers and offices	140	144	1,076	1,285	9	31,885	33,457	39,902	48,930
5052 Coal and other minerals and ores	4	4	35	39	10	49,486	48,513	2,589	3,469
5063 Electrical apparatus and equipment	266	242	2,528	2,339	10	38,828	41,330	101,035	99,737
5064 Electrical appliances, TV & radios	65	65	1,835	1,631	25	43,259	49,194	88,525	92,200
5065 Electronic parts and equipment	550	579	7,355	7,813	13	44,019	48,388	345,945	407,660
5072 Hardware	142	147	1,620	1,721	12	31,560	35,042	58,233	62,424
5074 Plumbing & hydronic heating supplies	94	87	873	987	11	33,269	35,299	29,990	36,347
5075 Warm air heating & air conditioning	39	36	391	410	11	33,064	32,000	14,537	14,388
5078 Refrigeration equipment and supplies	15	15	108	101	7	34,519	36,634	3,871	4,075
5082 Construction and mining machinery	25	19	203	182	10	36,690	41,429	9,314	9,393
5083 Farm and garden machinery	33	32	240	276	9	26,550	29,188	8,304	8,718
5084 Industrial machinery and equipment	412	415	3,737	3,486	8	36,604	40,327	148,426	146,678
5085 Industrial supplies	180	181	1,644	1,629	9	36,187	39,114	66,313	68,220
5087 Service establishment equipment	87	79	890	878	11	29,137	29,772	27,895	27,861
5088 Transportation equipment & supplies	82	77	661	644	8	36,224	39,522	28,790	30,192
5091 Sporting & recreational goods	152	170	1,985	2,349	14	28,337	28,289	88,434	92,932
5092 Toys and hobby goods and supplies	63	64	781	906	14	22,761	22,208	19,804	22,137
5093 Scrap and waste materials	66	75	885	1,071	14	18,169	23,813	19,831	28,766
5094 Jewelry & precious stones	63	65	430	432	7	32,037	31,657	13,399	14,248
5099 Durable goods, nec	140	156	958	871	6	27,203	30,517	27,746	28,496
5111 Printing and writing paper	48	48	606	400	8	44,158	62,580	26,217	23,979
5112 Stationery and office supplies	158	130	8,862	8,322	64	9,890	11,963	94,028	104,033
5113 Industrial & personal service paper	107	114	890	1,203	11	40,966	39,538	38,336	48,401
5120 Drugs, proprietaries, and sundries	130	135	2,390	2,605	19	42,536	48,811	102,474	136,448
5131 Piece goods & notions	69	75	580	738	10	28,786	32,417	27,581	25,238
5136 Men's and boys' clothing	83	69	1,134	1,317	19	28,801	28,583	36,846	40,549
5137 Women's and children's clothing	95	91	1,190	1,113	12	16,013	19,975	23,087	22,089
5139 Footwear	37	38	386	338	9	40,394	39,680	14,681	13,783
5141 Groceries, general line	55	58	833	897	15	26,339	25,512	22,745	24,065
5142 Packaged frozen food	40	36	798	742	21	31,985	33,725	24,183	26,027
5143 Dairy products, exc. dried or canned	18	15	288	202	13	45,694	51,030	14,921	10,061
5144 Poultry and poultry products	6	6	38	35	6	39,684	41,486	1,511	1,425
5145 Confectionery	22	22	554	541	25	26,282	28,954	15,282	15,349
5146 Fish and seafoods	15	13	77	96	7	28,000	25,333	2,368	2,418
5147 Meats and meat products	34	34	328	312	9	55,061	53,038	16,443	17,642
5148 Fresh fruits and vegetables	62	61	1,037	1,120	18	24,397	25,129	30,027	31,433
5149 Groceries and related products, nec	172	177	3,753	3,957	22	32,897	36,621	133,452	151,421
5159 Farm-product raw materials, nec	3	3	9	9	3	52,000	55,556	715	811
5162 Plastics materials & basic shapes	84	83	899	1,035	12	31,924	37,302	34,139	42,797
5169 Chemicals & allied products, nec	128	136	1,396	1,925	14	52,029	46,020	71,711	96,001
5171 Petroleum bulk stations & terminals	24	22	548	528	24	44,686	47,735	24,238	25,585
5172 Petroleum products, nec	31	29	182	185	6	62,593	55,503	12,220	10,420
5181 Beer and ale	11	10	903	780	78	39,650	35,733	40,021	25,601
5182 Wine and distilled beverages	18	16	620	671	42	40,342	55,034	31,302	37,363
5191 Farm supplies	39	34	238	279	8	30,739	36,186	7,131	11,194
5192 Books, periodicals, & newspapers	51	52	912	1,047	20	30,947	34,900	31,256	40,537
5193 Flowers & florists' supplies	63	56	708	649	12	16,220	16,641	13,102	11,933
5194 Tobacco and tobacco products	4	-	22	-	-	19,273	-	226	-
5198 Paints, varnishes, and supplies	50	46	586	602	13	39,788	37,654	23,626	23,383
5199 Nondurable goods, nec	395	442	2,510	2,986	7	23,538	22,260	66,984	73,967
52- Retail trade	13,895	13,829	210,968	218,749	16	16,068	16,371	3,566,131	4,029,777
5210 Lumber and other building materials	134	121	3,744	3,741	31	21,548	22,909	88,063	87,564
5230 Paint, glass, and wallpaper stores	93	85	509	556	7	23,662	28,043	13,167	16,033

Continued on next page.

ORANGE COUNTY, CA PMSA - [continued]

Wholesale and Retail Trade USA	Establishments		Employment		Emp / Est	Pay / Employee		Annual Payroll ($ 000)	
	1994	1995	1994	1995	1995	1994	1995	1994	1995
5250 Hardware stores	85	61	699	605	10	17,104	17,825	13,078	10,917
5260 Retail nurseries and garden stores	66	65	671	627	10	15,255	14,494	11,431	10,775
5270 Mobile home dealers	28	34	81	107	3	17,531	16,150	1,824	2,549
5310 Department stores	81	81	15,098	17,244	213	12,956	12,713	212,528	217,678
5330 Variety stores	16	14	164	151	11	12,805	12,848	1,993	1,927
5390 Misc. general merchandise stores	88	98	3,838	3,635	37	15,547	17,369	63,284	63,048
5410 Grocery stores	700	691	19,136	21,056	30	19,736	20,220	397,561	447,644
5420 Meat and fish markets	56	51	430	570	11	13,023	12,961	6,142	8,183
5430 Fruit and vegetable markets	16	17	110	136	8	10,691	9,735	1,312	1,415
5440 Candy, nut, and confectionery stores	48	53	287	302	6	9,017	9,470	2,989	3,189
5450 Dairy products stores	26	23	122	118	5	5,607	5,356	743	727
5460 Retail bakeries	301	281	1,724	1,614	6	10,077	10,984	19,797	18,238
5490 Miscellaneous food stores	152	157	868	883	6	10,300	11,243	11,617	11,080
5510 New and used car dealers	161	157	8,737	9,128	58	35,944	36,048	341,405	353,543
5520 Used car dealers	67	73	229	298	4	20,716	22,846	5,558	7,615
5530 Auto and home supply stores	400	372	3,106	2,908	8	18,438	19,403	64,299	57,190
5540 Gasoline service stations	617	600	4,765	4,735	8	12,013	12,089	59,843	61,463
5550 Boat dealers	44	50	288	292	6	20,792	22,288	7,341	7,340
5560 Recreational vehicle dealers	31	29	313	309	11	25,252	30,084	9,507	9,613
5570 Motorcycle dealers	41	42	348	372	9	20,678	21,462	8,944	8,441
5590 Automotive dealers, nec	12	10	123	54	5	17,854	18,444	2,542	1,023
5610 Men's & boys' clothing stores	148	131	1,197	1,113	8	13,109	14,286	16,273	16,561
5620 Women's clothing stores	433	385	3,601	3,317	9	10,858	11,610	41,113	39,271
5630 Women's accessory & specialty stores	103	97	621	613	6	10,325	10,976	7,605	7,981
5640 Children's and infants' wear stores	62	58	481	508	9	7,726	8,724	4,754	4,611
5650 Family clothing stores	167	151	5,445	5,741	38	14,335	14,257	81,664	84,520
5660 Shoe stores	321	293	1,871	1,831	6	13,529	13,903	26,323	25,487
5690 Misc. apparel & accessory stores	109	112	680	696	6	12,129	12,552	9,674	9,153
5712 Furniture stores	269	264	1,793	1,966	7	19,835	19,837	39,845	42,242
5713 Floor covering stores	144	135	875	1,017	8	22,025	24,802	22,748	26,344
5714 Drapery and upholstery stores	34	32	168	158	5	12,143	15,165	2,217	2,330
5719 Misc. homefurnishings stores	225	210	1,635	1,695	8	13,260	14,029	25,020	24,824
5720 Household appliance stores	63	56	289	327	6	20,969	21,554	6,590	7,492
5731 Radio, TV, & electronic stores	179	185	1,765	1,963	11	20,560	20,950	38,970	43,233
5734 Computer and software stores	156	175	1,219	1,860	11	24,335	27,213	34,581	50,646
5735 Record & prerecorded tape stores	131	123	1,552	1,737	14	8,415	8,090	13,361	13,474
5736 Musical instrument stores	38	40	230	227	6	16,539	17,727	3,783	4,016
5812 Eating places	4,015	3,827	74,125	74,316	19	8,741	9,190	699,217	712,296
5813 Drinking places	300	278	2,543	2,455	9	7,286	7,826	20,197	20,452
5910 Drug stores and proprietary stores	367	360	5,440	5,580	16	20,782	20,798	125,591	115,120
5920 Liquor stores	226	213	779	762	4	10,983	11,302	9,077	9,312
5930 Used merchandise stores	133	129	1,131	1,078	8	12,813	14,011	16,986	12,956
5941 Sporting goods and bicycle shops	265	259	2,727	2,682	10	13,498	13,199	37,190	35,777
5942 Book stores	125	126	1,029	1,010	8	11,926	13,853	12,738	13,990
5943 Stationery stores	68	84	617	1,026	12	11,650	13,598	7,982	14,240
5944 Jewelry stores	247	243	1,153	1,146	5	18,317	19,668	21,584	22,058
5945 Hobby, toy, and game shops	131	128	1,277	1,437	11	10,534	10,550	16,105	16,815
5946 Camera & photographic supply stores	44	43	288	276	6	14,694	16,957	4,439	4,349
5947 Gift, novelty, and souvenir shops	317	321	1,932	1,936	6	9,186	9,787	19,224	20,268
5948 Luggage and leather goods stores	15	16	132	145	9	18,697	21,241	2,611	3,318
5949 Sewing, needlework, and piece goods	71	76	610	620	8	10,164	9,381	6,431	6,191
5961 Catalog and mail-order houses	82	97	507	941	10	17,712	22,708	11,777	27,174
5962 Merchandising machine operators	39	41	332	323	8	22,361	23,307	8,084	8,431
5963 Direct selling establishments	138	123	1,916	1,682	14	20,808	24,794	43,170	39,066
5980 Fuel dealers	4	5	38	45	9	26,316	20,267	1,033	1,199
5992 Florists	230	236	1,110	1,080	5	9,038	9,959	10,571	11,410
5993 Tobacco stores and stands	10	9	68	86	10	10,706	12,791	911	1,206
5994 News dealers and newsstands	12	12	77	60	5	9,714	13,400	731	838
5995 Optical goods stores	96	98	482	556	6	15,710	17,158	8,204	11,398
5999 Miscellaneous retail stores, nec	550	562	2,917	3,210	6	12,868	14,126	41,803	49,097

Source: County Business Patterns 1994/95, CBP-94/95, U.S. Department of Commerce, Washington DC, November 1997. The employment column represents mid-March employment in the year. Pay per employee is calculated by dividing 1st Quarter payroll, annualized, by mid-March employment. The column headed 'Emp / Est' shows 'employees per establishment'. A dash (-) means that data are unavailable or cannot be calculated. nec means not elsewhere classified. *Notes:* 1. 1994 data incomplete; unavailable or withheld. 2. 1995 data incomplete; unavailable or withheld. 3. 1994 and 1995 data incomplete; unavailable or withheld.

ORLANDO, FL MSA

Wholesale and Retail Trade USA	Establishments		Employment		Emp / Est	Pay / Employee		Annual Payroll ($ 000)	
	1994	1995	1994	1995	1995	1994	1995	1994	1995
50 - Wholesale trade	3,232	3,330	36,158	37,549	11	28,448	30,492	1,079,187	1,174,086
5012 Automobiles and other vehicles	98	99	2,379	2,439	25	21,834	23,769	58,402	59,180
5013 Motor vehicle supplies and new parts	164	137	1,640	1,508	11	21,902	23,525	37,998	37,030
5014 Tires and tubes [3]	19	15	153	155	10	33,098	33,135	4,930	4,939
5015 Motor vehicle parts, used	38	48	206	264	6	18,680	19,712	4,506	5,697
5021 Furniture	53	54	374	379	7	25,422	25,636	11,115	11,730
5023 Homefurnishings	79	80	571	608	8	25,163	29,796	15,335	17,840
5031 Lumber, plywood, and millwork	53	59	794	927	16	28,821	30,265	22,786	26,573
5032 Brick, stone, & related materials [3]	31	25	167	161	6	24,838	25,888	4,860	4,168
5033 Roofing, siding, & insulation [3]	26	25	316	257	10	23,380	28,125	7,179	6,879
5039 Construction materials, nec	31	51	258	385	8	27,380	34,857	7,944	13,938
5043 Photographic equipment & supplies [3]	10	11	103	103	9	17,903	19,301	2,287	2,318
5044 Office equipment [3]	52	50	988	1,028	21	34,692	36,000	33,931	32,028
5045 Computers, peripherals, & software	166	157	2,098	1,747	11	48,065	52,245	91,805	88,270
5046 Commercial equipment, nec	43	47	248	267	6	20,097	25,648	5,285	7,069
5047 Medical and hospital equipment	104	100	875	750	8	32,699	35,344	29,779	27,170
5048 Ophthalmic goods [3]	10	12	114	145	12	17,930	20,028	2,562	3,117
5049 Professional equipment, nec [3]	31	28	110	129	5	25,927	23,318	2,715	3,035
5051 Metals service centers and offices [3]	57	61	79	515	8	21,468	27,992	1,941	15,322
5063 Electrical apparatus and equipment [3]	122	114	1,484	1,426	13	38,189	43,167	59,427	65,210
5064 Electrical appliances, TV & radios [3]	16	17	117	87	5	16,752	24,230	2,127	2,604
5065 Electronic parts and equipment	200	213	1,915	2,058	10	36,919	39,532	73,240	82,454
5072 Hardware [3]	59	60	552	638	11	28,551	29,467	19,030	21,546
5074 Plumbing & hydronic heating supplies	75	76	549	612	8	29,719	30,065	16,837	19,470
5075 Warm air heating & air conditioning	50	55	410	581	11	30,761	30,706	14,100	19,225
5078 Refrigeration equipment and supplies [2]	6	5	30	47	9	30,933	32,936	1,465	1,743
5082 Construction and mining machinery	36	36	375	427	12	30,901	34,407	12,808	15,636
5083 Farm and garden machinery	49	46	529	526	11	26,556	28,570	15,318	16,060
5084 Industrial machinery and equipment	151	151	1,118	1,220	8	31,259	34,452	39,168	44,358
5085 Industrial supplies	54	62	409	428	7	31,413	31,364	13,236	13,553
5087 Service establishment equipment	37	41	214	236	6	19,757	20,136	4,519	4,762
5088 Transportation equipment & supplies	35	36	129	176	5	33,209	29,341	4,682	6,076
5091 Sporting & recreational goods	52	46	323	296	6	30,786	25,865	10,091	8,075
5092 Toys and hobby goods and supplies	21	20	118	110	6	23,525	24,473	2,883	2,880
5093 Scrap and waste materials [3]	37	40	312	331	8	18,974	23,057	7,020	8,114
5094 Jewelry & precious stones	38	40	161	171	4	21,466	20,398	4,258	4,110
5099 Durable goods, nec	61	78	211	218	3	17,517	18,972	4,424	5,550
5111 Printing and writing paper [3]	15	15	149	119	8	36,161	41,042	4,831	5,073
5112 Stationery and office supplies	70	68	988	1,148	17	18,964	22,014	20,794	25,589
5113 Industrial & personal service paper [3]	28	26	387	424	16	28,661	32,783	12,042	14,971
5120 Drugs, proprietaries, and sundries	46	57	571	619	11	29,394	30,132	17,631	19,866
5131 Piece goods & notions [3]	17	19	61	71	4	20,852	20,507	1,369	1,293
5136 Men's and boys' clothing	23	19	153	126	7	17,804	18,921	3,096	2,737
5137 Women's and children's clothing [3]	17	19	38	43	2	18,105	22,977	804	1,218
5141 Groceries, general line [3]	21	22	993	992	45	27,215	28,657	27,708	27,248
5142 Packaged frozen food [3]	19	18	389	344	19	27,609	27,709	11,884	9,845
5143 Dairy products, exc. dried or canned [3]	15	16	375	339	21	30,517	29,817	10,859	9,972
5144 Poultry and poultry products [3]	3	3	60	69	23	26,200	19,014	1,874	1,549
5145 Confectionery [3]	11	10	412	446	45	31,194	28,054	12,436	12,843
5146 Fish and seafoods [3]	10	10	173	144	14	15,445	16,750	3,066	2,408
5147 Meats and meat products [3]	20	21	251	267	13	23,888	25,064	6,444	6,909
5148 Fresh fruits and vegetables	46	44	1,417	1,353	31	19,181	21,605	29,624	31,564
5149 Groceries and related products, nec	80	80	865	913	11	27,681	30,256	23,779	28,472
5150 Farm-product raw materials	-	9	-	15	2	-	12,533	-	363
5162 Plastics materials & basic shapes [1]	13	14	84	64	5	29,143	36,875	2,681	2,187
5169 Chemicals & allied products, nec [3]	66	61	891	996	16	34,622	44,406	32,203	44,366
5171 Petroleum bulk stations & terminals	32	29	326	307	11	26,773	26,606	8,914	8,098
5172 Petroleum products, nec [3]	9	10	111	77	8	29,658	33,299	2,641	2,669
5181 Beer and ale [3]	5	4	515	581	145	26,664	25,969	14,853	15,663
5182 Wine and distilled beverages [3]	6	6	499	478	80	37,379	40,117	16,398	15,998
5191 Farm supplies	51	40	393	252	6	27,064	27,508	11,345	6,992
5192 Books, periodicals, & newspapers	31	30	405	417	14	24,415	27,050	11,299	11,272
5193 Flowers & florists' supplies	82	82	663	608	7	18,486	18,816	13,353	12,196
5198 Paints, varnishes, and supplies	44	42	225	287	7	25,973	23,024	6,527	7,181
5199 Nondurable goods, nec	114	121	466	534	4	17,597	18,809	9,878	10,821
52 - Retail trade	8,883	9,002	137,006	143,917	16	13,321	13,944	1,953,844	2,058,608
5210 Lumber and other building materials	122	110	3,041	3,092	28	17,820	18,146	59,329	56,479
5230 Paint, glass, and wallpaper stores	57	55	214	201	4	17,607	18,189	4,027	3,752
5250 Hardware stores	81	60	571	428	7	15,699	16,673	9,019	7,285
5260 Retail nurseries and garden stores	77	80	404	477	6	14,129	12,436	5,865	7,278
5270 Mobile home dealers	26	25	243	199	8	13,432	14,915	3,529	3,233

Continued on next page.

ORLANDO, FL MSA - [continued]

Wholesale and Retail Trade USA	Establishments		Employment		Emp / Est	Pay / Employee		Annual Payroll ($ 000)	
	1994	1995	1994	1995	1995	1994	1995	1994	1995
5310 Department stores	65	64	10,091	10,783	168	11,541	13,284	125,932	138,536
5330 Variety stores	67	53	478	502	9	9,105	8,916	5,284	4,729
5390 Misc. general merchandise stores	58	77	1,774	2,035	26	14,956	16,210	28,390	31,802
5410 Grocery stores	685	671	19,500	19,315	29	10,894	11,927	215,436	235,087
5420 Meat and fish markets	27	24	179	180	8	15,307	15,778	2,794	2,854
5430 Fruit and vegetable markets	24	22	110	108	5	11,600	11,222	1,611	1,403
5440 Candy, nut, and confectionery stores	27	27	141	150	6	8,936	7,467	1,449	1,229
5450 Dairy products stores	9	8	28	19	2	4,429	7,789	161	141
5460 Retail bakeries	61	59	626	436	7	12,294	13,303	7,741	5,715
5490 Miscellaneous food stores	56	63	239	267	4	12,820	11,985	2,975	3,578
5510 New and used car dealers	108	114	5,758	6,174	54	31,539	31,611	201,916	213,666
5520 Used car dealers	187	173	924	872	5	22,199	23,330	20,099	22,002
5530 Auto and home supply stores	258	250	2,055	1,960	8	18,846	19,035	41,087	38,920
5540 Gasoline service stations	509	508	3,420	3,633	7	12,235	12,570	42,653	46,386
5550 Boat dealers	38	36	196	257	7	18,265	18,755	4,508	5,439
5560 Recreational vehicle dealers [3]	14	15	237	228	15	29,300	33,368	7,663	7,325
5570 Motorcycle dealers	25	23	186	231	10	20,645	21,506	5,473	6,422
5590 Automotive dealers, nec	-	10	-	145	15	-	28,303	-	5,293
5610 Men's & boys' clothing stores	89	86	756	805	9	10,926	11,896	8,917	9,363
5620 Women's clothing stores	253	228	2,554	2,282	10	10,069	9,723	26,819	23,518
5630 Women's accessory & specialty stores	49	47	341	370	8	10,545	11,016	3,807	4,157
5640 Children's and infants' wear stores [3]	29	31	272	341	11	8,324	8,223	2,517	3,022
5650 Family clothing stores	127	131	2,276	2,243	17	9,991	11,189	24,810	27,214
5660 Shoe stores	199	205	1,219	1,368	7	12,289	11,795	15,419	15,532
5690 Misc. apparel & accessory stores	85	85	530	547	6	11,842	12,197	6,555	6,899
5712 Furniture stores	207	209	1,564	1,552	7	17,361	18,216	28,622	29,745
5713 Floor covering stores	70	78	332	371	5	20,410	23,957	7,268	8,009
5714 Drapery and upholstery stores [2]	18	16	61	55	3	12,525	13,964	787	778
5719 Misc. homefurnishings stores	117	115	728	735	6	11,396	11,995	8,793	9,473
5720 Household appliance stores	40	41	175	198	5	19,017	18,687	4,307	4,470
5731 Radio, TV, & electronic stores	101	106	836	1,051	10	19,278	19,246	18,281	21,165
5734 Computer and software stores	49	68	213	281	4	14,967	18,292	3,483	5,812
5735 Record & prerecorded tape stores	51	52	339	342	7	11,009	10,070	3,833	3,512
5736 Musical instrument stores	20	18	99	89	5	15,879	16,135	1,577	1,556
5812 Eating places	1,889	1,753	48,961	50,444	29	9,363	9,591	488,585	488,760
5813 Drinking places	167	145	1,330	1,374	9	8,382	8,969	11,611	12,332
5910 Drug stores and proprietary stores	196	199	3,009	3,167	16	16,941	17,334	54,658	58,002
5920 Liquor stores	104	96	518	496	5	11,050	11,185	5,738	5,220
5930 Used merchandise stores	177	173	726	803	5	11,697	12,518	8,682	9,688
5941 Sporting goods and bicycle shops	135	127	969	1,170	9	15,199	12,574	16,301	15,196
5942 Book stores	83	76	574	505	7	11,101	11,850	6,430	6,394
5943 Stationery stores	19	23	49	93	4	17,469	18,022	865	1,721
5944 Jewelry stores	160	158	947	1,021	6	15,235	16,215	15,245	16,091
5945 Hobby, toy, and game shops	57	58	585	679	12	9,730	11,429	6,960	8,082
5946 Camera & photographic supply stores [3]	24	23	158	146	6	15,823	16,849	2,633	2,694
5947 Gift, novelty, and souvenir shops	323	327	2,050	2,139	7	10,603	10,942	24,097	25,504
5948 Luggage and leather goods stores [3]	19	18	76	72	4	10,474	12,167	832	847
5949 Sewing, needlework, and piece goods	40	40	287	291	7	7,331	7,258	2,257	2,016
5961 Catalog and mail-order houses	34	41	457	759	19	28,105	26,387	9,665	16,751
5962 Merchandising machine operators	35	45	160	181	4	19,775	20,044	3,377	4,073
5963 Direct selling establishments	95	98	1,091	1,243	13	18,002	18,436	19,360	21,770
5983 Fuel oil dealers [1]	7	10	35	36	4	28,000	28,889	1,105	1,133
5984 Liquefied petroleum gas dealers	22	20	114	93	5	21,509	22,796	2,533	2,219
5992 Florists [1]	134	129	424	593	5	12,302	12,108	5,593	7,278
5993 Tobacco stores and stands [3]	6	7	11	16	2	9,818	10,250	112	163
5994 News dealers and newsstands [1]	5	-	24	-	-	13,500	-	454	-
5995 Optical goods stores	87	90	500	456	5	14,776	17,789	7,420	8,026
5999 Miscellaneous retail stores, nec	343	378	1,725	2,133	6	12,334	13,853	24,811	32,774

Source: County Business Patterns 1994/95, CBP-94/95, U.S. Department of Commerce, Washington DC, November 1997. The employment column represents mid-March employment in the year. Pay per employee is calculated by dividing 1st Quarter payroll, annualized, by mid-March employment. The column headed 'Emp / Est' shows 'employees per establishment'. A dash (-) means that data are unavailable or cannot be calculated. nec means not elsewhere classified. *Notes:* 1. 1994 data incomplete; unavailable or withheld. 2. 1995 data incomplete; unavailable or withheld. 3. 1994 and 1995 data incomplete; unavailable or withheld.

OWENSBORO, KY MSA

Wholesale and Retail Trade USA	Establishments		Employment		Emp / Est	Pay / Employee		Annual Payroll ($ 000)	
	1994	1995	1994	1995	1995	1994	1995	1994	1995
50 - Wholesale trade	185	193	2,051	2,214	11	20,607	21,787	46,841	51,999
5013 Motor vehicle supplies and new parts	15	14	132	123	9	17,515	20,098	2,542	2,631

Continued on next page.

OWENSBORO, KY MSA - [continued]

Wholesale and Retail Trade USA	Establishments		Employment		Emp / Est	Pay / Employee		Annual Payroll ($ 000)	
	1994	1995	1994	1995	1995	1994	1995	1994	1995
5014 Tires and tubes	-	3	-	26	9	-	26,154	-	733
5015 Motor vehicle parts, used	6	-	40	-	-	13,400	-	538	-
5020 Furniture and homefurnishings	4	-	12	-	-	17,000	-	240	-
5039 Construction materials, nec	-	3	-	10	3	-	18,800	-	187
5044 Office equipment	5	6	28	27	5	22,000	22,222	674	785
5051 Metals service centers and offices	3	3	1	8	3	20,000	14,500	36	90
5063 Electrical apparatus and equipment	4	4	60	62	16	29,067	23,355	1,649	2,260
5072 Hardware	-	3	-	24	8	-	15,833	-	353
5074 Plumbing & hydronic heating supplies	3	3	16	14	5	14,500	20,857	293	298
5083 Farm and garden machinery	-	4	-	30	8	-	19,067	-	665
5084 Industrial machinery and equipment	6	6	67	69	12	24,836	27,246	1,918	1,706
5085 Industrial supplies	13	15	102	121	8	29,765	31,107	3,316	4,361
5087 Service establishment equipment	5	-	26	-	-	29,231	-	882	-
5093 Scrap and waste materials	5	6	59	85	14	15,390	13,976	1,810	2,584
5110 Paper and paper products	5	5	44	48	10	13,636	14,667	719	768
5149 Groceries and related products, nec	5	5	122	128	26	28,951	30,625	3,776	3,494
5159 Farm-product raw materials, nec	8	7	137	84	12	4,292	4,381	373	288
5169 Chemicals & allied products, nec	-	5	-	41	8	-	21,951	-	985
5171 Petroleum bulk stations & terminals	7	6	95	129	22	18,274	17,984	2,241	2,680
5172 Petroleum products, nec	3	3	16	18	6	26,000	26,000	362	447
5180 Beer, wine, and distilled beverages	6	6	84	74	12	26,952	35,297	2,232	2,432
5191 Farm supplies	10	10	149	166	17	17,772	19,711	3,605	4,196
5199 Nondurable goods, nec	9	9	47	53	6	18,298	17,283	928	967
52- Retail trade	616	591	7,963	8,033	14	10,211	11,400	89,726	96,563
5210 Lumber and other building materials	14	11	255	244	22	15,514	17,377	4,255	4,419
5230 Paint, glass, and wallpaper stores	6	7	23	22	3	12,522	25,455	307	401
5250 Hardware stores	3	-	40	-	-	10,100	-	471	-
5260 Retail nurseries and garden stores	3	-	39	-	-	8,308	-	623	-
5270 Mobile home dealers	6	-	28	-	-	36,143	-	1,413	-
5310 Department stores	7	7	1,057	1,045	149	9,612	12,253	11,440	12,952
5330 Variety stores	8	4	65	45	11	8,431	9,867	682	516
5390 Misc. general merchandise stores	6	6	80	96	16	11,350	10,917	927	1,088
5410 Grocery stores	47	43	1,099	1,088	25	9,871	10,537	11,144	11,701
5460 Retail bakeries	7	7	60	70	10	8,067	7,886	527	490
5510 New and used car dealers	11	11	322	316	29	23,739	24,494	8,518	8,302
5520 Used car dealers	8	9	53	62	7	20,679	20,452	1,274	1,607
5530 Auto and home supply stores	18	16	128	123	8	16,094	16,943	1,994	2,056
5540 Gasoline service stations	38	35	285	276	8	8,996	9,449	2,775	2,824
5550 Boat dealers	3	3	20	22	7	8,000	11,455	217	302
5610 Men's & boys' clothing stores	4	4	29	30	8	12,828	8,267	339	166
5620 Women's clothing stores	20	17	146	131	8	7,370	7,756	1,244	912
5630 Women's accessory & specialty stores	4	3	18	13	4	8,222	9,231	120	108
5640 Children's and infants' wear stores	4	4	15	16	4	5,067	4,000	68	68
5650 Family clothing stores	4	4	18	18	5	9,111	10,000	167	177
5660 Shoe stores	14	13	78	75	6	10,923	11,093	804	775
5712 Furniture stores	13	14	114	110	8	18,105	16,327	1,943	1,876
5713 Floor covering stores	7	9	56	62	7	13,786	17,806	819	1,083
5720 Household appliance stores	6	7	46	101	14	15,739	15,644	1,328	1,814
5731 Radio, TV, & electronic stores	10	10	33	42	4	16,242	15,429	514	635
5734 Computer and software stores	3	3	23	26	9	18,435	17,077	566	633
5735 Record & prerecorded tape stores	5	5	39	41	8	6,974	9,463	302	309
5812 Eating places	138	123	2,542	2,589	21	6,727	7,873	19,393	21,421
5813 Drinking places	15	14	75	77	6	5,973	8,883	439	717
5910 Drug stores and proprietary stores	26	26	233	226	9	14,901	17,133	3,852	4,176
5920 Liquor stores	19	17	134	126	7	9,791	8,984	1,346	1,280
5930 Used merchandise stores	16	15	44	46	3	7,182	7,304	363	353
5941 Sporting goods and bicycle shops	-	10	-	47	5	-	7,489	-	465
5942 Book stores	4	4	22	22	6	12,182	9,818	231	217
5944 Jewelry stores	15	14	96	90	6	8,667	10,533	955	978
5945 Hobby, toy, and game shops	-	6	-	13	2	-	8,308	-	288
5947 Gift, novelty, and souvenir shops	9	9	48	42	5	7,000	8,286	375	389
5949 Sewing, needlework, and piece goods	3	-	15	-	-	10,400	-	124	-
5960 Nonstore retailers	8	9	218	236	26	13,339	14,712	3,193	3,517
5980 Fuel dealers	5	6	18	37	6	17,111	20,216	366	744
5992 Florists	12	13	85	83	6	9,176	10,169	818	778
5995 Optical goods stores	-	4	-	16	4	-	10,750	-	191
5999 Miscellaneous retail stores, nec	17	-	57	-	-	10,526	-	737	-

Source: County Business Patterns 1994/95, CBP-94/95, U.S. Department of Commerce, Washington DC, November 1997. The employment column represents mid-March employment in the year. Pay per employee is calculated by dividing 1st Quarter payroll, annualized, by mid-March employment. The column headed 'Emp / Est' shows 'employees per establishment'. A dash (-) means that data are unavailable or cannot be calculated. nec means not elsewhere classified. *Notes:* 1. 1994 data incomplete; unavailable or withheld. 2. 1995 data incomplete; unavailable or withheld. 3. 1994 and 1995 data incomplete; unavailable or withheld.

PANAMA CITY, FL MSA

Wholesale and Retail Trade USA	Establishments		Employment		Emp / Est	Pay / Employee		Annual Payroll ($ 000)	
	1994	1995	1994	1995	1995	1994	1995	1994	1995
50 - Wholesale trade	210	217	1,508	1,611	7	20,414	21,120	32,722	35,139
5012 Automobiles and other vehicles	5	5	15	13	3	24,267	24,923	330	335
5013 Motor vehicle supplies and new parts	12	11	180	171	16	17,667	18,737	3,549	3,083
5015 Motor vehicle parts, used	6	6	32	27	5	12,375	13,037	430	514
5023 Homefurnishings	5	6	23	32	5	13,391	17,000	335	551
5031 Lumber, plywood, and millwork	6	5	28	19	4	19,714	24,000	676	477
5039 Construction materials, nec	-	5	-	43	9	-	16,744	-	926
5044 Office equipment	7	7	50	58	8	23,520	16,207	890	914
5045 Computers, peripherals, & software	-	4	-	6	2	-	14,000	-	63
5046 Commercial equipment, nec	3	-	5	-	-	12,000	-	68	-
5047 Medical and hospital equipment	5	3	28	19	6	17,714	16,421	475	305
5051 Metals service centers and offices	5	5	29	33	7	25,103	26,303	965	1,032
5063 Electrical apparatus and equipment	9	12	70	89	7	20,457	22,427	1,476	2,090
5064 Electrical appliances, TV & radios	4	3	15	13	4	16,533	20,308	269	284
5065 Electronic parts and equipment	4	4	8	9	2	33,500	35,556	439	372
5072 Hardware	5	5	12	15	3	20,333	21,867	277	290
5074 Plumbing & hydronic heating supplies	6	6	32	39	7	27,625	25,436	809	942
5075 Warm air heating & air conditioning	6	6	45	49	8	22,044	24,163	1,172	1,299
5085 Industrial supplies	6	5	38	33	7	20,632	25,333	871	796
5087 Service establishment equipment	3	3	27	27	9	18,667	18,222	550	561
5088 Transportation equipment & supplies	-	3	-	12	4	-	20,667	-	289
5092 Toys and hobby goods and supplies	3	3	9	13	4	23,556	20,615	285	331
5094 Jewelry & precious stones	4	4	19	26	7	12,632	12,923	326	455
5099 Durable goods, nec	9	9	69	78	9	26,145	32,667	2,012	2,218
5110 Paper and paper products	7	6	52	62	10	28,308	19,097	1,046	1,094
5130 Apparel, piece goods, and notions	5	3	12	7	2	13,333	14,286	140	105
5142 Packaged frozen food	3	3	39	38	13	26,051	23,579	745	649
5146 Fish and seafoods	11	11	78	110	10	16,359	14,655	1,849	1,621
5149 Groceries and related products, nec	9	8	156	152	19	19,128	22,132	3,432	3,743
5171 Petroleum bulk stations & terminals	4	4	30	28	7	30,533	30,143	819	901
5172 Petroleum products, nec	6	6	38	20	3	15,474	17,200	440	313
5181 Beer and ale	3	3	88	108	36	27,636	28,296	3,096	3,537
5191 Farm supplies	-	3	-	9	3	-	13,333	-	134
5198 Paints, varnishes, and supplies	-	3	-	8	3	-	35,500	-	285
5199 Nondurable goods, nec	7	7	30	31	4	15,467	20,000	510	603
52 - Retail trade	1,196	1,204	15,445	16,269	14	10,034	10,955	180,301	196,231
5210 Lumber and other building materials	17	20	431	427	21	14,905	17,199	6,966	8,046
5230 Paint, glass, and wallpaper stores	11	8	63	49	6	15,492	15,510	1,181	779
5250 Hardware stores	6	5	41	39	8	10,439	11,385	485	465
5260 Retail nurseries and garden stores	7	6	24	20	3	12,167	14,400	353	358
5270 Mobile home dealers	7	11	88	71	6	20,500	22,592	2,199	1,899
5310 Department stores	10	10	1,526	1,864	186	11,180	12,648	18,494	22,107
5330 Variety stores	11	6	61	62	10	9,246	9,548	724	630
5390 Misc. general merchandise stores	7	11	181	186	17	12,287	13,355	2,391	2,463
5410 Grocery stores	126	125	2,195	2,471	20	8,718	10,422	22,316	25,891
5420 Meat and fish markets	12	8	69	42	5	8,812	11,333	614	550
5460 Retail bakeries	8	8	44	50	6	7,818	8,640	399	431
5490 Miscellaneous food stores	8	8	16	25	3	12,250	9,280	185	243
5510 New and used car dealers	12	13	583	579	45	27,561	29,693	19,023	20,897
5520 Used car dealers	24	27	115	133	5	19,165	20,241	2,548	2,709
5530 Auto and home supply stores	35	45	246	314	7	15,919	16,051	4,246	5,664
5540 Gasoline service stations	51	50	225	245	5	9,156	9,796	2,446	2,562
5550 Boat dealers	16	15	83	88	6	15,133	15,136	1,372	1,414
5560 Recreational vehicle dealers	3	3	59	72	24	26,508	18,556	1,698	1,643
5610 Men's & boys' clothing stores	7	7	51	45	6	6,667	7,378	390	343
5620 Women's clothing stores	32	24	232	178	7	7,966	7,191	1,891	1,284
5630 Women's accessory & specialty stores	10	10	26	50	5	9,538	8,160	307	457
5640 Children's and infants' wear stores	4	4	13	17	4	8,923	8,471	134	123
5650 Family clothing stores	19	19	159	188	10	8,352	9,191	1,919	1,864
5660 Shoe stores	23	24	107	129	5	9,495	9,054	1,145	1,237
5690 Misc. apparel & accessory stores	33	35	162	184	5	8,765	8,457	1,972	2,156
5712 Furniture stores	31	34	199	241	7	14,392	15,071	3,188	3,698
5713 Floor covering stores	13	13	69	65	5	20,348	25,538	1,655	1,907
5719 Misc. homefurnishings stores	9	9	60	71	8	12,267	12,000	666	817
5720 Household appliance stores	4	3	8	25	8	13,000	6,560	67	282
5731 Radio, TV, & electronic stores	11	10	61	66	7	17,180	15,333	1,091	949
5734 Computer and software stores	8	7	27	21	3	10,667	15,810	324	375
5735 Record & prerecorded tape stores	5	5	29	27	5	7,862	8,741	245	235
5736 Musical instrument stores	3	3	16	17	6	13,500	15,529	235	284
5812 Eating places	270	248	5,934	5,651	23	6,725	7,468	47,830	50,776
5813 Drinking places	36	36	321	422	12	6,106	5,848	2,259	2,601

Continued on next page.

PANAMA CITY, FL MSA - [continued]

Wholesale and Retail Trade USA	Establishments		Employment		Emp / Est	Pay / Employee		Annual Payroll ($ 000)	
	1994	1995	1994	1995	1995	1994	1995	1994	1995
5910 Drug stores and proprietary stores	29	27	321	289	11	14,654	16,484	5,278	5,309
5920 Liquor stores	26	27	126	119	4	7,333	8,437	849	947
5930 Used merchandise stores	23	24	87	90	4	5,287	5,511	623	699
5941 Sporting goods and bicycle shops	23	21	89	99	5	10,921	11,556	1,141	1,257
5942 Book stores	10	9	51	38	4	7,922	10,737	439	424
5944 Jewelry stores	17	19	78	61	3	11,436	15,475	861	1,001
5945 Hobby, toy, and game shops	-	7	-	9	1	-	11,556	-	594
5947 Gift, novelty, and souvenir shops	29	27	331	412	15	10,779	10,233	4,293	4,763
5949 Sewing, needlework, and piece goods	5	-	32	-	-	6,250	-	901	-
5960 Nonstore retailers	8	8	84	99	12	14,333	11,636	1,102	1,147
5984 Liquefied petroleum gas dealers	4	4	23	23	6	18,609	20,000	391	368
5992 Florists	12	-	61	-	-	9,049	-	604	-
5995 Optical goods stores	-	7	-	53	8	-	13,208	-	684
5999 Miscellaneous retail stores, nec	43	45	136	166	4	12,529	13,060	2,088	2,497

Source: County Business Patterns 1994/95, CBP-94/95, U.S. Department of Commerce, Washington DC, November 1997. The employment column represents mid-March employment in the year. Pay per employee is calculated by dividing 1st Quarter payroll, annualized, by mid-March employment. The column headed 'Emp / Est' shows 'employees per establishment'. A dash (-) means that data are unavailable or cannot be calculated. nec means not elsewhere classified. *Notes:* 1. 1994 data incomplete; unavailable or withheld. 2. 1995 data incomplete; unavailable or withheld. 3. 1994 and 1995 data incomplete; unavailable or withheld.

PARKERSBURG – MARIETTA MSA (OH PART)

Wholesale and Retail Trade USA	Establishments		Employment		Emp / Est	Pay / Employee		Annual Payroll ($ 000)	
	1994	1995	1994	1995	1995	1994	1995	1994	1995
50 – Wholesale trade	97	92	1,115	1,160	13	19,659	21,107	25,521	26,644
5013 Motor vehicle supplies and new parts	9	9	223	224	25	18,583	20,214	4,857	5,094
5044 Office equipment	6	-	57	-	-	19,088	-	1,246	-
5060 Electrical goods	5	5	76	86	17	16,895	16,651	1,607	1,961
5074 Plumbing & hydronic heating supplies	-	3	-	6	2	-	18,000	-	111
5083 Farm and garden machinery	-	4	-	15	4	-	8,800	-	135
5084 Industrial machinery and equipment	-	5	-	248	50	-	23,387	-	5,625
5093 Scrap and waste materials	-	5	-	31	6	-	13,419	-	342
5140 Groceries and related products	-	5	-	53	11	-	18,868	-	1,135
5170 Petroleum and petroleum products	-	5	-	56	11	-	27,500	-	1,516
5191 Farm supplies	-	4	-	52	13	-	17,769	-	1,012
52 – Retail trade	363	370	4,392	4,686	13	10,308	11,137	52,555	56,089
5210 Lumber and other building materials	10	11	97	116	11	17,773	20,655	2,022	2,662
5230 Paint, glass, and wallpaper stores	4	5	8	17	3	13,500	15,294	135	291
5250 Hardware stores	4	-	9	-	-	8,444	-	94	-
5260 Retail nurseries and garden stores	3	5	11	22	4	5,091	5,455	181	201
5270 Mobile home dealers	4	4	29	42	11	13,931	15,714	672	917
5310 Department stores	3	3	424	434	145	6,811	11,088	4,275	5,051
5410 Grocery stores	36	35	873	911	26	10,914	10,854	10,041	10,269
5510 New and used car dealers	9	10	218	231	23	21,505	24,623	5,472	5,909
5520 Used car dealers	10	12	64	68	6	23,563	20,235	1,994	1,685
5530 Auto and home supply stores	14	16	70	86	5	16,743	17,209	1,342	1,808
5540 Gasoline service stations	42	41	276	268	7	9,826	9,955	3,013	2,823
5570 Motorcycle dealers	3	-	22	-	-	9,636	-	326	-
5620 Women's clothing stores	6	3	45	21	7	9,156	11,619	435	244
5660 Shoe stores	5	5	17	18	4	9,412	8,444	169	163
5710 Furniture and homefurnishings stores	12	11	106	98	9	16,566	19,143	1,998	2,018
5720 Household appliance stores	3	-	7	-	-	9,143	-	79	-
5730 Radio, television, & computer stores	5	-	18	-	-	14,000	-	232	-
5812 Eating places	88	82	1,384	1,560	19	7,058	7,372	11,760	12,516
5813 Drinking places	13	11	38	45	4	6,421	6,667	280	304
5910 Drug stores and proprietary stores	8	8	100	104	13	15,840	16,423	1,764	1,792
5920 Liquor stores	-	5	-	26	5	-	6,923	-	191
5930 Used merchandise stores	5	-	18	-	-	8,889	-	176	-
5942 Book stores	4	4	11	16	4	8,364	8,000	95	117
5944 Jewelry stores	4	4	27	25	6	16,889	15,360	382	368
5947 Gift, novelty, and souvenir shops	3	8	9	10	1	6,222	6,000	55	82
5960 Nonstore retailers	3	6	6	22	4	8,667	12,545	68	304
5995 Optical goods stores	4	4	12	13	3	10,667	13,231	147	176
5999 Miscellaneous retail stores, nec	6	9	14	18	2	6,571	9,778	195	303

Source: County Business Patterns 1994/95, CBP-94/95, U.S. Department of Commerce, Washington DC, November 1997. The employment column represents mid-March employment in the year. Pay per employee is calculated by dividing 1st Quarter payroll, annualized, by mid-March employment. The column headed 'Emp / Est' shows 'employees per establishment'. A dash (-) means that data are unavailable or cannot be calculated. nec means not elsewhere classified. *Notes:* 1. 1994 data incomplete; unavailable or withheld. 2. 1995 data incomplete; unavailable or withheld. 3. 1994 and 1995 data incomplete; unavailable or withheld.

PARKERSBURG - MARIETTA MSA (WV PART)

Wholesale and Retail Trade USA	Establishments		Employment		Emp / Est	Pay / Employee		Annual Payroll ($ 000)	
	1994	1995	1994	1995	1995	1994	1995	1994	1995
50- Wholesale trade	-	146	-	1,949	13	-	28,265	-	57,767
5013 Motor vehicle supplies and new parts	-	6	-	51	9	-	19,216	-	912
5030 Lumber and construction materials	-	8	-	92	12	-	28,087	-	2,900
5044 Office equipment	-	7	-	46	7	-	21,652	-	1,029
5045 Computers, peripherals, & software	-	4	-	26	7	-	38,000	-	821
5063 Electrical apparatus and equipment	-	5	-	65	13	-	25,969	-	1,785
5074 Plumbing & hydronic heating supplies	-	4	-	47	12	-	20,851	-	932
5075 Warm air heating & air conditioning	-	3	-	15	5	-	18,133	-	395
5082 Construction and mining machinery	-	4	-	44	11	-	35,273	-	1,613
5083 Farm and garden machinery	-	4	-	12	3	-	20,333	-	238
5085 Industrial supplies	-	8	-	67	8	-	26,328	-	2,038
5091 Sporting & recreational goods	-	4	-	66	17	-	11,636	-	873
5093 Scrap and waste materials	-	8	-	130	16	-	9,569	-	1,509
5099 Durable goods, nec	-	4	-	5	1	-	24,800	-	137
5110 Paper and paper products	-	5	-	49	10	-	23,673	-	1,329
5148 Fresh fruits and vegetables	-	3	-	38	13	-	14,526	-	626
5160 Chemicals and allied products	-	8	-	192	24	-	51,083	-	10,584
5170 Petroleum and petroleum products	-	4	-	42	11	-	14,762	-	582
5190 Misc., nondurable goods	-	10	-	245	25	-	21,290	-	4,781
52- Retail trade	-	626	-	9,199	15	-	11,351	-	110,639
5210 Lumber and other building materials	-	10	-	173	17	-	18,428	-	3,554
5230 Paint, glass, and wallpaper stores	-	4	-	20	5	-	13,800	-	289
5250 Hardware stores	-	6	-	34	6	-	13,176	-	523
5310 Department stores	-	8	-	1,243	155	-	11,820	-	15,044
5410 Grocery stores	-	56	-	958	17	-	12,710	-	12,935
5460 Retail bakeries	-	5	-	19	4	-	8,211	-	127
5510 New and used car dealers	-	14	-	583	42	-	22,950	-	14,140
5520 Used car dealers	-	15	-	30	2	-	11,867	-	471
5530 Auto and home supply stores	-	23	-	162	7	-	16,346	-	2,412
5540 Gasoline service stations	-	42	-	362	9	-	8,199	-	3,169
5620 Women's clothing stores	-	13	-	103	8	-	7,223	-	745
5650 Family clothing stores	-	9	-	174	19	-	10,598	-	1,796
5660 Shoe stores	-	20	-	82	4	-	10,732	-	880
5712 Furniture stores	-	15	-	109	7	-	16,771	-	2,034
5713 Floor covering stores	-	12	-	88	7	-	16,591	-	1,646
5720 Household appliance stores	-	6	-	25	4	-	11,040	-	281
5731 Radio, TV, & electronic stores	-	8	-	93	12	-	22,108	-	1,787
5736 Musical instrument stores	-	3	-	9	3	-	8,000	-	32
5812 Eating places	-	132	-	3,133	24	-	7,177	-	24,520
5813 Drinking places	-	27	-	110	4	-	5,673	-	662
5910 Drug stores and proprietary stores	-	18	-	293	16	-	12,778	-	4,178
5930 Used merchandise stores	-	7	-	23	3	-	10,435	-	284
5941 Sporting goods and bicycle shops	-	10	-	30	3	-	11,867	-	416
5942 Book stores	-	5	-	84	17	-	5,143	-	489
5944 Jewelry stores	-	15	-	78	5	-	17,641	-	1,246
5945 Hobby, toy, and game shops	-	8	-	36	5	-	11,444	-	517
5947 Gift, novelty, and souvenir shops	-	9	-	60	7	-	6,400	-	440
5960 Nonstore retailers	-	8	-	101	13	-	14,337	-	1,381
5992 Florists	-	9	-	79	9	-	9,165	-	734
5995 Optical goods stores	-	10	-	45	5	-	10,844	-	634
5999 Miscellaneous retail stores, nec	-	21	-	72	3	-	11,500	-	885

Source: County Business Patterns 1994/95, CBP-94/95, U.S. Department of Commerce, Washington DC, November 1997. The employment column represents mid-March employment in the year. Pay per employee is calculated by dividing 1st Quarter payroll, annualized, by mid-March employment. The column headed 'Emp / Est' shows 'employees per establishment'. A dash (-) means that data are unavailable or cannot be calculated. nec means not elsewhere classified. *Notes:* 1. 1994 data incomplete; unavailable or withheld. 2. 1995 data incomplete; unavailable or withheld. 3. 1994 and 1995 data incomplete; unavailable or withheld.

PARKERSBURG - MARIETTA, WV - OH MSA

Wholesale and Retail Trade USA	Establishments		Employment		Emp / Est	Pay / Employee		Annual Payroll ($ 000)	
	1994	1995	1994	1995	1995	1994	1995	1994	1995
50- Wholesale trade [1]	97	238	1,115	3,109	13	19,659	25,594	25,521	84,411
5013 Motor vehicle supplies and new parts [1]	9	15	223	275	18	18,583	20,029	4,857	6,006
5030 Lumber and construction materials	-	12	-	92	8	-	28,087	-	2,900
5044 Office equipment [1]	6	12	57	46	4	19,088	21,652	1,246	1,029
5045 Computers, peripherals, & software	-	7	-	26	4	-	38,000	-	821
5063 Electrical apparatus and equipment	-	9	-	65	7	-	25,969	-	1,785
5074 Plumbing & hydronic heating supplies	-	7	-	53	8	-	20,528	-	1,043
5075 Warm air heating & air conditioning	-	5	-	15	3	-	18,133	-	395
5082 Construction and mining machinery	-	6	-	44	7	-	35,273	-	1,613

Continued on next page.

PARKERSBURG - MARIETTA, WV - OH MSA - [continued]

Wholesale and Retail Trade USA	Establishments		Employment		Emp / Est	Pay / Employee		Annual Payroll ($ 000)	
	1994	1995	1994	1995	1995	1994	1995	1994	1995
5083 Farm and garden machinery	-	8	-	27	3	-	13,926	-	373
5084 Industrial machinery and equipment	-	12	-	248	21	-	23,387	-	5,625
5085 Industrial supplies	-	11	-	67	6	-	26,328	-	2,038
5091 Sporting & recreational goods	-	5	-	66	13	-	11,636	-	873
5093 Scrap and waste materials	-	13	-	161	12	-	10,311	-	1,851
5099 Durable goods, nec	-	7	-	5	1	-	24,800	-	137
5110 Paper and paper products	-	8	-	49	6	-	23,673	-	1,329
5148 Fresh fruits and vegetables	-	4	-	38	10	-	14,526	-	626
5160 Chemicals and allied products	-	9	-	192	21	-	51,083	-	10,584
5170 Petroleum and petroleum products	-	9	-	98	11	-	22,041	-	2,098
5191 Farm supplies	-	6	-	52	9	-	17,769	-	1,012
52 - Retail trade [1]	363	996	4,392	13,885	14	10,308	11,279	52,555	166,728
5210 Lumber and other building materials [1]	10	21	97	289	14	17,773	19,322	2,022	6,216
5230 Paint, glass, and wallpaper stores [1]	4	9	8	37	4	13,500	14,486	135	580
5250 Hardware stores [1]	4	7	9	34	5	8,444	13,176	94	523
5260 Retail nurseries and garden stores [1]	3	8	11	22	3	5,091	5,455	181	201
5270 Mobile home dealers [1]	4	6	29	42	7	13,931	15,714	672	917
5310 Department stores [1]	3	11	424	1,677	152	6,811	11,630	4,275	20,095
5410 Grocery stores [1]	36	91	873	1,869	21	10,914	11,805	10,041	23,204
5460 Retail bakeries	-	8	-	19	2	-	8,211	-	127
5510 New and used car dealers [1]	9	24	218	814	34	21,505	23,425	5,472	20,049
5520 Used car dealers [1]	10	27	64	98	4	23,563	17,673	1,994	2,156
5530 Auto and home supply stores [1]	14	39	70	248	6	16,743	16,645	1,342	4,220
5540 Gasoline service stations [1]	42	83	276	630	8	9,826	8,946	3,013	5,992
5570 Motorcycle dealers [1]	3	-	22	-	-	9,636	-	326	-
5620 Women's clothing stores [1]	6	16	45	124	8	9,156	7,968	435	989
5650 Family clothing stores	-	11	-	174	16	-	10,598	-	1,796
5660 Shoe stores [1]	5	25	17	100	4	9,412	10,320	169	1,043
5712 Furniture stores	-	24	-	109	5	-	16,771	-	2,034
5713 Floor covering stores	-	13	-	88	7	-	16,591	-	1,646
5720 Household appliance stores [1]	3	8	7	25	3	9,143	11,040	79	281
5731 Radio, TV, & electronic stores	-	12	-	93	8	-	22,108	-	1,787
5736 Musical instrument stores [2]	-	3	-	9	3	-	8,000	-	32
5812 Eating places [1]	88	214	1,384	4,693	22	7,058	7,241	11,760	37,036
5813 Drinking places [1]	13	38	38	155	4	6,421	5,961	280	966
5910 Drug stores and proprietary stores [1]	8	26	100	397	15	15,840	13,733	1,764	5,970
5920 Liquor stores	-	6	-	26	4	-	6,923	-	191
5930 Used merchandise stores [1]	5	13	18	23	2	8,889	10,435	176	284
5941 Sporting goods and bicycle shops	-	14	-	30	2	-	11,867	-	416
5942 Book stores [1]	4	9	11	100	11	8,364	5,600	95	606
5944 Jewelry stores [1]	4	19	27	103	5	16,889	17,087	382	1,614
5945 Hobby, toy, and game shops	-	10	-	36	4	-	11,444	-	517
5947 Gift, novelty, and souvenir shops [1]	3	17	9	70	4	6,222	6,343	55	522
5960 Nonstore retailers [1]	3	14	6	123	9	8,667	14,016	68	1,685
5992 Florists	-	16	-	79	5	-	9,165	-	734
5995 Optical goods stores [1]	4	14	12	58	4	10,667	11,379	147	810
5999 Miscellaneous retail stores, nec [1]	6	30	14	90	3	6,571	11,156	195	1,188

Source: County Business Patterns 1994/95, CBP-94/95, U.S. Department of Commerce, Washington DC, November 1997. The employment column represents mid-March employment in the year. Pay per employee is calculated by dividing 1st Quarter payroll, annualized, by mid-March employment. The column headed 'Emp / Est' shows 'employees per establishment'. A dash (-) means that data are unavailable or cannot be calculated. nec means not elsewhere classified. *Notes:* 1. 1994 data incomplete; unavailable or withheld. 2. 1995 data incomplete; unavailable or withheld. 3. 1994 and 1995 data incomplete; unavailable or withheld.

PENSACOLA, FL MSA

Wholesale and Retail Trade USA	Establishments		Employment		Emp / Est	Pay / Employee		Annual Payroll ($ 000)	
	1994	1995	1994	1995	1995	1994	1995	1994	1995
50 - Wholesale trade	527	516	5,996	5,991	12	21,162	23,364	137,381	143,695
5012 Automobiles and other vehicles	12	10	344	208	21	12,128	12,365	4,487	2,618
5013 Motor vehicle supplies and new parts	41	32	368	280	9	16,467	17,171	6,466	4,813
5014 Tires and tubes	6	-	23	-	-	28,000	-	837	-
5015 Motor vehicle parts, used	20	19	42	12	1	10,952	20,333	478	148
5021 Furniture	8	7	46	64	9	22,870	25,250	1,199	1,460
5023 Homefurnishings [3]	8	5	132	126	25	14,303	17,111	2,267	2,322
5031 Lumber, plywood, and millwork	16	16	254	300	19	21,480	25,800	6,068	7,213
5032 Brick, stone, & related materials [3]	5	5	39	36	7	28,923	29,111	1,207	944
5033 Roofing, siding, & insulation [1]	4	6	26	23	4	21,231	25,217	584	644
5039 Construction materials, nec	7	10	57	53	5	21,123	20,226	1,369	1,137
5044 Office equipment [3]	14	16	230	259	16	23,287	20,371	5,311	5,509
5045 Computers, peripherals, & software	23	20	155	158	8	33,600	50,810	5,252	5,290

Continued on next page.

PENSACOLA, FL MSA - [continued]

Wholesale and Retail Trade USA	Establishments		Employment		Emp / Est	Pay / Employee		Annual Payroll ($ 000)	
	1994	1995	1994	1995	1995	1994	1995	1994	1995
5046 Commercial equipment, nec	5	4	56	64	16	26,000	20,063	1,794	2,138
5047 Medical and hospital equipment	14	13	77	89	7	22,182	19,461	1,986	1,873
5049 Professional equipment, nec	7	6	35	24	4	16,914	20,833	635	369
5051 Metals service centers and offices	7	7	53	65	9	21,509	21,785	1,550	1,647
5063 Electrical apparatus and equipment	20	17	238	213	13	25,950	33,427	7,077	7,134
5064 Electrical appliances, TV & radios [1]	4	-	34	-	-	26,235	-	1,094	-
5065 Electronic parts and equipment	8	-	35	-	-	33,600	-	1,216	-
5074 Plumbing & hydronic heating supplies [1]	6	7	85	90	13	32,941	31,467	2,619	2,233
5075 Warm air heating & air conditioning	16	16	80	78	5	22,150	24,410	2,273	2,207
5082 Construction and mining machinery [3]	6	6	67	83	14	25,672	25,976	1,982	2,393
5083 Farm and garden machinery	5	6	88	92	15	21,500	20,217	1,942	1,925
5084 Industrial machinery and equipment	29	30	163	171	6	25,840	29,520	4,953	6,224
5085 Industrial supplies	25	24	198	204	9	26,788	27,922	5,249	5,838
5087 Service establishment equipment	11	10	50	45	5	19,280	20,089	1,079	1,115
5088 Transportation equipment & supplies	5	5	47	57	11	24,085	27,228	1,680	2,034
5093 Scrap and waste materials	7	8	109	86	11	19,413	20,744	2,302	1,780
5094 Jewelry & precious stones [2]	-	4	-	8	2	-	13,500	-	79
5099 Durable goods, nec [1]	8	-	19	-	-	18,947	-	265	-
5112 Stationery and office supplies	16	14	125	138	10	22,816	17,536	2,782	2,110
5120 Drugs, proprietaries, and sundries	-	6	-	28	5	-	24,429	-	805
5130 Apparel, piece goods, and notions	6	6	73	63	11	12,384	16,127	1,039	986
5143 Dairy products, exc. dried or canned	6	6	67	115	19	22,567	24,278	1,509	2,744
5148 Fresh fruits and vegetables [2]	6	4	265	234	59	13,464	15,026	3,996	3,924
5149 Groceries and related products, nec	13	13	380	525	40	21,179	24,830	8,803	14,145
5150 Farm-product raw materials	5	5	14	8	2	13,143	21,500	227	143
5169 Chemicals & allied products, nec	9	-	10	-	-	53,600	-	593	-
5171 Petroleum bulk stations & terminals	10	9	88	91	10	20,455	19,648	1,931	2,046
5172 Petroleum products, nec	4	4	22	7	2	17,818	26,857	363	236
5180 Beer, wine, and distilled beverages [3]	6	6	621	367	61	26,203	27,924	16,463	10,310
5191 Farm supplies	15	14	82	81	6	12,000	13,383	1,150	1,224
5192 Books, periodicals, & newspapers [3]	6	7	61	83	12	20,590	15,470	1,340	1,482
5193 Flowers & florists' supplies [3]	6	5	50	38	8	14,560	16,737	748	685
5199 Nondurable goods, nec	12	12	191	211	18	12,398	13,498	2,547	2,968
52 - Retail trade	2,163	2,168	28,392	29,631	14	10,976	11,636	336,062	356,500
5210 Lumber and other building materials	40	32	616	772	24	16,292	15,953	9,832	13,362
5230 Paint, glass, and wallpaper stores	14	16	55	81	5	18,255	20,691	1,068	1,851
5250 Hardware stores	23	21	139	141	7	10,964	12,199	1,537	1,847
5260 Retail nurseries and garden stores	15	16	84	84	5	10,905	9,667	1,086	939
5270 Mobile home dealers	7	7	24	26	4	20,833	16,923	551	536
5310 Department stores [3]	19	18	2,801	2,849	158	11,576	13,390	35,169	37,887
5330 Variety stores	21	20	168	172	9	8,786	8,977	1,693	1,685
5390 Misc. general merchandise stores	12	13	339	349	27	13,192	15,014	4,754	4,826
5410 Grocery stores	177	189	3,982	3,811	20	9,431	10,480	39,918	39,849
5420 Meat and fish markets	8	10	8	17	2	7,000	7,529	67	145
5460 Retail bakeries	15	15	86	109	7	8,047	9,468	979	1,100
5490 Miscellaneous food stores	10	14	31	49	4	10,194	10,286	388	526
5510 New and used car dealers	29	31	1,523	1,455	47	27,199	28,014	45,273	46,166
5520 Used car dealers	51	49	239	259	5	19,983	25,575	5,409	5,797
5530 Auto and home supply stores	63	69	555	661	10	15,712	15,897	9,558	10,759
5540 Gasoline service stations	158	147	1,077	1,167	8	10,344	10,540	12,176	12,843
5550 Boat dealers	16	19	98	142	7	15,918	16,761	2,142	2,945
5560 Recreational vehicle dealers	5	5	60	67	13	18,200	22,687	1,217	1,132
5570 Motorcycle dealers [3]	5	5	25	29	6	11,360	15,310	405	498
5610 Men's & boys' clothing stores [3]	11	12	98	88	7	9,388	9,818	916	870
5620 Women's clothing stores	65	61	448	406	7	8,420	7,419	4,015	3,164
5630 Women's accessory & specialty stores [3]	11	11	81	73	7	8,296	9,041	702	635
5640 Children's and infants' wear stores [3]	3	4	8	15	4	6,500	3,467	43	92
5650 Family clothing stores	12	17	234	238	14	11,145	11,513	2,825	2,843
5660 Shoe stores	45	40	187	181	5	10,610	11,315	2,069	1,977
5690 Misc. apparel & accessory stores	18	17	81	75	4	11,160	12,373	973	1,048
5712 Furniture stores	61	63	418	429	7	16,545	16,858	7,046	7,119
5713 Floor covering stores	29	31	225	222	7	11,467	13,315	2,968	3,207
5714 Drapery and upholstery stores	7	8	6	9	1	6,000	6,222	48	68
5719 Misc. homefurnishings stores	20	21	130	144	7	8,492	8,833	1,480	1,526
5720 Household appliance stores	20	18	174	132	7	12,023	16,848	2,157	1,839
5731 Radio, TV, & electronic stores	27	28	216	229	8	16,963	17,066	3,814	4,231
5734 Computer and software stores	9	11	27	44	4	11,259	13,636	347	681
5735 Record & prerecorded tape stores [1]	10	10	48	51	5	9,667	10,275	518	541
5736 Musical instrument stores [3]	6	6	38	37	6	16,526	16,000	637	643
5812 Eating places	409	390	9,146	10,097	26	7,208	7,371	71,360	76,378
5813 Drinking places	68	55	676	580	11	7,154	7,945	4,908	4,869

Continued on next page.

PENSACOLA, FL MSA - [continued]

Wholesale and Retail Trade USA	Establishments		Employment		Emp / Est	Pay / Employee		Annual Payroll ($ 000)	
	1994	1995	1994	1995	1995	1994	1995	1994	1995
5910 Drug stores and proprietary stores	76	68	831	810	12	17,396	17,659	14,743	15,140
5920 Liquor stores [3]	26	24	149	125	5	8,671	8,832	1,391	1,251
5930 Used merchandise stores	44	48	176	137	3	10,636	12,730	1,729	1,615
5941 Sporting goods and bicycle shops	47	43	195	191	4	13,231	13,403	2,864	2,715
5942 Book stores	23	25	123	167	7	8,715	8,862	1,120	1,531
5944 Jewelry stores	47	47	224	234	5	13,161	14,923	3,199	3,927
5945 Hobby, toy, and game shops	11	13	106	121	9	10,189	9,256	1,302	1,366
5947 Gift, novelty, and souvenir shops	47	42	224	213	5	7,304	8,676	1,777	1,971
5949 Sewing, needlework, and piece goods	12	11	88	75	7	7,273	7,680	628	530
5961 Catalog and mail-order houses [3]	3	4	3	21	5	16,000	53,714	105	860
5962 Merchandising machine operators [3]	4	4	9	11	3	9,778	8,727	90	102
5963 Direct selling establishments	17	14	59	52	4	13,695	16,615	837	826
5984 Liquefied petroleum gas dealers	8	8	18	18	2	17,778	18,222	312	318
5992 Florists	51	46	182	188	4	8,681	9,021	1,681	1,654
5995 Optical goods stores [3]	20	20	132	140	7	14,909	14,886	2,006	2,103
5999 Miscellaneous retail stores, nec	84	89	354	375	4	11,356	13,280	4,508	4,749

Source: County Business Patterns 1994/95, CBP-94/95, U.S. Department of Commerce, Washington DC, November 1997. The employment column represents mid-March employment in the year. Pay per employee is calculated by dividing 1st Quarter payroll, annualized, by mid-March employment. The column headed 'Emp / Est' shows 'employees per establishment'. A dash (-) means that data are unavailable or cannot be calculated. nec means not elsewhere classified. *Notes:* 1. 1994 data incomplete; unavailable or withheld. 2. 1995 data incomplete; unavailable or withheld. 3. 1994 and 1995 data incomplete; unavailable or withheld.

PEORIA – PEKIN, IL MSA

Wholesale and Retail Trade USA	Establishments		Employment		Emp / Est	Pay / Employee		Annual Payroll ($ 000)	
	1994	1995	1994	1995	1995	1994	1995	1994	1995
50- Wholesale trade	647	632	9,441	10,459	17	32,067	40,237	303,272	407,944
5012 Automobiles and other vehicles	9	10	162	207	21	15,901	14,744	3,137	3,614
5013 Motor vehicle supplies and new parts [1]	36	31	175	281	9	18,629	21,395	3,600	5,937
5014 Tires and tubes [1]	8	-	79	-	-	20,962	-	2,341	-
5015 Motor vehicle parts, used [1]	7	-	40	-	-	21,100	-	1,077	-
5021 Furniture [2]	-	10	-	239	24	-	26,594	-	6,820
5023 Homefurnishings [2]	-	5	-	24	5	-	21,000	-	529
5031 Lumber, plywood, and millwork [3]	10	8	71	104	13	19,099	24,231	1,726	2,454
5032 Brick, stone, & related materials [1]	5	-	16	-	-	28,750	-	600	-
5033 Roofing, siding, & insulation [3]	5	8	93	69	9	15,355	30,609	1,786	1,840
5039 Construction materials, nec [3]	4	13	32	113	9	18,875	21,027	1,090	3,224
5044 Office equipment [3]	10	9	107	173	19	26,467	27,283	2,781	4,626
5045 Computers, peripherals, & software [3]	20	16	234	198	12	42,462	59,394	10,087	9,141
5046 Commercial equipment, nec [3]	4	4	31	27	7	14,968	18,519	519	559
5047 Medical and hospital equipment	9	7	52	63	9	27,769	36,000	1,851	2,750
5049 Professional equipment, nec [3]	4	5	59	62	12	18,576	25,161	1,237	1,800
5051 Metals service centers and offices [3]	10	10	121	133	13	27,074	28,932	3,559	4,127
5063 Electrical apparatus and equipment	24	26	303	325	13	31,248	41,588	9,541	12,075
5064 Electrical appliances, TV & radios [3]	6	6	97	97	16	31,052	34,680	4,062	4,385
5065 Electronic parts and equipment [3]	12	14	144	147	11	39,111	45,497	6,170	6,147
5072 Hardware [1]	8	9	83	119	13	39,759	35,597	4,072	4,824
5074 Plumbing & hydronic heating supplies [3]	18	16	164	175	11	38,854	36,274	5,400	5,135
5075 Warm air heating & air conditioning [1]	11	13	113	117	9	41,558	48,786	4,601	5,092
5078 Refrigeration equipment and supplies [3]	4	4	10	12	3	22,800	22,000	274	339
5083 Farm and garden machinery	22	-	102	-	-	25,765	-	2,985	-
5084 Industrial machinery and equipment	55	51	491	470	9	29,238	31,396	17,947	19,344
5085 Industrial supplies [3]	28	26	103	101	4	30,641	34,653	3,306	3,864
5087 Service establishment equipment	16	14	124	121	9	24,484	25,983	3,387	3,683
5093 Scrap and waste materials [1]	8	7	158	149	21	34,962	37,664	6,113	6,989
5111 Printing and writing paper [3]	5	4	101	69	17	27,683	43,826	2,365	2,961
5112 Stationery and office supplies [3]	14	14	145	174	12	24,276	25,701	3,902	4,890
5113 Industrial & personal service paper [3]	4	4	38	55	14	27,474	24,364	1,303	1,526
5130 Apparel, piece goods, and notions [1]	5	-	18	-	-	7,556	-	125	-
5141 Groceries, general line [1]	4	-	44	-	-	16,091	-	667	-
5143 Dairy products, exc. dried or canned [3]	4	4	9	5	1	36,444	24,800	337	119
5147 Meats and meat products [3]	5	5	51	49	10	13,804	15,347	818	1,017
5149 Groceries and related products, nec [1]	18	19	507	550	29	25,602	25,462	13,581	15,000
5153 Grain and field beans [3]	36	34	108	125	4	25,370	27,552	3,045	3,260
5162 Plastics materials & basic shapes [3]	3	3	33	33	11	27,758	28,970	980	1,011
5169 Chemicals & allied products, nec [3]	12	12	103	103	9	32,194	36,233	3,607	3,957
5171 Petroleum bulk stations & terminals	16	-	57	-	-	28,211	-	2,024	-
5172 Petroleum products, nec [1]	6	-	12	-	-	21,333	-	235	-
5180 Beer, wine, and distilled beverages [3]	8	8	166	168	21	29,036	27,738	5,026	5,064
5191 Farm supplies	39	38	390	426	11	22,595	24,160	10,641	11,679

Continued on next page.

PEORIA – PEKIN, IL MSA - [continued]

Wholesale and Retail Trade USA	Establishments		Employment		Emp / Est	Pay / Employee		Annual Payroll ($ 000)	
	1994	1995	1994	1995	1995	1994	1995	1994	1995
5192 Books, periodicals, & newspapers [3]	6	6	123	123	21	12,553	13,984	1,674	1,776
5198 Paints, varnishes, and supplies [3]	9	9	58	54	6	16,897	20,444	1,105	1,151
5199 Nondurable goods, nec [3]	10	9	148	161	18	18,649	21,043	3,154	3,520
52 – Retail trade	2,148	2,138	30,400	30,636	14	11,063	11,858	372,393	391,963
5210 Lumber and other building materials	43	37	836	782	21	18,239	16,363	17,045	13,368
5230 Paint, glass, and wallpaper stores [3]	8	7	19	26	4	22,316	18,462	502	468
5250 Hardware stores	35	26	266	246	9	12,406	13,350	3,549	3,501
5260 Retail nurseries and garden stores	16	17	72	39	2	11,000	14,564	955	594
5310 Department stores [3]	19	19	3,043	3,028	159	9,928	11,893	33,279	35,493
5330 Variety stores [2]	19	15	152	120	8	7,763	8,367	1,267	1,036
5390 Misc. general merchandise stores	12	21	412	404	19	10,252	12,040	4,601	4,791
5410 Grocery stores	97	91	3,371	3,066	34	11,247	12,194	39,254	37,488
5420 Meat and fish markets [3]	8	9	35	54	6	9,257	9,481	402	433
5440 Candy, nut, and confectionery stores [2]	-	6	-	28	5	-	7,000	-	185
5450 Dairy products stores [2]	-	3	-	12	4	-	5,000	-	80
5460 Retail bakeries [3]	26	22	266	210	10	8,045	8,724	2,077	1,835
5490 Miscellaneous food stores [3]	9	11	42	104	9	7,810	7,192	439	734
5510 New and used car dealers	45	44	1,956	1,977	45	24,836	26,778	57,863	57,919
5520 Used car dealers [3]	28	21	101	79	4	15,168	18,987	1,619	1,562
5530 Auto and home supply stores	39	41	414	429	10	13,227	14,984	5,910	6,953
5540 Gasoline service stations [3]	166	167	1,060	1,025	6	9,302	10,185	10,254	10,669
5560 Recreational vehicle dealers [2]	-	7	-	5	1	-	30,400	-	183
5570 Motorcycle dealers [3]	6	6	29	41	7	16,276	15,317	875	969
5610 Men's & boys' clothing stores [3]	10	9	117	111	12	8,274	9,297	1,034	1,047
5620 Women's clothing stores	51	43	583	429	10	6,552	6,443	4,059	2,649
5630 Women's accessory & specialty stores	12	14	55	69	5	8,509	9,043	548	682
5640 Children's and infants' wear stores [3]	5	5	34	45	9	6,471	5,867	250	254
5650 Family clothing stores [3]	21	19	329	334	18	8,073	7,569	3,065	2,357
5660 Shoe stores [3]	44	40	220	236	6	10,218	11,492	2,581	2,643
5690 Misc. apparel & accessory stores	13	13	64	49	4	8,000	13,878	532	608
5712 Furniture stores	39	37	402	389	11	15,731	15,907	6,245	6,194
5713 Floor covering stores	19	20	143	162	8	19,972	20,469	3,437	3,409
5720 Household appliance stores	18	18	97	87	5	16,866	19,632	1,970	1,867
5731 Radio, TV, & electronic stores	29	30	188	285	10	14,872	13,502	2,924	3,852
5734 Computer and software stores [2]	-	5	-	7	1	-	18,857	-	174
5735 Record & prerecorded tape stores [3]	8	9	32	24	3	8,750	13,667	340	350
5736 Musical instrument stores [3]	5	4	26	21	5	12,308	12,762	292	294
5812 Eating places	567	540	9,945	10,064	19	6,739	7,191	75,613	78,598
5813 Drinking places	159	141	639	652	5	6,861	7,252	4,580	4,691
5910 Drug stores and proprietary stores	63	66	808	844	13	16,302	17,066	14,154	15,409
5920 Liquor stores [1]	36	33	86	131	4	8,279	8,733	759	1,247
5930 Used merchandise stores	25	26	82	110	4	9,854	10,109	834	1,199
5941 Sporting goods and bicycle shops	42	41	214	251	6	8,916	8,892	2,557	2,541
5942 Book stores	19	17	113	102	6	8,779	8,745	952	962
5943 Stationery stores [3]	4	3	14	12	4	5,714	8,333	119	128
5944 Jewelry stores	29	29	191	216	7	14,848	15,444	3,005	3,335
5945 Hobby, toy, and game shops [1]	13	17	131	176	10	7,817	8,136	1,629	1,633
5947 Gift, novelty, and souvenir shops	63	57	341	337	6	5,701	6,077	2,064	2,201
5949 Sewing, needlework, and piece goods [3]	12	9	107	82	9	4,897	5,805	537	500
5962 Merchandising machine operators	-	11	-	6	1	-	6,000	-	36
5963 Direct selling establishments [3]	23	24	629	85	4	13,641	29,694	9,933	2,315
5992 Florists	44	50	224	252	5	9,786	9,571	2,511	2,566
5999 Miscellaneous retail stores, nec	56	59	285	320	5	13,628	13,700	4,350	4,744

Source: County Business Patterns 1994/95, CBP-94/95, U.S. Department of Commerce, Washington DC, November 1997. The employment column represents mid-March employment in the year. Pay per employee is calculated by dividing 1st Quarter payroll, annualized, by mid-March employment. The column headed 'Emp / Est' shows 'employees per establishment'. A dash (-) means that data are unavailable or cannot be calculated. nec means not elsewhere classified. *Notes:* 1. 1994 data incomplete; unavailable or withheld. 2. 1995 data incomplete; unavailable or withheld. 3. 1994 and 1995 data incomplete; unavailable or withheld.

PHILADELPHIA PMSA (NJ PART)

Wholesale and Retail Trade USA	Establishments		Employment		Emp / Est	Pay / Employee		Annual Payroll ($ 000)	
	1994	1995	1994	1995	1995	1994	1995	1994	1995
50 – Wholesale trade [2]	2,392	2,405	35,028	34,323	14	32,187	35,106	1,220,373	1,246,060
5012 Automobiles and other vehicles [1]	64	65	1,509	1,761	27	29,254	29,233	48,099	51,455
5013 Motor vehicle supplies and new parts	120	110	1,546	1,521	14	24,582	26,632	42,507	41,110
5014 Tires and tubes	20	16	203	208	13	36,493	36,365	7,529	7,890
5015 Motor vehicle parts, used	36	41	166	209	5	16,265	19,579	2,962	4,124
5021 Furniture	43	41	638	477	12	38,182	46,507	23,612	20,826
5023 Homefurnishings [3]	43	41	724	684	17	33,972	38,421	26,201	25,714

Continued on next page.

PHILADELPHIA PMSA (NJ PART) - [continued]

Wholesale and Retail Trade USA	Establishments		Employment		Emp / Est	Pay / Employee		Annual Payroll ($ 000)	
	1994	1995	1994	1995	1995	1994	1995	1994	1995
5031 Lumber, plywood, and millwork [3]	36	31	724	588	19	27,320	32,878	22,943	20,770
5032 Brick, stone, & related materials [2]	18	15	161	28	2	26,534	39,571	5,606	2,283
5033 Roofing, siding, & insulation [3]	23	18	216	116	6	27,611	32,552	7,255	4,243
5039 Construction materials, nec [1]	28	36	400	582	16	28,170	29,649	13,170	18,440
5043 Photographic equipment & supplies [1]	6	-	45	-	-	44,178	-	1,931	-
5044 Office equipment	36	35	836	761	22	35,005	38,045	29,836	27,950
5045 Computers, peripherals, & software [3]	96	101	1,653	1,639	16	45,580	47,097	71,706	72,228
5046 Commercial equipment, nec [3]	23	24	380	386	16	31,958	35,782	13,919	14,485
5047 Medical and hospital equipment [3]	70	67	666	692	10	33,207	35,064	24,486	26,729
5048 Ophthalmic goods [1]	12	-	70	-	-	26,857	-	1,443	-
5049 Professional equipment, nec [3]	18	20	57	54	3	28,632	26,519	1,697	1,506
5051 Metals service centers and offices [3]	74	71	572	460	6	35,119	35,122	23,158	19,129
5063 Electrical apparatus and equipment	99	82	1,248	1,013	12	37,929	34,665	50,866	35,537
5064 Electrical appliances, TV & radios [3]	17	16	167	208	13	48,000	46,346	7,815	8,974
5065 Electronic parts and equipment	137	147	1,400	1,673	11	39,931	49,296	57,618	87,552
5072 Hardware [3]	39	42	336	319	8	24,869	25,881	10,508	9,694
5074 Plumbing & hydronic heating supplies	52	46	592	532	12	26,581	28,812	18,292	17,553
5075 Warm air heating & air conditioning [3]	25	27	168	85	3	27,214	31,859	5,558	3,152
5078 Refrigeration equipment and supplies [1]	8	-	65	-	-	23,077	-	1,532	-
5082 Construction and mining machinery	19	22	151	168	8	30,013	33,000	5,642	6,631
5083 Farm and garden machinery	15	13	44	35	3	18,182	18,171	931	659
5084 Industrial machinery and equipment	133	138	1,063	1,203	9	36,237	38,364	41,690	48,904
5085 Industrial supplies	75	75	653	666	9	32,447	31,754	25,051	24,418
5087 Service establishment equipment [3]	31	36	282	279	8	24,582	26,968	7,594	8,319
5088 Transportation equipment & supplies [3]	13	12	202	42	4	45,366	44,381	9,130	1,908
5091 Sporting & recreational goods [3]	22	22	306	486	22	25,503	36,453	11,086	20,213
5092 Toys and hobby goods and supplies [2]	-	9	-	94	10	-	75,404	-	5,590
5093 Scrap and waste materials	53	54	505	530	10	26,004	31,298	14,850	18,145
5094 Jewelry & precious stones [3]	13	9	6	17	2	12,667	13,647	73	212
5099 Durable goods, nec [3]	32	37	70	74	2	30,629	32,270	2,275	2,429
5111 Printing and writing paper [3]	23	21	178	174	8	30,135	35,954	6,402	6,906
5112 Stationery and office supplies [2]	62	57	971	794	14	28,445	29,647	27,979	23,828
5113 Industrial & personal service paper [3]	38	36	130	201	6	33,508	49,612	5,543	9,397
5120 Drugs, proprietaries, and sundries [3]	27	30	997	888	30	47,410	44,090	49,084	40,134
5131 Piece goods & notions [3]	13	18	167	125	7	24,263	31,168	5,947	6,716
5136 Men's and boys' clothing [3]	6	8	32	34	4	45,875	50,706	1,568	1,514
5137 Women's and children's clothing [2]	18	19	109	52	3	32,661	22,692	3,589	1,647
5139 Footwear [3]	10	8	140	84	11	28,886	46,000	4,188	2,534
5141 Groceries, general line [3]	23	26	212	210	8	28,132	35,790	7,618	6,141
5142 Packaged frozen food [3]	23	22	561	586	27	30,317	31,952	18,247	20,926
5143 Dairy products, exc. dried or canned	18	16	181	198	12	33,171	30,404	5,839	6,115
5144 Poultry and poultry products [3]	7	7	36	37	5	35,556	37,730	1,937	2,131
5145 Confectionery [3]	21	21	241	290	14	28,149	27,531	6,857	8,233
5146 Fish and seafoods	12	12	57	82	7	28,912	32,000	2,095	2,724
5147 Meats and meat products [3]	15	18	274	340	19	23,066	21,541	7,107	8,130
5148 Fresh fruits and vegetables	28	29	720	262	9	19,083	28,626	12,233	7,735
5149 Groceries and related products, nec [3]	78	79	1,977	2,027	26	26,877	29,462	58,716	60,188
5150 Farm-product raw materials	-	9	-	37	4	-	17,622	-	662
5162 Plastics materials & basic shapes	23	25	194	236	9	28,124	32,542	6,375	8,002
5169 Chemicals & allied products, nec [3]	65	65	622	610	9	38,740	41,220	25,734	25,637
5171 Petroleum bulk stations & terminals [1]	24	19	279	208	11	35,599	42,827	9,560	8,378
5172 Petroleum products, nec	19	17	74	55	3	31,189	33,018	2,286	2,207
5180 Beer, wine, and distilled beverages [1]	15	14	198	225	16	34,889	38,453	9,397	9,759
5191 Farm supplies	31	26	300	247	10	24,733	27,498	8,250	6,756
5192 Books, periodicals, & newspapers [3]	21	20	1,011	486	24	23,632	27,514	26,171	13,138
5193 Flowers & florists' supplies [3]	20	13	100	107	8	17,720	24,075	2,222	2,756
5194 Tobacco and tobacco products [3]	12	11	170	239	22	20,259	10,159	3,710	4,795
5198 Paints, varnishes, and supplies [1]	17	15	49	147	10	21,796	23,755	1,108	4,083
5199 Nondurable goods, nec	58	59	927	803	14	24,526	31,298	29,355	23,156
52- Retail trade [2]	6,613	6,664	88,118	87,596	13	13,590	14,432	1,320,275	1,318,885
5210 Lumber and other building materials	110	105	1,597	2,106	20	19,649	21,956	38,037	47,381
5230 Paint, glass, and wallpaper stores	47	40	189	177	4	18,349	20,565	3,734	3,729
5250 Hardware stores	67	57	471	435	8	12,943	13,811	6,419	6,222
5260 Retail nurseries and garden stores	58	58	449	511	9	14,049	14,286	9,616	9,732
5310 Department stores [3]	54	54	9,058	9,271	172	10,103	11,731	105,069	113,366
5330 Variety stores	40	46	418	429	9	11,254	10,266	4,768	5,065
5390 Misc. general merchandise stores	44	38	1,035	1,083	29	11,807	12,968	12,980	14,458
5410 Grocery stores	647	592	13,460	14,112	24	14,931	14,378	210,467	210,318
5420 Meat and fish markets	45	40	258	219	5	14,357	14,868	3,768	3,430
5430 Fruit and vegetable markets [2]	30	23	188	183	8	10,638	11,738	2,529	3,797
5440 Candy, nut, and confectionery stores	28	27	193	142	5	6,694	8,620	1,280	1,287

Continued on next page.

PHILADELPHIA PMSA (NJ PART) - [continued]

Wholesale and Retail Trade USA	Establishments		Employment		Emp / Est	Pay / Employee		Annual Payroll ($ 000)	
	1994	1995	1994	1995	1995	1994	1995	1994	1995
5450 Dairy products stores [3]	12	12	9	7	1	4,000	6,286	72	174
5460 Retail bakeries	114	111	863	812	7	10,762	11,118	10,319	9,475
5490 Miscellaneous food stores	55	57	280	296	5	10,014	11,176	3,069	3,435
5510 New and used car dealers	119	114	4,895	5,125	45	30,958	33,062	179,375	177,954
5520 Used car dealers [1]	58	66	228	279	4	21,123	23,025	5,991	6,983
5530 Auto and home supply stores	147	151	1,148	1,255	8	17,951	19,643	24,192	26,438
5540 Gasoline service stations	419	434	3,056	3,069	7	12,209	12,855	39,418	39,980
5550 Boat dealers	17	16	174	213	13	15,816	16,300	3,544	3,931
5560 Recreational vehicle dealers [3]	8	7	25	19	3	15,680	22,737	428	446
5570 Motorcycle dealers [3]	9	10	53	91	9	20,755	22,286	1,389	2,510
5610 Men's & boys' clothing stores [3]	56	56	453	503	9	10,464	11,062	4,830	5,408
5620 Women's clothing stores	202	186	2,382	2,060	11	8,322	8,730	23,185	18,756
5630 Women's accessory & specialty stores [3]	42	41	229	226	6	11,162	12,460	2,676	2,872
5640 Children's and infants' wear stores [3]	29	28	267	352	13	7,446	9,375	2,251	3,417
5650 Family clothing stores	57	57	1,044	1,102	19	9,985	10,152	11,933	12,801
5660 Shoe stores	195	186	1,012	991	5	11,577	12,416	12,682	12,218
5690 Misc. apparel & accessory stores	46	47	245	200	4	8,751	9,540	2,225	2,016
5712 Furniture stores	121	123	884	841	7	19,869	21,308	18,778	18,136
5713 Floor covering stores	59	59	262	283	5	19,802	22,473	5,774	6,570
5714 Drapery and upholstery stores [3]	12	11	45	24	2	16,533	12,000	644	304
5719 Misc. homefurnishings stores [2]	74	69	364	139	2	11,659	12,547	5,117	1,926
5720 Household appliance stores	44	43	213	279	6	18,385	23,097	5,316	6,226
5731 Radio, TV, & electronic stores	62	61	457	524	9	16,079	15,580	8,205	8,177
5734 Computer and software stores [3]	32	35	275	349	10	15,724	15,817	4,870	5,610
5735 Record & prerecorded tape stores [1]	46	45	245	364	8	11,984	11,857	3,147	4,389
5736 Musical instrument stores [3]	10	11	83	121	11	19,277	20,496	1,712	2,226
5812 Eating places	1,418	1,357	22,993	23,241	17	8,362	9,006	211,829	221,031
5813 Drinking places	221	207	1,258	1,357	7	9,068	9,250	12,777	12,996
5910 Drug stores and proprietary stores	250	248	3,407	3,519	14	14,437	15,024	52,225	52,890
5920 Liquor stores	190	187	1,300	1,260	7	12,338	12,790	16,999	16,584
5930 Used merchandise stores	35	37	248	216	6	7,597	9,537	2,154	2,340
5941 Sporting goods and bicycle shops	88	91	641	749	8	12,524	12,652	8,860	9,857
5942 Book stores [3]	41	43	394	427	10	10,386	13,077	4,144	5,348
5943 Stationery stores [3]	15	16	13	154	10	18,462	12,468	259	1,807
5944 Jewelry stores	99	111	414	459	4	16,106	18,031	7,269	8,459
5945 Hobby, toy, and game shops [3]	45	45	507	578	13	10,335	10,630	6,344	6,863
5946 Camera & photographic supply stores	25	27	108	40	1	11,481	12,900	1,301	513
5947 Gift, novelty, and souvenir shops	153	155	798	869	6	7,689	8,235	7,908	8,313
5948 Luggage and leather goods stores [3]	5	7	21	23	3	12,952	13,043	253	272
5949 Sewing, needlework, and piece goods	22	22	132	193	9	7,545	7,565	1,197	1,410
5961 Catalog and mail-order houses [3]	21	27	239	273	10	18,778	22,256	5,397	9,806
5962 Merchandising machine operators	22	23	256	230	10	20,563	22,730	5,556	5,106
5963 Direct selling establishments	71	70	656	528	8	13,921	15,947	9,407	8,388
5983 Fuel oil dealers [3]	78	81	563	609	8	28,306	26,522	15,844	15,696
5984 Liquefied petroleum gas dealers [3]	9	10	110	140	14	24,364	25,343	2,798	3,724
5992 Florists	118	127	628	610	5	10,000	11,338	6,755	7,220
5993 Tobacco stores and stands [3]	16	15	54	52	3	7,111	7,538	381	396
5994 News dealers and newsstands	24	23	85	76	3	13,129	12,737	1,125	950
5995 Optical goods stores [3]	64	70	337	335	5	16,843	18,472	6,064	6,503
5999 Miscellaneous retail stores, nec	181	189	876	943	5	13,553	13,943	13,603	14,222

Source: County Business Patterns 1994/95, CBP-94/95, U.S. Department of Commerce, Washington DC, November 1997. The employment column represents mid-March employment in the year. Pay per employee is calculated by dividing 1st Quarter payroll, annualized, by mid-March employment. The column headed 'Emp / Est' shows 'employees per establishment'. A dash (-) means that data are unavailable or cannot be calculated. nec means not elsewhere classified. *Notes:* 1. 1994 data incomplete; unavailable or withheld. 2. 1995 data incomplete; unavailable or withheld. 3. 1994 and 1995 data incomplete; unavailable or withheld.

PHILADELPHIA PMSA (PA PART)

Wholesale and Retail Trade USA	Establishments		Employment		Emp / Est	Pay / Employee		Annual Payroll ($ 000)	
	1994	1995	1994	1995	1995	1994	1995	1994	1995
50 – Wholesale trade	-	7,665	-	106,040	14	-	38,835	-	4,340,934
5012 Automobiles and other vehicles	-	105	-	1,647	16	-	32,005	-	53,708
5013 Motor vehicle supplies and new parts	-	310	-	4,318	14	-	24,048	-	107,570
5014 Tires and tubes	-	47	-	543	12	-	32,516	-	18,480
5015 Motor vehicle parts, used	-	97	-	563	6	-	20,710	-	12,302
5021 Furniture	-	148	-	2,269	15	-	32,067	-	71,288
5023 Homefurnishings	-	105	-	1,229	12	-	32,778	-	40,536
5031 Lumber, plywood, and millwork	-	89	-	1,593	18	-	32,352	-	55,247
5032 Brick, stone, & related materials	-	41	-	261	6	-	30,084	-	9,475
5033 Roofing, siding, & insulation	-	58	-	706	12	-	32,346	-	28,765

Continued on next page.

PHILADELPHIA PMSA (PA PART) - [continued]

Wholesale and Retail Trade USA	Establishments		Employment		Emp / Est	Pay / Employee		Annual Payroll ($ 000)	
	1994	1995	1994	1995	1995	1994	1995	1994	1995
5039 Construction materials, nec	-	108	-	988	9	-	34,753	-	32,012
5043 Photographic equipment & supplies [2]	-	16	-	154	10	-	27,662	-	4,824
5044 Office equipment	-	145	-	2,967	20	-	35,803	-	98,316
5045 Computers, peripherals, & software	-	299	-	4,220	14	-	57,229	-	230,973
5046 Commercial equipment, nec	-	79	-	589	7	-	27,083	-	16,863
5047 Medical and hospital equipment	-	206	-	2,806	14	-	52,004	-	146,000
5048 Ophthalmic goods	-	25	-	61	2	-	34,623	-	2,870
5049 Professional equipment, nec	-	57	-	548	10	-	34,431	-	19,852
5051 Metals service centers and offices [2]	-	234	-	1,856	8	-	41,246	-	82,817
5063 Electrical apparatus and equipment	-	303	-	4,010	13	-	35,745	-	148,726
5064 Electrical appliances, TV & radios	-	52	-	438	8	-	30,941	-	15,304
5065 Electronic parts and equipment	-	314	-	4,017	13	-	47,418	-	190,946
5072 Hardware	-	147	-	1,586	11	-	33,914	-	55,956
5074 Plumbing & hydronic heating supplies	-	178	-	2,477	14	-	33,431	-	92,366
5075 Warm air heating & air conditioning	-	83	-	1,205	15	-	39,436	-	49,474
5078 Refrigeration equipment and supplies	-	26	-	133	5	-	28,722	-	5,232
5082 Construction and mining machinery	-	48	-	723	15	-	36,835	-	28,300
5083 Farm and garden machinery	-	34	-	393	12	-	33,242	-	12,339
5084 Industrial machinery and equipment	-	541	-	4,866	9	-	38,130	-	198,406
5085 Industrial supplies	-	278	-	3,080	11	-	38,492	-	124,257
5087 Service establishment equipment	-	119	-	1,076	9	-	30,781	-	35,183
5088 Transportation equipment & supplies	-	37	-	189	5	-	33,947	-	6,834
5091 Sporting & recreational goods	-	69	-	946	14	-	27,340	-	35,148
5092 Toys and hobby goods and supplies	-	46	-	365	8	-	36,734	-	12,850
5093 Scrap and waste materials	-	157	-	1,604	10	-	30,359	-	55,118
5094 Jewelry & precious stones	-	82	-	536	7	-	27,970	-	16,861
5099 Durable goods, nec	-	135	-	1,269	9	-	25,998	-	38,830
5111 Printing and writing paper	-	56	-	899	16	-	59,835	-	56,879
5112 Stationery and office supplies	-	151	-	1,506	10	-	29,958	-	48,615
5113 Industrial & personal service paper	-	120	-	1,599	13	-	43,212	-	76,822
5120 Drugs, proprietaries, and sundries [2]	-	105	-	3,830	36	-	65,411	-	298,268
5131 Piece goods & notions	-	92	-	1,592	17	-	30,839	-	49,948
5136 Men's and boys' clothing	-	62	-	723	12	-	22,313	-	19,217
5137 Women's and children's clothing	-	93	-	960	10	-	36,267	-	29,853
5139 Footwear	-	22	-	102	5	-	41,804	-	3,826
5141 Groceries, general line	-	54	-	1,559	29	-	28,639	-	55,848
5142 Packaged frozen food [2]	-	48	-	1,377	29	-	33,267	-	47,910
5143 Dairy products, exc. dried or canned	-	42	-	972	23	-	30,963	-	29,655
5144 Poultry and poultry products	-	21	-	172	8	-	31,023	-	5,700
5145 Confectionery	-	43	-	382	9	-	32,482	-	13,667
5146 Fish and seafoods [2]	-	29	-	270	9	-	30,341	-	8,860
5147 Meats and meat products	-	76	-	1,517	20	-	31,214	-	48,981
5148 Fresh fruits and vegetables	-	103	-	2,217	22	-	27,973	-	67,987
5149 Groceries and related products, nec	-	188	-	4,249	23	-	31,340	-	152,531
5153 Grain and field beans [2]	-	6	-	21	4	-	72,000	-	1,095
5154 Livestock [2]	-	7	-	11	2	-	12,000	-	140
5159 Farm-product raw materials, nec [2]	-	8	-	11	1	-	16,364	-	130
5162 Plastics materials & basic shapes	-	85	-	977	11	-	41,777	-	44,591
5169 Chemicals & allied products, nec	-	175	-	3,207	18	-	50,708	-	168,245
5171 Petroleum bulk stations & terminals [2]	-	47	-	3,503	75	-	36,514	-	126,843
5172 Petroleum products, nec	-	30	-	215	7	-	36,112	-	7,945
5181 Beer and ale	-	66	-	1,083	16	-	29,861	-	42,297
5182 Wine and distilled beverages	-	31	-	337	11	-	31,228	-	11,136
5191 Farm supplies	-	61	-	744	12	-	29,016	-	23,451
5192 Books, periodicals, & newspapers	-	87	-	1,490	17	-	28,558	-	43,703
5193 Flowers & florists' supplies	-	55	-	811	15	-	24,385	-	21,187
5194 Tobacco and tobacco products	-	21	-	213	10	-	26,836	-	5,783
5198 Paints, varnishes, and supplies	-	74	-	682	9	-	38,252	-	30,789
5199 Nondurable goods, nec	-	373	-	2,107	6	-	25,338	-	52,464
52- Retail trade	-	21,599	-	285,581	13	-	15,114	-	4,542,902
5210 Lumber and other building materials	-	244	-	5,357	22	-	20,670	-	115,363
5230 Paint, glass, and wallpaper stores	-	134	-	476	4	-	20,118	-	9,850
5250 Hardware stores	-	141	-	1,061	8	-	13,712	-	13,971
5260 Retail nurseries and garden stores	-	147	-	1,231	8	-	16,101	-	23,666
5310 Department stores	-	118	-	24,301	206	-	11,277	-	289,304
5330 Variety stores	-	183	-	1,903	10	-	10,583	-	25,474
5390 Misc. general merchandise stores	-	143	-	2,914	20	-	12,612	-	38,907
5410 Grocery stores	-	1,560	-	37,780	24	-	14,732	-	576,068
5420 Meat and fish markets	-	219	-	1,279	6	-	13,717	-	17,955
5430 Fruit and vegetable markets	-	82	-	516	6	-	11,620	-	7,114
5440 Candy, nut, and confectionery stores	-	80	-	415	5	-	6,834	-	2,910

Continued on next page.

PHILADELPHIA PMSA (PA PART) - [continued]

Wholesale and Retail Trade USA	Establishments		Employment		Emp / Est	Pay / Employee		Annual Payroll ($ 000)	
	1994	1995	1994	1995	1995	1994	1995	1994	1995
5450 Dairy products stores	-	54	-	288	5	-	7,375	-	2,340
5460 Retail bakeries	-	341	-	2,758	8	-	9,595	-	27,030
5490 Miscellaneous food stores	-	189	-	897	5	-	12,771	-	11,890
5510 New and used car dealers	-	303	-	14,080	46	-	30,549	-	460,796
5520 Used car dealers	-	157	-	638	4	-	24,966	-	17,723
5530 Auto and home supply stores	-	325	-	6,298	19	-	15,080	-	123,752
5540 Gasoline service stations	-	1,068	-	6,264	6	-	13,837	-	89,194
5550 Boat dealers	-	11	-	45	4	-	23,644	-	1,172
5560 Recreational vehicle dealers [2]	-	13	-	113	9	-	26,195	-	4,251
5570 Motorcycle dealers	-	22	-	176	8	-	16,909	-	3,617
5610 Men's & boys' clothing stores	-	212	-	2,148	10	-	15,618	-	35,425
5620 Women's clothing stores	-	650	-	6,670	10	-	9,914	-	68,079
5630 Women's accessory & specialty stores	-	151	-	799	5	-	11,009	-	8,471
5640 Children's and infants' wear stores	-	113	-	1,216	11	-	8,961	-	11,449
5650 Family clothing stores	-	228	-	4,414	19	-	11,475	-	53,907
5660 Shoe stores	-	589	-	3,021	5	-	12,719	-	39,670
5690 Misc. apparel & accessory stores	-	121	-	685	6	-	11,801	-	10,167
5712 Furniture stores	-	435	-	3,459	8	-	19,393	-	67,724
5713 Floor covering stores	-	181	-	990	5	-	23,394	-	24,805
5714 Drapery and upholstery stores	-	44	-	185	4	-	12,519	-	2,324
5719 Misc. homefurnishings stores	-	229	-	1,586	7	-	13,347	-	21,405
5720 Household appliance stores	-	128	-	1,885	15	-	16,414	-	30,386
5731 Radio, TV, & electronic stores	-	188	-	1,596	8	-	17,847	-	28,763
5734 Computer and software stores	-	126	-	890	7	-	19,285	-	19,025
5735 Record & prerecorded tape stores	-	154	-	1,049	7	-	10,349	-	11,352
5736 Musical instrument stores [2]	-	37	-	242	7	-	25,174	-	6,337
5812 Eating places	-	4,639	-	75,548	16	-	9,286	-	737,680
5813 Drinking places	-	1,162	-	4,796	4	-	9,078	-	45,729
5910 Drug stores and proprietary stores	-	913	-	12,026	13	-	14,617	-	187,278
5920 Liquor stores	-	403	-	1,872	5	-	19,735	-	37,312
5930 Used merchandise stores	-	202	-	986	5	-	14,929	-	15,806
5941 Sporting goods and bicycle shops	-	296	-	2,467	8	-	12,767	-	34,240
5942 Book stores	-	208	-	1,611	8	-	12,276	-	20,677
5943 Stationery stores	-	74	-	1,004	14	-	17,056	-	22,091
5944 Jewelry stores	-	451	-	1,983	4	-	18,749	-	37,237
5945 Hobby, toy, and game shops	-	139	-	1,665	12	-	10,897	-	20,620
5946 Camera & photographic supply stores	-	95	-	485	5	-	14,499	-	7,422
5947 Gift, novelty, and souvenir shops	-	462	-	2,694	6	-	8,833	-	25,565
5948 Luggage and leather goods stores	-	46	-	191	4	-	17,571	-	3,467
5949 Sewing, needlework, and piece goods	-	78	-	717	9	-	9,791	-	7,227
5961 Catalog and mail-order houses [2]	-	81	-	2,226	27	-	41,511	-	75,890
5962 Merchandising machine operators [2]	-	87	-	2,041	23	-	18,111	-	37,609
5963 Direct selling establishments [2]	-	146	-	1,272	9	-	14,632	-	20,850
5983 Fuel oil dealers [2]	-	168	-	1,266	8	-	29,567	-	33,897
5984 Liquefied petroleum gas dealers	-	32	-	264	8	-	33,061	-	8,961
5992 Florists	-	335	-	1,704	5	-	12,045	-	21,889
5993 Tobacco stores and stands [2]	-	21	-	88	4	-	17,182	-	1,822
5994 News dealers and newsstands	-	64	-	200	3	-	9,360	-	1,822
5995 Optical goods stores	-	273	-	1,234	5	-	17,750	-	24,075
5999 Miscellaneous retail stores, nec	-	662	-	3,890	6	-	16,110	-	73,486

Source: County Business Patterns 1994/95, CBP-94/95, U.S. Department of Commerce, Washington DC, November 1997. The employment column represents mid-March employment in the year. Pay per employee is calculated by dividing 1st Quarter payroll, annualized, by mid-March employment. The column headed 'Emp / Est' shows 'employees per establishment'. A dash (-) means that data are unavailable or cannot be calculated. nec means not elsewhere classified. *Notes:* 1. 1994 data incomplete; unavailable or withheld. 2. 1995 data incomplete; unavailable or withheld. 3. 1994 and 1995 data incomplete; unavailable or withheld.

PHILADELPHIA, PA–NJ PMSA

Wholesale and Retail Trade USA	Establishments		Employment		Emp / Est	Pay / Employee		Annual Payroll ($ 000)	
	1994	1995	1994	1995	1995	1994	1995	1994	1995
50- Wholesale trade [3]	2,392	10,070	35,028	140,363	14	32,187	37,923	1,220,373	5,586,994
5012 Automobiles and other vehicles [1]	64	170	1,509	3,408	20	29,254	30,573	48,099	105,163
5013 Motor vehicle supplies and new parts [1]	120	420	1,546	5,839	14	24,582	24,721	42,507	148,680
5014 Tires and tubes [1]	20	63	203	751	12	36,493	33,582	7,529	26,370
5015 Motor vehicle parts, used [1]	36	138	166	772	6	16,265	20,404	2,962	16,426
5021 Furniture [1]	43	189	638	2,746	15	38,182	34,575	23,612	92,114
5023 Homefurnishings [3]	43	146	724	1,913	13	33,972	34,796	26,201	66,250
5031 Lumber, plywood, and millwork [3]	36	120	724	2,181	18	27,320	32,493	22,943	76,017
5032 Brick, stone, & related materials [3]	18	56	161	289	5	26,534	31,003	5,606	11,758
5033 Roofing, siding, & insulation [3]	23	76	216	822	11	27,611	32,375	7,255	33,008

Continued on next page.

PHILADELPHIA, PA-NJ PMSA - [continued]

Wholesale and Retail Trade USA	Establishments		Employment		Emp / Est	Pay / Employee		Annual Payroll ($ 000)	
	1994	1995	1994	1995	1995	1994	1995	1994	1995
5039 Construction materials, nec [1]	28	144	400	1,570	11	28,170	32,861	13,170	50,452
5043 Photographic equipment & supplies [3]	6	20	45	154	8	44,178	27,662	1,931	4,824
5044 Office equipment [1]	36	180	836	3,728	21	35,005	36,261	29,836	126,266
5045 Computers, peripherals, & software [3]	96	400	1,653	5,859	15	45,580	54,395	71,706	303,201
5046 Commercial equipment, nec [3]	23	103	380	975	9	31,958	30,527	13,919	31,348
5047 Medical and hospital equipment [3]	70	273	666	3,498	13	33,207	48,653	24,486	172,729
5048 Ophthalmic goods [3]	12	35	70	61	2	26,857	34,623	1,443	2,870
5049 Professional equipment, nec [3]	18	77	57	602	8	28,632	33,721	1,697	21,358
5051 Metals service centers and offices [3]	74	305	572	2,316	8	35,119	40,029	23,158	101,946
5063 Electrical apparatus and equipment [1]	99	385	1,248	5,023	13	37,929	35,527	50,866	184,263
5064 Electrical appliances, TV & radios [3]	17	68	167	646	10	48,000	35,901	7,815	24,278
5065 Electronic parts and equipment [1]	137	461	1,400	5,690	12	39,931	47,970	57,618	278,498
5072 Hardware [3]	39	189	336	1,905	10	24,869	32,569	10,508	65,650
5074 Plumbing & hydronic heating supplies [1]	52	224	592	3,009	13	26,581	32,614	18,292	109,919
5075 Warm air heating & air conditioning [3]	25	110	168	1,290	12	27,214	38,936	5,558	52,626
5078 Refrigeration equipment and supplies [3]	8	32	65	133	4	23,077	28,722	1,532	5,232
5082 Construction and mining machinery [1]	19	70	151	891	13	30,013	36,112	5,642	34,931
5083 Farm and garden machinery [1]	15	47	44	428	9	18,182	32,009	931	12,998
5084 Industrial machinery and equipment [1]	133	679	1,063	6,069	9	36,237	38,176	41,690	247,310
5085 Industrial supplies [1]	75	353	653	3,746	11	32,447	37,294	25,051	148,675
5087 Service establishment equipment [3]	31	155	282	1,355	9	24,582	29,996	7,594	43,502
5088 Transportation equipment & supplies [3]	13	49	202	231	5	45,366	35,844	9,130	8,742
5091 Sporting & recreational goods [3]	22	91	306	1,432	16	25,503	30,433	11,086	55,361
5092 Toys and hobby goods and supplies [2]	-	55	-	459	8	-	44,654	-	18,440
5093 Scrap and waste materials [1]	53	211	505	2,134	10	26,004	30,592	14,850	73,263
5094 Jewelry & precious stones [3]	13	91	6	553	6	12,667	27,530	73	17,073
5099 Durable goods, nec [3]	32	172	70	1,343	8	30,629	26,344	2,275	41,259
5111 Printing and writing paper [3]	23	77	178	1,073	14	30,135	55,963	6,402	63,785
5112 Stationery and office supplies [3]	62	208	971	2,300	11	28,445	29,850	27,979	72,443
5113 Industrial & personal service paper [3]	38	156	130	1,800	12	33,508	43,927	5,543	86,219
5120 Drugs, proprietaries, and sundries [3]	27	135	997	4,718	35	47,410	61,398	49,084	338,402
5131 Piece goods & notions [3]	13	110	167	1,717	16	24,263	30,863	5,947	56,664
5136 Men's and boys' clothing [3]	6	70	32	757	11	45,875	23,588	1,568	20,731
5137 Women's and children's clothing [3]	18	112	109	1,012	9	32,661	35,569	3,589	31,500
5139 Footwear [3]	10	30	140	186	6	28,886	43,699	4,188	6,360
5141 Groceries, general line [3]	23	80	212	1,769	22	28,132	29,488	7,618	61,989
5142 Packaged frozen food [3]	23	70	561	1,963	28	30,317	32,874	18,247	68,836
5143 Dairy products, exc. dried or canned [1]	18	58	181	1,170	20	33,171	30,868	5,839	35,770
5144 Poultry and poultry products [3]	7	28	36	209	7	35,556	32,211	1,937	7,831
5145 Confectionery [3]	21	64	241	672	11	28,149	30,345	6,857	21,900
5146 Fish and seafoods [3]	12	41	57	352	9	28,912	30,727	2,095	11,584
5147 Meats and meat products [3]	15	94	274	1,857	20	23,066	29,443	7,107	57,111
5148 Fresh fruits and vegetables [1]	28	132	720	2,479	19	19,083	28,042	12,233	75,722
5149 Groceries and related products, nec [3]	78	267	1,977	6,276	24	26,877	30,734	58,716	212,719
5153 Grain and field beans [2]	-	8	-	21	3	-	72,000	-	1,095
5154 Livestock [2]	-	11	-	11	1	-	12,000	-	140
5159 Farm-product raw materials, nec [2]	-	11	-	11	1	-	16,364	-	130
5162 Plastics materials & basic shapes [1]	23	110	194	1,213	11	28,124	39,980	6,375	52,593
5169 Chemicals & allied products, nec [3]	65	240	622	3,817	16	38,740	49,192	25,734	193,882
5171 Petroleum bulk stations & terminals [3]	24	66	279	3,711	56	35,599	36,868	9,560	135,221
5172 Petroleum products, nec [1]	19	47	74	270	6	31,189	35,481	2,286	10,152
5181 Beer and ale [2]	-	69	-	1,083	16	-	29,861	-	42,297
5182 Wine and distilled beverages [2]	-	40	-	337	8	-	31,228	-	11,136
5191 Farm supplies [1]	31	87	300	991	11	24,733	28,638	8,250	30,207
5192 Books, periodicals, & newspapers [3]	21	107	1,011	1,976	18	23,632	28,302	26,171	56,841
5193 Flowers & florists' supplies [3]	20	68	100	918	14	17,720	24,349	2,222	23,943
5194 Tobacco and tobacco products [3]	12	32	170	452	14	20,259	18,018	3,710	10,578
5198 Paints, varnishes, and supplies [1]	17	89	49	829	9	21,796	35,682	1,108	34,872
5199 Nondurable goods, nec [1]	58	432	927	2,910	7	24,526	26,983	29,355	75,620
52- Retail trade [3]	6,613	28,263	88,118	373,177	13	13,590	14,954	1,320,275	5,861,787
5210 Lumber and other building materials [1]	110	349	1,597	7,463	21	19,649	21,033	38,037	162,744
5230 Paint, glass, and wallpaper stores [1]	47	174	189	653	4	18,349	20,239	3,734	13,579
5250 Hardware stores [1]	67	198	471	1,496	8	12,943	13,741	6,419	20,193
5260 Retail nurseries and garden stores [1]	58	205	449	1,742	8	14,049	15,568	9,616	33,398
5310 Department stores [3]	54	172	9,058	33,572	195	10,103	11,402	105,069	402,670
5330 Variety stores [1]	40	229	418	2,332	10	11,254	10,525	4,768	30,539
5390 Misc. general merchandise stores [1]	44	181	1,035	3,997	22	11,807	12,709	12,980	53,365
5410 Grocery stores [1]	647	2,152	13,460	51,892	24	14,931	14,636	210,467	786,386
5420 Meat and fish markets [1]	45	259	258	1,498	6	14,357	13,885	3,768	21,385
5430 Fruit and vegetable markets [3]	30	105	188	699	7	10,638	11,651	2,529	10,911
5440 Candy, nut, and confectionery stores [1]	28	107	193	557	5	6,694	7,289	1,280	4,197

Continued on next page.

PHILADELPHIA, PA - NJ PMSA - [continued]

Wholesale and Retail Trade USA	Establishments		Employment		Emp / Est	Pay / Employee		Annual Payroll ($ 000)	
	1994	1995	1994	1995	1995	1994	1995	1994	1995
5450 Dairy products stores [3]	12	66	9	295	4	4,000	7,349	72	2,514
5460 Retail bakeries [1]	114	452	863	3,570	8	10,762	9,942	10,319	36,505
5490 Miscellaneous food stores [1]	55	246	280	1,193	5	10,014	12,376	3,069	15,325
5510 New and used car dealers [1]	119	417	4,895	19,205	46	30,958	31,220	179,375	638,750
5520 Used car dealers [1]	58	223	228	917	4	21,123	24,375	5,991	24,706
5530 Auto and home supply stores [1]	147	476	1,148	7,553	16	17,951	15,838	24,192	150,190
5540 Gasoline service stations [1]	419	1,502	3,056	9,333	6	12,209	13,514	39,418	129,174
5550 Boat dealers [1]	17	27	174	258	10	15,816	17,581	3,544	5,103
5560 Recreational vehicle dealers [3]	8	20	25	132	7	15,680	25,697	428	4,697
5570 Motorcycle dealers [3]	9	32	53	267	8	20,755	18,742	1,389	6,127
5610 Men's & boys' clothing stores [3]	56	268	453	2,651	10	10,464	14,754	4,830	40,833
5620 Women's clothing stores [1]	202	836	2,382	8,730	10	8,322	9,635	23,185	86,835
5630 Women's accessory & specialty stores [3]	42	192	229	1,025	5	11,162	11,329	2,676	11,343
5640 Children's and infants' wear stores [3]	29	141	267	1,568	11	7,446	9,054	2,251	14,866
5650 Family clothing stores [1]	57	285	1,044	5,516	19	9,985	11,211	11,933	66,708
5660 Shoe stores [1]	195	775	1,012	4,012	5	11,577	12,644	12,682	51,888
5690 Misc. apparel & accessory stores [1]	46	168	245	885	5	8,751	11,290	2,225	12,183
5712 Furniture stores [1]	121	558	884	4,300	8	19,869	19,767	18,778	85,860
5713 Floor covering stores [1]	59	240	262	1,273	5	19,802	23,189	5,774	31,375
5714 Drapery and upholstery stores [3]	12	55	45	209	4	16,533	12,459	644	2,628
5719 Misc. homefurnishings stores [3]	74	298	364	1,725	6	11,659	13,282	5,117	23,331
5720 Household appliance stores [1]	44	171	213	2,164	13	18,385	17,275	5,316	36,612
5731 Radio, TV, & electronic stores [1]	62	249	457	2,120	9	16,079	17,287	8,205	36,940
5734 Computer and software stores [3]	32	161	275	1,239	8	15,724	18,308	4,870	24,635
5735 Record & prerecorded tape stores [1]	46	199	245	1,413	7	11,984	10,737	3,147	15,741
5736 Musical instrument stores [3]	10	48	83	363	8	19,277	23,614	1,712	8,563
5812 Eating places [1]	1,418	5,996	22,993	98,789	16	8,362	9,220	211,829	958,711
5813 Drinking places [1]	221	1,369	1,258	6,153	4	9,068	9,116	12,777	58,725
5910 Drug stores and proprietary stores [1]	250	1,161	3,407	15,545	13	14,437	14,709	52,225	240,168
5920 Liquor stores [1]	190	590	1,300	3,132	5	12,338	16,941	16,999	53,896
5930 Used merchandise stores [1]	35	239	248	1,202	5	7,597	13,960	2,154	18,146
5941 Sporting goods and bicycle shops [1]	88	387	641	3,216	8	12,524	12,740	8,860	44,097
5942 Book stores [3]	41	251	394	2,038	8	10,386	12,444	4,144	26,025
5943 Stationery stores [3]	15	90	13	1,158	13	18,462	16,446	259	23,898
5944 Jewelry stores [1]	99	562	414	2,442	4	16,106	18,614	7,269	45,696
5945 Hobby, toy, and game shops [3]	45	184	507	2,243	12	10,335	10,828	6,344	27,483
5946 Camera & photographic supply stores [1]	25	122	108	525	4	11,481	14,377	1,301	7,935
5947 Gift, novelty, and souvenir shops [1]	153	617	798	3,563	6	7,689	8,687	7,908	33,878
5948 Luggage and leather goods stores [3]	5	53	21	214	4	12,952	17,084	253	3,739
5949 Sewing, needlework, and piece goods [1]	22	100	132	910	9	7,545	9,319	1,197	8,637
5961 Catalog and mail-order houses [3]	21	108	239	2,499	23	18,778	39,408	5,397	85,696
5962 Merchandising machine operators [3]	22	110	256	2,271	21	20,563	18,579	5,556	42,715
5963 Direct selling establishments [3]	71	216	656	1,800	8	13,921	15,018	9,407	29,238
5983 Fuel oil dealers [3]	78	249	563	1,875	8	28,306	28,578	15,844	49,593
5984 Liquefied petroleum gas dealers [3]	9	42	110	404	10	24,364	30,386	2,798	12,685
5992 Florists [1]	118	462	628	2,314	5	10,000	11,858	6,755	29,109
5993 Tobacco stores and stands [3]	16	36	54	140	4	7,111	13,600	381	2,218
5994 News dealers and newsstands [1]	24	87	85	276	3	13,129	10,290	1,125	2,772
5995 Optical goods stores [3]	64	343	337	1,569	5	16,843	17,904	6,064	30,578
5999 Miscellaneous retail stores, nec [1]	181	851	876	4,833	6	13,553	15,687	13,603	87,708

Source: County Business Patterns 1994/95, CBP-94/95, U.S. Department of Commerce, Washington DC, November 1997. The employment column represents mid-March employment in the year. Pay per employee is calculated by dividing 1st Quarter payroll, annualized, by mid-March employment. The column headed 'Emp / Est' shows 'employees per establishment'. A dash (-) means that data are unavailable or cannot be calculated. nec means not elsewhere classified. *Notes:* 1. 1994 data incomplete; unavailable or withheld. 2. 1995 data incomplete; unavailable or withheld. 3. 1994 and 1995 data incomplete; unavailable or withheld.

PHOENIX - MESA, AZ MSA

Wholesale and Retail Trade USA	Establishments		Employment		Emp / Est	Pay / Employee		Annual Payroll ($ 000)	
	1994	1995	1994	1995	1995	1994	1995	1994	1995
50 - Wholesale trade	4,979	5,154	62,133	66,799	13	29,458	32,169	1,967,505	2,232,314
5012 Automobiles and other vehicles [3]	88	87	1,719	1,834	21	21,475	24,883	41,561	44,921
5013 Motor vehicle supplies and new parts	243	222	2,473	2,703	12	20,277	21,517	54,541	60,581
5014 Tires and tubes	47	43	432	508	12	27,139	29,724	13,686	14,377
5015 Motor vehicle parts, used	65	76	353	417	5	19,671	22,456	7,394	9,740
5021 Furniture [3]	106	104	986	1,186	11	23,740	24,992	28,725	31,986
5023 Homefurnishings	98	98	1,116	1,232	13	25,265	25,529	33,419	34,505
5031 Lumber, plywood, and millwork [1]	75	79	1,299	1,278	16	33,318	43,368	44,395	44,205
5032 Brick, stone, & related materials	64	66	540	439	7	23,726	28,237	15,369	14,789
5033 Roofing, siding, & insulation [3]	25	28	453	459	16	27,382	26,466	13,424	12,177

Continued on next page.

PHOENIX – MESA, AZ MSA - [continued]

Wholesale and Retail Trade USA	Establishments		Employment		Emp / Est	Pay / Employee		Annual Payroll ($ 000)	
	1994	1995	1994	1995	1995	1994	1995	1994	1995
5039 Construction materials, nec[1]	64	97	647	1,090	11	27,641	29,207	19,589	34,862
5043 Photographic equipment & supplies[3]	10	10	104	121	12	25,923	24,099	2,855	3,275
5044 Office equipment	91	102	1,905	1,768	17	30,005	35,201	63,396	63,178
5045 Computers, peripherals, & software	255	257	4,260	4,878	19	41,117	40,774	190,030	218,827
5046 Commercial equipment, nec[3]	56	61	410	464	8	22,371	23,129	10,674	11,933
5047 Medical and hospital equipment[1]	135	135	1,445	1,213	9	35,637	39,641	54,614	48,285
5048 Ophthalmic goods[3]	20	22	277	268	12	25,415	36,119	6,893	7,677
5049 Professional equipment, nec[3]	31	34	252	298	9	32,937	33,651	9,993	11,226
5051 Metals service centers and offices	75	87	888	845	10	26,171	30,078	23,324	26,517
5052 Coal and other minerals and ores[1]	6	-	44	-	-	53,455	-	2,007	-
5063 Electrical apparatus and equipment	237	199	2,231	2,035	10	31,200	40,680	77,791	82,552
5064 Electrical appliances, TV & radios[3]	49	47	560	673	14	32,886	34,264	19,545	23,487
5065 Electronic parts and equipment	343	361	3,477	3,619	10	36,441	36,955	129,044	138,575
5072 Hardware[3]	90	99	1,134	1,176	12	23,086	28,395	28,612	34,259
5074 Plumbing & hydronic heating supplies[3]	97	94	855	920	10	26,704	30,235	25,511	28,625
5075 Warm air heating & air conditioning[3]	58	63	551	636	10	37,009	41,484	21,763	25,900
5078 Refrigeration equipment and supplies[3]	20	20	139	147	7	29,496	34,122	4,430	5,020
5082 Construction and mining machinery	70	68	1,120	1,244	18	34,025	37,678	42,136	48,978
5083 Farm and garden machinery	58	61	618	777	13	27,107	30,837	18,955	25,387
5084 Industrial machinery and equipment	254	267	2,137	2,446	9	30,124	31,228	69,892	84,098
5085 Industrial supplies	118	117	1,004	1,043	9	27,542	30,961	31,919	38,847
5087 Service establishment equipment[2]	96	98	1,059	1,103	11	23,494	24,780	26,498	27,958
5088 Transportation equipment & supplies[3]	47	47	816	403	9	40,779	35,355	35,920	16,361
5091 Sporting & recreational goods[3]	62	63	414	426	7	18,541	20,244	8,888	9,306
5092 Toys and hobby goods and supplies[3]	27	28	93	90	3	16,258	15,778	1,743	1,658
5093 Scrap and waste materials	79	88	801	1,241	14	17,783	17,138	18,003	25,377
5094 Jewelry & precious stones	69	76	392	402	5	20,765	22,537	8,861	9,855
5099 Durable goods, nec	80	88	871	961	11	34,742	37,136	33,963	39,576
5112 Stationery and office supplies	103	99	1,409	1,777	18	19,577	22,663	27,320	39,845
5120 Drugs, proprietaries, and sundries	97	108	1,396	1,839	17	42,226	64,522	59,786	126,123
5131 Piece goods & notions[3]	30	28	131	137	5	25,588	25,109	2,936	3,020
5136 Men's and boys' clothing[3]	29	29	524	513	18	19,550	20,842	12,007	12,290
5137 Women's and children's clothing[3]	32	29	218	245	8	17,688	19,722	4,313	5,076
5141 Groceries, general line	54	49	3,024	3,000	61	30,476	30,856	94,639	91,200
5142 Packaged frozen food[3]	29	26	627	616	24	33,876	34,948	20,829	20,832
5143 Dairy products, exc. dried or canned[2]	35	30	669	665	22	30,081	31,621	21,226	20,560
5144 Poultry and poultry products[1]	9	-	95	-	-	19,874	-	1,982	-
5145 Confectionery[3]	16	16	400	432	27	28,330	26,352	11,244	11,055
5147 Meats and meat products[3]	33	33	490	474	14	24,931	27,207	13,325	14,086
5148 Fresh fruits and vegetables[3]	49	47	735	749	16	19,701	21,688	18,103	20,483
5149 Groceries and related products, nec	139	150	2,667	3,267	22	27,024	27,545	72,805	89,229
5154 Livestock[3]	7	9	45	36	4	14,400	14,444	687	683
5159 Farm-product raw materials, nec[3]	10	12	49	56	5	28,898	45,786	1,890	3,050
5162 Plastics materials & basic shapes[3]	33	40	363	443	11	24,209	26,149	9,655	12,612
5169 Chemicals & allied products, nec	92	96	915	1,032	11	33,202	34,566	32,284	36,748
5171 Petroleum bulk stations & terminals	39	35	718	618	18	27,426	31,528	20,859	21,160
5172 Petroleum products, nec	22	23	491	522	23	13,923	14,000	9,288	7,893
5181 Beer and ale	9	11	712	874	79	29,438	33,373	24,821	34,991
5182 Wine and distilled beverages[3]	15	14	731	766	55	32,137	35,906	24,337	27,533
5191 Farm supplies	97	81	646	711	9	25,319	37,181	16,837	25,125
5192 Books, periodicals, & newspapers[1]	36	41	518	569	14	22,139	25,989	11,708	14,092
5193 Flowers & florists' supplies[1]	57	51	573	553	11	13,243	14,503	8,334	8,585
5194 Tobacco and tobacco products[1]	7	-	418	-	-	25,053	-	11,770	-
5198 Paints, varnishes, and supplies	44	-	299	-	-	24,187	-	7,955	-
5199 Nondurable goods, nec	170	187	1,079	1,078	6	17,294	21,473	21,603	24,539
52 - Retail trade	13,300	13,543	211,962	223,792	17	13,583	14,692	3,068,821	3,387,984
5210 Lumber and other building materials	137	110	3,736	3,996	36	18,219	21,276	77,379	82,353
5230 Paint, glass, and wallpaper stores	63	59	304	367	6	21,724	21,787	7,158	8,411
5250 Hardware stores	91	73	928	727	10	13,552	13,920	13,814	10,818
5260 Retail nurseries and garden stores	78	82	701	782	10	13,581	13,565	10,505	12,261
5270 Mobile home dealers	46	52	289	375	7	26,796	28,213	10,374	12,127
5310 Department stores[3]	100	102	15,580	17,916	176	11,558	12,737	198,751	228,225
5330 Variety stores	39	37	208	181	5	9,346	9,238	1,873	1,611
5390 Misc. general merchandise stores	72	82	2,736	3,205	39	14,830	16,766	45,270	53,844
5410 Grocery stores	904	901	26,607	27,257	30	15,037	16,786	419,231	459,451
5420 Meat and fish markets[1]	21	18	84	89	5	12,143	12,719	1,111	1,349
5430 Fruit and vegetable markets[2]	15	14	63	72	5	9,206	9,278	605	794
5440 Candy, nut, and confectionery stores[3]	39	42	218	215	5	9,009	9,526	1,994	2,025
5450 Dairy products stores[3]	16	21	134	158	8	5,701	6,430	937	1,226
5460 Retail bakeries	105	100	1,001	787	8	9,051	9,931	9,337	7,555
5490 Miscellaneous food stores	136	149	656	897	6	13,037	13,333	8,843	11,618

Continued on next page.

PHOENIX – MESA, AZ MSA - [continued]

Wholesale and Retail Trade USA	Establishments		Employment		Emp / Est	Pay / Employee		Annual Payroll ($ 000)	
	1994	1995	1994	1995	1995	1994	1995	1994	1995
5510 New and used car dealers	141	143	11,426	12,535	88	31,607	33,013	417,777	469,353
5520 Used car dealers	148	143	762	837	6	21,438	25,128	18,834	23,060
5530 Auto and home supply stores	382	408	4,002	3,999	10	16,786	18,015	74,965	77,191
5540 Gasoline service stations	587	555	5,963	6,447	12	11,991	12,452	76,470	84,115
5550 Boat dealers[3]	22	21	185	192	9	20,000	23,729	4,277	4,461
5560 Recreational vehicle dealers	52	50	557	546	11	21,989	26,784	13,138	14,058
5570 Motorcycle dealers[3]	35	36	302	318	9	19,391	21,962	7,782	8,790
5590 Automotive dealers, nec[3]	11	12	80	95	8	16,950	17,305	2,072	1,964
5610 Men's & boys' clothing stores	116	116	776	949	8	12,015	12,341	9,916	11,902
5620 Women's clothing stores	371	336	3,517	3,107	9	10,036	10,038	36,333	29,278
5630 Women's accessory & specialty stores	67	68	366	418	6	10,087	10,689	3,840	4,299
5640 Children's and infants' wear stores	34	31	277	347	11	7,913	7,988	2,053	2,927
5650 Family clothing stores	171	172	2,640	2,682	16	9,127	9,824	25,991	26,889
5660 Shoe stores	288	281	1,470	1,413	5	12,065	13,081	17,948	18,299
5690 Misc. apparel & accessory stores	135	135	784	739	5	9,459	10,766	7,669	7,939
5712 Furniture stores	338	338	2,902	3,126	9	19,966	20,591	60,286	66,906
5713 Floor covering stores	140	129	659	645	5	19,102	21,960	14,914	15,655
5714 Drapery and upholstery stores[3]	26	24	146	163	7	14,630	18,380	2,656	3,225
5719 Misc. homefurnishings stores	197	212	1,157	1,574	7	14,019	13,911	19,616	24,102
5720 Household appliance stores	74	73	575	440	6	14,136	19,891	8,783	8,912
5731 Radio, TV, & electronic stores	180	186	1,840	2,449	13	17,876	16,438	37,586	41,973
5734 Computer and software stores	90	114	814	748	7	19,258	22,636	16,203	17,601
5735 Record & prerecorded tape stores	79	77	775	736	10	9,383	10,500	7,948	7,760
5736 Musical instrument stores	37	40	222	216	5	18,649	20,648	4,666	5,308
5812 Eating places	3,600	3,472	75,538	76,789	22	8,075	8,796	620,917	676,276
5813 Drinking places	493	433	4,741	4,368	10	6,556	7,408	32,532	32,117
5910 Drug stores and proprietary stores	233	231	4,536	4,555	20	19,701	21,265	88,699	93,730
5920 Liquor stores	101	108	294	332	3	10,082	9,530	3,220	3,359
5930 Used merchandise stores	215	202	1,687	1,617	8	10,207	11,255	20,168	19,507
5941 Sporting goods and bicycle shops	243	249	1,768	2,196	9	11,242	11,508	22,964	26,930
5942 Book stores	134	129	858	944	7	11,012	12,148	9,780	11,457
5943 Stationery stores	54	58	289	473	8	12,111	12,770	4,009	6,860
5944 Jewelry stores	285	292	1,324	1,436	5	18,867	20,549	25,659	28,560
5945 Hobby, toy, and game shops	97	101	1,071	1,232	12	10,289	10,029	12,876	14,240
5946 Camera & photographic supply stores[3]	38	36	195	201	6	15,508	17,453	3,489	3,855
5947 Gift, novelty, and souvenir shops[1]	345	345	2,154	2,157	6	9,064	9,519	20,398	21,443
5948 Luggage and leather goods stores	22	26	130	114	4	11,446	12,000	1,551	1,756
5949 Sewing, needlework, and piece goods	71	66	640	607	9	8,194	8,837	5,295	5,236
5961 Catalog and mail-order houses	80	93	1,531	2,117	23	18,615	17,291	31,315	37,029
5962 Merchandising machine operators	80	77	331	392	5	18,683	19,122	7,681	8,050
5963 Direct selling establishments	121	127	1,889	1,897	15	17,453	17,986	33,606	36,648
5984 Liquefied petroleum gas dealers	20	18	164	193	11	22,634	22,632	3,489	3,799
5992 Florists	175	178	1,036	1,207	7	9,313	9,823	10,271	12,169
5993 Tobacco stores and stands	19	20	157	151	8	12,051	13,007	2,225	2,525
5995 Optical goods stores	167	165	777	787	5	16,607	17,698	13,433	13,556
5999 Miscellaneous retail stores, nec	552	592	2,774	3,204	5	14,787	15,453	45,579	55,229

Source: County Business Patterns 1994/95, CBP-94/95, U.S. Department of Commerce, Washington DC, November 1997. The employment column represents mid-March employment in the year. Pay per employee is calculated by dividing 1st Quarter payroll, annualized, by mid-March employment. The column headed 'Emp / Est' shows 'employees per establishment'. A dash (-) means that data are unavailable or cannot be calculated. nec means not elsewhere classified. *Notes:* 1. 1994 data incomplete; unavailable or withheld. 2. 1995 data incomplete; unavailable or withheld. 3. 1994 and 1995 data incomplete; unavailable or withheld.

PINE BLUFF, AR MSA

Wholesale and Retail Trade USA	Establishments		Employment		Emp / Est	Pay / Employee		Annual Payroll ($ 000)	
	1994	1995	1994	1995	1995	1994	1995	1994	1995
50- Wholesale trade	119	114	1,123	1,120	10	19,569	21,082	24,483	26,104
5013 Motor vehicle supplies and new parts	6	6	34	32	5	14,471	15,375	508	473
5015 Motor vehicle parts, used	4	4	9	11	3	12,889	13,455	137	155
5030 Lumber and construction materials	5	5	129	131	26	19,411	22,443	3,436	3,364
5046 Commercial equipment, nec	-	3	-	12	4	-	17,000	-	330
5060 Electrical goods	8	7	56	46	7	18,643	21,739	1,289	1,304
5074 Plumbing & hydronic heating supplies	3	3	23	23	8	21,217	20,870	432	453
5083 Farm and garden machinery	4	4	32	20	5	18,750	25,600	632	462
5084 Industrial machinery and equipment	5	5	64	69	14	17,250	17,275	1,290	1,221
5085 Industrial supplies	6	8	36	48	6	26,778	26,000	994	1,181
5090 Miscellaneous durable goods	5	-	27	-	-	14,370	-	435	-
5110 Paper and paper products	6	4	59	60	15	21,966	25,533	1,443	1,519
5149 Groceries and related products, nec	3	3	88	82	27	22,818	24,488	1,920	1,988
5159 Farm-product raw materials, nec	-	4	-	8	2	-	27,000	-	210

Continued on next page.

PINE BLUFF, AR MSA - [continued]

Wholesale and Retail Trade USA	Establishments		Employment		Emp / Est	Pay / Employee		Annual Payroll ($ 000)	
	1994	1995	1994	1995	1995	1994	1995	1994	1995
5169 Chemicals & allied products, nec	3	3	35	39	13	19,314	22,256	981	1,254
5171 Petroleum bulk stations & terminals	6	5	103	114	23	16,932	14,842	1,827	1,967
5181 Beer and ale	3	3	58	54	18	22,138	24,889	1,475	1,584
5191 Farm supplies	10	8	74	68	9	19,297	20,471	1,390	1,477
52 – Retail trade	510	510	6,062	6,306	12	10,499	11,080	68,963	72,688
5210 Lumber and other building materials	10	9	156	133	15	13,795	16,692	2,294	2,408
5230 Paint, glass, and wallpaper stores	3	3	17	14	5	20,941	25,143	351	339
5250 Hardware stores	4	3	27	15	5	25,333	10,933	518	162
5270 Mobile home dealers	-	3	-	39	13	-	23,077	-	1,435
5310 Department stores	5	5	844	866	173	10,512	12,005	9,696	10,435
5330 Variety stores	4	-	24	-	-	8,667	-	294	-
5390 Misc. general merchandise stores	3	-	35	-	-	9,371	-	387	-
5410 Grocery stores	50	55	917	985	18	10,111	9,982	10,022	10,507
5420 Meat and fish markets	6	6	11	13	2	10,182	11,692	126	192
5460 Retail bakeries	3	3	22	21	7	9,455	12,190	225	238
5490 Miscellaneous food stores	3	3	17	14	5	5,882	7,143	104	110
5510 New and used car dealers	8	8	311	340	43	24,695	27,294	8,526	9,213
5520 Used car dealers	11	12	45	41	3	17,333	18,732	851	956
5530 Auto and home supply stores	13	12	126	115	10	13,238	15,130	1,822	1,896
5540 Gasoline service stations	43	41	307	324	8	9,003	9,519	3,118	3,014
5550 Boat dealers	3	3	36	43	14	13,889	14,512	578	677
5610 Men's & boys' clothing stores	5	5	20	26	5	12,800	12,000	275	289
5620 Women's clothing stores	22	21	167	164	8	8,311	7,439	1,441	1,142
5630 Women's accessory & specialty stores	-	3	-	14	5	-	5,714	-	98
5640 Children's and infants' wear stores	3	3	15	15	5	5,333	5,067	105	96
5650 Family clothing stores	6	6	204	180	30	7,706	9,178	1,677	1,584
5660 Shoe stores	15	12	71	73	6	9,296	8,712	610	709
5690 Misc. apparel & accessory stores	-	3	-	13	4	-	10,769	-	126
5710 Furniture and homefurnishings stores	20	21	126	132	6	16,952	19,182	2,413	2,617
5731 Radio, TV, & electronic stores	7	7	37	34	5	15,459	15,882	550	463
5735 Record & prerecorded tape stores	3	3	19	21	7	8,000	8,000	173	171
5736 Musical instrument stores	3	3	24	26	9	13,167	13,846	393	459
5812 Eating places	103	101	1,669	1,772	18	6,085	6,142	10,825	11,467
5813 Drinking places	9	8	55	48	6	6,036	6,083	322	251
5910 Drug stores and proprietary stores	18	15	104	111	7	13,192	13,297	1,556	1,481
5920 Liquor stores	23	21	72	90	4	9,722	7,511	735	732
5930 Used merchandise stores	-	15	-	30	2	-	11,067	-	325
5941 Sporting goods and bicycle shops	5	4	14	11	3	10,286	10,545	156	112
5942 Book stores	4	5	25	30	6	10,560	10,133	278	323
5944 Jewelry stores	12	12	108	117	10	20,704	23,145	2,260	2,445
5945 Hobby, toy, and game shops	-	3	-	12	4	-	9,000	-	138
5947 Gift, novelty, and souvenir shops	5	6	30	19	3	7,467	6,737	273	135
5949 Sewing, needlework, and piece goods	3	-	12	-	-	7,333	-	105	-
5960 Nonstore retailers	7	5	110	113	23	13,236	13,805	1,005	1,639
5992 Florists	5	6	40	45	8	12,800	12,889	622	665
5999 Miscellaneous retail stores, nec	12	13	44	42	3	11,636	14,190	642	761

Source: County Business Patterns 1994/95, CBP-94/95, U.S. Department of Commerce, Washington DC, November 1997. The employment column represents mid-March employment in the year. Pay per employee is calculated by dividing 1st Quarter payroll, annualized, by mid-March employment. The column headed 'Emp / Est' shows 'employees per establishment'. A dash (-) means that data are unavailable or cannot be calculated. nec means not elsewhere classified. *Notes:* 1. 1994 data incomplete; unavailable or withheld. 2. 1995 data incomplete; unavailable or withheld. 3. 1994 and 1995 data incomplete; unavailable or withheld.

PITTSBURGH, PA MSA

Wholesale and Retail Trade USA	Establishments		Employment		Emp / Est	Pay / Employee		Annual Payroll ($ 000)	
	1994	1995	1994	1995	1995	1994	1995	1994	1995
50 – Wholesale trade	-	4,315	-	56,535	13	-	33,906	-	1,961,754
5012 Automobiles and other vehicles	-	73	-	1,484	20	-	27,224	-	39,292
5013 Motor vehicle supplies and new parts	-	229	-	2,228	10	-	22,903	-	54,388
5014 Tires and tubes	-	34	-	402	12	-	23,184	-	9,176
5015 Motor vehicle parts, used	-	77	-	328	4	-	19,415	-	6,822
5021 Furniture [2]	-	44	-	433	10	-	24,684	-	12,292
5023 Homefurnishings [2]	-	50	-	861	17	-	25,069	-	21,974
5031 Lumber, plywood, and millwork	-	60	-	703	12	-	31,562	-	22,641
5032 Brick, stone, & related materials [2]	-	35	-	191	5	-	29,654	-	5,764
5033 Roofing, siding, & insulation [2]	-	29	-	322	11	-	55,267	-	15,228
5039 Construction materials, nec	-	70	-	1,195	17	-	30,882	-	38,353
5043 Photographic equipment & supplies [2]	-	10	-	74	7	-	27,297	-	2,058
5044 Office equipment	-	64	-	1,416	22	-	40,907	-	52,010
5045 Computers, peripherals, & software [2]	-	148	-	1,929	13	-	55,494	-	101,349

Continued on next page.

PITTSBURGH, PA MSA - [continued]

Wholesale and Retail Trade USA	Establishments		Employment		Emp / Est	Pay / Employee		Annual Payroll ($ 000)	
	1994	1995	1994	1995	1995	1994	1995	1994	1995
5046 Commercial equipment, nec	-	59	-	347	6	-	30,571	-	11,063
5047 Medical and hospital equipment	-	89	-	1,465	16	-	41,423	-	62,679
5048 Ophthalmic goods [2]	-	15	-	239	16	-	23,782	-	6,267
5049 Professional equipment, nec [2]	-	29	-	386	13	-	35,617	-	14,399
5051 Metals service centers and offices [2]	-	200	-	2,284	11	-	49,173	-	114,983
5052 Coal and other minerals and ores	-	39	-	174	4	-	44,989	-	8,668
5063 Electrical apparatus and equipment	-	184	-	2,420	13	-	44,436	-	101,971
5064 Electrical appliances, TV & radios [2]	-	24	-	296	12	-	32,622	-	9,379
5065 Electronic parts and equipment	-	120	-	1,202	10	-	36,403	-	45,927
5072 Hardware [2]	-	80	-	1,017	13	-	27,229	-	31,678
5074 Plumbing & hydronic heating supplies	-	125	-	994	8	-	28,523	-	27,853
5075 Warm air heating & air conditioning	-	65	-	488	8	-	36,680	-	18,456
5078 Refrigeration equipment and supplies [2]	-	11	-	65	6	-	35,569	-	2,669
5082 Construction and mining machinery [2]	-	63	-	1,398	22	-	32,461	-	44,329
5083 Farm and garden machinery	-	36	-	284	8	-	19,620	-	6,080
5084 Industrial machinery and equipment	-	368	-	3,579	10	-	37,722	-	141,936
5085 Industrial supplies	-	219	-	2,167	10	-	38,525	-	88,250
5087 Service establishment equipment	-	78	-	614	8	-	27,453	-	17,284
5088 Transportation equipment & supplies [2]	-	7	-	33	5	-	28,121	-	960
5091 Sporting & recreational goods [2]	-	35	-	215	6	-	23,981	-	6,358
5092 Toys and hobby goods and supplies [2]	-	18	-	126	7	-	13,968	-	1,807
5093 Scrap and waste materials	-	150	-	1,706	11	-	34,317	-	63,950
5094 Jewelry & precious stones [2]	-	33	-	171	5	-	25,123	-	4,509
5099 Durable goods, nec [2]	-	71	-	313	4	-	23,629	-	7,393
5111 Printing and writing paper [2]	-	12	-	139	12	-	29,496	-	4,151
5112 Stationery and office supplies [2]	-	87	-	1,264	15	-	25,937	-	32,836
5113 Industrial & personal service paper [2]	-	40	-	366	9	-	42,896	-	16,170
5120 Drugs, proprietaries, and sundries [2]	-	33	-	1,033	31	-	37,464	-	40,280
5136 Men's and boys' clothing [2]	-	15	-	202	13	-	25,624	-	5,144
5141 Groceries, general line [2]	-	48	-	957	20	-	27,390	-	28,483
5142 Packaged frozen food [2]	-	33	-	837	25	-	23,384	-	20,323
5143 Dairy products, exc. dried or canned	-	12	-	110	9	-	23,818	-	2,569
5144 Poultry and poultry products [2]	-	6	-	22	4	-	26,182	-	727
5145 Confectionery	-	33	-	322	10	-	24,248	-	7,909
5147 Meats and meat products [2]	-	27	-	166	6	-	33,181	-	6,263
5148 Fresh fruits and vegetables [2]	-	37	-	552	15	-	24,167	-	14,780
5149 Groceries and related products, nec	-	84	-	2,074	25	-	30,864	-	63,566
5150 Farm-product raw materials [2]	-	8	-	26	3	-	30,000	-	691
5162 Plastics materials & basic shapes [2]	-	23	-	229	10	-	28,087	-	7,357
5169 Chemicals & allied products, nec	-	116	-	1,351	12	-	47,994	-	65,404
5171 Petroleum bulk stations & terminals [2]	-	56	-	664	12	-	33,645	-	23,889
5172 Petroleum products, nec	-	25	-	151	6	-	39,311	-	5,890
5181 Beer and ale	-	76	-	774	10	-	26,052	-	20,747
5182 Wine and distilled beverages [2]	-	12	-	65	5	-	24,492	-	1,649
5191 Farm supplies	-	52	-	392	8	-	19,204	-	8,846
5192 Books, periodicals, & newspapers [2]	-	30	-	379	13	-	30,121	-	12,033
5193 Flowers & florists' supplies	-	26	-	275	11	-	17,207	-	4,850
5194 Tobacco and tobacco products	-	20	-	440	22	-	20,655	-	9,612
5198 Paints, varnishes, and supplies	-	25	-	109	4	-	27,046	-	2,922
5199 Nondurable goods, nec	-	139	-	504	4	-	21,889	-	13,640
52 – Retail trade	-	14,158	-	202,758	14	-	11,951	-	2,567,480
5210 Lumber and other building materials	-	218	-	4,203	19	-	18,306	-	81,413
5230 Paint, glass, and wallpaper stores	-	75	-	298	4	-	15,745	-	5,183
5250 Hardware stores	-	152	-	1,279	8	-	11,418	-	15,641
5260 Retail nurseries and garden stores	-	125	-	673	5	-	9,967	-	10,596
5270 Mobile home dealers	-	25	-	74	3	-	17,459	-	1,634
5310 Department stores	-	121	-	18,709	155	-	11,739	-	230,114
5330 Variety stores [2]	-	115	-	1,024	9	-	8,789	-	9,407
5390 Misc. general merchandise stores [2]	-	58	-	1,540	27	-	12,117	-	18,405
5410 Grocery stores	-	995	-	29,938	30	-	10,740	-	339,812
5420 Meat and fish markets [2]	-	65	-	412	6	-	11,981	-	5,164
5430 Fruit and vegetable markets	-	30	-	198	7	-	6,990	-	1,477
5440 Candy, nut, and confectionery stores	-	73	-	498	7	-	7,382	-	3,603
5450 Dairy products stores [2]	-	37	-	175	5	-	4,549	-	963
5460 Retail bakeries	-	208	-	2,254	11	-	8,128	-	19,017
5490 Miscellaneous food stores	-	88	-	489	6	-	8,074	-	4,536
5510 New and used car dealers	-	289	-	10,880	38	-	23,460	-	286,341
5520 Used car dealers	-	142	-	495	3	-	15,087	-	8,457
5530 Auto and home supply stores	-	369	-	2,352	6	-	17,265	-	43,439
5540 Gasoline service stations	-	813	-	5,895	7	-	9,855	-	61,527
5550 Boat dealers [2]	-	19	-	78	4	-	11,026	-	1,227

Continued on next page.

PITTSBURGH, PA MSA - [continued]

Wholesale and Retail Trade USA	Establishments		Employment		Emp / Est	Pay / Employee		Annual Payroll ($ 000)	
	1994	1995	1994	1995	1995	1994	1995	1994	1995
5560 Recreational vehicle dealers [2]	-	14	-	82	6	-	17,268	-	1,777
5570 Motorcycle dealers	-	39	-	239	6	-	13,305	-	4,299
5610 Men's & boys' clothing stores	-	106	-	743	7	-	14,681	-	9,885
5620 Women's clothing stores	-	395	-	4,346	11	-	12,152	-	48,899
5630 Women's accessory & specialty stores	-	78	-	487	6	-	9,758	-	4,836
5640 Children's and infants' wear stores [2]	-	40	-	341	9	-	7,730	-	2,562
5650 Family clothing stores	-	123	-	2,242	18	-	9,513	-	21,031
5660 Shoe stores	-	343	-	1,701	5	-	11,577	-	19,544
5690 Misc. apparel & accessory stores	-	91	-	647	7	-	11,066	-	6,200
5712 Furniture stores	-	244	-	2,410	10	-	17,650	-	44,317
5713 Floor covering stores	-	133	-	683	5	-	19,578	-	16,480
5714 Drapery and upholstery stores [2]	-	18	-	48	3	-	9,667	-	576
5719 Misc. homefurnishings stores	-	122	-	821	7	-	11,074	-	9,645
5720 Household appliance stores	-	78	-	435	6	-	14,685	-	6,625
5731 Radio, TV, & electronic stores	-	126	-	1,009	8	-	20,119	-	18,336
5734 Computer and software stores	-	62	-	489	8	-	17,726	-	9,789
5735 Record & prerecorded tape stores	-	88	-	532	6	-	9,639	-	4,695
5736 Musical instrument stores	-	38	-	118	3	-	15,356	-	2,300
5812 Eating places	-	3,065	-	62,651	20	-	7,690	-	509,762
5813 Drinking places	-	890	-	3,540	4	-	7,202	-	26,735
5910 Drug stores and proprietary stores	-	555	-	6,945	13	-	13,667	-	100,451
5920 Liquor stores	-	315	-	1,353	4	-	16,216	-	22,305
5930 Used merchandise stores	-	115	-	906	8	-	9,174	-	8,872
5941 Sporting goods and bicycle shops	-	228	-	1,451	6	-	11,088	-	18,828
5942 Book stores [2]	-	108	-	759	7	-	8,769	-	7,300
5943 Stationery stores	-	28	-	94	3	-	8,426	-	1,011
5944 Jewelry stores	-	243	-	1,294	5	-	15,737	-	21,925
5945 Hobby, toy, and game shops	-	102	-	917	9	-	8,209	-	9,030
5946 Camera & photographic supply stores [2]	-	25	-	134	5	-	14,448	-	1,960
5947 Gift, novelty, and souvenir shops	-	311	-	1,946	6	-	8,199	-	17,024
5948 Luggage and leather goods stores [2]	-	14	-	106	8	-	15,623	-	1,670
5949 Sewing, needlework, and piece goods	-	62	-	517	8	-	7,095	-	3,597
5961 Catalog and mail-order houses [2]	-	37	-	1,219	33	-	21,011	-	28,439
5962 Merchandising machine operators	-	77	-	1,117	15	-	15,527	-	17,863
5963 Direct selling establishments	-	96	-	1,583	16	-	12,354	-	20,355
5983 Fuel oil dealers	-	36	-	112	3	-	15,107	-	1,607
5984 Liquefied petroleum gas dealers [2]	-	17	-	12	1	-	19,333	-	228
5992 Florists	-	333	-	1,637	5	-	9,349	-	16,027
5993 Tobacco stores and stands [2]	-	25	-	71	3	-	8,789	-	706
5994 News dealers and newsstands	-	64	-	243	4	-	7,901	-	1,931
5995 Optical goods stores	-	144	-	734	5	-	15,548	-	12,081
5999 Miscellaneous retail stores, nec	-	397	-	1,946	5	-	13,328	-	28,853

Source: County Business Patterns 1994/95, CBP-94/95, U.S. Department of Commerce, Washington DC, November 1997. The employment column represents mid-March employment in the year. Pay per employee is calculated by dividing 1st Quarter payroll, annualized, by mid-March employment. The column headed 'Emp / Est' shows 'employees per establishment'. A dash (-) means that data are unavailable or cannot be calculated. nec means not elsewhere classified. *Notes:* 1. 1994 data incomplete; unavailable or withheld. 2. 1995 data incomplete; unavailable or withheld. 3. 1994 and 1995 data incomplete; unavailable or withheld.

PORTLAND - VANCOUVER PMSA (OR PART)

Wholesale and Retail Trade USA	Establishments		Employment		Emp / Est	Pay / Employee		Annual Payroll ($ 000)	
	1994	1995	1994	1995	1995	1994	1995	1994	1995
50- Wholesale trade	-	4,049	-	60,875	15	-	35,955	-	2,221,063
5012 Automobiles and other vehicles [2]	-	76	-	1,462	19	-	37,376	-	55,087
5013 Motor vehicle supplies and new parts	-	165	-	2,548	15	-	25,706	-	71,258
5014 Tires and tubes [2]	-	28	-	253	9	-	31,905	-	7,472
5015 Motor vehicle parts, used [2]	-	57	-	303	5	-	24,172	-	7,511
5021 Furniture [2]	-	56	-	398	7	-	30,864	-	13,106
5023 Homefurnishings [2]	-	81	-	824	10	-	26,738	-	24,517
5031 Lumber, plywood, and millwork [2]	-	207	-	3,100	15	-	63,418	-	147,803
5032 Brick, stone, & related materials [2]	-	24	-	204	9	-	31,765	-	7,238
5033 Roofing, siding, & insulation [2]	-	27	-	335	12	-	29,600	-	11,387
5039 Construction materials, nec [2]	-	62	-	930	15	-	31,613	-	29,667
5043 Photographic equipment & supplies [2]	-	12	-	55	5	-	28,509	-	1,497
5044 Office equipment [2]	-	61	-	1,365	22	-	35,209	-	47,273
5045 Computers, peripherals, & software [2]	-	180	-	2,022	11	-	49,096	-	101,201
5046 Commercial equipment, nec [2]	-	58	-	695	12	-	28,167	-	21,183
5047 Medical and hospital equipment	-	90	-	672	7	-	38,173	-	26,292
5048 Ophthalmic goods [2]	-	17	-	128	8	-	22,406	-	3,263
5049 Professional equipment, nec [2]	-	29	-	209	7	-	25,952	-	5,884

Continued on next page.

PORTLAND - VANCOUVER PMSA (OR PART) - [continued]

Wholesale and Retail Trade USA	Establishments		Employment		Emp / Est	Pay / Employee		Annual Payroll ($ 000)	
	1994	1995	1994	1995	1995	1994	1995	1994	1995
5051 Metals service centers and offices [2]	-	71	-	132	2	-	26,394	-	4,316
5063 Electrical apparatus and equipment [2]	-	139	-	1,712	12	-	35,643	-	62,813
5064 Electrical appliances, TV & radios [2]	-	28	-	428	15	-	31,897	-	11,206
5065 Electronic parts and equipment [2]	-	194	-	2,121	11	-	40,036	-	93,826
5072 Hardware [2]	-	93	-	925	10	-	28,947	-	29,419
5074 Plumbing & hydronic heating supplies [2]	-	69	-	1,070	16	-	35,024	-	39,166
5075 Warm air heating & air conditioning [2]	-	32	-	574	18	-	34,383	-	19,571
5078 Refrigeration equipment and supplies [2]	-	8	-	78	10	-	36,000	-	2,634
5082 Construction and mining machinery	-	53	-	953	18	-	43,824	-	42,758
5083 Farm and garden machinery	-	37	-	342	9	-	25,801	-	9,696
5084 Industrial machinery and equipment	-	255	-	2,736	11	-	36,887	-	106,652
5085 Industrial supplies [2]	-	152	-	1,845	12	-	34,047	-	66,225
5087 Service establishment equipment [2]	-	62	-	651	11	-	28,233	-	19,262
5088 Transportation equipment & supplies [2]	-	37	-	492	13	-	29,154	-	15,412
5091 Sporting & recreational goods [2]	-	72	-	528	7	-	27,545	-	15,906
5092 Toys and hobby goods and supplies [2]	-	19	-	193	10	-	14,902	-	3,868
5093 Scrap and waste materials	-	68	-	1,248	18	-	25,994	-	32,046
5094 Jewelry & precious stones [2]	-	26	-	128	5	-	17,188	-	2,568
5099 Durable goods, nec	-	88	-	535	6	-	30,490	-	17,456
5111 Printing and writing paper [2]	-	25	-	352	14	-	44,693	-	15,479
5112 Stationery and office supplies [2]	-	79	-	1,427	18	-	31,512	-	40,798
5113 Industrial & personal service paper [2]	-	38	-	259	7	-	48,154	-	13,186
5120 Drugs, proprietaries, and sundries [2]	-	61	-	932	15	-	30,283	-	28,356
5136 Men's and boys' clothing [2]	-	29	-	54	2	-	20,815	-	818
5137 Women's and children's clothing [2]	-	16	-	340	21	-	46,988	-	16,066
5141 Groceries, general line [2]	-	47	-	1,930	41	-	32,184	-	62,082
5142 Packaged frozen food [2]	-	28	-	593	21	-	31,609	-	20,053
5143 Dairy products, exc. dried or canned	-	18	-	311	17	-	26,071	-	9,511
5145 Confectionery [2]	-	16	-	381	24	-	27,087	-	11,379
5146 Fish and seafoods [2]	-	12	-	155	13	-	22,477	-	3,663
5147 Meats and meat products [2]	-	36	-	458	13	-	28,541	-	13,831
5148 Fresh fruits and vegetables [2]	-	36	-	869	24	-	22,283	-	23,121
5149 Groceries and related products, nec [2]	-	110	-	1,991	18	-	27,379	-	56,199
5153 Grain and field beans [2]	-	28	-	263	9	-	47,103	-	11,919
5162 Plastics materials & basic shapes	-	32	-	218	7	-	31,615	-	7,575
5169 Chemicals & allied products, nec [2]	-	79	-	800	10	-	32,510	-	28,235
5171 Petroleum bulk stations & terminals [2]	-	40	-	368	9	-	41,380	-	13,209
5172 Petroleum products, nec [2]	-	17	-	145	9	-	27,421	-	4,685
5181 Beer and ale [2]	-	9	-	434	48	-	27,779	-	13,570
5182 Wine and distilled beverages [2]	-	23	-	300	13	-	23,547	-	7,892
5191 Farm supplies	-	62	-	648	10	-	26,728	-	17,638
5192 Books, periodicals, & newspapers [2]	-	47	-	539	11	-	30,486	-	16,146
5193 Flowers & florists' supplies	-	34	-	327	10	-	16,183	-	5,281
5198 Paints, varnishes, and supplies [2]	-	26	-	169	7	-	30,864	-	4,986
5199 Nondurable goods, nec	-	106	-	1,003	9	-	19,741	-	23,225
52- Retail trade	-	8,945	-	132,809	15	-	15,241	-	2,122,800
5210 Lumber and other building materials	-	135	-	2,586	19	-	20,957	-	58,727
5230 Paint, glass, and wallpaper stores	-	58	-	319	6	-	22,144	-	7,940
5250 Hardware stores [2]	-	53	-	478	9	-	13,824	-	6,448
5260 Retail nurseries and garden stores	-	76	-	527	7	-	14,338	-	9,312
5270 Mobile home dealers	-	23	-	278	12	-	32,000	-	9,600
5310 Department stores [2]	-	54	-	10,808	200	-	14,161	-	162,798
5330 Variety stores [2]	-	23	-	198	9	-	9,939	-	2,064
5390 Misc. general merchandise stores	-	48	-	1,969	41	-	21,410	-	43,952
5410 Grocery stores	-	683	-	13,389	20	-	15,407	-	210,299
5420 Meat and fish markets [2]	-	24	-	87	4	-	15,448	-	1,516
5430 Fruit and vegetable markets	-	13	-	97	7	-	16,165	-	1,858
5440 Candy, nut, and confectionery stores [2]	-	34	-	165	5	-	9,673	-	1,758
5450 Dairy products stores [2]	-	23	-	72	3	-	6,556	-	625
5460 Retail bakeries	-	65	-	509	8	-	11,749	-	6,261
5490 Miscellaneous food stores [2]	-	98	-	614	6	-	10,215	-	6,730
5510 New and used car dealers	-	123	-	6,176	50	-	30,895	-	218,182
5520 Used car dealers	-	72	-	476	7	-	24,319	-	13,373
5530 Auto and home supply stores	-	235	-	2,024	9	-	24,462	-	46,873
5540 Gasoline service stations	-	350	-	4,348	12	-	10,727	-	49,140
5550 Boat dealers [2]	-	33	-	203	6	-	21,596	-	4,934
5560 Recreational vehicle dealers	-	39	-	419	11	-	21,833	-	12,246
5570 Motorcycle dealers [2]	-	25	-	135	5	-	19,704	-	3,123
5590 Automotive dealers, nec [2]	-	10	-	55	6	-	33,964	-	1,801
5610 Men's & boys' clothing stores	-	66	-	417	6	-	14,935	-	6,448
5620 Women's clothing stores	-	176	-	1,514	9	-	10,473	-	16,020

Continued on next page.

PORTLAND - VANCOUVER PMSA (OR PART) - [continued]

Wholesale and Retail Trade USA	Establishments		Employment		Emp / Est	Pay / Employee		Annual Payroll ($ 000)	
	1994	1995	1994	1995	1995	1994	1995	1994	1995
5630 Women's accessory & specialty stores [2]	-	41	-	221	5	-	11,710	-	2,636
5640 Children's and infants' wear stores [2]	-	28	-	426	15	-	16,103	-	6,776
5650 Family clothing stores	-	110	-	4,251	39	-	12,784	-	55,574
5660 Shoe stores	-	123	-	830	7	-	12,670	-	10,508
5690 Misc. apparel & accessory stores [2]	-	52	-	296	6	-	12,189	-	4,245
5712 Furniture stores	-	187	-	1,687	9	-	22,293	-	36,125
5713 Floor covering stores	-	91	-	638	7	-	22,219	-	15,068
5714 Drapery and upholstery stores [2]	-	12	-	31	3	-	16,903	-	579
5719 Misc. homefurnishings stores	-	154	-	1,044	7	-	13,245	-	14,570
5720 Household appliance stores	-	56	-	471	8	-	20,875	-	10,741
5731 Radio, TV, & electronic stores	-	113	-	1,311	12	-	18,783	-	26,166
5734 Computer and software stores	-	60	-	336	6	-	22,310	-	8,422
5735 Record & prerecorded tape stores [2]	-	46	-	388	8	-	12,918	-	5,429
5736 Musical instrument stores [2]	-	38	-	205	5	-	16,780	-	4,481
5812 Eating places	-	2,341	-	43,416	19	-	8,952	-	410,373
5813 Drinking places	-	335	-	2,821	8	-	9,414	-	28,170
5910 Drug stores and proprietary stores	-	141	-	1,845	13	-	17,455	-	33,286
5920 Liquor stores	-	142	-	413	3	-	11,864	-	5,156
5930 Used merchandise stores	-	158	-	1,178	7	-	11,800	-	14,538
5941 Sporting goods and bicycle shops	-	164	-	1,485	9	-	12,762	-	19,758
5942 Book stores	-	109	-	1,012	9	-	13,798	-	13,986
5943 Stationery stores [2]	-	25	-	46	2	-	18,087	-	694
5944 Jewelry stores	-	116	-	742	6	-	22,706	-	16,258
5945 Hobby, toy, and game shops	-	75	-	976	13	-	10,176	-	11,673
5946 Camera & photographic supply stores [2]	-	12	-	21	2	-	18,286	-	468
5947 Gift, novelty, and souvenir shops [2]	-	202	-	1,136	6	-	9,852	-	11,697
5948 Luggage and leather goods stores [2]	-	20	-	106	5	-	16,377	-	2,470
5949 Sewing, needlework, and piece goods	-	44	-	441	10	-	8,916	-	3,981
5961 Catalog and mail-order houses [2]	-	67	-	994	15	-	25,252	-	26,805
5962 Merchandising machine operators	-	39	-	424	11	-	21,311	-	9,542
5963 Direct selling establishments [2]	-	110	-	727	7	-	15,818	-	12,388
5983 Fuel oil dealers [2]	-	18	-	164	9	-	27,244	-	4,309
5992 Florists	-	147	-	712	5	-	9,590	-	6,936
5993 Tobacco stores and stands [2]	-	13	-	57	4	-	17,825	-	984
5994 News dealers and newsstands [2]	-	9	-	23	3	-	18,087	-	435
5995 Optical goods stores [2]	-	96	-	423	4	-	19,697	-	8,946
5999 Miscellaneous retail stores, nec	-	290	-	1,570	5	-	15,279	-	25,403

Source: County Business Patterns 1994/95, CBP-94/95, U.S. Department of Commerce, Washington DC, November 1997. The employment column represents mid-March employment in the year. Pay per employee is calculated by dividing 1st Quarter payroll, annualized, by mid-March employment. The column headed 'Emp / Est' shows 'employees per establishment'. A dash (-) means that data are unavailable or cannot be calculated. nec means not elsewhere classified. *Notes:* 1. 1994 data incomplete; unavailable or withheld. 2. 1995 data incomplete; unavailable or withheld. 3. 1994 and 1995 data incomplete; unavailable or withheld.

PORTLAND - VANCOUVER PMSA (WA PART)

Wholesale and Retail Trade USA	Establishments		Employment		Emp / Est	Pay / Employee		Annual Payroll ($ 000)	
	1994	1995	1994	1995	1995	1994	1995	1994	1995
50 - Wholesale trade	-	469	-	3,588	8	-	32,107	-	126,176
5013 Motor vehicle supplies and new parts	-	18	-	147	8	-	19,619	-	3,534
5015 Motor vehicle parts, used	-	8	-	22	3	-	19,818	-	431
5021 Furniture	-	4	-	75	19	-	16,000	-	1,348
5031 Lumber, plywood, and millwork	-	19	-	94	5	-	42,383	-	3,899
5032 Brick, stone, & related materials	-	6	-	78	13	-	19,897	-	1,817
5033 Roofing, siding, & insulation	-	4	-	33	8	-	36,364	-	1,307
5039 Construction materials, nec	-	16	-	153	10	-	22,588	-	3,717
5044 Office equipment	-	4	-	21	5	-	40,381	-	817
5045 Computers, peripherals, & software	-	20	-	172	9	-	37,023	-	6,561
5046 Commercial equipment, nec	-	6	-	67	11	-	27,701	-	2,151
5047 Medical and hospital equipment	-	10	-	102	10	-	33,451	-	5,118
5050 Metals and minerals, except petroleum	-	16	-	161	10	-	34,360	-	5,874
5065 Electronic parts and equipment	-	16	-	136	9	-	40,176	-	6,791
5072 Hardware	-	10	-	63	6	-	26,540	-	2,236
5074 Plumbing & hydronic heating supplies	-	9	-	109	12	-	29,138	-	3,214
5082 Construction and mining machinery	-	5	-	54	11	-	35,630	-	2,193
5083 Farm and garden machinery	-	6	-	29	5	-	52,276	-	1,266
5084 Industrial machinery and equipment	-	43	-	221	5	-	37,756	-	9,941
5085 Industrial supplies	-	17	-	103	6	-	48,660	-	4,059
5087 Service establishment equipment	-	9	-	43	5	-	16,651	-	723
5091 Sporting & recreational goods	-	5	-	64	13	-	21,875	-	1,571
5093 Scrap and waste materials	-	12	-	77	6	-	21,766	-	1,672

Continued on next page.

PORTLAND - VANCOUVER PMSA (WA PART) - [continued]

Wholesale and Retail Trade USA	Establishments		Employment		Emp / Est	Pay / Employee		Annual Payroll ($ 000)	
	1994	1995	1994	1995	1995	1994	1995	1994	1995
5099 Durable goods, nec	-	9	-	31	3	-	16,129	-	510
5111 Printing and writing paper	-	4	-	21	5	-	38,476	-	754
5113 Industrial & personal service paper	-	8	-	21	3	-	37,905	-	797
5120 Drugs, proprietaries, and sundries	-	8	-	246	31	-	34,114	-	7,924
5130 Apparel, piece goods, and notions	-	6	-	37	6	-	13,189	-	479
5145 Confectionery	-	3	-	27	9	-	29,926	-	987
5146 Fish and seafoods	-	4	-	11	3	-	18,545	-	194
5147 Meats and meat products	-	6	-	45	8	-	21,422	-	1,128
5149 Groceries and related products, nec	-	10	-	154	15	-	32,727	-	5,429
5162 Plastics materials & basic shapes	-	3	-	43	14	-	20,837	-	1,077
5171 Petroleum bulk stations & terminals	-	5	-	40	8	-	36,300	-	1,537
5181 Beer and ale	-	5	-	107	21	-	27,215	-	3,267
5191 Farm supplies	-	12	-	100	8	-	20,920	-	2,326
5192 Books, periodicals, & newspapers	-	6	-	17	3	-	17,412	-	445
5199 Nondurable goods, nec	-	17	-	52	3	-	14,846	-	819
52- Retail trade	-	1,320	-	18,868	14	-	13,090	-	260,315
5210 Lumber and other building materials	-	24	-	442	18	-	21,864	-	9,977
5230 Paint, glass, and wallpaper stores	-	13	-	71	5	-	21,634	-	1,677
5250 Hardware stores	-	9	-	41	5	-	9,756	-	425
5260 Retail nurseries and garden stores	-	14	-	64	5	-	13,188	-	1,258
5270 Mobile home dealers	-	9	-	53	6	-	26,717	-	1,706
5310 Department stores	-	11	-	2,042	186	-	13,753	-	29,565
5410 Grocery stores	-	126	-	2,596	21	-	16,374	-	42,314
5440 Candy, nut, and confectionery stores	-	4	-	16	4	-	11,250	-	183
5450 Dairy products stores	-	3	-	65	22	-	13,415	-	928
5460 Retail bakeries	-	9	-	59	7	-	12,407	-	734
5510 New and used car dealers	-	14	-	1,308	93	-	21,737	-	33,268
5520 Used car dealers	-	9	-	33	4	-	20,242	-	928
5530 Auto and home supply stores	-	43	-	332	8	-	25,506	-	8,442
5540 Gasoline service stations	-	55	-	439	8	-	12,565	-	5,672
5560 Recreational vehicle dealers	-	5	-	57	11	-	22,105	-	1,069
5620 Women's clothing stores	-	19	-	133	7	-	8,331	-	1,125
5630 Women's accessory & specialty stores	-	4	-	19	5	-	7,368	-	147
5650 Family clothing stores	-	14	-	432	31	-	12,111	-	5,055
5660 Shoe stores	-	14	-	49	4	-	11,673	-	681
5690 Misc. apparel & accessory stores	-	4	-	8	2	-	8,500	-	72
5712 Furniture stores	-	34	-	244	7	-	18,902	-	4,718
5719 Misc. homefurnishings stores	-	18	-	94	5	-	11,660	-	1,428
5720 Household appliance stores	-	10	-	21	2	-	21,524	-	446
5731 Radio, TV, & electronic stores	-	11	-	49	4	-	14,776	-	704
5735 Record & prerecorded tape stores	-	9	-	104	12	-	9,462	-	1,070
5812 Eating places	-	348	-	6,684	19	-	7,963	-	56,056
5813 Drinking places	-	54	-	416	8	-	8,990	-	3,627
5910 Drug stores and proprietary stores	-	31	-	652	21	-	18,086	-	11,681
5930 Used merchandise stores	-	28	-	178	6	-	14,112	-	2,676
5941 Sporting goods and bicycle shops	-	20	-	126	6	-	10,952	-	1,658
5942 Book stores	-	15	-	54	4	-	10,000	-	558
5944 Jewelry stores	-	16	-	89	6	-	12,584	-	1,283
5945 Hobby, toy, and game shops	-	10	-	109	11	-	10,275	-	1,017
5947 Gift, novelty, and souvenir shops	-	23	-	137	6	-	8,380	-	1,302
5949 Sewing, needlework, and piece goods	-	8	-	82	10	-	7,756	-	601
5961 Catalog and mail-order houses	-	10	-	67	7	-	20,537	-	1,400
5962 Merchandising machine operators	-	5	-	13	3	-	5,846	-	88
5963 Direct selling establishments	-	18	-	56	3	-	13,286	-	972
5983 Fuel oil dealers	-	4	-	21	5	-	31,429	-	847
5984 Liquefied petroleum gas dealers	-	4	-	25	6	-	18,400	-	442
5992 Florists	-	22	-	133	6	-	8,571	-	1,154
5995 Optical goods stores	-	7	-	34	5	-	16,000	-	501
5999 Miscellaneous retail stores, nec	-	41	-	275	7	-	13,687	-	4,213

Source: County Business Patterns 1994/95, CBP-94/95, U.S. Department of Commerce, Washington DC, November 1997. The employment column represents mid-March employment in the year. Pay per employee is calculated by dividing 1st Quarter payroll, annualized, by mid-March employment. The column headed 'Emp / Est' shows 'employees per establishment'. A dash (-) means that data are unavailable or cannot be calculated. nec means not elsewhere classified. *Notes:* 1. 1994 data incomplete; unavailable or withheld. 2. 1995 data incomplete; unavailable or withheld. 3. 1994 and 1995 data incomplete; unavailable or withheld.

PORTLAND – VANCOUVER, OR – WA PMSA

Wholesale and Retail Trade USA	Establishments		Employment		Emp / Est	Pay / Employee		Annual Payroll ($ 000)	
	1994	1995	1994	1995	1995	1994	1995	1994	1995
50 – Wholesale trade	-	4,518	-	64,463	14	-	35,741	-	2,347,239
5012 Automobiles and other vehicles [2]	-	77	-	1,462	19	-	37,376	-	55,087
5013 Motor vehicle supplies and new parts	-	183	-	2,695	15	-	25,374	-	74,792
5014 Tires and tubes [2]	-	32	-	253	8	-	31,905	-	7,472
5015 Motor vehicle parts, used [2]	-	65	-	325	5	-	23,877	-	7,942
5021 Furniture [2]	-	60	-	473	8	-	28,507	-	14,454
5023 Homefurnishings [2]	-	83	-	824	10	-	26,738	-	24,517
5031 Lumber, plywood, and millwork [2]	-	226	-	3,194	14	-	62,799	-	151,702
5032 Brick, stone, & related materials [2]	-	30	-	282	9	-	28,482	-	9,055
5033 Roofing, siding, & insulation [2]	-	31	-	368	12	-	30,207	-	12,694
5039 Construction materials, nec [2]	-	78	-	1,083	14	-	30,338	-	33,384
5043 Photographic equipment & supplies [2]	-	12	-	55	5	-	28,509	-	1,497
5044 Office equipment [2]	-	65	-	1,386	21	-	35,287	-	48,090
5045 Computers, peripherals, & software [2]	-	200	-	2,194	11	-	48,149	-	107,762
5046 Commercial equipment, nec [2]	-	64	-	762	12	-	28,126	-	23,334
5047 Medical and hospital equipment	-	100	-	774	8	-	37,550	-	31,410
5048 Ophthalmic goods [2]	-	18	-	128	7	-	22,406	-	3,263
5049 Professional equipment, nec [2]	-	31	-	209	7	-	25,952	-	5,884
5051 Metals service centers and offices [2]	-	86	-	132	2	-	26,394	-	4,316
5063 Electrical apparatus and equipment [2]	-	159	-	1,712	11	-	35,643	-	62,813
5064 Electrical appliances, TV & radios [2]	-	31	-	428	14	-	31,897	-	11,206
5065 Electronic parts and equipment [2]	-	210	-	2,257	11	-	40,044	-	100,617
5072 Hardware [2]	-	103	-	988	10	-	28,794	-	31,655
5074 Plumbing & hydronic heating supplies [2]	-	78	-	1,179	15	-	34,480	-	42,380
5075 Warm air heating & air conditioning [2]	-	36	-	574	16	-	34,383	-	19,571
5078 Refrigeration equipment and supplies [2]	-	9	-	78	9	-	36,000	-	2,634
5082 Construction and mining machinery	-	58	-	1,007	17	-	43,384	-	44,951
5083 Farm and garden machinery	-	43	-	371	9	-	27,871	-	10,962
5084 Industrial machinery and equipment	-	298	-	2,957	10	-	36,952	-	116,593
5085 Industrial supplies [2]	-	169	-	1,948	12	-	34,819	-	70,284
5087 Service establishment equipment [2]	-	71	-	694	10	-	27,516	-	19,985
5088 Transportation equipment & supplies [2]	-	40	-	492	12	-	29,154	-	15,412
5091 Sporting & recreational goods [2]	-	77	-	592	8	-	26,932	-	17,477
5092 Toys and hobby goods and supplies [2]	-	22	-	193	9	-	14,902	-	3,868
5093 Scrap and waste materials	-	80	-	1,325	17	-	25,748	-	33,718
5094 Jewelry & precious stones [2]	-	29	-	128	4	-	17,188	-	2,568
5099 Durable goods, nec	-	97	-	566	6	-	29,703	-	17,966
5111 Printing and writing paper [2]	-	29	-	373	13	-	44,343	-	16,233
5112 Stationery and office supplies [2]	-	82	-	1,427	17	-	31,512	-	40,798
5113 Industrial & personal service paper [2]	-	46	-	280	6	-	47,386	-	13,983
5120 Drugs, proprietaries, and sundries [2]	-	69	-	1,178	17	-	31,083	-	36,280
5136 Men's and boys' clothing [2]	-	31	-	54	2	-	20,815	-	818
5137 Women's and children's clothing [2]	-	17	-	340	20	-	46,988	-	16,066
5141 Groceries, general line [2]	-	47	-	1,930	41	-	32,184	-	62,082
5142 Packaged frozen food [2]	-	30	-	593	20	-	31,609	-	20,053
5143 Dairy products, exc. dried or canned	-	20	-	311	16	-	26,071	-	9,511
5145 Confectionery [2]	-	19	-	408	21	-	27,275	-	12,366
5146 Fish and seafoods [2]	-	16	-	166	10	-	22,217	-	3,857
5147 Meats and meat products [2]	-	42	-	503	12	-	27,905	-	14,959
5148 Fresh fruits and vegetables [2]	-	38	-	869	23	-	22,283	-	23,121
5149 Groceries and related products, nec [2]	-	120	-	2,145	18	-	27,763	-	61,628
5153 Grain and field beans [2]	-	29	-	263	9	-	47,103	-	11,919
5162 Plastics materials & basic shapes	-	35	-	261	7	-	29,839	-	8,652
5169 Chemicals & allied products, nec [2]	-	86	-	800	9	-	32,510	-	28,235
5171 Petroleum bulk stations & terminals [2]	-	45	-	408	9	-	40,882	-	14,746
5172 Petroleum products, nec [2]	-	17	-	145	9	-	27,421	-	4,685
5181 Beer and ale [2]	-	14	-	541	39	-	27,667	-	16,837
5182 Wine and distilled beverages [2]	-	23	-	300	13	-	23,547	-	7,892
5191 Farm supplies	-	74	-	748	10	-	25,952	-	19,964
5192 Books, periodicals, & newspapers [2]	-	53	-	556	10	-	30,086	-	16,591
5193 Flowers & florists' supplies	-	35	-	327	9	-	16,183	-	5,281
5198 Paints, varnishes, and supplies [2]	-	29	-	169	6	-	30,864	-	4,986
5199 Nondurable goods, nec	-	123	-	1,055	9	-	19,500	-	24,044
52 – Retail trade	-	10,265	-	151,677	15	-	14,974	-	2,383,115
5210 Lumber and other building materials	-	159	-	3,028	19	-	21,090	-	68,704
5230 Paint, glass, and wallpaper stores	-	71	-	390	5	-	22,051	-	9,617
5250 Hardware stores [2]	-	62	-	519	8	-	13,503	-	6,873
5260 Retail nurseries and garden stores	-	90	-	591	7	-	14,213	-	10,570
5270 Mobile home dealers	-	32	-	331	10	-	31,154	-	11,306
5310 Department stores [2]	-	65	-	12,850	198	-	14,096	-	192,363
5330 Variety stores [2]	-	31	-	198	6	-	9,939	-	2,064

Continued on next page.

PORTLAND - VANCOUVER, OR - WA PMSA - [continued]

Wholesale and Retail Trade USA	Establishments		Employment		Emp / Est	Pay / Employee		Annual Payroll ($ 000)	
	1994	1995	1994	1995	1995	1994	1995	1994	1995
5390 Misc. general merchandise stores	-	51	-	1,969	39	-	21,410	-	43,952
5410 Grocery stores	-	809	-	15,985	20	-	15,564	-	252,613
5420 Meat and fish markets [2]	-	26	-	87	3	-	15,448	-	1,516
5430 Fruit and vegetable markets [2]	-	13	-	97	7	-	16,165	-	1,858
5440 Candy, nut, and confectionery stores [2]	-	38	-	181	5	-	9,812	-	1,941
5450 Dairy products stores [2]	-	26	-	137	5	-	9,810	-	1,553
5460 Retail bakeries	-	74	-	568	8	-	11,817	-	6,995
5490 Miscellaneous food stores [2]	-	109	-	614	6	-	10,215	-	6,730
5510 New and used car dealers	-	137	-	7,484	55	-	29,294	-	251,450
5520 Used car dealers	-	81	-	509	6	-	24,055	-	14,301
5530 Auto and home supply stores	-	278	-	2,356	8	-	24,610	-	55,315
5540 Gasoline service stations	-	405	-	4,787	12	-	10,895	-	54,812
5550 Boat dealers [2]	-	35	-	203	6	-	21,596	-	4,934
5560 Recreational vehicle dealers	-	44	-	476	11	-	21,866	-	13,315
5570 Motorcycle dealers [2]	-	27	-	135	5	-	19,704	-	3,123
5590 Automotive dealers, nec [2]	-	11	-	55	5	-	33,964	-	1,801
5610 Men's & boys' clothing stores	-	72	-	417	6	-	14,935	-	6,448
5620 Women's clothing stores	-	195	-	1,647	8	-	10,300	-	17,145
5630 Women's accessory & specialty stores [2]	-	45	-	240	5	-	11,367	-	2,783
5640 Children's and infants' wear stores [2]	-	29	-	426	15	-	16,103	-	6,776
5650 Family clothing stores	-	124	-	4,683	38	-	12,722	-	60,629
5660 Shoe stores	-	137	-	879	6	-	12,614	-	11,189
5690 Misc. apparel & accessory stores [2]	-	56	-	304	5	-	12,092	-	4,317
5712 Furniture stores	-	221	-	1,931	9	-	21,864	-	40,843
5713 Floor covering stores	-	102	-	638	6	-	22,219	-	15,068
5714 Drapery and upholstery stores [2]	-	14	-	31	2	-	16,903	-	579
5719 Misc. homefurnishings stores	-	172	-	1,138	7	-	13,114	-	15,998
5720 Household appliance stores	-	66	-	492	7	-	20,902	-	11,187
5731 Radio, TV, & electronic stores	-	124	-	1,360	11	-	18,638	-	26,870
5734 Computer and software stores	-	73	-	336	5	-	22,310	-	8,422
5735 Record & prerecorded tape stores [2]	-	55	-	492	9	-	12,187	-	6,499
5736 Musical instrument stores [2]	-	39	-	205	5	-	16,780	-	4,481
5812 Eating places	-	2,689	-	50,100	19	-	8,821	-	466,429
5813 Drinking places	-	389	-	3,237	8	-	9,359	-	31,797
5910 Drug stores and proprietary stores	-	172	-	2,497	15	-	17,620	-	44,967
5920 Liquor stores	-	154	-	413	3	-	11,864	-	5,156
5930 Used merchandise stores	-	186	-	1,356	7	-	12,103	-	17,214
5941 Sporting goods and bicycle shops	-	184	-	1,611	9	-	12,621	-	21,416
5942 Book stores	-	124	-	1,066	9	-	13,606	-	14,544
5943 Stationery stores [2]	-	33	-	46	1	-	18,087	-	694
5944 Jewelry stores	-	132	-	831	6	-	21,622	-	17,541
5945 Hobby, toy, and game shops	-	85	-	1,085	13	-	10,186	-	12,690
5946 Camera & photographic supply stores [2]	-	15	-	21	1	-	18,286	-	468
5947 Gift, novelty, and souvenir shops [2]	-	225	-	1,273	6	-	9,694	-	12,999
5948 Luggage and leather goods stores [2]	-	21	-	106	5	-	16,377	-	2,470
5949 Sewing, needlework, and piece goods	-	52	-	523	10	-	8,734	-	4,582
5961 Catalog and mail-order houses [2]	-	77	-	1,061	14	-	24,954	-	28,205
5962 Merchandising machine operators	-	44	-	437	10	-	20,851	-	9,630
5963 Direct selling establishments [2]	-	128	-	783	6	-	15,637	-	13,360
5983 Fuel oil dealers [2]	-	22	-	185	8	-	27,719	-	5,156
5984 Liquefied petroleum gas dealers [2]	-	10	-	25	3	-	18,400	-	442
5992 Florists	-	169	-	845	5	-	9,430	-	8,090
5993 Tobacco stores and stands [2]	-	13	-	57	4	-	17,825	-	984
5994 News dealers and newsstands [2]	-	9	-	23	3	-	18,087	-	435
5995 Optical goods stores [2]	-	103	-	457	4	-	19,422	-	9,447
5999 Miscellaneous retail stores, nec	-	331	-	1,845	6	-	15,042	-	29,616

Source: County Business Patterns 1994/95, CBP-94/95, U.S. Department of Commerce, Washington DC, November 1997. The employment column represents mid-March employment in the year. Pay per employee is calculated by dividing 1st Quarter payroll, annualized, by mid-March employment. The column headed 'Emp / Est' shows 'employees per establishment'. A dash (-) means that data are unavailable or cannot be calculated. nec means not elsewhere classified. *Notes:* 1. 1994 data incomplete; unavailable or withheld. 2. 1995 data incomplete; unavailable or withheld. 3. 1994 and 1995 data incomplete; unavailable or withheld.

PROVO - OREM, UT MSA

Wholesale and Retail Trade USA	Establishments		Employment		Emp / Est	Pay / Employee		Annual Payroll ($ 000)	
	1994	1995	1994	1995	1995	1994	1995	1994	1995
50- Wholesale trade	-	377	-	6,737	18	-	23,860	-	182,661
5013 Motor vehicle supplies and new parts	-	17	-	147	9	-	13,252	-	2,178
5031 Lumber, plywood, and millwork	-	7	-	97	14	-	15,464	-	1,866
5032 Brick, stone, & related materials	-	9	-	72	8	-	19,722	-	1,603

Continued on next page.

PROVO – OREM, UT MSA - [continued]

Wholesale and Retail Trade USA	Establishments		Employment		Emp / Est	Pay / Employee		Annual Payroll ($ 000)	
	1994	1995	1994	1995	1995	1994	1995	1994	1995
5045 Computers, peripherals, & software	-	32	-	377	12	-	25,337	-	12,218
5050 Metals and minerals, except petroleum	-	8	-	245	31	-	30,482	-	8,925
5063 Electrical apparatus and equipment	-	6	-	116	19	-	39,966	-	4,352
5064 Electrical appliances, TV & radios	-	4	-	17	4	-	12,706	-	313
5065 Electronic parts and equipment	-	15	-	195	13	-	17,251	-	4,133
5072 Hardware	-	4	-	71	18	-	23,606	-	1,341
5074 Plumbing & hydronic heating supplies	-	11	-	103	9	-	29,981	-	2,904
5082 Construction and mining machinery	-	6	-	35	6	-	23,086	-	958
5083 Farm and garden machinery	-	8	-	205	26	-	21,444	-	5,085
5084 Industrial machinery and equipment	-	6	-	45	8	-	29,156	-	1,297
5085 Industrial supplies	-	6	-	21	4	-	36,190	-	702
5087 Service establishment equipment	-	6	-	43	7	-	25,953	-	1,191
5088 Transportation equipment & supplies	-	3	-	184	61	-	18,326	-	3,380
5091 Sporting & recreational goods	-	9	-	102	11	-	14,706	-	1,465
5093 Scrap and waste materials	-	8	-	54	7	-	22,148	-	1,621
5099 Durable goods, nec	-	7	-	73	10	-	20,219	-	2,212
5112 Stationery and office supplies	-	7	-	82	12	-	10,683	-	1,086
5120 Drugs, proprietaries, and sundries	-	17	-	1,270	75	-	26,532	-	42,577
5131 Piece goods & notions	-	5	-	62	12	-	13,677	-	961
5136 Men's and boys' clothing	-	3	-	49	16	-	8,898	-	504
5141 Groceries, general line	-	4	-	14	4	-	20,000	-	400
5148 Fresh fruits and vegetables	-	5	-	125	25	-	11,904	-	1,576
5149 Groceries and related products, nec	-	12	-	468	39	-	23,915	-	10,870
5160 Chemicals and allied products	-	14	-	192	14	-	31,396	-	6,537
5171 Petroleum bulk stations & terminals	-	6	-	158	26	-	20,354	-	3,467
5172 Petroleum products, nec	-	8	-	277	35	-	11,336	-	3,247
5191 Farm supplies	-	14	-	106	8	-	17,660	-	2,549
5199 Nondurable goods, nec	-	6	-	94	16	-	8,255	-	1,155
52- Retail trade	-	1,232	-	20,371	17	-	10,527	-	234,109
5210 Lumber and other building materials	-	21	-	545	26	-	16,059	-	10,717
5230 Paint, glass, and wallpaper stores	-	11	-	64	6	-	17,750	-	1,198
5250 Hardware stores	-	12	-	235	20	-	10,451	-	2,873
5310 Department stores	-	13	-	2,032	156	-	10,337	-	22,584
5410 Grocery stores	-	60	-	2,638	44	-	12,638	-	35,821
5440 Candy, nut, and confectionery stores	-	3	-	20	7	-	8,800	-	150
5460 Retail bakeries	-	21	-	235	11	-	6,400	-	1,452
5490 Miscellaneous food stores	-	13	-	129	10	-	9,023	-	1,255
5510 New and used car dealers	-	24	-	770	32	-	24,582	-	21,482
5520 Used car dealers	-	21	-	90	4	-	17,778	-	1,604
5530 Auto and home supply stores	-	42	-	364	9	-	17,066	-	6,423
5540 Gasoline service stations	-	93	-	1,124	12	-	8,189	-	9,680
5560 Recreational vehicle dealers	-	5	-	40	8	-	18,000	-	626
5610 Men's & boys' clothing stores	-	9	-	77	9	-	13,818	-	1,151
5620 Women's clothing stores	-	29	-	224	8	-	6,714	-	1,587
5640 Children's and infants' wear stores	-	8	-	68	9	-	7,294	-	511
5650 Family clothing stores	-	18	-	239	13	-	9,205	-	2,527
5660 Shoe stores	-	33	-	148	4	-	10,946	-	1,626
5690 Misc. apparel & accessory stores	-	9	-	57	6	-	7,018	-	501
5712 Furniture stores	-	18	-	341	19	-	19,894	-	6,965
5713 Floor covering stores	-	17	-	70	4	-	17,429	-	1,307
5714 Drapery and upholstery stores	-	4	-	14	4	-	11,143	-	293
5719 Misc. homefurnishings stores	-	9	-	77	9	-	8,571	-	656
5720 Household appliance stores	-	14	-	57	4	-	14,386	-	963
5731 Radio, TV, & electronic stores	-	10	-	109	11	-	20,514	-	2,867
5734 Computer and software stores	-	22	-	180	8	-	22,511	-	5,740
5735 Record & prerecorded tape stores	-	10	-	128	13	-	10,188	-	1,003
5736 Musical instrument stores	-	7	-	67	10	-	15,045	-	1,121
5812 Eating places	-	278	-	5,871	21	-	6,387	-	40,775
5813 Drinking places	-	12	-	88	7	-	6,000	-	496
5910 Drug stores and proprietary stores	-	23	-	303	13	-	13,914	-	4,367
5930 Used merchandise stores	-	11	-	61	6	-	9,246	-	659
5941 Sporting goods and bicycle shops	-	32	-	322	10	-	13,938	-	3,408
5942 Book stores	-	18	-	144	8	-	9,500	-	1,328
5943 Stationery stores	-	5	-	14	3	-	12,857	-	210
5944 Jewelry stores	-	22	-	128	6	-	16,500	-	2,246
5945 Hobby, toy, and game shops	-	15	-	367	24	-	10,420	-	4,167
5947 Gift, novelty, and souvenir shops	-	28	-	138	5	-	6,145	-	1,223
5949 Sewing, needlework, and piece goods	-	10	-	135	14	-	6,163	-	832
5961 Catalog and mail-order houses	-	11	-	119	11	-	17,983	-	2,553

Continued on next page.

PROVO – OREM, UT MSA - [continued]

Wholesale and Retail Trade USA	Establishments		Employment		Emp / Est	Pay / Employee		Annual Payroll ($ 000)	
	1994	1995	1994	1995	1995	1994	1995	1994	1995
5992 Florists	-	26	-	126	5	-	6,095	-	822
5995 Optical goods stores	-	20	-	77	4	-	18,130	-	1,408
5999 Miscellaneous retail stores, nec	-	42	-	438	10	-	11,543	-	5,372

Source: County Business Patterns 1994/95, CBP-94/95, U.S. Department of Commerce, Washington DC, November 1997. The employment column represents mid-March employment in the year. Pay per employee is calculated by dividing 1st Quarter payroll, annualized, by mid-March employment. The column headed 'Emp / Est' shows 'employees per establishment'. A dash (-) means that data are unavailable or cannot be calculated. nec means not elsewhere classified. *Notes:* 1. 1994 data incomplete; unavailable or withheld. 2. 1995 data incomplete; unavailable or withheld. 3. 1994 and 1995 data incomplete; unavailable or withheld.

PUEBLO, CO MSA

Wholesale and Retail Trade USA	Establishments		Employment		Emp / Est	Pay / Employee		Annual Payroll ($ 000)	
	1994	1995	1994	1995	1995	1994	1995	1994	1995
50 – Wholesale trade	134	133	1,352	1,551	12	20,959	24,477	31,189	38,632
5013 Motor vehicle supplies and new parts	9	7	71	61	9	19,775	18,295	1,505	1,096
5015 Motor vehicle parts, used	12	12	85	88	7	13,224	13,500	1,249	1,305
5030 Lumber and construction materials	-	4	-	66	17	-	20,970	-	1,488
5044 Office equipment	8	6	40	37	6	14,500	15,243	571	516
5046 Commercial equipment, nec	3	3	14	15	5	18,286	26,400	291	313
5051 Metals service centers and offices	4	4	105	121	30	23,429	18,678	2,713	2,631
5063 Electrical apparatus and equipment	5	6	44	55	9	27,000	26,109	1,668	1,941
5065 Electronic parts and equipment	8	7	101	113	16	34,455	48,389	3,594	4,411
5074 Plumbing & hydronic heating supplies	6	6	86	99	17	23,721	28,646	2,441	3,096
5083 Farm and garden machinery	3	3	28	29	10	20,000	21,379	666	642
5084 Industrial machinery and equipment	5	7	13	78	11	20,000	43,795	285	3,036
5085 Industrial supplies	6	6	94	101	17	24,170	26,337	2,642	2,984
5087 Service establishment equipment	5	5	31	31	6	19,097	19,097	732	619
5093 Scrap and waste materials	5	-	59	-	-	25,085	-	1,281	-
5110 Paper and paper products	4	3	51	50	17	15,529	15,520	823	873
5141 Groceries, general line	4	4	118	110	28	19,932	20,727	2,539	2,514
5171 Petroleum bulk stations & terminals	6	5	77	57	11	12,052	15,789	1,127	1,195
5191 Farm supplies	4	-	22	-	-	13,636	-	358	-
52 – Retail trade	828	857	10,879	11,653	14	11,177	11,826	137,379	146,027
5210 Lumber and other building materials	13	9	222	210	23	15,117	15,295	3,945	3,439
5230 Paint, glass, and wallpaper stores	6	-	35	-	-	12,000	-	498	-
5250 Hardware stores	6	4	20	17	4	8,000	9,176	184	192
5270 Mobile home dealers	4	5	33	43	9	18,545	17,953	1,099	1,084
5310 Department stores	10	10	1,314	1,519	152	11,291	11,637	16,652	18,245
5410 Grocery stores	55	59	1,137	1,230	21	16,992	17,164	20,988	22,044
5420 Meat and fish markets	4	4	29	32	8	11,172	10,000	333	349
5440 Candy, nut, and confectionery stores	5	6	31	30	5	5,677	5,733	192	200
5450 Dairy products stores	-	3	-	3	1	-	8,000	-	25
5460 Retail bakeries	-	9	-	48	5	-	8,750	-	502
5490 Miscellaneous food stores	6	5	13	15	3	11,692	14,133	202	223
5510 New and used car dealers	11	13	438	461	35	29,890	30,221	15,410	14,824
5520 Used car dealers	18	15	51	48	3	14,196	16,917	911	1,039
5530 Auto and home supply stores	26	28	178	192	7	15,371	16,667	3,103	3,408
5540 Gasoline service stations	47	45	269	282	6	10,468	10,837	2,973	3,104
5570 Motorcycle dealers	4	4	23	27	7	11,478	12,296	369	513
5610 Men's & boys' clothing stores	6	5	36	33	7	13,667	14,909	551	380
5620 Women's clothing stores	22	17	156	127	7	7,897	5,984	1,244	817
5660 Shoe stores	22	21	81	102	5	9,827	8,549	968	1,004
5690 Misc. apparel & accessory stores	5	7	25	20	3	12,640	18,800	252	284
5712 Furniture stores	14	17	100	100	6	18,360	18,640	2,115	2,220
5713 Floor covering stores	10	10	68	64	6	13,765	17,188	1,142	1,155
5720 Household appliance stores	-	5	-	30	6	-	26,400	-	735
5731 Radio, TV, & electronic stores	7	6	42	26	4	16,286	18,000	672	448
5735 Record & prerecorded tape stores	8	8	29	63	8	9,241	12,190	360	704
5736 Musical instrument stores	5	-	12	-	-	7,333	-	102	-
5812 Eating places	194	194	3,806	3,758	19	5,842	6,756	24,906	27,630
5813 Drinking places	66	59	333	334	6	6,378	6,347	2,143	2,145
5910 Drug stores and proprietary stores	19	18	179	188	10	14,659	16,766	2,677	2,678
5920 Liquor stores	26	25	112	100	4	8,214	9,000	1,101	1,031
5930 Used merchandise stores	18	20	212	82	4	6,792	10,537	1,402	920
5941 Sporting goods and bicycle shops	11	9	68	72	8	8,294	10,556	693	701
5942 Book stores	6	-	61	-	-	5,508	-	282	-
5944 Jewelry stores	13	13	73	66	5	14,630	17,515	1,250	1,281
5945 Hobby, toy, and game shops	-	8	-	61	8	-	11,607	-	775
5947 Gift, novelty, and souvenir shops	14	15	42	49	3	7,048	8,082	369	432
5962 Merchandising machine operators	-	6	-	17	3	-	9,412	-	173

Continued on next page.

PUEBLO, CO MSA - [continued]

Wholesale and Retail Trade USA	Establishments		Employment		Emp / Est	Pay / Employee		Annual Payroll ($ 000)	
	1994	1995	1994	1995	1995	1994	1995	1994	1995
5984 Liquefied petroleum gas dealers	3	3	13	14	5	12,000	14,000	188	192
5992 Florists	8	8	60	61	8	8,933	9,770	697	665
5995 Optical goods stores	13	12	64	58	5	12,250	11,517	707	713
5999 Miscellaneous retail stores, nec	20	18	73	63	4	9,479	11,619	760	849

Source: County Business Patterns 1994/95, CBP-94/95, U.S. Department of Commerce, Washington DC, November 1997. The employment column represents mid-March employment in the year. Pay per employee is calculated by dividing 1st Quarter payroll, annualized, by mid-March employment. The column headed 'Emp / Est' shows 'employees per establishment'. A dash (-) means that data are unavailable or cannot be calculated. nec means not elsewhere classified. *Notes:* 1. 1994 data incomplete; unavailable or withheld. 2. 1995 data incomplete; unavailable or withheld. 3. 1994 and 1995 data incomplete; unavailable or withheld.

PUNTA GORDA, FL MSA

Wholesale and Retail Trade USA	Establishments		Employment		Emp / Est	Pay / Employee		Annual Payroll ($ 000)	
	1994	1995	1994	1995	1995	1994	1995	1994	1995
50- Wholesale trade	97	108	497	545	5	19,042	21,431	9,961	11,910
5013 Motor vehicle supplies and new parts	8	8	48	38	5	15,417	15,789	766	617
5015 Motor vehicle parts, used	-	4	-	27	7	-	17,333	-	550
5020 Furniture and homefurnishings	4	3	6	6	2	12,667	10,000	82	112
5030 Lumber and construction materials	4	5	41	61	12	19,317	21,049	1,185	1,283
5047 Medical and hospital equipment	3	-	9	-	-	24,889	-	187	-
5060 Electrical goods	7	9	40	55	6	24,900	23,636	1,051	1,373
5072 Hardware	3	3	19	20	7	18,105	23,000	393	505
5074 Plumbing & hydronic heating supplies	-	3	-	8	3	-	23,000	-	147
5075 Warm air heating & air conditioning	-	4	-	8	2	-	23,500	-	185
5084 Industrial machinery and equipment	4	5	16	23	5	19,250	16,174	323	379
5088 Transportation equipment & supplies	5	6	17	17	3	15,294	25,647	279	507
5092 Toys and hobby goods and supplies	-	3	-	21	7	-	9,333	-	193
5141 Groceries, general line	4	4	3	4	1	14,667	28,000	81	107
5149 Groceries and related products, nec	5	4	25	35	9	10,240	9,714	250	437
5191 Farm supplies	3	3	6	9	3	19,333	17,333	136	139
52- Retail trade	694	667	9,366	9,218	14	11,571	12,269	108,040	110,765
5210 Lumber and other building materials	16	14	393	397	28	18,198	19,587	7,598	7,903
5230 Paint, glass, and wallpaper stores	5	5	32	36	7	21,750	22,444	717	608
5250 Hardware stores	10	10	81	79	8	12,691	11,848	1,157	1,007
5260 Retail nurseries and garden stores	11	10	36	33	3	9,333	9,455	418	398
5270 Mobile home dealers	5	5	14	12	2	16,286	15,667	207	207
5310 Department stores	10	10	1,279	1,262	126	11,287	12,995	14,813	16,504
5330 Variety stores	7	5	33	30	6	11,273	11,600	379	303
5390 Misc. general merchandise stores	4	5	258	213	43	11,225	16,038	2,610	2,777
5410 Grocery stores	39	35	1,646	1,682	48	11,397	11,377	18,526	18,634
5420 Meat and fish markets	3	4	7	68	17	10,857	7,765	165	441
5440 Candy, nut, and confectionery stores	4	-	11	-	-	7,636	-	76	-
5460 Retail bakeries	5	-	39	-	-	4,615	-	173	-
5490 Miscellaneous food stores	9	9	29	90	10	19,724	9,511	649	859
5510 New and used car dealers	6	5	316	317	63	32,532	34,397	10,494	11,117
5520 Used car dealers	4	5	7	8	2	22,857	22,500	170	132
5530 Auto and home supply stores	13	16	75	105	7	18,880	18,400	1,465	2,056
5540 Gasoline service stations	37	37	341	287	8	10,581	12,627	3,698	3,370
5550 Boat dealers	7	7	28	40	6	16,571	17,400	504	559
5620 Women's clothing stores	30	24	189	160	7	8,593	8,525	1,604	1,273
5630 Women's accessory & specialty stores	7	7	33	35	5	7,879	8,343	287	302
5650 Family clothing stores	9	11	192	196	18	12,250	12,939	2,397	2,443
5660 Shoe stores	18	19	63	68	4	11,111	10,941	716	703
5690 Misc. apparel & accessory stores	5	5	25	22	4	6,720	8,727	191	181
5712 Furniture stores	20	19	159	172	9	15,346	15,721	2,202	2,582
5713 Floor covering stores	11	9	60	30	3	13,467	16,667	756	627
5719 Misc. homefurnishings stores	13	10	35	34	3	13,143	15,059	502	501
5720 Household appliance stores	7	7	14	14	2	16,000	18,000	219	242
5731 Radio, TV, & electronic stores	11	10	45	47	5	18,667	17,106	722	654
5734 Computer and software stores	4	3	14	17	6	24,857	18,824	347	164
5812 Eating places	150	128	2,873	2,529	20	8,000	8,229	21,075	20,487
5813 Drinking places	6	4	30	17	4	5,867	5,882	145	93
5910 Drug stores and proprietary stores	17	17	219	211	12	17,187	19,280	4,004	3,835
5920 Liquor stores	10	7	38	33	5	8,632	13,091	338	387
5930 Used merchandise stores	11	10	54	47	5	12,741	12,596	831	634
5941 Sporting goods and bicycle shops	13	13	24	27	2	21,333	14,963	433	372
5942 Book stores	4	3	20	22	7	8,000	7,455	178	185
5943 Stationery stores	3	-	5	-	-	9,600	-	75	-
5944 Jewelry stores	6	9	22	43	5	18,000	15,163	380	598
5945 Hobby, toy, and game shops	6	6	60	57	10	8,867	10,386	738	598

Continued on next page.

PUNTA GORDA, FL MSA - [continued]

Wholesale and Retail Trade USA	Establishments		Employment		Emp / Est	Pay / Employee		Annual Payroll ($ 000)	
	1994	1995	1994	1995	1995	1994	1995	1994	1995
5947 Gift, novelty, and souvenir shops	18	16	60	58	4	8,733	10,207	562	566
5949 Sewing, needlework, and piece goods	4	3	25	32	11	9,280	7,250	191	204
5963 Direct selling establishments	-	5	-	31	6	-	17,677	-	551
5992 Florists	15	13	61	71	5	9,049	9,127	614	583
5999 Miscellaneous retail stores, nec	27	24	77	68	3	13,403	13,118	1,118	859

Source: County Business Patterns 1994/95, CBP-94/95, U.S. Department of Commerce, Washington DC, November 1997. The employment column represents mid-March employment in the year. Pay per employee is calculated by dividing 1st Quarter payroll, annualized, by mid-March employment. The column headed 'Emp / Est' shows 'employees per establishment'. A dash (-) means that data are unavailable or cannot be calculated. nec means not elsewhere classified. *Notes:* 1. 1994 data incomplete; unavailable or withheld. 2. 1995 data incomplete; unavailable or withheld. 3. 1994 and 1995 data incomplete; unavailable or withheld.

RACINE, WI PMSA

Wholesale and Retail Trade USA	Establishments		Employment		Emp / Est	Pay / Employee		Annual Payroll ($ 000)	
	1994	1995	1994	1995	1995	1994	1995	1994	1995
50 - Wholesale trade	-	267	-	3,416	13	-	24,816	-	94,605
5012 Automobiles and other vehicles	-	13	-	554	43	-	13,935	-	7,009
5013 Motor vehicle supplies and new parts	-	20	-	363	18	-	27,956	-	12,021
5015 Motor vehicle parts, used	-	7	-	58	8	-	15,310	-	953
5020 Furniture and homefurnishings	-	5	-	40	8	-	16,600	-	806
5033 Roofing, siding, & insulation	-	4	-	15	4	-	12,800	-	262
5045 Computers, peripherals, & software	-	8	-	69	9	-	18,841	-	1,507
5048 Ophthalmic goods	-	3	-	44	15	-	18,545	-	918
5051 Metals service centers and offices	-	5	-	57	11	-	22,737	-	1,432
5063 Electrical apparatus and equipment	-	8	-	108	14	-	31,370	-	3,443
5065 Electronic parts and equipment	-	6	-	76	13	-	19,000	-	1,574
5072 Hardware	-	10	-	68	7	-	20,588	-	1,637
5084 Industrial machinery and equipment	-	24	-	190	8	-	35,053	-	7,477
5085 Industrial supplies	-	16	-	195	12	-	30,831	-	5,710
5087 Service establishment equipment	-	6	-	76	13	-	25,263	-	1,939
5093 Scrap and waste materials	-	10	-	84	8	-	23,286	-	2,031
5099 Durable goods, nec	-	3	-	9	3	-	17,778	-	177
5110 Paper and paper products	-	9	-	120	13	-	19,667	-	2,577
5148 Fresh fruits and vegetables	-	4	-	70	18	-	34,400	-	3,053
5169 Chemicals & allied products, nec	-	3	-	22	7	-	24,545	-	541
5172 Petroleum products, nec	-	3	-	20	7	-	19,600	-	408
5180 Beer, wine, and distilled beverages	-	6	-	111	19	-	22,054	-	2,477
5191 Farm supplies	-	5	-	64	13	-	27,063	-	1,850
5198 Paints, varnishes, and supplies	-	3	-	10	3	-	18,400	-	200
5199 Nondurable goods, nec	-	8	-	10	1	-	20,000	-	359
52 - Retail trade	-	1,003	-	14,163	14	-	10,967	-	167,741
5210 Lumber and other building materials	-	17	-	374	22	-	17,070	-	6,566
5230 Paint, glass, and wallpaper stores	-	4	-	12	3	-	19,333	-	226
5250 Hardware stores	-	15	-	252	17	-	10,635	-	2,834
5260 Retail nurseries and garden stores	-	9	-	282	31	-	11,518	-	4,048
5310 Department stores	-	10	-	1,581	158	-	9,508	-	15,907
5410 Grocery stores	-	82	-	1,889	23	-	11,557	-	23,610
5420 Meat and fish markets	-	9	-	153	17	-	9,516	-	1,700
5440 Candy, nut, and confectionery stores	-	3	-	27	9	-	3,407	-	105
5460 Retail bakeries	-	13	-	205	16	-	11,454	-	2,741
5490 Miscellaneous food stores	-	6	-	52	9	-	6,923	-	400
5510 New and used car dealers	-	16	-	588	37	-	28,673	-	19,258
5520 Used car dealers	-	14	-	59	4	-	20,136	-	1,372
5530 Auto and home supply stores	-	24	-	339	14	-	15,009	-	5,643
5540 Gasoline service stations	-	60	-	408	7	-	10,422	-	4,359
5550 Boat dealers	-	5	-	28	6	-	16,857	-	624
5570 Motorcycle dealers	-	4	-	18	5	-	18,889	-	354
5610 Men's & boys' clothing stores	-	7	-	30	4	-	10,000	-	273
5620 Women's clothing stores	-	23	-	221	10	-	6,624	-	1,493
5630 Women's accessory & specialty stores	-	4	-	18	5	-	7,333	-	146
5650 Family clothing stores	-	8	-	53	7	-	7,547	-	729
5660 Shoe stores	-	22	-	122	6	-	9,934	-	1,213
5690 Misc. apparel & accessory stores	-	3	-	40	13	-	10,000	-	421
5712 Furniture stores	-	22	-	219	10	-	17,973	-	3,727
5713 Floor covering stores	-	16	-	79	5	-	22,532	-	1,980
5714 Drapery and upholstery stores	-	5	-	23	5	-	11,826	-	294
5719 Misc. homefurnishings stores	-	5	-	43	9	-	11,628	-	447
5720 Household appliance stores	-	3	-	13	4	-	20,615	-	283
5736 Musical instrument stores	-	4	-	15	4	-	13,867	-	200
5812 Eating places	-	196	-	4,161	21	-	7,102	-	31,241

Continued on next page.

RACINE, WI PMSA - [continued]

Wholesale and Retail Trade USA	Establishments		Employment		Emp / Est	Pay / Employee		Annual Payroll ($ 000)	
	1994	1995	1994	1995	1995	1994	1995	1994	1995
5813 Drinking places	-	69	-	273	4	-	6,667	-	1,785
5910 Drug stores and proprietary stores	-	26	-	510	20	-	16,941	-	9,671
5920 Liquor stores	-	21	-	79	4	-	11,646	-	880
5930 Used merchandise stores	-	19	-	106	6	-	8,264	-	930
5941 Sporting goods and bicycle shops	-	10	-	53	5	-	18,113	-	887
5942 Book stores	-	7	-	66	9	-	6,182	-	446
5944 Jewelry stores	-	25	-	119	5	-	14,622	-	1,801
5945 Hobby, toy, and game shops	-	7	-	114	16	-	6,596	-	1,150
5947 Gift, novelty, and souvenir shops	-	16	-	98	6	-	7,306	-	713
5962 Merchandising machine operators	-	6	-	23	4	-	16,522	-	391
5980 Fuel dealers	-	5	-	36	7	-	23,000	-	1,236
5992 Florists	-	14	-	109	8	-	9,468	-	1,103
5995 Optical goods stores	-	16	-	88	6	-	21,318	-	2,184
5999 Miscellaneous retail stores, nec	-	33	-	144	4	-	10,306	-	1,544

Source: County Business Patterns 1994/95, CBP-94/95, U.S. Department of Commerce, Washington DC, November 1997. The employment column represents mid-March employment in the year. Pay per employee is calculated by dividing 1st Quarter payroll, annualized, by mid-March employment. The column headed 'Emp / Est' shows 'employees per establishment'. A dash (-) means that data are unavailable or cannot be calculated. nec means not elsewhere classified. *Notes:* 1. 1994 data incomplete; unavailable or withheld. 2. 1995 data incomplete; unavailable or withheld. 3. 1994 and 1995 data incomplete; unavailable or withheld.

RALEIGH - DURHAM - CHAPEL HILL, NC MSA

Wholesale and Retail Trade USA	Establishments		Employment		Emp / Est	Pay / Employee		Annual Payroll ($ 000)	
	1994	1995	1994	1995	1995	1994	1995	1994	1995
50- Wholesale trade	1,906	1,946	24,573	27,701	14	32,934	36,074	860,284	1,037,677
5012 Automobiles and other vehicles [3]	25	23	494	384	17	20,453	20,802	10,583	8,138
5013 Motor vehicle supplies and new parts	143	97	1,158	737	8	21,081	21,997	26,274	17,627
5014 Tires and tubes [3]	15	12	153	113	9	28,497	27,646	4,334	3,148
5015 Motor vehicle parts, used [1]	23	24	193	190	8	18,777	19,895	3,734	3,878
5021 Furniture [3]	27	31	279	240	8	29,649	28,783	9,393	6,851
5023 Homefurnishings [3]	29	29	217	167	6	25,088	36,096	5,849	6,886
5031 Lumber, plywood, and millwork [1]	37	42	754	989	24	26,472	26,063	20,542	26,151
5032 Brick, stone, & related materials [3]	21	24	163	144	6	34,135	34,639	5,570	5,511
5033 Roofing, siding, & insulation [3]	14	14	85	80	6	22,965	26,600	2,260	2,408
5039 Construction materials, nec [3]	12	29	63	268	9	34,476	31,478	2,421	8,444
5044 Office equipment [3]	45	49	821	818	17	31,990	39,936	26,718	31,061
5045 Computers, peripherals, & software [3]	101	118	1,699	1,751	15	47,447	56,041	81,908	93,293
5046 Commercial equipment, nec [3]	17	16	118	92	6	32,441	31,348	4,448	3,492
5047 Medical and hospital equipment [3]	50	48	635	681	14	40,000	44,781	31,158	33,037
5049 Professional equipment, nec [3]	20	20	287	189	9	28,878	37,206	9,469	7,338
5051 Metals service centers and offices [3]	18	19	133	137	7	38,617	46,394	6,017	6,600
5063 Electrical apparatus and equipment [1]	106	92	991	1,379	15	33,950	38,083	40,846	52,604
5064 Electrical appliances, TV & radios [3]	11	11	95	103	9	24,126	26,058	2,532	2,703
5065 Electronic parts and equipment [3]	144	154	2,023	2,500	16	46,531	46,733	96,238	122,015
5072 Hardware	28	28	192	232	8	27,792	24,017	5,401	5,927
5074 Plumbing & hydronic heating supplies [1]	34	37	212	236	6	31,849	33,814	7,638	9,335
5075 Warm air heating & air conditioning [3]	38	40	392	438	11	36,653	35,096	14,134	16,785
5078 Refrigeration equipment and supplies [2]	-	7	-	23	3	-	26,435	-	572
5082 Construction and mining machinery [3]	25	24	555	568	24	38,004	40,627	19,673	22,622
5083 Farm and garden machinery	21	22	385	389	18	43,584	41,604	18,323	20,611
5084 Industrial machinery and equipment [3]	82	89	999	1,087	12	37,361	39,588	38,433	43,193
5085 Industrial supplies [3]	36	41	263	302	7	31,103	32,305	8,585	9,452
5087 Service establishment equipment [3]	28	29	406	238	8	25,754	23,765	12,783	6,502
5088 Transportation equipment & supplies [3]	6	7	27	44	6	50,222	59,273	1,482	2,486
5091 Sporting & recreational goods [3]	20	17	125	136	8	22,368	22,971	2,816	3,406
5092 Toys and hobby goods and supplies [3]	4	6	9	11	2	12,889	16,000	116	326
5093 Scrap and waste materials	24	24	114	159	7	20,561	20,201	2,657	3,601
5094 Jewelry & precious stones [3]	8	9	29	32	4	13,241	13,375	594	940
5099 Durable goods, nec [1]	37	49	142	202	4	26,817	27,069	4,858	6,908
5111 Printing and writing paper [3]	13	13	136	166	13	37,000	45,759	4,665	7,557
5112 Stationery and office supplies [3]	39	40	591	678	17	21,110	24,201	13,326	17,783
5113 Industrial & personal service paper [3]	19	19	236	346	18	31,203	33,237	7,763	12,046
5120 Drugs, proprietaries, and sundries [3]	20	20	587	755	38	74,269	73,192	41,327	67,392
5131 Piece goods & notions [3]	15	17	240	283	17	19,483	20,792	5,559	6,289
5136 Men's and boys' clothing [3]	14	13	145	194	15	13,379	13,381	2,351	2,968
5137 Women's and children's clothing	-	12	-	9	1	-	13,333	-	175
5141 Groceries, general line [3]	20	17	596	615	36	27,490	26,556	17,430	17,177
5143 Dairy products, exc. dried or canned [3]	6	6	60	67	11	18,400	18,507	1,081	1,322
5144 Poultry and poultry products [3]	10	9	93	111	12	29,591	33,153	3,585	4,075
5145 Confectionery [1]	8	-	233	-	-	31,639	-	7,540	-

Continued on next page.

RALEIGH - DURHAM - CHAPEL HILL, NC MSA - [continued]

Wholesale and Retail Trade USA	Establishments		Employment		Emp / Est	Pay / Employee		Annual Payroll ($ 000)	
	1994	1995	1994	1995	1995	1994	1995	1994	1995
5147 Meats and meat products[3]	8	8	35	31	4	21,143	28,000	803	879
5148 Fresh fruits and vegetables[3]	20	18	298	281	16	23,302	25,708	8,573	8,923
5149 Groceries and related products, nec[3]	29	28	632	625	22	22,323	23,213	15,537	13,353
5159 Farm-product raw materials, nec[3]	14	12	1	19	2	4,000	30,105	375	1,194
5162 Plastics materials & basic shapes[3]	15	14	140	134	10	26,571	30,060	3,867	4,068
5169 Chemicals & allied products, nec[3]	40	39	520	593	15	46,400	49,302	21,929	25,847
5171 Petroleum bulk stations & terminals	42	35	305	187	5	26,138	31,551	10,093	5,355
5172 Petroleum products, nec[3]	4	4	17	19	5	11,059	11,368	408	308
5181 Beer and ale[3]	8	9	260	297	33	27,062	30,330	7,460	8,815
5182 Wine and distilled beverages[3]	11	14	189	230	16	27,534	28,417	5,810	7,270
5191 Farm supplies[3]	48	45	417	397	9	34,676	41,048	14,422	16,238
5192 Books, periodicals, & newspapers[3]	15	15	33	151	10	53,091	31,232	2,015	4,587
5193 Flowers & florists' supplies[3]	13	14	44	57	4	19,273	15,088	863	932
5194 Tobacco and tobacco products[3]	6	8	52	51	6	18,923	24,706	903	1,186
5198 Paints, varnishes, and supplies[3]	18	20	77	90	5	24,104	24,711	1,878	2,278
5199 Nondurable goods, nec[2]	90	88	402	475	5	23,453	27,579	11,267	14,653
52- Retail trade	6,373	6,445	88,638	92,993	14	11,618	12,653	1,126,813	1,246,215
5210 Lumber and other building materials	95	87	2,115	2,167	25	16,836	20,031	37,309	41,967
5230 Paint, glass, and wallpaper stores[3]	36	33	159	138	4	16,906	16,812	2,931	2,513
5250 Hardware stores[2]	59	38	392	345	9	12,071	12,487	4,932	4,301
5260 Retail nurseries and garden stores	45	47	317	322	7	10,675	13,130	4,316	4,476
5270 Mobile home dealers[3]	20	25	127	206	8	22,677	25,398	3,652	6,895
5310 Department stores[3]	51	49	7,330	6,974	142	9,532	11,479	74,396	81,915
5330 Variety stores	57	52	247	271	5	8,680	7,911	2,361	2,439
5390 Misc. general merchandise stores	48	59	1,108	1,361	23	10,253	11,688	12,578	16,151
5410 Grocery stores[2]	540	525	11,725	12,401	24	10,040	11,323	130,591	146,589
5420 Meat and fish markets[2]	22	16	35	48	3	12,457	8,333	457	460
5430 Fruit and vegetable markets[3]	5	6	1	1	-	8,000	8,000	23	27
5440 Candy, nut, and confectionery stores[3]	9	10	29	23	2	4,828	5,565	151	126
5460 Retail bakeries[3]	43	35	414	339	10	8,039	8,850	3,944	2,937
5490 Miscellaneous food stores[3]	32	28	113	173	6	7,469	8,647	1,135	1,360
5510 New and used car dealers	77	77	3,473	3,775	49	31,327	32,659	122,131	138,817
5520 Used car dealers	86	80	178	335	4	18,831	21,218	4,631	7,728
5530 Auto and home supply stores[3]	207	182	1,351	1,540	8	16,198	19,603	24,974	31,959
5540 Gasoline service stations	390	391	2,540	2,577	7	12,809	13,788	35,401	38,139
5550 Boat dealers[3]	9	7	41	40	6	16,780	19,200	997	1,033
5570 Motorcycle dealers[3]	12	12	101	102	9	16,040	18,235	2,246	2,582
5610 Men's & boys' clothing stores[3]	75	80	527	628	8	13,465	13,312	6,512	7,992
5620 Women's clothing stores	221	198	1,981	2,017	10	7,800	7,770	17,042	16,001
5630 Women's accessory & specialty stores[3]	33	33	212	237	7	7,736	8,911	1,842	2,101
5640 Children's and infants' wear stores[3]	22	23	129	173	8	6,915	6,844	1,029	1,230
5650 Family clothing stores	78	83	1,517	1,589	19	9,097	9,231	15,306	15,605
5660 Shoe stores	159	154	922	1,120	7	9,935	8,957	9,716	9,853
5690 Misc. apparel & accessory stores[3]	31	33	157	195	6	10,395	10,215	1,881	2,264
5712 Furniture stores	174	185	1,299	1,346	7	16,348	18,071	24,820	28,104
5713 Floor covering stores[3]	54	57	202	301	5	21,624	19,854	5,361	6,733
5714 Drapery and upholstery stores[3]	15	15	51	51	3	13,882	13,490	729	728
5719 Misc. homefurnishings stores	87	90	627	659	7	10,526	11,533	7,817	8,090
5720 Household appliance stores	49	51	175	197	4	17,234	19,553	3,326	3,790
5731 Radio, TV, & electronic stores	57	68	437	532	8	17,986	18,045	9,121	12,078
5734 Computer and software stores[3]	53	61	258	298	5	19,349	23,141	5,993	7,897
5735 Record & prerecorded tape stores[3]	48	51	328	448	9	8,671	6,768	3,315	3,246
5736 Musical instrument stores[3]	19	18	117	123	7	17,436	19,805	2,253	2,664
5812 Eating places	1,459	1,344	30,142	29,503	22	7,725	8,454	250,689	261,539
5813 Drinking places[2]	65	51	649	566	11	6,274	8,601	4,527	5,185
5910 Drug stores and proprietary stores	196	190	2,730	2,906	15	11,411	12,208	34,220	36,274
5920 Liquor stores	52	51	92	95	2	20,478	20,126	1,857	1,977
5930 Used merchandise stores	117	111	534	553	5	14,734	13,020	7,598	7,835
5941 Sporting goods and bicycle shops[2]	114	111	778	935	8	12,149	11,773	10,973	12,171
5942 Book stores[3]	72	72	536	640	9	8,590	9,875	5,228	6,096
5943 Stationery stores[3]	24	23	169	98	4	12,521	14,694	1,720	1,472
5944 Jewelry stores	127	135	653	713	5	14,217	15,512	10,096	11,298
5945 Hobby, toy, and game shops	58	59	443	474	8	8,749	9,443	4,527	5,031
5946 Camera & photographic supply stores[3]	9	15	67	38	3	12,537	15,053	925	714
5947 Gift, novelty, and souvenir shops	137	146	735	853	6	7,331	8,122	6,221	7,494
5948 Luggage and leather goods stores[3]	9	9	52	51	6	11,077	11,294	624	601
5949 Sewing, needlework, and piece goods[3]	32	31	170	173	6	7,906	9,434	1,649	1,893
5961 Catalog and mail-order houses[3]	27	27	1,104	1,225	45	15,851	16,408	21,184	20,585
5962 Merchandising machine operators[3]	20	20	149	162	8	16,295	16,988	2,721	2,908
5963 Direct selling establishments[3]	55	57	418	406	7	16,450	18,828	7,774	8,009
5983 Fuel oil dealers	15	17	66	147	9	16,121	17,986	1,279	3,238

Continued on next page.

RALEIGH – DURHAM – CHAPEL HILL, NC MSA - [continued]

Wholesale and Retail Trade USA	Establishments		Employment		Emp / Est	Pay / Employee		Annual Payroll ($ 000)	
	1994	1995	1994	1995	1995	1994	1995	1994	1995
5984 Liquefied petroleum gas dealers [3]	31	31	98	165	5	31,265	24,970	2,450	3,656
5992 Florists	123	115	393	457	4	11,247	12,210	4,788	5,676
5993 Tobacco stores and stands [3]	5	6	15	11	2	11,467	13,818	170	221
5994 News dealers and newsstands [3]	16	16	27	28	2	10,519	10,143	296	333
5995 Optical goods stores [3]	57	62	321	293	5	11,751	12,928	3,676	3,551
5999 Miscellaneous retail stores, nec	176	188	810	840	4	12,652	13,957	11,875	13,573

Source: County Business Patterns 1994/95, CBP-94/95, U.S. Department of Commerce, Washington DC, November 1997. The employment column represents mid-March employment in the year. Pay per employee is calculated by dividing 1st Quarter payroll, annualized, by mid-March employment. The column headed 'Emp / Est' shows 'employees per establishment'. A dash (-) means that data are unavailable or cannot be calculated. nec means not elsewhere classified. *Notes:* 1. 1994 data incomplete; unavailable or withheld. 2. 1995 data incomplete; unavailable or withheld. 3. 1994 and 1995 data incomplete; unavailable or withheld.

RAPID CITY, SD MSA

Wholesale and Retail Trade USA	Establishments		Employment		Emp / Est	Pay / Employee		Annual Payroll ($ 000)	
	1994	1995	1994	1995	1995	1994	1995	1994	1995
50 - Wholesale trade	-	204	-	2,338	11	-	26,595	-	64,115
5012 Automobiles and other vehicles	-	4	-	54	14	-	21,407	-	1,255
5013 Motor vehicle supplies and new parts	-	13	-	150	12	-	21,787	-	3,409
5014 Tires and tubes	-	3	-	60	20	-	32,133	-	1,614
5015 Motor vehicle parts, used	-	9	-	73	8	-	18,247	-	1,397
5020 Furniture and homefurnishings	-	6	-	91	15	-	20,264	-	1,822
5031 Lumber, plywood, and millwork	-	3	-	79	26	-	41,873	-	2,433
5044 Office equipment	-	8	-	73	9	-	26,904	-	2,097
5045 Computers, peripherals, & software	-	7	-	54	8	-	21,778	-	1,218
5063 Electrical apparatus and equipment	-	8	-	77	10	-	27,532	-	2,354
5065 Electronic parts and equipment	-	7	-	62	9	-	23,548	-	1,500
5074 Plumbing & hydronic heating supplies	-	10	-	67	7	-	41,493	-	2,312
5083 Farm and garden machinery	-	3	-	26	9	-	41,846	-	819
5084 Industrial machinery and equipment	-	8	-	107	13	-	37,495	-	3,633
5099 Durable goods, nec	-	9	-	49	5	-	20,980	-	1,100
5140 Groceries and related products	-	10	-	291	29	-	22,268	-	8,473
5150 Farm-product raw materials	-	5	-	23	5	-	18,087	-	417
5169 Chemicals & allied products, nec	-	4	-	36	9	-	20,222	-	895
5170 Petroleum and petroleum products	-	11	-	111	10	-	24,180	-	3,062
5180 Beer, wine, and distilled beverages	-	5	-	82	16	-	42,341	-	2,955
5190 Misc., nondurable goods	-	13	-	127	10	-	16,472	-	2,402
52 - Retail trade	-	775	-	10,688	14	-	12,208	-	140,392
5210 Lumber and other building materials	-	8	-	194	24	-	17,155	-	3,750
5230 Paint, glass, and wallpaper stores	-	4	-	23	6	-	21,391	-	486
5250 Hardware stores	-	5	-	78	16	-	15,333	-	1,158
5260 Retail nurseries and garden stores	-	7	-	23	3	-	11,304	-	352
5270 Mobile home dealers	-	7	-	90	13	-	21,333	-	2,429
5310 Department stores	-	7	-	1,236	177	-	11,540	-	14,553
5330 Variety stores	-	4	-	9	2	-	10,667	-	149
5390 Misc. general merchandise stores	-	7	-	83	12	-	8,482	-	901
5410 Grocery stores	-	33	-	1,135	34	-	10,936	-	13,515
5440 Candy, nut, and confectionery stores	-	5	-	12	2	-	7,667	-	128
5510 New and used car dealers	-	12	-	606	51	-	28,125	-	18,678
5520 Used car dealers	-	15	-	56	4	-	12,857	-	709
5530 Auto and home supply stores	-	22	-	169	8	-	20,426	-	3,616
5540 Gasoline service stations	-	47	-	366	8	-	11,464	-	4,722
5560 Recreational vehicle dealers	-	6	-	31	5	-	28,903	-	859
5610 Men's & boys' clothing stores	-	8	-	60	8	-	14,133	-	871
5620 Women's clothing stores	-	18	-	95	5	-	9,684	-	818
5630 Women's accessory & specialty stores	-	5	-	15	3	-	12,800	-	199
5650 Family clothing stores	-	13	-	150	12	-	10,480	-	1,690
5660 Shoe stores	-	15	-	107	7	-	10,505	-	1,005
5690 Misc. apparel & accessory stores	-	7	-	21	3	-	4,381	-	147
5712 Furniture stores	-	14	-	166	12	-	21,301	-	2,815
5719 Misc. homefurnishings stores	-	5	-	7	1	-	25,714	-	234
5731 Radio, TV, & electronic stores	-	8	-	91	11	-	21,846	-	1,995
5734 Computer and software stores	-	6	-	16	3	-	18,750	-	335
5812 Eating places	-	149	-	3,200	21	-	7,156	-	25,713
5813 Drinking places	-	35	-	316	9	-	6,772	-	2,437
5910 Drug stores and proprietary stores	-	11	-	232	21	-	16,983	-	4,768
5920 Liquor stores	-	4	-	14	4	-	7,714	-	113
5930 Used merchandise stores	-	24	-	104	4	-	12,808	-	1,388
5941 Sporting goods and bicycle shops	-	20	-	160	8	-	14,725	-	1,894
5944 Jewelry stores	-	24	-	141	6	-	14,496	-	2,298

Continued on next page.

RAPID CITY, SD MSA - [continued]

Wholesale and Retail Trade USA	Establishments		Employment		Emp / Est	Pay / Employee		Annual Payroll ($ 000)	
	1994	1995	1994	1995	1995	1994	1995	1994	1995
5945 Hobby, toy, and game shops	-	12	-	104	9	-	14,962	-	1,445
5946 Camera & photographic supply stores	-	3	-	22	7	-	16,909	-	412
5947 Gift, novelty, and souvenir shops	-	36	-	117	3	-	7,624	-	1,320
5961 Catalog and mail-order houses	-	4	-	12	3	-	19,000	-	317
5962 Merchandising machine operators	-	4	-	15	4	-	18,667	-	218
5963 Direct selling establishments	-	13	-	60	5	-	30,800	-	1,242
5980 Fuel dealers	-	5	-	16	3	-	17,250	-	271
5992 Florists	-	13	-	78	6	-	10,564	-	762
5999 Miscellaneous retail stores, nec	-	23	-	84	4	-	13,000	-	1,130

Source: County Business Patterns 1994/95, CBP-94/95, U.S. Department of Commerce, Washington DC, November 1997. The employment column represents mid-March employment in the year. Pay per employee is calculated by dividing 1st Quarter payroll, annualized, by mid-March employment. The column headed 'Emp / Est' shows 'employees per establishment'. A dash (-) means that data are unavailable or cannot be calculated. nec means not elsewhere classified. *Notes:* 1. 1994 data incomplete; unavailable or withheld. 2. 1995 data incomplete; unavailable or withheld. 3. 1994 and 1995 data incomplete; unavailable or withheld.

READING, PA MSA

Wholesale and Retail Trade USA	Establishments		Employment		Emp / Est	Pay / Employee		Annual Payroll ($ 000)	
	1994	1995	1994	1995	1995	1994	1995	1994	1995
50- Wholesale trade	-	514	-	8,900	17	-	32,178	-	294,743
5012 Automobiles and other vehicles	-	13	-	132	10	-	25,121	-	3,448
5013 Motor vehicle supplies and new parts	-	25	-	204	8	-	20,725	-	4,283
5014 Tires and tubes	-	5	-	59	12	-	30,780	-	2,071
5015 Motor vehicle parts, used	-	11	-	60	5	-	21,133	-	1,088
5021 Furniture	-	5	-	77	15	-	36,156	-	2,525
5023 Homefurnishings	-	8	-	45	6	-	21,333	-	950
5031 Lumber, plywood, and millwork	-	9	-	120	13	-	28,267	-	3,641
5032 Brick, stone, & related materials	-	4	-	50	13	-	31,440	-	1,778
5033 Roofing, siding, & insulation	-	9	-	147	16	-	39,075	-	5,936
5039 Construction materials, nec	-	9	-	103	11	-	29,709	-	2,904
5044 Office equipment	-	12	-	239	20	-	31,079	-	6,981
5045 Computers, peripherals, & software	-	20	-	263	13	-	48,030	-	9,172
5046 Commercial equipment, nec	-	5	-	145	29	-	30,317	-	4,739
5047 Medical and hospital equipment	-	12	-	137	11	-	43,766	-	7,803
5048 Ophthalmic goods	-	3	-	26	9	-	14,154	-	413
5051 Metals service centers and offices	-	12	-	139	12	-	33,007	-	4,520
5063 Electrical apparatus and equipment	-	12	-	221	18	-	30,462	-	9,775
5065 Electronic parts and equipment	-	13	-	257	20	-	34,553	-	9,001
5072 Hardware	-	10	-	235	24	-	39,234	-	7,734
5074 Plumbing & hydronic heating supplies	-	7	-	96	14	-	44,625	-	4,306
5083 Farm and garden machinery	-	10	-	86	9	-	22,372	-	1,935
5084 Industrial machinery and equipment	-	33	-	499	15	-	35,399	-	18,551
5085 Industrial supplies	-	27	-	297	11	-	37,616	-	11,460
5087 Service establishment equipment	-	9	-	214	24	-	28,542	-	5,950
5091 Sporting & recreational goods	-	3	-	68	23	-	22,412	-	1,621
5093 Scrap and waste materials	-	15	-	230	15	-	22,887	-	5,751
5094 Jewelry & precious stones	-	3	-	7	2	-	15,429	-	110
5099 Durable goods, nec	-	8	-	38	5	-	19,474	-	913
5113 Industrial & personal service paper	-	5	-	104	21	-	29,423	-	3,460
5136 Men's and boys' clothing	-	12	-	816	68	-	35,662	-	27,419
5141 Groceries, general line	-	9	-	1,340	149	-	29,349	-	39,394
5143 Dairy products, exc. dried or canned	-	3	-	23	8	-	16,348	-	395
5145 Confectionery	-	5	-	87	17	-	15,954	-	1,391
5146 Fish and seafoods	-	3	-	12	4	-	17,333	-	274
5148 Fresh fruits and vegetables	-	3	-	8	3	-	22,000	-	214
5149 Groceries and related products, nec	-	19	-	548	29	-	30,102	-	18,384
5162 Plastics materials & basic shapes	-	4	-	10	3	-	108,000	-	475
5169 Chemicals & allied products, nec	-	11	-	209	19	-	47,081	-	10,552
5171 Petroleum bulk stations & terminals	-	4	-	26	7	-	38,769	-	975
5172 Petroleum products, nec	-	3	-	23	8	-	20,174	-	498
5181 Beer and ale	-	9	-	122	14	-	32,230	-	3,837
5191 Farm supplies	-	8	-	208	26	-	30,000	-	6,663
5198 Paints, varnishes, and supplies	-	6	-	42	7	-	29,905	-	1,127
5199 Nondurable goods, nec	-	19	-	73	4	-	26,301	-	2,696
52- Retail trade	-	2,123	-	30,026	14	-	13,215	-	416,191
5210 Lumber and other building materials	-	32	-	559	17	-	18,741	-	10,693
5230 Paint, glass, and wallpaper stores	-	8	-	26	3	-	21,692	-	600
5250 Hardware stores	-	19	-	123	6	-	20,390	-	2,555
5260 Retail nurseries and garden stores	-	26	-	135	5	-	12,711	-	2,231
5270 Mobile home dealers	-	6	-	27	5	-	31,704	-	889

Continued on next page.

READING, PA MSA - [continued]

Wholesale and Retail Trade USA	Establishments		Employment		Emp / Est	Pay / Employee		Annual Payroll ($ 000)	
	1994	1995	1994	1995	1995	1994	1995	1994	1995
5310 Department stores	-	16	-	2,915	182	-	12,148	-	36,957
5330 Variety stores	-	8	-	122	15	-	8,590	-	1,184
5390 Misc. general merchandise stores	-	10	-	419	42	-	14,243	-	5,457
5410 Grocery stores	-	131	-	3,781	29	-	11,623	-	42,938
5420 Meat and fish markets	-	23	-	132	6	-	10,818	-	1,510
5430 Fruit and vegetable markets	-	10	-	21	2	-	6,667	-	187
5440 Candy, nut, and confectionery stores	-	12	-	45	4	-	5,333	-	241
5460 Retail bakeries	-	24	-	140	6	-	8,086	-	1,207
5490 Miscellaneous food stores	-	10	-	76	8	-	9,789	-	708
5510 New and used car dealers	-	47	-	1,666	35	-	27,325	-	49,257
5520 Used car dealers	-	38	-	151	4	-	20,450	-	3,181
5530 Auto and home supply stores	-	36	-	245	7	-	18,155	-	4,624
5540 Gasoline service stations	-	127	-	1,024	8	-	11,762	-	12,272
5550 Boat dealers	-	4	-	25	6	-	20,320	-	542
5570 Motorcycle dealers	-	5	-	43	9	-	12,558	-	562
5610 Men's & boys' clothing stores	-	31	-	393	13	-	8,346	-	3,251
5620 Women's clothing stores	-	66	-	568	9	-	7,958	-	4,627
5630 Women's accessory & specialty stores	-	18	-	103	6	-	9,631	-	1,964
5640 Children's and infants' wear stores	-	4	-	22	6	-	6,909	-	152
5650 Family clothing stores	-	25	-	660	26	-	11,436	-	8,755
5660 Shoe stores	-	58	-	401	7	-	10,334	-	4,227
5690 Misc. apparel & accessory stores	-	20	-	115	6	-	10,922	-	1,300
5712 Furniture stores	-	30	-	262	9	-	16,229	-	4,570
5713 Floor covering stores	-	17	-	110	6	-	17,564	-	1,986
5714 Drapery and upholstery stores	-	7	-	19	3	-	9,684	-	196
5719 Misc. homefurnishings stores	-	26	-	204	8	-	10,157	-	2,243
5720 Household appliance stores	-	16	-	101	6	-	16,990	-	1,950
5731 Radio, TV, & electronic stores	-	16	-	185	12	-	16,584	-	3,007
5734 Computer and software stores	-	5	-	19	4	-	14,947	-	388
5735 Record & prerecorded tape stores	-	14	-	101	7	-	9,030	-	869
5736 Musical instrument stores	-	8	-	75	9	-	19,307	-	1,506
5812 Eating places	-	500	-	8,259	17	-	7,884	-	68,274
5813 Drinking places	-	81	-	395	5	-	9,286	-	3,774
5910 Drug stores and proprietary stores	-	51	-	742	15	-	15,628	-	11,880
5920 Liquor stores	-	37	-	124	3	-	18,387	-	2,322
5930 Used merchandise stores	-	22	-	87	4	-	8,460	-	818
5941 Sporting goods and bicycle shops	-	32	-	157	5	-	11,287	-	1,796
5942 Book stores	-	19	-	104	5	-	9,000	-	1,029
5944 Jewelry stores	-	37	-	179	5	-	13,385	-	2,387
5945 Hobby, toy, and game shops	-	14	-	124	9	-	10,548	-	1,363
5947 Gift, novelty, and souvenir shops	-	47	-	235	5	-	8,102	-	2,087
5948 Luggage and leather goods stores	-	9	-	60	7	-	9,600	-	682
5949 Sewing, needlework, and piece goods	-	10	-	58	6	-	11,517	-	698
5961 Catalog and mail-order houses	-	10	-	130	13	-	17,600	-	2,271
5962 Merchandising machine operators	-	15	-	225	15	-	24,320	-	5,573
5963 Direct selling establishments	-	24	-	219	9	-	12,073	-	2,827
5983 Fuel oil dealers	-	31	-	544	18	-	26,206	-	14,274
5992 Florists	-	39	-	182	5	-	11,055	-	2,209
5995 Optical goods stores	-	25	-	104	4	-	16,615	-	1,710
5999 Miscellaneous retail stores, nec	-	59	-	265	4	-	13,585	-	3,923

Source: County Business Patterns 1994/95, CBP-94/95, U.S. Department of Commerce, Washington DC, November 1997. The employment column represents mid-March employment in the year. Pay per employee is calculated by dividing 1st Quarter payroll, annualized, by mid-March employment. The column headed 'Emp / Est' shows 'employees per establishment'. A dash (-) means that data are unavailable or cannot be calculated. nec means not elsewhere classified. *Notes:* 1. 1994 data incomplete; unavailable or withheld. 2. 1995 data incomplete; unavailable or withheld. 3. 1994 and 1995 data incomplete; unavailable or withheld.

REDDING, CA MSA

Wholesale and Retail Trade USA	Establishments		Employment		Emp / Est	Pay / Employee		Annual Payroll ($ 000)	
	1994	1995	1994	1995	1995	1994	1995	1994	1995
50- Wholesale trade	283	279	2,640	2,648	9	31,500	32,363	90,968	81,555
5012 Automobiles and other vehicles	4	5	86	95	19	30,930	30,526	2,519	2,651
5013 Motor vehicle supplies and new parts	15	17	175	189	11	21,623	21,037	4,364	4,511
5014 Tires and tubes	5	-	24	-	-	41,333	-	652	-
5015 Motor vehicle parts, used	7	-	85	-	-	15,294	-	1,592	-
5020 Furniture and homefurnishings	4	6	24	44	7	25,333	25,182	666	1,062
5031 Lumber, plywood, and millwork	19	16	315	301	19	92,571	99,442	32,682	20,751
5039 Construction materials, nec	3	6	15	41	7	21,867	18,439	300	984
5044 Office equipment	13	15	108	90	6	18,074	20,933	2,045	1,925
5045 Computers, peripherals, & software	7	7	19	16	2	13,053	16,250	265	206

Continued on next page.

REDDING, CA MSA - [continued]

Wholesale and Retail Trade USA	Establishments		Employment		Emp / Est	Pay / Employee		Annual Payroll ($ 000)	
	1994	1995	1994	1995	1995	1994	1995	1994	1995
5046 Commercial equipment, nec	3	3	24	27	9	17,500	17,926	501	582
5047 Medical and hospital equipment	6	6	27	28	5	26,815	25,571	1,211	1,070
5051 Metals service centers and offices	8	7	99	107	15	29,576	29,495	3,012	3,030
5063 Electrical apparatus and equipment	10	8	145	116	15	27,448	27,966	3,986	3,116
5065 Electronic parts and equipment	9	9	67	79	9	18,149	17,114	1,537	1,514
5074 Plumbing & hydronic heating supplies	10	12	86	93	8	21,674	25,892	2,188	2,645
5075 Warm air heating & air conditioning	5	5	23	10	2	29,739	18,800	736	224
5082 Construction and mining machinery	4	3	46	46	15	38,957	38,087	1,790	2,012
5083 Farm and garden machinery	-	7	-	31	4	-	18,581	-	678
5084 Industrial machinery and equipment	5	6	51	55	9	29,176	27,709	1,590	1,538
5085 Industrial supplies	10	10	72	67	7	47,500	31,642	2,217	1,988
5091 Sporting & recreational goods	3	-	21	-	-	12,000	-	319	-
5093 Scrap and waste materials	10	9	81	75	8	15,852	18,773	1,944	2,172
5099 Durable goods, nec	-	7	-	28	4	-	17,714	-	1,059
5112 Stationery and office supplies	9	-	85	-	-	14,871	-	1,516	-
5147 Meats and meat products	5	5	37	36	7	18,270	20,222	792	775
5148 Fresh fruits and vegetables	3	-	22	-	-	34,545	-	319	-
5149 Groceries and related products, nec	11	10	52	60	6	34,154	33,000	1,837	2,083
5170 Petroleum and petroleum products	11	12	184	188	16	22,304	23,894	4,921	5,066
5191 Farm supplies	12	12	59	72	6	12,203	12,556	837	1,050
52 – Retail trade	1,029	997	11,329	11,773	12	12,477	12,793	154,311	156,810
5210 Lumber and other building materials	25	24	471	449	19	18,786	18,833	9,814	8,442
5230 Paint, glass, and wallpaper stores	12	9	59	53	6	21,559	24,226	1,312	1,345
5250 Hardware stores	19	12	83	97	8	13,687	15,299	1,899	1,425
5260 Retail nurseries and garden stores	7	-	25	-	-	8,640	-	243	-
5270 Mobile home dealers	4	-	16	-	-	20,750	-	362	-
5310 Department stores	7	7	1,000	1,036	148	10,936	11,421	11,754	12,132
5330 Variety stores	6	3	16	8	3	11,250	6,500	102	82
5390 Misc. general merchandise stores	13	12	245	300	25	19,037	19,160	5,533	5,937
5410 Grocery stores	89	87	1,683	1,828	21	15,356	15,442	28,540	29,837
5460 Retail bakeries	11	9	49	46	5	5,306	6,870	357	365
5490 Miscellaneous food stores	7	8	45	57	7	7,111	8,070	361	504
5510 New and used car dealers	12	12	458	448	37	29,249	29,732	13,340	13,704
5520 Used car dealers	11	9	45	62	7	19,556	23,226	1,118	1,477
5530 Auto and home supply stores	34	36	191	225	6	21,173	23,449	5,063	5,640
5540 Gasoline service stations	67	66	544	601	9	12,059	12,433	7,018	6,455
5550 Boat dealers	7	7	58	58	8	14,759	17,655	1,193	1,382
5560 Recreational vehicle dealers	-	5	-	36	7	-	18,000	-	713
5570 Motorcycle dealers	-	5	-	25	5	-	21,920	-	749
5610 Men's & boys' clothing stores	8	9	52	57	6	7,538	8,281	500	496
5620 Women's clothing stores	25	21	130	104	5	9,600	8,769	1,299	819
5630 Women's accessory & specialty stores	3	3	20	13	4	5,400	8,000	105	88
5640 Children's and infants' wear stores	-	3	-	3	1	-	24,000	-	67
5650 Family clothing stores	12	9	122	139	15	11,082	15,137	1,441	1,814
5660 Shoe stores	21	20	93	90	5	10,495	11,067	1,111	1,059
5690 Misc. apparel & accessory stores	8	8	27	37	5	9,333	10,595	314	472
5712 Furniture stores	19	17	105	118	7	16,152	16,915	1,723	2,015
5713 Floor covering stores	14	11	71	56	5	17,634	21,143	1,380	1,276
5720 Household appliance stores	4	4	6	28	7	15,333	13,143	206	425
5731 Radio, TV, & electronic stores	14	12	83	101	8	15,325	12,634	1,193	1,142
5734 Computer and software stores	7	9	18	26	3	15,556	15,692	377	462
5735 Record & prerecorded tape stores	5	6	40	42	7	7,200	7,238	346	365
5736 Musical instrument stores	5	4	12	11	3	12,667	14,909	158	160
5812 Eating places	255	241	3,539	3,641	15	7,140	6,996	27,146	27,477
5813 Drinking places	39	29	212	206	7	7,717	7,612	1,519	1,522
5910 Drug stores and proprietary stores	27	27	414	405	15	20,676	20,346	8,730	8,183
5920 Liquor stores	12	13	42	34	3	9,714	11,294	418	395
5930 Used merchandise stores	20	18	105	93	5	9,257	9,634	1,004	955
5941 Sporting goods and bicycle shops	22	18	160	132	7	11,475	12,000	1,906	1,795
5942 Book stores	7	6	51	53	9	10,039	9,736	550	632
5944 Jewelry stores	9	8	37	36	5	18,919	20,889	692	695
5945 Hobby, toy, and game shops	9	10	94	104	10	10,383	10,077	1,145	1,151
5946 Camera & photographic supply stores	4	-	25	-	-	17,280	-	395	-
5947 Gift, novelty, and souvenir shops	12	12	130	120	10	5,692	6,067	836	753
5949 Sewing, needlework, and piece goods	-	4	-	51	13	-	7,216	-	349
5961 Catalog and mail-order houses	5	5	18	20	4	14,000	16,200	320	339
5962 Merchandising machine operators	5	5	16	15	3	9,500	8,533	156	189
5963 Direct selling establishments	14	14	93	90	6	14,108	13,111	1,306	1,255
5980 Fuel dealers	8	9	47	48	5	20,766	19,917	1,041	1,062

Continued on next page.

REDDING, CA MSA - [continued]

Wholesale and Retail Trade USA	Establishments		Employment		Emp / Est	Pay / Employee		Annual Payroll ($ 000)	
	1994	1995	1994	1995	1995	1994	1995	1994	1995
5992 Florists	11	11	57	53	5	7,930	8,830	441	454
5995 Optical goods stores	3	4	30	36	9	9,333	9,333	274	523
5999 Miscellaneous retail stores, nec	32	39	110	127	3	10,873	11,118	1,265	1,474

Source: County Business Patterns 1994/95, CBP-94/95, U.S. Department of Commerce, Washington DC, November 1997. The employment column represents mid-March employment in the year. Pay per employee is calculated by dividing 1st Quarter payroll, annualized, by mid-March employment. The column headed 'Emp / Est' shows 'employees per establishment'. A dash (-) means that data are unavailable or cannot be calculated. nec means not elsewhere classified. *Notes:* 1. 1994 data incomplete; unavailable or withheld. 2. 1995 data incomplete; unavailable or withheld. 3. 1994 and 1995 data incomplete; unavailable or withheld.

RENO, NV MSA

Wholesale and Retail Trade USA	Establishments		Employment		Emp / Est	Pay / Employee		Annual Payroll ($ 000)	
	1994	1995	1994	1995	1995	1994	1995	1994	1995
50 - Wholesale trade	-	722	-	8,924	12	-	31,982	-	295,716
5012 Automobiles and other vehicles	-	9	-	223	25	-	31,587	-	8,915
5013 Motor vehicle supplies and new parts	-	37	-	404	11	-	26,109	-	11,624
5014 Tires and tubes	-	6	-	84	14	-	36,667	-	3,391
5015 Motor vehicle parts, used	-	9	-	84	9	-	22,905	-	1,619
5021 Furniture	-	9	-	114	13	-	37,754	-	3,701
5023 Homefurnishings	-	12	-	90	8	-	20,089	-	2,308
5031 Lumber, plywood, and millwork	-	18	-	141	8	-	27,121	-	4,355
5039 Construction materials, nec	-	12	-	140	12	-	34,657	-	5,882
5044 Office equipment	-	17	-	142	8	-	39,859	-	4,397
5045 Computers, peripherals, & software	-	37	-	393	11	-	35,165	-	13,773
5047 Medical and hospital equipment	-	16	-	137	9	-	34,102	-	5,236
5049 Professional equipment, nec	-	5	-	88	18	-	20,091	-	1,979
5063 Electrical apparatus and equipment	-	22	-	230	10	-	58,330	-	9,148
5064 Electrical appliances, TV & radios	-	4	-	40	10	-	43,700	-	1,140
5065 Electronic parts and equipment	-	36	-	356	10	-	31,326	-	13,050
5074 Plumbing & hydronic heating supplies	-	12	-	303	25	-	32,898	-	11,852
5078 Refrigeration equipment and supplies	-	4	-	11	3	-	25,455	-	263
5082 Construction and mining machinery	-	21	-	542	26	-	35,756	-	20,322
5083 Farm and garden machinery	-	4	-	36	9	-	34,333	-	1,289
5084 Industrial machinery and equipment	-	30	-	217	7	-	48,258	-	10,057
5085 Industrial supplies	-	27	-	196	7	-	29,551	-	6,655
5087 Service establishment equipment	-	19	-	166	9	-	25,157	-	4,701
5088 Transportation equipment & supplies	-	5	-	8	2	-	39,500	-	318
5091 Sporting & recreational goods	-	17	-	388	23	-	25,258	-	9,085
5093 Scrap and waste materials	-	9	-	139	15	-	23,655	-	4,453
5099 Durable goods, nec	-	17	-	187	11	-	26,011	-	5,279
5110 Paper and paper products	-	28	-	333	12	-	23,279	-	7,559
5120 Drugs, proprietaries, and sundries	-	15	-	97	6	-	29,278	-	3,601
5130 Apparel, piece goods, and notions	-	20	-	190	10	-	23,495	-	4,405
5143 Dairy products, exc. dried or canned	-	5	-	26	5	-	22,923	-	582
5147 Meats and meat products	-	5	-	96	19	-	24,667	-	2,661
5149 Groceries and related products, nec	-	24	-	430	18	-	29,581	-	13,030
5162 Plastics materials & basic shapes	-	5	-	29	6	-	17,793	-	569
5169 Chemicals & allied products, nec	-	13	-	115	9	-	31,374	-	4,188
5172 Petroleum products, nec	-	3	-	22	7	-	24,182	-	524
5180 Beer, wine, and distilled beverages	-	5	-	301	60	-	38,804	-	11,570
5192 Books, periodicals, & newspapers	-	5	-	360	72	-	21,222	-	6,371
5198 Paints, varnishes, and supplies	-	8	-	97	12	-	23,216	-	2,454
5199 Nondurable goods, nec	-	22	-	91	4	-	22,330	-	2,755
52 - Retail trade	1,862	1,861	25,288	27,225	15	15,295	15,363	424,946	443,958
5210 Lumber and other building materials	29	29	587	723	25	23,101	21,632	14,138	15,885
5230 Paint, glass, and wallpaper stores	15	15	90	147	10	23,600	24,735	2,580	4,299
5250 Hardware stores	14	10	187	176	18	18,545	16,932	3,638	2,936
5260 Retail nurseries and garden stores	13	12	139	150	13	13,669	15,360	2,735	3,373
5270 Mobile home dealers	14	14	85	107	8	21,788	19,850	2,059	2,411
5310 Department stores	16	17	2,388	2,845	167	13,121	12,370	34,834	37,708
5410 Grocery stores	118	122	2,897	3,063	25	18,448	18,891	55,846	57,679
5440 Candy, nut, and confectionery stores	11	9	61	52	6	11,869	11,769	714	653
5460 Retail bakeries	21	15	91	84	6	8,484	7,667	946	709
5490 Miscellaneous food stores	-	14	-	67	5	-	10,269	-	715
5510 New and used car dealers	20	18	1,071	978	54	39,234	39,072	48,429	42,347
5520 Used car dealers	29	27	102	122	5	16,353	21,180	2,352	2,967
5530 Auto and home supply stores	54	48	402	363	8	18,159	19,625	7,892	7,831
5540 Gasoline service stations	80	77	1,012	1,160	15	14,107	14,686	16,029	17,878
5550 Boat dealers	5	-	29	-	-	20,414	-	681	-
5560 Recreational vehicle dealers	10	7	102	111	16	19,216	19,063	2,390	2,424

Continued on next page.

RENO, NV MSA - [continued]

Wholesale and Retail Trade USA	Establishments		Employment		Emp / Est	Pay / Employee		Annual Payroll ($ 000)	
	1994	1995	1994	1995	1995	1994	1995	1994	1995
5570 Motorcycle dealers	-	5	-	70	14	-	18,229	-	1,560
5620 Women's clothing stores	48	42	372	350	8	8,634	8,080	3,474	2,757
5650 Family clothing stores	24	24	277	314	13	11,610	10,892	3,261	3,255
5660 Shoe stores	39	35	185	188	5	13,081	12,277	2,511	2,256
5690 Misc. apparel & accessory stores	21	18	109	99	6	11,486	12,970	1,352	1,360
5712 Furniture stores	38	37	322	316	9	17,280	19,076	5,983	6,607
5713 Floor covering stores	13	12	89	89	7	23,416	22,831	2,233	2,516
5731 Radio, TV, & electronic stores	19	19	226	275	14	25,593	23,709	6,128	7,095
5734 Computer and software stores	22	19	84	78	4	16,381	18,974	1,407	1,448
5812 Eating places	446	428	7,105	7,503	18	8,806	8,878	67,962	71,158
5813 Drinking places	110	101	547	620	6	8,921	8,632	5,127	5,302
5910 Drug stores and proprietary stores	25	23	425	416	18	18,965	20,702	8,191	8,421
5920 Liquor stores	14	15	66	65	4	18,970	19,138	1,491	1,591
5930 Used merchandise stores	42	42	348	336	8	17,080	17,333	6,397	6,070
5941 Sporting goods and bicycle shops	45	44	278	317	7	14,475	16,189	4,675	5,624
5942 Book stores	14	13	73	103	8	11,123	11,068	858	1,200
5943 Stationery stores	3	-	7	-	-	9,143	-	76	-
5944 Jewelry stores	34	34	185	193	6	20,108	19,876	3,910	3,953
5945 Hobby, toy, and game shops	12	12	124	144	12	17,129	12,417	2,310	1,850
5946 Camera & photographic supply stores	5	-	28	-	-	18,857	-	610	-
5947 Gift, novelty, and souvenir shops	59	56	329	398	7	10,298	10,332	3,772	4,231
5948 Luggage and leather goods stores	4	4	23	24	6	8,696	10,167	310	233
5949 Sewing, needlework, and piece goods	10	-	88	-	-	7,864	-	694	-
5961 Catalog and mail-order houses	-	16	-	1,203	75	-	19,036	-	24,409
5962 Merchandising machine operators	9	7	52	47	7	21,154	21,532	1,095	947
5963 Direct selling establishments	-	19	-	160	8	-	20,750	-	3,272
5980 Fuel dealers	13	14	102	111	8	26,941	27,784	2,888	3,260
5992 Florists	23	23	142	156	7	12,761	13,410	2,050	2,189
5993 Tobacco stores and stands	-	5	-	66	13	-	12,788	-	759
5995 Optical goods stores	-	15	-	81	5	-	17,679	-	1,385
5999 Miscellaneous retail stores, nec	70	74	403	443	6	13,002	15,413	5,931	7,409

Source: County Business Patterns 1994/95, CBP-94/95, U.S. Department of Commerce, Washington DC, November 1997. The employment column represents mid-March employment in the year. Pay per employee is calculated by dividing 1st Quarter payroll, annualized, by mid-March employment. The column headed 'Emp / Est' shows 'employees per establishment'. A dash (-) means that data are unavailable or cannot be calculated. nec means not elsewhere classified. *Notes:* 1. 1994 data incomplete; unavailable or withheld. 2. 1995 data incomplete; unavailable or withheld. 3. 1994 and 1995 data incomplete; unavailable or withheld.

RICHLAND - KENNEWICK - PASCO, WA MSA

Wholesale and Retail Trade USA	Establishments		Employment		Emp / Est	Pay / Employee		Annual Payroll ($ 000)	
	1994	1995	1994	1995	1995	1994	1995	1994	1995
50 - Wholesale trade	-	270	-	2,938	11	-	22,588	-	74,015
5013 Motor vehicle supplies and new parts	-	10	-	73	7	-	23,014	-	1,832
5015 Motor vehicle parts, used	-	10	-	11	1	-	16,364	-	167
5039 Construction materials, nec	-	4	-	7	2	-	18,286	-	175
5044 Office equipment	-	8	-	76	10	-	21,632	-	1,755
5063 Electrical apparatus and equipment	-	6	-	25	4	-	43,840	-	940
5065 Electronic parts and equipment	-	7	-	28	4	-	24,000	-	775
5072 Hardware	-	5	-	23	5	-	21,739	-	523
5074 Plumbing & hydronic heating supplies [2]	-	5	-	98	20	-	24,082	-	2,398
5083 Farm and garden machinery	-	15	-	208	14	-	27,519	-	6,157
5084 Industrial machinery and equipment	-	9	-	85	9	-	22,447	-	2,087
5085 Industrial supplies	-	16	-	148	9	-	29,946	-	4,470
5087 Service establishment equipment	-	5	-	10	2	-	14,000	-	147
5093 Scrap and waste materials	-	8	-	45	6	-	16,889	-	1,285
5099 Durable goods, nec	-	7	-	8	1	-	40,000	-	500
5112 Stationery and office supplies [2]	-	5	-	28	6	-	15,857	-	596
5149 Groceries and related products, nec	-	7	-	51	7	-	24,078	-	1,280
5150 Farm-product raw materials	-	9	-	66	7	-	22,848	-	1,543
5169 Chemicals & allied products, nec	-	5	-	17	3	-	33,412	-	562
5171 Petroleum bulk stations & terminals	-	5	-	66	13	-	20,667	-	2,561
5180 Beer, wine, and distilled beverages [2]	-	5	-	144	29	-	16,139	-	2,554
5191 Farm supplies [2]	-	31	-	72	2	-	24,444	-	2,028
52 - Retail trade	-	958	-	12,237	13	-	13,753	-	178,107
5210 Lumber and other building materials	-	13	-	338	26	-	21,172	-	7,849
5250 Hardware stores	-	8	-	96	12	-	12,250	-	1,237
5270 Mobile home dealers [2]	-	8	-	75	9	-	43,307	-	2,895
5300 General merchandise stores	-	14	-	1,806	129	-	14,319	-	28,507
5410 Grocery stores [2]	-	73	-	1,124	15	-	16,520	-	19,449
5420 Meat and fish markets [2]	-	3	-	27	9	-	7,556	-	230

Continued on next page.

RICHLAND – KENNEWICK – PASCO, WA MSA - [continued]

Wholesale and Retail Trade USA	Establishments		Employment		Emp / Est	Pay / Employee		Annual Payroll ($ 000)	
	1994	1995	1994	1995	1995	1994	1995	1994	1995
5440 Candy, nut, and confectionery stores [2]	-	5	-	24	5	-	7,833	-	175
5460 Retail bakeries	-	12	-	92	8	-	8,478	-	791
5490 Miscellaneous food stores [2]	-	4	-	31	8	-	13,548	-	493
5510 New and used car dealers	-	13	-	739	57	-	30,766	-	24,364
5520 Used car dealers [2]	-	14	-	52	4	-	22,615	-	1,257
5530 Auto and home supply stores	-	43	-	309	7	-	24,026	-	7,254
5540 Gasoline service stations	-	57	-	449	8	-	11,278	-	5,175
5560 Recreational vehicle dealers	-	5	-	15	3	-	27,467	-	379
5570 Motorcycle dealers [2]	-	6	-	21	4	-	12,190	-	358
5610 Men's & boys' clothing stores	-	7	-	43	6	-	7,814	-	322
5620 Women's clothing stores	-	22	-	129	6	-	6,822	-	849
5630 Women's accessory & specialty stores [2]	-	4	-	13	3	-	9,231	-	129
5650 Family clothing stores	-	15	-	181	12	-	9,547	-	1,893
5660 Shoe stores	-	20	-	80	4	-	11,300	-	999
5690 Misc. apparel & accessory stores [2]	-	5	-	15	3	-	7,467	-	129
5712 Furniture stores	-	24	-	108	5	-	22,222	-	2,615
5713 Floor covering stores	-	14	-	73	5	-	17,808	-	1,195
5720 Household appliance stores	-	14	-	51	4	-	14,353	-	637
5731 Radio, TV, & electronic stores	-	8	-	45	6	-	18,489	-	749
5736 Musical instrument stores [2]	-	6	-	32	5	-	16,375	-	542
5812 Eating places	-	209	-	3,657	17	-	7,916	-	30,088
5813 Drinking places	-	37	-	235	6	-	9,974	-	2,211
5910 Drug stores and proprietary stores	-	21	-	391	19	-	18,148	-	7,444
5930 Used merchandise stores	-	15	-	95	6	-	8,042	-	836
5941 Sporting goods and bicycle shops	-	22	-	132	6	-	11,394	-	1,910
5942 Book stores	-	13	-	70	5	-	8,686	-	598
5944 Jewelry stores [2]	-	13	-	81	6	-	14,272	-	2,079
5945 Hobby, toy, and game shops	-	14	-	88	6	-	12,136	-	961
5947 Gift, novelty, and souvenir shops	-	20	-	71	4	-	7,268	-	525
5949 Sewing, needlework, and piece goods	-	9	-	76	8	-	5,632	-	433
5963 Direct selling establishments	-	12	-	128	11	-	11,000	-	1,338
5992 Florists	-	15	-	106	7	-	8,340	-	861
5995 Optical goods stores	-	10	-	39	4	-	14,872	-	523
5999 Miscellaneous retail stores, nec	-	28	-	133	5	-	8,511	-	1,498

Source: County Business Patterns 1994/95, CBP-94/95, U.S. Department of Commerce, Washington DC, November 1997. The employment column represents mid-March employment in the year. Pay per employee is calculated by dividing 1st Quarter payroll, annualized, by mid-March employment. The column headed 'Emp / Est' shows 'employees per establishment'. A dash (-) means that data are unavailable or cannot be calculated. nec means not elsewhere classified. *Notes:* 1. 1994 data incomplete; unavailable or withheld. 2. 1995 data incomplete; unavailable or withheld. 3. 1994 and 1995 data incomplete; unavailable or withheld.

RICHMOND – PETERSBURG, VA MSA

Wholesale and Retail Trade USA	Establishments		Employment		Emp / Est	Pay / Employee		Annual Payroll ($ 000)	
	1994	1995	1994	1995	1995	1994	1995	1994	1995
50- Wholesale trade	-	2,001	-	29,166	15	-	32,793	-	983,290
5012 Automobiles and other vehicles [2]	-	37	-	769	21	-	27,792	-	23,089
5013 Motor vehicle supplies and new parts [2]	-	114	-	1,141	10	-	23,351	-	27,187
5014 Tires and tubes [2]	-	17	-	170	10	-	21,953	-	3,945
5015 Motor vehicle parts, used [2]	-	35	-	101	3	-	23,208	-	2,398
5021 Furniture [2]	-	41	-	373	9	-	27,560	-	10,762
5023 Homefurnishings [2]	-	29	-	193	7	-	23,171	-	5,276
5031 Lumber, plywood, and millwork [2]	-	48	-	788	16	-	27,888	-	22,715
5032 Brick, stone, & related materials [2]	-	10	-	34	3	-	55,529	-	1,350
5033 Roofing, siding, & insulation [2]	-	22	-	314	14	-	41,210	-	12,151
5039 Construction materials, nec [2]	-	37	-	275	7	-	26,836	-	8,489
5043 Photographic equipment & supplies [2]	-	5	-	64	13	-	27,250	-	1,920
5044 Office equipment [2]	-	38	-	561	15	-	42,610	-	20,470
5045 Computers, peripherals, & software [2]	-	63	-	968	15	-	65,438	-	52,830
5046 Commercial equipment, nec [2]	-	23	-	117	5	-	21,504	-	3,221
5047 Medical and hospital equipment [2]	-	64	-	563	9	-	37,741	-	22,424
5049 Professional equipment, nec [2]	-	12	-	125	10	-	26,656	-	2,822
5051 Metals service centers and offices [2]	-	35	-	338	10	-	34,710	-	12,048
5052 Coal and other minerals and ores [2]	-	9	-	5	1	-	53,600	-	613
5063 Electrical apparatus and equipment [2]	-	102	-	1,011	10	-	38,679	-	40,613
5064 Electrical appliances, TV & radios [2]	-	14	-	253	18	-	37,708	-	8,569
5065 Electronic parts and equipment [2]	-	60	-	512	9	-	48,656	-	23,860
5072 Hardware [2]	-	30	-	404	13	-	27,168	-	11,408
5074 Plumbing & hydronic heating supplies [2]	-	51	-	278	5	-	30,619	-	8,901
5075 Warm air heating & air conditioning [2]	-	45	-	373	8	-	34,874	-	13,669
5082 Construction and mining machinery [2]	-	34	-	359	11	-	36,524	-	13,654

Continued on next page.

RICHMOND - PETERSBURG, VA MSA - [continued]

Wholesale and Retail Trade USA	Establishments 1994	Establishments 1995	Employment 1994	Employment 1995	Emp / Est 1995	Pay / Employee 1994	Pay / Employee 1995	Annual Payroll ($ 000) 1994	Annual Payroll ($ 000) 1995
5083 Farm and garden machinery [2]	-	27	-	292	11	-	20,068	-	6,664
5084 Industrial machinery and equipment [2]	-	159	-	1,359	9	-	38,472	-	54,628
5085 Industrial supplies [2]	-	76	-	704	9	-	37,131	-	28,064
5087 Service establishment equipment [2]	-	28	-	305	11	-	24,787	-	7,813
5091 Sporting & recreational goods [2]	-	12	-	45	4	-	25,333	-	1,100
5092 Toys and hobby goods and supplies [2]	-	7	-	40	6	-	21,200	-	942
5093 Scrap and waste materials [2]	-	32	-	460	14	-	27,461	-	12,065
5094 Jewelry & precious stones [2]	-	13	-	75	6	-	20,640	-	1,708
5099 Durable goods, nec [2]	-	38	-	268	7	-	28,313	-	8,102
5111 Printing and writing paper [2]	-	9	-	229	25	-	37,590	-	9,527
5112 Stationery and office supplies [2]	-	51	-	706	14	-	27,598	-	19,103
5113 Industrial & personal service paper [2]	-	22	-	129	6	-	49,953	-	5,093
5120 Drugs, proprietaries, and sundries [2]	-	22	-	423	19	-	42,582	-	19,405
5136 Men's and boys' clothing [2]	-	10	-	150	15	-	17,760	-	2,589
5141 Groceries, general line [2]	-	18	-	329	18	-	22,188	-	7,255
5143 Dairy products, exc. dried or canned [2]	-	8	-	229	29	-	32,052	-	4,792
5145 Confectionery [2]	-	11	-	54	5	-	33,185	-	2,042
5147 Meats and meat products [2]	-	6	-	47	8	-	23,234	-	1,119
5148 Fresh fruits and vegetables [2]	-	10	-	140	14	-	24,229	-	4,199
5149 Groceries and related products, nec [2]	-	43	-	1,458	34	-	21,904	-	34,083
5150 Farm-product raw materials [2]	-	19	-	5	-	-	55,200	-	288
5162 Plastics materials & basic shapes [2]	-	12	-	99	8	-	40,485	-	4,024
5169 Chemicals & allied products, nec [2]	-	49	-	642	13	-	46,237	-	32,493
5171 Petroleum bulk stations & terminals [2]	-	27	-	290	11	-	35,655	-	9,610
5172 Petroleum products, nec [2]	-	14	-	21	2	-	28,190	-	725
5181 Beer and ale [2]	-	11	-	67	6	-	23,343	-	1,740
5191 Farm supplies [2]	-	24	-	217	9	-	19,465	-	4,496
5192 Books, periodicals, & newspapers [2]	-	12	-	116	10	-	24,828	-	2,724
5193 Flowers & florists' supplies [2]	-	11	-	77	7	-	18,390	-	1,465
5198 Paints, varnishes, and supplies [2]	-	22	-	103	5	-	24,272	-	2,610
5199 Nondurable goods, nec [2]	-	69	-	449	7	-	23,857	-	11,170
52- Retail trade	-	5,562	-	89,417	16	-	13,892	-	1,302,654
5210 Lumber and other building materials [2]	-	61	-	1,176	19	-	19,796	-	25,869
5230 Paint, glass, and wallpaper stores [2]	-	34	-	132	4	-	19,212	-	2,600
5250 Hardware stores [2]	-	30	-	213	7	-	12,845	-	2,829
5260 Retail nurseries and garden stores [2]	-	37	-	223	6	-	15,587	-	3,842
5270 Mobile home dealers [2]	-	11	-	27	2	-	22,667	-	818
5310 Department stores [2]	-	37	-	6,011	162	-	10,739	-	64,289
5330 Variety stores [2]	-	37	-	293	8	-	8,437	-	2,752
5390 Misc. general merchandise stores [2]	-	43	-	1,314	31	-	16,237	-	21,051
5410 Grocery stores [2]	-	536	-	12,591	23	-	11,231	-	145,181
5420 Meat and fish markets [2]	-	25	-	91	4	-	12,923	-	1,265
5440 Candy, nut, and confectionery stores [2]	-	9	-	22	2	-	6,364	-	146
5460 Retail bakeries [2]	-	48	-	419	9	-	10,902	-	4,578
5490 Miscellaneous food stores [2]	-	35	-	198	6	-	8,646	-	1,849
5510 New and used car dealers [2]	-	75	-	3,856	51	-	29,976	-	127,501
5520 Used car dealers [2]	-	83	-	494	6	-	22,073	-	10,967
5530 Auto and home supply stores [2]	-	149	-	1,185	8	-	18,336	-	22,945
5540 Gasoline service stations [2]	-	350	-	2,942	8	-	13,608	-	41,930
5550 Boat dealers [2]	-	14	-	59	4	-	20,475	-	1,508
5570 Motorcycle dealers [2]	-	10	-	71	7	-	17,183	-	1,450
5610 Men's & boys' clothing stores [2]	-	85	-	779	9	-	13,094	-	9,920
5620 Women's clothing stores [2]	-	179	-	1,905	11	-	8,376	-	15,668
5630 Women's accessory & specialty stores [2]	-	37	-	202	5	-	10,634	-	2,329
5640 Children's and infants' wear stores [2]	-	25	-	261	10	-	8,628	-	2,151
5650 Family clothing stores [2]	-	52	-	823	16	-	9,536	-	7,665
5660 Shoe stores [2]	-	132	-	804	6	-	11,448	-	9,087
5690 Misc. apparel & accessory stores [2]	-	26	-	138	5	-	9,652	-	1,623
5712 Furniture stores [2]	-	151	-	1,306	9	-	17,354	-	23,070
5719 Misc. homefurnishings stores [2]	-	72	-	555	8	-	12,274	-	7,108
5720 Household appliance stores [2]	-	32	-	217	7	-	20,774	-	4,969
5731 Radio, TV, & electronic stores [2]	-	61	-	652	11	-	23,436	-	16,454
5734 Computer and software stores [2]	-	34	-	142	4	-	21,465	-	3,673
5735 Record & prerecorded tape stores [2]	-	35	-	235	7	-	11,557	-	2,855
5736 Musical instrument stores [2]	-	19	-	90	5	-	19,244	-	1,894
5812 Eating places	-	1,330	-	26,142	20	-	8,170	-	224,119
5813 Drinking places [2]	-	19	-	282	15	-	5,844	-	1,524
5910 Drug stores and proprietary stores [2]	-	197	-	2,370	12	-	15,364	-	38,918
5920 Liquor stores [2]	-	44	-	178	4	-	13,483	-	2,194
5930 Used merchandise stores [2]	-	76	-	502	7	-	13,116	-	5,536
5941 Sporting goods and bicycle shops [2]	-	82	-	616	8	-	13,058	-	8,208

Continued on next page.

RICHMOND – PETERSBURG, VA MSA - [continued]

Wholesale and Retail Trade USA	Establishments		Employment		Emp / Est	Pay / Employee		Annual Payroll ($ 000)	
	1994	1995	1994	1995	1995	1994	1995	1994	1995
5942 Book stores [2]	-	62	-	301	5	-	10,764	-	3,803
5943 Stationery stores [2]	-	21	-	161	8	-	11,155	-	1,698
5944 Jewelry stores [2]	-	99	-	605	6	-	16,939	-	10,605
5945 Hobby, toy, and game shops [2]	-	44	-	563	13	-	9,726	-	6,406
5946 Camera & photographic supply stores [2]	-	14	-	20	1	-	14,400	-	301
5947 Gift, novelty, and souvenir shops [2]	-	124	-	642	5	-	7,340	-	5,320
5948 Luggage and leather goods stores [2]	-	6	-	31	5	-	8,387	-	249
5949 Sewing, needlework, and piece goods [2]	-	28	-	154	6	-	8,416	-	1,321
5961 Catalog and mail-order houses [2]	-	21	-	252	12	-	20,937	-	5,271
5962 Merchandising machine operators [2]	-	23	-	215	9	-	19,498	-	4,654
5963 Direct selling establishments [2]	-	54	-	409	8	-	11,188	-	4,415
5983 Fuel oil dealers [2]	-	30	-	51	2	-	22,275	-	1,143
5984 Liquefied petroleum gas dealers [2]	-	10	-	26	3	-	24,462	-	624
5992 Florists [2]	-	89	-	445	5	-	12,162	-	5,664
5995 Optical goods stores [2]	-	63	-	280	4	-	19,571	-	5,500
5999 Miscellaneous retail stores, nec [2]	-	166	-	855	5	-	12,262	-	11,878

Source: County Business Patterns 1994/95, CBP-94/95, U.S. Department of Commerce, Washington DC, November 1997. The employment column represents mid-March employment in the year. Pay per employee is calculated by dividing 1st Quarter payroll, annualized, by mid-March employment. The column headed 'Emp / Est' shows 'employees per establishment'. A dash (-) means that data are unavailable or cannot be calculated. nec means not elsewhere classified. *Notes:* 1. 1994 data incomplete; unavailable or withheld. 2. 1995 data incomplete; unavailable or withheld. 3. 1994 and 1995 data incomplete; unavailable or withheld.

RIVERSIDE – SAN BERNARDINO, CA PMSA

Wholesale and Retail Trade USA	Establishments		Employment		Emp / Est	Pay / Employee		Annual Payroll ($ 000)	
	1994	1995	1994	1995	1995	1994	1995	1994	1995
50- Wholesale trade	3,077	3,112	37,797	39,193	13	26,642	27,864	1,079,915	1,136,469
5012 Automobiles and other vehicles	62	64	1,702	1,854	29	21,149	23,661	39,721	47,111
5013 Motor vehicle supplies and new parts	202	196	2,423	2,425	12	22,511	24,414	60,263	62,268
5014 Tires and tubes	30	27	384	319	12	26,667	33,016	10,813	9,998
5015 Motor vehicle parts, used	62	76	426	520	7	16,714	17,392	7,784	10,103
5021 Furniture	45	49	574	582	12	22,397	21,265	13,971	12,705
5023 Homefurnishings	54	50	603	591	12	23,774	24,115	16,105	15,322
5031 Lumber, plywood, and millwork	92	86	1,650	1,427	17	29,130	32,373	55,066	50,286
5032 Brick, stone, & related materials	42	44	494	561	13	24,818	25,996	14,416	13,182
5033 Roofing, siding, & insulation	16	11	440	156	14	27,773	30,538	12,436	5,489
5039 Construction materials, nec	36	50	315	565	11	28,089	26,478	9,883	15,382
5043 Photographic equipment & supplies	8	8	66	95	12	37,879	39,958	3,053	3,940
5044 Office equipment	60	60	669	690	12	27,928	29,768	19,504	20,819
5045 Computers, peripherals, & software	93	86	719	704	8	36,245	34,460	26,232	24,191
5046 Commercial equipment, nec	27	28	217	247	9	25,419	24,243	6,026	8,176
5047 Medical and hospital equipment	78	60	1,100	1,019	17	32,375	31,859	38,203	34,596
5048 Ophthalmic goods	16	15	38	59	4	18,000	16,881	822	1,277
5049 Professional equipment, nec	17	15	137	135	9	24,292	27,111	3,970	3,642
5051 Metals service centers and offices	74	68	869	1,017	15	26,697	26,037	25,899	29,242
5063 Electrical apparatus and equipment	103	99	1,019	1,052	11	31,176	32,985	32,902	33,161
5064 Electrical appliances, TV & radios	19	20	144	160	8	27,000	26,875	4,268	4,427
5065 Electronic parts and equipment	86	95	667	1,030	11	32,678	35,386	22,256	38,431
5072 Hardware	64	63	648	710	11	25,556	26,169	19,284	19,751
5074 Plumbing & hydronic heating supplies	68	64	515	434	7	26,283	26,258	13,855	11,402
5075 Warm air heating & air conditioning	39	38	373	389	10	32,043	30,458	12,904	13,028
5078 Refrigeration equipment and supplies	15	16	440	315	20	49,673	44,965	19,718	13,707
5082 Construction and mining machinery	31	35	447	475	14	36,465	37,381	15,776	17,453
5083 Farm and garden machinery	49	51	405	447	9	27,714	27,696	12,070	13,573
5084 Industrial machinery and equipment	139	145	984	1,086	7	31,663	32,663	32,174	35,996
5085 Industrial supplies	83	85	654	744	9	25,841	27,651	18,454	21,172
5087 Service establishment equipment	48	44	421	469	11	19,867	20,094	8,259	9,943
5088 Transportation equipment & supplies	21	25	123	131	5	25,821	25,435	3,835	4,068
5091 Sporting & recreational goods	46	53	377	382	7	18,844	21,298	9,028	8,351
5092 Toys and hobby goods and supplies	19	19	423	473	25	20,775	22,782	9,184	11,424
5093 Scrap and waste materials	80	83	913	1,046	13	20,329	21,740	20,797	25,131
5094 Jewelry & precious stones	14	12	47	89	7	16,085	20,360	766	2,128
5099 Durable goods, nec	43	54	212	283	5	21,509	20,650	4,460	6,236
5111 Printing and writing paper	14	16	140	158	10	33,800	30,633	4,639	4,511
5112 Stationery and office supplies	60	50	699	561	11	21,700	28,799	15,906	15,765
5113 Industrial & personal service paper	34	33	434	469	14	37,180	41,493	16,461	19,444
5120 Drugs, proprietaries, and sundries	44	43	729	731	17	30,140	33,209	25,859	25,698
5131 Piece goods & notions	23	20	234	212	11	15,915	23,679	5,602	5,842
5136 Men's and boys' clothing	20	17	142	134	8	21,042	22,269	3,519	3,527
5137 Women's and children's clothing	30	25	120	132	5	17,233	15,576	2,064	1,949

Continued on next page.

RIVERSIDE - SAN BERNARDINO, CA PMSA - [continued]

Wholesale and Retail Trade USA	Establishments		Employment		Emp / Est	Pay / Employee		Annual Payroll ($ 000)	
	1994	1995	1994	1995	1995	1994	1995	1994	1995
5139 Footwear	8	8	83	81	10	22,554	24,395	2,405	1,991
5141 Groceries, general line	44	42	1,254	1,300	31	26,954	26,212	35,018	34,839
5142 Packaged frozen food	12	12	379	461	38	39,377	34,751	16,775	17,260
5143 Dairy products, exc. dried or canned	20	16	609	621	39	29,314	31,414	19,804	20,904
5144 Poultry and poultry products	17	11	213	204	19	24,864	25,353	5,529	5,118
5145 Confectionery	8	8	248	266	33	28,161	27,880	7,022	7,578
5146 Fish and seafoods	6	8	13	18	2	28,308	31,556	313	557
5147 Meats and meat products	23	23	350	361	16	18,480	19,501	6,871	6,030
5148 Fresh fruits and vegetables	41	37	1,125	1,082	29	21,006	20,566	23,983	23,752
5149 Groceries and related products, nec	97	94	2,026	2,204	23	25,315	26,829	54,843	65,398
5153 Grain and field beans	7	6	183	185	31	19,126	22,724	3,940	2,692
5154 Livestock	-	8	-	4	1	-	21,000	-	118
5159 Farm-product raw materials, nec	8	-	51	-	-	19,765	-	954	-
5162 Plastics materials & basic shapes	26	26	239	277	11	28,134	28,780	7,578	8,708
5169 Chemicals & allied products, nec	51	56	373	434	8	36,150	37,465	13,669	15,733
5171 Petroleum bulk stations & terminals	37	34	552	500	15	33,833	35,008	20,026	18,393
5172 Petroleum products, nec	17	19	130	136	7	31,077	25,088	3,294	3,533
5180 Beer, wine, and distilled beverages	16	16	875	708	44	30,126	31,153	24,077	22,951
5191 Farm supplies	100	92	1,027	777	8	23,291	26,574	27,300	24,202
5192 Books, periodicals, & newspapers	21	21	266	296	14	20,797	23,649	5,596	11,639
5193 Flowers & florists' supplies	30	34	278	458	13	16,388	19,738	5,470	8,173
5198 Paints, varnishes, and supplies	31	26	189	186	7	24,063	26,108	5,473	5,746
5199 Nondurable goods, nec	137	152	1,041	1,365	9	23,727	23,959	28,026	31,432
52- Retail trade	12,069	11,994	171,817	178,332	15	13,900	14,593	2,551,510	2,678,688
5210 Lumber and other building materials	202	182	4,194	4,455	24	19,312	20,606	88,234	92,040
5230 Paint, glass, and wallpaper stores	93	88	448	462	5	21,179	21,437	9,808	9,398
5250 Hardware stores	93	67	602	502	7	13,528	14,821	8,952	7,710
5260 Retail nurseries and garden stores	71	72	383	361	5	13,859	14,404	5,824	5,495
5270 Mobile home dealers	37	32	128	108	3	17,781	15,148	2,397	1,932
5310 Department stores	119	121	18,481	19,613	162	11,202	12,193	226,127	239,828
5330 Variety stores	34	26	207	102	4	10,763	10,980	1,792	1,102
5390 Misc. general merchandise stores	90	86	3,533	3,875	45	14,363	16,840	58,324	66,305
5410 Grocery stores	853	857	19,729	20,134	23	19,578	20,526	404,557	423,996
5420 Meat and fish markets	39	40	340	250	6	12,812	10,400	4,525	2,946
5430 Fruit and vegetable markets	16	18	126	134	7	9,365	11,552	1,593	1,604
5440 Candy, nut, and confectionery stores	42	43	215	226	5	8,949	9,186	2,167	2,271
5450 Dairy products stores	24	28	93	126	5	4,860	6,952	696	1,097
5460 Retail bakeries	224	213	985	909	4	10,014	10,130	9,616	8,878
5490 Miscellaneous food stores	71	74	306	283	4	12,248	14,912	4,689	4,721
5510 New and used car dealers	182	179	8,067	8,563	48	30,919	31,639	279,051	299,072
5520 Used car dealers	85	86	354	516	6	18,565	19,574	7,571	12,478
5530 Auto and home supply stores	525	515	3,974	4,168	8	16,140	16,438	70,928	71,517
5540 Gasoline service stations	752	745	6,424	6,590	9	10,959	11,512	74,085	78,022
5550 Boat dealers	14	19	101	147	8	17,228	18,122	2,609	3,512
5560 Recreational vehicle dealers	51	51	598	615	12	25,284	26,628	16,942	17,202
5570 Motorcycle dealers	42	41	366	425	10	17,399	18,024	7,158	9,006
5590 Automotive dealers, nec	8	9	39	34	4	19,795	22,471	811	810
5610 Men's & boys' clothing stores	119	118	843	975	8	11,122	10,901	9,824	10,214
5620 Women's clothing stores	387	346	3,227	2,567	7	10,415	10,422	34,297	26,631
5630 Women's accessory & specialty stores	67	68	349	338	5	10,201	9,893	4,015	3,677
5640 Children's and infants' wear stores	51	50	319	323	6	9,367	9,746	3,098	3,259
5650 Family clothing stores	152	133	2,960	3,218	24	11,300	11,193	34,264	35,416
5660 Shoe stores	327	319	1,644	1,773	6	11,849	11,695	20,698	21,065
5690 Misc. apparel & accessory stores	73	74	370	417	6	11,395	11,415	4,187	4,895
5712 Furniture stores	244	228	1,436	1,330	6	18,265	20,171	28,326	28,847
5713 Floor covering stores	111	118	529	674	6	18,541	19,780	11,518	14,774
5714 Drapery and upholstery stores	16	17	64	62	4	12,375	13,548	871	744
5719 Misc. homefurnishings stores	163	158	924	965	6	12,446	12,775	11,473	14,077
5720 Household appliance stores	66	59	1,583	1,588	27	12,106	14,574	21,205	21,133
5731 Radio, TV, & electronic stores	150	156	1,224	1,436	9	18,232	17,721	24,381	30,348
5734 Computer and software stores	60	69	436	436	6	13,358	16,835	6,633	7,266
5735 Record & prerecorded tape stores	76	76	836	881	12	8,785	8,722	7,420	7,311
5736 Musical instrument stores	31	30	125	100	3	14,016	11,360	1,783	1,370
5812 Eating places	3,291	3,070	56,174	55,770	18	8,046	8,341	465,206	473,918
5813 Drinking places	278	242	1,694	1,565	6	7,837	8,680	14,678	14,616
5910 Drug stores and proprietary stores	302	293	4,621	4,988	17	22,593	21,524	107,567	106,898
5920 Liquor stores	245	247	795	754	3	9,917	9,958	7,961	7,765
5930 Used merchandise stores	118	127	1,145	1,210	10	10,407	10,516	13,020	14,047
5941 Sporting goods and bicycle shops	195	188	1,624	1,832	10	13,507	13,814	23,763	25,894
5942 Book stores	107	108	708	804	7	9,000	8,219	8,424	8,920
5943 Stationery stores	45	53	234	514	10	12,188	14,825	2,914	7,233

Continued on next page.

RIVERSIDE - SAN BERNARDINO, CA PMSA - [continued]

Wholesale and Retail Trade USA	Establishments		Employment		Emp / Est	Pay / Employee		Annual Payroll ($ 000)	
	1994	1995	1994	1995	1995	1994	1995	1994	1995
5944 Jewelry stores	177	173	900	840	5	19,413	20,319	17,450	16,599
5945 Hobby, toy, and game shops	89	84	982	1,026	12	10,065	9,088	12,815	10,642
5946 Camera & photographic supply stores	22	21	89	95	5	16,360	17,474	1,609	1,541
5947 Gift, novelty, and souvenir shops	241	238	1,225	1,160	5	8,069	8,255	10,827	10,403
5948 Luggage and leather goods stores	21	24	122	142	6	10,918	11,887	1,513	1,728
5949 Sewing, needlework, and piece goods	67	61	626	572	9	8,895	7,860	5,445	4,410
5961 Catalog and mail-order houses	39	47	1,368	1,826	39	14,140	16,793	21,063	26,910
5962 Merchandising machine operators	22	22	135	172	8	18,104	16,233	2,706	2,936
5963 Direct selling establishments	68	65	762	871	13	17,454	16,629	14,373	16,102
5983 Fuel oil dealers [3]	4	4	21	31	8	9,714	9,677	255	333
5984 Liquefied petroleum gas dealers [3]	34	33	138	153	5	22,435	21,961	2,929	3,228
5992 Florists	185	187	845	893	5	9,288	9,178	7,963	8,037
5993 Tobacco stores and stands	10	11	45	52	5	7,644	7,615	414	431
5994 News dealers and newsstands	10	11	23	23	2	8,000	9,913	238	190
5995 Optical goods stores	94	89	430	389	4	15,795	16,165	6,728	6,828
5999 Miscellaneous retail stores, nec	406	419	1,873	2,267	5	12,444	12,669	26,106	29,858

Source: County Business Patterns 1994/95, CBP-94/95, U.S. Department of Commerce, Washington DC, November 1997. The employment column represents mid-March employment in the year. Pay per employee is calculated by dividing 1st Quarter payroll, annualized, by mid-March employment. The column headed 'Emp / Est' shows 'employees per establishment'. A dash (-) means that data are unavailable or cannot be calculated. nec means not elsewhere classified. *Notes:* 1. 1994 data incomplete; unavailable or withheld. 2. 1995 data incomplete; unavailable or withheld. 3. 1994 and 1995 data incomplete; unavailable or withheld.

ROANOKE, VA MSA

Wholesale and Retail Trade USA	Establishments		Employment		Emp / Est	Pay / Employee		Annual Payroll ($ 000)	
	1994	1995	1994	1995	1995	1994	1995	1994	1995
50 - Wholesale trade	-	605	-	8,055	13	-	28,260	-	236,532
5012 Automobiles and other vehicles	-	14	-	237	17	-	27,544	-	6,894
5013 Motor vehicle supplies and new parts	-	40	-	565	14	-	19,363	-	11,645
5014 Tires and tubes [2]	-	10	-	132	13	-	25,758	-	4,068
5015 Motor vehicle parts, used	-	11	-	45	4	-	20,000	-	893
5021 Furniture [2]	-	10	-	75	8	-	34,613	-	2,066
5023 Homefurnishings [2]	-	8	-	44	6	-	25,091	-	1,245
5031 Lumber, plywood, and millwork [2]	-	13	-	98	8	-	24,490	-	2,217
5033 Roofing, siding, & insulation [2]	-	6	-	50	8	-	23,040	-	1,247
5044 Office equipment	-	18	-	227	13	-	36,987	-	7,614
5045 Computers, peripherals, & software [2]	-	20	-	136	7	-	53,765	-	5,968
5046 Commercial equipment, nec	-	7	-	37	5	-	26,270	-	1,125
5047 Medical and hospital equipment	-	18	-	124	7	-	48,677	-	4,913
5049 Professional equipment, nec [2]	-	3	-	25	8	-	41,600	-	848
5051 Metals service centers and offices [2]	-	10	-	82	8	-	23,463	-	2,160
5052 Coal and other minerals and ores [2]	-	8	-	17	2	-	54,118	-	1,020
5063 Electrical apparatus and equipment [2]	-	27	-	259	10	-	32,880	-	8,786
5064 Electrical appliances, TV & radios [2]	-	4	-	73	18	-	22,192	-	1,711
5065 Electronic parts and equipment [2]	-	17	-	90	5	-	29,467	-	2,778
5072 Hardware [2]	-	14	-	203	15	-	26,463	-	5,582
5074 Plumbing & hydronic heating supplies [2]	-	7	-	96	14	-	31,708	-	2,945
5075 Warm air heating & air conditioning [2]	-	15	-	186	12	-	33,462	-	6,336
5078 Refrigeration equipment and supplies [2]	-	3	-	19	6	-	28,000	-	620
5082 Construction and mining machinery [2]	-	15	-	590	39	-	34,597	-	21,025
5084 Industrial machinery and equipment	-	46	-	503	11	-	27,475	-	15,032
5085 Industrial supplies	-	32	-	156	5	-	31,385	-	5,393
5087 Service establishment equipment [2]	-	19	-	154	8	-	21,974	-	3,492
5088 Transportation equipment & supplies [2]	-	6	-	12	2	-	11,667	-	163
5091 Sporting & recreational goods [2]	-	4	-	10	3	-	14,800	-	124
5093 Scrap and waste materials	-	10	-	188	19	-	23,000	-	5,267
5112 Stationery and office supplies [2]	-	13	-	27	2	-	25,778	-	770
5130 Apparel, piece goods, and notions [2]	-	5	-	11	2	-	13,455	-	157
5141 Groceries, general line [2]	-	7	-	103	15	-	21,903	-	2,793
5150 Farm-product raw materials [2]	-	4	-	7	2	-	20,571	-	193
5169 Chemicals & allied products, nec	-	21	-	35	2	-	23,429	-	852
5170 Petroleum and petroleum products [2]	-	9	-	150	17	-	32,240	-	4,765
5199 Nondurable goods, nec [2]	-	11	-	41	4	-	18,049	-	926
52 - Retail trade	-	1,693	-	26,616	16	-	12,910	-	361,403
5210 Lumber and other building materials	-	27	-	494	18	-	19,247	-	9,981
5250 Hardware stores	-	15	-	103	7	-	12,311	-	1,318
5260 Retail nurseries and garden stores [2]	-	15	-	27	2	-	10,963	-	334
5310 Department stores [2]	-	15	-	1,794	120	-	11,775	-	19,894
5330 Variety stores [2]	-	13	-	156	12	-	8,564	-	1,511
5390 Misc. general merchandise stores [2]	-	14	-	395	28	-	13,782	-	6,972

Continued on next page.

ROANOKE, VA MSA - [continued]

Wholesale and Retail Trade USA	Establishments		Employment		Emp / Est	Pay / Employee		Annual Payroll ($ 000)	
	1994	1995	1994	1995	1995	1994	1995	1994	1995
5410 Grocery stores	-	183	-	3,351	18	-	10,570	-	36,330
5430 Fruit and vegetable markets[2]	-	6	-	3	1	-	6,667	-	58
5440 Candy, nut, and confectionery stores[2]	-	5	-	12	2	-	7,000	-	94
5460 Retail bakeries[2]	-	10	-	47	5	-	9,702	-	467
5490 Miscellaneous food stores[2]	-	7	-	32	5	-	5,750	-	213
5510 New and used car dealers	-	27	-	1,123	42	-	30,205	-	37,290
5520 Used car dealers	-	27	-	56	2	-	18,071	-	1,009
5530 Auto and home supply stores	-	41	-	355	9	-	17,780	-	7,607
5540 Gasoline service stations	-	96	-	893	9	-	12,255	-	11,214
5610 Men's & boys' clothing stores[2]	-	18	-	115	6	-	13,774	-	1,592
5620 Women's clothing stores	-	66	-	504	8	-	7,762	-	3,833
5630 Women's accessory & specialty stores[2]	-	8	-	42	5	-	8,762	-	344
5640 Children's and infants' wear stores[2]	-	3	-	15	5	-	8,267	-	153
5650 Family clothing stores[2]	-	17	-	331	19	-	8,326	-	2,618
5660 Shoe stores[2]	-	44	-	219	5	-	11,580	-	2,478
5690 Misc. apparel & accessory stores	-	16	-	75	5	-	11,627	-	839
5712 Furniture stores[2]	-	41	-	377	9	-	17,156	-	6,572
5713 Floor covering stores[2]	-	18	-	124	7	-	29,355	-	3,198
5719 Misc. homefurnishings stores[2]	-	22	-	15	1	-	12,800	-	246
5720 Household appliance stores[2]	-	12	-	48	4	-	16,167	-	858
5731 Radio, TV, & electronic stores[2]	-	23	-	246	11	-	18,585	-	4,633
5735 Record & prerecorded tape stores[2]	-	13	-	64	5	-	10,938	-	697
5812 Eating places	-	373	-	7,303	20	-	7,933	-	61,741
5813 Drinking places[2]	-	15	-	81	5	-	8,000	-	696
5910 Drug stores and proprietary stores	-	48	-	1,720	36	-	8,030	-	15,180
5930 Used merchandise stores	-	31	-	100	3	-	14,480	-	1,470
5941 Sporting goods and bicycle shops	-	23	-	167	7	-	12,886	-	2,169
5942 Book stores[2]	-	18	-	131	7	-	9,496	-	1,176
5943 Stationery stores[2]	-	10	-	66	7	-	13,697	-	857
5944 Jewelry stores[2]	-	31	-	250	8	-	17,840	-	4,697
5945 Hobby, toy, and game shops[2]	-	14	-	120	9	-	10,033	-	1,460
5947 Gift, novelty, and souvenir shops	-	40	-	171	4	-	9,637	-	1,670
5961 Catalog and mail-order houses	-	14	-	952	68	-	11,849	-	13,087
5992 Florists	-	29	-	147	5	-	11,156	-	1,532
5993 Tobacco stores and stands[2]	-	4	-	6	2	-	11,333	-	95
5995 Optical goods stores[2]	-	23	-	104	5	-	18,692	-	2,035
5999 Miscellaneous retail stores, nec	-	51	-	222	4	-	14,468	-	3,823

Source: County Business Patterns 1994/95, CBP-94/95, U.S. Department of Commerce, Washington DC, November 1997. The employment column represents mid-March employment in the year. Pay per employee is calculated by dividing 1st Quarter payroll, annualized, by mid-March employment. The column headed 'Emp / Est' shows 'employees per establishment'. A dash (-) means that data are unavailable or cannot be calculated. nec means not elsewhere classified. *Notes:* 1. 1994 data incomplete; unavailable or withheld. 2. 1995 data incomplete; unavailable or withheld. 3. 1994 and 1995 data incomplete; unavailable or withheld.

ROCHESTER, MN MSA

Wholesale and Retail Trade USA	Establishments		Employment		Emp / Est	Pay / Employee		Annual Payroll ($ 000)	
	1994	1995	1994	1995	1995	1994	1995	1994	1995
50- Wholesale trade	163	160	1,485	1,639	10	25,274	26,804	41,465	45,795
5012 Automobiles and other vehicles	4	5	68	81	16	28,118	25,679	2,395	2,631
5013 Motor vehicle supplies and new parts	10	7	119	107	15	18,487	20,561	2,212	2,247
5014 Tires and tubes	4	-	22	-	-	19,636	-	427	-
5015 Motor vehicle parts, used	3	-	18	-	-	16,222	-	351	-
5020 Furniture and homefurnishings	-	5	-	55	11	-	22,836	-	1,481
5031 Lumber, plywood, and millwork	4	5	9	16	3	28,889	34,500	189	347
5044 Office equipment	6	6	85	82	14	30,541	28,146	2,536	2,500
5045 Computers, peripherals, & software	11	12	119	146	12	29,916	44,192	3,917	5,818
5047 Medical and hospital equipment	7	7	65	98	14	20,862	20,735	1,720	2,182
5063 Electrical apparatus and equipment	8	7	69	67	10	27,304	30,567	2,052	2,120
5065 Electronic parts and equipment	6	7	37	41	6	31,351	33,463	1,196	1,333
5074 Plumbing & hydronic heating supplies	5	5	81	78	16	24,889	29,385	1,909	2,009
5085 Industrial supplies	4	4	60	62	16	28,600	35,419	1,746	2,091
5087 Service establishment equipment	4	3	21	25	8	21,524	19,200	467	624
5090 Miscellaneous durable goods	6	7	40	37	5	16,300	21,838	690	751
5110 Paper and paper products	10	6	74	87	15	24,973	14,437	2,217	1,301
5143 Dairy products, exc. dried or canned	3	3	19	20	7	34,737	39,400	983	879
5153 Grain and field beans	4	-	44	-	-	20,182	-	1,257	-
5170 Petroleum and petroleum products	8	8	27	33	4	23,704	22,788	706	924
5180 Beer, wine, and distilled beverages	4	4	73	67	17	31,123	38,448	2,290	2,415
5191 Farm supplies	9	7	59	23	3	21,695	12,000	1,435	368
52- Retail trade	744	738	12,675	12,309	17	10,529	11,371	145,639	149,903

Continued on next page.

ROCHESTER, MN MSA - [continued]

Wholesale and Retail Trade USA	Establishments		Employment		Emp / Est	Pay / Employee		Annual Payroll ($ 000)	
	1994	1995	1994	1995	1995	1994	1995	1994	1995
5210 Lumber and other building materials	18	15	302	273	18	18,874	19,634	5,857	5,404
5230 Paint, glass, and wallpaper stores	4	-	31	-	-	12,903	-	401	-
5250 Hardware stores	9	7	94	92	13	10,894	8,870	1,114	910
5260 Retail nurseries and garden stores	9	7	54	52	7	22,519	22,769	1,497	1,518
5310 Department stores	10	10	1,791	1,729	173	9,485	10,790	18,674	19,575
5410 Grocery stores	18	18	1,944	1,532	85	10,031	10,102	20,017	16,179
5440 Candy, nut, and confectionery stores	6	6	29	24	4	4,138	5,833	128	134
5460 Retail bakeries	13	12	105	106	9	6,514	8,566	778	1,012
5510 New and used car dealers	10	11	627	687	62	26,080	25,729	18,065	19,622
5520 Used car dealers	8	6	36	28	5	13,778	20,571	616	560
5530 Auto and home supply stores	13	13	127	131	10	16,945	17,924	2,287	2,467
5540 Gasoline service stations	53	51	459	452	9	10,806	11,628	5,332	5,469
5560 Recreational vehicle dealers	4	4	49	52	13	11,918	12,000	1,060	1,047
5610 Men's & boys' clothing stores	7	7	60	41	6	12,000	14,537	651	502
5620 Women's clothing stores	37	35	356	319	9	7,674	7,937	3,029	2,596
5630 Women's accessory & specialty stores	10	11	43	55	5	9,023	7,855	404	479
5640 Children's and infants' wear stores	-	3	-	20	7	-	10,400	-	201
5650 Family clothing stores	9	9	150	125	14	11,200	10,752	1,759	1,518
5660 Shoe stores	21	21	120	114	5	8,767	9,930	1,074	1,158
5690 Misc. apparel & accessory stores	-	3	-	30	10	-	10,133	-	243
5712 Furniture stores	15	15	107	108	7	19,140	19,185	2,290	2,201
5713 Floor covering stores	10	8	86	91	11	25,070	31,341	2,598	2,868
5714 Drapery and upholstery stores	3	3	6	6	2	6,000	8,000	39	61
5719 Misc. homefurnishings stores	14	13	89	109	8	11,730	11,303	1,259	1,331
5720 Household appliance stores	7	6	45	31	5	18,044	16,258	659	397
5731 Radio, TV, & electronic stores	5	5	90	108	22	15,067	13,630	1,387	1,489
5734 Computer and software stores	4	5	38	66	13	10,000	12,061	462	813
5735 Record & prerecorded tape stores	5	5	45	37	7	7,911	10,054	379	376
5736 Musical instrument stores	3	3	22	22	7	16,727	14,727	329	326
5812 Eating places	169	154	3,662	3,646	24	6,967	7,874	28,063	30,468
5813 Drinking places	14	14	94	169	12	7,957	7,858	956	1,161
5910 Drug stores and proprietary stores	15	16	290	273	17	11,600	12,498	3,569	3,792
5920 Liquor stores	18	16	134	138	9	9,134	8,638	1,324	1,285
5930 Used merchandise stores	14	15	54	57	4	8,667	9,053	575	643
5941 Sporting goods and bicycle shops	15	18	94	126	7	7,915	9,746	1,045	1,370
5944 Jewelry stores	17	20	77	89	4	15,325	13,843	1,096	1,108
5945 Hobby, toy, and game shops	8	11	60	70	6	7,800	8,800	622	731
5947 Gift, novelty, and souvenir shops	32	31	156	184	6	6,231	6,087	1,028	1,248
5949 Sewing, needlework, and piece goods	9	7	109	65	9	5,908	6,585	672	441
5962 Merchandising machine operators	6	5	113	75	15	9,381	14,507	1,142	1,106
5984 Liquefied petroleum gas dealers	4	4	21	23	6	20,952	20,000	423	426
5992 Florists	14	13	130	124	10	9,446	9,968	1,320	1,329
5999 Miscellaneous retail stores, nec	27	28	203	190	7	13,025	12,695	3,019	3,009

Source: County Business Patterns 1994/95, CBP-94/95, U.S. Department of Commerce, Washington DC, November 1997. The employment column represents mid-March employment in the year. Pay per employee is calculated by dividing 1st Quarter payroll, annualized, by mid-March employment. The column headed 'Emp / Est' shows 'employees per establishment'. A dash (-) means that data are unavailable or cannot be calculated. nec means not elsewhere classified. *Notes:* 1. 1994 data incomplete; unavailable or withheld. 2. 1995 data incomplete; unavailable or withheld. 3. 1994 and 1995 data incomplete; unavailable or withheld.

ROCHESTER, NY MSA

Wholesale and Retail Trade USA	Establishments		Employment		Emp / Est	Pay / Employee		Annual Payroll ($ 000)	
	1994	1995	1994	1995	1995	1994	1995	1994	1995
50- Wholesale trade	1,825	1,814	24,245	22,922	13	35,787	39,321	859,015	874,949
5012 Automobiles and other vehicles	21	26	350	474	18	23,703	24,473	8,582	11,566
5013 Motor vehicle supplies and new parts	119	106	967	838	8	20,232	21,547	20,957	19,225
5014 Tires and tubes [2]	16	12	120	117	10	20,767	23,453	2,749	3,038
5015 Motor vehicle parts, used [3]	17	19	125	142	7	16,480	16,563	2,181	2,496
5021 Furniture [3]	23	24	214	225	9	30,318	27,218	6,084	6,031
5023 Homefurnishings [3]	19	19	78	80	4	21,949	22,300	1,977	2,138
5031 Lumber, plywood, and millwork [3]	28	30	472	369	12	24,585	26,547	14,469	11,249
5032 Brick, stone, & related materials [3]	14	14	142	127	9	27,296	30,079	4,494	4,216
5033 Roofing, siding, & insulation [3]	18	17	218	173	10	30,477	34,012	8,043	6,671
5039 Construction materials, nec [3]	13	29	36	363	13	19,111	24,529	894	10,825
5044 Office equipment [3]	31	31	588	577	19	42,252	56,028	21,182	26,161
5045 Computers, peripherals, & software [3]	81	86	1,373	967	11	48,632	58,581	58,310	59,592
5047 Medical and hospital equipment [3]	39	37	412	385	10	28,495	40,197	13,652	14,078
5048 Ophthalmic goods [3]	23	23	393	420	18	47,552	47,505	17,849	19,469
5049 Professional equipment, nec [3]	16	17	404	358	21	28,901	34,123	11,321	10,331
5051 Metals service centers and offices [2]	-	29	-	380	13	-	32,032	-	12,896

Continued on next page.

ROCHESTER, NY MSA - [continued]

Wholesale and Retail Trade USA	Establishments		Employment		Emp / Est	Pay / Employee		Annual Payroll ($ 000)	
	1994	1995	1994	1995	1995	1994	1995	1994	1995
5063 Electrical apparatus and equipment	97	88	945	874	10	29,410	33,890	30,467	31,196
5064 Electrical appliances, TV & radios[3]	11	12	45	47	4	16,711	18,723	783	806
5065 Electronic parts and equipment[3]	102	105	862	1,528	15	40,195	47,678	35,854	72,954
5072 Hardware[3]	34	32	291	305	10	29,924	34,361	9,608	11,558
5074 Plumbing & hydronic heating supplies	53	49	401	350	7	29,257	31,520	11,984	10,770
5075 Warm air heating & air conditioning[3]	26	28	152	175	6	36,211	37,966	5,865	6,850
5078 Refrigeration equipment and supplies[3]	3	3	53	52	17	24,906	32,308	1,741	1,725
5082 Construction and mining machinery[3]	15	15	192	191	13	31,083	36,942	6,783	6,928
5083 Farm and garden machinery[1]	36	33	197	344	10	21,239	25,116	4,961	9,200
5084 Industrial machinery and equipment[2]	147	151	950	1,014	7	35,642	35,677	37,121	41,995
5085 Industrial supplies[3]	73	71	726	678	10	34,733	36,785	25,837	26,250
5087 Service establishment equipment[3]	28	27	218	260	10	22,257	23,908	5,448	5,870
5088 Transportation equipment & supplies[2]	-	5	-	8	2	-	109,000	-	686
5091 Sporting & recreational goods[3]	24	22	203	197	9	27,764	27,797	5,888	5,112
5092 Toys and hobby goods and supplies[3]	8	8	18	19	2	24,667	34,947	485	485
5093 Scrap and waste materials	29	30	314	296	10	23,771	23,108	11,243	11,325
5094 Jewelry & precious stones[3]	12	12	60	73	6	23,867	23,507	1,526	1,673
5099 Durable goods, nec	35	34	193	193	6	21,036	23,668	4,687	4,876
5111 Printing and writing paper[3]	14	13	141	137	11	38,894	40,672	5,017	5,222
5112 Stationery and office supplies[3]	36	35	377	335	10	26,334	35,415	9,776	11,160
5113 Industrial & personal service paper[3]	26	26	342	220	8	33,158	47,727	12,452	9,767
5120 Drugs, proprietaries, and sundries[3]	12	12	524	181	15	32,962	31,757	17,881	6,004
5131 Piece goods & notions[3]	9	8	56	88	11	27,143	31,273	1,784	2,235
5136 Men's and boys' clothing[2]	-	6	-	12	2	-	15,000	-	173
5137 Women's and children's clothing[3]	4	5	15	12	2	15,733	11,667	223	155
5141 Groceries, general line[3]	18	18	229	284	16	22,865	20,310	5,243	6,458
5142 Packaged frozen food[3]	10	10	152	162	16	29,868	30,370	4,923	4,860
5143 Dairy products, exc. dried or canned[3]	14	15	36	47	3	22,889	23,234	999	1,209
5145 Confectionery[3]	4	3	38	54	18	22,421	17,481	917	990
5146 Fish and seafoods[1]	5	-	116	-	-	19,828	-	2,300	-
5147 Meats and meat products[3]	21	18	286	265	15	33,497	33,449	9,932	10,851
5148 Fresh fruits and vegetables	22	21	166	237	11	19,157	20,675	3,500	3,934
5149 Groceries and related products, nec[2]	50	46	619	621	14	28,491	29,726	18,811	18,812
5150 Farm-product raw materials	28	25	168	162	6	16,071	15,852	3,081	2,740
5162 Plastics materials & basic shapes[3]	21	24	171	165	7	32,655	36,048	6,117	6,160
5169 Chemicals & allied products, nec[3]	28	33	242	244	7	40,793	45,311	10,885	11,760
5171 Petroleum bulk stations & terminals[3]	24	21	211	197	9	28,569	31,919	7,028	6,614
5172 Petroleum products, nec[2]	-	8	-	53	7	-	26,189	-	2,081
5181 Beer and ale[3]	8	9	196	85	9	27,020	18,024	7,048	1,881
5182 Wine and distilled beverages[1]	7	-	231	-	-	25,195	-	7,562	-
5191 Farm supplies	45	36	199	46	1	21,487	21,130	4,996	1,387
5192 Books, periodicals, & newspapers[3]	13	14	114	87	6	23,719	34,943	2,964	3,356
5193 Flowers & florists' supplies[3]	16	11	102	78	7	15,137	17,436	1,640	1,516
5194 Tobacco and tobacco products[3]	6	4	68	59	15	18,647	19,051	1,673	1,596
5198 Paints, varnishes, and supplies[3]	12	10	110	51	5	21,309	29,882	2,382	1,438
5199 Nondurable goods, nec[3]	38	34	115	127	4	22,991	23,402	2,921	3,380
52- Retail trade	5,941	5,851	84,915	84,723	14	11,649	12,366	1,101,573	1,121,951
5210 Lumber and other building materials	105	99	2,105	2,359	24	15,073	13,312	33,878	32,248
5230 Paint, glass, and wallpaper stores	31	29	142	155	5	16,141	18,658	2,567	2,919
5250 Hardware stores	74	55	445	335	6	14,822	16,131	6,721	5,228
5260 Retail nurseries and garden stores	50	56	285	355	6	16,154	17,217	7,402	8,699
5270 Mobile home dealers[3]	15	13	58	36	3	18,759	17,556	1,251	686
5310 Department stores[3]	49	46	6,502	5,337	116	9,896	12,179	72,281	71,422
5330 Variety stores	39	31	184	161	5	10,783	9,292	2,040	1,512
5390 Misc. general merchandise stores[2]	45	37	1,526	1,064	29	11,641	13,357	17,763	14,625
5410 Grocery stores	398	380	16,415	16,888	44	10,681	10,621	183,264	189,407
5420 Meat and fish markets[3]	31	30	147	149	5	9,660	10,094	1,529	1,564
5430 Fruit and vegetable markets[3]	14	15	16	18	1	11,250	11,111	271	368
5440 Candy, nut, and confectionery stores[3]	27	24	139	63	3	6,705	6,667	868	444
5450 Dairy products stores[3]	13	11	2	29	3	12,000	8,276	21	282
5460 Retail bakeries[3]	93	93	923	744	8	8,893	8,242	9,074	6,623
5490 Miscellaneous food stores[3]	26	27	138	165	6	10,464	9,600	1,574	1,618
5510 New and used car dealers	126	119	4,467	4,374	37	25,054	27,225	129,994	127,134
5520 Used car dealers	57	59	169	176	3	15,479	16,659	2,939	3,199
5530 Auto and home supply stores	119	113	674	908	8	17,460	17,278	14,570	16,589
5540 Gasoline service stations	432	402	3,159	3,161	8	11,440	11,753	38,197	38,486
5550 Boat dealers[3]	18	20	89	112	6	19,416	17,964	2,331	2,527
5560 Recreational vehicle dealers	18	17	46	46	3	18,522	18,261	996	916
5570 Motorcycle dealers[3]	14	14	14	32	2	20,000	17,875	358	664
5610 Men's & boys' clothing stores	68	66	342	390	6	9,404	10,636	3,693	4,541
5620 Women's clothing stores	155	142	1,902	1,463	10	7,630	7,593	15,960	11,462

Continued on next page.

ROCHESTER, NY MSA - [continued]

Wholesale and Retail Trade USA	Establishments		Employment		Emp / Est	Pay / Employee		Annual Payroll ($ 000)	
	1994	1995	1994	1995	1995	1994	1995	1994	1995
5630 Women's accessory & specialty stores [3]	26	25	128	132	5	7,563	9,061	1,148	1,210
5640 Children's and infants' wear stores [3]	15	16	147	137	9	6,667	7,591	1,005	1,133
5650 Family clothing stores [3]	68	64	1,275	1,647	26	9,757	9,107	13,076	15,232
5660 Shoe stores	160	144	754	647	4	11,125	11,777	8,900	7,804
5690 Misc. apparel & accessory stores [3]	33	33	128	131	4	9,344	12,427	1,173	1,324
5712 Furniture stores	117	114	832	864	8	17,226	17,940	15,069	15,591
5713 Floor covering stores	55	64	211	212	3	19,773	23,755	5,196	5,657
5714 Drapery and upholstery stores [2]	-	6	-	17	3	-	11,294	-	242
5719 Misc. homefurnishings stores [3]	52	42	64	287	7	8,188	9,951	629	3,086
5720 Household appliance stores	31	32	145	138	4	20,634	21,478	3,150	3,175
5731 Radio, TV, & electronic stores	70	65	317	370	6	16,757	17,503	4,659	6,845
5734 Computer and software stores [3]	24	31	188	240	8	14,234	16,667	3,328	4,291
5735 Record & prerecorded tape stores [3]	27	33	154	299	9	9,091	10,247	1,656	2,635
5736 Musical instrument stores [3]	17	14	102	94	7	14,510	17,319	1,787	1,754
5812 Eating places	1,573	1,501	24,599	24,185	16	7,548	8,175	207,469	212,663
5813 Drinking places	279	255	1,364	1,317	5	7,762	8,161	11,004	10,853
5910 Drug stores and proprietary stores	163	157	2,522	2,580	16	12,630	13,102	35,776	36,015
5920 Liquor stores	110	109	398	410	4	11,568	12,605	5,109	5,569
5930 Used merchandise stores	54	50	280	229	5	11,957	14,533	3,789	3,370
5941 Sporting goods and bicycle shops	91	94	686	840	9	11,464	11,124	8,805	9,906
5942 Book stores [2]	57	55	571	564	10	9,226	11,851	5,438	7,322
5943 Stationery stores [3]	21	19	102	171	9	8,353	10,129	1,094	1,646
5944 Jewelry stores	87	94	500	530	6	13,352	15,608	7,717	8,444
5945 Hobby, toy, and game shops [3]	43	45	421	377	8	9,283	9,432	4,546	4,314
5946 Camera & photographic supply stores [3]	9	9	57	60	7	12,772	13,533	819	892
5947 Gift, novelty, and souvenir shops	110	106	613	637	6	7,321	8,446	5,212	6,228
5948 Luggage and leather goods stores [3]	4	3	14	12	4	8,286	10,333	125	150
5949 Sewing, needlework, and piece goods	25	21	328	253	12	5,963	7,510	2,156	1,944
5961 Catalog and mail-order houses [3]	24	25	372	603	24	19,935	18,362	8,220	11,542
5962 Merchandising machine operators [3]	17	24	135	116	5	19,526	22,276	2,523	2,619
5963 Direct selling establishments [3]	51	50	214	212	4	16,000	15,000	3,611	3,494
5983 Fuel oil dealers	-	21	-	84	4	-	24,286	-	1,975
5984 Liquefied petroleum gas dealers [2]	-	10	-	30	3	-	18,400	-	615
5992 Florists	91	93	373	414	4	11,088	11,894	4,425	5,093
5994 News dealers and newsstands [3]	22	20	57	71	4	20,772	16,507	1,269	1,233
5995 Optical goods stores	90	89	485	486	5	18,400	19,078	8,624	7,922
5999 Miscellaneous retail stores, nec [2]	138	141	730	715	5	12,592	13,220	10,224	11,133

Source: County Business Patterns 1994/95, CBP-94/95, U.S. Department of Commerce, Washington DC, November 1997. The employment column represents mid-March employment in the year. Pay per employee is calculated by dividing 1st Quarter payroll, annualized, by mid-March employment. The column headed 'Emp / Est' shows 'employees per establishment'. A dash (-) means that data are unavailable or cannot be calculated. nec means not elsewhere classified. *Notes:* 1. 1994 data incomplete; unavailable or withheld. 2. 1995 data incomplete; unavailable or withheld. 3. 1994 and 1995 data incomplete; unavailable or withheld.

ROCKFORD, IL MSA

Wholesale and Retail Trade USA	Establishments		Employment		Emp / Est	Pay / Employee		Annual Payroll ($ 000)	
	1994	1995	1994	1995	1995	1994	1995	1994	1995
50- Wholesale trade	703	717	9,131	9,712	14	26,327	28,979	264,663	296,124
5012 Automobiles and other vehicles [3]	8	7	264	275	39	28,318	26,545	8,251	7,856
5013 Motor vehicle supplies and new parts	28	26	323	353	14	21,412	24,782	7,707	8,810
5014 Tires and tubes [3]	7	5	55	35	7	30,764	34,743	1,546	1,074
5015 Motor vehicle parts, used	10	15	37	51	3	20,000	17,255	811	1,035
5021 Furniture [3]	6	6	58	34	6	21,379	25,176	1,387	1,092
5023 Homefurnishings [3]	10	10	83	105	11	42,458	44,686	3,043	4,804
5031 Lumber, plywood, and millwork [3]	14	10	200	139	14	22,760	26,158	4,903	3,402
5032 Brick, stone, & related materials [3]	6	4	48	44	11	23,583	21,545	1,186	784
5033 Roofing, siding, & insulation [2]	-	7	-	68	10	-	33,765	-	2,750
5039 Construction materials, nec	-	9	-	80	9	-	28,850	-	2,416
5043 Photographic equipment & supplies [3]	3	3	16	15	5	14,750	11,200	220	130
5044 Office equipment [3]	12	14	145	137	10	30,234	35,036	4,771	4,691
5045 Computers, peripherals, & software [1]	20	19	135	113	6	39,022	47,257	5,077	4,353
5046 Commercial equipment, nec [3]	7	9	103	96	11	22,913	26,125	2,962	2,987
5047 Medical and hospital equipment [3]	5	5	107	125	25	29,981	33,952	3,521	4,092
5048 Ophthalmic goods [3]	3	3	25	22	7	21,760	23,818	513	508
5049 Professional equipment, nec [3]	4	4	24	21	5	28,000	38,286	762	748
5051 Metals service centers and offices	20	21	599	435	21	31,947	32,920	22,467	18,181
5063 Electrical apparatus and equipment [3]	26	25	248	196	8	29,290	34,449	8,443	6,686
5064 Electrical appliances, TV & radios [3]	3	3	3	2	1	14,667	30,000	36	54
5065 Electronic parts and equipment [3]	17	22	133	190	9	30,887	32,632	4,657	6,140
5072 Hardware [3]	20	21	321	400	19	26,318	24,790	9,237	10,963

Continued on next page.

ROCKFORD, IL MSA - [continued]

Wholesale and Retail Trade USA	Establishments		Employment		Emp / Est	Pay / Employee		Annual Payroll ($ 000)	
	1994	1995	1994	1995	1995	1994	1995	1994	1995
5074 Plumbing & hydronic heating supplies [2]	-	11	-	182	17	-	25,363	-	4,556
5075 Warm air heating & air conditioning [1]	10	-	109	-	-	34,936	-	3,902	-
5082 Construction and mining machinery [3]	9	8	96	106	13	41,958	52,604	3,508	4,255
5083 Farm and garden machinery	21	18	152	163	9	30,763	32,123	4,367	4,962
5084 Industrial machinery and equipment [1]	99	102	975	1,023	10	31,717	37,114	35,677	39,879
5085 Industrial supplies [3]	41	39	526	444	11	27,597	29,973	15,507	14,452
5087 Service establishment equipment [3]	15	14	101	90	6	21,743	26,622	2,745	2,803
5091 Sporting & recreational goods	6	6	75	87	15	11,520	12,276	1,149	1,144
5092 Toys and hobby goods and supplies [1]	3	-	7	-	-	58,857	-	908	-
5093 Scrap and waste materials	15	13	101	102	8	27,525	49,608	3,392	5,758
5099 Durable goods, nec	12	-	24	-	-	27,333	-	834	-
5111 Printing and writing paper [2]	-	3	-	40	13	-	28,800	-	1,172
5112 Stationery and office supplies [2]	-	13	-	142	11	-	23,042	-	3,204
5113 Industrial & personal service paper [3]	10	10	159	142	14	29,006	34,197	4,698	5,539
5130 Apparel, piece goods, and notions [2]	-	3	-	3	1	-	10,667	-	48
5143 Dairy products, exc. dried or canned [1]	4	-	11	-	-	28,364	-	311	-
5147 Meats and meat products [1]	5	-	48	-	-	11,750	-	684	-
5149 Groceries and related products, nec [3]	16	16	331	317	20	21,523	27,457	7,815	8,942
5153 Grain and field beans	24	25	127	119	5	21,858	22,891	2,981	2,993
5162 Plastics materials & basic shapes [3]	11	10	184	222	22	28,065	26,739	6,248	6,846
5169 Chemicals & allied products, nec	15	15	62	91	6	25,097	25,626	2,731	3,319
5171 Petroleum bulk stations & terminals	18	17	185	174	10	33,751	38,138	6,199	6,921
5172 Petroleum products, nec [3]	4	4	5	12	3	57,600	32,667	261	517
5181 Beer and ale [3]	6	7	99	103	15	31,960	64,311	3,790	5,017
5182 Wine and distilled beverages [3]	3	3	97	92	31	33,979	38,391	3,370	3,564
5191 Farm supplies	30	23	121	88	4	24,397	22,045	2,352	1,981
5193 Flowers & florists' supplies [3]	5	5	72	88	18	20,778	18,182	1,568	1,652
5199 Nondurable goods, nec [3]	14	13	64	45	3	20,500	22,489	1,624	1,708
52– Retail trade	1,991	1,997	27,878	28,356	14	11,022	12,083	336,909	354,971
5210 Lumber and other building materials	37	35	738	872	25	20,710	17,390	17,010	15,223
5230 Paint, glass, and wallpaper stores [1]	10	12	28	51	4	13,714	20,941	456	1,065
5250 Hardware stores	29	25	237	248	10	9,030	9,306	2,344	2,051
5260 Retail nurseries and garden stores	16	18	125	151	8	12,736	13,987	2,111	2,831
5270 Mobile home dealers [3]	6	6	25	32	5	23,840	20,500	711	847
5310 Department stores [3]	18	19	2,517	2,570	135	9,015	10,313	25,268	27,616
5330 Variety stores [3]	13	14	99	106	8	7,192	8,377	893	949
5390 Misc. general merchandise stores	22	18	661	629	35	11,637	13,113	8,028	7,790
5410 Grocery stores [3]	99	95	3,480	3,522	37	12,024	13,020	41,884	46,520
5420 Meat and fish markets	8	8	42	46	6	10,000	10,348	487	530
5440 Candy, nut, and confectionery stores [2]	-	5	-	36	7	-	6,444	-	236
5460 Retail bakeries	22	24	113	103	4	8,566	7,728	1,038	909
5490 Miscellaneous food stores [3]	12	13	46	63	5	13,739	11,302	587	759
5510 New and used car dealers	36	36	1,236	1,259	35	25,576	27,835	36,427	36,885
5520 Used car dealers [2]	35	41	109	120	3	18,092	18,800	2,287	2,892
5530 Auto and home supply stores	46	48	413	602	13	16,814	16,824	7,984	10,640
5540 Gasoline service stations	151	153	1,150	1,167	8	9,336	10,043	11,494	12,462
5550 Boat dealers [3]	7	7	38	33	5	12,105	14,424	644	551
5560 Recreational vehicle dealers [3]	5	5	59	58	12	20,881	21,034	1,412	1,451
5570 Motorcycle dealers [3]	9	8	41	37	5	15,707	16,757	737	722
5610 Men's & boys' clothing stores [3]	12	13	84	83	6	8,048	12,145	1,029	1,051
5620 Women's clothing stores	56	49	492	353	7	7,593	7,864	3,903	2,843
5630 Women's accessory & specialty stores [3]	11	12	35	35	3	10,400	11,771	362	397
5640 Children's and infants' wear stores [3]	6	5	40	42	8	5,300	6,476	262	265
5650 Family clothing stores	23	21	206	212	10	8,330	9,075	1,920	2,007
5660 Shoe stores	41	38	191	201	5	9,801	10,786	1,958	2,128
5690 Misc. apparel & accessory stores [3]	10	13	32	44	3	8,750	8,727	357	419
5712 Furniture stores	45	46	347	364	8	16,703	17,857	6,579	6,676
5713 Floor covering stores [1]	16	21	123	143	7	20,163	22,993	3,034	3,538
5719 Misc. homefurnishings stores [2]	-	17	-	78	5	-	11,436	-	989
5720 Household appliance stores	20	20	147	126	6	16,463	17,810	2,515	2,518
5731 Radio, TV, & electronic stores	28	29	344	458	16	18,314	15,878	6,627	7,847
5734 Computer and software stores [3]	7	6	29	12	2	7,862	11,333	224	212
5735 Record & prerecorded tape stores [3]	10	7	166	132	19	6,819	8,333	1,054	996
5736 Musical instrument stores [3]	6	5	36	37	7	15,333	15,459	577	593
5812 Eating places	522	493	8,985	8,663	18	6,815	7,646	68,788	69,295
5813 Drinking places	97	90	483	360	4	7,130	7,800	3,090	2,953
5910 Drug stores and proprietary stores	46	40	812	825	21	15,823	18,187	14,230	14,759
5920 Liquor stores	30	29	142	126	4	10,310	12,794	1,634	1,786
5930 Used merchandise stores [3]	15	15	62	61	4	13,742	6,754	767	421
5941 Sporting goods and bicycle shops	34	36	212	241	7	10,604	11,237	2,472	2,957
5942 Book stores [3]	15	15	109	147	10	8,697	7,755	1,067	1,300

Continued on next page.

ROCKFORD, IL MSA - [continued]

Wholesale and Retail Trade USA	Establishments		Employment		Emp / Est	Pay / Employee		Annual Payroll ($ 000)	
	1994	1995	1994	1995	1995	1994	1995	1994	1995
5944 Jewelry stores [3]	30	31	174	196	6	10,598	11,551	2,219	2,469
5945 Hobby, toy, and game shops	24	24	194	185	8	6,825	7,286	1,633	1,530
5946 Camera & photographic supply stores [1]	5	-	25	-	-	20,640	-	550	-
5947 Gift, novelty, and souvenir shops	49	47	288	288	6	6,389	7,264	2,165	2,314
5949 Sewing, needlework, and piece goods	10	9	77	44	5	6,182	7,545	504	328
5961 Catalog and mail-order houses [3]	7	9	45	53	6	19,200	26,642	862	1,074
5962 Merchandising machine operators [3]	13	13	227	227	17	17,057	18,537	3,955	4,275
5963 Direct selling establishments	18	16	194	198	12	12,722	13,313	2,816	2,601
5992 Florists	31	31	202	213	7	15,960	16,094	2,667	2,896
5999 Miscellaneous retail stores, nec	55	56	219	228	4	10,247	12,158	2,760	3,138

Source: County Business Patterns 1994/95, CBP-94/95, U.S. Department of Commerce, Washington DC, November 1997. The employment column represents mid-March employment in the year. Pay per employee is calculated by dividing 1st Quarter payroll, annualized, by mid-March employment. The column headed 'Emp / Est' shows 'employees per establishment'. A dash (-) means that data are unavailable or cannot be calculated. nec means not elsewhere classified. *Notes:* 1. 1994 data incomplete; unavailable or withheld. 2. 1995 data incomplete; unavailable or withheld. 3. 1994 and 1995 data incomplete; unavailable or withheld.

ROCKY MOUNT, NC MSA

Wholesale and Retail Trade USA	Establishments		Employment		Emp / Est	Pay / Employee		Annual Payroll ($ 000)	
	1994	1995	1994	1995	1995	1994	1995	1994	1995
50- Wholesale trade	211	205	2,812	2,822	14	27,329	28,536	83,842	84,711
5012 Automobiles and other vehicles	6	8	64	79	10	28,875	27,241	1,803	2,045
5013 Motor vehicle supplies and new parts	10	11	20	17	2	16,800	18,824	355	357
5020 Furniture and homefurnishings	6	6	96	89	15	31,500	35,281	2,497	2,598
5031 Lumber, plywood, and millwork	7	8	81	69	9	24,000	27,884	2,139	1,959
5032 Brick, stone, & related materials [1]	3	-	11	-	-	16,000	-	179	-
5044 Office equipment	6	5	35	33	7	30,400	23,758	859	721
5045 Computers, peripherals, & software [2]	-	6	-	40	7	-	29,400	-	1,324
5060 Electrical goods	9	-	62	-	-	26,194	-	1,721	-
5074 Plumbing & hydronic heating supplies [2]	-	4	-	57	14	-	32,561	-	1,753
5083 Farm and garden machinery	7	5	102	66	13	23,725	26,000	2,599	1,827
5084 Industrial machinery and equipment	6	7	92	94	13	24,913	28,809	2,840	3,085
5085 Industrial supplies	-	8	-	41	5	-	30,146	-	1,312
5099 Durable goods, nec	5	7	6	9	1	20,667	19,111	147	257
5112 Stationery and office supplies	7	8	11	43	5	16,000	13,488	188	629
5130 Apparel, piece goods, and notions	5	-	144	-	-	18,139	-	3,036	-
5148 Fresh fruits and vegetables [3]	3	3	9	7	2	82,667	96,000	336	331
5153 Grain and field beans	6	7	35	57	8	22,400	32,982	718	1,997
5159 Farm-product raw materials, nec	7	8	16	20	3	16,000	17,600	399	482
5169 Chemicals & allied products, nec	-	5	-	10	2	-	37,200	-	357
5171 Petroleum bulk stations & terminals	11	7	49	48	7	15,429	17,083	776	797
5191 Farm supplies	13	10	77	81	8	26,494	20,938	2,540	2,135
5199 Nondurable goods, nec [2]	7	5	27	55	11	19,111	21,455	626	1,360
52- Retail trade	893	904	11,758	12,003	13	13,068	13,836	162,951	178,977
5210 Lumber and other building materials	15	17	320	319	19	16,663	18,545	5,937	6,574
5250 Hardware stores	6	5	26	11	2	17,692	20,727	511	295
5260 Retail nurseries and garden stores	4	5	10	16	3	9,600	11,750	99	196
5270 Mobile home dealers	12	11	75	86	8	27,040	32,326	2,565	4,227
5310 Department stores	9	8	1,101	1,163	145	9,835	9,954	11,276	11,636
5330 Variety stores	11	11	52	44	4	6,385	8,455	385	404
5390 Misc. general merchandise stores	12	13	54	103	8	14,667	10,097	763	1,139
5410 Grocery stores	133	133	1,521	1,544	12	9,865	10,756	15,939	17,307
5420 Meat and fish markets	-	4	-	19	5	-	8,211	-	151
5460 Retail bakeries	5	6	20	22	4	7,600	8,000	169	172
5510 New and used car dealers	19	19	515	505	27	24,784	25,457	13,858	14,904
5520 Used car dealers	21	23	46	66	3	14,783	16,182	814	1,110
5530 Auto and home supply stores	32	35	214	216	6	13,907	15,185	3,309	3,533
5540 Gasoline service stations	67	64	315	321	5	12,267	12,698	4,084	4,112
5610 Men's & boys' clothing stores	8	8	37	61	8	10,054	9,508	370	508
5620 Women's clothing stores	29	25	206	189	8	6,330	7,302	1,316	1,291
5630 Women's accessory & specialty stores [3]	3	4	12	14	4	11,000	10,571	167	229
5650 Family clothing stores	8	10	208	224	22	8,365	8,143	1,837	1,882
5660 Shoe stores	27	27	145	150	6	8,993	9,573	1,373	1,374
5712 Furniture stores	34	32	247	221	7	12,470	15,005	3,423	3,664
5713 Floor covering stores [1]	9	-	24	-	-	23,667	-	483	-
5719 Misc. homefurnishings stores	8	8	28	57	7	10,429	9,965	318	563
5720 Household appliance stores	5	-	11	-	-	6,545	-	75	-
5731 Radio, TV, & electronic stores	11	11	30	34	3	17,867	20,000	632	575
5735 Record & prerecorded tape stores [3]	3	3	17	24	8	10,824	7,000	179	188
5812 Eating places	165	155	3,852	3,723	24	6,931	7,162	27,926	28,425

Continued on next page.

ROCKY MOUNT, NC MSA - [continued]

Wholesale and Retail Trade USA	Establishments		Employment		Emp / Est	Pay / Employee		Annual Payroll ($ 000)	
	1994	1995	1994	1995	1995	1994	1995	1994	1995
5910 Drug stores and proprietary stores	28	29	335	357	12	12,394	14,006	5,019	5,652
5930 Used merchandise stores	9	10	34	34	3	9,529	11,294	368	357
5941 Sporting goods and bicycle shops	7	8	26	30	4	7,846	7,200	216	240
5942 Book stores	9	9	78	67	7	10,821	12,179	887	924
5944 Jewelry stores	13	12	102	98	8	12,549	13,469	1,642	1,654
5945 Hobby, toy, and game shops [1]	7	-	55	-	-	7,418	-	437	-
5947 Gift, novelty, and souvenir shops	19	18	53	53	3	5,434	5,660	351	337
5949 Sewing, needlework, and piece goods	-	6	-	26	4	-	7,385	-	183
5983 Fuel oil dealers	5	4	13	20	5	22,769	19,800	289	373
5984 Liquefied petroleum gas dealers	-	9	-	42	5	-	25,524	-	949
5992 Florists	15	16	91	63	4	9,275	10,159	863	632
5995 Optical goods stores [2]	-	3	-	5	2	-	17,600	-	89
5999 Miscellaneous retail stores, nec	18	19	12	60	3	8,333	9,267	80	691

Source: County Business Patterns 1994/95, CBP-94/95, U.S. Department of Commerce, Washington DC, November 1997. The employment column represents mid-March employment in the year. Pay per employee is calculated by dividing 1st Quarter payroll, annualized, by mid-March employment. The column headed 'Emp / Est' shows 'employees per establishment'. A dash (-) means that data are unavailable or cannot be calculated. nec means not elsewhere classified. *Notes:* 1. 1994 data incomplete; unavailable or withheld. 2. 1995 data incomplete; unavailable or withheld. 3. 1994 and 1995 data incomplete; unavailable or withheld.

SACRAMENTO, CA PMSA

Wholesale and Retail Trade USA	Establishments		Employment		Emp / Est	Pay / Employee		Annual Payroll ($ 000)	
	1994	1995	1994	1995	1995	1994	1995	1994	1995
50- Wholesale trade	1,984	2,002	23,672	25,291	13	28,919	32,192	736,945	809,871
5012 Automobiles and other vehicles [3]	20	24	511	469	20	18,043	23,275	10,203	10,421
5013 Motor vehicle supplies and new parts	129	112	1,415	1,252	11	20,746	22,843	30,903	29,827
5014 Tires and tubes [3]	12	11	158	77	7	14,481	24,831	2,681	2,077
5015 Motor vehicle parts, used	59	53	378	389	7	18,042	18,098	7,308	7,796
5021 Furniture [1]	30	33	500	476	14	20,328	25,689	10,744	13,314
5023 Homefurnishings	35	31	279	200	6	23,384	23,280	7,188	4,970
5031 Lumber, plywood, and millwork	64	56	1,213	1,115	20	29,319	27,085	38,792	30,966
5032 Brick, stone, & related materials	17	23	125	167	7	24,704	22,659	2,609	3,629
5033 Roofing, siding, & insulation [3]	16	12	149	110	9	27,248	23,745	4,994	2,886
5039 Construction materials, nec [3]	25	35	193	455	13	30,073	32,809	6,264	16,910
5044 Office equipment [3]	45	43	925	1,047	24	35,079	38,025	33,861	36,942
5045 Computers, peripherals, & software	105	104	1,807	2,416	23	47,880	50,041	92,193	100,765
5046 Commercial equipment, nec [3]	24	28	202	205	7	29,327	38,459	6,305	6,952
5047 Medical and hospital equipment	51	48	563	646	13	34,494	37,845	21,350	26,930
5049 Professional equipment, nec [3]	12	12	61	67	6	20,984	23,522	1,337	1,888
5051 Metals service centers and offices	29	26	285	259	10	26,863	30,903	8,617	8,513
5063 Electrical apparatus and equipment	71	78	680	660	8	33,418	36,127	24,257	23,687
5064 Electrical appliances, TV & radios [3]	13	15	165	180	12	24,752	27,200	4,875	5,490
5065 Electronic parts and equipment	72	85	693	904	11	45,605	48,854	28,030	42,364
5072 Hardware	36	38	582	829	22	23,223	24,154	14,632	20,144
5074 Plumbing & hydronic heating supplies	55	55	369	342	6	25,322	28,725	10,872	10,629
5075 Warm air heating & air conditioning	28	28	252	259	9	36,746	38,440	11,590	11,933
5078 Refrigeration equipment and supplies [3]	5	4	24	22	6	35,333	35,455	702	738
5082 Construction and mining machinery	27	26	249	226	9	32,032	36,035	9,095	9,642
5083 Farm and garden machinery	26	26	220	205	8	25,218	29,580	6,724	7,024
5084 Industrial machinery and equipment	89	91	701	846	9	31,994	32,236	23,680	28,400
5085 Industrial supplies	41	41	371	365	9	26,383	29,797	10,966	10,800
5087 Service establishment equipment	47	43	304	303	7	26,842	27,657	8,290	8,172
5088 Transportation equipment & supplies [2]	14	12	115	119	10	26,017	24,739	3,516	3,156
5091 Sporting & recreational goods	26	27	181	180	7	22,762	24,333	4,740	4,480
5092 Toys and hobby goods and supplies [3]	8	10	41	46	5	24,293	26,087	1,199	1,333
5093 Scrap and waste materials	38	39	370	401	10	22,486	27,461	8,764	11,124
5094 Jewelry & precious stones	14	16	50	60	4	20,560	19,467	1,406	1,445
5099 Durable goods, nec	45	44	223	241	5	24,215	25,427	6,749	6,265
5111 Printing and writing paper [3]	13	15	100	103	7	38,840	45,709	3,579	4,668
5112 Stationery and office supplies	66	60	1,109	1,082	18	23,690	25,760	26,956	26,693
5113 Industrial & personal service paper	23	25	109	121	5	27,706	27,074	3,375	3,205
5120 Drugs, proprietaries, and sundries	22	21	660	724	34	31,576	32,337	20,439	23,316
5131 Piece goods & notions [3]	9	9	50	40	4	22,720	37,900	1,075	1,222
5136 Men's and boys' clothing	16	13	103	76	6	11,767	16,526	2,002	2,256
5137 Women's and children's clothing [1]	5	7	5	5	1	16,000	15,200	78	83
5139 Footwear [3]	4	3	9	14	5	18,667	15,429	210	231
5141 Groceries, general line	17	17	202	217	13	31,782	31,834	6,884	7,321
5142 Packaged frozen food [3]	8	8	113	129	16	25,522	26,605	3,151	3,340
5143 Dairy products, exc. dried or canned	21	18	228	189	11	28,877	29,989	6,616	5,658
5145 Confectionery [3]	8	8	333	359	45	27,471	30,396	10,104	11,987

Continued on next page.

SACRAMENTO, CA PMSA - [continued]

Wholesale and Retail Trade USA	Establishments 1994	Establishments 1995	Employment 1994	Employment 1995	Emp / Est 1995	Pay / Employee 1994	Pay / Employee 1995	Annual Payroll ($ 000) 1994	Annual Payroll ($ 000) 1995
5147 Meats and meat products	14	13	122	148	11	17,967	16,649	2,455	2,735
5148 Fresh fruits and vegetables	23	21	522	474	23	23,678	26,709	13,063	14,258
5149 Groceries and related products, nec	48	55	839	833	15	27,213	29,580	22,087	27,175
5154 Livestock[3]	4	4	32	41	10	11,250	9,268	453	430
5162 Plastics materials & basic shapes[3]	14	14	53	63	5	29,434	31,746	1,688	2,432
5169 Chemicals & allied products, nec[3]	28	28	457	371	13	30,179	31,105	13,191	12,646
5171 Petroleum bulk stations & terminals	21	16	206	157	10	36,194	35,898	7,485	6,001
5172 Petroleum products, nec[3]	15	16	149	110	7	43,919	40,691	5,823	4,707
5181 Beer and ale	9	9	303	323	36	22,653	22,291	7,108	7,544
5182 Wine and distilled beverages	7	8	34	35	4	49,765	48,914	1,548	1,880
5191 Farm supplies	46	47	347	412	9	28,196	31,689	10,757	12,712
5192 Books, periodicals, & newspapers	18	15	471	387	26	13,665	16,465	7,399	7,020
5193 Flowers & florists' supplies	26	24	331	281	12	13,245	13,238	5,086	4,369
5198 Paints, varnishes, and supplies[2]	17	13	98	85	7	22,612	23,765	2,461	2,115
5199 Nondurable goods, nec	81	89	365	421	5	19,901	21,311	7,925	9,856
52- Retail trade	7,687	7,669	107,517	109,860	14	13,829	14,408	1,592,399	1,652,529
5210 Lumber and other building materials	134	114	2,636	2,701	24	18,499	20,364	56,253	54,787
5230 Paint, glass, and wallpaper stores	65	68	367	365	5	22,975	25,184	8,176	9,358
5250 Hardware stores	84	68	635	557	8	14,482	15,454	10,044	9,125
5260 Retail nurseries and garden stores	42	45	352	429	10	15,966	14,816	7,485	7,994
5270 Mobile home dealers	16	15	58	63	4	15,655	16,952	967	1,468
5310 Department stores[3]	44	45	7,478	7,936	176	12,086	12,548	99,288	100,164
5390 Misc. general merchandise stores[2]	-	57	-	507	9	-	14,043	-	7,940
5410 Grocery stores	524	522	13,548	13,772	26	19,698	20,177	281,977	290,247
5420 Meat and fish markets[2]	14	15	64	93	6	13,125	14,409	972	1,595
5430 Fruit and vegetable markets	7	6	4	11	2	4,000	1,455	36	38
5440 Candy, nut, and confectionery stores	32	33	174	159	5	9,218	10,390	1,765	1,824
5450 Dairy products stores[1]	10	11	33	54	5	4,121	3,704	221	253
5460 Retail bakeries	129	101	946	647	6	9,400	8,482	9,116	5,762
5490 Miscellaneous food stores	63	79	330	454	6	9,394	9,251	3,503	4,701
5510 New and used car dealers	102	97	5,518	5,733	59	33,913	36,163	207,076	224,280
5520 Used car dealers	55	58	202	232	4	17,782	20,310	4,191	5,014
5530 Auto and home supply stores	251	256	2,418	2,466	10	16,868	17,729	43,760	45,813
5540 Gasoline service stations	343	335	2,947	3,190	10	12,789	12,607	41,003	42,064
5550 Boat dealers	26	27	163	164	6	17,595	15,488	3,447	3,321
5560 Recreational vehicle dealers[3]	24	27	123	152	6	21,854	20,553	3,062	3,724
5570 Motorcycle dealers	23	19	165	176	9	18,909	18,455	3,556	4,131
5590 Automotive dealers, nec[2]	-	6	-	4	1	-	34,000	-	163
5610 Men's & boys' clothing stores	63	63	459	443	7	12,941	15,521	6,149	6,316
5620 Women's clothing stores	201	178	1,803	1,480	8	8,781	8,303	16,871	12,326
5630 Women's accessory & specialty stores	35	36	176	187	5	9,409	10,289	1,711	1,879
5640 Children's and infants' wear stores	27	28	206	218	8	9,495	9,780	2,095	2,087
5650 Family clothing stores	82	83	1,992	2,035	25	11,972	12,242	24,719	25,452
5660 Shoe stores	149	138	769	789	6	11,163	11,113	8,882	8,774
5690 Misc. apparel & accessory stores	67	65	343	370	6	11,860	13,232	4,167	4,483
5712 Furniture stores	145	139	1,251	1,211	9	17,237	18,253	23,640	23,549
5713 Floor covering stores	84	84	350	420	5	21,314	22,390	9,042	9,778
5714 Drapery and upholstery stores	18	18	57	83	5	18,035	14,795	1,059	1,322
5719 Misc. homefurnishings stores	96	98	813	770	8	12,207	12,940	10,929	10,580
5720 Household appliance stores	50	52	451	430	8	21,543	20,344	9,476	8,999
5731 Radio, TV, & electronic stores	88	95	887	1,356	14	21,799	17,941	19,552	24,041
5734 Computer and software stores	61	56	473	485	9	21,184	20,981	10,754	10,789
5735 Record & prerecorded tape stores	41	39	454	512	13	9,304	9,602	4,337	4,713
5736 Musical instrument stores	23	21	110	102	5	13,200	14,745	1,529	1,939
5812 Eating places	2,316	2,164	37,942	37,776	17	7,976	8,321	317,921	325,127
5813 Drinking places	240	213	1,796	1,730	8	7,989	8,368	14,776	14,752
5910 Drug stores and proprietary stores	143	140	2,859	3,037	22	20,437	21,453	60,727	65,966
5920 Liquor stores	112	108	322	324	3	8,894	8,494	3,047	2,624
5930 Used merchandise stores	86	79	699	546	7	10,272	10,784	7,679	6,478
5941 Sporting goods and bicycle shops	157	162	1,301	1,421	9	11,022	11,389	15,234	15,942
5942 Book stores	72	79	534	543	7	10,300	11,337	5,839	5,864
5943 Stationery stores	29	26	132	108	4	11,545	13,889	1,499	1,540
5944 Jewelry stores	115	118	664	602	5	21,259	19,176	14,468	11,406
5945 Hobby, toy, and game shops	63	57	552	567	10	9,420	9,453	6,070	6,223
5946 Camera & photographic supply stores	12	11	43	40	4	13,395	19,900	673	715
5947 Gift, novelty, and souvenir shops	152	153	960	988	6	9,921	10,393	10,279	10,637
5948 Luggage and leather goods stores	18	19	68	64	3	13,882	15,688	989	968
5949 Sewing, needlework, and piece goods	42	42	400	368	9	8,410	8,630	3,130	3,002
5961 Catalog and mail-order houses	33	35	146	146	4	17,973	22,822	3,387	3,343
5962 Merchandising machine operators	28	29	151	173	6	17,060	16,185	2,865	3,252
5963 Direct selling establishments	72	90	650	738	8	19,015	19,995	13,508	15,677

Continued on next page.

SACRAMENTO, CA PMSA - [continued]

Wholesale and Retail Trade USA	Establishments		Employment		Emp / Est	Pay / Employee		Annual Payroll ($ 000)	
	1994	1995	1994	1995	1995	1994	1995	1994	1995
5984 Liquefied petroleum gas dealers	28	-	83	-	-	22,843	-	1,822	-
5989 Fuel dealers, nec	8	-	8	-	-	12,000	-	42	-
5992 Florists	119	122	513	537	4	9,045	9,601	4,726	5,181
5993 Tobacco stores and stands[3]	6	7	27	20	3	9,037	10,800	262	237
5994 News dealers and newsstands	9	12	17	19	2	10,824	11,579	182	203
5995 Optical goods stores	55	53	284	276	5	15,296	15,261	4,221	4,555
5999 Miscellaneous retail stores, nec	273	286	1,366	1,523	5	13,953	14,374	20,271	23,187

Source: County Business Patterns 1994/95, CBP-94/95, U.S. Department of Commerce, Washington DC, November 1997. The employment column represents mid-March employment in the year. Pay per employee is calculated by dividing 1st Quarter payroll, annualized, by mid-March employment. The column headed 'Emp / Est' shows 'employees per establishment'. A dash (-) means that data are unavailable or cannot be calculated. nec means not elsewhere classified. *Notes:* 1. 1994 data incomplete; unavailable or withheld. 2. 1995 data incomplete; unavailable or withheld. 3. 1994 and 1995 data incomplete; unavailable or withheld.

SAGINAW – BAY CITY – MIDLAND, MI MSA

Wholesale and Retail Trade USA	Establishments		Employment		Emp / Est	Pay / Employee		Annual Payroll ($ 000)	
	1994	1995	1994	1995	1995	1994	1995	1994	1995
50 – Wholesale trade	566	566	6,542	6,694	12	25,880	28,429	193,837	203,313
5012 Automobiles and other vehicles	11	12	198	225	19	27,354	29,227	6,023	6,526
5013 Motor vehicle supplies and new parts	41	32	509	388	12	21,540	22,485	12,264	9,796
5014 Tires and tubes	8	8	38	37	5	24,211	27,027	1,115	1,108
5015 Motor vehicle parts, used	14	19	43	37	2	11,814	11,568	540	459
5020 Furniture and homefurnishings	9	12	9	49	4	43,111	31,510	345	1,947
5031 Lumber, plywood, and millwork[2]	19	13	258	221	17	30,403	38,299	9,146	8,560
5032 Brick, stone, & related materials[2]	11	7	27	42	6	24,296	26,190	1,052	1,525
5033 Roofing, siding, & insulation[3]	8	9	78	85	9	28,513	30,918	2,408	2,658
5039 Construction materials, nec[1]	4	10	5	18	2	27,200	22,667	200	447
5044 Office equipment	10	10	81	86	9	29,086	29,860	2,561	2,711
5045 Computers, peripherals, & software	14	14	117	123	9	26,222	28,650	3,182	3,609
5047 Medical and hospital equipment[3]	8	8	106	102	13	29,887	34,824	3,729	3,711
5051 Metals service centers and offices	-	6	-	24	4	-	28,167	-	694
5063 Electrical apparatus and equipment	19	18	152	160	9	33,211	37,125	5,772	6,411
5064 Electrical appliances, TV & radios[3]	3	3	15	12	4	13,333	15,000	213	208
5065 Electronic parts and equipment	13	14	72	103	7	33,667	38,097	2,394	3,557
5074 Plumbing & hydronic heating supplies	17	17	50	48	3	29,200	29,000	1,399	1,346
5075 Warm air heating & air conditioning[3]	8	9	69	68	8	22,667	24,706	1,987	1,927
5082 Construction and mining machinery[3]	5	5	59	57	11	47,729	48,140	2,897	3,080
5083 Farm and garden machinery[1]	10	11	116	126	11	20,724	21,714	2,817	2,931
5084 Industrial machinery and equipment	35	35	347	374	11	31,666	36,588	12,814	14,779
5085 Industrial supplies	28	29	298	251	9	29,114	31,410	10,334	9,653
5087 Service establishment equipment	14	13	98	93	7	19,959	21,505	2,200	2,113
5093 Scrap and waste materials	16	16	172	199	12	22,907	25,327	4,384	4,551
5112 Stationery and office supplies[3]	17	14	27	27	2	12,296	15,852	415	432
5120 Drugs, proprietaries, and sundries[1]	5	-	17	-	-	18,353	-	382	-
5141 Groceries, general line[3]	8	8	184	198	25	32,522	28,808	6,093	2,916
5142 Packaged frozen food[3]	5	5	20	21	4	28,400	28,571	607	596
5143 Dairy products, exc. dried or canned	7	7	62	75	11	19,226	17,493	1,546	1,599
5148 Fresh fruits and vegetables[3]	5	4	18	19	5	35,556	31,158	970	1,320
5149 Groceries and related products, nec	20	20	774	761	38	26,300	30,265	23,222	25,280
5153 Grain and field beans	15	17	57	198	12	27,719	26,869	1,867	5,502
5169 Chemicals & allied products, nec	13	14	193	224	16	29,679	35,911	5,810	7,681
5171 Petroleum bulk stations & terminals	15	13	64	45	3	21,938	26,844	1,759	1,429
5180 Beer, wine, and distilled beverages	7	6	196	198	33	22,878	27,980	6,195	6,745
5191 Farm supplies	21	20	121	134	7	21,322	17,701	3,132	3,230
5193 Flowers & florists' supplies[1]	4	-	15	-	-	24,800	-	481	-
5198 Paints, varnishes, and supplies	6	5	44	26	5	25,727	29,385	1,503	809
5199 Nondurable goods, nec[3]	5	5	12	12	2	13,667	14,333	220	275
52 – Retail trade	2,632	2,655	37,039	38,388	14	10,458	11,077	437,354	464,471
5210 Lumber and other building materials	42	43	621	699	16	15,414	19,273	13,304	15,373
5230 Paint, glass, and wallpaper stores	13	15	56	47	3	12,000	17,702	812	961
5250 Hardware stores	33	26	265	242	9	12,589	14,264	3,950	3,871
5260 Retail nurseries and garden stores	23	26	318	250	10	8,553	12,784	3,595	3,846
5270 Mobile home dealers	11	10	76	62	6	17,526	21,032	1,839	1,503
5310 Department stores	23	23	5,190	5,396	235	10,516	11,297	61,241	66,741
5330 Variety stores	17	16	189	171	11	7,238	7,673	1,574	1,530
5390 Misc. general merchandise stores	11	13	259	261	20	9,143	11,510	2,927	3,029
5410 Grocery stores	266	271	3,661	4,017	15	9,455	9,097	38,799	39,065
5420 Meat and fish markets	21	18	162	141	8	9,309	10,780	1,644	1,638
5430 Fruit and vegetable markets	11	10	43	34	3	9,395	8,941	448	384
5440 Candy, nut, and confectionery stores	14	14	63	67	5	4,762	5,134	580	626

Continued on next page.

SAGINAW - BAY CITY - MIDLAND, MI MSA - [continued]

Wholesale and Retail Trade USA	Establishments		Employment		Emp / Est	Pay / Employee		Annual Payroll ($ 000)	
	1994	1995	1994	1995	1995	1994	1995	1994	1995
5450 Dairy products stores	8	6	16	16	3	5,250	5,000	120	97
5460 Retail bakeries	29	25	222	217	9	8,216	7,631	1,984	1,640
5490 Miscellaneous food stores	11	10	39	38	4	8,103	8,211	302	327
5510 New and used car dealers	45	47	1,758	1,810	39	26,687	27,735	53,987	54,551
5520 Used car dealers	19	20	77	86	4	21,195	22,140	2,146	2,020
5530 Auto and home supply stores	59	54	434	532	10	15,382	19,301	7,380	11,209
5540 Gasoline service stations	153	159	1,430	1,428	9	8,990	9,585	14,698	14,795
5550 Boat dealers	8	6	96	98	16	19,083	21,755	2,663	3,125
5560 Recreational vehicle dealers	7	8	35	41	5	13,600	14,634	653	711
5570 Motorcycle dealers[3]	3	3	45	51	17	18,578	17,961	957	1,048
5610 Men's & boys' clothing stores	33	34	219	277	8	10,100	9,126	2,588	2,843
5620 Women's clothing stores	105	101	888	851	8	8,279	7,929	8,444	7,459
5630 Women's accessory & specialty stores	17	16	63	56	4	9,016	9,643	610	595
5640 Children's and infants' wear stores	13	13	71	67	5	7,380	8,478	551	643
5650 Family clothing stores	48	51	847	938	18	8,538	9,608	8,542	9,293
5660 Shoe stores	67	68	372	422	6	10,656	11,441	4,380	4,747
5690 Misc. apparel & accessory stores	16	18	71	100	6	9,239	8,280	714	977
5712 Furniture stores	46	51	469	539	11	18,090	18,746	9,327	9,994
5713 Floor covering stores	23	23	191	228	10	18,136	18,386	4,111	4,474
5714 Drapery and upholstery stores[3]	5	6	9	8	1	6,222	8,000	66	60
5719 Misc. homefurnishings stores	42	40	247	236	6	9,684	10,525	2,785	2,932
5720 Household appliance stores	25	23	198	193	8	14,101	15,130	2,957	2,852
5731 Radio, TV, & electronic stores	38	35	233	280	8	14,558	14,443	3,768	4,326
5734 Computer and software stores	-	6	-	15	3	-	18,933	-	257
5735 Record & prerecorded tape stores	22	18	88	71	4	8,682	10,197	758	1,046
5736 Musical instrument stores	-	5	-	21	4	-	15,238	-	328
5812 Eating places	481	472	11,722	11,912	25	6,824	7,033	88,486	93,160
5813 Drinking places	140	126	786	744	6	6,412	6,419	4,970	4,843
5910 Drug stores and proprietary stores	76	74	870	873	12	13,379	15,033	11,721	13,560
5920 Liquor stores	30	28	131	119	4	9,160	9,042	1,308	1,090
5930 Used merchandise stores	20	17	80	53	3	10,350	9,736	869	527
5941 Sporting goods and bicycle shops	45	42	245	258	6	9,894	12,264	2,993	3,525
5942 Book stores	18	21	103	81	4	9,825	9,383	1,046	822
5944 Jewelry stores	37	41	243	253	6	18,156	20,190	3,955	4,348
5945 Hobby, toy, and game shops	25	25	156	167	7	9,821	9,749	1,959	1,973
5947 Gift, novelty, and souvenir shops	79	75	741	737	10	10,726	11,294	9,117	9,505
5948 Luggage and leather goods stores[2]	-	6	-	34	6	-	12,353	-	410
5949 Sewing, needlework, and piece goods	25	21	159	96	5	6,138	7,708	1,026	861
5961 Catalog and mail-order houses	-	7	-	124	18	-	13,065	-	1,767
5962 Merchandising machine operators[2]	9	6	60	49	8	19,800	22,694	1,231	1,341
5963 Direct selling establishments	24	22	51	136	6	9,412	11,029	689	1,832
5984 Liquefied petroleum gas dealers	7	-	21	-	-	22,476	-	458	-
5992 Florists	44	47	238	265	6	8,739	8,498	2,234	2,412
5995 Optical goods stores	23	22	96	22	1	19,958	26,364	1,914	597
5999 Miscellaneous retail stores, nec	70	73	336	355	5	13,024	13,837	5,538	6,113

Source: County Business Patterns 1994/95, CBP-94/95, U.S. Department of Commerce, Washington DC, November 1997. The employment column represents mid-March employment in the year. Pay per employee is calculated by dividing 1st Quarter payroll, annualized, by mid-March employment. The column headed 'Emp / Est' shows 'employees per establishment'. A dash (-) means that data are unavailable or cannot be calculated. nec means not elsewhere classified. *Notes:* 1. 1994 data incomplete; unavailable or withheld. 2. 1995 data incomplete; unavailable or withheld. 3. 1994 and 1995 data incomplete; unavailable or withheld.

ST. CLOUD, MN MSA

Wholesale and Retail Trade USA	Establishments		Employment		Emp / Est	Pay / Employee		Annual Payroll ($ 000)	
	1994	1995	1994	1995	1995	1994	1995	1994	1995
50- Wholesale trade	308	307	4,855	5,152	17	25,558	26,635	139,666	143,776
5012 Automobiles and other vehicles[3]	5	5	126	119	24	24,698	28,336	3,029	3,364
5013 Motor vehicle supplies and new parts	23	23	234	236	10	24,274	24,508	6,113	6,305
5031 Lumber, plywood, and millwork[3]	6	8	11	35	4	21,455	10,286	245	401
5044 Office equipment[1]	6	-	70	-	-	22,286	-	1,601	-
5045 Computers, peripherals, & software	-	9	-	192	21	-	27,542	-	6,117
5048 Ophthalmic goods[3]	7	7	178	167	24	15,933	18,659	3,113	3,141
5063 Electrical apparatus and equipment[3]	4	4	50	52	13	34,080	37,000	1,786	1,976
5065 Electronic parts and equipment[3]	4	5	16	17	3	34,250	40,235	582	741
5074 Plumbing & hydronic heating supplies[2]	10	7	54	57	8	22,519	25,053	1,331	1,374
5082 Construction and mining machinery[2]	-	3	-	42	14	-	37,714	-	1,767
5083 Farm and garden machinery	29	27	215	251	9	18,940	19,538	5,705	6,332
5084 Industrial machinery and equipment	-	9	-	33	4	-	27,394	-	994
5085 Industrial supplies	8	8	49	49	6	29,388	29,143	1,699	1,723
5087 Service establishment equipment[2]	4	5	10	24	5	24,800	14,333	237	401

Continued on next page.

ST. CLOUD, MN MSA - [continued]

Wholesale and Retail Trade USA	Establishments		Employment		Emp / Est	Pay / Employee		Annual Payroll ($ 000)	
	1994	1995	1994	1995	1995	1994	1995	1994	1995
5091 Sporting & recreational goods	4	4	26	26	7	21,077	22,154	724	536
5093 Scrap and waste materials [3]	10	11	149	149	14	14,201	15,060	2,201	2,565
5110 Paper and paper products	9	6	54	52	9	13,111	12,769	654	656
5130 Apparel, piece goods, and notions [1]	3	-	6	-	-	10,000	-	72	-
5143 Dairy products, exc. dried or canned [3]	5	6	24	76	13	16,500	14,105	433	1,192
5146 Fish and seafoods	4	-	20	-	-	12,200	-	196	-
5149 Groceries and related products, nec [3]	9	9	358	400	44	20,559	21,670	8,216	9,025
5153 Grain and field beans [3]	7	7	42	48	7	18,000	17,417	871	1,006
5154 Livestock [2]	-	3	-	43	14	-	8,093	-	313
5171 Petroleum bulk stations & terminals	17	15	50	47	3	14,960	16,681	751	823
5181 Beer and ale	4	4	44	41	10	20,273	23,317	1,146	1,177
5190 Misc., nondurable goods	45	47	1,260	1,370	29	36,406	34,409	50,693	47,543
52- Retail trade	1,043	1,044	19,897	21,297	20	12,230	12,558	276,166	276,740
5210 Lumber and other building materials	29	27	584	549	20	18,774	20,051	13,597	12,499
5230 Paint, glass, and wallpaper stores [2]	-	4	-	18	5	-	18,889	-	450
5250 Hardware stores	17	13	77	67	5	10,286	10,687	943	940
5260 Retail nurseries and garden stores [1]	6	-	23	-	-	8,870	-	379	-
5310 Department stores [3]	11	11	1,883	2,058	187	9,534	10,103	20,376	21,210
5330 Variety stores [3]	4	3	23	20	7	10,261	9,000	287	193
5390 Misc. general merchandise stores [2]	13	10	285	286	29	14,498	15,231	4,806	4,845
5410 Grocery stores [3]	57	57	1,523	1,522	27	9,371	9,829	15,663	16,386
5420 Meat and fish markets	7	6	36	36	6	14,000	14,889	552	567
5460 Retail bakeries	14	12	97	97	8	8,866	9,031	896	936
5490 Miscellaneous food stores [3]	6	6	26	29	5	11,846	11,034	298	327
5510 New and used car dealers	26	28	662	701	25	22,550	22,208	17,758	17,955
5520 Used car dealers [3]	16	18	65	84	5	18,400	16,810	1,396	1,469
5530 Auto and home supply stores	20	23	113	122	5	17,310	18,754	2,098	2,595
5540 Gasoline service stations	74	76	679	685	9	9,596	9,974	6,487	6,953
5560 Recreational vehicle dealers [2]	-	3	-	53	18	-	24,000	-	1,618
5610 Men's & boys' clothing stores [3]	9	8	54	62	8	14,370	14,000	797	808
5620 Women's clothing stores [3]	24	21	264	242	12	6,455	5,868	1,702	1,442
5650 Family clothing stores	9	9	101	101	11	7,723	7,881	838	1,001
5660 Shoe stores [3]	19	19	116	118	6	9,103	10,847	1,079	1,359
5690 Misc. apparel & accessory stores [3]	6	7	24	51	7	10,333	7,686	217	332
5712 Furniture stores	28	30	187	208	7	18,417	20,481	3,633	4,227
5713 Floor covering stores [3]	10	9	38	30	3	16,632	18,667	855	633
5719 Misc. homefurnishings stores	7	7	22	31	4	8,000	7,097	184	229
5720 Household appliance stores	10	12	63	54	5	11,238	13,481	786	818
5731 Radio, TV, & electronic stores	11	10	145	203	20	13,738	13,399	2,372	2,586
5735 Record & prerecorded tape stores [3]	5	5	138	131	26	7,333	7,603	1,019	941
5812 Eating places	222	211	4,734	4,825	23	6,430	6,810	32,959	34,266
5813 Drinking places	76	72	417	462	6	5,343	5,472	2,425	2,651
5910 Drug stores and proprietary stores	24	22	238	231	11	13,798	13,558	3,340	3,303
5920 Liquor stores [1]	34	33	17	134	4	8,941	8,030	164	1,103
5930 Used merchandise stores [1]	9	11	51	51	5	9,647	10,039	584	648
5941 Sporting goods and bicycle shops	24	29	155	208	7	12,387	12,654	1,909	2,786
5942 Book stores	-	8	-	17	2	-	5,647	-	158
5944 Jewelry stores	18	19	99	94	5	14,222	17,660	1,681	1,763
5945 Hobby, toy, and game shops	6	7	92	132	19	10,217	8,152	1,076	1,194
5947 Gift, novelty, and souvenir shops	19	18	127	99	6	5,260	6,586	647	670
5949 Sewing, needlework, and piece goods [1]	3	-	42	-	-	7,333	-	305	-
5962 Merchandising machine operators [3]	9	7	94	135	19	24,809	17,896	2,528	2,653
5984 Liquefied petroleum gas dealers	10	11	19	23	2	22,947	25,217	453	522
5995 Optical goods stores	19	20	277	285	14	16,910	19,256	5,076	5,028
5999 Miscellaneous retail stores, nec	20	25	159	117	5	14,138	15,316	2,497	2,033

Source: County Business Patterns 1994/95, CBP-94/95, U.S. Department of Commerce, Washington DC, November 1997. The employment column represents mid-March employment in the year. Pay per employee is calculated by dividing 1st Quarter payroll, annualized, by mid-March employment. The column headed 'Emp / Est' shows 'employees per establishment'. A dash (-) means that data are unavailable or cannot be calculated. nec means not elsewhere classified. *Notes:* 1. 1994 data incomplete; unavailable or withheld. 2. 1995 data incomplete; unavailable or withheld. 3. 1994 and 1995 data incomplete; unavailable or withheld.

ST. JOSEPH, MO MSA

Wholesale and Retail Trade USA	Establishments		Employment		Emp / Est	Pay / Employee		Annual Payroll ($ 000)	
	1994	1995	1994	1995	1995	1994	1995	1994	1995
50- Wholesale trade	199	197	1,878	2,302	12	23,474	25,896	47,832	66,084
5013 Motor vehicle supplies and new parts	12	10	70	58	6	14,971	19,448	1,354	1,257
5030 Lumber and construction materials [3]	7	4	78	61	15	26,256	22,098	2,148	1,408
5044 Office equipment [3]	11	10	74	69	7	19,405	19,362	1,543	1,413
5063 Electrical apparatus and equipment [3]	6	7	57	87	12	30,667	23,770	1,898	2,178

Continued on next page.

ST. JOSEPH, MO MSA - [continued]

Wholesale and Retail Trade USA	Establishments		Employment		Emp / Est	Pay / Employee		Annual Payroll ($ 000)	
	1994	1995	1994	1995	1995	1994	1995	1994	1995
5065 Electronic parts and equipment[3]	3	3	9	10	3	17,333	18,800	181	196
5074 Plumbing & hydronic heating supplies[3]	4	4	35	36	9	18,286	22,222	702	765
5082 Construction and mining machinery[2]	-	3	-	42	14	-	29,619	-	1,356
5084 Industrial machinery and equipment[1]	3	-	33	-	-	16,848	-	530	-
5085 Industrial supplies[3]	5	5	29	35	7	25,793	26,857	936	1,060
5093 Scrap and waste materials[3]	9	10	72	106	11	16,611	14,642	1,559	1,899
5113 Industrial & personal service paper[1]	4	-	24	-	-	16,500	-	445	-
5120 Drugs, proprietaries, and sundries[3]	6	7	148	448	64	31,703	38,509	5,231	22,534
5149 Groceries and related products, nec[3]	7	7	100	102	15	24,200	27,176	2,644	2,956
5153 Grain and field beans[3]	6	7	49	63	9	21,469	23,175	1,180	1,509
5154 Livestock	15	14	88	92	7	16,045	15,217	1,424	1,372
5169 Chemicals & allied products, nec[1]	3	-	14	-	-	20,286	-	319	-
5171 Petroleum bulk stations & terminals	7	7	52	78	11	22,769	22,154	1,323	1,459
5181 Beer and ale[3]	5	5	65	68	14	25,538	27,235	1,897	2,021
5191 Farm supplies	22	21	241	268	13	24,183	24,284	5,766	6,233
5198 Paints, varnishes, and supplies[1]	3	-	10	-	-	16,800	-	177	-
52- Retail trade	614	633	7,636	8,182	13	10,525	11,039	89,033	95,835
5210 Lumber and other building materials	12	15	43	71	5	18,791	24,338	1,065	1,702
5230 Paint, glass, and wallpaper stores[3]	3	3	15	15	5	13,867	13,867	229	197
5260 Retail nurseries and garden stores[3]	5	4	53	42	11	8,830	10,857	629	600
5310 Department stores	9	9	1,182	1,397	155	10,298	12,198	14,424	16,936
5330 Variety stores[1]	5	-	54	-	-	8,963	-	531	-
5410 Grocery stores	39	39	954	822	21	12,528	12,959	11,380	10,797
5420 Meat and fish markets[2]	-	4	-	6	2	-	12,667	-	89
5460 Retail bakeries[3]	8	8	52	41	5	5,923	7,024	333	299
5510 New and used car dealers	12	12	337	398	33	20,582	20,965	7,511	9,188
5520 Used car dealers[3]	14	16	53	61	4	14,491	15,607	905	1,021
5530 Auto and home supply stores[1]	17	18	127	156	9	17,827	18,154	2,653	3,116
5540 Gasoline service stations	58	55	406	426	8	9,360	9,315	4,210	4,352
5610 Men's & boys' clothing stores[3]	4	4	16	18	5	17,750	15,778	287	273
5620 Women's clothing stores[3]	15	13	109	93	7	7,670	6,796	939	601
5660 Shoe stores[3]	14	14	60	60	4	18,200	18,333	1,056	901
5712 Furniture stores[1]	7	8	74	84	11	17,243	17,714	1,701	1,944
5719 Misc. homefurnishings stores[3]	3	5	12	12	2	13,000	13,667	165	198
5720 Household appliance stores[3]	4	4	19	20	5	18,105	18,600	364	391
5731 Radio, TV, & electronic stores	9	-	27	-	-	16,593	-	590	-
5734 Computer and software stores[3]	4	4	34	52	13	11,412	13,923	453	719
5735 Record & prerecorded tape stores[2]	-	5	-	65	13	-	6,585	-	460
5812 Eating places	139	122	2,632	2,675	22	6,948	7,257	20,289	20,901
5813 Drinking places	30	28	92	91	3	7,087	7,297	672	663
5910 Drug stores and proprietary stores	15	16	196	188	12	13,592	14,532	2,929	2,862
5930 Used merchandise stores[3]	18	18	69	69	4	10,899	10,725	898	874
5941 Sporting goods and bicycle shops[2]	7	8	20	23	3	10,400	12,000	256	353
5942 Book stores[3]	3	4	21	19	5	10,667	10,737	251	273
5944 Jewelry stores[3]	6	7	39	42	6	15,385	16,571	783	872
5945 Hobby, toy, and game shops[3]	6	5	59	48	10	9,966	12,500	661	684
5947 Gift, novelty, and souvenir shops[3]	13	13	51	42	3	5,647	7,619	295	321
5949 Sewing, needlework, and piece goods[3]	5	5	27	33	7	6,370	4,970	179	179
5963 Direct selling establishments[1]	7	-	40	-	-	19,300	-	747	-
5992 Florists[3]	13	14	59	56	4	8,407	8,571	520	513
5995 Optical goods stores[3]	11	11	38	33	3	15,158	15,030	581	449
5999 Miscellaneous retail stores, nec[2]	-	15	-	43	3	-	17,581	-	805

Source: County Business Patterns 1994/95, CBP-94/95, U.S. Department of Commerce, Washington DC, November 1997. The employment column represents mid-March employment in the year. Pay per employee is calculated by dividing 1st Quarter payroll, annualized, by mid-March employment. The column headed 'Emp / Est' shows 'employees per establishment'. A dash (-) means that data are unavailable or cannot be calculated. nec means not elsewhere classified. *Notes:* 1. 1994 data incomplete; unavailable or withheld. 2. 1995 data incomplete; unavailable or withheld. 3. 1994 and 1995 data incomplete; unavailable or withheld.

ST. LOUIS MSA (IL PART)

Wholesale and Retail Trade USA	Establishments		Employment		Emp / Est	Pay / Employee		Annual Payroll ($ 000)	
	1994	1995	1994	1995	1995	1994	1995	1994	1995
50- Wholesale trade	703	725	7,067	7,433	10	24,834	26,530	187,910	202,529
5012 Automobiles and other vehicles[3]	15	16	263	277	17	32,000	35,567	8,298	8,663
5013 Motor vehicle supplies and new parts	47	50	265	330	7	18,974	18,812	5,240	6,381
5014 Tires and tubes[3]	7	4	50	58	15	28,960	27,931	1,536	1,594
5015 Motor vehicle parts, used[3]	22	23	122	137	6	17,311	17,869	2,651	2,659
5020 Furniture and homefurnishings[3]	6	6	21	25	4	13,333	21,440	327	603
5031 Lumber, plywood, and millwork[1]	9	14	151	143	10	43,762	34,266	5,614	4,489
5032 Brick, stone, & related materials[1]	7	-	39	-	-	12,923	-	558	-

Continued on next page.

ST. LOUIS MSA (IL PART) - [continued]

Wholesale and Retail Trade USA	Establishments		Employment		Emp / Est	Pay / Employee		Annual Payroll ($ 000)	
	1994	1995	1994	1995	1995	1994	1995	1994	1995
5033 Roofing, siding, & insulation [1]	6	-	30	-	-	20,267	-	966	-
5039 Construction materials, nec [3]	8	9	79	99	11	22,127	22,869	1,859	2,380
5044 Office equipment [3]	8	8	15	19	2	17,867	14,105	261	289
5045 Computers, peripherals, & software [3]	10	15	7	73	5	14,857	30,411	121	2,301
5046 Commercial equipment, nec [3]	7	7	27	30	4	13,185	13,200	393	416
5047 Medical and hospital equipment [3]	11	7	84	39	6	28,952	36,718	2,958	1,589
5051 Metals service centers and offices [1]	22	-	296	-	-	28,676	-	8,784	-
5063 Electrical apparatus and equipment [3]	22	22	110	111	5	24,218	24,541	2,816	2,814
5065 Electronic parts and equipment [3]	16	19	112	102	5	28,357	33,529	3,250	3,657
5072 Hardware [3]	6	8	21	25	3	17,524	16,320	379	507
5074 Plumbing & hydronic heating supplies [3]	16	14	154	146	10	22,052	26,274	4,037	4,148
5075 Warm air heating & air conditioning [3]	13	13	62	36	3	23,226	30,333	1,532	1,242
5078 Refrigeration equipment and supplies [1]	3	-	40	-	-	24,600	-	1,536	-
5083 Farm and garden machinery	36	35	287	291	8	21,226	20,619	7,499	6,967
5084 Industrial machinery and equipment [3]	31	27	232	250	9	27,914	31,232	6,900	7,290
5085 Industrial supplies [3]	26	28	163	169	6	24,982	28,852	4,544	5,382
5087 Service establishment equipment [3]	12	13	169	161	12	10,130	11,453	1,757	1,960
5088 Transportation equipment & supplies [2]	-	4	-	41	10	-	26,439	-	1,344
5093 Scrap and waste materials [3]	26	31	172	385	12	27,698	30,068	4,894	11,827
5112 Stationery and office supplies [3]	18	12	48	31	3	16,417	17,677	781	528
5142 Packaged frozen food [3]	6	6	85	91	15	32,424	27,429	2,861	2,565
5147 Meats and meat products [2]	-	4	-	57	14	-	21,474	-	1,083
5149 Groceries and related products, nec [3]	19	19	159	186	10	17,358	14,495	3,030	2,911
5153 Grain and field beans	35	33	229	254	8	24,961	35,071	5,855	8,292
5154 Livestock [3]	9	9	36	33	4	17,556	17,818	674	649
5169 Chemicals & allied products, nec [2]	-	14	-	25	2	-	24,960	-	581
5171 Petroleum bulk stations & terminals	27	24	262	262	11	32,763	31,038	9,335	8,927
5172 Petroleum products, nec [3]	10	12	34	38	3	45,529	41,579	1,557	1,724
5181 Beer and ale [3]	11	12	46	52	4	28,000	29,231	1,980	1,930
5191 Farm supplies	38	40	174	188	5	22,874	18,660	5,046	3,721
5199 Nondurable goods, nec [1]	24	23	89	86	4	17,483	19,907	1,756	2,123
52 - Retail trade	3,254	3,290	41,852	41,969	13	10,653	11,468	491,441	507,266
5210 Lumber and other building materials	71	70	750	909	13	19,269	21,571	17,296	19,768
5230 Paint, glass, and wallpaper stores [3]	18	22	75	104	5	14,773	15,462	1,288	1,724
5250 Hardware stores [3]	45	32	511	318	10	13,957	13,082	5,566	4,392
5260 Retail nurseries and garden stores [3]	25	25	140	150	6	10,086	10,853	1,880	2,101
5270 Mobile home dealers [3]	13	14	76	84	6	12,737	12,810	1,310	1,273
5310 Department stores [3]	33	33	4,868	4,941	150	10,403	12,303	56,754	60,530
5330 Variety stores [3]	32	15	237	87	6	7,747	6,851	2,102	673
5390 Misc. general merchandise stores [3]	11	28	352	344	12	13,977	13,674	5,127	4,381
5410 Grocery stores [3]	249	244	4,651	4,481	18	12,040	12,550	58,695	58,940
5420 Meat and fish markets [3]	29	26	124	122	5	13,548	13,639	1,883	1,788
5430 Fruit and vegetable markets [3]	9	13	36	106	8	9,111	9,811	418	1,368
5440 Candy, nut, and confectionery stores [2]	-	4	-	18	5	-	5,333	-	105
5460 Retail bakeries [3]	41	43	272	357	8	7,912	8,515	2,594	3,479
5490 Miscellaneous food stores [3]	12	12	38	37	3	8,737	6,270	434	272
5510 New and used car dealers	75	74	2,043	1,980	27	26,829	29,267	65,158	65,090
5520 Used car dealers [3]	42	43	138	131	3	19,971	18,229	2,615	2,424
5530 Auto and home supply stores	86	86	582	602	7	15,045	16,698	9,858	10,440
5540 Gasoline service stations	239	237	1,762	1,924	8	11,124	11,008	20,573	22,038
5550 Boat dealers [3]	11	11	63	69	6	19,048	20,870	1,437	1,632
5560 Recreational vehicle dealers [3]	6	5	12	21	4	20,667	18,476	248	420
5570 Motorcycle dealers [3]	11	10	51	58	6	14,745	15,655	1,203	1,371
5610 Men's & boys' clothing stores [3]	23	22	80	97	4	9,650	9,608	911	1,031
5620 Women's clothing stores [3]	92	78	750	596	8	7,525	7,295	6,056	4,413
5630 Women's accessory & specialty stores [3]	12	14	62	23	2	7,290	9,913	466	198
5640 Children's and infants' wear stores [2]	-	6	-	28	5	-	7,571	-	249
5650 Family clothing stores [2]	35	35	403	335	10	9,439	9,970	4,166	3,759
5660 Shoe stores [3]	62	57	295	293	5	9,383	9,884	2,951	2,996
5690 Misc. apparel & accessory stores [3]	13	14	58	72	5	8,207	8,167	484	589
5712 Furniture stores	61	59	408	521	9	17,147	15,900	8,636	9,033
5713 Floor covering stores	38	46	150	208	5	19,440	17,577	3,544	4,332
5714 Drapery and upholstery stores [3]	7	7	5	6	1	7,200	8,667	35	30
5719 Misc. homefurnishings stores [3]	23	23	50	60	3	10,000	10,267	489	492
5720 Household appliance stores [3]	24	25	132	142	6	14,273	15,549	2,188	2,280
5731 Radio, TV, & electronic stores [3]	27	27	255	265	10	14,855	14,113	4,099	4,108
5734 Computer and software stores [3]	9	13	27	52	4	7,852	8,077	248	455
5735 Record & prerecorded tape stores [3]	15	13	74	81	6	8,865	11,160	768	828
5736 Musical instrument stores [3]	12	13	59	65	5	12,678	12,492	745	855
5812 Eating places	722	684	15,014	14,560	21	6,639	7,106	107,005	109,332
5813 Drinking places	291	283	1,267	1,326	5	7,646	7,910	10,870	10,839

Continued on next page.

ST. LOUIS MSA (IL PART) - [continued]

Wholesale and Retail Trade USA	Establishments		Employment		Emp / Est	Pay / Employee		Annual Payroll ($ 000)	
	1994	1995	1994	1995	1995	1994	1995	1994	1995
5910 Drug stores and proprietary stores	95	92	948	1,022	11	17,181	17,926	17,052	18,510
5920 Liquor stores	57	55	335	298	5	9,063	8,993	3,249	2,850
5930 Used merchandise stores[3]	37	40	108	94	2	10,185	11,447	1,144	1,085
5941 Sporting goods and bicycle shops[3]	37	36	213	217	6	11,042	11,668	2,499	2,634
5942 Book stores[3]	18	20	81	86	4	10,222	10,651	842	966
5943 Stationery stores[1]	9	-	18	-	-	14,222	-	236	-
5944 Jewelry stores	46	47	318	339	7	13,585	14,183	4,932	4,987
5945 Hobby, toy, and game shops[1]	16	24	106	122	5	8,415	8,689	1,246	1,300
5947 Gift, novelty, and souvenir shops	61	61	319	374	6	9,129	8,973	3,409	3,577
5949 Sewing, needlework, and piece goods[3]	17	16	70	117	7	8,629	7,214	601	886
5961 Catalog and mail-order houses[3]	9	15	37	56	4	7,568	11,786	342	753
5962 Merchandising machine operators[3]	17	17	60	65	4	15,333	16,615	1,103	1,229
5963 Direct selling establishments[3]	20	26	74	74	3	19,243	18,162	1,384	1,469
5984 Liquefied petroleum gas dealers	14	-	23	-	-	21,913	-	500	-
5992 Florists[3]	76	68	136	144	2	8,765	8,611	1,388	1,374
5994 News dealers and newsstands[3]	4	4	5	4	1	8,000	12,000	39	40
5995 Optical goods stores[3]	25	25	175	183	7	15,703	18,011	3,272	3,501
5999 Miscellaneous retail stores, nec	95	99	515	528	5	10,082	11,629	5,556	6,676

Source: County Business Patterns 1994/95, CBP-94/95, U.S. Department of Commerce, Washington DC, November 1997. The employment column represents mid-March employment in the year. Pay per employee is calculated by dividing 1st Quarter payroll, annualized, by mid-March employment. The column headed 'Emp / Est' shows 'employees per establishment'. A dash (-) means that data are unavailable or cannot be calculated. nec means not elsewhere classified. *Notes:* 1. 1994 data incomplete; unavailable or withheld. 2. 1995 data incomplete; unavailable or withheld. 3. 1994 and 1995 data incomplete; unavailable or withheld.

ST. LOUIS MSA (MO PART)

Wholesale and Retail Trade USA	Establishments		Employment		Emp / Est	Pay / Employee		Annual Payroll ($ 000)	
	1994	1995	1994	1995	1995	1994	1995	1994	1995
50- Wholesale trade	4,800	4,835	64,121	67,455	14	34,241	36,749	2,331,478	2,521,510
5012 Automobiles and other vehicles[3]	69	68	1,342	1,612	24	26,525	30,759	39,067	49,083
5013 Motor vehicle supplies and new parts	230	227	2,912	3,322	15	27,367	31,616	85,029	106,696
5014 Tires and tubes[3]	25	21	270	268	13	26,622	27,672	8,083	6,921
5015 Motor vehicle parts, used	56	63	291	348	6	19,478	22,092	7,386	8,660
5021 Furniture[3]	79	78	868	1,022	13	30,553	34,458	27,552	36,368
5023 Homefurnishings[3]	83	73	807	1,033	14	27,301	27,051	26,088	30,160
5031 Lumber, plywood, and millwork[3]	77	59	879	624	11	30,093	32,590	29,604	21,517
5032 Brick, stone, & related materials[3]	43	36	356	312	9	33,674	40,436	12,028	11,254
5033 Roofing, siding, & insulation[3]	42	40	381	328	8	30,005	31,061	14,475	11,809
5039 Construction materials, nec[3]	43	59	406	834	14	23,951	29,386	12,506	28,195
5043 Photographic equipment & supplies[3]	17	16	404	422	26	35,881	40,929	13,986	15,510
5044 Office equipment[3]	77	76	1,808	1,910	25	31,861	36,846	62,066	67,264
5045 Computers, peripherals, & software[3]	160	169	2,447	2,171	13	49,703	60,018	117,709	121,108
5046 Commercial equipment, nec[3]	70	76	644	705	9	25,043	26,241	17,872	20,070
5047 Medical and hospital equipment[3]	180	169	2,536	2,328	14	39,938	42,144	105,940	99,625
5048 Ophthalmic goods[3]	18	15	175	188	13	20,366	19,851	3,637	3,638
5049 Professional equipment, nec[3]	33	28	415	414	15	26,747	29,816	11,875	12,746
5051 Metals service centers and offices[3]	163	165	138	1,339	8	26,377	46,641	4,010	57,804
5052 Coal and other minerals and ores[2]	-	6	-	4	1	-	13,000	-	864
5063 Electrical apparatus and equipment[1]	219	192	2,401	2,337	12	34,302	36,977	90,575	90,744
5064 Electrical appliances, TV & radios[3]	34	38	520	596	16	35,623	31,537	17,903	19,043
5065 Electronic parts and equipment[1]	179	190	2,130	2,754	14	39,585	41,606	89,569	114,023
5072 Hardware[3]	81	83	935	951	11	26,913	32,925	27,055	31,387
5074 Plumbing & hydronic heating supplies[3]	109	101	536	855	8	31,627	34,756	17,792	29,611
5075 Warm air heating & air conditioning[3]	61	61	678	696	11	36,419	37,971	27,427	28,050
5078 Refrigeration equipment and supplies[3]	22	26	142	252	10	55,183	42,635	6,914	9,382
5082 Construction and mining machinery[3]	47	45	773	923	21	33,247	31,801	36,143	30,890
5083 Farm and garden machinery	37	37	227	270	7	27,947	24,119	6,838	7,132
5084 Industrial machinery and equipment[3]	316	327	2,984	3,255	10	33,594	37,872	116,804	141,265
5085 Industrial supplies[3]	191	196	2,213	2,139	11	35,617	37,030	86,084	87,683
5087 Service establishment equipment[3]	94	97	622	665	7	23,916	24,986	16,242	17,761
5088 Transportation equipment & supplies[3]	46	43	312	246	6	44,449	32,065	14,701	9,497
5091 Sporting & recreational goods[3]	57	56	476	535	10	25,790	25,966	13,797	14,620
5092 Toys and hobby goods and supplies[3]	27	24	160	104	4	24,825	31,192	5,143	3,932
5093 Scrap and waste materials[3]	82	81	1,231	1,468	18	24,162	26,981	35,301	42,909
5094 Jewelry & precious stones[3]	59	62	678	444	7	24,083	24,865	15,508	11,337
5099 Durable goods, nec[3]	82	91	354	381	4	26,520	27,906	10,829	12,243
5111 Printing and writing paper[3]	34	35	267	487	14	33,079	44,715	8,383	31,449
5112 Stationery and office supplies[3]	122	121	1,858	2,082	17	24,624	26,079	47,984	56,908
5113 Industrial & personal service paper[3]	77	80	940	997	12	34,238	35,823	35,436	38,985
5120 Drugs, proprietaries, and sundries[3]	65	66	1,704	1,653	25	46,331	49,246	82,224	74,617

Continued on next page.

ST. LOUIS MSA (MO PART) - [continued]

Wholesale and Retail Trade USA	Establishments		Employment		Emp / Est	Pay / Employee		Annual Payroll ($ 000)	
	1994	1995	1994	1995	1995	1994	1995	1994	1995
5131 Piece goods & notions[3]	33	34	362	380	11	24,840	29,011	11,214	11,831
5136 Men's and boys' clothing[3]	37	41	468	463	11	20,983	24,726	12,428	16,716
5137 Women's and children's clothing[3]	37	38	722	716	19	27,812	29,894	20,035	20,516
5139 Footwear[3]	56	53	732	674	13	46,923	54,534	37,048	37,534
5141 Groceries, general line[3]	41	38	1,273	1,248	33	31,321	32,003	41,480	44,098
5142 Packaged frozen food[3]	26	25	660	616	25	29,582	32,565	20,435	20,345
5143 Dairy products, exc. dried or canned[3]	25	26	361	393	15	40,122	41,374	14,920	15,897
5145 Confectionery[3]	20	20	425	475	24	25,788	25,204	11,641	12,996
5146 Fish and seafoods[3]	7	7	68	56	8	22,471	24,000	1,460	1,224
5147 Meats and meat products[3]	24	25	382	429	17	24,031	24,970	11,008	11,408
5148 Fresh fruits and vegetables[3]	48	46	490	473	10	31,322	32,017	16,975	17,541
5149 Groceries and related products, nec[3]	119	120	1,816	2,146	18	30,211	30,925	59,592	70,984
5153 Grain and field beans[3]	28	26	131	95	4	30,260	35,116	3,730	3,017
5162 Plastics materials & basic shapes[3]	42	44	370	461	10	31,741	34,707	13,431	17,221
5169 Chemicals & allied products, nec[3]	133	134	1,366	1,464	11	39,734	42,202	61,017	65,489
5171 Petroleum bulk stations & terminals	54	47	697	780	17	32,608	35,456	25,102	27,090
5172 Petroleum products, nec[3]	23	27	424	418	15	30,321	35,627	12,788	14,614
5181 Beer and ale[3]	19	18	58	219	12	38,069	49,425	2,627	10,301
5182 Wine and distilled beverages[3]	13	13	128	151	12	23,094	42,570	3,073	7,315
5191 Farm supplies	65	64	864	618	10	86,208	29,935	58,099	18,784
5192 Books, periodicals, & newspapers[3]	43	48	869	1,023	21	22,545	23,175	18,683	24,614
5193 Flowers & florists' supplies[3]	33	26	271	277	11	17,550	21,747	5,892	6,150
5194 Tobacco and tobacco products[3]	11	11	229	172	16	18,690	21,116	4,587	3,254
5198 Paints, varnishes, and supplies[3]	53	53	310	323	6	22,426	27,616	7,690	9,180
5199 Nondurable goods, nec	162	170	943	1,840	11	24,963	24,309	27,837	44,691
52 - Retail trade	11,279	11,230	177,062	179,439	16	13,491	14,229	2,604,205	2,717,864
5210 Lumber and other building materials	183	161	2,800	2,746	17	20,034	21,777	69,504	62,000
5230 Paint, glass, and wallpaper stores[3]	65	68	272	274	4	16,456	17,854	5,210	5,370
5250 Hardware stores[2]	124	98	2,054	1,519	16	16,358	16,787	25,558	21,856
5260 Retail nurseries and garden stores	89	90	676	768	9	12,580	11,583	11,471	11,951
5270 Mobile home dealers[3]	27	27	186	242	9	23,183	22,992	5,693	7,425
5310 Department stores[3]	85	84	16,409	17,654	210	12,182	12,852	217,956	234,671
5330 Variety stores[2]	83	56	730	506	9	7,666	8,134	6,528	4,722
5390 Misc. general merchandise stores[3]	57	83	1,918	1,574	19	12,023	13,654	23,440	21,729
5410 Grocery stores[3]	690	686	19,128	18,159	26	13,220	14,001	268,991	255,588
5420 Meat and fish markets[3]	46	47	213	229	5	14,441	13,520	3,364	3,073
5430 Fruit and vegetable markets	27	23	57	48	2	13,263	8,667	914	485
5440 Candy, nut, and confectionery stores[3]	52	52	340	336	6	6,529	7,107	2,624	2,505
5450 Dairy products stores[3]	18	21	48	64	3	4,917	5,875	306	543
5460 Retail bakeries[3]	156	166	1,089	1,698	10	9,587	9,267	12,296	16,994
5490 Miscellaneous food stores[3]	64	64	267	274	4	8,974	10,263	2,498	2,807
5510 New and used car dealers	172	180	8,059	8,380	47	31,107	32,620	283,600	308,813
5520 Used car dealers	140	134	616	608	5	22,117	26,447	16,575	18,314
5530 Auto and home supply stores	304	307	2,318	2,586	8	17,060	18,398	44,348	49,537
5540 Gasoline service stations	787	755	6,511	6,525	9	12,321	13,072	83,345	88,886
5550 Boat dealers[3]	27	29	156	158	5	25,282	27,316	4,471	4,920
5560 Recreational vehicle dealers[3]	14	18	78	108	6	26,462	24,815	3,311	3,987
5570 Motorcycle dealers[3]	29	29	176	188	6	17,273	17,936	3,692	4,420
5610 Men's & boys' clothing stores[3]	139	131	1,007	988	8	11,130	11,830	13,149	12,157
5620 Women's clothing stores	357	328	3,961	3,748	11	8,517	8,464	35,788	32,372
5630 Women's accessory & specialty stores[3]	81	78	421	435	6	10,907	11,338	4,885	4,983
5640 Children's and infants' wear stores[3]	37	37	318	362	10	7,686	8,254	2,480	2,943
5650 Family clothing stores[3]	121	116	1,846	1,662	14	8,368	9,461	17,403	16,881
5660 Shoe stores[2]	278	261	1,714	1,636	6	10,476	11,396	18,559	18,961
5690 Misc. apparel & accessory stores[3]	85	86	474	522	6	10,734	10,621	6,124	6,675
5712 Furniture stores[1]	224	219	1,955	1,931	9	20,205	20,673	42,905	43,182
5713 Floor covering stores[3]	103	109	626	686	6	19,744	23,259	14,339	17,419
5714 Drapery and upholstery stores[3]	33	32	101	107	3	14,772	14,916	1,752	1,687
5719 Misc. homefurnishings stores	149	148	974	1,119	8	13,446	16,054	14,637	16,891
5720 Household appliance stores[3]	68	69	283	277	4	16,636	18,686	5,315	5,562
5731 Radio, TV, & electronic stores[3]	123	116	1,554	1,757	15	14,849	16,920	25,322	31,979
5734 Computer and software stores[3]	53	60	373	361	6	19,249	19,812	7,486	8,451
5735 Record & prerecorded tape stores[3]	81	87	635	749	9	8,687	8,876	5,792	6,655
5736 Musical instrument stores[3]	25	24	162	162	7	19,062	19,531	3,477	3,810
5812 Eating places	2,589	2,456	59,887	58,559	24	7,707	8,345	505,937	522,226
5813 Drinking places	403	336	2,246	2,047	6	7,544	7,930	17,354	16,104
5910 Drug stores and proprietary stores	239	229	3,905	3,888	17	17,636	20,003	69,305	77,724
5920 Liquor stores	149	138	517	452	3	10,391	11,186	5,464	5,217
5930 Used merchandise stores[3]	167	164	720	781	5	11,628	12,999	10,423	11,188
5941 Sporting goods and bicycle shops[1]	197	189	1,298	1,610	9	12,533	12,887	18,083	22,158
5942 Book stores[3]	106	98	869	967	10	8,612	8,368	8,340	8,920

Continued on next page.

ST. LOUIS MSA (MO PART) - [continued]

Wholesale and Retail Trade USA	Establishments		Employment		Emp / Est	Pay / Employee		Annual Payroll ($ 000)	
	1994	1995	1994	1995	1995	1994	1995	1994	1995
5943 Stationery stores[3]	38	26	147	29	1	13,333	13,931	1,677	410
5944 Jewelry stores	198	212	1,108	1,188	6	17,097	17,455	20,071	21,763
5945 Hobby, toy, and game shops[3]	94	85	910	1,040	12	8,369	7,969	8,909	9,389
5946 Camera & photographic supply stores[3]	16	16	96	62	4	17,417	19,935	1,941	1,402
5947 Gift, novelty, and souvenir shops[3]	267	256	1,833	1,811	7	6,959	8,373	14,840	15,919
5948 Luggage and leather goods stores[1]	16	-	88	-	-	13,500	-	867	-
5949 Sewing, needlework, and piece goods[3]	63	61	573	593	10	8,551	8,546	4,993	4,870
5961 Catalog and mail-order houses[3]	44	50	580	1,541	31	17,028	23,515	11,755	38,772
5962 Merchandising machine operators[1]	66	67	300	619	9	16,653	17,493	5,908	11,826
5963 Direct selling establishments[3]	150	151	1,357	1,364	9	15,360	17,346	24,166	26,552
5984 Liquefied petroleum gas dealers[3]	28	30	74	117	4	22,000	25,402	1,602	2,803
5992 Florists	151	158	799	828	5	11,895	12,179	10,182	10,940
5993 Tobacco stores and stands[3]	28	30	66	88	3	11,515	12,591	768	1,214
5994 News dealers and newsstands[3]	13	16	82	46	3	7,220	13,478	675	657
5995 Optical goods stores[3]	132	132	646	670	5	17,789	19,672	14,502	13,857
5999 Miscellaneous retail stores, nec	366	392	1,969	2,130	5	14,369	14,830	30,340	33,267

Source: County Business Patterns 1994/95, CBP-94/95, U.S. Department of Commerce, Washington DC, November 1997. The employment column represents mid-March employment in the year. Pay per employee is calculated by dividing 1st Quarter payroll, annualized, by mid-March employment. The column headed 'Emp / Est' shows 'employees per establishment'. A dash (-) means that data are unavailable or cannot be calculated. nec means not elsewhere classified. *Notes:* 1. 1994 data incomplete; unavailable or withheld. 2. 1995 data incomplete; unavailable or withheld. 3. 1994 and 1995 data incomplete; unavailable or withheld.

ST. LOUIS, MO – IL MSA

Wholesale and Retail Trade USA	Establishments		Employment		Emp / Est	Pay / Employee		Annual Payroll ($ 000)	
	1994	1995	1994	1995	1995	1994	1995	1994	1995
50- Wholesale trade	5,503	5,560	71,188	74,888	13	33,307	35,735	2,519,388	2,724,039
5012 Automobiles and other vehicles[3]	84	84	1,605	1,889	22	27,422	31,464	47,365	57,746
5013 Motor vehicle supplies and new parts	277	277	3,177	3,652	13	26,667	30,459	90,269	113,077
5014 Tires and tubes[3]	32	25	320	326	13	26,988	27,718	9,619	8,515
5015 Motor vehicle parts, used[3]	78	86	413	485	6	18,838	20,899	10,037	11,319
5021 Furniture[3]	82	81	868	1,022	13	30,553	34,458	27,552	36,368
5023 Homefurnishings[3]	86	76	807	1,033	14	27,301	27,051	26,088	30,160
5031 Lumber, plywood, and millwork[3]	86	73	1,030	767	11	32,097	32,902	35,218	26,006
5032 Brick, stone, & related materials[3]	50	42	395	312	7	31,625	40,436	12,586	11,254
5033 Roofing, siding, & insulation[3]	48	44	411	328	7	29,294	31,061	15,441	11,809
5039 Construction materials, nec[3]	51	68	485	933	14	23,654	28,695	14,365	30,575
5043 Photographic equipment & supplies[3]	17	16	404	422	26	35,881	40,929	13,986	15,510
5044 Office equipment[3]	85	84	1,823	1,929	23	31,745	36,622	62,327	67,553
5045 Computers, peripherals, & software[3]	170	184	2,454	2,244	12	49,604	59,055	117,830	123,409
5046 Commercial equipment, nec[3]	77	83	671	735	9	24,566	25,709	18,265	20,486
5047 Medical and hospital equipment[3]	191	176	2,620	2,367	13	39,586	42,055	108,898	101,214
5048 Ophthalmic goods[3]	20	15	175	188	13	20,366	19,851	3,637	3,638
5049 Professional equipment, nec[3]	35	30	415	414	14	26,747	29,816	11,875	12,746
5051 Metals service centers and offices[3]	185	190	434	1,339	7	27,945	46,641	12,794	57,804
5052 Coal and other minerals and ores[2]	-	9	-	4	-	-	13,000	-	864
5063 Electrical apparatus and equipment[3]	241	214	2,511	2,448	11	33,861	36,413	93,391	93,558
5064 Electrical appliances, TV & radios[3]	37	41	520	596	15	35,623	31,537	17,903	19,043
5065 Electronic parts and equipment[3]	195	209	2,242	2,856	14	39,024	41,318	92,819	117,680
5072 Hardware[3]	87	91	956	976	11	26,707	32,500	27,434	31,894
5074 Plumbing & hydronic heating supplies[3]	125	115	690	1,001	9	29,490	33,518	21,829	33,759
5075 Warm air heating & air conditioning[3]	74	74	740	732	10	35,314	37,596	28,959	29,292
5078 Refrigeration equipment and supplies[3]	25	29	182	252	9	48,462	42,635	8,450	9,382
5082 Construction and mining machinery[3]	48	46	773	923	20	33,247	31,801	36,143	30,890
5083 Farm and garden machinery	73	72	514	561	8	24,195	22,303	14,337	14,099
5084 Industrial machinery and equipment[3]	347	354	3,216	3,505	10	33,184	37,398	123,704	148,555
5085 Industrial supplies[3]	217	224	2,376	2,308	10	34,887	36,432	90,628	93,065
5087 Service establishment equipment[3]	106	110	791	826	8	20,971	22,349	17,999	19,721
5088 Transportation equipment & supplies[3]	50	47	312	287	6	44,449	31,261	14,701	10,841
5091 Sporting & recreational goods[3]	60	59	476	535	9	25,790	25,966	13,797	14,620
5092 Toys and hobby goods and supplies[3]	27	24	160	104	4	24,825	31,192	5,143	3,932
5093 Scrap and waste materials[3]	108	112	1,403	1,853	17	24,596	27,622	40,195	54,736
5094 Jewelry & precious stones[3]	62	65	678	444	7	24,083	24,865	15,508	11,337
5099 Durable goods, nec[3]	90	101	354	381	4	26,520	27,906	10,829	12,243
5111 Printing and writing paper[3]	35	36	267	487	14	33,079	44,715	8,383	31,449
5112 Stationery and office supplies[3]	140	133	1,906	2,113	16	24,418	25,956	48,765	57,436
5113 Industrial & personal service paper[3]	80	84	940	997	12	34,238	35,823	35,436	38,985
5120 Drugs, proprietaries, and sundries[3]	68	69	1,704	1,653	24	46,331	49,246	82,224	74,617
5131 Piece goods & notions[3]	34	35	362	380	11	24,840	29,011	11,214	11,831
5136 Men's and boys' clothing[3]	39	42	468	463	11	20,983	24,726	12,428	16,716

Continued on next page.

ST. LOUIS, MO - IL MSA - [continued]

Wholesale and Retail Trade USA	Establishments		Employment		Emp / Est	Pay / Employee		Annual Payroll ($ 000)	
	1994	1995	1994	1995	1995	1994	1995	1994	1995
5137 Women's and children's clothing [3]	38	39	722	716	18	27,812	29,894	20,035	20,516
5139 Footwear [3]	56	54	732	674	12	46,923	54,534	37,048	37,534
5141 Groceries, general line [3]	44	40	1,273	1,248	31	31,321	32,003	41,480	44,098
5142 Packaged frozen food [3]	32	31	745	707	23	29,906	31,904	23,296	22,910
5143 Dairy products, exc. dried or canned [3]	29	29	361	393	14	40,122	41,374	14,920	15,897
5145 Confectionery [3]	21	21	425	475	23	25,788	25,204	11,641	12,996
5146 Fish and seafoods [3]	8	9	68	56	6	22,471	24,000	1,460	1,224
5147 Meats and meat products [3]	27	29	382	486	17	24,031	24,560	11,008	12,491
5148 Fresh fruits and vegetables [3]	52	50	490	473	9	31,322	32,017	16,975	17,541
5149 Groceries and related products, nec [3]	138	139	1,975	2,332	17	29,177	29,614	62,622	73,895
5153 Grain and field beans [3]	63	59	360	349	6	26,889	35,083	9,585	11,309
5154 Livestock [3]	13	12	36	33	3	17,556	17,818	674	649
5162 Plastics materials & basic shapes [3]	44	48	370	461	10	31,741	34,707	13,431	17,221
5169 Chemicals & allied products, nec [3]	147	148	1,366	1,489	10	39,734	41,913	61,017	66,070
5171 Petroleum bulk stations & terminals	81	71	959	1,042	15	32,651	34,345	34,437	36,017
5172 Petroleum products, nec [3]	33	39	458	456	12	31,450	36,123	14,345	16,338
5181 Beer and ale [3]	30	30	104	271	9	33,615	45,550	4,607	12,231
5182 Wine and distilled beverages [3]	16	16	128	151	9	23,094	42,570	3,073	7,315
5191 Farm supplies	103	104	1,038	806	8	75,592	27,305	63,145	22,505
5192 Books, periodicals, & newspapers [3]	45	50	869	1,023	20	22,545	23,175	18,683	24,614
5193 Flowers & florists' supplies [3]	37	31	271	277	9	17,550	21,747	5,892	6,150
5194 Tobacco and tobacco products [3]	15	15	229	172	11	18,690	21,116	4,587	3,254
5198 Paints, varnishes, and supplies [3]	54	55	310	323	6	22,426	27,616	7,690	9,180
5199 Nondurable goods, nec [1]	186	193	1,032	1,926	10	24,318	24,112	29,593	46,814
52- Retail trade	14,533	14,520	218,914	221,408	15	12,948	13,706	3,095,646	3,225,130
5210 Lumber and other building materials	254	231	3,550	3,655	16	19,873	21,726	86,800	81,768
5230 Paint, glass, and wallpaper stores [3]	83	90	347	378	4	16,092	17,196	6,498	7,094
5250 Hardware stores [3]	169	130	2,565	1,837	14	15,880	16,146	31,124	26,248
5260 Retail nurseries and garden stores [3]	114	115	816	918	8	12,152	11,464	13,351	14,052
5270 Mobile home dealers [3]	40	41	262	326	8	20,153	20,368	7,003	8,698
5310 Department stores [3]	118	117	21,277	22,595	193	11,775	12,732	274,710	295,201
5330 Variety stores [3]	115	71	967	593	8	7,686	7,946	8,630	5,395
5390 Misc. general merchandise stores [3]	68	111	2,270	1,918	17	12,326	13,658	28,567	26,110
5410 Grocery stores [3]	939	930	23,779	22,640	24	12,990	13,714	327,686	314,528
5420 Meat and fish markets [3]	75	73	337	351	5	14,113	13,561	5,247	4,861
5430 Fruit and vegetable markets [3]	36	36	93	154	4	11,656	9,455	1,332	1,853
5440 Candy, nut, and confectionery stores [3]	58	56	340	354	6	6,529	7,017	2,624	2,610
5450 Dairy products stores [3]	22	24	48	64	3	4,917	5,875	306	543
5460 Retail bakeries [3]	197	209	1,361	2,055	10	9,252	9,137	14,890	20,473
5490 Miscellaneous food stores [3]	76	76	305	311	4	8,944	9,788	2,932	3,079
5510 New and used car dealers	247	254	10,102	10,360	41	30,242	31,979	348,758	373,903
5520 Used car dealers [3]	182	177	754	739	4	21,724	24,991	19,190	20,738
5530 Auto and home supply stores	390	393	2,900	3,188	8	16,655	18,077	54,206	59,977
5540 Gasoline service stations	1,026	992	8,273	8,449	9	12,066	12,602	103,918	110,924
5550 Boat dealers [3]	38	40	219	227	6	23,489	25,357	5,908	6,552
5560 Recreational vehicle dealers [3]	20	23	90	129	6	25,689	23,783	3,559	4,407
5570 Motorcycle dealers [3]	40	39	227	246	6	16,705	17,398	4,895	5,791
5610 Men's & boys' clothing stores [3]	162	153	1,087	1,085	7	11,021	11,631	14,060	13,188
5620 Women's clothing stores [3]	449	406	4,711	4,344	11	8,359	8,304	41,844	36,785
5630 Women's accessory & specialty stores [3]	93	92	483	458	5	10,443	11,266	5,351	5,181
5640 Children's and infants' wear stores [3]	42	43	318	390	9	7,686	8,205	2,480	3,192
5650 Family clothing stores [3]	156	151	2,249	1,997	13	8,560	9,546	21,569	20,640
5660 Shoe stores [3]	340	318	2,009	1,929	6	10,316	11,166	21,510	21,957
5690 Misc. apparel & accessory stores [3]	98	100	532	594	6	10,459	10,323	6,608	7,264
5712 Furniture stores [1]	285	278	2,363	2,452	9	19,677	19,659	51,541	52,215
5713 Floor covering stores [3]	141	155	776	894	6	19,686	21,937	17,883	21,751
5714 Drapery and upholstery stores [3]	40	39	106	113	3	14,415	14,584	1,787	1,717
5719 Misc. homefurnishings stores [3]	172	171	1,024	1,179	7	13,277	15,759	15,126	17,383
5720 Household appliance stores [3]	92	94	415	419	4	15,884	17,623	7,503	7,842
5731 Radio, TV, & electronic stores [3]	150	143	1,809	2,022	14	14,850	16,552	29,421	36,087
5734 Computer and software stores [3]	62	73	400	413	6	18,480	18,334	7,734	8,906
5735 Record & prerecorded tape stores [3]	96	100	709	830	8	8,705	9,099	6,560	7,483
5736 Musical instrument stores [3]	37	37	221	227	6	17,357	17,515	4,222	4,665
5812 Eating places	3,311	3,140	74,901	73,119	23	7,493	8,098	612,942	631,558
5813 Drinking places	694	619	3,513	3,373	5	7,581	7,922	28,224	26,943
5910 Drug stores and proprietary stores	334	321	4,853	4,910	15	17,547	19,571	86,357	96,234
5920 Liquor stores	206	193	852	750	4	9,869	10,315	8,713	8,067
5930 Used merchandise stores [3]	204	204	828	875	4	11,440	12,832	11,567	12,273
5941 Sporting goods and bicycle shops [3]	234	225	1,511	1,827	8	12,323	12,742	20,582	24,792
5942 Book stores [3]	124	118	950	1,053	9	8,749	8,555	9,182	9,886
5943 Stationery stores [3]	47	33	165	29	1	13,430	13,931	1,913	410

Continued on next page.

ST. LOUIS, MO – IL MSA - [continued]

Wholesale and Retail Trade USA	Establishments		Employment		Emp / Est	Pay / Employee		Annual Payroll ($ 000)	
	1994	1995	1994	1995	1995	1994	1995	1994	1995
5944 Jewelry stores	244	259	1,426	1,527	6	16,314	16,728	25,003	26,750
5945 Hobby, toy, and game shops [3]	110	109	1,016	1,162	11	8,374	8,045	10,155	10,689
5946 Camera & photographic supply stores [3]	19	19	96	62	3	17,417	19,935	1,941	1,402
5947 Gift, novelty, and souvenir shops [3]	328	317	2,152	2,185	7	7,281	8,476	18,249	19,496
5948 Luggage and leather goods stores [1]	17	-	88	-	-	13,500	-	867	-
5949 Sewing, needlework, and piece goods [3]	80	77	643	710	9	8,560	8,327	5,594	5,756
5961 Catalog and mail-order houses [3]	53	65	617	1,597	25	16,460	23,103	12,097	39,525
5962 Merchandising machine operators [3]	83	84	360	684	8	16,433	17,409	7,011	13,055
5963 Direct selling establishments [3]	170	177	1,431	1,438	8	15,561	17,388	25,550	28,021
5984 Liquefied petroleum gas dealers [3]	42	46	97	117	3	21,979	25,402	2,102	2,803
5992 Florists [3]	227	226	935	972	4	11,440	11,650	11,570	12,314
5993 Tobacco stores and stands [3]	29	32	66	88	3	11,515	12,591	768	1,214
5994 News dealers and newsstands [3]	17	20	87	50	3	7,264	13,360	714	697
5995 Optical goods stores [3]	157	157	821	853	5	17,345	19,315	17,774	17,358
5999 Miscellaneous retail stores, nec	461	491	2,484	2,658	5	13,480	14,194	35,896	39,943

Source: County Business Patterns 1994/95, CBP-94/95, U.S. Department of Commerce, Washington DC, November 1997. The employment column represents mid-March employment in the year. Pay per employee is calculated by dividing 1st Quarter payroll, annualized, by mid-March employment. The column headed 'Emp / Est' shows 'employees per establishment'. A dash (-) means that data are unavailable or cannot be calculated. nec means not elsewhere classified. *Notes:* 1. 1994 data incomplete; unavailable or withheld. 2. 1995 data incomplete; unavailable or withheld. 3. 1994 and 1995 data incomplete; unavailable or withheld.

SALEM, OR PMSA

Wholesale and Retail Trade USA	Establishments		Employment		Emp / Est	Pay / Employee		Annual Payroll ($ 000)	
	1994	1995	1994	1995	1995	1994	1995	1994	1995
50- Wholesale trade	-	461	-	4,568	10	-	23,915	-	116,836
5012 Automobiles and other vehicles [2]	-	9	-	22	2	-	16,000	-	369
5013 Motor vehicle supplies and new parts	-	23	-	254	11	-	22,441	-	6,414
5014 Tires and tubes	-	8	-	136	17	-	22,000	-	3,117
5015 Motor vehicle parts, used	-	14	-	72	5	-	13,333	-	1,127
5020 Furniture and homefurnishings	-	11	-	58	5	-	25,448	-	1,364
5031 Lumber, plywood, and millwork	-	23	-	126	5	-	24,444	-	3,032
5032 Brick, stone, & related materials [2]	-	4	-	21	5	-	58,286	-	774
5033 Roofing, siding, & insulation [2]	-	3	-	58	19	-	22,966	-	1,508
5039 Construction materials, nec	-	6	-	10	2	-	31,200	-	263
5044 Office equipment [2]	-	5	-	76	15	-	28,421	-	2,269
5045 Computers, peripherals, & software [2]	-	10	-	99	10	-	42,707	-	3,374
5063 Electrical apparatus and equipment	-	11	-	76	7	-	24,579	-	1,947
5072 Hardware [2]	-	11	-	150	14	-	20,693	-	3,606
5083 Farm and garden machinery	-	18	-	251	14	-	22,104	-	5,763
5084 Industrial machinery and equipment	-	19	-	58	3	-	23,931	-	1,568
5085 Industrial supplies	-	13	-	142	11	-	29,437	-	5,203
5087 Service establishment equipment [2]	-	6	-	44	7	-	27,636	-	1,387
5091 Sporting & recreational goods	-	4	-	25	6	-	22,880	-	664
5093 Scrap and waste materials	-	12	-	52	4	-	19,385	-	1,516
5099 Durable goods, nec	-	13	-	63	5	-	24,063	-	1,822
5110 Paper and paper products	-	11	-	119	11	-	17,479	-	2,014
5120 Drugs, proprietaries, and sundries [2]	-	4	-	17	4	-	19,765	-	337
5141 Groceries, general line [2]	-	4	-	34	9	-	26,471	-	780
5145 Confectionery	-	5	-	35	7	-	17,257	-	859
5148 Fresh fruits and vegetables [2]	-	6	-	146	24	-	15,616	-	2,180
5149 Groceries and related products, nec	-	13	-	318	24	-	17,786	-	6,867
5150 Farm-product raw materials	-	8	-	9	1	-	16,000	-	168
5160 Chemicals and allied products [2]	-	3	-	12	4	-	31,333	-	386
5171 Petroleum bulk stations & terminals	-	11	-	171	16	-	27,228	-	4,979
5172 Petroleum products, nec [2]	-	3	-	11	4	-	17,455	-	207
5181 Beer and ale [2]	-	3	-	137	46	-	28,380	-	3,990
5191 Farm supplies	-	47	-	485	10	-	25,014	-	13,567
5193 Flowers & florists' supplies	-	19	-	128	7	-	32,031	-	3,580
5199 Nondurable goods, nec	-	11	-	17	2	-	23,765	-	478
52- Retail trade	-	1,670	-	23,348	14	-	13,014	-	327,197
5210 Lumber and other building materials	-	34	-	554	16	-	22,231	-	12,659
5230 Paint, glass, and wallpaper stores	-	12	-	64	5	-	18,750	-	1,307
5250 Hardware stores	-	12	-	77	6	-	11,169	-	1,328
5260 Retail nurseries and garden stores	-	23	-	139	6	-	12,719	-	2,047
5270 Mobile home dealers	-	9	-	127	14	-	34,425	-	5,926
5310 Department stores [2]	-	16	-	2,600	163	-	12,632	-	33,732
5390 Misc. general merchandise stores [2]	-	17	-	106	6	-	11,887	-	2,472
5410 Grocery stores	-	115	-	2,979	26	-	13,903	-	43,873
5420 Meat and fish markets [2]	-	4	-	16	4	-	11,500	-	222

Continued on next page.

SALEM, OR PMSA - [continued]

Wholesale and Retail Trade USA	Establishments		Employment		Emp / Est	Pay / Employee		Annual Payroll ($ 000)	
	1994	1995	1994	1995	1995	1994	1995	1994	1995
5440 Candy, nut, and confectionery stores [2]	-	4	-	18	5	-	7,556	-	159
5460 Retail bakeries	-	13	-	131	10	-	9,435	-	1,195
5490 Miscellaneous food stores	-	18	-	112	6	-	8,607	-	1,129
5510 New and used car dealers	-	22	-	976	44	-	28,057	-	31,533
5520 Used car dealers	-	27	-	84	3	-	23,857	-	2,158
5530 Auto and home supply stores	-	42	-	313	7	-	27,885	-	8,290
5540 Gasoline service stations	-	76	-	821	11	-	11,337	-	9,962
5560 Recreational vehicle dealers [2]	-	6	-	83	14	-	28,675	-	2,760
5570 Motorcycle dealers [2]	-	9	-	148	16	-	10,405	-	2,035
5610 Men's & boys' clothing stores [2]	-	7	-	45	6	-	15,733	-	682
5620 Women's clothing stores	-	22	-	137	6	-	7,182	-	1,089
5630 Women's accessory & specialty stores [2]	-	7	-	25	4	-	10,080	-	256
5650 Family clothing stores	-	18	-	517	29	-	12,805	-	6,980
5660 Shoe stores	-	20	-	109	5	-	11,046	-	1,288
5690 Misc. apparel & accessory stores [2]	-	5	-	19	4	-	10,526	-	219
5712 Furniture stores	-	32	-	167	5	-	20,551	-	3,515
5713 Floor covering stores	-	22	-	104	5	-	33,923	-	2,901
5714 Drapery and upholstery stores [2]	-	3	-	11	4	-	12,364	-	146
5719 Misc. homefurnishings stores	-	18	-	74	4	-	12,378	-	947
5720 Household appliance stores	-	13	-	77	6	-	17,455	-	2,463
5731 Radio, TV, & electronic stores	-	22	-	161	7	-	16,696	-	2,743
5734 Computer and software stores [2]	-	11	-	49	4	-	13,878	-	718
5735 Record & prerecorded tape stores [2]	-	10	-	38	4	-	11,579	-	628
5736 Musical instrument stores [2]	-	9	-	42	5	-	18,762	-	827
5812 Eating places	-	437	-	8,063	18	-	7,730	-	64,247
5813 Drinking places	-	67	-	545	8	-	9,350	-	5,615
5910 Drug stores and proprietary stores	-	32	-	432	14	-	18,481	-	7,757
5930 Used merchandise stores	-	31	-	186	6	-	10,194	-	2,051
5941 Sporting goods and bicycle shops	-	30	-	123	4	-	13,626	-	1,764
5942 Book stores	-	19	-	144	8	-	9,389	-	1,322
5943 Stationery stores [2]	-	4	-	24	6	-	12,500	-	307
5944 Jewelry stores	-	22	-	106	5	-	20,113	-	2,302
5945 Hobby, toy, and game shops	-	16	-	121	8	-	10,479	-	1,356
5947 Gift, novelty, and souvenir shops [2]	-	30	-	127	4	-	7,307	-	1,070
5949 Sewing, needlework, and piece goods [2]	-	13	-	96	7	-	7,250	-	658
5963 Direct selling establishments	-	18	-	82	5	-	16,195	-	1,438
5984 Liquefied petroleum gas dealers [2]	-	3	-	23	8	-	18,609	-	472
5992 Florists	-	30	-	128	4	-	9,094	-	1,199
5993 Tobacco stores and stands [2]	-	5	-	27	5	-	22,074	-	856
5995 Optical goods stores [2]	-	14	-	74	5	-	14,378	-	1,102
5999 Miscellaneous retail stores, nec	-	55	-	295	5	-	11,322	-	3,930

Source: County Business Patterns 1994/95, CBP-94/95, U.S. Department of Commerce, Washington DC, November 1997. The employment column represents mid-March employment in the year. Pay per employee is calculated by dividing 1st Quarter payroll, annualized, by mid-March employment. The column headed 'Emp / Est' shows 'employees per establishment'. A dash (-) means that data are unavailable or cannot be calculated. nec means not elsewhere classified. *Notes:* 1. 1994 data incomplete; unavailable or withheld. 2. 1995 data incomplete; unavailable or withheld. 3. 1994 and 1995 data incomplete; unavailable or withheld.

SALINAS, CA MSA

Wholesale and Retail Trade USA	Establishments		Employment		Emp / Est	Pay / Employee		Annual Payroll ($ 000)	
	1994	1995	1994	1995	1995	1994	1995	1994	1995
50- Wholesale trade	540	536	7,237	7,906	15	28,784	33,297	227,852	283,577
5013 Motor vehicle supplies and new parts	35	31	299	303	10	20,896	22,205	6,995	7,451
5015 Motor vehicle parts, used	4	5	21	19	4	20,000	17,474	445	379
5021 Furniture	6	6	48	50	8	25,000	28,000	1,462	1,792
5023 Homefurnishings	7	7	38	36	5	20,105	16,889	787	578
5031 Lumber, plywood, and millwork	4	-	26	-	-	32,769	-	546	-
5032 Brick, stone, & related materials	4	4	14	13	3	30,857	40,308	436	500
5044 Office equipment	12	11	162	159	14	27,556	32,956	4,867	4,905
5045 Computers, peripherals, & software	14	12	133	96	8	45,203	30,208	5,572	3,324
5063 Electrical apparatus and equipment	13	13	106	384	30	28,755	36,823	2,857	13,124
5072 Hardware	-	6	-	46	8	-	21,739	-	1,024
5074 Plumbing & hydronic heating supplies	10	9	85	102	11	29,224	30,745	2,628	3,123
5078 Refrigeration equipment and supplies	4	-	44	-	-	32,273	-	1,265	-
5083 Farm and garden machinery	25	25	276	284	11	31,043	29,972	8,910	9,503
5084 Industrial machinery and equipment	12	12	53	54	5	32,755	37,185	1,977	2,339
5085 Industrial supplies	12	11	73	66	6	23,288	30,121	1,992	2,063
5093 Scrap and waste materials	9	9	121	183	20	19,669	16,284	2,747	3,278
5094 Jewelry & precious stones	5	-	57	-	-	10,947	-	911	-
5099 Durable goods, nec	-	7	-	59	8	-	20,203	-	1,428

Continued on next page.

SALINAS, CA MSA - [continued]

Wholesale and Retail Trade USA	Establishments		Employment		Emp / Est	Pay / Employee		Annual Payroll ($ 000)	
	1994	1995	1994	1995	1995	1994	1995	1994	1995
5112 Stationery and office supplies	12	10	131	159	16	19,115	19,371	2,777	2,890
5113 Industrial & personal service paper	10	12	52	59	5	47,231	48,068	2,236	2,604
5136 Men's and boys' clothing	3	3	71	60	20	8,507	15,067	678	852
5137 Women's and children's clothing	5	3	4	13	4	29,000	22,462	155	308
5141 Groceries, general line	4	4	21	20	5	30,286	30,400	605	570
5142 Packaged frozen food	13	14	611	565	40	7,817	6,676	4,894	4,452
5143 Dairy products, exc. dried or canned	9	8	72	76	10	31,444	32,737	2,458	2,743
5146 Fish and seafoods	3	5	52	17	3	7,231	23,765	497	724
5148 Fresh fruits and vegetables	100	95	2,134	1,950	21	36,731	38,753	84,802	88,837
5149 Groceries and related products, nec	24	21	493	318	15	25,063	25,535	12,767	8,924
5153 Grain and field beans	3	3	52	55	18	31,692	29,455	2,173	2,316
5159 Farm-product raw materials, nec	4	4	7	11	3	64,000	44,364	477	378
5162 Plastics materials & basic shapes	4	3	10	11	4	34,400	61,091	801	1,881
5169 Chemicals & allied products, nec	-	6	-	22	4	-	42,000	-	1,068
5171 Petroleum bulk stations & terminals	9	10	132	127	13	25,000	26,740	3,734	3,930
5180 Beer, wine, and distilled beverages	8	7	108	128	18	54,519	55,156	6,284	7,194
5191 Farm supplies	37	35	815	855	24	34,366	34,737	32,136	34,206
5192 Books, periodicals, & newspapers	6	-	29	-	-	30,897	-	1,043	-
5193 Flowers & florists' supplies	15	-	123	-	-	16,943	-	2,684	-
5199 Nondurable goods, nec	19	22	113	106	5	22,832	27,057	2,930	3,357
52 - Retail trade	2,251	2,193	24,395	23,750	11	13,537	14,283	359,785	362,104
5210 Lumber and other building materials	24	25	525	501	20	20,000	21,246	11,528	11,151
5230 Paint, glass, and wallpaper stores	18	17	89	73	4	23,281	23,288	2,077	1,732
5250 Hardware stores	17	12	216	206	17	11,278	12,000	2,707	2,865
5310 Department stores	12	11	1,889	1,971	179	11,718	11,963	23,851	24,315
5330 Variety stores	12	8	55	49	6	7,345	8,000	510	483
5390 Misc. general merchandise stores	11	11	321	321	29	19,402	21,533	6,763	6,686
5410 Grocery stores	141	139	2,535	2,542	18	20,622	21,637	54,599	56,475
5420 Meat and fish markets	14	12	75	81	7	10,987	10,173	761	1,033
5430 Fruit and vegetable markets	11	10	24	27	3	21,500	38,963	661	1,055
5440 Candy, nut, and confectionery stores	16	17	66	73	4	9,273	9,425	712	795
5450 Dairy products stores	-	4	-	4	1	-	7,000	-	64
5460 Retail bakeries	49	45	361	302	7	9,307	9,417	3,781	3,315
5490 Miscellaneous food stores	21	23	86	121	5	13,674	12,595	1,219	1,363
5510 New and used car dealers	32	33	1,056	1,029	31	29,636	32,362	38,063	37,484
5520 Used car dealers	14	13	37	51	4	30,811	19,294	810	933
5530 Auto and home supply stores	47	47	384	358	8	14,417	18,492	5,963	6,340
5540 Gasoline service stations	106	100	753	684	7	13,360	14,386	10,562	10,722
5550 Boat dealers	-	3	-	18	6	-	10,889	-	239
5560 Recreational vehicle dealers	4	4	18	20	5	18,667	19,800	397	432
5570 Motorcycle dealers	7	7	43	38	5	18,326	20,842	1,134	1,218
5610 Men's & boys' clothing stores	25	20	158	154	8	14,101	13,844	2,272	2,272
5620 Women's clothing stores	82	77	660	580	8	10,630	12,497	7,399	6,615
5630 Women's accessory & specialty stores	13	12	90	72	6	9,911	11,667	878	800
5640 Children's and infants' wear stores	13	13	85	74	6	8,800	10,162	696	662
5650 Family clothing stores	43	39	392	376	10	12,847	10,968	4,897	4,113
5660 Shoe stores	49	45	253	231	5	11,352	11,654	2,704	2,768
5690 Misc. apparel & accessory stores	22	23	138	145	6	10,319	10,345	1,561	1,591
5712 Furniture stores	37	38	170	147	4	16,871	16,136	3,097	2,916
5713 Floor covering stores	21	21	125	147	7	21,216	23,973	3,024	3,796
5719 Misc. homefurnishings stores	43	38	202	169	4	17,366	17,538	3,493	2,568
5720 Household appliance stores	6	6	28	27	5	21,143	20,889	605	609
5731 Radio, TV, & electronic stores	19	20	170	169	8	18,259	19,905	3,252	3,446
5734 Computer and software stores	12	13	59	74	6	18,644	24,324	1,460	1,946
5735 Record & prerecorded tape stores	15	14	130	132	9	8,031	8,212	1,071	1,043
5736 Musical instrument stores	5	-	16	-	-	14,000	-	234	-
5812 Eating places	610	564	9,129	8,609	15	9,258	9,571	94,283	91,502
5813 Drinking places	49	42	251	215	5	8,382	8,930	2,091	2,010
5910 Drug stores and proprietary stores	47	48	865	886	18	18,007	18,817	16,507	17,184
5920 Liquor stores	49	45	191	178	4	12,126	11,281	2,546	2,179
5930 Used merchandise stores	39	37	155	160	4	12,310	12,850	2,029	2,111
5941 Sporting goods and bicycle shops	42	43	271	252	6	10,391	11,444	3,223	3,164
5942 Book stores	22	22	193	184	8	9,575	10,196	1,924	1,911
5943 Stationery stores	8	8	44	57	7	7,545	12,281	431	920
5944 Jewelry stores	63	61	265	240	4	17,328	18,367	5,006	4,739
5945 Hobby, toy, and game shops	22	21	179	157	7	10,994	10,293	2,090	1,832
5946 Camera & photographic supply stores	6	6	41	40	7	15,902	17,100	709	714
5947 Gift, novelty, and souvenir shops	80	80	258	280	4	9,922	9,786	2,914	3,138
5948 Luggage and leather goods stores	6	6	35	32	5	10,514	12,375	362	384
5949 Sewing, needlework, and piece goods	11	11	97	87	8	8,866	9,425	851	809
5961 Catalog and mail-order houses	7	8	38	46	6	10,105	9,130	432	499

Continued on next page.

SALINAS, CA MSA - [continued]

Wholesale and Retail Trade USA	Establishments		Employment		Emp / Est	Pay / Employee		Annual Payroll ($ 000)	
	1994	1995	1994	1995	1995	1994	1995	1994	1995
5962 Merchandising machine operators	4	3	30	19	6	13,600	20,211	456	294
5963 Direct selling establishments	23	24	130	125	5	22,431	27,328	3,201	3,740
5984 Liquefied petroleum gas dealers	5	4	29	36	9	19,586	16,667	593	707
5992 Florists	29	27	128	125	5	9,938	11,104	1,337	1,432
5995 Optical goods stores	14	14	61	68	5	12,787	13,588	755	969
5999 Miscellaneous retail stores, nec	90	87	441	472	5	16,027	16,246	7,513	8,155

Source: County Business Patterns 1994/95, CBP-94/95, U.S. Department of Commerce, Washington DC, November 1997. The employment column represents mid-March employment in the year. Pay per employee is calculated by dividing 1st Quarter payroll, annualized, by mid-March employment. The column headed 'Emp / Est' shows 'employees per establishment'. A dash (-) means that data are unavailable or cannot be calculated. nec means not elsewhere classified. *Notes:* 1. 1994 data incomplete; unavailable or withheld. 2. 1995 data incomplete; unavailable or withheld. 3. 1994 and 1995 data incomplete; unavailable or withheld.

SALT LAKE CITY – OGDEN, UT MSA

Wholesale and Retail Trade USA	Establishments		Employment		Emp / Est	Pay / Employee		Annual Payroll ($ 000)	
	1994	1995	1994	1995	1995	1994	1995	1994	1995
50– Wholesale trade	-	2,642	-	38,315	15	-	28,834	-	1,162,185
5012 Automobiles and other vehicles	-	42	-	1,450	35	-	27,948	-	42,963
5013 Motor vehicle supplies and new parts	-	124	-	1,843	15	-	24,050	-	46,150
5014 Tires and tubes	-	21	-	266	13	-	34,872	-	8,954
5015 Motor vehicle parts, used	-	29	-	199	7	-	14,995	-	3,223
5021 Furniture	-	40	-	278	7	-	21,799	-	8,051
5023 Homefurnishings	-	50	-	636	13	-	27,855	-	14,615
5031 Lumber, plywood, and millwork	-	41	-	803	20	-	38,042	-	27,053
5032 Brick, stone, & related materials [2]	-	25	-	150	6	-	32,027	-	5,182
5033 Roofing, siding, & insulation	-	24	-	247	10	-	25,344	-	6,915
5039 Construction materials, nec	-	45	-	789	18	-	24,183	-	21,384
5044 Office equipment	-	47	-	829	18	-	35,189	-	31,318
5045 Computers, peripherals, & software	-	127	-	1,478	12	-	45,066	-	65,706
5046 Commercial equipment, nec	-	30	-	368	12	-	23,076	-	9,354
5047 Medical and hospital equipment	-	84	-	585	7	-	34,154	-	20,526
5049 Professional equipment, nec [2]	-	10	-	124	12	-	21,613	-	3,434
5051 Metals service centers and offices [2]	-	49	-	73	1	-	26,685	-	1,865
5063 Electrical apparatus and equipment	-	114	-	1,256	11	-	32,592	-	40,737
5064 Electrical appliances, TV & radios	-	25	-	212	8	-	28,736	-	7,199
5065 Electronic parts and equipment	-	106	-	1,672	16	-	39,289	-	78,293
5072 Hardware	-	59	-	736	12	-	23,495	-	19,186
5074 Plumbing & hydronic heating supplies [2]	-	54	-	612	11	-	31,667	-	21,071
5075 Warm air heating & air conditioning	-	34	-	332	10	-	34,060	-	12,521
5082 Construction and mining machinery	-	38	-	1,180	31	-	37,553	-	47,678
5083 Farm and garden machinery	-	19	-	215	11	-	28,949	-	6,243
5084 Industrial machinery and equipment	-	178	-	1,798	10	-	31,384	-	58,640
5085 Industrial supplies	-	81	-	898	11	-	33,345	-	29,235
5087 Service establishment equipment	-	68	-	661	10	-	25,785	-	16,923
5091 Sporting & recreational goods	-	45	-	308	7	-	22,519	-	8,775
5092 Toys and hobby goods and supplies	-	15	-	105	7	-	23,619	-	1,989
5093 Scrap and waste materials	-	35	-	499	14	-	23,503	-	13,123
5094 Jewelry & precious stones	-	20	-	376	19	-	69,223	-	25,580
5099 Durable goods, nec [2]	-	46	-	310	7	-	22,697	-	7,838
5112 Stationery and office supplies	-	54	-	722	13	-	18,626	-	13,433
5120 Drugs, proprietaries, and sundries	-	57	-	1,012	18	-	23,735	-	24,550
5131 Piece goods & notions	-	14	-	136	10	-	19,147	-	2,856
5136 Men's and boys' clothing	-	19	-	90	5	-	16,711	-	1,739
5137 Women's and children's clothing [2]	-	14	-	259	19	-	18,564	-	4,456
5141 Groceries, general line	-	30	-	1,955	65	-	28,403	-	62,347
5143 Dairy products, exc. dried or canned [2]	-	12	-	133	11	-	18,015	-	2,524
5144 Poultry and poultry products [2]	-	5	-	38	8	-	30,842	-	909
5147 Meats and meat products [2]	-	15	-	283	19	-	21,442	-	6,596
5148 Fresh fruits and vegetables	-	24	-	409	17	-	30,103	-	12,019
5149 Groceries and related products, nec [2]	-	111	-	1,868	17	-	24,582	-	52,096
5150 Farm-product raw materials [2]	-	17	-	150	9	-	13,440	-	1,982
5162 Plastics materials & basic shapes [2]	-	23	-	199	9	-	38,271	-	7,535
5169 Chemicals & allied products, nec	-	72	-	639	9	-	27,750	-	19,736
5171 Petroleum bulk stations & terminals	-	22	-	462	21	-	39,835	-	20,880
5172 Petroleum products, nec	-	10	-	46	5	-	24,261	-	1,229
5181 Beer and ale [2]	-	7	-	227	32	-	26,026	-	5,101
5191 Farm supplies	-	29	-	206	7	-	20,893	-	4,684
5192 Books, periodicals, & newspapers	-	32	-	586	18	-	24,314	-	13,178
5193 Flowers & florists' supplies	-	30	-	520	17	-	13,369	-	7,370
5198 Paints, varnishes, and supplies	-	22	-	111	5	-	20,721	-	2,605

Continued on next page.

SALT LAKE CITY - OGDEN, UT MSA - [continued]

Wholesale and Retail Trade USA	Establishments 1994	Establishments 1995	Employment 1994	Employment 1995	Emp / Est 1995	Pay / Employee 1994	Pay / Employee 1995	Annual Payroll ($ 000) 1994	Annual Payroll ($ 000) 1995
5199 Nondurable goods, nec	-	62	-	466	8	-	18,172	-	9,118
52- Retail trade	-	6,343	-	106,952	17	-	13,879	-	1,549,676
5210 Lumber and other building materials	-	90	-	2,498	28	-	21,050	-	55,059
5230 Paint, glass, and wallpaper stores	-	55	-	424	8	-	20,660	-	8,842
5250 Hardware stores [2]	-	21	-	541	26	-	14,425	-	7,668
5260 Retail nurseries and garden stores	-	40	-	458	11	-	7,485	-	5,455
5270 Mobile home dealers [2]	-	6	-	76	13	-	16,263	-	1,616
5310 Department stores	-	60	-	10,010	167	-	10,815	-	114,429
5330 Variety stores	-	23	-	188	8	-	7,383	-	1,603
5390 Misc. general merchandise stores [2]	-	43	-	1,416	33	-	14,698	-	25,570
5410 Grocery stores	-	346	-	12,426	36	-	13,902	-	179,373
5420 Meat and fish markets	-	12	-	51	4	-	6,118	-	436
5440 Candy, nut, and confectionery stores	-	27	-	189	7	-	8,190	-	1,674
5460 Retail bakeries	-	74	-	743	10	-	9,637	-	6,832
5490 Miscellaneous food stores	-	45	-	141	3	-	8,255	-	1,548
5510 New and used car dealers	-	90	-	5,082	56	-	28,965	-	165,099
5520 Used car dealers	-	97	-	921	9	-	22,662	-	22,651
5530 Auto and home supply stores	-	176	-	1,649	9	-	16,684	-	31,029
5540 Gasoline service stations	-	378	-	3,097	8	-	10,662	-	35,934
5550 Boat dealers	-	21	-	151	7	-	19,682	-	3,654
5560 Recreational vehicle dealers	-	26	-	269	10	-	19,896	-	7,501
5570 Motorcycle dealers	-	16	-	196	12	-	16,857	-	4,286
5610 Men's & boys' clothing stores	-	48	-	358	7	-	11,240	-	4,579
5620 Women's clothing stores	-	142	-	1,283	9	-	6,931	-	9,216
5630 Women's accessory & specialty stores	-	38	-	197	5	-	10,843	-	1,985
5640 Children's and infants' wear stores	-	27	-	202	7	-	8,218	-	1,574
5650 Family clothing stores	-	81	-	2,566	32	-	10,589	-	28,794
5660 Shoe stores	-	143	-	679	5	-	11,641	-	8,421
5690 Misc. apparel & accessory stores	-	53	-	341	6	-	8,622	-	2,944
5712 Furniture stores	-	135	-	2,585	19	-	22,861	-	62,134
5713 Floor covering stores	-	60	-	328	5	-	22,220	-	7,833
5714 Drapery and upholstery stores	-	14	-	20	1	-	12,200	-	258
5719 Misc. homefurnishings stores	-	70	-	455	7	-	11,912	-	5,745
5720 Household appliance stores	-	49	-	354	7	-	15,299	-	5,895
5731 Radio, TV, & electronic stores	-	79	-	669	8	-	19,785	-	15,301
5734 Computer and software stores	-	59	-	740	13	-	22,838	-	17,716
5735 Record & prerecorded tape stores	-	65	-	1,048	16	-	14,023	-	14,571
5736 Musical instrument stores	-	29	-	262	9	-	17,679	-	4,902
5812 Eating places	-	1,622	-	34,335	21	-	7,672	-	278,287
5813 Drinking places	-	149	-	1,165	8	-	6,651	-	7,843
5910 Drug stores and proprietary stores	-	89	-	1,083	12	-	16,809	-	20,181
5930 Used merchandise stores	-	82	-	441	5	-	11,628	-	5,303
5941 Sporting goods and bicycle shops	-	160	-	1,578	10	-	11,970	-	19,775
5942 Book stores	-	64	-	623	10	-	10,973	-	6,256
5943 Stationery stores	-	26	-	131	5	-	10,962	-	1,586
5944 Jewelry stores	-	104	-	554	5	-	19,646	-	11,405
5945 Hobby, toy, and game shops	-	82	-	819	10	-	8,405	-	7,901
5946 Camera & photographic supply stores	-	16	-	111	7	-	20,072	-	2,437
5947 Gift, novelty, and souvenir shops	-	148	-	909	6	-	9,417	-	8,897
5948 Luggage and leather goods stores [2]	-	4	-	79	20	-	13,418	-	1,193
5949 Sewing, needlework, and piece goods	-	55	-	538	10	-	6,654	-	3,549
5961 Catalog and mail-order houses [2]	-	34	-	247	7	-	14,364	-	4,115
5962 Merchandising machine operators	-	29	-	219	8	-	17,790	-	4,068
5963 Direct selling establishments [2]	-	85	-	864	10	-	18,125	-	16,441
5984 Liquefied petroleum gas dealers [2]	-	5	-	34	7	-	18,941	-	674
5992 Florists	-	101	-	729	7	-	8,044	-	5,872
5995 Optical goods stores	-	69	-	342	5	-	17,860	-	6,344
5999 Miscellaneous retail stores, nec	-	238	-	1,243	5	-	13,229	-	18,273

Source: County Business Patterns 1994/95, CBP-94/95, U.S. Department of Commerce, Washington DC, November 1997. The employment column represents mid-March employment in the year. Pay per employee is calculated by dividing 1st Quarter payroll, annualized, by mid-March employment. The column headed 'Emp / Est' shows 'employees per establishment'. A dash (-) means that data are unavailable or cannot be calculated. nec means not elsewhere classified. *Notes:* 1. 1994 data incomplete; unavailable or withheld. 2. 1995 data incomplete; unavailable or withheld. 3. 1994 and 1995 data incomplete; unavailable or withheld.

SAN ANGELO, TX MSA

Wholesale and Retail Trade USA	Establishments 1994	Establishments 1995	Employment 1994	Employment 1995	Emp / Est 1995	Pay / Employee 1994	Pay / Employee 1995	Annual Payroll ($ 000) 1994	Annual Payroll ($ 000) 1995
50- Wholesale trade	-	175	-	1,667	10	-	21,694	-	40,219
5012 Automobiles and other vehicles	-	3	-	45	15	-	22,844	-	1,098

Continued on next page.

SAN ANGELO, TX MSA - [continued]

Wholesale and Retail Trade USA	Establishments		Employment		Emp / Est	Pay / Employee		Annual Payroll ($ 000)	
	1994	1995	1994	1995	1995	1994	1995	1994	1995
5013 Motor vehicle supplies and new parts	-	14	-	82	6	-	22,732	-	2,130
5044 Office equipment	-	6	-	47	8	-	18,468	-	911
5046 Commercial equipment, nec	-	4	-	54	14	-	18,000	-	1,210
5051 Metals service centers and offices	-	7	-	41	6	-	20,390	-	1,405
5063 Electrical apparatus and equipment	-	6	-	54	9	-	22,444	-	1,235
5065 Electronic parts and equipment	-	8	-	49	6	-	57,061	-	3,363
5074 Plumbing & hydronic heating supplies	-	5	-	40	8	-	12,800	-	532
5083 Farm and garden machinery	-	4	-	49	12	-	23,020	-	1,352
5084 Industrial machinery and equipment	-	10	-	37	4	-	35,243	-	1,403
5085 Industrial supplies	-	4	-	17	4	-	20,471	-	408
5090 Miscellaneous durable goods	-	5	-	40	8	-	17,000	-	851
5110 Paper and paper products	-	6	-	82	14	-	22,488	-	2,130
5120 Drugs, proprietaries, and sundries	-	4	-	6	2	-	16,667	-	141
5149 Groceries and related products, nec	-	3	-	163	54	-	25,129	-	4,134
5154 Livestock	-	4	-	94	24	-	18,043	-	1,733
5159 Farm-product raw materials, nec	-	10	-	39	4	-	27,077	-	974
5170 Petroleum and petroleum products	-	6	-	127	21	-	16,157	-	2,054
5180 Beer, wine, and distilled beverages	-	4	-	81	20	-	23,259	-	2,032
5191 Farm supplies	-	5	-	28	6	-	17,429	-	494
52- Retail trade	-	645	-	8,590	13	-	12,782	-	116,970
5210 Lumber and other building materials	-	8	-	121	15	-	19,471	-	3,921
5250 Hardware stores	-	3	-	43	14	-	16,465	-	712
5260 Retail nurseries and garden stores	-	4	-	50	13	-	8,480	-	585
5310 Department stores	-	7	-	1,161	166	-	12,968	-	14,780
5410 Grocery stores	-	58	-	1,177	20	-	12,697	-	15,015
5460 Retail bakeries	-	6	-	67	11	-	5,313	-	436
5510 New and used car dealers	-	12	-	411	34	-	28,993	-	15,113
5520 Used car dealers	-	22	-	78	4	-	17,538	-	1,583
5530 Auto and home supply stores	-	22	-	161	7	-	18,733	-	3,279
5540 Gasoline service stations	-	41	-	250	6	-	11,968	-	2,723
5610 Men's & boys' clothing stores	-	4	-	10	3	-	15,600	-	151
5620 Women's clothing stores	-	25	-	173	7	-	8,301	-	1,382
5630 Women's accessory & specialty stores	-	4	-	15	4	-	7,200	-	108
5650 Family clothing stores	-	12	-	204	17	-	11,902	-	2,406
5660 Shoe stores	-	13	-	55	4	-	11,564	-	606
5690 Misc. apparel & accessory stores	-	3	-	8	3	-	3,000	-	43
5712 Furniture stores	-	16	-	139	9	-	12,719	-	1,863
5713 Floor covering stores	-	6	-	39	7	-	12,923	-	620
5714 Drapery and upholstery stores	-	5	-	29	6	-	12,000	-	377
5719 Misc. homefurnishings stores	-	6	-	26	4	-	11,077	-	303
5720 Household appliance stores	-	5	-	26	5	-	11,385	-	315
5731 Radio, TV, & electronic stores	-	7	-	40	6	-	19,800	-	750
5735 Record & prerecorded tape stores	-	3	-	46	15	-	10,696	-	461
5812 Eating places	-	120	-	2,564	21	-	8,591	-	23,492
5813 Drinking places	-	14	-	102	7	-	5,686	-	589
5910 Drug stores and proprietary stores	-	13	-	109	8	-	20,147	-	1,771
5920 Liquor stores	-	10	-	41	4	-	9,073	-	383
5930 Used merchandise stores	-	11	-	48	4	-	15,250	-	770
5942 Book stores	-	7	-	44	6	-	7,818	-	345
5944 Jewelry stores	-	13	-	115	9	-	13,426	-	1,413
5945 Hobby, toy, and game shops	-	7	-	65	9	-	9,662	-	800
5947 Gift, novelty, and souvenir shops	-	15	-	95	6	-	7,326	-	557
5949 Sewing, needlework, and piece goods	-	4	-	17	4	-	9,412	-	152
5960 Nonstore retailers	-	5	-	70	14	-	13,771	-	827
5984 Liquefied petroleum gas dealers	-	3	-	16	5	-	14,750	-	217
5995 Optical goods stores	-	10	-	39	4	-	15,897	-	536
5999 Miscellaneous retail stores, nec	-	19	-	151	8	-	11,046	-	2,014

Source: County Business Patterns 1994/95, CBP-94/95, U.S. Department of Commerce, Washington DC, November 1997. The employment column represents mid-March employment in the year. Pay per employee is calculated by dividing 1st Quarter payroll, annualized, by mid-March employment. The column headed 'Emp / Est' shows 'employees per establishment'. A dash (-) means that data are unavailable or cannot be calculated. nec means not elsewhere classified. *Notes:* 1. 1994 data incomplete; unavailable or withheld. 2. 1995 data incomplete; unavailable or withheld. 3. 1994 and 1995 data incomplete; unavailable or withheld.

SAN ANTONIO, TX MSA

Wholesale and Retail Trade USA	Establishments		Employment		Emp / Est	Pay / Employee		Annual Payroll ($ 000)	
	1994	1995	1994	1995	1995	1994	1995	1994	1995
50- Wholesale trade	-	2,267	-	28,534	13	-	28,184	-	836,048
5012 Automobiles and other vehicles [2]	-	29	-	633	22	-	29,150	-	18,596
5013 Motor vehicle supplies and new parts	-	130	-	1,410	11	-	22,099	-	30,139

Continued on next page.

SAN ANTONIO, TX MSA - [continued]

Wholesale and Retail Trade USA	Establishments		Employment		Emp / Est	Pay / Employee		Annual Payroll ($ 000)	
	1994	1995	1994	1995	1995	1994	1995	1994	1995
5014 Tires and tubes [2]	-	21	-	121	6	-	22,777	-	2,807
5015 Motor vehicle parts, used [2]	-	45	-	171	4	-	29,918	-	5,051
5021 Furniture [2]	-	32	-	399	12	-	30,677	-	11,757
5023 Homefurnishings [2]	-	40	-	416	10	-	22,308	-	9,577
5031 Lumber, plywood, and millwork [2]	-	33	-	797	24	-	25,561	-	20,720
5032 Brick, stone, & related materials [2]	-	27	-	283	10	-	24,749	-	8,168
5033 Roofing, siding, & insulation [2]	-	16	-	200	13	-	25,220	-	6,396
5039 Construction materials, nec [2]	-	50	-	574	11	-	26,230	-	15,232
5043 Photographic equipment & supplies [2]	-	3	-	26	9	-	24,308	-	580
5044 Office equipment [2]	-	51	-	917	18	-	35,019	-	29,410
5045 Computers, peripherals, & software [2]	-	90	-	897	10	-	44,285	-	45,156
5046 Commercial equipment, nec [2]	-	31	-	289	9	-	25,647	-	8,033
5047 Medical and hospital equipment [2]	-	68	-	548	8	-	37,161	-	21,872
5048 Ophthalmic goods [2]	-	12	-	56	5	-	23,786	-	1,287
5049 Professional equipment, nec [2]	-	13	-	91	7	-	23,912	-	3,312
5051 Metals service centers and offices [2]	-	42	-	452	11	-	29,478	-	17,826
5063 Electrical apparatus and equipment [2]	-	86	-	678	8	-	38,059	-	24,160
5064 Electrical appliances, TV & radios [2]	-	22	-	210	10	-	32,819	-	6,693
5065 Electronic parts and equipment [2]	-	75	-	869	12	-	33,947	-	30,265
5072 Hardware [2]	-	37	-	321	9	-	25,421	-	9,571
5074 Plumbing & hydronic heating supplies [2]	-	38	-	429	11	-	29,837	-	14,311
5075 Warm air heating & air conditioning [2]	-	38	-	582	15	-	30,110	-	18,324
5078 Refrigeration equipment and supplies [2]	-	12	-	183	15	-	32,459	-	5,710
5082 Construction and mining machinery [2]	-	28	-	351	13	-	34,473	-	12,452
5083 Farm and garden machinery [2]	-	23	-	261	11	-	27,126	-	6,984
5084 Industrial machinery and equipment	-	114	-	1,112	10	-	32,155	-	36,270
5085 Industrial supplies [2]	-	51	-	390	8	-	28,872	-	11,718
5087 Service establishment equipment [2]	-	37	-	260	7	-	19,000	-	5,263
5088 Transportation equipment & supplies	-	39	-	534	14	-	29,655	-	18,075
5091 Sporting & recreational goods [2]	-	21	-	131	6	-	24,763	-	3,586
5092 Toys and hobby goods and supplies [2]	-	11	-	79	7	-	19,899	-	2,397
5093 Scrap and waste materials [2]	-	30	-	287	10	-	24,084	-	8,360
5094 Jewelry & precious stones [2]	-	25	-	155	6	-	17,084	-	2,583
5099 Durable goods, nec [2]	-	45	-	449	10	-	27,724	-	12,450
5111 Printing and writing paper [2]	-	11	-	149	14	-	31,973	-	5,012
5112 Stationery and office supplies [2]	-	56	-	707	13	-	21,680	-	15,326
5113 Industrial & personal service paper [2]	-	25	-	297	12	-	29,239	-	9,870
5120 Drugs, proprietaries, and sundries [2]	-	26	-	596	23	-	38,248	-	21,099
5131 Piece goods & notions [2]	-	9	-	32	4	-	12,375	-	407
5136 Men's and boys' clothing [2]	-	18	-	168	9	-	14,738	-	2,969
5137 Women's and children's clothing [2]	-	13	-	180	14	-	27,311	-	4,236
5139 Footwear [2]	-	3	-	8	3	-	33,500	-	1,357
5141 Groceries, general line [2]	-	21	-	1,311	62	-	28,522	-	37,125
5142 Packaged frozen food [2]	-	16	-	454	28	-	23,322	-	11,170
5143 Dairy products, exc. dried or canned [2]	-	11	-	101	9	-	22,653	-	2,771
5144 Poultry and poultry products [2]	-	10	-	85	9	-	24,471	-	2,414
5145 Confectionery [2]	-	18	-	529	29	-	26,836	-	14,768
5146 Fish and seafoods [2]	-	7	-	91	13	-	18,330	-	1,466
5147 Meats and meat products [2]	-	25	-	596	24	-	24,047	-	14,146
5148 Fresh fruits and vegetables [2]	-	46	-	891	19	-	18,433	-	18,129
5149 Groceries and related products, nec [2]	-	62	-	1,217	20	-	29,417	-	35,268
5153 Grain and field beans [2]	-	7	-	24	3	-	24,167	-	605
5154 Livestock [2]	-	12	-	51	4	-	11,137	-	762
5159 Farm-product raw materials, nec [2]	-	7	-	49	7	-	20,898	-	1,113
5162 Plastics materials & basic shapes [2]	-	15	-	117	8	-	29,231	-	3,281
5169 Chemicals & allied products, nec [2]	-	49	-	419	9	-	36,506	-	15,298
5171 Petroleum bulk stations & terminals	-	23	-	155	7	-	36,671	-	5,783
5172 Petroleum products, nec [2]	-	15	-	114	8	-	32,526	-	3,736
5181 Beer and ale	-	13	-	900	69	-	29,111	-	27,124
5182 Wine and distilled beverages [2]	-	5	-	467	93	-	38,167	-	19,265
5191 Farm supplies [2]	-	38	-	271	7	-	18,303	-	5,286
5192 Books, periodicals, & newspapers [2]	-	28	-	251	9	-	18,996	-	7,106
5193 Flowers & florists' supplies [2]	-	20	-	206	10	-	16,097	-	3,544
5198 Paints, varnishes, and supplies [2]	-	13	-	140	11	-	25,457	-	3,680
5199 Nondurable goods, nec	-	73	-	431	6	-	19,174	-	7,696
52- Retail trade	-	7,634	-	124,638	16	-	13,742	-	1,787,197
5210 Lumber and other building materials [2]	-	70	-	1,806	26	-	19,181	-	36,988
5230 Paint, glass, and wallpaper stores [2]	-	40	-	203	5	-	17,734	-	3,862
5250 Hardware stores [2]	-	36	-	231	6	-	10,909	-	2,599
5260 Retail nurseries and garden stores [2]	-	43	-	483	11	-	10,617	-	5,907
5270 Mobile home dealers [2]	-	17	-	165	10	-	33,988	-	6,774

Continued on next page.

SAN ANTONIO, TX MSA - [continued]

Wholesale and Retail Trade USA	Establishments 1994	Establishments 1995	Employment 1994	Employment 1995	Emp / Est 1995	Pay / Employee 1994	Pay / Employee 1995	Annual Payroll ($ 000) 1994	Annual Payroll ($ 000) 1995
5310 Department stores [2]	-	52	-	9,053	174	-	13,107	-	122,370
5330 Variety stores [2]	-	42	-	309	7	-	8,531	-	2,797
5390 Misc. general merchandise stores	-	59	-	1,457	25	-	12,994	-	19,037
5410 Grocery stores	-	643	-	16,951	26	-	11,479	-	202,904
5420 Meat and fish markets	-	30	-	152	5	-	15,079	-	1,961
5430 Fruit and vegetable markets [2]	-	7	-	8	1	-	10,000	-	239
5440 Candy, nut, and confectionery stores [2]	-	22	-	133	6	-	6,677	-	923
5460 Retail bakeries	-	86	-	503	6	-	8,732	-	4,794
5490 Miscellaneous food stores [2]	-	47	-	175	4	-	12,549	-	3,024
5510 New and used car dealers	-	77	-	6,773	88	-	29,932	-	213,247
5520 Used car dealers	-	106	-	573	5	-	19,525	-	12,073
5530 Auto and home supply stores	-	248	-	2,243	9	-	17,025	-	39,455
5540 Gasoline service stations	-	438	-	2,551	6	-	12,897	-	34,710
5550 Boat dealers	-	14	-	101	7	-	22,574	-	2,667
5560 Recreational vehicle dealers [2]	-	12	-	91	8	-	20,308	-	1,815
5570 Motorcycle dealers [2]	-	10	-	125	13	-	23,776	-	3,028
5610 Men's & boys' clothing stores [2]	-	69	-	569	8	-	16,120	-	8,946
5620 Women's clothing stores	-	226	-	2,175	10	-	10,284	-	23,523
5630 Women's accessory & specialty stores [2]	-	53	-	292	6	-	9,808	-	2,760
5640 Children's and infants' wear stores [2]	-	25	-	119	5	-	8,571	-	1,117
5650 Family clothing stores	-	99	-	1,937	20	-	10,088	-	20,108
5660 Shoe stores [2]	-	180	-	1,002	6	-	12,419	-	11,920
5690 Misc. apparel & accessory stores [2]	-	69	-	331	5	-	9,801	-	3,635
5712 Furniture stores	-	151	-	1,389	9	-	19,041	-	27,261
5713 Floor covering stores [2]	-	43	-	237	6	-	21,840	-	6,023
5714 Drapery and upholstery stores [2]	-	16	-	43	3	-	15,163	-	616
5719 Misc. homefurnishings stores [2]	-	77	-	469	6	-	12,068	-	6,017
5720 Household appliance stores [2]	-	33	-	217	7	-	20,055	-	4,675
5731 Radio, TV, & electronic stores [2]	-	80	-	773	10	-	14,924	-	13,294
5734 Computer and software stores [2]	-	41	-	185	5	-	22,184	-	3,921
5735 Record & prerecorded tape stores [2]	-	44	-	401	9	-	7,252	-	2,924
5736 Musical instrument stores [2]	-	15	-	112	7	-	18,464	-	2,067
5812 Eating places	-	1,790	-	42,453	24	-	8,983	-	397,702
5813 Drinking places [2]	-	223	-	1,680	8	-	7,800	-	12,766
5910 Drug stores and proprietary stores	-	161	-	2,140	13	-	16,733	-	37,065
5920 Liquor stores	-	94	-	339	4	-	10,678	-	4,294
5930 Used merchandise stores [2]	-	205	-	1,114	5	-	13,074	-	14,999
5941 Sporting goods and bicycle shops [2]	-	103	-	841	8	-	12,419	-	11,792
5942 Book stores [2]	-	61	-	407	7	-	10,880	-	4,468
5943 Stationery stores [2]	-	16	-	61	4	-	10,361	-	686
5944 Jewelry stores [2]	-	142	-	771	5	-	17,613	-	12,322
5945 Hobby, toy, and game shops [2]	-	55	-	675	12	-	9,079	-	7,495
5946 Camera & photographic supply stores [2]	-	16	-	89	6	-	18,427	-	1,661
5947 Gift, novelty, and souvenir shops	-	189	-	960	5	-	8,521	-	8,829
5948 Luggage and leather goods stores [2]	-	8	-	31	4	-	11,613	-	366
5949 Sewing, needlework, and piece goods [2]	-	25	-	281	11	-	9,110	-	2,351
5961 Catalog and mail-order houses [2]	-	22	-	1,642	75	-	8,300	-	14,651
5962 Merchandising machine operators	-	28	-	220	8	-	18,655	-	4,240
5963 Direct selling establishments	-	57	-	450	8	-	19,236	-	8,210
5984 Liquefied petroleum gas dealers	-	14	-	144	10	-	21,556	-	2,643
5992 Florists	-	119	-	497	4	-	9,964	-	4,977
5993 Tobacco stores and stands [2]	-	3	-	16	5	-	14,500	-	272
5994 News dealers and newsstands [2]	-	6	-	47	8	-	12,766	-	699
5995 Optical goods stores [2]	-	106	-	555	5	-	15,798	-	8,501
5999 Miscellaneous retail stores, nec	-	253	-	1,347	5	-	14,667	-	21,228

Source: County Business Patterns 1994/95, CBP-94/95, U.S. Department of Commerce, Washington DC, November 1997. The employment column represents mid-March employment in the year. Pay per employee is calculated by dividing 1st Quarter payroll, annualized, by mid-March employment. The column headed 'Emp / Est' shows 'employees per establishment'. A dash (-) means that data are unavailable or cannot be calculated. nec means not elsewhere classified. *Notes:* 1. 1994 data incomplete; unavailable or withheld. 2. 1995 data incomplete; unavailable or withheld. 3. 1994 and 1995 data incomplete; unavailable or withheld.

SAN DIEGO, CA MSA

Wholesale and Retail Trade USA	Establishments 1994	Establishments 1995	Employment 1994	Employment 1995	Emp / Est 1995	Pay / Employee 1994	Pay / Employee 1995	Annual Payroll ($ 000) 1994	Annual Payroll ($ 000) 1995
50 – Wholesale trade	4,175	4,261	46,391	51,404	12	29,987	33,379	1,506,467	1,813,303
5012 Automobiles and other vehicles	56	56	823	882	16	23,198	25,274	22,641	23,754
5013 Motor vehicle supplies and new parts	204	194	1,908	1,832	9	22,046	23,382	46,645	43,817
5014 Tires and tubes	26	28	213	215	8	28,394	29,377	8,110	6,335
5015 Motor vehicle parts, used	66	76	276	346	5	17,377	18,717	5,296	7,023

Continued on next page.

SAN DIEGO, CA MSA - [continued]

Wholesale and Retail Trade USA	Establishments		Employment		Emp / Est	Pay / Employee		Annual Payroll ($ 000)	
	1994	1995	1994	1995	1995	1994	1995	1994	1995
5021 Furniture	72	72	720	850	12	27,211	25,327	23,630	23,762
5023 Homefurnishings	96	88	917	989	11	23,555	29,739	22,784	23,943
5031 Lumber, plywood, and millwork	55	50	725	586	12	29,324	27,939	21,452	16,242
5032 Brick, stone, & related materials	40	29	317	132	5	24,416	29,333	7,997	3,931
5033 Roofing, siding, & insulation	14	10	169	111	11	28,189	32,541	4,938	3,899
5039 Construction materials, nec	21	51	126	495	10	29,429	29,939	4,553	15,836
5043 Photographic equipment & supplies	15	16	107	127	8	29,271	27,402	3,262	4,152
5044 Office equipment	82	84	1,436	1,380	16	32,031	36,806	48,092	47,988
5045 Computers, peripherals, & software	233	238	3,236	3,584	15	41,946	46,517	146,191	173,665
5046 Commercial equipment, nec	38	38	266	252	7	25,173	27,175	6,881	7,285
5047 Medical and hospital equipment	128	121	1,143	1,231	10	36,703	37,989	49,089	48,605
5048 Ophthalmic goods	13	16	253	237	15	26,372	26,852	6,124	6,736
5049 Professional equipment, nec	30	31	165	179	6	23,055	24,827	3,946	5,243
5051 Metals service centers and offices	48	45	280	308	7	27,729	29,844	8,504	9,938
5063 Electrical apparatus and equipment	156	135	1,601	1,537	11	32,377	36,523	54,821	53,986
5064 Electrical appliances, TV & radios	29	26	264	275	11	32,076	31,913	8,849	9,387
5065 Electronic parts and equipment	269	283	5,139	7,443	26	43,065	46,064	247,907	396,205
5072 Hardware	73	74	748	871	12	32,326	35,853	25,487	34,562
5074 Plumbing & hydronic heating supplies	59	58	696	710	12	26,046	26,986	18,529	21,602
5075 Warm air heating & air conditioning	30	30	225	247	8	35,200	35,773	8,415	9,193
5078 Refrigeration equipment and supplies	18	18	91	83	5	27,385	28,482	2,606	2,566
5082 Construction and mining machinery	35	35	355	366	10	32,631	33,749	12,171	13,530
5083 Farm and garden machinery	41	39	344	291	7	28,047	29,251	10,356	9,872
5084 Industrial machinery and equipment	162	177	1,178	1,692	10	30,506	45,629	37,000	64,905
5085 Industrial supplies	93	88	994	1,015	12	25,968	28,674	28,885	32,235
5087 Service establishment equipment	67	58	676	645	11	25,497	28,633	19,043	23,608
5088 Transportation equipment & supplies	35	35	405	335	10	26,993	32,155	10,095	11,042
5091 Sporting & recreational goods	94	89	717	794	9	23,448	26,892	19,778	22,354
5092 Toys and hobby goods and supplies	34	33	248	318	10	32,694	30,365	7,767	9,403
5093 Scrap and waste materials	57	74	409	612	8	17,340	19,477	9,609	13,734
5094 Jewelry & precious stones	71	70	319	323	5	24,401	29,907	8,583	12,227
5099 Durable goods, nec	79	94	458	475	5	24,245	28,682	12,259	14,300
5111 Printing and writing paper	19	18	189	169	9	37,397	39,385	6,448	6,388
5112 Stationery and office supplies	91	83	1,381	1,266	15	23,012	26,044	31,917	32,646
5113 Industrial & personal service paper	44	39	337	383	10	30,944	34,715	11,673	14,376
5120 Drugs, proprietaries, and sundries	76	79	1,112	1,341	17	37,665	40,495	46,486	69,247
5131 Piece goods & notions	38	37	198	172	5	19,859	20,023	4,339	3,465
5136 Men's and boys' clothing	33	34	421	439	13	22,945	30,232	10,787	13,031
5137 Women's and children's clothing	60	52	1,082	891	17	22,059	25,230	25,000	22,894
5139 Footwear	27	27	153	161	6	27,425	27,205	5,282	8,880
5141 Groceries, general line	52	54	829	833	15	23,682	24,269	20,005	19,432
5142 Packaged frozen food	22	21	489	363	17	22,928	46,182	11,323	12,636
5143 Dairy products, exc. dried or canned	24	24	177	178	7	32,949	38,292	6,293	7,019
5145 Confectionery	23	20	428	373	19	20,458	21,330	8,148	7,389
5146 Fish and seafoods	24	20	229	230	12	20,856	23,722	5,323	5,771
5147 Meats and meat products	22	24	519	747	31	26,220	27,679	14,416	20,213
5148 Fresh fruits and vegetables	66	65	815	753	12	23,946	27,039	21,849	22,439
5149 Groceries and related products, nec	137	140	1,903	2,061	15	31,891	31,457	58,628	62,214
5153 Grain and field beans	3	-	4	-	-	13,000	-	48	-
5162 Plastics materials & basic shapes	25	30	234	331	11	28,496	37,414	6,422	10,253
5169 Chemicals & allied products, nec	59	56	545	555	10	34,165	37,816	19,580	21,323
5171 Petroleum bulk stations & terminals	30	25	310	277	11	35,148	39,032	12,239	11,617
5172 Petroleum products, nec	10	8	42	34	4	21,905	19,882	838	696
5181 Beer and ale	11	10	823	810	81	26,872	30,874	24,760	26,868
5182 Wine and distilled beverages	7	6	229	71	12	37,555	54,310	9,135	3,532
5191 Farm supplies	64	60	446	481	8	31,013	31,651	14,340	15,464
5192 Books, periodicals, & newspapers	53	53	946	1,052	20	25,835	30,665	25,477	33,220
5193 Flowers & florists' supplies	87	84	1,086	1,206	14	15,028	14,617	18,985	17,891
5194 Tobacco and tobacco products	6	6	97	94	16	19,134	19,404	1,925	1,960
5198 Paints, varnishes, and supplies	23	25	128	212	8	25,094	28,472	4,551	7,748
5199 Nondurable goods, nec	232	245	1,754	2,209	9	19,683	20,406	39,255	49,789
52 - Retail trade	13,687	13,571	187,673	191,559	14	13,892	14,364	2,801,750	2,867,401
5210 Lumber and other building materials	145	141	4,031	4,599	33	20,372	22,147	91,742	100,918
5230 Paint, glass, and wallpaper stores	84	77	450	491	6	23,449	22,582	11,362	12,010
5250 Hardware stores	68	44	524	358	8	16,580	14,503	8,856	6,053
5260 Retail nurseries and garden stores	61	67	539	535	8	14,649	15,477	9,205	9,168
5270 Mobile home dealers	14	13	49	45	3	19,673	15,644	1,243	730
5310 Department stores	78	81	13,792	15,250	188	11,881	12,476	173,994	192,051
5330 Variety stores	46	40	444	304	8	10,243	9,921	4,286	3,102
5390 Misc. general merchandise stores	84	88	3,426	3,393	39	16,027	18,190	63,248	61,901
5410 Grocery stores	934	898	18,911	18,538	21	18,035	18,879	357,622	362,543

Continued on next page.

SAN DIEGO, CA MSA - [continued]

Wholesale and Retail Trade USA	Establishments		Employment		Emp / Est	Pay / Employee		Annual Payroll ($ 000)	
	1994	1995	1994	1995	1995	1994	1995	1994	1995
5420 Meat and fish markets	33	37	252	254	7	12,317	13,370	3,169	3,924
5430 Fruit and vegetable markets	29	32	176	167	5	8,000	7,281	1,821	1,259
5440 Candy, nut, and confectionery stores	46	44	275	272	6	10,138	10,279	3,097	3,066
5450 Dairy products stores	26	23	74	148	6	6,054	4,811	597	724
5460 Retail bakeries	283	255	1,748	1,613	6	9,105	8,303	17,546	13,370
5490 Miscellaneous food stores	137	158	845	1,088	7	10,272	10,982	9,401	13,911
5510 New and used car dealers	161	160	9,209	9,535	60	30,835	31,178	315,679	328,973
5520 Used car dealers	97	99	345	413	4	15,246	17,743	6,069	8,126
5530 Auto and home supply stores	358	357	3,075	3,243	9	16,990	17,580	55,939	59,623
5540 Gasoline service stations	574	572	4,894	5,186	9	12,317	12,339	64,934	67,674
5550 Boat dealers	39	37	246	279	8	21,593	22,968	6,318	6,888
5560 Recreational vehicle dealers	39	35	495	582	17	21,640	21,732	13,574	14,652
5570 Motorcycle dealers	52	50	355	333	7	18,299	20,601	7,201	7,542
5590 Automotive dealers, nec	5	4	29	20	5	18,897	23,000	748	623
5610 Men's & boys' clothing stores	150	135	1,327	1,200	9	13,272	15,007	18,210	18,497
5620 Women's clothing stores	415	364	3,304	2,968	8	9,764	10,093	33,197	28,328
5630 Women's accessory & specialty stores	71	70	427	400	6	9,508	10,290	4,451	4,186
5640 Children's and infants' wear stores	62	54	353	321	6	7,728	8,735	3,054	2,805
5650 Family clothing stores	182	180	5,097	5,067	28	12,743	13,285	68,293	69,159
5660 Shoe stores	326	311	1,907	1,686	5	12,306	12,410	23,472	20,147
5690 Misc. apparel & accessory stores	106	103	641	704	7	8,281	11,926	6,606	8,934
5712 Furniture stores	280	273	2,149	1,982	7	19,594	21,104	45,029	42,680
5713 Floor covering stores	123	118	759	780	7	19,889	21,744	18,130	22,258
5714 Drapery and upholstery stores	27	23	111	90	4	13,189	13,733	1,536	1,283
5719 Misc. homefurnishings stores	161	145	1,116	1,052	7	12,140	13,262	14,600	14,539
5720 Household appliance stores	67	75	432	428	6	17,833	18,178	7,969	8,106
5731 Radio, TV, & electronic stores	178	175	1,906	2,033	12	19,024	19,970	40,582	43,408
5734 Computer and software stores	111	119	831	1,077	9	22,291	23,057	17,704	22,845
5735 Record & prerecorded tape stores	97	88	1,083	1,233	14	9,448	9,719	10,661	11,892
5736 Musical instrument stores	48	50	260	274	5	19,031	17,635	5,196	4,938
5812 Eating places	3,818	3,589	67,501	66,845	19	8,518	8,872	612,613	628,211
5813 Drinking places	372	336	3,075	3,099	9	7,634	8,234	25,698	25,637
5910 Drug stores and proprietary stores	305	298	4,848	5,533	19	22,244	21,155	114,355	116,250
5920 Liquor stores	272	278	893	967	3	9,904	10,374	9,834	9,985
5930 Used merchandise stores	177	184	1,548	1,497	8	11,362	12,248	19,166	19,501
5941 Sporting goods and bicycle shops	279	276	2,090	2,143	8	12,103	12,670	28,117	29,219
5942 Book stores	181	164	1,420	1,282	8	11,068	11,248	16,416	14,855
5943 Stationery stores	64	78	442	540	7	10,869	11,652	4,655	7,227
5944 Jewelry stores	272	251	1,248	1,125	4	18,144	19,979	23,268	22,641
5945 Hobby, toy, and game shops	106	108	1,080	1,127	10	9,615	9,668	11,860	12,406
5946 Camera & photographic supply stores	25	26	133	140	5	14,947	16,857	2,219	2,470
5947 Gift, novelty, and souvenir shops	367	359	2,204	2,085	6	8,848	9,759	20,932	21,189
5948 Luggage and leather goods stores	30	26	150	146	6	14,800	16,110	2,342	2,529
5949 Sewing, needlework, and piece goods	86	79	713	759	10	10,031	9,718	7,419	7,756
5961 Catalog and mail-order houses	81	96	916	1,056	11	19,306	21,318	21,924	23,240
5962 Merchandising machine operators	43	39	332	299	8	18,590	18,154	6,641	6,396
5963 Direct selling establishments	131	131	2,070	1,485	11	15,202	16,975	31,468	26,486
5984 Liquefied petroleum gas dealers	-	15	-	180	12	-	26,933	-	4,654
5989 Fuel dealers, nec	-	3	-	2	1	-	10,000	-	20
5992 Florists	218	207	1,006	1,021	5	9,058	10,045	9,678	10,622
5993 Tobacco stores and stands	7	9	15	14	2	8,800	8,000	140	146
5994 News dealers and newsstands	11	13	36	55	4	8,111	7,345	425	445
5995 Optical goods stores	108	103	699	789	8	17,419	18,824	12,274	14,558
5999 Miscellaneous retail stores, nec	535	540	2,465	2,755	5	13,345	14,412	37,804	44,770

Source: County Business Patterns 1994/95, CBP-94/95, U.S. Department of Commerce, Washington DC, November 1997. The employment column represents mid-March employment in the year. Pay per employee is calculated by dividing 1st Quarter payroll, annualized, by mid-March employment. The column headed 'Emp / Est' shows 'employees per establishment'. A dash (-) means that data are unavailable or cannot be calculated. nec means not elsewhere classified. *Notes:* 1. 1994 data incomplete; unavailable or withheld. 2. 1995 data incomplete; unavailable or withheld. 3. 1994 and 1995 data incomplete; unavailable or withheld.

SAN FRANCISCO, CA PMSA

Wholesale and Retail Trade USA	Establishments		Employment		Emp / Est	Pay / Employee		Annual Payroll ($ 000)	
	1994	1995	1994	1995	1995	1994	1995	1994	1995
50- Wholesale trade	4,510	4,641	50,794	52,767	11	41,346	47,228	2,130,098	2,490,294
5012 Automobiles and other vehicles	26	30	130	181	6	37,908	47,182	8,793	9,369
5013 Motor vehicle supplies and new parts	99	94	1,024	1,029	11	24,797	26,173	26,882	28,385
5014 Tires and tubes	17	15	137	162	11	40,467	33,160	5,077	5,298
5015 Motor vehicle parts, used	15	22	97	146	7	14,763	20,904	1,515	3,135
5021 Furniture	150	140	1,156	1,197	9	33,768	34,730	42,276	44,793

Continued on next page.

SAN FRANCISCO, CA PMSA - [continued]

Wholesale and Retail Trade USA	Establishments		Employment		Emp / Est	Pay / Employee		Annual Payroll ($ 000)	
	1994	1995	1994	1995	1995	1994	1995	1994	1995
5023 Homefurnishings	138	129	1,658	1,762	14	28,432	27,532	50,866	51,856
5031 Lumber, plywood, and millwork	42	34	464	461	14	38,009	38,551	19,570	19,556
5032 Brick, stone, & related materials	28	24	119	79	3	26,387	29,519	3,308	2,586
5033 Roofing, siding, & insulation	11	13	58	78	6	28,138	29,538	1,809	2,466
5039 Construction materials, nec	30	37	159	217	6	42,943	31,668	6,781	7,146
5043 Photographic equipment & supplies[3]	22	19	155	107	6	47,148	62,654	6,555	5,981
5044 Office equipment	63	67	1,294	1,394	21	37,629	42,284	48,820	56,479
5045 Computers, peripherals, & software	269	285	5,265	5,548	19	55,024	63,421	286,956	350,475
5046 Commercial equipment, nec	38	40	345	397	10	28,858	27,587	10,841	12,534
5047 Medical and hospital equipment	105	104	1,167	1,033	10	43,873	51,423	54,979	54,480
5048 Ophthalmic goods[1]	16	18	204	264	15	25,216	30,864	6,008	8,482
5049 Professional equipment, nec	28	27	348	280	10	37,011	39,343	12,687	13,249
5051 Metals service centers and offices[1]	51	48	65	340	7	33,292	45,953	2,444	16,387
5063 Electrical apparatus and equipment	130	123	1,279	1,270	10	37,898	42,643	66,119	55,469
5064 Electrical appliances, TV & radios	45	48	597	587	12	32,576	37,738	20,999	22,436
5065 Electronic parts and equipment	154	165	1,980	2,349	14	46,917	51,864	90,895	124,062
5072 Hardware	65	69	625	686	10	31,104	33,020	21,768	25,651
5074 Plumbing & hydronic heating supplies	55	56	417	446	8	36,537	36,664	15,278	15,612
5075 Warm air heating & air conditioning[1]	17	16	164	150	9	46,561	62,187	6,426	7,685
5078 Refrigeration equipment and supplies	14	12	38	30	3	31,684	38,133	1,153	1,208
5082 Construction and mining machinery	20	20	67	60	3	51,164	44,933	2,914	2,830
5083 Farm and garden machinery	16	17	155	161	9	26,168	29,118	5,057	5,768
5084 Industrial machinery and equipment	176	181	1,154	1,181	7	39,400	42,039	50,359	53,013
5085 Industrial supplies	83	86	632	724	8	34,266	37,287	24,309	30,055
5087 Service establishment equipment	40	42	421	401	10	27,059	31,222	12,140	13,251
5088 Transportation equipment & supplies	38	37	194	269	7	41,918	45,309	9,811	12,839
5091 Sporting & recreational goods	55	53	498	529	10	34,827	36,877	18,198	19,037
5092 Toys and hobby goods and supplies	52	55	506	649	12	46,972	76,857	22,050	36,049
5093 Scrap and waste materials	38	42	502	572	14	28,582	30,091	15,216	17,981
5094 Jewelry & precious stones	164	165	754	731	4	25,729	26,123	20,716	20,309
5099 Durable goods, nec	110	117	682	854	7	73,625	89,799	41,697	73,598
5111 Printing and writing paper	26	28	454	422	15	36,238	44,284	14,318	18,522
5112 Stationery and office supplies	112	92	1,849	1,367	15	28,684	29,800	55,358	39,723
5113 Industrial & personal service paper	31	30	234	248	8	37,726	40,919	9,745	11,230
5120 Drugs, proprietaries, and sundries	62	64	996	964	15	52,012	54,037	55,641	52,370
5131 Piece goods & notions	72	73	605	645	9	27,154	27,665	16,812	18,120
5136 Men's and boys' clothing	53	51	436	453	9	39,844	40,053	17,228	17,695
5137 Women's and children's clothing	120	108	1,606	1,539	14	28,339	31,977	50,654	53,024
5139 Footwear[2]	24	20	255	129	6	33,835	37,891	9,919	5,253
5141 Groceries, general line	64	61	778	763	13	30,015	32,771	26,408	27,394
5142 Packaged frozen food	57	55	823	1,020	19	31,149	32,349	25,948	29,794
5143 Dairy products, exc. dried or canned	21	19	274	187	10	34,000	36,535	9,834	7,146
5144 Poultry and poultry products[3]	14	12	290	274	23	23,090	24,832	7,663	7,463
5145 Confectionery	15	15	79	97	6	29,722	25,237	2,450	2,390
5146 Fish and seafoods	68	61	557	495	8	20,345	23,055	12,511	12,472
5147 Meats and meat products	31	31	348	440	14	34,713	34,464	12,136	15,930
5148 Fresh fruits and vegetables	100	99	1,087	1,114	11	33,785	34,427	40,856	44,729
5149 Groceries and related products, nec	241	232	2,479	2,641	11	31,403	33,624	85,996	92,288
5153 Grain and field beans	13	13	69	41	3	38,319	35,512	2,877	1,314
5159 Farm-product raw materials, nec[3]	8	9	41	58	6	32,976	46,966	1,476	2,333
5162 Plastics materials & basic shapes	34	32	314	301	9	25,860	32,824	9,114	9,301
5169 Chemicals & allied products, nec	41	47	325	369	8	51,200	50,829	17,106	19,032
5171 Petroleum bulk stations & terminals[1]	18	16	50	234	15	34,080	63,077	1,558	14,993
5172 Petroleum products, nec	15	15	96	105	7	36,833	42,933	4,251	5,416
5181 Beer and ale	18	17	572	525	31	32,077	30,651	19,910	17,375
5182 Wine and distilled beverages[2]	56	57	658	470	8	42,000	45,770	28,901	21,343
5191 Farm supplies	28	29	168	207	7	38,881	44,657	7,413	11,682
5192 Books, periodicals, & newspapers	80	83	1,148	1,517	18	40,282	49,192	47,085	71,113
5193 Flowers & florists' supplies	67	60	736	603	10	21,696	20,524	18,225	13,585
5194 Tobacco and tobacco products	10	8	145	146	18	33,214	34,959	5,098	4,810
5198 Paints, varnishes, and supplies	23	21	165	152	7	27,661	30,526	4,938	4,762
5199 Nondurable goods, nec	354	393	1,847	2,081	5	25,598	28,484	56,266	65,425
52- Retail trade	12,210	12,181	151,216	155,453	13	17,374	18,171	2,713,580	2,855,488
5210 Lumber and other building materials	115	109	1,692	1,736	16	24,700	26,954	45,461	49,601
5230 Paint, glass, and wallpaper stores[3]	52	58	162	221	4	26,593	22,172	4,567	5,609
5250 Hardware stores	94	74	1,118	950	13	16,522	16,017	20,479	15,886
5260 Retail nurseries and garden stores	72	76	487	556	7	15,105	18,374	8,467	11,642
5310 Department stores[3]	32	31	5,217	5,337	172	13,284	13,481	73,703	74,336
5330 Variety stores[3]	27	29	133	129	4	10,767	10,512	1,639	1,457
5390 Misc. general merchandise stores	62	58	2,075	2,294	40	18,668	21,264	43,879	48,272
5410 Grocery stores	800	790	13,354	13,049	17	20,829	21,977	282,331	291,023

Continued on next page.

SAN FRANCISCO, CA PMSA - [continued]

Wholesale and Retail Trade USA	Establishments 1994	Establishments 1995	Employment 1994	Employment 1995	Emp / Est 1995	Pay / Employee 1994	Pay / Employee 1995	Annual Payroll ($ 000) 1994	Annual Payroll ($ 000) 1995
5420 Meat and fish markets	107	100	496	497	5	15,895	16,217	8,384	8,240
5430 Fruit and vegetable markets	48	47	233	251	5	16,326	14,327	3,997	4,029
5440 Candy, nut, and confectionery stores	60	59	454	473	8	13,930	14,461	6,921	7,237
5450 Dairy products stores [1]	18	17	105	130	8	6,743	6,585	831	1,036
5460 Retail bakeries	292	252	2,467	2,141	8	11,588	11,144	31,824	26,326
5490 Miscellaneous food stores	185	190	1,380	1,623	9	11,119	10,923	16,587	18,932
5510 New and used car dealers	110	106	5,047	4,930	47	36,025	38,227	192,780	205,424
5520 Used car dealers	27	24	43	76	3	17,767	19,000	937	1,756
5530 Auto and home supply stores	131	134	1,021	1,065	8	20,223	21,213	22,099	22,991
5540 Gasoline service stations	390	382	3,120	3,158	8	14,319	14,391	47,015	47,410
5550 Boat dealers	22	23	140	161	7	18,714	23,081	2,703	3,683
5560 Recreational vehicle dealers [2]	-	4	-	17	4	-	15,765	-	294
5570 Motorcycle dealers	24	23	181	179	8	20,796	22,436	4,395	4,689
5610 Men's & boys' clothing stores	151	152	1,102	1,122	7	20,294	21,451	23,373	24,122
5620 Women's clothing stores	386	347	3,307	3,121	9	13,216	13,792	43,834	44,115
5630 Women's accessory & specialty stores	75	80	449	411	5	11,724	12,944	5,765	5,503
5640 Children's and infants' wear stores	48	47	346	389	8	9,353	9,296	3,566	3,648
5650 Family clothing stores	190	182	5,618	5,533	30	14,240	15,505	89,760	88,739
5660 Shoe stores	215	200	1,142	1,201	6	18,441	18,714	20,116	21,334
5690 Misc. apparel & accessory stores	85	77	414	441	6	14,164	15,410	6,237	7,345
5712 Furniture stores	215	206	1,552	1,426	7	24,691	24,168	38,140	36,406
5713 Floor covering stores	96	93	486	460	5	20,691	22,765	11,440	11,855
5714 Drapery and upholstery stores	28	27	95	100	4	20,000	18,560	2,111	2,196
5719 Misc. homefurnishings stores	186	182	1,480	1,400	8	13,116	15,669	22,330	22,915
5720 Household appliance stores	46	48	278	276	6	19,942	20,145	5,793	6,273
5731 Radio, TV, & electronic stores	167	162	1,392	1,551	10	23,264	22,466	32,797	38,151
5734 Computer and software stores	130	137	797	988	7	27,804	29,466	24,356	33,412
5735 Record & prerecorded tape stores	87	91	998	1,170	13	12,044	11,391	13,067	13,253
5736 Musical instrument stores	33	31	213	194	6	20,432	21,216	4,564	4,346
5812 Eating places	3,769	3,534	57,931	58,909	17	11,059	11,831	703,310	742,254
5813 Drinking places	424	415	3,264	3,144	8	9,137	10,247	31,580	33,274
5910 Drug stores and proprietary stores	260	255	4,597	4,393	17	24,729	22,396	117,571	104,361
5920 Liquor stores	168	154	630	578	4	13,454	14,422	8,810	8,837
5930 Used merchandise stores	209	207	1,176	1,383	7	14,656	14,456	18,467	21,333
5941 Sporting goods and bicycle shops	193	197	1,569	1,728	9	12,681	12,778	21,411	23,772
5942 Book stores	170	161	1,540	1,681	10	12,966	12,892	20,608	22,412
5943 Stationery stores	51	51	352	354	7	14,023	14,588	5,118	5,565
5944 Jewelry stores	263	246	1,078	961	4	22,134	23,829	23,873	22,283
5945 Hobby, toy, and game shops	73	71	767	804	11	12,188	13,010	10,767	11,604
5946 Camera & photographic supply stores	50	52	240	260	5	16,317	18,046	4,333	4,806
5947 Gift, novelty, and souvenir shops	380	374	2,400	2,321	6	9,993	11,647	26,879	29,860
5948 Luggage and leather goods stores	39	33	207	201	6	16,850	18,408	3,943	4,719
5949 Sewing, needlework, and piece goods	56	47	531	489	10	12,384	13,415	7,061	7,014
5961 Catalog and mail-order houses	91	97	1,378	1,477	15	24,792	25,246	38,745	39,078
5962 Merchandising machine operators	23	25	114	80	3	15,825	19,350	1,805	1,573
5963 Direct selling establishments	82	85	965	1,133	13	18,740	17,582	18,857	21,646
5980 Fuel dealers [1]	9	10	39	83	8	23,795	21,253	1,028	1,893
5992 Florists	200	200	793	830	4	12,121	11,860	9,858	10,225
5993 Tobacco stores and stands [3]	14	16	65	65	4	12,923	14,215	939	1,065
5994 News dealers and newsstands [3]	22	19	71	86	5	11,831	11,256	917	942
5995 Optical goods stores	89	87	496	615	7	15,863	15,037	8,585	10,740
5999 Miscellaneous retail stores, nec	415	444	1,997	2,113	5	17,424	18,904	37,284	42,649

Source: County Business Patterns 1994/95, CBP-94/95, U.S. Department of Commerce, Washington DC, November 1997. The employment column represents mid-March employment in the year. Pay per employee is calculated by dividing 1st Quarter payroll, annualized, by mid-March employment. The column headed 'Emp / Est' shows 'employees per establishment'. A dash (-) means that data are unavailable or cannot be calculated. nec means not elsewhere classified. *Notes:* 1. 1994 data incomplete; unavailable or withheld. 2. 1995 data incomplete; unavailable or withheld. 3. 1994 and 1995 data incomplete; unavailable or withheld.

SAN JOSE, CA PMSA

Wholesale and Retail Trade USA	Establishments 1994	Establishments 1995	Employment 1994	Employment 1995	Emp / Est 1995	Pay / Employee 1994	Pay / Employee 1995	Annual Payroll ($ 000) 1994	Annual Payroll ($ 000) 1995
50 - Wholesale trade	3,524	3,633	67,592	70,877	20	46,912	51,752	3,292,956	3,805,136
5012 Automobiles and other vehicles	27	26	423	368	14	38,156	36,707	15,076	14,994
5013 Motor vehicle supplies and new parts	108	102	1,328	1,356	13	26,955	27,041	42,253	40,131
5014 Tires and tubes	19	21	128	134	6	28,938	28,687	4,019	3,918
5015 Motor vehicle parts, used	36	44	210	304	7	22,590	21,579	5,454	6,678
5021 Furniture	48	45	789	876	19	39,787	42,146	32,302	38,517
5023 Homefurnishings	35	35	600	538	15	26,520	27,472	15,494	15,649
5031 Lumber, plywood, and millwork	26	22	355	291	13	30,118	33,402	11,566	10,663

Continued on next page.

SAN JOSE, CA PMSA - [continued]

Wholesale and Retail Trade USA	Establishments		Employment		Emp / Est	Pay / Employee		Annual Payroll ($ 000)	
	1994	1995	1994	1995	1995	1994	1995	1994	1995
5032 Brick, stone, & related materials	18	21	121	148	7	30,579	32,919	3,889	5,365
5033 Roofing, siding, & insulation	14	10	173	118	12	32,324	38,237	6,258	5,358
5039 Construction materials, nec	16	27	183	442	16	31,475	35,919	6,306	13,036
5043 Photographic equipment & supplies	6	8	66	153	19	34,303	51,948	2,273	6,712
5044 Office equipment	56	50	1,080	1,006	20	43,326	51,551	46,780	48,487
5045 Computers, peripherals, & software	696	698	17,179	17,309	25	54,083	54,565	951,156	998,451
5046 Commercial equipment, nec	20	26	209	204	8	30,794	37,490	6,642	7,901
5047 Medical and hospital equipment	66	63	881	895	14	41,598	40,340	37,785	40,910
5048 Ophthalmic goods	9	8	161	173	22	33,217	69,318	4,833	7,186
5049 Professional equipment, nec	39	38	672	681	18	39,143	41,040	28,936	29,727
5051 Metals service centers and offices	33	-	485	-	-	34,730	-	18,237	-
5063 Electrical apparatus and equipment	142	125	3,700	3,518	28	50,661	61,786	204,399	215,525
5064 Electrical appliances, TV & radios	23	24	482	556	23	45,975	46,892	25,636	37,826
5065 Electronic parts and equipment	641	668	12,349	14,584	22	46,717	59,644	611,329	950,038
5072 Hardware	51	53	1,060	1,130	21	29,453	33,232	36,797	43,038
5074 Plumbing & hydronic heating supplies	25	20	322	276	14	32,435	32,449	10,942	9,159
5075 Warm air heating & air conditioning	20	16	245	222	14	41,453	46,901	10,977	11,886
5078 Refrigeration equipment and supplies	9	8	46	44	6	29,304	30,727	1,500	1,461
5082 Construction and mining machinery	8	9	70	88	10	45,086	41,955	3,752	4,180
5083 Farm and garden machinery	15	10	100	89	9	24,720	27,281	2,590	2,586
5084 Industrial machinery and equipment	164	166	1,262	1,836	11	41,185	42,466	62,669	99,261
5085 Industrial supplies	68	66	1,002	1,107	17	45,441	52,267	50,966	65,388
5087 Service establishment equipment	33	27	260	216	8	28,800	37,981	8,198	8,482
5088 Transportation equipment & supplies	15	14	90	79	6	32,489	33,519	3,024	2,620
5091 Sporting & recreational goods	34	35	456	546	16	31,149	37,377	16,098	20,449
5092 Toys and hobby goods and supplies	19	17	107	108	6	46,841	72,889	4,706	6,224
5093 Scrap and waste materials	48	49	663	724	15	28,821	32,878	19,890	23,985
5094 Jewelry & precious stones	22	22	128	166	8	35,875	27,687	4,083	4,911
5099 Durable goods, nec	54	65	256	294	5	42,078	37,102	11,007	12,769
5111 Printing and writing paper	11	12	89	190	16	44,584	122,316	4,173	11,051
5112 Stationery and office supplies	65	60	974	1,021	17	20,476	22,601	20,410	24,016
5113 Industrial & personal service paper	32	31	965	748	24	19,337	29,016	20,944	22,550
5120 Drugs, proprietaries, and sundries	30	32	855	848	27	39,677	40,448	36,909	35,669
5131 Piece goods & notions	15	16	112	107	7	24,286	26,355	2,652	2,968
5136 Men's and boys' clothing	12	9	58	64	7	34,759	41,563	2,653	3,049
5137 Women's and children's clothing	16	19	52	70	4	14,077	17,200	1,351	1,501
5141 Groceries, general line	29	26	510	506	19	27,569	30,704	15,473	16,843
5142 Packaged frozen food	17	16	442	375	23	25,756	25,173	12,794	10,784
5143 Dairy products, exc. dried or canned	9	10	225	231	23	35,751	29,714	8,375	7,440
5144 Poultry and poultry products	4	4	38	33	8	24,105	28,242	946	944
5145 Confectionery	7	7	169	127	18	29,964	28,945	2,821	2,969
5146 Fish and seafoods	10	9	113	127	14	22,265	22,677	2,495	3,030
5147 Meats and meat products	12	12	195	209	17	30,646	30,297	7,258	7,618
5148 Fresh fruits and vegetables	29	26	390	373	14	29,128	32,300	13,693	12,663
5149 Groceries and related products, nec	70	72	1,369	1,544	21	30,983	32,148	44,135	50,411
5153 Grain and field beans	-	6	-	30	5	-	24,400	-	829
5162 Plastics materials & basic shapes	22	25	270	295	12	35,852	34,088	9,401	11,945
5169 Chemicals & allied products, nec	49	46	638	647	14	49,103	68,835	33,078	39,779
5171 Petroleum bulk stations & terminals	16	14	228	237	17	42,000	40,000	9,718	11,378
5172 Petroleum products, nec	10	10	87	97	10	24,460	30,474	2,514	3,161
5181 Beer and ale	6	6	467	440	73	34,090	40,545	17,096	19,574
5182 Wine and distilled beverages	9	7	167	194	28	32,359	28,392	7,071	6,832
5191 Farm supplies	20	17	320	343	20	39,588	46,029	10,878	13,979
5192 Books, periodicals, & newspapers	25	24	530	545	23	51,336	42,371	24,456	23,068
5193 Flowers & florists' supplies	21	25	289	213	9	15,488	18,685	4,915	4,341
5198 Paints, varnishes, and supplies	16	15	170	191	13	28,871	28,482	5,393	5,555
5199 Nondurable goods, nec	127	149	665	773	5	24,415	30,070	18,775	26,277
52- Retail trade	8,222	8,194	117,183	122,111	15	15,159	15,540	1,882,856	1,983,882
5210 Lumber and other building materials	89	72	1,599	1,619	22	22,054	23,965	38,749	40,092
5230 Paint, glass, and wallpaper stores	52	44	305	318	7	24,092	20,969	7,778	7,413
5250 Hardware stores	45	40	1,228	1,201	30	12,023	13,232	15,582	17,153
5260 Retail nurseries and garden stores	40	41	398	357	9	15,236	16,986	6,493	6,669
5270 Mobile home dealers	6	7	35	32	5	22,286	23,250	996	967
5310 Department stores	46	48	8,983	10,384	216	14,095	13,293	136,740	143,815
5330 Variety stores	19	15	235	215	14	10,298	10,847	2,957	2,635
5390 Misc. general merchandise stores	35	37	1,755	1,400	38	17,377	19,394	30,611	28,055
5410 Grocery stores	485	482	12,036	11,803	24	20,671	22,124	254,695	262,850
5420 Meat and fish markets	26	24	226	247	10	12,779	14,186	3,582	4,255
5430 Fruit and vegetable markets	26	25	202	207	8	13,129	13,585	3,088	2,975
5440 Candy, nut, and confectionery stores	33	34	185	198	6	10,184	11,010	1,986	2,265
5450 Dairy products stores	17	15	103	94	6	3,262	4,383	443	531

Continued on next page.

SAN JOSE, CA PMSA - [continued]

Wholesale and Retail Trade USA	Establishments		Employment		Emp / Est	Pay / Employee		Annual Payroll ($ 000)	
	1994	1995	1994	1995	1995	1994	1995	1994	1995
5460 Retail bakeries	155	139	1,116	1,107	8	11,287	10,298	13,051	11,993
5490 Miscellaneous food stores	80	90	415	588	7	12,492	10,673	6,135	6,683
5510 New and used car dealers	97	98	5,263	5,243	54	37,168	38,576	211,053	223,552
5520 Used car dealers	38	47	102	120	3	20,275	20,300	2,173	2,796
5530 Auto and home supply stores	222	227	1,750	1,965	9	21,378	22,599	40,087	44,148
5540 Gasoline service stations	363	341	2,619	2,720	8	13,451	13,188	36,060	37,391
5550 Boat dealers	5	4	57	55	14	27,719	26,982	1,676	1,656
5560 Recreational vehicle dealers	18	16	230	256	16	21,983	26,891	7,161	7,496
5570 Motorcycle dealers	26	25	158	165	7	21,038	23,685	3,817	4,315
5590 Automotive dealers, nec	5	5	26	29	6	26,308	22,483	732	829
5610 Men's & boys' clothing stores	102	101	810	767	8	15,422	17,398	12,356	12,399
5620 Women's clothing stores	258	209	2,460	2,037	10	10,829	11,175	27,211	19,586
5630 Women's accessory & specialty stores	42	41	261	302	7	9,870	10,715	3,061	3,160
5640 Children's and infants' wear stores	26	28	225	227	8	7,698	9,286	1,989	2,069
5650 Family clothing stores	107	104	3,667	3,811	37	19,798	13,020	56,163	50,444
5660 Shoe stores	198	183	1,026	1,203	7	13,653	12,020	15,039	14,769
5690 Misc. apparel & accessory stores	58	61	268	367	6	9,104	9,907	3,367	4,335
5712 Furniture stores	152	149	1,062	1,049	7	22,637	23,840	25,504	26,471
5713 Floor covering stores	67	59	402	391	7	22,458	24,092	10,109	10,482
5714 Drapery and upholstery stores	11	13	85	77	6	13,459	14,909	1,148	1,070
5719 Misc. homefurnishings stores	120	122	1,099	1,199	10	11,982	14,289	14,595	15,630
5720 Household appliance stores	45	43	287	320	7	29,882	30,425	8,695	10,414
5731 Radio, TV, & electronic stores	103	105	1,377	1,342	13	24,813	28,787	36,404	40,394
5734 Computer and software stores	145	160	1,981	2,239	14	25,347	28,447	54,872	69,200
5735 Record & prerecorded tape stores	60	57	701	899	16	10,573	9,148	7,938	7,645
5736 Musical instrument stores	27	29	173	213	7	18,150	21,333	3,415	4,732
5812 Eating places	2,497	2,321	42,029	42,785	18	9,166	9,505	414,876	427,284
5813 Drinking places	204	175	1,682	2,207	13	8,476	13,675	18,610	30,389
5910 Drug stores and proprietary stores	167	163	3,898	4,082	25	20,382	20,936	84,078	86,210
5920 Liquor stores	148	146	375	358	2	11,285	12,179	4,458	4,607
5930 Used merchandise stores	89	85	716	669	8	12,587	13,172	9,824	9,467
5941 Sporting goods and bicycle shops	163	168	1,532	1,673	10	13,193	12,987	21,476	21,718
5942 Book stores	112	99	1,531	1,511	15	11,070	12,463	17,279	19,103
5943 Stationery stores	24	26	206	264	10	10,000	9,333	2,239	3,373
5944 Jewelry stores	144	142	697	663	5	20,838	21,882	14,918	14,981
5945 Hobby, toy, and game shops	72	66	1,070	1,120	17	13,619	14,086	15,344	16,018
5946 Camera & photographic supply stores	49	53	580	513	10	11,476	12,546	7,426	7,002
5947 Gift, novelty, and souvenir shops	168	160	1,037	906	6	7,803	8,795	8,700	8,535
5948 Luggage and leather goods stores	26	27	128	169	6	12,063	12,852	2,010	2,473
5949 Sewing, needlework, and piece goods	41	39	488	430	11	7,566	8,642	3,826	3,645
5961 Catalog and mail-order houses	41	47	431	559	12	27,248	27,664	13,334	17,107
5962 Merchandising machine operators	34	33	465	444	13	16,456	13,865	7,816	6,168
5963 Direct selling establishments	99	104	597	702	7	21,173	20,137	14,205	14,284
5980 Fuel dealers	7	7	58	53	8	24,345	23,698	1,331	1,310
5992 Florists	125	124	545	539	4	10,488	10,100	6,155	5,765
5993 Tobacco stores and stands	5	5	18	22	4	8,222	7,818	169	216
5994 News dealers and newsstands	9	8	55	45	6	11,200	13,511	616	579
5995 Optical goods stores	66	74	411	425	6	14,268	14,682	5,984	6,900
5999 Miscellaneous retail stores, nec	276	290	1,486	1,754	6	14,156	15,129	24,013	29,164

Source: County Business Patterns 1994/95, CBP-94/95, U.S. Department of Commerce, Washington DC, November 1997. The employment column represents mid-March employment in the year. Pay per employee is calculated by dividing 1st Quarter payroll, annualized, by mid-March employment. The column headed 'Emp / Est' shows 'employees per establishment'. A dash (-) means that data are unavailable or cannot be calculated. nec means not elsewhere classified. *Notes:* 1. 1994 data incomplete; unavailable or withheld. 2. 1995 data incomplete; unavailable or withheld. 3. 1994 and 1995 data incomplete; unavailable or withheld.

SAN LUIS OBISPO - ATASCADERO - PASO ROBLES, CA MSA

Wholesale and Retail Trade USA	Establishments		Employment		Emp / Est	Pay / Employee		Annual Payroll ($ 000)	
	1994	1995	1994	1995	1995	1994	1995	1994	1995
50 - Wholesale trade	285	277	2,198	2,337	8	21,592	19,793	48,762	47,837
5013 Motor vehicle supplies and new parts	16	16	104	108	7	21,000	19,519	2,140	2,254
5015 Motor vehicle parts, used	5	5	26	27	5	12,462	13,926	358	250
5020 Furniture and homefurnishings	4	4	22	14	4	19,636	32,286	486	461
5031 Lumber, plywood, and millwork	5	-	25	-	-	21,120	-	593	-
5032 Brick, stone, & related materials	4	-	17	-	-	16,000	-	304	-
5044 Office equipment	5	5	70	78	16	28,057	27,282	1,931	1,422
5045 Computers, peripherals, & software	9	7	44	50	7	21,182	22,240	1,014	1,066
5047 Medical and hospital equipment	4	5	38	32	6	20,211	23,375	845	906
5051 Metals service centers and offices	3	3	37	22	7	21,514	19,091	743	763
5063 Electrical apparatus and equipment	12	-	48	-	-	18,333	-	896	-

Continued on next page.

SAN LUIS OBISPO – ATASCADERO – PASO ROBLES, CA MSA - [continued]

Wholesale and Retail Trade USA	Establishments		Employment		Emp / Est	Pay / Employee		Annual Payroll ($ 000)	
	1994	1995	1994	1995	1995	1994	1995	1994	1995
5064 Electrical appliances, TV & radios	3	-	16	-	-	24,750	-	413	-
5065 Electronic parts and equipment	6	9	55	90	10	28,364	24,222	2,065	2,187
5072 Hardware	5	5	39	36	7	26,667	32,222	929	948
5074 Plumbing & hydronic heating supplies	5	7	21	38	5	27,619	22,316	624	956
5075 Warm air heating & air conditioning	4	4	16	15	4	17,000	18,933	297	270
5083 Farm and garden machinery	3	3	10	11	4	32,400	26,909	273	319
5084 Industrial machinery and equipment	-	4	-	21	5	-	23,238	-	633
5087 Service establishment equipment	9	-	38	-	-	21,053	-	741	-
5091 Sporting & recreational goods	12	-	35	-	-	25,371	-	1,036	-
5093 Scrap and waste materials	8	8	99	84	11	12,525	9,476	1,135	961
5094 Jewelry & precious stones	-	3	-	5	2	-	7,200	-	39
5112 Stationery and office supplies	13	12	63	54	5	14,984	16,000	851	777
5120 Drugs, proprietaries, and sundries	-	4	-	32	8	-	19,500	-	214
5130 Apparel, piece goods, and notions	6	7	74	105	15	16,000	16,305	1,432	2,138
5141 Groceries, general line	4	5	31	37	7	29,548	26,811	974	1,065
5142 Packaged frozen food	-	3	-	14	5	-	70,286	-	606
5143 Dairy products, exc. dried or canned	-	3	-	11	4	-	7,273	-	92
5146 Fish and seafoods	6	6	127	144	24	14,740	12,333	1,820	1,704
5148 Fresh fruits and vegetables	-	7	-	55	8	-	17,673	-	1,466
5149 Groceries and related products, nec	9	11	60	62	6	23,000	25,161	1,427	1,592
5171 Petroleum bulk stations & terminals	-	6	-	48	8	-	25,667	-	1,228
5180 Beer, wine, and distilled beverages	7	7	59	52	7	25,153	29,846	1,643	1,603
5191 Farm supplies	21	16	157	161	10	24,433	24,398	3,858	3,771
5199 Nondurable goods, nec	9	-	95	-	-	17,263	-	2,205	-
52 - Retail trade	1,622	1,624	17,847	18,817	12	11,837	12,176	232,553	245,281
5210 Lumber and other building materials	30	25	337	314	13	18,896	19,885	7,052	6,870
5230 Paint, glass, and wallpaper stores	14	19	65	91	5	18,954	21,714	1,180	1,860
5250 Hardware stores	18	18	303	282	16	10,904	13,475	3,840	3,943
5260 Retail nurseries and garden stores	12	18	49	72	4	8,000	9,278	535	845
5270 Mobile home dealers	6	3	17	15	5	36,235	16,800	414	304
5310 Department stores	8	7	896	1,124	161	9,339	11,399	10,809	13,358
5330 Variety stores	9	-	71	-	-	8,451	-	646	-
5390 Misc. general merchandise stores	4	-	15	-	-	15,467	-	234	-
5410 Grocery stores	105	105	2,351	2,428	23	18,389	19,267	43,383	49,874
5420 Meat and fish markets	7	8	30	31	4	9,600	8,258	312	311
5430 Fruit and vegetable markets	4	6	13	18	3	8,000	4,889	99	108
5440 Candy, nut, and confectionery stores	7	5	39	25	5	6,462	8,000	245	205
5460 Retail bakeries	30	26	144	128	5	6,694	7,500	1,115	972
5490 Miscellaneous food stores	14	14	65	83	6	7,015	9,060	661	781
5510 New and used car dealers	20	21	558	649	31	30,100	29,411	18,943	20,870
5530 Auto and home supply stores	40	38	290	297	8	15,310	16,323	4,826	4,765
5540 Gasoline service stations	76	71	612	594	8	11,301	11,030	7,156	6,948
5550 Boat dealers	-	4	-	9	2	-	18,667	-	305
5570 Motorcycle dealers	4	4	29	21	5	13,655	15,429	443	374
5610 Men's & boys' clothing stores	18	17	44	166	10	11,000	8,096	665	1,366
5620 Women's clothing stores	47	47	258	255	5	9,132	9,773	2,708	2,755
5630 Women's accessory & specialty stores	6	5	20	14	3	7,800	9,429	167	170
5640 Children's and infants' wear stores	7	6	26	16	3	5,846	7,750	167	165
5650 Family clothing stores	14	18	119	144	8	9,748	9,472	1,180	1,612
5660 Shoe stores	30	27	115	186	7	12,348	10,108	1,641	1,735
5690 Misc. apparel & accessory stores	7	8	44	45	6	6,545	7,556	307	353
5712 Furniture stores	46	43	195	236	5	14,667	14,492	3,098	3,465
5713 Floor covering stores	16	14	69	61	4	15,072	16,656	1,057	1,172
5714 Drapery and upholstery stores	4	-	12	-	-	8,667	-	118	-
5719 Misc. homefurnishings stores	16	18	60	98	5	8,667	9,673	759	1,155
5720 Household appliance stores	12	11	62	55	5	15,097	18,764	1,025	1,010
5731 Radio, TV, & electronic stores	21	20	131	134	7	12,855	15,015	1,641	1,809
5734 Computer and software stores	6	6	16	18	3	9,250	8,444	134	295
5735 Record & prerecorded tape stores	7	7	100	109	16	8,360	8,183	904	846
5736 Musical instrument stores	4	5	9	10	2	12,889	15,600	135	180
5812 Eating places	469	450	7,440	7,652	17	7,930	7,840	67,272	65,941
5813 Drinking places	36	35	190	185	5	6,779	6,703	1,386	1,282
5910 Drug stores and proprietary stores	41	40	696	743	19	20,580	18,622	14,323	13,808
5920 Liquor stores	39	39	206	202	5	7,864	8,772	1,828	1,853
5930 Used merchandise stores	21	25	72	77	3	5,444	6,286	467	663
5941 Sporting goods and bicycle shops	35	36	490	243	7	6,808	9,613	6,299	2,542
5942 Book stores	19	19	73	107	6	7,890	9,121	673	987
5943 Stationery stores	5	5	28	33	7	10,000	10,667	319	506
5944 Jewelry stores	29	28	94	95	3	12,298	11,158	1,245	1,081
5945 Hobby, toy, and game shops	13	9	71	52	6	8,620	9,385	569	518
5947 Gift, novelty, and souvenir shops	62	55	290	240	4	7,200	8,050	2,272	2,056

Continued on next page.

SAN LUIS OBISPO - ATASCADERO - PASO ROBLES, CA MSA - [continued]

Wholesale and Retail Trade USA	Establishments		Employment		Emp / Est	Pay / Employee		Annual Payroll ($ 000)	
	1994	1995	1994	1995	1995	1994	1995	1994	1995
5949 Sewing, needlework, and piece goods	8	7	54	67	10	6,370	4,955	376	363
5963 Direct selling establishments	14	14	123	150	11	16,715	18,160	2,715	3,014
5984 Liquefied petroleum gas dealers	7	8	50	63	8	29,040	27,048	1,548	1,850
5992 Florists	24	27	126	119	4	5,937	6,521	712	749
5995 Optical goods stores	-	14	-	50	4	-	15,280	-	819
5999 Miscellaneous retail stores, nec	55	59	192	230	4	12,063	10,661	2,325	2,562

Source: County Business Patterns 1994/95, CBP-94/95, U.S. Department of Commerce, Washington DC, November 1997. The employment column represents mid-March employment in the year. Pay per employee is calculated by dividing 1st Quarter payroll, annualized, by mid-March employment. The column headed 'Emp / Est' shows 'employees per establishment'. A dash (-) means that data are unavailable or cannot be calculated. nec means not elsewhere classified. *Notes:* 1. 1994 data incomplete; unavailable or withheld. 2. 1995 data incomplete; unavailable or withheld. 3. 1994 and 1995 data incomplete; unavailable or withheld.

SANTA BARBARA - SANTA MARIA - LOMPOC, CA MSA

Wholesale and Retail Trade USA	Establishments		Employment		Emp / Est	Pay / Employee		Annual Payroll ($ 000)	
	1994	1995	1994	1995	1995	1994	1995	1994	1995
50- Wholesale trade	561	548	5,277	5,774	11	25,810	25,648	149,844	159,522
5013 Motor vehicle supplies and new parts	31	28	271	258	9	19,808	23,705	6,116	6,333
5014 Tires and tubes	5	6	65	78	13	21,169	18,923	1,636	1,800
5021 Furniture	-	9	-	56	6	-	25,714	-	1,830
5023 Homefurnishings	-	4	-	24	6	-	14,500	-	293
5031 Lumber, plywood, and millwork	7	8	35	42	5	28,571	29,810	1,090	1,161
5032 Brick, stone, & related materials	9	-	60	-	-	24,067	-	1,558	-
5039 Construction materials, nec	-	7	-	16	2	-	28,250	-	484
5044 Office equipment	12	14	109	114	8	32,183	37,123	3,516	3,572
5045 Computers, peripherals, & software	23	22	166	130	6	43,735	45,015	6,703	5,803
5046 Commercial equipment, nec	9	-	41	-	-	20,976	-	963	-
5047 Medical and hospital equipment	11	9	65	53	6	28,185	28,604	2,165	1,846
5049 Professional equipment, nec	6	5	90	94	19	23,067	23,574	2,290	2,451
5051 Metals service centers and offices	4	3	7	22	7	18,857	15,818	301	438
5063 Electrical apparatus and equipment	-	12	-	83	7	-	50,361	-	2,855
5064 Electrical appliances, TV & radios	-	4	-	25	6	-	7,200	-	450
5065 Electronic parts and equipment	18	22	155	171	8	38,555	39,368	6,451	7,938
5072 Hardware	5	5	54	50	10	26,667	30,800	1,500	1,627
5074 Plumbing & hydronic heating supplies	18	16	221	237	15	32,308	33,688	7,654	8,015
5082 Construction and mining machinery	-	3	-	22	7	-	28,364	-	779
5083 Farm and garden machinery	11	10	117	114	11	31,761	29,684	3,411	3,630
5084 Industrial machinery and equipment	22	18	190	157	9	32,463	29,248	6,549	4,859
5085 Industrial supplies	9	10	78	97	10	23,385	24,330	2,233	2,537
5087 Service establishment equipment	11	10	90	116	12	23,511	22,379	2,180	2,736
5091 Sporting & recreational goods	6	5	51	77	15	15,608	13,143	1,058	1,735
5092 Toys and hobby goods and supplies	4	4	7	9	2	18,286	17,333	154	169
5093 Scrap and waste materials	8	9	46	53	6	17,739	19,245	915	1,159
5094 Jewelry & precious stones	6	6	42	37	6	20,571	22,811	929	869
5099 Durable goods, nec	11	12	88	73	6	23,818	21,589	1,987	1,406
5111 Printing and writing paper	3	4	11	14	4	32,364	43,143	156	603
5112 Stationery and office supplies	12	10	75	123	12	17,227	20,520	1,276	2,620
5120 Drugs, proprietaries, and sundries	8	9	116	125	14	20,655	21,184	2,764	2,935
5137 Women's and children's clothing	11	9	39	34	4	26,051	18,471	1,096	753
5139 Footwear	6	4	119	81	20	28,000	31,654	3,651	2,148
5141 Groceries, general line	4	4	40	59	15	29,400	28,000	1,281	1,677
5143 Dairy products, exc. dried or canned	8	8	54	55	7	29,111	28,582	1,602	1,661
5146 Fish and seafoods	6	5	63	69	14	19,810	19,594	1,307	1,265
5148 Fresh fruits and vegetables	24	20	242	266	13	23,157	22,917	6,839	7,071
5149 Groceries and related products, nec	22	22	366	426	19	28,000	28,300	11,467	13,274
5159 Farm-product raw materials, nec	-	3	-	18	6	-	25,556	-	568
5160 Chemicals and allied products	12	10	88	75	8	23,000	32,427	2,563	2,822
5170 Petroleum and petroleum products	10	12	61	67	6	23,541	27,403	1,562	1,868
5181 Beer and ale	7	7	210	184	26	23,886	26,196	5,609	4,807
5182 Wine and distilled beverages	3	3	28	8	3	29,286	32,500	679	294
5191 Farm supplies	26	22	279	262	12	33,018	36,000	10,244	10,798
5192 Books, periodicals, & newspapers	7	7	57	60	9	22,175	21,000	1,485	1,627
5193 Flowers & florists' supplies	17	12	163	158	13	13,252	17,468	2,720	2,915
5198 Paints, varnishes, and supplies	-	4	-	19	5	-	31,579	-	596
5199 Nondurable goods, nec	22	20	200	229	11	14,920	14,865	3,650	3,745
52- Retail trade	2,476	2,404	29,891	30,272	13	12,821	13,213	408,734	426,221
5210 Lumber and other building materials	33	34	513	537	16	22,979	23,300	12,034	12,893
5230 Paint, glass, and wallpaper stores	-	17	-	59	3	-	21,831	-	1,432
5250 Hardware stores	26	19	262	270	14	14,290	15,081	4,411	4,309
5260 Retail nurseries and garden stores	26	27	120	126	5	13,800	14,063	1,941	2,007

Continued on next page.

SANTA BARBARA – SANTA MARIA – LOMPOC, CA MSA - [continued]

Wholesale and Retail Trade USA	Establishments		Employment		Emp / Est	Pay / Employee		Annual Payroll ($ 000)	
	1994	1995	1994	1995	1995	1994	1995	1994	1995
5310 Department stores	15	15	2,315	2,430	162	10,343	10,823	25,837	27,022
5330 Variety stores	5	4	38	25	6	7,579	9,280	336	254
5390 Misc. general merchandise stores	12	13	325	307	24	18,671	21,303	6,775	6,624
5410 Grocery stores	154	146	3,332	3,303	23	19,646	19,874	67,010	71,122
5420 Meat and fish markets	11	10	73	80	8	8,986	8,200	779	773
5440 Candy, nut, and confectionery stores	19	19	93	103	5	8,688	7,922	819	899
5450 Dairy products stores	4	4	13	16	4	4,923	5,250	99	104
5460 Retail bakeries	51	49	412	357	7	9,864	8,571	4,300	3,273
5490 Miscellaneous food stores	21	21	126	129	6	10,222	11,938	1,406	1,523
5510 New and used car dealers	25	24	1,149	1,152	48	31,064	32,997	37,387	39,365
5520 Used car dealers	9	7	27	24	3	20,296	20,167	561	455
5530 Auto and home supply stores	53	55	371	358	7	17,024	19,229	6,850	7,154
5540 Gasoline service stations	117	113	935	1,012	9	11,286	12,862	11,489	13,405
5550 Boat dealers	3	3	8	7	2	19,000	16,571	142	103
5570 Motorcycle dealers	9	8	42	33	4	14,476	17,939	705	811
5590 Automotive dealers, nec	4	3	13	19	6	29,846	26,316	437	571
5610 Men's & boys' clothing stores	23	22	167	174	8	11,401	13,471	2,019	2,149
5620 Women's clothing stores	82	67	619	616	9	9,409	10,104	6,789	6,552
5630 Women's accessory & specialty stores	19	19	81	77	4	8,741	8,416	712	693
5640 Children's and infants' wear stores	19	18	90	114	6	9,911	10,175	1,039	1,156
5650 Family clothing stores	40	37	867	827	22	13,153	13,843	11,984	11,666
5660 Shoe stores	59	56	294	297	5	12,014	12,269	3,643	3,622
5690 Misc. apparel & accessory stores	18	25	46	80	3	9,739	10,100	597	990
5712 Furniture stores	42	32	234	181	6	18,803	19,006	4,186	3,484
5713 Floor covering stores	17	17	109	141	8	24,147	21,333	2,909	3,182
5714 Drapery and upholstery stores	4	4	5	4	1	12,800	15,000	75	75
5719 Misc. homefurnishings stores	50	47	320	291	6	10,925	12,137	4,004	3,385
5720 Household appliance stores	16	13	56	58	4	15,857	16,414	925	939
5731 Radio, TV, & electronic stores	27	26	239	221	9	19,364	20,525	4,329	4,707
5734 Computer and software stores	15	22	88	125	6	19,909	34,144	2,398	5,450
5735 Record & prerecorded tape stores	13	15	159	243	16	8,528	9,449	1,342	2,100
5736 Musical instrument stores	11	9	111	47	5	14,775	13,957	1,671	596
5812 Eating places	671	622	10,985	10,824	17	8,437	8,591	101,486	98,686
5813 Drinking places	59	52	351	305	6	7,852	8,289	3,077	2,587
5910 Drug stores and proprietary stores	58	56	958	974	17	20,104	19,211	19,879	19,736
5920 Liquor stores	54	52	305	344	7	9,521	9,163	3,431	3,612
5930 Used merchandise stores	43	39	371	365	9	9,445	10,027	3,635	3,705
5941 Sporting goods and bicycle shops	53	55	316	376	7	9,215	9,532	3,538	4,792
5942 Book stores	30	27	370	311	12	10,076	13,055	4,041	4,168
5943 Stationery stores	7	7	42	71	10	11,714	11,211	441	726
5944 Jewelry stores	47	44	220	195	4	16,509	17,005	3,981	3,724
5945 Hobby, toy, and game shops	20	18	144	157	9	9,333	10,140	1,838	1,764
5946 Camera & photographic supply stores	6	5	18	16	3	10,667	10,250	205	195
5947 Gift, novelty, and souvenir shops	80	74	364	326	4	8,330	9,706	3,191	3,218
5948 Luggage and leather goods stores	4	4	24	27	7	8,833	13,333	209	386
5949 Sewing, needlework, and piece goods	18	18	188	173	10	8,043	8,416	1,533	1,486
5961 Catalog and mail-order houses	19	17	221	288	17	26,498	25,361	5,449	9,548
5962 Merchandising machine operators	7	8	32	31	4	14,125	14,710	476	416
5963 Direct selling establishments	21	21	139	110	5	13,755	9,964	1,946	1,222
5980 Fuel dealers	6	6	30	29	5	22,133	26,621	722	806
5992 Florists	28	35	230	221	6	11,322	11,276	2,380	2,337
5995 Optical goods stores	19	19	91	112	6	10,418	10,179	1,279	1,802
5999 Miscellaneous retail stores, nec	89	80	428	378	5	13,860	13,545	6,030	5,531

Source: County Business Patterns 1994/95, CBP-94/95, U.S. Department of Commerce, Washington DC, November 1997. The employment column represents mid-March employment in the year. Pay per employee is calculated by dividing 1st Quarter payroll, annualized, by mid-March employment. The column headed 'Emp / Est' shows 'employees per establishment'. A dash (-) means that data are unavailable or cannot be calculated. nec means not elsewhere classified. *Notes:* 1. 1994 data incomplete; unavailable or withheld. 2. 1995 data incomplete; unavailable or withheld. 3. 1994 and 1995 data incomplete; unavailable or withheld.

SANTA CRUZ – WATSONVILLE, CA PMSA

Wholesale and Retail Trade USA	Establishments		Employment		Emp / Est	Pay / Employee		Annual Payroll ($ 000)	
	1994	1995	1994	1995	1995	1994	1995	1994	1995
50 – Wholesale trade	393	379	4,435	4,622	12	26,280	29,533	132,522	153,979
5012 Automobiles and other vehicles	3	3	25	27	9	19,200	21,185	507	614
5013 Motor vehicle supplies and new parts	14	12	125	111	9	21,216	21,910	3,049	2,780
5014 Tires and tubes	3	3	21	20	7	22,857	25,200	497	540
5015 Motor vehicle parts, used	5	4	10	14	4	15,200	13,429	137	187
5021 Furniture	4	5	18	21	4	22,667	25,333	442	404
5023 Homefurnishings	5	4	72	128	32	15,444	12,750	2,224	2,515

Continued on next page.

SANTA CRUZ - WATSONVILLE, CA PMSA - [continued]

Wholesale and Retail Trade USA	Establishments		Employment		Emp / Est	Pay / Employee		Annual Payroll ($ 000)	
	1994	1995	1994	1995	1995	1994	1995	1994	1995
5031 Lumber, plywood, and millwork	6	5	30	44	9	31,067	27,545	929	1,268
5044 Office equipment	7	5	61	44	9	19,148	21,364	1,075	977
5045 Computers, peripherals, & software	31	25	390	179	7	43,056	46,905	17,406	9,822
5046 Commercial equipment, nec	-	4	-	12	3	-	18,667	-	239
5047 Medical and hospital equipment	6	6	100	126	21	38,680	41,016	4,068	5,511
5065 Electronic parts and equipment	21	24	197	387	16	34,619	58,026	6,652	27,027
5074 Plumbing & hydronic heating supplies	6	9	40	62	7	32,100	31,419	1,471	1,964
5083 Farm and garden machinery	5	5	55	53	11	23,345	29,208	1,672	1,774
5084 Industrial machinery and equipment	7	7	35	36	5	30,514	49,111	1,344	1,541
5085 Industrial supplies	4	4	14	14	4	28,571	28,857	501	503
5091 Sporting & recreational goods	9	10	125	152	15	17,312	16,184	2,442	2,805
5094 Jewelry & precious stones	8	7	34	53	8	20,000	27,094	1,031	1,607
5099 Durable goods, nec	8	8	18	33	4	28,889	28,606	701	927
5113 Industrial & personal service paper	4	4	82	88	22	33,122	34,909	3,976	3,943
5120 Drugs, proprietaries, and sundries	9	10	351	439	44	20,581	21,339	7,894	10,410
5136 Men's and boys' clothing	4	-	6	-	-	21,333	-	613	-
5137 Women's and children's clothing	5	-	13	-	-	16,308	-	229	-
5142 Packaged frozen food	14	13	254	265	20	35,433	38,596	10,791	11,246
5143 Dairy products, exc. dried or canned	4	3	31	19	6	31,097	27,368	921	596
5146 Fish and seafoods	4	4	14	14	4	20,857	23,714	333	353
5147 Meats and meat products	5	4	14	22	6	23,429	15,273	478	600
5148 Fresh fruits and vegetables	23	23	486	392	17	20,856	33,347	14,287	14,511
5149 Groceries and related products, nec	24	26	367	377	15	25,166	24,265	9,214	10,522
5160 Chemicals and allied products	4	5	18	21	4	29,778	34,667	589	572
5170 Petroleum and petroleum products	7	7	62	31	4	22,323	37,548	1,739	1,421
5180 Beer, wine, and distilled beverages	7	7	361	346	49	22,648	26,116	8,802	9,131
5191 Farm supplies	12	11	105	89	8	23,848	30,202	3,158	2,909
5192 Books, periodicals, & newspapers	4	4	17	21	5	22,353	23,429	552	551
5193 Flowers & florists' supplies	21	22	236	282	13	23,492	17,702	5,713	5,868
5199 Nondurable goods, nec	15	15	75	78	5	13,547	19,077	1,384	1,977
52- Retail trade	1,518	1,490	18,360	18,418	12	12,938	13,559	255,689	267,825
5210 Lumber and other building materials	25	25	445	452	18	26,607	27,150	13,375	14,053
5230 Paint, glass, and wallpaper stores	13	17	53	61	4	20,906	19,541	1,139	1,413
5250 Hardware stores	14	10	248	236	24	11,855	12,119	3,305	3,009
5260 Retail nurseries and garden stores	4	8	18	35	4	10,000	12,114	199	528
5310 Department stores	8	7	1,132	1,072	153	9,226	11,179	11,654	12,491
5330 Variety stores	7	-	64	-	-	10,125	-	642	-
5390 Misc. general merchandise stores	9	9	53	283	31	9,736	17,527	2,447	5,230
5410 Grocery stores	100	97	2,223	2,327	24	19,496	19,147	44,922	47,250
5420 Meat and fish markets	12	10	67	72	7	14,388	13,778	913	1,273
5430 Fruit and vegetable markets	8	6	49	43	7	8,653	9,302	513	360
5440 Candy, nut, and confectionery stores	7	5	24	22	4	10,500	11,818	280	288
5460 Retail bakeries	30	24	383	203	8	15,561	12,552	6,262	2,682
5490 Miscellaneous food stores	15	18	172	136	8	8,930	10,176	1,464	1,533
5510 New and used car dealers	12	13	496	564	43	34,274	30,468	17,744	19,056
5520 Used car dealers	7	9	43	57	6	23,628	24,842	1,254	1,700
5530 Auto and home supply stores	34	35	234	254	7	20,410	21,433	4,545	5,134
5540 Gasoline service stations	65	67	479	481	7	14,113	14,037	7,099	7,202
5550 Boat dealers	8	6	21	21	4	13,524	17,143	275	321
5560 Recreational vehicle dealers	3	-	8	-	-	71,500	-	260	-
5570 Motorcycle dealers	5	-	25	-	-	20,000	-	575	-
5610 Men's & boys' clothing stores	9	10	58	55	6	13,310	15,636	850	851
5620 Women's clothing stores	47	41	324	250	6	8,704	8,976	3,056	2,451
5630 Women's accessory & specialty stores	13	10	63	54	5	8,254	9,185	567	508
5640 Children's and infants' wear stores	6	5	14	14	3	9,143	9,714	142	157
5650 Family clothing stores	22	19	204	188	10	9,863	11,511	2,047	2,081
5660 Shoe stores	35	35	187	202	6	11,679	12,139	2,317	2,471
5690 Misc. apparel & accessory stores	6	8	81	69	9	4,691	6,725	804	702
5712 Furniture stores	24	21	130	94	4	16,831	16,553	2,138	2,135
5713 Floor covering stores	16	18	88	101	6	15,955	18,574	1,532	2,035
5720 Household appliance stores	6	7	22	32	5	16,909	16,125	403	524
5731 Radio, TV, & electronic stores	10	10	57	55	6	18,035	19,782	1,011	1,149
5734 Computer and software stores	11	9	49	22	2	11,184	18,364	651	341
5735 Record & prerecorded tape stores	11	11	93	103	9	8,688	8,738	917	944
5736 Musical instrument stores	6	9	22	29	3	19,455	18,483	429	553
5812 Eating places	440	410	6,780	6,642	16	7,668	8,094	57,546	59,357
5813 Drinking places	49	43	286	247	6	7,916	8,243	2,540	2,277
5910 Drug stores and proprietary stores	33	34	768	718	21	18,755	20,184	15,097	14,142
5920 Liquor stores	31	35	162	164	5	15,086	14,634	2,091	2,202
5930 Used merchandise stores	18	21	176	226	11	11,318	10,372	2,195	2,507
5941 Sporting goods and bicycle shops	32	34	228	274	8	12,193	12,686	3,317	3,703

Continued on next page.

SANTA CRUZ–WATSONVILLE, CA PMSA - [continued]

Wholesale and Retail Trade USA	Establishments		Employment		Emp / Est	Pay / Employee		Annual Payroll ($ 000)	
	1994	1995	1994	1995	1995	1994	1995	1994	1995
5942 Book stores	21	17	405	415	24	9,096	9,619	4,008	4,203
5943 Stationery stores	4	5	78	70	14	8,410	13,029	683	975
5944 Jewelry stores	29	29	118	105	4	20,407	16,571	2,464	1,892
5945 Hobby, toy, and game shops	13	14	65	50	4	8,615	10,800	584	584
5946 Camera & photographic supply stores	-	3	-	18	6	-	18,444	-	321
5947 Gift, novelty, and souvenir shops	40	37	189	205	6	8,783	8,995	1,957	2,192
5948 Luggage and leather goods stores	-	3	-	9	3	-	10,667	-	49
5949 Sewing, needlework, and piece goods	9	8	78	81	10	7,846	7,951	616	732
5961 Catalog and mail-order houses	12	10	93	82	8	27,613	37,317	2,276	2,443
5962 Merchandising machine operators	6	7	25	39	6	7,360	7,487	222	268
5963 Direct selling establishments	16	13	68	33	3	8,765	15,758	563	568
5980 Fuel dealers	9	8	73	66	8	21,479	24,606	1,587	1,834
5992 Florists	27	27	112	120	4	8,000	8,233	965	1,062
5995 Optical goods stores	-	9	-	42	5	-	14,857	-	635
5999 Miscellaneous retail stores, nec	44	46	242	247	5	12,810	13,571	3,340	3,521

Source: County Business Patterns 1994/95, CBP-94/95, U.S. Department of Commerce, Washington DC, November 1997. The employment column represents mid-March employment in the year. Pay per employee is calculated by dividing 1st Quarter payroll, annualized, by mid-March employment. The column headed 'Emp / Est' shows 'employees per establishment'. A dash (-) means that data are unavailable or cannot be calculated. nec means not elsewhere classified. *Notes:* 1. 1994 data incomplete; unavailable or withheld. 2. 1995 data incomplete; unavailable or withheld. 3. 1994 and 1995 data incomplete; unavailable or withheld.

SANTA FE, NM MSA

Wholesale and Retail Trade USA	Establishments		Employment		Emp / Est	Pay / Employee		Annual Payroll ($ 000)	
	1994	1995	1994	1995	1995	1994	1995	1994	1995
50– Wholesale trade	195	203	1,565	1,648	8	22,459	24,794	39,370	44,226
5010 Motor vehicles, parts, and supplies[3]	8	6	55	50	8	19,418	24,320	1,189	1,364
5020 Furniture and homefurnishings[3]	5	5	18	76	15	18,222	21,316	381	1,898
5032 Brick, stone, & related materials[3]	7	8	25	32	4	10,080	14,625	608	554
5039 Construction materials, nec[3]	3	4	27	28	7	23,407	28,143	891	993
5044 Office equipment[3]	7	9	86	82	9	30,512	24,634	2,778	1,877
5045 Computers, peripherals, & software	-	10	-	25	3	-	92,320	-	1,788
5063 Electrical apparatus and equipment[3]	7	7	54	57	8	33,407	36,351	1,725	1,816
5065 Electronic parts and equipment	4	6	9	10	2	21,778	22,800	367	324
5070 Hardware, plumbing & heating equipment[3]	7	6	47	66	11	37,277	38,667	1,535	2,010
5087 Service establishment equipment[3]	5	5	25	24	5	20,640	23,500	520	586
5088 Transportation equipment & supplies[3]	3	3	7	5	2	20,000	15,200	165	165
5094 Jewelry & precious stones[3]	12	11	137	106	10	15,737	17,396	2,176	1,950
5110 Paper and paper products	8	8	72	18	2	16,000	16,667	1,522	399
5137 Women's and children's clothing[2]	-	3	-	5	2	-	10,400	-	215
5143 Dairy products, exc. dried or canned[3]	7	7	71	71	10	19,718	25,296	1,635	2,077
5148 Fresh fruits and vegetables[3]	3	3	14	15	5	20,000	34,133	503	543
5149 Groceries and related products, nec[3]	12	13	228	276	21	20,246	17,551	5,272	5,460
5171 Petroleum bulk stations & terminals[3]	3	3	31	27	9	26,581	31,111	963	1,083
5180 Beer, wine, and distilled beverages[3]	6	6	111	124	21	20,505	20,452	2,520	2,831
5191 Farm supplies[2]	5	4	87	59	15	4,690	17,288	636	1,075
5192 Books, periodicals, & newspapers[2]	-	5	-	31	6	-	15,613	-	488
5199 Nondurable goods, nec[1]	14	-	30	-	-	17,600	-	645	-
52– Retail trade	1,185	1,184	13,324	13,177	11	12,886	14,207	192,507	199,303
5210 Lumber and other building materials[3]	10	10	209	235	24	17,340	21,719	4,185	4,652
5230 Paint, glass, and wallpaper stores[3]	9	7	54	35	5	17,407	30,286	1,034	1,100
5250 Hardware stores	10	-	73	-	-	23,397	-	1,879	-
5270 Mobile home dealers[2]	-	5	-	7	1	-	21,714	-	293
5310 Department stores[3]	7	7	982	961	137	11,629	14,422	12,418	13,223
5410 Grocery stores	36	41	1,245	1,259	31	15,415	17,560	21,594	23,115
5460 Retail bakeries	6	7	68	73	10	9,235	11,945	768	710
5490 Miscellaneous food stores	8	8	39	27	3	12,205	13,037	407	257
5510 New and used car dealers[3]	12	10	508	472	47	26,992	29,559	15,043	16,167
5530 Auto and home supply stores	17	18	160	141	8	17,650	19,943	3,097	3,210
5540 Gasoline service stations	37	36	133	217	6	14,316	10,820	2,091	2,800
5570 Motorcycle dealers[3]	3	5	9	3	1	8,889	20,000	67	123
5610 Men's & boys' clothing stores[3]	7	6	25	41	7	17,280	15,902	494	670
5620 Women's clothing stores	61	56	368	314	6	12,359	13,032	4,667	4,277
5630 Women's accessory & specialty stores[3]	9	8	30	32	4	17,733	14,875	577	538
5640 Children's and infants' wear stores[3]	4	3	14	10	3	6,857	5,600	70	62
5650 Family clothing stores	26	24	253	236	10	11,921	12,203	3,105	2,896
5660 Shoe stores	34	31	132	150	5	12,848	14,213	1,980	2,191
5690 Misc. apparel & accessory stores[3]	18	18	56	62	3	13,500	10,968	796	775
5712 Furniture stores[3]	27	28	210	226	8	18,190	22,336	4,677	4,848
5719 Misc. homefurnishings stores	41	39	237	231	6	16,641	15,481	4,259	4,272

Continued on next page.

SANTA FE, NM MSA - [continued]

Wholesale and Retail Trade USA	Establishments		Employment		Emp / Est	Pay / Employee		Annual Payroll ($ 000)	
	1994	1995	1994	1995	1995	1994	1995	1994	1995
5720 Household appliance stores[3]	8	6	44	23	4	12,182	20,000	679	470
5731 Radio, TV, & electronic stores	13	14	74	63	5	17,297	16,444	1,102	933
5735 Record & prerecorded tape stores	6	7	97	110	16	10,021	9,745	926	1,046
5812 Eating places	265	252	5,209	4,929	20	9,298	10,512	55,379	55,144
5813 Drinking places[3]	14	12	156	130	11	8,359	9,538	1,448	1,158
5910 Drug stores and proprietary stores	16	16	224	202	13	17,161	20,020	4,140	4,021
5920 Liquor stores[3]	14	9	72	51	6	9,611	12,627	804	767
5930 Used merchandise stores[3]	25	24	118	110	5	20,441	18,655	2,599	1,988
5941 Sporting goods and bicycle shops	20	18	157	139	8	12,306	13,007	1,949	1,692
5942 Book stores	26	23	188	201	9	9,043	8,915	1,817	1,742
5944 Jewelry stores	53	49	254	269	5	14,630	15,688	4,542	4,950
5945 Hobby, toy, and game shops	12	11	60	85	8	13,000	9,976	1,223	973
5946 Camera & photographic supply stores[3]	3	3	21	24	8	22,476	22,833	453	551
5947 Gift, novelty, and souvenir shops	42	35	159	156	4	11,296	11,103	1,909	1,951
5948 Luggage and leather goods stores[3]	6	7	26	27	4	16,769	13,926	448	418
5949 Sewing, needlework, and piece goods	5	6	43	37	6	11,628	15,459	565	588
5961 Catalog and mail-order houses	13	13	48	52	4	17,500	17,923	887	914
5980 Fuel dealers[3]	9	8	55	47	6	29,527	31,915	1,159	1,054
5992 Florists	12	14	43	55	4	22,791	18,909	1,253	974
5995 Optical goods stores	13	15	68	58	4	12,765	14,345	803	895
5999 Miscellaneous retail stores, nec	130	142	487	488	3	17,503	20,066	10,916	10,911

Source: County Business Patterns 1994/95, CBP-94/95, U.S. Department of Commerce, Washington DC, November 1997. The employment column represents mid-March employment in the year. Pay per employee is calculated by dividing 1st Quarter payroll, annualized, by mid-March employment. The column headed 'Emp / Est' shows 'employees per establishment'. A dash (-) means that data are unavailable or cannot be calculated. nec means not elsewhere classified. *Notes:* 1. 1994 data incomplete; unavailable or withheld. 2. 1995 data incomplete; unavailable or withheld. 3. 1994 and 1995 data incomplete; unavailable or withheld.

SANTA ROSA, CA PMSA

Wholesale and Retail Trade USA	Establishments		Employment		Emp / Est	Pay / Employee		Annual Payroll ($ 000)	
	1994	1995	1994	1995	1995	1994	1995	1994	1995
50- Wholesale trade	698	687	7,268	7,212	10	27,487	29,271	214,102	224,945
5012 Automobiles and other vehicles	10	9	92	91	10	31,565	34,418	5,478	5,453
5013 Motor vehicle supplies and new parts	33	31	291	282	9	20,577	22,440	6,587	6,462
5014 Tires and tubes	7	6	78	50	8	30,103	26,640	2,716	1,481
5015 Motor vehicle parts, used	7	7	43	38	5	18,047	18,947	724	696
5021 Furniture	9	9	73	77	9	26,685	25,610	2,438	2,869
5023 Homefurnishings	12	10	94	38	4	22,128	27,474	2,190	872
5031 Lumber, plywood, and millwork	26	20	466	405	20	27,639	31,723	14,248	13,204
5032 Brick, stone, & related materials	6	8	50	65	8	25,600	25,538	1,427	2,040
5033 Roofing, siding, & insulation	4	3	47	30	10	30,383	30,533	1,494	1,163
5039 Construction materials, nec	8	8	61	119	15	24,197	27,395	1,840	3,246
5044 Office equipment	10	11	206	178	16	30,466	33,438	5,437	5,087
5045 Computers, peripherals, & software	19	20	163	125	6	42,356	55,232	6,568	6,321
5046 Commercial equipment, nec	8	8	61	60	8	23,934	27,867	1,828	1,922
5047 Medical and hospital equipment	11	8	98	83	10	28,408	27,084	2,532	2,358
5051 Metals service centers and offices	-	8	-	50	6	-	28,480	-	1,689
5063 Electrical apparatus and equipment	23	20	206	234	12	35,320	32,359	7,058	7,492
5064 Electrical appliances, TV & radios	3	4	16	23	6	23,000	26,609	412	591
5065 Electronic parts and equipment	24	20	232	242	12	37,828	40,628	9,856	11,810
5072 Hardware	-	10	-	44	4	-	29,273	-	1,414
5074 Plumbing & hydronic heating supplies	13	15	131	121	8	29,924	31,934	3,975	3,781
5075 Warm air heating & air conditioning	7	5	30	17	3	30,000	24,471	1,093	427
5082 Construction and mining machinery	7	7	99	92	13	38,707	35,348	3,597	3,893
5083 Farm and garden machinery	11	11	87	94	9	30,713	28,213	2,955	2,954
5084 Industrial machinery and equipment	36	37	203	235	6	31,330	33,498	7,492	8,824
5085 Industrial supplies	14	15	107	149	10	29,981	23,409	3,377	3,205
5087 Service establishment equipment	8	9	106	107	12	27,170	28,673	3,025	3,350
5088 Transportation equipment & supplies	4	3	13	8	3	63,077	71,000	630	584
5091 Sporting & recreational goods	7	7	64	62	9	39,000	33,226	2,279	2,631
5094 Jewelry & precious stones	8	8	149	123	15	18,738	22,016	2,689	2,613
5099 Durable goods, nec	15	14	52	59	4	19,000	19,322	1,320	1,489
5112 Stationery and office supplies	22	23	352	317	14	19,841	24,416	7,290	7,395
5120 Drugs, proprietaries, and sundries	8	8	69	62	8	15,536	16,903	1,228	1,018
5131 Piece goods & notions	5	4	38	41	10	25,053	24,976	977	1,000
5137 Women's and children's clothing	7	6	75	92	15	11,840	12,652	1,126	1,183
5139 Footwear	-	3	-	21	7	-	20,952	-	505
5142 Packaged frozen food	4	5	156	159	32	28,154	27,547	4,908	5,642
5143 Dairy products, exc. dried or canned	10	10	218	229	23	33,431	35,755	8,017	8,758
5144 Poultry and poultry products	7	5	65	56	11	20,923	23,214	1,482	1,419

Continued on next page.

SANTA ROSA, CA PMSA - [continued]

Wholesale and Retail Trade USA	Establishments		Employment		Emp / Est	Pay / Employee		Annual Payroll ($ 000)	
	1994	1995	1994	1995	1995	1994	1995	1994	1995
5147 Meats and meat products	5	5	123	130	26	25,789	26,154	3,251	3,247
5148 Fresh fruits and vegetables	-	6	-	16	3	-	16,250	-	294
5149 Groceries and related products, nec	47	45	662	639	14	27,456	27,919	19,264	19,543
5154 Livestock	4	4	21	26	7	5,905	3,538	137	117
5162 Plastics materials & basic shapes	-	4	-	34	9	-	23,647	-	1,009
5169 Chemicals & allied products, nec	-	10	-	23	2	-	83,304	-	1,326
5171 Petroleum bulk stations & terminals	10	9	145	133	15	24,690	27,639	3,806	3,473
5172 Petroleum products, nec	3	3	11	10	3	5,455	14,400	158	139
5180 Beer, wine, and distilled beverages	33	34	664	733	22	36,211	38,319	25,317	28,648
5191 Farm supplies	30	29	153	161	6	22,745	22,658	4,195	4,594
5192 Books, periodicals, & newspapers	9	8	75	90	11	16,107	19,822	1,236	1,664
5193 Flowers & florists' supplies	12	9	121	86	10	11,702	14,930	1,508	1,420
5194 Tobacco and tobacco products	3	-	42	-	-	22,000	-	931	-
5198 Paints, varnishes, and supplies	-	3	-	23	8	-	32,522	-	761
5199 Nondurable goods, nec	32	32	183	187	6	19,541	19,679	3,823	3,941
52 - Retail trade	2,601	2,624	31,391	31,703	12	13,993	14,720	478,281	504,328
5210 Lumber and other building materials	44	50	925	1,052	21	24,130	22,506	23,822	24,670
5230 Paint, glass, and wallpaper stores	32	26	154	124	5	21,714	20,742	3,385	2,854
5250 Hardware stores	34	24	380	265	11	17,495	15,049	7,806	4,435
5260 Retail nurseries and garden stores	32	36	131	151	4	11,878	12,159	2,022	2,166
5270 Mobile home dealers	4	4	17	14	4	27,529	29,714	508	443
5310 Department stores	13	13	2,388	2,336	180	12,432	13,082	31,977	31,979
5330 Variety stores	9	4	60	67	17	9,933	7,045	540	524
5390 Misc. general merchandise stores	13	16	493	511	32	17,785	20,689	9,668	11,016
5410 Grocery stores	193	187	4,211	4,327	23	19,180	20,131	84,585	89,924
5420 Meat and fish markets	10	11	63	64	6	7,302	7,188	512	503
5430 Fruit and vegetable markets	8	8	96	75	9	10,167	12,267	1,077	1,024
5440 Candy, nut, and confectionery stores	12	13	56	56	4	9,000	9,929	540	659
5450 Dairy products stores	8	7	32	26	4	4,125	4,462	150	151
5460 Retail bakeries	53	50	410	268	5	9,707	8,642	4,444	2,385
5490 Miscellaneous food stores	27	28	207	296	11	9,411	10,973	2,450	3,402
5510 New and used car dealers	36	37	1,540	1,625	44	30,953	31,801	55,228	61,529
5520 Used car dealers	23	23	84	91	4	21,238	20,703	1,921	2,240
5530 Auto and home supply stores	65	74	487	537	7	17,708	20,037	9,354	11,492
5540 Gasoline service stations	106	108	724	737	7	14,674	13,959	11,191	11,382
5550 Boat dealers	7	6	47	50	8	19,404	19,120	1,115	1,260
5560 Recreational vehicle dealers	9	9	89	96	11	22,966	23,958	2,242	2,366
5570 Motorcycle dealers	10	11	52	53	5	20,538	21,585	1,173	1,372
5610 Men's & boys' clothing stores	23	24	134	183	8	12,806	11,650	1,734	2,065
5620 Women's clothing stores	78	64	446	430	7	8,628	7,712	4,287	3,483
5630 Women's accessory & specialty stores	9	7	40	42	6	9,800	9,333	403	390
5640 Children's and infants' wear stores	8	7	50	50	7	6,080	6,720	334	322
5650 Family clothing stores	25	26	368	329	13	9,207	11,295	3,700	3,627
5660 Shoe stores	45	45	211	222	5	14,882	13,910	3,105	3,227
5690 Misc. apparel & accessory stores	13	14	55	67	5	8,873	10,090	650	872
5712 Furniture stores	72	72	395	461	6	17,104	19,358	8,531	9,905
5713 Floor covering stores	21	21	128	174	8	21,000	20,207	2,907	4,003
5714 Drapery and upholstery stores	3	-	12	-	-	10,000	-	119	-
5719 Misc. homefurnishings stores	41	-	253	-	-	11,842	-	3,209	-
5720 Household appliance stores	16	18	96	97	5	19,333	21,113	1,981	2,190
5731 Radio, TV, & electronic stores	32	35	310	337	10	20,619	21,234	6,747	7,335
5734 Computer and software stores	19	23	91	131	6	17,978	19,053	1,770	2,275
5735 Record & prerecorded tape stores	18	18	152	123	7	8,553	13,496	1,345	1,698
5736 Musical instrument stores	11	11	71	74	7	12,732	17,027	1,048	1,255
5812 Eating places	678	649	10,462	10,393	16	7,954	8,363	91,503	94,202
5813 Drinking places	75	67	471	438	7	9,316	9,689	4,519	4,378
5910 Drug stores and proprietary stores	49	48	1,179	1,142	24	19,478	20,070	23,440	22,977
5920 Liquor stores	33	30	215	252	8	13,730	18,063	3,281	4,532
5930 Used merchandise stores	34	30	218	218	7	11,284	11,780	2,757	2,879
5941 Sporting goods and bicycle shops	57	55	357	315	6	11,317	13,029	4,325	4,556
5942 Book stores	40	39	258	299	8	11,395	12,455	3,144	3,762
5943 Stationery stores	8	8	38	36	5	10,421	14,667	375	449
5944 Jewelry stores	44	43	187	171	4	18,310	18,082	3,508	3,303
5945 Hobby, toy, and game shops	27	27	179	176	7	8,760	8,136	1,673	1,567
5946 Camera & photographic supply stores	8	7	41	39	6	16,488	17,641	747	717
5947 Gift, novelty, and souvenir shops	71	69	346	318	5	8,694	7,686	3,287	2,561
5948 Luggage and leather goods stores	5	4	7	19	5	16,571	10,105	115	215
5949 Sewing, needlework, and piece goods	11	13	108	101	8	8,000	11,723	863	919
5961 Catalog and mail-order houses	24	20	382	366	18	15,277	16,863	6,204	6,372
5962 Merchandising machine operators	5	6	38	42	7	24,316	24,952	1,106	1,219
5963 Direct selling establishments	26	30	190	206	7	16,421	20,505	3,503	4,870

Continued on next page.

SANTA ROSA, CA PMSA - [continued]

Wholesale and Retail Trade USA	Establishments		Employment		Emp / Est	Pay / Employee		Annual Payroll ($ 000)	
	1994	1995	1994	1995	1995	1994	1995	1994	1995
5984 Liquefied petroleum gas dealers	13	-	103	-	-	27,845	-	2,992	-
5989 Fuel dealers, nec	3	-	6	-	-	4,667	-	28	-
5992 Florists	41	37	155	148	4	9,368	8,459	1,557	1,305
5994 News dealers and newsstands	-	3	-	32	11	-	14,000	-	449
5995 Optical goods stores	19	20	110	89	4	12,509	14,202	1,098	1,307
5999 Miscellaneous retail stores, nec	89	113	428	452	4	15,439	15,531	6,705	8,398

Source: County Business Patterns 1994/95, CBP-94/95, U.S. Department of Commerce, Washington DC, November 1997. The employment column represents mid-March employment in the year. Pay per employee is calculated by dividing 1st Quarter payroll, annualized, by mid-March employment. The column headed 'Emp / Est' shows 'employees per establishment'. A dash (-) means that data are unavailable or cannot be calculated. nec means not elsewhere classified. *Notes:* 1. 1994 data incomplete; unavailable or withheld. 2. 1995 data incomplete; unavailable or withheld. 3. 1994 and 1995 data incomplete; unavailable or withheld.

SARASOTA - BRADENTON, FL MSA

Wholesale and Retail Trade USA	Establishments		Employment		Emp / Est	Pay / Employee		Annual Payroll ($ 000)	
	1994	1995	1994	1995	1995	1994	1995	1994	1995
50 - Wholesale trade	826	831	5,743	5,742	7	25,688	25,376	154,161	145,789
5012 Automobiles and other vehicles	18	19	114	212	11	7,825	26,075	1,276	4,462
5013 Motor vehicle supplies and new parts	34	29	285	251	9	15,958	17,482	4,795	4,451
5015 Motor vehicle parts, used	8	9	33	8	1	12,242	14,500	463	140
5021 Furniture	16	16	82	69	4	34,878	27,188	2,485	1,820
5023 Homefurnishings	27	24	165	177	7	21,721	24,181	3,660	3,456
5031 Lumber, plywood, and millwork	14	17	221	242	14	26,226	24,959	5,614	6,242
5032 Brick, stone, & related materials	18	16	103	88	6	25,010	28,864	2,861	2,573
5033 Roofing, siding, & insulation	7	8	32	29	4	20,875	23,310	657	708
5039 Construction materials, nec	6	23	44	127	6	34,273	30,740	1,926	4,286
5044 Office equipment	13	14	126	139	10	27,365	26,014	3,621	3,669
5045 Computers, peripherals, & software	25	20	122	142	7	31,934	25,859	4,143	3,354
5046 Commercial equipment, nec	6	5	14	14	3	28,286	29,143	379	335
5047 Medical and hospital equipment	29	21	115	161	8	33,009	28,075	4,730	4,861
5048 Ophthalmic goods	8	9	83	107	12	32,048	28,336	2,664	2,887
5051 Metals service centers and offices	15	12	8	11	1	22,000	40,364	228	357
5063 Electrical apparatus and equipment	32	23	326	204	9	30,564	32,314	11,626	6,525
5064 Electrical appliances, TV & radios	8	8	66	59	7	17,636	17,966	1,363	1,174
5065 Electronic parts and equipment	23	26	92	101	4	26,217	26,772	2,794	3,114
5072 Hardware	17	17	97	106	6	21,814	18,830	2,148	2,105
5074 Plumbing & hydronic heating supplies	18	18	82	148	8	27,707	28,297	2,077	4,205
5075 Warm air heating & air conditioning	15	13	41	50	4	24,098	23,680	1,075	1,271
5082 Construction and mining machinery	5	4	20	23	6	25,200	30,609	641	701
5083 Farm and garden machinery	13	10	127	104	10	24,409	33,692	3,483	3,189
5084 Industrial machinery and equipment	40	40	168	220	6	22,643	27,800	4,698	5,451
5085 Industrial supplies	16	14	60	60	4	33,667	36,133	2,152	2,365
5087 Service establishment equipment	6	6	27	30	5	21,037	20,400	621	635
5088 Transportation equipment & supplies	13	12	141	128	11	23,121	29,813	3,389	3,387
5091 Sporting & recreational goods	18	18	104	128	7	19,846	20,875	2,374	2,460
5092 Toys and hobby goods and supplies	-	4	-	7	2	-	15,429	-	166
5093 Scrap and waste materials	11	13	17	51	4	25,882	21,098	473	1,097
5094 Jewelry & precious stones	9	10	46	61	6	13,391	11,934	812	757
5099 Durable goods, nec	20	19	108	151	8	23,519	22,225	2,853	3,974
5111 Printing and writing paper	-	4	-	3	1	-	17,333	-	82
5112 Stationery and office supplies	19	17	157	197	12	13,936	16,122	2,151	3,075
5113 Industrial & personal service paper	-	6	-	28	5	-	26,857	-	738
5120 Drugs, proprietaries, and sundries	12	11	38	45	4	16,737	26,667	885	1,153
5131 Piece goods & notions [3]	8	6	12	22	4	14,667	13,636	231	339
5136 Men's and boys' clothing	7	6	75	22	4	15,947	21,091	866	443
5137 Women's and children's clothing	8	10	23	25	3	21,565	24,960	703	783
5139 Footwear [2]	-	3	-	3	1	-	28,000	-	41
5142 Packaged frozen food	6	5	45	47	9	30,133	29,787	1,453	1,501
5145 Confectionery	-	4	-	11	3	-	15,273	-	120
5146 Fish and seafoods	-	6	-	26	4	-	14,462	-	574
5148 Fresh fruits and vegetables	17	15	107	91	6	25,084	25,407	3,830	2,876
5149 Groceries and related products, nec [1]	23	19	138	134	7	21,797	25,194	3,001	2,950
5159 Farm-product raw materials, nec [2]	-	3	-	18	6	-	23,111	-	401
5162 Plastics materials & basic shapes	8	8	25	22	3	38,400	44,909	912	870
5169 Chemicals & allied products, nec	19	21	58	61	3	22,276	27,869	1,535	2,040
5171 Petroleum bulk stations & terminals	12	10	115	100	10	24,139	26,520	3,055	2,712
5172 Petroleum products, nec [3]	6	6	23	25	4	16,000	18,240	387	508
5180 Beer, wine, and distilled beverages	6	7	165	174	25	32,800	33,885	5,926	5,927
5191 Farm supplies	16	13	131	155	12	38,962	32,877	4,927	4,885
5192 Books, periodicals, & newspapers	10	12	85	123	10	12,612	15,415	1,070	1,802

Continued on next page.

SARASOTA – BRADENTON, FL MSA - [continued]

Wholesale and Retail Trade USA	Establishments		Employment		Emp / Est	Pay / Employee		Annual Payroll ($ 000)	
	1994	1995	1994	1995	1995	1994	1995	1994	1995
5193 Flowers & florists' supplies	18	15	130	137	9	18,585	17,606	2,485	2,316
5198 Paints, varnishes, and supplies	11	11	246	58	5	15,154	20,414	2,517	1,292
5199 Nondurable goods, nec	27	31	119	139	4	17,008	17,583	2,189	2,597
52- Retail trade	3,621	3,588	49,602	52,224	15	12,719	13,453	648,424	688,685
5210 Lumber and other building materials	61	54	1,230	1,256	23	17,626	19,369	22,511	23,830
5230 Paint, glass, and wallpaper stores	45	39	148	141	4	20,865	21,333	3,212	3,028
5250 Hardware stores	31	21	238	173	8	10,521	11,792	2,552	1,971
5260 Retail nurseries and garden stores	31	32	192	198	6	15,104	15,434	2,897	3,216
5270 Mobile home dealers	12	14	43	47	3	26,884	22,298	1,381	991
5310 Department stores	27	27	3,752	3,901	144	11,856	13,012	45,899	50,919
5330 Variety stores	26	17	222	164	10	9,279	9,463	2,178	1,608
5390 Misc. general merchandise stores	14	20	560	512	26	11,529	14,508	6,351	6,620
5410 Grocery stores	196	193	7,786	8,213	43	11,561	11,907	89,461	96,294
5420 Meat and fish markets	22	19	82	82	4	11,268	13,171	956	1,097
5430 Fruit and vegetable markets	10	10	22	13	1	12,182	9,538	181	71
5440 Candy, nut, and confectionery stores	12	11	47	35	3	6,383	6,743	305	258
5460 Retail bakeries	18	20	114	65	3	8,561	7,385	808	464
5490 Miscellaneous food stores	27	28	185	183	7	12,195	12,437	2,209	2,327
5510 New and used car dealers	43	44	2,373	2,398	55	31,203	32,901	78,593	85,437
5520 Used car dealers	47	47	180	213	5	18,622	18,873	3,800	3,405
5530 Auto and home supply stores	76	76	514	545	7	18,272	18,503	10,110	10,711
5540 Gasoline service stations	183	174	1,236	1,165	7	12,113	12,786	15,964	14,545
5550 Boat dealers	34	32	261	306	10	20,812	22,118	5,934	7,099
5560 Recreational vehicle dealers	9	9	46	45	5	18,348	16,356	785	758
5570 Motorcycle dealers	10	8	88	82	10	19,455	22,537	1,865	1,890
5610 Men's & boys' clothing stores	38	34	222	229	7	10,991	10,900	2,624	2,502
5620 Women's clothing stores	153	143	1,048	938	7	9,935	9,437	9,879	8,515
5630 Women's accessory & specialty stores	24	23	107	93	4	9,196	10,409	1,017	944
5640 Children's and infants' wear stores	10	11	35	48	4	8,686	8,500	349	469
5650 Family clothing stores	67	65	1,186	1,133	17	11,521	12,621	14,675	13,961
5660 Shoe stores	85	82	428	429	5	11,271	11,543	4,789	4,670
5690 Misc. apparel & accessory stores	32	30	207	299	10	10,222	11,037	2,602	3,485
5712 Furniture stores	114	112	905	925	8	19,744	20,406	17,373	17,878
5713 Floor covering stores	57	53	347	375	7	19,977	21,621	7,190	7,933
5714 Drapery and upholstery stores	13	15	37	37	2	15,892	15,459	596	593
5719 Misc. homefurnishings stores	62	61	339	408	7	12,885	13,127	4,543	5,625
5720 Household appliance stores	27	31	118	113	4	18,271	20,885	2,124	2,305
5731 Radio, TV, & electronic stores	35	35	283	301	9	19,746	19,734	5,370	5,471
5734 Computer and software stores	20	24	46	50	2	12,957	17,680	710	1,080
5735 Record & prerecorded tape stores	19	19	116	106	6	10,345	10,264	1,162	1,060
5736 Musical instrument stores	11	14	38	46	3	21,684	22,087	874	1,044
5812 Eating places	707	633	15,777	15,556	25	9,420	10,106	139,729	141,109
5813 Drinking places	72	61	451	479	8	7,672	7,858	3,742	3,417
5910 Drug stores and proprietary stores	94	91	1,329	1,265	14	17,020	18,817	23,574	23,580
5920 Liquor stores	44	46	206	228	5	10,951	10,842	2,328	2,510
5930 Used merchandise stores	82	74	374	349	5	9,765	9,742	3,694	3,484
5941 Sporting goods and bicycle shops	66	62	281	299	5	14,562	15,064	4,567	4,824
5942 Book stores	38	36	211	244	7	8,777	9,607	1,991	2,236
5943 Stationery stores	12	10	43	74	7	8,930	12,595	354	827
5944 Jewelry stores	84	83	1,743	2,896	35	10,678	10,988	26,593	33,134
5945 Hobby, toy, and game shops	22	25	187	173	7	8,257	9,202	1,882	1,804
5946 Camera & photographic supply stores	9	8	74	90	11	21,784	18,711	1,644	1,549
5947 Gift, novelty, and souvenir shops	103	99	449	443	4	8,454	9,318	4,093	4,268
5948 Luggage and leather goods stores	6	5	32	19	4	9,375	9,474	306	182
5949 Sewing, needlework, and piece goods	15	-	66	-	-	8,121	-	564	-
5961 Catalog and mail-order houses	22	23	119	149	6	11,529	17,369	1,206	2,688
5962 Merchandising machine operators	13	15	109	132	9	20,771	20,758	2,659	2,749
5963 Direct selling establishments	31	33	118	102	3	15,153	18,392	1,990	1,840
5984 Liquefied petroleum gas dealers	7	7	60	64	9	22,600	18,750	1,267	1,229
5992 Florists	69	63	247	236	4	11,126	11,932	2,798	2,721
5995 Optical goods stores	44	46	205	209	5	14,185	15,923	2,858	2,903
5999 Miscellaneous retail stores, nec	152	161	597	690	4	13,032	14,638	8,586	10,665

Source: County Business Patterns 1994/95, CBP-94/95, U.S. Department of Commerce, Washington DC, November 1997. The employment column represents mid-March employment in the year. Pay per employee is calculated by dividing 1st Quarter payroll, annualized, by mid-March employment. The column headed 'Emp / Est' shows 'employees per establishment'. A dash (-) means that data are unavailable or cannot be calculated. nec means not elsewhere classified. *Notes:* 1. 1994 data incomplete; unavailable or withheld. 2. 1995 data incomplete; unavailable or withheld. 3. 1994 and 1995 data incomplete; unavailable or withheld.

SAVANNAH, GA MSA

Wholesale and Retail Trade USA	Establishments		Employment		Emp / Est	Pay / Employee		Annual Payroll ($ 000)	
	1994	1995	1994	1995	1995	1994	1995	1994	1995
50- Wholesale trade	476	466	4,963	4,929	11	27,249	28,099	140,728	143,489
5012 Automobiles and other vehicles [3]	7	7	92	137	20	27,130	24,117	2,630	3,382
5013 Motor vehicle supplies and new parts [2]	44	41	276	253	6	21,130	22,213	6,118	5,944
5014 Tires and tubes [3]	6	6	63	67	11	22,032	23,164	1,556	1,471
5015 Motor vehicle parts, used [3]	7	8	63	73	9	19,619	21,863	1,796	2,015
5021 Furniture [1]	4	-	19	-	-	20,632	-	611	-
5023 Homefurnishings [1]	4	-	34	-	-	31,294	-	993	-
5031 Lumber, plywood, and millwork [3]	14	14	136	120	9	27,500	23,067	3,919	2,991
5032 Brick, stone, & related materials [2]	-	7	-	32	5	-	29,750	-	1,008
5033 Roofing, siding, & insulation [3]	5	5	77	112	22	27,325	34,857	2,382	4,184
5039 Construction materials, nec [2]	-	7	-	114	16	-	26,877	-	3,359
5044 Office equipment [3]	12	11	139	157	14	22,532	23,465	3,505	3,926
5045 Computers, peripherals, & software [3]	12	12	169	160	13	47,811	50,375	7,143	6,068
5046 Commercial equipment, nec [3]	8	8	29	28	4	18,345	19,429	611	666
5047 Medical and hospital equipment [1]	7	-	43	-	-	35,256	-	1,553	-
5050 Metals and minerals, except petroleum [3]	11	11	197	178	16	32,690	35,685	7,084	7,180
5063 Electrical apparatus and equipment [3]	15	15	132	146	10	26,727	38,438	3,765	5,496
5064 Electrical appliances, TV & radios [3]	4	4	15	19	5	22,133	29,895	373	605
5065 Electronic parts and equipment [3]	13	12	129	131	11	28,620	28,794	3,986	4,019
5074 Plumbing & hydronic heating supplies [3]	13	14	115	126	9	25,043	29,524	3,234	3,814
5075 Warm air heating & air conditioning [3]	8	8	69	75	9	30,203	33,067	2,229	2,487
5082 Construction and mining machinery [3]	9	10	143	170	17	33,455	32,682	5,203	6,110
5084 Industrial machinery and equipment	30	31	193	188	6	56,891	36,149	8,950	7,416
5085 Industrial supplies [3]	18	18	176	186	10	27,364	30,108	5,298	5,505
5087 Service establishment equipment [3]	12	12	87	65	5	21,609	25,477	1,804	1,580
5088 Transportation equipment & supplies [2]	-	3	-	8	3	-	58,000	-	468
5093 Scrap and waste materials	13	11	128	101	9	19,250	20,634	3,087	2,259
5099 Durable goods, nec [3]	7	7	97	83	12	27,010	33,446	2,434	2,472
5113 Industrial & personal service paper [3]	5	4	94	88	22	29,745	27,955	2,951	2,605
5120 Drugs, proprietaries, and sundries [3]	5	5	159	118	24	39,472	31,051	6,897	4,775
5142 Packaged frozen food [3]	4	4	28	29	7	17,000	17,379	630	635
5143 Dairy products, exc. dried or canned [1]	5	-	32	-	-	20,625	-	621	-
5145 Confectionery [3]	3	3	61	61	20	27,475	24,721	1,449	1,569
5146 Fish and seafoods [3]	6	6	22	24	4	13,455	14,000	360	412
5147 Meats and meat products [3]	3	3	82	74	25	15,951	16,703	1,419	1,222
5149 Groceries and related products, nec [3]	7	8	242	258	32	20,446	19,938	5,258	5,428
5169 Chemicals & allied products, nec [2]	-	12	-	59	5	-	28,746	-	1,886
5171 Petroleum bulk stations & terminals [3]	15	12	106	103	9	34,340	39,922	4,036	4,534
5172 Petroleum products, nec [3]	6	5	32	30	6	26,750	29,467	871	821
5181 Beer and ale [3]	3	3	170	169	56	23,106	24,781	4,814	5,351
5182 Wine and distilled beverages [3]	5	6	116	123	21	28,379	28,228	3,390	3,397
5191 Farm supplies	11	-	12	-	-	27,667	-	436	-
5192 Books, periodicals, & newspapers [1]	3	-	16	-	-	20,250	-	423	-
5193 Flowers & florists' supplies [3]	4	3	38	30	10	17,789	19,600	755	555
5198 Paints, varnishes, and supplies [3]	5	4	27	20	5	23,556	25,800	603	479
5199 Nondurable goods, nec [3]	11	12	137	131	11	22,190	25,099	3,133	3,245
52- Retail trade	1,819	1,849	24,678	26,653	14	10,772	11,295	291,821	321,982
5210 Lumber and other building materials [2]	29	26	626	614	24	13,700	19,036	8,391	11,475
5230 Paint, glass, and wallpaper stores [1]	13	15	58	54	4	19,862	21,481	1,173	1,116
5250 Hardware stores	20	12	114	61	5	10,912	12,787	1,329	727
5260 Retail nurseries and garden stores [1]	16	20	37	61	3	11,243	13,967	477	936
5270 Mobile home dealers [3]	9	10	41	56	6	16,293	19,000	1,162	1,598
5310 Department stores [3]	14	15	2,431	2,311	154	10,083	11,818	25,866	27,425
5330 Variety stores	17	13	119	80	6	8,706	9,600	1,146	770
5390 Misc. general merchandise stores [3]	9	10	316	312	31	12,937	13,628	4,466	4,329
5410 Grocery stores [3]	142	150	3,078	3,744	25	9,418	8,536	31,459	33,584
5420 Meat and fish markets [3]	13	12	50	57	5	13,360	12,772	691	697
5440 Candy, nut, and confectionery stores [3]	7	6	78	64	11	6,205	10,563	779	1,042
5460 Retail bakeries [1]	10	-	131	-	-	6,595	-	960	-
5490 Miscellaneous food stores [2]	-	8	-	58	7	-	6,966	-	416
5510 New and used car dealers [3]	22	23	998	1,088	47	26,938	29,585	31,152	38,013
5520 Used car dealers	32	25	131	188	8	16,855	17,234	2,849	3,694
5530 Auto and home supply stores	40	49	302	391	8	19,894	20,113	6,400	8,218
5540 Gasoline service stations	113	107	726	730	7	10,584	12,592	8,185	9,362
5550 Boat dealers [3]	10	12	59	93	8	16,475	16,387	1,107	1,576
5570 Motorcycle dealers [2]	-	5	-	44	9	-	22,818	-	932
5610 Men's & boys' clothing stores [3]	24	26	209	211	8	8,000	7,943	1,798	1,777
5620 Women's clothing stores [3]	68	63	560	535	8	7,421	7,477	4,233	4,100
5630 Women's accessory & specialty stores [3]	14	13	75	82	6	8,000	8,585	655	729
5640 Children's and infants' wear stores [3]	11	12	115	108	9	8,243	7,963	1,022	1,041
5650 Family clothing stores [3]	18	15	334	317	21	9,006	10,032	3,494	3,361

Continued on next page.

SAVANNAH, GA MSA - [continued]

Wholesale and Retail Trade USA	Establishments		Employment		Emp / Est	Pay / Employee		Annual Payroll ($ 000)	
	1994	1995	1994	1995	1995	1994	1995	1994	1995
5660 Shoe stores [3]	52	45	302	317	7	10,464	10,599	3,428	3,089
5690 Misc. apparel & accessory stores [3]	15	14	91	75	5	7,868	9,387	859	797
5712 Furniture stores [3]	43	47	371	416	9	16,852	15,798	6,764	7,708
5713 Floor covering stores [3]	14	17	93	102	6	18,237	21,059	1,998	2,108
5719 Misc. homefurnishings stores [2]	-	26	-	144	6	-	11,750	-	1,827
5720 Household appliance stores [3]	12	11	72	53	5	17,111	17,736	1,184	1,000
5731 Radio, TV, & electronic stores [3]	21	21	163	260	12	16,687	13,538	3,758	3,412
5734 Computer and software stores [3]	7	8	17	20	3	9,882	17,600	272	386
5735 Record & prerecorded tape stores [3]	12	13	58	94	7	10,414	7,787	608	833
5736 Musical instrument stores [3]	4	4	78	76	19	18,103	20,158	1,463	1,555
5812 Eating places	393	376	8,500	8,903	24	7,712	7,812	70,017	72,271
5813 Drinking places [3]	38	34	244	241	7	7,836	8,996	2,147	2,525
5910 Drug stores and proprietary stores	43	45	482	511	11	16,365	16,869	8,441	9,524
5920 Liquor stores [3]	44	46	182	171	4	11,209	12,585	2,183	2,241
5930 Used merchandise stores [3]	47	47	162	204	4	12,864	15,804	2,851	3,251
5941 Sporting goods and bicycle shops [3]	20	22	74	75	3	14,486	15,627	1,350	1,278
5942 Book stores [3]	23	18	117	112	6	8,821	8,679	1,079	1,062
5943 Stationery stores [3]	4	3	13	12	4	7,692	7,667	103	88
5944 Jewelry stores [3]	37	39	272	294	8	18,309	16,844	4,360	4,930
5945 Hobby, toy, and game shops [3]	13	13	127	156	12	9,417	8,000	1,399	1,585
5946 Camera & photographic supply stores [3]	4	4	26	18	5	13,385	17,778	375	364
5947 Gift, novelty, and souvenir shops	54	59	361	328	6	6,150	10,927	2,384	3,338
5948 Luggage and leather goods stores [3]	5	6	25	30	5	12,320	11,200	348	373
5949 Sewing, needlework, and piece goods [3]	8	9	53	66	7	7,019	6,000	397	433
5963 Direct selling establishments [3]	14	17	55	105	6	21,891	15,695	1,219	1,686
5984 Liquefied petroleum gas dealers	8	9	18	22	2	22,444	21,091	375	424
5992 Florists	34	32	112	96	3	9,250	9,667	1,050	1,006
5995 Optical goods stores [3]	17	18	108	90	5	14,148	18,133	1,553	1,612
5999 Miscellaneous retail stores, nec [3]	39	37	143	157	4	12,084	12,764	1,974	2,344

Source: County Business Patterns 1994/95, CBP-94/95, U.S. Department of Commerce, Washington DC, November 1997. The employment column represents mid-March employment in the year. Pay per employee is calculated by dividing 1st Quarter payroll, annualized, by mid-March employment. The column headed 'Emp / Est' shows 'employees per establishment'. A dash (-) means that data are unavailable or cannot be calculated. nec means not elsewhere classified. *Notes:* 1. 1994 data incomplete; unavailable or withheld. 2. 1995 data incomplete; unavailable or withheld. 3. 1994 and 1995 data incomplete; unavailable or withheld.

SCRANTON - WILKES-BARRE - HAZLETON, PA MSA

Wholesale and Retail Trade USA	Establishments		Employment		Emp / Est	Pay / Employee		Annual Payroll ($ 000)	
	1994	1995	1994	1995	1995	1994	1995	1994	1995
50- Wholesale trade	-	942	-	12,487	13	-	22,996	-	305,295
5012 Automobiles and other vehicles [2]	-	22	-	173	8	-	24,717	-	4,509
5013 Motor vehicle supplies and new parts	-	69	-	1,153	17	-	21,141	-	25,138
5014 Tires and tubes [2]	-	11	-	171	16	-	16,538	-	2,973
5015 Motor vehicle parts, used [2]	-	22	-	149	7	-	18,604	-	3,553
5021 Furniture [2]	-	11	-	122	11	-	23,246	-	2,928
5023 Homefurnishings [2]	-	16	-	167	10	-	21,437	-	4,058
5031 Lumber, plywood, and millwork [2]	-	21	-	305	15	-	25,482	-	8,170
5032 Brick, stone, & related materials [2]	-	12	-	75	6	-	23,627	-	2,124
5033 Roofing, siding, & insulation [2]	-	5	-	98	20	-	26,041	-	3,651
5039 Construction materials, nec [2]	-	10	-	113	11	-	23,009	-	2,717
5044 Office equipment [2]	-	28	-	358	13	-	27,743	-	9,103
5045 Computers, peripherals, & software [2]	-	15	-	52	3	-	29,769	-	1,421
5046 Commercial equipment, nec [2]	-	13	-	53	4	-	18,189	-	1,000
5047 Medical and hospital equipment [2]	-	15	-	302	20	-	24,914	-	7,665
5049 Professional equipment, nec [2]	-	4	-	19	5	-	15,789	-	305
5051 Metals service centers and offices [2]	-	14	-	114	8	-	24,807	-	3,160
5052 Coal and other minerals and ores [2]	-	9	-	45	5	-	26,222	-	1,166
5063 Electrical apparatus and equipment [2]	-	27	-	319	12	-	29,467	-	9,522
5064 Electrical appliances, TV & radios [2]	-	6	-	9	2	-	20,444	-	224
5065 Electronic parts and equipment [2]	-	20	-	123	6	-	33,431	-	4,081
5072 Hardware [2]	-	15	-	251	17	-	25,052	-	7,466
5074 Plumbing & hydronic heating supplies	-	33	-	394	12	-	24,609	-	9,497
5082 Construction and mining machinery	-	18	-	345	19	-	31,745	-	11,151
5083 Farm and garden machinery [2]	-	10	-	21	2	-	8,762	-	276
5084 Industrial machinery and equipment	-	35	-	292	8	-	27,658	-	9,624
5085 Industrial supplies [2]	-	26	-	143	6	-	26,573	-	4,166
5087 Service establishment equipment [2]	-	17	-	139	8	-	20,518	-	2,791
5093 Scrap and waste materials	-	24	-	259	11	-	21,313	-	6,654
5099 Durable goods, nec [2]	-	11	-	12	1	-	18,333	-	252
5111 Printing and writing paper [2]	-	5	-	67	13	-	27,224	-	1,868

Continued on next page.

SCRANTON – WILKES-BARRE – HAZLETON, PA MSA - [continued]

Wholesale and Retail Trade USA	Establishments		Employment		Emp / Est	Pay / Employee		Annual Payroll ($ 000)	
	1994	1995	1994	1995	1995	1994	1995	1994	1995
5112 Stationery and office supplies [2]	-	17	-	176	10	-	18,841	-	3,273
5113 Industrial & personal service paper	-	10	-	32	3	-	29,000	-	1,173
5120 Drugs, proprietaries, and sundries [2]	-	12	-	162	14	-	32,099	-	5,806
5131 Piece goods & notions [2]	-	7	-	74	11	-	11,730	-	958
5136 Men's and boys' clothing [2]	-	4	-	21	5	-	19,048	-	405
5141 Groceries, general line [2]	-	12	-	394	33	-	26,701	-	10,771
5143 Dairy products, exc. dried or canned [2]	-	6	-	34	6	-	19,882	-	778
5145 Confectionery [2]	-	14	-	349	25	-	18,544	-	6,013
5146 Fish and seafoods [2]	-	6	-	24	4	-	11,000	-	238
5147 Meats and meat products [2]	-	12	-	183	15	-	17,290	-	3,647
5148 Fresh fruits and vegetables [2]	-	17	-	204	12	-	25,196	-	5,659
5149 Groceries and related products, nec [2]	-	35	-	532	15	-	24,383	-	14,294
5154 Livestock [2]	-	3	-	8	3	-	10,500	-	97
5160 Chemicals and allied products [2]	-	15	-	187	12	-	27,936	-	5,405
5171 Petroleum bulk stations & terminals	-	24	-	321	13	-	15,564	-	5,061
5172 Petroleum products, nec [2]	-	5	-	76	15	-	16,368	-	1,882
5181 Beer and ale [2]	-	27	-	141	5	-	20,113	-	3,218
5191 Farm supplies [2]	-	10	-	121	12	-	18,413	-	2,160
5192 Books, periodicals, & newspapers [2]	-	10	-	251	25	-	16,940	-	4,513
5193 Flowers & florists' supplies	-	16	-	132	8	-	15,636	-	2,447
5198 Paints, varnishes, and supplies [2]	-	10	-	24	2	-	9,167	-	219
5199 Nondurable goods, nec [2]	-	39	-	230	6	-	15,913	-	4,741
52 – Retail trade	-	4,145	-	53,374	13	-	10,988	-	619,189
5210 Lumber and other building materials	-	79	-	975	12	-	19,696	-	19,992
5230 Paint, glass, and wallpaper stores [2]	-	23	-	76	3	-	19,158	-	1,577
5250 Hardware stores	-	27	-	174	6	-	12,966	-	2,364
5260 Retail nurseries and garden stores	-	36	-	133	4	-	10,977	-	1,857
5270 Mobile home dealers [2]	-	12	-	90	8	-	14,667	-	1,810
5310 Department stores [2]	-	43	-	6,219	145	-	11,110	-	72,764
5330 Variety stores	-	39	-	539	14	-	6,701	-	3,598
5390 Misc. general merchandise stores	-	17	-	530	31	-	12,521	-	6,000
5410 Grocery stores	-	307	-	8,647	28	-	9,817	-	91,727
5420 Meat and fish markets [2]	-	18	-	80	4	-	10,550	-	868
5440 Candy, nut, and confectionery stores [2]	-	26	-	92	4	-	6,261	-	560
5450 Dairy products stores [2]	-	12	-	51	4	-	8,000	-	488
5460 Retail bakeries	-	69	-	689	10	-	7,112	-	5,136
5490 Miscellaneous food stores	-	24	-	106	4	-	12,981	-	1,402
5510 New and used car dealers	-	88	-	2,248	26	-	23,237	-	56,157
5520 Used car dealers [2]	-	81	-	289	4	-	16,277	-	4,915
5530 Auto and home supply stores	-	101	-	837	8	-	18,055	-	15,515
5540 Gasoline service stations	-	255	-	1,678	7	-	10,055	-	17,978
5550 Boat dealers [2]	-	6	-	12	2	-	12,333	-	213
5560 Recreational vehicle dealers [2]	-	10	-	18	2	-	13,111	-	339
5570 Motorcycle dealers [2]	-	9	-	28	3	-	13,143	-	454
5610 Men's & boys' clothing stores [2]	-	33	-	155	5	-	11,510	-	1,714
5620 Women's clothing stores	-	111	-	925	8	-	7,892	-	7,283
5630 Women's accessory & specialty stores [2]	-	21	-	85	4	-	8,847	-	768
5640 Children's and infants' wear stores [2]	-	15	-	103	7	-	10,330	-	1,002
5650 Family clothing stores	-	34	-	510	15	-	9,435	-	4,911
5660 Shoe stores	-	103	-	512	5	-	10,898	-	5,132
5690 Misc. apparel & accessory stores	-	20	-	84	4	-	10,762	-	1,054
5712 Furniture stores	-	76	-	628	8	-	16,777	-	11,354
5713 Floor covering stores	-	43	-	205	5	-	17,990	-	3,863
5714 Drapery and upholstery stores [2]	-	7	-	3	-	-	13,333	-	38
5719 Misc. homefurnishings stores	-	20	-	75	4	-	10,400	-	756
5720 Household appliance stores	-	20	-	76	4	-	12,000	-	1,035
5731 Radio, TV, & electronic stores [2]	-	35	-	120	3	-	16,700	-	1,989
5734 Computer and software stores [2]	-	13	-	64	5	-	17,875	-	1,057
5735 Record & prerecorded tape stores [2]	-	22	-	132	6	-	9,364	-	1,315
5736 Musical instrument stores [2]	-	6	-	23	4	-	10,783	-	229
5812 Eating places	-	931	-	14,925	16	-	7,336	-	115,853
5813 Drinking places	-	198	-	673	3	-	7,031	-	5,169
5910 Drug stores and proprietary stores	-	180	-	1,951	11	-	14,327	-	28,611
5920 Liquor stores	-	87	-	393	5	-	15,145	-	6,008
5930 Used merchandise stores	-	27	-	163	6	-	8,613	-	1,654
5941 Sporting goods and bicycle shops [2]	-	50	-	236	5	-	11,627	-	2,734
5942 Book stores	-	28	-	188	7	-	10,362	-	2,068
5943 Stationery stores [2]	-	9	-	49	5	-	15,673	-	751
5944 Jewelry stores	-	62	-	352	6	-	12,580	-	4,452
5945 Hobby, toy, and game shops [2]	-	33	-	221	7	-	8,833	-	2,280
5947 Gift, novelty, and souvenir shops	-	66	-	460	7	-	6,626	-	3,246

Continued on next page.

SCRANTON – WILKES-BARRE – HAZLETON, PA MSA - [continued]

Wholesale and Retail Trade USA	Establishments		Employment		Emp / Est	Pay / Employee		Annual Payroll ($ 000)	
	1994	1995	1994	1995	1995	1994	1995	1994	1995
5949 Sewing, needlework, and piece goods [2]	-	8	-	57	7	-	6,596	-	386
5961 Catalog and mail-order houses [2]	-	7	-	24	3	-	21,333	-	544
5962 Merchandising machine operators [2]	-	19	-	204	11	-	18,078	-	3,885
5963 Direct selling establishments [2]	-	38	-	200	5	-	15,500	-	3,285
5983 Fuel oil dealers	-	51	-	232	5	-	18,655	-	4,216
5984 Liquefied petroleum gas dealers	-	16	-	96	6	-	21,958	-	2,067
5989 Fuel dealers, nec [2]	-	6	-	14	2	-	13,714	-	208
5992 Florists	-	72	-	287	4	-	10,383	-	3,077
5993 Tobacco stores and stands [2]	-	7	-	17	2	-	7,765	-	181
5994 News dealers and newsstands [2]	-	9	-	16	2	-	8,500	-	198
5995 Optical goods stores	-	39	-	188	5	-	15,766	-	3,409
5999 Miscellaneous retail stores, nec	-	113	-	471	4	-	15,032	-	8,374

Source: County Business Patterns 1994/95, CBP-94/95, U.S. Department of Commerce, Washington DC, November 1997. The employment column represents mid-March employment in the year. Pay per employee is calculated by dividing 1st Quarter payroll, annualized, by mid-March employment. The column headed 'Emp / Est' shows 'employees per establishment'. A dash (-) means that data are unavailable or cannot be calculated. nec means not elsewhere classified. *Notes:* 1. 1994 data incomplete; unavailable or withheld. 2. 1995 data incomplete; unavailable or withheld. 3. 1994 and 1995 data incomplete; unavailable or withheld.

SEATTLE – BELLEVUE – EVERETT, WA PMSA

Wholesale and Retail Trade USA	Establishments		Employment		Emp / Est	Pay / Employee		Annual Payroll ($ 000)	
	1994	1995	1994	1995	1995	1994	1995	1994	1995
50 – Wholesale trade	-	6,311	-	77,154	12	-	35,722	-	2,849,589
5012 Automobiles and other vehicles [2]	-	86	-	1,410	16	-	31,376	-	44,158
5013 Motor vehicle supplies and new parts	-	206	-	2,545	12	-	29,389	-	78,712
5014 Tires and tubes [2]	-	21	-	241	11	-	34,075	-	7,697
5015 Motor vehicle parts, used	-	49	-	501	10	-	21,493	-	11,227
5021 Furniture [2]	-	118	-	1,249	11	-	29,915	-	40,048
5023 Homefurnishings [2]	-	171	-	1,847	11	-	30,805	-	57,413
5031 Lumber, plywood, and millwork	-	189	-	2,037	11	-	37,133	-	78,235
5032 Brick, stone, & related materials [2]	-	47	-	462	10	-	31,810	-	15,185
5033 Roofing, siding, & insulation [2]	-	43	-	447	10	-	33,441	-	16,501
5039 Construction materials, nec [2]	-	132	-	1,312	10	-	32,439	-	45,430
5043 Photographic equipment & supplies [2]	-	14	-	101	7	-	31,010	-	3,119
5044 Office equipment [2]	-	90	-	1,671	19	-	43,624	-	73,457
5045 Computers, peripherals, & software	-	322	-	3,956	12	-	51,902	-	209,570
5046 Commercial equipment, nec	-	88	-	740	8	-	31,519	-	24,413
5047 Medical and hospital equipment [2]	-	141	-	1,514	11	-	42,502	-	65,210
5048 Ophthalmic goods [2]	-	20	-	198	10	-	29,091	-	5,522
5049 Professional equipment, nec [2]	-	37	-	330	9	-	35,988	-	12,333
5051 Metals service centers and offices [2]	-	119	-	1,547	13	-	35,462	-	55,498
5063 Electrical apparatus and equipment [2]	-	215	-	2,416	11	-	38,270	-	90,095
5064 Electrical appliances, TV & radios [2]	-	51	-	756	15	-	35,381	-	28,583
5065 Electronic parts and equipment [2]	-	278	-	3,100	11	-	39,568	-	127,712
5072 Hardware	-	121	-	1,175	10	-	31,037	-	40,399
5074 Plumbing & hydronic heating supplies [2]	-	93	-	1,114	12	-	29,709	-	34,635
5075 Warm air heating & air conditioning [2]	-	54	-	610	11	-	40,905	-	25,321
5078 Refrigeration equipment and supplies [2]	-	20	-	197	10	-	50,741	-	8,444
5082 Construction and mining machinery [2]	-	59	-	730	12	-	43,348	-	31,984
5083 Farm and garden machinery [2]	-	24	-	196	8	-	28,878	-	5,831
5084 Industrial machinery and equipment	-	340	-	3,030	9	-	36,910	-	120,718
5085 Industrial supplies	-	181	-	1,855	10	-	37,229	-	71,243
5087 Service establishment equipment [2]	-	75	-	722	10	-	28,903	-	22,139
5088 Transportation equipment & supplies [2]	-	170	-	1,754	10	-	36,775	-	69,972
5091 Sporting & recreational goods	-	118	-	1,326	11	-	30,833	-	44,409
5092 Toys and hobby goods and supplies [2]	-	46	-	1,204	26	-	33,834	-	47,042
5093 Scrap and waste materials	-	83	-	1,046	13	-	24,600	-	27,905
5094 Jewelry & precious stones [2]	-	74	-	482	7	-	27,967	-	13,986
5099 Durable goods, nec [2]	-	175	-	1,175	7	-	41,283	-	47,711
5111 Printing and writing paper [2]	-	27	-	366	14	-	43,760	-	14,846
5112 Stationery and office supplies	-	104	-	1,687	16	-	26,696	-	45,646
5113 Industrial & personal service paper [2]	-	70	-	897	13	-	36,905	-	34,872
5120 Drugs, proprietaries, and sundries [2]	-	77	-	1,811	24	-	42,893	-	80,353
5131 Piece goods & notions [2]	-	53	-	271	5	-	44,133	-	12,276
5136 Men's and boys' clothing [2]	-	87	-	1,467	17	-	35,970	-	48,502
5137 Women's and children's clothing	-	57	-	378	7	-	22,148	-	9,079
5139 Footwear [2]	-	27	-	265	10	-	35,411	-	10,150
5141 Groceries, general line [2]	-	81	-	3,565	44	-	36,784	-	134,525
5142 Packaged frozen food [2]	-	70	-	624	9	-	43,224	-	29,137
5143 Dairy products, exc. dried or canned [2]	-	37	-	596	16	-	29,785	-	19,079

Continued on next page.

SEATTLE - BELLEVUE - EVERETT, WA PMSA - [continued]

Wholesale and Retail Trade USA	Establishments		Employment		Emp / Est	Pay / Employee		Annual Payroll ($ 000)	
	1994	1995	1994	1995	1995	1994	1995	1994	1995
5144 Poultry and poultry products [2]	-	11	-	240	22	-	31,267	-	6,877
5145 Confectionery [2]	-	27	-	405	15	-	26,262	-	11,114
5146 Fish and seafoods	-	122	-	1,762	14	-	39,473	-	69,889
5147 Meats and meat products [2]	-	45	-	498	11	-	30,900	-	17,194
5148 Fresh fruits and vegetables [2]	-	51	-	965	19	-	29,256	-	33,355
5149 Groceries and related products, nec [2]	-	209	-	3,405	16	-	30,978	-	106,408
5153 Grain and field beans [2]	-	13	-	121	9	-	27,174	-	3,833
5159 Farm-product raw materials, nec [2]	-	8	-	155	19	-	23,613	-	3,088
5162 Plastics materials & basic shapes [2]	-	36	-	290	8	-	38,138	-	11,068
5169 Chemicals & allied products, nec [2]	-	81	-	730	9	-	38,493	-	29,700
5171 Petroleum bulk stations & terminals [2]	-	43	-	639	15	-	40,163	-	27,146
5172 Petroleum products, nec	-	16	-	65	4	-	40,677	-	2,898
5181 Beer and ale [2]	-	15	-	954	64	-	32,369	-	32,552
5182 Wine and distilled beverages [2]	-	28	-	596	21	-	44,940	-	26,244
5191 Farm supplies	-	64	-	576	9	-	27,708	-	16,585
5192 Books, periodicals, & newspapers [2]	-	56	-	1,129	20	-	29,562	-	36,243
5193 Flowers & florists' supplies [2]	-	52	-	704	14	-	23,602	-	17,448
5198 Paints, varnishes, and supplies [2]	-	64	-	420	7	-	27,067	-	13,682
5199 Nondurable goods, nec	-	192	-	1,292	7	-	24,217	-	34,794
52 - Retail trade	-	14,116	-	201,192	14	-	16,302	-	3,398,276
5210 Lumber and other building materials	-	160	-	3,371	21	-	21,635	-	83,806
5230 Paint, glass, and wallpaper stores	-	69	-	384	6	-	21,823	-	8,951
5250 Hardware stores	-	91	-	1,666	18	-	15,959	-	25,215
5260 Retail nurseries and garden stores	-	96	-	967	10	-	18,225	-	20,026
5270 Mobile home dealers	-	20	-	146	7	-	27,699	-	4,374
5310 Department stores [2]	-	60	-	11,951	199	-	15,578	-	199,638
5330 Variety stores	-	39	-	259	7	-	9,776	-	2,721
5390 Misc. general merchandise stores	-	66	-	2,433	37	-	21,111	-	56,930
5410 Grocery stores	-	958	-	23,291	24	-	18,086	-	418,032
5420 Meat and fish markets	-	49	-	263	5	-	23,757	-	8,743
5430 Fruit and vegetable markets [2]	-	34	-	134	4	-	13,552	-	2,314
5440 Candy, nut, and confectionery stores [2]	-	42	-	312	7	-	10,462	-	3,725
5450 Dairy products stores [2]	-	20	-	102	5	-	7,922	-	748
5460 Retail bakeries	-	196	-	1,401	7	-	10,335	-	16,086
5490 Miscellaneous food stores	-	172	-	1,232	7	-	10,114	-	14,523
5510 New and used car dealers	-	162	-	8,018	49	-	34,403	-	298,421
5520 Used car dealers	-	126	-	770	6	-	24,945	-	22,417
5530 Auto and home supply stores	-	369	-	2,878	8	-	22,164	-	64,423
5540 Gasoline service stations	-	518	-	4,701	9	-	13,247	-	64,371
5550 Boat dealers	-	87	-	501	6	-	27,042	-	14,032
5560 Recreational vehicle dealers [2]	-	33	-	558	17	-	23,412	-	15,753
5570 Motorcycle dealers [2]	-	30	-	306	10	-	21,516	-	8,821
5590 Automotive dealers, nec [2]	-	8	-	36	5	-	34,444	-	1,344
5610 Men's & boys' clothing stores	-	97	-	1,016	10	-	14,449	-	13,833
5620 Women's clothing stores	-	268	-	1,921	7	-	9,980	-	19,834
5630 Women's accessory & specialty stores [2]	-	46	-	226	5	-	10,655	-	2,373
5640 Children's and infants' wear stores [2]	-	33	-	329	10	-	8,717	-	2,782
5650 Family clothing stores	-	155	-	7,955	51	-	14,499	-	116,006
5660 Shoe stores	-	186	-	972	5	-	13,704	-	14,050
5690 Misc. apparel & accessory stores [2]	-	80	-	364	5	-	10,890	-	4,813
5712 Furniture stores	-	303	-	2,298	8	-	22,698	-	50,288
5713 Floor covering stores	-	139	-	645	5	-	24,521	-	16,430
5714 Drapery and upholstery stores [2]	-	16	-	76	5	-	21,211	-	1,558
5719 Misc. homefurnishings stores [2]	-	222	-	1,641	7	-	15,569	-	26,961
5720 Household appliance stores	-	98	-	565	6	-	19,207	-	11,684
5731 Radio, TV, & electronic stores	-	147	-	1,679	11	-	22,339	-	37,006
5734 Computer and software stores	-	134	-	1,213	9	-	23,014	-	29,289
5735 Record & prerecorded tape stores	-	90	-	819	9	-	11,951	-	10,927
5736 Musical instrument stores	-	66	-	422	6	-	17,270	-	7,795
5812 Eating places	-	3,742	-	67,154	18	-	9,907	-	697,922
5813 Drinking places	-	449	-	3,233	7	-	9,726	-	32,041
5910 Drug stores and proprietary stores	-	322	-	5,260	16	-	17,963	-	96,117
5920 Liquor stores	-	120	-	549	5	-	19,497	-	10,987
5930 Used merchandise stores	-	298	-	1,868	6	-	13,411	-	26,413
5941 Sporting goods and bicycle shops	-	290	-	2,711	9	-	13,574	-	37,975
5942 Book stores	-	193	-	1,654	9	-	12,699	-	21,053
5943 Stationery stores	-	49	-	314	6	-	15,720	-	5,505
5944 Jewelry stores	-	204	-	1,280	6	-	21,513	-	26,893
5945 Hobby, toy, and game shops	-	138	-	1,167	8	-	10,108	-	14,643
5946 Camera & photographic supply stores	-	50	-	286	6	-	19,273	-	5,676
5947 Gift, novelty, and souvenir shops	-	358	-	1,953	5	-	10,355	-	21,985

Continued on next page.

SEATTLE – BELLEVUE – EVERETT, WA PMSA - [continued]

Wholesale and Retail Trade USA	Establishments		Employment		Emp / Est	Pay / Employee		Annual Payroll ($ 000)	
	1994	1995	1994	1995	1995	1994	1995	1994	1995
5948 Luggage and leather goods stores [2]	-	19	-	173	9	-	13,503	-	2,126
5949 Sewing, needlework, and piece goods	-	94	-	937	10	-	9,336	-	8,848
5961 Catalog and mail-order houses	-	92	-	1,723	19	-	18,595	-	35,532
5962 Merchandising machine operators [2]	-	41	-	349	9	-	21,238	-	7,395
5963 Direct selling establishments	-	213	-	2,153	10	-	16,529	-	38,859
5983 Fuel oil dealers [2]	-	27	-	849	31	-	37,263	-	31,007
5984 Liquefied petroleum gas dealers	-	14	-	183	13	-	34,142	-	6,627
5992 Florists	-	217	-	1,338	6	-	10,912	-	15,114
5993 Tobacco stores and stands [2]	-	15	-	38	3	-	14,526	-	617
5994 News dealers and newsstands	-	12	-	122	10	-	12,426	-	1,655
5995 Optical goods stores	-	137	-	708	5	-	21,090	-	15,814
5999 Miscellaneous retail stores, nec	-	507	-	2,622	5	-	15,120	-	45,795

Source: County Business Patterns 1994/95, CBP-94/95, U.S. Department of Commerce, Washington DC, November 1997. The employment column represents mid-March employment in the year. Pay per employee is calculated by dividing 1st Quarter payroll, annualized, by mid-March employment. The column headed 'Emp / Est' shows 'employees per establishment'. A dash (-) means that data are unavailable or cannot be calculated. nec means not elsewhere classified. *Notes:* 1. 1994 data incomplete; unavailable or withheld. 2. 1995 data incomplete; unavailable or withheld. 3. 1994 and 1995 data incomplete; unavailable or withheld.

SHARON, PA MSA

Wholesale and Retail Trade USA	Establishments		Employment		Emp / Est	Pay / Employee		Annual Payroll ($ 000)	
	1994	1995	1994	1995	1995	1994	1995	1994	1995
50 – Wholesale trade	-	161	-	1,947	12	-	23,043	-	46,652
5012 Automobiles and other vehicles	-	3	-	7	2	-	18,286	-	138
5013 Motor vehicle supplies and new parts	-	12	-	173	14	-	21,780	-	3,180
5031 Lumber, plywood, and millwork	-	7	-	30	4	-	15,333	-	544
5032 Brick, stone, & related materials	-	3	-	12	4	-	43,333	-	450
5039 Construction materials, nec	-	4	-	83	21	-	20,627	-	2,029
5040 Professional & commercial equipment	-	7	-	25	4	-	40,480	-	657
5050 Metals and minerals, except petroleum	-	14	-	187	13	-	33,283	-	5,844
5063 Electrical apparatus and equipment	-	7	-	256	37	-	26,656	-	6,874
5065 Electronic parts and equipment	-	3	-	11	4	-	18,545	-	197
5070 Hardware, plumbing & heating equipment	-	6	-	67	11	-	25,134	-	2,143
5083 Farm and garden machinery	-	7	-	115	16	-	14,922	-	2,188
5084 Industrial machinery and equipment	-	5	-	55	11	-	27,345	-	1,773
5085 Industrial supplies	-	5	-	49	10	-	19,755	-	1,001
5099 Durable goods, nec	-	7	-	117	17	-	15,795	-	2,450
5110 Paper and paper products	-	4	-	70	18	-	14,743	-	1,058
5130 Apparel, piece goods, and notions	-	3	-	58	19	-	10,828	-	715
5149 Groceries and related products, nec	-	6	-	51	9	-	19,216	-	1,104
5169 Chemicals & allied products, nec	-	5	-	137	27	-	35,766	-	5,373
5170 Petroleum and petroleum products	-	6	-	42	7	-	16,952	-	737
5181 Beer and ale	-	8	-	44	6	-	16,727	-	915
5191 Farm supplies	-	8	-	39	5	-	10,564	-	473
52 – Retail trade	-	785	-	10,328	13	-	10,717	-	118,220
5210 Lumber and other building materials	-	14	-	261	19	-	16,920	-	4,275
5250 Hardware stores	-	8	-	92	12	-	12,478	-	1,138
5260 Retail nurseries and garden stores	-	8	-	137	17	-	15,504	-	2,063
5310 Department stores	-	9	-	1,199	133	-	11,186	-	13,546
5330 Variety stores	-	7	-	62	9	-	8,323	-	574
5390 Misc. general merchandise stores	-	6	-	89	15	-	10,921	-	1,041
5410 Grocery stores	-	49	-	1,257	26	-	10,861	-	14,751
5420 Meat and fish markets	-	7	-	28	4	-	9,143	-	276
5460 Retail bakeries	-	6	-	35	6	-	7,086	-	315
5510 New and used car dealers	-	24	-	544	23	-	26,360	-	15,620
5520 Used car dealers	-	4	-	24	6	-	15,333	-	365
5530 Auto and home supply stores	-	20	-	149	7	-	13,477	-	2,398
5540 Gasoline service stations	-	49	-	297	6	-	9,172	-	2,935
5550 Boat dealers	-	3	-	9	3	-	15,111	-	193
5610 Men's & boys' clothing stores	-	20	-	205	10	-	7,259	-	1,551
5620 Women's clothing stores	-	30	-	299	10	-	8,669	-	2,584
5630 Women's accessory & specialty stores	-	3	-	16	5	-	10,250	-	216
5650 Family clothing stores	-	11	-	136	12	-	10,147	-	1,682
5660 Shoe stores	-	18	-	282	16	-	9,390	-	2,752
5712 Furniture stores	-	12	-	143	12	-	16,643	-	2,394
5713 Floor covering stores	-	8	-	25	3	-	9,600	-	306
5719 Misc. homefurnishings stores	-	13	-	100	8	-	9,080	-	1,062
5720 Household appliance stores	-	4	-	14	4	-	13,143	-	191
5731 Radio, TV, & electronic stores	-	14	-	116	8	-	18,034	-	2,101
5812 Eating places	-	172	-	3,331	19	-	6,636	-	24,096

Continued on next page.

SHARON, PA MSA - [continued]

Wholesale and Retail Trade USA	Establishments		Employment		Emp / Est	Pay / Employee		Annual Payroll ($ 000)	
	1994	1995	1994	1995	1995	1994	1995	1994	1995
5813 Drinking places	-	49	-	158	3	-	6,278	-	1,006
5910 Drug stores and proprietary stores	-	31	-	309	10	-	14,058	-	4,583
5920 Liquor stores	-	14	-	41	3	-	19,317	-	784
5930 Used merchandise stores	-	9	-	53	6	-	6,566	-	478
5941 Sporting goods and bicycle shops	-	8	-	24	3	-	13,667	-	340
5944 Jewelry stores	-	13	-	64	5	-	14,875	-	921
5945 Hobby, toy, and game shops	-	4	-	27	7	-	5,778	-	193
5947 Gift, novelty, and souvenir shops	-	17	-	94	6	-	5,319	-	565
5949 Sewing, needlework, and piece goods	-	3	-	23	8	-	7,304	-	187
5963 Direct selling establishments	-	6	-	12	2	-	5,333	-	108
5983 Fuel oil dealers	-	4	-	28	7	-	21,857	-	673
5992 Florists	-	8	-	30	4	-	6,800	-	211
5995 Optical goods stores	-	7	-	22	3	-	15,273	-	400
5999 Miscellaneous retail stores, nec	-	22	-	132	6	-	19,364	-	2,350

Source: County Business Patterns 1994/95, CBP-94/95, U.S. Department of Commerce, Washington DC, November 1997. The employment column represents mid-March employment in the year. Pay per employee is calculated by dividing 1st Quarter payroll, annualized, by mid-March employment. The column headed 'Emp / Est' shows 'employees per establishment'. A dash (-) means that data are unavailable or cannot be calculated. nec means not elsewhere classified. *Notes:* 1. 1994 data incomplete; unavailable or withheld. 2. 1995 data incomplete; unavailable or withheld. 3. 1994 and 1995 data incomplete; unavailable or withheld.

SHEBOYGAN, WI MSA

Wholesale and Retail Trade USA	Establishments		Employment		Emp / Est	Pay / Employee		Annual Payroll ($ 000)	
	1994	1995	1994	1995	1995	1994	1995	1994	1995
50- Wholesale trade	-	168	-	2,479	15	-	26,401	-	73,057
5013 Motor vehicle supplies and new parts	-	9	-	82	9	-	21,171	-	1,767
5021 Furniture	-	3	-	12	4	-	24,333	-	345
5030 Lumber and construction materials	-	8	-	164	21	-	30,220	-	5,717
5044 Office equipment	-	4	-	26	7	-	19,385	-	514
5045 Computers, peripherals, & software	-	5	-	61	12	-	26,230	-	1,439
5050 Metals and minerals, except petroleum	-	7	-	70	10	-	27,200	-	1,850
5060 Electrical goods	-	4	-	68	17	-	25,353	-	1,918
5074 Plumbing & hydronic heating supplies	-	3	-	76	25	-	28,368	-	2,468
5083 Farm and garden machinery	-	7	-	55	8	-	18,327	-	1,124
5084 Industrial machinery and equipment	-	11	-	53	5	-	29,962	-	1,642
5099 Durable goods, nec	-	4	-	16	4	-	10,000	-	238
5110 Paper and paper products	-	9	-	94	10	-	21,149	-	2,102
5149 Groceries and related products, nec	-	6	-	117	20	-	28,171	-	3,491
5160 Chemicals and allied products	-	7	-	171	24	-	32,023	-	5,746
5171 Petroleum bulk stations & terminals	-	3	-	67	22	-	25,313	-	1,880
5191 Farm supplies	-	7	-	74	11	-	26,270	-	1,971
5199 Nondurable goods, nec	-	8	-	92	12	-	21,174	-	1,994
52- Retail trade	-	568	-	8,192	14	-	10,688	-	94,658
5210 Lumber and other building materials	-	6	-	195	33	-	18,585	-	3,879
5250 Hardware stores	-	9	-	91	10	-	9,890	-	857
5260 Retail nurseries and garden stores	-	5	-	65	13	-	11,815	-	953
5310 Department stores	-	9	-	1,091	121	-	10,676	-	12,184
5410 Grocery stores	-	34	-	1,432	42	-	8,919	-	14,263
5420 Meat and fish markets	-	5	-	37	7	-	14,162	-	439
5460 Retail bakeries	-	10	-	70	7	-	8,343	-	637
5510 New and used car dealers	-	19	-	572	30	-	25,476	-	15,097
5520 Used car dealers	-	12	-	64	5	-	19,188	-	1,631
5530 Auto and home supply stores	-	6	-	68	11	-	14,765	-	1,132
5540 Gasoline service stations	-	47	-	403	9	-	11,027	-	5,258
5620 Women's clothing stores	-	16	-	122	8	-	7,148	-	904
5660 Shoe stores	-	13	-	50	4	-	11,040	-	625
5713 Floor covering stores	-	8	-	37	5	-	25,838	-	1,062
5720 Household appliance stores	-	8	-	85	11	-	14,541	-	1,358
5731 Radio, TV, & electronic stores	-	6	-	17	3	-	16,235	-	284
5735 Record & prerecorded tape stores	-	3	-	18	6	-	6,222	-	132
5812 Eating places	-	114	-	2,200	19	-	6,358	-	14,887
5813 Drinking places	-	44	-	266	6	-	5,639	-	1,596
5910 Drug stores and proprietary stores	-	19	-	277	15	-	14,874	-	4,348
5920 Liquor stores	-	8	-	60	8	-	8,200	-	510
5930 Used merchandise stores	-	4	-	33	8	-	10,182	-	343
5941 Sporting goods and bicycle shops	-	10	-	40	4	-	9,600	-	463
5942 Book stores	-	6	-	44	7	-	9,000	-	446
5944 Jewelry stores	-	10	-	44	4	-	16,909	-	722
5947 Gift, novelty, and souvenir shops	-	6	-	34	6	-	6,941	-	253
5960 Nonstore retailers	-	8	-	96	12	-	18,125	-	1,866

Continued on next page.

SHEBOYGAN, WI MSA - [continued]

Wholesale and Retail Trade USA	Establishments		Employment		Emp / Est	Pay / Employee		Annual Payroll ($ 000)	
	1994	1995	1994	1995	1995	1994	1995	1994	1995
5980 Fuel dealers	-	3	-	21	7	-	22,286	-	402
5995 Optical goods stores	-	10	-	54	5	-	18,519	-	991
5999 Miscellaneous retail stores, nec	-	18	-	44	2	-	8,818	-	423

Source: County Business Patterns 1994/95, CBP-94/95, U.S. Department of Commerce, Washington DC, November 1997. The employment column represents mid-March employment in the year. Pay per employee is calculated by dividing 1st Quarter payroll, annualized, by mid-March employment. The column headed 'Emp / Est' shows 'employees per establishment'. A dash (-) means that data are unavailable or cannot be calculated. nec means not elsewhere classified. *Notes:* 1. 1994 data incomplete; unavailable or withheld. 2. 1995 data incomplete; unavailable or withheld. 3. 1994 and 1995 data incomplete; unavailable or withheld.

SHERMAN – DENISON, TX MSA

Wholesale and Retail Trade USA	Establishments		Employment		Emp / Est	Pay / Employee		Annual Payroll ($ 000)	
	1994	1995	1994	1995	1995	1994	1995	1994	1995
50 – Wholesale trade	-	159	-	1,047	7	-	23,790	-	27,759
5013 Motor vehicle supplies and new parts	-	15	-	65	4	-	19,200	-	1,550
5030 Lumber and construction materials	-	7	-	29	4	-	16,966	-	674
5045 Computers, peripherals, & software	-	4	-	17	4	-	20,941	-	371
5063 Electrical apparatus and equipment	-	9	-	57	6	-	20,491	-	1,268
5065 Electronic parts and equipment	-	3	-	9	3	-	22,222	-	269
5074 Plumbing & hydronic heating supplies	-	4	-	37	9	-	30,595	-	1,072
5075 Warm air heating & air conditioning	-	3	-	11	4	-	28,000	-	305
5083 Farm and garden machinery	-	7	-	57	8	-	33,123	-	2,337
5084 Industrial machinery and equipment	-	7	-	44	6	-	20,182	-	1,093
5085 Industrial supplies	-	6	-	43	7	-	25,860	-	1,134
5091 Sporting & recreational goods	-	5	-	11	2	-	11,273	-	194
5099 Durable goods, nec	-	6	-	22	4	-	15,455	-	572
5112 Stationery and office supplies	-	3	-	19	6	-	16,842	-	345
5149 Groceries and related products, nec	-	6	-	157	26	-	22,803	-	3,954
5150 Farm-product raw materials	-	5	-	24	5	-	17,667	-	461
5181 Beer and ale	-	4	-	53	13	-	34,189	-	1,944
5190 Misc., nondurable goods	-	16	-	80	5	-	15,600	-	1,447
52 – Retail trade	-	608	-	8,202	13	-	12,666	-	113,583
5210 Lumber and other building materials	-	17	-	252	15	-	17,778	-	5,844
5230 Paint, glass, and wallpaper stores	-	6	-	31	5	-	22,194	-	751
5310 Department stores	-	7	-	1,124	161	-	13,313	-	15,911
5410 Grocery stores	-	55	-	1,240	23	-	12,023	-	15,509
5460 Retail bakeries	-	11	-	40	4	-	7,800	-	348
5510 New and used car dealers	-	14	-	586	42	-	25,836	-	17,378
5520 Used car dealers	-	8	-	43	5	-	13,767	-	590
5530 Auto and home supply stores	-	19	-	91	5	-	16,352	-	1,589
5540 Gasoline service stations	-	45	-	388	9	-	11,237	-	4,841
5550 Boat dealers	-	4	-	16	4	-	14,750	-	223
5620 Women's clothing stores	-	14	-	91	7	-	7,516	-	689
5650 Family clothing stores	-	5	-	60	12	-	9,467	-	612
5660 Shoe stores	-	9	-	51	6	-	9,804	-	480
5712 Furniture stores	-	12	-	99	8	-	18,020	-	2,208
5713 Floor covering stores	-	9	-	28	3	-	18,286	-	603
5719 Misc. homefurnishings stores	-	4	-	40	10	-	15,800	-	710
5731 Radio, TV, & electronic stores	-	12	-	79	7	-	16,203	-	1,349
5735 Record & prerecorded tape stores	-	4	-	41	10	-	9,951	-	390
5812 Eating places	-	123	-	2,352	19	-	8,009	-	20,922
5813 Drinking places	-	7	-	57	8	-	7,509	-	417
5910 Drug stores and proprietary stores	-	31	-	268	9	-	15,642	-	4,400
5920 Liquor stores	-	13	-	72	6	-	10,444	-	813
5930 Used merchandise stores	-	18	-	125	7	-	11,424	-	1,463
5941 Sporting goods and bicycle shops	-	4	-	6	2	-	2,000	-	35
5942 Book stores	-	6	-	30	5	-	7,867	-	253
5944 Jewelry stores	-	10	-	31	3	-	13,419	-	470
5947 Gift, novelty, and souvenir shops	-	5	-	24	5	-	7,000	-	165
5961 Catalog and mail-order houses	-	3	-	3	1	-	8,000	-	39
5992 Florists	-	4	-	14	4	-	11,429	-	158
5995 Optical goods stores	-	7	-	28	4	-	16,143	-	442
5999 Miscellaneous retail stores, nec	-	19	-	57	3	-	13,474	-	967

Source: County Business Patterns 1994/95, CBP-94/95, U.S. Department of Commerce, Washington DC, November 1997. The employment column represents mid-March employment in the year. Pay per employee is calculated by dividing 1st Quarter payroll, annualized, by mid-March employment. The column headed 'Emp / Est' shows 'employees per establishment'. A dash (-) means that data are unavailable or cannot be calculated. nec means not elsewhere classified. *Notes:* 1. 1994 data incomplete; unavailable or withheld. 2. 1995 data incomplete; unavailable or withheld. 3. 1994 and 1995 data incomplete; unavailable or withheld.

SHREVEPORT – BOSSIER CITY, LA MSA

Wholesale and Retail Trade USA	Establishments		Employment		Emp / Est	Pay / Employee		Annual Payroll ($ 000)	
	1994	1995	1994	1995	1995	1994	1995	1994	1995
50 – Wholesale trade	730	724	8,412	8,790	12	25,062	26,214	227,442	241,066
5012 Automobiles and other vehicles [3]	12	15	115	135	9	27,061	26,904	3,207	3,664
5013 Motor vehicle supplies and new parts	42	37	320	314	8	19,888	20,268	6,571	6,909
5014 Tires and tubes [3]	7	10	54	60	6	21,926	22,067	1,273	1,591
5015 Motor vehicle parts, used	15	15	64	64	4	16,750	18,313	1,153	1,107
5023 Homefurnishings	-	13	-	119	9	-	23,261	-	3,872
5031 Lumber, plywood, and millwork	13	12	185	146	12	22,205	21,397	4,426	3,464
5032 Brick, stone, & related materials [3]	6	5	29	26	5	21,379	20,462	636	641
5033 Roofing, siding, & insulation [1]	6	-	35	-	-	21,600	-	951	-
5039 Construction materials, nec [3]	8	10	55	160	16	22,545	28,450	1,463	4,512
5044 Office equipment	24	22	237	218	10	29,992	32,881	6,892	6,596
5045 Computers, peripherals, & software [1]	18	20	142	162	8	40,366	47,333	5,508	6,433
5046 Commercial equipment, nec [3]	6	7	99	139	20	17,091	16,489	2,162	2,662
5047 Medical and hospital equipment [3]	22	16	231	176	11	29,004	29,136	6,937	5,323
5051 Metals service centers and offices [3]	16	16	263	281	18	23,985	24,228	6,602	7,019
5063 Electrical apparatus and equipment [2]	32	30	331	304	10	30,417	31,934	10,836	10,267
5064 Electrical appliances, TV & radios [3]	6	5	51	42	8	18,039	22,286	1,035	1,043
5065 Electronic parts and equipment [3]	14	16	69	84	5	27,304	28,095	1,959	2,323
5072 Hardware [3]	14	14	149	138	10	21,852	25,942	3,428	3,571
5074 Plumbing & hydronic heating supplies	15	15	77	10	1	23,636	13,600	1,958	129
5075 Warm air heating & air conditioning [3]	15	14	132	122	9	30,606	39,803	5,169	5,753
5078 Refrigeration equipment and supplies [1]	3	-	14	-	-	21,429	-	319	-
5082 Construction and mining machinery [3]	7	8	125	135	17	28,448	29,956	3,852	4,522
5083 Farm and garden machinery	6	8	21	31	4	26,286	18,452	572	580
5084 Industrial machinery and equipment	89	91	734	816	9	25,248	26,005	21,791	24,542
5085 Industrial supplies	40	38	395	409	11	27,818	29,359	11,028	12,395
5087 Service establishment equipment [1]	14	16	95	86	5	23,368	23,674	2,105	1,846
5091 Sporting & recreational goods	-	9	-	50	6	-	15,120	-	834
5093 Scrap and waste materials [1]	10	9	49	50	6	22,531	23,120	1,221	2,207
5099 Durable goods, nec [3]	10	10	30	23	2	15,333	38,435	461	805
5111 Printing and writing paper [3]	4	4	58	60	15	31,172	37,533	1,549	2,086
5112 Stationery and office supplies	14	14	191	180	13	20,670	24,911	4,278	4,474
5113 Industrial & personal service paper	6	6	36	35	6	31,778	31,314	1,120	1,215
5120 Drugs, proprietaries, and sundries [1]	10	-	457	-	-	27,519	-	13,507	-
5131 Piece goods & notions [3]	4	5	15	12	2	12,000	15,333	182	189
5141 Groceries, general line [1]	6	-	120	-	-	25,167	-	2,725	-
5142 Packaged frozen food [2]	-	6	-	176	29	-	24,500	-	5,092
5147 Meats and meat products [3]	4	4	108	117	29	15,074	14,393	1,726	1,687
5149 Groceries and related products, nec	15	16	155	314	20	28,181	33,618	4,530	10,781
5150 Farm-product raw materials	6	6	4	4	1	33,000	44,000	194	196
5160 Chemicals and allied products	24	24	154	145	6	32,000	35,641	4,775	5,577
5171 Petroleum bulk stations & terminals [3]	20	20	295	318	16	22,319	21,761	7,382	7,780
5172 Petroleum products, nec	12	-	109	-	-	24,183	-	2,647	-
5180 Beer, wine, and distilled beverages [3]	7	7	270	281	40	25,511	27,260	8,037	8,303
5191 Farm supplies	18	17	80	79	5	21,850	22,886	1,985	1,980
5193 Flowers & florists' supplies [2]	7	5	19	24	5	23,158	22,500	504	613
5198 Paints, varnishes, and supplies [3]	6	7	29	39	6	21,103	19,487	608	806
5199 Nondurable goods, nec [3]	13	14	87	73	5	18,943	16,767	2,058	1,818
52 – Retail trade	2,121	2,079	28,432	28,229	14	11,243	12,337	350,850	364,496
5210 Lumber and other building materials	30	24	708	598	25	16,983	18,448	12,643	11,499
5230 Paint, glass, and wallpaper stores	17	17	18	74	4	13,778	17,730	281	1,447
5250 Hardware stores	25	16	121	36	2	12,926	12,222	1,886	416
5260 Retail nurseries and garden stores	22	21	123	152	7	9,886	10,395	1,419	1,863
5270 Mobile home dealers	-	7	-	40	6	-	29,800	-	2,586
5310 Department stores [3]	20	19	2,732	2,695	142	11,092	13,127	33,120	35,366
5330 Variety stores	26	16	94	82	5	8,723	8,049	925	752
5390 Misc. general merchandise stores	23	23	545	522	23	10,686	12,199	6,319	6,074
5410 Grocery stores	230	225	3,649	3,412	15	10,590	11,742	40,948	42,346
5420 Meat and fish markets	10	-	40	-	-	11,700	-	487	-
5440 Candy, nut, and confectionery stores [3]	6	4	27	24	6	4,741	5,667	131	119
5460 Retail bakeries	14	13	135	100	8	10,785	8,440	1,567	900
5490 Miscellaneous food stores [3]	6	6	37	37	6	10,270	10,595	384	389
5510 New and used car dealers	30	31	1,667	1,814	59	25,636	28,695	50,443	58,676
5520 Used car dealers	28	27	119	90	3	10,555	12,400	1,252	1,147
5530 Auto and home supply stores	68	67	547	516	8	15,547	18,194	9,620	10,100
5540 Gasoline service stations	167	160	1,319	1,240	8	10,062	11,326	14,521	14,727
5550 Boat dealers [2]	-	8	-	42	5	-	18,952	-	768
5560 Recreational vehicle dealers	-	5	-	41	8	-	19,512	-	831
5570 Motorcycle dealers [3]	7	7	66	75	11	10,848	17,813	929	1,201
5610 Men's & boys' clothing stores	20	19	126	119	6	11,111	11,563	1,433	1,382
5620 Women's clothing stores	72	66	601	535	8	8,386	8,135	5,382	4,244

Continued on next page.

SHREVEPORT–BOSSIER CITY, LA MSA - [continued]

Wholesale and Retail Trade USA	Establishments		Employment		Emp / Est	Pay / Employee		Annual Payroll ($ 000)	
	1994	1995	1994	1995	1995	1994	1995	1994	1995
5630 Women's accessory & specialty stores [3]	9	10	32	67	7	10,000	12,060	356	766
5640 Children's and infants' wear stores	6	7	12	10	1	10,667	12,000	134	124
5650 Family clothing stores	29	30	442	395	13	9,385	10,724	4,340	5,303
5660 Shoe stores	57	53	328	269	5	10,183	11,703	3,237	3,021
5690 Misc. apparel & accessory stores [3]	10	9	44	56	6	10,091	9,643	626	692
5712 Furniture stores	51	51	459	512	10	19,120	22,453	9,226	10,015
5713 Floor covering stores	19	19	54	57	3	11,852	19,649	644	1,058
5714 Drapery and upholstery stores [3]	6	8	36	33	4	9,444	10,303	356	361
5719 Misc. homefurnishings stores [1]	20	20	118	77	4	7,729	11,688	981	808
5720 Household appliance stores [3]	14	14	35	40	3	9,829	9,000	409	290
5731 Radio, TV, & electronic stores	27	25	88	95	4	33,409	21,011	3,233	1,435
5734 Computer and software stores [3]	7	8	57	65	8	14,246	16,615	935	867
5735 Record & prerecorded tape stores [1]	12	12	53	93	8	8,000	8,086	495	681
5736 Musical instrument stores [3]	4	4	40	35	9	12,600	13,829	508	507
5812 Eating places	404	374	9,124	8,777	23	7,236	7,430	71,622	70,425
5813 Drinking places	40	32	183	187	6	7,301	6,588	1,422	1,350
5910 Drug stores and proprietary stores	73	73	698	830	11	16,550	17,012	12,165	14,267
5920 Liquor stores	47	42	225	233	6	11,609	11,948	2,849	2,846
5930 Used merchandise stores	32	29	210	217	7	9,810	10,212	2,391	2,250
5941 Sporting goods and bicycle shops	19	15	132	148	10	11,242	10,622	1,600	1,633
5942 Book stores [3]	17	19	91	136	7	9,055	8,676	882	1,213
5944 Jewelry stores	43	45	171	176	4	15,415	15,682	2,637	2,808
5945 Hobby, toy, and game shops [3]	14	15	148	168	11	8,459	8,095	1,425	1,756
5947 Gift, novelty, and souvenir shops	37	38	196	198	5	7,857	8,788	1,730	2,050
5949 Sewing, needlework, and piece goods [2]	8	6	72	39	7	7,278	9,949	396	389
5963 Direct selling establishments [3]	19	18	238	229	13	16,739	16,175	4,024	3,893
5992 Florists	45	44	133	139	3	9,083	9,151	1,245	1,267
5993 Tobacco stores and stands [3]	6	10	5	20	2	11,200	8,600	57	218
5995 Optical goods stores	26	27	138	149	6	14,638	14,738	2,164	2,290
5999 Miscellaneous retail stores, nec	54	62	196	256	4	12,245	14,891	2,952	3,440

Source: County Business Patterns 1994/95, CBP-94/95, U.S. Department of Commerce, Washington DC, November 1997. The employment column represents mid-March employment in the year. Pay per employee is calculated by dividing 1st Quarter payroll, annualized, by mid-March employment. The column headed 'Emp / Est' shows 'employees per establishment'. A dash (-) means that data are unavailable or cannot be calculated. nec means not elsewhere classified. *Notes:* 1. 1994 data incomplete; unavailable or withheld. 2. 1995 data incomplete; unavailable or withheld. 3. 1994 and 1995 data incomplete; unavailable or withheld.

SIOUX CITY MSA (IA PART)

Wholesale and Retail Trade USA	Establishments		Employment		Emp / Est	Pay / Employee		Annual Payroll ($ 000)	
	1994	1995	1994	1995	1995	1994	1995	1994	1995
50– Wholesale trade	273	264	3,050	3,251	12	27,845	28,576	90,021	94,391
5012 Automobiles and other vehicles	6	7	180	223	32	23,756	29,220	5,238	6,762
5013 Motor vehicle supplies and new parts	17	15	212	234	16	18,547	19,641	4,212	4,611
5021 Furniture	3	-	55	-	-	23,200	-	2,139	-
5039 Construction materials, nec	3	-	38	-	-	17,263	-	940	-
5044 Office equipment	7	6	116	89	15	21,517	25,034	2,678	2,439
5045 Computers, peripherals, & software	6	6	99	106	18	20,202	31,208	2,079	3,087
5046 Commercial equipment, nec	4	-	20	-	-	24,400	-	519	-
5049 Professional equipment, nec	3	3	30	33	11	27,067	23,394	893	987
5051 Metals service centers and offices	-	4	-	72	18	-	22,111	-	3,792
5063 Electrical apparatus and equipment	9	9	91	86	10	35,121	39,674	3,454	3,333
5072 Hardware	4	-	40	-	-	26,000	-	1,368	-
5074 Plumbing & hydronic heating supplies	9	9	94	103	11	22,255	27,573	2,440	2,810
5075 Warm air heating & air conditioning	5	-	12	-	-	20,667	-	238	-
5082 Construction and mining machinery	4	5	33	37	7	28,121	29,838	1,190	1,273
5083 Farm and garden machinery	7	7	47	43	6	21,702	21,953	995	1,047
5084 Industrial machinery and equipment	12	10	78	82	8	22,667	25,610	1,962	2,484
5085 Industrial supplies	8	8	66	78	10	27,939	26,256	2,041	2,171
5087 Service establishment equipment	6	5	16	22	4	17,750	16,000	316	517
5093 Scrap and waste materials	8	9	102	126	14	18,902	20,032	2,450	2,747
5112 Stationery and office supplies	7	7	76	99	14	20,316	20,848	1,574	2,426
5148 Fresh fruits and vegetables	3	3	66	71	24	20,909	20,394	2,023	1,749
5149 Groceries and related products, nec	5	4	55	52	13	15,127	18,000	1,025	1,114
5153 Grain and field beans	9	8	115	121	15	20,835	22,612	2,879	2,958
5154 Livestock	14	-	58	-	-	18,138	-	993	-
5160 Chemicals and allied products	7	9	36	40	4	23,222	24,600	989	1,110
5171 Petroleum bulk stations & terminals	5	-	36	-	-	24,333	-	939	-
5172 Petroleum products, nec	7	-	43	-	-	31,628	-	1,435	-
5180 Beer, wine, and distilled beverages	4	5	87	110	22	20,138	20,982	2,038	2,314
5191 Farm supplies	18	21	133	184	9	29,594	35,739	3,431	5,917

Continued on next page.

SIOUX CITY MSA (IA PART) - [continued]

Wholesale and Retail Trade USA	Establishments		Employment		Emp / Est	Pay / Employee		Annual Payroll ($ 000)	
	1994	1995	1994	1995	1995	1994	1995	1994	1995
5192 Books, periodicals, & newspapers	-	4	-	3	1	-	4,000	-	12
52- Retail trade	716	717	10,756	10,727	15	9,909	10,950	118,356	125,083
5210 Lumber and other building materials	14	17	369	426	25	15,545	16,291	7,184	7,570
5250 Hardware stores	14	11	99	77	7	8,848	9,610	971	806
5260 Retail nurseries and garden stores	5	5	31	31	6	10,323	10,839	379	423
5310 Department stores	8	8	1,200	1,289	161	9,710	10,600	13,094	13,918
5410 Grocery stores	47	43	1,749	1,728	40	9,153	9,477	16,950	17,700
5440 Candy, nut, and confectionery stores	-	3	-	22	7	-	5,091	-	113
5460 Retail bakeries	8	7	69	44	6	9,391	9,091	705	459
5490 Miscellaneous food stores	3	-	19	-	-	7,789	-	139	-
5510 New and used car dealers	10	8	423	420	53	25,504	26,962	12,059	12,820
5520 Used car dealers	11	12	56	59	5	17,929	16,881	1,125	1,129
5530 Auto and home supply stores	14	13	127	137	11	13,102	12,964	1,795	1,894
5540 Gasoline service stations	59	56	497	457	8	8,893	10,451	4,746	5,156
5610 Men's & boys' clothing stores	9	9	83	73	8	11,373	14,685	1,048	1,070
5620 Women's clothing stores	28	27	273	233	9	6,711	6,541	2,048	1,589
5630 Women's accessory & specialty stores	3	3	12	13	4	8,667	8,923	111	109
5650 Family clothing stores	5	4	57	56	14	7,649	7,429	457	427
5660 Shoe stores	19	17	115	133	8	10,330	10,105	1,308	1,350
5712 Furniture stores	18	18	90	118	7	15,333	15,492	1,628	1,926
5713 Floor covering stores	8	7	56	45	6	19,357	21,867	1,172	1,138
5720 Household appliance stores	7	5	73	22	4	20,274	19,636	807	571
5731 Radio, TV, & electronic stores	7	8	40	46	6	21,900	23,217	846	932
5734 Computer and software stores	-	3	-	46	15	-	13,652	-	675
5735 Record & prerecorded tape stores	3	4	29	34	9	8,966	8,824	252	273
5736 Musical instrument stores	-	3	-	14	5	-	8,000	-	144
5812 Eating places	155	148	3,084	3,046	21	6,497	7,410	22,772	24,064
5813 Drinking places	45	44	143	123	3	7,552	7,935	1,084	1,034
5910 Drug stores and proprietary stores	14	13	175	166	13	13,486	15,060	2,571	2,709
5920 Liquor stores	7	6	35	34	6	11,771	13,294	394	471
5930 Used merchandise stores	-	12	-	35	3	-	8,686	-	365
5941 Sporting goods and bicycle shops	13	13	114	133	10	12,246	13,714	1,328	1,650
5942 Book stores	10	10	58	60	6	7,931	9,533	524	593
5944 Jewelry stores	17	18	141	147	8	15,887	20,272	2,603	3,035
5945 Hobby, toy, and game shops	9	10	101	86	9	7,248	9,395	877	958
5947 Gift, novelty, and souvenir shops	17	15	97	114	8	7,258	8,000	822	972
5963 Direct selling establishments	16	16	259	265	17	13,266	14,415	3,513	4,012
5984 Liquefied petroleum gas dealers	-	3	-	10	3	-	12,800	-	149
5992 Florists	-	6	-	47	8	-	7,234	-	350
5994 News dealers and newsstands	-	3	-	2	1	-	4,000	-	9
5995 Optical goods stores	10	13	80	99	8	12,500	12,323	1,043	1,205
5999 Miscellaneous retail stores, nec	20	21	79	76	4	9,620	10,947	918	1,013

Source: County Business Patterns 1994/95, CBP-94/95, U.S. Department of Commerce, Washington DC, November 1997. The employment column represents mid-March employment in the year. Pay per employee is calculated by dividing 1st Quarter payroll, annualized, by mid-March employment. The column headed 'Emp / Est' shows 'employees per establishment'. A dash (-) means that data are unavailable or cannot be calculated. nec means not elsewhere classified. *Notes:* 1. 1994 data incomplete; unavailable or withheld. 2. 1995 data incomplete; unavailable or withheld. 3. 1994 and 1995 data incomplete; unavailable or withheld.

SIOUX CITY MSA (NE PART)

Wholesale and Retail Trade USA	Establishments		Employment		Emp / Est	Pay / Employee		Annual Payroll ($ 000)	
	1994	1995	1994	1995	1995	1994	1995	1994	1995
50- Wholesale trade	29	31	403	480	15	30,422	31,333	11,891	13,791
5010 Motor vehicles, parts, and supplies	6	6	63	69	12	18,222	17,855	1,328	1,254
5030 Lumber and construction materials	-	4	-	28	7	-	9,714	-	596
5080 Machinery, equipment, and supplies	4	4	39	45	11	23,077	23,644	985	1,389
5150 Farm-product raw materials	5	6	81	93	16	21,778	23,097	1,982	2,390
52- Retail trade	108	112	1,328	1,380	12	9,488	10,884	14,227	15,602
5200 Building materials & garden supplies	9	9	51	51	6	11,922	10,510	617	570
5400 Food stores	8	9	281	298	33	9,765	10,336	2,902	3,308
5520 Used car dealers	4	4	15	18	5	15,200	13,111	237	250
5530 Auto and home supply stores	3	3	11	14	5	14,909	12,857	185	205
5540 Gasoline service stations	11	10	114	120	12	8,702	7,800	998	966
5812 Eating places	28	31	526	512	17	7,019	8,070	4,212	4,489
5813 Drinking places	6	4	13	17	4	10,154	11,529	231	193
5920 Liquor stores	9	8	34	28	4	8,235	8,571	291	252
5990 Retail stores, nec	5	7	9	13	2	6,667	6,154	64	121

Source: County Business Patterns 1994/95, CBP-94/95, U.S. Department of Commerce, Washington DC, November 1997. The employment column represents mid-March employment in the year. Pay per employee is calculated by dividing 1st Quarter payroll, annualized, by mid-March employment. The column headed 'Emp / Est' shows 'employees per establishment'. A dash (-) means that data are unavailable or cannot be calculated. nec means not elsewhere classified. *Notes:* 1. 1994 data incomplete; unavailable or withheld. 2. 1995 data incomplete; unavailable or withheld. 3. 1994 and 1995 data incomplete; unavailable or withheld.

SIOUX CITY, IA–NE MSA

Wholesale and Retail Trade USA	Establishments		Employment		Emp / Est	Pay / Employee		Annual Payroll ($ 000)	
	1994	1995	1994	1995	1995	1994	1995	1994	1995
50– Wholesale trade	302	295	3,453	3,731	13	28,146	28,931	101,912	108,182
5012 Automobiles and other vehicles	7	8	180	223	28	23,756	29,220	5,238	6,762
5013 Motor vehicle supplies and new parts	20	17	212	234	14	18,547	19,641	4,212	4,611
5021 Furniture [1]	3	-	55	-	-	23,200	-	2,139	-
5039 Construction materials, nec	4	-	38	-	-	17,263	-	940	-
5044 Office equipment [3]	7	6	116	89	15	21,517	25,034	2,678	2,439
5045 Computers, peripherals, & software [3]	6	6	99	106	18	20,202	31,208	2,079	3,087
5046 Commercial equipment, nec	5	-	20	-	-	24,400	-	519	-
5049 Professional equipment, nec [3]	3	3	30	33	11	27,067	23,394	893	987
5051 Metals service centers and offices	-	5	-	72	14	-	22,111	-	3,792
5063 Electrical apparatus and equipment [3]	9	9	91	86	10	35,121	39,674	3,454	3,333
5072 Hardware [1]	4	-	40	-	-	26,000	-	1,368	-
5074 Plumbing & hydronic heating supplies [3]	9	9	94	103	11	22,255	27,573	2,440	2,810
5075 Warm air heating & air conditioning [1]	5	-	12	-	-	20,667	-	238	-
5082 Construction and mining machinery [3]	4	5	33	37	7	28,121	29,838	1,190	1,273
5083 Farm and garden machinery	9	9	47	43	5	21,702	21,953	995	1,047
5084 Industrial machinery and equipment	13	11	78	82	7	22,667	25,610	1,962	2,484
5085 Industrial supplies	9	9	66	78	9	27,939	26,256	2,041	2,171
5087 Service establishment equipment [3]	6	5	16	22	4	17,750	16,000	316	517
5093 Scrap and waste materials [3]	8	9	102	126	14	18,902	20,032	2,450	2,747
5112 Stationery and office supplies [3]	7	7	76	99	14	20,316	20,848	1,574	2,426
5148 Fresh fruits and vegetables [3]	3	3	66	71	24	20,909	20,394	2,023	1,749
5149 Groceries and related products, nec	6	5	55	52	10	15,127	18,000	1,025	1,114
5153 Grain and field beans	13	13	115	121	9	20,835	22,612	2,879	2,958
5154 Livestock [1]	14	-	58	-	-	18,138	-	993	-
5160 Chemicals and allied products [3]	7	9	36	40	4	23,222	24,600	989	1,110
5171 Petroleum bulk stations & terminals [1]	5	-	36	-	-	24,333	-	939	-
5172 Petroleum products, nec [1]	7	-	43	-	-	31,628	-	1,435	-
5180 Beer, wine, and distilled beverages [3]	4	5	87	110	22	20,138	20,982	2,038	2,314
5191 Farm supplies	21	24	133	184	8	29,594	35,739	3,431	5,917
5192 Books, periodicals, & newspapers [2]	-	4	-	3	1	-	4,000	-	12
52– Retail trade	824	829	12,084	12,107	15	9,863	10,942	132,583	140,685
5210 Lumber and other building materials	16	19	369	426	22	15,545	16,291	7,184	7,570
5250 Hardware stores	16	13	99	77	6	8,848	9,610	971	806
5260 Retail nurseries and garden stores	7	7	31	31	4	10,323	10,839	379	423
5310 Department stores [3]	9	9	1,200	1,289	143	9,710	10,600	13,094	13,918
5410 Grocery stores [3]	53	50	1,749	1,728	35	9,153	9,477	16,950	17,700
5440 Candy, nut, and confectionery stores [2]	-	3	-	22	7	-	5,091	-	113
5460 Retail bakeries	9	8	69	44	6	9,391	9,091	705	459
5490 Miscellaneous food stores	4	-	19	-	-	7,789	-	139	-
5510 New and used car dealers	11	9	423	420	47	25,504	26,962	12,059	12,820
5520 Used car dealers	15	16	71	77	5	17,352	16,000	1,362	1,379
5530 Auto and home supply stores	17	16	138	151	9	13,246	12,954	1,980	2,099
5540 Gasoline service stations	70	66	611	577	9	8,858	9,899	5,744	6,122
5610 Men's & boys' clothing stores [3]	9	9	83	73	8	11,373	14,685	1,048	1,070
5620 Women's clothing stores	29	28	273	233	8	6,711	6,541	2,048	1,589
5630 Women's accessory & specialty stores [3]	3	3	12	13	4	8,667	8,923	111	109
5650 Family clothing stores [3]	5	4	57	56	14	7,649	7,429	457	427
5660 Shoe stores [3]	19	17	115	133	8	10,330	10,105	1,308	1,350
5712 Furniture stores	20	20	90	118	6	15,333	15,492	1,628	1,926
5713 Floor covering stores [3]	8	7	56	45	6	19,357	21,867	1,172	1,138
5720 Household appliance stores [2]	8	5	73	22	4	20,274	19,636	807	571
5731 Radio, TV, & electronic stores [3]	7	8	40	46	6	21,900	23,217	846	932
5734 Computer and software stores	-	4	-	46	12	-	13,652	-	675
5735 Record & prerecorded tape stores [3]	3	4	29	34	9	8,966	8,824	252	273
5736 Musical instrument stores [2]	-	3	-	14	5	-	8,000	-	144
5812 Eating places	183	179	3,610	3,558	20	6,573	7,505	26,984	28,553
5813 Drinking places	51	48	156	140	3	7,769	8,371	1,315	1,227
5910 Drug stores and proprietary stores	17	15	175	166	11	13,486	15,060	2,571	2,709
5920 Liquor stores	16	14	69	62	4	10,029	11,161	685	723
5930 Used merchandise stores	-	14	-	35	3	-	8,686	-	365
5941 Sporting goods and bicycle shops	14	14	114	133	10	12,246	13,714	1,328	1,650
5942 Book stores [3]	10	10	58	60	6	7,931	9,533	524	593
5944 Jewelry stores [3]	17	18	141	147	8	15,887	20,272	2,603	3,035
5945 Hobby, toy, and game shops [3]	9	10	101	86	9	7,248	9,395	877	958
5947 Gift, novelty, and souvenir shops [3]	17	15	97	114	8	7,258	8,000	822	972
5963 Direct selling establishments	17	17	259	265	16	13,266	14,415	3,513	4,012
5984 Liquefied petroleum gas dealers	-	4	-	10	3	-	12,800	-	149
5992 Florists	-	8	-	47	6	-	7,234	-	350

Continued on next page.

SIOUX CITY, IA–NE MSA - [continued]

Wholesale and Retail Trade USA	Establishments		Employment		Emp / Est	Pay / Employee		Annual Payroll ($ 000)	
	1994	1995	1994	1995	1995	1994	1995	1994	1995
5994 News dealers and newsstands [2]	-	3	-	2	1	-	4,000	-	9
5995 Optical goods stores [3]	10	13	80	99	8	12,500	12,323	1,043	1,205
5999 Miscellaneous retail stores, nec	23	26	79	76	3	9,620	10,947	918	1,013

Source: County Business Patterns 1994/95, CBP-94/95, U.S. Department of Commerce, Washington DC, November 1997. The employment column represents mid-March employment in the year. Pay per employee is calculated by dividing 1st Quarter payroll, annualized, by mid-March employment. The column headed 'Emp / Est' shows 'employees per establishment'. A dash (-) means that data are unavailable or cannot be calculated. nec means not elsewhere classified. *Notes:* 1. 1994 data incomplete; unavailable or withheld. 2. 1995 data incomplete; unavailable or withheld. 3. 1994 and 1995 data incomplete; unavailable or withheld.

SIOUX FALLS, SD MSA

Wholesale and Retail Trade USA	Establishments		Employment		Emp / Est	Pay / Employee		Annual Payroll ($ 000)	
	1994	1995	1994	1995	1995	1994	1995	1994	1995
50– Wholesale trade	-	496	-	6,752	14	-	27,074	-	186,121
5012 Automobiles and other vehicles	-	12	-	246	21	-	31,756	-	7,232
5013 Motor vehicle supplies and new parts [2]	-	22	-	405	18	-	22,765	-	9,981
5014 Tires and tubes [2]	-	5	-	82	16	-	28,146	-	2,506
5015 Motor vehicle parts, used	-	6	-	54	9	-	18,074	-	1,031
5021 Furniture [2]	-	4	-	34	9	-	27,765	-	1,170
5031 Lumber, plywood, and millwork [2]	-	11	-	269	24	-	25,398	-	6,210
5044 Office equipment [2]	-	11	-	135	12	-	24,059	-	3,300
5045 Computers, peripherals, & software [2]	-	25	-	209	8	-	45,397	-	8,203
5047 Medical and hospital equipment [2]	-	13	-	112	9	-	32,143	-	4,035
5049 Professional equipment, nec [2]	-	5	-	57	11	-	30,807	-	1,649
5063 Electrical apparatus and equipment [2]	-	12	-	222	19	-	29,748	-	7,250
5072 Hardware [2]	-	8	-	90	11	-	21,956	-	2,279
5074 Plumbing & hydronic heating supplies [2]	-	12	-	126	11	-	27,587	-	3,860
5075 Warm air heating & air conditioning [2]	-	8	-	56	7	-	34,357	-	2,045
5078 Refrigeration equipment and supplies [2]	-	5	-	44	9	-	28,636	-	1,930
5082 Construction and mining machinery [2]	-	12	-	284	24	-	35,704	-	9,346
5083 Farm and garden machinery	-	22	-	113	5	-	25,593	-	4,314
5084 Industrial machinery and equipment [2]	-	19	-	241	13	-	25,095	-	5,717
5085 Industrial supplies [2]	-	12	-	82	7	-	61,854	-	3,518
5087 Service establishment equipment	-	7	-	59	8	-	26,102	-	1,507
5093 Scrap and waste materials [2]	-	13	-	95	7	-	17,432	-	1,921
5094 Jewelry & precious stones	-	8	-	63	8	-	24,317	-	2,677
5099 Durable goods, nec [2]	-	6	-	14	2	-	28,571	-	577
5110 Paper and paper products [2]	-	18	-	284	16	-	23,761	-	6,957
5137 Women's and children's clothing [2]	-	3	-	9	3	-	7,556	-	72
5149 Groceries and related products, nec [2]	-	7	-	256	37	-	20,359	-	5,074
5153 Grain and field beans	-	22	-	167	8	-	25,916	-	5,141
5160 Chemicals and allied products [2]	-	10	-	51	5	-	21,725	-	1,295
5170 Petroleum and petroleum products	-	17	-	102	6	-	29,922	-	3,159
5180 Beer, wine, and distilled beverages [2]	-	5	-	166	33	-	27,807	-	5,444
5191 Farm supplies	-	26	-	158	6	-	25,367	-	4,123
5199 Nondurable goods, nec [2]	-	12	-	92	8	-	16,652	-	1,481
52– Retail trade	-	1,153	-	20,103	17	-	11,626	-	243,063
5210 Lumber and other building materials	-	23	-	510	22	-	16,102	-	7,486
5230 Paint, glass, and wallpaper stores	-	8	-	45	6	-	18,578	-	1,077
5250 Hardware stores	-	12	-	123	10	-	10,114	-	1,324
5260 Retail nurseries and garden stores [2]	-	8	-	48	6	-	14,083	-	1,225
5270 Mobile home dealers [2]	-	6	-	81	14	-	20,296	-	2,389
5310 Department stores [2]	-	14	-	1,964	140	-	10,874	-	23,140
5410 Grocery stores	-	60	-	2,443	41	-	9,505	-	25,204
5420 Meat and fish markets	-	6	-	12	2	-	11,333	-	177
5440 Candy, nut, and confectionery stores [2]	-	4	-	20	5	-	6,200	-	120
5460 Retail bakeries	-	14	-	59	4	-	7,458	-	477
5490 Miscellaneous food stores [2]	-	3	-	21	7	-	7,429	-	168
5510 New and used car dealers	-	20	-	1,245	62	-	27,730	-	33,204
5520 Used car dealers	-	17	-	85	5	-	21,553	-	2,215
5530 Auto and home supply stores	-	28	-	252	9	-	21,063	-	5,355
5540 Gasoline service stations	-	93	-	811	9	-	10,481	-	8,532
5560 Recreational vehicle dealers	-	7	-	53	8	-	22,415	-	1,389
5570 Motorcycle dealers [2]	-	4	-	50	13	-	16,880	-	933
5610 Men's & boys' clothing stores [2]	-	11	-	105	10	-	15,124	-	1,318
5620 Women's clothing stores [2]	-	31	-	342	11	-	9,123	-	2,738
5630 Women's accessory & specialty stores [2]	-	7	-	46	7	-	8,609	-	413
5640 Children's and infants' wear stores [2]	-	6	-	55	9	-	6,982	-	398
5650 Family clothing stores	-	10	-	105	11	-	8,762	-	933
5660 Shoe stores [2]	-	24	-	122	5	-	12,623	-	1,459

Continued on next page.

SIOUX FALLS, SD MSA - [continued]

Wholesale and Retail Trade USA	Establishments		Employment		Emp / Est	Pay / Employee		Annual Payroll ($ 000)	
	1994	1995	1994	1995	1995	1994	1995	1994	1995
5690 Misc. apparel & accessory stores [2]	-	7	-	38	5	-	6,737	-	277
5712 Furniture stores	-	28	-	325	12	-	18,289	-	6,383
5713 Floor covering stores	-	11	-	56	5	-	20,429	-	1,451
5714 Drapery and upholstery stores [2]	-	4	-	13	3	-	9,538	-	137
5719 Misc. homefurnishings stores [2]	-	12	-	56	5	-	11,571	-	687
5720 Household appliance stores [2]	-	9	-	58	6	-	21,241	-	1,281
5731 Radio, TV, & electronic stores [2]	-	16	-	235	15	-	12,477	-	2,990
5734 Computer and software stores [2]	-	6	-	32	5	-	20,625	-	681
5735 Record & prerecorded tape stores [2]	-	8	-	58	7	-	13,517	-	764
5736 Musical instrument stores [2]	-	5	-	33	7	-	16,727	-	533
5812 Eating places	-	238	-	6,391	27	-	7,220	-	49,314
5813 Drinking places	-	59	-	629	11	-	7,860	-	5,491
5910 Drug stores and proprietary stores	-	26	-	592	23	-	12,169	-	7,306
5920 Liquor stores	-	21	-	181	9	-	7,934	-	1,319
5930 Used merchandise stores [2]	-	23	-	121	5	-	10,083	-	1,429
5941 Sporting goods and bicycle shops [2]	-	20	-	364	18	-	17,418	-	5,506
5942 Book stores [2]	-	9	-	97	11	-	7,918	-	852
5944 Jewelry stores [2]	-	15	-	107	7	-	17,794	-	1,865
5945 Hobby, toy, and game shops	-	17	-	125	7	-	9,152	-	1,258
5947 Gift, novelty, and souvenir shops [2]	-	23	-	184	8	-	6,717	-	1,400
5961 Catalog and mail-order houses [2]	-	9	-	134	15	-	19,701	-	2,867
5980 Fuel dealers	-	6	-	44	7	-	13,909	-	643
5992 Florists	-	17	-	17	1	-	4,000	-	64
5995 Optical goods stores [2]	-	12	-	56	5	-	15,929	-	844
5999 Miscellaneous retail stores, nec [2]	-	38	-	177	5	-	13,153	-	2,674

Source: County Business Patterns 1994/95, CBP-94/95, U.S. Department of Commerce, Washington DC, November 1997. The employment column represents mid-March employment in the year. Pay per employee is calculated by dividing 1st Quarter payroll, annualized, by mid-March employment. The column headed 'Emp / Est' shows 'employees per establishment'. A dash (-) means that data are unavailable or cannot be calculated. nec means not elsewhere classified. *Notes:* 1. 1994 data incomplete; unavailable or withheld. 2. 1995 data incomplete; unavailable or withheld. 3. 1994 and 1995 data incomplete; unavailable or withheld.

SOUTH BEND, IN MSA

Wholesale and Retail Trade USA	Establishments		Employment		Emp / Est	Pay / Employee		Annual Payroll ($ 000)	
	1994	1995	1994	1995	1995	1994	1995	1994	1995
50- Wholesale trade	573	575	7,524	7,709	13	26,409	28,229	217,675	227,785
5012 Automobiles and other vehicles	17	16	305	281	18	23,384	27,160	8,007	7,693
5013 Motor vehicle supplies and new parts	44	38	483	449	12	30,874	25,363	15,970	11,636
5014 Tires and tubes	8	7	255	236	34	27,671	35,797	8,057	8,557
5015 Motor vehicle parts, used	10	10	72	76	8	12,833	16,947	924	1,362
5021 Furniture	7	5	117	40	8	23,385	26,600	2,884	943
5023 Homefurnishings	-	9	-	51	6	-	18,196	-	1,187
5031 Lumber, plywood, and millwork	13	8	114	35	4	27,965	20,000	3,873	951
5032 Brick, stone, & related materials	7	6	95	22	4	13,137	25,091	1,694	899
5033 Roofing, siding, & insulation	6	8	45	63	8	26,311	26,286	1,665	1,916
5039 Construction materials, nec	5	12	29	119	10	16,828	27,664	693	3,794
5043 Photographic equipment & supplies	3	3	19	18	6	17,263	17,556	351	337
5044 Office equipment	26	26	377	349	13	31,809	34,923	12,138	11,436
5045 Computers, peripherals, & software	25	25	234	227	9	38,291	48,441	9,394	9,499
5046 Commercial equipment, nec	9	8	79	92	12	26,684	28,826	2,394	2,678
5047 Medical and hospital equipment	9	11	62	122	11	26,774	22,328	1,781	2,812
5051 Metals service centers and offices	18	17	410	452	27	28,029	30,327	12,960	14,392
5063 Electrical apparatus and equipment	21	24	249	289	12	30,233	32,678	7,827	8,887
5064 Electrical appliances, TV & radios	3	3	33	28	9	22,788	23,286	675	602
5065 Electronic parts and equipment	25	26	204	232	9	24,275	25,034	5,516	6,437
5072 Hardware	8	8	42	44	6	19,048	28,273	987	1,194
5074 Plumbing & hydronic heating supplies	7	9	173	170	19	25,711	25,059	5,033	4,999
5075 Warm air heating & air conditioning	8	7	94	83	12	40,766	47,373	4,254	4,487
5078 Refrigeration equipment and supplies	3	3	34	30	10	30,824	32,933	1,036	1,103
5082 Construction and mining machinery	5	5	236	170	34	23,797	30,306	5,899	6,379
5083 Farm and garden machinery	6	5	54	73	15	30,963	34,849	1,851	2,295
5084 Industrial machinery and equipment	42	40	285	286	7	24,070	24,140	7,765	8,025
5085 Industrial supplies	22	25	256	355	14	36,219	32,417	9,718	11,054
5087 Service establishment equipment	12	11	86	106	10	19,488	19,774	1,818	2,142
5093 Scrap and waste materials	7	8	133	184	23	28,842	25,217	4,248	5,482
5099 Durable goods, nec	10	12	23	29	2	20,696	18,207	513	560
5111 Printing and writing paper	7	7	59	59	8	37,831	41,153	2,325	2,614
5112 Stationery and office supplies	21	20	236	313	16	19,271	21,725	5,198	6,907
5113 Industrial & personal service paper	3	3	94	93	31	24,383	26,366	2,445	2,376
5120 Drugs, proprietaries, and sundries	16	16	375	422	26	23,904	24,531	9,793	11,342

Continued on next page.

SOUTH BEND, IN MSA - [continued]

Wholesale and Retail Trade USA	Establishments		Employment		Emp / Est	Pay / Employee		Annual Payroll ($ 000)	
	1994	1995	1994	1995	1995	1994	1995	1994	1995
5136 Men's and boys' clothing	3	4	19	14	4	16,842	27,143	438	272
5141 Groceries, general line	3	3	450	368	123	25,609	28,065	12,323	11,025
5145 Confectionery	3	3	20	20	7	17,400	17,000	371	386
5149 Groceries and related products, nec	12	13	274	282	22	26,409	29,631	8,344	9,816
5150 Farm-product raw materials	3	-	60	-	-	9,867	-	588	-
5162 Plastics materials & basic shapes	7	9	58	65	7	29,586	29,908	2,096	2,404
5169 Chemicals & allied products, nec	18	17	163	119	7	31,362	50,992	4,961	5,541
5170 Petroleum and petroleum products	11	11	176	168	15	25,136	27,167	5,140	5,123
5180 Beer, wine, and distilled beverages	4	4	214	265	66	27,159	28,800	6,434	8,166
5191 Farm supplies	4	4	30	34	9	18,133	16,706	716	740
5192 Books, periodicals, & newspapers	3	3	113	113	38	15,257	16,142	1,978	1,818
5193 Flowers & florists' supplies	5	3	60	36	12	15,000	17,111	796	841
5198 Paints, varnishes, and supplies	3	4	12	19	5	32,667	24,211	409	436
5199 Nondurable goods, nec	14	13	68	85	7	31,941	30,588	2,481	2,157
52 - Retail trade	1,558	1,570	24,721	25,455	16	10,568	11,367	289,096	307,442
5210 Lumber and other building materials	31	31	512	707	23	20,766	20,487	12,008	13,559
5250 Hardware stores	21	14	124	115	8	11,613	10,435	1,634	1,191
5260 Retail nurseries and garden stores	17	18	116	123	7	10,000	13,333	1,836	1,901
5310 Department stores	16	17	2,862	3,673	216	10,423	10,407	33,258	40,830
5330 Variety stores	15	12	202	145	12	8,198	9,076	1,546	1,292
5390 Misc. general merchandise stores	7	8	724	783	98	11,359	10,273	8,465	9,133
5410 Grocery stores	87	88	2,982	3,006	34	11,019	11,658	34,324	36,185
5420 Meat and fish markets	5	5	34	32	6	10,941	12,250	424	352
5440 Candy, nut, and confectionery stores	9	10	54	60	6	5,333	5,467	333	363
5460 Retail bakeries	29	27	193	198	7	7,979	8,505	1,738	1,763
5490 Miscellaneous food stores	4	4	19	21	5	9,053	9,905	223	238
5510 New and used car dealers	14	17	957	1,075	63	29,024	29,920	33,679	36,834
5520 Used car dealers	33	29	115	113	4	18,678	20,106	2,429	2,874
5530 Auto and home supply stores	37	41	219	257	6	15,543	15,222	3,542	4,605
5540 Gasoline service stations	91	90	774	725	8	10,295	10,919	8,422	8,461
5610 Men's & boys' clothing stores	15	17	131	131	8	9,008	9,099	1,268	1,184
5620 Women's clothing stores	49	46	551	446	10	6,947	7,220	4,170	3,302
5630 Women's accessory & specialty stores	10	10	56	54	5	9,571	10,889	571	586
5650 Family clothing stores	15	14	165	165	12	7,927	8,897	1,411	1,480
5660 Shoe stores	32	30	219	180	6	9,315	11,578	2,101	2,030
5690 Misc. apparel & accessory stores	7	9	23	24	3	9,043	8,833	224	227
5712 Furniture stores	28	29	356	360	12	18,921	19,100	6,943	6,792
5713 Floor covering stores	16	15	103	104	7	17,786	18,423	1,981	1,994
5714 Drapery and upholstery stores	5	5	22	18	4	9,636	15,111	261	283
5719 Misc. homefurnishings stores	12	10	113	110	11	10,088	10,182	1,089	1,046
5720 Household appliance stores	6	6	87	78	13	14,299	17,744	1,367	1,560
5731 Radio, TV, & electronic stores	16	16	191	224	14	13,529	13,750	2,549	2,866
5734 Computer and software stores	11	11	55	50	5	24,364	20,880	1,110	1,190
5735 Record & prerecorded tape stores	9	8	50	61	8	11,040	11,213	552	602
5736 Musical instrument stores	4	4	13	18	5	16,308	13,556	208	272
5812 Eating places	395	384	8,381	8,069	21	6,541	7,363	61,427	62,530
5813 Drinking places	80	76	584	536	7	7,493	8,104	4,556	4,460
5910 Drug stores and proprietary stores	42	45	701	700	16	15,258	17,046	12,069	11,952
5920 Liquor stores	38	38	181	195	5	8,729	9,579	1,854	2,014
5930 Used merchandise stores	21	19	380	304	16	10,011	13,882	4,197	4,525
5941 Sporting goods and bicycle shops	25	24	147	135	6	10,449	13,363	1,832	1,945
5942 Book stores	14	16	121	153	10	6,182	8,366	814	1,270
5943 Stationery stores	4	3	29	31	10	7,172	7,355	217	234
5944 Jewelry stores	27	29	152	169	6	12,684	12,024	2,106	2,270
5945 Hobby, toy, and game shops	11	10	122	135	14	8,492	8,296	1,211	1,350
5946 Camera & photographic supply stores	5	4	20	27	7	15,200	12,889	347	374
5947 Gift, novelty, and souvenir shops	39	38	211	196	5	5,801	6,755	1,273	1,541
5949 Sewing, needlework, and piece goods	6	5	75	71	14	7,040	6,479	560	439
5961 Catalog and mail-order houses	9	8	184	158	20	19,870	18,203	4,118	3,210
5962 Merchandising machine operators	10	10	153	150	15	23,948	25,280	3,877	3,767
5963 Direct selling establishments	16	20	191	168	8	9,508	11,262	2,216	1,905
5980 Fuel dealers	4	4	12	19	5	19,333	29,474	380	577
5992 Florists	29	31	209	209	7	7,789	8,134	1,708	1,749
5993 Tobacco stores and stands	-	3	-	12	4	-	4,667	-	167
5995 Optical goods stores	16	15	124	120	8	15,742	18,833	2,114	2,316
5999 Miscellaneous retail stores, nec	46	51	290	335	7	10,814	9,946	3,557	3,834

Source: County Business Patterns 1994/95, CBP-94/95, U.S. Department of Commerce, Washington DC, November 1997. The employment column represents mid-March employment in the year. Pay per employee is calculated by dividing 1st Quarter payroll, annualized, by mid-March employment. The column headed 'Emp / Est' shows 'employees per establishment'. A dash (-) means that data are unavailable or cannot be calculated. nec means not elsewhere classified. *Notes:* 1. 1994 data incomplete; unavailable or withheld. 2. 1995 data incomplete; unavailable or withheld. 3. 1994 and 1995 data incomplete; unavailable or withheld.

SPOKANE, WA MSA

Wholesale and Retail Trade USA	Establishments		Employment		Emp / Est	Pay / Employee		Annual Payroll ($ 000)	
	1994	1995	1994	1995	1995	1994	1995	1994	1995
50 - Wholesale trade	-	954	-	12,289	13	-	27,697	-	361,039
5012 Automobiles and other vehicles	-	20	-	383	19	-	26,068	-	10,786
5013 Motor vehicle supplies and new parts	-	46	-	558	12	-	25,047	-	13,997
5014 Tires and tubes	-	9	-	93	10	-	29,032	-	2,430
5015 Motor vehicle parts, used	-	18	-	212	12	-	20,038	-	4,596
5021 Furniture	-	12	-	132	11	-	21,606	-	3,259
5023 Homefurnishings	-	21	-	347	17	-	25,072	-	10,181
5031 Lumber, plywood, and millwork	-	24	-	353	15	-	28,351	-	10,491
5032 Brick, stone, & related materials	-	14	-	68	5	-	31,706	-	2,530
5033 Roofing, siding, & insulation	-	13	-	130	10	-	42,185	-	5,833
5039 Construction materials, nec	-	20	-	146	7	-	27,644	-	3,816
5044 Office equipment	-	26	-	282	11	-	31,929	-	10,087
5045 Computers, peripherals, & software	-	32	-	291	9	-	42,680	-	12,026
5046 Commercial equipment, nec	-	12	-	116	10	-	21,793	-	2,771
5047 Medical and hospital equipment	-	16	-	211	13	-	40,360	-	8,251
5049 Professional equipment, nec	-	6	-	55	9	-	29,091	-	1,314
5050 Metals and minerals, except petroleum	-	23	-	295	13	-	28,719	-	9,947
5063 Electrical apparatus and equipment	-	41	-	409	10	-	31,403	-	12,039
5065 Electronic parts and equipment	-	29	-	238	8	-	28,504	-	7,966
5072 Hardware	-	16	-	326	20	-	32,994	-	9,695
5074 Plumbing & hydronic heating supplies	-	12	-	128	11	-	32,688	-	4,122
5075 Warm air heating & air conditioning	-	18	-	177	10	-	25,130	-	4,678
5082 Construction and mining machinery	-	24	-	411	17	-	39,134	-	15,498
5083 Farm and garden machinery	-	12	-	112	9	-	25,143	-	2,947
5084 Industrial machinery and equipment	-	52	-	489	9	-	31,092	-	16,325
5085 Industrial supplies	-	23	-	310	13	-	32,942	-	10,503
5087 Service establishment equipment	-	23	-	152	7	-	23,947	-	3,951
5088 Transportation equipment & supplies	-	4	-	16	4	-	49,500	-	757
5091 Sporting & recreational goods	-	14	-	135	10	-	20,444	-	3,165
5093 Scrap and waste materials	-	18	-	114	6	-	14,281	-	2,151
5099 Durable goods, nec	-	19	-	112	6	-	24,393	-	3,042
5111 Printing and writing paper	-	3	-	58	19	-	39,448	-	2,579
5112 Stationery and office supplies	-	21	-	276	13	-	19,739	-	5,459
5113 Industrial & personal service paper	-	7	-	66	9	-	33,091	-	2,253
5120 Drugs, proprietaries, and sundries	-	9	-	168	19	-	27,310	-	4,690
5130 Apparel, piece goods, and notions	-	3	-	11	4	-	13,818	-	185
5141 Groceries, general line	-	15	-	1,147	76	-	30,312	-	39,200
5142 Packaged frozen food	-	3	-	30	10	-	20,533	-	711
5143 Dairy products, exc. dried or canned	-	4	-	78	20	-	23,641	-	2,147
5145 Confectionery	-	7	-	267	38	-	26,412	-	9,063
5147 Meats and meat products	-	7	-	243	35	-	19,407	-	5,164
5148 Fresh fruits and vegetables	-	6	-	378	63	-	23,598	-	9,508
5149 Groceries and related products, nec	-	38	-	638	17	-	24,665	-	17,774
5153 Grain and field beans	-	14	-	87	6	-	25,609	-	2,881
5162 Plastics materials & basic shapes	-	6	-	19	3	-	25,895	-	529
5169 Chemicals & allied products, nec	-	10	-	99	10	-	29,091	-	3,107
5171 Petroleum bulk stations & terminals	-	16	-	189	12	-	26,138	-	5,429
5172 Petroleum products, nec	-	7	-	30	4	-	26,533	-	1,133
5180 Beer, wine, and distilled beverages	-	11	-	296	27	-	24,635	-	7,777
5191 Farm supplies	-	27	-	301	11	-	26,246	-	8,155
5192 Books, periodicals, & newspapers	-	12	-	107	9	-	20,710	-	1,418
5193 Flowers & florists' supplies	-	7	-	109	16	-	19,083	-	2,157
5199 Nondurable goods, nec	-	33	-	173	5	-	19,399	-	3,961
52 - Retail trade	-	2,473	-	35,679	14	-	14,202	-	531,267
5210 Lumber and other building materials	-	33	-	745	23	-	19,699	-	16,752
5230 Paint, glass, and wallpaper stores	-	19	-	63	3	-	18,603	-	1,295
5250 Hardware stores	-	23	-	347	15	-	14,202	-	5,493
5260 Retail nurseries and garden stores	-	21	-	212	10	-	14,717	-	3,778
5270 Mobile home dealers	-	9	-	103	11	-	27,301	-	2,690
5310 Department stores	-	17	-	2,913	171	-	13,107	-	41,561
5330 Variety stores	-	9	-	180	20	-	8,156	-	1,500
5390 Misc. general merchandise stores	-	10	-	586	59	-	22,853	-	14,326
5410 Grocery stores	-	152	-	4,122	27	-	15,953	-	68,853
5420 Meat and fish markets	-	7	-	27	4	-	10,074	-	333
5440 Candy, nut, and confectionery stores	-	14	-	57	4	-	9,333	-	544
5450 Dairy products stores	-	4	-	8	2	-	17,000	-	76
5460 Retail bakeries	-	20	-	171	9	-	11,719	-	2,129
5490 Miscellaneous food stores	-	23	-	160	7	-	9,225	-	1,631
5510 New and used car dealers	-	41	-	1,875	46	-	30,803	-	60,635
5520 Used car dealers	-	53	-	177	3	-	21,785	-	4,088
5530 Auto and home supply stores	-	66	-	541	8	-	20,673	-	11,484

Continued on next page.

SPOKANE, WA MSA - [continued]

Wholesale and Retail Trade USA	Establishments		Employment		Emp / Est	Pay / Employee		Annual Payroll ($ 000)	
	1994	1995	1994	1995	1995	1994	1995	1994	1995
5540 Gasoline service stations	-	115	-	997	9	-	12,706	-	12,864
5550 Boat dealers	-	9	-	82	9	-	26,049	-	2,337
5560 Recreational vehicle dealers	-	14	-	112	8	-	22,214	-	3,262
5570 Motorcycle dealers	-	10	-	83	8	-	16,675	-	1,830
5590 Automotive dealers, nec	-	3	-	11	4	-	17,091	-	203
5610 Men's & boys' clothing stores	-	19	-	122	6	-	15,738	-	1,871
5620 Women's clothing stores	-	41	-	386	9	-	8,694	-	3,408
5630 Women's accessory & specialty stores	-	9	-	49	5	-	9,143	-	500
5640 Children's and infants' wear stores	-	7	-	35	5	-	10,057	-	411
5650 Family clothing stores	-	23	-	938	41	-	12,026	-	11,704
5660 Shoe stores	-	46	-	223	5	-	11,695	-	2,662
5690 Misc. apparel & accessory stores	-	18	-	92	5	-	11,783	-	993
5712 Furniture stores	-	51	-	432	8	-	22,296	-	9,686
5713 Floor covering stores	-	27	-	153	6	-	18,536	-	3,231
5714 Drapery and upholstery stores	-	6	-	38	6	-	12,842	-	512
5719 Misc. homefurnishings stores	-	26	-	132	5	-	12,303	-	1,773
5720 Household appliance stores	-	22	-	143	7	-	15,441	-	2,368
5731 Radio, TV, & electronic stores	-	26	-	240	9	-	20,750	-	4,811
5734 Computer and software stores	-	20	-	125	6	-	20,064	-	2,490
5735 Record & prerecorded tape stores	-	14	-	209	15	-	10,029	-	1,961
5736 Musical instrument stores	-	12	-	92	8	-	22,304	-	2,208
5812 Eating places	-	597	-	12,092	20	-	8,100	-	102,933
5813 Drinking places	-	99	-	546	6	-	8,374	-	4,647
5910 Drug stores and proprietary stores	-	46	-	721	16	-	19,307	-	13,525
5930 Used merchandise stores	-	53	-	365	7	-	11,485	-	4,713
5941 Sporting goods and bicycle shops	-	62	-	548	9	-	13,416	-	7,580
5942 Book stores	-	29	-	150	5	-	10,027	-	1,790
5943 Stationery stores	-	4	-	29	7	-	15,310	-	385
5944 Jewelry stores	-	32	-	232	7	-	16,966	-	4,138
5945 Hobby, toy, and game shops	-	22	-	147	7	-	10,558	-	1,706
5947 Gift, novelty, and souvenir shops	-	52	-	263	5	-	9,597	-	2,799
5949 Sewing, needlework, and piece goods	-	10	-	129	13	-	7,721	-	1,025
5963 Direct selling establishments	-	39	-	284	7	-	13,211	-	3,148
5983 Fuel oil dealers	-	4	-	103	26	-	24,854	-	3,095
5992 Florists	-	38	-	159	4	-	8,226	-	1,305
5995 Optical goods stores	-	27	-	109	4	-	15,339	-	1,894
5999 Miscellaneous retail stores, nec	-	91	-	574	6	-	11,638	-	6,487

Source: County Business Patterns 1994/95, CBP-94/95, U.S. Department of Commerce, Washington DC, November 1997. The employment column represents mid-March employment in the year. Pay per employee is calculated by dividing 1st Quarter payroll, annualized, by mid-March employment. The column headed 'Emp / Est' shows 'employees per establishment'. A dash (-) means that data are unavailable or cannot be calculated. nec means not elsewhere classified. *Notes:* 1. 1994 data incomplete; unavailable or withheld. 2. 1995 data incomplete; unavailable or withheld. 3. 1994 and 1995 data incomplete; unavailable or withheld.

SPRINGFIELD, IL MSA

Wholesale and Retail Trade USA	Establishments		Employment		Emp / Est	Pay / Employee		Annual Payroll ($ 000)	
	1994	1995	1994	1995	1995	1994	1995	1994	1995
50- Wholesale trade	347	352	4,431	4,608	13	29,690	33,206	141,436	149,407
5012 Automobiles and other vehicles[3]	7	7	286	295	42	27,315	27,675	9,248	8,550
5013 Motor vehicle supplies and new parts	16	15	164	169	11	18,683	19,314	3,247	2,981
5014 Tires and tubes	4	-	40	-	-	27,600	-	1,132	-
5015 Motor vehicle parts, used[1]	4	-	12	-	-	17,333	-	306	-
5020 Furniture and homefurnishings[3]	8	9	49	61	7	28,980	25,705	2,224	2,439
5031 Lumber, plywood, and millwork[3]	7	5	65	11	2	29,415	21,091	1,996	269
5032 Brick, stone, & related materials[3]	4	3	25	6	2	15,360	22,667	472	198
5033 Roofing, siding, & insulation[2]	-	5	-	48	10	-	52,167	-	1,806
5039 Construction materials, nec[2]	-	6	-	100	17	-	26,400	-	2,909
5044 Office equipment[3]	11	13	171	235	18	39,158	51,557	9,634	10,878
5045 Computers, peripherals, & software[3]	23	23	343	345	15	44,362	48,835	14,181	13,747
5047 Medical and hospital equipment[2]	-	4	-	29	7	-	51,724	-	1,715
5051 Metals service centers and offices[3]	4	4	66	95	24	14,303	15,453	1,267	1,784
5063 Electrical apparatus and equipment	10	11	149	175	16	45,718	41,349	5,672	6,217
5065 Electronic parts and equipment[2]	-	9	-	133	15	-	34,075	-	4,920
5074 Plumbing & hydronic heating supplies[1]	6	-	59	-	-	33,559	-	2,486	-
5075 Warm air heating & air conditioning[3]	5	4	153	169	42	36,026	30,959	5,395	4,995
5078 Refrigeration equipment and supplies[2]	-	4	-	34	9	-	25,529	-	725
5082 Construction and mining machinery[3]	10	10	209	220	22	35,177	41,709	7,291	7,909
5083 Farm and garden machinery	8	10	86	52	5	32,791	23,077	2,673	1,612
5084 Industrial machinery and equipment[3]	10	11	79	95	9	22,835	24,253	2,345	3,366
5085 Industrial supplies[2]	-	4	-	24	6	-	26,667	-	667

Continued on next page.

SPRINGFIELD, IL MSA - [continued]

Wholesale and Retail Trade USA	Establishments		Employment		Emp / Est	Pay / Employee		Annual Payroll ($ 000)	
	1994	1995	1994	1995	1995	1994	1995	1994	1995
5087 Service establishment equipment [3]	7	7	69	65	9	19,768	24,123	1,289	1,496
5093 Scrap and waste materials [2]	-	6	-	54	9	-	23,481	-	1,357
5094 Jewelry & precious stones [1]	4	-	29	-	-	12,828	-	396	-
5099 Durable goods, nec [3]	6	5	23	26	5	17,739	15,692	432	472
5110 Paper and paper products [3]	12	11	283	261	24	29,852	32,444	8,750	9,187
5120 Drugs, proprietaries, and sundries [3]	4	4	112	106	27	38,000	33,170	4,672	4,289
5142 Packaged frozen food [1]	3	-	148	-	-	27,459	-	4,215	-
5145 Confectionery [3]	3	3	51	40	13	19,137	21,400	1,137	800
5147 Meats and meat products [2]	-	3	-	39	13	-	19,282	-	815
5148 Fresh fruits and vegetables [3]	5	3	56	81	27	36,071	37,235	2,183	2,420
5149 Groceries and related products, nec [3]	11	11	244	268	24	31,213	30,806	7,345	7,724
5153 Grain and field beans [1]	30	28	31	123	4	18,710	23,350	534	3,389
5171 Petroleum bulk stations & terminals	8	8	188	91	11	19,809	25,626	4,001	2,749
5172 Petroleum products, nec	5	5	27	28	6	23,556	25,429	755	760
5180 Beer, wine, and distilled beverages [3]	6	7	152	179	26	33,842	30,034	5,185	5,562
5191 Farm supplies	25	24	182	202	8	21,978	54,040	5,039	8,760
5193 Flowers & florists' supplies [3]	3	4	23	28	7	15,652	15,143	294	342
5199 Nondurable goods, nec [3]	8	10	75	85	9	21,067	21,976	1,888	2,051
52 – Retail trade	1,322	1,343	18,192	18,572	14	10,866	11,772	220,833	227,545
5210 Lumber and other building materials [3]	25	19	624	570	30	16,583	19,502	12,006	11,682
5230 Paint, glass, and wallpaper stores	8	8	29	25	3	17,517	17,120	525	445
5250 Hardware stores	14	9	132	126	14	9,848	11,048	1,504	1,408
5260 Retail nurseries and garden stores	7	7	48	37	5	13,083	11,676	825	778
5270 Mobile home dealers [3]	6	6	26	33	6	16,000	16,606	544	647
5310 Department stores [3]	13	13	2,171	2,129	164	9,658	11,337	23,138	24,580
5330 Variety stores	10	5	80	46	9	6,950	9,565	643	484
5390 Misc. general merchandise stores	6	12	359	394	33	9,337	9,888	3,733	3,888
5410 Grocery stores	60	60	1,721	1,835	31	11,984	12,035	20,575	22,895
5440 Candy, nut, and confectionery stores [3]	9	10	50	59	6	8,560	8,271	435	477
5460 Retail bakeries [3]	15	13	74	95	7	9,027	9,811	884	973
5490 Miscellaneous food stores [3]	9	8	122	116	15	13,934	17,897	1,725	2,145
5510 New and used car dealers	23	28	764	740	26	27,969	30,838	24,221	22,496
5520 Used car dealers [3]	21	20	68	62	3	19,176	21,032	1,513	1,265
5530 Auto and home supply stores	27	26	235	245	9	18,145	18,743	4,667	4,996
5540 Gasoline service stations	70	70	497	591	8	10,318	11,838	5,462	7,544
5550 Boat dealers [3]	3	3	4	7	2	17,000	11,429	100	108
5570 Motorcycle dealers [3]	6	5	29	32	6	12,966	18,250	502	636
5610 Men's & boys' clothing stores [3]	12	12	111	107	9	11,892	11,776	1,142	1,089
5620 Women's clothing stores	36	30	422	361	12	7,725	7,524	3,166	2,600
5630 Women's accessory & specialty stores [3]	9	10	52	41	4	7,231	8,683	370	319
5640 Children's and infants' wear stores [3]	4	4	65	63	16	8,123	9,143	486	513
5650 Family clothing stores [3]	13	16	162	192	12	9,753	10,000	1,766	1,981
5660 Shoe stores [3]	38	34	222	234	7	9,604	10,034	2,232	2,546
5690 Misc. apparel & accessory stores [3]	8	8	40	47	6	7,400	8,255	370	410
5712 Furniture stores [3]	23	26	216	244	9	16,722	17,590	4,423	4,389
5713 Floor covering stores [2]	-	11	-	71	6	-	23,380	-	1,798
5719 Misc. homefurnishings stores [1]	13	-	52	-	-	8,692	-	438	-
5720 Household appliance stores [3]	9	10	119	124	12	18,252	19,613	2,518	2,493
5731 Radio, TV, & electronic stores [3]	14	15	167	215	14	12,766	10,902	2,320	3,215
5734 Computer and software stores [2]	-	7	-	66	9	-	15,152	-	1,048
5735 Record & prerecorded tape stores [2]	-	6	-	38	6	-	8,947	-	286
5736 Musical instrument stores [3]	6	6	47	44	7	16,085	21,091	711	739
5812 Eating places	324	310	6,249	6,187	20	7,479	8,037	52,225	51,855
5813 Drinking places	101	97	532	492	5	7,060	7,350	3,910	3,674
5910 Drug stores and proprietary stores	42	43	551	581	14	15,034	17,274	9,371	10,314
5920 Liquor stores [3]	15	12	68	67	6	7,529	8,418	613	672
5930 Used merchandise stores	21	21	90	106	5	8,000	8,340	636	873
5941 Sporting goods and bicycle shops [3]	22	25	81	101	4	10,222	10,772	994	1,171
5942 Book stores [3]	14	13	128	127	10	7,500	8,031	4,104	1,031
5944 Jewelry stores [3]	17	18	113	118	7	14,938	17,695	1,628	1,926
5945 Hobby, toy, and game shops [3]	9	11	106	145	13	9,170	9,517	1,423	1,504
5947 Gift, novelty, and souvenir shops	26	28	142	144	5	6,789	7,167	1,180	1,237
5949 Sewing, needlework, and piece goods [3]	7	7	67	64	9	6,388	5,813	425	354
5961 Catalog and mail-order houses [3]	3	5	7	11	2	9,143	11,636	82	136
5962 Merchandising machine operators [3]	8	11	39	43	4	19,692	20,465	882	942
5963 Direct selling establishments	24	22	276	283	13	15,899	16,212	4,280	4,601
5984 Liquefied petroleum gas dealers [3]	4	3	31	26	9	23,613	24,769	806	689
5992 Florists [3]	23	20	165	140	7	9,455	10,829	1,568	1,432
5995 Optical goods stores [3]	10	9	67	54	6	13,433	14,815	926	805
5999 Miscellaneous retail stores, nec	48	52	227	260	5	11,330	10,985	3,044	3,423

Source: County Business Patterns 1994/95, CBP-94/95, U.S. Department of Commerce, Washington DC, November 1997. The employment column represents mid-March employment in the year. Pay per employee is calculated by dividing 1st Quarter payroll, annualized, by mid-March employment. The column headed 'Emp / Est' shows 'employees per establishment'. A dash (-) means that data are unavailable or cannot be calculated. nec means not elsewhere classified. *Notes:* 1. 1994 data incomplete; unavailable or withheld. 2. 1995 data incomplete; unavailable or withheld. 3. 1994 and 1995 data incomplete; unavailable or withheld.

SPRINGFIELD, MO MSA

Wholesale and Retail Trade USA	Establishments		Employment		Emp / Est	Pay / Employee		Annual Payroll ($ 000)	
	1994	1995	1994	1995	1995	1994	1995	1994	1995
50- Wholesale trade	725	750	10,387	11,553	15	22,752	23,723	273,591	309,178
5012 Automobiles and other vehicles [3]	30	23	833	641	28	22,723	24,406	19,522	15,817
5013 Motor vehicle supplies and new parts	31	45	704	1,142	25	19,983	19,096	15,245	24,689
5014 Tires and tubes [3]	6	6	53	62	10	20,226	21,484	1,159	1,363
5015 Motor vehicle parts, used [3]	17	19	90	106	6	17,200	22,642	1,715	2,625
5021 Furniture [3]	6	7	46	58	8	19,304	20,966	965	1,164
5023 Homefurnishings [3]	14	14	131	112	8	19,725	22,286	2,824	2,564
5031 Lumber, plywood, and millwork [1]	15	17	357	369	22	24,796	26,862	9,379	9,809
5032 Brick, stone, & related materials [2]	-	6	-	39	7	-	17,231	-	791
5033 Roofing, siding, & insulation [3]	9	7	169	159	23	20,213	21,535	4,045	2,903
5039 Construction materials, nec [1]	11	14	81	105	8	21,679	29,067	1,864	3,100
5044 Office equipment [3]	21	22	225	277	13	23,591	24,520	6,290	7,226
5045 Computers, peripherals, & software [3]	18	19	172	179	9	29,395	32,179	5,362	5,839
5046 Commercial equipment, nec [3]	9	6	90	83	14	20,667	23,036	2,105	2,154
5047 Medical and hospital equipment [3]	10	10	68	62	6	36,235	40,581	2,561	2,543
5049 Professional equipment, nec [3]	6	6	62	75	13	25,226	24,907	1,697	1,801
5051 Metals service centers and offices [3]	15	15	107	141	9	22,243	22,014	3,075	3,461
5063 Electrical apparatus and equipment [3]	23	18	293	100	6	24,983	31,040	8,098	2,907
5064 Electrical appliances, TV & radios [3]	3	3	55	28	9	8,655	14,857	478	395
5065 Electronic parts and equipment [3]	24	26	168	183	7	30,405	31,847	4,549	5,615
5072 Hardware [3]	14	15	91	90	6	28,220	32,844	2,620	2,589
5074 Plumbing & hydronic heating supplies [3]	9	15	90	318	21	22,667	22,717	2,566	8,281
5075 Warm air heating & air conditioning [3]	12	13	55	50	4	24,218	29,440	1,554	1,549
5078 Refrigeration equipment and supplies [3]	3	3	41	46	15	23,220	24,261	2,068	1,895
5082 Construction and mining machinery [3]	9	8	185	189	24	27,957	31,196	6,190	6,568
5083 Farm and garden machinery	27	26	197	198	8	19,127	20,465	4,412	4,275
5084 Industrial machinery and equipment [3]	29	31	258	287	9	26,837	29,603	8,398	9,335
5085 Industrial supplies [3]	21	19	214	149	8	29,346	27,839	6,634	4,347
5087 Service establishment equipment [3]	18	19	98	122	6	19,673	18,951	2,228	2,697
5091 Sporting & recreational goods	14	15	162	174	12	15,259	18,069	2,653	3,226
5092 Toys and hobby goods and supplies [3]	5	5	82	75	15	19,220	19,253	1,728	1,648
5093 Scrap and waste materials	7	8	75	99	12	16,907	16,040	1,643	1,763
5094 Jewelry & precious stones [3]	4	5	2	2	-	8,000	10,000	25	56
5099 Durable goods, nec [3]	13	13	78	77	6	18,103	24,779	5,070	4,882
5111 Printing and writing paper [3]	4	4	51	54	14	32,235	34,296	1,712	1,984
5112 Stationery and office supplies [3]	21	23	232	226	10	17,259	21,150	4,214	4,955
5113 Industrial & personal service paper [3]	8	7	65	75	11	21,292	21,547	1,485	1,780
5120 Drugs, proprietaries, and sundries [3]	6	7	112	140	20	28,464	26,600	4,059	4,388
5136 Men's and boys' clothing [3]	5	5	44	43	9	13,455	16,651	808	635
5141 Groceries, general line [3]	11	9	1,270	1,265	141	29,915	32,243	41,691	44,745
5142 Packaged frozen food [3]	8	9	168	183	20	20,357	22,470	4,268	4,525
5144 Poultry and poultry products [3]	6	5	66	526	105	25,939	16,510	2,068	9,796
5145 Confectionery [3]	5	5	35	39	8	7,771	9,949	282	412
5147 Meats and meat products [3]	8	7	75	90	13	21,280	20,444	1,861	1,934
5149 Groceries and related products, nec [3]	19	20	454	490	25	27,013	27,951	12,939	14,048
5154 Livestock [3]	8	8	71	61	8	5,521	6,230	408	365
5162 Plastics materials & basic shapes [3]	8	8	45	52	7	15,111	15,077	808	919
5169 Chemicals & allied products, nec	20	22	143	210	10	28,699	31,486	4,295	6,996
5171 Petroleum bulk stations & terminals	12	12	83	16	1	21,831	26,000	2,118	440
5172 Petroleum products, nec [1]	7	-	115	-	-	21,635	-	3,533	-
5181 Beer and ale [3]	3	3	142	150	50	26,254	26,987	4,631	4,906
5182 Wine and distilled beverages [3]	3	3	103	99	33	25,165	28,000	2,773	2,786
5191 Farm supplies	38	34	395	421	12	15,544	16,304	7,617	7,078
5192 Books, periodicals, & newspapers [2]	-	5	-	51	10	-	11,529	-	649
5193 Flowers & florists' supplies [3]	6	8	70	88	11	25,200	23,136	1,769	2,008
5199 Nondurable goods, nec [3]	18	19	111	97	5	19,171	20,701	2,573	2,727
52- Retail trade	2,032	2,082	29,458	30,488	15	11,317	12,225	367,135	395,253
5210 Lumber and other building materials	50	43	965	878	20	18,802	23,011	17,925	16,968
5230 Paint, glass, and wallpaper stores [3]	19	19	98	125	7	14,449	21,248	1,990	2,713
5250 Hardware stores	20	14	103	83	6	12,505	11,325	1,412	968
5260 Retail nurseries and garden stores	16	16	180	147	9	9,156	13,007	2,348	2,440
5270 Mobile home dealers [3]	13	12	92	114	10	29,913	29,719	3,453	3,994
5310 Department stores [3]	17	16	2,975	3,477	217	10,969	12,372	35,776	42,538
5390 Misc. general merchandise stores	-	18	-	403	22	-	13,221	-	5,167
5410 Grocery stores [3]	111	118	2,578	2,757	23	12,678	13,577	34,738	38,861
5420 Meat and fish markets [3]	5	3	7	18	6	9,143	12,000	302	183
5440 Candy, nut, and confectionery stores [3]	6	7	38	45	6	5,474	5,244	300	276
5460 Retail bakeries [3]	15	12	143	66	6	6,517	9,030	1,337	555
5490 Miscellaneous food stores [3]	11	8	63	40	5	7,746	9,400	523	473
5510 New and used car dealers	32	33	1,306	1,324	40	29,400	29,456	44,128	41,089
5520 Used car dealers	50	50	136	186	4	20,618	20,043	3,890	3,928

Continued on next page.

SPRINGFIELD, MO MSA - [continued]

Wholesale and Retail Trade USA	Establishments		Employment		Emp / Est	Pay / Employee		Annual Payroll ($ 000)	
	1994	1995	1994	1995	1995	1994	1995	1994	1995
5530 Auto and home supply stores	56	63	351	334	5	15,806	16,910	6,114	6,555
5540 Gasoline service stations	161	151	1,015	1,005	7	11,389	12,068	12,784	12,828
5550 Boat dealers [3]	9	8	123	106	13	14,797	17,132	2,225	1,937
5560 Recreational vehicle dealers	5	6	15	16	3	13,333	15,250	234	235
5570 Motorcycle dealers [3]	8	10	36	40	4	14,111	13,600	642	659
5610 Men's & boys' clothing stores [3]	17	18	131	129	7	9,496	10,109	1,316	1,312
5620 Women's clothing stores [3]	51	47	515	435	9	8,070	8,478	4,395	4,136
5630 Women's accessory & specialty stores [3]	11	11	57	60	5	10,035	11,000	600	639
5640 Children's and infants' wear stores [3]	7	6	33	32	5	6,909	6,000	264	223
5650 Family clothing stores [3]	18	19	210	218	11	8,267	8,844	1,764	1,954
5660 Shoe stores [3]	46	47	310	273	6	8,232	8,821	2,719	2,583
5690 Misc. apparel & accessory stores [3]	17	14	121	150	11	10,512	7,813	1,361	1,347
5712 Furniture stores	49	53	281	316	6	17,623	16,557	5,537	6,156
5713 Floor covering stores	23	28	165	159	6	19,952	21,786	4,024	4,101
5714 Drapery and upholstery stores [1]	5	-	6	-	-	17,333	-	141	-
5719 Misc. homefurnishings stores [1]	17	-	91	-	-	10,242	-	1,076	-
5720 Household appliance stores [3]	15	14	51	59	4	12,627	16,814	823	1,043
5731 Radio, TV, & electronic stores [2]	31	28	353	409	15	17,394	17,222	7,048	7,685
5734 Computer and software stores [3]	8	10	31	35	4	16,903	17,714	704	589
5735 Record & prerecorded tape stores [3]	6	7	40	48	7	11,700	9,417	459	743
5736 Musical instrument stores [3]	6	6	30	24	4	17,200	20,667	562	567
5812 Eating places	418	414	9,721	9,981	24	6,729	7,249	71,056	80,688
5813 Drinking places [3]	65	53	607	510	10	6,649	6,980	4,146	3,705
5910 Drug stores and proprietary stores	30	39	321	384	10	14,604	14,719	4,977	5,733
5920 Liquor stores	36	34	156	146	4	7,846	8,904	1,389	1,641
5930 Used merchandise stores	49	49	159	145	3	8,881	9,821	1,542	1,485
5941 Sporting goods and bicycle shops [2]	34	36	541	539	15	10,906	12,267	7,023	7,105
5942 Book stores [3]	24	20	113	106	5	8,496	10,830	1,176	1,237
5944 Jewelry stores [3]	29	30	158	153	5	15,544	17,987	2,804	3,284
5945 Hobby, toy, and game shops [3]	22	22	261	245	11	7,540	8,327	2,347	2,357
5947 Gift, novelty, and souvenir shops	48	47	234	227	5	7,470	8,317	1,898	2,160
5949 Sewing, needlework, and piece goods [3]	7	6	58	52	9	8,207	8,538	433	400
5961 Catalog and mail-order houses [2]	-	9	-	41	5	-	16,976	-	754
5962 Merchandising machine operators [2]	-	11	-	124	11	-	13,484	-	1,787
5963 Direct selling establishments [3]	34	36	184	130	4	10,500	15,169	2,432	2,329
5984 Liquefied petroleum gas dealers	24	24	111	126	5	19,640	18,413	2,198	2,219
5992 Florists	34	37	149	157	4	9,477	9,860	1,513	1,664
5995 Optical goods stores [3]	15	18	108	115	6	14,259	15,096	1,661	1,814
5999 Miscellaneous retail stores, nec	67	70	310	343	5	14,826	14,880	5,267	5,208

Source: County Business Patterns 1994/95, CBP-94/95, U.S. Department of Commerce, Washington DC, November 1997. The employment column represents mid-March employment in the year. Pay per employee is calculated by dividing 1st Quarter payroll, annualized, by mid-March employment. The column headed 'Emp / Est' shows 'employees per establishment'. A dash (-) means that data are unavailable or cannot be calculated. nec means not elsewhere classified. *Notes:* 1. 1994 data incomplete; unavailable or withheld. 2. 1995 data incomplete; unavailable or withheld. 3. 1994 and 1995 data incomplete; unavailable or withheld.

STATE COLLEGE, PA MSA

Wholesale and Retail Trade USA	Establishments		Employment		Emp / Est	Pay / Employee		Annual Payroll ($ 000)	
	1994	1995	1994	1995	1995	1994	1995	1994	1995
50– Wholesale trade	-	132	-	1,443	11	-	24,130	-	36,264
5013 Motor vehicle supplies and new parts	-	17	-	175	10	-	21,966	-	4,104
5015 Motor vehicle parts, used	-	3	-	9	3	-	12,889	-	136
5021 Furniture	-	3	-	55	18	-	21,236	-	1,109
5032 Brick, stone, & related materials	-	3	-	10	3	-	16,000	-	239
5045 Computers, peripherals, & software	-	9	-	135	15	-	40,296	-	4,718
5063 Electrical apparatus and equipment	-	3	-	49	16	-	23,347	-	1,172
5065 Electronic parts and equipment	-	4	-	33	8	-	20,606	-	755
5074 Plumbing & hydronic heating supplies	-	6	-	48	8	-	16,667	-	829
5082 Construction and mining machinery	-	6	-	43	7	-	24,465	-	1,164
5085 Industrial supplies	-	3	-	22	7	-	23,818	-	525
5087 Service establishment equipment	-	3	-	20	7	-	21,400	-	442
5140 Groceries and related products	-	8	-	148	19	-	19,081	-	3,756
5169 Chemicals & allied products, nec	-	3	-	46	15	-	28,261	-	1,224
5170 Petroleum and petroleum products	-	7	-	157	22	-	22,293	-	3,569
5181 Beer and ale	-	4	-	62	16	-	24,903	-	2,131
5199 Nondurable goods, nec	-	6	-	20	3	-	34,400	-	961
52– Retail trade	-	818	-	11,349	14	-	10,737	-	128,338
5210 Lumber and other building materials	-	13	-	349	27	-	18,086	-	6,333
5250 Hardware stores	-	6	-	47	8	-	13,702	-	744
5260 Retail nurseries and garden stores	-	9	-	34	4	-	13,647	-	632

Continued on next page.

STATE COLLEGE, PA MSA - [continued]

Wholesale and Retail Trade USA	Establishments		Employment		Emp / Est	Pay / Employee		Annual Payroll ($ 000)	
	1994	1995	1994	1995	1995	1994	1995	1994	1995
5310 Department stores	-	9	-	1,074	119	-	11,292	-	13,297
5330 Variety stores	-	6	-	50	8	-	8,560	-	525
5390 Misc. general merchandise stores	-	4	-	110	28	-	8,145	-	1,480
5410 Grocery stores	-	57	-	1,459	26	-	9,280	-	14,789
5420 Meat and fish markets	-	3	-	19	6	-	8,211	-	146
5440 Candy, nut, and confectionery stores	-	5	-	39	8	-	4,205	-	145
5490 Miscellaneous food stores	-	4	-	32	8	-	11,375	-	328
5510 New and used car dealers	-	16	-	511	32	-	23,194	-	12,472
5520 Used car dealers	-	6	-	30	5	-	17,467	-	557
5530 Auto and home supply stores	-	16	-	92	6	-	18,739	-	1,757
5540 Gasoline service stations	-	62	-	614	10	-	9,935	-	6,267
5570 Motorcycle dealers	-	3	-	22	7	-	16,182	-	377
5610 Men's & boys' clothing stores	-	10	-	64	6	-	12,313	-	721
5620 Women's clothing stores	-	28	-	222	8	-	7,604	-	1,690
5630 Women's accessory & specialty stores	-	4	-	26	7	-	8,000	-	207
5650 Family clothing stores	-	15	-	213	14	-	7,117	-	1,459
5660 Shoe stores	-	20	-	112	6	-	12,321	-	1,393
5690 Misc. apparel & accessory stores	-	7	-	59	8	-	6,712	-	493
5712 Furniture stores	-	14	-	117	8	-	15,624	-	2,014
5713 Floor covering stores	-	9	-	26	3	-	14,923	-	392
5719 Misc. homefurnishings stores	-	9	-	38	4	-	8,947	-	329
5720 Household appliance stores	-	6	-	16	3	-	14,000	-	226
5731 Radio, TV, & electronic stores	-	9	-	51	6	-	18,275	-	1,070
5735 Record & prerecorded tape stores	-	10	-	62	6	-	10,065	-	586
5812 Eating places	-	167	-	3,529	21	-	6,978	-	25,889
5813 Drinking places	-	26	-	286	11	-	6,643	-	1,959
5910 Drug stores and proprietary stores	-	29	-	288	10	-	15,569	-	4,783
5920 Liquor stores	-	11	-	61	6	-	16,131	-	976
5930 Used merchandise stores	-	4	-	15	4	-	5,600	-	145
5941 Sporting goods and bicycle shops	-	19	-	85	4	-	6,965	-	697
5942 Book stores	-	8	-	148	19	-	11,135	-	2,022
5943 Stationery stores	-	4	-	16	4	-	6,250	-	110
5944 Jewelry stores	-	17	-	98	6	-	13,837	-	1,506
5945 Hobby, toy, and game shops	-	5	-	21	4	-	7,238	-	197
5946 Camera & photographic supply stores	-	4	-	21	5	-	14,476	-	322
5947 Gift, novelty, and souvenir shops	-	22	-	166	8	-	7,012	-	1,238
5949 Sewing, needlework, and piece goods	-	3	-	18	6	-	8,000	-	134
5963 Direct selling establishments	-	5	-	15	3	-	7,733	-	164
5980 Fuel dealers	-	6	-	94	16	-	17,660	-	1,667
5992 Florists	-	15	-	67	4	-	8,896	-	659
5995 Optical goods stores	-	12	-	31	3	-	12,387	-	506
5999 Miscellaneous retail stores, nec	-	16	-	55	3	-	8,000	-	462

Source: County Business Patterns 1994/95, CBP-94/95, U.S. Department of Commerce, Washington DC, November 1997. The employment column represents mid-March employment in the year. Pay per employee is calculated by dividing 1st Quarter payroll, annualized, by mid-March employment. The column headed 'Emp / Est' shows 'employees per establishment'. A dash (-) means that data are unavailable or cannot be calculated. nec means not elsewhere classified. *Notes:* 1. 1994 data incomplete; unavailable or withheld. 2. 1995 data incomplete; unavailable or withheld. 3. 1994 and 1995 data incomplete; unavailable or withheld.

STEUBENVILLE - WEIRTON MSA (OH PART)

Wholesale and Retail Trade USA	Establishments		Employment		Emp / Est	Pay / Employee		Annual Payroll ($ 000)	
	1994	1995	1994	1995	1995	1994	1995	1994	1995
50- Wholesale trade	99	99	920	977	10	22,509	21,928	23,015	23,368
5013 Motor vehicle supplies and new parts	10	10	48	51	5	13,500	16,863	769	1,029
5015 Motor vehicle parts, used	3	3	10	10	3	13,200	17,600	132	155
5050 Metals and minerals, except petroleum	5	5	68	79	16	53,118	33,620	3,515	2,815
5065 Electronic parts and equipment	-	3	-	67	22	-	13,552	-	805
5074 Plumbing & hydronic heating supplies	-	3	-	30	10	-	22,800	-	734
5084 Industrial machinery and equipment	-	4	-	29	7	-	22,897	-	787
5085 Industrial supplies	-	4	-	21	5	-	26,095	-	537
5093 Scrap and waste materials	-	8	-	153	19	-	25,098	-	3,968
5140 Groceries and related products	-	8	-	101	13	-	21,109	-	2,274
5170 Petroleum and petroleum products	-	8	-	62	8	-	22,129	-	1,722
5180 Beer, wine, and distilled beverages	-	4	-	66	17	-	24,424	-	1,717
5190 Misc., nondurable goods	-	7	-	57	8	-	20,491	-	1,228
52- Retail trade	502	502	5,412	5,546	11	9,303	10,123	55,902	60,199
5210 Lumber and other building materials	4	6	128	94	16	7,094	11,872	1,032	1,102
5250 Hardware stores	4	5	43	50	10	9,023	8,160	432	527
5260 Retail nurseries and garden stores	6	6	39	40	7	9,231	10,700	484	505
5310 Department stores	5	5	716	657	131	8,263	11,050	6,978	7,649

Continued on next page.

STEUBENVILLE – WEIRTON MSA (OH PART) - [continued]

Wholesale and Retail Trade USA	Establishments		Employment		Emp / Est	Pay / Employee		Annual Payroll ($ 000)	
	1994	1995	1994	1995	1995	1994	1995	1994	1995
5410 Grocery stores	54	54	1,081	1,123	21	9,943	9,820	11,496	11,533
5440 Candy, nut, and confectionery stores	3	5	17	11	2	5,176	7,273	95	102
5460 Retail bakeries	6	6	57	63	11	7,158	7,746	483	534
5490 Miscellaneous food stores	-	3	-	15	5	-	15,467	-	247
5510 New and used car dealers	13	13	330	352	27	18,291	19,523	6,738	7,415
5520 Used car dealers	5	6	14	17	3	9,429	8,941	162	200
5530 Auto and home supply stores	10	13	77	85	7	16,156	14,212	1,321	1,345
5540 Gasoline service stations	41	37	200	185	5	8,340	8,541	1,741	1,709
5610 Men's & boys' clothing stores	3	3	28	22	7	11,429	14,182	316	291
5620 Women's clothing stores	9	6	92	70	12	9,783	7,086	923	505
5650 Family clothing stores	3	3	39	31	10	8,000	8,774	331	326
5660 Shoe stores	9	8	36	34	4	10,222	11,529	376	364
5690 Misc. apparel & accessory stores	-	3	-	4	1	-	3,000	-	45
5712 Furniture stores	12	12	70	70	6	10,457	12,229	855	1,008
5713 Floor covering stores	8	9	33	32	4	9,576	8,875	364	309
5720 Household appliance stores	7	6	15	15	3	6,933	9,067	142	148
5731 Radio, TV, & electronic stores	7	8	87	80	10	10,115	20,300	875	1,497
5812 Eating places	109	105	1,356	1,485	14	6,493	6,836	10,083	10,494
5813 Drinking places	37	34	84	88	3	6,524	6,500	600	603
5910 Drug stores and proprietary stores	21	22	206	234	11	12,214	12,718	2,886	3,158
5920 Liquor stores	-	3	-	9	3	-	4,000	-	37
5941 Sporting goods and bicycle shops	-	5	-	9	2	-	8,444	-	100
5942 Book stores	3	-	18	-	-	5,333	-	102	-
5944 Jewelry stores	12	10	79	77	8	11,342	10,442	954	937
5945 Hobby, toy, and game shops	6	5	22	25	5	6,000	5,440	187	141
5947 Gift, novelty, and souvenir shops	9	8	46	40	5	6,087	10,700	339	464
5962 Merchandising machine operators	-	4	-	19	5	-	15,368	-	305
5983 Fuel oil dealers	4	4	12	18	5	12,333	10,889	168	207
5992 Florists	9	10	48	44	4	7,667	8,727	392	407
5995 Optical goods stores	6	6	25	29	5	12,960	12,690	371	388
5999 Miscellaneous retail stores, nec	14	14	37	39	3	10,703	14,051	506	697

Source: County Business Patterns 1994/95, CBP-94/95, U.S. Department of Commerce, Washington DC, November 1997. The employment column represents mid-March employment in the year. Pay per employee is calculated by dividing 1st Quarter payroll, annualized, by mid-March employment. The column headed 'Emp / Est' shows 'employees per establishment'. A dash (-) means that data are unavailable or cannot be calculated. nec means not elsewhere classified. *Notes:* 1. 1994 data incomplete; unavailable or withheld. 2. 1995 data incomplete; unavailable or withheld. 3. 1994 and 1995 data incomplete; unavailable or withheld.

STEUBENVILLE – WEIRTON MSA (WV PART)

Wholesale and Retail Trade USA	Establishments		Employment		Emp / Est	Pay / Employee		Annual Payroll ($ 000)	
	1994	1995	1994	1995	1995	1994	1995	1994	1995
50– Wholesale trade	-	38	-	231	6	-	22,234	-	4,729
5010 Motor vehicles, parts, and supplies	-	6	-	30	5	-	26,133	-	568
5040 Professional & commercial equipment	-	4	-	8	2	-	13,000	-	104
5060 Electrical goods	-	5	-	27	5	-	12,889	-	247
5090 Miscellaneous durable goods	-	6	-	32	5	-	23,750	-	720
5100 Wholesale trade-nondurable goods	-	10	-	91	9	-	23,077	-	2,010
52– Retail trade	-	341	-	3,328	10	-	10,498	-	39,655
5200 Building materials & garden supplies	-	11	-	91	8	-	16,879	-	2,156
5300 General merchandise stores	-	7	-	368	53	-	12,598	-	4,588
5410 Grocery stores	-	41	-	629	15	-	10,989	-	8,925
5510 New and used car dealers	-	7	-	135	19	-	17,570	-	2,466
5520 Used car dealers	-	7	-	5	1	-	3,200	-	29
5540 Gasoline service stations	-	26	-	134	5	-	9,075	-	1,237
5660 Shoe stores	-	4	-	6	2	-	10,667	-	63
5730 Radio, television, & computer stores	-	4	-	8	2	-	16,500	-	123
5812 Eating places	-	76	-	1,100	14	-	7,531	-	8,948
5813 Drinking places	-	37	-	131	4	-	5,527	-	719
5910 Drug stores and proprietary stores	-	17	-	148	9	-	17,676	-	2,940
5941 Sporting goods and bicycle shops [2]	-	3	-	4	1	-	7,000	-	62
5944 Jewelry stores	-	5	-	12	2	-	13,333	-	255
5992 Florists	-	14	-	27	2	-	6,815	-	181
5999 Miscellaneous retail stores, nec	-	5	-	13	3	-	13,538	-	123

Source: County Business Patterns 1994/95, CBP-94/95, U.S. Department of Commerce, Washington DC, November 1997. The employment column represents mid-March employment in the year. Pay per employee is calculated by dividing 1st Quarter payroll, annualized, by mid-March employment. The column headed 'Emp / Est' shows 'employees per establishment'. A dash (-) means that data are unavailable or cannot be calculated. nec means not elsewhere classified. *Notes:* 1. 1994 data incomplete; unavailable or withheld. 2. 1995 data incomplete; unavailable or withheld. 3. 1994 and 1995 data incomplete; unavailable or withheld.

STEUBENVILLE - WEIRTON, OH - WV MSA

Wholesale and Retail Trade USA	Establishments		Employment		Emp / Est	Pay / Employee		Annual Payroll ($ 000)	
	1994	1995	1994	1995	1995	1994	1995	1994	1995
50 - Wholesale trade [1]	99	137	920	1,208	9	22,509	21,987	23,015	28,097
5013 Motor vehicle supplies and new parts [1]	10	14	48	51	4	13,500	16,863	769	1,029
5015 Motor vehicle parts, used [3]	3	4	10	10	3	13,200	17,600	132	155
5040 Professional & commercial equipment	-	6	-	8	1	-	13,000	-	104
5050 Metals and minerals, except petroleum [3]	5	5	68	79	16	53,118	33,620	3,515	2,815
5065 Electronic parts and equipment	-	7	-	67	10	-	13,552	-	805
5074 Plumbing & hydronic heating supplies [2]	-	5	-	30	6	-	22,800	-	734
5084 Industrial machinery and equipment [2]	-	5	-	29	6	-	22,897	-	787
5085 Industrial supplies [2]	-	4	-	21	5	-	26,095	-	537
5093 Scrap and waste materials	-	11	-	153	14	-	25,098	-	3,968
5140 Groceries and related products [2]	-	8	-	101	13	-	21,109	-	2,274
5170 Petroleum and petroleum products [2]	-	9	-	62	7	-	22,129	-	1,722
5180 Beer, wine, and distilled beverages	-	8	-	66	8	-	24,424	-	1,717
5190 Misc., nondurable goods [2]	-	11	-	57	5	-	20,491	-	1,228
52 - Retail trade [1]	502	843	5,412	8,874	11	9,303	10,264	55,902	99,854
5210 Lumber and other building materials [1]	4	11	128	94	9	7,094	11,872	1,032	1,102
5250 Hardware stores [3]	4	6	43	50	8	9,023	8,160	432	527
5260 Retail nurseries and garden stores [1]	6	8	39	40	5	9,231	10,700	484	505
5310 Department stores [3]	5	7	716	657	94	8,263	11,050	6,978	7,649
5410 Grocery stores [1]	54	95	1,081	1,752	18	9,943	10,240	11,496	20,458
5440 Candy, nut, and confectionery stores [3]	3	5	17	11	2	5,176	7,273	95	102
5460 Retail bakeries [1]	6	12	57	63	5	7,158	7,746	483	534
5490 Miscellaneous food stores [2]	-	3	-	15	5	-	15,467	-	247
5510 New and used car dealers [1]	13	20	330	487	24	18,291	18,982	6,738	9,881
5520 Used car dealers [1]	5	13	14	22	2	9,429	7,636	162	229
5530 Auto and home supply stores [1]	10	22	77	85	4	16,156	14,212	1,321	1,345
5540 Gasoline service stations [1]	41	63	200	319	5	8,340	8,765	1,741	2,946
5610 Men's & boys' clothing stores [3]	3	3	28	22	7	11,429	14,182	316	291
5620 Women's clothing stores [1]	9	10	92	70	7	9,783	7,086	923	505
5650 Family clothing stores [1]	3	5	39	31	6	8,000	8,774	331	326
5660 Shoe stores [1]	9	12	36	40	3	10,222	11,400	376	427
5690 Misc. apparel & accessory stores [2]	-	4	-	4	1	-	3,000	-	45
5712 Furniture stores [1]	12	18	70	70	4	10,457	12,229	855	1,008
5713 Floor covering stores [3]	8	9	33	32	4	9,576	8,875	364	309
5720 Household appliance stores [1]	7	9	15	15	2	6,933	9,067	142	148
5731 Radio, TV, & electronic stores [3]	7	10	87	80	8	10,115	20,300	875	1,497
5812 Eating places [1]	109	181	1,356	2,585	14	6,493	7,132	10,083	19,442
5813 Drinking places [1]	37	71	84	219	3	6,524	5,918	600	1,322
5910 Drug stores and proprietary stores [1]	21	39	206	382	10	12,214	14,639	2,886	6,098
5920 Liquor stores	-	6	-	9	2	-	4,000	-	37
5941 Sporting goods and bicycle shops [2]	-	8	-	13	2	-	8,000	-	162
5942 Book stores [1]	3	-	18	-	-	5,333	-	102	-
5944 Jewelry stores [1]	12	15	79	89	6	11,342	10,831	954	1,192
5945 Hobby, toy, and game shops [1]	6	7	22	25	4	6,000	5,440	187	141
5947 Gift, novelty, and souvenir shops [1]	9	11	46	40	4	6,087	10,700	339	464
5962 Merchandising machine operators [2]	-	4	-	19	5	-	15,368	-	305
5983 Fuel oil dealers [3]	4	5	12	18	4	12,333	10,889	168	207
5992 Florists [1]	9	24	48	71	3	7,667	8,000	392	588
5995 Optical goods stores [3]	6	6	25	29	5	12,960	12,690	371	388
5999 Miscellaneous retail stores, nec [1]	14	19	37	52	3	10,703	13,923	506	820

Source: County Business Patterns 1994/95, CBP-94/95, U.S. Department of Commerce, Washington DC, November 1997. The employment column represents mid-March employment in the year. Pay per employee is calculated by dividing 1st Quarter payroll, annualized, by mid-March employment. The column headed 'Emp / Est' shows 'employees per establishment'. A dash (-) means that data are unavailable or cannot be calculated. nec means not elsewhere classified. *Notes:* 1. 1994 data incomplete; unavailable or withheld. 2. 1995 data incomplete; unavailable or withheld. 3. 1994 and 1995 data incomplete; unavailable or withheld.

STOCKTON - LODI, CA MSA

Wholesale and Retail Trade USA	Establishments		Employment		Emp / Est	Pay / Employee		Annual Payroll ($ 000)	
	1994	1995	1994	1995	1995	1994	1995	1994	1995
50 - Wholesale trade	659	653	8,954	9,030	14	27,952	30,263	272,229	285,002
5012 Automobiles and other vehicles	13	13	204	230	18	32,608	33,061	6,902	8,320
5013 Motor vehicle supplies and new parts	35	33	501	356	11	22,363	20,101	13,185	7,936
5015 Motor vehicle parts, used	16	17	60	71	4	16,333	18,817	1,212	1,371
5021 Furniture	5	6	9	14	2	23,556	30,857	379	539
5023 Homefurnishings	8	5	102	46	9	20,745	26,087	2,142	1,223
5031 Lumber, plywood, and millwork	13	15	178	144	10	27,978	27,444	4,843	4,006
5032 Brick, stone, & related materials	14	15	99	84	6	34,141	37,714	3,347	2,897
5044 Office equipment	12	12	164	193	16	24,317	49,886	4,807	6,206
5045 Computers, peripherals, & software	10	8	138	141	18	28,522	31,007	3,626	3,996

Continued on next page.

STOCKTON - LODI, CA MSA - [continued]

Wholesale and Retail Trade USA	Establishments 1994	Establishments 1995	Employment 1994	Employment 1995	Emp / Est 1995	Pay / Employee 1994	Pay / Employee 1995	Annual Payroll ($ 000) 1994	Annual Payroll ($ 000) 1995
5046 Commercial equipment, nec	9	-	49	-	-	24,653	-	1,343	-
5047 Medical and hospital equipment	8	7	128	127	18	22,375	23,843	3,381	3,540
5051 Metals service centers and offices	15	15	301	335	22	30,671	33,696	10,018	11,194
5063 Electrical apparatus and equipment	19	18	197	194	11	33,157	31,753	6,289	5,871
5064 Electrical appliances, TV & radios	7	5	43	49	10	9,581	11,592	474	562
5065 Electronic parts and equipment	4	8	28	51	6	29,571	33,255	921	1,679
5072 Hardware	6	6	76	73	12	24,368	24,767	1,860	1,904
5074 Plumbing & hydronic heating supplies	9	9	77	92	10	26,130	25,391	2,196	2,302
5082 Construction and mining machinery	8	8	85	107	13	34,024	31,589	3,186	3,925
5083 Farm and garden machinery	27	24	313	312	13	32,102	30,577	8,943	9,308
5084 Industrial machinery and equipment	34	37	403	431	12	31,782	31,777	13,721	14,950
5085 Industrial supplies	25	24	226	221	9	30,195	31,946	7,061	7,956
5087 Service establishment equipment	12	14	125	145	10	22,688	22,124	2,998	3,922
5088 Transportation equipment & supplies	3	3	40	52	17	19,700	20,462	926	957
5092 Toys and hobby goods and supplies	5	4	19	14	4	8,421	10,000	138	140
5093 Scrap and waste materials	17	16	113	119	7	18,832	19,765	2,420	2,328
5099 Durable goods, nec	10	10	133	81	8	22,376	20,790	3,361	1,801
5111 Printing and writing paper	6	6	34	106	18	26,471	30,491	3,039	3,358
5112 Stationery and office supplies	13	14	165	157	11	15,564	18,166	2,561	3,093
5113 Industrial & personal service paper	7	6	109	109	18	47,193	47,670	5,016	5,080
5120 Drugs, proprietaries, and sundries	-	4	-	193	48	-	25,658	-	2,367
5137 Women's and children's clothing	4	4	11	25	6	7,636	5,120	151	81
5142 Packaged frozen food	9	9	595	644	72	37,304	37,410	24,383	25,877
5143 Dairy products, exc. dried or canned	11	10	76	39	4	17,579	27,692	1,443	1,114
5144 Poultry and poultry products	5	6	152	130	22	27,132	31,446	4,582	4,330
5147 Meats and meat products	4	5	124	130	26	22,968	24,431	3,011	3,131
5148 Fresh fruits and vegetables	27	26	540	429	17	12,030	21,072	14,505	13,743
5149 Groceries and related products, nec	27	24	422	385	16	26,701	30,992	11,997	12,305
5153 Grain and field beans	10	10	78	99	10	58,103	53,414	3,835	4,586
5154 Livestock	4	4	50	38	10	6,080	6,316	310	494
5159 Farm-product raw materials, nec	5	6	42	133	22	24,762	14,617	975	2,271
5160 Chemicals and allied products	8	7	73	58	8	32,000	37,034	2,750	2,499
5171 Petroleum bulk stations & terminals	16	16	173	157	10	31,746	34,803	6,046	6,220
5172 Petroleum products, nec	6	6	47	49	8	30,894	31,837	1,308	1,424
5181 Beer and ale	3	3	182	191	64	29,099	29,613	5,229	5,588
5182 Wine and distilled beverages	3	3	294	290	97	40,190	41,834	11,253	11,162
5191 Farm supplies	40	37	427	538	15	29,068	31,472	14,139	18,964
5193 Flowers & florists' supplies	8	-	26	-	-	16,923	-	456	-
5198 Paints, varnishes, and supplies	10	7	67	60	9	22,567	27,400	1,633	1,586
5199 Nondurable goods, nec	14	20	127	139	7	23,811	19,856	3,008	3,077
52 - Retail trade	2,320	2,306	28,692	29,599	13	13,301	13,989	415,316	437,936
5210 Lumber and other building materials	35	28	430	536	19	20,660	20,925	9,025	11,158
5230 Paint, glass, and wallpaper stores	17	18	69	87	5	20,754	19,632	1,407	1,752
5250 Hardware stores	27	16	428	351	22	13,626	13,652	6,454	5,260
5260 Retail nurseries and garden stores	12	15	58	87	6	12,828	14,759	787	1,427
5270 Mobile home dealers	4	4	33	21	5	17,697	27,238	606	535
5310 Department stores	20	22	3,342	3,359	153	10,406	12,266	38,381	42,451
5330 Variety stores	6	-	58	-	-	10,138	-	573	-
5390 Misc. general merchandise stores	11	11	347	330	30	17,153	19,818	6,637	6,571
5410 Grocery stores	245	229	3,552	3,497	15	18,003	18,967	68,123	67,991
5420 Meat and fish markets	18	16	115	93	6	13,009	14,710	1,437	1,272
5430 Fruit and vegetable markets	3	3	10	12	4	6,800	6,333	148	145
5440 Candy, nut, and confectionery stores	7	8	24	27	3	11,167	9,630	320	334
5460 Retail bakeries	40	36	274	223	6	11,372	11,390	3,192	2,628
5490 Miscellaneous food stores	16	17	89	73	4	6,921	11,123	753	1,008
5510 New and used car dealers	38	38	1,491	1,509	40	29,427	30,592	49,201	50,577
5520 Used car dealers	28	32	120	199	6	23,067	19,317	3,186	4,138
5530 Auto and home supply stores	79	82	671	744	9	16,465	18,317	12,269	14,668
5540 Gasoline service stations	114	118	952	1,106	9	10,941	10,268	10,955	12,170
5550 Boat dealers	4	4	18	38	10	19,778	19,684	636	1,017
5560 Recreational vehicle dealers	10	11	128	176	16	19,375	19,477	3,192	4,663
5570 Motorcycle dealers	6	9	49	50	6	19,510	19,680	1,131	1,272
5610 Men's & boys' clothing stores	27	30	159	192	6	10,767	11,917	2,026	2,318
5620 Women's clothing stores	55	51	423	355	7	8,265	8,225	3,847	2,851
5630 Women's accessory & specialty stores	15	17	65	84	5	9,662	10,667	705	842
5640 Children's and infants' wear stores	5	5	18	20	4	6,444	8,000	137	149
5650 Family clothing stores	24	21	295	293	14	9,492	10,416	3,037	3,098
5660 Shoe stores	49	51	240	255	5	10,183	10,212	2,526	2,590
5690 Misc. apparel & accessory stores	11	13	53	58	4	10,340	10,138	573	641
5712 Furniture stores	43	43	210	188	4	17,905	16,915	4,075	4,156
5713 Floor covering stores	18	19	165	184	10	27,248	25,457	4,688	5,390

Continued on next page.

STOCKTON - LODI, CA MSA - [continued]

Wholesale and Retail Trade USA	Establishments		Employment		Emp / Est	Pay / Employee		Annual Payroll ($ 000)	
	1994	1995	1994	1995	1995	1994	1995	1994	1995
5714 Drapery and upholstery stores	5	5	30	25	5	12,933	15,040	426	400
5719 Misc. homefurnishings stores	24	22	88	107	5	9,591	11,402	1,047	1,249
5720 Household appliance stores	13	16	72	70	4	14,833	15,943	1,116	1,186
5731 Radio, TV, & electronic stores	25	26	182	205	8	20,791	19,941	3,952	4,008
5734 Computer and software stores	8	9	21	22	2	10,667	12,000	227	397
5735 Record & prerecorded tape stores	8	9	90	112	12	8,756	8,929	810	962
5736 Musical instrument stores	8	7	31	32	5	38,581	15,125	1,191	540
5812 Eating places	612	580	9,257	9,468	16	7,418	7,854	74,714	76,420
5813 Drinking places	87	73	279	276	4	8,143	8,507	2,469	2,171
5910 Drug stores and proprietary stores	87	82	1,263	1,183	14	20,019	20,686	25,387	25,287
5920 Liquor stores	46	44	170	140	3	9,553	9,829	1,535	1,422
5930 Used merchandise stores	22	19	229	252	13	10,638	10,206	3,137	3,666
5941 Sporting goods and bicycle shops	38	38	286	286	8	8,755	9,930	2,543	2,899
5942 Book stores	12	12	90	89	7	9,333	10,697	967	1,005
5943 Stationery stores	9	9	58	63	7	11,241	10,286	611	575
5944 Jewelry stores	40	40	172	168	4	18,023	18,000	3,136	3,092
5945 Hobby, toy, and game shops	17	15	205	223	15	7,766	7,641	1,870	1,751
5946 Camera & photographic supply stores	-	3	-	66	22	-	19,152	-	1,160
5947 Gift, novelty, and souvenir shops	31	33	175	174	5	7,840	7,402	1,498	1,374
5948 Luggage and leather goods stores	-	4	-	20	5	-	8,800	-	215
5949 Sewing, needlework, and piece goods	7	-	104	-	-	6,692	-	636	-
5961 Catalog and mail-order houses	8	-	24	-	-	9,833	-	253	-
5962 Merchandising machine operators	5	-	32	-	-	20,500	-	770	-
5963 Direct selling establishments	15	15	68	81	5	25,412	24,790	2,135	2,802
5980 Fuel dealers	8	8	95	115	14	24,084	24,209	2,473	3,238
5992 Florists	39	37	179	175	5	8,961	8,960	1,619	1,561
5994 News dealers and newsstands	6	5	34	32	6	6,235	6,875	215	217
5995 Optical goods stores	24	20	69	61	3	16,638	19,344	1,204	1,288
5999 Miscellaneous retail stores, nec	69	72	423	381	5	12,586	13,239	5,955	5,288

Source: County Business Patterns 1994/95, CBP-94/95, U.S. Department of Commerce, Washington DC, November 1997. The employment column represents mid-March employment in the year. Pay per employee is calculated by dividing 1st Quarter payroll, annualized, by mid-March employment. The column headed 'Emp / Est' shows 'employees per establishment'. A dash (-) means that data are unavailable or cannot be calculated. nec means not elsewhere classified. *Notes:* 1. 1994 data incomplete; unavailable or withheld. 2. 1995 data incomplete; unavailable or withheld. 3. 1994 and 1995 data incomplete; unavailable or withheld.

SUMTER, SC MSA

Wholesale and Retail Trade USA	Establishments		Employment		Emp / Est	Pay / Employee		Annual Payroll ($ 000)	
	1994	1995	1994	1995	1995	1994	1995	1994	1995
50- Wholesale trade	-	105	-	1,235	12	-	24,282	-	29,430
5013 Motor vehicle supplies and new parts	-	9	-	112	12	-	30,607	-	2,101
5030 Lumber and construction materials	-	7	-	149	21	-	21,718	-	3,559
5051 Metals service centers and offices	-	4	-	65	16	-	16,554	-	1,008
5063 Electrical apparatus and equipment	-	4	-	26	7	-	21,846	-	620
5070 Hardware, plumbing & heating equipment	-	10	-	63	6	-	22,222	-	1,482
5084 Industrial machinery and equipment	-	7	-	36	5	-	31,111	-	1,038
5093 Scrap and waste materials	-	6	-	53	9	-	20,528	-	1,228
5099 Durable goods, nec	-	3	-	9	3	-	3,556	-	32
5140 Groceries and related products	-	7	-	72	10	-	25,111	-	1,881
5160 Chemicals and allied products	-	7	-	239	34	-	27,314	-	5,634
5171 Petroleum bulk stations & terminals	-	4	-	53	13	-	29,962	-	1,337
5172 Petroleum products, nec	-	3	-	21	7	-	17,905	-	376
5180 Beer, wine, and distilled beverages	-	5	-	63	13	-	25,651	-	2,006
5199 Nondurable goods, nec	-	3	-	14	5	-	18,571	-	230
52- Retail trade	-	518	-	6,884	13	-	10,916	-	80,504
5210 Lumber and other building materials	-	5	-	114	23	-	18,351	-	2,176
5250 Hardware stores	-	6	-	74	12	-	14,595	-	1,102
5260 Retail nurseries and garden stores	-	5	-	12	2	-	11,333	-	127
5270 Mobile home dealers	-	10	-	137	14	-	26,803	-	4,536
5310 Department stores	-	4	-	514	129	-	12,568	-	6,282
5330 Variety stores	-	7	-	75	11	-	8,907	-	744
5390 Misc. general merchandise stores	-	3	-	67	22	-	10,687	-	691
5410 Grocery stores	-	76	-	1,503	20	-	7,470	-	11,529
5460 Retail bakeries	-	3	-	16	5	-	6,250	-	83
5510 New and used car dealers	-	14	-	374	27	-	27,519	-	11,936
5530 Auto and home supply stores	-	22	-	221	10	-	16,217	-	3,845
5540 Gasoline service stations	-	32	-	258	8	-	8,543	-	2,264
5570 Motorcycle dealers	-	4	-	13	3	-	17,231	-	239
5610 Men's & boys' clothing stores	-	6	-	37	6	-	10,270	-	415
5620 Women's clothing stores	-	22	-	134	6	-	8,000	-	1,249

Continued on next page.

SUMTER, SC MSA - [continued]

Wholesale and Retail Trade USA	Establishments		Employment		Emp / Est	Pay / Employee		Annual Payroll ($ 000)	
	1994	1995	1994	1995	1995	1994	1995	1994	1995
5630 Women's accessory & specialty stores	-	3	-	10	3	-	8,800	-	89
5650 Family clothing stores	-	6	-	128	21	-	8,906	-	1,223
5660 Shoe stores	-	10	-	64	6	-	10,250	-	546
5712 Furniture stores	-	19	-	136	7	-	17,176	-	3,083
5713 Floor covering stores	-	5	-	19	4	-	17,684	-	287
5720 Household appliance stores	-	5	-	15	3	-	20,800	-	336
5731 Radio, TV, & electronic stores	-	3	-	37	12	-	10,703	-	370
5734 Computer and software stores	-	5	-	15	3	-	19,200	-	508
5812 Eating places	-	87	-	2,013	23	-	7,354	-	15,251
5813 Drinking places	-	4	-	24	6	-	4,333	-	105
5910 Drug stores and proprietary stores	-	11	-	99	9	-	18,222	-	1,951
5920 Liquor stores	-	9	-	25	3	-	12,480	-	330
5930 Used merchandise stores	-	7	-	19	3	-	10,947	-	259
5944 Jewelry stores	-	7	-	80	11	-	15,250	-	1,173
5947 Gift, novelty, and souvenir shops	-	15	-	61	4	-	7,148	-	466
5949 Sewing, needlework, and piece goods	-	3	-	14	5	-	5,429	-	100
5980 Fuel dealers	-	3	-	63	21	-	21,841	-	1,401
5992 Florists	-	7	-	29	4	-	7,586	-	229

Source: County Business Patterns 1994/95, CBP-94/95, U.S. Department of Commerce, Washington DC, November 1997. The employment column represents mid-March employment in the year. Pay per employee is calculated by dividing 1st Quarter payroll, annualized, by mid-March employment. The column headed 'Emp / Est' shows 'employees per establishment'. A dash (-) means that data are unavailable or cannot be calculated. nec means not elsewhere classified. *Notes:* 1. 1994 data incomplete; unavailable or withheld. 2. 1995 data incomplete; unavailable or withheld. 3. 1994 and 1995 data incomplete; unavailable or withheld.

SYRACUSE, NY MSA

Wholesale and Retail Trade USA	Establishments		Employment		Emp / Est	Pay / Employee		Annual Payroll ($ 000)	
	1994	1995	1994	1995	1995	1994	1995	1994	1995
50- Wholesale trade	1,509	1,494	18,482	18,021	12	28,253	31,072	555,860	577,996
5012 Automobiles and other vehicles	25	28	462	463	17	26,848	23,957	13,407	11,809
5013 Motor vehicle supplies and new parts	104	93	818	855	9	20,919	22,704	18,029	19,187
5014 Tires and tubes [3]	16	17	100	123	7	25,240	25,106	2,740	2,946
5015 Motor vehicle parts, used	17	21	70	73	3	14,686	19,233	1,195	1,461
5021 Furniture [3]	21	21	208	224	11	26,115	26,125	6,063	6,399
5023 Homefurnishings [3]	19	18	131	149	8	26,015	25,396	3,764	3,713
5031 Lumber, plywood, and millwork [3]	22	23	409	346	15	26,484	29,376	11,297	9,081
5032 Brick, stone, & related materials [2]	12	10	126	72	7	28,381	38,444	4,189	3,027
5033 Roofing, siding, & insulation [3]	18	16	124	113	7	33,452	34,619	5,442	4,675
5039 Construction materials, nec [2]	17	30	64	225	8	22,875	31,556	1,845	7,095
5043 Photographic equipment & supplies [3]	4	4	41	42	11	28,878	34,476	1,344	1,486
5044 Office equipment	34	32	610	549	17	31,443	38,142	18,412	18,954
5045 Computers, peripherals, & software [3]	51	56	696	807	14	42,471	46,364	31,787	37,395
5046 Commercial equipment, nec [3]	16	14	131	127	9	23,023	24,472	3,387	3,465
5047 Medical and hospital equipment [2]	33	29	222	331	11	36,306	36,423	8,422	12,263
5048 Ophthalmic goods [3]	8	8	49	47	6	23,510	28,681	1,432	1,451
5049 Professional equipment, nec [3]	8	9	137	134	15	24,672	23,582	3,059	3,106
5051 Metals service centers and offices [1]	24	-	13	-	-	6,462	-	98	-
5063 Electrical apparatus and equipment	93	87	755	700	8	33,330	35,989	25,864	26,039
5064 Electrical appliances, TV & radios [3]	11	10	76	77	8	29,211	29,403	2,375	2,226
5065 Electronic parts and equipment	76	83	1,163	1,136	14	30,064	47,606	37,452	54,534
5072 Hardware [3]	33	30	316	322	11	28,557	31,366	9,330	9,766
5074 Plumbing & hydronic heating supplies	38	42	336	403	10	28,298	28,298	9,890	11,585
5075 Warm air heating & air conditioning [3]	32	32	587	204	6	53,622	49,373	29,865	10,075
5078 Refrigeration equipment and supplies [3]	6	7	78	88	13	33,179	32,318	2,873	2,992
5082 Construction and mining machinery [1]	23	21	406	406	19	33,044	35,665	14,529	14,288
5083 Farm and garden machinery	36	40	234	328	8	20,188	23,841	5,472	7,914
5084 Industrial machinery and equipment	100	98	779	799	8	30,685	32,010	24,746	27,613
5085 Industrial supplies [3]	53	53	657	652	12	31,951	34,865	23,310	25,404
5087 Service establishment equipment [3]	27	26	229	193	7	18,568	17,865	4,577	3,621
5091 Sporting & recreational goods	20	18	64	64	4	28,375	32,750	2,276	2,435
5092 Toys and hobby goods and supplies [1]	5	-	76	-	-	19,316	-	1,936	-
5093 Scrap and waste materials	19	19	209	206	11	20,459	27,301	5,359	6,264
5094 Jewelry & precious stones [1]	7	-	28	-	-	18,000	-	574	-
5099 Durable goods, nec	25	27	100	115	4	20,640	23,304	2,276	2,592
5111 Printing and writing paper [1]	4	-	81	-	-	30,963	-	2,498	-
5112 Stationery and office supplies [3]	46	43	321	312	7	24,885	25,654	8,107	8,336
5113 Industrial & personal service paper [3]	14	12	81	75	6	24,000	26,987	2,079	2,043
5120 Drugs, proprietaries, and sundries [3]	9	9	216	259	29	30,556	27,367	6,089	7,382
5131 Piece goods & notions [2]	-	5	-	29	6	-	13,931	-	467
5136 Men's and boys' clothing [2]	-	4	-	17	4	-	10,824	-	240

Continued on next page.

SYRACUSE, NY MSA - [continued]

Wholesale and Retail Trade USA	Establishments		Employment		Emp / Est	Pay / Employee		Annual Payroll ($ 000)	
	1994	1995	1994	1995	1995	1994	1995	1994	1995
5141 Groceries, general line[3]	19	15	625	607	40	30,490	33,397	19,752	23,340
5142 Packaged frozen food[3]	8	9	98	95	11	25,796	28,463	2,714	3,194
5143 Dairy products, exc. dried or canned[3]	15	15	362	299	20	32,994	31,786	13,037	8,336
5144 Poultry and poultry products[1]	6	-	23	-	-	20,348	-	515	-
5145 Confectionery[3]	9	9	167	166	18	24,743	26,699	4,524	5,152
5146 Fish and seafoods[1]	8	-	56	-	-	14,286	-	791	-
5147 Meats and meat products[3]	13	13	174	172	13	22,828	25,349	4,582	4,939
5148 Fresh fruits and vegetables	25	22	153	131	6	21,542	24,641	3,303	3,299
5149 Groceries and related products, nec[3]	38	33	1,156	982	30	30,388	33,303	35,692	32,666
5150 Farm-product raw materials[2]	8	6	39	9	2	16,308	17,778	526	154
5162 Plastics materials & basic shapes[3]	11	12	61	72	6	28,000	26,111	1,901	2,056
5169 Chemicals & allied products, nec[3]	26	24	186	194	8	35,484	36,206	6,532	6,524
5170 Petroleum and petroleum products	21	18	156	107	6	34,897	40,972	5,422	4,115
5181 Beer and ale[3]	10	10	346	364	36	23,306	22,165	9,389	9,509
5182 Wine and distilled beverages[3]	5	4	255	276	69	31,169	29,420	8,908	9,372
5191 Farm supplies	37	33	252	201	6	21,079	19,761	6,003	4,256
5192 Books, periodicals, & newspapers[3]	14	12	72	70	6	19,444	22,743	2,089	1,494
5193 Flowers & florists' supplies[3]	10	9	92	91	10	17,000	19,429	1,703	1,729
5194 Tobacco and tobacco products[3]	4	5	1,017	698	140	16,547	29,628	19,317	21,482
5198 Paints, varnishes, and supplies[3]	9	9	47	39	4	21,872	25,641	1,077	910
5199 Nondurable goods, nec	32	33	83	107	3	15,566	19,738	1,588	2,476
52- Retail trade	4,532	4,468	61,470	61,227	14	11,933	12,485	829,687	821,844
5210 Lumber and other building materials	86	77	1,208	1,318	17	15,377	16,883	21,775	23,683
5230 Paint, glass, and wallpaper stores	28	24	127	85	4	20,598	18,824	2,982	1,886
5250 Hardware stores	55	41	379	276	7	13,858	13,217	6,265	3,895
5260 Retail nurseries and garden stores	34	31	220	186	6	9,055	12,409	3,477	3,601
5270 Mobile home dealers[3]	13	12	29	51	4	24,552	36,549	850	1,932
5310 Department stores[3]	38	38	3,903	4,201	111	8,745	11,386	41,763	49,328
5330 Variety stores	21	18	167	193	11	9,701	8,953	1,808	1,821
5390 Misc. general merchandise stores	28	27	1,153	1,098	41	10,935	12,444	13,829	13,812
5410 Grocery stores	344	352	9,745	10,304	29	12,195	11,404	124,603	124,862
5420 Meat and fish markets[3]	24	21	111	114	5	9,730	10,491	1,178	1,343
5430 Fruit and vegetable markets	6	8	12	3	-	3,667	4,000	150	131
5440 Candy, nut, and confectionery stores	18	16	78	67	4	6,308	7,284	479	478
5450 Dairy products stores[1]	26	27	89	87	3	11,910	14,575	1,257	1,403
5460 Retail bakeries	65	55	515	500	9	8,482	7,776	4,528	4,068
5490 Miscellaneous food stores[3]	26	25	108	128	5	9,704	8,656	1,131	1,145
5510 New and used car dealers	92	94	2,995	3,012	32	23,153	24,910	83,353	80,761
5520 Used car dealers	49	42	125	116	3	16,672	19,828	2,290	2,459
5530 Auto and home supply stores	99	98	761	788	8	20,625	19,015	15,484	15,997
5540 Gasoline service stations	264	257	1,790	1,754	7	11,088	11,779	21,012	20,829
5550 Boat dealers	15	15	51	48	3	11,137	12,500	1,145	1,113
5560 Recreational vehicle dealers[3]	12	11	55	55	5	17,745	15,782	1,298	1,158
5570 Motorcycle dealers	10	9	41	46	5	15,220	17,826	903	1,082
5610 Men's & boys' clothing stores	42	39	275	312	8	9,571	10,308	2,640	3,032
5620 Women's clothing stores	127	113	1,342	1,141	10	7,207	7,057	10,226	8,031
5630 Women's accessory & specialty stores[3]	30	27	172	143	5	7,535	9,119	1,428	1,337
5640 Children's and infants' wear stores[3]	13	11	128	130	12	6,188	6,615	884	911
5650 Family clothing stores[3]	61	60	1,028	994	17	9,233	8,901	9,608	9,999
5660 Shoe stores	119	103	506	468	5	9,976	10,453	5,342	5,006
5690 Misc. apparel & accessory stores[3]	31	34	159	191	6	9,107	9,843	1,618	1,913
5712 Furniture stores	70	66	653	731	11	16,300	17,505	11,372	13,369
5713 Floor covering stores	41	43	272	236	5	19,500	22,424	6,113	5,545
5719 Misc. homefurnishings stores[1]	34	-	7	-	-	4,000	-	36	-
5720 Household appliance stores	20	19	40	40	2	12,200	13,000	564	566
5731 Radio, TV, & electronic stores	36	33	207	190	6	16,580	16,295	3,864	3,528
5734 Computer and software stores	13	20	38	42	2	9,474	9,619	359	685
5735 Record & prerecorded tape stores	33	31	221	293	9	6,769	9,119	1,890	2,351
5736 Musical instrument stores[3]	9	10	43	54	5	15,628	14,889	766	859
5812 Eating places	1,227	1,121	18,241	17,966	16	7,375	8,090	151,815	154,212
5813 Drinking places	261	231	1,165	1,092	5	6,493	6,850	7,802	7,207
5910 Drug stores and proprietary stores	133	135	2,829	2,351	17	11,852	13,443	34,262	33,180
5920 Liquor stores	64	67	236	261	4	9,492	8,935	2,360	2,407
5930 Used merchandise stores	47	52	155	127	2	9,006	9,071	1,522	1,253
5941 Sporting goods and bicycle shops	72	71	484	534	8	10,570	10,015	5,789	5,669
5942 Book stores	40	38	292	335	9	9,301	10,233	2,830	3,500
5943 Stationery stores	13	18	108	132	7	9,852	11,030	1,201	1,687
5944 Jewelry stores	59	57	373	368	6	14,155	14,467	5,393	5,249
5945 Hobby, toy, and game shops	27	28	160	204	7	10,275	8,941	2,172	2,531
5946 Camera & photographic supply stores[3]	9	9	31	31	3	14,065	13,161	536	457
5947 Gift, novelty, and souvenir shops	73	74	431	477	6	6,561	6,985	3,324	3,609

Continued on next page.

SYRACUSE, NY MSA - [continued]

Wholesale and Retail Trade USA	Establishments		Employment		Emp / Est	Pay / Employee		Annual Payroll ($ 000)	
	1994	1995	1994	1995	1995	1994	1995	1994	1995
5948 Luggage and leather goods stores [3]	3	4	13	15	4	12,923	13,600	188	209
5949 Sewing, needlework, and piece goods	23	23	198	163	7	5,131	5,816	1,145	972
5961 Catalog and mail-order houses	12	16	27	64	4	14,370	18,313	434	1,346
5962 Merchandising machine operators [3]	30	27	157	176	7	18,369	21,182	3,284	4,035
5963 Direct selling establishments [3]	33	36	276	192	5	16,986	21,708	5,283	4,234
5983 Fuel oil dealers	19	18	123	141	8	16,520	13,730	2,143	1,603
5984 Liquefied petroleum gas dealers [3]	9	9	26	25	3	21,846	22,400	531	551
5992 Florists	72	68	306	328	5	9,438	9,512	3,108	3,181
5993 Tobacco stores and stands [3]	7	6	36	29	5	6,000	7,310	233	216
5994 News dealers and newsstands [3]	12	13	58	92	7	8,759	8,696	563	791
5995 Optical goods stores	54	59	290	360	6	20,262	21,667	6,592	7,505
5999 Miscellaneous retail stores, nec	91	106	499	545	5	12,008	11,802	6,404	7,362

Source: County Business Patterns 1994/95, CBP-94/95, U.S. Department of Commerce, Washington DC, November 1997. The employment column represents mid-March employment in the year. Pay per employee is calculated by dividing 1st Quarter payroll, annualized, by mid-March employment. The column headed 'Emp / Est' shows 'employees per establishment'. A dash (-) means that data are unavailable or cannot be calculated. nec means not elsewhere classified. *Notes:* 1. 1994 data incomplete; unavailable or withheld. 2. 1995 data incomplete; unavailable or withheld. 3. 1994 and 1995 data incomplete; unavailable or withheld.

TACOMA, WA PMSA

Wholesale and Retail Trade USA	Establishments		Employment		Emp / Est	Pay / Employee		Annual Payroll ($ 000)	
	1994	1995	1994	1995	1995	1994	1995	1994	1995
50- Wholesale trade	-	853	-	11,402	13	-	29,521	-	341,237
5012 Automobiles and other vehicles	-	17	-	213	13	-	33,634	-	6,491
5013 Motor vehicle supplies and new parts	-	46	-	499	11	-	24,168	-	12,924
5014 Tires and tubes	-	13	-	92	7	-	26,304	-	2,612
5015 Motor vehicle parts, used	-	16	-	96	6	-	18,917	-	1,763
5021 Furniture	-	16	-	199	12	-	23,859	-	5,216
5023 Homefurnishings	-	13	-	97	7	-	25,361	-	2,797
5031 Lumber, plywood, and millwork	-	45	-	556	12	-	35,007	-	19,710
5032 Brick, stone, & related materials	-	13	-	60	5	-	40,867	-	2,130
5033 Roofing, siding, & insulation	-	10	-	174	17	-	27,770	-	5,955
5039 Construction materials, nec	-	27	-	315	12	-	27,225	-	9,901
5044 Office equipment	-	17	-	159	9	-	38,541	-	3,717
5045 Computers, peripherals, & software	-	26	-	208	8	-	26,942	-	5,466
5046 Commercial equipment, nec	-	6	-	98	16	-	20,245	-	2,257
5047 Medical and hospital equipment	-	11	-	241	22	-	41,643	-	8,777
5049 Professional equipment, nec	-	3	-	14	5	-	28,286	-	509
5051 Metals service centers and offices	-	21	-	293	14	-	32,041	-	10,266
5063 Electrical apparatus and equipment	-	23	-	232	10	-	36,000	-	7,910
5072 Hardware	-	21	-	252	12	-	25,175	-	6,734
5074 Plumbing & hydronic heating supplies	-	13	-	152	12	-	31,395	-	5,005
5075 Warm air heating & air conditioning	-	9	-	165	18	-	32,388	-	6,442
5078 Refrigeration equipment and supplies	-	3	-	14	5	-	34,571	-	331
5082 Construction and mining machinery	-	5	-	149	30	-	39,168	-	6,322
5083 Farm and garden machinery	-	5	-	29	6	-	24,000	-	723
5084 Industrial machinery and equipment	-	38	-	367	10	-	35,270	-	11,598
5085 Industrial supplies	-	19	-	252	13	-	31,667	-	7,924
5087 Service establishment equipment	-	17	-	120	7	-	23,900	-	2,908
5088 Transportation equipment & supplies	-	13	-	75	6	-	29,013	-	2,332
5091 Sporting & recreational goods	-	22	-	114	5	-	33,439	-	3,302
5092 Toys and hobby goods and supplies	-	6	-	38	6	-	23,053	-	935
5093 Scrap and waste materials	-	23	-	387	17	-	27,628	-	11,441
5094 Jewelry & precious stones	-	5	-	6	1	-	20,667	-	126
5099 Durable goods, nec	-	22	-	210	10	-	46,114	-	9,729
5112 Stationery and office supplies	-	17	-	191	11	-	23,518	-	4,569
5136 Men's and boys' clothing	-	7	-	24	3	-	17,000	-	484
5141 Groceries, general line	-	6	-	34	6	-	25,412	-	964
5142 Packaged frozen food	-	7	-	287	41	-	40,321	-	11,716
5145 Confectionery	-	6	-	53	9	-	24,226	-	1,375
5146 Fish and seafoods	-	8	-	325	41	-	12,197	-	2,942
5147 Meats and meat products	-	11	-	137	12	-	24,934	-	3,817
5148 Fresh fruits and vegetables	-	7	-	88	13	-	26,773	-	2,612
5149 Groceries and related products, nec	-	22	-	530	24	-	31,404	-	17,915
5162 Plastics materials & basic shapes	-	5	-	33	7	-	26,303	-	959
5169 Chemicals & allied products, nec	-	15	-	110	7	-	30,364	-	3,706
5170 Petroleum and petroleum products	-	10	-	145	15	-	34,510	-	5,105
5180 Beer, wine, and distilled beverages	-	6	-	325	54	-	29,354	-	10,036
5191 Farm supplies	-	13	-	123	9	-	10,667	-	1,376
5193 Flowers & florists' supplies	-	14	-	228	16	-	21,123	-	4,531

Continued on next page.

TACOMA, WA PMSA - [continued]

Wholesale and Retail Trade USA	Establishments		Employment		Emp / Est	Pay / Employee		Annual Payroll ($ 000)	
	1994	1995	1994	1995	1995	1994	1995	1994	1995
5198 Paints, varnishes, and supplies	-	12	-	68	6	-	20,765	-	1,404
5199 Nondurable goods, nec	-	27	-	239	9	-	20,887	-	5,730
52 - Retail trade	-	3,360	-	43,091	13	-	14,421	-	657,427
5210 Lumber and other building materials	-	41	-	973	24	-	22,804	-	22,347
5230 Paint, glass, and wallpaper stores	-	16	-	89	6	-	20,989	-	1,963
5250 Hardware stores	-	30	-	652	22	-	14,049	-	9,975
5260 Retail nurseries and garden stores	-	30	-	230	8	-	13,183	-	3,380
5270 Mobile home dealers	-	17	-	174	10	-	26,046	-	4,676
5310 Department stores	-	21	-	3,708	177	-	14,594	-	58,074
5390 Misc. general merchandise stores	-	16	-	792	50	-	17,369	-	14,287
5410 Grocery stores	-	268	-	5,512	21	-	16,803	-	93,395
5420 Meat and fish markets	-	13	-	64	5	-	15,563	-	1,197
5430 Fruit and vegetable markets	-	6	-	4	1	-	6,000	-	314
5440 Candy, nut, and confectionery stores	-	8	-	23	3	-	10,957	-	305
5450 Dairy products stores	-	6	-	13	2	-	8,308	-	89
5460 Retail bakeries	-	26	-	246	9	-	10,081	-	2,550
5490 Miscellaneous food stores	-	31	-	245	8	-	9,224	-	4,422
5510 New and used car dealers	-	48	-	2,251	47	-	33,795	-	87,013
5520 Used car dealers	-	54	-	175	3	-	21,623	-	4,497
5530 Auto and home supply stores	-	126	-	884	7	-	21,027	-	20,065
5540 Gasoline service stations	-	145	-	1,238	9	-	11,069	-	14,559
5550 Boat dealers	-	13	-	111	9	-	26,775	-	2,988
5560 Recreational vehicle dealers	-	24	-	361	15	-	23,435	-	10,087
5570 Motorcycle dealers	-	10	-	70	7	-	20,400	-	1,615
5590 Automotive dealers, nec	-	5	-	27	5	-	23,704	-	796
5610 Men's & boys' clothing stores	-	20	-	84	4	-	15,143	-	1,384
5620 Women's clothing stores	-	56	-	433	8	-	8,231	-	3,660
5630 Women's accessory & specialty stores	-	14	-	72	5	-	8,333	-	580
5640 Children's and infants' wear stores	-	4	-	9	2	-	6,222	-	64
5650 Family clothing stores	-	33	-	540	16	-	10,578	-	5,762
5660 Shoe stores	-	50	-	208	4	-	13,462	-	2,791
5690 Misc. apparel & accessory stores	-	14	-	73	5	-	12,219	-	904
5712 Furniture stores	-	79	-	683	9	-	21,019	-	13,599
5713 Floor covering stores	-	34	-	139	4	-	19,827	-	3,182
5714 Drapery and upholstery stores	-	6	-	8	1	-	10,500	-	86
5719 Misc. homefurnishings stores	-	40	-	197	5	-	13,746	-	2,740
5720 Household appliance stores	-	23	-	131	6	-	18,840	-	2,320
5731 Radio, TV, & electronic stores	-	32	-	237	7	-	23,004	-	4,964
5734 Computer and software stores	-	25	-	214	9	-	14,897	-	3,324
5735 Record & prerecorded tape stores	-	16	-	141	9	-	12,085	-	1,624
5736 Musical instrument stores	-	16	-	115	7	-	26,783	-	3,919
5812 Eating places	-	815	-	14,303	18	-	8,824	-	130,178
5813 Drinking places	-	130	-	988	8	-	8,684	-	8,700
5910 Drug stores and proprietary stores	-	65	-	927	14	-	16,764	-	16,567
5930 Used merchandise stores	-	85	-	587	7	-	10,944	-	6,675
5941 Sporting goods and bicycle shops	-	68	-	550	8	-	13,927	-	7,597
5942 Book stores	-	39	-	283	7	-	10,417	-	3,070
5943 Stationery stores	-	10	-	58	6	-	13,586	-	803
5944 Jewelry stores	-	62	-	302	5	-	20,848	-	6,055
5945 Hobby, toy, and game shops	-	24	-	246	10	-	13,187	-	3,243
5946 Camera & photographic supply stores	-	6	-	22	4	-	21,091	-	401
5947 Gift, novelty, and souvenir shops	-	83	-	390	5	-	9,262	-	3,692
5949 Sewing, needlework, and piece goods	-	22	-	212	10	-	8,283	-	1,844
5961 Catalog and mail-order houses	-	18	-	252	14	-	14,429	-	3,838
5962 Merchandising machine operators	-	10	-	97	10	-	27,546	-	2,545
5963 Direct selling establishments	-	45	-	284	6	-	18,042	-	5,603
5983 Fuel oil dealers	-	8	-	65	8	-	38,954	-	2,168
5992 Florists	-	59	-	319	5	-	11,473	-	3,654
5993 Tobacco stores and stands	-	9	-	103	11	-	14,252	-	1,720
5994 News dealers and newsstands	-	4	-	12	3	-	9,333	-	83
5995 Optical goods stores	-	40	-	230	6	-	20,870	-	5,308
5999 Miscellaneous retail stores, nec	-	104	-	480	5	-	13,067	-	7,747

Source: County Business Patterns 1994/95, CBP-94/95, U.S. Department of Commerce, Washington DC, November 1997. The employment column represents mid-March employment in the year. Pay per employee is calculated by dividing 1st Quarter payroll, annualized, by mid-March employment. The column headed 'Emp / Est' shows 'employees per establishment'. A dash (-) means that data are unavailable or cannot be calculated. nec means not elsewhere classified. *Notes:* 1. 1994 data incomplete; unavailable or withheld. 2. 1995 data incomplete; unavailable or withheld. 3. 1994 and 1995 data incomplete; unavailable or withheld.

TALLAHASSEE, FL MSA

Wholesale and Retail Trade USA	Establishments		Employment		Emp / Est	Pay / Employee		Annual Payroll ($ 000)	
	1994	1995	1994	1995	1995	1994	1995	1994	1995
50- Wholesale trade	347	345	3,849	3,711	11	26,885	27,805	105,461	106,777
5012 Automobiles and other vehicles [3]	8	6	78	78	13	19,077	19,385	2,085	2,028
5013 Motor vehicle supplies and new parts	32	22	179	104	5	15,844	16,385	3,047	1,976
5021 Furniture [2]	-	5	-	42	8	-	24,762	-	1,143
5023 Homefurnishings	-	4	-	8	2	-	15,000	-	91
5031 Lumber, plywood, and millwork	10	9	110	99	11	25,018	23,798	2,629	2,363
5032 Brick, stone, & related materials	6	5	19	24	5	26,737	27,167	527	606
5033 Roofing, siding, & insulation [3]	4	4	22	39	10	16,364	25,333	366	957
5039 Construction materials, nec	7	15	56	176	12	22,643	24,659	1,620	4,341
5044 Office equipment [3]	19	19	266	243	13	26,226	22,979	7,753	6,313
5045 Computers, peripherals, & software	24	23	296	236	10	62,757	62,000	13,661	13,382
5046 Commercial equipment, nec [2]	-	3	-	9	3	-	26,222	-	251
5047 Medical and hospital equipment [2]	11	9	110	120	13	30,727	31,500	3,801	4,510
5048 Ophthalmic goods [1]	3	-	16	-	-	18,500	-	328	-
5051 Metals service centers and offices [3]	4	3	18	16	5	21,556	26,500	371	377
5063 Electrical apparatus and equipment [3]	18	18	158	170	9	24,203	32,306	4,133	5,059
5064 Electrical appliances, TV & radios [2]	-	3	-	10	3	-	18,400	-	190
5065 Electronic parts and equipment [2]	-	9	-	73	8	-	16,877	-	1,191
5072 Hardware [1]	6	-	36	-	-	18,889	-	787	-
5074 Plumbing & hydronic heating supplies [1]	7	7	58	46	7	22,000	23,652	1,459	1,349
5075 Warm air heating & air conditioning [2]	-	8	-	60	8	-	32,000	-	2,173
5084 Industrial machinery and equipment [3]	7	6	64	65	11	17,688	18,646	1,392	1,470
5085 Industrial supplies [3]	8	7	53	54	8	22,113	25,333	1,324	1,315
5087 Service establishment equipment	7	6	51	44	7	24,314	27,909	1,205	1,236
5093 Scrap and waste materials [3]	5	6	51	69	12	15,686	22,667	1,234	1,540
5099 Durable goods, nec	5	7	18	13	2	10,444	14,769	393	277
5112 Stationery and office supplies [3]	19	17	180	165	10	19,333	20,412	3,335	3,208
5130 Apparel, piece goods, and notions [3]	6	7	80	80	11	15,050	16,450	1,367	1,359
5143 Dairy products, exc. dried or canned [3]	4	3	60	35	12	20,867	29,600	1,403	552
5149 Groceries and related products, nec	10	13	218	199	15	23,982	26,131	5,870	5,499
5169 Chemicals & allied products, nec [3]	5	5	27	39	8	32,000	26,667	1,193	1,303
5170 Petroleum and petroleum products	9	10	60	71	7	23,533	26,535	1,512	1,792
5180 Beer, wine, and distilled beverages [3]	4	4	158	187	47	24,354	23,914	4,344	4,874
5191 Farm supplies	-	7	-	24	3	-	9,333	-	214
5192 Books, periodicals, & newspapers [3]	5	4	81	82	21	23,556	28,878	2,065	2,284
5198 Paints, varnishes, and supplies [2]	-	3	-	7	2	-	32,571	-	211
52- Retail trade	1,517	1,514	24,745	24,749	16	9,889	10,862	265,714	280,027
5210 Lumber and other building materials	27	24	632	565	24	16,551	19,009	12,417	11,773
5230 Paint, glass, and wallpaper stores [3]	10	9	38	44	5	16,632	14,636	676	692
5250 Hardware stores	10	5	56	10	2	9,714	11,200	598	173
5260 Retail nurseries and garden stores	11	10	99	111	11	14,869	13,946	1,577	1,635
5270 Mobile home dealers [1]	9	14	46	63	5	37,652	30,921	1,815	2,382
5310 Department stores [3]	15	14	2,510	2,494	178	11,065	12,276	29,050	29,937
5330 Variety stores	11	8	47	46	6	6,723	5,478	384	296
5390 Misc. general merchandise stores	9	12	338	353	29	10,071	12,261	4,153	4,051
5410 Grocery stores	148	141	4,109	4,035	29	9,016	9,888	39,466	40,817
5420 Meat and fish markets	10	12	46	53	4	13,739	14,491	638	655
5460 Retail bakeries [3]	9	9	75	70	8	9,867	10,343	893	926
5490 Miscellaneous food stores [2]	9	9	116	108	12	5,931	8,333	799	949
5510 New and used car dealers	24	22	824	868	39	29,830	31,364	28,884	30,451
5520 Used car dealers	19	24	57	88	4	21,754	25,364	1,970	3,100
5530 Auto and home supply stores	48	54	290	378	7	15,807	18,286	5,316	7,060
5540 Gasoline service stations	89	83	681	676	8	11,477	11,657	8,264	8,200
5550 Boat dealers [2]	5	4	26	24	6	19,692	23,500	409	419
5560 Recreational vehicle dealers [1]	3	-	29	-	-	16,000	-	391	-
5570 Motorcycle dealers [1]	3	-	16	-	-	11,250	-	257	-
5610 Men's & boys' clothing stores	19	15	132	106	7	9,515	8,491	1,271	1,047
5620 Women's clothing stores	44	41	495	410	10	7,475	7,015	3,836	2,865
5630 Women's accessory & specialty stores [3]	10	8	69	69	9	6,841	7,652	504	529
5640 Children's and infants' wear stores [2]	-	4	-	37	9	-	7,568	-	312
5650 Family clothing stores	17	17	382	405	24	9,843	10,311	4,284	4,132
5660 Shoe stores	43	42	204	230	5	10,882	9,530	2,322	1,908
5690 Misc. apparel & accessory stores [3]	8	10	63	86	9	10,730	9,674	791	977
5712 Furniture stores	42	40	297	342	9	14,923	17,251	5,087	6,001
5713 Floor covering stores	-	13	-	93	7	-	17,290	-	1,999
5719 Misc. homefurnishings stores	20	-	136	-	-	9,647	-	1,540	-
5720 Household appliance stores [2]	8	7	56	62	9	19,214	19,871	1,153	1,334
5731 Radio, TV, & electronic stores [1]	18	20	132	206	10	18,636	14,932	2,480	2,972
5734 Computer and software stores [3]	11	12	72	65	5	17,833	24,000	1,596	1,778
5735 Record & prerecorded tape stores	12	14	90	118	8	10,800	9,627	1,047	1,110
5736 Musical instrument stores [3]	6	6	51	50	8	9,725	11,360	557	609

Continued on next page.

TALLAHASSEE, FL MSA - [continued]

Wholesale and Retail Trade USA	Establishments		Employment		Emp / Est	Pay / Employee		Annual Payroll ($ 000)	
	1994	1995	1994	1995	1995	1994	1995	1994	1995
5812 Eating places	328	309	9,149	8,630	28	6,315	7,149	60,322	61,508
5813 Drinking places [3]	11	13	157	177	14	5,732	6,576	1,035	1,149
5910 Drug stores and proprietary stores	36	36	644	677	19	13,609	12,892	9,110	9,606
5920 Liquor stores	28	29	201	249	9	9,831	8,530	2,109	2,169
5930 Used merchandise stores	36	35	113	124	4	9,699	11,452	1,128	1,280
5941 Sporting goods and bicycle shops	34	32	127	148	5	12,598	12,378	1,847	2,168
5942 Book stores [3]	19	19	291	274	14	9,595	10,146	3,129	3,185
5944 Jewelry stores	27	28	179	178	6	11,732	14,090	2,163	2,480
5945 Hobby, toy, and game shops [3]	7	7	39	57	8	8,308	8,912	514	571
5947 Gift, novelty, and souvenir shops	30	31	163	158	5	8,123	9,443	1,404	1,571
5949 Sewing, needlework, and piece goods [3]	11	9	60	76	8	7,267	5,789	398	537
5961 Catalog and mail-order houses [1]	7	-	17	-	-	15,059	-	250	-
5963 Direct selling establishments	14	12	10	8	1	5,200	5,500	46	49
5984 Liquefied petroleum gas dealers	9	9	16	20	2	19,250	19,800	320	429
5992 Florists [1]	28	26	5	135	5	5,600	8,948	27	1,194
5995 Optical goods stores	16	16	126	119	7	14,095	17,076	1,741	2,007
5999 Miscellaneous retail stores, nec	48	54	252	285	5	11,397	10,302	2,982	3,263

Source: County Business Patterns 1994/95, CBP-94/95, U.S. Department of Commerce, Washington DC, November 1997. The employment column represents mid-March employment in the year. Pay per employee is calculated by dividing 1st Quarter payroll, annualized, by mid-March employment. The column headed 'Emp / Est' shows 'employees per establishment'. A dash (-) means that data are unavailable or cannot be calculated. nec means not elsewhere classified. *Notes:* 1. 1994 data incomplete; unavailable or withheld. 2. 1995 data incomplete; unavailable or withheld. 3. 1994 and 1995 data incomplete; unavailable or withheld.

TAMPA - ST. PETERSBURG - CLEARWATER, FL MSA

Wholesale and Retail Trade USA	Establishments		Employment		Emp / Est	Pay / Employee		Annual Payroll ($ 000)	
	1994	1995	1994	1995	1995	1994	1995	1994	1995
50- Wholesale trade	4,554	4,650	55,251	55,048	12	28,599	30,155	1,660,799	1,714,469
5012 Automobiles and other vehicles	95	91	1,433	1,490	16	21,845	20,969	32,327	33,615
5013 Motor vehicle supplies and new parts	219	193	2,187	2,138	11	20,285	21,497	48,137	46,817
5014 Tires and tubes [3]	23	21	179	180	9	29,899	33,244	5,333	5,614
5015 Motor vehicle parts, used [3]	62	64	290	321	5	18,952	22,555	6,557	7,692
5021 Furniture	68	68	448	449	7	25,938	27,341	12,350	13,818
5023 Homefurnishings	77	76	329	376	5	22,553	23,564	8,667	9,321
5031 Lumber, plywood, and millwork [1]	76	71	1,007	1,000	14	30,097	29,348	29,103	28,844
5032 Brick, stone, & related materials	55	53	455	325	6	27,640	26,548	12,758	9,682
5033 Roofing, siding, & insulation [3]	35	30	514	366	12	24,872	31,301	13,884	12,071
5039 Construction materials, nec	40	68	503	857	13	27,308	25,592	15,356	23,339
5043 Photographic equipment & supplies [3]	14	15	319	334	22	44,690	56,886	13,341	16,463
5044 Office equipment	89	113	1,497	1,653	15	30,309	34,773	48,227	55,854
5045 Computers, peripherals, & software	182	179	3,123	3,931	22	39,768	41,211	127,961	159,764
5046 Commercial equipment, nec	65	63	670	573	9	22,746	25,201	16,328	14,912
5047 Medical and hospital equipment [3]	174	155	3,546	2,712	17	31,311	35,867	108,892	96,145
5048 Ophthalmic goods [3]	26	27	391	436	16	29,453	33,486	13,114	13,975
5049 Professional equipment, nec [3]	17	18	57	76	4	32,772	32,579	1,899	2,807
5051 Metals service centers and offices [3]	73	78	8	798	10	7,500	33,629	78	27,685
5063 Electrical apparatus and equipment	201	173	1,835	1,934	11	31,592	35,324	60,646	67,105
5064 Electrical appliances, TV & radios [3]	42	38	569	538	14	26,362	26,967	15,434	14,680
5065 Electronic parts and equipment	192	204	1,932	2,246	11	33,969	30,760	72,042	80,505
5072 Hardware [3]	79	79	881	847	11	26,370	24,911	23,797	21,898
5074 Plumbing & hydronic heating supplies	88	95	709	624	7	29,591	27,878	21,639	18,150
5075 Warm air heating & air conditioning	76	78	604	639	8	29,934	34,541	21,185	22,833
5078 Refrigeration equipment and supplies	13	15	107	126	8	32,486	29,079	3,558	3,591
5082 Construction and mining machinery	36	31	674	663	21	31,911	38,021	23,176	25,145
5083 Farm and garden machinery [3]	34	34	220	231	7	21,018	21,472	5,202	4,884
5084 Industrial machinery and equipment	247	242	1,963	2,092	9	30,280	31,685	65,972	72,821
5085 Industrial supplies	109	109	944	1,018	9	29,504	32,173	31,811	35,834
5087 Service establishment equipment [3]	54	57	752	423	7	21,282	20,936	16,482	10,922
5088 Transportation equipment & supplies	62	61	333	365	6	27,327	30,937	10,239	11,948
5091 Sporting & recreational goods	68	67	370	564	8	23,222	33,617	9,831	20,595
5092 Toys and hobby goods and supplies	27	30	331	329	11	12,495	16,328	5,805	5,568
5093 Scrap and waste materials	60	59	560	634	11	23,864	25,735	14,830	18,484
5094 Jewelry & precious stones [3]	52	59	325	378	6	26,043	28,646	9,674	11,148
5099 Durable goods, nec	97	107	409	498	5	19,765	21,622	9,716	12,693
5111 Printing and writing paper [3]	24	24	392	381	16	33,827	41,438	12,622	14,456
5112 Stationery and office supplies	101	78	1,341	1,042	13	20,552	24,637	28,465	24,791
5113 Industrial & personal service paper	57	60	379	421	7	28,538	28,485	11,666	12,446
5120 Drugs, proprietaries, and sundries	92	91	1,215	1,083	12	24,813	29,333	32,461	33,101
5131 Piece goods & notions [3]	24	24	215	237	10	19,609	21,485	4,641	5,044
5136 Men's and boys' clothing	24	25	409	371	15	18,269	22,803	7,371	8,280

Continued on next page.

TAMPA - ST. PETERSBURG - CLEARWATER, FL MSA - [continued]

Wholesale and Retail Trade USA	Establishments		Employment		Emp / Est	Pay / Employee		Annual Payroll ($ 000)	
	1994	1995	1994	1995	1995	1994	1995	1994	1995
5137 Women's and children's clothing[3]	27	28	149	176	6	13,047	13,523	2,387	2,566
5141 Groceries, general line[3]	33	36	1,118	1,027	29	22,612	25,449	24,407	29,024
5142 Packaged frozen food	50	45	906	941	21	27,872	28,349	24,497	27,441
5143 Dairy products, exc. dried or canned[3]	24	25	439	523	21	34,633	39,686	14,624	21,017
5144 Poultry and poultry products[3]	15	15	135	174	12	22,281	19,655	3,450	3,770
5145 Confectionery[3]	22	22	315	414	19	23,048	28,348	7,419	11,177
5146 Fish and seafoods[3]	51	57	472	547	10	20,602	23,320	11,971	14,016
5147 Meats and meat products	32	31	441	429	14	27,810	25,818	12,012	11,710
5148 Fresh fruits and vegetables	80	77	1,448	1,451	19	20,144	21,932	33,062	34,236
5149 Groceries and related products, nec[2]	126	108	2,781	2,801	26	28,209	30,322	82,865	83,486
5153 Grain and field beans[3]	5	5	29	31	6	23,448	30,581	796	949
5162 Plastics materials & basic shapes[3]	31	35	342	374	11	27,696	31,144	10,832	12,561
5169 Chemicals & allied products, nec	116	118	1,022	1,113	9	28,751	32,187	35,069	38,811
5171 Petroleum bulk stations & terminals[3]	55	49	768	699	14	28,339	27,960	20,769	21,085
5172 Petroleum products, nec[3]	23	23	178	168	7	24,742	27,786	4,903	5,747
5181 Beer and ale[3]	13	13	726	742	57	31,262	34,075	23,229	26,077
5182 Wine and distilled beverages[3]	16	17	873	946	56	39,963	43,463	29,394	34,924
5191 Farm supplies	76	77	677	809	11	29,359	31,051	22,780	29,139
5192 Books, periodicals, & newspapers[3]	32	30	442	535	18	23,638	25,249	10,516	12,881
5193 Flowers & florists' supplies[3]	50	41	640	454	11	12,275	19,031	8,475	9,231
5194 Tobacco and tobacco products[3]	14	14	359	396	28	24,958	30,040	11,113	13,207
5198 Paints, varnishes, and supplies	35	42	232	320	8	26,845	25,288	7,601	8,752
5199 Nondurable goods, nec	168	190	723	812	4	19,463	20,005	14,885	17,546
52- Retail trade	12,929	12,842	184,361	191,015	15	12,954	13,701	2,516,219	2,691,026
5210 Lumber and other building materials	173	157	3,897	4,589	29	16,049	16,865	67,172	82,824
5230 Paint, glass, and wallpaper stores	95	89	356	406	5	18,438	18,512	6,931	7,758
5250 Hardware stores	105	77	604	488	6	13,026	13,205	8,518	7,031
5260 Retail nurseries and garden stores	104	102	606	577	6	11,822	12,388	7,368	7,892
5270 Mobile home dealers	52	57	258	276	5	18,419	18,826	6,263	6,258
5310 Department stores	93	96	14,312	14,924	155	11,462	13,148	173,670	197,402
5330 Variety stores	108	76	982	939	12	9,369	9,321	10,321	8,999
5390 Misc. general merchandise stores	83	98	2,917	2,804	29	11,349	13,138	34,852	33,946
5410 Grocery stores	1,027	1,007	28,447	30,059	30	11,229	11,216	323,598	340,330
5420 Meat and fish markets	72	72	407	430	6	12,069	13,367	5,382	6,456
5430 Fruit and vegetable markets	32	38	443	364	10	9,968	12,714	3,537	3,229
5440 Candy, nut, and confectionery stores[3]	20	23	87	107	5	6,023	6,056	561	744
5450 Dairy products stores[3]	17	14	31	14	1	8,000	11,714	241	100
5460 Retail bakeries	121	107	885	844	8	11,747	10,905	11,106	9,425
5490 Miscellaneous food stores	97	106	405	742	7	12,919	11,342	5,440	7,853
5510 New and used car dealers	139	145	9,704	10,423	72	30,340	30,796	324,763	347,419
5520 Used car dealers	222	209	1,041	882	4	20,995	21,964	21,467	18,845
5530 Auto and home supply stores	314	318	2,222	2,462	8	18,043	18,167	43,152	47,252
5540 Gasoline service stations	727	716	4,717	4,432	6	12,205	13,421	59,541	60,057
5550 Boat dealers	75	75	543	530	7	20,074	21,977	15,132	14,192
5560 Recreational vehicle dealers	34	37	473	523	14	27,848	30,264	13,315	14,822
5570 Motorcycle dealers	26	26	174	159	6	17,080	20,252	3,400	4,036
5590 Automotive dealers, nec[3]	8	7	14	10	1	23,714	22,400	348	269
5610 Men's & boys' clothing stores[3]	111	98	642	599	6	11,533	12,167	7,476	6,938
5620 Women's clothing stores	400	342	3,184	2,721	8	9,102	8,672	29,505	23,681
5630 Women's accessory & specialty stores	72	68	347	360	5	8,934	9,122	3,338	3,400
5640 Children's and infants' wear stores	35	28	175	207	7	8,206	11,150	1,565	2,110
5650 Family clothing stores	164	166	2,421	2,422	15	9,532	10,813	25,491	26,810
5660 Shoe stores	279	280	1,360	1,446	5	11,206	11,162	15,956	15,624
5690 Misc. apparel & accessory stores	109	104	475	478	5	8,059	9,632	4,544	4,736
5712 Furniture stores	329	331	2,714	2,867	9	19,515	21,176	55,170	61,542
5713 Floor covering stores	140	138	609	704	5	18,213	20,682	11,786	14,295
5714 Drapery and upholstery stores	28	27	102	101	4	13,647	14,970	1,377	1,490
5719 Misc. homefurnishings stores	161	160	865	894	6	10,488	12,013	10,490	11,094
5720 Household appliance stores	81	76	572	577	8	17,476	17,948	11,055	10,466
5731 Radio, TV, & electronic stores	144	153	1,135	1,215	8	18,019	18,960	20,697	22,548
5734 Computer and software stores[2]	83	102	503	522	5	16,716	18,444	8,668	9,939
5735 Record & prerecorded tape stores	80	82	544	666	8	9,882	9,117	5,667	5,914
5736 Musical instrument stores	35	34	251	290	9	18,343	19,821	5,129	6,440
5812 Eating places	2,710	2,457	55,926	56,693	23	8,406	8,744	473,533	487,579
5813 Drinking places	344	295	2,271	2,067	7	9,108	8,995	19,509	17,069
5910 Drug stores and proprietary stores	334	313	5,668	5,357	17	16,500	17,728	97,738	98,826
5920 Liquor stores	168	153	853	739	5	11,114	11,020	10,121	8,315
5930 Used merchandise stores	237	235	944	937	4	10,263	11,863	10,519	11,330
5941 Sporting goods and bicycle shops	194	183	1,059	1,305	7	13,005	12,549	15,630	16,563
5942 Book stores	94	89	554	602	7	10,325	11,807	6,479	7,272
5943 Stationery stores	31	36	56	325	9	14,571	16,234	990	5,092

Continued on next page.

TAMPA - ST. PETERSBURG - CLEARWATER, FL MSA - [continued]

Wholesale and Retail Trade USA	Establishments		Employment		Emp / Est	Pay / Employee		Annual Payroll ($ 000)	
	1994	1995	1994	1995	1995	1994	1995	1994	1995
5944 Jewelry stores	228	237	1,068	1,163	5	15,700	15,976	17,635	18,132
5945 Hobby, toy, and game shops [2]	79	80	606	879	11	11,637	10,048	8,488	9,643
5946 Camera & photographic supply stores [3]	17	17	108	62	4	14,926	12,516	1,708	982
5947 Gift, novelty, and souvenir shops	360	335	1,517	1,630	5	8,609	9,193	14,399	15,772
5948 Luggage and leather goods stores [3]	12	14	50	61	4	9,040	10,361	430	625
5949 Sewing, needlework, and piece goods	62	59	529	517	9	8,537	9,803	4,928	4,891
5961 Catalog and mail-order houses [3]	53	58	2,103	1,880	32	24,274	32,502	57,738	63,218
5962 Merchandising machine operators [3]	45	50	66	76	2	18,424	18,105	1,214	1,463
5963 Direct selling establishments	126	124	1,472	1,471	12	16,429	19,007	25,878	29,133
5983 Fuel oil dealers [3]	10	9	25	19	2	13,120	10,526	312	193
5984 Liquefied petroleum gas dealers	26	28	265	111	4	21,404	17,117	5,165	1,922
5992 Florists	228	225	889	917	4	10,520	10,678	9,676	10,026
5993 Tobacco stores and stands [3]	15	16	63	69	4	9,905	9,913	718	829
5994 News dealers and newsstands [3]	16	15	55	68	5	10,182	9,118	628	613
5995 Optical goods stores	195	189	949	1,016	5	15,958	16,500	14,687	15,665
5999 Miscellaneous retail stores, nec	519	565	2,553	2,852	5	13,022	13,698	36,728	43,952

Source: County Business Patterns 1994/95, CBP-94/95, U.S. Department of Commerce, Washington DC, November 1997. The employment column represents mid-March employment in the year. Pay per employee is calculated by dividing 1st Quarter payroll, annualized, by mid-March employment. The column headed 'Emp / Est' shows 'employees per establishment'. A dash (-) means that data are unavailable or cannot be calculated. nec means not elsewhere classified. *Notes:* 1. 1994 data incomplete; unavailable or withheld. 2. 1995 data incomplete; unavailable or withheld. 3. 1994 and 1995 data incomplete; unavailable or withheld.

TERRE HAUTE, IN MSA

Wholesale and Retail Trade USA	Establishments		Employment		Emp / Est	Pay / Employee		Annual Payroll ($ 000)	
	1994	1995	1994	1995	1995	1994	1995	1994	1995
50- Wholesale trade	211	213	2,460	2,350	11	21,180	23,362	56,516	58,585
5012 Automobiles and other vehicles [3]	5	5	128	103	21	9,344	13,087	1,501	1,683
5013 Motor vehicle supplies and new parts	13	13	70	79	6	17,371	16,810	1,178	1,349
5020 Furniture and homefurnishings [3]	4	3	32	53	18	15,125	32,302	635	2,320
5030 Lumber and construction materials [2]	9	10	43	66	7	18,698	22,788	1,093	1,584
5044 Office equipment [3]	9	11	65	97	9	24,308	19,835	1,851	2,424
5045 Computers, peripherals, & software [3]	6	4	35	22	6	40,114	32,182	853	576
5050 Metals and minerals, except petroleum [3]	5	5	33	41	8	22,909	24,780	860	1,048
5060 Electrical goods [3]	11	13	87	121	9	20,230	26,479	1,732	2,960
5075 Warm air heating & air conditioning [3]	4	4	28	29	7	17,143	19,448	575	671
5084 Industrial machinery and equipment [1]	7	-	96	-	-	25,417	-	2,952	-
5085 Industrial supplies [3]	15	14	122	126	9	23,934	26,286	3,256	3,506
5093 Scrap and waste materials [2]	-	5	-	56	11	-	19,714	-	1,410
5110 Paper and paper products [3]	8	7	129	129	18	38,915	41,209	4,631	5,018
5148 Fresh fruits and vegetables [1]	4	-	179	-	-	13,073	-	2,651	-
5149 Groceries and related products, nec [3]	5	5	138	121	24	22,174	26,612	3,243	3,417
5153 Grain and field beans	12	12	56	56	5	20,571	22,071	1,401	1,435
5160 Chemicals and allied products [2]	-	3	-	45	15	-	27,022	-	1,295
5170 Petroleum and petroleum products [2]	7	6	48	51	9	21,750	20,549	1,132	1,095
5191 Farm supplies	8	7	151	59	8	8,848	22,847	1,520	1,580
5192 Books, periodicals, & newspapers [3]	4	4	31	30	8	14,710	15,733	524	535
5193 Flowers & florists' supplies [1]	3	-	20	-	-	14,800	-	324	-
5199 Nondurable goods, nec [3]	5	5	2	5	1	4,000	15,200	15	54
52- Retail trade	964	973	16,646	17,733	18	12,221	12,577	217,961	227,623
5210 Lumber and other building materials	21	16	426	369	23	14,742	17,583	7,123	6,711
5250 Hardware stores	10	9	113	107	12	12,248	13,383	1,597	1,051
5260 Retail nurseries and garden stores [3]	10	10	55	59	6	15,055	19,186	961	967
5310 Department stores [3]	11	11	1,405	1,327	121	9,851	11,078	14,885	15,936
5330 Variety stores	9	-	57	-	-	8,211	-	522	-
5390 Misc. general merchandise stores [1]	7	-	392	-	-	11,224	-	4,529	-
5410 Grocery stores [3]	61	62	1,027	1,622	26	13,418	13,036	16,047	21,160
5440 Candy, nut, and confectionery stores [1]	3	-	19	-	-	5,895	-	123	-
5460 Retail bakeries	11	12	68	82	7	9,824	8,829	710	741
5510 New and used car dealers	20	21	704	733	35	22,813	23,454	18,215	17,890
5520 Used car dealers [2]	24	22	64	65	3	17,313	15,815	1,176	1,094
5530 Auto and home supply stores	27	27	129	168	6	17,023	17,714	2,235	2,859
5540 Gasoline service stations	70	72	713	630	9	10,614	11,924	8,282	7,941
5570 Motorcycle dealers [2]	-	3	-	10	3	-	21,600	-	255
5610 Men's & boys' clothing stores [3]	6	6	42	37	6	10,095	12,000	487	465
5620 Women's clothing stores	30	23	298	183	8	5,544	5,923	1,790	1,103
5630 Women's accessory & specialty stores [3]	4	3	16	15	5	8,250	8,267	127	115
5650 Family clothing stores [1]	10	11	41	89	8	9,756	9,573	529	872
5660 Shoe stores [3]	22	19	122	123	6	9,967	10,862	1,401	1,561
5690 Misc. apparel & accessory stores [3]	4	5	5	25	5	6,400	7,520	106	178

Continued on next page.

TERRE HAUTE, IN MSA - [continued]

Wholesale and Retail Trade USA	Establishments		Employment		Emp / Est	Pay / Employee		Annual Payroll ($ 000)	
	1994	1995	1994	1995	1995	1994	1995	1994	1995
5712 Furniture stores	19	22	98	99	5	15,469	17,859	1,799	1,910
5713 Floor covering stores[1]	6	-	53	-	-	15,623	-	1,015	-
5719 Misc. homefurnishings stores[2]	-	8	-	26	3	-	10,000	-	348
5720 Household appliance stores	15	16	104	118	7	17,038	16,373	1,924	2,484
5731 Radio, TV, & electronic stores[3]	7	6	38	35	6	16,105	14,514	545	482
5735 Record & prerecorded tape stores[3]	7	7	118	117	17	19,898	24,684	2,593	2,711
5812 Eating places	237	222	5,224	5,519	25	6,985	7,203	39,653	40,293
5813 Drinking places	51	49	189	206	4	6,603	6,835	1,419	1,466
5910 Drug stores and proprietary stores[2]	24	26	314	104	4	15,962	14,385	5,635	1,619
5930 Used merchandise stores	-	14	-	9	1	-	5,333	-	47
5941 Sporting goods and bicycle shops[3]	13	15	49	49	3	11,265	12,653	500	605
5942 Book stores[3]	6	5	59	56	11	9,559	9,286	556	604
5944 Jewelry stores	13	15	97	91	6	17,196	18,769	1,695	1,586
5945 Hobby, toy, and game shops[3]	5	5	34	66	13	9,529	14,667	557	881
5947 Gift, novelty, and souvenir shops[3]	18	19	81	85	4	6,617	7,576	636	754
5962 Merchandising machine operators[2]	-	6	-	58	10	-	16,759	-	954
5963 Direct selling establishments[3]	6	6	62	61	10	11,677	11,869	734	661
5992 Florists	22	21	134	135	6	11,970	12,948	1,800	1,861
5995 Optical goods stores[2]	-	5	-	42	8	-	14,381	-	602
5999 Miscellaneous retail stores, nec	27	26	100	126	5	10,960	9,778	1,582	1,579

Source: County Business Patterns 1994/95, CBP-94/95, U.S. Department of Commerce, Washington DC, November 1997. The employment column represents mid-March employment in the year. Pay per employee is calculated by dividing 1st Quarter payroll, annualized, by mid-March employment. The column headed 'Emp / Est' shows 'employees per establishment'. A dash (-) means that data are unavailable or cannot be calculated. nec means not elsewhere classified. *Notes:* 1. 1994 data incomplete; unavailable or withheld. 2. 1995 data incomplete; unavailable or withheld. 3. 1994 and 1995 data incomplete; unavailable or withheld.

TEXARKANA MSA (AR PART)

Wholesale and Retail Trade USA	Establishments		Employment		Emp / Est	Pay / Employee		Annual Payroll ($ 000)	
	1994	1995	1994	1995	1995	1994	1995	1994	1995
50 - Wholesale trade	65	68	1,003	918	14	17,850	21,464	19,526	21,440
5013 Motor vehicle supplies and new parts	8	6	45	41	7	12,889	12,585	572	398
5015 Motor vehicle parts, used	4	5	19	17	3	10,526	15,059	244	238
5040 Professional & commercial equipment	-	3	-	5	2	-	13,600	-	87
5085 Industrial supplies	5	6	27	36	6	29,481	23,556	771	811
5090 Miscellaneous durable goods	5	6	40	38	6	21,000	22,000	1,078	1,564
5140 Groceries and related products	4	-	44	-	-	24,000	-	881	-
5170 Petroleum and petroleum products	-	4	-	46	12	-	22,522	-	1,066
5181 Beer and ale	3	3	62	58	19	21,613	26,345	1,532	1,561
5194 Tobacco and tobacco products	3	3	172	163	54	12,209	14,454	2,062	2,206
52 - Retail trade	229	226	2,578	2,738	12	10,377	10,799	28,772	29,718
5200 Building materials & garden supplies	5	6	138	123	21	17,217	19,024	2,651	2,582
5410 Grocery stores	29	29	420	431	15	10,952	11,842	4,964	5,188
5520 Used car dealers	3	3	7	11	4	10,286	12,000	99	118
5530 Auto and home supply stores	6	6	70	57	10	14,629	20,772	1,044	1,143
5540 Gasoline service stations	23	24	187	205	9	10,203	9,873	1,984	2,109
5610 Men's & boys' clothing stores	3	3	15	16	5	10,933	9,500	188	166
5620 Women's clothing stores	-	4	-	13	3	-	8,923	-	131
5660 Shoe stores	3	3	12	13	4	10,333	13,846	145	149
5719 Misc. homefurnishings stores	3	3	8	11	4	11,500	8,727	105	111
5812 Eating places	62	54	1,046	1,141	21	7,954	7,618	8,706	8,670
5813 Drinking places	9	7	26	48	7	7,385	6,167	206	277
5910 Drug stores and proprietary stores	5	5	49	50	10	19,755	21,280	1,119	1,188
5920 Liquor stores	19	20	91	86	4	9,714	10,605	954	984
5930 Used merchandise stores	7	8	17	17	2	7,765	7,765	173	144
5944 Jewelry stores	4	5	20	25	5	27,800	25,920	568	692
5984 Liquefied petroleum gas dealers	3	3	16	14	5	15,000	20,000	237	274
5992 Florists	-	4	-	15	4	-	12,000	-	166
5999 Miscellaneous retail stores, nec	3	-	19	-	-	9,684	-	242	-

Source: County Business Patterns 1994/95, CBP-94/95, U.S. Department of Commerce, Washington DC, November 1997. The employment column represents mid-March employment in the year. Pay per employee is calculated by dividing 1st Quarter payroll, annualized, by mid-March employment. The column headed 'Emp / Est' shows 'employees per establishment'. A dash (-) means that data are unavailable or cannot be calculated. nec means not elsewhere classified. *Notes:* 1. 1994 data incomplete; unavailable or withheld. 2. 1995 data incomplete; unavailable or withheld. 3. 1994 and 1995 data incomplete; unavailable or withheld.

TEXARKANA MSA (TX PART)

Wholesale and Retail Trade USA	Establishments		Employment		Emp / Est	Pay / Employee		Annual Payroll ($ 000)	
	1994	1995	1994	1995	1995	1994	1995	1994	1995
50– Wholesale trade	-	184	-	2,420	13	-	24,007	-	63,074
5012 Automobiles and other vehicles	-	7	-	187	27	-	33,989	-	6,847
5013 Motor vehicle supplies and new parts	-	15	-	101	7	-	15,683	-	1,927
5031 Lumber, plywood, and millwork	-	6	-	47	8	-	20,000	-	932
5032 Brick, stone, & related materials	-	4	-	29	7	-	14,621	-	497
5044 Office equipment	-	8	-	50	6	-	18,880	-	946
5047 Medical and hospital equipment	-	5	-	21	4	-	24,762	-	572
5063 Electrical apparatus and equipment	-	7	-	83	12	-	34,313	-	2,348
5072 Hardware	-	4	-	20	5	-	30,800	-	655
5084 Industrial machinery and equipment	-	5	-	28	6	-	16,000	-	459
5085 Industrial supplies	-	12	-	122	10	-	26,689	-	3,376
5087 Service establishment equipment	-	3	-	18	6	-	14,000	-	241
5093 Scrap and waste materials	-	4	-	70	18	-	17,829	-	764
5112 Stationery and office supplies	-	5	-	39	8	-	16,718	-	699
5149 Groceries and related products, nec	-	4	-	104	26	-	27,385	-	2,947
5150 Farm-product raw materials	-	7	-	94	13	-	14,638	-	1,419
5169 Chemicals & allied products, nec	-	3	-	70	23	-	42,229	-	4,293
5170 Petroleum and petroleum products	-	9	-	85	9	-	20,094	-	1,739
5193 Flowers & florists' supplies	-	4	-	29	7	-	11,586	-	319
5199 Nondurable goods, nec	-	4	-	11	3	-	9,091	-	84
52– Retail trade	-	506	-	7,293	14	-	13,381	-	98,529
5210 Lumber and other building materials	-	10	-	133	13	-	16,752	-	2,010
5230 Paint, glass, and wallpaper stores	-	3	-	21	7	-	47,429	-	555
5260 Retail nurseries and garden stores	-	6	-	35	6	-	11,200	-	540
5270 Mobile home dealers	-	4	-	30	8	-	23,600	-	819
5310 Department stores	-	8	-	1,392	174	-	13,063	-	16,796
5410 Grocery stores	-	46	-	905	20	-	11,885	-	11,003
5460 Retail bakeries	-	3	-	17	6	-	5,647	-	109
5510 New and used car dealers	-	12	-	449	37	-	28,463	-	14,551
5520 Used car dealers	-	15	-	59	4	-	15,864	-	1,131
5530 Auto and home supply stores	-	14	-	86	6	-	17,302	-	1,548
5540 Gasoline service stations	-	36	-	341	9	-	9,982	-	3,465
5620 Women's clothing stores	-	19	-	113	6	-	7,575	-	864
5630 Women's accessory & specialty stores	-	3	-	12	4	-	9,000	-	104
5640 Children's and infants' wear stores	-	5	-	17	3	-	11,529	-	186
5650 Family clothing stores	-	10	-	359	36	-	9,359	-	3,615
5660 Shoe stores	-	10	-	58	6	-	12,000	-	720
5690 Misc. apparel & accessory stores	-	6	-	18	3	-	11,111	-	197
5712 Furniture stores	-	13	-	83	6	-	22,313	-	1,800
5720 Household appliance stores	-	4	-	26	7	-	21,077	-	603
5731 Radio, TV, & electronic stores	-	7	-	58	8	-	14,759	-	843
5735 Record & prerecorded tape stores	-	4	-	20	5	-	11,000	-	250
5812 Eating places	-	99	-	1,819	18	-	8,194	-	15,798
5910 Drug stores and proprietary stores	-	14	-	96	7	-	25,667	-	1,733
5930 Used merchandise stores	-	5	-	8	2	-	12,000	-	100
5941 Sporting goods and bicycle shops	-	5	-	13	3	-	14,769	-	218
5942 Book stores	-	4	-	15	4	-	5,067	-	86
5944 Jewelry stores	-	8	-	45	6	-	20,800	-	985
5947 Gift, novelty, and souvenir shops	-	10	-	50	5	-	7,360	-	377
5949 Sewing, needlework, and piece goods	-	5	-	22	4	-	6,364	-	150
5992 Florists	-	13	-	48	4	-	7,833	-	400
5995 Optical goods stores	-	5	-	18	4	-	12,889	-	247
5999 Miscellaneous retail stores, nec	-	20	-	144	7	-	16,250	-	1,377

Source: County Business Patterns 1994/95, CBP-94/95, U.S. Department of Commerce, Washington DC, November 1997. The employment column represents mid-March employment in the year. Pay per employee is calculated by dividing 1st Quarter payroll, annualized, by mid-March employment. The column headed 'Emp / Est' shows 'employees per establishment'. A dash (-) means that data are unavailable or cannot be calculated. nec means not elsewhere classified. *Notes:* 1. 1994 data incomplete; unavailable or withheld. 2. 1995 data incomplete; unavailable or withheld. 3. 1994 and 1995 data incomplete; unavailable or withheld.

TEXARKANA, TX–TEXARKANA, AR MSA

Wholesale and Retail Trade USA	Establishments		Employment		Emp / Est	Pay / Employee		Annual Payroll ($ 000)	
	1994	1995	1994	1995	1995	1994	1995	1994	1995
50– Wholesale trade [1]	65	252	1,003	3,338	13	17,850	23,307	19,526	84,514
5012 Automobiles and other vehicles	-	10	-	187	19	-	33,989	-	6,847
5013 Motor vehicle supplies and new parts [1]	8	21	45	142	7	12,889	14,789	572	2,325
5015 Motor vehicle parts, used [1]	4	11	19	17	2	10,526	15,059	244	238
5031 Lumber, plywood, and millwork	-	7	-	47	7	-	20,000	-	932
5032 Brick, stone, & related materials	-	5	-	29	6	-	14,621	-	497
5044 Office equipment [2]	-	8	-	50	6	-	18,880	-	946

Continued on next page.

TEXARKANA, TX – TEXARKANA, AR MSA - [continued]

Wholesale and Retail Trade USA	Establishments		Employment		Emp / Est	Pay / Employee		Annual Payroll ($ 000)	
	1994	1995	1994	1995	1995	1994	1995	1994	1995
5047 Medical and hospital equipment [2]	-	5	-	21	4	-	24,762	-	572
5063 Electrical apparatus and equipment	-	9	-	83	9	-	34,313	-	2,348
5072 Hardware [2]	-	7	-	20	3	-	30,800	-	655
5084 Industrial machinery and equipment	-	7	-	28	4	-	16,000	-	459
5085 Industrial supplies [1]	5	18	27	158	9	29,481	25,975	771	4,187
5087 Service establishment equipment	-	4	-	18	5	-	14,000	-	241
5093 Scrap and waste materials	-	6	-	70	12	-	17,829	-	764
5112 Stationery and office supplies [2]	-	5	-	39	8	-	16,718	-	699
5149 Groceries and related products, nec	-	5	-	104	21	-	27,385	-	2,947
5150 Farm-product raw materials [2]	-	7	-	94	13	-	14,638	-	1,419
5169 Chemicals & allied products, nec	-	4	-	70	18	-	42,229	-	4,293
5170 Petroleum and petroleum products	-	13	-	131	10	-	20,947	-	2,805
5181 Beer and ale [3]	3	3	62	58	19	21,613	26,345	1,532	1,561
5193 Flowers & florists' supplies	-	5	-	29	6	-	11,586	-	319
5194 Tobacco and tobacco products [1]	3	4	172	163	41	12,209	14,454	2,062	2,206
5199 Nondurable goods, nec [2]	-	4	-	11	3	-	9,091	-	84
52 – Retail trade [1]	229	732	2,578	10,031	14	10,377	12,676	28,772	128,247
5210 Lumber and other building materials [2]	-	13	-	133	10	-	16,752	-	2,010
5230 Paint, glass, and wallpaper stores	-	5	-	21	4	-	47,429	-	555
5260 Retail nurseries and garden stores [2]	-	6	-	35	6	-	11,200	-	540
5270 Mobile home dealers [2]	-	4	-	30	8	-	23,600	-	819
5310 Department stores [2]	-	9	-	1,392	155	-	13,063	-	16,796
5410 Grocery stores [1]	29	75	420	1,336	18	10,952	11,871	4,964	16,191
5460 Retail bakeries	-	4	-	17	4	-	5,647	-	109
5510 New and used car dealers [2]	-	12	-	449	37	-	28,463	-	14,551
5520 Used car dealers [1]	3	18	7	70	4	10,286	15,257	99	1,249
5530 Auto and home supply stores [1]	6	20	70	143	7	14,629	18,685	1,044	2,691
5540 Gasoline service stations [1]	23	60	187	546	9	10,203	9,941	1,984	5,574
5610 Men's & boys' clothing stores [1]	3	5	15	16	3	10,933	9,500	188	166
5620 Women's clothing stores	-	23	-	126	5	-	7,714	-	995
5630 Women's accessory & specialty stores [2]	-	3	-	12	4	-	9,000	-	104
5640 Children's and infants' wear stores [2]	-	5	-	17	3	-	11,529	-	186
5650 Family clothing stores	-	11	-	359	33	-	9,359	-	3,615
5660 Shoe stores [1]	3	13	12	71	5	10,333	12,338	145	869
5690 Misc. apparel & accessory stores [2]	-	6	-	18	3	-	11,111	-	197
5712 Furniture stores	-	16	-	83	5	-	22,313	-	1,800
5719 Misc. homefurnishings stores [1]	3	8	8	11	1	11,500	8,727	105	111
5720 Household appliance stores	-	5	-	26	5	-	21,077	-	603
5731 Radio, TV, & electronic stores	-	10	-	58	6	-	14,759	-	843
5735 Record & prerecorded tape stores [2]	-	4	-	20	5	-	11,000	-	250
5812 Eating places [1]	62	153	1,046	2,960	19	7,954	7,972	8,706	24,468
5813 Drinking places [3]	9	7	26	48	7	7,385	6,167	206	277
5910 Drug stores and proprietary stores [1]	5	19	49	146	8	19,755	24,164	1,119	2,921
5920 Liquor stores [1]	19	21	91	86	4	9,714	10,605	954	984
5930 Used merchandise stores [1]	7	13	17	25	2	7,765	9,120	173	244
5941 Sporting goods and bicycle shops	-	6	-	13	2	-	14,769	-	218
5942 Book stores [2]	-	4	-	15	4	-	5,067	-	86
5944 Jewelry stores [1]	4	13	20	70	5	27,800	22,629	568	1,677
5947 Gift, novelty, and souvenir shops [2]	-	10	-	50	5	-	7,360	-	377
5949 Sewing, needlework, and piece goods	-	6	-	22	4	-	6,364	-	150
5984 Liquefied petroleum gas dealers [1]	3	4	16	14	4	15,000	20,000	237	274
5992 Florists	-	17	-	63	4	-	8,825	-	566
5995 Optical goods stores [2]	-	5	-	18	4	-	12,889	-	247
5999 Miscellaneous retail stores, nec [1]	3	23	19	144	6	9,684	16,250	242	1,377

Source: County Business Patterns 1994/95, CBP-94/95, U.S. Department of Commerce, Washington DC, November 1997. The employment column represents mid-March employment in the year. Pay per employee is calculated by dividing 1st Quarter payroll, annualized, by mid-March employment. The column headed 'Emp / Est' shows 'employees per establishment'. A dash (-) means that data are unavailable or cannot be calculated. nec means not elsewhere classified. *Notes:* 1. 1994 data incomplete; unavailable or withheld. 2. 1995 data incomplete; unavailable or withheld. 3. 1994 and 1995 data incomplete; unavailable or withheld.

TOLEDO, OH MSA

Wholesale and Retail Trade USA	Establishments		Employment		Emp / Est	Pay / Employee		Annual Payroll ($ 000)	
	1994	1995	1994	1995	1995	1994	1995	1994	1995
50 – Wholesale trade	1,169	1,180	15,276	16,332	14	27,966	29,356	466,366	517,242
5012 Automobiles and other vehicles [1]	18	19	203	324	17	25,970	24,370	7,037	9,431
5013 Motor vehicle supplies and new parts [2]	71	72	992	737	10	22,355	30,469	24,379	21,467
5014 Tires and tubes [2]	15	12	203	216	18	24,552	27,148	5,674	5,975
5015 Motor vehicle parts, used	23	24	107	133	6	22,766	23,639	2,714	3,561
5021 Furniture	10	12	25	92	8	24,800	22,609	694	2,706

Continued on next page.

TOLEDO, OH MSA - [continued]

Wholesale and Retail Trade USA	Establishments		Employment		Emp / Est	Pay / Employee		Annual Payroll ($ 000)	
	1994	1995	1994	1995	1995	1994	1995	1994	1995
5023 Homefurnishings	15	11	159	151	14	23,019	26,252	4,575	4,342
5031 Lumber, plywood, and millwork	16	17	236	269	16	20,305	22,156	5,371	6,571
5032 Brick, stone, & related materials [1]	11	10	69	91	9	24,000	27,341	2,663	3,696
5033 Roofing, siding, & insulation [3]	9	12	268	354	30	26,940	40,034	7,671	18,264
5039 Construction materials, nec [3]	13	21	149	250	12	26,738	26,352	5,910	8,043
5044 Office equipment	22	21	333	282	13	33,538	36,894	9,027	9,105
5045 Computers, peripherals, & software [1]	28	26	523	501	19	39,740	46,834	20,606	22,800
5046 Commercial equipment, nec [3]	14	14	87	113	8	26,391	29,522	2,433	3,704
5047 Medical and hospital equipment [3]	24	21	230	284	14	25,409	30,549	6,806	8,915
5049 Professional equipment, nec [3]	10	10	53	55	6	23,698	23,782	1,478	1,579
5051 Metals service centers and offices [3]	51	49	68	71	1	27,529	36,451	2,050	2,187
5063 Electrical apparatus and equipment	53	49	496	523	11	34,669	35,228	17,399	19,696
5064 Electrical appliances, TV & radios [3]	3	3	48	49	16	14,667	15,918	816	823
5065 Electronic parts and equipment	38	39	272	317	8	28,294	28,972	8,383	10,754
5072 Hardware	18	19	218	208	11	55,284	29,981	9,656	6,747
5075 Warm air heating & air conditioning [3]	26	26	298	296	11	28,416	34,108	9,909	10,295
5082 Construction and mining machinery	-	12	-	193	16	-	31,088	-	7,006
5083 Farm and garden machinery	-	24	-	282	12	-	24,128	-	7,052
5084 Industrial machinery and equipment	-	114	-	1,183	10	-	33,873	-	40,262
5085 Industrial supplies	-	59	-	818	14	-	34,460	-	31,344
5087 Service establishment equipment [2]	-	25	-	448	18	-	24,616	-	11,777
5088 Transportation equipment & supplies [2]	-	3	-	9	3	-	16,889	-	176
5091 Sporting & recreational goods [2]	-	7	-	52	7	-	22,769	-	1,211
5093 Scrap and waste materials	-	23	-	345	15	-	35,652	-	15,069
5099 Durable goods, nec [2]	-	26	-	128	5	-	20,969	-	3,785
5111 Printing and writing paper [2]	-	7	-	80	11	-	35,250	-	2,966
5112 Stationery and office supplies	-	23	-	301	13	-	17,316	-	5,354
5113 Industrial & personal service paper [2]	-	8	-	104	13	-	33,808	-	4,389
5120 Drugs, proprietaries, and sundries [2]	-	10	-	409	41	-	22,807	-	9,645
5136 Men's and boys' clothing [2]	-	6	-	46	8	-	26,783	-	1,745
5141 Groceries, general line [2]	-	15	-	219	15	-	22,064	-	4,962
5145 Confectionery [2]	-	6	-	30	5	-	26,933	-	816
5147 Meats and meat products [2]	-	7	-	92	13	-	26,565	-	1,836
5148 Fresh fruits and vegetables [2]	-	7	-	211	30	-	20,588	-	5,344
5149 Groceries and related products, nec	-	24	-	775	32	-	26,379	-	21,224
5153 Grain and field beans [2]	-	31	-	187	6	-	28,513	-	5,595
5154 Livestock [2]	-	3	-	42	14	-	14,095	-	595
5160 Chemicals and allied products	-	36	-	402	11	-	31,194	-	12,689
5171 Petroleum bulk stations & terminals	-	15	-	78	5	-	35,436	-	2,841
5172 Petroleum products, nec [2]	-	8	-	30	4	-	29,333	-	934
5180 Beer, wine, and distilled beverages [2]	-	9	-	305	34	-	29,875	-	10,146
5191 Farm supplies	-	24	-	242	10	-	26,380	-	6,485
5192 Books, periodicals, & newspapers [2]	-	6	-	81	14	-	14,667	-	1,305
5193 Flowers & florists' supplies [2]	-	11	-	72	7	-	17,611	-	1,707
5198 Paints, varnishes, and supplies [2]	-	11	-	70	6	-	22,057	-	1,614
5199 Nondurable goods, nec [2]	-	35	-	256	7	-	28,922	-	7,804
52- Retail trade	3,723	3,657	58,045	59,315	16	10,764	11,492	693,748	721,268
5210 Lumber and other building materials	54	51	1,027	982	19	18,056	18,941	19,988	19,032
5230 Paint, glass, and wallpaper stores [3]	26	26	96	79	3	15,250	17,873	1,604	1,555
5250 Hardware stores	34	25	202	163	7	12,238	10,748	2,667	2,023
5260 Retail nurseries and garden stores	23	24	273	293	12	11,179	12,655	3,881	4,318
5270 Mobile home dealers	5	6	26	33	6	18,308	15,152	652	761
5310 Department stores	37	38	6,763	6,947	183	10,087	10,608	75,745	78,927
5330 Variety stores	40	32	331	366	11	9,208	8,262	3,518	3,352
5390 Misc. general merchandise stores	21	27	2,478	2,454	91	9,280	10,044	25,317	25,215
5410 Grocery stores	297	281	6,585	6,711	24	11,113	11,838	79,744	78,598
5420 Meat and fish markets	21	21	154	170	8	12,390	15,506	2,512	3,121
5430 Fruit and vegetable markets [3]	7	6	15	28	5	5,333	4,000	163	260
5440 Candy, nut, and confectionery stores [3]	15	12	61	47	4	5,115	6,128	311	302
5450 Dairy products stores [3]	6	6	25	23	4	6,400	7,652	327	399
5460 Retail bakeries	32	29	153	157	5	9,830	8,637	1,667	1,432
5490 Miscellaneous food stores [3]	9	10	84	95	10	8,714	9,642	797	1,022
5510 New and used car dealers	60	59	2,572	2,637	45	27,865	29,509	84,369	84,836
5520 Used car dealers	38	47	122	152	3	16,393	20,211	2,508	3,438
5530 Auto and home supply stores	80	81	658	792	10	18,134	17,131	13,171	14,413
5540 Gasoline service stations	251	242	2,262	1,905	8	8,654	10,690	20,490	20,637
5550 Boat dealers [3]	6	7	48	33	5	14,667	8,242	637	384
5560 Recreational vehicle dealers	9	8	55	51	6	16,073	19,373	1,343	1,328
5570 Motorcycle dealers	6	-	29	-	-	17,517	-	632	-
5590 Automotive dealers, nec [2]	-	4	-	9	2	-	3,111	-	65
5610 Men's & boys' clothing stores	30	29	183	164	6	9,683	10,951	1,967	2,032

Continued on next page.

TOLEDO, OH MSA - [continued]

Wholesale and Retail Trade USA	Establishments		Employment		Emp / Est	Pay / Employee		Annual Payroll ($ 000)	
	1994	1995	1994	1995	1995	1994	1995	1994	1995
5620 Women's clothing stores	101	78	1,009	780	10	7,592	7,426	8,217	5,761
5630 Women's accessory & specialty stores[3]	21	21	124	127	6	9,387	10,331	1,197	1,283
5640 Children's and infants' wear stores[2]	11	10	103	103	10	8,699	9,748	855	883
5650 Family clothing stores	29	32	383	390	12	8,313	9,272	3,619	3,688
5660 Shoe stores	88	86	460	439	5	10,652	11,317	5,218	4,993
5690 Misc. apparel & accessory stores	15	15	72	84	6	14,611	12,524	749	812
5712 Furniture stores	67	69	514	502	7	20,397	20,566	11,150	11,269
5713 Floor covering stores	29	33	202	241	7	17,663	18,307	4,138	5,046
5719 Misc. homefurnishings stores[3]	32	32	10	10	-	9,200	10,000	94	102
5720 Household appliance stores	23	22	147	174	8	14,449	16,000	3,148	3,735
5731 Radio, TV, & electronic stores	45	43	464	508	12	17,138	16,850	8,276	8,934
5734 Computer and software stores[3]	15	17	84	66	4	17,000	20,909	1,462	1,504
5735 Record & prerecorded tape stores[3]	32	31	276	232	7	7,391	8,759	2,041	1,874
5736 Musical instrument stores[3]	12	12	37	42	4	15,027	16,857	635	709
5812 Eating places	953	883	19,999	20,422	23	6,881	7,234	150,127	154,542
5813 Drinking places	228	203	1,105	1,138	6	6,371	6,162	6,926	7,277
5910 Drug stores and proprietary stores	109	107	1,597	1,626	15	13,202	14,433	22,302	24,134
5920 Liquor stores	33	33	92	82	2	19,783	17,854	1,659	1,451
5930 Used merchandise stores	44	40	234	193	5	9,299	8,041	2,082	1,661
5941 Sporting goods and bicycle shops	51	53	255	282	5	10,525	11,447	3,229	3,516
5942 Book stores	35	32	333	303	9	8,877	10,970	3,069	3,483
5943 Stationery stores[2]	9	7	47	33	5	13,106	15,758	676	508
5944 Jewelry stores	58	62	359	364	6	14,184	15,527	5,286	5,522
5945 Hobby, toy, and game shops	31	32	217	307	10	9,456	8,691	3,013	3,361
5947 Gift, novelty, and souvenir shops	66	64	443	451	7	7,196	7,565	3,412	3,845
5949 Sewing, needlework, and piece goods	17	17	128	104	6	5,469	6,615	728	683
5961 Catalog and mail-order houses[3]	14	17	158	219	13	17,342	19,032	4,685	5,280
5962 Merchandising machine operators	16	16	308	401	25	15,792	19,092	5,885	8,043
5963 Direct selling establishments[3]	32	34	519	485	14	18,775	21,344	9,812	9,665
5984 Liquefied petroleum gas dealers	14	12	35	25	2	17,143	23,520	838	653
5992 Florists	76	75	538	546	7	8,773	9,934	5,291	5,503
5993 Tobacco stores and stands[2]	-	4	-	8	2	-	7,500	-	132
5994 News dealers and newsstands[2]	-	5	-	14	3	-	13,143	-	182
5995 Optical goods stores[3]	33	37	163	153	4	14,528	18,118	2,522	3,065
5999 Miscellaneous retail stores, nec	122	127	669	699	6	11,880	13,064	10,148	10,914

Source: County Business Patterns 1994/95, CBP-94/95, U.S. Department of Commerce, Washington DC, November 1997. The employment column represents mid-March employment in the year. Pay per employee is calculated by dividing 1st Quarter payroll, annualized, by mid-March employment. The column headed 'Emp / Est' shows 'employees per establishment'. A dash (-) means that data are unavailable or cannot be calculated. nec means not elsewhere classified. *Notes:* 1. 1994 data incomplete; unavailable or withheld. 2. 1995 data incomplete; unavailable or withheld. 3. 1994 and 1995 data incomplete; unavailable or withheld.

TOPEKA, KS MSA

Wholesale and Retail Trade USA	Establishments		Employment		Emp / Est	Pay / Employee		Annual Payroll ($ 000)	
	1994	1995	1994	1995	1995	1994	1995	1994	1995
50 - Wholesale trade	267	267	3,357	3,188	12	26,083	26,248	86,212	83,793
5012 Automobiles and other vehicles	7	9	117	107	12	14,222	16,561	1,685	1,734
5013 Motor vehicle supplies and new parts	17	20	184	206	10	20,283	20,058	3,259	4,040
5014 Tires and tubes	4	3	43	20	7	23,721	21,800	1,120	475
5015 Motor vehicle parts, used	10	9	79	58	6	16,405	25,379	1,470	1,025
5021 Furniture	4	-	46	-	-	22,435	-	1,267	-
5023 Homefurnishings	5	-	48	-	-	39,500	-	1,425	-
5039 Construction materials, nec	4	3	35	28	9	21,143	24,286	812	766
5044 Office equipment	11	9	162	136	15	24,469	26,706	4,349	3,691
5045 Computers, peripherals, & software	14	14	176	192	14	47,909	47,896	7,798	8,508
5047 Medical and hospital equipment	6	6	27	28	5	37,630	30,143	899	1,035
5063 Electrical apparatus and equipment	11	12	117	132	11	32,684	32,636	3,935	4,136
5074 Plumbing & hydronic heating supplies	-	5	-	41	8	-	28,488	-	866
5082 Construction and mining machinery	8	8	189	209	26	33,651	34,545	7,247	7,427
5083 Farm and garden machinery	6	6	51	55	9	16,863	17,091	976	1,048
5084 Industrial machinery and equipment	7	10	71	129	13	28,732	20,217	2,308	2,743
5085 Industrial supplies	9	11	72	80	7	24,833	25,550	2,006	2,121
5093 Scrap and waste materials	4	7	26	36	5	17,385	17,667	491	689
5099 Durable goods, nec	3	3	10	9	3	15,200	12,444	143	140
5110 Paper and paper products	10	10	184	182	18	23,543	18,242	3,086	3,138
5149 Groceries and related products, nec	5	4	104	104	26	23,000	24,423	2,503	2,670
5150 Farm-product raw materials	9	7	104	103	15	25,038	23,845	2,744	2,528
5169 Chemicals & allied products, nec	5	-	7	-	-	9,714	-	92	-
5171 Petroleum bulk stations & terminals	-	7	-	48	7	-	17,333	-	935
5180 Beer, wine, and distilled beverages	7	7	196	168	24	23,000	26,405	4,931	4,656

Continued on next page.

TOPEKA, KS MSA - [continued]

Wholesale and Retail Trade USA	Establishments		Employment		Emp / Est	Pay / Employee		Annual Payroll ($ 000)	
	1994	1995	1994	1995	1995	1994	1995	1994	1995
5191 Farm supplies	10	10	96	85	9	17,375	18,306	2,044	1,629
5192 Books, periodicals, & newspapers	3	3	98	115	38	16,000	16,696	1,585	1,806
52- Retail trade	1,114	1,108	17,306	18,583	17	13,630	14,443	269,916	293,449
5210 Lumber and other building materials	13	16	463	454	28	15,577	17,885	8,807	8,338
5230 Paint, glass, and wallpaper stores	7	8	40	43	5	20,700	18,605	1,011	1,296
5250 Hardware stores	10	-	92	-	-	10,783	-	1,126	-
5260 Retail nurseries and garden stores	7	8	110	128	16	12,800	13,344	1,645	1,773
5270 Mobile home dealers	3	-	10	-	-	28,000	-	327	-
5310 Department stores	13	14	2,212	2,368	169	10,461	11,338	24,502	28,067
5410 Grocery stores	52	48	1,498	1,594	33	12,772	13,019	19,780	21,232
5420 Meat and fish markets	-	3	-	14	5	-	13,429	-	259
5440 Candy, nut, and confectionery stores	4	4	19	16	4	5,053	7,250	120	107
5460 Retail bakeries	9	6	36	17	3	10,111	8,235	353	156
5490 Miscellaneous food stores	6	-	25	-	-	4,800	-	126	-
5510 New and used car dealers	14	14	799	766	55	23,539	26,240	21,869	22,634
5520 Used car dealers	22	22	41	46	2	14,634	16,522	725	879
5530 Auto and home supply stores	31	30	208	239	8	17,192	17,757	4,098	4,382
5540 Gasoline service stations	84	85	602	730	9	10,731	10,132	7,044	8,162
5560 Recreational vehicle dealers	3	3	22	24	8	17,273	18,500	481	484
5570 Motorcycle dealers	3	3	26	33	11	18,769	18,061	622	735
5610 Men's & boys' clothing stores	5	6	54	59	10	7,111	6,034	377	344
5620 Women's clothing stores	33	28	268	201	7	6,567	6,587	1,937	1,382
5630 Women's accessory & specialty stores	8	-	34	-	-	8,353	-	296	-
5650 Family clothing stores	10	11	134	122	11	8,687	10,590	1,087	1,176
5660 Shoe stores	30	28	223	198	7	20,807	23,515	5,235	5,436
5712 Furniture stores	16	14	179	173	12	20,179	23,006	3,631	3,690
5713 Floor covering stores	9	12	45	50	4	16,267	16,640	883	993
5714 Drapery and upholstery stores	4	3	9	10	3	8,000	9,200	98	110
5719 Misc. homefurnishings stores	15	17	62	68	4	7,355	7,647	495	515
5720 Household appliance stores	-	4	-	27	7	-	19,259	-	584
5731 Radio, TV, & electronic stores	8	8	117	140	18	12,889	12,829	1,717	1,933
5734 Computer and software stores	5	4	20	14	4	10,000	11,429	181	175
5735 Record & prerecorded tape stores	8	7	71	77	11	9,239	9,506	584	717
5736 Musical instrument stores	6	7	41	59	8	16,390	14,169	778	1,015
5812 Eating places	279	262	5,793	5,692	22	7,192	7,341	43,606	44,868
5813 Drinking places	56	47	246	278	6	6,293	6,101	1,851	2,107
5910 Drug stores and proprietary stores	22	22	369	363	17	17,377	18,105	6,807	7,009
5920 Liquor stores	48	46	150	173	4	5,920	5,988	941	1,067
5930 Used merchandise stores	33	27	98	106	4	21,959	23,887	1,339	1,492
5941 Sporting goods and bicycle shops	19	19	98	127	7	12,408	9,953	1,391	1,461
5942 Book stores	9	10	59	69	7	5,763	7,304	368	528
5944 Jewelry stores	19	17	116	122	7	16,103	17,738	2,001	2,113
5945 Hobby, toy, and game shops	14	13	153	144	11	9,438	10,472	1,615	1,651
5947 Gift, novelty, and souvenir shops	29	32	179	169	5	6,056	6,462	1,250	1,306
5949 Sewing, needlework, and piece goods	6	7	55	54	8	6,400	6,963	353	330
5963 Direct selling establishments	11	10	90	87	9	13,689	14,851	1,330	1,233
5992 Florists	14	-	90	-	-	11,600	-	981	-
5995 Optical goods stores	-	11	-	70	6	-	19,086	-	1,272
5999 Miscellaneous retail stores, nec	36	43	168	221	5	10,381	11,765	1,955	3,165

Source: County Business Patterns 1994/95, CBP-94/95, U.S. Department of Commerce, Washington DC, November 1997. The employment column represents mid-March employment in the year. Pay per employee is calculated by dividing 1st Quarter payroll, annualized, by mid-March employment. The column headed 'Emp / Est' shows 'employees per establishment'. A dash (-) means that data are unavailable or cannot be calculated. nec means not elsewhere classified. *Notes:* 1. 1994 data incomplete; unavailable or withheld. 2. 1995 data incomplete; unavailable or withheld. 3. 1994 and 1995 data incomplete; unavailable or withheld.

TRENTON, NJ PMSA

Wholesale and Retail Trade USA	Establishments		Employment		Emp / Est	Pay / Employee		Annual Payroll ($ 000)	
	1994	1995	1994	1995	1995	1994	1995	1994	1995
50- Wholesale trade	556	561	7,673	9,263	17	35,387	43,070	280,857	383,718
5012 Automobiles and other vehicles	11	12	101	104	9	23,683	28,231	2,801	3,118
5013 Motor vehicle supplies and new parts	22	21	219	230	11	22,886	24,348	5,782	5,903
5014 Tires and tubes	4	3	47	34	11	26,809	30,471	1,331	1,114
5015 Motor vehicle parts, used	4	6	18	27	5	21,111	20,000	422	468
5021 Furniture	8	10	70	74	7	28,629	38,541	2,327	3,927
5023 Homefurnishings	17	14	692	680	49	30,301	45,276	22,099	26,193
5031 Lumber, plywood, and millwork	8	5	71	53	11	32,338	36,604	2,618	2,213
5032 Brick, stone, & related materials	5	4	25	17	4	23,360	25,882	728	462
5033 Roofing, siding, & insulation	-	3	-	39	13	-	36,103	-	1,335
5039 Construction materials, nec	-	11	-	65	6	-	29,169	-	2,012

Continued on next page.

TRENTON, NJ PMSA - [continued]

Wholesale and Retail Trade USA	Establishments		Employment		Emp / Est	Pay / Employee		Annual Payroll ($ 000)	
	1994	1995	1994	1995	1995	1994	1995	1994	1995
5044 Office equipment	13	15	617	585	39	46,898	58,844	27,020	27,891
5045 Computers, peripherals, & software	29	31	215	281	9	46,772	46,491	10,381	11,238
5046 Commercial equipment, nec	6	-	66	-	-	14,727	-	1,906	-
5049 Professional equipment, nec	8	11	292	296	27	41,315	54,135	12,060	14,401
5051 Metals service centers and offices	12	10	190	192	19	33,200	39,625	6,166	6,312
5052 Coal and other minerals and ores	3	3	63	63	21	47,238	53,143	3,313	3,583
5063 Electrical apparatus and equipment	23	18	208	177	10	33,192	38,621	6,672	6,169
5072 Hardware	14	14	79	76	5	26,684	27,158	2,057	1,900
5074 Plumbing & hydronic heating supplies	20	12	217	125	10	23,558	29,216	5,865	3,765
5075 Warm air heating & air conditioning	5	7	22	25	4	32,182	41,440	941	1,127
5083 Farm and garden machinery	-	3	-	24	8	-	18,333	-	515
5084 Industrial machinery and equipment	23	23	294	263	11	36,639	48,304	10,911	13,307
5087 Service establishment equipment	13	13	204	180	14	27,333	31,311	5,678	4,874
5091 Sporting & recreational goods	6	-	47	-	-	44,596	-	1,961	-
5092 Toys and hobby goods and supplies	4	-	28	-	-	15,857	-	468	-
5093 Scrap and waste materials	9	9	85	84	9	20,329	23,143	1,946	2,459
5094 Jewelry & precious stones	8	9	25	29	3	23,040	21,517	729	694
5099 Durable goods, nec	6	8	47	52	7	19,660	19,615	1,624	1,647
5111 Printing and writing paper	5	-	91	-	-	29,055	-	1,294	-
5112 Stationery and office supplies	14	11	143	104	9	17,287	21,654	2,584	2,147
5113 Industrial & personal service paper	6	-	52	-	-	26,615	-	1,733	-
5120 Drugs, proprietaries, and sundries	6	4	136	76	19	48,559	42,105	7,435	3,664
5131 Piece goods & notions	4	6	5	6	1	137,600	62,000	639	618
5136 Men's and boys' clothing	8	9	34	96	11	151,412	59,667	8,007	5,783
5137 Women's and children's clothing	7	6	106	149	25	26,566	24,644	3,438	4,781
5139 Footwear	3	-	21	-	-	25,524	-	647	-
5148 Fresh fruits and vegetables	7	7	71	74	11	21,746	25,297	1,702	1,870
5149 Groceries and related products, nec	22	21	266	277	13	31,850	35,711	11,657	10,586
5150 Farm-product raw materials	4	4	17	15	4	16,941	17,067	349	324
5162 Plastics materials & basic shapes	6	6	26	46	8	32,308	30,174	1,014	1,605
5169 Chemicals & allied products, nec	19	21	121	126	6	48,264	57,810	5,918	6,555
5170 Petroleum and petroleum products	7	7	55	73	10	43,782	42,685	2,822	3,705
5180 Beer, wine, and distilled beverages	6	5	311	395	79	37,608	36,891	13,113	14,129
5191 Farm supplies	7	-	97	-	-	39,546	-	4,449	-
5192 Books, periodicals, & newspapers	4	5	216	1,193	239	52,500	53,713	8,023	61,725
5193 Flowers & florists' supplies	5	6	10	14	2	26,000	28,000	304	414
5194 Tobacco and tobacco products	5	5	52	88	18	22,692	21,045	1,352	2,223
5198 Paints, varnishes, and supplies	4	4	14	13	3	33,714	30,769	399	423
5199 Nondurable goods, nec	23	23	89	124	5	25,124	27,032	2,728	4,259
52 - Retail trade	2,033	2,053	24,728	25,474	12	13,819	14,793	373,859	395,506
5210 Lumber and other building materials	20	19	270	552	29	24,148	22,232	9,065	13,078
5230 Paint, glass, and wallpaper stores	14	13	74	71	5	23,459	22,310	1,722	1,522
5250 Hardware stores	16	10	92	72	7	18,304	18,611	1,877	1,323
5260 Retail nurseries and garden stores	12	13	54	61	5	11,926	14,361	1,418	1,489
5310 Department stores	11	9	2,107	2,024	225	11,389	11,617	25,369	24,593
5330 Variety stores	11	9	195	152	17	12,246	11,474	2,182	1,997
5390 Misc. general merchandise stores	12	12	255	217	18	10,416	14,691	2,693	7,054
5410 Grocery stores	146	147	3,913	3,761	26	14,711	15,882	59,521	60,407
5420 Meat and fish markets	13	14	70	84	6	11,086	12,048	969	1,081
5430 Fruit and vegetable markets	4	-	16	-	-	11,250	-	173	-
5440 Candy, nut, and confectionery stores	7	-	34	-	-	5,647	-	286	-
5460 Retail bakeries	43	47	394	407	9	13,340	13,346	5,619	5,552
5490 Miscellaneous food stores	6	7	49	50	7	12,816	19,280	769	930
5510 New and used car dealers	30	31	1,084	1,182	38	33,716	35,919	45,203	43,156
5520 Used car dealers	10	9	25	27	3	25,120	28,593	716	763
5530 Auto and home supply stores	33	35	282	273	8	20,298	22,286	6,292	6,431
5540 Gasoline service stations	139	123	818	802	7	14,068	15,217	12,421	12,758
5550 Boat dealers	3	-	27	-	-	16,296	-	548	-
5570 Motorcycle dealers	5	4	50	46	12	10,000	14,435	709	770
5610 Men's & boys' clothing stores	32	28	239	236	8	15,682	14,831	3,304	2,926
5620 Women's clothing stores	74	66	814	695	11	7,754	8,167	6,993	5,525
5630 Women's accessory & specialty stores	15	14	92	91	7	10,348	10,418	1,091	941
5640 Children's and infants' wear stores	14	14	135	148	11	7,970	8,378	1,177	1,219
5650 Family clothing stores	26	28	328	421	15	9,159	11,886	4,130	4,964
5660 Shoe stores	59	55	362	357	6	11,635	12,515	4,571	4,751
5690 Misc. apparel & accessory stores	13	15	71	75	5	9,972	10,987	776	850
5712 Furniture stores	34	33	263	279	8	22,144	22,136	5,878	6,205
5713 Floor covering stores	19	20	98	117	6	24,531	25,368	2,564	2,916
5714 Drapery and upholstery stores	8	7	54	58	8	15,111	16,828	837	915
5719 Misc. homefurnishings stores	30	31	274	263	8	12,204	13,567	3,840	3,702
5720 Household appliance stores	10	11	162	116	11	14,914	24,379	2,936	3,034

Continued on next page.

TRENTON, NJ PMSA - [continued]

Wholesale and Retail Trade USA	Establishments		Employment		Emp / Est	Pay / Employee		Annual Payroll ($ 000)	
	1994	1995	1994	1995	1995	1994	1995	1994	1995
5731 Radio, TV, & electronic stores	17	17	246	268	16	16,927	16,687	4,207	4,463
5734 Computer and software stores	16	16	82	98	6	18,390	20,531	1,747	1,967
5735 Record & prerecorded tape stores	14	17	85	131	8	8,518	13,313	766	1,888
5736 Musical instrument stores	6	7	48	48	7	19,083	25,750	1,135	1,301
5812 Eating places	492	482	6,910	7,147	15	9,813	10,230	73,518	77,367
5813 Drinking places	74	68	320	275	4	8,813	9,222	2,921	2,568
5910 Drug stores and proprietary stores	71	78	991	1,146	15	14,349	14,625	15,316	17,687
5920 Liquor stores	64	61	329	339	6	14,444	14,041	4,924	4,831
5930 Used merchandise stores	18	17	184	155	9	9,935	11,974	2,506	2,215
5941 Sporting goods and bicycle shops	40	43	390	406	9	11,897	11,724	5,095	5,301
5942 Book stores	20	20	240	330	17	11,733	12,691	3,044	4,162
5943 Stationery stores	4	4	45	56	14	10,667	14,357	494	726
5944 Jewelry stores	40	40	339	279	7	14,360	21,204	4,714	5,816
5945 Hobby, toy, and game shops	15	14	201	194	14	9,731	11,216	2,321	2,558
5947 Gift, novelty, and souvenir shops	44	51	269	305	6	8,625	9,115	2,589	3,029
5949 Sewing, needlework, and piece goods	6	4	64	46	12	7,188	9,217	460	442
5961 Catalog and mail-order houses	13	14	80	92	7	18,750	23,348	2,072	2,589
5962 Merchandising machine operators	8	7	47	24	3	21,702	21,333	754	522
5963 Direct selling establishments	11	9	55	60	7	21,455	23,600	1,413	1,462
5980 Fuel dealers	25	22	231	219	10	33,420	32,950	7,439	6,889
5992 Florists	34	29	168	157	5	11,429	11,771	2,054	2,001
5993 Tobacco stores and stands	-	3	-	4	1	-	34,000	-	147
5994 News dealers and newsstands	-	7	-	14	2	-	8,857	-	144
5995 Optical goods stores	17	19	100	100	5	16,480	19,840	1,610	2,131
5999 Miscellaneous retail stores, nec	49	56	183	229	4	14,295	16,559	2,802	3,741

Source: County Business Patterns 1994/95, CBP-94/95, U.S. Department of Commerce, Washington DC, November 1997. The employment column represents mid-March employment in the year. Pay per employee is calculated by dividing 1st Quarter payroll, annualized, by mid-March employment. The column headed 'Emp / Est' shows 'employees per establishment'. A dash (-) means that data are unavailable or cannot be calculated. nec means not elsewhere classified. *Notes:* 1. 1994 data incomplete; unavailable or withheld. 2. 1995 data incomplete; unavailable or withheld. 3. 1994 and 1995 data incomplete; unavailable or withheld.

TUCSON, AZ MSA

Wholesale and Retail Trade USA	Establishments		Employment		Emp / Est	Pay / Employee		Annual Payroll ($ 000)	
	1994	1995	1994	1995	1995	1994	1995	1994	1995
50- Wholesale trade	1,060	1,090	10,259	11,266	10	23,370	25,099	264,459	290,869
5012 Automobiles and other vehicles	21	23	107	245	11	16,336	12,147	2,004	3,135
5013 Motor vehicle supplies and new parts	65	61	564	547	9	18,035	20,088	10,990	11,444
5014 Tires and tubes	11	10	111	130	13	22,595	27,908	2,849	3,760
5015 Motor vehicle parts, used	27	32	120	138	4	15,633	15,797	1,801	2,104
5021 Furniture	13	12	141	144	12	19,745	18,694	2,911	2,828
5023 Homefurnishings	20	23	359	439	19	20,423	19,882	8,227	8,624
5031 Lumber, plywood, and millwork	21	16	334	349	22	22,072	23,977	7,983	9,602
5032 Brick, stone, & related materials	21	-	180	-	-	21,889	-	4,770	-
5039 Construction materials, nec	-	20	-	244	12	-	23,639	-	6,496
5043 Photographic equipment & supplies	3	3	9	13	4	23,556	15,385	212	217
5044 Office equipment	23	28	377	406	15	27,968	29,823	10,846	11,525
5045 Computers, peripherals, & software	57	58	675	558	10	34,963	34,423	22,845	17,866
5047 Medical and hospital equipment	27	24	186	201	8	21,935	23,383	4,680	4,649
5051 Metals service centers and offices	-	15	-	141	9	-	25,220	-	3,310
5063 Electrical apparatus and equipment	48	40	514	485	12	25,743	29,237	14,556	14,959
5064 Electrical appliances, TV & radios	5	5	10	11	2	37,200	44,727	304	377
5065 Electronic parts and equipment	41	43	353	410	10	29,983	30,771	10,277	13,717
5072 Hardware	21	25	222	185	7	20,468	24,843	4,668	4,910
5074 Plumbing & hydronic heating supplies	22	21	183	189	9	27,082	27,280	4,983	5,047
5082 Construction and mining machinery	36	32	362	396	12	32,906	41,475	16,274	16,626
5083 Farm and garden machinery	8	-	63	-	-	23,175	-	1,783	-
5084 Industrial machinery and equipment	46	47	400	471	10	20,670	22,760	10,039	12,564
5085 Industrial supplies	23	27	139	184	7	22,561	25,391	3,871	5,087
5087 Service establishment equipment	22	22	215	223	10	21,656	21,830	4,881	4,951
5088 Transportation equipment & supplies	8	-	75	-	-	33,387	-	2,339	-
5091 Sporting & recreational goods	18	17	83	100	6	20,000	19,600	1,828	1,856
5093 Scrap and waste materials	19	19	178	226	12	14,090	16,265	3,718	4,370
5094 Jewelry & precious stones	19	-	155	-	-	33,239	-	8,377	-
5099 Durable goods, nec	-	15	-	70	5	-	15,486	-	1,037
5112 Stationery and office supplies	31	27	363	351	13	13,388	16,308	5,025	5,257
5120 Drugs, proprietaries, and sundries	10	11	61	76	7	26,885	24,526	1,942	2,222
5136 Men's and boys' clothing	5	-	50	-	-	12,720	-	750	-
5137 Women's and children's clothing	5	5	29	34	7	7,448	6,588	246	189
5141 Groceries, general line	9	9	93	86	10	30,538	33,767	3,027	3,217

Continued on next page.

TUCSON, AZ MSA - [continued]

Wholesale and Retail Trade USA	Establishments		Employment		Emp / Est	Pay / Employee		Annual Payroll ($ 000)	
	1994	1995	1994	1995	1995	1994	1995	1994	1995
5143 Dairy products, exc. dried or canned	5	5	58	64	13	13,379	14,625	799	896
5145 Confectionery	8	7	123	158	23	21,854	19,114	3,073	3,486
5148 Fresh fruits and vegetables	6	8	144	177	22	20,333	23,390	3,428	4,329
5149 Groceries and related products, nec	36	41	465	611	15	20,740	18,802	11,050	11,621
5150 Farm-product raw materials	4	4	10	9	2	12,400	14,667	233	268
5160 Chemicals and allied products	32	30	219	272	9	40,548	43,691	8,766	10,868
5170 Petroleum and petroleum products	14	13	159	162	12	28,252	28,074	4,694	4,633
5180 Beer, wine, and distilled beverages	8	8	450	425	53	24,347	28,659	11,664	12,943
5191 Farm supplies	18	15	81	63	4	17,630	17,206	1,709	1,211
5192 Books, periodicals, & newspapers	10	12	127	198	17	22,614	21,051	3,367	4,316
5193 Flowers & florists' supplies	15	12	178	79	7	8,449	13,316	1,792	1,074
5199 Nondurable goods, nec	40	43	199	219	5	19,075	20,895	4,178	5,026
52 - Retail trade	3,997	3,992	62,046	62,022	16	11,993	12,957	792,507	822,294
5210 Lumber and other building materials	44	36	1,157	1,071	30	16,927	19,533	21,092	19,328
5230 Paint, glass, and wallpaper stores	23	26	111	123	5	21,081	21,724	2,435	2,820
5250 Hardware stores	42	39	427	458	12	15,101	15,860	7,424	8,202
5260 Retail nurseries and garden stores	20	23	146	283	12	12,219	9,300	2,025	2,996
5270 Mobile home dealers	19	23	207	270	12	23,652	25,200	6,793	7,248
5310 Department stores	32	26	5,409	4,757	183	10,940	13,113	62,856	61,459
5330 Variety stores	10	-	93	-	-	9,333	-	920	-
5390 Misc. general merchandise stores	20	-	813	-	-	15,449	-	14,169	-
5410 Grocery stores	271	275	7,771	8,669	32	15,077	15,949	125,322	137,964
5420 Meat and fish markets	9	10	64	61	6	14,188	14,426	866	869
5430 Fruit and vegetable markets	6	-	26	-	-	6,154	-	175	-
5440 Candy, nut, and confectionery stores	-	6	-	22	4	-	13,818	-	271
5450 Dairy products stores	5	6	24	45	8	4,000	3,200	126	180
5460 Retail bakeries	48	40	421	280	7	8,504	7,557	3,737	1,992
5490 Miscellaneous food stores	28	34	124	129	4	8,419	9,116	1,135	1,374
5510 New and used car dealers	35	34	2,369	2,483	73	30,320	31,447	78,883	84,907
5520 Used car dealers	44	48	397	396	8	24,897	24,980	10,522	11,045
5530 Auto and home supply stores	130	131	1,190	1,097	8	15,082	16,985	20,088	20,354
5540 Gasoline service stations	156	158	1,454	1,438	9	12,204	13,363	18,850	19,489
5560 Recreational vehicle dealers	10	10	239	282	28	30,628	29,560	7,365	8,266
5570 Motorcycle dealers	16	16	121	105	7	16,992	18,590	2,195	2,265
5590 Automotive dealers, nec	-	5	-	5	1	-	20,000	-	126
5610 Men's & boys' clothing stores	34	33	267	222	7	9,094	11,982	2,358	2,698
5620 Women's clothing stores	128	106	1,138	882	8	8,780	9,465	10,343	8,331
5630 Women's accessory & specialty stores	23	24	129	148	6	9,333	9,351	1,343	1,330
5640 Children's and infants' wear stores	9	10	55	60	6	5,673	6,733	576	723
5650 Family clothing stores	49	51	706	701	14	9,819	10,414	7,334	7,017
5660 Shoe stores	88	78	429	385	5	11,021	12,104	4,716	4,527
5690 Misc. apparel & accessory stores	29	27	146	127	5	8,192	10,520	1,377	1,341
5712 Furniture stores	108	106	1,056	1,055	10	18,080	17,653	19,327	18,978
5713 Floor covering stores	31	33	253	284	9	19,194	20,606	4,982	6,214
5714 Drapery and upholstery stores	10	9	35	62	7	10,857	10,516	490	535
5719 Misc. homefurnishings stores	36	38	258	249	7	12,171	14,538	3,486	3,893
5720 Household appliance stores	17	15	83	118	8	14,795	17,661	1,565	2,257
5731 Radio, TV, & electronic stores	63	62	787	625	10	14,618	18,522	12,755	11,720
5734 Computer and software stores	24	31	145	98	3	12,414	17,306	1,787	2,217
5735 Record & prerecorded tape stores	30	28	270	255	9	9,526	9,161	2,835	2,374
5736 Musical instrument stores	19	18	144	149	8	15,000	17,477	2,417	2,594
5812 Eating places	1,075	1,039	21,569	22,630	22	7,865	7,976	172,784	181,154
5813 Drinking places	163	137	1,721	1,628	12	6,173	6,162	10,968	10,282
5910 Drug stores and proprietary stores	62	57	1,363	1,285	23	18,911	21,099	26,411	27,206
5920 Liquor stores	33	30	130	114	4	7,723	8,070	1,013	1,001
5930 Used merchandise stores	74	75	621	701	9	8,432	8,970	5,918	6,429
5941 Sporting goods and bicycle shops	89	90	691	712	8	10,999	11,096	8,146	9,106
5942 Book stores	52	50	441	469	9	11,519	12,699	5,622	5,980
5943 Stationery stores	10	10	55	66	7	12,582	14,545	841	935
5944 Jewelry stores	90	92	464	530	6	16,595	16,657	7,687	8,698
5945 Hobby, toy, and game shops	37	37	361	353	10	8,920	9,802	3,783	4,141
5946 Camera & photographic supply stores	11	10	53	42	4	12,377	12,857	527	557
5947 Gift, novelty, and souvenir shops	113	116	717	685	6	8,151	9,571	6,424	7,439
5948 Luggage and leather goods stores	8	7	50	48	7	9,920	10,417	497	473
5949 Sewing, needlework, and piece goods	21	21	213	200	10	8,507	9,500	1,912	1,756
5961 Catalog and mail-order houses	30	28	653	535	19	12,429	14,228	8,920	7,042
5962 Merchandising machine operators	14	16	77	94	6	15,065	14,723	1,338	1,561
5963 Direct selling establishments	51	48	371	357	7	15,849	18,095	6,044	6,931
5980 Fuel dealers	5	4	82	87	22	19,122	21,425	1,526	1,526
5992 Florists	58	56	360	357	6	9,400	10,532	3,664	3,936
5993 Tobacco stores and stands	7	7	26	38	5	16,308	13,895	483	561

Continued on next page.

TUCSON, AZ MSA - [continued]

Wholesale and Retail Trade USA	Establishments		Employment		Emp / Est	Pay / Employee		Annual Payroll ($ 000)	
	1994	1995	1994	1995	1995	1994	1995	1994	1995
5994 News dealers and newsstands	4	4	12	10	3	7,667	8,800	94	96
5995 Optical goods stores	47	46	219	240	5	15,050	16,400	3,621	4,249
5999 Miscellaneous retail stores, nec	154	169	809	950	6	13,508	13,886	12,170	13,464

Source: County Business Patterns 1994/95, CBP-94/95, U.S. Department of Commerce, Washington DC, November 1997. The employment column represents mid-March employment in the year. Pay per employee is calculated by dividing 1st Quarter payroll, annualized, by mid-March employment. The column headed 'Emp / Est' shows 'employees per establishment'. A dash (-) means that data are unavailable or cannot be calculated. nec means not elsewhere classified. *Notes:* 1. 1994 data incomplete; unavailable or withheld. 2. 1995 data incomplete; unavailable or withheld. 3. 1994 and 1995 data incomplete; unavailable or withheld.

TULSA, OK MSA

Wholesale and Retail Trade USA	Establishments		Employment		Emp / Est	Pay / Employee		Annual Payroll ($ 000)	
	1994	1995	1994	1995	1995	1994	1995	1994	1995
50- Wholesale trade	-	1,871	-	24,765	13	-	32,723	-	825,672
5012 Automobiles and other vehicles [2]	-	27	-	619	23	-	22,637	-	14,340
5013 Motor vehicle supplies and new parts	-	85	-	781	9	-	20,994	-	17,490
5014 Tires and tubes [2]	-	8	-	117	15	-	26,359	-	3,709
5015 Motor vehicle parts, used [2]	-	24	-	109	5	-	18,349	-	1,937
5021 Furniture [2]	-	16	-	387	24	-	28,961	-	10,698
5023 Homefurnishings [2]	-	22	-	191	9	-	22,911	-	4,818
5031 Lumber, plywood, and millwork [2]	-	21	-	315	15	-	26,337	-	8,560
5032 Brick, stone, & related materials [2]	-	20	-	154	8	-	25,636	-	4,454
5033 Roofing, siding, & insulation [2]	-	10	-	103	10	-	29,825	-	3,205
5039 Construction materials, nec [2]	-	33	-	317	10	-	24,202	-	8,012
5043 Photographic equipment & supplies [2]	-	4	-	71	18	-	25,239	-	2,394
5044 Office equipment [2]	-	48	-	543	11	-	28,302	-	15,078
5045 Computers, peripherals, & software [2]	-	70	-	993	14	-	39,263	-	34,965
5046 Commercial equipment, nec [2]	-	14	-	128	9	-	28,750	-	3,899
5047 Medical and hospital equipment [2]	-	46	-	333	7	-	33,237	-	11,027
5048 Ophthalmic goods [2]	-	5	-	26	5	-	15,538	-	487
5049 Professional equipment, nec [2]	-	8	-	71	9	-	21,183	-	1,644
5051 Metals service centers and offices [2]	-	77	-	159	2	-	32,755	-	5,334
5063 Electrical apparatus and equipment [2]	-	90	-	657	7	-	33,041	-	21,477
5064 Electrical appliances, TV & radios [2]	-	7	-	78	11	-	19,026	-	1,550
5065 Electronic parts and equipment [2]	-	56	-	620	11	-	40,052	-	23,868
5072 Hardware [2]	-	36	-	1,000	28	-	38,704	-	38,391
5074 Plumbing & hydronic heating supplies [2]	-	30	-	213	7	-	24,563	-	5,251
5075 Warm air heating & air conditioning [2]	-	24	-	133	6	-	32,241	-	4,578
5082 Construction and mining machinery [2]	-	28	-	425	15	-	30,814	-	14,161
5083 Farm and garden machinery [2]	-	20	-	120	6	-	23,500	-	3,564
5084 Industrial machinery and equipment	-	231	-	2,409	10	-	36,955	-	90,776
5085 Industrial supplies	-	115	-	998	9	-	35,415	-	34,449
5087 Service establishment equipment [2]	-	27	-	272	10	-	24,265	-	6,298
5088 Transportation equipment & supplies [2]	-	26	-	227	9	-	23,841	-	6,079
5091 Sporting & recreational goods [2]	-	23	-	176	8	-	16,727	-	3,072
5093 Scrap and waste materials	-	25	-	187	7	-	26,738	-	5,444
5094 Jewelry & precious stones [2]	-	23	-	169	7	-	21,325	-	3,927
5111 Printing and writing paper [2]	-	8	-	125	16	-	43,648	-	5,063
5112 Stationery and office supplies [2]	-	39	-	431	11	-	22,784	-	9,806
5113 Industrial & personal service paper [2]	-	12	-	222	19	-	31,964	-	7,974
5120 Drugs, proprietaries, and sundries [2]	-	14	-	159	11	-	23,447	-	3,932
5137 Women's and children's clothing [2]	-	8	-	67	8	-	19,701	-	1,488
5141 Groceries, general line [2]	-	14	-	855	61	-	28,566	-	24,587
5142 Packaged frozen food [2]	-	4	-	202	51	-	29,822	-	6,748
5147 Meats and meat products [2]	-	9	-	117	13	-	20,068	-	2,846
5148 Fresh fruits and vegetables [2]	-	9	-	135	15	-	19,763	-	3,092
5149 Groceries and related products, nec [2]	-	36	-	527	15	-	25,412	-	13,881
5150 Farm-product raw materials [2]	-	13	-	101	8	-	14,178	-	1,339
5162 Plastics materials & basic shapes [2]	-	11	-	55	5	-	14,036	-	989
5169 Chemicals & allied products, nec [2]	-	51	-	418	8	-	47,589	-	17,411
5171 Petroleum bulk stations & terminals	-	40	-	183	5	-	30,077	-	5,824
5172 Petroleum products, nec [2]	-	40	-	287	7	-	42,146	-	13,836
5180 Beer, wine, and distilled beverages [2]	-	10	-	322	32	-	22,981	-	8,234
5191 Farm supplies	-	32	-	128	4	-	34,188	-	5,166
5192 Books, periodicals, & newspapers [2]	-	11	-	192	17	-	19,271	-	3,863
5193 Flowers & florists' supplies [2]	-	9	-	68	8	-	19,529	-	1,364
5198 Paints, varnishes, and supplies [2]	-	15	-	103	7	-	23,068	-	2,736
5199 Nondurable goods, nec [2]	-	39	-	310	8	-	19,174	-	6,811
52- Retail trade	-	4,481	-	60,325	13	-	13,048	-	812,448
5210 Lumber and other building materials	-	65	-	1,301	20	-	18,862	-	25,498

Continued on next page.

TULSA, OK MSA - [continued]

Wholesale and Retail Trade USA	Establishments		Employment		Emp / Est	Pay / Employee		Annual Payroll ($ 000)	
	1994	1995	1994	1995	1995	1994	1995	1994	1995
5230 Paint, glass, and wallpaper stores [2]	-	34	-	208	6	-	18,558	-	4,375
5250 Hardware stores [2]	-	18	-	76	4	-	10,526	-	825
5260 Retail nurseries and garden stores [2]	-	31	-	266	9	-	11,293	-	3,330
5270 Mobile home dealers [2]	-	11	-	75	7	-	28,533	-	2,450
5310 Department stores [2]	-	37	-	5,918	160	-	12,927	-	76,676
5330 Variety stores [2]	-	24	-	139	6	-	9,237	-	1,258
5390 Misc. general merchandise stores [2]	-	42	-	758	18	-	13,953	-	10,130
5410 Grocery stores [2]	-	322	-	6,526	20	-	13,690	-	92,155
5420 Meat and fish markets [2]	-	6	-	36	6	-	12,667	-	481
5440 Candy, nut, and confectionery stores [2]	-	12	-	77	6	-	6,442	-	495
5460 Retail bakeries [2]	-	66	-	271	4	-	7,897	-	2,440
5490 Miscellaneous food stores [2]	-	22	-	127	6	-	8,189	-	1,208
5510 New and used car dealers	-	63	-	3,614	57	-	27,558	-	108,893
5520 Used car dealers [2]	-	56	-	217	4	-	18,120	-	4,422
5530 Auto and home supply stores	-	155	-	956	6	-	18,724	-	19,057
5540 Gasoline service stations	-	287	-	1,768	6	-	15,100	-	24,928
5550 Boat dealers [2]	-	14	-	42	3	-	17,714	-	758
5560 Recreational vehicle dealers [2]	-	9	-	142	16	-	22,394	-	3,366
5570 Motorcycle dealers [2]	-	10	-	95	10	-	20,758	-	2,252
5590 Automotive dealers, nec [2]	-	5	-	55	11	-	20,000	-	1,158
5610 Men's & boys' clothing stores [2]	-	31	-	172	6	-	13,698	-	2,426
5620 Women's clothing stores [2]	-	103	-	891	9	-	10,101	-	9,450
5630 Women's accessory & specialty stores [2]	-	23	-	125	5	-	7,680	-	1,025
5640 Children's and infants' wear stores [2]	-	16	-	190	12	-	9,032	-	1,543
5650 Family clothing stores	-	65	-	1,028	16	-	11,307	-	10,245
5660 Shoe stores [2]	-	78	-	388	5	-	11,608	-	4,641
5690 Misc. apparel & accessory stores [2]	-	17	-	92	5	-	9,565	-	1,037
5712 Furniture stores [2]	-	69	-	511	7	-	23,796	-	12,595
5713 Floor covering stores [2]	-	40	-	233	6	-	21,425	-	5,359
5714 Drapery and upholstery stores [2]	-	8	-	39	5	-	10,769	-	801
5719 Misc. homefurnishings stores [2]	-	44	-	379	9	-	12,127	-	4,787
5720 Household appliance stores	-	37	-	144	4	-	16,472	-	2,537
5731 Radio, TV, & electronic stores [2]	-	47	-	471	10	-	16,331	-	8,857
5734 Computer and software stores [2]	-	37	-	145	4	-	19,476	-	3,139
5735 Record & prerecorded tape stores [2]	-	16	-	188	12	-	9,468	-	1,632
5736 Musical instrument stores [2]	-	19	-	103	5	-	15,922	-	2,129
5812 Eating places	-	1,144	-	21,263	19	-	7,731	-	171,700
5813 Drinking places	-	105	-	558	5	-	8,452	-	4,549
5910 Drug stores and proprietary stores	-	128	-	1,473	12	-	15,066	-	22,879
5920 Liquor stores	-	73	-	200	3	-	8,100	-	1,652
5930 Used merchandise stores	-	113	-	547	5	-	11,634	-	6,629
5941 Sporting goods and bicycle shops [2]	-	71	-	439	6	-	11,007	-	5,244
5942 Book stores [2]	-	45	-	275	6	-	10,851	-	2,985
5943 Stationery stores [2]	-	12	-	90	8	-	12,933	-	1,242
5944 Jewelry stores [2]	-	65	-	332	5	-	24,988	-	6,982
5945 Hobby, toy, and game shops [2]	-	33	-	424	13	-	8,651	-	4,222
5947 Gift, novelty, and souvenir shops	-	90	-	540	6	-	7,985	-	4,738
5949 Sewing, needlework, and piece goods [2]	-	20	-	159	8	-	7,145	-	1,129
5961 Catalog and mail-order houses [2]	-	20	-	49	2	-	25,388	-	1,647
5962 Merchandising machine operators [2]	-	19	-	125	7	-	19,200	-	2,425
5963 Direct selling establishments [2]	-	37	-	298	8	-	15,020	-	4,564
5984 Liquefied petroleum gas dealers	-	15	-	60	4	-	19,333	-	1,163
5992 Florists	-	90	-	292	3	-	10,151	-	2,983
5993 Tobacco stores and stands	-	21	-	118	6	-	10,949	-	1,346
5995 Optical goods stores [2]	-	33	-	229	7	-	15,284	-	3,758
5999 Miscellaneous retail stores, nec	-	142	-	793	6	-	13,614	-	11,249

Source: County Business Patterns 1994/95, CBP-94/95, U.S. Department of Commerce, Washington DC, November 1997. The employment column represents mid-March employment in the year. Pay per employee is calculated by dividing 1st Quarter payroll, annualized, by mid-March employment. The column headed 'Emp / Est' shows 'employees per establishment'. A dash (-) means that data are unavailable or cannot be calculated. nec means not elsewhere classified. *Notes:* 1. 1994 data incomplete; unavailable or withheld. 2. 1995 data incomplete; unavailable or withheld. 3. 1994 and 1995 data incomplete; unavailable or withheld.

TUSCALOOSA, AL MSA

Wholesale and Retail Trade USA	Establishments		Employment		Emp / Est	Pay / Employee		Annual Payroll ($ 000)	
	1994	1995	1994	1995	1995	1994	1995	1994	1995
50- Wholesale trade	211	211	2,193	2,420	11	22,926	25,193	55,875	64,658
5012 Automobiles and other vehicles	9	8	85	82	10	20,471	23,951	1,996	2,095
5013 Motor vehicle supplies and new parts	18	16	113	109	7	16,956	20,514	2,238	2,674
5014 Tires and tubes	3	3	35	42	14	27,657	24,762	1,110	1,217

Continued on next page.

TUSCALOOSA, AL MSA - [continued]

Wholesale and Retail Trade USA	Establishments		Employment		Emp / Est	Pay / Employee		Annual Payroll ($ 000)	
	1994	1995	1994	1995	1995	1994	1995	1994	1995
5015 Motor vehicle parts, used	7	7	66	74	11	15,333	18,865	1,129	1,463
5020 Furniture and homefurnishings	4	3	2	4	1	10,000	15,000	47	73
5031 Lumber, plywood, and millwork	9	10	78	71	7	20,205	23,099	1,888	1,685
5044 Office equipment	6	7	53	49	7	14,491	17,796	857	865
5046 Commercial equipment, nec	3	-	19	-	-	13,895	-	331	-
5047 Medical and hospital equipment	6	5	62	32	6	16,839	15,000	1,103	522
5051 Metals service centers and offices	3	-	42	-	-	20,571	-	954	-
5052 Coal and other minerals and ores	3	-	4	-	-	65,000	-	300	-
5063 Electrical apparatus and equipment	5	8	60	96	12	22,067	28,417	1,688	2,686
5065 Electronic parts and equipment	-	4	-	16	4	-	25,000	-	426
5074 Plumbing & hydronic heating supplies	8	6	100	107	18	27,240	30,168	3,017	2,864
5082 Construction and mining machinery	4	4	296	308	77	32,473	33,831	10,564	10,970
5083 Farm and garden machinery	-	3	-	16	5	-	19,500	-	392
5084 Industrial machinery and equipment	9	-	37	-	-	26,919	-	1,035	-
5085 Industrial supplies	7	7	88	99	14	24,182	26,869	2,251	2,826
5093 Scrap and waste materials	3	3	30	34	11	16,800	18,941	562	618
5099 Durable goods, nec	6	8	27	27	3	11,852	12,593	392	429
5110 Paper and paper products	14	10	94	113	11	21,149	21,699	2,852	2,515
5140 Groceries and related products	15	18	159	256	14	19,673	18,563	3,549	5,107
5169 Chemicals & allied products, nec	-	4	-	5	1	-	55,200	-	258
5171 Petroleum bulk stations & terminals	5	5	108	125	25	20,407	18,240	2,294	2,332
5172 Petroleum products, nec	3	3	55	45	15	11,055	13,956	646	797
5181 Beer and ale	3	-	84	-	-	24,095	-	2,225	-
5182 Wine and distilled beverages	3	-	20	-	-	19,400	-	393	-
5199 Nondurable goods, nec	5	5	54	52	10	29,111	35,000	1,711	2,015
52 - Retail trade	951	985	14,096	15,382	16	10,263	10,671	159,369	177,764
5210 Lumber and other building materials	19	19	411	430	23	17,635	18,800	7,959	8,748
5230 Paint, glass, and wallpaper stores	8	10	32	39	4	21,375	19,282	709	797
5250 Hardware stores	9	8	66	41	5	16,121	14,927	1,126	575
5260 Retail nurseries and garden stores	7	6	56	64	11	12,500	12,938	845	907
5270 Mobile home dealers	10	12	71	142	12	21,239	27,746	2,864	5,363
5310 Department stores	7	7	1,513	1,558	223	10,824	12,005	18,120	18,601
5330 Variety stores	6	6	54	57	10	6,296	5,544	380	378
5390 Misc. general merchandise stores	8	9	293	307	34	10,157	11,075	3,296	5,060
5410 Grocery stores	77	90	1,940	2,095	23	8,111	8,894	16,355	19,912
5460 Retail bakeries	9	4	120	76	19	9,200	9,895	797	586
5490 Miscellaneous food stores	-	4	-	19	5	-	11,368	-	244
5510 New and used car dealers	14	14	531	550	39	25,348	25,964	15,342	16,095
5520 Used car dealers	26	25	67	86	3	13,910	16,791	1,202	1,535
5530 Auto and home supply stores	35	37	271	309	8	15,675	16,595	4,811	5,745
5540 Gasoline service stations	69	70	688	659	9	9,238	9,414	6,924	6,691
5610 Men's & boys' clothing stores	8	10	53	48	5	11,170	12,667	686	668
5620 Women's clothing stores	34	31	271	225	7	7,232	7,360	2,080	1,621
5630 Women's accessory & specialty stores	3	4	9	47	12	9,333	4,766	117	228
5650 Family clothing stores	9	11	268	305	28	12,821	12,249	3,806	3,770
5660 Shoe stores	20	22	120	179	8	10,267	9,006	1,337	1,660
5712 Furniture stores	33	30	213	218	7	15,192	16,239	3,289	3,592
5713 Floor covering stores	9	10	80	86	9	16,500	18,326	1,579	1,740
5719 Misc. homefurnishings stores	11	13	71	115	9	11,662	10,261	1,067	1,271
5720 Household appliance stores	5	7	61	67	10	9,246	9,313	917	957
5731 Radio, TV, & electronic stores	15	16	98	110	7	19,184	17,600	1,917	1,846
5734 Computer and software stores	5	8	30	28	4	13,733	16,571	487	541
5735 Record & prerecorded tape stores	6	5	39	49	10	8,923	6,939	352	346
5736 Musical instrument stores	4	4	10	10	3	14,000	14,400	152	128
5812 Eating places	174	170	3,995	4,583	27	6,492	6,573	27,795	31,622
5813 Drinking places	17	16	135	144	9	6,074	5,806	910	1,018
5910 Drug stores and proprietary stores	38	38	546	530	14	11,766	11,758	6,736	6,465
5920 Liquor stores	5	8	32	40	5	9,250	13,700	405	593
5930 Used merchandise stores	18	17	59	69	4	11,932	10,551	760	737
5941 Sporting goods and bicycle shops	16	18	115	147	8	10,435	8,680	1,267	1,470
5942 Book stores	16	15	95	118	8	10,779	10,644	1,141	1,414
5944 Jewelry stores	21	19	127	118	6	11,811	13,356	1,436	1,537
5945 Hobby, toy, and game shops	8	7	61	48	7	8,787	12,917	614	714
5947 Gift, novelty, and souvenir shops	22	19	89	73	4	5,438	7,562	575	624
5949 Sewing, needlework, and piece goods	7	5	28	28	6	7,143	8,286	235	276
5963 Direct selling establishments	7	6	62	50	8	13,097	8,160	768	478
5984 Liquefied petroleum gas dealers	3	3	17	22	7	22,824	20,545	439	498
5992 Florists	21	18	79	93	5	9,823	9,290	799	847
5995 Optical goods stores	11	9	50	46	5	12,880	11,739	620	561
5999 Miscellaneous retail stores, nec	23	21	86	82	4	10,558	12,341	979	1,051

Source: County Business Patterns 1994/95, CBP-94/95, U.S. Department of Commerce, Washington DC, November 1997. The employment column represents mid-March employment in the year. Pay per employee is calculated by dividing 1st Quarter payroll, annualized, by mid-March employment. The column headed 'Emp / Est' shows 'employees per establishment'. A dash (-) means that data are unavailable or cannot be calculated. nec means not elsewhere classified. *Notes:* 1. 1994 data incomplete; unavailable or withheld. 2. 1995 data incomplete; unavailable or withheld. 3. 1994 and 1995 data incomplete; unavailable or withheld.

TYLER, TX MSA

Wholesale and Retail Trade USA	Establishments		Employment		Emp / Est	Pay / Employee		Annual Payroll ($ 000)	
	1994	1995	1994	1995	1995	1994	1995	1994	1995
50- Wholesale trade	-	365	-	3,510	10	-	27,324	-	103,278
5012 Automobiles and other vehicles	-	11	-	142	13	-	26,169	-	4,309
5013 Motor vehicle supplies and new parts	-	16	-	166	10	-	17,807	-	3,154
5015 Motor vehicle parts, used	-	8	-	57	7	-	12,561	-	747
5020 Furniture and homefurnishings	-	8	-	38	5	-	27,789	-	1,149
5031 Lumber, plywood, and millwork	-	5	-	67	13	-	28,478	-	2,050
5044 Office equipment	-	17	-	103	6	-	33,903	-	3,565
5045 Computers, peripherals, & software	-	14	-	93	7	-	50,366	-	3,671
5047 Medical and hospital equipment	-	8	-	50	6	-	28,800	-	1,447
5051 Metals service centers and offices	-	5	-	129	26	-	36,992	-	5,677
5063 Electrical apparatus and equipment	-	11	-	74	7	-	29,189	-	2,415
5072 Hardware	-	10	-	116	12	-	21,103	-	2,726
5074 Plumbing & hydronic heating supplies	-	9	-	68	8	-	23,059	-	1,803
5075 Warm air heating & air conditioning	-	3	-	13	4	-	20,000	-	283
5082 Construction and mining machinery	-	6	-	66	11	-	30,182	-	2,488
5083 Farm and garden machinery	-	6	-	39	7	-	21,128	-	900
5084 Industrial machinery and equipment	-	29	-	199	7	-	35,095	-	7,055
5085 Industrial supplies	-	15	-	117	8	-	30,632	-	3,498
5087 Service establishment equipment	-	6	-	35	6	-	22,057	-	805
5088 Transportation equipment & supplies	-	4	-	12	3	-	51,667	-	596
5093 Scrap and waste materials	-	9	-	88	10	-	18,182	-	2,198
5094 Jewelry & precious stones	-	3	-	10	3	-	12,800	-	101
5099 Durable goods, nec	-	6	-	25	4	-	33,280	-	825
5112 Stationery and office supplies	-	9	-	133	15	-	30,015	-	3,333
5120 Drugs, proprietaries, and sundries	-	7	-	52	7	-	22,923	-	1,223
5130 Apparel, piece goods, and notions	-	6	-	24	4	-	18,667	-	711
5142 Packaged frozen food	-	4	-	93	23	-	23,914	-	2,461
5149 Groceries and related products, nec	-	13	-	257	20	-	29,868	-	7,765
5150 Farm-product raw materials	-	3	-	4	1	-	19,000	-	90
5162 Plastics materials & basic shapes	-	3	-	36	12	-	21,667	-	693
5169 Chemicals & allied products, nec	-	5	-	33	7	-	28,364	-	922
5171 Petroleum bulk stations & terminals	-	6	-	50	8	-	37,520	-	1,777
5172 Petroleum products, nec	-	6	-	60	10	-	36,000	-	2,668
5191 Farm supplies	-	11	-	67	6	-	19,343	-	1,558
5193 Flowers & florists' supplies	-	7	-	294	42	-	16,367	-	5,553
5198 Paints, varnishes, and supplies	-	3	-	11	4	-	26,182	-	339
5199 Nondurable goods, nec	-	11	-	50	5	-	18,400	-	1,164
52- Retail trade	-	1,066	-	14,540	14	-	14,229	-	224,186
5210 Lumber and other building materials	-	22	-	402	18	-	18,925	-	8,244
5230 Paint, glass, and wallpaper stores	-	7	-	42	6	-	16,667	-	718
5250 Hardware stores	-	7	-	46	7	-	13,826	-	640
5260 Retail nurseries and garden stores	-	7	-	35	5	-	13,714	-	509
5270 Mobile home dealers	-	10	-	53	5	-	33,434	-	2,284
5310 Department stores	-	9	-	1,558	173	-	13,533	-	21,073
5330 Variety stores	-	7	-	55	8	-	7,855	-	435
5390 Misc. general merchandise stores	-	9	-	315	35	-	14,883	-	4,332
5410 Grocery stores	-	70	-	1,368	20	-	14,401	-	21,182
5460 Retail bakeries	-	12	-	40	3	-	8,200	-	413
5490 Miscellaneous food stores	-	7	-	29	4	-	9,931	-	298
5510 New and used car dealers	-	14	-	597	43	-	30,901	-	20,609
5520 Used car dealers	-	28	-	69	2	-	23,072	-	2,242
5530 Auto and home supply stores	-	35	-	315	9	-	17,206	-	5,962
5540 Gasoline service stations	-	96	-	469	5	-	13,160	-	6,548
5550 Boat dealers	-	6	-	28	5	-	17,714	-	463
5560 Recreational vehicle dealers	-	3	-	11	4	-	15,636	-	288
5570 Motorcycle dealers	-	4	-	32	8	-	18,375	-	760
5590 Automotive dealers, nec	-	4	-	15	4	-	12,800	-	379
5610 Men's & boys' clothing stores	-	10	-	76	8	-	14,895	-	1,251
5620 Women's clothing stores	-	37	-	259	7	-	8,216	-	2,214
5630 Women's accessory & specialty stores	-	7	-	35	5	-	9,600	-	339
5640 Children's and infants' wear stores	-	3	-	35	12	-	10,171	-	335
5650 Family clothing stores	-	12	-	230	19	-	8,765	-	1,972
5660 Shoe stores	-	26	-	173	7	-	12,786	-	2,192
5690 Misc. apparel & accessory stores	-	15	-	96	6	-	10,417	-	1,095
5712 Furniture stores	-	22	-	194	9	-	19,072	-	4,881
5713 Floor covering stores	-	11	-	34	3	-	24,118	-	992
5714 Drapery and upholstery stores	-	3	-	8	3	-	18,500	-	152
5719 Misc. homefurnishings stores	-	7	-	42	6	-	9,714	-	456
5720 Household appliance stores	-	8	-	40	5	-	15,400	-	736
5731 Radio, TV, & electronic stores	-	14	-	216	15	-	13,815	-	2,951
5734 Computer and software stores	-	6	-	15	3	-	12,000	-	173

Continued on next page.

TYLER, TX MSA - [continued]

Wholesale and Retail Trade USA	Establishments		Employment		Emp / Est	Pay / Employee		Annual Payroll ($ 000)	
	1994	1995	1994	1995	1995	1994	1995	1994	1995
5735 Record & prerecorded tape stores	-	4	-	80	20	-	10,800	-	736
5736 Musical instrument stores	-	5	-	31	6	-	18,839	-	636
5812 Eating places	-	187	-	4,213	23	-	8,320	-	36,759
5813 Drinking places	-	6	-	44	7	-	5,182	-	101
5910 Drug stores and proprietary stores	-	34	-	294	9	-	16,367	-	4,702
5930 Used merchandise stores	-	24	-	85	4	-	12,565	-	1,167
5941 Sporting goods and bicycle shops	-	24	-	124	5	-	12,806	-	1,598
5942 Book stores	-	9	-	69	8	-	12,116	-	1,086
5943 Stationery stores	-	3	-	19	6	-	9,474	-	205
5944 Jewelry stores	-	17	-	93	5	-	12,430	-	1,099
5945 Hobby, toy, and game shops	-	4	-	105	26	-	9,371	-	1,205
5947 Gift, novelty, and souvenir shops	-	15	-	82	5	-	10,780	-	948
5962 Merchandising machine operators	-	8	-	67	8	-	20,836	-	1,365
5980 Fuel dealers	-	9	-	62	7	-	19,935	-	1,415
5995 Optical goods stores	-	12	-	66	6	-	18,667	-	1,264
5999 Miscellaneous retail stores, nec	-	31	-	207	7	-	17,778	-	3,504

Source: County Business Patterns 1994/95, CBP-94/95, U.S. Department of Commerce, Washington DC, November 1997. The employment column represents mid-March employment in the year. Pay per employee is calculated by dividing 1st Quarter payroll, annualized, by mid-March employment. The column headed 'Emp / Est' shows 'employees per establishment'. A dash (-) means that data are unavailable or cannot be calculated. nec means not elsewhere classified. *Notes:* 1. 1994 data incomplete; unavailable or withheld. 2. 1995 data incomplete; unavailable or withheld. 3. 1994 and 1995 data incomplete; unavailable or withheld.

UTICA - ROME, NY MSA

Wholesale and Retail Trade USA	Establishments		Employment		Emp / Est	Pay / Employee		Annual Payroll ($ 000)	
	1994	1995	1994	1995	1995	1994	1995	1994	1995
50 - Wholesale trade	409	375	4,218	4,051	11	22,051	23,350	102,794	102,051
5012 Automobiles and other vehicles	10	10	155	178	18	21,006	21,685	4,392	4,170
5013 Motor vehicle supplies and new parts	39	34	250	175	5	19,984	20,183	5,283	3,448
5014 Tires and tubes[2]	4	3	19	20	7	21,474	21,600	444	464
5015 Motor vehicle parts, used	14	14	69	97	7	13,681	16,825	984	1,796
5021 Furniture[3]	8	6	105	102	17	24,800	27,490	2,697	2,804
5023 Homefurnishings[2]	8	6	100	132	22	23,040	16,212	2,178	2,382
5031 Lumber, plywood, and millwork	9	7	78	51	7	20,410	22,745	1,767	1,242
5033 Roofing, siding, & insulation[3]	3	3	30	32	11	26,133	23,500	909	858
5044 Office equipment	11	10	98	133	13	22,694	23,098	2,644	3,307
5045 Computers, peripherals, & software[3]	10	9	77	81	9	27,896	30,617	2,429	2,890
5047 Medical and hospital equipment[3]	7	7	109	93	13	26,239	29,290	3,012	2,755
5051 Metals service centers and offices	5	5	70	69	14	26,629	28,058	1,934	2,066
5063 Electrical apparatus and equipment[2]	11	10	72	79	8	27,333	26,886	2,183	2,451
5064 Electrical appliances, TV & radios[3]	4	4	18	18	5	19,778	23,778	472	556
5065 Electronic parts and equipment	19	15	172	169	11	24,558	22,178	4,426	4,304
5072 Hardware[2]	-	3	-	26	9	-	26,923	-	802
5074 Plumbing & hydronic heating supplies	16	17	88	131	8	19,818	19,237	1,850	2,548
5075 Warm air heating & air conditioning[2]	-	3	-	6	2	-	55,333	-	305
5083 Farm and garden machinery	12	12	124	114	10	22,323	27,333	3,154	3,122
5084 Industrial machinery and equipment	13	12	87	101	8	19,632	19,327	1,820	2,128
5085 Industrial supplies[3]	13	12	82	88	7	25,415	26,409	2,279	2,410
5091 Sporting & recreational goods[3]	7	6	78	82	14	15,692	15,073	1,304	1,356
5093 Scrap and waste materials	11	12	140	175	15	15,743	20,869	3,085	4,689
5099 Durable goods, nec[2]	8	7	103	97	14	15,961	18,639	1,889	2,047
5112 Stationery and office supplies	10	8	24	26	3	24,667	25,846	589	637
5120 Drugs, proprietaries, and sundries[3]	6	5	35	15	3	20,457	23,733	762	371
5142 Packaged frozen food[2]	-	3	-	43	14	-	25,860	-	1,309
5143 Dairy products, exc. dried or canned	7	7	143	153	22	20,783	20,758	3,301	3,592
5147 Meats and meat products[3]	4	4	45	51	13	16,800	17,490	876	1,020
5148 Fresh fruits and vegetables[2]	6	4	39	33	8	17,744	22,182	899	960
5149 Groceries and related products, nec	13	10	190	172	17	27,347	27,791	5,405	5,154
5154 Livestock	-	4	-	3	1	-	16,000	-	42
5169 Chemicals & allied products, nec[3]	6	6	73	64	11	31,562	40,688	2,463	2,402
5171 Petroleum bulk stations & terminals[3]	11	9	190	108	12	19,537	26,185	3,382	2,671
5172 Petroleum products, nec[3]	5	6	55	63	11	25,309	23,619	1,916	1,813
5181 Beer and ale[2]	5	4	177	212	53	25,017	23,717	4,524	5,712
5191 Farm supplies	19	15	127	97	6	19,685	17,485	2,709	1,899
5193 Flowers & florists' supplies[1]	3	4	13	12	3	20,308	22,667	343	331
5199 Nondurable goods, nec	6	-	34	-	-	10,941	-	505	-
52 - Retail trade	1,939	1,903	20,897	22,587	12	11,097	11,630	264,554	281,689
5210 Lumber and other building materials	37	40	427	480	12	20,000	20,767	9,746	10,416
5230 Paint, glass, and wallpaper stores[1]	10	10	47	39	4	18,894	21,128	964	977
5250 Hardware stores	31	24	134	131	5	11,612	12,366	1,651	1,668

Continued on next page.

UTICA – ROME, NY MSA - [continued]

Wholesale and Retail Trade USA	Establishments		Employment		Emp / Est	Pay / Employee		Annual Payroll ($ 000)	
	1994	1995	1994	1995	1995	1994	1995	1994	1995
5260 Retail nurseries and garden stores	22	21	84	76	4	9,667	11,895	1,096	1,095
5270 Mobile home dealers	10	11	41	53	5	14,634	15,623	933	1,198
5310 Department stores[3]	15	16	1,417	2,073	130	9,098	10,921	15,787	24,379
5330 Variety stores	17	16	111	82	5	9,369	8,488	1,017	782
5390 Misc. general merchandise stores	9	7	337	370	53	11,300	10,649	4,236	4,522
5410 Grocery stores	159	154	3,556	3,279	21	11,740	10,994	45,848	36,755
5420 Meat and fish markets[3]	10	8	67	61	8	11,522	11,279	738	700
5430 Fruit and vegetable markets[1]	4	4	10	8	2	11,200	13,000	166	190
5460 Retail bakeries	51	40	420	344	9	8,010	9,372	3,611	3,486
5490 Miscellaneous food stores[2]	11	14	68	84	6	18,882	15,714	1,456	1,375
5510 New and used car dealers	36	35	906	785	22	17,779	21,264	18,847	17,642
5520 Used car dealers	30	29	89	84	3	13,798	15,810	1,318	1,687
5530 Auto and home supply stores	39	39	216	259	7	13,741	13,838	3,444	3,555
5540 Gasoline service stations	105	104	656	714	7	9,854	10,616	7,086	7,737
5550 Boat dealers	-	5	-	8	2	-	16,000	-	136
5560 Recreational vehicle dealers	4	-	11	-	-	15,636	-	193	-
5610 Men's & boys' clothing stores	10	8	148	127	16	13,378	14,110	2,823	2,343
5620 Women's clothing stores	51	40	467	377	9	6,912	6,143	3,367	2,355
5630 Women's accessory & specialty stores[2]	-	11	-	56	5	-	8,857	-	595
5650 Family clothing stores	19	18	238	238	13	8,134	7,882	2,251	2,049
5660 Shoe stores	40	32	178	129	4	9,775	12,155	1,981	1,615
5690 Misc. apparel & accessory stores	8	-	36	-	-	8,667	-	355	-
5712 Furniture stores	27	26	137	129	5	17,343	17,457	2,425	2,208
5713 Floor covering stores	28	28	95	158	6	14,021	18,937	1,766	3,270
5714 Drapery and upholstery stores	7	7	16	8	1	11,750	13,000	194	77
5719 Misc. homefurnishings stores	9	8	62	57	7	11,677	8,561	765	549
5720 Household appliance stores	16	16	61	57	4	18,820	20,982	1,173	1,246
5731 Radio, TV, & electronic stores	20	20	67	76	4	17,851	17,211	1,099	1,162
5734 Computer and software stores[3]	6	7	36	31	4	9,000	8,645	311	277
5735 Record & prerecorded tape stores	12	12	55	45	4	5,891	9,067	365	366
5736 Musical instrument stores[3]	5	5	19	16	3	12,211	13,500	233	223
5812 Eating places	511	478	5,879	6,395	13	6,922	7,182	48,529	51,966
5813 Drinking places	111	100	317	308	3	7,420	6,922	2,564	2,263
5910 Drug stores and proprietary stores	69	69	1,137	1,158	17	12,081	13,465	14,123	16,477
5920 Liquor stores	20	23	85	88	4	9,459	9,727	853	964
5930 Used merchandise stores	8	6	29	26	4	8,690	8,308	295	220
5941 Sporting goods and bicycle shops	40	36	163	245	7	14,675	12,751	2,927	3,113
5942 Book stores	14	16	65	67	4	9,415	9,731	652	713
5944 Jewelry stores	19	22	128	138	6	16,313	17,072	2,131	2,377
5945 Hobby, toy, and game shops	8	9	56	70	8	11,929	10,571	865	910
5946 Camera & photographic supply stores[3]	5	6	19	15	3	8,632	10,933	167	161
5947 Gift, novelty, and souvenir shops	32	29	152	148	5	7,842	7,405	1,234	1,286
5949 Sewing, needlework, and piece goods[2]	7	6	69	45	8	4,696	7,022	381	298
5961 Catalog and mail-order houses[2]	-	7	-	164	23	-	14,634	-	3,610
5962 Merchandising machine operators	-	12	-	88	7	-	17,455	-	1,452
5963 Direct selling establishments	22	24	218	268	11	15,468	12,090	3,860	3,509
5980 Fuel dealers	30	30	262	272	9	20,443	20,456	5,406	5,356
5992 Florists	34	33	129	131	4	9,891	9,863	1,324	1,376
5995 Optical goods stores	20	22	89	115	5	23,056	20,452	2,026	2,233
5999 Miscellaneous retail stores, nec	33	34	154	172	5	9,247	10,744	2,346	2,647

Source: County Business Patterns 1994/95, CBP-94/95, U.S. Department of Commerce, Washington DC, November 1997. The employment column represents mid-March employment in the year. Pay per employee is calculated by dividing 1st Quarter payroll, annualized, by mid-March employment. The column headed 'Emp / Est' shows 'employees per establishment'. A dash (-) means that data are unavailable or cannot be calculated. nec means not elsewhere classified. *Notes:* 1. 1994 data incomplete; unavailable or withheld. 2. 1995 data incomplete; unavailable or withheld. 3. 1994 and 1995 data incomplete; unavailable or withheld.

VALLEJO – FAIRFIELD – NAPA, CA PMSA

Wholesale and Retail Trade USA	Establishments		Employment		Emp / Est	Pay / Employee		Annual Payroll ($ 000)	
	1994	1995	1994	1995	1995	1994	1995	1994	1995
50 – Wholesale trade	486	487	5,546	5,963	12	31,606	35,866	188,282	208,492
5012 Automobiles and other vehicles	11	12	149	172	14	20,483	37,395	3,764	6,659
5013 Motor vehicle supplies and new parts	28	25	308	325	13	19,364	19,963	6,563	6,695
5020 Furniture and homefurnishings[1]	14	13	141	141	11	22,099	24,255	4,126	2,774
5031 Lumber, plywood, and millwork	12	9	166	203	23	34,313	28,690	6,289	6,372
5032 Brick, stone, & related materials	8	8	43	64	8	18,977	28,375	1,091	2,204
5033 Roofing, siding, & insulation	4	5	20	27	5	27,200	27,704	673	858
5039 Construction materials, nec	9	10	71	50	5	30,986	36,640	2,839	1,661
5044 Office equipment	7	5	43	42	8	13,581	14,476	967	1,062
5045 Computers, peripherals, & software	18	19	124	286	15	26,710	54,839	3,530	6,999

Continued on next page.

VALLEJO - FAIRFIELD - NAPA, CA PMSA - [continued]

Wholesale and Retail Trade USA	Establishments		Employment		Emp / Est	Pay / Employee		Annual Payroll ($ 000)	
	1994	1995	1994	1995	1995	1994	1995	1994	1995
5047 Medical and hospital equipment	6	-	20	-	-	38,000	-	614	-
5063 Electrical apparatus and equipment	16	13	87	20	2	26,253	25,200	2,338	407
5065 Electronic parts and equipment	-	18	-	92	5	-	25,478	-	3,568
5074 Plumbing & hydronic heating supplies	7	6	44	52	9	43,636	40,385	1,419	1,813
5082 Construction and mining machinery[2]	7	6	150	116	19	34,000	32,138	5,321	4,387
5083 Farm and garden machinery	15	13	156	111	9	25,128	33,369	3,928	3,172
5084 Industrial machinery and equipment	27	30	263	261	9	40,837	42,222	9,695	10,137
5085 Industrial supplies	20	21	129	221	11	28,682	19,367	3,850	4,515
5087 Service establishment equipment	12	12	111	64	5	20,937	27,188	2,401	2,017
5088 Transportation equipment & supplies	10	9	60	61	7	41,000	41,902	2,216	2,321
5091 Sporting & recreational goods[1]	4	-	18	-	-	33,556	-	627	-
5093 Scrap and waste materials	-	9	-	26	3	-	33,846	-	1,232
5099 Durable goods, nec	12	13	5	75	6	8,000	19,947	57	1,985
5112 Stationery and office supplies	11	13	301	243	19	28,625	45,267	8,630	11,040
5137 Women's and children's clothing	5	5	22	21	4	33,273	33,524	728	818
5145 Confectionery[2]	4	6	9	8	1	28,444	18,500	201	108
5148 Fresh fruits and vegetables	9	7	34	26	4	14,706	20,308	533	446
5149 Groceries and related products, nec[1]	16	18	88	364	20	27,227	40,341	2,369	15,785
5153 Grain and field beans[3]	3	3	36	32	11	24,000	25,750	867	910
5162 Plastics materials & basic shapes[1]	4	-	10	-	-	18,400	-	228	-
5169 Chemicals & allied products, nec	8	-	33	-	-	42,061	-	1,360	-
5171 Petroleum bulk stations & terminals[2]	5	5	13	14	3	29,846	33,143	462	498
5180 Beer, wine, and distilled beverages	29	30	297	399	13	31,286	38,887	10,481	14,260
5191 Farm supplies	13	11	134	23	2	24,687	26,435	4,660	839
5193 Flowers & florists' supplies	4	-	2	-	-	16,000	-	49	-
5199 Nondurable goods, nec	28	25	271	304	12	22,244	22,000	6,643	6,463
52- Retail trade	2,413	2,437	32,341	32,700	13	13,870	14,393	479,253	491,803
5210 Lumber and other building materials	44	43	884	936	22	20,864	22,910	20,068	22,993
5230 Paint, glass, and wallpaper stores	27	24	57	52	2	23,158	22,846	1,437	1,239
5250 Hardware stores	16	11	340	225	20	15,965	17,778	5,499	3,905
5260 Retail nurseries and garden stores	17	15	80	83	6	14,350	14,120	1,194	1,047
5310 Department stores[3]	20	19	2,725	2,735	144	11,476	12,534	33,189	32,785
5390 Misc. general merchandise stores	15	16	623	640	40	16,809	18,869	11,501	12,030
5410 Grocery stores	176	189	4,827	4,890	26	22,058	22,271	109,351	111,433
5420 Meat and fish markets	10	11	36	15	1	11,111	7,467	304	131
5440 Candy, nut, and confectionery stores	10	11	56	51	5	8,214	8,392	421	512
5460 Retail bakeries	26	28	277	214	8	10,801	10,486	3,119	3,020
5490 Miscellaneous food stores	27	28	99	145	5	5,697	8,359	771	1,248
5510 New and used car dealers	38	42	1,373	1,358	32	32,827	32,810	48,192	49,262
5520 Used car dealers	11	8	10	14	2	15,600	13,143	157	166
5530 Auto and home supply stores	80	87	693	862	10	16,098	17,555	13,305	15,729
5540 Gasoline service stations	130	127	991	997	8	11,156	11,811	11,898	12,555
5550 Boat dealers[2]	-	4	-	12	3	-	27,333	-	432
5560 Recreational vehicle dealers	10	10	75	67	7	19,947	24,000	1,904	1,734
5570 Motorcycle dealers	6	6	55	64	11	27,273	26,938	1,626	1,866
5610 Men's & boys' clothing stores	35	34	253	307	9	12,822	11,726	3,192	3,536
5620 Women's clothing stores	90	78	607	489	6	9,430	9,767	6,058	4,847
5630 Women's accessory & specialty stores	9	9	63	52	6	9,905	11,231	626	590
5640 Children's and infants' wear stores	10	11	52	51	5	9,308	7,922	439	433
5650 Family clothing stores	32	30	428	414	14	9,888	11,546	4,660	4,496
5660 Shoe stores	54	54	266	292	5	11,729	11,397	3,104	3,259
5690 Misc. apparel & accessory stores	21	24	89	130	5	9,258	8,277	960	1,237
5712 Furniture stores	46	50	263	265	5	16,669	15,442	4,774	4,686
5713 Floor covering stores	-	23	-	35	2	-	8,571	-	368
5719 Misc. homefurnishings stores	44	39	251	246	6	10,693	11,675	2,834	2,984
5720 Household appliance stores	22	23	130	140	6	13,385	14,371	1,929	2,040
5731 Radio, TV, & electronic stores	29	30	209	244	8	20,344	17,672	4,359	4,443
5734 Computer and software stores	-	10	-	17	2	-	12,235	-	169
5735 Record & prerecorded tape stores	8	-	92	-	-	7,957	-	710	-
5812 Eating places	652	622	11,524	11,284	18	8,178	8,570	101,887	103,768
5813 Drinking places	80	74	381	427	6	6,982	7,063	2,990	3,132
5910 Drug stores and proprietary stores	43	42	902	891	21	21,379	22,236	20,442	20,406
5920 Liquor stores	40	43	134	158	4	13,403	12,937	1,912	2,182
5930 Used merchandise stores	34	32	237	108	3	10,498	11,148	2,633	1,277
5941 Sporting goods and bicycle shops	50	45	264	307	7	9,485	10,124	2,934	3,226
5942 Book stores	21	20	91	100	5	8,835	10,040	964	1,003
5943 Stationery stores	8	9	17	25	3	10,118	9,600	203	242
5944 Jewelry stores	40	36	167	136	4	18,299	19,529	3,394	2,589
5945 Hobby, toy, and game shops	28	25	209	260	10	10,565	9,662	2,731	2,639
5947 Gift, novelty, and souvenir shops	59	55	311	271	5	7,781	8,428	2,508	2,551
5949 Sewing, needlework, and piece goods	16	16	140	136	9	7,743	8,382	1,093	1,134

Continued on next page.

VALLEJO - FAIRFIELD - NAPA, CA PMSA - [continued]

Wholesale and Retail Trade USA	Establishments		Employment		Emp / Est	Pay / Employee		Annual Payroll ($ 000)	
	1994	1995	1994	1995	1995	1994	1995	1994	1995
5961 Catalog and mail-order houses [2]	6	4	19	18	5	10,316	9,333	230	221
5962 Merchandising machine operators	-	11	-	44	4	-	15,182	-	662
5963 Direct selling establishments	15	15	39	38	3	24,821	30,632	1,131	1,230
5980 Fuel dealers	5	4	14	27	7	24,286	16,000	378	547
5992 Florists	36	36	168	163	5	9,071	9,276	1,561	1,603
5999 Miscellaneous retail stores, nec	81	86	314	315	4	10,293	11,505	3,354	3,853

Source: County Business Patterns 1994/95, CBP-94/95, U.S. Department of Commerce, Washington DC, November 1997. The employment column represents mid-March employment in the year. Pay per employee is calculated by dividing 1st Quarter payroll, annualized, by mid-March employment. The column headed 'Emp / Est' shows 'employees per establishment'. A dash (-) means that data are unavailable or cannot be calculated. nec means not elsewhere classified. *Notes:* 1. 1994 data incomplete; unavailable or withheld. 2. 1995 data incomplete; unavailable or withheld. 3. 1994 and 1995 data incomplete; unavailable or withheld.

VENTURA, CA PMSA

Wholesale and Retail Trade USA	Establishments		Employment		Emp / Est	Pay / Employee		Annual Payroll ($ 000)	
	1994	1995	1994	1995	1995	1994	1995	1994	1995
50- Wholesale trade	1,108	1,115	12,772	12,795	11	31,233	33,945	426,299	451,607
5012 Automobiles and other vehicles	17	17	252	260	15	48,095	59,646	11,538	14,441
5013 Motor vehicle supplies and new parts	48	42	436	410	10	24,459	27,893	12,038	14,755
5014 Tires and tubes	7	7	104	101	14	25,538	29,030	2,983	2,767
5015 Motor vehicle parts, used	9	15	58	78	5	15,310	13,949	1,081	1,247
5021 Furniture	14	15	127	123	8	27,150	26,992	3,743	3,553
5023 Homefurnishings	25	24	201	173	7	26,448	31,006	5,825	5,126
5031 Lumber, plywood, and millwork	15	14	108	171	12	30,778	26,877	4,099	5,112
5032 Brick, stone, & related materials	15	8	79	60	8	24,253	27,400	2,265	1,868
5044 Office equipment	24	20	199	222	11	28,623	24,649	6,013	5,994
5045 Computers, peripherals, & software	67	61	491	507	8	36,220	44,821	18,779	24,418
5046 Commercial equipment, nec	4	6	20	26	4	25,600	23,846	597	643
5047 Medical and hospital equipment	22	27	383	280	10	38,339	28,329	15,487	8,608
5048 Ophthalmic goods	7	8	59	56	7	20,000	19,571	1,181	1,327
5051 Metals service centers and offices	15	19	106	117	6	26,264	30,051	3,171	4,267
5063 Electrical apparatus and equipment	39	29	355	230	8	38,175	36,313	14,678	7,613
5064 Electrical appliances, TV & radios	8	7	19	17	2	48,632	44,471	709	723
5065 Electronic parts and equipment	65	60	1,219	930	16	47,997	41,123	60,100	37,617
5072 Hardware	20	20	266	227	11	31,865	39,471	9,545	9,984
5074 Plumbing & hydronic heating supplies	20	26	124	139	5	26,903	25,237	3,587	3,720
5075 Warm air heating & air conditioning	13	11	60	45	4	27,400	32,089	1,692	1,550
5078 Refrigeration equipment and supplies	4	3	11	6	2	21,455	25,333	241	200
5082 Construction and mining machinery	8	9	274	157	17	39,796	38,471	9,378	6,316
5083 Farm and garden machinery	15	13	114	116	9	29,053	34,034	3,545	4,923
5084 Industrial machinery and equipment	61	62	414	409	7	29,691	34,103	13,055	14,553
5085 Industrial supplies	24	25	204	201	8	27,529	37,393	6,176	7,741
5087 Service establishment equipment	12	11	103	80	7	14,447	23,800	2,011	2,029
5088 Transportation equipment & supplies	29	29	240	249	9	39,483	56,048	10,423	12,024
5091 Sporting & recreational goods	23	25	236	245	10	34,576	37,665	9,386	9,121
5092 Toys and hobby goods and supplies	10	14	97	121	9	24,701	27,471	2,614	2,906
5093 Scrap and waste materials	15	18	163	233	13	18,994	21,631	4,716	6,613
5094 Jewelry & precious stones	7	7	37	35	5	18,595	22,857	903	847
5099 Durable goods, nec	27	28	378	424	15	24,825	23,311	10,963	11,493
5111 Printing and writing paper	9	9	41	42	5	28,293	29,714	1,174	1,244
5112 Stationery and office supplies	30	23	337	288	13	19,478	22,181	6,930	6,184
5113 Industrial & personal service paper	10	10	87	71	7	32,000	34,761	2,281	2,408
5120 Drugs, proprietaries, and sundries	29	31	376	389	13	40,298	41,296	16,201	15,238
5131 Piece goods & notions	7	10	106	119	12	70,340	65,950	6,683	6,914
5136 Men's and boys' clothing	11	13	519	594	46	21,464	24,209	16,007	17,251
5137 Women's and children's clothing	7	10	42	47	5	18,000	23,660	836	1,192
5141 Groceries, general line	9	-	123	-	-	21,691	-	2,770	-
5143 Dairy products, exc. dried or canned	7	6	62	41	7	22,516	27,317	1,312	1,163
5145 Confectionery	3	3	30	37	12	25,733	24,432	877	989
5146 Fish and seafoods	6	4	30	16	4	8,267	13,250	503	208
5148 Fresh fruits and vegetables	29	26	1,229	1,234	47	22,171	23,592	27,418	29,252
5149 Groceries and related products, nec	31	32	481	794	25	28,225	46,398	14,590	38,650
5153 Grain and field beans	4	4	17	17	4	18,353	19,059	691	2,530
5162 Plastics materials & basic shapes	7	6	40	46	8	23,900	26,174	1,048	1,293
5169 Chemicals & allied products, nec	28	24	209	146	6	41,321	43,836	7,325	6,053
5171 Petroleum bulk stations & terminals	14	14	116	114	8	32,310	28,877	3,505	3,754
5172 Petroleum products, nec	5	4	60	62	16	27,600	22,839	1,614	1,504
5181 Beer and ale	4	4	228	241	60	29,281	31,386	7,826	8,469
5191 Farm supplies	26	26	268	253	10	28,179	32,775	9,261	9,827
5193 Flowers & florists' supplies	18	22	162	230	10	15,827	25,826	3,282	4,849

Continued on next page.

VENTURA, CA PMSA - [continued]

Wholesale and Retail Trade USA	Establishments		Employment		Emp / Est	Pay / Employee		Annual Payroll ($ 000)	
	1994	1995	1994	1995	1995	1994	1995	1994	1995
5198 Paints, varnishes, and supplies	11	11	57	56	5	23,860	25,571	1,617	1,557
5199 Nondurable goods, nec	49	58	327	432	7	24,061	29,926	11,191	13,310
52- Retail trade	3,416	3,416	45,431	46,918	14	14,067	14,796	697,476	723,191
5210 Lumber and other building materials	47	45	1,024	1,186	26	20,031	21,572	23,592	25,639
5230 Paint, glass, and wallpaper stores	20	19	117	139	7	20,513	23,309	3,141	3,365
5250 Hardware stores	31	23	197	194	8	15,005	14,515	3,304	3,120
5260 Retail nurseries and garden stores	18	19	164	188	10	21,512	20,511	4,405	4,070
5270 Mobile home dealers	5	4	22	24	6	14,364	16,833	429	428
5310 Department stores	24	24	4,358	4,607	192	11,637	12,132	55,975	55,491
5330 Variety stores	7	6	51	58	10	11,294	9,586	556	578
5390 Misc. general merchandise stores	26	24	931	817	34	13,955	17,141	13,800	14,205
5410 Grocery stores	201	199	4,840	4,899	25	21,003	21,472	102,975	107,893
5420 Meat and fish markets	20	19	126	112	6	9,746	9,643	1,289	1,142
5430 Fruit and vegetable markets	5	-	73	-	-	10,466	-	1,620	-
5440 Candy, nut, and confectionery stores	8	9	36	36	4	13,222	13,111	524	566
5450 Dairy products stores	3	3	6	6	2	7,333	7,333	46	42
5460 Retail bakeries	84	78	375	322	4	11,584	9,267	4,783	3,230
5490 Miscellaneous food stores	34	39	190	213	5	7,958	9,784	1,694	2,465
5510 New and used car dealers	61	60	2,856	2,979	50	32,136	33,717	102,592	108,731
5520 Used car dealers	13	14	75	86	6	27,253	24,186	2,154	2,366
5530 Auto and home supply stores	118	107	752	832	8	19,106	19,303	16,021	16,950
5540 Gasoline service stations	172	175	1,065	1,194	7	11,835	11,353	13,777	14,227
5550 Boat dealers	18	18	88	91	5	12,773	15,780	1,368	1,578
5560 Recreational vehicle dealers	8	9	119	135	15	23,731	22,667	3,431	3,313
5570 Motorcycle dealers	14	15	76	77	5	20,158	21,403	1,832	1,956
5590 Automotive dealers, nec	4	5	14	16	3	18,000	15,500	238	225
5610 Men's & boys' clothing stores	30	34	204	284	8	11,196	11,113	2,816	3,216
5620 Women's clothing stores	109	97	759	636	7	9,165	9,226	7,365	6,079
5630 Women's accessory & specialty stores	18	16	79	79	5	10,785	10,582	961	972
5640 Children's and infants' wear stores	19	18	122	165	9	8,623	9,745	1,374	1,617
5650 Family clothing stores	32	30	482	517	17	9,776	10,035	5,020	5,113
5660 Shoe stores	82	85	414	429	5	12,928	12,858	5,844	5,757
5690 Misc. apparel & accessory stores	25	24	95	113	5	12,884	14,230	1,446	1,810
5712 Furniture stores	49	52	350	361	7	20,571	22,294	8,024	8,333
5713 Floor covering stores	30	33	165	207	6	21,745	23,961	4,920	5,672
5714 Drapery and upholstery stores	5	8	50	40	5	9,280	16,000	583	839
5719 Misc. homefurnishings stores	43	44	300	365	8	12,280	11,847	4,352	4,930
5720 Household appliance stores	18	17	83	117	7	14,795	18,974	1,466	2,428
5731 Radio, TV, & electronic stores	41	43	438	494	11	20,648	19,684	9,822	10,808
5734 Computer and software stores	26	30	167	199	7	17,030	17,508	3,250	4,133
5735 Record & prerecorded tape stores	26	26	303	338	13	9,347	10,118	2,881	3,091
5736 Musical instrument stores	-	9	-	39	4	-	10,359	-	397
5812 Eating places	905	857	16,506	16,047	19	7,871	8,760	141,721	146,905
5813 Drinking places	87	82	522	440	5	6,682	6,273	3,562	2,743
5910 Drug stores and proprietary stores	89	89	1,372	1,612	18	22,050	18,228	32,491	28,744
5920 Liquor stores	137	133	336	352	3	9,488	9,500	3,400	3,561
5930 Used merchandise stores	44	41	251	265	6	9,386	10,143	2,685	2,819
5941 Sporting goods and bicycle shops	61	66	453	554	8	11,196	12,852	5,626	8,052
5942 Book stores	43	40	221	252	6	10,045	10,365	2,620	2,604
5943 Stationery stores	15	18	115	151	8	12,348	10,225	1,478	1,497
5944 Jewelry stores	51	49	262	279	6	17,756	18,724	4,918	5,320
5945 Hobby, toy, and game shops	24	27	278	357	13	9,094	9,165	3,347	3,723
5946 Camera & photographic supply stores	14	14	60	52	4	17,000	19,385	1,085	1,083
5947 Gift, novelty, and souvenir shops	79	76	405	415	5	7,328	7,460	3,278	3,387
5948 Luggage and leather goods stores	5	8	27	47	6	13,630	10,894	404	549
5949 Sewing, needlework, and piece goods	19	16	201	226	14	8,736	5,858	1,778	1,262
5961 Catalog and mail-order houses	17	18	383	596	33	26,621	23,242	11,017	12,956
5962 Merchandising machine operators	9	7	66	40	6	26,606	24,700	1,441	1,121
5963 Direct selling establishments	26	29	158	185	6	31,190	24,541	4,751	4,671
5984 Liquefied petroleum gas dealers	-	4	-	39	10	-	23,692	-	965
5992 Florists	67	58	210	214	4	8,171	7,776	1,865	1,738
5994 News dealers and newsstands	8	7	44	46	7	7,455	6,870	274	344
5995 Optical goods stores	21	19	121	139	7	13,289	15,309	1,780	2,174
5999 Miscellaneous retail stores, nec	112	121	568	540	4	14,049	17,393	9,228	10,363

Source: County Business Patterns 1994/95, CBP-94/95, U.S. Department of Commerce, Washington DC, November 1997. The employment column represents mid-March employment in the year. Pay per employee is calculated by dividing 1st Quarter payroll, annualized, by mid-March employment. The column headed 'Emp / Est' shows 'employees per establishment'. A dash (-) means that data are unavailable or cannot be calculated. nec means not elsewhere classified. *Notes:* 1. 1994 data incomplete; unavailable or withheld. 2. 1995 data incomplete; unavailable or withheld. 3. 1994 and 1995 data incomplete; unavailable or withheld.

VICTORIA, TX MSA

Wholesale and Retail Trade USA	Establishments		Employment		Emp / Est	Pay / Employee		Annual Payroll ($ 000)	
	1994	1995	1994	1995	1995	1994	1995	1994	1995
50- Wholesale trade	-	180	-	1,822	10	-	23,870	-	48,249
5013 Motor vehicle supplies and new parts	-	8	-	103	13	-	24,699	-	2,611
5015 Motor vehicle parts, used	-	4	-	15	4	-	14,933	-	204
5030 Lumber and construction materials	-	6	-	66	11	-	17,939	-	1,383
5044 Office equipment	-	9	-	73	8	-	19,397	-	1,292
5045 Computers, peripherals, & software	-	5	-	62	12	-	24,000	-	1,504
5051 Metals service centers and offices	-	3	-	51	17	-	37,569	-	1,609
5065 Electronic parts and equipment	-	3	-	8	3	-	21,500	-	284
5072 Hardware	-	3	-	30	10	-	16,267	-	475
5074 Plumbing & hydronic heating supplies	-	4	-	37	9	-	31,676	-	1,207
5075 Warm air heating & air conditioning	-	7	-	13	2	-	23,077	-	333
5083 Farm and garden machinery	-	5	-	57	11	-	22,807	-	1,778
5084 Industrial machinery and equipment	-	36	-	280	8	-	27,671	-	7,983
5085 Industrial supplies	-	9	-	84	9	-	27,810	-	2,849
5087 Service establishment equipment	-	4	-	42	11	-	12,952	-	575
5093 Scrap and waste materials	-	4	-	51	13	-	17,647	-	1,066
5110 Paper and paper products	-	4	-	70	18	-	21,429	-	1,657
5149 Groceries and related products, nec	-	3	-	91	30	-	26,549	-	2,311
5160 Chemicals and allied products	-	7	-	18	3	-	27,333	-	575
5170 Petroleum and petroleum products	-	6	-	51	9	-	38,275	-	2,395
5181 Beer and ale	-	4	-	96	24	-	25,083	-	2,546
5191 Farm supplies	-	5	-	21	4	-	14,286	-	317
52- Retail trade	-	539	-	7,211	13	-	12,673	-	92,768
5210 Lumber and other building materials	-	10	-	140	14	-	17,143	-	3,445
5230 Paint, glass, and wallpaper stores	-	5	-	15	3	-	17,067	-	235
5260 Retail nurseries and garden stores	-	5	-	34	7	-	19,765	-	491
5300 General merchandise stores	-	10	-	1,070	107	-	13,335	-	13,670
5410 Grocery stores	-	46	-	1,145	25	-	12,622	-	14,614
5460 Retail bakeries	-	8	-	90	11	-	7,289	-	694
5490 Miscellaneous food stores	-	3	-	22	7	-	7,091	-	163
5510 New and used car dealers	-	12	-	384	32	-	27,875	-	11,095
5520 Used car dealers	-	18	-	57	3	-	18,246	-	1,080
5530 Auto and home supply stores	-	16	-	148	9	-	20,054	-	3,129
5540 Gasoline service stations	-	48	-	258	5	-	12,403	-	3,220
5550 Boat dealers	-	4	-	29	7	-	11,448	-	357
5570 Motorcycle dealers	-	4	-	12	3	-	16,333	-	227
5610 Men's & boys' clothing stores	-	4	-	23	6	-	14,261	-	432
5620 Women's clothing stores	-	17	-	132	8	-	9,879	-	1,330
5650 Family clothing stores	-	9	-	185	21	-	9,211	-	1,765
5660 Shoe stores	-	13	-	68	5	-	9,294	-	605
5712 Furniture stores	-	8	-	86	11	-	19,395	-	1,624
5720 Household appliance stores	-	4	-	22	6	-	11,636	-	301
5734 Computer and software stores	-	5	-	15	3	-	16,000	-	257
5735 Record & prerecorded tape stores	-	4	-	50	13	-	10,400	-	386
5812 Eating places	-	102	-	2,064	20	-	8,019	-	16,848
5813 Drinking places	-	13	-	113	9	-	6,301	-	578
5910 Drug stores and proprietary stores	-	12	-	150	13	-	14,027	-	2,166
5920 Liquor stores	-	4	-	9	2	-	9,778	-	80
5930 Used merchandise stores	-	11	-	47	4	-	14,383	-	677
5941 Sporting goods and bicycle shops	-	4	-	21	5	-	7,619	-	153
5944 Jewelry stores	-	15	-	73	5	-	11,726	-	894
5945 Hobby, toy, and game shops	-	4	-	73	18	-	9,534	-	847
5947 Gift, novelty, and souvenir shops	-	8	-	61	8	-	6,754	-	408
5949 Sewing, needlework, and piece goods	-	3	-	30	10	-	6,667	-	206
5960 Nonstore retailers	-	8	-	26	3	-	21,538	-	591
5980 Fuel dealers	-	3	-	15	5	-	17,600	-	236
5992 Florists	-	6	-	48	8	-	10,917	-	495
5995 Optical goods stores	-	7	-	32	5	-	15,125	-	452
5999 Miscellaneous retail stores, nec	-	13	-	54	4	-	10,593	-	701

Source: County Business Patterns 1994/95, CBP-94/95, U.S. Department of Commerce, Washington DC, November 1997. The employment column represents mid-March employment in the year. Pay per employee is calculated by dividing 1st Quarter payroll, annualized, by mid-March employment. The column headed 'Emp / Est' shows 'employees per establishment'. A dash (-) means that data are unavailable or cannot be calculated. nec means not elsewhere classified. *Notes:* 1. 1994 data incomplete; unavailable or withheld. 2. 1995 data incomplete; unavailable or withheld. 3. 1994 and 1995 data incomplete; unavailable or withheld.

VINELAND - MILLVILLE - BRIDGETON, NJ PMSA

Wholesale and Retail Trade USA	Establishments		Employment		Emp / Est	Pay / Employee		Annual Payroll ($ 000)	
	1994	1995	1994	1995	1995	1994	1995	1994	1995
50 - Wholesale trade	227	226	2,468	2,477	11	26,308	28,334	75,507	76,590
5012 Automobiles and other vehicles	5	5	51	67	13	27,608	27,164	1,574	1,841
5013 Motor vehicle supplies and new parts	6	6	66	70	12	18,000	17,714	1,285	1,331
5015 Motor vehicle parts, used	-	5	-	19	4	-	15,789	-	303
5020 Furniture and homefurnishings	10	10	186	205	21	41,828	42,068	7,077	7,749
5039 Construction materials, nec	4	-	74	-	-	21,568	-	1,985	-
5047 Medical and hospital equipment	4	5	126	135	27	28,540	26,993	3,935	3,947
5060 Electrical goods	15	15	109	113	8	35,046	39,080	3,732	4,058
5074 Plumbing & hydronic heating supplies	7	8	105	109	14	16,419	19,596	2,777	3,081
5083 Farm and garden machinery	7	7	70	69	10	23,429	26,087	2,418	2,573
5084 Industrial machinery and equipment	9	9	103	131	15	30,951	30,107	3,687	3,953
5093 Scrap and waste materials	7	7	88	99	14	16,909	22,141	1,932	2,549
5110 Paper and paper products	8	6	131	121	20	19,634	20,860	2,966	3,439
5130 Apparel, piece goods, and notions	-	5	-	29	6	-	25,517	-	705
5146 Fish and seafoods	-	4	-	37	9	-	21,081	-	786
5148 Fresh fruits and vegetables	23	23	175	164	7	28,823	34,659	8,468	8,135
5149 Groceries and related products, nec	10	-	122	-	-	24,426	-	3,189	-
5169 Chemicals & allied products, nec	7	7	121	99	14	21,355	20,970	2,302	1,772
5171 Petroleum bulk stations & terminals	5	4	82	68	17	32,683	32,235	2,683	2,394
5172 Petroleum products, nec	6	7	48	40	6	29,083	30,300	1,875	1,269
5193 Flowers & florists' supplies	-	4	-	14	4	-	14,857	-	297
52 - Retail trade	780	815	7,894	8,751	11	13,653	14,170	119,004	130,120
5210 Lumber and other building materials	15	17	134	247	15	24,448	24,324	4,280	6,329
5230 Paint, glass, and wallpaper stores	6	7	13	45	6	23,692	23,733	320	1,320
5250 Hardware stores	6	5	27	26	5	16,741	15,231	456	422
5260 Retail nurseries and garden stores	4	5	27	27	5	11,704	11,259	418	363
5310 Department stores	7	7	552	812	116	11,725	12,768	7,751	10,532
5330 Variety stores	8	8	66	75	9	9,152	9,013	573	782
5390 Misc. general merchandise stores	7	6	94	25	4	8,979	5,920	685	163
5410 Grocery stores	83	86	1,556	1,631	19	15,889	15,674	26,411	26,274
5420 Meat and fish markets	8	7	41	39	6	12,195	11,590	550	492
5430 Fruit and vegetable markets	3	5	17	13	3	8,000	12,308	423	384
5460 Retail bakeries	19	18	196	195	11	9,388	9,682	1,973	1,974
5490 Miscellaneous food stores	3	3	11	17	6	8,364	9,412	121	215
5510 New and used car dealers	18	17	450	488	29	30,276	30,623	15,218	15,625
5520 Used car dealers	15	16	57	58	4	18,877	18,966	1,216	1,186
5530 Auto and home supply stores	24	24	224	250	10	17,518	18,672	4,357	4,712
5540 Gasoline service stations	48	54	244	323	6	9,770	12,867	2,688	4,444
5550 Boat dealers	-	3	-	20	7	-	17,200	-	337
5570 Motorcycle dealers	4	4	17	22	6	17,647	16,909	463	555
5610 Men's & boys' clothing stores	13	13	59	39	3	12,475	14,872	737	721
5620 Women's clothing stores	17	17	187	137	8	7,914	7,387	1,570	1,026
5630 Women's accessory & specialty stores	3	3	8	9	3	12,000	9,333	97	82
5650 Family clothing stores	5	6	121	112	19	8,264	10,750	1,080	1,077
5660 Shoe stores	22	22	107	124	6	11,140	11,097	1,386	1,459
5712 Furniture stores	15	15	88	86	6	20,227	19,442	1,805	1,702
5713 Floor covering stores	9	8	26	27	3	13,846	13,926	387	394
5714 Drapery and upholstery stores	-	4	-	9	2	-	15,111	-	190
5720 Household appliance stores	9	8	66	66	8	15,455	19,333	1,267	1,247
5731 Radio, TV, & electronic stores	-	6	-	26	4	-	18,308	-	421
5736 Musical instrument stores	3	3	6	7	2	25,333	24,000	165	159
5812 Eating places	166	157	1,767	1,980	13	7,724	8,018	15,229	16,598
5813 Drinking places	23	26	89	125	5	8,764	9,088	961	1,221
5910 Drug stores and proprietary stores	22	20	521	557	28	12,583	13,774	7,444	8,151
5920 Liquor stores	25	27	141	139	5	11,262	11,799	1,781	1,684
5930 Used merchandise stores	6	3	79	23	8	4,152	8,870	430	261
5941 Sporting goods and bicycle shops	8	8	21	24	3	10,476	13,333	272	368
5942 Book stores	5	4	27	27	7	10,222	12,000	322	330
5944 Jewelry stores	14	15	70	67	4	14,629	16,179	1,058	1,172
5945 Hobby, toy, and game shops	6	7	28	32	5	12,143	10,250	389	646
5947 Gift, novelty, and souvenir shops	18	21	97	105	5	7,340	6,933	720	718
5963 Direct selling establishments	7	8	42	45	6	26,286	26,933	1,073	1,156
5980 Fuel dealers	14	14	206	197	14	33,301	31,533	6,519	6,117
5992 Florists	14	14	73	72	5	10,137	10,667	745	768
5995 Optical goods stores	8	8	15	21	3	22,133	20,190	395	467
5999 Miscellaneous retail stores, nec	22	22	106	102	5	11,962	11,529	1,475	1,351

Source: County Business Patterns 1994/95, CBP-94/95, U.S. Department of Commerce, Washington DC, November 1997. The employment column represents mid-March employment in the year. Pay per employee is calculated by dividing 1st Quarter payroll, annualized, by mid-March employment. The column headed 'Emp / Est' shows 'employees per establishment'. A dash (-) means that data are unavailable or cannot be calculated. nec means not elsewhere classified. *Notes:* 1. 1994 data incomplete; unavailable or withheld. 2. 1995 data incomplete; unavailable or withheld. 3. 1994 and 1995 data incomplete; unavailable or withheld.

VISALIA – TULARE – PORTERVILLE, CA MSA

Wholesale and Retail Trade USA	Establishments		Employment		Emp / Est	Pay / Employee		Annual Payroll ($ 000)	
	1994	1995	1994	1995	1995	1994	1995	1994	1995
50- Wholesale trade	425	397	5,579	5,737	14	23,274	23,543	134,308	135,231
5013 Motor vehicle supplies and new parts	30	16	401	413	26	19,382	20,203	8,366	8,832
5015 Motor vehicle parts, used	7	6	13	13	2	16,615	11,692	214	168
5020 Furniture and homefurnishings	7	5	104	51	10	22,885	21,020	2,616	1,144
5032 Brick, stone, & related materials	5	3	20	13	4	36,000	17,538	581	400
5039 Construction materials, nec	-	3	-	22	7	-	18,000	-	274
5044 Office equipment	9	9	64	80	9	26,000	25,350	1,707	1,973
5045 Computers, peripherals, & software	3	4	14	14	4	18,286	27,714	254	435
5046 Commercial equipment, nec	-	3	-	10	3	-	23,200	-	219
5063 Electrical apparatus and equipment	8	6	67	58	10	34,806	34,759	1,905	1,624
5064 Electrical appliances, TV & radios	-	3	-	6	2	-	13,333	-	34
5065 Electronic parts and equipment	-	8	-	39	5	-	44,205	-	1,558
5074 Plumbing & hydronic heating supplies	8	6	121	93	16	24,264	24,258	3,286	2,551
5083 Farm and garden machinery	31	31	412	439	14	29,058	28,219	11,299	11,417
5084 Industrial machinery and equipment	15	13	62	86	7	28,065	19,023	1,870	1,647
5085 Industrial supplies	11	11	70	68	6	28,343	29,647	1,914	2,009
5087 Service establishment equipment	6	6	37	34	6	14,270	14,471	594	580
5093 Scrap and waste materials	12	13	122	161	12	12,000	12,348	1,700	2,093
5099 Durable goods, nec	5	4	20	13	3	7,400	12,615	95	146
5110 Paper and paper products	8	10	65	61	6	15,200	31,869	1,111	2,084
5120 Drugs, proprietaries, and sundries	7	9	157	135	15	17,911	18,578	2,728	2,864
5141 Groceries, general line	5	5	117	116	23	21,128	20,207	2,063	1,923
5143 Dairy products, exc. dried or canned	-	3	-	2	1	-	20,000	-	46
5147 Meats and meat products	3	3	9	11	4	21,333	12,364	228	202
5148 Fresh fruits and vegetables	56	54	1,851	2,088	39	21,266	20,916	40,923	41,536
5149 Groceries and related products, nec	12	12	221	163	14	15,891	20,859	4,074	3,396
5153 Grain and field beans	4	-	18	-	-	47,333	-	655	-
5154 Livestock	9	8	67	65	8	11,164	10,585	742	806
5159 Farm-product raw materials, nec	4	-	37	-	-	21,838	-	525	-
5162 Plastics materials & basic shapes	3	3	13	10	3	18,769	25,200	375	290
5171 Petroleum bulk stations & terminals	14	14	166	169	12	25,783	28,710	4,929	5,406
5172 Petroleum products, nec	3	3	36	40	13	45,444	51,400	1,358	1,469
5191 Farm supplies	45	44	364	384	9	38,714	40,094	14,996	14,338
5193 Flowers & florists' supplies	7	-	22	-	-	17,636	-	509	-
5198 Paints, varnishes, and supplies	4	-	22	-	-	27,091	-	559	-
5199 Nondurable goods, nec	6	5	49	71	14	16,408	13,859	1,382	1,871
52- Retail trade	1,537	1,566	18,569	18,464	12	12,599	13,525	250,770	257,537
5210 Lumber and other building materials	27	18	467	401	22	16,403	18,683	8,518	7,856
5250 Hardware stores	18	16	201	184	12	16,637	17,283	2,727	2,611
5260 Retail nurseries and garden stores	15	13	64	60	5	13,875	12,600	881	832
5310 Department stores	16	16	2,256	2,276	142	10,158	11,910	25,628	27,385
5330 Variety stores	7	-	59	-	-	9,288	-	510	-
5390 Misc. general merchandise stores	9	-	212	-	-	18,925	-	4,361	-
5410 Grocery stores	205	206	3,078	2,744	13	15,101	16,487	48,050	45,860
5420 Meat and fish markets	4	4	9	8	2	8,444	9,000	163	178
5430 Fruit and vegetable markets	6	5	10	12	2	7,200	13,667	103	172
5440 Candy, nut, and confectionery stores	-	4	-	10	3	-	12,000	-	131
5460 Retail bakeries	32	27	134	100	4	7,134	7,400	935	774
5490 Miscellaneous food stores	9	10	28	22	2	10,143	10,727	279	315
5510 New and used car dealers	29	31	738	868	28	25,398	25,912	20,313	23,783
5520 Used car dealers	27	29	118	111	4	21,695	23,676	1,875	1,908
5530 Auto and home supply stores	76	86	512	615	7	15,219	16,631	9,163	11,387
5540 Gasoline service stations	78	76	492	497	7	11,301	11,340	5,662	6,060
5560 Recreational vehicle dealers	5	5	50	55	11	15,040	16,218	905	1,041
5570 Motorcycle dealers	4	4	28	29	7	17,857	16,828	536	557
5610 Men's & boys' clothing stores	12	-	51	-	-	12,941	-	683	-
5620 Women's clothing stores	39	35	287	192	5	7,749	6,958	2,516	1,405
5630 Women's accessory & specialty stores	5	6	24	18	3	7,167	9,333	165	167
5640 Children's and infants' wear stores	7	8	29	29	4	6,897	7,448	216	214
5650 Family clothing stores	15	17	195	182	11	7,426	8,527	1,563	1,653
5660 Shoe stores	27	31	131	136	4	10,565	10,059	1,446	1,529
5690 Misc. apparel & accessory stores	6	7	54	25	4	6,815	8,480	216	251
5712 Furniture stores	32	34	274	251	7	14,467	16,255	4,741	5,176
5713 Floor covering stores	17	17	116	141	8	12,793	17,617	1,819	3,126
5719 Misc. homefurnishings stores	10	-	32	-	-	7,625	-	230	-
5720 Household appliance stores	9	9	40	32	4	12,400	14,625	601	564
5731 Radio, TV, & electronic stores	20	17	145	154	9	17,903	19,117	2,856	2,790
5734 Computer and software stores	4	7	58	48	7	22,621	26,500	1,300	1,130
5735 Record & prerecorded tape stores	5	5	42	35	7	9,619	10,743	390	321
5812 Eating places	378	371	5,056	5,044	14	7,013	7,556	38,194	40,246
5813 Drinking places	36	31	177	190	6	5,876	5,642	1,080	1,103

Continued on next page.

VISALIA – TULARE – PORTERVILLE, CA MSA - [continued]

Wholesale and Retail Trade USA	Establishments		Employment		Emp / Est	Pay / Employee		Annual Payroll ($ 000)	
	1994	1995	1994	1995	1995	1994	1995	1994	1995
5910 Drug stores and proprietary stores	51	48	678	765	16	19,257	17,621	13,047	13,307
5920 Liquor stores	17	16	63	52	3	11,238	12,000	722	670
5930 Used merchandise stores	19	19	102	108	6	8,039	8,556	976	1,036
5941 Sporting goods and bicycle shops	25	26	210	201	8	10,038	10,229	2,242	2,017
5942 Book stores	8	-	38	-	-	8,211	-	334	-
5943 Stationery stores	-	11	-	60	5	-	13,133	-	768
5944 Jewelry stores	28	29	118	107	4	22,712	24,897	2,135	1,973
5945 Hobby, toy, and game shops	8	8	81	92	12	10,074	8,652	818	951
5947 Gift, novelty, and souvenir shops	17	20	72	69	3	8,389	9,681	647	702
5949 Sewing, needlework, and piece goods	5	5	71	53	11	7,437	8,226	507	471
5961 Catalog and mail-order houses	-	4	-	20	5	-	46,400	-	889
5962 Merchandising machine operators	-	6	-	35	6	-	12,800	-	533
5963 Direct selling establishments	13	14	65	124	9	24,738	10,677	1,651	1,326
5980 Fuel dealers	6	6	69	59	10	21,623	25,898	1,508	1,798
5992 Florists	22	27	128	130	5	7,969	8,892	1,048	1,098
5995 Optical goods stores	-	8	-	18	2	-	18,222	-	544
5999 Miscellaneous retail stores, nec	43	45	117	210	5	16,581	19,771	2,224	4,384

Source: County Business Patterns 1994/95, CBP-94/95, U.S. Department of Commerce, Washington DC, November 1997. The employment column represents mid-March employment in the year. Pay per employee is calculated by dividing 1st Quarter payroll, annualized, by mid-March employment. The column headed 'Emp / Est' shows 'employees per establishment'. A dash (-) means that data are unavailable or cannot be calculated. nec means not elsewhere classified. *Notes:* 1. 1994 data incomplete; unavailable or withheld. 2. 1995 data incomplete; unavailable or withheld. 3. 1994 and 1995 data incomplete; unavailable or withheld.

WACO, TX MSA

Wholesale and Retail Trade USA	Establishments		Employment		Emp / Est	Pay / Employee		Annual Payroll ($ 000)	
	1994	1995	1994	1995	1995	1994	1995	1994	1995
50 – Wholesale trade	-	396	-	4,696	12	-	23,842	-	119,921
5012 Automobiles and other vehicles	-	7	-	76	11	-	22,158	-	2,213
5013 Motor vehicle supplies and new parts	-	15	-	146	10	-	21,151	-	3,006
5014 Tires and tubes	-	3	-	27	9	-	23,111	-	631
5015 Motor vehicle parts, used	-	13	-	141	11	-	20,993	-	3,589
5021 Furniture	-	3	-	8	3	-	14,500	-	126
5023 Homefurnishings	-	4	-	10	3	-	49,600	-	344
5032 Brick, stone, & related materials	-	5	-	60	12	-	23,333	-	1,460
5039 Construction materials, nec	-	9	-	95	11	-	19,705	-	2,001
5044 Office equipment	-	13	-	132	10	-	21,212	-	2,988
5045 Computers, peripherals, & software	-	13	-	180	14	-	37,200	-	5,825
5046 Commercial equipment, nec	-	7	-	35	5	-	19,886	-	702
5047 Medical and hospital equipment	-	10	-	72	7	-	25,056	-	2,130
5051 Metals service centers and offices	-	8	-	61	8	-	20,328	-	2,010
5063 Electrical apparatus and equipment	-	7	-	104	15	-	24,654	-	2,845
5072 Hardware	-	8	-	110	14	-	20,582	-	2,224
5074 Plumbing & hydronic heating supplies	-	8	-	67	8	-	43,164	-	2,563
5082 Construction and mining machinery	-	4	-	101	25	-	32,832	-	3,555
5083 Farm and garden machinery	-	13	-	136	10	-	28,588	-	4,048
5084 Industrial machinery and equipment	-	16	-	221	14	-	28,163	-	7,543
5085 Industrial supplies	-	10	-	128	13	-	30,344	-	3,680
5087 Service establishment equipment	-	11	-	92	8	-	16,609	-	1,418
5091 Sporting & recreational goods	-	8	-	61	8	-	22,164	-	1,523
5093 Scrap and waste materials	-	5	-	203	41	-	22,286	-	6,994
5112 Stationery and office supplies	-	8	-	73	9	-	19,014	-	1,327
5120 Drugs, proprietaries, and sundries	-	4	-	65	16	-	18,215	-	1,478
5130 Apparel, piece goods, and notions	-	7	-	65	9	-	15,508	-	1,762
5143 Dairy products, exc. dried or canned	-	4	-	167	42	-	22,778	-	3,787
5148 Fresh fruits and vegetables	-	4	-	55	14	-	15,418	-	734
5149 Groceries and related products, nec	-	10	-	281	28	-	27,972	-	7,736
5153 Grain and field beans	-	8	-	35	4	-	18,857	-	659
5154 Livestock	-	3	-	81	27	-	8,840	-	763
5160 Chemicals and allied products	-	7	-	67	10	-	19,164	-	1,229
5171 Petroleum bulk stations & terminals	-	15	-	88	6	-	18,500	-	1,400
5172 Petroleum products, nec	-	12	-	107	9	-	18,243	-	2,239
5181 Beer and ale	-	4	-	183	46	-	28,590	-	5,092
5191 Farm supplies	-	30	-	281	9	-	19,089	-	6,000
5192 Books, periodicals, & newspapers	-	5	-	124	25	-	17,677	-	2,147
5199 Nondurable goods, nec	-	11	-	73	7	-	21,699	-	1,983
52 – Retail trade	-	1,183	-	16,107	14	-	12,780	-	209,744
5210 Lumber and other building materials	-	17	-	286	17	-	19,902	-	7,333
5230 Paint, glass, and wallpaper stores	-	7	-	63	9	-	22,286	-	1,337
5250 Hardware stores	-	7	-	41	6	-	11,512	-	475

Continued on next page.

WACO, TX MSA - [continued]

Wholesale and Retail Trade USA	Establishments		Employment		Emp / Est	Pay / Employee		Annual Payroll ($ 000)	
	1994	1995	1994	1995	1995	1994	1995	1994	1995
5260 Retail nurseries and garden stores	-	15	-	113	8	-	13,239	-	1,553
5270 Mobile home dealers	-	4	-	37	9	-	23,784	-	1,026
5310 Department stores	-	10	-	1,844	184	-	12,642	-	21,606
5330 Variety stores	-	7	-	52	7	-	6,923	-	389
5390 Misc. general merchandise stores	-	17	-	255	15	-	12,925	-	3,252
5410 Grocery stores	-	132	-	2,570	19	-	12,675	-	32,856
5440 Candy, nut, and confectionery stores	-	3	-	8	3	-	4,500	-	22
5460 Retail bakeries	-	8	-	47	6	-	5,872	-	218
5490 Miscellaneous food stores	-	5	-	20	4	-	10,400	-	131
5510 New and used car dealers	-	21	-	865	41	-	28,943	-	30,086
5520 Used car dealers	-	25	-	71	3	-	16,056	-	1,259
5530 Auto and home supply stores	-	43	-	317	7	-	15,470	-	5,428
5540 Gasoline service stations	-	78	-	406	5	-	11,172	-	4,660
5550 Boat dealers	-	3	-	25	8	-	20,800	-	527
5590 Automotive dealers, nec	-	4	-	36	9	-	14,111	-	715
5610 Men's & boys' clothing stores	-	8	-	58	7	-	12,552	-	560
5620 Women's clothing stores	-	27	-	193	7	-	7,627	-	1,416
5630 Women's accessory & specialty stores	-	6	-	34	6	-	9,765	-	430
5650 Family clothing stores	-	14	-	201	14	-	9,990	-	2,060
5660 Shoe stores	-	22	-	104	5	-	12,654	-	1,179
5690 Misc. apparel & accessory stores	-	8	-	37	5	-	8,649	-	397
5712 Furniture stores	-	26	-	220	8	-	26,400	-	4,910
5713 Floor covering stores	-	10	-	75	8	-	18,987	-	1,187
5720 Household appliance stores	-	9	-	27	3	-	10,815	-	318
5731 Radio, TV, & electronic stores	-	16	-	156	10	-	14,282	-	2,598
5734 Computer and software stores	-	4	-	17	4	-	13,412	-	164
5735 Record & prerecorded tape stores	-	6	-	65	11	-	5,108	-	711
5736 Musical instrument stores	-	4	-	42	11	-	19,524	-	951
5812 Eating places	-	239	-	5,345	22	-	7,996	-	44,254
5813 Drinking places	-	32	-	188	6	-	7,596	-	1,459
5910 Drug stores and proprietary stores	-	21	-	266	13	-	16,632	-	4,154
5920 Liquor stores	-	18	-	68	4	-	11,059	-	814
5930 Used merchandise stores	-	36	-	190	5	-	13,853	-	2,761
5941 Sporting goods and bicycle shops	-	8	-	29	4	-	9,379	-	277
5942 Book stores	-	8	-	95	12	-	9,221	-	881
5943 Stationery stores	-	5	-	34	7	-	11,176	-	373
5944 Jewelry stores	-	20	-	93	5	-	12,215	-	1,150
5945 Hobby, toy, and game shops	-	7	-	120	17	-	8,600	-	1,105
5947 Gift, novelty, and souvenir shops	-	20	-	103	5	-	6,563	-	704
5949 Sewing, needlework, and piece goods	-	4	-	40	10	-	7,400	-	290
5963 Direct selling establishments	-	8	-	46	6	-	22,174	-	917
5980 Fuel dealers	-	4	-	42	11	-	19,333	-	970
5992 Florists	-	19	-	81	4	-	9,333	-	738
5995 Optical goods stores	-	10	-	45	5	-	14,489	-	693
5999 Miscellaneous retail stores, nec	-	28	-	122	4	-	13,475	-	1,652

Source: County Business Patterns 1994/95, CBP-94/95, U.S. Department of Commerce, Washington DC, November 1997. The employment column represents mid-March employment in the year. Pay per employee is calculated by dividing 1st Quarter payroll, annualized, by mid-March employment. The column headed 'Emp / Est' shows 'employees per establishment'. A dash (-) means that data are unavailable or cannot be calculated. nec means not elsewhere classified. *Notes:* 1. 1994 data incomplete; unavailable or withheld. 2. 1995 data incomplete; unavailable or withheld. 3. 1994 and 1995 data incomplete; unavailable or withheld.

WASHINGTON PMSA (MD PART)

Wholesale and Retail Trade USA	Establishments		Employment		Emp / Est	Pay / Employee		Annual Payroll ($ 000)	
	1994	1995	1994	1995	1995	1994	1995	1994	1995
50- Wholesale trade	2,389	2,452	37,716	37,204	15	41,702	40,674	1,463,569	1,464,744
5012 Automobiles and other vehicles [3]	38	35	807	662	19	42,364	48,453	35,191	32,287
5013 Motor vehicle supplies and new parts	138	134	1,475	1,477	11	23,444	23,775	38,393	36,761
5014 Tires and tubes [3]	20	16	129	199	12	27,411	26,935	4,246	5,650
5015 Motor vehicle parts, used [3]	27	31	566	602	19	22,587	25,309	14,639	15,742
5021 Furniture	79	80	738	606	8	31,973	34,812	25,172	20,388
5023 Homefurnishings [1]	70	72	526	612	9	30,152	33,948	18,379	20,056
5031 Lumber, plywood, and millwork	36	42	688	863	21	29,250	29,103	22,833	26,775
5032 Brick, stone, & related materials [3]	22	25	151	218	9	32,450	35,523	6,158	8,090
5033 Roofing, siding, & insulation [3]	20	19	420	510	27	31,686	35,545	14,852	18,579
5039 Construction materials, nec	27	54	444	828	15	37,784	30,396	19,014	26,241
5043 Photographic equipment & supplies [3]	10	13	102	112	9	33,686	31,143	3,811	3,757
5044 Office equipment	52	57	1,109	1,132	20	36,941	40,081	39,558	34,911
5045 Computers, peripherals, & software	213	208	8,724	6,917	33	74,586	70,236	484,581	424,199
5046 Commercial equipment, nec [3]	30	33	373	363	11	27,925	33,719	11,431	12,590

Continued on next page.

WASHINGTON PMSA (MD PART) - [continued]

Wholesale and Retail Trade USA	Establishments		Employment		Emp / Est	Pay / Employee		Annual Payroll ($ 000)	
	1994	1995	1994	1995	1995	1994	1995	1994	1995
5047 Medical and hospital equipment [3]	66	52	500	525	10	40,008	38,781	20,631	20,342
5048 Ophthalmic goods [3]	9	9	100	116	13	29,920	34,379	3,542	4,403
5049 Professional equipment, nec [3]	29	29	195	217	7	43,446	35,171	9,190	11,719
5051 Metals service centers and offices [3]	18	20	274	283	14	29,168	31,505	8,582	10,646
5063 Electrical apparatus and equipment [1]	96	92	874	789	9	32,160	38,707	30,929	29,348
5064 Electrical appliances, TV & radios [3]	30	28	312	343	12	33,872	33,971	12,865	13,217
5065 Electronic parts and equipment [3]	130	134	2,079	2,190	16	45,206	50,037	89,633	103,980
5072 Hardware [3]	38	39	166	288	7	24,867	30,014	4,405	9,046
5074 Plumbing & hydronic heating supplies [2]	54	49	500	376	8	28,296	30,011	15,596	12,330
5075 Warm air heating & air conditioning [3]	53	48	390	301	6	30,708	36,930	13,232	11,669
5078 Refrigeration equipment and supplies [3]	7	7	65	62	9	37,477	45,484	2,862	3,382
5082 Construction and mining machinery [3]	20	24	135	146	6	36,652	42,329	5,846	7,159
5083 Farm and garden machinery	25	27	329	330	12	22,881	23,636	9,007	8,304
5084 Industrial machinery and equipment	63	64	657	607	9	34,624	34,096	24,684	22,602
5085 Industrial supplies [1]	27	30	156	170	6	28,385	30,165	5,703	5,840
5087 Service establishment equipment [3]	48	45	838	813	18	29,303	31,223	27,216	26,163
5088 Transportation equipment & supplies [3]	20	19	73	62	3	46,521	36,710	3,617	2,824
5091 Sporting & recreational goods [3]	17	17	48	68	4	26,250	22,471	1,486	1,867
5092 Toys and hobby goods and supplies [3]	10	12	28	66	6	15,714	11,333	463	946
5093 Scrap and waste materials [3]	36	36	504	597	17	23,230	29,474	15,001	16,977
5094 Jewelry & precious stones [3]	41	40	121	102	3	21,719	21,059	3,098	2,421
5099 Durable goods, nec [3]	42	37	309	314	8	34,498	37,847	11,934	12,842
5111 Printing and writing paper [3]	15	14	508	511	37	40,764	45,229	19,937	23,888
5112 Stationery and office supplies [3]	87	69	1,100	854	12	26,720	32,211	32,212	28,671
5113 Industrial & personal service paper [3]	21	21	401	432	21	38,643	40,204	15,202	16,318
5120 Drugs, proprietaries, and sundries [3]	29	32	805	827	26	47,260	50,781	35,253	39,885
5131 Piece goods & notions [3]	9	10	46	41	4	22,435	28,488	1,099	1,116
5136 Men's and boys' clothing [3]	12	12	96	88	7	17,458	21,591	2,070	2,897
5137 Women's and children's clothing [3]	17	16	64	84	5	19,313	19,190	1,480	1,559
5141 Groceries, general line [3]	14	15	132	172	11	24,727	29,023	3,742	3,718
5142 Packaged frozen food [3]	9	10	88	66	7	24,182	26,788	2,168	1,972
5143 Dairy products, exc. dried or canned [3]	9	9	225	242	27	28,978	32,165	7,038	7,460
5144 Poultry and poultry products [3]	4	5	205	175	35	26,049	33,143	5,992	5,744
5145 Confectionery [3]	10	11	128	143	13	56,000	35,469	3,854	4,720
5146 Fish and seafoods	10	10	31	34	3	25,677	27,412	867	852
5147 Meats and meat products [3]	11	9	157	167	19	30,726	30,563	6,178	7,657
5148 Fresh fruits and vegetables [1]	6	-	7	-	-	22,286	-	174	-
5149 Groceries and related products, nec [3]	69	68	2,001	1,932	28	26,695	28,110	55,661	54,922
5154 Livestock [3]	5	5	44	18	4	3,818	6,222	174	134
5162 Plastics materials & basic shapes [3]	9	8	41	108	14	41,073	37,148	1,125	3,262
5169 Chemicals & allied products, nec [3]	32	30	346	317	11	33,827	34,322	12,666	10,461
5171 Petroleum bulk stations & terminals [3]	24	19	150	46	2	29,200	31,652	4,479	1,740
5172 Petroleum products, nec [1]	4	-	26	-	-	15,538	-	373	-
5181 Beer and ale [3]	10	9	232	289	32	35,621	37,024	9,979	11,605
5182 Wine and distilled beverages [3]	8	7	33	38	5	27,394	32,737	1,048	876
5191 Farm supplies	36	28	360	286	10	25,956	27,636	10,321	8,563
5192 Books, periodicals, & newspapers [3]	30	50	713	927	19	27,203	23,055	20,356	22,258
5193 Flowers & florists' supplies [3]	21	19	203	230	12	19,094	18,452	4,269	4,631
5198 Paints, varnishes, and supplies [3]	41	41	317	303	7	34,095	29,426	11,599	9,500
5199 Nondurable goods, nec [3]	89	93	439	490	5	28,929	32,384	14,653	16,729
52- Retail trade	9,563	9,678	151,173	156,252	16	15,156	16,471	2,497,115	2,687,348
5210 Lumber and other building materials	123	110	3,683	3,757	34	18,066	18,812	73,535	72,714
5230 Paint, glass, and wallpaper stores	42	35	156	171	5	21,974	22,409	4,276	4,285
5250 Hardware stores	63	45	608	353	8	15,243	17,598	9,673	5,693
5260 Retail nurseries and garden stores	63	68	530	640	9	11,374	12,538	8,130	10,208
5310 Department stores [3]	65	65	13,101	13,031	200	10,284	11,250	150,276	152,247
5330 Variety stores	75	63	1,021	717	11	8,823	8,781	9,950	6,790
5390 Misc. general merchandise stores [2]	58	57	2,001	1,720	30	13,611	14,572	28,621	25,146
5410 Grocery stores	701	701	18,895	19,303	28	19,523	19,847	378,424	393,148
5420 Meat and fish markets	55	53	408	472	9	13,353	13,517	6,275	6,879
5430 Fruit and vegetable markets [1]	7	-	24	-	-	9,500	-	373	-
5440 Candy, nut, and confectionery stores [3]	21	22	120	70	3	8,567	12,171	865	816
5450 Dairy products stores [3]	14	13	23	16	1	8,870	6,500	217	127
5460 Retail bakeries	121	114	992	794	7	10,109	11,783	11,029	10,051
5490 Miscellaneous food stores [1]	56	56	285	245	4	9,572	11,412	2,697	3,279
5510 New and used car dealers	144	139	9,666	10,545	76	30,341	31,660	344,222	353,809
5520 Used car dealers [3]	50	56	165	225	4	18,788	21,440	3,745	5,101
5530 Auto and home supply stores	211	219	1,931	2,022	9	17,678	17,939	39,677	36,946
5540 Gasoline service stations	611	608	5,194	5,145	8	14,970	15,602	82,494	83,282
5550 Boat dealers	15	14	46	61	4	10,174	13,967	651	986
5560 Recreational vehicle dealers [3]	7	8	75	86	11	17,120	18,279	1,730	1,724

Continued on next page.

WASHINGTON PMSA (MD PART) - [continued]

Wholesale and Retail Trade USA	Establishments		Employment		Emp / Est	Pay / Employee		Annual Payroll ($ 000)	
	1994	1995	1994	1995	1995	1994	1995	1994	1995
5570 Motorcycle dealers[3]	13	13	93	122	9	14,968	22,295	2,078	3,152
5590 Automotive dealers, nec[3]	6	8	23	14	2	15,652	34,857	155	653
5610 Men's & boys' clothing stores[3]	105	107	1,078	1,126	11	13,269	13,368	14,533	14,749
5620 Women's clothing stores	326	288	4,042	3,595	12	9,584	9,895	42,599	36,541
5630 Women's accessory & specialty stores[3]	72	64	452	407	6	11,929	12,658	5,666	5,042
5640 Children's and infants' wear stores[3]	49	49	428	558	11	7,963	9,047	3,982	5,374
5650 Family clothing stores	121	119	2,938	2,866	24	11,398	12,342	34,910	35,580
5660 Shoe stores	304	274	1,921	1,758	6	11,286	11,229	22,925	19,533
5690 Misc. apparel & accessory stores[3]	58	59	274	280	5	11,810	16,743	3,359	4,528
5712 Furniture stores	219	213	1,864	2,147	10	18,313	19,475	40,121	43,865
5713 Floor covering stores	140	152	557	651	4	23,993	27,429	15,331	18,091
5714 Drapery and upholstery stores[3]	22	22	145	117	5	15,807	17,299	2,464	2,052
5719 Misc. homefurnishings stores[3]	120	122	928	949	8	11,233	13,526	12,664	13,326
5720 Household appliance stores	64	60	215	234	4	20,093	22,479	4,794	6,029
5731 Radio, TV, & electronic stores	133	134	1,301	1,591	12	19,099	19,475	28,184	31,664
5734 Computer and software stores	89	107	526	790	7	21,932	22,081	13,125	19,734
5735 Record & prerecorded tape stores	86	90	627	660	7	9,250	9,970	6,433	6,281
5736 Musical instrument stores[3]	36	33	339	436	13	22,844	20,514	9,495	10,150
5812 Eating places	2,387	2,299	43,463	44,341	19	8,537	9,347	412,447	438,439
5813 Drinking places	95	82	902	848	10	7,401	8,028	7,299	7,308
5910 Drug stores and proprietary stores	229	220	4,031	3,942	18	14,643	15,560	60,079	61,488
5920 Liquor stores	329	331	2,380	2,435	7	12,817	12,646	31,535	31,432
5930 Used merchandise stores	125	133	1,065	1,361	10	14,156	12,914	17,639	18,336
5941 Sporting goods and bicycle shops	184	159	1,244	1,392	9	12,177	12,152	17,506	18,424
5942 Book stores	85	86	733	771	9	10,587	11,585	7,799	8,383
5943 Stationery stores	30	37	83	424	11	22,313	16,292	2,047	7,342
5944 Jewelry stores	193	197	1,019	1,150	6	16,385	17,082	18,336	18,991
5945 Hobby, toy, and game shops	64	66	1,017	1,183	18	10,144	10,316	13,631	13,942
5946 Camera & photographic supply stores[3]	19	18	104	100	6	19,731	21,120	2,031	2,147
5947 Gift, novelty, and souvenir shops	209	192	1,254	1,157	6	7,589	8,857	10,692	11,457
5948 Luggage and leather goods stores[3]	17	14	69	79	6	10,899	11,544	802	960
5949 Sewing, needlework, and piece goods[3]	49	48	655	570	12	9,631	11,740	6,905	6,664
5961 Catalog and mail-order houses[3]	48	56	324	393	7	22,136	24,723	9,534	11,895
5962 Merchandising machine operators[3]	24	27	457	494	18	24,875	25,134	13,402	13,806
5963 Direct selling establishments	97	159	630	1,063	7	21,721	16,113	13,711	18,099
5983 Fuel oil dealers[2]	-	28	-	145	5	-	31,531	-	3,977
5992 Florists	126	117	647	571	5	12,971	13,534	9,074	8,184
5994 News dealers and newsstands	-	26	-	104	4	-	8,385	-	974
5995 Optical goods stores	130	138	625	677	5	17,702	18,747	11,634	13,378
5999 Miscellaneous retail stores, nec	333	355	2,078	2,212	6	14,768	16,107	33,090	36,746

Source: County Business Patterns 1994/95, CBP-94/95, U.S. Department of Commerce, Washington DC, November 1997. The employment column represents mid-March employment in the year. Pay per employee is calculated by dividing 1st Quarter payroll, annualized, by mid-March employment. The column headed 'Emp / Est' shows 'employees per establishment'. A dash (-) means that data are unavailable or cannot be calculated. nec means not elsewhere classified. *Notes:* 1. 1994 data incomplete; unavailable or withheld. 2. 1995 data incomplete; unavailable or withheld. 3. 1994 and 1995 data incomplete; unavailable or withheld.

WASHINGTON PMSA (VA PART)

Wholesale and Retail Trade USA	Establishments		Employment		Emp / Est	Pay / Employee		Annual Payroll ($ 000)	
	1994	1995	1994	1995	1995	1994	1995	1994	1995
50- Wholesale trade	-	2,481	-	38,208	15	-	40,706	-	1,579,684
5012 Automobiles and other vehicles[2]	-	39	-	333	9	-	40,264	-	14,927
5013 Motor vehicle supplies and new parts	-	160	-	1,275	8	-	24,442	-	31,865
5015 Motor vehicle parts, used[2]	-	28	-	139	5	-	23,770	-	3,466
5021 Furniture[2]	-	55	-	330	6	-	42,473	-	16,550
5023 Homefurnishings[2]	-	49	-	369	8	-	31,241	-	13,290
5031 Lumber, plywood, and millwork[2]	-	46	-	913	20	-	29,174	-	27,628
5032 Brick, stone, & related materials[2]	-	28	-	103	4	-	30,951	-	3,440
5033 Roofing, siding, & insulation[2]	-	20	-	141	7	-	32,709	-	4,484
5039 Construction materials, nec[2]	-	37	-	328	9	-	40,537	-	13,071
5043 Photographic equipment & supplies[2]	-	7	-	116	17	-	55,345	-	7,337
5044 Office equipment[2]	-	71	-	2,096	30	-	49,273	-	100,748
5045 Computers, peripherals, & software[2]	-	302	-	5,772	19	-	50,945	-	293,732
5046 Commercial equipment, nec[2]	-	25	-	145	6	-	25,986	-	3,904
5047 Medical and hospital equipment[2]	-	46	-	465	10	-	45,686	-	21,522
5051 Metals service centers and offices[2]	-	11	-	43	4	-	35,163	-	1,848
5063 Electrical apparatus and equipment[2]	-	80	-	961	12	-	45,544	-	45,795
5064 Electrical appliances, TV & radios[2]	-	17	-	185	11	-	29,449	-	5,609
5065 Electronic parts and equipment[2]	-	150	-	2,400	16	-	54,225	-	137,950
5074 Plumbing & hydronic heating supplies[2]	-	47	-	299	6	-	38,154	-	11,682

Continued on next page.

WASHINGTON PMSA (VA PART) - [continued]

Wholesale and Retail Trade USA	Establishments		Employment		Emp / Est	Pay / Employee		Annual Payroll ($ 000)	
	1994	1995	1994	1995	1995	1994	1995	1994	1995
5075 Warm air heating & air conditioning [2]	-	46	-	191	4	-	44,377	-	8,668
5082 Construction and mining machinery [2]	-	24	-	195	8	-	42,031	-	7,574
5083 Farm and garden machinery [2]	-	28	-	135	5	-	20,415	-	2,952
5084 Industrial machinery and equipment [2]	-	74	-	464	6	-	44,767	-	20,044
5085 Industrial supplies [2]	-	34	-	151	4	-	37,616	-	5,682
5087 Service establishment equipment [2]	-	28	-	50	2	-	26,800	-	1,175
5088 Transportation equipment & supplies [2]	-	48	-	546	11	-	52,689	-	28,722
5091 Sporting & recreational goods [2]	-	28	-	109	4	-	28,294	-	3,390
5092 Toys and hobby goods and supplies [2]	-	11	-	52	5	-	25,154	-	1,294
5093 Scrap and waste materials [2]	-	28	-	123	4	-	27,545	-	4,663
5094 Jewelry & precious stones [2]	-	23	-	78	3	-	36,821	-	2,971
5099 Durable goods, nec [2]	-	29	-	55	2	-	32,800	-	1,835
5112 Stationery and office supplies [2]	-	78	-	590	8	-	30,610	-	18,863
5113 Industrial & personal service paper [2]	-	11	-	81	7	-	26,963	-	2,989
5120 Drugs, proprietaries, and sundries [2]	-	22	-	144	7	-	42,000	-	5,447
5136 Men's and boys' clothing [2]	-	16	-	32	2	-	16,500	-	447
5137 Women's and children's clothing [2]	-	14	-	30	2	-	20,133	-	615
5141 Groceries, general line [2]	-	18	-	56	3	-	22,714	-	1,423
5142 Packaged frozen food [2]	-	16	-	31	2	-	27,484	-	821
5146 Fish and seafoods [2]	-	6	-	99	17	-	15,515	-	1,635
5149 Groceries and related products, nec [2]	-	56	-	2,612	47	-	14,738	-	39,395
5160 Chemicals and allied products [2]	-	33	-	157	5	-	35,592	-	5,982
5171 Petroleum bulk stations & terminals [2]	-	30	-	71	2	-	33,408	-	2,246
5181 Beer and ale [2]	-	16	-	602	38	-	41,568	-	23,684
5182 Wine and distilled beverages [2]	-	13	-	218	17	-	34,752	-	9,134
5191 Farm supplies [2]	-	31	-	180	6	-	22,111	-	4,914
5192 Books, periodicals, & newspapers [2]	-	48	-	435	9	-	36,846	-	16,110
5193 Flowers & florists' supplies [2]	-	14	-	104	7	-	21,808	-	2,456
5198 Paints, varnishes, and supplies [2]	-	36	-	101	3	-	25,505	-	2,627
5199 Nondurable goods, nec [2]	-	98	-	591	6	-	26,200	-	17,342
52- Retail trade	-	10,970	-	167,861	15	-	15,070	-	2,666,043
5210 Lumber and other building materials [2]	-	111	-	3,344	30	-	19,020	-	65,869
5230 Paint, glass, and wallpaper stores [2]	-	47	-	159	3	-	15,975	-	2,717
5250 Hardware stores [2]	-	54	-	322	6	-	13,106	-	4,245
5260 Retail nurseries and garden stores [2]	-	69	-	761	11	-	14,008	-	15,221
5310 Department stores [2]	-	64	-	12,214	191	-	12,647	-	159,029
5330 Variety stores [2]	-	50	-	212	4	-	11,566	-	2,490
5390 Misc. general merchandise stores [2]	-	90	-	1,872	21	-	15,231	-	28,357
5410 Grocery stores [2]	-	865	-	18,292	21	-	19,691	-	372,276
5420 Meat and fish markets [2]	-	29	-	71	2	-	12,000	-	974
5440 Candy, nut, and confectionery stores [2]	-	24	-	166	7	-	7,012	-	1,172
5450 Dairy products stores [2]	-	11	-	54	5	-	4,667	-	285
5460 Retail bakeries [2]	-	114	-	1,035	9	-	10,257	-	11,107
5490 Miscellaneous food stores [2]	-	104	-	643	6	-	9,661	-	6,567
5510 New and used car dealers [2]	-	146	-	9,889	68	-	31,945	-	354,117
5520 Used car dealers [2]	-	96	-	328	3	-	24,585	-	8,616
5530 Auto and home supply stores [2]	-	205	-	1,788	9	-	20,633	-	38,378
5540 Gasoline service stations	-	606	-	5,246	9	-	16,024	-	86,332
5550 Boat dealers [2]	-	14	-	129	9	-	21,860	-	3,334
5570 Motorcycle dealers [2]	-	18	-	120	7	-	29,267	-	3,645
5610 Men's & boys' clothing stores [2]	-	120	-	1,547	13	-	14,583	-	22,184
5620 Women's clothing stores [2]	-	328	-	3,623	11	-	9,750	-	35,071
5630 Women's accessory & specialty stores [2]	-	84	-	610	7	-	11,089	-	6,658
5640 Children's and infants' wear stores [2]	-	44	-	568	13	-	8,085	-	4,895
5650 Family clothing stores [2]	-	152	-	5,330	35	-	12,907	-	72,408
5660 Shoe stores [2]	-	264	-	1,590	6	-	11,726	-	17,975
5690 Misc. apparel & accessory stores [2]	-	71	-	279	4	-	11,369	-	3,345
5712 Furniture stores [2]	-	266	-	2,427	9	-	20,061	-	49,766
5713 Floor covering stores [2]	-	144	-	538	4	-	23,056	-	12,986
5714 Drapery and upholstery stores [2]	-	26	-	89	3	-	14,787	-	852
5719 Misc. homefurnishings stores [2]	-	221	-	2,059	9	-	12,274	-	26,484
5720 Household appliance stores [2]	-	61	-	263	4	-	21,612	-	5,985
5731 Radio, TV, & electronic stores [2]	-	149	-	1,695	11	-	17,017	-	28,637
5734 Computer and software stores [2]	-	134	-	941	7	-	19,439	-	18,776
5735 Record & prerecorded tape stores [2]	-	89	-	570	6	-	10,625	-	5,186
5736 Musical instrument stores [2]	-	35	-	145	4	-	15,310	-	2,492
5812 Eating places	-	2,830	-	55,347	20	-	9,811	-	579,623
5813 Drinking places [2]	-	19	-	69	4	-	11,884	-	750
5910 Drug stores and proprietary stores	-	214	-	3,413	16	-	15,794	-	56,909
5920 Liquor stores [2]	-	72	-	355	5	-	13,882	-	4,746
5930 Used merchandise stores [2]	-	166	-	692	4	-	12,618	-	9,353

Continued on next page.

WASHINGTON PMSA (VA PART) - [continued]

Wholesale and Retail Trade USA	Establishments		Employment		Emp / Est	Pay / Employee		Annual Payroll ($ 000)	
	1994	1995	1994	1995	1995	1994	1995	1994	1995
5941 Sporting goods and bicycle shops [2]	-	200	-	2,059	10	-	11,746	-	25,086
5942 Book stores [2]	-	127	-	1,179	9	-	10,456	-	12,271
5943 Stationery stores [2]	-	35	-	343	10	-	13,924	-	4,713
5944 Jewelry stores [2]	-	216	-	1,192	6	-	18,074	-	21,215
5945 Hobby, toy, and game shops [2]	-	128	-	1,647	13	-	8,891	-	16,981
5946 Camera & photographic supply stores [2]	-	25	-	145	6	-	12,028	-	1,834
5947 Gift, novelty, and souvenir shops [2]	-	321	-	1,940	6	-	8,243	-	17,539
5948 Luggage and leather goods stores [2]	-	31	-	126	4	-	11,016	-	1,516
5949 Sewing, needlework, and piece goods [2]	-	63	-	510	8	-	8,102	-	4,126
5961 Catalog and mail-order houses [2]	-	57	-	179	3	-	19,285	-	4,643
5962 Merchandising machine operators [2]	-	25	-	207	8	-	19,691	-	4,295
5963 Direct selling establishments [2]	-	162	-	1,430	9	-	21,206	-	28,847
5980 Fuel dealers [2]	-	33	-	197	6	-	29,604	-	5,673
5992 Florists [2]	-	188	-	901	5	-	12,737	-	11,996
5993 Tobacco stores and stands [2]	-	11	-	41	4	-	9,561	-	499
5994 News dealers and newsstands [2]	-	23	-	34	1	-	12,353	-	506
5995 Optical goods stores [2]	-	129	-	519	4	-	18,181	-	9,672
5999 Miscellaneous retail stores, nec	-	357	-	2,151	6	-	14,741	-	32,875

Source: County Business Patterns 1994/95, CBP-94/95, U.S. Department of Commerce, Washington DC, November 1997. The employment column represents mid-March employment in the year. Pay per employee is calculated by dividing 1st Quarter payroll, annualized, by mid-March employment. The column headed 'Emp / Est' shows 'employees per establishment'. A dash (-) means that data are unavailable or cannot be calculated. nec means not elsewhere classified. *Notes:* 1. 1994 data incomplete; unavailable or withheld. 2. 1995 data incomplete; unavailable or withheld. 3. 1994 and 1995 data incomplete; unavailable or withheld.

WASHINGTON PMSA (WV PART)

Wholesale and Retail Trade USA	Establishments		Employment		Emp / Est	Pay / Employee		Annual Payroll ($ 000)	
	1994	1995	1994	1995	1995	1994	1995	1994	1995
50- Wholesale trade	-	89	-	1,438	16	-	38,220	-	60,875
5015 Motor vehicle parts, used	-	6	-	23	4	-	12,870	-	296
5030 Lumber and construction materials	-	7	-	67	10	-	23,821	-	1,596
5060 Electrical goods	-	7	-	16	2	-	18,250	-	275
5085 Industrial supplies [2]	-	4	-	16	4	-	15,750	-	269
5091 Sporting & recreational goods [2]	-	4	-	27	7	-	15,704	-	403
5171 Petroleum bulk stations & terminals [2]	-	4	-	62	16	-	27,226	-	1,625
5180 Beer, wine, and distilled beverages [2]	-	4	-	54	14	-	24,741	-	1,995
5190 Misc., nondurable goods	-	8	-	25	3	-	16,320	-	416
52- Retail trade	-	629	-	7,224	11	-	10,471	-	80,676
5210 Lumber and other building materials	-	12	-	168	14	-	17,810	-	3,027
5260 Retail nurseries and garden stores	-	6	-	26	4	-	8,769	-	275
5270 Mobile home dealers [2]	-	4	-	19	5	-	11,579	-	250
5310 Department stores	-	5	-	641	128	-	12,343	-	7,552
5330 Variety stores	-	5	-	52	10	-	8,231	-	472
5390 Misc. general merchandise stores	-	10	-	49	5	-	7,918	-	378
5410 Grocery stores	-	58	-	1,182	20	-	10,135	-	12,115
5510 New and used car dealers	-	11	-	278	25	-	22,259	-	7,234
5520 Used car dealers	-	10	-	10	1	-	30,000	-	265
5530 Auto and home supply stores	-	13	-	74	6	-	17,459	-	1,384
5540 Gasoline service stations	-	34	-	307	9	-	10,814	-	3,821
5610 Men's & boys' clothing stores [2]	-	10	-	142	14	-	6,620	-	913
5620 Women's clothing stores	-	21	-	162	8	-	7,827	-	1,417
5630 Women's accessory & specialty stores [2]	-	4	-	17	4	-	7,765	-	143
5650 Family clothing stores	-	17	-	207	12	-	10,512	-	2,114
5660 Shoe stores	-	17	-	88	5	-	9,136	-	800
5712 Furniture stores	-	9	-	29	3	-	13,931	-	383
5719 Misc. homefurnishings stores	-	12	-	73	6	-	8,384	-	662
5720 Household appliance stores	-	4	-	14	4	-	18,000	-	281
5735 Record & prerecorded tape stores [2]	-	3	-	16	5	-	10,500	-	160
5812 Eating places	-	130	-	2,253	17	-	6,926	-	17,212
5813 Drinking places	-	31	-	95	3	-	8,337	-	836
5910 Drug stores and proprietary stores	-	15	-	170	11	-	17,082	-	3,218
5930 Used merchandise stores	-	12	-	15	1	-	5,867	-	115
5941 Sporting goods and bicycle shops [2]	-	6	-	21	4	-	12,000	-	289
5942 Book stores	-	7	-	24	3	-	6,333	-	169
5944 Jewelry stores	-	12	-	53	4	-	13,208	-	658
5947 Gift, novelty, and souvenir shops	-	17	-	64	4	-	6,875	-	453
5948 Luggage and leather goods stores [2]	-	4	-	15	4	-	10,400	-	169
5962 Merchandising machine operators	-	6	-	10	2	-	12,800	-	141
5980 Fuel dealers	-	8	-	114	14	-	17,439	-	1,951
5992 Florists	-	13	-	31	2	-	11,742	-	365

Continued on next page.

WASHINGTON PMSA (WV PART) - [continued]

Wholesale and Retail Trade USA	Establishments		Employment		Emp / Est	Pay / Employee		Annual Payroll ($ 000)	
	1994	1995	1994	1995	1995	1994	1995	1994	1995
5995 Optical goods stores	-	5	-	30	6	-	16,667	-	514
5999 Miscellaneous retail stores, nec	-	20	-	71	4	-	11,155	-	943

Source: County Business Patterns 1994/95, CBP-94/95, U.S. Department of Commerce, Washington DC, November 1997. The employment column represents mid-March employment in the year. Pay per employee is calculated by dividing 1st Quarter payroll, annualized, by mid-March employment. The column headed 'Emp / Est' shows 'employees per establishment'. A dash (-) means that data are unavailable or cannot be calculated. nec means not elsewhere classified. *Notes:* 1. 1994 data incomplete; unavailable or withheld. 2. 1995 data incomplete; unavailable or withheld. 3. 1994 and 1995 data incomplete; unavailable or withheld.

WASHINGTON, DC-MD-VA-WV PMSA

Wholesale and Retail Trade USA	Establishments		Employment		Emp / Est	Pay / Employee		Annual Payroll ($ 000)	
	1994	1995	1994	1995	1995	1994	1995	1994	1995
50- Wholesale trade[3]	2,389	5,022	37,716	76,850	15	41,702	40,644	1,463,569	3,105,303
5012 Automobiles and other vehicles[3]	38	75	807	995	13	42,364	45,713	35,191	47,214
5013 Motor vehicle supplies and new parts[3]	138	301	1,475	2,752	9	23,444	24,084	38,393	68,626
5014 Tires and tubes[3]	20	28	129	199	7	27,411	26,935	4,246	5,650
5015 Motor vehicle parts, used[3]	27	65	566	764	12	22,587	24,654	14,639	19,504
5021 Furniture[3]	79	136	738	936	7	31,973	37,513	25,172	36,938
5023 Homefurnishings[3]	70	122	526	981	8	30,152	32,930	18,379	33,346
5031 Lumber, plywood, and millwork[3]	36	92	688	1,776	19	29,250	29,140	22,833	54,403
5032 Brick, stone, & related materials[3]	22	54	151	321	6	32,450	34,056	6,158	11,530
5033 Roofing, siding, & insulation[3]	20	39	420	651	17	31,686	34,931	14,852	23,063
5039 Construction materials, nec[3]	27	93	444	1,156	12	37,784	33,273	19,014	39,312
5043 Photographic equipment & supplies[3]	10	20	102	228	11	33,686	43,456	3,811	11,094
5044 Office equipment[3]	52	130	1,109	3,228	25	36,941	46,050	39,558	135,659
5045 Computers, peripherals, & software[3]	213	511	8,724	12,689	25	74,586	61,461	484,581	717,931
5046 Commercial equipment, nec[3]	30	58	373	508	9	27,925	31,512	11,431	16,494
5047 Medical and hospital equipment[3]	66	98	500	990	10	40,008	42,024	20,631	41,864
5048 Ophthalmic goods[3]	9	12	100	116	10	29,920	34,379	3,542	4,403
5049 Professional equipment, nec[3]	29	52	195	217	4	43,446	35,171	9,190	11,719
5051 Metals service centers and offices[3]	18	32	274	326	10	29,168	31,988	8,582	12,494
5063 Electrical apparatus and equipment[3]	96	177	874	1,750	10	32,160	42,462	30,929	75,143
5064 Electrical appliances, TV & radios[3]	30	45	312	528	12	33,872	32,386	12,865	18,826
5065 Electronic parts and equipment[3]	130	286	2,079	4,590	16	45,206	52,227	89,633	241,930
5072 Hardware[3]	38	75	166	288	4	24,867	30,014	4,405	9,046
5074 Plumbing & hydronic heating supplies[3]	54	97	500	675	7	28,296	33,618	15,596	24,012
5075 Warm air heating & air conditioning[3]	53	95	390	492	5	30,708	39,821	13,232	20,337
5078 Refrigeration equipment and supplies[3]	7	12	65	62	5	37,477	45,484	2,862	3,382
5082 Construction and mining machinery[3]	20	49	135	341	7	36,652	42,158	5,846	14,733
5083 Farm and garden machinery[3]	25	56	329	465	8	22,881	22,701	9,007	11,256
5084 Industrial machinery and equipment[3]	63	141	657	1,071	8	34,624	38,719	24,684	42,646
5085 Industrial supplies[3]	27	68	156	337	5	28,385	32,819	5,703	11,791
5087 Service establishment equipment[3]	48	74	838	863	12	29,303	30,966	27,216	27,338
5088 Transportation equipment & supplies[3]	20	67	73	608	9	46,521	51,059	3,617	31,546
5091 Sporting & recreational goods[3]	17	49	48	204	4	26,250	24,686	1,486	5,660
5092 Toys and hobby goods and supplies[3]	10	24	28	118	5	15,714	17,424	463	2,240
5093 Scrap and waste materials[3]	36	65	504	720	11	23,230	29,144	15,001	21,640
5094 Jewelry & precious stones[3]	41	63	121	180	3	21,719	27,889	3,098	5,392
5099 Durable goods, nec[3]	42	68	309	369	5	34,498	37,095	11,934	14,677
5111 Printing and writing paper[3]	15	20	508	511	26	40,764	45,229	19,937	23,888
5112 Stationery and office supplies[3]	87	149	1,100	1,444	10	26,720	31,557	32,212	47,534
5113 Industrial & personal service paper[3]	21	33	401	513	16	38,643	38,113	15,202	19,307
5120 Drugs, proprietaries, and sundries[3]	29	56	805	971	17	47,260	49,479	35,253	45,332
5131 Piece goods & notions[3]	9	15	46	41	3	22,435	28,488	1,099	1,116
5136 Men's and boys' clothing[3]	12	28	96	120	4	17,458	20,233	2,070	3,344
5137 Women's and children's clothing[3]	17	30	64	114	4	19,313	19,439	1,480	2,174
5141 Groceries, general line[3]	14	34	132	228	7	24,727	27,474	3,742	5,141
5142 Packaged frozen food[3]	9	27	88	97	4	24,182	27,010	2,168	2,793
5143 Dairy products, exc. dried or canned[3]	9	13	225	242	19	28,978	32,165	7,038	7,460
5144 Poultry and poultry products[3]	4	6	205	175	29	26,049	33,143	5,992	5,744
5145 Confectionery[3]	10	17	128	143	8	56,000	35,469	3,854	4,720
5146 Fish and seafoods[3]	10	16	31	133	8	25,677	18,556	867	2,487
5147 Meats and meat products[3]	11	12	157	167	14	30,726	30,563	6,178	7,657
5148 Fresh fruits and vegetables[1]	6	-	7	-	-	22,286	-	174	-
5149 Groceries and related products, nec[3]	69	125	2,001	4,544	36	26,695	20,423	55,661	94,317
5154 Livestock[3]	5	8	44	18	2	3,818	6,222	174	134
5162 Plastics materials & basic shapes[3]	9	14	41	108	8	41,073	37,148	1,125	3,262
5169 Chemicals & allied products, nec[3]	32	57	346	317	6	33,827	34,322	12,666	10,461
5171 Petroleum bulk stations & terminals[3]	24	53	150	179	3	29,200	30,816	4,479	5,611
5172 Petroleum products, nec[1]	4	-	26	-	-	15,538	-	373	-

Continued on next page.

WASHINGTON, DC – MD – VA – WV PMSA - [continued]

Wholesale and Retail Trade USA	Establishments		Employment		Emp / Est	Pay / Employee		Annual Payroll ($ 000)	
	1994	1995	1994	1995	1995	1994	1995	1994	1995
5181 Beer and ale [3]	10	28	232	891	32	35,621	40,094	9,979	35,289
5182 Wine and distilled beverages [3]	8	21	33	256	12	27,394	34,453	1,048	10,010
5191 Farm supplies [3]	36	64	360	466	7	25,956	25,502	10,321	13,477
5192 Books, periodicals, & newspapers [3]	30	101	713	1,362	13	27,203	27,460	20,356	38,368
5193 Flowers & florists' supplies [3]	21	33	203	334	10	19,094	19,497	4,269	7,087
5198 Paints, varnishes, and supplies [3]	41	77	317	404	5	34,095	28,446	11,599	12,127
5199 Nondurable goods, nec [3]	89	191	439	1,081	6	28,929	29,003	14,653	34,071
52- Retail trade [3]	9,563	21,277	151,173	331,337	16	15,156	15,630	2,497,115	5,434,067
5210 Lumber and other building materials [3]	123	233	3,683	7,269	31	18,066	18,885	73,535	141,610
5230 Paint, glass, and wallpaper stores [3]	42	87	156	330	4	21,974	19,309	4,276	7,002
5250 Hardware stores [3]	63	102	608	675	7	15,243	15,455	9,673	9,938
5260 Retail nurseries and garden stores [3]	63	143	530	1,427	10	11,374	13,253	8,130	25,704
5270 Mobile home dealers [2]	-	16	-	19	1	-	11,579	-	250
5310 Department stores [3]	65	134	13,101	25,886	193	10,284	11,936	150,276	318,828
5330 Variety stores [3]	75	118	1,021	981	8	8,823	9,354	9,950	9,752
5390 Misc. general merchandise stores [3]	58	157	2,001	3,641	23	13,611	14,821	28,621	53,881
5410 Grocery stores [3]	701	1,624	18,895	38,777	24	19,523	19,477	378,424	777,539
5420 Meat and fish markets [3]	55	82	408	543	7	13,353	13,319	6,275	7,853
5430 Fruit and vegetable markets [1]	7	-	24	-	-	9,500	-	373	-
5440 Candy, nut, and confectionery stores [3]	21	49	120	236	5	8,567	8,542	865	1,988
5450 Dairy products stores [3]	14	25	23	70	3	8,870	5,086	217	412
5460 Retail bakeries [3]	121	231	992	1,829	8	10,109	10,920	11,029	21,158
5490 Miscellaneous food stores [3]	56	161	285	888	6	9,572	10,144	2,697	9,846
5510 New and used car dealers [3]	144	296	9,666	20,712	70	30,341	31,670	344,222	715,160
5520 Used car dealers [3]	50	162	165	563	3	18,788	23,425	3,745	13,982
5530 Auto and home supply stores [3]	211	437	1,931	3,884	9	17,678	19,170	39,677	76,708
5540 Gasoline service stations [3]	611	1,248	5,194	10,698	9	14,970	15,672	82,494	173,435
5550 Boat dealers [3]	15	28	46	190	7	10,174	19,326	651	4,320
5560 Recreational vehicle dealers [3]	7	16	75	86	5	17,120	18,279	1,730	1,724
5570 Motorcycle dealers [3]	13	31	93	242	8	14,968	25,752	2,078	6,797
5590 Automotive dealers, nec [3]	6	11	23	14	1	15,652	34,857	155	653
5610 Men's & boys' clothing stores [3]	105	237	1,078	2,815	12	13,269	13,695	14,533	37,846
5620 Women's clothing stores [3]	326	637	4,042	7,380	12	9,584	9,778	42,599	73,029
5630 Women's accessory & specialty stores [3]	72	152	452	1,034	7	11,929	11,652	5,666	11,843
5640 Children's and infants' wear stores [3]	49	94	428	1,126	12	7,963	8,561	3,982	10,269
5650 Family clothing stores [3]	121	288	2,938	8,403	29	11,398	12,655	34,910	110,102
5660 Shoe stores [3]	304	555	1,921	3,436	6	11,286	11,405	22,925	38,308
5690 Misc. apparel & accessory stores [3]	58	133	274	559	4	11,810	14,061	3,359	7,873
5712 Furniture stores [3]	219	488	1,864	4,603	9	18,313	19,749	40,121	94,014
5713 Floor covering stores [3]	140	304	557	1,189	4	23,993	25,450	15,331	31,077
5714 Drapery and upholstery stores [3]	22	48	145	206	4	15,807	16,214	2,464	2,904
5719 Misc. homefurnishings stores [3]	120	355	928	3,081	9	11,233	12,567	12,664	40,472
5720 Household appliance stores [3]	64	125	215	511	4	20,093	21,910	4,794	12,295
5731 Radio, TV, & electronic stores [3]	133	287	1,301	3,286	11	19,099	18,207	28,184	60,301
5734 Computer and software stores [3]	89	242	526	1,731	7	21,932	20,645	13,125	38,510
5735 Record & prerecorded tape stores [3]	86	182	627	1,246	7	9,250	10,276	6,433	11,627
5736 Musical instrument stores [3]	36	68	339	581	9	22,844	19,215	9,495	12,642
5812 Eating places [3]	2,387	5,259	43,463	101,941	19	8,537	9,546	412,447	1,035,274
5813 Drinking places [3]	95	132	902	1,012	8	7,401	8,320	7,299	8,894
5910 Drug stores and proprietary stores [3]	229	449	4,031	7,525	17	14,643	15,700	60,079	121,615
5920 Liquor stores [3]	329	406	2,380	2,790	7	12,817	12,803	31,535	36,178
5930 Used merchandise stores [3]	125	311	1,065	2,068	7	14,156	12,764	17,639	27,804
5941 Sporting goods and bicycle shops [3]	184	365	1,244	3,472	10	12,177	11,910	17,506	43,799
5942 Book stores [3]	85	220	733	1,974	9	10,587	10,847	7,799	20,823
5943 Stationery stores [3]	30	75	83	767	10	22,313	15,233	2,047	12,055
5944 Jewelry stores [3]	193	425	1,019	2,395	6	16,385	17,490	18,336	40,864
5945 Hobby, toy, and game shops [3]	64	197	1,017	2,830	14	10,144	9,487	13,631	30,923
5946 Camera & photographic supply stores [3]	19	44	104	245	6	19,731	15,739	2,031	3,981
5947 Gift, novelty, and souvenir shops [3]	209	530	1,254	3,161	6	7,589	8,440	10,692	29,449
5948 Luggage and leather goods stores [3]	17	49	69	220	4	10,899	11,164	802	2,645
5949 Sewing, needlework, and piece goods [3]	49	113	655	1,080	10	9,631	10,022	6,905	10,790
5961 Catalog and mail-order houses [3]	48	115	324	572	5	22,136	23,021	9,534	16,538
5962 Merchandising machine operators [3]	24	58	457	711	12	24,875	23,376	13,402	18,242
5963 Direct selling establishments [3]	97	324	630	2,493	8	21,721	19,034	13,711	46,946
5983 Fuel oil dealers [2]	-	48	-	145	3	-	31,531	-	3,977
5992 Florists [3]	126	318	647	1,503	5	12,971	13,019	9,074	20,545
5993 Tobacco stores and stands [2]	-	16	-	41	3	-	9,561	-	499
5994 News dealers and newsstands [2]	-	50	-	138	3	-	9,362	-	1,480
5995 Optical goods stores [3]	130	272	625	1,226	5	17,702	18,457	11,634	23,564
5999 Miscellaneous retail stores, nec [3]	333	732	2,078	4,434	6	14,768	15,365	33,090	70,564

Source: County Business Patterns 1994/95, CBP-94/95, U.S. Department of Commerce, Washington DC, November 1997. The employment column represents mid-March employment in the year. Pay per employee is calculated by dividing 1st Quarter payroll, annualized, by mid-March employment. The column headed 'Emp / Est' shows 'employees per establishment'. A dash (-) means that data are unavailable or cannot be calculated. nec means not elsewhere classified. *Notes:* 1. 1994 data incomplete; unavailable or withheld. 2. 1995 data incomplete; unavailable or withheld. 3. 1994 and 1995 data incomplete; unavailable or withheld.

WATERLOO – CEDAR FALLS, IA MSA

Wholesale and Retail Trade USA	Establishments		Employment		Emp / Est	Pay / Employee		Annual Payroll ($ 000)	
	1994	1995	1994	1995	1995	1994	1995	1994	1995
50 – Wholesale trade	224	217	2,888	2,943	14	23,284	26,082	73,929	78,955
5013 Motor vehicle supplies and new parts	14	11	100	77	7	15,600	16,883	1,578	1,239
5015 Motor vehicle parts, used	6	7	36	42	6	49,333	44,381	963	1,019
5031 Lumber, plywood, and millwork	8	7	179	163	23	24,894	27,534	4,966	4,045
5044 Office equipment	6	7	102	109	16	22,863	24,110	2,412	3,388
5045 Computers, peripherals, & software	5	5	27	25	5	20,741	29,920	697	787
5063 Electrical apparatus and equipment	7	7	66	73	10	24,909	30,849	1,666	2,018
5072 Hardware	-	6	-	58	10	-	30,069	-	1,836
5074 Plumbing & hydronic heating supplies	8	7	67	67	10	21,134	21,970	1,621	1,572
5075 Warm air heating & air conditioning	-	5	-	24	5	-	26,167	-	611
5083 Farm and garden machinery	9	6	107	97	16	20,374	27,876	2,688	2,666
5084 Industrial machinery and equipment	16	15	206	218	15	21,534	22,550	4,904	5,229
5085 Industrial supplies	10	10	120	135	14	33,067	37,452	3,891	4,386
5091 Sporting & recreational goods	5	6	43	45	8	34,512	55,644	1,515	1,873
5093 Scrap and waste materials	10	11	103	94	9	21,592	30,681	2,632	2,750
5099 Durable goods, nec	-	4	-	7	2	-	13,143	-	328
5110 Paper and paper products	7	6	122	126	21	23,246	23,333	2,949	2,648
5149 Groceries and related products, nec	-	5	-	286	57	-	27,287	-	8,824
5153 Grain and field beans	14	-	202	-	-	24,277	-	5,431	-
5169 Chemicals & allied products, nec	-	3	-	10	3	-	14,000	-	193
5170 Petroleum and petroleum products	9	7	62	57	8	23,548	24,842	1,607	1,399
5181 Beer and ale	3	3	130	101	34	21,200	21,545	3,296	2,495
5191 Farm supplies	8	8	104	108	14	23,846	25,889	2,736	2,988
5192 Books, periodicals, & newspapers	3	3	41	21	7	5,854	12,000	243	250
5193 Flowers & florists' supplies	-	4	-	93	23	-	15,355	-	1,298
5199 Nondurable goods, nec	4	4	6	9	2	14,000	12,889	101	127
52 – Retail trade	856	841	12,424	13,099	16	10,232	11,041	139,054	151,934
5210 Lumber and other building materials	13	13	271	348	27	16,000	18,368	4,793	6,410
5230 Paint, glass, and wallpaper stores	8	-	37	-	-	13,730	-	528	-
5250 Hardware stores	11	9	98	71	8	8,653	10,028	968	768
5260 Retail nurseries and garden stores	5	6	41	40	7	9,951	10,900	457	493
5310 Department stores	11	11	1,600	1,600	145	10,140	11,715	18,199	18,751
5410 Grocery stores	63	57	1,856	1,959	34	9,369	9,940	18,329	19,583
5440 Candy, nut, and confectionery stores	5	3	17	13	4	5,176	5,231	79	62
5460 Retail bakeries	12	13	104	117	9	8,500	7,863	948	962
5490 Miscellaneous food stores	5	4	21	24	6	11,810	10,000	217	214
5510 New and used car dealers	17	17	748	785	46	24,872	26,023	21,489	22,088
5520 Used car dealers	14	14	42	40	3	13,333	13,900	598	583
5530 Auto and home supply stores	20	21	195	204	10	16,062	16,667	3,603	3,715
5540 Gasoline service stations	57	57	461	479	8	10,308	11,190	5,154	5,624
5550 Boat dealers	-	3	-	19	6	-	14,947	-	342
5570 Motorcycle dealers	3	3	35	47	16	11,886	12,596	563	764
5610 Men's & boys' clothing stores	6	6	47	49	8	15,149	13,224	590	589
5620 Women's clothing stores	28	25	259	210	8	8,046	7,733	2,154	1,603
5630 Women's accessory & specialty stores	5	6	19	23	4	10,105	9,739	204	230
5650 Family clothing stores	9	10	71	65	7	7,155	8,062	493	551
5660 Shoe stores	20	17	106	107	6	11,887	11,178	1,297	1,104
5712 Furniture stores	17	21	163	168	8	15,804	17,429	2,938	3,225
5713 Floor covering stores	8	9	48	55	6	16,167	20,945	1,039	1,498
5719 Misc. homefurnishings stores	6	6	24	25	4	7,667	8,000	207	259
5720 Household appliance stores	8	8	41	118	15	16,683	14,746	1,100	1,620
5734 Computer and software stores	7	8	36	56	7	13,556	13,357	553	885
5735 Record & prerecorded tape stores	6	-	33	-	-	10,545	-	340	-
5812 Eating places	190	181	3,951	4,073	23	6,565	7,034	27,777	31,002
5813 Drinking places	65	53	385	396	7	4,862	4,687	2,013	1,925
5910 Drug stores and proprietary stores	15	14	223	237	17	16,359	16,034	3,773	3,887
5920 Liquor stores	5	-	15	-	-	11,467	-	169	-
5930 Used merchandise stores	19	17	84	81	5	6,952	7,704	683	715
5941 Sporting goods and bicycle shops	18	17	173	175	10	13,410	14,560	1,933	2,195
5942 Book stores	11	8	96	95	12	10,958	11,032	1,163	1,180
5944 Jewelry stores	22	22	111	127	6	11,279	14,268	1,567	1,868
5945 Hobby, toy, and game shops	9	8	47	86	11	7,915	8,372	399	810
5947 Gift, novelty, and souvenir shops	27	26	138	162	6	6,377	6,617	1,059	1,034
5949 Sewing, needlework, and piece goods	3	3	42	32	11	7,238	9,750	310	304
5961 Catalog and mail-order houses	5	4	64	85	21	19,250	20,706	1,554	1,608
5980 Fuel dealers	3	4	22	24	6	25,091	25,833	555	631
5992 Florists	15	15	76	92	6	9,842	9,522	783	895
5995 Optical goods stores	11	10	60	40	4	11,400	12,300	641	543
5999 Miscellaneous retail stores, nec	23	25	125	170	7	17,280	16,212	2,232	2,884

Source: County Business Patterns 1994/95, CBP-94/95, U.S. Department of Commerce, Washington DC, November 1997. The employment column represents mid-March employment in the year. Pay per employee is calculated by dividing 1st Quarter payroll, annualized, by mid-March employment. The column headed 'Emp / Est' shows 'employees per establishment'. A dash (-) means that data are unavailable or cannot be calculated. nec means not elsewhere classified. *Notes:* 1. 1994 data incomplete; unavailable or withheld. 2. 1995 data incomplete; unavailable or withheld. 3. 1994 and 1995 data incomplete; unavailable or withheld.

WAUSAU, WI MSA

Wholesale and Retail Trade USA	Establishments		Employment		Emp / Est	Pay / Employee		Annual Payroll ($ 000)	
	1994	1995	1994	1995	1995	1994	1995	1994	1995
50 – Wholesale trade	-	293	-	4,569	16	-	24,363	-	121,285
5012 Automobiles and other vehicles	-	5	-	180	36	-	19,600	-	3,386
5013 Motor vehicle supplies and new parts	-	14	-	99	7	-	22,101	-	2,040
5014 Tires and tubes	-	4	-	28	7	-	24,571	-	588
5015 Motor vehicle parts, used	-	4	-	29	7	-	19,172	-	553
5020 Furniture and homefurnishings	-	6	-	31	5	-	21,806	-	732
5031 Lumber, plywood, and millwork	-	13	-	172	13	-	19,512	-	3,692
5032 Brick, stone, & related materials	-	4	-	24	6	-	15,500	-	808
5033 Roofing, siding, & insulation	-	4	-	74	19	-	32,378	-	2,609
5039 Construction materials, nec	-	6	-	197	33	-	28,731	-	5,940
5044 Office equipment	-	10	-	245	25	-	17,192	-	4,433
5045 Computers, peripherals, & software	-	11	-	179	16	-	37,587	-	7,204
5051 Metals service centers and offices	-	6	-	173	29	-	30,613	-	5,468
5063 Electrical apparatus and equipment	-	6	-	88	15	-	33,773	-	2,983
5065 Electronic parts and equipment	-	9	-	60	7	-	23,333	-	1,537
5072 Hardware	-	3	-	11	4	-	34,182	-	344
5074 Plumbing & hydronic heating supplies	-	8	-	109	14	-	32,147	-	3,639
5082 Construction and mining machinery	-	5	-	69	14	-	27,188	-	2,247
5083 Farm and garden machinery	-	18	-	139	8	-	22,043	-	3,497
5084 Industrial machinery and equipment	-	17	-	226	13	-	23,540	-	5,746
5085 Industrial supplies	-	13	-	106	8	-	30,377	-	3,324
5087 Service establishment equipment	-	5	-	66	13	-	27,576	-	2,081
5093 Scrap and waste materials	-	9	-	138	15	-	9,420	-	1,686
5110 Paper and paper products	-	6	-	81	14	-	24,395	-	2,208
5149 Groceries and related products, nec	-	17	-	244	14	-	23,541	-	7,101
5160 Chemicals and allied products	-	4	-	36	9	-	28,111	-	1,130
5171 Petroleum bulk stations & terminals	-	7	-	47	7	-	29,617	-	1,580
5181 Beer and ale	-	3	-	77	26	-	27,844	-	2,418
5191 Farm supplies	-	19	-	209	11	-	20,153	-	4,630
52 – Retail trade	-	716	-	10,981	15	-	10,694	-	126,894
5210 Lumber and other building materials	-	16	-	262	16	-	17,802	-	4,721
5230 Paint, glass, and wallpaper stores	-	3	-	18	6	-	22,667	-	335
5250 Hardware stores	-	8	-	65	8	-	11,323	-	798
5260 Retail nurseries and garden stores	-	7	-	38	5	-	9,579	-	464
5270 Mobile home dealers	-	6	-	43	7	-	19,349	-	1,113
5310 Department stores	-	10	-	1,310	131	-	11,685	-	15,308
5410 Grocery stores	-	29	-	1,325	46	-	9,820	-	13,708
5420 Meat and fish markets	-	3	-	29	10	-	10,897	-	340
5440 Candy, nut, and confectionery stores	-	4	-	15	4	-	5,067	-	98
5460 Retail bakeries	-	8	-	42	5	-	8,095	-	366
5510 New and used car dealers	-	18	-	528	29	-	24,523	-	14,967
5520 Used car dealers	-	4	-	5	1	-	12,800	-	119
5530 Auto and home supply stores	-	11	-	99	9	-	15,475	-	1,676
5540 Gasoline service stations	-	55	-	446	8	-	10,583	-	4,981
5570 Motorcycle dealers	-	4	-	13	3	-	16,308	-	372
5610 Men's & boys' clothing stores	-	7	-	25	4	-	15,680	-	578
5620 Women's clothing stores	-	24	-	213	9	-	6,817	-	1,562
5630 Women's accessory & specialty stores	-	4	-	13	3	-	12,308	-	155
5650 Family clothing stores	-	7	-	67	10	-	5,731	-	412
5660 Shoe stores	-	19	-	125	7	-	9,120	-	1,227
5690 Misc. apparel & accessory stores	-	4	-	42	11	-	12,476	-	529
5712 Furniture stores	-	15	-	145	10	-	24,414	-	3,712
5713 Floor covering stores	-	7	-	39	6	-	14,872	-	607
5719 Misc. homefurnishings stores	-	8	-	41	5	-	9,561	-	443
5720 Household appliance stores	-	9	-	32	4	-	13,250	-	589
5731 Radio, TV, & electronic stores	-	6	-	30	5	-	12,533	-	322
5734 Computer and software stores	-	4	-	15	4	-	13,867	-	148
5812 Eating places	-	140	-	3,411	24	-	6,425	-	22,047
5813 Drinking places	-	55	-	221	4	-	5,394	-	1,189
5910 Drug stores and proprietary stores	-	14	-	124	9	-	16,581	-	2,193
5930 Used merchandise stores	-	8	-	38	5	-	13,684	-	570
5941 Sporting goods and bicycle shops	-	11	-	44	4	-	12,000	-	551
5942 Book stores	-	6	-	49	8	-	9,469	-	464
5944 Jewelry stores	-	14	-	79	6	-	12,861	-	1,085
5945 Hobby, toy, and game shops	-	6	-	21	4	-	8,762	-	257
5947 Gift, novelty, and souvenir shops	-	14	-	73	5	-	6,356	-	526
5949 Sewing, needlework, and piece goods	-	6	-	34	6	-	4,353	-	171
5961 Catalog and mail-order houses	-	6	-	747	125	-	11,052	-	11,433
5962 Merchandising machine operators	-	5	-	47	9	-	33,957	-	1,390
5963 Direct selling establishments	-	10	-	64	6	-	20,750	-	1,249
5980 Fuel dealers	-	5	-	49	10	-	23,755	-	1,127

Continued on next page.

WAUSAU, WI MSA - [continued]

Wholesale and Retail Trade USA	Establishments		Employment		Emp / Est	Pay / Employee		Annual Payroll ($ 000)	
	1994	1995	1994	1995	1995	1994	1995	1994	1995
5992 Florists	-	12	-	55	5	-	6,545	-	365
5999 Miscellaneous retail stores, nec	-	25	-	134	5	-	13,343	-	1,869

Source: County Business Patterns 1994/95, CBP-94/95, U.S. Department of Commerce, Washington DC, November 1997. The employment column represents mid-March employment in the year. Pay per employee is calculated by dividing 1st Quarter payroll, annualized, by mid-March employment. The column headed 'Emp / Est' shows 'employees per establishment'. A dash (-) means that data are unavailable or cannot be calculated. nec means not elsewhere classified. *Notes:* 1. 1994 data incomplete; unavailable or withheld. 2. 1995 data incomplete; unavailable or withheld. 3. 1994 and 1995 data incomplete; unavailable or withheld.

WEST PALM BEACH – BOCA RATON, FL MSA

Wholesale and Retail Trade USA	Establishments		Employment		Emp / Est	Pay / Employee		Annual Payroll ($ 000)	
	1994	1995	1994	1995	1995	1994	1995	1994	1995
50– Wholesale trade	2,203	2,269	21,278	23,082	10	37,479	39,393	850,830	904,933
5012 Automobiles and other vehicles	49	45	581	570	13	21,411	20,723	13,563	14,257
5013 Motor vehicle supplies and new parts	83	82	639	603	7	18,967	22,023	13,374	13,328
5014 Tires and tubes	21	19	144	131	7	27,000	29,069	3,930	4,056
5015 Motor vehicle parts, used	13	20	120	152	8	18,333	17,474	2,375	2,757
5021 Furniture	71	75	301	297	4	25,993	29,212	8,436	8,401
5023 Homefurnishings	64	58	290	246	4	23,917	21,821	7,665	5,937
5031 Lumber, plywood, and millwork	34	38	360	346	9	26,167	29,954	10,302	10,628
5032 Brick, stone, & related materials	24	29	179	184	6	31,039	28,565	5,690	5,171
5033 Roofing, siding, & insulation	10	14	90	124	9	27,289	27,677	2,552	3,398
5039 Construction materials, nec	23	42	121	437	10	25,025	26,352	3,852	12,533
5043 Photographic equipment & supplies	5	-	18	-	-	50,444	-	1,150	-
5044 Office equipment	34	33	500	454	14	34,088	39,233	16,933	16,587
5045 Computers, peripherals, & software	93	88	4,290	3,508	40	66,608	66,165	278,926	204,028
5046 Commercial equipment, nec	26	23	189	186	8	21,291	25,828	4,223	5,469
5047 Medical and hospital equipment	74	65	538	636	10	36,015	41,748	20,913	30,879
5048 Ophthalmic goods	9	-	151	-	-	73,934	-	10,774	-
5049 Professional equipment, nec	8	10	41	65	7	19,024	53,231	974	2,414
5051 Metals service centers and offices	32	34	204	253	7	34,922	40,348	9,347	11,934
5052 Coal and other minerals and ores	5	3	18	17	6	45,556	48,000	1,214	1,641
5063 Electrical apparatus and equipment	77	70	521	577	8	29,029	32,132	16,656	19,095
5064 Electrical appliances, TV & radios	16	19	159	162	9	40,277	44,272	6,637	7,826
5065 Electronic parts and equipment	91	95	887	672	7	35,067	33,887	31,246	23,855
5072 Hardware	25	29	197	232	8	30,741	29,741	6,471	7,578
5074 Plumbing & hydronic heating supplies	39	43	235	295	7	28,391	30,739	7,059	9,319
5075 Warm air heating & air conditioning	19	18	103	100	6	29,864	31,960	3,693	3,599
5078 Refrigeration equipment and supplies	8	7	37	36	5	27,243	31,778	1,341	1,436
5082 Construction and mining machinery	10	10	164	181	18	29,195	28,685	5,518	6,776
5083 Farm and garden machinery	28	27	344	341	13	27,349	28,880	10,935	10,162
5084 Industrial machinery and equipment	64	71	1,254	1,147	16	37,748	50,389	51,076	57,453
5085 Industrial supplies	30	35	140	167	5	23,657	27,186	3,581	4,534
5087 Service establishment equipment	31	31	206	220	7	19,825	21,145	5,143	5,170
5088 Transportation equipment & supplies	37	36	651	597	17	44,492	45,688	28,463	28,828
5091 Sporting & recreational goods	28	31	101	137	4	18,178	23,620	2,207	3,119
5092 Toys and hobby goods and supplies	16	17	34	40	2	26,706	24,800	1,098	1,543
5093 Scrap and waste materials	32	32	206	222	7	25,262	23,532	6,208	6,573
5094 Jewelry & precious stones	56	52	134	154	3	26,896	31,351	5,306	8,093
5099 Durable goods, nec	42	49	133	227	5	25,925	25,568	3,837	7,016
5111 Printing and writing paper	12	12	56	73	6	33,571	35,616	1,926	2,632
5112 Stationery and office supplies	43	37	542	522	14	17,306	16,713	9,908	9,529
5113 Industrial & personal service paper	17	16	107	134	8	22,766	28,269	2,887	3,895
5120 Drugs, proprietaries, and sundries	53	60	278	422	7	54,518	36,626	18,699	15,943
5131 Piece goods & notions	14	17	18	27	2	13,778	17,185	454	480
5136 Men's and boys' clothing	25	21	93	100	5	15,226	19,960	1,892	2,091
5137 Women's and children's clothing	36	39	260	158	4	19,169	22,962	4,458	4,935
5139 Footwear	8	8	24	43	5	52,000	40,930	1,148	1,808
5141 Groceries, general line	25	22	613	636	29	41,214	47,296	46,623	41,869
5142 Packaged frozen food	16	16	184	370	23	33,130	22,778	6,427	8,540
5143 Dairy products, exc. dried or canned	12	14	164	134	10	30,659	36,776	4,485	4,685
5144 Poultry and poultry products	3	-	133	-	-	19,850	-	2,949	-
5145 Confectionery	13	13	28	48	4	22,143	33,083	1,030	1,979
5146 Fish and seafoods	15	14	97	94	7	17,938	20,426	1,554	1,844
5147 Meats and meat products	20	19	104	111	6	36,154	26,486	3,428	3,075
5148 Fresh fruits and vegetables	45	44	774	754	17	18,171	19,416	16,275	16,367
5149 Groceries and related products, nec	64	56	896	832	15	35,205	38,370	32,103	32,438
5150 Farm-product raw materials	4	-	36	-	-	27,667	-	1,128	-
5162 Plastics materials & basic shapes	9	9	60	42	5	35,867	41,048	2,014	1,855
5169 Chemicals & allied products, nec	52	50	204	233	5	42,510	40,532	8,468	9,847

Continued on next page.

WEST PALM BEACH – BOCA RATON, FL MSA - [continued]

Wholesale and Retail Trade USA	Establishments		Employment		Emp / Est	Pay / Employee		Annual Payroll ($ 000)	
	1994	1995	1994	1995	1995	1994	1995	1994	1995
5171 Petroleum bulk stations & terminals	17	12	168	123	10	26,881	29,041	4,912	3,594
5172 Petroleum products, nec	8	7	26	20	3	32,308	32,600	810	306
5181 Beer and ale	5	-	357	-	-	33,479	-	13,685	-
5182 Wine and distilled beverages	9	-	73	-	-	37,205	-	3,192	-
5191 Farm supplies	39	32	159	127	4	25,887	23,622	4,409	2,985
5192 Books, periodicals, & newspapers	16	14	183	149	11	38,317	49,074	7,164	7,410
5193 Flowers & florists' supplies	40	34	425	316	9	14,955	14,089	6,883	4,820
5194 Tobacco and tobacco products	4	4	19	29	7	14,737	17,793	477	490
5198 Paints, varnishes, and supplies	17	18	138	141	8	27,362	30,610	3,838	3,895
5199 Nondurable goods, nec	101	95	360	370	4	17,856	20,130	8,065	8,063
52 – Retail trade	6,899	6,857	91,970	91,622	13	14,410	14,923	1,356,432	1,354,994
5210 Lumber and other building materials	91	66	1,955	1,855	28	20,252	20,209	42,413	38,867
5230 Paint, glass, and wallpaper stores	47	41	163	175	4	20,245	22,057	3,459	3,796
5250 Hardware stores	47	31	318	234	8	17,874	18,274	6,083	4,556
5260 Retail nurseries and garden stores	44	43	138	179	4	15,768	13,855	2,059	2,431
5270 Mobile home dealers	8	8	19	19	2	17,895	19,789	429	435
5310 Department stores	43	44	7,822	7,984	181	12,784	13,828	103,589	108,709
5330 Variety stores	27	29	317	341	12	10,549	9,572	3,760	3,560
5390 Misc. general merchandise stores	29	33	1,381	1,384	42	16,104	18,679	23,177	24,166
5410 Grocery stores	423	417	12,847	13,153	32	12,873	13,135	163,948	171,809
5420 Meat and fish markets	41	38	370	419	11	10,573	14,291	3,985	5,104
5430 Fruit and vegetable markets	22	24	184	211	9	12,109	12,171	2,266	2,615
5440 Candy, nut, and confectionery stores	25	22	156	179	8	9,231	8,291	1,406	1,332
5450 Dairy products stores	6	8	21	20	3	3,048	5,400	91	121
5460 Retail bakeries	75	75	587	590	8	8,831	9,573	5,058	5,197
5490 Miscellaneous food stores	60	71	286	446	6	10,671	12,233	3,458	5,609
5510 New and used car dealers	63	61	4,050	4,356	71	36,207	36,103	157,871	163,797
5520 Used car dealers	50	46	291	295	6	20,715	21,220	6,986	6,258
5530 Auto and home supply stores	135	139	903	960	7	20,625	22,375	19,181	22,082
5540 Gasoline service stations	319	302	2,040	1,982	7	12,431	13,873	26,205	26,605
5550 Boat dealers	42	44	194	208	5	19,299	20,577	4,298	4,783
5560 Recreational vehicle dealers	5	8	28	37	5	21,286	20,108	679	782
5570 Motorcycle dealers	10	11	55	63	6	16,873	18,921	1,285	1,406
5590 Automotive dealers, nec	9	9	47	59	7	22,213	25,627	1,352	1,580
5610 Men's & boys' clothing stores	78	70	489	475	7	13,145	13,078	6,377	6,347
5620 Women's clothing stores	330	301	2,899	2,623	9	14,466	15,204	39,033	36,383
5630 Women's accessory & specialty stores	63	63	339	313	5	11,493	13,482	4,055	3,873
5640 Children's and infants' wear stores	27	25	254	215	9	9,984	11,460	2,543	2,876
5650 Family clothing stores	99	93	1,512	1,396	15	10,960	12,281	16,661	16,964
5660 Shoe stores	175	170	842	877	5	14,014	13,966	11,639	12,104
5690 Misc. apparel & accessory stores	67	69	284	290	4	11,563	11,766	3,432	3,325
5712 Furniture stores	253	239	1,447	1,517	6	23,124	23,546	34,240	34,910
5713 Floor covering stores	83	79	296	261	3	18,149	21,824	5,328	5,619
5714 Drapery and upholstery stores	28	28	199	195	7	15,377	20,000	3,329	3,174
5719 Misc. homefurnishings stores	160	154	1,011	979	6	13,298	13,209	13,258	12,707
5720 Household appliance stores	26	27	129	136	5	18,481	17,735	2,393	2,816
5731 Radio, TV, & electronic stores	77	78	633	660	8	20,006	21,891	12,642	16,355
5734 Computer and software stores	44	45	260	300	7	15,508	19,427	4,661	6,724
5735 Record & prerecorded tape stores	33	29	211	204	7	8,701	10,098	1,986	2,246
5736 Musical instrument stores	14	14	64	59	4	18,688	19,729	1,233	1,217
5812 Eating places	1,391	1,212	30,215	28,121	23	10,160	10,802	283,985	274,380
5813 Drinking places	94	84	844	689	8	9,564	11,048	7,949	8,581
5910 Drug stores and proprietary stores	165	162	2,632	2,536	16	15,587	17,833	43,956	45,740
5920 Liquor stores	82	80	358	333	4	11,587	12,721	4,180	4,295
5930 Used merchandise stores	147	147	497	567	4	14,141	14,991	8,005	9,634
5941 Sporting goods and bicycle shops	145	150	620	746	5	15,084	15,646	11,200	12,550
5942 Book stores	48	41	401	448	11	9,556	10,634	4,158	4,799
5943 Stationery stores	18	19	62	71	4	13,355	15,662	909	1,110
5944 Jewelry stores	194	182	807	786	4	20,902	23,293	17,043	17,270
5945 Hobby, toy, and game shops	37	36	425	517	14	11,228	9,950	5,534	5,900
5946 Camera & photographic supply stores	13	13	77	116	9	18,545	18,000	1,746	2,008
5947 Gift, novelty, and souvenir shops	156	144	845	831	6	8,852	9,006	7,684	7,733
5948 Luggage and leather goods stores	21	20	100	99	5	14,520	14,343	1,459	1,356
5949 Sewing, needlework, and piece goods	35	33	215	247	7	9,433	9,862	2,146	2,318
5961 Catalog and mail-order houses	34	42	1,073	1,293	31	20,917	24,189	26,253	35,179
5962 Merchandising machine operators	18	21	23	40	2	15,478	15,300	403	632
5963 Direct selling establishments	60	54	730	686	13	12,132	12,111	8,580	7,455
5980 Fuel dealers	10	11	101	132	12	19,406	22,939	2,543	3,357
5992 Florists	108	104	483	499	5	13,391	13,820	6,136	6,607
5993 Tobacco stores and stands	5	7	31	30	4	8,258	9,200	409	469
5994 News dealers and newsstands	9	9	30	69	8	12,400	10,319	472	841

Continued on next page.

WEST PALM BEACH – BOCA RATON, FL MSA - [continued]

Wholesale and Retail Trade USA	Establishments		Employment		Emp / Est	Pay / Employee		Annual Payroll ($ 000)	
	1994	1995	1994	1995	1995	1994	1995	1994	1995
5995 Optical goods stores	110	113	503	573	5	16,922	16,140	8,612	10,167
5999 Miscellaneous retail stores, nec	322	338	1,220	1,368	4	16,089	17,158	21,770	23,730

Source: County Business Patterns 1994/95, CBP-94/95, U.S. Department of Commerce, Washington DC, November 1997. The employment column represents mid-March employment in the year. Pay per employee is calculated by dividing 1st Quarter payroll, annualized, by mid-March employment. The column headed 'Emp / Est' shows 'employees per establishment'. A dash (-) means that data are unavailable or cannot be calculated. nec means not elsewhere classified. *Notes:* 1. 1994 data incomplete; unavailable or withheld. 2. 1995 data incomplete; unavailable or withheld. 3. 1994 and 1995 data incomplete; unavailable or withheld.

WHEELING MSA (OH PART)

Wholesale and Retail Trade USA	Establishments		Employment		Emp / Est	Pay / Employee		Annual Payroll ($ 000)	
	1994	1995	1994	1995	1995	1994	1995	1994	1995
50- Wholesale trade	83	83	705	734	9	20,579	22,654	15,500	16,532
5013 Motor vehicle supplies and new parts	11	11	101	97	9	26,535	26,680	2,065	1,913
5044 Office equipment	5	5	17	8	2	16,471	26,500	304	209
5050 Metals and minerals, except petroleum	5	5	25	34	7	38,720	33,882	1,245	1,235
5070 Hardware, plumbing & heating equipment	-	5	-	91	18	-	34,725	-	2,952
5087 Service establishment equipment	-	3	-	15	5	-	14,667	-	276
5093 Scrap and waste materials	-	3	-	22	7	-	15,091	-	309
5140 Groceries and related products	-	9	-	116	13	-	14,897	-	1,896
5170 Petroleum and petroleum products	-	6	-	49	8	-	20,245	-	862
5191 Farm supplies	-	3	-	37	12	-	15,676	-	602
52- Retail trade	498	501	6,035	6,026	12	9,831	10,795	67,266	69,655
5210 Lumber and other building materials	8	6	86	58	10	14,047	18,966	1,287	1,061
5250 Hardware stores	8	9	55	51	6	10,764	10,824	748	694
5260 Retail nurseries and garden stores	5	4	25	17	4	7,520	12,471	240	239
5310 Department stores	6	6	932	857	143	8,464	10,432	8,935	9,715
5410 Grocery stores	38	39	1,191	1,241	32	10,186	10,221	12,969	13,323
5460 Retail bakeries	4	6	16	14	2	5,000	6,857	97	108
5510 New and used car dealers	9	9	304	287	32	17,408	20,070	6,355	6,047
5520 Used car dealers	14	14	39	54	4	14,564	13,926	712	807
5530 Auto and home supply stores	9	12	57	54	5	16,982	19,556	1,094	1,122
5540 Gasoline service stations	54	54	249	242	4	8,835	9,140	2,327	2,303
5610 Men's & boys' clothing stores	5	5	30	23	5	5,600	6,261	165	253
5620 Women's clothing stores	18	16	183	146	9	6,776	6,521	1,331	949
5630 Women's accessory & specialty stores	3	3	12	11	4	8,333	9,455	96	90
5650 Family clothing stores	12	12	118	125	10	8,305	7,840	1,334	970
5660 Shoe stores	18	14	67	63	5	10,806	10,476	811	618
5690 Misc. apparel & accessory stores	3	-	8	-	-	10,500	-	85	-
5712 Furniture stores	-	7	-	50	7	-	16,720	-	1,063
5713 Floor covering stores	5	-	35	-	-	10,514	-	504	-
5731 Radio, TV, & electronic stores	4	5	24	29	6	18,333	27,034	390	1,202
5735 Record & prerecorded tape stores	-	4	-	21	5	-	11,810	-	214
5812 Eating places	102	94	1,400	1,463	16	6,909	7,005	11,602	11,723
5813 Drinking places	24	21	53	64	3	5,887	5,813	357	368
5910 Drug stores and proprietary stores	17	16	230	217	14	12,104	13,493	3,053	3,097
5920 Liquor stores	7	7	26	29	4	11,692	12,552	343	386
5941 Sporting goods and bicycle shops	-	5	-	16	3	-	8,250	-	149
5944 Jewelry stores	8	10	54	49	5	12,741	14,857	662	644
5945 Hobby, toy, and game shops	6	7	102	91	13	9,804	11,121	1,103	1,195
5947 Gift, novelty, and souvenir shops	10	9	38	43	5	6,105	6,884	299	367
5949 Sewing, needlework, and piece goods	3	-	12	-	-	7,667	-	73	-
5960 Nonstore retailers	-	6	-	53	9	-	11,547	-	704
5980 Fuel dealers	4	5	22	23	5	20,545	19,304	406	436
5992 Florists	8	-	17	-	-	6,118	-	159	-
5995 Optical goods stores	7	7	35	33	5	14,629	18,909	547	608
5999 Miscellaneous retail stores, nec	-	11	-	33	3	-	9,333	-	320

Source: County Business Patterns 1994/95, CBP-94/95, U.S. Department of Commerce, Washington DC, November 1997. The employment column represents mid-March employment in the year. Pay per employee is calculated by dividing 1st Quarter payroll, annualized, by mid-March employment. The column headed 'Emp / Est' shows 'employees per establishment'. A dash (-) means that data are unavailable or cannot be calculated. nec means not elsewhere classified. *Notes:* 1. 1994 data incomplete; unavailable or withheld. 2. 1995 data incomplete; unavailable or withheld. 3. 1994 and 1995 data incomplete; unavailable or withheld.

WHEELING MSA (WV PART)

Wholesale and Retail Trade USA	Establishments		Employment		Emp / Est	Pay / Employee		Annual Payroll ($ 000)	
	1994	1995	1994	1995	1995	1994	1995	1994	1995
50- Wholesale trade	-	150	-	2,101	14	-	21,782	-	48,477
5013 Motor vehicle supplies and new parts	-	9	-	97	11	-	23,794	-	2,242

Continued on next page.

WHEELING MSA (WV PART) - [continued]

Wholesale and Retail Trade USA	Establishments		Employment		Emp / Est	Pay / Employee		Annual Payroll ($ 000)	
	1994	1995	1994	1995	1995	1994	1995	1994	1995
5020 Furniture and homefurnishings	-	8	-	68	9	-	18,471	-	1,371
5046 Commercial equipment, nec [2]	-	3	-	22	7	-	19,636	-	448
5063 Electrical apparatus and equipment	-	9	-	56	6	-	32,643	-	1,811
5074 Plumbing & hydronic heating supplies	-	5	-	41	8	-	15,902	-	734
5075 Warm air heating & air conditioning [2]	-	3	-	29	10	-	21,655	-	674
5085 Industrial supplies [2]	-	6	-	96	16	-	30,417	-	3,053
5087 Service establishment equipment [2]	-	4	-	15	4	-	15,733	-	272
5093 Scrap and waste materials	-	8	-	19	2	-	26,526	-	500
5110 Paper and paper products	-	8	-	53	7	-	21,358	-	1,324
5149 Groceries and related products, nec [2]	-	6	-	70	12	-	24,229	-	1,643
5170 Petroleum and petroleum products	-	8	-	105	13	-	17,295	-	1,721
5181 Beer and ale [2]	-	3	-	40	13	-	35,200	-	1,528
5190 Misc., nondurable goods	-	10	-	135	14	-	27,141	-	3,433
52- Retail trade	-	546	-	6,762	12	-	11,503	-	81,139
5210 Lumber and other building materials	-	7	-	97	14	-	20,000	-	2,059
5230 Paint, glass, and wallpaper stores	-	5	-	13	3	-	15,385	-	225
5260 Retail nurseries and garden stores	-	6	-	44	7	-	8,182	-	460
5310 Department stores [2]	-	4	-	279	70	-	9,978	-	2,925
5410 Grocery stores	-	56	-	1,207	22	-	9,674	-	12,211
5510 New and used car dealers	-	13	-	333	26	-	20,781	-	7,603
5520 Used car dealers	-	6	-	5	1	-	24,000	-	129
5530 Auto and home supply stores	-	22	-	194	9	-	18,206	-	4,101
5540 Gasoline service stations	-	30	-	317	11	-	11,256	-	3,776
5620 Women's clothing stores	-	7	-	64	9	-	4,375	-	335
5660 Shoe stores	-	8	-	21	3	-	9,524	-	227
5690 Misc. apparel & accessory stores	-	4	-	11	3	-	6,182	-	78
5712 Furniture stores	-	12	-	140	12	-	17,514	-	2,599
5713 Floor covering stores	-	8	-	71	9	-	9,803	-	650
5719 Misc. homefurnishings stores [2]	-	3	-	22	7	-	8,727	-	224
5731 Radio, TV, & electronic stores	-	9	-	25	3	-	12,320	-	314
5736 Musical instrument stores [2]	-	5	-	38	8	-	9,263	-	366
5812 Eating places	-	121	-	2,248	19	-	7,530	-	17,512
5813 Drinking places	-	46	-	156	3	-	5,949	-	940
5910 Drug stores and proprietary stores	-	21	-	198	9	-	14,061	-	3,112
5930 Used merchandise stores	-	10	-	28	3	-	12,714	-	378
5941 Sporting goods and bicycle shops	-	6	-	9	2	-	8,889	-	71
5942 Book stores [2]	-	4	-	31	8	-	9,548	-	322
5944 Jewelry stores	-	9	-	23	3	-	16,348	-	386
5947 Gift, novelty, and souvenir shops	-	13	-	65	5	-	9,662	-	721
5962 Merchandising machine operators [2]	-	3	-	19	6	-	12,000	-	234
5963 Direct selling establishments	-	6	-	25	4	-	19,200	-	638
5992 Florists	-	9	-	27	3	-	9,037	-	255
5999 Miscellaneous retail stores, nec	-	14	-	57	4	-	13,123	-	845

Source: County Business Patterns 1994/95, CBP-94/95, U.S. Department of Commerce, Washington DC, November 1997. The employment column represents mid-March employment in the year. Pay per employee is calculated by dividing 1st Quarter payroll, annualized, by mid-March employment. The column headed 'Emp / Est' shows 'employees per establishment'. A dash (-) means that data are unavailable or cannot be calculated. nec means not elsewhere classified. *Notes:* 1. 1994 data incomplete; unavailable or withheld. 2. 1995 data incomplete; unavailable or withheld. 3. 1994 and 1995 data incomplete; unavailable or withheld.

WHEELING, WV - OH MSA

Wholesale and Retail Trade USA	Establishments		Employment		Emp / Est	Pay / Employee		Annual Payroll ($ 000)	
	1994	1995	1994	1995	1995	1994	1995	1994	1995
50- Wholesale trade [1]	83	233	705	2,835	12	20,579	22,008	15,500	65,009
5013 Motor vehicle supplies and new parts [1]	11	20	101	194	10	26,535	25,237	2,065	4,155
5020 Furniture and homefurnishings	-	9	-	68	8	-	18,471	-	1,371
5044 Office equipment [3]	5	11	17	8	1	16,471	26,500	304	209
5046 Commercial equipment, nec [2]	-	3	-	22	7	-	19,636	-	448
5050 Metals and minerals, except petroleum [3]	5	7	25	34	5	38,720	33,882	1,245	1,235
5063 Electrical apparatus and equipment [2]	-	9	-	56	6	-	32,643	-	1,811
5074 Plumbing & hydronic heating supplies	-	8	-	41	5	-	15,902	-	734
5075 Warm air heating & air conditioning [2]	-	3	-	29	10	-	21,655	-	674
5085 Industrial supplies [2]	-	9	-	96	11	-	30,417	-	3,053
5087 Service establishment equipment [2]	-	7	-	30	4	-	15,200	-	548
5093 Scrap and waste materials	-	11	-	41	4	-	20,390	-	809
5110 Paper and paper products	-	12	-	53	4	-	21,358	-	1,324
5149 Groceries and related products, nec [2]	-	6	-	70	12	-	24,229	-	1,643
5170 Petroleum and petroleum products	-	14	-	154	11	-	18,234	-	2,583
5181 Beer and ale [2]	-	5	-	40	8	-	35,200	-	1,528
5191 Farm supplies [2]	-	4	-	37	9	-	15,676	-	602

Continued on next page.

WHEELING, WV - OH MSA - [continued]

Wholesale and Retail Trade USA	Establishments		Employment		Emp / Est	Pay / Employee		Annual Payroll ($ 000)	
	1994	1995	1994	1995	1995	1994	1995	1994	1995
52- Retail trade [1]	498	1,047	6,035	12,788	12	9,831	11,169	67,266	150,794
5210 Lumber and other building materials [1]	8	13	86	155	12	14,047	19,613	1,287	3,120
5230 Paint, glass, and wallpaper stores	-	6	-	13	2	-	15,385	-	225
5250 Hardware stores [1]	8	14	55	51	4	10,764	10,824	748	694
5260 Retail nurseries and garden stores [1]	5	10	25	61	6	7,520	9,377	240	699
5310 Department stores [3]	6	10	932	1,136	114	8,464	10,320	8,935	12,640
5410 Grocery stores [1]	38	95	1,191	2,448	26	10,186	9,951	12,969	25,534
5460 Retail bakeries [1]	4	11	16	14	1	5,000	6,857	97	108
5510 New and used car dealers [1]	9	22	304	620	28	17,408	20,452	6,355	13,650
5520 Used car dealers [1]	14	20	39	59	3	14,564	14,780	712	936
5530 Auto and home supply stores [1]	9	34	57	248	7	16,982	18,500	1,094	5,223
5540 Gasoline service stations [1]	54	84	249	559	7	8,835	10,340	2,327	6,079
5610 Men's & boys' clothing stores [3]	5	6	30	23	4	5,600	6,261	165	253
5620 Women's clothing stores [1]	18	23	183	210	9	6,776	5,867	1,331	1,284
5630 Women's accessory & specialty stores [3]	3	4	12	11	3	8,333	9,455	96	90
5650 Family clothing stores [1]	12	15	118	125	8	8,305	7,840	1,334	970
5660 Shoe stores [1]	18	22	67	84	4	10,806	10,238	811	845
5690 Misc. apparel & accessory stores [1]	3	6	8	11	2	10,500	6,182	85	78
5712 Furniture stores	-	19	-	190	10	-	17,305	-	3,662
5713 Floor covering stores [1]	5	15	35	71	5	10,514	9,803	504	650
5719 Misc. homefurnishings stores [2]	-	5	-	22	4	-	8,727	-	224
5731 Radio, TV, & electronic stores [1]	4	14	24	54	4	18,333	20,222	390	1,516
5735 Record & prerecorded tape stores [2]	-	4	-	21	5	-	11,810	-	214
5736 Musical instrument stores [2]	-	7	-	38	5	-	9,263	-	366
5812 Eating places [1]	102	215	1,400	3,711	17	6,909	7,323	11,602	29,235
5813 Drinking places [1]	24	67	53	220	3	5,887	5,909	357	1,308
5910 Drug stores and proprietary stores [1]	17	37	230	415	11	12,104	13,764	3,053	6,209
5920 Liquor stores [3]	7	8	26	29	4	11,692	12,552	343	386
5930 Used merchandise stores	-	11	-	28	3	-	12,714	-	378
5941 Sporting goods and bicycle shops	-	11	-	25	2	-	8,480	-	220
5942 Book stores [2]	-	7	-	31	4	-	9,548	-	322
5944 Jewelry stores [1]	8	19	54	72	4	12,741	15,333	662	1,030
5945 Hobby, toy, and game shops [3]	6	8	102	91	11	9,804	11,121	1,103	1,195
5947 Gift, novelty, and souvenir shops [1]	10	22	38	108	5	6,105	8,556	299	1,088
5949 Sewing, needlework, and piece goods [1]	3	-	12	-	-	7,667	-	73	-
5962 Merchandising machine operators [2]	-	5	-	19	4	-	12,000	-	234
5963 Direct selling establishments	-	9	-	25	3	-	19,200	-	638
5980 Fuel dealers [3]	4	6	22	23	4	20,545	19,304	406	436
5992 Florists [1]	8	20	17	27	1	6,118	9,037	159	255
5995 Optical goods stores [3]	7	9	35	33	4	14,629	18,909	547	608
5999 Miscellaneous retail stores, nec	-	25	-	90	4	-	11,733	-	1,165

Source: County Business Patterns 1994/95, CBP-94/95, U.S. Department of Commerce, Washington DC, November 1997. The employment column represents mid-March employment in the year. Pay per employee is calculated by dividing 1st Quarter payroll, annualized, by mid-March employment. The column headed 'Emp / Est' shows 'employees per establishment'. A dash (-) means that data are unavailable or cannot be calculated. nec means not elsewhere classified. *Notes:* 1. 1994 data incomplete; unavailable or withheld. 2. 1995 data incomplete; unavailable or withheld. 3. 1994 and 1995 data incomplete; unavailable or withheld.

WICHITA FALLS, TX MSA

Wholesale and Retail Trade USA	Establishments		Employment		Emp / Est	Pay / Employee		Annual Payroll ($ 000)	
	1994	1995	1994	1995	1995	1994	1995	1994	1995
50- Wholesale trade	-	263	-	2,145	8	-	23,373	-	53,684
5012 Automobiles and other vehicles [2]	-	6	-	60	10	-	26,067	-	1,879
5013 Motor vehicle supplies and new parts [2]	-	12	-	83	7	-	15,422	-	1,349
5020 Furniture and homefurnishings [2]	-	4	-	33	8	-	19,152	-	726
5032 Brick, stone, & related materials [2]	-	3	-	10	3	-	15,600	-	208
5039 Construction materials, nec	-	5	-	23	5	-	45,217	-	846
5045 Computers, peripherals, & software [2]	-	7	-	37	5	-	17,297	-	725
5047 Medical and hospital equipment [2]	-	5	-	41	8	-	16,293	-	739
5051 Metals service centers and offices [2]	-	6	-	44	7	-	27,000	-	1,212
5063 Electrical apparatus and equipment [2]	-	10	-	95	10	-	23,789	-	2,427
5065 Electronic parts and equipment [2]	-	6	-	41	7	-	33,659	-	1,678
5074 Plumbing & hydronic heating supplies [2]	-	3	-	43	14	-	24,186	-	940
5075 Warm air heating & air conditioning [2]	-	4	-	29	7	-	20,138	-	678
5084 Industrial machinery and equipment	-	43	-	198	5	-	24,020	-	4,886
5085 Industrial supplies [2]	-	11	-	116	11	-	26,345	-	3,186
5087 Service establishment equipment [2]	-	5	-	85	17	-	29,412	-	2,749
5091 Sporting & recreational goods [2]	-	3	-	24	8	-	12,833	-	387
5093 Scrap and waste materials [2]	-	5	-	52	10	-	18,923	-	1,153
5110 Paper and paper products [2]	-	8	-	102	13	-	27,490	-	2,753

Continued on next page.

WICHITA FALLS, TX MSA - [continued]

Wholesale and Retail Trade USA	Establishments		Employment		Emp / Est	Pay / Employee		Annual Payroll ($ 000)	
	1994	1995	1994	1995	1995	1994	1995	1994	1995
5149 Groceries and related products, nec	-	5	-	59	12	-	25,695	-	1,535
5150 Farm-product raw materials [2]	-	5	-	65	13	-	11,138	-	1,534
5160 Chemicals and allied products	-	6	-	28	5	-	32,714	-	874
5171 Petroleum bulk stations & terminals	-	12	-	67	6	-	25,015	-	1,682
5172 Petroleum products, nec [2]	-	3	-	20	7	-	19,200	-	401
5180 Beer, wine, and distilled beverages [2]	-	4	-	116	29	-	24,517	-	3,579
5191 Farm supplies	-	7	-	53	8	-	39,094	-	2,091
5199 Nondurable goods, nec [2]	-	3	-	2	1	-	12,000	-	30
52- Retail trade	-	872	-	11,080	13	-	12,016	-	137,888
5210 Lumber and other building materials [2]	-	21	-	272	13	-	16,338	-	5,399
5230 Paint, glass, and wallpaper stores [2]	-	5	-	37	7	-	24,973	-	859
5260 Retail nurseries and garden stores [2]	-	8	-	79	10	-	11,494	-	932
5270 Mobile home dealers [2]	-	3	-	61	20	-	18,295	-	1,178
5310 Department stores [2]	-	9	-	1,268	141	-	13,117	-	16,323
5330 Variety stores [2]	-	3	-	45	15	-	10,578	-	510
5390 Misc. general merchandise stores	-	14	-	307	22	-	12,339	-	3,384
5410 Grocery stores	-	84	-	1,421	17	-	11,657	-	16,714
5460 Retail bakeries	-	16	-	82	5	-	6,878	-	569
5490 Miscellaneous food stores [2]	-	5	-	7	1	-	9,714	-	68
5510 New and used car dealers	-	14	-	545	39	-	28,822	-	18,446
5520 Used car dealers [2]	-	18	-	56	3	-	13,500	-	834
5530 Auto and home supply stores	-	28	-	171	6	-	16,281	-	3,021
5540 Gasoline service stations	-	58	-	300	5	-	11,627	-	3,742
5570 Motorcycle dealers [2]	-	3	-	22	7	-	18,545	-	528
5610 Men's & boys' clothing stores [2]	-	8	-	47	6	-	8,000	-	378
5620 Women's clothing stores [2]	-	26	-	164	6	-	8,878	-	1,352
5650 Family clothing stores [2]	-	12	-	97	8	-	8,742	-	936
5660 Shoe stores [2]	-	12	-	59	5	-	10,644	-	621
5690 Misc. apparel & accessory stores [2]	-	11	-	46	4	-	8,435	-	353
5712 Furniture stores [2]	-	21	-	123	6	-	17,854	-	1,757
5719 Misc. homefurnishings stores [2]	-	4	-	15	4	-	12,533	-	161
5720 Household appliance stores [2]	-	7	-	88	13	-	19,318	-	1,849
5731 Radio, TV, & electronic stores [2]	-	12	-	57	5	-	15,860	-	898
5735 Record & prerecorded tape stores [2]	-	5	-	57	11	-	8,912	-	474
5812 Eating places	-	165	-	3,598	22	-	9,012	-	31,680
5813 Drinking places [2]	-	26	-	215	8	-	7,088	-	1,549
5910 Drug stores and proprietary stores	-	24	-	243	10	-	19,654	-	4,279
5920 Liquor stores	-	15	-	48	3	-	11,167	-	607
5930 Used merchandise stores [2]	-	14	-	51	4	-	14,745	-	792
5941 Sporting goods and bicycle shops [2]	-	6	-	18	3	-	11,556	-	241
5944 Jewelry stores [2]	-	14	-	77	6	-	14,701	-	1,166
5945 Hobby, toy, and game shops [2]	-	8	-	111	14	-	9,189	-	1,135
5947 Gift, novelty, and souvenir shops [2]	-	14	-	87	6	-	8,092	-	875
5949 Sewing, needlework, and piece goods [2]	-	4	-	28	7	-	8,857	-	242
5962 Merchandising machine operators [2]	-	5	-	47	9	-	14,809	-	678
5995 Optical goods stores [2]	-	12	-	58	5	-	12,069	-	701
5999 Miscellaneous retail stores, nec	-	27	-	92	3	-	12,174	-	1,196

Source: County Business Patterns 1994/95, CBP-94/95, U.S. Department of Commerce, Washington DC, November 1997. The employment column represents mid-March employment in the year. Pay per employee is calculated by dividing 1st Quarter payroll, annualized, by mid-March employment. The column headed 'Emp / Est' shows 'employees per establishment'. A dash (-) means that data are unavailable or cannot be calculated. nec means not elsewhere classified. *Notes:* 1. 1994 data incomplete; unavailable or withheld. 2. 1995 data incomplete; unavailable or withheld. 3. 1994 and 1995 data incomplete; unavailable or withheld.

WICHITA, KS MSA

Wholesale and Retail Trade USA	Establishments		Employment		Emp / Est	Pay / Employee		Annual Payroll ($ 000)	
	1994	1995	1994	1995	1995	1994	1995	1994	1995
50- Wholesale trade	1,091	1,107	12,546	13,382	12	26,972	28,959	359,665	394,879
5012 Automobiles and other vehicles [3]	20	20	399	402	20	24,190	27,065	11,873	12,120
5013 Motor vehicle supplies and new parts	63	55	680	588	11	24,759	26,048	18,274	16,366
5014 Tires and tubes [3]	9	9	89	94	10	19,326	23,447	1,667	2,377
5015 Motor vehicle parts, used	35	36	185	204	6	14,811	18,980	2,838	4,076
5021 Furniture [3]	13	13	164	151	12	29,171	34,146	4,757	5,068
5023 Homefurnishings [2]	18	17	204	250	15	23,176	19,152	4,624	5,136
5031 Lumber, plywood, and millwork [2]	21	18	239	342	19	33,975	31,556	9,235	11,878
5032 Brick, stone, & related materials [3]	9	13	49	85	7	23,673	21,694	1,391	2,140
5033 Roofing, siding, & insulation [3]	10	13	92	100	8	25,522	28,600	2,715	3,189
5039 Construction materials, nec [2]	18	23	263	207	9	18,692	25,990	5,487	5,870
5044 Office equipment [2]	25	20	351	293	15	29,128	36,027	10,085	8,854
5045 Computers, peripherals, & software	41	34	411	425	13	46,579	44,856	18,127	17,310

Continued on next page.

WICHITA, KS MSA - [continued]

Wholesale and Retail Trade USA	Establishments		Employment		Emp / Est	Pay / Employee		Annual Payroll ($ 000)	
	1994	1995	1994	1995	1995	1994	1995	1994	1995
5046 Commercial equipment, nec [2]	20	18	105	272	15	24,952	24,544	2,812	8,159
5047 Medical and hospital equipment [3]	23	19	147	146	8	39,238	37,507	6,021	5,835
5048 Ophthalmic goods [3]	4	3	20	15	5	16,200	16,267	359	274
5049 Professional equipment, nec [3]	9	12	60	63	5	21,267	21,270	1,187	1,472
5051 Metals service centers and offices [3]	20	19	261	292	15	25,349	27,192	7,135	8,350
5063 Electrical apparatus and equipment [1]	41	40	364	360	9	28,769	30,489	10,719	10,870
5064 Electrical appliances, TV & radios [3]	8	9	46	69	8	18,348	24,348	905	1,768
5065 Electronic parts and equipment	23	24	137	136	6	32,847	37,559	4,850	4,891
5072 Hardware [3]	14	14	88	91	7	25,455	29,451	2,403	2,836
5074 Plumbing & hydronic heating supplies [3]	15	19	191	379	20	20,649	20,982	4,740	8,023
5075 Warm air heating & air conditioning [3]	18	18	143	139	8	36,587	39,942	5,107	5,590
5078 Refrigeration equipment and supplies [3]	7	6	58	43	7	19,241	24,837	1,176	1,269
5082 Construction and mining machinery [3]	13	13	304	305	23	25,776	32,551	8,694	10,730
5083 Farm and garden machinery	28	27	287	281	10	20,530	22,776	7,062	7,151
5084 Industrial machinery and equipment [1]	56	62	376	413	7	28,106	29,860	11,452	13,053
5085 Industrial supplies [1]	49	48	557	520	11	30,700	33,869	17,595	17,790
5087 Service establishment equipment [3]	26	27	295	328	12	21,180	21,341	7,389	7,789
5088 Transportation equipment & supplies	44	47	1,054	1,178	25	37,374	38,102	41,737	44,574
5091 Sporting & recreational goods [2]	-	7	-	74	11	-	18,054	-	1,533
5092 Toys and hobby goods and supplies [1]	4	-	83	-	-	13,542	-	1,437	-
5093 Scrap and waste materials	21	21	254	290	14	16,772	20,869	5,127	7,343
5099 Durable goods, nec [2]	12	12	62	69	6	20,452	19,884	1,461	1,478
5112 Stationery and office supplies [1]	19	21	305	324	15	18,387	20,630	5,803	6,684
5120 Drugs, proprietaries, and sundries [3]	17	20	93	140	7	27,914	27,314	3,473	4,606
5137 Women's and children's clothing [3]	10	10	56	46	5	15,929	21,565	1,001	902
5142 Packaged frozen food [3]	5	5	84	85	17	18,143	20,047	1,770	1,665
5145 Confectionery [3]	6	7	178	189	27	23,079	21,757	4,608	4,723
5147 Meats and meat products [2]	12	10	115	133	13	30,852	35,820	3,001	4,208
5149 Groceries and related products, nec [2]	24	26	521	547	21	24,008	24,878	12,492	13,707
5153 Grain and field beans [3]	24	24	67	71	3	22,866	22,873	1,667	1,717
5162 Plastics materials & basic shapes [3]	5	6	38	49	8	20,526	21,796	850	994
5169 Chemicals & allied products, nec [3]	29	29	283	335	12	28,113	38,245	8,576	11,408
5171 Petroleum bulk stations & terminals	21	20	273	200	10	24,850	28,860	6,902	6,220
5172 Petroleum products, nec [1]	20	19	76	138	7	35,947	21,420	3,164	3,103
5181 Beer and ale [3]	5	5	169	165	33	28,781	33,697	5,209	5,420
5182 Wine and distilled beverages [3]	4	5	79	102	20	23,494	24,745	1,868	2,901
5191 Farm supplies	29	30	410	360	12	26,351	29,789	11,401	10,622
5192 Books, periodicals, & newspapers [3]	8	7	83	79	11	17,349	16,506	1,422	1,248
5193 Flowers & florists' supplies [3]	6	6	109	103	17	17,284	17,553	1,853	1,860
5198 Paints, varnishes, and supplies [2]	-	11	-	48	4	-	23,417	-	1,161
5199 Nondurable goods, nec [2]	19	24	97	94	4	21,567	22,936	2,052	2,212
52 - Retail trade	3,183	3,151	45,491	45,548	14	12,422	13,408	615,395	655,138
5210 Lumber and other building materials	47	42	1,330	1,334	32	17,263	17,742	26,619	23,962
5230 Paint, glass, and wallpaper stores	22	23	85	96	4	16,000	19,333	1,300	1,849
5250 Hardware stores	36	32	242	199	6	11,686	13,126	3,140	2,843
5260 Retail nurseries and garden stores	25	25	244	261	10	9,852	11,954	3,435	4,026
5270 Mobile home dealers [3]	12	13	67	89	7	25,851	26,921	2,030	3,087
5310 Department stores [3]	23	24	3,892	3,762	157	10,956	12,846	47,100	48,153
5330 Variety stores	19	-	104	-	-	8,500	-	1,252	-
5390 Misc. general merchandise stores	23	32	847	968	30	10,569	11,525	9,981	11,000
5410 Grocery stores [1]	173	167	5,016	5,181	31	13,455	14,107	65,193	79,508
5420 Meat and fish markets	10	10	35	34	3	11,200	11,059	432	392
5440 Candy, nut, and confectionery stores [3]	10	9	73	57	6	6,849	7,579	485	409
5460 Retail bakeries	45	40	343	150	4	8,397	8,080	3,861	1,439
5490 Miscellaneous food stores [1]	15	15	60	82	5	10,533	10,049	744	914
5510 New and used car dealers	40	40	2,043	2,122	53	26,485	27,508	58,760	63,385
5520 Used car dealers [2]	42	46	274	288	6	26,642	27,903	7,902	7,943
5530 Auto and home supply stores	79	80	553	642	8	17,374	17,146	10,394	12,166
5540 Gasoline service stations	220	196	1,591	1,341	7	10,602	11,967	17,632	16,733
5550 Boat dealers [3]	10	8	37	30	4	16,108	17,467	652	605
5560 Recreational vehicle dealers [3]	8	8	64	64	8	22,938	24,125	1,801	1,587
5570 Motorcycle dealers [3]	6	7	44	52	7	16,364	16,000	1,035	1,443
5590 Automotive dealers, nec [3]	11	8	12	37	5	13,000	8,216	310	338
5610 Men's & boys' clothing stores	25	24	190	182	8	12,779	14,989	2,418	2,442
5620 Women's clothing stores	76	75	748	619	8	7,888	8,213	6,384	5,334
5630 Women's accessory & specialty stores [3]	17	15	79	65	4	7,595	10,154	681	727
5640 Children's and infants' wear stores [3]	6	6	23	27	5	10,261	7,704	238	238
5650 Family clothing stores	31	33	406	479	15	9,626	10,789	4,781	5,209
5660 Shoe stores	71	71	441	425	6	9,324	10,372	4,260	4,535
5690 Misc. apparel & accessory stores [3]	18	21	83	94	4	11,229	10,936	987	995
5712 Furniture stores	59	54	386	371	7	19,275	20,345	7,925	7,917

Continued on next page.

WICHITA, KS MSA - [continued]

Wholesale and Retail Trade USA	Establishments		Employment		Emp / Est	Pay / Employee		Annual Payroll ($ 000)	
	1994	1995	1994	1995	1995	1994	1995	1994	1995
5713 Floor covering stores	22	20	82	98	5	20,293	21,633	2,146	2,342
5714 Drapery and upholstery stores [3]	5	5	13	17	3	10,462	11,529	173	178
5719 Misc. homefurnishings stores [3]	24	26	151	131	5	9,536	10,595	1,591	1,611
5720 Household appliance stores	19	22	59	78	4	16,475	19,026	1,025	1,597
5731 Radio, TV, & electronic stores	45	50	395	479	10	13,144	13,562	5,722	6,653
5734 Computer and software stores [3]	14	12	67	68	6	15,821	16,294	1,165	1,453
5735 Record & prerecorded tape stores [3]	15	15	127	160	11	8,819	10,675	1,234	1,792
5736 Musical instrument stores [3]	8	7	67	66	9	18,030	18,667	1,255	1,238
5812 Eating places	904	803	16,661	16,096	20	7,293	7,928	128,416	132,344
5813 Drinking places	122	98	752	740	8	6,761	7,535	6,125	5,062
5910 Drug stores and proprietary stores	66	63	692	699	11	17,636	18,850	13,439	13,084
5920 Liquor stores	105	108	373	404	4	7,292	7,030	2,898	3,105
5930 Used merchandise stores	69	69	449	481	7	10,343	10,661	5,246	5,287
5941 Sporting goods and bicycle shops	47	53	256	335	6	8,922	9,349	2,773	3,448
5942 Book stores [3]	18	18	333	354	20	9,946	10,260	3,466	3,500
5943 Stationery stores [1]	5	-	25	-	-	8,000	-	227	-
5944 Jewelry stores	44	43	209	227	5	17,895	18,396	3,740	4,027
5945 Hobby, toy, and game shops	27	29	286	297	10	8,825	8,754	2,995	3,271
5947 Gift, novelty, and souvenir shops	83	89	365	390	4	7,759	8,267	3,288	3,891
5949 Sewing, needlework, and piece goods [2]	20	18	132	131	7	6,667	6,840	894	815
5961 Catalog and mail-order houses [3]	9	13	148	137	11	9,730	13,343	1,761	1,934
5962 Merchandising machine operators [3]	7	8	119	113	14	22,622	22,867	2,687	2,671
5963 Direct selling establishments	29	25	125	104	4	21,344	21,615	2,404	2,364
5984 Liquefied petroleum gas dealers	-	9	-	23	3	-	19,130	-	478
5992 Florists	49	45	278	298	7	9,957	10,013	2,682	2,860
5993 Tobacco stores and stands [3]	7	6	36	34	6	11,889	15,059	431	462
5994 News dealers and newsstands [1]	3	-	22	-	-	6,545	-	160	-
5995 Optical goods stores [3]	29	31	139	145	5	18,072	16,966	2,452	2,486
5999 Miscellaneous retail stores, nec	96	111	459	679	6	12,209	11,399	7,123	8,878

Source: County Business Patterns 1994/95, CBP-94/95, U.S. Department of Commerce, Washington DC, November 1997. The employment column represents mid-March employment in the year. Pay per employee is calculated by dividing 1st Quarter payroll, annualized, by mid-March employment. The column headed 'Emp / Est' shows 'employees per establishment'. A dash (-) means that data are unavailable or cannot be calculated. nec means not elsewhere classified. *Notes:* 1. 1994 data incomplete; unavailable or withheld. 2. 1995 data incomplete; unavailable or withheld. 3. 1994 and 1995 data incomplete; unavailable or withheld.

WILLIAMSPORT, PA MSA

Wholesale and Retail Trade USA	Establishments		Employment		Emp / Est	Pay / Employee		Annual Payroll ($ 000)	
	1994	1995	1994	1995	1995	1994	1995	1994	1995
50 - Wholesale trade	-	192	-	2,300	12	-	22,871	-	53,609
5013 Motor vehicle supplies and new parts	-	15	-	68	5	-	22,000	-	1,486
5031 Lumber, plywood, and millwork	-	4	-	26	7	-	28,462	-	1,015
5044 Office equipment	-	6	-	52	9	-	21,692	-	1,081
5045 Computers, peripherals, & software	-	8	-	134	17	-	20,776	-	2,953
5047 Medical and hospital equipment	-	5	-	31	6	-	23,871	-	723
5063 Electrical apparatus and equipment	-	5	-	50	10	-	22,720	-	1,210
5074 Plumbing & hydronic heating supplies	-	6	-	32	5	-	21,125	-	728
5083 Farm and garden machinery	-	7	-	57	8	-	15,158	-	898
5084 Industrial machinery and equipment	-	8	-	124	16	-	32,258	-	3,115
5085 Industrial supplies	-	9	-	55	6	-	22,618	-	1,412
5093 Scrap and waste materials	-	7	-	103	15	-	24,583	-	2,831
5110 Paper and paper products	-	5	-	52	10	-	16,308	-	831
5149 Groceries and related products, nec	-	10	-	319	32	-	17,655	-	7,339
5181 Beer and ale	-	6	-	85	14	-	24,000	-	2,055
5191 Farm supplies	-	6	-	37	6	-	25,838	-	1,135
5199 Nondurable goods, nec	-	9	-	14	2	-	10,000	-	186
52 - Retail trade	-	832	-	10,284	12	-	12,049	-	131,366
5210 Lumber and other building materials	-	12	-	263	22	-	20,837	-	5,621
5230 Paint, glass, and wallpaper stores	-	4	-	20	5	-	14,000	-	307
5250 Hardware stores	-	7	-	57	8	-	13,965	-	849
5260 Retail nurseries and garden stores	-	7	-	19	3	-	10,947	-	225
5270 Mobile home dealers	-	4	-	20	5	-	13,800	-	344
5310 Department stores	-	7	-	922	132	-	11,584	-	11,840
5330 Variety stores	-	10	-	92	9	-	8,826	-	886
5390 Misc. general merchandise stores	-	7	-	34	5	-	6,588	-	284
5410 Grocery stores	-	57	-	1,640	29	-	9,305	-	16,257
5420 Meat and fish markets	-	11	-	67	6	-	13,015	-	907
5460 Retail bakeries	-	7	-	83	12	-	8,337	-	866
5490 Miscellaneous food stores	-	6	-	37	6	-	9,838	-	424
5510 New and used car dealers	-	25	-	711	28	-	22,706	-	17,766

Continued on next page.

WILLIAMSPORT, PA MSA - [continued]

Wholesale and Retail Trade USA	Establishments		Employment		Emp / Est	Pay / Employee		Annual Payroll ($ 000)	
	1994	1995	1994	1995	1995	1994	1995	1994	1995
5520 Used car dealers	-	17	-	59	3	-	15,186	-	930
5530 Auto and home supply stores	-	18	-	99	6	-	18,424	-	1,935
5540 Gasoline service stations	-	40	-	229	6	-	10,341	-	2,490
5610 Men's & boys' clothing stores	-	5	-	19	4	-	10,316	-	178
5620 Women's clothing stores	-	20	-	160	8	-	7,825	-	1,254
5630 Women's accessory & specialty stores	-	3	-	16	5	-	9,000	-	129
5650 Family clothing stores	-	11	-	222	20	-	11,135	-	2,392
5660 Shoe stores	-	17	-	90	5	-	10,933	-	987
5690 Misc. apparel & accessory stores	-	4	-	17	4	-	10,353	-	188
5712 Furniture stores	-	10	-	81	8	-	18,074	-	1,684
5713 Floor covering stores	-	12	-	39	3	-	19,590	-	771
5714 Drapery and upholstery stores	-	3	-	5	2	-	14,400	-	77
5720 Household appliance stores	-	8	-	80	10	-	20,250	-	1,711
5731 Radio, TV, & electronic stores	-	9	-	40	4	-	18,300	-	727
5812 Eating places	-	179	-	2,648	15	-	6,583	-	18,783
5813 Drinking places	-	53	-	202	4	-	6,812	-	1,465
5910 Drug stores and proprietary stores	-	33	-	319	10	-	15,900	-	5,628
5920 Liquor stores	-	15	-	73	5	-	12,767	-	983
5930 Used merchandise stores	-	7	-	21	3	-	6,857	-	199
5941 Sporting goods and bicycle shops	-	10	-	34	3	-	12,118	-	439
5942 Book stores	-	3	-	27	9	-	9,630	-	263
5944 Jewelry stores	-	20	-	109	5	-	12,440	-	1,362
5945 Hobby, toy, and game shops	-	9	-	66	7	-	8,667	-	661
5947 Gift, novelty, and souvenir shops	-	14	-	69	5	-	6,435	-	459
5949 Sewing, needlework, and piece goods	-	5	-	25	5	-	8,640	-	210
5961 Catalog and mail-order houses	-	6	-	90	15	-	24,622	-	2,203
5962 Merchandising machine operators	-	3	-	145	48	-	18,841	-	2,804
5963 Direct selling establishments	-	9	-	50	6	-	18,160	-	905
5983 Fuel oil dealers	-	5	-	78	16	-	9,846	-	786
5992 Florists	-	19	-	83	4	-	8,145	-	691
5994 News dealers and newsstands	-	5	-	17	3	-	7,529	-	127
5995 Optical goods stores	-	7	-	31	4	-	14,452	-	534
5999 Miscellaneous retail stores, nec	-	21	-	81	4	-	13,630	-	1,258

Source: County Business Patterns 1994/95, CBP-94/95, U.S. Department of Commerce, Washington DC, November 1997. The employment column represents mid-March employment in the year. Pay per employee is calculated by dividing 1st Quarter payroll, annualized, by mid-March employment. The column headed 'Emp / Est' shows 'employees per establishment'. A dash (-) means that data are unavailable or cannot be calculated. nec means not elsewhere classified. *Notes:* 1. 1994 data incomplete; unavailable or withheld. 2. 1995 data incomplete; unavailable or withheld. 3. 1994 and 1995 data incomplete; unavailable or withheld.

WILMINGTON - NEWARK PMSA (DE PART)

Wholesale and Retail Trade USA	Establishments		Employment		Emp / Est	Pay / Employee		Annual Payroll ($ 000)	
	1994	1995	1994	1995	1995	1994	1995	1994	1995
50- Wholesale trade	770	798	12,654	12,950	16	39,501	46,341	497,681	545,858
5012 Automobiles and other vehicles	16	15	249	274	18	29,012	27,255	7,426	7,575
5013 Motor vehicle supplies and new parts	43	37	519	490	13	27,746	30,098	15,379	14,790
5020 Furniture and homefurnishings	28	30	382	199	7	32,859	32,563	12,182	7,623
5031 Lumber, plywood, and millwork	15	18	237	316	18	26,481	30,253	7,951	9,718
5032 Brick, stone, & related materials	-	9	-	75	8	-	27,520	-	2,924
5033 Roofing, siding, & insulation	11	11	127	151	14	35,339	33,616	4,746	5,210
5039 Construction materials, nec	-	12	-	144	12	-	28,833	-	4,049
5044 Office equipment	17	22	441	432	20	43,737	49,676	17,867	20,949
5045 Computers, peripherals, & software	40	39	579	606	16	40,746	47,881	20,940	30,096
5047 Medical and hospital equipment	14	-	132	-	-	21,788	-	9,402	-
5051 Metals service centers and offices	-	13	-	290	22	-	35,366	-	9,165
5063 Electrical apparatus and equipment	33	24	482	371	15	33,344	37,563	17,104	13,206
5064 Electrical appliances, TV & radios	7	7	19	19	3	25,895	26,737	484	519
5065 Electronic parts and equipment	24	27	196	182	7	42,633	43,407	6,862	7,540
5072 Hardware	16	-	155	-	-	34,116	-	6,555	-
5074 Plumbing & hydronic heating supplies	19	20	183	180	9	25,858	32,756	5,278	5,878
5082 Construction and mining machinery	14	14	115	91	7	30,539	50,242	4,401	4,200
5083 Farm and garden machinery	5	6	71	70	12	24,225	27,771	1,882	2,184
5084 Industrial machinery and equipment	42	40	280	285	7	36,657	42,091	11,052	12,555
5085 Industrial supplies	29	29	307	338	12	34,489	34,296	11,145	10,698
5087 Service establishment equipment	-	15	-	80	5	-	26,150	-	1,990
5093 Scrap and waste materials	17	18	118	130	7	21,492	23,662	2,867	3,066
5094 Jewelry & precious stones	4	-	5	-	-	4,000	-	172	-
5099 Durable goods, nec	-	12	-	32	3	-	31,375	-	1,079
5111 Printing and writing paper	-	4	-	35	9	-	17,943	-	545
5112 Stationery and office supplies	19	15	249	138	9	27,438	35,710	6,912	5,272

Continued on next page.

WILMINGTON – NEWARK PMSA (DE PART) - [continued]

Wholesale and Retail Trade USA	Establishments		Employment		Emp / Est	Pay / Employee		Annual Payroll ($ 000)	
	1994	1995	1994	1995	1995	1994	1995	1994	1995
5113 Industrial & personal service paper	-	6	-	107	18	-	22,692	-	2,776
5137 Women's and children's clothing	6	7	26	37	5	20,923	19,243	682	844
5146 Fish and seafoods	-	6	-	39	7	-	26,154	-	1,229
5148 Fresh fruits and vegetables	3	3	26	29	10	39,538	62,759	1,135	1,598
5149 Groceries and related products, nec	22	23	379	417	18	27,420	31,789	10,942	13,007
5160 Chemicals and allied products	41	48	2,468	2,170	45	73,519	104,131	155,304	180,088
5171 Petroleum bulk stations & terminals	6	6	108	130	22	42,444	33,477	4,003	3,896
5180 Beer, wine, and distilled beverages	7	-	468	-	-	27,889	-	13,985	-
5191 Farm supplies	7	6	44	33	6	17,818	29,212	934	848
5199 Nondurable goods, nec	28	29	145	165	6	22,262	25,333	3,727	4,210
52 – Retail trade	2,852	2,856	41,846	43,881	15	12,403	13,277	577,810	613,814
5210 Lumber and other building materials	51	41	760	758	18	18,158	20,517	15,361	15,579
5250 Hardware stores	22	15	224	189	13	13,857	12,254	3,503	2,510
5260 Retail nurseries and garden stores	30	25	165	185	7	14,230	14,378	3,525	3,713
5310 Department stores	22	23	4,762	4,977	216	10,610	11,249	54,240	58,706
5330 Variety stores	24	25	295	283	11	11,471	10,940	3,404	3,136
5390 Misc. general merchandise stores	16	19	626	679	36	10,990	12,465	8,407	8,853
5410 Grocery stores	183	185	5,332	5,370	29	15,965	16,057	88,065	85,634
5420 Meat and fish markets	23	22	190	183	8	11,368	11,891	2,503	2,350
5430 Fruit and vegetable markets	7	7	71	78	11	10,479	9,231	1,304	1,173
5460 Retail bakeries	51	44	456	460	10	9,833	9,974	4,713	4,943
5490 Miscellaneous food stores	22	21	91	120	6	12,132	11,933	1,187	1,494
5510 New and used car dealers	41	40	2,157	2,468	62	27,681	29,580	72,321	77,854
5520 Used car dealers	20	21	82	68	3	24,976	27,824	2,125	2,137
5530 Auto and home supply stores	49	48	468	487	10	18,709	19,499	9,763	9,941
5540 Gasoline service stations	148	150	1,096	1,091	7	12,599	13,624	14,375	14,546
5560 Recreational vehicle dealers	-	3	-	29	10	-	24,552	-	991
5570 Motorcycle dealers	5	6	53	64	11	17,057	18,875	1,257	1,701
5610 Men's & boys' clothing stores	24	19	274	240	13	9,504	10,350	2,689	2,414
5620 Women's clothing stores	76	65	877	793	12	7,840	7,864	7,586	6,348
5630 Women's accessory & specialty stores	13	15	83	82	5	8,530	9,707	839	845
5640 Children's and infants' wear stores	19	16	185	187	12	6,616	7,316	2,265	2,408
5650 Family clothing stores	26	23	391	325	14	8,399	9,674	3,764	3,240
5660 Shoe stores	72	67	405	424	6	11,032	11,094	4,624	4,746
5690 Misc. apparel & accessory stores	13	15	125	131	9	10,208	9,771	1,272	1,340
5712 Furniture stores	63	59	485	564	10	17,823	19,113	10,266	11,490
5713 Floor covering stores	29	34	213	218	6	18,291	20,092	4,556	4,659
5714 Drapery and upholstery stores	-	8	-	42	5	-	16,381	-	784
5719 Misc. homefurnishings stores	-	33	-	189	6	-	12,614	-	2,249
5720 Household appliance stores	23	24	542	521	22	13,690	17,597	8,964	9,335
5731 Radio, TV, & electronic stores	39	38	264	348	9	17,621	17,805	5,205	7,351
5734 Computer and software stores	17	22	161	208	9	19,404	19,077	3,304	4,020
5735 Record & prerecorded tape stores	22	21	167	191	9	10,898	10,932	2,033	2,006
5812 Eating places	677	670	13,524	13,763	21	7,876	8,782	120,725	128,358
5813 Drinking places	70	63	496	516	8	7,427	8,744	4,174	4,898
5910 Drug stores and proprietary stores	88	83	1,584	1,516	18	13,490	12,367	21,968	18,911
5920 Liquor stores	147	142	687	653	5	9,933	10,273	7,223	6,967
5930 Used merchandise stores	27	27	160	169	6	10,225	11,456	1,557	1,672
5941 Sporting goods and bicycle shops	59	64	413	533	8	11,429	11,820	5,497	6,573
5942 Book stores	28	30	158	262	9	8,937	9,695	1,545	2,534
5944 Jewelry stores	48	50	312	334	7	17,487	18,611	5,881	6,145
5945 Hobby, toy, and game shops	24	18	289	258	14	10,727	12,729	4,056	3,398
5947 Gift, novelty, and souvenir shops	71	62	407	419	7	6,811	9,394	3,670	4,241
5949 Sewing, needlework, and piece goods	-	13	-	127	10	-	9,228	-	1,153
5961 Catalog and mail-order houses	9	14	71	174	12	16,394	20,805	1,213	3,851
5962 Merchandising machine operators	8	6	117	109	18	22,085	25,284	2,871	2,852
5963 Direct selling establishments	27	20	89	103	5	15,640	16,117	1,543	1,553
5983 Fuel oil dealers	19	-	215	-	-	28,781	-	6,423	-
5992 Florists	49	46	255	292	6	11,106	10,781	3,414	3,406
5993 Tobacco stores and stands	17	16	92	102	6	8,565	10,784	973	1,159
5994 News dealers and newsstands	13	13	65	62	5	10,892	11,355	762	727
5995 Optical goods stores	36	32	174	152	5	16,115	16,632	2,940	2,795
5999 Miscellaneous retail stores, nec	89	94	465	549	6	15,458	16,714	8,946	10,612

Source: County Business Patterns 1994/95, CBP-94/95, U.S. Department of Commerce, Washington DC, November 1997. The employment column represents mid-March employment in the year. Pay per employee is calculated by dividing 1st Quarter payroll, annualized, by mid-March employment. The column headed 'Emp / Est' shows 'employees per establishment'. A dash (-) means that data are unavailable or cannot be calculated. nec means not elsewhere classified. *Notes:* 1. 1994 data incomplete; unavailable or withheld. 2. 1995 data incomplete; unavailable or withheld. 3. 1994 and 1995 data incomplete; unavailable or withheld.

WILMINGTON - NEWARK PMSA (MD PART)

Wholesale and Retail Trade USA	Establishments		Employment		Emp / Est	Pay / Employee		Annual Payroll ($ 000)	
	1994	1995	1994	1995	1995	1994	1995	1994	1995
50- Wholesale trade	60	61	550	659	11	23,898	26,586	15,790	17,789
5013 Motor vehicle supplies and new parts	8	7	72	77	11	16,444	16,623	1,302	1,333
5070 Hardware, plumbing & heating equipment	3	3	16	17	6	25,500	32,941	554	610
5083 Farm and garden machinery	5	3	41	39	13	22,439	23,897	1,043	978
5084 Industrial machinery and equipment	4	4	9	12	3	29,778	24,667	273	285
5090 Miscellaneous durable goods	3	4	31	35	9	16,903	20,686	636	729
5140 Groceries and related products	5	6	139	176	29	20,576	23,705	4,016	3,981
5170 Petroleum and petroleum products	5	5	51	51	10	25,098	23,922	1,318	1,147
5190 Misc., nondurable goods	-	6	-	23	4	-	12,522	-	415
52- Retail trade	401	394	4,940	5,085	13	11,279	12,131	62,263	64,509
5210 Lumber and other building materials	8	8	124	156	20	22,323	27,564	3,607	4,128
5250 Hardware stores	-	3	-	29	10	-	12,828	-	372
5260 Retail nurseries and garden stores	-	5	-	11	2	-	21,818	-	279
5270 Mobile home dealers	4	4	18	16	4	13,778	17,000	376	374
5310 Department stores	3	-	379	-	-	9,879	-	4,432	-
5390 Misc. general merchandise stores	-	5	-	66	13	-	8,909	-	720
5410 Grocery stores	55	53	689	707	13	13,016	12,622	9,261	9,107
5510 New and used car dealers	8	8	194	252	32	22,990	22,460	5,650	6,154
5520 Used car dealers	-	4	-	26	7	-	13,385	-	383
5530 Auto and home supply stores	5	5	52	50	10	13,308	15,520	777	788
5540 Gasoline service stations	31	29	455	441	15	13,732	14,222	6,339	5,576
5550 Boat dealers	7	8	69	71	9	17,913	19,549	1,620	1,798
5570 Motorcycle dealers	-	3	-	5	2	-	15,200	-	142
5610 Men's & boys' clothing stores	4	5	18	60	12	8,000	7,133	195	389
5620 Women's clothing stores	13	14	131	123	9	9,282	9,268	1,352	1,225
5650 Family clothing stores	8	7	106	93	13	7,132	9,161	800	835
5660 Shoe stores	7	8	54	73	9	9,630	7,014	533	578
5719 Misc. homefurnishings stores	7	-	30	-	-	11,200	-	427	-
5812 Eating places	89	87	1,566	1,588	18	7,157	7,834	13,608	13,829
5813 Drinking places	11	9	63	73	8	6,476	7,836	552	688
5910 Drug stores and proprietary stores	9	8	125	111	14	15,232	16,793	1,965	1,950
5920 Liquor stores	29	25	249	247	10	9,703	9,765	2,691	2,607
5947 Gift, novelty, and souvenir shops	8	7	45	39	6	6,489	8,718	355	336
5948 Luggage and leather goods stores	3	-	17	-	-	8,941	-	140	-
5961 Catalog and mail-order houses	4	-	62	-	-	9,806	-	874	-
5963 Direct selling establishments	3	-	9	-	-	11,556	-	109	-
5983 Fuel oil dealers	4	4	28	24	6	20,000	23,500	511	544
5984 Liquefied petroleum gas dealers	3	3	27	28	9	54,370	49,571	1,442	1,405
5992 Florists	9	7	43	46	7	9,488	8,087	425	409
5999 Miscellaneous retail stores, nec	-	9	-	34	4	-	10,118	-	350

Source: County Business Patterns 1994/95, CBP-94/95, U.S. Department of Commerce, Washington DC, November 1997. The employment column represents mid-March employment in the year. Pay per employee is calculated by dividing 1st Quarter payroll, annualized, by mid-March employment. The column headed 'Emp / Est' shows 'employees per establishment'. A dash (-) means that data are unavailable or cannot be calculated. nec means not elsewhere classified. *Notes:* 1. 1994 data incomplete; unavailable or withheld. 2. 1995 data incomplete; unavailable or withheld. 3. 1994 and 1995 data incomplete; unavailable or withheld.

WILMINGTON - NEWARK, DE - MD PMSA

Wholesale and Retail Trade USA	Establishments		Employment		Emp / Est	Pay / Employee		Annual Payroll ($ 000)	
	1994	1995	1994	1995	1995	1994	1995	1994	1995
50- Wholesale trade	830	859	13,204	13,609	16	38,851	45,385	513,471	563,647
5012 Automobiles and other vehicles	19	18	249	274	15	29,012	27,255	7,426	7,575
5013 Motor vehicle supplies and new parts	51	44	591	567	13	26,369	28,268	16,681	16,123
5020 Furniture and homefurnishings	29	31	382	199	6	32,859	32,563	12,182	7,623
5031 Lumber, plywood, and millwork	16	20	237	316	16	26,481	30,253	7,951	9,718
5032 Brick, stone, & related materials[2]	-	9	-	75	8	-	27,520	-	2,924
5033 Roofing, siding, & insulation[3]	11	11	127	151	14	35,339	33,616	4,746	5,210
5039 Construction materials, nec[2]	-	12	-	144	12	-	28,833	-	4,049
5044 Office equipment	18	23	441	432	19	43,737	49,676	17,867	20,949
5045 Computers, peripherals, & software[3]	40	39	579	606	16	40,746	47,881	20,940	30,096
5047 Medical and hospital equipment	15	-	132	-	-	21,788	-	9,402	-
5051 Metals service centers and offices	-	14	-	290	21	-	35,366	-	9,165
5063 Electrical apparatus and equipment	34	25	482	371	15	33,344	37,563	17,104	13,206
5064 Electrical appliances, TV & radios[3]	7	7	19	19	3	25,895	26,737	484	519
5065 Electronic parts and equipment[3]	24	27	196	182	7	42,633	43,407	6,862	7,540
5072 Hardware	17	-	155	-	-	34,116	-	6,555	-
5074 Plumbing & hydronic heating supplies	20	21	183	180	9	25,858	32,756	5,278	5,878
5082 Construction and mining machinery[3]	14	14	115	91	7	30,539	50,242	4,401	4,200
5083 Farm and garden machinery	10	9	112	109	12	23,571	26,385	2,925	3,162
5084 Industrial machinery and equipment	46	44	289	297	7	36,443	41,387	11,325	12,840

Continued on next page.

WILMINGTON – NEWARK, DE – MD PMSA - [continued]

Wholesale and Retail Trade USA	Establishments		Employment		Emp / Est	Pay / Employee		Annual Payroll ($ 000)	
	1994	1995	1994	1995	1995	1994	1995	1994	1995
5085 Industrial supplies	30	30	307	338	11	34,489	34,296	11,145	10,698
5087 Service establishment equipment	-	16	-	80	5	-	26,150	-	1,990
5093 Scrap and waste materials	18	19	118	130	7	21,492	23,662	2,867	3,066
5094 Jewelry & precious stones [1]	4	-	5	-	-	4,000	-	172	-
5099 Durable goods, nec	-	13	-	32	2	-	31,375	-	1,079
5111 Printing and writing paper [2]	-	4	-	35	9	-	17,943	-	545
5112 Stationery and office supplies	20	16	249	138	9	27,438	35,710	6,912	5,272
5113 Industrial & personal service paper [2]	-	6	-	107	18	-	22,692	-	2,776
5137 Women's and children's clothing [2]	7	7	26	37	5	20,923	19,243	682	844
5146 Fish and seafoods [2]	-	6	-	39	7	-	26,154	-	1,229
5148 Fresh fruits and vegetables [3]	3	3	26	29	10	39,538	62,759	1,135	1,598
5149 Groceries and related products, nec	23	24	379	417	17	27,420	31,789	10,942	13,007
5160 Chemicals and allied products	43	50	2,468	2,170	43	73,519	104,131	155,304	180,088
5171 Petroleum bulk stations & terminals	10	10	108	130	13	42,444	33,477	4,003	3,896
5180 Beer, wine, and distilled beverages	10	-	468	-	-	27,889	-	13,985	-
5191 Farm supplies	10	9	44	33	4	17,818	29,212	934	848
5199 Nondurable goods, nec	30	31	145	165	5	22,262	25,333	3,727	4,210
52- Retail trade	3,253	3,250	46,786	48,966	15	12,284	13,158	640,073	678,323
5210 Lumber and other building materials	59	49	884	914	19	18,742	21,720	18,968	19,707
5250 Hardware stores	25	18	224	218	12	13,857	12,330	3,503	2,882
5260 Retail nurseries and garden stores	34	30	165	196	7	14,230	14,796	3,525	3,992
5270 Mobile home dealers	6	7	18	16	2	13,778	17,000	376	374
5310 Department stores [2]	25	25	5,141	4,977	199	10,556	11,249	58,672	58,706
5330 Variety stores	30	28	295	283	10	11,471	10,940	3,404	3,136
5390 Misc. general merchandise stores	18	24	626	745	31	10,990	12,150	8,407	9,573
5410 Grocery stores	238	238	6,021	6,077	26	15,627	15,657	97,326	94,741
5420 Meat and fish markets [3]	23	22	190	183	8	11,368	11,891	2,503	2,350
5430 Fruit and vegetable markets	8	8	71	78	10	10,479	9,231	1,304	1,173
5460 Retail bakeries	55	46	456	460	10	9,833	9,974	4,713	4,943
5490 Miscellaneous food stores	23	22	91	120	5	12,132	11,933	1,187	1,494
5510 New and used car dealers	49	48	2,351	2,720	57	27,294	28,921	77,971	84,008
5520 Used car dealers	24	25	82	94	4	24,976	23,830	2,125	2,520
5530 Auto and home supply stores	54	53	520	537	10	18,169	19,128	10,540	10,729
5540 Gasoline service stations	179	179	1,551	1,532	9	12,931	13,796	20,714	20,122
5550 Boat dealers	18	18	69	71	4	17,913	19,549	1,620	1,798
5560 Recreational vehicle dealers [2]	-	3	-	29	10	-	24,552	-	991
5570 Motorcycle dealers	7	9	53	69	8	17,057	18,609	1,257	1,843
5610 Men's & boys' clothing stores	28	24	292	300	13	9,411	9,707	2,884	2,803
5620 Women's clothing stores	89	79	1,008	916	12	8,028	8,052	8,938	7,573
5630 Women's accessory & specialty stores	16	18	83	82	5	8,530	9,707	839	845
5640 Children's and infants' wear stores [2]	20	16	185	187	12	6,616	7,316	2,265	2,408
5650 Family clothing stores	34	30	497	418	14	8,129	9,560	4,564	4,075
5660 Shoe stores	79	75	459	497	7	10,867	10,495	5,157	5,324
5690 Misc. apparel & accessory stores	14	16	125	131	8	10,208	9,771	1,272	1,340
5712 Furniture stores	66	62	485	564	9	17,823	19,113	10,266	11,490
5713 Floor covering stores	32	37	213	218	6	18,291	20,092	4,556	4,659
5714 Drapery and upholstery stores [2]	-	8	-	42	5	-	16,381	-	784
5719 Misc. homefurnishings stores [1]	41	40	30	189	5	11,200	12,614	427	2,249
5720 Household appliance stores	25	27	542	521	19	13,690	17,597	8,964	9,335
5731 Radio, TV, & electronic stores	40	40	264	348	9	17,621	17,805	5,205	7,351
5734 Computer and software stores [3]	17	22	161	208	9	19,404	19,077	3,304	4,020
5735 Record & prerecorded tape stores	23	22	167	191	9	10,898	10,932	2,033	2,006
5812 Eating places	766	757	15,090	15,351	20	7,802	8,684	134,333	142,187
5813 Drinking places	81	72	559	589	8	7,320	8,632	4,726	5,586
5910 Drug stores and proprietary stores	97	91	1,709	1,627	18	13,617	12,669	23,933	20,861
5920 Liquor stores	176	167	936	900	5	9,872	10,133	9,914	9,574
5930 Used merchandise stores	28	29	160	169	6	10,225	11,456	1,557	1,672
5941 Sporting goods and bicycle shops	64	69	413	533	8	11,429	11,820	5,497	6,573
5942 Book stores [3]	28	30	158	262	9	8,937	9,695	1,545	2,534
5944 Jewelry stores	50	51	312	334	7	17,487	18,611	5,881	6,145
5945 Hobby, toy, and game shops	25	20	289	258	13	10,727	12,729	4,056	3,398
5947 Gift, novelty, and souvenir shops	79	69	452	458	7	6,779	9,336	4,025	4,577
5948 Luggage and leather goods stores	6	-	17	-	-	8,941	-	140	-
5949 Sewing, needlework, and piece goods [2]	-	13	-	127	10	-	9,228	-	1,153
5961 Catalog and mail-order houses	13	18	133	174	10	13,323	20,805	2,087	3,851
5962 Merchandising machine operators [3]	8	6	117	109	18	22,085	25,284	2,871	2,852
5963 Direct selling establishments	30	24	98	103	4	15,265	16,117	1,652	1,553
5983 Fuel oil dealers [2]	23	24	243	24	1	27,770	23,500	6,934	544
5984 Liquefied petroleum gas dealers	10	9	27	28	3	54,370	49,571	1,442	1,405
5992 Florists	58	53	298	338	6	10,872	10,414	3,839	3,815
5993 Tobacco stores and stands [3]	17	16	92	102	6	8,565	10,784	973	1,159

Continued on next page.

WILMINGTON – NEWARK, DE – MD PMSA - [continued]

Wholesale and Retail Trade USA	Establishments		Employment		Emp / Est	Pay / Employee		Annual Payroll ($ 000)	
	1994	1995	1994	1995	1995	1994	1995	1994	1995
5994 News dealers and newsstands	15	15	65	62	4	10,892	11,355	762	727
5995 Optical goods stores [3]	36	32	174	152	5	16,115	16,632	2,940	2,795
5999 Miscellaneous retail stores, nec	97	103	465	583	6	15,458	16,329	8,946	10,962

Source: County Business Patterns 1994/95, CBP-94/95, U.S. Department of Commerce, Washington DC, November 1997. The employment column represents mid-March employment in the year. Pay per employee is calculated by dividing 1st Quarter payroll, annualized, by mid-March employment. The column headed 'Emp / Est' shows 'employees per establishment'. A dash (-) means that data are unavailable or cannot be calculated. nec means not elsewhere classified. *Notes:* 1. 1994 data incomplete; unavailable or withheld. 2. 1995 data incomplete; unavailable or withheld. 3. 1994 and 1995 data incomplete; unavailable or withheld.

WILMINGTON, NC MSA

Wholesale and Retail Trade USA	Establishments		Employment		Emp / Est	Pay / Employee		Annual Payroll ($ 000)	
	1994	1995	1994	1995	1995	1994	1995	1994	1995
50- Wholesale trade	404	420	4,033	4,025	10	23,370	25,338	102,913	107,119
5012 Automobiles and other vehicles	8	6	67	77	13	23,701	25,403	1,908	2,073
5013 Motor vehicle supplies and new parts	20	17	155	150	9	19,045	16,880	2,941	2,609
5014 Tires and tubes [3]	6	5	83	74	15	21,928	22,270	1,866	1,708
5015 Motor vehicle parts, used	6	7	31	25	4	14,323	19,520	447	432
5021 Furniture [3]	4	4	16	21	5	18,500	25,143	437	548
5023 Homefurnishings [3]	5	4	8	12	3	11,000	20,667	188	266
5031 Lumber, plywood, and millwork	9	14	129	128	9	23,814	25,469	3,068	3,607
5032 Brick, stone, & related materials [3]	8	6	35	33	6	22,971	27,030	898	891
5033 Roofing, siding, & insulation [3]	3	5	13	22	4	25,538	27,636	403	590
5039 Construction materials, nec [2]	-	4	-	32	8	-	24,125	-	848
5044 Office equipment [3]	8	9	77	80	9	17,610	24,100	1,438	1,696
5045 Computers, peripherals, & software [1]	9	-	54	-	-	24,963	-	1,359	-
5046 Commercial equipment, nec [3]	7	8	89	111	14	19,775	20,324	2,170	2,327
5047 Medical and hospital equipment	6	-	30	-	-	24,800	-	841	-
5048 Ophthalmic goods [3]	3	4	87	91	23	17,563	19,429	1,423	1,625
5049 Professional equipment, nec [3]	6	6	84	93	16	28,857	34,409	2,931	3,151
5051 Metals service centers and offices [2]	-	6	-	195	33	-	23,836	-	4,234
5063 Electrical apparatus and equipment	15	13	155	167	13	27,458	28,862	4,552	4,941
5072 Hardware	-	8	-	27	3	-	20,148	-	621
5074 Plumbing & hydronic heating supplies	9	9	85	92	10	25,553	25,391	2,351	2,496
5075 Warm air heating & air conditioning [3]	9	12	36	47	4	38,222	31,574	1,211	1,489
5078 Refrigeration equipment and supplies [2]	-	4	-	4	1	-	15,000	-	83
5082 Construction and mining machinery	7	8	83	89	11	28,675	34,112	2,569	2,995
5084 Industrial machinery and equipment	23	22	119	118	5	27,160	33,119	3,405	4,281
5085 Industrial supplies	25	26	204	219	8	26,824	29,279	5,716	6,426
5087 Service establishment equipment [3]	7	9	36	68	8	17,333	21,941	801	1,614
5091 Sporting & recreational goods [2]	-	3	-	11	4	-	21,818	-	346
5093 Scrap and waste materials	-	7	-	42	6	-	39,524	-	1,585
5099 Durable goods, nec	10	10	77	69	7	17,922	18,609	1,823	1,655
5110 Paper and paper products	15	15	149	154	10	23,570	26,442	3,598	3,928
5130 Apparel, piece goods, and notions	13	13	473	344	26	20,533	25,826	9,796	9,122
5143 Dairy products, exc. dried or canned [3]	4	3	48	40	13	16,250	16,700	780	669
5146 Fish and seafoods	17	18	89	104	6	9,663	8,885	956	976
5149 Groceries and related products, nec	10	12	51	64	5	32,078	28,625	2,693	3,242
5160 Chemicals and allied products	7	7	27	70	10	25,926	37,543	1,032	2,909
5171 Petroleum bulk stations & terminals	-	9	-	113	13	-	36,071	-	4,152
5172 Petroleum products, nec	-	6	-	25	4	-	24,800	-	679
5181 Beer and ale [3]	4	4	191	185	46	23,079	25,708	5,292	5,238
5182 Wine and distilled beverages [3]	4	4	51	45	11	19,059	22,133	1,042	1,140
5191 Farm supplies	7	6	70	33	6	24,514	27,636	1,731	851
5198 Paints, varnishes, and supplies [2]	-	3	-	17	6	-	31,765	-	517
5199 Nondurable goods, nec	22	24	137	149	6	22,248	22,201	3,327	3,396
52- Retail trade	1,688	1,726	20,401	21,138	12	10,851	11,735	249,799	278,044
5210 Lumber and other building materials	27	23	772	683	30	15,674	19,133	11,035	13,689
5230 Paint, glass, and wallpaper stores	7	9	24	42	5	18,500	19,429	492	974
5250 Hardware stores	24	20	84	102	5	11,619	12,000	1,264	1,509
5260 Retail nurseries and garden stores	16	17	77	86	5	12,935	15,070	1,288	1,724
5270 Mobile home dealers	12	10	45	48	5	25,156	26,250	1,225	1,557
5310 Department stores [3]	11	12	1,636	1,566	131	10,313	12,340	18,113	20,248
5330 Variety stores	20	21	166	164	8	7,181	7,512	1,472	1,579
5390 Misc. general merchandise stores	16	16	364	346	22	13,143	13,272	5,035	4,439
5410 Grocery stores	129	121	2,320	2,676	22	9,448	9,655	25,229	28,907
5420 Meat and fish markets	14	13	37	41	3	8,541	8,000	425	535
5460 Retail bakeries	13	13	95	128	10	12,884	9,938	1,265	1,356
5490 Miscellaneous food stores	9	11	28	36	3	12,143	10,889	406	419
5510 New and used car dealers	21	21	785	838	40	31,918	32,730	28,001	31,220

Continued on next page.

WILMINGTON, NC MSA - [continued]

Wholesale and Retail Trade USA	Establishments		Employment		Emp / Est	Pay / Employee		Annual Payroll ($ 000)	
	1994	1995	1994	1995	1995	1994	1995	1994	1995
5520 Used car dealers	26	25	87	94	4	14,759	22,511	1,236	2,603
5530 Auto and home supply stores	32	34	252	253	7	13,683	15,257	3,886	4,157
5540 Gasoline service stations	96	99	567	555	6	11,026	12,620	6,769	7,208
5550 Boat dealers	18	21	137	159	8	18,891	22,340	3,235	3,719
5560 Recreational vehicle dealers [3]	3	3	28	36	12	15,857	17,222	631	765
5570 Motorcycle dealers [3]	5	5	37	43	9	17,081	19,907	884	1,006
5610 Men's & boys' clothing stores [2]	14	13	104	108	8	10,462	11,519	1,043	1,223
5620 Women's clothing stores	58	61	421	414	7	7,876	8,135	4,222	4,122
5630 Women's accessory & specialty stores	8	6	29	29	5	10,345	10,069	301	292
5640 Children's and infants' wear stores	7	9	31	34	4	6,194	5,882	211	224
5650 Family clothing stores	26	26	215	243	9	12,837	13,037	2,731	3,064
5660 Shoe stores	36	35	183	193	6	11,585	10,528	2,259	2,148
5690 Misc. apparel & accessory stores	18	17	54	57	3	6,889	7,579	509	541
5712 Furniture stores	50	55	375	416	8	13,579	15,240	5,770	6,637
5713 Floor covering stores	16	22	107	111	5	14,654	18,378	1,844	2,488
5714 Drapery and upholstery stores [3]	3	4	15	29	7	10,667	7,586	173	255
5719 Misc. homefurnishings stores	25	24	86	134	6	7,488	8,000	739	1,152
5720 Household appliance stores	9	9	30	27	3	12,667	14,667	430	452
5731 Radio, TV, & electronic stores	18	25	80	75	3	16,600	17,973	1,369	1,644
5734 Computer and software stores	9	11	27	27	2	19,556	22,519	572	611
5735 Record & prerecorded tape stores [3]	6	7	40	46	7	11,600	12,609	532	575
5736 Musical instrument stores [1]	3	-	9	-	-	17,333	-	187	-
5812 Eating places	360	340	7,326	7,140	21	6,732	7,122	58,095	59,513
5813 Drinking places	33	26	73	95	4	6,575	6,905	634	925
5910 Drug stores and proprietary stores	46	46	519	542	12	14,790	15,513	8,490	9,162
5920 Liquor stores	21	21	76	70	3	14,842	15,086	1,080	1,129
5930 Used merchandise stores	27	17	108	74	4	13,852	17,946	1,607	1,413
5941 Sporting goods and bicycle shops	34	33	116	128	4	11,931	13,500	1,711	1,915
5942 Book stores	17	14	60	75	5	8,200	7,200	512	556
5943 Stationery stores [3]	5	4	36	15	4	9,333	13,333	267	191
5944 Jewelry stores	26	27	144	181	7	13,500	14,144	2,163	2,530
5945 Hobby, toy, and game shops [1]	8	11	108	128	12	13,074	15,250	1,554	2,420
5947 Gift, novelty, and souvenir shops	49	50	205	240	5	7,473	7,667	2,389	2,669
5949 Sewing, needlework, and piece goods	8	9	39	45	5	10,051	8,444	410	439
5963 Direct selling establishments	14	13	60	59	5	28,133	26,983	1,592	1,686
5984 Liquefied petroleum gas dealers	-	8	-	50	6	-	20,320	-	1,020
5992 Florists	26	23	96	115	5	9,417	8,730	968	1,155
5995 Optical goods stores [3]	12	13	72	89	7	14,056	13,798	965	1,094
5999 Miscellaneous retail stores, nec	58	69	204	230	3	9,294	10,522	2,280	2,836

Source: County Business Patterns 1994/95, CBP-94/95, U.S. Department of Commerce, Washington DC, November 1997. The employment column represents mid-March employment in the year. Pay per employee is calculated by dividing 1st Quarter payroll, annualized, by mid-March employment. The column headed 'Emp / Est' shows 'employees per establishment'. A dash (-) means that data are unavailable or cannot be calculated. nec means not elsewhere classified. *Notes:* 1. 1994 data incomplete; unavailable or withheld. 2. 1995 data incomplete; unavailable or withheld. 3. 1994 and 1995 data incomplete; unavailable or withheld.

YAKIMA, WA MSA

Wholesale and Retail Trade USA	Establishments		Employment		Emp / Est	Pay / Employee		Annual Payroll ($ 000)	
	1994	1995	1994	1995	1995	1994	1995	1994	1995
50- Wholesale trade	-	368	-	5,621	15	-	23,546	-	140,322
5012 Automobiles and other vehicles	-	8	-	127	16	-	31,244	-	4,050
5013 Motor vehicle supplies and new parts	-	22	-	201	9	-	25,413	-	5,278
5021 Furniture	-	4	-	28	7	-	15,714	-	464
5030 Lumber and construction materials	-	7	-	132	19	-	28,727	-	4,270
5044 Office equipment	-	12	-	71	6	-	24,676	-	1,898
5046 Commercial equipment, nec	-	3	-	24	8	-	30,167	-	804
5063 Electrical apparatus and equipment	-	11	-	116	11	-	31,241	-	3,763
5072 Hardware	-	7	-	118	17	-	21,085	-	2,647
5074 Plumbing & hydronic heating supplies	-	7	-	63	9	-	26,540	-	1,300
5082 Construction and mining machinery	-	5	-	47	9	-	27,064	-	1,488
5083 Farm and garden machinery	-	21	-	375	18	-	19,701	-	8,404
5084 Industrial machinery and equipment	-	14	-	81	6	-	29,383	-	2,238
5085 Industrial supplies	-	12	-	117	10	-	28,923	-	3,338
5087 Service establishment equipment	-	6	-	66	11	-	25,939	-	1,989
5099 Durable goods, nec	-	5	-	213	43	-	16,939	-	4,332
5112 Stationery and office supplies	-	8	-	53	7	-	24,679	-	1,580
5113 Industrial & personal service paper	-	3	-	122	41	-	75,148	-	8,186
5130 Apparel, piece goods, and notions	-	3	-	24	8	-	21,000	-	565
5141 Groceries, general line	-	4	-	38	10	-	19,158	-	891
5147 Meats and meat products	-	5	-	97	19	-	39,381	-	3,975

Continued on next page.

YAKIMA, WA MSA - [continued]

Wholesale and Retail Trade USA	Establishments		Employment		Emp / Est	Pay / Employee		Annual Payroll ($ 000)	
	1994	1995	1994	1995	1995	1994	1995	1994	1995
5148 Fresh fruits and vegetables	-	50	-	1,947	39	-	17,948	-	38,369
5149 Groceries and related products, nec	-	7	-	48	7	-	30,667	-	1,573
5150 Farm-product raw materials	-	8	-	107	13	-	13,121	-	1,593
5170 Petroleum and petroleum products	-	12	-	250	21	-	23,184	-	6,463
5180 Beer, wine, and distilled beverages	-	5	-	148	30	-	24,000	-	4,095
5191 Farm supplies	-	37	-	295	8	-	28,122	-	8,694
5199 Nondurable goods, nec	-	6	-	41	7	-	19,317	-	913
52- Retail trade	-	1,166	-	14,057	12	-	13,563	-	197,896
5210 Lumber and other building materials	-	12	-	244	20	-	21,098	-	5,872
5230 Paint, glass, and wallpaper stores	-	6	-	50	8	-	23,760	-	1,471
5250 Hardware stores	-	13	-	121	9	-	12,595	-	1,744
5260 Retail nurseries and garden stores	-	7	-	44	6	-	6,727	-	426
5270 Mobile home dealers	-	9	-	91	10	-	68,440	-	3,862
5310 Department stores	-	12	-	1,751	146	-	12,503	-	23,231
5330 Variety stores	-	6	-	30	5	-	8,133	-	276
5390 Misc. general merchandise stores	-	12	-	348	29	-	21,862	-	8,119
5410 Grocery stores	-	115	-	2,054	18	-	15,287	-	32,668
5420 Meat and fish markets	-	7	-	29	4	-	11,172	-	381
5430 Fruit and vegetable markets	-	5	-	8	2	-	19,500	-	197
5450 Dairy products stores	-	5	-	5	1	-	8,000	-	37
5460 Retail bakeries	-	6	-	23	4	-	6,783	-	159
5490 Miscellaneous food stores	-	10	-	91	9	-	14,813	-	1,484
5510 New and used car dealers	-	18	-	657	37	-	27,896	-	19,992
5520 Used car dealers	-	48	-	177	4	-	18,780	-	3,455
5530 Auto and home supply stores	-	49	-	327	7	-	20,685	-	6,868
5540 Gasoline service stations	-	45	-	473	11	-	10,537	-	5,072
5550 Boat dealers	-	4	-	19	5	-	18,105	-	404
5560 Recreational vehicle dealers	-	3	-	28	9	-	20,571	-	796
5570 Motorcycle dealers	-	6	-	29	5	-	20,000	-	675
5610 Men's & boys' clothing stores	-	7	-	28	4	-	10,286	-	278
5620 Women's clothing stores	-	20	-	80	4	-	8,750	-	635
5630 Women's accessory & specialty stores	-	5	-	18	4	-	7,111	-	116
5650 Family clothing stores	-	16	-	368	23	-	11,598	-	4,394
5660 Shoe stores	-	16	-	81	5	-	10,420	-	816
5690 Misc. apparel & accessory stores	-	4	-	22	6	-	20,000	-	334
5712 Furniture stores	-	14	-	141	10	-	17,191	-	2,426
5713 Floor covering stores	-	10	-	102	10	-	18,275	-	1,993
5714 Drapery and upholstery stores	-	3	-	9	3	-	7,556	-	66
5719 Misc. homefurnishings stores	-	7	-	49	7	-	12,898	-	747
5720 Household appliance stores	-	10	-	70	7	-	21,429	-	1,361
5731 Radio, TV, & electronic stores	-	10	-	24	2	-	20,500	-	475
5735 Record & prerecorded tape stores	-	6	-	41	7	-	8,000	-	350
5812 Eating places	-	269	-	4,384	16	-	7,985	-	36,523
5813 Drinking places	-	53	-	276	5	-	7,232	-	1,975
5910 Drug stores and proprietary stores	-	26	-	400	15	-	15,560	-	6,214
5930 Used merchandise stores	-	17	-	133	8	-	11,910	-	1,558
5941 Sporting goods and bicycle shops	-	26	-	112	4	-	15,000	-	1,676
5942 Book stores	-	9	-	42	5	-	9,333	-	383
5944 Jewelry stores	-	13	-	76	6	-	17,316	-	1,270
5945 Hobby, toy, and game shops	-	10	-	60	6	-	12,800	-	949
5947 Gift, novelty, and souvenir shops	-	20	-	59	3	-	7,593	-	482
5949 Sewing, needlework, and piece goods	-	4	-	48	12	-	7,667	-	374
5960 Nonstore retailers	-	15	-	100	7	-	20,360	-	2,066
5980 Fuel dealers	-	7	-	53	8	-	21,585	-	1,164
5992 Florists	-	17	-	99	6	-	9,697	-	1,028
5995 Optical goods stores	-	11	-	71	6	-	18,873	-	1,032
5999 Miscellaneous retail stores, nec	-	29	-	127	4	-	13,480	-	1,958

Source: County Business Patterns 1994/95, CBP-94/95, U.S. Department of Commerce, Washington DC, November 1997. The employment column represents mid-March employment in the year. Pay per employee is calculated by dividing 1st Quarter payroll, annualized, by mid-March employment. The column headed 'Emp / Est' shows 'employees per establishment'. A dash (-) means that data are unavailable or cannot be calculated. nec means not elsewhere classified. *Notes:* 1. 1994 data incomplete; unavailable or withheld. 2. 1995 data incomplete; unavailable or withheld. 3. 1994 and 1995 data incomplete; unavailable or withheld.

YOLO, CA PMSA

Wholesale and Retail Trade USA	Establishments		Employment		Emp / Est	Pay / Employee		Annual Payroll ($ 000)	
	1994	1995	1994	1995	1995	1994	1995	1994	1995
50- Wholesale trade	304	298	5,860	6,301	21	29,407	30,461	182,297	198,400
5012 Automobiles and other vehicles	15	14	258	289	21	29,178	30,173	8,215	9,575
5013 Motor vehicle supplies and new parts	26	23	287	270	12	24,460	25,200	7,518	6,879

Continued on next page.

YOLO, CA PMSA - [continued]

Wholesale and Retail Trade USA	Establishments		Employment		Emp / Est	Pay / Employee		Annual Payroll ($ 000)	
	1994	1995	1994	1995	1995	1994	1995	1994	1995
5014 Tires and tubes	-	7	-	117	17	-	35,316	-	3,662
5015 Motor vehicle parts, used	-	3	-	16	5	-	12,750	-	243
5023 Homefurnishings	5	-	58	-	-	22,828	-	1,280	-
5031 Lumber, plywood, and millwork	8	4	128	107	27	31,719	30,879	4,018	3,350
5045 Computers, peripherals, & software	-	6	-	59	10	-	48,881	-	3,666
5046 Commercial equipment, nec	3	-	26	-	-	18,769	-	503	-
5051 Metals service centers and offices	-	5	-	48	10	-	26,667	-	1,405
5063 Electrical apparatus and equipment	6	6	20	24	4	25,200	27,500	504	647
5065 Electronic parts and equipment	8	8	156	133	17	40,462	42,165	6,509	4,573
5070 Hardware, plumbing & heating equipment	8	10	223	268	27	27,785	27,388	6,227	7,663
5082 Construction and mining machinery	6	4	33	28	7	33,697	28,286	1,218	1,286
5083 Farm and garden machinery	15	15	163	182	12	25,988	29,736	5,677	6,171
5084 Industrial machinery and equipment	32	30	390	396	13	34,585	38,576	14,464	15,032
5085 Industrial supplies	9	10	73	81	8	23,671	26,272	2,038	2,160
5093 Scrap and waste materials	5	6	75	82	14	19,520	22,098	1,519	1,580
5099 Durable goods, nec	5	5	399	698	140	20,050	21,112	9,154	15,695
5110 Paper and paper products	6	-	131	-	-	39,908	-	5,445	-
5120 Drugs, proprietaries, and sundries	3	4	289	292	73	34,242	29,877	11,200	9,973
5148 Fresh fruits and vegetables	9	7	158	313	45	30,025	28,754	6,832	9,815
5149 Groceries and related products, nec	11	11	182	206	19	35,451	39,748	5,662	6,808
5153 Grain and field beans	5	5	40	44	9	22,600	22,000	1,176	1,198
5160 Chemicals and allied products	7	7	65	54	8	30,954	34,889	1,969	1,797
5171 Petroleum bulk stations & terminals	9	7	264	256	37	30,258	31,594	8,035	8,202
5172 Petroleum products, nec	6	-	160	-	-	24,400	-	3,868	-
5191 Farm supplies	17	13	174	126	10	27,885	33,905	5,424	6,159
5192 Books, periodicals, & newspapers	3	-	40	-	-	18,700	-	893	-
5199 Nondurable goods, nec	8	-	39	-	-	18,667	-	649	-
52 – Retail trade	677	689	11,729	12,220	18	15,015	15,950	195,691	212,388
5210 Lumber and other building materials	8	10	124	161	16	30,065	23,727	4,096	4,075
5230 Paint, glass, and wallpaper stores	8	-	30	-	-	15,333	-	512	-
5250 Hardware stores	8	6	100	81	14	14,480	16,049	1,642	1,373
5260 Retail nurseries and garden stores	4	4	44	40	10	11,909	12,600	509	459
5270 Mobile home dealers	3	-	7	-	-	55,429	-	185	-
5310 Department stores	5	5	497	508	102	9,996	10,827	5,360	5,812
5330 Variety stores	3	-	18	-	-	6,889	-	158	-
5390 Misc. general merchandise stores	5	-	72	-	-	8,944	-	686	-
5410 Grocery stores	63	66	1,421	1,427	22	19,313	20,118	28,866	29,040
5440 Candy, nut, and confectionery stores	3	3	6	8	3	15,333	9,500	163	128
5460 Retail bakeries	10	6	83	41	7	5,012	5,561	479	194
5490 Miscellaneous food stores	-	6	-	29	5	-	10,759	-	414
5510 New and used car dealers	13	12	389	367	31	26,571	29,068	11,269	11,736
5520 Used car dealers	4	5	11	21	4	21,818	23,810	385	527
5530 Auto and home supply stores	24	23	159	198	9	15,170	15,071	2,894	3,370
5540 Gasoline service stations	42	46	384	439	10	12,448	12,601	5,169	5,612
5560 Recreational vehicle dealers	4	4	62	73	18	31,742	32,658	2,326	2,102
5610 Men's & boys' clothing stores	3	-	10	-	-	10,800	-	121	-
5620 Women's clothing stores	11	10	89	77	8	7,596	7,636	783	569
5630 Women's accessory & specialty stores	-	3	-	13	4	-	5,538	-	61
5650 Family clothing stores	8	8	77	88	11	8,831	9,500	777	628
5660 Shoe stores	14	14	69	65	5	8,638	9,477	649	767
5690 Misc. apparel & accessory stores	5	4	15	12	3	9,067	8,333	207	123
5712 Furniture stores	6	4	37	33	8	18,595	18,424	663	626
5713 Floor covering stores	3	-	18	-	-	9,111	-	176	-
5719 Misc. homefurnishings stores	4	-	8	-	-	8,500	-	64	-
5720 Household appliance stores	5	4	30	39	10	21,600	18,154	617	393
5734 Computer and software stores	3	5	16	20	4	8,500	13,800	149	309
5735 Record & prerecorded tape stores	6	8	67	69	9	6,806	7,420	585	568
5812 Eating places	189	180	3,719	3,594	20	7,122	7,687	29,386	29,119
5813 Drinking places	20	20	104	117	6	6,962	6,803	739	834
5910 Drug stores and proprietary stores	11	11	293	492	45	20,314	18,065	5,840	9,070
5920 Liquor stores	10	11	21	13	1	11,048	10,769	215	203
5930 Used merchandise stores	9	10	119	132	13	9,277	13,000	1,351	1,106
5941 Sporting goods and bicycle shops	17	18	177	125	7	9,356	10,528	1,572	1,491
5942 Book stores	10	9	78	87	10	9,333	9,977	787	983
5944 Jewelry stores	12	12	53	39	3	15,019	16,718	769	803
5945 Hobby, toy, and game shops	5	-	15	-	-	9,067	-	165	-
5947 Gift, novelty, and souvenir shops	12	10	112	94	9	6,821	7,319	717	656
5949 Sewing, needlework, and piece goods	-	3	-	35	12	-	6,971	-	272
5960 Nonstore retailers	8	9	40	57	6	21,200	16,211	839	956

Continued on next page.

YOLO, CA PMSA - [continued]

Wholesale and Retail Trade USA	Establishments		Employment		Emp / Est	Pay / Employee		Annual Payroll ($ 000)	
	1994	1995	1994	1995	1995	1994	1995	1994	1995
5992 Florists	10	11	47	58	5	12,851	10,621	551	597
5995 Optical goods stores	5	4	11	11	3	14,182	15,273	149	173
5999 Miscellaneous retail stores, nec	15	19	62	58	3	11,419	10,414	771	622

Source: County Business Patterns 1994/95, CBP-94/95, U.S. Department of Commerce, Washington DC, November 1997. The employment column represents mid-March employment in the year. Pay per employee is calculated by dividing 1st Quarter payroll, annualized, by mid-March employment. The column headed 'Emp / Est' shows 'employees per establishment'. A dash (-) means that data are unavailable or cannot be calculated. nec means not elsewhere classified. *Notes:* 1. 1994 data incomplete; unavailable or withheld. 2. 1995 data incomplete; unavailable or withheld. 3. 1994 and 1995 data incomplete; unavailable or withheld.

YORK, PA MSA

Wholesale and Retail Trade USA	Establishments		Employment		Emp / Est	Pay / Employee		Annual Payroll ($ 000)	
	1994	1995	1994	1995	1995	1994	1995	1994	1995
50- Wholesale trade	-	546	-	8,344	15	-	29,789	-	248,558
5012 Automobiles and other vehicles	-	12	-	522	44	-	16,245	-	9,392
5013 Motor vehicle supplies and new parts	-	38	-	336	9	-	20,702	-	7,197
5014 Tires and tubes	-	5	-	28	6	-	22,286	-	599
5015 Motor vehicle parts, used	-	17	-	79	5	-	20,152	-	1,618
5021 Furniture	-	6	-	48	8	-	20,417	-	1,056
5023 Homefurnishings	-	6	-	416	69	-	35,077	-	14,626
5031 Lumber, plywood, and millwork	-	12	-	342	29	-	24,807	-	9,494
5033 Roofing, siding, & insulation	-	6	-	39	7	-	25,744	-	956
5044 Office equipment	-	11	-	155	14	-	24,155	-	4,247
5045 Computers, peripherals, & software	-	18	-	168	9	-	38,714	-	5,037
5047 Medical and hospital equipment	-	7	-	73	10	-	36,658	-	2,877
5050 Metals and minerals, except petroleum	-	10	-	273	27	-	30,388	-	8,966
5063 Electrical apparatus and equipment	-	25	-	480	19	-	44,842	-	19,842
5064 Electrical appliances, TV & radios	-	3	-	12	4	-	25,667	-	368
5065 Electronic parts and equipment	-	13	-	206	16	-	41,689	-	8,974
5072 Hardware	-	12	-	144	12	-	24,639	-	3,643
5074 Plumbing & hydronic heating supplies	-	8	-	79	10	-	24,000	-	1,643
5075 Warm air heating & air conditioning	-	7	-	78	11	-	39,128	-	2,456
5082 Construction and mining machinery	-	6	-	382	64	-	28,513	-	10,629
5083 Farm and garden machinery	-	13	-	78	6	-	18,513	-	1,451
5084 Industrial machinery and equipment	-	42	-	549	13	-	34,324	-	18,725
5085 Industrial supplies	-	34	-	692	20	-	32,283	-	22,444
5087 Service establishment equipment	-	12	-	97	8	-	15,052	-	1,488
5091 Sporting & recreational goods	-	7	-	69	10	-	17,217	-	1,261
5093 Scrap and waste materials	-	13	-	206	16	-	27,204	-	5,766
5099 Durable goods, nec	-	12	-	69	6	-	16,812	-	1,796
5111 Printing and writing paper	-	4	-	30	8	-	29,333	-	976
5112 Stationery and office supplies	-	12	-	143	12	-	17,566	-	2,660
5113 Industrial & personal service paper	-	6	-	172	29	-	31,279	-	5,228
5120 Drugs, proprietaries, and sundries	-	5	-	181	36	-	25,459	-	4,835
5130 Apparel, piece goods, and notions	-	4	-	27	7	-	14,815	-	507
5145 Confectionery	-	6	-	72	12	-	13,333	-	1,002
5146 Fish and seafoods	-	4	-	21	5	-	24,762	-	547
5148 Fresh fruits and vegetables	-	5	-	47	9	-	18,298	-	869
5149 Groceries and related products, nec	-	14	-	550	39	-	32,844	-	17,806
5160 Chemicals and allied products	-	13	-	111	9	-	21,333	-	2,440
5171 Petroleum bulk stations & terminals	-	12	-	248	21	-	40,210	-	9,847
5172 Petroleum products, nec	-	6	-	53	9	-	24,377	-	1,337
5180 Beer, wine, and distilled beverages	-	9	-	129	14	-	27,907	-	3,913
5191 Farm supplies	-	19	-	172	9	-	18,465	-	4,029
5194 Tobacco and tobacco products	-	4	-	46	12	-	18,087	-	907
5198 Paints, varnishes, and supplies	-	5	-	71	14	-	20,676	-	1,431
5199 Nondurable goods, nec	-	10	-	33	3	-	27,636	-	966
52- Retail trade	-	1,968	-	30,918	16	-	13,344	-	423,792
5210 Lumber and other building materials	-	35	-	750	21	-	20,192	-	14,451
5230 Paint, glass, and wallpaper stores	-	11	-	57	5	-	16,070	-	918
5250 Hardware stores	-	17	-	126	7	-	9,937	-	1,329
5260 Retail nurseries and garden stores	-	31	-	256	8	-	15,719	-	5,110
5270 Mobile home dealers	-	7	-	46	7	-	22,174	-	1,244
5310 Department stores	-	21	-	2,910	139	-	11,309	-	34,050
5330 Variety stores	-	19	-	198	10	-	8,263	-	1,648
5390 Misc. general merchandise stores	-	11	-	374	34	-	14,332	-	5,620
5410 Grocery stores	-	168	-	5,201	31	-	9,707	-	52,253
5420 Meat and fish markets	-	17	-	58	3	-	10,621	-	578
5430 Fruit and vegetable markets	-	4	-	4	1	-	4,000	-	21
5440 Candy, nut, and confectionery stores	-	11	-	88	8	-	4,636	-	473

Continued on next page.

YORK, PA MSA - [continued]

Wholesale and Retail Trade USA	Establishments		Employment		Emp / Est	Pay / Employee		Annual Payroll ($ 000)	
	1994	1995	1994	1995	1995	1994	1995	1994	1995
5460 Retail bakeries	-	19	-	118	6	-	7,559	-	829
5490 Miscellaneous food stores	-	10	-	60	6	-	9,667	-	686
5510 New and used car dealers	-	43	-	1,745	41	-	25,197	-	46,892
5520 Used car dealers	-	44	-	168	4	-	17,643	-	3,305
5530 Auto and home supply stores	-	41	-	296	7	-	18,365	-	5,646
5540 Gasoline service stations	-	114	-	792	7	-	11,374	-	8,866
5550 Boat dealers	-	4	-	18	5	-	19,556	-	404
5560 Recreational vehicle dealers	-	7	-	24	3	-	14,500	-	455
5570 Motorcycle dealers	-	10	-	60	6	-	15,667	-	1,234
5610 Men's & boys' clothing stores	-	12	-	59	5	-	12,271	-	704
5620 Women's clothing stores	-	41	-	392	10	-	7,408	-	2,772
5630 Women's accessory & specialty stores	-	9	-	48	5	-	8,667	-	394
5640 Children's and infants' wear stores	-	4	-	27	7	-	8,296	-	194
5650 Family clothing stores	-	15	-	280	19	-	11,114	-	3,225
5660 Shoe stores	-	47	-	275	6	-	10,560	-	2,864
5690 Misc. apparel & accessory stores	-	7	-	47	7	-	10,979	-	544
5712 Furniture stores	-	39	-	289	7	-	17,772	-	4,749
5713 Floor covering stores	-	22	-	116	5	-	18,655	-	2,235
5720 Household appliance stores	-	12	-	66	6	-	17,394	-	1,171
5731 Radio, TV, & electronic stores	-	25	-	108	4	-	19,852	-	1,934
5734 Computer and software stores	-	9	-	53	6	-	12,755	-	660
5735 Record & prerecorded tape stores	-	13	-	92	7	-	10,565	-	847
5736 Musical instrument stores	-	5	-	46	9	-	19,913	-	990
5812 Eating places	-	421	-	8,634	21	-	7,300	-	65,957
5813 Drinking places	-	67	-	287	4	-	7,749	-	2,294
5910 Drug stores and proprietary stores	-	61	-	593	10	-	15,798	-	10,034
5941 Sporting goods and bicycle shops	-	34	-	282	8	-	12,426	-	4,155
5942 Book stores	-	13	-	97	7	-	8,371	-	877
5943 Stationery stores	-	3	-	45	15	-	13,778	-	614
5944 Jewelry stores	-	39	-	197	5	-	12,629	-	2,437
5945 Hobby, toy, and game shops	-	18	-	179	10	-	8,648	-	1,749
5946 Camera & photographic supply stores	-	8	-	24	3	-	15,333	-	643
5947 Gift, novelty, and souvenir shops	-	55	-	291	5	-	7,478	-	2,324
5948 Luggage and leather goods stores	-	3	-	8	3	-	8,500	-	46
5949 Sewing, needlework, and piece goods	-	8	-	92	12	-	7,957	-	744
5963 Direct selling establishments	-	19	-	114	6	-	17,509	-	2,004
5983 Fuel oil dealers	-	13	-	119	9	-	16,034	-	2,078
5992 Florists	-	21	-	199	9	-	11,457	-	2,041
5994 News dealers and newsstands	-	7	-	49	7	-	10,776	-	551
5995 Optical goods stores	-	26	-	134	5	-	20,687	-	2,691
5999 Miscellaneous retail stores, nec	-	63	-	365	6	-	11,879	-	4,744

Source: County Business Patterns 1994/95, CBP-94/95, U.S. Department of Commerce, Washington DC, November 1997. The employment column represents mid-March employment in the year. Pay per employee is calculated by dividing 1st Quarter payroll, annualized, by mid-March employment. The column headed 'Emp / Est' shows 'employees per establishment'. A dash (-) means that data are unavailable or cannot be calculated. nec means not elsewhere classified. *Notes:* 1. 1994 data incomplete; unavailable or withheld. 2. 1995 data incomplete; unavailable or withheld. 3. 1994 and 1995 data incomplete; unavailable or withheld.

YOUNGSTOWN–WARREN, OH MSA

Wholesale and Retail Trade USA	Establishments		Employment		Emp / Est	Pay / Employee		Annual Payroll ($ 000)	
	1994	1995	1994	1995	1995	1994	1995	1994	1995
50- Wholesale trade	875	866	11,042	11,225	13	23,596	25,461	294,936	305,522
5012 Automobiles and other vehicles	29	32	506	597	19	24,909	28,268	17,535	19,049
5013 Motor vehicle supplies and new parts	47	45	419	435	10	20,420	23,623	8,364	9,413
5014 Tires and tubes [3]	7	5	65	24	5	20,492	17,000	1,518	450
5015 Motor vehicle parts, used	25	26	71	77	3	14,817	15,844	1,156	1,258
5021 Furniture [3]	12	11	112	128	12	24,321	27,875	2,892	3,128
5023 Homefurnishings [3]	9	10	29	42	4	25,241	21,619	835	923
5031 Lumber, plywood, and millwork	19	17	227	164	10	21,885	23,512	5,348	3,968
5032 Brick, stone, & related materials	9	9	357	383	43	18,611	20,146	10,895	13,047
5033 Roofing, siding, & insulation [3]	6	7	51	55	8	35,059	34,618	2,257	2,351
5039 Construction materials, nec	9	12	44	101	8	18,091	21,901	1,025	2,616
5044 Office equipment [3]	13	14	145	130	9	24,910	20,738	3,920	2,839
5045 Computers, peripherals, & software [2]	12	11	123	133	12	39,122	35,910	5,114	5,480
5046 Commercial equipment, nec	14	12	115	47	4	18,783	24,000	2,192	1,122
5047 Medical and hospital equipment [3]	19	17	227	200	12	25,445	30,600	5,598	5,085
5049 Professional equipment, nec [2]	-	5	-	25	5	-	9,760	-	340
5051 Metals service centers and offices [3]	56	55	509	534	10	27,819	31,079	16,918	18,207
5052 Coal and other minerals and ores [1]	4	-	13	-	-	36,923	-	430	-
5063 Electrical apparatus and equipment	25	24	242	229	10	22,083	28,105	6,352	6,454

Continued on next page.

YOUNGSTOWN - WARREN, OH MSA - [continued]

Wholesale and Retail Trade USA	Establishments		Employment		Emp / Est	Pay / Employee		Annual Payroll ($ 000)	
	1994	1995	1994	1995	1995	1994	1995	1994	1995
5064 Electrical appliances, TV & radios	7	7	21	22	3	39,619	44,000	681	715
5065 Electronic parts and equipment	21	22	168	161	7	20,238	24,199	3,696	4,664
5072 Hardware	8	12	42	59	5	27,238	22,102	1,240	1,488
5074 Plumbing & hydronic heating supplies [3]	23	24	174	190	8	26,161	25,011	5,025	5,314
5075 Warm air heating & air conditioning [3]	9	9	62	67	7	27,871	28,299	2,165	2,361
5078 Refrigeration equipment and supplies [3]	4	4	51	38	10	25,490	26,632	1,410	1,228
5082 Construction and mining machinery	-	7	-	67	10	-	39,104	-	2,363
5083 Farm and garden machinery	-	14	-	113	8	-	22,796	-	2,907
5084 Industrial machinery and equipment	-	55	-	730	13	-	33,956	-	26,772
5085 Industrial supplies	-	45	-	448	10	-	31,946	-	16,565
5087 Service establishment equipment	-	9	-	75	8	-	19,253	-	1,455
5093 Scrap and waste materials	-	39	-	445	11	-	20,009	-	11,727
5099 Durable goods, nec	-	22	-	106	5	-	20,113	-	2,464
5110 Paper and paper products	-	22	-	262	12	-	17,237	-	4,580
5120 Drugs, proprietaries, and sundries	-	18	-	672	37	-	21,357	-	10,525
5141 Groceries, general line	-	10	-	173	17	-	27,538	-	3,024
5148 Fresh fruits and vegetables	-	6	-	127	21	-	20,283	-	3,684
5149 Groceries and related products, nec	-	24	-	480	20	-	30,575	-	15,240
5160 Chemicals and allied products	-	13	-	119	9	-	18,286	-	2,565
5170 Petroleum and petroleum products	-	22	-	268	12	-	24,313	-	6,899
5180 Beer, wine, and distilled beverages [2]	-	9	-	268	30	-	24,373	-	7,383
5191 Farm supplies	-	20	-	169	8	-	15,716	-	3,358
5192 Books, periodicals, & newspapers	-	8	-	54	7	-	35,926	-	1,074
5193 Flowers & florists' supplies	-	7	-	118	17	-	8,610	-	1,100
5199 Nondurable goods, nec	-	25	-	82	3	-	14,732	-	1,543
52- Retail trade	3,611	3,658	50,043	50,881	14	10,471	11,292	581,517	615,510
5210 Lumber and other building materials	59	52	1,066	1,011	19	11,737	15,039	15,087	15,786
5230 Paint, glass, and wallpaper stores	20	21	58	41	2	15,241	13,268	970	597
5250 Hardware stores	50	37	509	336	9	10,798	10,988	6,473	3,659
5260 Retail nurseries and garden stores	27	30	152	222	7	10,105	11,495	2,199	3,270
5310 Department stores	31	32	4,683	4,525	141	9,261	11,648	49,530	53,866
5330 Variety stores	40	34	483	406	12	8,290	8,660	4,329	3,864
5390 Misc. general merchandise stores	25	29	634	691	24	11,621	11,693	7,660	7,849
5410 Grocery stores	338	337	6,488	6,733	20	10,215	10,657	71,688	76,777
5420 Meat and fish markets	18	16	32	28	2	7,625	6,714	214	207
5440 Candy, nut, and confectionery stores	15	15	22	29	2	5,273	4,966	124	142
5450 Dairy products stores [1]	4	-	10	-	-	7,200	-	75	-
5460 Retail bakeries	46	46	362	418	9	10,232	8,718	3,497	3,503
5490 Miscellaneous food stores	14	13	58	55	4	9,448	13,891	630	774
5510 New and used car dealers	70	71	2,602	2,637	37	22,781	25,106	71,140	73,994
5520 Used car dealers	56	54	190	209	4	15,347	16,517	3,255	3,831
5530 Auto and home supply stores	110	121	689	743	6	13,962	16,393	11,014	13,410
5540 Gasoline service stations	264	269	2,058	1,876	7	8,468	9,539	17,908	18,706
5550 Boat dealers [3]	10	9	29	24	3	11,586	14,167	373	332
5560 Recreational vehicle dealers	8	7	12	14	2	18,667	20,000	281	298
5570 Motorcycle dealers	10	9	23	69	8	13,739	13,797	502	1,157
5610 Men's & boys' clothing stores	35	34	224	228	7	9,321	10,228	2,418	2,351
5620 Women's clothing stores	110	92	978	802	9	7,387	7,327	7,900	5,947
5630 Women's accessory & specialty stores	18	16	60	91	6	7,200	8,264	486	783
5640 Children's and infants' wear stores [3]	5	5	33	30	6	7,030	8,533	280	264
5650 Family clothing stores	33	34	466	415	12	8,876	9,243	4,108	4,106
5660 Shoe stores	80	72	391	414	6	10,015	10,097	4,105	4,017
5690 Misc. apparel & accessory stores	18	23	49	63	3	9,878	10,286	450	609
5712 Furniture stores	62	63	702	654	10	15,840	18,373	13,258	13,353
5713 Floor covering stores	34	37	184	183	5	15,152	16,437	3,308	3,632
5719 Misc. homefurnishings stores [1]	30	30	138	408	14	17,362	10,980	2,855	5,109
5720 Household appliance stores	16	19	76	79	4	10,947	12,253	991	1,109
5731 Radio, TV, & electronic stores	48	45	380	430	10	17,295	16,000	5,954	6,653
5734 Computer and software stores [2]	13	11	63	72	7	12,254	15,222	886	1,117
5735 Record & prerecorded tape stores	14	11	152	144	13	6,816	7,278	1,015	944
5736 Musical instrument stores	10	10	31	29	3	9,161	11,310	315	309
5812 Eating places	818	788	15,571	16,186	21	6,402	6,660	111,913	116,461
5813 Drinking places	191	183	751	679	4	6,072	6,233	4,626	4,347
5910 Drug stores and proprietary stores	130	134	1,604	1,619	12	13,239	14,873	22,420	24,368
5920 Liquor stores	52	45	165	199	4	9,455	9,769	1,603	2,082
5930 Used merchandise stores	35	34	259	250	7	8,216	10,416	2,356	2,906
5941 Sporting goods and bicycle shops	46	48	205	265	6	12,390	11,789	2,837	3,341
5942 Book stores	25	23	133	139	6	8,150	8,863	1,125	1,312
5943 Stationery stores	5	6	9	11	2	8,000	9,818	88	214
5944 Jewelry stores	63	66	333	355	5	14,727	15,031	5,148	5,503
5945 Hobby, toy, and game shops	19	19	201	246	13	10,667	9,089	2,650	2,582

Continued on next page.

YOUNGSTOWN - WARREN, OH MSA - [continued]

Wholesale and Retail Trade USA	Establishments		Employment		Emp / Est	Pay / Employee		Annual Payroll ($ 000)	
	1994	1995	1994	1995	1995	1994	1995	1994	1995
5947 Gift, novelty, and souvenir shops	64	68	350	336	5	7,509	7,952	3,033	3,040
5949 Sewing, needlework, and piece goods	20	19	132	133	7	5,879	6,406	865	992
5961 Catalog and mail-order houses	10	14	183	396	28	16,852	13,818	3,085	5,387
5962 Merchandising machine operators[3]	18	19	58	57	3	18,000	20,070	1,153	1,220
5963 Direct selling establishments	27	27	88	98	4	7,773	7,878	805	877
5983 Fuel oil dealers	10	12	18	68	6	15,556	15,235	287	1,217
5984 Liquefied petroleum gas dealers	9	9	11	46	5	11,273	19,130	283	996
5992 Florists	68	63	380	369	6	7,695	7,957	3,154	3,057
5994 News dealers and newsstands	13	13	38	34	3	6,000	7,412	233	245
5995 Optical goods stores	43	47	168	172	4	14,524	16,163	2,548	2,818
5999 Miscellaneous retail stores, nec	88	93	392	492	5	11,286	12,846	4,795	6,543

Source: County Business Patterns 1994/95, CBP-94/95, U.S. Department of Commerce, Washington DC, November 1997. The employment column represents mid-March employment in the year. Pay per employee is calculated by dividing 1st Quarter payroll, annualized, by mid-March employment. The column headed 'Emp / Est' shows 'employees per establishment'. A dash (-) means that data are unavailable or cannot be calculated. nec means not elsewhere classified. *Notes:* 1. 1994 data incomplete; unavailable or withheld. 2. 1995 data incomplete; unavailable or withheld. 3. 1994 and 1995 data incomplete; unavailable or withheld.

YUBA CITY, CA MSA

Wholesale and Retail Trade USA	Establishments		Employment		Emp / Est	Pay / Employee		Annual Payroll ($ 000)	
	1994	1995	1994	1995	1995	1994	1995	1994	1995
50- Wholesale trade	151	145	1,242	1,205	8	24,805	28,050	33,329	36,038
5013 Motor vehicle supplies and new parts	11	11	31	33	3	15,613	15,030	515	505
5015 Motor vehicle parts, used	6	-	21	-	-	13,333	-	327	-
5032 Brick, stone, & related materials[2]	-	3	-	52	17	-	15,923	-	951
5040 Professional & commercial equipment	6	6	21	16	3	15,810	16,500	311	210
5051 Metals service centers and offices[3]	4	4	27	27	7	23,556	20,741	683	611
5060 Electrical goods[2]	10	6	97	23	4	17,402	29,391	867	545
5072 Hardware	4	4	15	9	2	9,067	11,556	127	136
5082 Construction and mining machinery	-	4	-	144	36	-	43,639	-	6,453
5083 Farm and garden machinery[3]	7	7	86	85	12	26,372	26,588	2,971	3,001
5084 Industrial machinery and equipment	-	5	-	36	7	-	35,556	-	1,273
5085 Industrial supplies	-	5	-	35	7	-	39,429	-	1,293
5087 Service establishment equipment[2]	-	6	-	7	1	-	12,000	-	86
5090 Miscellaneous durable goods	9	9	24	35	4	8,833	16,000	236	570
5110 Paper and paper products	6	-	32	-	-	13,625	-	849	-
5149 Groceries and related products, nec	7	6	33	36	6	28,606	30,778	949	1,095
5153 Grain and field beans[3]	4	4	28	27	7	29,857	31,259	1,067	1,061
5170 Petroleum and petroleum products	7	6	26	24	4	20,615	21,500	520	515
5191 Farm supplies	17	15	123	162	11	21,789	31,136	3,379	5,312
52- Retail trade	599	577	7,184	6,941	12	12,344	13,354	94,927	96,292
5210 Lumber and other building materials	12	8	208	152	19	20,346	19,447	4,881	3,626
5250 Hardware stores	5	-	115	-	-	11,722	-	1,436	-
5260 Retail nurseries and garden stores	4	4	26	15	4	12,154	13,333	296	211
5310 Department stores[3]	8	8	818	842	105	10,381	12,290	9,522	10,429
5390 Misc. general merchandise stores	6	6	218	221	37	12,330	13,991	2,972	3,163
5410 Grocery stores	76	84	1,098	1,084	13	17,446	19,284	20,677	20,718
5440 Candy, nut, and confectionery stores	4	-	8	-	-	10,500	-	93	-
5460 Retail bakeries[2]	10	7	36	30	4	8,333	7,067	246	202
5510 New and used car dealers	8	9	330	338	38	24,218	24,473	8,605	9,039
5520 Used car dealers	10	10	6	23	2	14,667	19,826	135	431
5530 Auto and home supply stores	24	22	180	185	8	12,622	13,600	2,562	2,553
5540 Gasoline service stations	29	30	170	199	7	10,847	10,231	2,082	2,212
5550 Boat dealers[2]	-	3	-	8	3	-	10,000	-	87
5620 Women's clothing stores	15	10	105	67	7	7,390	5,493	829	383
5650 Family clothing stores	5	5	41	38	8	7,512	8,421	351	376
5660 Shoe stores[3]	13	12	48	67	6	12,417	9,672	703	642
5712 Furniture stores	15	15	71	69	5	18,761	17,043	1,330	1,156
5713 Floor covering stores	8	-	38	-	-	19,789	-	781	-
5719 Misc. homefurnishings stores[2]	-	7	-	21	3	-	12,000	-	216
5720 Household appliance stores	5	4	18	14	4	14,667	15,143	272	206
5731 Radio, TV, & electronic stores	7	7	25	26	4	14,720	15,538	364	393
5734 Computer and software stores	4	-	13	-	-	11,385	-	112	-
5735 Record & prerecorded tape stores	4	-	28	-	-	9,000	-	260	-
5812 Eating places	149	131	2,241	2,003	15	6,718	7,696	16,742	16,712
5813 Drinking places	21	20	74	93	5	6,811	10,237	519	807
5910 Drug stores and proprietary stores	11	11	214	217	20	22,692	23,263	4,992	5,151
5920 Liquor stores	8	-	9	-	-	10,222	-	76	-
5930 Used merchandise stores	6	7	48	33	5	21,333	8,970	738	381
5941 Sporting goods and bicycle shops	9	11	42	29	3	8,095	9,655	398	324

Continued on next page.

YUBA CITY, CA MSA - [continued]

Wholesale and Retail Trade USA	Establishments		Employment		Emp / Est	Pay / Employee		Annual Payroll ($ 000)	
	1994	1995	1994	1995	1995	1994	1995	1994	1995
5944 Jewelry stores	9	10	46	46	5	19,391	21,130	894	865
5945 Hobby, toy, and game shops	5	6	53	45	8	9,962	11,111	596	544
5947 Gift, novelty, and souvenir shops	10	8	46	40	5	5,913	6,700	308	261
5963 Direct selling establishments	5	5	7	5	1	9,714	9,600	55	61
5984 Liquefied petroleum gas dealers	4	-	13	-	-	14,769	-	227	-
5992 Florists	7	7	17	19	3	12,471	10,947	205	202
5999 Miscellaneous retail stores, nec	23	22	74	88	4	8,378	9,000	757	901

Source: County Business Patterns 1994/95, CBP-94/95, U.S. Department of Commerce, Washington DC, November 1997. The employment column represents mid-March employment in the year. Pay per employee is calculated by dividing 1st Quarter payroll, annualized, by mid-March employment. The column headed 'Emp / Est' shows 'employees per establishment'. A dash (-) means that data are unavailable or cannot be calculated. nec means not elsewhere classified. *Notes:* 1. 1994 data incomplete; unavailable or withheld. 2. 1995 data incomplete; unavailable or withheld. 3. 1994 and 1995 data incomplete; unavailable or withheld.

YUMA, AZ MSA

Wholesale and Retail Trade USA	Establishments		Employment		Emp / Est	Pay / Employee		Annual Payroll ($ 000)	
	1994	1995	1994	1995	1995	1994	1995	1994	1995
50- Wholesale trade	164	166	3,061	3,014	18	19,638	16,027	47,763	45,666
5013 Motor vehicle supplies and new parts	12	10	76	62	6	15,368	17,742	1,139	1,114
5015 Motor vehicle parts, used	-	3	-	13	4	-	18,154	-	239
5039 Construction materials, nec	-	5	-	23	5	-	17,391	-	429
5040 Professional & commercial equipment	10	8	71	58	7	15,944	17,241	1,254	880
5065 Electronic parts and equipment	5	5	28	29	6	29,714	34,897	656	1,358
5074 Plumbing & hydronic heating supplies	5	-	48	-	-	14,250	-	820	-
5083 Farm and garden machinery	12	11	129	139	13	25,674	28,691	3,791	4,578
5084 Industrial machinery and equipment	-	3	-	18	6	-	23,556	-	529
5085 Industrial supplies	-	3	-	6	2	-	26,667	-	200
5087 Service establishment equipment	5	-	33	-	-	14,061	-	444	-
5090 Miscellaneous durable goods	-	5	-	16	3	-	5,750	-	83
5120 Drugs, proprietaries, and sundries	-	3	-	12	4	-	19,333	-	265
5141 Groceries, general line	5	4	36	24	6	21,222	25,333	672	598
5148 Fresh fruits and vegetables	8	8	1,530	1,611	201	17,744	9,281	11,910	9,334
5149 Groceries and related products, nec	10	10	107	106	11	20,374	22,264	2,242	2,304
5169 Chemicals & allied products, nec	4	4	25	30	8	10,880	12,000	370	313
5170 Petroleum and petroleum products	5	5	81	80	16	29,235	32,700	3,063	3,174
5191 Farm supplies	-	29	-	343	12	-	27,102	-	10,334
52- Retail trade	652	659	8,962	9,712	15	12,217	12,321	105,360	112,049
5210 Lumber and other building materials	6	5	98	86	17	18,082	18,930	1,659	1,498
5230 Paint, glass, and wallpaper stores	7	10	33	36	4	13,333	13,667	485	493
5250 Hardware stores	6	5	93	83	17	10,065	11,036	1,029	1,048
5260 Retail nurseries and garden stores	7	7	44	51	7	19,727	19,294	966	1,132
5270 Mobile home dealers	8	9	86	70	8	24,884	18,000	1,784	1,020
5310 Department stores	7	6	1,228	928	155	10,736	12,280	14,006	10,557
5410 Grocery stores	55	50	1,168	1,766	35	14,301	12,988	15,031	21,181
5460 Retail bakeries	-	7	-	53	8	-	7,094	-	335
5490 Miscellaneous food stores	4	-	13	-	-	17,231	-	250	-
5510 New and used car dealers	10	9	408	400	44	27,578	29,630	11,425	12,144
5520 Used car dealers	11	14	38	60	4	14,211	14,533	748	962
5530 Auto and home supply stores	31	29	277	271	9	13,617	15,557	4,305	4,561
5540 Gasoline service stations	50	46	385	390	8	11,439	11,446	4,291	4,287
5560 Recreational vehicle dealers	12	12	180	225	19	31,644	30,667	3,062	3,373
5570 Motorcycle dealers	-	3	-	35	12	-	14,629	-	584
5610 Men's & boys' clothing stores	-	4	-	22	6	-	11,455	-	257
5620 Women's clothing stores	20	15	101	83	6	8,396	7,084	842	459
5650 Family clothing stores	9	8	149	140	18	7,544	7,171	1,043	956
5660 Shoe stores	14	13	59	50	4	9,627	12,320	625	547
5690 Misc. apparel & accessory stores	7	7	18	19	3	8,000	8,211	154	138
5712 Furniture stores	20	21	122	105	5	16,557	16,838	2,226	2,095
5713 Floor covering stores	4	-	12	-	-	14,333	-	217	-
5719 Misc. homefurnishings stores	7	10	9	34	3	14,667	12,353	145	413
5731 Radio, TV, & electronic stores	9	8	65	75	9	16,985	16,373	1,096	1,256
5735 Record & prerecorded tape stores	5	-	54	-	-	8,593	-	406	-
5736 Musical instrument stores	-	3	-	5	2	-	9,600	-	42
5812 Eating places	148	148	2,994	3,248	22	8,067	8,046	22,402	23,494
5813 Drinking places	32	27	160	150	6	8,150	7,707	1,257	1,116
5910 Drug stores and proprietary stores	11	11	233	256	23	18,953	20,609	4,407	4,843
5920 Liquor stores	6	7	23	25	4	6,261	7,680	137	193
5930 Used merchandise stores	4	4	23	23	6	7,304	8,696	167	209
5941 Sporting goods and bicycle shops	10	10	86	79	8	11,349	12,759	931	1,018
5942 Book stores	5	-	13	-	-	6,462	-	145	-

Continued on next page.

YUMA, AZ MSA - [continued]

Wholesale and Retail Trade USA	Establishments		Employment		Emp / Est	Pay / Employee		Annual Payroll ($ 000)	
	1994	1995	1994	1995	1995	1994	1995	1994	1995
5944 Jewelry stores	9	11	43	126	11	16,651	6,730	707	924
5945 Hobby, toy, and game shops	9	8	29	28	4	8,000	8,143	258	858
5947 Gift, novelty, and souvenir shops	12	10	46	47	5	7,739	10,298	355	483
5949 Sewing, needlework, and piece goods	4	-	40	-	-	7,700	-	247	-
5960 Nonstore retailers	6	7	27	33	5	23,704	24,364	677	819
5984 Liquefied petroleum gas dealers	4	4	33	38	10	20,606	16,211	506	540
5992 Florists	10	10	56	58	6	8,643	12,483	485	561

Source: County Business Patterns 1994/95, CBP-94/95, U.S. Department of Commerce, Washington DC, November 1997. The employment column represents mid-March employment in the year. Pay per employee is calculated by dividing 1st Quarter payroll, annualized, by mid-March employment. The column headed 'Emp / Est' shows 'employees per establishment'. A dash (-) means that data are unavailable or cannot be calculated. nec means not elsewhere classified. *Notes:* 1. 1994 data incomplete; unavailable or withheld. 2. 1995 data incomplete; unavailable or withheld. 3. 1994 and 1995 data incomplete; unavailable or withheld.

SIC INDEX

The SIC Index shows all 4-digit SICs covered in *Wholesale and Retail Trade USA* in numerical order. A separate section, listing the industries in alphabetical order, follows. In the alphabetical section, each industry name is followed by the SIC number (in parentheses) and then by one or more page numbers. This SIC structure is based on the 1987 definitions published in *Standard Industrial Classification Manual*, 1987, Office of Management and Budget. The abbreviation 'nec' stands for 'not elsewhere classified'.

Wholesale Trade - Durable Goods

Wholesale Trade - Nondurable Goods

Retail Trade - Building Materials & Garden Supplies

General Merchandise Stores

Food Stores

Automotive Dealers & Service Stations

Apparel & Accessory Stores

Furniture & Homefurnishing Stores

Eating & Drinking Places

Miscellaneous Retail

Alphabetical Listing

SUBJECT INDEX

The Subject Index holds references to more than 2,400 products or types of enterprises. The page of the industry in which the product or enterprise is covered follows index term. The SIC is shown in brackets.

Subject Index

Auto service station equipment, 6 [SIC 5013]
Auto service stations, 264 [SIC 5541]
Auto tire dealers, 261 [SIC 5531]
Auto tires and tubes, 9 [SIC 5014]
Autograph supplies, 399 [SIC 5999]
Automatic merchandising units, 372 [SIC 5962]
Automats (eating places), 327 [SIC 5812]
Automobile parts, 261 [SIC 5531]
Automobiles, passenger, 3 [SIC 5012]
Automotive accessories, 6 [SIC 5013]
Automotive air-conditioners, 75 [SIC 5075]
Automotive engines, new, 6 [SIC 5013]
Automotive equipment, 276 [SIC 5599]
Automotive parts, 12 [SIC 5015]
Automotive parts, new, 6 [SIC 5013]
Automotive stampings, 6 [SIC 5013]
Automotive supplies, 6, 276 [SICs 5013, 5599]
Automotive vehicles, 276 [SIC 5599]
Automotive wrecking for scrap, 105 [SIC 5093]
Autos, 3, 255 [SICs 5012, 5511]
Autos, new and used, 255 [SIC 5511]
Autos, used, 258 [SIC 5521]
Awning shops, 399 [SIC 5999]
Awnings, 30 [SIC 5039]

Baby carriages, 399 [SIC 5999]
Baby goods, 132 [SIC 5137]
Backpacking, 342 [SIC 5941]
Bag reclaiming, 105 [SIC 5093]
Bagel stores, 249 [SIC 5461]
Bagging, 207 [SIC 5199]
Bagging of tea, 162 [SIC 5149]
Bags, 120 [SIC 5113]
Bags, textile, 207 [SIC 5199]
Bait, artificial, 99 [SIC 5091]
Bait and tackle shops, 342 [SIC 5941]
Bakeries, 249 [SIC 5461]
Bakery goods, 138 [SIC 5141]
Bakery goods, purchased, 375 [SIC 5963]
Bakery products, 141, 162, 249 [SICs 5142, 5149, 5461]
Balances, 42 [SIC 5046]
Bale ties, wire, 54 [SIC 5051]
Balloon shops, 360 [SIC 5947]
Banana ripening for the trade, 159 [SIC 5148]
Bananas, 159 [SIC 5148]
Bandages, 123 [SIC 5122]
Bank automatic teller machines, 36 [SIC 5044]
Banner shops, 399 [SIC 5999]
Bar furniture, 15 [SIC 5021]
Barber shop equipment and supplies, 93 [SIC 5087]
Barbershop equipment, 93 [SIC 5087]
Barley, 165 [SIC 5153]
Barrels, new and reconditioned, 90 [SIC 5085]
Bars, alcoholic beverages, 330 [SIC 5813]
Bars, concrete reinforcing, 54 [SIC 5051]
Bars, metal, 54 [SIC 5051]
Bars (drinking places), 330 [SIC 5813]
Baskets, 207 [SIC 5199]
Baskets, rattan, 207 [SIC 5199]
Baskets, reed, 207 [SIC 5199]
Baskets, willow, 207 [SIC 5199]
Baskets, wood, 207 [SIC 5199]
Bathing suit stores, 297 [SIC 5699]
Bathing suits, 297 [SIC 5699]
Baths, whirlpool, 45 [SIC 5047]
Batteries, 6, 255, 261, 264 [SICs 5013, 5511, 5531, 5541]
Batteries, automotive, 6 [SIC 5013]
Batteries, except automotive, 60 [SIC 5063]
Battery dealers, auto, 261 [SIC 5531]
Beachwear, 129 [SIC 5136]
Beaneries, 327 [SIC 5812]
Beans, dry, 165 [SIC 5153]
Beans, field, 165 [SIC 5153]
Beans, inedible, 165 [SIC 5153]
Beans, unshelled, 165 [SIC 5153]
Bearing piles, iron and steel, 54 [SIC 5051]
Bearings, 90 [SIC 5085]
Beauty parlor equipment, 93 [SIC 5087]
Bedding, 309 [SIC 5719]
Beds, 300 [SIC 5712]
Beds, hospital, 45 [SIC 5047]
Beds and springs, 15, 300 [SICs 5021, 5712]
Bedspreads, 18 [SIC 5023]
Beekeeping supplies, 192 [SIC 5191]
Beer, 186 [SIC 5181]
Beer, packaged, 336 [SIC 5921]
Beer gardens, parlors, taverns, 330 [SIC 5813]
Belt and buckle assembly kits, 126 [SIC 5131]
Belting, hose and packing, 90 [SIC 5085]
Belts, apparel, 297 [SIC 5699]
Beverage concentrates, 162 [SIC 5149]
Beverage coolers, 78 [SIC 5078]
Bibles, house-to-house selling, 375 [SIC 5963]
Bicycle accessories, 342 [SIC 5941]
Bicycle and bicycle parts dealers, 342 [SIC 5941]
Bicycle parts, 342 [SIC 5941]
Bicycle tires and tubes, 99 [SIC 5091]
Bicycles, 99, 342 [SICs 5091, 5941]
Bicycles, motorized, 273 [SIC 5571]
Billiard supplies, 99 [SIC 5091]
Billiard table stores, 342 [SIC 5941]
Billiards equipment, 99 [SIC 5091]
Binders, 117 [SIC 5112]
Binding, textile, 126 [SIC 5131]
Binoculars, 399 [SIC 5999]
Biologicals and allied products, 123 [SIC 5122]
Bituminous processing equipment, 81 [SIC 5082]
Black plate, iron and steel, 54 [SIC 5051]
Blankbooks, 117, 348 [SICs 5112, 5943]
Blankets, 18, 309 [SICs 5023, 5719]
Blanks, tips and inserts, 87 [SIC 5084]
Blinds, venetian, 309 [SIC 5719]
Blocks, building, 24 [SIC 5032]
Blood plasma, 123 [SIC 5122]
Blouse stores, 285 [SIC 5632]
Blouses, 132, 285 [SICs 5137, 5632]
Blueprinting equipment, 36 [SIC 5044]
Boat dealers, 267 [SIC 5551]
Boats, 96, 99 [SICs 5088, 5091]
Bodies, automotive, 3 [SIC 5012]
Boilers, 72 [SIC 5074]
Boilers, power, 72 [SIC 5074]
Boilers, steam, 72 [SIC 5074]
Bolts, 69 [SIC 5072]
Book clubs, 369 [SIC 5961]
Book clubs, mail-order, 369 [SIC

Subject Index

5812]
Dining rooms, 327 [SIC 5812]
Dinner theaters, 327 [SIC 5812]
Dinners, frozen, 141 [SIC 5142]
Diodes, 66 [SIC 5065]
Direct selling organizations, 375 [SIC 5963]
Discotheques, alcoholic beverage, 330 [SIC 5813]
Dishes, disposable, 120 [SIC 5113]
Dishes, paper and disposable plastics, 120 [SIC 5113]
Dishwashers, household, 63 [SIC 5064]
Disk drives, 39 [SIC 5045]
Diskettes, 66 [SIC 5065]
Disks, music and video, 321 [SIC 5735]
Dispensing machine sale of products, 372 [SIC 5962]
Display cases, refrigerated, 78 [SIC 5078]
Distilled spirits, 189 [SIC 5182]
Distribution equipment, 60 [SIC 5063]
Dog and cat food, 162 [SIC 5149]
Dogs, 207 [SIC 5199]
Dolls, 102 [SIC 5092]
Door frames, all materials, 21 [SIC 5031]
Door locks, 216 [SIC 5251]
Door locks and lock sets, 216 [SIC 5251]
Doors, 21, 210 [SICs 5031, 5211]
Doughnut shops, 249 [SIC 5461]
Drafting instruments, 51 [SIC 5049]
Drafting instruments and tables, 51 [SIC 5049]
Draperies, 18 [SIC 5023]
Drapery, 306 [SIC 5714]
Drapery material, 126 [SIC 5131]
Drapery stores, 306 [SIC 5714]
Dredges and draglines, except ships, 81 [SIC 5082]
Dress shops, 282 [SIC 5621]
Dressed lumber, 210 [SIC 5211]
Dresses, 132, 282 [SICs 5137, 5621]
Dresses made to order, 297 [SIC 5699]
Dressmakers' shops, custom, 297 [SIC 5699]
Dried beet pulp, 171 [SIC 5159]
Drilling bits, 87 [SIC 5084]
Drilling mud, 177 [SIC 5169]
Drinking places, alcoholic beverages, 330 [SIC 5813]
Drinking water coolers, 78 [SIC 5078]
Drinking water coolers, mechanical, 78 [SIC 5078]
Drive-in restaurants, 327 [SIC 5812]
Drug proprietaries, 123 [SIC 5122]
Drug stores, 333 [SIC 5912]
Druggists' sundries, 123 [SIC 5122]
Drugs, 123 [SIC 5122]
Drugs, prescription, 333 [SIC 5912]
Drugs, proprietary, 333 [SIC 5912]
Drums, new and reconditioned, 90 [SIC 5085]
Dry goods, 126 [SIC 5131]
Dry ice, 177 [SIC 5169]
Drycleaning equipment, 93 [SIC 5087]
Drycleaning plant equipment, 93 [SIC 5087]
Dryers, beauty shop, 93 [SIC 5087]
Dryers, clothes, 63 [SIC 5064]
Dryers, laundry, 300 [SIC 5712]
Ducks, 147 [SIC 5144]
Dunebuggies, 276 [SIC 5599]
Dunnage (marine supplies), 96 [SIC 5088]
Duplicating machines, 36 [SIC 5044]
Dust collection equipment, 75 [SIC 5075]
Dyestuffs, 177 [SIC 5169]

Earthenware, 18 [SIC 5023]
Eating utensils, 120 [SIC 5113]
Eating utensils, disposable, 120 [SIC 5113]
Egg dealers, 252 [SIC 5499]
Eggs, 147, 252 [SICs 5144, 5499]
Electric appliances, household, 63 [SIC 5064]
Electric construction materials, 60 [SIC 5063]
Electric energy, 60 [SIC 5063]
Electric household appliance stores, 312 [SIC 5722]
Electric housewares and fans, 63 [SIC 5064]
Electric irons, 63, 312 [SICs 5064, 5722]
Electric ranges, 63 [SIC 5064]
Electric razor shops, 399 [SIC 5999]
Electric razors, 63 [SIC 5064]
Electric refrigerators, 312 [SIC 5722]
Electric washing machines, 63 [SIC 5064]
Electrical appliances, 63 [SIC 5064]
Electrical equipment, 60 [SIC 5063]
Electrical generators, 60 [SIC 5063]
Electrical household goods, 18 [SIC 5023]
Electrical signs, 42 [SIC 5046]
Electrical testing equipment, 6 [SIC 5013]
Electromedical equipment, 45 [SIC 5047]
Electronic coils and transformers, 66 [SIC 5065]
Electronic communications equipment, 39 [SIC 5045]
Electronic connectors, 66 [SIC 5065]
Electronic equipment, 66 [SIC 5065]
Electronic parts, 66 [SIC 5065]
Electronic tubes, 66 [SIC 5065]
Electronics, audio, 315 [SIC 5731]
Electronics, video, 315 [SIC 5731]
Elevators, 87 [SIC 5084]
Enameled iron, 72 [SIC 5074]
Enameled tileboard, 21 [SIC 5031]
Enamels, 204 [SIC 5198]
Enamelware stores, 309 [SIC 5719]
Encyclopedias, 375 [SIC 5963]
Energy, electric, 60 [SIC 5063]
Engine electrical equipment, 6 [SIC 5013]
Engine testing equipment, 6 [SIC 5013]
Engineers' equipment, 51 [SIC 5049]
Engines, automobile, 12 [SIC 5015]
Engines, automotive, 6 [SIC 5013]
Engines and parts, diesel, 87 [SIC 5084]
Engraved stationery, 348 [SIC 5943]
Envelope paper, 114 [SIC 5111]
Envelopes, 117 [SIC 5112]
Equipment, air-conditioning, 75 [SIC 5075]
Equipment, automotive, 276 [SIC 5599]
Equipment, broadcasting, 66 [SIC 5065]
Equipment, commercial, 42 [SIC 5046]
Equipment, communications, 66 [SIC 5065]
Equipment, computer peripheral, 39 [SIC 5045]
Equipment, computer peripherals, 318 [SIC 5734]
Equipment, construction, 81 [SIC

Subject Index

Gift shops, 360 [SIC 5947]
Gifts and novelties, 207 [SIC 5199]
Giftware shops, 360 [SIC 5947]
Glass, 213, 216 [SICs 5231, 5251]
Glass, automotive, 6 [SIC 5013]
Glass, flat, 30 [SIC 5039]
Glass, medical, 123 [SIC 5122]
Glass, prefabricated, 30 [SIC 5039]
Glass bottles, 90 [SIC 5085]
Glass stores, 213 [SIC 5231]
Glassware, 18, 309 [SICs 5023, 5719]
Glassware, antique, 339 [SIC 5932]
Glassware, household, 18 [SIC 5023]
Glassware, novelty, 207 [SIC 5199]
Glassware stores, 309 [SIC 5719]
Gloves, 129, 132, 294 [SICs 5136, 5137, 5661]
Gloves, women's, 285 [SIC 5632]
Glue, 177 [SIC 5169]
Go-carts , 276 [SIC 5599]
Goats, 168 [SIC 5154]
Gocarts, 99, 276 [SICs 5091, 5599]
Gold, 108 [SIC 5094]
Gold ore, 57 [SIC 5052]
Golf carts, 96, 99 [SICs 5088, 5091]
Golf equipment, 99 [SIC 5091]
Golf goods, 342 [SIC 5941]
Golf professionals, 342 [SIC 5941]
Graders, motor, 81 [SIC 5082]
Grain, 165 [SIC 5153]
Grain elevators, 165 [SIC 5153]
Grain storage bins, 30 [SIC 5039]
Grains, 165 [SIC 5153]
Granite building stone, 24 [SIC 5032]
Grave markers, 111 [SIC 5099]
Gravel, 24, 210 [SICs 5032, 5211]
Gravestones, finished, 399 [SIC 5999]
Greases, animal and vegetable, 207 [SIC 5199]
Greeting card shops, 360 [SIC 5947]
Greeting cards, 117, 360 [SICs 5112, 5947]
Grills (eating places), 327 [SIC 5812]
Grocer stores, 234 [SIC 5411]
Groceries, 138, 162 [SICs 5141, 5149]
Groceries, general line, 138 [SIC 5141]
Grocery stores, 234 [SIC 5411]
Grommets, 90 [SIC 5085]
Growing plants, 387 [SIC 5992]
Guided missiles, 96 [SIC 5088]
Guided missiles , 96 [SIC 5088]
Gum and wood chemicals, 177 [SIC 5169]
Gymnasium equipment, 342 [SIC 5941]

Haberdashery stores, 279 [SIC 5611]
Hair, animal, 171 [SIC 5159]
Hair accessories, 126 [SIC 5131]
Hair preparations, 123 [SIC 5122]
Hairbrushes, 207 [SIC 5199]
Hamburger stands, 327 [SIC 5812]
Handbag stores, 285 [SIC 5632]
Handbags, 132, 285, 294 [SICs 5137, 5632, 5661]
Handkerchiefs, 129, 132 [SICs 5136, 5137]
Handsaws, 69 [SIC 5072]
Handtools, 69, 216 [SICs 5072, 5251]
Hanging devices, 60 [SIC 5063]
Hardboard, 21 [SIC 5031]
Hardware, 69, 210, 216 [SICs 5072, 5211, 5251]
Hardware, automotive, 6 [SIC 5013]
Hardware, heavy, 69 [SIC 5072]
Hardware, pole line, 60 [SIC 5063]
Hardware, shelf or light, 69 [SIC 5072]
Hardware stores, 216 [SIC 5251]
Harness equipment, 192 [SIC 5191]
Harness made to individual order, 192 [SIC 5191]
Harvesting machinery, 84 [SIC 5083]
Hat and cap material, 126 [SIC 5131]
Hat stores, 279 [SIC 5611]
Hats, 129, 132 [SICs 5136, 5137]
Hay, 192 [SIC 5191]
Haying machinery, 84 [SIC 5083]
Health food stores, 252 [SIC 5499]
Health foods, 162, 252 [SICs 5149, 5499]
Hearing aids, 45, 399 [SICs 5047, 5999]
Heat exchange equipment, 87 [SIC 5084]
Heating equipment, 72, 75 [SICs 5074, 5075]
Heating equipment, warm air, 75 [SIC 5075]
Herbs, 252 [SIC 5499]
Hides (may include curing), 171 [SIC 5159]
High fidelity (hi-fi) equipment, 63, 315 [SICs 5064, 5731]
Hiking, 342 [SIC 5941]
Hobby goods, 102 [SIC 5092]
Hobby kits, 102, 354 [SICs 5092, 5945]
Hobby shops, 354 [SIC 5945]
Hobs, 87 [SIC 5084]
Hogs, 168 [SIC 5154]
Hoists, 87 [SIC 5084]
Holiday decorations, 360 [SIC 5947]
Homefurnishing stores, 339 [SIC 5932]
Homefurnishings, 18, 300, 309, 339 [SICs 5023, 5712, 5719, 5932]
Homes, motor, 270 [SIC 5561]
Honey, 162 [SIC 5149]
Hop extract, 162 [SIC 5149]
Hops, 171 [SIC 5159]
Horses, 171 [SIC 5159]
Hose, belting, and packing, 90 [SIC 5085]
Hosiery, 129, 132, 294 [SICs 5136, 5137, 5661]
Hosiery, women's, 285 [SIC 5632]
Hosiery stores, 285 [SIC 5632]
Hospital equipment, 45 [SIC 5047]
Hospital furniture, 45 [SIC 5047]
Hospital gowns, 132 [SIC 5137]
Hot dog (frankfurter) stands, 327 [SIC 5812]
Hot plates, 312 [SIC 5722]
Hot tubs, 99, 399 [SICs 5091, 5999]
House delivery of purchased milk, 375 [SIC 5963]
House-to-house merchandising, 375 [SIC 5963]
Household appliance stores, 312 [SIC 5722]
Household appliances, 312, 315 [SICs 5722, 5731]
Household furniture, 15, 300 [SICs 5021, 5712]
Housewares, 18, 216, 375 [SICs 5023, 5251, 5963]
Housewares stores, 309 [SIC 5719]
Hucksters, 375 [SIC 5963]
Humidifiers and dehumidifiers, 63, 75 [SICs 5064, 5075]
Hunters' equipment, 342 [SIC 5941]
Hydraulic valves, 90 [SIC 5085]
Hydronic heating equipment, 72 [SIC 5074]
Hydronics, 72 [SIC 5074]

Ice, manufactured or natural, 207 [SIC 5199]
Ice cream, 144 [SIC 5143]

Ice cream and ices, 144 [SIC 5143]
Ice cream cabinets, 78 [SIC 5078]
Ice cream making machines, 78 [SIC 5078]
Ice cream (packaged) stores, 246 [SIC 5451]
Ice cream stands, 327 [SIC 5812]
Ice cream wagons, 375 [SIC 5963]
Ice dealers, 399 [SIC 5999]
Ice making machines, 78 [SIC 5078]
Identity recorders, 33 [SIC 5043]
Indicating instruments, 87 [SIC 5084]
Industrial chemicals, 177 [SIC 5169]
Industrial feeding, 327 [SIC 5812]
Industrial fittings, 90 [SIC 5085]
Industrial gases, 177 [SIC 5169]
Industrial machinery, 87 [SIC 5084]
Industrial motor controls, 60 [SIC 5063]
Industrial paper, 120 [SIC 5113]
Industrial safety devices, 45 [SIC 5047]
Industrial salts, 177 [SIC 5169]
Industrial sewing thread, 90 [SIC 5085]
Industrial supplies, 90 [SIC 5085]
Industrial wheels, 90 [SIC 5085]
Industrial yarn, 207 [SIC 5199]
Industrial yarns, 207 [SIC 5199]
Infants' accessories, 288 [SIC 5641]
Infants' clothing, 132, 288 [SICs 5137, 5641]
Infants' furnishings, 288 [SIC 5641]
Infants' wear, 132 [SIC 5137]
Infants' wear stores, 288 [SIC 5641]
Ingots, 54 [SIC 5051]
Ink, printers', 90 [SIC 5085]
Ink, writing, 117 [SIC 5112]
Inked ribbons, 117 [SIC 5112]
Insecticides, 192 [SIC 5191]
Instruments, drafting, 51 [SIC 5049]
Instruments, musical, 324 [SIC 5736]
Instruments, scientific, 51 [SIC 5049]
Insulation, thermal, 27 [SIC 5033]
Insulation material, building, 210 [SIC 5211]
Insulation materials, 27 [SIC 5033]
Insulators, electrical, 60 [SIC 5063]
Intercommunications equipment, 66 [SIC 5065]
Iron, 57 [SIC 5052]
Iron, pig, 54 [SIC 5051]
Iron and steel flat products, 54 [SIC 5051]
Iron and steel products, 54 [SIC 5051]
Iron and steel scrap, 105 [SIC 5093]
Iron ore, 57 [SIC 5052]
Ironers, household, 63 [SIC 5064]
Irons, electric, 312 [SIC 5722]
Irrigation equipment, 84 [SIC 5083]

Jams, 162 [SIC 5149]
Janitors' supplies, 93 [SIC 5087]
Jeans stores, 291 [SIC 5651]
Jellies, 162 [SIC 5149]
Jewelers' findings, 108 [SIC 5094]
Jewelry, 108, 351, 369 [SICs 5094, 5944, 5961]
Jewelry boxes, 207 [SIC 5199]
Jewelry stores, 285, 351 [SICs 5632, 5944]
Jigs, 87 [SIC 5084]
Juices, frozen, 141 [SIC 5142]
Junk and scrap, general line, 105 [SIC 5093]
Jute piece goods, 126 [SIC 5131]
Juvenile furniture, 300 [SIC 5712]

Karate uniforms, 132 [SIC 5137]
Kerosene, 183 [SIC 5172]
Keying equipment, 39 [SIC 5045]
Kitchen cabinets, 21, 300 [SICs 5031, 5712]
Kitchen tools, 18 [SIC 5023]
Kitchens, 312 [SIC 5722]
Kitchenware stores, 309 [SIC 5719]
Kite (toy) stores, 354 [SIC 5945]
Knit fabrics, 126 [SIC 5131]
Knit goods, 126 [SIC 5131]
Knitting yarn shops, 366 [SIC 5949]

Labels, woven, 126 [SIC 5131]
Laboratory equipment, 45, 51 [SICs 5047, 5049]
Lace fabrics, 126 [SIC 5131]
Lacquers, 204 [SIC 5198]
Ladders, 87 [SIC 5084]
Ladies' handkerchiefs, 132 [SIC 5137]
Ladies' purses, 132 [SIC 5137]
Lamp and shade shops, 309 [SIC 5719]
Lamp bulbs, 60 [SIC 5063]
Lamps, 18 [SIC 5023]
Lamps, household, 309 [SIC 5719]
Land preparation machinery, 84 [SIC 5083]
Lapidary equipment, 90 [SIC 5085]
Lard, 156 [SIC 5147]
Laundry equipment, 63, 93 [SICs 5064, 5087]
Laundry soap, chips, and powder, 177 [SIC 5169]
Lawn and garden stores, 219 [SIC 5261]
Lawn furniture, 15 [SIC 5021]
Lawn machinery, 84 [SIC 5083]
Lawnmowers, 219 [SIC 5261]
Lead, 54, 57 [SICs 5051, 5052]
Lead ore, 57 [SIC 5052]
Leather and cut stock, 207 [SIC 5199]
Leather and sheep-lined clothing, 129, 132 [SICs 5136, 5137]
Leather belting, packing, 90 [SIC 5085]
Leather goods, 207, 363 [SICs 5199, 5948]
Legal forms, 348 [SIC 5943]
Lenses, contact, 396 [SIC 5995]
Lenses, eyeglasses, 48 [SIC 5048]
Lenses, ophthalmic, 48 [SIC 5048]
Lenses, sunglasses, 48 [SIC 5048]
Lift trucks, 87 [SIC 5084]
Light bulbs, electric, 60 [SIC 5063]
Lighters, cigar and cigarette, 207 [SIC 5199]
Lighting fixtures, 60 [SIC 5063]
Limbs, artificial, 399 [SIC 5999]
Limbs, orthopedic, 399 [SIC 5999]
Lime, 24 [SIC 5032]
Lime, agricultural, 192 [SIC 5191]
Lime, except agricultural, 24 [SIC 5032]
Lime and plaster dealers, 210 [SIC 5211]
Limestone, 24 [SIC 5032]
Limited price variety stores, 228 [SIC 5331]
Linen, 309 [SIC 5719]
Linen piece goods, 126 [SIC 5131]
Linen shops, 309 [SIC 5719]
Linens, 18 [SIC 5023]
Lingerie, 132, 285 [SICs 5137, 5632]
Lingerie stores, 285 [SIC 5632]
Linoleum, 18 [SIC 5023]
Linoleum stores, 303 [SIC 5713]
Linseed oil, 207 [SIC 5199]
Liquefied petroleum gas (LPG), 180 [SIC 5171]
Liquefied petroleum (LP), 381 [SIC 5984]
Liquid petroleum gas, 381 [SIC

5984]
Liquor, packaged, 336 [SIC 5921]
Liquors, distilled, 189 [SIC 5182]
Livestock, 168 [SIC 5154]
Livestock, except horses and mules, 168 [SIC 5154]
Lock sets, 216 [SIC 5251]
Lockers, 15, 42 [SICs 5021, 5046]
Lockers, not refrigerated, 42 [SIC 5046]
Locks and related materials, 69 [SIC 5072]
Logging equipment, 81 [SIC 5082]
Logs, hewn ties, posts, and poles, 111 [SIC 5099]
Looseleaf binders, 117 [SIC 5112]
Lounges, cocktail, 330 [SIC 5813]
Lubricants, 183, 264 [SICs 5172, 5541]
Lubricating oils and greases, 183 [SIC 5172]
Luggage, 111, 363 [SICs 5099, 5948]
Luggage and leather goods stores, 363 [SIC 5948]
Lugs and connectors, 60 [SIC 5063]
Lumber, 21, 210 [SICs 5031, 5211]
Lumber and building materials dealers, 210 [SIC 5211]
Lumber dealers, 210 [SIC 5211]
Lunch bars, 327 [SIC 5812]
Lunch counters, 327, 333 [SICs 5812, 5912]
Lunch wagons, mobile, 375 [SIC 5963]
Luncheonettes, 327 [SIC 5812]
Lunchrooms, 327 [SIC 5812]

Macaroni, 162 [SIC 5149]
Machine guns, 111 [SIC 5099]
Machine tool accessories, 87 [SIC 5084]
Machine tools, 87 [SIC 5084]
Machinery, 81 [SIC 5082]
Machinery, industrial, 87 [SIC 5084]
Machines, ice cream making, 78 [SIC 5078]
Machines, vending, 372 [SIC 5962]
Machines, X-ray, 45 [SIC 5047]
Machinists' measuring tools, 87 [SIC 5084]
Magazine stands, 393 [SIC 5994]
Magazine subscription sales, 375 [SIC 5963]
Magazines, 195, 345, 375, 393 [SICs 5192, 5942, 5963, 5994]
Magazines, mail-order, 369 [SIC 5961]
Magnetic recording tape, 66 [SIC 5065]
Mail-order book clubs, 369 [SIC 5961]
Mail-order cheese, 369 [SIC 5961]
Mail-order computer software, 369 [SIC 5961]
Mail-order houses, 369 [SIC 5961]
Mail-order merchandising, 369 [SIC 5961]
Mail-order record clubs, 369 [SIC 5961]
Mailing machines, 36 [SIC 5044]
Major appliances, 300 [SIC 5712]
Malt, 162 [SIC 5149]
Malt beverages, 186 [SIC 5181]
Malt extract, 162 [SIC 5149]
Manifold business forms, 117 [SIC 5112]
Manmade fibers, 177 [SIC 5169]
Mannequins, 42 [SIC 5046]
Manuscripts, rare, 339 [SIC 5932]
Marble building stone, 24 [SIC 5032]
Margarine, 162 [SIC 5149]
Marine propulsion machinery, 96 [SIC 5088]
Marine service stations, 264 [SIC 5541]
Marine supplies, 267 [SIC 5551]
Marine supplies (dunnage), 96 [SIC 5088]
Marine supply dealers, 267 [SIC 5551]
Marking devices, 117 [SIC 5112]
Masons' materials, 24 [SIC 5032]
Matches, 207 [SIC 5199]
Materials, 306 [SIC 5714]
Materials, construction, 30, 60 [SICs 5039, 5063]
Materials, electric construction, 60 [SIC 5063]
Materials, fiberglass, 27 [SIC 5033]
Materials, insulation, 27 [SIC 5033]
Materials, quilting, 366 [SIC 5949]
Materials, roofing, 27 [SIC 5033]
Materials, siding, 27 [SIC 5033]
Materials, upholstery, 306 [SIC 5714]
Materials handling equipment, 87 [SIC 5084]
Maternity shops, 282 [SIC 5621]
Mattress stores, 300 [SIC 5712]
Mattresses, 15, 300 [SICs 5021, 5712]
MDF (Medium density fiberboard), 21 [SIC 5031]
Measuring equipment, 87 [SIC 5084]
Meat, 138 [SIC 5141]
Meat, frozen, 141 [SIC 5142]
Meat markets, 237 [SIC 5421]
Meat pies, frozen, 141 [SIC 5142]
Meat stores, 237 [SIC 5421]
Meats, 156 [SIC 5147]
Meats, cured or smoked, 156 [SIC 5147]
Meats, fresh, 156 [SIC 5147]
Meats, frozen, 141 [SIC 5142]
Medallions, 108 [SIC 5094]
Medical equipment, 45 [SIC 5047]
Medical glass, 45 [SIC 5047]
Medical rubber goods, 123 [SIC 5122]
Medicinals and botanicals, 123 [SIC 5122]
Medicine cabinet sundries, 123 [SIC 5122]
Medicines, nonprescription, 333 [SIC 5912]
Medium density fiberboard, 21 [SIC 5031]
Men's clothing, 279 [SIC 5611]
Men's footwear, 294 [SIC 5661]
Men's wearing apparel, 279 [SIC 5611]
Merchandise, novelty, 333 [SIC 5912]
Merchandise, used, 339 [SIC 5932]
Merchandise stores, general, 231 [SIC 5399]
Merchandising, automatic, 372 [SIC 5962]
Merchandising, automatic units, 372 [SIC 5962]
Merchandising, catalog, 369 [SIC 5961]
Merchandising, house-to-house, 375 [SIC 5963]
Merchandising, mail-order, 369 [SIC 5961]
Merchandising, telephone, 375 [SIC 5963]
Merchandising, television, 369 [SIC 5961]
Merchandising, temporary locations, 375 [SIC 5963]
Merchandising machines, 42 [SIC 5046]
Merchant tailors, 297 [SIC 5699]

Subject Index

COMPANY INDEX

This index shows, in alphabetical order, the 4,300 companies in *Wholesale and Retail Trade USA*. Organizations may be public or private companies, subsidiaries or divisions of companies, joint ventures or affiliates, or corporate groups. Each company entry is followed by one or more page numbers. One or more SIC codes under which the company appears follow the page numbers in brackets.

Company Index

Company Index

Company Index

METROPOLITAN AREA INDEX

This index shows the 370 metropolitan areas listed in *Wholesale and Retail Trade USA, 2nd Edition.* Two arrangements are provided: an alphabetical listing by name of the metro area and an alphabetical listing by state. Metro areas that span more than one state are listed under each of the states in which a part of them appears. Each metro area name is followed by a page reference.

Metro Area Index

Alphabetically by State

Alabama

Alaska

Arizona

Arkansas

California

Colorado

Delaware

District of Columbia

Florida

Georgia

Hawaii

Idaho

Illinois

Indiana

Iowa

Oregon

Pennsylvania

South Carolina

South Dakota

Tennessee

Texas

Utah

Virginia

Washington

West Virginia

Wisconsin

Wyoming

OCCUPATION INDEX

This index lists those occupations in Wholesale and Retail that account for 1 percent or more of employment. This limitation excludes many occupations employed in the sectors in small numbers. After the name of each occupation, a value in parentheses shows the number of 3-digit service industry groups in which the occupation occurs. One or more page numbers follow. After the page numbers, the 3-digit SICs are shown inside brackets. *Please note:* page and SIC references are sorted so that they point to industry groups with descending employment (the first page reference is to the largest employing industry group). Only the top ten industry groups are referenced.

Accountants (1) 181 [SIC 517]
Accounting clerks (25) 298, 337, 241, 220, 214, 373, 229, 379, 217, 223 [SICs 569, 592, 543, 526, 523, 596, 533, 598, 525, 527]
Adjustment clerks (2) 376, 226 [SICs 596, 531]
Advertising managers (2) 223, 256 [SICs 527, 551]
Agricultural, forestry, fishing workers nec (1) 154 [SIC 514]
Air conditioning mechanics (1) 382 [SIC 598]
Assemblers, fabricators, hand workers nec (6) 298, 211, 10, 340, 91, 19 [SICs 569, 521, 501, 593, 508, 502]
Assistants, pharmacy (1) 334 [SIC 591]
Attendants, service station (3) 385, 184, 265 [SICs 598, 517, 554]
Auditing clerks (25) 298, 337, 241, 220, 214, 373, 229, 379, 217, 223 [SICs 569, 592, 543, 526, 523, 596, 533, 598, 525, 527]
Auditors (1) 181 [SIC 517]
Automotive body & related repairers (2) 214, 256 [SICs 523, 551]
Automotive mechanics (6) 379, 223, 13, 265, 262, 256 [SICs 598, 527, 501, 554, 553, 551]

Bakers, bread & pastry (3) 241, 250, 235 [SICs 543, 546, 541]
Bar attendants (1) 328 [SIC 581]
Bartenders (2) 337, 328 [SICs 592, 581]
Bicycle repairers (1) 355 [SIC 594]
Billing, cost, & rate clerks (2) 379, 256 [SICs 598, 551]
Blue collar worker supervisors (7) 184, 313, 7, 262, 154, 88, 19 [SICs 517, 572, 501, 553, 514, 508, 502]
Bookkeeping, accounting, & auditing clerks (25) 298, 337, 241, 220, 214, 373, 229, 379, 217, 223 [SICs 569, 592, 543, 526, 523, 596, 533, 598, 525, 527]
Bread bakers (3) 241, 250, 235 [SICs 543, 546, 541]
Bus & truck mechanics (2) 85, 4 [SICs 508, 501]
Butchers (3) 238, 154, 235 [SICs 542, 514, 541]
Buyers, wholesale & retail (14) 238, 220, 298, 337, 241, 217, 313, 310, 340, 280 [SICs 542, 526, 569, 592, 543, 525, 572, 571, 593, 561]

Cafeteria attendants (1) 328 [SIC 581]
Carpenters (1) 211 [SIC 521]
Carpet installers (1) 301 [SIC 571]
Cash register servicers (1) 16 [SIC 502]
Cashiers (27) 214, 223, 379, 370, 298, 238, 220, 295, 304, 184 [SICs 523, 527, 598, 596, 569, 542, 526, 566, 571, 517]
Cleaners (5) 223, 250, 310, 256, 331 [SICs 527, 546, 571, 551, 581]
Clerical supervisors & managers (11) 298, 223, 181, 262, 370, 307, 7, 148, 85, 256 [SICs 569, 527, 517, 553, 596, 571, 501, 514, 508, 551]
Clerks (25) 298, 337, 241, 220, 214, 373, 229, 379, 217, 223 [SICs 569, 592, 543, 526, 523, 596, 533, 598, 525, 527]
Clerks, adjustment (2) 376, 226 [SICs 596, 531]
Clerks, billing, cost, & rate (2) 379, 256 [SICs 598, 551]
Clerks, counter & rental (1) 217 [SIC 525]
Clerks, information (2) 82, 19 [SICs 508, 502]
Clerks, office (25) 238, 298, 220, 214, 217, 223, 229, 334, 181, 385 [SICs 542, 569, 526, 523, 525, 527, 533, 591, 517, 598]
Clerks, order (5) 7, 139, 97, 376, 19 [SICs 501, 514, 508, 596, 502]
Clerks, stock (28) 223, 181, 238, 214, 250, 298, 220, 373, 262, 295 [SICs 527, 517, 542, 523, 546, 569, 526, 596, 553, 566]
Clerks, traffic & shipping (15) 214, 298, 217, 229, 313, 280, 301, 373, 364, 211 [SICs 523, 569, 525, 533, 572, 561, 571, 596, 594, 521]
Coin & vending machine servicers & repairers (1) 373 [SIC 596]
Cooks, restaurant (1) 328 [SIC 581]
Cooks, short order & fast food (3) 238, 265, 328 [SICs 542, 554, 581]
Cosmetologists (1) 226 [SIC 531]
Cost clerks (2) 379, 256 [SICs 598, 551]
Counter & rental clerks (1) 217 [SIC 525]
Custom tailors & sewers (2) 298, 280 [SICs 569, 561]
Cutters, metal (1) 82 [SIC 508]

Data entry keyers, except composing (1) 370 [SIC 596]

Occupation Index

Appendix: SIC Descriptions

WHOLESALE TRADE

SIC 5012 - Motor Vehicles and Motor Vehicle Parts and Supplies

Establishments primarily engaged in the wholesale distribution of new and used passenger automobiles, trucks, trailers, and other motor vehicles, including motorcycles, motor homes, and snowmobiles. Automotive distributors primarily engaged in selling at retail to individual consumers for personal use, and also selling a limited amount of new and used passenger automobiles and trucks at wholesale, are classified in Retail Trade, SIC 5511.

SIC 5013 - Motor Vehicle Supplies and New Parts

Establishments primarily engaged in the wholesale distribution of motor vehicle supplies, accessories, tools, and equipment; and new motor vehicle parts. Supplies include: automotive engines, batteries, stampings, seat belts, and automobile glass. Equipment covers garage service equipment, electrical testing equipment, and pumps that measure and dispense gasoline. Parts include both automotive and motorcycle, as well as automotive hardware.

SIC 5014 - Tires and Tubes

Establishments primarily engaged in the wholesale distribution of tires and tubes for passenger and commercial vehicles. This also includes new tires and tubes, repair materials, and used tires.

SIC 5015 - Motor Vehicle Parts, Used

Establishments primarily engaged in the distribution at wholesale or retail of used motor vehicle parts. This industry includes establishments primarily engaged in dismantling motor vehicles, including automobile engines, automotive and motor vehicle parts. Establishments primarily engaged in dismantling motor vehicles for scrap are classified in SIC 5093.

SIC 5021 - Furniture

Establishments primarily engaged in the wholesale distribution of furniture, including bedsprings, mattresses, and other household furniture; office furniture; and furniture for public parks and buildings. Establishments primarily engaged in the wholesale distribution of partitions, shelving, lockers, and store fixtures are classified in SIC 5046.

SIC 5023 - Homefurnishings

Establishments primarily engaged in the wholesale distribution of homefurnishings and housewares, including antiques; china; glassware and earthenware; lamps (including electric); curtains and draperies; linens and towels; and carpets, linoleum, and all other types of hard and soft surface floor coverings. Establishments primarily engaged in the wholesale distribution of other electrical household goods are classified in SIC 5064, and those distributing precious metal flatware are classified in SIC 5094.

SIC 5031 - Lumber, Plywood, Millwork, and Wood Panels

Establishments with or without yards, primarily engaged in the wholesale distribution of rough, dressed, and finished lumber (but not timber); plywood; reconstituted wood fiber products, such as medium density fiberboard; doors and windows and their frames (all materials); wood fencing; and other wood or metal millwork.

SIC 5032 - Brick, Stone, and Related Construction Materials

Establishments primarily engaged in the wholesale distribution of stone, cement, lime, construction sand, and gravel; brick (except refractory); asphalt and concrete mixtures; and concrete, stone, and structural clay products (other than refractories). Distributors of industrial sand and of refractory materials are classified in SIC 5085. Establishments primarily engaged in producing ready-mixed concrete are classified in Manufacturing, SIC 3273.

SIC 5033 - Roofing, Siding, and Insulation Materials

Establishments primarily engaged in the wholesale distribution of roofing and siding (except wood) and insulation materials. Roofing and siding materials include asphalt felts and coatings, tarred felts, and shingles. Insulation includes fiberglass materials, thermal insulation, and mineral wool insulation materials.

SIC 5039 - Construction Materials, Not elsewhere Classified

Establishments primarily engaged in the wholesale distribution of mobile homes and construction materials, not elsewhere classified, including prefabricated buildings and glass. Establishments selling construction materials to the general public, such as fencing and accessories, and known as retail in the trade are classified in Retail Trade, SIC 5211. Establishments primarily engaged in marketing heavy structural metal products are classified in SIC 5051.

SIC 5043 - Photographic Equipment and Supplies

Establishments primarily engaged in the wholesale distribution of photographic equipment and supplies. Equipment includes cameras, darkroom equipment, motion picture cameras, and printing and projecting apparatus. Establishments primarily engaged in the wholesale distribution of photography, microfilm, and similar equipment are classified in SIC 5044.

SIC 5044 - Office Equipment

Establishments primarily engaged in the wholesale distribution of office machines and related equipment, including photography and microfilm equipment and safes and vaults. These establishments frequently also sell office supplies. However, establishments primarily engaged in wholesaling most office supplies are classified in SIC 511. Establishments primarily engaged in wholesaling office furniture are classified in SIC 5021, and those wholesaling computers and peripheral equipment are classified in SIC 5045.

SIC 5045 - Computers and Computer Peripheral Equipment and Software

Establishments primarily engaged in the wholesale distribution of computers, computer peripheral equipment, and computer software. These establishments frequently also may sell related supplies, but establishments primarily engaged in wholesaling supplies are classified according to the individual product (for example, computer paper in SIC 5112). Establishments primarily engaged in the wholesale distribution of modems and other electronic communications equipment are classified in SIC 5065. Establishments primarily engaged in selling computers and computer peripheral equipment and software for other than business or professional use are classified in Retail Trade, SIC 5734.

SIC 5046 - Commercial Equipment, Not Elsewhere Classified

Establishments primarily engaged in the wholesale distribution of commercial and related machines and equipment, not elsewhere classified, such as commercial cooking and food service equipment, including coffee urns; partitions, shelving, lockers, and store fixtures, such as mannequins; electrical signs; and balances and scales, except laboratory.

SIC 5047 - Medical, Dental, and Hospital Equipment and Supplies

Establishments primarily engaged in the wholesale distribution of surgical and other medical instruments, apparatus, and equipment; dentist equipment; artificial limbs; operating room and hospital equipment; X-ray machines; and other electromedical equipment and apparatus used by physicians and in hospitals. Also included in this SIC are establishments primarily engaged in the wholesale distribution of professional supplies used by medical and dental practitioners.

SIC 5048 - Ophthalmic Goods

Establishments primarily engaged in the wholesale distribution of professional equipment and goods used, prescribed, or sold by ophthalmologists, optometrists, and opticians, including ophthalmic frames, lenses, and sunglass lenses.

SIC 5049 - Professional Equipment and Supplies, Not Elsewhere Classified

Establishments primarily engaged in the wholesale distribution of professional equipment and supplies, not elsewhere classified, such as drafting instruments, laboratory equipment, and scientific instruments such as analytical instruments, architects' and engineers' equipment.

SIC 5051 - Metals Service Centers and Offices

Establishments primarily engaged in marketing semifinished metal products, except precious metals. Establishments in this SIC may operate with warehouses (metals service centers) or without warehouses (metals sales offices). Establishments primarily engaged in marketing precious metals are classified in SIC 5094.

SIC 5052 - Coal and Other Minerals and Ores

Establishments primarily engaged in the wholesale distribution of coal and coke; copper, iron, lead, and other metallic ores, including precious metal ores; and crude nonmetallic minerals (including concentrates), except crude petroleum. Establishments primarily engaged in the wholesale distribution of nonmetallic minerals used in construction, such as sand and gravel, are included in SIC 5032.

SIC 5063 - Electrical Apparatus and Equipment, Wiring Supplies, and Construction Materials

Establishments primarily engaged in the wholesale distribution of electrical power equipment for the generation, transmission, distribution, or control of electric energy; electrical construction materials for outside power transmission lines and for electrical systems; and electric light fixtures and bulbs. Construction contractors primarily engaged in installing electrical systems and equipment from their own stock are classified in Construction, SIC 1731.

SIC 5064 - Electrical Appliances, Television and Radio Sets

Establishments primarily engaged in the wholesale distribution of radio and television receiving sets, other household electronic sound or video equipment, self-contained air-conditioning room units, and household electrical appliances. Also included are establishments primarily engaged in the wholesale distribution of household nonelectric laundry equipment and refrigerators and freezers.

SIC 5065 - Electronic Parts and Equipment, Not Elsewhere Classified

Establishments primarily engaged in the wholesale distribution of electronic parts and electronic communications equipment, not elsewhere classified, such as telephone and telegraph equipment; radio and television broadcasting and communications equipment; and intercommunications equipment. Establishments primarily engaged in the wholesale distribution of radio and television receiving sets, phonographs, and other household sound or video equipment are classified in SIC 5064.

SIC 5072 - Hardware

Establishments primarily engaged in the wholesale distribution of cutlery and general hardware, including handsaws; saw blades; brads, staples, and tacks; and bolts, nuts, rivets, and screws. Establishments primarily engaged in the wholesale distribution of nails, noninsulated wire, and screening are classified in SIC 5051.

SIC 5074 - Plumbing and Heating Equipment and Supplies (Hydronics)

Establishments primarily engaged in the wholesale distribution of hydronic plumbing and heating equipment and supplies. Plumbing equipment and supplies include boilers, plumbers' brass goods, fittings, valves, and plumbing fixtures. Heating equipment includes boilers, burners, oil burners, and stoves. Construction contractors primarily engaged in installing plumbing and heating equipment from their own stock are classified in SIC 1711.

SIC 5075 - Warm Air Heating and Air-Conditioning Equipment and Supplies

Establishments primarily engaged in the wholesale distribution of warm air heating and air-conditioning equipment and supplies. Construction contractors primarily engaged in installing warm air heating and air- conditioning equipment, including air pollution control equipment, are classified in Construction, SIC 1711.

SIC 5078 - Refrigeration Equipment and Supplies

Establishments primarily engaged in the wholesale distribution of refrigeration equipment and supplies. Refrigeration equipment includes beverage coolers, display cases, drinking water coolers, ice cream making machines, and soda fountain fixtures. Construction contractors primarily engaged in the installation of refrigeration equipment from their own stock are classified in Construction, SIC 1711.

SIC 5082 - Construction and Mining (Except Petroleum) Machinery and Equipment

Establishments primarily engaged in the wholesale distribution of construction or mining cranes, excavating machinery and equipment, power shovels, road construction and maintenance machinery, tractor-mounting equipment and other specialized machinery and equipment used in the construction, mining, and logging industries. Establishments engaged in marketing oil well machinery and equipment are classified in SIC 5084.

SIC 5083 - Farm and Garden Machinery and Equipment

Establishments primarily engaged in the wholesale distribution of agricultural machinery and equipment for use in the preparation and maintenance of the soil, the planting and harvesting of crops, and other operations and processes pertaining to work on the farm or the lawn or garden; and dairy and other livestock equipment.

SIC 5084 - Industrial Machinery and Equipment

Establishments primarily engaged in the wholesale distribution of industrial machinery and equipment, not elsewhere classified. Includes the entire range of machinery used in industrial production.

SIC 5085 - Industrial Supplies

Establishments primarily engaged in the wholesale distribution of industrial supplies such as abrasives, bearings, boxes and crates (other than paper), cork, gears, and seals, gaskets, and packaging not elsewhere classified.

SIC 5087 - Service Establishment Equipment and Supplies

Establishments primarily engaged in the wholesale distribution of equipment and supplies for barber shops, beauty parlors, power laundries, dry-cleaning plants, upholsterers, undertakers, and related personal service establishments.

SIC 5088 - Transportation Equipment and Supplies, Except Motor Vehicles

Establishments primarily engaged in the wholesale distribution of transportation equipment and supplies. This category includes aircraft, combat vehicles, guided missiles, railroad equipment, etc. Those establishments primarily engaged in the wholesale distribution of motor vehicles and motor vehicle parts are classified in SIC 501, and those distributing pleasure boats are classified in SIC 5091.

SIC 5091 - Sporting and Recreational Goods and Supplies

Establishments primarily engaged in the wholesale distribution of sporting goods and accessories; billiard and pool supplies; sporting firearms and ammunition; and marine pleasure craft, equipment, and supplies. Establishments primarily engaged in the wholesale distribution of motor vehicles and trailers are classified in SIC 5012; those distributing self-propelled golf carts are classified in SIC 5088; and those distributing athletic apparel and footwear are classified in SIC 513.

SIC 5092 - Toys and Hobby Goods and Supplies

Establishments primarily engaged in the wholesale distribution of games, toys, hobby goods and supplies, and related goods such as fireworks and playing cards. This would include items such as dolls, model kits, philatelist stamps, and children's vehicles.

SIC 5093 - Scrap and Waste Materials

Establishments primarily engaged in assembling, breaking up, sorting, and wholesale distribution of scrap and waste materials. This industry includes auto wreckers engaged in dismantling automobiles for scrap. However, those engaged in dismantling cars for the purpose of selling secondhand parts are classified in SIC 5015.

SIC 5094 - Jewelry, Watches, Precious Stones, and Precious Metals

Establishments primarily engaged in the wholesale distribution of jewelry, precious stones and metals, costume jewelry, watches, clocks, silverware, and jewelers' findings. Those establishments primarily engaged in the wholesale distribution of precious metal ores are classified in SIC 5052.

SIC 5099 - Durable Goods, Not Elsewhere Classified

Establishments primarily engaged in the wholesale distribution of durable goods, not elsewhere classified, such as musical instruments and forest products, except lumber. This also includes ammunition (except sporting), audio prerecorded cassettes, fire extinguishers, coin-operated game machines, monuments, and grave markers.

SIC 5111 - Printing and Writing Paper

Establishments primarily engaged in the wholesale distribution of printing and writing paper, including envelope paper; fine paper; and groundwood paper.

SIC 5112 - Stationery and Office Supplies

Establishments primarily engaged in the wholesale distribution of stationery and office supplies, including computer and photocopy supplies, envelopes, typewriter paper, file cards and folders, pens, pencils, social stationery, photo albums, loose-leaf binders, manifold business forms, scrapbooks, and greeting cards.

SIC 5113 - Industrial and Personal Service Paper

Establishments primarily engaged in the wholesale distribution of wrapping and other coarse paper, paperboard, and converted paper and related disposable plastics products, such as bags, boxes, dishes, eating utensils, napkins, and shipping supplies.

SIC 5122 - Drugs, Drug Proprietaries, and Druggists' Sundries

Establishments primarily engaged in the wholesale distribution of prescription drugs, proprietary drugs, druggists' sundries, and toiletries. Those establishments primarily engaged in the wholesale distribution of surgical, dental, and hospital equipment are classified in SIC 5047.

SIC 5131 - Piece Goods, Notions, and Other Dry Goods

Establishments primarily engaged in the wholesale distribution of piece goods or yard goods of natural or manmade fibers, notions (sewing and hair accessories, etc.), and other dry goods. Converters who buy fabric goods (except knit goods) in the grey, have them finished on contract, and sell at wholesale are included here. Converters of knit goods are classified in Manufacturing, SIC 225. This SIC does not include establishments primarily engaged in the wholesale distribution of homefurnishings which are classified in SIC 5023.

SIC 5136 - Men's and Boys' Clothing and Furnishings

Establishments primarily engaged in the wholesale distribution of men's and boys' apparel and furnishings, sportswear, hosiery, underwear, nightwear, and work clothing, including gloves, hats, and overcoats.

SIC 5137 - Women's, Children's, and Infants' Clothing and Accessories

Establishments primarily engaged in the wholesale distribution of women's, children's, and infants' clothing and accessories, including hosiery, lingerie, millinery, outerwear, purses, scarves, underwear, uniforms, and furs.

SIC 5139 - Footwear

Establishments primarily engaged in the wholesale distribution of footwear (including athletic) of leather, rubber, and other materials. Also includes shoe accessories.

SIC 5141 - Groceries, General Line

Establishments primarily engaged in the wholesale distribution of a general line of groceries. Those establishments primarily engaged in roasting coffee, blending tea, or grinding and packaging spices are classified in Manufacturing, Major Group SIC 20.

SIC 5142 - Packaged Frozen Foods

Establishments primarily engaged in the wholesale distribution of packaged quick-frozen vegetables, juices, meats, fish, poultry, pastries, and other "deep freeze" products. The establishments primarily engaged in the wholesale distribution of frozen dairy products are classified in SIC 5143, and those distributing frozen poultry, fish, and meat which are not packaged are classified in SICs 5144, 5146, and 5147, respectively.

SIC 5143 - Dairy Products, Except Dried or Canned

Establishments primarily engaged in the wholesale distribution of dairy products such as butter, cheese, ice cream and ices, and fluid milk and cream. This SIC does not include establishments primarily engaged in pasteurizing and bottling milk, which are classified in Manufacturing, SIC 202. Establishments primarily engaged in the wholesale distribution of dried or canned dairy products are classified in SIC 5149.

SIC 5144 - Poultry and Poultry Products

Establishments primarily engaged in the wholesale distribution of poultry and poultry products, except canned and packaged frozen products. This industry does not include establishments primarily engaged in the killing and dressing of poultry, which are classified in Manufacturing, SIC 2015. Establishments primarily engaged in the wholesale distribution of packaged frozen poultry are classified in SIC 5142, and those distributing canned poultry are classified in SIC 5149.

SIC 5145 - Confectionery

Establishments primarily engaged in the wholesale distribution of confectionery and related products, such as candy, chewing gum, fountain fruits, salted or roasted nuts, popcorn, fountain syrups, soda fountain toppings, and potato, corn, and similar chips.

SIC 5146 - Fish and Seafoods

Establishments primarily engaged in the wholesale distribution (but not packaging) of fresh, cured, or frozen fish and seafoods, except canned or packaged frozen. The preparation of fresh or frozen packaged fish and other seafood, and the shucking and packaging of fresh oysters in nonsealed containers, are classified in Manufacturing, SIC 2092. Establishments primarily engaged in the wholesale distribution of canned seafood are classified in SIC 5149, and those distributing packaged frozen foods are classified in SIC 5142.

SIC 5147 - Meats and Meat Products

Establishments primarily engaged in the wholesale distribution of fresh, cured, and processed (but not canned) meats and lard. The establishments primarily engaged in the wholesale distribution of frozen packaged meats are classified in SIC 5142, and those distributing canned meats are classified in SIC 5149.

SIC 5148 - Fresh Fruits and Vegetables

Establishments primarily engaged in the wholesale distribution of fresh fruits and vegetables, including banana ripening for the trade, and potatoes.

SIC 5149 - Groceries and Related Products, Not Elsewhere Classified

Establishments primarily engaged in the wholesale distribution of groceries and related products, not elsewhere classified. Those establishments primarily engaged in the wholesale distribution of soft drinks, and in bottling and distributing natural spring and mineral waters, are classified in this SIC, but establishments primarily engaged in bottling soft drinks are classified in Manufacturing, SIC 20. This SIC does not include establishments primarily engaged in the wholesale distribution of farm-product raw materials classified in SIC 515, nor those distributing beer, wine, and distilled alcoholic beverages of SIC 518.

SIC 5153 - Grain and Field Beans

Establishments primarily engaged in buying and/or marketing grain (such as corn, wheat, oats, barley, and unpolished rice); dry beans; soybeans, and other inedible beans. Country grain elevators primarily engaged in buying or receiving grain from farmers are included, as well as terminal elevators and other merchants marketing grain. Establishments primarily engaged in the wholesale distribution of field and garden seeds are classified in SIC 5191.

SIC 5154 - Livestock

Establishments primarily engaged in buying and/or marketing cattle, hogs, sheep, and goats, but does not include horses and mules. This SIC also includes the operation of livestock auction markets.

SIC 5159 - Farm-Product Raw Materials, Not Elsewhere Classified

Establishments primarily engaged in buying and/or marketing farm products, not elsewhere classified. Included are animal hair, bristles, chicks, raw cotton, feathers, horses, mules, pelts, and raw wool. Those establishments primarily engaged in the wholesale distribution of milk are classified in SIC 5143, and those distributing live poultry are classified in SIC 5144.

SIC 5162 - Plastics Materials and Basic Forms and Shapes

Establishments primarily engaged in the wholesale distribution of plastics materials, and of unsupported plastics film, sheets, sheeting, rods, tubes, and other basic forms and shapes.

SIC 5169 - Chemicals and Allied Products, Not Elsewhere Classified

Establishments primarily engaged in the wholesale distribution of chemicals and allied not elsewhere classified, such as acids, industrial and heavy chemicals, dyestuffs, industrial salts, rosin, and turpentine. The establishments primarily engaged in the wholesale distribution of ammunition are classified in SIC 509; those distributing agricultural chemicals and pesticides are classified in SIC 5191; those distributing drugs are classified in SIC 5122; and those distributing pigments, paints, and varnishes are classified in SIC 5198.

SIC 5171 - Petroleum Bulk Stations and Terminals

Establishments primarily engaged in the wholesale distribution of crude petroleum and petroleum products, including liquefied petroleum gas, from bulk liquid storage facilities.

SIC 5172 - Petroleum and Petroleum Products Wholesalers, Except Bulk Stations and Terminals

Establishments primarily engaged in the wholesale distribution of petroleum and petroleum products, except those with bulk liquid storage facilities. Included are packaged and bottled petroleum products distributors, truck jobbers, and others marketing petroleum and its products at wholesale, but without bulk liquid storage facilities.

SIC 5181 - Beer and Ale

Establishments primarily engaged in the wholesale distribution of beer, ale, porter, and other fermented malt beverages.

SIC 5182 - Wine and Distilled Alcoholic Beverages

Establishments primarily engaged in the wholesale distribution of distilled spirits, including neutral spirits and ethyl alcohol used in blended wines and distilled liquors. Included are bottling wines and liquors, brandy and brandy spirits, premixed alcoholic cocktails, and alcoholic wine coolers.

SIC 5191 - Farm Supplies

Establishments primarily engaged in the wholesale distribution of animal feeds, fertilizers, agricultural chemicals, pesticides, seeds, and other farm supplies, except grains. Establishments primarily engaged in the wholesale distribution of pet food are classified in SIC 5149, and those distributing pet supplies are classified in SIC 5199.

SIC 5192 - Books, Periodicals, and Newspapers

Establishments primarily engaged in the wholesale distribution of books, periodicals, and newspapers. Also includes magazines and newspaper agencies.

SIC 5193 - Flowers, Nursery Stock, and Florists' Supplies

Establishments primarily engaged in the wholesale distribution of flowers, nursery stock, and florists' supplies. This includes artificial flowers, potted plants, and fresh flowers.

SIC 5194 - Tobacco and Tobacco Products

Establishments primarily engaged in the wholesale distribution of tobacco and its products. Included are chewing tobacco, cigarettes, cigars, snuff, and smoking tobacco. Leaf tobacco wholesalers are classified in SIC 5159, and establishments primarily engaged in stemming and redrying tobacco are classified in Manufacturing, SIC 2141.

SIC 5198 - Paints, Varnishes, and Supplies

Establishments primarily engaged in the wholesale distribution of paints, varnishes, wallpaper, and supplies (such as paint brushes, rollers, and sprayers). Those establishments selling to the general public and known as retail in the trade are classified in Retail Trade, SIC 5231.

SIC 5199 - Nondurable Goods, Not Elsewhere Classified

Establishments primarily engaged in the wholesale distribution of nondurable goods, not elsewhere classified, such as art goods, industrial yarns, textile bags, and bagging and burlap. Also includes advertising specialties, baskets (reed, rattan, willow, and wood), candles, charcoal, plant food, sheet music, and wigs.

RETAIL TRADE

SIC 5211 - Lumber and Other Building Materials Dealers

Establishments engaged in selling primarily lumber, or lumber and a general line of building materials, to the general public. While these establishments may sell primarily to construction contractors, they are known as retail in the trade. The lumber which they sell may include rough and dressed lumber, flooring, molding, doors, sashes, frames, and other millwork. The building materials may include roofing, siding, shingles, wallboard, paint, brick, tile, cement, sand, gravel, and other building materials and supplies. Hardware is often an important line sold by retail lumber and building materials dealers. Establishments which do not sell to the general public and those which are known in the trade as wholesale are classified in Wholesale Trade, SIC 503.

SIC 5231 - Paint, Glass, and Wallpaper Stores

Establishments engaged in selling primarily paint, glass, and wallpaper, or any combination of these lines, to the general public. While these establishments may sell primarily to construction contractors, they are known as retail in the trade. Establishments which do not sell to the general public or are known in the trade as wholesale are classified in Wholesale Trade, SIC 503.

SIC 5251 - Hardware Stores

Establishments primarily engaged in the retail sale of a number of basic hardware lines, such as tools, builders' hardware, chainsaws, handtools, paint and glass, door locks and lock sets, housewares and household appliances, and cutlery.

SIC 5261 - Retail Nurseries, Lawn and Garden Supply Stores

Establishments primarily engaged in selling trees, shrubs, other plants, seeds, bulbs, mulches, soil conditioners, fertilizers, pesticides, garden tools, and other garden supplies to the general public. These establishments primarily sell products purchased from others, but may sell some plants which they grow themselves. Establishments primarily engaged in growing trees (except Christmas trees), shrubs, other plants, seeds, and bulbs are classified in Agriculture, SIC 01 and those growing Christmas trees are classified in SIC 0811.

SIC 5271 - Mobile Home Dealers

Establishments primarily engaged in the retail sale of new and used mobile homes, parts, and equipment. The establishments primarily selling travel trailers and campers are classified in SIC 5561.

SIC 5311 - Department Stores

Retail stores generally carrying a general line of apparel, such as suits, coats, dresses, and furnishings; homefurnishings, such as furniture, floor coverings, curtains, draperies, linens, and major household appliances; and housewares, such as tables and kitchen appliances, dishes, and utensils. These stores must carry men's and women's apparel and either major household appliances or other home furnishings. These and other merchandise lines are normally arranged in separate sections or departments with the accounting on a departmentalized basis. The department and functions are integrated under a single management. The stores usually provide their own charge accounts, deliver merchandise, and maintain open stocks. These stores normally have 50 employees or more. Establishments which sell a similar range of merchandise with less than 50 employees are classified in SIC 5399. Establishments which do not carry these general lines of merchandise are classified according to their primary activity.

SIC 5331 - Variety Stores

Establishments primarily engaged in the retail sale of a variety of merchandise in the low and popular price ranges. Sales usually are made on a cash-and-carry basis, with the open-selling method of display and customer selection of merchandise. These stores generally do not carry a complete line of merchandise, are not departmentalized, do not carry their own charge service, and do not deliver merchandise.

SIC 5399 - Miscellaneous General Merchandise Stores

Establishments primarily engaged in the retail sale of a general line of apparel, dry goods, hardware, housewares or homefurnishings, groceries, and other lines in limited amounts. Stores selling commodities covered in the definition for department stores, but normally having less than 50 employees, and stores usually known as country general stores are included in this SIC. Establishments primarily engaged in the retail sale of merchandise by television, catalog, and mail-order are classified in SIC 5961.

SIC 5411 - Grocery Stores

Stores, commonly known as supermarkets, food stores, and grocery stores, primarily engaged in the retail sale of all sorts of canned foods and dry goods, such as tea, coffee, spices, sugar, and flour; fresh fruits and vegetables; and fresh and prepared meats, fish and poultry.

SIC 5421 - Meat and Fish (Seafood) Markets, Including Freezer Provisioners

Establishments primarily engaged in the retail of fresh, frozen, or cured meats, fish, shellfish, and other seafoods. This SIC includes establishments primarily engaged in the retail sale, on a bulk basis, of meat for freezer storage and in providing home freezer plans. Meat markets may butcher animals on their own account, or they may buy from others. Food locker plants primarily engaged in renting locker space for the storage of food products for individual households are classified in SIC 4222. Establishments primarily engaged in the retail sale of poultry are classified in SIC 5499.

SIC 5431 - Fruit and Vegetable Markets

Establishments primarily engaged in the retail sale of fresh fruits and vegetables. They are frequently found in public or municipal markets or as roadside stands. However, establishments which grow fruits and vegetables and sell them at roadside stands are classified in Agriculture, Major Group 01.

SIC 5441 - Candy, Nut, and Confectionery Stores

Establishments primarily engaged in the retail sale of candy, nuts, popcorn, and other confections. This also includes candy stores, confectionery produced for direct sale on the premises, retail confectionery stores, nut stores, and popcorn stands.

SIC 5451 - Dairy Products Stores

Establishments primarily engaged in the retail sale of packaged dairy products to over-the-counter customers. Ice cream and frozen custard stands are classified in SIC 5812, and establishments selling ice cream and similar products from trucks or wagons are classified in SIC 5963. Establishments primarily engaged in processing and distributing milk and cream are classified in Manufacturing, SIC Group 202.

SIC 5461 - Retail Bakeries

Establishments primarily engaged in the retail sale of bakery products. The products may be purchased from others or made on the premises. Establishments manufacturing bakery products for the trade are classified in Manufacturing, SIC Group 205, and those purchasing bakery products and selling house-to-house are classified in SIC 5963.

SIC 5499 - Miscellaneous Food Stores

Establishments primarily engaged in the retail sale of specialized foods, not elsewhere classified, such as eggs, poultry, health foods, spices, herbs, coffee, and tea. The poultry stores may sell live poultry, slaughter and clean poultry for their own account, and sell dressed fowls, or sell fowls cleaned and dressed by others.

SIC 5511 - Motor Vehicle Dealers (New and Used)

Establishments primarily engaged in the retail sale of new automobiles or new and used automobiles. These establishments frequently maintain repair departments and carry stock of replacement parts, tires, batteries, and automotive accessories. These establishments also frequently sell pickups and vans at retail.

SIC 5521 - Motor Vehicle Dealers (Used Only)

Establishment primarily engaged in the retail sale of used cars only, with no sales of new automobiles. These establishments also frequently sell antique autos and used pickups and vans.

SIC 5531 - Auto and Home Supply Stores

Establishments primarily engaged in the retail sale of new automobile tires, batteries, and other automobile parts and accessories. Such establishments frequently sell a substantial amount of home appliances, radios, and television sets. Establishments dealing primarily in used parts are classified in Wholesale Trade, SIC 5015. Establishments primarily engaged in both selling and installing such automotive parts as transmissions, mufflers, brake linings, and glass are classified in Services, SIC Group 753.

SIC 5541 - Gasoline Service Stations

Gasoline service stations primarily engaged in selling gasoline and lubricating oils. These establishments frequently sell other merchandise, such as tires, batteries, and other automobile parts, or perform minor repair work. Gasoline stations combined with other activities, such as grocery stores, convenience stores, or carwashes, are classified according to the primary activity.

SIC 5551 - Boat Dealers

Establishments primarily engaged in the retail sale of new and used motorboats and other watercraft, marine supplies, and outboard motors.

SIC 5561 - Recreational Vehicle Dealers

Establishments primarily engaged in the retail sale of new and used motor homes, recreational trailers, and campers (pickup coaches). The establishments primarily engaged in retail sale of mobile homes are classified in SIC 5271, and those selling utility trailers are classified in SIC 5599.

SIC 5571 - Motorcycle Dealers

Establishments primarily engaged in the retail sale of new and used motorcycles, including motor scooters, mopeds, motorized bicycles, motorcycle parts, and all-terrain vehicles.

SIC 5599 - Automotive Dealers, Not Elsewhere Classified

Establishments primarily engaged in the retail sale of new and used automotive vehicles, utility trailers, and automotive equipment and supplies, not elsewhere classified, such as snowmobiles, dunebuggies, and go-carts. Also included in this SIC are establishments primarily engaged in the retail sale of aircraft.

SIC 5611 - Men's and Boys' Clothing and Accessory Stores

Establishments primarily engaged in the retail sale of men's and boys' ready-to-wear clothing and accessories. Including retail men's and boys' clothing stores, haberdashery stores, and tie shops.

SIC 5621 - Women's Clothing Stores

Establishments primarily engaged in the retail sale of a general line of women's ready-to-wear clothing. This SIC also includes establishments primarily engaged in the specialized retail sale of women's coats, suits, and dresses. Custom tailors primarily engaged in making women's clothing to individual order are classified in SIC 5699.

SIC 5632 - Women's Accessory and Specialty Stores

Establishments primarily engaged in the retail sale of women's clothing accessories and specialties, such as millinery, blouses, foundation garments, lingerie, hosiery, costume jewelry, gloves, handbags, and furs (including custom-made furs).

SIC 5641 - Children's and Infants' Wear Stores

Establishments primarily engaged in the retail sale of children's and infants' clothing, furnishings, and accessories. Such establishments may specialize in either children's or infants' wear or they may sell a combination of children's and infants' wear.

SIC 5651 - Family Clothing Stores

Establishments primarily engaged in the retail sale of clothing, furnishings, and accessories for men, women, and children, without specializing in sales for an individual sex or age group, such as family clothing stores, jeans stores, and unisex clothing stores.

SIC 5661 - Shoe Stores

Establishments primarily engaged in the retail sale of men's, women's, and children's footwear, including athletic footwear. These establishments frequently carry accessory lines, such as hosiery, gloves, and handbags.

SIC 5699 - Miscellaneous Apparel and Accessory Stores

Establishments primarily engaged in the retail sale of specialized lines of apparel and accessories, not elsewhere classified, such as uniforms, bathing suits, raincoats, riding apparel, sports apparel, umbrellas, wigs, and toupees. This SIC also includes custom tailors primarily engaged in making and selling men's and women's clothing, except fur apparel. Establishments primarily engaged in making fur apparel to custom order are classified in SIC 5632.

SIC 5712 - Furniture Stores

Establishments primarily engaged in the retail sale of household furniture. These stores may also sell homefurnishings, major appliances, and floor coverings. Household furniture may include beds and springs, custom-made furniture, waterbeds, and outdoor furniture. Home furnishings may include kitchen cabinets (not built in), cabinet work on a custom basis to individual order, and mattress stores.

SIC 5713 - Floor Covering Stores

Establishments primarily engaged in the retail sale of floor coverings. Establishments included in this SIC may incidentally perform installation, but contractors primarily engaged in installing floor coverings for others are classified in Construction, SIC 1752.

SIC 5714 - Drapery, Curtain, and Upholstery Stores

Establishments primarily engaged in the retail sale of draperies, curtains, and upholstery materials. Included are drapery stores, curtain stores, slipcover stores, and upholstery materials stores. Those establishments primarily engaged in reupholstering or repairing furniture are classified in Services, SIC 7641.

SIC 5719 - Miscellaneous Homefurnishings Stores

Establishments primarily engaged in the retail sale of miscellaneous homefurnishings, such as china, glassware, and metalware for kitchen and table use; bedding and linen; brooms and brushes; lamps and shades; mirrors and pictures; venetian blinds; and window shades. Establishments primarily engaged in the retail sale of miscellaneous homefurnishings by house-to-house canvass or by party-plan merchandising are classified in SIC 5963.

SIC 5722 - Household Appliance Stores

Establishments primarily engaged in the retail sale of electric and gas refrigerators, stoves, and other household appliances, such as electric irons, percolators, hot plates, and vacuum cleaners. Many such stores also sell radios and television sets. Retail stores operated by public utility companies and primarily engaged in the sale of electric and gas appliances for household use are classified in this SIC.

SIC 5731 - Radio, Television, and Consumer Electronics Stores

Establishments primarily engaged in the retail sale of radios, television sets, record players, stereo equipment, sound reproducing equipment, and other consumer audio and video electronics equipment (including automotive). Such establishments may also sell additional lines, such as household appliances; computers, computer peripheral equipment, and software; musical instruments; or records and prerecorded tapes. Establishments in this SIC may perform incidental installation and repair work on radios, television sets, and other consumer electronic equipment. Establishments primarily engaged in the installation and repair of these products are classified in Services, SIC 7622. Establishments primarily engaged in the retail sale of computer equipment are classified in SIC 5734, and those selling electronic toys are classified in SIC 5945.

SIC 5734 - Computer and Computer Software Stores

Establishments primarily engaged in the retail sale of computers, computer peripheral equipment, such as computer printer stores, and software. Those establishments primarily engaged in the sale of computers, computer peripheral equipment, and software for business or professional use are classified in Wholesale Trade, SIC 5045.

SIC 5735 - Record and Prerecorded Tape Stores

Establishments primarily engaged in the retail sale of phonograph records and prerecorded audio and video tapes and disks. Establishments primarily engaged in the retail sale of computer software are classified in SIC 5734, and those primarily engaged in the rental of video tapes are classified in Services, SIC 7841.

SIC 5736 - Musical Instrument Stores

Establishments primarily engaged in the retail sale of musical instruments, such as pianos, sheet music, and similar supplies.

SIC 5812 - Eating and Drinking Places

Establishments primarily engaged in the retail sale of prepared food and drinks for on-premises or immediate consumption. Included are buffets (eating places), cafes, commissary restaurants, concession stands (in airports and sports arenas), hamburger stands, and tea rooms. Caterers and industrial and institutional food service establishments are also included in this SIC.

SIC 5813 - Drinking Places (Alcoholic Beverages)

Establishments primarily engaged in the retail sale of alcoholic drinks, such as beer, ale, wine, and liquor, for consumption on the premises. The sale of food frequently accounts for a substantial portion of these establishments. Includes bars, beer taverns, cabarets, night clubs, and saloons.

SIC 5912 - Drug Stores and Proprietary Stores

Establishments engaged in the retail sale of prescription drugs, proprietary drugs, and nonprescription medicines, and which may also carry a number of related lines, such as cosmetics, toiletries, tobacco, and novelty merchandise. These stores are included on the basis of their usual trade designation rather than on the stricter interpretation of commodities handled. This SIC includes drug stores which also operate a soda fountain or lunch counter.

SIC 5921 - Liquor Stores

Establishments primarily engaged in the retail sale of packaged alcoholic beverages, such as ale, beer, wine, and liquor, for consumption off the premises. Stores selling prepared drinks for consumption on the premises are classified in SIC 5813.

SIC 5932 - Used Merchandise Stores

This industry includes stores primarily engaged in the retail sale of used merchandise, antiques, and secondhand goods, such as clothing and shoes; furniture; books and rare manuscripts; musical instruments; office furniture; phonographs and phonograph records; and store fixtures and equipment. This SIC also includes pawnshops. Dealers primarily engaged in selling used motor vehicles, trailers, and boats are classified in Major Group 55, and those selling used mobile homes are classified in SIC 5271. Establishments primarily selling used automobile parts and accessories are classified in Wholesale Trade, SIC 5015, and scrap and waste dealers are classified in SIC 5093. Establishments primarily engaged in automotive repair are classified in Services, SIC Group 753.

SIC 5941 - Sporting Goods Stores and Bicycle Shops

Establishments primarily engaged in the retail sale of sporting goods, sporting equipment, and bicycles, bicycle parts, and accessories. Retail establishments primarily engaged in selling motorized bicycles are classified in SIC 5571, and those engaged in the retail sale of athletic footwear are classified in SIC 5661. Establishments primarily engaged in repairing bicycles are classified in Services, SIC 7699, and those renting bicycles are classified in SIC 7999.

SIC 5942 - Book Stores

Establishments primarily engaged in the retail sale of new books and magazines, including religious book stores. Those establishments primarily engaged in the retail sale of used books are classified in SIC 5932.

SIC 5943 - Stationery Stores

Establishments primarily engaged in the retail sale of stationery, such as paper and paper products (including printing and engraving), postcards, and paper novelties. These establishments may also sell additional lines of office type supplies, such as accounting and legal forms, blankbooks and forms, and office forms and supplies. Establishments primarily engaged in selling office forms and supplies are classified in Wholesale Trade, SIC 5112. Establishments primarily engaged in the retail sale of greeting cards are classified in SIC 5947.

SIC 5944 - Jewelry Stores

Establishments primarily engaged in the retail sale of any combination of the lines of jewelry, such as diamonds and other precious stones mounted in precious metals as rings, bracelets, and broaches; sterling and plated silverware; and watches and clocks. Stores primarily engaged in watch and jewelry repair are classified in Services, SIC 7631. Establishments primarily engaged in selling costume jewelry are classified in SIC 5632.

SIC 5945 - Hobby, Toy, and Game Shops

Establishments primarily engaged in the retail sale of toys, games, and hobby and craft kits and supplies. Includes ceramic supplies, game shops, and hobby shops. Establishments primarily engaged in selling artists' supplies or collectors' items, such as coins, stamps, and autographs, are classified in SIC 5999.

SIC 5946 - Camera and Photographic Supply Stores

Establishments primarily engaged in the retail sale of cameras, film, and other photographic supplies and equipment. Establishments primarily engaged in the retail sale of video cameras are classified in SIC 5731, and those engaged in finishing films are classified in Services, SIC 7384.

SIC 5947 - Gift, Novelty, and Souvenir Shops

Establishments primarily engaged in the retail sale of combined lines of gifts and novelty merchandise, souvenirs, greeting cards, holiday decorations, and miscellaneous small art goods. Includes balloon shops, curio shops, gift shops, greeting card shops, novelty shops, and souvenir shops.

SIC 5948 - Luggage and Leather Goods Stores

Establishments primarily engaged in the retail sale of luggage, trunks, and leather goods. Leather goods includes goods made to individual order.

SIC 5949 - Sewing, Needlework, and Piece Goods Stores

Establishments primarily engaged in the retail sale of sewing supplies, fabrics, patterns, yarn, and other needlework accessories. SIC includes fabric shops, mill end stores, notion stores, quilting materials and supplies stores, and remnant stores.

SIC 5961 - Catalog and Mail-Order Houses

Establishments primarily engaged in the retail sale of products by television, catalog, and mail-order. These establishments do not ordinarily maintain stock for sale on the premises. Separate stores operated by catalog and mail-order houses for the retail sale of products on the premises are classified according to the product sold. Includes mail-order book clubs, mail-order cheese, mail-order computer software, and record clubs.

SIC 5962 - Automatic Merchandising Machine Operators

Establishments primarily engaged in the retail sale of products by means of automatic merchandising units, also referred to as vending machines. This SIC does not include the operation of coin-operated service machines, such as music machines, amusement and game machines, and lockers and scales. Insurance policies sold through vending machines are classified in Insurance, Major Group 63 or 64. Establishments primarily engaged in operating music machines, amusement and game machines, lockers and scales, and most other coin-operated service machines, are classified in Services, Division I.

SIC 5963 - Direct Selling Establishments

Establishments primarily engaged in the retail sale of merchandise by telephone; by house-to-house canvass; or from trucks or wagons or other temporary locations. Included in this SIC are individuals who sell products by these methods and who are not employees of the organization which they represent, and establishments which are retail sales offices from which employees operate to sell merchandise from door-to-door.

SIC 5983 - Fuel Oil Dealers

Establishments primarily engaged in the retail sale of fuel oil. Establishments primarily engaged in selling fuel oil burners are classified in Wholesale Trade, SIC 5074; those primarily engaged in installing and servicing fuel oil burners are classified in Construction, SIC 1711; and those engaged in fuel oil repair service only are classified in Services, SIC 7699.

SIC 5984 - Liquefied Petroleum Gas (Bottled Gas) Dealers

Establishments primarily engaged in the retail sale of bottled or bulk liquefied petroleum (LP) gas. Includes bottled gas, bottled Butane gas, liquefied petroleum (LP) gas delivered to customers' premises, and bottled propane gas.

SIC 5989 - Fuel Dealers, Not Elsewhere Classified

Establishments primarily engaged in the retail sale of coal, wood, or other fuels, not elsewhere classified.

SIC 5992 - Florists

Establishments primarily engaged in the retail sale of cut flowers and growing plants. Establishments primarily engaged in the retail sale of seeds, bulbs, and nursery stock are classified in SIC 5261, and greenhouses and nurseries primarily engaged in growing seeds, bulbs, flowers, and nursery stock are classified in Agriculture, SIC 0181.

SIC 5993 - Tobacco Stores and Stands

Establishments primarily engaged in the retail sale of cigarettes, cigars, tobacco, and smokers' supplies. Includes cigar stores and stands, tobacco stores, and tobacconists.

SIC 5994 - News Dealers and Newsstands

Establishments primarily engaged in the retail sale of newspapers, magazines, and other periodicals. Home delivery of newspapers by other than printers or publishers is classified in SIC 5963.

SIC 5995 - Optical Goods Stores

Establishments primarily engaged in the retail sale of eyeglasses and contact lenses to prescription for individuals. Offices of oculists, ophthalmologists, and optometrists are classified in Services, Major Group 80, even if a majority of their revenues comes from retail sales. Establishments primarily engaged in the retail sale of binoculars, telescopes, and opera glasses are classified in SIC 5999.

SIC 5999 - Miscellaneous Retail Stores, Not Elsewhere Classified

Establishments primarily engaged in the retail sale of specialized lines of merchandise, not elsewhere classified, such as artists' supplies; orthopedic and artificial limbs; rubber stamps; pets; religious goods; and monuments and tombstones. This SIC also includes establishments primarily engaged in selling a general line of their own or consigned merchandise at retail on an auction basis. Establishments primarily engaged in auctioning tangible personal property of others on a contract or fee basis are classified in Services, SIC 7389.